# shakespearean criticism

"Thou art a Monument without a tomb,
And art alive still while thy Book doth
    live
And we have wits to read and praise to
    give."

*Ben Jonson, from the preface
to the First Folio, 1623.*

# Mr. WILLIAM
# SHAKESPEARES

## COMEDIES,
## HISTORIES, &
## TRAGEDIES.

Published according to the True Originall Copies.

Martin Droeshout sculpsit London.

## LONDON
Printed by Isaac Iaggard, and Ed. Blount. 1623.

*Frontispiece to the First Folio (1623). By permission of the Folger Shakespeare Library.*

ISSN 0883-9123

Volume 5

# shakespearean criticism

Excerpts from the Criticism of
William Shakespeare's Plays and Poetry,
from the First Published Appraisals
to Current Evaluations

**Mark W. Scott**

Editor

Gale Research Company
Book Tower
Detroit, Michigan 48226

# STAFF

Mark W. Scott, *Editor*

Sandra L. Williamson, *Senior Assistant Editor*

Kathleen M. Aro, Cappy Beins, James P. Draper, K. R. Krolicki, *Assistant Editors*

Carolyn Bancroft, Phyllis Carmel Mendelson, *Contributing Editors*

Melissa Reiff Hug, Debra A. Wells, *Contributing Assistant Editors*

Jeanne A. Gough, *Permissions & Production Manager*
Lizbeth A. Purdy, *Production Supervisor*
Denise Michlewicz Broderick, *Production Coordinator*
Kathleen M. Cook, *Assistant Production Coordinator*
Maureen Duffy, Suzanne Powers, Jani Prescott, *Editorial Assistants*
Linda M. Pugliese, *Manuscript Coordinator*
Donna Craft, *Assistant Manuscript Coordinator*
Jennifer E. Gale, Maureen A. Puhl, Rosetta Irene Simms, *Manuscript Assistants*

Victoria B. Cariappa, *Research Supervisor*
Maureen R. Richards, *Assistant Research Coordinator*
Daniel Kurt Gilbert, Kent Graham, Michele R. O'Connell,
Keith E. Schooley, Filomena Sgambati, Vincenza G. Tranchida,
Mary D. Wise, *Research Assistants*

Janice M. Mach, *Text Permissions Supervisor*
Susan D. Battista, Sandra C. Davis, Kathy J. Grell, *Assistant Permissions Coordinators*
Mabel Gurney, Josephine M. Keene, Mary M. Matuz, *Senior Permissions Assistants*
Margaret A. Carson, H. Diane Cooper, *Permissions Assistants*
Eileen H. Baehr, Anita Ransom, Kimberly Smilay, *Permissions Clerks*

Patricia A. Seefelt, *Picture Permissions Supervisor*
Margaret A. Chamberlain, *Assistant Permissions Coordinator*
Colleen M. Crane, *Permissions Assistant*
Lillian Tyus, *Permissions Clerk*

Frederick G. Ruffner, *Chairman*
J. Kevin Reger, *President*
Dedria Bryfonski, *Publisher*
Ellen T. Crowley, *Associate Editorial Director*
Laurie Lanzen Harris, *Director, Literary Criticism Division*
Dennis Poupard, *Senior Editor, Literary Criticism Series*

Since this page cannot legibly accommodate all the copyright notices,
the Appendix constitutes an extension of the copyright notice.

Copyright © 1987 by Gale Research Company

ISBN 0-8103-6129-9
ISSN 0883-9123

Computerized photocomposition by
Typographics, Incorporated
Kansas City, Missouri

Printed in the United States

# Contents

# Preface

The works of William Shakespeare have delighted audiences and inspired scholars for nearly four hundred years. Shakespeare's appeal is universal, for in its depth and breadth his work evokes a timeless insight into the human condition.

The vast amount of Shakespearean criticism is a testament to his enduring popularity. Critics of each epoch have contributed to this critical legacy, responding to the comments of their forebears, bringing the moral and intellectual atmosphere of their own era to the works, and suggesting interpretations that continue to inspire critics of today. Thus, to chart the history of criticism on Shakespeare is to note the changing aesthetic philosophies of the past four centuries.

## The Scope of the Work

The success of Gale's four existing literary series, *Contemporary Literary Criticism (CLC), Twentieth-Century Literary Criticism (TCLC), Nineteenth-Century Literature Criticism (NCLC),* and *Children's Literature Review (CLR),* suggested an equivalent need among students and teachers of Shakespeare. Moreover, since the criticism of Shakespeare's works spans four centuries and is larger in size and scope than that of any author, a prodigious amount of critical material confronts the student.

*Shakespearean Criticism (SC)* presents significant passages from published criticism on the works of Shakespeare. Eight volumes of the series will be devoted to aesthetic criticism of the plays. Performance criticism will be treated in separate special volumes. Other special volumes will be devoted to such topics as Shakespeare's poetry, the authorship controversy and the apocrypha, stage history of the plays, and other general subjects, such as Shakespeare's language, religious and philosophical thought, and characterization. The first eight volumes will each contain criticism on four to six plays, with an equal balance of genres and an equal balance of plays based on their critical importance. Thus, volume 5 contains criticism on one major tragedy *(Romeo and Juliet),* one history *(Henry V),* one major comedy *(As You Like It),* and one minor comedy *(The Merry Wives of Windsor).*

The length of each entry is intended to represent the play's critical reception in English, including those works which have been translated into English. The editors have tried to identify only the major critics and lines of inquiry for each play. Each entry represents a historical overview of the critical response to the play: early criticism is presented to indicate initial responses and later selections represent significant trends in the history of criticism on the play. We have also attempted to identify and include excerpts from the seminal essays on each play by the most important Shakespearean critics. We have directed our series to students in late high school and early college who are beginning their study of Shakespeare. Thus, ours is not a work for the specialist, but is rather an introduction for the researcher newly acquainted with the works of Shakespeare.

## The Organization of the Book

Each entry consists of the following elements: play heading, an introduction, excerpts of criticism (each followed by a bibliographical citation), and an additional bibliography for further reading.

The *introduction* begins with a discussion of the date, text, and sources of the play. This section is followed by a critical history which outlines the major critical trends and identifies the prominent commentators on the play.

*Criticism* is arranged chronologically within each play entry to provide a perspective on the changes in critical evaluation over the years. For purposes of easier identification, the critic's name and the date of the essay are given at the beginning of each piece. For an anonymous essay later attributed to a critic, the critic's name appears in brackets at the beginning of the excerpt and in the bibliographical citation. Within the text, all act, scene, and line designations have been changed to conform to *The Riverside*

*Shakespeare,* published by Houghton Mifflin Company, which is a standard text used in many high school and college English classes. All of the individual essays are prefaced with *explanatory notes* as an additional aid to students using *SC.* The explanatory notes provide several types of useful information, including: the importance of the critics in literary history, the critical schools with which they are identified, if any, and the importance of their comments on Shakespeare and the play discussed. The explanatory notes also identify the main issues in the commentary on each play and provide previous publication information, such as original title and date, for reprinted and translated publications.

A complete *bibliographical citation* designed to facilitate the location of the original essay or book follows each piece of criticism.

Within each play entry are *illustrations,* such as facsimiles of title pages taken from the quarto and First Folio editions of the plays as well as pictures drawn from such sources as early editions of the collected works and artists' renderings of some of the famous scenes and characters. The captions following each illustration indicate act, scene, characters, and the artist and date, if known. The illustrations are arranged chronologically and, as a complement to the criticism, provide a historical perspective on Shakespeare throughout the centuries.

The *additional bibliography* appearing at the end of each play entry suggests further reading on the play. This section includes references to the major discussions of the date, the text, and the sources of each play.

At the request of librarians, beginning with volume 4 *SC* provides a list of Shakespeare's plays covered in the series, indicating which works of the canon are treated in each existing or future volume. This is referred to as the List of Plays and can be found following the Preface.

To help students locate essays by certain commentators, *SC* includes a cumulative index to critics; under each critic's name are listed the plays on which the critic has written and the volume and page where the criticism appears. Beginning with volume 5, *SC* will also include a cumulative index to topics. This new feature identifies the principal topics of debate in the criticism of each play; the topics are arranged alphabetically and indicate the initial page number of each excerpt that offers substantial commentary on that topic.

As an additional aid to students, beginning with volume 3 *SC* provides a glossary of terms relating to date, text, and source information frequently mentioned by critics and used throughout the introductions to the plays. The glossed terms and source names are identified by small capital letters when they first appear in the introductions.

An appendix is also included that lists the sources from which the material in the volume is reprinted. It does not, however, list every book or periodical consulted for the volume.

## Acknowledgments

No work of this scope can be accomplished without the cooperation of many people. The editors wish to thank the copyright holders of the excerpts included in this volume, the permissions managers of the book and magazine publishing companies for assisting us in securing reprint rights, and the staffs of the Detroit Public Library, the University of Michigan libraries, and the Wayne State University Library for making their resources available to us. We would especially like to thank the staff of the Rare Book Room of the University of Michigan Library for their research assistance and the Folger Shakespeare Library for their help in picture research. We would also like to thank Jeri Yaryan and Anthony J. Bogucki for assistance with copyright research.

## Suggestions Are Welcome

The editors welcome the comments and suggestions of readers to expand the coverage and enhance the usefulness of the series.

# List of Plays Covered in *SC*

[The year or years in parentheses indicate the composition date of the
play as determined by G. Blakemore Evans in *The Riverside Shakespeare*]

**Volume 1**

*The Comedy of Errors* (1592-94)
*Hamlet* (1600-01)
*1* and *2 Henry IV* (1596-98)
*Timon of Athens* (1607-08)
*Twelfth Night* (1601-02)

**Volume 2**

*Henry VIII* (1612-13)
*King Lear* (1605)
*Love's Labour's Lost* (1594-95)
*Measure for Measure* (1604)
*Pericles* (1607-08)

**Volume 3**

*1, 2,* and *3 Henry VI* (1589-91)
*Macbeth* (1606)
*A Midsummer Night's Dream* (1595-96)
*Troilus and Cressida* (1601-02)

**Volume 4**

*Cymbeline* (1609-10)
*The Merchant of Venice* (1596-97)
*Othello* (1604)
*Titus Andronicus* (1593-94)

**Volume 5**

*As You Like It* (1599)
*Henry V* (1599)
*The Merry Wives of Windsor* (1597)
*Romeo and Juliet* (1595-96)

**In Forthcoming Volumes:**

*All's Well That Ends Well* (1602-03)
*Antony and Cleopatra* (1606-07)
*Coriolanus* (1607-08)
*Julius Caesar* (1599)
*King John* (1594-96)
*Much Ado about Nothing* (1598-99)
*Richard II* (1595)
*Richard III* (1592-93)
*The Taming of the Shrew* (1593-94)
*The Tempest* (1611)
*The Two Gentlemen of Verona* (1594)
*The Two Noble Kinsmen* (1613)
*The Winter's Tale* (1610-11)

# As You Like It

**DATE:** Scholars generally agree that *As You Like It* was written and first performed sometime between 1598 and 1600, probably in 1599 or 1600. Although the play does not appear by its present title in the list of Shakespeare's comedies in FRANCIS MERES's *Palladis Tamia* (1598), it does appear as an entry in the STATIONERS' REGISTER for August 1600. Some critics have suggested that Meres's allusion to a play titled *Loue Labours Wonne* may refer to *As You Like It* in its present or, perhaps, an earlier version, but their arguments are speculative; in fact, almost no one assigns *As You Like It,* as we have it, to a date earlier than 1598. Further evidence for a composition date just after 1598 is the popularity of two Robin Hood plays, *The Downfall of Robert, Earl of Huntington,* by Anthony Munday, and *The Death of Robert, Earl of Huntington,* by Munday and Henry Chettle, which in 1598 were performed before large audiences by the LORD ADMIRAL'S MEN at the ROSE THEATRE. Some scholars have suggested that *As You Like It* may represent the GLOBE THEATRE's attempt to match the success of these works and to satisfy the public's taste for forest outlaws. Additional arguments for dating the play's composition between 1598 and 1600 are also based on the theatrical milieu of the time. Shakespeare's decision to dramatize a pastoral novel has sometimes been seen as a response to revivals from 1597 to 1600 of the pastoral plays of John Lyly and their like, which provided suitable material for the reconstituted boys' companies. In addition, some critics have suggested that the part of Touchstone may have been expressly written for Robert Armin, who joined the LORD CHAMBERLAIN'S MEN in 1599 and specialized in such roles.

Scholars have occasionally noted possible allusions in *As You Like It* to books published in or around 1598, most notably to John Lyly's *The Woman in the Moon* (1597), Christopher Marlowe's *Hero and Leander* (1598), and Bartholemew Yonge's 1598 translation of Jorge de Montemayor's *Diana*. Also, there appeared a new edition of Thomas Lodge's *Rosalynde*—the major source of *As You Like It*—in 1598. Allusions in the play to the events of the 1590s are generally considered tenuous and offer little help in proving or disproving the accepted 1598-1600 composition date; however, several critics have discerned in the figure of Jaques an oblique allusion to one historical event, namely, the Bishop's Edict of 1599 forbidding the publication of certain types of satire. One notable stylistic test for dating *As You Like It* suggests the possibility of an earlier version of the play, assigned by J. Dover Wilson to 1593, of which the present text is a revision. However, the evidence adduced for this hypothesis—the appearance of blank verse lines or "verse fossils" embedded in the prose—has not been widely accepted.

**TEXT:** The FIRST FOLIO of 1623 is the sole authority for the text of *As You Like It*. This FOLIO text is generally agreed to be a very good one, most likely printed from a PROMPT-BOOK or an excellent transcript of one. There are no notable instances of false starts or loose ends, and the few textual inconsistencies detected have not always been accepted or, if so, are usually explained as COMPOSITOR's or scribal errors. Although several theories have been put forward that the First Folio text of *As You Like It* contains inconsistencies due to haste or rewriting, as well as evidence of interpolations by Shakespeare or some

*Title page of As You Like It taken from the First Folio (1623).*

other writers, the strong likelihood that the Folio text of the play derives from a very neat transcript by a playhouse scribe has never been seriously challenged.

**SOURCES:** As previously mentioned, the primary source of *As You Like It* is Thomas Lodge's novel or pastoral romance *Rosalynde,* first published in 1590 and reprinted three times before the beginning of the seventeenth century. *Rosalynde* provided Shakespeare with most of his play's plot and characters, and a comparison of the two works shows that he followed Lodge's narrative fairly closely. Among Shakespeare's most important inventions in the play, according to scholars, are the characters Jaques, Touchstone, Audrey, William, Amiens, Le Beau, and Sir Oliver Martext. In addition, Shakespeare's altering of the sequence of events in *Rosalynde* to provide the smoother, swifter action of *As You Like It* has also attracted commentary. Because *Rosalynde* is based in part on the mid-fourteenth-century narrative poem *The Tale of Gamelyn,* some critics, discerning events in *As You Like It* that seem closer to *Gamelyn* than to Lodge's work, have argued that Shakespeare may have used the older story in addition to *Rosalynde* as a direct source for his comedy. Most scholars, however, have found such evidence inconclusive.

Shakespeare drew on a variety of contemporary events, incidents, and literary works and traditions in shaping *As You Like It.* For Jaques, he adopted the generic traits of the late-sixteenth-century melancholy man. Touchstone—as both a type and a personality—is commonly believed to have originated in the court fool of Shakespeare's day and in the conventional stage jester. Scholars have found parallels for the country clowns of *As You Like It*—Corin, William, and Audrey—in, among other works, Sir Philip Sidney's *Arcadia* (1590) and the anonymous *Historie of Sir Clyomon and Clamydes,* published in 1599 but written during the 1580s. A mixture of Robin Hood legends is thought by many critics to have significantly affected the pastoral quality of the play, while such works as Jorge de Montemayor's *Diana,* published in English in 1598, are often credited with contributing to Shakespeare's handling of the pastoral ideal. John Lyly's drama *Gallathea*—performed in 1586, but not published until 1592—is usually named as the immediate source of Rosalind's proposed "love-cure" to Orlando, and a number of other English works of the period have been cited with varying certainty as the sources of one or another of the incidents or passages in *As You Like It.* Finally, critics often point to OVID's *Metamorphoses* as a direct source for, among other things, Shakespeare's notion of the Golden Age as a perpetual spring, and a variety of other Renaissance Italian influences have also been detected.

**CRITICAL HISTORY:** Critical commentary on *As You Like It* has been concerned primarily with four major issues: the play's theme, characters, dramatic technique, and tone. Within these broad areas, critics have treated a variety of smaller concerns. These include, among other interests, the meaning and function of pastoralism in the play, the purpose and effect of Rosalind's sexual disguise, the nature of Jaques's melancholy, Touchstone's comic role, the play's structure and dramatic elements, the importance of self-knowledge as a central motif, the thematic significance of love, Shakespeare's mixture of verse and prose, the concept of time in Arden, the self-reflexive nature of the comedy, and, finally, the meaning of its Christian and religious elements. Rarely treated separately, these issues have usually been discussed as interrelated themes in Shakespeare's overall design.

According to available evidence, *As You Like It* enjoyed little or no critical recognition during the seventeenth century. With the possible exception of a performance in 1603 before James I and his court at Wilton House, no critical or historical record of the play is known from the time it was entered in the Stationers' Register until the beginning of the eighteenth century. In 1710, Charles Gildon raised in his brief remarks several thematic and technical issues that were to assume fundamental importance in *As You Like It* studies, such as the questions of verisimilitude and probability in the play, Shakespeare's depiction of art and nature, his adaptation of his sources, the contrasting worlds of court and country, Duke Senior's "moral reflections," and the depiction, meaning, and function of time in the play. Gildon found *As You Like It* generally satisfying, singling out for special praise both Oliver's "artful and natural" management of the provoking of Charles the wrestler and Touchstone's metaphor of rotting humankind through the passage of time. Nearly four decades later, William Warburton initiated the aesthetic study of the comedy's sources with his close analysis of the sense and origin of Touchstone's description of the degrees of polite quarrelling. Richard Hurd, Warburton's contemporary, also studied the sources of *As You Like It,* finding in Torquato Tasso's works the model for the play's conventional pastoral details. Concentrating on the drama's

form, characters, and language, Samuel Johnson regretted that Shakespeare lost the opportunity to draw a moral lesson from the reported dialogue between "the usurper and the hermit." Nevertheless, Johnson praised the play's "very sprightly" comic language and called its story "wild and pleasing."

Later in the eighteenth century, Francis Gentleman noted that, although "there is not a more agreeable piece on the stage," *As You Like It* ends imperfectly and includes an "invasion" of the Aristotelian and other unities—specifically, those rigid principles of dramatic structure involving action, time, and setting so fundamental to Neoclassical doctrine. Approaching the play as essentially didactic, Elizabeth Griffith concentrated almost exclusively on the "moral" subjects it treats, citing and praising passages that exemplify such virtues as affection, gratitude, nobility, honesty, and love. Most notably, she commended Adam's example of the "virtue and sobriety of the antient Peasantry of England" and extolled the banished duke's contrast between "sincere country life" and "false city life." Several years later, William Richardson initiated the critical study of the characters in *As You Like It* with his close evaluation of Jaques's manner, temper, and psychological motivation. Finding the figure at once "solitary and morose" and "strongly disposed to compassion," Richardson—mirroring a major interest of his age—praised the way Jaques's keen remarks and shrewd observation instruct and amuse. The critic also argued that it is through adverse circumstances, and not by natural inclination, that Jaques turns melancholic and disgusted by all those forms of enjoyment he cannot share. Toward the end of the century, Walter Whiter—in the first extended commentary on *As You Like It*—helped pioneer the exploration of Shakespeare's imagination by examining idiosyncratic linkings in the play. Applying historical, aesthetic, interpretive, and what he called "associative" techniques to his study of the passage containing Orlando's "indirect" allusions to Helen, Cleopatra, Atalanta, and Lucretia (III. ii. 145-48), Whiter argued that Shakespeare's imagery here derived not from "abstract consideration of general qualities," but from his visual impressions of the principal traits of these four women derived from the tapestry or pictorial renderings popular during the sixteenth century and earlier.

The early years of the nineteenth century saw not only the advancement and revaluation of the existing issues in *As You Like It* criticism, but also the beginning and evolution of several new approaches to the play. A major nineteenth-century commentator, the German critic August Wilhelm Schlegel, regarded *As You Like It* as romantic drama, a genre separate from but equal to the ancient genres of tragedy and comedy. Anticipating an interest of later critics, among them George Daniel and Hippolyte A. Taine, Schlegel discussed the play's subordination of plot and action to dialogue, maintaining that "what is done is not so essential as what is said." Prefiguring a significant twentieth-century concern, he also argued that, "of all the human passions, love alone has found an entrance" into Arden. Narrowing his focus, he praised the pastoral ideal in the comedy, singling out the "natural shepherds and shepherdesses" as examples of the "native inhabitants" that populate the "shady, dark-green landscape" of the forest. Schlegel's contemporary, the English critic Samuel Taylor Coleridge, admired both the "beauty" and suggestiveness of Oliver's use of the word "boy" in addressing Orlando in Act I, Scene i, and, detecting a possible lack of verisimilitude—a "want of truth to nature"—he described Oliver's evaluation of Orlando (I. i. 163-73) as "one of the most un-Shakespearean speeches in all (the genuine works of) Shakespeare." Also early in the nineteenth century, William Hazlitt commented on the plot, setting, structure, and characters, noting, like Schlegel, the play's subordination of "actions and situations" to "sentiments and characters." Hazlitt also discussed Jaques and Touchstone; he called the former "the only purely contemplative character" in Shakespeare's works, and the latter he regarded as part ancient philosopher, part buffoon, who "turns folly into wit, and wit into folly."

Throughout the nineteenth century, critics repeatedly addressed the issue of Jaques's character and psychological motivation; chief among their interests was the genuineness of his melancholy. Hazlitt concurred with Richardson's description of the character as solitary, morose, beneficent, and "addicted to social enjoyment." This remained the common view of Jaques until it was challenged by William Maginn in 1837. Maginn described the melancholy Jaques as "a dresser forth in sweet language of . . . ordinary common-places" and claimed that his happiest days are those in the forest. Shortly thereafter, Hermann Ulrici, a German critic noted for his Christian aesthetics, contended that Jaques is best regarded as a "comic, foolish character," who, unlike Touchstone, is profoundly superficial. In another original view, G. G. Gervinus disputed the assumption that Jaques's melancholy is "mild, human, and attractive," asserting instead that it is "rooted in bitterness and ill-humour." Like Ulrici, Charles Cowden Clarke characterized Jaques not as a melancholiac, but as "tinged with the *affectation* of melancholy," a "satire upon your pretenders to wisdom." H. N. Hudson passed no judgment on the genuineness of Jaques's melancholy, but, like Richardson, detected in him both a fondness for solitude and an interest in society. In addition, Hudson concluded that Jaques's melancholy is not malignant, but is the product of self-love and "an excess of generative virtue." Later in the century, Edward Dowden found no "real melancholy" in the play at all, calling Jaques "self-indulgent" and "no more than a curious experimenter in libertinism." Denton J. Snider, like some of his predecessors, suspected that Jaques affects the misanthropic role he chooses to play "to the bitter end." Frederick S. Boas shared Dowden's conclusion, pointing to Jaques's "ennui" amidst a "flux of sensations." One of the nineteenth-century's last commentators on Jaques, the Danish critic George Brandes, synthesized his predecessors' remarks. Describing Jaques's melancholy as "a poetic dreaminess," a "bitterness [that] springs from a too tender sensibility," Brandes nevertheless warned against taking Jaques's dark behavior too seriously. This concentration on Jaques's "too tender sensibility" rather than the genuineness of his melancholy anticipated a major twentieth-century approach to the character.

Touchstone's role was also one of the leading topics in nineteenth-century criticism of *As You Like It*. Hazlitt, the first to comment on Touchstone's dramatic function, saw him not only as a stock fool, but also as the possessor of a privileged insight arising from the conflation of wit and folly. Likewise, Maginn also praised this character's worldly wisdom. Ulrici called Touchstone the play's "merry fool," claiming that he alone knows his mind throughout the drama and, unlike Jaques, shows "a truly noble disinterestedness and fidelity." Similarly, Gervinus described Touchstone as "a fool of a somewhat more elevated nature" than Shakespeare's earlier fools, adding that this humorous figure provided the dramatist with the means to comment ironically on the play's pastoral ideal. Later in the century, Charles Cowden Clarke contended that Touchstone is "not in the least a buffoon"; the critic added that the motley figure shows "genuine qualities of affection" and is able "to

draw truth and beauty, as well as fine humour, out of passing life." Following Gervinus's suggestion, Boas maintained that Touchstone serves to temper the "lusciousness of the conventional pastoral" with the "acid flavour" of his wit.

Another critical issue raised in the nineteenth century, which was more fully developed in the twentieth, concerns Rosalind's characterization. Among the early commentators, George Daniel described Rosalind as "gentle and confiding." In a more rigorous assessment, Anna Brownell Jameson analyzed Rosalind as both a dramatic character and a woman. Finding her less forceful than Beatrice in *Much Ado about Nothing,* but a superior female, Jameson claimed that she possesses more of the feminine qualities than Beatrice and that her pastoral surroundings offer her more scope to exhibit her womanly traits. In a similar reading, Clarke admired Rosalind's "womanly vivacity," comparing her as well to Beatrice in *Much Ado*. Brandes also discussed Rosalind, comparing her "gaiety without a sting" with Beatrice's "rapier" wit. Lastly, Bernard Shaw not only found Rosalind's language and character both admirable and appropriate, but also praised her aggressive approach to love.

Shakespeare's presentation of Arden and the pastoral ideal in *As You Like It*—first studied in detail in the mid-eighteenth century by Richard Hurd—was another major concern of nineteenth-century critics. Schlegel merely referred to it as the "shady, dark-green landscape" inhabited by "ideal and natural shepherds and shepherdesses," while Hazlitt described the Forest of Arden as a place infused with "a spirit of philosophical poetry." In his source study of *As You Like It*, Gervinus contended that "on the whole, Shakespeare has completely eradicated the pastoral mannerisms" of his major source. Unlike his predecessors, Gervinus considered the play close to ordinary reality, adding that Arden's scenery serves to attune the reader's imagination "gently and tenderly." Similarly, Hippolyte A. Taine described the forest as "a fit spot in which to listen to love-talk" and commended the pastoral setting chiefly for the way it adds to the play's "illusion and charm." In one of the century's more innovative readings of *As You Like It*, Denton J. Snider objected to labelling the play a pastoral, maintaining that Shakespeare intended to show the limitations of pastoralism. This view, taken up by several twentieth-century critics, was shared near the end of the nineteenth century by Boas, who not only saw Touchstone's "acid" wit as a foil to pastoral conventions, but also regarded the natives of Arden as part of Shakespeare's contrasting parodies of town and country life.

Often related to the pastoralism issue, critical consideration of the play's fantastic tone and numerous improbabilities—first raised in the eighteenth century by Gildon—continued throughout most of the nineteenth century, although in time the discussion centered slightly less on such issues as the appropriateness, or "naturalness," of the play's characters and incidents than on their dramatic function and complementary relationships. As noted above, Coleridge examined Oliver's description of Orlando in Act I, Scene i for its apparent "want of truth to nature." Maginn, noting the play's fantastic and improbable elements which troubled so many eighteenth-century commentators, asserted that nothing was wrong with the presence of "a tropical lion and a serpent" in Arden, suggesting that "all the prodigies spawned in Africa" might be found in a forest inhabited by Rosalind, Touchstone, and Jaques. Later, Ulrici, pointing to a "decided preponderance of the fanciful element in *As You Like It*," stated that Shakespeare did not intend to portray ''ordinary reality'' in Arden. Rather, he continued, in presenting a ''mirror of irony and humour'' that exhibits ''the eternal order of things,'' primarily through the dialectical reversal of the characters' fortunes, Shakespeare was providing ''a view of life taken from a peculiar poetic position.'' In contrast, Gervinus considered the play close to ordinary reality, claiming that it ''only borders on the limits of the fantastical.'' During the remainder of the nineteenth century, the debate over the play's fantastic nature was not prominent in *As You Like It* criticism. However, it was revived in the twentieth century with, among other issues, the discussion of Shakespeare's use of disguise in the play.

Searching *As You Like It* for evidence of Shakespeare's own life and thought also constituted a notable, if limited, current in nineteenth-century criticism of the play. In a brief autobiographical assessment, Daniel claimed that Orlando and Adam's ''divine lesson of humanity'' must have come from ''the sentiment in [Shakespeare's] own bosom.'' Similarly, Taine not only described Jaques as Shakespeare's ''transparent mask,'' but also argued that such lines as ''the shade of melancholy boughs'' (II. vii. 111-12) express the dramatist's ''delicate soul, bruised by the shocks of social life.'' Dowden disputed the view that *As You Like It* was ''an early attempt by [Shakespeare] to control the dark spirit of melancholy in himself,'' offering instead his own theory that the play reflects the dramatist's ''repose'' from ''the trumpet-tones'' of his earlier histories. Later, Brandes regarded the play's pastoral setting as Shakespeare's expression of his longing ''to get away from the unnatural city life,'' and, like Taine, he perceived in Jaques evidence that Shakespeare, in moods of humorous melancholy, must have felt as though he himself were ''one of his jesters.'' Although confined for the most part to the nineteenth century, the autobiographical assessment of *As You Like It* can also be discerned in the studies of such twentieth-century critics as E. K. Chambers and Warren Staebler.

Several other issues in nineteenth-century criticism of *As You Like It* are noteworthy. One of these is the question of the play's dramatic deficiencies, an issue first raised in the eighteenth century by Francis Gentleman. Anticipating the stance of the twentieth-century critic Arthur Quiller-Couch, Algernon Charles Swinburne, writing in 1880, regretted Shakespeare's ''unlucky slip of the brush'' in putting stage conventions ahead of moral beauty and spiritual harmony by marrying Oliver to Celia. Similarly, Bernard Shaw found the play didactically inadequate and aesthetically lazy, criticizing, among other faults, Shakespeare's ''missed chance'' in not developing the ''pregnant metaphor'' of Jaques's ''Seven Ages of Man'' speech (II. vii. 139-66). Shaw also ridiculed the ''canting, snivelling, hypocritical unctuousness'' following Orlando's description of time in Act II, Scene vii. Nevertheless, he maintained that ''the fascination of *As You Like It* is still very great'' and, anticipating several twentieth-century critics, praised the prose in the play, particularly the ''energy of exposition'' in the opening act. In addition to its plot deficiencies, nineteenth-century critics also evaluated the thematics and structure of *As You Like It*. As mentioned earlier, Ulrici identified the comedy's ''ground idea'' in its ironical or dialectical presentation of ''the eternal order of things''—the fact that although the characters do just what they like, God's ''harmony and law'' ensure that discordant elements eventually ''destroy themselves'' and all things turn out right. Gervinus discerned the play's central ''moral'' in its depiction of the power of ''self-mastery, equanimity, and self-control'' to withstand ''outward suffering and inward passion.'' Later in the century, Henry A. Clapp and Horace How-

ard Furness advanced separately their views of dramatic time in *As You Like It*. On internal evidence alone, both critics found the play's progress of time logical and consistent, although Furness noted that Shakespeare employed a ''double time'' scheme in the opening acts of his play in order to overcome certain dramatic problems his source story presented. Concerning the structure of *As You Like It*, Snider, prefiguring the twentieth-century scholar G. K. Hunter, postulated that the comedy follows three distinct movements involving separation, mediation, and return—what he termed as the ''Real World of Wrong,'' the ''Idyllic Realm,'' and the ''restored Real World of Right.'' Snider added that within these movements operate ''threads'' or elements of action, all of which are brought together by the theme of love.

Critics of the twentieth century continued addressing many of the same issues outlined above, reevaluating previous assumptions and focusing more intently on such concerns as Shakespeare's pastoral ideal in *As You Like It*, the themes of love and self-knowledge, and the significance of Rosalind's disguise. One of the first reappraisals was that of the melancholy Jaques. On largely historical grounds, Elmer Edgar Stoll argued in his study of 1906 that Jaques is a specific type of malcontent. Calling him ''a professional cynic and censor'' who moves about in the ''professional garb of cynicism and melancholy,'' Stoll saw affinities between Shakespeare's character and other Elizabethan malcontents, especially John Marston's Malevole, and he posited a direct relationship between them. Several years later, Oscar James Campbell disputed Stoll's argument, contending that Jaques is not modeled on the conventional figure of the malcontent, but is ''an amusing representative of the English satirists who wrote from 1590 to 1600''—a ''satirically drawn portrait of a familiar dramatic type'' characterized by a ''moderately adust temperament'' and phlegmatic constitution. Campbell's view was similar to that voiced a few years earlier by J. B. Priestley, who called Jaques ''the pure seeker after sensations'' and noted that, among the character's genuine defects, his ''sickly mind'' and ''hardness of the chronic querulous invalid'' are prominent. However, Priestley justified Jaques's melancholic behavior by stating that his ''whimsical self-indulgence'' accords well with the antics of the other characters. Offering yet another approach, G. F. Bradby maintained that Shakespeare initially created Jaques as a foil to the romantic characters in *As You Like It*, but then used him without much regard for consistency. Bradby also detected in the figure elements of the ''travelled *poseur*'' and stated that he invariably talks nonsense, ''as is befitting in a comedy.'' Several years later, echoing Bradby's argument, Z. S. Fink attributed Jaques's cynicism to his many peregrinations, adding that, unlike the usual traveler in sixteenth-century literature, Jaques is not crudely drawn, but is transformed by Shakespeare into a more humane figure. Likewise, Thomas Marc Parrott considered Jaques an example of a malcontent traveler-type, but claimed that Shakespeare individualized him by making him a traveler who sneers at all things English. Arguing, like Bradby, that Jaques is essentially a poseur, Enid Welsford regarded the character as the play's superficial critic of society, a self-indulgent commentator whose critical function both complements and contrasts with Touchstone's truly impartial role. Mark Van Doren similarly considered Jaques's melancholy indicative of vanity and self-love that serves ''none of wisdom's purposes.'' In 1949, Warren Staebler opposed this growing perception of Jaques as a superficial figure, maintaining that the character is free of malice and suspicion, and that he is ''a philosopher with the true philosopher's detachment toward things.'' Unlike many of the earlier critics, especially those of the nineteenth century, S. C. Sen Gupta argued that Jaques's dark temperament is not an affectation, but is essential to his character. In addition, the critic averred that Jaques's melancholy is integral to the play, in that it tempers the romantic view of Duke Senior and Rosalind and thus provides a broader perspective on life. Most subsequent commentators have similarly regarded the melancholic Jaques as providing a critical perspective on—or, at least, a balance to—the romantic and pastoral ideals presented in *As You Like It.*

Closely related to the question of the nature and role of Jaques's melancholy in the play is the issue of Touchstone's significance and function. During the twentieth century, commentators rarely shared the nineteenth century's interest in this character's personal attributes, but considered instead the larger question of his place within Shakespeare's presentation of wisdom and folly. Commenting on the fool's comic purpose, Arthur Quiller-Couch described Touchstone as "piquantly out of place, while most picturesquely in place" with respect to his forest surroundings; he also stressed Touchstone's function as a "critic" of the play's pastoral conventions. Priestley, contrasting Jaques as the "cynical-sentimental-moralistic chorus" in the drama with Touchstone as the "comic chorus," noted that both of these characters observe and mock the main action. But Priestley added that since Touchstone, though external to the main action, does not completely detach himself from his fellow human beings, he is a better critic than Jaques. During the next fifty years, several commentators, including P. V. Kreider, Thomas Marc Parrott, S. C. Sen Gupta, Helen Gardner, Harold Jenkins, J. Dover Wilson, and Jan Kott, continued to describe Touchstone as the detached critic of the comedy. In addition, others augmented or revised this view. In an important discussion of folly and wisdom in *As You Like It,* Welsford called Touchstone an intermediary between the playwright and the audience; she argued that he is literally what his name implies: a test of the quality of people and manners. As a privileged truth-teller, Welsford continued, Touchstone is Shakespeare's critical spokesman on prevailing literary fashion and, thanks to his occasional cutting quality, saves the narrative from inanity. Some atypical and less favorable assessments of Touchstone have also been voiced in modern commentary on *As You Like It.* Writing in 1951, Harold C. Goddard regarded the character as neither wise nor witty, describing him as callous, profane, and condescending. More recently, Patrick Swinden argued that both Jaques and Touchstone express a "reductive humor" and an exaggerated attachment to the critical mode. Although Swinden noted that the fool is the only other character beside Rosalind to see "things from two points of view simultaneously," unlike her he is unable to affirm these opposing perspectives, and thus "the two sides of his nature remain polarized." Perhaps the most innovative approach to Touchstone in the present century is that of Robert Wilcher, who placed the character at the center of what he calls the play's "double-act routine." Describing Touchstone as the first act's "sustaining jester to the nobility," Wilcher contended that the fool is unable to cope with the "total licence" of the pastoral world in Arden, mismanaging his role as a jester in two significant encounters: those with Corin and William. Wilcher concluded that Touchstone remains out of place until the play's end, where the return to court signals as well a return of the fool's proper role.

One of the major concerns of twentieth-century commentary on *As You Like It* has been the study of the play's pastoral setting and its treatment of the pastoral ideal in general. Early

in the century, E. K. Chambers described Arden as a restorative, "a spiritual force, bringing medicine to the hurt souls of men," an assessment echoed in various forms by many subsequent commentators. Like Snider and Boas in the nineteenth century, Walter W. Greg maintained that in *As You Like It* Shakespeare passes judgment on, and reveals his opinion of, the pastoral ideal. He claimed that Shakespeare created from conventional material three types of pastoral characters: "courtly characters" like Rosalind and Celia; "polished Arcadians of pastoral tradition," including Phebe and Silvius; and such "farcical rustics" as Audrey and William, who exhibit "inimitable humanity." Arguing that Shakespeare here uses pastoralism chiefly as "a delicate colouring, an old-world fragrance," Greg further averred that the dramatist depicts the genre as "unsuited in its evanescent charm to be the serious business of art and life." P. V. Kreider also divided the play's "pastoral folk" into three groups, but, unlike Greg, related them closely to their satirical functions within the pastoral tradition. Noting pastoral life's "literary and social trumpery," Kreider suggested that Shakespeare managed in *As You Like It* both to expose the conventional material's falsity and preserve his comedy's integrity. In partial contrast to Kreider, Mark Van Doren regarded the play as "a criticism of the pastoral sentiment," but he asserted that it is not a satire, for "its examination is conducted without prejudice." C. L. Barber, in his influential study of 1942, agreed that the comic humor of *As You Like It* is not satirical or critical of the play's pastoral and romantic ideals, saying that it is "precisely the reverse of satire" in its contribution of a broader perspective. Near the middle of the century, Helen Gardner offered a new perception of Arden. Claiming that the forest is not entirely amiable, she argued that, like Lear's place of exile in *King Lear,* Arden is a place where bitter lessons can be learned, not a "place where . . . roses are without their thorns."

The view of Arden as a testing-ground, a world which fosters the characters' self-knowledge and sexual awareness even promoting those human values that form the foundation of life, has been addressed by nearly all subsequent commentators on *As You Like It.* Essentially initiated in 1949 by Staebler, this assessment often involves—as Chambers and others suggested in another context—the forest's nurturing effect on its inhabitants. Staebler averred that the forest's "at-oneness," its "humanizing, harmonizing influence"—in short, its "magical power"—promotes self-knowledge and thus heals Duke Frederick and Oliver of their villainy. Likewise, Geoffrey Bush argued that Arden is a place where self-knowledge is both possible and desirable, claiming that it acts as "a natural persuasion that leads us first to ourselves and then . . . to one another." In his essay on love's ordering principle in the forest, John Russell Brown noted that Arden is hardly the golden Arcadia we might expect, since there, as at the court, "content" or peace of mind can only be achieved through a character's proper acceptance of life. In his analysis of Shakespeare's depiction of time in *As You Like It,* Jay L. Halio described Arden as a timeless world, a refuge where past and present merge and people flourish. Jan Kott, in one of the most pessimistic or nihilistic readings of *As You Like It,* called Arden "Shakespeare's Bitter Arcadia," a place where lovers go through "the dark sphere of animal eroticism." He added that the dramatist both "makes mockery of Arcadia" and his pastoral romance and demonstrates the necessity of such ideals as Arden represents. In his study of 1970, D. J. Palmer argued that the forest represents nature as art; according to the critic, Arden functions within the play as an unreal pastoral world having the properties of both a teacher and a restorer of nature's equilibrium, for "those who enter there, and encounter each other under its auspices, are cast by reflection into their natural roles." Albert R. Cirillo, like Halio, emphasized the mythic quality of Shakespeare's forest, maintaining that Arden acts as a "second world" or fiction which most of the characters enter temporarily and from which they emerge with a new, revitalized perspective on life. Stressing the subjectivity and relativity of the Arden forest, noting how it changes "in each contact with a separate imagination," David Young declared that it is also a source of self-knowledge in the play: it "gives back to its inhabitants and visitors the images of their own selves and preoccupations." In his comment on the juxtaposed views of time in *As You Like It,* Alexander Leggatt described Arden as a place where "old values," such as those of Adam, can be recovered and where time can be temporarily cheated of its sting through the establishment of a new order.

More recent discussions of Shakespeare's presentation of Arden and the pastoral ideal in *As You Like It* have been offered by Elliot Krieger, Louis Adrian Montrose, Alice-Lyle Scoufos, and Peter Erickson. In his Marxist reading of the comedy, Krieger disputed the view that Arden promotes self-discovery among the characters, averring instead that Shakespeare's forest exists only as a "style" projected by his courtiers out of their own subjective desires. Krieger determined that the aristocracy used its own vision of nature—what he termed its "second-world strategy"—to "justify its freedom from labour and the subordination of . . . other social classes." Examining the issue of primogeniture in *As You Like It,* Montrose claimed that Arden "miraculously assuages" tensions in the "nuclear family and in the body politic," that it depicts brotherhood as the ideal of social as well as sibling male relationships, and that it reaffirms fatherhood as a positive, nurturing force. Scoufos described the forest as an "Eden made harsh by post-Lapsarian Nature," a place for love's development and fruition, and she traced as evidence of its powers the transformation of Orlando, as a result of his experience there, from an unwise, violent man into one with proven fidelity, virtue, and courage. Lastly, Erickson, like Montrose, stressed the masculine, nurturing force of Arden, but, unlike the earlier critic, contended that Shakespeare's forest is based on "an idealized male community" and that the play itself is primarily a defensive work against female power rather than a celebration of it in the figure of Rosalind.

The theme of love in *As You Like It*—also linked with the issue of self-knowledge, but usually discussed in relation to Rosalind's characterization—has also received a considerable amount of attention from twentieth-century critics. In 1905, Stopford A. Brooke identified "many forms" of love in the comedy, emphasizing most the passion "between man and woman." He described three versions of this kind of "enchanted" love: that of Rosalind and Orlando, who are "kindled into brightness" by love; Celia and Oliver's "swift, mutual passion, more of the senses than the soul"; and Silvius and Phebe's "conventional love of the Elizabethan Pastoral." Half a century later, Harold C. Goddard argued that Shakespeare's central concern in *As You Like It* is "the relation of love and wisdom"—specifically, that "true love" imparts "true wisdom" and that knowledge or learning without love is barren. Goddard considered Rosalind the "instrument" of this idea, claiming that she, more than any other character, combines "wit with love" and, in her "reconciliation of opposites," demonstrates the ability of love to provide insight and to increase "the wisdom of the race." As mentioned above, John Russell Brown focused as well on love's ordering principle in the comedy,

identifying Rosalind as the source of the play's "generosity and confidence." Brown added that the heroine, in her role as an exponent of "love's doubts and faith, love's obedience and freedom," prevents Shakespeare's ideal of love's ordering power from being merely a cold theorem in the drama. G. K. Hunter, like Goddard, linked the themes of self-knowledge and love in his commentary on *As You Like It,* stating that the principal characters "face the deviations of folly" with "an air of effortless superiority" because of their "humanely poised love" and the self-awareness such love engenders. Hunter considered Rosalind "the central and normative figure" in this design, the only one able to affirm the centrality of absurd love to human experience. In a related reading, Peter G. Phialas claimed that *As You Like It* explores the concept of self-awareness and that it expresses, through Rosalind, a balanced view of the ideals of romantic love and "the realism of the working-day world."

Other twentieth-century scholars who have discussed the importance of love in *As You Like It,* either in relation to Rosalind's characterization or to the theme of self-knowledge, include Patrick Swinden, Alexander Leggatt, Alice-Lyle Scoufos, and Robert Kimbrough. In his examination of the manner in which Shakespeare structured his play through the interaction of various viewpoints, Swinden maintained that Rosalind—in part because of her disguise—possesses the greatest ability for synthesizing both the skeptical and the romantic attitudes toward love. Again, focusing on Shakespeare's juxtaposition of various "styles" and attitudes in *As You Like It,* Leggatt asserted that the play's final impression resides not in these comic dislocations, but in Rosalind herself, a fact dramatized when the heroine turns from the conventions of satire to those of romantic love—both of which she incorporated in her role as Ganymede—and moves to synthesize the ceremonial and the practical in the act of the final marriages. As previously noted, Scoufos examined the theme of love's testing in *As You Like It,* stressing the Platonic nature of Shakespeare's presentation of love in the play and concluding that as Orlando learns to channel his energy into proper, selfless action, "the cosmic forces return tenfold the frail harmony established in Arden by human love." Kimbrough, in his study of sexual disguise in the comedy, concluded that the "magic" Rosalind employs "to make all this matter even" in the final moments of the play is love.

Another major issue in twentieth-century commentary on *As You Like It* is the relation of Rosalind's sexual disguise to Shakespeare's thematic concerns. Interest in this issue was enhanced for many commentators because of the fact that in Shakespeare's Elizabethan theater boy actors were employed in women's roles, thereby complicating further the multiple identities Rosalind assumes. In his 1937 essay on *As You Like It,* Elmer Edgar Stoll was among the first commentators to examine fully Shakespeare's use here of the disguise convention. Stoll pointed out how the play's concern with romantic love is "facilitated by the conventions of disguise and impersonation," adding that the Rosalind/Ganymede device not only enriches the narrative, but also broadens its emotional range. It was not until the 1960s and 1970s that the study of Shakespeare's disguise convention was revived and given greater attention. Calling Rosalind's impersonation a "dangerous game," Jan Kott explored its overtones of eroticism, orgy, and "chaos," and its "double significance" of the intellectual and the sensual. He also argued that disguise contributes to the play's impression of concurrent falseness and genuineness, of illusion and reality. As previously stated, Peter G. Phialas underscored the importance of Rosalind's disguise to Shakespeare's themes of self-knowledge and love, claiming that the device not only accounts for the richness of the heroine's role, but that it also enables her to take on different points of view simultaneously and to bring about the final synthesis of the play's chief ideas. Discussing Shakespeare's "alliance" of the artificial and the natural in *As You Like It*, Palmer declared that these two realms confront each other in the play at a number of different levels, but perhaps most visibly in Rosalind's disguise as Ganymede. Albert R. Cirillo examined Rosalind's role in the comedy in relation to the Arcadian experience itself, asserting that it is through her "mythical generic" disguise that the "magic circle" of Arden takes effect. Focusing on Rosalind's "kaleidoscopic identity," Hugh M. Richmond investigated Elizabethan stage conventions and argued that Rosalind—through her successive roles as herself, as Ganymede, as Ganymede playing herself, as herself again, and finally, in the play's epilogue, as the boy actor—not only gains insight into male psychology, but also reflects the comedy's concern with "the interaction between the conscious mind with its emotional drives and the physiological equipment with which it finds itself arbitrarily endowed." In his study of Shakespeare's comic juxtapositions in *As You Like It*, as previously mentioned, Alexander Leggatt considered Rosalind's "genuinely liberating" disguise one of the principal means by which the dramatist exploits his play's comic effect, as well as the technique by which he establishes, then rejects, the satiric view of love. In yet another reading, Nancy K. Hayles averred that Rosalind's disguise expresses the heroine's right to be herself, not Orlando's idealized fantasy of her. Hayles added that, in separate movements involving disguise's "layering-on" and "layering-off," conflict and reconciliation are respectively created, leading to the resolution of the "traditional tension beneath the needs of the female and the desires of the male." Elliot Krieger regarded sexual disguise in *As You Like It* as Rosalind's own form of "style" which she subjectively creates and projects onto the outside world, allowing her to act as if she controls her own emotions and those of others. The heroine's example, Krieger continued, mirrors the play's overriding proposition that material problems may be solved by translating external conditions into stylistic propositions, thus transcending, or at least transforming, the material world. Objecting to Hayles's argument, Robert Kimbrough stated that Rosalind's disguise allows her to grow into her "fuller human self"; the critic added that Rosalind's androgyny makes her wit "in essence and choice . . . both masculine and feminine . . . [and] therefore, more fully human than a gender designation would indicate." Finally, in his discussion of Shakespeare's depiction of "an idealized male community" in *As You Like It*, Peter Erickson countered a number of prevailing views of Rosalind's disguise. Most importantly, he contended that in her role as Ganymede, Rosalind never integrates the male-female perspectives, as some commentators claim, but always remains aware that she, as a woman, must eventually yield her temporary control to Orlando and the duke if she is to fulfill her love. Erickson also asserted that it is not Rosalind who experiences the benefits of androgyny in the play, for she must eventually surrender her male characteristics, but the courtiers of the duke's banished kingdom, who in creating their ideal community permanently adopt feminine nurturing tendencies, such as gentleness, pity, and love.

Two other major concerns of modern critics of *As You Like It* are the play's language and its structural design. Concerning the former, Arthur Quiller-Couch was among the first commentators to discuss what he called the "false sparkle," the "dull, level, chop-logic repetitive rhythm" of the dialogue between Rosalind and Celia in the play's opening act. Quiller-Couch attributed the weakness of the language here to the likelihood that Shakespeare, "impatient . . . and ardent for Arden," did not give Act I much attention. On the other hand, Stoll, in his 1937 essay on *As You Like It*, commended Rosalind's language throughout the play, especially what he referred to as the "untrammelled liberties of wording" of her prose passages. In a digression from his examination of Arden's harmonizing influence and the characters in *As You Like It*, Warren Staebler praised the comedy's prose, identifying as its principal qualities "warmth," "luminousness," and "earthy substantiality." Thomas Marc Parrott attributed the play's success less to its action than its speech, maintaining that in this work Shakespeare's "free and . . . almost careless mastery of language" surpasses that of most of his earlier comedies. Parrott also lauded the excellence of Rosalind's prose as one element exhibiting "the happy and carefree ease" of the entire play. In 1951, Milton Crane continued the study of Shakespeare's use of prose and verse in *As You Like It*, noting that although prose is the norm here, the two maintain a close balance. According to Crane, verse is for "scenes of higher emotional tension, for the idyllic atmosphere of the forest," for "Jaques's moralizing and melancholy reflections, and for the burlesqued pastoral amours of Phebe and Silvius." Prose, on the other hand, is the play's "normal, flexible, and colloquial mode of speech," most often used to undercut the pastoral linguistic conventions of the romantic characters. More recently, Patrick Swinden has put forth a similar assessment of the comedy's "verbal strategies," stating that prose functions as a corrective to the occasional "inflated and vulnerable romantic verse."

One of the leading discussions of Shakespeare's structure and dramatic technique in *As You Like It* is that of C. L. Barber. Barber introduced a new approach to the study of the play, claiming that it is less a comedy than a romance with comic accompaniment and that its humor not only provides pleasure, but also implements a wider awareness. He added that this comic humor is in no manner critical or evaluative of the play's pastoral and romantic ideals, but that it serves only to balance the one-sidedness of these conventional views of life. Since 1960, a host of other critics have addressed the issue of Shakespeare's dramatic technique in *As You Like It*. Bertrand Evans assessed what he calls discrepant awarenesses in the comedy—points in the action where the characters, or the characters and the audience, possess conflicting levels of perception. He concluded that although this technique is not so complex or extensive here as in Shakespeare's other comedies—he noted, in fact, instances where the device is initiated but never developed—it does exert a crucial influence on the plot at one point, namely, the scenes between Rosalind and Orlando in Arden, leading to the so-called wooing episode in Act IV, Scene i. Recalling Denton J. Snider in the nineteenth century, G. K. Hunter divided *As You Like It* into separate movements: he described Act I as a simple escape from evil, while the central episodes he identified as a series of contrasting attitudes toward love and the pastoral ideal; the final movement, Hunter concluded, begins with Shakespeare's introduction of the Masque of Hymen, which both resolves the previous confusions and suggests the presence of a life force behind Rosalind's "control" over the other characters. A number of modern critics—such as Barber, Harold Jenkins, Peter G. Phialas, Patrick Swinden, and Alexander Leggatt—have maintained that the overriding structural design of *As You Like It* is based on a synthesis or balance of antithetical, conflicting styles and viewpoints.

One recent commentator, D. J. Palmer, has disputed this thesis, claiming that the relationship of the artificial and the natural at every level in the play—that of the characters, the Arden forest, Rosalind's disguise, and so on—is not antithetical or conflicting, but is "an alliance in which each justifies the other."

As the above review indicates, many of the interpretive problems in *As You Like It* criticism have not received what might be termed definitive solutions. It is clear, however, that while there is little consensus on the play's more troubling aspects, most commentators agree that *As You Like It* is one of Shakespeare's most successful comedies, even though it is often difficult to explain exactly why. Toward the end of the nineteenth century, Edward Dowden could have spoken for most of his predecessors when he claimed, "Upon the whole, *As You Like It* is the sweetest and happiest of all Shakespeare's comedies." Since Dowden's time, that assessment has met with few detractors, and it is telling that Bernard Shaw, who brought all his pejorative wit to bear on the play, could only conclude that "the fascination of *As You Like It* still is very great."

---

**[CHARLES GILDON]**   (essay date 1710)

*[Gildon was the first critic to write extended commentary on the entire Shakespearean dramatic canon. Like many other neoclassicists, he regarded Shakespeare as an imaginative playwright who nevertheless frequently violated the dramatic "rules" necessary for correct writing. In the following excerpt, Gildon shows an interest in versimilitude in* As You Like It *by admiring Oliver's management of the provoking of Charles against Orlando in Act I, Scene ii., calling it both "artful and natural." Anticipating the moral interpretations of many later critics, Gildon also notices the "moral reflections" in Duke Senior's speech at the beginning of Act II, and he further comments on time in the play, noting especially Jaques's account of Touchstone's metaphor of rotting humankind at II. vii. 20-33.]*

[The story of *As You Like It*] has nothing Dramatic in it, yet *Shakespear* has made as good use of it as possible.

The Scene betwixt *Orlando* and his Brother *Oliver* in the opening of the Play is well manag'd, discovering something, that goes before in the Quarrel between them; and *Oliver's* Management of the provoking *Charles* the Wrestler against *Orlando* is artful and natural. . . .

The old Dukes Speech [in II. i.] preferring that Solitude to the World is full of moral Reflections. . . . That Pleasantry [at II. vii. 20-33] of the different Motion of Time is [also] worth remarking. And *Rosalinda's* Character of a Man in Love [in III. ii.] is very pretty. (p. 326)

> [Charles Gildon], "Remarks on the Plays of Shakespear," in The Works of Mr. William Shakespear, Vol. 7, 1710. Reprint by AMS Press, Inc., 1967, pp. 325-26.

**WILLIAM WARBURTON**   (essay date 1747)

*[Warburton, a controversial eighteenth-century English theologian and literary scholar, edited the works of Alexander Pope and William Shakespeare. His edition of Shakespeare, based primarily on the work of Lewis Theobald, contained many unsub-*

*stantiated and questionable emendations. Because of this, subsequent scholars severely criticized and generally rejected his work. However, Warburton did contribute a few significant textual emendations which are accepted by scholars today. In the following excerpt from the "Comments and Notes, Critical and Explanatory" to his* The Works of Shakespeare in Eight Volumes *(1747), Warburton posits a source for Touchstone's description of the "degrees" of polite quarrelling at V. iv. 90-103 of* As You Like It, *locating in this passage verbal, syntactical, and sense parallels to Vincentio Saviolo's* Of Honour and Honourable Quarrels *(1594).]*

The Poet has, in [*As You Like It*, V. iv. 90-103], rallied the mode of formal dueling then so prevalent with the highest humour and address; nor could he have treated it with a happier contempt than by making his *Clown* so knowing in the forms and preliminaries of it. The particular book . . . alluded to [at V. iv. 90] is a very ridiculous treatise of one *Vincentio Saviolo*, intitled *Of honour and honourable quarrels*. . . , 1594. The first part of this tract he intitles *A discourse most necessary for all gentlemen that have in regard their honors, touching the giving and receiving the lye, whereupon the* Duello *and the* Combat *in divers forms doth ensue; and many other inconveniences, for lack only of true knowledge of honor, and the* RIGHT UNDERSTANDING OF WORDS, *which here is set down.* . . . In the chapter of *conditional lies* speaking of the particle IF, [Saviolo] says—*Conditional lies be such as are given conditionally thus*—IF *thou hast said so or so, then thou liest. Of these kind of lies, given in this manner, often arise much contention, whereof no sure conclusion can arise.* By which he means they cannot proceed to cut one another's throats while there is an IF between. Which is the reason of *Shakespeare's* making the *Clown* say, *I knew when seven justices could not make up a quarrel: but when the parties were met themselves, one of them thought but of an IF, as if you said so, then I said so, and they shook hands, and swore brothers. Your IF is the only peacemaker; much virtue in IF* [V. iv. 98-103]. (p. 234)

> William Warburton, in an extract from Shakespeare, the Critical Heritage: 1733-1752, Vol. 3, edited by Brian Vickers, Routledge & Kegan Paul, 1975, pp. 223-58.

**RICHARD HURD**   (essay date 1753)

*[Hurd was an eighteenth-century English theologian and man of letters who made his career in the Church of England. A friend of William Mason and Thomas Gray, Hurd was encouraged in his scholarly pursuits by his literary acquaintances, particularly the Shakespearean scholar William Warburton, who greatly admired the "Notes on the Art of Poetry" accompanying Hurd's 1749 edition of Horace's* Ars Poetica. *In the following excerpt, originally published in his* Q. Horatti Flacci Epistolae ad Pisones et Augustum *(1753), Hurd raises an issue of fundamental importance in* As You Like It *studies: the play's pastoralism. Citing the works of Torquato Tasso (1544-95) as the source of pastoral drama, Hurd praises the "natural sylvan manners" and "sylvan scenes" in* As You Like It. *He also suggests the appropriateness of pastoral subjects to comic drama and commends Shakespeare for his awareness of this as well.]*

The famous Tasso, by an effort of genius which hath done him more honour than even his epic talents, produced a new kind of pastoral, by engrafting it on the drama. And under this form, pastoral poetry became all the vogue. The charming *Amintas* was even commented by the greatest scholars and critics. It was read, admired, and imitated by all the world.

There is no need to depreciate the fine copies that were taken of it, in Italy. But those by our own poets were, by far, the best. Shakespeare had, indeed, set the example of something like pastoral dramas, in our language; and in his *Winter's Tale, As ye like it,* and some other of his pieces, has enchanted every body with his natural sylvan manners, and sylvan scenes. But Fletcher set himself, in earnest, to emulate the Italian, yet still with an eye of reverence towards the English, poet. In his *faithful shepherdess* he surpasses the *former,* in the variety of his paintings and the beauty of his scene; and only falls short of the *latter,* in the truth of manners, and a certain original grace of invention which no imitation can reach. (pp. 215-16)

In this new form of the pastoral, what was childish before, is readily admitted and excused. A simple *moral* tale being the groundwork of the piece, the charms of description and all the embellishments of the scene are only subservient to the higher purpose of picturing the manners, or touching the heart.

But the good sense of Shakespeare, or perhaps the felicity of his genius, was admirable. Instead of the deep tragic air of Tasso (which has been generally followed) and his continuance of the pastoral strain, even to satiety, through *five* acts, he only made use of these playful images to enrich his comic scenes. He saw, I suppose, that pastoral subjects were unfit to bear a tragic distress. And besides when the distress rises to any height, the wantonness of pastoral imagery grows distasteful. Where as the genius of comedy admits of humbler distresses; and leaves us at leisure to recreate ourselves with these images, as no way interfering with the draught of characters, or the management of a comic tale. But to make up in *surprize* what was wanting in *passion,* Shakespeare hath, with great judgment, adopted the popular system of Faeries; which, while it so naturally supplies the place of the old sylvan theology, gives a wildness to this sort of pastoral painting which is perfectly inimitable.

In a word; if Tasso had the honour of inventing the *pastoral drama,* properly so called, Shakespeare has shewn us the just application of *pastoral poetry;* which, however amusing to the imagination, good sense will hardly endure, except in a short dialogue, or in some occasional dramatic scenes; and in *these* only, as it serves to the display of characters and the conduct of the poet's plot. (pp. 216-17)

> Richard Hurd, "Epistola ad Pisones: With an English Commentary and Notes," in his The Works of Richard Hurd, Vol, I, 1811. Reprint by AMS Press, Inc., 1967, pp. 27-278.

## SAMUEL JOHNSON   (essay date 1765)

[*Johnson has long held an important place in the history of Shakespearean criticism. He is considered the foremost representative of moderate English neoclassicism and is credited by some literary historians with freeing Shakespeare from the strictures of the three unities valued by strict neoclassicists: that dramas should have a single setting, take place in less than twenty-four hours, and have a causally connected plot. More recent scholars portray him as a critic who was able to synthesize existing critical theory rather than as an innovative theoretician. Johnson was a master of Augustan prose style and a personality who dominated the literary world of his epoch. The following excerpt is taken from Johnson's endnote to* As You Like It, *originally published in the 1765 edition of his* The Plays of William Shakespeare. *Johnson regards the "fable" of* As You Like It *as "wild and pleasing" and the character of Jaques as "natural and well preserved." He also praises the comic dialogue with its restrained use of "low buf-*]

*foonery," as well as the "graver" issues in the play, but faults Shakespeare for failing to exact a moral in "the dialogue between the usurper and the hermit."*]

Of [*As You Like It*] the fable is wild and pleasing. I know not how the ladies will approve the facility with which both Rosalind and Celia give away their hearts. To Celia much may be forgiven for the heroism of her friendship. The character of Jaques is natural and well preserved. The comick dialogue is very sprightly, with less mixture of low buffoonery than in some other plays; and the graver part is elegant and harmonious. By hastening to the end of his work Shakespeare suppressed the dialogue between the usurper and the hermit, and lost an opportunity of exhibiting a moral lesson in which he might have found matter worthy of his highest powers. (pp. 264-65)

> Samuel Johnson, "Notes on Shakespeare's Plays: 'As You Like It'," in his The Yale Edition of the Works of Samuel Johnson: Johnson on Shakespeare, Vol. VII, edited by Arthur Sherbo, Yale University Press, 1968, pp. 242-65.

## FRANCIS GENTLEMAN   (essay date 1770)

[*Gentleman, an Irish actor and playwright, was the author of* The Dramatic Censor; or, Critical Companion *(1770) and contributed the introduction to John Bell's 1774 edition of Shakespeare's plays. In the following excerpt from* The Dramatic Censor, *he discusses, among other matters, Shakespeare's handling of the Aristotelian and other unities in* As You Like It. *Acknowledging that "with all its faults, there is not a more agreeable piece on the stage," Gentleman nevertheless criticizes the imperfections of the play's plot and structure, noting in particular the "imperfect catastrophe" toward which the plot is hurried. The critic also faults Shakespeare for not including in his comedy an "interview" between the two dukes, but praises the play's characters as "well supported" and the incidents as pleasing if not striking. In his concluding remarks, Gentleman touches on a particularly Neoclassical issue by stating approvingly that the play affords "considerable instruction from attentive perusal."*]

[*As You Like It*] considered at large has a very romantic air, the unities suffer severe invasion, several scenes are very trifling, and the plot is hurried on to an imperfect catastrophe: we hear something of Oliver's being punished as an unnatural, abominable brother, but have a strong objection to crowning such a monster with fortune and love. An interview between the dukes would have afforded an opportunity for genius and judgment to exert themselves commendably; however, with all its faults, there is not a more agreeable piece on the stage; the characters are various, and all well supported; the incidents, if not striking, are certainly pleasing; the sentiments, with very few exceptions, are pregnant with useful meaning; and the language, though quaint in some places, shews in general strength and spirit worthy of SHAKESPEARE's pen.

Duke Senior is an amiable character, sustained with philosophical dignity, turning the frowns of fortune, as every man should do, into the means and motives of instruction: what he says is not of sufficient length to constitute a very conspicuous part in action, but if a performer has any declamatory merit, he may shew it to advantage here. (pp. 474-75)

It is almost needless to remark, that as not one of SHAKESPEARE's pieces is without abundant beauties, so not one can claim the praise of being free from egregious faults; however, in *As You Like It,* the latter fall very short of the former; and we make no scruple to affirm, that this piece will afford considerable instruction from attentive perusal, with great addition of pleasure from adequate representation. (p. 478)

*Francis Gentleman, "'As You Like It'," in his* The Dramatic Censor; or, Critical Companion, Vol. I, *1770. Reprint by AMS Press Inc., 1975, pp. 460-79.*

## ELIZABETH GRIFFITH  (essay date 1775)

[*Griffith exemplifies the seventeenth- and eighteenth-century preoccupation with searching through Shakespeare's plays for set speeches and passages that could be read out of dramatic context for their own sake. Griffith, however, avoided the more usual practice of collecting and commenting on poetic "beauties" and concentrated instead on the "moral" subjects treated in the text. This interest in moral issues is apparent in the following excerpt, in which she comments on Shakespeare's treatment of manners and morals in* As You Like It. *Griffith cites and praises passages in the play that exemplify or comment on such virtues as affection, gratitude, nobility, honesty, sincerity, and love. More significantly, she recognizes the wholesomeness of the pastoral element in the play, especially as it is reflected in Duke Senior's preference for a "sincere country life" to a "false city life" in II. i., and admires Adam's example in II. iii. of the "virtue and sobriety of the antient Peasantry of England."*]

[*As You Like It*] begins with a reflection on the *first*, and I may add the *principal*, concern in life, the education of children. Men are often more sedulous in training the brutes of their kennels, their mews and their stables, than they seem to be about the heirs of their blood, their fortunes, or their honours. In sad truth may it be said, that we seldom meet with a jockey, an huntsman, or a sportsman, who is half so *well-bred* as his horses, his hawks, or his hounds. (p. 69)

There are some passages very tender, generous, and affecting, in the first part of the dialogue [in I. iv.] between Rosalind and Celia, who had been bred up from their infancy in friendship together; the first, daughter to the exiled Duke; and the other, child to his brother, the Usurper. (p. 70)

The first speech in [II. i.] is rich in reflection upon the new-moulding faculty of use or habit, the preference of a *sincere* country life to a *false* city one, the advantages of adversity, and the benefits of retired contemplation. (p. 72)

[In the same scene], some humane sentiments are thrown out on the subject of hunting, with an affecting description given of a wounded deer; and also some moral allusions from human life to the different circumstances and situations of the poor victim, which must equally engage the thought and feeling of the reader. (p. 73)

When Adam counsels [Orlando in II. iii.] to fly from the persecution of his cruel brother, his answer expresses a noble and virtuous acquiescence in any state of misery or danger, rather than submit to support himself by base or dishonest means. . . .

There is a charming glow of affection, gratitude, and spirit, in the reply made by Adam; with a pleasing description of the virtue and sobriety of the antient Peasantry of England; and the difference of manners and morals between those times and the more modern ones, is well remarked upon. (p. 75)

There is no passion which Shakespeare more frequently, or so poetically describes, as that of love; and as it is the one which, by its despotism in our youthful years, often forms the destiny of our future life, and holds so immediate a relation to morals, we should suffer [no such occasion as in IV. v.] to pass un-

noticed, however humorously or ludicrously expressed, which either defines its nature, or remarks upon its effects. (p. 87)

*Elizabeth Griffith, "'As You Like It'," in her* The Morality of Shakespeare's Drama Illustrated, *1775. Reprint by Frank Cass & Co. Ltd., 1971, pp. 69-89.*

## WILLIAM RICHARDSON  (essay date 1780)

[*Richardson was a Scottish author and educator whose philosophical leanings led him to focus on the psychological and moral aspects of Shakespeare's major characters, drawing from each a philosophical lesson, or what he termed a "ruling principle." For Richardson, such guiding principles served to establish the psychological aspects of Shakespeare's characters—their motives, fears, delusions—and in the process defined the action of each play. In the following excerpt from his* Philosophical Analysis and Illustration of Some of Shakespeare's Remarkable Characters (1780), *Richardson evaluates Jaques's manner, character, temper, and psychological motivation. Focusing on a common Neoclassical concern, the critic praises the way Jaques's keen remarks and shrewd observation instruct and amuse. Richardson considers Jaques a realistic blend of "melancholy and misanthropy," emphasizing the character's "sensibility" and "compassion." He further proposes reasons for Jaques's rejection of society. Critical interest in Jaques—essentially initiated here by Richardson—has continued steadily and can be noted in the commentary on* As You Like It *throughout the nineteenth and twentieth centuries.*]

Jaques, in *As You Like It,* is exhibited to us in extraordinary circumstances, and in a situation very romantic. (p. 144)

The most striking character in the mind of Jaques, according to [the] description [of him at II. i. 29-57], is extreme sensibility. He discovers a heart strongly disposed to compassion, and susceptible of the most tender impressions of friendship: for he who can so feelingly deplore the absence of kindness and humanity, must be capable of relishing the delight annexed to their exercise. But sensibility is the soil where nature has planted social and sweet affections: by sensibility they are cherished, and grow mature. Social dispositions produce all those amiable and endearing connections that alleviate the sorrows of human life, adorn our nature, and render us happy. Now Jaques, avoiding society, and burying himself in the lonely forest, seems to act inconsistently with his constitution. He possesses sensibility; sensibility begets affection; and affection begets the love of society. But Jaques is unsocial. Can these inconsistent qualities be reconciled? Or has Shakespeare exhibited a character of which the parts are incongruous, and discordant? In other words, how happens it that a temper disposed to beneficence, and addicted to social enjoyment, becomes solitary and morose? (pp. 145-47)

Aversion from society proceeds from dislike to mankind, and from an opinion of the inefficacy, and uncertainty of external pleasure. Let us consider each of these apart: let us trace the progress by which they established themselves in the mind of Jaques, and gave his temper an unnatural colour.

The gratification of our social affections supposes friendship and esteem for others; and these dispositions suppose in their object virtues of a corresponding character: for every one values his own opinion, and fancies the person to whom he testifies esteem actually deserves it. If beneficent affections, ardent and undisciplined, predominate in our constitution, and govern our opinions, we enter into life strongly prepossessed in favour of mankind, and endeavour, by a generous and disinterested conduct, to render ourselves worthy of their regard. (pp. 147-48)

Though melancholy rules the mind of Jaques, he partakes of the leaven of human nature, and, moved by a sense of injury and disappointment,

> Most invectively he pierceth through
> The body of the country, city, court.
>
> [II. i. 58-9]

Instigated by sentiments of self-respect, if not of pride, he treats the condition of humanity, and the pursuits of mankind, as insignificant and uncertain. His invectives, therefore, are mingled with contempt, and expressed with humour. At the same time, he shows evident symptoms of a benevolent nature. He is interested in the improvement of mankind, and inveighs, not entirely to indulge resentment, but with a desire to correct their depravity [II. vii. 11-61]. (pp. 157-58)

This mixture of melancholy and misanthropy in the character of Jaques, is more agreeable to human nature than the representation of either of the extremes; for a complete misanthrope is as uncommon an object as a man who suffers injury without resentment. Mankind hold a sort of middle rank, and are in general too good for the one, and too bad for the other. As benevolence and sensibility are manifest in the temper of Jaques, we are not offended with his severity. By the oddity of his manner, by the keenness of his remarks, and shrewdness of his observations, while we are instructed, we are also amused. He is precisely what he himself tells us, "often wrapped in a most humourous sadness" [IV. i. 19-20]. His sadness, of a mild and gentle nature, recommends him to our regard; his humour amuses.

A picture of this kind shews the fertility of Shakespeare's genius, his knowledge of human nature, and the accuracy of his pencil, much more than if he had represented in striking colours either of the component parts. By running them into one another, and by delineating their shades where they are gradually and almost imperceptibly blended together, the extent and delicacy of his conceptions, and his amazing powers of execution are fully evident. Violent and impetuous passions are obvious, their colours are vivid, their features strongly marked, they may easily be discerned and easily copied. But the sensibility of the soul flows out in a variety of emotions and feelings, whose impulses are less apparent, and whose progress and operation may escape the notice of superficial observers; but whose influence in governing the conduct, and fashioning the tempers of mankind, is more extensive than we are apt to imagine. (pp. 159-61)

That Jaques, on account of disappointments in friendship, should become reserved and censorious, is consistent with human nature: but is it natural that he should abjure pleasure, and consider the world and every enjoyment of sense as frivolous and inexpedient? Ought he not rather to have recurred to them for consolation, and to have sought in them wherewithal to have relieved and solaced him? On the contrary, [at II. vii. 139-66] he expatiates with satisfaction on the insufficiency of human happiness, and on the insignificance of our pursuits. (pp. 162-63)

That the heart, sorrowful and dejected by the repulse of an ardent passion, is averse to pleasure of every kind, has been often observed. The mind, in a gay and healthful state, receives hope and enjoyment from every object around us. The same objects, if we languish and despond, are regarded with disgust or indifference. . . . Morose and splenetic moments are transient; the soul recovers from them as from a lethargy, exerts her activity, and pursues enjoyment: but, in the temper of Jaques, moroseness is become habitual: he abandons the world,

he contemns its pleasures, and buries himself in a cloister. The cause of this excessive severity requires a particular explanation.

Among the various desires and propensities implanted by nature in the constitution of every individual, some one passion, either by original and superior vigour, or by reiterated indulgence, gains an ascendant in the soul. . . . The ruling passion, blended with others, augments their vehemence, and consequently enhances their pleasure: for the pleasure arising from the gratification of any passion, is proportioned to its force. . . . Suppose the ruling passion thwarted: it ceases to operate with success. . . . [If] social and beneficent affections, by gaining a superiority in the constitution, have heightened every other enjoyment, and if their exercise is suspended by disappointment, all the pleasures of sense or of ambition that formerly contributed to our felicity, though in themselves they are still the same; yet, being reft of their better part, of the spirit that enlivened them, they strike the mind so feebly, as only to awaken its attention to the loss it hath sustained; and, instead of affording comfort, they aggravate our misfortune. (pp. 164-68)

To the foregoing observations, and to the consistency of Jaques's character, one thing may be objected: he is fond of music. But surely music is an enjoyment of sense; it affords pleasure; it is admitted to every joyous scene, and augments their gaiety. How can this be explained? (p. 171)

[If] we are languid and desponding, if melancholy diffuses itself through the soul, we no longer cherish the gay illusions of hope; no pleasure seems worthy of our attention; we reject consolation, and brood over the images of our distress. . . . Precisely agreeable to this description, is the character of melancholy music. The sounds, that is, the ideas it conveys to the mind, move slowly; they partake of little variety, or, if they are considerably varied, it is by a contrast that heightens the expression. The idea of a sound has certainly no resemblance to that of a misfortune: yet, as they may affect us in a similar manner, it is probable they have some common qualities: and those . . . consist in the manner by which they enter the mind. Slow sounds, gentle zephyrs, and murmuring streams, are agreeable to the afflicted lover. And the dreary whistling of the midnight wind through the crevices of a darksome cloister, cherisheth the melancholy of the trembling nun, and disposes her to a gloomy and austere devotion. Thus, the desire of Jaques seems perfectly suited to his character; for the music he requires is agreeable to his present temper. (pp. 172-74)

Thus we have endeavoured to illustrate, how social dispositions, by being excessive, and by suffering painful repulse, may render us unsocial and morose. . . . (p. 175)

> *William Richardson, "On the Character of the Melancholy Jaques," in his* A Philosophical Analysis and Illustration of Some of Shakespeare's Remarkable Characters, *revised edition, 1780. Reprint by AMS Press, Inc., 1966, pp. 144-76.*

## WALTER WHITER (essay date 1794)

[*A little-known Cambridge scholar, Whiter wrote* A Specimen of a Commentary on Shakspeare (1794), *the first extended commentary on* As You Like It. *Undertaking "to explain and illustrate the various passages* [*in Shakspeare's works*] *. . . on a new principle of criticism derived from Mr. Locke's doctrine of the association of ideas," Whiter pioneered the exploration of Shakespeare's imagination by considering idiosyncratic linkings "which have no natural alliance or relation to each other." He tested* *his "new principle" on* As You Like It. *In the following excerpt from* A Specimen, *Whiter closely analyzes the passage in the play at III. ii. 145-48, combining historical, aesthetic, interpretive, and "associative" techniques to demonstrate Shakespeare's "indirect" allusions here to certain aspects of Helen, Cleopatra, Atalanta, and Lucretia. He determines that the imagery of the passage "was not derived from the abstract consideration of their general qualities," but from Shakespeare's visual impressions of the principal traits of these women derived from the tapestry or pictorial renderings popular during the sixteenth century and earlier.]*

> Helen's cheek, but not her heart;
> Cleopatra's majesty;
> *Atalanta's better part;*
> Sad Lucretia's modesty.

[III. ii. 145-48]

There is no passage in Shakspeare which has more embarrassed his Commentators than this celebrated line, which enumerates among the perfections of a beauty *the better part of Atalanta.* Dr. Johnson observes, that the *better part of Atalanta* "seems to have been her heels;" yet he is inclined to think that our Poet, though no despicable mythologist, has mistaken some other character for that of Atalanta [see excerpt above, 1765].— Dr. Farmer is of opinion, that her *better part* is her *wit,* that is, the *swiftness of her mind* [see Additional Bibliography]; and Mr. Malone observes, that a passage in Marston's *Insatiate Countesse* might lead us to suppose that the *better part* of Atalanta was her *lips.* Mr. Tollet remarks, that "perhaps the poet means her beauty and graceful elegance of shape, which he would prefer to her swiftness;" but he afterwards asks, whether *Atalanta's better part* may not mean "her virtue or virgin chastity."

The explication of Mr. Tollet is the only one, which affords any suitable sense to this disputed expression; yet I am persuaded that the genuine spirit of the image is yet perfectly unknown. The reader of taste, who is ardent in the study of our Poet, will, I hope, be considerably gratified when I shall have placed before him the whole passage with a new vein of illustration; nor will he, I trust, be of opinion that I have been too laboured or minute in the discussion of a principle, which refers not only to the present instance, but may be frequently applied with singular success in the elucidation of Shakspeare. It is well known and acknowledged, that our old Poets derived many of their allusions and descriptions from *pictures and representations in Tapestry,* which were then equally familiar to themselves and to their readers. We must not therefore be astonished if their imagery should sometimes be deficient in that *abstraction of sentiment,* which we have been so accustomed to admire in the delineations of other Poets; nor is it difficult to imagine, that their colourings would be often marked by some peculiar allusions, which can now only be understood by conceiving, that the works of the Artist were still present to the mind of the Poet, and that the operations of the fancy were controuled by the impressions of the eye. This observation, which is rigorously applicable to our ancient bards, *Chaucer, Gower,* and *Lydgate,* may be extended likewise with considerable truth to the Poets of succeeding times, and will afford the intelligent critic a very important principle in illustrating the writers of the sixteenth century. It has been remarked by our Commentators, that Shakspeare has himself borrowed many of his images from *prints—statues—paintings*—and *exhibitions in tapestry;* and we may observe, that some allusions of this sort are to be found in the play before us, and especially in those places which describe the beauties of Rosalind. (pp. 29-32)

Let us now examine whether the present passage may not be illustrated by a principle which has been allowed universally to operate on our ancient Poets; and which has been proved in various instances to have acted on the imagination of Shakspeare. I have always been firmly persuaded, that the *imagery,* which our Poet has selected to discriminate the more prominent perfections of *Helen, Cleopatra, Atalanta,* and *Lucretia,* was not derived from the abstract consideration of their general qualities; but was caught from those *peculiar traits* of beauty and character, which are impressed on the mind of him who contemplates their portraits. It is well known, that these celebrated heroines of romance were in the days of our Poet the favourite subjects of popular representation, and were alike visible in the coarse hangings of the poor and the magnificent arras of the rich.—In the portraits of *Helen,* whether they were produced by the skilful artist, or his ruder imitator, though her face would certainly be delineated as eminently beautiful, yet she appears not to have been adorned with any of those charms which are allied to *modesty;* and we accordingly find that she was generally depicted with a loose and insidious countenance, which but too manifestly betrayed the inward wantonness and perfidy of her heart. (pp. 34-5)

With respect to the *Majesty of Cleopatra,* it may be observed, that this notion is not derived from Classical authority, but from the more popular store-house of legend and romance. . . . When our Poet had afterwards occasion in his *Antony and Cleopatra* to delineate her portrait at full length from a Classical original, we do not find that the idea of her *Majesty* is particularly inculcated. I infer therefore that the *familiarity* of this image was impressed both on the Poet and his reader from pictures and representations in tapestry, which were the lively and faithful mirrors of popular romances.—*Atalanta,* we know, was considered likewise by our antient Poets as a celebrated beauty; and we may be assured therefore that her portraits were every where to be found. . . . Since the story of *Atalanta* represents that heroine as possessed of singular beauty, zealous to preserve her virginity even with the death of her lovers, and accomplishing her purposes by extraordinary swiftness in running, we may be assured that the skill of the artist would be employed in displaying the most perfect expressions of *virgin purity,* and in delineating the *fine proportions and elegant symmetry of her person.*—"*Lucretia*" (we know) "was the grand example of conjugal fidelity throughout the Gothic ages;" and it is this spirit of unshaken chastity, which is here celebrated under the title of *modesty.* The epithet *sad* is but ill calculated to represent the abstract notion of *conjugal virtue,* and we may be assured therefore that it was forced upon the mind of our Poet from a very different impression. (pp. 36-7)

Let us suppose therefore that the portraits of these celebrated beauties, *Helen—Cleopatra—Atalanta*—and *Lucretia,* were delineated as I have above described—that in the days of Shakspeare they continued to be the favourite subjects of popular representation, and that consequently they were familiarly impressed on the mind of the Poet and on the memory of his audience. Let us now investigate what the bard, or the lover, under the influence of this impression, would select as the *better parts* of these celebrated heroines, which he might wish to be transferred to his own mistress as the perfect model of female excellence. In contemplating the portrait of *Helen,* he is attracted only by those charms which are at once the most distinguished, and at the same time are the least employed in expressing the feelings of the heart. He wishes therefore for that rich bloom of beauty, which glowed upon her *cheek,* but he rejects those lineaments of her countenance which betrayed the loose inconstancy of her mind—the insidious smile and the wanton brilliancy of her eye. Impressed with the effect, he passes instantly to the cause. He is enamoured with the *better part* of the beauty of *Helen;* but he is shocked at the depravity of that *heart,* which was too manifestly exhibited by the worse. To convince the intelligent reader, that *cheek* is not applied to *beauty in general;* but that it is here used in its appropriate and original sense, we shall produce a very curious passage from one of our Author's Sonnets, by which it will appear that the portraits of Helen were distinguished by the consummate beauty which was displayed upon *her cheek.*

> Describe Adonis, and the \**counterfeit* (\**i.e. picture*)
> Is poorly imitated after you;
> On Helen's *cheek* all art of beauty set,
> And you in Grecian tires are *painted* new.
>
> [Sonnet 53]

—In viewing the *portrait* of Cleopatra, we should all naturally agree in admiring the stately air and majestic appearance of her person; though in the bare contemplation of her *character,* we should not have equally concurred in speaking familiarly of her majesty as the most eminent and distinguished of her qualities.—In surveying the portrait of *Atalanta,* and in reflecting on the character which it displayed, the lover would not find it difficult to select the *better part* both of her mind and of her form, which he might wish to be transfused into the composition of his mistress. He would not be desirous of that perfection in her person, which contributed nothing to the gratification of his passion, and he would reject that principle of her soul which was adverse to the object of his wishes. He would be enamoured with the fine proportions and elegant symmetry of her limbs; though his passion would find but little reason to be delighted with the quality of *swiftness,* with which that symmetry was connected.—He would be captivated with the blushing charms of unsullied virginity; but he would abhor that unfeeling coldness, which resisted the impulse of love; and that unnatural cruelty which rejoiced in the murder of her lovers.—The Poet lastly wishes for the Modesty of the *sad Lucretia*—that firm and deep-rooted principle of female chastity, which is so visibly depicted in the *sadness* of her countenance lamenting for its involuntary loss; and which has rendered her through all ages the pride and pattern of conjugal fidelity.—Such then are the wishes of the lover in the formation of his mistress, that the *ripe* and *brilliant beauties* of *Helen* should be united to the *elegant symmetry* and *virgin graces* of *Atalanta;* and that this union of charms should be still dignified and ennobled by the *majestic mien* of *Cleopatra* and the *matron modesty* of *Lucretia.*

Finally; it is extremely observable, and will indeed considerably confirm the diligent reader of our Poet in the truth of this new interpretation, that *allusions to Pictures,* or at least *terms,* which are on all hands acknowledged to be *derived from Painting,* are found to accompany the passage which is the subject of our present commentary. . . . (pp. 39-41)

[I] have not hesitated to be thus minute and circumstantial in the explanation of this passage, that the reader might be at once possessed with a general notion of a species of *indirect* allusion, which occurs perpetually in our ancient poets, and which, when duly understood, will afford us a new and uniform light in discovering the peculiar spirit of their descriptions, and the *associating* principle of their imagery. (p. 43)

> *Walter Whiter, "Notes on 'As You Like It'," in his*
> A Specimen of a Commentary on Shakspeare, *edited*
> *by Alan Over and Mary Bell, revised edition, Methuen & Co. Ltd., 1967, pp. 7-56.*

## SAMUEL TAYLOR COLERIDGE　(essay date 1808-18)

[*Coleridge's lectures and writings on Shakespeare form a major chapter in the history of English Shakespearean criticism. As the channel for the critical ideas of the German Romantics and as an original interpreter of Shakespeare in the new spirit of Romanticism, Coleridge played a strategic role in overthrowing the last remains of the Neoclassical approach to Shakespeare and in establishing the modern view of the dramatist as a conscious artist and masterful portrayer of human character. Coleridge's remarks on Shakespeare come down to posterity largely as fragmentary notes, marginalia, and reports by auditors on the lectures, rather than in polished essays. In the following excerpt, drawn from marginalia and other notes first published in 1836 but written between 1808 and 1818, Coleridge comments on two passages in* As You Like It. *In the first case, he admires the "beauty" of Oliver's use of the word "boy" in addressing his younger brother in I. i. 52-5. The second comment concerns I. i. 163-73, Oliver's evaluation of his younger brother's character. Finding this passage "one of the most un-Shakespearean speeches in all (the genuine works of) Shakespeare," Coleridge points to its "want of truth to nature."*]

> *Oli.* What, boy!
> *Orl.* Come, come, elder brother, you are too young in this.
> *Oli.* Wilt thou lay hands on me, villain?
>
> [I. i. 52-5]

There is a beauty here. The word 'boy' naturally provokes and awakens in Orlando the sense of his manly powers: and with the retort, 'elder brother,' he grasps him with firm hands, and makes him feel that he is no *boy.*

> *Oli.* Farewell, good Charles. . . . Now will I stir this gamester: I hope I shall see an end of him; for my soul, yet I know not why, hates nothing more than he. Yet he's gentle; never schooled, and yet learned; full of noble device; of all sorts enchantingly beloved; and indeed so much in the heart of the world, and especially of my own people, who best know him, that I am altogether misprized; but it shall not be so long; this wrestler shall clear all: nothing remains but that I kindle the boy thither; which now I'll go about.
>
> [I. i. 163-73]

This has always *appeared* to me one of the most un-Shakespearian speeches in all (the genuine works of) Shakespeare. Yet I shall be nothing surprised, and greatly pleased, to find it hereafter a fresh beauty, as has so often happened with me with the supposed defects of the great. . . . (p. 93).

It is too venturous to charge a speech in Shakespeare with want of truth to nature. And yet at first sight this speech of Oliver's *expresses* truths which it almost seems impossible that any mind should so distinctly and so livelily have voluntarily presented to itself in connection with feelings and intentions so malignant and so contrary to those which the qualities expressed would naturally have called forth. But I dare not say that this *unnaturalness* is not in the nature of an abused *wilfulness* when united with a strong intellect. In such characters there is sometimes a gloomy self-gratification in making the *absoluteness* of the will . . . evident to themselves by setting the reason and conscience in full array against it. (pp. 93-4)

Samuel Taylor Coleridge, "Notes on the Comedies of Shakespeare: 'As You Like It'," in his Shakespearean Criticism, Vol. 1, edited by Thomas Middleton Raysor, second edition, Dutton, 1960, pp. 93-5.

## AUGUST WILHELM SCHLEGEL   (essay date 1811)

[*A prominent German Romantic critic, Schlegel holds a key place in the history of Shakespeare's reputation in European criticism. His translations of thirteen of the plays are still considered the best German editions of Shakespeare. Schlegel was also a leading spokesman for the Romantic movement, which permanently overthrew the neoclassical contention that Shakespeare was a child of nature whose plays lacked artistic form. The excerpt below was originally part of a lecture delivered by Schlegel in Vienna in 1808 and later revised and published in his Über dramatische Kunst und Literatur (1811). Schlegel focuses on the plot and content of* As You Like It, *maintaining that "what is done [in the play] is not so essential as what is said." He praises the drama's pastoral element, singling out the "ideal and natural shepherds and shepherdesses" as examples of the "native inhabitants" of the "shady, dark-green landscape in the background." He also touches on the theme of love and its importance in the play, stating that "of all the human passions, love alone has found an entrance" into Arden.*]

It would be difficult to bring the contents [of *As You Like It*] within the compass of an ordinary narrative; nothing takes place, or rather what is done is not so essential as what is said; even what may be called the *dénouement* is brought about pretty arbitrarily. Whoever can perceive nothing but what can as it were be counted on the fingers, will hardly be disposed to allow that it has any plan at all. Banishment and flight have assembled together, in the forest of Arden, a strange band: a Duke dethroned by his brother, who, with the faithful companions of his misfortune, lives in the wilds on the produce of the chase; two disguised Princesses, who love each other with a sisterly affection; a witty court fool; lastly, the native inhabitants of the forest, ideal and natural shepherds and shepherdesses. These lightly-sketched figures form a motley and diversified train; we see always the shady dark-green landscape in the background, and breathe in imagination the fresh air of the forest. The hours are here measured by no clocks, no regulated recurrence of duty or of toil: they flow on unnumbered by voluntary occupation or fanciful idleness, to which, according to his humour or disposition, every one yields himself, and this unrestrained freedom compensates them all for the lost conveniences of life. One throws himself down in solitary meditation under a tree, and indulges in melancholy reflections on the changes of fortune, the falsehood of the world, and the self-inflicted torments of social life; others make the woods resound with social and festive songs, to the accompaniment of their hunting-horns. Selfishness, envy, and ambition, have been left behind in the city; of all the human passions, love alone has found an entrance into this wilderness, where it dictates the same language alike to the simple shepherd and the chivalrous youth, who hangs his love-ditty to a tree. A prudish shepherdess falls at first sight in love with Rosalind, disguised in men's apparel; the latter sharply reproaches her with her severity to her poor lover, and the pain of refusal, which she feels from experience in her own case, disposes her at length to compassion and requital. The fool carries his philosophical contempt of external show, and his raillery of the illusion of love so far, that he purposely seeks out the ugliest and simplest country wench for a mistress. Throughout the whole picture, it seems to be the poet's design to show that to

call forth the poetry which has its indwelling in nature and the human mind, nothing is wanted but to throw off all artificial constraint, and restore both to mind and nature their original liberty. In the very progress of the piece, the dreamy carelessness of such an existence is sensibly expressed: it is even alluded to by Shakspeare in the title. Whoever affects to be displeased, if in this romantic forest the ceremonial of dramatic art is not duly observed, ought in justice to be delivered over to the wise fool, to be led gently out of it to some prosaical region. (pp. 391-92)

August Wilhelm Schlegel, "Criticisms on Shakspeare's Comedies," in his A Course of Lectures on Dramatic Art and Literature, edited by Rev. A. J. W. Morrison, translated by John Black, revised edition, 1846. Reprint by AMS Press, Inc., 1965, pp. 379-99.

## WILLIAM HAZLITT   (essay date 1817)

[*Hazlitt is considered a leading Shakespearean critic of the English Romantic movement. A prolific essayist and critic on a wide range of subjects, Hazlitt remarked in the preface to his* Characters of Shakespear's Plays, *first published in 1817, that he was inspired by the German critic August Wilhelm Schlegel, and was determined to supplant what he considered the pernicious influence of Samuel Johnson's Shakespearean criticism. Hazlitt's criticism is typically Romantic in its emphasis on character studies. His experience as a drama critic was an important factor in shaping his descriptive, as opposed to analytical, interpretations of Shakespeare. In the following excerpt from* Characters of Shakespear's Plays, *Hazlitt comments on the plot, structure, setting, and characters of* As You Like It. *Opening with brief remarks on the pastoral nature of Arden—it "breathes a spirit of philosophical poetry"—and a declaration of the play's dramatic subordination of "actions or situations" to "sentiments and characters," Hazlitt proceeds to analyze a selection of the play's characters. He finds Jaques to be "the only purely contemplative character" in Shakespeare's works and offers a brief, early view of Celia's character and function as "silent and retired," a "necessary relief to the provoking loquacity" of Rosalind. He describes Touchstone as part ancient philosopher, part buffoon, who "turns folly into wit, and wit into folly." Considering the comedy as a whole, Hazlitt calls it "the most ideal of any of [Shakespear's] plays."*]

Shakespear [in *As You Like It* has] converted the forest of Arden into another Arcadia, where they "fleet the time carelessly, as they did in the golden world" [I. i. 118-19]. It is the most ideal of any of this author's plays. It is a pastoral drama, in which the interest arises more out of the sentiments and characters than out of the actions or situations. It is not what is done, but what is said, that claims our attention. Nursed in solitude, "under the shade of melancholy boughs" [II. vii. 111], the imagination grows soft and delicate, and the wit runs riot in idleness, like a spoiled child, that is never sent to school. Caprice and fancy reign and revel here, and stern necessity is banished to the court. The mild sentiments of humanity are strengthened with thought and leisure; the echo of the cares and noise of the world strikes upon the ear of those "who have felt them knowingly" [*Cymbeline*, III. iii. 46], softened by time and distance. "They hear the tumult, and are still." The very air of the place seems to breath a spirit of philosophical poetry: to stir the thoughts, to touch the heart with pity, as the drowsy forest rustles to the sighing gale. Never was there such beautiful moralising, equally free from pedantry or petulance. (p. 187)

Jaques is the only purely contemplative character in Shakespear. He thinks, and does nothing. His whole occupation is to amuse his mind, and he is totally regardless of his body and his fortunes. He is the prince of philosophical idlers; his only passion is thought; he sets no value upon any thing but as it serves as food for reflection. He can "suck melancholy out of a song, as a weasel sucks eggs" [II. v. 12-13]; the motley fool, "who morals on the time" [II. vii. 29], is the greatest prize he meets with in the forest. He resents Orlando's passion for Rosalind as some disparagement of his own passion for abstract truth; and leaves the Duke, as soon as he is restored to his sovereignty, to seek his brother out who has quitted it, and turned hermit. (pp. 187-88)

Within the sequestered and romantic glades of the forest of Arden, they find leisure to be good and wise, or to play the fool and fall in love. Rosalind's character is made up of sportive gaiety and natural tenderness: her tongue runs the faster to conceal the pressure at her heart. She talks herself out of breath, only to get deeper in love. The coquetry with which she plays with her lover in the double character which she has to support is managed with the nicest address. How full of voluble, laughing grace is all her conversation with Orlando—

—In heedless mazes running
With wanton haste and giddy cunning.

How full of real fondness and pretended cruelty is her answer to him when he promises to love her "For ever and a day!" [IV. i. 145]. (p. 188)

The silent and retired character of Celia is a necessary relief to the provoking loquacity of Rosalind, nor can any thing be better conceived or more beautifully described than the mutual affection between the two cousins. . . . (pp. 188-89)

The unrequited love of Silvius for Phebe shews the perversity of this passion in the commonest scenes of life, and the rubs and stops which nature throws in its way, where fortune has placed none. Touchstone is not in love, but he will have a mistress as a subject for the exercise of his grotesque humour, and to shew his contempt for the passion, by his indifference about the person. He is a rare fellow. He is a mixture of the ancient cynic philosopher with the modern buffoon, and turns folly into wit, and wit into folly, just as the fit takes him. His courtship of Audrey not only throws a degree of ridicule on the state of wedlock itself, but he is equally an enemy to the prejudices of opinion in other respects. (p. 189)

There is hardly any of Shakespear's plays that contains a greater number of passages that have been quoted in books of extracts, or a greater number of phrases that have become in a manner proverbial. If we were to give all the striking passages, we should give half the play. We will only recall a few of the most delightful to the reader's recollection. Such are the meeting between Orlando and Adam, the exquisite appeal of Orlando to the humanity of the Duke and his company to supply him with food for the old man, and their answer, the Duke's description of a country life, and the account of Jaques moralising on the wounded deer, his meeting with Touchstone in the forest, his apology for his own melancholy and his satirical vein, and the well-known speech on the stages of human life, the old song of "Blow, blow, thou winter's wind," Rosalind's description of the marks of a lover and the progress of time with different persons, the picture of the snake wreathed round Oliver's neck while the lioness watches her sleeping prey, and Touchstone's lecture to the shepherd, his defence of cuckolds, and panegyric on the virtues of "an If."—All of these are familiar to the reader: there is one passage of equal delicacy and beauty which may have escaped him, and with [mention

of] it we shall close our account of As You Like It. It is Phebe's description of Ganimed at the end of the third act [III. v. 109-29]. (pp. 189-90)

*William Hazlitt, "'As You Like It',"* in his Characters of Shakespear's Plays & Lectures on the English Poets, *The Macmillan Company, 1903, pp. 187-90.*

### GEORGE DANIEL   (essay date 1829)

[*A nineteenth-century English miscellaneous writer and book collector, Daniel is chiefly remembered for the numerous editions of plays he prepared for John Cumberland's* British Theatre, With Remarks Biographical and Critical, Printed from the Acting Copies as Performed at the Theatres Royal, London *(1823-31). In the following excerpt from the "Remarks" preceding his 1829 serial edition of* As You Like It, *Daniel surveys the play's plot and characters. Praising the work as "the most perfect specimen of Shakespeare's various powers," Daniel attributes its excellence not to its plot, of which he says there is "little . . . to arrest attention," but to its sentiments, "clothed in language the most choice and appropriate." Daniel also comments on the various characters in the comedy, especially Jaques, Touchstone, and Rosalind. Further, the critic notes one of the play's central concerns in the benefits of adversity, and he introduces a somewhat autobiographical reading with his suggestion that the "divine lessons of humanity" to be found in Orlando and Adam must have come from "the sentiment in [Shakespeare's] own bosom."*]

"As You Like It" is the most perfect specimen of Shakspeare's various powers, that is to be found in all his writings. Some exceptions to *general* excellence may be discovered in many of his productions; but this drama presents one uniform picture of surpassing beauty. Every line teems with humanity. There is the philosophy of love, of mirth, and of melancholy. Of love, in all the delicacy and refinement of that exquisite passion—of mirth, sparkling with the utmost exuberance of wit and fancy—of melancholy, . . . a spirit deeply stricken with the baseness and ingratitude of the world—moralising on the various conditions and pursuits of men, not with cynical asperity, but sorrowful regret, chequered with the caustic and satirical humour that may serve to distinguish a disciple of Democritus. There is little plot to arrest attention, or to create suspense: the spell lies in the sentiments, which are clothed in language the most choice and appropriate, and in the grace and propriety of the characters.

This play is founded on the novel of *Rosalynde* . . . written by *Thomas Lodge*, an elegant and somewhat prolific author of the Elizabethan age. From this origin has Shakspeare borrowed not only many of the incidents, but some of his principal characters, with the exception of Jaques, Touchstone, and Audrey, which are his own. The scene is chiefly laid in the forest of Arden. We have the primitive simplicity of the pastoral age, with the wisdom of the schools—the quaint sallies of a court fool amidst the glories of paradise.

The character of Jacques bears a certain resemblance to that of Timon [in *Timon of Athens*]. Jacques has fled, not from the society of men, but from their follies and their vices; he still joins in fellowship with his brothers in exile; nor has his love of solitude given him a disrelish for humour in the pointed jests of the clown. Not so with Timon—his turbulent passions are only forced into a different channel: he *hates* with the same violence that he once *revelled*—his spirit, so far from being subdued by adversity, has become more furious by being opposed—and he lives and dies a hideous example of impotent malice and disappointed ambition. Such are the shades that distinguish these two celebrated characters, which, though they bear some analogy in certain features, are, nevertheless, perfectly individualised and distinct.

The ancient clown, or fool (which characters have been strangely confounded with each other), was a domestic buffoon, whose peculiar province was to divert his lord. He had the privilege of saying that which from other lips would have been accounted treason or heresy; satirising the follies of all present, not sparing even his lord, with the utmost keenness of sarcastic wit. . . . Such [a figure] is Touchstone, in whom shrewdness and humour contend for the mastery. He is a *material* fool, as Jacques aptly describes him [III. iii. 32]. His folly, like Hamlet's madness, has both matter and method in it. His description of the knight who swore by his honour the mustard was naught—his scenes of courtship with Audrey—his dissertation upon horns, and upon the lie seven times removed, are alternate jest and apotheghm. The character is worked up to the highest pitch of grotesque humour without any approach to vulgar buffoonery.

The disposition of Rosalind is gentle and confiding—sprightly as youth and innocence can make it—tinged with occasional sadness for the banishment of her father—and shaded with that most exquisite of all sensations, the melancholy of true love. Nor is the character of Celia scarcely less interesting, from her heroic friendship in following the fortunes of Rosalind; in soothing and supporting her amidst the perils of their flight; and in whimsically becoming the victim of that very passion which she rallies with such agreeable playfulness in her friend.

Orlando and Adam, the generous lord and the attached servant, exhibit human nature in that elevated point of view in which it is both useful and delightful to contemplate it. The poet who could thus inculcate such divine lessons of humanity, must have surely found the sentiment in his own bosom! (pp. 5-6)

Sylvius is a love-lorn shepherd, whose amorous expostulations have much of the quaintness of elegance and refinement. He pleads with considerable point and antithesis, and must have learnt his lesson in some other school than the forest of Arden. If Pope has made his swains talk like knights and scholars, he may plead the authority of Sir Philip Sydney and Shakspeare.

Phoebe displays the caprice and fickleness that have been common to her sex, whether in crowded cities, or in the Vales of Arcady. Audrey is a butt, against whom the mad wag, Touchstone, aims his sharpest arrows of satirical wit. She is a rich conception of comic humour, though the gods have not made her poetical.

Among the many noble passages which this drama contains— the speech of the duke—

> Now, my co-mates, and brothers in exile,
>
> [II. i. 1]

Jacques' description of the wounded stag, and his far-famed speech on the seven ages of man are the most prominent. The song *"Under the greenwood tree"* [II. v. 1], is a beautiful pastoral. *"Blow, blow, thou winter wind"* [II. vii. 174], is sublime.

Johnson regrets that Shakspeare, by hurrying this play to a close, lost the opportunity of inculcating some fine moral sentiments, through the medium of a dialogue between the usurper and the hermit [see excerpt above, 1765]. We regret it, too—

injustice had then received a still sterner rebuke, and the following sentiment of the poet a more ample illustration:—

> Sweet are the uses of adversity,
> Which, like the toad, ugly and venomous,
> Wears yet a precious jewel in its head.
>
> [II. i. 12-14]

In contemplating this romantic and beautiful drama, all opinion necessarily rises into panegyric. Every part is so perfect—the philosophy, the humour, the sentiments, and the imagery— that to rise from it without delight and improvement, would betray an obliquity of feeling wholly inconsistent with just perception and moral rectitude. We are taught by the noblest examples, that adversity is not in reality a bane to man, but to his pride and ambition. That its uses are sweet and consolatory; and while with rude hand it arrests the career of his unlicensed passions, it restores his mind to that state of healthful serenity, which, when the vain blandishments of life are past and gone, is the remaining friend and companion of virtue. The schools dedicated to morals and philosophy, the holy temples of religion, never echoed with more divine precepts than the solitudes of Arden. Mirth never sounded a merrier note, nor music a more enchanting strain, than those which glad the hearts, and sooth the cares, of these banished foresters. (pp. 6-7)

> *George Daniel, in remarks in* As You Like It: A Comedy *by William Shakspeare, G. H. Davidson, 1829, pp. 5-7.*

## ANNA BROWNELL JAMESON   (essay date 1833)

[*Jameson was a well-known nineteenth-century English essayist whose essays and criticism span the end of the Romantic age and the beginning of Victorian realism. She is best remembered for her study* Shakespeare's Heroines *(1833), which was originally published in a slightly different form in 1832 as* Characteristics of Women: Moral, Poetical, and Historical. *This work demonstrates both her historical interests and her sympathetic appreciation of Shakespeare's female characters. In the following excerpt from* Shakspeare's Heroines, *Jameson analyzes Rosalind as a dramatic character. Finding her ''inferior in force'' to Beatrice in* Much Ado about Nothing *but superior as a woman, Jameson claims that she possesses more of the feminine qualities of playfulness, sensibility, and naiveté, and that her pastoral surroundings offer her more scope to exhibit these traits.*]

[I should rank Rosalind] before Beatrice [in *Much Ado about Nothing*], inasmuch as the greater degree of her sex's softness and sensibility, united with equal wit and intellect, give her the superiority as a woman; but that as a dramatic character she is inferior in force. The portrait is one of infinitely more delicacy and variety, but of less strength and depth. It is easy to seize on the prominent features in the mind of Beatrice, but extremely difficult to catch and fix the more fanciful graces of Rosalind. She is like a compound of essences, so volatile in their nature, and so exquisitely blended, that on any attempt to analyse them they seem to escape us. . . . [Her] genial spirit touches into life and beauty whatever it shines on!

But this impression, though produced by the complete development of the character, and in the end possessing the whole fancy, is not immediate. The first introduction of Rosalind is less striking than interesting; we see her a dependant, almost a captive, in the house of her usurping uncle; her genial spirits are subdued by her situation, and the remembrance of her banished father; her playfulness is under a temporary eclipse—

I pray thee, Rosalind, sweet my coz, be merry!

[I. ii. 1-2]

is an adjuration which Rosalind needed not when once at liberty, and sporting "under the greenwood tree." The sensibility and even pensiveness of her demeanour in the first instance render her archness and gaiety afterwards more graceful and more fascinating.

Though Rosalind is a princess, she is a princess of Arcady; and, notwithstanding the charming effect produced by her first scenes, we scarcely ever think of her with a reference to them, or associate her with a court and the artificial appendages of her rank. She was not made to "lord it o'er a fair mansion" [*The Merchant of Venice*, III. ii. 167-68], and take state upon her, like the all-accomplished Portia; but to breathe the free air of heaven, and frolic among green leaves. She was not made to stand the siege of daring profligacy, and oppose high action and high passion to the assaults of adverse fortune, like Isabel [in *Henry V*]; but to "fleet the time carelessly as they did i' the golden age" [I. i. 118-19]. She was not made to bandy wit with lords, and tread courtly measures with plumed and warlike cavaliers, like Beatrice; but to dance on the greensward, and "murmur among living brooks a music sweeter than their own."

Though sprightliness is the distinguishing characteristic of Rosalind, as of Beatrice, yet we find her much more nearly allied to Portia in temper and intellect. The tone of her mind is, like Portia's, genial and buoyant: she has something, too, of her softness and sentiment; there is the same confiding abandonment of self in her affections: but the characters are otherwise as distinct as the situations are dissimilar. The age, the manners, the circumstance, in which Shakspeare has placed his Portia, are not beyond the bounds of probability; nay, have a certain reality and locality. We fancy her a contemporary of the Raffaelles and the Ariostos; the sea-wedded Venice, its merchants and Magnificos, the Rialto and the long canals—rise up before us when we think of her. But Rosalind is surrounded with the purely ideal and imaginative; the reality is in the characters and in the sentiments, not in the circumstances or situation. Portia is dignified, splendid, and romantic, Rosalind is playful, pastoral, and picturesque: both are in the highest degree poetical, but the one is epic and the other lyric.

Everything about Rosalind breathes of "youth and youth's sweet prime." She is fresh as the morning, sweet as the dew-awakened blossoms, and light as the breeze that plays among them. She is as witty, as voluble, as sprightly, as Beatrice; but in a style altogether distinct. In both the wit is equally unconscious: but in Beatrice it plays about us like the lightning, dazzling but also alarming; while the wit of Rosalind bubbles up and sparkles like the living fountain, refreshing all around. Her volubility is like the bird's song; it is the outpouring of a heart filled to overflowing with life, love, and joy, and all sweet and affectionate impulses. She has as much tenderness as mirth, and in her most petulant raillery there is a touch of softness—"By this hand, it will not hurt a fly" [IV. i. 111]. As her vivacity never lessens our impression of her sensibility, so she wears her masculine attire without the slightest impugnment of her delicacy. Shakspeare did not make the modesty of his women depend on their dress. . . . Rosalind has in truth "no doublet and hose in her disposition" [III. ii. 195-96]. How her heart seems to throb and flutter under her page's vest! What depth of love in her passion for Orlando! whether disguised beneath a saucy playfulness, or breaking forth with a fond impatience, or half betrayed in that beautiful scene where

she faints at the sight of the kerchief stained with his blood! Here her recovery of her self-possession—her fears lest she should have revealed her sex—her presence of mind, and quick-witted excuse—

I pray you, tell your brother how well I counterfeited—

[IV. iii. 166-67]

and the characteristic playfulness which seems to return so naturally with her recovered senses—are all as amusing as consistent. Then how beautifully is the dialogue managed between herself and Orlando! how well she assumes the airs of a saucy page, without throwing off her feminine sweetness! How her wit flutters free as air over every subject! with what a careless grace, yet with what exquisite propriety! (pp. 78-81)

And if the freedom of some of the expressions used by Rosalind or Beatrice be objected to, let it be remembered that this was not the fault of Shakspeare or the women, but generally of the age. Portia, Beatrice, Rosalind, and the rest, lived in times when more importance was attached to things than to words; now we think more of words than of things; and happy are we in these later days of super-refinement, if we are to be saved by our verbal morality. But this is meddling with the province of the melancholy Jaques, and our argument is Rosalind.

The impression left upon our hearts and minds by the character of Rosalind—by the mixture of playfulness, sensibility, and what the French (and we for lack of a better expression) call *naïveté*—is like a delicious strain of music. There is a depth of delight, and a subtlety of words to express that delight, which is enchanting. Yet when we call to mind particular speeches and passages, we find that they have a relative beauty and propriety, which renders it difficult to separate them from the context without injuring their effect. She says some of the most charming things in the world, and some of the most humorous; but we apply them as phrases rather than as maxims, and remember them rather for their pointed felicity of expression and fanciful application, than for their general truth and depth of meaning. (pp. 81-2)

Rosalind has not the impressive eloquence of Portia, nor the sweet wisdom of Isabella. Her longest speeches are not her best; nor is her taunting address to Phebe, beautiful and celebrated as it is, equal to Phebe's own description of her. The latter, indeed, is more in earnest.

Celia is more quiet and retired; but she rather yields to Rosalind than is eclipsed by her. She is as full of sweetness, kindness, and intelligence, quite as susceptible, and almost as witty, though she makes less display of wit. She is described as less fair and less gifted; yet the attempt to excite in her mind a jealousy of her lovelier friend by placing them in comparison . . . fails to awaken in the generous heart of Celia any other feeling than an increased tenderness and sympathy for her cousin. To Celia, Shakspeare has given some of the most striking and animated parts of the dialogue; and in particular, that exquisite description of the friendship between her and Rosalind [at I. iii. 72-6]. (p. 83)

The feeling of interest and admiration . . . excited for Celia at the first, follows her through the whole play. We listen to her as to one who has made herself worthy of our love, and her silence expresses more than eloquence.

Phebe is quite an Arcadian coquette; she is a piece of pastoral poetry. Audrey is only rustic. A very amusing effect is produced by the contrast between the frank and free bearing of

*Act III. Scene ii. Rosalind as Ganymed, Touchstone, and Celia as Aliena. Frontispiece to the Rowe edition (1709). By permission of the Folger Shakespeare Library.*

the two princesses in disguise and the scornful airs of the real shepherdess. In the speeches of Phebe, and in the dialogue between her and Sylvius, Shakspeare has anticipated all the beauties of the Italian pastoral, and surpassed Tasso and Guarini. We find two among the most poetical passages of the play appropriated to Phebe—the taunting speech to Sylvius, and the description of Rosalind in her page's costume; which last is finer than the portrait of Bathyllus in Anacreon. (pp. 83-4)

> Anna Brownell Jameson, ''Rosalind,'' in her Shak-
> speare's Heroines: Characteristics of Women, Moral,
> Poetical, & Historical, *George Newnes, Limited, 1897,
> pp. 78-84.*

**WILLIAM MAGINN** (essay date 1837)

[*Maginn was a nineteenth-century Anglo-Irish essayist, poet, short story writer, and literary critic who helped to establish* Black-wood's Edinburgh Magazine *and* Fraser's Magazine. *In the following excerpt, he discusses Jaques's ''Seven Ages of Man'' speech at II. vii. 139-66. Disagreeing with critics who see in this passage an expression of true melancholy, Maginn instead claims that it demonstrates Jaques's general contentment and good fortune—verbal proof that the character has nothing to be melancholy about. According to Maginn, Jaques is merely ''a dresser forth*

*in sweet language of . . . ordinary common-places,'' and he maintains that the fool Touchstone evidences more worldly wisdom in his acceptance of the natural process of life. In his concluding remarks, Maginn claims to find no problem with the presence of a ''tropical lion and a serpent'' in Arden, suggesting that ''all the prodigies spawned in Africa'' might properly be found in a forest ''inhabited by such characters as Rosalind, Touchstone, and Jaques.''*]

[Jaques] is nothing more than an idle gentleman given to musing, and making invectives against the affairs of the world, which are more remarkable for the poetry of their style and expression than the pungency of their satire. His famous description of the seven ages of man is that of a man who has seen but little to complain of in his career through life. The sorrows of his infant are of the slightest kind, and he notes that it is taken care of in a nurse's lap. The griefs of his schoolboy are confined to the necessity of going to school; and he, too, has had an anxious hand to attend to him. His shining morning face reflects the superintendence of one—probably a mother—interested in his welfare. The lover is tortured by no piercing pangs of love, his woes evaporating themselves musically in a ballad of his own composition, written not to his mistress, but fantastically addressed to her eyebrow. The soldier appears in all the pride and the swelling hopes of his spirit-stirring trade. . . . The fair round belly of the justice lined with good capon lets us know how he has passed his life. He is full of ease, magisterial authority, and squirely dignity. The lean and slippered pantaloon, and the dotard sunk into second childishness, have suffered only the common lot of humanity, without any of the calamities that embitter the unavoidable malady of old age. All the characters in Jaques's sketch are well taken care of. The infant is nursed; the boy educated; the youth tormented with no greater cares than the necessity of hunting after rhymes to please the ear of a lady, whose love sits so lightly upon him as to set him upon nothing more serious than such a self-amusing task; the man in prime of life is engaged in gallant deeds, brave in action, anxious for character, and ambitious of fame; the man in declining years has won the due honours of his rank, he enjoys the luxuries of the table and dispenses the terrors of the bench; the man of age still more advanced is well to do in the world. If his shank be shrunk, it is not without hose and slipper,—if his eyes be dim, they are spectacled,—if his years have made him lean, they have gathered for him wherewithal to fatten the pouch by his side. And when this strange eventful history is closed by the penalties paid by men who live too long, Jaques does not tell us that the helpless being . . . is left unprotected in his helplessness.

Such pictures of life do not proceed from a man very heavy at heart. Nor can it be without design that they are introduced into this especial place. The moment before, the famished Orlando has burst in upon the sylvan meal of the Duke, brandishing a naked sword, demanding with furious threat food for himself and his helpless companion. . . . The Duke, struck with his earnest appeal, cannot refrain from comparing the real suffering which he witnesses in Orlando with that which is endured by himself and his ''co-mates, and partners in exile'' [II. i. 1]. Addressing Jaques, he says,

> Thou seest we are not all alone unhappy.
> This wide and universal theatre
> Presents more woful pageants than the scene
> Wherein we play in.
>
> [II. vii. 136-39]

But the spectacle and the comment upon it lightly touch Jaques, and he starts off at once into a witty and poetic comparison of the real drama of the world with the mimic drama of the stage, in which, with the sight of well-nurtured youth driven to the savage desperation of periling his own life, and assailing that of others,—and of weakly old age lying down in the feeble but equally resolved desperation of dying by the wayside, driven to this extremity by sore fatigue and hunger,—he diverts himself and his audience, whether in the forest or theatre, on the stage or in the closet, with graphic descriptions of human life; not one of them, proceeding as they do from the lips of the *melancholy* Jaques, presenting a single point on which true melancholy can dwell. Mourning over what cannot be avoided must be in its essence common-place: and nothing has been added to the lamentations over the ills brought by the flight of years since Moses, the man of God, declared the concluding period of protracted life to be a period of labour and sorrow. . . . Abate these unavoidable misfortunes, and the catalogue of Jaques is that of happy conditions. In his visions there is no trace of the child doomed to wretchedness before its very birth; no hint that such a thing could occur as its being made an object of calculation, one part medical, three parts financial, to the starveling surgeon, whether by the floating of the lungs, or other test equally fallacious and fee-producing, the miserable mother may be convicted of doing that which, before she had attempted, all that is her soul of woman must have been torn from its uttermost roots, when in an agony of shame and dread the child that was to have made her forget her labour was committed to the cesspool. No hint that the days of infancy should be devoted to the damnation of a factory, or to the tender mercies of a parish beadle. No hint that philosophy should come forward armed with the panoply offensive and defensive of logic and eloquence, to prove that the inversion of all natural relations was just and wise,—that the toil of childhood was due to the support of manhood,—that those hours, the very labours of which even the etymologists give to recreation, should be devoted to those wretched drudgeries which seem to split the heart of all but those who derive from them blood-stained money, or blood-bedabbled applause. Jaques sees not Greensmith squeezing his children by the throat until they die. He hears not the supplication of the hapless boy begging his still more hapless father for a moment's respite, ere the fatal handkerchief is twisted round his throat by the hand of him to whom he owed his being. Jaques thinks not of the baby deserted on the step of the inhospitable door, of the shame of the mother, of the disgrace of the parents, of the misery of the forsaken infant. His boy is at school, his soldier in the breach, his elder on the justice-seat. Are these the woes of life? Is there no neglected creature left to himself or to the worse nurture of others, whose trade it is to corrupt,—who will teach him what was taught to swaggering Jack Chance, found on Newgate steps, and educated at the venerable seminary of St. Giles's Pound. . . . Is the soldier melancholy in the storm and whirlwind of war? Is the gallant confronting of the cannon a matter to be complained of? The dolorous flight, the trampled battalion, the broken squadron, the lost battle, the lingering wound, the ill-furnished hospital, the unfed blockade, hunger and thirst, and pain, and fatigue, and mutilation, and cold, and rout, and scorn, and slight,—services neglected, unworthy claims preferred, life wasted, or honour tarnished,—are all passed by! In peaceful life we have no deeper misfortune placed before us than that it is not unusual that a justice of peace may be prosy in remark and trite in illustration. Are there no other evils to assail us through the agony of life? And when the conclusion comes, how far less tragic is the portraiture of mental imbecility, if considered as a state of misery than as

one of comparative happiness, as escaping a still worse lot! (pp. 552-55)

If what he here sums up as the result of his life's observations on mankind be all that calls forth the melancholy of the witty and eloquent speaker, he had not much to complain of. . . . Jaques has just seen the aspect of famine, and heard the words of despair; the Duke has pointed out to him the consideration that more woful and practical calamities exist than even the exile of princes and the downfall of lords; and he breaks off into a light strain of satire, fit only for jesting comedy. (p. 555)

Shakspeare designed [Jaques] to be a maker of fine sentences,—a dresser forth in sweet language of the ordinary common-places or the common-place mishaps of mankind, and he takes care to show us that he did not intend him for anything beside. With what admirable art he is confronted with Touchstone. He enters merrily laughing at the pointless philosophising of the fool in the forest. His lungs crow like chanticleer when he hears him moralizing over his dial, and making the deep discovery that ten o'clock has succeeded nine, and will be followed by eleven. When Touchstone himself appears, we do not find in his own discourse any touches of such deep contemplation. He is shrewd, sharp, worldly, witty, keen, gibing, observant. It is plain that he has been mocking Jaques; and, as is usual, the mocked thinks himself the mocker. If one has moralized the spectacle of a wounded deer into a thousand similes, comparing his weeping into the stream to the conduct of worldlings in giving in their testaments the sum of more to that which had too much,—his abandonment, to the parting of the flux of companions from misery,—the sweeping by of the careless herd full of the pasture, to the desertion of the poor and broken bankrupt by the fat and greasy citizens,—and so forth; if such have been the common-places of Jaques, are they not fitly matched by the common-places of Touchstone upon his watch?. . . The motley fool is as wise as the melancholy lord whom he is parodying. The shepherd Corin, who replies to the courtly quizzing of Touchstone by such apophthegms as that "it is the property of rain to wet, and of fire to burn" [III. ii. 26-7], is unconsciously performing the same part to the clown, as *he* had been designedly performing to Jaques. Witty nonsense is answered by dull nonsense, as the emptiness of poetry had been answered by the emptiness of prose. There was nothing sincere in the lamentation over the wounded stag. It was only used as a peg on which to hang fine conceits. (pp. 556-57)

Whether he would or not, [Jaques] departs from the stage with the grace and easy elegance of a gentleman in heart and manners. He joins his old antagonist the usurping Duke in his fallen fortunes; he had spurned him in his prosperity: his restored friend he bequeaths to his former honour, deserved by his patience and his virtue,—he compliments Oliver on his restoration to his land, and love, and great allies,—wishes Silvius joy of his long-sought and well-earned marriage,—cracks upon Touchstone one of those good-humoured jests to which men of the world on the eve of marriage must laughingly submit,—and makes his bow. Some sage critics have discovered as a great geographical fault in Shakspeare, that he introduces the tropical lion and serpent into Arden, which, it appears, they have ascertained to lie in some temperate zone. I wish them joy of their sagacity. Monsters more wonderful are to be found in that forest; for never yet, since water ran and tall tree bloomed, were there gathered together such a company as those who compose the *dramatis personae* of "As You Like it." All the prodigies spawned by Africa . . . might well have teemed in a forest, wherever situate, that was inhabited by such creatures as Rosalind, Touchstone, and Jaques. (p. 560)

*William Maginn, "Shakspeare Papers, No. II: Jaques," in* Bentley's Miscellany, *Vol. I, No. VI, June, 1837, pp. 550-60.*

## HERMANN ULRICI (essay date 1839)

[*A German scholar, Ulrici was a professor of philosophy and the author of works on Greek poetry and Shakespeare. The following excerpt is from an English translation of his* Über Shakespeares dramatische Kunst, und sein Verhältniss zu Calderon und Göthe, *a work first published in 1839. This study exemplifies the "philosophical criticism" developed in Germany during the nineteenth century. The immediate sources of Ulrici's critical approach appear to be August Wilhelm Schlegel's conception of the play as an organic, interconnected whole and Georg Wilhelm Friedrich Hegel's view of drama as an embodiment of the conflict of historical forces and ideas. Unlike his fellow German Shakespearean critic G. G. Gervinus, Ulrici sought to develop a specifically Christian aesthetics, but one which, as he carefully points out in the introduction to the work mentioned above, in no way intrudes on "that unity of idea, which preeminently constitutes a work of art a living creation in the world of beauty." In his study of* As You Like It, *Ulrici is primarily concerned with the play's verisimilitude, its so-called ground idea, and the characteristics of Jaques and Touchstone. Noting a "decided preponderance of the fanciful element" in the comedy, Ulrici dismisses the notion that Shakespeare was interested in portraying "ordinary reality." Instead, he discerns in the play "a view of life taken from a peculiar poetic position," a "mirror of irony and humour" exhibiting "the eternal order of things" through a dialectical reversal of the characters' fortunes and behavior. Within this eternal order, and reflecting the play's title, Ulrici continues, "every one does just as he likes," but at the same time God's "harmony and law" ensure that disruptive elements "destroy themselves" and all things turn out well. Further, Ulrici studies the "dialect of irony" exemplified by the play's "two fools": Touchstone, the "merry fool," shows "a truly noble disinterestedness and fidelity" and is alone in knowing "his own mind throughout"; on the contrary, Jaques is characterized as superficial and profound, a "comic, foolish character."*]

The noble comedy of "As You Like It" is . . . of the mixed class, but with a decided preponderance of the fanciful element. Of two princely brothers, one is in possession of the ducal throne, of which—we are not told how—he has unjustly dispossessed the other, who, with his followers, are leading a wild and fantastic sort of life in the Forest of Arden; of another pair of noble brothers, the younger is persecuted by the elder, and takes refuge in the forest with the banished Duke; two princesses, the daughters of the two dukes, are deeply attached to each other, so that upon the banishment of one the other accompanies her in her flight also to the forest; a merry and a melancholy fool, with shepherds and shepherdesses, drawn to the truth of nature, with a few light touches—such are the principal personages of the piece, which, in harmonious and graceful grouping, and pleasing contrasts, animate the wilds of the wood of Arden, and by their diversified situations, relations, and character, condition every thing, and of themselves bring about whatever happens in the piece. Separately considered nothing appears directly to contradict nature; no being or event singly is supernatural or unusual; viewed singly, each character, situation, and transaction, might belong to the most ordinary reality. It is only by the presence of lions and serpents in an European forest, that we are gently reminded that we are standing within the intellectual domain of poetical fancy. But still more strongly does the whole, as it organically develops

itself, and by the action of the several parts on each other, and *their* relation to the whole—in short, the sum of the circumstances, situations, transactions, and incidents, give us to understand that it is by no means the purpose of the drama to exhibit ordinary reality, but, on the contrary, a view of life taken from a peculiar poetic position—in other words, a fanciful reflection of it in the mirror of irony and humour. For, when we take a closer look at the whole, we are soon compelled to admit that the like does not and could not come to pass in reality, but that such a romantic mode of living, in the solitude of a forest, is but a poetical dream; that caprice and humour do not so absolutely rule human life; that a character like that of the unjust Duke would not be so easily converted by the religious old hermit, nor a man like Oliver de Boys be suddenly diverted from his hatred by one magnanimous action of his persecuted and injured brother.

But it will be asked, where, then, amid this apparent want of nature and reality, is the poetic truth of the piece, and what is the position from which it contemplates human life? To answer this question it must be borne in mind, that the general comic view of things forms the basis of the whole piece, and that, consequently, it is by means of contrast, and not directly, that human life is here illustrated, and that by chance, humour, and caprice, being made to annihilate and subvert each other, the true director of human life, which is nothing less than the eternal order of things, is brought to light. This becomes clearly manifest, when we behold the arbitrary caprice which led to the banishment of the good old Duke, brought to an end by a like capricious whim; and how, in like measure, fickle humour restores a good understanding between the two brothers Oliver and Orlando de Boys; and how the fanciful loves of Rosalind and Orlando, of Celia and Oliver, which owed their origin to a singular concurrence of circumstances, are rendered happy by a no less arbitrary play of caprice and accident; and how, in the same way, the coyness of the shepherdess Phebe is overcome, and she is united to her faithful and good-humoured simpleton of a lover.

Thus is the general comic view reflected in the whole, and thus does it form the foundation and platform on which all moves. When, then, we come to ask what *special* position the poet has here taken, and what is the *special* ground-idea of the piece, the title of the play will, in the first place, afford us some information on this head. The words "As You Like It," are but a phrase of courtesy, which says and means but little. This title, like "What You Will," [the subtitle of *Twelfth Night*], has also been referred to the relation between the piece and the public . . . , and been so interpreted as to be made to convey the sense that the poem might assume any form and appearance at the pleasure of the spectator. But, as already remarked, this is not and cannot be the case. On the other hand, it is quite possible that the title may . . . contain an allusion to Ben Jonson's unreasonable attacks on Shakspeare's easy and apparently irregular and arbitrary compositions. But, on the one hand, the allusion does not hold exactly; Jonson's words are, "If You Like It," whereas the superscription to Shakspeare's piece is, "As You Like It'. . . . On the other hand, any subordinate allusion which the title may convey of this kind, will not by any means exclude a reference to the contents and ground-idea of the whole. Shakspeare might possibly choose or alter the title of his comedy, with a sidelong look of derision at the pedantic assumption of his adversary; but, at the same time, I am confident he would never have adopted it, if it did not possess an objective justification in its applicability to the subject-matter of the drama. And, in fact, it is easy enough to point out this reference, as soon as we have apprehended the whole in its life-giving and animating ground-idea. In this comedy, life itself is contemplated in the light it would appear, if it were presented to a man, as it were, on a salver, with the courteous invitation to take it as he likes it. Throughout the whole piece, every one does just as he likes; every one, with unrestrained wilfulness and caprice, gives himself up either to evil or to good as the fit strikes him; every one looks upon, turns, and shapes life as he fancies. The forest of Arden is the stage, and with its fresh and free forest air, and its mysterious gloom, at the same time the fitting scene for the realisation of such a view of life. That out of which the whole action proceeds, on which the entire representation is based, and on which likewise the fantastic character of the whole consists, is not so much any external objective, as an internal and subjective contingency—the humour and caprice of the acting personages in their influence on one another.

It is true that on this account the whole cannot be justifiable, except within the comic view of things; such a view of life, in truth, can be nothing but irony; such a position for the contemplation of life is at best an isolated and exclusive one; such a view is not the whole truth. However, irony, on the other hand, does not consist merely in taking and exhibiting the absolutely false for the truth; but the essence of irony depends on that sharp dialectic of the mind, which seizes a matter, or a one-sided view in its naked onesidedness, and shews how in such exclusiveness it becomes its direct opposite. In fact, the above view of life conveys the profound truth, that the mind of man, by its free-will and faculty of self-determination, can really shape, turn, and direct his own life as he likes. But, however true this may be, still it is only one side of the truth that is here brought forward; its other equally important aspect, which exhibits the eternal harmony and law— the everlasting counsels of God, ruling and superintending the history of the world, and every individual life,—is entirely overlooked, and like the reverse of a coin, turned away from our regard in darkness and obscurity. But, although Shakspeare has set forward the first side in full light, still it was far from his intention to offer it as the full and perfect truth. On the contrary, he places the whole on the airy summit of the comic point of view, and while he allows it to unfold itself, to develope itself in its full and sharp exclusiveness, the dialectic of irony which it involves within itself urges it forward till it passes into its direct contrary. Contradictions, humour, caprice, and folly, destroy themselves, and at last the good and the rational prevail, and the whole terminates in an intrinsic harmony which is only possible in the empire of true liberty, and not in that of caprice and humour.

This dialectic of irony, and therein the fundamental meaning of the whole drama, appears at its greatest height in the two fools. The melancholy Jaques is not drawn as a fool by profession; he appears merely as a comic, foolish character; but his profound superficiality, his witty sentimentality, his merry sadness, have struck root so deeply in his inmost being, that it shews throughout but the one stamp of folly and perversity. All these contrasts are in fact found in his character; his profoundness is really profound, but at the same time, when held up to the light, very superficial; his soft, tender sensitiveness is however full of sharp hooks and edges, and his melancholy in fact is in the highest degree merry and sportive. While all the other characters seem to regard life as a gay toy and merry pomp, he, with similar one-sidedness, takes it for a sombre funeral train, in which every mourner, weeping and wailing, is advancing to his own grave. The gay and festive play of the others bears, however, in itself, and eventually passes over into, a deep seriousness; so in like manner, in this case, the dull melancholy funeral train changes insensibly and involuntarily into a procession of fools. The merry fool, Touchstone, on the other hand, is the genuine English clown—the fool with the jingling cap-and-bells, who is and professes to be a fool, and so makes sport of himself and all the rest of the world. In this personification of irony, all the perversities and contradictions of the represented view of life are collected together; but on this obverse is stamped the profound truth and wisdom which lies hidden on the reverse of the whole. While the other lovers are in chase of some fancied ideal of beauty, amiability, and virtue, and yet, after all, run into the arms of very ordinary and every-day sort of beings, he takes for himself an ill-favoured piece of flesh of a country girl—he loves her because he chooses her—and he chooses her because he loves her. This is, indeed, the wilfulness of love, as it is depicted by Shakspeare in his comedies, in its full force. But it is even this very unreasonableness that renders it the wonderful and fatal power which seizes upon the heart and life of man without his knowledge or consent; while at the same time it represents that higher power, which, uninfluenced by human caprice and subjectivity, guides the life and history of mankind with unseen hand. Lastly, while all the other personages have adopted the solitary and free life of the forest, either through external circumstances or internal impulse—in short, on good reason, and of their free-will—he alone has come there without adequate cause or occasion, and even against his natural inclinations, which disposed him to prefer the ease and comforts of a court. Thus, beneath the outer shell of folly, he evinces a truly noble disinterestedness and fidelity. Lastly, while all the other characters appear more or less the playthings of their own caprice and wilfulness, he is the only one who makes a play both of himself and others, and thereby maintains a real independence and liberty; and in that he knowingly and intentionally makes himself a fool, he at least shews that he is possessed of the first necessary element of true intellectual freedom—the mastery over himself. One might almost pronounce the professed fool to be clearly the most rational of all this singular company, for he alone knows his own mind throughout; and while he takes every thing to be sheer folly, he at the same time views it all with the profound irony that is its due. A striking contrast to Touchstone is furnished by Sir Oliver Martext—the very embodying of the common prose of life, which suffers nothing in the world to lead it away from the text of the actual living reality, and which ever mars the profound, eternal meaning of the book of life.

It is hardly necessary to dwell on the skill and truthfulness with which all the other characters are conceived and worked out, or the lovely harmony and vivid contrast in which they are arranged and grouped together. It will be enough to allude to the deep feeling and nimble wit and intellect which are associated with Rosalind's fascinating archness—her saucy yet maidenly petulance—to the noble candour and openness, and the indestructible energy of a good disposition, which shew themselves in Orlando—to the bright colours in which the high-minded and good old Duke appears, as taught and softened by the sweet uses of adversity. In spite of all caprices, all perversities and inconsistencies, how much of what is truly noble and beautiful in humanity is here again displayed to us! It is obvious that all the characters are conceived and worked out in perfect keeping with the ground-idea of the whole; in the highest and most excellent, as well as in the basest and meanest, there reigns the same fantastic wilfulness, though under manifold modifications, occurring at one time as the inner motive, at another as the outward occasion of their resolves and actions. The arbitrary dethronement of the good Duke forms the basis and ground plan of the plot; the causeless persecution of Orlando by his brother; his sudden whim to try a fall with the Duke's wrestler; and the equally unmerited banishment of Rosalind, are the chief springs for the march of the action. In the wood of Arden all abandon themselves to the most unrestrained and diversified play of humour and fancy, which goes on until the wicked Oliver and the usurping Duke are suddenly converted, and Rosalind throws aside her disguise. Thus the principal moments of the action are in perfect keeping with the ground-idea of the whole. The whole is a deep pervading harmony, while sweet and soul-touching melodies play around; all is so ethereal, so tender and affecting, so free, fresh, and joyous, and so replete with a genial sprightliness, that I have no hesitation in pronouncing this comedy to be one of the most excellent compositions in the whole wide domain of poesy. (pp. 253-59)

> Hermann Ulrici, "Criticisms of Shakspeare's Dramas: 'As You Like It'—'Comedy of Errors'—'Winter's Tale'," in his Shakspeare's Dramatic Art: And His Relation to Calderon and Goethe, translated by Rev. A. J. W. Morrison, Chapman, Brothers, 1846, pp. 253-69.

## G. G. GERVINUS   (essay date 1849-50)

[One of the most widely read Shakespearean critics of the latter half of the nineteenth century, the German critic Gervinus was praised by such eminent contemporaries as Edward Dowden, F. J. Furnivall, and James Russell Lowell; however, he is little known in the English-speaking world today. Like his predecessor Hermann Ulrici, Gervinus wrote in the tradition of the "philosophical criticism" developed in Germany in the mid-nineteenth century. Under the influence of August Wilhelm Schlegel's literary theory and Georg Wilhelm Friedrich Hegel's philosophy, German critics like Gervinus tended to focus their analyses around a search for the literary work's organic unity and ethical import. Gervinus believed that Shakespeare's works contained a rational ethical system independent of any religion—in contrast to Ulrici, for whom Shakespeare's morality was basically Christian. The excerpt below is taken from the English translation of Gervinus's Shakespeare Commentaries, originally published in German in 1849-50. Comparing As You Like It with Thomas Lodge's Rosalynde, Gervinus contends that "on the whole, Shakespeare has completely eradicated the pastoral mannerism" and simplified the motives in his source, but has kept intact Lodge's principal moral, which Gervinus defines as the merits of "self-mastery, equanimity, and self-control in outward suffering and inward passion." He maintains that As You Like It is close to ordinary reality and that it "only borders on the limits of the fantastical." Concerning the characters, Gervinus objects to appraisals of Jaques's melancholy as "mild, human, and attractive"; it is, he claims, "rooted in bitterness and ill-humour." As a "shaming contrast to the calumniator Jaques," Gervinus points to Orlando, a "healthful, self-contained" youth who "promises [to be] a perfect man." In closing, the critic echoes a number of earlier commentators in describing Touchstone as "a fool of a somewhat more elevated nature" than Shakespeare's earlier fools, adding that this humorous figure also provided Shakespeare with the means to comment ironically on the traditional romanticized view of the pastoral ideal presented in his play.]

We may consider [As You Like It] as probably intended for a masque, a style of drama in which the poet, whether by the introduction of wonderful machinery or by the display of all kinds of pageantry, permitted himself somewhat more license than elsewhere, but in no wise a license which interfered with the truth of his grounds for action or the just unravelling of his plot. Thus we are here transported to a romantic Arcadia, into which the forest of Arden is metamorphosed. . . . If with respect to the locality a slightly fanciful feature is . . . introduced, this is also the case with respect to the characters of the play in Rosalind's pretence . . . of having learned witchcraft from an uncle. But this feature, also, borders so closely on the limits of ordinary reality that it might be completely effaced by clever management in the performance. . . . In this manner, the comedy only borders on the limits of the fantastical. And the justification of this lies in the style itself, whether it be that the poet composed the work as a masque, or as a pastoral drama, or as a play uniting the two styles. (p. 387)

Shakespeare met with the design of the story of this comedy in Lodge's pastoral romance [Rosalynde]. . . . Many of the Ovid-like reminiscences, and much of the mythological learning with which the romance abounds, still adhere to Shakespeare's play; but, on the whole, he has completely eradicated the pastoral mannerism, and, according to his wont, he simplifies the motives of the actions and ennobles the actions themselves. The rude enmity between Oliver and Orlando, which results in acts of violence in the romance, is properly moderated by our poet. He has removed the unnaturalness of Celia's banishment by her father on her protest against the banishment of Rosalind. The war, by which the exiled prince regains his throne, and the rescue of the ladies from robbers, with which in the romance Celia's love for Oliver is introduced, have been omitted by the dramatist in order that he might not disturb the peace and merry sports of his rural life by any discords. The play between Orlando and Rosalind is in the romance only a pastoral song, but Shakespeare has made it a link for the continuation of the action in the last act. In all the rest the poet adheres faithfully to the course of the story in the novel, without much addition and omission. He even kept closely before him the moral of the narrative, which in the romance is declared by perpetual repetitions, and is well adapted to the nature and position of the characters. . . . If we concentrate this moral reflection into one idea, we shall find that the intention of the narrative is to extol self-mastery, equanimity, and self-command in outward suffering and inward passion. We should scarcely imagine, at the first glance, that this idea lies also at the root of Shakespeare's comedy, so completely is every reflection avoided, and so entirely in the lightest and freest play of action and conversation is a mere picture sketched for our contemplation.

The author of the romance of Rosalind contrasts town and court life with rural and pastoral life, the one as a natural source of evil and misery, which finds its natural remedy in the other. . . . In the same manner [Shakespeare] appears to let the sorrows which arise at the court in the first and second acts find their cure in the pastoral life of the last three acts. In the same manner he imputes the cause of the disasters created there to the vices which belong to courts and to worldly life, to the envy and hatred arising from covetousness and ambition, and in the same manner he seeks the remedy for the wounds inflicted there in that moderation and simple contentment to which a life of solitude invites or even compels. The first acts begin therefore like a tragedy; they exhibit the actors in a state of war, from which they subsequently escape or are driven away to the merry sports of pleasure and peace which await them in the forest of Arden, with its hunting-life, and in the shepherds' cottages on its border. Duke Frederick is called even by his daughter a man of harsh and envious mind; he appears to be perpetually actuated by gloomy fancies, by suspicion and mistrust, and to be urged on by covetousness. . . . [In Oliver] there flows the same vein of avarice and envy as in the Duke. He strives to plunder his brother of his poor inheritance, he undermines his education and gentility, he first endeavours to stifle his mind, and then he lays snares for his life; all this he does from an undefined hatred of the youth, whom he is obliged to confess is 'full of noble device' [I. i. 167], but who for this very reason draws away the love of all his people from Oliver to himself; and on this account excites his envious jealousy. Both the Duke and Oliver equally forfeit the happiness which they seek, the one the heritage of his usurped dukedom, the other his lawful and unlawful possessions. And in this lies the primary impulse and the material motive for their subsequent renunciation of the world; a more moral incentive to this change of mind is given to Oliver in the preservation of his life by Orlando, and to the Duke in the warning voice of a religious man who speaks to his conscience and his fear. These are only sketches of characters, not intended to play conspicuous parts; but we see that they are drawn by the same sure hand which we have seen at work throughout Shakespeare's works.

The misery which proceeds from these two covetous and ambitious men, who were not even contented in and with their prosperity, affects in the first place the deposed Duke. He took flight with 'a many merry men' [I. i. 115] to the forest of Arden. . . . Thus withdrawn from the dangers of the 'envious court' [II. i. 4], they have learned to love exile beyond the painted pomp of the palace; endowed with patience and contentment, they have translated 'the stubbornness of fortune into so quiet and so sweet a style' [II. i. 19-20]. . . . The fragrance of the country, the scent of the wood, the tone of solitude in this part of the piece, have been always justly admired; colouring and scenery gently and tenderly attune the imagination of the reader, they make us understand how hermits in such a region feel impelled to fill up the leisure and void with meditation and reflection, and to open the heart to every soft emotion; the noise of the world falls only from afar on the ear of the happy escaped ones, and the poet has carefully avoided in any way inharmoniously to disturb this profound peace. When the starved Orlando introduces the only discord, by frightening the Duke and his companions at their meal, how wonderfully is this discord resolved at once by the loving gentleness with which they meet and help the needy one!

Only the one danger does this life possess, that by its monotony it awakes, in one and another, ennui, melancholy, and ill-humour. In the hunting circle round the Duke, Jaques is in this condition. He shares with the Duke and his companions the propensity for drawing wisdom and philosophy from the smallest observation and consideration; he has to excess the gift of linking reflections to the smallest event, and in this seclusion from the world these reflections have assumed a touch of despondency. The melancholy which this man imbibes from every occasion has always appeared to most readers . . . as mild, human, and attractive . . . ; but it is rooted, on the contrary, in a bitterness and ill-humour which render the witty and sententious worldling far rather a rude fault-finder than a contented sufferer like the rest. He is of that class of men to whom Bacon addresses this sentence:—'He who is prudent may seek to have desire; for he who does not strive after something with eagerness, finds everything burdensome and tedious.' In his hypochondriacal mood and in his spirit of contradiction—the remembrance of his travels and his former worldly life having left a sting behind—Jaques finds this forest life equally foolish as that of the court which they have quitted; he carries the state of nature and peace too far; he considers the chase of the

animals of the forest to be greater usurpation than that of the unlawful Duke; he flees from the solitary company into still greater solitude, and likes to hide his thoughts, the fruit of his former experience and of his present leisure; then again with eagerness he goes in quest of society and cheerful company. Wholly 'compact of jars' [II. vii. 5], he is blunted to all friendly habits, he is discontented with all, and even with the efforts of others to satisfy him; angry at his own birth and at his fortune, he rails against 'all the first-born of Egypt' [II. v. 61], he blames the whole world, finds matter for censure in the great system of the world, and stumbles over every grain of dust in his path. Long experienced in sin, he has learned to find out the shadow side of every age of man; he has satiated himself with the world, and has not entered upon this life of retirement furnished with the patience and contentment of the others, but from a natural passion for the contrary. If his satire is directed more against things in general, and is free from bitterness towards stated individuals, this is only a result of his inactive nature, which is rather calculated for observation and reflection than for work and action, and of his isolated position in this idyllic and peaceful life, in which moreover the poet will suffer no discord to arise. This character is entirely Shakespeare's property and addition. It furnishes a fresh instance to us of the two-sidedness of the poet's mind, with which so many proofs have made us familiar. Shakespeare does not imitate the trivial tradition of the pastoral poets, who praise the quiet life of nature in itself as a school for wisdom and contentment. He shows, in the contrast between Jaques and the Duke, that those who would desire enjoyment and advantage from this life must in themselves have a natural disposition for moderation and self-mastery; they must be able to disarm misfortune and to do without happiness. But this Jaques, according to the Duke, has been himself a libertine, leading a sensual and dissolute life, and he has now leaped from one extreme to another—a blasé man, an exhausted epicurean, an outcast from life. The sensible Orlando with true instinct perceives his censoriousness, regarding him as a fool or a cipher; Rosalind discovers it, and in the poet's own meaning with regard to those who are in extremity of either joy or sorrow, she calls the fools who are ever laughing, and those who carry melancholy to excess, 'abominable fellows who betray themselves to every modern censure, worse than drunkards' [IV. i. 6-7]. Thus carrying to excess his gloomy love of calumny, Jaques rebounds in the opposite extreme when he wishes to be invested in the fool's motley, to have 'as large a charter as the wind, to blow on whom he pleases' [II. vii. 48-9], and to cleanse 'the foul body of the infected world' [II. vii. 60]. Completely mistaking the inoffensive vocation of the fool, he wishes to 'disgorge' into the general world the poison he has caught from his evil experience [II. vii. 69]. As no opportunity for this is offered, he turns at last, retaining his former part, to the hermit Frederick, because, 'out of these convertites there is much matter to be heard and learned' [V. iv. 184-85].

We have seen how the banished Duke has converted his misery into smiling happiness. He is joined subsequently by the two ladies, Rosalind and Celia, and by Orlando. In them the poet has shown us what qualities caused them to spend the time in the 'golden world' [I. i. 118-19] of Arden more pleasurably than the melancholy Jaques. A more than sisterly bond inseparably chains the two cousins; in the romance they are compared with Orestes and Pylades; and in their fervent friendship alone we see the gift of self-renunciation, which renders them strangers to all egotism. Innocent and just, Celia solemnly promises at a future time to restore to Rosalind her withdrawn inheritance; she demands of her in return to be as merry as she is herself; she would, she says to her, had their positions been different, have been happier; and she proves this subsequently, when, a better friend than daughter, she follows the banished cousin into exile. Rosalind for a long time disarms her uncle's envy and suspicion by her innocent nature, which even in thought wishes no evil to an enemy; he was overcome by the universal impression of her character, which won for her the praise and pity of the people. She bore her sorrow in 'smoothness, silence, and patience' [I. iii. 77-9]. . . . We recognise plainly . . . the disposition to command herself and to deprive misfortune of its sting. But for this we must not consider her cold and heartless. She feels deeply that fortune has punished her with disfavour; and when in the person of Orlando she meets one equally struck by fate, her heart, taken unawares, betrays how accessible she is to the most lively feelings. The similarly hapless circumstances which Orlando announces to her, his combat with the wrestler, his descent from an old friend of her father's, all this, added to his attractive manner, helps to conquer *her,* who has already vanquished *him.* 'Her pride fell with her fortunes' [I. ii. 252]; she gives the victor a chain which seals at once her fate and her almost hereditary love; she rashly and involuntarily reveals her feelings, having only moments in which to see him; she turns back to him, and once again she even says to him that he has 'overthrown more than his enemies' [I. ii. 254]; and immediately afterwards we find her fallen 'fathom-deep in love' [IV. i. 206]. We see indeed that a violent passion has to be mastered; *how* she masters it is afterwards the problem which she has to solve in her subsequent meeting with Orlando. In this Orlando, on the other side, we perceive just as readily the same naturally excitable temperament, and, at the same time, the power of self-command which knows how to restrain it. He has been 'trained like a peasant' [I. i. 68] by his brother, and treated like a slave; he feels the disadvantage of his deficient education more than the crushed nobility of his birth; the 'spirit of his father grows strong in him' [I. i. 70-1]; he will no longer endure the unworthy treatment; and when Oliver insults in him the honour of his father, he attacks his elder brother, not so far, however, as, according to [Lodge's] romance, to forget himself in acts of violence or to lay snares for revenge, but even in anger he is master of himself. The feeling of his nothingness struggles in his mind with an ambitious striving. He seeks the combat with the feared wrestler Charles, contented to meet death, since he has no honour to lose and no friends to wrong, but still hoping to recommend himself by victory, and to secure himself from his brother. Instead of this, he provokes the Duke to suspicion and excites Oliver to designs against his life; and although he has just tested his own strength, he prefers to wander away rather than to meet the malice of his brother. So in the wood afterwards, with the anxiety of childlike fidelity and the strength of an irritated wild beast, he is quickly resolved to maintain with sword and violence the life of his fainting old servant, but he is gentle as a lamb again when he meets with friendly courteousness. Subsequently, when he sees his brother sleeping in the arms of danger, he is not untempted to revenge, but fraternal love prevails. Throughout we see the healthful, self-contained, calm nature of a youth, which promises a perfect man. Everything in him bespeaks a child of nature, who has remained pure and uninjured in the midst of a corrupt world. What a shaming contrast to the calumniator Jaques, whom he thus answers, when he invites him to rail with him against the deceitful world: 'I will chide no breather in the world but myself, against whom I know most faults!' [III. ii. 280-81]. How innocent does the young Hercules appear in his laconic bashfulness, when love has 'overthrown' him [I. ii. 259], when

Rosalind makes him her valuable gift and her still more valuable confession, and he finds no words to thank her for the one and to reply to the other!

In all these characteristics, in all three individuals, we cannot overlook the predisposition to a natural power of resistance against the overwhelming force of outward evil and of inward emotion. Endowed with this gift, they bear about with them a spring of happiness, as is proved by the ladies in their merry league in the very scene of hatred and persecution. This spring, however, will of course flow more richly as soon as it is set free from hindrances, and freed from the intricate and manifold passions of a rude and intriguing society; when it is, as it were, left to itself and thrown on its own affections and feelings. (pp. 390-96)

In Touchstone, Shakespeare has for the first time produced a fool of a somewhat more elevated nature. In all the earlier comedies there have been only clowns introduced, natural fools whose wit is either studied and mechanically prepared or is given out in droll unconsciousness. The fool alone in *All's Well that Ends Well* has somewhat of the 'prophetic' vein in him, which he ascribes to himself according to the general notion of the age that fools, in virtue of their capacity for speaking 'the truth the next way' [*All's Well That End's Well*, I. iii. 58-9], possessed something of a divine and foretelling character. Shakespeare, at any rate in his artistic efforts, rendered complete homage to this notion of the age respecting the higher significance of fools. He left to the Ben Jonsons and the Malvolios that over-wisdom, which from learned haughtiness and pedantry, or from self-love or corrupt taste, looks down contemptuously or censuringly on these characters of comedy. As we [often see in his plays], he invested even the simple clowns with a deeper significance, from the relation in which he always placed them to the action of the piece, without fearing to place constraint on nature and truth; for who has not often witnessed, in living examples, how mother-wit solves unconsciously and easily problems over which the wise labour, and how a childlike mind executes in simplicity that which no understanding of the intelligent perceives? But a higher value than this is attributed by Shakespeare to the men of wit, to the real fools who play their part with knowledge, to whom full power is given to speak the truth, to rend asunder, as often as they will, the veil of mere propriety and hypocrisy, and wittily to unmask the folly of others under cover of their own. This appeared to Shakespeare 'a practice as full of labour as a wise man's art' [*Twelfth Night,* III. i. 65-6], and as useful as a chaplain's discourse. For it appeared to him to belong to the most expert knowledge of the world and of men, of the 'quality of persons and the time' [*Twelfth Night,* III. i. 63], to use appropriately and wisely the sting of seeming folly; and he admired the watchful and acute mind, which was quick enough to discover the veiled weaknesses of men and understood how like 'the haggard to check at every feather that comes before his eye' [*Twelfth Night,* III. i. 64-5]. . . . [Touchstone] is not quite so expert nor so sensible of his wit as the fools in *Twelfth Night* and *Lear;* but he is also not on the same ground with Costard, Launce, and Launcelot. He stands on the doubtful limit between instinct and consciousness, where this character is the most acceptable. Jaques regards him as a clown, who has 'crammed' the strange places of his dry brain with observation, which 'he vents in mangled forms' [II. vii. 40-2]; he considers him as one of those 'natural philosophers' . . . of whom Touchstone himself says that they have learned no wit by nature nor art [III. ii. 32]. The two ladies call him by turns a natural and a fool; Celia, in his face, ascribes to him the dulness of the fool, which is the whetstone of the witty, while to the true fool the folly of others is the whetstone of his wit. And Touchstone himself assumes the appearance of being wiser than he himself knew; he shall, he says, ne'er be 'ware of his own wit, till he breaks his shins against it. On the other hand, from his expressions in other passages, he regards himself as far superior to the clown and the natural philosopher, and the Duke readily perceives his design behind his interposing folly; 'he uses his folly,' he says, 'like a stalking-horse, and under the presentation of that he shoots his wit' [V. iv. 106-07].

Entirely corresponding with this two-sided capacity are his actions and language throughout the piece. He performs his tricks in the manner of the clowns, with whom roguish acts pass for wit. On the other hand, the poet has consigned to him the part of the comic chorus in the comedy, in which the fool should always be employed. . . . Shakespeare has employed the mouth of his fool as his stalking-horse, to express his opinion of the customary idealising of shepherd life in pastoral poetry, in the same sense as it appears in his play and in the scenes it contains. On Corin's question, as to how he likes this shepherd's life, Touchstone answers him: 'Truly, shepherd, in respect of itself it is a good life; but in respect that it is a shepherd's life it is naught. In respect that it is solitary, I like it very well; but in respect that it is private, it is a very vile life. Now, in respect it is in the fields, it pleaseth me well; but in respect it is not in the court, it is tedious. As it is a spare life, look you, it fits my humour well; but as there is no more plenty in it, it goes much against my stomach. Hast any philosophy in thee, shepherd?' [III. ii. 13-22]. It seems to me that perhaps all pastoral poetry put together scarcely contains so much real wisdom as this philosophy of the fool. He finds nothing to say against the shepherd's life, but nothing also against the contrary manner of living; and the homely simplicity of Corin himself is on his side in this, that he leaves courtly manners to the court and country ones to the country. Shakespeare knew nothing of the one-sidedness which condemned or rejected either life in the world or life in retirement, the one for the sake of the other. Rather does the fool's wit consider him who merely knows the one, or, as the meaning is, merely esteems the one, as 'damned, like an ill-roasted egg, all on one side' [III. ii. 37-8]. In Shakespeare's play, no expression of preference rests on either of the two kinds of life. In neither of the two circles does he find the condition of happiness or virtue in itself, but he sees happiness most surely dwelling, not in this or that place, but in the beings who have a capacity and a natural share of qualification for either or for every other kind of existence; in those beings who, exiled from the world, do not feel themselves miserable, just as little so as when they are recalled to the world from their solitude. The poet knows nothing of a certain situation, condition, or age, which would be a sure source of happiness; but he knows that there are men in all classes and generations, like his Duke, his Rosalind, and his old Adam Spencer, who bear in their bosoms that equanimity and contentment which is the only fruitful soil of all true inner happiness, and who carry with them wherever they go a smiling Eden and a golden age. (pp. 402-05)

> G. G. Gervinus, "Second Period of Shakespeare's Dramatic Poetry, Comedies: 'As You Like It'," in his Shakespeare Commentaries, translated by F. E. Bunnètt, revised edition, 1877. Reprint by AMS Press Inc., 1971, pp. 386-405.

## HIPPOLYTE A. TAINE   (essay date 1863)

[Taine was a nineteenth-century French philosopher, literary critic, and historian who gained a wide reputation for his theories of the interdependence of physical and psychological factors in human development. He applied these theories—adding emphasis to the importance, for historians and critics, of studying the physical and psychological factors responsible for cultural and social development—to the study of English literature in his monumental Histoire de la Littérature Anglaise (1863). In the following excerpt from an English translation of this work, Taine admires As You Like It for "the pleasantness of [its] puerilities" and its refreshing "absence of the serious." Like earlier commentators, he imagines Shakespeare deliberately downplaying his narrative—"there are no events, and there is no plot"—suggesting that what makes the play enjoyable is the beauty of the setting and the attractiveness of the love poetry. Taine also discerns an autobiographical element in As You Like It, suspecting that such lines as "the shade of melancholy boughs" at II. vii. 111-12 express Shakespeare's "delicate soul, bruised by the shocks of social life," just as Jaques is a "transparent mask" of the poet.]

As you Like it is a caprice. Action there is none; interest barely; likelihood still less. And the whole is charming. Two cousins, princes' daughters, come to a forest with a court clown, Celia disguised as a shepherdess, Rosalind as a boy. They find here the old duke, Rosalind's father, who, driven out of his duchy, lives with his friends like a philosopher and a hunter. They find amorous shepherds, who with songs and prayers pursue intractable shepherdesses. They discover or they meet with lovers who become their husbands. Suddenly it is announced that the wicked Duke Frederick, who had usurped the crown, has just retired to a cloister, and restored the throne to the old exiled duke. Every one gets married, every one dances, everything ends with a "rustic revelry" [V. iv. 177]. Where is the pleasantness of these puerilities? First, the fact of its being puerile; the absence of the serious is refreshing. There are no events, and there is no plot. We gently follow the easy current of graceful or melancholy emotions, which takes us away and moves us about without wearying. The place adds to the illusion and charm. It is an autumn forest, in which the sultry rays permeate the blushing oak leaves, or the half-stript ashes tremble and smile to the feeble breath of evening. The lovers wander by brooks that "brawl" [II. i. 32] under antique roots. As you listen to them, you see the slim birches, whose cloak of lace grows glossy under the slant rays of the sun that gilds them, and the thoughts wander down the mossy vistas in which their footsteps are not heard. What better place could be chosen for the comedy of sentiment and the play of heart-fancies? Is not this a fit spot in which to listen to love-talk? Some one has seen Orlando, Rosalind's lover, in this glade; she hears it and blushes. "Alas the day! . . . What did he, when thou sawest him? What said he? How looked he? Wherein went he? What makes he here? Did he ask for me? Where remains he? How parted he with thee? and when shalt thou see him again?" [III. ii. 219-24]. Then, with a lower voice, somewhat hesitating: "Looks he as freshly as he did the day he wrestled?" [III. ii. 230-31]. She is not yet exhausted: "Do you not know I am a woman? When I think, I must speak. Sweet, say on" [III. ii. 249-50]. One question follows another, she closes the mouth of her friend, who is ready to answer. At every word she jests, but agitated, blushing, with a forced gaiety; her bosom heaves, and her heart beats. Nevertheless she is calmer when Orlando comes; bandies words with him; sheltered under her disguise, she makes him confess that he loves Rosalind. Then she plagues him, like the frolic, the wag, the coquette she is. "Why, how now, Orlando, where have you been all this while? You a lover?" [IV. i. 38-40]. Orlando repeats that he loves Rosalind, and she pleases herself by making him repeat it more than once. She sparkles with wit, jests, mischievous pranks; pretty fits of anger, feigned sulks, bursts of laughter, deafening babble, engaging caprices. "Come, woo me, woo me; for now I am in a holiday humour, and like enough to consent. What would you say to me now, an I were your very very Rosalind?" [IV. i. 68-71]. And every now and then [in IV. i.] she repeats with an arch smile, "And I am your Rosalind; am I not your Rosalind?" Orlando protests that he would die. Die! Who ever thought of dying for love! Leander? He took one bath too many in the Hellespont; so poets have said he died for love. Troilus? A Greek broke his head with a club; so poets have said he died for love. Come, come, Rosalind will be softer. And then she plays at marriage with him, and makes Celia pronounce the solemn words. She irritates and torments her pretended husband; tells him all the whims she means to indulge in, all the pranks she will play, all the teasing he will have to endure. The retorts come one after another like fireworks. At every phrase we follow the looks of these sparkling eyes, the curves of this laughing mouth, the quick movements of this supple figure. It is a bird's petulance and volubility. "O coz, coz, coz, my pretty little coz, that thou didst know how many fathom deep I am in love" [IV. i. 205-07]. Then she provokes her cousin Celia, sports with her hair, calls her by every woman's name. Antitheses without end, words all a-jumble, quibbles, pretty exaggerations, word-racket; as you listen, you fancy it is the warbling of a nightingale. The trill of repeated metaphors, the melodious roll of the poetical gamut, the summer-warbling rustling under the foliage, change the piece into a veritable opera. The three lovers end by chanting a sort of trio [at V. ii. 83-8, 94-102]. The first throws out a fancy, the others take it up. Four times this strophe is renewed; and the symmetry of ideas, added to the jingle of the rhymes, makes of a dialogue a concerto of love.... The necessity of singing is so urgent, that a minute later songs break out of themselves. The prose and the conversation end in lyric poetry. We pass straight on into these odes. We do not find ourselves in a new country. We feel the emotion and foolish gaiety as if it were a holiday. We see the graceful couple whom the song of the two pages brings before us, passing in the misty light "o'er the green corn-field" [V. iii. 18], amid the hum of sportive insects, on the finest day of the flowering spring-time. Unlikelihood grows natural, and we are not astonished when we see Hymen leading the two brides by the hand to give them to their husbands.

Whilst the young folks sing, the old folk talk. Their life also is a novel, but a sad one. Shakspeare's delicate soul, bruised by the shocks of social life, took refuge in contemplations of solitary life. To forget the strife and annoyances of the world, he must bury himself in a wide silent forest, and

> Under the shade of melancholy boughs,
> Loose and neglect the creeping hours of time.

We look at the bright images which the sun carves on the white beech-boles, the shade of trembling leaves flickering on the thick moss, the long waves of the summit of the trees; then the sharp sting of care is blunted; we suffer no more, simply remembering that we suffered once; we feel nothing but a gentle misanthropy, and being renewed, we are the better for it. The old duke is happy in his exile. Solitude has given him rest, delivered him from flattery, reconciled him to nature. He pities the stags which he is obliged to hunt for food:

> Come, shall we go and kill us venison?
> And yet it irks me the poor dappled fools,
> Being native burghers of this desert city,
> Should in their own confines with forked heads
> Have their round haunches gored.

Nothing sweeter than this mixture of tender compassion, dreamy philosophy, delicate sadness, poetical complaints, and rustic songs.... Amongst [the] lords is found a soul that suffers more, Jaques the melancholy, one of Shakspeare's best-loved characters, a transparent mask behind which we perceive the face of the poet. He is sad because he is tender; he feels the contact of things too keenly, and what leaves others indifferent, makes him weep. He does not scold, he is sad; he does not reason, he is moved; he has not the combative spirit of a reforming moralist; his soul is sick and weary of life. Impassioned imagination leads quickly to disgust. Like opium, it excites and shatters. It leads man to the loftiest philosophy, then lets him down to the whims of a child. Jaques leaves other men abruptly, and goes to the quiet nooks to be alone. He loves his sadness, and would not exchange it for joy.... He has the fancies of a nervous woman. He is scandalised because Orlando writes sonnets on the forest trees. He is eccentric, and finds subjects of grief and gaiety, where others would see nothing of the sort.... Jacques hearing [Touchstone moralise in II. vii.] begins to laugh "sans intermission" that a fool could be so meditative [II. vii. 33, 42-3].... The next minute he returns to his melancholy dissertations, bright pictures whose vivacity explains his character, and [in his "All the world's a stage" speech at II. vii. 139-66,] betrays Shakspeare, hiding under his name.... (pp. 128-34)

*Hippolyte A. Taine, "The Normans," in his* History of English Literature, Vol. I, *translated by H. van Laun, Grosset & Dunlap, Publishers, 1908, pp. 95-169.*

## CHARLES COWDEN CLARKE (essay date 1863)

[*Clarke was a scholar, critic, and public lecturer on the arts and drama. His Shakespeare lectures, which he began in 1834, proved to be one of the major factors in the renewed interest in Shakespeare's works during the Victorian era. Clarke also edited, with his wife, Mary,* The Shakespearean Key *(1879), a kind of topical concordance, and a multivolumed edition of Shakespeare's plays. In the following excerpt, Clarke evinces a Christian, moral approach in his study of the characters in* As You Like It. *Unlike most earlier critics, he regards Jaques not as a melancholic figure, but as "tinged with the* affectation *of melancholy," a "satire upon your pretenders to wisdom." Clarke characterizes Orlando as "the very perfection of gentleness in manliness" and praises his "inherent nobleness and high spirit." Concerning Rosalind, the critic admires the "womanly vivacity of her character," comparing her with Beatrice in* Much Ado about Nothing. *And in his discussion of Touchstone, Clarke emphasizes the character's "genuine qualities of ... affection," describing him as "not in the least a buffoon" or mere jester, but a good-natured individual able "to draw truth and beauty, as well as fine humour, out of passing life."*]

The exiled Duke [in "As You Like It"] is a perfect exemplar of what should comprise a Christian's course—a cheerful gratitude for the benefits that have been showered upon him; a calm, yet firm endurance of adversity; a tolerance of unkindness; and a promptitude to forgive injuries. How sweet, and yet how strong is his moral nature! It seems as though no trial, social or physical, could change the current of his gracious wisdom. In a scene subsequent to that containing his celestial confession of moral faith, we have the proof that his philosophy is no cold profession merely,—no lip-deep ostentation,—no barren theory without practice. His conduct shows that his cheerful morality nestles in his heart, and inspires his actions. It is the seventh Scene of the second Act, where he and his followers are about to sit down to their woodland meal, when

Orlando rushes in with his drawn sword, and demands food. There is in every point of the Duke's behaviour on this occasion, the forbearance, the gentleness, the charity, and the cordial courtesy which grow out of such philosophy as his—that of unaffected contentment. "Sweet are the uses of adversity" [II. i. 12], indeed, when they teach such lessons as these! We cannot fancy that this true-hearted gentleman could have so perfected his native character had he never known the reverse of fortune, which exiled him from his court, and sent him among the forest-trees to learn wisdom from all-bounteous Nature; to know the worth of his true friends, who forsook land and station to share his seclusion; and to secure a peace of soul seldom known to those who live perpetually in the turmoil of public life. (pp. 36-7)

When we design to change our course of the moralising in this most perfect of Arcadian plays, we will accompany the "melancholy Jaques"—albeit not an especial favourite with us, for he is somewhat tinged with the *affectation* of melancholy and philosophy. Besides, we recognise no more affinity with "melancholy" than did Shakespeare himself, who never misses an opportunity of girding at your pompous and affectedly pensive character, and of proclaiming the superior qualifications of cheerfulness and good-humour. (p. 37)

Jaques, nevertheless, is a great character in his way, and good too; as, indeed, says the Duke, "there is good" (more or less) "in everything" [II. i. 17]. His chuckling account of the court fool, whom he stumbles upon in one of his rambles through the forest, is choicely good, and is as famous; both as giving a capital sketch of the man described, and as affording a characteristic picture of the mind of him who is describing. Jaques finds the fool-jester's conventional affectations irresistibly comic, while he betrays his own individual affectations even in the act of laughing at the other's.

Jaques is the model of a man addicted to self-contemplation; he always appears to be before his own mental looking-glass. He has inherited or acquired the tact to discern the worthlessness of artificial society, but he has not carried that tact into the wisdom of turning his philosophy the sunny side outwards. (p. 38)

From [the Duke's rebuke of Jaques at II. vii. 58-69], it appears clear that Shakespeare had in view the overweening mouth-moralist; for, with all the reflections and sarcasms he has put into the mouth of this self-asserting philosopher, and which have the air of being gleanings from the harvests of other men rather than the result of his own growth, it is to be remarked that he never brings him point to point in contest of wit with any of the other characters of the play, but he is foiled; they, being natural people, outwit the artificial one. (p. 39)

[An instance] (to my mind at least) that Shakespeare intended Jaques for a grave coxcomb, appears with some strength in that short parley between him and Amiens, after the sprightly song, "Under the greenwood tree." Observe the pomposity and patronising air with which the philosopher condescends to encourage the ballad-singer:—

More, more, I prithee, more.

*Am.* It will make you *melancholy*, Monsieur Jaques.

[II. v. 9-11]

Amiens is hoaxing him. What is there in a merry roundelay to make a man melancholy? Jaques, however, is so engrossed

with himself that he takes the songster gravely and literally. (pp. 41-2)

Shakespeare certainly intended the character of Jaques to be a satire upon your pretenders to wisdom; and I have [thus] rather enlarged and insisted on this reading of it, because the world (both literary and theatrical) appear to have misunderstood the poet's intention. (p. 42)

In the character of Orlando, Shakespeare has depicted the very perfection of gentleness in manliness—modesty in manhood. He is an exemplar of the power of gentleness, and the gentleness of power. His inadequate training and breeding—the result of his despotic brother's tyrannous restraint and miserly allowance—induces a withdrawing, a self-mistrust, that is only counterbalanced by his inherent nobleness and high spirit. Orlando is by nature generous, warm, eager, without one spark of conceit or presumption. He is by conformation robust, athletic—a model of manly vigour—and yet, as old Chaucer hath it, "Meek of his port as is a maid." The dramatist has markedly and vividly kept before us this point of Orlando's personal strength as a counterbalance to the extreme mildness of his disposition. He perpetually reminds us of his might of frame, his might and command of limb, and his bodily force, in order that his tenderness of heart and modesty of deportment may in no wise show like effeminacy, or an undue softness, but in their full advantage and truth of manly gentleness.

His consciousness of a too homely and unworthy nature is well set off by his spirited remonstrance to his ungenerous and unjust elder brother; his signal encounter with Charles, the wrestler, and complete overthrow of the "strong man," enhance the pathos of his self-resigned speech, uttered immediately before he enters upon his athletic trial; and his firm yet courteous reply to Duke Frederick, and his self-possessed bearing to the courtier, Le Beau, heighten by contrast the diffidence and touching emotion of his address to the two princesses—or rather of his *reception* of the words which they address to *him*. (pp. 43-4)

The most manifest display of Orlando's combined qualities of personal force and courage with moral suavity is in the scene where he rushes with drawn sword to the greenwood table of the banished Duke, to demand food for his faithful old servitor; and where, upon being received with that mild inquiry—

What would you have? Your gentleness shall force
More than your force move us to gentleness;

[II. vii. 102-03]

he at once resumes the bearing natural to him; and after explaining his urgent need, concludes with,

Let gentleness my strong enforcement be:
In the which hope, *I blush*, and hide my sword;

[II. vii. 118-19]

a perfect illustration of manly diffidence. But the triumph of Orlando's generous nature—at once capable of revenging itself by force of arms, yet incapable of revenge by force of gentle-heartedness—shines forth in his slaying the lioness that would have killed his sleeping brother: that brother who had dealt so unjustly by his orphaned youth; and, indeed, who had treacherously sought his life. (pp. 44-5)

Rosalind is one of the most enchanting among jocund-spirited heroines. Her first scene shows the womanly sentiment, as well as the womanly vivacity of her character. We see her natural cheerfulness clouded by sympathy for her banished father; revived at the instance of her cousin, the crystal-hearted Celia, who cannot endure to see her cast down. Their opening dialogue well displays the affectionate nature and playful wit of both women; for Celia is hardly inferior to Rosalind in witty accomplishment, though rarely displaying it, in order, with a generous prodigality, that her cousin's may shine forth uninterruptedly. But, perhaps, the two most gifted of Shakespeare's women, with that peculiar power of fancy and instinct called "wit," are Rosalind and Beatrice [in *Much Ado about Nothing*]. But how individually and distinctively has he characterised the wit of the respective heroines! That of Beatrice is sarcastic—that of Rosalind, playful. The one is biting, pointed, keen; the other is sprightly, sportive, sympathetic. The one is like the lightning, sudden, dazzling, startling, and sometimes scathing; the other is like the sunshine, cheerful, beaming full of life, and glow, and warmth, and animation. We are apt to shrink from the wit of Beatrice; we *bask* in that of Rosalind. (pp. 45-6)

[Of Celia], I must take leave to descant *at will;* for she is of inestimable worth. Celia is one of those characters that pass through society in almost unrecognised perfection. They are beloved for their tempers, and respected for their understandings and attainments. They make no display of their qualities; and yet they are an unfailing resource when a friend needs assistance or advice—domestic or mental. It is difficult, upon demand, to indicate any prominent example of their intellectual or social excellences—the impression in their favour is general and unequivocal. And so with the career of Celia in this play: it leaves a bland and gratified impression upon the mind of the reader; with a sense of uncertainty as to what scene we should quote as a specimen of more than quiet excellence. (p. 46)

Celia is a worshipper of her cousin; and yet so pure in her loving idolatry, that neither the idol appears conscious of superiority, nor does the idolater become inferior. Celia accompanies and attends her friend implicitly, but so genuine and spontaneous is her personal attachment that she scarcely seems to *follow* Rosalind. She is, in fact, her double, her very shadow; yet so clear and lustrous is her own affectionate nature that it is never thrown into shadow, even by the effulgence of Rosalind's wit. The very generosity with which she constantly, and as if involuntarily, cedes the precedence to Rosalind's keener intellect, only serves to heighten the effect of her own fine understanding and just perception. Indeed, Celia would be a wit and heroine of the first water in any other play, and as a character by herself. But seen by the side of Rosalind— to whom her own modesty (the modesty of loving-kindness) chooses to yield the palm, in standing silently by, while her cousin keeps up the ball of wit-raillery with others—she does not display to the same brilliant advantage. What she does say, however, amply testifies that, if she chose, she could shine to the full as brightly as the gifted Rosalind: by which means the poet has ingeniously conveyed to us the impression that hers is a *voluntary non*-speech,—a silence arising from preference to hear her cousin, and from no deficiency on her own part. (p. 48)

It is a glowing instance of Shakespeare's prodigality of loving resources, and his potency, as well as plenitude of means to inspire infinity of liking, that he makes us admire and love Rosalind the more for her vicinity to the sweethearted Celia, and Celia the more for hers to the bewitching Rosalind. We love and esteem each the better for the other's sake. Shakespeare has this in common with Nature—and how many qualities does he *not* possess in common with her? The love he

causes us to feel for his several characters—individually distinct and dissimilar as they may be, or sympathetic and analogous one with the other as they may be—never interferes with your love for them all. In teaching us to see the enchanting qualities that embellish a Rosalind, he never lets us lose sight of the tender devotion and unselfish beauty that distinguish a Celia. In making us feel the full value of a gentle, affectionate being like Celia, he never suffers us to overlook the grace and fascination of her cousin. Like the love which Nature puts into our heart—with its own bounteous magic, it fills our soul for one selected object, while it still affords room for loving regard and estimation towards all existing human merit. Nay, the exclusive preference for the *one* beloved, but expands our capacity for perceiving excellence elsewhere, and for yielding it our admiration and our loving-kindness.

We have . . . proof of the estimation in which Shakespeare held a cheerful philosophy, in the personal qualities he has given to Touchstone, the clown. Touchstone—the universal favourite—the man of mirth and good-humour; but who, nevertheless, can tang out a sarcasm with any professor of cynicism. Touchstone is a fellow possessing genuine qualities of attachment and affection. When Rosalind is expelled the court by the usurping Duke, and Celia, in that gentle speech, resolves to share her fortunes, the question is started, whether it were not good to have the Fool for their safeguard; and she says, "He'll go along o'er the wide world with me: leave me alone to woo him" [I. iii. 132-33]. . . . The court-life was to him a second nature; nevertheless, it becomes a second object in his choice when his young mistress is to leave it. And although it may be said that he was ignorant of what he had to encounter in following a woodland life, subject to the shrewd caprice of the elements; yet, when he does encounter them, he bears the change from that he prefers, with all the playfulness and sweet temper of the wiseliest ordered mind. (pp. 53-4)

Touchstone has good and gentlemanly feeling; witness his rebuke to the courtier Le Beau, who gives a description of the hurts and wounds of the three young fellows who have been overthrown by Charles the wrestler, and the moan made over them by their poor old father; and which encounter he details with a cruel relish and enjoyment as "sport," and expressing regret that the ladies have missed seeing it. (pp. 54-5)

Touchstone has also *right* feeling; for, although his worldly-reaped terrors of matrimony give him a qualm or two, and a momentary thought of availing himself of the hedge-parson's services to wed him, that so slip-knot a marriage might give him a chance of retreating, in case of repenting at leisure; yet his good faith and "right feeling" hold good, and he determines to act honourably by the trusting and doating Audrey.

He has a keen eye for pretension; for he sees through Professor Jaques's pretended immaculacy, and his assumption in moral philosophy. He treats him with a kind of old-glove easiness of familiarity,—a negligent, dressing-gown air of equality, as amusing in effect as it is warranted in fact. . . . (p. 55)

He has the delightful quality (quite that of a sweet-natured person,—one who is at once good-hearted, good-humoured, and good-minded,) of being able to make himself happy and contented wherever fortune chances to cast him. He is gay and easy at court;—he is good-tempered and at ease in the forest. He makes himself at home anywhere and everywhere; for he carries his own sunshine about with him. Touchstone is not a mere jester—a mere extracter of *fun* from what occurs around him; and he is not in the least a buffoon:—there is nothing low or common in his composition. He has excellent sense, and the good feeling to draw truth and beauty, as well as fine humour, out of passing life. (pp. 55-6)

It was a happy thought to introduce the court-jester among the shepherds and shepherdesses of a pastoral drama. His pert railleries and waggishness come with the best possible relief to the honey-dew sentimentalities of the writers of love-verses. His quizzing of Rosalind is in the best style of light o' love, and mock romance. ''I remember when I was in love,'' he says, ''I broke my sword upon a stone, and bid him take that for coming a-nigh to Jane Smile. We that are true lovers run into strange capers; but, as all is mortal in nature, so is all nature in love mortal in folly'' [II. iv. 46-8, 54-6]. Rosalind tells him that he has ''spoken more wisdom than he was aware of;'' and he answers with amusing conceit and mock humility: ''Nay, I shall never be aware of my own wit, till I break my shins against it'' [II. iv. 58-9]. (pp. 56-7)

It was good, also, to pay that compliment to rural simplicity, that the court-bred clown should become honestly attracted by a primitive clod of mother-earth; and most true to nature that the country-wench should have her head turned by the wooing of a gentleman, who had been the companion of princes. Audrey is the most perfect specimen of a wondering she-gawky. She thanks the gods she is foul; and if to be poetical is not to be honest, she thanks the gods also that she is not poetical. (pp. 57-8)

She would be anything that her new lover might require of her. She casts off William, as if he were a broken patten, and gallops away with his rival, as she would to a harvest-home, or a wake at a fair. She has no idea of marriage beyond a merry-making,—a new gown and ribands, cakes and ale, and a rousing country-dance. Audrey is a homely type of human nature—a rough clod turned off the great lathe, untrimmed, unglazed. Happy for her that she made choice of one who did not make a goddess of her at first, and a broken-spirited drudge afterwards. (p. 58)

We must not pass over unregarded that beautiful little sketch of a character in old Adam, with his heart of fourteen, and his body of fourscore years. He must have honourable mention, if it be only for the lovely homily put into his simple and confiding mouth, when he spares with his young master, Orlando, his little ''all'' of savings, trusting for the hereafter to Him, that ''doth the ravens feed, yea, providently caters for the sparrow'' [II. iii. 43-4]. (p. 59)

''As You Like It'' has been denominated a ''Pastoral Drama.'' I have no objection to the term, and have no inclination to discuss the principles of the pastoral:—in this instance, suffice to me to arrive at the conclusion, that no composition of the same class will bear comparison with it, for the combination of exquisite poetry,—both descriptive and moral, fanciful, playful, and passionate; for variety and amiability of character; for gravity, wit, and broad humour. It is altogether so perfect a piece of homage to the happy state of a rural, unartificial life, that every scene in it, untainted with bad passions, occurs amid the pomp and garniture of God's creation—the green fields and the forest glades. (p. 60)

> *Charles Cowden Clarke, ''''As You Like It','' in his*
> Shakespeare-Characters: Chiefly Those Subordinate,
> *Smith, Elder, & Co., 1863, pp. 33-60.*

*Act I. Scene ii. Adam, Duke Frederick, Rosalind, Celia, Charles, Orlando, and Courtiers. Frontispiece to the Hanmer edition by Francis Hayman (1744). By permission of the Folger Shakespeare Library.*

### REV. H. N. HUDSON   (essay date 1872)

[*Hudson was a nineteenth-century American clergyman and literary scholar whose Harvard edition of Shakespeare's works, published in twenty volumes between 1880 and 1881, contributed substantially to the growth of Shakespeare's popularity in America. He also issued two critical works on Shakespeare, one a collection of lectures, the other—and the more successful—a biographical and critical study entitled* Shakespeare, His Life, Art, and Characters *(1872). In the following excerpt from the last-named work, Hudson is principally interested in finding examples of ''Christian discipline'' and moral behavior among the characters in* As You Like It. *He begins his study by warning against attributing to nature—as many critics have—''the goodness which proceeds from habits generated under Gospel culture,'' stating that the characters could not act as virtuous as they do were it not for their contacts with civilization. Hudson then examines the various figures in the play. He describes Orlando as ''one of the highest results of Christian discipline,'' noting in him ''plenty of heroic stuff'' of the kind that grows from ''free and spontaneous'' virtue. Of the other male characters, Hudson continues, Duke Senior is ''built up with Christian discipline,'' Touchstone demonstrates Shakespeare's ''human-heartedness,'' and Jaques, though fond of solitude, is ''nevertheless far from being unsocial.'' Unlike many previous commentators, Hudson also contends that Jaques's melancholy is not malignant, but is the product of self-love and ''an excess of generative virtue.'' Hudson asserts that Shakespeare's ''geographical license''—the strange combination of lions and other elements—is appropriate to the general tone of the play.*]

*As You Like It* is exceedingly rich and varied in character. The several persons stand out round and clear in themselves, yet their distinctive traits in a remarkable degree sink quietly into the feelings without reporting themselves in the understanding; for which cause the clumsy methods of criticism are little able to give them expression. Subtile indeed must be the analysis that should reproduce them to the intellect without help from the Dramatic Art.

Properly speaking, the play has no hero; for, though Orlando occupies the foreground, the characters are mainly co-ordinate; the design of the work precluding any subordination among them. Diverted by fortune from all their cherished plans and purposes, they pass before us in just that moral and intellectual dishabille which best reveals their indwelling graces of mind and heart. Schlegel remarks that "the Poet seems to have aimed, throughout, at showing that nothing is wanting, to call forth the poetry that has its dwelling in Nature and the human mind, but to throw off all artificial restraint, and restore both to their native liberty" [see excerpt above, 1811]. This is well said; but it should be observed withal that the persons have already been "purified by suffering"; and that it was under the discipline of social restraint that they developed the virtues which make them go right without such restraint, as indeed they do, while we are conversing with them. Because they have not hitherto been altogether free to do as they would, therefore it is that they are good and beautiful in doing as they have a mind to now. Let us beware of attributing to Nature, as we call it, that goodness which proceeds from *habits* generated under Gospel culture and the laws of Christian society.... The liberty that goes by unknitting the bands of reverence and dissolving the ties that draw and hold men together in the charities of a common life, is not the liberty for me, nor is it the liberty that Shakespeare teaches.... It is true, however, that in this play the better transpirations of character are mainly conducted in the eye of Nature, where the passions and vanities that so much disfigure human life find little to stir them into act. In the freedom of their woodland resort, and with the native inspirations of the place to kindle and gladden them, the persons have but to live out the handsome thoughts which they have elsewhere acquired. Man's tyranny has indeed driven them into banishment; but their virtues are much more the growth of the place they are banished from than of the place they are banished to.

Orlando is altogether such a piece of young-manhood as it does one good to be with. He has no special occasion for heroism, yet we feel that there is plenty of heroic stuff in him. Brave, gentle, modest, and magnanimous; never thinking of his high birth but to avoid dishonouring it; in his noble-heartedness, forgetting, and causing others to forget, his nobility of rank; he is every way just such a man as all true men would choose for their best friend. His persecuting brother, talking to himself, describes him as "never school'd, and yet learned; full of noble device; of all sorts enchantingly beloved; and indeed so much in the heart of the world, and especially of my own people, who best know him, that I am altogether misprised" [I. i. 166-71]; and this description is amply justified by his behavior. The whole intercourse between him and his faithful old servant Adam is replete on both sides with that full-souled generosity in whose eye the nobilities of Nature are always sure of recognition.

Shakespeare evidently delighted in a certain natural harmony of character wherein virtue is free and spontaneous, like the breathing of perfect health. And such is Orlando. He is therefore good without effort; nay, it would require some effort for him to be otherwise; his soul gravitating towards goodness as of its own accord.... And perhaps the nearest he comes to being aware of his virtue is when his virtue triumphs over a mighty temptation; that is, when he sees his unnatural brother in extreme peril;

> But kindness, nobler ever than revenge,
> And nature, stronger than his just occasion,
>                                              [IV. iii. 128-29]

made him risk his own life to save him; and even in this case the divine art of overcoming evil with good seems more an instinct than a conscious purpose with him. This is one of the many instances wherein the Poet delivers the highest results of Christian discipline as drawing so deeply and so creatively into the heart, as to work out with the freedom and felicity of native, original impulse. (pp. 337-40)

The banished Duke exemplifies the best sense of nature as thoroughly informed and built up with Christian discipline and religious efficacy; so that the asperities of life do but make his thoughts run the smoother. How sweet, yet how considerative and firm, is every thing about his temper and moral frame! He sees all that is seen by the most keen-eyed satirist, yet is never moved to be satirical, because he looks with wiser and therefore kindlier eyes. The enmity of Fortune is fairly disarmed by his patience; her shots are all wasted against his breast, garrisoned as it is with the forces of charity and peace: his soul is made storm-proof by gentleness and truth: exile, penury, the ingratitude of men, the malice of the elements, what are they to him? he has the grace to sweeten away their venom, and to smile the sting out of them. He loves to stay himself upon the compensations of life, and to feed his gentler affections by dwelling upon the good which adversity opens to him, or the evil from which it withdraws him; and so he rejoices in finding "these woods more free from peril than the envious Court" [II. i. 3-4]. In his philosophy, so bland, benignant, and contemplative, the mind tastes the very luxury of rest, and has an antepast of measureless content.

Touchstone, though he nowhere strikes so deep a chord within us as the poor Fool in *King Lear,* is, I think, the most entertaining of Shakespeare's privileged characters. And he is indeed a mighty delectable fellow! wise too, and full of the most insinuative counsel. How choicely does his grave, acute nonsense moralize the scenes wherein he moves! Professed clown though he be, and as such ever hammering away with artful awkwardness at a jest, a strange kind of humorous respect still waits upon him notwithstanding. It is curious to observe how the Poet takes care to let us know from the first, that beneath the affectations of his calling some precious sentiments have been kept alive; that far within the Fool there is laid up a secret reserve of the man, ready to leap forth and combine with better influences as soon as the incrustations of art are thawed and broken up. This is partly done in the scene where Rosalind and Celia arrange for their flight from the usurper's Court [I. iii. 129-33]....

[Here] we learn that some remnants, at least, of a manly heart in him have asserted their force in the shape of unselfish regards, strong as life, for whatever is purest and loveliest in the characters about him. He would rather starve or freeze, with Celia near him, than feed high and lie warm where his eye cannot find her. If, with this fact in view, our honest esteem does not go out towards him, then we, I think, are fools in a worse sense than he is.

So much for the substantial manhood of Touchstone, and for the Poet's human-heartedness in thus putting us in communication with it. As for the other points of his character, I scarce know how to draw a reader into them by any turn of analysis. Used to a life cut off from human sympathies; stripped of the common responsibilities of the social state; living for no end but to make aristocratic idlers laugh; one therefore whom nobody heeds enough to resent or be angry at any thing he says;—of course his habit is to speak all for effect, nothing for truth: instead of reflecting the natural force and image of things, his vocation is to wrest and transshape them from their true form and pressure. Thus a strange wilfulness and whimsicality has wrought itself into the substance of his mind. He takes nothing for what it is in itself, but only for the odd quirks of thought he can twist out of it. Yet his nature is not so "subdued to what it works in" but that, amidst the scenes and inspirations of the Forest, the Fool quickly slides into the man; the supervenings of the place so running into and athwart what he brings with him, that his character comes to be as dappled and motley as his dress. Even the new passion which there overtakes him has a touch of his wilfulness in it: when he falls in love, as he really does, nothing seems to inspire and draw him more than the unloveliness of the object; thus approving that even so much of nature as survives in him is not content to run in natural channels.

Jaques is, I believe, an universal favourite, as indeed he well may be, for he is certainly one of the Poet's happiest conceptions. Without being at all unnatural, he has an amazing fund of peculiarity. Enraptured out of his senses at voice of a song; thrown into a paroxysm of laughter at sight of the motley-clad and motley-witted Fool; and shedding the twilight of his merry-sad spirit over all the darker spots of human life and character; he represents the abstract and sum-total of an utterly useless yet perfectly harmless man, seeking wisdom by abjuring its first principle. An odd choice mixture of reality and affectation, he does nothing but think, yet avowedly thinks to no purpose; or rather thinking is with him its own end. On the whole, if in Touchstone there is much of the philosopher in the Fool, in Jaques there is not less of the fool in the philosopher; so that the German critic, Ulrici, is not so wide of the mark in calling them "two fools" [see excerpt above, 1839].

Jaques is equally wilful, too, with Touchstone, in his turn of thought and speech, though not so conscious of it; and as he plays his part more to please himself, so he is proportionally less open to the healing and renovating influences of Nature. We cannot justly affirm, indeed, that "the soft blue sky did never melt into his heart," as Wordsworth says of his Peter Bell; but he shows more of resistance than all the other persons to the poetries and eloquences of the place. Tears are a great luxury to him: he sips the cup of woe with all the gust of an epicure. Still his temper is by no means sour: fond of solitude, he is nevertheless far from being unsocial. The society of good men, provided they be in adversity, has great charms for him. He likes to be with those who, though deserving the best, still have the worst: virtue wronged, buffeted, oppressed, is his special delight; because such moral discrepancies offer the most salient points to his cherished meditations. He himself enumerates nearly all the forms of melancholy except his own, which I take to be the melancholy of self-love. And its effect in his case is not unlike that of Touchstone's art; inasmuch as he

greatly delights to see things otherwise than as they really are, and to make them speak out some meaning that is not in them; that is, their plain and obvious sense is not to his taste. Nevertheless his melancholy is grateful, because free from any dash of malignity. His morbid habit of mind seems to spring from an excess of generative virtue. And how racy and original is everything that comes from him! as if it bubbled up from the centre of his being; while his perennial fulness of matter makes his company always delightful. The Duke loves especially to meet him in his "sullen fits" [II. i. 68], because he then overflows with his most idiomatic humour. After all, the worst that can be said of Jaques is, that the presence of men who are at once fortunate and deserving corks him up; which may be only another way of saying that he cannot open out and run over, save where things are going wrong.

It is something uncertain whether Jaques or Rosalind be the greater attraction: there is enough in either to make the play a continual feast; though her charms are less liable to be staled by use, because they result from health of mind and symmetry of character; so that in her presence the head and the heart draw together perfectly. I mean that she never starts any moral or emotional reluctances in our converse with her: all our sympathies go along with her freely, because she never jars upon them, or touches them against the grain.

For wit, this strange, queer, lovely being is fully equal to Beatrice [ in *Much Ado about Nothing*], yet nowise resembling her. A soft, subtile, nimble essence, consisting in one knows not what, and springing up one can hardly tell how, her wit neither stings nor burns, but plays briskly and airily over all things within its reach, enriching and adorning them; insomuch that one could ask no greater pleasure than to be the continual theme of it. In its irrepressible vivacity it waits not for occasion, but runs on for ever, and we wish it to run on for ever: we have a sort of faith that her dreams are made up of cunning, quirkish, graceful fancies; her wits being in a frolic even when she is asleep. And her heart seems a perennial spring of affectionate cheerfulness: no trial can break, no sorrow chill, her flow of spirits; even her sighs are breathed forth in a wrappage of innocent mirth; an arch, roguish smile irradiates her saddest tears. No sort of unhappiness can live in her company: it is a joy even to stand her chiding; for, "faster than her tongue doth make offence, her eye doth heal it up" [III. v. 116-17].

So much for her choice idiom of wit. But I must not pass from this part of the theme without noting also how aptly she illustrates the Poet's peculiar use of humour. For I suppose the difference of wit and humour is too well understood to need any special exposition. But the two often go together; though there is a form of wit, much more common, that burns and dries the juices all out of the mind, and turns it into a kind of sharp, stinging wire. Now Rosalind's sweet establishment is thoroughly saturated with humour, and this too of the freshest and wholesomest quality. And the effect of her humour is, as it were, to *lubricate* all her faculties, and make her thoughts run brisk and glib even when grief has possession of her heart. Through this interfusive power, her organs of play are held in perfect concert with her springs of serious thought. Hence she is outwardly merry and inwardly sad at the same time. We may justly say that she laughs out her sadness, or plays out her seriousness: the sorrow that is swelling her breast puts her wits and spirits into a frolic; and in the mirth that overflows through her tongue we have a relish of the grief with which her heart is charged. And our sympathy with her inward state is the more divinely moved, forasmuch as she thus, with indescribable delicacy, touches it through a masquerade of play-fulness. Yet, beneath all her frolicsomeness, we feel that there is a firm basis of thought and womanly dignity; so that she never laughs away our respect.

It is quite remarkable how, in respect of her disguise, Rosalind just reverses the conduct of Viola [in *Twelfth Night*], yet with much the same effect. For, though she seems as much at home in her male attire as if she had always worn it, this never strikes us otherwise than as an exercise of skill for the perfecting of her masquerade. And on the same principle her occasional freedoms of speech serve to deepen our sense of her innate delicacy; they being manifestly intended as a part of her disguise, and springing from the feeling that it is far less indelicate to go a little out of her character, in order to prevent any suspicion of her sex, than it would be to hazard such a suspicion by keeping strictly within her character. In other words, her free talk bears much the same relation to her character as her dress does to her person, and is therefore becoming to her even on the score of feminine modesty.—Celia appears well worthy of a place beside her whose love she shares and repays. Instinct with the soul of moral beauty and female tenderness, the friendship of these more-than-sisters "mounts to the seat of grace within the mind." (pp. 340-46)

The general drift and temper, or, as some of the German critics would say, the ground-idea of this play, is aptly hinted by the title. As for the beginnings of what is here represented, these do not greatly concern us; most of them lie back out of our view, and the rest are soon lost sight of in what grows out of them; but the issues, of which there are many, are all exactly to our mind; we feel them to be just about right, and would not have them otherwise. For example, touching Frederick and Oliver, our wish is that they should repent, and repair the wrong they have done, in brief, that they should become good; which is precisely what takes place; and as soon as they do this, they naturally love those who were good before. Jaques, too, is so fitted to moralize the discrepancies of human life, so happy and at home, and withal so agreeable, in that exercise, that we would not he should follow the good Duke when in his case those discrepancies are composed. The same might easily be shown in respect of the other issues. Indeed I dare ask any genial, considerate reader, Does not every thing turn out just *as you like it?* Moreover there is an indefinable something about the play that puts us in a receptive frame of mind; that opens the heart, soothes away all querulousness and fault-finding, and makes us easy and apt to be pleased. Thus the Poet here disposes us to like things as they come, and at the same time takes care that they shall come as we like. The whole play indeed is *as you like it*.

Much has been said by one critic and another about the improbabilities in this play. I confess they have never troubled me; and, as I have had no trouble here to get out of, I do not well know how to help others out. (pp. 346-47)

[The] bringing of lions, serpents, palm-trees, rustic shepherds, and banished noblemen together in the Forest of Arden, is a strange piece of geographical license, which certain critics have not failed to make merry withal. Perhaps they did not see that the very grossness of the thing proves it to have been designed. The Poet keeps his geography true enough whenever he has cause to do so. He knew, at all events, that lions did not roam at large in France. By this irregular combination of actual things, he informs the whole with ideal effect, giving to this charming issue of his brain "a local habitation and a name" [*A Midsummer Night's Dream*, V. i. 17], that it may link-in

with our flesh-and-blood sympathies, and at the same time turning it into a wild, wonderful, remote, fairy-land region, where all sorts of poetical things may take place without the slightest difficulty. Of course Shakespeare would not have done thus, but that he saw quite though the grand critical humbug which makes the proper effect of a work of art depend upon our belief in the actual occurrence of the thing represented. (p. 348)

As far as I can determine the matter, *As You Like It* is, upon the whole, my favourite of Shakespeare's comedies. Yet I should be puzzled to tell why; for my preference springs not so much from any particular points or features, wherein it is surpassed by several others, as from the general toning and effect. The whole is replete with a beauty so delicate yet so intense, that we feel it everywhere, but can never tell especially where it is, or in what it consists. For instance, the descriptions of forest scenery come along so unsought, and in such easy, quiet, natural touches, that we take in the impression without once noticing what it is that impresses us. Thus there is a certain woodland freshness, a glad, free naturalness, that creeps and steals into the heart before we know it. And the spirit of the place is upon its inhabitants, its genius within them: we almost breathe with them the fragrance of the Forest. . . . Even the Court Fool, notwithstanding all the crystallizing process that has passed upon him, undergoes, as we have seen, a sort of rejuvenescence of his inner man, so that his wit catches at every turn the fresh hues and odours of his new whereabout. (pp. 348-49)

To all which add, that the kindlier sentiments here seem playing out in a sort of jubilee. Untied from set purposes and definite aims, the persons come forth with their hearts already tuned, and so have but to let off their redundant music. Envy, jealousy, avarice, revenge, all the passions that afflict and degrade society, they have left in the city behind them. And they have brought the intelligence and refinement of the Court without its vanities and vexations; so that the graces of art and the simplicities of nature meet together in joyous, loving sisterhood. A serene and mellow atmosphere of thought encircles and pervades the actors in this drama. . . . Nature throws her protecting arms around them; Beauty pitches her tents before them; Heaven rains its riches upon them: with "no enemy but Winter and rough weather" [II. v. 7-8], Peace hath taken up her abode with them; and they have nothing to do but to "fleet the time carelessly, as they did in the golden world" [I. i. 118-19].

But no words of mine, I fear, will justify to others my own sense of this delectable workmanship. I can hardly think of any thing else in the whole domain of Poetry so inspiring of the faith that "every flower enjoys the air it breathes." The play, indeed, abounds in wild, frolicsome graces which cannot be described; which can only be seen and felt; and which the hoarse voice of Criticism seems to scare away, as the crowing of the cocks is said to have scared away the fairy spirits from their nocturnal pastimes. (pp. 349-50)

*Rev. H. N. Hudson, "Shakespeare's Characters: 'As You Like It'," in his* Shakespeare: His Life, Art, and Characters, Vol. I, *fourth revised edition, Ginn & Company, 1872, pp. 330-50.*

## ALGERNON CHARLES SWINBURNE (essay date 1880)

[*Swinburne was an English poet, dramatist, and critic who devoted much of his literary career to the study of Shakespeare and other Elizabethan writers. His three books on Shakespeare—A Study of Shakespeare (1880), Shakespeare (1909), and Three Plays of Shakespeare (1909)—all demonstrate his keen interest in Shakespeare's poetic talents and, especially, his major tragedies. Swinburne's literary commentary is frequently conveyed in a style that is markedly intense and effusive. In the following excerpt from A Study of Shakespeare, Swinburne demonstrates this effusive style in his study of As You Like It. The critic particularly regrets Shakespeare's "unlucky slip of the brush" in marrying Oliver to Celia, by which, he argues, Shakespeare put stage conventions ahead of the play's "moral beauty or spiritual harmony." Swinburne can cite only two other comedies in which Shakespeare made this mistake: Measure for Measure and Much Ado about Nothing.]*

[It cannot] well be worth any man's while to say or to hear for the thousandth time that *As You Like It* would be one of those works which prove, as Landor said long since, the falsehood of the stale axiom that no work of man's can be perfect, were it not for that one unlucky slip of the brush which has left so ugly a little smear in one corner of the canvas as the betrotal of Oliver to Celia. . . . Once elsewhere, or twice only at the most, is any such other sacrifice of moral beauty or spiritual harmony to the necessities and traditions of the stage discernible in all the world-wide work of Shakespeare. In the one case it is unhappily undeniable; no man's conscience, no conceivable sense of right and wrong, but must more or less feel as did Coleridge's the double violence done it in the upshot of *Measure for Measure*. Even in the much more nearly spotless [*Much Ado about Nothing*] . . . , some readers have perhaps not unreasonably found a similar objection to the final good fortune of such a pitiful fellow as Count Claudio. It will be observed that in each case the sacrifice is made to comedy. The actual or hypothetical necessity of pairing off all the couples after such a fashion as to secure a nominally happy and undeniably matrimonial ending is the theatrical idol whose tyranny exacts this holocaust of higher and better feelings than the mere liquorish desire to leave the board of fancy with a palatable morsel of cheap sugar on the tongue. (pp. 151-53)

> Algernon Charles Swinburne, "Second Period: Comic and Historic," in his A Study of Shakespeare, R. Worthington, 1880, pp. 66-169.

### EDWARD DOWDEN   (essay date 1881)

[*Dowden was an Irish critic and biographer whose* Shakspere: A Critical Study of His Mind and Art, *first published in 1875 and revised in 1881, was the leading example of the biographical criticism popular in the English-speaking world near the end of the nineteenth century. Biographical critics like Dowden sought in the plays and poems a record of Shakespeare's personal development. As that approach gave way in the twentieth century to aesthetic theories with greater emphasis on the constructed, artificial nature of literary works, the biographical analysis of Dowden and other critics came to be regarded as limited and often misleading. In the following excerpt from the work mentioned above, Dowden maintains that Jaques's melancholy in* As You Like It *is unproved if not false. Calling the character "self-indulgent" and "no more than a curious experimenter in libertinism," he argues that "of real melancholy there is none in the play." Dowden also disputes the view that* As You Like It *was "an early attempt made by [Shakspere] to control the dark spirit of melancholy in himself," offering his own autobiographical assessment that the play reflects Shakespeare's "repose" from "the trumpet-tones" of his earlier histories.*]

[*As You Like It*] has been represented by [C. E. Moberly, in his 1872 edition of the play] as an early attempt made by the

poet to control the dark spirit of melancholy in himself "by thinking it away." The characters of the banished Duke, of Orlando, of Rosalind, are described as three gradations of cheerfulness in adversity, with Jaques placed over them in designed contrast. But no real adversity has come to any one of them. Shakspere, when he put into the Duke's mouth the words "Sweet are the uses of adversity" [II. i. 12], knew something of deeper affliction than a life in the golden leisure of Arden. Of real melancholy there is none in the play; for the melancholy of Jaques is not grave and earnest, but sentimental, a self-indulgent humor, a petted foible of character, melancholy prepense and cultivated; "it is a melancholy of mine own, compounded of many simples, extracted from many objects; and indeed the sundry contemplation of my travels, in which my often rumination wraps me in a most humorous sadness" [IV. i. 15-20]. The Duke declares that Jaques has been "a libertine, as sensual as the brutish sting itself" [II. vii. 65-6]; but the Duke is unable to understand such a character as that of Jaques. Jaques has been no more than a curious experimenter in libertinism, for the sake of adding an experience of madness and flly to the store of various superficial experiences which constitute his unpractical foolery of wisdom. The haunts of sin have been visited as a part of his travel. (pp. 68-9)

Upon the whole, *As You Like It* is the sweetest and happiest of all Shakspere's comedies. No one suffers; no one lives an eager intense life; there is no tragic interest in it as there is in *The Merchant of Venice*, as there is in *Much Ado about Nothing*. It is mirthful, but the mirth is sprightly, graceful, exquisite; there is none of the rollicking fun of a Sir Toby [in *Twelfth Night*] here; the songs are not "coziers' catches" shouted in the night-time, "without any mitigation or remorse of voice" [*Twelfth Night*, II. iii. 90-1], but the solos and duets of pages in the wild-wood, or the noisier chorus of foresters. The wit of Touchstone is not mere clownage, nor has it any indirect serious significance; it is a dainty kind of absurdity worthy to hold comparison with the melancholy of Jaques. And Orlando, in the beauty and strength of early manhood, and Rosalind—

> A gallant curtle-axe upon her thigh,
> A boar-spear in her hand,
>
> [I. iii. 117]

and the bright, tender, loyal womanhood within—are figures which quicken and restore our spirits, as music does which is neither noisy nor superficial, and yet which knows little of the deep passion and sorrow of the world.

Shakspere, when he wrote this idyllic play, was himself in his Forest of Arden. He had ended one great ambition—the historical plays—and not yet commenced his tragedies. It was a resting-place. He sends his imagination into the woods to find repose. Instead of the courts and camps of England and the embattled plains of France, here was this woodland scene, where the palm-tree, the lioness, and the serpent are to be found; possessed of a flora and fauna that flourish in spite of physical geographers. There is an open-air feeling throughout the play. The dialogue, as has been observed, catches freedom and freshness from the atmosphere. . . . After the trumpet-tones of *Henry V.* comes the sweet pastoral strain, so bright, so tender. Must it not be all in keeping? Shakspere was not trying to control his melancholy. When he needed to do that, Shakspere confronted his melancholy very passionately, and looked it full in the face. Here he needed refreshment, a sunlight tempered by forest-boughs, a breeze upon his forehead, a stream murmuring in his ears. (pp. 70-2)

Edward Dowden, "Growth of Shakspere's Mind and Art, in his Shakspere: A Critical Study of His Mind and Art," third edition, Harper & Brothers Publishers, 1881, pp. 37-83.

## HELENA FAUCIT, LADY MARTIN (letter date 1884)

[*Faucit was a highly respected and greatly admired English actress whose stage career began in 1833 and lasted until 1879. Her* On Some of Shakespeare's Female Characters *(1882) presents studies of seven Shakespearean heroines, together with recollections of her performances of these roles. In the following excerpt from a letter to Robert Browning, first published in a subsequently revised edition of the above-named work (1893), Faucit is one of the few nineteenth-century critics to stress the thematic importance of the love element in* As You Like It, *comparing the play with* Romeo and Juliet *but noting this difference:* As You Like It *"deals with happy love."*]

To me, *As You Like It* seems to be essentially as much a love-poem as *Romeo and Juliet,* with this difference—that it deals with happy love, while the Veronese story deals with love crossed by misadventure and crowned with death. It is as full of imagination, of the glad rapture of the tender passion, of its impulsiveness, its generosity, its pathos. No "hearse-like airs," indeed, come wailing by, as in the tale of those "star-crossed lovers," to warn us of their too early tragic "overthrow." All is blended into a rich harmonious music, which makes the heart throb, but never makes it ache. Still the love is not less deep, less capable of proving itself strong as death; neither are the natures of Orlando and Rosalind less touched to all the fine issues of that passion than those of "Juliet and her Romeo."

Is not love, indeed, the pivot on which the action of the play turns—love, too, at first sight? Does it not seem that the text the poet meant to illustrate was that which he puts into Phebe's mouth—

> Dead shepherd, now I find thy saw of might—
> 'Who ever loved, that loved not at first sight?' . . .
> [III. v. 81-2]

Love at first sight, like that of Juliet and Romeo, is the love of Rosalind and Orlando, of Celia and Oliver, and of Phebe herself for Ganymede. The two latter pairs of lovers are perhaps but of little account; but is not the might of Marlowe's saw as fully exemplified in Rosalind and Orlando as in the lovers of Verona? (pp. 237-38)

*Helena Faucit, Lady Martin, in a letter to Robert Browning in September, 1884, in her* On Some of Shakespeare's Female Characters, *fifth edition, William Blackwood and Sons, 1893, pp. 225-85.*

## HENRY A. CLAPP (essay date 1885)

[*Clapp was a nineteenth-century American lawyer and drama critic whose recollections and reviews were collected in his* Reminiscences of a Dramatic Critic *(1902). In the following excerpt from his 1885 essay "Time in Shakespeare's Comedies," Clapp provides the first published analysis of the time scheme of* As You Like It. *On the basis of internal evidence alone, he finds no inconsistencies or problems with the progress of time from incident to incident in the play. Clapp locates two separate days in Act I, followed by a "new starting point of interest" at the beginning of Act II, succeeded by, in II. ii., the "beginning of the third day of the regular action." There follow, he argues, several intervals, "all quite short," leading to III. iv., "the actual last* day but one" of the comedy. The final scene of Act V is said to begin the next day.]

*As You Like It* opens in Oliver's orchard, and its first scene stands by itself, occupying a part of the first day of the action of the piece. "To-morrow," before the new Duke, Charles, the professional athlete, is to "wrestle for his credit" [I. i. 126-27], as in this scene he warns Orlando's malevolent brother. The second day, therefore, is that of the second scene, in which Orlando trips up the wrestler's heels and Rosalind's heart, both in an instant. The third scene closely follows the encounter of the lovers, and is occupied with Celia's prompt teasing of her friend, then with the usurping Duke's appearance and sentence of banishment upon Rosalind, and finally with the resolution of the young maids to go into exile together. Scene 1, Act II., is with the Banished Duke in the forest of Arden, and makes a new starting-point of interest. . . . Scene 2 of this act marks the beginning of the third day of the regular action, inasmuch as the attendant ladies in the palace have just found Celia's "bed untreasured of their mistress" [II. ii. 7]. The following scene also belongs to the third day, for in it Orlando, just returned from the short journey to court, meets Adam before Oliver's house, and with the old man sets forth for the forest, to which all roads in *As You Like It* lead. There are divers unknown intervals, all quite short, between the scenes which succeed until Scene 4 of Act III. is reached. Shakespeare does not inform us how long Rosalind, Celia, and Touchstone were in making the journey, the close of which in Scene 4, Act II., finds them so weary in spirits and in legs; nor how much time Orlando and Adam consumed upon the way; nor what period elapsed before the usurper, Frederick, turned Oliver out-of-doors to bring back Orlando, "dead or living" [III. i. 6], to his court; nor how long Orlando lived in the forest before he began to abuse the "young plants with carving Rosalind on their barks," and to hang "odes upon hawthorns and elegies on brambles" [III. ii. 360-62]. But many slight hints in the text show that these periods were very short. In Scene 2, Act III., Orlando first sees Rosalind in her disguise, and then and there makes that contract for substituted wooing, the story of which, at the end of three centuries, comes filled with the scent of the wild rose and the note of the nightingale, and both as fresh and sweet as if they were breathed out but yesterday. An undisclosed interval then occurs, which is doubtless filled by Rosalind with love-making and by Orlando with love-thinking. Rosalind evidently fritters away no part of the time in cultivating acquaintance with her father, the Banished Duke, though she meets him once, and bestows some of her sweet sauciness upon him; not that she lacked filial affection, but that she was in a state of mind which many maidens have experienced, though not many have had the courage to put it frankly into words, and say there is no use in "talking of fathers" "when there is such a man as Orlando" [III. iv. 38-9]. The interval is a short one, we may be sure, for Rosalind's heart beats as fast as her wit moves and her tongue trips; and Orlando has been well and much, if briefly, tutored in the art of love when Scene 4 of Act III. opens, and with it the actual last day but one of the comedy. Scenes 4 and 5 of Act III., the whole of Act IV., and the whole of Act V. except its final scene are compressed within this one day, the progress of which is marked almost to the point of distinguishing its hours. Scene 4, Act III., opens at about the hour of ten in the forenoon,—as will be presently verified,—with Rosalind's lament over Orlando's broken promise to "come this morning" [III. iv. 18-19]; thence Rosalind, Celia, and Corin pass directly to Scene 5, and the contemplation of the misery of Silvius and the coquetry of Phebe; and in Scene 1 of Act IV. Orlando appears, and in response to Rosalind's peevish "How now, Orlando! where have you been all this while?" [IV. i. 39-40] replies that he comes "within an hour of" his "promise" [IV. i. 42-3]. This enchanting scene begins at about eleven and ends at noon, when Orlando departs to attend the Duke at dinner, promising to be with Rosalind again by two o'clock. The two hours which follow, though not included in the action of the play, are very important. After dinner, Orlando, "chewing the food of sweet and bitter fancy" [IV. iii. 101], takes a walk in the forest, discovers Oliver asleep upon the ground, and saves him, at the cost of a wound, from the paw of the "sucked and hungry lioness" [IV. iii. 126]; and, upon Oliver's showing a sudden but complete change of heart, the brothers are reconciled. The story of this adventure is told by the elder brother to Rosalind and Celia in an interview which begins in the latter part of Scene 3, Act IV., the opening hour of which—as fixed by Rosalind, again impatient of her lover's tardiness—was "past two o'clock" [IV. iii. 1-2]; and by the time Rosalind has revived from her counterfeit of faintness the afternoon must be pretty well advanced. In Scene 1 of Act V. it is "good even" [V. i. 13, 14, 15, 16], and at the same time, or a little later, in the sequent scene Rosalind tells Orlando the tale of Oliver's and Celia's love, which, beginning in an introduction a few hours before, has developed with such extraordinary rapidity that Rosalind plainly feels called upon to make a little humorous apology for it ("Your brother and my sister no sooner met but they looked; no sooner looked but they loved," etc. [V. ii. 32-4]); and the scene closes with Rosalind's promise to make everything "on the morrow" [V. ii. 112, 114, 116, 118] as everybody likes it. Scene 3 comes as a queer little postscript. "To-morrow" is to be "the joyful day" [V. iii. 1] also for Touchstone and Audrey, and with some of the Clown's exquisite fooling the night falls and the great day ends. In the last scene of Act V. the famous "to-morrow" and promise-keeping Rosalind arrive together. Her tongue now for the first time finds but little to do,—it being remembered that she has a last opportunity in the epilogue,—and with five charming words, where, if her heart were less full, a hundred would not have sufficed, she makes her lover and her father happy. (pp. 399-400)

*Henry A. Clapp, "Time in Shakespeare's Comedies," in* The Atlantic Monthly, *Vol. LV, No. CCCXXIX, March, 1885, pp. 386-403.*

## HORACE HOWARD FURNESS    (essay date 1890)

[*Furness was an American lawyer who abandoned law to devote his life to Shakespearean studies. In 1871 he became the first editor of the New Variorum edition of Shakespeare's works with the publication of* Romeo and Juliet. *Eighteen volumes appeared under his editorship, all of which draw heavily on the First Folio of 1623. The value of Furness's work rests on his extensive textual, critical, and annotative notes derived from the best authorities of the time. In the following excerpt from his appendix to the New Variorum edition of* As You Like It *(1890), Furness examines Shakespeare's use of double time in the opening acts of the play. He notes that it is necessary for the dramatist to suggest that Duke Senior's banishment was recent, so that the new duke "feels his grasp of the sceptre most insecure" and we comprehend the reason for his sudden suspicion of Rosalind; yet, it is equally important that Shakespeare implies that this banishment happened long ago—for two reasons, according to Furness: one, so that no "chill air of [recent] tragedy" might disturb the serenity of the Arden forest; and two, so that we do not question why no one from the duke's court immediately recognizes Touchstone.*]

When [*As You Like It*] opens it is necessary that the senior Duke's banishment should be recent, so recent that the usurping Duke feels his grasp of the sceptre most insecure. Time can have given to the traitor no prescriptive right. 'What is the new news at the new court?' asks Oliver. 'There's no news,' answers Charles, 'but the old news: that is, the old Duke is banished by his younger brother, the new Duke, and three or four loving lords have put themselves into voluntary exile with him' [I. i. 96-102]. The impression here conveyed is clear enough. The banishment is spoken of almost in the present tense. And if the news is called 'old,' it may be so called on the assumption that its limit of life is nine days. At any rate, it is not so 'old' but that the 'younger brother' is called the 'new Duke,' and the report of the banishment has not yet had time (and such news travels fast) to reach Oliver in all its details. Oliver's residence cannot be far removed from the ducal court, the wrestling match was quite in his neighborhood, and yet Oliver neither knows where the banished Duke has gone, nor whether Rosalind has accompanied her father. 'She is at the court,' Charles informs him, 'and no less beloved of her uncle than his own daughter' [I. i. 110-11]. 'Where will the old Duke live?' asks Oliver. '*They say,*' replies Charles, 'he is already in the Forest of Arden,—*they say,* many young gentlemen flock to him every day' [I. i. 113-14, 116-17]. There can be no shadow of a doubt that the Duke's banishment is most recent. Sufficient time has not elapsed wherein to obtain exact information of his whereabouts. Had the Duke's banishment lasted many months, or even many weeks, some authentic reports would have come back from him, and the public would be fully aware whether he were acquiescing in his exile or gathering forces to resist. The vagueness of the information concerning his movements or his habitation proves conclusively that he had only just been driven from his throne. The 'new court' cannot be many weeks old. It is so 'new' that the only news in it is the event which created it. (p. 390)

Accepting then, as Shakespeare intended we should, the Duke's banishment to be recent, it will be manifest that sufficient time has not elapsed to allow the social upheaval to subside, and there will be no need to tell us that the treacherous usurper eats his meal in fear and sleeps in the affliction of terrible dreams that shake him nightly. This follows as of course, and gives us the clue to understand why the mere mention to the usurping Duke by Orlando of Sir Rowland de Boys's name is sufficient to kindle the spark which blazes into a fury of suspicion against Rosalind. . . . [This suspicion against Rosalind] is an indispensable element. It is one of the main springs. [Such a] suspicion against a gentle girl can be accounted for only by the usurper's extreme terror. This extreme terror is accounted for by his feeling of insecurity. His insecurity arises from the newness of his position. And the newness of his position is due solely to the fact that his elder brother has only just been banished. This recent banishment supplies the motive which drives Rosalind from court to the Forest of Arden. It is vital to the movement of the First Act. But how long are its effects to last? Clearly, not long. Social upheavals are dangerous to meddle with, on or off the stage. . . . [If] their memories were kept up here, the turbulence of the times would show its effects on the exiled Duke, and we should find him in the Forest of Arden still distraught and dishevelled after his compulsory banishment. The peaceful quiet of a woodland comedy cannot breathe amid such scenes. Therefore after the explosion of wrath and suspicion from the usurper which drives forth both Rosalind and Oliver, there is no longer need of this present impression of the recent civil strife; indeed, it would be destructive of the comedy; and so, having woven its spell around us and solved dramatic difficulties, it is gently effaced by vague, misty allusions to the past; and that which happened but yesterday begins to recede into the dark backward of time; days take the place of hours, and months of days, and we count the time by the chimes of another clock which the cunning conjurer, before our very eyes but without our seeing it, has substituted for the old one.

Perhaps the first faint intimation of the lapse of time—and it is very faint but still marked enough to create an impression—is after the wrestling, when the usurping Duke says to Orlando, 'The world esteemed thy father honourable, But I did find him still mine enemy' [I. ii. 225-26]. This must refer to old Sir Rowland's loyalty to the senior Duke and his hostility to the usurper during the recent crisis, the only time as far as we know when any proofs of enmity could have been evoked. But the first impression concerning old Sir Rowland which we receive, in the very opening of the play, is that he has been dead several years, at least long enough to account for Orlando's neglected education. This passing reference, then, to Sir Rowland's enmity during his lifetime to the usurping Duke weakens the impression that the *coup d'état* is so very recent, and for one second carries that event with it back into the past, and there is a fleeting vision of unflinching loyalty long years ago to the exiled Duke in the stress that then drove him from his throne.

This allusion, which has swiftly come and swiftly gone, is closely followed by another allusion to time long past, more marked, as it ought to be, than the former, and which can scarcely fail to leave a still more decided impression. Le Beau says to Orlando immediately after the wrestling: 'But I can tell you that *of late* this duke Hath ta'en displeasure 'gainst his gentle niece, Grounded upon no other argument But that *the people praise her for her virtues*' [I. ii. 277-80]. Charles, the Wrestler, told us that Rosalind was 'no less beloved of her uncle than his own daughter' [I. i. 111]. To turn love thus deep into 'displeasure' time will be required; and visions arise before us of a blameless life lived by Rosalind in the sight of all men, week by week, and month by month, full of patient submission and deeds of gentle kindness, and not alone winning all hearts but winning them so strongly that the murmurs of applause swell till at last they reach the throne.

Deep as this impression is of the slow flight of time, and remote as the banishment of the Duke is beginning to grow, this impression is followed up by another still deeper. When the usurping Duke, half crazed by suspicion, wrathfully banishes Rosalind, Celia intercedes for her cousin, and recalls to her cruel father that when he 'stay'd Rosalind,' and she had not 'with her father ranged along' [I. iii. 67-8], he had done it out of pity and of love for his own daughter, but, pleads Celia, 'I was TOO YOUNG THAT TIME to value her; But NOW I know her' [I. iii. 71-2], and then she goes on to picture *the years that have passed* since that time in her unconscious childhood when the Duke was banished, and how since then she and Rosalind have grown up together, how they had learned their lessons together, played together, slept together, rose at an instant, ate together, and wherever we went 'like Juno's swans still we went coupled and inseparable' [I. iii. 75-6]. It is necessary only to cite this passage; comment on it is impertinent; no one can evade the impression of years, passing and passed, which it conveys.

But to one fact attention must be called, and this is, the extreme importance, dramatically, of making, just at this point, the time of the Duke's banishment recede into the past. As a present

active force its power is spent. It was of vital importance to quicken the usurper's suspicion and to cause him to drive Rosalind forth. It is now equally important that it should recede into the past and, for two reasons, grow dim through a vista of years. First, the next Act is to open in the Forest of Arden; there for the first time we see the banished Duke. No chill air of tragedy can be suffered to disturb the repose of that 'immortal umbrage,' and all traces of a brother's perfidy and treachery must be obliterated; in things evil we must discern the soul of goodness, and recognize it in that philosophic calm which years of exile have brought to the Duke; all thoughts of recent turbulence or of recent violence, so necessary in the first Act, must here, when we first see the exiled Duke, give place to that imperturbable serenity and acquiescence with fate which is the benison of time. Hence it is that the Second Act opens with the immortal lines:

> Now, my co-mates and brothers in exile,
> Hath not *old custom* made this life more sweet
> Than that of painted pomp? Are not these woods
> More free from peril than the envious court?
> Here feel we not the penalty of Adam,
> The *seasons' difference*.
>
> [II. i. 1-6]

Are not 'old custom' and 'the seasons' difference' 'the very lime-twigs' of Shakespeare's spell? Why else are they here mentioned, if not to catch us with memories of years gone by? Can it be doubted for a moment that Shakespeare did not here intend us to believe that the Duke had lived through many a seasons' difference, or that custom to him had not grown old? (pp. 390-92)

Henceforth there is but little need of any allusion either to fast or to slow movement of time, other than to make us believe that Orlando has been long enough in the Forest of Arden to write love-songs in the bark of the trees, and that he goes wooing every day to Rosalind's sheep-cote.

I have just said that there are two reasons why, dramatically, it is necessary for us to suppose that the Duke has been long an exile in Arden; the reason which has just been given is, I think, of itself quite sufficient. But there is yet another, which renders a long sojourn there by the Duke, at least of many, many months, if not of years, almost, if not absolutely, imperative. Unless the impressions are obliterated that the Duke's exile is 'new news,' and that Jaques and Amiens and the rest have only just fled from the court and flocked to Arden,—unless, I say, these impressions are obliterated, how can we possibly understand why Jaques or the Duke, when they met Touchstone in the Forest, did not instantly recognise him, familiar to them as he must have been in and about the court. . . . The conclusion, therefore, is to me inevitable, that the impression which Shakespeare wished to make on us is that the Duke and Jaques and the rest had been so long fleeting the time carelessly in the Forest of Arden that a new set of courtiers had arisen in their old court at home, almost a new generation since their exile had begun. (p. 393)

*Horace Howard Furness, "Duration of the Action," in* A New Variorum Edition of Shakespeare: As You Like It, Vol. 8, *edited by Horace Howard Furness, 1890. Reprint by Dover Publications, Inc., 1963, pp. 388-93.*

### DENTON J. SNIDER (essay date 1890?)

[*Snider was an American scholar, philosopher, and poet who closely followed the precepts of the German philosopher Georg*

*Wilhelm Friedrich Hegel and contributed greatly to the dissem-
ination of his dialectical philosophy in America. Snider's critical
writings include studies on Homer, Dante, and Goethe, as well
as Shakespeare. Like Hermann Ulrici and G. G. Gervinus, Snider
sought the dramatic unity and ethical import in Shakespeare's
plays, but he presented a more rigorous Hegelian interpretation
than those two German philosophical critics. In the introduction
to his three-volume work* The Shakespearian Drama: A Commentary *(1887-90), Snider states that Shakespeare's plays present
various ethical principles which, in their differences, come into
"Dramatic Collision," but are ultimately resolved and brought
into harmony. He claims that these collisions can be traced in
the plays' various "Dramatic Threads" of action and thought,
which together form a "Dramatic Movement," and that the analysis of these threads and movements—"the structural elements of
the drama"—reveal the organic unity of Shakespeare's art. Snider
observes two basic movements in the tragedies—guilt and retribution—and three in the comedies—separation, mediation, and
return. In the excerpt below, Snider identifies three movements
in* As You Like It: *1) the Real World of Wrong; 2) the Idyllic
Realm; and 3) the restored Real World of Right. These movements,
he continues, correspond to the corrupt court, the Forest of Arden,
and the renewed political and social organization. Within these
movements, Snider argues, operate "threads" or elements of
action, all of which are brought together by Love, "the grand
social organizer" that enables healing to take place. Snider also
comments on the play's genre, concentrating especially on Shakespeare's use of inherited material. Objecting to earlier descriptions of* As You Like It *as a pastoral, or as a comedy of intrigue
and love, Snider maintains that Shakespeare is here depicting the
inadequacies of the pastoral ideal, both as a system of thought
and as a literary convention.]*

In [*As You Like It*] we see placed in striking contrast the actual
and the idyllic world. The former contains society, state, business, and their manifold interests and complications; the latter
is the simple pastoral existence, without care, struggle, or
occupation—almost without want. The former is the world of
Reason, and exhibits man in his rational development, and for
this very cause has within it the deepest and most terrific contradictions. The loftier the summit the greater the fall; the more
highly organized a society the mightier are the collisions slum-
bering or struggling in its bosom. But an idyllic existence is
almost without contradiction, and, hence, it happens that men
sometimes flee from a more concrete social life, in order to
get rid of its difficulties, and betake themselves to the simple
state of the shepherd. (p. 339)

[This consciousness of the idyllic existence]—so general, so
deeply grounded in human nature—the Poet proposes to make
the subject of a comedy. That it is capable of a comic treatment
is manifest when we reflect that the very realization of the
ideal world must be its annihilation, for then it is real and no
longer ideal. Thus the pursuit of such an end, as absolute and
final, is contradictory and null in itself, since it must terminate
in just the opposite of that which is sought. Now, Comedy
exhibits the individual pursuing ends which are nugatory, and,
therefore, destroy themselves in their realization. That the Poet
had this consciousness in mind is clear from his allusions to
Robin Hood, the English ideal hero of the forest [I. i. 114-16];
and still more plainly does the same fact appear when he speaks
of "those who fleet the time carelessly as they did in the golden
world" [I. i. 117-19], an obvious reference to the Greek ideal
realm. To this latter he likens the Forest of Arden, a comparison
by which he lets us know what he meant by that forest.

But it is through beholding the organization of the drama that
the purpose of the Poet will be most clearly revealed. There
are three movements, which, however, are merely the essential

phases of one and the same general process. The first movement
depicts the Real World of Wrong, in which institutions have
fallen into conflict, and in which the individual is assailed in
his personal rights. Here there are two threads, of which the
central figures are, respectively, a man and a woman—Orlando
and Rosalind. Both are the victims of wrong in this unsettled
society; both have to flee from domestic and political oppression; they also become enamored of one another—the common
bond of misfortune easily changes to the common bond of
love. The second movement portrays the Idyllic Realm to which
the individual has fled in order to get rid of the institutional
world and its injustice; it is the simple pastoral and sylvan life
before society. Here also there are essentially two threads; the
first is the banished Duke and lords, who have been driven off
by the existing wrongs of the civilized State and have gone to
the woods, there to dwell in the primitive peace of nature; the
second thread is made up of three groups, which must be
considered together—that of Orlando and his servant, and his
brother; that of Rosalind and Celia, and the clown; and, finally,
that of the native shepherds. The third movement is the restoration of the Real World of Right—the idyllic realm dissolves
of its own inherent necessity, and there is a complete return
of the banished members to society, which is healed of its
wrong by the departure and repentance of the usurping Duke.

We shall now glance at the incidents of the play, and trace the
first movement through its various parts. This unfolds, as before said, the Real World of Wrong. . . . Here two leading
characters are introduced, a man and a woman, who are able
to endure insult and injustice, and to draw from their discipline
the true result of life. Wrong cannot destroy, but can only bring
out and confirm their integrity of soul. Both Orlando and Rosalind have this indestructible germ of character, each in a different way; they become the heroes not only of their own, but
of society's rescue.

Another fact is brought out in this movement. The world is
truly in a state of wrong and dissolution, yet the opposite force
is also setting in; under destruction reconstruction is in the act
of being born. The principle of it is Love, the grand social
organizer, and primal founder of all institutions; here it appears
in its first beautiful, all-subduing shape, the love of man and
woman. It leads straightway to the Family; the Family rises to
the State, gives the primitive basis for the Church, in fact begets
and nourishes with its mother's milk the whole realm of institutional life, as it begets and nourishes man himself. Over
this social ruin, then, we see floating the form of Love, as
winged Eros, in the old fable, was the first to rise out of
primeval Chaos. The harbinger of the new society thus appears
amid the successful violence of the old, in the very victory of
wrong lurks its defeat. This result is now to be shown in the
two leading characters, each of which can be unfolded on its
own line, till they come together.

Orlando has been deprived of his share in the paternal estate
by his brother Oliver, and, what is much worse, his education
has been utterly neglected, in violation of the will of his father.
Here is shown the wrong in the Family; but this is not all. The
rightful Duke has been expelled from his government by his
brother, and thus we see that the wrong extends into the State;
it is not only in the reigning family but in the subject family.
The play does not unfold, but rather presupposes, these two
great acts of injustice, and, hence, society is portrayed as in
condition of strife and contradiction. (pp. 340-44)

[Soon] this world of injustice comes into full activity and manifests its inherent character. The Duke, as the violator of all

individual right, must naturally become jealous of all individuals; accordingly he has banished a number of lords who seemed dangerous to his power. And so this process must continue as long as anybody is left in the country, since the existence of one man must be a continual source of fear to such a tyrant. . . . Hence Orlando, as the son of an old enemy, excites his suspicion, and has to leave the court with precipitation. (p. 345)

But the wrongs of Orlando do not end with his departure from court. He returns to his brother's estate only to find his life conspired against there, and his condition more hopeless than ever. Accompanied by his trusty servant, Adam, a second time he betakes himself to flight. It is impossible to mistake the meaning of these scenes. The Poet has here portrayed society in contradiction with its fundamental object; it has driven off those whom, by every tie of blood and of right, it was bound to protect; both State and Family have become the instruments of the direst injustice; on all sides we behold the *world of wrong.*

Such is the first thread of this movement; the second thread has its central figure, Rosalind, daughter of the former Duke, who has been driven off by his brother, the present usurper. (pp. 345-46)

Rosalind . . . meets with the same treatment from the suspicious Duke that Orlando has received. She is driven out of his dominions in the most wanton manner, but is accompanied by the daughter of the usurper—a just retribution upon his own family for the wrong done his brother's. The two young ladies now disguise themselves for their journey. Rosalind assumes the garb of a man, which she retains through all her adventures in the idyllic land. Here we have the chief instrumentality of comic situation—Disguise— which furnishes the intrigue of the play, though this is by no means its sole, or even its leading, element. This disguise, too, lies in [Rosalind's] character, nay, in her womanly character; in a time of violence, the good, being weak, is preserved by concealment; Rosalind, the woman, must show her skill by mastering destiny and maintaining her inner worth by an outer artifice.

Both Orlando and Rosalind have, therefore, to flee; each is the victim of wrong in the Family and in the State. Moreover, we see in the background the general condition of society. There is no rightful authority; the true Duke has been expelled by an usurper; many lords have been compelled to leave their country. Such is the first movement. We are now prepared to make the transition to the second movement, in which will be portrayed the Idyllic World—the sphere of mediation.

These people have betaken themselves to flight; but whither are they to go? Society has wronged them, has banished them; their object must now be to find a place where the injustice of society does not reach them, where there is no civil order. They cannot pass to another State, since, logically, the same collision would arise. The Poet's image, though particular, represents an universal truth; it would be no solution, but an evasion of the poetic problem, if these people should simply run from one country to another of the same social grade. A double process is to take place: the State is to be purified of its wrong against the individual, and the individual is to be purified of his conflict with the State. The institution is to protect man, and man is to live in harmony with the institution. Both sides must pass through the discipline; man, wronged in civilized society, quits it and goes to its opposite, which is here the Forest of Arden. . . . It shows the innocent pastoral life, free of the conflicts of civilization; its nature is well indicated by the Poet when

*Act IV. Scene iii. Oliver, Celia as Aliena, Rosalind as Ganymed. Frontispiece to the Bell edition (1773).*

he likens it to the Golden Age [I. i. 117-19]. Its essential character is determined by the fact that it is the negation of the social organism, is the simple primitive condition of man in the simple primitive society. Such is this world of mediation, in which both man and society are turned back to their very beginning, and are made to bathe afresh in the primeval fountains of their being, till they be cured of their disease. The whole movement is healing, remedial, not tragic but comic in the deeper sense of the word.

But who are here? Four groups we note, which are to be duly ordered. The first group is made up of the banished Duke and his company. . . . They form, in the forest, the living background upon which the comedy of love is to play. This is the first thread. The three other groups—two are composed of newcomers and one of native shepherds—are in the main, lovers, and may be classified together as the second thread, as they are intimately connected both in meaning and incident. (pp. 346-49)

The banished Duke is supremely the optimist. He finds even "the uses of adversity" [II. i. 12] to be sweet, and draws out of them comfort and instruction; he prefers the woods to the court, and winter's icy fang to civilized luxury. Here he feels not "the penalty of Adam" [II. i. 5]; he is, like the unfallen first man, dwelling in Paradise still, which is this Forest of Arden. (p. 349)

But hold! A disagreeable contrast arises. The Duke feels that even in this new life he has not wholly avoided the old difficulty, for there still remains the struggle with the animal world—the burghers of the wood—for physical maintenance. Nay, there is one of these lords who cannot find here any solution of the trouble—who declares that injustice is as rife in the Forest of Arden as in society. Witness the slaughter of the innocent beasts of the field, and that same usurpation of their domains by the banished Duke and lords, of which they themselves were the victims in society. This is Jaques, whose negative character can find repose nowhere; he even sees in Nature herself only discord and evil; the deer is as bad as man—it leaves its wounded neighbor to perish, while it passes haughtily on. Thus is our Idyllic World, from which we had thought to shut out all negation, disturbed by its reappearance, like a ghost among children. (pp. 350-51)

If the Duke be the optimist, Jaques is the pessimist of the Forest of Arden; if the Duke find "good in everything" [II. i. 17], Jaques is sure to find the bad in everything; even here in the Duke's Paradise, he discovers an Inferno. The simple reason is because it is in him and he carries it along for his own punishment. . . . Jaques, in his banishment, refuses to accept his discipline, the purgatorial training of the Forest of Arden, and so lapses into pessimistic hate which finds expression in a sort of universal blasphemy. He has no fortitude, no inner prop against the outer burden; his disposition is soured and melancholy; for the man who refuses to bear the trial of fortune, though it be fiery, and to draw from it the true lesson of patience, must become a misanthrope, hateful to man and to himself. (pp. 351-52)

Jaques thus sneers at the old-comers, and their idyllic life; he bemocks their principle, their patience in adverse fortune. We are also to see him turn his ridicule upon the other set, the lovers, and their principle. He comes upon them in his rambles through the Forest at various times; but the fact is that he, the wit-cracker and professional satirist, is put down by the lovers, one after another; Rosalind, Orlando, even Touchstone, manifestly beat him at his own game. They indeed show that their love is a positive thing, and may sharpen the intellect into superiority over the scoffer. Love, then, in the Idyllic Realm, triumphs over Jaques, its keen-tongued enemy. Yet we feel that in all his cynicism, there is a vein of affectation; he has assumed a part and is going to play it to the bitter end. (pp. 353-54)

These persons the play presupposes to have already gone to the Idyllic Realm, but now behold the new arrivals. First, Rosalind and Celia, in their disguise, appear at [the forest]. . . . Strange to say, Orlando and his old, devoted servant, Adam, have arrived in another part of the same territory, a proceeding which seems at first somewhat arbitrary on the part of the Poet. Yet, whither else had they to go? They have fled society, and, hence, must proceed to a place where social order is unknown, which place has been identified as the Forest of Arden. . . . [Thus, with] the end of the Second Act we find everybody fairly established in the new country.

The next question which arises is: What are they to do here? What is to be the business of their lives? We are not long left in ignorance, for soon we find Orlando wholly occupied with love, carving the name of his fair one upon the bark of trees, making love-ditties and hanging them upon the bushes—in fine, consumed with the most intense passion. Nor is Rosalind much better off, though she preserves her disguise in his presence. Touchstone—the clown—too, becomes infected with the

prevailing frenzy, and the native Shepherd Silvius, who is also heart-stricken, is again introduced, together with the disdainful shepherdess, Phebe, who, in her turn, falls in love with the disguised Rosalind. The result of the Third Act is that we have three pairs of lovers, native and foreign, to whom one pair is added in the following Acts. Thus our Ideal Realm is, for the new-comers, transformed into a sort of love-land, where the young people seem wholly occupied with their passion, though the old-comers are not so affected, but are engaged in transmuting adversity into sweetness.

That such a state of existence should take this form is in the natural order of things. Let us analyze this remarkable transition. Man without society is without the substantial element of his life. Here society exists not, business is impossible, ambition in the State is cut off, the physical wants are reduced to the smallest compass and are satisfied with the smallest amount of exertion. Without occupation, without incentive—in general, without content to his life—man is reduced to the *natural individual*. Thus left alone to himself, his finitude begins to show itself in every direction; for man, single, is one-sided—a half—as is manifest by reflecting a moment on the sexual diremption [separation]. He is thus the half, yet would be the whole, and his entire nature drives him to overcome the contradiction; for, in truth, he is not himself; his existence is in and through another, namely, one of the opposite sex. Such is the feeling of love, for it is here not conscious, not in reflection, but the impulse of the natural individual to cancel his own finitude. (pp. 354-57)

Thus they all in this idyllic life reach Love, which is the bedrock of social organization. Love is the essential discipline, the primal sacrifice of self, whereby society becomes possible. It is true that they have fled from society, but the comedy of the poem lies in the fact that they bring about just the opposite of what they intend. They are really going towards what they think they are leaving. By flight from family and society, they are not getting rid of them, but running back into them, actually creating them again.

Thus we see that not only the single characters, but the whole movement of the poem is comic, representing a phase of the comic world; it is self-annulling, is but an appearance which vanishes with its own fulfillment. And it is well that people do not succeed in such a plan, it would end them and the race. They are saved from their own design by a higher design; Providence lets them play, yet in beneficence overrules their scheme; through free-will they bring to pass the opposite of what they will. (pp. 358-59)

We have now reached the third movement, which shows the outcome of the drama in both its threads. It reveals the restoration, the return to institutional life, with which the break originally occurred. Not the individual alone has been cured by this trip to the Idyllic World; society also is healed of its wound, of that wrong which caused the first flight, being turned back to its very source in the love of man and woman, and ideally built up again from the beginning.

First, let us note what becomes of the lovers. Their complications, which rest wholly in the disguise of Rosalind, are solved by her appearance in woman's clothes; she is the mediatorial center of the drama, and, as a bride, brings all to a happy end in wedlock. Hymen can be now introduced as the divine magician who reconciles these collisions of love-land, and the result of the pastoral world is marriage, the Family, which again results directly in Society. So, viewed on this side, the Idyllic World cancels itself, and passes over into a system of social order. (pp. 359-60)

But the banished Duke and lords cannot thus return out of their idyllic existence, for it is supposed that they are too old for passion, or have previously entered the family relation. It is the State which has driven them off, and through the State they must be brought back. So the Poet introduces a new—and, of course, the true—motive for their return. The world of wrong, of which the usurping Duke is the representative, must continue its assaults upon the individual, since it is based upon the destruction of personal right. The result must be that soon a majority—or, if injustice be carried to its extreme logical end, all—of the people will be driven off to the Forest of Arden, where the rightful Duke resides. In such case the Idyllic Realm is at once converted into the same State from which they have fled, lacking only the soil and the usurping Duke. But the return must be complete—must be to the old territory. Hence the usurper is made to repent when he sees that he is deserted, and the old ruler and his attendant lords are restored *peacefully*—an important point, for it would ill comport with their peaceful character, and their simple, unoffending life in the woods, to come back by violence. Thus the reconciliation is complete; harmony is restored; the world of wrong dissolves of its own accord, the world of right returns with the rightful Duke. The disruption with which the play begins is now healed over, the Ideal World being the means whereby the regeneration takes place.

It will be noticed, however, that there is one of the company who does not return. Jaques is the completely negative character, who believes in society as little as in anything else. . . . He does not return, therefore, with the rest, but goes to the new convert, the Duke's brother, who has now "left the world" in his turn, but whose career in the world was also negative. Jaques is one of those psychological characterizations of Shakespeare which are true to the most rigid logic, yet are so completely vitalized that we never feel the abstraction. Such is the third movement of the play.

To sum up, this drama gives a poetic statement and solution of the problem of the Real and Ideal. First comes the struggle of the individual with the actual world, whereby he is trampled into the dust, his rights taken away, his life endangered. It becomes the Real World of Wrong, and destroys that which it was called into existence to protect, and thus has the contradiction within itself which must bring about its destruction. Secondly, the individual, therefore, must flee; abandon State and Society, which oppress and try to destroy him, and go—whither? Not to another State, for the thought in its universality is that the State as such assails him; hence he must find some spot quite out of its reach. The simple primitive life must, therefore, be sought; he has to betake himself to the woods—the Forest of Arden—where only a few scattered shepherds eke out a scanty existence. Thus the individual is established in his Ideal Realm, far away from institutions, from the conventional usages and the struggles of society, in simple unity with nature and the beasts of the field. But, in the third place, this mode of life is found to be of very short duration—is, hence, not a true and permanent condition of the human race. There arises simultaneously a twofold movement for its dissolution. On the one hand, the members of this ideal land are still natural individuals—hence must love, and, what is more, must marry; thus the Family appears, which again in good time brings forth the State, and the Ideal Realm vanishes into thin air. On the other hand, the Real World of Wrong continues its warfare with the individual until it drives all away into the Forest of Arden; for its principle is the destruction of the individual, who has, of course, to flee. The ideal land thereby is converted into the old State minus the tyrant, since the citizens of the one have become inhabitants of the other. So, by a double process, this realm cancels itself and passes into the higher form of civil and social organization. The Poet, therefore, indicates that such an idyllic life is an irrational abstraction; that man's rational existence is in the State and in Society, whose collisions he must endure, bitter though they be. The absurd notion that a pastoral, dreamy existence is the highest finds here no toleration—is, in fact, reduced to a comedy, which shows it dissolving in its own absurdity.

Such is the lesson for life; but the Poet's work cuts wider, since it includes the literary and artistic products of the same consciousness. All those ideal commonwealths of which literature is full may here obtain their final judgment. But particularly the nature, extent, and limits of pastoral poetry—the art-form of such a life—are brought out with a hey-dey of laughter. For this species of poetry also must end with the entrance into society; it belongs only to the simple shepherd on his native hills; it is the first and least concrete—and, hence, least interesting—of all poetry, being without the presupposition of society. The course of the drama, therefore, is the contradiction in the world of reality which results in the wrongs done to the individual; the mediation is through the Ideal World, whereby a reconciliation is brought about and the individual is restored to the world of reality. The three steps may be generalized as the Separation, the Mediation and the Return. They exhibit a totality of society, with its corresponding Art and a hint of its Literature.

Some have considered this play to be a mere caprice—a wild and irregular sport of fancy. But, if we have succeeded in our interpretation, we have shown it to be an inherent and necessary development out of one fundamental thought. Again, it has been taken for a pastoral drama. But its very aim, its comic germ, is to show the limits of pastoral poetry—in fact, of idyllic life generally—and consequently, of the poetic form which springs from such a life. Still more frequently it is held to be an ordinary comedy of situation, of intrigue and love, as if the incidents connected with the disguise of Rosalind were alone to be considered. It has, undoubtedly, a pastoral element—it has also intrigue; but both are subordinate—are only means to bring forth the grand result. It is thus a comedy within a comedy, or, rather, two comedies within a comedy. The pursuit of an idyllic life calls forth the pastoral, the love gives the basis of the intrigue. But the third and highest comic element is to be found in the return to society; in the fact that these people of the Ideal Realm are, in reality, doing just the opposite of what they think they are doing—they are trying to accomplish ends which are in themselves contradictory and null. In general, this play may be called the comedy of the Phantasy, as against the Reason, or of the abstract Ideal as against the Actual, wherein the Phantasy in pursuing an object is at the same time destroying it. Its content thus reaches deep into the history of the world. (pp. 363-68)

*Denton J. Snider, " 'As You Like It', " in his* The Shakespearian Drama, a Commentary: The Comedies, *Sigma Publishing Co., 1890? pp. 339-77.*

## GEORGE BRANDES   (essay date 1895-96)

[*Brandes was a distinguished scholar and the most influential literary critic of late nineteenth-century Denmark. His three-vol-*

ume study of *Shakespeare*, William Shakespeare *(1895-96; translated into English under the same title in 1898), was at the time of its appearance regarded by critics as one of the most important and original non-English language works on Shakespeare. The following excerpt from this work epitomizes the biographical approach to Shakespeare's plays. In his comments on* As You Like It, *Brandes discerns in the play's pastoral setting an expression of "Shakespeare's longing . . . to get away from the unnatural city life," and he finds in Jaques evidence that, "in moods of humorous and melancholy, it must have seemed to Shakespeare as though he himself were one of [his] jesters." The critic adds that we hear Shakespeare's mood in many of Jaques's lines, asserting, "The voice is [Shakespeare's]." Brandes also describes Jaques's melancholy as "a poetic dreaminess," a "bitterness [that] springs from a too tender sensibility," but, like many earlier critics, warns against taking this melancholy too seriously. In addition, Brandes discusses Rosalind and Celia, comparing the former's "gaiety without a sting" with Beatrice's "rapier" wit in* Much Ado about Nothing.]

First and foremost, [*As You Like It*] typifies Shakespeare's longing, the longing of this great spirit, to get away from the unnatural city life, away from the false and ungrateful city folk, intent on business and on gain, away from flattery and falsehood and deceit, out into the country, where simple manners still endure, where it is easier to realise the dream of full freedom, and where the scent of the woods is so sweet. There the babble of the brooks has a subtler eloquence than any that is heard in cities; there the trees and even the stones say more to the wanderer's heart than the houses and streets of the capital; there he finds "good in everything" [II. i. 17].

The roving spirit has reawakened in his breast—the spirit which in bygone days sent him wandering with his gun through Charlcote Park—and out yonder in the lap of Nature, but in a remoter, richer Nature than that which he has known, he dreams of a communion between the best and ablest men, the fairest and most delicate women, in ideal fantastic surroundings, far from the ugly clamours of a public career, and the oppression of everyday cares. A life of hunting and song, and simple repasts in the open air, accompanied with witty talk; and at the same time a life full to the brim with the dreamy happiness of love. And with this life, the creation of his roving spirit, his gaiety and his longing for Nature, he animates a fantastic Forest of Arden.

But with this he is not content. He dreams out the dream, and feels that even such an ideal and untrammelled life could not satisfy that strange and unaccountable spirit lurking in the inmost depths of his nature, which turns everything into food for melancholy and satire. From this rib, then, taken from his own side, he creates the figure of Jaques . . . and sets him wandering through his pastoral comedy, lonely, retiring, self-absorbed, a misanthrope from excess of tenderness, sensitiveness, and imagination.

Jaques is like the first light and brilliant pencil-sketch for Hamlet. Taine, and others after him, have tried to draw a parallel between Jaques and Alceste—of all Molière's creations, no doubt, the one who contains most of his own nature. But there is no real analogy between them. In Jaques everything wears the shimmering hues of wit and fantasy, in Alceste everything is bitter earnest. Indignation is the mainspring of Alceste's misanthropy. He is disgusted at the falsehood around him, and outraged to see that the scoundrel with whom he is at law, although despised by every one, is nevertheless everywhere received with open arms. He declines to remain in bad company, even in the hearts of his friends; therefore he withdraws from them. (pp. 222-23)

The melancholy of Jaques is a poetic dreaminess. (p. 223)

His bitterness springs from a too tender sensibility, a sensibility like that of Sakya Mouni before him, who made tenderness to animals part of his religion, and like that of Shelley after him, who, in his pantheism, realised the kinship between his own soul and that of the brute creation. . . .

In moods of humorous melancholy, it must have seemed to Shakespeare as though he himself were one of [his] jesters, who had the privilege of uttering truths to great people and on the stage, if only they did not blurt them out directly, but disguised them under a mask of folly. (p. 224)

Therefore it is that Shakespeare makes Jaques exclaim—

> O, that I were a fool!
> I am ambitious for a motley coat.
>
> [II. vii. 42-3]

When the Duke answers, "Thou shalt have one" [II. vii. 43], he declares that it is the one thing he wants, and that the others must "weed their judgments" [II. vii. 45] of the opinion that he is wise:

> I must have liberty
> Withal, as large a charter as the wind,
> To blow on whom I please; for so fools have:
> And they that are most galled with my folly,
> They most must laugh. . . .
> Invest me in my motley: give me leave
> To speak my mind, and I will through and through
> Cleanse the foul body of the infected world,
> If they will patiently receive my medicine.
>
> [II. vii. 47-51, 58-61]

It is Shakespeare's own mood that we hear in these words. The voice is his. The utterance is far too large for Jaques: he is only a mouthpiece for the poet. Or let us say that his figure dilates in such passages as this, and we see in him a Hamlet *avant la lettre* [before the letter].

When the Duke, in answer to this outburst, denies Jaques' right to chide and satirise others, since he has himself been "a libertine, As sensual as the brutish sting itself" [II. vii. 65-6], the poet evidently defends himself in the reply which he places in the mouth of the melancholy philosopher:—

> Why, who cries out on pride,
> That can therein tax any private party?
> Doth it not flow as hugely as the sea,
> Till that the weary very means do ebb?
> What woman in the city do I name,
> When that I say, the city-woman bears
> The cost of princes on unworthy shoulders?
> Who can come in, and say that I mean her,
> When such a one as she, such is her neighbour? . . .
>
> [II. vii. 70-8]

The poet is evidently rebutting a common prejudice against his art. And as he makes Jaques an advocate for the freedom which poetry must claim, so also he employs him as a champion of the actor's misjudged calling, in placing in his mouth the magnificent speech on the Seven Ages of Man. (p. 225)

This same Jaques, who gives evidence of so wide an outlook over human life, is in daily intercourse . . . nervously misanthropic and formidably witty. He is sick of polite society, pines for solitude, takes leave of a pleasant companion with the words: "I thank you for your company; but, good faith, I had as lief have been myself alone'' [III. ii. 253-54]. Yet we must not take his melancholy and his misanthropy too seriously. His melancholy is a comedy-melancholy, his misanthropy is only the humourist's craving to give free vent to his satirical inspirations.

And there is . . . only a certain part of Shakespeare's inmost nature in this Jaques, a Shakespeare of the future, a Hamlet in germ, but not that Shakespeare who now bathes in the sunlight and lives in uninterrupted prosperity, in growing favour with the many, and borne aloft by the admiration and goodwill of the few. We must seek for this Shakespeare in the interspersed songs, in the drollery of the fool, in the lovers' rhapsodies, in the enchanting babble of the ladies. He is, like Providence, everywhere and nowhere.

When Celia says [I. ii. 31-2], ''Let us sit and mock the good housewife, Fortune, from her wheel, that her gifts may henceforth be bestowed equally,'' she strikes, as though with a tuning-fork, the keynote of the comedy. The sluice is opened for that torrent of jocund wit, shimmering with all the rainbows of fancy, which is now to rush seething and swirling along.

The Fool is essential to the scheme: for the Fool's stupidity is the grindstone of wit, and the Fool's wit is the touchstone of character. Hence his name.

The ways of the real world, however, are not forgotten. The good make enemies by their very goodness, and the words of the old servant Adam (Shakespeare's own part) to his young master Orlando [at II. iii. 9-15], sound sadly enough. . . . (p. 226)

But soon the poet's eye is opened to a more consolatory life-philosophy, combined with an unequivocal contempt for school-philosophy. There seems to be a scoffing allusion to a book of the time, which was full of the platitudes of celebrated philosophers, in Touchstone's speech to William [at V. i. 32-6], ''The heathen philosopher, when he had desire to eat a grape, would open his lips when he put it into his mouth, meaning thereby that grapes were made to eat and lips to open;'' but no doubt there also lurks in this speech a certain lack of respect for even the much-belauded wisdom of tradition. The relativity of all things, at that time a new idea, is expounded with lofty humour by the Fool in his answer to the question what he thinks of this pastoral life [III. ii. 13-22]. . . . (p. 227)

The two cousins, Rosalind and Celia, seem at first glance like variations of the two cousins, Beatrice and Hero, in the play Shakespeare has just finished [*Much Ado about Nothing*]. Rosalind and Beatrice in particular are akin in their victorious wit. Yet the difference between them is very great; Shakespeare never repeats himself. The wit of Beatrice is aggressive and challenging; we see, as it were, the gleam of a rapier in it. Rosalind's wit is gaiety without a sting . . . ; her sportive nature masks the depth of her love. Beatrice can be brought to love because she is a woman, and stands in no respect apart from her sex; but she is not of an amatory nature. Rosalind is seized with a passion for Orlando the instant she sets eyes on him. From the moment of Beatrice's first appearance she is defiant and combative, in the highest of spirits. We are introduced to Rosalind as a poor bird with a drooping wing; her father is banished, she is bereft of her birthright, and is living on sufferance as companion to the usurper's daughter, being, indeed, half a prisoner in the palace, where till lately she reigned as princess. It is not until she has donned the doublet and hose, appears in the likeness of a page, and wanders at her own sweet will in the open air and the greenwood, that she recovers her

radiant humour, and roguish merriment flows from her lips like the trilling of a bird.

Nor is the man she loves, like Benedick [in *Much Ado about Nothing*] an overweening gallant with a sharp tongue and an unabashed bearing. This youth, though brave as a hero and strong as an athlete, is a child in inexperience, and so bashful in the presence of the woman who instantly captivates him, that it is she who is the first to betray her sympathy for him, and has even to take the chain from her own neck and hang it around his before he can so much as muster up courage to hope for her love. So, too, we find him passing his time in hanging poems to her upon the trees, and carving the name of Rosalind in their bark. She amuses herself, in her page's attire, by making herself his confidant, and pretending, as it were in jest, to be his Rosalind. She cannot bring herself to confess her passion, although she can think and talk (to Celia) of no one but him, and although his delay of a few minutes in keeping tryst with her sets her beside herself with impatience. She is as sensitive as she is intelligent, in this differing from Portia [in *The Merchant of Venice*], to whom, in other respects, she bears some resemblance, though she lacks her persuasive eloquence, and is, on the whole, more tender, more virginal. She faints when Oliver, to excuse Orlando's delay, brings her a handkerchief stained with his blood; yet has sufficient self-mastery to say with a smile the moment she recovers, ''I pray you tell your brother how well I counterfeited'' [IV. iii. 166-67]. She is quite at her ease in her male attire, like Viola [in *Twelfth Night*] and Imogen [in *Cymbeline*] after her. (pp. 227-28)

What Rosalind says of women in general applies to herself in particular: you will never find her without an answer until you find her without a tongue. And there is always a bright and merry fantasy in her answers. She is literally radiant with youth, imagination, and the joy of loving so passionately and being so passionately beloved. And it is marvellous how thoroughly feminine is her wit. Too many of the witty women in books written by men have a man's intelligence. Rosalind's wit is tempered by feeling.

She has no monopoly of wit in this Arcadia of Arden. Every one in the play is witty, even the so-called simpletons. It is a festival of wit. At some points Shakespeare seems to have followed no stricter principle than the simple one of making each interlocutor outbid the other in wit (see, for example, the conversation between Touchstone and the country wench whom he befools). The result is that the piece is bathed in a sunshiny humour. And amid all the gay and airy wit-skirmishes, amid the cooing love-duets of all the happy youths and maidens, the poet intersperses the melancholy solos of his Jaques. . . .

[His] is the melancholy which haunts the thinker and the great creative artist; but in Shakespeare it as yet modulated with ease into the most engaging and delightful merriment. (p. 230)

*George Brandes, ''The Interval of Serenity—'As You Like It'—The Roving Spirit—The Longing for Nature—Jaques and Shakespeare—The Play a Feast of Wit,'' translated by William Archer, in his* William Shakespeare, *William Heinemann, 1920, pp. 221-30.*

**BERNARD SHAW** (essay date 1896)

*[Shaw, an Irish dramatist and critic, was the major English playwright of his generation. In his Shakespearean criticism, he consistently attacked what he considered to be Shakespeare's inflated reputation as a dramatist. Shaw did not hesitate to judge the characters in the plays by the standards of his own values and*

*prejudices, and much of his commentary is presented—as the prominent Shaw critic Edwin Wilson once remarked—"with an impudence that had not been seen before, nor is likely to be seen again." Shaw's hostility toward Shakespeare's work was due in large measure to his belief that it was interfering with the acceptance of Henrik Ibsen and the new social theater he so strongly advocated. In the following excerpt from a dramatic review originally published in 1896, Shaw brings all his pejorative wit to bear on As You Like It. He finds the play didactically inadequate and aesthetically lazy, criticizing, among other things, its "sham moralizing" and lamenting that Shakespeare missed his chance to develop the "pregnant metaphor" in Jaques's "Seven Ages of Man" speech in II. vii. In spite of his criticisms, Shaw maintains that "the fascination of As You Like It is still very great" and praises the play's prose, particularly the "energy and exposition" of the first act's language. He also recognizes the comedy's "vital parts"—its "genuine story-telling, the fun, the poetry, the drama"— and regrets only that Shakespeare included a mass of "putrescence" along with them. Finally, Shaw admires Rosalind, not only for her language and character, but also for her aggressive approach to love.*]

[What] a play! It was in "As You Like It" that the sententious William first began to openly exploit the fondness of the British Public for sham moralizing and stage "philosophy." It contains one passage that specially exasperates me. Jaques, who spends his time, like Hamlet, in vainly emulating the wisdom of Sancho Panza, comes in laughing in a superior manner because he has met a fool in the forest who

Says very wisely, It is ten o'clock.
Thus we may see [quoth he] how the world wags.
'Tis but an hour ago since it was nine;
And after one hour more 'twill be eleven.
And so, from hour to hour, we ripe and ripe;
And then, from hour to hour, we rot and rot;
And thereby hangs a tale.

[II. vii. 22-8]

Now, considering that this fool's platitude is precisely the "philosophy" of Hamlet, Macbeth ("To-morrow and to-morrow and to-morrow," &c. [*Macbeth*, V. v. 19]), Prospero [in *The Tempest*], and the rest of them, there is something unendurably aggravating in Shakespeare giving himself airs with Touchstone, as if he, the immortal, ever, even at his sublimest, had anything different or better to say himself. Later on he misses a great chance. Nothing is more significant than the statement that "all the world's a stage" [II. vii. 139]. The whole world *is* ruled by theatrical illusion. Between the Cæsars, the emperors, the Christian heroes, the Grand Old Men, the kings, prophets, saints, heroes and judges, of the newspapers and the popular imagination, and the actual Juliuses, Napoleons, Gordons, Gladstones, and so on, there is the same difference as between Hamlet and Sir Henry Irving. The case is not one of fanciful similitude, but of identity. The great critics are those who penetrate and understand the illusion: the great men are those who, as dramatists planning the development of nations, or as actors carrying out the drama, are behind the scenes of the world instead of gaping and gushing in the auditorium after paying their taxes at the doors. And yet Shakespeare, with the rarest of opportunities of observing this, lets his pregnant metaphor slip, and, with his usual incapacity for pursuing any idea, wanders off into a grandmotherly Elizabethan edition of the advertisement of Cassell's "Popular Educator." How anybody over the age of seven can take any interest in a literary toy so silly in its conceit and common in its ideas as the Seven Ages of Man passes my understanding. Even the great metaphor itself is inaccurately expressed; for

the world is a playhouse, not merely a stage; and Shakespeare might have said so without making his blank verse scan any worse than Richard's exclamation, "All the world to nothing!" [*Richard III*, I. ii. 237].

And then Touchstone with his rare jests about the knight that swore by his honor they were good pancakes! Who would endure such humor from any one but Shakespeare?—an Eskimo would demand his money back if a modern author offered him such fare. And the comfortable old Duke, symbolical of the British villa dweller, who likes to find "sermons in stones and good in everything" [II. i. 17], and then to have a good dinner! This unvenerable impostor, expanding on his mixed diet of pious twaddle and venison, rouses my worst passions. Even when Shakespeare, in his efforts to be a social philosopher, does rise for an instant to the level of a sixth-rate Kingsley, his solemn self-complacency infuriates me. And yet, so wonderful is his art, that it is not easy to disentangle what is unbearable from what is irresistible. Orlando one moment says:

Whate'er you are
That in this desert inaccessible
Under the shade of melancholy boughs
Lose and neglect the creeping hours of time;

[II. vii. 109-12]

which, though it indicates a thoroughly unhealthy imagination, and would have been impossible to, for instance, Chaucer, is yet magically fine of its kind. The next moment he tacks on lines which would have revolted Mr. Pecksniff:

If ever you have looked on better days,
If ever been where bells have knolled to church,
    [*How perfectly the atmosphere of the rented
        pew is caught in this incredible line!*]
If ever sat at any good man's feast,
If ever from your eyelids wiped—

[II. vii. 113-16]

I really shall get sick if I quote any more of it. Was ever such canting, snivelling, hypocritical unctuousness exuded by an actor anxious to show that he was above his profession, and was a thoroughly respectable man in private life? Why cannot all this putrescence be cut out of the play, and only the vital parts—the genuine storytelling, the fun, the poetry, the drama, be retained? Simply because, if nothing were left of Shakespeare but his genius, our Shakespearolaters would miss all that they admire in him.

Notwithstanding these drawbacks, the fascination of "As You Like It" is still very great. It has the overwhelming advantage of being written for the most part in prose instead of in blank verse, which any fool can write. And such prose! The first scene alone, with its energy of exposition, each phrase driving its meaning and feeling in up to the head at one brief, sure stroke, is worth ten acts of the ordinary Elizabethan sing-song. It cannot be said that the blank verse is reserved for those passages which demand a loftier expression, since Le Beau and Corin drop into it, like Mr. Silas Wegg, on the most inadequate provocation; but at least there is not much of it. The popularity of Rosalind is due to three main causes. First, she only speaks blank verse for a few minutes. Second, she only wears a skirt for a few minutes (and the dismal effect of the change at the end to the wedding-dress ought to convert the stupidest champion of petticoats to rational dress). Third, she makes love to the man instead of waiting for the man to make love to her—a piece of natural history which has kept Shakespeare's heroines alive, whilst generations of properly governessed young ladies, taught to say "No" three times at least, have miserably perished. (pp. 116-19)

*Bernard Shaw, "Toujours Shakespeare," in his* Dramatic Opinions and Essays with an Apology, Vol. 2, *Brentano's, 1906, pp. 116-22.*

### FREDERICK S. BOAS (essay date 1896)

[*Boas was a nineteenth- and early twentieth-century scholar specializing in Elizabethan and Tudor drama. In his Shakespearean criticism, he focuses on both the biographical elements and the historical influence apparent in Shakespeare's works. For this reason, many scholars today regard him as occupying a transitional position in Shakespearean criticism between the biographical and historical approaches to the plays. In the following excerpt from* Shakspere and His Predecessors, *first published in 1896, Boas focuses on the pastoralism in* As You Like It. *He discusses Shakespeare's adaptation of Thomas Lodge's* Rosalynde, *observing that the dramatist's "series of entirely novel creations" accounts for the "profoundly original and . . . unique character" of the play. Boas discerns the most decisive evidence of Shakespeare's skill as an adapter in the "forest dialogue between the lovers,' and he particularly admires his "prodigal use of metaphor" in portraying Rosalind's "lambent" wit. Commenting on the Silvius and Phebe episode, Boas praises Shakespeare's parody of town and country life, noting that it preserves "all that is really true in the contrast." The critic also touches on Jaques and Touchstone, finding in the former evidence of "dilettante" libertinism—of "ennui" amidst a "flux of sensations"—and describing the latter's "acid flavour" wit as an ingredient that "tempers the lusciousness of the conventional pastoral."*]

[*As You Like It* has] features which make it peculiarly representative of Shakspere in the most joyous period of his art, and it may therefore fittingly stand as the climax of his greater comedies, though in compact structure of plot it cannot vie with *Twelfth Night,* and still less with *Much Ado about Nothing.*This looseness of texture is due to the source of the play, a novel by Thomas Lodge, called *Rosalind, Euphues' Golden Legacy.* . . . (p. 328)

[Shakspere] has followed the framework of Lodge's attractive though somewhat prolix tale with unusual fidelity. All the more remarkable therefore is it that by readjustments of the perspective, and by the addition of a series of entirely novel creations, the dramatist has given to his work a profoundly original and, in respect of his epoch, unique character. For the broad result of his treatment is to substitute for the artificial atmosphere of the Renaissance pastoral the open-air freshness, the breeze and blue of the old English ballad-poetry. . . . [By] a masterstroke of skill, a single episode, that of Silvius and Phebe, is worked up into an exaggerated form of the conventional pastoral method, so that the contrast between it and the natural charm of the simple woodland life is the most effective satire upon this growth of the literary forcing-house. Thus Shakspere preserves all that is really true in the contrast between town and country while parodying its exaggerations. Not indeed that *As You Like It* takes us back to the homely, realistic Warwickshire or Windsor scenery of *Love's Labour's Lost* or *The Merry Wives.* Rather we find ourselves in an atmosphere akin to that of *A Midsummer Night's Dream,* truly English in the main, but with added features unfamiliar to the traveller's eye. (p. 332)

It is in [the] forest dialogues between the lovers that Shakspere's skill in transforming Lodge's romance is most decisively shown. The novelist had put into the mouth of Rosalind

moralizing reflections on the dangers of love, containing some pretty turns of phrase, but growing oppressive in their heavy Euphuistic brocade. For this Shakspere substituted a gushing stream of wit that carries foam and freshness into the close atmosphere of the conventional Arcadia. But this wit of Rosalind is of peculiar quality. Unlike that of Beatrice [in *Much Ado about Nothing*], it is lambent rather than pungent, and does not spring so much from a penetrating intellect as from a fertile fancy. It shows a far-off touch of kinship in its prodigal use of metaphor to the Euphuistic passion for similes, which appears indiscriminately in the speeches of all Lodge's characters. This leisurely forest life allows ample time for weaving imaginative embroidery round not too serious themes, and thus we get Rosalind's charming little lecture on the divers paces in which time travels with divers persons, and her comparison of love to a madness, which deserves a dark house and a whip, and only escapes because the whippers share the lunacy. In a similar vein is her modernized version of the romantic stories of Troilus and Cressida, and Hero and Leander, in support of her assertion that 'men have died from time to time, and worms have eaten them, but not for love' [IV. i. 106-08]. Of this painful raillery it may be said in her own words that it would not kill a fly. It is a weapon merely of self-defence, and the pictures that she draws for Orlando's benefit of the changeable humours of a coquette and of a wife's wayward moods are in ironical antithesis to the passionate devotion with which her own heart swells almost to bursting. (pp. 336-37)

Amongst the couples whom Hymen unites are Silvius and Phebe, who had already made their appearance in Lodge's romance. The novelist had censured Phebe for her excessive scorn, and had emphasized the retribution in kind that falls upon her head. But his picture of the self-forgetting devotion of Silvius was, on the whole, sympathetic, and neither of the characters moved in a different plane from the remaining figures in the story. But in the drama this is exactly what they do, for, by a number of minute touches, Shakspere transposes them into the region of caricature. Unlike the other lovers, they speak uniformly in verse instead of prose, and this in itself gives a distinctively idealistic flavour to their sentiments. Silvius' recital in strophic form to Corin of the signs of true love, ending with the triple invocation of the name of Phebe, prepares us for the pageant played between him and his disdainful mistress. Phebe has all the 'regulation' charms of a pastoral nymph—inky brows, black silk hair, bugle eyeballs, and cheeks of cream; but these are turned into burlesque by the addition of 'a leathern hand, a free-stone coloured hand' [IV. iii. 24-5]. She has been allowed a very pretty gift of language, and her process of proof to Silvius that eyes, 'the frailest, softest things, who shut their coward gates on atomies' [III. v. 12-13], cannot be called butchers or murderers, is a charming piece of filigree logic. But her dainty terms become ridiculous when they are used to express her love for Ganymede; and the poetical epistle in which she questions the supposed youth whether he is a 'god to shepherd turned' [IV. iii. 40], and promises, if her passion is fruitless, to 'study how to die' [IV. iii. 63], is a glaring travesty of the sentimental effusions of the conventional love-lorn Phyllises and Chloes. Similarly the 'tame snake' [IV. iii. 70], Silvius, who is satisfied to live upon a 'scattered smile' [III. v. 104] loosed now and then by his mistress, and who bears her letter to Ganymede in the fond belief that it has an angry tenor, is a parody of that true loyalty of heart which, as seen in Orlando, is no enemy to either cheerfulness or self-respect. At the end of the comedy, when they have served the dramatist's purpose, they are united in marriage like the other lovers; but this similarity of fate does not annul the contrast between the Dresden-china couple, and the true children of nature, Orlando and Rosalind.

To throw Silvius and Phebe into yet bolder relief Shakspere has set beside them one or two genuinely rustic figures, drawn probably from his personal observation in Warwickshire. Corin, the shepherd to a churlish master, had already appeared in Lodge's novel. With his primitive philosophy, that 'good pasture makes fat sheep, and that a great cause of the night is lack of the sun' [III. ii. 27-8], he puts to shame the extravagances of morbid fancies, and instead of sighing and weeping after the fashion of mock swains, he finds in the honest toil of a country life an abiding content.... To the same genuinely rustic species, though of coarser mould, belongs Audrey, a creation completely of the dramatist. She is, as she does not hesitate to admit, an ill-favoured thing, without any touch of the beauty in which the idyllic shepherdess is habitually arrayed. And that she is better versed in a plain country morality than in lyrical flights of passion is sufficiently proved by her inquiry what it is to be poetical. 'Is it honest in deed and word? Is it a true thing?' [III. iii. 17-18]. This bucolic simplicity delivers her completely into the hands of the artful Touchstone, for whom apparently she forsakes a former lover William.

Touchstone is another figure due to Shakspere's invention, and together with Feste [in *Twelfth Night*] he stands far above the other Fools in the comedies. He entirely lacks Feste's tender lyrical vein, and the few snatches of rhyme that fall from his lips are only jingling parodies. Feste's good humour had not been seriously ruffled even by the contemptuous ill-will of Malvolio [in *Twelfth Night*], but Touchstone's wit takes always and with every one a caustic turn, and though he gives practical proof of his attachment to Celia by following her to the forest, he spares her with his tongue as little as the rest. Thus while, like Feste, he has to do with each of the characters in turn, he notes their special disposition, not in order to chime in with it, or to gently hint a cure for its defects, but to throw it up in all its worst lights. The acid flavour of his wit is another of the ingredients with which Shakspere tempers the lusciousness of the conventional pastoral, and his readiness to rail against both town and country goes far to keep the balance evenly swung between the two. (pp. 338-40)

The addition of a Fool to the personages found in the original romance is in no way surprising, but far different is it with another Shaksperean creation whom we encounter within the groves of Arden. What has the melancholy Jaques to do there, and why is he drawn with such elaborate finish? In him, from yet another and more subtle point of view, the dramatist makes war against the idea that in an idyllic life every nature will find an anodyne for its peculiar malady. Under the influences of Arcadia the unhappy may become cheerful, and even the wicked may turn to good, but real sorrow and real evil imply stability of character, and a recognition of the facts and laws of life. There is one type of nature which never for a moment plants its foot on the solid rock-bed of things as they are, but which sees in existence only a constant flux of sensations after which it constantly flies. Of this type Jaques is the consummate representative, and to him Arcadia is merely a fresh field for the chase of new experiences. In men of his class the inward fever begets a corresponding physical restlessness which drives them from pole to pole in search of an elusive satisfaction—with the result of profound *ennui*.... He has experimented on life under all its phases, and this, as we gather from the Duke, has included a deep plunge into vicious pleasures; but we think of him as merely a dilettante libertine, who has gone through

a course of iniquity that he may be more qualified to inveigh against the dark side of all things human. Everywhere and always he pores morbidly upon the hollow and petty phases of existence. The world to him is a stage, and nothing more: the men and women are merely players, with their exits and their entrances, mechanically regulated movements, in an ephemeral pageant. (pp. 341-42)

*Frederick S. Boas, "The Golden Prime of Comedy," in his* Shakspere and His Predecessors, *Charles Scribner's Sons, 1896, pp. 292-343.*

## E. K. CHAMBERS   (essay date 1905)

[*Chambers occupies a transitional position in Shakespearean criticism, one which connects the biographical sketches and character analyses of the nineteenth century with the historical, technical, and textual criticism of the twentieth century. While a civil servant in the British Education Department, Chambers earned his reputation as a scholar with his multivolume works,* The Medieval Stage *(1903) and* The Elizabethan Stage *(1923), while he also edited* The Red Letter Shakespeare *(1904-08). Chambers investigated both the purpose and limitations of each dramatic genre as Shakespeare presented it and speculated on how the dramatist's work was influenced by contemporary historical issues and his own frame of mind. In the following excerpt from his* Shakespeare: A Survey, *originally published in his introduction to the Red Letter edition of* As You Like It *(1905), Chambers offers an early view of the play as a romance—a "romance incarnate"—describing it as a gathering of "all the wonderful elements of the secular tradition." Chambers also discusses the function and meaning of the Arden forest, the role of women in the play, and Jaques's melancholy. He characterizes Arden as a "spiritual force, bringing medicine to the hurt souls of men," and, in an autobiographical comment, regards Shakespeare's interest in pastoral as "a reaction against urban life" and an expression of his own longing for the country. Noting that* As You Like It *is "dominated" by women, Chambers credits to Rosalind the play's "special human charm" and its "note of ... joyous vitality." Like many earlier critics, he labels Jaques a "poseur" and a "professional cynic." Also of importance, Chambers argues that the pastoral vision is not entirely idealized, for Shakespeare ultimately directs his satire "as much against as for the romantic ideals that the play sets out to expound."*]

Before *As You Like It* Zoilus is disarmed. The temper of the play is so perfect, its poetry so mellow and so golden, that the critic would fain hold his hand in fear that, when all has been said, he shall but seem in his curiosity to have rubbed off the marvellous dust from the wings of a butterfly. Here you have a Shakespeare, the conscious lord of his art, launched triumphantly once for all upon the high tide of romance. He has come to the plenitude of his powers. He has found his characteristic formula; and we have nothing to do but to listen to the bugles blown as he hunts the quarry of his theme through the intricate glades and tangles of his bosky imagination. *As You Like It* is romance incarnate. All the wonderful elements of the secular tradition are gathered together there in its lighthearted compass. There is the romance of friendship in Rosalind and Celia, 'like Juno's swans, still coupled and inseparable' [I. iii. 75-6]; the romance of Adam's loyalty, 'the constant service of the antique world' [II. iii. 57]; the romance of love at first sight, acknowledged in words by the smitten Phebe's quotation of dead Marlowe's saw, and acknowledged as the mainspring of the whole plot when young Orlando wrestled and overthrew more than his enemies, and witty Rosalind, for all her cousin's warning, fell deeper in love than with safety of a pure blush she might in honour come off again. Then you have Orlando as the typical lover of romance, the love-shaked sonnetteer, hanging his odes upon hawthorns and his elegies upon brambles, and abusing the young plants with carving 'Rosalind' upon their barks. You have the conventional issues of romance in the wind-up of the story; the sudden changes of fortune which betray a beneficent disposer of events, the repentance of Oliver and the conversion of Frederick to a religious life, whereby the banished duke returns from exile and Orlando wins his father's inheritance, and earthly things made even atone together beneath the blessing of Hymen. Above all, you have the romantic spirit of adventure with which the play is filled; and never more high-spirited and picturesque company of knight-errant and squire and dwarf set out on their enterprise in *Palmerin of England* and *Amadis of Gaul,* than this of Rosalind with curtle-axe upon her thigh, and Celia smirched with umber, and the roynish clown. *As You Like It* is one of the plays, so numerous above all at the midmost stage of Shakespeare's development, which are dominated by their women; and if one polled the company of readers for their choice of a heroine, although some would swear fealty to Imogen's endurance [in *Cymbeline*] or Beatrice's ardent soul [in *Much Ado about Nothing*], and I myself make my reserve of devotion to Portia [in *The Merchant of Venice*], yet it can hardly be doubted that the majority of suffrages would be Rosalind's. Witty and brave, audacious and tender, with a grace that her doublet and hose cannot pervert, and a womanhood that they cannot conceal, it is indeed she that gives the piece its special human charm, its note of sane and joyous vitality.

And yet, splendid as is Rosalind's, there is an even greater part in *As You Like It.* And that is the part of the Forest of Arden. Commentators dispute whether Arden is a duchy on the confines of France and Germany, or whether it lies north of the Avon in Warwickshire, just as they dispute whether the island of *The Tempest* is this or that little nook of land in the Mediterranean. Actually, of course, it too is the essential forest of romance, with its strange fauna and flora, its possibilities of a lioness beneath every bush, its olive-trees and its osiers, its palms and its oaks growing together. It is here that men live like the old Robin Hood of England, fleeting the time carelessly as they did in the golden world. We have travelled through it already, in *The Two Gentlemen of Verona.* Then it stood between Milan and Mantua, and the outlaws swore in it 'by the bare scalp of Robin Hood's fat friar' [*The Two Gentlemen of Verona,* IV. i. 36]. In its purlieus lie the pleasant pastoral lands which Theocritus invented, and after him Virgil and Mantuan sang of, where peaceful shepherds feed their flocks, careless of the court, and vexed only by the pains of love and the cruelty of a disdainful mistress. We are always conscious of the forest in *As You Like It.* It is something more than a mere scenic background; a spiritual force, bringing medicine to the hurt souls of men. The banished duke has the sentiment of it—

> Hath not old custom made this life more sweet
> Than that of painted pomp? Are not these woods
> More free from peril than the envious court?
>
> [II. i. 2-4]

Thus *As You Like It* does for the Elizabethan drama what the long string of pastoral poets, Spenser and Sidney, Lodge and Greene, Drayton and Browne, and the rest, had already done, or were still to do, for Elizabethan lyric. The temper of it is not strictly the temper of the actual country-dweller as that has filled our later literature for the last century. It is rather the temper of urban disillusion, the instinctive craving of the man

who has been long in cities pent for green fields and quiet nights. And no doubt it yields rather a mirage of the country than a sober and realistic vision of the country as it really is. Yet it is a temper to be accounted with, and insistent upon its expression. There are those who speak of pastoral as if it were only a fashion of writing, a literary convention which filtered from the classics through the Italians to the literatures of the west. There is an element of truth in this, of course, but upon the whole it is more false than true. It is parallel to the misreading of Shakespeare's *Sonnets* which sees in them merely an exercise in the manner of Petrarch. Poets are not really so inhuman as all that; and why does a literary fashion have its vogue at a given moment in a people's history, if not because, just then and there, it answers to some natural necessity in the hearts of men? The pastoral impulse of the end of the sixteenth century in England means that at the end of the sixteenth century Englishmen were learning to feel the oppression of cities. . . . The monstrous nightmare of the modern city had not yet made its appearance; but there was already reason enough, especially in days when court intrigue was merciless and none too savoury, for the finer souls to dream their dreams of Arcady or of Arden.

And if Shakespeare dreamed, one is tempted to ask whether he dreamed for others only, or for himself as well. Does *As You Like It* disclose the first stirrings of an impulse back to the land, which may be held to account for his ultimate return to Stratford in 1611 while he was still but a man of middle age and in the full enjoyment of fame and fortune? Did Arden mean for him the woods and parks in which he had wandered as a boy and taken his share, if tradition errs not, in goring the round haunches of the poor dappled fools? Such questions can hardly be answered. One likes to think that Shakespeare never became at heart a Londoner. But all that is certain is that he never wholly cut himself adrift from Stratford interests, since two or three years before he wrote *As You Like It* he had already bought the fine house there in which he was to end his days; and that in *As You Like It* itself there breathes more of the country than in any other play between *A Midsummer Night's Dream* and the group which immediately preceded his retirement.

The fact that its theme is inspired by the reaction against urban life naturally makes *As You Like It* a comedy as well as a romance. Its criticism is not only implied but direct. Consider the proceedings of Touchstone. Touchstone has been a courtier; he has proof indisputable of it. 'I have trod a measure; I have flattered a lady; I have been politic with my friend, smooth with mine enemy; I have undone three tailors; I have had four quarrels, and like to have fought one' [V. iv. 46-7]. He gives himself airs accordingly; but, when he finds himself amongst the shepherds and shepherdesses, like the most capricious poet, honest Ovid, among the Goths, he certainly does not commend the court by the good sense or the decency of his love-making. He behaves, indeed, much like 'Arry in Epping. It is, however, to Jaques, rather than to Touchstone, that the function of voicing the satire of the play upon contemporary civilization chiefly belongs. Jaques is the professional cynic, always ready to rail against all the first-born of Egypt and to pierce with his invective the body of the country, city, court. It is, however, fair to note that the utterances of Jaques must not be taken as summing up the meaning of the play. Jaques is jaundiced, a *poseur;* he has the traveller's melancholy, which consists in disabling all the benefits of his own country. To the wholesome natures of Rosalind and Orlando he is plainly antipathetic. The duke, who finds entertainment in his humours, declines to take him seriously, and tells him to his face that his cynicism is but the reaction of his own evil life. . . . Shakespeare's judgment of life is, indeed, too sane to let him even maintain the pretence that the perfection which is lacking at court will be found in the forest. Herein is the significance of the episode of the shepherdess Phebe, for Phebe is as vain and disdainful and wanton, and as remorseless in the prosecution of her selfish intrigues, as the finest lady of them all. She, no less than Oliver and Frederick, must learn her lesson.

And so we come to the point that the satire of the play is, after all, as much against as for the romantic ideals that the play sets out to expound; which is as much as to say, that the satire is converted into essential humour. Does Orlando stand for the romantic love of the sonnetteers? By the end of his encounters with the wicked wit of Rosalind, he is . . . dry-beaten with pure scoff . . . ; and even the faithful Celia must complain that her cousin has simply misused their sex in her love-prate. Once more an investigation of Touchstone is illuminating as to the intention of the dramatist. Touchstone, the court fool, is the first example of that dramatic type which was afterwards to yield the Feste of *Twelfth Night,* the Lavache of *All's Well that Ends Well,* and the nameless fool of *King Lear.* . . . [It] has often been observed that the fools of Shakespeare's plays have a sort of choric function. They are commentators rather than actors, and if you read them aright, you may catch in their fantastic utterance some reflection of the maker's own judgment upon his puppets. Herein Shakespeare is but true to an historic model. In mediaeval courts, where, as in all courts, the serious man must needs dissemble, it was always the privilege of those that wore the motley to speak a shrewd word in jest, to use their folly like a stalking-horse and under the presentation of that to shoot their wit. Touchstone, however, must, I think, be regarded as something of a variation upon the type. He embodies Shakespeare's comment upon romance, but it is rather by what he is, than by anything that he consciously says. For how can romance more readily be made ridiculous than by the disconcerting contact of the natural gross man, who blurts out in every crisis precisely those undesirable facts which it is the whole object of romance to refine away? Adventure brings us to Arden, and it is left for the fool to realize that when he was at home he was in a better place; nor can the literary graces of love at first sight hold their own against Touchstone's ready offer to 'rime you so, eight years together, dinners and suppers and sleeping hours excepted' [III. ii. 96-7]. It is doubtless only an accident of chronology, that Touchstone performs exactly the same office of disillusion to the knight-errantry of Rosalind and Orlando, as is performed by Sancho Panza to that of the almost precisely contemporary Don Quixote de la Mancha. (pp. 155-63)

> *E. K. Chambers, "'As You Like It'," in his* Shakespeare: A Survey, *1925. Reprint by Oxford University Press, 1926, pp. 155-63.*

## STOPFORD A. BROOKE (essay date 1905)

*[Brooke was an Anglo-Irish clergyman, poet, critic, and educator, whose* Primer of English Literature *(1876) was popular with generations of students. Among his other notable works on literature are* Theology in the English Poets *(1874) and* Naturalism in English Poetry *(1920). In the following excerpt from his* On Ten Plays of Shakespeare *(1905), Brooke provides the first extended commentary on the various forms of love in* As You Like It. *The love "between man and woman" is the most important to Shakespeare, he says, and in this play it is "always modest, chaste, true, faithful, . . . full of fire and joy." He cites three examples*

*of this "enchanted" love: 1) that of Rosalind and Orlando, who are "kindled into brightness" by love; 2) that of Celia and Oliver, who enjoy a "swift, mutual passion, more of the senses than the soul"; and 3) the "conventional love of the Elizabethan Pastoral" of Silvius and Phebe. Brooke also discusses three kinds of beauty in the play: 1) the "delightful charm" and "finished execution" of the play itself; 2) the beauty of character, exemplified by Rosalind and Orlando, who are "charming" and "ennobling"; and 3) the physical beauty of the scenery of Arden.]*

The solemn professor, the most solid moralist, will not be able to assert that Shakespeare wrote [*As You Like It*] with a moral purpose, or from a special desire to teach mankind. He wrote it as he liked it, for his own delight. He hoped men would listen to it for their pleasure, and take it just as they liked best to take it. It is true there is much matter in it, as there is in human life, which the prophets and moralists may use for their own purposes, but Shakespeare did not write these things for their ethical ends. He wrote them because they were the right things in their places; and he smiled, as he wrote them, with pleasure in them. (p. 155)

In this play love lives in many forms: in Orlando and Rosalind, Celia and Oliver, Silvius and Phoebe, Touchstone and Audrey. We see also other forms of love: the love of two girls for one another, of Adam for his master and his master for him, of Touchstone for Celia and Rosalind. Even a few touches are given to us of a daughter's affection for her father. But these kinds of love, outside the passion of youthful love, are but side-issues, due to the love of Shakespeare for lovingness. Of them all, in comparison with the enchanted drawing of love between man and woman, Rosalind's phrase may be said, 'But what talk we of fathers, when there is such a man as Orlando?' [III. iv. 38-9].

In this play also the lovers love one another at first sight.

> Dead shepherd, now I find thy saw of might:
> Who ever lov'd that lov'd not at first sight?
>
> [III. v. 81-2]

is the cry of Phoebe when she sees Rosalind, and thinks she is a man. Rosalind is smitten the moment she sees Orlando, Orlando when he sees Rosalind. When Oliver and Celia meet, they 'no sooner saw one another but they loved' [V. ii. 33-4]. . . . It was like [Shakespeare's] naturalness to believe in love at first sight, like a man who lived in that swift and undelaying time, like the southern warmth of his temperament, like his reverence for passion as a native goodness in human nature. And love, in his work, even when it breaks at once into the full-blown rose, is always modest, chaste, true, faithful, and full of fire and joy. Moreover, when circumstance is not dark, it is not isolating, selfish, foolish, or sentimental. It thinks of others; it sees things clearly, and is quick to meet them. It has fine intellect at hand to use, and uses it. And it is full of common-sense.

There is not a word of this which might not be proved from the love-play of Orlando and Rosalind. That is one of the gayest things in Shakespeare. The wit which flashes through their conversation does not lessen its clean brightness from the beginning to the end, neither does the pleasant humour which plays innocuous over every circumstance, over every character, and over the natural world. Nor is the humour forced or conventional or derived from others. It is the natural bubbling up of the fountain of happy youth into gracious gaiety of temper, into self-delighting joy. We, who listen, cannot enjoy the humour of the situation when, dressed as a gallant hunter Rosalind meets Orlando, half as much as she enjoys it herself. She plays with it as a kitten with a ball. Her love develops, does not check or dim, her humour. As to her natural intellect, it is the same with that. Love has not impaired it. It is as swift and various as summer lightning; and though it flashes here and there and everywhere, it always strikes the point at issue. It sees into the centre of all masked conventions. It understands Jaques in a moment, though he is a man of the world and she a girl; and lays him bare to himself. Yet all the time this clear-eyed intellect is working on life, she is so deep in love that it cannot be sounded. In her, emotion and intellect are equal powers. (pp. 156-58)

Orlando's love is of the same quality, full of gaiety, even though—for he cannot find Rosalind—it be dashed with a shade of natural melancholy: amusing itself with delightful verses hung on happy trees, ready to play with the pretty youth he is pleased to call his Rosalind; witty enough to make the talk lively, not witty enough to displease the girl who would not wish him to be brilliant when he thought he was away from her; of a grave intelligence also when he chooses; able, like Rosalind, to overcome Jaques with his own weapons.

Love, with him, is no mournful, depressing companion. It kindles into brightness all his powers, as it does with Rosalind. There is no fading in its rose, no false sentiment, none of the marks of a dying lover. (pp. 158-59)

In both, their love enkindles, not only itself to finer loving, but all their natural qualities. To read of it is pleasure. It gives almost as much pleasure as it has.

The love of Celia and Oliver is of a different kind, a swift, mutual passion, more of the senses than the soul. Rosalind does not like it, as we hear from her account of it. She is more scornful than pleased. It jars on her dignity, on her humorous nature. There is no play in it, such as she has had with Orlando, to keep it healthy. And we do not expect it of Celia; this kind of passion does not lie in her character as we have seen it; and I think Shakespeare has been betrayed into inventing something which is not quite in nature by his desire to wind up his play by such a reconciliation of Oliver and Orlando as will make everything comfortable for Rosalind and Orlando in the future. It is against probability that Oliver should change in a moment from the scoundrel he is in the first act to a high-bred gentleman, only because his brother did not allow him to be killed by a serpent and a lioness. The invention of the lioness and the fight becomes improbable because of the main improbability. And, moreover, I cannot get over the matching of Celia to a man whose nature has been for many years that of a ruffian, a murderer, and a greedy dog. It stains her pleasant image. Oliver has repented, but we are sorry for Celia. Shakespeare ought not to have made him so very bad in the beginning, if he was to be so good in the end. It is out of tune. (pp. 159-60)

The love of Silvius and Phoebe is the conventional love of the Elizabethan Pastoral; and it may be, in this love-drama, a satire on that academic, literary love. He who conceived the natural love of Orlando and Rosalind would see no reality [in artificial love] . . . ; and it would be quite like Shakespeare to make a picture of it, partly for the sake of pleasant mockery of it, and partly in order to contrast it with natural love in Rosalind and Orlando. But, as he is in earnest all through this play, and as love of whatever kind is at root serious as well as gay to him, he touches the love of Silvius with reality. Its expression goes far beyond the conventional phrasing of the Pastoral. It seems a pity that Silvius is almost too great a fool for any woman to care for. But he is in earnest, and Rosalind sees that he is; and

while she strives to lash him into rebellion against Phoebe, she also takes some pains to get his sweetheart for him in the end. She does not pity him, for his want of manliness deserves no pity; but she uses Phoebe's love for her (as a man) to soften her heart, to make her understand what Silvius has suffered; and, in that new temper, Phoebe takes Silvius because he has been faithful. The conventional love is led into the natural; and the way it is managed is as pretty a piece of work as is to be found in Shakespeare.

The best characteristic of the play is beauty. I am not sure that it is not the most beautiful of all the comedies, because the beautiful in it is so joyous, and distributed with so equal a hand over the whole. It is pervasive, like a sweet air in which all things are seen delicately. There may be lovelier or grander passages of poetry in other comedies than any we find here, but no other comedy has the same equality of poetry, the same continuity of lovely emotion, of delightful charm, and of finished execution. And though the poetry in the tragic plays may have more of fire and sensuousness, of emotion breaking into ideal form, of thought on the verge of the eternal intelligence, yet here, where the gentle note of gaiety naturally eludes these supreme qualities, there is abundance of good matter, of the stuff of thought, of what Arnold would call the criticism of life. Few plays are wiser, more full of affectionate experience of human nature. And without that element of human wisdom and affection there is no great poetry.

A greater beauty even than this is the beauty of character. Rosalind and Orlando! could any one desire to have more charming, more ennobling companions than these two enchanting persons? To live with them is to live with moral beauty, but it is not a beauty which the pharisaic moralist will like at all. Their life will do good to every one they meet. Rosalind even lifts her thought, at times, into a spiritual beauty, and then returns to the natural, like the lark who soars in song and then drops downward to her nest. The characters of Celia, and of almost all the rest, are lower than Rosalind's, but they have a steady sweetness of nature. Of course, Jaques is set over against them, but even he is better than the cynic. There is a sadness in him which is real; he is not so bad a man as he has been; he is meditative, and has at times the gentleness of pensiveness. Then the banished Duke is a noble gentleman; worldly-wise but enjoying the woods, pleased even with Jaques when in his sullen fits he is full of matter; taking all his misfortunes with a gallant air, and turning them into good fortune; translating the stubbornness of ill-luck into so 'quiet and so sweet a style' [II. i. 20] that all the banished lords are happy with him; finding good in everything, and as kind in his thoughts of animals as of men. Amiens, the other lords, even the pages, are courteous, good-humoured, musical, and ready to help. Silvius is not intelligent, but he is good; Phoebe turns out very graciously; Audrey is an honest creature; Touchstone loves his mistresses with fidelity, though he is naughty enough; Corin is not only an honest labourer, he has also loved and can feel with those in love. As to Orlando, he is as good as gold. The mantle of Rosalind's sweetness and goodness is over them all. We dwell in a world of moral beauty. Its characters soothe and heal the trouble of the world.

Lastly, on this matter of beauty, how fair is the scenery, when we have left the Court! Shakespeare builds it up by suggestions on the lips of the actors into lovely landscape. The forest of Arden, by a lucky coincidence of name, puts us in mind of an English forest; and seems to transfer the action to our own land. And Shakespeare, no doubt, with his patriotic passion,

*Act I. Scene ii. Charles, Duke Frederick, Celia, Rosalind, Touchstone, Orlando, and others. By Daniel Maclise.*

would have desired this. Whether he desired it or no, he played into this idea. He used, as material, his youthful wanderings in the glades and by the streams of Warwickshire. (pp. 160-63)

> Stopford A. Brooke, "'As You Like It'," in his On Ten Plays of Shakespeare, 1905. Reprint by Constable and Company Ltd., 1925, pp. 155-79.

**ELMER EDGAR STOLL**   (essay date 1906)

[*Stoll was one of the earliest critics to attack the method of character analysis that had dominated nineteenth-century Shakespearean criticism. Instead, he maintained that Shakespeare was primarily a man of the professional theater and that his works had to be interpreted in the light of Elizabethan stage conventions and understood for their theatrical effects, rather than their psychological insight. Stoll has in turn been criticized for seeing only one dimension of Shakespeare's art. In the following excerpt, Stoll introduces a new element to* As You Like It *criticism by arguing, on largely historical grounds, that Jaques is a specific type of "malcontent." Noting that the melancholic figure is the "only 'humorous' character in the play" and a "professional cynic and censor," Stoll claims that Jaques is based on the type-character portrayed by Malevole in John Marston's* The Malcontent *(first published in 1604). Both Jaques and Malevole, Stoll maintains, move about in the "professional garb of cynicism and melancholy"; they are both on excellent terms with the fool in*

*their plays; and both are "at home in the set, isolated speech or soliloquy." Ultimately, Stoll continues, they are of the type later described by Robert Burton in his* Anatomy of Melancholy *(1621).*]

Is Jaques a recast of the title-hero, Malevole [in John Marston's *Malcontent*]? Jaques, too, is a Malcontent—a melancholy figure conceived in the Elizabethan "humorous" manner, a professional fantastic meditator, a professional cynic and censor. He is the only "humorous" character in the play—practically the only one since *Love's Labor's Lost*—and in the prominence of this quality, as well as in other respects, he is unlike any character of Shakspere's before or after him. And he is a figure (and name) utterly unknown to the source from which Shakspere drew his plot, Lodge's novel of *Rosalind*. There is reason, then, in the question we ask, and we shall see that there is reason for not asking the converse of it—is Malevole a recast of Jaques?—instead.

The points of similarity between Jaques and Malevole are many. Both appear constantly, not as plain human beings, but as "humorous" Malcontents in their professional garb of cynicism and melancholy: of this, directly or indirectly, they and their interlocutors never fail to remind us. As such, they, like the Fool, hold a privileged position: they are "as free as air, and blow on whom they please" [II. vii. 49]. Freest they are with their master the Duke, and he in return is fondest of them;

and with the other persons of the drama they are pretty uniformly blunt and cynical, or ironically friendly. With the Fool, however—Passarello in the *Malcontent* and Touchstone in *As You Like It*—they are on excellent terms. They draw him out, revel in his grotesque wisdom, and eagerly fling it in the face of the more foolish world. Their conversation is alike lively, abrupt, fantastically phrased; but both are most at home in the set, isolated speech or soliloquy. Here appear their essentially melancholy and Malcontent bias, their railing at the follies and abuses of society, at classes like courtiers and ladies, and at "the world" in general, and their contemplation—in picturesque fashion—of the vanity and transitoriness of human pretensions, distinctions, and existence itself.

There are details which, with the above points, make connection between the plays seem pretty probable. The Duke, Jaques's master, has been deposed, as has Duke Altofront, who is disguised as Malevole; and in the end both come to their own. Here the only discrepancy lies in the very Shaksperean separation of the disguise-character, or Malevole, from the true character of the Duke. That, genetically, this disguise is represented by Jaques—Altofront and Malevole, though one person, are, in Marston's hands, almost as separate—becomes circumstantially evident at the end. Like Malevole, after a fashion unique in Shakspere, and in keeping only with a duke or sovereign, he portions off their lot of weal or woe to the various persons of the drama in one similarly phrased, final speech [in V. iv.]. . . . The purport of Jaques's wish [in Act II]—

> I must have liberty
> Withal, as large a charter as the wind,
> To blow on whom I please—
>
> [II. vii. 47-9]

moreover, is quite that of the character which Pietro gives Malevole,

> Now shall you hear the extremity of a malcontent: he is as free as air; he blows on every man;

and as Jaques continues [in II. vii.], in praise of the privileges of motley, . . . his thought is like Malevole's in his self-gratulation on the advantages of his disguise. . . . And Touchstone's satirical retort [V. iv. 43-50], being similarly provoked, may possibly be an echo of Malevole's. . . . All these, together with Jaques's and Malevole's delight in jarring sounds, which I have not found in the contemporary descriptions of melancholy, and which is inconsistent with Jaques's sucking of melancholy from a song, are points of contact such as would come about quite naturally from Shakspere's seeing Marston's play on the boards.

There is, however, a material objection to our theory. Malevole's humor is never once called melancholy, but that of a Malcontent, and Jaques's is always called melancholy. But to the Elizabethan mind the word "malcontent" implied melancholy—denoted, like "cynicism" with us today, an exacerbated form of it. The only proof I have to offer (but, I think, a conclusive one) is a comparison of the characteristics of Malevole with the symptoms of melancholy as given by [Robert Burton in his *Anatomy of Melancholy*]—collected in 1621, but all of them, being from authorities almost as venerable as Galen, certainly as well known to any Elizabethan as the symptoms of small-pox or diphtheria to the Englishman of today. . . . [Melancholy as described by Burton is, certainly,] the humor of Malevole. Here are his leanness, wakefulness, and fearful

or absurd dreams; his excellent apprehensions, abrupt changes from sobriety to mirth, and uncouth ejaculations; his howling like a beast; his corrupt imaginations and continual meditations; his surliness, his repinings, and his quarrel with the course of the world at large. One other symptom, his love of jarring sounds, which reappears in Jaques, is not noticed by Burton—the melancholy are expressly said to be fond of music—and is, I am persuaded, a popular or a Marstonian invention, in keeping poetically rather than physiologically or psychologically; but enough, surely, has already been adduced to show that Malevole's humor is as much that of melancholy as is Jaques's itself.

As always, there are the three alternatives—Marston may be indebted to Shakspere, Shakspere to Marston, or both to a common source.

The first alternative is improbable, and for two reasons: the main features of Malevole are all at hand in the Feliche of the First Part of Marston's *Antonio and Mellida*, acted in 1599; and of the two portrayals of the Malcontent—Jaques and Malevole—the latter is the cruder, the more popular and primitive. (pp. 281-86)

As to the other reason, we have seen already how much more "humorous" Malevole is than Jaques—how many more signs of melancholy he bears and how much more glaringly and popularly he is painted. . . . He has, moreover, none of the milder, more human symptoms of Jaques—also noticed by Burton—the sentimentality, the morbid delight in music and solitariness, the aversion to love matters and pastimes. Picturesque as Jaques, his is a louder-mouthed humor, meant to delight the popular Elizabethan heart; it is not psychologized, or tamed and mellowed down within the limits of decency and plausible humanity. To the author of such a character what could Jaques have been? . . . The relation inverted—the finished, humanly significant Jaques as prototype—would have been an anomaly in the evolution of the drama.

The third alternative—that Shakspere and Marston drew from a common source—is equally improbable, and thus the second—that Shakspere drew from Marston—is alone left open. For not only is there no such source now to be found, but, as it appears, there could hardly have ever been one. There are skits at melancholy in the contemporary plays, there are melancholy characters treated satirically, but those are different matters. And the only melancholy characters treated sympathetically, the only characters in function or in temper at all like Malevole, Feliche, or Jaques, . . . are scarcely like Jaques, and yet are so much like Feliche and Malevole as to be, very certainly, their sources. How, then, is there place for a *common* source?

Malevole was not influenced by Jaques, both were not conceivably derived from a common source, and shall we not infer that Jaques was influenced by Malevole? At least—what is almost as interesting—Jaques, born into the world of fancy the same year as Malevole, belongs like him to the Malcontent type, which is a Marstonian creation, and was influenced—directly or indirectly, through Malevole or through Feliche—by Marston. (pp. 287-88)

*Elmer Edgar Stoll, "Shakspere, Marston, and the Malcontent Type," in* Modern Philology, *Vol. III, No. 3, January, 1906, pp. 281-303.*

**WALTER W. GREG** (essay date 1906)

[*An English literary scholar and librarian, Greg was a pioneer in establishing modern Shakespearean bibliographical scholar-*

*ship. Combining bibliographical and critical methods, he developed a methodological approach to the text of Shakespeare's works that examines the physical evidence of external documents, such as the Stationers' Register and private journals, and the mechanical errors in the composition of the quartos in an effort to establish the nature and authority of certain texts in their original form. In the following excerpt from his best-known work of aesthetic criticism,* Pastoral Poetry and Pastoral Drama *(1906), Greg maintains that* As You Like It *passes judgment on and reveals Shakespeare's opinion of the pastoral ideal. Like many earlier critics, Greg recognizes in the Forest of Arden an adaptation of largely conventional material, but he adds a new element by dividing the forest-dwellers into categories. Celia and Rosalind he calls "courtly characters"; Phebe and Silvius he describes as "polished Arcadians of pastoral tradition"; and Audrey and William, he notes, are Shakespeare's own addition— "farcical rustics" combined with "inimitable humanity." Together, he continues, these characters, as well as other elements in the play, reveal "Shakespeare's appreciation of pastoral as a deliberate colouring, an old-world fragrance, a flower from wild hedgerows or cultured garden . . . , unsuited in its evanescent charm to be the serious business of art or life."*]

[There] is one play which more than any other illustrates the nature of the influence exerted by pastoral tradition over the romantic drama and the relation subsisting between the two. This is *As You Like It;* for if in one sense Shakespeare was but following [Thomas Lodge's *Rosalynde*] in the traditional blending of pastoral elements with those of court and chivalry, in another sense he has in this play revealed his opinion of, and passed judgement upon, the whole pastoral ideal. This must necessarily happen whenever a great creative artist adopts, for reasons of his own, and takes into his work any merely outward and formal convention. It was rarely that in his plays Shakespeare showed any inclination to connect himself even remotely with pastoral tradition. The *Two Gentlemen of Verona* traces its origin, indeed, to the *Diana* of Montemayor; but all vestige of pastoral colouring has vanished, and Shakespeare may even have been himself ignorant of the parentage of the story he treated. A more apparent element of pastoral found its way many years later into the *Winter's Tale;* but it is characteristic of the shepherd scenes of that play, written in the full maturity of Shakespeare's genius, that, in spite of their origin in Greene's romance of *Pandosto,* they owe nothing of their treatment to pastoral tradition, nothing to convention, nothing to aught save life as it mirrored itself in the magic glass of the poet's imagination. They represent solely the idealization of Shakespeare's own observation, and in spite of the marvellous and subtle glamour of golden sunlight that overspreads the whole, we may yet recognize in them the consummation towards which many sketches of natural man and woman, as he found them in the English fields and lanes, seem in a less certain and conscious manner to be striving in plays of an earlier date. It was characteristic of Shakespeare, as it has been of other great artists, to introduce into his early writings incidental sketches which serve as studies for further work of a later period. In much the same manner the varied, but at times uncertain, melody of the early love comedies seems to aspire towards the full sonority and magic of lyric feeling and utterance in *Romeo and Juliet.*

Thus it is neither to the mellow autumn of his art, when he had cast aside as unworthy all the trivialities of convention, nor yet to the storm and stress of adolescence, the immaturity of pettiness and exaggeration, that we must look if we would discover Shakespeare's attitude towards pastoral tradition. *As You Like It* belongs to his middle period. . . . [In] this play Shakespeare substantially followed the story of Rosalind as narrated by Lodge, to whom we owe the introduction of a

pastoral element into the old tale of Gamelyn. The pastoral characters of the play may be roughly analysed as follows. Celia and Rosalind, the latter disguised as a youth, are courtly characters; Phebe and Silvius represent the polished Arcadians of pastoral tradition; while Audrey and William combine the character of farcical rustics with the inimitable humanity which distinguishes Shakespeare's creations. It is noteworthy that this last pair is the dramatist's own addition to the cast. Thus we have all the various types—all the degrees or variations of idealization—brought side by side and co-existent in the fairyland of the poet's fancy. The details of the play are too well known for there to be any call to outrage the delicate interweaving of character and incident by translating the perfect scenes into clumsy prose. Nor would such analysis throw any light upon Shakespeare's attitude towards pastoral. That must be sought elsewhere. We may seek it in the fanciful mingling of ideals and idealizations—of courtly masking, of the conventional naturalism of polished dreamers, and of a rusticity more genuine at once and more sympathetic than that of Lorenzo, all of which act by their very natures as touchstones to one another. We may seek it in the uncertainty and hovering between belief and scepticism, earnest and play, reality and imagination—such as can only exist in art, or in life when life approaches to the condition of an art—which we find in the scenes where Orlando courts his mistress in the person of the youth who is but his mistress in disguise. We may seek it lastly in the manner in which the firm structure of the piece is fashioned of the non-pastoral elements; in the happiness of the art by which the pastoral incidents and business appear but as so much fair and graceful ornament upon this structure, bringing with them a smack of the free, rude, countryside, or a faint perfume of the polished Utopia of courtly makers. It is here that we may trace Shakespeare's appreciation of pastoral, as a delicate colouring, an old-world fragrance, a flower from wild hedgerows or cultured garden, a thing of grace and beauty, to be gathered, enjoyed, and forgotten, unsuited in its evanescent charm to be the serious business of art or life. (pp. 411-13)

> Walter W. Greg, "Masques and General Influence," in his Pastoral Poetry & Pastoral Drama, A. H. Bullen, 1906, pp. 369-422.

## SIR ARTHUR QUILLER-COUCH (essay date 1917)

[*Quiller-Couch was editor with J. Dover Wilson of the New Cambridge edition of Shakespeare's works. In his study* Shakespeare's Workmanship, *and in his Cambridge lectures on Shakespeare, Quiller-Couch based his interpretations on the assumption that Shakespeare was mainly a craftsman attempting, with the tools and materials at hand, to solve particular problems central to his plays. In the excerpt below, after locating the Arden forest in Stoneleigh Deer Park, not far from Shakespeare's native town of Stratford-upon-Avon, Quiller-Couch comments on the language and technique of* As You Like It. *He finds "carelessness of detail" in Act I, criticizing the "false sparkle," the "dull, level, choplogic, repetitive" rhythm of the bantering between Rosalind and Celia, claiming that, being "impatient . . . and ardent for Arden," Shakespeare did not give Act I much attention. Quiller-Couch also comments on Jaques and Touchstone, regarding them as "both piquantly out of place, while most picturesquely in place," and pointing out how each serves as a "critic" of the pastoral lifestyle. On other matters, the critic agrees with many earlier commentators that the marriage of Oliver and Celia is "unsatisfactory"; but to him the more glaring fault is the Hymen episode in V. iv., which he describes as "sheer botchwork."*]

Some years ago, in hope to get a better understanding of Shakespeare, a friend and I tracked the Warwickshire Avon together, from its source on Naseby battlefield down to Tewkesbury, where, by a yet more ancient battlefield, it is gathered to the greater Severn. (p. 121)

On the second day, after much pulling through reed beds and following for many miles Avon's always leisurely meanders, we came to the upper bridge of Stoneleigh Deer Park. (p. 122)

[We] looked to right and left, amazed. We had passed from a sluggish brook, twisting among water-plants and willows, to a pleasant, expanded river, flowing between wide lawns, by slopes of bracken, by the roots of gigantic trees—oaks, Spanish oaks, wych-elms, stately firs, sweet chestnuts, backed by filmy larch coppices.

This was Arden, the forest of Arden, actually Stoneleigh-in-Arden, and Shakespeare's very Arden. (pp. 122-23)

This (I repeat) is verily and historically Arden. We know that Arden—a lovely word in itself—was endeared to Shakespeare by scores of boyish memories; Arden was his mother's maiden name. I think it arguable of the greatest creative artists that, however they learn and improve, they are always trading on the stored memories of childhood. I am sure that, as Shakespeare turned the pages of Lodge's *Rosalynde*—as sure as if my ears heard him—he cried to himself, "Arden? This made to happen in a Forest of Arden, in France? But I have wandered in a Forest of Arden ten times lovelier; and, translated thither, ten times lovelier shall be the tale!"

And he is in such a hurry to get to it!

The opening Act of *As You Like It* (we shall find) abounds in small carelessness of detail. Rosalind is taller than Celia in one passage, shorter in another. A name, "Jaques," is bestowed on an unimportant character, forgotten, and later used again for an important one. In one passage there is either confusion in the name of the two Dukes, exiled and regnant, or the words are given to the wrong speaker. Orlando's protasis is a mere stage trick. The persiflage between Rosalind and Celia has a false sparkle. Actually it is dull, level, chop-logic, repetitive in the rhythm of its sentences. In fact, the whole of the language of this Act, when we weigh it carefully, is curiously monotonous. It affects to be sprightly, but lacks true wit. Until he gets to Arden, Touchstone never finds himself. All goes to show that Shakespeare, while laying out his plot, was impatient of it and ardent for Arden.

Now, in Stoneleigh Deer Park, in Arden, I saw the whole thing. . . . [I] saw the whole thing for what the four important Acts of it really are—not as a drama, but as a dream, or rather a dreamy delicious fantasy, and especially a fantasy in colour.

I want to make this plain: and that the play, not my criticism, is fanciful. I had always thought of *As You Like It*—most adorable play of boyhood, in those days not second even to *The Tempest*—in terms of colour, if I may so put it. Shakespeare, improving on Lodge, invented Jaques and Touchstone. Both are eminently piquant figures under the forest boughs; both piquantly out of place, while most picturesquely in place; both critics, and contrasted critics, of the artificial-natural life ("the simple life" is our term nowadays) in which the exiled Duke and his courtiers profess themselves to revel. Hazlitt says of Jaques that "he is the only purely contemplative character in Shakespeare" [see excerpt above, 1817]. Well, with much more going on about him, Horatio, in *Hamlet,* is just as inactive—the static, philosophical man . . . set in the midst of tragic aberrations. This function of the critic amid the comic aberrations of *As You Like It,* Jaques and Touchstone share

between them. Jaques moralises; Touchstone comments and plays the fool, his commentary enlightening common sense, his folly doing common sense no less service by consciously caricaturing all prevalent folly around it.

As contrast of character indicated by colour, can we conceive anything better than Jaques' sad-coloured habit opposed to Touchstone's gay motley? With what a whoop of delight the one critic happens on the other [at II. v. 12-43]. . . . (pp. 123-25)

Well then, to pass from Jaques' to our own appreciation of motley, can we not see Touchstone's suit—scarlet, we will say, down one side, and green down the other—illustrating his own contrast of wit and conduct, in speech after speech! Take, for example, his answer [at III. ii. 13-21] to Corin's query, "And how like you this shepherd's life, Master Touchstone?" [III. ii. 11-12] and see him exhibiting one side of himself, then the other. . . . (pp. 126-27)

The comedy . . . is less a comedy of dramatic event than a playful fantastic criticism of life: wherein a courtly society being removed to the greenwood, to picnic there, the Duke Senior can gently moralise on the artificiality he has left at home, and his courtiers—being courtiers still, albeit loyal ones—must ape his humours. But this in turn, being less than sincere, needs salutary mockery: wherefore Shakespeare invents Jaques and Touchstone, critics so skilfully opposed, to supply it. But yet again, Jaques' cynicism being something of a pose, he must be mocked at by the Fool; while the Fool, being professionally a fool, must be laughed at by Jaques, and, being betrayed to real folly by human weakness, laughed at by himself. Even Rosalind, being in love, must play with love. Even honest Orlando, being in love, must write ballads and pin them on oaks; but he writes them so very ill that we must allow him honest. Otherwise I should maintain his ancient servant Adam . . . to be the one really serious figure on the stage. It is at any rate observable that while, as we should expect, the play contains an extraordinary number of fanciful and more or less rhetorical moralisings—such as the Duke's praise of a country life, Jaques' often-quoted sermon on the wounded deer and his "All the world's a stage" [II. vii. 139-66], Rosalind's lecture on the marks of a lover, Touchstone's on the virtue in an "If," on the Lie Circumstantial, and on horns (to name but a few), it is Orlando who speaks out from the heart . . . while to Adam it falls to utter the sincerest, most poignant, line in the play:

> And unregarded age in corners thrown.
>
> [II. iii. 42]

An exquisite instance of Shakespeare's habitual stroke!—with which the general idea, "unregarded age," is no sooner presented than (as it were) he stabs the concrete into it, drawing blood: "unregarded age *in corners thrown.*"

But in truth all the rest of our bright characters are not in earnest. They do but *play* at life in Arden. As Touchstone knew, "cat will after kind" [III. ii. 103]; and, as Shakespeare knew, the world is the world as man made it for man to live in. These courtiers are not *real* Robin Hoods. When the *ducdame, ducdame* has been played out [in III. v.], yet not so as to over-weary, Shakespeare gathers up his "fashionables"—as afterwards in *The Tempest* he gathers up the Neapolitan courtiers—and restores them, like so many fish, to their proper element; even as he himself, after living with shows and making himself a motley to the view, returned to his native Stratford, bought land, and lived doucely. The Duke regains his dukedom, his followers are restored to their estates. By a pretty turn of workmanship, Orlando, who started with a patrimony of "poor a thousand crowns" [I. i. 2-3], dependent on an unjust brother, returns as heir-apparent and that brother's prospective liege-lord. By an equally pretty turn of irony, the one man—the usurping Duke—who reaches Arden on his own impulse, moved by a ferocious idea to kill somebody, is the only one left there in the end, when the sentimental moralists have done with the Forest, to use it as a school of religious contemplation.

Some critics have held it for a blot on the play that Oliver, his brotherly crime condoned, is allowed to marry a Celia. Shakespeare merely neglects the excuse found for it in Lodge's story, where the repentant elder brother helps to rescue Aliena (Celia) from a band of robbers. It *is* unsatisfactory, if we will. The play, according to Swinburne, would be perfect "were it not for that one unlucky slip of the brush which has left so ugly a little smear in one corner of the canvas as the betrothal of Oliver to Celia" [see excerpt above, 1880]. (pp. 127-30)

But "perfect," after all, is a word we should keep in hand for perfection: and full though *As You Like It* is of life and gaiety and exquisite merriment, on other points than Oliver's betrothal (I have instanced the mechanical introduction, and the rather pointless chop-logic of the First Act), it does not quite reach perfection. And, after all, a fantasy is a fantasy, and forgiveness Christian. I cannot feel my soul greatly perturbed over the mercy shown to Oliver; and I will give Celia to him, any day of the week, to save her from Jaques. The only possible wife for Jaques was one that Shakespeare omitted to provide. She should have to be an arrant shrew, to talk him dumb: and so he and Touchstone might have expiated their criticism together on a fair balance of folly. Rosalind herself would have cured him; but Rosalind, of course, is by miles too good for Jaques. She is reserved to be loved by an honest man his life through; and, like many another dear woman, to nag him his life through.

Rosalind herself is not perfect; but she is in a way the better for it, being adorable: at once honest and wayward, "true brow and fair maid" [III. ii. 214-15], and infinitely tantalising. She means to be the Nut Brown Maid of the Greenwood, as the whole play seems trying, over and again, to be a Robin Hood play. She means this, I repeat; but being courtly bred she has to play with it before admitting it. Yet she is honest, and confesses her love almost from the first, to herself and to Celia. She does not, as Imogen does [in *Cymbeline*], lift the heart out of us, ready to break for her: but she bewitches us, and hardly the less because all the while she allows us to know that the witchery is conscious and intentional. (pp. 130-31)

Having said this in praise of a piece of good workmanship, I must in fairness mention a piece of sheer botchwork. I mean the introduction of Hymen in the last Act. To explain away this botch as an imposition upon Shakespeare by another hand—to conjecture it as some hasty alternative to satisfy the public censor, who objected to Church rites of marriage on the stage—would be as easy as it were accordant with the nice distinctions of critical hypocrisy, were it not that Shakespeare, almost if not quite to the end of his days, was capable of similar ineptitudes, such as the vision of Posthumus [in *Cymbeline*] and the scroll dropped into his lap. You can explain away one such lapse by an accident; but two scarcely, and three or four not at all. That kind of artistic improbability runs almost in harmonical progression. Hymen in *As You Like It* is worse than Hecate in *Macbeth*. (pp. 132-33)

*Sir Arthur Quiller-Couch, "'As You Like It'," in his* Shakespeare's Workmanship, *1917. Reprint by T. Fisher Unwin Ltd., 1918, pp. 117-33.*

## J. B. PRIESTLEY   (essay date 1925)

[*A prolific English man of letters, Priestley wrote a number of popular novels depicting the world of everyday, middle-class England. His most notable critical work is* Literature and Western Man *(1960), a survey of Western literature from the invention of moveable type through the mid-twentieth century. In the following excerpt, Priestley comments principally on Touchstone, but also on Jaques. He defends the latter against previous attacks on his self-conscious melancholic behavior, stating that Jaques's "whimsical self-indulgence" accords with the antics of the other characters, who are just as much play-acting in Arden. Despite this justification, however, Priestley notices, among the character's defects, his "sickly" mind and the "hardness of the chronic querulous invalid" he exhibits, describing him as a "pure seeker after sensations." Maintaining that Jaques "plays the part of the cynical-sentimental-moralistic chorus," Priestley points to Touchstone as the supplier of "the comic chorus," adding that the clown is a better critic than the melancholic fool because he "does not completely detach himself from his fellow mortals." Together, Priestley continues, they are the critics in* As You Like It, *"detached from the main action, observing, mocking."*]

[Touchstone] is no ordinary comic figure; he is the representative, and easily the best representative . . . , of a special class of comic figures. Unlike most other humorous characters, he has no unconscious absurdities, and that is why he cannot be counted among those who wear the fine flower of the ridiculous; he is not laughable in himself, he is only droll by vocation. Although he is a Clown, a Fool, he is obviously a superior member of his order; he is no common buffoon making the most of some natural deformity and finding his fun in bladder play and monkey tricks, but the first of Shakespeare's great Fools, a professional wit and humorist, who publishes his jests and sarcasms daily at the dinner-table instead of bringing them out in octavo in the spring and autumn publishing seasons. Our laughter is his applause. It may be sometimes necessary for him to turn himself into a butt, a target for his witty superiors, for, as Celia remarks, "the dulness of the fool is the whetstone of the wits" [I. ii. 54-5]; but actually there is little of Celia's or anyone's wit that is whetted on the dullness of Touchstone. Certainly for us he is no mere butt, for we laugh with him and not at him. Even when he is gabbling nonsense, and that is not often, he is, of course, angling for a laugh and usually preparing to launch some shrewd home-truth. Nor must it be forgotten that the fashion in wit changes, and that the poor nonsense that Touchstone occasionally achieves once passed for wit. (pp. 21-2)

[Jaques] bears witness to the quality of Touchstone. In that famous speech [in II. vii.], describing their meeting in the forest, he recognises a fellow philosopher, in his new acquaintance. . . . And ever afterwards, he pursues Touchstone through the greenwood as the lovers pursue their ladies, and it is doubtful if some of Touchstone's escapades are not staged purely for his amusement; though Touchstone, with the detachment of the genuine humorist, is quite capable of acting foolishly merely for the satisfaction of enjoying his own folly. There is, of course, a strain of patronage, of easy contempt, in Jaques' attitude towards Touchstone; but then rank has not been forgotten even in Arden, where the courtiers are only playing at adversity, are only staging a pastoral. Moreover, this same strain is discovered in Jaques' attitude towards everything and everybody. This cynic-sentimentalist deserves a word to himself. Ever since the delighted commentators have made the discovery that Jaques is not merely the poet's mouthpiece but a distinct character like the rest of the personages in the comedy, they have pressed hard upon him and abused him without stint. He is almost regarded as the villain of the piece. One would suppose that critics are themselves men of thought rather than men of action, even though they are often more active than thoughtful, and yet, oddly enough, the very sight of a contemplative character, such as Jaques, always sends them into a rage. From their diatribes it would be easy to imagine that all the harm in the world is done by the few eccentric persons who stand on one side to watch the tragi-comedy of existence and are content to find entertainment in their own thoughts. That the melancholy of Jaques is not a very serious business, that it is a piece of whimsical self-indulgence, half play-acting, goes without saying; but there is room in Arden for his whims just as there is for the antics of the Duke, the courtiers, and the lovers. Though Duke Senior criticises Jaques somewhat roughly, actually there is as much to be said for the one as for the other. Indeed, Jaques is the more consistent, for at the very end, hearing that the usurping Duke has taken to religion, he decides to join him:

> Out of these convertites
> There is much matter to be heard and learned. . . .
> [V. iv. 184-85]

Whereas Duke Senior, for all his comfortable talk after lunch, surrounded by his admiring courtiers, of "sermons in stones, and good in everything" [II. i. 17], shows no great reluctance to return to "the envious court" [II. i. 4] when his time comes. But though we preach tolerance for Jaques, we need not be blind to his defects. His attitude of mind is sickly. And as he has the apparent softness, so too he has the real hardness of the chronic querulous invalid. Although he can weep over wounded deer, we feel, and rightly too, that there is really something hard, inelastic, griping about his mind. This is because he is that not unfamiliar type, the pure seeker after sensations: he does not identify himself with anything in the whole world, but uses experience as if it were merely a restaurant to dine in; he can enjoy, for he enjoys his cynicism, his tears, his exquisite disillusion, and not least, for it gives support to all the rest, his massive feeling of superiority, but it is impossible for him to be really happy because never for a single moment can he forget himself. (pp. 23-6)

Now, as we have seen, Jaques and Touchstone stand in somewhat similar relation to the rest of the company. They are "the critics," detached from the main action, observing, mocking. Whatever departs from sincerity receives a flick of the whip from them; or, if you will, they supply the chorus to the piece; one, the sad-suited gentleman, this somewhat eighteenth-century figure with his exquisite sensibility and his lack of real warm human sympathy, plays the part of cynical-sentimental-moralistic chorus; the other, motleying for more than mere beef and ale, an embassy from the Spirit of Comedy, supplies the comic chorus. But while these two seem to run together most of the way, Touchstone parodying to Jaques' applause, there is a very real and very important difference in their respective attitudes. Motley is a better critic than Melancholy. He is a better critic because, unlike Jaques, he does not completely detach himself from his fellow mortals but identifies himself with them; he does not say, in effect, "What beasts you are!" but "What fools we are!"; and so, like a true comic genius, he is universal. He does not stand entirely apart, but plays the courtier and the pastoral lover like the rest, only taking care that everything he does shall be plunged into his own atmosphere of exaggeration and absurdity; he parodies humanity, which looked at from one angle is fundamentally ridiculous, in his own activities and in his own person; and he

does this not simply because he is a Fool, a professional humorist, but also because he is by temperament and inclination a kind of comic philosopher. In this leafy republic of Arden, with its moralising gentlemen, rhyming lovers, passionate shepherds, where so many moods and whims are being dandled throughout the long golden days, the Comic Spirit, scenting profitable negotiations, has established its embassy, and Touchstone, full-dressed in his motley, is the ambassador.

The two persons who know him best and who are responsible for his being in the forest at all, Rosalind and Celia, rather miss his real character: they see the Fool but are blind to the comic philosopher. To them he is "the clownish fool" [I. iii. 130]. (pp. 27-8)

But if Rosalind and Celia hardly testify to Touchstone's quality as a humorist, they do show us, in one flash, something of his quality as a man. They pay him a magnificent compliment, for they single him out to be their companion in their flight to Arden. . . . This shows us a new Touchstone. Companions for such a journey are not lightly chosen, even by a Rosalind: our comic philosopher is clearly a man to be depended on; Motley covers a stout heart. And if Rosalind's suggestion tells us much, Celia's reply tells us even more. "He'll go along o'er the wide world with me" [I. iii. 132]; this demure young lady knows her power; she has the Fool in thrall. He is not then altogether in the service of the Comic Spirit; his detachment is not complete, for now, it seems, he shows himself to be a romantic at heart, ready to exchange his comfortable berth at court, that dinner-table which is the field of glory for the humorist, for the discomforts and dangers of secret flight. . . . He has flung away safety and comfort and applause for a lady's whim, and has thereby betrayed his genial cynicism. Remove the motley, the cap and the bells, the irreverent jests and sarcasms, the ripe disillusionment, and there remains Touchstone the romantic, set wandering by a glance from his lady's eye, a wave of her hand. Thus he arrives in Arden.

Romance, however, having enticed him into her own green Arcadia, has to be content with that and nothing more, for once there, Touchstone returns to his ancient loyalties and promptly goes about his own business of parody and mockery, of clowning illuminated by criticism. The chief targets for his wit are the pastoral life, which the Duke and his companions are busy praising with suspicious enthusiasm, and the passion of love, which is leading so many of the gentle foresters into delightful affectations and whimsies. Touchstone brings scepticism into the greenwood. . . . [He lays] a finger, not merely upon the defects of a pastoral life, but upon those human limitations that prevent our declaring, with any sincerity, that any way of life is perfect; we cannot—more's the pity!—be in two places at once, cannot have our cake and eat it too; so every gain enumerated by Touchstone is quickly followed by its corresponding loss, every positive by its negative, and all cancels out. Well might he conclude by asking, "Hast any philosophy in thee, shepherd?" [III. ii. 21-2]. (pp. 30-3)

He can indite verses as good as, if not better than, those of Orlando, and he certainly has more wit, but—alas!—his lady, being no Rosalind but a genuine creature of the countryside, can understand neither. . . . Audrey, good soul, cannot even pretend to poetry, and has, indeed, a most disarming knowledge of her own limitations, even confessing to a want of beauty, which may be joined in time, in Touchstone's opinion, by other defects, notably sluttishness. None of this, however, disturbs the ironist in motley for an instant: he revels in the incongruity of it all. And while the other lovers, triple-dyed in romance, are swearing eternal constancy, he is calmly welcoming a doubtful ceremony by a doubtful parson because "he is not like to marry me well; and not being well married, it will be a good excuse for me hereafter to leave my wife" [III. iii. 92-4]. But he is only seeing all round the question. Just as there is a possibility that, after all, the romantic lovers may not be true to one another for ever, so too it is possible that Touchstone may cleave to his Audrey a little longer than a couple of months or so.... The relation between Touchstone and his stolid mistress is really nothing but the reverse side, the unpoetical, comic, gross side, of the relation between Orlando and Rosalind, all ardour and bloom and young laughter, beyond the reach of disillusion. Shake them up together and out of them both could be fashioned the actual relations between most men and women in this world; and Shakespeare, who knew most things, knew this too, and so gave us both sides of the question. By the time he came to create Touchstone, his comic relief had become something more than buffoonery flung in at random, it had become comment, criticism.

That Touchstone's courtship of Audrey, as Hazlitt remarks, "throws a degree of ridicule on the state of wedlock itself" [see excerpt above, 1817], must be admitted, but both his vocation and his natural bent of mind urge Touchstone towards ridicule, and there is, in the last resort, more to be said about his queer courtship than this, more, indeed, than has apparently been said anywhere. That he is not seriously in love is obvious enough, but this is probably only because he cannot be entirely serious about anything. Even his surprisingly romantic devotion to his young mistress Celia, probably has a comical air: we have not heard him on the subject. Yet it is quite possible that a lapse of time that would find Oliver deserting Celia and taking to the forest again, to haunt the neighbourhood of Phebe, now the bored wife of Silvius, would also find Touchstone and Audrey still jogging along together, the gentleman still making mysterious jests and criticisms, and the lady fixing her stolid gaze upon the solid fruits of his jesting and not troubling her head about his whims and fancies.... And consider, before we leave him, Touchstone's introduction of his Audrey to the Duke: "A poor virgin, sir, an ill-favour'd thing, sir, but mine own" [V. iv. 57-8]. This, it will be said, is not the speech of a man in love; nor is it, but it might very well be the speech of a humorist, a dry, sceptical humorist, who is as near to being in love as he is likely to be.... This world being what it is—and how well Motley knows the world—it describes with more accuracy than all the honeyed, golden speeches of our Romeos and Antonies the actual feelings that men and women, not poets and born lovers, ever ready to shower glittering words upon any newly found deity, but workaday men and women, have for one another.... And no matter which colouring your mood takes on, you will find some correspondence in colour, some answer, in Touchstone, deep in Arden, for is he not particoloured, being in Motley? A rare fellow. (pp. 38-42)

*J. B. Priestley, "Touchstone," in his* The English Comic Characters, *Dodd, Mead and Company, 1925, pp. 20-42.*

## G. F. BRADBY (essay date 1929)

[*Bradby was an English scholar, poet, novelist, and academic who is perhaps best remembered for his school story,* The Lanchester Tradition *(1913). In the following excerpt from his* Short Studies in Shakespeare *(1929), he claims that Jaques is "not one of the characters whom Shakespeare has thought out most deeply." Bradby argues that Shakespeare conceived Jaques as simply "a*

*foil" to the optimism and romantic ideals of the other characters, but that he used him "without any great regard for consistency." Like many other critics, Bradby finds elements of the "disillusioned rake" as well as the "travelled poseur" in Jaques, but adds a new element, that the melancholic figure invariably talks nonsense, "as is befitting in a comedy."*]

Jaques is a character of Shakespeare's own creation. He does not belong to the story which is dramatised in *As You Like It*, and he takes no part in the development of the plot. Shakespeare was therefore able to do with him exactly as he pleased, and it is particularly interesting to observe how he treats him.

The reason why Jaques came into being is perfectly clear: he is needed as a foil, as a contrast. In a world of convinced optimists like the banished Duke, who finds life in the forest of Arden "more sweet than that of painted pomp" [II. i. 2-3], and of high-spirited lovers, like Orlando and Rosalind, he speaks the language of disillusion. But, as is befitting in a Comedy, his disillusionment does not go very deep, and the speaker is invariably shown to be talking nonsense; or, to use an expressive schoolboy phrase, he is invariably "scored off." He is "scored off," rather ponderously, by the Duke Senior in [II. vii. 64-9]; more wittily by Rosalind in [IV. i. 1-29]; and too easily to be convincing, by Orlando in [III. ii. 285-90]:

> JAQ. By my troth, I was seeking for a fool when
> I found you.
> ORL. He is drowned in the brook: look but in,
> and you shall see him.
> JAQ. There I shall see mine own figure.
> ORL. Which I take to be either a fool or a cipher.

The dullest schoolboy would not have fallen into so obvious a trap, and Jaques was very far from being dull. There is much internal evidence to show that this play was written at more than the usual speed, and this is one of the places in which haste may have led to carelessness.

And not only is Jaques "scored off" by the other characters in the play, but his cynicism is proved to be ridiculous by the facts of life. In [II. vii. 139-66] he has been developing, with much gusto, his theme that "All the world's a stage," on which mankind plays a series of contemptible parts. (pp. 87-8)

At this moment Orlando re-enters with Adam. Now, Adam is eighty years old [II. iii. 71], and ought by rights to be a typical example of the "last stage of all" "sans *teeth*, sans taste," etc. In reality, of course, he is nothing of the kind....

The Duke says to Orlando, "Welcome. Set down your venerable burthen"; and then, with a sly glance at Jaques, adds "and let him *feed*" [II. vii. 167-68].

We are told one or two things about Jaques in the course of the play. Audrey [V. i. 4] calls him "the old gentleman." (p. 89)

The Duke tells us [II. vii. 65] that Jaques has been "a libertine," and Jaques himself [IV. i. 18] informs us that he has been a traveller. Our first introduction to him is at second-hand through the report of the First Lord, who relates how he and "my Lord of Amiens" overheard the soliloquy on the wounded deer [II. i. 47-59].... And finally he is left "*weeping* and commenting upon the sobbing deer" [II. i. 65].

This seems a rather more poetical and sentimental Jaques than the one with whom we become familiar in the play, and who, moreover, likes to have an audience for his tirades. Possibly Shakespeare had not determined, at this stage of the play, the exact quality of Jaques' melancholy, or perhaps he was carried by the nature of the incident (as he not infrequently is) out of drama into poetry. At all events, in the rest of the play Jaques generally affects prose; he parodies the lovely little lyric, "Under the greenwood tree" [II. v. 50-7]. . . . And he objects to poetical language in others [IV. i. 31-2]. . . . Nor does he show any feeling for the *dead* deer [IV. ii. 1-6]. (pp. 89-91)

To all the dwellers in the forest he is known as "the melancholy Jaques," and he is proud of the title. It is not, as he explains to Rosalind . . . , the ordinary kind of melancholy, but something peculiar to himself, "compounded of many simples, extracted from many objects; and indeed the sundry contemplation of my travels, in which my often rumination wraps me in a most humorous sadness" [IV. i. 16-20].

It is a self-conscious melancholy. There is no echo in it of Hamlet's cry:

> O God! God!
> How weary, stale, flat and unprofitable
> Seem to me all the uses of this world!
>
>                              [*Hamlet*, I. ii. 132-34]

It displays itself in caustic comments on lovers and the voices of singers, in a good-natured interchange of insults with Orlando, and, generally speaking, in a cynical attitude towards life, which finds a zest in its littlenesses and absurdities. Hence his delight in Touchstone, the fool apeing the philosopher [II. vii. 12-13, 28-33]. (pp. 91-2)

This "melancholy" was combined with a dry humour. He answers Orlando's melodramatic "Forbear and eat no more," with "Why, I have eat none yet" [II. vii. 87-8], and, immediately afterwards, to the equally melodramatic

> But forbear, I say:
> He dies that touches any of this fruit
> Till I and my affairs are answered,
>
>                              [II. vii. 97-9]

he replies in prose:

> An you will not be answered with reason, I
> must die.
>
>                              [II. vii. 100-01]

Apt and witty too is his simile of the ark, when the various couples are approaching the trysting place [V. iv. 35-8]. (p. 92)

Once only in the excitement of his discovery of "the fool i' the forest" [II. vii. 12], does Jaques claim for himself a more ambitious role than that of licensed "grouser."

> Invest me in my motley; give me leave
> To speak my mind, and I will through and through
> Cleanse the foul body of the infected world,
> If they will patiently receive my medicine.
>
>                              [II. vii. 58-61]

The idea of Jaques as a minor prophet in motley would certainly have amused any other of his friends and acquaintances; but the Duke, who always remains ducal and has not a light touch, turns on him with an asperity which seems hardly justified by the occasion, and which is in strange contrast with the general tone and temper of the play. . . . After this we are not surprised that Jaques has been trying to avoid the Duke "all this day," as being "too disputable" for his company [II. v. 34-5]. He does not defend himself against the charge of having been a rake; but, when he explains [II. vii. 60-1] with what kind of "medicine" he is going to "cleanse the foul body of the in-

fected world," we find that he has nothing more drastic in view than to tell city women and men "of basest function" [II. vii. 79] that they dress extravagantly.

In reality Jaques' "melancholy" is more than half a conscious and cultivated pose. When he says to Rosalind, "Why, 'tis good to be sad and say nothing" [IV. i. 8], we know that he is describing a felicity to which he has never attained and that his "I'll go sleep, if I can; if I cannot, I'll rail against all the first-born of Egypt" [II. v. 60-1], and (to Orlando) "Will you sit down with me? and we two will rail against our mistress the world, and all our misery" [III. ii. 277-79], correspond more closely with his practice. Indeed, what Jaques most dearly loves is to "rail" to an audience, and explain that the world is or ought to be a "miserable" world, and that they are all fools.

But his cynicism is only skin-deep, and it does not survive the test of action. Touchstone has arranged to be married to Audrey by a hedge-priest, Sir Oliver Martext, in an ambiguous manner, which will make the validity of the marriage uncertain. Sir Oliver insists that there must be someone to "give" the woman. Jaques, who has been watching, unseen, steps forward, and says:

> Proceed, proceed; I'll give her.
>
>                              [III. iii. 71-2]

But, a moment later, better thoughts prevail, and he says, abruptly:

> And will you, being a man of your breeding,
> be married under a bush like a beggar? Get you
> to church, and have a good priest that can tell
> you what marriage is: this fellow will but join
> you together as they join wainscot; then one of
> you will prove a shrunk panel, and like green
> timber warp, warp.
>
>                              [III. iii. 83-9]

There is no cynicism here; the Duke Senior could not have spoken better. (pp. 93-5)

Jaques is not one of the character whom Shakespeare has thought out most deeply. He was needed as a foil, and he is used, as occasion serves, without any great regard for consistency. But he is an arresting character, partly because he is very much alive, and partly because in him Shakespeare for the first time touches on the problem of disillusionment. To treat it seriously would have been out of place in a Comedy, yet there are moments when he seems on the point of probing a little deeper, and giving us the disillusioned rake, instead of the travelled *poseur*. His sense of comedy restrained him; the temper of *As You Like It* is not the temper of *Measure for Measure*. But *As You Like It* stands on the borderline of the tragic period, and, perhaps, we may see in the sudden and unexpected outburst of the Duke Senior an indication of the mood which was soon to become the dominant one, and which was to lead the dramatist himself to other than to dancing measures. (pp. 96-7)

> *G. F. Bradby, "Jaques," in his* Short Studies in Shakespeare, *John Murray, 1929, pp. 87-97.*

## JOHN W. DRAPER (essay date 1934)

[*An American critic, editor, and poet, Draper is best known for his studies of the historical background of Shakespeare's plays, particularly with respect to Elizabethan character-types. These include* The Hamlet of Shakespeare's Audience *(1938), The Hu-*

mours and Shakespeare's Characters *(1945), and* The "Twelfth Night" of Shakespeare's Audience *(1950). All of these studies stress the influence of contemporary life and thought on Shakespeare's drama and thus attempt to provide new interpretations unavailable to the strictly aesthetic or psychological critic. Draper's efforts reflect the popularity during the mid-twentieth century of historical interpretations of Shakespeare's plays, an approach also apparent in the works of E. E. Stoll and E. M. W. Tillyard. In the following excerpt from his essay "Orlando, the Younger Brother" (1934), Draper discusses the issue of primogeniture in* As You Like It, *discerning in the play Shakespeare's special concern for the trials and hardships of younger sons in Elizabethan times. Draper argues that, because Orlando is the younger son, he is effectively deprived by law of both assistance and fortune, and thus must seek his own way. He further contends that Shakespeare's substitution of "greater realism" for the "melodramatic incident" in his principal source—Thomas Lodge's* Rosalynde— *makes* As You Like It *a "high comedy" in which meaning is as important as entertainment. In support of his argument, Draper cites differences in* As You Like It *from Lodge's* Rosalynde, *noting the overall deeper significance of the former that makes it more compelling than farce.]*

The Mediaeval youngster of good family was either put out as a page to do "hard service" in the household of his father's overlord so that he might in time become a knight; or he was forced upon some monastery to grow up into a monkish worldling like Chaucer's; or perhaps he was apprenticed to a rich merchant. In the Renaissance, however, arms became a career for professional mercenaries skilled in the mathematics of gunnery; the monasteries in England were dissolved; and trade was more and more considered "utterly vnfit for Gentlemen." Thus, unless his father provided the son with lands and income, he could hardly rise above the place of armed retainer, or "servingman" in the household of his patron; and, as the tranquility of Tudor times made retainers less and less necessary, and as the rising cost of living made them more and more a burden, the servingman generally sank to a mere menial servant; and, even if he escaped being cast out upon the highway by the "incertaintie of service," he could look forward only to a "contemptible" old age. . . . The system that in feudal times had fitted and introduced a young man to his livelihood was acutely dislocated without as yet an adequate substitute; and Peacham might well complain of the neglected education of Elizabethan youth.

Family honor and future policy required that what money there was should be spent on the eldest son; for primogeniture was an established custom consecrated in the Bible and in the laws of England. The stress of the times, therefore, left the younger brother unprovided for. (pp. 72-3)

This situation must have been notorious; and, in *As You Like It,* Shakespeare portrays Orlando as faced with the typical problems of the younger son. In the very first scene, the audience is told and re-told that he is a younger brother; and he delivers himself of a whole speech on his status in the family [I. i. 43-6]. The second scene introduces him to the Duke as "the youngest sonne of Sir *Roland de Boys*" [I. ii. 223]; and he later declares that he is "proud to be Sir *Rolands* sonne, His yongest sonne" [I. ii. 232-33]. Celia is made to overhear and remember this remark, and later refers to him as "old Sir *Roulands* yongest sonne." [I. iii. 28]; and, in the third and in the fourth acts, Rosalind twits him with the fact that mere manhood ("your having in beard" [III. ii. 377]) was the only "reuenew" of a younger brother [III. ii. 378]. His father had left Orlando a thousand crowns; but, as his elder brother refuses him even this patrimony, he is no better off than the average

younger son: he feeds with his brothers "Hindes" [I. i. 19]; and he bitterly complains: "I am not taught to make [do] anything" [I. i. 30], and again: ". . . you have train'd me like a pezant, obscuring and hiding from me all gentleman-like qualities" [I. i. 68-70]. Thus he is sinking to the rank of menial; and the dramatic value of Adam in the play is largely his vivid illustration of Orlando's future fate, unless the young man makes a break for freedom; and, indeed, Adam's "constant service" [II. iii. 57] has brought him to be turned off as an "olde dogge" [I. i. 81] in his "vnregarded" [II. iii. 42] old age. If Orlando leaves his brother's roof, however, he has no choice but the beggary that Oliver taunts him with, or "A theeuish liuing on the common rode" [II. ii. 33], and he is saved from this dilemma only by the little money that the faithful Adam gives him [II. iii. 38-45]. Not content with setting forth this theme in the virtuous and beloved Orlando, Shakespeare shows it also in the wicked younger brother, the usurping Duke of Burgundy. Like King Claudius and Edmund in *Lear,* and the false Duke in *The Tempest,* he has yielded to temptation, but Orlando, great as was his provocation, never dreams of supplanting his brother on the ancestral lands. He will not offend against the divine law of primogeniture; but rather, full of youth and spirits, he tries to do something "notable" to win his way. His first effort is the wrestling match; and, though the wicked usurping Duke gave him no reward, yet his strength and valor "tript vp the Wrastlers heeles" and the heart of Rosalind "both in an instant" [III. ii. 212-13]; and so, finally, like the impoverished Bassanio [in *The Merchant of Venice*], he achieves a rich heiress, to the applause of all good Elizabethans. Indeed, this close reflection of the current problem of the younger son must have given Shakespeare's audience an immediacy of interest in the play.

An examination of Lodge's *Rosalynde,* from which Shakespeare seems to have drawn his plot, shows that he himself supplied most of the realistic details that link the old story to contemporary life. In Lodge, the father, against all Elizabethan decency and custom, gives the chief share of his land to the youngest son; in Shakespeare, the eldest inherits the actual land; and Orlando is to get "a poore thousand Crownes" [I. i. 2-3]. . . . In both versions, the elder brother refuses him his legacy. In Lodge, the younger is degraded for "two or three years" to the "seruile subiection" of a "foote boy"; in Shakespeare, he is allowed mere board and keep, and so sinks uneducated to the companionship and the life of his brother's menials—just the situation that would actually develop. In Lodge, the younger is made a prisoner and a public show before his brother's friends, actions that family pride would hardly have allowed in fact; and finally he escapes to Arden by stratagems and feats of strength that suggest the hero of a Mediaeval romance rather than a probable human being. Shakespeare suppresses these crudities. In Lodge, he is kept at home by force; in Shakespeare, by economic necessity. The Elizabethan dramatists, and Shakespeare in particular, were bound rather closely by the stories that they used; for their audience would feel cheated if the play left out any favorite episode; and the fact that Shakespeare courted this danger by omitting the fisticuffs between the brothers, implies some strong reason on his part. This sacrifice of melodramatic incident, the present writer would impute to the dramatist's desire for greater realism of detail and so for more telling immediacy of theme: Shakespeare, indeed, turned the broad farce of his source into high comedy, written not only for its fun but for its meaning.

These changes clearly deepen the significance, not only of the three or four Adam-Orlando scenes, but also of the entire play.

The most obvious result is condensation of plot and concentration on the later scenes in Arden. The setting and style also achieve a finer unity; for these scenes of realistic prose are reduced to a mere introductory link with actual life and a touch or two of contrast in the later pastoralism. Character, likewise, is refined, and given truer motives: from a romantic swashbuckler, Orlando is transformed into an Elizabethan country gentleman, fit to espouse the charming Rosalind; and Adam typifies at once the impending fate of Orlando and the sufferings of a class for which Shakespeare elsewhere expresses the popular sympathy. The addition of realism to these scenes, however, affects chiefly the theme of the play as a whole: the scion of a noble house, newly come up from the country, wins at court both fame and fortune, first by besting the wrestler of the usurping Duke, and later, as a consequence of this success, by gaining the heart and hand of the true Duke's daughter.

The plays of Shakespeare's first period, largely imitative of the so-called "University wits," are clearly studies in the technique of his art, and show only sporadic and superficial elements of contemporary realism. In the second period, he more and more enlivens the English history of his chronicle plays with such vivid additions as the Falstaff scenes [in *1* and *2 Henry IV*]; and, into the folk-stories and Italian tales that were the sources of his comedies, he not only introduced Elizabethan local color, but even re-interpreted one or more aspects of the plot to give the tale a timely meaning: the old story of the merchant who signs a bond for a friend, he assimilated by numerous changes in *The Merchant of Venice* to the contemporary abuses of usury; and, in *As You Like It,* he reads a new significance into Orlando's youthful struggles. These plays are still "romantic" comedies in the sense that the old tale still dominates the plot; but the growing power of the theme that Shakespeare is reading into the given episodes leads directly to the "bitter comedies," more happily termed problem-plays. Here, in *Measure for Measure, All's Well,* and *Timon,* the theme gains predominance, and the plot moves largely at its behest. In some of the tragedies also, this is true—in *Othello,* for instance, on military honor, in *Macbeth,* on the dreadful effects of regicide, and in *Lear,* on the evils of abdication. Shakespeare's art grows more and more a commentary on current problems, social, economic and political. The constantly deepening realism and the constantly increasing intellectual significance of the plays of his first three periods go hand in hand—a natural evolution in a dramatist who purveyed increasingly to the tastes of the court, and who preferred the praise of the "judicious" to that of "a whole theatre of others." Thus, at the end of his second period, even amidst the unrealities of a pastoral romance that combines Corin and Silvius with verses cut upon palm-trees and the spirit of Robin Hood, Shakespeare has introduced a current social theme that looks forward to the problem comedies that immediately follow. Indeed, the theatre must have been full of young gentlemen of fortune, younger sons of county families who had come up to court to make their careers, and surely they especially enjoyed seeing a younger son marry the rightful heiress to the crown, and felt that a play with so pat a theme and so pleasing a denouement might be most properly entitled *As You Like It.* (pp. 73-7)

John W. Draper, "Orlando, the Younger Brother,"
in Philological Quarterly, Vol. XIII, No. 4, October,
1934, pp. 72-7.

## Z. S. FINK (essay date 1935)

[*Fink is an American scholar and literary critic who has written extensively on English literature, chiefly the Elizabethan and Ro-*

*mantic periods. In the following excerpt, Fink joins the critical controversy over Jaques's melancholy by maintaining that Shakespeare's character is derived from—and is in part an example of—the typical foreign traveler depicted in sixteenth-century literature, but unlike the usual traveler of the time, he is not "crudely drawn"; instead, the critic claims, he is transmuted by Shakespeare. His bitterness is typical of those wanderers, Fink explains, and thus "we cannot dismiss [Jaques's melancholy] as merely a pose." Fink further suggests that Shakespeare's delineation of Jaques's type is "softened" by the fact that, by the time* As You Like It *was written, traveler's melancholy was widespread, a "disillusion shared by the age . . . and by Shakespeare."*]

Shakespeare's Jaques in *As You Like It* has provoked an extraordinary diversity of critical opinion. Anyone who will glance through the introductions of various editors, and through the estimates of the character in the Variorum edition of the play, will be told that he is a misanthrope; that he is not a misanthrope, but is profoundly melancholy; that he is not really melancholy at all; that Shakespeare is laughing at him; that he is doing nothing of the sort; that Jaques is satirized in one scene, but not in the play as a whole; that his character contrasts most favorably with that of the exiled Duke; that exactly the opposite is true; that he is a sated libertine, that he is not, and never really has been a libertine; that he has been a libertine, but is an earnest teacher of virtue as he appears in the play; that he is a mere lip moralist; that he finds the forest a pleasant escape for a man tired of the corruptions of courts and cities; that he discovers in Arden the same cruelty, folly, and usurpation that have disillusioned him in the great world; that he "has seen but little to complain of in his career through life"; that he is angry at his birth and fortune and discontented with everything; that he is "amiable, gentle, and humane"; that he is churlish and ill-natured; that he loves music; that he is fond of discords; that he is perfectly normal; and that he displays signs of incipient insanity. Nor is there any agreement as to the cause of his melancholy among those critics who assume that he is genuinely melancholy.

In view of this diversity of opinion, it is rather surprising that more attention has not been paid to the sources of the character, and to the possibility that Jaques might be a delineation of the contemporary figure of the foreign traveler. (pp. 237-38)

The traveler who is significant in connection with Jaques had something in common with the usual foreign traveler in the literature of the time, but on the whole was rather different from him. (p. 238)

He was, however, closely related to the terrible Italianated Englishman of the late sixties, with whom Ascham's famous diatribe in *The Scholemaster* has made everyone interested in the period familiar. In fact, we can say that, as a literary figure, our traveler was the Italianated Englishman as developed in some respects, and modified in others, in the period between 1570 and 1585 or 1590, the development and modification coming about because of the actual appearance in England in the late eighties of a type of traveler who in the life approximated the literary figure which resulted from him. (pp. 238-39)

[This new traveler of the time] is one who dresses in black and affects melancholy. He has lived a licentious life abroad and has picked up the characteristic vices of all nations. He is so corrupted that he sees even nature as tainted. Either because of this fact, or because of what he conceives to be the world's neglect, or because he has become a Catholic or an atheist and lost his love of his native country and his faith in life, he is also genuinely melancholy and discontented with everything.

He rails at the abuses of the world when he is himself thoroughly polluted. Nor are his railings and lamentations necessarily for the benefit of others. Sometimes he avoids company and seeks a solitary spot where he quarrels with himself. In other respects, for one reason or another, his deportment varies. He either affects the gravity of the Italians or, like Ascham's Italianate, assumes a skulking behavior calculated to impress others with the fact that he is a dangerous Italianated duelist. Sometimes he alternates the one behavior with the other. Occasionally he carries a "picktooth" and affects French negligence in dress. (pp. 244-45)

Now to come to Jaques. It is obvious that our traveler as delineated by the satirists was often a crude figure and that Jaques is not crudely drawn; and that some of the characteristics of the traveler do not appear, or are not prominent, in Jaques. We have no reason to expect that the case would be otherwise; every reason to expect that what the transmuting and transforming genius of Shakespeare did with the originals of other characters, it would do with the original of Jaques. We are not looking, therefore, for a crude satirical portrait. It will be enough if we can show that in creating Jaques, at whom he is laughing, Shakespeare drew heavily on the contemporary Italianated and malcontent type of foreign traveler, and that this fact indicates that the character was intended to be taken in a way decidedly different from that in which many Shakespearean critics have taken him.

The characteristics in common between Jaques and the melancholy traveler are many and arresting. It is clear in the first place that he has traveled and that he has been to Italy. He is "Monsieur Traveler" to Rosalind [IV. i. 33]. . . . We are told specifically that his life abroad has been licentious. He has been a libertine, and is described as one who "with license of free foot" has caught "all the embossed sores and headed evils" of the various countries he has visited [II. vii. 65-9]. In this connection his very name is significant, for as is well known, the word *jakes* in Elizabethan times meant a privy. In one of his melancholy complainings when he is unaware that anyone is near, he implies that he is a "poor and broken bankrupt" [II. i. 57]. At times he avoids company, and like Tahureau's melancholy gentlemen [in his *Dialogues*], seeks out secluded spots where he complains to himself and rails against the world. Railing, in fact, is one of Jaques's chief characteristics. To Orlando he proposes that they should "rail against our mistress the world, and all our misery" [III. ii. 278-79]. To Amiens he says that if he cannot sleep, he will "rail against all the first-born of Egypt" [II. v. 60-1]. The First Lord finds him railing "most invectively" not only at court and country, but "at this our life" [II. i. 58-60]. Like Marston's Bruto, he inveighs against the corruptions of the age when he is himself one of the most polluted of men, and boasts that he would bring about a reformation in things if the world would but listen to him. And the rebuke which the Duke gives him [at II. vii. 59-69] is precisely the rebuke which Marston administers to Bruto. . . . Furthermore, Jaques's melancholy has exactly the ambiguity of the melancholy of the foreign traveler. It is partly a cultivated pose; he is proud of the fact that he can "suck melancholy" [II. v. 13] out of the various experiences of life. He tells us explicitly [at IV. i. 10-20] that his melancholy is the product of his travels. . . . If any clue to the interpretation of [his speech here] were necessary, it is to be found in Rosalind's immediate exclamation, "A Traveler" [IV. i. 21]. The melancholy which is explained for us is exactly the kind of melancholy which was affected by the foreign traveler. But in spite of the distinguished assurance of Dowden

to the contrary [see excerpt above, 1881], we cannot dismiss it as merely a pose. Jaques's invectives against life are by no means confined to times when there are others around to hear them. The truth is that his melancholy is both an affectation and a reality. He is cynical and pessimistic; he has lost any real faith in life; it is the futility of existence, not the goodness and sweetness of it, that is the burden of his complaining. As has been often pointed out, the Duke finds in the forest a relief from the corruptions of courts and cities; but to Jaques Arden is no more satisfactory in any respect than is the great world; in both he sees the same misery, cruelty and folly. It is not merely that mankind is corrupt, but that all nature and the whole order of existence seem tainted. Hence, the wounded stag speeches, which, if they have been not infrequently correctly interpreted, have been as often described as being everything but what they really are. At this point Jaques coincides exactly with those foreign travelers who are so vituperatively attacked in [the anonymous late-sixteenth-century tract] *The English Ape* on the ground that they saw even "nature and her diuine creation" as tainted and out of order. Finally, the action of the play and the attitudes of the other characters towards Jaques contain definite indications as to how he was intended to be taken. His cynicism and pessimism are negated at every turn. Orlando comes in carrying Adam as a counterblast to the "Seven Ages" speech [II. vii. 167]. Rosalind makes fun of Jaques [IV. i. 5-38], Orlando has no time for him [III. ii. 293]. Touchstone mimics him [II. vii. 12ff.], the Duke rebukes him [II. vii. 62ff.] and expresses it as his opinion that Jaques is one who has been "transformed into a beast" [II. vii. 1]. And the end of the play is a justification, not of the pessimism and cynicism of Jaques, but of the cheerfulness and optimism of the Duke.

Jaques, then, is based on the traveler. He is, moreover, based primarily on the complaining and railing type . . . rather than on the active Machiavellian. . . . But it is important to note that the Duke's second speech [at II. vii. 64-9], makes clear that if Jaques were to act, he would, because of his corrupted nature, be a vicious and dangerous man. He would, be it noted, "disgorge into the general world" all "the embossed sores and headed evils" which he had picked up in his travels. To appreciate fully the force of this statement, one needs only to recall what the vices brought home by the traveler were alleged to be. Imagine Jaques active, or grown more cankered through long meditation over his woes, and he would not be so far removed from the type represented by [the] Machiavellian corrupter as might at first appear. The Duke, in fact, in the speech to which I have referred, in effect accuses Jaques of wanting to be a corrupter.

There remains one important question. If Jaques is based on the traveler and Shakespeare is laughing at him, how is one to account for the fact that there are moments in the play when he is more than the mere railer against life, moments when his questioning of life and destiny seems to be the anxious inquiry of a disillusioned, but not unsympathetically treated man? The answer to this question is, I believe, that Shakespeare's delineation of the type was softened by the fact that Jaques's melancholy was rapidly becoming in 1600 a disillusion shared by the age, and shared, furthermore, by Shakespeare. A few years earlier, the melancholy and cynicism of the traveler had been material for satire and laughter, and they still were in 1600, but the laughter was becoming increasingly difficult. To accept this explanation, we need not assume that Shakespeare's middle period was clouded by personal sorrow and grief; we need only

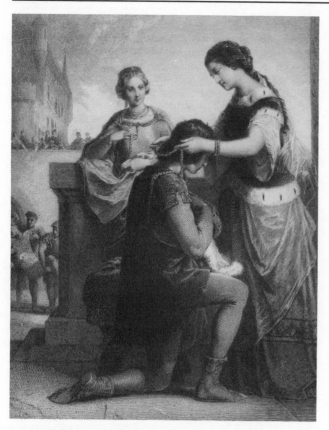

*Act I. Scene ii. Celia, Orlando, and Rosalind. By Schwoerer. The Department of Rare Books and Special Collections, The University of Michigan Library.*

assume that Shakespeare was not impervious to the main currents of thought and feeling in his own time. (pp. 248-52)

> Z. S. Fink, *"Jaques and the Malcontent Traveler,"* in Philological Quarterly, *Vol. XIV, No. 2, April, 1935, pp. 237-52.*

## OSCAR JAMES CAMPBELL   (essay date 1935)

[*An American scholar and critic, Campbell is best known for his* Comicall Satyre and Shakespeare's "Troilus and Cressida" *(1938), an influential study in which he argues that in* Troilus and Cressida *Shakespeare was imitating a new genre invented by Ben Jonson. In his following publication,* Shakespeare's Satire *(1943), Campbell continued his emphasis on the satiric elements in Shakespeare's plays and established himself as an innovative interpreter of Elizabethan drama, particularly with his characterization of Timon of Athens* as a tragic satire, rather than a tragedy. *Campbell was also the editor of* The Living Shakespeare, *an edition of twenty-one of Shakespeare's most popular plays, and* The Reader's Encyclopedia of Shakespeare, *an indispensable guide to features of the poet's life and work. In the following excerpt from his 1935 study of Jaques, Campbell argues against Elmer Edgar Stoll's view that Jaques is modeled on the conventional figure of the "malcontent" in Elizabethan literature (see excerpt above, 1906). Maintaining that the word "malcontent" had too many different connotations in the sixteenth century to apply usefully to Jaques, Campbell instead regards Shakespeare's character as "an amusing representative of the English satirists who wrote from 1590 to 1600," a "satirically drawn portrait of a familiar dramatic type." As such, Campbell continues, Jaques represents*

Shakespeare's "first clear effort" to use "devices that had appeared in the recently initiated satiric drama."]

Since 1906 most competent critics have regarded Jaques as that type of melancholy man which the Elizabethans called "malcontent." In that year Professor E. E. Stoll attempted to fix its distinguishing marks and to show that Jaques possessed most of these characteristics [see excerpt above, 1906]. The author of the present essay believes this to be a mistaken view. An examination of the occurrences of the term in English literature of the late sixteenth century convinces him that the word, although then widely current, was so inexactly used that it could not have suggested to Shakespeare's contemporaries any clearly defined type of eccentric. Yet Jaques' state of mind would almost surely have been recognized as something more specific than mere vague sadness and general discontent. It would probably have been identified with some of the carefully differentiated forms of melancholy scientifically described in many of the medical treatises of the sixteenth century—volumes which served also as handbooks of the psychological notions of the age. (p. 71)

Professor Stoll derived his term from Marston's play called *The Malcontent.* The title describes Malevole, a name which Altofronto, a deposed Duke of Genoa, gives to a disguise which he assumes. Stoll believes that Malevole is the most completely drawn portrait of the type to which both he and Jaques belong. He enumerates what he conceives to be their more important resemblances. . . . (pp. 71-2)

Some of the similarities enumerated [by Stoll] may be questioned. It is doubtful, for example, whether Jaques wears a professional garb of cynicism in any such fashion as does Malevole. The former's melancholy has not been donned, but is an inevitable product of his unbalanced nature. But many of the characteristics mentioned by Stoll are clearly common to Malevole and Jaques. Yet the similarities are of different kinds. Some are qualities of their personalities and some, such as their relation to other characters in the play, are those of dramatic function. Indeed, it is seldom clear whether Mr. Stoll believed the term "malcontent" to describe an Elizabethan personality or a conventional dramatic type.

Furthermore, Malevole and Jaques are as often unlike as alike. The former calls himself "a desperate malcontent," and adopts many attitudes and performs many actions which resemble those of a professed cynic—sometimes, in fact, they are as extreme as those of Shakespeare's Timon of Athens. At Malevole's initial appearance he expresses extravagant pessimism. We first hear discordant music off stage, evidently of his own making, and then his voice railing at Ferrardo. The vituperative terms he applies to him—"Duke's Ganymede," "shadow of a woman," and "smooth-chinned catamite"—show Malevole to be a railing misanthropist. (pp. 72-3)

[The] most important of his dramatic functions [is] his devotion to corrective satire. He expresses the spirit which Marston rescued from his forbidden formal satires and introduced into his plays that succeeded them. Consequently, Malevole is a new vehicle for his author's persistent zeal for reform, particularly of licentiousness. On occasion the satire degenerates into moral exhortation appropriate to the latest mouthpiece of Marston, the satirist, but foreign to the character of the whimsical and remote Jaques. (p. 73)

Shakespeare . . . during the 1590's, when the word ["malcontent"] was fashionable, employed it a number of times, never with a more precise meaning than a "general feeling of dissatisfaction.'' In every case, however [as, for example, in *Love's Labors Lost*, III. i. 179-83, and *The Two Gentlemen of Verona*, II. i. 17-20], he expects it to have a ludicrous connotation, as though it had become a cant term, likely to produce laughter in its own right.

Uses of the word similar to those of Shakespeare began to become conventional. It came to be applied to affectations of manner or of apparel. For example, Greene presents himself in *The Repentance of Robert Greene* as thrown into a deep and permanent boredom by the wild, unsettled life that he lived after leaving Cambridge. He traveled in Italy and Spain, where he "sawe and practizde such villainie as is abhominable to declare.'' ... His scorn for England, real or affected, after his life on the Continent and the resulting moroseness and dissatisfaction with everything at home, were symptoms of a melancholy with which the dissolute traveler abroad was often afflicted. But only his costume, not his state of mind, is described by the adjective "malcontent.''

Nashe, in *Pierce Penilesse* (1592), describes an upstart who despises England and her customs for the same ostensible reason as did Greene. But he only pretends to have traveled widely, having really been no farther away from home than Dieppe. However, it is part of his affectation to regard civilization in England as barbarous compared to what he has seen abroad, and that notion fills him with melancholy.... (pp. 76-7)

The counterfeit politician whom Nashe depicts in *Pierce Penilesse*, among those exhibiting the sins of pride, has an equally fundamental quarrel with life. His scornful melancholy has been caused by the failure of the Commonwealth to recognize and employ the political genius which he fancies he possesses.... (p. 78)

These examples establish one fact beyond doubt—that the Elizabethans recognized no "malcontent type" and that to define Jaques by putting him into a class of characters so denominated throws no light upon Shakespeare's conception, either of his nature or of his dramatic function....

Jaques would much more easily be recognized as a type by an Elizabethan audience if he were presented as suffering from one of the carefully differentiated forms of melancholy described in the medical treatises of the age. The main tenets of the theory of humors, in which melancholy played the most prominent part, are too well known to require explanation here. However, in most of the modern expositions of the subject, the important place given to those forms of melancholy caused by the so-called adustion or burning of each one of the four humors has been neglected. Yet this conception was axiomatic in every treatment of the subject. (p. 79)

It may be that the fine distinctions between the various sorts of melancholy were recognized only by physicians. Men of letters might have been acquainted with merely the most prominent and picturesque symptoms of the general disease, without knowing precisely which form they characterized. Therefore, a melancholy man in a work of fiction might exhibit a combination of peculiarities that, from the medical point of view, would be quite impossible. However, there is reason to believe that Shakespeare, at least, possessed more than an uninformed layman's knowledge of the subject. The convincing evidence that Miss Lily B. Campbell has presented [in her 1930 study *Shakespeare's Tragic Heroes: Slaves of Passion*] to prove that Hamlet is an accurately conceived type of the sanguine adust temperament makes it probable that by 1600 Shakespeare was familiar with the standard scientific analyses of melancholy.

Hence, it should not prove wasted labor to discover whether Jaques is a figure drawn closely upon a scientifically accurate model.

Natural melancholy—that produced by a considerable excess of this humor—was commonly called "ass-like melancholy" and rendered its victim, above all, sluggish.... Jaques displays none of the symptoms characteristic of either the man who by nature is predominantly melancholy or of the sufferer who is so overburdened with his humor as to exhibit unmistakable signs of mental pathology. He is clearly not suffering from any form of so-called "Natural Melancholy.''

To understand the second, or unnatural, sort of melancholy—that produced by adustion—one must remember that, ideally, the humors were supposed not only to preserve an equilibrium among themselves, but also, as expressions of the vital moisture, to maintain, severally and collectively, a properly balanced relationship to natural physiological heat. When any humor was subjected to excessive heat, it became transformed into an unnatural humor called phlegm-, choler-, melancholy-, or blood-adust, as the case might be. Moreover, all of these states were regarded as forms of melancholy and frequently called by the general term "choler adust,'' as a short equivalent of the phrase "melancholy formed by adustion.'' (pp. 80-1)

Jaques' prevailing humor obviously has not been burned so deeply as to reduce it to any form of madness. But he does exhibit the emotional variability characteristic of the moderately adust temperament. He takes equal delight in weeping over the hunted deer and in laughing at Touchstone's sallies. Yet he is enough master of his mind to enlist his volatile powers of intelligence and imagination in the service of his figurative sententiousness. These are the most prominent features of his character, and of all types of the unnaturally melancholy.

The initial description of Jaques [in II. i.], developed with more than ordinary fulness and circumstance, suggests that Shakespeare wishes his audience to regard his eccentric as a representative of one specific form of adustion.... This report would suggest to anyone who possessed the most elementary knowledge of the humors that Jaques was a phlegmatic person of some sort. Being a cold and moist humor, phlegm was associated in everyone's mind with water. The phlegmatic were attracted to water in both their waking and dreaming hours. (pp. 83-4)

A character who was introduced to an Elizabethan audience poring over a brook and there weeping and meditating, would write himself down at once as a phlegmatic person who had been rendered melancholy.

Jaques, then, was presented at first in a way which would inevitably suggest to an Elizabethan audience a man of natural phlegmatic temperament. Some of his original sluggishness appears in his aversion to practical life and to all forms of useful activity. Yet his phlegm, through his licentious life, has been heated to a temperature at which the brain is stimulated to ingenious exercise of the imagination. Abstention from action gives him leisure for incessant meditation upon the ways of man. The unnaturally produced melancholy renders him incapable of being delighted by anything that he sees and hears. Instead, all life seems to be a manifestation of folly and futility. Finally, his particular form of burnt phlegm has heated his mind to a temperature at which it is automatically stimulated to sententious comment upon ridiculous aspects of life—in other words, he moralizes every spectacle. These characteristics would be immediately recognized by intelligent Elizabethans as the identifying marks of a familiar type of mildly abnormal individual. They would have realized at once that his was the unnatural melancholy produced by the adustion of phlegm.

Whatever insight our examination may have given us into the essential character of Jaques will be of importance largely as it facilitates understanding of his dramatic function. Representing no figure in Lodge's novel [*Rosalynde*] of which the play is a dramatization, Jaques renders no service to the plot. His entertainment is offered in interludes to the story, and the critics agree that it is a form of satire. Yet it is a moot question whether the author's shafts of ridicule are aimed against Jaques or whether he serves as the mouthpiece for Shakespeare's own satiric comment. (pp. 84-5)

[In] the dramas written just before *As You Like It* two sorts of melancholy figures appeared. One was the preposterous gull or social would-be, who affected melancholy because he regarded it as almost the essential quality of an Elizabethan gentleman. The other was the man of native intellectual power, the equilibrium of whose mental constitution has been upset by too great an infusion of the humor of melancholy into his system. The consequence is an accentuation of his critical attitude toward the social world in which he lives. All his utterances thus take inevitably some form of satire. Certain of his speeches are just enough restrained to gain our assent and to induce us to adopt his hostile point of view. Others are so clearly the product of his jaundiced eye that their exaggerations make him absurd. This second type of melancholy man performs a twofold comic service: he is at once the agent and the object of the writer's satire.

Jaques belongs, I believe, to this second class of humorous melancholics. That he is an abnormal type, defined and universally recognized by Renaissance experts in internal medicine, establishes this fact. He, too, serves the double satiric purpose. Through the invasion of melancholy, his native intellectual keenness has been put into the service of a misanthropic spirit. His insight enables him to ferret out hidden abuses in society and absurdities in personality; his pessimism impels him to comment on his discoveries with bitterness, often so overdrawn as to become ludicrous. His dramatic function can thus be said to be wholly satiric—a fact which renders him important as marking the first clear effort on the part of Shakespeare to employ some of the devices that had appeared in the recently initiated satiric drama.

Jaques is introduced to the audience not only as a phlegmatic person afflicted with unnatural melancholy, but also as a figure to be laughed at. The Duke immediately recognizes possibilities of entertainment in a fellow who is automatically stimulated by a wounded deer to pessimistic generalities delivered to the vacant air. He longs to encounter him when he is in one of these sullen fits, for then he furnishes him with rich food for laughter. To transform a character thus introduced into a mouthpiece of the author's philosophy later in the play, would be to confuse an audience in a way that Shakespeare, the practical dramatist, would unquestionably have avoided. (pp. 90-1)

However induced, Jaques' irresistible impulse to moralize every spectacle [is] . . . presented as food for laughter. He wishes all those he meets to join with him in a chorus of misanthropic comment. (p. 93)

Jaques, then, during most of the play is a satirically drawn portrait of a familiar dramatic type. He is, to be sure, comic

without ever becoming downright ridiculous. His abstention from any form of grotesque folly enables him on occasions to be . . . an agent of satire. Indeed, he serves as an amusing representative of the English satirists who wrote from 1590 to 1600, so that we find him enunciating some of the critical doctrines which, by 1600, they had made official for the group. (p. 94)

*Oscar James Campbell, "Jaques," in* The Huntington Library Bulletin, *No. 8, October, 1935, pp. 71-102.*

## P. V. KREIDER (essay date 1935)

[*In the excerpt below, Kreider discusses Shakespeare's literary satire in* As You Like It. *He divides the "pastoral folk" in the play into three groups, and relates them to their satirical functions within the pastoral convention: 1) Ganymede and Aliena, who "typify the social aspects of the pastoral convention"; 2) Phebe, Corin, and Silvius, who, as Theocritan types, embody the literary tradition; and 3) William and Audrey, the only realistic rustics, who represent a counterpoint to the romantic, ideal state which the court members, "in their ignorance, believe they should like to revert." Kreider also maintains that, in shaping the conventions of the romance and the pastoral for use in* As You Like It, *Shakespeare managed both to expose the falsity of the conventional material and to preserve the integrity of his comedy. Touchstone, who belongs to none of the three groups of pastoral characters, sees through the "literary and social trumpery" of their way of life. Touchstone's satirical function, Kreider continues, is reinforced by Rosalind, who reveals herself to be both amused by and attracted to the romantic conventions as she exposes the artificiality of the other lovers' utterances and attitudes.*]

In *As You Like It* Shakspere freely satirizes his own language, his own characters, his own situations, and his own devices. There is no other comedy into which he inserts so much criticism of the literary genre represented by the piece itself. Among Shakspere's characters Falstaff is unique at least partly because he is possessed of the unusual ability to laugh at his own absurd pretense even while enacting, with the utmost external gravity, his artificial little dramas with himself as hero. Similarly—as if, indeed, the fat roysterer and none other had composed this play—the author of *As You Like It* chuckles merrily through most of the action, and now and then even bursts into riotous guffaws as he contemplates the soul-wrenching solemnity with which his puppets perform their conventional gyrations. In this comedy Shakspere may write as well as ever he can, he may compose lyrical passages of surpassing beauty and utter philosophic observations of unquestionable truth, he may bring his personages gloriously to life and into their mouths he may put inspired expressions of genuine feeling; but he will not regard these amusing automata and all their stereotyped, perfunctory business seriously. He creates in exquisite verse a comedy which presents the emotions of appalling persons, and then he subjects his own methods to mild ridicule. He shakes his head over his figures and studies them, as if they were only first rough drafts of human characters, and he discredits their attempts at self-expression as ludicrous and unsatisfactory. As if intent upon establishing the reputation that "hee never blotted out line," he lets what he has "penn'd" stand; but by subjecting it to critical scrutiny and declaring it less than it should be, he establishes a thesis for realism as opposed to unintelligent tradition in drama. The result of the author's examination of his work is that his characters and situations acquire increased life-likeness; but it is a daring experiment. Only a rare genius could successfully perform a feat so astounding—so impudent. To say that Shakspere was a superb artist is not enough: he must also have been confident of his own power.

Inasmuch as *As You Like It* is written in the pastoral tradition, it represents a series of episodes occurring in woodland and shepherd life and carried out by shepherds, genuine and feigned. The pastoral folk may be classified in three groups. There are, first, Ganymede and Aliena, who never seriously think of themselves as shepherds; they are ladies of the Court masking as rustics and merely playing at pastoral life. They typify the social aspects of the pastoral convention, the romantic enthusiasm which induces people who know nothing about country life to indulge in a synthetic pastoralism. Then there are Phebe, Corin, and Silvius, products of the literary tradition based ultimately upon Theocritus. Corin of course is the mild, contented, astute old herdsman; Silvius is the love-sick, rejected swain; and Phebe is the beautiful but cold and haughty shepherdess. Last there are William and Audrey, the only approaches to realistic rustics in the play, the results neither of an urban idealization of rural life nor of a literary vogue based upon an extinct Mediterranean culture. Essentially products of the contemporary English countryside, somewhat exaggerated for increased effectiveness, they are a contradiction to the claims of both the social and the literary bucolic conventions, not merely a denial but a defamation of the traditional, artificial pastoralism. These bumpkins are, in effect, actual shepherds whom, in delusion, the élite social groups are imitating; and the crude life, gross manners, and dull wits of these uncouth simpletons represent the state of society to which courtly ladies and gentlemen, in their ignorance, believe they should like to revert.

Not content with merely picturing the contrast between the illusion and the truth about shepherds, Shakspere estimates the virtues of the convention in fairly extensive dialogue between Touchstone and Corin. The Fool, it may be said, belongs with none of the three groups of rustics, although by profession he is associated with the pretenders and by fleshly appetite he is led to attach himself to unattractive reality; at the same time he sees through the literary and social trumpery which surrounds the pastoral life. At first Touchstone judiciously evaluates pastoralism as represented in literature—Corin's type—by carefully balancing disadvantage against advantage, and in the end he finds it more pleasing to the fancy than to the judgment. Much of the appeal of the fad, he intimates [in III. ii.], may be ascribed to an error, to the tendency to call conditions by approximately correct but actually misleading names, as privation and grim hunger are concealed under the euphonious caption, "spare life" [III. ii. 19], which suggests such romantic ideals as simplicity, contentment, mild asceticism, and self-discipline.... Then there is the delightful comparison [at III. ii. 32-85] of court and country manners and customs, in which the Jester, mockingly stating the opinion of the cultured group, declares that Corin is damned out of hand for his bad manners if he has never visited the Court, and in which Corin, a satisfactorily philosophical conventional herdsman, contends with admirable stubbornness that the ways of the field and of the Court would be equally inappropriate if transplanted into each other's territory.... In his heart Touchstone must know very well, as does Corin, that the courtiers, accustomed to the soft, clean, perfumed hands of their comrades, would never countenance in their society the horny, stained, and vile-smelling hands of the shepherd, the goatherd, or the neatherd. Yet it is to make contact with, indeed to acquire, such hands that those who dream pastoral dreams imagine ladies and gen-

tlemen deliberately converting themselves into shepherds.... If this argument of Touchstone's be not intended to ridicule those pleasure- and sensation-seeking idlers, and those enthusiastic but inexperienced writers, whose susceptibilities make them silly victims of an unnatural pastoralism, then the Jester's humor is entirely on the surface, and there is no depth or subtlety in it.

Shakspere can so expose the falsity of his conventional material without damaging his comedy because whenever he sweeps away tradition he uncovers some kind of actuality. Beneath extravagant language and theatrical poses are genuine feelings that have been not quite truthfully expressed; and beneath the brightly-colored, picturesque litter of "ink-pot" pastoralism is a world which is friendly, beautiful, and wholesome, and at the same time primarily simple and sincere. In the attempt to reclaim this calmer life and world from the tawdry allurements of fictitious pastoralism, there is no bludgeoning or vituperation. Even in the comments of the melancholy philosopher, Jaques, the satire is sympathetic and genial. Though this grumbler describe the seven ages of man in none too attractive terms, and though he insist upon the unreality of human life, yet his fellows in Arden will refuse to be saddened by his exposition; for Duke Senior and Jaques himself are ready with their plausible if varied explanations of his sadness, and the history of his case is such that none of the other characters need duplicate it in their own lives. Nor will the audience be misled as to Shakspere's basic interpretation of life, for he successfully establishes a serene atmosphere before he allows Jaques, an alien spirit, to intrude. In fact, the glad world of the comedy is made brighter by contrast with the dark spirit of this philosopher. He is out of place not only among such persons as surround him, but in the very air of Arden; and were he to reappear at the Court, he would be equally uncomfortable. Thus it is by no mere chance, but by a subtle inevitability, that Jaques feels nothing but irritation in the presence of such sentimentalists as Orlando, and finally retreats from the Forest in which unrestrained romance can flourish. It is likewise inevitable that he should refuse to return to the Court presided over by Duke Senior, who, philosophizing his misfortunes into blessings, more than anyone else puts into words the conception of the pleasant world in which all the action occurs.... (pp. 212-16)

It is well to note the courtier's praise [at II. i. 18-20] of the Duke's felicity of expression, for never again in this comedy will Shakspere pass favorable comment upon, or even show reasonable respect for, the rhetorical accomplishments of his creatures. Elsewhere he ridicules all effort at elegance. In a moment, when Rosalind and her companions reach the outskirts of the Forest, Shakspere has no relish for the poetic line. "O Jupiter," complains Rosalind in the vein conventionally ascribed to the romantic sufferer, "how weary are my spirits!" [II. iv. 1]. But her ornate phrase is rudely translated into realistic prose by the Jester, who knows nothing about spirits and prefers always to interpret experience in fundamental physical terms. "I care not for my spirits," says he, "if my legs were not weary" [II. iv. 2-3]. Thus while the arrival of the enamored, vivacious, and eloquent maiden indicates that there will be romance in Arden, yet Touchstone's prosaic utterance serves notice that it will be contemplated only with amusement—as is often the result when the matter-of-fact is superimposed upon the poetic.

Touchstone, indeed, has no illusions about poetic language. By the time the "sonneteering" of Orlando is in full flower, the nectar of his saccharine verses drips from every bough. But the Fool is unappreciative. . . . Touchstone knows poetry not only from the point of view of the critic, but likewise from that of the composer: [in III. ii.] he emphasizes his stricture of the love-lorn wrestler's lines by reciting, extempore, a dozen more of the same pattern and of approximately the same slight value, and later he declares that he has written lyrics to win the heart of Audrey. Unfortunately for him, however, the unlettered wench is not susceptible to rhymed sentiment. (pp. 217-18)

But it is not only in writing that Orlando is poetical, nor is Touchstone the only woodlander to jeer at those who are more lyrically amorous. Jaques will not stay in the same part of the Forest with such a person. At the end of a long prose dialogue between Rosalind and Jaques, Orlando enters with the salutation, "Good-day and happiness, dear Rosalind!" [IV. i. 30]. To express his contempt for such nonsense, the usually loquacious philosopher can find no words: simply, as he departs, he mutters, "Nay, then, God buy you, and you talk in blank verse" [IV. i. 31-2]. (pp. 218-19)

Shakspere makes fun of Orlando and other lovers not because they are in love, but because in all that they do as lovers they are thoroughly conventionalized. Not only do they speak the orthodox lines; they also indulge in the extravagant pretenses, heartfelt rather than rational, which constitute the self-deceptive attitudinizing of Cupid's victims in all contemporary amorous literature. Regardless of whether Shakspere or someone else be the author, the lover upon the stage, in the sonnets, and in the prose and verse romances is always pictured as Jaques describes him:

> Sighing like furnace, with a woeful ballad
> Made to his mistress' eyebrow.
>
> [II. vii. 148-49]

Rosalind twice asserts that Orlando cannot possibly be sincere in his protestations of affection, since he does not fulfil the requirements of the popular formula. When he tells her that he cannot say what hour it is, since there is no clock in the Forest, she retorts, "Then there is no true lover in the forest; else sighing every minute and groaning every hour would detect the lazy foot of Time as well as a clock" [II. vii. 148-49]. Orlando's protest against this deduction elicits from his tutor an elaboration upon the discrepancy between her own dapper, athletic suitor and the stereotyped figure—a man much more suggestive of the actor Hamlet, in whom the naïve Ophelia and her formalist parent recognize the lover because he runs true to the standard. . . . (p. 221)

The fact is that Rosalind, like Shakspere, is both attracted and amused by the romantic conventions. Concealed under the whimsicality that is Ganymede, reposes the substantial Rosalind; but she can be Rosalind only to Celia, while to all others she must be Ganymede—and if a game must be played in romantic disguise, why should it not be played in a romantic manner? Indeed, Orlando knew exactly what he was getting when he accepted Rosalind's offer to pose as his lady. She explained to him that she would be a mistress in all details like those pictured in the sonnet sequences and the romances [III. ii. 407-24]. . . . This counterfeit personality Rosalind attempts to preserve later, even though in order to do so she must fall back upon the convention of death for love. To her it makes no difference that she condemned this same fiction when Orlando proposed it, less than a hundred lines earlier in the same scene. (pp. 222-23)

The most complete and out-spoken attack upon the amorous convention, however, occurs [in III. v.] in a discussion between Silvius and Phebe, in which Rosalind finally becomes involved. At first Silvius strikes the approved attitude and speaks the prescribed lines; but Phebe, as disdainful and intractable as any lady a sonneteer might visualize, subjects her suitor's trite complaint to the test of fact and thus shows how vapid and false the whole conceit is. Then Rosalind, who, despite her foibles as Ganymede, is actually far from the coy mistress of the verse-makers, points out that Phebe differs in every detail of appearance from the fanciful, idealized literary representation of the desirable one whose eyes are grey and sparkling like the stars, whose hair is golden wire, whose brow is ivory, and whose cheeks are like the rose. One evil of this irresponsible scribbling amorousness, says Rosalind, is that it induces self-love among maidens who are in fact quite ordinary. . . . (p. 223)

Actually Rosalind can ill afford to rail at other lovers, for she is herself amusing to Touchstone and Celia. Coming upon Corin and Silvius in the Forest, she overhears the young shepherd lamenting his cruel fate in a conventional manner; but instead of abusing him, she indorses all he has said because it might well be an expression of her own passion. To the Jester, however, the episode is simply funny, and he cannot resist the temptation to enact a lugubrious parody upon it:

| | |
|---|---|
| *Sil.* | If thou rememb'rest not the slightest folly<br>That ever love did make thee run into,<br>Thou hast not lov'd;<br>Or if thou hast not sat as I do now,<br>Wearing thy hearer in thy mistress' praise,<br>Thou hast not lov'd;<br>Or if thou hast not broke from company<br>Abruptly, as my passion now makes me,<br>Thou hast not lov'd.<br>O Phebe, Phebe, Phebe!               [*Exit.* |
| *Ros.* | Alas, poor shepherd! searching of thy wound,<br>I have by hard adventure found mine own. |
| *Touch.* | And I mine. I remember, when I was in love<br>I broke my sword upon a stone, and bid him<br>take that for coming a-night to Jane Smile;<br>and I remember the kissing of her batlet and<br>the cow's dugs that her pretty chopt hands<br>had milk'd; and I remember the wooing of a<br>peascod instead of her; from whom I took<br>two cods and, giving her them again, said<br>with weeping tears, "Wear these for my<br>sake." We that are true lovers run into<br>strange capers; but as all is mortal in nature,<br>so is all nature in love mortal in folly. |
| *Ros.* | Thou speakest wiser than thou art ware of. |
| *Touch.* | Nay, I shall ne'er be ware of mine own wit<br>till I break my shins against it. |
| *Ros.* | Jove, Jove! this shepherd's passion<br>Is much upon my fashion. |
| *Touch.* | And mine; but it grows something stale with<br>me. |

> [II. iv. 34-63]
> (pp. 224-25)

As Shakspere ridicules the unrealistic pastoral atmosphere in which his action occurs, the poetic language in which his characters now and then incline to express themselves, and the sentimental attitudinizing in which they indulge, so too does he make fun of his plot. For purely practical reasons a dramatist often is compelled to base his action upon love at first sight; yet the fact that the device is necessary does not persuade Shakspere that it is convincing. Phebe, Orlando, Rosalind, Celia, and Oliver all succumb to love literally with the twinkling of an eye, and Phebe states the literary justification for swift surrender to feeling:

> Dead shepherd, now I find thy saw of might,
> "Who ever loved that loved not at first sight?"
>                                      [III. v. 81-2]

For the romantic shepherdess perhaps the process is natural enough. . . . But the dramatist seems unconvinced: for Rosalind and Celia are fundamentally sensible; Orlando, despite his verse-making folly and his readiness to make love to a shepherd boy, is manly and sane; and Oliver is by no means a flabby sentimentalist. Moreover, the first three of these four characters have a sterling sense of humor, which should save them from most arrant nonsense. Since Shakspere could not take time to allow all these persons to fall in love slowly, he did follow the established method, but at the same time he branded it patently inadequate. (pp. 226-27)

> *P. V. Kreider, "Genial Literary Satire in the Forest of Arden," in* The Shakespeare Association Bulletin, *Vol. 10, No. 4, October, 1935, pp. 212-31.*

## ENID WELSFORD  (essay date 1935)

[*The following excerpt is taken from one of the most important discussions of the purpose of the fool, and to a larger extent the purpose of folly and wisdom, in* As You Like It. *Welsford regards Touchstone as a "privileged truth-teller," stating that he both expresses Shakespeare's criticism of prevailing literary fashion and, by his occasional cutting quality, saves the narrative from inanity. Welsford regards Touchstone as a kind of intermediary between the playwright and the audience, who is literally what his name implies: a "test of the quality of men and manners." While the critic considers Touchstone, as well as Jaques, a critic of society, she argues that the latter is a poseur, a superficial critic whose chief interest is in his own, not society's, reactions, while Touchstone is both sympathetic and truly impartial.*]

In *As You Like It* the fool's name indicates his dramatic rôle: he serves as a touchstone or test of the quality of men and manners, and so helps to poise an otherwise somewhat kaleidoscopic play. For here, as elsewhere, Shakespeare expresses a complex point of view, making the most of the comic as well as of the romantic possibilities of his theme, and even at times burlesquing the pastoral convention in which his play is written. In such a play as this, where so much depends on a skilful use of allusion, contrast, and a variety produced by constant shift of focus, the rôle of the court-jester can be turned to very useful account. As privileged truth-teller, he can both serve as a mouthpiece for his author's criticism of prevailing literary fashions, and also by an occasional tartness preserve the play from the insipidity which so often mars pastoral literature. As an onlooker by profession he can supply us with that *punctum indifferens*, or point of rest, which, as Coventry Patmore has well remarked, is particularly necessary for the enjoyment of a complicated work of art.

The plan of *As You Like It* is indeed unexpectedly subtle. Touchstone is, as it were, the authorized commentator, but he has a rival in the person of that self-constituted critic of society, the melancholy Jaques. It is as though, the curtain which veils Arcadia having been drawn aside, two of the inhabitants sep-

arate themselves from the rest, and step forward to the front of the stage offering themselves as guides to the spectators in the auditorium. Both of them are equally ready to act as showmen, but in every other respect they are sharply contrasted: the one a sophisticated traveller, professedly intellectual, melancholy and dressed in black, the other a natural court-jester, professionally mad, merry and dressed in motley. This contrast of colour is not unimportant in a play which derives much of its charm from its picturesque qualities, and has many affinities with masque and ballet. But the contrast of outward appearances corresponds to a contrast of critical attitudes, which is still more significant. In spite of his varied experiences, Jaques is a superficial critic of life, because his apparent curiosity as to the doings of other people is really only an intense interest in his own reactions. He is essentially a poseur. Touchstone, on the other hand, exposes affectation; but he is capable of sympathy as well as of criticism, and his judgments are really impartial because his mental peculiarities and his degraded social position prevent him from having any private axe to grind. So, although Jaques and Touchstone stand side by side as showmen, their points of view are not equally valid; and it is the fool, not the cynic, who is the touchstone of the play. But although, like the shepherd whom he twits, 'such an one is a natural philosopher' [III. ii. 32], he is not to be taken oversadly; for, after all, he jests in an evanescent world of romantic freedom where the only touchstones are beauty and delight. For all his protests the fool is at home in Arden . . . , and it is only the over-clever, introverted victim of ennui who excludes himself from the jovial harmony and hymeneal mirth 'when earthly things made even, atone together' [V. iv. 109-10].

The use made of the fool in the play is a striking illustration of Shakespeare's successful craftsmanship. Ben Jonson's verdict that 'Shakespeare wanted arte' becomes amusing when we compare the subtly conceived rôle of Touchstone with the repulsive clowns of *Volpone*, who may well be life-like portraits of the more unpleasant inmates of an Italian palace, but contribute practically nothing to the meaning of the comedy. In fact, although Shakespeare's fecundity was too great to allow him to be over-meticulous, he excelled his fellow-playwrights not only as a poet and student of human nature, but also as a thinker and as an artist. He was the only dramatist of the time to make use of the technical peculiarities of the dramatic tradition which he inherited, and in the creation of Touchstone he did very nearly, though not quite, succeed in making the fool's rôle as potent a theatrical device as the Greek chorus. (pp. 249-51)

> *Enid Welsford, "The Court-Fool in Elizabethan Drama," in his* The Fool: His Social and Literary History, *1935. Reprint by Farrar & Rinehart Incorporated, 1936, pp. 243-72.*

## ELMER EDGAR STOLL  (essay date 1937)

[*In the following excerpt from his* Shakespeare's Young Lovers *(1937), originally delivered in an earlier version as part of a series of lectures on "The Maidens of Shakespeare's Prime," Stoll praises Rosalind's personal virtues and discusses the disguise convention in* As You Like It. *He calls Rosalind "the heartiest, the most abundant and exuberant" of Shakespeare's later heroines, comparing her in her superior womanliness to Beatrice in* Much Ado about Nothing. *In addition, Stoll comments on the play's romantic love, noticing how it is "facilitated by the conventions of disguise and impersonation." He adds that the Rosalind/Ganymede device not only enriches the narrative, but also broadens its emotional range. In his closing remarks, Stoll touches on Rosalind's language, commending, especially, the appropriateness—the "untrammelled liberties of wording"—of the heroine's prose passages.]*

Rosalind is the heartiest, the most abundant and exuberant [of the maidens of Shakespeare's prime]. In her, for once, Aphrodite, goddess of love and laughter, flew up into the North, and by her if not by others the 'laureate of love' wins his laurels. Beatrice [in *Much Ado about Nothing*] when most moved contracts to seriousness; Rosalind unfolds and expands. For her wit has no trace of a sting in it—like her frown, which Orlando fears would kill him,—'By this hand,' she, in her disguise, reassures him, 'it will not kill a fly' [IV. i. 111]. Wit and humour are both the mask and the indirect utterance of her passion, the effervescence of her happiness. Indeed, love and merriment are in her fairly inseparable, even when happiness is still in doubt. 'But is all this for your father?' [I. iii. 10] Celia asks her cousin when after the first sight of Orlando she is in the dumps.

> No, some of it is for my child's father. . . .
>
> [I. iii. 11]

And this glorious, romantic reunion of love and laughter Shakespeare has facilitated by the conventions of disguise and impersonation. As Rosalind and Orlando pretend that in her man's clothing she is Rosalind, she plays only a part that she feels, and eagerly notes as he woos her how much—and says mockingly, how little—he feels the part he plays. Fact and fiction here merge, and her joy in the fact overflows in her merriment over the fiction.

This is a remarkable case of an improbable convention being employed to enrich the situation, to broaden the emotional range; for it is the high ambition and privilege of art not to reproduce reality but without conspicuously offending against it to enlarge its confines. Her disguise is like the feigning of Hamlet, whereby, under the cover of madness, he can, as he bides his time, say out what he thinks and feels. It is like the convention of calumny credited, whereby the spirit of jealous vengeance coils round Othello's trustful love. And there, and often elsewhere in art, the end justifies the means. . . . [The] spirit of wit and humour, and the taking of the initiative by a newly enamoured but sweet and innocent young woman, though rightly treated, they heighten the romantic effect, decidedly imperil it; but here both are given full warrant by a device that is improbability itself. Orlando, for whom to see her was to love her, a day or two ago, would surely know her in any costume conceivable, to their days' end. But without the armour of disguise Rosalind could not profit by full knowledge on her part or by ignorance on his; and, certain of his love though she has not yet received a proposal, she would not be in a position, as she is, to coax him into making it, under the mocking eyes of Celia, in words that are enough to pull the soul out of his body:

> Come, woo me, woo me: for now I am in a
> holiday humour and like enough to consent.
> What would you say to me now, an I were your
> very very Rosalind?
>
> [IV. i. 68-71]

Spoken in skirts and stomacher, at a time when, off the stage, women no more laid bare their hearts than they then did their bodies, such words would never do. Spoken in disguise or without, by the enlightened and enfranchised female of today, they would do well enough but lack their startling charm. They would lend themselves to psychology, not drama. By the con-

vention of disguise Rosalind is given the advantages of merriment and audacity without the disadvantages, and thus what a breadth of emotion she, and we in turn, enjoy! Before taking on this role of Rosalind the beloved, she, as the youth instructed by his lovelorn uncle, is sceptical—Orlando has not the symptoms—

> A lean cheek, which you have not; a blue eye
> and sunken, which you have not . . .
>
> [III. ii. 373-74]

and she merrily enumerates the many signs of careless desolation that she half-ruefully misses. The wooing begun, she cries out, for the pure joy of saying it, 'Am I not your Rosalind?' [IV. i. 88] flinging her arms wide in her hose and doublet, but thereupon, in her pretended person in skirts, refuses him. He then, in his own person, is for dying:

> No faith, die by attorney. The poor world is
> almost six thousand years old, and in all this
> time there was not any man died in his own
> person, videlicit, in a love-cause. Troilus . . .
> Leander . . . But thése are àll líes. Mén have
> diéd from time to time, and wórms have eáten
> them, but nót for lóve.
>
> [IV. i. 94-108]

His right Rosalind Orlando would not have of this mind; she is far enough from it, to the point of letting Celia play the priest and marry them; and before the scene is over, her counterfeiting is pretty nearly like that when she swoons at the sight of the bloody napkin. 'For these two hours, Rosalind,' sighs Orlando, 'I will leave thee' [IV. i. 177-78]. 'Alas, dear love,' she whimpers, in her hose and doublet, 'I cannot lack thee two hours!' [IV. i. 179]. It is a jest between them, and another jest for herself and Celia, and underneath no jest at all.

Her voice—words of my own here fail me and I have recourse to the infallible Hazlitt: 'How full of voluble, laughing grace!' [see excerpt above, 1817]. At her best, with her lover, she talks prose, like Beatrice but unlike Portia [in *The Merchant of Venice*] and Viola [in *Twelfth Night*], in whom wit and humour yield priority to the lyric or sentimental mood. For these impetuous, effervescent spirits, in the midst of verse, prose alone will do, with its untrammelled liberties of wording and of rhythm; and how marvelously the medium responds to them both! It is poetry, but neither bastard prose nor free verse; it is drama, as it falls in with the pulsations of human utterance, laughing or rallying, but coaxing—half teasing, half caressing. 'For ever and a day,' murmurs Orlando [IV. i. 145].

> Ros.  Say 'a day,' without the 'ever.' No, no,
>       Orlando. Men are April when they woo,
>       December when they wed; maids are May
>       when they are maids, but the sky changes
>       when they are wives. I will be more jealous
>       of thee than a Barbary cock-pigeon over
>       his hen, more clamorous than a parrot
>       against rain, more new-fangled than an
>       ape, more giddy in my desires than a
>       monkey. I will weep for nothing, like
>       Diana in the fountain, and I will do that
>       when you are dispos'd to be merry. I will
>       laugh like a hyen, and that when thou art
>       inclin'd to sleep.
> Orl.  But will my Rósalind do so?
> Ros.  By my life, she will do as Í do.
>
> [IV. i. 146-58]

What a change and fresh precipitate running start at 'I will be more jealous of thee than a Barbary cock-pigeon over his hen,' what giddiness of rhythm in 'more giddy in my desires than a monkey,' and what a curvet and toss of the mane in 'By my life, she will do as I do'!

One of the most charming of Rosalind's traits is her affection for Celia, and no speech ever expressed more happily the affection that runs over into another:

> O coz, coz, coz, my pretty little coz, that thou
> didst know how many fathom deep I am in love.
>
> [IV. i. 205-07]

Repetitions such as these are as characteristic of her voluble exuberance as her rhythms. Beatrice has repetitions of her own, but high spirits rather than affection are behind them. (pp. 70-5)

> Elmer Edgar Stoll, "The Maidens of Shakespeare's Prime," in his Shakespeare's Young Lovers, Oxford University Press, 1937, pp. 45-84.


## MARK VAN DOREN    (essay date 1939)

[Van Doren was an American educator, editor, novelist, and Pulitzer Prize-winning poet. In the introduction to his Shakespeare (1939), he states that he "ignored the biography of Shakespeare, the history and character of his time, the conventions of his theater, the works of his contemporaries" to concentrate on the interest of the plays and their relevance to the modern reader or spectator. In the following excerpt on As You Like It, Van Doren discusses the play's pastoralism, Touchstone's and Rosalind's functions, and the nature of Jaques's melancholy. He argues that Shakespeare intended As You Like It to be "a criticism of the pastoral sentiment," but denies that it is satire, since "its examination is conducted without prejudice." Enlarging on this interpretation, Van Doren notes how Touchstone undermines the pastoral ideal through his "dialect" and dry humor, but he cites Rosalind as "the most searching critic of [the play's] theme," crediting her commentary with saving the comedy from absurdity. As the philosopher of the play, Van Doren continues, Rosalind exhibits intelligence and integrity, while Jaques wallows in self-serving melancholy "that serves none of wisdom's purposes."]

The airiness of "As You Like It" is as much the work of thought as the reward of feeling. The comedy seems to balance like a bubble on a point of thin space; yet space in its neighborhood has not worn thin, and the bubble is as tough as eternity, it does not break. This, doubtless, is because the sentiments of its author were at the moment in a state of rare equilibrium, and because his nerves were happy in an unconscious health. Also, however, it is because his mind was tuned to its task. "As You Like It" is so charming a comedy that in order to enjoy it we need not think about it at all. But if we do think about it we become aware of intellectual operations noiselessly and expertly performed. We see an idea anatomized until there is nothing left of it save its original mystery. We watch an attitude as it is taken completely apart and put completely together again. And all of this is done without visible effort. Shakespeare's understanding of his subject increases until the subject is exhausted, until there is no more to understand; and still there are no signs of labor or fatigue. Shakespeare has been denied an intellect. But whatever it took to write "As You Like It" was among other things mental, and the exact like of it, as well as the exact degree, has never been seen in literature again.

"As You Like It" is a criticism of the pastoral sentiment, an examination of certain familiar ideas concerning the simple life and the golden age. It is not satire; its examination is conducted without prejudice. For once in the world a proposition is approached from all of its sides, and from top and bottom. The proposition is perhaps multiple: the country is more natural than the court, shepherds live lives of enviable innocence and simplicity, the vices that devour the heart of civilized man will drop from him as soon as he walks under a greenwood tree, perversion and malice cannot survive in the open air, the shade of beech trees is the only true Academy, one impulse from the vernal wood will teach us more than all the sages can. Yet it is single too, and pastoral literature has monotonously intoned it. Shakespeare relieves the monotony by statement which is also understanding, by criticism which is half laughter and half love—or, since his laughter is what it is, all love. The result is something very curious. When Rosalind has made her last curtsy and the comedy is done, the pastoral sentiment is without a leg to stand on, yet it stands; and not only stands but dances. The idea of the simple life has been smiled off the earth and yet here it still is, smiling back at us from every bough of Arden. The Forest of Arden has been demonstrated not to exist, yet none of its trees has fallen; rather the entire plantation waves forever, and the sun upon it will not cease. The doctrine of the golden age has been as much created as destroyed. We know there is nothing in it, and we know that everything is in it. We perceive how silly it is and why we shall never be able to do without it. We comprehend the long failure of cynicism to undo sentiment. Here there is neither sentiment nor cynicism; there is understanding. An idea is left hanging in free air, without contamination or support. That is the place for ideas, as Shakespeare the comic poet seems to have known without being told.

"Where will the old Duke live?" asks Orlando's villainous brother of the still more villainous wrestler Charles [I. i. 113]. The unscrupulous bruiser answers in terms that may surprise us by their prettiness:

> They say he is already in the forest of Arden,
> and a many merry men with him; and there
> they live like the old Robin Hood of England.
> They say many young gentlemen flock to him
> every day, and fleet the time carelessly, as they
> did in the golden world.
>
> [I. i. 114-19]

That is the text to be annotated, the idea to be analyzed in the comedy to come. But analysis has already taken place, a cross-glance has already been shot by one whose mind will go on to draw lines in every direction athwart the theme. Shakespeare's first operation consists of putting such a speech into such a mouth, and letting it be ground between great molars there, unsympathetically. We get the doctrine, but we get it crooked, as comedy prefers: through the most unlikely medium, and the most unconscious. The first act is for the most part mechanically introductory to what follows; its business is to push everybody off to Arden, and Shakespeare writes it without much interest, since his sole interest is Arden. Rosalind is introduced, and of course it is important that we should find her from the first a gallant and witty girl, as we do. But she too is being saved for the forest. Charles's speech is the one memorable thing we have heard before we plunge into the depths of Arden at the beginning of the second act. But it is distinctly memorable, and it modifies the music which plays for us in the old Duke's mind.

> Now, my co-mates and brothers in exile,
> Hath not old custom made this life more sweet
> Than that of painted pomp? Are not these woods
> More free from peril than the envious court? . . .
> Sweet are the uses of adversity,
> Which, like the toad, ugly and venomous,
> Wears yet a precious jewel in his head;
> And this our life, exempt from public haunt,
> Finds tongues in trees, books in the running brooks,
> Sermons in stones, and good in every thing.
>
> [II. i. 1-17]

There is the text once more, translated into so quiet and so sweet a style that we may be tempted to believe it is the author speaking. But he was speaking as well in Charles; or rather he speaks in both—in their relation, which is only one of many relations the play will explore. The simple text will receive further statement through four pleasant acts. Good old Adam reminds Orlando of "the antique world" which was so much purer than "the fashion of these times" [II. iii. 57-9]. Shepherds appear named Corin and Silvius, and one of them goes sighing through the forest for love of his Phebe. A member of the Duke's retinue in exile knows how to be philosophical about everything; the humorous sadness of Jaques promises to ripen into wisdom now that ingratitude is forgotten and ambition can be shunned. We look to him for the sermons that so far have remained silent in their stones.

> Give me leave
> To speak my mind, and I will through and through
> Cleanse the foul body of the infected world,
> If they will patiently receive my medicine.
>
> [II. vii. 58-61]

So radical a boast in such emancipated terms, delivered by one who sees through the mummery of manners and considers compliment to be but the encounter of two dog-apes [II. v. 26-7], leads us to expect that in Jaques if in no one else the doctrine of the Duke will yield edifying fruit. Glimpses of a paradisal landscape are not withheld—boughs mossed with age, antique oaks whose roots peep out at brawling brooks, and purlieus of the forest where stand sheep-cotes fenced about with olive trees. And Shakespeare by no means stops short of miraculous conversions under the influence of this place. It seems to work. Oliver's transformation tastes sweetly to him, making him the thing he is; he will live and die a shepherd. The base Duke Frederick scarcely sets foot in the forest before an old religious man, harmonious with the wild wood, turns him not only from his hatred for the old Duke but from the world. The text is given every opportunity to state itself, and nowhere does the comedy overtly contradict it.

All the while, however, it is being subtly undermined and sapped of its simplicity. Touchstone shreds it with the needle of his dialectic, with the razor of his parody. . . . Encountering Corin in the forest and receiving from him the pastoral gospel—that courts are corrupt and manners unnatural—he juggles it till he has proved that courtiers are indistinguishable from shepherds, for tar on the hands of the one class is equivalent to civet on the hands of the other, and both substances are lowly born. . . . [Touchstone] is without illusion; so much so that he will not claim he can do without it. His dryness touches the pastoral text throughout, and alters it; the detachment of his wit gives everything perspective, including himself. He is in-

tellect afield; contemptuous of what he sees so far from home, but making the thin best of what is there. Not much is there when his withering, somewhat bored glance has circled the horizon. (pp. 151-56)

But nothing is more characteristic of the comedy than the fact that its heroine is the most searching critic of its theme. Rosalind's laughter is neither dry nor wry; it is high and clear, it has a silver sound, and the sun dances among its fiery, impalpable particles. Her disguise as a man does not explain the quality of this laughter. There are as many kinds of men as of women, and a different girl would have become a different boy; one, for instance, who moped and sighed and languished in the purlieus of romance. Rosalind has no difficulty with the language of scoffing youth. To such a fellow the poems of Orlando are tedious homilies of love. "I was never so berhym'd since Pythagoras' time, that I was an Irish rat, which I can hardly remember" [III. ii. 176-78]. Her vocabulary is as tart and vernacular as that of Mercutio [in *Romeo and Juliet*], Faulconbridge [in *King John*], or Hotspur [in *Richard II* and *Henry IV, Part 1*]. The skirts of the forest are for her the "fringe upon a petticoat" [III. ii. 336-37], love is a madness deserving the dark house and the whip, if Orlando will accept her as his physician she will wash his liver "as clean as a sound sheep's heart" [III. ii. 422-23], Phebe has no more beauty than without candle may go dark to bed, when lovers lack words they should kiss as orators in the same predicament spit, she will be as jealous over Orlando as a Barbary cock-pigeon over his hen, her affection hath an unknown bottom like the bay of Portugal, love hath made Silvius a tame snake. Language like this is not learned by putting on man's apparel, nor is there any sign that it goes against Rosalind's grain to jest about incontinence, your neighbor's bed, and the inevitable horns; there is a rank reality in her speech, as in the speech of Shakespeare's best women always. And she would appear to be without any understanding whatever of the rare states to which lovers can be reduced. . . . The tone [of her account of Oliver and Celia at V. ii. 32-41] is unsympathetic, logically enough for a young woman whose diatribe [at IV. i. 94-108] against the doctrine of the broken heart has become classic. . . . The realism is uproarious, as the prose is artful and the wit is incessant. "You shall never take her without her answer," she warns Orlando of the true Rosalind, "unless you take her without her tongue" [IV. i. 172-73]. Her gaiety runs like quicksilver, and is as hard to head off. She is of great value for that reason to her author, who can so easily use her as a commentator on his play when it grows absurd—as, being a pastoral play, it must. (pp. 156-58)

[Rosalind,] not Jaques, is the philosopher of the play. Hers is the only mind that never rests; his bogs down in the mire of melancholy, in the slough of self-love. He is too fond of believing he is wise to be as wise as he sounds, either in the set speech he makes about man's seven ages [II. vii.] or in the insults he considers himself privileged at all times to deliver. His distrust of manners turns out to be the disaffection of a boor. His melancholy, like his wit, is an end in itself, a dyspeptic indulgence, an exercise of vanity that serves none of wisdom's purposes. "Motley's the only wear," he decides [II. vii. 34], but when he is dressed in it he has no place to go. "I can suck melancholy out of a song as a weasel sucks eggs," he tells Amiens [II. v. 12-13], and the figure is better than he knows. He slithers through Arden, in love with his own sad eyes. "Will you sit down with me?" he asks Orlando, "and we two will rail against our mistress the world, and all our misery" [III. ii. 277-79]. Orlando's answer is priggish, but it

*Act I. Scene ii. Orlando, Rosalind, and Celia. By John Downman. The Department of Rare Books and Special Collections, The University of Michigan Library.*

is nearer to the meaning of the play. "I will chide no breather in the world but myself, against whom I know most faults" [III. ii. 280-81]. Jaques is a fat and greasy citizen of the world of easy words. He is a fine poet at this stage of Shakespeare's career, but he will degenerate into Thersites and Apemantus. Rosalind it is who knows his weakness best. . . . Jaques has seen much and can say anything, but he has nothing. Experience has made him sad. The more experience Rosalind has the merrier she grows. She too is a traveler, but she has not sold her own lands. She has taken her integrity with her to Arden, tucked under her three-cornered cap. It is proper that the limitations of Jaques should be stated by her, for if in him we have the pastoral sentiment criticized we have in her the only intelligence capable of judging the criticism. She judges with more than intelligence—with, for instance, instinct and love—but that again is proper to the comedy of Shakespeare's prime. (pp. 159-60)

> *Mark Van Doren, "'As You Like It'," in his* Shakespeare, *Henry Holt and Company, 1939, pp. 151-60.*

## C. L. BARBER   (essay date 1942)

[*An American scholar, Barber is one of the most important contemporary critics of Shakespearean comedy. In his influential study* Shakespeare's Festive Comedy (1959), *he examined the parallels between Elizabethan holiday celebrations and Shakespeare's comedies. In the introduction to this work, Barber states that the festival customs and the comic plays both contain a saturnalian pattern involving "a basic movement which can be summarized in the formula, through release to clarification." He defines release as a revelry, a mirthful liberation, "an accession of wanton vitality" over the restraint imposed by everyday life; the clarification that follows he characterizes as a "heightened awareness of the relation between man and 'nature'," which in comedy "puts holiday in perspective with life as a whole." In the following excerpt from his 1942 essay on the use of comedy in* As You Like It, *Barber introduces a new approach to the study of the play. He argues that* As You Like It *is less a comedy than a romance with comic accompaniment. As such, it dramatizes a central experience and has a serious theme, and its humor functions as a device which not only provides pleasure, but also implements a wider awareness. Barber claims that this humor is in no manner critical or evaluative of the play's pastoral and romantic ideals, but that it serves to balance the one-sidedness of these conventional views of life. The critic also disputes those assessments of* As You Like It *as a satire, stating that the "comic method" here is "precisely the reverse of satire." With respect to the characters, Barber considers Rosalind "the principal comic agency" in the play, noting how she embodies its opposing attitudes towards love, both the conventional and the humorous; he also stresses the importance of Touchstone and Jaques, calling them the "vehicles" of the comic method which Shakespeare has placed beside his serious theme.*]

Most criticism of Shakespeare's comedy has been impression-istic and appreciative rather than analytical. Since there is plenty to be serious about in the tragedies, critics have made it a virtue to be gay and glancing about "creatures of the woods and wilds." . . . The consequence of such spotty treatment has been to make the comedy appear casual and miscellaneous. Shake-speare did indeed write a great many different kinds of comedy, and often in a happy-go-lucky spirit which produced plays relatively loosely organized. Actually, however, we can re-peatedly see in his works a method, not in the least casual, of using humor as an element in a larger, serious dramatic whole; and we can find in this method the organizing principles, not of all his comedy, but of his best comedy. . . . In reality the finest comedy is not a diversion from serious themes but an alternative mode of developing them: not only the placing of the humor but also its content is determined by its function in the whole play. A close examination of the way the comedy functions in one of the plays where it is most successfully used can perhaps define principles of dramatic construction which will have a general application in discriminating between casual and motivated humor, and between those plays where comic and serious material are organically united and those where Shakespeare fell back on the formula of throwing in a little of both.

*As You Like It* is a good choice for this purpose because it is one of the plays which appear at first glance most casual. A good way to begin is to ask the simple but much-begged ques-tion "What is the comedy in *As You Like It* about? What does Shakespeare ridicule?" At times one gets the impression that it doesn't matter very much what the characters make fun of so long as they make fun. The wit seems directed almost at random, not criticism by laughter, but a buoyant sort of game, high spirits overflowing in high jinks with language. Certainly we cannot find the point of the humor in satire; it does not cut into the real world of Elizabethan men and manners. . . . Jaques, in response to a topical interest at the time when the play appeared, talks a good deal about satire, and proposes to "cleanse the foul body of th' infected world" [II. vii. 60] with the fool's medicine of ridicule. But neither Jaques, the amateur fool, nor Touchstone, the professional, ever really gets around to doing the satirist's work of ridiculing life as it is. . . . After all, they are in Arden, not in Jonson's London: the infected body of the world is far away out of range.

What they make fun of instead is what they can find in Arden—pastoral innocence and romantic love, life as it might be rather than life as it is. And this is true throughout the play. When the comedy is examined with an eye to what it is about, we find that by far the greater portion of it is not really introduced at random, but ridicules precisely the sentiments and behavior which are expressed or represented seriously in the play as a whole. The play as a whole is not comic, though we call it a comedy; the comical matter is a mocking accompaniment to a serious action, romantic and pastoral in character, which enlists our sympathetic participation. Touchstone's affair with Au-drey, to mention the most obvious case in point, is a burlesque of the other love-affairs. As a preliminary example of the way the comedy mocks the serious action, recall his famous remarks to the good duke, when he comes on with Audrey to take his grotesque part in the multiple marriage: "I press in here, sir, amongst the rest of the country copulatives, to swear and to forswear, according as marriage binds and blood breaks" [V. iv. 55-7]. This baldly reduces the pastoral lovers, with their highflown sentiments of devotion, to "country copulatives." And Touchstone suggests, by his pat antithesis, that the eternal

faith they pledge is nonsense, that blood will surely break what marriage binds. Yet these lines are spoken just after the au-dience has heard, and heard sympathetically, the lovers' pro-testations, and just before romantic faith reaches full tide in the finale of marriage.

This practice of making fun of something which is presented seriously a moment before or a moment after is standard throughout the play. It raises the question whether the play is divided against itself. But the humor is not really critical of the ideals on which the serious action is founded: its contri-bution is of a different kind. Touchstone's remarks make fun of the ideal of marriage, not as a bad ideal, but as an ideal which life does not live up to. His humor thus expresses the difference between the ideal existence represented in the play and life as a whole, which so frequently is not ideal. The fool is throughout a representative of the side of human nature which runs counter to the idyllic and romantic. . . . [His remarks] imply that the ideal is ideal, that an important phase of human nature runs counter to it. Their presence in the play thus makes for an inclusive objectivity concerning its serious theme.

This comic method is precisely the reverse of satire. The satirist presents life as it is and ridicules it because it is not ideal, as we would like it to be and as it should be. Shakespeare goes the other way about: he represents or evokes ideal life, and then makes fun of it because it does not square with life as it ordinarily is. Similar comic presentation of what is not ideal in man is characteristic of Medieval fool humor, where the humorist, by his gift of long ears to the long-robed dignitaries, makes the point that, despite their official perfection, they are human too. . . . Shakespeare's affinities in comedy are medi-eval rather than modern. Not that his point of view was me-dieval: his ideal was very different. But his plays are primarily concerned with giving form to ideal life, whether romantic or heroic; and his comedy is a response, a counter-movement, to this artistic idealization, as medieval burlesque was a response to the ingrained idealism of the culture. . . . [This] kind of comedy is by nature an accompaniment, achieving its greatest effects by humorously modifying and controlling our attitude towards dominant serious themes.

The comedy consequently implies a point of vantage outside the serious action, as the humorous tone of a seriously couched remark implies a detached valuation by the speaker of what he is saying. In *As You Like It*, where the serious material is particularly fragile, founded on ideals elaborated by literature rather than by society as a whole, the action is never out of humorous perspective for very long. Rosalind's sense of humor is the principal comic agency; but the detachment fundamental to the comedy is most obvious in Touchstone and Jaques, whose whole function is to be its vehicles. Once or twice these mockers seem to stand altogether outside the play, as when Jaques responds to Orlando's romantic greeting: "Good day and happiness, dear Rosalind!" with "Nay then, God b'wi' you, an you talk in blank verse!"

Although both Jaques and Touchstone are connected with the action well enough at the level of plot, their real position is generally mediate between the audience and the play. Jaques's factitious melancholy, which critics have made too much of as a "psychology," serves primarily to set him at odds with Arden and so motivate a "contemplative" mockery from out-side. Touchstone is put outside by his special status as a fool. As a fool, incapable, at least for professional purposes, of doing anything right, he is beyond the pale of normal achievements. In anything he tries to do he is comically disabled, as, for example, in falling in love. All he achieves is a burlesque of love. And yet, just because he is an outcast, he has none of the illusions of those who try to be ideal, and so is in a position to make a business of being dryly objective. . . . In *As You Like It* the court fool for the first time takes over the work of comic commentary and burlesque from the clown of the earlier plays; in Jaques's praise of Touchstone and the corrective virtues of fooling, Shakespeare can be heard crowing with delight at his discovery. The figure of the jester, with his recognized social rôle and rich traditional meaning, enabled the dramatist to embody in a character and his relations with other characters the relation of his comic to his serious action, to make explicit the comedy's purpose of maintaining objectivity. The fact that Shakespeare created both Jaques and Touchstone out of whole cloth, adding them to the story as it appears in Lodge's *Rosalynde,* is the best index to what he did in dramatizing the prose romance. . . . Shakespeare scarcely changes the story at all, but where in Lodge it is presented in the flat, he brings alive the dimension of its relation to life as a whole. The control of this dimension makes his version solid as well as delicate.

Indeed, the manipulation of our attitude towards the imagined conditions of life becomes more important than the plot which unrolls under those conditions. The best analogies for the play's structure are in music. *As You Like It* is composed in two movements, of about equal length, the first developing the pastoral theme, the second the romantic. Since the essence of pastoral is to feel the country, not as it is in itself, but in contrast to the court, the first half of the play is poised around this contrast, moving from the opening statement of jealousy and conflict to a resolution in the freedom of Arden. The smaller units of the action recapitulate the same movement from tension to release. A revealing example of the dominance of this rhythm of feeling is Orlando's entrance, sword in hand, to interrupt the duke's gracious banquet by a threatening demand for food. Such behavior on his part is quite out of character (in Lodge he is most courteous); but his brandishing entrance gives Shakespeare occasion to resolve the attitude of struggle once again, this time by a lyric invocation of "what 'tis to pity and be pitied" [II. vii. 117]. When this recurrent rhythm has brought us securely into the golden world, and its limitations, in their turn, have been suggested by the humor of Jaques and Touchstone, the pastoral motif as such drops into the background; Rosalind finds Orlando's verses in the second scene of Act III, and the rest of the play elaborates the theme of love. This second movement is like a theme and variations. The love affairs of the three pairs of lovers, Silvius and Phoebe and Touchstone and Audrey, as well as the hero and heroine, succeed one another in the easy-going sequence of scenes, while the dramatist deftly plays each off against the others. In each case the humor lies in making us aware of a version of the incongruity between the reality of love and the illusions (in poetry, the hyperboles) which it creates and by which it is expressed. The comic variations are centered around the seriously-felt love of Rosalind and Orlando. The final effect is to enchance the reality of this love by making it independent of illusions, whose incongruity with life is recognized and laughed off. (pp. 354-59)

Romantic participation in love and humorous detachment from its follies, the two polar attitudes which are balanced against each other in the action as a whole, meet and are reconciled in Rosalind's personality. Because she remains always aware of love's illusions while she herself is swept along delightfully by its deepest currents, she possesses as an attribute of character the power of combining whole-hearted feeling and undistorted

judgment which gives the play its value. Shakespeare exploits her situation in disguise to permit her to furnish the humorous commentary on her own ardent love affair, thus keeping comic and serious actions going at the same time. In her pretended rôle of saucy shepherd youth, she can mock at romance and burlesque its gestures while playing the game of putting Orlando through his paces as a suitor, to "cure" him of love. But for the audience, her disguise is transparent, and through it they see the very ardor which she mocks. When, for example, she stages [in IV. i.] a gayly overdone take-off of the conventional impatience of the lover, her own real impatience comes through the burlesque; yet the fact that she makes fun of exaggerations of the feeling conveys an awareness that it has limits, that there is a difference between romantic hyperbole and human nature. . . . (p. 362)

One effect of this indirect, humorous method of conveying feeling is that Rosalind is not committed to the conventional language and attitudes of love, loaded as these inevitably are with sentimentality. . . . [In] expressing her own love, [Rosalind] conveys by her humorous tone a valuation of her sentiments, and so realizes her own personality for herself, without being indebted to another for the favor. She uses the convention where Phoebe, being unaware of its exaggerations, abuses it, and Silvius, equally naïve about hyperbole, lets it abuse him. This control of tone is one of the great contributions of Shakespeare's comedy to his dramatic art as a whole. In his early plays we can see him struggling, often with indifferent success, to differentiate his characters from their sentiments by external devices of plot and situation, for example, Richard III's "hypocrisy." Later, the discipline of comedy in controlling the humorous potentialities of a remark enables the dramatist to express the relation of a speaker to his lines, including the relation of naïvete. The focus of attention is transferred from the outward action of saying something to the shifting, uncrystalized life which motivates what is said.

Without this technical resource, Rosalind could never have been created; for her peculiar charm lies less in what she does as a lover than in her attitude towards being in love. The full realization of this attitude in the great scene of disguised wooing marks the climax of the play's romantic movement. It is achieved when Rosalind is able, in the midst of her golden moment, to look beyond it and mock its illusions, including the master illusion that love is an ultimate and final experience, a matter of life and death. (pp. 362-63)

In connection with Marvell and the metaphysical poets, T. S. Eliot has made familiar an "alliance of levity and seriousness," "by which the seriousness is intensified." What he has said about the contribution of wit to this poetry is strikingly applicable to the function of Shakespeare's comedy in *As You Like It*: wit conveys "a recognition, implicit in the expression of every experience, of other kinds of experience which are possible." The likeness does not consist in the fact that the wit of certain of Shakespeare's characters at times is like the wit of Donne and his school. The real similarity is in the way the humor functions to implement a wider awareness, maintaining proportion where less disciplined and coherent art falsifies by presenting a part as though it were the whole. (p. 365)

By no means all of Shakespeare's burlesque and mocking comedy is as closely integrated by its function in the dramatic whole as that in *As You Like It*. He often introduced such humor more or less at random because no serious theme emerged from his material as the object for comic commentary. *Twelfth Night* is a case in point: taken part by part, it is as fine, or finer, than

*As You Like It;* yet it is distinctly inferior as a play, because the comedy does not bear on a central experience. The playwright, moreover, wrote a great deal of plain and fancy farce, where the amusement springs entirely from manipulating situations and no object for the humor is in question. (p. 366)

The traditional division into Comedies, Histories and Tragedies has obscured the way Shakespeare really put his plays together, for his use of burlesque cuts right across these categories. He wrote only three whole comedies: *The Comedy of Errors, The Taming of the Shrew,* and *The Merry Wives of Windsor;* and these three pieces are predominantly farce. Elsewhere, he always had serious matters in hand: most of the other plays called Comedies are better described as romances with more or less of comic accompaniment. And his practice, once he had reached maturity, was to use comedy wherever there was occasion for it, not simply in connection with romance. By and large, there is more, though not better, comedy in the romances than in plays of the other categories, because a romantic theme and a happy ending usually called for a more extensive comic response to strike a balance. (pp. 366-67)

> C. L. Barber, "The Use of Comedy in 'As You Like It'," in Philological Quarterly, Vol. XXI, No. 4, October, 1942, pp. 353-67.

## WARREN STAEBLER (essay date 1949)

[*In the following excerpt, Staebler argues that Shakespeare wrote* As You Like It *as an expression of atonement or "perfect adjustment." He regards Rosalind, Jaques, Duke Senior, and Touchstone as endowed with composure and self-knowledge: they "know themselves and in their knowledge are at-one with themselves." This concept, Staebler explains, involves the "humanizing, harmonizing influence of the Forest of Arden upon all who enter it." Staebler also comments on the treatment of time and sex in the play, Jaques's melancholy, and the general issues of motive, language, and imagery. Most importantly, the critic dissents from the rather unfavorable view of Jaques voiced by most commentators, maintaining that the character is free of malice and suspicion toward other people, and that he is "a philosopher, with the true philosopher's detachment toward things." Lastly, Staebler praises the prose in* As You Like It, *stating that it is characterized by "luminousness," "warmth," and "earthy substantiality."*]

[*As You Like It*] is unique in its atmosphere, for it is suffused with a singular combination of autumnal mellowness and spring freshness and vivacity. But the extraordinary thing is that its atmosphere is not the result of poetic virtuosity or imaginative fancy as is that of *Love's Labors Lost* or *A Midsummer Night's Dream,* but the reflection of an attitude toward life, the emanation of a spirit, the aura of a mind. It is not a funny play, for it is high comedy, not a comedy of jokes. Yet although it is not funny, it includes fun along with other things—wit, sentiment, sentimentality, and pathos. It is the product of a being all of whose faculties were in equipoise. It is serene because it was created by Shakespeare when he was at-one with life; it is therefore, in the Elizabethan sense of the word, a play of atonement, or, to use a modern word, a play of perfect adjustment. For this reason a unique harmony pervades it.

The principal characters are at-one with themselves, with their fellows, and with nature. There is extraordinary wisdom and maturity in the way they look at life. To be so wise and mature and "atoned" demands that they see things as they are; they are, in fact, admirably disillusioned for theirs is a disillusionment untainted by cynicism. Even Corin the shepherd, lowly and inconsequential though he is, exhibits this atonement for he is content with earning what he eats and getting what he wears and owes no man hate, envies no man's happiness, is glad of other men's good, and undisturbed by his own harm. . . .

There is no evidence in *As You Like It* that Rosalind, Jaques, the banished Duke, and Touchstone have either patiently or zealously striven all their lives to know themselves, but the fact is that they do know themselves and in their knowledge are at-one with themselves. They accept, and can laugh at, themselves. The miracle is that so young (for none of them are old) and so little exercised by life, they are what they are. (p. 92)

Jaques passes for a melancholy fellow, but his is a consciously cultivated melancholy of a highly eclectic brand and he describes for Rosalind the many simples of which it is compounded. The feelings which he has studied how to indulge sensitively and aesthetically afford him a connoisseur's pleasure. He knows this and admits it and therefore can say with truth that he can suck melancholy out of a song as a weasel sucks eggs. But he does not while away his earthly time only by playing the man of variegated sentiment; he is also a philosopher, with the true philosopher's detachment toward things. Moved by Touchstone's laconic simplification of life to a ripening from hour to hour followed by a rotting from hour to hour, and inspired by a sudden perception of folly, or satirical laughter, as the one effectual means of reforming human beings and getting them to lead reasonable lives, he thinks of himself, invested with a fool's prerogatives, wandering over the globe, through and through cleansing its foul infected body. But his ardor has not carried him away or befogged his perspective. An important "if" attaches to the success which he, or anyone, as moral physician can attain. He can purify human beings only *if* they will patiently receive his medicine! What balance, what absence of illusion!

The principal characters are as much at-one with their fellow human beings as with themselves. The most conspicuous examples of close, affectionate, but unselfish ties are the friendships of Rosalind and Celia and of Adam and Orlando. But the relation between Jaques and the Duke is perhaps almost as close, though much less demonstratively so. They value each other's company for the play of mind it affords, the Duke loving most to "cope" Jaques in his "sullen fits," since he finds him then "full of matter." Jaques, however, finds the Duke occasionally disputatious in their exchanges, and caring too much for their friendship (as well as for his own privacy of mind) to allow it to be endangered by prolonged controversy, not seldom takes pains like a reasonable man to avoid his company. . . . Toward others with whom he is less intimate, Jaques is good-natured, although sometimes his sense of irony and quickness of perception lead him to be impudent in his replies to them. Even so, he is never guilty of malice. . . . In his regenerated state he is essentially a man of reason unable to communicate with anybody whose responses to life have ceased to be rational. But he does not damn those who are irrational, or exploit them; he ignores them, without contempt. Since they do not enter his sphere there is no danger of collision with them. Nor does he deride those who like himself have undergone regeneration but now live by a different discipline and evaluate life through a different medium. . . . He has been redeemed by reason and the light he has seen is that of luminous intelligence. . . . As he tells Rosalind, the one important thing about his life, the thing which compensates for all losses, is what he has gained in the way of experience. And in his amused eyes humanity is not to be despised for it is always affording the stuff out of which new experience, no matter how slight, can be shaped.

As for Orlando, stereotyped character though he is, it is significant that in spite of the indignities he has suffered, he bears no malice against humanity, or as we should say, society, and is not out to get even with the world. In his speech to Rosalind and Celia just before his wrestling match with Charles [I. ii. 183-93], he reveals his dispassionate adaptation to his lot. In its expression, true, part of this may be a little fulsome, for he was after all unschooled in such things, but what it reveals of his modesty and fortunate disposition cannot be gainsaid. (pp. 93-6)

As for the at-onement of the characters with nature, as much as can be said has already been said about the humanizing, harmonizing influence of the Forest of Arden upon all who enter it. The beneficence of nature in this play is as romantically idealized by Shakespeare as it was ever to be two centuries later by Wordsworth or Byron or Shelley. Indeed the Forest is much like a prototype of the blessed isle-haven of which Shelley dreams in his "Lines Written Among the Euganean Hills," where "the love which heals all strife" is so operative as instantaneously to transform any of "the polluting multitude" who find their way there and set foot upon its shores. It is because the Forest provides such magical power that the two villains in *As You Like It,* Oliver and the usurping Duke, are healed of their villainy as soon as they reach it and harmony restored between them and those they have wronged, so that the two discords sounded early in the play are at its close resolved into perfect concord. . . . When I say that the characters of *As You Like It* are at-one with nature, I have in mind the physical facts of life, the flux of things of which they themselves are part. They accept their animal, vegetable selves and the end as well as the functions by which they are inevitably characterized. The most important physical fact of life is growth followed by decay and dissolution, or death; and to this the characters of *As You Like It* are reconciled genially and compassionately. Touchstone voices most succinctly, at once tender and amused, his acceptance of this fact, and Jaques, marveling as he listens, subscribes to it:

> And so, from hour to hour, we ripe and ripe,
> And then, from hour to hour, we rot and rot;
> And thereby hangs a tale.
>
> [II. vii. 26-8]

A few minutes later Jaques himself, in his "All the world's a stage," in more detail, describes the subtle changes which overtake the flesh in its brief, arc-like voyage through time [II. vii. 139-66]. . . . The passage has been justly famous. Although it is not explicitly voiced by them, this attitude is essentially that of the other major characters; and even Adam, lesser figure though he is, in accepting his age as a frosty but kindly winter, shows us that he shares it. Indeed on the theme of time, touched eloquently in every play, Shakespeare has woven a number of variations in *As You Like It.* In addition to Jaques' speech on the seven ages of man and Touchstone's observation on ripening and rotting, there are Rosalind's elucidation to Orlando of Time traveling "in divers paces with divers persons" [III. ii. 308-09] and the sounding of "carpe diem" [seize the day] in the songs, notably in "It was a lover and his lass" at the end [V. iii. 16-33].

The chief fact of animal existence is sex, and to this, no less than to the mutability and death of earthly things, the men and

women of *As You Like It* are reconciled, Rosalind and Touchstone having most to say about it. In short, living in the body they are not at all reluctant to say they are of the body, with its appetites and instincts. It may be that Elizabethans spoke more frankly, or less self-consciously, about their bodies and about sex than we do now, but even if this were so, the wholesome, rounded candor of *As You Like It* could not be accounted for simply by this fact. There is frank talk, too, among men and women in the other comedies, much more sophisticated, but it does not bear the same relation to everything that is said as does that of *As You Like It*—it does not grow naturally out of an underlying view of things uniform among the characters. We see in the other comedies the brilliant plucked petals of the flower as they are scattered here and there by the poet; but in *As You Like It* we see the complete flower, the petals and the stem to which they are attached, flourishing serenely in the sunlit air. The lesser functions of the body, even that of perspiration, when they are mentioned, are touched on with good-natured humor.

Love for Touchstone is a phenomenon of the blood, an impulsion of the body toward an object which, because of a crystallization of certain substances within the flesh, has become desirable to it. . . . At the end of the play in joining with Audrey what he calls "the rest of the country copulatives" [V. iv. 55-6], he is honest and informs us that he is both swearing and forswearing, for although marriage binds, blood breaks. . . . And for Rosalind, too, for she knows to what extent it is chemical in its nature. . . . To the great legendary fictions about romantic love she cannot subscribe; there is for her no grand passion. Such tales as those of the suicide of Troilus over love of Cressida and of the martyrdom through drowning of Leander for love of Hero

> . . . are all lies.
> Men have died from time to time and worms
> have eaten them, but not for love.
>
> [IV. i. 106-08]

Troilus simply "had his brains dash'd out with a Grecian club" [IV. i. 97-8], and Leander, while taking a bath in the Hellespont, was simply stricken with cramps. But there is no bitterness, no sourness in her disbelief. On the contrary, it is with sympathy that she smiles at the credulity of a world by which such myths are perpetuated from generation to generation to delude the minds of young men like Orlando and young women like Phebe. As for marriage as a man-made institution for the confinement of sexual love, with something of his amused eye for human absurdities, she believes it to be generally as little stable and lasting as Touchstone himself. She has seen too many tempers run out, too many vows weaken—in short, too much conjugal passion die and too much infidelity take its place to see it under any glamor. (pp. 96-9)

And so all the absurd, the distasteful, the sad, even the ugly, things of life are openly faced and serenely accepted by the memorable figures of *As You Like It.* The elusiveness of time, the ephemerality of beauty and love and life are touched in this play with a warmth and compassion which recall Ecclesiastes. Dust we are, and dust to dust we return. Purged by the sympathy and clear vision of Jaques, Touchstone, and Rosalind, the gross is no longer gross. They are reconciled to their mortality. And yet it is this same mortality which constitutes the rock on which later protagonists in the tragedies are to be wrecked. (p. 100)

[Considering] the October sunlight which lights up and warms its atmosphere, it is not at all un-apt to call *As You Like It* a play of the golden mean. The characters are thinking beings and Jaques is not alone in feeling it imperative to say in a crisis with another human being: "An you be not answered with reason, I must die" [II. vii. 100-01]. (p. 101)

Jaques is sometimes thought to be an individual wrapped up in himself, devoid of instinctual trust or love. He certainly appears unsusceptible to love—erotic love, that is—but this may be because he has outgrown it. But it is surely wrong to say that he is without instinctual trust or affection. Adherent of reason though he is, his heart is not in the least atrophied. He is not only free of malice or suspicion toward people in general; he is affectionately disposed to those in particular among whom he has chosen to make his lot. Shakespeare after all gives him what is really the last word—a series of benedictions as he disposes of the various male characters who have been involved in the complications of the play. These are spoken with affectionate good will, even though it means recommending some of them to their marriage beds.

Indeed *As You Like It* is the most human and down-to-earth of all Shakespeare's comedies, for it deals exclusively with human beings and their relation to themselves and to the good earth. It is free of the preciosity of *Love's Labors Lost*, the fantasy of *A Midsummer Night's Dream*, the barbed wit and sinister undertones of *Much Ado About Nothing*, the cruelty of *Twelfth Night*, and the magic of *The Tempest*. There is nothing in it of our relation to powers suprahuman—nothing of astral determinism, nothing of any divinity, and only a few mentions of Fortune, or chance, the most important occurring in the second scene of the play when Rosalind and Celia playfully distinguish between the offices of Fortune and those of Nature as they affect their state. God, I believe, is mentioned only once, and then inconsequentially, in Jaques' "Nay, then, God buy you, an you talk in blank verse" [IV. i. 31-2], as he takes leave of Rosalind following their first meeting. And "heaven" occurs only occasionally, in hardly more significant fashion, as when Touchstone tells Jaques [at II. vii. 19] that he is not to be called fool until heaven has sent him fortune. . . . It is out of their deep regard for their common humanity that the Duke and his fellows are ready to give succor to Adam and Orlando, and not for any professed kinship with a supernatural Being; and indeed it is to their humanity that Orlando appeals. It is as if for Shakespeare in *As You Like It* the human condition contained fullness enough, as if he had surveyed it with a loving eye and found it wholly good.

Coherent in its outlook on life from beginning to end, *As You Like It* is as consistent in its tone as it is uniform in its atmosphere. With whatever technical faults exist in the manipulation of the plot, or whatever overstrainings of coincidence there are, I am not concerned here. The cast of the language in which the story is projected, however, and the aptness of it at every turn deserve at least a glance by way of consideration. The verse is no more rich or ornate than the prose. Splendor and luxuriance have given place to luminousness and warmth and earthy substantiality. The best known passages from *As You Like It* are not distinguished by either richness of sound or striking imagery. . . . This is not to say that there are no images. There are, but they are of a different nature from those which highlight much of the verse in the other comedies; and furthermore the fabric in which they are embedded has been cut more nearly all from the same cloth. Extravagance and magnificence are forsworn in *As You Like It*. So, too, is imagery deriving from classical myth. The characteristic image of this play grows out of homely, warm, fruitful nature—from the

friendly English countryside of spring or autumn, with its flocks and lowly human habitations. And its dimensions are small. For Rosalind, early in the play, the working-day world is full of briers, or burs, which she can shake off her coat but not off her heart; adversity, says the Duke in his first speech, has its sweet uses after all for like the toad it hides a precious jewel in its head; Orlando humbly tells Adam, who has faith in him, that he is pruning a rotten tree which cannot yield so much as a blossom . . . ; Jaques sucks melancholy out of a song as a weasel sucks eggs; Touchstone tells Corin he is damn'd "like an ill roasted egg all on one side" [III. ii. 37-8]; Celia finds Orlando under a tree like a dropped acorn; Rosalind as Ganymede tells Orlando she lives with her sister "in the skirts of the forest, like fringe upon a petticoat" [III. ii. 335-37]; she engages to wash his "liver as clean as a sound sheep's heart, that there shall not be one spot of love in't" [III. ii. 422-24]; Celia tells Rosalind that, considering Orlando's "verity in love," she thinks him as "concave as a covered goblet or a worm-eaten nut" [III. iv. 23-5]; Jaques tells Touchstone that Sir Oliver Martext in marrying him and Audrey will only join them "together as they join wainscot" so that one of them "will prove a shrunk panel and like green timber, warp" [III. iii. 87-9]; etc., etc. Once in a while, rarely, the figure is on a scale which approaches the grand, as when Rosalind reproaches Silvius for following Phebe

> Like foggy south, puffing with wind and rain.
>
> [III. v. 50]

Through the images of *As You Like It* we get glimpses into the quiet, rustic life of 16th-century England just as through the Homeric similes of *The Iliad* we have flashbacks to the pastoral life left behind by the Achaeans warring on the fields of Troy. The difference is one of scale.

The wit in *As You Like It* is never ostentatious or extraneous, but grows directly out of the dramatic circumstances framing the incidents in which it occurs and is in keeping with the characters who voice it. There is much thoughtful laughter about life, but little playing with words and no playing with words solely for the play as in other comedies. Even when a passage of wit is prolonged beyond the bounds of what the immediate circumstances seem to justify, it can be seen to possess an organic connection with the deep, underlying theme of man and his destiny on earth, creature of curious imperfections and practices. The most conspicuous illustration of this is in Touchstone's disquisition almost at the very end of the play on the seven degrees of the lie, culminating in his pronouncement of "If" as the "only peace-maker" [V. iv. 102-03]. In his expatiating he says nothing related to what has happened before his appearance or to the action which follows at once. But what felicitous laughter about a branch of human behavior! And how in keeping with the substance and tone of the play!

Indeed it is a marvel that young as he was at the time of *As You Like It*, Shakespeare should have had an image of life in his mind so complete, so rounded, so congenial, and so harmonious. In his play of atonement he has drawn men and women with a humanity akin to that of the Mozart of *Don Giovanni*, the Wagner of *Die Meistersinger*, and the Strauss of *Don Quixote*. (pp. 102-05)

*Warren Staebler, "Shakespeare's Play of Atonement," in* The Shakespeare Association Bulletin, *Vol. XXIV, No. 2, April, 1949, pp. 91-105.*

## THOMAS MARC PARROTT (essay date 1949)

[*An American scholar and academic, Parrott wrote several critical studies of Shakespeare's works and edited a collection of*

*Shakespeare's plays and sonnets. In the following excerpt from his* Shakespearean Comedy *(1949), he examines Shakespeare's changes from his source, Lodge's* Rosalynde, *identifying the most significant alteration in the dramatist's parody—as opposed to Lodge's wholehearted acceptance—of the pastoral convention. Parrott focuses on the principal contributors to this parodic design in* As You Like It: *Jaques, Touchstone, and the rustics. The first he describes as a "malcontent," but more than a type character, claiming that Shakespeare took pains to individualize Jaques by making him a traveler who sneers at English things. Parrott sees Touchstone's principal function in* As You Like It *as an exposer of folly; his contribution to the action is not great, but, through his skillful handling of exaggeration and parody, he functions as an amusing commentator on the events around him. And the rustics Corin, William, and Audrey, the critic contends, provide an element of realism, thereby exposing "the fantastic figment of the pastoral." On a different matter, Parrott attributes much of the play's success less to its action than to its speech, maintaining that here Shakespeare's "free and . . . almost careless mastery of language" surpasses that of most of his earlier comedies.*]

In the main [Shakespeare] followed his source very closely [in *As You Like It*]; it takes a comparative study of the romance and the play to show how many minor incidents Shakespeare took over from Lodge. But it is still more interesting to note the changes he made. In the first place he cuts down the introductory matter; the long narrative of Rosader's strife with his brother is reduced to a brief physical encounter and to the mere mention of a plot against Orlando's life. Shakespeare wanted to get his characters to Arden as soon as possible. In the same way he shortens Lodge's conclusion; the detailed account of the loves of Saladyne and Aliena is cut down to Rosalind's mocking report of their sudden infatuation. The marriage of Oliver and Celia—Saladyne and Alinda in Lodge—has been called 'the one unlucky slip of the brush' in Shakespeare's play, but it was given him by his source and was, in fact, demanded by the convention of Elizabethan comedy that all eligible maidens should be married off in the last act. The Masque of Hymen, which winds up the play, is perhaps a less happy ending than *Rosalynde's* pretty revelation of herself in woman's dress to her father. There is, however, some reason to believe that this episode was not part of Shakespeare's original plan, but was inserted later to give a bit of spectacle with music when the play was performed at some noble wedding.

Yet it would be wrong to suppose that Shakespeare merely threw Lodge's narrative into dramatic form. He did much more; he transformed the tone of the romance as thoroughly as Lodge had done that of the tale of Gamelyn. Shakespeare called his play *As You Like It,* perhaps with a smiling admission that a pastoral romance of this sort was the dear delight of his Elizabethan audience; he himself, certainly, was too much of a realist to accept its absurdities.

By way of corrective he introduces into his play various characters whose sole business it is to comment on, often indeed to expose, the fantastic figment of the pastoral. One of these characters, the shepherd Corin, comes over from Lodge's Corydon, but while in the romance he is a singing shepherd like one of Spenser's, in the play he is a simple representative of the shepherd's life as it really is, the hired servant of a churlish master, his hands hard and greasy with handling his ewes, a 'natural philosopher' [III. ii. 32]. To Corin Shakespeare added the country wench, Audrey, and her rustic lover, William. All three give a background of realism to the pastoral scene.

Jaques, another of Shakespeare's inventions, is a more important character. He takes no part in the action, yet *As You Like It* would be the poorer without him. Jaques is first of all

a 'humor' character such as Jonson had lately introduced on Shakespeare's stage. His 'humor' is that of a somewhat cynical melancholy; in the phrase of that day he is a 'malcontent.' Yet he is more than a type figure; Shakespeare has taken some pains to individualize him. He is the traveler returned from the Continent . . .—the Duke calls him 'a libertine as sensual as the brutish sting itself' [II. vii. 65-6]—and he has come home to sneer at all things English. Rosalind's gibe hits him off exactly: 'Farewell, Monsieur Traveller: look you lisp, and wear strange suits, disable all the benefits of your own country, be out of love with your nativity, and almost chide God for making you that countenance you are; or I will scarce think you have swam in a gondola' [IV. i. 33-8]. A professed satirist he demands the liberty of caustic criticism of society, of all human life in fact; his famous 'All the world's a stage' oration [at II. vii. 139-66] is the cynic's picture of man's life in all its periods. There is no fear that we shall take the pastoral seriously while Jaques is there to comment on it. (pp. 167-68)

Touchstone's role is that of the Court Jester, the 'all-licensed fool.' It is as such that he first appears at Duke Frederick's court, using the Fool's license to mock at the Knight who swore by his honor that the pancakes were good, and indulging himself at the same time with a side thrust at the Duke, who loves this honorless Knight. He is threatened, to be sure, with a whipping, the customary penalty for the Fool who overstepped his bounds . . . , but he is clever enough to sidestep the danger at Court, and once he is in Arden all danger blows away in the forest air. Here he is free to practice, unchecked, his vocation, the exposure of folly. That, presumably, is the significance of his name; he is the touchstone that distinguishes pure from base metal. He contributes to the action of the play as little as Jaques, but he is an even more amusing commentator. He comments mainly by exaggeration and by parody. We have examples of his art in his reminiscence of his early love for Jane Smile, a wild caricature of the fantastic passion of Silvius for Phebe, and in his impromptu parody of Orlando's 'false gallop of verses' [III. ii. 113]. He is even able to win a laugh from the cynic Jaques by ranting on Lady Fortune 'in good set terms' [II. vii. 17], really a mockery, though Jaques does not recognize it, of that railer's own habitual practice. His story of a quarrel with a courtier, which ran through all the degrees from the Retort Courteous to the Countercheck Quarrelsome, is a satiric parody of the behavior of gentlemen who wrangled, as they dressed, 'by the book,' the book, that is, of an Elizabethan Emily Post. This speech, by the way, looks like an afterthought on Shakespeare's part, written in, perhaps, at a rehearsal, to . . . amuse the audience while the costumes and the music for the coming Masque were being made ready offstage. Touchstone's one contribution to the action of the play is his wooing of Audrey. This, of course, is Shakespeare's invention; there was no place for such a courtship in Lodge's pastoral. Yet this very wooing is Touchstone's comment on the whole business of lovemaking in Arden. Silvius and Phebe are fantastic lovers in the pastoral convention; the sudden mutual passion of Oliver and Celia is quite incredible; Rosalind and Orlando are romantic lovers *par excellence*. Touchstone and his girl, on the other hand, present this relation of the sexes in its simplest realistic form: 'man hath his desires; and as pigeons bill, so wedlock would be nibbling' [III. iii. 80-2]. Touchstone's courtship is not only comment, but parody.

Apart from characters already mentioned, the figures of any importance in the play—the two Dukes, the brothers, Orlando and Oliver, the cousins, Rosalind and Celia, along with Phebe and her lover—have all stepped out of Lodge's romance onto

Shakespeare's stage. One of these characters, however, has been so transformed by Shakespeare's magic as to have become a new creation. This, of course, is Rosalind. (pp. 170-71)

For Rosalind plays a far more important part in *As You Like It* than her namesake does in the source, where the heroine divides the interest with Saladyne and Alinda, with Montanus and Phoebe. As a matter of fact, once Shakespeare gets his characters to Arden the whole action of the play revolves about Rosalind in her disguise as Ganymede. Not only that, but she has become quite a different person from Lodge's lady. Rosalynde is the conventional heroine of romance, 'the paragon of all earthly perfection.' (p. 171)

Shakespeare's Rosalind, on the contrary, is a creature of a natural and almost divine simplicity. She first appears saddened for her banished father, a striking contrast to the resplendent Rosalynde at the usurper's court. Her dawning passion for Orlando is motivated, in part at least, by the fact that he is the son of her father's old friend, a matter passed over in silence by Lodge. . . . Of all the heroines of Shakespearean comedy, Rosalind in Arden is the gayest, because she is the happiest, and the happiest because she knows her lover loves her, while yet she need not confess her own passion. There is no trace of this light-hearted gaiety in Lodge's Rosalynde, any more than there is that trace of feminine weakness which Rosalind shows when she faints at the sight of her lover's blood.

This atmosphere of happiness breathes through all the scenes in Arden. The threat of danger or of death which hangs over various characters in earlier comedies is soon dispelled in this play. Duke Senior, Orlando, and Rosalind all have to fly for their lives, but they are all happier in exile than ever they were at home. (pp. 171-73)

Enough has been said of the characters who contribute to, who constitute in fact, the comic element in this delightful play. It may, however, be noted that their contribution is less a matter of action than of speech. Jaques and Touchstone reveal themselves as figures of comedy less by what they do than by what they say, and while Rosalind's action follows in the main the pattern laid down by the source, it is, after all, her speech that matters. It is in his free and, as it were, almost careless mastery of language in *As You Like It* that Shakespeare surpasses most of his earlier works in comedy. There is a more even balance of prose and verse in this play than in *Much Ado*. That was a comedy of character revealed in action, and for that purpose Shakespeare used mainly prose. Here, however, where action in itself is less important, verse regains some of the lost ground. About two-fifths of *As You Like It* is in verse—apart from the songs almost entirely in blank verse. The rhymed couplet, so frequent in the early comedies, has disappeared except in isolated cases like Phebe's quotation from Marlowe, Orlando's imperfect sonnet, and tag-ends of scenes and speeches. What is of more importance, the blank verse recovers not only in extent, but in poetic quality. It is not easy to find in *Much Ado* a memorable passage of more than a few lines of verse; *As You Like It* is 'thick inlaid' [*The Merchant of Venice*, V. i. 59] with stars. The best-known passage, the Seven ages of man, is a set speech, written, perhaps, to let Jaques hold the stage while Orlando goes off to bring in old Adam. It is rhetorical rather than lyric, which is appropriate to the speaker. In general, the lyric strain of *A Midsummer Night's Dream* is, except for the songs, seldom heard in this play. Its music is graver and more equable, nearer, perhaps, to that of *The Merchant.* . . . It is not far wrong to say that when sentiment predominates, verse prevails in *As You Like It*. When the stress

lies on character, character contrast, satiric comment, or the play of the comic spirit, Shakespeare reverts to prose. Touchstone regularly speaks prose; that is the proper dialect of the Jester. Rosalind swings back and forth from verse to prose—and what a prose! (pp. 174-75)

It is not easy to pass final judgment on a play at once so delightful and so provoking. It is the work of a playwright fully master of his art, yet contemptuous of probability and recklessly careless of construction. It has always been a favorite with lovers of the romantic. . . . Hazlitt, most romantic of critics, has been its most enthusiastic admirer [see excerpt above, 1817]. A realist like Shaw, on the contrary, sees in its very title the author's contempt of a public he stooped to entertain [see excerpt above, 1896]. This, to be sure, seems as wilfully perverse as much of Shaw's comment on Shakespeare, for it is hardly possible to read *As You Like It* without feeling that Shakespeare thoroughly enjoyed writing it. (p. 176)

In no play of Shakespeare's do we feel so plainly this sense of happy and carefree ease. It cost him little intellectual effort to transform *Rosalynde* into a stage-play; there were few dramatic problems to be met and mastered. The core of Lodge's romance was a pleasant story of young love; it was an easy matter to strip off its conventional absurdities and to substitute for its stock figures creatures of real flesh and blood. Even these creatures may mean less in the play than the atmosphere of Arden. Once he sat down to write this play Shakespeare left the noisy crowded town with all the demands it made on him, to forget the world for a while in the shade of this legendary wood. *As You Like it* is of all Shakespeare's plays most visibly a comedy of escape. As he shakes off the briers of this working-day world, his pen runs swiftly without pause or check through scene after scene. . . . Properly to appreciate *As You Like It* we must forget for a time all matters of dramatic technique, all conceptions of a 'well-made' play, and be content, like the inhabitants of Arden to 'fleet the time carelessly' [I. i. 118]. (pp. 177-78)

> *Thomas Marc Parrott, "The Master Craftsman," in his* Shakespearean Comedy, *Oxford University Press, 1949, pp. 134-90.*

## S. C. SEN GUPTA   (essay date 1950)

[*An important Indian critic, Sen Gupta has written extensively on Shakespearean drama, particularly Shakespeare's tragedies and comedies. In the following excerpt from his* Shakespearian Comedy *(1950), he emphasizes the variety and importance of the large cast of characters in* As You Like It, *asserting that each is a facet of a broadly envisioned, "intricate and iridescent world." He thus maintains that Jaques's melancholy is no "mere pose," for it adds to the broad perspective Shakespeare sought; and Touchstone, though inconsistent to some commentators, is meant to be "both a critic and a clown." Overall, Sen Gupta claims, to achieve his larger vision Shakespeare sacrificed "subtlety and delicacy" in plot and characterization.*]

It is mere speculation whether Shakespeare liked *As You Like It,* but the title of the play is particularly appropriate, because it is a comedy which is expected to please all tastes, one which you will all like. The play is characterized by largeness rather than by intensity, by diffuseness rather than by concentration. Rosalind is as brilliant as Portia [in *The Merchant of Venice*], but she cannot have a decisive victory over anybody because she has no antagonist like Shylock, and there is nothing in this drama which can claim the poignant interest aroused by the trial scene in *The Merchant of Venice*. But there is no comedy in which the minor characters are more important than in *As You Like It*. Jaques, as Hazlitt points out [see excerpt above, 1817], 'does nothing', but his musings run like a dark thread across the cheery world of Arden. Touchstone is a mere clown, but occupies a more important place in this play than Feste in *Twelfth Night* or Lavache in *All's Well that Ends Well*. Corin stands for real pastoral life and is thus distinguished from Silvius and Phebe who represent the artificial life of pastoral literature, the romance grafted on pastoral life by the pastoral convention. The Dukes do not play a very important part in the central episodes of the comedy, but they are not without distinctive features of their own. The Elder is a philosopher who finds books in running brooks and sermons in stones, but hastens to take possession of his lost dukedom as soon as he gets it back, without casting a longing, lingering look behind at the simple life he seemed to prize above princedom. The Usurper is a 'humorous' man whose conduct is a succession of caprices, the last of which is the most unexpected, although most pleasant. The most remarkable thing in *As You Like It* is thus the amplitude and variety of its portraiture. It exhibits a many-sided world which includes the court as well as the forest, four pairs of lovers who have their own ways of wooing, shepherds and courtiers, philosophers and fools, treacherous brothers and faithful servants. The largeness of this world is enhanced by the presence of the vaster forces of Nature which form a fitting background to the pastoral romance. It is, indeed, an intricate and iridescent world that Shakespeare portrays in this comedy. We may take it as *we* like it.

The complexity which is the principal feature of Shakespearian drama is seen not only in the multiplicity of the incidents described in this comedy or in the large number of characters represented in it, but also in the total impression conveyed by the interweaving of its incidents and the interplay of its characters. On a superficial view, it appears that Shakespeare's play is little more than a rehash of a Euphuist story written by Lodge, which contains almost all the incidents described by Shakespeare and most of the characters introduced by him. Shakespeare, however, so changes the characters and the story that his play is, like Lodge's *Rosalynde,* a pastoral romance, and also, what Lodge's novel most certainly is not, a criticism of it. It provides both a pastoral romance and an ironical commentary on it—a commentary that works itself out through the cynicism of Jaques, the pungent humour of Touchstone and the sentimental exaggeration of the Silvius-Phebe episode. The protagonists can be seen in a proper perspective only when they confront people who are not directly connected with them. Rosalind, the brilliant heroine who carries everything before her sprightliness of manner and sharpness of wit, gets the better of Jaques, the melancholy cynic, in the one or two encounters she has with him. But Jaques is not as irrelevant to the action as he seems to be; although he is worsted by Rosalind, he helps to orientate us with regard to the meaning of the drama and realize the limitations of the aspect of life of which Rosalind is a symbol. We feel that Rosalind gives us only a brilliant picture of the sunny surface of life, and that there are dark depths of which she is totally ignorant. Jaques' melancholy is not, as some critics have assumed, an affectation; it is different from all other types of melancholy, because it is a melancholy of his own, ingrained in his nature and reinforced by the sundry contemplation of his travels. But we are constantly reminded that this melancholy, although not a pose, reveals only one aspect of the many-coloured dome of life. He desired to be better acquainted with Ganymede, but is anxious to leave as soon as Orlando comes forward with his silly verses. He gives Rosalind his blessing on her marriage, but does not consider

it worth his while to accompany her and her father back to the court. Corin's simple wisdom is a refreshing contrast to the sophistries of Jaques and Touchstone. Shakespeare parodies the artificiality of pastoral convention in the episode of Silvius the love-sick swain and Phebe the country belle, and enlarges the scope of his comedy by introducing William and Audrey, whose unredeemed rusticity is a reminder that the pastoral world represented by the other characters from the Duke to the shepherds is only a poetical make-believe. It is a wide and many-sided world which Shakespeare represents in this comedy, and we shall be mistaken if we emphasize this or that facet of it.

Shakespeare pays the penalty for this largeness of vision by sacrificing the subtlety and delicacy he might have attained in the working out of the component episodes or the individual characters. To take the most prominent example, Rosalind the heroine falls in love with Orlando at first sight, is banished from her uncle's court, and on reaching the forest meets her beloved, who, she is pleased to find, is in a frenzy of passion for her. She encounters no obstacle to the fulfilment of her marital ambition, and there seems to be no reason why she should not anticipate her cousin Celia's method and get married at once. As Rosalind is not Celia, she loves to be in love and plays a cat-and-mouse game with Orlando. These tactics enable her to give many exhibitions of her wit and passion, but they also betray the essential emptiness of the central episode in the story. Rosalind's reflections on love and life show that she is possessed of keen insight and is capable of strong emotion, but neither the sharpness of her intellect nor the depth of her passion has been put to any real test. She seems to be brilliant but superficial. The defect lies neither in the conception of the character, which is original, nor in the dialogue, which is sparkling, but in the attempt to express character through a plot that is thin of content, and in the sacrificing of subtlety to breadth.

The story of Celia suffers from the opposite defect. Here Shakespeare has the substance of drama, but he disposes of it before he has even touched the core of the problem. As Celia is acquainted with the full details of Oliver's villainy she must have had to overcome a strong prejudice before accepting Oliver for her husband. But Shakespeare skips this part of his work and we do not have any direct picture of the growth of love in Celia's heart; the nearest we get to the secret of Celia's love is in Rosalind's humorous account of the meeting of Celia and Oliver [at V. ii. 30-7]. . . . In this description—very characteristic of the witty Rosalind—we have Shakespeare's own apology for not taking us through all the stages in a courtship in which love had first to conquer prejudice. Probably it is not merely a love for mechanical symmetry that makes Shakespeare marry Celia to Oliver, for there is no reason why Celia should not fall in love—and with Oliver. But we feel dissatisfied, and even speculate about an ideal husband for Celia, only because Shakespeare has not made the story convincing enough by revealing all the stages in the courtship even though these stages were got through as quickly as Caesar's victory at Zela. If he had done this or endowed the Orlando-Ganymede-Rosalind story with a real plot, he would have had to sacrifice comprehensiveness of vision to subtle and detailed workmanship; he would have lost sight of the wood in the trees. The play shows that romantic sentiment is intrepid, exuberant and irrational and that its significance and value may be appreciated if only it is seen in relation to the cynicism of Jaques, which is itself sentimentalism turned inside out . . . , and the salt humour of Touchstone. Though *As You Like It* belongs to the same group as *The Merchant of Venice* and *Much Ado about Nothing* and has affinities with them, the technique it adopts is peculiar to itself; it is a technique of synthesis rather than of analysis.

Not that this play is lacking in action. The peculiarity is rather that here a particular action or a particular character is not represented for its or his own sake; but character and incident are both subordinated to the ultimate end—the juxtaposition of different attitudes so as to give us a large and total view of things. There are banishment, restoration, crime, repentance, courtship, marriage, but more important than any one of these items is the general impression produced by their co-operation and contrast. A peculiar feature of *As You Like It* is that two important figures—Jaques and, in a lesser degree, Touchstone—stand aloof from the main action in order to be free to comment on it. The Duke mockingly refers to Jaques' salacious past, but we are not given any clear glimpse of what it was actually like, for in the drama we are concerned more with the total effect of his manifold experiences on his character than with the experiences themselves. His cynicism, which is temperamental, has been aggravated by his experiences, and by the time he retires to the forest of Arden he has acquired the capacity of sucking melancholy out of a song as a weasel sucks eggs. Critics, who find such deep-seated melancholy intolerable, ridicule it as a mere pose, but if it had been a mere pose he would have betrayed signs of discomfort and, at unguarded moments, slipped out of it into a cheerful mood. His melancholy is so essential a part of his character that except on the one occasion when he blesses almost everybody [V. iv. 184-93], he is always wrapped in a most humorous sadness and feels uncomfortable in the presence of Rosalind and Orlando. The motley clown arouses his admiration, but even here his enthusiasm is checked by the sad wisdom he has learnt from experience. He interrupts the sham marriage Touchstone intends going through, but he does not prevent it altogether; he does not disillusion Audrey, and when the ceremony is actually performed, he is content to dismiss the couple with the characteristic prophecy:

> And you to wrangling; for thy loving voyage
> Is but for two months victual'd.
>
> [V. iv. 191-92]

It is true that Jaques' reflections on life are one-sided and exaggerated; but exaggeration must not be mistaken for artificiality. Jaques represents a point of view opposed to that of Duke Senior and Rosalind, and it is only when we make a synthesis of these different points of view that we approach a complete understanding of life.

Touchstone, the other critic in the play, is different from Jaques. 'Motley,' says Priestley, 'is a better critic than Melancholy. He is a better critic because, unlike Jaques, he does not detach himself from his fellow mortals but identifies himself with them; he does not say, in effect, "What beasts you are!" but "What fools we are!" and so, like a true comic genius, he is universal' [see excerpt above, 1925]. Touchstone participates in two episodes in the play, namely the flight of Rosalind and Celia in which he is their trusted companion, and the marriage of Audrey in which he is the protagonist. As these episodes bring out contradictory traits in his character, he seems to be a critical puzzle. Some readers exalt him as a noble philosopher, illuminating both the court and the forest, while others look upon him as a rapscallion 'equally devoid of the morality of the town and the country'. How is it possible that the man on whom Celia depends so unquestioningly should marry Audrey with the intention of abandoning her whenever it suits his

convenience? Is not his loyalty to Celia and Rosalind incompatible with his intended infidelity to Audrey? Priestley, who tries to reconcile these apparently contradictory features in his character, warns us against taking an exaggerated view either of his loyalty or of his unfaithfulness. He suggests that the 'romantic lovers may not be true to one another for ever' and that 'it is possible that Touchstone may cleave to his Audrey a little longer than a couple of months or so'. Priestley's comments, though suggestive, are all conjectures; they do not explain the real Touchstone. . . . The play contains three 'romantic' episodes—of Rosalind and Orlando, Celia and Oliver, and Phebe and Silvius. It seems to have been a part of the dramatist's intention that in Touchstone's wooing of Audrey there should be a burlesque of romantic love-making so that the play might carry with it its own ironical commentary.

The peculiarity of Touchstone is that he is nothing if not a critic. He has been called a philosopher, but has no positive philosophy. Critical by temperament, he has had the training of a professional jester whose business it is to flout the world. He possesses a sharp insight and also a capacity for searching analysis, and it is this intellectual acumen which makes him critical of human absurdities in all spheres of life. He knows the weaknesses of courtiers whom he satirizes with relentless thoroughness. He is acquainted with their pomposity, their extravagance, and their cowardice. With his remarkable command of the grotesque, he easily reduces all exuberance to absurdity. His keen sense of humour does not spare even Rosalind whenever she transgresses the bounds of normality. When Rosalind says that by Silvius' wound she has by hard adventure found her own, Touchstone, keenly aware of the awkwardness of the comparison, conjures up ludicrous images in order to burlesque Rosalind's romance [II. iv. 46-56]. His comic sense is so acute and pervasive that it not only brings out the ludicrous element in the fantastic vagaries of love-lorn maidens or forsworn knights but reveals a core of absurdity even in the most normal and universal thing, the passage of time [II. vii. 20-8]. Poets discover the source of beauty in everything; Touchstone, whose gifts are the reverse of the poetical, travesties all that he comes across so that from his point of view life appears to be essentially ludicrous and grotesque. That is what makes him both a critic and a clown. (pp. 154-62)

*S. C. Sen Gupta, "Middle Comedies," in his* Shakespearian Comedy, *Oxford University Press, Indian Branch, 1950, pp. 129-73.*

## HAROLD C. GODDARD  (essay date 1951)

[*In the following excerpt from his* The Meaning of Shakespeare *(1951), Goddard offers some innovative views of* As You Like It *that oppose, in many ways, previous assessments of the play. First, he states that the central theme of the drama is "the relation of love and wisdom"—specifically, that "true love" imparts "true wisdom" and that knowledge or learning without love is barren. The critic regards Rosalind as the "instrument" of this idea, claiming that she, more than any other character, combines "wit with love" and, in her "balance" and "reconciliation of opposites," demonstrates the ability of love to provide insight and to increase "the wisdom of the race." Second, Goddard considers all of the other characters incomplete beside Rosalind; he especially condemns Jaques and Touchstone, noting the shallowness of the cynic's professed wit and wisdom and, interestingly, regarding the fool as callous, profane, condescending, and lacking in love. In both of these figures, Goddard discerns the worldly wisdom which he considers inadequate as a provider of self-knowledge.*]

*As You Like It* is far from being one of Shakespeare's greatest plays, but it is one of his best-loved ones. "I know nothing better than to be in the forest," says a character in Dostoevsky, "though all things are good." We are in a forest, the Forest of Arden, during four-fifths of *As You Like It,* but it is a forest that by some magic lets in perpetual sunshine. And not only do we have a sense of constant natural beauty around us; we are in the presence, too, almost continuously, of a number of the other supremely good things of life, song and laughter, simplicity and love; while to guard against surfeit and keep romance within bounds, there is a seasoning of caustic and even cynical wit, plenty of foolishness as a foil for the wisdom, and, for variety, an intermingling of social worlds from courtiers and courtly exiles to shepherds and country bumpkins. In this last respect *As You Like It* repeats the miracle of *A Midsummer-Night's Dream.*

As might be expected of a work that is a dramatized version of a pastoral romance . . . , the play is the most "natural" and at the same time one of the most artificial of the author's. Yet we so surrender ourselves after a little to its special tone and atmosphere that there is no other work of Shakespeare's in which coincidences, gods from the machine, and what we can only call operatic duets, trios, and quartettes trouble us less or seem less out of place. The snake and lioness that figure in Oliver's sudden conversion might be thought to be enough for one play, but when on top of that in the twinkling of an eye an old religious man turns the cruel usurping Duke, who is on the march with an army against his enemies, into a humble and forgiving hermit, instead of questioning the psychology we accept it meekly and merely observe inwardly that the magic of the Forest of Arden is evidently even more potent than we had supposed. (pp. 281-82)

There is generally an Emersonian sentence that comes as close to summing up a Shakespearean play as anything so brief as a sentence can. "A mind might ponder its thought for ages and not gain so much self-knowledge as the passion of love shall teach it in a day." There, compressed, is the essence of *As You Like It,* and, positively or negatively, almost every scene in it is contrived to emphasize that truth. As *Love's Labour's Lost,* to which Emerson's sentence is almost equally pertinent, has to do with the relation of love and learning, *As You Like It* has to do with the relation of love and wisdom. Rosalind is the author's instrument for making clear what that relation is.

In no other comedy of Shakespeare's is the heroine so all-important as Rosalind is in this one; she makes the play almost as completely as Hamlet does *Hamlet.* She seems ready to transcend the rather light piece in which she finds herself and, if only the plot would let her, to step straight into tragedy. (p. 282)

*As You Like It* has no lack of interesting characters, but most of them grow pretty thin in Rosalind's presence, like match flames in the sun. However less brilliant, Celia suffers less than she otherwise would because of her loyalty and devotion to her cousin and freedom from jealousy of her. Adam, Corin, and Rosalind's father are characters in their own right, but minor ones. Orlando at his best is thoroughly worthy of the woman he loves, but by and large she sets him in the shade. For the rest, Rosalind exposes, without trying to, their one-sidedness or inferiority, whether by actual contact or in the mind of the reader. . . . It is this wholeness of hers by which the others are tried, and in the comparison Touchstone himself (so named possibly for that very reason) fades into a mere

manipulator of words, while that other favorite of the commentators, Jaques, is totally eclipsed.

One way of taking Jaques is to think of him as a picture, duly attenuated, of what Shakespeare himself might have become if he had let experience sour or embitter him, let his critical powers get the better of his imagination, "philosophy" of poetry. As traveler-libertine Jaques has had his day. Now he would turn spectator-cynic and revenge himself on a world that can no longer afford him pleasure, by proving it foul and infected. The more his vision is darkened the blacker, naturally, what he sees becomes in his eyes. He would withdraw from society entirely if he were not so dependent on it for audience. That is his dilemma. So he alternately retreats and darts forth from his retreat to buttonhole anyone who will listen to his railing. But when he tries to rationalize his misanthropy and pass it off as medicine for a sick world, the Duke Senior administers a deserved rebuke. Your very chiding of sin, he tells him, is "mischievous foul sin" [II. vii. 64] itself.

Jaques prides himself on his wit and wisdom. But he succeeds only in proving how little wit and even "wisdom" amount to when indulged in for their own sakes and at the expense of life. His jests and "philosophy" give the effect of having been long pondered in solitude. But the moment he crosses swords with Orlando and Rosalind, the professional is hopelessly outclassed by the amateurs. Extemporaneously they beat him at his own carefully rehearsed game. Being out of love with life,

*Act II. Scene iii. Orlando and Adam. By Robert Smirke (1798).*

Jaques thinks of nothing but himself. Being in love with Rosalind, Orlando thinks of himself last and has both the humility and the insight that love bequeaths. When the two men encounter, Jaques' questions and answers sound studied and affected, Orlando's spontaneous and sincere.

> JAQ.:   Rosalind is your love's name?
> ORL.:   Yes, just.
> JAQ.:   I do not like her name.
> ORL.:   There was no thought of pleasing you when she was christened.
> JAQ.:   What stature is she of?
> ORL.:   Just as high as my heart.
> JAQ.:   You are full of pretty answers. Have you not been acquainted with goldsmiths' wives, and conn'd them out of rings?
> ORL.:   Not so; but I answer you right painted cloth, from whence you have studied your questions.
> JAQ.:   You have a nimble wit: I think 'twas made of Atalanta's heels. Will you sit down with me? and we two will rail against our mistress the world, and all our misery.
> ORL.:   I will chide no breather in the world but myself, against whom I know most faults.
>
> [III. ii. 263-81]

There is not a trace of any false note in that answer. It has the ring of the true modesty and true wisdom that only true love imparts. (pp. 283-84)

Love bestows on those who embrace it the experience and wisdom of the race, compared with which the knowledge schools and foreign lands can offer is at the worst a mere counterfeit and at the best a mere beginning. What wonder that Jaques, after being so thoroughly trounced by the pretty youth whose acquaintance he was seeking a moment before, is glad to sneak away as Orlando enters (what would they have done to him together?), or that Rosalind, after a "Farewell, Monsieur Traveller" [IV. i. 33], turns with relief to her lover.

Even Jaques' most famous speech, his "Seven Ages of Man" as it has come to be called [II. vii. 139-66], which he must have rehearsed more times than the modern schoolboy who declaims it, does not deserve its reputation for wisdom. It sometimes seems as if Shakespeare had invented Adam (that grand reconciliation of servant and man) as Jaques' perfect opposite and let him enter this scene, pat, at the exact moment when Jaques is done describing the "last scene of all" [II. vii. 163], as a living refutation of his picture of old age. How Shakespeare loved to let life obliterate language in this way! And he does it here prospectively as well as retrospectively, for the Senior Duke a second later, by his hospitable welcome of Adam and Orlando, obliterates or at least mitigates Amiens' song of man's ingratitude ("Blow, blow, thou winter wind" [II. vii. 174-90]) that immediately follows.

When I read the commentators on Touchstone, I rub my eyes. You would think to hear most of them that he is a genuinely wise and witty man and that Shakespeare so considered him. That Shakespeare knew he could pass him off for that in a theater may be agreed. What he is is another matter. A "dull fool" [III. ii. 115] Rosalind calls him on one occasion. "O noble fool! a worthy fool!" [II. vii. 33-4] says Jaques on another. It is easy to guess with which of the two Shakespeare came nearer to agreeing. The Elizabethan groundlings had to have their clown. At his best, Touchstone is merely one more

and one of the most inveterate of the author's word-jugglers, and at his worst (as a wit) precisely what Rosalind called him. What he is at his worst as a man justifies still harsher characterization.

In her first speech after he enters the play in the first act, Rosalind describes him as "the cutter-off of Nature's wit" [I. ii. 49-50], and his role abundantly justifies her judgment. "Thou speakest wiser than thou art ware of," she says to him on another occasion, and as if expressly to prove the truth of what she says, Touchstone obligingly replies, "Nay, I shall ne'er be ware of mine own wit till I break my shins against it" [II. iv. 57-9]. Which is plainly Shakespeare's conscious and Touchstone's unconscious way of stating that his wit is low. And his manners are even lower, as he shows when he first accosts Corin and Rosalind rebukes him for his rude tone. . . . Nothing could show more succinctly Rosalind's "democracy" in contrast to Touchstone's snobbery. (No wonder the people thought highly of her, as they did of Hamlet.) The superiority in wisdom of this "clown" to the man who condescends to him comes out, as we might predict it would, a little later.

> TOUCH.:   Wast ever in court, shepherd?
> COR.:     No, truly.
> TOUCH.:   Then thou art damned.
> COR.:     Nay, I hope.
> TOUCH.:   Truly, thou art damned, like an ill-roasted egg all on one side.
>
> [III. ii. 33-8]

It is an almost invariable rule in Shakespeare, as it is in life, that when one man damns another, even in jest, he unconsciously utters judgment on himself, and the rest of the scene, like Touchstone's whole role, is dedicated to showing that he himself is his own ill-roasted egg, all "wit" and word-play and nothing else. (pp. 285-86)

But even with all this mauling, Shakespeare is not done with Touchstone. Having demonstrated to the hilt that his wit instead of sharpening has dulled his wits, he proceeds to show that his wit has also withered his heart. It is in his interlude with Audrey that we see Touchstone at his moral nadir. It will be said, of course, that this episode is pure farce and that to take it seriously is to show lack of humor. The objection need disturb nobody but the man who makes it. For of all the strange things about this man William Shakespeare one of the most remarkable is the fact that he could contrive no scene so theatrical, no stage effect so comic or dialogue so nonsensical, as to protect himself from the insertion right in the midst of it of touches of nature scientific in their veracity. Such was the grip that truth seems to have had on him.

Audrey is generally dismissed as a country wench expressly set up as a butt for Touchstone. And a theater audience can be duly counted on to roar with laughter at her. She is indeed just a goatherd, plain in appearance (though doubtless not as plain as Touchstone would make out) and so unlettered that most words of more than one syllable bewilder her simple wits. Touchstone's literary and mythological puns and allusions are naturally lost on her. But the attentions of this stranger from the court have awakened unwonted emotions and aspirations in her breast, and nothing could be clearer than her desire to be modest and true and pure. Love is the great leveler as well as the great lifter, and Audrey, perhaps for the first time in her life, feels that even she may have a place in God's world. And this is the way Touchstone deals with the emotion he has awakened:

| | |
|---|---|
| TOUCH.: | Truly, I would the gods had made thee poetical. |
| AUD.: | I do not know what ''poetical'' is. Is it honest in deed and word? Is it a true thing? |
| TOUCH.: | No, truly, for the truest poetry is the most feigning; and lovers are given to poetry, and what they swear in poetry may be said as lovers they do feign. |
| AUD.: | Do you wish then that the gods had made me poetical? |
| TOUCH.: | I do, truly; for thou swearest to me thou art honest; now, if thou wert a poet, I might have some hope thou didst feign. |
| AUD.: | Would you not have me honest? |
| TOUCH.: | No, truly, unless thou wert hard-favour'd; for honesty coupled to beauty is to have honey a sauce to sugar. |
| JAQ.: | (Aside): A material fool. |
| AUD.: | Well, I am not fair, and therefore I pray the gods make me honest. |
| TOUCH.: | Truly, and to cast away honesty upon a foul slut were to put good meat into an unclean dish. |
| AUD.: | I am not a slut, though I thank the gods I am foul. |
| TOUCH.: | Well, praised be the gods for thy foulness! sluttishness may come hereafter. |

[III. iii. 15-41]

As ''theater'' this is doubtless what a modern director might call ''surefire stuff.'' As life it comes close to being the sin against the Holy Ghost. Touchstone of course is planning to marry Audrey (''to take that that no man else will'' [V. iv. 59]) and abandon her as soon as he is sick of his bargain, and when Sir Oliver Martext, a marrying parson, enters, he is ready to go ahead with the ceremony then and there. Jaques, who has been eavesdropping, coming forward offers at first to ''give the woman'' [III. iii. 67-72]. But on second thought the scandalous procedure is too much for even him to stomach and he rebukes Touchstone roundly for his conduct, about the best thing Jaques does in the play:

> And will you, being a man of your breeding,
> be married under a bush like a beggar? Get you
> to church, and have a good priest that can tell
> you what marriage is.
>
> [III. iii. 83-6]

But a good priest and a binding marriage are precisely what Touchstone does not want.

Later, Shakespeare treats us to a little encounter between Touchstone and William, the forest youth who ''lays claim'' to Audrey. Setting out to make a fool of him, Touchstone asks him if he is wise.

| | |
|---|---|
| WILL.: | Ay, sir, I have a pretty wit. |
| TOUCH.: | Why, thou sayest well. I do now remember a saying, ''The fool doth think he is wise, but the wise man knows himself to be a fool.'' |

[V. i. 29-32]

But in that case Touchstone stands condemned as a fool by his own rule, for about twenty lines back in this same scene he had said, ''By my troth, we that have good wits have much to answer for'' [V. i. 11-12]. And about ten lines farther on he again convicts himself by his own rule even more convincingly:

| | |
|---|---|
| TOUCH.: | You do love this maid? |
| WILL.: | I do, sir. |
| TOUCH.: | Give me your hand. Art thou learned? |
| WILL.: | No, sir. |
| TOUCH.: | Then learn this of me. . . . |

[V. i. 36-40]

Whereupon, addressing William as ''you clown'' [V. i. 47], he announces that he, Touchstone, is the man who is to marry Audrey, and orders his rival on pain of death to abandon her company, meanwhile drowning him under such a flood of unfamiliar words that the bewildered youth is only too glad to decamp. ''Oh, but Touchstone's threats to kill are just jest,'' it will be said, ''and his superiority and condescension just mock-heroics and mock-pedantics. Again you are guilty of taking seriously what is mere fooling, making a mountain out of a molehill of the text, and treating William as if he were a real human being instead of the theatrical puppet that he is.'' (As if Shakespeare did not make even his most minor characters human beings!) Granted that to Touchstone the whole thing is a huge joke; that does not make his torrent of talk any less perplexing or menacing to William, nor the theft of Audrey any less mean or immoral. It is merely a consummation of what this man in motley has revealed throughout; his snobbery and bad manners, and ultimately his hard heart. Touchstone, if you insist, is making a fool of this rustic simpleton, William. It is another William who is making a fool of Touchstone.

So even the tormented comes off better than the tormentor. Indeed nearly everybody in the play does who comes in contact with Touchstone. ''A touchstone,'' says the dictionary, is ''a black siliceous stone used to test the purity of gold and silver by the streak left on the stone when rubbed by the metal.'' Not precious itself, it reveals preciousness in what touches it. That seems to be precisely the function assigned to Touchstone in this play, so perhaps its author knew what he was doing when he named him. Near the end two of the banished Duke's pages enter and Touchstone asks them for a song. They comply with his request by singing:

> It was a lover and his lass,
>
> [V. iii. 16ff.]

and when they are done Touchstone rewards them by remarking, ''Truly, young gentlemen, though there was no great matter in the ditty, yet the note was very untuneable'' [V. iii. 34-6]. ''You are deceived, sir,'' the First Page protests, ''we kept time; we lost not our time'' [V. iii. 37-8]. ''By my troth, yes,'' Touchstone persists, ''I count it but time lost to hear such a foolish song'' [V. iii. 39-40]. Here again Shakespeare lets Touchstone judge himself in judging others, for though as manikin he will doubtless long continue to entertain the crowd in the theater, as man he is even more empty of both matter and music than the foolish song he counts it time lost to listen to. Touchstone is ''wit'' without love.

And Rosalind is wit with love, which is humor, humor being what wit turns into when it falls in love. But humor is almost a synonym for many-sidedness and reconciliation of opposites, and in her versatility, her balance of body, mind, and spirit, Rosalind reminds us of no less a figure than Hamlet himself, the uncontaminated Hamlet. As there is a woman within the Prince of Denmark, so there is a man within this Duke's daughter, but never at the sacrifice of her dominant feminine nature. ''Do you not know I am a woman? when I think, I must speak,'' she says to Celia [III. ii. 249-50]. She changes color when she first suspects that the verses on the trees are Orlando's, and cries "Alas the day! what shall I do with my doublet and hose?" [III. ii. 219-20] when the fact that he is in the Forest is confirmed. And she swoons when she hears he is wounded. Yes, Rosalind is a woman in spite of the strength and courage of the man within her. All of which makes her disguise as a boy immeasurably more than a merely theatrical matter. . . . Rosalind is . . . fair and wise and strong and rich (except in a worldly sense) and generous. But not in vain. For she has also, as her name betokens, the untaught strain that sheds beauty on a rose. The Forest of Arden, for all its trees, is, as we remarked, forever flooded with sunshine. There is no mystery about it. Rosalind is in the Forest and she supplies it with an internal light. "Be like the sun," says Dostoevsky. Rosalind is. She attracts everything that comes within her sphere and sheds a radiance over it. She is the pure gold that needs no touchstone.

Rosalind has the world at her feet not just for what she is but because, being what she is, she so conducts her love with Orlando as to make it a pattern for all true love-making. Unimaginative love, whether sentimental or overpassionate, overreaches and defeats itself because it cannot keep its secret. Intentionally or otherwise, it spills over—confesses or gives itself away. . . . The love of Silvius for Phebe and of Phebe for Ganymede in this play are examples. Imaginative love is wiser. Taking its cue from the arts, of which it is one and perhaps the highest, it creates a hypothetical case in its own image, a kind of celestial trap under cover of which (only the maddest mixture of metaphors can do it justice) it extorts an unconscious confession from the loved one, all the while keeping a line of retreat fully open in case the confession should be unfavorable, in order that no humiliation may ensue.

In this play Rosalind undertakes to cure Orlando of his love by having him come every day to woo her under the illusion that she is just the boy Ganymede impersonating Rosalind. Thus the love between the two is rehearsed in the kingdom of the imagination, where all true love begins, before any attempt is made to bring it down to the level of everyday life, a situation that permits both lovers to speak now as boldly, now as innocently, as though they were angels or children. (pp. 288-92)

Again we are reminded of the Prince of Denmark. In *Hamlet* a literal play within the play becomes a device (inspired or infernal according to your interpretation of the play) whereby to catch the guilty conscience of a murderer. Here a metaphorical "play" within the play becomes a celestial trap in which to expose the tender heart of a lover. Heaven and hell are at opposite poles, but the one is a model of the other. "Upward, downward," says Heraclitus, "the way is the same." It is not chance that *As You Like It* and *Hamlet* were written not far apart in time.

Love between man and woman having the importance that it does in life, what wonder that a drama that depicts it in perfect action under its happiest aspect should be popular, even though not one in a hundred understands the ground of its fascination. (p. 292)

Harold C. Goddard, "'As You Like It'," in his *The Meaning of Shakespeare, The University of Chicago Press,* 1951, pp. 281-93.

## MILTON CRANE   (essay date 1951)

[*In the following excerpt, Crane describes Shakespeare's use of verse and prose in* As You Like It, *claiming that, in this work, prose is the norm and verse the exception. Nevertheless, he continues, the two maintain a close balance: verse is for "scenes of higher emotional tension, for the idyllic atmosphere of the forest," for "Jaques's moralizing and melancholy reflections, and for the burlesqued pastoral amours of Phebe and Silvius." Prose, on the other hand, is the play's "normal, flexible, and colloquial mode of speech," most often used to undercut the pastoral linguistic conventions of the romantic characters. Like many earlier critics, Crane singles out Rosalind's prose passages for special praise, maintaining that Rosalind "thinks in prose terms" and is never really comfortable in verse. The reason for this, he suggests, is that verse is uncongenial to her satrical humor, prose being the natural expression of the "detached and skeptical intellectual."*]

The prose of *As You Like It* . . . , as Rosalind says of Time, ambles, trots, gallops and—rarely, to be sure—stands still. It has great variety of movement because virtually every character in the play makes use of it at one time or another. Prose, both at the court and in the Forest of Arden, is the normal, flexible, and colloquial mode of speech; verse usually brings an unfamiliar and serious tone into the otherwise light-hearted play.

The play opens with a prose speech by Orlando, briefly summarizing his situation. It is one of the shortest and lamest exposition-scenes in any of the plays; but one is not permitted to dwell on its shortcomings (including the absurdity of telling Adam what the old man already knows) because the entrance of Oliver at once brings violent action. Further exposition is provided, after the brothers' fight, by the conversation of Charles and Oliver.

The second scene opens with the witty prose dialogue of Rosalind and Celia, which continues with the entrance of Touchstone. After Orlando's triumph, the Duke asks the victor his name, and shows his heightened emotional tension by changing to verse. He leaves at the end of the speech, but the scene continues in its new tone and in verse to the end. A similar pattern is followed in the next scene: the cousins chat together in prose until the Duke and his lords come to banish Rosalind, after which all speak verse.

In II, iv, Rosalind, Celia, and Touchstone have arrived at the Forest, and joke in prose about the discomfort of their journey. Corin and Silvius have a short verse interlude to discuss the latter's love-pains. Touchstone resumes his clown's function and breaks into Rosalind's romantic musing by describing in prose his courting of Jane Smile. Here, in a single scene, is the play's division of media.

Orlando addresses a formal invocation to the poem which he pins on a tree (III, ii); the speech consists of two quatrains, alternately rhymed, and a final couplet. If Shakespeare gives Orlando so elaborate and artificial a form, it is with a double purpose: an extremely long and witty prose scene is to follow, providing the maximum contrast in form and idea to the lover's words and actions; and echoes of Orlando's speech will recur in the poems later found and read aloud by Rosalind and Celia. Orlando, then, is permitted to state a theme which will later be parodied in his own mode, and mocked in the prose which Rosalind will always find her more natural medium.

Parody and burlesque are not the prerogative of the clown alone in this play, but they find more direct expression in Touchstone than in Rosalind. His account of the wooing of Jane Smile assumes flesh in the courting of Audrey, which is placed neatly between the beginning of the Orlando-Rosalind romance and the introduction of Silvius and Phebe. For the latter plot of the swooning lover and cruel charmer, Shakespeare employs his lushest verse—and unmercifully makes it in Rosalind's prose.

Rosalind and Jaques' prose discussion of melancholy, at the beginning of Act IV, is broken by Orlando's entrance. His one line of verse, "Good day and happiness, dear Rosalind!" elicits Jaques' sarcastic rejoinder, "Nay then, God b'wi' you, an you talk in blank verse!" [IV. i. 30-2]—a further indication of the equation of prose with naturalness.

Silvius interrupts the prose dialogue of Rosalind and Celia in IV, iii, to discuss in verse the unhappy errand on which Phebe has sent him. As soon as Rosalind begins to read the verse letter, she punctuates it with waspish prose comments, and, at last, breaks out in a prose tirade. The realism of prose is employed to criticize the lover's foolishness. Oliver's story brings verse for a heightening of tension which is not dispelled by Rosalind's later jesting in prose.

V, ii, has a formal little verse masque in which Silvius states a theme and is echoed by the other three lovers. But Rosalind's ironic participation cannot long amuse her, and she restores common sense in prose:

> Pray you, no more of this; 'tis like the howling
> of Irish wolves against the moon.
>
> [V. ii. 109-10]

The final scene introduces prose, after Rosalind's promise of a satisfactory conclusion, for Touchstone's extended *jeu d'esprit* [witticism] on the punctilio of the quarrel. The revelation of identity and the short masque are naturally in verse, as are Jaques de Boys' news and Jaques' general summation. But Rosalind, as always, has the last word in her prose Epilogue.

Looking back on this play, which rests on a solid base of prose, one finds a closer balance between verse and prose than one might expect. There is verse for the scenes of higher emotional tension, for the idyllic atmosphere of the forest as dominated by Duke Senior, for Jaques' moralizing and melancholy reflections, and for the burlesqued pastoral amours of Phebe and Silvius—but, when the play seeks its level, it returns inevitably to prose. Rosalind must in large part be thanked for the dominance of prose, because she is never really comfortable in verse, a medium quite uncongenial to her satirical humour. She is the reasonable woman, for all her weakness, and what she wants to say she can hardly express in verse. She is the woman who is uniquely privileged in being able to assume an unparalleled objectivity in discussing her love with her lover; the quality of that discussion demands prose. Rosalind rules the play and thereby makes prose supreme. But the rest have discovered the trick without waiting for her lead. Orlando's prose is better than his verse, although there is little to choose between them. Even Charles the wrestler can use the form brilliantly:

> They say he is already in the Forest of Arden,
> and a many merry men with him; and there
> they live like the old Robin Hood of England.
> They say many young gentlemen flock to him
> every day, and fleet the time carelessly as they
> did in the golden world.
>
> [I. i. 114-19]

Both in the golden world and in the Forest, all can express themselves in this admirable and facile prose. And the verse, however good, must doubly justify itself—as it does—to gain entrance.

The large body of prose is present in the play not merely because this is a comedy, but because it is a very special sort of comedy. Rosalind's unique license in the play explains her oscillation between the poles of romantic love and her realistic, occasionally cynical comic attitude. It must further be said that Rosalind, even at her most romantic, is never completely free from skepticism. When she is deeply concerned at Orlando's tardiness at the first meeting of the course in love, she seems as much amused at her own fits of passion as she is at Orlando's. Rosalind's great charm lies in this combination of elements, yet one cannot for a moment doubt the supremacy of the skepticism.

She is not utterly disillusioned like Jaques, to whom she is opposed; his skepticism has reached the final stage of self-consuming melancholy. There are definite bounds to Rosalind's cynicism: no more obvious proof could be asked than the fact of her marriage to Orlando. Jaques' delight in melancholy is perverse; Rosalind seeks only a humorous objectivity which will let her see the world in the only terms that her healthy and realistic mind will tolerate. This mind thinks in prose terms; for prose, in Shakespeare, is necessarily the expression of the detached and skeptical intellectual. Rosalind's position in the play permits her to give the freest possible rein to these qualities. Her disguise puts her at a remove from all the characters. It is small wonder that, in this comedy, a detached mind in a detached situation is given some of Shakespeare's most brilliant comic prose to speak. *Hamlet* will show the reverse of this coin: the skeptical mind fettered by circumstances and by itself. (pp. 101-04)

*Milton Crane, "Shakespeare: The Comedies," in his* Shakespeare's Prose, *The University of Chicago Press, 1951, pp. 66-127.*

## HAROLD JENKINS (lecture date 1953)

[*Jenkins is an English academic and scholar who has written extensively on English Renaissance literature, especially Shakespeare's drama, and has served as a general editor of the New Arden Shakespeare. In the following excerpt, he examines Shakespeare's comic method in* As You Like It. *He argues that, compared with* Twelfth Night *and* Much Ado about Nothing, *"As You Like It is conspicuously lacking in comedy's more robust and boisterous elements." Action, he continues, does not seem to be the "first essential" of* As You Like It, *in that the play lacks big theatrical scenes and its events are not usually linked "by the logical intricacies of cause and effect." However, a partial exception, he points out, is Act I, which, although perfunctory, is nevertheless crucial to our proper understanding of the Arden scenes. Jenkins then compares* As You Like It *to* Love's Labour's Lost, *finding the "constant little shifts and changes" in the former more complex than the latter's "formal parallelisms." Commenting on these comic juxtapositions in* As You Like It, *Jenkins especially praises Jaques's and Touchstone's antithetical contributions to Shakespeare's pastoral theme. But the critic notes that each judgment in the play, even those of Touchstone and Jaques, is always modified by another permitting "an all-embracing view far larger and more satisfying than any one [judgment] in itself." Jenkins's essay was originally delivered as a lecture before the Shakespeare Conference at Stratford-upon-Avon, August 18, 1953.*]

A masterpiece is not to be explained, and to attempt to explain it is apt to seem ridiculous. I must say at once that I propose nothing so ambitious. I merely hope, by looking at one play, even in what must necessarily be a very fragmentary way and with my own imperfect sight, to illustrate something of what Shakespeare's method in comedy may be. And I have chosen *As You Like It* because it seems to me to exhibit, most clearly of all the comedies, Shakespeare's characteristic excellences in this kind. This is not to say that *As You Like It* is exactly a representative specimen. Indeed I am going to suggest that it is not. In this play, what I take to be Shakespeare's distinctive virtues as a writer of comedy have their fullest scope; but in order that they may have it, certain of the usual ingredients of Shakespeare's comedy, or indeed of any comedy, have to be— not of course eliminated, but very much circumscribed. In *As You Like It,* I suggest, Shakespeare took his comedy in one direction nearly as far as it could go. And then, as occasionally happens in Shakespeare's career, when he has developed his art far in one direction, in the comedy which succeeds he seems to readjust his course.

If our chronology is right, after *As You Like It* comes, among the comedies, *Twelfth Night.* . . . [In] some important respects, [this comedy] returns to the method and structure of the previous comedy of *Much Ado About Nothing.* Sandwiched between these two, *As You Like It* is conspicuously lacking in comedy's more robust and boisterous elements—the pomps of Dogberry [in *Much Ado about Nothing*] and the romps of Sir Toby [in *Twelfth Night*]. More significantly, it has nothing which corresponds to the splendid theatricalism of the church scene in *Much Ado,* nothing which answers to those crucial bits of trickery by which Benedick and Beatrice in turn are hoodwinked into love. . . . The slandering of Hero in *Much Ado* also is to have its counterpart in *Twelfth Night.* For the slandering of Hero, with its culmination in the church scene, forces one pair of lovers violently apart while bringing another pair together. And in *Twelfth Night* the confusion of identities holds one pair of lovers—Orsino and Viola— temporarily apart, yet forces another pair—Olivia and Sebastian—with some violence together. A satisfactory outcome in *Much Ado* and *Twelfth Night* depends on such embroilments; and the same is even more true in an earlier comedy like *A Midsummer Night's Dream.* In *As You Like It* I can hardly say that such embroilments do not occur, but they are not structural to anything like the same degree. Without the heroine's masculine disguise Phebe would not have married Silvius any more than in *Twelfth Night* Olivia would have married Sebastian; but the confusions of identity in *As You Like It* have no influence whatever upon the ultimate destiny of Rosalind and Orlando, or of the kingdom of Duke Senior, or of the estate of Sir Rowland de Boys. Yet these are the destinies with which the action of the play is concerned. It is in the defectiveness of its action that *As You Like It* differs from the rest of the major comedies—in its dearth not only of big theatrical scenes but of events linked together by the logical intricacies of cause and effect. Of comedy, as of tragedy, action is the first essential; but *As You Like It* suggests that action is not, if I may adapt a phrase of Marston's, "the life of these things". It may be merely the foundation on which they are built. And *As You Like It* further shows that on a very flimsy foundation, if only you are skilful enough, a very elaborate structure may be poised. (pp. 40-1)

A man has died and left three sons. Three is the inevitable number, and though Shakespeare . . . forgets to do much with the middle one, he is not therefore unimportant. The eldest brother is wicked, the youngest virtuous—and does fabulous feats of strength, notably destroying a giant in the shape of Charles the wrestler, who has torn other hopeful youths to pieces. Orlando therefore wins the princess, herself the victim of a wicked uncle, who has usurped her father's throne. This is the *story* of *As You Like It.* And Shakespeare . . . gets most of it over in the first act. That is what is remarkable. By the time we reach the second act Rosalind has already come safe to the Forest of Arden, by the aid of her man's disguise. From

this disguise, as everybody knows, springs the principal comic situation of the play. But such is the inconsequential nature of the action that this comic situation develops only when the practical need for the disguise is past. The course of true love has not run smooth. But most of its obstacles have really disappeared before the main comedy begins. It only remains for the wicked to be converted, as they duly are at the end, all in comedy's good but arbitrary time, when the wicked eldest brother makes a suitable husband for the second princess. Or a most *un*suitable husband, as all the critics have complained. But this, I think, is to misunderstand. Instead of lamenting that Celia should be thrown away on Oliver, he having been much too wicked to deserve her, we should rather see that Oliver's getting this reward is a seal set on his conversion, and a sign of how good he has now become.

The first act of *As You Like It* has to supply the necessary minimum of event. But, Quiller-Couch notwithstanding, this first act is something more than mechanical [see excerpt above, 1918]. It is for one thing a feat of compression, rapid, lucid and, incidentally, theatrical. In fifty lines we know all about the three brothers and the youngest is at the eldest's throat. In three hundred more we know all about the banished Duke and where and how he lives, and the giant has been destroyed before our eyes. But there is more to the first act than this. Before we enter Arden, to "fleet the time carelessly, as they did in the golden world" [I. i. 118-19], we must be able to contrast its simple life with the brittle refinement of the court. This surely is the point of some of what [Quiller-Couch] called the "rather pointless chop-logic"; and also of the courtier figure of Le Beau, a little sketch for Osric [in *Hamlet*], with his foppery of diction and his expert knowledge of sport. Le Beau's notion of sport provokes Touchstone's pointed comment on the courtier's values: "Thus men may grow wiser every day: it is the first time that ever I heard breaking of ribs was sport for ladies" [I. ii. 138-39]. This *is* the callousness one learns at a court ruled by a tyrannous Duke, whose malevolent rage against Rosalind and Orlando not only drives them both to Arden but completes the picture of the world they leave behind.

This first act, then, shows some instinct for dramatic preparation, though we may grant that Shakespeare's haste to get ahead makes him curiously perfunctory. He is in two minds about when Duke Senior was banished; and about which Duke is to be called Frederick; and whether Rosalind or Celia is the taller. He has not quite decided about the character of Touchstone. I do not think these are signs of revision. They simply show Shakespeare plunging into his play with some of its details still but half-shaped in his mind. The strangest of these details is the mysterious middle brother, called Fernandyne by Lodge but merely "Second Brother" in *As You Like It,* when at length he makes his appearance at the end. Yet in the fifth line of the play he was already christened Jaques. And Shakespeare of course afterwards gave this name to someone else. It seems clear enough that these two men with the same name were originally meant to be one. As things turned out Jaques could claim to have acquired his famous melancholy from travel and experience; but I suspect that it really began in the schoolbooks which were studied with such profit by Jaques de Boys. Though he grew into something very different, Jaques surely had his beginnings in the family of De Boys and in such an academy as that in Navarre [in *Love's Labour's Lost*] where four young men turned their backs on love and life in the belief that they could supply the want of experience by study and contemplation.

Interesting as it might be to develop this idea, the important point of comparison between *As You Like It* and *Love's Labour's Lost* is of another kind. . . . *Love's Labour's Lost* is the most formally constructed of all the comedies. When the ladies and gentlemen temporarily exchange partners, this is done symmetrically and to order. Indeed the movement of the whole play is like a well-ordered dance in which each of the participants repeats the steps of the others. But this is exactly what does *not* happen in *As You Like It,* where the characters do *not* keep in step. When they *seem* to be doing the same thing they are really doing something different, and if they ever echo one another they mean quite different things by what they say—as could easily be illustrated from the little quartet of lovers in the fifth act (''And so am I for Phebe.—And I for Ganymede.—And I for Rosalind.—And I for no woman'' [V. ii. 99-102]), where the similarity of the tune they sing conceals their different situations. The pattern of *As You Like It* comes not from a mere repetition of steps, but from constant little shifts and changes. The formal parallelisms of *Love's Labour's Lost* are replaced by a more complex design, one loose enough to hold all sorts of asymmetries within it. (pp. 41-3)

In *As You Like It* the art of comic juxtaposition is at its subtlest. It is to give it fullest scope that the action can be pushed up into a corner, and the usual entanglements of plotting, though not dispensed with altogether, can be loosened. Freedom, of course, is in the hospitable air of Arden. . . . This is ''the golden world'' to which, with the beginning of his second act, Shakespeare at once transports us, such a world as has been the dream of poets since at least the time of Virgil when, wearied with the toilings and wranglings of society, they yearn for the simplicity and innocence of what they choose to think man's natural state. It is of course a very literary tradition that Shakespeare is here using, but the long vogue of the pastoral suggests that it is connected with a universal impulse of the human mind, to which Shakespeare in *As You Like It* gives permanent expression. But this aspect of the play is merely the one which confronts us most conspicuously. There are many others. *As You Like It* has been too often praised for its idyllic quality alone, as though it were some mere May-morning frolic prolonged into a lotos-eating afternoon. A contrast with the ideal state was necessitated by the literary tradition itself, since the poet seeking an escape into the simple life was expected to hint at the ills of the society he was escaping from. That meant especially the courts of princes, where life—it was axiomatic—was at its most artificial. And the vivid sketching in of the courtly half of the antithesis is, as I have shown, an important function of *As You Like It*'s maligned first act. With the first speech of the banished Duke at the opening of the second act, the complete contrast is before us; for, while introducing us to Arden, this speech brings into sharp focus that first act which has just culminated in the usurper's murderous malice. ''Are not these woods more free from peril than the envious court?'' [II. i. 3-4] Though the contrast is traditional, it comes upon us here, like so many things in Shakespeare, with the vitality of fresh experience. The Forest of Arden comes to life in numerous little touches of the country-side, and the heartless self-seeking of the outer world is concentrated into phrases which have the force of permanent truth. The line that [Quiller-Couch] admired—''And unregarded age in corners thrown'' [II. iii. 42]—might have come from one of the sonnets, and when Orlando observes how ''none will sweat but for promotion'' [II. iii. 60] we recognize the fashion of our times as well as his. As the play proceeds, it is easy enough for Shakespeare to keep us ever aware of the forest, what with Amiens to sing for us, the procession home after the killing of the deer,

an empty cottage standing ready for Rosalind and Celia, surrounded by olive-trees beyond a willow stream, and a good supply of oaks for Orlando or Oliver to lie under. It cannot have been quite so easy to keep us in touch with the court life we have now abandoned; but nothing is neater in the construction of the play than those well-placed little scenes which, by despatching first Orlando and then Oliver to the forest, do what is still required by the story and give the illusion that an action is still going briskly forward, while at the same time they renew our acquaintance with the wicked world. After the first scene in the ideal world of Arden and a sentimental discourse on the deer, there is Frederick again in one of his rages, sending for Oliver, who, an act later, when we are well acclimatized to the forest, duly turns up at court. Then occurs a scene of eighteen lines, in which Shakespeare gives as vivid a sketch of the unjust tyrant as one could hope to find. (pp. 43-4)

The contrast between court and country is thus presented and our preference is very plain. Yet as a counterpoise to all this, there is one man in the country-side who actually prefers the court. Finding himself in Arden, Touchstone decides: ''When I was at home, I was in a better place'' [II. iv. 17]. It is no doubt important that he is a fool, whose values may well be topsy-turvy. But in one word he reminds us that there are such things as domestic comforts. And presently we find that the old man whom society throws into the corner is likely in the ''uncouth forest'' [II. vi. 6] to die of hunger and exposure to the ''bleak air'' [II. vi. 15]. There is clearly something to be said on the other side; the fool may anatomize the wise man's folly. And there is also Jaques to point out that the natural life in Arden, where men usurp the forest from the deer and kill them in their ''native dwelling-place'' [II. i. 63], while deer, like men, are in distress abandoned by their friends, is as cruel and unnatural as the other. When Amiens sings under the greenwood tree and turns ''his merry note unto the sweet bird's throat'' [II. v. 3-4], inviting us to shun ambition and be pleased with what we get, Jaques adds a further stanza to the song which suggests that to leave your ''wealth and ease'' is the act of an ass or a fool [II. v. 52]. Most of us, I suppose, have moods in which we would certainly agree with him, and it is a mark of Shakespeare's mature comedy that he permits this criticism of his ideal world in the very centre of it. The triumphal procession after the killing of the deer, a symbolic ritual of the forester's prowess, is accompanied by a mocking song, while the slayer of the deer is given its horns to wear as a somewhat ambiguous trophy.

It is Jaques, mostly, with the touch of the medieval buffoon in him, who contributes this grotesque element to the songs and rituals of Arden. Like Touchstone he is not impressed by Arden, but unlike Touchstone he does not prefer the court. Indeed, as we have seen, he is able to show that they are very much alike, infected by the same diseases. No doubt his is a jaundiced view of life, and it is strange that some earlier critics should have thought it might be Shakespeare's. Shakespeare's contemporaries would hardly have had difficulty in recognizing in Jaques a variant of the Elizabethan melancholy man—the epithet is applied to him often enough—though I remain a little sceptical when I am told by O. J. Campbell that from the first moment they heard Jaques described, the Elizabethans would have perceived ''the unnatural melancholy produced by the adustion of phlegm'' [see excerpt above, 1935]. Whatever its physiological kind, the important thing about his melancholy is that it it is not the fatigue of spirits of the man who has found the world too much for him, but an active principle manifesting itself in tireless and exuberant antics. Far from being a morose man, whether he is weeping with the stag or jeering at the huntsman, he throws himself into these things with something akin to passion. His misanthropy is a form of self-indulgence, as is plain enough in his very first words. . . . His own comparison with a weasel sucking eggs suggests what a ferocious and life-destroying thing this passion is. Shakespeare's final dismissal of Jaques is profound. Far from making Celia a better husband than Oliver . . . , he is the one person in the play who could not be allowed to marry anyone, since he can have nothing to do with either love or generation. His attempt to forward the nuptials of Touchstone and Audrey serves only to postpone them. He is of course the one consistent character in the play in that he declines to go back with the others to the court that they have scorned. Yet how *can* he go back when the court has been converted? Jaques's occupation's gone. And he will not easily thrive away from the social life on which he feeds. It is notable that the place he really covets, or affects to, is that of the motley fool, licensed to mock at society, indulged by society but not of it. Yet, seeking for a fool, he has only to look in the brook to find one; and it is the romantic hero who will tell him so.

Shakespeare, then, builds up his ideal world and lets his idealists scorn the real one. But into their midst he introduces people who mock their ideals and others who mock *them*. One must not say that Shakespeare never judges, but one judgement is always being modified by another. Opposite views may contradict one another, but of course they do not cancel out. Instead they add up to an all-embracing view far larger and more satisfying than any one of them in itself. (pp. 44-5)

So far I have dealt only with the immigrants to Arden. There is of course a native population. The natural world of the poet's dreams has always been inhabited by shepherds, who from the time of Theocritus have piped their songs of love. And Rosalind and Celia have been in the forest for only twenty lines when two shepherds appear pat before them. In an earlier comedy perhaps these might have been a similar pair singing comparable love-ditties. But in *As You Like It*—Shakespeare making the most of what is offered him by Lodge—they are a contrasting pair. One is young and one is old, one is in love and one is not. The lover is the standard type. But the notion of love has undergone a change since classical times and the shepherds of Renaissance pastorals have all been bred in the schools of courtly love. So young Silvius is the faithful abject lover who finds disdain in his fair shepherdess's eye and sighs "upon a midnight pillow" [II. iv. 27]—Shakespeare always fixes on a detail in which a whole situation is epitomized. There are of course many other lovers in the play, but the story of Silvius and Phebe is of the pure pastoral world, the familiar literary norm against which all the others may be measured. First against Silvius and Phebe are set Rosalind and Orlando, and the immediate result of this is that Rosalind and Orlando, though they clearly belong to the pastoral world, seem much closer to the ordinary one. Indeed, since Silvius and Phebe relieve them of the necessity of displaying the lovers' more extravagant postures, Rosalind and Orlando are freer to act like human beings. Rosalind need only play at taunting her adorer while allowing her real woman's heart to be in love with him in earnest. In an earlier comedy like *The Two Gentlemen of Verona* the heroes themselves had to undergo those "bitter fasts, with penitential groans, With nightly tears and daily heart-sore sighs" [*The Two Gentlemen of Verona*, II. iv. 131-32]. . . . But with Silvius to take this burden from him, Orlando can really be a hero, performing the traditional hero's fabulous feats, and upon occasion may even be a common man

like ourselves. He has, for example, the very human trait of unpunctuality; he is twice late for an appointment. And although on one occasion he has the perfect excuse of a bloody accident, on the other he has nothing to say, beyond "My fair Rosalind, I come within an hour of my promise" [IV. i. 42-3]. Such engaging casualness is of course outside Silvius's range. And although Orlando has his due share of lovers' sighs and is indeed the "unfortunate he" who hangs the verses on the trees [III. ii. 395], in so human a creature these love-gestures appear not as his *raison d'être* but as an aberration. A delightful aberration, no doubt—"I would not be cured, youth", he says [III. ii. 425]—but still an aberration that can be the legitimate subject of our mockery. Lying contemplating his love under an oak, he seems to Celia "like a dropped acorn" [III. ii. 235], and both the ladies smile at his youthful lack of beard. But Orlando is robust enough to stand their mockery and ours, and Shakespeare's superb dramatic tact arranges that Orlando shall draw our laughter towards him so that he may protect the fragile Silvius from the ridicule which would destroy *him*. Rosalind alone is privileged to make fun of Silvius; and that because searching his wounds, she finds her own. The encounters which do not occur have their significance as well as those which do: Touchstone is only once, and Jaques never, allowed a sight of Silvius before the final scene of the play. Silvius has not to be destroyed or the play will lack something near its centre.

If in a pastoral play the ideal shepherd is satirized it must be indirectly. But that he is, through his complete unreality, a likely target for satire has been commonly recognized by the poets, who have therefore had a habit of providing him with a burlesque counterpart to redress the balance and show that they did know what rustics were like in real life. As Gay was to put it in his proem to *The Shepherd's Week*, the shepherd "sleepeth not under myrtle shades, but under a hedge"; and so when Gay's shepherd makes love it is in a sly kiss behind a haycock to the accompaniment of the lady's yells of laughter. This may have been the method of Shakespeare's William, for, far from inditing verses to his mistress, William is singularly tongue-tied; though he is "five and twenty" [V. i. 19] and thinks he has "a pretty wit" [V. i. 29], the biggest of his eleven speeches is only seven words long. And his partner is just as much a contrast to the shepherdess of pastoral legend. She thanks the gods she is not beautiful, does not even know the meaning of "poetical", and her sheep, alas, are goats.

Shakespeare, then, presents the conventional pastoral, and duly burlesques it. But with a surer knowledge of life than many poets have had, he seems to suspect that the burlesque as well as the convention may also miss the truth. Do shepherds really sleep under hedges? In order to be unsophisticated, must they be stupid too? So among his varied array of shepherds, Silvius and Ganymede and William, Shakespeare introduces yet another shepherd, the only one who knows anything of sheep, whose hands even get greasy with handling them. . . . [Corin] speaks at once of grazing and shearing and an unkind master; and when he talks about the shepherd's life he shows that he knows the value of money and that fat sheep need good pasture. His greatest pride is to see his ewes graze and his lambs suck. This is the note of his philosophy, and if it has its limitations, it is far from despicable and is splendidly anchored to fact. His attitude to love is that of the fully sane man undisturbed by illusions. Being a man, he has been in love and can still guess what it is like; but it is so long ago he has forgotten all the details. . . . In *As You Like It* perpetual youth is the happiness of Silvius, and his fate. *That* much of the difference between Silvius and Corin is apparent from the short dialogue of twenty lines which first introduces them together to us.

In Corin Shakespeare provides us with a touchstone with which to test the pastoral. Corin's dialogue with the Touchstone of the court, dropped into the middle of the play, adds to the conventional antithesis, between courtier and countryman a glimpse of the real thing. Our picture of the court as a place of tyranny, ambition and corruption is no doubt true enough. But its colours are modified somewhat when Touchstone gives us the court's plain routine. For him, as he lets us know on another occasion, the court is the place where he has trod a measure, flattered a lady, been smooth with his enemy and undone three tailors. Though Touchstone seeks to entangle Corin in the fantastications of his wit, his arguments to show that the court is better than the sheepfarm have a way of recoiling on himself. What emerges from the encounter of these two realists is that ewe and ram, like man and woman, are put together and that though the courtier perfumes his body it sweats like any other creature's. In city or country, *all* ways of life are at bottom the same, and we recognize a conclusion that Jaques, by a different route, has helped us to reach before.

The melancholy moralizings of Jaques and the Robin Hood raptures of the Duke, though in contrast, are equally the product of man's spirit. There has to be someone in Arden to remind us of the indispensable flesh. It was a shrewd irony of Shakespeare's to give this office to the jester. Whether he is wiser or more foolish than other men it is never possible to decide, but Touchstone is, as well as the most artificial wit, the most natural man of them all; and the most conscious of his corporal needs. . . . This preoccupation with the physical makes Touchstone the obvious choice for the sensual lover who will burlesque the romantic dream. So Touchstone not only deprives the yokel William of his mistress, but steals his part in the play, making it in the process of infinitely greater significance. (pp. 46-8)

The fool is not only a material touchstone; he is also the time-keeper of the play. At least, in the forest, where "there's no clock" [III. ii. 300-01], he carries a time-piece with him; and it provokes the reflection: "It is ten o'clock . . . 'Tis but an hour ago since it was nine, And after one hour more 'twill be eleven" [II. vii. 22, 24-5]. The people of Arcadia will do well to take note of this, but if all you can do with your hours is to count them, this undeniable truth may seem a trifle futile. Touchstone, to do him justice, goes on: "And so, from hour to hour, we ripe and ripe, And then, from hour to hour, we rot and rot" [II. vii. 26-7]. He dares to speak in Arcadia, where one can never grow old, of Time's inevitable processes of maturity and decay. By this the ideal life of the banished Duke is mocked, and since Touchstone's words are repeated by Jaques with delighted and uproarious laughter, the mockery is double. Yet, in accordance with the play's principle of countering one view with another, there are two things that may be noted: first, that in a later scene Touchstone, who sums up life as riping and rotting, is compared by Rosalind to a medlar, which is rotten before it is ripe; and second, that it is at this very point, when the ideal life is doubly mocked, that the Duke administers to the mocker Jaques a direct and fierce rebuke, charging the mocker of the world's vices with having lived a vicious life himself.

The satirist, of course, is far from silenced; it is now that he ridicules the romantic hero, and presently he delivers his famous speech on the seven ages of man, brilliantly summing up the course of human life, but omitting to notice anything in it that is noble or even pleasant. However, as has often been observed, though the seven ages speech ends with a description of man's final decrepitude—"sans teeth, sans eyes, sans taste, sans everything" [II. vii. 166]—it has not yet left the speaker's tongue when an aged man appears who is at once addressed as "venerable" [II. vii. 167]. There is always this readjustment of the point of view. Senility and venerableness—are they different things or different ways of looking at the same? Certainly the entry of the venerable Adam does not disprove what Jaques says; Shakespeare seeks no cheap antithesis. "Sans teeth"—Adam himself has admitted to being toothless, Orlando has called him "a rotten tree" [II. ii. 63], and his helplessness is only too visible when he is *carried* on to the stage. Yet he *is* carried, tenderly, by the master whom he has followed "to the last gasp, with truth and loyalty" [II. iii. 70]. Here is the glimpse of human virtue that the seven ages speech omitted. And then it is upon this moving spectacle of mutual affection and devotion that Amiens sings his song, "Blow, blow, thou winter wind, Thou art not so unkind As man's ingratitude" [II. vii. 174-90]. Placed here, this lovely lyric, blend of joy and pathos, has a special poignancy.

The arrangement of the play depends upon many such piquant but seemingly casual juxtapositions. *As You Like It* contemplates life within and without Arden, with numerous shifts of angle, alternating valuations, and variations of mood. As for action, incident—life in the Forest of Arden does not easily lend itself to those. I have suggested that Shakespeare does something to supply this want by a glance or two back at what is happening at court. And departures from the court are matched by arrivals in the forest. For events, of course, even in Arden do sometimes occur. Orlando arrives dramatically, even melodramatically. Presently Rosalind learns that he is about. A little later on they meet. Later still Oliver arrives and is rescued from a lioness. Shakespeare still keeps up a sense of things going on. But the manner of the play, when once it settles down in the forest, is to let two people drift together, talk a little, and part, to be followed by two more. Sometimes a pair will be watched by others, who will sometimes comment on what they see. Sometimes of course there is a larger group, once or twice even a crowded stage; but most often two at a time. When they part they may arrange to meet again, or they may not. Through the three middle acts of the play, though there are two instances of love at first sight (one of them only reported), it is rare that anything happens in any particular encounter between these people of the sort that changes the course of their lives, anything, that is to say, that goes to make what is usually called a plot. Yet the meetings may properly be called "encounters", because of the impact the contrasting characters make on one another and the sparkle of wit they kindle in one another. What is important in each meeting is our impression of those who meet and of their different attitudes to one another or to one another's views of life, an impression which is deepened or modified each time they reappear with the same or different partners. As I describe it, this may all sound rather static, but such is the ease and rapidity with which pairs and groups break up, re-form, and succeed one another on the stage that there is a sense of fluid movement. All is done with the utmost lightness and gaiety, but as the lovers move through the forest, part and meet again, or mingle with the other characters in their constantly changing pairs and groups, every view of life that is presented seems, sooner or later, to find its opposite. Life is "but a flower in spring time, the only pretty ring time" [V. iii. 19], but for the unromantic Touchstone there is "no great matter in the ditty" [V. iii. 35] and he counts it but time lost—his eye no doubt still on his timepiece—"to hear such a foolish song" [V. iii. 40]. A quartet of lovers avowing their lover is broken up when one of them says

> Pray you, no more of this; 'tis like the howling
> of Irish wolves against the moon.
>
> [V. ii. 109-10]

And the one who says this is she who cannot tell "how many fathom deep" she is in love [IV. i. 206]. Dominating the centre of the play, playing both the man's and woman's parts, counsellor in love and yet its victim, Rosalind gathers up into herself many of its roles and many of its meanings. Around her in the forest, where the banished Duke presides, is the perfect happiness of the simple life, an illusion, much mocked at, but still cherished. She herself, beloved of the hero, has all the sanity to recognize that "love is merely a madness" [III. ii. 400] and that lovers should be whipped as madmen are, but admits that "the whippers are in love too" [III. ii. 403-04]. Heroine of numerous masquerades, she is none the less always constant and never more true than when insisting that she is counterfeiting. For she is an expert in those dark riddles which mean exactly what they say. Though things are rarely what they seem, they may sometimes be so in a deeper sense. What is wisdom and what is folly is of course never decided—you may have it "as you like it". Or, as Touchstone rejoined to Rosalind, after her gibe about the medlar, "You have said; but whether wisely or no, let the forest judge" [III. ii. 121-22].

It may be possible to suggest that the forest gives its verdict. For if *As You Like It* proclaims no final truth, its ultimate effect is not negative. Longing to escape to our enchanted world, we are constantly brought up against reality; sanity, practical wisdom sees through our illusions. Yet in *As You Like It* ideals, though always on the point of dissolving, are for ever recreating themselves. They do not delude the eye of reason, yet faith in them is not extinguished in spite of all that reason can do. "I would not be cured, youth" [III. ii. 425]. (pp. 49-51)

> *Harold Jenkins, "'As You Like It'," in* Shakespeare Survey: An Annual Survey of Shakepearian Study and Production, *Vol. 8, 1955, pp. 40-51.*

**HELEN GARDNER**   (lecture date 1954-58?)

[*Gardner was an English academic, scholar, and literary critic whose many works of critical theory and writings on English literature have brought her international recognition. She edited, along with F. P. Wilson,* Shakespeare and the New Bibliography *(1970), and her* King Lear *(1967) is widely regarded as one of the seminal studies of that play. In the following excerpt from the text of a lecture delivered sometime between 1954 and 1958 at the Shakespeare Memorial Theatre's Summer School on Shakespeare, Gardner argues that* As You Like It, *as its title proclaims, is a play designed "to please all tastes." In accord with this view, she cites Harold Jenkins's study of the play (see excerpt above, 1953), agreeing that Shakespeare here juxtaposes various perceptions to present "a balance of sweet against sour, of the cynical against the idealistic." She emphasizes how the dramatist consistently opposes the one-sided view of things in* As You Like It, *noting that Arden is not entirely amiable, but is, as is Lear's place of exile in* King Lear, *a place where bitter lessons can be learned. Gardner also points out how Touchstone's parodic commentary—in touch as it is with the processes of life—balances Jaques's cynical criticism; but like other critics, she adds that Jaques, despite his shallowness balances the otherwise "too sweet" portrayal of Arden. Gardner also touches on a rarely discussed element in the comedy, saying that the Christian ideals of "loving-*

*kindness, gentleness, pity and humility," though unobtrusive, inform Shakespeare's vision throughout.*]

As its title declares, [*As You Like It*] is a play to please all tastes. It is the last play in the world to be solemn over. . . . The play itself provides its own ironic comment on anyone who attempts to speak about it: "You have said; but whether wisely or no, let the forest judge" [III. ii. 121-22].

For the simple, it provides the stock ingredients of romance: a handsome, well-mannered young hero, the youngest of three brothers, two disguised princesses to be wooed and wed, and a banished, virtuous Duke to be restored to his rightful throne. For the more sophisticated, it propounds, in the manner of the old courtly literary form of the *débat*, a question which is left to us to answer: Is it better to live in the court or the country? "How like you this shepherd's life, Master Touchstone?," asks Corin, and receives a fool's answer: "Truly, shepherd, in respect of itself, it is a good life; but in respect that it is a shepherd's life, it is naught. In respect that it is solitary, I like it very well; but in respect that it is private, it is a very vile life" [III. ii. 11-16]. Whose society would you prefer, Le Beau's or Audrey's? Would you rather be gossiped at in the court or gawped at in the country? The play has also the age-old appeal of the pastoral, and in different forms. The pastoral romance of princesses playing at being a shepherd boy and his sister is combined with the pastoral love-eclogue in the wooing of Phoebe, with the burlesque of this in the wooing of Audrey, and with the tradition of the moral eclogue, in which the shepherd is the wise man, in Corin. For the learned and literary this is one of Shakespeare's most allusive plays, uniting old traditions and playing with them lightly. Then there are the songs—the forest is full of music—and there is spectacle: a wrestling match to delight lovers of sport, the procession with the deer, which goes back to old country rituals and folk plays, and finally the masque of Hymen, to end the whole with courtly grace and dignity. This is an image of civility and true society, for Hymen is a god of cities. . . . The only thing the play may be said to lack, when compared with Shakespeare's other comedies, is broad humor, the humor of gross clowns. William makes only a brief appearance. The absence of clowning may be due to an historic reason, the loss of Kempe, the company's funny man. But if this was the original reason for the absence of pure clowning, Shakespeare has turned necessity to glorious gain and made a play in which cruder humors would be out of place. *As You Like It* is the most refined and exquisite of the comedies, the one which is most consistently played over by a delighted intelligence. It is Shakespeare's most Mozartian comedy.

The basic story is a folk tale. . . . Lodge retained some traces of the boisterous elements of this old story [in *Rosalynde*, his version of it]; but Shakespeare omitted them. His Orlando is no bully, threatening and blustering and breaking down the doors to feast with his boon companions in his brother's house. He is brave enough and quick-tempered; but he is above all gentle. . . . Shakespeare added virtually nothing to the plot of Lodge's novel. There is no comedy in which, in one sense, he invents so little. He made the two Dukes into brothers. Just as in *King Lear* he put together two stories of good and unkind children, so here he gives us two examples of a brother's unkindness. This adds to the fairy-tale flavor of the plot, because it turns the usurping Duke into a wicked uncle. But if he invents no incidents, he leaves out a good deal. Besides omitting the blusterings of Rosader (Orlando), he leaves out a final battle and the death in battle of the usurping Duke, preferring to have him converted off-stage by a chance meeting with a convenient and persuasive hermit. In the same way he handles very cursorily the repentance of the wicked brother and his good fortune in love. In Lodge's story, the villain is cast into prison by the tyrant who covets his estates. In prison he repents, and it is as a penitent that he arrives in the forest. Shakespeare also omits the incident of the attack on Ganymede and Aliena by robbers, in which Rosader is overpowered and wounded and Saladyne (Oliver) comes to the rescue and drives off the assailants. As has often been pointed out, this is both a proof of the genuineness of his repentance and a reason, which many critics of the play have felt the want of, for Celia's falling in love. Maidens naturally fall in love with brave young men who rescue them. But Shakespeare needs to find no "reasons for loving" in this play in which a dead shepherd's saw is quoted as a word of truth: "Whoever lov'd that lov'd not at first sight" [III. v. 82]. He has far too much other business in hand at the center and heart of his play to find time for mere exciting incidents. He stripped Lodge's plot down to the bare bones, using it as a kind of frame, and created no subplot of his own. But he added four characters. Jaques, the philosopher, bears the same name as the middle son of Sir Rowland de Boys—the one whom Oliver kept at his books—who does not appear in the play until he turns up casually at the end as a messenger. It seems possible that the melancholy Jaques began as this middle son and that his melancholy was in origin a scholar's melancholy. If so, the character changed as it developed, and by the time that Shakespeare had fully conceived his cynical spectator he must have realized that he could not be kin to Oliver and Orlando. The born solitary must have no family: Jaques seems the quintessential only child. To balance Jaques, as another kind of commentator, we are given Touchstone, critic and parodist of love and lovers and of court and courtiers. And, to make up the full consort of pairs to be mated, Shakespeare invented two rustic lovers, William and Audrey, dumb yokel and sluttish goat-girl. These additional characters add nothing at all to the story. If you were to tell it you would leave them out. They show us that story was not Shakespeare's concern in this play; its soul is not to be looked for there. If you were to go to *As You Like It* for the story you would, in Johnson's phrase, "hang yourself." (pp. 58-60)

[Here] the plot is handled in the most perfunctory way. Shakespeare crams his first act with incident in order to get everyone to the forest as soon as he possibly can and, when he is ready, he ends it all as quickly as possible. A few lines dispose of Duke Frederick, and leave the road back to his throne empty for Duke Senior. As for the other victim of a wicked brother, it is far more important that Orlando should marry Rosalind than that he should be restored to his rights. (p. 61)

The Forest of Arden ranks with the wood near Athens [in *A Midsummer Night's Dream*] and Prospero's island [in *The Tempest*] as a place set apart, even though, unlike them, it is not ruled by magic. It is set over against the envious court ruled by a tyrant, and a home which is no home because it harbors hatred, not love. Seen from the court it appears untouched by the discontents of life, a place where "they fleet the time carelessly, as they did in the golden age" [I. i. 118-19], the gay greenwood of Robin Hood. But, of course, it is no such Elysium. It contains some unamiable characters. Corin's master is churlish and Sir Oliver Martext is hardly sweet-natured; William is a dolt and Audrey graceless. Its weather, too, is by no means always sunny. It has a bitter winter. To Orlando, famished with hunger and supporting the fainting Adam, it is

"an uncouth forest" [II. vi. 6] and a desert where the air is bleak. He is astonished to find civility among men who

in this desert inaccessible,
Under the shade of melancholy boughs,
Lose and neglect the creeping hours of time.
[II. vii. 110-12]

In fact Arden does not seem very attractive at first sight to the weary escapers from the tyranny of the world. Rosalind's "Well, this is the forest of Arden" [II. iv. 15] does not suggest any very great enthusiasm; and to Touchstone's "Ay, now I am in Arden; the more fool I: when I was at home, I was in a better place: but travellers must be content," she can only reply "Ay, be so, good Touchstone" [II. iv. 16-19]. It is as if they all have to wake up after a good night's rest to find what a pleasant place they have come to. Arden is not a place for the young only. Silvius, for ever young and for ever loving, is balanced by Corin, the old shepherd, who reminds us of that other "penalty of Adam" beside "the seasons' difference" [II. i. 5-6]: that man must labor to get himself food and clothing. Still, the labor is pleasant and a source of pride: "I am a true laborer: I earn that I eat, get that I wear, owe no man hate, envy no man's happiness, glad of other men's good, content with my harm; and the greatest of my pride is to see my ewes graze and my lambs suck" [III. ii. 73-7]. Arden is not a place where the laws of nature are abrogated and roses are without their thorns. If, in the world, Duke Frederick has usurped on Duke Senior, Duke Senior is aware that he has in his turn usurped upon the deer, the native burghers of the forest. If man does not slay and kill man, he kills the poor beasts. Life preys on life. Jaques, who can suck melancholy out of anything, points to the callousness that runs through nature itself as a mirror of the callousness of men. The herd abandons the wounded deer, as prosperous citizens pass with disdain the poor bankrupt, the failure. The race is to the swift. But this is Jaques's view. Orlando, demanding help for Adam, finds another image from nature:

Then but forbear your food a little while,
Whiles, like a doe, I go to find my fawn
And give it food. There is a poor old man,
Who after me hath many a weary step
Limp'd in pure love: till he be first suffic'd,
Oppress'd with two weak evils, age and hunger,
I will not touch a bit.
[II. vii. 127-33]

The fact that they are both derived ultimately from folk tale is not the only thing that relates *As You Like It* to *King Lear*. Adam's sombre line, "And unregarded age in corners thrown" [II. iii. 42], which Quiller-Couch said might have come out of one of the greater sonnets [see excerpt above, 1918], sums up the fate of Lear:

Dear daughter, I confess that I am old;
Age is unnecessary: on my knees I beg
That you'll vouchsafe me raiment, bed, and food.
[*King Lear*, II. iv. 154-56]

At times Arden seems a place where the same bitter lessons can be learnt as Lear has to learn in his place of exile, the blasted heath. Corin's natural philosophy, which includes the knowledge that "the property of rain is to wet" [III. ii. 26], is something which Lear has painfully to acquire:

When the rain came to wet me once and the
wind to make me chatter, when the thunder

would not peace at my bidding, there I found
'em, there I smelt 'em out. Go to, they are not
men o' their words: they told me I was everything; 'tis a lie, I am not ague-proof.

[*King Lear,* IV. vi. 100-05]

He is echoing Duke Senior, who smiles at the "icy fang and
churlish chiding of the winter's wind" [II. i. 6-7], saying:

This is no flattery: these are counselors
That feelingly persuade me what I am.

[II. i. 10-11]

Amiens's lovely melancholy song:

Blow, blow, thou winter wind,
Thou are not so unkind
As man's ingratitude. . . .
Freeze, freeze, thou bitter sky,
That dost not bite so nigh
As benefits forgot . . . ,

[II. vii. 174-76, 184-86]

is terribly echoed in Lear's outburst:

Blow, winds, and crack your cheeks! rage! blow! . . .
Rumble thy bellyful! Spit, fire! spout, rain!
Nor rain, wind, thunder, fire, are my daughters:

*Act II. Scene iv. Rosalind as Ganymed, Celia as Aliena,
and Touchstone. By J. Walter West.*

I tax not you, you elements, with unkindness;
I never gave you kingdom, call'd you children. . . .

[*King Lear,* III. ii. 1, 14-17]

And Jaques's reflection that "All the world's a stage" [II. vii.
139] becomes in Lear's mouth a cry of anguish:

When we are born, we cry that we are come
To this great stage of fools.

[*King Lear,* IV. vi. 182-83]

It is in Arden that Jaques presents his joyless picture of human
life, passing from futility to futility and culminating in the
nothingness of senility—"sans everything" [II. vii. 166]; and
in Arden also a bitter judgment on human relations is lightly
passed in the twice repeated "Most friendship is feigning, most
loving mere folly" [II. vii. 181]. But then one must add that
hard on the heels of Jaques's melancholy conclusion Orlando
enters with Adam in his arms, who, although he may be "sans
teeth" and at the end of his usefulness as a servant, has, beside
his store of virtue and his peace of conscience, the love of his
master. And the play is full of signal instances of persons who
do not forget benefits: Adam, Celia, Touchstone—not to mention the lords who chose to leave the court and follow their
banished master to the forest. . . . Professor Harold Jenkins has
pointed out how points of view put forward by one character
find contradiction or correction by another, so that the whole
play is a balance of sweet against sour, of the cynical against
the idealistic, and life is shown as a mingling of hard fortune
and good hap [see excerpt above, 1953]. The lords who have
"turned ass," "leaving their wealth and ease a stubborn will
to please" [II. v. 51-3], are happy in their gross folly, as
Orlando is in a lovesickness which he does not wish to be cured
of. What Jacques has left out of his picture of man's strange
eventful pilgrimage is love and companionship, sweet society,
the banquet under the boughs to which Duke Senior welcomes
Orlando and Adam. Although life in Arden is not wholly idyllic, and this place set apart from the world is yet touched by
the world's sorrows and can be mocked at by the worldly wise,
the image of life which the forest presents is irradiated by the
conviction that the gay and the gentle can endure the rubs of
fortune and that this earth is a place where men can find happiness in themselves and in others.

The Forest of Arden is, as has often been pointed out, a place
which all the exiles from the court, except one, are only too
ready to leave at the close. As, when the short midsummer
night is over [in *A Midsummer Night's Dream*], the lovers
emerge from the wood, in their right minds and correctly paired,
and return to the palace of Theseus; and, when Prospero's
magic has worked the cure [in *The Tempest*], the enchanted
island is left to Caliban and Ariel, and its human visitors return
to Naples and Milan; so the time of holiday comes to an end
in Arden. The stately masque of Hymen marks the end of this
interlude in the greenwood, and announces the return to a court
purged of envy and baseness. Like other comic places, Arden
is a place of discovery where the truth becomes clear and where
each man finds himself and his true way. This discovery of
truth in comedy is made through errors and mistakings. The
trial and error by which we come to knowledge of ourselves
and of our world is symbolized by the disguisings which are
a recurrent element in all comedy, but are particularly common
in Shakespeare's. Things have, as it were, to become worse
before they become better, more confused and farther from the
proper pattern. By misunderstandings men come to understand,
and by lies and feignings they discover truth. If Rosalind, the
princess, had attempted to "cure" her lover Orlando, she might

have succeeded. As Ganymede, playing Rosalind, she can try him to the limit in perfect safety, and discover that she cannot mock or flout him out of his "mad humor of love to a living humor of madness," and drive him "to forswear the full stream of the world, and to live in a nook merely monastic" [III. ii. 418-21]. By playing with him in the disguise of a boy, she discovers when she can play no more. By love of a shadow, the mere image of a charming youth, Phoebe discovers that it is better to love than to be loved and scorn one's lover. This discovery of truth by feigning, and of what is wisdom and what folly by debate, is the center of *As You Like It*. It is a play of meetings and encounters, of conversations and sets of wit: Orlando versus Jaques, Touchstone versus Corin, Rosalind versus Jaques, Rosalind versus Phoebe, and above all Rosalind versus Orlando. The truth discovered is, at one level, a very "earthy truth": Benedick's discovery that "the world must be peopled" [*Much Ado about Nothing*, II. iii. 242]. The honest toil of Corin, the wise man of the forest, is mocked at by Touchstone as "simple sin" [III. ii. 78]. He brings "the ewes and the rams together" and gets his living "by the copulation of cattle" [III. ii. 78-80]. The goddess Fortune seems similarly occupied in this play: "As the ox hath his bow, the horse his curb, and the falcon her bells, so man hath his desires; and as pigeons bill, so wedlock would be nibbling" [III. iii. 79-82]. Fortune acts the role of a kindly bawd. Touchstone's marriage to Audrey is a mere coupling. Rosalind's advice to Phoebe is brutally frank: "Sell when you can, you are not for all markets" [III. v. 60]. The words she uses to describe Oliver and Celia "in the very wrath of love" [V. ii. 40] are hardly delicate, and after her first meeting with Orlando she confesses to her cousin that her sighs are for her "child's father" [I. iii. 11]. Against the natural background of the life of the forest there can be no pretence that the love of men and women can "forget the He and She." But Rosalind's behavior is at variance with her bold words. Orlando has to prove that he truly is, as he seems at first, the right husband for her, and show himself gentle, courteous, generous and brave, and a match for her in wit, though a poor poet. In this, the great coupling of the play, there is a marriage of true minds. The other couplings run the gamut downwards from it, until we reach Touchstone's image of "a she-lamb of a twelvemonth" and "a crooked-pated, old, cuckoldy ram" [III. ii. 81-2], right at the bottom of the scale. As for the debate as to where happiness is to be found, the conclusion come to is again, like all wisdom, not very startling or original: that "minds innocent and quiet" can find happiness in court or country:

Happy is your Grace,
That can translate the stubbornness of fortune
Into so quiet and so sweet a style.

[II. i. 18-20]

And, on the contrary, those who wish to can "suck melancholy" out of anything, "as a weasel sucks eggs" [II. v. 13].

In the pairing one figure is left out. "I am for other than for dancing measures" [V. iv. 193], says Jaques. Leaving the hateful sight of revelling and pastime, he betakes himself to the Duke's abandoned cave, on his way to the house of penitents where Duke Frederick has gone. The two commentators of the play are nicely contrasted. Touchstone is the parodist, Jaques the cynic. The parodist must love what he parodies. We know this from literary parody. All the best parodies are written by those who understand, because they love, the thing they mock. Only poets who love and revere the epic can write mock-heroic. . . . In everything that Touchstone says and does

gusto, high spirits, and a zest for life ring out. Essentially comic, he can adapt himself to any situation in which he may find himself. Never at a loss, he is life's master. The essence of clowning is adaptability and improvisation. The clown is never baffled and is marked by his ability to place himself at once *en rapport* with his audience, to be all things to all men, to perform the part which is required at the moment. Touchstone sustains many different roles. After hearing Silvius's lament and Rosalind's echo of it, he becomes the maudlin lover of Jane Smile; with the simple shepherd Corin he becomes the cynical and worldly-wise man of the court; with Jaques he is a melancholy moralist, musing on the power of time and the decay of all things; with the pages he acts the lordly amateur of the arts, patronising his musicians. It is right that he should parody the rest of the cast, and join the procession into Noah's ark with his Audrey. Jaques is his opposite. He is the cynic, the person who prefers the pleasures of superiority, cold-eyed and cold-hearted. The tyrannical Duke Frederick and the cruel Oliver can be converted; but not Jaques. He likes himself as he is. He does not wish to plunge into the stream, but prefers to stand on the bank and "fish for fancies as they pass." Sir Thomas Elyot said that dancing was an image of matrimony: "In every daunse, of a most auncient custome, there daunseth together a man and a woman, holding eche other by the hande or the arme, which betokeneth concorde." There are some who will not dance, however much they are piped to, any more than they will weep when there is mourning. "In this theatre of man's life," wrote Bacon, "it is reserved only for God and angels to be lookers on." Jaques arrogates to himself the divine role. He has opted out from the human condition.

It is characteristic of Shakespeare's comedies to include an element that is irreconcilable, which strikes a lightly discordant note, casts a slight shadow, and by its presence questions the completeness of the comic vision of life. . . . It is characteristic of the delicacy of temper of *As You Like It* that its solitary figure, its outsider, Jaques, does nothing whatever to harm anyone, and is perfectly satisfied with himself and happy in his melancholy. Even more, his melancholy is a source of pleasure and amusement to others. The Duke treats him as virtually a court entertainer, and he is a natural butt for Orlando and Rosalind. Anyone in the play can put him down and feel the better for doing so. All the same his presence casts a faint shadow. His criticism of the world has its sting drawn very early by the Duke's rebuke to him as a former libertine, discharging his filth upon the world, and he is to some extent discredited before he opens his mouth by the unpleasant implication of his name. But he cannot be wholly dismissed. A certain sour distaste for life is voided through him, something most of us feel at some time or other. If he were not there to give expression to it, we might be tempted to find the picture of life in the forest too sweet. His only action is to interfere in the marriage of Touchstone and Audrey; and this he merely postpones. His effect, whenever he appears, is to deflate: the effect does not last and cheerfulness soon breaks in again. Yet as there is a scale of love, so there is a scale of sadness in the play. It runs down from the Duke's compassionate words:

Thou seest we are not all alone unhappy:
This wide and universal theatre
Presents more woeful pageants than the scene
Wherein we play in,

[II. vii. 136-39]

through Rosalind's complaint "O, how full of briers is this working-day world" [I. iii. 11-12], to Jaques's studied refusal to find anything worthy of admiration or love.

One further element in the play I would not wish to stress, because though it is pervasive it is unobtrusive: the constant, natural and easy reference to the Christian ideal of loving-kindness, gentleness, pity and humility and to the sanctions which that ideal finds in the commands and promises of religion. In this fantasy world, in which the world of our experience is imaged, this element in experience finds a place with others, and the world is shown not only as a place where we may find happiness, but as a place where both happiness and sorrow may be hallowed. The number of religious references in *As You Like It* has often been commented on, and it is striking when we consider the play's main theme. Many are of little significance and it would be humorless to enlarge upon the significance of the "old religious man" [V. iv. 160], who converted Duke Frederick, or of Ganymede's "old religious uncle" [III. ii. 344]. But some are explicit and have a serious, unforced beauty: Orlando's appeal to outlawed men,

> If ever you have look'd on better days,
> If ever been where bells have knoll'd to church . . . ;
>
> [II. vii. 113-14]

Adam's prayer,

> He that doth the ravens feed,
> Yea, providently caters for the sparrow,
> Be comfort to my age!
>
> [II. iii. 43-5]

and Corin's recognition, from St. Paul, that we have to find the way to heaven by doing deeds of hospitality. These are all in character. But the God of Marriage, Hymen, speaks more solemnly than we expect and his opening words with their New Testament echo are more than conventional:

> Then is there mirth in heaven,
> When earthly things made even
> Atone together.
>
> [V. iv. 108-10]

The appearance of the god to present daughter to father and to bless the brides and grooms turns the close into a solemnity, an image of the concord which reigns in Heaven and which Heaven blesses on earth. But this, like much else in the play, may be taken as you like it. There is no need to see any more in the god's appearance with the brides than a piece of pageantry which concludes the action with a graceful spectacle and sends the audience home contented with a very pretty play. (pp. 64-71)

> *Helen Gardner, " 'As You Like It'," in* Shakespeare, the Comedies: A Collection of Critical Essays, *edited by Kenneth Muir, Prentice-Hall, Inc., 1965, pp. 58-71.*

## GEOFFREY BUSH   (lecture date 1955)

[*In the following excerpt from a lecture delivered in January 1955, Bush discusses the nature of the comic vision in* As You Like It, *claiming that the Forest of Arden functions as a "picture of order" in the play. The forest is, he asserts, a place in which self-knowledge is both possible and desirable; it acts as "a natural persuasion that leads us first to ourselves and then . . . to one another." Bush further maintains that the humanizing influence of Arden not only allows a choice to be made between the "artificial court" and the "natural forest," but ends as well in the discovery that, by returning to the court without a loss, the "fact and the dream" of these two realms may be had at once.*]

To be ourselves, in the vision of comedy, is to realize a perfect idea of ourselves, and return to our original natural goodness.

The Forest of Arden, in *As You Like It,* is like the golden world; it is a natural persuasion that leads us first to ourselves and then, in the happy notion of comedy, to one another. The Forest is not a natural paradise; there is winter and rough weather in it; but it is a picture of order that addresses the Duke Senior to teach him "what I am" [II. i. 11], and the shepherd Corin, who has lived in the Forest all his life, is a "natural philosopher" [III. ii. 32]—though it is Touchstone who says so, and to be a natural philosopher is to be something of a fool.

Rosalind needs no instruction in who she is or whom she will marry; it is the women of comedy who by their own natural philosophy arrange the happy endings. But Orlando and Oliver are instructed in nature, and like the Duke Senior they are taught to know and to be themselves. At the beginning Orlando complains that his brother Oliver denies him any education; Orlando would be "a gentleman" [I. i. 9], he speaks of "gentility" [I. i. 21], the "gentle condition of blood" [I. i. 44-5], and "gentlemanlike qualities" [I. i. 69-70]. Gentleness, he thinks, has been kept from him; but his brother Oliver confesses in puzzled hatred: "Yet he's gentle; never school'd and yet learned" [I. i. 166-67]. Orlando has a natural gentleness, and when he enters the Forest his natural education is completed. The Forest at first seems a desert, the air seems bleak, and he advances upon the Duke Senior with a drawn sword; but the Duke tells him: "Your gentleness shall force" [II. vii. 102-03], and when Orlando replies abashed: "I thought that all things had been savage here" [II. vii. 107], the Duke bids him sit down "in gentleness" [II. vii. 124]. Pacing through the woods, Orlando comes upon Oliver asleep beside a lioness. Orlando might have turned away, but nature addresses him with the lesson of affection:

> Twice did he turn his back and purpos'd so;
> But kindness, nobler ever than revenge,
> And nature, stronger than his just occasion,
> Made him give battle to the lioness,
> Who quickly fell before him.
>
> [IV. iii. 127-31]

Orlando's gentleness, as it was before, is his by nature; his goodness, like the goodness of trees and stones and running brooks, is natural. And Oliver, who before was the "most unnatural" brother among men [IV. iii. 122], is no longer what he was; he has become himself. . . . The Forest has taught them who they are, and they are ready to be married.

The Forest is not perfect, and in *As You Like It* there are adverse judgments of the world. Orlando, pinning poems on every tree, attaches some that tell

> how brief the life of man
> Runs his erring pilgrimage.
>
> [III. ii. 129-30]

But on the fairest boughs he will write "Rosalinda" [III. ii. 137]. The comic vision can permit touches of sorrow in a world capable of arranging a natural happiness that so far transcends them. When Rosalind exclaims: "O, how full of briers is this working-day world!" Celia answers: "They are but burrs, cousin, thrown upon thee in holiday foolery" [I. iii. 11-14]. The comic vision is a holiday of the fancy that repudiates from the start the more pressing and dangerous natural adversities. Comedy accepts the penalty of Adam into the Forest of Arden, admitting imperfection into a world assured to be more good than bad; and whatever cannot be shaped to fit the vision is happily disregarded. For the end of *As You Like It,* no matter what happens, will be marriage, a moment whose natural perfection is so certain that Touchstone, adjuring Audrey to bear her body more seeming, does no more than demonstrate how wide an area the moment of natural perfection embraces. Shallow villains and sleeping lions fall quickly before it; enemies are sweetly converted to themselves; and even heaven is glad. . . . Hymen remarks, of the simultaneous union of eight people, that these are ''strange events'' [V. iv. 127]. They are indeed; but comedy, like Rosalind, can do strange things. The natural perfection of marriage disarms adversity, and finally adversity disarms itself. The Duke Senior and his men find their lands and fortune restored, and, to our philosophic dismay, they take it: they return to the envious court as joyfully as they had commended their absence from it. The artificial court and the natural Forest turn out, in the best of all possible worlds, not to be opposites after all; the choice ends in the pleasant discovery that both the fact and the dream can be had at once. Jaques's seven ages of man are a ''strange eventful history'' [II. vii. 164], but in *As You Like It* they are a history that breaks off with an unconquerably happy ending. (pp. 27-9)

> *Geoffrey Bush, ''Comedy and the Perfect Image,''*
> *in his* Shakespeare and the Natural Condition, *Cambridge, Mass.: Harvard University Press, 1956, pp. 23-52.*

## JOHN RUSSELL BROWN   (essay date 1957)

[*In the following excerpt from his* Shakespeare and His Comedies, *originally published in 1957, Brown traces Shakespeare's treatment in* As You Like It *of three ideas: social disorder, Arden's subjective order, and love's order. He considers these ideas interrelated parts of Shakespeare's principal theme of love's order, within which Jaques functions as the completely negative character and the exposer of disorder. On other matters, Brown finds the source of the play's ''generosity and confidence'' not in the interaction of all the lovers, but chiefly in Rosalind, who, he claims, acts to prevent Shakespeare's ideal of the ordering power of love from being ''presented as a cold theorem.'' Within Rosalind, Brown continues, coexist ''love's doubts and faith, love's obedience and freedom.'' Brown also maintains that, because Shakespeare is concerned with society as well as love, the disorder of the court and city are contrasted with the ''subjective order'' of Arden; but he adds that the forest is hardly the golden Arcadia we at first expect, since there—as in the city—peace and ''content'' must be achieved through the characters' proper acceptance of life.*]

Alone among [Shakespeare's] comedies, *As You Like It* starts with a single prose speech of over two hundred words; the words are simple enough but the speech is so involved with parenthetical qualifications and elaborations that it has to be delivered slowly and deliberately. Before the play can quicken into action, the audience must hear Orlando reiterate [at I. i. 1-25] how Oliver, his guardian and eldest brother, keeps him in 'servitude', 'bars' him the 'place of a brother', and treats him as one of his 'hinds' or 'animals'. Oliver's entry interrupts this protestation, but only momentarily, for the two brothers start at once to quarrel in earnest. When Adam, an old servant, begs them, in their father's name, to 'be at *accord*' [I. i. 64], Oliver orders him away as an 'old dog' [I. i. 81]. The whole exchange is a picture of disorder in a family. Left alone, Oliver asks for Charles, the 'duke's wrestler', and in direct terms— 'what's the new news at the new court?' [I. i. 96-7]—calls forth still more direct exposition. There follows a second picture of disorder in society, for 'the old duke', says Charles, 'is banished by his younger brother the new duke' [I. i. 99-100];

our attention is turned from a 'tyrant brother' in the country, to a 'tyrant duke' at the court [I. ii. 288].

It is clear that, in this comedy, Shakespeare is concerned with society as well as with love, and at this point anyone who knows Shakespeare's history-plays might expect some criticism of these two disorders. It comes at once from Charles, the professional wrestler, who in his dispassionate, professional way tells how 'three or four loving lords' have given up 'lands and revenues' to go to the forest of Arden and live there with the old duke in 'voluntary exile' [I. i. 100-02]. Objectively he recounts the common notion of this other court:

> they say many young gentlemen flock to him
> every day, and fleet the time carelessly, as they
> did in the golden world.
>
> [I. i. 116-19]

After this momentary contrast, the action continues with Oliver persuading Charles to attempt the life of Orlando who intends to wrestle for a prize at court. But when the scene changes there is a further contrast and we are shown Celia, the tyrant duke's daughter, promising Rosalind, the banished duke's daughter, that she will restore all as soon as she is able—she would count herself a '*monster*' if she failed to do this [I. ii. 22].

After these contrasts the tyrant's court is presented more directly. First Touchstone talks, jestingly as befits a clown, of its lack of true honour and wisdom, and then the duke himself enters to watch the wrestling match between Charles and Orlando. Orlando wins but when he says that he is the youngest son of Sir Rowland de Boys, he receives no honour for his victory; although the 'world esteem'd' Sir Rowland 'honourable', the tyrant had found that he was always his enemy and therefore he cannot welcome the son [I. ii. 225-26]. This example of court life comes pat upon Touchstone's moralizing.

The action of the comedy is now well under way, for Rosalind and Orlando have fallen in love, but Shakespeare is still not finished with social disorder. Into the story which he found in Lodge's *Rosalynde*, he has already introduced two characters; the first, Touchstone the clown, has been used to comment on the corruptions of the court, and the second, Le Beau the courtier, is now used likewise. As a messenger from the tyrant, he had spoken with marked lack of feeling about the sport which, for his master's entertainment, had killed the three sons of an old father—the incongruity of this entertainment was quickly underlined with a jest from Touchstone—but now, in his own person, he feels such warm friendship for Orlando that he neglects attendance on the duke to counsel him to leave the court. Le Beau recognizes the 'malice' of his master, but, as Touchstone had hinted earlier, the 'little wit' that he has has been 'silenc'd' at court [I. ii. 89]; he breaks off his hurried meeting with—

> Sir, fare you well:
> Hereafter, in a better world than this,
> I shall desire more love and knowledge of you.
>
> [I. ii. 283-85]

From this world, Rosalind and Celia escape to Arden, and, because she fears the unordered 'thieves' of the forest [I. iii. 108-10], Rosalind decides to disguise herself as a page, Ganymede, and they agree to ask Touchstone to accompany them. Thus weakly and foolishly protected, they leave the court's travesty of order and security, going—

> . . . in content
> To *liberty* and not to banishment.
>
> [I. iii. 137-38]

On this cue the scene changes for the first time to the forest of Arden, and, at once, our expectations are dashed; it is neither the careless golden world of the people's imagination nor the ruffian world of Rosalind's. We do indeed find contentment there, but it has only been won by *searching* for

> . . . tongues in trees, books in the running brooks,
> Sermons in stones and good in every thing.
>
> [II. i. 16-17]

There is an 'adversity' [II. i. 12], or 'stubborness of fortune', which has to be 'translated' into peace and quiet [II. i. 19-20]; order and tranquillity are subjective only, and not easily maintained. The banished duke has deliberated so curiously that he is 'irked' because the deer, 'poor dappled fools' and 'native burghers of this desert city', have to be 'gored' to provide him with sustenance [II. i. 22-3]. This appears to be a new scruple—there's nothing to suggest that he had thought of being a vegetarian while at court—but he is immediately echoed by a jesting report of how Jaques, a lord who seeks to 'pierce' to the truth about life in 'country, city, court', has found that in killing deer the duke does 'more *usurp*' than did his brother who banished him [II. i. 25-63]. This short scene concludes with the duke going to hear Jaques' philosophizing. The pastoral and courtly worlds had been compared a thousand times before Shakespeare wrote this play, but here the comparison is unexpected and strangely baffling; it raises issues without answering them, issues clearly related to those of earlier scenes by the direct comparison of the 'woods' with the 'envious court' [II. i. 3-4].

The action returns to the court to show the usurping duke hearing of the princesses' escape and reacting with nervous suspicion and vindictiveness. Then Adam is seen encountering Orlando and persuading him to fly from his brother who is again plotting to take his life. Adam laments in words that partly echo and partly amplify those of Le Beau:

> O, what a world is this, when what is comely
> Envenoms him that bears it.
>
> [II. iii. 14-15]

Under Oliver's unnatural tyranny, his 'house is but a *butchery*' [II. iii. 27], but Orlando swears that he would rather stay there than beg. . . . As Rosalind found comfort in Celia and Touchstone, so Orlando does in Adam who, trusting in the One who 'providently caters for the sparrow' [II. iii. 44], gives to his master all the savings of his thrifty, well-ordered youth, and offers to go with him into exile. . . . Together they leave Oliver's tyranny and seek, instead, 'some settled low content' [II. iii. 68].

The preliminary pictures of disordered society are now almost complete—there is only one more direct view which comes four scenes later [in II. i.] and shows the tyrant sending Oliver 'out of doors' [III. i. 14-15] to seek his brother while seizing into his own hands the lands and revenues which Oliver had sought to augment. Shakespeare has created these pictures in 'primitive' outline and colour, a technique which has enabled him to isolate and contrast significant and typical actions. By a series of recurrent words, actions, and images, and by additions to his source, he has shown how generous loyalty and affection cannot purge a disordered world but can at least give to fugitives some measure of personal order and content.

The 'primitive' technique of these early scenes has led some critics to think that Shakespeare was only interested in getting to Arden as quickly as possible, but once the action is centred in the forest, he is still not wholly concerned with its delights; repeatedly these early scenes are echoed in theme if not in manner, and their careful contrasts and emphases are made to contribute to the final resolution. For example, the preliminary scene in Arden had stressed the need for a personal acceptance of the 'stubbornness of fortune' [II. i. 19]—the pastoral world was not an easy substitute for the corrupt court—and this is the point which Shakespeare reiterates as each fugitive enters the forest. Rosalind, Celia, and Touchstone are the first to arrive, weary in body and spirit. The clown says frankly that it were better to be at court, while Rosalind, asking the old shepherd Corin for help, hardly dares to hope that such a 'desert place' can yield 'entertainment' [II. iv. 72]. When Corin rejoins that he is a 'shepherd to another man', a master of *churlish disposition* [II. iv. 78-80] who

> . . . little recks to find the way to heaven
> By doing deeds of hospitality. . . .
>
> [II. iv. 81-2]

their fears seem confirmed. But Rosalind discovers a kinship with the suffering, amorous shepherd, Silvius, and Corin promises to help them, and at once their spirits rise; Rosalind offers to buy the master's cottage and Celia forgets both her weariness and the unfriendly aspect of Arden—she will 'mend' Corin's wages and 'willingly could waste' her time in the forest [II. iv. 94-5]. (pp. 142-47)

Arden is not necessarily or unequivocally the 'golden world' of the people's imagination, but 'gentleness', '*kind*-ness', the duke's philosophy, or the willingness to serve submissively and patiently for love can translate the 'stubbornness of fortune' into a sweet and quiet style. This is the point at which the pictures of social disorder and of newfound order in Arden are contrasted and related, and thereby illuminate each other. At court or in Oliver's household, affection and faith could only bring 'content' in the 'liberty' of banishment, but once in Arden, content is at command: the forest mirrors one's mind; if peace and order are found there, the forest will reflect them.

And at this point too, order and disorder are related to the love stories which are about to take the main focus in the drama. Contentment in love is, like content in Arden, subjective; it is as one's self likes it. Phoebe's eyes have power to act against Silvius as 'tyrants, butchers, murderers' [III. v. 14], but that is only because Silvius sees her in that way; when [at III. v. 36-56] she tries to 'entame' Ganymede, she is for Rosalind a 'tyrant' who 'exults' in a power which only Silvius recognizes: "'Tis not her glass, but you, that flatters her', she tells the youth—

> And out of you she sees herself more *proper*
> Than any of her lineaments can show her.
>
> [III. v. 55-6]

This private, subjective truth is sufficient for the lovers, as the subjective order must be for the fugitives in Arden; Silvius can only answer Phoebe's refusal with renewed vows of generous service.

And as each of Arden's citizens and each of its lovers finds content in his or her own manner, so both citizens and lovers find it in terms of the 'gentleness', service or order which has been neglected in the world outside. For Silvius love is

> . . . to be all made of faith and service . . .
> All adoration, duty, and observance,
> All humbleness, all patience and impatience,
> All purity, all trial, all observance.
>
> [V. ii. 89, 96-8]

As in the 'antique world' of good order, he 'sweats for duty not for meed' [II. iii. 57-8]. And when Phoebe finds she has been fooled by the appearance of a man in Ganymede, she accepts the suit of Silvius because of his belief in an order in which she herself believes. . . . Oliver and Celia establish their mutual content more rapidly and confidently, but it is still in terms of order; as Caesar established his kingdoms, so they both 'came, saw, and overcame' [V. ii. 35]. Rosalind and Orlando had met for the first time at court but their love was not fully expressed there. They had done what they could—Rosalind had given him a favour to wear and both had confessed that they were 'thrown down' [I. ii. 250], 'overthrown' [I. ii. 259], disordered by a new 'master' and new duties of service—yet more was expressed in their hesitations than in words or deeds, and it is only in Arden that they learn the full strength of their new order, of their mutual defeat and mastery. In the forest they learn to make their love explicit in the very words by which Silvius vows his service, observance, and faith. On one level the story of Rosalind and Orlando is easily appreciated, but it should be seen in the context of the whole play, of the tyrannies outside Arden, of the subjective content which can be won within Arden, and of the other stories; all these are informed by Shakespeare's ideal of order and all these contribute to the implicit judgement of the play, and to the full significance of any part of it.

Arden's pleasures and love's order do not recommend themselves to all comers. Touchstone does not readily give way to such enthusiasms: he is 'Nature's natural' [I. ii. 49] who cares not for his 'spirits' if his legs are not 'weary' [II. iv. 2-3]. The excitement of a lover, the zeal of a scholar, the business of a lawyer do not affect, for him, the pace of Time; for him, Time travels regularly:

'Tis but an hour ago since it was nine,
And after one hour more 'twill be eleven;
And so, from hour to hour, we ripe and ripe,
And then, from hour to hour, we rot and rot. . . .
[II. vii. 24-7]

Determined to treat a spade only as a spade, Touchstone will not be carried away by any subjective idealization of life in Arden. . . . In the affairs of love he reckons, like Costard, on the 'simplicity of man' [*Love's Labour's Lost*, I. i. 217]; he notices the 'strange capers' which lovers run into [II. iv. 55], but he quickly accounts for such vagaries:

If a hart do lack a hind,
Let him seek out Rosalind.
If the cat will after kind,
So be sure will Rosalind. . . .
[III. ii. 101-04]

Yet once Touchstone finds Audrey his attitude changes; the desire to possess involves him, by degrees, in the mutual order of love. The first time we see them together, he is offering to 'fetch up' her goats and is already impatient of Time, questioning 'Am I the man yet? doth my simple feature *content* you?' [III. iii. 1-4]. . . . When Jaques tells him that Sir Oliver Martext can only wed them like badly joined wainscot, Touchstone professes himself content, for, in due time, this will give him the better excuse to leave his wife. But he is further in than he admits, and, to Audrey's surprise, he fails to take advantage of Sir Oliver but goes with Jaques to find a 'good priest that can tell . . . what marriage is' [III. iii. 85-6]. He now remembers, not merely that 'cat will after kind' [III. ii.

103], but also something which is above man's apparent 'simplicity'; he recollects that

As the ox hath his *bow*, . . . the horse his *curb*
and the falcon her *bells*, so man hath his desires;
and as pigeons bill, so *wedlock* will be nibbling.
[III. iii. 79-82]

The 'yoke', 'curb', or order of love also seems to be 'necessary', even for a man of 'a fearful heart' [III. iii. 48-9].

Touchstone falls in with the ordered dance of the lovers as best he may. First he jousts with William a youth of the forest who lays claim to Audrey and, asserting his new-found possessiveness, routs the complacent, good-natured clown. Then he is ready to press in 'amongst the rest of the country copulatives' [V. iv. 55-6]. Knowing that 'marriage binds and blood breaks', he expects to 'swear and to forswear' [V. iv. 56-7], but he makes what show he can. Audrey may not cut a fine figure in the eyes of other people but love is ever 'as you like it'; 'a poor virgin, sir', he explains, 'an ill-favoured thing, sir, but mine own' [V. iv. 57-8]. And as he is now disposed to dignify any complaisance with the formality of honour and good manners, so he commands Audrey—and his concern for this draws laughter from everyone—to 'bear' her 'body more seeming' [V. iv. 68-9]. Touchstone may yet find the 'pearl' in his 'foul oyster' [V. iv. 61]; at least he knows something of the terms—the mutual order of love—on which such treasure is discovered.

By adding Touchstone to the story that he had found in Lodge's *Rosalynde*, Shakespeare has emphasized the implicit judgement of this play; by contrast and relationship with other characters, Touchstone illuminates the main theme in each of its three branches—social disorder, Arden's subjective order, and love's order. And Shakespeare's preoccupation with these ideas becomes even clearer when we notice that Jaques, his other major addition to Lodge, is used in the same threefold manner.

Jaques' talent is for the exposure of disorder, not the affirmation of order; we first hear [of him in II. i. in] a report of his whimsically extravagant denunciation of the duke's 'tyranny' over the deer, and then we see him 'sucking' melancholy from Amiens' song, as 'a weasel sucks eggs' [II. v. 12-14]. Jaques rightly uses a destructive image to describe his pleasure, for he finds no joy in the song's harmony nor in its simple, complaisant reconciliation with Arden. . . . The 'young' [I. i. 117] foresters join in with Amiens' second stanza [of "Under the greenwood tree"], but Jaques thinks of the 'grossness', the lack of complexity, which their song represents. He offers another stanza of his own:

If it do come to pass
That any men turn ass,
Leaving his wealth and ease,
A stubborn will to please,
Ducdame, ducdame, ducdame:
Here shall he see
Gross fools as he,
An if he will come to me.
[II. v. 50-7]
(pp. 149-54)

Jaques will not risk being a fool on his own account—he prefers to rail against others—but he feels a kinship with the clown Touchstone who sees life as a mere 'simplicity' of ripening and rotting. He is at once ambitious for a fool's licence to speak his mind and so, as he believes,—

. . . through and through
Cleanse the *foul* body of the *infected* world.
[II. vii. 59-60]

Given his liberty he would sing no song, but rail against disorder, against the city woman who bears the 'cost of princes on *unworthy* shoulders' and against the upstart courtier of '*basest* function' [II. vii. 74-82]. When Orlando enters, desperate with hunger, Jaques has only 'reason' to offer as a cure [II. vii. 100-01]; and then, while Orlando goes to fetch Adam at the duke's invitation, he proceeds to amplify Touchstone's wisdom and to speak of the seven ages of man as of a mere mutation in response to Time's ordering—of man's own ordering vision, he makes no account. At this point Shakespeare fully demonstrates Jaques' limitations, for as soon as he has called old age a 'second childishness and mere oblivion' [II. vii. 165], Orlando re-enters with the aged Adam whose 'constant service' [II. iii. 57] has made him the 'venerable burden' [II. vii. 167] which the duke at once recognizes. Following this reminder of all that Jaques had forgotten, Amiens sings of man's ingratitude; respect for virtue is not forgetfulness.

Jaques' negative, reasonable, and unenthusiastic attitude towards men and society, which decries disorder but neglects to praise and appreciate such order as men have achieved, is matched by his attitude to lovers. With Orlando, conversation is almost impossible. Jaques reproves him for 'marring' the trees by 'writing love-songs in their barks', and Orlando reproves Jaques for reading them so 'ill-favouredly' [III. i. 259-62]. Jaques does not like the name of Rosalind, and Orlando does not defend it; these matters are 'as you like it' and there was 'no thought of pleasing [him] when she was christened' [III. ii. 266-67]. Jaques invites him to rail 'against our mistress the world and all our misery', and Orlando, mindful of another mistress, answers that he will 'chide no breather in the world' but himself, against whom he knows 'most faults' [III. ii. 277-81]. Orlando's love leads him into absurdities which appear as 'faults' to others, but they are faults that Orlando would not change for the 'best virtue' that Jaques can boast of [III. ii. 283-84].

Jaques has more to say to Touchstone, for he must denounce the iniquities of Martext, but with Rosalind he can only once more manifest his ignorance of love's inward order and joy. He is neither scholar, musician, courtier, soldier, lawyer nor lover, and he feels none of their emotions; he merely contemplates their exploits and failures, and gains a 'most humourous sadness' [IV. i. 19-20]. This is his only possession. Orlando interrupts his talk with Rosalind, or rather with Ganymede, by addressing the seeming boy with 'Good day and happiness, dear Rosalind' [IV. i. 30]; to Jaques this is doubly nonsense and he leaves, baffled by their mutual, private pleasure.

When the duke is restored to his true place in society by the sudden conversion of his tyrant brother, Jaques cannot join the dance which celebrates the new order of the lovers; unappeased, he must seek more matter for his contemplation. But having seen them all endure 'shrewd days and nights' [V. iv. 173], he accepts this as testimony of their inward virtues, and, for the first time in the play, sees promise of order, not of disorder. He speaks formally and in due order—to the duke:

> You to your former honour I bequeath;
> Your patience and your virtue well deserves it:

then to Orlando, Oliver, and Silvius in turn, dismissing them:

> You to a love that your true faith doth merit:
> You to your land and love and great allies:
> You to a long and well-deserved bed.
>
> [V. iv. 186-90]

For Touchstone he foresees 'wrangling', for the clown has only given proof of 'victual' for some two months of 'loving voyage' with Audrey [V. iv. 191-92]. This is a rational appraisement of their several chances of creating love's order in the more complex, less subjective, world of society at large.

A detached critic who rails at the follies or 'disorders' of others sounds a tiresome character for any comedy, but even when Jaques criticizes those who affirm individual visions of order, the effect on them is only to add to their happiness; his 'sullen fits' [II. i. 67] are sport for the philosophical duke, his encounters with Rosalind and Orlando encourage them to be more confident in their own happiness, and his mockery of the young foresters for 'conquering' the deer, sends them singing through the forest. His strictures on corrupt society can give pleasure by the seasoned wit with which he, like a true satirist, affirms the value of order by recognizing and describing disorder; as he himself says, his 'sadness' is one, limited, kind of 'good' [IV. i. 8]. Without Jaques, *As You Like It* would be a far less subtle play, for besides showing the limitations of his own disinterested judgement, he makes us aware of the limitations of subjective order and content; he shows us that the philosophical duke is 'too disputable' for some company [II. v. 35], that the young foresters are content because they are easily so, that Orlando does not care to mend his most obvious absurdities. And indirectly Jaques affirms the complexity of love's order, for as the couples come together at the close of the play, he reminds us that they are not merely servants of each others' excellencies, but also 'couples . . . coming to the Ark', some of them very 'strange beasts' [V. iv. 36-7].

To follow Jaques through the play is to become aware of Shakespeare's preoccupation with the ideal of order in society, in Arden, and in love, and of the subtlety and range of his consequent judgements. But Jaques alone cannot suggest the light-footed gaiety, the warmth, and the confidence with which this comedy is written. Some of these qualities derive from the apparently easy interplay between the varied and individually conceived characters; for example, the absurdly single-minded Silvius is first introduced talking to the simply and sensibly satisfied Corin, and overheard by Rosalind and Touchstone, and then, later, Touchstone and Corin meet and compare their individual 'simplicities'. But the play's generosity and confidence spring chiefly from the characterization of Rosalind. She ensures that Shakespeare's ideal of love's order is not presented as a cold theorem; in her person love's doubts and faith, love's obedience and freedom, co-exist in delightful animation.

The lively characterization of Rosalind is not an added, irrelevant pleasure, but arises from, and continually illuminates, the thematic structure of the whole play. This is perhaps Shakespeare's greatest triumph in *As You Like It*: from the moment when she is disordered by the claims of love to the moment when she makes Orlando reiterate their 'compact' [V. iv. 5] for the last, unnecessary time, she invites our understanding as well as our enthusiasm. She delights to 'play the knave' with Orlando [III. ii. 296-97], for the more she casts doubts upon whether he is truly 'sick' of an unsatisfied love the more assurance she receives that he is indeed so, and the more outrageously she pictures women the more strongly he affirms his faith in her own virtue. Yet while his faith permits her to enjoy this freedom, she is careful to offer no more alluring 'cure' for his 'sickness' than the prospect of living 'in a nook merely monastic' [III. ii. 420-21]. Love's order has its justice, and Rosalind must pay for the advantage she delights to take; Orlando, protected by the belief that she is Ganymede, can come 'within an hour' of his promise and be quite easy in mind [IV. i. 42], but for Rosalind, to 'break but a part of the thousandth part of a minute' [IV. i. 46] has its torments. She may 'disable' all the fabled heroics of other lovers, but that is only because her own love is too great to be spoken, because she 'cannot be out of the sight of Orlando' [IV. i. 215].

In the two central scenes between Orlando and Rosalind, Shakespeare shows us the growing assurance of their mutual love, its generosity, truth, and order. And at the close of the play, he directs that they should take hands in the forefront of the other lovers and, after the final dance affirming the creation of mutual order, that they should go back with the duke to the court, away from purely subjective content—they go to play their part on the great stage of society and to affirm order and harmony there.

And then Rosalind steps forward:

> It is not the fashion to see the lady the epilogue;
> but it is no more unhandsome than to see the
> lord the prologue. . . .
>
> [Epilogue, 1-3]

She will not beg for applause for the play; her 'way is to conjure':

> I charge you, O women, for the love you bear
> to men, to like as much of this play as please
> you: and I charge you, O men, for the love you
> bear to women—as I perceive by your simper-
> ing, none of you hates them—that between you
> and the women the play may please.
>
> [Epilogue, 12-17]

'Between the men and the women' the play *can* please, for it mirrors the 'mutual ordering' of love. If we answer its 'conjuration', we shall, consciously or unconsciously, be 'pleased' with its ideal of harmony. We may, of course, allow the trick to retain all its mystery, but if we wish, by tracing the implicit judgements of the play, we may realize that it succeeds not merely by some sleight of hand, but also by reason of the ideals which inform it. (pp. 154-59)

> *John Russell Brown, "Love's Order and the Judge-*
> *ment of 'As You Like It',*" *in his* Shakespeare and
> His Comedies, *second edition, Methuen & Co. Ltd.,*
> *1962, pp. 124-59.*

## BERTRAND EVANS (essay date 1960)

[*In two studies of Shakespearean drama,* Shakespeare's Comedies *(1960) and* Shakespeare's Tragic Practice *(1979), Evans examines what he calls Shakespeare's use of "discrepant awarenesses." He claims that Shakespeare's dramatic technique makes extensive use of "gaps" between the different levels of awareness the characters and audience possess concerning the circumstances of the plot. In the following excerpt from the earlier work, Evans discusses the level of discrepant awarenesses in* As You Like It, *claiming that the technique in this play is less complex and less extensive than in Shakespeare's other comedies and noting many points where the device is initiated but never developed. But the critic also maintains that the central instance where a conflict in awarenesses does exert influence on the plot—namely, the scenes between Rosalind as Ganymede and Orlando in Arden, leading to the "wooing" episode (IV. i.)—is, though apparently simplistic, crucial to the entire comedy and just as compelling as in Shakespeare's other works. In fact, Evans contends, the wooing of Ganymede by Orlando is the "climactic" moment in* As You*

Like It, *the point "which the rest of the play, including Jaques and all the golden world of the Forest of Arden itself, supports."*]

The worlds of *Much Ado about Nothing* and *As You Like It* contrast in notable ways, even as do their inhabitants. In the world of *Much Ado* all is astir, for its people will not suffer it to stand motionless for a moment. Twelve active practisers, nine amateur, three professional, deceiving one another and being deceived in turn, keep Messina bustling. Beside it the world of *As You Like It* is still and golden, and most of its inhabitants would be content if some of its moments endured for ever: Jaques weeping with the stricken deer, 'Ganymede' being wooed by Orlando, Duke Senior hearing Amiens sing, Phebe being chided by 'Ganymede'. While Oliver sleeps, the serpent will not sting nor the lioness claw him. Although the first two acts are much given to contrasting good and evil in country and court, old times and new, and the motives of men, the ultimate criticism of life is gentle: it is the mellowest of Shakespeare's many worlds. Here a brilliant heroine, a duke's daughter, driven into the forest, finds such joy in the shepherd's life that she does not trouble to seek out her banished father: 'What talk we of fathers, when there is such a man as Orlando?' [III. iv. 38-9]. Here a stalwart hero wins the heart of a princess by cracking a professional wrestler's bones and gains a fortune by felling a 'suck'd and hungry lioness' [IV. iii. 126] with his bare hands. Here hardened villainy simply cannot endure, but is dissolved and absorbed by the goodness of environment. Here Melancholy grows lean, finding nothing left to nourish itself on, and at last banishes itself. . . . (p. 87)

From the point of view of the disposition and uses of awareness the two plays stand in marked contrast also. In the first place, *As You Like It* depends far less than *Much Ado about Nothing* upon discrepant awarenesses for its movement and effects. Although we are given advantage over certain participants in eleven of twenty-two scenes, the gap between awareness is rarely the central dramatic fact in these scenes and is sometimes left quite unexploited; moreover, in several of these scenes our advantage functions during only a portion of the action. Further, the play exhibits no very complex arrangement of awarenesses at any time; usually, in scenes in which we hold any advantage, it is a single one, which we share with one or two persons at the expense of one or two others. Near-universal ignorance is exploited only in the closing moments. In *Much Ado*, swarming with practisers, many secrets are shared by many persons and hidden from many more. *As You Like It* has only two notable practisers, Rosalind and Celia, and the only notable secret concerns their identities. All in all, then, *As You Like It* makes less use of the difference between advantage and disadvantage than any other mature comedy except *The Merchant of Venice*.

Nevertheless both the effects and the action of the climactic scenes of *As You Like It* depend on this difference quite as much as do those of the comparable scenes in *Much Ado about Nothing*. In that play the scene of Hero's denunciation could not occur but for Claudio's error in thinking Hero false; in *As You Like It* the scene of Orlando's wooing could not occur but for Orlando's error in thinking Rosalind to be Ganymede. In their degree of dependence on a gap for the central action, then, the two plays are alike even though the complexity of the patterns differs widely. No less significantly, the plays are related, as are both to *The Merry Wives of Windsor* and *Twelfth Night*, in the love of practising exhibited by certain participants. Again the difference is in complexity rather than degree: in the other plays virtually all persons are incorrigibly addicted to the art whereas in *As You Like It* only Rosalind and Celia are devoted to it. But their zeal for the game compensates for their numerical deficiency. In Rosalind the holiday spirit of the dedicated practiser has its most exuberant expression. 'I will speak to him like a saucy lackey,' she says to Celia, 'and under that habit play the knave with him' [III. ii. 295-97]. It is with no better excuse that she begins her sport with poor Orlando.

Her practice produces no important consequence until Act III, however, and we hold no great advantage over anyone until then. Aside from the heroines, Oliver is the only practiser, and his two devices, like those that fill the opening scenes of *Much Ado*, yield no noteworthy effects, though they bear significantly on subsequent action. Our first advantage is over Charles the wrestler, deceived by Oliver's description of Orlando [I. i. 147-55]. . . . But although we hold brief advantage over both contestants, nothing comes either of Charles's ignorance of Orlando's true nature or of Orlando's ignorance that Charles, in his error, is determined to 'give him his payment' [I. i. 160] so decisively that he will never walk again. For Orlando proves competent to hold his own in muscular terms with man or beast, and presumably if he knew of Charles's intent he would throw him no harder than he does in ignorance: 'Bear him away' [I. ii. 221]. Oliver's second device, even wickeder, comes to no more than the first in terms of an exploitable situation, since Orlando learns from Adam as soon as we of his brother's intent to burn Orlando's lodging 'where you use to lie / And you within it' [II. iii. 23-4]. For subsequent action, of course, this practice proves indispensable: it precipitates Orlando's flight to the forest, after which Oliver's own departure in pursuit is occasioned by the error of Duke Frederick in supposing that Orlando, for whose act he holds Oliver responsible, aided the flight of the princesses.

A few other moments of participants' unawareness are either represented or alluded to during the first two acts, but all are left unexploited. Thus Duke Senior appears at the opening of Act II, directly after we have learned that Celia and Rosalind are coming to the forest to seek him, and our knowledge of their decision inevitably casts special light upon him; but he is busily contrasting court and forest life, and Shakespeare gives him no mention of Rosalind or otherwise capitalizes on his ignorance that she is coming. Little more is made of Orlando's ignorance that he is in the presence of a great Duke when in the last scene of Act II he bursts upon the forest camp, sword drawn, demanding food. Some sparks of irony do indeed flash from his ignorance: 'If ever you have look'd on better days, / If ever been where bells have knoll'd to church' [II. vii. 113-14], he tells the Duke, 'Let gentleness my strong enforcement be; / In the which hope I blush, and hide my sword' [II. vii. 118-19]. In return, there is a quiet flash from the Duke's reply: 'True is it that we have seen better days' [II. vii. 120]. The period of Orlando's unawareness extends to a hundred lines, until the Duke ends it with an abrupt 'I am the Duke / That lov'd your father' [II. vii. 195-96]. But except for the quick flashes of irony, the unconscious and the conscious, the fact of the hero's ignorance is not essential to the action itself or to the main dramatic effects of the scene. Finally, in the first encounter of Rosalind and Celia in their masked identities with a resident of Arden, Corin, little is made of the gap between awarenesses. The purposes of this scene (II. iv) are mainly preparatory: to introduce the rural lovers, Silvius and Phebe, to show us that the heroines are in their disguises, and to get them settled in the forest. The fact that Corin does not know he is in the presence of princesses is irrelevant to these purposes, and it is uncapitalized. Besides,

old Corin is a rooted element of the country-side, and revelation of their identity would presumably make no difference to him: whether for the churlish old master or for the new, and whether the new be master or mistress, of royal blood or common, he will continue to feed the sheep and shear the fleeces.

Exploitation of the great central secret of the play, then, takes its real start in Act III—the point at which the heart of the play begins to beat—and does not reach a climax until IV. i, with the wooing of 'Ganymede'. The approach to this scene is made by degrees, as Rosalind, acting her masquerade in a spirit of pure mischief, meets successively Orlando, Phebe and Silvius, and Jaques. She meets her father also during this period, but the hilarity of their interview Shakespeare leaves to the imagination, merely having Rosalind report the incident in passing to greater matters [III. iv. 35-8]. . . . No more is made of her encounter with Jaques, with which Act IV opens. Jaques's ignorance of her identity, like Corin's, is irrelevant and is therefore appropriately left unexploited. It is, then, primarily through the interview with Phebe and Silvius and the preliminary interview with Orlando himself that Shakespeare prepares the climate for the great scene.

'I'll prove a busy actor in their play' [III. iv. 59], Rosalind promises Corin, who has invited her to witness the 'pageant truly play'd' [III. iv. 52] between Silvius and Phebe. The line reminds of Oberon's when he enlists himself in the service of true love for Helena's sake: 'Fare thee well, nymph. Ere he do leave this grove, / Thou shalt fly him and he shall seek thy love' [*A Midsummer Night's Dream*, II. i. 245-46]. It is the first clear placement of Rosalind in the line of Oberon, Duke Vincentio, and Prospero. Later, when the denouement nears, as we shall observe, she takes upon herself increasingly the role of the omniscient, omnipotent controlling force. Further, the present interview with Silvius and Phebe anticipates the interviews of Viola with Olivia in *Twelfth Night;* but it has striking contrasts with those scenes also, for Rosalind's temperament is as far from Viola's as Phebe's from Olivia's. Rosalind's is a zestful, mischievous, even mildly wicked delight in the masquerade; with a keen relish like Prospero's, of her role and her advantage, she lashes Phebe with words meant to sting:

> No, faith, proud mistress, hope not after it.
> 'Tis not your inky brows, your black silk hair,
> Your bugle eyeballs, nor your cheek of cream
> That can entame my spirits to your worship.
>
> [III. v. 45-8]

And, again:

> Down on your knees,
> And thank heaven, fasting, for a good man's love;
> For I must tell you friendly in your ear,
> Sell when you can; you are not for all markets.
>
> [III. v. 57-60]

Phebe is the first real victim of Rosalind's mockery. She looks on to Olivia, innocent victim of Viola's disguise, but she differs from Olivia in deserving to be humiliated. Presumptuous, pretentious, proud, she scorns the poor slave of a shepherd who dotes on her, killing him over and over with darted looks—all the while insisting that 'there is no force in eyes / That can do hurt' [III. v. 26-7]. When Olivia falls in love with 'Cesario', the gentle Viola pities her and strains to avoid hurting her; not so Rosalind, when she perceives Phebe's error: 'Why do you look on me? / I see no more in you than in the ordinary / Of nature's sale-work' [III. v. 41-3]. Olivia's declaration of love invites no derision but only compassion: 'A cypress, not a bosom, / Hides my heart' [*Twelfth Night*, III. i. 121-22]. In contrast, Phebe deserves the corrective medicine of ridicule which Rosalind, of all Shakespeare's heroines, is best qualified to administer.

Yet it is not Phebe who occupies the lowest vantage-point in this scene, or in any scene in which the shepherd lovers participate. Here, as elsewhere, that place is reserved for the hapless male. Ignorant of 'Ganymede's' sex and rank, Silvius fails to comprehend the more obvious and equally significant fact, that Phebe has fallen in love. 'There be some women, Silvius, had they mark'd him / In parcels as I did,' asserts Phebe, 'would have gone near / To fall in love with him; but, for my part, / I love him not nor hate him not' [III. v. 124-27]. Seeing nothing in this but a plain statement, Silvius gladly agrees to bear to Ganymede Phebe's 'very taunting letter' [III. v. 134]. The display of Silvius's masculine oblivion in the presence of Phebe is prelude to the full-scale exhibition of the same condition in the climactic scene, when Orlando is pitted in unequal combat with Rosalind. Indeed, the entire scene of Rosalind's encounter with Silvius and Phebe, presenting the first real exploitation of the gulf between her awareness and the ignorance of the persons she meets in the forest and overthrows one by one, serves as an approach, itself climactic, to that summit of the comedy.

The scene is not the only preparation for the climactic period of some 200 lines that immediately follows Jaques's departure at the opening of Act IV: every preceding scene in which either Orlando or Rosalind appears is preparation in that it builds our sense of the *rightness* of these two for their roles in the climactic scene and thus increases the comic potentiality of that scene. For certainly the great scene does not exploit an ordinary discrepancy between the awarenesses of two ordinary lovers. It is in large part because these two are precisely as they are, with a wider gap between their awarenesses than between just any two lovers, that the climactic scene is so memorable.

The width of this discrepancy is due not only to the fact of Rosalind's disguise, although of course that is essential. Nor is it attributable wholly to the fact that she possesses, besides the disguise that hides her identity, extraordinary native gifts that make her the most circumspect of heroines. Without disguise, her natural gifts would set her above everyone else in the play. 'She is too subtle for thee,' says Duke Frederick to Celia in banishing Rosalind [I. iii. 77]. 'She robs thee of thy name, / And thou wilt show more bright and seem more virtuous / When she is gone' [I. iii. 80-2]. With disguise to supplement her gifts, hers is a towering advantage, and not only Orlando but all the persons she meets in the forest are reduced to a state of oblivion when they encounter her. The cream of the cream of the jest is that such a one is confronted in the climactic scene with precisely such a one as Orlando.

Rosalind is the brightest of Shakespeare's bright heroines, and Orlando is the least conscious of his unconscious heroes. The gap between them is that between omniscience and oblivion. It is not that Orlando is a stupid man. . . . [In] our view, Orlando is more admirable as a human being than Shakespeare's other heroes of comedy—than Proteus, the incipient rapist [in *The Two Gentlemen of Verona*], Bassanio, the fleece hunter [in *The Merchant of Venice*], Claudio, the sadistic prig [in *Much Ado about Nothing*], Bertram, the liar and ready adulterer [in *All's Well That Ends Well*]. But though good, and not stupid, Orlando is afflicted to an extraordinary degree with that obliviousness that is common to the heroes. Perhaps Orsino of *Twelfth*

*Night* stands nearest him in this respect—but Orsino has only to deal with gentle Viola, and Orlando is at the mercy of Rosalind.

Orlando is right for the great scene just as Bottom, equipped with an ass's head, is right for the profoundly ironic moments with Titania [in *A Midsummer Night's Dream*]. Despite the deserved praise which Oliver heaps upon Orlando as reason for getting rid of him—'he's gentle, never schooled and yet learned, full of noble device, of all sorts enchantingly beloved, and indeed so much in the heart of the world, and especially of my own people, who best know him, that I am altogether misprised' [I. i. 166-71]—Shakespeare begins early to qualify his hero for his miserable role with brilliant Rosalind. Orlando is exposed repeatedly in situations of which the truth eludes him. Ludicrous comments, outrageously damaging to his heroic prestige, are made about him when he is absent: 'I found him under a tree, like a dropp'd acorn' [III. ii. 234-35], says Celia—and the image stays. His abrupt disposal of Charles the wrestler; his first tongue-tied meeting with Rosalind; his sword-brandishing, valiant, but frightfully unaware entrance to demand food of Duke Senior—all these are parts of the preparation. By III. ii, when he runs about the forest, scattering bad verses and blemishing trees—'Run, run, Orlando; carve on every tree / The fair, the chaste, the unexpressive she' [III. ii. 9-10]—he has been readied for the climactic moment. But there is even more preparation—indeed, 300 lines of it—after which, entering, Orlando can seem only a sturdy booby. First, samples of his verse, at its simultaneous best and worst, are exposed [III. ii. 109-12]. . . . Next the verse and the man are subjected to the biting wit, in turn, of Touchstone, Rosalind, Celia, and Jaques. 'This is the very false gallop of verses,' says the fool. 'Why do you infect yourself with them?' [III. ii. 113-14]. And Rosalind to Celia: '. . . look here what I found on a palm tree. I was never so berhym'd since Pythagoras' time, that I was an Irish rat, which I can hardly remember' [III. ii. 175-78]. At what exact instant in the course of this universal belittlement Rosalind learns that the maker of these verses is Orlando, it is impossible to tell. Evidently she knows by the time of Celia's comment, 'And a chain, that you once wore, about his neck. Change you colour?' [III. ii. 181-82]. Probably we are expected to understand that she guesses the truth at the outset, when she enters reading aloud: 'From the east to western Ind, / No jewel is like Rosalind' [III. ii. 88-9]. In any event, during part of the scene she feigns ignorance of the poet's identity, and, true to her nature, uses her pretended ignorance as an excuse for adding wicked touches to the growing portrait of Orlando: 'Is he of God's making? What manner of man? Is his head worth a hat or his chin worth a beard?' [III. ii. 205-07]. It is at the height of this discussion that Celia adds the definitive stroke: 'I found him under a tree, like a dropp'd acorn' [III. ii. 234-35].

It is an Orlando whom the dramatist has subjected to such levity that we are next shown conversing with Jaques, while Rosalind and Celia observe unseen. And it is with the departure of Jaques, when the disguised princesses move in on their victim—'I will speak to him like a saucy lackey, and under that habit play the knave with him' [III. ii. 295-97]—that the main action commences. The first interview of Orlando and 'Ganymede', ending with her promise to wash his liver 'as clean as a sound sheep's heart, that there shall not be one spot of love in 't' [III. ii. 422-24], is itself a prelude to the climactic scene of the wooing of 'Ganymede'. The scene of 200 lines, after Jaques leaves at the opening of Act IV, is the climactic peak, the point which the rest of the play, including Jaques and all the golden world of the Forest of Arden itself, supports.

*Act III. Scene iii. Audrey and Touchstone. By John Pettie.*

Though it lacks the fullness and complexity of corresponding moments in *The Merchant of Venice, Much Ado about Nothing, Twelfth Night,* and *Measure for Measure,* the scene deserves its crowning place. It has one distinction: it is the only cloudless climactic scene in Shakespeare's romantic comedies. The others are characterized by a complex disposition of awarenesses, and exploitation produces multiple effects, some pleasant, some painful. But here are only two levels—Rosalind's (and ours) and Orlando's—and the result of exploitation is unadulterated fun. Our equipment for the climactic scenes of other mature comedies includes a heavy burden of advantages, some over all participants, some shared with a few. Our equipment for the wooing scene is a single advantage, which we share with Rosalind alone over Orlando alone. Lacking the typical tensions and conflicting appeals of the others, the climactic scene of *As You Like It* is structurally simple. Indeed, having but one matter to exploit—the discrepancy between the lovers' awarenesses—it is unique as a climactic scene not only among the comedies but among all Shakespeare's plays. Complexity in both cause and effect being his favoured way, the climactic scene of *As You Like It* might be expected to be inferior; instead, it is a magnificent exercise in simplicity.

Inferior it might be if there were no compensation for the lack of complexity. The compensating factor is the width of the discrepancy, so carefully prepared, between the awarenesses of the lovers. Though single, this gulf is wider than that between any other lovers in the comedies—as wide as that between any other two persons in any play. Even Bottom and Titania are not so separated as these, for though Bottom's understanding approximates Orlando's, Titania's eyes, bewitched by the juice of the little western flower, lack the clarity of Rosalind's. Neither are Hero and Claudio so far apart, since Don John's practice has blinded the callow youth, and Hero is ignorant that she has been defamed. The awarenesses of Bassanio and Portia, in the court scene, are far apart with respect only to a minor aspect of the situation; the court scene does not exist primarily to exploit the discrepancy resulting from Bassanio's ignorance of Portia's identity: its main business is the trial of Antonio, and the facts of the case are known to both. In Act V, however, when the affair of the rings becomes central, division of awarenesses of Portia-Bassanio and Nerissa-Gratiano is both wide and central.

The exclusive business of the wooing scene of *As You Like It* is exploitation of the gap between the awarenesses of Orlando and Rosalind; but for this gap the scene could not exist. Though extended, the exploitation is not thin; it is a virtuoso piece played on one string, as is no other major scene in Shakespeare. Neither the relation of the participants nor the situation changes at all during the action. At the beginning Rosalind knows everything and Orlando nothing; at the end, the same. So wide is the space between them that Rosalind can repeatedly insist that she is 'very very Rosalind' [IV. i. 70-1] without risk of losing her advantage. She plays one game, and Orlando, thinking it all one, another. . . . Rarely flattering to his comic heroes, Shakespeare treats Orlando abominably! An open-hearted and open-minded innocent, incapable of suspecting that reality might differ from appearance, he is permitted no glimpse of the truth. Even Bottom has moments of dim wonder, finding his face hairy and his stomach wanting hay; and Orsino, though without realizing the fact, comes to the edge of truth in remarking that 'Cesario's' voice 'is as the maiden's organ' [*Twelfth Night*, I. iv. 33]. Orlando is made to play out the scene without even touching the truth unaware. Ironical flashes are sparked by Orsino's and Bottom's near approaches; Orlando's utterances, despite Rosalind's repeated assertions that she is Rosalind, flare up in irony only when they illuminate his remoteness from the truth: 'Who could be out, standing before his beloved mistress?' [IV. i. 81-2] he inquires—standing before her.

Since Orlando has learned nothing to the purpose at the end of the scene and since the time of a second meeting is fixed, the same discrepancy remains the principal exploitable condition up to the time we learn that Orlando cannot keep the two o'clock appointment. In the interim occurs a scene in which Silvius briefly replaces Orlando as Rosalind's victim—and Phebe's unawareness of 'Ganymede's' identity is capitalized also, through her 'very taunting' letter borne to Rosalind by Silvius [III. v. 134]. 'Can a woman rail thus?' asks Rosalind, starting to read her admirer's love poem [IV. iii. 42]; and Silvius, supposing himself wise indeed, alarmed that 'Ganymede' has stolen his love, replies, 'Call you this railing?' [IV. iii. 43]. The tangle of awarenesses that involves Rosalind, Phebe, and Silvius is more complicated than is the knot that involves Rosalind and Orlando. For Phebe, ignorant of Rosalind's sex, is in love with her; and Silvius, ignorant also of Rosalind's sex, at first does not realize that Phebe has fallen in love and therefore gladly bears the 'chiding' letter [IV. iii. 64], and then, perceiving the lesser truth—that Phebe is in love—but not the greater—that 'Ganymede' is no formidable rival—is needlessly distressed. 'Alas, poor shepherd' [IV. iii. 65], says Celia—not, certainly, because he has lost Phebe, but because he has been doubly deluded.

Rosalind's next victim is Oliver—who, however, is victim only of her disguise and not her mockery, for she is briefly too unhappy to play games. Indeed, for about fifty lines the dramatist gives us advantage over both Rosalind and Celia, since we and not they know that their visitor is Orlando's brother; it is an insignificant advantage, however, and is left unexploited. The main advantage remains with the disguised heroines. Orlando has described them to Oliver, and in doing so has transmitted his own error to his brother, thus Oliver:

> If that an eye may profit by a tongue,
> Then should I know you by description:
> Such garments and such years. 'The boy is fair,
> Of female favour, and bestows himself
> Like a ripe sister; the woman low,
> And browner than her brother.'
>
> [IV. iii. 83-8]

The femininity of Rosalind is manifest in her swooning at sight of the napkin red with Orlando's blood; very briefly at this point she anticipates Viola of *Twelfth Night*, who has greater difficulty than other heroines in maintaining her masquerade. Yet Rosalind recovers quickly and resumes her role even as she reopens her eyes. Oliver is doubly deceived: not only does he, like his brother, take Rosalind to be 'Ganymede' pretending to be Rosalind, but he takes Celia for no more than the pro-

prietor of 'the cottage and the bounds / That the old carlot once was master of' [III. v. 107-08], and as such woos and wins her.

It is Oliver's success in wooing and the setting of the wedding date for 'Tomorrow' [V. ii. 42] that abruptly terminates Rosalind's sport, which she might otherwise continue indefinitely, and precipitates the denouement. For Orlando, seeing his brother's success, 'can live no longer by thinking' [V. ii. 50]: 'Ganymede' will no longer serve. Finding it impossible to perpetuate the static situation, Rosalind takes upon herself the role of the external, controlled force. As 'Ganymede' she has enjoyed an advantage in awareness, overpeering all Arden. But even omniscience will no longer serve; so upon her practice as 'Ganymede' she grafts a second practice. . . . Earlier, going with Corin to watch the 'pageant truly play'd' [III. iv. 52] between Silvius and Phebe, she had promised to 'prove a busy actor in their play' [III. iv. 59], identifying herself with the role played by Oberon in the affairs of the Athenian lovers [in *A Midsummer Night's Dream*]. She now identifies herself more explicitly with this role. Her omnipotence—which seems magical to the participants—is, of course, only feigned, where Oberon's, and later Vincentio's [in *Measure for Measure*] and Prospero's [in *The Tempest*], is real. In our view it is a patent fraud. Even so, we know also that she can do all she promises—and she promises infinitely:

> *(To Phe.)* I will marry you, if ever I marry woman, and I'll be married to-morrow. *(To Orl.)* I will satisfy you, if ever I satisfi'd man, and you shall be married to-morrow. *(To Sil.)* I will content you, if what pleases you contents you, and you shall be married to-morrow. *(To Orl.)* As you love Rosalind, meet. *(To Sil.)* As you love Phebe, meet. And as I love no woman, I'll meet. So, fare you well. I have left you commands.
>
> [V. ii. 113-21]

Portia of *The Merchant of Venice*, coming to Antonio's trial dressed as 'a young doctor of Rome' [*The Merchant of Venice*, IV. i. 153], resolves the dilemma of the court without magic or pretence of magic. Her superior awareness is leagued with merely mortal power—her own brilliance and the 'opinion' of the learned Bellario of Padua. Rosalind, in affecting to have been 'tutor'd in the rudiments / Of many desperate studies' [V. iv. 31-2] by a 'great magician / Obscured in the circle of this forest' [V. iv. 33-4], moves well beyond Portia toward Prospero: in effect, if not fact, her control of the world of Arden and the destinies of its inhabitants is as complete as Oberon's control of the enchanted woods outside Athens and Prospero's control of his island, its winds, waters, residents, and visitors.

To accomplish all the miracles she has promised to perform by magical acts, she need really only reveal her own identity. She surrenders her advantage spectacularly, in a burst of music and mystic song, a kind of magic in itself—and somehow, magically perhaps, she does manage to produce Hymen in person for the occasion. In this denouement, which has only one gap to close, the discrepancy in awarenesses vanishes as suddenly as a burst bubble; our own advantage over the inhabitants of the Forest is lost at the same instant Rosalind surrenders hers. In this as in other great final moments, Shakespeare sharply limits the comments of participants for whom dark has suddenly become light. 'If there be truth in sight,' says the Duke, 'you are my daughter' [V. iv. 118]. 'If there

be truth in sight,' says Orlando—who has had cause to doubt—
'you are my Rosalind' [V. iv. 119]. Shakespeare gives the
Duke four additional speeches, the hero not another word.
Another kind of man, now seeing what a game was played
with him—recalling the outlandish spectacle he had been tricked
into making—would bide his time until fast married to this
Rosalind and then would beat her until she begged for mercy.
Orlando, of course, will not do so. Even from the first, he was
as other heroes of the comedies are at the end—hooked and
gasping for air. At last, then, Rosalind having ended her sport
with him, he is properly left speechless. (pp. 87-98)

> Bertrand Evans, *"For the Love of Mockery: Ap-*
> *proach to the Summit,"* in his Shakespeare's Com-
> edies, *Oxford at the Clarendon Press, Oxford, 1960,*
> *pp. 68-117.*

## JAY L. HALIO  (essay date 1962)

[*In the following excerpt, Halio describes time's two functions in*
As You Like It: *as a foil whose two extremes—timelessness and
time-consciousness—favorably contrast pastoral life in Arden with
court and city life; and, as timelessness alone, as a link between
life in the present and life in an earlier, less corrupt, largely
better time. Halio maintains that in Shakespeare's view, the city
and the court are ruthless and degenerate, threatening places
from which Arden's timeless world is a refuge, a world "where
past and present merge" and people flourish. Citing dramatic
and thematic juxtapositions between these two worlds, Halio focuses on Rosalind's awareness of time, noting how, unlike Touchstone's fascination with time's power to ripen things then rot them,
Rosalind's preoccupation is with time's regenerative power alone,
especially as it concerns lovers.*]

In *As You Like It* Shakespeare exploits timelessness as a convention of the pastoral ideal along with other conventions taken
from pastoralism, but unlike his treatment, say, of Silvius and
Phebe, his treatment of time is not so thoroughly satirical.
Though neither will quite do, timelessness in Arden (on the
whole) contrasts favorably to the time-consciousness of court
and city life which Touchstone, for example, brings to the
forest. In addition, timelessness links life in Arden with the
ideal of an older, more gracious way of life that helps regenerate
a corrupt present.

Orlando's first speech immediately voices several aspects of
the time theme. Speaking to Adam, he recalls his father's will
and its provision that Oliver, the eldest son, should educate
the younger brothers. This Oliver has failed to do, at least with
respect to Sir Rowland's youngest son; but despite his enforced
rusticity, Orlando reveals an innate gentility so wonderful that
even his tyrannical brother is brought to remark: "Yet he's
gentle, never schooled, and yet learned, full of noble device,
of all sorts enchantingly beloved . . ." [I. i. 166-68]. These
innate qualities derive directly from old Sir Rowland, for the
identification between Orlando and his father, as we shall see,
is repeatedly and pointedly made. Moreover, Orlando twice
remarks in this scene that it is his father's spirit within him
that prompts him to revolt against his present humiliation—a
revelation which has more than ordinary implications later.
(p. 197)

[We] need not go outside the play to discover what Sir Rowland
represents. Adam, the old retainer of the de Boys household
and himself a living reminder of the former age, provides some
important clues. When Oliver apparently consents to his brother's departure, he throws Adam out, too:

*Oliver*. Get you with him, you old dog.
*Adam*. Is "old dog" my reward? Most true, I
have lost teeth in your service. God be with
my old master! He would not have spoke such
a word.

> [I. i. 81-4]

Later, when Adam warns Orlando to run from Oliver's treachery and even offers his life's savings—and his life—to assist
in the escape, Orlando recognizes the gesture for what it is—
the product of a gracious ideal:

> O good old man, how well in thee appears
> The constant service of the antique world,
> When service sweat for duty, not for need!
> Thou art not for the fashion of these times,
> Where none will sweat but for promotion,
> And having that do choke their service up
> Even with the having. It is not so with thee.
> [II. iii. 56-62]

The two dukes also furnish evidence of the esteem in which
Sir Rowland was universally held: Duke Frederick, villain-
ously, found him an enemy, but Duke Senior (to Rosalind's
evident gratification) "loved Sir Rowland as his soul" [I. ii.
235]. Orlando, who functions in the play partly to bear out the
spirit of his father, naturally attracts similar feelings. It is not
for nothing that he attaches to himself repeatedly the clumsy-
naive epithet "old Sir Rowland's youngest son" [I. iii. 28];
besides, his name is both an anagram of Rowland and its Italian
translation. The predicament in which the young man eventually discovers himself will test his true mettle and, more
importantly, the worth of all that he and his name may symbolize. (pp. 198-99)

Orlando's world of court and city is a far different world from
his father's. It is a perverse world, where brother plots against
brother and virtues become "sanctified and holy traitors" [II.
iii. 13]. It is a world ruled over by the usurping Frederick (the
"new" Duke), who banishes his elder brother (the "old" Duke)
and keeps his niece only so long as convenience allows. When
he fears Rosalind as a threat to the fame and popularity of his
own daughter, he drives her out also—just as Oliver plans to
kill the brother he fears he can no longer suppress. In short,
it is a world based on expediency and the lust for power (III.
i. 15-18), not a brave new world, but a degenerate new one.
With no obligation to tradition—to the past—it is ruthless in
its self-assertion. But while this "new" world may banish its
principal threats, Rosalind and Orlando, it does not thus destroy
them (we are, after all, in the realm of romantic comedy). In
the timeless pastoral world of the Forest of Arden, where past
and present merge, they find refuge and there flourish.

The first mention of the life led by Duke Senior and his fellows
in the Forest of Arden occurs early in the play in the dialogue
between Charles and Oliver. Oliver has decided to use the
wrestler to rid himself of Orlando (thus perverting the intention
of Charles's visit), but first he inquires into the "new news at
the new Court" [I. i. 96-7]. Charles recounts what Oliver
already knows: the new Duke has driven out the old Duke,
and a number of lords have voluntarily accompanied him into
exile. For no apparent reason, Oliver next inquires into Rosalind's position, and then asks where the old Duke will live.
Charles replies:

> They say he is already in the Forest of Arden,
> and a many merry men with him; and there
> they live like the old Robin Hood of England.

> They say many young gentlemen flock to him
> every day, and fleet their time carelessly as they
> did in the golden world.
>
> [I. i. 114-19]

Here Oliver abruptly changes the subject to the next day's wrestling match. Now, merely as dramatic exposition this dialogue is at least ingenuous—if not downright clumsy. Obviously it must serve another function to justify itself; that is, by describing the conflict between the two dukes, it provides a parallel to the decisive quarrel between Orlando and Oliver which has just taken place. The inversion of roles played by the younger and older brothers is merely a superficial variation of the plot; the point is to suggest an alignment between Duke Senior and Sir Rowland de Boys, between the "golden world" and the "antique world," which coalesce in the fabulous Robin Hood life now led by the banished Duke. Should we require any further evidence of this significance, the change in Sir Rowland's name from its source is clear enough. The anagram *Rowland-Orlando* has already been explained, but the change from *de Bordeaux* is otherwise meaningful: *de Boys* is simply *de Bois*, "of the forest." Elizabethan spelling commonly substitutes *y* for *i*, as everyone knows, but the pronunciation is the same. . . . And Dover Wilson's note [in his edition of the play], recording the fact that the de Boyses were an old Arden family, gives us more light than it perhaps suspects—or intends.

Lest there be any mistake about the kind of forest in which Duke Senior and (later) Orlando, Rosalind, and the others find themselves, we must listen carefully to the Duke's first speech. . . . Its theme is "Sweet are the uses of adversity"; only in this way can he and his followers discover "tongues in trees, books in the running brooks / . . . and good in everything." Here, unlike the conventional pastoral, others besides unrequited lovers may feel the shrewdness of the winter wind; shepherds will confess to smelling of sheep dip; and a Sir Oliver Martex is available for weddings as well as Hymen. The forest may be enchanted—the appearance of a god is only the least subtle indication that it is—but the enchantment is of an unusual kind; the forest still admits of other, qualifying realities. For the right apprehension of a natural, humane order of life, which emerges as Shakespeare's standard, takes account of both the ideal (what should or could be) and the actual (what is). By contrast, the standard of life in court and city is unnatural insofar as it stifles the ideal aspirations of the human imagination and sinks to the level of a crude, animal existence. If Duke Senior finally returns along with the others to his dukedom (despite his earlier assertion that he would not change his "life exempt from public haunt" [II. i. 15]), he returns not only because his dukedom is ready to receive him, but also (we must infer) because he is prepared to resume his proper role. Tempered by adversity, his virtue matures. To provide this temper, or balance, is the true function of the forest, its real "magic." Neither the Duke nor anyone else who comes to Arden emerges the same.

The trip to the forest is itself exhausting and fraught with danger. Rosalind and her little company are quite unable to take another step. Similarly, Adam is close to expiring when he arrives with Orlando. But on each occasion the forest at once works its charm. Corin and Silvius are at hand to entertain Rosalind and her friends and to provide them with a gentle welcome and a home. At the end of the scene even the fainting Celia quickens to remark, "I like this place, / And willingly could waste my time in it" [II. iv. 94-5]. Orlando, seeking food in what he calls an "uncouth" desert [II. vi. 6], comes upon the banquet of the banished Duke. Showing the valor of his heritage, he opposes single-handed the entire host of the Duke and his men. Under the conventions of this romance, this show of valor is not quixotic—it fits rather with Orlando's defeat of Charles. But, though hardly despised (except by Jaques), it is misdirected; and Orlando is made to recognize the code that here reigns [II. vii. 106-19]. . . . Gentleness joins with gentleness; golden world merges with antique world—at least through their modern representatives. If the parvenu at first mistakes the appearance of his surroundings, he is soon instructed: this is no ordinary forest. At the same time, he reminds us of what civilization *might* be like, or once was. Certainly he perceives another aspect of his new environment accurately, one he will quickly cultivate: the meaninglessness of time in the forest.

For unlike the life of the court and the city, "men fleet the time carelessly" in Arden, as Charles earlier remarked. Here are no power-seekers like Oliver and Duke Frederick, impatient to rid themselves of encumbrances . . . , but men who love to lie under the greenwood tree seeking—only the food they eat. Appropriately, this casualness is the theme of many of their songs. Touchstone's comment on the last—"I count it but lost time to hear such a foolish song" [V. iii. 39-40]—briefly expresses the opposing attitude brought from court into the forest. The attitude is shared by the malcontent Jacques, his fellow satirist, and in some respects by Rosalind. Touchstone is, in fact, the play's timekeeper, as Harold Jenkins has called him [see excerpt above, 1953], and his most extended disquisition on time is fittingly recounted by Jaques [II. vii. 20-8]. . . . Later in the same scene Jaques *in propria persona* also "morals on the time" in his speech on the Seven Ages of Man, calling our attention to the broader divisions of time's progress and pageant. Between these speeches, it should be noted, occur Orlando's entrance and his words . . . on the neglect of time by the Duke and his foresters. Clearly, Shakespeare throughout the play contrasts the timelessness of the forest world with the time-ridden preoccupations of court and city life, but here the juxtaposition is both dramatically and thematically emphasized. For the court and city habitués, time is a measured progress to the grave—or worse! But for the foresters, is merely "the stream we go a-fishing in" (to borrow the phrase of a later pastoralist). Neither attitude, of course, will quite do in this sublunary world; hence, to present a more balanced view of time—as of love, pastoralism, and poetry—Shakespeare uses the dialectic characteristic of this play and centers it upon his hero and heroine.

For Rosalind's awareness of time, however related to the preoccupation imported from the "outside" world, is different from Touchstone's obsession with "riping and rotting." It is, partly, the awareness of a girl in love and impatient for the attentions of her lover, a healthy consciousness that recalls Juliet's except as it is undarkened by tragic fate. But her awareness has further implications. When she and Orlando first meet in the forest, their dialogue, appropriately enough, is itself about time. Rosalind's question, "I pray you, what is't o'clock?" [III. ii. 299], although banal, suits the occasion; for despite her boast that she will speak like a saucy lackey, she is momentarily confused by confronting Orlando and scarcely knows how to begin. What follows in her account of Time's "divers paces" [III. ii. 308-33], however, is something more than a verbal smokescreen to help her collect her wits, detain her lover, and make sure he keeps coming back: it is a development of Jaques' Seven Ages speech with important thematic variations. Jaques' speech describes a man in his time playing many parts and suggests that his speed, or "pace," will vary along with his role; the series of vignettes illustrates the movement of a person *in* time. Rosalind not only adds appreciably to Jaques' gallery, but showing profounder insight, she shifts the emphasis from the movement *of a person,* to the movement *of time* as apprehended, for example, by the young maid "between the contract of her marriage and the day it is solemniz'd. If the interim be but a se'ennight, Time's pace is so hard that it seems the length of seven year" [III. ii. 314-17]. In this way, she more thoroughly accounts for *duration,* or the perception of time, which, unlike Jaques' portrait of our common destiny, is not the same for everyone.

Naturally, Rosalind is most concerned with the perception of time by the lover, and here her behavior is in marked contrast to Orlando's. Quite literally—and like any fiancée, or wife— she is Orlando's timekeeper. When he fails to keep his appointments, she suffers both pain and embarrassment (III. iv) that are relieved only by the greater follies of Silvius and Phebe that immediately follow. When he finally does turn up an hour late—as if to dramatize his belief that "there's no clock in the forest" [III. ii. 300-01]—Rosalind rebukes him severely [IV. i. 38-52]. . . . Rosalind's time-consciousness goes beyond the mere moment: she knows the history of love—witness her speech on Troilus and Leander [IV. i. 94-108]—and she predicts its future, as she warns Orlando of love's seasons after marriage [IV. i. 146-49]. Her ardent impulse is thus in comic juxtaposition with her realistic insight, just as Orlando's "point-device" attire and time-unconsciousness comically contrast with his rimes and other protestations of love.

In this fashion we arrive at the theme's center, or balance. If Orlando, as we have seen, is an agent of regeneration, he appears through his forgetfulness of time to be in some danger of not realizing his function. He might like Silvius, were it not for Rosalind, linger through an eternity of unconsummated loving; certainly, like the Duke, he feels in the forest no urgency about his heritage—at least not until he comes upon his brother sleeping beneath an ancient oak tree and menaced by a starved lioness (the symbolism is obvious). Oliver's remarkable conversion after his rescue and his still more remarkable engagement to Celia pave the way for Rosalind's resolution of the action, for under the pressure of his brother's happiness, Orlando can play at games in love no longer. And despite the play's arbitrary finale—Duke Frederick's conversion and the end of exile, in all of which she has had no hand—nevertheless, it is again Rosalind who has had an important share in preparing the principals for this chance. Like her less attractive counterpart Helena in *All's Well That Ends Well,* she remains a primary agent for the synthesis of values that underlies regeneration in Shakespeare's comedy. At the very outset we see her, the daughter of Duke Senior at the court of Duke Frederick, as a link between two worlds, not unlike Orlando's representative linking of two generations. In love, she is realistic rather than cynical, but not without a paradoxical—and perfectly human—romantic bias. So, too, with regard to time she moves with Orlando to a proper balance of unharried awareness. For all of these functions—as for others—the timeless world of the forest, with its complement of aliens, serves as a haven; but more importantly, it serves as a school.

Neither the extremes of idealism nor those of materialism, as they are variously represented, emerge as "the good life" in *As You Like It.* That life is seen rather as a mean of natural human sympathy educated—since that is a major theme in the play—by the more acceptable refinements of civilization (II.

vii) and the harsh realities of existence ("winter and rough weather" [II. v. 8]). The "antique world" stands for a timeless order of civilization still in touch with natural human sympathy that, under the "new" regime (while it lasted), had been forced underground. To the forest, the repository of natural life devoid of artificial time barriers, the champions of regeneration repair in order to derive new energy for the task before them. There they find refuge, gain strength, learn—and return. (pp. 199-207)

*Jay L. Halio, "'No Clock in the Forest': Time in 'As You Like It,'" in* Studies in English Literature, 1500-1900, *Vol. II, No. 2, Spring, 1962, pp. 197-207.*

## JOHN DOVER WILSON (essay date 1962)

[*Dover Wilson was a highly regarded Shakespearean scholar who was involved in several aspects of Shakespeare studies. As an editor of the* New Cambridge Shakespeare, *he made numerous contributions to twentieth-century textual criticism of Shakespeare, making use of the scientific bibliography developed by W. W. Greg and Charlton Hinman. As a critic, Dover Wilson combines several contemporary approaches and does not fit easily into any one critical "school." He is concerned with character analysis in the tradition of A. C. Bradley; he delves into Elizabethan culture like the historical critics, but without their usual emphasis on hierarchy and the Great Chain of Being; and his interest in visualizing possible dramatic performances of the plays links him with his contemporary, Harley Granville-Barker. In the following excerpt from* Shakespeare's Happy Comedies (1962), *Dover Wilson continues a dominant view of* As You Like It *by arguing that a strong "vein of mockery" runs throughout the play. Like many earlier critics, he regards Jaques and Touchstone as the principal figures through whom Shakespeare parodies his pastoral design—especially Touchstone, whom he compares to Dull and Costard in* Love's Labour's Lost, *asserting that, like these characters, the fool contributes the "rich, rank, scent of Mother Earth to the synthetic airs of . . . love in Arcadia." Concerning love, Dover Wilson also points out that this passion "is the main industry of Arden."*]

[As] everyone knows, Shakespeare took the *story* of *As You Like It* from a little pastoral novel by Thomas Lodge, entitled *Rosalynde, or Euphues' Golden Legacy.* . . . This slender tale is however the least important part of the play; it gets it going and finishes it off. But all the middle portion is taken up with encounters and talk, songs and jests, in the forest of Arden, which Shakespeare sets before the eyes of our imagination by a hundred little touches. The forest makes the play, and the forest is a blend of two elements: (i) the delightful scenery of [Montemayor's *Diana*], and (ii) Shakespeare's memories of the Warwickshire scenery round about his native home—his own forest of Arden, in fact.

His success in the creation of this atmosphere, of this 'golden world' in which his characters 'fleet the time carelessly' [I. i. 118-19] for so many scenes, is all the greater when we call to mind that he wrote for the bare Elizabethan stage. And yet, it was just the bareness of that stage which put him to his task and challenged him. Shakespeare's scenery is in the verse he writes. His earliest success of the kind is *A Midsummer Night's Dream,* and we [find] him bettering that in the last Act of *The Merchant.* *As You Like It* goes one better still, in atmospheric effect, to be excelled only by the night of *Macbeth,* the storm of *Lear,* and the music-laden air of Prospero's island [in *The Tempest*].

But, while the forest is a triumph of dramatic scene-painting and the play as a whole the very distillation of pastoral romance, the more judicious among Shakespeare's audience would not miss the vein of mockery that runs throughout.

First of all, Arden takes a good deal of getting to. Rosalind, Celia and Touchstone reach it utterly dead-beat; old Adam cannot walk a step further, so that Orlando is forced to carry him in his arms; Oliver, Orlando's brother, arrives footsore, in rags, and so dog-tired that when he falls asleep even a snake coiling about his throat is not able to wake him. Moreover, though eternal summer reigns in the lands of pastoral romance, our first glimpse of Arden is in wintertime. The exiled Duke is bravely making the best of it, and welcoming

> the icy fang
> And churlish chiding of the winter's wind,
> Which, when it bites and blows upon my body,
> Even till I shrink with cold, I smile and say
> 'This is no flattery: these are counsellors
> That feelingly persuade me what I am.'
> Sweet are the uses of adversity.
>
> [II. i. 6-12]

And the emphasis upon winter and its trials is continued in the song, 'Under the greenwood tree' with its refrain of

> No enemy
> But winter and rough weather
>
> [II. v. 7-8]

and the later 'Blow, blow thou winter wind', the second verse of which begins

> Freeze, freeze, thou bitter sky.
>
> [II. vii. 184-85]

Only in the fifth Act does spring arrive with 'It was a lover and his lass' [V. iii. 16-33].

And in the third place, there is a touch of irony about most of the characters. The exiled Duke and his co-mates are slightly ridiculous in their enforced stoicism, and were intended, I have little doubt, to recall the attitude of so many of Elizabeth's courtiers, like Ralegh and Essex, who when they fell out of the Queen's favour, as they not infrequently did, retired to their own estates in the provinces and sulked in voluntary or involuntary exile. (pp. 150-52)

The presence of such a character as Jaques, for whom there is no parallel in Lodge or Montemayor, is also highly significant. Jaques is Shakespeare's misanthrope—though a very different one from Molière's Alceste. We are not told why he has accompanied the Duke into exile, but it is clear that while he rails at his fellow-exiles for being fools, he despises the world so much that he prefers the country to the court. It is for instance noteworthy that he does not return to court with the Duke at the end of the play, but joins the 'convertite' brother usurper [V. iv. 184]. His famous 'All the world's a stage' [II. vii. 139-66] . . . is of course sheer cynicism. (p. 153)

Yet Jaques, who can suck melancholy out of a song, as a weasel sucks eggs, laughs at least once in the play. For the fool can make even him merry. The incident is not shown upon the stage; but Jaques reports it to the Duke at great length in the beginning of II, vii. . . . [His words here are as familiar] as 'All the world's a stage'—and like them as often misunderstood. Jaques laughs at the melancholy Touchstone; it does not occur to him that the Fool, who has not a true note of melancholy in him, is really laughing at him—is shooting at his melancholy from behind the stalking-horse of his wit.

Touchstone mocks Jaques as he mocks all the other characters he encounters in Arden. He is the second critic of the pastoral world and like Jaques an addition by Shakespeare to the characters Lodge gave him. He is the realist of the play, or one of the two realists (for Rosalind is another). As his name implies, he *tests* all that the world takes for gold, especially the gold of the golden world of pastoralism. And he had made up his mind about Arden directly he arrives . . . :

> ROSALIND. Well, this is the forest of Arden!
> TOUCH. Ay, now I am in Arden, the more
> fool I. When I was at home, I was in a better
> place, but travellers must be content.
>
> [II. iv. 15-18]

Mr. Aldous Huxley has an essay upon travel somewhere entitled 'Why not stay at home?' which is little more than an expansion of that.

But what raised most laughter, no doubt, with Shakespeare's original audience was Touchstone's lording it as a courtier, a gentleman and a philosopher, over the simple rustics of Arden—he 'the roynish clown' [II. ii. 8]! His long discussion with Corin, the old shepherd, on the comparative merits of life in the court and life in the country leaves little to be said in defence of either state. But the humour of it is in the superior airs which the Fool puts on—as of a thinker and a wit, leaving the poor simpleton before him damned, 'like an ill-roasted egg all on one side' [III. ii. 37-8].

Or mark how he puts down William, his rival for the hand of Audrey [at V. i. 10-51]. . . . (pp. 155-57)

If Corin is ill roasted on one side, the Duke and Jaques are equally ill roasted on the other. And when Touchstone finds himself in the Duke's court at the end of the play, he not only assumes the courtier's style with a ludicrous grace all his own, but delivers himself of the most brilliant burlesque of the preliminaries to a court duel which the literature of the period affords [V. iv. 64-82].

Yet we must never forget . . . that Touchstone is a *Fool*. 'And in his brain', as Jaques tells us,

> Which is as dry [i.e. stupid] as the remainder biscuit
> After a voyage, he hath strange places crammed
> With observation, the which he vents
> In mangled forms.
>
> [II. vii. 39-42]

He possessed, in the educational jargon of our time, a better *background* than Launcelot Gobbo; but he was just as much the 'natural'. His stiff mechanical gait, his drawling speech, his wooden face (all the more so for the flashes of intelligence, released as it were by a hidden spring, which passed across it), together with the motley of his profession, combined to mark him off from the other characters as something less than human.

In the shimmering air of Romance which the inhabitants of Arden breathe, love . . . is the main industry, love the course of which 'never did run smooth' [A Midsummer Night's Dream, I. i. 134]. Touchstone must perforce press in amongst the rest of the country folk 'to swear or to forswear, according as marriage binds and blood breaks' [V. iv. 56-7], and his pairing off with Audrey, the half-witted goatherd, is at once a parody of the love-making of the others and a symptom of his own nature.

For he is 'a material fool' [III. iii. 32], and this materialism, gross as it is, is itself a touchstone; it helps to keep the balance of the play and its atmosphere sane. For as he himself had originally put it:

> As the ox hath his bow, sir, the horse his curb,
> and the falcon her bells, so man hath his de-
> sires.
>
> [III. iii. 79-81]

What Dull and Costard supply in *Love's Labour's Lost,* Touchstone gives to *As You Like It.* They, who had not 'ate paper as it were' and 'not drunk ink' [*Love's Labour's Lost,* IV. ii. 25-6], who were only 'animals, only sensible in the duller parts'; and he, with Audrey upon his arm—'A poor virgin, sir, an ill-favoured thing, sir, but mine own—a poor humour of mine, sir, to take that that no man else will' [V. iv. 57-9]— contribute the rich, rank, scent of Mother Earth to the synthetic airs of Learning's academe and Love in Arcadia. (pp. 157-59)

*As You Like It* is Shakespeare's Arcadia, his escape-play; it is also Shakespeare's criticism of Arcadia and escape literature. (p. 162)

> *John Dover Wilson, "'As You Like It',' in his* Shakespeare's Happy Comedies, *1962. Reprint by Faber and Faber, 1969, pp. 141-62.*

## G. K. HUNTER   (essay date 1962)

[*In the following excerpt, Hunter discusses the importance of "humanely poised and socially accepted love" in* As You Like It, *emphasizing as well the related themes of self-knowledge and self-discipline. He notes that the play's principal figures—Rosalind, Celia, and Orlando—'face the deviations of folly" with "an air of effortless superiority" made possible by the "conquering good" of love and the self-awareness such a love engenders. Rosalind, Hunter argues, has a "terrifyingly accurate perception of shams and follies." More than Touchstone, he continues, she is the "central and normative figure" in the play, able, as in Act III, Scene ii, to affirm the importance of absurd love to human experience. Hunter also suggests that the play is based on a three-part movement. He sees Act I as a simple escape from evil, and the central episodes, he states, depict a series of contrasting attitudes to love and to country life that "becalm" the play and make a satisfactory conclusion difficult. This problem is allayed, Hunter concludes, by Shakespeare's introduction of the Masque of Hymen, which functions as an appropriate expression of both the life force behind Rosalind's "control" over the other characters and the life-as-play theme, which Hunter claims is a "recurrent emphasis throughout"* As You Like It.]

Of all Shakespeare's comedies, *As You Like It* is the most completely centred on the vision of the happiness that is available in this world through personally satisfying, humanely poised and socially accepted love. This does not mean that the play contains no evil or foolish characters: Frederick, the usurping duke who displaces and exiles his elder brother, and Oliver, who seeks to kill and forces into exile *his* brother, are violent and destructive in their attitudes. Even in the Forest of Arden, which provides a space temporarily free from the operations of vice, and so available for the comic and romantic manipulations of Rosalind—even here Jaques the forest moralist and retired libertine, and Phebe the ungentle shepherdess are unbalanced enough in their attitudes to make the equation of Arden with Eden an absurd over-simplification. The point is not that folly and vice do not exist in this comic world, but that the central figures, Rosalind, Celia and Orlando, can face the reality of vice and yet escape contamination, can face the

deviations of folly and yet, through self-knowledge and self-discipline, dismiss them with an air of effortless superiority. (p. 32)

The central image of the love which can effortlessly see through and put aside folly, and yet retain its own exuberant vision of happiness, is found in Rosalind, and around her. (p. 34)

The easy assurance of love and the bubbling vision of happiness that it offers are seen as the basis of Rosalind's unassertive but terrifyingly accurate perception of shams and follies. As we have suggested, the Forest of Arden is no mere haunt of sentimental self-indulgence, where self-control is unnecessary. The ease with which Rosalind detects the follies of Phebe and Jaques is directly connected with her self-awareness and capacity for self-mockery. Her disguise as Ganymede gives Shakespeare a unique opportunity to make this point. In stressing the force and independence of Beatrice's mind [in *Much Ado about Nothing*] Shakespeare made her into something dangerously close to a shrew; but Rosalind, in order to sustain her role as a quasi-man, *must* play a swaggering part of this kind, and there is no danger that we will take her play-role as an infringement of her true personality, or have difficulty in separating out the mocking part from the loving part. Indeed, the golden assurance of the conquering good in love that this play presents is necessarily connected with the assumption that lovers are absurd; to know one's own absurdity, yet not to be oppressed by it, indeed to enjoy it, is the basis of romantic heroism as the play shows it.

The scene in which we can most clearly see Shakespeare balancing the wonder against the absurdity of love is Act III, scene ii, and a look at the details of this scene may indicate the methods by which the effect is built up. Here Shakespeare puts the poet, the lover and the madman together (once again), but here, if not in *A Midsummer-Night's Dream,* it is clear what he means by the conjunction. The scene opens with Orlando as pastoral poet-lover hanging his verses on a tree. There is much that is inherently absurd here: the very action of tying love-verses on trees takes us far away from practical behaviour; then there are the verses themselves, which reflect the attempt to be poetical rather than the success; the central image of Orlando 'abusing young plants with carving Rosalind on their barks' [III. ii. 360-61] leads forward to the climactically absurd lines:

> Run, run, Orlando; carve on every tree
> The fair, the chaste and unexpressive she,
>
> [III. ii. 9-10]

where the idea of the fervent lover sprinting from tree to tree, with his jack-knife at the ready, seeking to express what he knows already is inexpressible ('unexpressive' [III. ii. 10]), cannot possibly be taken seriously. But though the poet-lover is shown as absurd here, he is not really satirized; he is lovably absurd; we sympathize with the noble and poetical madness, whose victim he is, and whose name he bears.

Orlando's poeticizing makes the prologue to the scene, and the verses remain dangling from the stage tree to remind the audience what has passed. For what follows has no obvious continuity with what we have seen: Corin and Touchstone enter and debate the traditional topic of court versus country. Shakespeare, as is usual in his handling of debates, does not prefer one side to another; he is content to establish the social and psychological backgrounds which give coherence to the separate views. Most important for the development and balance of the scene is the view of Touchstone that emerges: against

Corin, his slick wit and uncommitted cleverness are clear enough, but it is also clear that his lack of commitment to any way of life makes him incomplete as a man. . . . [The] 'placing' of Touchstone [at III. ii. 73-85] is important to the economy of the scene, for it is Touchstone who appears in the next episode as the chief critic of Orlando's verses. We have already seen that these are delightfully absurd. Now we hear Touchstone scoffing at them while Rosalind demurs; but having observed already that Touchstone is more clever than understanding we are in a position to enjoy Touchstone's parodies:

> If a hart do lack a hind
> Let him seek out Rosalind, etc.
>
> [III. ii. 101-02]

knowing that they reflect on the parodist at least as much as on the poet. Likewise we can enjoy Rosalind's embarrassment when still more poems appear, and at the same time share her delight in being praised. Rosalind (in so far as she is a lover) is also absurd, and the dialogue which follows between Rosalind and Celia [at III. ii. 219-24], makes this point abundantly clear. . . . In [Rosalind's] situation we laugh *at* her, but we laugh with her as well, for she takes us on to her side by laughing at herself.

The climax of this scene is the confrontation of the self-aware but passionate Rosalind and the noble but absurd Orlando; but before Shakespeare moves on to this he interposes another of those interlude-like dialogues (we have already seen one involving Corin and Touchstone) which prolong the pleasure of anticipated resolutions, and at the same time prepare us for, give depth to, the characteristics about to be displayed. This time we meet Orlando, not as a pastoral poet-lover, but, in contrast to Jaques, as a well-balanced *Man,* contemptuous of affection. Jaques' ridicule of Orlando, like Touchstone's earlier ridicule of the verses, reflects back on himself: love may be absurd, but compared to melancholy it is not at all disabling.

Now comes the climax which all that has gone before has prepared for; Jaques having slunk away, Rosalind takes up the challenge and issues forth herself:

> *Ros.* [*Aside to Celia*] I will speak to him like
> a saucy lackey, and under that habit play the
> knave with him.
>
> [III. ii. 295-96]

Her wit succeeds where Jaques' had failed; it is quicker than Orlando's on the turn, and more acute in its social reference. Without ever reversing our impression that she is deeply in love she is able to keep Orlando at wit's distance, to play the opposing role of 'A very beadle to a humorous sigh' [*Love's Labour's Lost*, III. i. 175], and remain in control of the situation, while revealing (to us) how far she is emotionally involved in it. The scene ends with the preparations for further interviews in which the lover will give his mistress (and us) the pleasures of romantic wooing, without ever knowing how far his play of love with 'Ganymede' is the reality of love with Rosalind.

This scene we have been looking at is not only beautifully balanced in itself, but reflects the central achievement of the play—the achievement of a point of view in which love is known for its absurdity, and yet retained with laughing certainty at the centre of human experience, able to put aside the self-indulgent anti-love jaundice of Jaques, and the self-regarding and prettified love of Phebe. It is sometimes supposed that Touchstone's name indicates that *he* is the central and

normative figure in the play, but this would seem to be a confusion of his role with that of Feste in *Twelfth Night.* Touchstone is, of course, though a jester, no fool; he is faithful to the ladies and he sees through Jaques. But his deliberate downgrading of his desires to what he can get cheaply, his sophisticated version of earthiness, is seen by the play as only a very restricted kind of virtue; the dialogue with Corin reveals his shallowness, and even the clodhopping William shows him up. Set beside Rosalind, Touchstone is no touchstone at all.

The first part of the play is concerned with the escape from evil; the central episodes (of which I hope the scene I have chosen—III. ii—is sufficiently representative) show a series of contrasting attitudes to love and to the country; these are developed through the meaningful *play* of Rosalind (pretending to be 'Ganymede' pretending to be Rosalind) and Orlando. This *play* is a uniquely powerful way of presenting the richness and complexity of a relationship; but it requires a suspension of place, time and intrigue, and this becalming of the play makes it difficult to steer it to a satisfactory conclusion. Shakespeare has to rescue his characters from their 'dream' or 'holiday' at the end of the play, and to tie up the various strands of interest and intention, and do so in such a way that we can believe that the knots will last.

He solves the problem in an unexpected way. He achieves the fulfilment of a character as real as Rosalind by keeping his *play* motif open, and deliberately exploiting its theatrical naivety. The couples are paired off with comic efficiency:

> *Jaques.* There is, sure, another flood toward,
> and these couples are coming to the ark.
>
> [V. iv. 35-6]

Rosalind acts as impresario, not only for their wedding but also for her own, seeing as well as enjoying the naivety that underlies the proper ceremonial of a great social occasion:

> *Rosalind.* Pray you, no more of this; 'tis like
> the howling of Irish wolves against the moon.
> [*To Silvius*] I will help you if I can. [*To Phebe*]
> I would love you if I could.—Tomorrow meet
> me all together. [*To Phebe*] I will marry you
> if ever I marry woman, and I'll be married
> tomorrow. [*To Orlando*] I will satisfy you if
> ever I satisfied man, and you shall be married
> tomorrow. [*To Silvius*] I will content you if
> what pleases you contents you, and you shall
> be married tomorrow. [*To Orlando*] As you
> love Rosalind, meet. [*To Silvius*] As you love
> Phebe, meet;—and as I love no woman, I'll
> meet.
>
> [V. ii. 109-20]

Shakespeare wishes to emphasize his heroine's control over the environment, and she hangs on to her role as impresario for as long as possible; but even she has to step down eventually and join the Dance of Life. . . . (pp. 35-40)

The formal arrangement of the lovers and the final appearance of Hymen, to bless and organize, only reflect the formality which life, no less than art, thinks appropriate to the presentation of marriage. Hymen admits that these are 'strange events' and instructs the bystanders (including the theatre audience):

> Whiles a wedlock-hymn we sing,
> Feed yourselves with questioning;
> That reason wonder may diminish,
> How thus we met, and these things finish.
>
> [V. iv. 137-40]

But this *wonder* is not a new or unprepared element in the play; it has sustained Rosalind throughout the action, not only in the sense that the world shows itself extraordinarily amenable to her control and full of most convenient coincidences . . . , but also in the sense that her control seems to be supported by a force outside herself or a tendency in the world—call it the Life-force if you will; Hymen is as good a name as any, and Shakespeare does not seem too anxious to make definitions—which can emerge and take charge on their own account, when this is required. We may see the formality of Hymen as only the emergence of a subdued current which has run through the play.

What is more, the Masque of Hymen serves to bring to the surface an idea which has had recurrent emphasis throughout the play, the idea of life itself as a 'play', which only the most poised can master, and in which the others are tied to stage-struck or incoherent roles. It is no accident that the most famous and perhaps even the 'keynote' speech of the play is Jaques' 'All the world's a stage' [II. vii. 139-66] which is so well-known that we have ceased to ask what it means in the play. . . .

A tradition of reciters and of 'speeches from Shakespeare' has taught us to accent this, 'All the *world's* a stage', but in the context it must be, '*All* the world's a stage'; that is, 'not only are we not alone in presenting a "woeful pageant", but we are in fact only doing what *everyone* must do—playing a part'. The words are given to Jaques, and the instances are presented with his characteristic bile, but the idea is appropriate to the play as a whole; it is Rosalind, not Jaques, who exemplifies in the dramatic action the knowledge that *play* is itself a mode (and often the most accessible mode) of reality.

Jaques himself is in some ways a frustrated impresario. . . . It is [his] constant effort to find or invent or organize occasions which he can moralize into food for melancholy, but he fails to convince others, for he has his eye fixed constantly on his own obsessions. Touchstone, on the other hand, is disabled by precisely the opposite defect: his life is organized too obviously with an eye fixed on an audience that can be amused by wit. His wooing of Audrey is conducted in the same spirit as his memory of Jane Smile [II. iv. 46-50]. . . . Touchstone is imprisoned in his detachment as surely as Jaques is imprisoned in his obsession. It is the . . . final scene that shows us the superiority of Rosalind in these terms by making her step down from her role as presenter and stand in line with the other country copulatives. She has as much wit as Touchstone and as much morality as Jaques, but her wit is a function of her feeling heart, and her morality springs from the experience or expectation of being one in the final dance of comedy. (pp. 40-3)

> G. K. Hunter, "'As You Like It'," in his William Shakespeare, the Later Comedies: "A Midsummer-Night's Dream," "Much Ado About Nothing," "'As You Like It," "Twelfth Night," *The British Council, 1962, pp. 32-43.*

## JAN KOTT (essay date 1964)

[*Kott is a Polish-born critic and professor of English and comparative literature now residing in the United States. In his well-known study* Shakespeare, Our Contemporary, *originally published in Polish as* Szkice o Szekspirze *in 1964, he interprets several of the plays as presenting a tragic vision of history. Kott calls this historical pattern the Grand Mechanism. The following excerpt from* Shakespeare, Our Contemporary *is one of the most pessimistic or nihilistic readings of* As You Like It *and a notably*

*original departure from the body of criticism preceding it. Kott treats four issues in his discussion of Shakespeare's comedy: 1) disguise; 2) the nature of Arden; 3) the play's rustic figures and the clown Touchstone; and 4) Jaques's role and character. Calling disguise in* As You Like It *"a dangerous game," Kott explores its overtones of eroticism, orgy, and "chaos," and its "double significance" of the "intellectual and the sensual"; he also argues that disguise contributes to the play's concurrent falseness and genuineness, its illusion and reality. Kott calls Arden "Shakespeare's Bitter Arcadia"; it is, he claims, a place where lovers go through "the dark sphere of animal eroticism." He also avers, like earlier critics, that Shakespeare both "makes mockery of Arcadia" and his pastoral romance and demonstrates the necessity of such ideals or illusions. Extending this argument, Kott focuses on Jaques and Touchstone, emphasizing how both provide the critical commentary in Arden.*]

Rosalind assumed the name of Ganymede when she escaped to the Forest of Arden. Shakespeare adopted this from Lodge's story which served him as material for the plot of *As You Like It.* The choice and assumption of this name was not a matter of chance.

> I'll have no worse a name than Jove's own page,
> And therefore look you call me Ganymede.
> [I. iii. 124-25]

Rosalind, disguised as a boy, meets Orlando in the Forest of Arden. Orlando is in love with her and she is in love with him. But Orlando does not recognize Rosalind in the shape of Ganymede. Rosalind woos him with intensity, but she does it as a boy, or rather as a boy who in this relationship wants to be a girl for his lover. Rosalind plays Ganymede who in turn plays Rosalind. . . . (p. 269)

This is just the beginning. These scenes belong to the finest and most refined among Shakespeare's love dialogues and (but for the fact that the term "mannerism" has a certain traditional pejorative flavour) they should be recognized as a masterpiece of mannerism. On the surface of the dialogue, on the higher level of a disguise, identical with that of *Twelfth Night,* two youths, Ganymede and Orlando, play a love game. On the intermediate level we have Rosalind and Orlando in love with each other. But the real Rosalind happens to be a disguised boy.

The borderlines between illusion and reality, between an object and its reflection, are gradually lost. . . . [One] has to recall the theatrical aesthetics of Genet. The theatre represents in itself all human relationships, but not because it is their more or less successful imitation. The theatre is the image of all human relationships because it is based on falseness—original falseness, rather like original sin. The actor plays a character he is not. He is who he is not. He is not who he is. To be oneself means only to play one's own reflection in the eyes of strangers. (pp. 269-70)

In the love scenes of Arden Forest, just as in those of Illyria [in *Twelfth Night*], the theatrical form and the theme completely correspond with and penetrate each other, on condition, that is, that female parts are played, as they were on the Elizabethan stage, by boys. An actor disguised as girl plays a girl disguised as boy. Everything is real and unreal, false and genuine at the same time. And we cannot tell on which side of the looking glass we have found ourselves. As if everything were mere reflection. (p. 270)

Rosalind plays Ganymede who plays Rosalind. She plays herself being married to Orlando. At that wedding ceremony Celia will play the priest. The amazing poetics of these scenes has not yet been demonstrated. As if our contemporary theatre had no proper instrument! And yet these scenes contain Genet's theatre to the same degree that Beckett's theatre is contained in *King Lear,* except that they are sur-Genet, just as the quartet of madmen, real and feigned, in the third act of *Lear,* is sur-Beckett.

The love scenes in the Forest of Arden have the logic of dreams. Planes, persons, tenses—past, present, future—are intermingled; so is parody with poetry. (p. 271)

Disguise [here] is a dangerous game. It is a game in which one discards one's own shape and assumes, or at least borrows, a strange one. The Harlequin is a transformist, but he comes from the devil species. The evil spirit leads people astray because he continually assumes different shapes; the shape of a man, an animal, or even of an inkstand. (p. 272)

The most dangerous disguise of all is the one where sex is changed. Transvestism has two directions: sacral and sexual; liturgical and orgiastic. Orgy can also be part of a liturgical feast. In the Saturnalia boys and girls used to exchange their clothes. Laws and rules were suspended. Boys behaved like girls, girls behaved like boys. Values and judgements were mixed up. For one night everything was permitted. But in a liturgical disguise, laws and rules were only suspended, never revoked. Disguise was, as it were, a return to Chaos from which Law had emerged and in which there had as yet been no division into the male and the female.

Every disguise involves not only an invitation to Cytherea, a call to orgy; disguise is a diabolic invention in a much deeper sense. It is the realization of man's eternal dream about overcoming the boundaries of his own body and of his sex. It is a dream of an erotic experience in which one is one's own partner, in which one sees and experiences sensual pleasure, as it were, from the other side. One is oneself and at the same time someone else, someone like oneself and yet different.

Disguise has its metaphysical plane, a remnant perhaps from the periods when it was part of liturgy. That metaphysical plane could at any rate still be traced in it at the time of Renaissance. Not only was it an attempt at eroticism free from the limitations of the body. It was also a dream of love free from the limitations of sex; of love pervading the bodies of boys and girls, men and women, in the way light penetrates through glass.

In the closing scenes of *As You Like It* one can discern this double significance of disguise: the spiritual and the physical; the intellectual and the sensual. Everything has been mixed up: the bodies of boys and girls; desire and love. Silvius loves Phebe, the shepherdess; Phebe loves Ganymede; Ganymede loves Orlando; Orlando loves Rosalind. Ganymede is Rosalind, but it is Rosalind who is Ganymede, because Rosalind is a boy, just as Phebe is a boy. Love is an absolute value, and at the same time most absolutely a matter of chance. Eroticism goes through bodies like electric current and makes them tremble. Every Rosalind is Ganymede, and every Ganymede is Rosalind. (pp. 272-73)

The love scenes in *As You Like It* take place in the Forest of Arden. The Arden Forest is like all Shakespeare's forests, except that it is possibly more amazing, as if it contained, repeated, or foretold them all. Shakespearean forests are real and enchanted, tragic and grotesque; pathetic and lyrical scenes are performed in them. In Shakespeare's forest, life is speeded up, becomes more intense, violent, and at the same time, as it were, clearer. Everything acquires a double significance: the literal and the metaphorical. Everything exists for itself and is also its own reflection, generalization, archetype.

In a Shakespearean forest [in *A Midsummer Night's Dream*], the lovers in the course of a summer night went through the dark sphere of animal eroticism. They came to know the urgency of desire and possession. They exchanged partners. In another of Shakespeare's forests [in *King Lear*], four characters of *As You Like It* will pass through tempest and hurricane: the prince who has renounced his crown; the exiled minister; the exiled brother; and the clown. They will be reduced to bare existence, which must suffice for itself and in itself find reasons for being, as there can be no appeal from it, whether to empty heavens, to bloody history, or to nonrational nature. In the last of Shakespearean forests, on Prospero's island [in *The Tempest*], the history of the world will be performed in quick motion, in three hours.

First, the Forest of Arden means escape; escape from the cruel kingdom where, as always in Shakespeare, two themes obsessively repeat themselves: exile of the lawful prince and depriving the younger brother of his inheritance. For Shakespeare this is rudimentary social history in a nutshell. In *As You Like It* the daughter of the dethroned prince will also be exiled. The opening of the play has nothing of the calm and light-heartedness that, following the nineteenth-century pattern, critics still try to detect in *As You Like It* and *Twelfth Night*. It even seems singularly dark:

> O, what a world is this, when what is comely
> Envenoms him that bears it!
>
> [II. iii. 14-15]

A tyrant has ascended the throne, a brother persecutes a brother, love and friendship have been destroyed by ambition, the world is ruled by sheer force and money. From the Duke's feast wrestlers are being carried away with broken ribs. The opening of *As You Like It* has the atmosphere of the Histories; the air is stuffy and every one is afraid. The new prince is distrustful, suspicious, jealous of everything and everybody, unsure of his position, sensing the enemy in everyone. As in the Histories, the only hope of salvation is in escape; escape at any price and as fast as one can. (pp. 275-76)

The opening of the play is violent and brutal; the close, naïve and idyllic, written in a few lines, deliberately devoid of motivation. The bad duke meets a hermit and is converted. Brother restores brother his inheritance. (p. 276)

Between the dark prologue and the fairy-tale epilogue there is the Forest of Arden, the most English of all Shakespearean forests. It is like the one in Warwickshire, near Stratford. Tall oaks grow in it, there are many glades and clearings, streams flow down mossy stones. People wander among briers and thorns. In this forest birds sing; does, hares, and deer ("poor dappled fools" [II. i. 22]) run about. It is here that the exiled duke has taken refuge.... (pp. 276-77)

In this Forest of Arden good gentlemen play at free men and noble brigands; the priest is to marry the clown to the milkmaid; sheep are herded by peasants who declaim about love; girls dress up as boys; a melancholy courtier mocks himself and everyone around.

It is a strange kind of forest in which almost all the characters of Shakespeare's world meet. It is a real forest, as well as a feudal utopia and a sneering comment on that utopia. A lioness

*Act III. Scene iii. Touchstone and Audrey. By Steven Spurrier.*

with her cub has wandered into the forest, and snakes crawl on the moss.

> Now go we in content
> To liberty, and not to banishment.
>
> [I. iii. 137-38]

This is the coda of the first act. It is spoken by Celia to Rosalind before their escape into the forest. The kingdom of liberty is at the same time the kingdom of nature; idyllic, poeticized nature, reminding one of Theocritus. . . . (p. 277)

The kingdom of liberty and nature is contrasted with life at court; harmony and freedom, with captivity of mind, bondage of heart, insecurity of life. . . .

But from the very first scene the idyll is blurred. As in *Twelfth Night,* the instruments are in discord. The music of Arden Forest is all in disharmony.

> And yet it irks me the poor dappled fools,
> Being native burghers of this desert city,
> Should, in their own confines, with forked heads
> Have their round haunches gor'd.
>
> [II. i. 22-5]

To all appearances we seem to remain in the same poetic key. Hunting scenes traditionally include sentimental lamentations over a wounded stag deserted by its fellows. But here the tone is different. The kingdom of nature is as ruthless and egotistic as the world of civilization. There is no return to primeval harmony. It is the dispossessed who dispossess here, and they kill those who have themselves escaped with their lives. (p. 278)

In Arcadia all are equal. Unknown is the power of money and the advantage of superior birth. Law does not yield to force, and the only people who are unhappy are those whose love is unrequited. Rosalind has hardly arrived at the Forest of Arden than she overhears two shepherds talking, the younger of whom is complaining to the older that his love is not requited. Rosalind is hungry and sleepy. Like Homeric heroes, Shakespear-

ean heroes every now and then feel hunger and the need for sleep, even when they are unhappy in love, or engaged in a conspiracy.

Rosalind and Celia are looking for shelter and food. They will, of course, pay with gold. The romantic Rosalind is sober enough. Just as Shakespeare was. The Forest of Arden, where the golden age was to come anew, is ruled by the capitalist laws of hire.

> But I am shepherd to another man
> And do not shear the fleeces that I graze.
> My master is of churlish disposition.
>
> [II. iv. 78-80]

And even more to the point:

> Besides, his cote, his flocks, and bounds of feed
> Are now on sale. . . .
>
> [II. iv. 83-4]

Rosalind the Arcadian, Rosalind the heroine of romance, Rosalind the character of pastoral court comedy, buys the cottage, land, and sheep. . . . (pp. 278-79)

Arcadia has been turned into an estate, into landed property. Says the shepherd:

> . . . If you like, upon report,
> The soil, the profit, and this kind of life,
> I will your very faithful feeder be
> And buy it with your gold right suddenly.
>
> [II. iv. 97-100]

A lovely enumeration, and a lovely order: "the soil, the profit, and this kind of life." Lovely, and very English. Very Shakespearean, for that matter, because, of all we know about Shakespeare, only one thing is certain: he was a competent judge of houses and land, and knew how to buy them. (pp. 279-80)

Of all Shakespeare's works, *As You Like It* and *Twelfth Night* are closest to the spirit of Ariosto. There is a similar combination of pathos and irony, mockery and lyricism. This mixture of techniques and literary genres is something very modern, and the theatre is wrong to draw back from it. Even more modern, closer to our own time, is the ambiguous attitude to madness; or rather, to the escape into madness, into mythology, and into disguise. It is not only Rosalind who disguises herself as Ganymede. Elizabethan outlaws disguise themselves as noble brigands of Robin Hood's time. They are rather like Don Quixote, who put on an old suit of armour he had found in the attic. Shakespeare has no illusions; not even the illusion that one can live without illusions.

He takes us into the Forest of Arden in order to show that one must try to escape, although there is no escape; that the Forest of Arden does not exist, but those who do not run away will be murdered. Without her escape to the non-existent forest, Rosalind will not marry Orlando, and Orlando will not regain his paternal inheritance.

Two pairs of shepherds, real and invented, derived from English pastures and from pastoral Arcadia, serve as the system of mirrors that enables Shakespeare to discredit and ridicule courtly refinement with its code of honour, all the charms of the "natural state," and the conventions of pastoral romance.

> CORIN
> . . . and would you have us kiss tar? The courtier's hands are perfum'd with civet.

TOUCHSTONE
Most shallow man! . . . Civet is of a baser birth
than tar—the very uncleanly flux of a cat.
[III. ii. 63-5, 67-8]

A very similar device will be used in the future by Jonathan
Swift. The juxtaposition of the great and the small can be a
system of mirrors too. It is enough to reduce man a hundred
times in size for dynastic wars and endeavours to obtain court
preferment to become a flea circus. It is enough to magnify
him a hundred times for a kiss to become a monstrosity. Says
Touchstone to Corin:

That is another simple sin in you: to bring the
ewes and the rams together and to offer to get
your living by the copulation of cattle; to be
bawd to a bell-wether, and to betray a she-lamb
of a twelvemonth to a crooked-pated old cuckoldly ram, out of all reasonable match.
[III. ii. 78-83]

It is not just the mechanism of ridicule that is Swiftian here.
Shakespeare is the forerunner of Swift in his slowly and consistently growing disgust at nature. His anti-physis, directed
above all at the sphere of reproduction and sexual instinct, will
find its apogee in *King Lear* and *Othello*. But already here, in
the calm landscape of Arden Forest, the word "natural" begins
to acquire the meaning we give it when referring to "natural
functions".

. . . 'Tis such fools as you
That makes the world full of ill-favour'd children.
[III. v. 52-3]

It might have been a line spoken by the Fool in *King Lear*. In
*As You Like It* it is not spoken by Touchstone. This is the
sweet, tender, passionate Rosalind mocking Silvius, who is in
love with Phebe. Rosalind, Phebe, Audrey are also the successive mirrors in which love sees itself. Idyllic shepherds and
shepherdesses had always been beautiful. In *As You Like It*
only Ganymede-Rosalind, the youth-girl, has the right to beauty.
In the mocked-at Arcadia shepherdesses are plain. (pp. 280-82)

Phebe is plain to Rosalind and beautiful to Silvius [III. v.].
Phebe is plain only in one of the mirrors. Audrey is plain in
all of them. Audrey is meant to be plain and stupid. Audrey
is natural. The clown wants to marry a girl who is plain and
stupid, so as not to have any illusions. The marriage ceremony
is to be performed by Sir Oliver Martext whose parish is, of
course, also to be found in the Forest of Arden. But the clown
will chase the priest away. They will be joined according to
the laws of nature; natural nature, that is.

Phebe is poetic and behaves in the Petrarchan manner. Phebe
wears pastoral costume. But in Shakespeare even shepherdesses from fictional Arcadia suddenly become real. Phebe had
dressed herself up as shepherdess, so let her have the red hands
of a swineherd. Shakespeare leaves nothing of the over-sweet-
ened and over-aestheticized pastoral nature. (pp. 282-83)

The clowns in *As You Like It* and *Twelfth Night* are Shakespeare's most original addition to his inherited plots. If wisdom
becomes clowning, then clowning becomes wisdom. If the
world has come to stand on its head, one can adopt the right
attitude to it only by turning somersaults. These are the pre-
suppositions of clownish logic. The world makes clowns of
everybody, except clowns. They are the only ones to have
escaped general buffoonery by hiding under their fool's caps.
Feste [in *Twelfth Night*] and Touchstone are not clowns any

more; their jokes have ceased to be funny. They are disagreeable. Disintegration is their function. They live in a bare world,
bereft of myths, reduced to knowledge without illusions.

The clownish echo in the Forest of Arden is a double one. Not
only Touchstone echoes the characters of the play. The other
critical echo is provided by Jaques. . . . (pp. 284-85)

*As You Like It* and *Twelfth Night* are close in time to *Hamlet*.
In the figure of Jaques Shakespearean scholars long ago perceived the first outline of the Prince of Denmark. Before Jaques
turns into Hamlet he must first go through the school of clowning. Feste and Touchstone are philosophical clowns already.
But they are only clowns. When they have taken off their fool's
caps, they cease to exist. Before a philosophical clown can
become Hamlet, he must find personal reasons for his bitterness. He must first be a man. (p. 285)

At the beginning Jaques is a repentant libertine; or at least this
is how the Duke describes him. He is a melancholiac pure and
simple, the essence of melancholy, as if he were filled with
bile, according to the Elizabethan classification of humours.
He is even sentimental at first, sorry for a wounded stag. But
he soon fastens his look upon the clown:

. . . O noble fool!
A worthy fool! Motley's the only wear!
[II. vii. 33-4]

Like King Lear in his wanderings to the far end of the cold
night, Jaques undergoes in the Forest of Arden a lesson of
clownish education. Soon he envies the clown his freedom:

. . . I must have liberty
Withal, as large a charter as the wind,
To blow on whom I please; for so fools have.
[II. vii. 47-9]

The Forest of Arden is a return to the golden age, the only
place in the feudal world where alienation has ceased to operate. And in this Forest of Arden, it is Jaques who feels his
alienation most fully and is, to use our terminology, most
thoroughly frustrated. (pp. 285-86)

Jaques has learned from the Fool not only his philosophy, but
also his language; the language Hamlet will speak. At the end
of the play everyone will leave the Forest of Arden, except
Jaques. He is the only one who has no reason to leave the
Forest, because he has never believed in the Forest, has never
entered Arcadia. (p. 286)

The Forest of Arden makes mockery of Arcadia and constitutes
a new Arcadia. Love is escape from cruel history to an invented
forest. Shakespeare is like a Bible; he creates his own myths.
The Forest of Arden is a place in which all dreams meet; it is
a dream and the awakening from a dream.

*Coincidentia oppositorum!* The unification of all opposites! In
the Forest of Arden love is both earthly and platonically sublimated. Rosalind is Ganymede and the most girlish of girls.
Constant-fickle, calm-violent, fair-dark, shy-impudent, pru-
dent-rash, tender-mocking, childish-grownup, cowardly-cou-
rageous, bashful-passionate. As in Leonardo, she is an almost
perfect androgyny and personifies the same longing for the lost
Paradise where there had as yet been no division into male and
female elements.

All this the world well knows; yet none knows well
To shun the heaven that leads men to this hell.
[Sonnet 129]
(p. 292)

Jan Kott, ''Shakespeare's Bitter Arcadia,'' in his Shakespeare, Our Contemporary, *translated by Boleslaw Taborski, new edition, Anchor Books, 1966, pp. 237-92.*

**PETER G. PHIALAS** (essay date 1966)

[*In the following excerpt, Phialas argues that* As You Like It *represents the ''fruition'' of Shakespeare's experiments in the comic form, expressing, through Rosalind, a balanced view of the ideals of romance and ''the realism of the working-day world.'' Noting the importance of self-awareness or self-knowledge in the play, Phialas claims that it is Rosalind's disguise that accounts not only for the richness of her role, but also enables her to take on different points of view simultaneously and to bring about the ''final synthesis of the play's chief ideas.'' Rosalind, the critic maintains, is therefore capable of an analogical self-irony and reflexive scrutiny that applies equally to the play's pastoral and romantic elements, for at one moment she deflates romantic or pastoral conventions with strong and direct satire, and at another she is the embodiment of romantic love.*]

With *As You Like It* Shakespeare reached a significant milestone in his career as comic dramatist, and here his mode of romantic comedy achieved so successful a form that further development of it seemed impossible. In *As You Like It* a number of experiments and trials carried out in earlier comedies find their full fruition. This is particularly true of Shakespeare's unceasing search for a harmonious relationship of idea or theme and the story or metaphor with which to give it expression. He had already attempted this metaphorical dramatization of his theme in such plays as *The Two Gentlemen of Verona, Love's Labour's Lost,* and most especially in *A Midsummer Night's Dream* and *The Merchant of Venice.* But in none of these earlier plays had he achieved the perfect agreement of idea and symbol that we find in *As You Like It.* In addition to achieving this just relationship of story and theme, *As You Like It* is the first comedy in which the chief idea in the play is enshrined in the temperament and attitudes of the heroine. And this is no small matter, seeing that the dramatist had travailed long to bring into agreement the psychological realism necessary to the creation of character and that character's expression in word and deed of Shakespeare's long-standing theme of romantic comedy. Rosalind surpasses Shakespeare's earlier romantic heroines precisely in this very point. The story of her flight to Arden and her adventures there may not be of the most absorbing interest; the story may be, as some students of the play believe, of minor importance. But Rosalind is realized on the stage as a living character, one possessed of so much that is verifiable by experience that we never question the genuineness of her being. But she is more than that. Her temperament, as we shall see, is of a special sort, like that of no other heroine before or after in Shakespearean comedy. And what makes her unique is the special but true-to-character combination in her of certain attitudes towards love and life, towards herself and her fellow human beings. (pp. 209-10)

In her first appearance onstage Rosalind exhibits briefly the sort of melancholy proper to the daughter of an exiled Duke, but such concession to simple realism is soon replaced by a hint of more characteristic complexities. For instance, the note of self-pity revealed in her initial speech disappears when Touchstone joins her and Celia a few lines later. A moment thereafter, upon Orlando's arrival, Rosalind is swept by love at first sight, and during the remainder of the scene behaves in the conventional way of romantic lovers. But the way of romantic lovers, though amusing even to Rosalind in the bal-

ance of the play, is here presented as something actual and true. What is recorded in the episode is that Orlando and Rosalind fall in love; what among other things will be recorded later, mostly through Rosalind's agency, is that the way of lovers, including these two, whether they follow literary convention or not, is amusing and not infrequently ridiculous. After establishing this most necessary fact that Rosalind and Orlando are in love and that both have behaved in the way of romantic lovers, Shakespeare may proceed to the far more entertaining and meaningful complexities of Rosalind's role in the play. By way of bridging the simplicity of the early episode with those complexities of later action, Shakespeare in Act I, scene 3, shows a Rosalind on her way to that self-awareness which is one of the most characteristic and most necessary features of her temperament. When the scene opens Rosalind is so sad that she has not a word ''to throw at a dog'' [III. i. 3].

| Celia. | But is all this for your father? |
| Rosalind. | No, some of it is for my child's father. O, how full of briers is this working-day world! |

[I. iii. 10-12]

The concluding line recalls the heroine's melancholy revealed upon her first appearance on the stage, but Shakespeare has already injected a note of self-awareness in her speech which gives it a lightness and flexibility and in addition a special quality of humor. Her reply that some of her sadness is ''for [her] child's father'' illustrates at this early stage the comic tone of her language, a very individual tone which distinguishes her not only from the rest of the *dramatis personae* but also from Shakespeare's earlier comic heroines as well. ''Is it possible,'' Celia asks a moment later, ''on such a sudden you should fall into so strong a liking with old Sir Roland's youngest son?'' [I. iii. 26-8]. And Rosalind replies: ''The Duke my father lov'd his father dearly'' [I. iii. 29-30]. Although very brief, Rosalind's reply illustrates in this early episode both an attitude and a tone of speech which enable her to convey at once her deepest feeling and her comic valuation of it.

When Rosalind and Celia, accompanied by Touchstone, reach Arden, they first encounter Silvius and Corin who are engaged in a sort of debate on the most likely pastoral theme, love. When a few moments later the tearful Silvius, acting the role of the pastoral unrequited lover, leaves the stage, Rosalind responds with the sympathy of one suffering like pain.

> Alas, poor shepherd! searching of thy wound,
> I have by hard adventure found mine own.

[II. iv. 44-5]

The lines strike us as sentimental, and we may find it difficult to relate their tone to the Rosalind we know from the rest of the play. Furthermore, Shakespeare makes sure that the passage, as well as Silvius' complaint preceding it, are gently mocked by Touchstone's own reminiscence of his affair with Jane Smile. But although the sentimental passages are thus vulnerable, they nevertheless record the fact that lovers, including Rosalind, no matter how they express or exaggerate their feelings, do indeed suffer this pleasurable pain. Although she will never again reveal her emotions in this manner, and although she will later severely reprimand Silvius' sentimental self-abandonment, Rosalind here lends significant support to the romantic aspect of love. In the rest of the play she may comment upon her own love and that of others in a far richer, more complex tone, but Rosalind remains a romantic lover to the end, even though in the wooing scenes with Orlando she seems to mock everything we associate with romantic love. The outstanding thing about her is that she is capable of expressing both attitudes simultaneously and with equal conviction.

This complex attitude, already hinted at earlier, is revealed in full in the first of the wooing scenes between Orlando and Rosalind. The scene opens most appropriately with Orlando affixing upon the trunks of trees in Arden love poems addressed to the "fair, the chaste, and unexpressive she" [III. ii. 10]. It is this Petrarchism of Orlando's and his insistence upon wooing by the romantic book, so to speak, that Rosalind will deflate later in the scene, but she will do this without for a moment abandoning her own romantic sentiments. After the intervening debate between Corin and Touchstone . . . , Rosalind enters reading one of Orlando's love poems. Her gentle mockery of the lines gives way to Touchstone's sexual realism in the poem he recites in answer to Orlando's. What is of interest in the clown's rhymes is that they bluntly qualify Orlando's blazon of the "chaste and unexpressive she."

> If a hart do lack a hind,
> Let him seek out Rosalind.
> If the cat will after kind,
> So be sure will Rosalind.
>
> [III. ii. 101-04]

These lines are in shocking contrast to Orlando's but Rosalind offers no defense. On the contrary, her allusion to grafting and medlars momentarily sustains the sexual context created by Touchstone. At that point Celia enters with more of Orlando's lines, and there follows her revelation that Orlando is the author and that he is in the forest. To this, Rosalind responds in the breathless manner of the romantic lover: "Alas the day! what shall I do with my doublet and hose? What did he when thou saw'st him? What said he? How look'd he? Wherein went he? What makes he here? Did he ask for me? Where remains he? How parted he with thee? And when shalt thou see him again? Answer me in one word" [III. ii. 219-24]. And she maintains this romantic attitude throughout the episode. . . . Although her lines sustain the romantic approach to love, the tone Rosalind employs in speaking them lends a new complexity to her role. We may, of course, see these lines as "straight" and flat, but we would be nearer Shakespeare's intention, I believe, if we admit a hint of self-irony in Rosalind's tone. And this would fit well her deportment later in the scene when she accosts Orlando, for there her tone is nothing if not ironic.

After the interlude between Jaques and Orlando, and as soon as Jaques has left the stage, Rosalind, now in the simultaneous role of herself as well as Ganymede, opens her long conference with Orlando. Immediately she broaches the theme of love, and in her very first reference to it she voices that complexity of attitude already hinted at in earlier episodes. If there is no clock in the forest, she says, then "there is no true lover in the forest; else sighing every minute and groaning every hour would detect the lazy foot of Time as well as a clock" [III. ii. 302-05]. While she longs to know if Orlando is a true lover she simultaneously mocks the conventional lover's "sighing every minute and groaning every hour." She is at once Rosalind and Ganymede, or rather Rosalind and Rosalind as Ganymede, at once in love and insisting upon her lover's romantic posturing and also gently mocking both that very romantic posturing as well as her twin attitudes to it. As Ganymede she can recall her uncle's "many lectures" against love and also the "many giddy offenses" women are "touched with" [III.

ii. 347-49]. When Orlando begs her to recount some of those offenses, she protests she will not "cast away . . . physic but on those that are sick" [III. ii. 358-59], that is, men in love. And she adds that she would give "some good counsel" to the "fancy-monger" who has been abusing "our young plants with carving Rosalind on their barks" and hanging "odes upon hawthorns and elegies on brambles; all, forsooth, deifying the name of Rosalind" [III. ii. 359-64]. Here the complexity of simultaneous attitudes is at last expressed by both the dramatic situation and what might seem an arbitrary tone. But the tone, already emerging in earlier episodes, is here triumphantly united with the dramatic or stage contrivance in the meeting of Orlando and the disguised Rosalind. . . . [Her] disguise enables Rosalind to include in her disquisition on love not only the alleged attitudes of Ganymede but also those of the Rosalind he is soon to impersonate. And all this gives extraordinary richness to the heroine's role and allows her to bring about that final synthesis of the play's chief ideas.

Orlando gladly admits that he is the guilty one "that is so love-shak'd" [III. ii. 367], whereupon Rosalind announces, to his considerable distress, that he cannot be in love, for he exhibits none of her "uncle's marks" upon him [III. ii. 369]. Those marks of the conventional lover, she tells him, are a lean cheek, a blue eye and sunken, an "unquestionable" spirit, a beard neglected, a hose ungartered, a bonnet unbanded, a sleeve unbuttoned, a shoe untied, and so on [III. ii. 373-81]. But none of these are to be seen in Orlando, for he is, she tells him, "rather point-device in your accoustrements, as loving yourself than seeming the lover of any other" [III. ii. 382-84]. Though she is here gently mocking the convention, Rosalind also aims at eliciting from Orlando the assurance he so eagerly voices in his reply. "Fair youth, I would I could make thee believe I love" [III. ii. 385-86]. And now, content with that for the moment, she returns to her gentle censure of her sex in matters of love, and as always she includes herself. . . . In sharp contrast to Rosalind's awareness, Orlando keeps in the beaten path of the conventional lover. When she inquires again if he is the author of the verses hanging on the trees, he replies in predictable language:

> I swear to thee, youth, by the white hand of
> Rosalind, I am that he, that unfortunate he.
> *Rosalind.* But are you so much in love as your
> rhymes speak?
> *Orlando.* Neither rhyme nor reason can express
> how much.
>
> [III. ii. 394-99]

It is this flatly conventional language and the attitude it expresses that Rosalind essays to change when she offers to "cure" Orlando of his love sickness. That cure consists simply in exposing her sex's tyranny of their lovers and offering it in corrective contrast to the Petrarchan blazon to which Orlando is totally dedicated. Again her gentle ridicule of her sex, herself included, is made obliquely through a double impersonation which softens its effect. She has cured a lover in this fashion: "He was to imagine me his love, his mistress, and I set him every day to woo me; at which time would I, being but a moonish youth, grieve, be effeminate, changeable, longing and liking, proud, fantastical, apish, shallow, inconstant, full of tears, full of smiles; for every passion something and for no passion truly any thing, as boys and women are for the most part cattle of this colour . . ." [III. ii. 407-15]. But all this is lost upon Orlando, who when they meet again, as promised, in IV, i, returns to his romantic ways. And Rosalind on her part resumes the lesson or cure, but not without first revealing her own deepest longing for reassurance that Orlando loves her:

> *Orlando*. My fair Rosalind, I come within an hour of my promise.
> *Rosalind*. Break an hour's promise in love! He that will divide a minute into a thousand parts, and break but a part of the thousandth part of a minute in the affairs of love, it may be said of him that Cupid hath clapp'd him o' th' shoulder but I'll warrant him heartwhole.
>
> [IV. i. 42-9]

In a moment she will turn to a stronger and more direct satire of romantic conventions but always with an immediate reference to something Orlando has said and especially the manner of his saying it. After her passing allusion to the snail's horns and Orlando's avowal that his "Rosalind is virtuous" [IV. i. 63-4], she asks him to woo her. And when she says she will not have him, he replies "Then in mine own person I die" [IV. i. 93]. To this she offers her strongest "cure," a brief anatomy of two classical archetypes [Troilus and Leander] of romantic love. . . . This, too, is lost upon Orlando, who continues his wooing by the book, insisting that Rosalind's frown would kill him, that "all thoughts . . . are winged" [IV. i. 142], that he would love and have Rosalind for "ever and a day" [IV. i. 145]. To this last, Rosalind offers yet another anti-romantic lecture, this one half-mockingly warning him against the wifely tyranny which she places by the side of his own romantic illusions about her, though she cherishes those illusions even as she mocks them. . . . And she follows this with allusions to wayward wives, concluding that "that woman that cannot make her fault her husband's occasion, let her never nurse her child herself, for she will breed it like a fool" [IV. i. 173-76]. No wonder Celia complains a moment later that Rosalind has "simply misused our sex in your love-prate" [IV. i. 201-02]. But it is all to a purpose, though it comes short of immediate fulfillment, for Orlando will not be "cured." Nor should we take Rosalind's "misuse" of her sex at its face value. It is but a half-serious, half-mocking, anti-romantic lecture, delivered by one who a moment after Orlando's departure admits herself hopelessly in love: "O coz, coz, coz, my pretty little coz, that thou didst know how many fathom deep I am in love!" [IV. i. 205-07]. And just as her grave matter turns out to be half-jesting, so her jest and double jest is in the end all too serious. When Orlando bids her farewell, saying for "these two hours, Rosalind, I will leave thee" [IV. i. 177-78], she replies: "Alas, dear love, I cannot lack thee two hours!" [IV. i. 179]. It is, as E. E. Stoll remarks, "a jest between them, and another jest for herself and Celia, and underneath no jest at all" [see excerpt above, 1937].

Orlando is not the only character in the play whose romantic approach to love engages Rosalind. . . . [She also] has a great deal to say about Silvius' sentimental self-abandonment to Phoebe's disdain. On the one hand, Rosalind responds to his plaints in the manner of one also in love and in like pain, but this is only one side of her attitude towards his love affair. Because neither Silvius nor Phoebe can see themselves or each other in any sort of perspective, Rosalind essays to qualify their single-minded attachment to the convention. Just as in her wooing scenes with Orlando she refuses to be what he and convention say she is, so in her counsel to Silvius and Phoebe Rosalind insists that they abandon their self-deception and look at themselves and each other as persons living in this "working-

day world." In order to shock them into such a change of outlook she employs strong language, some of the most harshly anti-romantic lines in the play.

> You foolish shepherd, wherefore do you follow her,
> Like foggy south, puffing with wind and rain?
> You are a thousand times a properer man
> Than she a woman. 'Tis such fools as you
> That makes the world full of ill-favour'd children.
> 'Tis not her glass, but you, that flatters her;
> And out of you she sees herself more proper
> Than any of her lineaments can show her.
> But, mistress, know yourself. Down on your knees,
> And thank heaven, fasting, for a good man's love;
> For I must tell you friendly in your ear,
> Sell when you can; you are not for all markets. . . .
>
> [III. v. 49-60]

More significant than her disdain of Silvius is Phoebe's rejection of love, for although that rejection inheres in her role of the disdainful shepherdess, it is one of the chief themes in Shakespearean comedy. It is true that Phoebe's falling in love with Ganymede recalls yet another feature of the pastoral convention. . . . But what is more relevant to Shakespeare's theme is that Phoebe not only falls in love at first sight with another shepherd but that she becomes enamored of Ganymede. This particular detail has point in providing the shock needed for Phoebe's conversion. It recalls a related motif in *Much Ado*, where those who mock and disdain love and each other suddenly discover that they are in love. And it anticipates the same circumstance in *Twelfth Night*, where the disdainful Olivia falls in love with the disguised Viola.

Even in this passive way Rosalind is made to affect and even control not only changes in a character's attitude but also the movement and direction of the play's action. . . . [Her] own love affair illustrates most clearly her adjustment of the ideal with the real; her comment upon the pastoral convention, direct and oblique, points to the same adjustment. In all her words and actions Rosalind reveals in herself, and recommends to others, a combination of sentiment and good sense, the ideal and the actual, yielding to neither sentimentality nor cynicism. . . . Whether in the wooing scenes with Orlando or in her colloquies with Celia, Jaques, or the Duke, or in the episodes with Silvius and Phoebe, whether deeply moved or amused, Rosalind maintains unclouded good judgment, a clarity of vision which, as many readers of the play have observed, is the chief value of the play.

In order to stress Rosalind's role Shakespeare comes very near to raising her speech and act to the level of symbol, and this is particularly true of the episode in which she promises the lovers that she will bring them together. She will join Orlando and Rosalind, Oliver and Celia, Silvius and Phoebe. "Believe then, if you please, that I can do strange things. I have, since I was three years old, convers'd with a magician, most profound in his art, and yet not damnable" [V. ii. 58-61]. And of course in the concluding scene she does as she here promises, "make all this matter even" [V. iv. 18]. There is no claim here that Rosalind is a symbolic character. She is far too recognizably human for that. But the concluding scene of the play forces us to admit that a symbolic element is surely present in the appearance, and particularly the words, of Hymen. This final scene concludes happily the two strands of the play's action: the conflict of the two pairs of brothers and the love affairs of the four couples. Both actions end in union and reconciliation, and as in all non-satiric comedy the wedding ceremony symbolizes the union not only of the lovers but of nearly all persons in the play. And here that union is dignified by Hymen himself as he sings:

> Then is there mirth in heaven,
> When earthly things made even
> Atone together.

> [V. iv. 108-10]

Surely here the dramatist, as other poets of his age and in particular Spenser, brings together Neoplatonist and Christian notions concerning the meaning and power of love. And in doing so he touches the very soul of romance. But we should remember that Shakespeare places romance in a comic context instead of merely reproducing it. To the cynic as well as the satiric poet or dramatist the theme of romance is at variance with reality and therefore unacceptable. To Shakespeare that same theme is not only acceptable but the chief subject for comic treatment. . . . In Shakespearean romantic comedy, though romance is its subject, the dramatist refuses to reproduce, merely to dramatize, romance. Instead, he chooses to present it in a comic mode, to place its longing for the ideal against the fact of human limitation. This is what Shakespearean romantic comedy is about, and failure to see this has often led critics astray. One often comes upon the comment, from Jonson to our own day, that romantic love, being at variance with the truth, is unfit for comic treatment. Such a notion overlooks the fact that in Shakespearean romantic comedy the truth, the actual, is as indispensable as romance itself. . . . [The] fusion or balance of these two is Shakespeare's chief concern in his comedies. And it is precisely because Rosalind is able to express this perfect equilibrium that she may be said to represent a culmination of Shakespeare's quest for the ideal comic heroine. For *As You Like It*, in its action generally, in its structure, in its variety of characters and their relationship, but most especially in the temperament of its heroine, expresses better than any other comedy the balance between the idealism of romance and the realism of the working-day world. The longing for ideal forms is qualified and balanced by the knowledge that full realization is impossible. (pp. 243-54)

> *Peter G. Phialas, "'As You Like It'," in his* Shakespeare's Romantic Comedies: The Development of Their Form and Meaning, *The University of North Carolina Press, 1966, pp. 209-55.*

## SYLVAN BARNET　(essay date 1968)

[*Barnet is an American critic and scholar and the general editor of the Signet edition of Shakespeare's works. In the following excerpt, he discusses the issue of probability and improbability in* As You Like It, *assessing, especially, the meaning and function of the deliberate "strangeness" of the Arden forest. Against the argument that Shakespeare introduced such improbable events as the immediate conversion of Frederick and Oliver because he was following "meaningless conventions" or in order to wind "things up quickly," the critic asserts that the character conversions and transformations resemble the renewal of suffering humanity exemplified by Ovid in his* Metamorphoses, *and that they even constitute "an element of marvel" indicative of divine will and intervention. As such, Barnet concludes, events in the play that seem implausible should not mislead us into thinking that the author of* As You Like It *was negligent.*]

*As You Like It*, for all of its gentle satire on pastoral life and literature, is nevertheless set in a world where, despite Touchstone's dial, there is "no clock i' th' forest" [III. ii. 301]. That is, this pastoral world is utterly different from the shepherd world that King Henry VI calls to mind when, like any of us trying to get through the working-day world, he enumerates a shepherd's chores [in *3 Henry VI*, II. v. 31-7]. . . . While it would be a mistake to say that nothing happens (as someone has remarked, dialogue is what characters *do* to one another), it is true to say that the characters in Arden are in a sort of suspended animation, waiting for the reformation of Oliver and of Frederick, and largely free from the need to make choices and to take effective action. Orlando, for example, defeats a wrestler and (on Adam's advice) runs away, but once in Arden he does very little until near the end, when he saves Oliver. Chance—or Providence—brings him to the good Duke and to Rosalind, and once there he gets what little direction he needs from Rosalind, who herself does very little, for she is in "a holiday mood" [IV. i. 69], until near the end when she presides over the denouement. It should be noted that although at the end she is the mistress of ceremonies, in fact she has contrived almost nothing when compared, say, to Portia [in *The Merchant of Venice*] or to Helena [in *All's Well That Ends Well*] or to Prospero [in *The Tempest*] or to the Duke in *Measure for Measure*. She does not arrange any of the meetings; at the end of the fifth act she runs things only because at the end of the first act she decided to adopt a man's attire. Even the decision to leave the court was forced upon her by her uncle, and the decision to adopt a disguise is a modification of Celia's idea. The characters, that is, live in a wonderful Eden-like world, and Shakespeare on three occasions calls attention to the improbability. Of her chance encounter with Orlando, Celia says, "O wonderful, wonderful, and most wonderful, and yet again wonderful, and after that out of all whooping" [III. ii. 191-93]. Commenting on Oliver's report of "Ganymede's" swoon, Orlando says he has heard of "greater wonders" [V. ii. 28], referring to the amazing swiftness with which Celia and Oliver fall in love. And near the end of the play, Hymen says:

> Whiles a wedlock hymn we sing,
> Feed yourselves with questioning,
> That reason wonder may diminish
> How thus we met, and these things finish.

> [V. iv. 137-40]

But reason will not be able to diminish the wonder by explaining "how thus we met," because there is no explanation, other than, perhaps, guidance by Him

> that doth the ravens feed,
> Yea, providently caters for the sparrow.

> [II. iii. 43-4]

Orlando had sought out neither the good Duke nor Rosalind, but he encountered both. The echo of *Luke*, xii. 24 and of *Psalms*, cxlvii. 9, evoked by the reference to the raven, and of *Luke*, xii. 6, evoked by the reference to the sparrow, is underscored by the explicit reference to Providence, and in the final scene Hymen twice speaks of heaven, suggesting that there is "mirth in heaven / When earthly things made even / Atone together" [V. iv. 108-10]. Jaques gives us a comic version of the wonder evoked by miracle when, looking at the paired lovers, he says, "There is, sure, another flood toward, and these are couples coming to the ark" [V. iv. 35-6]. This sense of wonder, with a concomitant hint of Providence, is of course found elsewhere, not only in the romances, where it has often been noticed, but also in the earlier comedies, for example in *The Merchant of Venice*, where Portia's revelations, like "manna," leave the characters "amazed," and where the audience itself cannot but wonder how Portia has news that Antonio's ships are safe. In *As You Like It*, Hymen himself is part of the wonder that concludes the play; he is never explained in the play, and those productions that make him recognizably one of the Duke's men, or a Corin whose Falstaffian girth reveals his identity beneath his sheet, do an injustice to this element in the play. Rosalind, I have said, really does very little, but one of the things she does do is mysteriously produce Hymen.

In keeping with the strangeness of this world, Shakespeare in several places *lessens* the motivation he found in Lodge's *Rosalynde*. It is customary in critical discussions of Shakespeare's use of his sources, to point out how he increases the probability of his actions, as though he were writing *pièces bien faites* [well-made fragments], or as though he felt compelled to heed Aristotle's comments on probability. Yet in fact he often lessens the probability. . . . [For example,] Shakespeare might have followed Lodge in having the eldest son envious of his young brother's ample possessions, but instead Shakespeare makes Oliver's conspiracy against Orlando *less* intelligible by giving Orlando only a "poor thousand crowns" [I. i. 2-3], a "poor allottery" [I. i. 73] that does not seem to interest Oliver. Near the end of the first scene, after we have witnessed the quarrel between the brothers but have been given no explanation for Oliver's treatment of Orlando, Oliver confesses he can offer no explanation, "for my soul, yet I know not why, hates nothing more than he" [I. i. 165-66]. He indeed goes on to pay tribute to Orlando's virtues, and then suggests that because of them "I am altogether misprized" [I. i. 170-71], but this explanation appears as an afterthought, and although Adam later says that Orlando's virtues "are sanctified and holy traitors" [II. iii. 13] because they arouse envy, it is clear that Oliver's motivation is thereby only the more mysterious. As Adam says of this wonder, "O, what a world is this, when what is comely / Envenoms him that bears it" [II. iii. 14-15]. The fact may be plain, but the motive remains mysterious. (pp. 120-22)

[Shakespeare, unlike Lodge,] does not bother to tell us why a wrestling match is being held; "Tomorrow, sir, I wrestle for my credit," Charles tells Oliver [I. ii. 126-27]. That is as much motive as we get, and while it tells us something about Charles, it tells us nothing at all about Frederick's reason for holding a tournament.

The reasons for Frederick's banishment of Rosalind are similarly less detailed and less plausible than those for Torismond's banishment of Rosalynde [in *Rosalynde*]. Le Beau has earlier warned Orlando (and us) that Frederick is unpredictable:

> Yet such is now the Duke's condition
> That he misconsters all that you have done.
> The Duke is humorous.
>
> [I. ii. 264-66]

In the following scene he enters, "his eyes full of anger" [I. iii. 40], and orders Rosalind to "get you from our court" [I. iii. 42]. When she asks how she has offended, he calls her a traitor, and when he is pressed for a more detailed explanation he answers, "Thou art thy father's daughter, there's enough" [I. iii. 58]. Rosalind points out that she was her father's daughter when Frederick first usurped the throne, and to Celia's interruption Frederick answers that he allowed Rosalind to remain for Celia's sake. But now, for some unstated reason, Rosalind is to be banished. When Celia protests further, Frederick at last offers something that can be called an explanation: Rosalind's very excellence is Celia's enemy because it diminishes Celia's excellence. This indeed is a reason, but it is a

bad one, and we can only echo Le Beau's earlier conclusion: "The Duke is humorous" [I. ii. 266]. But that is a conclusion, not an explanation. . . .

Celia's decision to flee with Rosalind marks a departure from Lodge, whose Alinda is banished by her father Torismond. Here we may at first glance feel that Shakespeare's action is more plausible: rather than have a father unnaturally banish his daughter, Shakespeare has the daughter leave the court in order to remain with her devoted friend. And yet again Shakespeare's action is more mysterious, more wonderful, for devotion of such magnitude is inexplicable. This is not to say that it is unreal, only that it cannot be explained in terms of cause and effect. (p. 124)

In yet another crucial episode Lodge's usurper behaves more plausibly than Shakespeare's. Torismond banishes Saladyne in order to gain possession of all the lands of Sir John of Bourdeaux, Saladyne having enlarged his own holdings by annexing Rosader's. Torismond first imprisons Saladyne on account of "the wrongs hee proffred to his brother" . . . , and then banishes him, explaining "I spare thy life for thy fathers sake". . . . Frederick, however, learning that Celia and Rosalind have fled the court, perhaps with Orlando, says [II. ii. 17-19] that if indeed Orlando is missing he will send Oliver to find him. Five scenes intervene before this subject is returned to, when in III.i Frederick orders Oliver to find Orlando and confiscates Oliver's property. In this scene nothing is said of the likelihood that Orlando is with the two girls, and nothing at all is said of the girls; without reference to the earlier brief discussion of this likelihood it is unclear why Frederick is concerned about Orlando. Again we get a sense that the Duke is "humorous," unpredictable, rather than a coherent perverse character.

But of course in *As You Like It* the most unpredictable happenings (from the point of view of psychology, not of literary conventions) are the instantaneous love affairs and the conversions of the villains. . . . Shakespeare assumes that beautiful young people fall in love for no apparent reason. This assumption is especially evident in the love exchanged between Celia and the reformed Oliver. . . . [Shakespeare] goes out of his way to insist upon the suddenness and the improbability of the love between Celia and Oliver. There is no rescue from brigands, nor any other stated reason for it. (Perhaps it should be mentioned that Shakespeare's Arden, however green or golden, could have harbored brigands as well as a lioness and snake.) Rosalind is our source for what happened between Celia and Oliver. . . . (pp. 125-26)

[Rosalind's] insistence on the suddenness and improbability of the experience suggests not that Shakespeare is winding things up quickly because (in Johnson's words) he is "in view of his reward," or that (in Paul V. Kreider's words) Shakespeare is mocking his "patently inadequate plot" [see excerpt above, 1935], but that suddenness and improbability are part of the meaning of the play. It will not do to take Johnson's or Kreider's positions. . . . Now, just as no one believes that the dialogue of a play is a transcript of real talk, or that the *dramatis personae* are real people, so no one believes that the plot is an exact reproduction of a chain of historical events. But plot, like dialogue and character, presumably has some sort of intimate connection with reality. One might say that plot, dialogue, and character are symbolic, standing for realities. In *As You Like It*, presumably the sudden alterations in Rosalind, Orlando, Celia, and Oliver suggest changes in personality of a sort suggested, say, in Ovid's *Metamorphoses*. In those legends, suffering humanity—usually consumed by guilt or fear—

is unable to continue its existence, the metamorphosis representing the sort of change that in life is accomplished by suicide, by retreat into a psychotic state, or by religious conversion. Tolstoi's conversion, preceded by enormous anxieties, contradictory actions and suicidal impulses, is a familiar example from life of the sort of thing that much of Ovid implies. And this brings us back to the matter of the conversion of Oliver, for he not only falls in love with Celia but first loses the hatred for Orlando that animated him when in the first act he said, "for my soul, yet I know not why, hates nothing more than he" [I. i. 165-66]. In Lodge, Saladyne repents while in Torismond's prison. There is nothing strange here. Whatever our modern doubts about the value of imprisonment, a stubborn part of our mind sees such a change as reasonable. . . . But, again, Shakespeare omits such motivation, heightening the abruptness of Oliver's conversion, making it (like love at first sight) a matter of minutes. Certainly it is understandable; Orlando nobly has saved Oliver's life, but Oliver in the first act had clearly perceived Orlando's nobility and had hated him for it. Now, in an instant, Oliver is a new man. Asked by Celia if he is the man "that did so oft contrive to kill" Orlando [IV. iii. 134], Oliver replies:

> 'Twas I. But 'tis not I. I do not shame
> To tell you what I was, since my conversion
> So sweetly tastes, being the thing I am.
>
> [IV. iii. 135-37]

Oliver explicitly speaks of his "conversion," and the experience he describes has obvious affinities with religious conversion, which utterly transforms one's personality, as, for example, on the road to Damascus Paul's personality was transformed. And as Paul, who persecuted Christ, finally yielded utterly to him, so Oliver, who persecuted Orlando, yields to him "all the revenue that was old Sir Rowland's" [V. ii. 10-11]. (pp. 126-28)

Shakespeare, it should be mentioned, did not need to convert Oliver merely to end the play; Oliver could have remained wicked, to be dealt with in an unwritten sixth act, as Don John in *Much Ado* is to be dealt with. Nor is Oliver's conversion necessary merely to provide Celia with a husband; one of Duke Senior's "loving lords" might have served. Similarly, Frederick might have been captured and pushed offstage. But Shakespeare gives us a different plot, and it is likely that his plot is meaningful rather than slipshod or perfunctory.

Frederick's conversion at the hands of "an old religious man" [V. iv. 160] is only the last of a series of implausible happenings that suggests the existence of a benevolent Providence. *As You Like It* is not devoid of oblique references to Providence, some of which have already been glanced at. But it is in the strange happenings, rather than in the oblique references in the dialogue, that one perceives most clearly that (to quote from *Cymbeline*)

> The fingers of the pow'rs above do tune
> The harmony of this peace. . . .
>
> [*Cymbeline*, V. v. 466-67]

Like Oliver's conversion, Frederick's is apparently triggered by a sudden experience, and it has "an element of marvel," to use words that William James in Lecture IX of *The Varieties of Religious Experience* used of conversion. But as James pointed out, conversion is often preceded by a hidden complex psychic state. . . . Early in the play, by means of references to Frederick's unpredictability and to Oliver's confession that his hatred was inexplicable, Shakespeare indicates that the villains' per-

sonalities were unstable, and therefore that they were open to sudden re-information, or reformation. One might add here that the melancholy Jaques—whose melancholy is inexplicable, for it is not the scholar's or the musician's or the courtier's or the soldier's or the lawyer's, and it does not really seem to be the traveler's either—is a similar figure, puzzling because his principle of behavior is unclear. (There have, or course, been various studies of his melancholy, but the scholarship adduced to prove it is due to one or another cause is not substantiated in the play.) That he will seek out Frederick, because "Out of these convertites / There is much matter to be heard and learned" [V. iv. 184-85], is not at all strange; earlier he was faintly associated with the humorous duke by virtue of being said to be "compact of jars" [II. vii. 5]. Jaques' discords, like Frederick's discordant actions, betoken a personality that has not become integrated, and at the conclusion of the play, after the report of Frederick's conversion, Jaques' intention to visit Frederick reminds us of this sort of anxious personality and it reminds us also of its great potentiality for change. In Jaques' statement that he hopes to learn "much matter" from the convertite, we may hear, very faintly, a voice like that of the jailer who asked Paul and Silas, "What must I do to be saved?" Zera Fink says Jaques "has lost any real faith in life" [see excerpt above, 1935], but the implication of the play is, I think, that his dissatisfaction with things as they are prepares him for the possibility of conversion of the sort experienced by Frederick and Oliver, by the lovers.

These remarks do not, I hope, resemble those on the girlhood of Shakespeare's heroines, the child-bearing of Lady Macbeth, or the heavenly or hellish destinations of the figures in the tragedies. The point is not that the characters have a life before the first act or after the fifth, but that in the play as we have it they engage in strange behavior because strange behavior is what Shakespeare is talking about, not because he is employing meaningless conventions or winding things up quickly. In the romances the working of grace is more prominent, but even as early as *The Comedy of Errors*, when Luciana's words cause Antipholus of Syracuse to say, "Would you create me new?" [*The Comedy of Errors*, III. ii. 39] we find in Shakespeare suggestions of powers that mysteriously transform nature into something higher. Such inexplicable and wonderful transformations are entirely in harmony with another thread that runs through comedy. . . . In comedy we find things absurd to reason. As the etymology indicates, the preposterous is that in which the natural order is broken, the first coming last, and the conversions we have been speaking of involve the unnatural, the implausible. But it should be noted, too, that although in the last act of *As You Like It* some of the chief characters return to the court from which they had been exiled, what we saw at first is not what we now see last. The court society at the end is not identical with the court society of the first act, where a capricious usurper ruled, and where ribs were cracked. As Northrop Frye says [in his *A Natural Perspective*], "The action of a Shakespearean comedy, then, is not simply cyclical but dialectical as well: the renewing power of the final action lifts us into a higher world, and separates that world from the world of the comic action itself." There is at the end a return to the court, but the court now will house the rightful duke and a Rosalind and an Orlando transformed by love. Moreover, two former court-figures, Frederick and Oliver, who have undergone the greatest transformations, will not be there; though Duke Senior is the ruler of no mean city, these two feel the claim of a higher city, and Jaques also indicates an awareness of it. That is, Shakespeare's pastoral world in *As You Like It* is not only a place where innocence is achieved through retreat, abstinence, and self-sufficiency as is common in pastoral literature; it is also a place where innocence is achieved through conversion, and, for Frederick and Oliver, through some degree of self-mortification.

Early in the play Jaques describes as a "strange eventful history" [II. vii. 164] man's unhappy progress through seven rather uneventful ages; in the last act, when conflicts have been wondrously reconciled through patently unreasonable (but not therefore perfunctory or meaningless) transformations, Hymen justly speaks of "strange events" [V. iv. 127]. Had Shakespeare wished to write a more plausible play, he needed only to have followed his source more closely. But he apparently took pains to make his play implausible, and we ought not to let our awareness of conventions, or our tolerance for occasional perfunctoriness, mislead us into thinking that the plot of *As You Like It* is negligible, or that the play is about anything less strange than "strange events." (pp. 128-30)

> Sylvan Barnet, " 'Strange Events': Improbability in
> 'As You Like It'," in Shakespeare Studies: An Annual
> Gathering of Research, Criticism, and Reviews, *Vol.
> IV*, 1968, pp. 119-31.

## D. J. PALMER  (essay date 1970)

[*In the following excerpt, Palmer discusses the concepts of art and nature in* As You Like It. *Arguing against C. L. Barber (1942) and Harold Jenkins (1953), who implied that the play's structure is based on antithesis, Palmer claims that the relationship of the artificial to the natural in* As You Like It *is not "an antithesis or conjunction of opposites, but an alliance in which each justifies the other." According to the critic, this explains the play's "simultaneous use and abuse of the pastoral." Additionally, Palmer argues, the artificial and the natural confront each other as much in Shakespeare's use of parody and disguise as they do in the encounters between the courtiers and rustics. Palmer further suggests that Duke Senior's discovery of "sermons in stones" shows that there is an art in nature, that the forest, in essence, represents nature as art; thus, according to the critic, Arden functions as an unreal pastoral world with the properties of both a teacher and a restorer of nature's equilibrium, for "those who enter there, and encounter each other under its auspices, are cast by reflection into their natural roles." Palmer ultimately relates this reflective process within the comedy to the play itself, which he states provides its audience with a reflection of its own nature.*]

When Rosalind steps forward to speak the Epilogue to *As You Like It*, she does so both as the heroine of the play just concluded, and as the boy actor of that part. Such an ambiguous coupling of art with reality is appropriate to any epilogue, which effects the transition from make-believe to truth, but it is especially fitting to a play with the self-conscious artifice of *As You Like It*. The Epilogue links the play to its spectators in the real world, by appealing to the men and women, for the love they bear to each other, to applaud this comedy of lovers. Rosalind's charge to the men, "that between you and the women the play may please" [Epilogue, 16-17], contains a bawdy pun on "play" which expresses in a word the correspondence between the lovers on the stage and those who have been watching them. The stage holds up a mirror to life, and the men and women whose favor is now solicited, as they like it, are reminded that they have seen their own image in the business of the play.

The Epilogue thus echoes Rosalind's previous confession that "the sight of lovers feedeth those in love" [III. iv. 57], when she was invited to witness the interview between Silvius and Phebe. There Rosalind stood in relation to the rustic couple as the spectators in the theatre do to all that takes place on the stage. This analogy was driven home in Corin's promise that she and Celia would see "a pageant truly play'd" [III. iv. 52], and again in Rosalind's intention to "prove a busy actor in their play" [III. iv. 59]. The parallel between this eavesdropping, with its stage metaphor, and the argument of the Epilogue, turns upon the conventional idea that Art reflects Nature. It has two important implications for the play as a whole, the first of which is that we are made aware of the interaction of the artificial and the natural at different levels of the play's structure, in the poetic and dramatic methods themselves as well as in the location and events of the story. Secondly, in recognizing the reference to a traditional conception of Art as Nature's mirror, we perceive that the relationship of the artificial to the natural in the play is not fundamentally an antithesis or conjunction of opposites, but an alliance in which each justifies the other. Rosalind's meeting with Silvius and Phebe is one of several encounters in the Forest of Arden of a similar kind, in which a character's own situation is counterfeited by those who confront him.

The twin concepts of Art and Nature, in their complex relations, were traditionally the controlling ideas of the pastoral genre, yet the blend of romantic and satirical comedy in *As You Like It* has caused some uncertainty about its connection with pastoralism.... [Previous critics have shared] an assumption that Shakespeare judged the pastoral from a point of view outside its conventions, but the problem of Shakespeare's attitude to the pastoral, and his apparent ability to have his cake and eat it, is made much clearer when we understand how he turned the pastoral concern with Art and Nature upon the convention itself. Recognizing this, our sense of the play's artistic unity is considerably enhanced. The artificial and the natural confront each other in Shakespeare's use of parody and counterfeiting... as much as they do in the meetings between sophisticated courtiers and simple rustics, or in the comparison of "man's ingratitude" with the "winter wind" [II. i. 7]. Art and Nature remain the controlling ideas, even when pastoralism is under attack, for Shakespeare's attitude to extravagant artifice accords well with the orthodox precepts of Elizabethan poetic theory.... Shakespeare's simultaneous use and abuse of the pastoral is also authorized by its own associations with poetic virtuosity and literary debate. By Shakespeare's day the roles of shepherd and poet had long been interchangeable in pastoral convention, and the shepherds of Lodge's romance, *Rosalynde*, which is the play's immediate source, devote themselves more to versifying than to tending their flocks. There is therefore no self-contradiction implied in the play's many-sided treatment of pastoralism, for the central theme of *As You Like It*, both in its stylistic self-consciousness and in its varied episodes, is always the relationship of Art with Nature.

Modern interpretations have drawn a good deal of attention to the innumerable contrasts and parallels developed in the action of the play. C. L. Barber, for instance, writes of the love-affairs which "succeed one another in the easy-going sequence of scenes, while the dramatist deftly plays each off against the others" [see excerpt above, 1942].... Harold Jenkins explores the subtlety of "the art of comic juxtaposition," and says of Shakespeare's method, "What Shakespeare characteristically does in his comedy is to set together the contrasting elements in human nature and leave them by their juxtaposition or interaction to comment on one another" [see excerpt above, 1953]. This emphasis in recent criticism upon contrasting and opposing sets of relationships in the play is particularly concerned with the meetings that take place in the forest. . . . The general tenor of these views, I think, may be questioned for their implication that the structure of the play is based on antithesis, and that the chief purpose of these encounters in the forest is to place a series of contrasting attitudes side by side. Certainly, the artificial and the natural are contrasted in the various exchanges which take place between characters in Arden, but there is usually more to be seen than the simple conflict of mutually contradictory attitudes. "Confrontations" might be a better word for such meetings, because for the characters involved they have a reflexive significance. Each sees his own image reflected in a "true" perspective. When paths cross in Arden, the audience may be less aware of the interplay between contrary or parallel points of view than they are of the strange way in which the forest brings its inhabitants face to face with their own shadows. These confrontations are comic counterparts to those situations in tragedy, where the leading figures discover their own circumstances reflected in some chance meeting with a stranger, as Hamlet identifies himself with the actor's passion for Hecuba, or with Fortinbras's quixotic sense of honor, or with the grief of Laertes, and as Lear sees his own image in "poor Tom" [*King Lear,* III. vi. 29].

As a pastoral world, the forest itself possesses this mirrorlike quality, and upon our first entry there the banished Duke describes its peculiar virtue for us:

> Here feel we not the penalty of Adam
> The seasons' difference?—as the icy fang
> And churlish chiding of the winter's wind,
> Which when it bites and blows upon my body,
> Even till I shrink with cold, I smile and say,
> "This is no flattery: these are counsellors
> That feelingly persuade me what I am."
>
> [II. i. 5-11]

The Duke's discovery of books in the running brooks, and sermons in stones, shows that there is an Art in Nature itself. Arden is a meeting-place of Art and Nature, a world whose inhabitants may recognize themselves more truly in the reflections that are cast back upon them.

The influence exerted by the forest upon its inmates is perhaps illustrated most strikingly in the sequence of events attending the arrival there of the "unnatural" Oliver. He is first discovered asleep by Orlando, and rescued from imminent death, as Orlando's natural feelings for his brother overcome the temptation to leave his enemy to his fate:

> Twice did he turn his back, and purpos'd so;
> But kindness, nobler ever than revenge,
> And nature, stronger than his just occasion,
> Made him give battle to the lioness.
>
> [IV. iii. 127-30]

So Oliver's "conversion" is brought about when his own long-suppressed nature responds to this "kindness" of Orlando: the Elizabethan connotation of "kindness" with "nature" is particularly strong here. But Shakespeare keeps this meeting of the brothers off-stage, because he has further revelations to make by allowing Oliver to report the episode to Celia and Rosalind. When he tells how Orlando fainted, Rosalind swoons herself, forgetting her swashing and martial outside; and we later learn that in this first meeting of Oliver and Celia, they "no sooner look'd than they lov'd" [V. ii. 33-4]. Such a threefold proof of the reciprocity of Nature is both patently artificial and at the same time evidence of the forest's powers

in drawing Nature to her bias, for such things could happen only in Arden.

Another and earlier confrontation which takes place off-stage is the first meeting between Touchstone and Jaques. By allowing Jaques to give his own account of this meeting, Shakespeare reveals both Jaques' identification of himself with the fool, and his inability to see how true the reflection is. There is an irony in Jaques' enthusiastic ambition for motley: "O that I were a fool" [II. vii. 42]. As Jaques reports the words of this "deep-contemplative" fool, they sound uncommonly like Jaques' own vein of melancholy moralizing, and indeed Jaques is quite unaware that he is repeating a parody of himself. . . . Jaques' natural foolishness is thus reflected by the artful fool Touchstone, though Jaques has so little self-knowledge that he fails to recognize the image of himself. The irony is deepened when Jaques goes on to raise this matter of how the fool "anatomizes" his victim:

> He that a fool doth very wisely hit
> Doth very foolishly, although he smart,
> Not to seem senseless of the bob; if not,
> The wise man's folly is anatomiz'd
> Even by the squand'ring glances of the fool.
>
> [II. vii. 53-7]

Being totally unaware of Touchstone's mimicry Jaques does not have to pretend to "seem" senseless of the way he himself has been "very wisely hit"; and another turn of the screw is given by the Duke's remonstrance that Jaques reflects himself in what he says of others:

> Most mischievous foul sin, in chiding sin:
> For thou thyself hast been a libertine.
>
> [II. vii. 64-5]

In a later scene, Orlando makes the same point when Jaques tries to score off him in the forest:

> *Jaques.* By my troth, I was seeking for a fool
> when I found you.
> *Orlando.* He is drown'd in the brook; look but
> in, and you shall see him.
> *Jaques.* There I shall see mine own figure.
> *Orlando.* Which I take to be either a fool or a
> cipher.
>
> [III. ii. 285-90]

The distinction between "naturals" and wise fools is directly related to the play's concern with Art and Nature, and Touchstone's motley is a visible reminder of this theme, for the motley coat was worn by congenital idiots as well as by professional fools: "The fool doth think he is wise, but the wise man knows himself to be a fool" [V. i. 31-2]. Touchstone's very name suggests his function in the play: to reflect the nature of those he confronts. His wit exposes folly, and his sophistication forces simplicity to know itself. As a fool by art, Touchstone holds a mirror to the whole world, since his favorite mode of speech and action is parody. Significantly, he is "the more fool" in Arden [II. iv. 16], for everyone becomes more fully himself in the forest. (pp. 30-5)

Rosalind's counterfeiting with Orlando is the most elaborate and artificial pageant of the play. It is a mock-courtship where each finds a reflection of his true love, and where reality and its counterfeit image are eventually revealed as one and the same. While Orlando plays himself as truth indivisible, Rosalind counterfeits herself through the medium of Ganymede, and so translates their wooing into the world of make-believe.

To Orlando, the whole forest reflects his love for Rosalind, literally so, since he has hung so many verses about her on the trees. He echoes the Duke in finding Arden his library. . . . He agrees to allow Ganymede to "cure" him of love only when he is invited to call "him" Rosalind, for in this counterfeit too he can continue to bear witness to her virtues. And for her part Rosalind can use her disguise as her "stalking-horse," as a kind of motley which makes jesting an image of truth. Such artifice in wooing is unlike Silvius's rhetorical artifice in his courting of Phebe, which, as Rosalind points out to the youth, only gives a false reflection of nature:

> 'Tis not her glass, but you, that flatters her;
> And out of you she sees herself more proper
> Than any of her lineaments can show her.
>
> [III. v. 54-6]

There is general agreement in the play that, as the song puts it, "most loving is folly," and accordingly Rosalind's counterfeit wooing is intended not merely to ridicule the foolishness of lovers, herself included, but to make such folly aware of itself in terms of a charade, a pretence in which it is foolish to be wise:

> Love is merely a madness; and, I tell you, de-
> serves as well a dark house and a whip as mad-
> men do; and the reason why they are not so
> punish'd and cured is that the lunacy is so or-
> dinary that the whippers are in love too. Yet I
> profess curing it by counsel.
>
> [III. ii. 400-05]

This of course is Ganymede speaking, not Rosalind in her true character, although the words reflect Rosalind's true situation as the physician who is herself sick. Her claim to cure love recalls the medical metaphor used by Jaques, when he spoke of his ambition to wear motley, and to speak his mind. . . . Jaques however is not aware that he has the infection himself, as the Duke tells him. Rosalind's counterfeit, on the other hand, allows her to speak truth as though Ganymede were jesting, and to jest when as Ganymede she seems to be in earnest. Much of the criticism that has been written on Rosalind's qualities of common sense and sanity as revealed in these scenes is really wide of the mark, since we know that Rosalind is far from sharing Ganymede's anti-romantic point of view. Ganymede professes to cure by counsel, but such counsel as "he" gives to Orlando has very little effect, and "his" advice to Phebe produces a result very different from its avowed intention, just as Phebe's own mockery of Silvius fans the very flames it would extinguish. (pp. 37-8)

Rosalind's counterfeiting . . . confirms Touchstone's paradox that "the truest poetry is the most feigning" [III. iii. 19-20], and in doing so it is an emblem of the play's own relationship with reality. Art and Nature are reconciled, with the characteristic Elizabethan fondness for turning these ideas inside out, because Nature is discovered through Art, an Art that is itself of Nature's making. The Forest of Arden represents Nature as Art, not only when we accept it as an unreal pastoral world, but equally in its properties as a teacher and as a restorer of Nature's equilibrium. For those who enter there, and encounter each other under its auspices, are cast by reflection into their natural roles. Such confrontations are analogues of the play in the theatre, as Art holding up the mirror to Nature, because "all the world's a stage, and all the men and women merely players" [II. vii. 139-40]. (p. 40)

*Act III. Scene iv. Celia as Aliena and Rosalind as Ganymed. By C. R. Leslie. The Department of Rare Books and Special Collections, The University of Michigan Library.*

D. J. Palmer, "Art and Nature in 'As You Like It'," in Philological Quarterly, Vol. XLIX, No. 1, January, 1970, pp. 30-40.

## ALBERT R. CIRILLO   (essay date 1971)

[*In the following excerpt, Cirillo claims that, by consistently undercutting the pastoral convention as a convention, Shakespeare suggests in* As You Like It *that the ideal of the pastoral is not an end in itself, but the "underlying substance of the real, the world of the possible which should inform the actual." Extending this thesis, he contends that the only real reconciliation in the play between the actual and the ideal is subjective and effected in the mind, and he maintains that Arden is a "second world," or fiction, within the play, which most of the characters enter temporarily and from which they emerge with a new, revitalized perspective on life. Cirillo also discusses Rosalind's role in the play, asserting that it is through her "mythical generic" disguise as Ganymede that the "magic circle" of Arden takes effect. Further, he suggests, Hymen functions as "a projection of Rosalind's magic, objectified in terms of music and harmony." Focusing on the metadramatical aspect of Shakespeare's comedy, Cirillo lastly points out the correspondence between the "second world" of the forest and the "second world" of the play itself, stating that "if the Forest has been a magic circle for the characters," providing them with the means to recover values and ideals "lost with the Fall," "so has the play been for the audience."*]

The shifting perspective between actual and ideal that is so integral a part of the pastoral world in Renaissance literature is infused with urbanity, wit, and mild but revealing cynicism in *As You Like It*. By the time Shakespeare wrote this delightful comedy the Elizabethan world was already yielding to the melancholy humor which was to predominate in a later age. This slight touch of malaise allows Shakespeare to maintain a healthy distance from the overtly sentimental possibilities of the pastoral material. In infusing the play with the romantic and idealistic glow virtually inherent in a *pastoral* romantic comedy, Shakespeare does not shrink from a simultaneously down-to-earth attitude toward the facts of real life which continuously undercuts the polite fictions of pastoral convention. In effect, he has . . . [made] the pastoral a necessarily ephemeral but educative experience for the characters of the comedy. By making the Forest of Arden a temporary retreat from the world of the Machiavellian court, Shakespeare suggests the ideal which should be the foundation of the real; but by consistently undercutting the pastoral convention *as a convention,* he also suggests that the ideal of the pastoral is not an end in itself—which would be unattainable in any case—but the underlying substance of the real, the world of the possible which should inform the actual. At its sophisticated best—as it is here—pastoral gives an image of the high ideals towards which life in the world should be aiming. (pp. 19-20)

The contrast between city and woods in [*As You Like It*] reverses that in *A Midsummer Night's Dream,* for example—another play in which the woods have a magical effect on characters. In the latter play, the woods are a place of confusion and madness, the world of the "dream," whereas in *As You Like It,* the Forest of Arden, though a temporary refuge, is the place where sanity is restored, where the possibility of order exists (as it does on Prospero's island [in *The Tempest*], for example)—so long as there is a Rosalind or a Touchstone to make the contrast meaningful, to jostle the characters out of their false dreams and illusions. The Forest of Arden forms a magic circle (the reference to the Forest as a magic circle is explicitly made in Act V, as we shall see) out of which issues a new order based on a more realistic attitude towards life and love (in its most inclusive sense of social justice as well as romantic love) effected by Rosalind in her almost mythical generic (i.e., man-woman) role of Ganymede.

The Forest of Arden represents the second world not simply as naïve pastoralism, but as a testing ground for love in a realm that is distinct from the world of Machiavellian politics. Yet, the synthesis which Shakespeare suggests by his parodic thrusts at the pastoral convention, made by characters in the forest, and by the final resolution of the play, indicates that while these worlds are dramatically separate, they are realistically one. The real world is not one *or* the other, but a combination of both, a world where the poses and postures of love are not adequately or accurately represented by the inane attitudes of Silvius or Phoebe, or by the absurdity of an Orlando's carving Rosalind's name on the trees of the forest. Nor is it one where the world of "business" (to give the milieu of the court a convenient tag) is one of motiveless villainy. The real world is Arden *and* the court fused, simply because the world of "business" . . . must be part of life since the Fall when man had to move out of his garden or rustic paradise. Thus, the movement in the play is from the court to the forest and then back again because these people—that is, real people—cannot live in a fictive Arcadia, though they can carry it back with them as an informative ideal for life. In *As You Like It* the return to the court, at the end, embodies this return to "life" in terms of a convenient happy ending expected in romantic comedy. (pp. 21-2)

[The courtly characters] need the Arcadian experience, with all of its ambiguity, to bring order and value to their lives. Once this has been achieved they can return to the court, taking with them the knowledge that they have gained in Arcadia-Arden. *As You Like It,* then, I take to be a Renaissance work which illustrates Sidney's concept of the *golden world* in romantic-dramatic terms. Here, the fiction—the apparent world of the ideal in the Forest of Arden—is a moral landscape which needs what is provided by the world outside of the forest for completion in two related ways. First, the Forest needs the contrast with the court and worldly values to clarify the consciousness of the audience as to the essential illusory quality of this pastoral world; and it needs it in this particular dramatic context to effect a transformation of the characters in the play, to awaken them to the true nature of their human situation. Needless to say, the manipulation of the characters' awakening parallels the dramatist's control of his audience's "awakening"; the former—i.e., the action of the play itself—is a microcosmic version, so to speak, of the affective force of the interaction between work and audience.

Only Corin, Sylvius, Phebe, William, and Audrey can be considered natives of the pastoral world of Arden. In one sense or another, all others are outsiders, there only for refuge. Within this context, the meaning of the pastoral is defined in terms of various love relationships: Phebe-Sylvius (and Phebe-Ganymede), Celia-Oliver, and Touchstone-Audrey, as well as Rosalind-Orlando. The play begins in a world in which order and justice have been subverted. The true Duke has fled to the forest, his position usurped by his brother, Frederick. In a parallel situation, Orlando is being denied the proper breeding and education of his class by his older brother. . . . Even so is Rosalind banished by her uncle—who has seized her father's dukedom—for no real reason ("Let it suffice thee that I trust thee not" [I. iii. 55]). Like her father, the true Duke, and like Orlando, she escapes to the pastoral world. Here, amidst the traditional trappings of the rustic retreat which the Renaissance knew well she assumes an important role which is central to the entire play and which makes her something of a *magus* or magician who controls nature and sets all things aright through her influence on the amorous relationships in the circle of the forest.

The amorous situation itself in the perspective provided by the Forest of Arden becomes a trial which leads to harmony. Rosalind is the instrument who effects this order and therein lies a great deal of the ironic humor of the play. For the name *Rosalind* had become, by the time Shakespeare wrote the play, almost a stock symbol for the loved-one in romantic situations; she was, almost in virtue of her name, the lovely lass for whom poetic shepherds pined, and her name evoked all of the sweet melancholy associated with literary lovers. By making the object of Orlando's youthful ardor a figure with inherent associations of romantic pastoral—a Rosalind who, somewhat paradoxically, acts as a cynical iconoclast towards the standard romantic convention—Shakespeare makes his play and its setting a self-reflective commentary on the unreality of the pastoral convention.

This is not to say that the play rejects the significance of the pastoral as a *symbol*; what it rejects is the naïve belief in the pastoral fiction as an attainable ideal in life. There are two worlds in the play, the court and the forest. At the beginning these worlds are distinct—the active life of the body politic, if you like, the civilized world where power politics is played; and the contemplative life of the country. . . . At the end of the play these worlds have become one in the consciousness of the principal characters (and in the consciousness of the audience) who, even though they return to the court, return having experienced "nature" as lived in the Forest of Arden; they and we have come to learn that the "pastoral" is a force, a principle which should be part of one's life although it is not life. Those who have come to the court to find refuge in the forest discover that it does not represent life any more than the court does. Both forest and court are polarities in the overall symbolism of the play (as, indeed, they are in the convention of Renaissance pastoral): the court is the active life of ambition and struggle, the world of "politics" and power; the forest is the garden, the world of pastoral ease and idyllic innocence, of guilelessness and faith—at least, these are the reverberations which Shakespeare is utilizing as his background motif. In the end, of course, we discover, as we are meant to, that real life is both, not one or the other.

This explains the wonderful comic technique and effect of the play; for Shakespeare educates his characters gently, through a lightly humorous coming-to-awareness of different values, all played against the audience's consciousness of the *données* [givens] of the convention. The juxtaposition of ideal and real for comic effect also explains the metamorphoses which take place in the forest symbolized most distinctly by Rosalind's reappearance, in the last scene, in her own person, in place of the presumably masculine Ganymede. The juxtaposition of one world with the other effects changes within the pastoral world itself by means of the interaction between the two worlds and their values. Every force which would lead to the acceptance of life in Arden as a perfect world is negated by the intrusion of a harsher reality. (pp. 24-7)

In all of the activity of the play it is Rosalind who remains the principal comic character. By this I mean that she is the spokesman for the central comic vision, although she herself is not left untouched by the satire. Rosalind can see things clearly enough, but she too plays a role that is important for the audience's point of view. I use the suggestion of "role-playing" in more than a casual sense. Rosalind literally assumes a disguise and thus consciously takes on a "role," that of the youth, Ganymede. Further, when she comes upon Orlando in the forest she persuades him to see her in still another role, that of Ganymede *as* Rosalind. On this double "role-playing" hinges much of the comedy of the play; but, what is perhaps more important is that fact that this "role-playing," this assumption of a masculine-feminine duality, permits Rosalind to put love to the test from both the masculine and feminine points of view. As Ganymede, she can perceive the pretentiousness of a Phebe's behaviour; as Rosalind (disguised as Ganymede), she can perceive, in both Silvius and Orlando, the ridiculousness of the masculine lover's dotage; and in her dual role she can, in the great climax of the play, "cure" these lovers as well as herself.... Part of the magic of her cure lies in the fact that throughout she has, in her satiric comments, been attempting to force these lovers to realize the ridiculousness of their positions. The paradox of her role is that while she is the spokesman for what might be termed a "rational" position on love and the pastoral tradition, she herself is not immune from it, as she realizes. (p. 28)

Rosalind's assumption of a dramatic role within Arden is her own way of "experiencing the operation of a high idea in the self" [Walter R. Davis, in his *Idea and Act in Elizabethan Fiction*]; she tests love as an "idea" and as an "ideal" and forces us to recognize, even as she does, the distance between

ideal and reality, theory and practice. What we learn in the forest, to quote Davis again, is "that the realm of love is the realm of heightened possibilities for good *or* evil, that love is a force rather than an ideal." In showing this, Rosalind becomes more of a magician than she knows (in the Forest of Arden she claims to be the relative of a great magician), making her own educative process a transforming one that affects both the characters she controls and us. Early in the play, for example, she suggests to Celia that love is a sport or a game [I. ii. 24-5], and so it would seem. Her assumption of the role of Ganymede in the Forest of Arden is, in its way, a carrying on of this game, but it is the kind of game or play which ... affirms both its limits and its power in a single gesture. The game that Rosalind plays is thus a double-edged one, revealing, as it does even in the fact of her own disguise, the ambiguity of "nature": as Ganymede she becomes the man-woman, a figure who seemingly takes on two roles or what might be regarded as the completeness of human nature. While this magical union of sexes, on the one hand, seems to restore balances, on the other, it upsets her own balance, paradoxically working its effects on her. (pp. 29-30)

[In] the magic that seems to take place in the forest Rosalind/Ganymede plays an important part to the very end. Part of her "role-playing" in the pastoral world has been her claim to be related to a magician ("I have, since I was three year old, convers'd with a magician most profound in his art, and yet not damnable" [V. ii. 59-62]). In reporting this fact to the Duke just before the final resolution, which Rosalind/Ganymede has promised ("... I can do strange things" [V. ii. 59]), Orlando puts the matter in interesting terms:

> But, my good lord, this boy is forest born
> And hath been tutor'd in the rudiments
> Of many desperate studies by his uncle,
> Whom he reports to be a great magician
> Obscured in the circle of this forest.
>
> [V. iv. 30-4]

The image of the circle, which is a standard one in magic or occult rites, becomes integral to the final resolution of the play and, in retrospect, casts light on all that has preceded. The Forest of Arden is indeed a circumscribed world; it is a second world *within* the fiction just as the entire fiction is a second world in relation to the audience: the magic of one parallels the magic of the other in terms of affective movement. Rosalind will later become a Prospero (the general resemblances between this play and *The Tempest*, which represents a more mature vision, are worth recognition); and she is here just as much a surrogate for Shakespeare, the artist, as that later magician is. Within the magic circle of the forest Rosalind/Ganymede can, like a true Renaissance *magus* [a practitioner of white magic], proceed to set everything according to nature; as the image of the circle suggests, she will bring everything to a harmonious conclusion. To this purpose we notice how, after claiming to be a magician herself [V. ii. 71], she gives directions, she organizes things in a supervisory manner when she directs all the lovers to meet her in order to have their desires answered.... (pp. 34-5)

With the emphasis on *marriage,* the harmonious conclusion of love, the play ends in an atmosphere of harmonious magic, in a series of rites keynoted by two songs. The first, the *carpe diem* [seize the day] verses of "It was a lover and his lass" [V. iii. 16-33], with its lightly bawdy overtones, with its ever so subtle allusions to the ephemeral quality of life and youth, brings reality and the harsh facts of life into Arcadia particularly against the background of the Audrey-Touchstone situation, which is the immediate context for the song. We are reminded once again that even in the apparently idyllic country of pastoral delight lovers lie together and time passes. The contrast between the song's jostling "With a hey, and a ho, and a hey nonino" refrain, its vivacious and infectious form and rhythm, and the slight, glancing melancholy of its allusion to the passing of youth and time, make it dramatically appropriate in the scheme of a play which suggests, in comic terms, that life is more than a pastoral idyll.

In conjunction with this song, however, we must read Hymen's, sung at the moment Rosalind enters *in propria persona* [as her proper self], as if metamorphosed, by her own magic, from Ganymede into the real Rosalind; for the song expresses in musical terms the great correspondence between earth and heaven, reasserting the concord and harmony that is symbolized by marriage (Hymen) and the circle. In effect, the circle of the forest has become the circle of correspondences and the circle of true love. . . . As Hymen says when Rosalind reveals herself to her father, gives herself to Orlando, and the other lovers are united:

> I bar confusion.
> 'Tis I must make conclusion
> Of these most strange events.
> Here's eight that must take hands
> To join in Hymen's bands. . . .
>                                    [V. iv. 125-29]

Hymen is a projection of Rosalind's magic, objectified in terms of music and harmony. This motif of the magical transformation of the self through disguise, music, and love has transformation of the self through disguise, music, and love has long been associated with "festive comedy" which is so closely related to ritual and the cycle of nature. The incantatory nature of magical rites which informs this scene, under the harmonic cover of the song, is reflected in the rhyming as Hymen brings the couples together. . . . (pp. 35-6)

The harmonious circle of marriage is the theme of the subsequent song [V. iv. 141-46], presumably sung by Rosalind and the others, with its references to "wedding" as "Juno's crown," and as "blessed bond of board and bed." What we are witnessing is a magical ritual, within the magic circle of the forest, which is restoring relationships and perspectives; it is an epitome of the action within the forest itself; and the symbolic catalyst of all of this magic, all of these metamorphoses, has been Rosalind in her "role-playing" of Ganymede, the nephew of a great magician. It is significant that these wedding festivities are immediately followed by the report of the last, and perhaps most important conversion—that of the usurping Duke Frederick who has come to the forest to kill his banished brother only to be "converted / Both from his enterprise and from the world" by an "old religious man" [V. iv. 160-62]. . . . The conversion of Duke Frederick is the fitting climax of these events because it is the ultimate indication that life has been reestablished in its proper perspective. Rosalind and Orlando can now return to the court, as can her father and his group, because they have, in effect, learned that though man cannot live in the Forest of Arden—that is, the Forest of Arden conceived as a golden world of ideal nature—as if it were the absolute condition of life, he can and should keep what the Forest represents within him, the *potentially* perfect other nature that was lost with the Fall and is now recoverable, not absolutely, but morally through the striving for order and justice.

But if the Forest has been a magic circle for the characters in the play, so has the play been for the audience. Again, it is Rosalind who makes this clear in her Epilogue. By stepping out of the play, as if out of the fiction, she exercises the genuine force of her magic on us by bringing us *into* the fictional. The play is our Arden. What Rosalind does in directly begging the audience for applause is to *invoke* us, to bring us into the circle of her magic. As she says, "My way is to conjure you . . ." [Epilogue, 11]. This is followed by orders to the men and women of the audience to like the play, commands phrased in terms of the love that exists between men and women: "I charge you, O women, for the love you bear to men. . . . And I charge you, O men, for the love you bear to women . . ." [Epilogue, 12-15]. The final charge to "when I make curtsy, bid me farewell" [Epilogue, 22-3] is a direct involvement of the audience by bringing her magic to it, by stepping out of the magic circle of the play. This is the artist as *magus* gently saying, "as you have been transformed by the Arcadian experience, by the second world, your applause will be an assent of approval." Applause will express the fact that we are conscious of what has happened, that we assent to it, that our wills have been affected; that this second world is not a never-never land of impossible illusion, as merely naïve pastoral is, but something in which we are all involved. What Shakespeare has done in this play with charm and humor, and in the most gently satiric terms possible, is to use a traditional landscape only to suggest that there is perhaps something wrong with an unquestioned acceptance of its values as an actual condition of existence. . . . The true "second world" or "second nature" here is not the Forest of Arden *per se*, but the ideal which it suggests and *is* not, the ideal which in a Renaissance Christian ethic, can only exist in the impetus for a conversion of the will that lets us see things, not necessarily as we like them, but as they should be, and as they are. (pp. 37-9)

> Albert R. Cirillo, "'As You Like It': Pastoralism Gone Awry," in ELH, *Vol. 38, No. 1, March, 1971, pp. 19-39.*

## HUGH M. RICHMOND (essay date 1971)

[*Richmond assesses the function of Rosalind's disguise in* As You Like It, *arguing that much of the play's importance depends almost entirely on the heroine's role-changing and "kaleidoscopic identity." This role-changing, as Rosalind appears first as herself, then as Ganymede, as Ganymede playing herself, as herself again, and finally, in the play's epilogue, as the boy actor in the theater, not only gives the character insight into male psychology "uncolored by the effects of sexual excitement," but also, Richmond asserts, is the means of the play's "investigation of the interaction of the conscious mind with its emotional drives and the physiological equipment with which it finds itself arbitrarily endowed." The critic adds that Rosalind's disguise also provides the heroine with an unusual opportunity for self-awareness and increased understanding of her own sexual identity; in fact, he declares, she alone of all the characters "knowingly develops her own nature" through the choices offered her as a result of her disguise.*]

Rosalind is Shakespeare's most delightful heroine, and her sexual experience anticipates the vagaries of our own age closely. Shakespeare's other female characters may be more passionate or heroic, more deeply moving to the audience, but Rosalind experiments most successfully with the range of amatory relationships open to both sexes. Her capacity for bisexuality seems to impress Shakespeare greatly, for he never shows her less than creatively alert and responsive to all the nuances of amatory feeling and action that surround her. By the end of *As You Like It*, her sexual insights are so potent that she anticipates Prospero's magical dominion over his environment [in *The Tempest*]: "Believe then . . . that I can do strange things . . . and yet not damnable . . . though I say I am a magician" [V. ii. 58-71]. However, she is never tyrannical in her authority over others' emotions. By comparison even Portia [in *The Merchant of Venice*] has a strain of the termagant (one might even say of the racist) in her contemptuous attitude to her foreign suitors, not to mention her cat-and-mouse treatment of Shylock and Bassanio. When Rosalind finally resolves all the emotional tangles which have grown up around her because of her fascination for both sexes, it is without false rhetoric or drastic action. Simply because she is able when she wishes to present herself as what she most conveniently should be, all the problems evaporate into mere absurdity. As a catharsis of incompetence in her victims this is one of the least painful in the comedies. Rosalind is thus all a woman can ever hope to be. Emotionally committed to femininity yet sexually experienced in both male and female attitudes, she remains witty and skeptical enough never to be trapped in an inexpedient role. She thus deserves our closest attention as the most successful model for women in Shakespeare.

She is the more impressive in that her proficiency is less artificial than that shown in the manipulations of any of the earlier comedies. . . . [The] evolution of Portia's personal awareness is far less evident and instructive than Shakespeare's delicate exposition of Rosalind's maturation. Far from centering on clever permutations of the pastoral mode, *As You Like It* is concerned to explore the crystallization of personality by building up a scintillating constellation of human types centered on Rosalind's own kaleidoscopic identity. Here for the first time we see a womanly figure plausibly capable of attaining St. Paul's heroic ideal of "being all things to all people." (pp. 137-38)

Rosalind's flight [to Arden] in male disguise is her salvation. . . . [Her] drastic reversal of sexual roles serves . . . to crystallize fully her awareness of the arbitrariness of the human lot, which the play commemorates so schematically in Jaques' speech about "the ages of man" [II. vii. 139-66]. Far more than Jaques, Rosalind is forced to surrender her established identity wholesale to the demands of threatening circumstances. Jaques merely affects to don the clown's motley, which his whimsical egotism has anyway largely earned him. But by disguising herself as a boy, Rosalind has to give up that very sexual pattern to which she has just committed herself in her avowal to Orlando.

It is this chastening of her sexual identity which makes Rosalind so interesting to moderns, for whom her ambivalent experience has become increasingly familiar in both sexes. We now are accustomed to trousered women and effeminate males. Rosalind's experiments as a male are an early prefiguration of Jung's sense of the creative possibilities of at least some awareness of bisexuality. In her exchange of sex we see how a maturation of personality like Katharina's [in *The Taming of the Shrew*] or Isabella's [in *Measure for Measure*] might be achieved without the arbitrary intervention of a magician like Petruchio or Duke Vincentio. Nor is this tempering process merely a latent theme in the play. Intending us to recognize fully how Rosalind attains that dazzling sexual finesse which finally allows her to secure the happiness not only of herself but of all the lovers in the play, Shakespeare permutes the sexual roles of Rosalind with a virtuosity exceeding that of a Petronius, or a Boccaccio, or even a Proust.

These roles of Rosalind require her portrayer to be a youthful Proteus, for her changes of identity are paradoxical in the extreme. We must start from the inescapable fact for an Elizabethan audience . . . : they are watching here a boy actor playing a girl's part, a fact Shakespeare insists on our recognizing also in Rosalind's Epilogue ("If I were a woman . . ." [Epilogue, 18]). Thus the play cannot invite us to see a realistic display of how women behave, with all their conventional lapses into human fallibility (such as Chekhov's *Three Sisters* shows us). Rather, it presents a girl's role boldly illuminated, heightened, even transcended, by exploitation of the unconventional vigor and wit that a boy must almost inevitably bring to it. Shakespeare's comic heroines (and Rosalind *par excellence*) thus map out the way for truly emancipated modern women to behave, precisely because these roles were *not* originally to be acted by women but by unusually vivacious males. The parts necessarily lack the easy sentimentality and the merely physical eroticism which all too often resulted from the introduction upon the stage of actresses (and hence of traditional ideals of femininity) in facile roles of the kind sometimes evident in the plays of Dryden, or even Wycherley.

Moreover, in *As You Like It* the boy originally playing Rosalind appears physically costumed as a girl only three brief times in the play. For Shakespeare's tact usually disdains to exploit any direct demonstrations of sexuality. All the physically erotic passages in his presentation of amatory themes are retrospective, and often second-hand. The physiological fascinations and sexual capacities of such women as Cleopatra or Imogen [in *Cymbeline*] are necessarily narrated, often by other characters than their lovers (such as Enobarbus or Iachimo). Still more than theirs, Rosalind's role as a young woman is deliberately deprived of even a retrospective physiological interest: she is costumed as a boy and "her" maleness is even finally acknowledged openly in the play's epilogue. By means of such devices "Rosalind" is forced to adopt a pattern of purely mental or inward femininity (which is, after all, true to the discipline of the actor playing the part). Further, the actor is obliged to sustain "her" feminine nature while continually performing in situations more appropriate to male virility, such as responding to the blunt erotic advances of the nymph Phoebe or playing a sexually jaded Mercutio [as in *Romeo and Juliet*] to Orlando's sentimental Romeo.

The surface form of this latter relationship of Rosalind with Orlando marks one of the most bizarre extremes of Shakespeare's sophistication of personality: the boy actor here plays a girl who is continually playing at being a boy, who in turn has to humor Orlando and "pretend" to be the girl (Rosalind) that he is supposed, by the conventions of the play, actually to be. The role of Rosalind thus dissolves into a chromatic spectrum of personae. As a boy actor she speaks as a male in the Epilogue; as avowedly a girl she speaks to Orlando in Act I, scene ii, only for a few moments; as a supposed male she masquerades as Ganymede thereafter, except when she "falsely" affects to be feminine for Orlando's instruction. Shakespeare produces many interesting results from this detachment of a rational mind from its wildly oscillating sexual identity. He suspends Rosalind's awareness precariously between the two poles of human eroticism formed by the conventional roles of men and women. As a maturing person, Rosalind eagerly investigates both sexual potentialities; and Shakespeare shows us this process with an assurance modern writers have only recovered since Jung asserted the presence of both the female-oriented persona (or anima) and the male animus in all human personalities, whatever their local physiological attributes.

From a very early moment Rosalind begins to analyze her relationship to her various sexual roles. She even starts out briskly by claiming many of the physical capacities of a male:

> Were it not better,
> Because that I am more than common tall,
> That I did suit me all points like a man?
> A gallant curtle-axe upon my thigh,
> A boar-spear in my hand; and—in my heart
> Lie there what hidden woman's fear there will—
> We'll have a swashing and a martial outside,
> As many other mannish cowards have
> That do outface it with their semblances.
>
> [I. iii. 114-22]

The choice is a common one for Shakespeare's women, always with tragic results if it is made without Rosalind's cool suspicion of affected virility. St. Joan and the Duchess of Gloucester (in *Henry VI*) both mistake the toughness and bellicosity of the male for absolute virtues, an error far more subtly developed in the character of Lady Macbeth. Rosalind, by contrast, does not ape the male out of envy, but through mere necessity. And in masquerading as a man she comes to recognize that what conventionally passes for virility is often little more than her own masquerade.

By virtue of that disguise she also acquires an insight into male psychology uncolored by the effects of sexual excitement. She can speak to Jaques, Silvio, and Orlando with the privileged bluntness of a fellow man when she sees their behavior uncensored by awareness of a female observer. Even more instructively, she is forced to recognize and cope with the classic aberrations of women's sexual behavior without the advantage of a softening screen of male sentimentality. She discovers not only much to reproach in the perverseness of her lover Phoebe, but also in herself. Moreover, her own wayward instincts can find no release with Orlando beyond their own censure in her objective exposition of women's responses to courtship [in III. ii.]. Rosalind's detachment from her identities is a magnificent school for self-awareness, as well as a unique pedagogic opportunity in her dealings with others. As with Prospero's feigned tempest, Rosalind is able to stage-manage a storm of emotional entanglements, confident of her power to resolve them because she is sharply aware of their artificiality and arbitrariness.

Phoebe is thus brought down from her role as Silvio's cruel deity by public proof that she is so indiscriminate as to focus her own sexual interests on Ganymede, a person not only physically unequipped to meet them, but indeed scarcely actual in any way at all. Orlando is purged of a lover's sentimental affectations by relentlessly authoritative instruction in female unpredictability. Paradoxically, he comes to know the nature of his mistress fully just because for a time he fails to recognize her as other than a discriminating friend. But of course the play's most creative display of personality development lies in showing what all this complication does to Rosalind and what she makes of the result, for she alone in the play (except, perhaps, for Jaques) knowingly develops her own nature by deliberate choices.

Early on in the forest her responses oscillate, and her estimates of her own nature are quite contradictory. On the one hand she asks: "Do you not know I am woman? When I think, I must speak" [III. ii. 249-50] and on the other, she asserts to Orlando: "Me believe it! you may as soon make her that you love believe it; which, I warrant, she is apter to do than to confess she does" [III. ii. 387-89]. The latter passage has the ingenious

dramatic irony so characteristic of Shakespeare. A mere two hundred lines of dialogue have advanced Rosalind from sentimental confusion at the approach of her lover ("Alas the day! what shall I do . . ." [III. ii. 219]) to wry self-judgment. The fatuous example of Phoebe's treatment of Silvio further increases her detachment from the conventional role of a mistress, while the whimsical egotism of Jaques' humor ("a melancholy of mine own . . . in which my often rumination wraps me in a most humorous sadness" [IV. i. 15-20]) serves as a further awful example of the dangers of complacency.

Thus, in affecting to flirt maliciously with Orlando, Rosalind attains a dual catharsis: enjoying perhaps a vestigial and harmless delight in female waywardness, yet also dramatizing for herself a role that she sees to be frivolous if not contemptible. (pp. 140-44)

As in all Shakespeare's comedies, the surface humor of *As You Like It* rises from the ridiculous behavior produced by intense emotions untempered by good sense. But more than most, the play organizes these eccentricities into a complex investigation of the interaction of the conscious mind with its emotional drives and the physiological equipment with which it finds itself arbitrarily endowed. The other characters in the play are merely the resultants of exterior pressures triggering predictable responses. They are "but stewards of their excellence" [Sonnet 94], ultimately guided to their own well-being largely by the will of Rosalind. She alone explores her own identity, faculties, and roles with creative intelligence. (p. 145)

If, as I believe, the distinction of drama lies in its capacity to show broadly meaningful changes in situations and characters, then *As You Like It* depends for its importance almost entirely on the role-changing of Rosalind. And in this it is a work of consummate virtuosity, for Shakespeare manages to convince us thoroughly of the plausibility of her emotional growth to womanhood, from her initial unawakened state, through casual sexual excitement, to wry self-awareness and tough recognition of her lover's conventionality, to which she reconciles herself in marriage. If I had my way the play would be required reading for every teenage girl, not as a charming pastoral fantasy about outlaws and country pleasures, but for this successful exposition of what the sexual maturing of feminine temperament ideally should be. The rest of the play may be charming or merely clever, but as a whole its richness and importance depend on its principal female role. (p. 146)

*Hugh M. Richmond, "Low Love and High Passion," in his* Shakespeare's Sexual Comedy: A Mirror for Lovers, The Bobbs-Merrill Company, Inc., *1971, pp. 102-76.*

### DAVID YOUNG   (essay date 1972)

[*Young is an American academic, scholar, anthologist, and poet whose writings on Shakespeare include* Something of Great Constancy: The Art of "A Midsummer Night's Dream" *(1966) and* The Heart's Forest: Shakespeare's Pastoral Plays *(1972). In the following excerpt from the latter work, Young surveys* As You Like It *for its stylistic and thematic relationship to the pastoral mode. Arguing that the comedy tends "to keep before us the artificial basis of the pastoral design," he focuses on the "essential subjectivity" of Arden by suggesting that it is "changeable in each contact with a separate imagination." In addition, Young maintains that Arden is a source of self-knowledge: it "gives back to its inhabitants and visitors the images of their own selves and preoccupations." The critic also comments on the relativity of Arden, saying that all the principal elements of the play are "seen as variables rather than constants." On related matters, Young discusses Touchstone and Jaques, describing the former as a deft reflector of others in the play, a "chameleon" in the forest who serves as a constant reminder of the relativity of things; the latter Young considers an enthusiast in his melancholy, and he warns against taking Jaques's behavior too seriously.]*

The tendency of *As You Like It* to keep before us the artificial basis of the pastoral design is closely linked to its stress on the relativity and subjectivity of the experience of sojourn. The forest is constant in its imaginary character and changeable in each contact with a separate imagination. The essential subjectivity of pastoral thus emerges with considerable force; and since each character's encounter with Arden differs, the play offers a growing awareness of the fundamental relativity of human experience. (p. 50)

The forest of Arden, like the theater or any art, can be likened to a special sort of mirror that reflects the subject under the guise of objects. It is not surprising that its viewers so seldom realize that they are seeing themselves when they look at it. Even as the Duke is declaring winds to be counselors and stones capable of sermons, we realize that he is finding in nature an image of his own tendency to moralize. Jaques is engaged in the same thing, and his forest differs as he himself differs from the Duke: he finds it a reflection of the world and an opportunity for invective, but the truth is nearer in his own resemblance to the sequestered stag, and the amusing mirror-image of him, "weeping and commenting / Upon the sobbing deer" [II. i. 65-6], with which the scene closes. Jaques may be, as the Duke says, "full of matter" [II. i. 68] at such moments, but the matter is whatever he has brought to the forest in his own person rather than anything he has learned there. This tendency to be imprisoned in one's own nature may not destroy the ideal of contemplation which informed the pastoral (reflection and contemplation were, and are, respectable cohorts), but it certainly gives it a comic and skeptical flavor which is largely Shakespeare's own contribution.

Everywhere this world gives back to its inhabitants and visitors the images of their own selves and preoccupations. Adam and Orlando find it hostile because they are lost and hungry; when they have had a square meal its savage character vanishes, to return for as long as it takes Orlando to forgive Oliver and dispatch the lioness. Corin sees in his flock the image of his own peace and contentment, while Touchstone, exercising his fascination with sexuality, turns it all into "the copulation of cattle" [III. ii. 80], with Corin as presiding pimp. Touchstone comes closest to acknowledging the subjectivity of pastoral experience. "Ay, now am I in Arden," he remarks on arrival, "the more fool I" [II. iv. 16]. And he goes on to demonstrate this intensification of selfhood, proving a much apter and funnier clown in the forest than he ever was at court.

It is not only in nature that the characters find themselves reflected, but in each other as well. Rosalind and her party have no sooner arrived than they have an opportunity to hear Silvius on the subject of his love for Phebe. Rosalind is immediately referred to her own passion for Orlando:

> Alas, poor shepherd! Searching of thy wound,
> I have by hard adventure found mine own.
>
> [II. iv. 44-5]

So has Touchstone, but with a characteristic difference:

> And I mine. I remember, when I was in love
> I broke my sword upon a stone and bid him
> take that for coming a-night to Jane Smile; and

> I remember the kissing of her batlet and the
> cow's dugs that her pretty chopt hands had
> milked; and I remember the wooing of a peas-
> cod instead of her, from whom I took two cods
> and, giving her them again, said with weeping
> tears "Wear these for my sake."
>
> [II. iv. 46-54]

This is the funnier for being so complicated. Touchstone is not only defacing literary landscape with genuine rusticity, real postures in real pastures, he is also participating in and simultaneously parodying everybody else's subjectivity. His "wooing . . . instead" even prefigures Orlando's hypothetical courtship of Ganymede.

Indeed, it is Touchstone, parodist supreme, who proves the deftest reflector of others in the play, partly because it is his professional role. Had he been merely "nature's natural" [I. ii. 49], a clown like Bottom [in *A Midsummer Night's Dream*], Sly [in *The Taming of the Shrew*], or Dogberry [in *Much Ado about Nothing*], he could have accomplished this only in part. But Shakespeare . . . made him a master stylist and wit, and his verbal adaptability gives him his astonishing range. He is as much a chameleon as the forest, although this fact seems to have escaped the commentators who have disapproved of him as a show-off, cynic, and lecher. Touchstone is either a grotesque reflection of those he encounters, as with Jaques, Silvius, and Orlando, or a reflection of what they think a courtier must be like, as with Corin, William, and Audrey. He exists to score off other characters and conventional attitudes, and as such he is a source of pure, and at times extremely subtle, enjoyment. If his grounding in the lost tradition of the licensed fool makes him a difficult character for a modern actor to re-create, he is nevertheless one of Shakespeare's happiest inspirations.

It is shortly after he has treated us to the story of Jane Smile that we hear of Touchstone's first encounter with Jaques, reported by Jaques himself. The special irony of this instance of reflection, with the "deep contemplative" [II. vii. 31] fool railing "on Lady Fortune" [II. vii. 16] and moralizing "In good set terms" [II. vii. 17], is that the resemblance never strikes the enthusiastic Jaques. He has been superbly mimicked, but his reaction is only:

> O that I were a fool!
> I am ambitious for a motley coat.
>
> [II. vii. 42-3]

Jaques does not fare very well in the holding up of mirrors which occupies so much of *As You Like It*. He is usually taken in. When Touchstone gives him some exaggerated euphuism, he takes it straight. And when he meets Orlando, and for a moment their two kinds of melancholy mirror each other, it is Orlando who points out their difference and scores off Jaques with a stale joke. . . .

> *Jaques.* . . . Will you sit down with me? and
> we two will rail against our mistress the world
> and all our misery.
> *Orlando.* I will chide no breather in the world
> but myself, against whom I know most faults.
>
> [III. ii. 277-81]

> *Jaques.* But my troth, I was seeking for a fool
> when I found you.
> *Orlando.* He is drowned in the brook. Look
> but in and you shall see him.

*Jaques.* There I shall see mine own figure.
*Orlando.* Which I take to be either a fool or a
cipher.

[III. ii. 285-90]

And so they part, addressing each other as ''Signior Love''
and ''Monsieur Melancholy'' [III. ii. 291-94]. Their encounter
is, in one sense, a contest between love and self-love, from
which love, not surprisingly, emerges victorious. The connection between reflection and illusory self-esteem is made elsewhere by Rosalind, in her criticism of Silvius' behavior to
Phebe:

'Tis not her glass, but you, that flatters her;
And out of you she sees herself more proper
Than any of her lineaments can show her.

[III. v. 54-6]

The answer to excessive subjectivity and self-love is love for
another, but it too sometimes requires the kind of corrective
glass that Rosalind holds up for Orlando when, as Ganymede,
she mirrors his love as something less perfect and ideal than
''The fair, the chaste, and unexpressive she'' [III. ii. 10] he
had posited while behaving like Silvius. Mirroring in Shakespearean comedy is always used to emphasize limitations of
awareness, introducing the audience to comic resemblances the
characters tend to miss. In *As You Like It* it seems particularly
linked to the subjectivity which threatens to nullify the contemplative ideal of the pastoral sojourn. What is the value, in
other words, of Jaques musing all day in the forest, if he cannot
see himself clearly and chide accordingly? Something else is
needed, something provided by Rosalind's experience and,
through her, in Orlando's.

Accompanying the emphasis on subjectivity is its natural concomitant, a sense of relativity. As the play progresses it becomes clear that blanket judgments and rigid categories will
not suffice in this world; they must be adapted to the characters
and situation in question. Thus, while we begin the play with
two of the familiar pairs of opposites from pastoral tradition—
Nature and Nurture, as an expression of Orlando's dilemma,
and Nature and Fortune as Rosalind's—we are not allowed to
use them for easy classification or to feel that they are immutable. Orlando, denied nurture, must fall back on nature,
but his case is not that simple, as his brother, who finds him
''never schooled and yet learned'' [I. i. 166-67], admits. His
blood and breeding, in this case ''the spirit of my father'' [I.
i. 22], assert themselves, and they partake, since breeding is
a kind of art, of both nurture and nature.

Rosalind, in turn, may be justified in describing herself to
Orlando as ''one out of suits with fortune'' [I. ii. 246], but
she has contributed to the witty disintegration of the Nature-
Fortune dichotomy a moment earlier. Celia has invited her to
''sit and mock the good housewife Fortune from her wheel''
[I. ii. 31-2], an image in which the mockery is already well
begun. Celia wants Fortune's gifts ''bestowed equally'' [I. ii.
33], and Rosalind agrees that the ''bountiful blind woman''
[I. ii. 35-6] is especially unfair to women:

*Celia.* 'Tis true, for those that she makes fair,
she scarce makes honest, and those that she
makes honest, she makes very ill-favoredly.
*Rosalind.* Nay, now thou goest from Fortune's
office to Nature's. Fortune reigns in gifts of
the world, not in the lineaments of Nature.

[I. ii. 37-42]

But the re-establishment of the distinction is merely a prelude
to further wordplay, as Celia seizes on the opportunity provided
by Touchstone's approach:

*Celia.* No; when Nature hath made a fair creature, may she not by Fortune fall into the fire?
Though Nature hath given us wit to flout at
Fortune, hath not Fortune sent in this fool to
cut off the argument?
*Rosalind.* Indeed, there is Fortune too hard for
Nature when Fortune makes Nature's natural
the cutter-off of Nature's wit.
*Celia.* Peradventure this is not Fortune's work
neither, but Nature's, who perceiveth our natural wits too dull to reason of such goddesses
and hath sent this natural for our whetstone.

[I. ii. 43-54]

The effect of this is not to deny that there is any valid distinction
between the two concepts, but to leave us feeling that they are
scarcely so hard and fast as some would like to believe, and
that heroines who can bandy them about in this fashion are
unlikely to exist merely as illustrations of their objective truth.

An even greater relativity comes to surround the opposition of
Nature and Art. Like all pastoral, *As You Like It* celebrates the
values of harmony with nature, uncomplicated living, and love
without artifice. At the same time . . . , it calls attention to the
artificial character of its natural setting, and its characters turn
continually to the stratagems of art to accomplish natural ends.
Orlando hangs poems on the trees, the foresters use song and
ritual to express their pastoral commitments, Rosalind maintains a disguise and becomes an actor to promote a more naturalistic courtship, and, at the end, that most artificial of forms,
a masque, is used to celebrate a series of natural truths. This
blurring of the Nature-Art distinction is hardly surprising in
view of the common Renaissance ideal that Nature and Art
should harmonize . . . , an ideal of which pastoral was the standard vehicle. Again, however, Shakespeare has gone further
than other writers of pastoral in making explicit the relativity
of nature and art as a precondition of pastoral; most writers
preferred to maintain the pretence that they were opting for
nature over art in theory, whatever they did in practice.

Characterization is affected by this unstable, mutable atmosphere as well. Several commentators have noted Rosalind's
ability to embody opposing points of view, mocking love at
one moment and confessing herself so deeply in love that ''it
cannot be sounded'' the next. Rather than a falsification, her
disguise is a means of revelation, allowing her to avoid con-
straining roles and give full expression to her contradictory
feelings. She is by no means the only character to do so.
Touchstone, as already noted, is like a chameleon, ready to
take on whatever coloration will provide the most amusement.
He is no more a courtier than he is a fool, and no more a fool
than he is a poet, but he is ready to impersonate all at a
moment's notice.

No character is more contradictory than Jaques, a fact which
has led to frequent misunderstandings. His melancholy must
not be taken too literally because it is in fact an enthusiasm.
No one has more zest for life than this declared solitary. He
can ''suck melancholy out of a song as a weasel sucks eggs''
[II. v. 13-14], an appropriate image, surely, in its suggestion
of furtive pleasure. His encounter with Touchstone arouses him
to a frenzy of happy excitement, and leads him on to a spirited
defense of satire and his Seven Ages speech. He admits to

Rosalind of his melancholy that "I do love it better than laughing" [IV. i. 4]. It is his own artful compound, in which he takes great pride and pleasure, and it would be wrong to find anything but complacent satisfaction in his account of the way his "often rumination" wraps him "in a most humorous sadness" [IV. i. 19-20]. The Duke is surely quite right to describe him as "compact of jars" [II. vii. 5], and we may perhaps pardon a man so largely composed of fads and fashions, enthusiastically taken up, if he is unusually lacking in self-knowledge.

There is scarcely an element in *As You Like It* unaffected by a sense of relativity. Sex, rank, fortune, the ages of man, the forest itself, are all seen as variables rather than constants. And so is Time, not only in the play as a whole, but quite particularly in Rosalind's opening gambit when she encounters Orlando in the forest. "Time," she tells him, "travels in divers paces with divers persons" [III. ii. 308-09], and ambles, trots, gallops, and stands still. She goes on to a detailed account that resembles Jaques' portrayal of the seven ages. Time ambles, for example,

> With a priest that lacks Latin and a rich man
> that hath not the gout, for the one sleeps easily
> because he cannot study, and the other lives
> merrily because he feels no pain.
>
> [III. ii. 319-22]

It is, in effect, Orlando's first lesson, and it is a good one, a lesson that the play takes to heart. We may suppose that the title is related to it, as a kind of warning against categorical judgments. Pastoral is not always true or always false or always anything; it is as you like it. And it is not just to pastoral that this applies, but to Time, to Nature, to Art, and to life itself. (pp. 50-8)

> *David Young, "Earthly Things Made Even: 'As You Like It'," in his* The Heart's Forest: A Study of Shakespeare's Pastoral Plays, *Yale University Press, 1972, pp. 38-72.*

**PATRICK SWINDEN**   (essay date 1973)

[*In the following excerpt, Swinden asserts that* As You Like It *is "the most perfect of Shakespeare's comedies." Like many earlier commentators, he downplays the narrative and structural importance of the play's plot, claiming instead that Shakespeare develops his comedy by "bringing together different members of different groups for purposes of dispute and argument." Swinden also discusses the play's "verbal strategies," noting how prose functions as a corrective to the occasional "inflated and vulnerable" romantic verse. In addition, he comments on Rosalind, Touchstone, and Jaques. Rosalind, the critic avers, has the "most visible initiative" of all the play's characters and, in part thanks to her disguise, the ability to synthesize both the skeptical and the sentimental attitudes toward love. At the same time, Swinden concludes, Touchstone and Jaques express a "reductive humor" and an exaggerated allegiance to the critical mode. Although Swinden notes that Touchstone is the only other character besides Rosalind "to see things from two points of view simultaneously," unlike her he is unable to affirm these opposing perspectives, and thus "the two sides of his nature remain polarized."*]

*As You Like It* may not be the most popular, but it is the most perfect of Shakespeare's comedies. (p. 110)

The most memorable scenes in [the play] have nothing to do with the plot. Orlando's intrusion into the Duke's conversation with Jaques at II, vii is brief and cursory. We are not concerned

with him or with Adam, whom he has left in the forest. What we are interested in is Jaques' melancholy and the Duke's response to it. When Orlando goes off to fetch Adam, we can sit back again and enjoy Jaques' speech on the seven ages of man. The debate between Corin and Touchstone in III, ii . . . is rightly one of the most admired passages in the play. It is followed by the scene in which Rosalind, disguised as Ganymede, persuades Orlando to take her for his mistress in rehearsing his address to her—a scene which does nothing to resolve the plot and everything to hold it up; to substitute for it a little game that will amuse her, and will amuse us, but will advance the narrative not a jot. . . . Similar scenes, in which much is done but little progress is made, are those involving Touchstone and Audrey, and Touchstone and Jaques at II, iii, and Silvius, Phebe and Rosalind at III, v. These are all conversation pieces on the absurdity of sex and the folly of courtly love. In each case either they make no contribution to the plot or they actually impede its progress.

The play develops in quite another way, in bringing together different members of different groups for purposes of dispute and argument—even going to the lengths of introducing William in Act V so as to give Touchstone a new butt to mock at during his courtship of Audrey. It is worthy of note that Touchstone doesn't meet Duke Senior until Act V, a delay that creates a new 'area' in which he and Jaques can conduct their argument. The form of *As You Like It* is therefore centrifugal—an ugly word, but the most appropriate I can find to describe this play. Characters belonging to different groups temporarily disperse and recombine talkatively with members of other groups. They are always moving outwards from their position within the group they were attached to at first to a new one at the circumference of a quite separate group. So Jaques meets Touchstone, Rosalind meets Phebe, Touchstone meets William, and each of them gets involved, in a mocking, detached sort of way, in an action which is not, and usually doesn't remain, his own. The dialogues and conversations that ensue are loosely held together by a spoof romance plot, the pivots of which take the form of wrestlers, lionesses, snakes and hermits. Neither the lionesses nor the lovers are taken terribly seriously. The lionesses, however, are absurd. At bottom, the lovers are not. Though they are treated lightly, they contrive to make a kind of sense out of the comic situation in which they are discovered. Though they are not serious in themselves, a seriousness of a kind can be made to emerge from a study of their fortunes. (pp. 114-15)

In [Shakespeare's] early comedies, the parts for the ladies were relatively small, especially those for the adult ladies, those who knew what they were about. The love affairs between Proteus and Julia and Valentine and Silvia in *Two Gentlemen of Verona* were subordinated to the theme of friendship as it was exemplified by the relationship between Proteus and Valentine. The French ladies in *Love's Labour's Lost* had less to say for themselves than their male counterparts. And Portia, in *The Merchant of Venice,* had to withdraw behind the caskets until Act IV of that play. As a result, most of the speeches about love were spoken by the men and (because of the immaturity of the men as compared with the women) from a position in the play in which they were bound to be criticised and mocked. Julia and Portia have their moments, but they are brief when set beside the opportunities given to Berowne and Bassanio. In *As You Like It,* however, the character with the greatest stage presence, with the most visible initiative, is a woman, Rosalind. This totally alters the bias of the play, the way it makes its pronouncements on courtship and love.

Rosalind is more mature, more poised, than love's spokesmen in the early comedies. She does not lay herself and what she speaks about open to ridicule, or at least gentle mockery, as Proteus, Berowne [in *Love's Labour's Lost*], Lysander and Demetrius [in *A Midsummer Night's Dream*] did. Rosalind does what none of these other protagonists managed to do. She creates a context for the statements she makes about love which, because it is itself mocking and witty, neutralises the mockery and wit with which we, and the other characters, might otherwise be tempted to attack what it contains. Hence the ambiguities and uncertainties that . . . exist at the centre of our response to love in, say, *Love's Labour's Lost,* are here thrust to one side. The absurdity, the 'more-strange-than-true' aspect of romance, is absorbed into the poised acceptance of love that Rosalind makes. . . . With the certainty about love that is guaranteed in Rosalind's person comes a new and comprehensive facility with wit, and an astringency that consorts well with the endorsement of sentiment at the heart of the play.

The wit is an expression of the poise given the three theoreticians of love—Rosalind, Touchstone, Jaques—to speak. Even Jaques' verse at II, vii has the colloquial dash-and-run of the prose, which is not altogether new in Shakespeare, though it is almost new to his comedies. Sly had used prose vigorously in *The Taming of the Shrew* and Launce had a good line in it in *The Two Gentlemen of Verona*. And, of course, there was Bottom in *A Midsummer Night's Dream*. But none of these could match the prose of Falstaff in *Henry IV* and, more to our purpose here, that of Benedick and Beatrice in *Much Ado about Nothing*. (pp. 116-17)

[In *As You Like It*,] prose is used as a corrective to the inflated and vulnerable romantic verse which is spoken by the other lovers—Orlando, Silvius, and Phebe. . . . The mock wooing of Rosalind/Ganymede by Orlando is at the centre of the play, and Rosalind's scene with Phebe is one of the wittiest. Indeed, *As You Like It* is constructed out of a series of contrasts between different kinds of verbal strategies—those proper to verse and those proper to prose. It is the culmination of a process that began with Titania's wooing of Bottom, in *A Midsummer Night's Dream*. Here prose and verse exist side by side, and when they move apart the prose, which for want of a better word I shall say expresses a realistic assessment of the value of sentiment and other things as well, is spoken by male and female parts, instead of by the clown, as it was in both *The Two Gentlemen of Verona* and *A Midsummer Night's Dream* (and later by Launcelot Gobbo in *The Merchant of Venice*). By the time we arrive at *As You Like It* the female lead has taken over the 'prose' role of the clown, and with it the critical temperament it expresses. . . . Love and a realistic critique of love co-exist within a single person, at the centre of the play.

This explains my reference to Rosalind creating the context within which she is to be appraised. It is a context made up

*Act IV. Scene ii. Jaques and the Lords as Foresters. The Department of Rare Books and Special Collections, The University of Michigan Library.*

equally of the romantic idealism that is rendered absurd by Orlando and Silvius and the different types of mockery and criticism of romantic idealism that are represented by Touchstone and Jaques. Rosalind creates it by taking over both alternatives and subordinating them to her own requirements. By this means they are got into proportion, the silliness contained in each in their unmixed forms disappears in the world of mature and 'unillusioned' love she embodies. The witty prose she speaks and thinks in allows Rosalind to see round both extremes and to 'place' them within the circle of her own judgement.

We can see the way she does this in respect of Touchstone and Jaques by looking at passages from two different scenes. The first is from III, ii, where Touchstone, having heard Rosalind read out one of the rhymes Orlando has written to her, replies with a rhyme of his own and asks:

> *Touchstone*: This is the very false gallop of verses. Why do you infect yourself with them?
> *Rosalind*: Peace, you dull fool, I found them on a tree.
> *Touchstone*: Truly, the tree yields bad fruit.
> *Rosalind*: I'll graff it with you, and then I shall graff it with a medlar; then it will be the earliest fruit i'the' country: for you'll be rotten ere you be half ripe, and that's the right virtue of the medlar.
> *Touchstone*: You have said; but whether wisely or no, let the forest judge.
>
> [III. ii. 113-22]

And the second is from IV, i, Rosalind's first (and only) meeting with Jaques:

> *Jaques*: I have neither the scholar's melancholy, which is emulation; nor the musician's, which is fantastical; nor the courtier's, which is proud; nor the soldier's, which is ambitious; nor the lawyer's, which is politic; nor the lady's, which is nice; nor the lover's, which is all these: but it is a melancholy of mine own, compounded of many simples, extracted from many objects, and indeed the sundry contemplation of my travels, in which my often rumination wraps me in a most humorous sadness.
> *Rosalind*: A traveller! By my faith, you have great reason to be sad. I fear you have sold your own lands to see other men's; then, to have seen much and to have nothing is to have rich eyes and poor hands.
> *Jaques*: Yes, I have gained my experience.
>
> *Enter Orlando.*
>
> *Rosalind*: And your experience makes you sad. I had rather have a fool to make me merry than experience to make me sad—and to travail for it too!
> *Orlando*: Good day, and happiness, dear Rosalind!
> *Jaques*: Nay then, God buy you, an you talk in blank verse.
>
> *Going.*
>
> *Rosalind*: (*as he goes*) Farewell, Monsieur Traveller. Look you lisp and wear strange suits; disable all the benefits of your own country; be out of love with your nativity, and almost chide God for making you that countenance you are;

or I will scarce think you have swam in a gondola.

> [IV. i. 10-38]

Rosalind does not attack Touchstone and Jaques head on. She corrects the criticism they make by attributing the nature of that criticism to distortions arising out of defects of character, and therefore of valuation, in each of their persons. She creates a firm basis for romantic love, not by providing any positive rationale—that is impossible—but by correcting the bias of its detractors. She exposes the limitations and distortions imposed on their powers of judgement by defects (mainly of self-knowledge) in their own characters.

That is one way she does it. Another is by her disguise as Ganymede, which enables her to give full expression to her love for Orlando whilst preserving a distancing effect, an obliquity, that removes any hint of the maudlin, the cloying, the overblown. . . . I shall limit my treatment [of Rosalind's disguise] to the use it is put to in the Phebe-Silvius affair.

The contrast between the earnest contrivances of the lovers and the elaborate banter of Rosalind brings out most of the advantages of the disguise. Romantic idealism has been transformed into a literary trick in Silvius's Arcadian speech, in spite of the sincerity of his love for Phebe which lies beneath the jumble of words he thinks he needs to express it. Or it is shrivelled up in Phebe's unimaginative and graceless common sense when she tells Silvius not to be a fool and stop supposing that anybody's eyes are capable of killing. Where to take your stand between fancy and sheer literalism, that is the problem. Rosalind's disguise shows her the way. In it she can combine superficial mockery and real passion, which Orlando may not be able to see, but we can (perhaps Celia can too). (pp. 118-21)

Mark Van Doren sums up Shakespeare's achievement with Rosalind very well. Her criticism of love and the pastoral life, he says, is unremitting, 'yet she has not annihilated them. Rather, she has preserved them by removing the flaws of their softness. . . . There is only one thing sillier than being in love, and that is thinking it is silly to be in love. Rosalind skips through both errors to wisdom' [see excerpt above, 1939]. Elegantly and succinctly put. Orlando, Silvius and William exemplify the first silliness. It is left to Touchstone and Jaques to exemplify the second. It is time now we took a look at the malcontent and the fool, to discover the different ways in which they do this. (p. 121)

Both Touchstone and Jaques are exponents of a reductive humour, that is to say of a temperament that delights in stripping away the fantasies and deceits that are believed to clothe the body of truth. Since truth appears to be made of clothes, however, the exercise is usually disastrous when taken to its extreme. . . . So in *As You Like It* neither of them is allowed to go to the furthest extremes, though Jaques comes near to it on occasion. His account of the seven ages of man is deeply cynical. Touchstone has a more ambivalent attitude, quizzically sceptical of both illusion and disillusion. His conversation with Corin at III, ii, is typical of him:

> *Corin*: And how like you this shepherd's life, Master Touchstone?
> *Touchstone*: Truly, shepherd, in respect of itself, it is a good life; but in respect that it is a shepherd's life, it is naught. In respect that it is solitary, I like it very well; but in respect that it is private, it is a very vile life. Now in respect it is in the fields, it pleaseth me well;

> but in respect it is not in the court, it is tedious.
> As it is a spare life, look you, it fits my humour
> well; but as there is no more plenty in it, it
> goes much against my stomach.
>
> [III. ii. 11-22]

His insistence on having it both ways is a linguistic reflection of the double landscape in which the dialogue takes place. The two ways of looking at nature are transposed into two ways of appraising a situation. Touchstone's ability to see things from two points of view simultaneously is like Rosalind's. The difference is that he cannot make the affirmation that locks them together somewhere half-way between.

In the speech the balanced antitheses and *exempla* of Euphuism are used with a critical intent. Van Doren sums up its object in a probing paradox. 'Touchstone is without illusion;' he says, 'so much so that he will not claim that he can do without it.' His 'fault' lies in the stance he takes up towards the world of love and sentiment. Even his romance with Audrey is something to be half involved with and half to be contemplated in the light of his dry, mocking intelligence. That intelligence remains dry. It doesn't combine with the sentiment it exercises itself upon. The two sides of his nature remain polarised, the one looking at the other across a void his own scepticism has created.

If Jaques is 'too fond of believing he is wise to be as wise as he sounds' [Van Doren], Touchstone is too sure of the terms according to which he has met illusion half way to convince us (and himself, perhaps) that such terms are not part of a greater illusion still. Only Rosalind has got it right and passed by on the other side of the struggle between sentiment and scepticism. This is why she can act as a norm around which the lovers and the cynics conduct their disputations and play out their scenes. But we should be mistaken if we supposed that as such she occupies a fixed position, an Aristotelian point of balance. Shakespeare knew that the norm is never fixed. It moves in strange ellipses around a central point that never existed. It is a principle of vitality, as well as judgement. (pp. 123-24)

> *Patrick Swinden, "'As You Like It'," in his* An Introduction to Shakespeare's Comedies, *1973. Reprint by Macmillan, 1979, pp. 110-24.*

## ALEXANDER LEGGATT   (essay date 1974)

[*In the following excerpt, Leggatt discusses Shakespeare's fusion of convention and reality in* As You Like It. *Arguing that Shakespeare uses art to conceal art in the play, he emphasizes the comedy's swift, unpredictable shifts in idiom from casual naturalism to high artifice as evidence of the "liberty" of mind that allows the playwright to mix dramatic styles. A juxtaposition of attitudes in* As You Like It, *Leggatt maintains, is effected not only by the "dislocating confrontations of different characters," but also by the comparing of different minds and experiences "purely for their own sake." Opportunities for these juxtapositions, the critic continues, are provided by both the forest itself and by such devices as Rosalind's "genuinely liberating" disguise. Ultimately, Leggatt argues, the swift interplay of perspectives supplies much of* As You Like It's *comic effect, but not the play's final impression. This he finds reflected in Rosalind's eventual acceptance of romantic love over the conventions of satire—both of which she incorporated in her role as Ganymede—and in her synthesis of the ceremonial and the practical as she moves to bring about the final marriages. On a related matter, Leggatt avers that just "as the play toys with and rejects the satiric view of love," so does it undercut "the realist's view of time as a* linear movement to inevitable decay"—*an attitude best expressed by Touchstone and Jaques. Shakespeare accomplishes this by depicting Arden as a place where "old values," such as those of Adam, can be recovered and by showing that through "one moment of happiness," such as marriage brings, we can "cheat" time and establish a new order.*]

At the start of *As You Like It*, we overhear what seems to be a casual conversation between a young man and a servant. But as we listen, it occurs to us that the situation unfolded in the dialogue, that of a young man oppressed by a wicked older brother, is familiar from old tales; and the fact that there are three brothers increases this feeling. At the same time we are bound to protest that Adam must already know everything Orlando is telling him. What looks at first like a realistic conversation is in fact a blatant theatrical trick: the machinery of exposition is unashamedly exposed. Yet throughout the opening scene the manner of the dialogue continues to be as natural and easy as in any of the realistic scenes of *The Merchant of Venice* or *Much Ado About Nothing*. And throughout the play this double-exposure effect persists: the characters converse in a convincingly natural manner within situations that are clearly the product of theatrical artifice. (p. 185)

[Throughout *As You Like It*], the blending of convention and human reality is so light, swift and subtle that we accept the fusion as natural. It is the art that conceals the art, and more than that it is a way of extending our sense of human possibilities, of suggesting that the distinction between ordinary experience and the conventionalized actions of storybook characters may be a false one. (p. 189)

The forest of Arden is itself the product of a fusion of conventions. At times it suggests the playwright's native landscape, at other times the forest of classical pastoral: Warwickshire is notably deficient in lions and olive trees, yet this forest has both. The mingling of conventions is to a great extent dependent on the mixed nature of the characters themselves: we hear of the olive trees, for example, once in a scene with Phebe [III. v. 75] and once in the scene of Oliver's conversion [IV. iii. 77]—the scene that also gives us the serpent and the lion. The native population of Arden is mixed indeed: for one kind of wedding, the forest can produce an Elizabethan hedge-priest, Sir Oliver Martext, whose very name suggests the real problems the church has always faced in country parishes; for another kind of wedding, it can produce Hymen himself. There is one shepherd, Corin, whose language, pungent and concrete, is rooted in his occupation, and who experiences the hard facts of social and economic reality: 'But I am shepherd to another man, / And do not shear the fleeces that I graze' [II. iv. 78-9]. There is another shepherd, Silvius, who 'little cares for buying anything' [II. iv. 90], and whose language has no particular roots in rural experience (pleading with Phebe, he uses a very urban image, drawn from public executions [III. v. 3-6]). There is nothing in the play to suggest that Silvius knows one end of a sheep from the other, and when he and Phebe are played with yokel accents it always sounds wrong. The female population is equally mixed: there is Phebe, a shepherdess who can quote Marlowe in a gracefully allusive manner: 'Dead shepherd, now I find thy saw of might: / "Who ever lov'd that lov'd not at first sight?"' [III. v. 81-2]. And there is Audrey, a country wench (a very distinct breed from the shepherdess) who finds the very word 'poetical' hard to understand [III. iii. 17-18]. These figures represent not simply different types of character, but different types of dramatic idiom. Yet they mingle freely—Corin and Silvius are first seen together—and no one coming to Arden remarks on the incongruity.

This may be because they themselves enjoy considerable imaginative freedom in the forest. The liberty of the mind that allows Shakespeare to mix dramatic styles is not only part of the play's manner, but part of its matter as well. We are often assured by critics that Arden is a place of testing and education, as though there were something suspect about pure holiday. But I do not feel this is a prominent issue: the characters may learn, perhaps, that the property of rain is to wet and fire to burn, and that if a cat will after kind, so be sure will Rosalind. But they are not under the severe and obvious pressure to learn that characters experience in, for example, *The Taming of the Shrew* and *Love's Labour's Lost* (where the cast includes a sprinkling of pedants, to emphasize the point). Rosalind may tease Orlando about his Petrarchanisms, but unlike Berowne [in *Love's Labour's Lost*] he is never shown repenting, and there is never any doubt that Rosalind wants him, bad verses and all. I think the keynote of the forest scenes is rather an imaginative freedom to explore ideas and play roles—on one's own terms, and for one's own amusement. There is a quality of relaxation, even in the way the forest is introduced. In *A Midsummer Night's Dream* we are firmly removed from the court, kept in the wood, and then just as firmly returned. Here, the forest fades into the play gradually, overlapping with lingering scenes in the court. The fact that the play opens in Oliver's orchard helps to blur the transition, suggesting that Shakespeare envisaged property trees as a permanent feature of the stage. The forest is introduced by a line at the end of a court scene, Celia's 'Now go we in content / To liberty, and not to banishment' [I. iii. 137-38], and in the scene that follows immediately we get some idea of what that liberty means. You can be master of your own mind in this forest in a way that is impossible in the enchanted wood near Athens. Duke Senior uses this freedom to draw philosophy from the weather and the landscape; and he lets his mind play over country and town, drawing them together imaginatively:

> Come, shall we go and kill us venison?
> And yet it irks me the poor dappled fools,
> Being native burghers of this desert city
> Should, in their own confines, with forked heads
> Have their round haunches gor'd.
>
> [II. i. 21-5]

Corin would never talk like this: to see the slaughter of animals as pitiful is the prerogative of the town-bred man. The countryman's view needs to be harder, and narrower.

Jaques, in his speech on the wounded deer, elaborates the incident into a fantasy about a bankrupt citizen, and releases his imagination to range even more freely than the Duke's:

> Thus most invectively he pierceth through
> The body of the country, city, court,
> Yea, and of this our life, swearing that we
> Are mere usurpers, tyrants, and what's worse,
> To fright the animals and to kill them up
> In their assign'd and native dwelling-place.
>
> [II. i. 58-63]

Affected it may be; but it shows also the free play of a civilized mind, unconfined by court or country. And while the Duke realizes the practical necessities of forest life, he is not limited by them; hearing that Jaques is in his moralizing vein, he postpones his hunting to seek him out [II. i. 66-8]. The playful elaboration of Jaques's fantasy, and the Duke's philosophizing, give us our first real taste of Arden; and the emphasis throughout is not on the tough, simple life Arden provides for the

natives (Corin is the spokesman for that) but rather on the fresh material it offers for the courtly figures to exercise their wits upon. (pp. 190-93)

[The] trouble with Frederick's court is that it is not civilized enough: it is a place where wits like Touchstone are suppressed, and denied their traditional privilege of attacking folly.... Duke Senior is more civilized in this respect, tolerating and even encouraging the satire of Jaques; and Touchstone enjoys as much licence as he wants in Arden. The court is also a place where 'breaking of ribs' is considered 'sport for ladies' [I. i. 138-39]. The oppression of the court is not a matter of whips and jackboots, but something more attuned to the spirit of the play—a stifling of genuine fun, and a crude idea of what constitutes sport; bad manners and bad taste, as opposed to the civilized liberty of Arden.

This oppression affects Rosalind and Orlando: their love dialogue at the court is hesitant, groping, and shy:

> ROSALIND: He calls us back. My pride fell with my
>                          fortunes;
>        I'll ask him what he would. Did you call,
>             sir?
>        Sir, you have wrestled well, and overthrown
>        More than your enemies.
> CELIA:                            Will you go, coz?
> ROSALIND: Have with you. Fare you well.
>             [*Exeunt Rosalind and Celia.*
> ORLANDO: What passion hangs these weights upon my
>             tongue?
>        I could not speak to her, yet she urg'd
>             conference.
>        O poor Orlando, thou art overthrown!
>        Or Charles or something weaker masters
>             thee.
>
> [I. ii. 252-60]

Here, as in *The Two Gentlemen of Verona*, love is more an oppressive than a liberating power—they both feel 'overthrown' by it.... The atmosphere of the court, in which both are 'out of suits with fortune' and Orlando in particular is denied his full development, may have something to do with this. But all this changes when the characters come to the forest. Throughout the opening scenes, Celia is the woman with the wit and initiative, and Rosalind merely follows along. It is Celia who suggests going to the forest; but once the notion of disguise is introduced, Rosalind starts developing her own ideas, and using her own wit [I. iii. 114-31]. And the change anticipated here becomes decisive in the forest, where Rosalind, wearing the disguise, comes into her own, and the earlier balance between the women is reversed. Orlando finds both his tongue and his spirits in Arden. (pp. 193-94)

The freedom of the forest provides a chance for those dislocating confrontations of different characters that provide one of Shakespeare's favourite comic effects. Harold Jenkins has written of the play's 'piquant but seemingly casual juxtapositions', and of 'the ease and rapidity with which pairs and groups break up, re-form, and succeed one another on the stage' [see excerpt above, 1953]. The play is unusually rich in such moments since, freed for the most part from the demands of developing an intrigue, Shakespeare can concentrate on juxtapositions of different minds and experiences purely for their own sake. One is tempted to say that the main action of the play takes place in its language, for confrontations of characters mean, as usual, confrontations of style. Up to a point the effect is that of *A Midsummer Night's Dream*—a series of mutual dislocations, rather than one controlling view that compromises all the others. In the earlier play, however, each group of characters was allowed, in turn, to take over the stage, and the dislocations were provided more by the sheer presence of other groups than by their direct intervention—the fairies watching the lovers, the lovers watching the clowns. In that respect *As You Like It* is a more active play, full of brisk local skirmishes:

| | |
|---|---|
| ROSALIND: | Jove! Jove! this shepherd's passion<br>Is much upon my fashion. |
| TOUCHSTONE: | And mine; but it grows something stale<br>with me. |
| CELIA: | I pray you, one of you question yond man<br>If he for gold will give us any food;<br>I faint almost to death. |

[II. iv. 60-6]

Here, two views of love are quickly juxtaposed—Rosalind's rhymed, romantic contemplation and Touchstone's wry, prosaic dismissal—and both are broken in on by the voice of Celia, who (like Speed) is uninterested in love or indeed anything that is not edible. Once the characters have been established, their mere physical juxtaposition will do the trick. . . . (pp. 195-96)

Touchstone is particularly useful for moments such as this, for he has a natural tendency to react against the person he is speaking with. Against Silvius's dreamy, disembodied view of love

> If thou rememb'rest not the slightest folly
> That ever love did make thee run into,
> Thou hast not lov'd.
>
> [II. iv. 34-6]

he offers concrete experience, seen with cynical detachment:

> I remember, when I was in love, I broke my
> sword upon a stone and bid him take that for
> coming a-night to Jane Smile; and I remember
> the kissing of her batler, and the cow's dugs
> that her pretty chopt hands had milk'd. . . .
>
> [II. iv. 46-50]

But the other shepherd finds Touchstone in a different vein. Corin's mind is simple, direct, and practical. He knows that 'the property of rain is to wet, and fire to burn; that good pasture makes fat sheep; and that a great cause of the night is lack of the sun' [III. ii. 26-8]. Faced with a mind as concrete as this, Touchstone's mind at once reacts by using words with a deliberate vagueness that allows him to play verbal tricks. . . . The most frequently discussed juxtapositions, however, involve Jaques and Orlando: when Orlando's heroic posture, with drawn sword, is deflated by Jaques's cool wit; and when in turn Jaques's view of old age as mere senile collapse is set against Orlando's entrance with old Adam. For the shrewdest discussion of these and similar moments we are indebted to Harold Jenkins, and it is worth recalling his warning that 'Shakespeare seeks no cheap antithesis'. There is no simple partisan laughter at any one figure; rather, we are gently reminded of the incompleteness of each character's view seen in isolation. No one attitude can be taken as absolute or final, for truth can always wear another face: it is dangerous to laugh too simply even at Silvius, for while Touchstone is unimpressed by him, Rosalind sees in his experience a reflection of her own [II. iv. 44-5, 60-1].

A sense of the relativity of experience is implied by these comic juxtapositions, as it was in *The Comedy of Errors*. But here it is more than implied: it is directly stated. Time, says Rosalind in her set piece on the subject, moves at different paces for different people. . . . When Touchstone and Corin discuss the merits of court and country life, no objective reality emerges. . . . A single quality can be a virtue or a fault, depending on one's point of view. Corin has a similar idea about good manners: 'Those that are good manners at the court are as ridiculous in the country, as the behaviour of the country is most mockable at the court' [III. ii. 45-8]. But lest we should settle too comfortably in the idea that at least the difference between court and country is a fixed truth, Touchstone insists that from some points of view they are identical: shepherds' and courtiers' hands are both greasy, and while the one is smeared with tar the other is no less disgustingly smeared with civet [III. ii. 52-69]. No fixed attitude to court or country emerges from this debate, unless it be the idea that everything is relative. But to state this idea so clearly—more clearly than in any previous comedy—is to bring it out into the open, and that makes it vulnerable. A Shakespearian comedy is a very dangerous place for an abstract idea to be wandering loose. And the idea that all experience is relative, that everything depends on your point of view, is no safer than any other.

In order to see how this idea is dealt with, we need first to examine the function of role-playing in the comedy. If a character's attitude is not final or absolute when seen against the world at large, possibly it is not final or absolute even for himself. There is often an element of pose in the statements the characters make. . . . Touchstone's set piece on time is certainly a calculated performance. We are told that he

> laid him down and bask'd him in the sun,
> And rail'd on Lady Fortune in good terms,
> In good set terms—and yet a motley fool.
>
> [II. vii. 15-17]

Nor is Touchstone the only one to employ 'good set terms'. Jaques's speech on the seven ages of man begins with a cliché and ends with a self-consciously rhetorical climax [II. vii. 164-66]. So does Duke Senior's lecture on the uses of adversity, with its balanced, alliterative conclusion. . . . It is not entirely mischievous, I think, to wonder how many times Duke Senior's followers have heard this speech before. And the ease with which he returns to the 'envious court' is notorious: the value of the simple life is an idea to be entertained, not a final commitment.

But not all the characters simply toy with attitudes, retaining the ultimate detachment the Duke seems to achieve: some are fully absorbed in the roles they play. Silvius and Phebe, in the parts of suffering lover and disdainful beauty, show no awareness that their behaviour is conventional. . . . [They] are absorbed in their roles, unconscious of the entertainment they provide for their onstage audience. Touchstone is more aware of his audience; yet in a different way he too is trapped by his role. He cannot turn off his professional, joking manner, and it is remarkable how often we find him 'wasting his sharpness on the desert air' [see excerpt above by D. J. Palmer, 1970]: some of his most elaborate performances are directed at Corin, Audrey and William, who are all in varying degrees too slow to appreciate them. (pp. 196-200)

Jaques presents a more complicated case. Behind the pose of melancholy we detect a genial interest in humanity. His lecture on the seven ages has a light, jocular tone that works against the cynicism of its content. And he seems gregarious by nature. . . . He collects people, prizing Touchstone in particular as a rare item. But while unlike the jester he allows us glimpses of the man behind the mask, he has no real freedom beyond his adopted role. We see this when he wishes to change his part, becoming not a light entertainer specializing in melancholy, but a fully-fledged satirist reforming the world. The Duke brings him sharply to heel, claiming that he would do

> Most mischievous foul sin, in chiding sin;
> For thou thyself hast been a libertine,
> As sensual as the brutish sting itself. . . .
>
> [II. vii. 64-6]

This sharp and surprisingly serious rebuke contrasts with the Duke's usual indulgence of Jaques—'I love to cope him in these sullen fits' [II. i. 67]. And it reveals more of Jaques than we might have expected to learn: a comic figure does not usually have a past. Jaques is tolerable as an entertainer if he keeps his satire light; but that satire has no value as a moral corrective, for it reflects merely his own experience of corruption. The Duke is telling him, in effect, that he can be tolerated only if he does not claim to be taken too seriously. Jaques's reply, offering the conventional argument that satire is general and not aimed at particular individuals, evades the Duke's charge; but for the rest of the play we hear nothing more of Jaques the reformer of the world. We have now seen that the lightening of his cynicism by conscious role-playing is a necessary tactic to preserve the social acceptability his gregarious nature requires. Like the type figures of his most famous speech, he has a part, and—like it or not—he must play it.

Arden gives Touchstone and Jaques freedom to exercise their wits, but that freedom is finally limited by their own adopted roles. Rosalind's disguise as Ganymede, on the other hand, is genuinely liberating. For one thing, there is a clear distinction between the role and the character behind the role; a different name, a different sex. This is not to say that Ganymede and Rosalind are utterly different beings, and that nothing Ganymede says can be taken as Rosalind's serious view. It is not so simple as that. Ganymede is part of Rosalind's nature, but clearly not the whole; rather the role is a device allowing Rosalind a freedom of comment impossible in a conventional love affair, while at the same time freeing her from any final commitment to Ganymede's point of view. Like the women of *Love's Labour's Lost* she can be properly scathing about her lover's attempts at poetry: 'O most gentle pulpiter! What a tedious homily of love have you wearied your parishioners withal, and never cried, "Have patience, good people" ' [III. ii. 155-57]. This is before she knows who wrote the verses; but even in direct conversation with Orlando she can be satiric about the way love is expressed in literature, poking fun at both the conventions of love poetry and the great love stories of the past:

> The poor world is almost six thousand years old, and in all this time there was not any man died in his own person, videlicet, in a love-cause. Troilus has his brains dash'd out with a Grecian club; yet he did what he could to die before, and he is one of the patterns of love. Leander, he would have liv'd many a fair year, though Hero had turn'd nun, if it had not been for a hot midsummer-night; for, good youth, he went but forth to wash him in the Hellespont, and, being taken with the cramp, was drown'd;

and the foolish chroniclers of that age found it was—Hero of Sestos. But these are all lies: men have died from time to time, and worms have eaten them, but not for love.

> [IV. i. 94-108]

While in *Pyramus and Thisbe* tragedy was dismissed as irrelevant, here it is rejected as untrue. Rosalind's speech is controlled by a cool sense of the world as it really is—men *do* die, but not for love.

But the paradox is that despite the conviction with which the satire is spoken, and the realism that appears to control it, the satire is itself conventional, just as Berowne's renunciation of rhetoric [in *Love's Labour's Lost*] was conventional (and rhetorical). . . . Ganymede's view of love is . . . second-hand, orthodox and not always in tune with the facts: contemplating Orlando, he cannot imagine him as a lover, for 'There is none of my uncle's marks upon you' [III. ii. 369]. In thus identifying the satiric role as conventional, Rosalind preserves herself from any final commitment to it, just as Ganymede swears 'by all pretty oaths that are not dangerous' [IV. i. 189-90]. In confessing her love directly—which she does over and over—she can be as extravagant as the old tales she mocks: 'his kissing is as full of sanctity as the touch of holy bread' [III. iv. 13-14]. After Ganymede has been particularly active, with an extended attack on women, love and marriage, Rosalind hastens to redress the balance:

> ROSALIND: O coz, coz, coz, my pretty little coz, that thou didst know how many fathom deep I am in love! But it cannot be sounded: my affection hath an unknown bottom, like the Bay of Portugal.
> CELIA: Or rather, bottomless; that as fast as you pour affection in, it runs out.
> ROSALIND: No; that same wicked bastard of Venus, that was begot of thought, conceiv'd of spleen, and born of madness; that blind rascally boy, that abuses everyone's eyes because his own are out—let him be judge how deep I am in love. I'll tell thee, Aliena, I cannot be out of the sight of Orlando. I'll go find a shadow, and sigh till he come.
> CELIA: And I'll sleep.
>
> [IV. i. 205-17]

Rosalind veers between frank confession and self-mockery, trying hard to keep her balance as her feelings are released. Celia meets her confession with pure mockery, and then with ostentatious indifference; her interventions help us to distinguish between the satire of the totally immune and the satire of a woman genuinely in love but trying to keep her poise. Celia's manner is cool, detached and simple; Rosalind's is more complex, showing a wry awareness of her own extravagance while insisting on that extravagance as the only adequate expression of her feelings. The play's open, flexible manner is nowhere better illustrated, or more eloquent. (pp. 200-04)

Rosalind has the range of feeling and expression [of] . . . some of the major figures of previous comedies. But she has more control over the wide possibilities of her nature than Berowne, with his unstable veering between self-indulgence and self-contempt, or Portia [in *The Merchant of Venice*], who is forced into imitating Shylock somewhat against the grain of her nature. She is closer to Petruchio [in *The Taming of the Shrew*], who turns one possibility of his nature—noisy bullying—into a comic performance, and thus exorcizes it to clear the way for domestic peace. Everything is relative, it all depends on your point of view—that idea depends on the comic confrontations of different figures, each of whom is locked in a fixed position, whether consciously like Jaques, or unconsciously like Silvius. Rosalind can take us beyond that idea by including in her nature several points of view. She can encompass the romanticism of Silvius, the realism of Touchstone, and even at times Corin's awareness of the working-day world. Having various attitudes at her command, she is in a position to pick and choose among them. 'It all depends on your point of view'— but if one is not to be paralysed by inactivity, one has to decide which point of view is worth acting on. On the question of love, Rosalind finally stands with Orlando: 'I would not be cured' [III. ii. 425]. The satiric point of view cannot be forgotten, for that would be to deny an important part of her nature. But it can be put in its place by being turned into a performance, acted out and thus exorcized. This could be seen as a last fling before the surrender of marriage—Rosalind giving free play to her individuality before . . . dwindling into a wife. But the satiric view of love is as conventional, as unoriginal, as the acceptance of it. Rosalind's freedom is rather her power to choose between conventions, to decide that one is to be treated as a game, and the other taken seriously. Unlike Jaques and Touchstone, she turns only part of her nature into a performance, and thus maintains the control and flexibility they lack. And this process of selection in Rosalind's nature is reflected in the play as a whole: beneath the shifting surface of *As You Like It* is a firm acceptance of the conventions of love. (pp. 206-07)

Much of the comic effect of *As You Like It* comes, as we have seen, from a swift interplay of perspectives. But that is not the play's final effect. In the forest scenes we seem for a while to be suspended beyond time, enjoying an endless afternoon. The only movement is a back-and-forth shuttling as the various characters wander in, confront each other and wander out again. But just as there is a controlling attitude behind the interplay of perspectives, so in the play as a whole there is a steady forward motion behind the apparent casualness. We can trace through the play two main ways of seeing time. One is the Jaques-Touchstone view of inevitable decay:

> And so, from hour to hour, we ripe and ripe,
> And then, from hour to hour, we rot and rot;
> And thereby hangs a tale.
>
> [II. vii. 26-8]

Jaques's set piece on the seven ages of man is essentially an elaboration of this view. Rosalind, in her satiric vein, shares it. The great mock courtship scene (IV. i) imitates the progress of a love affair through time, from disdain to acceptance to a re-enactment of the marriage service, and then to the disillusion of marriage itself. Man's life is linked with the seasons, and the process is seen as one of decay [IV. i. 146]. . . . This is the realist's view, and the satirist's view. But this view is part of the self-conscious role-playing of all three characters, and thus its seriousness is compromised. In the play itself we detect a different, less mechanical view of the changes of time, one that is embodied not in any one speech, but in the whole movement of the play.

The early scenes are dominated by a sense of an old order lost. The idea is centred on old Adam, whom Orlando addresses as the last survivor of better days. . . . Connected with this contrast between an idealized past and a corrupt present is the curious obsession with fathers that runs all through the early scenes.

Rosalind and Orlando both brood over their lost fathers. When attacked first by Oliver and then by Frederick, Orlando seems more concerned to defend his dead father's dignity than his own [I. i. 56-9; I. ii. 232-34]. Rosalind cannot be merry, 'unless you could teach me how to forget a banished father' [I. ii. 5-6]. (pp. 207-09)

But while passages like this may seem to confirm the idea of decay through time, the old order is not dead; it is recoverable in the forest of Arden. When Charles the wrestler describes the banished Duke's court, he speaks of it as though the past has come to life again:

> They say he is already in the Forest of Arden,
> and a many merry men with him; and there
> they live like the old Robin Hood of England.
> They say many young gentlemen flock to him
> every day, and fleet the time carelessly, as they
> did in the golden world.
>
> [I. i. 114-19]

Instead of seeing time as inevitable decay, this suggests that time's progress may be circular: the golden age we nearly always associate with the past can be recovered. . . . [When] Orlando comes to the forest these hints of the recovery of the old order are fulfilled. His appeal to the order and decency of the past meets with a responsive voice from the Duke:

> If ever you have look'd on better days,
> If ever been where bells have knoll'd to church,
> If ever sat at any good man's feast,
> If ever from your eyelids wip'd a tear,
> And know what 'tis to pity and be pitied,
> Let gentleness my strong enforcement be;
> In the which hope I blush, and hide my sword.
>
> DUKE: True is it that we have seen better days,
> And have with holy bells been knoll'd to church,
> And sat at good men's feasts, and wip'd our eyes
> Of drops that sacred pity hath engend'red;
> And therefore sit you down in gentleness,
> And take upon command what help we have
> That to your wanting may be minist'red.
>
> [II. vii. 113-26]

The Duke knows just what Orlando means; the young man has in a sense come home. The incantatory repetitions give a posed, formal dignity to this moment. . . . [It] is quiet, serious and free from the usual comic dislocation. It is also the last occasion in the play on which there is an appeal to the golden past. Having found a community where the old decency and order are maintained, the characters no longer find it necessary to look backwards. After the scene of the Duke's banquet, old Adam disappears from the play; he is not even referred to. His disappearance, like that of Lear's fool, is unexplained in plot terms, but in both cases the character's dramatic function has been fulfilled, and he is no longer needed.

In this respect the pivot on which the play turns is Rosalind's line 'But what talk we of fathers when there is such a man as Orlando?' [III. iv. 38-9]. The characters turn from nostalgia for the security of a father-dominated world to the decision to create their own kind of order in marriage. Here again, time is seen not as the medium of decay but as the medium of fulfilment. In the final movement of the play, there is an urgent drive forward. A transition from winter to spring is marked in the songs. . . . 'It was a lover and his lass' offers the traditional *carpe diem* theme, urging us to 'take the present time . . . For love is crowned with the prime' [V. iii. 30-2]. As usual in

Shakespearian comedy, human actions are connected with the rhythms of nature, and this song prepares us for the comic finale by providing the play's clearest images of spring and fertility. . . . [We] are moving towards the practical realities of love. In the process, Ganymede disappears; like old Adam, he has served his purpose. It is not just that Rosalind removes the disguise; it is rather that this aspect of her nature is gradually withdrawn, and the change is therefore subtler than the simple removal of a mask. . . . When she appears as herself in the finale, it is not just the winding up of a comic intrigue, but the end of a gradual transition from the games of satire to the ceremonies of love.

But as satire fades away, so too does the purely romantic contemplation of love. The litany of the four lovers in V. ii marks the transition. Silvius, chief spokesman for the romantic view, gives it a final, definitive statement, and the others join in, acknowledging the truth it has for them:

> It is to be all made of fantasy,
> All made of passion, and all made of wishes;
> All adoration, duty, and observance,
> All humbleness, all patience, and impatience,
> All purity, all trial, all observance;
> And so am I for Phebe.
> PHEBE:      And so am I for Ganymede.
> ORLANDO:  And so am I for Rosalind.
> ROSALIND:  And so am I for no woman.
>
> [V. ii. 94-102]

But the patient yearning suggested here would be sterile if not matched by action; and in the atmosphere of growing urgency at the end of the play, action cannot be delayed much longer. Rosalind, having joined in the litany, suddenly becomes impatient with it:

> Pray you, no more of this; 'tis like the howling
> of Irish wolves against the moon. . . .
>
> [V. ii. 109-10]

In turning from verse to prose, she turns from romantic contemplation to realistic action; but the prose is still patterned and formal, and the responses of the other characters echo the rhythm of the earlier litany. The ceremonial idiom is broken only to be redirected. In Rosalind's speech, the ceremonial and the practical come together; and thus we could say that the realism of Ganymede has also been broken only to be redirected. The result, in the final scene, is an image of love that is ceremonial but not disembodied, and practical but not satiric. (pp. 209-13)

The image of marriage at the end is . . . a complex one, bringing together a rich variety of attitudes. And the new world of marriage is fused with the old world of decency and order represented by the Duke: Rosalind greets her father and her husband with the same words, 'To you I give myself, for I am yours' [V. iv. 116-18]. There is a harmony of different generations suggested here, quite different from the conflict of youth and age so frequently found in comedy. . . . The harmony of the ending finally includes more than the joining of the sexes in marriage: it involves a full restoration of social order in the broadest terms. The Duke promises that

> every of this happy number,
> That have endur'd shrewd days and nights with us,
> Shall share the good of our returned fortune,
> According to the measure of their states.
>
> [V. iv. 172-75]

The last line in particular suggests a respect for the social decorum we saw so rudely violated earlier in the play. The old values, recovered in the forest, will now return to the court. Just as the play toys with and rejects the satiric view of love, so (through the speeches of Touchstone and Jaques) it has toyed with the realist's view of time as a linear movement to inevitable decay, but chosen in the end to focus on that one moment of happiness when we seem to have cheated time, when a new world and an old come together in permanent harmony, 'mirth in heaven' [V. iv. 108]. (pp. 215-16)

The choice of a female character to deliver the epilogue is peculiar, as [Rosalind] herself admits. . . . But the choice of Rosalind is deliberate. Throughout the play she is the character who makes the most creative use of role-playing, the one who is most careful to see the relation between performance and reality. And as in the play itself the conventions of love could be mocked while the love was accepted as real, so in the epilogue the play is admitted to be an illusion (and perhaps not even a good play). . . . [But] all we have to do is look at the audience to see the truth of its final vision of humanity walking to the Ark in pairs. This may be one more reason for the play's title. (p. 218)

The physical level of love [portrayed here] is the common one, the one we can all understand, and it dominates the epilogue: 'If I were a woman, I would kiss as many of you as had beards that pleas'd me, complexions that liked me, and breaths that I defied not' [Epilogue, 18-20]. This is the one clear bond between the play and the audience's own experience of life. It is also the one aspect of love whose power a satirist like Touchstone is prepared to admit, and the one interest shared by all four couples. If this play is peculiarly successful in showing the reality behind convention, this may be because it sees convention is strongest where it embodies recognizable, predictable experiences: in love in particular, all the clichés come true. Dispensing with the sort of intrigue he used in *The Merchant of Venice* and *Much Ado About Nothing*, Shakespeare avoids the distasteful narrowing of experience produced by such conventions as Shylock's bond and Don John's plotting. Instead, he concentrates on a convention—the Noah's Ark ending—which allows us in the audience to feel that we are not merely spectators but participants. We are entitled to poke fun at it if we wish. The liberty of Arden will admit almost any point of view. But if we do laugh, we must also recognize that, like Rosalind when she played Ganymede, we are laughing at ourselves. (p. 219)

> *Alexander Leggatt, " 'As You Like It'," in his* Shakespeare's Comedy of Love, *Methuen, 1974, pp. 185-219.*

### NANCY K. HAYLES   (essay date 1979)

[*In the following excerpt, Hayles discusses Shakespeare's use of sexual disguise in* As You Like It. *She argues that this device in the comedy proceeds in separate movements; layers of disguise are first added to Rosalind, then slowly removed as Ganymede abandons Rosalind's play-acting, and finally eliminated when the heroine abandons her disguise altogether. The layering-on movement, Hayles contends, suggests selfish control and creates conflict in the play, just as the layering-off movement fosters reconciliation. Further, the critic remarks, the unlayering resolves the "traditional tension beneath the needs of the female and the desires of the male," demonstrated in the play by the conflicting expectations of Orlando and Rosalind with respect to their love. Hayles extends this pattern of increased selfish control and reconciliation to Shakespeare and* As You Like It *itself, stating that*] *in the epilogue the dramatist, like his heroine, "relinquishes control of the audience" and achieves a reconciliation between men and women similar to that achieved in the play. In an interesting psychoanalytic diversion, Hayles claims that Oliver's account of the lioness and the snake suggests both female engulfment and phallic invasion, two different but related fears that Orlando overcomes, symbolically, by rescuing his brother.]*

*As You Like It* opens with scenes that emphasize rivalry and competition. Orlando has been mistreated by his brother Oliver, and Oliver in turn feels that Orlando has caused him to be 'altogether misprised' [I. i. 170-71] and undervalued by his own people. The rivalry that Duke Frederick still feels with the rightful Duke is also apparent. Moreover, the chief event of the opening scenes, the wrestling match between Charles and Orlando, is a formalized and ritualistic expression of male rivalry. Against the backdrop of male rivalry, the female intimacy between Celia and Rosalind makes a striking contrast. It is an intimacy, however, maintained at some cost. When Duke Frederick peremptorily orders Rosalind into banishment, Celia's protest is countered by her father's attempt to transform intimacy into rivalry between the two girls, too.

Thou art a fool; she robs thee of thy name,
And thou wilt show more bright and seem more virtuous
When she is gone. Then open not thy lips.

[I. iii. 80-2]

The opening scenes of the play, then, draw a society where intimacy among women is implicitly contrasted with the rivalry among men. When the scene changes to the forest, several incidents seem designed as signals that the forest is a world where co-operation rather than competition prevails. Orlando meets with civility instead of hostility when he seeks meat for the fainting Adam; Rosalind and Celia find the natives to be kind shepherds rather than would-be rapists; and the exiled Duke hails his followers as 'Co-mates and brothers' [II. i. 1]. But we soon discover that competition is not altogether absent from the Forest of Arden. Jaques accuses the Duke of himself usurping the forest from its rightful owners, the deer; Touchstone confronts and bests his country rival, William; and Silvius discovers that his beloved Phebe has fallen in love with a courtly newcomer. The situation is thus more complicated than a simple contrast between court competition and pastoral co-operation, or between female intimacy and male rivalry. The sexual disguise of Rosalind mirrors the complexities of these tensions.

We can consider the disguise as proceeding in two separate movements. First, the layers of disguise are added as Rosalind becomes Ganymede, and then as Ganymede pretends to be Orlando's Rosalind; second, the layers are removed as Ganymede abandons the play-acting of Rosalind, and then as Rosalind herself abandons the disguise of Ganymede. The layering-on movement creates conflict and the layering-off movement fosters reconciliation as the disguise confronts and then resolves the issue of competition versus co-operation.

In the most complex layering, Rosalind-as-Ganymede-as-Orlando's Rosalind, Rosalind presents Orlando with a version of his beloved very different from the one he imagines in his verses. When Rosalind-as-Ganymede insists that Orlando's Rosalind will have her own wit, her own will and her own way, implicit in the portrayal is Rosalind's insistence that Orlando recognize the discrepancy between his idealized version and the real Rosalind. In effect, Rosalind is claiming the right to be herself rather than to be Orlando's idealized version of her, as female reality is playfully set against male fantasy. In

playing herself (which she can apparently do only if she first plays someone else) Rosalind is able to state her own needs in a way she could not if she were simply herself. It is because she is disguised as Ganymede that she can be so free in portraying a Rosalind who is a flesh and blood woman instead of a Petrarchan abstraction. Rosalind's three-fold disguise is therefore used to accentuate the disparity between the needs of the heroine and the expectations of the hero.

Even the simpler layering of Rosalind-as-Ganymede accentuates conflict, though this time the couple being affected is Phebe and Silvius. Rosalind's guise as Ganymede causes Phebe to fall in love with her. Rosalind's on-layering, which inadvertently makes her Silvius's rival, causes Phebe's desires to be even more at variance with Silvius's hopes than before. It takes Ganymede's transformation into Rosalind to trick Phebe into accepting her swain, as the off-layering of Rosalind's disguise reconciles these two Petrarchan lovers. The Silvius-Phebe plot thus shows in simplified form the correlation between on-layering and rivalry, and off-layering and co-operation. It also gives us a standard by which we can measure the more complicated situation between Orlando and Rosalind.

Phebe and Silvius are caricatures of courtly love, and through them we are shown female manipulation and male idealization in a way that emphasizes the less pleasant side of the courtly love tradition. But it is important to see that this rustic couple merely exaggerates tendencies also present in Rosalind and Orlando. Rosalind's disguise creates an imbalance in her relationship with Orlando because it allows Rosalind to hear Orlando's love-confession without having to take any comparable risks herself. Rosalind's self-indulgence in demanding Orlando's devoted service without admitting anything in return could become a variation of the perversity that is anatomized for us in the relationship between Phebe and Silvius. Thus the expectations of Rosalind and the desires of Orlando are not only the responses of these two characters, but are also reflections of stereotypical male and female postures, familiar through the long tradition of courtly love. The layering of the disguise has served to accentuate the conflict between men and women; now the unlayering finally resolves that traditional tension between the needs of the female and the desires of the male.

The unlayering begins when Oliver appears to explain why Orlando is late. Oliver's tale reveals, in almost allegorical fashion, the struggle within Orlando when he sees his brother in peril, and the tale has as its point that Orlando put the needs of his brother before his own natural desire for revenge. More subtly, the tale with its depiction of the twin dangers of the snake and lioness hints at a symbolic nexus of male and female threats. The specificity of the imagery suggests that the details are important. The first beast is described as a lioness, not a lion; moreover, she is a lioness in suck, but now with teats sucked dry, her hunger presumably made more ferocious by her condition. The description thus links a specifically female animal, and a graphically specific female condition, with the threat of being eaten. The details, taken in sum, evoke the possibility of female engulfment. The snake about to enter the sleeping man's mouth, again a very specific image, suggests even to a non-Freudian the threat of phallic invasion. But perhaps most significant is simply the twinning of the threats itself, which suggests the presence of two different but related kinds of danger.

By overcoming the twin threats, Orlando conquers in symbolic form projections of both male and female fears. Rosalind responds to Oliver's account by swooning. Her faint is a literal relinquishing of conscious control; within the conventions of the play, it is also an involuntary revelation of female gender because fainting is a 'feminine' response. It is a subtle anticipation of Rosalind's eventual relinquishing of the disguise and the control that goes with it. The action surrounding the relation of the tale parallels its moral: Orlando performs a heroic and selfless act that hints at a triumph over threatening aspects of masculinity and femininity, and Rosalind responds to the dangers that Orlando faces with an unconscious gesture of sympathy that results, for a moment, in the loss of her conscious control over the disguise and with it, the loss of her manipulative control over Orlando. Rosalind's swoon thus provides a feminine counterpart to Orlando's selflessness.

Orlando's struggle and Rosalind's swoon mark a turning point. When they meet again, Rosalind tries at first to re-establish their old relationship, but when Orlando replies, 'I can live no longer by thinking' [V. ii. 50], she quickly capitulates and reassumes control only in order to be able to relinquish it. From this point on, the removal of the disguise signals the consummation of all the relationships as all four couples are married. The play suggests that control is necessary to state the legitimate needs of the self, but also that it must eventually be relinquished to accommodate the needs of another. Consummation is paradoxically achieved through an act of renunciation.

The way that sexual disguise is used reflects the play's overall concern with the tension between rivalry and co-operation. The disguise is first used to crystallize rivalry between the woman's self-image and the man's desires; in this sense it recognizes male-female discord and implicitly validates it. But because the disguise can be removed, it prevents the discord from becoming perpetual frustration. The workings of the disguise suggest that what appears to be a generous surrendering of self-interest can in fact bring consummation both to man and woman, so that rivalry can be transcended as co-operation brings fulfillment. In *As You Like It,* fulfillment of desire, contentment and peace of mind come when the insistence on self-satisfaction ceases. Duke Senior's acceptance of his forest exile and the subsequent unlooked-for restoration of his dukedom; the reconciliation between the sons of Rowland de Boys, in which Oliver resigns his lands to Orlando and finds forgiveness and happiness in love; the miraculous conversion of Duke Frederick by the old hermit and the voluntary abdication of his dukedom—all express the same paradox of consummation through renunciation that is realized in specifically sexual terms by the disguise.

When the boy actor who plays Rosalind's part comes forward to speak the epilogue, the workings of the sexual disguise are linked with the art of the playwright. The epilogue continues the paradox of consummation through renunciation that has governed sexual disguise within the play, as the final unlayering of the disguise coincides with a plea for the audience to consummate the play by applauding [Epilogue, 11-23]. . . . At this moment the playwright relinquishes control of the audience. As with Rosalind and Orlando, his success is marked by a control that finally renounces itself, a control which admonishes only to release as the audience is asked to 'like as much . . . as please you' [Epilogue, 13-14]. Our applause is a gesture of acceptance which encompasses both the working of sexual disguise within the play, and the art whose operation parallels it as the play ends. At the same time, the boy actor alludes to the fact that he is not after all the woman he plays ('*if* I were

a woman' [Epilogue, 18]), and so relinquishes the last level of the sexual disguise. For the last time, the unlayering of the disguise is linked with a reconciliation between the sexes as the boy actor speaking the epilogue appeals separately to the men and women in the audience. Within the play these two perspectives have been reconciled, and the joint applause of the men and women in the audience re-affirms that reconciliation and extends it to the audience.

The sexual disguise in *As You Like It* therefore succeeds in interweaving various motifs. Many of the problems considered in the play (Duke Frederick's tyranny, Oliver's unfair treatment of Orlando, Phebe's exultation over Silvius) stem from excessive control, and the heroine exercises extraordinary control over the disguise. The removal of the disguise signals a renunciation of control on her part, and this in turn is linked with a voluntary renunciation of control by others, so that the unlayering and the resolution of problems neatly correspond. Moreover, the sexual reversal inherent in the disguise, which itself implicitly promises a reconciliation of male and female perspectives, is used to reconcile the men and women in the play. Since the key to reconciliation has been the renunciation of control, the playwright uses his relinquishing of control over the play to signal a final reconciliation between the men and women in the audience. Because of the correspondence between Rosalind as controller of the disguise, and Shakespeare as controller of the disguised boy actor who plays Rosalind's part, Rosalind's control over her disguise is paradigmatic of the playwright's control over the play. Both use their control creatively and constructively, but for both the relinquishing of control corresponds with the consummation of their art.

The means by which resolution is achieved in *As You Like It* says a great deal about the kinds of problems the play considers. By having Rosalind as surrogate playmaker, the playwright must not pose problems that are beyond her power to solve. There are a few hints that Rosalind's control exceeds the merely human; she tells Orlando she possesses magical powers, and Hymen mysteriously appears to officiate at the wedding. The playwright likewise allows himself some hints of supernatural intervention—witness Duke Frederick's miraculous conversion. But positing a human problem-solver almost necessitates limiting the problems to human scale. Moreover, because the disguise is the key to Rosalind's ability to solve problems, the emphasis on male and female perspectives inherent in the sexual disguise places the problems in the context of the social roles of each sex. The disguise thus gives the play artistic unity, but it also imposes limitations on the play's thematic scope. The brilliance of *As You Like It* is that it so perfectly matches what the play attempts to the inherent limitations of its techniques that it makes us unaware there are limitations. (pp. 64-8)

Nancy K. Hayles, "*Sexual Disguise in 'As You Like It' and 'Twelfth Night'*," in Shakespeare Survey: An Annual Survey of Shakespearian Study and Production, *Vol. 32, 1979, pp. 63-72.*

**ELLIOT KRIEGER** (essay date 1979)

[*In an unexcerpted section of his* A Marxist Study of Shakespeare's Comedies *(1979), Krieger argues that the inability of the aristocratic characters in* As You Like It *to act within the realm of Fortune—here represented by the court—may be traced to their assumption that the hierarchic structure of nature justifies their social station and frees them from the forces of chance. Rosalind and Orlando, Krieger suggests, therefore see their problems as the result of an opposition between Fortune and Nature, not of the mutability of Fortune. Likewise, in Arden, the critic continues, outer Nature expresses inner Nature for the courtiers, in that their subjectivity transforms the objective conditions of the natural environment to recreate Fortune and Nature as a "style." In this manner, Krieger claims, a "second-world" strategy—that of the characters' own creation—is developed in order to confront and change the material conditions of the "primary world." In the following excerpt, Krieger enlarges these themes, adding to them a discussion of Rosalind's dramatic function in* As You Like It, *Arden's role in the play, and the comedy's ideology in general. Krieger argues that Rosalind's disguise is a form of style that allows her to feel and act as if she controls her own emotions and those of others. Her example, Krieger suggests, mirrors the play's proposition that material problems may be solved by translating material conditions into stylistic propositions, thus transcending the material world. Focusing his attention on Arden, Krieger objects to the view of many earlier critics that the forest "allows" self-discovery to take place. He offers a Marxist reading instead, contending that* As You Like It *dramatizes an ideological process, in which the ruling class in the forest uses its definition of nature to "justify its freedom from labour and the subordination of . . . other social classes."]*

[In the Forest of Arden], the gap between internal and external, or self and other, closes and disappears. The subjectivity of the protagonists merges with the objective conditions of the environment. This resolution, however, depends on a particular hierarchy of the definitions of *nature*: the protagonists do not perceive themselves, their own intrinsic qualities, as encompassed by or in terms of the out-of-doors; rather, they see the out-of-doors in their own terms: in short, they project. They therefore subordinate the out-of-doors to human needs and conditions, they stylize Nature. In a process typical of pastoral literature, the Nature to which the protagonists retreat becomes . . . its own opposite; the characters produce Nature, they re-create Nature as a style: Nature becomes art. Duke Senior's often-quoted speech, which introduces us to Arden, clearly illustrates the predominant pastoral tendency to see Nature in cultural or artistic terms:

> Here feel we not the penalty of Adam,
> The seasons' difference, as the icy fang
> And churlish chiding of the winter's wind,
> Which when it bites and blows upon my body
> Even till I shrink with cold, I smile and say,
> "This is no flattery: these are counsellors
> That feelingly persuade me what I am."
>
> [II. i. 5-11]

As some critics have noted, the Duke perceives Nature as a linguistic act. The physical conditions of his world work upon him stylistically and rhetorically, chide and persuade him. . . . By the end of the Duke's speech, Nature no longer has merely some of the qualities of language, such as the ability to persuade; the Duke has redefined Nature as fundamentally verbal, containing within itself tongues, books, and sermons. The Duke has transformed Nature into style. (pp. 75-6)

By translating banishment into Fortune, Fortune into style, the exiled courtiers have done more . . . than negate the necessity for action. Perhaps surreptitiously (thus exemplifying what William Empson would call one of the "tricks" of pastoral), they have also resolved the opposition between Fortune and Nature by creating a common denominator for the two terms. Because in the Forest of Arden the protagonists translate both Fortune and Nature into style, they can treat the two terms as if they were equivalent, as if they could be converted into each other. As a much more voluntary and subjective, and as a humanly created . . . quality, style gives the protagonists the

feeling, or illusion, that they control the external, objective forces of Fortune and Nature. As a consequence, the protagonists use style to express, as the predominant aspect of both Fortune and Nature, their own subjective treatment of or reaction to these external phenomena, rather than the innate qualities of the phenomena, rather than the effect the external phenomena have on the subject. (p. 77)

The effectiveness of the second-world strategy in *As You Like It* depends on the protagonists' ability to use style in [a] protective way, not just to protect themselves against cognizance of their disruptive position in Nature, but also to protect themselves against cognizance of their conflicts with a culture. Through recourse to style, the protagonists assert and maintain an autonomy, and thus they remain free, as subjects, from the determining, oppositional forces both of Nature and of Fortune, as mediated through human action. Rosalind and Celia's retreat to the forest aptly demonstrates how style protects the protagonists from the stubbornness of Fortune. Banished by the usurping Duke Frederick, the two women "devise" [I. iii. 100, 135] a plan for escape to the Forest of Arden, much as they had agreed, earlier, to "devise sports" [I. ii. 24-5]. As they plan to leave for Arden, Rosalind's banishment quickly becomes the occasion for both women to formulate a playful costume drama: before they have considered "the fittest time and safest way / To hide [themselves] from pursuit that will be made" [I. iii. 135-36], they have already selected roles, costumes, props, and pseudonyms, and they have agreed to take along the court fool for their diversion. Clearly, they give prominence to the adventurous, imaginative, and playful aspects of their retreat so as to avoid active recognition of, or to divert Rosalind's incipient discussion of, the pain of leaving home and the dangers they might face when travelling. In short, they convert actual "banishment" and self-exile into an expected "liberty" [I. iii. 138].

The liberty that they create depends, however, more on process than on completion, more on transition than on arrival. Although Celia initially proposed that they "fly" the court intending "to seek" Duke Senior "in the forest of Arden" [I. iii. 100, 107], once she and Rosalind arrive in Arden they no longer seek the Duke. In fact, the disguises, which they originally devised in order to protect themselves and to facilitate their safe passage to the exiled court, become, once they arrive in the forest, a protection against being incorporated into the Duke's society, against being recognized by the Duke. . . . [Rosalind's] unwillingness [at III. iv. 35-9] to speak with her father, or, in positive terms, her desire to remain in male disguise, exemplifies the same second-world strategy that the Duke himself has practiced. Were Rosalind to join her father in the forest and thus supply a terminus to her flight from the court, she would transform her exile into a process of running away from the authority of Duke Frederick. Rosalind does not acknowledge and verify the actual political power that Duke Frederick has over her life; rather, she translates her exile into a life that feels as if it were voluntarily chosen and whose rudiments and conditions can be determined solely by her own will. Like her father, she treats Duke Frederick's political actions as the stubbornness of Fortune so as to translate Fortune into a style.

So, although Rosalind remains in disguise long after the practical need for the disguise has passed, her disguise serves needs other than the practical. As a form of style, disguise allows her to feel and to act as if she controls her own emotions and the emotions of others. These qualities, the simultaneous participation and detachment for which so many have praised the character of Rosalind, do not so much distinguish a unique personality for Rosalind as they associate Rosalind's actions with the actions of the other protagonists. Duke Senior gains precisely the same effect by translating his exile, over which he has no control, into a style, which he does control. Consequently, we should not try to see Rosalind's particular style, the feigned homosexual courtship of Orlando, as a process through which she actually controls her own and others' fortunes; she uses style, rather, to translate her total lack of control into the feeling or illusion of complete control.

By this I mean that the motive for Rosalind's particular style of courting Orlando really has nothing to do with Orlando himself, nor with Rosalind's feelings toward him; Rosalind does not, as has often been argued, use disguise primarily to test Orlando's love or to educate him about love. Certainly the gaping wonder with which Orlando ultimately receives Rosalind . . . indicates that the courtship has confirmed rather than purged Orlando's idealization and over-valuation of Rosalind's powers; certainly Rosalind could most effectively have tested Orlando's love by offering him as the alternative to the "absent" Rosalind not a boy playing Rosalind but an eligible woman—Celia/Aliena. In fact, however, Rosalind's maintenance of the disguise, and particularly of the homosexual bearing of the disguise, stylistically embellishes her courtship of Orlando. The stylized courtship serves a psychodynamic function concerning Rosalind's relation to the court of Duke Frederick. . . . [It] keeps her from experiencing as persecution the actions of her antogonist, Duke Frederick.

Although Rosalind uses style as a protection, so long as her style remains bound to the disguised courtship of Orlando, it cannot resolve the initial problem that confronted Rosalind. The subjective, psychodynamic strategy that she creates works for her, but does not work upon the objective, material conditions of her world: her homosexual style leaves Duke Frederick's tyranny and Duke Senior's banishment intact. In order to respond to the real, primary-world persecution, Rosalind must give her subjective style its own real, objective status in a new environment; she must use her subjectivity to "create", as her father has done, a second world. To do so, Rosalind must project the control that her disguise enables her to feel out into the world, so that the internal feeling of control can return to her from without, be expressed *to* her through social relations. When Rosalind's style becomes objective, gets returned to her by another source, it appears that she has created a world based on the conditions and prerogatives of her own style, a second world, and that she thereby has negated the stubbornness of Fortune and reconciled her individual fortune with her own intrinsic nature.

Rosalind accomplishes this feat, removes herself from the limitations of her own disguise, by projecting her style and her control of others onto the figure of Hymen. In the last scene of *As You Like It*, Rosalind's style expands into ritual; she gives up her disguise to gain a wider and more profound control, no longer only over her courtship of Orlando, but now over the entire pastoral society. While still disguised as the boy Ganymed, and thus containing her own style, Rosalind claims to have "promis'd to make all this matter even" [V. iv. 18], and she repeats the phrase as she departs from the stage: "and from hence I go / To make these doubts all even" [V. iv. 24-5]. Rosalind returns to the stage, however, with her style split apart: she reappears *in propria persona* [as herself], but accompanied by "a person representing Hymen" (*Dra-

matis Personae*). This Hymen, presumably then a figure in disguise, claims to have taken on Rosalind's controlling or restorative functions, once more repeating Rosalind's phrasing:

> Then is there mirth in heaven
> When earthly things made even
>    Atone together.
> Good Duke, receive thy daughter,
> Hymen from heaven brought her,
>    Yea, brought her hither, . . .
>
> [V. iv. 108-13]

We experience a complex, ambiguous reaction here. Rosalind at once designates her control to someone else or to some other force, and at the same time increases our sense of the extent of her control. We hear that Hymen, not Rosalind, "must make conclusion / Of these most strange events" [V. iv. 126-27], yet by allowing her feeling of control to return to her from without, Rosalind expands our sense of her capacity to control, for we also know that Hymen constitutes a part of the ritualistic style by which Rosalind concludes the courtship she had begun as Ganymed. Further, by designating the resolution that we know she herself has created to the power of Hymen, Rosalind creates the illusion or the feeling that the "strange events" of the conclusion could not have taken place without heavenly intervention. The presence of Hymen, and the formal, ritualistic, incantatory language that he speaks and seems to inspire in others [at V. iv. 147-50] . . . , draws attention to itself as style, distracting us from the particular contents of the dramatic resolution: Rosalind appears to her father and to Orlando, which she could have elected to do at any time since arriving in Arden, and Phebe must "accord" herself to Sylvius [V. iv. 133], which could, as in *Twelfth Night*, be attributed to "Nature" drawing "to her bias" [*Twelfth Night*, V. i. 260]. Consequently, Rosalind's control, when returned to her from without by means of the exaggerated style of ritual, reappears in magnified form: the events that Rosalind finally allows to occur seem "supernatural", much more mysterious and difficult than they would have without Hymen's presence.

The surprising entry of Jaques de Boys, which really concludes the strange events in the forest, confirms and expands rather than resolves the ambiguity of the conclusion that Rosalind arranged and staged. Rosalind's conclusion felt ambiguous because while it attributed her real control of events to another force, it exaggerated our sense of the importance and difficulty of the events that were controlled. Jaques de Boys's announcement sustains this ambiguity, but with the emphasis reversed. By awakening the memory of the tyrannic Duke Frederick—note that as soon as Rosalind's homosexual courtship ends, the force of persecution returns—Jaques de Boys deflates the importance and the effect of the multiple marriages: his "tidings" [at V. iv. 151-66] at first remind us that the separation of a daughter from her father, or of a woman from her beloved, did not initiate the anxiety in *As You Like It*. The usurping Duke Frederick, Jaques de Boys reminds us, remains the real "problem" of the play, and, as a consequence, Rosalind's conclusion becomes, in its effect, impractical: the multiple marriages do not resolve the specific social tensions and oppositions with which the play, or the retreat to Arden, began. We almost feel as if Rosalind's conclusion uses the fantasy structure of wish-fulfillment in dreaming and that Jaques de Boys wakes us from the dream to confront, in the "real" world, the problem that the dreamworks tried, symbolically, to solve.

But, as a countermovement to their sense of awakening, Jaques de Boys's tidings also create a deeper sense of wish-fulfillment

*Oliver's description of Orlando rescuing him from the lion and the snake, Act IV. Scene iii. By Raphael West. The Department of Rare Books and Special Collections, The University of Michigan Library.*

and mystery, a sense that inevitably must be attached to, as though caused symbolically by, Rosalind's ceremonial conclusion. . . . The effect [of Jaques de Boys's words], which raises real fears of Duke Frederick only to dissolve them immediately without satisfactorily explaining Duke Frederick's conversion, first demonstrates the practical insufficiency of Rosalind's conclusion in isolation, then implies that a magical power does operate in Arden, a power that Rosalind's rituals may have inspired or activated through sympathetic magic. The immediate conjunction of Jaques de Boys's announcement with Rosalind's conclusion, then, makes us feel that contact coordinates the strange events. We feel as if the rituals celebrated by Hymen have extended their powers into other regions—of the forest, or of consciousness—so as to make the conclusion that Rosalind has accomplished occur both as a nuptial and a political fact.

In this sense, then, by its sympathetic association that primarily results from dramatic conjunction with the wedding ceremonies, Jaques de Boys's announcement extends and expands the power that we have attributed to Rosalind's style: because they juxtapose, we attribute the two conclusions to the same cause. The conclusion of *As You Like It* thus ties in the off-stage conversion of Duke Frederick with the predominant second-world strategy of the play: his conversion does not occur because of the vicissitudes of Fortune, but because of the magical effects of Rosalind's style. By translating Nature and Fortune

into the voluntary force of style, the conclusion of *As You Like It* places both terms under human control. The Fortune that brings Orlando to Rosalind and that converts Duke Frederick, the sexual nature that draws Phebe to Sylvius, Touchstone to Audrey, and the familial nature that draws Rosalind to her father, reconciles Oliver to his brother, all are subordinated because attributed to the power of Hymen, which appears to be a heavenly intervention but which we know to be a manifestation of Rosalind's style. The conclusion of *As You Like It* dramatizes the determinant effect that style has on both Nature and Fortune, and therefore the conclusion confirms the second-world strategy . . . associated with Duke Senior—the translation of Fortune and Nature into style—as a way to confront and to change, not merely to avoid, the threatening material conditions of the primary world.

In short, *As You Like It* concludes by elevating art to a position above the antithetic terms Nature and Fortune, by proposing style as the synthesis to the dialectical problem. The play therefore proposes that one solve problems in the material world by transcending them, or by transcending the material world, and translating material conditions into stylistic propositions. *As You Like It* further implies that the only true reconciliations occur not in the world or between the subject and the world but in the mind, purely subjectively. Consequently, to defend against objective opposition, assault from without, one should cultivate one's own subjectivity, should express and discover the self through style, and thereby know the self, achieve self-knowledge. And one could stop there, having identified *As You Like It* with the defense of style and artifice. Yet such a conclusion, one that advocates absorption in style and in self, has no meaning unless placed within a context, a qualification that escapes many critics of *As You Like It*. To conclude from the play [along with D. J. Palmer] that people discover Nature and thus become more fully themselves through art [see excerpt above, 1970] or that the "only real reconciliation between the actual and the ideal . . . is subjective, effected in the mind" [see excerpt above by Albert R. Cirillo, 1971], one must mistake the part for the whole: *As You Like It* contains and expresses these subjective ideas and ideals, but these ideas do not comprise the play. In fact, the play uses its own expression and dramatization of subjective ideals to explore the practical limitations of subjectivity, to confront subjectivity with real, material conditions.

Part of the difficulty with *As You Like It* arises because the play creates the illusion that the second-world society developed by the protagonists constitutes an entire "world". . . . In *As You Like It*, the pastoral society itself contains several sets of extremes (the isolated Jaques and the surrounded Duke Senior, the indecorous Touchstone and the fastidious Sylvius, for example), which make us feel, on one level, that the society of the exiled courtiers constitutes a complete world. At the same time, however, the play breaks down this illusion and shows the limitations or boundaries of the second-world society by also including a society of native foresters, "real" shepherds and country people. . . . *As You Like It* enforces a distinction—inevitably a class distinction—between those who come from the court and those who live in Arden. By maintaining a distinction between those who come to and those who live in the forest, *As You Like It* identifies the achievements of the second-world society, the stylistic transcendence of Nature and Fortune, with the particular strategies of one social class.

The encounters between the aristocrats in exile and the natives of Arden, the real shepherds, show us that the ideals of translating Fortune into style or of using art to learn about Nature require for their enactment the privileges, the freedom from material concerns, of the ruling class; or, put another way, the ruling class ideals contradict the material conditions in which other classes live. Rosalind and Celia's entry into Arden and their initial encounter with Corin (II. iv.) nicely demonstrate the native's limited access to the strategy of stylistic abstraction. (pp. 80-8)

Here we can see why it makes no sense to say, as many have, that the forest "allows" people in general to discover their own Nature: such a proposition ignores or abstracts from the material conditions that exist in and that the protagonists bring to the forest. Rosalind and Celia's gold, or, more precisely, their aristocratic poise that bespeaks their gold, enables them to translate their fortunes into the pastoral style of life:

> Corin:      . . . if you like upon report
> The soil, the profit, and this kind of life,
> I will your very faithful feeder be,
> And buy it with your gold right suddenly.
>
> [II. iv. 97-100]

Corin, however, explicitly points out that he is bound to his "fortunes" [II. iv. 77] by the material, or economic, circumstances within which he lives. Only benevolent new masters,

by "mending" Corin's wages [II. iv. 94], can improve, but hardly translate, *his* fortunes.

The play establishes here a distinction between what we could call fixed and variable, or else involuntary and voluntary, fortunes: Corin's fortunes depend on the actions, dispositions, and dispensations of others, whereas Rosalind and Celia control or translate their fortunes through and because of their access to gold. The characters experience this distinction between fixed and variable fortune as a class distinction in the most basic sense: because of their access to gold, explicitly *not* because of a "natural" hierarchy, Rosalind and Celia remain detached from any requirement that they work. Later in the play Sylvius and Phebe, who seem to live in the forest but who speak with the courtly rhetoric characteristic of the pastoral tradition, carry this detachment from labour to an extreme point. Sylvius, like Rosalind and Celia, has access to capital—he had planned to buy Corin's master's cottage until distracted by his love for Phebe—and therefore he can retain a separation from the explicitly pastoral labours: not only his place within a literary tradition but also his financial independence within the play frees Sylvius from physical toil. Although always referred to as a shepherd or a swain, Sylvius never works at tending flock; he works only at style, or as Phebe's appointed stylist. . . . Sylvius's detachment from material concerns enables him to express an ideal attitude toward labour and toward the materials of human subsistence:

> So holy and so perfect is my love,
> And I in such a poverty of grace,
> That I shall think it a most plenteous crop
> To glean the broken ears after the man
> That the main harvest reaps. Loose now and then
> A scatt'red smile, and that I'll live upon.
>
> [III. v. 94-104]

For Sylvius, both employment and food remain metaphoric and stylistic, separate and distinct from both actual physical engagement with and the material properties of his environment.

Rosalind and Celia's perception of their environment shows this same sense of detachment from the need for physical labour. As Celia's remark "I like this place, / And willingly could waste my time in it" [II. iv. 94-5] indicates, they perceive the environment as if it passively contains and nurtures them, allowing them the freedom to use time at will. Corin, however, perceives the environment as an object—"Assuredly the *thing* is to be sold" [II. iv. 96]—and as a place that requires human labour, as a place where sheep graze and are sheared [II. iv. 79]. Corin thus takes upon himself the active, nurturing role—"I will your very faithful feeder be" [II. iv. 99]—that Rosalind and Celia had, abstractly and unconsciously, attributed to the environment in general.

Corin, therefore, becomes identified with the materials of his environment, whereas Rosalind and Celia, who own those materials as property, can remain detached from their environment, free to see it subjectively, as an idea, free to translate the environment to suit their internal "nature". Corin's long discussion with Touchstone (III. ii.) displays his nearly tautological relation to Nature as the out-of-doors; Corin and Touchstone differ in that Touchstone can affect Nature with language, can use subjective perception to achieve a different perspective on life: whereas Corin sees Nature as a fixed condition, with laws of cause and effect independent of human will. . . . Corin must understand Nature objectively, as a part of real, material conditions independent of his consciousness, because his life depends upon his own physical relation to Nature. The courtiers use their bodies ceremonially, they kiss one another's hands, and appropriate Nature, "the very uncleanly flux of a cat" [III. ii. 68], as the accoutrements of their style, whereas Corin uses his body to work in and upon Nature: "we are still handling our ewes" [III. ii. 53]; "[Our hands] are aften tarr'd over with the surgery of our sheep" [III. ii. 62-3]; finally:

> Sir, I am a true laborer: I earn that I eat, get
> that I wear, owe no man hate, envy no man's
> happiness, glad of other men's good, content
> with my harm, and the greatest of my pride is
> to see my ewes graze and my lambs suck.
>
> [III. ii. 73-7]

The events of the play, of course, negate the feeling of independence that Corin's statement implies, which illustrates one of the paradoxes of the "independent" labourer: on one level, Corin's statement correctly asserts that Rosalind, Celia, and Touchstone, who do not earn that they eat, depend for their survival upon others; on another level, the level that the play as a whole explores, those who can depend on the true labour of others rather than on the objective conditions of their environment for their survival attain the *independence* of complete subjectivity, the freedom to change their environment. . . . (pp. 89-92)

By using language to shift his perspective on the forest, Touchstone hints at the subjective independence that the courtiers achieve, but we can see the actual freedom from, or freedom to change, material conditions developed more completely when the aristocrats discuss and use time and space. For example, when Rosalind first meets Orlando in Arden she diverts and charms him by trying to prove the relativity of time:

> Time travels in divers paces with divers persons. I'll tell you who Time ambles withal, who
> Time trots withal, who Time gallops withal,
> and who he stands still withal.
>
> [III. ii. 308-11]

In response to Orlando's questioning, she then proceeds to tell him with whom Time travels in each of these paces [III. ii. 312-33]. In effect, Rosalind proves—declares, actually—that one's subjective feelings, not objective, natural phenomena, determine the "time o'day" [III. ii. 300]—a pleasant conceit, but one that presupposes the capacity to subordinate time to the needs of one's ego. Rosalind's sense of the variability of time, and of the interdependence of time and the emotions, directly contradicts Corin's implicit sense of the fixed nature of time: Corin's sense of being, his sense of *his* subjectivity, derives from his accepting the conditions of Nature as objective realities. Corin's belief "that the property of rain is to wet and fire to burn; that good pasture makes fat sheep; and that a great cause of the night is lack of the sun" [III. ii. 26-8] implicitly opposes Rosalind's subjective attitude toward time in that he keeps natural conditions *distinct* from the emotions. By inference, Corin does not believe, for example, that rain imitates the lover's sorrow, or that the beloved's absense causes the night. Whereas for Rosalind, subjectivity determines the conditions of Nature, for Corin the conditions of Nature determine subjectivity.

The aristocratic protagonists further distort the natural, or in this case really social, conditions of the forest to satisfy their subjective needs, to purge Arden of an alien culture, through their repeated insistence that no people inhabit the forest. . . .

[We see], for example, that the Duke and his followers call the deer the "native burghers of this desert city" [II. i. 23], and that Rosalind refers to the forest as "this desert place" [II. iv. 72]. . . . [The] idea of the desert forest extends beyond mere stylistic conceit and affects the way some of the characters live in Arden: Duke Senior and the courtiers live almost barbarically in caves, although the forest contains enough of a civilization and an economy so that Rosalind and Celia can buy a cottage. The inability to perceive the actual country community, or—expressed another way—the projection of the subjective desire for an unpeopled forest on to the material world, works to determine the conditions of Nature, to control the courtiers' active relation to Nature in the forest. The courtiers purge Arden of people in order to fill the world with their pastoral style.

Here we can see how the generalization that the "forest mirrors one's mind" actually distorts the facts and conditions of the play, restricts the whole play to the privileged perceptions of one class. Only the aristocracy can appropriate the new environment as a subjective entity, an emblem of the mind. This same act of appropriation, while it brings about an accord between mind and Nature for the courtiers, also distorts the objective facts of Nature known and experienced by the country people, for whom the forest merely exists—as the material conditions of time and place, as environment. For Corin, Nature contains and produces the materials with which and conditions in which he works; Audrey, William, and Sir Oliver Martext, the characters most clearly designated as country-dwellers, are the *only* characters in the play who never mention either Nature in general or their environment in particular. The concept of the forest-as-mirror, therefore, attributes a quality to the forest environment, to Nature, that it does not possess: their freedom from labour allows the aristocrats to translate Nature into an aspect of mind, but Nature itself remains objective and other to the minds of the country people. The forest does not mirror William's mind, or Audrey's. The aristocratic protagonists incorporate the forest within their subjectivity, but they can do so only because they remain free from the need to work in the forest, free from the imposed objective conditions of Nature. For Corin, rain helps make good pasture, which makes fat sheep; for the Duke, the climate persuades him who he is.

By translating Nature into an aspect or expression of their own subjective style, the courtiers articulate a harmony between the divergent senses or definitions of *nature*: their intrinsic qualities or fundamental characteristics become identical with the physical world, the out-of-doors; their natures become identical with Nature. But, significantly, the aristocrats must achieve or create this harmony; the harmony does not come about "by nature". As an achieved quality, this harmony between two senses of *nature* also negates Nature in another sense: Nature becomes a phenomenon contrived through human effort, produced through purposive action; Nature becomes its own opposite, culture. The pastoral second-world functions, therefore, to create an environment in which the lineaments of Nature need not have been fixed and determined *a priori*, but in which Nature itself can be culturally determined so as to define the lineaments of a ruling class.

Consequently, the willed misperception of environment in *As You Like It* does not represent mere error, but represents a creative social act, the formation of an ideology. By creating the illusion that the forest mirrors the mind, the ruling class also creates the illusion that Nature certifies all of the social conditions in Arden. The illusion makes us feel that Corin's resignation to and contentment with labour and the ruling class presupposition of freedom from labour both derive from Nature, from an environment that expresses the intrinsic qualities of *all* of its inhabitants. . . . The extreme flexibility of *nature* . . . appears in *As You Like It* as a ruling-class identification of consciousness with Nature, which determines the relation of all other classes to Nature. Since the forest mirrors the mind, this ideology implies, the opposition between labour and freedom in Arden does not subject one class to another but helps determine those who have "superior natures" and who "by nature" should rule. Further, the ideology implies, the real shepherd, who does not rule, achieves his own form of superiority, a superiority resulting from his contentment with what he has, a superiority that, as Lawrence Lerner has written [in his 1972 study *The Uses of Nostalgia*] in reference to literary shepherds in general, "depends on his staying where he is". The shepherd's labour, presumably, expresses his nature, "the function for which he is 'by nature' adapted", while the freedom and style, the functions for which the aristocracy is "by nature" adapted, express the aristocratic nature. This opposition between labour and freedom, since each activity expresses the Nature of a particular class, appears to constitute a single social order whose qualities are, "by nature", good.

Beneath the romance and the comedy, *As You Like It* articulates an ideological process, whereby the ruling class uses Nature, or its own translation and redefinition of *nature,* to justify its freedom from labour and the subordination of, or struggle against, other social classes. By identifying the class opposition with Nature, and by using Nature to guarantee both its own autonomy and the subservience of others, the ruling class makes it appear as if its second-world strategy has no class contents at all: its ideology creates the feeling that, since each class expresses its own nature through its activity, an "implicitly multi-layered social contract" gets established, the feeling that "class difficulties" have been put "in the context of a view beyond them in the leveling power of nature and imagination". The critic I am quoting here, Harold E. Toliver [see Additional Bibliography], comes so close to the truth about *As You Like It,* yet, failing to see the fantasy or ideology that controls this truth, he misses the truth entirely: he does not realize that the ruling class uses Nature and the imagination to separate its freedom from others' labour while transcending all opposition as such between classes. The idea of a "contract" shrewdly implies that all classes have agreed to the separation of freedom from labour for the maintenance of a general social good, identical both with Nature and with the *status quo.* In fact, *As You Like It* establishes no such social contract; its aristocratic protagonists formulate and enact an ideology: they express the particular interests of their own class as if these were identical with universal interests, with the interests of the whole society. (pp. 92-6)

*Elliot Krieger, "'As You Like It','' in his* A Marxist Study of Shakespeare's Comedies, *Macmillan, 1979, pp. 70-96.*

## KENNETH MUIR  (essay date 1979)

[*In addition to his editions of* Richard II, King Lear, *and* Macbeth, *Muir also published numerous volumes of Shakespearean criticism and served as the editor of* Shakespeare Survey. *In the following excerpt from his* Shakespeare's Comic Sequence (1979), *he argues that Shakespeare intended* As You Like It *to be not a straight pastoral, but a pastoral work suited to his own dramatic*

*purposes. Muir recognizes such scenes in the comedy as I. i. 1-5, in which Orlando informs Adam of facts he already knows, as technically crude, but nevertheless in keeping with the tone of the tale. Muir also notes irony in our awareness throughout the play that Duke Senior and his entourage will return to court at their first opportunity, and he warns against taking Jaques's comments as authorial, for, he argues, they are consistently undercut. In addition, Muir perceives Shakespeare exploiting other literary conventions besides the pastoral, including the "love at first sight" notion and, in the cases of Oliver and Duke Frederick, the sudden conversion of a villain.*]

As *you* like it? Does the title suggest (as some critics have supposed) that Shakespeare was deploring the taste of his audience at the Globe, or was he happily proclaiming that their taste corresponded with his own? Most great writers begin by giving their public what it wants and end by making the public want what they choose to give. Before the end of the sixteenth century, Shakespeare was in this happy position, though he kept up the pretence in his titles and sub-titles—*As You Like It, Much Ado about Nothing, What You Will*—that the boot was on the other foot.

The same irony is apparent in his dramatisation of Thomas Lodge's *Rosalynde.* . . . Although Shakespeare follows Lodge's plot fairly closely, there are no verbal echoes of his dialogue. His aim, it soon becomes clear, was different from that of Lodge: he was not trying to write a straight pastoral, but to use it for his own dramatic purposes.

The very first speech should alert us to what he is doing. Orlando is informing Adam, his old retainer, of facts which he already knows, and which Orlando knows that he knows:

> As I remember, Adam, it was upon this fashion
> bequeathed me by will but poor a thousand
> crowns, and, as thou say'st, charged my brother,
> on his blessing, to breed me well; and there
> begins my sadness.
>
> [I. i. 1-5]

This violates one of the most elementary rules of play-writing. There is no other exposition in all Shakespeare's works which is so unashamedly crude. As he had already written some seventeen competent plays, and as a writer of comedy was at the height of his powers, we are entitled to wonder why he should revert to such an unashamedly primitive technique—more primitive than that of his earliest experimental plays. The speech is, in fact, a way of preparing us for the tone of the rest of the play. Shakespeare is pretending that he is presenting a corny tale of a bad elder brother and a good younger brother, a tale which will end, as such tales do, with the good brother marrying a princess and living happily ever after. For good measure he introduces a usurping Duke and his exiled brother who lives in the greenwood like Robin Hood. On the face of it, the play is naïve in the extreme; but it is really as sophisticated as those of Marivaux.

Orlando, of course, defeats Charles the wrestler, who has been bribed to break his neck; but Shakespeare is careful to remind us that we are in a world of fiction by making Celia comment on Le Beau's account of Charles's prowess, 'I could match this beginning with an old tale' [I. ii. 120]. Rosalind, with the initiative expected of a fairy-tale princess, hints to Orlando that she has fallen in love at first sight:

> Sir, you have wrestled well, and overthrown
> More than your enemies.
>
> [I. ii. 253-54]

Before long, Rosalind and Celia (disguised as Ganymede and Aliena), go off with Touchstone to the forest of Arden and Orlando, to escape being murdered by his brother, makes the same journey with Adam. Meanwhile we have been introduced to the exiled Duke and his entourage, and they are depicted not without irony. However much they profess to believe in the superiority of the forest life to that of the court, however much Amiens extols the greenwood and the jolliness of its life, we know that they will hurry back to court as soon as they get the chance. The only one of their number who does not, Jaques, has mocked the insincerity of his fellow-exiles.

Yet we are prevented from accepting Jaques's comments as authorial by the fact they are undercut by the Duke, by Orlando and by Rosalind. The Duke accuses him of being a reformed libertine, satirising the vices he once enjoyed; when Orlando is invited to rail against mankind, he gently reproves Jaques; and when Rosalind hears his affected account of his particular brand of melancholy, she laughs at him [IV. i. 21-5, 27-9]. . . . Even Jaques's set speech on the seven ages of man, suggested probably by the motto of the Globe theatre, cannot be taken as Shakespeare's considered opinion on human life; for its melancholy outlook is contradicted by the play as a whole, as well as by the situation which evokes it—for Orlando, courteously received by the outlaws, has gone out to fetch the exhausted Adam and courtesy, charity and fellow-feeling are apparently excluded from Jaques's philosophy of life.

The attitude we are forced to adopt to the outlaws is a complex one and the same complexity is apparent in the other versions of pastoral with which Shakespeare treats. The oldest matter of pastoral . . . is that of a love-sick shepherd in love with a scornful shepherdess. The love of Silvius for Phebe is in this convention, and it is in the scenes in which they appear that Shakespeare comes nearest to the spirit of his source. Yet he provides a suitable antidote to the convention in the very scene in which the pastoral lovers are introduced when Rosalind intervenes [at III. v. 34-60]. . . . (pp. 84-6)

Another form of pastoral convention is represented by Audrey and William, who are not real rustics but country bumpkins seen through urban eyes; they are illiterate, slow-witted and not very clean. Audrey does not know the meaning of 'poetical' and this provides Touchstone with the opportunity of telling her that 'the truest poetry is the most feigning' [III. iii. 19-20]— an ironical comment on the poetic conventions Shakespeare is exploiting in the play. Although Touchstone puts William to flight and goes through a form of marriage with Audrey, he does not intend it to be more than temporary. The simple-minded and 'foul' rustic is superior in some ways to the civilised fool. Indeed, when Touchstone attempts, by a series of quibbles, to prove that Corin is damned, that sensible and dignified shepherd gets the best of the argument.

The last kind of pastoral represented in the play is that of Rosalind and Celia, aristocrats who adopt the pastoral role. On the spur of the moment they decide to buy the farm belonging to Corin's master [II. iv. 91-5]. . . . They buy the farm without even seeing it, much less calling in a surveyor or scrutinising the accounts. We hear nothing more about the farm. Presumably Corin continues to do all the work.

Shakespeare exploits other literary conventions. His lovers— Rosalind, Orlando, Celia, Oliver and Phebe—would all make answer to Marlowe's question 'Who ever loved that loved not a first sight?' with a chorus of 'No one'. Shakespeare goes out

of his way to underline the absurdity, as when Rosalind tells Orlando of the match between Celia and Oliver:

> Nay, 'tis true. There was never anything so sudden, but the fight of two rams and Caesar's thrasonical brag of 'I came, saw, and over-came'. For your brother and my sister, no sooner met but they look'd; no sooner look'd but they lov'd; no sooner lov'd but they sigh'd; no sooner sigh'd but they asked one another the reason; no sooner knew the reason but they sought the remedy—and in these degrees have they made a pair of stairs to marriage, which they will climb incontinent, or else be incontinent before marriage.
>
> [V. ii. 29-39]

One other romantic convention may be mentioned—the sudden conversion of a villain. In the twinkling of an eye, Oliver is converted from being a murderous, avaricious scoundrel with no redeeming characteristics into a pleasant and acceptable husband for Celia. The usurping Duke is a cruel tyrant and in Act V is about to exterminate his brother and the other outlaws when he meets an old religious man, and, we are told,

> After some question with him, was converted
> Both from his enterprise and from the world.
> [V. iv. 161-62]

Some actors of these parts, conscious of the improbability of the conversions, have attempted to prepare the audience by presenting Frederick and Oliver as psychological wrecks, on the verge of nervous breakdowns. This is surely wrong, for Shakespeare was merely rounding off his comedy with a happy ending, the improbability being part of the fun. To force *As You Like It* into a naturalistic mode is to maim it. In the last act there is a scene which becomes almost operatic in its mock-ery of naturalism, with a quartet of wailing lovers [V. ii. 83-108]. . . . (pp. 87-9)

The finest scenes in the play are, of course, those in Arden between Orlando and Rosalind. Bernard Shaw ascribed their success to the fact that they were written in prose [see excerpt above, 1896] and there is a grain of truth in this paradox since . . . Shakespeare at this time in his career found it easier to express individualities of character in prose than in verse. Not wholly true, however, for Shaw himself complained that if you wreck the beauty of Shakespeare's lines 'by a harsh, jarring utterance, you will make your audience wince, as if you were singing Mozart out of tune'. . . . (p. 89)

Shaw's explanation of Rosalind's popularity need not be taken seriously—that she speaks blank verse for only a few minutes, that she soon gets into doublet and hose, and that like Shaw's Ann Whitefield, she takes the initiative and does not wait to be wooed. But Shaw was right to protest about the confusion of life and art by those critics who describe Rosalind as 'a perfect type of womanhood'. To him she was 'simply an extension into five acts of the most affectionate, fortunate, delightful five minutes in the life of a charming woman'. This is not quite true, however, because Rosalind is given misfortunes, as well as a wit that has never been excelled.

It is important to remember that the effect of these scenes in 1600 was rather different from that in the modern theatre. . . . His original audience would have seen a boy impersonating a woman who was also a princess; they then saw this princess pretending to be Ganymede, and Ganymede pretending to be

Rosalind, but in so doing guying the real Rosalind. . . . In Shakespeare's day there were a number of different images imposed one on the other. We have a boy pretending to be a woman, pretending to be a boy, pretending to be a woman, satirising feminine behaviour. Rosalind, moreover, though pretending to cure Orlando, is making certain she will fail; for she makes him love the pretended Rosalind, and love more the real one of which Ganymede is but the shadow.

In the scenes when Rosalind pretends to be Rosalind, Orlando is merely a feed to her brilliant improvisations. Luckily his character has been established early in the play. His name is that of a famous lover, Orlando Furioso . . . , and like his namesake he carves his love's name on tree trunks. He shows both dignity and courage in his struggles with his brother and Charles the wrestler; he saves the lives of Adam and of Oliver; he answers Jaques's cynicism good-humouredly and sensibly . . . ; it is only as a lover that he is at a loss.

Most of Shakespeare's comedy is a critique of love; and in *As You Like It* different kinds of love are examined—the lust of Touchstone, the self-love of Jaques, the pride and vanity of Phebe, and the sentimental idealism of Orlando—are all found wanting. It would be a mistake, then, to regard the play as a mere pot-boiler, although it is obvious from the triumphant epilogue that it made the pot boil merrily: it is a highly sophisticated play that uses all the stalest devices of romantic fiction and popular drama so as to satisfy what Hamlet called 'the judicious' [*Hamlet*, III. ii. 26].

Perhaps the judicious of Shakespeare's day appreciated Touchstone more than we can. He never comes up to Jaques's description of him. Shaw, with pardonable exaggeration, asked, 'Who would endure such humour from anyone but Shakespeare?—an Eskimo would demand his money back if a modern author offered him such fare.' The wit of Rosalind is undimmed by time; but Touchstone is dimmed. (pp. 90-1)

> Kenneth Muir, " 'As You Like It'," in his Shakespeare's Comic Sequence, *Barnes & Noble Books*, 1979, pp. 84-91.

**A. P. RIEMER**    (essay date 1980)

[*In the excerpt below, Riemer discusses Shakespeare's use of artifice and patterns of evasion in* As You Like It. *He comments on Arden's gratuitous fictions, claiming that the play is not meant to provide examples of social and moral responsibility, but that it merely demonstrates the literary freedom available in the pastoral mode. Maintaining that Arden is essentially an absurd place "filled with suspense," Riemer claims that the audience is both attracted to the forest world and impatient with its limitations, for its continued existence thwarts the union of Rosalind and Orlando. A happy outcome, he continues, "requires the return of the sympathetic characters to the [reality of the] social world." Riemer also discusses Jaques's "Seven Ages of Man" speech, arguing that it is neither a corrective to the play's pervasive jollity, nor an instance of despairing sadness. It is, he contends, "fundamentally operatic," a "performance," a "bravura display," a description he applies as well to Touchstone's commentary in the play. Riemer compares* As You Like It *to a musical composition, stating that it "resembles a set of variations on a ground-theme" and that its "commonplace topic"—the debate over whether idyllic solitude is preferable to society—"is embellished in a number of artful and elegant ways."*]

One of the problems in *As You Like It* is to what extent we are meant to discover moral and social values in the Forest of Arden. Stern critics have detected a measure of moral delin-

quency in some parts of the play: it has been suggested that Shakespeare was so enamoured with the freedom of the natural world that he came to recommend it as a panacea for the ills of society he depicted so memorably in the earlier scenes. But it is doubtful whether we may see this (or any other) play simply in such terms—these attitudes presume an artistic purpose for which the plays themselves offer little evidence. The green world of Arden is beguiling and fascinating; but it is to be doubted whether we are meant to discover in it a *regulum vitae* [rule of life] or a statement about social and moral responsibility.

Criticism has largely overlooked one important aspect of the pastoral in the play: the powerful suggestions it contains that we should, to some extent, yearn to escape from it. This is achieved in two ways. In the first place, no particularly cogent reason is given why Rosalind's masquerade should continue as long as it does, or why she does not declare herself to Orlando sooner. It may be taken as a 'testing' of the youth, or as a particularly keen insight into the psychological complexion of a personality requiring oblique and indirect relationships. But these represent surmise. The episodes, as they stand in the play, are a prolonged version of the comic mocktorment, akin to the gulling of Bassanio and Gratiano in the last scene of *The Merchant of Venice*. The prolongation of any aspect of a play's structure usually generates a sense of impatience in the audience: we desire to see its conclusion and culmination. The frustration and the tension in *As You Like It* arise, moreover, not merely because we wish to come to the conclusion of this particular theatrical device, but also because, while it is in operation, it stands so much in the way of the desired outcome: the happy union of Rosalind and Orlando. This desire to see the fortunes of the young people happily resolved is part of the second reason why the pastoral world, for all its allure, breeds impatience in the spectator. We observe in the first act of the play a number of instances of patent injustice—Oliver's denial of Orlando's patrimony, Duke Frederick's usurpation and his tyrannical banishment of Rosalind. As Dr Johnson remarked, an audience naturally finds justice pleasing; we desire, therefore, the righting of these wrongs, and, no matter how enjoyable the holiday sports of Arden might be, our expectations are not satisfied until these injustices are reversed. That, inevitably, requires the return of the sympathetic characters to the social world.

The Forest of Arden is, thus, a holiday world filled with suspense, an environment that is fantastical, gay, appealing and yet, for all that, unsatisfactory because of its limitations. Some of the characters do, indeed, discover there a degree of freedom not available in the ordinary world; but the audience's reaction to this freedom is ambivalent—we are made as conscious of the necessity of leaving the green world as of its allure. Consequently, the sojourn in Arden becomes a game—fantastic, at times exhilarating—but, like all games, basically unsatisfactory. It is as a result of theatrical expectations, not because of its moral implications, that the pastoral world breeds impatience. This essentially paradoxical response to the holiday world is, at times, captured by the characters themselves, usually with memorable effect, as at those moments when Rosalind's gaiety turns to a smiling sadness. . . . Later drama often vulgarized such effects—laughter-through-tears has become a totally debased currency. But in *As You Like It* it has freshness and gaiety: in the simultaneous presence of playfulness and sentiment an essential quality of the play is revealed.

These are some of the possibilities of the pastoral world. In it the dramatist may explore varieties of emotion and of human relationships with a freedom unavailable in the world of common experience. The courtship of Rosalind and Orlando is a curious mixture of charm, pathos and hilarity; Ganymede's education of the young swain is, by turns, fantastic and touching. The situation in which a girl disguised as a boy pretends (for 'pedagogic' purposes) to be a girl—especially when the character is impersonated by a boy-actor—is an instance of theatrical flamboyance, as well as a tactful suggestion of ambivalent sexuality. The pastoral landscape holds surprising and delightful potentialities. It is also a meeting-place for a variety of emotional and ethical attitudes. It contains not only the lovers, but also that philosophical melancholiac, the Duke Senior, an elder statesman cast into the Ovidian world of the golden age (only to discover that he has moral qualms about it), and the professional melancholiac, Jaques, who finds the *topoi* [common-places] of elegant disillusionment in his green exile. As the scenes set in this world unfold, so probability is left farther behind. When Rosalind and her friends arrive in Arden, she still retains some of the characteristics of the outside world. 'Well, this is the forest of Arden' [II. iv. 15] is a matter-of-fact, practical statement, only a little more practical than her subsequent decision to set up in farming. But the nature of this world gradually imposes itself on her: she enters into the dream-existence of ambivalences; half-plucky, half-vulnerable, she plays out her curious masquerade of courtship.

The events of the play (as already hinted) also come increasingly to be determined not so much by moral propositions or by the observation of a particular decorum of what is real, as by the exploitation of the freedom available to the artist when he depicts the ideal world of fantasy. The events of the last act, unexpected and unprepared, thrown off with that legerdemain Dr Johnson found so distressing [see excerpt above, 1765], are perfectly credible in such an imaginative environment. The measure of their viability is the ease with which Hymen's appearance to preside over the marriage of the 'country copulatives' [V. iv. 55-6] proves acceptable, natural and proper. In its last moments, the play leaves behind even the minimal decorum of 'reality' it had maintained until then. Even though it had depicted a fantastic landscape where lions roam the forests of northern Europe, where exiled dukes spend philosophically resigned lives in the wilderness, where the most extraordinary changes of heart occur, there is, until the play's last moments, a general insistence that this world is circumscribed by the natural and biological probabilities of life. But all this changes at the end. Hymen descends, mythology invades fantasy as the god among mankind blesses the happy occasion with a sidelong glance at numerology:

> Peace, ho! I bar confusion;
> 'Tis I must make conclusion
>   Of these most strange events.
> Here's eight that must take hands
> To join in Hymen's bands,
>   If truth holds true contents.
>                                        [V. iv. 125-30]

[A] little later, the preposterous dramatic event occurs: a new character, about whom we have been told only a little (and much earlier in the play at that) arrives on the scene with astonishing news, barely minutes before the end. Such improprieties may only occur in this version of the pastoral.

There is a naïve-sophisticated optimism in these turns and arabesques. Shakespeare creates, with certain limitations, a world of innocent make-believe where our fondest dreams may be indulged. But a special distinction of *As You Like It* (as of some other comedies) is that this pleasing indulgence is contained within an awareness of its own absurdity. Some characters are present here, as elsewhere, to remind us that this is cloud-cuckoo-land, and that these events are impossibilities. Touchstone and Jaques are sometimes seen as embodiments of Shakespeare's trenchant criticism of the green world, his disillusioned condemnation of these fancies. Their function is, however, somewhat different. The joyful sports are placed at an ironic distance by the acerbic comments of these two characters; yet this distancing and the changed perspective are as sportive as the revels against which they are contrasted. Jaques's well-known monologue on the seven ages of man expresses melancholic disillusionment. But its thematic function in the play is peculiar: it is neither a corrective to the pervasive jollity, nor an instance of despairing sadness which must be conquered. It is a performance, a bravura display, both within the fiction of the play and from the point of view of the theatrical audience. Just as Touchstone is the professional *farceur* [farce-player], so Jaques has some of the characteristics of the professional *déraciné* [uprooted]. His expression of profound melancholy follows the Duke Senior's remarks concerning the privations of old Adam:

> Thou seest we are not all alone unhappy:
> This wide and universal theatre
> Presents more woeful pageants than the scene
> Wherein we play in.
>                                        [II. vii. 136-39]

Jaques then embroiders this statement in a fanciful speech filled with well-known rhetorical flourishes and a series of elegantly witty conceits. The fundamentally operatic nature of the speech would not have been lost on Shakespeare's audience, and it would, no doubt, have been savoured for its qualities as a performance.

By such means, Shakespeare incorporates in his pastoral world views quite contrary to the play's basic attitudes. Yet there is no requirement that one set of views should be measured against the other. The most important characteristic of the ideal landscape created in comedies like *As You Like It* is that it is encyclopaedic: the pastoral offers an opportunity for the inclusion of a variety of effects and, at times, of contradictory possibilities. The inclusiveness might best be described through the use of a musical analogy: *As You Like It* resembles a set of variations on a ground-theme. Its theme is akin to the ancient debating topic that a life of solitude is preferable to the busy world of society. This commonplace topic is embellished in a number of artful and elegant ways; the emphasis (as in the musical genre of variations) comes to fall on the amplitude, inventiveness and even extravagance of the performance, not on the result of the debate or on the judicial decision. The nature of the impossible world implicit in the pastoral conceit makes this possible; heterogeneous material is capable of being contained within a unified work of art: the artist may enjoy a freedom not available in those fictions which retain a closer relationship with daily experience.

Touchstone's comments illustrate this dimension in *As You Like It*. Not since Costard's discovery in *Love's Labour's Lost* of the exact monetary values of guerdon and remuneration had Shakespeare given so many *mots justes* [appropriate words] to one of his clown-figures. His quibbles and gibes are, nevertheless, good-humoured, if not exactly good-natured—his rôle represents, once more, a bravura performance. He never forgets that he is a court-jester, even if an absconding one: his comments are barbed, but a large part of their intention is still to amuse. His various contests with Jaques bring together the professional clown and the gifted amateur; each, in his own way, demonstrates the extent of his skill. Jaques's description [at II. vii. 18-34] of his first encounter with Touchstone indicates the mutual recognition of two practitioners of the same craft.... The shudder that passes across the surface of the play in [Touchstone's] 'And then, from hour to hour, we rot and rot' [II. vii. 27] is transformed and converted by the multiplicity of perspectives—it reaches us through the filter of Jaques's fantastical, flamboyant report. Decay and death are registered at this moment in *As You Like It* (as they are elsewhere in the play) but their status is jesting and hypothetical. Because of their placement in this ideal world, the play is able to entertain these reminders of death and of the sadder, darker side of existence in a manner for which 'comic' is the only appropriate term. This is not a mocking, satiric or despairing comment on the vanity of human wishes; it is, rather, a recognition that maturation does, indeed, lead to decay and death; but in the comic world, even these may be transformed into 'something of great constancy' [*A Midsummer Night's Dream,* V. i. 26]. When Shakespeare's drama moves into the impossible and ideal landscape represented, in this instance, by the thorough employment of the pastoral mode, it becomes possible for these thematic strands to be liberated from their moral and emotional significances in 'ordinary' experience. The astonishing quality of this manner of comic drama is its ability to transform sadness into a species of hilarity. (pp. 76-81)

A. P. Riemer, "Ideal Landscapes," in his Antic Fables: Patterns of Evasion in Shakespeare's Comedies, St. Martin's Press, 1980, pp. 64-109.

## LOUIS ADRIAN MONTROSE (essay date 1981)

[*In the following excerpt, Montrose examines the issue of primogeniture and the conflict between younger and older brothers in* As You Like It. *Beginning with a discussion of the problems of the younger brother in Elizabethan England, Montrose turns to the structural and thematic significance of age categories in the play, chiefly as revealed through language, characterization, and plot. He claims that the action of* As You Like It *corresponds with the social process of youth in the Elizabethan world, to the extent that youth reflects a rite of passage between "physical puberty and social puberty," just as Arden in the comedy is the crucible where the hero and heroine overcome oppression and form new identities through marriage. Returning to his principal concern, Montrose regards the conflict between Orlando and Oliver as an oedipal struggle between father and son, brought about by a contradiction in "the categories of social status" often caused by primogeniture. The critic also comments on the forest's relation to the characters in the play; he avers that Arden "miraculously" assuages tensions in the "nuclear family and in the body politic," that it depicts brotherhood as the ideal of social as well as sibling male relationships, and that it reaffirms fatherhood as a positive, nurturing force. Montrose concludes by emphasizing the skillful manner in which Shakespeare reconciles "the social imperatives of hierarchy and difference," which his Elizabethan audience would have found proper and natural, "with the festive urges toward leveling and atonement," which his comic dramaturgy demanded.*]

In *As You Like It,* the initial conflict arises from the circumstances of inheritance by primogeniture. The differential relationship between the first born and his younger brothers is profoundly augmented at their father's death: the eldest son assumes a paternal relationship to his siblings; and the potential for sibling conflict increases when the relationship between brother and brother becomes identified with the relationship

between father and son. The transition of the father from life to death both fosters and obstructs the transition of his sons from childhood to manhood. In *As You Like It,* the process of comedy accomplishes successful passages between ages in the life cycle and ranks in the social hierarchy. By the end of the play, Orlando has been brought from an impoverished and powerless adolescence to the threshold of manhood and marriage, wealth and title. (p. 30)

Shakespeare's opening strategy is to plunge his characters and his audience into the controversy about a structural principle of Elizabethan personal, family, and social life. He is not merely using something topical to get his comedy off to a lively start: the expression and resolution of sibling conflict and its social implications are integral to the play's form and function. The process of comedy works against the seemingly inevitable prospect of social degradation suggested at the play's beginning, and against its literary idealization in conventions of humble pastoral retirement. In the course of *As You Like It,* Orlando's gentility is preserved and his material well-being is enhanced. Shakespeare uses the machinery of pastoral romance to remedy the lack of fit between deserving and having, between Nature and Fortune. Without actually violating the primary Elizabethan social frontier separating the gentle from the base, the play achieves an illusion of social leveling and of unions across class boundaries. Thus, people of every rank in Shakespeare's socially heterogeneous audience might construe the action as they liked it. (p. 33)

Shakespeare's plays are thickly populated by subjects, sons, and younger brothers who are ambivalently bound to their lords, genitors, and elder siblings—and by young women moving ambivalently between the lordships of father and husband. If this dramatic proliferation of patriarchs suggests that Shakespeare had a neurotic obsession, then it was one with a social context. To see father figures everywhere in Shakespeare's plays is not a psychoanalytic anachronism, for Shakespeare's own contemporaries seem to have seen father-figures everywhere.... This social context shaped Shakespeare's preoccupation with fathers; and it gave him the scope within which to reshape it into drama, satisfying his own needs and those of his paying audience. His plays explore the difficulty or impossibility of establishing or authenticating a self in a rigorously hierarchical and patriarchal society, a society in which full social identity tends to be limited to propertied adult males who are the heads of households.

Shakespeare's Sir Rowland de Boys is dead before the play begins. But the father endures in the power exerted by his memory and his will upon the men in the play—his sons, Adam, the dukes—and upon their attitudes toward each other. The play's very first words insinuate that Orlando's filial feeling is ambivalent "As I remember, Adam, it was upon this fashion bequeathed me by will but poor a thousand crowns, and, as thou sayst, charged my brother on his blessing to breed me well; and there begins my sadness" [I. i. 1-5]. Orlando's diction is curiously indirect; he conspicuously avoids naming his father.... There is an implied resentment against an unnamed father, who has left his son a paltry inheritance and committed him to an indefinite and socially degrading dependence upon his own brother. Ironically, Orlando's first explicit acknowledgment of his filial bond is in a declaration of personal *independence,* a repudiation of his bondage to his eldest brother: "The spirit of my father, which I think is within me, begins to mutiny against this servitude" [I. i. 22-4]. Orlando's assertions of filial piety are actually self-assertions, directed against his father's eldest son. As Sir Rowland's inheritor, Oliver perpetuates Orlando's subordination within the patriarchal order; he usurps Orlando's selfhood.

In a private family and household, the eldest son succeeds the father as patriarch. In a royal or aristocratic family, the eldest son also succeeds to the father's title and political authority. . . . [Oliver] is simultaneously a father and a brother to his own natural sibling; he is at once Orlando's master and his peer. Primogeniture conflates the generations in the person of the elder brother and blocks the generational passage of the younger brother. What might be described dispassionately as a contradiction in social categories is incarnated in the play, as in English social life, in family conflicts and identity crises.

Orlando gives bitter expression to his personal experience of this social contradiction: "The courtesy of nations allows you my better in that you are the firstborn, but that same tradition takes not away my blood, were there twenty brothers betwixt us. I have as much of my father in me as you, albeit I confess that your coming before me is nearer his reverence" [I. i. 46-51]. Here Orlando asserts that all brothers are equally their father's sons. Oliver might claim a special paternal relationship because he is the first born; but Orlando's own claim actually to incorporate their father renders insubstantial any argument based on age or birth order. Thus, Orlando can indict his brother and repudiate his authority: "You have trained me like a peasant, obscuring and hiding from me all gentlemanlike qualities. The spirit of my father grows strong in me, and I will no longer endure it" [I. i. 68-71]. Because the patriarchal family is the basic political unit of a patriarchal society, Orlando's protests suggest that primogeniture involves contradictions in the categories of social status as well as those of kinship. Orlando is subordinated to his sibling as a son to his father; and he is subordinated to a fellow gentleman as a peasant would be subordinated to his lord. (pp. 35-6)

Because fraternity is confused with filiation—because the generations have, in effect, been collapsed together—the conflict of elder and younger brothers also projects an oedipal struggle between father and son. In the second scene, the private violence between the brothers is displaced into the public wrestling match. Oliver tells Charles, the Duke's wrestler, "I had as lief thou didst break [Orlando's] neck as his finger" [I. i. 146-47]. Sinewy Charles, the "general challenger" [I ii. 170-71], has already broken the bodies of "three proper young men" [I. ii. 121] before Orlando comes in to try "the strength of [his] youth" [I. ii. 172]. In a sensational piece of stage business, Orlando and Charles enact a living emblem of the generational struggle. When Orlando throws Charles, youth is supplanting age, the son is supplanting the father. This contest is preceded by a remarkable exchange:

> *Cha.* Come, where is this young gallant that
> is so desirous to lie with his mother earth?
> *Orl.* Ready sir, but his will hath in it a more
> modest working.
>
> [I. ii. 200-03]

Charles's challenge gives simultaneous expression to a filial threat of incest and a paternal threat of filicide. In this conspicuously motherless play, the social context of reciprocal father-son hostility is a male struggle for identity and power fought between elders and youths, first-born and younger brothers.

Orlando's witty response to Charles suggests that he regards neither his fears nor his threats. Orlando's "will" is merely to come to man's estate and to preserve the status of a gentleman. At the beginning of *As You Like It,* then, Shakespeare sets himself the problem of resolving the consequences of a conflict between Orlando's powerful assertion of identity—his spiritual claim to be a true inheritor—and the social fact that he is a subordinated and disadvantaged younger son. In the forest, Oliver will be spiritually reborn and confirmed in his original inheritance. Orlando will be socially reborn as heir apparent to the reinstated Duke. Orlando will regain a brother by "blood" and a father by "affinity."

Orlando is not only a younger son but also a youth. And in its language, characterization, and plot, *As You Like It* emphasizes the significance of age categories. Most prominent, of course, is Jaques' disquisition on the seven ages of man. But the play's *dramatis personae* actually fall into the three functional age groups of Elizabethan society: youth, maturity, and old age. (pp. 37-8)

[In Elizabethan times, the] family was a source of social stability, but most families were short-lived and unstable. Youth was geographically mobile, but most youths were given no opportunity to enjoy their liberty. In schools and in households, the masters of scholars, servants, and apprentices were to be their surrogate fathers. . . . Most Elizabethan youths and maidens were in their mid or late twenties by the time they entered Hymen's bands. When Touchstone quips that "the forehead of a married man [is] more honourable than the bare brow of a bachelor" [III. iii. 60-1], he is giving a sarcastic twist to a fundamental mark of status. And when, late in his pseudo-mock-courtship of Ganymede, Orlando remarks ruefully that he "can live no longer by thinking" [V. ii. 50], he is venting the constrained libido of Elizabethan youth. . . . ["Youth"] was the Elizabethan age category separating the end of childhood from the beginning of adulthood. It was a social threshold whose transitional nature was manifested in shifts of residence, activity, sexual feeling, and patriarchal authority.

The dialectic between Elizabethan dramatic form and social process is especially conspicuous in the triadic romance pattern of exile and return that underlies *As You Like It*. Here the characters' experience is a fictional analogue of both the theatrical and the social experiences of its audience. . . . When they enter the special space-time of the theatre, the playgoers have voluntarily and temporarily withdrawn from "this working-day world" [I. iii. 12] and put on "a holiday humour" [IV. i. 69]. When they have been wooed to an atonement by the comedy, the Epilogue conducts them back across the threshold between the world of the theatre and the theatre of the world. The dramatic form of the characters' experience corresponds, then, not only to the theatrical experience of the play's audience but also to the social process of youth in the world that playwright, players, and playgoers share. In a play-world of romance, Orlando and Rosalind experience separation from childhood, journeying, posing and disguising, altered and confused relationships to parental figures, sexual ambiguity, and tension. The fiction provides projections for the past or ongoing youthful experiences of most of the people in Shakespeare's Elizabethan audience. The forest sojourn conducts Orlando and Rosalind from an initial situation of oppression and frustration to the threshold of interdependent new identities. . . . The characters' fictive experience is congruent with the ambiguous and therefore dangerous period of the Elizabethan life cycle that is betwixt and between physical puberty and social puberty.

*Act V. Scene iv. Touchstone, Jaques, Duke Senior, Celia, Oliver, Rosalind, Hymen, Orlando, Phebe, and Silvius. By William Hamilton. The Department of Rare Books and Special Collections, The University of Michigan Library.*

Not only relationships between offspring and their genitors, or between youths and their elders, but any relationship between subordinate and superior males might take on an oedipal character in a patriarchal society. Orlando is perceived as a troublemaker by Oliver and Frederick; his conflicts are with the men who hold power in his world, with its insecure and ineffectual villains. "The old Duke is banished by his younger brother the new Duke" [I. i. 99-100]. Old Adam has served Orlando's family "from seventeen years, till now almost fourscore" [II. iii. 71], but under Oliver he must endure "unregarded age in corners thrown" [II. iii. 42]. It is precisely the elders abused by Frederick and Oliver who ally themselves to Orlando's oppressed youth. Adam gives to Orlando the life savings that were to have been the "foster-nurse" [II. iii. 40] of his old age; he makes his "young master" [II. iii. 2] his heir. The idealized relationship of Orlando and his old servant compensates for the loss or corruption of Orlando's affective ties to men of his own kin and class. But Adam's paternity is only a phase in the reconstitution of Orlando's social identity. In the process of revealing his lineage to the old Duke, Orlando exchanges the father-surrogate who was his own father's servant for the father-surrogate who was his own father's lord [II. vii. 191-96]. . . . The living son replaces his dead father in the affections of their lord. The Duke, who has no natural son,

assumes the role of Orlando's patron, his social father: "Give me your hand / And let me all your fortunes understand" [II. vii. 199-200]. Orlando's previous paternal benefactor has been supplanted: Adam neither speaks nor is mentioned again. (pp. 39-41)

The old Duke who adopts Orlando in the forest has been disinherited by his own younger brother in the court; Frederick has forcibly made himself his brother's heir. In the course of the play, fratricide is attempted, averted, and repudiated in each sibling relationship. Tensions in the nuclear family and in the body politic are miraculously assuaged within the forest. The Duke addresses his first words to his "co-mates and brothers in exile" [II. i. 1]. The courtly decorum of hierarchy and deference may be relaxed in the forest, but it has not been abrogated; the Duke's "brothers in exile" remain courtiers and servants attendant upon his grace. An atmosphere of charitable community has been created among those who have temporarily lost or abandoned their normal social context; the sources of conflict inherent in the social order are by no means genuinely dissolved in the forest, but rather are translated into a quiet and sweet style. In the forest, the old usurped Duke is a co-mate and brother to his loyal subjects and a benevolent father to Orlando. The comedy establishes *brotherhood* as an ideal of social as well as sibling male relationships; at the same time, it reaffirms a positive, nurturing image of *fatherhood*. And because family and society are a synecdoche, the comedy can also work to mediate the ideological contradiction between spiritual fraternity and political patriarchy, between social communion and social hierarchy.

Like Richard of Gloucester [in *Richard III*], Claudius [in *Hamlet*], Edmund [in *King Lear*], and Antonio [in *The Tempest*], Frederick is a discontented younger brother whom Shakespeare makes the malevolent agent of his plot. Frederick generates action in *As You Like It* by banishing successively his elder brother, his niece, and his subject. Like his fellow villains, Frederick is the effective agent of a dramatic resolution which he himself does not intend; the tyrant's perverted will subserves the comic dramatist's providential irony. Frederick enforces the fraternal bond between Orlando and Oliver by holding Oliver responsible for Orlando on peril of his inheritance, forcing Oliver out to apprehend his brother. By placing Oliver in a social limbo akin to that suffered by Orlando, Frederick unwittingly creates the circumstances that lead to the brothers' reunion:

> *Duke F.*  Thy lands and all things that thou dost call thine,
> Worth seizure, do we seize into our hands,
> Till thou canst quit thee by thy brother's mouth
> Of what we think against thee.
> *Oli.*  O that your Highness knew my heart in this!
> I never lov'd my brother in my life.
> *Duke F.*  More villain thou.
>
> [III. i. 9-15]

Oliver has abused the letter and the spirit of Sir Rowland's will: "It was . . . charged my brother on his blessing to breed me well" [I. i. 1-4]. Frederick is Oliver's nemesis.

In the exchange I have just quoted, Frederick's attitude toward Oliver is one of *moral* as well as political superiority. His judgment of Oliver's villainy is sufficiently ironic to give us pause. Is the usurper in Frederick projecting onto Oliver his guilt for his own unbrotherliness? Or is the younger brother in him identifying with Orlando's domestic situation? In seizing Oliver's lands and all things that he calls his until Oliver's (younger) brother can absolve him, Frederick parodies his own earlier usurpation of his own elder brother. Frederick's initial seizure takes place before the play begins; its circumstances are never disclosed. We do better to observe Frederick's dramatic function than to search for his unconscious motives. Frederick actualizes the destructive consequences of younger brothers' deprivation and discontent, in the family and in society at large. The first scenes demonstrate that such a threat exists within Orlando himself. The threat is neutralized as soon as Orlando enters the good old Duke's comforting forest home; there his needs are immediately and bountifully gratified. . . . What is [thus] latent and potential within Orlando is displaced onto Frederick and realized in his violence and insecurity, his usurpation and tyranny.

Frederick sustains the role of villain until he too comes to Arden. . . . Like Orlando, [he] finds a loving father in the forest. And his conversion is the efficient cause of Orlando's elevation. In the denouement of Lodge's *Rosalynde*, the reunited brothers, Rosader and Saladyne, join the forces of the exiled King Gerismond; the army of the usurping King Torismond is defeated, and he is killed in the action. With striking formal and thematic economy, Shakespeare realizes his change

of plot as a change *within* a character; he gets rid of Frederick not by killing him off but by morally transforming him. Frederick gives all his worldly goods to his natural brother and goes off to claim his spiritual inheritance from a heavenly father.

The reunion of the de Boys brothers is narrated retrospectively by a reborn Oliver, in the alien style of an allegorical dream romance:

> . . . pacing through the forest,
> Chewing the food of sweet and bitter fancy,
> Lo what befell! He threw his eye aside,
> And mark what object did present itself.
> Under an old oak, whose boughs were moss'd with age
> And high top bald with dry antiquity,
> A wretched ragged man, o'ergrown with hair,
> Lay sleeping on his back.
>
> [IV. iii. 100-07]

These images of infirm age and impotence, of regression to wildness and ruin through neglect, form a richly suggestive emblem. Expounded in the context of the present argument, the emblem represents the precarious condition into which fratricidal feeling provoked by primogeniture has brought these brothers and their house. . . . Orlando, whose "having in beard is a younger brother's revenue" [III. ii. 377-78], confronts a hairy man asleep amidst icons of age and antiquity. The description suggests that, in confronting "his brother, his elder brother" [IV. iii. 120], young Orlando is confronting a personification of his patriline and of the patriarchal order itself. The brothers find each other under an *arbor consanguinitatis* [tree of kindred], at the de Boys "family tree." (pp. 41-3)

In constructing a romantic comedy of familial and sexual tension resolved in brotherhood and marriage, Shakespeare gives new complexity and cohesiveness to his narrative source. The struggle of elder and younger brothers is not simply duplicated; it is inverted. In the younger generation, the elder brother abuses the younger; in the older generation, the younger abuses the elder. The range of experience and affect is thereby enlarged, and the protest against primogeniture is firmly balanced by its reaffirmation. . . . Because in *As You Like It* the doubling and inversion of fraternal conflict links generations, the relationship of brother and brother can be linked to the relationship of father and son. In the process of atonement, the two families and two generations of men are doubly and symmetrically bound: the younger brother weds the daughter of the elder brother, and the elder brother weds the daughter of the younger brother. They create the figure of *chiasmus* [an inverted relationship between the syntactic elements of parallel phrases]. Whatever vicarious benefit *As You Like It* brings to younger brothers and to youths, it is not achieved by perverting or destroying the bonds between siblings and between generations, but by transforming and renewing them—*through marriage*. (pp. 47-8)

In the world of its Elizabethan audience, the form of Orlando's experience may indeed have functioned as a collective compensation, a projection for the wish-fulfillment fantasies of younger brothers, youths, and all who felt themselves deprived by their fathers or their fortunes. But Orlando's mastery of adversity could also provide support and encouragement to the ambitious individuals who identified with his plight. The play may have fostered strength and perseverance as much as it facilitated pacification and escape. For the large number of youths in Shakespeare's audience—firstborn and younger siblings, gentle and base—the performance may have been anal-ogous to a rite of passage, helping to ease their dangerous and prolonged journey from subordination to identity, their difficult transition from the child's part to the adult's.

My subject has been the complex interrelationship of brothers, fathers, and sons in *As You Like It*. But . . . the play's concern with relationships among men is only artificially separable from its concern with relationships between men and women. The androgynous Rosalind—boy actor and princess—addresses Shakespeare's heterosexual audience in an epilogue: "My way is to conjure you, and I'll begin with the women. I charge you, O women, for the love you bear to men, to like as much of this play as please you. And I charge you, O men, for the love you bear to women—as I perceive by your simpering none of you hates them—that between you and the women the play may please" [Epilogue, 11-17]. Through the subtle and flexible strategies of drama—in puns, jokes, games, disguises, songs, poems, fantasies—*As You Like It* expresses, contains, and dis-charges a measure of the strife between the men and the women. Shakespeare's comedy manipulates the differential social re-lationships between the sexes, between brothers, between fa-ther and son, master and servant, lord and subject. It is by the conjurer's art that Shakespeare manages to reconcile the social imperatives of hierarchy and difference with the festive urges toward leveling and atonement. The intense and ambivalent personal bonds upon which the play is focused—bonds between brothers and between lovers—affect each other reciprocally and become the means of each other's resolution. And as the actions within the play are dialectically related to each other, so the world of Shakespeare's characters is dialectically related to the world of his audience. *As You Like It* is both a theatrical *reflection* of social conflict and a theatrical *source* of social conciliation. (pp. 53-4)

*Louis Adrian Montrose, "'The Place of a Brother' in 'As You Like It': Social Process and Comic Form," in* Shakespeare Quarterly, *Vol. 32, No. 1, Spring, 1981, pp. 28-54.*

**ALICE-LYLE SCOUFOS** (essay date 1981)

[*In the following excerpt, Scoufos discusses the theme of love's testing as exemplified by Orlando's development in* As You Like It. *Arden, she claims, is "Eden made harsh by post-lapsarian Nature," a "place for love's development and fruition"; she adds that although love is ultimately successful in the play, this is only the case "after a series of tests in the forest." Scoufos maintains that Orlando is violent and unwise at the beginning of the play as a result of his being denied nurture, but by the end he is changed; "nurture in Arden has redefined his nature," and his fidelity, virtue, and courage have been proved. Scoufos points to Act IV, Scene iii in* As You Like It—*in which Orlando's virtuous nature triumphs over the villainous impulse to let the lioness destroy Oliver—as evidence of love's transforming power over selfishness; in saving Oliver, Orlando has channeled his energy into proper action, enabling "the cosmic forces [to] return tenfold the frail harmony established in Arden by human love." Scoufos emphasizes throughout her study the Platonic nature of Shake-speare's presentation of love in* As You Like It, *and she notes as well the Christian significance of the Arden forest, especially evident in the scene of Orlando's testing with the snake and the lion.*]

In Shakespeare's Arden we find an Eden made harsh by post-lapsarian Nature. The wind is cold, and the deer must be slaugh-tered to provide food for the inhabitants. At times Arden is called "uncouth" [II. vi. 6], and it has within it "a desert

inaccessibly" [II. vii. 110]. But Arden is paradoxical. Unlike Arcadia, where it is human disorder that mars the ideal garden, making men fight the elements as well as each other, Shake-speare's Arden provides a retreat from the human hostilities that are found in the outside world of the court. Arden, like Eden, is timeless, and Touchstone's watch becomes an object of laughter. Arden is also a place that mirrors truth. Nature's counselors "feelingly perswade me what I am" [II. i. 11], insists the exiled duke. But it is also a place where the inhab-itants no longer "feel the penaltie of Adam" [II. i. 5]. . . . Certainly the festive music and dancing that precede the ban-quet scene are indicative of pastoral delight. It is a place for love's development and fruition, we learn by the end of the comedy. We should not be surprised because love (as well as death) from the days of Theocritus onward was a subject for secular pastoral poetry. What is new in [Shakespeare's] sylvan settings is the success of love. But that success comes only after a series of tests in the forest or garden. In *As You Like It* these tests mount to a climax under the ancient tree as Orlando undergoes a severe temptation to let the lioness destroy his brother. The testing scenes in Arden, however, begin much earlier in the comedy. (p. 218)

At the beginning of the play we find Orlando a vigorous and violent young man in a state of rebellion because nurture is being denied him. He knocks Oliver down and apparently pounds his head in the dirt, an action that sets old Adam hopping in distress. A few scenes later Orlando breaks the neck of Charles the wrestler who is carried off the field unconscious.

For Orlando, virility means violence. His actions are not dis-ciplined by wisdom or good manners. His rebellion is under-standable, but his violence is not commendable. In Arden Or-lando must learn that violence and physical prowess are not ends in themselves nor are they instruments of revenge. In addition, he must learn that love is more than a passion for a beautiful woman; it includes civility, gratitude, understanding, and charity in its highest meanings. Orlando begins to learn this lesson with Duke Senior's response to his drawn sword: "What would you have? Your gentlenesse shall force, more then your force, Move us to gentlenesse" [II. vii. 102-03]. Orlando's chagrin only increases his embarrassment. His speech reverts to the high civility of liturgical rhythms as his thoughts turn instinctively to the vital conception of nurture:

> If ever you have look'd on better dayes:
> If ever beene where bels have knoll'd to Church:
> If ever sate at any good mans feast:
> If ever from your eye-lids wip'd a teare,
> And know what 'tis to pittie, and be pitted
> Let gentlenesse my strong enforcement be
> In which hope, I blush, and hide my sword.
>
> [II. vii. 113-19]

Shakespeare stresses the message as Duke Senior repeats Or-lando's statements. This moral exemplum is intended for Jaques's ears as well as Orlando's, for the moral lesson applies to Jaques's desire to gall and whip the world's follies under the license of the poet's cloak.

Orlando responds immediately to the lesson of gentleness; Jaques does not. The duke's speech merely opens the door to Jaques's famous oration, "All the world's a Stage, / And all the men and women meerely Players" [II. vii. 139-40]. In spite of his desire to reform the world, Jaques the dilettante believes that the human condition is one of static frustration without apparent meaning. . . . [He] looms large in the pastoral play as a symbol of the classical chauvinistic attitude toward sexual love: Plato had stated bluntly that ideal love was a rational, intelligent love capable of bringing immortality, and it was possible only between men; earthly love, on the other hand, was directed toward boys and women and was a kind of madness. Jaques is an extremely important part of the pastoral tradition. His disdain for the lovers reflects generations of minds that had rejected human love as a foolish and degrading emotion. Shakespeare has created this melancholic character to serve as a foil for Orlando's steady progression up the symbolic ladder of love.

The next major testing of Orlando comes in the temptation he faces when he agrees to meet the sprightly Ganymede and court him as though he were the beautiful Rosalind. He says as he accepts Ganymede's challenge, "Now by the *faith* of my love, I will" [III. ii. 428]. This test of the quality of his love is also a test of his capacity for fidelity, for virtuous choice. Rosalind begins the anatomy by proclaiming that "Love is meerely a madnesse" [III. ii. 400], and she uses the standard misogyny of the preceding two thousand years as she probes both love and human nature's idealistic centers. Orlando's position is unshaken. His views of Rosalind are presented in his poem on her image:

> Therefore heaven Nature charg'd
> that one bodie should be fill'd
> With all Graces wide enlarg'd
> Nature presently distill'd. . . .
>
> [III. ii. 141-44]

And we have a catalogue of feminine parts—from Helen's cheek to Lucretia's modesty. We should note, however, that in the first part of this poem the poet says he will also write songs about "how briefe the Life of man, runs his erring pilgrimage," and still others about "violated vowes twixt the soules of friend and friend" [III. ii. 129-30, 133-34]. Orlando is no saccharin fool.

The third test comes in that graphic tableau that Oliver describes for the girls at the end of Act IV. The ancient tree, the wild man, the green snake, the hungry lioness, and the sorely tempted Orlando are depicted. (pp. 219-21)

In this scene, which happens offstage as do the climactic actions of classical drama, archetypal images pull the pastoral setting suddenly into the mystical realm. Shakespeare intensifies the action with this mysticism that is an important part of the *paradiso terrestre* [earthly paradise] tradition. Shakespeare's images are dense with allusions, for when a Renaissance poet placed a tree and a snake in the center of a garden or woods, the Edenic reference was automatically created for his reader or audience. In the pastoral tradition stemming from Genesis, the human soul faces original temptation. The doctrine of original sin included not only the idea of mankind as Adam and Eve's progeny inheriting the flawed nature of the first couple, but also the idea that each human soul developing in this life must make a symbolic pilgrimage back to that forbidden tree in Eden and perform once again the fateful act of disobedience. When Orlando approaches the ancient oak that is "moss'd with age" and "bald with drie antiquitie" [IV. iii. 104-05], we note that the tree has been particularized for its setting in Arden, and we note also that Orlando is approaching a severe testing of his moral nature. We know that he is tempted to leave his infamous brother to the lioness, thus gaining his revenge. . . . [But] Orlando's virtuous nature triumphs over the villainous

impulse to let the lioness destroy Oliver. Why? The snake and the lioness offer us an answer.

The green and gilded snake is that attractive serpent of Eden, and it has all the sexual overtones that the medieval churchmen associated with Satan in the original temptation. But Shakespeare, the sophisticated artist, adds to the natural phallic symbolism. If we keep in mind that love is being tested in this pastoral comedy, the idea of sexual love's perversion is introduced in the detailed description:

> . . . about his neck
> A green and gilded snake had wreath'd itself,
> Who with her head nimble in threats approach'd
> The opening of his mouth; but suddenly
> Seeing Orlando, it unlink'd itself,
> And with indented glides did slip away
> Into a bush. . . .
>
> [IV. iii. 107-13]

Eroticism is not absent from Arden; it too can point a sensual finger and say, *"Et in Arcadia ego"* [I am in Arcadia]. But in Shakespeare's depiction of the Edenic experience, the snake slips into a bush. The snake is used to help identify the Edenic setting, but having done so, it disappears. Sensual temptation is not to be the character of this confrontation. It is no longer necessary because Orlando's love has proved faithful and pure. It is the predatory lioness that offers the dangerous testing in Arden.

The lioness, a symbol of royalty, comes from another meaning of the archetypal garden metaphor—this too from medieval usage. . . . The Eden-Arcadia-Arden metaphor contains broad social meanings. As in Sidney's symbolic pastoral, so too in Shakespeare's forest: love must move from the personal level upward to the social. This is the normal progression up the Neoplatonic ladder of love. Sensual love leads to social love which in turn leads to the brotherhood of man, and that universal human love leads to a love of God. Orlando's concern for himself, which was so strident at the beginning of the play, has now changed because he has fallen in love. And this love must grow to include the love of mankind—in this case, love for the wild man, his villainous brother.

Oliver is described as "a wretched ragged man, ore-growne with haire" who lies "sleeping on his back" near the tree [IV. iii. 106-07]. This is an image from emblematic literature. The image is also that of the ubiquitous wild man of the romance tradition who ducks in and out of dozens of medieval and Renaissance stories. He is usually interpreted as the symbol of humanity without divine grace. (pp. 221-22)

In addition to learning to love his wretched brother, Orlando must understand that passive love is not sufficient; ultimately, love must lead to virtuous action. And this is where Arden is severed from Arcadia. (pp. 222-23)

In this mystical scene Orlando learns his final and greatest lesson; his physical prowess must be disciplined into proper uses, not disciplined into passivity. Orlando learns this lesson only because he has discovered the true meaning of the first step in love, his love for Rosalind. If we let nineteenth-century Romanticism blind us with its doctrine of the preeminence of sexual love, we lose touch with the Renaissance hierarchy of values. In *As You Like It* sexual love leads to social harmony, and social harmony leads to a cosmic union between mankind and the cosmic powers.

Just as Adam faced temptation at the tree in Eden, Orlando faces temptation in Arden. Like Adam he has free will to succumb or to resist the impulse to evil, which in this case is self love that blinds man to the nature of true love. The struggle is powerful: ''Twice did he turne his backe, and purpos'd so'' (to desert Oliver) [IV. iii. 127]. But Orlando resists the temptation and hurtles with the lioness. We note with satisfaction that our hero, rather than being passive, which is the natural opposite of being violent, uses his prowess to defend his brother. He has channeled his energy into proper action, and in doing so, he is wounded. By spilling his blood for his brother, he resembles the Second Adam whose blood is the premier symbol of sacrifice and love in Christianity. (p. 223)

In Shakespeare's Arden we go beyond the philosophy found in Sidney's *Arcadia*. Shakespeare's conception of love is closer to Milton's grand philosophy in which deeds are added to the knowledge of love, love ''the soul of all the rest''.... Orlando's education in Arden-Eden is complete. He has proved his fidelity, his virtue, his courage. Nurture in Arden has refined his nature, and it is time for rewards. (p. 224)

When the characters have made the proper virtuous choices, exemplified in human action, the cosmic forces return tenfold the frail harmony established in Arden by human love, and Hymen speaks of the heavens smiling when men achieve accord [V. iv. 108-10]. The good fortune that follows quickly upon this statement is the result of harmony established by love in Arden. The news that Jaques de Boys brings of reformation and restoration is unexpected; in other words, it seems an artifical *deus ex machina*—unless we are attending to the intellectual statements . . . of the drama. The playwright has carefully integrated his final scene with the philosophical ideas upon which the play is structured. When human nature is properly nurtured, its moral and ethical choices will illuminate the inner virtue. Growth and enlightenment will be enhanced by cosmic harmony, and Dame Fortune herself will become magnanimous. The questions concerning the function of Fortune and Nature, posed in the witty comments of Rosalind and Celia in Act I, scene ii, are answered in this philosophical action at the end of the comedy. Nurture can modify human nature through the learning process, and human nature can influence the cosmic order, bringing harmony (in comedy) and dire disorder (in tragedy). Human responsibility, as well as ripeness, is all.

In this final scene of *As You Like It,* Jaques assumes a posture that duplicates that of Hymen. The god of marriage extends his hands in benediction as he blesses the four couples before him. A few lines later Jaques offers his benedictions to the men standing before him [V. iv. 186-92].... Has this dissipated malcontent reformed, or is Jaques humorously parodying Hymen's benedictions? Perhaps neither. I am of the opinion that we have contrasting values in the dramatic iconography of this final scene. I believe that Jaques is sincere in his statements (as sincere as a posturing malcontent can be), but we should note that the women are excluded from Jaques's formal benedictions. He does not become a part of the harmonic and symbolic circle forming at the end of the comedy. He wants only to seek out Duke Frederick, for ''out of these convertites, / There is much matter to be heard, and learn'd'' [V. iv. 184-85], and he retreats from the dancing to retire to the cave. In Sidney's pastoral romance the cave is an important locale in Arcadia, a place that depicts the ''subnatural world of tooth and nail.'' But I believe that Shakespeare had in mind the famous cave in Book VII of Plato's *Republic*. In that symbolic cave

the majority of mankind foolishly perceives the meaning of reality in the dancing images reflected on the wall by the fire. Jaques is preoccupied with these same false images; he has not yet learned the lesson of Arden. The true view of reality is revealed only by looking directly into the light of the Good, the True, the Beautiful—which ultimately is the light of love. (pp. 224-25)

*Alice-Lyle Scoufos, ''The 'Paradiso Terrestre' and the Testing of Love in 'As You Like It','' in* Shakespeare Studies: An Annual Gathering of Research, Criticism, and Reviews, *Vol. XIV, 1981, pp. 215-27.*

## ROBERT KIMBROUGH (essay date 1982)

[*In the following excerpt, Kimbrough discusses androgyny and disguise in* As You Like It. *Objecting to Nancy K. Hayles's argument that ''Shakespeare and his colleagues exploited girl-into-boy disguise'' because their female roles were played by boys ''and their audiences knew it'' (see excerpt above, 1979), Kimbrough maintains that Rosalind's disguise allows her to grow into her ''fuller human self.'' In Arden, Kimbrough claims, Rosalind is both male and female. As a male she is free from the conventions of society, able both to speak her mind and to encourage Orlando—who is relaxed in male company—to reveal his emotions. Rosalind's androgyny, Kimbrough continues, makes her wit ''in essence and choice . . . both masculine and feminine . . . [and] therefore, more fully human than a gender designation would indicate.'' Echoing an assessment voiced by earlier critics, Kimbrough attributes Rosalind's self-knowledge to her conscious use of her disguise to act in a way not normally allowed a woman. The critic also discusses Rosalind's role as a magician—in his analogy, an ''alchemist''—in the final moments of* As You Like It, *stating that the magic she employs ''to make all this matter even'' (V. iv. 18) is love.*]

''In dealing with the female page disguise in Renaissance drama, one is invariably struck by the complexity of the double sex reversal implied by the presence of the boy actor'' [see excerpt above by Nancy K. Hayles, 1979]. Sitting in a study, one may very well be so struck. But to allow oneself to be so prevents one from viewing Renaissance drama historically and theatrically. Indeed, critically blinding homage has too long been paid to the false assumption that Shakespeare and his colleagues readily exploited girl-into-boy disguise because their women were really men and their audiences knew it. We have too long assumed that writers were thus provided the essential ingredients to formulate easy, automatic situation-comedy.

In point of historical fact, there is little comically elaborated girl-into-boy disguise in Shakespearean and Elizabethan drama. And, from the standpoint of legitimate theatre, to maintain that there has ever been a comic device based on the actual sex of the actors is to fly in the face of a generic essential casually remarked upon by Sidney and Johnson: people going to the theatre check their literal-mindedness at the door and willingly believe anything they are asked to believe; the theatre is where illusion becomes reality. An actor in role is whatever sex, age, and cultural origin the playwright asserts. Thus, a speech assigned by Shakespeare to a woman in disguise as a boy can work in the theatre *only* if the audience knows and accepts that the speaker is really a woman—even in Elizabeth's day when, in an entirely different and dramatically extraneous mode of consciousness, the audience simultaneously knew and unconsciously accepted that the speaker was really a male actor. We do Shakespeare a disservice not to accept his women as women. We risk missing the full significance of the lines he gives them. (p. 17)

In *As You Like It,* in order to suggest the androgynous dimensions of the characterization of Rosalind, Shakespeare provides within the play three special audiences for her playing: Celia, Orlando, and Phebe. Alone with Celia, Rosalind can show her intellect and wit, which must be hidden in part from the male world, and she can be relaxed, giddy, and giggly, which in public would be very unladylike. With Orlando, she can be one of the boys: wisecracking, shoulder-thumping, slightly salacious, and pragmatically knowing, in an eye-winking way. And with Phebe, with her sex hidden, Rosalind is able to reveal the maturing range of her attractive human person. In disguise, Rosalind grows into a fuller human self.

At the outset of the play Rosalind reveals a kind of restlessness with her situation in life. From her first conversation with Celia in I. ii, she shows the witty, educated side of her nature along with this restlessness. It is she who suggests the game ''of falling in love'' [I. ii. 25], and it is she who, in agreeing with Celia that there is no equity in the world, feels that Fortune ''doth most mistake in her gifts to women'' [I. ii. 36]. Celia responds with an anti-female commonplace much older than ''The Wife of Bath's Tale'': '' 'Tis true, for those that she makes fair she scarce makes honest, and those that she makes honest she makes very ill-favoredly'' [I. ii. 37-9]. But Rosalind keeps the attention on her first remark: on inequities and the unfortunate lot of women. Celia's response concerns ''Nature,'' which causes one's birth as male or female, whereas ''Fortune reigns in gifts of the world'' [I. ii. 41]. Thus, when Rosalind is banished, it is almost with relief that she decides to put on an unnecessary but wished-for male disguise behind which she can escape not just the court, but in part what has been so far her Fortune-dealt restricted feminine self.

Three points support this bald assertion. When Celia suggests that to be less provocative during their journey to the Forest of Arden they put on ''poor and mean attire,'' Rosalind goes one step further:

> Were it not better,
> Because that I am more than common tall,
> That I did suit me all points like a man?
> A gallant curtle-axe upon my thigh,
> A boar-spear in my hand; and, in my heart
> Lie there what hidden woman's fear there will,
> We'll have a swashing and a martial outside,
> As many other mannish cowards have
> That do outface it with their semblances.
>
> [I. iii. 114-22]

Although there is some suggestion of a need for male protection, when Rosalind advises that they take Touchstone along she negates the actual need for a protective male disguise. The second point is more persuasive: once in the forest Rosalind makes no attempt to seek her father; she must, perforce, like the part she has created and cast. The third is conclusive: when Rosalind discovers from Celia in III. ii that Orlando is in the forest, she consciously elects to stay in disguise. Her first reaction to Celia's news is doubt and dismay: ''Alas the day! what shall I do with my doublet and hose?'' [III. ii. 219-20]. In her next speech, she asks, ''doth he know that I am in this forest, and in man's apparel?'' [III. ii. 229-30]. But after she sees him and after Jaques leaves, she comes to a clear decision; she tells Celia, ''I will speak to him like a saucy lackey, and *under that habit* play the knave with him'' [III. ii. 295-97]. . . . (pp. 23-4)

Up to this point, Shakespeare has given Rosalind lines emphasizing the woman within the knave's clothes in order to

maintain a sense of contrary doubleness. . . . Once she has spoken to Orlando, she must stay in her self-selected part. She mocks herself and mocks men by using her wit in the manner of men who belittle women's wit: ''Make the doors open a woman's wit, and it will out at the casement; shut that, and 'twill out at the keyhole; stop that, 'twill fly with the smoke out at the chimney'' [IV. i. 161-64]. So well does Rosalind swagger along in male assuredness of supremacy that she completely ignores Celia's touchstone comment on the contradiction between Rosalind's masculine, misogynous wit and her actual sex: ''You have simply misused our sex in your love-prate. We must have your doublet and hose plucked over your head, and show the world what the bird hath done to her own nest'' [IV. i. 201-04]. But alone with Celia, Rosalind can still be delightfully open and emotional: ''O coz, coz, coz, my pretty little coz, that you didst know how many fathom deep I am in love! But it cannot be sounded. My affection hath an unknown bottom, like the Bay of Portugal'' [IV. i. 205-08].

When Rosalind meets Orlando at court, she enters into a real game ''of falling in love'' [I. ii. 25]. When she discovers that he is in the forest, she decides to continue playing the game by forsaking father and clinging unto Orlando, as we can see after the one time Rosalind comes upon her father: ''I met the Duke yesterday and had much question with him. He asked me of what parentage I was. I told him, of as good as he; so he laughed and let me go. But what talk we of fathers when there is such a man as Orlando?'' [III. iv. 35-9]. In this speech both the giddy girl that she is and the saucy boy that she is able to play emerge. To this duality, because she is not sure that either she or Orlando is ready for an open, mutual commitment, she adds the role of ''Rosalind,'' which is a hidden way of being openly herself.

On the surface, then, Rosalind is now both male and female. As a man, she is freed from societal convention and can speak her *mind*. Also, because of her being a man, Orlando, relaxed in the presence of male company, can reveal his *emotions*. If Orlando knew he was in the presence of a woman, let alone Rosalind, he would once again become as tongue-tied as he had been at court. With Adam, and with Jaques, we see him to be a bluntly articulate, plain-spoken young man. Love is new to him, and with a stranger in a strange place he can show his befuddlement openly and honestly, with no need to be ''manly'': he has no past social or psychological investment regarding Ganymede to impede or embarrass him (as indeed that poetry should).

That Rosalind carries her double role with ease and accomplishment is attested by her confrontation with Phebe. Rosalind's gently chiding speech to Phebe regarding her treatment of Silvius is so full of good common sense that Phebe would not tolerate it from another woman. And, because Rosalind is a woman, the speech is delivered without a subtext of sexual threat: there is more safety for Phebe in Rosalind's aggressive passiveness than in Silvius' passive aggressiveness. Yet more than a defense mechanism is at work; Phebe could not fall into love at first sight were not the object of her love an attractive human being.

Thus, Rosalind's male behavior simply emphasizes the wit which governs that behavior, a wit which by strict definition is a ''woman's wit.'' But her wit is in essence and choice indivisibly both masculine and feminine; it is, therefore, more fully human than a gender designation would indicate. When Rosalind receives Phebe's letter, she is strategically and personally able to tease Silvius by toying with society's definitions of masculine and feminine because her own experience has taken her beyond the limitations of those definitions. . . . She has achieved a position as woman and man from which she can understand and mock the absurdity of the social restrictions caused by gender stereotyping.

Rosalind's "male" wisdom and common sense—"Men have died from time to time, and worms have eaten them, but not for love" [IV. i. 106-08]—have often been noted, but her seemingly anti-female jibes have not been understood as ways of wrestling with attributes created for women by society. In consciously using her disguise to act in a way that society will not allow a woman to act, she is more her real, essential self—or can move more easily to discovery and revelation of that essential self. As a saucy knave she can mock the very passions that she, Phebe, and Orlando are all subjected to; in testing and purging those two, she is testing and purging herself. Thus, by a directness allowed by an indirectness, Rosalind and Orlando find each other out and in their own way they (as do Celia and Oliver) by degrees make "a pair of stairs" [V. ii. 37-8] to marriage.

At the end, Rosalind claims that she will resolve all of the conflicts among the lovers through magic. As Albert R. Cirillo has pointed out, "she assumes an important role which is central to the entire play and which makes her something of a *magus* or magician who controls nature and sets all things aright through her influence on the amorous relationships in the circle of the forest" [see excerpt above, 1971]. Her magic is one of the world's oldest forces bringing harmony out of conflict—love. Not only is Rosalind the magician she claims to be; she is herself the product of her magic. More accurately, she is that special magician, the alchemist, who seeks to compound higher substances out of lesser, contrary elements, all of which are carefully divided under male and female headings. As a magician/alchemist, Rosalind will take the male-Rosalind and the female-Rosalind and merge them into a human-Rosalind. . . . (pp. 24-6)

Rosalind has been growing all during the course of the play. She started as a wise and witty young woman, became a wise and witty young man, and through her interactions with both a man, Orlando, and a woman, Phebe, has been able to reach toward a fuller realization of her humanhood, or potential for androgyny. The catalyst in the process is love. Once Rosalind knows herself and what she wants, she can remove what has been her self-protective disguise to come before lover and father, leaving her earlier restlessness behind. (p. 26)

The power of sex in human intercourse has been present in the play through Audrey and Touchstone and, by report, Celia and Oliver, but the emphasis in the main plot has been on gender differentiations. In the epilogue Shakespeare brings sex and gender together in order to give a final plea in behalf of androgynous behavior. Just as he had used Puck's epilogue to emphasize the handy-dandy of his illusion/reality motif within *A Midsummer Night's Dream,* Shakespeare now uses Rosalind's address to the audience to emphasize the androgynous element of *As You Like It.*

The plea in behalf of the play opens with a reference to a "lady" and a "lord" and goes on to address both the "women" and the "men" in the audience: "I charge you, O women, for the love you bear to men, to like as much of this play as please you; and I charge you, O men, for the love you bear to women (as I perceive by your simp'ring none of you hates them), that between you and the women the play may please" [Epilogue,

12-17]. This is most appropriate, for the play has celebrated the play between men and women. Now, the dramatic illusions of that play within the play must be made real, for Shakespeare's art celebrates life as the ultimate pleasure. In the end, the individuals in the audience are asked to enter into the sport "of falling in love." Rosalind before, during, and after disguise has shown them how. Just as an actor's role is a disguise, so also is gender a disguise, and all disguises must be removed for people to be themselves. Now, Rosalind as boy actor must push home that fact.

When Shakespeare has him say "What a case am I in" [Epilogue, 7], Rosalind's gown becomes a costume for a male actor. His "case" is both his costume and his problem because it is a female costume on a man presenting the epilogue: "If I were a woman, I would kiss as many of you as had beards that pleased me, complexions that liked me, and breaths that I defied not; and I am sure, as many as have good beards, or good faces, or sweet breaths, will, for my kind offer, when I make curtsy, bid me farewell" [Epilogue, 18-24].

His words are intended to startle us: "If I were a woman . . . when I make curtsy." When the man walks off the stage after executing a female gesture, the men and the women in the audience should be able in some small way to understand that while the differences between men and women are important and powerful, we are all most human under the surfaces. The play has shown us that if we can accept our sex instead of hiding it behind the disguise of gender, we will have established a base upon which to build human fulfillment. (pp. 26-7)

*Robert Kimbrough, "Androgyny Seen through Shakespeare's Disguise," in* Shakespeare Quarterly, *Vol. 33, No. 1, Spring, 1982, pp. 17-33.*

**ROBERT WILCHER**   (essay date 1982)

[*In an unexcerpted section of his "The Art of the Comic Duologue in Three Plays by Shakespeare" (1982), Wilcher states that three principal types of comic duologue occur in Shakespeare's plays: 1) self-conscious set-pieces or performances in which the lead clown sharpens his wit on a stooge of the same low social class; 2) duologues between characters from the main plot, in which there is no dominant partner and each holds his own in a mutual display of verbal cleverness; and 3) duologues in which a high-status character plays the "straight-man" to a socially inferior comedian. In the following excerpt, Wilcher argues that all three types of comic duologue occur in* As You Like It. *He claims that Touchstone is at the center of the play's "double-act routine," but he notes that, once removed from the court, the clown is initially unable to cope with the "total licence" of the pastoral world. In two encounters, those with William and Corin, Wilcher claims, Touchstone fails to adopt the proper, expected stance, breaking the "formal rules" of the double-act routine. Wilcher continues that Touchstone is essentially out of place until the play's end, when the problem of his mismanagement of his role as jester in the forest is finally resolved.*]

[Three] types of comic duologue occur in *As You Like It*. This play, indeed, more than any other of the mature plays, is built upon conversations between two characters, as the courtiers and the inhabitants of Arden light upon each other in the forest in a ballet of ever-changing partners. It is Touchstone, however, who will provide the main focus for a discussion of the use of the double-act routine in *As You Like It,* and we must begin by examining the immediate context that Shakespeare creates for him. The second scene of the play opens with Celia and Rosalind discussing the situation caused by the Duke's banishment and their determination to 'be merry' and 'devise sports' [I. ii. 23-5]. They begin to amuse themselves with banter about 'falling in love' [I. ii. 25] and mocking 'the good house-wife Fortune from her wheel' [I. ii. 31-2], and at that point reinforcements arrive in the person of the professional merry-maker. This is the cue for a mock-serious debate about the function of the fool, designed to draw Touchstone into their sport:

> *Celia.* Though Nature hath given us wit to flout at Fortune, hath not Fortune sent in this fool to cut off the argument?
> *Rosalind.* Indeed, there is Fortune too hard for Nature, when Fortune makes Nature's natural the cutter-off of Nature's wit.
> *Celia.* Peradventure this is not Fortune's work neither, but Nature's, who perceiveth our natural wits too dull to reason of such goddesses, and hath sent this natural for our whetstone; for always the dullness of the fool is the whetstone of the wits. How now, wit! Whither wander you?
>
> [I. ii. 45-56]

Shakespeare is here ringing the changes on a highly charged and ambiguous group of words, which the very person of 'the fool' throws into relief: Nature, Fortune, wit, and folly. 'Nature's natural' is a half-wit, a Poor Tom (which Touchstone manifestly is not); but as well as natural folly, there is also something that can be called 'natural wit', which makes it possible for Celia and Rosalind to 'flout at Fortune'. The culmination of Shakespeare's probing of the mysteries that surround the concept of folly will come in Lear's profound and agonized recognition: 'I am even the natural fool of Fortune' [*King Lear,* IV. vi. 190-91]. For the moment, he is content to tease at these shifting meanings in a comic vein, as Celia teases Touchstone by dubbing him a 'natural' fool and assuming an intellectually superior stance in relation to him. The fool's natural dullness, she declares, is the mere whetstone on which the wits of the naturally witty can be sharpened. This is not, in fact, how Celia and Rosalind *do* treat Touchstone. Knowing that he is an artificial fool, rather than a natural one, they quickly drop into their socially determined role as 'feeds', happy to allow his wit dominance in the dialogue that ensues:

> *Rosalind.* Where learned you that oath, fool?
> *Touchstone.* Of a certain knight that swore by his honour they were good pancakes, and swore by his honour the mustard was naught. Now I'll stand to it, the pancakes were naught and the mustard was good, and yet was not the knight forsworn.
> *Celia.* How prove you that, in the great heap of your knowledge?
> *Rosalind.* Ay, marry, now unmuzzle your wisdom.
>
> [I. ii. 62-70]

The proper behaviour in the face of social or intellectual inferiors is *not* to use them as butts for the display of one's own superior wit, and this the aristocratic girls know perfectly well. (pp. 90-1)

The three types of comic duologue [to be found in *As You Like It*] embody the range of approved witty relationships. In the low-comedy turn it is acceptable for the lead clown to sharpen his wits on the whetstone of his duller companion, because the audience recognizes the double-act as an extra-dramatic entertainment, performed for its benefit by two actors who are functioning as theatrical clowns rather than 'real' characters towards whom human sympathy should be extended. The bout of courtly repartee is self-entertainment among members of the same class, and mockery is in order if one participant descends into folly by ignoring the code that governs the game—as Thurio does [in *The Two Gentlemen of Verona*] by allowing personal animosity to intrude. The duologue between master and allowed fool requires the socially superior partner to take the comically inferior role as straight-man in the interests of lightening humour with 'merry jests'. From *As You Like It* onwards, Shakespeare becomes increasingly preoccupied with the consequences for the individual and for the human community at large when these conventional relationships within the duologue are disrupted. The breaking of the formal rules that govern the double-act is felt to be symptomatic of deeper disturbances.

Touchstone is a case in point. Alexander Leggatt is right in saying that 'Touchstone enjoys as much licence as he wants in Arden' [see excerpt above, 1974]; but it is also true, as D. J. Palmer notes, that 'Touchstone is out of his element in Arden' [see Additional Bibliography]. He is essentially a court fool, and we see him still performing his accustomed function of being, in Rosalind's words, 'a comfort to our travel' [I. iii. 131], as he and the two runaway girls approach the skirts of the forest:

> *Rosalind.* O Jupiter, how weary are my spirits!
> *Touchstone.* I care not for my spirits, if my legs were not weary. . . .
> *Celia.* I pray you, bear with me; I cannot go no further.
> *Touchstone.* For my part, I had rather bear with you than bear you; yet I should bear no cross if I did bear you; for I think you have no money in your purse.
>
> [II. iv. 1-14]

He is taking the initiative here, in trying to lighten their humour, in contrast with the earlier scene in which they prompted his witticisms. Another fool who follows his master into the wilderness will be seen, transposed into a tragic key, similarly labouring 'to out-jest / His heart-struck injuries' [*King Lear,* III. i. 16-17].

Once Touchstone has entered the forest, however, and been cut adrift from the social context that enables him to sustain his defining role as jester to the nobility, his behaviour becomes questionable. Shakespeare involves him in two set-piece duologues, which reveal that the 'all-licens'd fool' [*King Lear,* I. iv. 201] of the court cannot cope with the total licence of the pastoral world. In his encounters with two versions of the countryman—Corin, the realistic shepherd, and William, the conventional stage-yokel—Touchstone is in danger of forfeiting our sympathy because he fails to adopt the proper stance. The nature of his failure is indicated in the first words he flings at Corin in act 2, scene 4: 'Holla, you clown!' [II. iv. 66]. His assumption of superiority over the mere country 'clown' is immediately slapped down by Rosalind, who reminds him that he, too, is a clown, and therefore in no position to act the courtier: 'Peace, fool; he's not thy kinsman' [II. iv. 67]. That Touchstone does not learn this lesson in behaviour is obvious when he enters later in conversation with Corin. Throughout their duologue, he is trying to score points off the old man. His patronizing question is an attempt to get Corin to make a fool of himself by exposing his intellectual limitations: 'Hast any philosophy in thee, shepherd?' [III. ii. 21-2]. Corin's dignified reply puts Touchstone down, and he can only retort lamely with a quibble: 'Such a one is a natural philosopher' [III. ii. 32]. The intended scorn of this cuts back at Touchstone, since Corin's philosophy contains the common wisdom of one close to Nature, which is far from 'natural' in the derogatory sense of the word. The fool's next ploy is to mock the shepherd's lack of social sophistication:

> *Touchstone.* Wast ever in court, shepherd?
> *Corin.* No, truly.
> *Touchstone.* Then thou art damn'd.
> *Corin.* Nay, I hope.
> *Touchstone.* Truly, thou art damn'd, like an ill-roasted egg, all on one side.
> *Corin.* For not being at court? Your reason.
> *Touchstone.* Why, if thou never wast at court thou never saw'st good manners; if thou never saw'st good manners, then thy manners must be wicked; and wickedness is sin, and sin is damnation. Thou art in a parlous state, shepherd.

> [III. ii. 33-44]

Having trapped Corin into feeding him with a familiar prompt-line—'Your reason'—Touchstone launches into the triumphant sequence of chop-logic which will prove the old man's damnation. But Corin is no Jessica [in *The Merchant of Venice*], who was content to play along with Launcelot's similar line of jesting. He once more makes Touchstone look foolish with his earthy wisdom:

> Not a whit, Touchstone. Those that are good manners at the court are as ridiculous in the country as the behaviour of the country is most mockable at the court. You told me you salute not at the court, but you kiss your hands; that courtesy would be uncleanly if courtiers were shepherds.

> [III. ii. 45-51]

Touchstone has completely misjudged the situation. Corin is neither a dim-witted stooge, like Old Gobbo [in *The Merchant of Venice*] or Curtis [in *The Taming of the Shrew*], nor a sophisticated courtier prepared to indulge the jester's verbal fantasies. Unable to find any way of communicating with him outside the modes of his fool's repertoire, Touchstone continues to press him for 'instances' on which he can build further witticisms, only to be met with the apposite and deflating verdict: 'You have too courtly a wit for me' [III. ii. 70].

He has more success in a formal sense in his encounter with William, who naturally falls into the role of the bewildered butt of the jester's condescending mockery:

> *Touchstone.* Good ev'n, gentle friend. Cover thy head, cover thy head; nay, prithee be cover'd. How old are you, friend?
> *William.* Five and twenty, sir.
> *Touchstone.* A ripe age. Is thy name William?
> *William.* William, sir.
> *Touchstone.* A fair name. Wast born i' th' forest here?
> *William.* Ay, sir, I thank God.
> *Touchstone.* 'Thank God.' A good answer. Art rich?
> *William.* Faith, sir, so so.

> *Touchstone.* 'So so' is good, very good, very excellent good; and yet it is not; it is but so so. Art thou wise?
> *William.* Ay, sir, I have a pretty wit.
> *Touchstone.* Why, thou say'st well. I do now remember a saying: 'The fool doth think he is wise, but the wise man knows himself to be a fool'.

> [V. i. 16-32]

This follows the traditional method of the low-comedy turn, and is amusing for the audience. But there is a complicating factor, which is not present when Launcelot tips us the wink that he is about to 'try confusions' with his father [*The Merchant of Venice*, II. ii. 37]. The scene is not set up in such a way that we retain that half-awareness of the clowns as comic entertainers putting on a show for us. Audrey is present throughout, and the duologue ends with Touchstone crowing over his ousted rival for her affections:

> *Touchstone.* Now, you are not ipse, for I am he.
> *William.* Which he, sir?
> *Touchstone.* He, sir, that must marry this woman. Therefore, you clown, abandon—which is in the vulgar leave—the society—which in the boorish is company—of this female—which in the common is woman—which together is: abandon the society of this female; or, clown, thou perishest; or, to thy better understanding, diest; or, to wit, I kill thee, make thee away, translate thy life into death, thy liberty into bondage. . . .

> [V. i. 44-54]

[Touchstone's] easy triumph over the poor yokel is open to moral judgement, in a way that Launcelot's treatment of his father is not, because the fictional situation has weakened the 'traditional connexion between the clowning actor and the laughing spectator' [Robert Weimann, in his essay "Laughing with the Audience: 'The Two Gentlemen of Verona'"]. He is exulting in his superior wit for his own and Audrey's benefit, not for ours, and this gives an unpleasant edge to the whole sequence.

At the end of the play, the uncomfortable problem of Touchstone's mismanagement of his role as jester in the forest is resolved along with the other restorations of order. This resolution is marked by his final double-act before an appreciative on-stage audience, with Jaques as straight-man prompting him to his comic *tour de force* of the seven 'degrees of the lie'. The sense of relief, as we see the jester once more operating skilfully within his familiar context, contributes to the general feeling that things are returning to their proper places. (pp. 91-3)

*Robert Wilcher, "The Art of the Comic Duologue in Three Plays by Shakespeare," in* Shakespeare Survey: An Annual Survey of Shakespearian Study and Production, *Vol. 35, 1982, pp. 87-100.*

## PETER ERICKSON (essay date 1985)

[*In the following excerpt, Erickson contends that in* As You Like It *Shakespeare is principally concerned with establishing "an ideal male community based on 'sacred pity'" and with vindicating a patriarchal system as the foundation of social unity. Thus, the critic opposes many generally accepted views of the play.*

*First, he maintains that Rosalind's disguise, although it "gives her freedom of action and empowers her to take the initiative with Orlando," is a protective device that allows her to delay her role as a subservient wife. Erickson further claims that in her disguise as Ganymede, Rosalind never integrates or synthesizes the male-female perspectives, as some commentators have averred, but always remains aware that she is a woman who must eventually yield her temporary control to Orlando and the Duke if she is to fulfill her love. The critic also contends that it is not Rosalind who experiences the benefits of androgyny in the play, for she must eventually surrender her male characteristics, but the courtiers of the Duke's banished kingdom, who in creating their ideal community permanently adopt feminine nurturing tendencies, such as gentleness, pity, and love. Erickson provides much commentary on this "idealized male enclave" in* As You Like It, *demonstrating how it reestablishes paternal continuity in the case of Orlando and his brothers and how it receives consistent endorsement throughout the play. He concludes that* As You Like It *is primarily a defensive work against female power rather than a celebration of it, citing the epilogue as evidence that "not only are women to be subordinate; they can, if necessary, be imagined as non-existent."]*

Before entering the forest of Arden, Rosalind's companion Celia/Aliena [defines the] pastoral space to mean opportunity rather than punishment: "Now go we in content / To liberty, and not to banishment" [I. iii. 137-38]. This "liberty" implies overcoming the restrictions of the female role. The idea of the male disguise originates as a strategy for avoiding the normal vulnerability to male force: "Alas, what danger will it be to us, / Maids as we are, to travel forth so far! / Beauty provoketh thieves sooner than gold" [I. iii. 108-10]. Rosalind's male costume, as it evolves, expands her identity so that she can play both male and female roles. Yet the costume is problematic. Though it gives her freedom of action and empowers her to take the initiative with Orlando, it simultaneously serves as a protective device, which temptingly offers excessive security, even invulnerability. In order to love, Rosalind must reveal herself directly to Orlando, thereby making herself vulnerable. She must give up the disguise and appear—as she ultimately promises Orlando—"human as she is" [V. ii. 67]. But in giving up the disguise, she also gives up the strength it symbolizes. As the disguise begins to break down before its official removal, Rosalind's transparent femininity takes the form of fainting—a sign of weakness that gives her away: "You a man? / You lack a man's heart" [IV. iii. 163-64]. This loss of control signals that Rosalind can no longer deny her inner feminine self. The capacity for love that we find so admirable in Rosalind is compromised by the necessity that she resume a traditional female role in order to engage in love.

This traditional image has been present all along. Rosalind willingly confides to Celia that she remains a woman despite the male costume: "in my heart / Lie there what hidden woman's fear there will— / We'll have a swashing and a martial outside" [I. iii. 118-20]; "Good my complexion, dost thou think, though I am caparison'd like a man, I have a doublet and hose in my disposition?" [III. ii. 194-96]; and "Do you not know I am a woman?" [III. ii. 249]. By virtue of the costume, Rosalind does have access to both male and female attributes, but the impression she conveys of androgynous wholeness is misleading. Neither Rosalind nor the play questions the conventional categories of masculine and feminine. She does not reconcile gender definitions in the sense of integrating or synthesizing them. Her own insistence on the metaphor of exterior (male) and interior (female) keeps the categories distinct and separable. The liberation that Rosalind experiences in the forest has built into it the conservative coun-

termovement by which, as the play returns to the normal world, she will be reduced to the traditional woman who is subservient to men.

Rosalind is shown working out in advance the terms of her return. Still protected by her disguise yet allowing herself to come closer to the decisive moment, she instructs Orlando to "woo me" [IV. i. 68] and subsequently tells him what to say in a wedding rehearsal while she practises yielding. Though she teases Orlando with the wife's power to make him a cuckold and then to conceal her duplicity with her "wayward wit" [IV. i. 160-76], this is good fun, and it is only that. It is clear to the audience, if not yet to Orlando, that Rosalind's flaunting of her role as disloyal wife is a put-on rather than a genuine threat. She may playfully delay the final moment when she becomes a wife, but we are reassured that, once married, she will in fact be faithful. Her humor has the effect of exorcising and renouncing her potential weapon. The uncertainty concerns not her loyalty but Orlando's, as her sudden change of tone when he announces his departure indicates: "Alas, dear love, I cannot lack thee two hours!" [IV. i. 179]. Her exuberance and control collapse in fears of his betrayal: "Ay, go your ways, go your ways; I knew what you would prove" [IV. i. 182-83]. Her previous wit notwithstanding, for Rosalind the scene is less a demonstration of power than an exercise in vulnerability. She is once again consigned to anxious waiting for her tardy man: "But why did he swear he would come this morning, and comes not?" [III. iv. 18-19].

Rosalind's own behavior neutralizes her jokes about cuckoldry, but this point is sharply reinforced by the brief account of the male hunt that immediately follows act 4, scene 1. The expected negative meaning of horns as the sign of a cuckold is transformed into a positive image of phallic potency that unites men. Changing the style of his literary response to deer killing, Jaques replaces his earlier lament [II. i. 26-66] with a celebration of male hunt and conquest: "Let's present him to the Duke like a Roman conqueror, and it would do well to set the deer's horns upon his head, for a branch of victory" [IV. ii. 3-5]. The rousing song occasioned by this moment suggests the power of an all-male activity to provide a self-sufficient male heritage, thus to defend against male insecurity about humiliation by women.

The final scene, orchestrated by Rosalind, demonstrates her power in a paradoxical way. She is the architect of a resolution that phases out the control she has wielded and prepares the way for the patriarchal status quo. She accedes to the process by which, in the transition from courtship to marriage, power passes from the female to the male: the man is no longer the suitor who serves, obeys, and begs but is now the husband who commands. Rosalind's submission is explicit but not ironic, though her tone may be high-spirited. To each of the two men in her life she declares: "To you I give myself, for I am yours" [V. iv. 116-17]. Her casting herself in the role of male possession is all the more charming because she does not have to be forced to adopt it: her self-taming is voluntary. We may wish to give Rosalind credit for her cleverness in forestalling male rivalry between her father and her fiancé. Unlike Cordelia [in *King Lear*], she is smart enough to see that in order to be gratified, each man needs to feel that he is the recipient of all her love, not half of it. Yet Rosalind is not really in charge here because the potential hostility between the younger and older man has already been negotiated in the forest in act 2, scene 7, a negotiation that results in the formation of an idealized male alliance. Rosalind submits not only to two individual

*Act V. Scene iv. Oliver, Celia, Rosalind, Duke Senior, Orlando, and others. By J. Hatherell (1885).*
*The Department of Rare Books and Special Collections, The University of Michigan Library.*

men but also to the patriarchal society that they embody. Patriarchy is not a slogan smuggled in from the twentieth century and imposed on the play but an exact term for the social structure that close reading reveals within the play.

We are apt to assume that the green world is more free than it actually is. In the case of *As You Like It*, the green world cannot be interpreted as a space apart where a youthful rebellion finds a refuge from the older generation. The forest of Arden includes a strong parental presence: Duke Senior's is the first voice we hear there. Moreover, the green world has a clear political structure. Freed from the constraints of courtly decorum, Duke Senior can afford to address his companions as "brothers" [II. i. 1], but he nonetheless retains a fatherly command. Fraternal spirit is not equivalent to democracy, as is clarified when the duke dispenses favor on a hierarchical basis: "Shall share the good of our returned fortune, / According to the measure of their states" [V. iv. 174-75].

Although interpretations of *As You Like It* often stress youthful love, we should not neglect the paternal context in which the love occurs. Both Rosalind and Orlando acknowledge Duke Senior. Rosalind is aware, as she finds herself attracted to Orlando, that "My father lov'd Sir Rowland [Orlando's father] as his soul" [I. ii. 235] and hence that her affection is not incompatible with family approval. Orlando, for his part, does not go forward in pursuit of love until after he has become friends with Duke Senior. Rosalind and Orlando approach the forest in strikingly different ways. Rosalind's mission is love. Upon entering the forest, she discovers there the love "pas-

sion" she has brought with her: "Alas, poor shepherd, searching of thy wound, / I have by hard adventure found mine own" [II. iv. 44-5]. Orlando, by contrast, has two projects (though he does not consciously formulate them) to complete in the forest: the first is his quest to reestablish the broken connection with his father's legacy; the second is the quest for Rosalind. The sequence of these projects is an indication of priority. Orlando's outburst—"But heavenly Rosalind!" [I. ii. 289]—is not picked up again until he opens act 3, scene 2, with his love poem. The interim is reserved for his other, patriarchal business.

In the first scene of the play, Orlando makes it clear, in a melodramatic but nonetheless poignant way, that he derives his sense of identity from his dead father, an identity that is not yet fulfilled. In protesting against his older brother's mistreatment, Orlando asserts the paternal bond: "The spirit of my father grows strong in me, and I will no longer endure it" [I. i. 70-1]. His first step toward recovery of the connection with his lost father is the demolition of Charles the wrestler: "How dost thou, Charles?" / "He cannot speak, my lord" [I. ii. 219-20]. This victory earns Orlando the right to proclaim his father's name as his own:

> DUKE F. What is thy name, young man?
> ORL.    Orlando, my liege, the youngest son
>         of Sir Rowland de Boys. . . .
>         I am more proud to be Sir Rowland's
>         son.
>
> [I. ii. 221-22, 232]

Frederick's negative reaction to Orlando's statement of identity confirms the concept of heritage being evoked here: "Thou shouldst have better pleas'd me with this deed / Hadst thou descended from another house" [I. ii. 227-28]. The significance of the wrestling match is that Orlando has undergone a traditional male rite of passage, providing an established channel for the violence he has previously expressed by collaring Oliver in the opening scene. Yet aggression is the epitome of a rigid masculinity that Shakespeare characteristically condemns as too narrow a basis for identity. Orlando's aggressiveness is instantly rendered inappropriate by his falling in love. Moreover, his recourse to violence simply mirrors the technique of the tyrannical Duke Frederick. As it turns out, Orlando must give up violence in order to meet the "good father."

While Rosalind's confidante Celia provides the opportunity to talk about love, Orlando is accompanied by Adam, who serves a very different function since he is a living link to Orlando's father. The paternal inheritance blocked by Oliver is received indirectly from Adam when he offers the money "I sav'd under your father, / Which I did store to be my foster-nurse" [I. iii. 39-40]. The motif of nurturance implied by the "foster-nurse" image is continued as Orlando, through Adam's sudden collapse from lack of food, is led to Duke Senior's pastoral banquet. Treating this new situation as another trial of "the strength of my youth," Orlando imagines an all-or-nothing "adventure" [I. ii. 172, 177] similar to the wrestling match: "If this uncouth forest yield any thing savage, I will either be food for it, or bring it for food to thee" [II. vi. 6-8]. In act 2, scene 7, he enters with drawn sword. Unexpectedly finding a benevolent father figure, Orlando effects as gracefully as possible a transition from toughness to tenderness: "Let gentleness my strong enforcement be, / In the which hope I blush, and hide my sword" [II. vii. 118-19]. This display of nonviolence is the precondition for Orlando's recovery of patriarchal lineage. Duke Senior aids this recovery by his recognition of the father's reflection in the son and by his declaration of his own loving connection with Orlando's father [II. vii. 191-96]. (pp. 22-8)

The confirmation of Orlando's identity has the effect of a ritual blessing that makes this particular father-son relation the basis for social cohesion in general. There is much virtue in Orlando's "If":

ORL.    If ever you have look'd on better days,
      If ever been where bells have knoll'd to
        church,
      If ever sate at any good man's feast,
      If ever from your eyelids wip'd a tear,
      And know what 'tis to pity, and be pitied. . . .

DUKE S.  True is it that we have seen better days,
      And have with holy bell been knoll'd to
        church,
      And sat at good men's feasts, and wip'd our
        eyes
      Of drops that sacred pity hath engend'red.

                       [II. vii. 113-17, 120-23]

The liturgy of male utopia, ruthlessly undercut in *Love's Labor's Lost,* is here allowed to stand. Virgilian piety, founded on ideal father-son relations and evoked visually when, like Aeneas with Anchises, Orlando carries Adam on his back, can achieve what Navarre's academe with its spurious abstinence could not. Orlando's heroic language as he goes off to rescue Adam is as clumsy as any he uses in the poems to Rosalind, but whereas the play pokes fun at the love poetry, the expres-

sion of duty to Adam is not subject to irony: "Then but forbear your food a little while, / Whiles, like a doe, I go to find my fawn, / And give it food" [II. vii. 127-29]. We are invited simply to accept the doe-fawn metaphor that Orlando invokes for his obligation to reciprocate Adam's "pure love" [II. vii. 131].

Just as there is an unlimited supply of food in this scene, so there seems to be more than enough "pure love" to go around, Jaques excepted. Love is expressed in terms of food, and men gladly take on nurturant roles. Duke Senior's abundant provision of food and of "gentleness" creates an image of a self-sustaining patriarchal system. The men take over the traditional female prerogative of maternal nurturance, negatively defined by Jaques: "At first the infant, / Mewling and puking in the nurse's arms" [II. vii. 143-44]. Such discomfort has been purged from the men's nurturance as it is dramatized in this scene, which thus offers a new perspective on Duke Senior's very first speech in the play. We now see that it is the male feast, not the biting winter wind, that "feelingly persuades me what I am" [II. i. 11]. "Sweet are the uses of adversity" because, as Orlando discovers, adversity disappears when men's "gentleness" prevails, "translating the stubbornness of fortune / Into so quiet and sweet a style" [II. i. 12, 19-20]. This sweetness explains why "loving lords have put themselves into voluntary exile" with the duke and why "many young gentlemen flock to him every day" [I. i. 101-02, 117].

The idealized male enclave founded on "sacred pity" in act 2, scene 7, is not an isolated incident. The power of male pity extends beyond this scene to include the evil Oliver, who is threatened by a symbol of maternal nurturance made hostile by depletion: "A lioness, with udders all drawn dry" [IV. iii. 114] and "the suck'd and hungry lioness" [IV. iii. 126]. The motif of eating here creates a negative image that might disturb the comfortable pastoral banquet, but the lioness's intrusion is quickly ended. Responding with a kindness that can be traced back to his meeting with Duke Senior, Orlando rescues his brother: "But kindness, nobler ever than revenge, / And nature, stronger than his just occasion, / Made him give battle to the lioness" [IV. iii. 128-30]. Oliver's oral fulfillment follows: "my conversion / So sweetly tastes" [IV. iii. 136-37]. The tears "that sacred pity hath engend'red" [II. vii. 123] are reiterated by the brothers' reconciliation—"Tears our recountments had most kindly bath'd" [IV. iii. 140]—and their reunion confirmed by a recapitulation of the banquet scene: "he led me to the gentle Duke, / Who gave me fresh array and entertainment, / Committing me unto my brother's love" [IV. iii. 142-44]. Again the pattern of male reconciliation preceding love for women is seen in Oliver's confession of his desire to marry Celia [V. ii. 1-14] coming after his admission to the brotherhood.

The male community of act 2, scene 7, is also vindicated by the restoration of patriarchal normalcy in the play's final scene. In the end, as Rosalind's powers are fading, the relationship between Duke Senior and Orlando is reasserted and completed as the duke announces the inheritance to which marriage entitles Orlando: "A land itself at large, a potent dukedom" [V. iv. 169]. Like the "huswife Fortune" who "doth most mistake in her gifts to women" [I. ii. 31-2, 36], Rosalind plays her part by rehearsing the men in their political roles:

ROS.      You say, if I bring in your Rosalind,
           You will bestow her on Orlando here?
DUKE S.  That would I, had I kingdoms to give with
           her.

ROS.     And you say you will have her, when I bring
         her.
ORL.     That would I, were I of all kingdoms king.

                                                    [V. iv. 6-10]

The reference the two men make to kingdoms is shortly to be fulfilled, but this bounty is beyond Rosalind's power to give. For it is not her magic that produces the surprise entrance of Jaques de Boys with the news of Duke Senior's restoration. In completing the de Boys family reunion, the middle brother's appearance reverses the emblematic fate of the three sons destroyed by Charles the wrestler: "Yonder they lie, the poor old man, their father, making such pitiful dole over them that all the beholders take his part with weeping" [I. ii. 129-32]. The image of three de Boys sons reestablishes the proper generational sequence, ensuring continuity. (pp. 28-31)

[In] *As You Like It* the conservatism of comic form does not affect all characters equally. In the liberal opening out into the forest of Arden, both men and women are permitted an expansion of sexual identity that transcends restrictive gender roles. Just as Rosalind gains access to the traditional masculine attributes of strength and control through her costume, so Orlando gains access to the traditional female attributes of compassion and nurturance. However, the conservative countermovement built into comic strategy applies exclusively to Rosalind. Her possession of the male costume and of the power it symbolizes is only temporary. But Orlando does not have to give up the emotional enlargement he has experienced in the forest. Discussions of androgyny in *As You Like It* usually focus on Rosalind whereas in fact it is the men rather than the women who are the lasting beneficiaries of androgyny. It is Orlando, not Rosalind, who achieves a synthesis of attributes traditionally labeled masculine and feminine when he combines compassion and aggression in rescuing his brother from the lioness.

This selective androgyny demands an ambivalent response: it is a humanizing force for the men, yet it is based on the assumption that men have power over women. Because androgyny is available only to men, we are left with a paradoxical compatibility of androgyny with patriarchy, that is, benevolent patriarchy. In talking about male power in *As You Like It*, we must distinguish between two forms of patriarchy. The first and most obvious is the harsh, mean-spirited version represented by Oliver, who abuses primogeniture, and by Duke Frederick, who after usurping power holds on to it by arbitrary acts of suppression. Driven by greed, envy, suspicion, and power for power's sake, neither man can explain his actions. In an ironic demonstration of the consuming nature of evil, Duke Frederick expends his final rage against Oliver, who honestly protests: "I never lov'd my brother in my life" [III. i. 14]. In contrast to good men, bad men are incapable of forming alliances. Since Frederick's acts of banishment have now depopulated the court, he himself must enter the forest in order to seek the enemies so necessary to his existence [V. iv. 154-58]. But of course this patriarchal tyranny is a caricature and therefore harmless. Oliver and Frederick are exaggerated fairy-tale villains whose hardened characters are unable to withstand the wholesome atmosphere of the forest and instantly dissolve [IV. iii. 135-37; V. iv. 159-65]. The second, more serious version of patriarchy is the political structure headed by Duke Senior. To describe it, we seek adjectives like "benevolent," "humane," and "civilized." Yet we cannot leave it at that. A benevolent patriarchy still requires women to be subordinate, and Rosalind's final performance is her enactment of this subordination. (pp. 31-2)

[Rosalind] confronts her father in the final scene. [For her], paternal power is vigorously represented by Duke Senior and by the line of patriarchal authority established when Senior makes Orlando his heir. Festive celebration is now possible because a dependable, that is, patriarchal, social order is securely in place. It is Duke Senior's voice that legitimates the festive closure: "Play, music, and you brides and bridegrooms all, / With measure heap'd in joy, to th' measures fall" [V. iv. 178-79]. Orlando benefits from this social structure because . . . he has a solid political resource to offset the liability of a poetic convention that dictates male subservience. *As You Like It* achieves marital closure not by eliminating male ties but rather by strengthening them.

A further phasing out of Rosalind occurs in the Epilogue when it is revealed that she is male: "If I were a woman I would kiss as many of you as had beards that pleas'd me" [Epilogue, 18-19]. This explicit breaking of theatrical illusion forces us to reckon with the fact of an all-male cast. (pp. 33-4)

The convention of males playing female roles gives men the opportunity to imagine sex-role fluidity and flexibility. Built into the conditions of performance is the potential for male acknowledgment of a "feminine self" and thus for male transcendence of a narrow masculinity. In the particular case of *As You Like It*, the all-male cast provides a theatrical counterpart for the male community at Duke Senior's banquet in act 2, scene 7. This theatrical dimension reinforces the conservative effect of male androgyny within the play. Acknowledgment of the feminine within the male is one thing, the acknowledgment of individual women another: the latter does not automatically follow from the former. In the boy-actor motif, woman is a metaphor for the male discovery of the feminine within himself, of those qualities suppressed by a masculinity strictly defined as aggressiveness. Once the tenor of the metaphor has been attained, the vehicle can be discarded—just as Rosalind is discarded. The sense of the patriarchal ending in *As You Like It* is that male androgyny is affirmed whereas female "liberty" in the person of Rosalind is curtailed.

There is, finally, a studied ambiguity about heterosexual versus homoerotic feeling in the play, Shakespeare allowing himself to have it both ways. The Epilogue is heterosexual in its bringing together of men and women: "and I charge you, O men, for the love you bear to women (as I perceive by your simp'ring, none of you hates them), that between you and the women the play may please" [Epilogue, 14-17]. The "simp'ring" attributed to men in their response to women is evoked in a good-natured jocular spirit; yet the tone conveys discomfort as well. In revealing the self-sufficient male acting company, the Epilogue also offers the counterimage of male bonds based on the exclusion of women.

Though he is shown hanging love poems on trees only after achieving atonement with Rosalind's father, Orlando never tries . . . to avoid women. The social structure of *As You Like It*, in which political power is vested in male bonds, can include heterosexual love because marriage becomes a way of incorporating women since Rosalind is complicit in her assimilation by patriarchal institutions. However, in spite of the disarming of Rosalind, resistance to women remains. It is as though asserting the priority of relations between men over relations between men and women is not enough, as though a fall-back position is needed. The Epilogue is, in effect, a second ending that provides further security against women by preserving on stage the image of male ties in their pure form with women absent. Not only are women to be subordinate; they can, if necessary, be imagined as nonexistent. Rosalind's art does not, as is sometimes suggested, coincide with Shakespeare's: Shakespeare uses his art to take away Rosalind's female identity and thereby upstages her claim to magic power.

We can see the privileged status accorded to male bonds by comparing Shakespeare's treatment of same-sex relations for men and for women. Men originally divided are reunited as in the instance of Oliver and Orlando, but women undergo the reverse process. Rosalind and Celia are initially inseparable: "never two ladies lov'd as they do" [I. i. 112]; "whose loves / Are dearer than the natural bond of sisters" [I. ii. 275-76]; "And whereso'er we went, like Juno's swans, / Still we went coupled and inseparable" [I. iii. 75-6]; and "thou and I am one. / Shall we be sund'red? shall we part, sweet girl? / No, let my father seek another heir" [I. iii. 97-9]. Yet the effect of the play is to separate them by transferring their allegiance to husbands. Celia ceases to be a speaking character at the end of act 4, her silence coinciding with her new role as fiancée. The danger of female bonding is illustrated when Shakespeare diminishes Rosalind's absolute control by mischievously confronting her with the unanticipated embarrassment of Phebe's love for her. Rosalind is of course allowed to devise an escape from the pressure of this undesirable entanglement, but it is made clear in the process that such ardor is taboo and that the authorized defense against it is marriage. "And so am I for no woman," Rosalind insists [V. ii. 88]. A comparable prohibition is not announced against male friendship.

In conclusion, we must ask: what is Shakespeare's relation to the sexual politics of *As You Like It*? Is he taking an ironic and critical stance toward the patriarchal solution of his characters, or is he heavily invested in this solution himself? I think there are limits to Shakespeare's critical awareness in this play. The sudden conversions of Oliver and Duke Frederick have a fairytale quality that Shakespeare clearly intends as an aspect of the wish fulfillment to which he calls attention in the play's title. Similarly, Jaques's commentary in the final scene is a deliberate foil to the neatness of the ending that allows Shakespeare as well as Jaques a modicum of distance. However, in fundamental respects Shakespeare appears to be implicated in the fantasy he has created for his characters. (pp. 34-7)

We have too easily accepted the formulation that says that Shakespeare in the mature history plays concentrates on masculine development whereas in the mature festive comedies he gives women their due by allowing them to play the central role. *As You Like It* is primarily a defensive action against female power rather than a celebration of it. [In addition], Shakespeare portrays an ideal male community based on "sacred pity." This idealized vision of relationships between men can be seen as sentimental and unrealistic, but . . . Shakespeare is here thoroughly engaged and endorses the idealization. These two elements—female vitality kept manageable and male power kept loving—provided a resolution that at this particular moment was "As Shakespeare Liked It." (p. 37)

> Peter Erickson, *"Sexual Politics and Social Structure in 'As You Like It',"* in his Patriarchal Structures in Shakespeare's Drama, *University of California Press, 1985, pp. 15-38.*

---

## ADDITIONAL BIBLIOGRAPHY

Allen, Michael J. B. "Jaques against the Seven Ages of the Proclan Man." *Modern Language Quarterly* 42, No. 4 (December 1981): 331-46.

Analyzes Jaques's "Seven Ages of Man" speech (II. vii. 139-66) as a familiar antithesis precluding notions of nihilism and absurdity. Allen suggests that the portraits in the speech explicitly pervert the dominant astrological characteristics of each of the seven ages, painting a philosophical picture of "a sunless man in a sunless world."

"Characters in 'As You Like It': Rosalind and Orlando, before Their Meeting in the Forest." *The Athenaeum*, No. 872 (13 July 1844): 647-49.

Study of the portrayal of Rosalind and Orlando from Act I, Scene i to Act III, Scene ii, focusing on both Rosalind's "noble and tender graces" and the trials and incidents that reveal Orlando's inherent qualities.

Babb, Lawrence. "The Malcontent Types." In his *The Elizabethan Malady: A Study of Melancholia in English Literature from 1580 to 1642*, pp. 73-101. East Lansing: Michigan State College Press, 1951.

Overview of the "epidemic of melancholy" in Elizabethan and Jacobean literature, touching on Jaques, who is described here as "the best example in the drama of the malcontent in the role of philosophic critic."

Beckman, Margaret Boerner. "The Figure of Rosalind in *As You Like It*." *Shakespeare Quarterly* 29, No. 1 (Winter 1978): 44-51.

Argues that in *As You Like It* Shakespeare depicts humanity's "possible perfection" rather than its "certain imperfection" by presenting that perfection as a reconciliation of opposites. Beckman maintains that Rosalind is Shakespeare's chief instrument in presenting this view, for "to know Rosalind is to know that opposites can be reconciled."

Bennett, Josephine W. "Jaques' Seven Ages." *The Shakespeare Association Bulletin* XVIII, No. 4 (October 1943): 168-74.

Examines possible sources for Jaques's "Seven Ages of Man" speech at II. vii. 139-66. Bennett establishes a close verbal parallel between Jaques's speech and the *Onomasticon* of Julius Pollux and argues that Shakespeare drew on this work, either directly or indirectly. She concludes by rejecting the view that Jaques's speech is an expression of Shakespeare's personal disillusion, preferring to see it as "a set of rhetorical commonplaces such as a conventional malcontent of no great intellectual stature might offer."

Bennett, Robert B. "The Reform of a Malcontent: Jaques and the Meaning of *As You Like It*." *Shakespeare Studies* IX (1976): 183-204.

Postulates Shakespeare's dramatic intention in including a malcontent in the romantic world of Arden. Bennett regards Jaques as an essentially benign spirit whose presence in Arden provides both a needed balance in the forest-court debate and a tartness to counter the preciousness of the pastoral setting.

Berry, Ralph. "No Exit from Arden." *The Modern Language Review* 66, No. 1 (January 1971): 11-20.

Discusses the structure of *As You Like It* as a synthesis of romance and antiromance, in which overt hints that Arden is no paradise, such as the play's "discordant music," complement the evolving forest-court debate. Berry approaches the court versus country issue in terms of the larger theme of the romantic ideal challenged by realism, commonsense, and satire.

Birney, Alice Lotvin. "Jaques: The Pharmakos Railer of Comedy." In her *Satiric Catharsis in Shakespeare: A Theory of Dramatic Structure*, pp. 79-98. Berkeley: University of California Press, 1973.

Applies a semi-Aristotelian hypothesis of satiric catharsis to *As You Like It*, examining the tradition of the satirist as a kind of physician trying to cure society's moral diseases. Birney sees Jaques as such a *pharmakos* who fails to convert anyone to his own melancholic satire.

Bradford, Alan Taylor. "Jaques' Distortion of the Seven-Ages Paradigm." *Shakespeare Quarterly* 27, No. 2 (Spring 1976): 171-76.

Evaluates Shakespeare's alteration of astrological models in Jaques's "Seven Ages of Man" speech at II. vii. 139-66. Bradford sees the distorted paradigm operating as a "subtextual metaphor," reinforcing Jaques's view that life is without meaning, purpose, or value.

Brissenden, Alan. "The Dance in *As You Like It* and *Twelfth Night*." *Cahiers Elisabethains*, No. 13 (April 1978): 25-34.

Examines Shakespeare's use of dance in *As You Like It*. Noticing the combination of joy and solemnity following the marriages in Act V, Scene iv, Brissenden posits the likelihood of the couples dancing a patterned and harmonious pavan. Jaques's not joining the dance—he is "for other than dancing measures" (V. iv. 193)— is interpreted as further evidence of this character's deeply rooted melancholy.

Brown, John Russell. "*As You Like It*." In his *Shakespeare's Dramatic Style*, pp. 72-103. London: Heinemann, 1970.

Overview of several scenes in *As You Like It*. Brown suggests, "Incidental variety is related to a consistent dramatic development, and between each scene unifying elements can be seen shaping the play as a whole." He supports his argument by reviewing the language, entrances, exits, character groupings, and movements at I. ii. 216-89, IV. i. 123-218, and V. iv. 108-50.

Carroll, William C. "'Forget to Be a Woman'." In his *The Metamorphoses of Shakespearean Comedy*, pp. 103-37. Princeton: Princeton University Press, 1985.

Includes a discussion of "real and apparent" transformations in *As You Like It*, primarily those involving Rosalind. Carroll explores the direct and indirect influence of Ovid's *Metamorphoses* on selected incidents in the play, such as Rosalind's playacting, the transformations that occur in the marriages of the final scene, and Shakespeare's emphasis on the mutability of things.

Cole, Howard C. "The Moral Vision of *As You Like It*." *College Literature* III, No. 1 (Winter 1975): 17-32.

Examines the moral vision of *As You Like It*. Cole explores Shakespeare's use of Jaques and Touchstone to test the conventions of his source, concluding that the dramatist "at once emphasizes and undercuts the romantic conventions" never questioned in Thomas Lodge's *Rosalynde*. In the end, Cole suggests, Shakespeare begins to establish his own moral vision "that deals far more honestly with the inconvenient facts of human experience than [do] his philosophers' flights."

Collie, Rosalie L. "Perspectives on Pastoral: Romance, Comic, and Tragic." In her *Shakespeare's Living Art*, pp. 243-83. Princeton: Princeton University Press, 1974.

Examination of literary forms, conventions, and genres in *As You Like It*, stressing Shakespeare's adherence to, modification of, and departure from selected aspects of the pastoral mode. Collie is particularly concerned with demonstrating Shakespeare's reliance on "traditional implications within the mode" that remain valuable to the playwright "in spite of [their] manifest weakness."

Daley, A. Stuart. "Where Are the Woods in *As You Like It*?" *Shakespeare Quarterly* 34, No. 2 (Summer 1983): 172-80.

Warns that exaggerating the sylvan quality of *As You Like It* makes it difficult to understand the play as it was understood by its Elizabethan audience. Daley distinguishes between two Arden settings, one dark and perilous, the other characterized by sunny fields and a murmuring stream. He maintains that, in suggesting a "plenitude of classical, Biblical, and Christian symbols," the two Ardens function as academies where self-knowledge is taught by discourse, example, and experience.

Doebler, John. "Orlando: Athlete of Virtue." *Shakespeare Survey* 26 (1973): 111-17.

Historical assessment of Orlando's maturation. Doebler focuses chiefly on the sources and meaning of Orlando's bout with Charles in Act I, Scene ii, comparing his strength with that of Hercules and his victory with David's defeat of Goliath.

Doran, Madeleine. "'Yet am I inland bred'." *Shakespeare Quarterly* XV, No. 2 (Spring 1964): 99-114.

Detailed analysis of Orlando's epithet "Yet am I inland bred" at II. vii. 91-7 of *As You Like It*. Doran concludes that, as a man "inland bred," Orlando identifies himself with the other exiles in Arden who await their return to their proper places in the city or court, after it is purged of its corruption.

Draper, John W. "Shakespeare's Orlando Innamorato." *Modern Language Quarterly* 2, No. 1 (March 1941): 179-84.

Psychological evaluation of Orlando's physical humor and astral complexion which concludes that, because of his succession of pure luck, Orlando must be a sanguine type under Jupiter's influence. The physical effects of this type—strength and longevity—are seen by Draper to present "in the end the placid poise of a mind at peace with the world."

———. *Stratford to Dogberry: Studies in Shakespeare's Earlier Plays*. Pittsburgh: University of Pittsburgh Press, 1961, 320 p.

Useful collection of essays on the historical, intellectual, and social background of Shakespeare's early plays. Draper treats *As You Like It* in a chapter on "Country and Court"; he remarks on the lamentable fate and condition of Adam and discusses the comic irony in the love-making of Orlando and Rosalind.

Draper, R. P. "Shakespeare's Pastoral Comedy." *Etudes Anglaises* XI, No. 1 (January-March 1958): 1-17.

Examines the pastoral elements—chiefly classical—in *As You Like It*, arguing that it "almost seems a mistake" to call the play a pastoral, for "in so doing we range it with a genre that is noted . . . for its fantasy, lyrical sweetness, and sophisticated unreality." Draper maintains that, unlike the traditional pastoral, *As You Like It* is a means of "exploring instead of escaping from life."

Faber, M. D. "On Jaques: Psychoanalytic Remarks, Parts I and II." *The University Review* XXXVI, Nos. 2 and 3 (October 1969-March 1970): 89-96, 179-82.

Psychoanalytic study of Jaques, concentrating on his behavior in Act II of *As You Like It*. Faber regards Jaques as an oral-erotic who projects irrational, retaliatory aggression onto Duke Senior. In the second part of his study, Faber takes up Jaques's attitude toward "the feminine principle," connecting his fear of being wounded by a father or authority figure with his fear of becoming regressively involved with his mother.

Farmer, Richard. An extract from "*An Essay on the Learning of Shakespeare* (1767)." In *Shakespeare: The Critical Heritage, Vol. 5, 1765-1774*, edited by Brian Vickers, pp. 259-79. London: Routledge & Kegan Paul, 1979.

Maintains that Shakespeare—"no hunter of manuscripts"—drew only on printed texts for the story of *As You Like It*.

Forker, Charles R. "All the World's a Stage: Multiple Perspectives in Arden." *Iowa State Journal of Research* 54, No. 3 (February 1980): 421-30.

Comments on four sets of contrasting, complementary, and overlapping perspectives in *As You Like It*: Nature versus Grace, Life versus Art, Time versus Timelessness, and Subjectivity versus Objectivity. Forker discerns in these perspectives "the thematic fullness and complexity" of Shakespeare's pastoralism, pointing to "a comprehensiveness of vision characteristic of Shakespeare's mature comic art."

Fortin, René E. "'Tongues in Trees': Symbolic Patterns in *As You Like It*." *Texas Studies in Literature and Language* XIV, No. 4 (Winter 1973): 569-82.

Uses *As You Like It* to argue against the notion that we should not expect much meaning or significance in Shakespeare's comedies. Focusing on Act II, Scene i and Act IV, Scene iii, Fortin claims that Shakespeare has subtly transformed his sources to introduce "images . . . that charge these key scenes with symbolic significance." The critic interprets these images as part of a process in which classical and Christian images are "atoned," thereby enriching the play's meaning.

Goldsmith, Robert Hillis. "Touchstone: Critic in Motley." *PMLA* LXVIII, No. 4 (September 1953): 884-95.

Discusses Touchstone's dramatic function in *As You Like It*. Positing Shakespeare's indebtedness to the Italian theater for certain features of his play, Goldsmith compares Touchstone's burlesque of love to the *zanni* of Italian comedy. In his conclusion, he stresses the clown's fundamental wisdom, which allows him to function as "the critic inside the play."

———. "Shakespeare's Wise Fools." In his *Wise Fools in Shakespeare*, pp. 47-67. East Lansing: Michigan State University Press, 1955.

Claims that the discrepancy between Touchstone's portrayal as a simple fool in Act I and as a wise, ironical fool in Act V stems from Shakespeare's having written the part to suit the temper of a particular actor. Alternatively, Goldsmith suggests, Touchstone may have disguised his sophisticated wit in Act I out of prudent regard for Duke Frederick's authority.

Grennan, Eamon. "Telling the Trees from the Wood: Some Details of *As You Like It* Re-examined." *English Literary Renaissance* 7, No. 2 (Spring 1977): 197-206.

Scrutinizes details in *As You Like It* relating to its pastoralism, examining Shakespeare's possible debt to Edmund Spenser's Shepheardes *Calender* and *Faerie Queene*, and his likely links with Christopher Marlowe. Grennan credits these and other writers with helping Shakespeare to "greatly extend and enrich the limited nature of his major source."

Halio, Jay L., and Millard, Barbara C. *"As You Like It": An Annotated Bibliography, 1940-1980*. New York: Garland Publishing, 1985, 744 p.

Comprehensive listing, with descriptive notes, of 1,584 items of published commentary on *As You Like It*, chiefly from the period 1940 to 1980. The entries are organized in sections to reflect a variety of scholarly concerns, including aesthetic criticism, sources and background, textual studies, and performance criticism.

Harrison, G. B. "An Essay on Elizabethan Melancholy." In *Melancholike Humours*, by Nicholas Breton, edited by G. B. Harrison, pp. 49-89. London: The Scholartis Press, 1929.

Early and influential attempt to define the Elizabethan conception of melancholy. Harrison touches on Jaques in *As You Like It* as an example of a complex state of melancholy which combines an unwilling agnosticism, a morbid fear of death, the weariness of travel, and excessive sensitivity in a brutal world.

Hart, John A. "*As You Like It*: The Worlds of Fortune and Nature." In his *Dramatic Structure in Shakespeare's Romantic Comedies*, pp. 81-97. Pittsburgh: Carnegie-Mellon University Press, 1980.

Overview of the contrasting worlds in *As You Like It*. Hart examines the court and the forest, noting differences in the attitudes of the dominant characters in each world, significant differences in the settings, and behavior changes among those figures who exist in both worlds. The critic concludes that Duke Frederick's courtly world is shown to exist not so much for itself as to help us understand its successor.

Hassel, R. Chris, Jr. "'Most Faining': Foolish Wits and Wise Fools in *As You Like It*." In his *Faith and Folly in Shakespeare's Romantic Comedies*, pp. 110-48. Athens: The University of Georgia Press, 1980.

Examines *As You Like It* as "a banquet of the follies of human perception and human behavior." Hassel explores Shakespeare's treatment of the Erasmian and Pauline theme of the wisdom of folly, showing that—through the folly of the fools, the lovers, and the play itself—*As You Like It* probes the transcendent realities of feeling and truth beneath human conventions and rituals.

Hieatt, Charles W. "The Quality of Pastoral in *As You Like It*." *Genre* VII, No. 2 (June 1974): 164-82.

Maintains that the variety and complexity of Renaissance pastorals have been neglected in *As You Like It* studies. Hieatt elucidates the play's connection with the special form of "pastoral romance." He identifies a variety of combinations of pastoral conventions in the comedy, especially those involving the hero/shepherd motif, and determines that the irony of the Arden scenes is "alien to the pastoral mid-section of romance."

Howarth, Herbert. "1599: The Event and the Art." In his *The Tiger's Heart: Eight Essays on Shakespeare*, pp. 78-93. London: Chatto & Windus, 1970.

Hypothesizes that the taxation episode in *As You Like It*, Act II, Scene vii, is a response to the Bishops' Edict of 1599 banning

publication of certain types of satire. Howarth argues for the timeliness of the episode and the play, suggesting that "Shakespeare not only gave reasons why poets should satirize and their masters and victims should listen, but wrote an ingenious illustration of a new, subtler satire."

Hutchings, W. "'Exits and Entrances': Ways In and Out of Arden." *The Critical Quarterly* 21, No. 3 (Autumn 1979): 3-13.

Useful review essay focusing on recent studies of pastoralism in *As You Like It* criticism. Hutchings comments on the work of seventeen essayists who more or less treat Arden as "a landscape where objects may be held up for our contemplation."

Hyland, Peter. "Shakespeare's Heroines: Disguise in the Romantic Comedies." *Ariel: A Review of International English Literature* 9, No. 2 (April 1978): 23-39.

Examination of Shakespeare's disguised heroines which focuses specifically on their special intimacy with the audience and on the opportunity they provide the playwright to manipulate spectator response. Hyland regards the disguised Rosalind as both the creator and stage manager of much of the action in *As You Like It*, drawing the audience into the play and aligning its point of view with her own.

Iser, Wolfgang. "The Dramatization of Double Meaning in Shakespeare's *As You Like It*." *Theatre Journal* 35, No. 3 (October 1983): 307-32.

Explores the semiotics of *As You Like It*, emphasizing the interrelation of the pastoral and Arcadian worlds as well as the "clearly marked boundary" between them. Iser sees the play as based on the principle of doubling: the characters who pass from the court to the country are each split into two persons, acting out the difference between what they were and what they have become.

Kellogg, A. O. "Jaques." In his *Shakespeare's Delineations of Insanity, Imbecility, and Suicide*, pp. 87-102. New York: Hurd and Houghton, 1866.

Curious character study of Jaques by a staff physician of the State Lunatic Asylum of Utica, New York. Kellogg argues that Shakespeare intended to represent in Jaques "a certain delicate shade of incipient melancholia," adding that when "the disease becomes fairly fixed, the . . . melancholic is the greatest of egoists."

Kelly, Thomas. "Shakespeare's Romantic Heroes: Orlando Reconsidered." *Shakespeare Quarterly* XXIV, No. 1 (Winter 1973): 12-24.

Considers Orlando "a breed apart" from Shakespeare's usual romantic heroes, whom we are inclined to regard as peculiarly inept and slightly ridiculous. Kelly regards Orlando not only as generally self-possessed and able to control events in *As You Like It*, but also as demonstrating a wisdom that sets him apart as a "romantic hero of a new stamp."

Kernan, Alvin. "The English Satyr, 'The Tamberlaine of Vice'." In his *The Cankered Muse: Satire of the English Renaissance*, pp. 81-140. New Haven: Yale University Press, 1959.

Proposing that satire is a distinct artistic genre with a number of marked characteristics, Kernan examines Jaques as the embodiment of "the more twisted and diabolic features of the [English sixteenth-century] satyr." Kernan supports his claim by citing examples of Jaques's "exaggerated" melancholy and "extravagant pessimism."

Knight, Charles. Introduction to *As You Like It*, by William Shakespeare. In *The Comedies, Histories, Tragedies, and Poems of William Shakspere*, second edition, edited by Charles Knight, pp. 247-65. London: Charles Knight, 1842.

Surveys the sources of *As You Like It*, praising Shakespeare's adaptation of "a pastoral replete with quaintness, and antithesis, and pedantry" into "an imaginative drama, in which . . . the highest poetry appears to be as essentially natural as the most familiar gossip."

Knowles, Richard. "Myth and Type in *As You Like It*." *ELH* 33, No. 1 (March 1966): 1-22.

Mythical reading of *As You Like It* which emphasizes the play's "seriousness of mythological allusion" and the influence of myths on the audience's "comic apprehension" of the drama. Knowles argues that Ovidian and other allusions in the play cause the audience to react to "the collective fantasy of heroic success," revealing to them a "time-tested pattern of life as we would like it."

Kronenfeld, Judy Z. "Social Rank and the Pastoral Ideals of *As You Like It.*" *Shakespeare Quarterly* 29, No. 3 (Summer 1978): 333-48.

Approaches *As You Like It* "in the context of pastoral's potential for reconciling the different parts of society." Kronenfeld focuses on Duke Senior and Adam, regarding the former as a model of pastoral virtue who nevertheless enters into an exploitative relationship with the forest, the latter as an unsurpassed model of pastoral virtue. According to Kronenfeld, these two portraits suggest not that Shakespeare intended to "unmask" pastoral, but that he wanted to put pressure on its social vision in order to revivify it.

Kuhn, Maura Slattery. "Much Virtue in *If.*" *Shakespeare Quarterly* 28, No. 1 (Winter 1977): 40-50.

Close analysis of the staging, decorum, text, and dramatic recognition of Act V, Scene iv of *As You Like It*. Kuhn argues that Shakespeare's extensive use of "If" is a springboard that "propels the quester from the premise to a conclusion beyond." She adds that "If" permits the audience to yield its disbelief and therefore be pleased, for by defining the condition and shaping the consequence, "If saves the game."

Laroque, François. "No Assembly but Horn-Beasts—A Structural Study of Arden's Animal Farm." *Cahiers Elisabethains*, No. 11 (April 1977): 55-62.

Structural reading of *As You Like It*. Laroque concentrates on the physical, spatial, and metaphorical conventions of the animal images in the play, discerning in the ox and the deer Shakespeare's subversion of the pastoral model and its ideals.

Latham, Agnes. Introduction to *As You Like It*, by William Shakespeare, edited by Agnes Latham, pp. ix-xcv. The Arden Edition of the Works of William Shakespeare, edited by Harold F. Brooks and Harold Jenkins. London: Methuen, 1975.

Valuable introduction to the critical and historical issues surrounding *As You Like It*, containing brief surveys and summaries of the transmission of the text, its date, major plot sources, principal characters and themes, and an overview of the play's stage history.

Latimer, Elizabeth Wormeley. "*As You Like It.*" In her *Familiar Talks on Some of Shakspeare's Comedies*, pp. 231-87. Boston: Roberts Brothers, 1886.

Scene-by-scene commentary on *As You Like It*, touching on such issues as characterization, plot development, and motivation. Latimer is chiefly interested in Jaques and Rosalind; she finds the former's melancholy to be "simply discontent born of satiety" and the latter's pleading with her uncle in Act I, Scene iii "very beautiful."

Mares, F. H. "Viola and Other Transvestist Heroines in Shakespeare's Comedies." In *Stratford Papers, 1965-67*, edited by B. A. W. Jackson, pp. 96-109. Hamilton, Ontario: McMaster University Press, 1969.

Studies the girl-boy disguise as a special class of the disguise convention popular on the Elizabethan stage. Mares discusses Rosalind in *As You Like It*, who he claims, unlike Viola in *Twelfth Night*, "positively enjoys her disguise, flaunts it, [and] exploits its possibilities."

Martz, William J. "Rosalind and Incremental Development of Character in Comedy." In his *Shakespeare's Universe of Comedy*, pp. 84-99. New York: David Lewis, 1971.

Explores the development of Rosalind's character as "incremental in a manner appropriate to the purposes of comedy." Martz traces the evolution of Rosalind's experience from romantic to imaginative love, to loneliness and longing, to the wooing process as self-discovery, to the "lyric wonder of love," and finally to love as an earnest passion.

Masefield, John. "*As You Like It.*" In his *William Shakespeare*, pp. 93-4. London: William Heinemann, 1954.

Brief introduction to *As You Like It*, suggesting that, "as Rosalind is the play," the work was written "apparently for the triumph of some . . . boy-actor, a child of perhaps thirteen." Masefield describes the play as "the usual Shakespearean whirligig of Time," populated by an "odd and mixed assembly" in which Jaques stands out for his wit and grace of mind.

McFarland, Thomas. "For Other Than for Dancing Measures: The Complications of *As You Like It.*" In his *Shakespeare's Pastoral Comedy*, pp. 98-121. Chapel Hill: The University of North Carolina Press, 1972.

Proposes that *As You Like It* "involves the first massive assault of the forces of bitterness and alienation upon the pastoral vision of Shakespeare, and its action glances off the dark borders of tragedy." McFarland focuses on Arden's pastoral "complications"—its disharmony of verbal duels, tree carving, hunting, and so on—as evidence that the forest is less than the pastoral ideal. He considers these complications parallels to the dark tone and action of the Cain-and-Abel situations of Act I, preventing even Hymen's song from completely eradicating the play's nearly tragic tone.

Mincoff, Marco. "What Shakespeare Did to *Rosalynde.*" *Shakespeare Jahrbuch* 96 (1960): 78-89.

Careful study of Shakespeare's adaptation of Thomas Lodge's *Rosalynde*. Noting Shakespeare's downplaying of the pastoral atmosphere in *As You Like It*, Mincoff minimizes the importance of this aspect of the play. He also comments on Shakespeare's structural alterations, arguing that they provide smooth, swift action without breaks, permitting concurrent treatment of the various courtships.

Morris, Harry. "*As You Like It:* Et in Arcadia Ego." *Shakespeare Quarterly* XXVI, No. 3 (Summer 1975): 269-75.

Assesses the extent of the sombre element in *As You Like It* which Shakespeare used to counterpoint the vitality underlying Arden. Morris observes the play's images of death, decay, and time, concluding that Shakespeare introduced these dark elements among joy to reinforce the elegiac qualities of the concept *et in Arcadia ego*, "I am in Arcadia."

Nearing, Homer, Jr. "The Penaltie of Adam." *Modern Language Notes* LXII, No. 5 (May 1947): 336-38.

Historical and textual study of the meaning of "the penalty of Adam" comment by the Duke at II. i. 5 of *As You Like It*. Nearing avers that the phrase refers to Adam and Eve's knowledge of good and evil received through eating the forbidden fruit in Genesis 3. He adds that Duke Senior and his co-mates do not feel this penalty "because they are no longer exposed to the insidious flattery and intrigue of the court."

Nevo, Ruth. "Existence in Arden." In her *Comic Transformations in Shakespeare*, pp. 180-99. London and New York: Methuen & Co., 1980.

Treats *As You Like It* as a "meta-comedy," in which the underlying principles of Shakespearean practice "are drawn out for all to see and turned into the comic material itself." Arguing that the play exhibits a looser and more casual handling of the "orthodox" or "Terentian" formula than *Twelfth Night*, Nevo identifies its comic disposition in Shakespeare's presentation of the forest as a pastoral polemic of contraries.

Palmer, D. J. "*As You Like It* and the Idea of Play." *The Critical Quarterly* 13, No. 3 (Autumn 1971): 234-45.

Studies *As You Like It* as a demonstration of humanity's natural propensity for play. Defining play as "a civilizing impulse to create a better world," Palmer traces in Shakespeare's comedy a series of forest encounters presented within an apparently timeless realm, where narrative progression is suspended and the mating game becomes the principal concern of most of the characters.

Rea, John D. "Jaques in Praise of Folly." *Modern Philology* XVII, No. 8 (December 1919): 465-69.

Discusses Shakespeare's adaptation in *As You Like It* of Thomas Lodge's *Rosalynde*. Rea asserts that Shakespeare's addition of

Jaques to the characters may be traced directly to the dramatist's reading of Erasmus's *Praise of Folly.*

Ridley, M. R. *"As You Like It."* In his *Shakespeare's Plays: A Commentary,* pp. 121-24. London: J. M. Dent, 1937.
    Brief assessment of the merits of *As You Like It,* touching on aspects of the play that evidence "a period of rest and relaxation in Shakespeare's dramatic career." Ridley admires the play's "peculiar genial warmth," attributing this quality to the fact that, apart from Duke Frederick, Oliver, and Phebe, "there is not a character in the play who is not good-hearted."

Rossi, L. "As You Like It." In his *Side-Lights on Shakspere,* with E. M. Courbould, pp. 137-65. London: Swan Sonnenschein, 1897.
    Introductory survey of *As You Like It,* concentrating on characterization, dialogue, dramatic structure, and textual "inconsistencies." Rossi ranks *As You Like It* among Shakespeare's "best and brightest comedies," but unfavorably compares the conclusion's "sense of incompletion" with the last scenes of *The Merchant of Venice* and *Much Ado about Nothing.*

Salingar, Leo. *Shakespeare and the Traditions of Comedy.* Cambridge: Cambridge University Press, 1974, 356 p.
    Presents the history of Shakespearean comedy as a dramatic form. Salingar provides many passing references to *As You Like It,* and he discusses in the last chapter, "An Elizabethan Playwright," the debates, songs, conversations, and reportings of meetings which occur frequently in the play.

Scott, W. I. D. "Jaques—The Involutional." In his *Shakespeare's Melancholics,* pp. 61-72. London: Mills and Boon, 1962.
    Psychoanalytical examination of Jaques as an "involutional"—a lonely, introverted character engaged with the spiritual side of man's nature. Scott follows Jungian theory in describing Jaques's melancholy as "his persona covering deeper layers of the ego." Later, the critic applies Freudian techniques in analyzing the dialogue between Jaques and Orlando in Act II, Scene ii; here he determines that Jaques represents Orlando's super-ego—his critical father-substitute—from whom the hero hopes to derive a logical basis for love.

Shaw, John. "Fortune and Nature in *As You Like It.*" *Shakespeare Quarterly* VI, No. 1 (Winter 1955): 45-50.
    Argues that beneath *As You Like It*'s "gay romancing" there is "a basic philosophic strife between Fortune and Nature" that affects both character and plot. Shaw discerns a resolution to the conflict when Fortune is mocked from her wheel at the end of the play, allowing the gifts of the world to be bestowed on the deserving.

Smith, James. *"As You Like It."* *Scrutiny* IX, No. 1 (June 1940): 9-32.
    Contends that *As You Like It* is both unsentimental and unromantic, and that it therefore provides both a fitting preparation for Shakespeare's later problem plays and a close connection with the later tragedies, especially *Hamlet.*

Stoll, Elmer Edgar. "Jaques, and the Antiquaries." *Modern Language Notes* LIV, No. 2 (February 1939): 79-85.
    Stoll's spirited defense of his 1906 study of Jaques as a "malcontent," prompted by O. J. Campbell's argument that this term should not be applied to Jaques (see excerpts above, 1906 and 1935). Stoll adds little to his original thesis; rather, his defense is primarily a diatribe against purely historical—here called "antiquarian"—criticism of *As You Like It.*

Taylor, Donn Ervin. "'Try in Time in Despite of a Fall': Time and Occasion in *As You Like It.*" *Texas Studies in Literature and Language* 24, No. 2 (Summer 1982): 121-36.
    Investigates Shakespeare's depiction of time in *As You Like It.* Refuting those critics who contend that Arden is either timeless or a place where time is subjective, Taylor maintains that Shakespeare portrays time as an objective phenomenon, independent of both the individual characters' perception of it and the place in which it is perceived.

Taylor, Gary. "Touchstone's Butterwomen." *The Review of English Studies* XXXII, No. 126 (May 1981): 187-93.
    Close historical evaluation of Touchstone's remark at III. ii. 96-8: "I'll rhyme you so eight years together. . . . It is the right butterwomen's rank to market." Taylor contends that Touchstone is here unfavorably comparing Orlando's verse with the "crowding lines of voluble, foul-mouthed, lascivious, repetitive, ignorant marketwomen trotting to market. . . ."

Thorndike, A. H. "The Relation of 'As You Like It' to Robin Hood Plays." *The Journal of English and Germanic Philology* IV, No. 1 (1901): 59-69.
    Compares *As You Like It* with a selection of early Robin Hood plays, citing evidence of Shakespeare's indebtedness to these works for the "out-of-doors atmosphere" of his comedy.

Toliver, Harold E. "Shakespeare's Inner Plays and the Social Contract." In his *Pastoral Forms and Attitudes,* pp. 82-115. Berkeley: University of California Press, 1971.
    Includes a discussion of Shakespeare's harmonizing of social disorder in *As You Like It* by means of "satire, irony, and marked participation in opposites." Toliver argues that the forced integration of the lovers into the forest's social mixture enables them to rise above their egoistic natures and discover an "oppositional harmony," thus making way for the marriage rite and its "implicitly multilayered social contract."

Traci, Philip. "*As You Like It:* Homosexuality in Shakespeare's Play." *CLA Journal* XXV, No. 1 (September 1981): 91-105.
    Investigates the diversity of sexual preferences in *As You Like It,* focusing on the element of homosexuality in the play. Traci maintains that Rosalind's multiple identities—reinforced and enlarged by the fact that her original portrayal on the stage was by a young, probably effeminate, boy—suggests that homosexuality and pederasty are among the diverse sexual preferences Shakespeare is here exploring.

Turner, Frederick. "*As You Like It:* 'Subjective,' 'Objective,' and 'Natural' Time." In his *Shakespeare and the Nature of Time: Moral and Philosophical Themes in Some Plays and Poems of William Shakespeare,* pp. 28-44. Oxford: At the Clarendon Press, 1971.
    Explores Shakespeare's depiction of time in the Forest of Arden. Turner maintains that the human measurement of time is meaningless in Arden because measurable, social time is rendered absurd by the holiday setting of a poetic region. True love, he says, must reconcile itself to "historical" and "natural" time, as it does—with the idea of musical time—in the song "It Was a Lover and His Lass."

Uhlig, Claus. "'The Sobbing Deer': *As You Like It,* II. i. 21-66 and the Historical Context." *Renaissance Drama* n.s. III (1970): 79-109.
    Examines in detail the historical context of the sobbing deer episode in Act II, Scene i of *As You Like It.* Arguing that the passage is emblematic, Uhlig concludes that the deer symbolizes not love's agony, but the commonplace humanistic theme of the tyrannical cruelty of the hunt.

Van Den Berg, Kent Talbot. "Theatrical Fiction and the Reality of Love in *As You Like It.*" *PMLA* 90, No. 5 (October 1975): 885-93.
    Discusses Shakespeare's deliberate emphasis in *As You Like It* on "the artifice of theatrical fiction." Van Den Berg points to "mirroring relationships" among the characters that reflect the nature of the play itself as a mirror of love held up to the audience. These relationships, he claims, give the drama a "reflexive" or "metadramatic" capacity to interpret itself as theatrical fiction.

Waddington, Raymond B. "Moralizing the Spectacle: Dramatic Emblems in *As You Like It.*" *Shakespeare Quarterly* 33, No. 2 (Summer 1982): 155-63.
    Explores the historical basis of "iconic clusterings" in *As You Like It,* focusing on the play's "self-reflectiveness" and the "assertiveness of its illusionism." Tracing Shakespeare's use of emblems in the play, Waddington concludes that "the success of Rosalind's exploration . . . of love expresses itself generically in comedy and socially in the masque of the mass wedding."

Williamson, Marilyn L. "The Masque of Hymen in *As You Like It*." *Comparative Drama* II, No. 4 (Winter 1968-69): 248-58.

   Approaches the Masque of Hymen in *As You Like It* as a fitting resolution to, and a timely fulfillment of, the play's central theme of the relationship between time and permanence and the urgency of love. Williamson regards Duke Senior's restoration as the reclaiming of the past and a renewal of the future, complemented visually by the artistic order of the wedding dance.

Wilson, Rawdon. "The Way to Arden: Attitudes Toward Time in *As You Like It*." *Shakespeare Quarterly* XXVI, No. 1 (Winter 1975): 16-24.

   Refutes the idea that it is proper to regard the apparent lack of time in Arden as mere timelessness. Wilson discusses concepts of Aristotelian time in *As You Like It*, concluding that "the consciousness of time continues but is transferred to the interiority of the mind's aperception," causing the concern for "objective, public time" to be lost.

# Henry V

**DATE:** On the basis of what is generally perceived as a topical allusion in the play, it is widely agreed that *Henry V* was written and first performed in 1599. Gerard Langbaine, writing in 1691, was the first to suggest that the reference to "the general of our gracious Empress" in the Chorus preceding Act V is an allusion to the Earl of Essex, who led an English expedition to put down an Irish rebellion in March of 1599. Essex and his men returned to London in disgrace on September 28 of that same year, for the Irish campaign was a humiliating failure. Most modern scholars endorse the thesis that the description of a triumphant general "from Ireland coming / Bringing rebellion broached on his sword" (Chrous, V, 31-2)—if indeed it is a reference to Essex—would have been egregiously inappropriate after the Earl's actual return; thus, they conclude that Shakespeare must have composed *Henry V* sometime between March and early September 1599. Warren D. Smith (see Additional Bibliography) has proposed, however, that the reference is not to Essex but to Charles Blount, Lord Mountjoy, who led a subsequent—and successful—expedition against the Irish rebels in 1603. But Smith also maintains that the Chorus passages did not appear in the original text of *Henry V,* and he supports an original composition date of 1599 for the other portions of the play. Although FRANCIS MERES's *Palladis Tamia* (1598) offers an incomplete list of Shakespearean plays written to that time, commentators have found some significance in the absence of *Henry V* from his catalogue. The play was entered in the STATIONERS' REGISTER on August 4, 1600, apparently in an attempt, which proved unsuccessful, to prevent the printing of an unauthorized edition. There is no record of a performance of *Henry V* before January 7, 1605, when it was presented at Court by the King's Majesty's Players.

**TEXT:** The only authoritative text of *Henry V* is that of the FIRST FOLIO (F1), published in 1623. The play was originally issued in QUARTO form in 1600 (Q1). This version is regarded as a bad quarto; a majority of modern scholars believe that it was based on a MEMORIAL RECONSTRUCTION by one or more actors of an abridged version of *Henry V* prepared for a provincial tour by the LORD CHAMBERLAIN'S MEN, Shakespeare's acting company. Q1 was twice reprinted with some corrections in 1602 (Q2) and 1619 (Q3), the last under a false date of 1608 in order to circumvent a recent ruling by the Lord Chamberlain prohibiting the printing of any works belonging to the KING'S MEN without his permission. Bibliographers agree that there is some connection between the quarto versions—especially Q3—and F1, but there is no consensus on the nature of that relationship. It is generally accepted that F1 was printed from a manuscript in Shakespeare's own hand, most likely the dramatist's FOUL PAPERS. In addition, there is evidence that a quarto text was occasionally consulted by the F1 printers. Both John Dover Wilson and J. H. Walter, in their respective editions of *Henry V,* have held that Shakespeare's original version of the play included the character of Falstaff accompanying Henry to France. However, they posited, at some point in the composition process the dramatist altered his first intention and was therefore forced to make extensive revisions in his text, particularly in Act II. Dover Wilson argued that what Shakespeare could salvage of Falstaff's part he transferred to Pistol. The textual criticism of *Henry V* includes what is perhaps the most celebrated EMENDATION in Shakespearean scholarship. In

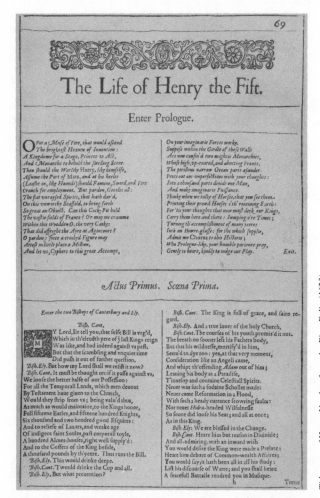

*Title page of Henry V taken from the First Folio (1623).*

response to Alexander Pope's reading of a phrase in Mistress Quickly's description of the death of Falstaff, Lewis Theobald proposed that the line should be emended to "'a' babled of green Fields" (II. iii. 16-17). A majority of modern editors have followed Theobald's suggestion, but a few scholars contend that the original Folio line, "A Table of green fields," is correct and understandable.

**SOURCES:** Perhaps because RAPHAEL HOLINSHED relied heavily on EDWARD HALL's *The Union of the Two Noble and Illustre Famelies of Lancastre and York* (2d ed., 1548) for his own *Chronicles of England, Scotlande, and Irelande* (1577; 1587), critics are divided on whether for *Henry V* Shakespeare was principally indebted to one or the other historiographer. But most modern scholars maintain that there is strong evidence in the play that the dramatist consulted both works. Commentators have noted that such passages as Canterbury's Salic law speech in Act I, Scene ii is a paraphrase in verse of Holinshed's narrative of this episode, with only minimal variations from the original. On the other hand, Shakespeare made no reference to many events that appear in Hall's and Holinshed's accounts of the reign of Henry V; in addition, the dramatist implied only a short passage of time between Agincourt and the achievement of a treaty with France, when in fact the two were separated by a period of nearly four years, and he provided details—such as Henry's declaration that mercy be shown to the citizens of Harfleur after their surrender—that have no basis in the chronicles. A lost and anonymous play from the 1580s, *The Famous Victories of Henry the Fifth,* survives only in a corrupt edition of 1598, so that it has proved difficult to determine the degree of Shakespeare's familiarity with this work. However, several commentators have noticed parallels between Shakespeare's *Henry V* and *The Famous Victories,* including similarities in structure, the prominence in each of the Dauphin's gift of tennis balls to Henry, and the inclusion in both of a wooing scene between Henry and Katherine. It has been proposed by some modern scholars that the resemblances between the two plays indicate that there was a third drama which served as a common source for *Henry V* and *The Famous Victories.* Three fifteenth-century biographical treatments of Henry have also been identified as possible sources: the *Gesta Henrici Quinti,* written by a chaplain in Henry's army; the *Vita et Gesta Henrici Quinti,* a work from the middle of the century that was once thought to have been written by Thomas of Elmham; and Titus Livius's *Vita Henrici Quinti,* of which an English translation first appeared in 1513. Scholars have discovered echoes in *Henry V* of incidents presented in each of these works. Finally, in the *Annals of Tacitus*—published in English in 1598—there is an account of the Roman emperor Germanicus disguising himself and moving about among his soldiers on the night before an important battle. Several commentators believe that this account influenced Shakespeare's depiction of Henry on the eve of Agincourt.

***CRITICAL HISTORY:*** From the early nineteenth century to the present, the central issue for commentators on *Henry V* has been the character of the king. Scholars have been deeply divided over whether Shakespeare intended to portray Henry as an ideal monarch and military hero or as a ruthless Machiavel. Although the latter reading is more prominent in modern studies, critics continue to share the former interpretation as well. In addition to this central question, there are a number of secondary issues. The lack of critical agreement over the principal thematic concerns raised in the play resembles the division among scholars over the character of Henry. Nineteenth- and twentieth-century critics have proposed a variety of themes, including war, governance, national unity, heroism, the conflict between passion and reason, right relation between subjects and king, order and harmony, enervation, and individual maturity, as paramount in the drama. Other significant critical questions center on *Henry V*'s often noted ironic elements, its portrayal of war and patriotism, Mistress Quickly's account of the death of Falstaff—together with the fat knight's absence from the play—, Canterbury's Salic law speech (I. ii. 33-95, 97-100) and his role in the decision to invade France, the function of the Chorus, and the epic nature of the drama. During almost three hundred years of commentary, many subsidiary issues have also been discussed, including Henry's courtship of Katherine, the significance of the play's comic elements, the characterization of Fluellen and members of the French nobility, and Shakespeare's dramatic style and structure.

The earliest recorded criticism of *Henry V* addresses some of these subordinate questions. In 1691, for example, Gerard Langbaine suggested that the lines at Chorus, V, 30-4 constitute a reference to the Earl of Essex and his Irish expedition of 1599 (see *DATE* section above). Langbaine also remarked on the mixture of historic and comic elements in Shakespeare's drama. Later in that decade, Jeremy Collier compared the death

of Falstaff to that of "a Rat behind the Hangings." But Nicholas Rowe, writing early in the following century, found the account of the knight's death as "diverting" as any episode in his life. Rowe also held that the scene in which Katherine attempts to learn English indicates that Shakespeare understood the French language. Another early eighteenth-century critic, Charles Gildon, judged it ludicrous that Katherine is unable to communicate with Henry in the courtship scene that concludes the play, for, he pointed out, all the other French characters in *Henry V* are able to speak English. Gildon's primary focus, however, was on the Chorus. He judged that the numerous apologies to the audience included in the choruses convey Shakespeare's uneasiness about the many violations in the play of Neoclassical rules concerning the unities of time and place. He was also the first critic to contend that the Chorus serves to bridge the gaps in time between otherwise unconnected actions and to narrate events not dramatized in the play; Gildon concluded that it generally functions to correct "the Lameness of the Representation." In 1723, Alexander Pope proposed his idiosyncratic reading of Mistress Quickly's account of the death of Falstaff, which prompted Lewis Theobald's famous emendation (see *TEXT* section above).

Among critics writing near the middle of the eighteenth century, Thomas Hanmer briefly discussed the so-called tutoring scene, which he described as "that wretched piece of ribaldry." Later, Richard Farmer challenged the authenticity of this episode. He insisted that the tutoring scene is an interpolation by another writer, claiming that Shakespeare would never have introduced "such obscenity and nonsense" into his play. Other commentators from this period raised more substantial questions about *Henry V.* Writing in 1754, Charlotte Lennox was the earliest to note that many passages in the play are either verbatim copies or very close rewordings of Holinshed's account of Henry's reign, and she further remarked that a comparison of the chronicler's description of the principal characters and Shakespeare's portrayal of them reveals "very little Variation." Additionally, Lennox faulted the lack of propriety and dignity in the final scene of the play, arguing that the conduct of Henry and Katherine is wholly inappropriate to their rank and stature. Samuel Johnson also dispraised this scene, judging Henry's behavior here as not only inconsistent with his conduct earlier in the play, but unfortunately reminiscent of Hotspur in *1 Henry IV.* Indeed, the critic described the whole of Act V as empty and narrow, contending that after the battle of Agincourt, there was little of dramatic interest in Henry's reign to depict; thus, when Shakespeare reached the concluding act of the play he was "glad to fill it up with what he could get." Johnson was also the first critic to comment on the conflicting reasons offered by the king and Gower for the order to kill the French prisoners—an episode discussed by many subsequent scholars. Further, he initiated the line of inquiry into Shakespeare's reasons for failing to include Falstaff in the dramatic events of *Henry V,* suggesting that the dramatist may have provided the account of Sir John's death in order to forestall other writers from attempting to incorporate this popular figure into their work.

Later in the eighteenth century, Richard Cumberland further questioned Falstaff's absence from *Henry V.* Cumberland was one of the few commentators on this issue to maintain that Sir John would not have been out of place in the dramatic world of this play. He noted that there are many comic passages throughout the play which feature the king's former Eastcheap cronies, adding that Fluellen himself appears to have "arisen out of the ashes of Falstaff." Two other commentators from this period, Francis Gentleman and Elizabeth Griffith, focused on Henry in their remarks on the play. Gentleman held that Shakespeare's presentation of the king's character and conduct is historically faithful and balances the portrayal of his youthful follies in *1* and *2 Henry IV*. Griffith, arguing that Henry is a completely estimable figure, included composure, courage, calm assurance, and piety in a catalogue of his principal virtues.

Nineteenth-century critics of *Henry V* offered a wide range of evaluations of the king and explored several other aspects of the play for the first time. In the earliest commentary from this period, August Wilhelm Schlegel considered Henry to be Shakespeare's "favourite hero in English history," but, like Johnson, he maintained that aside from the conquest of France Henry's reign provided little dramatic material for Shakespeare to develop. Schlegel regarded war as "an epic rather than a dramatic object" which could be of only secondary interest in the theater, and he maintained that Shakespeare introduced the Chorus to lend "epic pomp and solemnity" to the play, as well as to remind the spectators that they must improve the dramatic action with their own imaginations. He was also the first commentator to point out the irony of the allusion in Act V, Scene ii to the progeny of Henry and Katherine—who turned out to be not the heroic crusader the king envisions, but the hapless Henry VI. Also writing in the first quarter of the nineteenth century, William Hazlitt offered one of the most frequently cited essays on *Henry V*. He inaugurated the line of negative judgments of the king, disparaging him as "a very amiable monster" whose savage potential is not truly threatening in the theater where the horrible consequences of his war against France cannot be realistically conveyed. Following a suggestion of Schlegel, Hazlitt was also the first to question both Henry's motivation for instigating the war and the Archbishop of Canterbury's reasons for encouraging him to do so. In 1839, the German critic Hermann Ulrici contended that whatever the king's real motives for declaring war with France, the battle itself was a divine instrument—"essentially a *judgment of God*"—whose purpose was "to promote the development of the intellectual and moral vigour" of these two nations. Ulrici added that the war had another, "higher and nobler aim—the moral purification and amendment of man," primarily "in the person of Henry."

Other nineteenth-century critics concerned with both Shakespeare's portrayal of war in *Henry V* and the character of the king include Thomas Carlyle, Charles Knight, and G. G. Gervinus. Carlyle contended that the play reflects Shakespeare's own strongly held national sentiments, and he praised in particular the dramatization of the battle of Agincourt. Knight was the first critic to hold that the play offers no dramatic conflict because there is never any doubt about the outcome of the war against the French. He also argued that *Henry V* vividly portrays both "the fearful responsibilities" of leading a nation into war and the inevitable horrors that ensue. Gervinus provided the earliest extended commentary on Henry, stressing the king's "many-sided nature" and identifying piety as his principal trait. He was also the first scholar to argue that Henry's ambitiousness, occasional impatience and boasting, and zealous pursuit of honor are reminiscent of Hotspur; however, he maintained that on the eve of Agincourt Henry displays a gracious condescension to his soldiers and a serenity of mind that could never be exhibited by the irascible Hotspur.

Throughout the remaining decades of the nineteenth century, critics of *Henry V* continued to focus their analyses on the character of the king, offering opinions from one end of the critical spectrum to the other. In one of the most iconoclastic essays in the history of *Henry V* commentary, William Watkiss Lloyd contended that the king is manipulative, hypocritical, sanctimonious, and morally blind. He also offered one of the earliest discussions of the events of Act IV, Scene i—a scene which many twentieth-century scholars view as central to any interpretation of the play—, arguing that the king's exchange with Bates and Williams reveals that none of them possesses any intellectual or philosophical acuity and describing Henry's soliloquy as affected, self-pitying, and hypocritical. In an evaluation that recalls Gervinus's, Henry Norman Hudson (see Additional Bibliography) regarded Henry's piety as his most significant trait, but he also found him honest, affable, interested in honor for its own sake, and the very model of Shakespeare's own code of ethics. Algernon Charles Swinburne, however, held that the king displays serious flaws as well as pure and noble qualities. Declaring that Henry's chief motivation is "the principle of self-interest," Swinburne contended that the king's need for a "plausible excuse" to invade France is complemented by the "political sophistries" and self-interest of Canterbury and Ely. On the other hand, Denton J. Snider regarded Henry as "the ideal ruler" who promulgates harmony in his kingdom and "supremacy abroad." Snider also offered one of the earliest defenses of Henry's order to kill the French prisoners, asserting that it was necessary to ensure the English victory, and therefore the command was appropriately issued. The critic further related the characterization of the French nobles to the superior justness of that country's cause, suggesting that their exaggerated arrogance serves both to deter the audience from sympathizing with them and to provide a reason for their defeat—their humbling by "a leveling Nemesis." In the last decade of the century, Bernard Shaw foreshadowed many twentieth-century critics by dismissing Henry as "a Jingo hero" of limited ability and excessive chauvinism.

While critics of the present century have pursued a variety of questions concerning *Henry V,* interest has continued to center on the figure of the king. One of the most significant issues is whether he represents Shakespeare's ideal monarch. In general, twentieth-century critics have claimed that he does not. This assessment was initially put forth by A. C. Bradley, who acknowledged that although Henry possesses many admirable qualities, including modesty, piety, and an extraordinary talent for leadership, he is also superstitious, prone to manipulate others for his own purposes, and displays no indication "of a strong affection for any one." Similarly, W. B. Yeats declared that despite Henry's ability to inspire his forces and rule his kingdom, he lacks a transcendent vision, moving through the play like some "remorseless and undistinguished . . . natural force. "In the following decade, John Masefield described the king as a man who lacks sympathetic feelings for others and shows no capacity for understanding the spiritual significance of life. Stopford A. Brooke also expressed the belief that Henry is not a perfect monarch, claiming that he is a combination of political expediency, ruthlessness and mercy, humility, and self-deception. Gerald Gould was one of Henry's most vigorous detractors. He regarded the king as hypocritical, dishonest, and barbarous, noting that Shakespeare underscores his viciousness through the conduct of such secondary characters as Bardolph and Nym. Late in the 1930s, Mark Van Doren disparaged Henry as "a hearty undergraduate with enormous initials on his chest." Like Yeats and Masefield, he viewed the king as a simplistic figure devoid of vision and comprehension.

In the 1940s, three commentators offered divergent, but similarly unflattering estimations of Henry. Acknowledging that the king is calculating and ruthless, apt to evade responsibility for his actions, and motivated principally by political expediency, D. A. Traversi nevertheless contended that Henry's conduct is entirely consonant with the principles of effective leadership. John C. McCloskey emphatically denied that Henry represents the ideals of monarchy. He argued that the king's battle conduct is savage, displaying no evidence of Christian ethics or ordinary standards of civilization; he also viewed Henry's frequent allusions to God as "patronizingly familiar" attempts to associate his own interests with those of Providence. E. M. W. Tillyard adopted an autobiographical approach to Henry, suggesting that by this point in his career Shakespeare had lost interest in the historical figure esteemed by chroniclers and Elizabethans as one of England's greatest national heroes. He maintained that Henry is an inconsistent, "patchwork character," embodying no significant principle that would serve as a dramatic focal point.

Yet, despite these rather unfavorable assessments of King Henry, many twentieth-century critics found in him Shakespeare's ideal expression of monarchy. Although he did not label Henry an ideal king, John William Cunliffe nevertheless countered the negative appraisals of the character by emphasizing the historical accuracy of his representation. Similarly, Elmer Edgar Stoll recommended a historical interpretation of the play, contending that Shakespeare created Henry to reflect the Elizabethan notion of a perfect monarch; he added that the king's frequent allusions to God are thus the conventional demonstrations of a ruler's piety and morality. Stoll also noted that Shakespeare individualized and humanized Henry, providing us with a dramatic character that accurately portrays one of England's most popular heroes. In the mid-1930s, Charles Williams praised Henry for his "almost supernatural" ability to comfort and encourage his soldiers, adding that the king achieves an exalted sense of honor that permits him to remain calm toward the possibility of defeat and the certainty of his own mortality.

One of the most famous encomiums of Henry was presented by John Dover Wilson in 1947. Not only is the king an incomparable epic hero, Dover Wilson contended, but from the close of Act III to the conclusion of the play he demonstrates such admirable human qualities as generosity and gaiety of spirit. The critic further asserted that Henry's claim to the French throne is valid, that his speech at Harfleur should be perceived as a successful attempt to end the siege as quickly as possible, and that his order to kill the French prisoners reveals his decisiveness, strength, and self-possession in moments of crises. In the following decade, the New Arden editor J. H. Walter urged an equally favorable reading of Henry as the ideal epic hero. In his view, an Elizabethan audience would have unquestionably seen the king as "a leader of supreme genius"—stoical, high principled, and inspiring his countrymen at Agincourt by virtue of his piety and moral strength.

From 1960 to the present, commentators have continued to evaluate Henry as an ideal monarch. H. M. Richmond argued that *Henry V* traces the development of the king from bellicosity, deceit, and hypocrisy in the early scenes to moderation, responsibility, and humility at the close of the play. In Act IV, the critic held, Henry attains self-perception and, through this, a profound understanding of his role as king, together with a new appreciation of the need to trust in God. Similarly, Dorothy Cook maintained that while the early scenes of *Henry V* demonstrate that the king has the political and military virtues he needs to fulfill his role, in the final three acts of the play he

becomes increasingly governed by his private virtues—his mercy, humility, equity, and piety. In the critic's estimation, it is these private virtues that lead to Henry's victory at Agincourt and reveal that he is "the ideal king." Moody E. Prior contended that Henry embodies the qualities which contemporary religious and secular treatises on kingship required of an ideal ruler. However, Prior also believed that the play's allusions to the rejection of Falstaff and the "haunting" account of his death, together with the ironical reference in Act V to Henry VI, serve to undermine and question the myth of the exemplary monarch. Finally, C. G. Thayer viewed Henry as not only Shakespeare's ideal Christian king, but also as the model for "man-centered kingship." Everything he achieves is the result of human endeavor, the critic argued, rather than divine intervention or "political mysticism."

Reviewing the polarized assessments of Henry as an ideal and ruthless king, some modern commentators have claimed that Shakespeare's portrayal is intentionally ambiguous. Writing in 1951, Harold C. Goddard initiated this view, contending that there are two Henry V's: one is the supremely popular military hero, the other a disingenuous Machiavel. Although he suggested that Shakespeare leaves us "free to accept whichever of the two we prefer," Goddard pointed out that Henry's godlike stature and heroic accomplishments are repeatedly undermined by his Machiavellian behavior, and we thereby learn "the truth about him." In his Christian analysis of *Henry V*, Roy W. Battenhouse likewise postulated that Shakespeare presents the king as both a glorious national hero and a man motivated by greed, more concerned with his "public image" than with the religious or ethical bases of life. Norman Rabkin, writing in the late 1970s, also asserted that the play supports two opposing views of Henry—from one perspective he is a model Christian monarch who successfully combines spiritual and political virtues, from the other he is a brutal Machiavel whose principal motive is merciless expediency. There is no safe middle ground between these extreme interpretations, the critic maintained. He concluded that *Henry V* depicts the complex and unpredictable union of disparate realities, deliberately leaving us unsure of "what to think" about the play and its principal character.

Several commentators of the present century have held that the discrepancies in Henry's conduct are the result of a division between his public role and his private persona, between the qualities required of him as a king and those expected of him as an individual human being. Many of these critics have related this issue of the king's dual nature to Shakespeare's views of governance in the play. For example, H. B. Charlton, in his lecture of 1929, maintained that Shakespeare's attitude towards kingship in *Henry V* remains the same as that in *1* and *2 Henry IV*: "what is good in the world of politics is entirely unrelated to and generally the opposite of what makes for goodness in the moral life." Similarly, Traversi argued that in *Henry V* Shakespeare was predominantly interested in "the conditions of kingship" and "the sacrifice of common humanity" that a ruler must make if he is to succeed, even though this condition carries with it the possibility of tragedy. Una Ellis-Fermor asserted that Henry is a consummate statesman and leader with impeccable public conduct. But his personality has been effaced by his royal office, she maintained, leaving "no Henry, only a king." Peter G. Phialas held that Henry must constantly struggle to achieve a balance between the demands placed on him by his public role and his right as a human being to express personal feelings. While he acknowledged that Henry's human qualities are less evident than his public virtues of bravery, resolution, and impartiality, the critic averred that on the eve of Agincourt the king perceives a shared humanity with his soldiers and by the end of the play has successfully reconciled his personal yearnings and his public conduct. Like Ellis-Fermor, Alvin B. Kernan proposed that Henry is an unerring politician whose individual humanity has disappeared beneath his public role as monarch. Rather than insisting on categorizing the king as either hero or Machiavel, he argued, we should see that his behavior is governed by political considerations and that his principal motivation is the successful functioning of his kingdom. More recently, James L. Calderwood has contended that except for the doubts and uncertainties he experiences on the night before the battle, Henry suppresses all private feelings in order to gain his objective of national order and unity. In an examination of the Tudor theory of the King's Two Bodies—the "natural" one subject to frailty and error and the "politic" one "incapable of imperfection' '—, Thayer, as mentioned earlier, claimed that Henry succeeds because of human endeavor—through actions that underscore his personal identity—not because of "political mysticism."

In reaching these various assessments of Henry, twentieth-century critics have analyzed his correspondence to other Shakespearean characters and his relationships with other figures in *Henry V*. Like Johnson and Gervinus in previous centuries, H. M. Richmond and Marilyn L. Williamson discussed Henry's affinity to Hotspur. Richmond held that the king's attitude during the period when the French expedition is being readied closely resembles Hotspur's "intoxicated ambition," and Williamson contended that in the courtship scene Henry shows a strong similarity to Hotspur in his self-love, verbosity, and pretense of caring for other people. Henry's encounter with Williams and Bates has been examined by such critics as John C. McCloskey, Phialas, Brian Vickers, Robert Ornstein, and Thayer. McCloskey denigrated Henry's behavior towards Williams, judging it snobbish and condescending; he also characterized the king's exchange of gages with Williams as "a crude and humorless practical joke." Act IV, Scene i demonstrates the right relation between king and subject, Phialas argued, and further reveals, through Henry's inability to alleviate the discontent of his soldiers, Shakespeare's "tragic concept of kingship." Vickers noted that as the argument between the king and the common soldiers becomes more intense and forceful there is an increasing use of symmetries and parallelisms in Henry's syntax. Ornstein pointed out that Henry was not obligated to debate the justice of his cause with his men; the critic also believed that Williams and Bates are as eager to evade responsibility for the condition of their souls as Henry is to avoid liability for their deaths. Thayer held that Shakespeare does not present Henry as evading responsibility for the spiritual state of his soldiers, but instead emphasizes in this scene the importance of distinguishing between a monarch's secular and mystical identities. Thayer also argued that Henry's order to kill the French prisoners does not reflect negatively on his character; the critic asserted that the king's first order was never carried out and that his second one proceeds from a justifiable anger over the slaying of the boys.

Although it is the central issue in twentieth-century commentary on *Henry V*, the character of the king is by no means the only concern. Other important questions include the nature and function of the play's ironic elements, its thematic issues, and Shakespeare's attitudes toward patriotism and war. Beginning with Yeats early in the century and continuing to the present day, a large measure of critical attention has focused on the

ironic attitudes or devices in *Henry V*. Yeats believed that Shakespeare treats Henry with "tragic irony," for the dramatist and the audience share the knowledge that the French victories are short-lived and the conquered land will be lost by Henry VI. Gould subsequently asserted that the play is deeply ironic and provides a satirical treatment of monarchy, imperialism, "the baser kinds of 'patriotism'," and war. Goddard argued that irony is pervasive in *Henry V,* but particularly penetrating in Act I, Scene ii. As previously mentioned, Roy W. Battenhouse held that Shakespeare offers a deeply ironical view of history by presenting the king as both a national hero and a man motivated by greed and personal ambition. Northrop Frye also identified two points of view in the play. He maintained that the first is derived from the patriotic, uncritical Chorus and the other from an appreciation of Henry as a tragic figure, destined to die a short time after reaching the apex of his fortunes. In a similar vein, James Winny discerned a deep discrepancy between the Chorus's affirmation of heroic values and Shakespeare's treatment of those values, evident in several scenes, with "doubts and skepticism." He contended that the Chorus's description and evocation of martial glories are sharply undercut by Henry's "recurrent crises of belief," by the doubts of the soldiers, and by the reality that Pistol's attempt to extort ransom from a Frenchman is the sole instance of armed conflict in a work that purportedly celebrates the "glorious" battle of Agincourt.

From the 1940s to the present, another significant area of critical concern has been the identification of prominent thematic issues in *Henry V*, other than those of Henry's royal identity and the nature of governance. Traversi saw the struggle between a king's natural passion and his "controlling reason" as the central theme in *Henry V*, maintaining that the play presents a cold "indifference to humanity" as an essential quality in a successful monarch. Dover Wilson regarded heroism as the primary theme and the drama itself as a celebration of Henry's unmatched leadership and the "moral significance" of Agincourt. Rose A. Zimbardo contended that the preeminent idea in *Henry V* is the "harmonious operation of parts in an ordered whole," depicted in the king's achievement of control over his own potentially disruptive emotions and over opposing elements in his state. Winny argued that inertia or enervation is a recurring theme in the drama. Recalling the assessment of E. M. W. Tillyard, he hypothesized that Shakespeare was apathetic toward his dramatic material, never becoming fully engaged in the composition of the play, and thus the theme is a reflection of the dramatist's own indifference. Like H. M. Richmond before her, Dorothy Cook asserted that *Henry V* dramatizes "the theme of individual maturity" by showing the king's increasing realization of both his responsibility toward his subjects and the necessity of a humble trust in the will of God. The frequent references in the play to mercy and justice, Ornstein maintained, underscore the theme of kindness; but he further identified a contrasting theme of war that depicts humanity in its most merciless state. For Calderwood, national unity and a "concept of royal order" in which the monarchy is based on both the loyalty of its subjects and the approval of God are the principal ideas dramatized in the play.

Several twentieth-century critics have also been interested in the more pervasive concerns of war and patriotism in *Henry V*. Early in the 1900s, E. K. Chambers regarded the play as both a commemoration of "the dauntless spirit and invincible endurance of Englishmen"—reflecting the patriotic fervor of the closing years of the Elizabethan era—and a representation of the darker side of nationalism evident in Henry's obsessive concern with foreign conquest, his cruel treatment of Falstaff, and the frequent allusions to the horrors of war. In 1913, Brander Matthews disparaged what he saw as the fervid nationalism of the drama, complaining that it is "often perilously close to jingoism, if not to claptrap." In that same year, Stopford A. Brooke contended that on one hand the play celebrates the indomitable spirit of the courageous English army at Agincourt, but on the other it repeatedly emphasizes that the war against France is unjust. More than thirty years later, Dover Wilson held that in the first half of the play war is depicted as a great national enterprise, but that from Act III, Scene iii to the conclusion Shakespeare offers numerous examples of the suffering it inevitably produces. In 1972, Ornstein contended that the play represents war as brutal and dehumanizing and that Henry himself is an apocalyptic figure of "famine, sword, and fire" (Prologue, 7) with no true appreciation of the effects of war on ordinary citizens. In the following year, Moody E. Prior characterized *Henry V* as a dramatization of a national myth, but he also remarked that this myth is frequently undercut by allusions to the rejection and death of Falstaff and to the unfortunate heir of Henry and Katherine.

Many twentieth-century critics have examined the character of the king and other aspects of *Henry V* in light of such dramatic elements as Falstaff's absence from the play and Mistress Quickly's account of his death, the function of the Chorus, and the significance of the scene in which Canterbury expounds the bases of Henry's claim to the French throne. As previously mentioned, Chambers asserted that the king's cruel treatment of Falstaff is consonant with the play's depiction of the darker side of nationalism. Chambers also declared that, with the exception of the description of the fat knight's death, "there is nothing" in *Henry V* "that is intimate, nothing that touches the depths." Gould charged that Falstaff is victimized by the same crime of ingratitude which Henry accuses Cambridge, Scroop, and Grey of showing toward him. In a historical reading, Dover Wilson (see Additional Bibliography) proposed that Sir John is absent from *Henry V* because the actor who played the part in *1* and *2 Henry IV* left Shakespeare's company before this drama was first performed. Walter, however, argued that Falstaff's dramatic role as "corrupt flatterer" threatens the divine plan for national order and unity, asserting that he therefore cannot be a part of the glorious English victory at Agincourt. J. I. M. Stewart (see Additional Bibliography) related the death of Falstaff to the folk ritual of slaying "an old, impotent, and guilty king" in order to restore the health and fecundity of the community. Frye also discussed the folkloric implications of the character of Falstaff and likened him to a "martyred father." He further remarked that Falstaff's possible function in *Henry V* as ironic commentator has been taken by "a properly disciplined chorus," whose purpose is to ensure that the audience adopts an unquestioning attitude toward the dramatic events.

Among those who have discussed the role of the Chorus in *Henry V* are such twentieth-century commentators as Granville-Barker, Williams, Goddard, and Winny. Arguing that Shakespeare recognized that the king was an uninteresting character and that the attempt to depict momentous historic events was severely constrained by the limitations of his theater, Granville-Barker urged that the repeated apologies from the Chorus be viewed as Shakespeare's acknowledgement of the failure of his art. Williams held that the Chorus preceding Act IV contains intimations of Shakespeare's later tragedies, particularly in its evocation of universal night and the accompanying "spectral images of mankind." Goddard believed that one of the prin-

cipal functions of the Chorus is to convince us to see Henry as a godlike hero; but he also maintained that the dramatic action of the play subverts this intention. Similarly, as mentioned earlier, Winny claimed that not only are the Chorus's descriptions of English military prowess unrealized in the action of *Henry V*, but they are repeatedly undermined by dramatic events.

Canterbury's defense of that cause, together with Henry's conduct in the scene in which it is offered, has been analyzed by such twentieth-century critics as Brooke, Gould, Charlton, Dover Wilson, Goddard, and Battenhouse. In Brooke's view, both the king and the archbishop hypocritically pretend to be unaware of each other's motives; he also argued that Canterbury gives no consideration to the devastating effects on ordinary citizens of the war he wishes to instigate. Gould was the earliest critic to note—as have several others since—that if the arguments advanced by Canterbury in his Salic law speech are accepted as valid, they prove that Edmund Mortimer, not Henry, is the legitimate heir to the English throne. He also asserted that the multiple justifications for the French war are intentionally confused and often contradictory, and thus should be regarded as elements in Shakespeare's satire on imperialistic monarchies. Charlton held that by virtue of Henry's lack of intellectual acuity, the bishops maneuver him into declaring war on France; he doubted that the king possesses the "Machiavellian astuteness" required to see through their tactics and adapt them to his own advantage. Rejecting the view of critics who discern in the early scenes of *Henry V* the king's self-interestedness and the churchmen's political casuistry, Dover Wilson asserted that Act I clearly presents the war as just and Henry's claim to the French throne as valid. Although Goddard found Act I, Scene ii especially ironic and agreed that the Salic law speech demonstrates that Mortimer is the true heir to the throne, he also discovered in this scene some evidence of Henry's "nobler self" trying to gain ascendency over the dominant Machiavellian aspect of his character. Like Gould and Goddard, Battenhouse held that Canterbury's arguments ironically support Mortimer's claim to the English crown—not Henry's to the French; he regarded this scene as part of the recurring pattern of discrepancy between "shadow" and "substance" in *Henry V*.

Other scenes examined in detail by twentieth-century critics include Henry's courtship of Katherine, those in which Fluellen appears, and those featuring various members of the French aristocracy. Vickers, Prior, and Williamson have all assessed different aspects of the wooing scene. From an analysis of the syntactical patterns in Act V, Scene ii, Vickers concluded that this episode is designed to demonstrate that in addition to being a heroic soldier, Henry is also capable of wit and eloquence. Like some nineteenth-century commentators, Prior held that Henry's allusion to his and Katherine's future child has the effect of undercutting the play's representation of a great national victory, for that progeny, Henry VI, would lose all that his father had won in France. Williamson argued that Henry's wooing recapitulates a pattern of behavior that he has demonstrated both in this play and, as Prince Hal, in *1* and *2 Henry IV*; she characterized the king's actions in this scene as manipulative, self-justifying, and disingenuous. Turning to Shakespeare's depiction of Fluellen, both Gould and Van Doren regarded this figure as a counterpoise to Henry. Gould maintained that Fluellen is skeptical of Henry's pious comments after the battle of Agincourt, and Van Doren contended that one of the functions of the Welsh captain is to help deflate the theme of war. Brander Matthews complained of Shakespeare's portrayal of the French nobles, arguing that, in characterizing them as arrogant and inane, the dramatist had pandered ''to the prejudice of the insular rabble'' in the audience and betrayed his craft. Winny offered detailed analyses of Grandpré's description of the dispirited English army and of Burgundy's account of the ravaged French countryside, evaluating both as intensive expositions of the theme of enervation in *Henry V.*

Examinations of the dramatic language in *Henry V*, together with discussions of the play's structure and Shakespeare's mixture of epic and comic elements, constitute additional concerns in the twentieth century. Van Doren, Zimbardo, and Vickers have all offered analyses of the drama's linguistic elements. Van Doren maintained that although the poetry of the Chorus is ''always very fine,'' Shakespeare erred in narrating rather than dramatizing the events and actions recited by the Chorus. In his estimation, the play's language is frequently strained and inflated. Zimbardo commented on the ways in which the formality of Henry's rhetoric and the static design of the play underscore the theme of order and harmony. Vickers offered a close analysis of Shakespeare's unusual use of prose in the play, demonstrating that characters from every level of society—not just the low or humorous figures—speak in this manner; also unusual, in his estimation, is the appearance of prose in a broad range of dramatic situations, ''from serious argument to witty love talk.'' Dorothy Cook, James L. Calderwood, and Joanne Altieri have each recently examined the dramatic structure of *Henry V.* Cook argued that as the king undergoes triumphs and reversals, Shakespeare alternately quickens and slows the tempo of the dramatic action, balances the placement of psychologically important scenes, and, by the use of multiple plotting, provides contrasts to Henry's progress toward personal maturity. Calderwood compared Henry's search for political unity to Shakespeare's pursuit of an artistic unity that evolves naturally from the action of his drama. Just as the king must suppress his private feelings in order to perform his public function, the critic contended, so the dramatist had to constrain his personal views of the dramatic material in order to conform to the realities of English history, the expectations of his audience, and his depiction of Hal in *1* and *2 Henry IV.* Altieri analyzed the way in which Shakespeare employed the romance form to achieve an idealized view of Henry and his reign, and she pointed out how the dramatic action approximates the movement toward the ''green world'' of the romance tradition.

The relation of *Henry V* to the epic tradition has been discussed by Walter and Prior. As mentioned earlier, Walter regarded Henry as the ideal epic hero; he also emphasized the epic nature of the play and noted many parallels between Henry and Virgil's Aeneas. For Prior, *Henry V* dramatizes an epic theme and celebrates a legendary hero, rather than expressing Shakespeare's own perception of historical and political realities. In the present century, however, critics have focused more on the comic elements in the play than on the epic ones. Traversi pointed out how the careful juxtaposition of scenes which feature Henry's ''rhetorical incitations to patriotic feeling'' and those that demonstrate the darker, tragic effects of war on such common soldiers as Bardolph, Nym, and Pistol yields a more realistic, even tragic view of the effects of war on its participants. Tillyard saw no connection between the central plot and the comic scenes, but Goddard contended that several of the humorous incidents in the play—especially those involving Bardolph and Nym—function as ironical commentary on Henry's conduct. And in his analysis of prose passages in *Henry V*, Vickers discussed the syntax of Mistress Quickly's account

of the death of Falstaff and Shakespeare's employment of idiosyncratic prose patterns to help characterize such comic figures as Pistol, Nym, and Fluellen.

*Henry V* has been praised by many eminent scholars as a vigorous portrayal of one of England's most popular heroes and a commemoration of the spirit of Agincourt. Yet others, such as Tillyard, regarded it as distinctly inferior to Shakespeare's earlier English history plays. Although commentators have prized the speeches of the Chorus and Henry's exhortation before Agincourt, many more have judged Mistress Quickly's narrative of the death of Falstaff as the most emotive passage in the play. Modern critics have noted that no other Shakespearean protagonist has been the object of such drastically divergent opinions as Henry. Noting the current state of such ''incompatible and radically opposed views'' of the king, Norman Rabkin asserted that the drama is ''an extreme version of the fundamental ambiguity that many critics have found at the center of the Shakespearean vision.'' *Henry V* is as inscrutable as history itself, he suggested, and we should not look for a single angle of vision from a dramatist who has elsewhere demonstrated his clear understanding of the duality of nature.

---

### GERARD LANGBAINE   (essay date 1691)

[*Langbaine is generally acknowledged as the first historian of the English theater. He wrote several catalogues of dramatic history, including* An Account of the English Dramatick Poets *(1691), in which he provided biographical sketches of playwrights, lists of their works, and possible sources for the plots of their plays. In the following excerpt from this work, Langbaine is the first commentator of record to assert that the lines at Chorus, V, 30-4—describing a ''general of our gracious empress'' who is expected to put down a rebellion—is a reference to the Earl of Essex and his Irish campaign of 1599, thus establishing a composition date for the play. Although a majority of critics since Langbaine have also regarded these lines as an allusion to Essex, some twentieth-century scholars have disputed this conclusion. Langbaine also remarks on the combination of comic and historic elements in Shakespeare's play.*]

*Henry* the Fifth, his Life. This play is . . . writ and founded on History, with a Mixture of Comedy. The Play is continued from the beginning of his Reign, to his Marriage . . . with *Katherine* of *France.* . . . This Play was writ during the time that *Essex* was General in *Ireland*, as you may see in the beginning of the [fifth] Act, where our Poet, by a pretty Turn, compliments *Essex*, and seems to foretell Victory to Her Majesties Forces against the Rebels.

> *Gerard Langbaine, in an extract from* The Shakspere Allusion-Book: A Collection of Allusions to Shakspere from 1591 to 1700, Vol. II, *edited by John Munro, revised edition, 1932. Reprint by Books for Libraries Press, 1970; distributed by Arno Press, Inc., p. 362.*

### JEREMY COLLIER   (essay date 1698)

[*Collier, an English clergyman, is best remembered for his attack on the Restoration stage in a tract entitled* A Short View of the Immorality and Profaneness of the English Stage *(1698). Collier did not fully exempt Shakespeare from his condemnation of stage immorality, but he did find him a ''gentiler Enemy'' than the Restoration dramatists who were the critic's chief targets. In the following excerpt from the above-named work, Collier is the first critic to allude to the death of Falstaff in* Henry V, *maintaining that the knight "dies like a Rat behind the Hangings" after having been rejected by the young king at the close of* 2 Henry IV. *Throughout the critical history of* Henry V, *commentators have continued to speculate why Shakespeare chose this fate for the character often regarded as his most magnificent comic creation.*]

*Falstaffe* goes off in Disappointment. He is thrown out of Favour as being a *Rake*, and dies like a Rat behind the Hangings. The Pleasure he had given, would not excuse him. The *Poet* was not so partial, as to let his Humour compound for his Lewdness. If 'tis objected that this remark is wide of the Point, because *Falstaffe* is represented in Tragedy, where the Laws of Justice are more strickly observ'd. To this I answer, that you may call *Henry* the Fourth and Fifth, Tragedies if you please. But for all that, *Falstaffe* wears no *Buskins*, his Character is perfectly Comical from end to end. (p. 154)

> Jeremy Collier, "The Authority of Shakespear Against the Mockastrologer," in his A Short View of the Immorality and Profaneness of the English Stage, 1698. Reprint by Garland Publishing, Inc., 1972, pp. 153-54.

## NICHOLAS ROWE   (essay date 1709)

[*Rowe was the editor of the first critical edition of Shakespeare's plays (1709) and the author of the first authoritative Shakespeare biography. He was also one of the leading proponents of the view that Shakespeare had not read classical Greek and Roman playwrights and was thus unaware of classical rules of dramaturgy. The following excerpt is taken from the preface to his 1709 edition of Shakespeare's works. Like many subsequent critics, Rowe praises the account of Falstaff's death offered by Mistress Quickly, the Hostess, in Act II, Scene iii. He also holds that the scene written in French (Act III, Scene iv) clearly demonstrates Shakespeare's knowledge of that language. Like Gerard Langbaine (1691), Rowe believes that the Chorus beginning Act V contains a compliment to the Earl of Essex and thus provides a definite composition date for the play.*]

Whatever *Latin* [Shakespeare] had, 'tis certain he understood *French*, as may be observ'd from many Words and Sentences scatter'd up and down his Plays in that Language; and especially from one Scene in *Henry* the Fifth written wholly in it. (p. iv)

['Tho] the order of Time in which the several [plays] were written be generally uncertain, yet there are Passages in some few of them which seem to fix their Dates. So the *Chorus* in the beginning of the fifth Act of *Henry* V. by a Compliment very handsomly turn'd to the Earl of *Essex*, shews the Play to have been written when that Lord was General for the Queen in *Ireland*. . . . (p. vii)

*Falstaff* is allow'd by every body to be a Master-piece; the Character is always well-sustain'd, tho' drawn out into the length of three Plays; and even the Account of his Death, given by his Old Landlady Mrs. *Quickly*, in the first Act of *Henry* V. tho' it be extremely Natural, is yet as diverting as any Part of his Life. (pp. xvii-xviii)

> Nicholas Rowe, "Some Account of the Life, &c. of Mr. William Shakespear," in The Works of Mr. William Shakespear, Vol. 1, edited by Nicholas Rowe, 1709. Reprint by AMS Press, Inc., 1967, pp. i-xl.

## [CHARLES GILDON]   (essay date 1710)

[*Gildon was the first critic to write extended commentary on the entire Shakespearean dramatic canon. Like many other Neoclassicists, he regarded Shakespeare as an imaginative playwright who nevertheless frequently violated the dramatic "rules" necessary for correct writing. In the excerpt below, Gildon focuses on the role of the Choruses preceding each act. He views the Prologue as Shakespeare's apology to the audience for his "preposterous" attempt to "huddle so many Actions, so many Places, and so many Years into one Play, one Stage and two Hours"— an allusion by the critic to the drama's violation of the Neoclassical principles of unity of time and place. The subsequent Choruses, Gildon argues, serve to bridge the gaps in time between various actions, narrate events not dramatized in the play, and generally amend "the Lameness of the Representation." Since Gildon's commentary, the function and significance of the Chorus in* Henry V *have been addressed by a number of commentators. Gildon also remarks that Fluellen is both "extreamly comical" and admirable. Finally, he raises another important critical issue concerning Henry's wooing of Katherine in Act V, Scene ii: noting that all the French characters except Katherine can converse in English, he contends that the scene is "silly and unnatural."*]

The Prologue to [*Henry V*] is as remarkable as any thing in *Shakespear*, and is a Proof, that he was extremely sensible of the Absurdity, which then possess'd the Stage in bringing in whole Kingdoms, and Lives, and various Actions in one Piece; for he appologizes for it, and desires the Audience to perswade their Imaginations to help him out and promises a Chorus to help their Imagination.

> For 'tis your Thoughts (*says he*) that now must deck
>   our Kings,
> Carry them here and there, Jumping o'er Times;
> Turning the Accomplishments of many years
> Into an Hour-Glass; for the which supply
> Admit me *Chorus* to this History. &c.
>                                             [Prologue, I. 28-32]

He here and in the foregoing Lines expresses how preposterous it seem'd to him and unnatural to huddle so many Actions, so many Places, and so many Years into one Play, one Stage and two Hours. So that it is not to be doubted but that he wou'd have given us far more noble Plays if he had had the good Fortune to have seen but any one regular Performance of this Nature. The Beauty of Order wou'd have struck him immediately, and at once have made him more correct, and more excellent; and I do not at all doubt but that he wou'd have been the *Sophocles* of *England*, as he is now but little more, than the *Thespis* or at most the *Æschylus*. Tho' Tragedy in *Greece* was founded on Religion and came early under the Care of the Magistrate; yet by what I can discover, the Stage was as rude as ours till *Æschylus* gave it Majesty. But in *England* it had no such advantagious Foundation, nor any such nourishing Influence; yet *Shakespear* by his own Genius brought it so far as to leave it some Beauties which have never since been equal'd.

The Character of *Hen*. V. given by the Bishop of *Canterbury* [I. i. 24ff.] is very noble. His Discourse of the *Salique* Law is a Proof, that *Shakespear* was well acquainted with the History of modern Times. . . . (pp. 346-47)

The King's Answer to the French Ambassadours on the *Dauphine*'s Present is not only fine, but shews, that *Shakespear* understood Tennis very well, and is perfect in the Terms of the Art [I. ii. 261ff.]. The *Chorus* is found to come in [at the beginning of Act II] to fill up the Gap of Time and help the Imagination of the Audience with a Narration of what is not represented. In this *Chorus* are a few Lines of good Moral to the *English* and therefore I transcribe them.

> O! *England!* model to thy inward Greatness,
> Like little Body with a mighty Heart;
> What mightst thou do, that Honour wou'd thee do
> Were all thy Children kind and natural.
> > [Chorus, II, 16-19]

King *Henry* Vth's Speech to *Scroop* [II. ii. 126ff.], from this Line—*Oh! how hast thou with Jealousy infected the Sweetness of Affiance*—is very fine. The latter end of the Constable of *France*'s Speech; and Part of the *French* King's [II. iv. 34-40, 50ff.] worth perusing as giving a noble Character of two *English* Kings, and *Exeter*'s Answer to the *French* . . . shews the Spirit of an English Nobleman [II. iv. 76ff.]. The *Chorus* is necessitated to come in again to tell all that must be suppos'd to connect the Representation before to that, which follows. King *Henry*'s Encouragment of his Men [III. i. 1ff.] contains a great many fine Lines. Another *Chorus* begins the [fourth] Act to help out the Lameness of the Representation, and I wonder when *Shakespear* was sensible of the Absurdity of the bringing a Battle on the Stage he shou'd in some Measure do it notwithstanding.

> Where for Pity we shall much Disgrace
> With four or five most vile and ragged Foils
> (Right ill dispos'd in Brawl ridiculous)
> The Name of *Agin Court*. . . .
> > [Chorus, IV, 49-52]

Tho' the Discourses of the King to *Williams,* &c. are very good, and full of Reason and Morality, yet contain they nothing dramatic, and are indeed fitter for a Philosopher, than a King. . . . (pp. 348-49)

What I have already said of *Shakepear*'s being sensible of the Defect of these Historical Representations is confirm'd plainly in the *Chorus* of the fifth Act. . . .

> I humbly pray them to admit excuse
> Of Time, of Numbers, and due Course of things,
> Which cannot in their huge and proper Life
> Be here presented
> > [Chorus, V, 3-6]

He shows how sensible he is of this in the short Chorus that Ends this Play, saying,

> Thus far with rough and all unabled Pen
> Our bending Author hath pursued the Story
> In little Room confining mighty Men;
> Mangling *by Starts* the full Course of their Glory.
> > [Epilogue, 1-4]

And indeed all that can be done in these Cases, is only a Collection of so many Themes of different Subjects. As in *Burgundy*'s Speech [V. ii. 24ff.]. The Description of *Peace* and its Advantages.

The Character of *Fluellen* is extreamly comical, and yet so very happily touch'd, that at the same time when he makes us laugh he makes us value his Character. The Scene of Love betwixt *Henry* V. and *Catharine* is extravagantly silly and unnatural; for why he shou'd not allow her to speak in English as well as all the other *French* I cannot imagine since it adds no Beauty but gives a patch'd and pye-bald Dialogue of no Beauty or Force. (p. 350)

> [Charles Gildon], "Remarks on the Plays of Shakespear," *in* The Works of Mr. William Shakespear,

Vol. 7, 1710. Reprint by AMS Press, Inc., 1967, pp. 345-50.

## ALEXANDER POPE   (essay date 1723)

[*Pope was the foremost English poet of the first half of the eighteenth century, as well as a prolific author of satires written at the expense of his literary contemporaries. Between 1723 and 1725 he published a six-volume edition of the works of Shakespeare which was based upon the text of Nicholas Rowe. Pope was more concerned with poetics than with editorial scholarship, and thus his edition is replete with corruptions, principally interpolations and omissions that he believed would improve the metric patterns of Shakespeare's dramatic verse. In the following excerpt, he initiates one of the merriest and most famous controversies over an emendation in the history of Shakespearean textual studies. Pope explains that he has deleted the words "a Table of green fields" that appear in the First Folio version of Mistress Quickly's description of Falstaff's death, for he believes it is actually a stage direction mistakenly interpolated into the text. "Greenfield was the name of the Property-man," he contends, and a marginal note directed that a table be provided at this point in the action. Modern editions of* Henry V, *however, generally follow the lead of Lewis Theobald (1726) and emend the line to read "and a' [Falstaff] babbled of green fields" (II. iii. 16-17).*]

[*His*] nose was as sharp as a pen, and a table of green fields [II. iii. 16-17]. These words *and a table of green fields* are not to be found in the old editions [of *Henry V*] of 1600 and 1608. This nonsense got into all the following editions by a pleasant mistake of the Stage-editors, who printed from the common piecemeal-written Parts in the Play-house. A Table was here directed to be brought in, (it being a scene in a tavern where they drink at parting) and this direction crept into the text from the margin. *Greenfield* was the name of the Property man in that time who furnish'd implements &c. for the actors. A *Table* of *Greenfield*'s.

> Alexander Pope, in a footnote from The Works of Mr. William Shakespear: Historical Plays, Vol. III, edited by Alexander Pope, Jacob Tonson, 1723, p. 422.

## LEWIS THEOBALD   (essay date 1726)

[*Theobald, a dramatist and classical scholar, was one of the most important editors of Shakespeare's plays in the first half of the eighteenth century. Although his reputation as a Shakespearean editor declined after his death and the value of his work remains a question today, he nonetheless contributed significant emendations which have been adopted by many modern editors. His adaptations of Shakespeare's plays, revised to adhere to Neoclassical dramatic rules, have been less well received. In the excerpt below, Theobald challenges Alexander Pope's emendation of part of Mistress Quickly's narrative account of the death of Falstaff (see excerpt above, 1723), suggesting that the line be read as "a' babled of green Fields" (II. iii. 16-17). He concludes it is more probable that the phrase is part of Shakespeare's original text, not a compositor error, as Pope maintained, for Mistress Quickly is here reporting Falstaff's final moments of delirium before his death.*]

I'll now proceed to consider a Conjecture of the Editor's [Alexander Pope], which I am very free to own is *ingeniously* urg'd: But there is Something more than *Ingenuity* requir'd, to guess for the *Stage* rightly. His Conjecture is grounded upon a marginal Interpolation, that had crept into the Text of some later Editions, in Dame *Quickly*'s admirable Description of the Manner in which *Falstaffe* dy'd.

For after I saw him fumble with the Sheets,
and play with Flowers, and smile upon his Finger's End, I knew there was but one way; for
*his nose was as sharp as a Pen. [II. iii. 13-16]

*His nose was as sharp as a pen, and a table
of green fields.*

*These Words,* and a table of green fields, *are not to be found
in the old Editions of 1600 and 1608. This nonsense got into
all the following Editions by a pleasant mistake of the Stage-
Editors, who printed from the common piece-meal written Parts
in the Play-house. A Table was here directed to be brought
in, (it being a scene in a tavern where they drink at parting,)
and this Direction crept into the text from the margin.* Greenfield *was the name of the Property-man in that time who furnish'd implements, &c. for the actors. A Table of* Greenfield's
[see excerpt above, 1723].

So far, the Note of the EDITOR. Something more than *Ingenuity*
is wanting, as I said before, to make these Conjectures pass
current; and That is, a *competent Knowledge* of the *Stage* and
its *Customs.* As to the History of *Greenfield* being then Property-Man, whether it was really so, or it be only a *gratis dictum*
[a statement not supported by fact], is a Point which I shall
not contend about. But allowing the marginal Direction, and
supposing that a *Table* of *Greenfield*'s was wanting; I positively
deny that it ever was customary (or, that there can be any
Occasion for it) either in the *Promptor's* Book, or piece-meal
*Parts,* where any such Directions are marginally inserted for
the *Properties,* or *Implements* wanted, to add the *Property-
Man*'s Name whose Business it was to provide them. The
Stage-Necessaries are always furnish'd between the *Property-
Man* and the *Scene-Keeper;* and as the Direction is for the
*Promptor*'s Use, and issued from him, there can be no Oc-
casion, as I said, for inserting the Names either of the one, or
the other.

But there is a stronger Objection yet against this Conjecture
of the *Editor*'s, in the Manner he supposes it: Which he must
have foreseen, had he had that Acquaintance with Stage-Books,
which it has been my Fortune to have. Surely, Mr. POPE cannot
imagine, that when Implements are wanted in any Scene, the
Direction for them is mark'd in the Middle of that Scene, tho'
the Things are to be got ready against the Beginning of it. No;
the Directions for *Entrances,* and *Properties* wanting, are always mark'd in the Book at about a Page in Quantity before
the *Actors* quoted are to enter, or the *Properties* be carried on.
And therefore GREENFIELD'S *Table* can be of no Use to us for
this Scene.

I agree, indeed, with Mr. *Pope,* that these Words might be a
*Stage-Direction,* and so crept into the Text from the Margin:
But, I insist, that they must be a Direction then for the *subsequent* Scene, and not for the Scene in *Action.* I don't care
therefore if I venture my Conjecture too upon the Passage: I'll
be sure at least, if it be not altogether right, it shall not be
liable to the *Absurdity* of the *Objection* last struck at. I suppose,
with the Editor, that over-against the Words of the Text, there
might be this Marginal Quotation so close to them, that the
Ignorance of the Stage-Editors might easily give them Admittance into the Text:

--------- *his Nose was as*      *Chairs,* and a Table off.
*sharp as a Pen.*                Green Fields.

The Scene in Action is part of Dame *Quickly,* the Hostess, her
House; and Chairs and Table were here necessary: The fol-

lowing Scene carries us into the *French* Dominions. I therefore
believe This was intended as a Direction to the *Scene-Keepers,*
to be ready to remove the *Chairs* and *Table* so soon as the
*Actors* went off; and to shift the Scene, from the *Tavern,* to a
Prospect of *green Fields,* representing Part of the *French* Territories.

But what if it should be thought proper to retract both Mr.
POPE's and my own Conjecture, and to allow that these Words,
corrupt as they now are, might have belong'd to the Poet's
Text? I have an Edition of *Shakespeare* by Me with some
Marginal Conjectures of a Gentleman sometime deceas'd, and
he is of the Mind to correct this Passage thus;

for his Nose was as sharp as a Pen, and a'
talked *of green Fields.*

It is certainly observable of People near Death, when they are
delirious by a Fever, that they talk of moving; as it is of Those
in a Calenture, that they have their Heads run on green Fields.
The Variation from *Table* to *talked* is not of a very great
Latitude; tho' we may still come nearer to the Traces of the
Letters, by restoring it thus;

----- *for his Nose was as sharp as a Pen, and
a' babled of green Fields.*

To *bable,* or *babble,* is to mutter, or speak indiscriminately,
like Children that cannot yet talk; or dying Persons when they
are losing the Use of Speech. (pp. 137-38)

Lewis Theobald, "The Appendix," in his Shakespeare Restored or, a Specimen of the Many Errors
as Well Committed, as Unamended by Mr. Pope, *J.
Woodman and D. Lyon, 1726, pp. 133-94.*

### SIR THOMAS HANMER (essay date 1743)

[*An eminent member of Parliament during the first quarter of the
eighteenth century, Hanmer compiled a six-volume edition of
Shakespeare's plays (1743-44) that is remarkable for the superior
quality of its typography and engravings. The following excerpt
is taken from the preface to that edition. Hanmer acknowledges
that he has followed Alexander Pope in deleting many "spurious"
passages in* Henry V, *most particularly "that wretched piece of
ribaldry" between Katherine and Alice in Act III, Scene iv. The
only redeeming feature of this scene, the critic declares, is that,
because it is written in French, it is "not intelligible to an English
audience."*]

Most of those passages are here thrown to the bottom of the
page and rejected as spurious, which were stigmatized as such
in Mr. *Pope*'s Edition; and it were to be wished that more had
then undergone the same sentence. The promoter of the present
Edition hath ventured to discard but few more upon his own
judgment, the most considerable of which is that wretched
piece of ribaldry in King *Henry V.* put into the mouths of the
*French* Princess and an old Gentlewoman, improper enough
as it is all in *French* and not intelligible to an *English* audience,
and yet that perhaps is the best thing that can be said of it.
(p. iii)

*Sir Thomas Hanmer, in a preface to* The Works of
Mr. William Shakespear: Comedies, Vol. 1, *edited
by Sir Thomas Hanmer, n.p., 1743, pp. i-vi.*

### [CHARLOTTE LENNOX] (essay date 1754)

[*Lennox was a novelist and Shakespearean scholar who compiled*
Shakespear Illustrated *(1754), a three-volume edition of translated*

*texts of the sources used by Shakespeare in twenty-two of his plays, including some analyses of the ways in which he used these sources. In the excerpt below, taken from that work, Lennox discusses Shakespeare's indebtedness to Holinshed, the wooing scene in Act V, Scene ii, and the character of the Dauphin. She is the earliest commentator to note that many passages in Henry V are either verbatim copies from Holinshed or very close re-wordings and that there is "very little Variation" between the chronicler's description of the principal characters and Shakespeare's presentation of them. Yet, she contends, Shakespeare has made the Dauphin more humorous and animated than either Holinshed and Hall did. Further, Lennox harshly judges Shakespeare's portrayal of Henry's courtship of Katherine, saying that "the great Henry makes but a miserable Figure as a Lover" and the dialogue is more suitable to "a common Soldier making love to an aukward Country Girl."]*

The Transactions comprised in this Historical Play, commence about the latter End of the first, and terminate in the eighth Year of this King's Reign, when he married the Princess *Catharine* of *France*, and put an End to the Differences betwixt *England* and that Crown.

The Siege and taking of *Harfleur*, the Battle of *Agincourt*, the Peace concluded between King *Henry* and the *French* King, with the Marriage of the former to the Princess of *France*, are the principal Actions of this Play, and are taken from *Holingshed*'s Chronicle, after whom the Characters are likewise drawn, with very little Variation.

The Archbishop's Speech to King *Henry*, in the first Act, in which he explains his Title to the Crown of *France* [I. ii. 33-95], is closely copied from this Historian. . . . (pp. 127-28)

In *Shakespear*, when the Conspiracy of *Scroop, Cambridge,* and *Grey,* is discovered to the King, after expostulating with them on their Treachery, he gives them up to punishment and dismisses them from his Presence in the very Words of *Holingshed*. . . . (p. 132)

*Shakespear,* throughout this Play, has copied many of the Sentiments and even Words of *Holingshed,* sometimes almost literally . . . ; at others he has just taken Hints which the Force of his own Imagination improves into the most striking Beauties. . . . (p. 134)

In the first Act of this Play the Dauphin of *France* sends an insulting Message to King *Henry* accompanied with a Present of Tennis Balls as a Reproach for the wild Sallies of his Youth.

There is no Foundation either in *Hall* or *Holinshed* for this Circumstance, *Shakespear* indeed took the out-lines of the Dauphin's Character from these Historians who represent him to be a light, arrogant, and vain-glorious Prince; but he has painted at full Length what they only drew in Miniture; and by adding, with great Propriety some of the Characteristic Follies of his Nation, given us a lively and humerous Picture of a Coxcomb Prince.

The absurdity of making the Princess *Catharine* the only Person in the *French* Court, who does not understand *English,* has been already taken Notice of [see excerpt above by Charles Gildon, 1710]: And it must be confessed that the great *Henry* makes but a miserable Figure as a Lover; no Language can be coarser than that in which he addresses the Princess, the first Time he sees her, *Do you like me Kate, &c.* [V. ii. 107ff.]. Yet the Dialogue is not without wit, livliness, and humour; but so utterly void of Propriety that we lose all Idea of the Dignity of the Persons who manage it, and, are readier to imagine we hear a common Soldier making love to an aukward

Country Girl, than a King of *England* courting a Princess of *France*. (pp. 136-37)

[*Charlotte Lennox*], "The Life of 'King Henry the Fifth'," *in her* Shakespear Illustrated; or, the Novels and Histories, on Which the Plays of Shakespear Are Founded, Vol. III, *1754. Reprint by AMS Press Inc., 1973, pp. 127-41.*

## SAMUEL JOHNSON   (essay date 1765)

*[Johnson has long held an important place in the history of Shakespearean criticism. He is considered the foremost representative of moderate English Neoclassicism and is credited by some literary historians with freeing Shakespeare from the strictures of the three unities valued by strict Neoclassicists: that dramas should have a single setting, take place in less than twenty-four hours, and have a causally connected plot. More recent scholars portray him as a critic who was able to synthesize existing critical theory rather than as an innovative theoretician. Johnson was a master of Augustan prose style and a personality who dominated the literary world of his epoch. The excerpt below from Johnson's commentary on* Henry V *is taken from his 1765 edition of Shakespeare's plays and consists of remarks on individual lines and scenes, as well as a brief overview of the play. He asserts that the drama's principal flaw is "the emptiness and narrowness of the last act," maintaining that when Shakespeare reached this point there was little of substance remaining to be portrayed, and so he was "glad to fill it up with what he could get." Johnson judges Henry's wooing of Katherine to be clumsy and inconsistent with his earlier conduct in both this play and in 1 and 2 Henry IV—as well as reminiscent of Hotspur in 1 Henry IV—and he also notes the conflicting reasons offered by the king and Gower for the slaughter of the French prisoners. A number of nineteenth- and twentieth-century critics have discussed the significance of Henry's order to his soldiers to kill their prisoners. Johnson also raises the issue—subsequently addressed by many other commentators—of Shakespeare's failure to include the character of Falstaff in this play.]*

> QUICKLY. his nose was as sharp as a pen, and
> a' babled of green fields. . . .
>
> [II. iii. 16-17]

Upon this passage Mr. Theobald has a note that fills a page [see excerpt above, 1726], which I omit in pity to my readers, since he only endeavours to prove, what I think every reader perceives to be true, that at this time no "table" could be wanted. Mr. Pope, in an appendix to his own edition . . . seems to admit Theobald's emendation, which we would have allowed to be uncommonly happy, had we not been prejudiced against it by Mr. Pope's first note [see excerpt above, 1723], with which, as it excites merriment, we are loath to part.

> QUICKLY. I put my hand into the bed and felt
> them, and they were as cold as a stone; then I
> felt to his knees, and so upward, and upward,
> and all was as cold as any stone.
>
> [II. iii. 23-6]

Such is the end of Falstaff, from whom Shakespeare had promised us in his epilogue to *Henry IV* that we should receive more entertainment. It happened to Shakespeare as to other writers, to have his imagination crowded with a tumultuary confusion of images, which, while they were yet unsorted and unexamined, seemed sufficient to furnish a long train of incidents, and a new variety of merriment, but which, when he was to produce them to view, shrunk suddenly from him, or could not be accommodated to his general design. That he once designed to have brought Falstaff on the scene again, we know from himself; but whether he could contrive no train of adventures suitable to his character, or could match him with no companions likely to quicken his humour, or could open no new vein of pleasantry, and was afraid to continue the same strain lest it should not find the same reception, he has here for ever discarded him, and made haste to dispatch him, perhaps for the same reason for which Addison killed Sir Roger [de Coverly in *The Spectator*], that no other hand might attempt to exhibit him. (pp. 541-42)

> FLUELLEN. Kill the poyes and the luggage! 'tis expresly against the law of arms; 'tis as arrant a piece of knavery, mark you now, as can be desir'd in your conscience now, is it not?
> GOWER. 'Tis certain, there's not a boy left alive; and the cowardly rascals, that ran away from the battle, have done this slaughter. Besides, they have burn'd or carried away all that was in the King's tent; wherefore the King most worthily has caus'd ev'ry soldier to cut his prisoner's throat. O 'tis a gallant King! . . .
>
> [V. vii. 1-10]

Unhappily the King gives one reason for his order to kill the prisoners, and Gower another. The King killed his prisoners because he expected another battle, and he had not men sufficient to guard one army and fight another. Gower declares that the "gallant King" has "worthily" ordered the prisoners to be destroyed, because the luggage was plundered, and the boys were slain. (pp. 559-60)

> KING HENRY. I'faith, Kate, my wooing is fit for thy understanding; I am glad thou canst speak no better English, for if thou couldst, thou wouldst find me such a plain king, that thou wouldst think I had sold my farm to buy my crown.
>
> [V. ii. 122-26]

I know not why Shakespeare now gives the King nearly such a character as he made him formerly ridicule in Percy [in *Henry IV*]. This military grossness and unskilfulness in all the softer arts, does not suit very well with the gaieties of his youth, with the general knowledge ascribed to him at his accession, or with the contemptuous message sent him by the Dauphin, who represents him as fitter for the ball room than the field, and tells him that he is not "to revel into dutchies," or win provinces "with a nimble galliard" [I. ii. 252-53]. The truth is, that the poet's matter failed him in the fifth act, and he was glad to fill it up with whatever he could get; and not even Shakespeare can write well without a proper subject. It is a vain endeavour for the most skilful hand to cultivate barrenness, or to paint upon vacuity. (p. 565)

This play has many scenes of high dignity, and many of easy merriment. The character of the King is well supported, except in his courtship, where he has neither the vivacity of Hal, nor the grandeur of Henry. The humour of Pistol is very happily continued; his character has perhaps been the model of all the bullies that have yet appeared on the English stage.

The lines given to the chorus have many admirers; but the truth is, that in them a little may be praised, and much must be forgiven; nor can it be easily discovered why the intelligence given by the chorus is more necessary in this play than in many others where it is omitted. The great defect of this play is the emptiness and narrowness of the last act, which a very little diligence might have easily avoided. (p. 566)

*Samuel Johnson, "Notes on Shakespeare's Plays: 'Henry V'," in* The Yale Edition of the Works of Samuel Johnson: Johnson on Shakespeare, *Vol. VIII, edited by Arthur Sherbo, Yale University Press, 1968, pp. 527-66.*

### RICHARD FARMER   (essay date 1767)

[*Farmer was a prominent academic, classicist, and antiquarian whose most important publication,* An Essay on the Learning of Shakespeare *(1767), speculates that the dramatist's knowledge of classical history derived from reading translations of Greek and Latin works. In the following excerpt from that work, Farmer challenges the authenticity of the "early Editions" of* Henry V— *presumably the bad quartos published before the First Folio— and remarks on their evident signs of corruption. He especially maintains that Act III, Scene iv, in which Alice tutors Katherine in the English language, is an interpolation by another writer, for Shakespeare, he insists, "surely would not have admitted such obscenity and nonsense" into his play.*]

[Much] hath been said concerning *Shakespeare*'s acquaintance with the *French* language. In the Play of *Henry the fifth* we have a whole Scene in it [III. iv.]: and in other places it occurs familiarly in the Dialogue.

We may observe in general that the early Editions have not half the quantity, and every sentence, or rather every word most ridiculously blundered. These, for several reasons, could not possibly be published by the Author, and it is extremely probable that the *French* ribaldry was at first inserted by a different hand, as the many additions most certainly were after he had left the Stage.—Indeed, every friend to his memory will not easily believe that he was acquainted with the Scene between *Catharine* and the *old Gentlewoman;* or surely he would not have admitted such obscenity and nonsense. (pp. 277-78)

> *Richard Farmer, in an extract from* Shakespeare, the Critical Heritage: 1765-1774, *Vol. 5, edited by Brian Vickers, Routledge & Kegan Paul, 1979, pp. 259-79.*

### FRANCIS GENTLEMAN   (essay date 1774)

[*Gentleman, an Irish actor and playwright, was the author of* The Dramatic Censor; or Critical Companion *(1770) and contributed the introductions to John Bell's 1774 edition of Shakespeare's plays, from which the following excerpt on* Henry V *is taken. Gentleman asserts that Shakespeare's presentation of the character and conduct of the king is historically faithful and balances the picture of his youthful follies which the dramatist had offered in* 1 *and* 2 Henry IV.]

Our Fifth *Henry*, notwithstanding his unpardonable levity and dissipation, while a prince, shone with such resplendent lustre and dignity, when a monarch, that *Shakespeare*, who had shewn his foibles, was under a kind of necessity to produce him in an improved state, and if we judge by the outset of his prologue, he summoned all his powers, to do the hero justice; nor has he failed; the character is faithfully and ably drawn; it is furnished with language and sentiments suitable; being placed also in the most advantageous point of view. 'Tis true, the plot is irregular, and tainted with some low quibbling comedy, which, as we think, contrary to some idolators of *Shakespeare*, greatly disgrace the serious part; however, upon the whole, we may safely and cordially admit, that there are several passages in this piece, equal to any other the author ever wrote; it would be exceedingly painful to find fault, but that we have many more agreeable opportunities to praise.

*Francis Gentleman, in an introduction to "King Henry" in Bell's Edition of Shakespeare's Plays, Vol. IV, 1774. Reprint by Cornmarket Press, 1969, p. 3.*

## ELIZABETH GRIFFITH  (essay date 1775)

[*Griffith exemplifies the seventeenth- and eighteenth-century preoccupation with searching through Shakespeare's plays for set speeches and passages that could be read out of dramatic context for their own sake. However, she avoided the more usual practice of collecting and commenting on poetic "beauties" and concentrated instead on the "moral" subjects treated in the text. In the excerpt below, Griffith focuses on the character of Henry V. She emphasizes his courage and resolve, his composure, his piety, and the "careless spirit" with which he responds to the insolent taunts of the French, concluding that Shakespeare raises the king "to the highest pitch in our admiration and esteem." Unlike several critics who preceded her, Griffith is not offended by the wooing scene, finding Henry's conduct there entirely consistent with his earlier expressions of "humour, playful spirit, and careless ease."*]

After the surrender of Harfleur, when Henry is on his march to Calais, he is met by Mountjoy, the French Herald, who delivers an insolent defiance from the king of France, requiring to know what ransom he will compound to pay, for leave to retire alive out of the kingdom; to which he replies,

> Thou dost thy office fairly. Turn thee back,
> And tell thy king I do not seek him now,
> But could be willing to march on to Calais
> Without impeachment; for, to say the *sooth*,
> Though 'tis no wisdom to confess so much
> Unto an enemy of craft and vantage,
> My people are with sickness much enfeebled,
> My numbers lessened, and those few I have,
> *Almost no better than so many French;*
> Who, when they were in health, I tell thee, Herald,
> I thought upon one pair of English legs
> Did march three Frenchmen. . . .
>           and so, Mountjoy, fare you well.
> The sum of all our answer is but this:
> We would not seek a battle, as we are,
> Yet, as we are, we say, we will not shun it—
> So tell your master—
>
> [III. vi. 139-50, 162-66]

There is something extremely fine in Henry's reply to the French gasconading taunt above. It is uncommon to meet with so much carelessness and courage in the same character—There is no such description in history, nor have many people, probably, ever been acquainted with it among the living manners of men; and yet the representation of it appears to be so perfectly natural, that we must greatly admire the talents of a writer, who could thus realize, in effect, a mere idea.

The bravery of Henry scorned to deny the condition of his troops, either with regard to their health or numbers: these circumstances the enemy pretended to have been acquainted with already, or were determined to make an experiment of, at least; he therefore openly acknowledges the truth of his weak situation; and this with the same ease and humour, as he would

have delivered himself to Falstaff, had he been his aid-du-camp for the day.

> Upon his royal face there is no note,
> How dread an army have enrounded him
>
> [Chorus, IV, 35-6]

But, at the same time, he most resolutely declares his purpose of trying the event, at every hazard of life, claim, and liberty.

The contemptuous sarcasms he throws out, in this speech, against the French nation, besides shewing an admirable temper and composure of mind in such difficult circumstances, convey also an apt repartee to the scornful insolence of the Dauphin; who, in return to Henry's demanding his right of succession to the crown of France, sent him a parcel of tennis-balls to play with, in allusion to the slight repute of his former life and manners. Pertness is impertinence; but repartee has the *lex talionis*, or law of retaliation, on its side. (pp. 262-63)

> *Henry.*   I was not angry, since I came to France,
> Until this instant. Take a trumpet, Herald,
> Ride thou unto the horsemen on yon hill;
> If they will fight with us, bid them come down,
> Or void the field; they do offend our fight;
> If they'll do neither, we will come to them,
> And make them sker away, as swift as stones
> Enforced from the old Assyrian slings.
>
> [IV. vii. 55-62]

The first sentence in the above speech, is one among the many instances in which Shakespeare has manifested his thorough knowledge in human nature. Henry acts with an heroic resolution during the whole of this perilous conflict, and replies with a daring and careless spirit to all the insolence and contempt of a powerful enemy; but he expresses no rage, nor betrays the least manner of resentment, throughout. The dangers and difficulties of his situation required the utmost command and preservation of his temper. Distress and affliction are sovereign specifics for the pride and fierceness of man's nature. But these restraints being now removed, by his victory, he begins to yield the rein a little to passion, upon seeing the obstinacy of the enemy still continuing after their defeat. (p. 275)

Henry preserves the same spirit of piety after his victory, as he had expressed just before the action, in Scene the [Eighth] of . . . Act [Four]; in imputing his success to the arm and protection of Omnipotence alone.

Henry, Exeter, *and* Fluellin.

> *Henry.*   O God! thy arm was here!
> And not to us, but to thy arm alone,
> Ascribe we all. When without stratagem,
> But in plain shock and even play of battle,
> Was ever known so great, and little loss,
> On one part, and on t'other? Take it, God,
> For it is only thine.
> *Exeter.*   'Tis wonderful!
> *Henry.*   Come, go we in procession to the village;
> And be it death proclaimed through our host,
> To boast of this, or take that praise from God,
> Which is his only.
> *Fluellin.* Is it not lawful, an please your majesty, to tell how many are killed?
> *Henry.*   Yes, captain, but with this acknowledgment,
> That God fought for us.
>
> [IV. viii. 106-20]
> (pp. 276-77)

Shakespeare appears to be so fond of the personage of Henry, that though he has already raised him to the highest pitch in our admiration and esteem, he continues to recommend him to us still further, by introducing him in a new character and situation, that of a lover and a courtier. He did the same for Falstaff before, in the *Merry Wives of Windsor,* at the request of Queen Elizabeth; but here he enters a volunteer in the service. Had any other writer ventured on such an attempt, he would have rendered him a quite different man from himself . . . ; but Henry continues to be the same person still, only appearing in new circumstances; the same humour, playful spirit, and careless ease, remain in his courtship, as may be seen in his rallying of Falstaff, replying to Mountjoy, or exchanging gages with the soldier. (pp. 278-79)

> Elizabeth Griffith, "'Henry the Fifth'," in her The Morality of Shakespeare's Drama Illustrated, 1775. Reprint by Frank Cass & Co. Ltd., 1971, pp. 255-84.

## RICHARD CUMBERLAND   (essay date 1786)

[*Cumberland was a prolific dramatist whose most successful works were sentimental comedies, such as* The Brothers *(1769),* The West Indian *(1770), and* The Fashionable Lover *(1772). In the following excerpt from an essay entitled "Remarks upon the characters of Falstaff and his group," first published in* The Observer: being a Collection of Moral, Literary and Familiar Essays *(1786-91), he discusses the absence of Falstaff from* Henry V. *Unlike most other commentators on this subject, Cumberland does not believe that the fat knight would be out of place in this play. He remarks that there are comic passages even in the battle scenes and that Shakespeare found it appropriate to include such humorous characters as Pistol and Fluellen; interestingly, Cumberland describes the latter of these two figures as "arisen out of the ashes of Falstaff."*]

As it is impossible to ascertain the limits of Shakespeare's genius, I will not presume to say he could not have supported [Falstaff's] humour, had he chosen to have prolonged his existence thro' the succeeding drama of *Henry the Fifth.* We may conclude that no ready expedient presented itself to his fancy, and he was not apt to spend much pains in searching for such. He therefore put him to death, by which he fairly placed him out of the reach of his contemporaries, and got rid of the trouble and difficulty of keeping him up to his original pitch, if he had attempted to carry him through a third drama, after he had removed the Prince of Wales out of his company and seated him on the throne. I cannot doubt but there were resources in Shakespeare's genius, and a latitude of humour in the character of Falstaff, which might have furnished scenes of admirable comedy by exhibiting him in his disgrace, and both Shallow and Silence would have been accessaries to his pleasantry. Even the field of Agincourt, and the distress of the king's army before the action, had the poet thought proper to have produced Falstaff on the scene, might have been as fruitful in comic incidents as the battle of Shrewsbury. This we can readily believe from the humours of Fluellen and Pistol which he has woven into his drama; the former of whom is made to remind us of Falstaff in his dialogue with Captain Gower, when he tells him that— *As Alexander is kill his friend Clytus, being in his ales and his cups, so also Harry Monmouth, being in his right wits and his goot judgement, is turn away the fat Knight with the great pelly-doublet: He was full of jests and gypes and knaveries, and mocks; I am forget his name.—Sir John Falstaff.—That is he.* [IV. vii. 44-51]—This passage has ever given me a pleasing sensation, as it marks a regret in the poet to part with a favourite character, and is a tender farewell to his memory.

It is also with particular propriety that these words are put into the mouth of Fluellen, who stands here as his substitute, and whose humour, as well as that of Nym, may be said to have arisen out of the ashes of Falstaff. (pp. 459-60)

> *Richard Cumberland, in an extract from* Shakespeare, the Critical Heritage: 1774-1801, Vol. 6, *edited by Brian Vickers, Routledge & Kegan Paul, 1981, pp. 447-60.*

## AUGUST WILHELM SCHLEGEL   (essay date 1811)

[*A prominent German Romantic critic, Schlegel holds a key place in the history of Shakespeare's reputation in European criticism. His translations of thirteen of the plays are still considered the best German editions of Shakespeare. Schlegel was also a leading spokesman for the Romantic movement, which permanently overthrew the Neoclassical contention that Shakespeare was a child of nature whose plays lacked artistic form. In the following excerpt, taken from his* Course of Lectures on Dramatic Art and Literature, *originally published in German in 1811, the critic asserts that although Henry V was evidently Shakespeare's "favourite hero in English history . . . endowed with every chivalrous and kingly virtue," the attempt to dramatize his accomplishments was circumscribed by the fact that the conquest of France was the only significant event of his reign. Since "war is an epic rather than a dramatic object," in the theater it can only be a "means by which something else is accomplished," rather than a central interest. To compensate for the limited dramatic substance, the critic contends, Shakespeare introduced the Choruses to remind the spectators that they must amend "the deficiencies of the representation" with their own imaginations and to infuse the drama with "epic pomp and solemnity." Schlegel is also the earliest critic to identify an ironic element in the play; he finds the allusion in Act V, Scene ii to the future child of Henry and Katherine—who is supposed to bring happiness to their nations—intentionally ironic, for their son would be the irresolute and unstable Henry VI.*]

King Henry the Fifth is manifestly Shakspeare's favourite hero in English history: he paints him as endowed with every chivalrous and kingly virtue; open, sincere, affable, yet, as a sort of reminiscence of his youth, still disposed to innocent raillery, in the intervals between his perilous but glorious achievements. However, to represent on the stage his whole history subsequent to his accession to the throne, was attended with great difficulty. The conquests in France were the only distinguished event of his reign; and war is an epic rather than a dramatic object. For wherever men act in masses against each other, the appearance of chance can never wholly be avoided; whereas it is the business of the drama to exhibit to us those determinations which, with a certain necessity, issue from the reciprocal relations of different individuals, their characters and passions. In several of the Greek tragedies, it is true, combats and battles are exhibited, that is, the preparations for them and their results; and in historical plays war, as the *ultima ratio regum* [ultimate argument of kings], cannot altogether be excluded. Still, if we would have dramatic interest, war must only be the means by which something else is accomplished, and not the last aim and substance of the whole. For instance, in *Macbeth,* the battles which are announced at the very beginning merely serve to heighten the glory of Macbeth and to fire his ambition; and the combats which take place towards the conclusion, before the eyes of the spectator, bring on the destruction of the tyrant. It is the very same in the Roman pieces, in the most of those taken from English history, and, in short, wherever Shakspeare has introduced war in a dramatic combination. With great insight into the essence of his art, he never paints the fortune of war as a blind deity who sometimes favours one and sometimes another; without going into the details of the art of war, (though sometimes he even ventures on this), he allows us to anticipate the result from the qualities of the general, and their influence on the minds of the soldiers; sometimes, without claiming our belief for miracles, he yet exhibits the issue in the light of a higher volition: the consciousness of a just cause and reliance on the protection of Heaven give courage to the one party, while the presage of a curse hanging over their undertaking weighs down the other. In *Henry the Fifth* no opportunity was afforded Shakspeare of adopting the last mentioned course, namely, rendering the issue of the war dramatic; but he has skillfully availed himself of the first.—Before the battle of Agincourt he paints in the most lively colours the light-minded impatience of the French leaders for the moment of battle, which to them seemed infallibly the moment of victory; on the other hand, he paints the uneasiness of the English King and his army in their desperate situation, coupled with their firm determination, if they must fall, at least to fall with honour. He applies this as a general contrast between the French and English national characters; a contrast which betrays a partiality for his own nation, certainly excusable in a poet, especially when he is backed with such a glorious document as that of the memorable battle in question. He has surrounded the general events of the war with a fulness of individual, characteristic, and even sometimes comic features. A heavy Scotchman, a hot Irishman, a well-meaning, honourable, but pedantic Welchman, all speaking in their peculiar dialects, are intended to show us that the warlike genius of Henry did not merely carry the English with him, but also the other natives of the two islands, who were either not yet fully united or in no degree subject to him. Several good-for-nothing associates of Falstaff among the dregs of the army either afford an opportunity for proving Henry's strictness of discipline, or are sent home in disgrace. But all this variety still seemed to the poet insufficient to animate a play of which the subject was a conquest, and nothing but a conquest. He has, therefore, tacked a prologue (in the technical language of that day *a chorus*) to the beginning of each act. These prologues, which unite epic pomp and solemnity with lyrical sublimity, and among which the description of the two camps before the battle of Agincourt forms a most admirable night-piece, are intended to keep the spectators constantly in mind, that the peculiar grandeur of the actions described cannot be developed on a narrow stage, and that they must, therefore, supply, from their own imaginations, the deficiencies of the representation. As the matter was not properly dramatic, Shakspeare chose to wander in the form also beyond the bounds of the species, and to sing, as a poetical herald, what he could not represent to the eye, rather than to cripple the progress of the action by putting long descriptions in the mouths of the dramatic personages. (pp. 428-30)

However much Shakspeare celebrates the French conquest of Henry, still he has not omitted to hint, after his way, the secret springs of this undertaking. Henry was in want of foreign war to secure himself on the throne; the clergy also wished to keep him employed abroad, and made an offer of rich contributions to prevent the passing of a law which would have deprived them of the half of their revenues. His learned bishops consequently are as ready to prove to him his indisputable right to the crown of France, as he is to allow his conscience to be tranquillized by them. They prove that the Salic law is not, and never was, applicable to France; and the matter is treated in a more succinct and convincing manner than such subjects usually are in manifestoes. After his renowned battles, Henry

wished to secure his conquests by marriage with a French princess; all that has reference to this is intended for irony in the play. The fruit of this union, from which two nations promised to themselves such happiness in future, was the weak and feeble Henry VI., under whom every thing was so miserably lost. It must not, therefore, be imagined that it was without the knowledge and will of the poet that a heroic drama turns out a comedy in his hands, and ends in the manner of Comedy with a marriage of convenience. (p. 432)

> *August Wilhelm Schlegel, "Criticism on Shakespeare's Historical Dramas," in his* Course of Lectures on Dramatic Art and Literature, *edited by Rev. A. J. W. Morrison, translated by John Black, revised edition, 1846. Reprint by AMS Press, Inc., 1973, pp. 414-45.*

## WILLIAM HAZLITT (essay date 1817)

[*Hazlitt is considered a leading Shakespearean critic of the English Romantic movement. A prolific essayist and critic on a wide range of subjects, Hazlitt remarked in the preface to his* Characters of Shakespear's Plays, *first published in 1817, that he was inspired by the German critic August Wilhelm Schlegel and was determined to supplant what he considered the pernicious influence of Samuel Johnson's Shakespearean criticism. Hazlitt's criticism is typically Romantic in its emphasis on character studies. His experience as a drama critic was an important factor in shaping his descriptive, as opposed to analytical, interpretations of Shakespeare. In the following excerpt from* Characters of Shakespear's Plays, *Hazlitt initiates a long line of negative appraisals of the character of Henry V. He alternates between stinging indictments of the historical ruler and disparagement of the dramatic one, noting that Shakespeare's characterization is historically accurate. However, Hazlitt calls the dramatic Henry V "a very amiable monster" whose bellicose conduct fascinates rather than horrifies us, for the brutal consequences of war cannot be made real in the theater. The critic also charges Canterbury with self-interest and praises both Fluellen and the courtship scene.*]

Henry V. is a very favourite monarch with the English nation, and he appears to have been also a favourite with Shakespear, who labours hard to apologise for the actions of the king, by shewing us the character of the man, as "the king of good fellows" [V. ii. 242-43]. He scarcely deserves this honour. He was fond of war and low company:—we know little else of him. He was careless, dissolute, and ambitious;—idle, or doing mischief. In private, he seemed to have no idea of the common decencies of life, which he subjected to a kind of regal licence; in public affairs, he seemed to have no idea of any rule of right or wrong, but brute force, glossed over with a little religious hypocrisy and archiepiscopal advice. His principles did not change with his situation and professions. His adventure on Gadshill [in *1 Henry IV*] was a prelude to the affair of Agincourt, only a bloodless one; Falstaff was a puny prompter of violence and outrage, compared with the pious and politic Archbishop of Canterbury, who gave the king *carte blanche*, in a genealogical tree of his family, to rob and murder in circles of latitude and longitude abroad—to save the possessions of the Church at home. This appears in the speeches in Shakespear, where the hidden motives that actuate princes and their advisers in war and policy are better laid open than in speeches from the throne or woolsack. Henry, because he did not know how to govern his own kingdom, determined to make war upon his neighbours. Because his own title to the crown was doubtful, he laid claim to that of France. Because he did not know how to exercise the enormous power, which had just dropped into his hands, to any one good purpose, he immediately undertook (a cheap and obvious resource of sovereignty) to do all the mischief he could. Even if absolute monarchs had the wit to find out objects of laudable ambition, they could only ''plume up their wills'' in adhering to the more sacred formula of the royal prerogative, ''the right divine of kings to govern wrong,'' because will is only then triumphant when it is opposed to the will of others, because the pride of power is only then shewn, not when it consults the rights and interests of others, but when it insults and tramples on all justice and all humanity. Henry declares his resolution ''when France is his, to bend it to his awe, or break it all to pieces'' [I. ii. 224-25]—a resolution worthy of a conqueror, to destroy all that he cannot enslave; and what adds to the joke, he lays all the blame of the consequences of his ambition on those who will not submit tamely to his tyranny.... Henry V., it is true, was a hero, a king of England, and the conqueror of the king of France. Yet we feel little love or admiration for him. He was a hero, that is, he was ready to sacrifice his own life for the pleasure of destroying thousands of other lives: he was a king of England, but not a constitutional one, and we only like kings according to the law; lastly, he was a conqueror of the French king, and for this we dislike him less than if he had conquered the French people. How then do we like him? We like him in the play. There he is a very amiable monster, a very splendid pageant. As we like to gaze at a panther or a young lion in their cages in the Tower, and catch a pleasing horror from their glistening eyes, their velvet paws, and dreadless roar, so we take a very romantic, heroic, patriotic, and poetical delight in the boasts and feats of our younger Harry, as they appear on the stage and are confined to lines of ten syllables; where no blood follows the stroke that wounds our ears, where no harvest bends beneath horses' hoofs, no city flames, no little child is butchered, no dead men's bodies are found piled on heaps and festering the next morning—in the orchestra!

So much for the politics of this play; now for the poetry. Perhaps one of the most striking images in all Shakespear is that given of war in the first lines of the Prologue.

O for a muse of fire, that would ascend
The brightest heaven of invention,
A kingdom for a stage, princes to act,
And monarchs to behold the swelling scene!
Then should the warlike Harry, like himself,
Assume the port of Mars, and *at his heels*
*Leash'd in like hounds, should famine, sword, and fire*
*Crouch for employment.*

[Prologue, *1-8*]

Rubens, if he had painted it, would not have improved upon this simile.

The conversation between the Archbishop of Canterbury and the Bishop of Ely, relating to the sudden change in the manners of Henry V., is among the well-known *Beauties* of Shakespear. It is indeed admirable both for strength and grace. It has sometimes occurred to us that Shakespear, in describing ''the reformation'' of the Prince, might have had an eye to himself—

Which is wonder how his grace should glean it,
Since his addiction was to courses vain,
His companies unletter'd, rude and shallow,
His hours fill'd up with riots, banquets, sports;
And never noted in him any study,
Any retirement, any sequestration
From open haunts and popularity.

—*Ely*. The strawberry grows underneath the nettle,
And wholesome berries thrive and ripen best
Neighbour'd by fruit of baser quality:
And so the prince obscur'd his contemplation
Under the veil of wildness, which no doubt
Grew like the summer-grass, fastest by night,
Unseen, yet crescive in his faculty.

[I. i. 53-66]

This at least is as probable an account of the progress of the poet's mind as we have met with in any of the Essays on the Learning of Shakespear.

Nothing can be better managed than the caution which the king gives the meddling Archbishop, not to advise him rashly to engage in the war with France, his scrupulous dread of the consequences of that advice, and his eager desire to hear and follow it.

And God forbid, my dear and faithful lord,
That you should fashion, wrest, or bow your reading,
Or nicely charge your understanding soul
With opening titles miscreate, whose right
Suits not in native colours with the truth.
For God doth know how many now in health
Shall drop their blood, in approbation
Of what your reverence shall incite us to....
Under this conjuration, speak, my lord;
For we will hear, note, and believe in heart,
That what you speak, is in your conscience wash'd,
As pure as sin with baptism.

[I. ii. 13-20, 29-32]

Another characteristic instance of the blindness of human nature to everything but its own interests, is the complaint made by the king of ''the ill neighbourhood'' [I. ii. 154] of the Scot in attacking England when she was attacking France.

For once the eagle England being in prey,
To her unguarded nest the weazel Scot
Comes sneaking, and so sucks her princely eggs.

[I. ii. 169-71]

It is worth observing that in all these plays, which give an admirable picture of the spirit of the *good old times*, the moral inference does not at all depend upon the nature of the actions, but on the dignity or meanness of the persons committing them. ''The eagle England'' has a right ''to be in prey,'' but ''the weazel Scot'' has none ''to come sneaking to her nest,'' which she has left to pounce upon others. Might was right, without equivocation or disguise, in that heroic and chivalrous age. The substitution of right for might, even in theory, is among the refinements and abuses of modern philosophy.

A more beautiful rhetorical delineation of the effects of subordination in a commonwealth can hardly be conceived than the following:—

For government, though high and low and lower,
Put into parts, doth keep in one consent,
Congruing in a full and natural close,
Like music.
—Therefore heaven doth divide
The state of man in divers functions,
Setting endeavour in continual motion;
To which is fixed, as an aim or butt,

Obedience: for so work the honey-bees;
Creatures that by a rule in nature, teach
The art of order to a peopled kingdom. . . .
                                    I this infer,—
That many things, having full reference
To one consent, may work contrariously:
As many arrows, loosed several ways,
Come to one mark;
As many ways meet in one town;
As many fresh streams meet in one salt sea;
As many lines close in the dial's centre;
So may a thousand actions, once a-foot,
End in one purpose, and be all well borne
Without defeat.

                              [I. ii. 180-89, 204-13]

*Henry V.* is but one of Shakespeare's second-rate plays. Yet by quoting passages, like this, from his second-rate plays alone, we might make a volume "rich with his praise,"

    As is the oozy bottom of the sea
    With sunken wrack and sumless treasuries.
                                    [I. ii. 163-65]
                                    (pp. 156-61)

But we must have done with splendid quotations. The behaviour of the king, in the difficult and doubtful circumstances in which he is placed, is as patient and modest as it is spirited and lofty in his prosperous fortune. The character of the French nobles is also very admirably depicted; and the Dauphin's praise of his horse shews the vanity of that class of persons in a very striking point of view. Shakespear always accompanies a foolish prince with a satirical courtier, as we see in this instance. The comic parts of *Henry V.* are very inferior to those of *Henry IV.* Falstaff is dead, and without him, Pistol, Nym, and Bardolph are satellites without a sun. Fluellen the Welchman is the most entertaining character in the piece. He is good-natured, brave, choleric, and pedantic. His parallel between Alexander and Harry of Monmouth, and his desire to have "some disputations" with Captain Macmorris on the discipline of the Roman wars, in the heat of the battle, are never to be forgotten. His treatment of Pistol is as good as Pistol's treatment of his French prisoner. There are two other remarkable prose passages in this play: the conversation of Henry in disguise with the three centinels on the duties of a soldier, and his courtship of Katherine in broken French. We like them both exceedingly, though the first savours perhaps too much of the king, and the last too little of the lover. (p. 164)

> William Hazlitt, "'Henry V'," in his Characters of Shakespeare's Plays, *1817. Reprint by J. M. Dent & Sons Ltd., 1906, pp. 156-64.*

## HERMANN ULRICI   (essay date 1839)

[*A German scholar, Ulrici was a professor of philosophy and the author of works on Greek poetry and Shakespeare. The following excerpt is from an English translation of his* Über Shakespeares dramatische Kunst, und sein Verhältniss zu Calderon und Göthe, *a work first published in German in 1839. This study exemplifies the "philosophical criticism" developed in Germany during the nineteenth century. The immediate sources for Ulrici's critical approach appear to be August Wilhelm Schlegel's conception of the play as an organic, interconnected whole and Georg Wilhelm Friedrich Hegel's view of drama as an embodiment of the conflict of historical forces and ideas. Unlike his fellow German Shakespearean critic G. G. Gervinus, Ulrici sought to develop a specifically Christian aesthetics, but one which, as he carefully points*

*out in the introduction to the work mentioned above, in no way intrudes on "that unity of idea, which preeminently constitutes a work of art a living creation in the world of beauty." In the excerpt below, Ulrici, considering* Henry V *within the context of Shakespeare's other English histories, contends that this specific play dramatizes the "historical and poetical significance" of the war with France. Besides its historical causes, he asserts, this conflict—like all wars—is a "judgment of God," resulting not only in "the development of the intellectual and moral vigour" of these two nations, but also in "the moral purification and amendment of man." According to Ulrici, Henry emerges brave and splendid, and Falstaff's demise is morally, as well as dramatically, appropriate. The critic further claims that despite the numerous outcries against the so-called wooing scene, the episode properly establishes marriage as the foundation of national peace.*]

[Considering] "Henry the Fifth" as the centre of interest in the two parts of "Henry the Fourth," we are only the more ready to look upon the drama which bears his name as a continuation of the foregoing. In fact it is simply the *third* and next act of the great tragedy. The historical stability which, under Henry the Fourth, the house of Lancaster had yet to struggle for, gains a brief prescription under his son. His title to the crown is undisputed. On the contrary, the moral strength, and manly energy of his character, and his true kingly mind, defy all competition. Against so good an internal title to the throne, no one would be bold enough to set up a mere external claim. And yet the intrinsic rottenness of his historical position is still discernible, although in a different form. In the first place, the life of so upright and gracious a prince is constantly threatened by the treacherous and murderous designs of a few selfish and ambitious nobles; the blackest ingratitude and treachery embitter his kingly office, and disappoint his fairest hopes. This is the bearing of the conspiracy of the Earls of Cambridge, Grey, and Scrope, which is episodically interwoven with the general fable. In the next place, it is to divert the thoughts of the nobles and people from the internal affairs of the state, that Henry, in obedience to his dying father's advice, not more than to the dictates of his own judgment, enters upon plans of foreign conquest. Even though truly and properly speaking the war with France may have had a deeper and different origin, still this object was no doubt the motive which led him to commence the campaign so suddenly, and with so little preparation. Although the personal heroism of Henry, and the constitutional bravery of the English, brought it quickly to a glorious termination, it nevertheless proved at a later period the fruitful source of misery and disgrace to England, and gave the chief shock to the grandeur and stability of the House of Lancaster. For the reign of Henry the Sixth, which in peaceful times might have been beneficial, was in no wise fitted for the troublesome consequences of this war, and the renewed outbreak of the dispute with France. Amid circumstances of such difficulty its inherent weakness was laid bare, and served but to stimulate the pretensions of the other claimants of the royal house, as well as the restlessness of the powerful and ambitious nobles. In this manner the disturbance of history, begun in the reign of Richard, was carried through that of Henry the Fifth into the times of his feeble successor. With such wonderful tact has the poet illustrated the significant and intrinsic coherence which runs through a whole century of English history.

The war with France forms essentially the dramatic action of "Henry the Fifth." It exhibits in the strongest possible light [the] preponderance of the *Epic* element in the *historical* drama. . . . A war which is the death-struggle of two valiant and chivalric nations furnishes poetical materials such as preeminently belong to the Epos. To treat such a subject dramatically is in the highest degree difficult. It is a vulgar opinion that wars are *made* by kings at the mere impulses of their own private passions and interests. They are no doubt co-operating, and, to a superficial view, appear the immediate causes. But in truth, a national war, such as we have here depicted, is *never,* simply speaking, made, but is an organic growth, like every other historical phenomenon. In other words, it results by a certain intrinsic *necessity* from the past course of history, the present posture of political circumstances, and by the general spirit of the age. If, therefore, poesy would exhibit war in its true historical light, it must apprehend it as a necessary member of the organism of history. This is a task which for obvious reasons must be much easier for the narrative of an epos than the action of a drama to accomplish. And yet Shakspeare has succeeded in it, by the aid no doubt of an extrinsic, but nevertheless perfectly allowable and appropriate expedient. By the introduction of a chorus as prologue, he has given a narrative exposition of all such events as did not admit of being exhibited dramatically. Whatever, on the contrary, is of leading moment, such as the delineation of the spirit of the age in relation both to the past and the national characters of the two belligerent parties, is thrown out in truly dramatic style by the most vivid action. . . . [Shakspeare has] employed the different *characters* of the two *nations* as motives of the historical action. The modest practical patriotism of the English, conscious of their strength, is justly offended at the haughty arrogance of the French, which speaks forth so loudly in the Dauphin's contumelious message to Henry. Shakspeare has not left unnoticed, even in his "Richard the Second" and "Henry the Fourth," the rivalry which the proximity of the two nations, and their conflicting political interests, as well as the affinity and connection of the two royal houses, had fomented between France and England, from the reign of John, and even earlier, and which spreading from the throne to the very lowest of the people, had degenerated into national hatred. The war was as popular on both sides as it was inevitable.

But to depict a popular war with truth and justice, ample space must be given in the delineation to the co-operation and activity of the *people.* While, therefore, in "King John," the mutual relation of Church and State; in "Richard the Second," the kingly office and dignity; and in "Henry the Fourth" the true position and influence of a nobility and of chivalry, are brought prominently forward, as constituting the general condition of the historical development respectively, in "Henry the Fifth" it is the people in the narrower sense of the term that is presented to us, and its character and relation both to the State and the other members of the body politic, as well as the degree of its participation in, and mode of viewing historical events, that are distinctly laid open. The nobles and grandees of the kingdom fall as it were voluntarily into the background, and merge more and more into the general body of the people, whenever a great and ruling mind, like Henry the Fifth, is at the head of the State. This consideration furnishes the poetic justification of all the scenes, where we meet with private soldiers, camp servants, and officers,—where the Prince is represented as holding free intercourse with his people, or sitting in deliberation with his principal generals,—and where also the characters of the different races of his subjects are dramatically embodied in appropriate representations: such as Fluellen, Macmorris, and Jamy.

The genuine historical import of the war is however at the same time truly poetical; and I have no hesitation to declare it as my opinion, that this historical and poetical significance is the ground-idea of the whole drama. Every war is essentially a *judgment of God,* in the same sense that universal history is the tribunal of the world. Its commencement and its close are alike a divine Providence—a moment in that divine superintendence of the world's history, of which a sense pervades the whole drama, and which finds an utterance in the words of Henry: "We are in *God's* hand, brother, not in theirs" [III. vi. 169]. These words, spoken on the evening of the fatal day of Agincourt, which was to decide the fortunes of two great nations, and indeed the entire scene in which they occur, diffuse over the whole representation a deeply serious tone. They proclaim a high and solemn tribunal before which history and the world is judged. The drama gives rise insensibly to a calm feeling of religious awe. It elevates our reverence of God, to see a handful of tired and famished Englishmen, animated by their own and their king's heroism, and in full resignation to the will of God, attacking and routing three or four times as numerous an army of well-fed and well-equipped Frenchmen; and the hand of God aiding the mental and moral vigour of man, to defeat a power far superior outwardly, but weak from inward depravity. Justly, therefore, might Henry exclaim, after the battle:—

> ————————O God! thy arm was here,
> And not to us, but to thy arm alone
> Ascribe we all.
>
> [IV. viii. 106-08]

But the end of war is not only to promote the development of the intellectual and moral vigour of nations and their rulers—not merely to afford room to the most richly-gifted characters, such as the noble Henry V., to unfold all the riches of its inmost life, and to display in different lights its many capacities and qualities, which otherwise would never be manifest: it has a higher and nobler aim—the moral purification and amendment of man. Shakspeare has traced this amelioration in the English and French armies, but chiefly in the person of Henry, who, at first but a rough jewel, and only cleansed by his father's death from the filth with which it was encrusted, and first cut and polished by the great emergency, shines forth in native beauty and splendour. On the other hand, whatever is incapable of improvement must meet with punishment and destruction under the retributive scourge of heaven. Accordingly the poet has again introduced upon the scene Falstaff's *impure* companions, Bardolph, Nym, and Pistol, in order to shew forth their appropriate but shameful end. The very story of Falstaff's death, who cannot survive the loss of the King's favour, and his banishment from the court, which has blighted for him all the joys of life, is episodically introduced, in order that the least seed even of the great poetic creation might not be lost, but that every one should find his due, and every member of the great dramatic action have for himself a proper beginning, middle, and end.

Thus does the true import of war appear to be coincident with the end and essence of history itself. While the poet exhibits war, though springing in the first instance from the sinfulness of man, as a judgment of God, the executioner of divine justice, and the medium of His grace—and consequently a lever of the development of history, and a means of the advancement of the human race—in this fundamental idea of his poem, he has at the same time seized and depicted the most important moments of history itself.

But although we have hitherto left unnoticed the immediate external cause and the particular circumstances of this great national war, they have not been neglected by Shakspeare him-

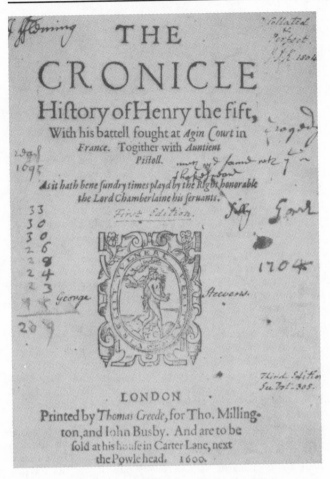

*Title page of the First Quarto of* Henry V *(1600).*

self. A questionable *right* led to the war. The drama accordingly opens with an examination of the title on which it is founded. However debateable Henry's legal claim may have been, his inward title was only the more indisputable. Accordingly, he gains and maintains the victory. But as the war had its external cause and beginning, it must also have a similar close; the contested claims must be decided finally. Historically this is accomplished by Henry's marriage with Catherine of France, with the reversion of the French throne on the death of Charles VI. With the same events the drama also closes. This conclusion has been frequently censured, on the ground that the love-making and espousals of the fifth act are, it is justly urged, little in unison with the serious, heroic, and epical subject-matter of the first four. But in truth the war itself is only *apparently* ended; it does not *really* come to end for several decades later, when Henry has long rested in the grave. But, on the other hand, it should be remembered, that the drama does not stand isolated by itself; and it is only a part of a greater whole, and with outstretched arms reaches far into the great trilogy which follows. On the other hand, the natural and intrinsic relation between war and marriage has been overlooked in the censure. It resembles that which subsists between life and death. As war springs out of peace, inasmuch as the collected forces of peace press outwardly under the action of constant collision; so war, whenever it is just, is in its turn the parent of peace. But now the most lively type of peace is marriage, the foundation of the family and the state, and the germ of a new and vigorous life. It is quite true that the peace

here made is no real pacification—it is an outward peace only; the princes, and not the nations, are reconciled. But is the poet to be blamed for this? If critics are determined to tear his work from its organic connexion with the following dramas, then the concluding peace may and must be taken for a true and genuine resting point, and it is the natural close both of the war and of the drama. If, on the other hand, it be considered in the connexion in which it really stands with the other pieces of the great historical drama, then its true close is "Henry the Sixth;" and the last act of "Henry the Fifth" is but a transition point, which conveys however the same important lesson which runs through the whole piece, teaching us that war and peace are not to be made arbitrarily at the caprices and humours of man. It is on this account that, as Schlegel has justly remarked, a decided tone of irony prevails in the fifth act [see excerpt above, 1811]. Moreover, all these objections have proceeded from the mistaken theory, that every historical drama ought to be simply a tragedy or a comedy. Now "Henry the Fifth" is manifestly neither the one nor the other; and this the sticklers of theory could not forgive. Most of these oblique and distorted judgments have been passed upon "Henry the Fifth" by those notion-mongers who reject every thing as false and blame-worthy that they find difficult to reconcile with their own factitious theories. (pp. 379-85)

*Hermann Ulrici, "'Henry V'," in his* Shakspeare's Dramatic Art: And His Relation to Calderon and Goethe, *translated by Rev. A. J. W. Morrison, Chapman, Brothers, 1846, pp. 379-85.*

**THOMAS CARLYLE** (lecture date 1840)

[*A noted nineteenth-century essayist, historian, critic, and social commentator, Carlyle was a central figure of the Victorian age in England and Scotland. In his writings, he advocated a Christian work ethic and stressed the importance of order, piety, and spiritual fulfillment. In the excerpt below from remarks first delivered as a lecture on May 12, 1840, Carlyle commends the epic qualities of Shakespeare's histories, particularly praising the dramatist's evocative portrayal of the battle of Agincourt in* Henry V.]

August Wilhelm Schlegel has a remark on [Shakespeare's] Historical Plays, *Henry Fifth* and the others, which is worth remembering. He calls them a kind of National Epic. Marlborough . . . said, he knew no English History but what he had learned from Shakspeare. There are really, if we look to it, few as memorable Histories. The great salient points are admirably seized; all rounds itself off, into a kind of rhythmic coherence; it is, as Schlegel says, *epic;*—as indeed all delineation by a great thinker will be. There are right beautiful things in those Pieces, which indeed together form one beautiful thing. That battle of Agincourt strikes me as one of the most perfect things, in its sort, we anywhere have of Shakspeare's. The description of the two hosts: the worn-out, jaded English; the dread hour, big with destiny, when the battle shall begin; and then that deathless valour: "Ye good yeomen, whose limbs were made in England!" [III. i. 25-6]. There is a noble Patriotism in it,—far other than the 'indifference' you sometimes hear ascribed to Shakspeare. A true English heart breathes, calm and strong, through the whole business; not boisterous, protrusive; all the better for that. There is a sound in it like the ring of steel. This man too had a right stroke in him, had it come to that! (pp. 101-02)

*Thomas Carlyle, "The Hero as a Poet: Dante, Shakspeare," in his* On Heroes, Hero-Worship and the

Heroic in History, *Chapman & Hall, Limited, 1840, pp. 73-106.*

## CHARLES KNIGHT  (essay date 1849)

[*Knight, an English educator and publisher, wrote numerous books and periodicals intended to educate the Victorian working class. Among these were his highly popular illustrated edition of Shakespeare's plays and a complementary illustrated biography of Shakespeare. In addition, Knight also produced a book of critical commentary on the plays,* Studies of Shakspere (1849), *and was a founder of the first Shakespeare Society. In the following excerpt from his 1849 study, he asserts that Shakespeare himself probably realized that the subject of* Henry V *was "essentially undramatic" and, without Falstaff, "extremely meagre and unsatisfying," but public demand obliged him to complete the story begun in 1 and 2* Henry IV. *Knight is the earliest commentator to maintain that the play offers no dramatic conflict, for we are never in any doubt about the outcome of the English campaign against the French and Shakespeare offers no subplot of human frailty and intrigue to divert our interests. However, he praises the dramatist for constructing a realistic yet patriotic portrayal of Henry and of the horrors of war.*]

"Shakspere," says Frederick Schlegel, "regarded the drama as entirely a thing for the people, and, at first, treated it throughout as such. He took the popular comedy as he found it, and whatever enlargements and improvements he introduced into the stage were all calculated and conceived according to the peculiar spirit of his predecessors, and of the audience in London" [in his *Lectures on the History of Literature*]. This is especially true with regard to Shakspere's Histories. In the case of the 'Henry V.' it appears to us that our great dramatic poet would never have touched the subject, had not the stage previously possessed it in the old play of 'The Famous Victories.' 'Henry IV.' would have been perfect as a dramatic whole, without the addition of 'Henry V.' The somewhat doubtful mode in which he speaks of continuing the story appears to us a pretty certain indication that he rather shrunk from a subject which appeared to him essentially undramatic. It is, however, highly probable that, having brought the history of Henry of Monmouth up to the period of his father's death, the demands of an audience, who had been accustomed to hail "the madcap Prince of Wales" as the conqueror of Agincourt, compelled him to "continue the story" [2 *Henry IV*, Epilogue, 27-8]. That he originally contemplated lending to it the interest of his creation of Falstaff is also sufficiently clear. It would be vain to speculate why he abandoned this intention; but it is evident that, without the interest which Falstaff would have imparted to the story, the dramatic materials presented by the old play, or by the circumstances that the poet could discover in the real course of events, were extremely meagre and unsatisfying. It is our belief, therefore, that, having hastily met the demands of his audience by the first sketch of 'Henry V.,' as it appears in the quarto editions, he subsequently saw the capacity which the subject presented for being treated in a grand lyrical spirit. Instead of interpolating an under-plot of petty passions and intrigues,—such, for the most part, as we find in the dramatic treatment of an heroic subject by the French poets,—he preserved the great object of his drama entire by the intervention of the chorus. Skilfully as he has managed this, and magnificent as the whole drama is as a great national song of triumph, there can be no doubt that Shakspere felt that in this play he was dealing with a theme too narrow for his peculiar powers. . . . The didactic lessons of moral prudence,—the brief sententious precepts,—the *descriptions* of high actions and high passions,—are alien from the whole spirit of Shakspere's drama.

The 'Henry V.' constitutes an exception to the general rules upon which he worked. "High actions" are here described as well as exhibited; and "high passions," in the Shaksperean sense of the term, scarcely make their appearance upon the scene. Here are no struggles between will and fate; no frailties of humanity dragging down its virtues into an abyss of guilt and sorrow,—no crimes,—no obduracy,—no penitence. We have the lofty and unconquerable spirit of national and individual heroism riding triumphantly over every danger; but the spirit is so lofty that we feel no uncertainty for the issue. We should know, even if we had no foreknowledge of the event, that it must conquer. We can scarcely weep over those who fall in that "glorious and well-foughten field" [IV. vi. 18], for "they kept together in their chivalry" [IV. vi. 19], and their last words sound as a glorious hymn of exultation. The subject is altogether one of lyric grandeur; but it is not one, we think, which Shakspere would have chosen for a drama.

And yet how exquisitely has Shakspere thrown his dramatic power into this undramatic subject! The character of the King is altogether one of the most finished portraits that has proceeded from this masterhand. It could, perhaps, only have been thoroughly conceived by the poet who had delineated the Henry of the Boar's Head, and of the Field of Shrewsbury. The surpassing union, in this character, of spirit and calmness, of dignity and playfulness, of an ever-present energy, and an almost melancholy abstraction,—the conventional authority of the king, and the deep sympathy, with the meanest about him, of the man,—was the result of the most philosophical and consistent appreciation by the poet of the moral and intellectual progress of his own Prince of Wales. And let it not be said that the picture which he has painted of his favourite hero is an exaggerated and flattering representation. The extraordinary merits of Henry V. were those of the individual; his demerits were those of his times. . . . At any rate, it was not for the poet to regard the most popular king of the feudal times with the cold and severe scrutiny of the philosophical historian. It was for him to embody in the person of Henry V. the principle of national heroism; it was for him to call forth "the spirit of patriotic reminiscence." . . . Frederick Schlegel says, "The feeling by which Shakspere seems to have been most connected with ordinary men is that of nationality." But how different is his nationality from that of ordinary men. It is reflective, tolerant, generous. It lives not in an atmosphere of falsehood and prejudice. Its theatre is war and conquest; but it does not hold up war and conquest as fitting objects for nationality to dedicate itself to, except under the pressure of the most urgent necessity. Neither does it attempt to conceal the fearful responsibilities of those who carry the principle of nationality to the last arbitrement of arms, nor the enormous amount of evil which always attends the rupture of that peace, in the cultivation of which nationality is best displayed. Shakspere, indeed, speaks proudly as a member of that English family

Whose blood is fet from fathers of war-proof;

[III. i. 18]

but he never forgets that he belongs to the larger family of the human race. When Henry tells the people of Harfleur,

The gates of mercy shall be all shut up,

[III. iii. 10]

and draws that most fearful picture of the horrors of a sacked city, the poet tells us, though not in sententious precepts, that nationality, when it takes the road of violence, may be driven to put off all the gentle attributes of social life, and, assuming the "action of the tiger" [III. i. 6] have the tiger's undiscriminating bloodthirstiness. When Henry, on the eve of the battle, walks secretly amidst his soldiers, the poet makes him hear that truth which kings seldom hear, and which, however the hero, in this instance, may contend with it, cannot be disguised or controverted:—"If the cause be not good, the king himself hath a heavy reckoning to make; when all those legs, and arms, and heads, chopped off in a battle, shall join together at the latter day, and cry all—we died at such a place; some, swearing; some, crying for a surgeon; some, upon their wives left poor behind them; some, upon the debts they owe; some, upon their children rawly left. I am afeard there are few die well that die in battle; for how can they charitably dispose of anything when blood is their argument?" [IV. i. 134-43]. Again, when Henry has won France, what a France does the poet present to the winner!—

 ——All her husbandry doth lie on heaps,
Corrupting in its own fertility.
Her vine, the merry cheerer of the heart,
Unpruned dies: her hedges even-pleach'd,
Like prisoners wildly overgrown with hair
Put forth disorder'd twigs: her fallow leas
The darnel, hemlock, and rank fumitory,
Doth root upon; while that the coulter rusts,
That should deracinate such savagery:
The even mead, that erst brought sweetly forth
The freckled cowslip, burnet, and green clover,
Wanting the scythe, all uncorrected, rank,
Conceives by idleness; and nothing teems
But hateful docks, rough thistles, kecksies, burs,
Losing both beauty and utility:
And as our vineyards, fallows, meads, and hedges,
Defective in their natures, grow to wildness;
Even so our houses, and ourselves, and children,
Have lost, or do not learn, for want of time,
The sciences that should become our country;
But grow, like savages,—as soldiers will,
That nothing do but meditate on blood,—
To swearing, and stern looks, diffused attire,
And everything that seems unnatural.

           [V. ii. 39-62]

Thoughts such as these, coming from the great poet of humanity and wisdom, are the correctives of a *false* nationality. (pp. 182-84)

    *Charles Knight, " 'King Henry V'," in his* Studies
    of Shakspere, *Charles Knight, 1849, pp. 180-85.*

### G. G. GERVINUS (essay date 1849-50)

[*One of the most widely read Shakespearean critics of the latter half of the nineteenth century, the German critic Gervinus was praised by such eminent contemporaries as Edward Dowden, F. J. Furnivall, and James Russell Lowell; however, he is little known in the English-speaking world today. Like his predecessor Hermann Ulrici, Gervinus wrote in the tradition of the "philosophical criticism" developed in Germany in the mid-nineteenth century. Under the influence of August Wilhelm Schlegel's literary theory and Georg Wilhelm Friedrich Hegel's philosophy, such German critics as Gervinus tended to focus their analyses around a search for the literary work's organic unity and ethical import. Gervinus believed that Shakespeare's works contained a rational ethical system independent of any religion—in contrast to Ulrici, for whom Shakespeare's morality was basically Christian. In the following excerpt, taken from* Shakespeare Commentaries, *a work which originally appeared in German in 1849-50, Gervinus offers*

*the earliest extended examination of the character of the king, emphasizing Henry's "many-sided nature" and his "pious humility and fear of God." He contends that the king's piety is the central feature of his character, noting the numerous occasions throughout the play when Henry gives to God all honor and glory for the English military successes. Gervinus is the first critic to contend that Henry's ambitiousness, his occasional impatience and boasting, and his zealous pursuit of honor recall the character of Percy in* 1 Henry IV, *but he also asserts that Henry's gracious condescension to his soldiers and the "tranquil repose" he displays on the eve of the battle of Agincourt distinguish him from the irascible Percy. On other matters, Gervinus maintains that the scenes which feature the French aristocrats "border on caricature." He also comments at length on Fluellen, whom he praises for his courage and integrity.*]

The whole interest of our play lies in the development of the ethical character of the hero. After the poet has delineated his careless youthful life in the first part of *Henry IV.*, and in the second part has shown the sting of reflection and consideration piercing his soul as the period of self-dependence approaches, he now displays Henry as arrived at the post of his vocation, and exhibits the king acting up to his resolutions for the future. At the very beginning of the play we are at once informed of the utter change which has passed over him. The sinful nature is driven out of him by reflection, the current of reformation has suddenly scoured away the old faults; as the wholesome strawberry ripens best 'neighboured by fruit of baser quality' [I. i. 62], so his active practice, his intercourse with lower life and simple nature, has matured in him all those gifts which etiquette and court ceremony would never have produced in him, and which those now around him perceive in him with admiration. The poet expressly tells us, through the prelates who discuss the king in the first scene, that there are no miracles, either in his poetry or the world, and that the natural grounds for this wonderful change are to be sought for really in the unpromising school of this apparently untutored man. There this many-sidedness was developed, which now astonishes them in him, and on account of which he now appears equally acquainted with all things, ecclesiastical and secular, in the cabinet as in the field. He no longer squanders his now valuable time, but weighs it to the last grain; the curb of mildness and mercy is now placed on his passions, and even foreign lands conjecture that

   his vanities fore-spent
Were but the outside of the Roman Brutus,
Covering discretion with a coat of folly.

          [II. iv. 36-8]

And *how* justly his systematic wickedness was calculated, how entirely according to his design the unexpected sunshine broke through the veil of clouds is excellently expressed in the scene in which the king first meets us again, discussing with his counsellors the important business of the wars with France. The force and courage of men, the success and the favour of Providence, is manifest in every word of this discussion. . . . Every one, in the suddenness of his gladly disappointed expectation, appears as if electrified. The thought of honour prevails in every breast. All classes are equally devoted to him in heroic unity; his family, his uncle and brothers, no less than the nobles, urge him to the war; the clergy give him the mightiest sum that they had ever granted to an English king; they depict to him the heroic age of the Edwards, and call him to renew their feats; everything breathes courage and good will. As if seized with a better spirit, even Bardolph, Nym, and Pistol seem to settle their quarrels among themselves, that as sworn brothers they may march against France. The Eumenides of the insurrection, who had disturbed and crossed the rule of Henry IV., are heard retreating in the distance. The Irish, who had rebelled against Richard II., and the Welsh and Scotch, with whom Henry IV. had to fight, appear together as countrymen in the king's army. The treachery of a few bribed nobles is easily frustrated. The words of the dying Henry IV. are fulfilled, that the crown seemed in him merely as 'an honour snatched with boisterous hand' [*2 Henry IV,* IV. v. 191], and the quarrel which arose in consequence was the argument of which his reign had been the scene. His death 'changed the mode.' The young king follows the home policy which his father had in dying commended to him; he leads those 'overproud with sap and blood' [*Richard II,* III. iv. 59] into foreign war, and turns their thoughts to new and greater things.

This policy urges Henry to the French war; he is urged to it by right and the well-grounded claim of which with religious conscientiousness he is convinced; he is urged to it by his ambition, which bids him compensate for his youth and its idleness by great deeds. His history, he desires, shall speak with full mouth freely of his acts, or else his grave 'shall have a tongueless mouth, not worship'd with a waxen epitaph' [I. ii. 232-33]. The scorn of the enemy and the mocking taunt at his madly-spent youth excite his passion for the righteous war, which he has undertaken with steadfast resolve, and to this passion he gives vent in an ambition equally scornful:—he never valued 'this poor seat of England' [I. ii. 269], but when he rouses himself in his throne of France, for which he has laid by his majesty, he will 'rise there with so full a glory, that he will dazzle all the eyes of France' [I. ii. 278-79]. It is in this war that he acknowledges himself the most offending soul alive if it be a sin to covet honour; for now he has the great object before him, as we have said before, in behalf of which it must seem to him noble to be roused. In his fight at Agincourt he has before him even to surpass the warlike Edwards, when, with a little, weak, famished band, he has to withstand the brilliant force of the French, at least five-fold more in number. And in this position he aspires truly after the wholly undiminished glory of a position so desperate; he prefers not to lose so much 'honour as one man more would share from him' [IV. iii. 31-2], who should come to his assistance from England.

In these expressions somewhat of that strained nature may seem to lie, which we [may observe] in Percy [in *1 Henry IV*] as opposed to Henry; and truly we see the king in this over-strained condition throughout the whole war. This would be a contradiction in his character, if anything were a contradiction in it; but . . . it belongs to his nature and essence to be everything when occasion calls him and necessity claims him. We found him indolent and idle amid the degeneracy of a corrupt period of peace; now that he is in the war he is a soldier, showing himself collected and eager, mighty and violent in word and deed, acquainted with the terrible ravages of war, and with unrestrained passions ready even at the right moment to unbridle them himself. In peace, he says himself, nothing so becomes a man as modest stillness and humility; but in war he must 'imitate the action of the tiger, stiffen the sinews, summon up the blood, and disguise fair nature with hard-favoured rage' [III. i. 6-8]. Just so, influenced less by principle than after his fashion by time and place, the king's behaviour at first towards the French ambassador is marked by resolute decision; he sends back defiance and contempt to the scornful Dauphin; he is announced by the French embassy as coming 'in thunder, and in earthquake, like a Jove' [II. iv. 100]; and thus we see him before Harfleur, threatening the citizens with

all the terrors of a besieged town. Once had *Prince* Henry said that he was 'not yet of Percy's mind' [*1 Henry IV,* II. iv. 101-02], but the *King* is so now. Just in the same way would Percy's impatient spirit have chafed before a besieged city; just in the same way as Henry does would Percy have broken out with boasting before the scornful French ambassadors, infected by the soil of the boastful nation; just in the same way did Vernon's words provoke Percy at Shrewsbury as the Dauphin's message now does the prince; and yet, at his subsequent wooing of Katherine, he is as entirely the soldier, as far from quibbling rhetoric and as free from all arts of verse and mincing as Percy ever could have appeared. The world now compares him, as the poet once had done Percy, to Cæsar and to Alexander. He appears now wrathful and terrible as the war-god, when, in the battle of Agincourt, furious at the plunder and slaughter committed by the flying French, he commands the death of the prisoners. His ambition now also, like Percy's, imperceptibly passes into a thirst for honour, which, when in hasty impatience it desires to obtain an object, weighs not means and ways.

But that which at once obliterates all these similarities to Percy is the contrast of circumstances, which at once draw in him those opposite qualities which Percy could not have possessed. Left to himself, and unprovoked, the braggart is all humility; in the pauses of rest the warlike tiger is peaceful and tame. He calls himself a man like every other, whose affections are indeed higher mounted, yet when they stoop they stoop with the like wing. Percy's affections did not do this. Never would he have been seen, least of all as king, in that condescension which marks Henry in his present position; never, in the moment of serious preparation for hot strife, would he have exhibited the tranquil repose which Henry manifested. In his courtship and on the day of battle Henry is just as plain a king as if he had 'sold his farm to buy his crown' [V. ii. 125-26]. He has shaken off his old dissolute companions, but the remembrances of that simple intercourse are recalled to our mind at every moment. The same inclination to rove about with the common man in his army, the old mildness and familiarity, and the same love for an innocent jest, exist in him now as then, without derogating in the least from his kingly dignity. He leaves his nobles waiting in his tent, while he visits the posts of his soldiers; the old habit of night-watching is of use to him now; he sounds the disposition of individuals; he encourages them without high-sounding words; he fortifies them without ostentation; he can preach to them and solve moral scruples, and can make himself intelligible to them; he contrives a trick quite of the old kind in the moment of most gloomy suspense; like a brother, he borrows the cloak of the old Erpingham; he familiarly allows his countryman Fluellen to join freely in his conversation with the herald, and in his short appeal before the battle he declares all to be his brothers who on this Crispin's day shed their blood with him.

This contrast between his repose and calmness and his martial excitement, between his plain homely nature and the kingly heroic spirit which in the moment of action exercises dominion over him, is, however, not the only one in which the poet has exhibited him. The night before and the day during the battle, which form the centre of our play, is a period so prominent, and one in which such manifold moods, emotions, and passions are roused and crossed, that the best opportunity was here afforded to the poet for exhibiting to our view this many-sided man in all the richness and the diversity of his nature. When the mind is quickened, he himself says, 'the organs break up their drowsy grave, and newly move with casted slough and fresh legerity' [IV. i. 21-3]: and thus is it with him in this great and decisive moment. We see him in a short time alternate between the most different emotions and positions, ever the same master over himself, or we may rather say, over the opportunity and the matter which lie for the moment before him. The French herald comes and challenges him to ransom himself from his unavoidable detention; he returns a proud bragging declaration; he repents it while he is speaking. He is seized with a moment of passion, as in that collision with the Chief Justice [in *2 Henry IV*], but at once he is again master of himself; nor was he so forgetful, even in the moment of excitement, as in any way to neglect the truthfulness of his nature; imprudently he conceals not from the enemy the critical condition of his little army. At night, well knowing the danger of his position, we find him in the most serious mood: he desires no other company, he and his bosom will debate awhile. This debating is disturbed by contact with all sorts of people belonging to his camp. He hears the scorn of the boaster, he listens to the voice of the pedantic lover of discipline, and he talks with the apprehensive who are better and braver than their words. That truth so incapable of dissimulation speaks in him even here. What would it have cost him to boast of the king, in the name of a third person, and to declare that he was cheerful and full of trust? But he does it not; he desires as little in the soldiers as in himself to extinguish the consciousness of danger, in order that he may spur them by the necessity to their utmost exertion. When he remarks this anxious expectation, he assures them truly that the king himself would not wish to be anywhere but where he is. The serious natures are occupied with the question as to whether they must answer with their souls for the possible injustice of the royal cause they fight for, or whether the king, if they die for him unprepared, will have to answer for their sins? He turns field preacher and explains to them; he falls into a quarrel on the matter with the coarse Williams; he takes up the jest as well as the edifying conversation, though the acting out of the matter is to be disturbed by the bloody seriousness of the battle. After the unexpected interruption and its half-constrained humorous turn the king sinks all the more completely into solemn deliberation with himself; meditation and seriousness overtake and overburden his soul. After the soldiers had just been laying their cares and burdens to the king's charge, how natural is the sequence of this same king's train of thought, that having known the happiness of private life he should recall it to his mind at this hour, when ceremony, the prerogative of kings from which he was ever escaping, must appear so empty to him. He, he says in the deepest self-consciousness of his real sterling value, he is a king who has found out this ceremony and its importance! How enviously (standing before the last pinnacle of his fame, as his father had done before in the moment of sickness and distress), how enviously he looks upon the healthful occupation of the peasant, who rises with the sun, 'sweats in the eye of Phoebus, and all night sleeps in Elysium' [IV. i. 273-74]—and how affecting and striking is it, and how completely in the spirit of this king by merit, that in sight of this happy toil of the poor, returning to his former idea, he sees the vocation of the king in this, that he, conscious and vigilant, with *his own* labour and exertions, establishes that security of the state and that peace which the poor man enjoys in unconscious happiness. His meditation upon the ideas thus aroused is followed by the perfect collectedness of mind exhibited in that fervent prayer, in which he prays God 'not to-day' [IV. i. 293] to think upon his father's fault. Then he rides forth to see the order of the battle. And as he meets his nobles, and hears Westmoreland's wish to have here 'one ten thousand of those men in England that do no

work' [IV. i. 17-18], he shows how seriously he means to gain for himself, out of this very necessity, the highest prize of honour without further help. How popular after his old fashion, and at the same time how sublime, is his encouragement to the battle! How calm his last words to the French herald! How far is he from being over-hasty in giving credit to the victory! When he hears of the touching death of the noble York, how near is he to tears! and at the same moment, alarmed by a new tumult, how steeled to a bloody command! how impatiently furious at the last resistance! and at the moment when victory decides for him, how pious and how humble! And again, a short time after this solemn elevation of mind, he concludes his joke with Williams, careful even then that no harm should result from it. The poet has continued in the fifth act to show us to the very last the many-sided nature of the king. The terrible warrior is transformed into the merry bridegroom, the humorous vein again rises within him; yet he is not so much in love with his happiness, or so happy in his love, that in the midst of his wooing, and with all his jest and repartee, he would relax the smallest article of the peace which his policy had designed.

But how is it? Has not the poet forgotten that grand feature in Henry's character, that profound modesty, which formerly, as if willfully, veiled all his brilliant qualities? Is it only expressed in the serious mood before the battle, which is however natural, even in the coarse, quarrelsome Williams, when in a similar position? Or was there no occasion to display this former characteristic of the prince, which appeared to us the very marrow of his virtue? Or did he cast it off for this once at this noble provocation for the exertion of all his powers. We saw him at the battle of Shrewsbury [in *1 Henry IV*] voluntarily yield one glorious deed to his inglorious friend; but here he has fought a battle, the whole glory of which falls on him alone, and which the poet with evident design has cast upon him alone, since he keeps the heroic forms of Bedford, Salisbury, and York so completely in the back-ground. What turn does his modesty take, if it retains its old character of avoiding after its fashion this glaring light of fame? The answer is this: it deepens in the same degree as his fame becomes more exalted; it becomes humility, and gives the honour to God. This sentence will shock many of Shakespeare's worshippers, who discover in him nothing but aesthetic and moral free-thinking, and who regard him as a man of disorderly and wild genius. But to our mind the truth of the sentence and the truth of the delineation of the character can be little disputed. Throughout the whole play, throughout the whole bearing of the king, sounds the key-note of a religious composure, of a severe conscientiousness, and of an humble modesty. The Chronicle itself, which extols Henry so highly that it placed him before the poet as an historical favourite, praises the king's piety at home and at every page in his campaign; Shakespeare accepted this historical hint in no mechanical manner, but wrought it appropriately into the characteristics of his hero. The clergy, at the very beginning of the play, call him a true friend of the Church, and have reason to rejoice over his respect for it, as well as over his knowledge of sacred things. When he is occupied with the plan of war, he charges the Archbishop of Canterbury with a solemn oath to take heed in his counsel; he 'will believe in heart,' that what he speaks as to his right to this war is in his 'conscience washed as pure as sin with baptism' [I. ii. 30, 31-2]. When he has no thought but France, those to God alone 'run before' his business. He receives it as a promising ordinance from God that the treason lurking in his way is 'brought to light' [II. ii. 185]. He delivers his 'puissance into the hand of God, putting it straight in expedition' [II. ii.

190-91]; 'God before,' he says several times, he will come to take his right. He orders his old friend Bardolph to be pitilessly executed for robbing a church; he wishes all such offenders to be cut off; for he knows well that when 'lenity and cruelty play for a kingdom, the gentler gamester is the soonest winner' [III. vi. 118]. We have seen him previous to the battle in solemn preparation, and engaged in edifying conversation with his soldiers. His first word on the certainty of the victory is— 'Praised be God, and not our strength, for it!' [IV. vii. 87]. When he reviews the greatness of the victory, he says again: 'Take it, God, for it is only thine!' [IV. viii. 111-12]. And that this is in earnest, he orders even death to be proclaimed to any who may boast of it or take the honour from God. At his triumphal entry into London he forbids the sword and helm, the trophies of his warlike deeds, to be borne before him; and the poet says expressly of him, in the prologue, what once the prince had said of himself on that day at Shrewsbury over Percy's body—that he was 'free from vainness and self-glorious pride, giving full trophy, signal, and ostent, quite from himself to God' [Chorus, V, 20-2]. The atonement which his father could not attain to, for want of energetic, persevering, inward stimulus, is accomplished by him. In his prayer to God before the battle, when he wishes that 'the sense of reckoning' may be taken from his soldiers and that his father's fault may not be thought upon, he declares that he has 'interred anew' Richard's body, has wept over it and has ordered masses to be said; that he has five hundred poor in yearly pay, 'who twice a day their withered hands hold up toward Heaven' for him [IV. i. 291, 295, 299-300]. The poet, we see plainly, adheres to the character of the age, and invests Henry with all that outward work of repentance which in that day was considered necessary for the expiation of a crime. To many he will appear to have gone too far in this, both as regards his hero, who is otherwise of so unshackled a mind, and himself, rising as he does generally so far above the narrow views of his own, to say nothing of older times. But above this objection, also, the poet soars victoriously in those excellent words which he puts into the mouth of the king at the close of that penitential prayer:—

> More will I do;
> Though all that I can do is nothing worth,
> Since that my penitence comes after all,
> Imploring pardon.
> [IV. i. 302-05]

Shakespeare has in no wise attributed to the king this pious humility and fear of God as an occasional quality, upon which he places no more value than upon any other; we see from the repeated reference to it, we see from the nature of the character and its consequent bearing in various circumstances, we see from the plan of the whole play, that this trait is intended to form the central point of the whole. The poet works with the same idea in which Æschylus wrote his warlike pieces, the Persians and the Seven before Thebes: namely, that terrible is the warrior who fears God, and that on the other hand the blossom of pride ripens into the fruit of evil and the harvest of tears. For entirely in this sense has Shakespeare depicted the camp of the French and their princes, in Xerxes-like arrogance and crime, in opposition to the little troop of Britons and their intrepid pious hero. He shows this arrogance in their dividing the lion's skin before the hunt; in the French king wishing to bring the English prince in a chariot captive to Rouen; in the Dauphin, in derision of his youthful tricks, sending a tun of tennis-balls to the man who is pondering with such anxious conscientiousness his articles of war; in their playing

at dice beforehand for 'the low-rated English' [Chorus, IV, 19]; in their bribing the English nobles with money to murder their king. Shakespeare's age designated that impious reliance on human power by the name of *security,* and this bold confidence in their number and this proud contempt of the enemy is imputed by the poet to the French camp. With arrogant desire they long for the day which the English are awaiting in suspense and doubt; they spend the night in noise and din which the English pass waking in uneasy calmness, and in edifying preparation; they sparkle with shining weapons, and they boast of splendid steeds, while 'the beggared host' [IV. ii. 43] of the Britons go in war-worn coats and ride famished horses; they look down with haughty boasting on the heads so heavily armed yet devoid of 'intellectual armour' [III. vii. 138], and compare their fool-hardy courage to that of their mastiffs; while the English, as if the king had imparted his soul to them, calm in their anxiety, gather rather fresh courage from necessity, self-respect, and fidelity. Among the French leaders there is hardly one who does not vie with another in empty boasting and bragging, not one who does not share the childish delight in dress and military decoration, not one whom the seriousness of things can draw away from insipid witticisms and vain debates, not one who showed even a tinge of the seriousness and of the calm courage and devotion of the English. But the Dauphin surpasses them all in shallow self-complacency, in frivolous arrogance, and in this merry bragging from natural narrowness of capacity. These scenes, if only from the broken French introduced, border on caricature; Shakespeare here, if anywhere, has fallen too easily into a weakness of the age. It seems to me more than probable that a jealous patriotic feeling actuated our poet in the entire representation of his Prince Henry: the intention, namely, of exhibiting by the side of his brilliant contemporary, Henry IV. of France, a Henry upon the English throne equal to him in greatness and originality. The greatness of his hero, however, would appear still more estimable if his enemies were depicted as less inestimable. It alone belonged to the ancients to honour even their enemies. Homer exhibits no depreciation of the Trojans, and Æschylus no trace of contempt of the Persians, even when he delineates their impiety and rebukes it. In this there lies a large-hearted equality of estimation, and a nobleness of mind, far surpassing in practical morality many subtle Christian theories of brotherly love. That Shakespeare distorts the French antagonists, and could not even get rid of his Virgil-taught hatred against the Greeks, is one of the few traits which we would rather not see in his works; it is a national narrow-mindedness, with which the Briton gained ground over the man. The nations of antiquity, who bore a far stronger stamp of nationality than any modern people, were strangers to this intolerant national pride; even the Romans were so; on their triumphal arches they fashioned the statues of captive barbarian monarchs, noble in outward form, and showing in their whole bearing all the hostile defiance of independence.

Shakespeare has in this play also brought the popular king Henry into close contact with the people; his society is, however, now wholly different to that of his youth. At that time extravagance and idleness, thieving and loitering, were placed by his side, in order to make the contrast more sensible of his own occasional participation in the wantonness of the others; now the poet has found it necessary to present a wholly different contrast, designed to show us that his new moral severity and religious character rest not on the mechanism of an ecclesiastical habit, and that the free-spirited youth has in no wise become an old devotee. Shakespeare could not dare to exhibit the plain contrast of a religious bigot; the religious spirit and puritanical strictness of the age did not permit it; the whole English stage of the period never ventured, to my knowledge, to portray a character even slightly tinged with religious bigotry. Shakespeare therefore has rather exhibited by the side of the king the worldly aspect of an austerity and conscientiousness of this kind; he displays it as grown into a habit, respectable but not too accountable, so that we at once feel the contrast to the unshackled mind of his hero, in whom religious fervour, like each of his qualities, was developed according to the nature of circumstances; in whom it became apparent before, over the body of Percy, at the tidings of his father's illness, and as early as at that first soliloquy upon the crown; in whom it now blazes forth more brightly on the great occasion of a war between two mighty states, at an undertaking in which the boldest is reminded of his dependence on external powers. Among the more serious popular characters—the steady, worthy Gower, the rough Williams, and the dry Bates—the Welshman Fluellen, the king's countryman, is the central point. He is, as the king himself says, a man of 'much care and valour,' but 'out of fashion' [IV. i. 84-5]. Compared with the former companions of the Prince, he is like discipline opposed to licence, like pedantry opposed to dissoluteness, conscientiousness to impiety, learning to rudeness, temperance to intoxication, and veiled bravery to concealed cowardice. Contrasted with those boasters, he appears at first a 'collier' who pockets every affront. In common with his royal countryman, he is not what he seems. Behind little caprices and awkward peculiarities is hidden an honest, brave nature, which should be exhibited by the actor . . . without playfulness or caricature. Open and true, he suffers himself to be deceived for a time by Pistol's bragging, then he seems coldly to submit to insult from him, but he makes him smart for it thoroughly after the battle, and then gives him 'a groat to heal his broken pate' [V. i. 58-9]. He settles the business on which Henry sets him against Williams and which brings him a blow, and when the king rewards Williams with a glove full of crowns, he will not be behind in generosity, and gives him a shilling. He speaks good and bad of his superiors, ever according to truth, deeply convinced of the importance of his praise and blame, but he would do his duty under each. He is talkative in the wrong place, takes the word from the lips of others, and is indignant when it is taken from him; but in the night before the battle he knows how to keep himself quiet and calm, for nothing surpasses to him the discipline of the Roman wars, in which this is enjoined. The cold man flashes forth warmly like the king when the French commit the act, so contrary to the law of arms, of killing the soldiers' boys. At the time of his respect for Pistol, the latter begs him to intercede for the church-robber Bardolph, but he made his appeal to the wrong man. It is a matter of dicipline, in which Fluellen is inexorable. Indeed he especially esteems his countryman king for having freed himself of these old companions. This is the essential point to him in his learned comparison between Henry V. and Alexander the Great, that the latter killed his friends in his intoxication, while the former turned away his when he was in 'his right wits' [IV. vii. 47]. Since then his countryman is inscribed in his honest scrupulous heart, though before he had certainly made little of the dissolute fellow; now he cares not who knows that he is the king's countryman, he needs not to be ashamed of him 'so long as his majesty is an honest man' [IV. vii. 114-15]. Happy it is that the noble Henry can utter a cordial amen to this remark, 'God keep me so' [IV. vii. 116]; his captain Fluellen would at once renounce his friendship if he learned from him his first dishonourable trick. The self-contentedness of an integrity,

unshaken indeed, but also never exposed to any temptation, is excellently designed in all the features of this character.

The pedantic-like discipline and love of order, the valour by line and level of the brave Fluellen, though it may appear in an old-fashioned light compared with the well-based and free virtue of the king, stands out on the other hand by its unassuming nature in advantageous contrast to the worthlessness of his boasting companions, Pistol, Nym, and Bardolph. The poet allows us through them to have another glimpse of the early intercourse of the prince. At the commencement of the important period they appear a little elevated, but circumstances again ruin them. Their seducer Falstaff is no longer with them; a better spirit accompanies them in the boy, whom we venture to take for the page in the second part of *Henry IV.*, and who honourably falls in battle with the boys. He characterises his three companions, whom he thought of leaving, so distinctly that we require no other analysis. They are soon again 'sworn brothers in filching' [III. ii. 44-5], and Bardolph and Nym bring themselves to the gallows. As a proof that Shakespeare has not made the king act inconsiderately to Falstaff . . . he makes him say expressly, at Bardolph's fall, that he 'would have all such offenders so cut off' [III. vi. 107-08]. Pistol is not so bold a thief as they, and he is, therefore, dismissed with the more lenient lesson from Fluellen, who makes him eat his Welsh leek, and 'cudgels his honour' from his limbs. The poet did not again introduce the fat Falstaff; we hear only of his death. From the epilogue to *Henry IV.* it was undoubtedly Shakespeare's intention to let him appear in this piece also. During the work itself he must have discovered that this was no longer practicable. He could only have exhibited him in ever greater debasement, and this would have destroyed the symmetry and the great design of the play. (pp. 340-52)

G. G. Gervinus, "'Henry V'," in his Shakespeare Commentaries, *translated by F. E. Bunnètt, revised edition, 1877. Reprint by AMS Press, Inc., 1971, pp. 339-52.*

### WILLIAM WATKISS LLOYD  (essay date 1856)

[Lloyd was a classical and Elizabethan scholar whose "The Life of the Poet and critical essays on the plays" was first published in S. W. Singer's edition of The Dramatic Works of William Shakespeare (1856); the study was subsequently reprinted independently in 1858 and the critical portions reissued in 1875. In the excerpt below, Lloyd identifies in Henry V a recurring pattern of hypocrisy, sanctimony, and moral blindness. He asserts that Henry V represents a world in which "wrangling princes trample upon humanity" and "cover all with the cloak of half-faced piety and spurious religion," and where the frequent references to God are more "sanctimonious than sincere, ostentatious and politic than truly pious." In Act I, Scene ii, Lloyd maintains, the king manipulates the clergymen into falsely believing that he is indifferent to the prospect of a French campaign; as a result, and to avoid the threat of church reform, they offer him lavish funding for his war and intentionally distorted opinions of the legality of his claim to the throne of France. Concerning Henry's exchange with Bates and Williams and his soliloquy at the close of Act IV, Scene i., the critic charges that the king understands no more than the soldiers the moral issues involved, and that Henry recognizes his complicity in the murder of Richard II, displays an affected and self-pitying discontent with his life, and exhibits "at least as much of weakness of mind and superstition as of hypocrisy." Lloyd's assessment of the world of Henry V is one of the most negative in the critical history of the play.]

The historical drama of Henry the Fifth is . . . by no means an independent whole, rounded off and complete within itself from commencement to end. Much of its contents, the purport of incidents, the characters of agents, cannot be felt, cannot even be understood, unless as following up impressions and remembrances of former plays. And so the entire moral of the action can scarcely be gathered from the action itself, and is only salient in the story of *Henry VI.* . . . True it is that Falstaff, now dying and soon dead, never comes in presence on the stage, but the play cannot open and show the new king in dignified state without some thoughts reverting to his disgraced companion, and the recollection is indulged and addressed accordingly. So, again, we shall be in danger of misconstruing the spirit of the play both historically and personally, if we do not retain from the anterior play [*2 Henry IV*], the thought of the counsel of the dying Bolingbroke to his son, to busy his nobility with foreign wars and so fence his title; and the thought, also, from the general disposition evinced by the Prince of Wales, of how far a sage counsel was likely to sink into his mind, and with what steady self-restraint and reserve he could at once conceal and act upon it. Nay, we must be retentive of warnings still further back, and entertain the argument of the immediate story, with remembrance how far it is but episodical to a more comprehensive movement that was set in motion in the play of *Richard II.* It is there that the Bishop of Carlisle's prophecy foretells the horrors of the civil wars, and the contested succession of the divided house, consequent on the usurpation of Bolingbroke. . . . In the mind of the spectator of the present play, as in that of the king, there is therefore the latent sense, the half suspended consciousness, that a back account of original misdoing may be at any time, and must at last be brought forward; but, meanwhile, the mere vigour of personal character of the occupant of the throne defers the catastrophe, holds the realm well together and perfectly in hand, and launches its whole power with such effect as to make an era in the history of the country, and establish a precedent of chivalrous achievement and pretension, from which it must ever after be loath to recede.

At the conclusion of the former play, it was intimated that the direction in which the new king designed to carry out his father's policy of external enterprise, was not the Holy Land but France; and forward as the war-exciting zeal of the bishops appears, the poet does not permit us to regard the king as duped or directed by them; the subsidy they propose to furnish is in regard of causes already in hand, and they only lend their eager aid to push on the prosecution of those causes, in order that the aid by which they buy their immunity from reform may be indispensable. The king, by their own account, affects so much indifference in the question they fear, as to whet their anxiety, and thus he obtains from them not only pecuniary supply, but all the important diplomatic furtherance that is gained by the holy sanction and perverted colour of historical traditions, of the law not only of nations and of Holy Writ, but of nature,— citations of half obliterated genealogies, the book of Numbers, and the order and analogies of the human microcosm and the honey bees.

The poet leaves no uncertainty as to the motives of the Archbishop; and when he makes him, in his second speech, read from a draft of the bill for the civil application of Church temporalities, the advantages are so expressed as to engage the sympathy of the spectators for its design as both politic and charitable, and very decidedly against its opposers. When, therefore, from the same lips we receive the overstrained eulogium of the king, some suspicion is aroused which assuredly is not, or should not, be dispersed when, with an air of solemn conscientiousness, he invokes a holy and disinterested state-

ment of his French claims, and is so easily satisfied with what is so glibly provided for him. . . . [The] dignitary proves what he is called and required to prove, and follows up with exhortations to the king to unwind his "bloody flag," and when a military nobleman avouches that the hearts of Englishmen lie pavilioned in the fields of France, the Christian churchman takes up the cue with overdone and somewhat revolting animation:—

> O! let their bodies follow, my dear liege,
> With blood, and sword, and fire to win your right!
>                                                        [I. ii. 130-31]

In the same scene we have also conveyed to us a sense of the complete command of the king over the military element of his power, founded on the confidence and respect he inspires, and on hearty sympathy with the enterprise of which he puts himself at the head.

It is under these conditions of questionable motives, questionable because dynastic rather than patriotic, and because faced and guarded with holy pretences and assumed conscientiousness, that the war is commenced, and its course does not belie the falsities of its origin. It carries us along with all the interest excited by the prowess of fellow-countrymen, who reply to shallow taunts with dignified retort and challenge, oppose discipline to irregularity and coolness to flightiness, and when hemmed in by fivefold odds, reject indignantly every suggestion of surrender, and looking forward to the peril at once collectedly and cheerfully, respond to the gallant incitements of their leader in a spirit and accents like his own; and whether for the assault of the perilous breach, or the reception of an out-numbering charge, acquit themselves so manfully, that even private soldiers rise to the height of heroic achievement and bravery. In this there is no little glory, and a glory that it ever behoves a country, with independence and authority to be defended, to be eager for, jealous of, proud of; but here this glory, otherwise susceptible of far higher enrichment, simply ends. The cause at issue is not so exalted, as to continue the excitement to the height after the decision of the pitched field. The enterprise was commenced with a frequency of reference to the Divine name, which in such a connection seems rather sanctimonious than sincere, ostentatious and politic than truly pious. In the king's soliloquy, however, before the battle, it appears that there is at least as much of weakness of mind and superstition as of hypocrisy in the case. He stands truly in awe of Divine Power, but in truth this seems to be the only divine attribute he recognizes. The very terms of his prayer prove his consciousness that he is at heart still guilty of consent to the terms by which his crown was purchased, the murder of Richard; and hopeless of immunity from the consequent penalty, he presses for the postponement of it. With anxiety and urgency he pleads the merit of pompous and ceremonial reparation, and even while he promises still more, is brought back to the confession that true penitence has scarcely been his motive and remains at last to pay. Knowing as the spectator is supposed to know and must remember,—for Shakespeare, when a main point has been sufficiently impressed, does not lower his demand of attention by reminding of it or repeating it,—what relation the expedition bears to the retention of the murder-purchased sovereignty, the prayer of Henry sounds to him but as deprecation of the descent of divine vengeance for a crime, while he aims at securing the results of it by commission of another. Side by side with the blaze of heroism throughout the play, we have lively allusion to the havoc and atrocities of war, and side by side also appeals to God; and it is shame and pity if we cannot see the native blackness of ambition all the more distinctly, when the very picture and figure of mangled peace and desolated society lies bleeding before us, and wrangling princes trample upon humanity to resent a mock and found ill-gotten power, and cover all with the cloak of half-faced piety and spurious religion. (pp. 251-54)

[By] the very conditions of the subject theme, when the battle is won and the excitement of danger and the admiration of resolution is exhausted, the triumph and sequel are likely to be somewhat tame; the spirits have been exalted throughout, but the heart, we are surprised to find, remains comparatively unmoved, and we are relieved from impending disappointment when the course of the play strikes into comedy, and the still living appetite for excitement is slaked by the indulgence of an afterpiece, for such we may consider the concluding act.

In Harry the Fifth, . . . the active energies are more powerful . . . than the reflective; engrossed by a pursuit or a passion, his whole nature is promptly co-operant in furtherance of it, but he can never, even for a moment, so far disengage himself from it as to take any other point of view. In his night talk with the soldiers the limitations of minds, sophisticated by station and unsophisticated, mutually define each other. Private Williams and private John Bates have a clear and honest sense of royal responsibility; their own duty is to obey and to fight bravely, but it is for the king to look to the justice of the cause and be answerable for it—and answerable moreover, for some unrepented sins of those whom a false quarrel may bring to death prematurely and in ill blood;—a clear principle enough and palpable to plain sense, and, in fact, the very touchstone of the moral position of Henry in the action of the play. His reply at the moment, and his soliloquy after, are sufficiently in harmony to evince the sincerity of his reply, and thus to prove that he is as unconsciously blind when he answers with plausible detail a different question to that which is proposed, as the questioners who accept his conclusions and leave satisfied. With lucid exposition he proves that if a sinful servant miscarry on a lawful errand, the imputation of his wickedness cannot justly lie on the master who so dispatched him, whereas the hypothesis laid out that the errand was unlawful, and made no question of the servant not answering for himself, but of his damnation aggravating that of his master, not being transferred to him. The soldiers are not acute enough to check this logic, and freely admit the new case stated. Williams, however, has still a genuine English jealousy of royal sincerity, and the renewed difference leads to the challenge. The king left alone reverts to the earlier discussion, and a careless reader, interpreting by his own impulses, too often assumes in the opening reflections, that suddenly alone, the awful sense of regal responsibility rushes upon his mind and finds his feeling conscience. No such thing; in mingling indignation and discontent he reflects on the ingratitude of the subject, commiserates the hardship of his own, the royal lot, runs through the evils of the station with which dignity is coupled, and then contrasting, as his father had done before him, the superior happiness and ease of the lowly, he slides insensibly into such a description with such epithets, of a state of existence divided between toil and mere insensibility, as convicts his complaint of self-imposing affectation at last. (pp. 254-55)

*William Watkiss Lloyd, "Critical Essays on 'King Henry V'," in his* Critical Essays on the Plays of Shakespeare, *1875. Reprint by George Bell and Sons, 1909, pp. 251-67.*

**ALGERNON CHARLES SWINBURNE**   (essay date 1880)

[*Swinburne was an English poet, dramatist, and critic who devoted much of his literary career to the study of Shakespeare and other Elizabethan writers. His three books on Shakespeare—*A Study of Shakespeare *(1880),* Shakespeare *(1909), and* Three Plays of Shakespeare *(1909)—all demonstrate his keen interest in Shakespeare's poetic talents and, especially, his major tragedies. Swinburne's literary commentary is frequently conveyed in a style that is markedly intense and effusive. In the excerpt below, taken from* A Study of Shakespeare, *the critic contends that Shakespeare has drawn Henry with serious flaws as well as pure and noble qualities. Swinburne maintains that Henry and the churchmen are chiefly motivated by "the principle of self-interest."*]

Henry V. is the first as certainly as he is the noblest of those . . . daring and calculating statesmen-warriors whose two most terrible, most perfect, and most famous types are Louis XI. and Caesar Borgia. Gain, "commodity," the principle of self-interest, . . . is . . . evidently the mainspring of Henry's enterprise and life. . . . The supple and shameless egotism of the churchmen on whose political sophistries he relies for external support is needed rather to varnish his project than to reassure his conscience. Like Frederic the Great before his first Silesian war, the future conqueror of Agincourt has practically made up his mind before he seeks to find as good reason or as plausible excuse as were likewise to suffice the future conqueror of Rosbach. In a word, Henry is doubtless not the man . . . to do the devil's work without his wages; but neither is he, on the like unprofitable terms, by any manner of means the man to do God's. No completer incarnation could be shown us of the militant Englishman—*Anglais pur sang* [pure-blooded Englishman]; but it is not only, as some have seemed to think, with the highest, the purest, the noblest quality of English character that his just and far-seeing creator has endowed him. The godlike equity of Shakespeare's judgment, his implacable and impeccable righteousness of instinct and of insight, was too deeply ingrained in the very core of his genius to be perverted by any provincial or pseudo-patriotic prepossessions; his patriotism was too national to be provincial. . . . [Shakespeare] certainly was not "too English" to see and cleave to the main fact, the radical and central truth, of personal or national character, of typical history or tradition, without seeking to embellish, to degrade, in either or in any way to falsify it. (pp. 112-14)

*Algernon Charles Swinburne, "Second Period: Comic and Historic," in his* A Study of Shakespeare, *R. Worthington, 1880, pp. 66-169.*

**DENTON J. SNIDER**   (essay date 1890)

[*Snider was an American scholar, philosopher, and poet who closely followed the precepts of the German philosopher Georg Wilhelm Friedrich Hegel and contributed greatly to the dissemination of his dialectical philosophy in America. Snider's critical writings include studies on Homer, Dante, and Goethe, as well as Shakespeare. Like Hermann Ulrici and G. G. Gervinus, Snider investigated both the dramatic unity and ethical import in Shakespeare's plays, but he presented a more rigorous Hegelian interpretation than those two German philosophical critics. In the introduction to his three-volume work* The Shakespearian Drama: A Commentary *(1887-90), Snider states that Shakespeare's plays present various ethical principles which, in their differences, come into "Dramatic Collision," but are ultimately resolved and brought into harmony. He claims that these collisions can be traced in the plays' various "Dramatic Threads" of action and thought, which together form a "Dramatic Movement," and that the analysis of these threads and movements—"the structural elements of the drama''—reveals the organic unity of Shakespeare's art. Snider observes two basic movements in the tragedies—guilt and retribution—and three in the comedies—separation, mediation, and return. In the excerpt below from his* The Shakespearian Drama, a Commentary: The Histories *(1890), Snider views* Henry V *as the culmination of all Shakespeare's English history plays in its presentation of the king as ''the ideal ruler'' and of England ''in harmony at home and in supremacy abroad.'' The critic argues that Henry's aggressive militarism reflects popular national sentiment and that his order to murder the French prisoners should be regarded in terms of national supremacy, issued only because nothing must be allowed to jeopardize the English victory. The critic further interprets Shakespeare's portrayal of the French as haughtily confident as an attempt to justify their defeat—a device ultimately derived from ''an old Greek tragic motive—human arrogance humbled by a leveling Nemesis.'' Such a dramatic technique was necessary, he argues, for the English violated their own principle of nationality and their victory thus becomes ''a terrible defeat.'' Snider also assesses the structure of* Henry V, *maintaining that it lacks unity, thematic concentration, and ''organic completeness,'' suggesting, like several other critics, that Shakespeare was here struggling to join together an unwieldly variety and number of dramatic elements.*]

The structure of *Henry the Fifth* is without its like in Shakespeare. The employment of choruses or prologues to precede every Act, as is the case here, is unknown in any of his other works, if we except the doubtful play of *Pericles*. The object of these choruses seems, in the main, twofold; they announce the subject of the Acts which . . . are to follow, and mark with some care the large gaps of time which are to be passed over by the mind. Thus they try to connect somewhat more closely the disjointed parts of the drama. The Poet himself clearly sees the loose texture of his work; he is full of apologies, which imply his own judgment of its main weakness. He appears to feel that he has transcended quite the limits of Dramatic Art—the theme is too extensive for representation on a petty stage; he seems almost afraid of turning it into ridicule. Hence he is continually begging the spectator to use his imagination and forget the apparent caricature. In no other play is he seen to struggle so hard with his artistic form as here; he surges and frets against its bounds on every side. The great exploits of his hero are in danger of appearing farcical on the stage.

The whole action is of the moving, spectacular kind; it is a series of historical pictures selected from one great campaign, with a chorus to explain the general movement and to supply the omitted links. The play, therefore, is closely tied to the external realities of place and time, and is governed to a less extent than usual by an inner controlling thought; hence criticism, whose function it is to unfold this thought, has no very profound task at present. The result is that *Henry the Fifth*, judged by the Shakespearian standard, must be considered as one of the lesser stars of the Poet's dramatic constellation; it is lacking in unity, in concentration, in organic completeness. Still, it must not be esteemed too lightly. As the play moves in the external details of history, much has to be omitted, since the dramatic form is too narrow; such a manner of treatment demands the fullness and diversity of the Epic or of the Novel. The dramatic work must compress all into the one central, glowing point; only those events are to be taken, and only those things are to be said, which embody directly the thought.

As might be inferred from its spectacular character, the play has no inherent division into movements; indeed, the structure indicates that it is made up of five separate pictures, each of which is preceded by an explanatory prologue. Yet the entire action tends to one supreme event—the battle of Agincourt—in which single effort the conquest of France was accom-

plished. The drama may be externally divided into two movements. First, the preparation at home on both sides, comprising the first two Acts; secondly, the conflict and its results, terminating in the overwhelming success of Henry the Fifth. England, united within after a slight ripple of opposition, prepares herself for the struggle, passes over to the territory of her enemy, subjugates the country, and tries to confirm its possession by an alliance of marriage with the royal family of France.

The division into threads is, however, strictly maintained; they . . . may be called, the elevated or serious thread, and the low or comic thread. The first subdivides itself, according to nationality, into two groups—the French and the English—between whom lies the conflict, which is the main theme of the play. Here we must seek for the political elements which control the work. England claims the right to the throne of France, and makes good the claim by force of arms. The second or comic thread has not less than four groups; there are the remnants of the old Falstaffian company; the three English common soldiers who have the little intrigue with the King; the group of officers representing the several British nationalities—Welsh, Scotch, Irish, English; to these must be added the French Princess in her conversation with her attendant, Alice, and with the English King. The superabundance here is manifest; it branches out into so many directions that the unity of the work is in danger of being lost—the central thought seems not to be able to control the dramatic luxuriance springing out of the subject.

Beginning with the English side of the first thread, we notice at once the remarkable change in the life of the King. He is no longer the wild Prince Harry of Eastcheap, companion of thieves and revelers, but he has become a religious man; he has truly received the new birth, which has left ''his body as a paradise to envelop and contain celestial spirits'' [I. i. 30-1]. The caprice of youthful wantonness, ''hydra-headed willfullness'' [I. i. 35], has been completely laid aside, and there has been a full submission to the established order of the world. It is clergymen who are speaking; they praise especially his holy demeanor, and wonder at his sudden reformation. Indeed, the play throughout exalts the piety of the King as one of his main characteristics, and there is, perhaps, no other personage in Shakespeare's dramas who comes so near being a religious hero. The associate of Falstaff has, therefore, fully redeemed his promise of amendment.

His intellectual gifts, which were never dim, seem to be wonderfully brightened and quickened by his moral change. ''Hear him but reason in divinity,'' says the admiring Archbishop, ''you would desire the King were made a prelate'' [I. i. 38, 40]; he speaks of matters of policy with the knowledge and skill of the veteran statesman. But, when he comes to his supreme vocation, ''list to his discourse of war, and you shall hear a fearful battle rendered you in music'' [I. i. 43-4]. Still greater is his genius for action; he is the true practical man, who strikes boldly, yet at the same time thinks. In fine, he is the all-sufficient hero in whom intellect and will, the speculative and the active principles of man, are blended in the happiest harmony. Neither of these powers paralyzes the other, as is often the case, but each supports and intensifies the other to a supreme degree. And also he is the stronger and better for having passed through a wild period in his youth. ''Wholesome berries thrive and ripen best, neighbored by fruit of baser quality'' [I. i. 61-2], says the worthy Bishop of him, a clerical authority to which we may reasonably submit, though not without some surprise at the source.

Next there is revealed the chief object of his ambition, the object for which his whole career has been a long preparation—in fact, the object in which the Lancastrian Tetralogy culminates, namely, the conquest of France. But he will not proceed to it without being first assured of the justice of his cause. Accordingly he calls around himself his learned religious advisers, who state in full the grounds of his claim, and vindicate his title against the French doctrine of succession. The Clergy thus requite his favors to the Church; they even urge him to conquest, who needed no incitement; the Archbishop of Canterbury addresses him: "Stand for your own, unwind your bloody flag," and bids him take as a pattern his noble ancestors who once did "forage in blood of French nobility" [I. ii. 101, 110]. So speaks the primate of all England, the chief apostle of peace and good-will among men in the British isles.

It is manifest that the nation is for war; it is not merely sustaining, but even pushing, Henry to the struggle. Yet he is fired with the same ambition; he, therefore, most truly represents the spirit of the country. The Nobles are with him, the People have been always with him, now the Clergy have become the most urgent advisers of an invasion of France. All classes are in harmony; then there is the furious energy resulting from a common aspiration. It is a national enterprise, at the head of which is marching the national Hero; the outlook is ill for the object which offers resistance to their purpose. (pp. 410-16)

England—consolidated, as it were, into one body—is eager to be hurled across the channel into the heart of France, shouting with her monarch the popular war cry:—

No King of England if not King of France.

[II. ii. 193]

The French group, on the other hand, are introduced discussing the threatened invasion. Their monarch, with the circumspection of age, manifests no little anxiety; he recalls the many examples of English valor enacted on the soil of his own realm. But the Dauphin, with the impetuosity of youth, is eager for the conflict, having no fear of England now, because "she is so idly kinged" [II. iv. 26]. But the clear-headed Constable gives a well-timed warning to the young Prince; he has carefully noted the great transformation of King Henry's character, whose

—Vanities forespent
Were but the outside of the Roman Brutus,
Covering discretion with a coat of folly.

[II. iv. 36-7]

Of course the French emphatically reject the claims of England, and the messenger departs with the declaration of war. Thus we are prepared for the shock of armies which is to follow—two great nations are about to grapple in a terrific struggle—though the English predilection of the Poet has given a distinct hint of the result. Such is the faint outline of the leading French characters.

Passing now to the comic thread, we behold the Falstaffian group without Falstaff. At the first view this omission seems quite surprising, since the Poet has distinctly promised the reappearance of the jolly Fat Knight, at the end of *Henry the Fourth.* Why he is dropped can be only conjectured; but it is manifest that the Poet changed his mind only after mature deliberation. A little reflection on the part of the reader will fully justify the same conclusion; in fact, the dramatic possibilities of the character had been exhausted in the previous plays—nothing could well be added to the portraiture. Besides,

some repugnance to Falstaff must have been manifested by the more decent and moral portion of the audience, inasmuch as there are not a few persons of the present day who cannot endure his appearance and behavior. Personally, we would like to have seen his enormous bulk again on the stage and heard some of his monstrous lies, but, upon the second thought, it is well as it is; we, too, like the Prince, have had enough of his society for our own good, and should now consent to a permanent separation. Only the death of poor Jack is told; it looks as if he had experienced a hard struggle in his last hours, wrestling with repentance; and we repeat involuntarily the sigh of Prince Henry on the field of Shrewsbury: "I could have better spared a better man" [*1 Henry IV,* V. iv. 104].

The remaining members of this comic group are brought forward from *Henry the Fourth. . . .* It is still the reverse side of society—the immoral element—in the present case transmitted to a happier era from a period of civil discord. Its importance is much diminished; still, it is here, following in the track of war, and the whole company is about to cross the channel with the army, not for the purpose of patriotism, but of plunder. The contrast to the general feeling of the nation is most clearly seen in this group of debauched camp-followers. Every great enterprise, however righteous it may be, always has such vermin clinging to it on the outside, and trying to reach its vital juices, but they must be brushed off with the strong hand of merciless justice. The fate of these people in the present undertaking will be the same as that of the external enemy—the French.

In the second movement of the play, which now follows, the scene changes to France, where the struggle at once begins. The key-note is struck by the King in his famous address to his soldiers—the fierce blast of the English war bugle:—

Once more unto the breach, dear friends, once more,
Or close the wall up with our English dead.

[III. i. 1-2]

The sublime theme of the speech throughout is nationality, of which Henry is the most glorious representative in English History. The same spirit permeates this entire series of plays; here is its culmination. Hitherto England had been able to master her internal difficulties; now she is to measure herself with another nation, which it is her weighty enterprise to conquer. If she succeeds, then the English nationality has won the laurel among peoples. The strong appeal is, therefore, to Englishmen, their glory and superiority; it is a battle-prologue, nerving for the conflict which is to follow.

Great stress is laid by the Poet upon the behavior of the two armies just before the struggle comes on. The haughty confidence and fatuitous arrogance of the French are brought out in the strongest colors. It is, indeed, the only tragic ground of their fate; they seem to defy Heaven itself to keep them from their prey; on the pinnacle of insolence they are placed, to be hurled down by an avenging Nemesis. Even the cautious Constable gives way to arrogant boasting. A herald is sent to King Henry demanding ransom before the battle is fought; the common soldiers play at dice for English captives that are not yet taken. To the entire French army the victory seems to be won before the engagement; their camp is a scene of wild frolic and impatience. Very necessary and skillful is this motive of impious arrogance, in order to detach the sympathy of the hearer or reader from the side of the French, for they are really defending their nationality, while the English are assailing it; their cause is in every way the more rightful. Indeed, the

English are not only committing a wrong against a neighboring nation, but against themselves; they are logically destroying their own supreme principle in the present conflict, namely, nationality. All of which is felt by the Poet, and its effects artfully guarded against by introducing an old Greek tragic motive—human arrogance humbled by a leveling Nemesis.

In the strongest contrast to the action of the French is the conduct of the English; from the noble down to the private soldier there is a feeling of humility—indeed, of depression, though not of despair. They all think that the result will be very doubtful; gloomy forebodings haunt them; still, the staunchest resolution pervades the host. But there is one Englishman who is animated by the most exalted hope, who sees in the present emergency the greatest opportunity of his life or of his century—it is King Henry himself. He moves around among his soldiers, giving a word of encouragement to all; he is full of religious fervor—prayer is often on his lips; nor, on the other hand, does he forget even in the most trying hour of his life to play a good joke on a common soldier. He still has some of the former Prince Hal peering out of his conduct; he has not lost his sportiveness. Once, however, in a sudden fit of anger, he gives the most cruel order that every soldier should slay his prisoners—a fact which can be reconciled with his general character only by reflecting that his highest principle is the victory and supremacy of his nation, and whatever jeopardizes this supreme end must be removed at any cost. The day of Agincourt is won; King Henry the Fifth comes out of the battle the greatest of English national heroes; at one blow he utterly overwhelms and subjugates the ancient enemy of his country.

For France naught remains but submission; one people passes under the yoke of another. . . . [Such] a condition of affairs violates in the deepest manner the principle of nationality; there can result from it only perennial strife and calamity to both States. To avoid the difficulty inherent in the situation, to cement the bond between the two nations by domestic affection, the Family is now introduced into the political relation. Henry marries Catherine, daughter of the French King; but the royal woman is not here, as is often the case, made a sacrifice to the State. The famous wooing scene shows that their marriage had its true basis of love, notwithstanding the strong comic features. But the domestic ties of the Monarchs cannot control the destinies of two great people; the Family is a very imperfect bulwark against the Nation. The political object of the present matrimonial alliance is manifest from the beautiful expressions of the Queen-mother, who gives the true ground of royal intermarriage, in her earnest appeal to the happy pair:—

> As man and wife, being two, are one in love,
> So be there 'twixt your kingdoms such a spousal
> That never may ill office or fell jealousy,
> Which troubles oft the bed of blessed marriage,
> Thrust in between the paction of these kingdoms,
> To make divorce of their incorporate league,
> That English may as French, French Englishmen,
> Receive each other.

[V. ii. 361-68]

The comic thread of the second movement breaks up into four distinct groups. The first is composed of the old associates of Falstaff; they now meet the fit retribution of their deeds. The immoral company seems to be pretty much wiped out in the course of the war; Nym and Bardolph have been hung; "Nell is dead in the spital" [V. i. 81]; Pistol, ranter and coward, steals back in shame and punishment to England. Thus de-

bauchery from its first prominence in *Henry the Fourth* is quite brought to an end under the heroic King at the same time with his great national victory.

A second and new comic group is made up of representatives from the four British peoples—Welsh, Scotch, Irish, and English. They are all working for the common cause, though they have their little bickerings among themselves; they show how the heroic King had united every kind of subjects in his great foreign enterprise. In compliment to the birthplace and blood of Henry, the pedantic but valorous Welshman, Fluellen, is here the leading figure. The comic effect rests mainly upon the pronunciation of the English tongue in a different fashion by each of these persons, thus indicating with a laugh the checkered variety of speech and men in the English army—a motley gathering, but with the deepest purpose.

Another group is that of the three English soldiers, quite sober when talking together of the prospect of the battle, and not at all very comic figures at any time. But the King comes along in disguise, and they converse with him reprovingly; the result is, he exchanges gloves with one of them in token of a future settlement. From this incident springs a little comic intrigue, which ends in the King discovering himself to the soldier, who is overcome with confusion, but who receives a reward for his manly behavior generally. It is such a simple story as would be told among the common people of their beloved leader.

One more comic group can be distinguished, of which the French Princess, with her broken English, is the chief character. She makes the fourth person employing a brogue in the play. This slender comic instrumentality is quite worked to death; the tendency thereby is to drop down into a farce. (pp. 416-25)

These four groups, composing the second thread, have no very rigid central thought; they manifest rather the appearance of capricious diversity. Yet they all celebrate the internal or domestic triumphs of Henry, while the great battle of Agincourt, given in the first thread, celebrates the external or national triumph of the heroic King. It will hardly be questioned, however, that four comic groups here are too many; confusion results from excessive multiplicity always, and the feeling of the artistic Whole is obscured—or, even lost—in a labyrinth of details.

Such is the conclusion of the Lancastrian Tetralogy. Indeed, the present play . . . may be considered as the culminating point of the whole Historical Drama of Shakespeare; it delineates the ideal ruler in his personal, civil, and military character, and it portrays the ideal England in harmony at home and in supremacy abroad. This Tetralogy is, in the highest sense, a positive work, having a happy outcome; it begins with a revolution and passes through to final reconstruction. A Drama of the Nation it may be called, as distinct from the Drama of the Individual; for here it is a nation which after many conflicts and obstacles, reaches a happy destiny, at least for the time being. (pp. 425-26)

But there is, behind the bright skies of *Henry the Fifth* a dark, concealed background. A violation has taken place which will in its own time bring the penalty. Nationality is the spirit of England, of these English Historical plays of Shakespeare, of the modern world as distinguished from the Roman Empire, which sought to absorb all nations. But after the anguish and struggle of a thousand years, nationality has been restored to Europe, which now consists, not of one all-devouring Empire, but of a family of Nations, of which England and France have grown to be two members, independent, self-contained, with the same ultimate right, namely, that of nationality. It is this right which England assails in assailing France; it is the highest of all rights, above the right of inheritance specially to which the counselors of Henry appeal, but which cannot stand in the way of the nation, as Shakespeare himself has shown in two revolutionary plays, *King John* and *Richard the Second*. The political principle of modern times, the World-Spirit itself, is violated. The irony of the deed at once begins to show itself; England, in the pride of nationality, marches forth to destroy nationality, and thus aims a blow at herself, at her own greatest right and achievement. She obtains a transcendent victory which in the end will turn out a terrible defeat; Agincourt is really the loss of her own deepest principle. Such is the danger lurking in all victory; in the irony of history it is apt to change to the very opposite of itself. (pp. 429-30)

> *Denton J. Snider, "'Henry V'," in his* The Shake-spearian Drama, a Commentary: The Histories, *1890. Reprint by Indiana Publishing Co., 1894, pp. 407-30.*

## BERNARD SHAW   (essay date 1896)

[*Shaw, an Irish dramatist and critic, was the major English playwright of his generation. In his Shakespearean criticism, he consistently attacked what he considered to be Shakespeare's inflated reputation as a dramatist. Shaw did not hesitate to judge the characters in the plays by the standards of his own values and prejudices, and much of his commentary is presented—as the prominent Shaw critic Edwin Wilson once remarked—"with an impudence that had not been seen before, nor is likely to be seen again." Shaw's hostility towards Shakespeare's work was due in large measure to his belief that it was interfering with the acceptance of Henrik Ibsen and the new social theater he so strongly advocated. Shaw's brief remarks on* Henry V, *excerpted below, are taken from his review of a performance of* 1 Henry IV *at the Haymarket Theater which first appeared in the* Saturday Review *on May 16, 1896. Shaw disparages the chauvinism of the play's protagonist, describing him as "a Jingo hero," and he remarks that like similarly capable but limited young aristocrats, Henry "would have been quite in his place if he had been born a gamekeeper or a farmer."*]

One can hardly forgive Shakespeare quite for the worldly phase in which he tried to thrust such a Jingo hero as his Harry V down our throats. The combination of conventional propriety and brute masterfulness in his public capacity with a low-lived blackguardism in his private tastes is not a pleasant one. No doubt he is true to nature as a picture of what is by no means uncommon in English society, an able young Philistine inheriting high position and authority, which he holds on to and goes through with by keeping a tight grip on his conventional and legal advantages, but who would have been quite in his place if he had been born a gamekeeper or a farmer. (pp. 428-29)

> *Bernard Shaw, "Henry IV," in his* Dramatic Opinions and Essays with an Apology, Vol. 1, *Brentano's, 1928, pp. 423-34.*

## A. C. BRADLEY   (essay date 1902)

[*Bradley was a major Shakespearean critic whose work culminated the method of character analysis initiated in the Romantic era. He is best known for his* Shakespearean Tragedy (1904), *a close analysis of* Hamlet, Othello, King Lear, *and* Macbeth. *Bradley concentrated on Shakespeare as a dramatist, and particularly on his characters, excluding not only the biographical questions*

*so prominent in the works of his immediate predecessors but also the questions of poetic structure, symbolism, and thematics which became prominent in later criticism. He thus may be seen as a pivotal figure in the transition in Shakespearean studies from the nineteenth to the twentieth century. Although he has been a major target for critics reacting against Romantic criticism, he has continued to be widely read to the present day. In the following excerpt from an essay first published in the* Fortnightly Review, May 1, 1902, *Bradley observes that although Henry V has many admirable qualities, Shakespeare does not present him as an ideal hero. The critic argues that Henry's piety is marred by superstition, that he is too ready to manipulate other people for his own purposes, and that, like his father, Henry IV, there is "no sign in him of a strong affection for any one."*]

Both as prince and as king [Henry V] is deservedly a favourite, and particularly so with English readers, being, as he is, perhaps the most distinctively English of all Shakespeare's men. In *Henry V.* he is treated as a national hero. In this play he has lost much of the wit which in him seems to have depended on contact with Falstaff, but he has also laid aside the most serious faults of his youth. He inspires in a high degree fear, enthusiasm, and affection; thanks to his beautiful modesty he has the charm which is lacking to another mighty warrior, Coriolanus; his youthful escapades have given him an understanding of simple folk, and sympathy with them; he is the author of the saying, 'There is some soul of goodness in things evil' [IV. i. 4], and he is much more obviously religious than most of Shakespeare's heroes. Having these and other fine qualities, and being without certain dangerous tendencies which mark the tragic heroes, he is, perhaps, the most *efficient* character drawn by Shakespeare, unless Ulysses, in *Troilus and Cressida*, is his equal. And so he has been described as Shakespeare's ideal man of action; nay, it has even been declared that here for once Shakespeare plainly disclosed his own ethical creed, and showed us his ideal, not simply of a man of action, but of a man.

But Henry is neither of these. The poet who drew Hamlet and Othello can never have thought that even the ideal man of action would lack that light upon the brow which at once transfigures them and marks their doom. It is as easy to believe that, because the lunatic, the lover, and the poet are not far apart, Shakespeare would have chosen never to have loved and sung. Even poor Timon, the most inefficient of the tragic heroes, has something in him that Henry never shows. Nor is it merely that his nature is limited: if we follow Shakespeare and look closely at Henry, we shall discover with the many fine traits a few less pleasing. Henry IV describes him as the noble image of his own youth; and, for all his superiority to his father, he is still his father's son, the son of the man whom Hotspur called a 'vile politician' [*1 Henry IV*, I. iii. 241]. Henry's religion, for example, is genuine, it is rooted in his modesty; but it is also superstitious—an attempt to buy off supernatural vengeance for Richard's blood; and it is also in part political, like his father's projected crusade. Just as he went to war chiefly because, as his father told him, it was the way to keep factious nobles quiet and unite the nation, so when he adjures the Archbishop to satisfy him as to his right to the French throne, he knows very well that the Archbishop *wants* the war because it will defer and perhaps prevent what he considers the spoliation of the Church. This same strain of policy is what Shakespeare marks in the first soliloquy in *Henry IV.*, where the prince describes his riotous life as a mere scheme to win him glory later. It implies that readiness to use other people as means to his own ends which is a conspicuous feature in his father; and it reminds us of his father's plan of keeping himself out of the people's sight while Richard was making himself cheap by his incessant public appearances. And if I am not mistaken there is a further likeness. Henry is kindly and pleasant to every one as Prince, to every one deserving as King; and he is so not merely out of policy: but there is no sign in him of a strong affection for any one, such an affection as we recognise at a glance in Hamlet and Horatio, Brutus and Cassius [in *Julius Caesar*], and many more. We do not find this in *Henry V.*, not even in the noble address to Lord Scroop, and in *Henry IV.* we find, I think, a liking for Falstaff and Poins, but no more: there is no more than a liking, for instance, in his soliloquy over the supposed corpse of his fat friend, and he never speaks of Falstaff to Poins with any affection. The truth is, that the members of the family of Henry IV. have love for one another, but they cannot spare love for any one outside their family, which stands firmly united, defending its royal position against attack and instinctively isolating itself from outside influence. (pp. 256-58)

We wish Henry a glorious reign and much joy of his crew of hypocritical politicans, lay and clerical; but our hearts go with Falstaff to the Fleet, or, if necessary, to Arthur's bosom or wheresomever he is. (p. 260)

> A. C. Bradley, *"The Rejection of Falstaff,"* in his Oxford Lectures on Poetry, *revised edition, Macmillan and Co., Limited, 1909, pp. 247-75.*

## W. B. YEATS  (essay date 1903)

[*The leading figure of the Irish Renaissance and a major poet in twentieth-century literature, Yeats was also an active critic of his contemporaries' works. As a critic, he judged the works of others according to his own poetic values of sincerity, passion, and vital imagination. Yeats's remarks on* Henry V *are frequently cited by later commentators on the play. He maintains that Shakespeare treats Henry with "tragic irony," for behind the presentation of his French successes is the knowledge that these gains were short-lived, since England's foreign conquests would soon be lost by Henry VI. Henry's abilities to inspire and rule are evident, Yeats contends, but he lacks transcendent vision, proceeding on his way like some "remorseless and undistinguished . . . natural force."*]

The Greeks, a certain scholar has told me, considered that myths are the activities of Dæmons, and that the Dæmons shape our characters and our lives. I have often had the fancy that there is some one Myth for every man, which, if we but knew it, would make us understand all he did and thought. Shakespeare's Myth, it may be, describes a wise man who was blind from very wisdom, and an empty man who thrust him from his place, and saw all that could be seen from very emptiness. It is in the story of Hamlet, who saw too great issues everywhere to play the trivial game of life, and of Fortinbras, who came from fighting battles about 'a little patch of ground' [*Hamlet*, IV. iv. 18] so poor that one of his Captains would not give 'six ducats' to 'farm it,' and who was yet acclaimed by Hamlet and by all as the only befitting King. And it is in the story of Richard II., that unripened Hamlet, and of Henry V., that ripened Fortinbras. To poise character against character was an element in Shakespeare's art, and scarcely a play is lacking in characters that are the complement of one another, and so, having made the vessel of porcelain Richard II., he had to make the vessel of clay Henry V. He makes him the reverse of all that Richard was. He has the gross vices, the coarse nerves, of one who is to rule among violent people, and he is so little 'too friendly' to his friends that he bundles them out of doors when their time is over. He is as remorseless and

undistinguished as some natural force, and the finest thing in his play is the way his old companions fall out of it brokenhearted or on their way to the gallows; and instead of that lyricism which rose out of Richard's mind like the jet of a fountain to fall again where it had risen, instead of that phantasy too enfolded in its own sincerity to make any thought the hour had need of, Shakespeare has given him a resounding rhetoric that moves men, as a leading article does to-day. His purposes are so intelligible to everybody that everybody talks of him as if he succeeded, although he fails in the end, as all men great and little fail in Shakespeare, and yet his conquests abroad are made nothing by a woman turned warrior [Joan of Arc] and that boy he and Katherine were to 'compound,' 'half French, half English,' 'that' was to 'go to Constantinople and take the Turk by the beard' [V. ii. 208-09] turns out a Saint, and loses all his father had built up at home and his own life.

Shakespeare watched Henry V. not indeed as he watched the greater souls in the visionary procession, but cheerfully, as one watches some handsome spirited horse, and he spoke his tale, as he spoke all tales, with tragic irony. (pp. 161-64)

> W. B. Yeats, *"At Stratford-on-Avon,"* in his Ideas of Good and Evil, *A. H. Bullen, 1903, pp. 142-67.*

## E. K. CHAMBERS  (essay date 1905)

[*Chambers occupies a transitional position in Shakespearean criticism, one which connects the biographical sketches and character analyses of the nineteenth century with the historical, technical, and textual criticism of the twentieth century. While a member of the education department at Oxford University, Chambers earned his reputation as a scholar with his multivolume works,* The Medieval Stage *(1903) and* The Elizabethan Stage *(1923); Chambers investigated both the purpose and limitations of each dramatic genre as Shakespeare presented it and speculated on how the dramatist's work was influenced by contemporary historical issues and his own frame of mind. In the following excerpt, taken from his introduction to The Red Letter edition of* Henry V *(1905), Chambers contends that the play celebrates "the dauntless spirit and invincible endurance of Englishmen" and reflects the patriotic fervor of the late Elizabethan era. But Shakespeare has also depicted the darker side of nationalism, the critic adds, in Henry's obsession with foreign conquest, his cruel treatment of Falstaff, and the grim descriptions of the horrors of war. Chambers concludes that the play is relatively limited and that, with the exception of Mistress Quickly's description of the death of Falstaff, "there is nothing that is intimate, nothing that touches the depths."*]

Patriotism . . . is the keynote of [*Henry the Fifth*]. One may fairly regard it as the most complete expression of that heightened national self-consciousness, which is so characteristic a feature of the latter years of Elizabeth's chequered and anxious reign. It sums up, once and for all, the whole of that dramatic tendency, which took its origin in the enthusiasms of the Armada year and is responsible for the vogue and elaboration of the chronicle play. Ten years had elapsed since the Armada; and it is tempting to connect the immediate inspiration of *Henry the Fifth* with the renewed stimulus given to the patriotic order of ideas by the exploits of the Earl of Essex and his gallant company during the filibustering expedition to Cadiz in 1596 and the less successful island voyage to the Azores in 1597. Essex is of course 'the general of our gracious empress' [Chorus, V, 30], the hope of whose glorious return from Ireland—

Bringing rebellion broached upon his sword,

[Chorus, V, 32]

gives occasion for one of Shakespeare's comparatively rare direct allusions to contemporary history in the prologue to the Fifth Act.... [From] 1596 to 1599 Essex was the centre and focus of national feeling, the darling hope of all those who looked to see England a power upon the seas and the champion of the Protestant cause in Europe. A few months after *Henry the Fifth* was put upon the stage, Essex had returned indeed from Ireland, but not gloriously, and at his fall the star of nationalism waned, hardly to lighten again through the long days of James and his cloud of Spanish intrigues. Drayton's fine ode of *Agincourt,* printed not later than 1606, sounds already like a faint and far-off echo of the forgotten Elizabethan dream.

But the dream is still a reality in *Henry the Fifth*. It is a pæan which Shakespeare comes singing, in glorification of the dauntless spirit and invincible endurance of Englishmen, of the folk at unity with itself, among whom king and nobles, yeomen and peasants, vie with one another to show the mettle of their pasture. Even the arrogant French cannot withhold their admiration from the 'nook-shotten isle of Albion' [III. v. 14], whose barley-broth can decoct cold blood to such a heat. 'This island of England,' says the Dauphin, 'breeds very valiant creatures; their mastiffs are of unmatchable courage' [III. vii. 140-42]. And in the front of all is Henry himself, 'the mirror of all Christian kings' [Chorus, II, 6], one who goes to battle as to a sacrament, and would rather be on the weaker than the stonger side, for—

> If it be a sin to covet honour,
> I am the most offending soul alive.
>
> [IV. iii. 28-9]

Henry's secret is that he is so fully representative of his fellow-countrymen. The Dauphin taunts him with his wilder days—

> Not measuring what use we made of them.
>
> [I. ii. 268]

But in reality his 'humorous youth' has been his period of training for kingship. 'Unseen, yet crescive in his faculty' [I. i. 66], he has come, through close contact with what is bad as well as what is good among his kind, to exercise a sure empire over the souls of men, and to be their true leader in the day of stress. Even the incorrigible ruffian and cur, Pistol, feels the finer influence, and cries amazed, 'I love the lovely bully!' [IV. i. 48] and his mere presence as he rides through the camp is sufficient to knit men's sinews and steel their hearts—

> That every wretch, pining and pale before,
> Beholding him, plucks comfort from his looks.
> A largess universal like the sun
> His liberal eye doth give to every one,
> Thawing cold fear, that mean and gentle all
> Behold, as may unworthiness define,
> A little touch of Harry in the night.
>
> [Chorus, IV, 41-7]

Harry sets the spirit of the play; and this spirit is pure English. As if with some deliberate intention to make his picture representative, Shakespeare has filled the canvas with figures which typify every element in the mixed blood of the race. Fluellen the Welshman, Macmorris the Irishman, and Jamy the Scots captain jostle in the field of valour with honest Saxon Williams. And with the virtues of nationalism go its defects. To our modern thinking the lust of conquest is at once base and terrible. A spirited foreign policy has its reaction in the ineradicable tendency to regard mere matters of domestic concern as not

*Frontispiece to the Rowe edition (1709). By permission of the Folger Shakespeare Library.*

worth taking thought for. The king tells the French ambassador how—

> We never valued this poor seat of England,
>
> [I. ii. 269]

and one recognizes the prototype of the blatant modern imperialist, with his insolent talk of 'little England.' Henry himself can do a cruel thing in the pursuit of his high purpose. One cannot quite forget poor Jack Falstaff, whose heart was fracted and corroborate, before he died, by the bad humours which had been run upon him; and the treatment of Jack Falstaff remains a stain even upon 'the mirror of all Christian kings.' One need not suppose that Shakespeare was blind to all this, or regarded his ideal king as a being necessarily exempt from all criticism. Certainly he is by no means unaware of the dark shadows that edge what a later poet has called 'the sound and splendour of England's war,' of—

> The widows' tears, the orphans' cries,
> The dead men's blood, the pining maidens' groans;
>
> [II. iv. 106-107]

and of the desolation of a land wherein—

> All her husbandry doth lie on heaps,
> Corrupting in its own fertility.
> Her vine, the merry cheerer of the heart,
> Unpruned dies; her hedges even-pleached,

Like prisoners wildly overgrown with hair,
Put forth disordered twigs; her fellow leas
The darnel, hemlock, and rank fumitory
Doth root upon, while that the coulter rusts
That should deracinate such savagery.
The even mead, that erst brought sweetly forth
The freckled cowslip, burnet and green clover,
Wanting the scythe, all uncorrected, rank,
Conceives by idleness and nothing teems
But hateful docks, rough thistles, keckses, burs,
Losing both beauty and utility.

[V. ii. 39-53]

Obviously, too, a dramatist who can include Pistol, Nym, and Bardolph in the same army with a Henry and a Williams has not failed to look upon the seamy side of imperialism.

Such a theme as that of *Henry the Fifth*, when put upon the stage, naturally calls for some elaboration of scenic setting. Patriotism loves the blare of trumpets and drums, glittering coats and the pomp and circumstance of alarums and excursions. It is always interesting when Shakespeare becomes his own critic, and the choruses to *Henry the Fifth* betray him as preoccupied with the inadequacy of his limited methods of production to answer to the stage-manager's ideal—

Pardon, gentles all,
The flat unraised spirits that hath dared
On this unworthy scaffold to bring forth
So great an object! Can this cockpit hold
The vasty fields of France? Or may we cram
Within this wooden O the very casques
That did affright the air at Agincourt?

[Prologue, 8-14]

Or again—

And so our scene must to the battle fly;
Where—O for pity!—we shall much disgrace
With four or five most vile and ragged foils,
Right ill disposed in brawl ridiculous,
The name of Agincourt.

[Chorus, IV, 48-52]

So Shakespeare provides the refutation of those who deny the propriety of calling in the stage-carpenter and costume-designer to do their share, in such a degree as discretion and a sense of proportion may suggest, in the presentation of his plays. It was his poverty and not his will that consented to the primitive arrangements which an archæological fantasy of our day has elevated into an artistic gospel. He disposes you his ragged foils with an apology. But it is the art of the dramatist to sting the imagination of his audience into supplying for itself what may be lacking in the visual illusion. Hence the martial ring and hard brilliance of so much of the verse of the play, in which Shakespeare's style reaches its zenith of objectivity and rhetoric. Hence the unfailing imagery, the abundant eloquence, the swelling phrase. Hence, above all, the choruses themselves, which endeavour by strenuous description to add what the action must needs omit, and through which the total impression left upon the spectator has something of an epic, rather than of a strictly dramatic character. Within its limits all is magnificent; but the limits are unmistakable. Here you have a Shakespeare playing on the surface of life, much occupied with externalities and the idols of the forum. And with the exception of a few unconsidered words that fall from the mouth of a woman of no reputation, there is nothing that is intimate, nothing that touches the depths. (pp. 139-45)

*E. K. Chambers, "Henry the Fifth'," in his* Shakespeare: A Survey, *1925. Reprint by Hill and Wang, 1959?, pp. 136-45.*

## JOHN MASEFIELD  (essay date 1911)

[*Masefield was an English poet, dramatist, and novelist who was appointed poet laureate in 1930. Although not a scholar, he wrote* William Shakespeare *(1911), an introductory overview of the entire canon intended to stimulate the study of Shakespeare by the general public. In his 1924 lecture entitled "Shakespeare and the Spiritual Life," Masefield was one of the earliest commentators to address the issue of symbolism in Shakespearean drama. In the following brief remarks on* Henry V, *Masefield stresses the significance of judging the play in relation to Shakespeare's other English histories. He notes that Henry is unique among the protagonists of these dramas, for he is the only one who "enjoys success and worldly happiness." Masefield characterizes the king as a man who lacks sympathetic feelings for others, prefers plain blunt speech, and generally "has the knack of life that fits human beings for whatever is animal in human affairs."*]

[*Henry V*] bears every mark of having been hastily written. Though it belongs to the great period of Shakespeare's creative life, it contains little either of clash of character, or of that much tamer thing, comparison of character. It is a chronicle or procession, eked out with soldiers' squabbles. It seems to have been written to fill a gap in the series of the historical plays. Perhaps the management of the Globe Theatre, where the play was performed, wished to play the series through, from *Richard II* to *Richard III*, and persuaded Shakespeare to write this play to link *Henry IV* to *Henry VI*. The lines of the epilogue show that Shakespeare meant the play to give an image of worldly success between the images of failure in the other plays.

The play ought to be seen and judged as a part of the magnificent tragic series. Detached from its place, as it has been, it loses all its value. It is not greatly poetical in itself. It is popular. It is about a popular hero who is as common as those who love him. But in its place it is tremendous. Henry V is the one commonplace man in the eight plays. He alone enjoys success and worldly happiness. He enters Shakespeare's vision to reap what his broken-hearted father sowed. He passes out of Shakespeare's vision to beget the son who dies broken-hearted after bringing all to waste again.

Hear him but reason in divinity,

[I. i. 38]

cries the admiring archbishop. Yet this searcher of the spirit woos his bride like a butcher, and jokes among his men like a groom. He has the knack of life that fits human beings for whatever is animal in human affairs.

His best friend, Scroop, plots to kill him, but is detected and put to death. Henry accuses Scroop of cruelty and ingratitude. He forgets those friends whom his own cruelty has betrayed to death and dishonour. Falstaff dies broken-hearted. Bardolph, whose faithfulness redeems his sins, is hanged. Pistol becomes a cutpurse. They were the prince's associates a few months before. He puts them from his life with as little feeling as he shows at Agincourt, when he orders all the prisoners to be killed.

He has a liking for knocks. Courage tempered by stupidity (as in the persons of Fluellen, etc.) is what he loves in a man. He, himself, has plenty of his favourite quality. His love of plainness and bluntness makes him condemn sentiment in his one profound speech—

> All other devils that suggest by treasons
> Do botch and bungle up damnation
> With patches, colours, and with forms being fetch'd
> From glistering semblances of piety.
>
> [II. ii. 114-17]

The scenes between Nym and Pistol, and the account of Falstaff's death, are the last of the great English scenes. This (or the next) was Shakespeare's last English play, for Lear and Cymbeline are British, not English. When he laid down his pen after writing the epilogue to this play he had done more than any English writer to make England sacred in the imaginations of her sons. (pp. 120-23)

> John Masefield, "'King Henry V',' in his William Shakespeare, Henry Holt and Company, 1911, pp. 120-23.

## BRANDER MATTHEWS    (essay date 1913)

[*An American scholar, educator, and novelist whose academic training was in the law, Matthews began his literary career by lecturing, contributing extensively to various periodicals, and writing plays. In 1900 he was appointed professor of dramatic literature at Columbia University, becoming the first person to hold such a title at any American university. His published works, including* The Development of the Drama *(1903),* Molière *(1910),* Shakspere as a Playwright *(1913), and* The Principles of Playmaking *(1919), reflect his interest in the practical as opposed to theoretical aspects of drama, and his writing on Shakespeare focuses on the dramatist's stagecraft and his theatrical rather than literary abilities. Although he was an academician for many years, Matthews had a wide influence on playwrights, critics, and the general public. In the excerpt below, taken from* Shakspere as a Playwright, *he offers a negative appraisal of Shakespeare's dramatic technique in* Henry V, *asserting that the play shows little sign of artistry. Matthews also disparages what he sees as the fervid nationalism of the drama, charging that it is "often perilously close to jingoism, if not to claptrap." He further complains of Shakespeare's portrayal of the French, arguing that the dramatist betrayed his craft by "pandering to the prejudice of the insular rabble" in his Elizabethan audience.*]

['Henry V'] is a mere drum-and-trumpet history, with alarums and cannon-shots, sieges and battles, the defiance of heralds, and the marching of armies. As a specimen of playmaking it is indefensibly artless. Furnivall frankly admitted that "a siege and a battle, with one bit of light love-making, cannot form a drama, whatever amount of historical patriotic speeches and comic relief are introduced"; and Brandes is equally plain-spoken, dismissing this piece as "an epic in dialogue, without any sort of dramatic structure, development or conflict." Possibly Shakspere was getting dissatisfied with the chronicle-play as a form which made too little demand upon him; and, in fact, 'Henry V' is the last of his histories, with the exception only of 'Henry VIII' (which is not wholly his handiwork). In 'Henry V' he does not hesitate to avail himself of the medieval device of the expositor, whose narrative served to link together the separate incidents of the long-drawn mystery-play. Chorus is sent on the stage not only to speak propitiatory prologue, but to reappear again and again for the sole purpose of bridging over the yawning gaps of the action by telling the spectators what is supposed to have taken place during the intervals.

As Prince Hal was contrasted with Hotspur in the first part of 'Henry IV,' so he is provided with a foil in 'Henry V,' but with far less effect, since the Dauphin is only a vain braggart, whose boastings are hollow even in the ears of his own countrymen. Throughout the play Shakspere is grossly unfair to the French, pandering to the prejudice of the insular rabble in a fashion quite unworthy of a great poet. Indeed, the value of Henry's victory is diminished by the needless doubts cast on the valor of the foes the English king overcame. The play burns with patriotic fervor and bristles with patriotic appeals, often perilously close to jingoism, if not to claptrap.

The king himself is provided with unending speeches of a swelling eloquence, superb specimens of declamation for its own sake, examples of bravura rhetoric which afford rich histrionic opportunities, even if they are sometimes devoid of dramatic significance. High-flown as these orations are, we need not doubt Shakspere's sincerity in penning them, even if we may suspect also his consciousness that they would appeal directly to the hearts of his hearers. (pp. 122-24)

> Brander Matthews, "The Falstaff Plays," in his Shakspere as a Playwright, Charles Scribner's Sons, 1913, pp. 117-41.

## STOPFORD A. BROOKE    (essay date 1913)

[*A noted English ecclesiastic, Brooke was also a literary critic and historian, as well as an eminent lecturer and writer on English poetry. In the excerpt below, he asserts that in* Henry V *Shakespeare offers a superbly balanced view of war and patriotism. According to the critic, Shakespeare here celebrates the indomitable spirit of the valorous Englishmen, victorious although hopelessly outnumbered. Yet, Brooke claims, Shakespeare also repeatedly emphasizes that the war against France is unjust; further, he adds, Act I, Scene ii is "steeped in irony," for it reveals the self-serving hypocrisy of both the king and the archbishop. Shakespeare's balanced presentation is similarly evident in the characterization of Henry V, the critic notes, for he is not "the perfect king," but rather a combination of political expediency, ruthlessness, and mercy, equally capable of humility and self-deception; however, when the situation is most desperate, as on the field at Agincourt, he clearly demonstrates "all his manhood, fortitude, courage, and goodness."*]

Henry V. is the natural conclusion of Henry IV., and yet its spirit is quite different from that of its predecessor. We feel that Shakespeare was glad to emerge in it from English questions of statecraft, from civil wars and dissensions among the nobility, into one plain issue—a war with France, with which, as he wrote, he could sympathise more than he could with civil war; by which, though in an unjust war, the various parties in England (when Scroop, Cambridge, and Grey were executed) were united in one aim under one King. It had been difficult to give a full swing to his patriotic feeling, when he had to feel blame for both sides in the civil wars of Henry IV. It was not difficult now, but joyful, to let himself loose on the honour and greatness of England; and he has done it in this play. The play is a song, with trumpets, to the glory of England, and it is full to the brim not only with the exultation of the patriot, but also with the spirit of joy in the artist. This side of the play I state fully; but it was tempered and modified by thoughts of the immoral side of war. (p. 294)

Shakespeare, leaving with pleasure behind him the civil broils of the last reign, came with eagerness to tell of a King whom, at least in a great portion of the play, and in contrast with Henry IV., he represents as an open-hearted, bluff, plain-spoken, fighting King; and of a victory, not over brother Englishmen, but over a foreign foe. It is plain that he enjoyed this part of his task. He was not a fighter himself, but he who had lived with Essex, Raleigh, Sidney, Drake and Howard could not avoid the thrill of war, the leaping of his blood when he heard of the great deeds of England in past wars, against heavy odds; when, among the shouting crowd, he welcomed the news of the singeing of Philip's beard in Spain, or saw the ships of Drake and the adventurers come up the Thames with their bellies filled with the ill-got gold of Spain. This temper runs through all his historical plays, and rings on them like steel on steel. It is a temper which has never been otherwise than powerful, chiefly for good, sometimes for evil, in this realm of England.

It is mixed up with the temper of patriotism—that is, the love of our country as our Mother and our Home; our love of her Honour in the past; our faith in her as the refuge of our children and of liberty in the future. Our duty, indeed our passion, is to keep her national traditions free for noble development, her indwellers free from oppression, and her coasts free from the invader. War for these duties and this love, war in defence of all we hold dear, is part of a just patriotism; and all Shakespeare's set outbursts of patriotic feeling in the historical plays, on the lips of Gaunt, Faulconbridge, Hereford, and others, are directed to this aspect of patriotism—defence of England against the foreigner—a view of love of country which the attempt of the Armada must have driven home to the heart of Shakespeare and of every Englishman.

Nothing of this special emotion of patriotism could have filled the soul of Shakespeare as he wrote this play, for in it England was not invaded, but the invader. She was, in war, doing the very thing to another nation, which it was part of her high patriotism not to permit being done to her. The war was a wicked because an aggressive war; and its only result was to sow the dragon seed of the wars in France, and of the renewed civil wars in England, when punishment of it fell on the House of Lancaster in direful ruin, and then on the House of York. Shakespeare knew this well. He never forgets this woeful aspect of the war he pictures.

In what way then could patriotism speak? How could Shakespeare, in this play, exalt the glory of England, when the war was, he knew, first unjust, and then fatal?

Well, the natural, the inevitable feeling of the mass of any people is to wish passionately that its folk may have the better of its opponents. One might as well try to push back the tidal wave as the swell of this national emotion. It has the force of a natural law. Now and then, men to whom Justice is dearer than this desire for the victory of their people rise so far above nature as to wish that their countrymen should be beaten in battle. They are brushed away by the national passion of which I speak. Shakespeare shared in that passion. Whatever origin the war had, he wished his people to win. And *Henry V.* is full of that common excitement. It is not a lofty element in patriotism, but it is a natural and inevitable part of it.

Again, patriotism, when it is ill-married to the weakness of national vanity, gives birth to national contempts. Each nation, while extolling itself, laughs the other to scorn. This is natural enough, but it is a fruitful source of wrong and folly. It has been thought for centuries in England to be a part of patriotism. The spirit of Nelson's sailors was the spirit of Englishmen towards the French, from the days of Creçi almost to the present day. Shakespeare himself is guilty of it in his picture of the French Dauphin and nobles before the battle. He enhances the glory of England when he sets the boastful splashing of the

French over against the modest steadfastness of the English. It is a piece of his patriotism, but not a wise or useful one.

The third element in this patriotism of war was the most natural, the most useful to the nation, and the most noble. It was founded on admiration and affection for those qualities in the English which, in moments of tremendous trial, against the overwhelming odds, enable them to win the victory. The French at Agincourt were five times more numerous than the English. They were well fed, their army was in good trim. The English were half-starved, ill-clad, and in retreat. But they had great steadfastness, unfaltering courage, belief in their leaders, unquestioning obedience, discipline, and the modesty of brave men. With these they won the battle. To praise and be proud of such a victory, to remember it for ever as a national encouragement, an inspiring tradition; to keep up in a people the honour and practice of the high qualities that won it; to scorn death rather than be false to its spirit—that would be part of a true patriotism, and of its praise from generation to generation, even if the war in which it was proved was in its origin unjust or in its aim unworthy. For these are qualities which exist in a people, independently of the follies and greed of the rulers who have caused the war.

And it is on these deep-set, noble qualities in the nature of his countrymen that Shakespeare most dwells in this patriotic poem. He embodies them all in the King before and after that battle-day; for he knew the weight of a single representative figure. But he does not neglect to show them in the great gentlemen of the kingdom—in York and Suffolk, Exeter and Sir Thomas Erpingham; in the captains and officers like Fluellen, in Welsh and Scotch and Irish, united in war, if divided in peace; and in the common soldiers like John Bates, Alexander Court, and Michael Williams. Each, in his several character, represents those typical elements of the English character which won, against enormous odds, the fight at Agincourt. (pp. 296-99)

The splendour and national inspiration of such steadfast valour break forth in the words of Henry before the battle; and their spirit is the spirit which makes nations great in peace as well as in war. It issues, as a bright stream, from days of heavy battle; but it is not the spirit of mere fighting; it is not born of the false glory of war. It is in the soul of men; and to praise it and urge it into act deserves the name of patriotism. Shakespeare put that spirit on the lips of Henry, and touched it with a grave humility; and the noble words arose out of the spiritual depth of a patriot King's emotion, rejoicing in his people's character. So far he is the patriot of war; so far Henry is his hero.

But he does not leave the other side of war unrepresented, nor is his hero free from its evils. The war Henry waged with France was an unjust and cruel war; base also in its origin. Shakespeare does not shirk that aspect of it. He seems to have had a steady but prudent hatred of all war which sacrificed the people to the advantage of kites and crows, of kings and nobles. At least, I hold that to be the underdrift of the historical plays and of *Coriolanus*.

He represents the Church, the King, and the Palace clique as the sources of the War, and each acting for his own advantage. The play opens with a conversation between the Bishop of Ely and the Archbishop of Canterbury. It seems the Commons had brought forward a bill which would strip the Church of half its temporal lands, and bring the proceeds to the State. 'What is to be done?' they ask. 'Why, get round the King. He is a true lover of holy Church; he is miraculously changed; he can even reason in divinity. With regard to the bill itself he is, alas! indifferent. But he is not indifferent to war. If we can prove he has some claim of descent to heirships in France, he will let this bill alone, and take our part; and we will offer him an immense sum for the expenses of the war. Let us then get up the war, and save the temporalities of the Church.' This is the remarkable conduct of the Church; and the whole representation of the ecclesiastical hypocrisy and trickery of these mitred rascals is a masterpiece of sugared scorn and indignation.

Then the Archbishop, in council, proves to the King's satisfaction, and on the flimsiest ground, that Henry is the rightful heir to France; and urges war, bloody war. He paints the Black Prince at Creçi, how he foraged in blood of French nobility; he blows the trumpet of English fame and bids the King awake his blood and courage. The men of England, he cries, long for the battle. Take them to France,

> With blood, and sword, and fire, to win your right:
> In aid whereof, we of the spiritual'ty
> Will raise your highness such a mighty sum
> As never did the clergy at one time
> Bring in to any of your ancestors.
>
> [I. ii. 131-35]

A vile Christian, but a good politician! Without one thought of pity for the miseries war will bring on the French and English people, without one prophetic glance into the future, the Archbishop of the Christian Church of England unleashes, for the sake of gain, famine, sword, and fire, the three dark hounds of war; and then, when he has got his wicked way, assumes the philosopher, wears the statesman's air, and delivers that famous speech which compares the divers functions of men in a kingdom to the ordered polity of the bees. Shakespeare displays a master-hypocrite. How far the tale is historically true, I do not know. But that is his picture of the matter, and a splendid piece of irony it is.

And now, how is the King made by Shakespeare to behave in this question of war? He also starts this bloody business for the sake of policy, not for any just cause. He fears the nobility and all the feuds left behind by his father's seizure of the crown. War will occupy their minds; they love war, and they shall have it. His father, dying, recommended that.

> Therefore, my Harry,
> Be it thy course to busy giddy minds
> With foreign quarrels; that action, hence borne out,
> May waste the memory of the former days.
>
> [*2 Henry IV*, IV. v. 212-15]

And the last words of the play of *Henry IV*. show that the new King, to secure his power, had already resolved on war with France. I will lay odds, says Lancaster,

> that, ere this year expire,
> We bear our civil swords and native fire
> As far as France. I heard a bird so sing,
> Whose music, to my thinking, pleased the king.
>
> [*2 Henry IV*, V. v. 105-08]

So, as Shakespeare puts it, the Archbishop of Canterbury knew the King's mind before he made his solemn argument; and the King's speech, warning the Archbishop not to let loose the dogs of war unless on the gravest ground, was really a piece of hypocrisy, spoken to play the part of a temperate, just, and thoughtful monarch, while all the time his craft had resolved on war. This is what Shakespeare represents, and he disap-

proved of it. He makes that clear by the subtle address to the Archbishop with which the King opens the council. While the King speaks, he knows the Archbishop wants war, and he himself is resolved on war. The whole passage is steeped in irony, and the last lines (again remembering that war was already settled on between them) are really Shakespeare's gird with bitter scorn at the Archbishop—

> Under this conjuration speak, my lord;
> For we will hear, note and believe in heart
> That what you speak is in your conscience wash'd
> As pure as sin with baptism.
>
> [I. ii. 29-32]

Nevertheless, the King in the midst of his crafty policy is supposed by Shakespeare to have something of a conscience. The Church is represented as having none at all.

Many think that Shakespeare painted Henry as the perfect king; as almost the perfect man. I am surprised when I read that view. Shakespeare sat far too close to fact to represent Henry as entirely noble. He painted him as he was: the crafty politician, the steadfast, masterly leader of men; England's hero-warrior; merciful in peace, ruthless and resolute in war, mild to his own, fierce to his foes as long as they fought against him. His speech to the burghers of Harfleur is the speech of one who will not spare, to get his ends, one jot of the horrors of war to a conquered town.

His soldiers, if the town does not yield, shall have their full and savage way with women and children and old men. When, in the year after Agincourt, at the siege of Rouen, the town turned out twelve thousand men, women and children who would have weakened the defence, Henry would not let them pass through his lines. These innocent defenceless folk, down to the helpless children, died of starvation. It is well to remember that story when this English king is exalted into a perfect character; and it was well that Shakespeare should ask his imagination what lay beneath the glory of war. He replied by recording its horrors, and he puts them into the mouth of Henry at several points in the play; and with a certain irony, for Henry has made the war for his own purposes. He records them even more clearly when Burgundy, at the end of the play, describes what France had suffered from the curse of war—

> What rub or what impediment there is,
> Why that the naked, poor and mangled Peace,
> Dear nurse of arts, plenties and joyful births,
> Should not in this best garden of the world,
> Our fertile France, put up her lovely visage?
> Alas, she hath from France too long been chased,
> And all her husbandry doth lie on heaps,
> Corrupting in its own fertility. . . .
> And as our vineyards, fallows, meads and hedges,
> Defective in their natures, grow to wildness,
> Even so our houses and ourselves and children
> Have lost, or do not learn for want of time,
> The sciences that should become our country;
> But grow like savages,—as soldiers will
> That nothing do but meditate on blood,—
> To swearing and stern looks, diffused attire
> And everything that seems unnatural.
> Which to reduce into our former favour
> You are assembled: and my speech entreats
> That I may know the let, why gentle Peace
> Should not expel these inconveniences
> And bless us with her former qualities.
>
> [V. ii. 33-40, 54-67]

The picture is pitiful, but it does not move Henry in the least from his unjust demand. He will have his pound of flesh—

> If, Duke of Burgundy, you would have peace,
> . . . you must buy that peace
> With full accord to all our just demands;
>
> [V. ii. 68, 69-70]

and the just demand is that he should be acknowledged as heir to the kingdom of France. This is to be the mere conqueror, not the hero. Two years afterwards he was dead, dead at the height of his conquering glory.

Where Shakespeare does make the King heroic, is in his conduct before and after the battle. He enforces discipline on his soldiers. He insists that all goods taken shall be paid for. He hangs those followers of his who steal from the churches or the country-folk, and poor Nym and Bardolph perish in that fashion. He will have mercy shown to the captives. As long as he is not in actual battle, he is temperate in counsel. And when he is brought to bay, when, as the great war-leader, he is face to face with almost certain defeat and death, his attitude is indeed heroic. The desperate situation brings out all his manhood, fortitude, courage, and goodness. He is gentle, good-humoured, wearing a face of joy like a man inspired, full of trust in himself and his men, almost looking for victory! He will not ask another man from England. Proud of his brave soldiers, he is humble before God in whom he trusts. 'Not in our hands,' he cries, 'O Lord, lies victory, but in thine.' The way God is used by priests and kings in war is as irritating as it is impertinent, but still to confess Him as master of history (and not ourselves as Shakespeare represents France doing), has at least some grace, some humility, and therefore a nobler war-temper than to confess no power but our own. In all this Shakespeare does draw a hero.

But, again, he does not leave this splendid picture without painting another, of his own proper invention, to balance its effect. The King, going in disguise through the camp, meets three of the common soldiers who are in arms for his cause, and know nothing about it. They question his responsibility. 'We are,' they say, 'the King's subjects. We know not why he brings us into battle. If his cause be wrong, our obedience to the King wipes the crime of it out of us. If the cause be not good, the King has a heavy reckoning to make. All the slain will testify against him at the judgment day.' The soldier suffers in obedience to the warring King. Let the King look to it that his cause is just, else he makes every soldier sin—and that may be a black reckoning for the King. Henry's answer is so sophistical that I see in it another example of Shakespeare's irony. But the King has listened, and is left alone to think on what he has heard. And in an hour of revelation, when he is alone with God and his soul, Shakespeare makes the King see what he really is; and what difference there is between him and the peasant he had made his soldier. Policy has slipped from him, kingship has left him, the fiery fever of the great captain of war is dead in his heart. He is only a man among men. He shows the same temper as he shows in his speech to his father on his death-bed, so closely does Shakespeare keep the unity of his characters. He continues the thought with which he was full when he began his talk with Bates and Will—

> I think the king is but a man, as I am: the violet
> smells to him as it doth to me; the element
> shows to him as it doth to me: all his senses
> have but human conditions: his ceremonies laid
> by, in his nakedness he appears but a man, and

> though his affections are higher mounted than
> ours, yet, when they stoop, they stoop with the
> like wing.
>
> [IV. i. 101-07]

It is a noble, thoughtful temper, full of humanity, of apartness from his self, but it creeps back into self-consideration. The sense of kingship and the resolution to keep the powers of a king, which he has forgotten at the beginning, rise to the surface towards the end of the soliloquy. Conscience and kingcraft, as often before, meet at the end of it again. The soliloquy is a grave piece of thoughtful poetry. It is Shakespeare's vision of the finer nature of the man within the trappings of the king. But see how it ends—with a piece of self-deceit! 'The peasant,' Henry says, 'sleeps at ease, the king wakes; the peasant has the vantage of the king, but he little knows

> What watch the king keeps to maintain the peace,
> Whose hours the peasant most advantages.
>
> [IV. i. 283-84]

Yet, it was not peace that Henry had maintained, but war. (pp. 301-08)

I may say one word more on this representation of the 'for and against' of war. It was a habit, almost a trick, of Shakespeare's to parody—sometimes for the sake of humour, sometimes to strengthen a main issue of thought or action—the doings of the great by the doings of the common folk. He had done this, for example, in *Richard III.*, in *Coriolanus*, and in the *Tempest*. Here, in the ridiculous dialogue between Pistol and his French prisoner, the action and the motives of Henry's invasion of France are parodied. The greed of the King is echoed by the greed of Pistol. The war is a bandit's war. Pistol will have his ransom of two hundred crowns; if not, death to his captive. Henry will have the whole of France; if not, France shall perish.

Yet, while we have all these contrasted issues of the war-question presented to us, one thing remains supreme—the uplifting passion with which Shakespeare remembered and praised the mighty deed of Agincourt; the spiritual glory of facing with hope and valiancy of heart enormous odds, for the sake of the ideals and memories of England. That rings through the whole play, and it still rings in our hearts. The splendid war-chorus at the beginning of the fourth Act tells us, with uplifted passion, how Shakespeare felt when he looked back on the days of England's steadfastness and valour; how he felt when he heard the news of the great sea-fight in the narrow seas against the boasting odds of the Armada.

And now, as we look back on this treatment in art and by the artist-imagination of the question of war and the glory of war—not treated in a discussion, not from the point of view either of morality or philosophy or even of philanthropy, but embodied and explained by the art-creation of men of different types who, with no conscious reference to that question, nevertheless set it forth in different lights by speaking as their characters, their place in life, their interests and circumstances urge them—are we not amazed with the extraordinary balance of the poet's judgment? Some have seen nothing in this play but what we should vulgarly call Jingoism. They must be blind, or only read the Act in which Agincourt is fought. Yet, even in that Act, how much is said against the temper of the Jingo! The whole representation of war, by Shakespeare, is a miracle of quiet, temperate, austere judgment. A just and equal hand holds the balance. (pp. 309-10)

On one side, he reveals, with irony, the picture of a ruthless war waged for a cause not just, but unjust; set on foot, not for defence but for aggression; begun not even for glory, but for selfish policy; and the judgment is a condemnation. But, on the other side, he paints another picture. In the course of the war the King and his English are at death's door, devoid of all things but the courage of the soul, but love of the honour of England. Their King is great-minded, and so are they, in this overmastering hour, in which all that makes the heart of England great is tried to the uttermost. And Shakespeare, while he does not forget the wrongs of the war, feels the magnificence and magnanimity of this, records it in words which shall never be forgotten, himself thrills with it, and thrills his readers, and sends its glory down to us, to inspire our valour, our stead-fastness, and our love of the noble soul of England. For it was the soul which conquered at Agincourt. (pp. 310-11)

> Stopford A. Brooke, " 'Henry V'," in his Ten More plays of Shakespeare, *Constable and Company Ltd.*, *1913, pp. 294-313*.

## JOHN WILLIAM CUNLIFFE (essay date 1916)

[*Cunliffe was an Anglo-American literary critic, journalist, and educator. In the following excerpt, Cunliffe contends that Shakespeare intended to provide a "generous appreciation" of the character of the king in* Henry V, *and he seeks to explain the prevailing "attitude of cold or hostile criticism" of Henry by A. C. Bradley (1902), W. B. Yeats (1903), and John Masefield (1911). Without the proper historical perspective, the critic maintains, twentieth-century commentators have failed to understand that the king's pietism, political and moral expediency, practical temperament, and heavy-handed humor would not have offended an Elizabethan audience; he adds that these personal traits should be viewed as expressions of Henry's "appreciation of the value of common virtues and common things." However, one advantage that Cunliffe recognizes in the modern interpretation of Henry is that it may lead us to regard him as "more human, more vivid, [and] more interesting."*]

The three views [of A. C. Bradley, W. B. Yeats, and John Masefield; see excerpts above, 1902, 1903, and 1911] have obviously much in common, and it will be convenient . . . to suggest some of the reasons that underlie the change from the generous appreciation of Henry's character as Shakspere depicts it, to this attitude of cold or hostile criticism. In the first place, we are no longer sensible of "the divinity that doth hedge a king" [*Hamlet*, IV. v. 124], and we apply to Henry the same standards as to other men. When his father deplores the "indirect crook'd ways" by which he gained the crown and Henry replies:

> You won it, wore it, kept it, gave it me;
> Then plain and right must my possession be,
> [*Henry IV*, IV. v. 221-22]

it is a position we can understand; but when in answer to Henry's adjuration, the Archbishop of Canterbury enters into an elaborate argument as to Henry's claim to the throne of France, the plea does not move us—does not even interest us. We cannot forget that the reigning French king's right rests upon the same foundation as Henry's own right to the crown of England, the right of possession and continuance, and the acquiescence of his subjects. We are conscious too, that neither the Archbishop's nor Henry's view is disinterested. In the case of the Archbishop, Shakspere has devoted the opening scene to making this abundantly clear. In the case of Henry, his father's dying advice was "to busy giddy minds with foreign

quarrels" [*2 Henry IV*, IV. v. 213-14], and Lancaster's closing speech in '2 Henry IV' is equally significant:

> *Lan.* I will lay odds that, ere this year expire,
> We bear our civil swords and native fire
> As far as France: I heard a bird so sing,
> Whose music, to my thinking, pleas'd the king.
> [*2 Henry IV*, V. v. 105-08]

To us, Henry's attack upon France is merely a war of conquest—no more and no less—and his valor, whether as prince or king, stirs us simply as a warlike quality without regard to the cause in which it is displayed. We can not regard the rebellion of the Percies [in *Henry IV*] as a heinous offence, and the terrible threats Henry utters against the citizens of Harfleur only provoke our sympathy for them; so far as he himself is concerned, we can only hope that he did not mean what he said, but was using guileful rhetoric to cow the burghers into prompt submission. (pp. 322-23)

Again in the fine soliloquy before Agincourt, ending:

> And but for ceremony, such a wretch,
> Winding up days with toil and nights with sleep,
> Had the fore-hand and vantage of a king.
> The slave, a member of the country's peace,
> Enjoys it; but in gross brain little wots
> That watch the king keeps to maintain the peace,
> Whose hours the peasant best advantages.
> [IV. i. 278-84]

we are keenly conscious of the fact that Henry thoroughly enjoys being king and is doing everything in his power to seat himself firmly on the throne; he does not really wish to change places with the peasant, any more than the great landowner or manufacturer wishes to change places with the people who work for him, however much envy he may sometimes express of their freedom from responsibility.

Another element in Henry's character which the modern reader takes very differently from the generation for which the play was written is his religiosity—I can find no more accurate word for the mixture of official piety with what Professor Bradley describes as superstition. Certainly, such passages as

> O God of battles! steel my soldiers' hearts;
> [IV. i. 289]

and

> . . . O God, thy arm was here;
> And not to us, but to thy arm alone,
> Ascribe we all!
> [IV. viii. 106-08]

strike us with a sense of incongruity when we remember Henry's command just before:

> Then every soldier kill his prisoners
> [IV. vi. 37]

and his threat:

> Besides, we'll cut the throats of those we have
> And not a man of them that we shall take
> Shall taste our mercy. . . .
> [IV. vii. 63-5]

No doubt Henry's religious fervor is thoroughly in character, and was a historical fact, but it no longer appeals to us as it did to the men of Shakspere's own day.

Another and perhaps more debatable point is his humour, as to which Mr. Masefield is especially severe. . . . He says . . . :

> Henry V is the one commonplace man in the eight plays. He alone enjoys success and worldly happiness. He enters Shakspere's vision to reap what his broken-hearted father sowed. He passes out of Shakspere's vision to beget the son who dies broken-hearted after bringing all to waste again.
>
> "Hear him but reason in divinity,"
>
> cries the admiring archbishop. Yet this searcher of the spirit woos his bride like a butcher, and jokes among his men like a groom. He has the knack of life that fits human beings for whatever is animal in human affairs.

It must be confessed that to a modern taste Henry's sallies of wit, whether as prince or king, are not of the most refined sort. He has a love for that most detestable kind of joke called practical; and his wooing of Katharine, though full of humor and a certain bluff overbearing hilarity, has nothing princely about it. For an ideal hero, even for an ideal sovereign, thinking people of our age would demand something different.

When all these deductions and exceptions are allowed, what is there left for us of "the mirror of all Christian kings" [Chorus, II, 6]? Obviously nothing that has been said detracts from Shakspere's portrayal of the character, which still stands foursquare to all the winds of heaven. On the contrary, while the esteem in which such a character is held has changed, the character as Shakspere has portrayed it becomes on closer consideration more human, more vivid, more interesting. When we regard Henry no longer as an ideal hero but as a man subject to the limitations of his time and with some personal shortcomings of his own to boot, he becomes all the more real to us, and the more worthy of our attention. For the predominant feature in his individuality Professor Bradley has, I think, hit upon the right word when he describes Henry as "the most *efficient* character drawn by Shakspere." The word carries with it familiar connotations and limitations which are by no means out of place in this connection. Henry is efficient after the manner of a modern captain of industry, although his efficiency is directed not to the management of a great railroad or trade combination or financial enterprise, but to the ruling of a kingdom. (pp. 324-26)

His energy and ambition find a natural outlet in the war with France, and he is doubtless fully aware of the political expediency of the course recommended by his father, "to busy giddy minds with foreign quarrels" [2 *Henry IV*, IV. v. 213-14]. He seeks the official sanction of the Archbishop, no doubt . . . as a political expedient rather than to solve any doubt in his own mind—his mind was not given to doubt; he knows beforehand the answer the Archbishop will make and the special reasons he has for making it. To admit this is not to accuse Henry of hypocrisy. He is not troubled, any more than a modern capitalist on the eve of a great undertaking, with moral misgivings; he accepts the law as it is expounded by the traditional authorities, all the more readily, no doubt, because it falls in with his own inclinations and interests. In the conduct of the campaign he shows the same practical temper. He uses horrible threats to induce the citizens of Harfleur to yield promptly, but enjoins mercy to all when they do yield. He knows that "when lenity and cruelty play for a kingdom, the gentler gamester is the soonest winner," and therefore gives express charge that

"in all our marches through the country, there be nothing compelled from the villages, nothing taken but paid for, none of the French upbraided or abused in disdainful language" [III. vi. 112-13, 108-11]. But when at Agincourt the defeated enemy threatens to gather head again, he bids "every soldier kill his prisoners" [IV. vi. 37]. He sees directly to the aim he wishes to attain and takes without hesitation the means necessary to accomplish it.

Henry's religion is of a piece with his morals. It is the conventional religion of his time. Why should one expect it to be otherwise? It would be idle to expect from him the philosophical subtleties of Hamlet or the profound reflections of Prospero [in *The Tempest*] or the poetic vision of Macbeth. His conversation with the soldiers as he wanders through the camp in disguise on the eve of Agincourt and his subsequent meditations in private run on the familiar theme of the responsibilities of kingship, and hardly rise above the commonplace. The horrors of war indeed obtain a passing reference in the adjuration to the Archbishop before the campaign, already planned, is entered upon. They are effectively used by Henry as a means of bringing the citizens of Harfleur to prompt submission. But when one of the soldiers before Agincourt proposes to call the king to a reckoning for "their wives left poor behind them . . . their children rawly left" [IV. i. 139-40, 141], Henry answers with an argument conceived in the spirit of medieval theology, "Every subject's duty is the King's, but every subject's soul is his own" [IV. i. 176-77]. It is the soldier's account of heaven that occupies Henry's mind, not the bereavement and suffering of their families; and the moment he is left alone he throws off the burden of spiritual responsibility for himself as decisively as he has rejected it in argument.

> Upon the king! let us our lives, our souls,
> Our debts, our careful wives,
> Our children and our sins lay on the king!
> We must bear all. O hard condition,
> Twin-born with greatness, subject to the breath
> Of every fool, whose sense no more can feel
> But his own wringing! What infinite heart's ease
> Must kings neglect, that private men enjoy!
> And what have kings, that privates have not too,
> Save ceremony, save general ceremony!
>
> [IV. i. 230-39]

Although Shakspere has not endowed Henry with any deep spiritual insight, he has given him a common sense appreciation of the value of common virtues and common things; he is not deceived by mere appearances. He is not blind to the penalties of high office, and his consciousness of kingship does not mislead him into an exaggerated estimate of his own personality. "All his senses have but human conditions: his ceremonies laid by, in his nakedness he appears but a man; and though his affections are higher mounted than ours, yet, when they stoop, they stoop with the like wing" [IV. i. 103-07]. It is this essential humility which redeems Henry's conventional piety as expressed in his prayer before battle and his ascription of the victory to the special interposition of Providence.

> Come, go we in procession through the village
> And be it death proclaimed through our host
> To boast of this or take that praise from God
> Which is his only.
>
> [IV. viii. 113-16]

Fluellen's matter-of-fact reference in this passage to the help of the Deity, "Yes, my conscience, he did us great good"

[IV. viii. 121], suggests that Shakspere was not himself oblivious of the human elements of the great struggle. There is nothing to justify us in assuming that in ascribing this attitude to Henry, Shakspere did more than follow historical tradition and invest his hero with qualities which he knew would be acceptable to his audience. Shakspere has indeed clothed Henry's commonplace thoughts with beauty, just as he has expressed Henry's patriotism in imperishable lines which still stir the blood. In both cases he was the dramatic artist appealing to current religious and political sentiment, and the charm and vigor of the expression keep their emotional hold on people whose minds are no longer affected by the intellectual assumptions which the passages imply.

Henry's humor, as has been already suggested, is somewhat too robust "for this refined age." But the wooing scene is undoubtedly effective. With Katharine as an equal in rank—and, moreover, one who does not entirely understand what he is saying—Henry is more himself than in any previous scene, and we get a glimpse of him as a man which rounds out our appreciation of him as prince and king. Masefield's strictures on Henry in this situation seem to me much exaggerated. He is masterful, downright, bluff, good-natured; he is not delicate or refined, but he is not indelicate, according to the less squeamish standard of Shakspere's time. The dramatic irony of the passage about the "boy, half French, half English, that shall go to Constantinople and take the Turk by the beard" [V. ii. 208-09], takes the edge off its directness; and Katharine's reply leaves it doubtful whether this long speech was supposed or intended to be understood by her. Henry was enjoying an unaccustomed freedom of letting himself talk. Shakspere had promised his audience at the end of 'Henry IV,' Part II, to make them merry with fair Katharine of France, and he fulfilled his promise in a fashion still highly effective with the unsophisticated, and of added interest because of the light it throws on Henry's character.

Finally, as a matter of literary curiosity rather than as a necessary factor in the appreciation of the play, one may ask the question, "How far did Shakspere approve of Henry's character, regarded not as an artistic achievement but as a living soul he had himself created?" Shakspere was not in the habit of labelling his characters or their qualities for the moral edification of his audience, and the question may be unanswerable in any definite, precise way. There is nothing to show that Shakspere drew Henry lovingly, as we are inclined to fancy he did his great tragic characters, Hamlet and Othello and Macbeth, because he seems to us to have put into them something of himself. It appears rather that he accepted Henry as a national hero, and presented him as such to the public of his day. Henry's character has solid qualities which Shakspere must have admired, and he has made him the instrument of a ringing rhetoric which resounds through the long avenues of time. . . . When we remember that 'Henry V' addressed itself in a peculiar fashion to the spirit of the Elizabethan age, when we recall the enormous changes in political, social and religious opinion that have taken place since, the amazing thing is that the play still appeals to a modern audience and that the breath of life with which Shakspere inspired Henry's heroic figure has preserved him, not indeed as an ideal, but as a human personality with striking resemblances to people whom, under very different conditions, we see about us at the present day. It is his common humanity that endears him to us, his high courage, his modesty, his plain-speaking, his good-humor, and his practical commonsense. (pp. 327-31)

*John William Cunliffe, "The Character of 'Henry V' as Prince and King," in Shaksperian Studies, edited by Brander Matthews and Ashley Horace Thorndike, 1916. Reprint by Russell & Russell, Inc., 1962, pp. 313-31.*

### GERALD GOULD  (essay date 1919)

[*Gould asserts that* Henry V *is deeply ironic, "a satire on monarchical government, on imperialism, on the baser kinds of 'patriotism,' and on war." The multiple justifications for the war against France are intentionally confusing and often contradictory, he contends, adding that if the arguments advanced by Canterbury in Act I, Scene ii are accepted as valid, they prove that Edmund Mortimer, not Henry, is the legitimate heir to the French throne. Gould regards the king himself as hypocritical, dishonest, unscrupulous, and barbarous, and he maintains that Henry's viciousness is underscored by the conduct and reactions of several secondary characters, such as Bardolph, Nym, and Fluellen.*]

None of Shakespeare's plays is so persistently and thoroughly misunderstood as *Henry V.,* and one is tempted to think that there is no play which it is more important to understand. Irony is an awkward weapon. No doubt the irony of *Henry V.* was meant to "take in" the groundlings when it was first produced: had it failed to take them in, it would have invited bitter and immediate unpopularity. But Shakespeare can scarcely have intended that the force of preconception should, hundreds of years after his death, still be preventing the careful, the learned, and the sympathetic from seeing what he so definitely put down. *The play is ironic:* that is, I venture to think, a fact susceptible of detailed proof. Yet we still find, for instance, Mr. J.A.R. Marriott taking it at its face value as an example of "patriotism" [see Additional Bibliography]; while the critics who counter this error by a reminder of the more hideous "Prussianisms" with which Shakespeare has endowed his Henry fail to press the argument home, and are content with a sort of compromise reading.

That Shakespeare was a patriot there is neither reason nor excuse for denying. What must be denied is that *Henry V.* is patriotic. Precisely because Shakespeare *was* patriotic, he must have felt revolted by Henry's brutal and degrading "militarism." The question of how far Shakespeare's reading of Henry is historically accurate does not arise: Shakespeare chose Henry, as he chose Antony, to illustrate and enforce a certain reading of life. And he never allowed himself to be limited by his materials.

The misunderstandings of *Henry V.* have varied. Hazlitt was bitterly opposed to the conventional interpretation [see excerpt above, 1817]. He detested Henry, and said so: but he made the mistake of supposing that that detestable character was a "favourite" character of Shakespeare's. Dr. A. C. Bradley, as is his habit, has come nearest to the detection and exposition of the essential [see excerpt above, 1902]: and to differ from Dr. Bradley on any point of Shakespearean criticism is an act of presumption which no one will venture lightly. Yet even he declares to be inconceivable that reading of *Henry V.* which is demonstrably the right one: and it is impossible, if one is wrong about *Henry V.,* to be altogether right about the rest of Shakespeare. *Henry V.* is central and conclusive, and that in spite of the fact that it is certainly not one of the best plays. It is central actually in time: and this in itself makes us mildly wonder why it is *not* one of the best plays. It happens to be one of the few whose date can be determined with certainty and precision. It belongs to 1599: that is to say, it comes between Shakespeare's greatest comic period, the period which saw the creation of Falstaff, and his greatest tragic period, the period which began with *Julius Caesar* and *Hamlet*. Is it not odd that work so circumstanced should be so largely lacking in indications of Shakespeare's tragic or comic greatness? Touches of greatness, certainly, there are: the death of Falstaff is in the high sense "Shakespearean." But for the most part the serious scenes are full of a loud clanging rhetoric, which lacks almost wholly the intensity and profundity of tragic poetry, and the humours are mainly crude and verbal. The play, both in its "serious" parts and in its comedy, is specially popular with schoolboys. Some of the more miserable jocosities are, it is true, borrowed from an old play: but that is neither excuse nor (to anyone who has studied Shakespeare's ways of using his materials) explanation. On the other hand, this particular argument must not be pushed too far. It is certain that the middle period of Shakespeare saw, at any rate, some other work of inferior character, and consequently we cannot pretend that the inferiority of *Henry V.* was necessarily intentional and "tendencious."

Again, if the examination of the play shows us—as it does—various discrepancies and contradictions, we must hesitate as to how far we press the argument from these. The contradictions in Shakespeare vary in kind. In the early plays they seem often to be nothing but the results of technical carelessness and incompetence. The contradictions of time in *Othello,* on the other hand, seem to be carefully inserted in order to secure the dramatic effect of "double time," while, as against that, when we go on to *Lear,* we find confusions and discrepancies for which no critical scheme can account. The contradictions in *Henry V.,* then, must be judged on their own merits, and brought to one simple test: the test of whether they do or do not appear to follow a definite line, illustrate a definite tendency, and fix a definite character. If they do so appear, it will scarcely be fair to dismiss them as technical errors. Rather, we shall have to consider them as the means of Shakespeare's irony. *Henry V.* is a satire on monarchical government, on imperialism, on the baser kinds of "patriotism," and on war. This can be proved by quotation from the play itself, even if we consider the play itself in isolation. But we ought not to consider it in isolation. It is definitely the concluding portion of a trilogy. The character of Henry V. is perfectly consistent throughout: both in the two parts of *Henry IV.* and in *Henry V.* he puts forward consistent and convincing explanations of his apparent "wildness" and the change from that to his assumption of public dignity. His explanations differ only when they have different objects to subserve. He is the perfect hypocrite. Even in soliloquy he sometimes keeps up the pretences which he uses elsewhere to deceive his acquaintances or the public: the fact being that his pretences have penetrated to the subconscious deeps of his character. (It is instructive to compare the soliloquies of Iago, in which that supreme villain searches about in his consciousness, of course unsuccessfully, for motives which are not there at all—motives which ought rather to be sought in the subconscious "urge" of an unrealised moral jealousy.) Never once, throughout the three plays in which he figures, the trilogy of which he is the unifying centre, does Henry perform an act of spontaneous generosity or kindliness. When he displays magnanimity, as towards the Lord Chief Justice [in *2 Henry IV*], it is always in order to reap some return in political advantage. His "magnanimity" to the Lord Chief Justice is in sharp, immediate, and intentional contrast to his rejection of Falstaff. There was nothing to be "got" by being magnanimous, or even fair, to Falstaff: quite the contrary. Octavius in *Antony and Cleopatra* displays a mag-

nanimity similar to Henry's both in manner and in motive. Shakespeare, in short, was constantly preoccupied with the contrast between cold successfulness and the generous infirmities of human nature. He recurred again and again to this theme. In such "militarism" as Henry's he saw an outstanding example of what cold successfulness means in the political and international sphere, and this impression was fortified by his reading of the characters of Henry's father and brother. In devoting the play of *Henry V.,* which is both a complete play in itself and the conclusion of a trilogy, to a satire on "militarism," he was providing a central and conclusive example of a constant theme. (pp. 42-5)

[*Henry V.*] is about war. The King makes war—war which, whether it is justifiable or not, is admittedly not thrust upon him. In war lies the whole glory of the play and its hero, such as that glory is. We can scarcely, therefore, shut our eyes to the irony with which Shakespeare makes Henry declare . . . :

> The slave, a member of the country's peace,
> Enjoys it; but in gross brain little wots
> What watch the King keeps to maintain the peace,
> Whose hours the peasant best advantages.
> [IV. i. 281-84]

It may well be said here that the "peace" referred to is not international peace, but legal and domestic. Even so, the contrast is sufficiently striking, and none the less so if we accept the view that Henry's war-making can somehow be justified. But can it?

The actual words used in *Henry V.* about the French war are foreshadowed at the end of *Henry IV.* in the speech of Prince John of Lancaster (and as to Shakespeare's view of *his* cynicism there can be no doubt):

> I will lay odds that, ere this year expire,
> We bear our civil swords and native fire
> As far as France: I heard a bird to sing,
> Whose music, to my thinking, pleased the King.
> [*2 Henry IV*, V. v. 105-08]

"Pleased the King"—that is the point. That forestalls all the arguments by which, in the early part of *Henry V.,* the justification of a war against France is urged. But even earlier there has been an indication of the militarist motive. In *Henry IV.,* Part II., Act iv., sc. 5, the dying Henry IV. says to his son, who is to succeed him:

> Therefore, my Harry,
> Be it thy course to busy giddy minds
> With foreign quarrels; that action, hence borne out,
> May waste the memory of the former days.
> [*2 Henry IV*, IV. v. 212-15]

The pleas of justification for the war, with which we are bound to begin any detailed examination of *Henry V.,* are open to two main criticisms. Even if they were convincing on their merits, they would prove only that the war was justified as a *dynastic* war. And are dynastic wars ever justified?—seeing that they cost the blood of the common people who have nothing to do with dynasties. To say this is not to import "modern" ideas into Shakespeare; the point was fully appreciated, long before Shakespeare, by Sir Thomas More. So much, however, is conjecture: the sound and unanswerable criticism is that, even *as* a dynastic claim, Henry's claim to the French crown could be justified as he indeed seeks to justify it, by his descent from Edward III. and by that only: and *since he was not descended in the eldest line, the claim had no shadow of justi-*

*fication*. He held the English throne by vote of Parliament; but even he could scarcely think that the English Parliament could vote him the French crown. Nor can it be said that we are here going outside Shakespeare to mere historical fact: Henry himself admits his position as a usurper's son . . . :

> Not to-day, O Lord,
> O, not to-day, think not upon the fault
> My father made in compassing the crown!
>
> [IV. i. 292-94]

All the Archbishop's talk about the "Salic law" (Act i., sc. 2) is utterly beside the point. Granted the refutation of the "Salic law," granted Edward III.'s claim, still the heir was not Henry but Mortimer. (pp. 48-9)

It is Act i., sc. I, which at once gives the game away. Two prelates are discussing how they may avert a threatened law for the disendowment of the Church:

> If it pass against us,
> We lose the better half of our possession,
>
> [I. i. 7-8]

says the Archbishop of Canterbury, and proposes to buy off the King by offering him an unprecedentedly large sum towards the expenses of a war with France—and *to explain to him*

> The severals and unhidden passages
> Of his true titles to some certain dukedoms,
> And generally to the crown and seat of France.
>
> [I. i. 86-8]

The cynicism of this, in the forefront of the play, needs no elaboration—it is only amazing that it should ever have been missed. Bear in mind that there is artistically, in dramatic construction, no reason or excuse whatever for this scene: unless its intention is the obvious cynical one, there is no intention at all. A later speech of Henry's own, again (Act i., sc. 2) admits of only one reading. He is explaining the wild courses of his youth, and advances an argument so obviously outrageous for a seriously patriotic play that one wonders even the "rabble" could swallow it:

> We never valued this poor seat of England;
> And therefore, living hence, did give ourself
> To barbarous licence; as 'tis ever common
> That men are merriest when they are from home.
> But tell the Dauphin I will keep my state,
> Be like a king and show my sail of greatness
> When I do rouse me in my throne of France.
>
> [I. ii. 269-75]

If this is not a plain statement that the war with France was intended from long before, it is (to say nothing of the quaint "patriotism" of the first line!) utterly meaningless. Then what are we to say of the hypocrisy which seeks to put the decision upon the Archbishop of Canterbury? Henry cannot have it both ways within three hundred lines. The Archbishop is adjured:

> And God forbid, my dear and faithful lord,
> That you should fashion, wrest, or bow your reading,
> Or nicely charge your understanding soul
> With opening titles miscreate, whose right
> Suits not in native colours with the truth;
> For God doth know how many now in health
> Shall drop their blood in approbation

> Of what your reverence shall incite us to.
> Therefore take heed how you impawn our person,
> How you awake our sleeping sword of war:
> We charge you, in the name of God, take heed. . . .
>
> [I. ii. 13-23]

Then follows the Archbishop's exposition of the Salic law— an exposition which is, in any case, . . . wholly irrelevant and certainly known to be insincere. Later, different suggestions of motives are allowed to peep out—not, we must suppose, without deliberate intention of contrast. Thus Ely urges:

> . . . my thrice puissant liege
> Is in the very May-morn of his youth,
> Ripe for exploits and mighty enterprises.
>
> [I. ii. 119-21]

And Exeter:

> Your brother kings and monarchs of the earth
> Do all expect that you should rouse youself,
> As did the former lions of your blood.
>
> [I. ii. 122-24]

Henry's tendency, indulged already at great length, to deplore the waste of innocent blood in war, does not here move him to rebuke these "militarist" incitements! Is there, again, no hint of irony in the Prologue to Act ii.?

> Now thrive the armourers, and honour's thought
> Reigns solely in the breast of every man.
>
> [Chorus, II, 3-4]

Perhaps not. But can a king who has so recently been unsure of his own claim be credited with sincerity when he tries to put on those who resist it the whole blame of the war? Yet Henry's emissary, Exeter, speaking to the French king . . . , thus defines his master's attitude:

>        . . . he
> . . . bids you, in the bowels of the Lord,
> Deliver up the crown, and to take mercy
> On the poor souls for whom this hungry war
> Opens his vasty jaws; and on your head
> Turning the widows' tears, the orphans' cries,
> The dead men's blood, the pining maidens' groans,
> For husbands, fathers, and betrothed lovers,
> That shall be swallow'd in this controversy.
>
> [II. iv. 101, 102-09]

It is important to notice the extraordinary accumulation and contradiction of motives with which the whole question of the war's origin is confused. In the negotiation scene (Act ii., sc. 4) the Dauphin's earlier and provocative message is admitted by implication to be a mere side-issue. Now this message of the Dauphin's was in answer to a demand of Henry's, not indeed for the crown of France, but for "some certain dukedoms": and *those* were claimed "in the right of your great predecessor, King Edward the Third" [I. ii. 247-48]. That claim was made, then, long before the King had received the Archbishop of Canterbury's decision about the Salic law and the right of succession—and yet the Archbishop makes no distinction between the two claims when . . . he speaks of Henry's

> . . . true titles to some certain dukedoms,
> And generally to the crown and seat of France,
> Derived from Edward, his great-grandfather.
>
> [I. i. 87-9]

Besides, before the war irretrievably begins, the French King relents from the Dauphin's attitude, and fruitlessly offers Henry his daughter's hand and what the Prologue to Act iii. describes as

> Some petty and unprofitable dukedoms.
>
> [Chorus, III, 31]

Confusion on confusion! Leaving aside the fact that Henry had no claim to the French crown at all, and judging only the English case as presented by the English in the play, what do we find? The claim to certain dukedoms is identical with the claim to the whole French Kingdom: both depend on the inheritance from Edward: yet the former claim is put forward irrespective of the latter, and is refused by the Dauphin. The Dauphin's refusal is made the occasion of violent threats against the French people—threats which are later in a slightly different form repeated to the French King as the penalty of refusing the *second* claim, not the first. Indeed, as has been said, the French King is willing to depart from the Dauphin's attitude and to compromise: but it is too late. Why, since the Dauphin's insult is admitted to be irrelevant? Because the Archbishop has decided that Henry has a claim, not merely to the dukedoms which he *had* claimed, but to the Kingdom of France. But Henry had previously intended to conquer the Kingdom of France anyway: the whole course of his youth is explained by that single intention. Yet the responsibility of his enterprise is to rest, firstly, on the Archbishop, who gives Henry the advice which he has already acted on before receiving it, and secondly on the King of France, who refuses a claim about which Henry himself has been extremely doubtful. War is a glorious thing, irrespective of its cause or object—a "mighty enterprise" in which a King is expected to engage; yet it is so inglorious that the responsibility of embarking on it has, at all costs of veracity and common sense, to be "shelved." It diverts men's minds from difficulties at home, and requires and receives the blessings of the Church! One can, of course, if one chooses, attribute all this wildness of contradiction and nonsense to carelessness or incompetence on Shakespeare's part. But to do so is an extreme step, in face of the satisfying completeness with which every contradiction, every absurdity, fits in with the further insincerities of Henry's character to make of that character a comprehensive and comprehensible whole.

The second main indictment against Henry is his unscrupulous brutality. This is so clear, so insistent, that it can be neither missed nor explained away. Commentators have sometimes taken the discreet course of ignoring it. It should, alone, be sufficient to silence the suggestion that we are meant to admire Henry. But it does not stand alone. It is inextricably mingled with the old hypocrisy, the continual confusion of motive. In Act iv., sc. 6 every soldier is ordered to kill his prisoners, merely as a precautionary measure ("Give the word through" [IV. vi. 38]); yet in the next scene we find, first, that this measure *has* been adopted for quite a different reason, and, secondly, that the threat of such a measure (had the word not been "given through"?) is to be used in negotiation, and that as a preface to it Henry says:

> I was not angry since I came to France
> Until this instant.
>
> [IV. vii. 55-6]

Unfortunately, the anger of such cold-blooded worldlings can be produced to order, like their magnanimity, when "profits will accrue" [II. i. 112]. One wonders how, if not by anger,

Henry can have excused his previous ravings, almost incredible in their mingled brutality and hypocrisy, before Harfleur:

> . . . as I am a soldier,
> A name that in my thoughts becomes me best,
> If I begin the battery once again,
> I will not leave the half-achieved Harfleur
> Till in her ashes she lie buried.
> The gates of mercy shall be all shut up,
> And the flesh'd soldier, rough and hard of heart,
> In liberty of bloody hand shall range
> With conscience wide as hell, mowing like grass
> Your fresh-fair virgins and your flowering infants.
> What is it then to me, if impious war,
> Array'd in flames like to the prince of fiends,
> Do, with his smirch'd complexion, all fell feats
> Enlink'd to waste and desolation?
> What is 't to me, when you yourselves are cause,
> If your pure maidens fall into the hand
> Or hot and forcing violation? . . .
>          Therefore you men of Harfleur,
> Take pity of your town and of your people
> Whiles yet my soldiers are in my command. . . .
> If not, why, in a moment look to see
> The blind and bloody soldier with foul hand
> Defile the locks of your shrill-shrieking daughters;
> Your fathers taken by the silver beards,
> And their most reverend heads dash'd to the walls,
> Your naked infants spitted upon pikes. . . .
>
> [III. iii. 5-21, 27-9, 33-8]

Is it seriously maintained that Shakespeare means us to admire Henry *here*?

The scene in which the King, disguised, talks with the soldiers is very much to my purpose: it is too famous to bear much quotation, but I may point out how completely and deliberately Henry confuses the issue. Bates and Williams argue that there is heavy responsibility on the King *"if the cause be not good"* [IV. i. 134], and that they, having no choice but to obey, do not know whether the cause is good or not. Williams says:

> I am afeard there are few die well that die in
> a battle; for how can they charitably dispose of
> anything, when blood is their argument?
>
> [IV. i. 141-43]

to which Henry replies with an irrelevant and hypocritical discourse on the sins that may have been committed *before* the war. What do those who take Henry seriously as a patriot argue here? Do they suggest Shakespeare was so obtuse as not to know when he was making one of his characters argue dishonestly? Follows the famous speech on Kingship, closely parallel to a similar outbreak, in a previous play, of the archhumbug, Henry IV., who there deplored the crown which he had won by such ill means. The ground on which, in the present scene, Henry defends war reveals the very grotesqueness of insincerity, especially when contrasted with his own previous expatiation on its horrors. Consider this:

> Therefore should every soldier in the wars do
> as every sick man in his bed, wash every mote
> out of his conscience; and dying so, death is to
> him advantage; or not dying, the time was
> blessedly lost wherein such preparation was
> gained.
>
> [IV. i. 178-82]

The inglorious and "profiteering" side of war is hit off in two lines delivered by Pistol in Act ii., sc. I:

> . . . for I shall sutler be
> Unto the camp, and profits will accrue.
>
> [II. i. 111-12]

So later, on the death of Falstaff, Pistol says:

> Yoke fellows in arms,
> Let us to France; like horse-leeches, my boys,
> To suck, to suck, the very blood to suck!
>
> [II. iii. 54-6]

Nor, when in Act iv., sc. 4, we find Bardolph and Nym hanged for stealing, can we forbear the reflection that they have only done on a small scale what Henry has done on a large.

The part played by Fluellen as ironic commentator is highly significant. He is unimpressed by Henry's characteristic comment after victory . . . :

> O God, thy arm was here;
> And not to us, but to thy arm alone,
> Ascribe we all!
>
> [IV. viii. 106-08]

—with which we may profitably compare Prince John's epilogue to his own successful but contemptible treachery . . . :

> God, and not we, hath safely fought to-day.
>
> [*2 Henry IV*, IV. ii. 121]

When Fluellen asks:

> Is it not lawful, an't please your majesty, to
> tell how many is killed?
>
> [IV. viii. 117-18]

the King replies:

> Yes, captain, but with this acknowledgment,
> That God fought for us.
>
> [IV. viii. 119-20]

Is there anyone who will contend that Fluellen's rejoinder—"Yes, my conscience, he did us great good" [IV. viii. 121]—is not ironic? Nor is the same note hard to discern in his reference to Falstaff:

> As Alexander killed his friend Cleitus, being
> in his ales and his cups; so also Harry Monmouth, being in his right wits and his good
> judgments, turned away the fat knight with the
> great-belly doublet.
>
> [IV. vii. 44-8]

About Fluellen, however, opinions may easily vary. They cannot easily vary about the treatment of Falstaff. . . . The two scenes, Act ii., sc. 2 and 3, are in this connection decisive. They comprise the unmasking of the treachery of Cambridge, Scroop, and Grey, *with enormous stress laid on the sin of ingratitude towards a former comrade*—and the death of Falstaff, the victim of *the King's ingratitude towards a former comrade*. The irony of the contrast is unmistakable—it is indeed "laid on almost too thick." The whole character of Henry "pivots," as it were, on his relation to Falstaff. It is the familiar antithesis—cold success and sinful humanity—which runs through the whole trilogy and through the whole of Shakespeare. It runs through the play of *Henry V*. like a rhythm. "Nay," says Exeter, speaking, not of the King's treachery towards Falstaff, but of a conspirator towards the King:

*Act IV. Scene iii. Salisbury, Henry V, Exeter, Montjoy, and others. Frontispiece to the Hanmer edition by Francis Hayman (1744). By permission of the Folger Shakespeare Library.*

> Nay, but the man that was his bedfellow,
> Whom he hath dull'd and cloy'd with gracious
> favours. . . .
>
> [II. ii. 8-9]

The King thanks God for having graciously intervened on his behalf—and it is then that we go on to the famous and touching scene in which Falstaff's death is described. Those whom the fat knight has wronged stay by him: only the King has proved a false friend. It is Shakespeare's final moral judgment. (pp. 49-55)

> Gerald Gould, "A New Reading of 'Henry V'," in The English Review, *Vol. XXIX, July, 1919, pp. 42-55.*

### ELMER EDGAR STOLL (lecture date 1921)

[*Stoll was one of the earliest critics to attack the method of character analysis that had dominated nineteenth-century Shakespearean criticism. Instead, he maintained that Shakespeare was primarily a man of the professional theater and that his works had to be interpreted in the light of Elizabethan stage conventions and understood for their theatrical effects, rather than their psychological insight. Stoll has in turn been criticized for seeing only one dimension of Shakespeare's art. His remarks on Henry V, excerpted below, were originally delivered as a lecture before the Shakespeare Association at Kings College, London, in 1921. Stoll focuses on the characterization of Henry, asserting that Shakespeare dramatized not necessarily his own but "his country's notion" of an ideal hero-king. The critic finds no evidence of irony in Henry's characterization and proclaims that an Elizabethan audience would have unreservedly approved this portrait of one of England's most popular monarchs. For modern readers who are skeptical of the king's frequent allusions to God, Stoll recommends that we recognize that "on the Elizabethan stage piety and morality are as inseparable from the ideal king as the crown on his head."]*

[*Henry V*] interests us most as a picture of life and character. The patriotism, though ardent, is not highly enlightened. The war is for no good cause; Henry's claim to the throne is, for all that he believes in it, unfounded. And the ideal of the English is, so far as it is expressed, honor and glory, not love of country, or liberty, or devotion to one's faith. It is a feudal, chivalric war, waged, not for a cause like a crusade, but like a tournament for a victor's crown. (p. 36)

Chief of the characters is, of course, the King. He is, on the whole, done according to historical and popular tradition; he is the Hal of *Henry IV,* reclaimed and sobered. He has the manliness, the physical strength and ability, the personal courage, the generalship, the ruthlessness (as well as the mercifulness toward the poor and the weak), the piety (though not the bigotry and intolerance), and the exalted patriotic temper, which the chronicler Holinshed had attributed to the great popular hero of the land. But the mere transcription of traits will not go far towards making a character; and Shakespeare gave him many other features, and put in his nostrils the breath of life besides.

The most remarkable thing about him is the way that Shakespeare reforms him and yet contrives to keep him human and recognizable. Reformations are ticklish things to handle on the stage; edifying, but alienating, they ordinarily lead beyond the province of art and poetry into the dry and sterile air of morals or the dank atmosphere of sentimentality. This on the whole the royal reformation does not do. Henry is a knight and a hero, a king and a wise ruler, and a general who has put almost all petty personal considerations under his feet; but he is still a friendly good fellow, has his joke before battle and in the midst of battle, and woos the French princess in no silken terms of gallantry, but more like a captain of cavalry than a king, though more like a king than a suitor, with fire in his heart though with a twinkle in his eye. (pp. 38-9)

Some readers may object a little to Henry's obtrusive morality and his familiarity with the Most High. They may be reminded of later czars and kaisers, likewise engaged in wars of aggression, and be inclined to call it all hypocrisy or official cant. Shakespeare surely did not mean it so; the Elizabethans would not have taken it so; and such monarchs, . . . like their parties, are specimens of times and manners, now long out of date, but not out of date in the age of Elizabeth. In any case, Shakespeare has deliberately brushed away much of the piety clinging to him in Holinshed. He has added, to be sure, the prayer the night before the battle, in which he speaks of King Richard's death. But that really is a relief; Henry is not so pious as penitent, and would make amends for his father's wrong, by which he profits. (p. 40)

Was Henry, then, as some have thought, Shakespeare's ideal? Gervinus [see excerpt above, 1849-50] and other German critics have declared he was, being the antithesis of Richard II and Hamlet. Some of them have even gone so far as to say that Henry is Shakespeare himself, with his practical genius

and well-balanced nature, his taste for the low as well as the lofty, and his sense of humor in the midst of duty—his liking for play when at work. Mr. W. B. Yeats holds just the contrary [see excerpt above, 1903]. Poet of the Celtic twilight, of them that went forth to battle but always fell, he thinks that Shakespeare infinitely preferred Richard; and that Henry is given the "gross vices and coarse nerves," and "the resounding rhetoric, as of a leading article," which befit a man who succeeds, though his success was really failure. "Shakespeare watched Henry V, not indeed as he watched the greater souls in the visionary procession, but cheerfully, as one watches some handsome spirited horse, and he spoke his tale, as he spoke all tales, with tragic irony." But when Shakespeare—when any popular dramatist—is ironical, we the people must needs know it; or else his popular art has failed him and missed the mark. Here is no evidence of either. Instead of being sly, or insinuating, or pregnant of innuendo, he is more exuberant and enthusiastic than usual; the choruses, which are the authentic voice of the poet himself, put that beyond the peradventure of a doubt. And the likelihood is that Professor Dowden is nearer the truth; Henry V, at least in some measure, approaches Shakespeare's ideal of the practical man, which is not his highest ideal. Shakespeare, no doubt, admired success, though without worshipping it; he himself succeeded, not inconsiderably in his brief two score and ten; but the men he admired most, I daresay, were the finer spirits such as Hamlet, Brutus, or Prospero [in *Julius Caesar* and *The Tempest*], whether they succeeded or failed. It was their devotion and gallantry that he admired, not (pessimistically or sentimentally) their devotion and gallantry foiled or thrown away.

It is more to the point to say that Henry is the ideal of England, not Shakespeare's but his country's notion of their hero-king. He is the king that audiences at the Globe would have him be. This is particularly true as regards what we nowadays consider his bragging, his priggishness and cant. The obtrusive morality and piety were expected; for that matter they are like the sort of thing you find in a Speech from the Throne or our American Presidential Thanksgiving proclamations at the present day. (pp. 41-2)

And on the Elizabethan stage piety and morality are as inseparable from the ideal king as the crown on his head, the royal "we" in his mouth, or the "strut" . . . with which his royal legs must tread the stage. There is in all Elizabethan dramatic art something naïve—something self-descriptive—in the lines, which in the three centuries of evolution towards the more purely and strictly dramatic has nearly disappeared. The wicked, like Richard III in his first soliloquy, know that they are wicked; the good, that they are good; heroes like Julius Caesar boast and vaunt their prowess; and a king, like a god on the stage, must every minute remember, and make us remember too, that he is nothing less. Henry's preaching, swaggering, and swinging of the scepter may repel us a bit today; but that is because as we read we democratically take him for no more than a man, as people at the Globe did not nor were expected to do. (p. 43)

Or if Henry's blatant piety still offend us, surely we should find relief from it in his bragging and swearing. For these efface any impression of sanctimoniousness—these are royal, too, in the genuine antique style. Fancy William the Conqueror, Richard the Lion-hearted, or a king of Henry of Lancaster's kidney, shorn of all these high privileges and immunities of utterance, particularly on the stage. A medieval king can hardly be expected to talk like a gentleman in top hat and gaiters. The lion must not speak small—leviathan must not speak soft words unto thee—but have his roar. Despite our enlightenment, most of us, I suppose, have a sneaking notion of a king as one who talks and does, with a superlatively grand air, pretty much as he pleases. At the theater—at the Elizabethan theater far more than at ours—many, for the time being, have hardly any other notion of him at all. "We are the makers of manners," says Henry himself [V. ii. 270-71]. And something of this loftiness and liberty of utterance must be granted him even in his morality and piety.

For through it all the man appears. Like Shakespeare's other characters Henry has an individual tone, his own voice, not just anybody's, and one unmistakably human. It swells and subsides, pulses and undulates, alive as a limb in a Rubens or a Raphael. Here are both man and king, both individual and Englishman, in Henry's mingled downrightness and moderation, as he flings his cards upon the table, though ready enough for all that to play on:

> There's for thy labour, Montjoy.
> Go bid thy master well advise himself,
> If we may pass, we will; if we be hind'red,
> We shall your tawny ground with your red blood
> Discolour; and so, Montjoy, fare you well.
> The sum of all our answer is but this:
> We would not seek a battle, as we are;
> Nor as we are, we say we will not shun it.
> So tell your master.
>
> [III. vi. 158-66]

That's the voice of a king, a man, an Englishman, and yet not quite that of any other that I know.

As a king, Henry is made to suit the Globe; as a man, to suit the English people. How English he is,—so practical, sportsmanlike, moral and pious; so manly and stalwart, and yet free and easy; so self-assertive and yet modest and generous; so fierce against his enemies, and yet merciful towards women and the weak; so serious, and yet simple and humorous; and so bluff and downright, and hearty and genuine, in the avowal of his love. And how instinctively an English audience must have taken to him! His wildness in youth gave him an added flavor, as it did to Richard the Lion-hearted before him and to Edward VII since; and his skill at leapfrog—a game which had not yet passed over into the hands of boys . . . fitted him even then to be a hero in this land of sport. The wooing scene itself, in which he refers to this and other accomplishments, must have been enough to float the play. If there is anything that the English take to, it is the unconventional and plain-spoken, especially when combined with humor and genuine affection at the core. "A character" the combination is called, as you find it throughout English literature, from Dekker down to Fielding and Dickens. And this character has the further charm of a king and soldier trying—and yet scorning—to be a suitor; unconventional in part because he cannot help it, in part because he would not help it if he could; wooing, and overruling, a conventional and coquettish princess, in a language that he cannot speak and she will not understand. All that is simple and English, all that is affected and French, and all that is mannish and womanish, too, comes out in the lively encounter between them; and how hugely an English audience must have been tickled with the contrast! (pp. 43-5)

*Elmer Edgar Stoll, " 'Henry V'," in his* Poets and Playwrights: Shakespeare, Jonson, Spenser, Milton, *The University of Minnesota Press, 1930, pp. 31-54.*

## H. B. CHARLTON   (lecture date 1929)

[*An English scholar, Charlton is best known for his* Shakespearian Comedy *(1938) and* Shakespearian Tragedy *(1948)—two important studies in which he argued that the proponents of New Criticism, particularly T. S. Eliot and I. A. Richards, were reducing Shakespeare's drama to its poetic elements and in the process losing sight of his characters. In his introduction to* Shakespearian Tragedy, *Charlton described himself as a "devout" follower of A. C. Bradley, and like his mentor he adopted a psychological, character-oriented approach to Shakespeare's work. The excerpt below is taken from a 1929 address to the Leeds Branch of the English Association. In it, Charlton maintains that* Henry V *is not only a study of a king, but one of governance as well. The critic holds that Shakespeare's attitude towards kingship in* Henry V *remains the same as that in* 1 *and* 2 Henry IV: *"what is good in the world of politics is entirely unrelated to and generally the opposite of what makes for goodness in the moral life." Charlton credits Henry V with political instincts that lead to national and personal success, but he also argues that the king's "ingratiating commonplaceness of mind" permits him to avoid the "immoral implications" of his choices. The critic further contends that the bishops exploit Henry's lack of intellectual acuity and maneuver him into declaring war on France, and he doubts that the king possesses the "Machiavellian astuteness" to see through their tactics and adapt them to his own advantage.*]

[*Henry IV* and *Henry V*] are perhaps the only perfect specimens of a dramatic type which, even in an age of creative dramatists, only Shakespeare's genius could invent. They are not chronicle-pageants: they are not tragedies, nor are they comedies, though they come closer to comedy than to other recognized types, and indeed curiously so, since the traditional affinities of the chronicle play had been with tragedy. They are history-plays. A better name would be political plays, for they are plays in which the prevailing dramatic interest is in the fate of a nation. Since that is their nature, there will be in them much of what Shakespeare's insight had apprehended of the forces which shape a nation's destiny.

The plot of both of them is specifically political, and the nominal hero of each is elected to the office in his capacity as a political agent, a wielder of government. To an Elizabethan, the welfare of England was in the hands of its sovereign. These two history-plays are representations of two kings, each contributing his particular service to the good of his country by virtue of his gifts, his principles, and his personality. At the end of them, England is what it has become in each, because this or that trait in its king has visibly produced these political consequences. They are, psychologically, studies in kings; but, dramatically, they are views of kingship. (pp. 13-14)

In popular estimation Shakespeare's Henry V is probably a more perfect king than Henry IV. Admittedly he is a far more likeable fellow—once he has ceased to explain his wild oats. And what enterprises of kingship he undertakes he performs no less successfully than did his father. But Shakespeare can only allow him to purchase our personal affection by considerably reducing his duties as a king. His father had to exercise the whole art of government, maintaining peace at home and securing glory abroad. It was in the more exacting office of governing at home that his subtlest craft was needed. But Hal is largely relieved of these routine trials, and for the most part his kingship is circumscribed to military leadership. At the head of his army, in embarkation, in siege, and in battle, he treads the surest of traditional ways to popular acclamation. He is a great commander whose greatness as a king is tacitly and sentimentally assumed. In a field-command he can keep so much of the humanity he would perforce have to leave outside the door of civil office. Soldiers are much more obviously human than clerks of the Treasury.

But on the rare occasions when Hal is called upon for a definitely political decision, are the factors determining political wisdom different from what they were in his father's case? Hal's mode of leading his army to victory is his most obvious national asset. But it was, so to speak, a secondary achievement, and the good it did was entirely dependent on the prior decision to make war on France. The first scene of *Henry V*— a scene which critics curiously pass by—unmistakably deprives Hal of all personal credit for that decision. He is trapped into declaration of war by the machinations of a group of men whose sole and quite explicit motive is to preserve their own revenues; and the political implication is more flagrant in that these men are an ecclesiastical synod. Hal, in fact, owes his political achievement, not as did his father, to his own insight, but rather to something so near to intellectual dullness that it permits of his being jockeyed into his opportunities. He can be saved from such imputation only by the assumption that he saw through the bishops' subtlety and quietly used them as an excuse to embark on a foreign war with the idea of securing domestic peace, even as his father in his dying words had advised him to do. But such Machiavellian astuteness does not fit in with the indubitable traits of Hal's nature. On one occasion, and on one occasion only, there is a faint suspicion of political sophistication. In [*1 Henry IV*], Hotspur contributed to his own political ruin by a noble gesture of bravado. Too eager to await reinforcements, he joined immediate battle with the vaunt that the reduction of his forces

> lends a lustre and more great opinion
> A larger dare to our great enterprise.
>                          [*1 Henry IV*, IV. i. 77-8]

As a moral attitude its effect is magnificent; as a political decision it is disastrous. But on a similar occasion, Henry V displays a like temper. When, on the night before Agincourt, Westmoreland wishes that they had but one ten thousand more recruits from England, Henry will have none of it.

> The fewer men, the greater share of honour,
> . . . Wish not a man from England.
> God's peace, I would not lose so great an honour
> As one man more methinks would share from me.
>                          [IV. iii. 22, 30-2]

He exceeds Hotspur in moral generosity and in thirst for glory: he would even reduce the army he has:

> Rather proclaim it, Westmoreland, through my host,
> That he which hath no stomach to this fight,
> Let him depart: his passport shall be made
> And crowns for convoy put into his purse—
>                          [IV. iii. 34-7]

and all because

> we would not die in that man's company
> That fears his fellowship to die with us.
>                          [IV. iii. 38-9]

But his gesture does not lead to defeat. It is not in fact a proclamation and a firm offer to the army. It is merely a remark to one of his chiefs of staff. Nor would there have been much opportunity for wholesale demobilization on the very eve of battle. The offer, which was no offer, was either a piece of strategy or the natural outcome of Henry's military enthusiasm. Either his guardian spirit once more urges Henry to make what,

in spite of first appearances, proves in the end to be the politic move, or Henry is sounder in the theory of military numbers than he appears in this speech to be. There is more of the general's acumen in another of his battle-prayers:

> O God of battles, steel my soldiers' hearts,
> Possess them not with fear; take from them now
> The sense of reckoning, if the opposed numbers
> Pluck their hearts from them.
>                          [IV. i. 289-92]

Altogether, then, the play of *Henry V* does not really imply substantial modifications in Shakespeare's apprehension of the political life. There remains in it the sense that what is good in the world of politics is entirely unrelated to and generally the opposite of what makes for goodness in the moral life. It is the distinction between Machiavelli's *virtu* and the moralist's virtue, or, as Mr. G. B. Shaw puts it, between virtue and goodness. . . . Henry IV achieves political greatness and proves his political worth by the deliberate exercise of his political acumen: whence our coldness to him as a man. To a large extent, Henry V is thrust into political greatness by sheer instinct. His genius leads him to take steps his moral nature would have prohibited his taking; and his ingratiating commonplaceness of mind hides from him their immoral implications or even glosses them with conventional moral sanctions. He is secured in our affections, because he is dispensed by Shakespeare from requiring such intellectual greatness as his father had. He stands before us always as the great plain man, and there is a sort of gratification felt by Shakespeare, as by most of us, in installing the plain man in high political office. Illogical, it probably is; a mere gamble with fate. We trust that a blind instinct will prompt the plain man to do those things the competent politician would clearly see to be necessary; and we are willing to take our chance, though at such very long odds against us, because, as human beings and unpolitical animals, we prefer to sacrifice the probability of good government to secure ourselves against the fear of exploitation by the expert. A pledge to do nothing at all is not without advantages as an electioneering cry. Henry V wins our hearts as the greatest of plain men. His common text is that the king is but a man; that all his senses have but human conditions, and that, his ceremonies laid by, in his nakedness he appears but a man. Note, however, how his guardian angel saw to it that he should preserve his incognito whilst preaching this sermon. Henry has all the admirable propensities of the average Englishman, his conventions, his manners, and his opportune lack of them, his prejudices, and even his faith. He would have welcomed Robinson Crusoe as a brother in God. In all except generalship, he is that most attractive and delightful being, the magnificent commonplace, and we needs must love the glorified image of ourselves.

Thus did Shakespeare sweeten the savour of the political life, without giving the lie to what he had apprehended of its sordid necessities. Though it may be largely hidden, the truth as Shakespeare grasped it, remains even in *Henry V*: the sense that not only is politics a nasty business, but that a repugnant unscrupulousness is an invaluable asset in the art of government. That is the burden of the English History plays, jubilant as they are in pride of country and of race. (pp. 16-19)

> *H. B. Charlton, in his* Shakespeare, Politics and Politicians, *The English Association, Pamphlet No. 72, 1929, 24 p.*

## HARLEY GRANVILLE-BARKER   (essay date 1933)

[*Granville-Barker was a noted actor, playwright, director, and critic. His work as a Shakespearean critic is at all times informed by his experience as a director, for he treats Shakespeare's plays not as works of literature better understood divorced from the theater, as did many Romantic critics, but as pieces meant for the stage. As a director, he emphasized simplicity in staging, set design, and costuming. He believed that elaborate scenery obscured the poetry which was of central importance to Shakespeare's plays. Granville-Barker also eschewed the approach of directors who scrupulously reconstructed productions based upon Elizabethan stage techniques; he felt that this, too, detracted from the play's meaning. In the following excerpt taken from a revised version of a 1925 British Academy Lecture, Granville-Barker judges* Henry V *disappointing because he finds in it no "spiritually significant idea" and "very little that is dramatically interesting" in Henry himself. He avers that Shakespeare recognized the dramatic limitations of both his protagonist and his historical material and apologized for these deficiencies through the Chorus. Concerning Falstaff, Granville-Barker suggests that Shakespeare could not risk the fat knight's ironic comments on Henry's "new dignity."]*

In 1599 Shakespeare produced *Henry V*. He was at a height of success and popularity. He had never looked back since Marlowe died and left him, so to speak, the sceptre of heroic blank verse as a legacy. In *Henry V* he is wielding that sceptre—incomparably and with a difference—but it is that same sceptre still. The play was, no doubt, a contemporary success. But it bears signs, like many successes, of having brought its writer to a 'dead end'. (p. 51)

What is it, in this play, which disappoints us—which, as I believe, disappointed him . . .? (p. 58)

[Here] he is, an acknowledged master of his craft and in the full flush of success, setting out to write a fine play, a spacious play, with England as its subject, no less a thing. He is now to crown the achievement of the earlier histories and, above all, of the last two, in which he had so 'found himself'. He is to bring that popular favourite Prince Hal to a worthy completion; and to this obligation—though against his formal promise to the public—he sacrifices Falstaff. It is easy to see why. Could Falstaff reform and be brought back into the company of the reformed Henry? No. Once before Shakespeare has hinted to us that the fat knight, if he grow great shall grow less, purge, leave sack, and live cleanly. But not a bit of it. *Henry IV, Part II*, when it came, found him more incorrigible than ever. On the other hand, had Falstaff made his unauthorized way to France, how could Henry's new dignity suffer the old ruffian's ironic comments on it? He had run away with his creator once: better not risk it. So to his now unimpeachable hero Shakespeare has to sacrifice his greatest, his liveliest creation so far. Does the hero reward him? No one could say that Henry is ill-drawn or uninteresting. But, when it comes to the point, there seems to be very little that is dramatically interesting for him to do. Here is a play of action, and here is the perfect man of action. Yet all the while Shakespeare is apologizing—and directly apologizing—for not being able to make the action effective. Will the audience, for heaven's sake, help him out? One need not attach too much importance to the formal modesty of the prologue.

> O pardon! Since a crooked figure may
> Attest in little place a million,
> And let us, ciphers to this great accompt,
> On your imaginary forces work.
>
> [Prologue, 15-18]

This might be merely the plea of privilege that every playwright, ancient or modern, must tacitly make. But when we find the apology repeated and repeated again, and before Act

V most emphatically of all; when we find there the prayer to his audience

> . . . to admit the excuse
> Of time, of numbers, and due course of things
> Which cannot in their huge and proper life
> Be here presented—
>
> [Chorus, V, 3-6]

does it not sound a more than formal confession, and as if Shakespeare had distressfully realized that he had asked his theatre—mistakenly; because it must be mistakenly—for what it could not accomplish?

Turn now to Henry himself. When do we come closest to him? Not surely in the typical moments of the man of action, in

> Once more unto the breach, dear friends, once more . . .
>
> [III. i. 1ff.]

and upon like occasions. But in the night before Agincourt, when, on the edge of likely disaster, he goes out solitary into the dark and searches his own soul. This is, of course, no new turn to the character. Prince Hal at his wildest has never been a figure of mere fun and bombast. Remember the scenes with his father and with Hotspur. Still, soul-searching is—if one may use such a phrase of Majesty—not his long suit; and the passage, fine as it is, has the sound of a set piece. It is rhetoric rather than revelation.

In the later speech to Westmoreland:

> We few, we happy few, we band of brothers . . .
>
> [IV. iii. 60ff.]

Henry, set among his fellows, is more himself. But Shakespeare makes practically no further attempt to show us the inner mind of the man. The Henry of the rest of Act IV is the Henry of the play's beginning. While, since for Act V some new aspect of the hero really must be found, we are landed with a jerk (nothing in the character has prepared us for it) into a rollicking love scene. And this well-carpentered piece of work is finished. I daresay it was a success, and the Shakespeare who lived to please and had to please to live, may have been content with it. But the other, the daring, the creative Shakespeare, who had now known what it was to have Shylock, Mercutio, Hotspur [in, respectively, *The Merchant of Venice, Romeo and Juliet,* and *1 Henry IV*], and Falstaff come to life, and abound in unruly life, under his hands—was he satisfied? No doubt he could have put up as good a defence as many of his editors have obliged him with both for hero and play, for its epic quality and patriotic purpose. Though had he read in the preface to the admirable Arden edition that—

> Conscientious, brave, just, capable and tenacious, Henry stands before us the embodiment of wordly success, and as such he is entitled to our unreserved admiration . . . [see essay by H. A. Evans listed in the Additional Bibliography].

I think he would have smiled wryly. For he was not the poet to find patriotism an excuse for the making of fine phrases. And he knew well enough that neither in the theatre nor in real life is it these 'embodiments of worldly success' that we carry closest in our hearts, or even care to spend an evening with.

No, he had set himself this task, and he carried it through conscientiously and with the credit which is sound workmanship's due. But I detect disappointment with his hero, and—

not quite fancifully, I believe—a deeper disillusion with his art. The 'daemonic' Shakespeare, then, was only a lesson to the good. But it was a valuable lesson. He had learnt that for presenting the external pageantry of great events his theatre was no better than a puppet-show; and that though the art of drama might be the art of presenting men in action, your successful man of action did not necessarily make the most interesting of heroes. For behind the action, be the play farce or tragedy, there must be some spiritually significant idea, or it will hang lifeless. And this is what is lacking in *Henry V*. (pp. 58-61)

> Harley Granville-Barker, ''From 'Henry V' to 'Hamlet','' in Aspects of Shakespeare: Being British Academy Lectures, *Oxford at the Clarendon Press, Oxford, 1933, pp. 49-83.*

**CHARLES WILLIAMS**  (essay date 1936)

[*Williams was an English novelist, poet, biographer, and critic. In the following excerpt on* Henry V, *he contends that in Act IV Henry reveals for the first time that he has embraced the challenges that face him and has thereby achieved ''an almost supernatural'' capacity to comfort and rouse the spirits of his army. This acceptance signals, Williams asserts, that the king has attained a more highly developed sense of honor than that held by Hotspur in* 1 Henry IV, *resulting in his buoyant—almost careless—attitude toward ''darkness, danger, defeat, and death.'' The critic also discerns in the Chorus at the beginning of Act IV intimations of Shakespeare's later tragedies, particularly in its evocation of universal night and the accompanying ''spectral images of mankind.''*]

[*Henry V*] is at once a conclusion and a beginning. It is not primarily a patriotic play, for the First Chorus knows nothing of patriotism nor of England, but only of *a Muse of fire which would ascend the brightest heaven of invention* [Prologue, 1-2] by discovering a challenge between mighty monarchies. Patriotism certainly keeps breaking in, but rather like the army itself: the mass behind Henry is dramatically an English mass, and as the play proceeds he becomes more and more an English king. So much must be allowed to the patriots; it is, however, for them to allow that he becomes something else and more as well, and it is in that something more that his peculiar strength lies.

Before defining that, however, and his own words define it, it may be well to remark a few of the differences between *Henry V* and its precedent *Henry IV*. The newer manner of the blank verse itself is accentuated; it gains in speed. Less even than in *Henry IV* are there any involutions or adornments; its movements, like the action of the persons, admit of no delay. It has lost superfluity, though it has not yet gained analysis. No word blurs, but each word does not yet illuminate, as each was to illuminate in that later play of action and vision, *Antony and Cleopatra*. Here it is equivalent to the King's desire and the King's deed, and equals the one with the other. But there is, at first, no variation between the King and other characters, as there is variation between the Prince and Hotspur and Falstaff in *Henry IV*: what the King is, he is, and the others are apart from him. In fact, the next differences between the two plays are (i) the omission of Hotspur, and (ii) the omission of Falstaff. It will be said that Hotspur is dead before *Henry IV* ends and Falstaff dies soon after *Henry V* begins. But whatever historical necessity or moral convenience compelled those two deaths, the result is to leave the stage free not only for King Henry himself, but for something else—for the development of the

idea of honour. In *Henry IV* honour had been peculiarly the property of Hotspur, and it had seemed like being his property in a narrower sense. He had regarded it almost as if it were something he owned as he owned his armour, something that he could capture and possess.

> By heaven methinks it were an easy leap
> To pluck bright honour from the pale-fac'd moon,
> Or dive into the bottom of the deep,
> Where fathom-line could never touch the ground,
> And pluck up drowned honour by the locks;
> So he that doth redeem her thence might wear
> Without corrival all her dignities:
>> [*1 Henry IV*, I. iii. 201-07]

Against this splendid and egotistical figure is the figure of Falstaff. Up to the last act of *2 Henry IV* the distinction of Falstaff had been that, though he may want a lot for his comfort, he does not need it for his complacency. Hotspur, without a sense of his own honour, feels himself deficient; it is why he rebels. Falstaff, without the same sense, feels himself free; it is why he runs away or fights as circumstances and his own common sense dictate. Henry V might have been made like either of them; in fact, he was made like neither. Neither Hotspur nor Falstaff could suit the Muse of fire or the brightest heaven. Honour must for Henry in his own play be something consonant with that brightness, and that invention discovered a phrase which made honour more than reputation—whether for possession or repudiation.

> And those that leave their valiant bones in France,
> Dying like men, though buried in your dunghills,
> They shall be fam'd; for there the sun shall greet them,
> And draw their honours reeking up to heaven,
> Leaving their earthly parts to choke your clime.
>> [IV. iii. 98-102]

Their bodies are dead; their honours live, but not as fame upon earth. The heaven of invention is to suggest this other heaven; the honour of poetry is to show the honour of the spirit in challenge. It is a little reminiscent of [Milton's] *Lycidas* where also Fame is transmuted into something pleasing to 'all-judging Jove'. The honours which so live are the spirits and souls of the righteous—anyhow, of the righteous at Agincourt. It is to Henry that the identification is given; it is for him that honour is now a name for man's immortal part. If that venture of war which is the result of the challenge between two great worldly powers, two mighty monarchies, is defeated, this end at least is left to those who carry themselves well in that venture.

As far as the war itself is concerned, the play did not attempt any illusion. It put war 'in the round'. The causes of it are there; dynastic claims are the equivalent of the modern prestige of governments. The force of the verse carries the sincerity of the intention, and the tennis-balls are part of the cause of the war; that is, the other monarchy is also involved. Any insincerity is part of the way of things, but insufficient to cloud the glory of the change. In this sense Shakespeare threw over the diplomatic advice of the King in *Henry IV* as well as the martial egotism of Hotspur.

Besides the causes of war there is, in the first Harfleur scene, what a soldier-poet [Julian Grenfell] called 'Joy of Battle'; so, with a horrid faithfulness, in the second Harfleur scene, is the usual result of Joy of Battle. So, finally, in the field before Agincourt, is a kind of summing-up. War is not so very much more dangerous than peace; one is almost as likely to be killed one way as the other. 'Every soldier's duty is the King's, but every subject's soul is his own' [IV. i. 176-77], which if he keep clean, it does not very much matter whether he lives or dies. Death is not all that important—to Henry (who in the play was going to fight), to the lords, to the army, and, as a consequence, to the citizens of Harfleur. The Duke of Burgundy's oration in the last Act describes all the general advantages of peace, but it does not do more. Peace, as a general thing, is preferable to war, but life is pretty dangerous any way—pretty bloody, in every sense of the word—and a healthy male adult should be prepared for death at any moment. So what does it matter? It is not the modern view, but we are not Elizabethans, and our police are efficient.

Honour then—the capacity to challenge the world and to endure the result of challenge—is the state to be coveted.

> But if it be a sin to covet honour,
> I am the most offending soul alive.
>
> [IV. iii. 28-9]

Those lines come from the most famous of Henry's speeches. But there is another and much shorter and less famous speech which throws a stronger light on Henry. There had been a minor crisis—the conspiracy in the Second Act—before the great crisis of Agincourt. But as no one has the least interest in the Lord Scroop of Masham, and as no one can feel the King himself has had time to love him behind the scenes either in *Henry IV* or *Henry V*, the conspiracy fails to excite. We are left to listen to the King being merely vocal. When, however, the central crisis approached, Shakespeare had another way of being equivalent to it. This comes in the English camp by night before the battle, very soon after the greatest thing in the play, the sublime Fourth Chorus. In that Chorus a change had been presented as coming over the whole war. The venture had gone wrong, the challenge delivered to the world of the French had been accepted and that French world had trapped the English army and was on the point of destroying it. At the point of that pause the Fourth Chorus delivers its speech, describing the night, the gloom, and the danger. But its speech, if the words are literally followed, has two futures. The first is Agincourt; the second is the tragedies. There is not only a change in *Henry V;* there is a still darker change away from *Henry V.* The Muse of fire has been ascending her heaven—that is the poetry's own description of what it has been trying to do. But now it directly suggests that it is doing something quite different.

> Now entertain conjecture of a time
> When creeping murmur and the poring dark
> Fills the wide vessel of the universe.
>
> [Chorus, IV, 1-3]

The word 'universe' means, certainly, earth and heaven in that darkness before the battle. But there seems no reason why it should not also mean 'universe' in the accepted sense, the whole world and the whole heaven, including the brightest heaven of poetry with which we began. It is all this which is beginning to be filled with creeping murmur and the poring dark. Poetry and (so to speak) life are being occupied by this universal noise and night. It is not yet so fixed; it is but a guess and a wonder. 'Now entertain conjecture—' It is the prelude to all the plays that were to come.

From poetry thus conceiving of its own probable business, both locally at Agincourt and universally, and its future, two other enlargements follow. One concerns the English army; the other, the King.

The *Muse of Fire* is compelled to behold the army as 'so many horrid ghosts' [Chorus, IV, 28], and the description of the soldiers is that of men who are in the state she has described. It is an army but it is also humanity. To 'sit patiently and inly ruminate the morning's danger' [Chorus, IV, 24-5] is a situation familiar enough to us in peace as to them in war, if 'danger' also may be given a wider meaning than that of battle. Illness, unemployment, loneliness, these are the things that make sacrifices of 'the poor condemned English', that make them 'pining and pale' [Chorus, IV, 22, 41]. It is among such a host of spectral images of mankind that the King moves, and the Chorus imagines him as their contrast and support: 'the royal captain of this ruined band' [Chorus, IV, 29]. It remains true, however, that the Chorus has to do this without having had, up to that point, much support from the play itself. Henry has been cheerful and efficient and warlike and friendly, but he has not suggested to us his capacity for being an almost supernatural 'little touch of Harry in the night' [Chorus, IV, 47]. The wider and the darker the night, the more that gleam shines. But why?

The cause follows. When the King appears he is speaking, more or less lightly, of the advantages which evil chances bring with them. It is not a particularly original remark, not a moment of 'great insight', and we need not perhaps suppose it is meant to be solemn or serious. It is in the next speech that the sudden difference between Henry and all the rest appears.

> 'Tis good for men to love their present pains
> Upon example; so the spirit is eas'd:
> And when the mind is quicken'd, out of doubt,
> The organs, though defunct and dead before,
> Break up their drowsy grave, and newly move
> With casted slough and fresh legerity.
>
> [IV. i. 18-23]

This is the centre of Henry's capacity. He 'loves' his present pains, and his spirit is therefore eased. He has rather more than accepted darkness, danger, defeat, and death, and loves them. It is this which gives him a new quickening of the mind, new motions of the organs; it destroys sloth and the drowsy grave of usual life. It is this love and the resulting legerity of spirit which enable him to be what the Chorus describe, and what the rest of the Act accentuates.

> Upon his royal face there is no note
> How dread an army hath enrounded him;
>
> [Chorus, IV, 35-6]

how can there be when he loves being enrounded?

> But freshly looks and overbears attaint
> With cheerful semblance and sweet majesty.
>
> [Chorus, IV, 39-40]

It is precisely a description of what he has done within himself. Therefore every wretch 'plucks comfort from his looks' [Chorus, IV, 42], receiving the 'largess universal' from his liberal eye—from the eased spirit, the quickened mind, the moving organs, which are the effect of his love for present pains.

Perhaps this also was something of the explanation of the dead Falstaff; perhaps Henry was more like his old acquaintance than he altogether knew. Only the word 'love' can hardly be used of Falstaff in any sense; it was by no accident or haste that Shakespeare could not show him in more 'love' than the odd possibility of lechery excites. He enjoyed his dilemmas in the sense that he enjoyed being equal to them, but Henry enjoys them because he is careless of them.

There is a distinction, and it lies in the fact that the King's spirit is 'honour' whereas Falstaff's is the rejection of 'honour'. It also lies in the fact that Falstaff does die when he cannot conquer 'the King's unkindness'. If ever Falstaff's spirit was drawn reeking up to heaven, he would only enter it on his own terms, but Henry will enter it on Heaven's terms. It is Falstaff's greatness that we are delighted to feel heaven give way to him; Henry's that we are eased by his giving way to heaven. But the artistic difference is that there is no more to be done in the method of Falstaff—he is complete and final. He can be continually varied and repeated, but he cannot be developed. Henry is complete, but not final. For he, in whose honour there is no self-contradiction, could love his pains simply because there was nothing else to do except run away, and that the same honour forbade. The genius of Shakespeare proceeded, however, immediately to imagine an honour in which self-contradiction did passionately exist; it emerged as Brutus, and was set in front of a power which was more 'monstrous' than that of the French army; he called that monstrosity Caesar, and made another play out of those other conditions, in which the crisis is a more deeply interior thing, and the heaven of honour begins itself to be at odds.

Henry then has made of his crisis an exaltation of his experience; he has become gay. This gaiety—a 'modest' gaiety, to take another adjective from the Chorus—lasts all through the Act. It lightens and saves the speech on ceremony; more especially, it illuminates the speech to Westmoreland. In view of the King's capacity the stress there may well be on the adjective rather than the substantive: 'We few, we *happy* few' [IV. iii. 60]. His rejection of all those who have no stomach for the fight, his offer of crowns for convoy, is part of the same delight: so far as possible he will have no one there who does not love to be there. He makes jokes at the expense of the old men's 'tall stories' of the battle, and at the French demand for ransom. We are clean away from the solemn hero-king, and therefore much more aware of the Harry of the Chorus, and of the thing he is—the 'touch of Harry in the night'. The very last line of that scene—'how thou pleasest, God, dispose the day' [IV. iii. 133]—is not a prayer of resignation but a cry of complete carelessness. What does it matter what *happens*?

It is a legerity of spirit, the last legerity before the tragedies. Hamlet was to have a touch of it, but there is little else, in the greater figures, until, as from beyond a much greater distance, it is renewed by a phrase Kent uses of the Fool in *Lear*. Who, says a Gentleman on the moor, is with the King?

> None but the Fool, who labours to outjest
> His heart-struck injuries.
>
> [*King Lear*, III. i. 16-17]

Henry's injuries are not heart-struck; he is no tragic figure. But he deserves more greatly than has perhaps always been allowed. The muse, *entertaining conjecture* of a new and dreadful world, conjectured also a touch in the night, the thawing of fear, a royal captain of a ruined band, and conjectured the nature of the power of love and consequent lightness that thrills through the already poring dusk. (pp. 180-88)

> *Charles Williams, "'Henry V,'" in* Shakespeare Criticism, 1919-1935, *edited by Anne Bradby Ridler, 1936. Reprint by Oxford University Press, London, 1963, pp. 180-88.*

## MARK VAN DOREN (essay date 1939)

[*Van Doren was a Pulitzer prize-winning poet, critic, American educator, editor, and novelist. In the introduction to his Shake-speare (1939), he states that he "ignored the biography of Shakespeare, the history and character of his time, the conventions of his theater, the works of his contemporaries" to concentrate on the interest of the plays and their relevance to the modern reader or spectator. Arguing that Shakespeare's interest and imagination were only minimally engaged by the subject matter of* Henry V, *Van Doren offers in the following excerpt one of the twentieth century's most acerbic—and most frequently cited—appraisals of the play. He maintains that although the poetry of the Chorus is "always very fine," the substance of those verses should have been dramatized rather than narrated; he also charges that throughout the play the language is frequently strained and inflated. Van Doren further dispraises the king as "a hearty undergraduate with enormous initials on his chest" and contends that he is a simplistic figure who lacks vision and understanding. Finally, the critic briefly discusses comic elements in* Henry V, *judging that Bardolph's parody of the king's speech before the walls of Harfleur is unnecessary, for "Henry has already parodied himself," and contending that one of Fluellen's functions is to help deflate the theme of war.*]

"Henry IV" . . . both was and is a successful play; it answers the questions it raises, it satisfies every instinct of the spectator, it is remembered as fabulously rich and at the same time simply ordered. "Henry V" is no such play. It has its splendors and its secondary attractions, but the forces in it are not unified. The reason probably is that for Shakespeare they had ceased to be genuine forces. He marshals for his task a host of substitute powers, but the effect is often hollow. The style strains itself to bursting, the hero is stretched until he struts on tiptoe and is still strutting at the last insignificant exit, and war is emptied of its tragic content. The form of the historical drama had been the tragic form; its dress is borrowed here, but only borrowed. The heroic idea splinters into a thousand starry fragments, fine as fragments but lighted from no single source.

Everywhere efforts are made to be striking, and they succeed. But the success is local. "Henry V" does not succeed as a whole because its author lacks adequate dramatic matter; or because, veering so suddenly away from tragedy, he is unable to free himself from the accidents of its form; or because, with "Julius Caesar" and "Hamlet" on his horizon, he finds himself less interested than before in heroes who are men of action and yet is not at the moment provided with a dramatic language for saying so. Whatever the cause, we discover that we are being entertained from the top of his mind. There is much there to glitter and please us, but what pleases us has less body than what once did so and soon will do so with still greater abundance again.

The prologues are the first sign of Shakespeare's imperfect dramatic faith. Their verse is wonderful but it has to be, for it is doing the work which the play ought to be doing, it is a substitute for scene and action. "O for a Muse of fire" [Prologue, 1], the poet's apology begins. The prologues are everywhere apologetic; they are saying that no stage, this one or any other, is big enough or wealthy enough to present the "huge and proper life" [Chorus, V, 5] of Henry's wars; this cockpit cannot hold the vasty fields of France, there will be no veritable horses in any scene, the ship-boys on the masts and the campfires at Agincourt will simply have to be imagined. Which it is the business of the play to make them be, as Shakespeare has known and will know again. The author of "Romeo and Juliet" had not been sorry because his stage was a piece of London rather than the whole of Verona, and the storm in "King Lear" will begin without benefit of description. The description here is always very fine, as for example at the opening of the fourth act:

> Now entertain conjecture of a time
> When creeping murmur and the poring dark
> Fills the wide vessel of the universe.
> From camp to camp through the foul womb of night
> The hum of either army stilly sounds,
> That the fix'd sentinels almost receive
> The secret whispers of each other's watch;
> Fire answers fire, and through their paly flames
> Each battle sees the other's umber'd face;
> Steed threatens steed, in high and boastful neighs
> Piercing the night's dull ear; and from the tents
> The armourers, accomplishing the knights,
> With busy hammers closing rivets up,
> Give dreadful note of preparation.
>
> [Chorus, IV, 1-14]

But it is still description, and it is being asked to do what description can never do—turn spectacle into plot, tableau into tragedy.

The second sign of genius at loose ends is a radical and indeed an astounding inflation in the style. Passages of boasting and exhortation are in place, but even the best of them, whether from the French or from the English side, have a forced, shrill, windy sound, as if their author were pumping his muse for dear life in the hope that mere speed and plangency might take the place of matter. For a few lines like

> Familiar in his mouth as household words
>
> [IV. iii. 52]

> The singing masons building roofs of gold
>
> [I. ii. 198]

> I see you stand like greyhounds in the slips,
> Straining upon the start
>
> [III. i. 31-2]

there are hundreds like

> The native mightiness and fate of him
>
> [II. iv. 64]

> With ample and brim fullness of his force
>
> [I. ii. 150]

> That caves and womby vaultages of France
> Shall chide your trespass and return your mock.
>
> [II. iv. 124-25]

Mightiness and fate, ample and brim, caves and vaultages, trespass and mock—such couplings attest the poet's desperation, the rhetorician's extremity. They spring up everywhere, like birds from undergrowth: sweet and honey'd, open haunts and popularity, thrive and ripen, crown and seat, right and title, right and conscience, kings and monarchs, means and might, aim and butt, large and ample, taken and impounded, frank and uncurbed, success and conquest, desert and merit, weight and worthiness, duty and zeal, savage and inhuman, botch and bungle, garnish'd and deck'd, assembled and collected, sinister and awkward, culled and choice-drawn, o'erhang and jutty, waste and desolation, cool and temperate, flexure and low bending, signal and ostent, vainness and self-glorious pride. Shakespeare has perpetrated them before, as when in "Henry VI" he coupled ominous and fearful, trouble and disturb, substance and authority, and absurd and reasonless. But never has he perpetrated them with such thoughtless

frequency. Nor has he at this point developed the compound epithet into that interesting mannerism—the only mannerism he ever submitted to—which is to be so noticeable in his next half-dozen plays, including "Hamlet." The device he is to use will involve more than the pairing of adjectives or nouns; one part of speech will assume the duties of another, and a certain very sudden concentration of meaning will result. There is, to be sure, one approximation to the device in "Henry V"—"the quick forge and working-house of thought" [Chorus, V, 23]. But our attention is nowhere else held and filled by such lines as these in "Hamlet" ...:

> Unto the voice and yielding of that body
>
> [I. iii. 23]

> And in the morn and liquid dew of youth
>
> [I. iii. 41]

> The slings and arrows of outrageous fortune
>
> [III. i. 57]

> Which is not tomb enough and continent; . . .
>
> [IV. iv. 63]

In such lines there is not merely the freshness and the emphasis which an expert distortion of conventional meanings can give; there is a muscled cadence, an abrupt forward stride or plunge of sound. All this is lacking for the most part in the style of "Henry V," which is fatty rather than full, relaxed instead of restrung.

The third sign is a direct and puerile appeal to the patriotism of the audience, a dependence upon sentiments outside the play that can be counted on, once they are tapped, to pour in and repair the deficiencies of the action. Unable to achieve a dramatic unity out of the materials before him, Shakespeare must grow lyrical about the unity of England; politics must substitute for poetry. He cannot take England for granted as the scene of conflicts whose greatness will imply its greatness. It must be great itself, and the play says so—unconvincingly. There are no conflicts. The traitors Scroop, Cambridge, and Grey are happy to lose their heads for England (II, ii), and the battles in France, even though the enemy's host is huge and starvation takes its toll, are bound to be won by such fine English fellows as we have here. If the French have boasted beforehand, the irony of their doing so was obvious from the start. But it was patriotism, shared as a secret between the author and his audience, that made it obvious. It was not drama.

And a fourth sign is the note of gaiety that takes the place here of high passion. The treasure sent to Henry by the Dauphin is discovered at the end of the first act to be tennis-balls: an insult which the young king returns in a speech about matching rackets and playing sets—his idiom for bloody war. When the treachery of Scroop, Cambridge, and Grey is detected on the eve of his departure for France he stages their discomfiture somewhat as games are undertaken, and with a certain sporting relish watches their faces as they read their dooms. The conversation of the French leaders as they wait for the sun to rise on Agincourt is nervous as thoroughbreds are nervous, or champion athletes impatient for a tournament to commence; their camp is a locker room, littered with attitudes no less than uniforms (III, vii). The deaths of York and Suffolk the next day are images of how young knights should die. They kiss each other's gashes, wearing their red blood like roses in the field, and spending their last breath in terms so fine that Exeter, reporting to the King, is overcome by "the pretty and sweet manner of it" [IV. vi. 28]. And of course there are the scenes where Katharine makes fritters of English, waiting to be wooed (III, iv) and wooed at last (V, ii) by Henry Plantagenet, "king of good fellows" [V. ii. 242-43]. "The truth is," said Dr. Johnson, "that the poet's matter failed him in the fifth act, and he was glad to fill it up with whatever he could get; and not even Shakespeare can write well without a proper subject. It is a vain endeavour for the most skilful hand to cultivate barrenness, or to paint upon vacuity" [see excerpt above, 1765]. That is harsh, but its essence cannot be ignored. The high spirits in which the scenes are written have their attraction, but they are no substitute for intensity.

Nor do they give us the king we thought we had. "I speak to thee plain soldier" [V. ii. 149], boasts Henry in homespun vein. "I am glad thou canst speak no better English; for, if thou couldst, thou wouldst find me such a plain king that thou wouldst think I had sold my farm to buy my crown. I know no ways to mince it in love, but directly to say, 'I love you.' . . . These fellows of infinite tongue, that can rhyme themselves into ladies' favours, they do always reason themselves out again. . . . By mine honour, in true English, I love thee, Kate" [V. ii. 123-27, 155-58, 220-21]. "I know not," breaks in Dr. Johnson's voice once more, "why Shakespeare now gives the king nearly such a character as he made him formerly ridicule in Percy. This military grossness and unskillfulness in all the softer arts does not suit very well with the gaieties of his youth, with the general knowledge ascribed to him at his accession, or with the contemptuous message sent him by the Dauphin, who represents him as fitter for the ball room than the field, and tells him that he is not 'to revel into dutchies,' or win provinces 'with a nimble galliard'" [I. ii. 253, 252]. Shakespeare has forgotten the glittering young god whom Vernon described in "Henry IV"—plumed like an estridge or like an eagle lately bathed, shining like an image in his golden coat, as full of spirit as the month of May, wanton as a youthful goat, a feathered Mercury, an angel dropped down from the clouds. The figure whom he has groomed to be the ideal English king, all plumes and smiles and decorated courage, collapses here into a mere good fellow, a hearty undergraduate with enormous initials on his chest. The reason must be that Shakespeare has little interest in the ideal English king. He has done what rhetoric could do to give us a young heart whole in honor, but his imagination has already sped forward to Brutus and Hamlet: to a kind of hero who is no less honorable than Henry but who will tread on thorns as he takes the path of duty—itself unclear, and crossed by other paths of no man's making. Henry is Shakespeare's last attempt at the great man who is also simple. Henceforth he will show greatness as either perplexing or perplexed; and Hamlet will be both.

Meanwhile his imagination undermines the very eminence on which Henry struts. For the King and his nobles the war may be a handsome game, but an undercurrent of realism reminds us of the "poor souls" for whom it is no such thing. We hear of widows' tears and orphans' cries, of dead men's blood and pining maidens' groans [II. iv. 106-09]. Such horrors had been touched on in earlier Histories; now they are given a scene to themselves (IV, i). While the French leaders chaff one another through the night before Agincourt the English common soldiers have their hour. Men with names as plain as John Bates and Michael Williams walk up and down the dark field thinking of legs and arms and heads chopped off in battle, of faint cries for surgeons, of men in misery because of their children who will be rawly left. Henry, moving among them in the disguise of clothes like theirs, asks them to remember that the King's cause is just and his quarrel honorable. "That's more than we

know," comes back the disturbing cool voice of Michael Williams [IV. i. 129]. Henry answers with much fair prose, and the episode ends with a wager—sportsmanship again—which in turn leads to an amusing recognition scene (IV, viii). But the honest voice of Williams still has the edge on Henry's patronizing tone:

> Williams.    Your Majesty came not like yourself. You appear'd to me but as a common man; witness the night, your garments, your lowliness; and what your Highness suffer'd under that shape, I beseech you take it for your own fault and not mine. . . .
> King Henry.    Here, uncle Exeter, fill this glove with crowns,
> And give it to this fellow. Keep it, fellow;
> And wear it for an honour in thy cap
> Till I do challenge it.
>
> [IV. viii. 50-4, 57-60]

Henry has not learned that Williams knows. He is still the plumed king, prancing on oratory and waving wagers as he goes. That he finally has no place to go is the result of Shakespeare's failure to establish any relation between a hero and his experience. Henry has not absorbed the vision either of Williams or of Shakespeare. This shrinks him in his armor, and it leaves the vision hanging.

The humor of the play, rich as it sometimes is, suffers likewise from a lack of vital function. The celebrated scene (II, iii) in which the Hostess describes Falstaff's death shuts the door forever on "Henry IV" and its gigantic comedy. Pistol and Bardolph continue in their respective styles, and continue cleverly; the first scene of the second act, which finds them still in London, may be indeed the best one ever written for them—and for Nym in his pompous brevity.

> I cannot tell. Things must be as they may. Men may sleep, and they may have their throats about them at that time; and some say knives have edges. It must be as it may.
>
> [II. i. 20-3]

Pistol was never excited to funnier effect.

> O hound of Crete, think'st thou my spouse to get?
> No! to the spital go,
> And from the powdering-tub of infamy
> Fetch forth the lazar kite of Cressid's kind,
> Doll Tearsheet she by name, and her espouse.
> I have, and I will hold, the quondam Quickly
> For the only she; and—*pauca,* there's enough.
> Go to.
>
> [II. i. 73-80]

Yet this leads on to little in France beyond a series of rather mechanically arranged encounters in which the high talk of heroes is echoed by the rough cries of rascals. "To the breach, to the breach!" [III. ii. 1-2] yells Bardolph after Henry, and that is parody. But Henry has already parodied himself; the device is not needed, any more than the rascals are. Shakespeare seems to admit as much when he permits lectures to be delivered against their moral characters, first by the boy who serves them [III. ii. 28-53] and next by the sober Gower [III. vi. 67-81], and when he arranges bad ends for them as thieves, cutpurses, and bawds.

There is a clearer function for Fluellen, the fussy Welsh pedant who is for fighting wars out of books. Always fretting and out of breath, he mourns ''the disciplines of the wars'' [III. ii. 59], the pristine wars of the Romans, now in these latter days lost with all other learning. There was not this tiddle taddle and pibble pabble in Pompey's camp. The law of arms was once well known, and men—strong, silent men such as he fancies himself to be—observed it without prawls and prabbles. He has no shrewdness; he mistakes Pistol for a brave man because he talks bravely, and there is his classic comparison of Henry with Alexander because one lived in Monmouth and the other in Macedon and each city had a river and there were salmons in both. He has only his schoolmaster's eloquence; it breaks out on him like a rash, and is the one style here that surpasses the King's in fullness.

> *Fluellen*. It is not well done, mark you now,
> to take the tales out of my mouth, ere it is made
> and finished. I speak but in the figures and
> comparisons of it. As Alexander kill'd his friend
> Cleitus, being in his ales and his cups; so also
> Harry Monmouth, being in his right wits and
> his good judgements, turn'd away the fat knight
> with the great belly doublet. He was full of
> jests, and gipes, and knaveries, and mocks; I
> have forgot his name.
> *Gower*. Sir John Falstaff.
> *Fluellen*. That is he.
>
> [IV. vii. 42-52]

Fluellen reminds us of Falstaff. That is a function, but he has another. It is to let the war theme finally down. Agincourt is won not only by a tennis-player but by a school-teacher. Saint Crispin's day is to be remembered as much in the pibble pabble of a pedant as in the golden throatings of a hollow god. Fluellen is one of Shakespeare's most humorous men, and one of his best used. (pp. 170-79)

> *Mark Van Doren, '' 'Henry V','' in his* Shakespeare, *Henry Holt and Company, 1939, pp. 170-79.*

## D. A. TRAVERSI  (essay date 1941)

[*Traversi, a British scholar, has written a number of books on Shakespeare's plays, including* An Approach to Shakespeare *(1938),* Shakespeare: The Last Phase *(1954),* Shakespeare: From ''Richard II'' to ''Henry V'' *(1957), and* Shakespeare: The Roman Plays *(1963). In the introduction to the first of these studies, Traversi proposes to focus his interpretation of the plays on ''the word,'' stating that the experience which forms the impetus to each of Shakespeare's dramas ''will find its most immediate expression in the language and verse.'' In his analysis of* Henry V *excerpted below, he asserts that Shakespeare was predominantly interested in dramatizing ''the conditions of kingship'' and ''the sacrifice of common humanity'' that a ruler must make if he is to succeed. Traversi regards the struggle between a monarch's natural passions and his ''controlling reason'' as the central thematic issue in the play, declaring that* Henry V's *cold ''indifference to humanity'' is necessary to a successful ruler, even though this condition carries with it the possibility of tragedy. Although the critic views Henry as calculating and ruthless, motivated principally by expediency, and prone to shirk or pass off onto others responsibility for his conduct, he insists that the king is not portrayed as a hypocrite, for he is acting in accord with the precepts of effective leadership. Traversi also discusses the comic elements in the play, remarking on the juxtaposition of scenes which feature Henry's ''rhetorical incitations to patriotic feeling'' and those which realistically demonstrate the darker, tragic effects of war on such participants as Bardolph, Nym, and Pistol; in the critic's*

*opinion, the result is a somber and even pessimistic depiction of human nature.*]

*Henry V* does not stand alone. Shakespeare's interest in political conduct and its human implications was, at this period, intense and continuous. The general theme of *Henry V*, already approached in *Richard II* and developed in the two parts of *Henry IV*, is the establishment in England of an order based on consecrated authority and crowned successfully by action against France. The conditions of this order, which is triumphantly achieved by the new King, are moral as well as political. The crime of regicide which, by breeding internal scruples and nourishing external revolt, had stood between Bolingbroke and the attainment of peace, no longer hangs— unless as a disturbing memory—over Henry V, and the crusading purpose which had run as an unfulfilled nostalgia through the father's life is replaced by the reality, at once brilliant and ruthless, of the son's victorious campaign.

This, as critics have not always realized, is less a conclusion than a point of departure for the understanding of *Henry V*. It was the conditions of kingship, rather than its results, that really interested Shakespeare, whose emphasis falls, not upon the king's success, but upon the sacrifice of common humanity which it involves. It is significant that he takes up almost immediately the theme of Henry's 'miraculous' transformation

*Act IV. Scene iv. Pistol, French Soldier, and Boy. Frontispiece to the Bell edition (1773).*

from dissolute prince to accomplished monarch and gives it a setting of political intrigue which barely conceals the underlying irony. The opening scene is, in this respect, full of meaning. A bill is to be passed, as prelude to the new reign, which will deprive the Church of 'the better half' of her temporal possessions [I. i. 8]; and the bishops of Canterbury and Ely, with pondered diplomatic cunning, are debating the possibility of evading a measure which would 'drink deep,' which would, indeed, 'drink the cup and all' [I. i. 20]. The remedy lies, to Canterbury's mind, in the virtues of the King, who is 'full of grace and fair regard,' and moreover, most conveniently, 'a true lover of the holy church' [I. i. 22-3]. In words which deliberately underline the incredible, the unmotivated nature of the change so suddenly wrought in Henry, Canterbury proceeds to describe these virtues:

> Never was such a sudden scholar made;
> Never came reformation in a flood
> With such a heady currance, scouring faults;
> Nor never Hydra-headed wilfulness
> So soon did lose his seat, and all at once,
> As in this king.
>
> [I. i. 32-7]

Never, indeed; and there is something unreal, more than a hint of deliberate exaggeration in the studied artificial phrases with which the Archbishop proceeds to particularize the royal gifts:

> Turn him to any course of policy,
> The Gordian knot of it he will unloose,
> Familiar as his garter; that, when he speaks,
> The air, a chartered libertine, is still,
> And the mute wonder lurketh in men's ears,
> To steal his sweet and honey'd sentences.
>
> [I. i. 45-50]

The apparent servility of the prelate ends by casting an indefinable doubt upon the very reformation he is describing. That Henry should be able so suddenly to undo 'the Gordian knot' of policy may pass, but that he should do it negligently, 'familiar as his garter,' passes belief: and the suggestion of cloying persuasiveness behind the reference to 'his sweet and honey'd sentences' makes us question, not only the sincerity of the speaker, but that of Henry himself. The thing, to be true, must be a miracle; and 'miracles,' as Canterbury himself points out in a most damaging conclusion, 'are ceased.'

Shakespeare's treatment of Henry's transformation needs to be considered in the light thrown upon it by the preceding plays. Finding it, of course, in his sources, he seems to have fastened upon it from the first as peculiarly relevant to his purpose. Prince Hal's first soliloquy at once foreshadows it and explains its animating spirit:

> So, when this loose behaviour I throw off
> And pay the debt I never promised,
> By how much better than my word I am,
> By so much shall I falsify men's hopes;
> And like bright metal on a sullen ground,
> My reformation, glittering o'er my fault,
> Shall show more goodly and attract more eyes
> Than that which hath no foil to set it off.
> I'll so offend, to make offence a skill,
> Redeeming time when men least think I will.
>
> [1 Henry IV, I. ii. 208-17]

The note of calculation, therefore, is present from the first, and as the Prince's character develops through the two plays

dealing with his father's reign, it is most noticeably deepened and intensified by contrast with Falstaff. Shakespeare not only accepted the artistic difficulty involved in the Prince's rejection of his former friend, he wove it into the structure of his play. The cleavage between the two men is only a projection of one, fundamental to his purpose, between unbridled impulse, which degenerates into swollen disease, and the cold spirit of successful self-control, which inevitably becomes inhuman. . . . Prince Hal in Henry IV—Part II strikes a note of calculating vulgarity, which he regards as a necessary condition of his success. His remark to Poins—'My appetite was not princely got' [2 Henry IV, II. ii. 9-10]—is highly typical. It implies a contrast between the natural sensual processes ('appetite,' of course, in connection with the consuming desires of the 'blood,' is a word which constantly interested Shakespeare) and the indifference to humanity which is required of the princely state. This contrast, as it affects the mature King, is the theme of Henry V.

It is a theme . . . closely related to Shakespeare's maturing interests and destined to unfold itself progressively in his great series of tragedies. The problem of political unity, or 'degree,' and that of personal order are brought in the course of these historical plays into the closest relationship. Just as the state, already in Henry IV—Part II, is regarded in its divisions as a diseased body ravaged by a consuming fever of its various members, so is the individual torn between the violence of his passions and the direction of reason; and just as the political remedy lies in unquestioned allegiance to an authority divinely constituted, so does personal coherence depend upon the submission to reason of our uncontrolled desires. The link between the two states, political and personal, is provided in these plays by concentration upon the figure of the King. The problem of the state becomes, in a very real sense, that of the individual at its head. The King, who rightly demands unquestioning allegiance from his subjects, is first called upon to show, through the perfection of his self-control, a complete and selfless devotion to his office. The personal implications of that devotion are considered in Henry V.

It demands, in the first place, an absolute measure of self-domination. Called upon to exercise justice and shape policies for the common good, the King can allow no trace of selfishness or frailty to affect his decisions. He must continually examine his motives, subdue them in the light of reason; and this means that he is engaged in a continual struggle against his share of human weakness. This struggle, as I have already suggested, is presented in terms of one between passion and the controlling reason. The mastery of passion and its relation to action are themes which Henry V shares with most of the plays written by Shakespeare at this time. Such control, admittedly essential in a king, is infinitely dangerous in its possible consequences. . . . The virtuous man is he who, without exercising it, has 'power to hurt' [Sonnet 94], the man who is cold, slow, impassive as stone before the claims of his own humanity. He seems, indeed, in full possession of his impulses, but his control is only separated by a continual and conscious effort from cruelty and the satisfaction of desires which long denial has set increasingly on edge. The similarity of the King's position is obvious. He too has power to hurt and may easily abuse it: he too, whilst moving others, must keep the firmest check upon his impulses and watch sleeplessly over his judgment. And he too—we might add—may easily fall from his position of vigilance into an unrestrained and savage indulgence. If this is the just man, in short, Henry V is fairly representative of him.

The circumstances of Henry's first appearance before his court make this clear. The subject under discussion is the action shortly to be taken by the freshly united kingdom against the realm of France. The idea of war has obviously been already accepted. Henry does not, in reality, look for disinterested advice. He prompts the subservient Archbishop, at each step, not without a touch of irony, to the expected answer:

> My learned lord, we pray you to proceed
> And justly and religiously unfold
> Why the law Salique that they have in France
> Or should or should not bar us in our claim. . . .
>
> [I. ii. 9-12]

And then, when the matter has been expounded to his satisfaction:

> May I with right and conscience make this claim?
>
> [I. ii. 96]

The King's mind, in short, is already made up, and his decision only awaits public confirmation. The perfunctory flatness of Canterbury's exposition, which no one could possibly hear without indifference, contrasts most forcibly with the rhetoric with which he and his fellow-courtiers underline what is obviously a foregone conclusion:

> Gracious lord,
> Stand for your own; unwind your bloody flag;
> Look back into your mighty ancestors.
>
> [I. ii. 100-02]

Already, however, another theme of deeper significance has made itself felt in Henry's utterances: the theme of the horrors of war and, by implication, of the responsibility which weighs upon the king who would embark upon it:

> Therefore take heed how you impawn our person,
> How you awake our sleeping sword of war:
> We charge you, in the name of God, take heed;
> For never two such kingdoms did contend
> Without much fall of blood; whose guiltless drops
> Are everyone a woe, a sore complaint
> 'Gainst him whose wrongs give edge unto the swords
> That make such waste in brief mortality.
>
> [I. ii. 21-8]

Most of Shakespeare's conception of the King is already implicit in this speech. Throughout the play, Henry is not deaf to the voice of conscience. It pursues him, in fact, with almost superstitious insistence to the very eve of Agincourt, when the memory of his father's crime aginst his sovereign is still present in his mind:

> Not to-day, O Lord,
> O, not to-day, think not upon the fault
> My father made in compassing the crown.
>
> [IV. i. 292-94]

Bolingbroke's misdeed is by now only a memory, but here, at the outset of Henry's proposed enterprise in France, the same kind of misgiving is already present. The awareness that his victories must be bought at a terrible price in bloodshed and human suffering remains with him throughout the play; but— and here is the flaw essential to the character—so does his readiness to shift the responsibility upon others, to use their complacence to obtain the justification he continually, insistently requires. Take heed, he warns the prelate, 'how *you*

impawn our person,' 'how *you* awake the sleeping sword of war'; for

> we will hear, note, and believe in heart
> That what you speak is in *your* conscience wash'd
> As pure as sin in baptism.
>
> [I. ii. 30-2]

Henry's political success is definitely associated, in the mind of Shakespeare, with this ability to override his conscience. Once Canterbury has spoken, once the dutiful moral echo has been duly obtained, the very ruthlessness which seems to have disturbed him at the opening of the scene enters into his own rhetorical utterance:

> Now we are well resolved; and, by God's help,
> And yours, the noble sinews of our power,
> France being ours, we'll bend it to our awe,
> Or break it all to pieces.
>
> [I. ii. 222-25]

The reference to conscience, the inevitable preface to each of Henry's utterances, remains in the propitiatory aside 'by God's help'; but, once it has been uttered, the sense of power implied in the cumulative force of 'sinews' joined to the verbs 'bend' and 'break,' takes possession of the speech. This overriding— for in the last analysis it is nothing else—of conscience by the will to power is a process which constantly repeats itself in Henry's utterances.

But there is, in Shakespeare's interpretation of the character, a further subtlety of analysis. As the play proceeds, we become increasingly aware that there is in Henry an uneasy balance . . . between unbridled passion and cold self-control. The latter element, exercised even to the exclusion of normal human feeling, has been present in him from the first. Prince Hal shows it, as we have already noted, in his first soliloquy when he announces his utilitarian attitude to the company he is keeping, and it is strongly felt, of course, in the rejection of Falstaff. Such control is, indeed, an essential part of his political capacity; but it has behind it, in addition to the strain of inhumanity, an unmistakable sense of constraint which makes itself felt in his greeting to the French ambassador:

> We are no tyrant, but a Christian king;
> Unto whose grace our passion is as subject
> As are our wretches fettered in our prisons.
>
> [I. ii. 241-43]

The harshness of the comparison is, to say the least of it, remarkable. Such self-control is necessarily precarious; the passions, held in subjection, 'fettered,' treated with a disdain similar to that which, as Prince Hal, he has already displayed to normal human feelings when his success as monarch depended upon the renunciation of his past, may be expected to break out in forms not altogether creditable. Almost at once, in fact, they do so. The French ambassadors, in fulfilling their mission by presenting him with the Dauphin's tennis-balls, touch upon Henry's most noticeable weakness: they expose him to ridicule and, worst of all, they refer—by the observation that 'You cannot revel into dukedoms here' [I. ii. 253]—to the abjured, but not forgotten past. Henry's reaction, in spite of the opening affirmation of his self-control, takes the form of one of those outbursts which are habitual with him whenever his will is crossed. As when France was to be 'bent' or 'broken,' his rhetoric, measured and even cold on the surface, is full of accumulated, irrepressible passion:

> When we have match'd our rackets to these balls,
> We will in France, by God's grace, play a set
> Shall strike his father's crown into the hazard.
>
> [I. ii. 261-63]

The reference to 'God's grace,' rarely omitted from Henry's utterances, clearly befits a 'Christian king'; but the note of resentment which rises through the speech and finally takes complete control of it, is undeniably personal. It rankles in the utterance until the real motive, scarcely concealed from the first, becomes at last explicit:

> we understand him well,
> How he comes o'er us with our wilder days
> Not measuring what use we made of them.
>
> [I. ii. 266-68]

The personal offence, once mentioned, banishes every consideration of conscience. The horrors of war, the slaughter and misery attendant upon it, are mentioned once again, but only—as so often in Henry—that he may disclaim responsibility for them. The tone of the utterance rises to one of ruthless and triumphant egoism:

> But *I* will rise there with so full a glory
> That *I* will dazzle all the eyes of France,
> Yea, strike the Dauphin blind to look on us.
> And tell the pleasant prince this mock of his
> Hath turned his balls to gun-stones; and his soul
> Shall stand sore charged for the wasteful vengeance
> That shall fly with them: for many a thousand widows
> Shall this his mock mock out of their dear husbands;
> Mock mothers from their sons, mock castles down;
> And some are yet ungotten and unborn
> That shall have cause to curse the Dauphin's scorn.
>
> [I. ii. 278-88]

'*I* will rise there': '*I* will dazzle all the eyes of France.' The Dauphin's gibe has set free Henry's fettered passions and they express themselves frankly in a cumulative vision of destruction. . . . The responsibility for coming events, already assumed by the Archbishop, has now been further fastened upon the Dauphin, and Henry is in a position to wind up the picture of his coming descent upon France with a phrase that incorporates into his new vehemence the convenient certainty of righteousness—

> But all this lies within the will of God,
> To whom I do appeal.
>
> [I. ii. 289-90]

No doubt the conviction is, as far as it goes, sincere; for the will of God and the will of Henry, now fused in the egoistic passion released by the Dauphin's jest, have become identical.

It is not until the opening of the third Act that the characteristic qualities of Henry's utterances and preparations are openly translated into action. The poetry of war in this play deserves careful attention, for much of it is unmistakably associated with the element of constraint already noted in Henry himself. The rhetoric with which the King incites his men to battle before the walls of Harfleur has about it a strong flavour of artificiality and strain. There is about his picture of the warrior something grotesque and exaggerated, which almost suggests the caricature of a man:

> imitate the action of the tiger;
> Stiffen the sinews, summon up the blood,
> Disguise fair nature with hard-favour'd rage;
> Then lend the eye a terrible aspect;
> Let it pry through the portage of the head
> Like the brass cannon; let the brow o'erwhelm it

> As fearfully as doth a galled rock
> O'erhang and jutty his confounded base,
> Swill'd with the wild and wasteful ocean.
> Now set the teeth and stretch the nostril wide,
> Hold hard the breath and bend up every spirit
> To his full height.
>
> [III. i. 6-17]

There is about this incitation something forced, incongruous, even slightly absurd. The action of the warrior is an imitation, and an imitation of a wild beast at that, carried out by a deliberate exclusion of 'fair nature.' The blood is to be 'summoned up,' the sinews 'stiffened' to the necessary degree of artificial bestiality, whilst the involved rhetorical comparisons which follow the references to the 'brass cannon' and the 'galled rock' strengthen the impression of unreality. In stressing the note of inhumanity, Shakespeare does not deny the poetry of war which he expresses most fully in certain passages from the various prologues of this play; but . . . he balances the conception of the warrior in his triumphant activity as 'a greyhound straining at the leash' against that, not less forcible, of a ruthless and inhuman engine of destruction. (pp. 352-61)

Henry's treatment of the governor and citizens of Harfleur, immediately after this apostrophe, relates this conception of the warrior more clearly to strains already apparent in the King's own character. Shakespeare, not for the first time, places the two scenes together to enforce a contrast. The words in which Henry presents his ultimatum are full of that sense of conflict between control and passion which is so prominent in his first utterances. The grotesque inhumanity of his words is balanced, however, by a suggestion of tragic destiny. Beneath his callousness is a sense that the horrors of war, once unloosed, once freed from the sternest self-control, are irresistible. . . . In his catalogue of the horrors of unbridled war stress is laid continually upon rape and the crimes of 'blood.' The 'fresh-fair virgins' [III. iii. 14] of Harfleur will become the victims of the soldiery, whose destructive atrocities are significantly referred to in terms of 'liberty'—

> What rein can hold licentuous wickedness
> When down the hill he holds his fierce career?
>
> [III. iii. 22-3]

The process of evil, once unleashed, proceeds along courses fatally determined; but Henry, as usual, having described them in words which lay every emphasis upon their horror, disclaims all responsibility for them, just as he had once disclaimed all responsibility for the outbreak of the war. The whole matter, thus taken out of his hands, becomes indifferent to him:

> What is't to me, *when you yourselves are cause*,
> If your pure maidens fall into the hand
> Of hot and forcing violation?
>
> [III. iii. 19-21]

Yet this very assertion of indifference implies, at bottom, a sense of the tragedy of the royal position. Only this denial of responsibility, Shakespeare would seem to say, only the exclusion of humanity and the acceptance of a complete dualism between controlling 'grace' and the promptings of irresponsible passion, make possible that success in war which is, for the purposes of this play, the crown of kingship.

For it would be wrong to suppose that Shakespeare, in portraying Henry, intends to stress the note of hypocrisy. His purpose is rather to bring out certain contradictions, human and moral, which seem to be inherent in the notion of a successful king. As the play proceeds, Henry seems to be increasingly, at least in the moral sense, the victim of his position. The cunning calculations of the Archbishop, with which the play opens, have already given us a hint of the world in which he moves and which he has, as King, to mould to his own purposes; and the treasonable activities of Cambridge, Grey, and Scroop are further indications of the duplicity with which monarchs are fated by their position to deal. . . . Somewhere at the heart of this court . . . there is a fundamental fault which must constantly be allowed for by a successful king. It appears to Henry, in his dealings with the conspirators, as something deep-rooted enough to be associated with the original Fall of man:

> Seem they religious?
> Why, so did'st thou: or are they spare in diet,
> Free from gross passion or of mirth or anger,
> Constant in spirit, not swerving with the blood,
> Garnish'd and decked in modest complement,
> Not working with the eye without the ear,
> And put in purged judgment trusting neither?
> Such and so finely bolted didst thou seem:
> And thus thy fall hath left a kind of blot,
> To mark the full-fraught man and best indued
> With some suspicion. I will weep for thee;
> For this revolt of thine, methinks, is like
> Another fall of man.
>
> [II. ii. 130-42]

It is remarkable that Henry, in meditating upon this betrayal, should return once more to that theme of control, of freedom from passion, which is so prominent in his own nature. Much in the expression—notably the references to 'diet' and purging and the presence of adjectives like 'garnish'd' and 'bolted' drawn from material processes to express a moral content—recalls the problem plays. There is the same tendency to labour in the versification and the same struggle to convey by a difficult concentration of imagery a spiritual condition that obstinately refuses to clarify itself in the expression. By concentrating on the functioning of the body, and on the sense of mutual divergence between eye, ear, and judgment in the infinitely difficult balance of the personality, Shakespeare sets spiritual control in contrast with a sense of anarchy which proceeds, most typically, from his contemplation of physical processes. 'Gross passion'—the adjective is significant—is associated with the irrational 'swerving of the blood,' and the judgment which controls it needs to be 'purged' by fasting ('spare in diet') before it can attain a scarcely human freedom from 'mirth or anger.' By emphasizing the difficult and even unnatural nature of such control, Shakespeare casts doubt, at least by implication, upon that of Henry himself; but it is also seen to be necessary, inseparable from his office. The administration of justice, upon which depends order within the kingdom and success in its foreign wars, demands in the monarch an impersonality which is almost tragic and borders on the inhuman. The state must be purged of 'treason lurking in its way' before it can be led, with [a] single-mindedness of purpose which . . . [involves] in Henry a definite sacrifice of common humanity, to the victorious enterprise in France.

It will be clear by now that *Henry V* represents, however tentatively, a step in the realization of themes only fully developed in the tragedies. Inheriting from his material a conception of Henry as the victorious king, perfectly aware of his responsibilities and religiously devoted to the idea of duty, Shakespeare seems to emphasize the difficulties of the conception, the obstacles, both personal and political, which lie between it and fulfilment. These difficulties, however, never amount to a questioning of the royal judgment. Even in his decisive debate with Williams and Bates on the eve of Agincourt (IV, i), where the implications of his power are most searchingly discussed, the king's right to command is never in doubt. The claims of authority, which are as fundamental to the Shakespearean conception of the body politic as are those of judgment and control to the moral idea, must still be made and accepted. Henry's soldiers, in spite of their pessimistic view of the military situation, accept them without reserve. For Bates the duty of a subject lies simply in loyal execution of the royal will, and the responsibility for wrong action, if wrong there be, rests beyond the simple soldier with the king: 'we know enough if we know we are the king's subjects' [IV. i. 131-32]. Williams is more sceptical in his estimate of the king's judgment, but his scepticism, far from eating into the mind and sapping the will to action, is simply the reflection of a sturdy and independent character. It is, in other words, closer in spirit to Falstaff's unprejudiced observations upon 'honour' than to the corroding scepticism of the 'problem' plays. Replying to Henry's assertion that the cause is just with a doubtful 'that's more than we know' [IV. i. 129], he never really questions the postulate that the subject is bound to obedience. Indeed, he openly asserts that this is so. To disobey, as he puts it, 'were against all proportion of subjection' [IV. i. 146]; and the emphasis is still upon the 'proportion' to be observed in the relationship between king and subject, between the directing head and the executive body, and upon the proper submission necessary to successful military effort. Henry, of course, accepts this view of his position. Indeed, the temper of the play, still strictly political and patriotic, does not permit him to do otherwise: but the manner of his acceptance, modified as it is by a consistently sombre estimate of human possibilities, is decidedly tragic in spirit.

For the arguments of his followers, though they do not lead Henry to question his own authority, force him to reflect deeply upon the weaknesses which even kings cannot overcome. It is in the tone of these reflections that he approaches more nearly than ever before to the spirit of later plays: 'The king is but a man as I am; the violet smells to him as it doth to me; . . . all his senses have but human conditions: his ceremonies laid by, in his wickedness he appears but a man; and though his affections are higher mounted than ours, yet when they stoop they stoop with the like wing' [IV. i. 101-02, 103-07]. There is about the argument a universality which transcends the royal situation. Men, differentiated by vain 'ceremony,' are united in their common wickedness, and the most notable feature of human behaviour is its domination by sensual weakness, its helplessness before the universal stooping of the affections. In this respect, at least, the king shares the failings of his men; and just because he is so like them, just because 'his senses too have but human conditions,' are constantly liable to break through the guard of rigid self-control, there is something precarious and disproportionate in his absolute claim upon the allegiance of his followers. The royal isolation is further underlined by Williams when he points out the spiritual consequences of a conflict for which the king, as unquestioned head of his army, is alone responsible: 'For how can they' (soldiers) 'charitably dispose of anything when blood is their argument? Now, if these men do not die well, it will be a black matter for the king that led them to it' [IV. i. 142-45]. (pp. 362-66).

Henry counters the disturbing implications of Williams' argument by pointing out that soldiers 'purpose not their death, when they purpose their services' [IV. i. 157-58]. His sombre view of human nature, however, impresses itself upon the king, attaches itself to his own meditations, and is profoundly echoed in his own words. Connecting war with sin, and in particular with overriding passion, he repeats the tone of earlier statements: 'Besides, there is no king, be his cause never so spotless, if it come to the arbitrament of swords, can try it out with all unspotted soldiers: some peradventure have on them the guilt of premeditated and contrived murder; some, of beguiling virgins with the broken seals of perjury' [IV. i. 158-64]. The result is, in part, a fresh emphasis upon meticulous self-examination as a means of conserving spiritual health—'therefore should every soldier in the wars do as every sick man in his bed, wash every mote out of his conscience' [IV. i. 178-80]—and, in the soliloquy which brings the scene to an end, one of those outbursts of nostalgic craving for release which have appeared already in the Second Part of *Henry IV* and will be repeated with a new, more directly *physical* apprehension of existence in Hamlet's soliloquies and the Duke's incitations to Claudio in *Measure for Measure*.

> What infinite heart's ease
> Must kings neglect, that private men enjoy.
>
> [IV. i. 236-37]

The craving for 'heart's ease' in this long speech is still, generally speaking, what it is in *Henry IV*: a desire to be freed from the burden of an office in which human purposes seem fatally divorced from human achievement. . . . Greatness is a 'fiery fever' which consumes its royal victim like a bodily disease, and the contrasted peace of the humble subject is described with a curious ambiguity of tone:

> Not all these, laid in bed majestical,
> Can sleep so soundly as the wretched slave,
> Who with a body fill'd and vacant mind
> Gets him to rest, cramm'd with distressful bread.
>
> [IV. i. 267-70]

In the association of peace with bodily fulness and vacancy of mind, in the impression, harshly and directly physical, behind 'fill'd' and 'cramm'd,' there is a distinct suggestion of certain descriptions of satiated, idle contentment in plays as far apart as *Troilus and Cressida* and *Coriolanus*. Here already such imagery represents a kind of residue standing, intractable and irreducible, in direct contrast to the king's unceasing emphasis on the need for spiritual discipline. It is no more than a suggestion, unabsorbed as yet into the main imaginative design of the play; but, tentative as it is, it does stand in a certain relationship to the clash of flesh and spirit, 'passion' and 'grace' which exacts continual vigilance from Henry, and which is slowly moving through these developments of imagery towards more open realization.

A similar potential cleavage, and one which is given clearer dramatic expression, can be traced in the treatment of the two sides drawn up in battle at Agincourt. . . . In his treatment of the French nobility, Shakespeare seems to be turning a popular satirical conception to fresh purposes. The Dauphin's description of his horse (III, vii), which is typical of many French utterances, combines a certain elemental lightness with a deliberate Euphuistic hollowness of phrase: 'It is a beast for Perseus; he is pure air and fire, and the dull elements of earth and water never appear in him' [III. vii. 20-2]. The contrast between the opposed elements is typical, but so is the reference just below to the conventional love poetry of the courts. For the Dauphin goes on to say that he once wrote in praise of his

horse a sonnet beginning 'Wonder of nature,' to which Orleans retorts 'I have heard a sonnet begin so to one's mistress'; and the Dauphin, oblivious to the reversal of values involved, comments—'Then did they imitate that which I composed to my courser, for my horse is my mistress' [III. vii. 40-4]. The world implied by such remarks is clearly, in embryo, that of the early scenes of *Troilus:* a world far less seriously treated and with much less evidence of a dominating and clearly conceived purpose, but already light, sceptical, and revealing a fundamental moral carelessness, a society which views with cynicism the graceful phrase-making of its own members. . . . The French, trusting in a thin and rhetorical belief in their own aristocratic superiority, rush hastily and incompetently to their deaths; the English, deriving their spirit from their King, win the day by perseverance and self-control. Self-control, however, which is—as in Henry himself—not without a suggestion of harshness and inhumanity. Henry's righteousness does not prevent him from inflicting merciless reprisals on his prisoners, and there is something sardonic about Gower's comment that 'the king, most worthily, hath caused every soldier to cut his prisoner's throat. O 't is a gallant king' [IV. vii. 8-10]. By such excellence, Shakespeare would seem to say, must wars be won.

There is, indeed, a good deal of throat-cutting in this play. The King's ruthlessness, which is a logical consequence of his efficiency, needs to be seen against the human background which Shakespeare provides for it, most noticeably in the comic scenes which turn on the behaviour of the common soldiery. There is little room in *Henry V* for the distinctive note of comedy. Shakespeare's delineation of character is as clear-cut as ever, and his dialogue abundantly if discreetly flavoured with the sense of humanity; but there is about these humorous scenes a certain desiccated flatness that contrasts sharply with the exuberance of earlier plays. We may detect in these scenes, if we will, an increasing interest in Ben Jonson's handling of 'humour' to fit a new kind of moral purpose. Bardolph, Pistol, and the others, no longer enlivened by contact with Falstaff, quarrel like curs, and their jokes turn largely upon the bawdy-houses which will inevitably swallow them up when they return to England, and upon the cutting of throats. 'Men may sleep, and they may have their throats about them at that time; and some say knives have edges' [II. ii. 21-2]. Nym's remark, itself dark and enigmatic, is prefaced by a sombre, fatalistic 'things must be as they may' [II. ii. 20], which modifies the comic sententiousness of the speaker and implies a certain resigned acceptance of the ordering of things. The humorous conception of the character is toned down to fit in with a spirit no longer essentially humorous; and this applies not only to Nym, but to his companions in arms. Fluellen and Gower, Williams and Bates are distinguished, not by comic vitality or by the penetration of their comments on men and events, but by their qualities of common-sense, by a tough sense of loyalty and dedication to the work in hand; and it is by their devotion to the strictly practical virtues and by the definition of their various national idiosyncrasies that they live. This is no longer the world of *Henry IV—Part I*. Falstaff himself, out of place in such company, is remembered only in his death, serving as a kind of measure by contrast with which Shakespeare emphasizes his changing vision of humanity. His death—it is worth noting—is ascribed directly to the King, who 'has killed his heart' [II. i. 88]; and Nym, repeating that phrase of resignation which conveys so much more than he realizes of the spirit of this new world, relates Henry's treatment of him to an obscure, inherent fatality. 'The King is a good King; but it must be as it may; he passes some humours and careers' [II.

i. 125-26]. In a play where the touchstone of conduct is political success, and in which humanity has to accommodate itself continually to the claims of expediency, there is no place for Falstaff. Shakespeare had already recognized this and prepared for the necessary change in the 'rejection' which had brought the previous play to a close; and now, in *Henry V*, his death affects us tragically as the last glimpse of another and less sombre world. His companions who remain, and whose life in previous plays was largely a reflection of his vitality, must now accommodate themselves to the times. They do so—and this is significant in defining Shakespeare's attitude to Henry's war—by abandoning domestic crime to follow their King to France. War, and its prospects of plunder, are for them no more and no less than a means of livelihood and an alternative to preying upon one another. As Bardolph puts it—'We must to France together; why the devil should we keep knives to cut one another's throats?' [II. i. 90-2].

In the comic scenes which present Henry's campaign against a background of drab reality, Shakespeare sets this sober view of human nature against the King's rhetorical incitations to patriotic feeling. The arrangement of the scenes is, as usual, not accidental. The behaviour of Nym, Bardolph and Pistol before Harfleur (III, ii) reads with double force after Henry's stress on breeding and the patriotic virtues. The general tone of the soldierly meditations is familiar enough and recalls Falstaff's observations at Shrewsbury [in *1 Henry IV*]. 'The knocks are too hot'—as Nym puts it—'and for mine own part, I have not a case of lives'; whilst the Boy's comment—'I would give all my fame for a pot of ale and safety'—makes him the inheritor, at least for a moment, of the philosophy of his former master [III. ii. 3-5, 13]. But the Shakespearean attitude to war in this play implies, beyond this familiar appeal to common-sense, a further element scarcely suggested in *Henry IV—Part I*, although it is in process of development in the sequel to that play. The values towards which Shakespeare is now feeling his way are tragic and essentially moral. Even in Pistol's flamboyant bravado and evident cowardice, there is a new note of reflection, a serious reference to the wastage of invaluable human lives—'Knocks come and go; God's vessels'—the phrase, for all its comic solemnity, is not unaffected by the sense of religious seriousness—'drop and die' [III. i. 8]. Striking too, though in another direction, is the repeated emphasis upon stealing in the scenes which portray the invading army. Henry's Englishmen, 'the noblest English' who are to be a copy to 'men of grosser blood,' are the same who 'will steal anything and call it purchase' [III. i. 17, 24; III. ii. 42]. They steal, not in the spirit of the earlier Falstaff defying 'the rusty curb of old father antic the law' [*1 Henry IV*, I. ii. 61], but to keep body and soul together or in simple obedience to their innate cupidity; and in the intervals of stealing, there are abundant opportunities for the throat-cutting which is so great a part of the military vocation. As Macmorris reminds his fellows, 'there is throats to be cut and works to be done' [III. ii. 111-12], so that Henry's treatment of his prisoners in the hour of battle, far from being an isolated incident, simply gives a polite sanction to the common reality of war.

The presence of these elements in his army imposes certain necessities upon the King in the fulfilment of his responsibilities. Cupidity in man is balanced by uncompromising rigour in the maintenance of elementary moral law. Besides being ready to inflict suffering upon his enemies, Henry has to enforce good conduct among his own men. When Bardolph, adding sacrilege to theft, steals a pax from a French church, Henry has no hesitation in ordering him to be hanged (III, vi);

for discipline, as the faithful and competent Fluellen observes, 'is to be used,' and the offender should die, even 'if he were my brother' [III. vi. 56, 54]. In imposing discipline upon his men, Henry has to make the sacrifices called for by his office. Once more justice requires authority to be ready to cut across human feeling; and once more the dominating impression is one of political expediency. Even the enforcement of honesty in this play has its basis in sober calculation. Henry, in confirming the sentence passed upon the thief, leaves the last word to diplomacy: 'for when lenity and cruelty play for a kingdom, the gentler gamester is the soonest winner' [IV. vi. 112-13]. Moral principle, coming into contact with political reality, translates itself inevitably into a question of expediency; and it is expediency, the condition of successful leadership, which is—whatever his deepest desires—the touchstone of Henry's conduct.

Perhaps we can now understand why *Henry V*, as I suggested at the opening of this essay, has been most generally popular when imperfectly understood. Its concessions to human feeling are too few, its presiding spirit too discouraging to compel enthusiasm. It ends, on every level, in a decided pessimism which somehow fails to attain the note of tragedy. Pistol, speaking the last word for the cut-throats of the play, leaves us with a gloomy and uncompromisingly realistic vision of his future which the sober common-sense of Fluellen and the other soldiers does not sufficiently lighten:

Doth Fortune play the huswife with me now?
News have I, that my Doll is dead i' the spital
Of malady of France;
And there my rendezvous is quite cut off.
Old do I wax; and from my weary limbs
Honour is cudgelled. Well, bawd I'll turn,
And something lean to cutpurse of quick hand.
To England will I steal, and there I'll steal:
And patches will I get unto these cudgell'd scars,
And swear I got them in the Gallia wars.

[V. i. 80-9]

Nor is the political conclusion, which shows peace following on the English triumph, much more encouraging. Henry's wooing of Katharine, distant and consistently prosaic in tone, befits what is after all never more than a political arrangement undertaken in a spirit of sober calculation. It may have satisfied the demands of patriotic orthodoxy at Elizabeth's court; but Shakespeare had the gift of fulfilling obligations of this kind without being deterred from his deeper purposes, and this conclusion can hardly have been meant to do more. The inspiration of *Henry V* is, if anything, critical, analytic, exploratory. As we read it, a certain coldness takes possession of us as it took possession, step by step, of the limbs of the dying Falstaff; and we too, in finishing this balanced, sober study of political success, find ourselves in our own way 'babbling of green fields' [II. iii. 17]. (pp. 367-72)

*D. A. Traversi, "'Henry the Fifth',' in* Scrutiny, *Vol. IX, No. 4, March, 1941, pp. 352-74.*

**JOHN C. McCLOSKEY** (essay date 1944)

[*McCloskey disputes the description of Henry V as "the mirror of all Christian kings" (Chorus, II, 6). He contends that the king's conduct in battle is barbarous, revealing nothing of Christian ethics or ordinary standards of civilization, and he regards his frequent references to God as patronizingly familiar attempts to associate his own interests with divine will. McCloskey also cas-*

*tigates Henry's behavior towards Williams, judging it snobbish and condescending, and he describes the king's exchange of gloves with the common soldier as "a crude and humorless practical joke."*]

The final play of the Plantagenet cycle presents Henry V, the son of the usurper Bolingbroke made king by Parliament, as the great warrior-king of England, the brilliant conqueror at Agincourt, and the embodiment of the national spirit of England. As in Holinshed, Henry is a king loved by all men, humane and just in peace, valiant and hardy in war, humble and devout in victory, a king of qualities most praiseworthy and of virtues notable, "a pattern in princehood, a lodestar in honour, and a mirrour of magnificence" [Holinshed]. He is the ideal prince of the Renaissance. Early in the first scene the Archbishop of Canterbury eulogizes the reformed tavern prankster and long-familiar companion of Sir John Falstaff as suddenly learned in divinity, skillful in government, expert in warfare, and competent in statecraft. Henry V is, in the words of the Prologue, "the mirror of all Christian kings" [Chorus, II, 6]. The name of God is ever on his lips; and not only is God on his side as his cause is just, but it is to God that he generously gives the credit for the slaughter of ten thousand Frenchmen and fellow-Christians in one bloody day.

It is, of course, abundantly evident that this son of Henry Bolingbroke is an inspiring leader, a dauntless warrior, and a well-loved sovereign, yet it is evident, too, that far from being "the mirror of all Christian kings" in the conduct of warfare, to which the ethics of Christianity may presumably be applied if the warfare is between Christians, Henry V is a savage barbarian unrestrained by Christian ethics in his ruthless pursuit of victory in the war upon which he has embarked following out the politically expedient advice of his dying father to busy giddy minds with foreign quarrels.

In the siege of Harfleur, Henry practices what today we know as total war, about which no one is likely to assert that there is anything distinctively Christian. This king, who seeks ecclesiastical sanction for his war against France, who is patronizingly familiar with God, and who confidently identifies God's interests with his own, involves the terrors of murder, rape, and villainy to achieve his mind, the capitulation of Harfleur. Although it may be objected that this ideal king did not intend to follow out his threats, those threats constitute what may be regarded as "a war of nerves" and would be ineffectual as threats if their maker, no speaker of idle words, was not determined beforehand to enforce them. If the French of Harfleur do not immediately surrender, Henry shouts, not only will their soldiers be defeated and slain, but horrific vengeance will be wreaked upon the innocent non-combatants; and whatever happens, the guilt, according to the English king's self-interested ethics which justify violent deeds on the ground that if the victims do not peaceably submit, they are responsible for their own destruction, will rest not on Henry but on the French who resist. There is neither Christianity nor civilization in Henry's martial tactics. If he must begin the siege again, he will leave Harfleur in ashes, and the gates of mercy, one of the cardinal Christian virtues, shall be all shut up. His rough soldiers, calloused by bloodshed and hardened in heart, shall range with conscience wide as hell and in liberty of bloody hand shall mow like grass the fair French virgins and the flowering infants. What is it to him, Henry cries, if impious and hellish war perpetrates all fell feats linked to waste and desolation?

> What is't to me, when you yourselves are cause,
> If your pure maidens fall into the hand

> Of hot and forcing violation?
> What rein can hold licentious wickedness
> When down the hill he holds his fierce career?
>
> [III. iii. 19-23]

What if the French do not surrender at once in this "war of nerves" while Henry yet restrains his soldiers from "heady murder, spoil and villainy"? [III. iii. 32]. Then in a moment they may look to see:

> The blind and bloody soldier with foul hand
> Defile the locks of your shrill-shrieking daughters;
> Your fathers taken by the silver beards,
> And their most reverend heads dash'd to the walls,
> Your naked infants spitted upon pikes,
> Whiles the mad mothers with their howls confus'd
> Do break the clouds, as did the wives of Jewry
> At Herod's bloody-hunting slaughtermen.
> What say you? will you yield? and this avoid,
> Or, guilty in defence, be thus destroy'd?
>
> [III. iii. 34-43]

For cold ferocity this speech of the Christian king is unsurpassed. That these threats were made with ruthless coldness is attested by Henry's subsequent remark [IV. vi. 55-6] during the course of the battle at Agincourt: "I was not angry since I came to France until this instant." If it must be granted that warfare is, in general, un-Christian, then it must likewise be granted that at Harfleur, at least, Henry lays his Christianity aside in his ruthless practice of total war.

Despite the assertion of Henry later in the play that he has given express charge that in his army's marches through the country nothing be compelled from the villages, nothing taken but paid for, and none of the French upbraided or abused in disdainful language, this unpalatable scene is reinforced by other details inconsistent with the concept of "the mirror of all Christian kings." When after their initial defeat at Agincourt the French reorganize their forces and again threaten the English, Henry orders every English soldier to kill his French prisoners. That this command was carried out is evidenced in the following scene by the conversation of Fluellen and Gower, during the course of which we learn that in retaliation for the killing of the boys guarding the luggage by French stragglers and deserters the king has, "most worthily," caused every soldier to cut his prisoner's throat. "O, 'tis a gallant king!" [IV. vii. 10] Gower exclaims. In the same scene Henry dispatches a herald to some horsemen on a hill bidding them come down and fight or void the field. If they will do neither, Henry will come to them and make them skirr away as swift as stones cast from Assyrian slings.

> Besides, we'll cut the throats of those we have,
> And not a man of them that we shall take
> Shall taste our mercy. Go and tell them so.
>
> [IV. vii. 63-5]

Although the quality of mercy, which Portia lauds in *The Merchant of Venice,* is a fundamental virtue of Christian ethics, Henry time and again rejects it and conducts himself in battle more like a butcher than a warrior. In the light of these speeches, Henry's confident assignation to God of the credit for victory is in presumptuous bad taste, and his patronizing familiarity with the Deity is once more displayed in his twisted moral sense which inspires him to proclaim death to whoever of his own army shall boast of the victory or "take that praise from God which is his only" [IV. viii. 115-16].

Aside from these major flaws in the character of Henry V as "the mirror of all Christian kings," there are certain minor touches which detract from his greatness and make it difficult to admire his character as fully as his efficiency. He is a royal snob with an exalted concept of his greatness; he luxuriates in self-pity for the cares that the crown brings to him who wears it. Everyone, he says, lays his sins upon the king, who is subject to the breath of every fool. The only thing the king possesses which private men do not is ceremony. This sophistic rationalizing Henry carries on at some length, for he has not given a very satisfactory answer to the critical objections of the soldier Williams and must, therefore, reassure himself. Vain and empty are the shows of kingship, and not all its pomp and gorgeous ceremony can make the king sleep so soundly as the wretched slave with body filled and vacant mind. With characteristic royal snobbism Henry confuses the lowly and the wretched with the ignorant and the stupid. So conscious is this Henry of his royal differences from other men that he condescends (but not with humility) to point out his human similarities to them.

Finally, Henry's character is not displayed to advantage in his contacts with Williams, a courageous, manly, and independent common soldier. When Williams' realistic criticism of war is answered by Henry's presentation of the customary case made out for those responsible for war, Williams remained unconvinced and, chiding Henry somewhat too roundly, is involved in a quarrel with the disguised king. In the exchange of gages for this quarrel and in the subsequent events Henry exercises his immunity as a king for the sake of gratifying his exalted sense of royal greatness by playing a shabby and boorish trick upon a common soldier, who can call the man to account but not the king. Into this quarrel Henry enters as a common man, but the issue of it he evades as a king, and all that is left for Williams to do is to withdraw in embarrassed chagrin. But Henry's self-assured, kingly presumption that he can cancel out a crude and humorless practical joke by regal condescension and by a patronizing gratuity is rejected by the sturdy refusal of Williams, who is possessed of a democratic sense of man's intrinsic worth, to be so bought off. "I will none of your money" [IV. viii. 67], says Williams. To this common soldier, self-respect, dignity, and honor are greater virtues than humble submissiveness to mere kingship, even when embodied in the person of "the mirror of all Christian kings." (pp. 36-40)

*John C. McCloskey, "The Mirror of All Christian Kings," in* The Shakespeare Association Bulletin, *Vol. XIX, No. 1, January, 1944, pp. 36-40.*

### E. M. W. TILLYARD (essay date 1944)

[*Tillyard's* Shakespeare's History Plays *(1944), one of the most influential twentieth-century works in Shakespearean studies, is regarded by many scholars as the leading example of historical criticism. Tillyard's thesis, which is shared, with variations, by other historical critics, discerns a systematic world view in Shakespeare's plays—and one common to educated Elizabethans—in which reality is understood to be structured in a hierarchical Great Chain of Being. On a social level such a philosophy valued order, hierarchy, and civil peace as the chief political goals. Further, Tillyard notes a basic acceptance in Shakespeare's histories of "the Tudor myth," the critic's term for an interpretation of English history from Richard II to Henry VIII. According to this "myth," Henry IV was a usurper, and his usurpation set into motion the disastrous chain of events which culminated in the War of the Roses between 1455 and 1485. In the following excerpt from the work mentioned above, Tillyard regards* Henry V *as inferior to the earlier plays in the history cycle, arguing that at this stage in his career Shakespeare had little interest in the kind of man both the chroniclers and the Elizabethan audience esteemed as one of England's greatest national heroes. He contends that the king is a "patchwork character," inconsistent not only with the figure of Prince Hal in* 1 *and* 2 Henry IV, *but within this play as well; further, he embodies no significant principle upon which the dramatist could construct his play.* Henry V *lacks "intensity," Tillyard maintains, and he cites as evidence the dearth of cosmic or universal implications in the dramatic action, the "unevenness of the verse," and the disjunction between the central plot and the comic scenes.*]

Hall's chronicle caught Shakespeare's youthful imagination and impelled him to dramatise the whole stretch of English history from the prosperity of Edward III, through the disasters that succeeded, to the establishment of civil peace under the Tudors. In all the History Plays so far written (*King John* excepted, which is outside the sequence) he had fulfilled his obligation. But in the last three plays [*Richard II* and *1* and *2 Henry IV*] he had quite exceeded it by giving, concurrently with the strict historical theme, his epic picture of medieval and of contemporary England. But this excess could not cancel the residue of his obligation. He had created his picture of the great traditional villain king; he had still to create his picture of the great hero king. Richard III had figured in *2* and *3 Henry VI* and had declared his character. But that was not enough. Hall, by incorporating More's life of Richard III, dwells on that king with a special emphasis. Shakespeare fulfils his obligation to Hall by giving Richard a play to himself, in which his monstrosity is done full justice to. Hall, following the tradition established by Polydore Vergil, makes Henry V the second exceptional figure in his chronicle: the copy-book paragon of kingly virtue, to balance Richard the monstrous pattern of concentrated vice. If Shakespeare was to carry his work through he was obliged to treat Henry like Richard: to allow him a play to himself. There was a personal reason why Shakespeare should now acquiesce in the precedent of Hall: he had finished the theme of England or Respublica and was almost forced to allow a concrete hero to dominate his next History Play.

But Shakespeare also had his duty to the expectations of an Elizabethan audience. Having achieved popularity in showing Henry's youthful dissipation he could not, without scandal, refuse to show Henry in his traditional part of perfect king. And this traditional part contained factors not found in Hall: namely his sudden miraculous conversion when he came to the throne and his pre-eminence among English kings as the bluff hearty man and the good mixer. The legend of his conversion was powerful and of long standing. It began with the chronicler Walsingham, who said that Henry on coming to the throne was turned suddenly into another man, and persisted in the *Famous Victories of Henry V*, where only a miracle can account for the abrupt transition from waster to serious monarch. The tradition of good mixer finds typical expression in [Henry V's] dealing with Simon Eyre in Dekker's *Shoemaker's Holiday* [1600].

Here then were two obligations; and they were both impossible of worthy fulfilment. In creating his epic of England Shakespeare had set himself an exacting standard. His political hero, to be worthy of the standard just set, must be the symbol of some great political principle. And there was no principle he could symbolise. The pre-eminently successful political hero in great literature is Aeneas; and it was Virgil's powerful and steady belief in the missionary and civilising destiny of Rome that animated him. England had not yet reached the stage of

Virgil's Rome. She had preserved herself, had achieved union, had "rested true" to herself, but she did not yet stand consciously for any wide political idea. The Tudors were successful by personal astuteness rather than by exemplifying any principle. They were not for export, not oecumenical. Thus Henry V, who could at best stand for Elizabethan political principle, could only fail when great weight was put on him. (pp. 304-06)

To fulfil the second obligation in a manner worthy of the plays he had just written was also impossible. The whole point of the Prince's character was that his conversion was not sudden, that he had been preparing with much deliberation for the coming burden. And as for being the hearty man and the good mixer, the Prince may indeed have charmed his audience by the mere fact of his presence at Eastcheap; but his fundamental detachment and persistent irony are quite at odds with the popular conception of a simple forthright energetic man, transparent in character and separated from simple humble souls only by the accident of his exalted position. It would have been too risky to allow him to remain the ironist after he had come to the throne.

Shakespeare came to terms with this hopeless situation by jettisoning the character he had created and substituting one which, though lacking all consistency, satisfied the requirements both of the chroniclers and of popular tradition. No wonder if the play constructed round him shows a great falling off in quality.

Not that Shakespeare jettisoned his old creation without a struggle. He would hardly have begun his play with

> O for a Muse of fire, that would ascend
> The brightest heaven of invention,
>
> [Prologue, 1-2].

if he had felt quite hopeless of his genius soaring into the empyrean, and thus achieving a miraculous solution of the seemingly impossible. And in the first scene where Henry appears (I. 2) and once or twice later Shakespeare does try to invest his hero with a glamour that shall by its sheer blinding power make us insensible to any inconsistencies. The prelates and nobles who incite Henry to great deeds in France speak splendidly:

> Gracious lord,
> Stand for your own; unwind your bloody flag;
> Look back into your mighty ancestors:
> Go, my dread lord, to your great-grandsire's tomb,
> From whom you claim; invoke his warlike spirit
> And your great-uncle's, Edward the Black Prince,
> Who on the French ground play'd a tragedy,
> Making defeat on the full power of France,
> Whiles his most mighty father on a hill
> Stood smiling to behold his lion's whelp
> Forage in blood of French nobility.
>
> [I. ii. 100-10]

Ely reinforces these words of Canterbury with

> Awake remembrance of these valiant dead
> And with your puissant arm renew their feats.
> You are their heir, you sit upon their throne;
> The blood and courage that renowned them
> Runs in your veins; and my thrice-puissant liege
> Is in the very May-morn of his youth,
> Ripe for exploits and mighty enterprises.
>
> [I. ii. 115-21]

These lines not only dazzle us with their brilliance but they place Henry in the grand context of English history and make us forget the subtle personal touches of his previous character. And they do even more. They refer back to a specific passage in *Henry IV,* the reference to May suggesting the description of Henry and his companions before Shrewsbury,

> As full of spirit as the month of May.
>
> [*1 Henry IV,* IV. i. 101]

It looks as if Shakespeare was trying desperately, by creating casual links between Prince Hal and Henry V, to mask their fundamental discrepancy. Anyhow we cannot but be appeased for the moment; and when Exeter continues with

> Your brother kings and monarchs of the earth
> Do all expect that you should rouse yourself,
> As did the former lions of your blood,
>
> [I. ii. 122-24]

we are still more appeased, for Exeter here takes up Henry's promise, made at the end of the last play, that he will accept his due place among the other monarchs in the ocean of royalty, that his vanity will no longer beat idly on the rocks but that

> Now doth it turn and ebb back to the sea,
> Where it shall mingle with the state of floods
> And flow henceforth in formal majesty.
>
> [*2 Henry IV,* V. ii. 131-33]

Further questionings about Henry's character are held off by Exeter's noble commonplace on the order of government being like music:

> While that the armed hand doth fight abroad,
> The advised head defends itself at home;
> For government, though high and low and lower,
> Put into parts doth keep in one consent,
> Congreeing in a full and natural close,
> Like music—
>
> [I. ii. 178-83]

and by Canterbury's splendid comparison of the state to the beehive. But the truth cannot be withheld for ever and out it comes in Henry's speech to the French ambassador about the tennis balls: a speech whose heavy irony and orotundity compare poorly with the Prince's light ironies and truly Olympian grandeur in *Henry IV*. It is not the same man speaking. Later efforts to inflate Henry to greatness are no more successful. His reproof of the traitor, Lord Scroop, at Southampton, is wonderful poetry, possibly the finest thing in the play; yet it is queerly ineffective in its context. The Henry we knew was an unerring judge of human nature and never gave himself away. When he says of Scroop

> Thou that didst bear the key of all my counsels,
> That knew'st the very bottom of my soul,
> That almost mightst have coin'd me into gold,
>
> [II. ii. 96-8]

he speaks gloriously, he may charm us for the moment, but he ultimately bewilders us. He is utterly inconsistent with his old self and with any of the pieces of self that make up his patchwork character in the present play. Nor can one plead that his words are a sentamental passage spoken out of character: they are too emotional. One is tempted to suppose (as nowhere else in all Shakespeare's History Plays) that the poet, defeated in the real business of his drama, is drawing on personal experience and filling up the gap with an account of how someone at some time let him, Shakespeare, down. Once again Shakespeare tried to save his play in the scenes before Agincourt. Of Henry's conversation with Bates and Williams, Johnson wrote that "the whole argument is well followed, and properly concluded." This is a just comment, but the conversation does not get beyond the sober and the rational. It has the chill of Brutus's speech over Caesar's body rather than the warmth of the prose of the previous plays. Henry's following soliloquy "Upon the king!" [IV. i. 230ff.] is splendid poetry and yet somehow extrinsic to the play, a piece of detached eloquence on a subject on which Shakespeare had long meditated with interest and fervour.

Finally, there is a curious reference back to *Henry IV* near the end of the play, as if even then, when the game was lost, Shakespeare was still hankering after continuity with his late masterpiece. It is where Henry, courting Katharine, mentions his skill in vaulting onto his horse fully armed.

> If I could win a lady at leap-frog, or by vaulting
> into my saddle with my armour on my back,
> under correction of bragging be it spoken, I
> should quickly leap into a wife.
>
> [V. ii. 136-39]

Here is a clear reminiscence of the gay description in *I Henry IV* [IV. i. 104-10] of Prince Hal mounting his horse. But how alien the two passages are: the earlier a brilliant piece of Renaissance painting; the other, with its stately indecent double-meaning, a piece of sheer writing down to the populace. In spite of these efforts to manufacture connections and of the closeness with which its plot follows on, *Henry V* is as truly separated from the two parts of *Henry IV* as *Richard II* is allied to them.

But I need not deal exhaustively with the play's shortcomings, when they have been set forth in such masterly fashion by Mark Van Doren in his *Shakespeare* [see excerpt above, 1939]. I will rather point out how conscientiously Shakespeare fulfilled his double obligation: to the chroniclers and to his public. If his muse failed to ascend the brightest heaven of invention at least it tried to pay the debts it owed below the sphere of the moon.

First, Shakespeare through the mouth of the Archbishop prolongs the chronicle story of Henry's sudden conversion:

> Never was such a sudden scholar made;
> Never came reformation in a flood
> With such a heady currance, scouring faults.
> For never Hydra-headed wilfulness
> So soon did lose his seat, and all at once,
> As in this king.

To suppose that Shakespeare meant the Archbishop here to be wrong, just as Poins had been wrong, about Henry's true character is to introduce a subtlety quite alien to the rest of the play. Shakespeare is submitting to the popular tradition of the chronicles and going back on his own earlier creation. Another legacy of the chronicle tradition, Henry's rejection of his old companions, had been done justice to in the previous play. Yet Shakespeare is careful to bring it in again when he makes Fluellen say,

> So also Harry Monmouth, being in his right
> wits and his good judgements, turned away the
> fat knight with the great-belly doublet.
>
> [IV. vii. 46-8]

With this rejection was coupled the election of grave counsellors and the heed Henry gave them. And here Shakespeare pays his debt in full, and once again at his own expense. His Prince Hal had been an eminently self-reliant and self-sufficient young man, one who would never accept the advice of others without subjecting it to the closest scrutiny. In the debate in I. 2 on the French war Henry is a different person. He hardly interposes, much less argues. As a thinker he is quite passive, leaving the business to others. When these have pronounced their verdict, he accepts it without a word of comment but initiates action with

> Call in the messengers sent from the Dauphin.
>
> [I. ii. 221]

The perfect courtier in whom intellect and activity was finely balanced has given way to the pure man of action, whose thinking is done for him by his counsellors. His subsequent pedestrian thoughtfulness when he argues with Bates and Williams is inconsistent alike with Prince Hal's brilliant intellect and with the narrow activity he shows both in the scene with his counsellors and his courtship of Katharine. Then the chroniclers (Polydore Vergil and Hall) tell us that Henry was able to learn wisdom by historical precedent. Shakespeare makes his Henry refer to the past history of his country:

> For you shall read that my great-grandfather
> Never went with his forces into France
> But that the Scot on his unfurnish'd kingdom
> Came pouring.
>
> [I. ii. 146-49]

Finally, the chroniclers make much of Henry's piety, and Shakespeare follows them very conscientiously. He pays his debt; but at what a cost. We have only to compare Henry's pious comments on the miraculously low number of English casualties at Agincourt (twenty-five) and his orders for the *Non Nobis* and the *Te Deum* to be sung, with the last scenes of *Richard III* and certain parts of *Hamlet* to recognise how chilly they are. The platitudes of piety can become ultimate statements of overwhelming power if they issue from a worthy context. Occurring as they do here in a play which is constructed without intensity, they can only depress.

Other debts to the chroniclers concern not Henry's character but ideas about history. Before dealing with these I will speak of Shakespeare's fulfilling his debt to his audience by making Henry the hearty king, the good mixer. It was probably his sense of this debt that made him depress Henry's intellectual power in the debate about the French war referred to above. He fulfils it in Henry's familiarity with his "kinsman" Fluellen and his exchange of gages with Williams. But it is in his courtship of Katharine that Henry reaches his full degree of bluffness and heartiness. "I know not," says Johnson, "why Shakespeare now gives the king nearly such a character as he made him formerly ridicule in Percy" [see excerpt above, 1765]. Johnson may well ask; for the whole distance between the poles divides the lubberly wooer with his coarse complexion, who "could lay on like a butcher" [V. ii. 141], from the "king of courtesy" [*1 Henry IV*, II. iv. 10-11] of the earlier play. (pp. 306-11)

I wrote above that *Henry V* was constructed without intensity. It is worth mentioning one or two points in which this is true. After the Archbishop's fable of the bees there is little of the cosmic lore that marks the other History Plays. When Shakespeare's mind was working intensely it was aware of the whole range of the universe: events were not isolated but took place concurrently with other events on all the planes of existence. But the settings of the different scenes in this play are simple and confined. Even the battle of Agincourt evokes no correspondences in the heavens or elsewhere. A second sign of slack construction is the unevenness of the verse. There are passages of flatness among the rhetoric. The rhetoric has been better remembered than the flatness. But take the opening of II. 4 (the first scene showing the French court) up to the arrival of Exeter: it is written in the flattest verse, a relapse into the style of the more primitive parts of *1 Henry VI;* and, though Exeter proceeds to liven things a little, the verse remains lethargic. Nor is there much energy in the verse portions of the play's last scene. A third sign of weak construction is the casualness of the comic scenes. Whereas in *Henry IV* these were linked in all sorts of ways with the serious action, in *Henry V* they are mainly detached scenes introduced for mere variety. The farewell scene of Pistol and the Hostess in London is good enough in itself, but it is quite episodic. It would be unfair, however, not to mention the redeeming brilliance of Fluellen. For sheer original invention Shakespeare never made a better character. Had the rest of the play backed him up, he would (as his creator probably meant him to do) have filled the place of Falstaff not unworthily.

I fancy, too, that Fluellen helps us to understand Shakespeare's state of mind when he wrote *Henry V*. Fluellen is an entire innovation, like nobody else in Shakespeare before . . . ; and he suggests that Shakespeare was now wanting to do something fresh. Whenever Fluellen, the new character, is on the stage, Shakespeare's spirits seem to rise and he ceases to flog himself into wit or rhetoric. There are other things in the play that suggest Shakespeare's longing for a change. The coarseness of Henry's courtship of Katharine is curiously exaggerated; one can almost say hectic: as if Shakespeare took a perverse delight in writing up something he had begun to hate. Henry's reproof of Scroop, already noted as alien in tone to the norm of the play, has a quality as new as the character of Fluellen; for it is tragic and looks forward to Shakespeare's future bent of mind—

> May it be possible that foreign hire
> Could out of thee extract one spark of evil
> That might annoy my finger? 'tis so strange
> That, though the truth of it stands off as gross
> As black and white, my eye will scarcely see it.
>                                        [II. ii. 100-04]

That is one of the tragic themes: the unbelievable contradiction of appearance and reality; felt by Troilus about Cressida, by Hamlet about his mother, and by Othello about Desdemona. It has nothing to do with . . . politics, with patterns of history, with ancestral curses, with England's destiny and all the order of her society. It is a personal and not a public theme.

That Shakespeare was wanting to do something new is not at all to be wondered at. He had written his epic of England and had no more to say on the matter. In writing it he had developed characters of uncommon subtlety and in Prince Hal he had pictured a man, having indeed settled a conflict, but one in whom a genuine conflict had taken place. No wonder if Henry V, traditionally the man who knew exactly what he wanted and went for it with utter singleness of heart, was the very reverse of what Shakespeare was growing truly interested in. (pp. 312-14)

> E. M. W. Tillyard, "The Second Tetralogy: 'Henry
> V'," in his Shakespeare's History Plays, *Chatto &*
> *Windus, 1944, pp. 304-14.*

## UNA ELLIS-FERMOR   (essay date 1945)

[*An Irish scholar, critic, and editor, Ellis-Fermor devoted a considerable portion of her literary and academic career to the study of Shakespearean and Jacobean drama, although she also contributed studies on the Irish dramatic movement and on modern drama. She served on the advisory board of* Shakespeare Survey, *and from 1946 to 1958 was the General Editor of* The New Arden Shakespeare. *At the time of her death, Ellis-Fermor left unfinished her only full-length study of Shakespeare, portions of which were later published by Kenneth Muir in his* Shakespeare the Dramatist and Other Essays *(1961). The excerpt below is taken from an essay which first appeared in her* The Frontiers of Drama *(1945). Ellis-Fermor maintains that Henry V is a composite of the monarchs who preceded him in Shakespeare's other English history plays—the complete statesman and leader, with his impeccable public conduct, "his unflawed hereditary title and his assured possession of all kingly attributes." But his personality has been entirely subsumed under his public persona, she asserts, and it is useless to attempt to discover any signs of individuality in him: "There is no Henry, only a king." Ellis-Fermor theorizes that the play reveals Shakespeare's disillusion with the concept of the ideal king as one who suppresses all human desires and values.*]

In the sequence of the history plays, Shakespeare . . . achieved a reconciliation of epic material with dramatic form. . . . (p. 34)

The central and continuous image in these plays . . . is, I believe, a composite figure—that of the statesman-king, the leader and public man, which Shakespeare builds up gradually through the series of the political plays from *Henry VI* to *Henry V.* (p. 36)

The portrait of the statesman-king is the result of a series of explorations, now the study of a failure, now of a partial success; a vast, closely articulated body of thought imaged always in terms of actual character, yet completely incorporated in no one character. The figure that finally emerges is not Falconbridge or Theseus [in *King John* and *A Midsummer Night's Dream*] or Henry IV or Henry V, yet it would be incomplete if any one of them were taken away; nor is it the mere opposite of Henry VI or John or Richard III or Richard II, yet it would also be incomplete if one of these were destroyed. These separate images are but statements or qualifications contributing to that vaster image, no one of them in itself coextensive with the composite whole. It is this which gives coherence to the material of the history plays, which nevertheless remain individual works of art. (pp. 36-7)

Henry IV has all the qualities necessary to a king and avoids all the weaknesses of temperament. . . . He has shrewdness, tenacity, and self-command that already approaches self-concealment; he has the true Tudor sense of the value of discreet popularity. He is as astute as a badger and has very much the same tough courage. He is not self-indulgent, he is not vain, he is not self-absorbed. He is not even a saint or a poet. He is an exceedingly able, hard-working statesman whose career reveals gradually but clearly the main qualification for kingship, the king's sense of responsibility to his people, that sense of service which, while making him no more than the state's greatest servant, makes all his privileges and exemptions, even a measure of autocracy itself, no more than necessary means for that service. Domineering he is, at times, like Shakespeare's prototype of Tudor monarchy, but he has, in the main, decent intentions, and he possesses, through thick and thin, an unfailing, humorous sense of proportion. (pp. 42-3)

[However, the] flaw in Henry's title, the fatal act of usurpation [cripples] . . . his power and, through that, his mental stature, eating into his confidence and bringing down all loftiness of

gesture or intention to the necessity of cunning and circumspection. Character no less than tenure suffers thus under the
nemesis for an outrage done to the sacredness of inheritance.
Henry IV is in nearly all things a potential Henry V and,
trembling upon the verge of achievement, he looks into the
promised land, and, as so often happens, speaks more explicitly
of it than those who have dwelt in it familiarly. That is why
it is, I think, impossible to understand Henry V as Shakespeare
saw him, the Henry V who never speaks out, unless we can
see his position and his intentions through the eyes of Bolingbroke's frustration:

> Heaven knows, my son,
> By what by-paths, and indirect, crook'd ways
> I met this crown: and I myself know well
> How troublesome it sat upon my head.
> To thee, it shall descend with better quiet,
> Better opinion, better confirmation:
> For all the soil of the achievement goes
> With me, into the earth.
>
> [IV. v. 183-90]

It is left to Henry V to gather up in himself all that is fitting
and necessary to a king and to remain as the epitome of the
Elizabethan idea of the 'polliticke vertues'. Shakespeare has . . .
resolved his demands upon such a figure into certain clearly
defined qualifications and summed them all in Henry V, with
his unflawed, hereditary title and his assured possession of all
kingly attributes. With his broad-based popularity, his genuine
love of public service for its own sake, his strong sense of
responsibility, and his equally clear sense of its relation to
privilege, his shrewd statesman's brain, successfully masked
as that of a simple soldier, he stands where, perhaps, no king
in drama has stood before or after him. Church and state,
commoners and noblemen, soldiers and civilians, he knows
them all, with a knowledge rooted in the taverns of Eastcheap,
and holds them in his hand, too practised, popular, and secure
to make a show of mastery. He was a statesman fulfilling
Burke's demand—he knew how the whole world lived. He was
a monarch, modelled upon the greatest of the Tudors, Elizabeth
herself. It probably happens to every man to believe, at one
time or another, for a time at least, that the greatest of the arts
is conduct. And it is some such experience as this, in Shakespeare's career, that lies, I think, at the base of the great
historical studies culminating in the figure of Henry V.

But if this were all, the composite figure would be shorn of
half its subtlety and magnitude. We are aware already in this
play that Shakespeare has gone beyond the experience he is
primarily describing; that, implicit in this carefully balanced
study, this culmination of so long and careful an exploration,
is the germ of some later revulsion of thought which refutes
it, as the great destructive speeches of Timon refute Ulysses'
speech on the beauty of degree, of the ordered hierarchical
state [in *Troilus and Cressida*]. For a while, it may be, between
the writing of *Henry IV* and *Henry V*, Shakespeare believed
the highest achievement of man to be the ordered state he
afterwards described in *Troilus and Cressida*, the image of the
ordered universe, of the cosmos with its regulated spheres.

> The Heavens themselves, the planets, and this centre,
> Observe degree, priority, and place,
> Insisture, course, proportion, season, form,
> Office, and custom, in all line of order: . . .
>       But when the planets
> In evil mixture to disorder wander,
> What plagues, and what portents, what mutiny?
> What raging of the sea? Shaking of earth?

> Commotion in the winds, frights, changes, horrors,
> Divert and crack, rend and deracinate
> The unity and married calm of states
> Quite from their fixture? O, when degree is shak'd,
> (Which is the ladder to all high designs)
> The enterprise is sick. How could communities,
> Degrees in schools, and brotherhoods in cities,
> Peaceful commerce from dividable shores,
> The primogenitive and due of birth,
> Prerogative of age, crowns, sceptres, laurels,
> (But by degree) stand in authentic place?
> Take but degree away, untune that string,
> And hark what discord follows.
>
> [*Troilus and Cressida*, I. iii. 85-8, 95-110]

The keystone of this order was the figure of the perfect public
man, of Henry V. All the implications of the foregoing plays
point to this ultimate emergence of the complete figure. In all
the anticipations that lead up to him, and particularly in the
later scenes of the second part of *Henry IV*, Shakespeare has,
he would seem to imply, 'in this rough work, shaped out a
man' [*Timon of Athens*, I. i. 43]; the great art of conduct, and
of public conduct at that, is at last truly understood.

But has he? Or has he, as it were unawares, and led already
on to some perception beyond his immediate purpose, shaped
out instead something that is at once more and less than a man.
Henry V has indeed transformed himself into a public figure;
the most forbidding thing about him is the completeness with
which this has been done. He is solid and flawless. There is
no attribute in him that is not part of this figure, no desire, no
interest, no habit even that is not harmonized with it. He is
never off the platform; even when, alone in a moment of weariness and of intense anxiety, he sees with absolute clearness
the futility of privilege and the burden of responsibility, he still
argues his case in general terms, a king's life weighed against
a peasant's, peasant against king. No expression of personal
desire escapes him; . . . he is detached alike from king and
shepherd, commenting upon them, but wasting no more strength
on imagining what cannot be than on deluding himself . . . with
the empty glories of his state. He has inured himself so stead-
fastly to the life of a king, lived so long in councils and com-
mittees, weighing, sifting, deciding, commanding, that his brain
automatically delivers a public speech where another man utters
a cry of despair, of weariness or of prayer. It is in vain that
we look for the personality of Henry behind the king; there is
nothing else there. We know how his brain works upon any
one of half a dozen problems; the treachery of Cambridge,
Grey, and Scroop, the fomenting of wars abroad to preserve
peace at home, the disaffection in the army, the difficulties of
a formidable campaign, and the equally great dangers of a
crushing victory. We see the diplomacy, the soldiership, the
vigilant, astute eye upon the moods of people and barons, the
excellent acting of a part in court and camp and council-room,
and only when we try to look into the heart of the man do we
find that it is hardly acting, after all, that the character has
been converted whole to the uses of this function, the individual
utterly eliminated, sublimated, if you will. There is no Henry,
only a king.

I think Shakespeare was profoundly interested in this particular
study. Not, indeed, by the character, for there is no character,
but by the singular circumstances of its disappearance. Neither
we the readers nor Henry himself nor his God ever meets the
individual that had once underlain the outer crust that covers
a Tudor monarch, for there is nothing beneath the crust; all

has been converted into it; all desires, all impulses, all selfhood, all spirit. He is never alone, even with his God—least of all when he prays, for then he is more than ever in the council chamber driving an astute bargain, a piece of shrewd diplomacy, between one king and another.

> O God of battles, steel my soldiers' hearts,
> Possess them not with fear. Take from them now
> The sense of reckoning, if th' opposed numbers
> Pluck their hearts from them. Not to-day, O Lord,
> O, not to-day, think not upon the fault
> My father made, in compassing the crown.
> I Richard's body have interred new,
> And on it have bestowed more contrite tears,
> Than from it issued forced drops of blood.
> Five hundred poor I have in yearly pay.
> Who twice a day their wither'd hands hold up
> Toward Heaven, to pardon blood. And I have built
> Two chantries, where the sad and solemn priests
> Sing still for Richard's soul. More will I do,
> Though all that I can do is nothing worth;
> Since that my penitence comes after all,
> Imploring pardon.
>
>                              [IV. i. 289-305]

This king, as Shakespeare portrays him, is indeed 'a wondrous necessary man', the keystone upon which the sixteenth-century state depends, and individuality has at last been subjugated wholly to the demands of office. But it is not for nothing that generations of Shakespeare's readers have found little to love in this play. Unless we read it in the light of a certain bitter, underlying commentary, implicit in the orientation of the chief character, there is little there but that most grievous product of unremitting office, a dead man walking.

For the truth is that Shakespeare himself, now that he has built the figure with such care, out of the cumulative experience of eight plays, begins to recoil from it. It has been an experiment, an exploration, like, but for its larger scale, his brief but effective exploration of the system of Machiavelli, and, as he did with that system, so he does with this vast body of assembled evidence on public life: he rejects its findings as invalid before the deeper demands of the less explicit but immutable laws of man's spirit.

So much, then, for the Elizabethan phase of Shakespeare's portrait of the statesman-king, for the record of the period when he for a time believed that the wide canvas of public life was greater than the illimitable experience of the spirit. The contrast between the private and public virtues has been made clear, the qualifications of the great statesman have been slowly selected, tested, and built up into a single figure. Such characteristics as did not contribute to his public self have been eliminated (and they are seen, somewhat surprisingly, to be nearly co-terminous with character). More than this, certain of the loyalties, decencies, and ideals most prized in an individual are found to be incompatible with the public virtues. Henry, who rejected Falstaff in circumstances which cannot be forgiven, will also, in the moment of crisis, bargain with his God like a pedlar. His religion and his love for his people alike carry with them a tinge of expediency, a hint of the glib platform speaker.

It would seem, then, that in the very act of completing the figure, Shakespeare became aware of a certain insufficiency, and that dissatisfaction was already implicit in his treatment of Henry V, the culminating study of the series. (pp. 43-7)

Una Ellis-Fermor, "Shakespeare's Political Plays," in her *The Frontiers of Drama, 1945. Reprint by Methuen & Co. Ltd., 1964, pp. 34-55.*

## JOHN DOVER WILSON   (essay date 1947)

[*John Dover Wilson was a highly regarded Shakespearean scholar who was involved in several aspects of Shakespeare studies. As an editor of the* New Cambridge Shakespeare, *he made numerous contributions to twentieth-century textual criticism of Shakespeare, making use of the scientific bibliography developed by W. W. Greg and Charlton Hinman. As a critic, Dover Wilson combines several contemporary approaches and does not fit easily into any one critical "school." He is concerned with character analysis in the tradition of A. C. Bradley; he delves into Elizabethan culture like the historical critics, but without their usual emphasis on hierarchy and the Great Chain of Being; and his interest in visualizing possible dramatic performances of the plays links him with his contemporary, Harley Granville-Barker. Dover Wilson edited the Cambridge edition of* Henry V *(1947). In addition to the introduction—from which portions are reprinted below—, this work also offers a stage history of the play, commentary on likely sources and date of composition, and a discussion of textual issues. In the following excerpt, Dover Wilson provides one of the most notable twentieth-century defenses of the play and of the king himself. He argues that the central theme is heroism and that the play celebrates Henry's incomparable leadership and the "moral significance" of Agincourt, "a triumph which, under God, was due to the heroic spirit of the great King." Contending that modern commentators have mistakenly relied on Holinshed rather than on Shakespeare's text, Dover Wilson responds to what he considers misconceptions in the criticism of* Henry V, *reaching the following conclusions: Act I clearly presents the war as just and Henry's claim to the French throne as valid; the king's speech to the citizens of Harfleur in Act III, Scene iii is a successful attempt to end the siege so that the English forces may move on to Calais; and Henry's order to kill the French prisoners in Act IV shows his "strength, decision, and presence of mind at the crisis of the battle." Finally, the critic contends that in Act III, Scene iii Henry undergoes a subtle change as his heroic, epical stature is enriched by the expression of such human qualities as mercy and gaiety of spirit; at the same time, Dover Wilson concludes, there is a corresponding shift in dramatic atmosphere, in which Shakespeare provides repeated examples of the suffering war inevitably produces instead of depicting it as a great national enterprise.*]

What is the 'idea' of *Henry V*? Ever since 1817, when Hazlitt, in a fit of republican and anti-patriotic spleen, stigmatized Shakespeare's hero as a brute and a hypocrite [see excerpt above, 1817], Henry has been a subject of debate among critics. (p. xv)

'Brute force, glossed over with a little religious hypocrisy and archiepiscopal advice' is how Hazlitt saw Henry's 'Virtue'; and the words take us to the opening of the play and down to the roots of the modern difficulties about it. Practically every critic since Hazlitt has assumed that the invasion of France is an act of pure aggression, which is first suggested to Henry V by the Archbishop, who, in order to avoid a wholesale expropriation of church lands, cleverly directs his attention towards another victim. Swinburne, for example, expands Hazlitt as follows:

> The supple and shameless egotism of the churchmen on whose political sophistries he relies for external support is needed rather to varnish his project than to reassure his conscience [see excerpt above, 1880];

and Bradley, more temperate, though no less hostile, writes:

> When he adjures the Archbishop to satisfy him
> as to his right to the French throne, he knows
> very well that the Archbishop *wants* the war,
> because it will defer and perhaps prevent what
> he considers the spoliation of the Church [see
> excerpt above, 1902].

Now the actual invasion may have been quite unjustifiable by modern Anglo-Saxon standards, and it is possible to deduce the whole business of the Archbishop from Holinshed's version; while it was probably Holinshed who led many of the critics astray. But history is one thing, drama another; and Holinshed's version is certainly not Shakespeare's. On the contrary, this is one of the few occasions on which Shakespeare departs from the chronicles, with the intention, I do not doubt, of guarding his hero from the very charges which modern writers have brought against him. (pp. xviii-xx)

In the first place, it is clear from his text that before the Archbishop takes any hand in the affair at all, not only has the whole question of Henry's titles in France been broached, and, presumably in order to test the ground, a claim to 'certain dukedoms' already been lodged (the answer to which claim is brought by French ambassadors who arrive in the second scene), but the King's

> loyal subjects,
> Whose hearts have left their bodies here in England,
> And lie pavilioned in the fields of France,
>
> [I. ii. 127-29]

have long since decided for an invasion. Next, so far from initiating anything, the Archbishop's speech on the Salic Law is delivered at the invitation of the King, who, though the general validity of the English claims has been recognized since the time of Edward III, when they were first put forward, is anxious to leave no corner of the legal position unexplored before taking the final step. It is not the Archbishop who sets the King awork, but the King the Archbishop; and we gather a general impression, which is everything in drama, of an imminent war, for which the country is all afire, only delayed by the uprightness of the young King, who wishes first to be absolutely certain of the justice of his cause. This is brought out in Henry's solemn 'conjuration' to the Archbishop to take heed how he 'incites' him to shed blood, a speech given him by Shakespeare to mark the gravity of the occasion and the scrupulosity of the King's conscience.

Lastly, the sole connection between the subject of the Archbishop's speech and the question of Church lands is that both are spoken of in the conversation of the two bishops which constitutes the opening scene. From this we glean the following information: that a bill for the wholesale expropriation of Church property is before Parliament; that the King, though, 'as a true lover of the holy Church' [I. i. 23], not in normal times likely to countenance such proceedings, might be tempted to use an opportunity of thus filling his coffers for the French war; that the Archbishop, in the perfectly legitimate desire of removing the temptation from his path, waits upon him and offers, in the name of Convocation, a large subsidy towards the war; and that this offer naturally leads to talk between them about the diplomatic preliminaries, in the course of which Henry learns for the first time of the Archbishop's knowledge of French constitutional law, eagerly begs him to expound the matter, but is for the moment prevented from hearing him by the arrival of the French ambassadors. Not a hint of a bribe on the Arch-

bishop's part, still less of his provoking the King to war in order to protect Church property! Unhappy Shakespeare! He little dreamed that learned doctors would read their Holinshed or Holinshed's modern successors instead of his play, and so draw precisely those cynical conclusions, the evidence for which he had been at pains to erase from the record.

Yet he would not and could not dispense with the Archbishop and his speech. For one thing, some discussion of the young King's conversion was needed at the outset as a link with *Henry IV,* and who more apt for this than a couple of clergymen? Secondly, he wanted to preface his dramatic epic on an ideal King by some disquisition on the character of good government, with allusions to parallels in music and the world of nature; and for this a grave prelate would again be the natural speaker. But the discourse on the Salic Law is in a different category. Why did Shakespeare, generally ready to sacrifice almost anything in his sources likely to induce boredom in the audience, transplant therefrom this tiresome genealogical lecture, sixty-three lines long, and full of obscure names, some of which he did not even trouble to transcribe correctly? Our producers, quite wisely, cut it drastically; Shakespeare could no more do without something of the kind than a modern historian can omit Magna Carta from an account of the reign of John. To the Elizabethans France was a lost possession of the English crown; lost during the disastrous Wars of the Roses, which are the main theme of *Henry VI,* but never prescriptively abandoned, even after the bitter humiliation of the capture of Calais by the French in 1558. Moreover, the English title seemed to Englishmen self-evident.... Few, if any, of the theatre audience would know or care about the names in question; but most would expect to hear the case argued. And the Archbishop argues well. Being constitutionally litigious, Elizabethans loved a good pleader, while it flattered their national pride to hear it *proved* that France belonged to them.

When the Henry of the play, therefore, affirms that he puts forth his 'rightful hand in a well-hallowed cause' [I. ii. 293], he is speaking the simple truth. The war against France is a righteous war; and seemed as much so to Shakespeare's public as the war against the Nazis seems to us. Once this is realized, a fog of suspicion and detraction is lifted from the play; the mirror held up in 1599 shines bright once more; and we are at liberty to find a hero's face reflected within it. That face has been hitherto dimmed by other misconceptions also; but they are less serious than the one just considered, and may be dealt with as the occasion arises.

There are, however, heroes and heroes. Assuming that Shakespeare accepted the critical ideals of his age, what sort of hero is he likely to have set before men's eyes, so as to inflame their minds 'with desire to be worthy' and inform them 'with counsel how to be worthy'? One thing we can at any rate be certain of: he would be content with nothing less than a human being. The very nature of his genius, its instinctive drive and bias, assures us of something very wrong in a recent criticism of Henry's speeches as 'the golden throatings of a hollow god' [see excerpt above by Mark Van Doren, 1939]. And it was of 'hollow gods' that Johnson was thinking when he wrote: 'Shakespeare has no heroes; his scenes are occupied only by men, who act and speak as the reader thinks that he would himself have spoken or acted on the same occasion.' Yet the criticism is just to this extent, that not until towards the end of act 3, as we read the play, does the humanity of the King begin to engage our hearts. Is this because Shakespeare's creative imagination only at that point got to work upon his hero, that he took in fact some time to 'wind himself into his subject'? Or did he deliberately, and gradually, shift his focus as the action of the play developed? It is not easy to say. But a shift in the focus there certainly is, and it is one that might well have been adopted by a dramatist who set out to inflame an audience, prone to admire one kind of hero, with worship for another kind altogether.

To the ordinary Elizabethan . . . , Henry V was first and foremost a great conqueror, a popular national hero who had been 'outstretched', as Hamlet might say, by two centuries of acclamation. In the opening words of the play Shakespeare gives this public what it wants, and in the most magnificent manner possible:

> O for a Muse of fire, that would ascend
> The brightest heaven of invention:
> A kingdom for a stage, princes to act,
> And monarchs to behold the swelling scene.
> Then should the warlike Harry, like himself,
> Assume the port of Mars, and at his heels,
> Leashed in like hounds, should Famine, Sword and Fire
> Crouch for employment.
>
> [Prologue, 1-8]

The hero thus conjured up, in what Hazlitt, the admirer of Napoleon, calls 'perhaps one of the most striking images in all Shakespeare', springs from the Marlovian sphere; he is a kind of English Tamburlaine. We have the same Harry, once more outstretched against the bright epical background, in the message of Exeter, the English ambassador, which menaces the French King with

> Bloody constraint: for if you hide the crown
> Even in your hearts, there will he rake for it.
> Therefore in fierce tempest is he coming,
> In thunder and in earthquake, like a Jove:
> That, if requiring fail, he will compel.
>
> [II. iv. 97-101]

Nor is this vision of him in any way disturbed by his words and actions before he leaves England, by his dealings with the Archbishop and his Council, by his sarcastic 'merry message' in answer to the Dauphin's 'tun of tennis-balls', or even by the long speech of impassioned reproach to 'the man that was his bedfellow' [II. ii. 8]. The last ends in a sob indeed, but we feel that Friendship, not Harry, weeps. All this only teaches us that the great King is as much above the stature of ordinary men in statecraft as he is in conquest. Lastly, in his summons to Harfleur to surrender, one of the most dreadful speeches in Shakespeare, though based upon the book of Deuteronomy and no doubt reflecting contemporary Christian usage, we seem to hear the voice of Tamburlaine himself.

Up to the taking of Harfleur, Henry is what John Bailey calls 'the most royal, masterful, and victorious of Shakespeare's kings.' And the impression has been so firmly established that it remains with us for the rest of the play. Yet Harfleur is a turning-point. For no sooner does the governor yield than we become conscious that Henry's fierce intimidation is a mere device to bring an end to the siege, on the part of a commander anxious, because of sickness among his troops, to hurry on to Calais; while in the brief order, 'Use mercy to them all' [III. iii. 54], given to Exeter whom he leaves in temporary command of the town, we have the first glimpse of a real man behind the traditional heroic mask. From this moment we are brought closer and closer to him, until we come, if not to know him well, at least to do him homage, even to think of him with

affection. . . . And that this change of focus was not just accidental, or occasioned by a character suddenly 'taking charge' of its creator, is suggested by the fact that it coincides with another change, equally interesting and structurally closely connected, a change of atmosphere.

The background of Henry V is war; and its atmosphere, as in most epics, is determined by the poet's attitude towards war. Now war may be conceived in two ways: as man's greatest vocation, the pursuit of Glory, at the risk of one's own life or those of others, and through the ruthless exercise of power; or as one of the greatest of human evils, with its miserable train of blood and anguish, horror and tears. The first, on the whole that of the traditional epic, is once again Marlowe's; the second, represented by Hardy's Dynasts and Tolstoi's War and Peace, is on the whole modern. Shakespeare gives both, one after the other. Yet there is no sudden transition, no violent contrast or crude incongruity: the change is so natural and inevitable that a spectator will not realize it is taking place; it corresponds with the development of the campaign, and reflects the mood of the nation and the army. The first two acts are concerned with the preparation for the descent upon France; and, once the legal and diplomatic preliminaries have been dealt with, the aspects of the war most emphasized are the light-hearted enthusiasm of the nation, and ferocious descriptions by its accredited representatives of what is coming to the enemy. In other words, we see England going to war after the fashion of all times and all countries:

> Now all the youth of England are on fire,
> And silken dalliance in the wardrobe lies,
>
> [Chorus, II, 1-2]

says Shakespeare's Chorus;

> Now God be thanked Who has matched us with His
>   hour,
> And caught our youth, and wakened us from sleeping,

echoes an English youth, Rupert Brooke [in "Peace"], three hundred and fifteen years later; while the preliminary phase of bluster and threats, mirrored especially in [I. ii. 100-31, 274-97], has by now become so well known that in 'jingoism' we have invented a special word for it. There follows the sailing of the expeditionary force, brilliantly presented in the third Prologue. And then, suddenly, the audience is before Harfleur; and begins, with the army, to face the realities of war for the first time. For though Shakespeare quickens the pulse of every patriot by Henry's charge to his troops, a speech which opens,

> Once more unto the breach, dear friends, once more;
> Or close the wall up with our English dead,
>
> [III. i. 1-2]

shows that war is something more than 'a thing for an editorial—a triumphal parade' [Stephen Benét, in John Brown's Body]. And in the next scene but one Henry sets war before us in all its naked brutality, when he summons the town to surrender; while seeing that, as explained above, this speech has little relevance to character, I am persuaded that Shakespeare wrote it in order to bring home to his audience the meaning of war in terms of human agony.

Nor is this the only occasion on which he goes out of his way to do so. Honest Williams, concerned for the state of his soul before battle, gives us the following vivid glimpse of the stricken field:

But if the cause be not good, the king himself hath a heavy reckoning to make, when all those legs, and arms, and heads, chopped off in a battle, shall join together at the latter day, and cry all, 'We died at such a place'; some swearing, some crying for a surgeon; some upon their wives left poor behind them; some upon the debts they owe, some upon their children rawly left. . . . I am afeard there are few die well, that die in a battle.

[IV. i. 135-42]

Montjoy gives us another glimpse after the fight is over. And in the last scene of all Burgundy has a speech of forty lines describing the devastation which war has wrought upon the 'lovely visage' [V. ii. 37] of fair France, lest the spectators should go away imagining that victory means nothing but fresh territory and the joyful homecoming of the conquerors. Of course, there is jesting also; but at what period have English soldiers not made fun of war?—behaviour which nations, to whom war is a vocation, find it hard to understand. It must be added that the English are also prone, too prone, to make fun of their enemies; and *Henry V* faithfully reflects this national characteristic as well. In short, as a recent writer has observed, while fighting is incidental to many other Shakespeare plays, 'In *Henry V* war is itself a theme—its glories, humours and passions; its dutiful courage and proud cruelty; its brilliant surface and the horrors that lie beneath it' [see essay by John Palmer listed in the Additional Bibliography]. Yet when the same writer goes on to characterize the play as 'the glorification of a patriot king and an exposure of the wicked futility of his enterprise', and therefore a supreme instance of Shakespeare's 'ironic detachment', he misses the whole point. For, first, the 'brilliant surface and the horrors' represent, not the comment of some Epicurean divinity upon human strife, but what war has ever seemed, first in prospect and then in reality, and in particular what it looks like to Henry and his army before and after they have actual experience of it. And, second, the more they experience it, the greater they become. In a word, the 'idea' of *Henry V* is not Success, but Heroism.

The turning-point, I have said, is Harfleur. Up to then 'sits Expectation in the air' [Chorus, II, 8]; after, the English are dogged by sickness and despondency, utter weariness and sore peril, to say nothing of dilapidated boots, tattered garments and the discomfort of 'rainy marching in the painful field' [IV. iii. 111]; until, with their line of retreat to Calais cut off and forced to give battle,

The poor condemnèd English
Like sacrifices, by their watchful fires
Sit patiently, and inly ruminate
The morning's danger: and their gesture sad,
Investing lank-lean cheeks, and war-worn coats,
Presenteth them unto the gazing moon
So many horrid ghosts.

[Chorus, IV, 22-8]

Agincourt was a great victory; great in its decisive results, but greatest of all in its moral significance. For it was the triumph of a much inferior army, diseased, famished, weary, bedraggled, dispirited, over a mighty French array, fresh, magnificently equipped, and entirely confident; a triumph which, under God, was due to the heroic spirit of the great King. 'The most foolhardy and reckless adventure that ever an unreasoning pietist devised' is how a modern historian describes the march from Harfleur [James Hamilton Wylie in *The Reign of Henry*

*the Fifth*]. Yet the same writer calls it our English anabasis. And it is its heroic character which Shakespeare insists upon in scene after scene, speech after speech, and once even in a stage-direction, though the editors have obliterated it. For the zenith of the play is not the victory—that is lightly passed over, and (in itself miraculous) is ascribed to God alone—but the King's speeches before the battle is joined, the battle which all but the King think already lost. Every line of what Henry then says breathes the English temper, but one above all—

We few, we happy few, we band of brothers.

[IV. iii. 60]

If History never repeats itself, the human spirit often does: Henry's words before Agincourt, and Churchill's after the Battle of Britain, come from the same national mint.

It is thus not to glory, or even to pride in 'the expansion of England', that Shakespeare mainly appeals in *Henry V*, but to the admiration and homage which Englishmen and Scots, like the Greeks before them, instinctively pay to those who withstand an overwhelming force or power. Such battle, if fought to the death as at Thermopylae, or till victory as at Bannockburn, by a body of men united in affection and loyalty under an indomitable leader, has always appeared in their eyes the finest of war-plays. (pp. xx-xxxi)

Heroism is then the theme, and Henry the hero. In the humanizing of him that follows Harfleur Shakespeare breathes the spirit of Sidney's heroical 'worthy' into the lay figure he found in Hall; and adds the vitalizing touch of his own divine genius. 'No emperor in magnanimity ever him excelled', says Hall. We have seen his quality of mercy shown towards the inhabitants of Harfleur. It is still further stressed in the words, based upon Holinshed, which he utters after the arrest of Bardolph for plundering a church:

And we give express charge that in our marches
through the country there be nothing compelled
from the villages; nothing taken but paid for;
none of the French upbraided or abused in disdainful language; for when lenity and cruelty
play for a kingdom, the gentler gamester is the
soonest winner.

[III. vi. 108-13]

With such clemency his order for the slaying of the prisoners at the height of the battle seems in strange discord until it is realized that this episode, like the speech of the Archbishop on the Salic Law, has been altogether misapprehended by modern critics. Holinshed writes apologetically of the King's 'dolorous decree', and explains that it is 'contrary to his accustomed gentleness'; Shakespeare, who might have omitted it, offers no apologies, but sets the decree in a framework of circumstances which, when followed on the stage, in scenes 4. 4 to 4. 7, which are in fact one continuous battle-scene, makes it seem natural and inevitable. Once again the critics have read the chronicler instead of watching the dramatist at work; and bemused themselves with attempts to unravel Holinshed's tangled skein which Shakespeare had carefully straightened out.

The whole situation is dominated by the fact that the English are 'enrounded' by an army which outnumbers them five to one. Henry is indeed so short of men that, as we are informed at the end of 4. 4, he is obliged to leave his camp unguarded except by boys, while even at the moment of their ignominious flight, one of the French nobles declares in 4. 5,

> We are enow yet living in the field
> To smother up the English in our throngs,
> If any order might be thought upon.
>
> [IV. v. 19-21]

Encouraged by this recollection, and by the do-or-die determination of Bourbon, who recalls them to their duty, the French commanders, later in the same scene, return to the battle from which they had first fled, resolved to sell their lives dearly in some desperate counterstroke. It is a hazardous moment for the English, as spectators with any knowledge of warfare will be aware; since by a successful rally the French might not only offset their initial repulse, but, with the weight of numbers on their side, wrest the crown of victory from Henry's grasp. And Henry himself is well aware of this, as is shown us at the opening of 4. 6, when, congratulating his troops on what has so far been accomplished, he warns them at the same time

> But all's not done, yet keep the French the field.
>
> [IV. vi. 2]

Nor has he long to wait. The 'alarum' sounds, telling him of a rally, while we realize that some 'order' has been 'thought upon', and that Bourbon has managed to pull his men together for the counter-attack.

Henry's response is immediate and unhesitating. At the beginning of 4. 6 he had entered 'with prisoners', which on the stage should, I suggest, be represented as more numerous than the men who guard them. In any case an encumbrance, since it is not possible for the same soldiers to guard and to fight, prisoners become a grave embarrassment under attack. Moreover, if rescued, they would add dangerously, if not fatally, to the enemy's already excessive numbers. Accordingly, the King issues the only command possible under the circumstances. 'But hark!' he cries,

> What new alarum is this same?
> The French have reinforced their scattered men:
> Then every soldier kill his prisoners,
> Give the word through—
>
> [IV. vi. 35-8]

and at once hurries forward to the quarter from which the attack threatens. The order is one that, the security of his whole force being at stake, any general then would have given. Monstrelet, the contemporary Burgundian chronicler, explains the situation clearly, and never even suggests that the order requires justification. (pp. xxxii-xxxv)

*Act II. Scene ii. Cambridge, Grey, Scroop, Henry V, Exeter, Bedford, Westmoreland, and others. By Henry Fuseli. The Department of Rare Books and Special Collections, The University of Michigan Library.*

But Shakespeare had yet another point to make in favour of Henry's 'heroic spirit'. At the opening of 4. 7 he brings in Fluellen and Gower to tell us what the great counterstroke of the French had been. 'The cowardly rascals that ran from the battle' (i.e. Bourbon, the Constable, and the rest, whom we saw running in 4. 5) had 'reinforced their scattered men', and fallen—upon the undefended English camp, putting all the boys they found there to the sword [IV. vii. 6; IV. vi. 36]! The attack is historical; and Fluellen's exclamation, ''Tis expressly against the law of arms, 'tis as arrant a piece of knavery, mark you now, as can be offert!' [IV. vii. 2-3] is in accordance with much contemporary comment on the battle, which shows that the treacherous assault left a deep stain upon the chivalry of France. Thus any lingering doubt about Henry's action is blotted from the minds of even the most squeamish in the audience, while his blazing anger and further threats at the sight of other bands of Frenchmen galloping about the field, on his return from avenging the boys, are fully justified. In point of fact, it is only when the French herald appears and admits the victory to be an English one, that he can breathe freely at all. The slaughter of the prisoners might . . . have been omitted. Yet Shakespeare makes it central to his account of the battle. Indeed, it is almost the only aspect of it he sets upon the stage; for though the hubris of the French, which was the primary cause of their overthrow, is well brought out in scenes 3. 7 and 4. 2, strangely enough nothing whatever is said of the bowmen of England, who were the real victors. Clearly, Shakespeare's attention was concentrated upon Henry and he intended ours to be. Thus the general impression which the incident was designed to convey, and which I do not doubt was conveyed to the original audiences, is not one of brutality at all, but of a great commander's strength, decision, and presence of mind at the crisis of the battle. No wonder honest Gower cries, 'O, 'tis a gallant king!' [IV. vii. 110] and Fluellen goes on to speak of Alexander the Great. (pp. xxxvi-xxxvii)

[The] slaying of the prisoners is so famous and its misunderstanding is so generally entertained that it casts a baleful shadow over Henry's earlier actions. It is therefore well to have it out of the way before we consider him in those desperate hours on the eve of the battle when he rises to the supreme height of his heroic stature. As the ordeal draws near Shakespeare reveals more and more of the man to us, and his humanity is the argument at once of his conversation with the soldiers and of the soliloquy that follows. Where else, too, in English poetry is to be found our English notion of leadership better expressed than in the fourth Chorus, which describes him touring the camp throughout the night, and cheering the 'ruined band' by his mere presence, words of comfort being idle mockery in that awful predicament? Above all, the grimmer things seem, the gayer he becomes. Such gaiety is infectious; as recent experience has taught us, can even be caught by a whole nation from the example of one man. For, as Henry himself remarks,

> 'Tis good for men to love their present pains,
> Upon example—so the spirit is eased:
> And when the mind is quickened, out of doubt
> The organs, though defunct and dead before,
> Break up their drowsy grave, and newly move
> With casted slough and fresh legerity.
>
>             [IV. i. 18-23]

Those who miss the gaiety of act 4 have missed one of the finest effects of the play. It animates almost everything the King says or does before the battle. How light-heartedly does he give good-morrow to his brothers and old Erpingham! as if

it had been a huntsman's horn in England that makes them 'early stirrers'. Yet, as he tells the soldier Michael Williams not long after, the whole army knows that they are 'even as men wracked upon a sand, that look to be washed off the next tide' [IV. i. 97-8]. He is quite ready again to devise a jest against the same soldier through the exchange of gloves for a challenge, upon a morrow none of them may see. And though he is grave in the discourses on Kingship, he is merry enough in that on Crispin Crispian over the stories the veterans will tell 'in their flowing cups' and the thought of 'gentlemen in England, now a-bed' [IV. iii. 55, 64]. Gaiety of this kind belongs to the genius of heroic leadership, a genius which, likely enough, the historical Henry himself possessed. (pp. xxxvii-xxxix)

No doubt the source of this inspiration differs with different leaders; but many great English soldiers have found it in their religion; and Shakespeare makes it clear that Henry does so likewise. In the first two and a half acts his references to God sound a little official. But the dangers of the campaign bring out the real man here as in other respects. After the crossing of the Somme the plight of the English host is made evident for the first time in an interview between Henry and Montjoy, who is sent to bid him face the facts and surrender. Henry admits the facts; but rejects the consequence. The interview over, Gloucester expresses the fears of all present in a fervently uttered 'I hope they will not come upon us now!' To which the King simply, almost casually, replies, 'We are in God's hand, brother, not in theirs', and turns directly to the duties of the day [III. vi. 168, 169]. The words sound a deeper, humbler, more intimate note than we have heard hitherto, and suggest a Henry who bows spirit as well as knees, and finds in prayer a source of strength and confidence. Nor is it the only hint of the kind. We may infer that the implied counsel to his senior staff to 'dress' them 'fairly' for their 'end', and the more explicit counsel of the same sort to his soldiers later, would not have been offered had he not already performed a like action himself, as his historical counterpart is known to have done.

But he has yet another prayer to utter, this time on behalf of his army as king and leader; and that Shakespeare, as is fitting, allows us to overhear. . . . What I would stress here is the spirit in which the prayer is uttered. No claims of any kind are made; no reference to the justness of the cause; not even a petition for victory. All Henry asks is that courage be granted his soldiers to fight against overwhelming odds, and that the crime of his father, in compassing the throne by the deposition and death of Richard, be not weighed in the balance against them. And the attitude of the petitioner is evident from the closing words, in which, after speaking of what he has tried to do by way of expiation, he continues:

>              More will I do:
> Though all that I can do is nothing worth;
> Since that my penitence comes after all,
> Imploring pardon.
>
>             [IV. i. 302-05]

Is this bowed figure the 'warlike Harry' who 'assumes the port of Mars' [Prologue, 6] and hurls himself upon France

> In thunder and in earthquake, like a Jove?
>
>             [II. iv. 100]

It is the same, seen no longer from without but from within; and all the more a hero, because now known as a man. Yet Shakespeare has a still finer moment for him, the last before battle, into which he sends his soldiers, no longer as at Harfleur with the war-cry 'God for England, Harry and Saint George!' but with a petition, 'How thou pleasest, God, dispose the day!' [III. i. 34; IV. iii. 133]. The words are not to be taken as implying despondency or resignation; on the contrary, as Charles Williams has observed [see excerpt above, 1936], they are uttered gaily, like almost everything else the King says in the scene, and express the spiritual exaltation which inspires him, and through him the whole English army, at this crisis of their fate. One may paraphrase them roughly: 'Death or Victory, as God wills!—what matter which, since Honour comes either way, in heaven or on earth?' It is a statement of the ultimate heroic faith, a faith which, like that of the martyrs, puts him who holds it beyond reach of mortal man.

After Agincourt anti-climax was hardly to be avoided, and most critics have complained of the emptiness of the fifth act. Yet, the fine description of Henry's homecoming, the eating of the leek by Pistol, and the wooing of Katharine make a good mixture and the first two ingredients have generally been approved. So I believe the third would also have been, but for an unfortunate misunderstanding about it, which is the last this Introduction must remove. It was Dr Johnson who here first led the world astray; and his note, still being quoted with approval by critics, runs as follows:

> I know not why Shakespeare now gives the king nearly such a character as he made him formerly ridicule in Percy. This military grossness and unskilfuness in all the softer arts, does not suit very well with the gaieties of his youth, with the general knowledge ascribed to him at his accession, or with the contemptuous message sent him by the Dauphin, who represents him as fitter for the ball room than the field, and tells him that he is not *to revel into duchies,* or win provinces *with a nimble galliard* [see excerpt above, 1765].

Johnson is usually so level-headed in judgment, and so careful a reader of his text, that this criticism fills one with astonishment. For Prince Hal ridicules no such characteristics in Hotspur as he himself displays as King Henry; nor does Hotspur's off-hand treatment of his married Kate bear any real resemblance to Henry's forthright conversation with his unmarried one; while as for 'the gaieties of his youth', Johnson has forgotten that their venue was the tavern and the highway, not polite society, and that they brought him into the company of topers and wenches, not of ladies in ballrooms. The bishops, again, speak in 1.1 of his proficiency in divinity, statecraft, and military affairs, but say nothing at all of 'the softer arts'. Lastly, the Dauphin's 'contemptuous message' was clearly worded to show us that the French prince was totally ignorant of the youthful habits he affected to despise in the English one.

Yet Johnson's criticism serves to remind us of a fact that should never be forgotten, viz. that Henry is simply Hal grown up and grown wise, and that we have the story of his education in *Henry IV.* And is not the courtship of Katharine exactly the kind of wooing we might expect of the adult Hal, of a man who has had no experience or training in 'the softer arts', but despises what he knows of them, of a soldier genuinely in love, but to whom integrity of mind and plain dealing are the very pith of life? (pp. xxxix-xliii)

The courtship is written *con brio* [with spirit] because it was conceived *con amore* [with love]. For, so far from being dis-

appointed in his hero, Shakespeare had, I believe, fallen pretty deeply in love with him before he had done. And having taught his audience too to hold him in their hearts, he will now show them that he is the 'King of good fellows' [V. ii. 242-43], one whom they might 'even care to spend an evening with' [see excerpt above by Harley Granville-Barker, 1933]. The 'port of Mars'? This hero, when he walks, treads on the ground. (p. xlv)

> *John Dover Wilson, in an introduction to* King Henry V *by William Shakespeare, edited by John Dover Wilson, Cambridge at the University Press, 1947, pp. vii-xlvii.*

### HAROLD C. GODDARD   (essay date 1951)

[*Goddard argues that Shakespeare intentionally created two Henry V's—the supremely popular military hero and the disingenuous Machiavel—and left us "free to accept whichever of the two we prefer." He suggests that one of the principal functions of the Chorus is to promulgate the godlike stature and heroic achievements of the king, but that alternately with these passages Shakespeare reveals "the truth about him"; in the critic's judgment, these discrepancies are presented with a penetrating irony that "imparts intense dramatic value to practically every one of [the play's] main scenes." He finds Act I, Scene ii especially ironic, noting that Canterbury's arguments in defense of Henry's claim to the French throne actually demonstrate that the legitimate heir is Edmund Mortimer. Goddard further discovers in several of the comic scenes, especially those featuring Bardolph and Nym, Shakespeare's ironical commentary on the conduct of the play's protagonist.*]

There is near-unanimity among critics that *Henry V* is not a marked success as a play. For once, it is said, his material was too much even for Shakespeare. A great military victory is epic, or even lyric, rather than dramatic matter, and though the piece contains much that is splendid and picturesque, these merits cannot atone for its intellectual and dramatic poverty.... The play remains history, it seems to be agreed, instead of being history transmuted into drama. To make up for this lack of the dramatic, Shakespeare, it is intimated, was not above truckling to the patriotic emotions of his audience. To say right out what many have insinuated: the poet in this play proves himself something of a jingo. (p. 215)

That Shakespeare loved England, all his plays prove, and [the] historical ones in particular. But there is nothing, unless it be this play, to show that he was a flag-waver. (p. 216)

But there are the Choruses of *Henry V*, it will be said, which all in themselves, without going any further, prove the point.

The Choruses of *Henry V* are indeed full of a windy chauvinism. But who said they are Shakespeare? Who said, I mean, that they represent the author's ideas or attitude? A good many have said so, it is true, in the face of the fact that they are like nothing else in the poet's works that has ever been convincingly identified with his spirit.

The Chorus differentiates himself specifically from the author on his first appearance by asking the audience to

> Admit me Chorus to this history,
> Who prologue-like your humble patience pray....
>                                  [Prologue, 32-3]

"Me Chorus" is plainly not the author; and that the speaker of a prologue may be anything but the representative of the poet or the playwright is proved in most specific fashion by the Chorus-prologue of *Troilus and Cressida,* who says:

> hither am I come
> A prologue arm'd, *but not in confidence*
> *Of author's pen or actor's voice,* but suited
> In like conditions as our argument,
> To tell you, fair beholders, that our play
> Leaps o'er the vaunt and firstlings of those broils,
> Beginning in the middle.
> > [*Troilus and Cressida,* Prologue, 22-8]

And the words of the Chorus in the epilogue of *Henry V* confirm the distinction:

> Thus far, with rough and all-unable pen,
> Our bending author hath pursu'd the story.
> > [Epilogue, 1-2]

The poet would not refer to himself as "*our* bending author." It is somebody else who is speaking.

Who, then, is the Chorus? He appears to be a mixture of several things. He is in part History filling in the gaps of the story by making abridgments of what is necessarily left out in the theater. He is in part the stage manager apologizing for that necessity and for the general inadequacy of the stage to the poet's theme.... And, in accordance with one of the traditional functions of the Chorus, he is in part an abstract of average public opinion.

This last point is the crucial one. A military hero at the top of his success is always elevated by the populace into something like a god. And that is just the note that is struck with regard to the warlike Harry throughout these Choruses. But can anyone believe that Shakespeare in his own person would have called Henry "the mirror of all Christian kings" [Chorus, II, 6] and then let him threaten to allow his soldiers to impale French babies on their pikes and dash the heads of old men against the walls; or called him "this grace of kings" [Chorus, II, 28] and then let him declare of the prisoners,

> we'll cut the throats of those we have,
> And not a man of them that we shall take
> Shall taste our mercy;
> > [IV. vii. 63-5]

that he would have pronounced Henry "free from vainness and self-glorious pride" [Chorus, V, 20], after dedicating a good part of two plays to showing how he wanted to imitate the sun and astound the world by emerging suddenly from behind clouds—and not only wanted to, but did?

Soldiers before battle are exposed to martial music and often given even stronger intoxicants, that when they begin to fight they may not be coldly aware of the exact nature of what is before them. Shakespeare offers the martial music of a Chorus before each act of this play, possibly with a similar motive with regard to his auditors and readers. As word music and rhetoric, they are indeed intoxicating. But poetry in any high sense, except perhaps for a few touches, they are not. We have ourselves to blame if we let them put us in a condition in which we cannot see what is going on before us in the play. Shakespeare's procedure was quite justified. As playwright, he must get a hearing for his play. As poet, he must tell the truth. But to tell the truth about a great national hero at a time when patriotism is running high calls for courage. To tell it and to keep the piece in which you tell it popular calls for more than courage. Shakespeare did as life does. Life places both its facts

and its intoxicants before us and bids us make out of the resulting clash what we can and will. So does the author of *Henry V.* Through the Choruses, the playwright gives us the popular idea of his hero. In the play, the poet tells the truth about him. We are free to accept whichever of the two we prefer. God does not indicate what we shall think of his world or of the men and women he has created. He puts them before us. But he does not compel us to see them as they are. Neither does Shakespeare.

*Henry V* opens with war on France as good as decided on. Henry would have resented it if someone had told him that. Who doesn't resent being told that his mind is made up when he thinks it is still open? The resentment is a confession that it is closed. (pp. 216-18)

War being deemed desirable, the next thing is to find a reason for it. The opening of the play is dedicated to a search for sound moral ground for the attack on France. Fortunately for Henry, the Archbishop of Canterbury not only has such a sanction at hand but has a motive for bringing it forward.... The King begins by warning the Archbishop not to incite him to war on specious grounds. Think of the blood that will be spilt, he reminds him, every drop of which will be a just complaint against whoever begins an unrighteous conflict.

> We charge you in the name of God, take heed....
> Under this conjuration speak, my lord,
> And we will hear, note, and believe in heart,
> That what you speak is in your conscience wash'd
> As pure as sin with baptism.
> > [I. ii. 23, 29-32]

Nothing could sound more moral and humane (though a suspicious mind might find a Chaucerian ambiguity in that last phrase). But we must judge Henry by his acts, not by his words.

The King must have an irreproachable reason for making war. The one thing that his claim to the French throne must be is *clear.* But when the Archbishop goes on to expound that claim, clear is the one thing it does not seem to be. (pp. 218-20)

Canterbury's long argument and its conclusion, which he pronounces "as clear as is the summer's sun" [I. ii. 86], bewilder Henry as much as they do the reader. Or perhaps he prefers not to understand, that the responsibility may rest on the Archbishop. At any rate, quite as if he had not taken in a word of Canterbury's magnificent effort, he merely reiterates his original question:

> May I with right and conscience make this claim?
> > [I. ii. 96]

To which the Archbishop replies:

> The sin upon my head, dread sovereign!
> For in the book of Numbers it is writ,
> When the son dies, let the inheritance
> Descend unto the daughter.
> > [I. ii. 97-100]

The Book of Numbers! The Archbishop has been holding back his ace. All those tedious genealogical details, then, were only a foil against which the crowning precedent should shine forth. (Quite in Henry's own style.) It was a considerable step back to the King's great-great-grandmother. But Moses, or whoever wrote the Pentateuch, is an even more venerable authority. When, in the next act, Exeter, in Henry's name, demands that the French King resign the crown and adds, as he presents his sovereign's pedigree:

> That you may know
> 'Tis no sinister nor no awkward claim,
> Pick'd from the worm-holes of long-vanish'd days,
> Nor from the dust of old oblivion rak'd,
> He sends you this most memorable line,
> In every branch truly demonstrative,
>
> [II. iv. 84-9]

we remember the learned Archbishop's researches and the Book of Numbers, and perceive that Exeter's vehement denial that there is anything shady or far-fetched in Henry's claim is the poet's oblique way of telling us that shady and far-fetched is exactly what it is.

And there is irony in this scene at a still deeper level. Henry bases his title on inheritance through the female line. But by this very rule under which he claims the French, he must surrender the English throne, for, allow inheritance through the female, and Edmund Mortimer, who is descended from the third son of Edward III through his grandmother, has a prior claim over Henry, who is descended from the fourth son. Shakespeare leaves it to anyone who will to remember this little fact. With it, the play is one thing; without it, quite another. (pp. 221-22)

We interrupted the Archbishop at the Book of Numbers. Let us return to his speech. "Gracious lord," he exclaims, passing from learning to exhortation,

> Gracious lord,
> Stand for your own! Unwind your bloody flag!
> Look back into your mighty ancestors!
> Go, my dread lord, to your great-grandsire's tomb,
> From whom you claim.
>
> [I. ii. 100-04]

It is indeed a tombstone claim.

> For in his tomb lie my affections,
> [*2 Henry IV*, V. ii. 124]

Henry, we may recall, said of his father. Now they go still deeper into the family burial chambers. Could anything make clearer the atavistic character of the change that is coming over Henry than these references to blood and ancestry and graves? His nobler self is regressing not merely into his father but into "the fathers."

In what follows one might imagine that that nobler self makes a final attempt to assert itself, for Henry says nothing for forty lines, while Canterbury, Ely, Exeter, and Westmoreland vie with one another in urging him to rouse himself like "the former lions" of his blood to "forage in the blood of French nobility" as did that "lion's whelp," the Black Prince, in his great-grandfather's day [I. ii. 124, 110, 109]. Their verbal violence suggests both a suppressed thirst for blood on their own parts and a fear that Henry is hesitating to give the final word. Your subjects' hearts have already left their bodies and lie pavilioned on the fields of France, says Westmoreland.

> O, let their bodies follow, my dear liege,
> [I. ii. 130]

cries the Archbishop,

> With blood and sword and fire to win your right;
> In aid whereof we of the spiritualty
> Will raise your highness such a mighty sum
> As never did the clergy at one time
> Bring in to any of your ancestors.
>
> [I. ii. 131-35]

Fire, blood, lucre, and spiritualty! The witches' brew in *Macbeth* scarcely exceeds that.

It is evidently at just this moment that Henry overcomes any lingering scruples. With the tension removed, all these men, including the King, let themselves go a bit and their metaphors grow correspondingly revealing. The Scots, who are likely to attack England when her back is turned, are called petty thieves, snatchers, and weasels who suck princely eggs. England is an eagle in prey—and a cat. But the Archbishop's comparison is a worse giveaway than any of these. He likens human polity in a well-ordered state to that of the bees. The bees, it turns out, have nearly everything in their community that men have except archbishops and armies. No high churchmen of the hive are mentioned. And as for fighters, this is the way the Archbishop tries to squeeze them in:

> Others, like soldiers, armed in their stings,
> Make boot upon the summer's velvet buds,
> Which pillage they with merry march bring home
> To the tent-royal of their emperor.
>
> [I. ii. 193-96]

As if bees hovering above flowers, or the fruitful communion of the two, could be compared to the clash of enemies on the battlefield, or honey to the spoils of war! The Archbishop is as deficient in his science as in his symbolism. His childhood was plainly not spent in the meadows of Stratford. And his logic, that theological and ecclesiastical specialty, is no better. The bees are united and harmonious in a perfect division of labor, he says; "therefore" Henry should "divide" his forces into four parts, attack France with one, and leave the other three for home defense. What these two kinds of division have to do with each other only a mind more concerned with words than realities could figure out. What fun Shakespeare must have had making such a fool of his Archbishop, knowing all the while that his audience would swallow his utterances as grave political wisdom.

The King evidently accepts them as such, for as the Archbishop concludes, he gives the order:

> Call in the messengers sent from the Dauphin.
> Now are we well resolv'd.
>
> [I. ii. 221-22]

The French ambassadors enter and ask whether they shall speak their sovereign's intent plainly or veil it in diplomatic language.

Henry tells them to speak out:

> We are no tyrant, but a Christian king;
> Unto whose grace our passion is as subject
> As are our wretches fetter'd in our prisons:
> Therefore with frank and with uncurbed plainness
> Tell us the Dauphin's mind.
>
> [I. ii. 241-45]

The metaphor is worth noting, for it is presently going to escape, as prisoners sometimes do, and stab its user in the back. "Whatever praises itself but in the deed," Shakespeare was to write a year or two later, "devours the deed in the praise" [*Troilus and Cressida*, II. iii. 156-57]. He knew it already.

Accepting Henry's invitation not to mince their words, the ambassadors declare that the Dauphin thinks Henry's claims (to certain lands in France—they have not yet heard his claim to the throne) "savour too much of your youth" [I. ii. 250], a plain allusion to the part Hal had taken in *robberies;* that he cannot *dance* and *revel* himself into French dukedoms. Therefore he sends Henry, in satisfaction of his claims and as more appropriate to his spirit, a tun of treasure. The treasure turns out to be—tennis balls!

This allusion to his gay youth touches Henry where he is sorest. On the instant his passions, which a moment before he had boasted were his subjects and prisoners, break their chains in such a threat of violence that it sounds more like the barbarous license of some Goth or Norseman in the days of Beowulf than the utterance of a supposedly responsible monarch. Go tell the Dauphin that

> many a thousand widows
> Shall this his mock mock out of their dear husbands;
> Mock mothers from their sons, mock castles down;
> And some are yet ungotten and unborn
> That shall have cause to curse the Dauphin's scorn.
>
> [I. ii. 284-88]

Diplomatic insults have often precipitated wars, and it isn't easy even for the Mirror of all Christian Kings to be twitted in the presence of his court on the subject of his misspent youth. Yet somehow all those widows and mothers and unborn babes seem more than an equivalent for a few tennis balls. (pp. 222-25)

If Act I ends with a quarrel made, Act II opens with a quarrel composed. If there is to be war in France, there is peace for the moment at any rate in the tavern. The title that figures here is one not to a portion of the earth but to a woman. Pistol has married the Hostess of the Boar's Head, Mistress Quickly, to whom Corporal Nym was troth-plighted. But his legal claim has not allayed fears of a rival:

> O hound of Crete, think'st thou my spouse to get?
>
> [II. i. 73]

And his trepidation is deepened by a gambling debt that he owes Nym of no less than eight shillings. Bardolph, the red-nosed, seeks to prevent bloodshed and to bring the two angry men together: "I will bestow a breakfast to make you friends; and we'll be all three sworn brothers" [II. i. 11-12].

It is all very vulgar, if you will, food for the groundlings. But putting its vernacular simplicity of utterance (except of course for Pistol) and the good sense of its outcome over against the hypocrisy, the moralizing, and the rhetoric of the previous act, and their outcome, one is tempted to feel that wisdom has fled to the underworld.

"I dare not fight," Corporal Nym confesses, "but I will wink and hold out mine iron" [I. ii. 7-8]. His sword, he says, "will toast cheese" [II. i. 9]. A cheese-toaster is not a bad tavern-equivalent for the biblical pruning hook.

"Good Corporal Nym," cries Nell Quickly when she sees him about to go to it with her husband, "show thy valour and put up your sword" [II. i. 43-4]. It might be a motto for nations! (p. 226)

"Why the devil should we keep knives to cut one another's throats?" [II. i. 91-2] asks Bardolph, unconsciously condensing into a sentence the question of the centuries, as he seeks to compel the loud-mouthed and cowardly Pistol to keep the peace and pay his debt. "Base is the slave that pays" [II. i. 96], retorts Pistol, unaware that about twenty seconds later he will pay. "An thou wilt be friends, be friends," says Bardolph, "an thou wilt not, why then, be enemies with me too" [II. i. 102-04]. And a touch on his sword is enough to remind the

two that Bardolph means business and that his use for his weapon is to prevent a quarrel, not to prick one on. Whereat, Pistol meekly pays.

How far Shakespeare has juxtaposed intentionally the boastings of Pistol in this scene and those of Henry in the previous one, each reader must decide for himself. The fact is that he has juxtaposed them.

> O braggart vile and damned furious wight!
>
> [II. i. 60]

Shocking as it may sound to say it, that line is a vulgar, but nonetheless a psychologically accurate description of Henry, when, beside himself with anger, he resents the insults of the Dauphin. Not Henry, note, but Henry-beside-himself. ("Thou art essentially mad without seeming so" [*1 Henry IV*, II. iv. 492-93]). Shakespeare can never be trusted not to comment on his main plot in his underplot.

This seemingly casual little scene is also the one that brings the news of Falstaff's mortal illness, and in it we get the reaction of this group of his friends to Henry's rejection of him. "The king has killed his heart" [II. i. 88], laments Mistress Quickly. "The king hath run bad humours on the knight; that's the even of it" [II. i. 121-22], says Nym.

> Nym, thou hast spoke the right;
> His heart is fracted and corroborate,
>
> [II. i. 123-24]

echoes Pistol—and it is as if the invisible Falstaff were almost causing the two men who were about to fight each other to embrace. Dying, he makes peace, while Henry, living, makes war. "The king is a good king," Nym concludes fatalistically, "but it must be as it may; he passes some humours and careers" [II. i. 125-26].

It will be impossible to analyze in detail all the scenes that make up the underplot of this play. The little one we have just glanced at is typical of the way the author relates them to his main theme and so makes them immensely more than comic relief. There are those who hold that the sins of men in high places should be less stressed than the sins of those in private life. There is no evidence that to Shakespeare right and wrong are one thing for kings and another for commoners or even for the underworld. (pp. 226-27)

[At III. vi. 100ff.] Fluellen, the Welsh captain, [announces] that Bardolph is to be executed for robbing a church. Bardolph, we recall, was one of Hal's cronies of the wild-oats days, and time was when he and Hal went stealing together. Does Hal remember this at a moment so critical for his old friend? It is hard to see how he could have failed to. But he does not mention it. "We would have all such offenders so cut off" [III. vi. 107-08], is his laconic comment, whereupon he plunges in his next breath into his order against plundering. Much ink has been spilled over the rejection of Falstaff [in *2 Henry IV*]. This much briefer rejection of Bardolph has scarcely been noticed. But it is psychologically hardly less interesting. The King spares Bardolph (who indeed is not present) the sermon he preached on the other occasion. In place of it, he gives orders for lenity and mercy on his soldiers' part. Henry covers his unmerciful deed by his merciful words. "I give orders for the death of a friend, but let my soldiers beware of stealing a spoon from the enemy or even speaking impolitely to them." That is the compensatory logic of it. But as usual with Shakespeare, the most interesting thing is behind. Robbing a church! Had Henry, even in his wildest days, ever broken into a church edifice and stolen a pyx? There is no record of anything of the sort. But he had accepted the bribe of a large slice of ecclesiastical property for the purpose of launching his proposed conquest of France. It makes a difference whether you steal retail or wholesale, and whether you do it openly or slyly, legally or illegally. The plot and underplot of this play grow more and more mutually illuminating.

The fourth act of *Henry V* is dedicated to the Battle of Agincourt and what preceded it. The last scene of the previous act supplies the foil. In it we catch a glimpse of the French camp the night before the battle, with its mingled frivolity, light conversation about horses, mistresses, and sonnets, and wishes for the dawn of the morning that will summon them to the easy extinction of the English. It is all like some hopelessly overconfident university football squad contemptuous of the team of a backwoods college that by some freak of fortune they have been compelled to condescend to play.

And then, with the new act, the scene shifts to the English camp on the same night and we have one of the most dramatic and symbolic scenes that Shakespeare, up to that time, had conceived.

The King wraps himself in a borrowed cloak, and, Haroun-al-Raschid-like, mingles incognito with the common soldiers. And forthwith, a miracle! His royal habiliments hidden, Henry is at first almost the old Hal with whom we were formerly acquainted. The man had had to disguise himself to become a king; now the king must disguise himself to become a man. Wrapped in the double obscurity of his cloak and of night, he engages in conversation three of his soldiers, John Bates, Alexander Court, and Michael Williams. Their Christian names, in each case, I think, are intended to have significance, and in the case of Court the surname certainly does, for his first speech in the play turns out to be his last, possibly, in proportion to its length, as remarkable a role as is to be found in Shakespeare.

"Brother John Bates," he says "is not that the morning which breaks yonder?" [IV. i. 85-6]. Just eleven words—and the rest is silence. But those words let us into the secret thoughts of a man who never expects to see another dawn, and in his silence we hear his heartbeats. . . . Bates and Williams too are filled with dark forebodings, but they are at least able to speak. All three of them are plainly men of sincerity and worth. Somehow Shakespeare convinces us that it is of this stuff that England is made. The three men evoke a responsive sincerity from Henry. "I think the king is but a man" [IV. i. 101-02], he says—in words that are a clear echo of Shylock's memorable words on a similar theme—and we can feel the relief with which in the darkness he puts aside not merely the trappings but the very accent of state. "A little touch of Harry in the night" [Chorus, IV, 47]. Like the others, significantly, he speaks in prose.

This is the scene widely relied on by Henry's admirers to prove his simplicity, his modesty, his democracy. If only this *were* Henry! Those who think it is forget that it is night. This is the suppressed Henry. Which is real? The old man who lies in bed and remembers his youth or the youth the old man lies in bed and remembers? If only we were what we lie awake in the night and wish we were! It is what a man makes of himself in the daylight that he *is*. . . . [The] King is present in this scene as well as the ghost of Hal. In coming to the defense of the King, Hal begins to pass back into him.

BATES:       He may show what outward courage he will, but I believe, as cold a night as 'tis, he could wish himself in Thames up to the neck, and so I would he were, and I by him, at all adventures, so we were quit here.

K. HEN.:     By my troth, I will speak my conscience of the king: I think he would not wish himself any where but where he is.

BATES:       Then I would he were here alone; so should he be sure to be ransomed, and a many poor men's lives saved.

K. HEN.:     I dare say you love him not so ill to wish him here alone, howsoever you speak this to feel other men's minds. Methinks I could not die any where so contented as in the king's company,

[IV. i. 113-27]

and then, as if Bates' words had revived some old doubt, the ghost of Hal adds, "his cause being just and his quarrel honourable" [IV. i. 127-28].

"That's more than we know" [IV. i. 129], says Williams.

Bates assuages his conscience with the thought that, even if the King's cause is bad, the soldier's obedience wipes out the crime of it for him. But the more assertive Williams turns it the other way around and points out how heavy in that case is the responsibility of the king.

WILL.: But if the cause be not good, the king himself hath a heavy reckoning to make, when all those legs and arms and heads, chopped off in a battle, shall join together at the latter day and cry all "We died at such a place"; some swearing, some crying for a surgeon, some upon their wives left poor behind them, some upon the debts they owe, some upon their children rawly left. I am afeard there are few die well that die in a battle; for how can they charitably dispose of any thing, when blood is their argument? Now, if these men do not die well, it will be a black matter for the king that led them to it; whom to disobey were against all proportion of subjection.

[IV. i. 134-46]

It is an unanswerable argument. And does it not have a familiar ring? It should have. For it is the precise argument that Henry himself used when he told the Archbishop of Canterbury that it would be a black matter for him, the Archbishop, if he incited him, the King, to a bad war:

We charge you in the name of God, take heed;
For never two such kingdoms did contend
Without much fall of blood, whose guiltless drops
Are every one a woe, a sore complaint
'Gainst him whose wrongs give edge unto the swords
That make such waste in brief mortality.

[I. ii. 23-8]

The King was willing to put the responsibility on an archbishop but he is unwilling to let his soldiers put the responsibility on a king. . . . Henry is caught in his own trap. The King gives no sign that he remembers his former words, but if any proof were needed that he knows in his heart of hearts that this is a bad war we have it in the squirming sophistry . . . with which he vainly attempts to refute the simple and straightforward statement of Williams. (pp. 239-42)

If the events of this play be taken at face value, if Henry is accepted at his own estimate, or if we go even further and believe with the Chorus that he is the mirror of all Christian kings, or with the majority of critics that he is Shakespeare's portrait of the ideal king, then there is no contesting the view that the play is epic and lyrical rather than dramatic. There is in that case none of that disparity between inner and outer upon which all poetic drama depends for its effect. But grant that Henry is the golden casket of *The Merchant of Venice*, fairer to a superficial view than to a more searching perception, and instantly the play becomes pervaded with an irony that imparts intense dramatic value to practically every one of its main scenes. . . . It is all woven into a web of high psychological, political, symbolical, and (if so much be granted) dramatic value. And this does not take into account the "comic relief" which is enough in itself, with its oblique comments on the main plot, to relieve the play of the charge of being undramatic. If this play is undramatic, *Hamlet* itself, one is tempted to say, is undramatic. The difference is that Hamlet is at least partly conscious of psychological events which in Henry, except on rare occasions, take place below the threshold of apprehension. Whether *Henry V* is theatrical as well as dramatic is another question the answer to which will depend on the acting and the audience at a particular performance. It has been said that no actor can fail as Hamlet. Any actor can fail as Henry.

"It is well to seem merciful, faithful, humane, sincere, religious, and also to be so," says Machiavelli, prescribing right conduct to the ideal ruler in *The Prince*, "but you must have the mind so disposed that when it is needful to be otherwise you may be able to change to the opposite qualities. . . . A prince must take great care that nothing goes out of his mouth which is not full of the above-named five qualities, and, to see and hear him, he should seem to be all mercy, faith, integrity, humanity, and religion. And nothing is more necessary than to seem to have this last quality, for men in general judge more by the eyes than by the hands, for every one can see, but very few have [power] to feel. Everybody sees what you appear to be, few feel what you are."

Not maliciously and in cold blood but against the grain of his own nature and by insensible degrees, the man who began as Hal and ended as Henry V made himself into something that comes too close for comfort to Machiavelli's ideal prince. "Then why did not Shakespeare make it plain?" those will exclaim who hold that at any sacrifice everything must be clear in the theater. (That everything must seem to be clear may be readily granted.) But how, will they tell us, could Shakespeare draw a character whose first requisite is that he shall appear to be the opposite of what he is except by drawing a character who appears to be the opposite of what he is? "If Machiavelli had had a prince for disciple," wrote Voltaire in his *Memoirs,* "the first thing he would have recommended him to do would have been to write a book against Machiavellism." Samuel Butler has demonstrated in convincing detail that no art or mental process is perfect until it becomes unconscious. The perfect thief is the kleptomaniac, who steals as it were automatically. In that sense Henry V was possibly the perfect Machiavellian prince. (pp. 266-67)

*Harold C. Goddard, " 'Henry V'," in his* The Meaning of Shakespeare, *The University of Chicago Press, 1951, pp. 215-68.*

## J. H. WALTER    (essay date 1954)

[*Walter edited the New Arden edition of* Henry V *(1954), which contains discussions of the dates of composition, first performance, and first publication, of textual issues, and of possible sources. In the following excerpt from the introduction to that edition, Walter focuses on the epic nature of the play and the king as the ideal epic hero. From the viewpoint of an Elizabethan audience, he contends, Henry would appear as "a leader of supreme genius" who, like Virgil's Aeneas, is stoical and high principled. Walter maintains that the central significant idea of the play is Henry's ability, through the example of his "spiritual strength, his faith and moral courage," to inspire his countrymen to overcome the overwhelming military odds against them. In addition, the critic asserts that the drama "gains in epic strength and dignity from Falstaff's death," for in his role of "corrupt flatterer," Walter argues, Falstaff represents a threat to the divine plan for national order and unity, and thus he has no place "in Henry's tent on the eve of Agincourt."*]

Poor Henry! the chorus of critics sings both high and low, now as low as "Mars, his idiot", now as high as "This star of England" [Epilogue, 6]. It is strangely ironical that a play in which the virtue of unity is so held up for imitation should provoke so much disunity among its commentators. (p. xiv)

The reign of Henry V was fit matter for an epic. Daniel omits apologetically Henry's reign from his *Civil Wars,* but pauses to comment,

> O what eternal matter here is found
> Whence new immortal *Iliads* might proceed;

and there is little doubt that this was also the opinion of his contemporaries, for not only was its theme of proper magnitude, but it also agreed with Aristotle's pronouncement that the epic fable should be matter of history. (p. xv)

Shakespeare's task was not merely to extract material for a play from an epic story, but within the physical limits of the stage and within the admittedly inadequate dramatic convention to give the illusion of an epic whole. In consequence *Henry V* is daringly novel, nothing quite like it had been seen on the stage before. No wonder Shakespeare, after the magnificent epic invocation of the Prologue, becomes apologetic; no wonder he appeals most urgently to his audiences to use their imagination, for in daring to simulate the "best and most accomplished kinde of Poetry" [Sir Philip Sidney, *Apologie for Poetrie*] on the common stage he laid himself open to the scorn and censure of the learned and judicious.

Dover Wilson [see excerpt above, 1947] points out that Shakespeare accepted the challenge of the epic form by writing a series of historic tableaux and emphasizing the epical tone "by a Chorus, who speaks five prologues and an epilogue". Undoubtedly the speeches of the Chorus are epical in tone, but they have another epical function, for in the careful way they recount the omitted details of the well-known story, they secure unity of action. Shakespeare, in fact, accepts Sidney's advice to follow the ancient writers of tragedy and "by some *Nuncius* to recount thinges done in former time or other place". . . . Indeed, it is possible that the insistent emphasis on action in unity in [I. ii. 183-220], with illustrations drawn from music, bees, archery, sundials, the confluence of roads and streams, is, apart from its immediate context, a reflection of Shakespeare's concern with unity of action in the structure of the play.

The moral values of the epic will to a large extent depend on the character and action of the epic hero, who in renaissance theory must be perfect above the common run of men and of royal blood, in effect, the ideal king. (pp. xv-xvi)

Medieval and Tudor historians saw in the events they described the unfolding of God's plan, history for them was still a hand-maid to theology, queen of sciences. Henry V, the epic hero and the agent of God's plan, must therefore be divinely inspired and dedicated; he is every bit as dedicated as is [Virgil's] "pius Aeneas" to follow the divine plan of a transcendent God.

Within this all-embracing Christian Providence there was an acceptance of classical beliefs of the innate tendency of states to decay, and of the limitations and repetitions of human thoughts and emotions throughout the ages consequent on the sameness of the elements from which human bodies were formed. It was hoped that men would return to the brilliance of pagan achievement in classical times, that highest peak of human endeavour, since the conception of progress had not yet come to birth. In the meantime classical writers were models for imitation and touchstones of taste, classical figures were exemplars of human actions and passions, and the language of Cicero and Virgil, still current, foreshortened the centuries between. The modern was naturally compared with the ancient, Henry with Alexander. Calvary apart there could be no greater praise.

Only a leader of supreme genius bountifully assisted by Fortune and by the unity of his people could arrest this civic entropy and raise a state to prosperity. We do less than justice to Henry if we do not realize that in Elizabethan eyes he was just such a leader whose exploits were greater than those of other English kings, in Ralegh's words "None of them went to worke like a Conquerour: saue onely King *Henrie* the fift".

This is the man, and this his background. Let us now look more closely at Shakespeare's presentation of him in the major incidents of the play.

The conversation of Canterbury and Ely in the opening scene establishes economically the religious conversion of Henry on the highest authority in the country, Henry's support of the Church as a true Christian monarch, and his desire for guidance from learned churchmen, a procedure warmly recommended to kings by Erasmus, Chelidonius and Hooker. Later Canterbury demolishes the French objections to Henry's claim to the throne of France, and by his authority encourages Henry to undertake a righteous war. The characters of the two prelates have been heavily assailed, but Dover Wilson is surely right in his vindication of their integrity. . . . Moreover, to portray Henry as the dupe of two scheming prelates, or as a crafty politician skilfully concealing his aims with the aid of an un-scrupulous archbishop, is not consistent with claiming at the same time that he is the ideal king; indeed it is destructive of the moral epic purpose of the play.

Yet Henry has been so calumniated. His invasion of France has been stigmatized as pure aggression—though the word is somewhat worn—and Henry himself charged with hypocrisy. Now Henry does not, as Bradley alleges, adjure "the Arch-bishop to satisfy him as to his right to the French throne" [see excerpt above, 1902], he urges that the Archbishop should

> justly and religiously unfold
> Why the law Salic that they have in France
> Or should, or should not, bar us in our claim

and the remaining thirty-two lines of his speech are a most solemn warning to the Archbishop not to

> wrest, or bow your reading,
> Or nicely charge your understanding soul
> With opening titles miscreate, whose right
> Suits not in native colours with the truth.
>
> [I. ii. 10-12, 14-17]

This does not sound like hypocrisy or cynicism. The Arch-bishop discharges his duty faithfully, as it stands his reasoning is impeccable apart from any warrant given by the precedent of Edward III's claims. Henry is not initiating aggression, in fact Shakespeare omits from Exeter's speech in Hall the one argument that has a predatory savour, namely, that the fertility of France makes it a desirable addition to the English crown. (pp. xxii-xxv)

While with some insensitiveness to irony we in this modern age may excuse Henry's invasion of France as arising from his limited medieval horizons, many are less inclined to pardon his rejection of Falstaff. Although Shakespeare's original intention was to portray Falstaff larding the fields of France, no doubt discreetly distant from Henry, he must accept responsibility for the play as it is. If he were prohibited from introducing Falstaff in person into *Henry V*, why was it necessary to mention Falstaff at all? In some slight way it might be regarded as fulfilling the promise in the epilogue of *2 Henry IV* that Falstaff might "die of a sweat" [*2 Henry IV*, Epilogue, 30], or as containing a topical reference to the Oldcastle affairs, or as the best conclusion that could be made to cover the results of official interference; any or all of these might be offered as explanation. Surely the truth lies deeper. The "finer end" that Falstaff made changes the tone of the play, it deepens the emotion; indeed, it probably deepened the tone of the new matter in Act IV. The play gains in epic strength and dignity from Falstaff's death, even as the *Aeneid* gains from Dido's death, not only because both accounts are written from the heart with a beauty and power that have moved men's hearts in after time, but because Dido and Falstaff are sacrifices to a larger morality they both ignore. Some similarities too between Aeneas and Henry may be noted; both neglect their duties for pleasant dalliance; both are recalled to their duty by divine interposition; thenceforth both submit to the Divine Will—it is significant that in *Aeneid*, IV, 393, immediately after Dido's denunciation of him, Aeneas is "pius" for the first time in that book—both display a stoic self-control for which they have been charged with coldness and callousness.

Falstaff has given us medicines to make us love him, he has bewitched us with his company just as Dido bewitched the imagination of the Middle Ages. We have considered him at once too lightly and too seriously: too seriously in that we hold him in the balance against Henry and England, and too lightly in that as a corrupt flatterer he stands for the overthrow of the divinely ordained political order. Erasmus expresses the opinion of the age when he reserves his severest censures for those flatterers who corrupt a prince, the most precious possession a country has . . . , and whom he would punish with death. Falstaff is such a one. If Henry's conversion and acceptance of God's will mean anything at all, they must be viewed in the light of the period to see Henry's full stature, even as a reconsideration of Virgil's religion enlarges and dignifies the character of Aeneas. The medieval habit of mind did not disappear with the Renaissance and Copernicus, on the contrary it is no longer a paradox that the Renaissance was the most medieval thing the Middle Ages produced. For both Middle

Ages and Renaissance religion was planned, logical and integrated with everyday life, not as it is for many of their descendants a sentimental impulse to an occasional charity. So while a place may have been found for Falstaff with his crew of disreputable followers with Henry's army, there could be no room for him in Henry's tent on the eve of Agincourt. (pp. xxvi-xxvii)

It is in Act IV that we see the full picture of Henry as the heroic leader. The devotion and enthusiasm he inspires indeed begin earlier, before he set foot in France. His personality has united England as never before . . . , and already "the youth of England are on fire" eager to follow the "mirror of all Christian kings" [Chorus, II, 1, 6]. (p. xxviii)

Nobleman and common soldier alike are inspired by Henry's gay and gallant spirits. Among the English nobles there is a courteous loyalty to each other quite unlike the sparrow squabbling of the French nobles, their preoccupation with vain boasting and their lack of foresight and order. Salisbury, the "winter lion" of 2 Henry VI, goes "joyfully" into battle, and Westmoreland unwishes five thousand of the men he had previously desired. Henry himself sums up the heart of the matter in the memorable words,

> We few, we happy few, we band of brothers,
> [IV. iii. 60]

words that have come to stand for so much that is English. (p. xxix)

The words are English but the mood is older and universal, it is the note of epic heroism that sounded at Thermopylae, at Maldon, and in a pass by Rouncesvalles.

While Henry infuses courage into his men, he is not without unease of soul. The conversation with Bates, Court and Williams forces him to examine his conscience on his responsibility for those who are to die in the coming battle, and to complain how little his subjects understand the hard duties of a king in their interests. Militarily his position is desperate: his enemy has selected the time and place for battle, his men are heavily outnumbered, tired and weakened by disease and lack of food. His faith in the righteousness of his cause is strained to the uttermost, and in prayer he pleads that his father's sin of usurpation may not be remembered against him. His courage is magnificent, and his extraordinary self-control has not always been acknowledged. He does not unpack his heart and curse like a drab, nor flutter Volscian dovecots, nor unseam his enemies from the nave to the chaps, he is no tragic warrior hero, he is the epic leader strong and serene, the architect of victory.

For all his self-control he is moved to rage by the treacherous attack on the boys and lackeys in his tents, and, fearing for the safety of his army, gives the harsh order to kill the prisoners. Dover Wilson's comment is valuable:

> The attack is historical; and Fluellen's exclamation, 'Tis expressly against the law of arms, 'tis as arrant a piece of knavery, mark you now, as can be offert!' [IV. vii. 1-3], is in accordance with much contemporary comment on the battle, which shows that the treacherous assault left a deep stain upon the chivalry of France. Thus any lingering doubt about Henry's action is blotted from the minds of even the most squeamish in the audience. . . .

Gower's remark, "the king most worthily hath caused every soldier to cut his prisoner's throat. O! 'tis a gallant king" [IV. vii. 8-10], shows wholehearted approval of Henry's promptness in decision and his resolute determination. The rage of the epic hero leading to the slaughter of the enemy within his power is not without Virgilian precedent (see Aeneid, X and XII).

Exeter's account of the deaths of York and Suffolk also touches Henry to tears. The purpose of the description, for which there is no warrant in any of the sources of the play, seems to have been overlooked. . . . York and Suffolk die in the right epic way, their love "passing the love of women" [2 Samuel, i. 23] is fulfilled in death. The surviving heroes, in epic style, mourn their death at once so fitting, so sadly beautiful, so "pretty and sweet" [IV. vi. 28], a phrase recalling at once that other pair of heroes who "were lovely and pleasant in their lives, and in their death they were not divided" [2 Samuel, i. 23].

The Henry of Act V is to many a disappointment, indeed the whole act, it is suggested, is an anticlimax. Dover Wilson defends it rather unconvincingly as a good mixture, and, following Hudson [see Additional Bibliography], praises Henry's overflowing spirits and frankness in the wooing scene as a convincing picture of the humorous-heroic man in love. This is so, but the truth lies deeper. The Christian prince to complete his virtues must be married. (pp. xxix-xxxi)

This marriage in particular seals the union of two Christian countries with momentous possibilities for Christendom then divided by schism. (p. xxxi)

The Treaty of Troyes saw Henry as the most powerful monarch in Europe, he had built unity by force of arms, by his inspiring military genius, and by the grace of God. He was now the complete Christian monarch, "the mirror of christendom". It is this completion that necessitated Act V, it was not implicit in Agincourt. . . .

If Henry has proved less interesting a man than Richard [II], it is because his problems are mainly external. The virtuous man has no obvious strife within the soul, his faith is simple and direct, he has no frailties to suffer in exposure. It is just this rectitude and uprightness, this stoicism, this unswerving obedience to the Divine Will that links both Aeneas and Henry, and has laid them both open to charges of priggishness and inhumanity. (p. xxxii)

As for the play itself it has been roundly condemned as lacking spiritually significant ideas. This is curious. In hardly any other play of Shakespeare is there such interweaving of themes of the highest value to an Elizabethan. References, explicit and implicit, to "breed", "unity", "honour" (fame), "piety" abound throughout the play. It is noteworthy that the French display degenerate breeding, disunity, dishonour and impiety in waging a "bellum impium" [unholy war] against Henry the rightful inheritor. Shakespeare's description of the evils and devastation of war as having befallen or as likely to befall the French, it should be observed, is part of his insistence that war is God's scourge for securing justice among the nations: defeat and despoiling is the portion of those nations whose cause is unrighteous.

What does seem to have escaped notice is the unfolding of Henry's character. At the outset of the play his virtue after his conversion, complete though it may be, is yet cloistered, it has not sallied forth into the dust and heat. Though he makes decisions, he is dependent on the advice of others, and in spite of his self-control, the treachery of Scroop, his bedfellow, obviously hurts him and he finds it necessary to ease his mind in speech. At Harfleur his speech is an incitement to battle, very skilfully done, but with no deeper note. By Agincourt he no longer seeks advice, he acts, he directs. His physical courage, long since proved on Shrewsbury field [in *1 Henry IV*], is again apparent but not stressed. Shakespeare might have shown the famous combat with Alençon, but he did not; physical prowess in Henry was not at this point the most important quality. It is Henry's spiritual strength, his faith and moral courage which inspire and uphold his whole army. By sheer exaltation and power of spirit he compels his men to achieve the impossible. And this inspired mood does not leave him again, it carries him exuberantly through v. ii. to the union of England and France. No spiritual significance? Surely,

> The gods approve
> The depth, and not the tumult, of the soul.
> [William Wordsworth, *Laodamia*]
> (pp. xxxiii-xxxiv)

*J. H. Walter, in an introduction to "King Henry V" by William Shakespeare, edited by J. H. Walter, 1954. Reprint by Methuen & Co. Ltd., 1962, pp. xi-xlvii.*

### ROY W. BATTENHOUSE  (essay date 1962)

[*Battenhouse is well known for his studies on religion and literature and for his theory that Shakespeare's works embody a specifically Christian world view. In the following excerpt, he labels Henry V a "heroic comedy" or "comic history," claiming that in this work Shakespeare offers a deeply ironical, "double-edged" view of history by simultaneously presenting the king as a glorious national hero and as a man motivated by greed, more concerned with his "public image" than the religious or ethical bases of life. Battenhouse discovers a recurring discrepancy between "shadow" and "substance" in the play; he argues, for example, that the king's morality and piety are not deeply held principles, but mere counterfeits of genuine feeling. He remarks that Canterbury's arguments in favor of Henry's claim to the French throne ironically demonstrate that Edmund Mortimer is the true heir, and he also maintains that the only title Henry succeeds in winning is that of the French king's "son," which he achieves only through marriage and not through any legitimation of his claim. Battenhouse further avers that there is an implicit sense of chicanery in the bawdy exchanges between Katherine and Alice in Act III, Scene iv and a hovering "between suggestions of robbery and rape," claiming that the episode serves as an "epitome of the play itself."*]

H. C. Goddard, in a long and penetrating chapter in *The Meaning of Shakespeare* [see excerpt above, 1951], has developed the thesis that

> through the Choruses, the playwright gives us the popular idea of his hero. In the play, the poet tells the truth about him.

That truth, as Goddard sums it up, is that

> not maliciously and in cold blood but against the grace of his own nature and by insensible degrees, the man who began as Hal and ended as Henry V made himself into something that comes too close for comfort to Machiavelli's ideal prince.

Goddard sees not epic but irony. . . . He believes Shakespeare is quite aware of the analogy between highway robbery in *Henry IV* and imperialism in *Henry V,* and aware that the "unity" it forged was counterfeit, doomed soon to collapse under Henry VI. To these points Allan Gilbert has added a few, in a recent article suggesting that "satire" is interwoven with patriotism in the mixed fabric of the play [see Additional Bibliography]. . . .

It seems to me there is satire, but not of the "cankered-muse" type practiced by Shakespeare's rivals. Rather, Shakespeare's satire is Chaucerian, both gently sympathetic and covertly hilarious. It is grounded in irony; and in this case in an irony which is already present, although probably unwittingly, in the chronicles themselves. As expanded in drama, this irony gives rise to what I prefer to call "heroic comedy," or else "comic history." I see this mood and mode as controlling the entire action of *Henry V,* pervading all its strands and levels. (p. 165)

Now the chroniclers and Shakespeare agree in describing the popular view of Henry. Shakespeare, however, enlivens and punctuates it with [a] deeper insight. . . . It might perhaps be argued that Hall or Holinshed had some inklings of this deeper insight, but in their eulogies deliberately avoided it for safety's sake. That is possible, yet seems hardly likely. In any case, what their eulogies state is the popular portrait; and what I am suggesting is that Shakespeare could accept their statements as true within this framework. Thus when they say that Henry's "life" was "without spot," their words can be read as describing, not Henry's heart or soul, but his public behavior as seen by contemporaries. And when Hall says that Henry was the "apparent lantern in his days," this phrase can be read in the sense in which it would apply equally to Alexander the Great in his days. Further, to call Henry "the mirror of all Christendom" does not prohibit viewing all Christendom as, say, Dante did in *Purgatorio 32,* as a presently tattered realm to be sighed over. If Henry is "the flower of kings past," as Hall asserts, may he not then be the flower of Richard II's deceptive piety and of Henry IV's cold ambition? And, finally, when Hall says that no emperor ever excelled Henry in "magnanimity," this credits him merely with one of the sub-Christian virtues, the one particularly exalted by the Renaissance. Thus a strictly literal reading of Hall does not require anyone to impute to Henry an authentically Christian *spirit,* or the distinctively Christian virtues. I doubt that Hall or Holinshed saw this fact, yet the details which they recount of Henry's actions . . . imply this limitation quite plainly.

May not Shakespeare, therefore, have undertaken to portray a Henry—and indeed the whole society which he heads—as admittedly illustrious but bounded within the limits of sub-Christian virtue? Within such limits, Shakespeare can add appropriate detail to his sources without risk of contradicting them, so long as whatever behavior he adds does not imply the inner operation of any genuinely Christian motive in the persons portrayed. There can be "glistering semblances of piety" [II. ii. 117], yes. But the heart of the action will suggest no substantial Christianity. Thus reconstructed the history will be double-edged. It will allow some spectators, blinded by a surface patriotism, to admire as their own ideal its particular heroism. But it will permit others to discern, as various modern critics have, an ultimate emptiness in the pageantry, a suspicious fulsomeness in the rhetoric, and a kind of heroism in Henry more suggestive of "a very amiable monster" (Hazlitt's phrase [see excerpt above, 1817]), or of "some handsome spirited horse" (Yeats's phrase [see excerpt above, 1903]), than of a truly human being.

If we will recall that Dante placed Alexander below the min-
otaur in Hell's circle of the violent, we may have a key to
Shakespeare's moral estimate of Henry. For does not Fluellen
patriotically compare Henry to ''Alexander the Pig'' (adding
that this is all one with ''magnanimous'') in a comic scene
invented by Shakespeare? The pronunciation ''Pig,'' of course,
results from Fluellen's Welsh accent, but Shakespeare is making his own serious jest. Dante, in commenting on Alexander,
had cried out:

> O blind cupidity both wicked and foolish, which
> so incites us in the short life, and then, in the
> eternal, steeps us so bitterly.

Shakespeare, I think, saw this cupidity in Henry's career, as
an underside to the portrait drawn by the Tudor chronicles.
Without directly stating this judgment, he implies it repeatedly.
For example, he shows Henry invoking Alexander's name at
Harfleur, in a speech urging the English to fight like tigers and
pursue their game like greyhounds. And at the play's very
beginning, the Prologue speaks of crouching hounds and of
proud horses' hoofs, of a ''cockpit'' and of ''upreared and
abutting fronts.'' War as animal sport, clearly, is a theme in
the play's action. But will not a heroism thus blind to its own
cupidity inevitably have ''contradictions moral and human''
[see excerpt above by D. A. Traversi, 1941] inherent in it?

To achieve his purpose, Shakespeare has invoked a complex
dramatic structure. In his main characters he has delineated a
worldly professionalism, which continually confesses itself in
ironic evasions. Then, at a secondary level, he has invented
characters such as Fluellen and Macmorris, who by speaking
wiser than they know serve to reveal flaws in their leaders.
And finally, at the level of Pistol and company, he has provided
antic clowning which parodies the main action of the play.
Although epic and farce are technically polar opposites, Shakespeare by intertwining them has been able to write a history
which is also heroic comedy.

It is important to recognize that the chronicles themselves,
despite their high tone of eulogy, provide a basis for irony in
the very facts they report. There are ominous undertones, for
example, in Holinshed's details describing Henry IV's passing.
We are told how the son overhastily claimed the crown as his
''right,'' grasping for it on superficial evidence, careless of
the deeper truth of the situation. May not this action be symptomatic—of the way he will later grasp for the French crown?
(pp. 167-69)

Can Henry V's reign be different from his father's? The details
with which Holinshed ushers it in do not hint so:

> He was crowned the ninth of April being Pas-
> sion sundaie, which was a sore, ruggie, and
> tempestuous day, with wind, snow, and sleet;
> that men greatlie marvelled thereat, making di-
> verse interpretations what the same might sig-
> nifie. But this king even at first appointing with
> himselfe, to shew that in his person princelie
> honors should change public manners, he de-
> termined to put upon him the shape of a new
> man. For whereas aforetime he had made him-
> selfe a companion unto misrulie mates of dis-
> solute order and life, he now banished them all
> from his presence. . . .

Here what most critics have noted and applauded is Henry's
change in public manners. But does that differentiate him in

any way from his father? Rather, it marks a move toward
duplicating the father's kind of excellence. He will henceforth
put on the manners of respectability—the ''shape'' of a new
man. Not necessarily, however, the ''new man'' which Scrip-
ture recommends. There lies the significant irony, overlooked
by many readers of Holinshed and perhaps by Holinshed himself. But Shakespeare could have, and I think did, recognize
it. Surely he knew that the ''new man'' of which St. Paul
speaks is achieved not by putting on ''princelie honors'' but
by counting them as nothing; not by reshaping one's public
image but by being renewed in ''the spirit of the mind''; not
by banishing misruly companions but by suffering for them
and among them. Hence, the ''new man'' which Holinshed
has described is nothing new at all but simply old Henry *re-
divivus*. And like his father, young Henry is dedicating himself
to a counterfeit morality rather than a true morality, ignoring
duty's substance for duty's shadow. (pp. 170-71)

His launching of a quarrel with France, as Shakespeare presents
it, is managed with such an adroit show of ''right'' and of
''conscience'' that no one within the world of the play seems
to recognize the counterfeit of justice that is being fabricated.
By the end of Act I, Henry's ''well-hallowed cause'' [I. ii.
293] has taken on the color of a crusade, led by a ''Christian''
who goes forth ''by God's grace'' [I. ii. 262] and in His name—
to play a set of tennis for the rule or ruin of France! Surely
old Henry IV could have dreamt nothing finer. The magic of
it all is the product not merely of the ''muse of fire'' and
''heaven of invention'' [Prologue, 1, 2] invoked by the play's
Prologue, but also of subtle fires of cupidity and inventions of
piety which Shakespeare allows for in the characters of his
story.

Does his portrait distort Holinshed's facts? Rather, it incorporates them within a fuller context. The archbishop's two-
part argument for the war, so carefully reported in Holinshed,
is given conspicuous prominence. (p. 172)

One wonders how Holinshed, in detailing so carefully the archbishop's oration, could have failed to see its irony. The initial
argument against the Salic law boils down to a single point:
French *usurpers* have never accepted this law as a bar to *their*
kingship, therefore neither can it bar the ''princes of this realm
of England of their right and lawfull inheritance'' (Holinshed).
In strict logic, this must mean: either that the ''lawfull inheritance'' of English princes has no dependence whatever on
French law (which is true, but ruinous to any legal claim to
France), or else that English princes have as their ''lawfull
inheritance'' the task of emulating French usurpers (which turns
out ironically as a fact). . . . Shakespeare plays up the irony
by letting the archbishop play rhetorically on the word ''bar,''
while otherwise the syntax is getting so tangled that no one
can quite follow the logic by which the speaker pirouettes to
his triumphant conclusion.

Then comes the second argument, as overbrief as the first was
overlong. ''The archbishop,'' says Holinshed, ''further alleged
out of the booke of Numbers this saying: 'When a man dieth
without a sonne, let the inheritance descend to his daughter.' ''
That is all. But Shakespeare makes explicit the implied sequitur, when he lets the archbishop leapfrog his logic and
conclude:

> Gracious lord
> Stand for your own, unwind your bloody flag,
> Look back into your mighty ancestors. . . .
>                                        [I. ii. 100-02]

and invoke the "warlike spirit" of the Black Prince! The Black Prince, in such a context, becomes a veritable Prince of Darkness; and the archbishop's serpentine unreason goes beautifully with his golden rhetoric. (pp. 173-74)

And there is a deeper irony. In strict logic, if the "let descend" of *Numbers* is read as *must* descend in civil law, would it not justify first of all (as Goddard notes . . .), not Henry's antiquated claim to France, but rather Edmund Mortimer's claim to the English crown Henry now wears? To insist on inheritance through the female is to undermine Henry's own present position. Blindly, Henry does not see this. Nor apparently does Holinshed. Yet Holinshed mentions a parallel case in his reference, a page later, to the living wife of the Earl of Cambridge, a female in the royal line, through whom this Earl hoped to claim the English throne as his wife's "inheritance." This Earl is the very man we see in Act 2 of the play, there executed by Henry on the charge of selling out his country to the French, a charge which hides the Earl's real intention. Hence the huge irony of Act 2: with great show of piety Henry executes his rival—essentially for the treasonably English and all-too-Frenchified dream of inheriting through the female! Thus does the pot call the kettle black. And Henry's accompanying sermon on the "fall of man" [II. ii. 142] is double-edged irony: for it unwittingly describes not only his own moral fall from grace, but also his fall from manliness in yielding to a female ambition.

This episode prepares us for the crowning irony of Act 5. What Henry there achieves, as the reward of all his labors, is merely the title "heir." Henry never becomes "king" of France; and Shakespeare highlights the point by silence as to the lesser honor mentioned by Holinshed, "regent" of France. Henry gets, instead, the title of "son" to the French king (which rather diminishes Henry's former title); and he get this (as both Shakespeare and Holinshed carefully state) by marrying the *living* female Kate, not by reason of any dead great-great-grandmother's claim. In other words, he inherits through the female by marrying her—an appropriate answer, surely, to his demand in 2.4.103 (and in Holinshed) that France deliver up the crown "in the bowels of the Lord," thus taking "mercy on poor souls" for whom war opens the jaws [II. iv. 102, 103-04]. With ironic mercy, Henry's own jaws are fed a bride, while the crown is delivered from his threat and into France's safe keeping. In fact, in a bawdy sense, Kate becomes his "lord," whose bowels may deliver up to him a "French crown." (Her non-virginal status is hinted at in her kissing Henry after saying that "maids" do not [s. d., V. ii. 275].) Hence Kate's importance to Act 5. The marriage negotiations have overtones of a shotgun-marriage, with Henry holding the shotgun; but he ends up with no status other than as consort to the delicately bawdy Kate.

Earlier, according to the prologue to Act 3, Henry "likes not" the French offer of Kate together with some "petty and unprofitable dukedoms" [Chorus, III, 31]. Yet what else but this is he accepting at the play's ending? Is there not dramatic appropriateness, therefore, in opening Act 5 with a scene in which Pistol is made to eat the leek which he likes not? Surely this is a prophecy, through parody, of Henry's fate. (pp. 174-75)

And has not Shakespeare elsewhere, through parody, foreshadowed an overall reading of Henry's expedition to France? At the beginning of Act 2 he shows us Ancient Pistol preparing to carry away Nell Quickly from an intimidated Nym. Let us see if we cannot read Nym as an anticipatory symbol of the French, and in particular of Burgundy. Nym is being robbed

of his "troth-plight," but "when time shall serve there shall be smiles" [II. i. 6]. Why? Because "I dare not fight; but I will wink and hold out mine iron" [II. i. 7-8]. Recall Monsieur Le Fer in 4.4. Recall, also, Burgundy's yielding of Kate to Henry . . .: "I will wink on her to consent, my lord, if you will teach her to know my meaning" [V. ii. 306-07]. Like Nym, the French are ready to play at bragging and at dueling but know also how to yield when the opponent gets the upper hand—for "though patience be a tired mare, yet she will plod" [II. i. 23-4], just as Burgundy plods in the peace negotiations.

"Couple a gorge" [II. i. 71], shouts Pistol, a cry we shall often hear, at times accompanied by a "permafoy" [IV. iv. 37]. Does it not epitomize Henry's tactics? . . . At Agincourt he uses it conspicuously, when having killed one batch of prisoners he threatens to slit the throats of another batch unless the French surrender. "Fearing the sentence of so terrible a decree," says Holinshed, the French yielded "without further delaie." Wisely they might.

For what shall we say of Pistol's second theme, "Base is the slave that pays" [II. i. 96]? It parallels Henry's scorn of demands for ransom. Yet when it comes to making peace Pistol goes beyond Nym's request for "eight shillings," freely offering him a "noble" with "present pay," together with "liquor" and "brotherhood." For "I'll live by Nym, and Nym shall live by me. Is not this just?" [II. i. 110-11]. Let us say it is as just as what Henry offers France in Act 5. For note what is involved in Henry's insisting that France address him as "Notre très cher Henry, Roy d'Angleterre, Héritier de France" [V. ii. 339-40]. Together with "present pay" of homage, France gets a "noble" Henry as *our* Henry. And as for the "brotherhood," let us listen to Henry's words to Kate:

> take me by the hand, and say "Harry of England, I am thine": which word thou shalt no sooner bless mine ear withal, but I will tell thee aloud "England is thine, Ireland is thine, France is thine, and Henry Plantagenet is thine"; who, though I speak it before his face, if he be not fellow with the best king, thou shalt find the best king of good fellows.
>
> [V. ii. 236-43]

Precisely: he remains king of "good fellows," but Kate is being made Queen of all his lands. "Dat is as it shall please de roi mon père," says Kate [V. ii. 247].

Thus the patient fox has outwitted the valorous mastiff. Just so the French had predicted . . . that the "fat brained" English "curs" would "run winking into the mouth of the Russian bear and have their heads crushed" [III. vii. 143-44]. Or, let us recall Nym's warning to Pistol: "I will cut thy throat, one time or another, and *in fair terms;* that is the humour of it" [II. i. 69-70]. Or recall Fluellen's words . . .: "Th'athversary, look you, is digt himself four yard under the countermines" [III. ii. 61-3]. And to cap the humor, there is Henry's own jovial phrase to Kate: "St. Denis be my speed" [V. ii. 183]. Do readers remember St. Denis—the man who was reduced to carrying his severed head in his own hand?

The early scene between Pistol and Nym at Hostess Quickly's is, in fact, a mirror scene with reflections in other directions too. It reflects a light of analogy, for example, on Henry's dealings with Williams. Figuratively, Henry has Williams by the throat when, glove in hand, he claims: "'Twas I indeed thou promised'st to strike. . . . How can thou give me satisfaction?" [IV. viii. 41, 45]. Williams must bow and beseech pardon, whereupon Henry offers "fellow"-ship by extending, not his hand, but a glove full of crowns. In this case, of course, the analogy focuses on a contrast: Williams will have none of Henry's dishonorable "glove" or ransoming gold. Unlike Nym, Williams is no pander to Mistress Quickly, but instead true-plighted to Lady Honor. He is content to seem to lose, knowing himself to be the actual victor morally. Henry's triumph is merely verbal. Symbolically, the king now plainly has a "leek" in his cap, "For I am Welsh, you know . . ." [IV. vii. 105]. As a St. Davy he is no less ironic here than as a St. Denis later.

But the "mirror scene" of 2.1 looks in still another direction—backward, on the events of Act 1. Perhaps we should have carried through this analogy first, since it is the most immediate. Nym resembles Canterbury who, when Henry's gloved hand had threatened his throat, yielded gracefully. Also like Nym, Canterbury in due time outwits Pistol-Harry. For he maneuvers him into handing over to the prelates the office of magistrates in England during his absence. In a sense, then, there is truth in Henry's later boast at Agincourt: "It yearns me not if men my garments wear; such outward things dwell not in my desires" [IV. iii. 26-7]. Not Henry but the bishops have secured the garments of his authority within England, while Henry has carried off merely the "honor" he so sinfully covets [IV. iii. 28]—in this case, the honor of Mistress Sanctity, the church's hostess, whom the bishops have prostituted to their temporal gain.

The way in which Henry continues to prostitute sanctity can easily be seen at Agincourt. What "fellowship," for example, can Saints Crispin and Crispianus have with the work Henry is about? These brothers were humble shoemakers. They were martyred by Diocletian—perhaps because Diocletian did not like their efforts to shoe public actions with a "good" justice (obeying St. Paul's "feet shod with the preparation of the gospel of peace"). In William Shakespeare's play, the efforts of Williams are similarly unwelcome to Henry. For Henry has his own sense of what is fit and right: War is God's beadle. Or let the Irish Macmorris speak for Henry: "The trumpet call us to the breach; and we talk, and, by Chrish, *do* nothing: . . . It is a shame, by my hand; and there is throats to be cut and works to be done" [III. ii. 108-09, 111-12]. (pp. 176-78)

Shakespeare sees also, as Holinshed apparently does not, the ironic connection between Henry's murdering of the prisoners and his pious eagerness, immediately afterwards, to give God's "arm" the whole credit for the victory. "To thine arm alone, ascribe we all" [IV. viii. 107-08], says Shakespeare's Henry—and, in the next breath, proclaims a penalty of "death" on any soldier who boasts of a share in the victory. (p. 178)

We have critics, nevertheless, who wax enthusiastic over Henry's piety at Agincourt. Commenting on Henry's line, "How thou pleasest, God, dispose the day," Dover Wilson writes . . . : "It is a statement of the ultimate heroic faith, a faith which, like that of the martyrs, puts him who holds it beyond reach of mortal man" [see excerpt above, 1947]. Perhaps so. But just how like is it, really? As like as shadow to substance, is what Shakespeare's irony tells us. His drama makes plain whose arm disposed of the prisoners and also who disposed the French to yield.

By now my reader will scarcely need the help of a commentator on Henry's famous prayer before Agincourt. Its opening line, "O God of battles steel my soldiers' hearts" [IV. i. 289], distorts both God's nature (which is not *of* battles but *above*

them) and His work (which is to soften by grace, not to steel). Henry's petition is Turkish piety, in the spirit of an Amurath (despite *2 Henry IV* [V. ii. 48]). Moreover, what should be mentioned first in any Christian prayer—namely, penitence—comes at the tag-end of Henry's, and in the weasel form of "imploring pardon," not mercy. In this context his confession that "all that I can do is nothing worth" [IV. i. 303] is ironically correct. For all that he has been able to do is to boast of his philanthropies—exactly like the Pharisee in the biblical parable. And instead of "God be merciful to *me*, a sinner," there is the almost farcical plea that God *not think* on "my *father's* fault"—"Not today, O Lord, oh, not today" [IV. i. 292-93]. Only the pre-established rhythm of the blank verse hides the inner rhythm of blank panic.

Henry's language gives him away at other times too. Only once, and then as an insinuation from under disguise, does he term the war just—in the phrase "his cause being just" [IV. i. 127-28]. Williams at once moves toward the heart of this matter, only to be shuffled off by the king's evasive sermon in another direction. Holinshed had put the words "our just cause" and "our just quarrel" squarely into Henry's mouth at Agincourt. Shakespeare is a better psychologist; he understands the evasions of a guilty conscience. Also he knows its proneness to inadvertent self-revelation. Note, for example, Henry's reply to the French ambassadors:

> We never valued this poor seat of England;
> And therefore, loving hence, did give ourself
> To barbarous licence.
>
> [I. ii. 269-71]

Or notice, at Harfleur, his threatening of "infants" in the name of *"Herod's* bloody-hunting slaughtermen" [III. iii. 41]. Or at Agincourt, his threatening of the French with stones "from the old *Assyrian* slings" [IV. vii. 62]. Such allusions speak loud, louder than the direct "We are no tyrant but a Christian king" of Act 1. The same Henry who orders Bardolph hanged for stealing a "pax of little price" [III. vi. 45] will later swear, "by the mass," that his soldiers' hearts are in trim to steal French "new coats" [IV. iii. 115, 118]. Ah, yes, the new "coat." By the mass, that's what will make the New Man of St. Paul's teaching!

The comic language lesson in 3.4, located at a central point in the play's structure, is also pivotal for interpretation. Shakespeare does not waste scenes of farce; he makes them carry theme as well as immediate entertainment. Here the scene is placed between, on the one hand, Henry's "impious war" over Harfleur, replete with imagery of rape, and, on the other hand, a scene in which the French speak with bawdy innuendo of the "barbarous" English. What kind of "language," then, do the English speak? Katherine is about to find out. She discovers a body-language which amazes her, yet arouses her desire to repeat the lesson "une autre fois" [III. iv. 57].

The words Katherine asks about have an order suggestive of a progress in love-making, though devoid of any words for heart or soul. Beginning with attention to the hand, the focus of interest moves up the arm to the neck and chin (as if for a stolen kiss) and then downward to what we may call fundamental matters, adequately deciphered by Katherine's broad wit. Quite well enough she understands that the English tongue is bent on "sin" and, in the end, on things too naughty to mention in polite society. The wordplay of the dialogue, as if in epitome of the play itself, hovers between suggestions of robbery and rape. The connotations on this level prepare us for the later love-scene in Act 5, where Katherine professes to "understand well" when Henry talks of desiring to "possess" her by winning at "Leap-frogge" and getting her by "scambling." In that scene his request that she "mock me mercifully . . . because I love thee cruelly" [V. ii. 201-03] is as truly fulfilled as is the cruelty of his love. Indeed his proper match is Kate, who as Burgundy suggests is "well summered and warm" to "endure *hand*ling" [V. ii. 307-08, 310].

But besides overtones of bawdy in the language lesson, the fact that it starts out with vocabulary for the "hand" and its parts is itself significant. At Harfleur, let us recall, Henry has pictured his English army as a "blind and bloody soldier with foul hand" [III. iii. 34]; and one of his captains, Macmorris, goes around swearing characteristically "by my hand." Moreover, an undertone of legerdemain has been noticeable in the play from its beginning; and at the end we will overhear Henry's comic surrogate, Pistol, resolving to turn bawd and "something lean to cutpurse of quick hand" [V. i. 86]. Thus "hand" has a primary importance in understanding the English order of values. In the outreach of the hand's parts and powers may we not see delineated the ethos of Henry and his fellows? Katherine's lesson, through its farce, implies and plays on this truth. She is shown learning about (the) English, so to speak, from head to toe—which ironically in this case means from the nailed hand to the indecent foot, with nothing worth mentioning above the chin. The vignette is its own commentary. But of the various verbal puns which accompany it, Katherine's associating of the hand's "nails" with English "males" is particularly apt, since it amusingly links English men with claws or a bestial kind of manhood. Moreover, "nails" will be mentioned in a later scene . . . as characteristic of "the roaring devil in the old play" [IV. iv. 71].

Much of what the language lesson has hinted as to the English character we can find openly ascribed to Henry, later, in Pistol's eulogy. Valiant fist, beau-cock habits, and even dirty foot are here praised. In fact, the whole of Pistol's admiring tribute might well be engraved as Henry's epitaph:

> The king's a bawcock, and a heart of gold,
> A lad of life, an imp of Fame,
> Of parents good, of fist most valiant:
> I kiss his dirty shoe, and from heart-string
> I love the lovely bully. . . .
>
> [IV. i. 44-8]

As an imp of fame with a dirty shoe, our Harry-hero's version of John Bull does indeed deserve aesthetic admiration—the more so when *we* understand its marvelous incongruity with Christian heroism. Recognition of the obscene belongs to art's morality. Hence we may say likewise, with Nym: "The king is a good king; but it must be as it may; he passes some humors and careers" [II. i. 125-26].

And of course Henry's opponents in the play come off no better, or no worse. The French are repeatedly characterized as magnificently frivolous, shrewdly pusillanimous, and sinuously bawdy. They call themselves "bastard warriors," and Pistol calls one of them a "damned and luxurious mountain goat" [IV. iv. 19]. Thus the goatish and horsey French balance against the piggish and bullishly barking English. The whole play, in its undertones, is a splendid contest between London gunstones and Paris balls; between Greeks with an Achilles heel and Trojan Paris-lovers (the pun in [II. iv. 132]) with their Nell; between Ares and Aphrodite, between Jove and Europa—all the various aspects of Renaissance paganized Christendom.

Nor is such a spectacle really new within Christendom. The Epistle of St. Peter describes at length certain Christians who, after having known the way of righteousness, slide back into the defilements of the world, uttering "great and swelling words of vanity," and whose "last state is become worse than the first." In fact, St. Peter has an indelicate proverb for this: "The dog is returned to his own vomit again, and the sow that was washed to her own wallowing in the mire" *(2 Peter,* 2.22). Shakespeare tucks this proverb (in French) in the middle of his play . . . , with the added comment, "thou makest use of any thing" [III. vii. 64-6]. Could it be the play's motto?

Shakespeare's prologue to Act 4, provided we know how to read it, states well enough his dramatic purpose. The drama's pitiful and ridiculous "foils," says the Chorus, are "mockeries" by means of which we are invited to discern truth:

> And so our scene must to the battle fly;
> Where, O for pity! we shall much disgrace
> With four or five most ragged foils,
> Right ill-disposed to brawl ridiculous,
> The name of Agincourt. Yet sit and see
> Minding true things by what their mock'ries be.
>
> [Chorus, IV, 48-53]

Pity for the human imagination's mockeries of heroism and of grace: such is the Christian playwright's request of us as we read with him the history of Agincourt. A pitiful history of "foiled" cupidity is the comic theme. Or, ironically stated, the theme is: How to put off the old man and put on the New. The recipe for this is an heroic comedy. (pp. 178-82)

> *Roy W. Battenhouse, "'Henry V' as Heroic Comedy," in* Essays on Shakespeare and Elizabethan Drama in Honor of Hardin Craig, *edited by Richard Hosley, University of Missouri Press, 1962, pp. 163-82.*

## ROSE A. ZIMBARDO  (essay date 1964)

[*Zimbardo contends that "*Henry V *is a study in order and harmony; it does not record, but rather it celebrates the victory of form over disorder and chaos." The king is Shakespeare's perfect monarch, she argues, for he has achieved control over his own potentially disruptive emotions and over opposing forces in his state, so that his realm now reflects the cosmic "harmonious operation of parts in an ordered whole." Zimbardo also remarks on the ways in which the formality of Henry's rhetoric and the static design of the play—partly a result of the Chorus—underscore the theme of order and harmony.*]

*Henry V* is an almost perfect realization of meaning in form. Its thematic essence is to be found in the formalism of its style and architecture. In movement the play resembles a stately, ceremonial dance, each figure of which calls to life a different aspect of the hero's excellence. These figures, each retaining a degree of independence, each preserving its own boundaries, move in measured order to complete the design of the whole. The effect is of a universal harmony wherein each planet, exactly placed, has its proper movement and function. The thematic relevance of such a structure is obvious: the ideal king embodies in himself and projects upon his state the ideal metaphysical order. A harmonious operation of parts in an ordered whole is the design of the cosmos, of the state, of the perfect king,

> For government, though high and low and lower
> Put into parts, doth keep in one consent
> Congreeing in a full and natural close,
> Like music.
>
> [I. ii. 180-83]

And, as the object of art is to imitate such ideal forms as "nature often erring yet shewes she would faine make" [Philip Sidney, in his *Arcadia*], this is the design too of the imitative rhetorical construct, the play itself.

The first figure lays the groundwork for the whole. . . . Henry's recourse to religious authority to test the justice of his cause, his careful blend of wisdom, courage and temperance in exercising power, and the nice balance in his character of reason with passion outline the cosmic architecture of ideal kingship. The ideal kingdom realizes the kingdom of God on earth; the ideal king is the instrument and his own soul the medium through which that realization takes place. There is a confluence here of three planes of existence, the metaphysical, the political and the moral. In the world this can occur only when nature is tempered by an ordered formalism. Henry defines the relation of his office to his nature in terms of temperance.

> We are no tyrant [i.e., self-willed] but a Christian king
>     [i.e., God-willed]
> Unto whose grace our passion is as subject
> As is our wretches fett'red in our persons.
>
> > [I. ii. 241-43]

The interrelation of Christianity, kingship and personal morality is ordered and ordering.

Each of the succeeding figures displays in detail a facet of the kingly perfection outlined in the first. The second figure shows Henry's achievement in government of a golden mean between justice and clemency. The third measures the extent to which even his heroic valor is controlled by his perfect understanding of himself and his office (we might contrast here the irregular, Herculean heroism of Hotspur wherein the lust for glory overrules judgment). The last figure shows at once the simplicity and self-control of the hero in love.

The trappings of war that deck the play function as ornament, heroic conceit. There is no warlike clamor in the play; there is indeed no motion at all that is not controlled and measured. No moral tension is created by the war, for one knows from the beginning that God is with Henry. One knows before the battle that the English will win and would be no less confident had he never heard of Agincourt. Even the conspiracy, so quietly discovered and handled, on Henry's part with control and on the conspirators' with an almost grateful admission of guilt, creates no impression of faction. The army is displayed only that the comparison may be struck between its harmonious order and the disorder of the French army. The characters in the scene are types; like all the characters in the play they have no existence in themselves but serve only to illustrate some grace of Henry's. For example, the captains in Henry's army, Jamy, the Scot, Macmorris, the Irishman and Fluellen, the Welshman, are by design exaggerated almost into music-hall types. Their function is to illustrate the *concors discordia* [harmonious discord] which the ideal king makes of his state, and which is comparable to the *concors discordia* of the natural universe under God.

The battle is over before it has begun. There is no presentation here, as there is, for example, in *Henry IV*, of actual fighting. The only battle scene, in which the dying York kisses the dead Suffolk, is a conceit, an emblem of heroic conduct that invests the war with courtly formality. Yet even this scene does not occur before our eyes, but is related as action past. Shakespeare uses this device throughout the play. The chorus, for instance, in addition to bridging gaps in time and place and enlarging the scene to epic proportion, also translates action into de-

*Act III. Scene iii. Henry V, Exeter, and others. By Richard Westall.*

scription; movement related becomes static. The effect, however, is not of lifelessness but of motion arrested. We envision the English sailing to France, or the camp on the eve of battle as we see a huge canvas, all at once and with the figures caught, frozen in the middle of action. That they are as figures in a tapestry, almost moving yet still, enhances the formality of the scene.

Just as action is fitted to the careful, measured order of the design, so is style. In Henry's speech reviling the treason of Lord Scroop there is not the slightest suggestion of personal anger. Henry's emotions are not his own but are in the control of an order larger than his limited human self. That his emotion is enlarged and controlled is manifested in the formality of his rhetoric:

> . . . Show me men dutiful?
> Why, so did'st thou. Seem they grave and learned?
> Why, so did'st thou. Come they of noble family?
> Why, so did'st thou. Seem they religious?
> Why, so did'st thou. . . .
>
> > [II. ii. 127-31]

The stylistic devices—rhetorical question, repetition, parison, paramoron, symmetry—might have come straight from a Renaissance book of rhetoric. They are purposely exaggerated to emphasize the control of passion by an ordered, ordering judgment in the character of the king. The speech of the ideal king, like every other of his attributes is measured and controlled. At every juncture in the play where action or passion might threaten to disturb measured order, the agitating force is brought under control by a highly formal rhetorical style. Henry's exhortation to the troops (''Once more into the breach . . .'' etc. [III. i. 1ff.]), for example, arrests and formalizes movement. His challenge to the governor of Harfleur . . . is framed in such exaggerated rhetoric that it becomes Senecan—i.e., horrible subject matter is rendered as still as statuary by stylistic formality.

> [He] bids you, in the bowels of the Lord
> Deliver up the crown and to take mercy
> On the poor souls for whom this hungry war
> Opens his vasty jaws and on your head
> Turning the widow's tears, the orphan's cries
> The dead men's blood, the pining maidens' groans
> For husbands, fathers and betrothed lovers
> That shall be swallow'd in this controversy.
> This is his claim, his threatening, and my message.
>
> [II. iv. 102-10]

Here the formal measure achieved in such devices as balance, the use of triplets (''husbands,'' ''fathers,'' ''lovers,'' ''claim,'' ''threatening,'' ''message''), and paramoron is enhanced by elevation and conventionality of diction (''vasty jaws,'' ''bowels of the Lord,'' ''widow's tears,'' ''dead men's blood,'' ''pining maidens''). The threat has nothing of passion in it. It cannot be mistaken for the personal threat of Henry or a reflection of his own feelings or desires, because its formalism marks it as part of a controlling order of which Henry himself is merely the instrument.

When we have recognized that formalism is at once the structure, style and meaning of the play, the relation of Act V to the whole becomes apparent. The tone of the last figure is quite different from that of the others, but since each episode in some measure retains its independence, the shift in mood does not disturb, but rather completes the whole design. One cannot ignore Johnson's objection [see excerpt above, 1765] that Act V presents a break in the character of Henry, that here Shakespeare invests his hero with the very social awkwardness that he had so effectively ridiculed in Hotspur. How could a prince who once did ''Shine so brisk, and smell so sweet / And talk so like a waiting gentlewoman'' [1 Henry IV, I. iii. 54-5] grow into such a cloddish king? What would be a flaw in character development in a linear scheme, however, is perfectly consistent with the design of this play. The point to be considered is that character development has no place in such a design. Henry's character is fully developed when the play begins; the object here is to explore the operation of that character, to reveal the nature of its harmony and the harmony which grows out of it to control the state. For the sake of setting another balance for creating still another reconciliation of opposites, Shakespeare chooses here to make Henry a blunt English soldier, that he may the better contrast with the sprightly, Gallic Katherine. It is true that to do this he had to sacrifice altogether the facile, witty Hal, but he had made that sacrifice long ago. The function of Act V, as of the rest of the play, is to exhibit harmonious order, the reconciliation of contrasting elements that would be opposing forces were they not brought into harmony by formalism. In the exchanges between Henry and Katherine the courtly dance shows a lighter side, but it remains nonetheless courtly and still a part of the stately, ceremonial whole.

Considering the play itself, then, we find it to be a system of contrasts and balances that are brought into order by stylistic and structural formalism. When we consider it in relation to the rest of the tetralogy it assumes still greater significance. Once again a contrast is being struck—here between Richard II and Henry V. In Richard II order was torn down not by Bolingbroke, who was merely an instrument, but by Richard himself, for it is Richard who is ultimately responsible for his deposition. In Henry V order is restored and again the king alone is responsible. (pp. 16-21)

Henry V has from the beginning been aware that a virtuous king must be a virtuous man. So much is he the superior of his father that he has recognized his sins and vowed to reform them at the time when his father is merely urging that he put a good appearance on his behavior. His development in the Henry IV plays is a progress toward the attainment of virtue; before the beginning of Henry V he has reached his goal.

> Consideration like an angel came
> And whipped the offending Adam out of him
> Leaving his body as a paradise.
>
> [I. i. 28-30]

He has whipped sin out of his body in preparation for the sacrament of kingship. This does not, as Traversi maintains [see excerpt above, 1941], make him less human, unless we equate humanity with sin. So human is Henry that his achievement of virtue has cost him great pain and sacrifice. He knows by experience what it is to be king, ''what infinite heartsease/ Must kings reject that private men enjoy'' [IV. i. 236-37]. He knows too that mere ceremony would be an empty reward for such sacrifice. The only real reward of the true king is the harmony of self and state within the all-embracing harmony of God's order. Rather than lapsing, as Richard does, into the excuse of being human, Henry screws his humanity to the highest pitch of virtue to realize the perfection that ''king'' implies.

The critics argue that Falstaff dies because he has no place in the new order and that his death makes the final accusation of Henry's and the play's inhumanity. It is true that Falstaff (whose character is derived from the carnival figure The Lord of Misrule) has no place in the new order. But he is allowed to die only after his character has degenerated to the lowest ebb of venery and mean parasitism. Falstaff is one's warm, lively, much-loved self, but the path of self-indulgence can lead ultimately only to meanness and death. His death (which, significantly, does not ''happen'' but is merely reported) can be pathetic in this play because its necessity has been established before the play begins. Falstaff is the old Adam who has had to be whipped out before Prince Hal could become King Henry. In this play he is a memory, just as Henry's recollection of his father's guilt is a memory. Both recall the struggle that had to be undergone that right order might be achieved.

Henry V is a study in order and harmony; it does not record, but rather it celebrates the victory of form over disorder and chaos. As form governs every attribute of the king, so does it every aspect of the play that celebrates him—structure, characterization, style. Finally, it reaches beyond the limits of the play to invest the tetralogy with new meaning and to draw the circle closed. (pp. 22-3)

*Rose A. Zimbardo, ''The Formalism of 'Henry V','' in* Shakespeare Encomium, *edited by Anne Paolucci, The City College, 1964, pp. 16-24.*

## PETER G. PHIALAS  (essay date 1965)

[*Phialas views the nature of kingship and the ideal relation between a ruler and his subjects as the central thematic interests in* Henry V. *In* 1 *and* 2 Henry IV, *he contends, Prince Hal struggled to achieve a balance between "the demands of the public function" of a monarch and his right as a human being to express personal feelings, but he does not fully accomplish this reconciliation until the close of* Henry V. *Although Phialas acknowledges that Henry's human qualities are less in evidence than his bravery, firmness of intent, and impersonal dispensation of justice, he notes several instances where the king exhibits clemency, understanding, and mental anguish, and he maintains that in Act IV, Scene i Henry recognizes the common humanity he shares with Williams and Bates. This scene also demonstrates, Phialas claims, the right relation between king and subject and, through Henry's inability to fully assuage the discontent of his soldiers, Shakespeare's "tragic concept of kingship."*]

Some years ago Granville-Barker pointed to what many critics before and since have considered the most serious failure of *Henry V* [see excerpt above, 1933]. "For behind the action," he wrote, "be the play farce or tragedy, there must be some dramatically significant and fruitful idea, or it will hang lifeless. And this is what is lacking in *Henry V*." In serious drama this significant and fruitful idea is generally expressed in conflict, a struggle within the chief character or characters or between men or groups of men. And whereas the dramatization of a struggle between men or groups of men is not extraordinarily difficult, that of the conflict within an individual most assuredly is; and it is particularly so in a play like *Henry V* where such inner conflict must be represented in a plot concerned in the main with overt military action. Another reason contributing to this difficulty is the fact that the conflict within Henry is dramatized in three plays instead of one (for although *Henry V* and the two parts of *Henry IV* may be seen as independent artistic creations, in terms of theme and character they are bound together with the closest ties). For these reasons it is not surprising that the representation of conflict in the chief character is stretched somewhat long and thin and may thus be all too easily underestimated. On the other hand the same conflict is shown briefly in other characters of the tetralogy, in Richard, Gaunt, Bolingbroke, and York, and to some extent in Northumberland. And it is also the chief conflict in Shakespeare's Roman plays.

In terms of character, the most significant idea dramatized in Shakespeare's political plays is that success in public life depends on the ability to reconcile the demands of the public function with the claims of the individual life. It is this opposition of the two claims which forms the inner conflict of the second tetralogy, a conflict successfully resolved . . . only by Henry V. (pp. 158-59)

What a successful king must achieve is a balance, and Henry V does indeed achieve it but not in the *Henry IV* plays although it is forecast there. That balance begins to emerge in full in the early scenes of *Henry V*, particularly those leading to the invasion of France, during the battles there, and later still in the king's wooing of Katherine, so that only then can Henry be truly called "this star of England" [Epilogue, 6]. (pp. 165-66)

Prince Hal's response to the claims of royalty, his implicit search for balance, though moving forward, falls into occasional lapses from which it is wrenched by the shock of external events. Two such events, one in each of the *Henry IV* plays, stand out: the threat to the crown by reason of Hotspur's rebellion in part one and the king's illness and death in part two. The Prince's actions in response to these are the slaying of Hotspur and the rejection of Falstaff: in the one he saves the crown and the king's life and in the other he rejects vanity in favor of justice. . . .

No amount of ingenious defense of the king's treatment of Falstaff will satisfy those who fail to see that Henry's casting away of his old companion is an aspect of the tragic conception of royalty. Critics have gone to extraordinary pains to point out that Shakespeare prepares us for the rejection of Falstaff: he shows the gradual estrangement, the moral and physical deterioration of the old knight, particularly in the second part of *Henry IV;* and even a physical separation ordered by the king. All this helps us see that the rejection was coming, but it does not convince us that it had to come or that it had to be done in the manner in which the king does it. Even if we are convinced that Falstaff had to be rejected sooner or later, we are made very unhappy by that rejection when it comes. (p. 166)

Shakespeare, no doubt aware of our response to the episode, tries one last means of mollifying us: he announces in the Epilogue that in the next play he intends to "continue the story, with Sir John in it, and make [us] merry with fair Katherine of France; where . . . Falstaff shall die of a sweat" [*2 Henry IV*, Epilogue, 27-9, 30]. And in *Henry V*, though he does not keep his promise, he nevertheless gives us, if not Falstaff himself, at least two scenes about him, the first informing us of his illness and the second of his death. And in the space of four lines the king is at once blamed for Falstaff's illness and absolved of it.

| | |
|---|---|
| Nym. | The king hath run bad humours on the knight; that's the even of it. |
| Pistol. | Nym, thou hast spoke the right. His heart is fracted and corroborate. |
| Nym. | The king is a good king, but it must be as it may. |

[II. i. 121-26]

But of greater force than this comment is the position of the two scenes concerning Falstaff: between them Shakespeare places the unmasking of the traitors by the king shortly before he sails from Southampton. For Henry it is a most painful episode, particularly since one of the conspirators, Lord Scroop, had been his closest associate, a man dutiful, grave and learned, noble, religious, spare in diet, free from passions, constant in spirit, "garnish'd and deck'd in modest complement" [II. ii. 134]. The rehearsal by the king of Scroop's character sounds exaggerated even in a play bursting with superlatives: Scroop had been such a splendid man that the king had worn him in his heart of hearts. But the description of the traitor not only indicates the basis on which the youthful king had entrusted Scroop with high responsibility but also emphasizes those elements of character and temperament which Falstaff most obviously lacks. And so the description of Lord Scroop, his treason and execution, throw a significant light upon the king's relationship with Falstaff. And far more important Henry's words of judgment to Scroop show that the king is not the ruthless Machiavellian that some critics take him to be. He has no choice in the rejection of Falstaff or the execution of the traitor, but it does not follow that Henry fails to experience real pain in passing judgment upon those two. Both actions on the king's part are made to underscore the tragic element in Shakespeare's—and King Henry's—conception of the royal dilemma. That element resides . . . in the conflict between the impersonal necessities of the king's public function and the multiple needs of Henry the man. We, of course, demand that he be firm, impersonal, just and at the same time humane,

· merciful, understanding; and we insist that he display these qualities at all times and simultaneously. That Henry is capable of discharging effectively his public function with firmness and justice is made very clear in his dealing with the conspirators as well as in his disposing of Falstaff in 2 *Henry IV*. But what of his mercy, his understanding and humaneness? What of those other attitudes or qualities of character which must effect a balance in Henry's discharge of his royal duties? It must be admitted that these are less prominently shown in the plays, but they are nevertheless a most significant part of Shakespeare's conception of Henry, and critics of the king's character must take them into account. (pp. 167-68)

Early in *Henry V* the youthful king speaks of himself as "no tyrant, but a Christian king" [I. ii. 241]. Shortly before unmasking the conspirators at Southampton Henry forgives the drunkard who the day before had reviled him; and though he cannot overlook Lord Scroop's treason, he tells him that he will weep for him. After the surrender of Harfleur, King Henry, contrary to Holinshed's account, commands his subordinates to "use mercy to them all" [III. iii. 54]. And he repeats the order later after Bardolph's arrest and condemnation for stealing a pax: "We would have all such offenders so cut off: and we give express charge that . . . there be nothing compelled from the villages, . . . none of the French upbraided or abused in disdainful language" [III. vi. 107-108, 109-10, 110-11]. Nor is this mercy vitiated at Agincourt by what Holinshed calls Henry's "dolorous decree" to his soldiers to slay their prisoners after the French have regrouped and assaulted the "boys and the luggage." From a military point of view the decree is unavoidable; yet Shakespeare goes to the trouble of explaining and justifying it in the immediately following scene with Gower and Fluellen. And it is made very clear indeed, as Holinshed gives it, that Henry's order to kill the prisoners came *after* the French had slain the boys in the English camp.

> Gower. 'Tis certain there's not a boy left alive . . .
> wherefore the king most worthily hath caused
> every soldier to cut his prisoner's throat.
>
>                                    [IV. vii. 5, 8-10]

And the humorous Fluellen then proceeds to extol the virtues of his king above those of Alexander the Great, climaxing the contrast by pointing out that whereas the intoxicated Macedonian had slain his best friend Cleitus, King Henry "being in his right wits and his good judgments, turned away the fat knight" [IV. vii. 46-8].

These allusions to the king's mercy and wisdom and humaneness are, as we have noted, scattered through the play, but though singly their effect is limited, their cumulative impact attains considerable force. Their function is to keep fresh in our minds the *idea* of the king's humaneness, and to lead up to and support Henry's own exposition of his concept not only of his humanity but also—and because of it—of the tragic dilemma inherent in the role of kingship. And the exposition of that dilemma, that tension between the man with his individual "affects" and the king with his impersonal duties, climaxes the inner action of the climactic fourth play; and it is fittingly presented in the scenes which simultaneously mark the high point of the overt action, the victorious battle of Agincourt.

The Chorus to Act IV gives note of the grave matters at hand and in a generalized statement describes the king's concern with the fearful prospects of the morrow.

> For forth he goes and visits all his host,
> Bids them good-morrow with a modest smile

And calls them brothers, friends and countrymen.

                                    [Chorus, IV, 32-4]

In his own person, the Chorus tells us, the king moves about his army lending courage and comfort, but in the action itself Henry does much more than this. For he is concerned not merely with the dangers of the battle but more gravely with the moral issues which engage him as king and military commander. In this serious mood he declines Erpingham's offer to accompany him, for he wishes to be alone:

> I and my bosom must debate awhile,
> And then I would no other company.
>
>                                    [IV. i. 31-2]

With Erpingham's cloak thrown over his shoulders the king then moves about his army, seeing, overhearing, conversing. First he meets Pistol, with whom he exchanges lines reminiscent of the humour of *Henry IV*: he then overhears Fluellen severely reprimand Gower for not keeping "the true and aunchient prerogatifes and laws of the war" [IV. i. 67-8]. And finally Henry meets Bates, Court, and Williams, with whom he debates the king's responsibility for his soldiers' deaths. The first question is whether the king's cause is "just and his quarrel honourable" [IV. i. 128]: for if it is, the subject's and soldier's duty is to obey and if need be die for his king. But Williams turns to another and for him much more serious matter: that soldiers die unprepared, that as he puts it "there are few die well that die in battle" [IV. i. 141-42], and that for this non-Christian death of his soldiers the king bears sole responsibility. But this notion . . . Henry easily rejects, and in the end Williams admits that "'Tis certain, every man that dies ill, the ill upon his own head: the king is not to answer it" [IV. i. 186-87]. Nothing is said by the king on the justice of his cause: and indeed Bates dutifully avers that that question is "more than we should seek after" [IV. i. 130]. But to the Elizabethan audience the justice of the king's quarrel with France was a matter of course, which the early scenes of the play had sufficiently demonstrated. But though Bates will not pursue that argument, and though the king convinces Williams that every man that dies ill bears his own moral responsibility therefor, their parting with the king is not a happy one; and that discontent is yet another element in the tragic concept of kingship which Shakespeare's political plays dramatize. And Henry's soliloquy "Upon the King" which follows [IV. i. 230ff.], far from being extrinsic to the play (as Professor Tillyard believes [see excerpt above, 1944]), is a most necessary expression of Henry's mature insight into the nature of the crown. The difference between a king and his subjects is his greater care, his neglect of "infinite heart's ease," his suffering of "mortal griefs" [IV. i. 236, 242]. "Great greatness" is only a dream, for the king is but a man whose thrice-gorgeous ceremony can avail him nothing against the ills of common humanity.

>                     No, thou proud dream,
> That play'st so subtly with a king's repose;
> I am a king that find thee. . . .
>
>                                    [IV. i. 257-59]

This is precisely the point: Henry V has made the discovery early in his career as king, long before such characters as Richard II and Lear for instance do in their own. For them the crown had meant privilege, self-indulgence, a special immunity, a false sense of infallibility and omnipotence. Lear learns better too late. (pp. 168-71)

The king's mixing with his men on the eve of battle is Shakespeare's way of emphasizing at once Henry's humanity and the ideal relationship of king and subject. The incident is Shakespeare's own, as there is no record of it in the chronicles, and it is unique in Shakespearean drama. Throughout the episode Henry lays emphasis on his being a man like his soldiers and on his capacity and willingness to see things from their point of view.

> For though I speak it to you, I think the king
> is but a man, as I am: the violet smells to him
> as it doth to me; the element shows to him as
> it doth to me; all his senses have but human
> conditions.
>
> [IV. i. 100-04]

The king, says Henry, is but a man as I am, and the irony of his hidden identity doubles the force of his words. He is, he insists, a king and yet a man like themselves. And on the morrow when Henry tells Williams that it was the king he had abused, Williams retorts: "Your majesty came not like yourself: you appeared to me but as a common man; witness the night, your garments, your lowliness" [IV. viii. 50-2].The allusion to the king's garments and lowliness recalls the very image of Henry in the form and attitude of a common soldier on the eve of battle, and through the allusion the dramatist makes certain that the plain but effective symbolism of the episode is not lost upon us. Furthermore, this concept of the ideal relationship of king and subject is reinforced by Henry in his address to the army a few minutes before the great battle:

> And Crispin Crispian shall ne'er go by,
> From this day to the ending of the world,
> But we in it shall be remembered;
> We few, we happy few, we band of brothers.
> For he today that sheds his blood with me
> Shall be my brother.
>
> [IV. iii. 57-62]

It is a sentiment we would associate with neither Richard II nor Henry IV, and the French on their side offer meaningful contrast when after the battle their humbled herald appeals to the English king for "charitable license" to book and bury their dead:

> To sort our nobles from our common men.
> For many of our princes—woe the while!—
> Lie drown'd and soak'd in mercenary blood;
> So do our vulgar drench their peasant limbs
> In blood of princes.
>
> [IV. vii. 74-8]

Finally Henry's insistence on balancing the king and the man is stressed in the wooing scene, where he tells the fair Katherine that she would find him "such a plain king that thou wouldst think I had sold my farm to buy my crown" [V. ii. 124-26], a man no more adept in the badinage of love than a butcher.

In all these episodes Shakespeare stresses those attributes of royalty which are responsible for Henry's success, for it was not enough to dramatize success itself; what was of even greater significance was to isolate and underscore those aspects of character which make for success in public life. It is true that in *Henry V* Shakespeare paints with strong colors the scenes of Henry's triumphs, but he does much more. The play deals with many matters, not the least of these being the heroism of the diseased and hopelessly outnumbered English in the battle of Agincourt. But that heroism, Shakespeare shows, is the

response to great leadership: the miracle of Agincourt is the symbol of successful governance. For, in spite of Scroop's conspiracy and the soldiers' seeming discontent on the eve of the great battle, the English are devoted to their king, and the dramatist is most careful to reveal the reasons for that devotion and its effects in peace as well as war. That devotion, there can be no doubt, is inspired by the king's character. And this is precisely what Shakespeare found in his chief source. (pp. 171-73)

To the modern reader or critic, determined to find irony in all writing of whatever kind, Holinshed's portrait of Henry, though it may accord with Elizabethan estimates of the King's character, seems uncritical if not downright naive. And on the other hand it must be admitted that Shakespeare enriched and humanized the portrait in part by means of ironic overtones scattered throughout the plays and particularly *Henry V*. Shakespeare's Henry, it is true, is not quite Holinshed's. Nevertheless it is clear that the dramatist accepted and elaborated the chronicler's interpretation of Henry's achievement. Holinshed was convinced that the king's triumphs were due to good fortune but also to a happy balance of certain qualities in him; he was a brave and hardy soldier, a bold and imaginative strategist, a loyal friend, a "seuere iusticer" and at the same time "so humane withall" that he was beloved as well as obeyed by all. In general these are the virtues responsible for the success of Shakespeare's Henry too although the dramatist refuses to reproduce untouched the idealized portrait of the chronicles. But he takes great care to stress the same balance of attitudes in the king's character. His Henry is neither the embodiment of what is noblest in the English temperament nor the ruthless Machiavellian of rival critics. He is rather a king who combines military and political skills with an awareness of the just relationship of ruler and ruled, a man who can bring to a near balance the necessities of his royal vocation and the needs of his personal human relationships. (pp. 173-74)

*Peter G. Phialas, "Shakespeare's 'Henry V' and the Second Tetralogy," in* Studies in Philology, *Vol. LXII, No. 2, April, 1965, pp. 155-75.*

## NORTHROP FRYE (lecture date 1966)

*[Frye is considered one of the most important critics of the twentieth century and a leader of the anthropological or mythic approach to literature which gained prominence during the 1950s. As outlined in his seminal work* An Anatomy of Criticism *(1957), Frye views all literature as ultimately derived from certain myths or archetypes present in all cultures, and he therefore sees literary criticism as an unusual type of science in which the literary critic seeks only to decode the mythic structure inherent in a work of art. Frye's intention was to formulate a method of literary interpretation more universal and exact than that suggested in other critical approaches, such as New Criticism, biographical criticism, or historical criticism—all of which he finds valuable, but also limited in application. The excerpt below is taken from the written version of a lecture Frye delivered, in shortened form, at the University of Toronto in March 1966. He maintains that there are two points of view in* Henry V: *one may be derived from the patriotic, uncritical Chorus, the other from a recognition of Henry as a tragic figure. While the Chorus celebrates Henry's heroic military triumphs and his marriage to Katherine, Frye asserts, the play reveals his coldness to his former companions and the transitoriness of his achievements. The critic describes Henry as "Shakespeare's most complete example of the cyclical movement of the youthful tragic hero," a rare figure nearly exceeding what is natural or regular and destined to die a short time after reaching the apogee of his fortunes. Frye also discusses the folkloric im-*

*plications of the character of Falstaff, viewing him as a "martyred father" in this play; he further remarks that Falstaff's possible function as ironic commentator has been taken instead by "a properly disciplined chorus," whose function is "to put us into as uncritical a frame of mind as possible."*]

A tragic hero may be an older man or a younger man, a paternal or a filial figure: the tragedy of order is the typical Shakespearean form of the fall of the older man, and the tragedy of passion the typical Shakespearean form of the fall of the younger one. (p. 50)

Henry V is not a person that one would at first associate with the tragedy of passion, as he has probably less passion than any other major character in Shakespeare. But he is Shakespeare's most complete example of the cyclical movement of the youthful tragic hero, and so establishes the context for the group of passion-tragedies. Of the great conquerors of history, the most famous are Caesar and Alexander. Caesar had consolidated his power and was of mature years at the time of his death, hence his role in tragedy is that of an order-figure who has developed from the favourite of fortune into becoming part of the order of nature, and whose achievement becomes an even greater memory. Alexander died in youth, and his triumphs, dramatically speaking, instantly disappeared: he is the supreme example of the young hero raised by the wheel of fortune to its height and then thrown off. Henry is England's Alexander, the parallel being called to our attention by Fluellen. (p. 51)

If we think of Henry simply as a hero of action, that is, if we take the point of view of the chorus, we shall see him as a prince of the most radiant and triumphant glory. Alexander was much preoccupied with his resemblance to divinity: Henry is not, but several touches in the imagery make him a preternatural figure, a Messiah treading the winepress. . . . [When] he becomes king, according to Canterbury, he becomes an unfallen Adam:

> Consideration like an angel came
> And whipped th' offending Adam out of him,
> Leaving his body as a paradise
> T' envelop and contain celestial spirits.
>
> [I. i. 28-31]

He describes a conspiracy against him . . . in the familiar phrase "a second fall of man" [II. ii. 142], and his conquest of France has apocalyptic overtones. France is twice called the "world's best garden" [V. ii. 36; Epilogue, 7], and its cities turn into a "maid," like the New Jerusalem.

But of course other things are going on too. There is a markedly disapproving emphasis on what amounts to the killing of Falstaff. Fluellen, not a person temperamentally much in sympathy with Falstaff, compares his death to Alexander's murder of Clitus, which, being done in hot blood, under great provocation, and bitterly repented afterward, brings out the coldness of Henry all the more clearly. There is the gradual disappearance of our other old friends, as Bardolph and Nym are hanged and the disgraced and beaten Pistol, his wife dead, goes back to a life of begging and stealing. In a tyranny . . . there is often a sharp focus on a youthful victim: here, where the sense of tyranny is carefully muted and left only to implication, the Boy, whose shrewd comments make him a kind of infant Falstaff, simply vanishes, doubtless murdered by the enemy. The world's best garden, as Burgundy's speech shows, is a ruin, and Henry is appealed to do something about it as soon as it is, as he says, "all mine." But, as we know, he dies at once; the war goes on and on, and the only result of his marriage to

Katharine is Henry VI, the most pitiful creature in all Shakespeare. At the beginning of *Henry VI* La Pucelle says:

> With Henry's death the English circle ends:
> Dispersed are the glories it included.
>
> [*1 Henry VI*, I. ii. 136-37]

And, however many fiends La Pucelle may keep company with, she is dead right. What we see in the play from this point of view is an illustration of the remark in the Epilogue: "Fortune made his sword" [Epilogue, 6]. And Fortune, according to the useful Fluellen, is "painted also with a wheel, to signify to you, which is the moral of it, that she is turning, and inconstant, and mutability, and variation: and her foot, look you, is fixed upon a spherical stone, which rolls, and rolls, and rolls" [III. vi. 32-6]. Even at the beginning of the play we notice some oddly elegiac cadences. The sentimental Canterbury urges Henry to revive the glory of Edward III's time, when the chronicle of England was as full of praise

> As is the ooze and bottom of the sea
> With sunken wrack and sumless treasuries.
>
> [I. ii. 164-65]

The play does not build up to an attitude that we are expected to take, to a view that coincides with whatever Shakespeare "had in mind." Shakespeare is neither the mouth-piece of a jingoistic audience nor an over-subtle ironist. We are quite free to admire Henry or to regard him as detestable. There is plenty of textual evidence for both views, but neither view of him will alter the structure of the history play he is in. And what the structure of a history play says to us is: "This is the essential poetic significance of something that really happened." From the point of view of France, Henry is a rebel-figure, a Tamburlaine or scourge of God who explodes within a weak and demoralized social order and destroys it in a tragedy of blood. In France, Henry is an angel of death, which is what Coriolanus is also described as being to the enemies of Rome, in one of those many passages where the echoes and overtones of a statement sound very different from the context of the statement itself:

> He was a thing of blood, whose every motion
> Was timed with dying cries.
>
> [*Coriolanus*, II. ii. 109-10]

There is no incongruity, even from the French point of view, in Henry's making such a to-do over the legitimacy of his claim to the French throne when his claim to his own was so doubtful. Henry is repeating the legend of his patron St. George, coming over the sea and acquiring the country *de facto* by conquest, and *de jure* by marrying the king's daughter. From the point of view of England, Henry's story is not a tragedy, because it ends in triumph and marriage. But it is one episode of what is, in its totality, a tragic vision, the cycle of nature and of fortune, of which the victims of the passion-tragedies represent other episodes.

In the tragedies of order, it is the function of the nemesis-figure to re-establish a disrupted continuity. The continuity is personal as well as social: Hamlet and Malcolm are the sons of the kings they avenge, and Octavius is a Caesar. In the tragedies of passion there is a conflict between personal and social loyalties. Henry V has no nemesis problem, but when his father dies, he makes the crucial social transition from prince to king, using "prince" here in the sense of heir apparent, someone who is still technically a private citizen, and who can therefore be presented dramatically in a "madcap" role without stirring up the anxieties of censorship. As king, he is confronted with two surviving father-figures. One, the Chief Justice, is the symbol of Henry's new social duties in his Apollo role of sun-king; the other, Falstaff, is the symbol of his old night-time companionship of tavern and highroad. Henry wipes Falstaff out of his life, hence, as it is somewhat disconcerting to observe, the role of the martyred father in *Henry V* is taken by Falstaff, not an order-figure but a disorder-figure, a lord of misrule. In destroying Falstaff, Henry also destroys, along with his sense of humour, an inner tension within society itself, the resistance to what Falstaff calls "old father antic the law" [*1 Henry IV*, I. ii. 61]. This inner tension explodes in a far more sinister form as soon as Henry dies, and becomes, so to speak, a nemesis of misrule. Falstaff's whole being is in his relation to Prince Henry—"Before I knew thee, Hal, I knew nothing," he says [*1 Henry IV*, I. ii. 92-3]—and, as long as the Prince is a madcap, Falstaff is a parasite, a corrupt recruiting sergeant, and something of a brigand. As an attendant on a victorious king, he might well have settled into the role of professional jester, so important as a safety-valve in court life. He is given to drinking and wenching, but so are the jesters of the comedies. As it is, he has the role of rejected commentator on the action of *Henry V*, his place being taken by a properly disciplined chorus. For it is the function of the chorus in *Henry V* . . . to put us into as uncritical a frame of mind as possible. (pp. 52-6)

Northrop Frye, "The Tailors of the Earth: The Tragedy of Passion," in his Fools of Time: Studies in Shakespearean Tragedy, *University of Toronto Press, 1967, pp. 43-74.*

### H. M. RICHMOND (essay date 1967)

[*Richmond argues that* Henry V *traces the king's development from "bellicose exuberance," deceit, and hypocrisy in the early scenes to moderation, responsibility, and humility at the close. As the French expedition is being readied, the critic contends, Henry's attitude closely resembles Hotspur's "intoxicated ambition" in* 1 Henry IV *and he behaves more like "a young man's hero . . . than an ideal king"; however, Richmond continues, in Act IV Henry acquires a clearer perception of himself, achieving as well a deeper understanding of his role as king and the necessity of trusting in divine Providence. Additionally, the critic asserts that Shakespeare characterizes the world of* Henry V *as dark and sinister, particularly in the early scenes, and he notes that "Falstaff's venality appears almost innocent in comparison with the fatal depravity, directly murderous treason, and wholesale destruction" found in the dramatic action of this play.*]

It has not been adequately recognized that Falstaff's absence from *Henry V* makes as distinctive a contribution to its atmosphere as did his presence to *Henry IV*. This is not to say that the later play is thinner than its predecessors by the lack of his comic figure, but rather the reverse: the eclipse of many humane elements in the new king's personality is stressed by the way in which Falstaff's spirit haunts the play's dark texture, providing a necessary norm of reference in our response to Henry's "new" personality.

Henry's resolute harshness is evidenced by new black threads in the weave of the play, alongside the high colors of a few of the figures in its foreground. In view of this *chiaroscuro*, the play proves to be less simply epic than has usually been assumed, and to have somewhat more in common with the anti-epic overtones of *Troilus and Cressida*. In the first part of *Henry IV*, there had been relatively few sinister effects, apart from Worcester's treachery to Hotspur. In the second

part, we have a far more overtly diseased society, with the addition of the prostitute Doll Tearsheet to replace the attractive Lady Percy. In *Henry V*, this pattern of development reaches that harsh extreme that is to give its coloration, intermittently at least, to such plays as *Measure for Measure, King Lear,* and *Timon of Athens,* in which the images of venereal disease continually recur, along lines first crudely sketched by Pistol's acid advice to Nym, his rival for the hand of the Hostess:

> . . . to the spital go,
> And from the powdering-tub of infamy
> Fetch forth the lazar kite of Cressid's kind,
> Doll Tearsheet she by name, and her espouse:
> I have, and I will hold, the quondam Quickly.
>
> [II. i. 74-8]

Later, Pistol also announces:

> News have I, that my Nell is dead i' the spital
> Of malady of France;
> And there my rendezvous is quite cut off.
>
> [V. i. 81-3]

Not only is such English femininity as appears in the play thus shown to be fatally debauched, but the Frenchwomen of the highest rank are shown to conceal a treasonous lust for English virility beneath their affectation of prudery. We may feel that there is simply chivalric exaggeration in the Dauphin's account of the plight of the French nobility, who have been accepting the English invasion passively. He claims:

> By faith and honour,
> Our madams mock at us, and plainly say
> Our mettle is bred out and they will give
> Their bodies to the lust of English youth
> To new-store France with bastard warriors.
>
> [III. v. 27-31]

However, it is not by accident that only a few lines earlier, the French princess, Katherine, has herself been assiduously learning English; and while she pretends disgust at the sexual associations of some of the English words [III. iv. 52-6], this physiological awareness itself unmistakably indicates that she rightly expects, one way or another, to be exposed to the embraces of the English. The later scene of her surrender to Henry's courtship curiously echoes that of the seduction of Lady Anne by Richard III, for the French princess manages to overcome an analogous barrier of loyalty ("Is it possible dat I sould love de enemy of France?" [V. ii. 169-70]) by accepting a specious logic, which Henry shares with Richard:

> No; it is not possible you should love the enemy
> of France, Kate: but in loving me, you should
> love the friend of France; for I love France so
> well that I will not part with a village of it; I
> will have it all mine; and, Kate, when France
> is mine and I am yours, then yours is France
> and you are mine.
>
> [V. ii. 171-76]

This reveals the virtuosity of argument that Hal had learned from Falstaff, in such exchanges as the one in which Falstaff was challenged as to whether the prince owed him a thousand pounds as he had claimed, and replied: "A thousand pound, Hal! a million: thy love is worth a million: thou owest me thy love" [*1 Henry IV*, III. iii. 136-37]. An even more authentic echo of Falstaff occurs when the Boy exclaims at the battle of Harfleur: "Would I were in an alehouse in London! I would give all my fame for a pot of ale and safety" [III. ii. 12-13].

It is typical of the sinister tone of *Henry V* that the Boy and all his youthful fellows are slain by the "chivalric" French in revenge for their defeat at Agincourt by Henry V, "wherefore the king most worthily, hath caused every soldier to cut his prisoner's throat. O, 'tis a gallant king!" [IV. vii. 8-10]. After such an episode one may begin to sympathize with Fluellen's dry scholarly analogies between Henry and the ancient hero whom he clumsily calls "Alexander the Pig" [IV. vii. 13]. (pp. 175-78)

There is at least one other significant scene that reinforces Falstaff's changed role in *Henry V,* a scene in which he appears to illustrate many of the more intimate and less political values that Henry's public role requires him to sacrifice. Even before Falstaff's death, the Hostess has poignantly observed: "The king has killed his heart" [II. i. 88]. And in the moving account of his death, we must note that, through her garbled version of his last words, there appear clear indications that Falstaff died repentant; for Theobald's famous emendation "a' babbled of green fields" [II. iii. 16-17] [see excerpt above, 1726] confirms the impression of a serene death. . . . Henry's repudiation of Falstaff thus appears in the harshest light in *Henry V;* Falstaff's venality appears almost innocent in comparison with the fatal depravity, directly murderous treasons, and wholesale destruction that characterize the latest play in the series. And, while Henry has cast off the person and the outward vices of Falstaff, he has preserved that virtuosity of mind that Falstaff had devoted to the amusement of his friends, but which the king now devotes with terrifying efficiency to coldly political ends, in which it verges on equivocation—if not downright deceit and hypocrisy. (p. 179)

The opening scene of the play, of course, offers the most sententious recognition of the deceptive capacities of the new king, in the conversation between the two bishops:

> The strawberry grows underneath the nettle
> And wholesome berries thrive and ripen best
> Neighbour'd by fruit of baser quality:
> And so the prince obscured his contemplation
> Under the veil of wildness; which, no doubt,
> Grew like the summer grass, fastest by night,
> Unseen, yet crescive in his faculty.
>
> [I. i. 60-6]

The king is thus established from the start of the play as an elusive personality whose nature has defied prediction. Nor is there any reason to think that, with the assumption of regal dignity, he has also sacrificed the capacity for psychological disguise, any more than he has given up the physical deceptions under the cover of which he continues to explore the minds of his compatriots even after his accession.

Perhaps the most frightening illustration of Henry's mastery of psychological deception appears in his handling of the conspiracy to assassinate him. The evil nature of the intended crime of which the three treacherous English nobles have been accused has been carefully presented so as to justify any handling of their case, yet the fact remains that Henry chooses to play cat and mouse with them. He betrays them into unconsciously sentencing themselves mercilessly, by presenting them with the case of a slight misdemeanor committed against his dignity, which he is choosing to forgive. When they protest that in such cases mercy is unwise, he springs his trap on them and condemns them to death out of their own mouths:

> The mercy that was quick in us but late,
> By your own counsel is suppress'd and kill'd.
>
> [II. ii. 79-80]

Later in the play, and much more jestingly, the king is also to lay a little trap for the volatile and self-assured Welshman Fluellen, who will be tricked into a quarrel with Williams; but there the idea is essentially merciful—to save Williams from the dangerous act of striking the king, if he holds to his word and attacks the wearer of the king's favor.

In the case of the three traitors, the issue evolves far more significantly in ways that impugn the character of the king himself, who unconsciously traps himself by his speeches just as had the conspirators. For in his overlong and sententious diatribe against them, Henry marvels at the discrepancy between their conspicuous outward excellence and their unintelligible inward corruption:

> Such and so finely bolted didst thou seem:
> And thus thy fall hath left a kind of blot,
> To mark the full-fraught man and best indued
> With some suspicion. I will weep for thee;
> For this revolt of thine, methinks, is like
> Another fall of man.
>
> [II. ii. 137-42]

If one must thus necessarily regard even the "best indued with some suspicion," then Henry himself must be included in our doubtful scrutiny; and of course his allusion to Adam's fall, and the consequent doctrine of all men's involvement in this original sin, *requires* that Henry be recognized as no more infallible than other examples of English nobility. If Shakespeare regards Henry V as the ideal king, it is clearly not in such pagan epic terms as those that have been favored by his critics: the ruthless conquering hero whom the gods uniformly favor.

It is true that, before Harfleur, Henry sounds like Marlowe's Tamburlaine, utterly callous toward those who persist in opposing him:

> If I begin the battery once again,
> I will not leave the half-achieved Harfleur
> Till in her ashes she lie buried.
> The gates of mercy shall be all shut up,
> And the flesh'd soldier, rough and hard of heart,
> In liberty of bloody hand shall range
> With conscience wide as hell, mowing like grass
> Your fresh-fair virgins and your flowering infants.
>
> [III. iii. 7-14]

This hardly sounds like the Christian king which Henry rather too conscientiously insists that he is at other points in the play. He is probably once again affecting an attitude that he does not really accept, in order to attain by psychological means what he has failed to achieve by physical ones. For even his famous speech inciting his troops to return to the siege: "Once more unto the breach, dear friends . . ." [III. i. 1ff.] has already *failed* to carry his army to victory by mere force of arms. In fact, that very speech had been followed by a parody of it in the low-life terms of Bardolph and his companions [III. ii. 1ff.], and the same scene continues with an embittered debate between the experienced Scottish and Welsh captains about the inadequacy of the siege. (pp. 180-83)

Henry's rhetorical performance before the unconquered Harfleur is likely to be nothing more than another stroke of calculated policy. Yet even this is not the reason for Harfleur's surrender, which results simply from its having received news from the Dauphin that he cannot raise an army to relieve it [III. iii. 44-50]. Neither Henry's bravery nor his rhetoric is therefore the immediate cause of the town's surrender, and it is a chastened Henry who graciously accepts it:

> Open your gates. Come, uncle Exeter,
> Go you and enter Harfleur; there remain,
> And fortify it strongly 'gainst the French:
> Use mercy to them all. For us, dear uncle,
> The winter coming on and sickness growing
> Upon our soldiers, we will retire to Calais.
>
> [III. iii. 51-8]

The expedition has proven to be a success, but a precarious one from the very start; its ill-omened conspiracy had shown how necessary the distraction of foreign war still is for the preservation of Henry's authority in England.

In some ways, Henry is thus as guilty of "stealing the pax" as Bardolph—in so far as he has "broken the peace" for his own advantage.... Often the words of Bardolph and Pistol anticipate or caricature the nobler strains of Henry himself. We have already seen how Bardolph parodies Henry's futile invocation to renew the assault on Harfleur. Even before the expedition leaves England, Pistol (a low-life caricature of aristocratic bellicosity and sententiousness) has already given his version of the famous St. Crispin's Day speech:

> A noble shalt thou have, and present pay;
> And liquor likewise will I give to thee,
> And friendship shall combine, and brotherhood:
> I'll live by Nym, and Nym shall live by me;
> Is not this just? for I shall sutler be
> Unto the camp, and profits shall accrue.
> Give me thy hand.
>
> [II. i. 107-13]

This sordid fellow has the same relationship to Henry's aristocratic profiteering as Falstaff's robberies had to the supposedly "honorable" enterprises of Hotspur, which after all had only the dignity of stealing a kingdom instead of a purse. If only it is big enough, a theft seems to legitimize itself publicly, as Henry IV himself had demonstrated; but the personal moral issues remain the same as for Gadshill [in *1 Henry IV*] or Pistol: the exploitation of public issues for private gain, or at best as political expedients. (pp. 183-85)

Henry is certainly the most powerful personality in this tetralogy, and has most of the attributes of the successful ruler; but if he were always admirable, and never exposed to corrupting situations or learning painful lessons from them, we would have not a play but only the smug epic consecrated to English patriotism that we are sometimes advised to consider the play to be. Only a year or so later Shakespeare will write *Troilus and Cressida,* in which he refuses to treat the Trojan War in epic terms. In it he produces a portrait of the hero Achilles which he refuses to sentimentalize, for he shows us that the hero and the criminal attain their differing ends by a shared contempt for conventional values. The analogy may encourage us to recognize that Henry V is shown to us as a great leader, but not as an infallible one. Shakespeare never violates Christian theology to the point of presenting a portrait of unqualified human virtue in any of his heroes—and if he had attempted to do so, he would surely have falsified the essence of drama: conflict between two roughly equivalent but incompatible forces. Henry has all the defects of a great leader.

One may nevertheless feel inclined to doubt the validity of such a tension on any large scale in *Henry V.* The English seem to be too strongly favored, and their French opponents too contemptible for that. Yet we must recognize the recurrent polarity in the tetralogy between the idealizing romantic temperament on the one hand, and that of the narrowly political manipulator on the other. Richard II surrenders his picturesque but erratic government to Bolingbroke, whose chill and monochromatic rule antagonizes such romantic rebels as Hotspur. When Henry V inherits a pacified kingdom, he directs it by exploiting the traditional Lancastrian potentialities against the national entity that shares the archaic values of such figures as Richard and Hotspur: the high culture of medieval France. For all his sophistication as a politician, Henry knows that he is almost a barbarian in the eyes of the sophisticated French court: hence the affected bluntness of his courtship of Katharine. Henry and his followers thus stand in the same relationship to the French as the cunning and intellectual Greeks do to the witty and gallant Trojans in *Troilus and Cressida* (of which Shakespeare is perhaps already thinking, as Pistol's first quoted speech has shown us). But are the forces and associations of England and France sufficiently balanced to suggest a truly creative conflict in the Hegelian manner, so that the climactic marriage acquires symbolic overtones?

We must first consider the presentation of the situation in the opening scenes of *Henry V.* It is not enough simply to impose our knowledge of Henry IV's cunning advice to his son, in the earlier play, to pursue "foreign quarrels" [*2 Henry IV*, IV. v. 214], on the pious figure that the new king presents in the opening scenes of *Henry V.* For any interpretation to carry conviction, the play must make its point in its own terms. However, its opening scene does suggest the same political maneuvering as characterized *Henry IV.* (pp. 185-87)

Henry . . . obtains personally (instead of at the discretion of Parliament) the means to finance his French expedition, as well as the ecclesiastical sanctions that had seemed so vital to the mounting of the second rebellion against Henry IV. Parliament's hostility to the Church meanwhile remains a useful lever with which to control the bishops' responses to Henry's later intentions. Thus the long second scene of the play in which the king canvasses opinion about the proposed war with France is no less cunningly stage-managed than is Henry IV's striking opening speech at the start of the first part of *Henry IV.* (p. 188)

It now needs only the clumsy provocation of the Dauphin's mocking gift of tennis balls to lend the final edge of "legitimate" resentment to Henry's public intention—but even before the French ambassador's undiplomatic present, Henry has already firmly resolved to overturn the French monarchy:

> Call in the messengers sent from the Dauphin.
> Now are we well resolved; and, by God's help,
> And yours, the noble sinews of our power,
> France being ours, we'll bend it to our awe,
> Or break it all to pieces: or there we'll sit,
> Ruling in large and ample empery
> O'er France and all her almost kingly dukedoms,
> Or lay these bones in an unworthy urn.
>
> [I. ii. 221-28]

Are these really the words of "the ideal king"? "We'll bend it to our awe, / Or break it all to pieces" looks forward by contrast to such tragic figures as Macbeth and Lear. The choice of death or glory subsequently offered in this speech is an echo of Hotspur's suicidal heroism. Henry V is a young man's hero, at this point, rather than an ideal king: Alexander, indeed, rather than Augustus Caesar.

Even the Chorus introduces a hint of irony into his Prologue to Act II as he notes that "all the youth of England are on fire" and "sell the pasture now to buy the horse" [Chorus, II, 1, 5]. There is more than a hint here of proverbial reproach for youthful improvidence, and indeed the major part of Henry's expedition suggests that it is mounted in a state of mind comparable to Hotspur's intoxicated ambition before his dramatic assault on the English throne:

> Imagination of some great exploit
> Drives him beyond the bounds of patience.
>
> [*1 Henry IV*, I. iii. 199-200]

Not only does Henry at the start tend to talk of war with the same cheerful exuberance as if it were a game of tennis ("The game's afoot" [III. i. 32]), but his terms to the French king are so outrageous that Hotspur at his wildest would never have dared publicly to propose such demands as Exeter transmits on Henry's behalf:

> When you find him evenly derived
> From his most famed of famous ancestors,
> Edward the Third, he bids you then resign
> Your crown and kingdom, indirectly held
> From him the native and true challenger.
>
> [II. iv. 91-5]
> (pp. 189-90)

Henry thus appears not as the ideal ruler, but as the youthful hero, already tempered by a broader range of experience than Hotspur's, but still drawn (despite ulterior political motives) to the same dashing, risky, and destructive enterprises as his erstwhile enemy. The English cannot therefore be accurately seen by Shakespeare's audience as merely idealized compatriots. Even Henry in his speech before Harfleur recognizes that his army is full of men like Bardolph and Pistol, rather than romantic heroes like Suffolk and York (who die so picturesquely at Agincourt, IV.v.):

> What rein can hold licentious wickedness
> When down the hill he holds his fierce career?
> We may as bootless spend our vain command
> Upon the enraged soldiers in their spoil
> As send precepts to the Leviathan
> To come ashore.
>
> [III. iii. 22-7]

This pattern of analogy may well have suggested the title for Hobbes' study of the untamable viciousness of men once they are freed from strict discipline. Henry has turned on France those forces that he feared at home in England; but in the beginning he rides the crest of the rapidly breaking wave of the English invasion with a delight that is scarcely compatible with the issues involved—just as Antony is to gloat over the prospect of firing the civil wars in Rome through which Caesar's murder will be avenged, in *Julius Caesar* [III. ii. 260-61]. Both men are to pay a price for their satisfaction in the role of manipulator of human passions: Antony's will be his own destruction, Henry's the happier one of the sacrifice of his bellicose exuberance for a more sober humility. (pp. 190-91)

Henry has to learn moderation; his firm denunciation of Bardolph's minor theft in Act III, Scene vi, suggests how cautious he has become in the later phases of his campaign: "when lenity and cruelty play for a kingdom, the gentler gamester is the soonest winner" [III. vi. 112-13]. At this point the king has all but abandoned his hopes for the present expedition, which Shakespeare has shown us to be dignified alone by the isolated and insignificant surrender of Harfleur. Thus, when the French herald brings Henry news of the French intention to challenge his passage (in a speech full of the same bravado that had initially been cause for affront, in the presentation of the tennis balls), Henry is now willing to buckle down his pride and to ask with moderation for the opportunity to pass peacefully home to England:

> Thou dost thy office fairly. Turn thee back,
> And tell thy king I do not seek him now;
> But would be willing to march on to Calais
> Without impeachment: for to say the sooth,
> Though 'tis no wisdom to confess so much
> Unto an enemy of craft and vantage,
> My people are with sickness much enfeebled,
> My numbers lessened, and those few I have
> Almost no better than so many French.
>
> [III. vi. 139-47]

It is to this low pitch that the original wild hopes of the English invaders have been reduced; instead of:

> . . . crowns imperial, crowns and coronets,
> Promised to Harry and his followers
>
> [Chorus, II, 10-11]

there is left only the rueful recognition for Henry that:

> My ransom is this frail and worthless trunk,
> My army but a weak and sickly guard.
>
> [III. vi. 154-55]

The epic tone and the ruthless political finesse have been replaced by a new simplicity and candor. The threat of failure has increased Henry's stature as a man, even if he sounds less dazzling as a leader. He has learnt the bitter lesson of the need for moderation in one's demands which fate lays upon the invader of foreign soil, at least in the plays of Shakespeare. His retreat is indeed determined more by such hostile "acts of God" as sickness and disease than by the effective opposition of the French who, with unconscious wisdom, have played a waiting game.

It is at this point that a truer balance can be struck between the opposing forces. Henry's invasion of France may have been politically expedient domestically, but it was mounted in a spirit of brash confidence and chauvinistic indifference for the well-being of his intended kingdom. This well-being he has now come to respect, having found it impossible to maintain himself in France merely by armed might. The French inertia has thus already effectively defeated the hubristic energy of the invaders, rather as Tolstoy later shows us in *War and Peace* how the vastness of Russia swallows up Napoleon's Grand Army, without ever directly confronting it in decisive battle. But if the French are now effectively masters of the situation, the question remains whether they will ultimately handle this advantage wisely. The humiliation of invasion has increasingly made the discreet policy of the French king intolerable to such bellicose spirits as the Dauphin's. Thus, at the very moment when France, as "the gentler gamester," is winning the match, this policy is overthrown in favor of a more flamboyant one, aimed less at the expulsion of the English than at their total annihilation, which is gloatingly anticipated in a spirit no less hubristic than that of the original English enthusiasm for the invasion:

> Do but behold yon poor and starved band,
> And your fair show shall suck away their souls,
> Leaving them but the shales and husks of men. . . .

'Tis positive 'gainst all exceptions, lords,
That our superfluous lackeys and our peasants,
Who in unnecessary action swarm
About our squares of battle, were enow
To purge this field of such a hilding foe,
Though we upon this mountain's basis by
Took stand for idle speculation.

[II. iv. 16-18, 25-31]

The chivalric insolence of this speech provides us with both an echo of the earlier Henry V, and a contrast with his more recent frame of mind.

The center of the play lies in the scene (IV.i.) in which Henry V and his army review their fate soberly, man to man, without the intrusion of any of that aristocratic contempt for the common foot-soldier that is so marked in the speech of the Constable of France just noted. Indeed, Shakespeare cleverly uses the theme of Shylock's famous demonstration of the humanity of the despised Jewish race to demonstrate the equally mundane nature of kings, for Henry has been made to recognize that he has no more deserved unusual favor as a king than has the most wretched of his subjects:

I think the king is but a man, as I am: the violet smells to him as it doth to me; the element shows to him as it does to me; all his senses have but human conditions: his ceremonies laid by, in his nakedness he appears but a man; and though his affections are higher mounted than ours, yet, when they stoop, they stoop with the like wing.

[IV. i. 101-07]

It is no accident that it is precisely the lack of this knowledge of oneself to which Henry has attained that later provokes Lear's tragic misunderstanding of *his* kingly role; and its attainment through far more intense effort than Henry's constitutes the essential content of Lear's suffering in the storm. Williams' assumption that the king is wholly responsible for his followers' misfortunes [IV. i. 134ff.] adds a further disturbing consideration to Henry's anxieties. He answers bravely for himself, concealed by his disguise, maintaining that, "his cause being just and his quarrel honorable" (as the Archbishop had guaranteed), then "the king is not bound to answer the particular endings of his soldiers, the father of his son, nor the master of his servants; for they purpose not their death, when they purpose their services" [IV. i. 127-28, 155-58].

The king refuses responsibility for the spiritual condition of those who die in sin as a result of his orders, plausibly affirming that the proper regulation of their minds is as much their responsibility as their obligation to serve is the right of the just king: "Every subject's duty is the king's; but every subject's soul is his own" [IV. i. 176-77]. Again the recognition is an anticipation of Hobbes' insistence that the state's authority may not be publicly questioned, although a man's most private thoughts properly lie outside the scope of public concern. Henry thus painfully, and under acute personal and public pressure, labors toward a code of public and private responsibility. It is perhaps an unfashionable code nowadays intellectually; but the basis for all law and order still lies in respect for legally established practice, and Shakespeare will duly show in *Julius Caesar* (as Hobbes will also declare) that, once complete freedom of conscience and of consequent action is assumed, murderous anarchy alone can immediately result, with the ultimate

establishment of absolute tyranny as the only defense against individual men's assertion of endlessly conflicting aspirations.

At his moment of most intense political awareness, Henry V thus comes to conclusions that wholly destroy any justifications for those actions of his father to which Henry V ultimately owes his crown. The scene must inevitably end with Henry's recognition of this bitter truth:

Not today, O Lord,
O, not today, think not upon the fault
My father made in compassing the crown!
I Richard's body have interred new;
And on it have bestow'd more contrite tears
Than from it issued forced drops of blood: . . .
Though all that I can do is nothing worth,
Since that my penitence comes after all,
Imploring pardon.

[IV. i. 292-97, 303-05]

All that he had welcomed on his accession to the throne has thus been drastically impaired; his title and his authority dwindle to the sacrifice of private personality to public needs:

What infinite heart's ease
Must kings neglect, that private men enjoy!
And what have kings, that privates have not too,
Save ceremony, save general ceremony?

[IV. i. 236-39]

However, even at this moment of truth, Shakespeare characteristically does not hesitate to add a dash of irony in Henry's somewhat inappropriate reflection on the rigors of that "watch the king keeps to maintain the peace" [IV. i. 283]. Up to this point, Henry has certainly *not* "watched" enough to seek the means to peace—rather the reverse, though from this point on in the play he will not fail to seek it by all means, fighting only when battle is forced on him.

The logic of the French defeat at Agincourt is thus, from Shakespeare's point of view, fully apparent. (pp. 191-96)

Wisdom now rides with the English, as earlier it had ridden with the French king. Henry has shown to the full that power to fuse the loyalties of all the classes of English society that he had derived long before from drinking with the tapsters in Eastcheap. His troops may be ragged, but they are bound to him by a bond of community that his last speech to them on St. Crispin's Day has shown him to be able to draw to the tightest:

And Crispin Crispian shall ne'er go by,
From this day to the ending of the world,
But we in it shall be remembered;
We few, we happy few, we band of brothers;
For he today that sheds his blood with me
Shall be my brother; be he ne'er so vile,
This day shall gentle his condition.

[IV. iii. 57-63]

At this point, Henry's rhetoric touches true nobility, affirming his reacceptance of his erstwhile low-life companions on fair terms and expiating his cruelty to Falstaff. This markedly contrasts with the superciliousness of the aristocratic French and with their complacent assumption of victory, which fully justifies Henry's contemptuous allusion to the old fable:

The man that once did sell the lion's skin
While the beast lived, was killed with hunting him.

[IV. iii. 93-4]

The English victory becomes fully intelligible in this moral context—yet we must beware of simplifying its nature. The battle moves forward to a conclusion in which both sides are guilty of barbarities: the French murder the English boys, the English their French prisoners. Henry himself is censured by Williams for spying on his men in the guise of a private gentleman on the eve of the battle. Such darker notes tone down the splendor of the victory and legitimize the temperate response of Henry to the low English casualty list, which he discreetly ascribes to the Providence of God (as the Elizabethans did with the defeat of the Armada):

> O God, thy arm was here;
> And not to us, but to thy arm alone,
> Ascribe we all! When without stratagem,
> But in plain shock and even play of battle,
> Was ever known so great and little loss
> On one part and on the other? Take it, God,
> For it is none but thine.
>
> [IV. viii. 106-12]

Henry thus finally discards the heroic role which, at the start of the expedition, he had seemed to inherit from Hotspur. The subsequent humiliation of Pistol, the corrupt military "humor," symbolically completes the deflation of bellicosity, whose horrors are depicted by the Duke of Burgundy, when he declares that Peace

> . . . hath from France too long been chased,
> And all her husbandry doth lie on heaps
> Corrupting in its own fertility. . . .
> And as our vineyards, fallows, meads and hedges,
> Defective in their natures, grow to wildness,
> Even so our houses and ourselves and children
> Have lost, or do not learn for want of time,
> The sciences that should become our country;
> But grow like savages,—as soldiers will
> That nothing do but meditate on blood,—
> To swearing and stern looks, defused attire
> And every thing that seems unnatural.
>
> [V. ii. 38-40, 54-62]

It is to this condition that Henry's earlier relentless pursuit of a supposedly legal title has reduced the goal of his efforts.

In his pressing of the negotiations for peace, however, one feels a new gentleness and consideration in Henry's bearing. (pp. 197-99)

Henry abandons his extravagant claim to immediate succession to the French throne in favor of a diplomatic formula that promises his ultimate succession (a formula, incidentally, that is to lead to those disastrous wars during the reign of his juvenile and incompetent son and successor that were treated at length in *Henry VI*). Henry's title to both thrones is thus reinforced, without resort to extreme measures. Indeed, as the Chorus' last speech recognizes, it is ultimately less his unassisted merits that have won Henry victory than Providence:

> Fortune made his sword;
> By which the world's best garden he achieved,
> And of it left his son imperial lord.
>
> [Epilogue, 6-8]

The echo of Burgundy's plea for the arts of peace is unmistakable—just as unmistakable as the bitter moral of the succeeding references to the renewed collapse of this new order into a new chaos under Henry VI. All that will really be left is the lesson of the success of Henry V, which is based not on

the romantic bellicosity of a clever young hero masquerading as the ideal king, but on the ultimate steadiness attained by a mature man who knows his failures and, regretting them, puts his trust in Providence. If Henry were held to be a perfect ruler from the start of his reign, this maturation could scarcely be recognized, and the play would lack that central purpose that lends each Shakespearean drama its subtle integrity and evolution. (p. 200)

> *H. M. Richmond, " 'Henry V'," in his* Shakespeare's Political Plays, *Random House, 1967, pp. 175-200.*

## BRIAN VICKERS (essay date 1968)

[*Vickers is the author of* The Artistry of Shakespeare's Prose *(1968) and editor of the six-volume* Shakespeare: The Critical Heritage *(1974-1981), a comprehensive collection of Shakespearean commentary from 1623 to 1801. In the excerpt below, he offers a close analysis of Shakespeare's language in* Henry V, *demonstrating that characters from all levels of society are given prose speeches and that prose is employed in a wide variety of dramatic situations, "from serious argument to witty love talk." Vickers focuses on the syntactical patterns evident in Henry's exchange with Williams and Bates—where he finds an increasing use of symmetries and parallelisms as the king's argument becomes more intense and forceful—and in his wooing of Katherine—which he believes is designed to display Henry's wit and eloquence. He also discusses the syntax of Mistress Quickly's account of the death of Falstaff and Shakespeare's employment of idiosyncratic prose patterns to help characterize such comic figures as Pistol, Nym, and Fluellen.*]

Falstaff's association with this play is tenuous, more so than had been planned, for at some stage in its composition Shakespeare, having promised in the Epilogue to *2 Henry IV* a continuation 'with Sir John in it', decided to leave him out, and became involved in some hasty alterations. But his death is reported, his presence is often felt, and there is even a formal *apologia* for him given to Fluellen in his imitation of Plutarch's 'Parallel Lives':

> as Alexander killed his friend Cleitus, being in
> his cups; so also Harry Monmouth, being in
> his right wits, and his good judgements, turned
> away the fat knight with the great-belly doublet;
> he was full of jests, and gipes, and knaveries,
> and mocks; I have forgot his name.
>
> [IV. vii. 44-50]

So this is our last glimpse of Falstaff's world—not that anything has changed, for his cronies continue their downward paths while their styles remain the same. Nym, although he later revives his favourite 'that's the humour of it', now has a new catch-phrase, involving the ominous permissive 'as it *may*', but with the same enigmatic defiant brevities, each of which would be suitable to sum up a piece of rational speech, though they are now lumped together indifferently, with some sawn-off proverbs:

> I cannot tell. Things must be as they may. Men
> may sleep, and they may have their throats
> about them at that time, and some say, knives
> have edges. It must be as it may. Though patience be a tired mare, yet she will plod; there
> must be conclusions. Well, I cannot tell.
>
> [II. i. 20-5]

Pistol has his usual stiff armour-plated verse, with a touch in Cambises' vein which Falstaff had mocked: 'Go clear thy crystals' [II. iii. 54]; with more poetic inversions: 'I thee defy again' [II. i. 72], and with more internal line-pauses than ever, as if his note is getting higher and more ominous:

Let senses rule. The word is pitch and pay.
Trust none;
For oaths are straws, men's faiths are wafer-cakes. . . .
[II. iii. 49-51]

Shakespeare is always ready to make comedy out of linguistic deficiencies: 'It is not enough to speak, but to speak true,' and he involves Pistol in situations where his curiously corrupt view of language comes into collision with quite innocuous users. Thus he is as ignorant as ever of some phrases, as in his fury over Nym's use of 'solus', and as enamoured of others, as 'couple a gorge' (II, i). His distorted ear makes nonsense both of the King's 'Harry le Roy' ('a Cornish name'), and—still more amusing—of the captured prisoner's French ('. . . la force de ton bras?'—'Brass, cur? / Thou damned and luxurious mountain goat, / Offer'st me brass?' [IV. iv. 16-20]).

Mistress Quickly is the malapropist still: 'we shall see wilful adultery and murder committed', 'a burning quotidian tertian' [II. i. 37-8, 119]. But for her account of Falstaff's death Shakespeare puts her characteristic habits of speech to good dramatic purpose. The effect of our meeting in this sad context the eccentricities which we have previously laughed at is to create a curiously mixed mood, which may be less sentimental than that created by an unambiguously sorrowful epitaph, but which is in some respects more touching. In her first few sentences she mistakes 'Abraham' and 'chrisom', but the feeling behind the words comes through all the same:

Nay sure, he's not in hell; he's in Arthur's
bosom, if ever man went to Arthur's bosom.
'A made a finer end, an went away an it had
been any christom child.
[II. iii. 9-12]

Then the way she passes without distinction from direct reported speech to indirect would normally be amusing: 'How now Sir John, quoth I, what man, be o'good cheer: so 'a cried out, God, God, God, three or four times' [II. iii. 17-19]—but the report of Falstaff finally repenting does not make us laugh. And there would normally be more humour in the way she reports herself with a curious confusion at 'I hoped', as if it were a normal verb with which to report speech, like 'said' perhaps: 'now I, to comfort him, bid him a' should not think of God; I hoped there was no need to trouble himself with any such thoughts yet' [II. iii. 19-22]—but it also might convey her own hope. Her slightly ridiculous fondness for repetition is seen in the first sentence and again in the next with its doubling of 'even': ''a parted ev'n just between twelve an one, ev'n at the turning o'th'tide' [II. iii. 12-13]—but it is not ridiculous now. These mingled comic effects alternate with more straight-forwardly serious points, as in her listing of the symptoms of mortal decay, given more finality by the symmetry:

for after I saw him fumble with the sheets,
             and play    with the flowers,
             and smile    upon his finger's end,
I knew there was but one way; for his nose was as
                          sharp as a pen,
             and a'babbled of green fields.
[II. iii. 13-17]

In addition to these ominous details Shakespeare finds two images which suggest Falstaff's alteration, as they embody completely the qualities not found in him when he was alive: 'his nose was as sharp as a pen', 'and all was cold as any stone' [II. iii. 25-6].

Gradually moving away from this pathos, Shakespeare gives her more repetition for that reminiscence of the death of Socrates, but makes it tragicomic by her unwitting bawdy (the unconscious pun on 'stone'):

so 'a bade me lay more clothes on his feet: I
put my hand into the bed, and felt them, and
they were as cold as any stone; then I felt to
his knees, and so up'ard, and up'ard, and all
was as cold as any stone.
[II. iii. 22-7]

The incomprehending bawdy appears again: ''A did in some sort, indeed, handle women; but then he was rheumatic,' and her malapropism for the last time in her misunderstanding of 'devil incarnate'—''A could never abide carnation, 'twas a colour he never liked' [II. iii. 37-8, 33-4]. These mistakings would normally create a laugh, but one wonders if they do so now—even the recollection of one of the dead Falstaff's deflating similes for Bardolph is now pathetic:

BOY. Do you not remember 'a saw a flea stick
upon Bardolph's nose, and 'a said it was a black
soul burning in hell.
BARDOLPH. Well, the fuel is gone that maintained that fire.
[II. iii. 40-4]

So the transition to a less valedictory mood has been made. By the simple device of placing familiar linguistic characteristics in a dramatic context where they act both with and against the dominant mood, Shakespeare has created a wonderfully mixed feeling, and, keeping complete decorum with Mistress Quickly's character, has given Falstaff one of the most moving of epitaphs.

But though we lament his passing we are not encouraged to admire the milieu he has left behind, for just as in both parts of *Henry IV*, Shakespeare writes a choric scene here which leaves us in no doubt as to our proper attitude to roguery and corruption. After the 'three swashers' have been forcibly propelled towards the breach, their Boy steps forward to deliver a long, cool, and carefully structured anatomy of their crimes. He is first made to bring out their inversion of manliness and courage, placed more sharply into an *antimetabole* [inverting the order of repeated words] which becomes an antithesis (on 'boy' / 'man'):

I am boy to them all three, but all they three,
though they would serve me, could not be man
to me; for indeed three such antics do not amount
to a man.
[III. ii. 29-32]

He now reviews their characters separately, and together with the mockery of his puns a most carefully arranged parallel structure brings out the same vices and dissimulation in all three:

For Bardolph, he is white-livered,
            and red-faced;
by the means whereof 'a faces it out,
            but fights not.

For Pistol, he hath   a killing tongue,
                and a quiet sword;
by the means whereof, 'a   breaks words,
                and keeps whole weapons.
For Nym, he hath heard that men of few words
      are the best men, and therefore he scorns to say his
prayers,
lest 'a should be thought a coward: but his few bad
words
                  are matched with as few good
deeds;

[III. ii. 32-9]

The antithetical puns fix very clearly the gap between surface
and reality in Bardolph and Pistol, and the pattern set up for
those two was broken for Nym, the surprise effect of this
unsymmetrical movement being capped by the return of a pattern later than we had expected, and in a different form—'few
bad words . . . as few good deeds'. The clowns' list of ludicrous
human attributes from the early comedies is here applied to a
pungent anatomy of the dregs of war. After the clarity of that
exposure the Boy is given more naturalistic syntactical patterns,
but the puns reappear, simple yet grisly, to continue the moral
condemnation, culminating in the prophetic dismissal: 'Their
villainy goes against my weak stomach, and therefore I must
cast it up' [III. ii. 52-3]. Bardolph is deflated for ever with his
theft of the pyx, and Pistol is also brought down, but more
humorously, in his comic confrontation with Fluellen and in
the apt images applied to him by the Boy again in another
choric soliloquy: 'Bardolph and Nym had ten times more valour
than this roaring devil i'th'old play, that every one may pare
his nails with a wooden dagger' [IV. iv. 70-2]; and by Gower
just before he is humiliated: 'here he comes, swelling like a
turkey-cock' [V. i. 14-15].

The more genuine soldiers in the play are also individualized
in prose, but with the simple devices used in the *Merry Wives,*
mainly regional accents. The Irishman MacMorris is easily
caught by his pronunciation of 's' as 'sh': 'By Chrish la tish
ill done; the work ish give over,' by his repetition of these
phrases and by his haste to get on: 'there is throats to be cut,
and works to be done', and by the speed with which he takes
affront when Fluellen mentions his 'nation' [III. ii. 88-9, 111-12,
121]. The Scot Jamy is done with more variety of pronunciation: 'By the mess, ere theise eyes of mine take themselves
to slomber, ay'll do gud service, or ay'll lig i'th'grund for it;
ay, or go to death' [III. ii. 114-16]. Fluellen is clearly a martial
version of Sir Hugh Evans [in *The Merry Wives*], both in his
pronunciation: 'There is no tiddle-taddle nor pibble-pabble in
Pompey's camp' [IV. i. 70-1], and in his odd habit of equating
nouns and adjectives: Fortune is 'turning and inconstant and
mutability, and variation' [III. vi. 34-5]. But Fluellen is much
more of a character than anyone else in this milieu (the King
is made to praise his 'care and valour' [IV. i. 84]), and his
stylistic individualization is thus more complex. As a scholar
and lover of rhetoric he is much given to symmetrical syntax,
heaping up parallel clauses: 'you shall find the ceremonies of
the wars, and the cares of it, and the forms of it, and the
sobriety of it, and the modesty of it, to be otherwise' . . . [IV.
i. 72-4]. But the fluency and tautology of these repetitions
point to a rather over-inflated love of language which is seen
throughout, but particularly in his extravagant military analogies: Exeter is 'as magnanimous as Agamemnon', Pistol 'as
valiant a man as Mark Antony' [III. vi. 6-7, 13-14], a weakness
shown best in his ambitious and over-reaching comparison of
the King with Alexander (IV, vii)—but once again Shakespeare

puts a stylistic oddity to good dramatic purpose, for that rather
ludicrous comparison issues out into the apology for Falstaff,
and having reached that effective climax is broken off by the
entry of the King. . . . But if Fluellen's vanity is well applied
there, it is also quietly mocked through his fondness for catch-
phrases, which he is made to repeat in unsuitable contexts: so
one favourite phrase . . . is later undermined by the parts added
to it: 'an arrant traitor as any's in the universal world, *or in
France, or in England!*' [IV. viii. 9-10], and better still he
defends his mistaken respect for Pistol by using a phrase correctly: ''a uttered as prave words at the pridge, as you shall
see in a summer's day' ([III. vi. 63-4]—already 'see' is rather
silly), but when he discovers what he thinks to be Williams'
treasonous plot he is made to use the phrase ludicrously, for
something one would not desire to see: 'a most contagious
treason come to light, look you, as you shall desire in a summer's day' [IV. viii. 21-2]. (pp. 156-61)

Although prose is well fitted for these realistic lower levels of
the play, the world presented here is much wider than that of
*The Merry Wives of Windsor,* and prose is used across all strata
of society and to complex effects with a flexibility not seen
since *The Merchant of Venice.* Characters from the upper plot
are brought down to prose for some comic effects, most notably
for the French language-lesson between Katharine and Alice
(III, iv) which develops into that perennially amusing situation
of a foreigner unwittingly speaking bawdy, although here it is
reversed in that Katharine is merely suspecting bawdy (editors
are still rather coy about glossing this scene, and those who
do not understand the joke should consult Eric Partridge [in
his *Shakespeare's Bawdy*]). The French Lords normally speak
verse, but they are brought down to prose for the scene before
Agincourt (III, vii) to create an atmospheric effect and also for
stylistic contrast. They are shown breaking abusive images on
each other, and their bawdy repartee and destructive puns both
alienate our sympathies and suggest that the dissension in the
camp will be fatal. . . . [One] of the speakers is made to use
inflated images, which make him look ridiculous, as the Dauphin rhapsodizes on his horse:

He bounds from the earth, as if his entrails were
hares. . . . When I bestride him, I soar, I am a
hawk; he trots the air; the earth sings when he
touches it; the basest horn of his hoof is more
musical than the pipe of Hermes.

[III. vii. 13-14, 15-18]

[One] . . . of the other characters is given the sarcastic comment, as when the Dauphin launches into a sonnet written to
his horse, only for his affectation to be speedily brought to
earth (and to bawdy) by Orleans. Surrounded as this scene is
by majestic English heroic verse their petty quibbling prose
makes them seem more puerile still.

The same use of prose for a contrast to more dignified verse
had been applied in the previous scene, where the French herald
is made to deliver a speech in which the images are pallid and
ineffectual: 'Thus says my King. Say thou to Harry of England,
though we seemed *dead,* we did but *sleep; advantage* is a
better soldier than *rashness*' [III. vi. 118-20]. The images follow as prepared 'amplifiers' to the sense, and in the most
obvious, commonplace form: 'Tell him, we could have rebuked
him at Harfleur, but that we thought not good to *bruise* an
injury till it were full *ripe.* Now we *speak* upon our *cue,* and
our *voice* is imperial' [III. vi. 120-24]. Shakespeare uses two
other devices to make the speech ineffective: first, symmetries
which are so flat and formal that they are not worth quoting,

*Before Agincourt. By T. Grieve and T. Lloyd (1859). The Department of Rare Books and Special Collections, The University of Michigan Library.*

and secondly a curious use of reported speech (the same linguistic device as had been used to a totally different effect for Mistress Quickly's epitaph) by means of which the defiant words expressed are set back a stage and so seem like a rather mechanical recipe: 'To this add defiance; and tell him for conclusion, he hath betrayed his followers, whose condemnation is pronounced' . . . [III. vi. 133-35]. Thus Shakespeare has subtly applied several devices to take the wind out of the French sails even when they seem most threatening, and this dehydrated prose is a perfect foil for the King's vigorous and superior verse.

It is around the person of King Henry V that, suitably enough, the most varied application of prose is made. As he goes through the camp on the eve of Agincourt, dressed 'but as a common man', he puts aside his verse with his dignity, and as if in recognition of his disguise is made to speak prose to the soldiers (IV, i). But although this conversation begins in the semi-realistic language of conversation, a serious and complex issue is at stake and the King's prose is given all the appropriate devices to clarify the argument. To begin with, and for ironic effect to an audience knowing of his disguise, he establishes the King's humanity by comparing him to himself:

> I think the King is but a man, as I am;
>   the violet smells to him as it doth to me;
>   the element shows to him, as it doth to me.
>                           [IV. i. 101-03]

and so on through his human form, his passions, and his fears, all in this steady rational tone, the syntactical symmetries showing the correspondences in his argument. By contrast Williams, in his evocation of the horrors of battle, is made to appeal directly to the emotions with his parallel clauses listing the diverse fates of 'all those legs, and arms, and heads, chopped off in a battle' and their reactions if revived again:

> some swearing;
> some crying for a surgeon;
> some upon their wives, left poor behind them;
> some upon the debts they owe;
> some upon their children rawly left.
>                    [IV. i. 135-36, 138-41]

In reply to that powerful reminder of the horrors of war and the ruler's responsibility for it, Shakespeare deliberately gives the King a cool, non-emotional beginning, developing an analogy without any patterning:

> So, if a son that is by his father sent about
> merchandise, do sinfully miscarry upon the sea,
> the imputation of his wickedness, by your rule,
> should be imposed upon his father that sent
> him. Or if a servant, under his master's command, transporting a sum of money. . . .
>                         [IV. i. 147-52]

The function of this plain style is simply to be non-rhetorical, to establish an impersonal basis to the argument.

But as Henry begins to apply the comparisons, the tone of the argument begins to rise, and the symmetries appear:

> But this is not so.
> The King is not bound to answer
>      the particular endings of his soldiers,
>   the father                of his son,
> nor the master           of his servant;
> for they purpose not their death,
> when they purpose   their services.
>                             [IV. i. 154-58]

That last symmetrical clause sums up the first part of the argument, and the parallelism gives it the greatest possible clarity. The King now begins to attack Williams' argument directly, urging that 'no king, be his cause never so spotless' could have 'all unspotted soldiers' [IV. i. 159, 161], and in so doing he uses the soldier's weapon (*anaphora* on 'some') to list the diverse crimes:

> Some, peradventure, have on them the guilt
>   of premeditated and contrived murder;
> some, of beguiling virgins with the broken seals of
>   perjury;
> some, making the wars their bulwark, that have before
>   gored the gentle bosom of peace with pillage and
>   robbery.
>                             [IV. i. 161-66]

And in this dramatic context the force of the argument is increased by the presence . . . of several offenders in the last category. The argument moves on, built around logical conjuctions: 'So' — 'but' — 'for' — 'besides' — 'Now' — 'so that' — 'therefore' and using symmetry to reinforce its points, as for those criminals who have escaped the civil law:

> though they can outstrip men,
> they have no wings to fly from God.
>      War is his beadle,
>      war is his vengeance.
>                       [IV. i. 167-69]

The rhetorical structure becomes more concentrated as the King enlarges this point, with the antitheses matching the concept of the equality of Justice being expressed, and this second part of the argument is summed up in a sentence given inescapable clarity by its symmetry:

> Every subject's duty is the King's,
> but every subject's soul is his own.
>                    [IV. i. 176-77]

We may find the argument repugnant, and we may find the soldiers' consent to it dramatically unconvincing, but we must concede that the rhetorical symmetries of prose have been applied to this progression with considerable effect. Yet on the other side we must notice the restricted expressive potential of this prose by contrast with the King's powerful soliloquy which follows, as left alone he returns to verse and that theme of the discomfort of the individual holding great office which has been for Shakespeare a constant source of human sympathy—and thus of greater poetry—throughout the History Plays. In retrospect his prose seems cool, and again acts as a springboard for the intensity of verse.

But for one important scene in this play prose is used not as a contrast to verse but for its own potential, in the King's witty courtship of Katharine (V, ii). This is his longest prose scene, and Shakespeare has evidently taken considerable trouble with it. . . . [The] wit and brilliance of [Henry's] wooing language look forward to the high comedies which follow, and even to the gallantry of Restoration comedy. It seems that Shakespeare, having decided to show Henry actually wooing Kate, was intent on making this theatrically convincing—and also adding another string to this ideal ruler's bow—by showing him as the eloquent witty courtier. Furthermore, the dramatic situation forces him to develop Henry's wit more than would have been necessary if he had married an English Queen, for although we have seen Katharine trying to learn English we know just how much she has yet to learn, as their first exchanges confirm: 'You Majesty shall mock at me, I cannot speak your England. . . . Pardonnez moi, I cannot tell what is "like me" [V. ii. 102-03, 108]. So she is going to be the weak partner in the dialogue, and as it would not do for the King's success here to be cut down to some brief, possibly ambiguous victory, justice must be seen to have been done, and so the scene must be longer, and he must do all the talking. Thus the versatility which he displays with Shakespeare's verbal tools for lovemaking, wit and rhetoric, is not a sign of insincerity but rather one of excellence in the proper sphere, developed according to the needs of the play.

He begins with some simple courtly language: 'An angel is like you, Kate, and you are like an angel' [V. ii. 109-10], (a complimental *antimetabole*) but although the King protests his plainness—if she understood English better she would think he had 'sold my farm to buy my crown' [V. ii. 125-26]—he nevertheless produces several long and witty speeches (this contradiction is not a sign of dissimulation as it is for other Shakespeare characters who protest that they cannot 'cog' yet immediately proceed to do so—Richard III, say, or Falstaff to Mistress Ford). The effect of Henry's eloquence in terms of our reaction in the theatre is, I suppose, that we think that he rises to the occasion, producing eloquence when it is needed, as he has done in war. . . . The lightly mocking mood thus established is continued in the playful comparisons of his lovemaking to winning her at leap-frog or buffeting, and in the account of his face being so ugly that her eye must be her 'cook'. The syntactical patterning is here subdued to the imagery and wit, with only such simple balances as 'downright oaths, which I never use till urged, nor never break for urging' [V. ii. 144-46], but as he concludes the first part of his argument he produces a very complex sequence:

> I speak to thee plain soldier.
> If thou canst love me for this, take me;
> if not, to say to thee that I shall die, is true;
>           but for thy love, by the Lord no;
>           yet I love thee too.
>                      [V. ii., 149-52]

That riddling denial of Romantic infatuation keeps the mood light, not portentous.

In the second part of his speech he urges that his constancy will be strengthened by his lack of eloquence, because he will not have 'the gift to woo in other places', and he mocks poets for their fluency:

> for these fellows of infinite tongue,
>   that can rhyme themselves into ladies' favours,
> they do always reason themselves out again.
>                    [V. ii. 155-58]

If that is more than competent eloquence his next ploy is a remarkably eloquent deflation of all qualities except love and truth:

>               What, a speaker is but a prater;
>                    a rhyme is but a ballad;
>               a good leg    will fall,
>          a straight back    will stoop,
>           a black beard    will turn white,
>           a curled pate    will grow bald,
>               a fair face    will wither,
>                a full eye    will wax hollow;
>     but a good heart, Kate, is the sun and the moon,
>                                          [V. ii. 158-63]

There has not been such a long sequence of parallel clauses since the earlier comedies, but this is no display-piece, being quite in the character of a plain soldier, or indeed any lover.— However, it is remarkably eloquent, and the rhetoric becomes still more brilliant as he uses 'a pretty *Epanorthosis*' [correction of a word or phrase used previously] to correct that last image:

>     or rather the sun, and not the moon;
>          for it shines bright,
>          and never changes,
>               but keeps his course truly.
>                                          [V. ii. 163-64]

The crowning touch now is his very assured use of the figure *gradatio* [mounting by degrees], the chain effect which sums up the argument and relates it to his own person:

>     If thou wouldst have such a one, take me.
>          And take me, take a soldier.
>               Take a soldier, take a King.
>                                          [V. ii. 165-66]

That is as regal a piece of eloquence as you could wish for in a summer's day.

As the dialogue continues (and there is nearly two hundred lines more of it) the King does not reach those heights of eloquence again, but there are moments of witty elegance, as when his straightforward inversion: 'it is not possible you should love the enemy of France, Kate; but in loving me, you should love the friend of France' [V. ii. 171-73], then produces this dazzling sequence:

>     And Kate,  when France is mine,
>          and I        am yours;
>          then yours    is France,
>          and you      are mine.
>                                          [V. ii. 175-76]

—where any simply mathematical expectations we might have had of the symmetry are over-ridden by the meaning. The King's playful wit ensures that the mood does not cloy, as in the image with which he mocks his inability to speak French, and which is still more mocking in terms of his immediate situation: a language 'which I am sure will hang upon my tongue, like a new-married wife about her husband's neck, hardly to be shook off' [V. ii. 179-80]. This gaiety produces the most human reference to Bolingbroke yet: 'Now beshrew my father's ambition, he was thinking of civil wars when he got me, therefore was I created with a stubborn outside, with an aspect of iron, that when I come to woo ladies, I fright them' [V. ii. 224-28]. But for his final appeal rhetorical structure must lend a more formal and serious note:

>                    Thou hast me,
>          if      thou hast me, at the worst;
>          and    thou shalt wear me,
>          if      thou  wear me, better and better,
>                                          [V. ii. 231-33]

leading up to the proposal with *epistrophe* [repetition of a closing word or phrase at the end of several clauses, sentences or verses]: 'I am thine . . . England is thine . . . Ireland is thine', and so on, pressing his worth with *antimetabole* again:

>     if he be not fellow with the best King,
>          thou shalt find the best king of good fellows
>                                          [V. ii. 241-43]

and demanding a reply with a series of twists on 'broken English'. The courtship is successful, justice is seen to have been done, the lover has proved himself—and at this point Shakespeare brings Burgundy on to share a sparring-bout of bawdy with Henry, who as ever gets the better, but with some quite disillusioning images. The function of this sequence is partly anti-romantic, partly to establish Henry's superior wit, partly . . . to invoke and so release the normal sexuality of this situation, but also perhaps to complete an aspect of kingship which Henry touched on in his debate with the soldiers:

>     his ceremonies laid by, in his nakedness he
>     appears but a man; and though his affections
>     are higher mounted than ours, yet when they
>     stoop, they stoop with the like wing.
>                                          [IV. i. 104-07]

In this, as in everything, he is the complete Elizabethan, and the lowering truth implicit in that image having been established (and with wit) the King can revert to verse and to state dignity, while we are confident that he is more than a suit of robes.

The prose of *Henry V*, although the scenes in which it is used are often dispraised by critics, runs across all levels of society and across almost all the dramatic resources open to Shakespeare, from serious argument to witty love-talk. . . . *Henry V* is . . . significant in that it is an almost exact transition: schematic characterization by foreign accents and catch-phrases is used for the last time, and for the first time prose is used for witty love-talk at a high social and intellectual level. And in this respect it points directly on to the world of the comedies. (pp. 161-70)

> *Brian Vickers, "The World of Falstaff," in his* The Artistry of Shakespeare's Prose, *Methuen & Co. Ltd., 1968, pp. 89-170.*

### JAMES WINNY   (essay date 1968)

[*In the following excerpt, taken from a wide-ranging discussion of* Henry V, *Winny argues that there is a deep discrepancy between the Chorus's affirmation of heroic values and the "opposite impulse," evident in several scenes, to treat those values with "doubts and scepticism." He maintains that Shakespeare's imagination was not fully committed to the play's dramatic material; therefore, he contends, the Chorus's description and evocation of English military triumph are not only unrealized in the action of the play, but are sharply undercut by the portrayal of a king who undergoes "recurrent crises of belief" in his authority and by soldiers who doubt the justice of their monarch's cause. Winny points out that the "glorious" battle is only represented, in Act IV, Scene iv, "by the efforts of an illiterate braggart to extort ransom from a spineless coward." The critic proposes that Shakespeare's apathy toward his material is reflected in the recurring*] *theme of inertia or enervation, which he identifies especially in the scenes involving the French nobles before Agincourt, in Grandpre's description in Act IV, Scene ii of the dispirited English army, and in Burgundy's account in Act V, Scene ii of the neglected French countryside.*]

[*Henry V*] is both a surprise and a disappointment. Whatever qualities of good and bad may be claimed for it, *Henry V* is a work radically unlike any other of Shakespeare's history-plays in general style and structure. Instead of a continuous dramatic development, it offers its audience a disjointed succession of scenes or groups of scenes in chronicle fashion, related not by persistent imaginative themes but by common subject-matter; binding them loosely together through the commentary of a Chorus who presents the play. (p. 168)

[Little] suggests that Shakespeare was imaginatively committed to the characters and events of *Henry V*, or to whatever view of life it might contain. The presence of the Chorus as interpreter between the action and the audience, and his reminders that they are in the playhouse together, shows a disposition to regard the play as a piece of entertainment in which the spectators are not personally involved. Shakespeare seems to be standing away from the scenes which the Chorus presents; giving his presenter a dramatic immediacy and force not often found in the play itself, and then using his authority to urge the audience to participate imaginatively in dramatic events which have no such compulsion. However persuasively the Chorus paints the scene, it is difficult not to feel a sense of anxiety and strain beneath his repeated promptings to spectators who must devise elaborate scenic effects at the poet's bidding. The persistent imperatives of these speeches—'Piece out our imperfections', 'work, work your thoughts', 'grapple your minds' [Prologue, 23; Chorus, III, 25, 18]—suggest a degree of almost muscular effort as the poet struggles to set an unyielding train of ideas in motion. . . . The long set speeches of *Henry V*—those of the Archbishop in i. 2, the King in iv. 1, and of Burgundy in v. 2 are typical—suggest that despite its association with warfare, the character of the play is predominantly static. One may go further than this and assert that an imaginative awareness of inertia, of paralysed immobility, is one of the few realised poetic features of *Henry V:* a point which must be examined more closely later. While it would be absurd to suggest that the play never breaks out of lethargy into vigorous action, *Henry V* is never convincingly moved by the sense of developing events which gives other plays their dramatic life. (pp. 169-70)

It may be worth considering whether the admittedly virtuous character of Henry V could account for Shakespeare's evident difficulty in bringing his material to life. Unlike Richard II and Henry IV, the King is not involved in contradictions of character and moral identity; and however admirable he may appear by comparison with them, this integrity of being seems not to hold the imaginative interest which impels Shakespeare to create. . . . The episodes of *Henry V* in which the play becomes poetically alive are moments of uncertainty and doubt in the King, when his virtuousness seems of no help in solving the moral dilemmas to which he is exposed by kingship. (p. 174)

If *Henry V* cannot claim equality of rank with Shakespeare's previous plays about English history, the poet's evident disinclination to look critically into the King's behaviour and beliefs is chiefly responsible. This does not mean that the King is wilfully or unconsciously mistaken about the moral fitness of his policy, but that Shakespeare makes no attempt to establish through the action what standards of political behaviour the King should adopt. . . . Except in the one scene of self-examination, the King does not come under scrutiny. He is uncritically acknowledged and respected by his own people and by the French leaders, and Shakespeare gives him no reason to look into the legality of his title to a throne which should be occupied by Edmund Mortimer. The King has not inherited the talking starling which Hotspur was to have given Bolingbroke. There is in consequence no such working-out of moral standards as Shakespeare contrives through the action of *Henry IV,* and no character to take over Falstaff's satirical function by looking beneath the outward forms of dignity and grandeur. The lack of such critical questioning makes *Henry V* a much less intensely realised play than its predecessor, and a work on which Shakespeare's attention is seldom fully engaged.

The much lower level of critical awareness in *Henry V* is seen in the character of the King himself. . . . The treachery of his bosom friend Scroop,

> that didst bear the key of all my counsels,
> That knew'st the very bottom of my soul,
>
> [II. ii. 96-7]

takes the King completely by surprise, as though the savage trick he played on Falstaff had come home to roost. Not only is he entirely unprepared for the discovery, but so staggered by the disclosure that he can barely come to terms with his disillusion:

> 'Tis so strange
> That, though the truth of it stands off as gross
> As black and white, my eye will scarcely see it.
>
> [II. ii. 102-04]
> (pp. 177-78)

From the beginning of the play until the victory of Agincourt the King undergoes recurrent crises of belief which threaten to immobilise him if they are not satisfactorily cleared up. The first of these occurs before the King takes the decision to invade France in pursuit of his claim to the French throne. We are perhaps invited to contrast the King's careful and sober enquiry into the moral and legal force of his claim with the contempt for justice displayed by all Shakespeare's earlier aspirants to kingly power. There is opportunity, when the Archbishop speaks of the King's interest in

> his true titles to some certain dukedoms,
> And generally to the crown and seat of France,
> Derived from Edward, his great-grandfather
>
> [I. i. 87-9]

to hint at the disregarded issue of the inheritor's title to the English crown stolen by Bolingbroke; but the allusion has no ironic overtones. Instead of raising this issue, Shakespeare allows the King to build upon an unequivocal reference to his 'true titles' by telling the Archbishop to declare 'justly and religiously' [I. ii. 110] whether the Salic law obstructs his claim. At first reading it is difficult to believe that the King's warning against straining and misrepresenting facts . . . is not [a] virtuous protestation, meant to recoil upon the speaker; but again Shakespeare's irony is silent. 'God forbid,' the King tells the prelates,

> That you should fashion, wrest, or bow your reading,
> Or nicely charge your understanding soul
> With opening titles miscreate, whose right
> Suits not in native colours with truth.
>
> [I. ii. 14-17]

The speech turns upon a number of crucial terms—right, truth, conscience, baptism—and upon references to spurious claims which should establish a basis of moral judgement; but in *Henry V* such terms are inert. The King is sincere in wishing to be cleared by religious authority before undertaking war against France, and the Archbishop seems to be offering sincere advice. Because he is acting deliberately, the King is able to reflect dispassionately upon the likely consequences of making war, and to recognise what unforeseen dangers his decision may incur. His warning to the Archbishop admits hazards that are both moral and physical; from neither of which the King can dissociate himself:

> Take heed how you impawn our person,
> How you awake our sleeping sword of war:
> We charge you, in the name of God, take heed.
>
> [I. ii. 21-3]

It would be wrong to suppose that the King is merely satisfying his conscience over the justice of his claim before declaring war. Whether right is on his side or not, the destructive effects of war between England and France will be so terrible that the responsibility for opening the conflict must daunt any thoughtful ruler. The repeated warning, 'take heed', is not addressed only to the Archbishop: the King must himself be sure that both this advice and his own final decision are not swayed by interests that would condemn his military undertaking from the outset. . . . [He] denies himself the impulse of private interest, which provides an immediate spur to action; and feels his way uncertainly towards a judgement formed by weighing legal arguments and material considerations. This respect for moral law and humanity is in itself admirable; but although the outcome of the King's deliberations is never in doubt, we are made to feel an uncertainty and disquiet behind his search for assurance which—in some other dramatic circumstances—might have led to an *impasse*. The undue length of the Archbishop's recital of French history should suggest to any playgoer who remains awake the difficulty of disentangling from such a confusion of facts a plain answer to the King's simple question:

> May I with right and conscience make this claim?
>
> [I. ii. 96]

Like the Trojan princes in *Troilus and Cressida*, who discover when they try to debate the value of Helen that worth has no fixed standards, the King comes near to finding that right and wrong may be qualities impossible to determine. Shakespeare's plot does not allow his central character to become immobilised by uncertainty of this kind here, though later in the play the King will encounter a greater challenge to the beliefs which impel purposeful action. But this second scene of *Henry V* shows the King in some trouble; not merely obtaining religious approval for the course he intends to follow, but looking for answers to moral problems that are too weighty and complex for any simple solution to be adopted with complete confidence. (pp. 179-82)

Whether we are to see some incompletely realised crisis of personal outlook behind the King's questioning of moral right may be open to dispute; but there is no doubt that Scroop's defection, brought to light on the eve of the King's embarkation for France, undermines an area of belief on which much of his private security depends. Beside losing a trusted friend, the King discovers that a central assumption of his outlook is valueless. . . . By discrediting the system of belief which hitherto has guided the King, Scroop's treachery threatens to paralyse his ability to take decisive action. In consequence, it puts the success of the English expedition in hazard. What dumbfounds the King is not the cruelty of his betrayal but the seeming lack of motive in Scroop's treachery. 'He that tempered thee bade thee stand up,' the King tells him,

> Gave thee no instance why thou should'st do treason,
> Unless to dub thee with the name of traitor.
>
> [II. ii. 118-20]

Even with the proof in his hands, the King finds it impossible to assimilate the fact of Scroop's broken trust. To accommodate this unthinkable fact his mind must reconstruct its disordered pattern of beliefs upon a new basis; and meanwhile the King is denied the assurance of tried assumptions. 'I will weep for thee,' he tells Scroop;

> For this revolt of thine, methinks, is like
> Another fall of man.
>
> [II. ii. 140-42]

The remark is not simply hyperbolic, but an indication of how profoundly the King's security has been shaken. The full significance of his admission is not seen until it is set beside the Archbishop's reference to the spiritual reflections by which the King 'whipped the offending Adam out of him' [I. i. 29] when he succeeded to the throne. The innocence which the King acquired at his accession was both a freedom from sin and a state of unsuspecting trust, like that of a newly-made man who had yet to encounter evil. Scroop has now opened the King's eyes to the existence of moral corruption in the most unthinkable place and the most repulsive form. The disclosure strikes at the roots of the beliefs which have shaped the King's outlook and character, and so brings his personality under strain. The demands of the plot do not allow Shakespeare to develop the situation. At the end of his anguished reproach the King rapidly pulls himself together, commits the offenders to the course of law, and sets out for France with a cheerful enthusiasm that belies the shocked incredulity he has just expressed. (pp. 183-85)

[Although] Shakespeare does not explain how the King rapidly absorbs the double shock of Scroop's treachery and a disillusioning of private belief, he lets it appear that the King's resolution has been severely challenged, and that he has fought off a well-timed and potentially demoralising attack upon his royal purposes. In France he is to meet further challenges; not in the simple form of physical or tactical hazards which he has ample courage to resist, but in more insidious threats to his moral assurance. The first of these is presented by the French herald, who issues his challenges when the King knows himself to be heavily outnumbered, and his small army weakened by sickness. This military disadvantage is serious enough to give the King some anxiety, and Mountjoy's speech attempts to exploit this natural sense of misgiving by suggesting that rash leadership and insulting arrogance are about to be fittingly punished in the repulse of an ill-considered military adventure. 'England shall repent his folly, see his weakness, and admire our sufferance,' Mountjoy promises impressively;

> Bid him therefore consider of his ransom, which
> must proportion the losses we have borne, the
> subjects we have lost, the disgrace we have
> digested: which in weight to re-answer, his pet-
> tiness would bow under.
>
> [III. vi 124-29]

The verbal assault on the King's morale is most damaging in its final comment: 'Tell him, for conclusion, he hath betrayed his followers' [III. vi. 134-35]. The implication that he has behaved like Scroop might itself unsettle the King; and the knowledge that a sick and enfeebled army has been brought into peril through his decisions could check his confidence with the disheartening suggestion that his invasion of France was a foolhardy mistake. In the depressing circumstances of Mountjoy's challenge, the sober warning that the French are about to take full revenge for the hurts done to them must have an ominous ring of likelihood. The King's compliment to Mountjoy, 'Thou dost thine office fairly' [III. vi. 139], admits that the threat has been given teeth. But the form of the King's answer, which begins as though unconcernedly by asking the herald his name, proves him unshaken:

> If we may pass, we will; if we be hinder'd,
> We shall your tawny ground with your red blood
> Discolour.
>
> [III. vi. 160-62]

This calmly defiant statement of purpose disposes of Mountjoy's challenge to the King's belief in his cause; but as night falls upon his uneasy army a different form of threat begins to take shape. (pp. 186-87)

As he samples the morale of his army through his conversation with Bates and Williams, the King discovers that his men regard him as one of themselves in wishing to save his neck whatever happens. 'He may show what outward courage he will,' Bates remarks simply,

> but I believe, as cold a night as 'tis, he could
> wish himself in Thames up to the neck . . . so
> we were quit here.
>
> [IV. i. 113-15, 116-17]

His remark implies a total rejection of the noble standards which direct the King's behaviour; in particular his conduct as a soldier. Bates, in his forthright valuation of life, feels no respect for noble reputation: he will fight lustily for the King, but with the entirely realistic intention of keeping a whole skin; and without supposing that love of honour runs very deep. If the King enjoys his present danger, Bates continues, 'then I would he were here alone'; he would then be ransomed, and 'a many poor men's lives' would be spared [IV. i. 121, 122-23]. Hitherto, in his pursuit of military honour, the King has ignored the fate of the ordinary fighting-man whose uncomplaining service buttresses great reputations and famous victories. He is now being made to acknowledge how much such achievements depend upon the loyalty and personal sacrifice of men too poor and unimportant to merit ransoming; and who, unlike their leaders, cannot expect a painless outcome to defeat. Pushed home, this recognition must call into question assumptions that are fundamental to the King's active direction of an invading army; but the interrogation of his beliefs does not stop here. When the King answers Bates by asserting that he would be content to die in his sovereign's company, 'his cause being just and his quarrel honourable', Williams cuts in with an unanswerable comment,

> That's more than we know.
>
> [IV. i. 127-29]

The sense of the remark may be simply that issues of this kind are above the head of the common man; but the King can hardly avoid the suggestion that the problem of his moral right to invade France is being raised again, in the form of a direct challenge. Bates has no wish to hear the matter discussed: it is enough for him to know that they are the King's subjects,

bound to obedience whether or not his cause is just, and so not implicated in the guilt of wrongful proceeding:

> If his cause be wrong, our obedience to the
> king wipes the crime of it out of us.
>
> [IV. i. 132-33]

Williams takes up this point and develops it with some energy; arguing that unless the King has right on his side he will have a heavy reckoning to make at Judgement Day, when all the bodies dismembered in battle will join together to witness against him, crying, 'We died at such a place' [IV. i. 137-38]. To refute this argument might not be easy; but as Williams continues he shifts attention from the King's guilty responsibility for the deaths of his subjects, and speaks about the weight of private sin in soldiers who die unshriven. This change of subject allows the King to ignore the question of his general responsibility in a doubtful cause, and to answer only the suggestion that he is to blame when his soldiers die in battle with misdeeds on their consciences. This is a comparatively easy matter. 'If they die unprovided,' he tells Williams at the end of an extended reply,

> no more is the king guilty of their damnation
> than he was before guilty of those impieties for
> the which they are now visited. Every subject's
> duty is the king's; but every subject's soul is
> his own.
>
> [IV. i. 173-77]

The King has evaded the major issue; but the unanswered problem of his right to commit men to battle where justice cannot be determined continues to challenge his immediate purposes. The question drops out of sight, yet the discordant note introduced by Williams's comment, 'That's more than we know', has not been silenced. . . . The open dispute with Williams leaves the King badly shaken; and in the soliloquy which follows he shows himself for the first time doubtful of his royal authority and of the dignity which it confers upon him. The speech touches on a theme found elsewhere in Shakespeare, of the simple pleasures denied to kings yet granted to the poorest subject; but here the familiar commentary is sharpened by an angry anatomising of the privileged treatment which sets the king apart from the common body of men:

> And what art thou, thou idol ceremony?
> What kind of god art thou, that suffer'st more
> Of mortal griefs than do thy worshippers?
> What are thy rents? what are thy comings-in?
> O ceremony, show me but thy worth!
> What is thy soul of adoration?
> Art thou aught else but place, degree, and form,
> Creating awe and fear in other men?
>
> [IV. i. 240-47]

This sceptical bitterness is a mood not previously heard from the King; but he has only now recognised that his unique status rests upon this seemingly illusory basis. (pp. 189-95)

Like the disillusioning disclosure of Scroop's motiveless treachery, the King's recognition that only the trivial process of ceremony distinguishes him from other men does not fit naturally into the play outlined and presented by the Chorus. It seems worth remarking that the passages of *Henry V* which reveal the King's private feelings, and which were not drawn from Shakespeare's source-material, convey an impression of scepticism and disquiet strongly alien to the generally optimistic spirit of the play. These conflicting purposes are made to serve a single dramatic end when the King is first impeded by doubts and later released from his hesitation, triumphing over an opposing army and his own uncertainties in the same affirmation of self-confidence; yet the sense of disparity remains between the plain terms of patriotic chronicle-play and the occasional passages of satirical inquiry in which Shakespeare's imaginative commitment is more positively felt. (pp. 195-96)

This imaginative engagement is strongly felt in the images of fixity and inaction which recur throughout *Henry V*. In a play concerned with campaigns and battles the predominant mood might be one of energetic movement; and a persistent interest in stagnation and inertia could indicate that the physical events of the play did not contain the centre of imaginative attention. This seems the case here. Suggestions of an immobilised will, hard to set in motion, are present from the opening scenes. Although the King's refusal to be hurried into a declaration of war does credit to his moral circumspection, some of the terms he uses carry implications of a reluctance to move at all. His warning to the Archbishop,

> Take heed . . .
> How you awake our sleeping sword of war;
> [I. ii. 21, 22]

seems to admit a personal drowsiness which his counsellors urge to shake off: 'Awake remembrance . . . rouse yourself' [I. ii. 115, 123]. The Archbishop's promptings include a curious reference to the English victory at Cressy won by half an army, while the rest of the King's forces looked on unused,

> All out of work, and cold for action.
> [I. ii. 114]

The speaker's immediate intention is to suggest the laughable ease of this victory over the French; but the image of inactivity suggests a force which has only partly stirred itself out of lassitude. The idea of awakened vigour struggling to free itself of a clogging inertia is expressed later by the King, in remarking to Erpingham that when 'the mind is quickened',

> The organs, though defunct and dead before,
> Break up their drowsy grave, and newly move
> With casted slough and fresh legerity.
> [IV. i. 20, 21-3]

The remark follows a scene in the French camp which epitomises the languor and boredom of enforced idleness. The trivial bickering of the French lords, their wit as jaded as their yawning assurance of easy victory, is interrupted again and again by weary complaints about the sluggish passing of time—'Will it never be morning?' 'What a long night is this!' [III. vii. 6, 11]—which involve the audience in the same stagnation of spirit. Unlike the English, the French lords have no respect for their leader, and no expectation that his boastful promises will be translated into action. 'Doing is activity, and he will still be doing,' the Constable comments of the Dauphin; to which Orleans replies damningly,

> He never did harm, that I heard of.
> [III. vii. 99-100]

'Nor will do none tomorrow,' the Constable forecasts; but on the morning of the battle he himself assures the French lords that they need barely exert themselves to overwhelm so petty a foe:

> There is not work enough for all our hands.
> [IV. ii. 19]

The theme of inertia and futile activity continues to occupy Shakespeare's imagination as the Constable speaks of the throngs of servants and country people who swarm about the French army 'in unnecessary action', and suggests that these unwarlike followers could rout the English without help,

> Though we upon this mountain's basis by
> Took stand for idle speculation. . . .
> [IV. ii. 30-1]

The whole tendency of his address is to suggest a task so undemanding that the French need hardly trouble to brace themselves for battle: merely to make an appearance in the field will assure victory. Encouraged to be indolent and lazily casual, they deserve Grandpré's rebuke, 'Why do you stay so long?' [IV. ii. 38] though the description of the English which he brings must give them more cause to remain relaxed. His account of men and beasts in a state of dispirited lethargy and exhaustion has a poetic power which indicates an unusual degree of imaginative commitment on Shakespeare's part:

> The horsemen sit like fixed candlesticks,
> With torch-staves in their hand; and their poor jades
> Lob down their heads, dropping the hides and hips,
> The gum down-roping from their pale-dead eyes,
> And in their pale dull mouths the gimmal'd bit
> Lies foul with chaw'd grass, still and motionless.
> [IV. ii. 45-50]

Grandpré's report does not tally with the audience's view of the English army, which, however depleted, is in good heart and ready for battle; but his speech should not be read as an attempt to boost French morale. Whatever function it serves in respect of the plot of *Henry V*, within the poetic design of the play this extended metaphor of unresponsive apathy has an importance not determined by its part in the dramatic story. Because the French discover that Grandpré was badly mistaken, his picture of an army sunk in torpor does not cease to be imaginatively effective: it continues to exert the pressure of a fully realised concept upon the structure of ideas which Shakespeare builds up. While the plot moves towards its climax in military action, the overthrow of a great army by a weak and outnumbered force, the imaginative attention of *Henry V* pursues its own dissociated course by suggesting enervation and idleness on both sides. Westmoreland's wish to be reinforced by

> But one ten thousand of those men in England
> That do no work today!
> [IV. iii. 17-18]

is taken from Holinshed but placed appositely in the context of Shakespeare's unheroic battle-scenes, which give more prominence to Pistol's service as 'brave, vaillant, et trés distingué seigneur' [IV. iv. 56-7] than to the King's active personal contribution to the victory. It is curious that of all Shakespeare's stage battles, the most glorious for English audiences should be represented by the efforts of an illiterate braggart to extort ransom from a spineless coward; and a curious contradiction of the impulse that makes the Chorus speak with awed respect of

> the very casques
> That did affright the air at Agincourt.
> [Prologue, 13-14]

The apologies offered by the Chorus for the play's unworthy and inadequate attempts to bring Agincourt before the audience are not out of place; though what might need pardoning is the choice of ignoble and contemptible figures to represent the contending forces, and not a failure to give these scenes the heroic magnitude they deserve. The plea made in the first Chorus,

> Think, when we talk of horses, that you see them
> Printing their proud hoofs i' the receiving earth;
>
> [Prologue, 26-7]

is immediately effective; but the suggestions of noble endeavour in the speeches of the Chorus are only faintly borne out in the action. This splendid image of horses, and the associations of nobility which it evokes, have no place in the Agincourt scenes. The exhausted mounts described by Grandpré, broken-spirited and ill-conditioned, are more fairly representative of the terms of debased grandeur in which we are obliged to see much of the battle. (pp. 196-201)

When Grandpré describes the dwindled and impoverished state of the English army,

> Big Mars seems bankrupt in their beggar'd host,
> And faintly through a rusty beaver peeps;
>
> [IV. ii. 43-4]

embodying in 'peeps' the frightened reluctance of the English troops to face a hopeless situation, he stamps a clear impression of shaken morale which cannot be erased by making allowance for prejudice. 'Description cannot suit itself in words,' he concludes, doing Shakespeare less than justice,

> To demonstrate the life of such a battle
> In life so lifeless as it shows itself.
>
> [IV. ii. 53-5]

Grandpré might be making a satirical parody of the apologies offered by the Chorus for the dramatic inadequacies of the play. His speech certainly makes it difficult for an audience to retain a respectful image of the army through which the King must prove his great-hearted courage and resolute will. The French view of his forces as a thoroughly demoralised army, whose soldiers are empty effigies of men waiting to be bowled over, is not simply accountable as an over-confident error. On the English side the common soldiers are not alone in feeling the outcome of battle already decided by the great numerical superiority of the French. Exeter's comment,

> There's five to one; besides, they are all fresh
>
> [IV. iii. 4]

is a muted admission of fear confirmed by Salisbury: ''Tis a fearful odds' [IV. iii. 5]. In the temporary absence of the King, confidence does not hold up against the intimidating threats of 'most assured overthrow' [IV. iii. 81] which Mountjoy repeats once more before the battle. The King himself must be source and mainstay of his army's courage, fighting back the sense of inferiority expressed in Westmoreland's wish for reinforcements, and compelling them to believe in a victory which will make St Crispin's Day famous in the annals of war. The great challenge which confronts him is not so much the prospect of defeat as the task of transforming a small army, wearied and dispirited to the point of collapse, into a vigorous and self-assured fighting force capable of destroying an enemy several times larger than itself. This transformation must begin within the King. His natural buoyancy has been checked by Williams's contempt for the code of honourable behaviour which must sustain the King, and by his own realisation of the worthlessness of ceremony. His prayer, 'Not today,' admits a deeper sense of unease originating in his father's crime, which might

now be avenged in the ruin and humiliation of Bolingbroke's heir. That the King's physical courage is equal to the hazards of his exposed military position is not enough to secure him: his resolution is under attack from more insidious and demoralising forms of uncertainty. Unless he can overcome these misgivings within himself and reanimate his men, the army will remain sunk in the exhausted apathy which Grandpré describes, to be swept away with no more effort than the Constable calls for.

Thus it would be wrong to regard Grandpré as a prejudiced or wilfully optimistic observer; though his picture of an abject and inert English force cannot be accepted quite literally. We are not to suppose that the army looks as spiritless as Grandpré suggests, but to see his images of lifeless apathy representing a state of moral defeat in which fear takes body and mind captive. To this extent his speech is not 'true'; but its imaginative associations illuminate a level of meaning below the plane of dramatic events, where physical happenings acquire the significance of metaphor. The demoralised army which is made to exist imaginatively in Grandpré's speech has such a significance, chiefly for the King who should command its now immobilised power. It indicates the particular danger of the situation which confronts him, and the particular urgency of the need to release his forces from the sickly, trance-like paralysis of spirit which transfixes them. The King answers this crucial challenge in his address to the army, heartening his men by making their small numbers a point of noble credit, and then leading them to inflict a disastrous defeat upon a mangled and bewildered French host.

With Agincourt the play reaches its dramatic climax, and the King undergoes the last and severest of the personal crises which test his abilities as sovereign. He has now fought free of the impending doubts that repeatedly threaten to clog and hamper vigorous action; and after his culminating triumph over irresolution and inertia we might expect this running theme of *Henry V* to drop out of sight. But if the King has done with the subject, the play has not. In Act V the theme is re-introduced by Burgundy, in one of the long set speeches that characterise the play, supplying background comment rather than developing the action. Burgundy's topic, the wild and neglected state of France brought about by war, invites him to describe the desolation of a countryside left to grow unrestrained and unkempt. Among several curious features of this long and impressive speech is the sense of concern for France, which the audience is induced to share with Burgundy. Hitherto the play has treated the French with a good deal of contempt, openly suggesting that the devastation of their country is a well-deserved punishment for which the audience should feel no pity. By intervening between the combatants, Burgundy now reintroduces the impulse of compassionate feeling exiled by war, and turns attention to the productive labour of cultivation—human as well as agricultural—which warfare has interrupted for so long. Yet although his purpose is entirely constructive—both a knitting-together of his shattered country, and a peaceful alliance of the warring kingdoms—his speech limits attention to the widespread neglect of the French countryside, whose untended fields either waste themselves in unharvested crops or run wild, reverting to uncultivated nature. Part of Burgundy's appeal is directed against this purposeless wasting of creative energy; a protest which, in a long view of the dramatic series about to be concluded, may be read as a moral indictment of the causes which have led to such unproductive spending of human potential. But in his picture of unpopulated farms, where the plough rusts and the scythe lies unused, Burgundy evokes a melancholy impression of a deserted countryside where nothing moves, and weeds smother an abandoned cultivation:

> All her husbandry doth lie on heaps,
> Corrupting in its own fertility.
> Her vine, the merry cheerer of the heart,
> Unpruned dies; her hedges even-pleach'd,
> Like prisoners wildly overgrown with hair,
> Put forth disorder'd twigs; her fallow leas
> The darnel, hemlock and rank fumitory
> Doth root upon, while that the coulter rusts
> That should deracinate such savagery;
> The even mead, that erst brought sweetly forth
> The freckled cowslip, burnet, and green clover,
> Wanting the scythe, all uncorrected, rank,
> Conceives by idleness, and nothing teems
> But hateful docks, rough thistles, kecksies, burrs.
>
> [V. ii. 39-52]
> (pp. 201-05)

The mixture of entreaty and warning in Burgundy's speech has no parallel in Shakepeare's earlier history-plays. For the first time a strong moral rebuke is being uttered against war, for its encouragement of man's natural inclination towards brutishness, and for its destruction of the ordered life which he arduously brings about by civilising and cultivating the natural wildness of himself and his setting. (pp. 206-07)

The more immediate interest of Burgundy's speech is that, under cover of an appeal for France, it brings back the recurrent ideas of apathy and idleness. We expect this challenge to be met, as before, by a thrust of vigorous activity which breaks through the clogging depression and sets impeded life in motion again. So far as the dramatic circumstances allow this impulse of reinvigorating purpose to be represented, it is suggested in the King's wooing of Katherine and the political settlement which concludes the play. The wooing shows the King for the first time in a light-hearted, even frivolous mood; and the sombre emotional colour of Burgundy's speech is relieved by the playfulness of what follows. It would be absurd to argue that a scene as shallow and perfunctory in its dialogue could carry any imaginative conviction; but Shakespeare's intention of giving the last of the Histories the form of a happy ending makes itself apparent. Peace, political harmony and marriage are together to set a term to the waste and upheaval of war, and to allow the neglected arts of civilisation to be practised again. On this note the play and the historical series close.

But such an ending cannot resolve the interests which *Henry V* voices most strongly. It may justify the spirit of elation and confidence injected into the play by the Chorus; but those speeches are not compounded of rapturous exclamation alone. They admit as though for the author a sense of inadequacy and flagging invention which requires the audience to share the work of bringing heroic figures and momentous occasions to life. If these repeated appeals to the audience to work their thoughts are intended seriously, they are not prompted by the physical limitations of Shakespeare's playhouse, but by the evident unwillingness of his imagination to give full reality to the resplendent figures which the Chorus describes. The action of the play gives being to less noble characters: to a king whose royal dignity is compromised by the treachery of a trusted friend and by doubts of his own authority; to common soldiers who fight without belief in the justice of the King's cause, and to cowardly braggarts who bring disgrace on their times. Against the unsettled creative impulse that produces figures of this

unexalted kind, the lyrical excitement of the Chorus cannot assert itself to much purpose. His speeches, which express rather a wish than a promise to realise heroic conceptions in dramatic form, provide a generally misleading idea of the play to which he acts as presenter. (pp. 209-10)

A play whose poetic integrity is so doubtful resists the kind of interpretative criticism that can be usefully applied to a work which has consistent imaginative purpose. For this reason *Henry V* must remain a frustrating play. It declares contradictory interests, and does not maintain any single well-marked line of development. The popular opinion that it should be read as a splendid patriotic chronicle finds support in the Chorus's speeches and the King's address before Agincourt, but ignores the pointed evidence of an opposite impulse which calls heroic values into question. To argue that this sceptical purpose supplies the main energy of *Henry V* invites the same kind of objection; that much of the writing is fired by an enthusiastic acceptance of the values which elsewhere Shakespeare seems inclined to repudiate. Since the Chrous stands outside the play proper, we might perhaps discount the exalted feeling which his speeches inject into the work; seeing his function as an attempt to offset the satirical impulse which threatens heroic achievement in the play. In a critical summing-up of *Henry V* we may be finally influenced by the fact that while its heroic values form the subject of high rhetorical commentary, its doubts and scepticism are enacted in the few scenes that have the intensity of imaginative engagement. (p. 212)

> *James Winny, "The True Inheritor," in his* The Player King: A Theme of Shakespeare's Histories, *Chatto & Windus, 1968, pp. 168-216.*

### ALVIN B. KERNAN (essay date 1969)

[*In a portion of his essay not reprinted below, Kernan asserts that* Richard III, 1 *and* 2 Henry IV, *and* Henry V "*constitute an epic,* The Henriad," *and record "the passage from the Middle Ages to the Renaissance and the modern world." In the following excerpt, he describes* Henry V *as a consummate and unerring politician whose individual humanity has disappeared beneath his public role as monarch of England. Kernan finds "a curious ambiguity" in Henry's conduct and speeches, and he discusses his possible motives in several scenes, including the meeting with Williams and Bates on the eve of Agincourt, noting particularly the king's repeated evasions of responsibility for his actions. However, instead of regarding Henry as either hero or Machiavel, Kernan argues, we should recognize that his principal motive is to rule his kingdom efficiently.*]

Henry V has the public virtues of a great king, magnanimity, courage, resourcefulness, energy, efficiency, and a great public presence. At the same time, certain private traits seen in him [in *1* and *2 Henry IV*]—flat practicality, hard objectivity, a lack of complexity amounting almost to insensitivity, a sense of the uses of a public image, and an ability secretly to make and carry out long-range plans—persist and contribute much to his political efficiency, even while raising questions about him as a man. (p. 27)

As *Henry V* opens, the Bishop of Ely and the Archbishop of Canterbury tell us that Parliament has proposed to expropriate Church lands, but the King has not yet committed himself on the issue. Canterbury has offered a deal: if Henry will block the bill, the clergy will provide him with a great deal of money to support his proposed expedition to France. Rather than giving a direct answer, Henry asked the Archbishop what he thought about the English king's rights to the throne of France:

> The severals and unhidden passages
> Of his true titles to some certain dukedoms,
> And generally to the crown and seat of France,
> Deriv'd from Edward, his great-grandfather.
>
> [I. i. 86-9]

Taking up the hint, the Church is now here, in the persons of Canterbury and Ely, to interpret Henry's French title for him. Before the Archbishop begins to speak Henry charges him most solemnly to speak nothing but certain truth, for a war between great nations and the deaths of many men hang upon his words. Happily for Canterbury, Hal's title to the throne of France is "as clear as is the summer's sun" [I. ii. 86], but the proof he offers is an incredible jumble of ancient geography, the customs of the primitive Germans, the workings of something called the Salic Law prohibiting females from ruling in central Europe, and other obscure pedantries. The King, still not clear about his title, or wishing to declare himself again, asks plainly, "May I with right and conscience make this claim?" [I. ii. 96]. When reassured once more, all doubt dies and Henry determines to seize France as his right or obliterate it:

> Now are we well resolv'd; and, by God's help
> And yours, the noble sinews of our power,
> France being ours, we'll bend it to our awe,
> Or break it all to pieces;
>
> [I. ii. 222-25]

Nothing more is heard about the expropriation of Church lands. It would be most interesting to hear either Falstaff or Hotspur comment on these speeches and events, but their voices are no longer heard in Henry V's England. What Hal's thoughts are it is impossible to say—his motives are always as obscure as his father's—but it is equally impossible to forget the dying Henry IV's advice to his son, "To busy giddy minds / With foreign quarrels" [2 Henry IV, IV. v. 213-14].

This is not the only occasion on which there is something puzzling about Hal's motives, on which it is possible to see him acting as both the hero king and as an unscrupulous politician. Hal, in III. iii, has brought his army across the sea to the walls of Harfleur. The town at first resists siege, but the citizens then decide that there is no hope and ask for a parley. As the parley begins, Hal turns on the citizens and storms at them for defending their town so long and putting themselves and their dependents in such danger. Furthermore, if the town continues to resist he will batter it to pieces and burn it to ashes. His soldiers, inflamed by battle, will break loose into the town "with conscience wide as hell" [III. iii. 13] to murder, rape, and pillage. "What is it to me," the King shouts again and again [III. iii. 15, 19], if these dreadful things happen? What responsibility do I have if these animals run lusting for blood through your streets, since it is you, the citizens of Harfleur, who by your stubbornness endanger your people? The repeated rhetorical question, "what is it to me," with its implicit answer, "nothing," sounds very strange in this context. Considering the brutalities he is describing, it should be a great deal, and how does he think this army got across the English Channel and arrived before the walls of Harfleur? Who was it who assembled such cutthroats as Pistol and Nym and brought them to France "to suck, to suck, the very blood to suck" [II. iii. 56]? The very question by which the King disclaims responsibility, ironically forces a more profound consideration of the matter.

Whether Henry's words express indifference, ala a lack of moral sensitivity, or a sure sense of the usefulness of terror, it is impossible to say. His motives escape us. But we can see that while there seems to be a thinness of feeling, there is at the same time a sure political sense of what is required of a king and the leader of a great army engaged in the conquest of a kingdom. This ambivalence emerges again and again, to reach full statement on the night before the battle of Agincourt. The King puts aside his public role, covering himself with a dark cloak, and walks in the night among the army. He comes to the campfire . . . of three ordinary English soldiers, John Bates, Alexander Court, and Michael Williams. The soldiers are face to face on the eve of the battle with those existential questions which so many others have faced in *The Henriad*, and they voice these questions in a most simple way. The soldiers are frightened about dying and worried about their families and their own souls. Is the cause for which they fight a just one? If it is not, what happens to the soul of a man who dies hating and killing other men? How can a man reconcile his duty to his king and his duty as a Christian?

> But if the cause be not good, the King himself
> hath a heavy reckoning to make when all those
> legs and arms and heads, chopp'd off in a bat-
> tle, shall join together at the latter day and cry
> all 'We died at such a place'—some swearing,
> some crying for a surgeon, some upon their
> wives left poor behind them, some upon the
> debts they owe, some upon their children rawly
> left. I am afeard there are few die well that die
> in a battle; for how can they charitably dispose
> of anything when blood is their argument? Now,
> if these men do not die well, it will be a black
> matter for the King that led them to it; who to
> disobey were against all proportion of subjec-
> tion.
>
> [IV. i. 134-46]

Harry Plantagenet responds as authority must respond: the King's cause *is* just, and his quarrel honorable, and therefore the men are absolved of any responsibility before God for shedding blood. But, almost as if in doubt, he goes on to argue that "the King is not bound to answer the particular endings of his soldiers" [IV. i. 155-56] because he did not intend their deaths when he brought them to France. Here again, as before Harfleur, he is raising the questions he intends to settle: whether he intended death or not, he did bring his subjects to France, where they may die, and surely he bears some responsibility. And he continues to avoid and raise the full question of responsibility by arguing that many of the soldiers carry mortal sins upon their souls and that therefore if they die in battle the King bears no responsibility for their damnation: "Every subject's duty is the King's; but every subject's soul is his own" [IV. i. 176-77]. But this really does not answer Williams's objection that every man who dies in battle dies in sin trying to murder his fellow men, and he is doing so because his King has brought him to this place and ordered him to fight. In this brief scene in the middle of darkness on the edge of a great battle, Michael Williams has faced for himself and his King the most fundamental questions about the responsibility of rulers and men. But Henry does not answer the questions, either because he does not understand them or because no ruler of a state can ever answer such questions.

The actions and the speeches of King Henry V produce a curious ambiguity. On one hand he is the hero king, the restorer of England's glory, and the efficient manager of the realm; but he is at the same time, it would appear, a cunning Machiavel, a cynical politician, a man lacking in moral depth, perhaps even a limited intelligence. Our difficulties in understanding the King are intensified by the almost total absence from the play of speeches in which Henry speaks as a private man, directly revealing his own feelings. He lives in the full glare of public life, and even those usually private activities such as wooing a wife are carried out on the great stage of the world. Nor does his language yield insights into the depths of self of the kind found in the language of Richard II, Falstaff, Hotspur. Instead, Henry uses political and heroic rhetoric whose brightly polished surface allows no penetration.

Faced with the absence of motives, critics have resolved the problem by judging Henry according to their particular moral bias and concluding that he is either a good and efficient ruler who sacrifices himself for the good of the state, or a hypocritical and cunning politician who relentlessly seizes every opportunity to extend and consolidate his power. We must, however, take Henry as Shakespeare gives him to us: a man who has no private personal self, but only a public character, a character which is supremely, unerringly political, which chooses without hesitation that course of action which will make the kingdom function efficiently, balance the divisive powers within, and strengthen the ruler's grasp on the body politic.

Our own age shares with Shakespeare's some understanding of political man, and the following description of an American politician is at once a perfect description, even down to the small details, of Henry V:

> He is a totally political man, clever but not thoughtful, calculating more than reflective. He appears at once sentimental and ruthless, thin-skinned and imperious, remarkably attuned to public moods and utterly expert at the "game" of political maneuver. He is all of a piece, seemingly monolithic, not only completely *in* but totally *of* politics. Upon the devices and costs of political manipulation he is capable of looking with some irony, but toward the idea of the manipulation itself and the kind of life it entails he shows no irony whatever.
> [Irving Howe, in his essay "I'd Rather Be Wrong"]

Henry reverses the path taken by Richard II, who believed that kingship and rule were his reality but discovered under the battering of circumstance that he was only a mortal man,

> you have but mistook me all this while.
> I live with bread like you, feel want,
> Taste grief, need friends; subjected thus,
> How can you say to me I am a king?
> [*Richard II*, III. ii. 174-77]

At the other end of the cycle, the King who has known from the beginning that he is a man playing king—"Yet herein will I imitate the sun" [*I Henry IV*, I. ii. 197]—discovers, however briefly, the claims of his humanity, only to turn away and lock himself forever into the role.

*The Henriad* traces in its kings a great paradox: necessity forces man out of role into reality—necessity forces man back out of reality into role. The movement is much like that of the *Aeneid*, where the establishment of New Troy and, eventually, Augustan order requires the absorption of the man Aeneas into

the role of the founder of Rome, and the destruction of such turbulent energies as Dido and Turnus. In both the Roman and English epics the even balance of loss and gain create finally a tone of great sadness inextricably mixed with great triumph. (pp. 27-32)

*Alvin B. Kernan, "The Henriad: Shakespeare's Major History Plays," in* The Yale Review, *Vol. LIX, No. 1, October, 1969, pp. 3-32.*

## DOROTHY COOK  (essay date 1972)

[*Cook asserts that* Henry V *dramatizes "the theme of individual maturity" by demonstrating the king's growing realization of both his responsibility toward his subjects and the necessity of a humble reliance on the will of God. While the early scenes show that he has already acquired the requisite political and military virtues for his role as monarch, Cook contends, Henry's conduct from Act III onward is increasingly determined by his private virtues, and it is his mercy, humility, equity, and piety that account for his success at Agincourt and demonstrate that he is, indeed, "the ideal king." Cook also examines the structure of* Henry V. *She argues that as the king undergoes triumphs and reversals, Shakespeare alternately quickens and slows the tempo of the dramatic action, balances the placement of psychologically significant scenes, and, through the use of multiple plotting, provides contrasts to Henry's progress toward personal maturity.*]

If one does not naively require that what he reads and watches confirm his own beliefs, he may find Shakespeare's *Henry V* a very appealing and artistic play. Moreover, the meaning that grows out of the various structural complexities, particularly the skillful development of the play's hero, King Henry, possesses a kind of dramatic truth that can be disputed only on the somewhat petty grounds of taste. Like the sight lines in a magnificent painting, the more overt ordering of the narrative structure, together with the more organic structuring of the multiple plotting in *Henry V*, reinforce and enhance the principal action of Henry's progress and achievements throughout the play. They represent not only the culmination of Shakespeare's study of kingship in the second tetralogy but also, and, it seems, more importantly, a subtle study in the spiritual growth of a responsible leader. Because he is an amenable human being, Henry becomes in the course of the play a mature ruler, a man who succeeds in fulfilling, to his subjects' and his own satisfaction, the demands of the private and the public life.

On the surface, the division of *Henry V* into five acts, each preceded by an informative prologue or chorus, constitutes a clear narrative line. So ordered, the play moves climactically toward the confrontation of the "two mighty monarchies" [Prologue, 20] of England and France. The dramatic skill of this level of development deserves examination because it makes for a clarity of pattern that invites the reader to look beneath and consider deeper levels of design and meaning in the play.

The Prologue and choruses generally serve an expository purpose, bridging the gaps in time and space between the acts and binding together the various stages of Henry's physical and spiritual progress; the depiction of them in the acts themselves, represents a dramatic, almost cinematic, emphasis upon only the most decisive and meaningful occasions. (p. 111)

In addition to keeping the narrative line clearly before the audience, the Prologue and choruses provide the action with a suitable background mood of national excitement and an atmosphere of pomp and ceremony, reflecting especially the enthusiasm of the patriotic citizen. Hence the Prologue evokes an epic "Muse of fire" with which to paint the "swelling scene" [Prologue, 1, 4] and convey the portentousness of the coming battle. Preceding Act II, the chorus's comments on the preparations of England's fiery youth, selling "pasture now, to buy the horse" [Chorus, II, 5] and the reference to the French plot create a sense of tension that, since there is actually less fighting in this play than in *I Henry IV,* and particularly since Henry's life is never really shown to be in danger, suffice in themselves as sources of dramatic interest. By contrast they also stress the more significant psychological nature of the action. As preface to Act IV, the chorus is especially important in portraying a sympathetically striking picture of tired but depressed, disadvantaged English forces, "Proud of their numbers, and secure in soul," and an ominous as well as repulsive account of the "confident and over-lusty French" [Chorus, IV, 17, 18], whose superior numbers and dreadful proximity provide a contrast that heightens English heroism. Finally, the chorus before Act V conveys the jubilance and celebrations among the proud English people upon the return of their victorious king. All together, these descriptions arouse a sense of anticipation of the English adventure and accomplishment.

In addition to clarifying and, with a sense of historic destiny, underlining Henry's movements, the Prologue and choruses successively characterize the public Henry, again very largely from the viewpoint of the admiring general citizen. The "warlike Harry" is said to be master of the hounds of "famine, sword, and fire" [Prologue, 5, 7] and is bravely superior to the snakes of treachery. At Hampton pier this "well-appointed King" [Chorus, III, 4] proudly refuses the compromising offer of the French and embarks for France where, an example of fortitude in adversity, he assumes a "cheerful semblance and sweet majesty" [Chorus, IV, 40] to encourage his men. "Being free from vainness and self-glorious pride" [Chorus, V, 20], Henry returns to England, insisting that the victory belongs to God, thus climaxing the epic function of these links in forecasting Henry's progress throughout the play.

The order of the scenes and acts further reveals Shakespeare's structural skill in focusing upon Henry. Having chosen to concentrate mainly on dramatic, often psychological, moments in his story, Shakespeare not only builds through the reverses in Henry's good and bad fortunes toward his triumphant meeting with the King of France, but he also builds with steady climactic progress toward Henry's self-realization—both of which are climaxed in the last scene of the play. To begin with, Shakespeare utilizes the Bishop of Ely and the Archbishop of Canterbury to explain the immediate situation and by their praise of Henry's kingly qualities to prepare the audience for his behavior in the important council scene that follows and for the emphasis on the king throughout the play. Although the chorus to Act II omits any mention of its two scenes of low life, these interludes in the action serve to quicken the pace of the overall action and to set in relief the courtly activities of scenes ii and iv. The tempo is further increased by the succession of seven brief scenes in Act III. At the beginning of this act Henry's fortunes reach an early height. During the course of the next six scenes, however, they decline, so that by the end of Act III Henry and his exhausted forces are faced with virtual annihilation by the greater numbers of the French army. At this low point in Henry's outward progress, Shakespeare slows his pace to concentrate particularly on the individual Henry. The opening scene of Act IV is like an island among the surrounding briefer scenes; as such, it relates in stress alone to the earlier council scene and forecasts the final

reward scene. It invites a comparative look backward as well as forward. Appropriately, Henry's ascent to victory begins at this point. Like many of the scenes in Act III, the remaining scenes in Act IV take the audience horizontally back and forth between the French and English forces and vertically up and down through the English ranks, gradually blending lines of action in the exchanges between Henry, his leaders, his men, and the French envoy. The battle, as Henry once suggests, is not only the time of reckoning but also a point of structural unification. The fourth act ends with a reassertion of order, and the fifth act clearly establishes the return to peace. The resolution occurs in the form of Pistol's comeuppance in the opening scene and in the form of the concessions required of the French in the closing scene.

Aside from the use of the Prologue and choruses and the deft handling of conflict and resolution, *Henry V* is organically unified by the careful arrangement of several lines of action involving Pistol and the figures of low life, the French nobles and women, and Fluellen and the other soldiers. Whereas the paths of the soldiers and the French relate throughout to the main plot and eventually converge with it, the low-life characters hardly touch Henry in this play. Only twice does the king even appear in close proximity with Pistol, once in Act III when he commends Fluellen for refusing to take Pistol's side in behalf of his condemned fellow thief, Bardolph, and again in Act IV when Henry overhears Pistol briefly express faith in the king. Nevertheless, the action of this subplot, like everything else in the play, revolves around and points up Henry's progress. Specifically, it provides a contrast with Henry and his behavior, it relates ironically to the French and their values and activities, and it is governed by the Welshman Fluellen, who becomes Henry's agent. And thus in the relative stasis of the last act, where all action is completed and structurally balanced, Pistol, too, meets his justice. (pp. 112-14)

Although multiple plotting in *Henry V* greatly enhances its unity, Henry himself and his course constitute the chief source of the play's symmetry. For in his role Henry demonstrates compelling qualities of the political, judicial, and spiritual leader, both as king and as man. Behind his public composure is the craft of the king who wishes, while busying his country with wars, to fill its treasury, apparently using appeals to patriotism and to religion as means to his end. But Henry also displays a genuine, though at first secondary, concern for the life of the individual soldier and for his own worth and security as a king. Certainly the complexity of Henry's motives qualifies the surface bravado and patriotism that often makes *Henry V* unappealing, especially to modern audiences. Moreover, these deeper and more personal levels of interest are evident from the very outset when the patronizing and expedient Archbishop of Canterbury, worried that the bill before Parliament would strip the "better half of our possession" [I. i. 8] earnestly reports to his colleague, the Bishop of Ely, that the young king has reformed, the "offending Adam" having been "whipped" from him, and that he is "full of grace and fair regard" [I. i. 29, 22]. Thus, like all England, the Church must turn to the new king not merely for justice on this occasion but for proof of his ability as a leader. For although Henry is described as knowledgeable in the affairs of church and state, as well as in the "discourse of war" [I. i. 43], this anticipation of his first appearance nevertheless subtly recalls his youthful and wayward association with Falstaff. The praise is thus undercut by a critical vein of reservation, a subtle but effectively questioning attitude of wonder. Much dramatic interest in the play depends upon Henry's ability to live up to the good opinion of his subjects, proving himself to them, to those who sneer at him abroad, and to his own satisfaction, with the result that the play must be read not only as the record of a triumphant public campaign but also and primarily as a personal quest.

In the council scene Henry speaks well. Manifest particularly in his rhetoric, his control shows that he is able to elicit "just cause" for his war upon France from the highest officials of the Church and the government. With a kind of deadly confidence, Henry only asks questions, inquiring, "May I with right and conscience make this claim?" [I. ii. 96], thereby prompting the war-mongering rationalizations from the Archbishop. When Henry stresses the need for positive moral justification, he slyly appears as the better defender of the faith, whereas the head of the Church takes the position of scheming politician. Henry never openly acknowledges any motive but that of national honor, but his methods and his reasons are undeniably political. He obviously wishes to unite the country, as his father advised, and however historically right the Archbishop may be, both he and Henry are shown—the king much more subtly than the churchman—as arguing their own ends. (pp. 117-18)

The unappealing political motives of Henry are mitigated by his awareness of the great cost of war in terms of individuals' lives, by his faith, and by his own decision to accept the challenge to prove himself. By asking "May I with right and conscience make this claim?" . . . Henry has apparently sought the "justification" for his war, but he listens carefully to the reasons given, and the tone of his answers is generally serious. He is without the self-satisfaction that an egotistic and ambitious young king would display when he asks for surety and truth, ironically, from the Archbishop, and it is not merely in retrospect that his concern for life is revealed to be genuine. When Henry warns,

> God doth know how many now in health
> Shall drop their blood in approbation
> Of what your reverence shall incite us to,
>
> [I. ii. 18-20]

he may be evading his own responsibility for the war, but he speaks with a gravity and a persistent emphasis that conveys his sympathy and sincerity. (p. 119)

The question of why in his position of authority Henry tolerates the hypocrisy of the church is answered by his own sense of moral purpose, which includes not only his quest in France but his recognition of the necessity, particularly for the benefit of the country, of proving himself. The continuing theme of the test of maturity and merit in Henry, introduced by the reminders in scene i of his past, surfaces in the reinforcement Henry's nobles give to Ely's idea that the blood and courage of his forefathers is in Henry "Ripe for exploits and mighty enterprises" [I. ii. 121]. Exeter says, for example, that his "brother kings and monarchs" expect Henry to rouse himself in battle, "As did the former lions of your blood" [I. ii. 122, 124], and Westmoreland adds that the rich and loyal nobles themselves, whose hearts "lie pavilioned in the fields of France" [I. ii. 129] await his command. Hence when the Dauphin sends word that Henry savors too much of "youth" [I. ii. 250] and that he "cannot revel into dukedoms" [I. ii. 253] in France, and when he gives to the English king tennis balls to play with instead, Henry *must* take due notice of the seriously degrading reference to his "wilder days" and vow to "Be like a king, and show my sail of greatness" [I. ii. 267, 274] and "rise there with so full a glory / That I will dazzle all the eyes of

France" [I. ii. 278-79]. The campaign therefore largely assumes the significance of a test, with nearly the whole world watching. To avoid his challenge would be to call in question his own authority. He may have proved himself militarily in *I Henry IV*, and civilly in *II Henry IV*, but now he must prove himself king once and for all. A careful reader may well come away from the first act of *Henry V* with an awareness of the complexity of Henry's motives, some of which, such as his general concern with cause, appear to represent his effort to put the best face possible on a difficult but necessary campaign. Generally, his combination of political cunning and personal consideration here and throughout the play is arresting.

Having embarked on his campaign, Henry can now begin to exercise a kind of active control beyond that expected of him in the formal and somewhat restrictive atmosphere of the council chamber. In fact, his clever and ironic handling of the traitors, Scroop, Cambridge, and Grey at once demonstrates Henry's increasing autonomy. The tension in this scene does not lie, as the chorus rather sensationally suggests, in a dramatic confrontation between enemies, or in near escape, but rather in the king's judgment of the guilty. In his decision to free a man whose threat against him he considers the result of excessive drink, Henry allows the traitors to judge themselves, showing them more leniency than they deserve, as they themselves admit. In this unusual degree of mercy and in his passionate condemnation of their treachery, Henry rises, more fervidly than he does at the end of Act I, to a scourging indictment that further confirms the sincerity of his concern for his men and his country. "For this revolt of thine," he remarks, revealing the dismay of a man who seeks to be trustworthy and who is betrayed by his close associates, "is like / Another fall of man" [II. ii. 141-42]. Because Henry emphasizes moral justice against those who would have led his country to "desolation" [II. ii. 173], these men do not die with curses on their lips. Instead they repent and their last words recognize the authority of God and their king. Although Henry forgives them personally and joins them in asking God's pardon, his sentence requires their deaths as traitors to their country in time of war. This decision represents Henry's first victory over France; he must purge from his own ranks his enemy's insidious efforts at preventing his mission. . . . Exeter's remarks on Henry's prowess are proved by the king's firm yet just treatment of the conspirators. As a comment on Henry's progress, the English ambassador says of Henry,

> And be assured, you'll find a difference,
> As we his subjects have in wonder found,
> Between the promise of his greener days
> And these he masters now. Now he weighs time
> Even to the utmost grain. . . .
>
> [II. iv. 134-38]

With the famous rhetoric of "Once more unto the breach" [III. i. 1] in the opening scene of Act III, Henry's progress might be said to constitute additional proof of his kingly abilities and confirmation of his initial vows. The execution of the traitors established his political and military command. This demonstration of internal control is a preface to Exeter's appearance at the French court. Unlike the Dauphin, with whom Henry is from the first contrasted, Henry does not boast cavalierly or mince words. His threats are based, as the French king recognizes, on real potential. That his word is reliable both he and the play are concerned to demonstrate. In the gradual and, it is important to recognize, orderly realization of Henry's capacity, the appearance of an English ambassador before the French leaders is not only evidence of Henry's spare and incisive diplomacy but also a prelude in itself to his victory at Harfleur. The rousing encouragement of his speech before that city is another stage in his development, showing in particular Henry's military leadership, not at the initial charge, where it might be easy and expected, but at the crucial point where renewed effort is required. . . . The "Once more" speech is a call to arms appropriate to the freshness of the soldiers and to Henry's early good fortunes in his campaign. And as such it marks a kind of high point in his military success, but it also represents, because of his individual development, another stage in his progress of self-realization. It is the last of his rhetorically stirring speeches.

Politically and militarily, Henry has been more than equal to the early demands of his venture. Now that his forces have suffered loss of life and strength he must withstand the more demanding trials of adversity. It is his response to this test that really stresses Henry's best qualities, notably those of humane mercy, becoming humility, firm justice, honest pride, and sincere faith. Heretofore somewhat less apparent than his political and military skills, these private virtues now tend to dominate his action. He remains an effective soldier and king, but his more personal traits account more for his endurance and hence his victory. As the tempo of Act III increases, these qualities are manifest in Henry's remaining appearances: in the terms of "cool and temperate . . . grace" [III. iii. 30] that he offers the governor of Harfleur; in his disciplined occupation and brave defense of the city; and his proud but realistic reply to the French messenger, Mountjoy. Unlike the haughty French leaders, Henry is realistic and modest. His humility especially prepares the audience, despite the ominous plot line, for the English supremacy at Agincourt.

From the height of confidence and shrewd control of the council scene in Act I through his initial successes, Henry moves towards a depth of depression and enlightening humility expressed in his soliloquies at the conclusion of the pivotal first scene of Act IV. Henry admits at the beginning of this act that the English are in great danger, countering with the obvious call for greater courage. But he is no Hotspur. Even his poor attempt at grim humor cannot disguise his pessimism, and he speaks to Sir Thomas Erpingham as though the good old knight's death were almost a certainty, saying "A good soft pillow for that good white head / Were better than a churlish turf of France" [IV. i. 14-15]. . . . Sir Thomas replies heroically to Henry, and his good example somewhat cheers the discouraged king, who even as he goes off in disguise to debate awhile with himself is met by the encouraging good opinion of the king from Pistol and the admiring Fluellen. His spirit slightly eased, Henry next meets the soldiers Bates, Court, and Williams. Their sense of doom, cynicism, and irresponsibility prompt Henry, who is not necessarily to be held to consistency in behavior during this remarkable time of release from his authority, to defend himself and further motivate his men. First, he applies the lesson just learned from Sir Thomas that "no man should possess him with any appearance of fear, lest he, by showing it, should dishearten his army" [IV. i. 110-12]. He then asserts again the honor of his cause. Next, he rationalizes the degree of the king's responsibility. Alone, Henry soliloquizes in a rather self-pitying tone on the difficulties of being a king instead of a private "wretch" [IV. i. 278], and finally, he prays to God for help. Examined closely, these constitute an important turning point in the play.

On the key point of responsibility, Henry argues, like a sententious clergyman, that soldiers owe the king duty, whereas their souls, though they are, as he once told Falstaff, owed to God, are their own. This long and somewhat rambling prose speech in which Henry avoids obligation does not convince the soldiers of anything but the self-evident truth that they are responsible for their own sins. Henry clearly does not answer the charge against the king and his cause, and the fact that Henry's reply is largely circumlocution indicates, not necessarily that he deliberately misrepresents Bates, but possibly that he himself has not fully understood the gravity and extent of his own responsibility. He is on safer though no less important ground when he defends the king's word in the exchange of gloves with Williams. Yet the effect of his encounter with these men is to bruise and shake him inwardly, though he appears outwardly unaffected. For if he is to be the ideal king, Henry must accept the responsibility of the ruler, but facing up to this central matter of maturity naturally does not come easily. Having begun by putting the responsibility for the war on the Church, Henry has progressed to the stage where, as a sensitive and intelligent man, he cannot now avoid it himself. And the measure of his personal greatness lies in his wrestling with and taking on this difficult and weighty burden. Another figure might have escaped the issue of responsibility by passing it off with the defense of his personal honor, parting from his men with a subtle reminder, which Henry does make, of the spoils of victory. But Shakespeare has carefully developed the proper capacity of character in Henry, so that the concern for keeping his oath with Williams leads Henry plausibly back to the issue of the king's responsibility and, rather poignantly, to his indulgent questioning and lamentation of his "hard condition" [IV. i. 233]. Indeed, he comes to the very verge, at his most despairing stage, of rejecting "place, degree and form" [IV. i. 246] in his momentary envy of the irresponsible life of the common man. But Henry's crucial acceptance of full awareness of responsibility comes when he prays earnestly and privately not for himself alone but primarily for his soldiers. Repudiating his assumed role as God's champion and spokesman for His way, he humbly asks God to be his champion. He prays that both he and his men will be free from fear and "the sense of reck'ning" [IV. i. 291] that he has just invoked in speaking to the soldiers. Acknowledging his own father's guilt, Henry implores God's "pardon" [IV. i. 305]. At this point his humility becomes genuine. Previously he had claimed God as his ally, relying on the facile strength of the Church's argument; now he *asks* God, sincerely and deeply, for his alliance. When Tillyard speaks of Henry's "sudden miraculous conversion when he came to the throne" [see excerpt above, 1944], he overlooks, I think, this evolution of Henry's attitude from a sincere but interested and partly political alliance with God to a serious faith and gratitude.

Henry's emotional disclaimers to Bates, Court, and Williams are of course really a dramatically psychological recognition of the burden that is his, without which no ruler can pursue that most important virtue of magnanimity. From despair and excuse and self-righteousness and poignant weariness, Henry moves out of his nadir of depression into self-realization. When he concludes the scene with "The day, my friends, and all things stay for me" [IV. i. 308], he has not merely resumed a role; he has acquired a responsibility and a humble awareness. This tight-lipped recognition of his responsibility as crusading king and worthy individual marks the turning point in his fortunes and especially in his ability to govern. It is further manifest in his subsequent order to set free and provide with money any man who does not wish to fight. And it is heralded by his magnificent evocation in scene iii of the Old English warrior's code of pure honor in heroic behavior. These genuinely stirring lines speak to the "happy few" [IV. iii. 60], who understand that valor in battle has a worth of its own which rightly warrants fame. It is a great speech. Made by a king with his back to the wall, this appeal carries conviction and maturity as no other speech does in the play. At its conclusion Henry again rejects in humble but courageous terms the mocking French offer of ransom. So inspired, it is no wonder that the English leaders prove themselves the very antithesis of the bragging, cowardly, ignoble, and effeminate French. And so generalled, it is appropriate that the English are victorious. (pp. 120-25)

The vision that the various lines of action in *Henry V* convey is not merely the "establishment in England of an order based on consecrated authority and crowned successfully by action against France" [see excerpt above by D. A. Traversi, 1941]. In fact, Henry's victory is the means to a personal development that leads appropriately to marriage and the promise of an heir. Not just an act of policy, this contract dramatizes Henry's personal readiness to govern England and more importantly to perpetuate his line. Because the action of the play turns on Henry's acceptance of individual responsibility and culminates in the arrangement of marriage, the theme of individual maturity, which assures political peace within and without the country, becomes primary. And to look back over the play and the tetralogy after studying *Henry V* is to see that Henry's confidence rests on a capacity that has been—and as the Epilogue emphasizes, can only be—won by means of a great personal struggle. . . . Seen, therefore, as showing the gradual emergence of wisdom and humaneness over craft, *Henry V* becomes a very appealing play. It does not have to be made dark in tone to attract a modern audience nor does it convey the cynical belief that, as long as a king is an effective and calculating ruler his individual qualities are irrelevant. Politically cunning, militarily confident, Henry is an ideal king precisely because of his individual spiritual qualities. Neither man nor God is expendable to him . . . and thus Shakespeare's Henry becomes at last another man for all seasons. (pp. 127-28)

Dorothy Cook, "'Henry V': Maturing of Man and Majesty," in Studies in the Literary Imagination, Vol. V, No. 1, April, 1972, pp. 111-28.

## ROBERT ORNSTEIN (essay date 1972)

[*Ornstein is a twentieth-century American critic and scholar and the author of* A Kingdom for a Stage: The Achievement of Shakespeare's History Plays *(1972), which has been called one of the most important contributions to Shakespearean studies in recent years, as well as the most influential study of the history plays since E. M. W. Tillyard's* The Elizabethan World Picture *(1944). The purpose of Ornstein's book was to challenge the popular belief that Shakespeare's histories dramatize not such universal concerns as human nature and the effects of power, but the orthodox view of English history as championed by the Tudor monarchy. Ornstein's attempt to interpret the history plays as drama rather than historical documents contributed to a reappraisal of these works, specifically with regard to their political assumptions, and signified their return to the same standard of evaluation accorded the rest of the Shakespearean canon. In the following excerpt, he contends that despite allusions throughout* Henry V *to "justice and mercy and the talk of ancient disciplines and rules," Shakespeare here presents war as brutal and dehumanizing. The king himself, Ornstein argues, "is the very personification of War," an apocalyptic figure of "famine, sword, and fire" (Prologue, 7) who has a limited appreciation of the effects of war on common citizens. The critic maintains that the theme*

*of kindness is frequently juxtaposed with the theme of war, and he especially discerns a contrast between these two ideas in certain aspects or events of the play: the sympathetic judgment which the Chorus entreats from the audience; Henry's dispassionate and impersonal treatment of the traitors, the citizens of Harfleur, and Bardolph; and Mistress Quickly's forgiveness and charity toward Falstaff. Finally, in his analysis of Act IV, Scene i, Ornstein points out that although Henry resists "the thought that he will be accountable for all this suffering," he was not obliged to debate the justice of his cause with his soldiers; the critic adds that the men are as eager to "place the burden of their immortal souls on Henry" as he is to disclaim "responsibility for their deaths."*]

Did it never occur to Shakespeare that some would regard his "ideal king" as a blatant imperialist? Or did he, like Machiavelli, regard the empire-builder as the ideal prince? The acclamation of the King in *Henry V* is very explicit and very specific. Echoing the judgment of the Chroniclers, the Chorus declares him a "mirror of all Christian kings" [Chorus, II, 6], the princes of the Church admire his mastery of divinity and policy, and his captains praise his astuteness as a military commander. Such speeches do not prove, however, that Harry was an ideal ruler—one who brought to his nation the blessings of lasting peace and unity. Although characters speak of Harry's genius at rule, little of that genius is evident when he discusses the French campaign with his councilors, and still less when he leads his army to victory. Our hero is a man on horseback, not a statesman, a military leader who metes out summary judgments, not the bearer of the sacred sword of heaven. The opening Chorus invites us to imagine a "swelling scene" and a Harry as fierce as the Apocalypse, who, letting slip the dogs of war, licenses carnage:

> Then should the warlike Harry, like himself,
> Assume the port of Mars, and at his heels
> (Leash'd in, like hounds) should famine, sword, and
>   fire
> Crouch for employment.
>
> [Prologue, 5-8]

The portrait is emblematic, and the emblem is unmistakable—or at least was unmistakable to Shakespeare's audience, for Harry is the very personification of War, a figure described in the Induction to *The Mirror for Magistrates* as standing

> in glitterying arms yclad,
> With visage grym, sterne lookes, and blackely hewed;
> In his right hand a naked sworde he had,
> That to the hiltes was al with blud embrewed:
> And in his left, (that kinges and kingdomes rewed)
> Famine and fyer he held, and therewythall
> He razed townes and threwe downe towers and all.

The Chorus' vision of Harry in the port of Mars could be explained as just a bit of awe-struck rhetoric, except that the apocalyptic image returns again in the scenes where Harry plays the mighty huntsman of war. At Harfleur he describes his troops as "greyhounds in the slips, / Straining upon the start" [III. i. 31-2], and urges them to imitate the action of the tiger, even as he was urged by Canterbury to forage like his ancestors in French blood. When imagery of this kind appeared in the battle scenes of *King John*, one could precisely gauge the emotional effect Shakespeare intended because the Bastard was present to anatomize the senseless brutality and waste of life in the war. The Chorus to *Henry V*, who rejoices in Harry's employment of famine, sword, and fire, is a less obvious guide to Shakespeare's attitude. (pp. 177-78)

The Chorus is an interesting figure because in one aspect he is your average patriotic Elizabethan whose eyes moisten at the thought of his nation's triumphs, and in another aspect, he is the author's surrogate, a means by which Shakespeare reflects on his art as well as on England's history. The Chorus plays the latter role in a curious way, because where the Epilogues of Shakespeare's plays are appropriately deferential to his audience, the Chorus to *Henry V* is absolutely obsequious to the "gentles all" whom he addresses and astonishingly apologetic about the limitations of the playwright, the play, and the company. (p. 186)

Shakespeare, I think, never doubted for a moment his ability to deal with epic subjects in drama. What he does "honestly" apologize for through the Chorus is his inability to render on stage the destructiveness of war. Unable to present Harry the huntsman in all his apocalyptic horror—with famine, sword, and fire at his feet—the Chorus asks "pardon, gentles all" [Prologue, 8]. Once again before the third act, the Chorus apologizes for the inadequacy of the artistic representation when he asks the audience to imagine the cannon "with fatal mouths gaping" [Chorus, III, 27] on Harfleur. Since Harry likes not the French offer of terms,

> The nimble gunner
> With linstock now the devilish cannon touches,
> *Alarum, and chambers go off.*

And down goes all before them. Still be kind,
And eke out our performance with your mind.

[Chorus, III, 32-5]

If there is a subtle irony in the Chorus' innocent manner, it is directed, not so much against Harry and his men, as against the audience. Assuming that they want a realistic portrayal of patriotic gore, that they would like to hear the cannon's roar, to see the walls crumbling, the houses burning, the swords whistling through the air, the Chorus asks the "gentle" spectators nevertheless to "still be kind" He even promises to digest the "abuse of distance" so that the gentles present will have a gentle pass to France, because "we'll not offend one stomach with our play" [Chorus II, 32, 40].

The immediate juxtaposition of the plea for kindness and the cannon's roar and the recurrent appeals to the gentleness of the audience remind us that from the beginning of civilization war has been an aristocratic enterprise as well as an exalted literary theme. For centuries the hunt of battle has left an "unnatural" trail of devastation through the world, and for centuries the impulse to the hunt has been native to man—bred in his blood, enshrined in his history, and celebrated in his art. Before Agincourt, Canterbury recalls, there was Cressy; before Cressy there was the Norman Conquest, to which the French nobility refer; and long before the Norman Conquest were the

*Exeter's description of the deaths of Suffolk and York, Act IV. Scene vi. By H. Corbauld. The Department of Rare Books and Special Collections, The University of Michigan Library.*

"pristine wars of the Romans" [III. ii. 81-2], the campaigns of Caesar and Pompey, and the famous victories of Alexander the Great, which Fluellen learnedly cites. Since time immemorial the battlefield has provided the supreme test of nobility. Just as Harry proved his princeliness at Shrewsbury [in *I Henry IV*], he will prove at Agincourt his right to an imperial title, and those who shed their blood with him, he promises, will also gentle their condition, be they "ne'er so vile" [IV. iii. 62].

The Chorus bids us "gently to hear, kindly to judge the play" [Prologue, 34]. If we have any doubt what kindliness of judgment is we can take our cue from the King, who stands in judgment over the traitors at Southampton and over the citizens of Harfleur, who confirms the sentencing of Bardolph and pardons Williams. Unless we see that kindness is a theme in *Henry V*, we will wonder why Shakespeare allows so much space to the scene at Southampton and why he amplifies the Chronicle account of this episode by inventing the cat-and-mouse game which Harry plays with the traitors before he condemns them. Once again, as in the rejection of Falstaff, Harry's behavior is unimpeachably correct; the earls confess their shameful guilt, and their punishment exactly fits their crime. Once again, however, Harry's manner is somewhat priggish if not heartless. He entraps the traitors in their hypocrisy in very much the way that the Duke, at the end of *Measure for Measure,* entraps Angelo; but, unlike the Duke, Harry makes no attempt to reform the traitors, who, like Angelo, are stunned into confession and repentance. Where the Duke's game of cat and mouse has its moral and psychological purposes, Harry's game simply allows him to enjoy his mastery of those who would have betrayed him. Their crime he regards as a breach of personal faith, but his rage he considers wholly impersonal. It is the law, he explains (as Angelo does to Isabella) that condemns wrongdoers, not he; and he sees himself as the helpless instrument of the law, though just before he showed that he has the godlike office of charity. But even as he protests that he seeks no revenge "touching our person" [II. ii. 174], he turns on the traitors with a fury that is barely contained by the conventionalities of his pulpit rhetoric. Sixty-five lines are scarcely enough to express his outrage at their offence, which seems to him so hellish, so damned, so fiendish and unnatural that it can only be compared to the original disobedience in the Garden. Three times the mirror of all Christian kings calls on God to have mercy on the traitors because, though he promises that he will weep for them, he offers no mercy himself. Or, rather, he explains that he was filled with mercy for the drunken soldier who merely railed against his person, a mercy that was "suppress'd and kill'd" [II. ii. 80] by the traitors' own counsel. (pp. 186-88)

Immediately before and after this scene, the tavern crew gathers on stage to speak of the dying Falstaff, whose heart the King broke. Unless God is merciful, the traitors, Harry thinks, will end in hell. Where Falstaff will ultimately rest is a more dubious matter, but the Hostess, who sends him to his last reward, is sure that it will not be in hell. Like Harry, she also was betrayed; she was fobbed off, cheated, and mocked by the Falstaff whose last hours she tenderly comforted. Where Harry could enumerate every detail of the traitors' guilt, the foolish, forgetful Hostess cannot remember even the crimes Falstaff committed against her own person, though she reluctantly admits that Sir John "did in some sort, indeed, handle women" [II. iii. 37]. Where Harry invokes God's name repeatedly, the Hostess describes how she bid Falstaff not trouble himself before times with the thought of God:

So a' cried out, "God, God, God!" three or
four times. Now I, to comfort him, bid him a'
should not think of God; I hop'd there was no
need to trouble himself with such thoughts yet.
[II. iii. 18-22]

Are we to assume that the Hostess' muddle-headed sentiments are a foil to Harry's deeply religious and clear-sighted judgment? Or are we to wonder if there is not more tenderness of heart and Christian charity in this gross vessel than in the mirror for all Christian kings?

At his most self-righteous with the traitors, Harry is not quite John of Lancaster [in *2 Henry IV*], who sneered at the rebels' pose of piety and then betrayed them with pious protestations and finely spun casuistry. Where John could not see that good faith was at issue in his dealings at Gaultree Forest, Harry is well aware that mercy is the rarer action, but his moral awareness is of the mind, not of the heart. He knows intellectually the obligations he does not feel. Thus when he exhorts the citizens of Harfleur to surrender, he can describe the horror that threatens them with extraordinary detachment:

If I begin the batt'ry once again,
I will not leave the half-achieved Harfleur
Till in her ashes she lie buried.
The gates of mercy shall be all shut up,
And the flesh'd soldier, rough and hard of heart,
In liberty of bloody hand shall range
With conscience wide as hell, mowing like grass
Your fresh-fair virgins and your flow'ring infants.
What is it then to me if impious war,
Array'd in flames like to the prince of fiends,
Do with his smirch'd complexion, all fell feats
Enlink'd to waste and desolation?
What is't to me, when you yourselves are cause,
If your pure maidens fall into the hand
Of hot and forcing violation?
[III. iii. 7-21]

Just before, Harry had urged his men to imitate the action of the tiger; now he asks what it is to him if they act like raging beasts. He can promise Harfleur grace if he gets what he demands—and gets it immediately. Otherwise, he will turn his soldiers loose like dogs on a quarry and, once they taste blood, he will not be able to control them or be responsible for their savagery. Just as Harry could dissociate himself from the sentencing of the traitors, so too he can dissociate himself from the horror he threatens at Harfleur by abstracting the violence of war so that it seems to have a life and agency beyond his control. The raging beast will not be his army but "impious war." The women will be ravaged, not by his soldiers, but by "the hand of hot and forcing violation." And what rein, he asks, "can hold licentious wickedness / When down the hill he holds his fierce career"? [III. iii. 22-3] Here as always Harry sees the moral issue as a problem in casuistry. If he can find himself not guilty, he thinks his course justified, however many will suffer because of it. Some critics are confident that he would not have carried out his threat, and he does prove merciful to the citizens of the surrendered city. But the fact remains that Harry was capable of making the terrible threat— and in good conscience—because he does not see the horror of war feelingly.

Promising mercy and threatening destruction at Harfleur, Harry reminds modern readers (as he no doubt reminded Shakespeare) of Marlowe's Tamburlaine, who offered the citizens of Damascus the same choices. But where Tamburlaine has the simplistic morality of a mythological titan—his will is a universal law—Harry is all too human in his moral equivocations. Although he refers again and again during the play to his just and hallowed cause, and dedicates his victory to God, he speaks with conviction at Harfleur of the unholy desolation, and the hellish lusts and "liberties" of war. He describes the "filthy and contagious clouds / Of heady murther, spoil, and villany" [III. iii. 31-2] that o'er hang Harfleur and compares the impending slaughter of women and children to Herod's murder of the innocents. Yet even as the "base contagious clouds" [*1 Henry IV,* I. ii. 198] of his tavern cronies helped to create Harry's radiant future, so too the filthy and contagious clouds of murder, rapine, and villainy at Harfleur will bring him closer to a dazzling greatness. And whatever happens, the burden of guilt for the slaughter of innocents will be on the heads of the leaders of Harfleur if they persist in their "guilty defence."

Harry's ability to turn his consciousness of the horror of war into a weapon of coercion is fascinating. His men are not more tenderhearted, just less sensitive. Fluellen and the others beat their men into the breach, summarily condemn Bardolph to death for stealing, and adore their gallant king when he worthily commands them to cut their prisoners' throats.... Harry's followers, honest Christian men all, can give themselves to the bestiality of war in good conscience and go about the business of slaughtering their enemies, as Macmorris can at Harfleur, with the name of Christ on their lips:

> The town is beseech'd, and the trumpet calls
> us to the breach, and we talk, and be Crish, do
> nothing. 'Tis shame for us all. So God sa' me,
> 'tis shame to stand still, it is shame, by my
> hand! and there is throats to be cut, and works
> to be done, and there ish nothing done, so Crish
> sa' me, la!
>
> [III. ii. 107-13]

Such men do not disobey the Christian ethic; they are, like Harry, Christians as well as soldiers who, going about their good works on the field of battle, prove there is no activity so savage that men cannot reduce to sober order and to humane rules and disciplines. The discrimination of just and unjust wars was centuries old by Shakespeare's time. The rules of battle, which allowed captured populations to be expelled from cities and territories, to be sold into slavery or slaughtered, were carefully prescribed and scrupulously obeyed by honorable and courteous combatants. According to these rules, Harry's position at Harfleur was impeccable: a hopeless resistance to a siege was "guilty" because it needlessly cost the attackers' blood; and it thus gave the captors the right to slaughter or sell into captivity those who did not surrender. But, while the slaughter of babes at Harfleur would have been "right," the killing of the English camp boys was, as Fluellen remarked, "expressly against the law of arms" [IV. vii. 1-2], and angers the King.

Shall our guide to *Henry V* be medieval and Renaissance treatises on the proprieties of war? Or shall we see war feelingly through Shakespeare's eyes and recognize that, despite the appeals in *Henry V* to God and Christ, despite the references to justice and mercy and the talk of ancient disciplines and rules, war is an assault on the foundations of civilization. It is a breach in the structure of moral restraints, a hunt in which the pack as well as the quarry are dehumanized, and the most primitive bloodlusts and sexual appetites are unleashed. Armies have their camp followers; conquerors take their choice of

women, and maidenheads become as cheap as stinking mackerel, because women, caught up in the sexual excitements of war, are ready to offer their bodies even to the enemy soldiers. When what is animal in man is deliberately summoned forth and praised, other values, including that of mercy, are necessarily debased. Grace is equated, as in Harry's speeches to the French Ambassadors, not with angelic love but with a checked fury or a fettered passion. The King who mercifully spares the inhabitants of Harfleur shows equal "grace" at Agincourt when he allows the French to sort out their dead.

In his oration at Southampton, Harry equated treason with hell. In his oration at Harfleur he equates war with hell. Yet the slaughter of women and children at Harfleur, like the slaughter of the outnumbered English envisioned around the campfire on the eve of Agincourt, is a dread possibility that never materializes. By keeping the battle offstage, Shakespeare spares us the horror of war. Instead of hearing the moans of the dying, we listen to the good-natured wrangling of Fluellen, Gower, Macmorris, and Jamy. We are told that the French dead cover the field after Agincourt but we do not see them. They are part of the body count, of the statistics which testify to English courage and divine providence. Taking his cue directly from Holinshed, the author of *The Famous Victories* depicts ordinary French soldiers dicing for and gloating over the prisoners and booty they expect to win at Agincourt. Shakespeare, however, never allows his audience to see the French equivalents of Williams and Bates. Juxtaposing the wretchedness of simple English soldiers against the foppish overconfidence of French generals who wager on the number they will kill, he never shows the answering fires of the French camp where other men like Williams and Bates await the morrow. If an audience is to rejoice in the victory, it cannot feel too much for those who will litter the field. All that it can know is the hubris, folly, and effeteness of the French leaders, who, in the judgment of some historians, were nearly as incompetent as Shakespeare describes.

I do not mean that as we read *Henry V* we expect to see a French campfire scene on the eve of Agincourt and are conscious of its omission. Since our view of the English army has included from the beginning such volunteers as Bardolph and Pistol, it seems natural enough that we eavesdrop on Williams and Bates at Agincourt. We do not expect to see ordinary French men at arms because our view of the French is confined from the beginning to noblemen and princes. It is artistically appropriate, moreover, that the moral issue at Agincourt be debated among Englishmen and be focused on the fate of the English soldiers, because here as elsewhere in the History Plays the crucial question is the King's responsibility for the well-being of his subjects. Accused of malfeasance by Gaunt and York, Richard II literally stood trial before his peers at his deposition. In like manner Hal was accused of irresponsibility and disloyalty by his father in both *Henry IV* plays. Once again on trial in *Henry V,* he is indicted first by the French Herald, who accuses him of misleading and betraying his ragged army. Sharper still are the accusations of falsehood made by Williams and Bates, who doubt the King's statement that he refuses ransom. Now that the glittering chivalric adventure threatens to become a shambles there is cause for recriminations. The tables have turned; the hunters of crowns and coronets have become the prey. The once eager greyhounds who strained at the leash are lank-cheeked, hungry, sick; their coats are shabby and worn. As the Chorus describes them waiting like cattle to be slaughtered, we remember the wretched company Falstaff led to Shrewsbury and wonder at the irony of fate that finds the cautious, calculating Harry in the shoes of the reckless Hotspur. Like the harebrained Percy, Harry seems to rejoice at Agincourt in the odds that lend a greater luster to the enterprise, and he announces to his men that he covets the honor that will be won at such a risk.

In war as in peace the end crowns all: the reckless winner is balladed for his daring; the reckless loser is scorned for his folly. It would have been amazing, however, if Hotspur had won at Shrewsbury, because his cause was shabby, his allies unfaithful, his council of war divided, and his leadership faulty. Conversely, Harry's triumph at Agincourt is not a piece of incredible luck. His leadership is inspiring and his men are splendid soldiers, brave and faithful to one another unto the last. Although hungry and sick in body, the English army does not droop from the infection of spirit that sapped the rebel cause at Shrewsbury. The wrangling around the campfire expresses the anxieties of men who are determined to fight the next day as bravely as they can for themselves and their king. Furthermore, though Harry says that he welcomes the great odds, because the fewer the men the greater the share of honor, he does not, like Hotspur, call recklessness security or refuse to calculate the risk. Not one to court danger for its own sake, he tells the French Herald that he would rather not fight at Agincourt, even as he confesses to his men that they are like shipwrecked men who can expect to be washed away by the tide. Wanting no reluctant men by his side, he invites those who have "no stomach to this fight" [IV. iii. 35] to depart with passport and crowns for convoy in their purse. If there is an analogue to Hotspur at Agincourt it is not Harry; it is the Dauphin, who echoes Hotspur's contempt for Hal and who wagers with his barons for men's lives. Or rather, the Dauphin is a counterfeit Hotspur who chatters about his horse and armor and courtly mistresses but whose only gest is the slaughter of the English camp boys.

Shrewsbury was a personal victory for Hal, who, dressed in glittering armor and plumed like an estridge, slew Hotspur in single combat. Agincourt is a victory in which all England shares, a victory won by men who received from their leader on the dark night before the battle "a largesse universal" [Chorus, IV, 43] like the sun. Although he has his doubts about the morrow, Harry does not parade them, and though he feels the weight of responsibility for the fates of the men under him, he does not shrink from their presence. Not the greatest of military strategists, he can inspire those who follow him—plain, outspoken warriors for the working day. He has the very accent of their manly pride, their gruff good humor, and their understated courage. He knows how they observe their feast days, the words and ceremonies with which they commemorate their times of fellowship and victory. At Shrewsbury the King's body became again a mystical host because devoted men marched in Henry's suits and died for his sake. At Agincourt the bond between the King and his men is of a humbler sort; it is symbolized by the cloak which disguises Harry's royalty from Williams and Bates and which allows them to speak as equals and share for a while their common fears and hopes.

One would like to say that at the moment of supreme crisis Harry discovers his humanity or grows companionable again. But though he can disguise his majesty with a cloak, he cannot shrug off the consciousness of his majesty and of his soldiers' commonness. Even when he speaks to Bates of the King, with "his ceremonies laid by, in his nakedness" appearing "but a man," he cannot see himself as but a man [IV. i. 104-05, 101-02]. On the morrow he will proclaim to the army that those

who shed their blood with him will be his brothers; on the eve of the battle he expresses in soliloquy a very different point of view: a contempt and disgust for ordinary men which recalls his treatment of Francis, Poins, and Falstaff in the *Henry IV* plays. He bemoans the hard condition of greatness, "subject to the breath / Of every fool" [IV. i. 234-35]. He compares the uneasy sleep of kings with the sound sleep of "the wretched slave," "Who with a body fill'd, and vacant mind, / Gets him to rest, cramm'd with distressful bread" [IV. i. 268-70]. He meditates on the life of the "lackey," the "slave," the "gross brain," who does not know "What watch the king keeps to maintain the peace" [IV. i. 283].

Although he has learned the language of common men in the tavern, Harry cannot sympathize with the lowly born. He is not really moved by the prospect of his soldiers' fates, nor does he grieve for the lonely impoverished widows and orphaned children they will leave behind. What agonizes him is the thought that he will be accountable for all this suffering. He joins the men about the campfire partly to confess the anxieties he dare not reveal as King and partly to be absolved by them of guilt for the impending disaster. Much more honest about his situation than Hotspur, Harry nevertheless seeks out the soul of goodness in things evil and discovers the moral uses of adversity. Forgetting that his army has invaded France, he speaks to his commanders of the French as bad neighbors who make the peaceful English early risers. And he plays the King's counsel at the campfire as deftly as he played the prosecutor of the traitors at Southampton. Like a clever advocate, he can argue both sides of the same question. At Harfleur he spoke of impious war that carries its foul contagion of murder and rapine. At the campfire he describes war as God's beadle who takes vengeance upon the sinners killed in battle. On the morrow he will embrace his men as brothers, but now he meditates on their likely crimes of murder, seduction, riot, and robbery. Unable to accept his responsibility for having led them to the brink of disaster, he would like to attribute their fates to the fortunes of war, or, rather, to the risks of life, because he would compare their plight to that of men who miscarry at sea or are assailed by robbers.

To judge Harry fairly we must recognize that he did not have to debate this issue with his men, nor did he have to tolerate their insinuations about his honesty. Where a hypocrite would have had his revenge on Williams and walked away more convinced than ever of his righteousness, Harry is stricken by his soldiers' refusal to absolve him. At Southampton he had relished the role of the betrayed king—a role which Henry VI, Richard II, and Henry IV had played before him in the History Plays. But he cannot bear to be cast in the role of Judas by his own men when he was prepared to play Pilate and wash their blood from his hands. When they reject his facile arguments, he complains, as so often before, that he is misunderstood. Perhaps he is right, because his soldiers are at least as obtuse as he is. Just as he would shrug off responsibility for their deaths, they would place the burden of their immortal souls on him. He would forget that he led them to the edge of a catastrophe; they would forget their eagerness to be led. . . . [They] were not impressed; they were volunteers eager to seek their fortunes in France. Yet when Harry insists upon the righteousness of the King's cause—"his cause being just and his quarrel good"—they insist on their ignorance of such matters: "That's more than we know" [IV. i. 128, 129]. They cannot be duped by his talk of fathers and sons because they do not want a royal father or brother; they want a royal scapegoat. And though . . . they accuse Harry of untruth, they would not think of disobeying him, because obedience is their moral ab-solution: ''we know enough if we know we are the King's subjects. If his cause be wrong, our obedience to the King wipes the crime of it out of us'' [IV. i. 131-33].

For Williams and Bates ignorance of the King's cause is bliss. For Harry there is no comparable escape. Without a single confidant, he can only ruminate on the unfairness of life which makes the royal destiny so much harder than that of common men:

> And what have kings that privates have not too,
> Save ceremony, save general ceremony?
> And what art thou, thou idol Ceremony?
> What kind of god art thou, that suffer'st more
> Of mortal griefs than do thy worshippers?
> What are thy rents? what are thy comings-in?
> O Ceremony, show me but thy worth!
> What is thy soul of adoration?
> Art thou aught else but place, degree, and form,
> Creating awe and fear in other men?
> Wherein thou art less happy being fear'd,
> Than they in fearing.
> What drink'st thou oft, instead of homage sweet,
> But poison'd flattery? O! be sick, great greatness,
> And bid thy ceremony give thee cure!
>
> [IV. i. 238-52]
> (pp. 188-96)

In *Henry IV Part II* Harry spoke of the crown as a golden scalding care and protested his uneasiness in the gorgeous gar-ments of majesty. Now when he expounds the mockery of the Idol Ceremony, we are once more unconvinced because again and again he returns to the thought of those who stoop before him: he speaks of ''homage sweet,'' of ''flexure and low-bending,'' of commanding ''the beggar's knee'' [IV. i. 255, 256]. Even as he denies the satisfactions of power and the pleasure of rule, his rhetoric swells to a crescendo that pro-claims the oceanic splendor of majesty:

> 'Tis not the balm, the sceptre, and the ball,
> The sword, the mace, the crown imperial,
> The intertissued robe of gold and pearl,
> The farced title running fore the king,
> The throne he sits on, nor the tide of pomp
> That beats upon the high shore of this world—
>
> [IV. i. 260-65]

It is all vanity, every last drop of it, but Harry never thinks of renouncing it. Having led his army to the pit in search of empire and everlasting fame, he speaks with heavy heart at Agincourt of the thankless burden of keeping the peace.

While his father lived Harry avoided his presence. When his father lamented the way he met the crown, Harry seemed not to understand. On the eve of Agincourt, however, he begs God not to think ''upon the fault / My father made in compassing the crown!'' [IV. i. 293-94]. Characteristically, it does not occur to him that Agincourt may be a fitting retribution for his own vainglory. Insisting on his blamelessness, he can only attribute the impending catastrophe to the sins of his father. Hearing him speak of his father's guilt, one understands the rage with which he had turned upon his would-be assassins at Southampton; their plot to assassinate him would strike him as a primal and original sin, because just such a crime has ''left a kind of blot'' [II. ii. 138] on his own title, which had been gained by treason and murder. Accustomed to measuring out his moral obligations, Harry would strike a bargain with

God, but he is not so crass as to think that he can buy absolution. Even as he enumerates his acts of contrition and the prayers he has commissioned ''to pardon blood,'' he knows that these ceremonies are ''nothing worth'' [IV. i. 300, 303]. All is finally in God's hand and God's will; only from God can come the absolution of a miraculous victory.

The attempted communion about the campfire ends in bitter-ness. The next morning, however, Harry and his men stand together against the enemy, and though their fellowship cannot last, for the brief time of the battle they are the few, the happy few, the band of brothers. Finding his redemption in the great triumph, Harry is . . . at peace with himself and able to relax and joke with his men. He allows Fluellen and Williams to appeal one another and to hurl gauntlets of defiance and ac-cusations of treason at one another . . . ; but he makes certain that no blood is spilled in this last of his practical jokes. Fearing no treason from his subjects, and desiring no revenge on the loyal men who insulted his majesty, he fills Williams' glove with crowns and thus plays one last time the king of courtesy and good fellows. (pp. 196-97)

Harry has won a place for himself in Chronicles in time to come. He has not, however, called back yesterday; he has not recreated the stable political order which fell with Richard II. Where Richard's authority rested on the great pyramid of feudal privileges, Harry stands alone in the play as sovereign of En-gland; more like a Tudor than a Plantagenet monarch, he is adored by his followers as Elizabeth was adored, as a person not as a god. Fluellen tells the King that he need not be ashamed of him ''so long as your majesty is an honest man'' [IV. vii. 114-15], and whatever private thoughts Harry may have about his imperial greatness, he must publicly admit that with his ceremonies laid by, he is merely human. Defending himself against the charge of lese majesty, Williams claims that he did not insult the King on the eve of Agincourt, because Harry came to the campfire as a man, not as a king. In accepting this excuse, Harry implicitly admits that majesty is a garment worn, not (as Richard II imagined) an inherited mystery that exalts one man above other mortals. The royal office is anointed, not the man who fills it.

Like *Richard III, Henry V* concludes with a prayer that a royal marriage will make friends of foes and secure the blessings of peace for future generations, but it is hard to believe that Har-ry's marriage to Katherine was made in heaven when she is so obviously a political pawn. Although the hand of hot and forcing violation will never threaten her as it does the women of Harfleur, she will endure handling because she is a trophy of the hunt, a maiden princess identified with cities ''girdled with maiden walls that war hath never ent'red'' [V. ii. 322-23]. In possessing her, Harry possesses France. . . . (pp. 199-200)

No sooner does Harry win his empire than the Chorus enters to speak in the Epilogue of the ''small time'' of his greatness. Nevertheless, as Harry prophesied it would, the memory of Agincourt will endure as a precious reminder of the courage and determination that can sustain a people in the face of terrible adversity. ''Old men forget,'' says Harry to his troops at Agin-court, ''yet all shall be forgot'' [IV. iii. 49], but the memory of Agincourt will live. Its story

> shall the good man teach his son;
> And Crispin Crispian shall ne'er go by,
> From this day to the ending of the world,
> But we in it shall be remembered.
>
> [IV. iii. 56-9]

To the ending of the world is a long time, however, for feast-days to be observed, and no man can be absolutely certain how his fame will be bruited in future times. Just as Alexander is remembered in *Henry V* as the man who conquered the world and in a drunken rage killed his friend, Harry is remembered by Shakespeare and his readers as the hero king who triumphed at Agincourt and turned away the fat old knight. Although we are advised by critics not to linger over the rejection of Falstaff, Shakespeare refers to it a half dozen times or more in *Henry V*, and though we are warned not to sentimentalize Falstaff's fate, Shakespeare makes the Hostess' description of Falstaff's death the only moment in the play that touches the heart.

Where the last lines of *Richard III* look ahead to an Elizabethan present, the last lines of *Henry V* look back on a legendary past which the playwright's art has for a time restored to present memory. In a retrospective if not valedictory mood in his Epilogue, Shakespeare meditates not only on Harry's epic achievement but also on his own epic achievement in the History Plays. Recalling to his audience's minds the plays of the first tetralogy, "which oft our stage has shown" [Epilogue, 13], he whimsically begs his listeners to look kindly on *Henry V* for their sake. Apologize though he may for his "rough and all-unable pen" [Epilogue, 1], he must have known that his art would last longer than the small time of Harry's empire. He must also have suspected that if the memory of Agincourt were to last unto the ending doom, it would be because his powerful rhyme would outlive the gilded monuments to Harry's victories. As he came to the ending of *Henry V*, Shakespeare's thoughts returned to the sonnets in which he had posed the tender living memory of art against the speechless ironies of statues overturned. Appropriately enough, his last words about the king who wielded Fortune's sword are an Epilogue composed in sonnet form. (pp. 201-02)

> Robert Ornstein, "'Henry V'," in his A Kingdom for a Stage: The Achievement of Shakespeare's History Plays, *Cambridge, Mass.: Harvard University Press, 1972, pp. 175-202.*

## MOODY E. PRIOR   (essay date 1973)

[*Prior regards* Henry V *as a dramatization of a national myth, not a presentation of Shakespeare's own perception of historical and political realities. He claims that Henry is a composite of ideal qualities found in contemporary religious and secular treatises on kingship, noting that one means of dramatizing such a copy-book figure is to present him in a variety of situations, designed to demonstrate his possession of those qualities. However, the critic identifies two elements "which in a subtle way have the effect of undermining and questioning the myth itself": (1) the allusions to the rejection of Falstaff and the "haunting" account of his death; and (2) the ironical reference to the unfortunate progeny of Henry V and Katherine.*]

In the two *Henry IV* plays Shakespeare has given close attention to the prince, and from these plays there emerges a character that has been growing in interest and complexity, about whose charms and virtues we are not wholly certain, and who is not yet fully enough realized to enable us to enter into all his actions with understanding and sympathy. At the conclusion of Part 2, in his speech to the Chief Justice, he dedicates himself to his high office and resolves to become, with the help of others, the leader of "the best-governed nation" [2 *Henry IV*, V. ii. 137]. We can begin to feel that we are on the threshold of the fulfillment of a painstaking and potentially exciting dramatic development, and that the play to follow, announced in the

epilogue, will be the capstone to this remarkable series and will reveal the completed and fully rounded characterization of the prince now a king and grown to mature manhood. For many admirers of Shakespeare these expectations are not fulfilled, and they turn to the *Henry IV* plays for clues to a consistent understanding of the character of the king. When this approach is zealously applied, *Henry V* emerges as a deliberate undermining of a popular national myth and a devastating criticism of political man, and the best that can be said of its hero king is that he is a political genius whose Machiavellianism is so refined that he can delude a nation into accepting cynical power politics as a benevolent and humane administration of sovereignty. The play thus conceived is one which would defy realization in the theatre. Shakespeare provides no clear signs that he is subverting the image of Henry enshrined by the historians and national tradition, and he is explicit about the model on which he constructs the character of the king. Moreover, Shakespeare's dramatic strategy seems pointedly to suggest that most of what has been painstakingly built up in the characterization of the prince is set aside in *Henry V* in favor of the idol of the histories whose reformation and military success had become legendary. (pp. 316-17)

The character who becomes Henry V on the death of his father in *2 Henry IV* undergoes a fundamental change before appearing in *Henry V* as the legendary hero of Agincourt. And there is a commensurate change in dramatic conception: the candidly political and worldly conflicts of *Henry IV* are replaced by a series of stately pageants celebrating the hero of a national myth.

The model on which Shakespeare formed his portrayal of Henry is clearly announced in the chorus to act 2, where Henry is referred to as "the mirror of all Christian kings" [Chorus, II, 6]. The phrase calls to mind the extensive body of writings delineating the qualities of a good king and offering advice for his proper conduct. What, if any, specific work might have influenced Shakespeare in shaping the character of Henry V is not of itself important; the treatises on the ideal ruler tend to repeat each other, and the common elements of the type could be derived from almost any one of them. J. H. Walter, in his introduction to the Arden edition of the play [see excerpt above, 1954], has demonstrated how closely Shakespeare based his *Henry V* on such models in a point-by-point comparison between the qualities demanded by Erasmus and Chelidonius and Henry's principal characteristics as king. Henry is a good Christian and a religious man. He listens to his counselors, whom he has chosen for their learning and wisdom. He is just, and if necessary sternly so. But he can also be merciful. He knows the vanity of ceremony and pomp. His position is lonely and demanding, for though the Christian king should have a human capacity to know his people, he should not demean himself by associating with common persons or run the danger of being abused by flatterers. War is a grave matter and a great evil, and should not be lightly entered upon; Henry warns Canterbury of this and wants to make sure that his cause is just. These are the principal items. The correctness of Henry's conduct can also be supported by other, more secular, treatises of advice for kings. Henry's conduct in the first act conforms to Claude de Seysell's advice that before deciding on hostilities there should be serious consultation and debate concerning the reason for the war, the right to the territories to be claimed, and the justice of the cause, as well as meditation on God's justice against wrongdoers. When victory has been won, Henry, in a manner approved not only by Erasmus but by the best military manuals, attributes the victory to God and orders appropriate religious observances.

From the beginning of the play, Shakespeare points out the direction which his treatment of the story is to take. The opening invocation announces a play on a warlike theme. Canterbury's speech isolates the king from the prince and briefly sets forth the image of the national hero which the historians had established. The reference in the chorus to "the mirror of all Christian kings" points to the ideal qualities with which the monarch was to be endowed as a model king and warrior. It is a clearly defined conception which called for a different kind of play from any that had preceded.

In the first lines of the prologue, Shakespeare makes it clear that he had in mind a work lofty in tone and majestic in scope, for these lines do not derive from the idiom of theatrical prologues but have the unmistakable ring of an invocation to an epic: "O for a Muse of fire, that would ascend / The brightest heaven of invention" [Prologue, 1-2]. The theme he announces in the prologue is epic in character—a warrior king with "the port of Mars" [Prologue, 6], who is to lead his nation to a victory whose very name has become a legend. The invocation shifts rapidly to apology, as though to concede that the theatre is not a proper frame for an epic action and an epic theme. (pp. 323-25)

It is not primarily the physical limitations of the theatre which were troublesome, though Shakespeare refers to these:

> may we cram
> Within this wooden O the very casques
> That did affright the air at Agincourt?
>
> [Prologue, 12-14]

Dramatic magnitude does not depend significantly on grand spectacle, and the point has frequently been made that the wooden O which could contain *King Lear* needs no apology. A more serious problem lay in creating a drama around an image of perfection.

How does one dramatize a model hero who has become a national myth of royal greatness? . . . In a dramatic action, interest arises in large part from our becoming involved in how a character will meet a new situation, knowing that, being himself, he must respond in a particular way, but also that in making a choice he is in danger of making one that may lead to failure. A model character that meets each situation in a serious action by exercising exactly the right virtue to insure success and approbation is not responding to challenges with his total imperfect nature, but reacting predictably to opportunities. Narrative interest can be sustained by depicting the progress of such a character through a series of events, and interest in the character can be sustained by arranging a sequence of episodes to illustrate a number of distinctive qualities which together constitute the ideal he exemplifies. The method is not entirely suited to the drama, for while certain traits common to an ideal conception, such as a model king or courtier or man of learning, will all find a proper place in a single book on the subject, it does not follow that they can for that reason be convincingly associated with a single individual as a living man or a believable character. The character of Henry V is a composite.

In our first view of the king, we see him deciding the issue of the French war with his council and with the French ambassadors. In this setting, which is the only time we see him in his native land except for the scene before his departure, he exemplifies the ruler who has chosen grave counselors whose advice he listens to courteously and carefully, the just king who wants to be sure his procedure is lawful, and the patriot king who upholds the honor of his country against foreign insult. Where his rights and national honor are concerned he displays an unsentimental toughness and a disinclination to compromise: "France being ours, we'll bend it to our awe, / Or break it all to pieces" [I. ii. 224-25]. His clergy are shown to be politic, but he conspicuously is not. In this entire scene he is a model of correctness. Just before he leaves for France, Henry displays his sense of firm justice when the conspiracy is discovered and he has to condemn the three men to death, though all are well known to him and Scroop was a close friend and companion. Our next view of him is before Harfleur, urging his troops on with rousing martial rhetoric, and using the same rhetorical skill to threaten the city with all the brutal savagery and awful horrors of total war if it does not surrender peacefully. The tone of this is fiercely unchristian—it has a trace of Tamburlaine's threats before he sets up his black tents, and modern critics are reluctant to forgive the king. But his strategy succeeds, and he accepts the surrender of the city in all mildness: "Use mercy to them all," he proclaims [III. iii. 54]. Shakespeare shows Henry to better advantage here than he appears in Holinshed's account, where the city is sacked and Holinshed describes "the distress whereto the people, then expelled out of their habitations were driven: Inasmuch as parents with their children, young maids and old folk went out of the town gates with heavy hearts (God wot) as put to the present shifts to seek them a new abode." Shakespeare has taken pains here not to damage the impression of the Christian king as a warrior. He is similarly protective of our sensibilities in the matter of the later order to kill the French prisoners. We are not permitted to view, or even to reflect on, any of the unpleasant consequences to the French, whereas in Holinshed we are told of their agony:

> When this dolorous decree, and pitiful proclamation was pronounced, pity it was to see how some Frenchmen were suddenly sticked with daggers, some were brained with pole-axes, some slain with mails, other had their throats cut, and some their bellies paunched, so that in effect, having respect to the great number, few prisoners were saved.

In the scenes from Harfleur to Agincourt, Shakespeare pictures Henry as a tough and knowledgeable but thoroughly honorable soldier. And in the closing scene following Agincourt, he is shown as a religious and pious man.

With the fifth act, we meet Henry in still another guise. He opens the negotiations for peace in a speech of firmness and dignity, but when he is left alone with Katharine and begins to act the royal wooer, something surprising happens, and if there was any doubt that Shakespeare had left Prince Hal behind, this scene should dispel it. Johnson was puzzled: "I know not why Shakespeare now gives the King nearly such a character as made him formerly ridicule in Percy" [see excerpt above, 1765]. Quite unexpectedly, inexplicably, Henry becomes an awkward, blunt fellow—"thou wouldst think I had sold my farm to buy my crown" [V. ii. 125-26]. Even taken at his word he puzzles us in this scene, for the speech in which he protests that he is neither a poet nor a talker runs to some forty lines of coy prose. It does not matter whether one finds this scene charming or a bore. What is significant is that one cannot find the basis for this Henry anywhere in the play. This cannot be the Henry who replies smartly to the French ambassadors:

> We are glad the Dauphin is so pleasant with us;
> His present, and your pains, we thank you for.
> When we have matched our rackets to these balls,
> We will in France, by God's grace, play a set
> Shall strike his father's crown into the hazard.
>
> [I. ii. 259-63]

And we have certainly lost the Henry of the oration before Agincourt, whose splendid rhetoric might move one to lament that this play never quite soared into poetry. If we ask where this notion of an unhandsome, tongue-tied king comes from, the answer seems to be that he came directly out of contemporary accounts of the disabilities of soldiers as lovers, lacking in good looks and having no skill in words.

It may be said of this, as of the other attitudes Henry assumes, that it is a virtue in a talented and versatile hero to know what the proper line is under any circumstance, but such an interpretation sounds the note of politic expediency which leads to the ironic undermining of the heroic Christian king, even though the latter is the image indicated by all the signs in the play. It is possible to discern certain common elements in the several Henrys, but these are not enough to bind the character into a whole. There are characters in Shakespeare who utter a scant dozen lines and leave their mark on us, and his greatest characters sometimes speak lines which take us by surprise yet help to illuminate everything they have said or done. Henry does not act on us in that way. It is not the whole man we hear at any given moment, but some particular manifestation of an *exemplum*.

The king's actions sometimes produce offense rather than the reaction apparently intended, precisely because we have no deep insight into his character and cannot therefore enter sympathetically into his trials and dilemmas. To suggest a contrast, we do not hear or see Othello agonize over his decision to dismiss Cassio, but we have already been allowed to see enough into his character to understand what this act means to him and why he can do nothing else. We experience no such immediate response with, for example, Henry's order to kill the prisoners, or his refusal to intercede for Bardolph, or his trapping of the traitors, and therefore many readers entertain ill thoughts about the lack of Christian charity and plain humanity on the part of this much-heralded model of perfection. We see the gesture by which an act is accomplished but not the man behind it, and where it is possible to read an act in either of two ways it is more satisfying to see it as a manifestation of human imperfection. The very effortlessness of the king's actions arouses mistrust. Everything comes so easily and readily to this fortunate young man. We do not see him struggle against the dangers of great place, and when he calls for an earnest debate on the justice of his cause, it comes over like a ceremony required by his office. We do not see him tried by the dilemmas which great place imposes on the private man, and so when late in the play he soliloquizes on kingly burdens and the vanity of ceremony, the speech has the effect of an aria on an obligatory theme.... The defect of Henry V as a character in a political play is that he acts as though he has never personally known political sin, never been threatened, or sullied, or even seriously tempted by the evils of sovereign power. Where he must perform an act that might be thought to challenge his right to the title "the mirror of all Christian kings," it can always be shown that he has acted correctly according to the best authorities. The misleading notion of a sly Machiavellian

Henry V growing out of *Henry IV* is an understandable product of unsympathetic critics attempting to find a consistent center for this character. Since it is hard to believe in the paragon, it seems sensible to look for the smart operator. There is, one might more properly contend, too little of Prince Hal and his father in the character. All the rich if sometimes contradictory and even unpleasant possibilities which have been built up over two plays are largely set aside in the interest of the hero of Agincourt and the myth of the spotless Christian king who upon his coronation was made new. (pp. 326-31)

The making of the Henry V legend began almost immediately after his death, for his brief career lent itself to eulogy and embellishment; but the persistence of the myth was owing to the fact that subsequent events enhanced its appeal. To any later historian looking at the hundred-odd disordered years between the reign of Richard II and the coming of the Tudors, Henry would have appeared as Hall described him, a blazing comet; for during his brief and meteoric career, Henry V provided the one brilliant exemplification of the monarchical idea, a historic demonstration that, given even a dubious title with some popular support, a king who combined genius for rule, courage, love of justice, and the capacity to inspire loyalty could make the monarchical idea work and bring glory to his country. There are several clear signs early in *Henry V* that this is the idea which was to give direction to Shakespeare's dramatization of Henry's reign. Such a treatment of the legend would be consistent with the admiration for Henry as a king which runs through the *Henry VI* trilogy, at the very beginning of the cycle. However, by the time Shakespeare, in the course of writing the histories, had come to dramatize the reign of the hero king, he had already produced eight plays (including *King John*) in which political man and the world of power were presented from many angles with a thoroughness and imaginative vividness without parallel in the world's literature. In all these plays, the hard light of Shakespeare's political intelligence illumines every corner. And just ahead lay *Julius Caesar*. At this moment, the notion of an ideal king who had become a national symbol of monarchical perfection and success must have seemed to Shakespeare unreal and lacking in substance.

Shakespeare's sense of historical reality and political truth has little place in this celebration of the national myth of kingship, but it does intrude now and then; for instance, in the politicking of the bishops, the doings of Pistol and his companions who join Henry's expeditionary forces not out of patriotic fervor but to make a dishonest penny out of the opportunity, and in the treachery of the small group of nobles. Shakespeare manages for the most part to keep the king above and thus unsullied by these contaminating elements, though not so unequivocally in the matter of the bishops' offer of money for a war with France to avoid a shock at the very outset from which some readers do not recover. There are, however, two features of the play which in a subtle way have the effect of undermining and questioning the myth itself. The first of these is the references to Falstaff. Most allusions to Hal's riotous youth serve to emphasize the complete separation of the king from the prince, and this could be said even of the death of Falstaff: "Of Falstaff we read only concerning his death. It is a dramatic touch. The King's old life is dead in the person of his boon companion" [Beverley Warner, in his *English History in Shakespeare's Plays*]. But the reports of Falstaff's death are not to be so simply disposed of. They introduce, just before the king's departure for France, a haunting note—"The King has killed his heart" [II. i. 88]. Even the inspired malapropism of the Hostess, "he's in Arthur's bosom" [II. iii. 9-10], adds a wry pathos to her account of how Falstaff died. And this is not the end of the matter. Falstaff is referred to once again in the midst of the battle of Agincourt. Fluellen, in a laborious comparison between Alexander and Henry, explains to Gower that whereas Alexander the Great killed his friend Cleitus "in his ales and angers," in contrast, "Harry Monmouth, being in his right wits and his good judgments, turned away the fat knight with the great-belly doublet" [IV. vii. 37-8, 46-8]. The battle of Agincourt, where Henry is light-years away from his past and at his heroic best, is certainly an odd place to introduce a defense of Henry's rejection of Falstaff. Though Fluellen speaks it in praise of the king, it is nevertheless just one more pointed reminder, at the very moment of the king's greatest triumph, of the harsh personal act that was demanded by the hero's accession to power. . . . [A] shadow is allowed to pass over this model of royal perfection by the pointed recall of the *Henry IV* plays and a humanly disturbing consequence of that misspent youth which was so miraculously set aside and so should now have been forgotten.

In the concluding scene another and different sort of implied contrast turns the very glow of optimism and joyful success of the finale into an ironic comment on the myth itself. During the courtship of Katharine, Henry says, "Shall not thou and I, between Saint Dennis and Saint George, compound a boy, half French, half English, that shall go to Constantinople, and take the Turk by the beard?" [V. ii. 206-09]. With the marriage and the other terms agreed upon, the queen of France, just before Henry's final speech which concludes the play, pronounces a benediction on these doings. . . . [None] of the things hopefully anticipated by Henry and fervently prayed for by the queen ever happened, and anyone who had read history or had been attending plays at the Globe knew it. The son was feeble and a pathetic failure, and the two countries wore each other out in bitter and useless fighting. . . . As history, therefore, the happy optimism of the ending is totally unfounded and absurd.

If, however, for one moment, we set history aside and think of the play simply as a dramatic spectacle, we can recognize that, poetically speaking, such an ending is inevitable and dictated by the progress of the fable. . . . A legendary king, endowed by nature and favored by God, conquers a foreign land which he claims as his own, marries the beautiful princess of that realm, and makes an honorable peace with his foes; surely we must therefore grant that he lived happily ever after. That is what this heroic fairy tale imperatively calls for, and with a little help from our imagination we allow the dramatic myth to take us to its proper conclusion. But if we have permitted ourselves to be thus carried away, the epilogue is there to bring us back to earth and reality:

Thus far, with rough and all-unable pen,
    Our bending author hath pursued the story,
In little room confining mighty men,
    Mangling by starts the full course of their glory.
Small time, but in that small, most greatly lived
    This star of England. Fortune made his sword;
By which, the world's best garden he achieved;
    And of it left his son imperial lord.
Henry the Sixth, in infant bands crowned King
    Of France and England, did this king succeed;
Whose state so many had the managing,
    That they lost France, and made his England bleed:
Which oft our stage hath shown; and, for their sake,
In your fair minds let this acceptance take.

[Epilogue, 1-14]

That is the way things really turned out; the king's buoyant hopes for his future son, the queen's blessings on the peace and the marriage which was to seal it, and her prayers for the future are fit accompaniments for this heroic patriotic spectacle, but are inconsistent with reality. What we had been seeing was an insubstantial pageant. The strongest effects and the most moving moments in *Henry V* are those which arise from its preoccupation with war, and the subsequent need for peace, but it is not serious as dramatized history or as an image of the political world. (pp. 335-40)

*Richard III* is also the dramatic re-creation of a myth and a political idea, but it has its foundations in the realities of power, and its hero, monstrous as he is, represents a danger that continually threatens to come into being and calls to mind historic parallels too actual for comfort. *Henry V* derives from a different kind of myth. It celebrates in its hero a national ideal that bends the facts of history to the services of a concept which is out of touch with the realities of power and which in consequence evades experience and eludes expectation. In the perspective of the plays which preceded it, *Henry V* appears as a theatrically handsome fulfillment of an obligation, performed with skill but without deep conviction. (p. 341)

> *Moody E. Prior, "Two Political Myths: 'Henry V',"*
> *in his* The Drama of Power: Studies in Shakespeare's
> History Plays, *Northwestern University Press, 1973,*
> *pp. 311-41.*

## MARILYN L. WILLIAMSON   (essay date 1975)

[*Williamson argues that Henry's wooing of Katherine is consistent with his conduct earlier in* Henry V *and recapitulates a pattern of behavior that he has demonstrated both in this play and in 1 and 2 Henry IV. Characterizing the king's actions in this scene as manipulative, self-justifying, and disingenuous, she maintains that his courtship of the French princess demonstrates that no matter how sincerely he may wish to relate to other people "simply as a human being, he can no longer do so," for isolation is "a condition of [his] kingship." Williamson also pays tribute to Samuel Johnson (see excerpt above, 1765) for first calling attention to Henry's kinship with Hotspur in this scene, stating that in his self-love, verbosity, and pretense of caring for other people, the king bears a strong resemblance to the nobleman he despises in 1 Henry IV.*]

Ever since Dr. Johnson concluded that Shakespeare wrote it only because he had run out of material [see excerpt above, 1765], critics have glossed over or left unregarded the final episode of *Henry V*: the courtship of Katherine of France. The reasons for ignoring it are simple: it does not seem to fit with the rest of the action, for though the marriage of Henry and Katherine is necessary enough to assure peace and unity after the war, that wedding, as part of the treaty, needs hardly be made an instant love match, and so the wooing seems superfluous and "shallow." Moreover, Dr. Johnson's initial objection must, as always, be met; in this scene, he says, Shakespeare makes Henry "nearly such a character as he made him formerly ridicule in Percy. This military grossness and unskillfulness in all the softer arts does not suit very well with the gaieties of his youth, with the general knowledge ascribed to him at his accession, or with the contemptuous message sent him by the Dauphin, who represents him as fitter for the ballroom than the field." (p. 326)

I hope to show . . . that the wooing scene is more than a gratuitous crowd-pleaser, that the scene is integrated into the structure of the play and of the tetralogy because it repeats a basic pattern in Henry's behavior that reaches back to his madcap days, and that Henry's manner with Katherine is consonant with Shakespeare's total portrait of him and brings to completion tendencies which develop earlier in *Henry V. . . .* The courtship scene fulfills Henry's progression from Hal into Henry V; it clinches the revelation that now that he is king, he can no longer behave genuinely and simply as a man, despite a strong desire to do so. He is every inch a king, but one who contrives, as he often did when prince, carefully controlled situations in which he plays at being "the best king of good fellows" [V. ii. 242-43], a man who may be loved for himself alone. At the same time we are never more aware than in the courtship scene that Henry has become, as king, all that he disdained in his father and in Hotspur during his carefree youth.

First, we may observe that the contrivance of the scene is itself an echo of earlier practice. Katherine has been offered to Henry before, along with some "petty and unprofitable dukedoms" [Chorus, III, 31]. Henry's rejection of this offer, along with his later eagerness to have Katherine as his "capital demand" in the treaty after his conquest of France, may suggest that Henry is really more interested in Katherine for reasons of state than for personal ones. If she proves a good soldier-breeder, she will be the means whereby Henry will repeat history; like his father, he will leave his son a dubious title based primarily on force and popular appeal, but one legitimized, like his own claim to France, through the female, Katherine, in spite of the Salic Law or the mores of France. The princess seals the achievement; she is part of the conquest and assures its survival into the future. His father's dream had been a crusade to unify England, as well as to expiate the crime of Richard's murder; Henry's mind is now drawn to a similar notion, one that will unify the two kingdoms: "Shall not thou and I, between Saint Denis and Saint George, compound a boy, half French and half English, that shall go to Constantinople and take the Turk by the beard?" [V. ii. 206-09]. The courtship is entirely gratuitous because the match, a *fait accompli,* has already had progeny in Henry's mind. Moreover, Katherine too has earlier accepted this fact, as we know from the scene in which she begins to learn English, which is linked through its obscenities with the remarks of Burgundy and Henry after the courtship scene. By including the seemingly superfluous English lesson earlier in the action Shakespeare intensifies our sense that the courtship is play-acting or role-playing about a settled issue.

This pattern of toying with people within a framework of certainty, together with an expression of a strong desire to act as if he is a private individual, to pretend to be a good fellow, repeats Henry's behavior as we have seen it from the Eastcheap days to the eve of Agincourt. . . . Henry shows clear signs of continuing his old ways in his treatment of the traitors, Cambridge, Scroop, and Grey, and in his encounter with Williams during his disguise as Harry Le Roi on the eve of Agincourt. In both situations he pretends briefly that he can separate his private interests and feelings from the crown, while always depending on the kingship for certainty of the framework. The traitors trap themselves as they are led into Henry's self-justifying device, but Williams gives Henry a comeuppance that teaches us, if not him, that kings cannot pretend to be private men. We notice that Henry uses a similar technique in dealing with the Archbishop about the claim to France at the beginning of the play. As Coursen has pointed out [see Additional Bibliography], it seems clear to us that Henry has decided that he will invade France before the scene with the churchmen and has maneuvered them into simply justifying what he has already determined to do. This pattern of manipulating people or play-

acting within a context of [certainty] is repeated finally in the courtship of Katherine, where Henry pretends it really matters whether Katherine loves him, while all the time they both know that her father's wishes will settle the issue.

Why, we may ask ourselves, does Henry continue this pattern after his dramatic reformation, after he has achieved his goal of a virtually unassailable kingship? The answers which the tetralogy suggests are several. First, there is the inevitable result of the three crucial scenes already mentioned: that with the Archbishop, that with the traitors, and that with Katherine—self-justification is the result of Henry's maneuverings in each case. Perhaps Henry is still unsure of himself and of his title because of his father's usurpation, and so he creates situations in which others will justify his actions, which he has already decided to carry out, but which he likes others to seem to bring about because of his unease in the kingship: when he declares war, or executes traitors, or marries, all crucial actions of a monarch, he seeks support, even if it is spurious, in the behavior of others. Trying to get Katherine to say that she loves him may be relatively less critical to the marriage than is the support of the Archbishop for the war in France, but it seems to spring from the same motive or need. In fact, the superfluousness of the wooing calls our attention to Henry's almost compulsive need to seem that it does matter. (pp. 327-30)

What the scene with Bates and Williams and the plain-soldier pose with Katherine reveal is that Henry never loses his pleasure at playing the good fellow, despite the rejection of Falstaff and the Eastcheap comrades. So he wants to pretend, at first anyway, that he is actually a man in love persuading a woman who loves him to marry him. Henry's entire maneuver in getting Katherine to justify his demanding her as one of the treaty terms depends for its effect on the pretense that both are free as ordinary men and women to love and marry by choice. His pretense only serves to make us more aware of the fact that neither he nor Kate can escape one of the penalties of high place, little choice in marriage.

Katherine's attitude throughout the scene gives evidence that she never forgets that she has no choice about whether she will marry Henry; after several protestations on her part and several long speeches by Henry, she replies to his repeated proposals: "Dat is as it shall please de *roi mon pere,*" and when her "lover" pre-emptively asserts, "It shall please him, Kate," she counters mildly with, "Den it sall also content me" [V. ii. 247, 248-50]. A dutiful princess and an obedient daughter, she will do what is expected of her, but she will not pretend that she is doing anything else or that she loves Henry or that she can speak his language, as he attempts hers; in fact she greets his play-acting with a healthy skepticism: *"O bon Dieu, les langues des hommes sont pleines de tromperies"* [V. ii. 115-16]. Katherine's realistic acceptance of her role accents the pretense of her wooer.

Henry also talks too much to Katherine, a habit he has developed in his long orations as king, though his long soliloquy announcing his planned reformation shows symptoms of it, as do the speeches to his father in both *Part I* and *Part II* in which he seems similarly to protest too much. By the time of the wooing scene we are accustomed to his talking a great deal every time he feels defensive about an action or when he wants to be certain people will follow him: in the scenes when the invasion of France is determined; in the exposure of the traitors; in the orations to his men or to the Governor of Harfleur; in the scene with his soldiers on the eve of Agincourt and the soliloquy afterwards. And Katherine shows the same kind of resistance to playing the game of king-and-man that Williams has shown in the earlier episode: "Your majesty came not like yourself. You appear'd to me but as a common man" [IV. viii. 50-1]. Similarly, however much Henry may talk, Kate does not forget that her father will decide what she does and that she is talking to the enemy of France. Moreover, Shakespeare has been at pains to emphasize the fact that she cannot understand much of what Henry says, and so we can only conclude that his long, persuasive speeches are as much self-justification, given for his own benefit to rationalize his action, as they are made to affect his future queen.

Henry's final gesture in the wooing scene enables us to understand clearly that though he may often yield to his impulse to imitate the common man, Henry is unable—or perhaps unconsciously unwilling—to escape his kingship and the habits of mind and heart that go with it. In making Katherine kiss him, a small but significant violation of the customs of France, Henry asserts his will at the expense of the fair French maid he claims has saved many a French city, just as earlier he flouted the Salic Law in claiming the French throne:

> O Kate, nice customs cur'sy to great kings.
> Dear Kate, you and I cannot be confined within
> the weak list of a country's fashion. We are
> the makers of manners, Kate; and the liberty
> that follows our places stops the mouths of all
> find-faults, as I will do yours, for upholding
> the nice fashion of your country, in denying
> me a kiss. . . .
>
> [V. ii. 268-74]

However much he may call the princess, "Kate," and pose as the farmboy, the imperiousness eventually emerges, and by juxtaposing the two attitudes in one scene Shakespeare shows us vividly what Henry has become: all that he mocked earlier—a pompous Hotspur, without the saving bluntness and sincerity.

If Hal planned to use his traffic with ordinary men to advantage in assuming the kingship, this strategy is no longer available to him once he is actually king, but he never seems to realize it. He wants to react as a private person with Williams, Bates, and the other soldiers, but his need to justify his cause finally crops out and mars the encounter because he cannot keep his word as a man since he is king. Similarly, a kingly pomposity overwhelms whatever charm might have lain in the brief return to wit and unconventionality in the courtship scene. The episode with Katherine puts a cap on a process that has been developing throughout the tetralogy, whereby the prince's most attractive qualities of moving unpretentiously among his fellow men and a corresponding irreverence about high place disappear under the impact of his assuming the kingship and are replaced by qualities that isolate him from his fellow men. However much he may pretend—or actually desire—to relate to them simply as a human being, he can no longer do so. The early tensions, whenever the Eastcheap gang presume upon his position, presage the development, as do, in a different way, his several reformations in *Part I* and *Part II*. The rejection of Falstaff accelerates the process greatly, and so in *Henry V,* when Hal is king, we see it everywhere. Falstaff dies, "killed" by the king; the rest of the Eastcheap crowd die off, one by one, during the course of the action until only Pistol, the parody of Henry's *miles gloriosus* [braggart soldier] style is left. When the death of Bardolph is specifically brought to his attention, Henry's reaction is coldly official.

The King is, moreover, betrayed by his noble friends, one of whom, at least, has been a close personal attachment:

> What shall I say to thee, Lord Scroop, thou cruel,
> Ingrateful, savage, and inhuman creature?
> Thou that didst bear the key of all my counsels,
> That knew'st the very bottom of my soul,
> That (almost) mightst have coin'd me into gold,
> Wouldst thou have practic'd on me, for thy use?
>
> [II ii. 94-9]

Having himself rejected his low-life comrades and having been rejected by his noble friends, Henry assumes that he can still relate to his "band of brothers" [IV. iii. 60], and so he can, if he is acting as their leader, whose stirring orations inspire them to extraordinary achievements. But he can no longer move among them, even in disguise, simply as a man. His career thus has an inverse symmetry: if he used his lowlife friendships and a rejection of them to strengthen his kingship, it is now a condition of the kingship that he is isolated from his fellow man.

The inability of Henry and Kate to speak one another's language becomes a kind of figure, a paradigm, for his predicament as he is now so separated from the rest of humanity that he cannot even talk to his intended wife. But if in the episode with Williams we felt sympathy with Henry because as king he could not be true to his word with the soldier, we see in the wooing scene that he is too self-engrossed really to care whether the woman he is wooing can understand his long speeches, as they are made as much for himself as for her. He has the temperament of the hale fellow who does not really like people but who seems to. I suggest that it is to this quality in Henry and in Hotspur (think of how he alienates one ally after another) that Dr. Johnson alludes in his comment about the wooing scene, and the loquacity, that other symptom of self-love in both Hotspur and Henry. If we must disagree with Dr. Johnson about the integrity and function of the scene, we may be grateful to him for giving a clue to its significance: Henry has become like Hotspur and like much that as Hal he despised, including the kind of king his father was. Once we see this process as a basic pattern of the tetralogy, we can understand the importance and function of the courtship of Katherine in *Henry V.* (pp. 331-34)

*Marilyn L. Williamson, "The Courtship of Katherine and the Second Tetralogy," in* Criticism, *Vol. XVII, No. 4 (Fall, 1975), pp. 326-34.*

## NORMAN RABKIN (essay date 1977)

[*Rabkin claims that the wide discrepancy between critical estimations of* Henry V *may be traced to a "fundamental ambiguity" in the play. He compares those who see the king as a model Christian monarch and those who regard him as a brutal Machiavel to people who have looked at a clever gestalt drawing: some will say they have seen a rabbit and others will insist they have seen a duck. Shakespeare has provided evidence for both interpretations, Rabkin argues, on the one hand portraying the king as the combination of spiritual and political virtues promised in* 1 Henry IV, *and on the other as the ruthless and expedient ruler foreboded in* 2 Henry IV. *He concludes that it is impossible to find a middle ground between the two "extreme readings" of the play and its protagonist; instead, he asserts, if we view it as depicting the complex and unpredictable union of disparate realities—what Rabkin calls its "complementarity"—our reaction will be like that of "Shakespeare's best audience," who came away from its first performance knowing "terrifyingly that they did not know what to think."*]

[In] *Henry V* Shakespeare creates a work whose ultimate power is precisely the fact that it points in two opposite directions, virtually daring us to choose one of the two opposed interpretations it requires of us. In this deceptively simple play Shakespeare experiments, perhaps more shockingly than elsewhere, with a structure like the gestaltist's familiar drawing of a rare beast. [In *Art and Illusion: A Study of the Psychology of Pictorial Representation*, E. H.] Gombrich describes the experience of that creature in memorable terms:

> We can see the picture as either a rabbit or a duck. It is easy to discover both readings. It is less easy to describe what happens when we switch from one interpretation to the other. Clearly we do not have the illusion that we are confronted with a "real" duck or rabbit. The shape on the paper resembles neither animal very closely. And yet there is no doubt that the shape transforms itself in some subtle way when the duck's beak becomes the rabbit's ears and brings an otherwise neglected spot into prominence as the rabbit's mouth. I say "neglected," but does it enter our experience at all when we switch back to reading "duck"? To answer this question, we are compelled to look for what is "really there," to see the shape apart from its interpretation, and this, we soon discover, is not really possible. True, we can switch from one reading to another with increasing rapidity; we will also "remember" the rabbit while we see the duck, but the more closely we watch ourselves, the more certainly we will discover that we cannot experience alternative readings at the same time. Illusion, we will find, is hard to describe or analyze, for though we may be intellectually aware of the fact that any given experience *must* be an illusion, we cannot, strictly speaking, watch ourselves having an illusion.

If one considers the context of *Henry V*, one realizes that the play could scarcely have been anything but a rabbit-duck.

*Henry V* is, of course, not only a free-standing play but the last part of a tetralogy. (pp. 279-80)

In each of the first three plays the audience had been confronted at the beginning with a set of problems that seemed solved by the end of the preceding play but had erupted in different forms as soon as the new play began. Thus the meaning of each of the plays subsequent to *Richard II* had been enriched by the audience's recognition of the emergence of old problems in a new guise. By the time the cycle reached *Henry V*, the recurrent and interlocking set of problems had become so complex that a reflective audience must have found it impossible to predict how the last play could possibly resolve them.

The unresolved thematic issue at the end of *Richard II* is the conflict of values embodied in the two kings who are its protagonists: Bullingbrook's talent as opposed to Richard's legitimacy; Bullingbrook's extroverted energy and calculating pursuit of power as opposed to Richard's imagination, inwardness, and sense of mortality. . . . *Richard II* thus poses a question that arches over the entire tetralogy: can the manipulative qualities that guarantee political success be combined in one man

with the spiritual qualities that make one fully open and responsive to life and therefore fully human? Or, to put it more accurately, can political resourcefulness be combined with qualities more like those of an audience as it sees itself?

*1 Henry IV* moves the question to a new generation, asking in effect whether the qualities split between Richard and Bullingbrook can be united in Hal. And in the manner of a comedy, it suggests optimistically that indeed they can. (pp. 280-81)

But the end of *Henry IV*, Part One marks only the halfway point, both in this massive tetralogy and in the study of Prince Hal, and Part Two brutally denies the comic optimism we might have expected to encounter once again. (p. 282)

If *Henry V* had followed directly on *1 Henry IV*, we might have expected to be made merry by the comedy such critics as Dover Wilson have taken that play to be, for we have seen a Hal potentially larger than his father, possessing the force that politics requires without the sacrifice of imagination and range that Bullingbrook has had to pay. But Part Two has told us that Part One deceived us, for the day has had to come when Hal, no longer able to live in two worlds, would be required to make his choice, and the Prince has had to expel from his life the very qualities that made him better than his father. Have we not, after Part Two, good reason to expect in the play about Hal's kingship the study of an opportunist who has traded his humanity for his success, covering over the ruthlessness of the politician with the mere appearance of fellowship that his past has endowed him with? Surely this is what Goddard means when he calls Henry V "the golden casket of *The Merchant of Venice*, fairer to a superficial view than to a more searching perception" [see excerpt above, 1951].

As we watch the Prologue stride across the stage of the Curtain, then, we are ready for one of two opposed presentations of the reign of the fifth Henry. Perhaps we hope that the play now beginning will resolve our doubts, set us right, give us a single gestalt to replace the antithetical images before our mind's eye. And that, as is demonstrated by the unequivocal interpretations good critics continue to make, is exactly the force of the play. We are made to see a rabbit or a duck. In fact, if we do not try obsessively to cling to memories of past encounters with the play, we may find that each time we read it it turns from one shape to the other, just as it so regularly does in production. I want to show that *Henry V* is brilliantly capable of being read, fully and subtly, as each of the plays the two parts of *Henry IV* had respectively anticipated. Leaving the theatre at the end of the first performance, some members of the audience knew that they had seen a rabbit, others a duck. Still others, and I would suggest that they were Shakespeare's best audience, knew terrifyingly that they did not know what to think.

Think of *Henry V* as an extension of *1 Henry IV*. For the generation who came to know it under the spell of Olivier's great film [1944], it is hard to imagine *Henry V* any other way, but Olivier's distortions, deletions, and embellishments only emphasized what is already in the play. The structure of the entire cycle has led from the beginning of conflict in a quarrel to its end in a wedding, from the disruption of royal power to its unchallenged reassertion. If *Richard II* at the beginning transformed the normally episodic chronicle form into tragedy, *Henry V* at the end turns it into comedy: the plot works through the troubles of a threatening world to end in marriage and the promise of a green world. Its protagonist, like Benedick returned to Messina [in *Much Ado about Nothing*], puts aside military exploits for romance, and charms even his enemies with his effervescent young manhood. Its prologue insists, as the comedies always do, on the importance of imagination, a faculty which Bullingbrook, wise to the needs of a tragic world, had rejected in *Richard II* as dangerous. And as in all romantic comedy providence guides the play's events to their desired conclusion.

To be sure, Olivier's camera and Walton's music prettied up the atmosphere, transporting their war-weary audience to the fairy-tale world of the Duc de Berry. But they found their cues in the play—in the Chorus's epic romanticizations of land and sea, his descriptions of festooned fleets and nocturnal campfires and eager warriors, and his repeated invitations to imagine even more and better. Nor did Olivier invent his film's awe at the spectacle of the past. In *Henry V,* as nowhere before in the tetralogy, Shakespeare excites us by making us conscious that we are privileged to be watching the very moments at which event transforms itself into history:

> *Mont.* The day is yours.
> *K. Hen.* Praised be God, and not our strength, for it!
> What is this castle call'd that stands hard by?
> *Mont.* They call it Agincourt.
> *K. Hen.* Then call we this the field of Agincourt,
> Fought on the day of Crispin Crispianus.
>
> [IV. vii. 86-91]

Ultimately, it was not Olivier's pictures but the play's language that made his *Henry V* so overwhelming, and the rhetoric of the play is extraordinary, unprecedented even in Shakespeare. Think, for example, of the King's oration to his troops on Saint Crispin's day [IV. iii. 19-67]. Thematically, of course, the speech is a tour de force, subjecting motifs from the tetralogy to Aeschylean or Wagnerian transmutations. Like the dying John of Gaunt [in *Richard II*], Harry is inspired by a vision of England, but one characteristically his own, made as romantic by the fantasy of neighborhood legionnaires and domestic history lessons as by the magical names of England's leaders. Unlike Richard II, Harry disprizes trappings, "outward things." Like Hotspur, he cares only about honor and wants to fight with as few troops as possible in order to acquire more of it: "the fewer men, the greater share of honor." Like Falstaff, he is finicky about the kind of company he adventures with: "we would not die in that man's company / That fears his fellowship to die with us" [IV. iii. 38-9]. Again like Falstaff, he thinks of the "flowing cups" to come when the day's work is done and sees the day's events in festival terms. Gaily doing battle on the Feast of Crispian, he is literally playing at war like Hotspur, paradoxically uniting the opposed principles of the two most enchanting characters of the cycle.

Such echoes and allusions give Henry's speech a satisfying finality, a sense of closure. He is the man we have been waiting for, the embodiment of all the virtues the cycle has made us prize without the vices that had accompanied them before. "He is as full of valor as of kindness," we have heard just before the speech, "Princely in both" [IV. iii. 15-16], and the Crispin's day exhortation demonstrates precisely the combination of attributes that Sherman Hawkins has pointed out as belonging to the ideal monarch postulated by Elizabethan royalism [in his essay "Virtue and Kingship in Shakespeare's *Henry IV*"]. But even more powerful than its thematic content is the stunning rhetoric of the King's tirade: its movement from the King's honor to his people's; its crescendo variations on St. Crispin's day, reaching their climax in the last line; its rhythmic

patterns expanding repeatedly from broken lines to flowing periods in each section and concluding climactically in the coda that begins "We happy few" [IV. iii. 60]; its language constantly addressed to the pleasures, worries, and aspirations of an audience of citizens. (pp. 284-86)

The fourth act of *Henry V,* in the third scene of which this speech has its place, is a paradigm of the King's virtues. It begins with the Chorus's contrast between the "confident and over-lusty French" and the thoughtful and patient Englishmen at their watchful fires on the eve of Agincourt, visited by their generous, loving, brave, and concerned royal captain—"a little touch of Harry in the night" [Chorus, IV, 18, 47]. The act moves, first through contrasting scenes in the two camps, then through confrontations of various sorts between the opposing sides, to the victory at Agincourt and the King's call for the charitable treatment of the dead as he announces his return to England. In the course of the act we see Harry, constantly contrasted to the stupid and corrupt French, in a triumphant show of bravery and high spirits. But we see him also in a kind of inwardness we have seldom observed in his father, listening as neither Richard II nor Henry IV could have done to the complaints and fears of a common soldier who knows what kings impose on their subjects that they do not themselves have to risk. His response is a soliloquy as powerful in its thematic and rhetorical complexity as the public address we have just considered [IV. i. 230-84].

In some respects this soliloquy, which precedes by only a few moments the Crispin's day speech, is the thematic climax of the entire tetralogy, showing us that at last we have a king free of the crippling disabilities of his predecessors and wise in what the plays have been teaching. Recognizing that all that separates a king from private men is ceremony, Harry has escaped Richard's tragic confusion of ceremony with reality: "Is not the King's name twenty thousand names?" [*Richard II*, III. iii. 85]. Unwittingly reenacting his father's insomniac soliloquy in the third act of *2 Henry IV,* Harry too longs for the heart's ease of the commoner. But where the old King could conclude only, "Uneasy lies the head that wears a crown" [*1 Henry IV,* III. i. 31], recurring despairingly to his posture of perennial guiltiness and to his weary sense of mortality, his young son ends by remembering his responsibility, his life of service, and sees that—"what watch the King keeps to maintain the peace" [IV. i. 283]—as the defining mark of the King. Moreover, in his catechistic questioning of ceremony Harry shows that he has incorporated Falstaff's clearsightedness: like honor in Falstaff's catechism, ceremony consists only in what is conferred by others, bringing no tangible good to its bearer, unable to cure disease, no more than a proud dream. But the lesson is not only Falstaff's; for, in the dark backward and abysm of time, before Hal ever entered the scene, a young Bullingbrook had anticipated his son's "Thinks thou the fiery fever will go out / With titles blown from adulation?" [IV. i. 253-54] with a similar repudiation of comforting self-deception:

> O, who can hold a fire in his hand
> By thinking on the frosty Caucasus?
> Or cloy the hungry edge of appetite
> By bare imagination of a feast?
>
> [*Richard II*, I. iii. 294-97]

These multiple allusions force us to see in Henry V the epitome of what the cycle has taught us to value as best in a monarch, indeed in a man; and the King's ability to listen to the soldier Williams and to hear him suggests, like his subsequent fooling with Fluellen in the same fourth act, a king who is fully a man. All that is needed to complete him is mature sexuality, scarcely hinted at in the earlier portraits of Hal, and the wooing of Princess Katherine in the fifth act brings finality to a lively portrayal of achieved manhood, a personality integrated in itself and ready to bring unity and joy to a realm that has suffered long from rule by men less at ease with themselves and less able to identify their own interests with those of their country.

It was such a response to *Henry V* that led me years ago to write [in *Shakespeare and the Common Understanding*]:

> In only one play in his entire career does Shakespeare seem bent on making us believe that what is valuable in politics and in life can successfully be combined in a ruler as in his state. . . . There can be no doubt that [the play] is infectiously patriotic, or that the ideal of the harmonious commonweal . . . reflects the highest point of Shakespeare's civic optimism. And Henry is clearly presented as the kind of exemplary monarch that neither Richard II nor Henry IV could be, combining the inwardness and the sense of occasion of the one and the strength of the other with a generous humanity available to neither. . . . In *Henry V* Shakespeare would have us believe what hitherto his work in its genre has denied, that in the real world of the chronicles a man may live who embodies the virtues and experiences the fortune of the comic hero.

Reading the play thus optimistically, I had to note nevertheless how many readers respond otherwise to it, and I went on to observe that the play casts so many dark shadows—on England after Agincourt, for instance—that one can scarcely share its optimism, and that "in this respect *Henry V* is the most melancholy of the history plays." But I have now come to believe that my acknowledgment of that darker aspect of the play hardly suggested the terrible subversiveness with which Shakespeare undermines the entire structure.

Taking the play, as we have just done, to be an extension of the first part of *Henry IV*, we are almost inevitably propelled

*Act V. Scene i. Pistol and Fluellen. By John Thurston. The Department of Rare Books and Special Collections, The University of Michigan Library.*

to optimism. Taking it as the sequel of the second part of *Henry IV*, we are led to the opposite view held by critics as diverse as H. C. Goddard, Roy W. Battenhouse, Mark Van Doren, and H. M. Richmond [see excerpts above, 1951, 1962, 1939, and 1967]. Think of those dark shadows that cloud the comedy. The point of the stock ending of romantic comedy is, of course, its guarantee of the future: marriage secures and reinvigorates society while promising an extension of its happiness into a generation to come. Like *A Midsummer Night's Dream*, *Henry V* ends in a marriage whose blessing will transform the world:

> *K. Hen.* Now welcome, Kate; and bear me witness all,
> That here I kiss her as my sovereign queen. *Flourish.*
> *Q. Isa.* God, the best maker of all marriages,
> Combine your hearts in one, your realms in one!
> As man and wife, being two, are one in love,
> So be there 'twixt your kingdoms such a spousal,
> That never may ill office, or fell jealousy,
> Which troubles oft the bed of blessed marriage,
> Thrust in between the [paction] of these kingdoms,
> To make divorce of their incorporate league;
> That English may as French, French Englishmen,
> Receive each other, God speak this Amen!
> *All.* Amen!
> *K. Hen.* Prepare we for our marriage; on which day,
> My Lord of Burgundy, we'll take your oath,
> And all the peers', for surety of our leagues.
> Then shall I swear to Kate, and you to me,
> And may our oaths well kept and prosp'rous be!
> *Sennet. Exeunt.*
> [V. ii. 357-74]

We don't really know very much about what was to happen in Theseus's Athens. But we know a good deal about Plantagenet England; and in case any member of the audience has forgotten a history as familiar to Elizabethans as our Civil War is to us, the Chorus appears immediately to remind them—both of what would soon happen, and of the fact that they have already seen a cycle of Shakespearean plays presenting that dismal story:

> Small time, but in that small most greatly lived
> This star of England. Fortune made his sword;
> By which the world's best garden he achieved,
> And of it left his son imperial lord.
> Henry the Sixt, in infant bands crown'd King
> Of France and England, did this king succeed;
> Whose state so many had the managing,
> That they lost France, and made his England bleed;
> Which oft our stage hath shown; and for their sake,
> In your fair minds let this acceptance take.
> [Epilogue, 5-14]

"But if the cause be not good," Williams muses on the eve of Agincourt [IV. i. 134-42], "the King himself hath a heavy reckoning to make, when all those legs, and arms, and heads, chopp'd off in a battle, shall join together at the latter day and cry all, 'We died at such a place'—some swearing, some crying for a surgeon, some upon their wives left poor behind them, some upon the debts they owe, some upon their children rawly left. I am afeard there are few die well that die in a battle." Replying to Williams, the King insists that the state of a man's soul at the moment of his death is his own responsibility. . . . [The] King's answer evades the issue: the suffering he is capable of inflicting, the necessity of being sure that the burden is imposed for a worthy cause. The end of the play bleakly implies that there is no such cause; all that Harry has won will be lost within a generation. (pp. 287-89)

But the implication that the cause is not good disturbs us well before the aftermath of Agincourt. The major justification for the war is the Archbishop of Canterbury's harangue on the Salic Law governing hereditary succession, a law the French are said to have violated. The Archbishop's speech to the King follows immediately on his announcement to the Bishop of Ely that he plans to propose the war as a means of alleviating a financial crisis in the Church. The speech itself is long, legalistic, peppered with exotic genealogies impossible to follow; its language is involuted and syntactically loose. The very qualities that make its equivalent in Shakespeare's sources an unexceptionable instrument of statecraft make it sound on the stage like doubletalk, and Canterbury's conclusion that it is "as clear as is the summer's sun" [I. ii. 86] that King Henry is legitimate King of France is a sardonic bit of comedy. (p. 290)

Henry's insistence throughout the scene that the Archbishop reassure him as to his right to make the claim insures our suspicion that the war is not quite the selfless enterprise other parts of the play tempt us to see.

Our suspicions are deepened by what happens later. Harold C. Goddard has left us a devastating attack on Henry V as Shakespeare's model Machiavellian. Goddard's intemperate analysis, as right as it is one-sided, should be read by everyone interested in the play. (pp. 290-91)

Admittedly, Goddard's analysis is excessively partisan. He ignores the rhetoric we have admired, he sees only the King's hypocrisy on Agincourt eve, and he refuses the Chorus's repeated invitations to view the war as more glorious than what is shown. But the burden of Goddard's argument is difficult to set aside: the war scenes reinforce the unpleasant implications of the Salic Law episode. Consider the moment, before the great battle, when the King bullies the citizens of Harfleur, whose surrender he demands, with a rapacious violence that even J. H. Walter [see excerpt above, 1954] does not cite as an instance of "Henry's christian self-control":

> If I begin the batt'ry once again,
> I will not leave the half-achieved Harflew
> Till in her ashes she lies buried.
> The gates of mercy shall be all shut up,
> And the flesh'd soldier, rough and hard of heart,
> In liberty of bloody hand, shall range
> With conscience wide as hell, mowing like grass
> Your fresh fair virgins and your flow'ring infants.
> What is it then to me, if impious War,
> Arrayed in flames like to the prince of fiends,
> Do with his smirch'd complexion all fell feats
> Enlink'd to waste and desolation?
> What is't to me, when you yourselves are cause,
> If your pure maidens fall into the hand
> Of hot and forcing violation?
> What reign can hold licentious wickedness
> When down the hill he holds his fierce career?
>
> [III. iii. 7-23]

In such language as [Marlowe's] Tamburlaine styled his "working words," the King, like the kind of aggressor we know all too well, blames the rapine he solicits on his victims. The alacrity of his attack makes one understand Yeats's description of Henry V as a "ripened Fortinbras" [see excerpt above, 1903]; its sexual morbidity casts a disquieting light on

the muted but unmistakable aggressiveness of his sexual assault on Katherine in the fifth act.

Henry's killing of the French prisoners inspires similar uneasiness. Olivier justified this violation of the putative ethics of war by making it a response to the French killing of the English luggage boys, and one of the most moving moments of his film was the King's passionate response: "I was not angry since I came to France / Until this instant" [IV. vii. 55-6]. After such a moment one could hardly fault Henry's

> Besides, we'll cut the throats of those we have,
> And not a man of them that we shall take
> Shall taste our mercy.
>
> [IV. vii. 63-5]

In the same scene, indeed, Gower observes that it was in response to the slaughter of the boys that "the King, most worthily, hath caus'd every soldier to cut his prisoner's throat. O, 'tis a gallant king!" [IV. vii. 8-10]. But the timing is wrong: Gower's announcement came *before* the King's touching speech. In fact, Shakespeare had presented the decision to kill the prisoners as made at the end of the preceding scene, and while in the source it has a strategic point, in the play it is simply a response to the fair battlefield killing of some English nobles by the French. Thus the announcement comes twice, first as illegitimate, second as if it were a spontaneous outburst of forgivable passion when it actually is not. In such moments as this we feel an eloquent discrepancy between the glamor of the play's rhetoric and the reality of its action.

*Henry IV*, Part One is "about temperance and fortitude," Part Two is "about wisdom and justice," and Shakespeare's "plan culminates in *Henry V*." So argues Sherman Hawkins. "Henry's right to France—and by implication England—," he claims, "is finally vindicated by a higher power than the Archbishop of Canterbury." God's concern that France be governed by so ideal a monarch culminates, of course, in the ruins so movingly described in Act V by the Duke of Burgundy, to whose plea the King responds like the leader of a nation of shopkeepers with a demand that France "buy [the] peace" [V. ii. 70] it wants according to a contract Henry just happens to have had drawn up. What follows is the King's coarse wooing of his captive princess, with its sexual innuendo, its repeated gloating over Henry's possession of the realm for which he sues, and its arch insistence on his sudden lack of adequate rhetoric. Dr. Johnson's judgment is hardly too severe: the King "has neither the vivacity of Hal, nor the grandeur of Henry. . . . We have here but a mean dialogue for princes; the merriment is very gross, and the sentiments are very worthless" [see excerpt above, 1765].

Henry's treatment of France may suggest to the irreverent that one is better off when providence does not supply such a conqueror. And his impact on England is scarcely more salubrious. . . . England must pay a high price for the privilege of the returning veterans to show their wounds every October 25.

We do not have to wait for the Epilogue to get an idea of it. At the end of Act IV, as we saw, the King calls for holy rites for the dead and orders a return to England. The Chorus to the ensuing act invites us to fantasy the King's triumphant return, his modesty, and the outpouring of grateful citizens. But in the next scene we find ourselves still in France, where Fluellen gives Pistol, last of the company of the Boar's Head, the comeuppance he has long fended off with his shield of preposterous language. Forced to eat his leek, Pistol mutters one last feeble imprecation ("all hell shall stir for this" [V. i. 68]), listens to

Gower's final tonguelashing, and, alone on the stage at last, speaks in soliloquy:

> Doth Fortune play the huswife with me now?
> News have I that my Doll is dead i' th' spittle
> Of a malady of France,
> And there my rendezvous is quite cut off.
> Old do I wax, and from my weary limbs
> Honor is cudgell'd. Well, bawd I'll turn,
> And something lean to cutpurse of quick hand.
> To England will I steal, and there I'll steal;
> And patches will I get unto these cudgell'd scars,
> And [swear] I got them in the Gallia wars.
>
> [V. i. 80-9]

The pun on "steal" is the last faint echo of the great Falstaff scenes, but labored and lifeless now as Pistol's pathetic bravura. Pistol's *Exit* occasioned Dr. Johnson's most affecting critical comment: "The comick scenes of the history of Henry the Fourth and Fifth are now at an end, and all the comick personages are now dismissed. Falstaff and Mrs. Quickly are dead; Nym and Bardolph are hanged; Gadshill was lost immediately after the robbery; Poins and Peto have vanished since, one knows not how; and Pistol is now beaten into obscurity. I believe every reader regrets their departure." But our regret is for more than the end of some high comedy: it is for the reality of the postwar world the play so powerfully conjures up—soldiers returned home to find their jobs gone, falling to a life of crime in a seamy and impoverished underworld that scarcely remembers the hopes that accompanied the beginnings of the adventure.

It is the "duty of the ruler," Hawkins says, "to make his subjects good." For the failure of his subjects, the play tells us, we must hold Henry V and his worthless war responsible. Unsatisfactory though he was, Henry IV was still the victim of the revolution of the times, and our ultimate attitude toward him, hastened to his death by the unconscious ambition of his own son, took a sympathetic turn like that with which we came at the end to regard the luckless Richard. But Henry V, master manipulator of time, has by the end of the cycle immersed himself in the destructive element. The blows he has rained on his country are much more his than those of any enemy of the people, and all he has to offer his bleeding subjects for the few years that remain is the ceremonial posture which he himself has earlier had the insight to contemn. Like the Edmund of *King Lear,* another lusty and manipulative warrior who wins, woos, and dies young, Henry might have subscribed himself "in the ranks of death" [*King Lear,* IV. ii. 25].

Well, there it is. Should one see a rabbit or a duck? Along the way I've cited some critics who see an exemplary Christian monarch, who has attained, "in the language of Ephesians, both the 'age' and 'stature' of a perfect man" [Hawkins]. And I have cited others who see "the perfect Machiavellian prince" [Goddard], a coarse and brutal highway robber. Despite their obvious differences, these rival views are essentially similar, for each sees only a rabbit or a duck. (pp. 291-94)

A third response has been suggested by some writers of late: *Henry V* is a subtle and complex study of a king who curiously combines strengths and weaknesses, virtues and vices. One is attracted to the possibility of regarding the play unpolemically. Shakespeare is not often polemical, after all, and a balanced view allows for the inclusion of both positive and negative features in an analysis of the protagonist and the action. But sensitive as such analysis can be—and I especially admire

Robert Ornstein's study in *A Kingdom for a Stage* [see excerpt above, 1972]—it is oddly unconvincing, for two strong reasons. First, the cycle has led us to expect stark answers to simple and urgent questions: is a particular king good or bad for England? can one be a successful public man and retain a healthy inner life? has Hal lost or gained in the transformation through which he changes name and character? does political action confer any genuine benefit on the polity? what is honor worth, and who has it? The mixed view of Henry characteristically appears in critical essays that seem to fudge such questions, to see complication and subtlety where Shakespeare's art forces us to demand commitment, resolution, answers. Second, no real compromise is possible between the extreme readings I have claimed the play provokes. Our experience of the play resembles the experience Gombrich claims for viewers of the trick drawing: "We can switch from one reading to another with increasing rapidity; we will also 'remember' the rabbit while we see the duck, but the more closely we watch ourselves, the more certainly we will discover that we cannot experience alternative readings at the same time."

The kind of ambiguity I have been describing in *Henry V,* requiring that we hold in balance incompatible and radically opposed views each of which seems exclusively true, is only an extreme version of the fundamental ambiguity that many critics have found at the center of the Shakespearean vision and that some years ago, borrowing a bit of jargon from physics, I called "complementarity." What we are talking about is the perception of reality as intransigently multivalent. Though we are poignantly convinced of basic truths—complementarity is a far cry from skepticism—we know that rabbits are always turning into ducks before our eyes, bushes into bears. (p. 295)

[In] *Henry V,* it seems to me, Shakespeare's habitual recognition of the duality of things has led him, as it should lead his audience, to a point of crisis. Since by now virtually every other play in the canon has been called a problem play, let me add *Henry V* to the number. Suggesting the necessity of radically opposed responses to a historical figure about whom there would seem to have been little reason for anything but the simplest of views, Shakespeare leaves us at a loss.

Is it any wonder that *Julius Caesar* would follow in a few months, where Shakespeare would present one of the defining moments in world history in such a way that his audience cannot determine whether the protagonist is the best or the worst of men, whether the central action springs from disinterested idealism or vainglorious egotism, whether that action is virtuous and necessary or wicked and gratuitous? Nor is one surprised to see that the most romantic and comic of Shakespeare's history plays was created at the moment when he was about to abandon romantic comedy, poised for the flight into the great tragedies with their profounder questions about the meaning of action and heroism. The clash between the two possible views of the world of *Henry V* suggests a spiritual struggle in Shakespeare that he would spend the rest of his career working through. One sees a similar oscillation, magnified and reemphasized, in the problem plays and tragedies, and one is tempted to read the romances as a last profound effort to reconcile the irreconcilable. The terrible fact about *Henry V* is that Shakespeare seems equally tempted by both its rival gestalts. And he forces us, as we experience and reexperience and reflect on the play, as we encounter it in performances which inevitably lean in one direction or the other, to share his conflict.

*Henry V* is most valuable for us not because it points to a crisis in Shakespeare's spiritual life, but because it shows us something about ourselves: the simultaneity of our deepest hopes and fears about the world of political action. In this play, Shakespeare reveals the conflicts between the private selves with which we are born and the public selves we must become, between our longing that authority figures can be like us and our suspicion that they must have traded away their inwardness for the sake of power. The play contrasts our hope that society can solve our problems with our knowledge that society has never done so. The inscrutability of *Henry V* is the inscrutability of history. And for a unique moment in Shakespeare's work ambiguity is the heart of the matter, the single most important fact we must confront in plucking out the mystery of the world we live in. (p. 296)

> Norman Rabkin, ''Rabbits, Ducks, and 'Henry V','' in Shakespeare Quarterly, *Vol. 28, No. 3, Summer, 1977, pp. 279-96.*

## JAMES L. CALDERWOOD   (essay date 1979)

[*Calderwood has examined what he calls Shakespeare's ''metadrama'' in two studies,* Shakespearean Metadrama *(1971) and* Metadrama in Shakespeare's Henriad *(1979). In the introduction to his earlier book, Calderwood claims that Shakespeare's plays are not only concerned with various moral, social, and political themes, but are also self-reflexively concerned with dramatic art itself—''its materials, its media of language and theater, its generic forms and conventions, its relationship to truth and the social order.'' In the excerpt below, Calderwood discusses the parallels between Henry's quest for political unity and Shakespeare's search for an artistic unity that is not merely imposed on his material, but evolves naturally from the action of the drama. He compares the king's suppression of all private feelings in his public persona to the dramatist's need to constrain his personal viewpoint in light of the realities of English history, the expectations of his audience, and his portrayal of Prince Hal in* 1 *and* 2 Henry IV. *However, in Act IV, Scene i, according to the critic, Shakespeare ''introduces an element of thematic dissension into his previously untroubled drama,'' presenting Henry as doubting his claim to the throne, mistrusting ceremony, and uncertain about the outcome of the battle because he knows he cannot rely on divine intervention on his behalf. But at Agincourt, Calderwood concludes, Henry not only consolidates the disparate elements of his army and leads them to victory, he also reestablishes national unity and resurrects ''an old and long-neglected concept of royal order'' in which the monarchy is based on both the loyalty of its subjects and the approval of God.*]

That [*Henry V*] is an advance, a shaping of a new kind of dramatic order, is argued by its New Arden editor, J. H. Walter, who says:

> Shakespeare's task was not merely to extract material for a play from an epic story, but within the physical limits of the stage and within the admittedly inadequate dramatic convention to give the illusion of an epic whole. In consequence *Henry V* is daringly novel, nothing quite like it had been seen on the stage before [see excerpt above, 1954].

No wonder, then, Walter observes, that Shakespeare, after his epic invocation in the Prologue—''O for a Muse of fire . . .'' [Prologue, 1]—quickly grows apologetic about the inadequacies of the theater to represent the manifold of history. The same theme of apology runs through all the prologues and the epilogue. Since history in its ''huge and proper life'' cannot ''be here presented'' [Chorus, V, 5, 6], it must be re-presented, not in its wholeness but in its ''partness.'' A thousand men

are reduced to one man and ''the accomplishment of many years / Into an hour-glass'' [Prologue, 30-1]. The technique is essentially metaphoric and, since metaphor requires an act of imaginative completion by a reader, Shakespeare asks here not merely for his audience's indulgence but for their imaginative assistance in creating the ''tenor'' of English history by means of the ''vehicle'' of metaphoric theater. More specifically, however, the technique is synecdochic, using the dramatic part to stand for the historic whole.

The relation of part to whole is a cardinal issue in *Henry V*, for the illusion of epic unity that Shakespeare is seeking is sought also—and rather readily discovered—by King Harry in the political sphere. The ideological basis for political unity is supplied by the Archbishop of Canterbury's speech in act 1 about divine, natural, governmental, and military order [I. ii. 183-220]. The speech itself is curiously excessive to the problem of defending England from the Scots while Harry's armies are in France. Ultimately it is decided to divide Harry's forces into four parts, leave three in England, and take one to France. But this rather obvious solution comes only after some thirty-four lines by Exeter and Canterbury justifying such division on the grounds of unity of purpose. Illustrations of this kind of unity are drawn from music, sundials, archery, the confluence of roads and streams, and most expansively from bees— ''Creatures that by a rule of nature teach / The act of order to a peopled kingdom'' [I. ii. 188-89]. In this Platonic perspective the emphasis is upon transcendence. Particulars are of no value in themselves; a man achieves fulfillment not by cultivating singularity but by submerging himself in a larger scheme. Self-servers like Bardolph and Nym will be brought down, to the full stretch of hemp, and even Pistol will be demeaned—that sorry stand-in for the Great Gormandizer must come at last to dine on leeks. On the other hand, through personal sacrifice and useful service, the individual transcends himself to become a functional part of the greater whole. Thus the Many, whether bees or barons, become the One. (pp. 135-37)

As an exposition of order in nature and society Canterbury's speech is perfectly orthodox; it dominates the conduct of the English throughout the play. National unity is achieved by inclusion and by exclusion—by incorporating the Welsh Fluellen, the Irish Macmorris, and the Scottish Jamy into the English cause, for example, and by eliminating the English traitors, the disobedient Bardolph and Nym, and ultimately the opposing French. The French are, of course, poor imitators of God's confluent order. In 3.5 their preparations for battle seem largely to consist of a roll call of titled names: ''High dukes, great princes, barons, lords, and knights'' [III. v. 46]. Harry can cite noble names too [IV. iii. 51-5], but he can also give tribute to the worker bees and the cooperative hive:

> We few, we happy few, we band of brothers.
> For he today that sheds his blood with me
> Shall be my brother. Be he ne'er so vile,
> This day shall gentle his condition.
>
> [IV. iii. 60-3]

It is true that Harry has not so much established a happy democracy here as introduced upward mobility into the Great Chain of Being. Even so, in contrast to the feudal French, he proposes a ''gentling of condition'' that is earned rather than inherited, a brotherhood with the king that is achieved not through shared bloodlines but through shared blood losses. Then, during the final act, after the harsh dialectics of combat, we are given a glimpse of a transcendent synthesis. King Harry and Princess Katherine are to lose their individuality and, ''being two, are one in love'' [V. ii. 361]. Frenchmen and Englishmen are to lose their nationalities and mingle indistinguishably as members of God's international community [V. ii. 367-68], though we may take leave to doubt whether the conquering English are as anxious as the conquered French to dissolve all differences.

The demand for unity in England is fully honored by England's new king, whose own personality is a microcosm of the nation in this regard. Everyone has lamented the loss of Prince Hal in King Harry, nearly as much as the loss of Falstaff in *Henry V,* for the newly crowned king's famous ''I know thee not, old man'' [*2 Henry IV,* V. v. 47] seems also to have meant ''I know thee not, young prince.'' At any rate, the various-minded Hal, who moved gracefully between the worlds of court, tavern, and battlefield, who could speak prose as well as verse, who could say ''I am now of all humours that have showed themselves humours since the old days of goodman Adam to the pupil age of this present twelve o'clock midnight'' [*1 Henry IV,* II. iv. 92-5], has been succeeded by King Harry, single-mindedly pious, militant, even ruthless. Victories can not do without victims, and the victims add up: Falstaff (''I know thee not, old man''), Lord Scroop and his fellow traitors (''Touching our person seek we no revenge, / But we our kingdom's safety must so tender'' . . . [II. ii. 174-75]), the citizens of Harfleur whom Harry's armies will ravage (''What is it then to me. . . . What is't to me . . .?'' [III. iii. 15, 19]), Bardolph of the lantern nose (''We would have all such offenders so cut off'' [III. vi. 107-08]), the French prisoners at Agincourt (''Then every soldier kill his prisoners'' [IV. vi. 37]), and finally Katherine, who though only coyly resistant is nevertheless part of the spoils of war.

So thoroughly has Hal disappeared with Falstaff from *Henry V* that Una Ellis-Fermor has claimed it is futile to ''look for the personality of Henry behind the king; there is nothing else there. . . . There is no Henry, only a king'' [see excerpt above, 1945]. This is both true and untrue. It is true that, as Alvin Kernan says, our ''difficulties in understanding the King are intensified by the almost total absence from the play of speeches in which Henry speaks as a private man, directly revealing his own feelings,'' and that Harry ''lives in the full glare of public life'' [see excerpt above, 1969]. But it is not true that the crown never leaves Harry's head. Shakespeare is quite clear about that on the eve of Agincourt when he has Harry tell Bates:

> For, though I speak it to you, I think the King is but a man, as I am. The violet smells to him as it does to me; the element shows to him as it doth to me; all his senses have but human conditions. His ceremonies laid by, in his nakedness he appears but a man . . .
>
> [IV. i. 100-05]

Public office and private man are for Harry the reverse of what they were for Hal. As part of his sun-cloud strategy Hal suppressed his princeliness, making his office—or his training for office—private, and gave public expression to the wayward young man. Intending to prove ''better than [his] word,'' he has, as Henry V, become so. Harry the man is now kept private, suppressed in favor of Harry the king, who is nearly always on public display. In keeping with the theme of unity, the private man is subsumed by the public office. As for his motives, they are the motives of a king who consults England's welfare rather than his own feelings before rendering decisions. Not for himself but for the nation Harry declares war, executes

traitors, threatens Harfleur, refuses ransom, orders prisoners killed, gives credit for the victory to God, and marries Katherine. (pp. 137-41)

Harry's personality is united under his political office, and his conduct in office is designed to unite the nation in accordance with Canterbury's speech on order. As Harry's piety testifies, God stands in relation to Harry's well-ordered character as He does also to order in England, for God has been Englished by Canterbury's rhetoric. God created order in nature, the English and Harry imitate it and triumph, the French fail to do so and predictably suffer.

Cast in military form, Canterbury's confluent order appears as a united English army mowing down the French nobility. Cast in dramatic form, it would appear as a play all the parts of which yield to a unifying principle. Taken metadramatically, Canterbury's speech might be seen as an apologia for the playwright who, claiming a kind of divine authority, nationalizes his literary themes, suppresses internal dissent, and tailors his characters and actions to a partisan pattern. And this is partly the case. Shakespeare the English dramatist has to some degree imitated Harry the English king in suppressing private feeling in favor of national interest. He too achieves unity through inclusion and exclusion. If Harry has rejected Falstaff at Westminster, thus killing his heart, as the Hostess claims, Shakespeare has done the dramatic equivalent, writing Falstaff out of *Henry V* (despite his promise in . . . *2 Henry IV* to ''continue the story, with Sir John in it'' [Epilogue, 27-8]) and literally killing his heart offstage. . . . So too with the remaining low-life characters. If Harry eliminates the traitorous Grey, Scroop, and Cambridge, Shakespeare diminishes in his turn the comic rebels Bardolph, Nym, and Pistol. If they survive Falstaff, as though to inherit his role as parodist, they are granted a toothless parody at best. No sooner have they mimicked Harry's ''Once more unto the breach'' address at Harfleur [III. i. 1ff.]—in a scene of uninspired humor—than Fluellen arrives to pummel them into battle and the Boy lingers on to satirize the would-be satirists. Their villainies stem, the Boy claims, from a failure to match words with deeds—''For Pistol, he hath a killing tongue and a quiet sword'' and ''For Nym . . . his few bad words are matched with as few good deeds'' [III. ii. 34, 36, 39]. As a result their burlesque of the main plot succeeds only in degrading themselves. Instead of being made to seem foolish, Harry emerges as the one man whose words are more than matched by his deeds, as he declared they would be from the beginning: ''By how much better than my word I am, / By so much shall I falsify men's hopes'' [*1 Henry IV,* I. ii. 210-11]. In the remainder of this scene, having excluded the three self-serving parasites, Shakespeare underscores unity by inclusion with the three representatives of England's habitually churlish border nations—the Welsh Fluellen, the Irish Macmorris, and the Scottish Jamy—who, though contentious enough with one another, are united in their desire, as Jamy puts it, to ''de gud service'' against the French [III. ii. 115].

All that remains, then, now that the English are in harmony, is to do in the French. History having made the English victory a foregone conclusion, Shakespeare can busy himself to make it glorious. It is not enough that the French lose at Agincourt; they must also deserve to lose. Hence the Dauphin is made supercilious and arrogant, and the French in general, especially in 3.7 and 4.2, are presented as fatuously insolent. In them feudal chivalry has degenerated into a mannered doting on trivia, of which the Dauphin's sonnet in praise of his horse is emblematic.

Finally, having protected Harry and England from within by aggrandizing those who are "with" and either eliminating or degrading those who are "against" the national cause, Shakespeare takes pains to indemnify the epic-heroic mode against misinterpretation from without. In the Induction to *2 Henry IV* Rumour announced himself as running up and down England sowing dissension of understanding. In a play so prefaced, false expectations, ironic double meanings, and mistrust will afflict not merely the characters but the audience as well. But Rumour is succeeded in *Henry V* by the Chorus, whose name in itself implies musical unity and whose dramatic function is to secure unity of interpretation. We are told in unambiguous tones what to expect in this play and how to respond to it. As an English audience, we are told to identify with, to admire, and to yearn for the lost glories of Henry's reign.

Not only does the Chorus encourage unity of interpretation, it also helps create unity of structure in the play itself by building narrative bridges between the five acts whose discreteness has prompted from critics such adjectives as episodic and tableau-like. This structural unity to which the Chorus contributes reinforces the internal thematic unity of the play, which is so rigorous in behalf of the English, so disturbingly suggestive of a "God's on our side" chauvinism, that many critics have sought evidence of Shakespearean irony. (pp. 142-46)

The issue is larger than chauvinism and the question of Shakespeare's patriotic beliefs or theatrical opportunism. We encounter here an old critical problem that new critical attention has brought into sharper focus. If literary works consist of a marriage between parts and whole, which of the partners to this marriage must defer to the other? Should priority be given to unity and wholeness—to Apollonian order, Aristotelian form, Hegel's synthesis, Ransom's universal, Tate's intension, Frye's archetype? If so, how much Platonic oneness can the work permit without converting its marriage into a bleak domestic tyranny of the whole over the parts? On the other hand, will not too great a complexity of parts—Hegel's dialectical conflict, Empson's ambiguity, Brooks's paradox, Warren's impurity, Wimsatt's hateful contraries, Krieger's existential chaos, and so on—dissolve all order and unity in the work? How much Dionysiac dancing and rebellious individuality can the work permit without converting its marriage into a domestic insurrection of parts against whole? In this direction madness lies; in that, an arid sanity.

Chaos, strife, and irresolution come cheap. Any literary neophyte, mind boggling like Bottom's with inexpressible dreams, can strew a page with slices and shards of irreconcilable "life." Order is another matter. To cast the clutter of raw experience into even a trivial, third-hand, sentimental order takes a measure, however small, of literary skill. By its nature order must be imposed, and its price, the price of unity in the work, is necessarily the autonomy of the parts, of the division and strife that make for internal complexity. . . . But, on the other hand, to prevent the work from becoming a dizzying reproduction of life's disorder—Yvor Winters's "fallacy of imitative form"—we concede that these intramural complications must be resolvable.

With the notion of resolvable complications we seem to have got safely out of this winding dark wood of poetics. But alas, as Murray Krieger reminds us, resolvable complications come not by the grace of Manichaean chance but by authorial design, no less so than the preordained structure of meaning in the most rigid of allegories. For to introduce resolvable complications the writer must load his artistic dice and call upon all

his skill to disguise that fact. Instead of earning or achieving an order, instead of allowing a new order to emerge from the dialectical ordeal of the creative process, the writer will merely impose upon the work a preexistent order. And yet, what remedy? The literary dice are either loaded or they are not loaded; there are no degrees in between, such as their being only "slightly" loaded. If the writer plays for truth with loaded dice, he is patently dishonest. If he does not, he abandons the literary game to the randomness of chance. On the one hand he is not an honest artist, on the other he is not an artist at all.

I think Shakespeare was aware of these problems, indeed, this dilemma, and that we can see him exploring it in *Henry V*. Faced with the obligation of writing *Henry V*, in fact, he could hardly avoid such issues. For a play in which "this star of England" [Epilogue, 6] is to be studied at its zenith makes more than ordinary demands on its author. Shakespeare knows, for instance, that he is bound by history. Not *enslaved* by it—he can collapse history's four dauphins into one for his purposes—but bound by it nevertheless, and willing to admit as much in his prologues, as when the epilogue refers to "Our bending author [who] hath pursued the story" [Epilogue, 2]. Moreover, he knows that he is bound by his own immediate literary history, the three preceding plays in *The Henriad*. History alone would have authorized him to conclude *Henry V* with, say, Harry's death and funeral as readily as with Agincourt and a marriage. But the *Henry IV* plays have guaranteed us that *Henry V* will exhibit sovereignty in success, ending not with death but with triumph and a sense of national fulfillment. And, finally, Shakespeare knows that he is bound by his audience and the nationality he shares with them. How he presents Harry and his England depends less on his own inclinations than on the expectations of an English audience who may not know the details of history but are steeped in awe for the mythical magnificence of Harry and his times.

Having given hostages to English history, to his own tetralogy, and to the expectations of his English audience, Shakespeare might well have felt that writing *Henry V* was less an exercise in creative freedom than a discharge of obligations. Thus he seems to have written into the play a self-justifying rationale, a speech by the Archbishop of Canterbury emphasizing obedience to higher laws, self-sacrifice, all the virtues of the "act of order" [I. ii. 189]. Sanctified by the cause of national and dramatic unity, the play eliminates all dissension and advances toward Agincourt under God's banner.

But at this point Shakespeare seems to have suffered doubts. In any event, it is at this point that he inflicts doubts upon the previously self-assured King Harry. On the eve of Agincourt, when Harry goes disguised among his men, the foot-soldier Williams raises the question of royal responsibility and the rightness of the English cause in France:

> But if the cause be not good, the King himself
> hath a heavy reckoning to make when all those
> legs and arms and heads chopped off in battle
> shall join together at the latter day and cry all,
> "We died at such a place." . . . I am afeard
> there are few die well that die in a battle, for
> how can they charitably dispose of anything
> when blood is their argument. Now if these
> men do not die well it will be a black matter
> for the King that led them to it, who to disobey
> were against all proportion of subjection.
>
> [IV. i. 134-38, 141-46].

Williams asks, in effect, "Are my services to the king consistent with my obligations to God?" If they are, well and good; if they are not, the king must answer for it, since I am bound to his service. (pp. 146-50)

The gist of [Harry's] reply—which is long, consistent, well illustrated, and quite beside the point—lies in one sentence: "Every subject's duty is the king's, but every subject's soul is his own" [IV. i. 176-77]. Williams seems reassured, but he has small reason to be. At issue are not the private sins each soldier totals up in the general business of living—from that point of view, every subject's soul is indeed his own—but rather those sins he specifically commits "when blood is their argument," when he is, in the present case, piling up legs and arms and heads to support Harry's claims in France. From this standpoint, each subject's soul and duty are inevitably the king's responsibility, and the question comes back, "Is the king's cause also God's cause?"

That, however, is precisely the question Harry avoids. The reason for this avoidance is not far to seek. In his speech on Ceremony immediately following the departure of the soldiers Harry demythologizes kingship rather as Falstaff did honor at Shrewsbury. In contrast to Canterbury's thesis about God and His divine order standing surety for the king and his well-regulated state—in effect, the old Ricardian "divine right" view of politics—King Harry confesses that there is nothing inherently majestic about majesty. "Place, degree, and form" are not ways in which men participate in divine order but merely instruments of political expediency "creating awe and fear in other men" and lending dignity to the exercise of power [IV. i. 246, 247]. Then Harry addresses a prayer to the "God of battles" asking Him to "think not upon the fault / [His] father made in compassing the crown" [IV. i. 289, 293-94] and citing at length his own contrition for Richard's death and efforts in his spiritual behalf.

Despite Harry's regal confidence up to this point, we now see that he is uneasily aware that he owes his kingship not to God but to his usurping, regicidal father. Perhaps this uneasiness has been with him earlier. For if God *had* made him king, if he were graced with the Divine Right legitimacy of a Richard, Harry would not have had to rely on Canterbury to sanctify the invasion of France ("The sin upon my head, dread sovereign!" [I. ii. 97]). Nor would he have had to make others responsible for his decisions: the Dauphin and his father for the war [I. ii. 284-88; II. iv. 105-09]), the English traitors for their punishment ("The mercy that was quick in us but late, / By your own counsel is suppressed and killed" [II. ii. 79-80]), the citizens of Harfleur for atrocities done them ("What is it to me, when you yourselves are cause" [III. iii. 19]), and the foot-soldiers for the perils of their souls. As God's vicegerent, King Harry would legitimize his ventures by the act of announcing them. But how Harry's credit stands in heaven, heaven alone knows. Instead of inheriting Divine Right from Henry IV, he has inherited mere Ceremony—"titles blown from adulation" [IV. i. 254]—a showy but sorry substitute.

If Harry's regal insecurities account directly for the priests singing and the poor praying for Richard's soul, they also account for Harry's general oversupply of piety, his almost automatic qualification of every stated intention with a "God willing" or "God before" or "But this lies all within the will of God" [I. ii. 289]. These are symptoms not merely of routine religious deference but of Harry's quasi-fallen royalty. If the king cannot claim to speak *for* God as His appointed agent, he had better speak *to* Him as His devoted appellant.

Harry's speech on Ceremony and his prayer to the God of battles have no effect upon the English, who of course remain as united as before; but they do call into question the aesthetic and thematic unity of *Henry V*. However foreordained the outcome of Agincourt may be from the standpoint of the audience, Shakespeare takes unusual pains to assure us that from Harry's perspective there are no guarantees whatsoever. God will bring no legions to Agincourt in support of the beleaguered English. In His divine wisdom He may know in advance how the plot turns out—who wins, who loses, who's in, who's out—but in His divine inscrutability He keeps His intentions shrouded. Up until now it has seemed that God's role was that of a participant who had chosen a side to defend. Now it appears that He is in the role of a judge who will render a verdict after reviewing the military, and presumably the moral and spiritual, evidence on both sides.

With God's withdrawal from overt partisanship, what had seemed a sure thing takes on the character of a genuine contest, a true trial of the English cause. That means, for Harry and the English, an element of risk. The French, who are going to die at Agincourt but who cannot know that, take no risks beforehand; they ride the odds and their sleek horses toward an obvious victory. The English, on the other hand, most of whom are not going to die at Agincourt but who cannot know that, ponder on St. Crispian's Eve the dreary likelihood that their souls as well as their lives are in peril, and then soberly risk both on the morrow.

And the king whom they follow at such risk, he risks most of all. First, of course, his life. Refusing to avail himself of kingly privileges by accepting ransom, as Williams had feared he might, Harry hazards his life as extremely as his men do theirs: "Bid them achieve me," he cautions the French herald, "and then sell my bones" [IV. iii. 91]. Second, he risks his title, not only to France but to England as well, as he did not understand when he cried "No king of England, if not king of France!" [II. ii. 193]. God, we know, conferred kingship on Richard; and Bolingbroke, God knows, conferred it on himself, substituting Ceremony for Divine Right. With no claim to Divine Right and with no trust in Ceremony, Harry is afflicted with royal doubts. For if he remains tainted by his father's usurpation and regicide, then he is an impostor, and the English order descending from God is a fraud. If so, then Harry risks not only life and title but, as Williams feared, the lives and souls of all his soldiers as well. That most awesome risk Harry accepts as part of his own trial: "We must bear all" [IV. i. 233].

Thus at Agincourt Harry redeems from hazard not only his own life, and the lives and souls of his men, but English kingship too, which has been in pawn since Richard's reign. Instead of Richard's inherited Divine Right, however, Harry acquires an earned human right to the crown, gained through ordeal by combat, "in plain shock and even play of battle" [IV. viii. 109]. On the day of battle his royal authenticity is plainly evident. If at Shrewsbury in *1 Henry IV* the English sovereign was unrecognizable amid the (other) counterfeits dressed in his coats, at Agincourt no man walks in the king's coat but the king himself. Harry may pass unrecognized in Erpingham's cloak on St. Crispian's Eve, but on St. Crispian's Day every man knows who the King of England is.

At Agincourt King Harry also redeems the playwright Shakespeare from the charge of artistic despotism. As England and Harry's armies have banded together in self-righteous confidence of God's partisanship, so the play *Henry V* has been thematically unified by an act of order imposed on it by its partisan playwright. With God inside the play and Shakespeare outside it both bent on being fully English, *Henry V* exemplifies that tyranny of whole over parts, Apollo over Dionysus, thesis over antitheses, that we spoke of earlier. Or so it seems. From our present perspective, however, we can see that if Shakespeare framed Canterbury's speech on order as a justifying rationale not only for military unity in England but for an overbearing thematic unity in *Henry V* he at some point came to regard that speech with suspicion. Thus he subjects the Archbishop's routine recipes for national efficiency to a shrewd critique by the distraught King Harry, and in doing so he introduces an element of thematic dissension into his previously untroubled drama. What had seemed an uncontested whole is now challenged by a part, the very scene in which Harry's legitimacy is challenged by his fears of divine disfavor.

By rendering Harry's doubts so vividly at this point, Shakespeare in effect causes God to withdraw from apparent partisanship—and that emblemizes Shakespeare's own withdrawal from partisanship as omnipotent author, at least his withdrawal from the kind of naive, unexamined partisanship that seems to have characterized him thus far. Later on, as we know, when the battle is over, Harry will claim that God's "arm was here," that God was partisan after all. And we know too that Shakespeare's arm was certainly here, even though, like God, he seems to have announced his withdrawal. But if he has not totally withdrawn from the literary engagement—and of course how could he?—he has withdrawn from apparent chauvinism into a more sophisticated partisanship, making an honest playwright of himself, and an honest God of God, by bringing before us the very issue of honesty in art. From a too easy concept of literary order he wrests a new kind of order, tested in action and opposition, the dramatic ordeal by combat.

Harry undergoes his ordeal too. If his deepest fears hold true, then his royal legitimacy is no more valid than the gauds and trappings of office—mere Ceremony—and he is on his own. Say he is—what then? Harry has his look into the abyss, and what he sees there he takes in reasonable stride. If he cannot look to divine aid in battle, he will look to himself and his ragged followers. The battle is not won through divine interference but in familiar human ways—through courage, discipline, cooperative effort—and, to be sure, in familiar inhuman ways, through the proposed slaughter of French prisoners. His methods are no more legitimized in advance than is his kingship; they earn legitimacy in action, by proving successful in England's cause. The king will cut the throats of his prisoners if necessary, because he knows that God will not cut them for him. . . . So long as God voices judgment only after ordeals by combat, the king must do as he can—and find in his success a declaration of divine will:

> O God, thy arm was here
> And not to us, but to thy arm alone,
> Ascribe we all!
>
> [IV. viii. 106-08]
> (pp. 151-58)

In plain shock and even play of battle Harry has earned God's approval, and with it he has earned, not so much a new as an old and long-neglected concept of royal order. Ideally the English king derives his authority from God above and his subjects below, his own function being to mediate between the two. Richard, claiming his authority exclusively from on high, disregarded the downward direction of royal sway, lost touch with the commons, leased out the very land itself. . . . Unlike Rich-

ard, Harry has not been elected by the Lord. He has had a corporate majesty founded on shared English culture, English aspirations, English blood. Thus Fluellen says, "All the water in the Wye cannot wash your Majesty's Welsh plood out of your pody, I can tell you that" [IV. vii. 106-08], and adds:

> But Jeshu, I am your Majesty's countryman, I care not who know it. I will confess it to all the 'orld. I need not be ashamed of your Majesty, praised be God, so long as your Majesty's an honest man.
>
> [IV. vii. 111-15]

To which Harry replies, "God keep me so!" [IV. vii. 116].

Kingship, it is clear, has not descended on Harry; he has risen to it. But he has not risen to it in his father's fashion, Bolingbroke of the supple knees and usurping mind, whose overeager "In God's name, I'll ascend the regal throne" provoked Carlisle's righteous "Marry, God forbid!" [*Richard II*, IV. i. 113, 114]. If Richard owed all to heaven, and Bolingbroke all to himself, neither held full title to the crown. But Harry descends to the level of his soldiers and rises with them to heights of Agincourt, earning God's endorsement in the process. The divine and temporal dimensions of royal authority thus coalesce in English kingship as they have not done since before Richard's time. (pp. 159-60)

> *James L. Calderwood, "'Henry V': The Act of Order," in his* Metadrama in Shakespeare's Henriad: "Richard II" to "Henry V," *University of California Press, 1979, pp. 134-61.*

### JOANNE ALTIERI   (essay date 1981)

[*Altieri maintains that* Henry V *may be seen as Shakespeare's experiment in combining "an illusionistic portrayal of the political realities" with "an idealized perception of political order." As God's deputy, Henry possesses "transcendent" as well as "worldly power," she argues, and he succeeds—even if only for a brief time—in bringing about a restoration of hierarchical order and the return of society "to the garden state." Altieri analyzes the way in which Shakespeare employed the romance form to achieve this idealized view, pointing out that the dramatic action "follows roughly the pastoral 'green world' pattern common in romance." But she also believes that the mixture of epic, history, romance, and naturalism seriously impedes a coherent and satisfactory response to the action of the play or the character of Henry.*]

In the midst of the battle of Agincourt in *Henry V*, Shakespeare turns from the noblemen who conduct the war to a conversation between two of Henry's captains, Fluellen and Gower. They discuss the French slaughter of the luggage boys and Henry's order that the prisoners' throats be cut in retaliation for the boys' deaths and the destruction of "all that was in the king's tent" [IV. vii. 8]. Through their view of the events—or at least Fluellen's, Gower being a staider soul—they seek to understand Henry's decision by developing a parallel between Henry's nature and Alexander the Great's:

> *Flu.* If you mark Alexander's life well, Harry of Monmouth's life is come after it indifferent well; for there is figures in all things. Alexander, God knows and you know, in his rages, and his furies, and his wraths, and his cholers, and his moods . . . did, in his ales and his angers, look you, kill his best friend, Cleitus.
> *Gow.* Our king is not like him in that. He never kill'd any of his friends.

*Flu....* As Alexander kill'd his friend Cleitus, being in his ales and his cups, so also Harry Monmouth, being in his right wits and his good judgements, turn'd away the fat knight with the greatbelly doublet. He was full of jests, and gipes, and knaveries, and mocks. I have forgot his name.
*Gow.* Sir John Falstaff.

[IV. vii. 31-6, 37-41, 44-51]

The conversation is a good example of the problems inherent in the play as a whole. On the one side we see Henry in the best of all possible lights, an heroic Alexander, adored by his men; on the other we are reminded of his rejection of the man who loved him best (and we loved best in the plays that went before this one); and on yet another we, being less caught up in Henry's mystique than Fluellen is, have to wonder about the morality of the order to assassinate the prisoners. We wonder even more when Henry, who gave the order at [IV. vi. 37] as a reaction to French reinforcements coming on the field, gives it again at [IV. vii. 63]. This time the motive seems to be that imputed to him by Gower—revenge for the boys' slaughter and the tent's plundering. At least it is presented by Henry as a response generated by his Alexandrian anger.

While there are always textual hypotheses about the sort of repetition that occurs here in Henry's two orders—surely if Shakespeare had read proof he would have eliminated either [IV. vi. 37] or [IV. vii. 63]—the fact that both were written at all indicates the natures of the problem Shakespeare had before him in the characterization of the king. The first line is a straightforward practical military decision, the second, embedded as it is in a heroic speech, complete with trumpet and Assyrian sling, following the Fluellen-Gower Alexander parallel, is the infuriated, classically heroic extreme reaction of a feeling, indeed enraged, man. Neither is, I suppose, an admirable motive by modern standards, but responding to practical military necessity does have a calculated air about it quite different from the fury of an Alexander.

All the forces that swirl around Henry's character here—the practical decisive leader, the heroic conqueror, the betrayer of old friends, the beloved king—recur, recede, intensify throughout the play, but they never coalesce for the modern reader. We can find the reason for the lack of cohesion in the mixture of elements out of which Shakespeare has constructed both the play and the character, a mixture which has proved misleading, confusing, and at points self-contradictory. The play is in the first place a generic puzzle. Is it best understood as comedy, as part four of an epic that began with *Richard II,* or as an "implicit" tragedy? (pp. 223-25)

This paper attempts to regain the comic perspective. It does so by examining the mixture of major elements in the play and stressing one of the play's recognized generic resources, romance, which I believe has been neglected. While romance has been commented on by a number of critics, usually in a brief overview of the play's form as an adumbration of the romance mythos we are most familiar with in Northrop Frye's notion of the "green world" [in his *Anatomy of Criticism*], the extent of Shakespeare's reliance on romance in *Henry V* goes much further than that, a fact that our interest in Shakespeare's political naturalism has obscured. For romance exists here in somewhat uneasy solution with several other pervasive elements: a hero of classically epic proportion and characteristics, of Virgilian stature and destiny; an historical plot that, once taken beyond the limits of the play proper, creates a shape

opposite to comedy's; a political theme, far less readily definable than the other elements, emergent from them, and including a high degree of naturalism in its development. The crux of interpretation is, of course, what one makes of that theme.

Yet it seems pointless to go on simply providing thematic interpretations of the play when we already possess the means by which the two poles of current interpretation can be made equal partners in arriving at the ultimate indeterminacy of Shakespeare's vision. Presumably everything between the poles could be absorbed as well. Norman Rabkin has argued that *Henry V* is a supreme instance of Shakespearean "complementarity," ... presenting its audience with a gestalt of the world at once a "rabbit" and a "duck": upon seeing the play "Shakespeare's best audience knew terrifyingly that they did not know what to think" [see excerpt above, 1977]. The rest saw either the rabbit (centering on Henry as a perfect king) or the duck (Henry as prisoner-executing war-monger) and missed the meaning of the play's contrasting "our hope that society can solve our problems with our knowledge that society has never done so." ... Rabkin's interpretation depends upon a clear opposition between two strains which are neither as clear nor as clearly opposed as he suggests. What we now call the green world, given the hindsight bestowed on us by *The Winter's Tale* and *The Tempest,* was still in the process of development in this play by an extension into an explicitly political world. By imposing on the play a theme more appropriate to the tragedies, a theme which does not correlate with the obvious facts of dramatic structure, Rabkin avoids the problem of specific thematic evolution with an assertion: the play's darker aspects constitute a "terrible subversiveness with which Shakespeare undermines the entire structure."

By insisting upon a coherent intentional role for these "subversive" elements, Rabkin ignores not only this play's structure but also the experimental nature of Shakespeare's craftsmanship, which in *Henry V* seems intent upon bringing an illusionistic portrayal of the political realities (episcopal simony, the need for civil order even in war) into integral union with an idealized perception of political order, for such the implications of the romance form seem to be. That he tries to do this through the strength of his protagonist's characterization as an epic hero is not strange, for the Renaissance had already produced several effective mixed generic idealizations of the social world and its constructive hero by combining epic and romance; however no one had done so with the commitment to naturalism which marks Shakespeare's work. (pp. 226-28)

The naturalizing begins at the first level—of subject matter and plot. For the play, while it follows roughly the pastoral "green world" pattern common in romance (extrusion—sojourn in a natural environment—return in increased strength), does so through the least pastoral of subjects—war. Yet the war, quite paradoxically, serves the same function that life in the forest or the sheepcote serves in traditional pastoral: it is the restorative agent which recreates society in a sounder, more vigorous form, brings to all the characters (who survive it) a richer sense of the social order and their parts in the hierarchical world which pastoral takes as its norm. While the play focuses almost unremittingly on the central figure who both makes that order possible and embodies it in his role, it also expends a significant effort on depicting the layers of society that make up the "band of brothers" who miraculously defeat the French army because "O God, thy arm was here" [IV. iii. 60; IV. viii. 106].

Nor does Shakespeare show us very much of war itself, as the Chorus apologetically reminds us. Agincourt is at least as memorable in the play for its "little touch of Harry in the night" [Chorus, IV, 47] as for any battling we see. The "little touch" is justly celebrated, because it is the dramatic image of the incarnational model of kingship which is at the heart of *Henry V*. Released by his disguise from the heroic role, Henry is humanized for us to a greater degree than anywhere else in the play. . . . Henry here fulfills the practical need to know those whom he leads and serves, those whom he serves by leading, and they come to understand better what is involved not only in being a king, but also in being a subject. For some (Bates) conviction is immediate; for others (Williams) it requires the more elaborate stage-managing of the glove challenge; for one— the always present sole hold-out of Shakespearean comedy— it never comes: Pistol joins the ranks of Jaques, Malvolio [in *As You Like It* and *Twelfth Night*], et al. in exclusion from the vision of unity and harmony realized dramatically in the ultimate union of the whole. The union is made to embrace not just the disparate social and national elements of Henry's army, but France and England themselves in the concluding marriage. And after the wedding the cast will leave France to return to England's quotidian reality, rounding out the harmony of marriage and political unity with the re-entry into the "real world" we now expect of Shakespearean romance.

This description of the dramatic pattern, as is so often the case with mythic archetypes, may seem at best only partially relevant to the play because, while it traces the general movement accurately enough, it does so at the expense of a number of important specifics, not the least of which is the setting itself. Burgundy may see France as "this best garden of the world"; he also sees that the loss of peace has corrupted the garden "in its own fertility" [IV. ii. 36, 40], and we are led to see military and political France largely as embodied in the asinine Dauphin, whose main concern throughout the play seems to be his horse. (pp. 228-29)

The corruption in the garden lamented by Burgundy also finds its parallel in romance. The romantic epic is particularly fond of the garden as an image of the earthly paradise, an image that Shakespeare had dwelt upon in *Richard II* and returns to in the final Lancastrian play. Henry V is a far cry from Sir Guyon [in *The Faerie Queene*], the garden of good government from the Garden of Adonis, yet like Spenser's hero, Shakespeare's has been on a quest through three plays, in an often hostile world, a quest whose ultimate goal was not simply to realize Shakespeare's portrait of the perfect ruler but to return the polis to the garden state. Looked at in this way, the green world becomes less a place than a possibility, a band of brothers in a potential garden, or perhaps a band of brothers who themselves constitute a garden, stripped by its political weight of the solipsism of traditional romance, yet no less idealized. Such a reading is not out of keeping with Shakespeare's customary manipulation of the pastoral and of romance in general, which always involves naturalizing the artificialities of the genre and subjecting its underlying myths to critical scrutiny, yet usually concludes with a picture affirming the ideals involved.

Quite uncustomarily, this play provides us with a mediator who makes specific claims for the picture of reality that the play is developing. In a move we associate more with Jonson's distrust of the audience than with Shakespeare's celebrated self-containment, Shakespeare supplies *Henry V* with a Chorus, a figure who stands both within the play world and outside it, uniquely situated to comment on the relationship between the play's reality and our own. (p. 231)

When the drama is over, the Chorus . . . speaks an epilogue reminding us that what we have seen is a construct placed upon history, and that history was not so kind as "our bending author" [Epilogue, 2]. Just as the poet hopes to suggest "the full course of their glory," even having confined his heroes "in little room," so Henry's greatness was confined in "small time," yet in that time "the world's best garden he achieved" [Epilogue, 4, 3, 7]. The reference to the garden may remind us only of France in Burgundy's speech, which this echoes, or it may push us back further to the far more extensive gardening imagery of *Richard II,* which Burgundy echoed, or, since the garden is the "best," it may push us back to the Edenic analogue. At any rate, the quatrains parallelling the small space of the stage and the small time of Henry place the value of "this Star of England" [Epilogue, 6] outside of space and time, in the realm of the imagination. Like the stage, Henry is supposed to be something outside the merely real, a "true thing"; and while the turn of the sestet must admit that history destroyed it, the garden was "achieved," and that is the point the play itself ends on. (p. 232)

In at least one sense, the play is treating the world of history on the ideal plane of perfected principles (in terms of which it is as important for the Chorus to remind us that Henry returned between acts IV and V a "conqu'ring Caesar," "giving full trophy, signal and ostent / Quite from himself to God" [Chorus, V, 21-2] as that some time passed and certain events occurred in that interim). The dramatic mode which can best encompass this intention is romance, with its ability consistently to range beyond verisimilitude towards the ideal whose reality it seeks to mirror.

While the play in its form, then, and in a number of subsidiary motifs is dependent on that paradigm of the creative imagination we call romance, it extends romance into an area less susceptible to absorption into idealization than we (or the Renaissance?) are accustomed to. For in constructing Henry's romance, Shakespeare chose to include some constituents that strike us as antagonistic, that perhaps destroy the romance's consistency—most notably the naturalistic approach to the political. . . . The first point at which a modern reader usually experiences modal tension is in the scene with the Archbishop of Canterbury and the Bishop of Ely [I. ii. 7ff.]. It seems that the Archbishop has been cast in a role reminiscent of Northumberland's in *Richard II* or John of Lancaster's in *2 Henry IV,* that of the king's surrogate in political machinations. Heroic readers of the play often subtly assume any evil intentions are the Archbishop's. . . . But Shakespeare explicitly makes the latter an impossible interpretation when he gives Henry several speeches in the scene that develop the king's thinking in detail: the nobles and clergy urge undertaking the war, but Henry makes the choice [I. ii. 14ff., 115-42]; the clergy do not take all on their consciences, Henry puts it there:

> For God doth know how many, now in health,
> Shall drop their blood in approbation
> Of what your reverence shall incite us to.
>
> [I. ii. 18-20]

This may be sophistry, but Henry is fully cognizant of every move being made and remains fully in control of the proceedings.

Those who, at the other pole, concentrate on the subversive realities insist upon the sophistry and take the scene as an exposé of the worldliness of the clergy and Henry's complicity in it. And it is true that if one decides that both Henry and the

Archbishop are being negatively defined as Machiavellian politicians, there is nothing said in the scene that can't be integrated with that view. However, the total context makes such a position untenable: it fails to resolve the anomalies which surface with the French ambassador in whom Shakespeare introduces no worthy foe with a serious mission but a carrier of adolescent insults from the Dauphin, a reminder—one of many in the play—of the Hal we once thought so highly of. If the act to that point was ambiguous, the tennis balls knock us into Henry's court with a chauvinistic vengeance. And shortly God is to reappear, for the first time since *Richard II* in the history plays, as the king's only true cohort. Throughout the play, Henry's sense of his relationship to God is presented in a way that has to be taken seriously. To the suggestion that Henry is following Machiavelli's rules, one must reply that in soliloquy Henry appeals to God in exactly the tone and terms he uses publicly. Had Shakespeare intended us to see in this the manipulating Machiavel, he has gone about it in a way no Elizabethan, at least, could have recognized. What is more important, Henry's faith in God and his relation to Him is borne out by the play's movement and events. What we should recognize in this first act is neither an ironically conceived picture of a manipulative establishment nor a sheltered hero-king whose bishops do his dirty work. It is simply a naturalistic portrayal of political life into which a central figure is introduced who is conceived on a model at once heroic and romantic, a model too absolute to fit comfortably into its environment.

A second early instance of the same quality in Henry's characterization occurs in II.ii, the scene that establishes order at home before the movement to France. When the English traitors are marched before Henry to be tried, he is again absolute authority and sole actor, so he must personally—and not, like his father, through some Northumberland—unveil their guilt and pronounce their doom. . . . It is here that God comes back into play, Henry first committing the traitors to His mercy and then the country's strength into His hands—making himself God's lieutenant (a role he calls up frequently as the play progresses). Next, the traitors themselves "see the light": they go rather happily to death, thanking Henry for having discovered their faults in time to prevent an unfortunate murder. Perhaps only a Prospero could make a modern audience accept this as the way traitors would behave in such a situation. In fact, Prospero does just that. This mingling of heroic rigor and romantic idealism is based on God not because Shakespeare is intent upon giving dramatic form to a "Tudor myth," but because he has to ground his vision of political order on something capable of bearing the weight. If he is to successfully mythicize (some might say re-mystify) the king, he must do so through a conceptual pattern that can have meaning for his audience. As Ernst Kantorowicz has made eminently clear [in *The King's Two Bodies*], the natural place for an Elizabethan to go for such a concept is to that strange and elaborate nexus of political-theological-legal ideas that Tudor jurists elaborated ad infinitum: the separation of the king's body natural from the king's body politic and, more specifically, to the christological parallel that formed its basis. Two of the reigning images of Henry in the play—the dispenser of Justice (here in II. ii, at the gate of Harfleur, remarking upon the hanging of Bardolph) and the incarnated King (at Agincourt: the more than human become merely human, taking on man with Erpingham's cloak)—are readily available in that nexus. . . . The "king's body politic" was understood to be just such a "mystical body" as Shakespeare envisions in the union depicted in *Henry V*—both what it includes and what it rejects. That body depended for its validity upon the incarnational model of king-

ship, the king as *vicarius dei* [God's deputy] or *vicarius Christi* [Christ's deputy], the role Henry casts himself in and that Shakespeare casts him in as well, assimilating the godlike to the heroic in a secularization of the mystical notion quite parallel to the jurists' own.

Does this mean . . . that in *Henry V* Shakespeare turned his back on the knowledge implicit in his naturalistic treatment of politics in *Richard II* and *Henry IV* and returned to the political perspective of the Yorkist tetralogy? In a sense, yes, but only in a sense. Insofar as the original perspective depended upon a notion of the suprahuman in social order, he did. But he has transvalued the suprahuman and made it dependent, like all avowedly fictive orders, on the nature of its specific embodiment. Thus the play is not a preachment for divine right, but an idealized perception of an ideal political order; and thus, too, the play is at pains to define Henry as opposite to Richard II, the last Shakespearean king who called himself *vicarius dei*, but who proved a very ineffective deputy indeed.

Henry is nothing if not effective—to the limit of romantic idealization, in fact. Shakespeare constrains the idealization in two ways: by an effort to assimilate within it the troublesome historical facts and by forcibly including the remnants of Falstaff's cohorts in Henry's social context. As a major example of the first, Henry does order the slaughter of the French prisoners on the remarkably equivocal motivation we noted at the outset. Is it a military decision or revenge for the boys (and the tent)? Shakespeare apparently didn't decide, and neither can we. . . . All we can *know*, all the dramatic guidance we are given throws the weight of the action on the heroic parallel between Alexander's rage and Henry's. And right after Henry's expression of anger [IV. vii. 55-65], the victory of Agincourt is announced. So the great moment of the play, seen by Henry as the result of divine concern ("Praised be God and not our strength for it" [IV. vii. 87]), is seen by us as issuing from a combination of remarkable fortune (a romantic miracle, if you like) and a heroic leader endowed with the ability and strength of purpose to capitalize on both what fortune puts in his path and what he creates of fortune, thereby molding a national destiny.

It seems to dodge the issue at a point like this to say that the rabbit-seers among us behold an Alexander, the duck-seers an ex-bully king who now hangs those he once drank with, and the wise an effective ruler with his value undercut by our knowledge of his amoral expediency. All these possibilities are suggested one by one in the materials of this succession of scenes, but the materials remain disparate; they do not come together to form a coherent larger vision.

A similar disjunction occurs, though not so patently, around the part Prince Hal's old friends play—or fail to play—in *Henry V*. From the report of the death of Falstaff, through Pistol's plain-song with Nym, Bardolph, and the Boy, to the news of Bardolph's hanging, and finally the report of Nym's having joined him, Shakespeare cuts off all members of the old troup one by one, even stopping in the conversation between Henry and Pistol to remind us of the lost legendary good fellowship of "the lovely bully" and these men [IV. i. 44-8], a fellowship which it is notable that Pistol never, in fact, enjoyed. Because these characters retain their noisy naturalism, readers have often taken their dismissal as the sign of a kind of incipient totalitarianism in Shakespeare's garden-state, its leader having divorced himself from fellowship, good will, and the affection that he once had for men like Pistol. And perhaps it was a gamble that Shakespeare lost, bringing together his romantic

ruler and naturalistic subjects. . . . Yet it is reasonably evident
that if Henry is to be the personification of an ideal England,
then the communal bond which he engenders and supports must
itself be significant. What it means to Pistol is neatly expressed
in his abandoning the luggage to the boys—and the boys to
their subsequent slaughter [IV. iv. 74-7].

It has often been remarked that the replacement of Falstaff and
his remnant by Fluellen, Gower, Macmorris, and Jamy as the
group forming Henry's connection with the common man is
an unfortunate idealization of the kingly role. Whether or not
it is unfortunate, it is an idealization, as all essentially utopian
pictures are. Perhaps even the scent of totalitarianism inevitably
accompanies such dreams. The somewhat sanctimonious nature
of the new group has lost enormously in sheer humor and
intensity of effect compared to what was possible in Falstaff's
grittier world. (To mention the Boar's Head Tavern in the same
sentence as the weak practical joke of the glove incident seems
ridiculous.) Yet Shakespeare does try to create around Henry
and his cohorts a new sense of fellowship, honest to the constraints of the kingly role, but not devoid of human sympathy.

That we cannot accept the replacement says something about
either Shakespeare's success in dramatizing it or our own expectations about political drama, our unwillingness to entertain
seriously romantic conceptions of political subjects. Insofar as
our difficulty with the play is one of conflicting decorums, it
is a historical and theoretical problem. Shakespeare has tried
to do in this play what he continues to attempt for several years:
to bring a naturalistic representation of life's seamier qualities
under the idealizing umbrella of a comic perspective. (pp.
232-38)

Insofar, however, as our difficulties with the play spring from
a rejection of the play's idealism, we can only recognize that
that is the case or, at most, re-examine our own preconceptions.
We resent the idea that Caliban must go to school, Shylock to
church, and Bardolph to the gallows. But Shakespeare probably
thought they must. At least his plays say so. What imperfections this play contains—and there are some—are the result of
a relative failure in accommodating naturalistically conceived
characters and events to the fabric of the play, which is predominantly romantic. Romance is in many ways antipathetic
to verisimilitude, particularly when its symbolic structure runs
counter to what we "know" of the reality which makes up its
content. By leaning on the epic hero in order to form a political
romance without sacrificing political naturalism altogether,
Shakespeare created a play world with precisely the sorts of
fissures a post-Romantic critical generation would leap into.
Given the intensity of our belief in the indeterminate nature of
human reality and, therefore, the best literature, it was inevitable that what Una Ellis-Fermor first perceived as the beginning of Shakespeare's "recoil" from the perfect king [see
excerpt above, 1945], Alvin Kernan would go on to find a
picture of the loss of the "essential 'I' . . . as the man disappear[ed] in the role his work demands" [in his *Modern Shakespearean Criticism: Essays on Style, Dramaturgy, and the Major Plays*], from which it is a short leap to Rabkin's insistence
that ideal plus subversive equals gestalt, predictably a gestalt
that makes a virtue of confusion by declaring it indeterminacy.

The next step, not yet taken so far as I know, will probably
be the application of Howard Felperin's modernist method to
the play [in his *Shakespearean Representation*]. There are a
number of "archaic narrative forms" within the play from
which we will be able to witness Henry working himself free
to issue forth the tragic figure whose humanity is insured by

his achievement of indeterminacy. Such a reading will have
the virtue of accepting all those moments when Henry repels
us as warmonger or cold fish, moments which here are regarded
as the unfortunate result of jarring dramatic modes. What will
have been lost is not only the political romance—oxymoron
though that sound in a Shakespearean context, but also a crucial
step in the development of Shakespeare's manipulation of romantic materials. While it is certainly true that the history plays
introduced and elaborated themes and situations that required
the tragedies for their completion, it is also true that the Henry
plays, comic in themselves, are the source of comic ideas that
continued fruitful. Technically the most important seems to be
how to represent the "real" world, more broadly and more
naturalistically enacted than in the comedies through *Twelfth
Night,* in a comic shape. Part of the solution is prefigured in
the role Henry plays here, a role that is the progenitor of
Vincentio's [in *Measure for Measure*] and Prospero's. The shift
in the artificer's status from that of a Portia or Rosalind [in *As
You Like It*] to the ruler of the play world made it possible for
Shakespeare to expand enormously the content of his comedies,
the realms controlled by that central figure who legitimately
combines both worldly and transcendent power. (pp. 238-39)

Joanne Altieri, ''Romance in 'Henry V','' in *Studies
in English Literature, 1500-1900,* Vol. XXI, No. 2,
Spring, 1981, pp. 223-40.

## C. G. THAYER   (essay date 1983)

[*In a portion of his* Shakespearean Politics: Government and Misgovernment in the Great Histories *(1983) not reprinted here, Thayer
reviews the Tudor theory of the King's Two Bodies—the ''natural'' one subject to frailty and error and the ''politic'' one ''incapable of imperfection''—that was employed by Elizabethans to
uphold the doctrine of divine kingship. In the following excerpt,
the critic asserts that ''*Henry V* represents the triumph of man-
centered kingship,'' for while Henry is Shakespeare's ideal Christian monarch, everything he achieves is the result of human endeavor and ''has nothing to do with any kind of political mysticism.'' Indeed, in Thayer's estimation, such crucial episodes as
the encounter with Bates and Williams and the king's order to
kill the French prisoners emphasize Henry's personal identity.
Thayer further contends that Shakespeare does not represent Henry
on the eve of Agincourt as evading responsibility for the spiritual
state of his soldiers, but instead emphasizes the need to distinguish
between a ruler's temporal and transcendent attributes.*]

Books on governors and governing poured from the pens and
presses of Renaissance Europe and Tudor England, and it is
not surprising that Shakespeare made his contribution to the
deluge or that his contribution is among the most interesting
and the most lively. I suspect that the subject had a special
urgency for him at the end of the Tudor era. For the first time
in *his* life, England was going to have a new monarch, soon,
and of necessity that monarch was going to be *chosen,* as there
was no unquestioned successor; the succession was among the
most pressing issues of the last decade of the sixteenth century.
It was a good, if risky, time to take a long reflective look at
a brief and striking period of English history, at the reigns of
a king deposed, the problems of the ruler who deposed him,
and the stirring triumphs of that ruler's son and successor.
They were all the subjects of much contemporary attention,
and the Queen herself was occasionally compared with the first
of the three, Richard II, while the third, Henry V, was still a
model of English heroism against fearful odds. (p. viii)

With *Henry V* the great tetralogy comes to a triumphant close,
with a king who is, whether we like him or not, the precise

antithesis of King Richard II. Richard was utterly undone by the assumptions he made about kingship. He put his faith in divine right (although he was a little careless about his accountability to God and didn't understand the full meaning of hereditary right, even when it was explained to him); he had some idea of himself as a mystical corporation (King Body Politic); and he tended to think of his office in terms of a corrupt version of divine, Christ-centered kingship. (p. 143)

If Shakespeare's King Henry is the antithesis of his King Richard, what has happened to the four cardinal principles of the doctrine of the divine right of kings? If monarchy is ordained by God, here is a king who seems to have been born for just that sort of ordination; if hereditary right is indefeasible, here is a king who rules by hereditary right (a point vigorously made in *2 Henry IV*); if the king is accountable to God alone, here is a king who says that the success of his ventures lies in God's hands and who thanks God when his ventures succeed; if passive obedience is enjoined by God, here is a king who enjoys the loyal obedience of the overwhelming majority of his subjects, including those who must follow him into battle. In fact, here is a king who seems to enjoy all the advantages of divine right without making any of its claims and without having anyone else make them for him, a king with no professional problems, so to speak, whatever, who seems to have no notion of the King Body Politic or of divine kingship. It is almost as though Shakespeare were saying, "Let a king do his work well and the prerogatives will take care of themselves, or they will become irrelevant." Richard invoked divine right and divine kingship to buck himself up; Harry doesn't need to and wouldn't care to. (pp. 143-44)

If Shakespeare demonstrated the dangers of mystical, religiously oriented theories of kingship in *Richard II,* he replaced them with something far more satisfactory in *Henry IV* and *Henry V.* . . . *Henry V* represents the triumph of man-centered kingship, in which the standard by which a king is measured is human. He is not a god, not like a god, not compared to a god; he is not God's substitute, deputy, or lieutenant. He is, for Shakespeare anyhow, someone who inherited a crown: a king, the one we have in England. (pp. 144-45)

King Henry himself has no identifiable theory of kingship, only a series of pragmatic observations: kings are like other people except that they have greater responsibilities, wear better clothes, (probably) eat better, work harder, are flattered, sleep less, and are burdened with "ceremony" (most of this emerges in act IV, scene i). Such a theory, if that's what it is, does not guarantee a good king, but it increases the likelihood of a reasonably responsible one; and it prevents the misuse of religion to cow subjects into accepting, or enduring, tyranny or gross incompetence. King Harry is of course rather special, and Shakespeare holds him up for special examination.

*Act V. Scene ii. Alice, Katherine, and Henry V. By Friedrich Pecht. The Department of Rare Books and Special Collections, The University of Michigan Library.*

The great tetralogy began with a fascinating account of a king so obsessed with notions of his own divinity that he was unable to take the sort of actions one might expect of a mere prudent man or politician. It ends with an equally fascinating account of a man who is a king and who seems clearly to have worked hard and successfully to achieve the image and the qualities of a great king. (p. 145)

I believe that Shakespeare intended King Harry to be seen as a model, that the Chorus's description of him as "the mirror of all Christian kings" [Chorus, II, 6] is meant to be taken seriously, that the high adventures of this king are designed to bring the tetralogy to a triumphant close. It does seem to me that if Shakespeare had intended a contemporary audience to dislike King Henry, or to disapprove of his activities, he set about achieving his intention in a very strange way.

He gives us a King Harry who is frankly a winner (this is no doubt part of the problem), is seen by virtually everyone else in his play as a winner, and is almost universally applauded for it. He achieves everything he wants, on a superlative scale, with dash and flair; he wins the war, gets the girl, and will inherit her father's estate. In view of the status of Henry V in Shakespeare's time, this is not, on the face of it, surprising. He was, after all, a great national hero, perhaps England's greatest national hero, and he won one of England's two greatest military victories. In contemporary eyes, his greatest achievement was the victory at Agincourt, and so it was, in a special sense, for Shakespeare. . . . Anyone writing a play about Henry V in 1599 would have seemed more than a little eccentric if he did not deal with the famous victory and did not represent on the stage some of the qualities, kingly and military, that made it possible. (p. 146)

I think that Shakespeare has set about representing on the stage the quintessence of kingship, a mirror not only to be wondered at but also to be emulated. That is, he is the kind of ruler that we Englishmen want, right now, in 1599 (or as soon as possible), and the monarchy and civil polity over which he presides are the sort of monarchy and civil polity we want. It goes almost without saying that we won't get either, but our king-makers and our potential kings would do well to regard them as models, constituting an Idea.

The nature of the king-model is partly indicated by the epic tone of the Prologue. More is suggested by Canterbury's description of the King. . . . He is "full of grace and fair regard," and is, as Ely quickly adds, "a true lover of the holy Church" [I. i. 22, 23]. His body is as a Paradise, containing "celestial spirits." He is a scholar, a master of divinity, an authority on statecraft and "policy," and "his discourse of war" becomes "a fearful battle render'd you in music" [I. i. 43, 44]. When he speaks,

> . . . the mute wonder lurketh in men's ears,
> To steal his sweet and honey'd sentences;
> So that the art and practic part of life
> Must be the mistress to this theoric.
>
> [I. i. 49-52]

Even ignoring the apparent extravagance, this is all very surprising for the prelates "since his [youthful] addiction was to courses vain" [I. i. 54]. How did this astonishing transformation come about? Ely has an easy and simple-minded answer: "the prince obscur'd his contemplation / Under the veil of wildness" since "wholesome berries thrive and ripen best / Neighbour'd by fruit of baser quality" [I. i. 61-2]. Canterbury goes along with the homely analogy, although he would ap-

parently prefer to attribute the change in the young king to a miracle; but "miracles are ceas'd; / And therefore we must needs admit the means / How things are perfected" [I. i. 67-8]. (pp. 151-52)

Now, about the extravagant praise that Canterbury heaps on the King: it *is* extravagant—he sounds almost too good to be true. That, I think, is deliberate on Shakespeare's part. If Harry the fifth is to be our model, we will clean up an already well-laundered product. When we see the King in action, beginning with the play's second scene, it is obvious that he likes his work and that he is good at it; and, as Canterbury has said, he certainly talks well. But would it really be possible to write a play about a great king and show him demonstrating convincingly *all* the gifts that Canterbury ascribes to him? Theoretically, I suppose, it would, and Walter has shown [see excerpt above, 1954] that Shakespeare at least glances at virtually all of the sixteenth-century kingly qualities. But on purely practical grounds, the way to manage the problem is to have someone credible describe the virtues; then, perhaps, an audience will assume that those virtues make it possible for the King to function so exceedingly well in those actions in which we see him engaged. Canterbury and Ely are, I should think, talking about an ideal king who seems, almost miraculously, actually to have materialized. What we see in the play is a national hero devoting most of his energies to the great adventure that made him a national hero.

The first scene defines and describes the model: this is the kind of king we want. The rest of the play, except for one crucial episode, shows this kind of king in action, on public display, so to speak. Shakespeare does not give this king much time to himself; he wants us to see his paragon in action rather than in meditation; but the one meditation we get is pure gold. For the purposes of this play, the King is—as rulers must or should be—a very public sort of figure. What he is *personally,* Canterbury tells us; and what Canterbury tells us seems to be confirmed by what follows. But although we get a clear sense of the King's temperament and person, or personality, as the play goes on, it is a public personality. More than that, it is a highly polished and refined image, and polished quite consciously, we can hardly doubt, by the King himself. The image is the result of his conception of how kings should go about their business and how they should act, and speak, while doing it. He knows very well how a king should talk to an archbishop, to foreign ambassadors, to confessed traitors, to troops and officers before a battle, to an enemy's herald, to the princess he knows very well he is going to marry. And he knows how to talk to the people of a besieged city. His truly ferocious speech to the citizens of Harfleur [III. iii. 1-43] is a masterpiece of warlike rhetoric, describing in terrifying detail what happens when cities are sacked. The purpose of the speech, clearly, is to prevent what it so vividly describes; and we ought to remember that Holinshed's Harry, the historical Harry, *did* have the city sacked whereas Shakespeare's does not. Instead, when (naturally enough) the town surrenders, he orders Exeter to "use mercy to them all" [III. iii. 54]. The question of what *this* Harry would have done if the city had not surrendered does not arise: his oration *made* it surrender, and his soldiers in any case do not appear to be like those of Charles V sacking Rome in one of warfare's less edifying episodes. The perfected image of a conqueror can save a lot of bloodshed, and a proper conqueror should want to do just that.

But what if he gives the order that "every soldier kill his prisoners" [IV. vi. 37]? If Shakespeare puts the Harfleur speech to a special use, he does something similar with this famous, or notorious, order, about which, not surprisingly, much has been said. And, not incidentally, he cleans up what he found in Holinshed. Killing prisoners has always been a good deal worse than merely bad military etiquette, and a cold-blooded order to do so deserves more than mild censure. Holinshed gives a just barely digestible account of the killing of the prisoners at Agincourt . . . , and Shakespeare could hardly have overlooked it even though he does not use it. Can such an order ever be justified? Only, one would think, under the most desperate circumstances: if a sudden turn of battle should threaten the actual destruction of an army by making the prisoners themselves a prime danger. One can easily imagine conditions in which prisoners could rearm themselves with weapons discarded by men in retreat or by men killed or wounded. . . . (pp. 157-59)

What happens in the play is that the King hears a "new alarum" and thinks that the "French have reinforc'd their scatter'd men" [IV. vi. 35, 36]. Since the English are greatly outnumbered, it is not only the outcome of the battle that is at stake but, literally, the existence of the English army, the lives of most of its men. This is not necessarily an idle or exaggerated fear: the reader and audience will not have forgotten that the preceding scene (only forty lines earlier) had ended with Bourbon, the Constable, and Orleans preparing to return to battle like berserkers, to "die in arms," "on heaps go offer up our lives," "To smother up the English in our throngs" [IV. v. 18, 20]. Our knowledge must suggest that King Henry's instinct was correct: the French lords will not throw away their lives without taking some Englishmen with them—as many as possible.

It looks, however, as though the new alarum was *not* the French reinforcing their scatter'd men, but the French killing "the poys and the luggage," as Fluellen puts it, and that too is "expressly against the law of arms" [IV. vii. 1, 2]. The French lords achieve none of their aims. When we next see Bourbon, he is a prisoner [s.d., IV. vii. 55], and not the only one ("*Enter King Henry and* Bourbon *with prisoners*"). If the other French lords have regrouped, they have done it more prudently than their words in scene v might have led one to expect since they are now apparently "on yon hill" [IV. vii. 58], not obviously ready to fight and die.

In the desperate resolution of the French lords, Shakespeare has given the audience objective information about something that King Henry, no amateur general, grasps instinctively. If the order to kill the prisoners still seems unwarranted (to many critics it *is*—they know not "seems"), *ex post facto* warrant arrives, two lines after the King gives his order (a little hard to see how it could have arrived sooner), in Fluellen's outraged explosion. If King Harry did not have a wholly satisfactory reason for ordering the killing of the prisoners, the French gave him one on the instant.

If the slaughter at the baggage park will not satisfy a scrupulous notion of providence (and I do not insist that it should), providence seems nevertheless to have been at work: unless the stage direction "*with prisoners*" and the King's promise to "cut the throats of those we have" [IV. vii. 63] refer to prisoners remaining alive after the slaughter, or to new prisoners taken in an almost incredibly brief interim, the order to kill the prisoners was not carried out. . . . It would seem that Shakespeare, stuck with a famous historical fact about King Harry and the battle of Agincourt, has done everything possible to clean up the fact, to give solid justification to what in other circumstances would have been a cruel and discreditable order,

what Holinshed called "this dolorous decree and pitiful proclamation," . . . although it is not clear why Holinshed chose to offer an eyewitness account of something that didn't happen. Then, lest the mirror tarnish a bit anyhow, Shakespeare has implied, via a stage direction and a threatening speech, that in fact the order was not carried out. Thus the way is cleared for a brief reprise of the speech before Harfleur, although here it is genuine anger and not high rhetoric that is in control: one can hardly doubt that the King means exactly what he says:

> I was not angry since I came to France
> Until this instant. Take a trumpet, herald;
> Ride thou unto the horsemen on yon hill:
> If they will fight with us, bid them come down,
> Or void the field; they do offend our sight.
> If they do neither, we will come to them,
> And make them skirr away, as swift as stones
> Enforced from the old Assyrian slings.
> Besides, we'll cut the throats of those we have,
> And not a man of them that we shall take
> Shall taste our mercy. Go and tell them so.
>                                              [IV. vii. 55-65]

Few readers will question the rightness, or righteousness, of King Harry's wrath; the threat clearly works, and you cannot credibly threaten to kill your prisoners if they have been killed already. The King's original order to kill the prisoners may demonstrate that he is not infallible: he thought, wrongly but with good reason, that his army was in danger of destruction. The standard by which he is to be judged is merely human, and Shakespeare has gone out of his way to clean up a serious historical blemish.

King Henry has worked hard to achieve the image of a king (it should be clear enough that he was thinking precisely of that in the famous soliloquy in act I, scene ii of *1 Henry IV*). It is decidedly worth remembering that "image . . . is a vital, valid concern of anyone who hopes to govern. And image needs cultivation, attention, work" [Meg Greenfield in *Newsweek*]. In the speech quoted above, image and substance are inseparable; the image can't be a hollow one, like King Richard's. Harry's is substantial: if you work hard and intelligently at achieving the image of King Harry, you will be King Harry, no trivial achievement. If you are altogether successful, you might become (Shakespeare's) mirror (image) of all (Catholic) Christian kings. (pp. 159-61)

The mirror of all Christian kings is a paragon of man-centered kingship, and 1599 was a good year to write about him because, in addition to the reasons given earlier, in 1599 the likeliest successor to the crown had published the age's most uncompromising statement on the doctrine of divine right, *The Trew Law of Free Monarchies* (first published anonymously, but King James's style is about as anonymous as Henry James's). James espoused an idea of kingship already completely familiar in Tudor England, through the Homilies of 1547 and 1570 and through other official and unofficial pronouncements, an idea that Shakespeare had thoroughly battered about in *Richard II*. I do not suggest that, in 1595, Shakespeare was "showing" James Stuart the fractured face of divine kingship—although he was certainly showing it to *someone;* but in 1599, after the publication of *The Trew Law* and at a time when James's candidacy had been considerably strengthened, Shakespeare was representing on the stage the virtues of man-centered kingship with some reference to the monarch that most Englishmen expected would succeed to the throne and whose candidacy was being quietly but aggressively pushed by both Cecil and

Essex and was very likely accepted by the Queen herself. (pp. 162-63)

[The concept of man-centered kingship] helps explain why Shakespeare does more with King Harry than represent him as a king who shares the common humanity of those around him. It adds a dimension of meaning to the catalogue of virtues supplied by Canterbury in act I, scene i, and it underlines the point of Canterbury's beautiful speech on the orderly society of the bees [I. ii. 183-220]. . . . Canterbury's speech describes something like the conditions that we are to assume exist in Henry's kingdom, as I assume that the description of the King's virtues is to be taken as an account of an ideal king who has, somehow, actually materialized, seemingly like a miracle.

Canterbury's allegorical apiary is like Ulysses' universe [in *Troilus and Cressida*] when Degree has not been ''shak'd,'' and it is introduced, and elicited by, an observation of Exeter about government, an observation that seems intended to describe England under King Harry, an England well equipped to manage its affairs at home and abroad:

> While that the armed hand doth fight
> abroad
> Th'advised head defends itself at home;
> For government, though high and low and
> lower,
> Put into parts, doth keep in one consent,
> Congreeing in a full and natural close,
> Like music.
> *Canterbury.*        Therefore doth heaven divide
> The state of man in diverse functions,
> Setting endeavor in continual motion;
> To which is fixed, as an aim or butt,
> Obedience: for so work the honey-bees,
> Creatures that by a rule in nature teach
> The act of order to a peopled kingdom.
>                              [I. ii. 178-89]

(It is, I suppose, at this point unnecessary to call attention to Canterbury's, and hence the Church's, role in providing information and commentary, here supported by Exeter, for the King and the nobility. If we assume that Canterbury is merely venal, well, that's that.) Exeter and Canterbury are describing an ideal state of affairs that seems actually to have materialized—if it had not, then the enterprise of France could hardly be urged and would not be successful if undertaken.

The key word, I am afraid, is obedience. Where there is obedience, in Canterbury's and Shakespeare's sense, there is Justice. It is analogous to Exeter's and Shakespeare's music, and we are asked to accept the existence of the harmony of obedience, and therefore of Justice, in the monarchy over which King Harry presides. It is not a liberal blueprint, and it would be fatuous to expect it to be. Modern readers tend rather to dislike the way the King administers justice to the traitors at Southampton, but it is defective by standards that Shakespeare and his age would have found astonishing. And the fates of Bardolph and the others cause much resentment. But they violate an order based on the general's opposition to looting, which tends to cause resentment among the people with whom one expects one day to be at peace, and on his reverence for the Church. The King *is* willing to pardon an abusive drunk. (In the nether regions of scholarship, there is a circle the inmates of which condemn him for [a] pardoning the drunk and [b] executing the confessed traitors, but here I seem to lose the thread. . . .)

As a principle of Justice, obedience means obeying laws— e.g., laws against conspiring to murder the king, laws against theft, from churches or wherever. It means submission to rule or authority, and no society has ever been able to forego submission to some form of legitimate authority and survive. If the source and center of authority is itself corrupt, then of course Justice becomes an obscenity—endless instances come to mind. But for Shakespeare, at least, there seems to be some sense that Justice should be rational and not capricious, that it ought to be just by standards that almost anyone can comprehend: the authority that lies in government, ''Put into parts, doth keep in one consent, / Congreeing in a full and natural close, / Like music'' [I. ii. 181-83]. We are told in the play that King Harry has formidable virtues and that he presides over a just society, i.e., one whose parts are harmonious, like music. And we are *not* told that his kingship is hedged with divinity. Without *this* King, obviously, England would be very different; and that is the point on which man-centered kingship assumes its importance. When the Epilogue tells us that with his sword King Harry achieved ''the world's best garden'' [Epilogue, 7], we are being told that he achieved something like an earthly paradise, another Eden, demi-paradise. (pp. 164-66)

In connection with a theory of man-centered kingship, the importance of the achievement is that it has nothing to do with any kind of political mysticism. It was brought about by a particular king who assumed the throne legitimately on the death of his father and immediately committed himself to a principle of Justice that then permitted, or required, him to go to war and, with his sword, extend the boundaries of the world's best garden, the evidence consisting, as far as we can tell, of the double marriage of Harry and Kate, England and France (which probably signifies an inherently less unlikely union, between England and Scotland, and theoretically an end to the terrible succession of wars between the two countries). (pp. 166-67)

The idea of man-centered kingship gets its most concentrated treatment in Act IV, scene i, and I don't doubt that the Chorus speaks the playwright's sentiments:

> O, now, who will behold
> The royal captain of this ruin'd band
> Walking from watch to watch, from tent to tent,
> Let him cry, ''Praise and glory on his head!''
>                              [Chorus, IV, 28-31]

To old Sir Thomas Erpingham, King Harry is a fellow soldier, of a higher rank but still, for now, part of a band of brothers. He prefers having no good soft pillow for his good white head because he can say, ''Now lie I like a king'' [IV. i. 17]. It is to a fellow officer, exalted but familiar, that he can say without offense, ''The Lord in heaven bless thee, noble Harry!'' [IV. i. 33]—worth comparing, for the tone, with Falstaff's ''God save thee, my sweet boy!'' [2 *Henry IV*, V. v. 43]. Most important, with the remarkable Bates, Court, and Williams, those radically atypical soldiers, he is a soldier among soldiers. His famous remark, ''Every subject's duty is the king's; but every subject's soul is his own'' [IV. i. 176-77], sometimes thought of as an evasion of responsibility, in fact reaffirms a basic distinction between the temporal and the spiritual worlds. War may be God's beadle [IV. i. 169], but the King cannot absolve his subjects of their sins because he is not God's substitute or . . . the shepherd of his flock, except in a very remote sort of way. Quite the contrary: the King is but a man; the violet smells to him as it does to anyone else. ''All his senses have but human conditions: his ceremonies laid by, in his nakedness he appears but a man'' [IV. i. 103-05]: King Richard's opposite; King Harry has nothing to do with the King's Two Bodies.

A little too pleased with himself for the natural ease with which he plays the soldier, he permits himself a rather fatuous jest (''If I live to see it [the King allowing himself to be ransomed], I will never trust him after'' [IV. i. 195-96]); and when the highly intelligent Williams takes him up on it, he even allows himself a man's indulgence in anger. A major point of the whole episode in the camp is to underline the separateness between the temporal and the spiritual and to insist on the King's strictly secular and human identity. That is the point of the so-called practical joke on Williams. The King was angry, but he did not reveal his identity until after the battle. Then he can say, in effect, you couldn't recognize a king when you saw one and for good reason. To have gotten into a fight, however, while still in disguise, to have been struck by Williams, is probably something that even this king could not allow—and it would certainly have demoralized Williams.

The point of the great soliloquy [IV. i. 230-84] is, again, to place the strongest possible emphasis on the King as a man. If one believes that the King protests too much, the reply, I think, is that—even setting aside the impending battle—kings have fearful responsibilities that they must meet with purely human capacities, although capacities in this case of a very high order. They may and must pray, but they must also do the work. They won't know until the event whether or not they did the right work and did it well. King Harry cannot count on a descent of Lancastrian angels; but, as the great speech before the battle indicates [IV. iii. 19-67], he does have confidence in himself and in his men; and as his words to Westmoreland and Montjoy indicate, he loves his work.

He enjoys playing, too, but not all the year. His wooing of Kate is a marvelous bit of gallant relaxation and fun, but it is more than that. It may be that nothing tells us more about King Harry than the manner of his wooing. He is jolly well going to marry Kate; she is part of his price for peace; there is very little she or her parents can do about it; no marriage, no peace, and some French cities will be sacked. Not only must there be a marriage but the French king must, and finally does, agree to address the English King as ''Our very dear son Henry, King of England, heir of France.'' Yet Shakespeare has devoted almost two hundred lines just before the end of the play to a scene in which King Harry plays the ardent wooer, amusingly, masterfully, in prose as befits a hearty fellow, producing the rather attractive image of a king turned simple soldier and unskilled lover. The whole performance has aroused some resentment among students of the play: since Kate is part of the package, an article of the spoils of war, why bother to woo when he can wed without going to all that trouble? With a clear implication of hypocrisy—since she is part of Henry's price, he can't really love her, and it won't do to attempt to disguise the stern conqueror's face behind the lover's mask. But Harry the King *is* a man, and he *is* going to marry her; she *is* going to be his wife as well as his queen, and she does not seem to dislike the idea at all. The question should not be ''Why bother, since he is going to marry her anyhow?'' Why *not* bother? We know how noble and royal marriages were arranged, long before and long after the time of Henry V. But here is, shall we say an *inevitable* husband who actually shows some regard for the lady's wishes and feelings, who seems to have some regard for the lady herself. He knows she will have

to marry him, that she really has no choice unless he gives her a choice to make. He has some confidence that he can elicit the right choice, and the English lesson has told us that she is eager to marry the English King. This is the time to show some consideration for the lady's feelings, to be agreeable: since he is naturally agreeable, that is easy enough. And he presents himself as what he is in fact now becoming, a man who loves her and wants to know, ''Canst thou love me?'' [V. ii. 193-94]. If there are large political considerations, all the more reason to achieve them through love. This love might even extend to love between England and France; it is the French Queen's hope.

In wooing Kate as he does, King Harry is presenting himself, not for the first time, as a man, not a demigod. Perhaps Shakespeare had in mind Erasmus's injunction that kings should marry, but not merely for the sake of alliances—that might breed strife. . . . But King Harry is well beyond the textbook stage; he is also about as far as it is possible to get from mystical notions of kingship. The standard by which he is to be judged is both reasonable and familiar: it is human, and he knows it. In perfecting the image of a king, he has enhanced the image of a man and therefore stands well in the unique register of the human race. This seems to be what Shakespeare intended to show. (pp. 174-77)

*C. G. Thayer, "Preface" and "The Mirror of All Christian Kings," in his* Shakespearean Politics: Government and Misgovernment in the Great Histories, *Ohio University Press, 1983, pp. viii-x, 143-77.*

---

## ADDITIONAL BIBLIOGRAPHY

Akrigg, G. P. V. ''*Henry V*: The Epic Hero as Dramatic Protagonist.'' In *Stratford Papers: 1965-67*, edited by B. A. W. Jackson, pp. 186-207. Hamilton, Ontario, Canada: McMaster University Library Press, 1969.
　　Argues that Shakespeare strove to make his epic hero dramatically convincing, but that the character of Henry V never becomes ''a living figure.'' Akrigg believes that the dramatist himself recognized this and apologized to his audience in the Epilogue for his failure; the critic maintains, however, that it is to Shakespeare's credit that he failed, for ''the very concept of the epic hero is naive, primitive and immature in the modern world. And Shakespeare belongs with the modern world.''

Babula, William. ''Whatever Happened to Prince Hal?: An Essay on 'Henry V'.'' *Shakespeare Survey* 30 (1977): 47-59.
　　Contends that during the course of the play Henry learns the importance of moderation, honesty, and peace, thereby attaining a maturity that he lacks at the start of the drama. Babula argues that this process is reflected in the gradual change in Henry's language, which is characterized by artifice and ''epic rhetoric'' at the beginning but develops into a direct and ''simple prose'' style in the courtship of Katherine.

Barton, Anne. ''The King Disguised: Shakespeare's *Henry V* and the Comical History.'' In *The Triple Bond: Plays, Mainly Shakespearean, in Performance*, edited by Joseph G. Price, pp. 92-114. University Park: The Pennsylvania State University Press, 1975.
　　Analyzes Shakespeare's use in *Henry V* of the romantic motif of the disguised monarch recurrent in folk ballads and late sixteenth-century drama. Barton argues that members of an Elizabethan audience would be familiar with this tradition and would expect the meeting between Henry and Williams in Act IV, Scene i to lead to mutual understanding and accord. By representing the encounter between the two men as acrimonious and unenlightening for both of them, she maintains, Shakespeare rejected the romantic

view of the relationship between subject and king as "attractive but untrue."

Battenhouse, Roy. "The Relation of Henry V to Tamburlaine." *Shakespeare Survey* 27 (1974): 71-9.

Detailed analysis of the parallels between Henry and Christopher Marlowe's Tamburlaine and the way in which these echoes serve as instruments of the "dramatic patterning" of Shakespeare's play. Battenhouse contends that Henry treats himself as "an actor caught up in his own play" and thus he blinds himself to "the moral implications of his action." In his devotion to his role, the critic concludes, Henry is "basically more frivolous than Tamburlaine, more self-defined as 'actor' rather than an agent inspired by goals of missionary dimension."

Berman, Ronald S. "Shakespeare's Alexander: Henry V." *College English* 23, No. 7 (April 1962): 532-39.

Examines the parallels between Plutarch's Alexander and the protagonist of *Henry V,* especially their pragmatic and empirical personal philosophies, their resolute self-discipline, and their primary objective of restoring order and integrity in their political worlds. Both Plutarch and Shakespeare, Berman maintains, demonstrate through these central figures that the course of human history is essentially tragic, for the achievements of Alexander and Henry V were of short duration and, after their deaths, the states they governed lapsed into internecine wars; thus, they both represent "the eventual failure of nature to thrust back mortal limitations."

Berry, Edward I. "'True Things and Mock'ries': Epic and History in *Henry V.*" *Journal of English and Germanic Philology* LXXVIII, No. 1 (January 1979): 1-16.

Maintains that in *Henry V* Shakespeare "superimposed an epic form" upon "comic, realistic, and skeptical" content, thus providing the audience with a two-fold view of dramatic events and ideas. Berry argues that the dramatist urges us to accommodate the perspective of the idealized "golden world" of Elizabethan epic to "the actualities of history" so that we may apprehend "two different conceptions of truth."

Berry, Ralph. "*Henry V:* The Reason Why." In his *The Shakespearean Metaphor: Studies in Language and Form,* pp. 48-60. Totowa, N. J.: Rowman and Littlefield, 1978.

Asserts that Henry is no ideal king, but rather an extremely successful politician with an unusual talent for making "all that he wishes or does" appear inevitable. Berry argues that the Chorus functions as public relations for Henry, helps make possible a straightforward reading of the play, and serves to "redress the balance which would otherwise be heavily weighed down by the ironic possibilities in the main text."

Boas, Frederick S. "The Chief Group of Chronicle-History Plays: *King John—Richard II—Henry IV—Henry V.*" In his *Shakspere and His Predecessors,* pp. 235-91. London: John Murray, 1896.

Regards Henry V as the embodiment of English "national strength and glory." Boas contends that the king's soliloquy in Act IV, Scene i demonstrates Henry's piety, humility, and deeply held sense of responsibility as a ruler, but he can find no excuse—except for Shakespeare's strict adherence to historical accounts—for the massacre of the French prisoners, judging that this conduct "casts a stain" on the character of the king.

Boklund, Gunnar. "Henry V—a Hero for Our Time?" *The University of Denver Quarterly* 10, No. 2 (Summer 1975): 83-92.

Claims that Shakespeare has provided a "practical and pragmatic context in which everything in *Henry V*" is to be viewed. In such a context, Boklund maintains, the king's achievement is what is important and "niceties of motivation are of very little significance." The critic acknowledges that there are ironic possibilities in the play, but he emphasizes that Henry has wholeheartedly accepted his public responsibility—"largely at the expense of his human qualities"—and successfully plays the part that national and dynastic interests require of him.

Bromley, John C. "The Shakespearean Bestiary: *1* and *2 Henry IV* and *Henry V.*" In his *The Shakespearean Kings,* pp. 75-92. Boulder: Colorado Associated University Press, 1971.

Views Henry as uniting the lion's ferocity and the shrewd dissimulation of the fox. Bromley claims that Henry is a perversion of qualities demonstrated by the principal figures in *1* and *2 Henry IV:* to the rhetoric of the lord chief justice is added his own "native duplicity," to the statecraft of his father his own "lust for war," and to "Falstaff's joy" his own "brutal humor."

Bullough, Geoffrey. Introduction to *Henry V,* by William Shakespeare. In *Narrative and Dramatic Sources of Shakespeare,* Vol. IV, edited by Geoffrey Bullough, pp. 347-75. London: Routledge and Kegan Paul, 1962.

An overview of Shakespeare's likely sources for *Henry V* and a scene-by-scene analysis of the possible origins of specific passages and dramatic events in the play. Bullough maintains that Shakespeare consulted both Hall and Holinshed in writing *Henry V;* he also finds "many significant resemblances" between the anonymous drama *The Famous Victories of Henry the fifth* (c. 1598) and *Henry V* and compares the disguised king's visit to his soldiers in Act IV, Scene i to a very similar account of the Roman emperor Germanicus provided in *The Annals* of Tacitus.

Burckhardt, Sigurd. "'Swoll'n with Some Other Grief': Shakespeare's Prince Hal Trilogy." In his *Shakespearean Meanings,* pp. 144-205. Princeton: Princeton University Press, 1966.

Discusses *Henry V* in the context of the second tetralogy. Burckhardt contends that throughout these plays Shakespeare was searching for an ordering principle or model to explain universal human experience, the creative process, and English history. Royal succession, the critic argues, could be viewed as legitimized either by combat or by primogeniture, and in *Henry V* Shakespeare chose the combat model—which some Elizabethans held to be "an acceptable way of discovering God's will and verdict." Burckhardt declares that Henry's "title is legitimized largely by his self-nurtured qualities and by his achievements; when God 'crowns' him with victory, that legitimation is *ex post facto.*"

Candido, Joseph, and Forker, Charles R., eds. *"Henry V": An Annotated Bibliography.* The Garland Shakespeare Bibliographies, edited by William Godshalk, no. 4. New York and London: Garland Publishing, 1983, 815 p.

A comprehensive catalogue, with descriptive notes, of published commentary on *Henry V.* The listings include aesthetic criticism, adaptations, textual and bibliographical studies, analyses of the play's language and its sources, and a stage history.

Campbell, Lily B. "The Victorious Acts of King Henry V." In her *Shakespeare's "Histories": Mirrors of Elizabethan Policy,* pp. 255-305. San Marino, Calif.: The Huntington Library, 1947.

A discussion of *Henry V* in terms of "the Elizabethan philosophy of war," with particular reference to the respective responsibilities of king and soldiers. Through an extensive review of sixteenth-century public documents, military books, sermons, and philosophical treatises, Campbell demonstrates that the Elizabethans generally held that a Christian state might make war on another Christian state if the cause is just, but it "should not be undertaken lightly" nor for purposes of "private vengeance." The ultimate responsibility and power of declaring war resided in the king, she shows, and while his "chief concern must be the righteousness of his cause, for God determines the outcome," his soldiers, as such, are responsible to their monarch, though as men they are "responsible to God."

Champion, Larry S. "The Maturity of Perspective: *King John, 1, 2 Henry IV, Henry V.*" In his *Perspective in Shakespeare's English Histories,* pp. 92-165. Athens: The University of Georgia Press, 1980.

Argues that in *Henry V* Shakespeare methodically employed a unique structural principle, incorporating human elements into the stylized or "abstract design" of the play to achieve a two-fold perspective. Shakespeare deliberately distances the audience from the characters—through "the multiple plots, the diverse settings, the use of the chorus as a persistent pointing device, and the essentially fixed characterization''—to provide a broad historical viewpoint, Champion maintains. But the critic also remarks that throughout the play the dramatist repeatedly offers—through Henry's soliloquies and asides in Act IV, Scene i and from other characters' ''divergent angles of vision''—opportunities for us to see the king's sensitivity and vulnerability, thereby lending ''a dramatic viability to the characters and to the events.''

Coursen, Herbert R., Jr. "Henry V and the Nature of Kingship." *Discourse* XIII, No. 3 (Summer 1970): 279-305.

Contends that Henry V is an ingenious politician who, in the course of becoming a successful monarch, has lost the ability to ''play the part of mere man even if he wishes to.'' Shakespeare casts no moral judgment on the king, Coursen maintains, but instead demonstrates that limited vision and the ability to make morality subservient to politics are essential to the successful governor. Arguing that Henry, the master manipulator of others, finally becomes controlled by the role he has assumed, the critic concludes that the play ''is not so much concerned with patriotism as with the price of patriotism.''

Duthie, George Ian. "History." In his *Shakespeare*, pp. 115-56. London: Hutchinson's University Library, 1951.

Argues that Henry V is Shakespeare's ideal king, balancing ''policy'' and chivalric values in perfect equilibrium and thus exemplifying the best in his father and the best in Hotspur. Duthie judges that although the king's conduct in Act I, Scene ii may appear hypocritical if the scene is analyzed separately, throughout the remainder of the play he is consistently treated sympathetically; therefore, the critic concludes, it is reasonable ''to give him the benefit of the doubt and regard him as speaking perfectly sincerely'' to the churchmen about his claim to the French throne.

Egan, Robert. "A Muse of Fire: *Henry V* in the Light of *Tamburlaine*." *Modern Language Quarterly* XXIX (1968): 15-28.

Analyzes *Henry V* in terms of the convention of ''the conqueror play,'' a stylized drama—''most clearly typified by Marlowe's *Tamburlaine*''—in which the plot is predetermined, the structure is episodic, and the protagonist confronts the dilemma of his conflicting public and private personae. Egan regards *Henry V* as a subtle and complex treatment of this convention, and he contends that the king achieves both a profound understanding of ''the artificiality of his public role . . . when divorced from his humanity'' and an uneasy synthesis between his princely and Christian obligations.

Erickson, Peter B. "'The Fault / My Father Made': The Anxious Pursuit of Heroic Fame in Shakespeare's *Henry V*." *Modern Language Studies* X, No. 1 (Winter 1979-80): 10-25.

Proposes that Henry V's ''double roles as ideal king and ideal warrior'' produce a divisive ''struggle between compassion and aggression'' and a conflict between his ''feelings of pity and anger'' that is never fully resolved. Erickson also focuses on the Chorus, which he describes as ''a figure who poses, and fails to solve, the conflict of modes entailed by the idea of an 'epic-drama'.''

Evans, Herbert Arthur. Introduction to *The Life of King Henry the Fifth*, by William Shakespeare, edited by Herbert Arthur Evans, pp. ix-xlviii. London: Methuen and Co., 1903.

Judges that the characterization of Henry, although lacking in subtlety, is intended to evoke unqualified admiration from the audience. The king is ''the embodiment of worldly success,'' Evans argues, consistently resolute and practical throughout *1* and *2 Henry IV*, as well as *Henry V*. Evans also discusses questions relating to the date, text, and sources of the play; he describes the 1600 Quarto as ''a very imperfect and clumsy'' version—based on a reporter's transcription of an abbreviated performance—of Shakespeare's original work.

Gilbert, Allan. "Patriotism and Satire in *Henry V*." In *Studies in Shakespeare*, edited by Arthur D. Matthews and Clark M. Emery, pp. 40-64. University of Miami Publications in English and American Literature, vol. I. Coral Gables, Fla.: University of Miami Press, 1953.

Identifies an interdependence of three themes in *Henry V*: the king's superlative military heroism is balanced by the recurrent motif of ''the horrors of war,'' and both imply a third theme of the mutual responsibilities of ruler and subjects. Gilbert contends that many of the comic scenes parody the central action and provide ironic commentary on the portrayal of triumphant English militarism.

Godshalk, W. L. "Henry V's Politics of Non-Responsibility." *Cahiers Élisabéthains*, no. 17 (April 1980): 11-20.

Focuses on Henry's ''inability to accept responsibility.'' Godshalk argues that the king feels guilty about his father's usurpation of the crown and insecure with regard to the validity of the Lancastrian claim; thus—like a ''passive neurotic''—he thrusts responsibility for his actions onto others. But this personal frailty is also a central source of his political success, the critic contends, for by implicating others, he is able to walk ''through the holocaust untarnished—the perfect Christian king *and* the Machiavellian manipulator.''

Grennan, Eamon. " 'This Story Shall the Good Man Teach His Son': *Henry V* and the Art of History." *Papers on Language and Literature* 15, No. 4 (Fall 1979): 370-82.

Views *Henry V* as Shakespeare's nonjudgmental ''exposition of the nature of official history and official historiography, with the king and the chorus cast in analogous roles as self-conscious historymakers.'' Grennan proposes that the Chorus functions as a ''commissioned historiographer'' whose narrative reveals an unproblematic, uncritical sense of history; similarly, he claims, Henry is intent on promulgating a historical perspective that is most favorable to himself and, by virtue of ''his rhetorical genius,'' he succeeds in imposing ''upon his own historical career its official historiographical meaning.''

Hobday, C. H. "Imagery and Irony in 'Henry V'." *Shakespeare Survey* 21 (1968): 107-14.

Hypothesizes that Shakespeare's mind was deeply divided over the question of the character of Henry V. Although Shakespeare was obligated to portray the king as a great national hero, Hobday contends, ''in his heart he regarded him as a murderer.'' The critic finds supporting evidence for his thesis in the concentration of death imagery in the scenes depicting the outbreak of war and in the savage irony that results from the frequent juxtaposition of ''patriotic illusion'' and ''stark reality.''

Holderness, Graham. "Chronicles of Feudalism: *Richard II*, *Henry IV Part One* and *Henry V*." In his *Shakespeare's History*, pp. 40-144. Dublin: Gill and Macmillan, 1985.

Maintains that ''the heroic dimension'' of *Henry V* is presented ''as a purely *theatrical* reality, . . . impressive and exciting only in the theater.'' An important function of the Chorus, Holderness argues, is to focus audience attention on ''the *artificiality* of the dramatic event, placing a barrier between action and audience'' which impedes us from linking the action of the drama to ordinary reality. The critic also views Henry as ''a feudal overlord'' rather than a Renaissance monarch, and he declares that the king's achievement ''is not a peaceful and harmonious commonwealth, but a barren military triumph.''

Hotson, Leslie. "Ancient Pistol." *The Yale Review* XXXVIII, No. 1 (September 1948): 51-66.

Contends that throughout *1* and *2 Henry IV* and *Henry V* Pistol imagines himself to be a tragic hero-king. Citing evidence that he was immensely popular with Elizabethan audiences, Hotson argues that Shakespeare's contemporaries would have been enchanted by Pistol's susceptibility to human folly and his determination to sustain the self-image of ''his imagined greatness . . . through thick and thin.''

Hudson, H. N. "Historical Plays: *King Henry the Fifth*." In his *Shakespeare: His Life, Art, and Characters*, pp. 105-33. Boston: Ginn & Co., 1872.

Regards Henry's piety as his most significant trait, but also finds him honest, modest, affable, interested in honor for its own sake, and capable of ''harmless fun.'' Hudson asserts that in his depiction of the king Shakespeare revealed his own personal concept of "what is good and noble," together with the ethical system that guided his own conscience.

Jorgensen, Paul A. "Accidental Judgments, Casual Slaughters, and Purposes Mistook: Critical Reactions to Shakspere's *Henry the Fifth*." *Shakespeare Association Bulletin* XXII, No. 2 (April 1947): 51-61.

Evaluates the gap between "the reactions of many estimable critics" from the eighteenth century onward and Shakespeare's avowed intention "to glorify Henry." The dramatist's conscious purpose may have been foiled by his artistic integrity, Jorgensen argues, so that his attempt to celebrate realistically the virtues of a paragon produced instead an unsatisfying "panegyric."

———. "Military Rank." In his *Shakespeare's Military World*, pp. 63-119. Berkeley and Los Angeles: University of California Press, 1956.

Regards *Henry V* as "a sustained dramatization of Elizabethan ideas and procedures of war" and the king himself as "the mirror of a Christian general." Jorgensen demonstrates the close correspondence between Henry's conduct of the French campaign and the ideas set forth in sixteenth- and seventeenth-century treatises on military theory; but he also contends that as a consequence of his rigorous self-discipline and careful calculation, the king falls short of being an attractive human being.

Knight, G. Wilson. "Saint George for England." In his *The Olive and the Sword: A Study of England's Shakespeare*, pp. 12-40. London: Oxford University Press, 1944.

Asserts that Henry V represents Shakespeare's attempt to fuse Christian virtue with "martial prowess" in a single English king. First written in the early years of World War II, when England had suffered shattering reverses in its struggle against Germany, Knight's essay focuses on passages in *Henry V*—particularly, the king's Crispin's day speech—through which he believes his countrymen may find renewed hope and "national confidence."

Levin, Richard. "Clown Subplots: Foil, Parody, Magic—*Henry V, Doctor Faustus*." In his *The Multiple Plot in English Renaissance Drama*, pp. 116-23. Chicago and London: The University of Chicago Press, 1971.

Rejects the view that the comic subplot in *Henry V* parodies the main action. The scenes featuring Pistol, Bardolph, and Nym, Levin asserts, function as foils "to contrast with, and so render still more admirable, the exploits of the 'mirror of all Christian kings'."

Manheim, Michael. "New Thoughts to Deck Our Kings: *Henry V*." In his *The Weak King Dilemma in the Shakespearean History Play*, pp. 161-82. Syracuse, N. Y.: Syracuse University Press, 1973.

Maintains that Henry is intended to be both "a successful, admirable and heroic figure" and a perfect Machiavellian monarch. Shakespeare acknowledges, Manheim argues, that in order to produce "a sense of stability in the state and the illusion of personal security" among its citizens, the king must project an image of monarchic superiority that conceals his essential vulnerability, thus depending for his success as much on "effect and artifice as Shakespeare's theatre itself."

McFarland, Thomas. "A Babble of Green Fields: Falstaff as Pastoral Outcast." In his *Shakespeare's Pastoral Comedy*, pp. 177-211. Chapel Hill: The University of North Carolina Press, 1972.

Proposes that the account of Falstaff's death in *Henry V* underscores one aspect of the fat knight's character: "the disappointed idealist, outcast in a corrupt and alien world." Falstaff's true home, McFarland contends, is "the pastoral world of ideal social harmony," and thus it is appropriate that Mistress Quickly associates him with the Arthurian myth, speaks of his playing with flowers, and reports that he dies babbling of "the land of 'green fields'." The critic also argues that the similarity between Falstaff's death and Socrates's enhances Sir John's function as a critic of the Machiavellian society in which he is an alien and from which he disappears in *Henry V*.

Merrix, Robert P. "The Alexandrian Allusion in Shakespeare's *Henry V*." *English Literary Renaissance* 2, No. 3 (Winter 1972): 321-33.

Analyzes "the structural and thematic relationship" of Fluellen's comparison of Henry and Alexander to the play as a whole. Noting that Fluellen's comments directly follow Henry's order to kill the French prisoners and, in turn, are followed by the king's "appearance and violent rhetoric," Merrix concludes that the intention is to satirize Henry by juxtaposing him with the classical figure who represented, for medieval and Renaissance writers, "unbridled ambition" and "the grievous consequences of rash actions."

Palmer, John. "Henry of Monmouth." In his *Political Characters of Shakespeare*, pp. 180-249. London: Macmillan and Co., 1945.

Asserts that the simultaneous glorification of the hero-king and exposure of "the wicked futility of his enterprise" in *Henry V* demonstrate "Shakespeare's peculiar blend of moral detachment and imaginative sympathy." The dramatist neither censures nor commends his protagonist, Palmer contends, but appears to be more engaged by the character's human weaknesses than by his martial or royal roles. The critic proclaims that the deep division among critics on the nature of Henry V "is the best possible proof of Shakespeare's complete neutrality" on the question.

Pierce, Robert B. "*Henry V*." In his *Shakespeare's History Plays: The Family and the State*, pp. 225-40. Columbus: Ohio State University Press, 1971.

Argues that in *Henry V* such thematic issues as "the inheritance of virtue, the family as a symbol of unity, and public disorder as a threat to the family" regularly appear in the public rhetoric of the French and English leaders. But apart from its linguistic function as an enhancer of the political themes, Pierce maintains, "the family has no broader dramatic role"; he suggests that this is related to Henry's isolation as king, which requires him to be "inhumanly strong and wise" and to emphasize his public role at the expense of his private nature.

Reese, M. M. "Shakespeare's England: *Henry V*." In his *The Cease of Majesty: A Study of Shakespeare's History Plays*, pp. 317-32. London: Edward Arnold, 1961.

Argues that a true appreciation of Henry V requires that he be judged by Elizabethan rather than modern standards. Shakespeare viewed the king as a paragon, Reese declares, and he carefully directed the dramatic action of the play to portray him as "doing everything that the age expected of the perfect king."

Rossiter, A. P. "Ambivalence: the Dialectic of the Histories." In his *Angel with Horns and Other Shakespeare Lectures*, edited by Graham Storey, pp. 40-64. London: Longmans, Green and Co., 1961.

A discussion of the relationship between serious and comic elements in Shakespeare's history plays. Remarking only briefly on *Henry V*, Rossiter contends that in this play there is little significant interplay between comedy and serious matter, and he suggests that Falstaff must die because of the danger he poses of "killing the heroics with a jest." The critic also believes that *Henry V* is not an insightful account of English history, claiming that whatever Shakespeare's original intention with regard to the subject, "what he produced was a propaganda-play on National Unity: heavily orchestrated for brass."

Sen Gupta, S. C. "The Second Tetralogy." In his *Shakespeare's Historical Plays*, pp. 113-50. London: Oxford University Press, 1964.

Views Henry V as a decisive man of action who seldom questions his own assumptions, analyzes the bases of his claims, or considers "the subtler implications of his conduct." Sen Gupta considers the play a personal rather than a national epic, arguing that the English soldiers are inspired more by loyalty to the king than by any national ideal.

Shanker, Sidney. "*Henry V* as Ideological Vehicle." In his *Shakespeare and the Uses of Ideology*, pp. 68-80. The Hague and Paris: Mouton, 1975.

Asserts that there is no doubt of Shakespeare's ideological commitment to formulate in *Henry V* "a devoutly conceived plea for English unity and greatness, for governance by a transcendent king who could make the commons love him." Although the dramatist took great pains to represent Henry "in the best of all possible lights," Shanker maintains, we are made uneasy by the uncritical tone of the play, its portrayal of war as "glorious and heroic," the confusion of generic forms, and the disparate elements of epic and realistic comedy.

Smith, Gordon Ross. "Shakespeare's *Henry V:* Another Part of the Critical Forest." *Journal of the History of Ideas* XXXVII, No. 1 (January-March 1976): 3-26.

Argues that the speeches and characters in *Henry V* reflect the diverse variety of political thought in the Renaissance rather than a narrow Tudor orthodoxy. Although "the spirit of heroic patriotism" is clearly evident in the surface of the play, Smith contends, a sensitive audience will also detect elements of hypocrisy, exploitation, and rapacity.

Smith, Warren D. "The *Henry V* Choruses in the First Folio." *Journal of English and Germanic Philology* LIII, No. 1 (January 1954): 38-57.

Proposes that the Chorus passages in *Henry V* did not appear in the original text of 1599 but were added at a later date—perhaps by someone other than Shakespeare—when the play was privately performed at court. Smith notes that the Chorus's frequent apologies for the limitations of the stage would be appropriate if the play were being presented in a small, private theater before a sophisticated audience. He also maintains that the reference to "the general of our gracious Empress" in the Chorus preceding Act V is not to Essex, but to Charles Blount, Lord Mountjoy, who defeated the Irish rebels in the spring of 1603.

Soellner, Rolf. "*Henry V:* Patterning after Perfection." In his *Shakespeare's Patterns of Self-Knowledge,* pp. 113-28. Columbus: Ohio State University Press, 1972.

Argues that Henry V exemplifies the four cardinal virtues which Renaissance Christian humanists held were requisite in a good man: "fortitude, justice, prudence, and . . . temperance." Soellner contends that the king represents Shakespeare's "ideal or very nearly ideal character" and that there is "every reason to believe that it is a sympathetic portrait." Henry is not highly esteemed by modern critics, he concludes, because ours is an antiheroic age that values pacificism and is distrustful of success.

Spurgeon, Caroline F. E. "Leading Motives in the Histories." In her *Shakespeare's Imagery and What It Tells Us,* pp. 213-58. Cambridge: At the University Press, 1935.

Identifies a recurring pattern of images in *Henry V* related to birds and flight. Especially in the early parts of the play, Spurgeon suggests, these metaphors contribute to the sense of "swift and soaring movement" in the dramatic action.

Stewart, J. I. M. "The Birth and Death of Falstaff." In his *Character and Motive in Shakespeare: Some Recent Appraisals Examined,* pp. 111-39. London: Longmans, Green and Co., 1949.

Relates the death of Falstaff to the folk ritual of slaying "an old, impotent, and guilty king" in order to restore the health and fecundity of the community. Noting the implicit parallels in *Henry IV* between "Bolingbroke and his policies and Falstaff and *his* policies," Stewart proposes that instead of killing his father, Henry "kills" Falstaff, who, by displacement, stands for "all the accumulated sin of the reign, all the consequent sterility of the land."

Stříbrný, Zdeněk. "*Henry V* and History." In *Shakespeare in a Changing World,* edited by Arnold Kettle, pp. 84-101. London: Lawrence & Wishart, 1964.

Compares the contradiction inherent in the play's depiction of both "the glory and the horror of war" with the portrayal of Henry V as both the ideal "hearty soldier-king," on the one hand, and a self-righteous, opportunistic hypocrite, on the other. Shakespeare's realistic view of war, Stříbrný contends, is paralleled by his conception of Henry as "a conquering hero who has to pay a heavy human toll for his success."

Tolman, Albert H. "The Epic Character of Henry V." *Modern Language Notes* XXXIV, No. 1 (January 1919): 7-16.

Argues that Shakespeare intended to idealize the character of Henry V, but that such a portrayal is more appropriate to epic poetry than to drama. Tolman asserts that there is neither internal struggle nor development in Henry's character, nor any real external contest in the play; the result, he feels, is unrealistic and nondramatic, with the figure of Henry appealing "to our admiration more than our sympathy."

Wentersdorf, Karl P. "The Conspiracy of Silence in *Henry V*." *Shakespeare Quarterly* 27, No. 3 (Summer 1976): 264-87.

Focuses on Henry's discovery of Cambridge, Scroop, and Grey's efforts to secure the crown for Edmund Mortimer. Wentersdorf argues that the king insists on speaking of their plot against his life in terms of moral corruption—and is silent on their real motive—in order to avoid the fact that these men "are challenging Henry's right to the English throne on grounds at least as convincing as those justifying Henry's challenge to the French king." The conspirators themselves, the critic asserts, offer almost no justification for their conduct "because they do not want to jeopardize the survival of their families," who—as in all cases of treason—face the forfeiture of their titles and possessions.

Williamson, Marilyn L. "The Episode with Williams in *Henry V*." *Studies in English Literature 1500-1900* IX, No. 2 (Spring 1969): 275-82.

Maintains that in his encounter with Williams, Henry shows that he is still learning "what it is like to be a king." Williamson argues that Henry's assumption of a disguise and the trick of giving Fluellen the gage recall his behavior in *1* and *2 Henry IV*, but the trick backfires, she contends, because the king has not yet faced the reality which Williams comprehends—"that the king is not just another man"—and because what would have delighted his Eastcheap cronies in the earlier plays is wholly inappropriate in the episode with Williams.

Wilson, J. Dover. "The Choice and the Balance." In his *The Fortunes of Falstaff,* pp. 114-28. Cambridge: At the University Press, 1943.

Speculates that Shakespeare's intention to continue the story of Falstaff in *Henry V* was thwarted when William Kempe, the actor who had taken the role in *1* and *2 Henry IV*, left the Lord Chamberlain's Men early in 1599. Without Kempe, Dover Wilson hypothesizes, Shakespeare "was obliged to alter his plans" and explain Falstaff's absence by recounting his death. Mistress Quickly's description of the fat knight's end, he maintains, displays the dramatist employing "his full powers in an endeavour to win indulgence from the spectators for the disappointment of their hopes."

# The Merry Wives of Windsor

**DATE:** Although *The Merry Wives of Windsor* was not entered in the STATIONERS' REGISTER until January 18, 1602, most scholars believe that it was written in 1597 and first performed as part of the entertainment at a Feast of the Order of the Garter on April 23 of that year. These dates are based on topical allusions in the play and on Leslie Hotson's identification (see Additional Bibliography) of certain contemporary figures whom it is believed Shakespeare was satirizing in his portrayal of Shallow and Slender. Early in the eighteenth century, John Dennis reported a tradition that *The Merry Wives* was written in fourteen days at the command of Queen Elizabeth; similarly, Nicholas Rowe claimed to have learned that the queen had so enjoyed the character of Falstaff in *Henry IV* that she bade the dramatist compose a new play representing Falstaff "in Love." Many modern commentators hold that the play gives evidence of having been hastily composed, but there is no independent verification of the tradition of Elizabeth's role in the origin of the play. There is also no conclusive evidence as to where *The Merry Wives* belongs in relation to the chronology of the Henriad, but most scholars either place it after *2 Henry IV* or, like the New Arden editor H. J. Oliver (see Additional Bibliography), posit that Shakespeare interrupted his work on *2 Henry IV* to create the comedy.

**TEXT:** *The Merry Wives of Windsor* was first printed in QUARTO form in 1602 and reissued, also as a quarto edition, in 1619. As it appears in the FIRST FOLIO of 1623, the play is markedly different from the 1602 Quarto. Entire scenes are missing from the quarto edition, many of the speeches are radically compressed, and there are numerous confusions and conflations of situations and passages. W. W. Greg (see Additional Bibliography) was the first commentator to assert that the quarto was assembled on the basis of a MEMORIAL RECONSTRUCTION and was therefore less authoritative than the Folio; he contended that the actor who took the role of the Host of the Garter Inn sold the pirated version to the printer. Greg's hypothesis is generally endorsed by present-day scholars, some of whom have argued that more than one member of Shakespeare's company participated in the pirated reconstruction of the play. Various theories have been advanced regarding the transmission of the Folio text. Noting that the Folio omits stage directions, A. W. Pollard and John Dover Wilson jointly contended that it was based on a compilation of players' parts, but others have claimed that the copy for the Folio was a transcript prepared by Ralph Crane, a professional scribe. Modern editors, such as H. J. Oliver, generally regard the Folio as the superior text, but they also consult the quarto to clarify passages which appear garbled or corrupt in the Folio.

**SOURCES:** No definitive source for *The Merry Wives of Windsor* has been discovered, but scholars have postulated that perhaps because of the brief period of time allotted for its composition, Shakespeare drew upon a number of existing works. Frederick Gard Fleay, A. W. Pollard and John Dover Wilson, J. M. Nosworthy, and Oscar James Campbell (see Additional Bibliography) are among those commentators who have proposed that a lost play by an unknown dramatist—either the *Jealous Comedy* (1592) or some other domestic comedy that featured a duped husband—provided the basic plot and perhaps some of the characters for *The Merry Wives*. In addition, as

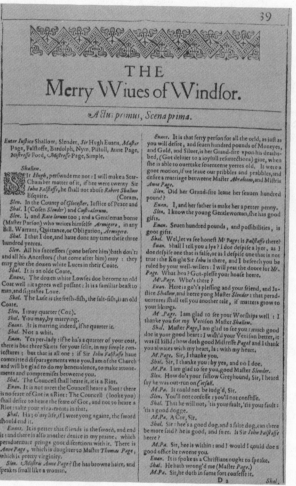

*Title page of The Merry Wives of Windsor taken from the First Folio (1623).*

Geoffrey Bullough (see Additional Bibliography) and others have pointed out, many situations and incidents in the play can be found in earlier English and Italian works. For example, the scenes in which Falstaff narrates for the benefit of Ford-Brook his alleged amorous progress with Mistress Ford and the incident of the knight's concealment in a buck-basket by the merry wives appear to be based on Ser Giovanni Fiorentino's *Il Pecorone* (1558). In this work, a young student informs his professor of the progress of his affair with a married woman, unaware that his mistress is the wife of the pedant; when the teacher finally comprehends the situation and tries to surprise the couple, the wife hides her lover in a basket of laundry. Also, Falstaff's attempt to woo two women simultaneously, his sending them identical letters, and their reactions to his advances may have their precursors in G. F. Straparola's *La Piacevoli Notti* (1550-53). In this Italian work, a young man makes seductive overtures to three women at a ball and subsequently writes identical letters to each; after the women disclose the contents of the letters to each other, they resolve to punish the would-be lover for his insolence. A possible inspiration for Falstaff's final humiliation in Act V, Scene v is John Lyly's *Endimion* (1591), which contains a scene in which a nobleman is punished for his lust by fairies who pinch and torment him. In addition, some commentators have compared Mistress Ford and Mistress Page to the two spirited women in Barnaby Riche's *Riche his Farewell to Militarie Profession* (1581). Further, E. K. Chambers has demonstrated that the realistic manner and tone of *The Merry Wives*, its satiric treatment of characters, and its instances of bawdy humor are all reminiscent of the medieval French verse form known as *fabliau*.

**CRITICAL HISTORY:** The figure of Sir John Falstaff has dominated the criticism of *The Merry Wives of Windsor* from the early eighteenth century to the present day. Much attention has been devoted to comparing his representation in this play with his portrayal in *1* and *2 Henry IV*. Until the second half of the twentieth century, critics almost unanimously expressed their disappointment with the character of Sir John in the comedy, judging him to be a witless caricature of the splendid fat knight in *Henry IV* and, in some cases, recoiling from the depiction of his serial humiliations. More recently, the trend toward comparison has been replaced by an interest in Falstaff as a ritualistic scapegoat figure and by a focus on his status as a knight and member of the feudal aristocracy. Other topics addressed by commentators on *The Merry Wives* include the play's dramatic structure, its central thematic issues, its language, and its dramatization of the historical conflict between the aristocracy and the new middle class which developed during the Renaissance with the rise of capitalism as the economic basis of Western society. Although discussions of characterization in Shakespeare's play have been limited for the most part to the figure of Falstaff, some have focused as well on Master Ford and, more recently, on the role of the women in the play.

Indeed, characterization was a principal issue in the earliest criticism of *The Merry Wives of Windsor*. In the third quarter of the seventeenth century, Samuel Pepys recorded his reaction to a performance of the play and alluded to Shakespeare's use of the Elizabethan literary convention of characterization based on temperament or disposition—also known as "humors"—in the depiction of Shallow and Doctor Caius. During that same period, John Dryden described Falstaff as a compilation of humors, but also noted that he is distinguished from similar characters in other plays by his unusual mental agility. Dryden also praised *The Merry Wives* for its adherence to regularity of dramatic structure. In the first decade of the eighteenth century, Nicholas Rowe commended the play for the variety and opposition of humors represented in the characters. Rowe also contended that the movement of the dramatic action hinges on the process by which Ford is cured of his irrational jealousy.

Dryden's and Rowe's concerns with the structure of *The Merry Wives* was shared to a degree by all eighteenth-century commentators. John Dennis argued that the dramatic structure is flawed by the lack of unity or interdependence among the three main plots; he asserted that some scenes appear to bear no relation to other parts of the play, and thus they effectively interrupt or stifle the movement of the action. Charles Gildon lauded the play for its taut construction, arguing that with the exception of the Latin lesson in Act IV, Scene i, no single incident may be deleted without impairing its structural unity. The critic also evaluated the exposure of Falstaff's attempt to woo two women simultaneously as the central dramatic action and the successful deception carried out by Anne Page and Fenton as the principal subplot. John Potter described *The Merry Wives* as "the most perfect" of Shakespeare's comedies

and similarly praised its skillful plot construction and highly finished characters. On the other hand, like Dennis, Samuel Johnson generally faulted the progress of the dramatic action in *The Merry Wives*, although he praised Shakespeare's masterful use of language and his capacity to amuse and entertain an audience in the play.

In their discussions of *The Merry Wives of Windsor*, both Dennis and Johnson foreshadowed the debate over the characterization of Falstaff in this play compared to that in *1* and *2 Henry IV*. Dennis, expressing what has remained a minority viewpoint, asserted that the fat knight in *The Merry Wives* is superior to or at least as dramatically effective as his representation in the histories. Johnson considered the Falstaff of the comedy less diverting than that of *1* and *2 Henry IV*; in addition, he was the first critic to voice the opinion shared by many subsequent commentators that Queen Elizabeth's command to see Falstaff in love was impossible to fulfill, for "Falstaff could not love, but by ceasing to be Falstaff."

The impossibility of showing Shakespeare's knight in love was iterated by several nineteenth-century critics, many of whom also focused their commentary, like Dennis and Johnson, on a comparison between Falstaff in the histories and Falstaff in *The Merry Wives*. Near the beginning of the century, August Wilhelm Schlegel maintained that it was inconceivable to portray the knight in love, adding that the most implausible element in the play is Falstaff's belief that he is capable of inspiring passionate love in two women. The critic argued that although the repeated dupings of Falstaff lead the audience to a lower estimate of his shrewdness than that evidenced in *1* and *2 Henry IV*, the scenes which depict the results of these deceptions are incomparably droll. William Hazlitt charged that Falstaff's wit and talent for manipulating language have deserted him in *The Merry Wives*, and he rated the knight and others in this play as pale representations of their originals in the histories. However, Hazlitt praised the characterization of several minor figures in the play, describing Slender as "a very potent piece of imbecility." Hartley Coleridge, son of the eminent Romantic poet and essayist, shared the view that Falstaff could not be depicted in love. His opinion of Queen Elizabeth for making such a request—which he claimed proved her to have been "a gross-minded old baggage"—was matched late in the century by George Brandes, who contended that Falstaff became the victim of the queen's "barbarous wish," since Shakespeare could not obey the royal command without degrading the knight and rendering him almost wholly inconsistent with his depiction in *1* and *2 Henry IV*. H. N. Hudson offered a generally sympathetic appraisal of the figure of the knight in *The Merry Wives*, expressing some dissatisfaction over his persecution by the Windsorites and stating that his humiliations are pitiable even though they are the result of his own misconduct. Near the end of the century, Frederick S. Boas argued that there were many points of resemblance between Falstaff's presentation in the histories and in *The Merry Wives* that had been overlooked by earlier critics, although he did conclude that the knight in this play is "Shakspere's literary crime; his caricature . . . of one of the mightiest of his own creations."

At the same time that Falstaff dominated nineteenth-century criticism of *The Merry Wives of Windsor*, several commentators began focusing on other issues in the play, including its representation of middle-class life, whether it dramatizes a satirical or didactic point of view, and its structure and language. Hermann Ulrici asserted that Shakespeare's objective was to satirize the comic principle, chiefly in the figure of Falstaff, but also in his portrayal of the other characters as conceited and mistaken about their infallibility. Ulrici also emphasized the significance of the many distinctions made in the play between the aristocratic and middle classes, contending that they underscore the dramatist's ridicule of the remnants of the chivalric convention that had survived into the Elizabethan age. Karl Kautsky viewed *The Merry Wives* as reflecting "the struggle between the decaying knighthood . . . and the aspiring middle class" and as accurately representing Elizabethan social conflict. George Brandes also called attention to the play's focus on the contemporary life of the English middle classes, styling it the most "prosaic and bourgeois" of all Shakespeare's plays.

G. G. Gervinus was among those nineteenth-century critics who discerned a strain of moral seriousness in *The Merry Wives*. Contending that the play demonstrates the ethical principle that honesty is superior to deviousness, he asserted that Shakespeare was disturbed by his audiences' fascination with Falstaff in *1* and *2 Henry IV*. Gervinus argued that by depriving the knight of his former intellectual acuity in the comedy, the dramatist intended us to focus on Falstaff's vanity and egotism and to condemn his morally reprehensible behavior. Later in the century, Boas disagreed with Gervinus and denied that Shakespeare had any didactic intent in this play, maintaining that there are so many differences in the character of Falstaff as presented in the histories and the comedy that his punishments here cannot be linked to his misconduct in the earlier dramas.

Towards the close of the nineteenth century, Denton J. Snider commented on the structure of the play, tracing a pattern of conflict, mediation, and reconciliation in the movement of its dramatic action. He noted that Anne Page and the mistresses Ford, Page, and Quickly are the agents of mediation, linking them to the more elevated female figures in Shakespeare's other plays. Snider further discussed linguistic elements in *The Merry Wives*, remarking that the use of prose and "perverted human speech" are highly appropriate to the spirit of caricature that pervades the play. Concerning the character of Falstaff, Snider emphasized the fat knight's sensuality and maintained that in the play's final scene Sir John admits the folly of his lust and repents—at least for a time—his foolish conduct.

Throughout the twentieth century, critics have continued to focus their analyses of *The Merry Wives* on the character of Falstaff; but since the late 1940s, some have perceived more serious implications in the knight's characterization and, like a small number of nineteenth-century commentators, have identified significant thematic issues in the play as well. Near the beginning of this century, A. C. Bradley described as "horrible" the tricks and indignities suffered by Falstaff at the hands of the Windsorites, and he lamented the presentation of the knight as repentant at the close of the play. Bradley further repeated the claim that it was impossible for Shakespeare to show Falstaff in love, concluding that Sir John in this play is a separate and distinct character from the Falstaff of *1* and *2 Henry IV*. Similarly, H. B. Charlton viewed Falstaff in *The Merry Wives* as a "contemptible caricature" of the knight in the histories. He contended, however, that there is evidence throughout *2 Henry IV* that Shakespeare was growing increasingly disillusioned with Falstaff as the ideal comic hero and that the discrediting of Sir John was complete even before the dramatist turned to the composition of *The Merry Wives*. Writing in the second half of the twentieth century, Bertrand Evans also expressed his unhappiness with the portrayal of Falstaff's degradation in the play, and he argued that Shakespeare's re-

sentment of Queen Elizabeth's command to show the fat knight in love is clearly evident. Deflecting the critical attention away from Falstaff, Ralph Berry contended that the knight himself has not changed in the comedy, but that the cooperation shown him by Prince Hal has been replaced by the outright hostility of the citizens of Windsor—a situation that significantly alters our perception of Sir John. Recently, Anne Barton has also remarked on the effect of the change in locale between *1* and *2 Henry IV* and *The Merry Wives* on our perception of Falstaff, arguing that Windsor is a wholly inimical setting for Sir John.

An innovative mode of approaching the character of Falstaff was initiated by Northrope Frye in 1948. Comparing the vicissitudes of the knight to the flogging and banishment of the winter or death figure in traditional folk rituals, Frye noted that by undergoing his repeated humiliations, Falstaff "had done about all that could reasonably be asked of any fertility spirit." Frye's identification of ritualistic elements in the play was significant, for it influenced such subsequent critics as Jeanne Addison Roberts, J. A. Bryant, Jr., Barbara Freedman, and Jan Lawson Hinely. Roberts likened Falstaff to a scapegoat figure who is sacrificed in order to reestablish a healthy society. She argued that Falstaff's lust represents a threat to the values of the society and that the entire community appears released from its "follies and anxieties" through his incapacitation by the merry wives in the ritual masque (Act V, Scene v). Thus, according to Roberts, the play concludes with a harmonious spirit of accommodation. Tracing the similarities between the three punishments inflicted on Falstaff and traditional fertility rituals, Bryant also compared the knight's final humiliation in Act V, Scene v to "the ancient castigation of the scapegoat," and he contended that this analogy deepens the significance of the Falstaff plot. Bryant further asserted that by offering a screen for the elopement of Anne Page and Fenton, the masque also serves to displace the older generation's preoccupation with the monetary implications of marriage and assures that procreation will ensue from the union of the young lovers. Unlike these critics, Freedman argued that the final punishment of Falstaff is not a reenactment of a scapegoating ceremony, but merely a "playful parody" of the ritual. And Hinely further modified this view of Falstaff by claiming that the citizens of Windsor are as vain and pretentious as the knight himself and that the festive ending of *The Merry Wives of Windsor* is unique in presenting not only the reintegration of the scapegoat figure into the community, but in demonstrating parallel recognitions of guilt by the townspeople as well. Most recently, Anne Barton has maintained that Falstaff is not a scapegoat figure and that the play does not dramatize a pattern of ritual renewal of society. In her view, Windsor is a society that generally upholds the traditional Shakespearean comic values and thus does not need to undergo a ritualistic cleansing.

Coinciding with the beginning of a deeper appreciation of Falstaff was a growing critical perception of serious thematic, even didactic, elements in *The Merry Wives of Windsor*. Like the nineteenth-century critic Gervinus, Donald A. Stauffer regarded the play as a work of moral instruction, intended to dramatize Shakespeare's belief that avarice, lust, and jealousy must be punished. Commenting on the theme of appearance and reality in the comedy, John Russell Brown asserted that most of the characters overly rely on their abilities to create or interpret reality, and he held that the play-within-the-play at Herne's Oak provides a merry exposure of the vanities and dangers inherent in such pretense. W. L. Godshalk maintained that Ford and Falstaff—as well as many of the secondary characters—fail to discern the "true worth" of others, and he identified the necessity of perceiving individual worth and value as a significant thematic element in the play. William Carroll contended that a central concern in *The Merry Wives* is "the use and abuse of imagination." Comparing the manipulations of illusion by Falstaff, Ford, Mistress Ford, and Mistress Page, the critic argued that the play depicts the power of imagination to subvert and delude us, as well as enrich our lives; he also compared the intrigues devised by the merry wives to vanquish Falstaff's threat to the community with the way in which a playwright shapes our perception of his dramatic world through similar tricks and deceptions. Richard F. Hardin examined several variations on the theme of honor in the play. In his profanation of his knightly vows, Hardin claimed, Falstaff represents "the nemesis of honor"; the critic further asserted that the knight's attempt to compromise the honor of Mistresses Ford and Page is only one of several assaults on the personal integrity of women in *The Merry Wives*, for all the men believe that young, marriageable women can be treated as chattel and, further, Ford dishonors his wife by suspecting her fidelity. Freedman viewed the play as demonstrating human limitations generally and, more specifically, as depicting the impending decline in physical and mental abilities that must be faced by all middle-aged males. She argued that Master Page possesses a self-confident, nondestructive sense of male sexuality and is thus able to serve as mediator between the inadequate old order of Windsor society and the chaotic forces which attack it. Marilyn French contended that "possession of property, possession of women, and fear of theft" are the central thematic issues in *The Merry Wives*, and she argued that Falstaff can never be fully accepted as a member of the Windsor community because his lack of money in a society where almost everyone views human relationships in terms of property and possession signifies a diminished status. Analyzing the way in which the play dramatizes the conflicts between men and women and between different social classes, Peter Erickson contended that while the class struggle is resolved in favor of the aristocracy, there is no parallel resumption of male dominance in Windsor and the play ends on a note of "residual male discontent"; this discontent, according to Erickson, reflects Shakespeare's resentment of the cult of Elizabeth and her supreme power in a patriarchal society.

Erickson's conception of the play as a reaffirmation of class hierarchy and of its ending as "a celebration of national identity that is aristocratic rather than egalitarian in orientation" was preceded by other twentieth-century considerations of class conflict or accommodation in *The Merry Wives*. Hardin argued that the marriage of Anne and Fenton underscores the view found throughout the play that an aristocrat who wishes to maintain the vestiges of family glory must come to terms with the new order represented by the Fords and Pages. French maintained that because they are members of the aristocracy, Falstaff and Fenton are the outsiders in this bourgeois society and both are initially perceived by the Windsorites as challenging the legitimate, proprietary interests of the community; although Fenton successfully integrates himself into the bourgeois community, she declared, Falstaff remains an outsider.

Other twentieth-century commentators on *The Merry Wives of Windsor* have focused on the play's genre, structure, and language. Early in this century, E. K. Chambers linked the play with the medieval French verse form known as *fabliau* and remarked on the "delightful contrast" between the realistic tone and manner of most of the play and the romantic mood of the final scene. John Dover Wilson evaluated the play as "a comedy of humours, i.e., a collection of whimsical char-

acters," all of whom—with the exception of Pistol and Nym—are endowed with human qualities that evoke our sympathy as well as our laughter. Because of its vivid portrayal of a small-town community, Muriel C. Bradbrook designated *The Merry Wives* a "citizen comedy"; she also argued that in order to complete the composition of the play within the two weeks alloted him by Queen Elizabeth, as tradition has it, Shakespeare synthesized elements from a variety of "theatrical genres" and recreated some of his most popular comic characters, including Mistress Quickly, Bardolph, Pistol, and Nym, in supporting roles for the resurrected Falstaff. Roberts argued that because its dramatic action follows a structural pattern of rational "cause and effect," and because it offers a hopeful view of life, *The Merry Wives* is a comedy rather than the simple farce most previous commentators assumed it to be. Ralph Berry, however, called the play a "brutal farce" in which the central motif of revenge evokes sadistic reactions from the audience, reflecting the hostility directed against Falstaff by the other characters. And in yet another reading of the play's genre, Ronald Huebert suggested that *The Merry Wives* may be seen as "sophisticated literary parody" of a variety of late sixteenth-century writers and dramatic conventions.

Both Bertrand Evans and Godshalk analyzed the dramatic structure of *The Merry Wives of Windsor*. Evans contended that the dramatic action is built upon a dazzling array of "practices and counter-practices" of various characters, and he demonstrated the varying degrees of awareness held by Falstaff, Ford, and the secondary characters. Evans particularly praised the way in which the disparate dramatic actions are drawn together in the final scene of the play. Godshalk contended that the central dramatic action and several of the subplots as well are shaped by a structural pattern of "offense, revenge of punishment, . . . and reconciliation." As both Falstaff and Ford undergo a course of purgation leading to understanding and regeneration, he argued, each is symbolically transformed "from man to beast," mirroring the way in which their transgressions have led to their alienation from human society. As mentioned above, Godshalk also asserted that *The Merry Wives* underscores the importance of distinguishing the "true worth" of others, and he asserted that the repeated instances of failed verbal communications between minor characters convey a sense of "linguistic alienation" that results from their misapprehensions about each other.

This interest in the language of *The Merry Wives of Windsor* can be noted in the studies of other twentieth-century critics. Mark Van Doren argued that Falstaff's speeches in *The Merry Wives* are distinctly inferior to those provided him in *1* and *2 Henry IV*. In fact, Van Doren maintained, the Host of the Garter Inn exhibits the kind of exuberant and forceful eloquence previously characteristic of Falstaff, whose wit in this play appears forced and whose humor relies heavily on puns and "monstrous circumlocutions." Brian Vickers contended that although most of the characters generally express themselves in unadorned, conversational prose speeches, Shakespeare achieved a remarkable degree of differentiation among the minor characters by assigning to each an idiosyncratic use of language. The critic singled out for particular praise the way in which "Ford's insane jealousy" is vividly conveyed through his rambling and disjointed prose style. Most recently, William Carroll has examined the unintended richness and creativity in the puns and malapropisms of such characters as Nym, Mistress Quickly, and the Host, remarking that language, like imagination, may break away from a speaker's intended significance "to lead a wayward life of its own."

Compared with Shakespeare's other comedies, even his early ones, there is a relatively small corpus of critical commentary on *The Merry Wives of Windsor*. In 1971, H. J. Oliver, editor of the New Arden edition of the play, pointed out that numerous books have been written on Shakespearean comedy which "either neglect the play altogether or mention it only in passing." Since that date there has been a dramatic increase in the number of studies focusing on *The Merry Wives*. Critics have begun to discern a deeper significance in Falstaff's role in the play, to note the importance of class struggle and human sexual relations, to identify Shakespeare's ongoing concern, in this work as well as his others, with true and false perception, and to analyze the subtle use of language beneath the comedy's prosaic surface. It would appear that nearly four hundred years after its composition, *The Merry Wives of Windsor* has begun to receive the intensive critical scrutiny common to Shakespeare's other plays. And although its literary merits continue to elicit debate, for many it remains one of the most exuberant and entertaining of Shakespeare's comedies.

---

### SAMUEL PEPYS   (diary date 1660)

[*A diversified background of travel, intellectual pursuits, and public service gave Pepys the opportunity to be a close observer of his society. His unique* Diary *is an unreserved study of the affairs and customs of his time. His personal revelations create a document of unusual psychological interest as well as providing a history of the Restoration theater. In the earliest surviving reference to* The Merry Wives of Windsor, *entered in his* Diary *for December 5, 1660, and excerpted below, Pepys generally disparages the specific performance of the play he had attended that evening. He also makes an oblique reference to "the humours" of Shallow and Doctor Caius, thus becoming the first critic to remark on Shakespeare's use of the Elizabethan literary convention of characterization based on temperament or disposition to represent the secondary figures in* The Merry Wives of Windsor.]

I dined at home, and after dinner I went to the new Theatre and there I saw "The Merry Wives of Windsor" acted, the humours of the country gentleman and the French doctor very well done, but the rest but very poorly, and Sir J. Falstaffe as bad as any.

> Samuel Pepys, in a diary entry of December 5, 1660, in his *The Diary of Samuel Pepys, Vol. I, edited by Henry B. Wheatley, Random House, 1924, p. 202.*

### JOHN DRYDEN   (essay date 1668)

[*Dryden, the leading poet and playwright of Restoration England, helped formulate the Neoclassical view of Shakespeare as an irregular genius whose native talent overcame his ignorance of the proper "rules" and language for serious drama. He was also instrumental in establishing Shakespeare's reputation as the foremost English dramatist, and his opinions influenced critics well into the following century. In the excerpt below, taken from a portion of Dryden's* Of Dramatic Poesy: An Essay *(1668) in which he discusses Ben Jonson's use of "humours" to portray dramatic characters, he describes Shakespeare's Falstaff as "a miscellany of humours or images." But in addition to such stock characteristics as obesity, cowardice, and vanity, the critic maintains, Falstaff demonstrates an unusual mental acuity that not only diverts us, but also serves to distinguish him from dramatic figures drawn with less individuality.*]

[Critics] say, it is not enough to find one man of [one particular] humour; it must be common to more, and the more common the more natural. To prove this, they instance in the best of comical characters, Falstaff: there are many men resembling him; old, fat, merry, cowardly, drunken, amorous, vain, and lying. But to convince these people, I need but tell them, that humour is the ridiculous extravagance of conversation, wherein one man differs from all others. If then it be common, or communicated to many, how differs it from other men's? or what indeed causes it to be ridiculous so much as the singularity of it? As for Falstaff, he is not properly one humour, but a miscellany of humours or images, drawn from so many several men: that wherein he is singular is his wit, or those things he says *praeter expectatum*, unexpected by the audience; his quick evasions, when you imagine him surprised, which, as they are extremely diverting of themselves, so receive a great addition from his person; for the very sight of such an unwieldy old debauched fellow is a comedy alone. (p. 84)

> John Dryden, "'Of Dramatic Poesy, an Essay'," in his Essays of John Dryden, Vol. I, *edited by W. P. Ker, 1900. Reprint by Russell & Russell, 1961, pp. 21-108.*

### JOHN DRYDEN   (essay date 1679)

[*In the following excerpt, taken from prefatory remarks to his adaptation of Shakespeare's* Troilus and Cressida *(1679), Dryden is the earliest critic to comment on the dramatic structure of* The Merry Wives of Windsor. *He maintains that although Ben Jonson was credited with being the first English dramatist to observe the Neoclassical unities of "Time, Place, and Action," the plot of Shakespeare's* The Merry Wives of Windsor *"was regular before him."*]

How defective Shakespeare and Fletcher have been in all their plots, Mr. Rymer has discovered in his criticisms: neither can we, who follow them, be excused from the same, or greater errors; which are the more unpardonable in us, because we want their beauties to countervail our faults. (pp. 211-12)

The difference between Shakespeare and Fletcher in their plotting seems to be this; that Shakespeare generally moves more terror, and Fletcher more compassion: for the first had a more masculine, a bolder and more fiery genius; the second, a more soft and womanish. In the mechanic beauties of the plot, which are the observation of the three Unities, Time, Place, and Action, they are both deficient; but Shakespeare most. Ben Johnson reformed those errors in his comedies, yet one of Shakespeare's was regular before him; which is, *The Merry Wives of Windsor*. (p. 212)

> John Dryden, "Preface to 'Troilus and Cressida', Containing the Grounds of Criticism in Tragedy (1679)," in his Essays of John Dryden, Vol. I, *edited by W. P. Ker, 1900. Reprint by Oxford at the Clarendon Press, Oxford, 1926, pp. 202-29.*

### GERARD LANGBAINE   (essay date 1691)

[*Langbaine is generally acknowledged as the first historian of the English theater. He wrote several catalogues of dramatic history, including* An Account of the English Dramatick Poets *(1691), in which he provided biographical sketches of playwrights, lists of their works, and possible sources for the plots of their plays. In the following excerpt from the work mentioned above, Langbaine is the first commentator to note that for* The Merry Wives of Windsor *Shakespeare borrowed from earlier novellas the devices*

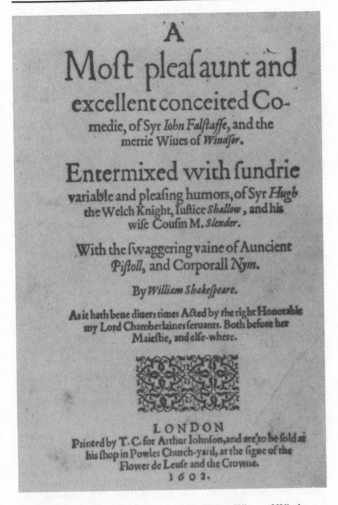

*Title page of the First Quarto of* The Merry Wives of Windsor *(1602).*

*of the buck-basket and the disguised husband learning of his wife's alleged affair. The critic's use of "Mr. Broom" rather than "Mr. Brooke" as the alias of Master Ford indicates that he is referring to the First Folio text rather than that of the First Quarto of 1602.*]

[*The Merry Wives of Windsor*] is not wholly without the Assistance of Novels; witness Mrs. *Ford*'s conveying out Sir *John Falstaff* in the Basket of Foul Clothes; and his declaring all the Intrigue to her Husband, under the Name of Mr. *Broom;* which Story is related in the first Novel of *The Fortunate Deceived, and Unfortunate Lovers.* (p. 459)

> Gerard Langbaine, "William Shakespear," in his
> An Account of the English Dramatick Poets, 1691.
> Reprint by Garland Publishing, Inc., 1973, pp. 453-69.

## JOHN DENNIS    (essay date 1702)

[*Dennis was an English essayist whose most important critical works are* The Usefulness of the Stage *(1698),* The Advancement and Reformation of Modern Poetry *(1701),* The Grounds of Criticism in Poetry *(1704), and* An Essay on the Genius and Writings of Shakespear *(1712). He held that a play's dramatic action must represent the operation of poetic justice, for the stage should serve as a medium of moral and religious instruction. Dennis also wrote many plays, none of which achieved much popular or crit-*

*ical success, including adaptations of Shakespeare's* The Merry Wives of Windsor *(1702) and* Coriolanus *(1720). In the excerpt below, taken from the epistle dedicatory to his version of* The Merry Wives of Windsor, *the critic becomes the earliest essayist to claim that Shakespeare wrote this play at the command of Queen Elizabeth. Dennis further asserts that the dramatist composed it in the space of fourteen days and that the queen was "very well pleas'd at the Representation." He also initiates what was to become the central critical concern for more than two hundred and fifty years by comparing the character of Falstaff in this play with the Falstaff in* 1 *and* 2 Henry IV. *Dennis contends that the figure of the knight in* The Merry Wives of Windsor *is superior to or at least as dramatically effective as his representation in these other plays—a judgment not shared by any subsequent commentator. Finally, the critic maintains that the dramatic structure of this play is flawed by the lack of unity or interdependence among the three main plots and that Shakespeare's inclusion of scenes which seem to bear no relation to other parts of the drama "is enough to obstruct and stifle the Action."*]

When I first communicated the design which I had of altering [*The Merry Wives of Windsor*], I found that I should have two sorts of People to deal with, who would equally endeavour to obstruct my success. The one believed it to be so admirable, that nothing ought to be added to it; the others fancied it to be so despicable, that any ones time would be lost upon it.

That this Comedy was not despicable, I guess'd for several Reasons: First, I knew very well, that it had pleas'd one of the greatest Queens that ever was in the World, great not only for her Wisdom in the Arts of Government, but for her knowledge of Polite Learning, and her nice taste of the Drama, for such a taste we may be sure she had, by the relish which she had of the Ancients. This Comedy was written at her Command, and by her direction, and she was so eager to see it Acted, that she commanded it to be finished in fourteen days; and was afterwards, as Tradition tells us, very well pleas'd at the Representation. In the second place, in the Reign of King *Charles* the Second, when People had an admirable taste of Comedy, all those men of extraordinary parts, who were the Ornaments of that Court; as the late Duke of *Buckingham,* my Lord *Normanby,* my Lord *Dorset,* my late Lord *Rochester,* Sir *Charles Sidley,* Dr *Frazer,* Mr *Savil,* Mr *Buckley,* were in Love with the Beauties of this Comedy. In the third place, I thought that after so long an acquaintance as I had with the best Comick Poets, among the Antients and Moderns, I might depend in some measure upon my own Judgment, and I thought I found here three or four extraordinary Characters, that were exactly drawn, and truly Comical; and that I saw besides in it some as happy touches as ever were in Comedy: Besides I had observed what success the Character of *Falstaffe* had had, in the first part of *Harry* the Fourth. And as the *Falstaffe* in the Merry Wives is certainly superiour to that of the second part of *Harry* the Fourth, so it can hardly be said be to inferior to that of the first.

For in the second part of *Harry* the Fourth, *Falstaffe* does nothing but talk, as indeed he does nothing else in the third and fourth Acts of the first part. Whereas in the Merry Wives, he every where Acts, and that action is more Regular, and more in compass than it is in the first part of *Harry* the Fourth. 'Tis true, what he says in *Harry* the Fourth is admirable; but action at last is the business of the Stage. The Drama is action itself, and it is action alone that is able to excite in any extraordinary manner the curiosity of mankind. What News, is the Question now adays ev'ry moment, but people by that question demand what is done, and not what is said upon the Great Stage of the World. In short, I defie any man to name me a Play that has ever succeeded without some sort of action or another. But I could if I pleased mention more than one, that has succeeded barely by the force of Action, without almost any thing else.

It was for the above-named reasons, that I thought this by no means a despicable Comedy. And it was for the Reasons which follow, that I believed it not so admirable, but that it might receive improvement. First, I knew very well, that in so short a time as this Play was writ, nothing could be done that is perfect. Secondly, I knew very well, that this Comedy had never upon Revivals had any great success, and that particularly when it was Revived in King *Charles* the Seconds time, the only Character that pleased to a height was *Slender* acted by *Wintershal*. And that tho something like this may very well happen to a living Author without any just Cause, yet that there must be reason for it, when it happens to an Author who has a long time been dead, and whose Reputation has been long established. And indeed the *Merry Wives of Windsor,* as it has great Beauties, so it has strange Defects, which tho they past at first for the sake of the Beauties, yet will come to be less endured as the Stage grows more Regular. For there are no less than three Actions in it that are independant of one another, which divide and distract the minds of an Audience, there is more than one insignificant Scene, which has nothing to do with any other part of the Play, which is enough to obstruct and stifle the Action. The Style in some places is stiff and forced and affected, whereas the Dialogue in Comedy ought to be as free as the air. This affectation is particularly remarkable in some part of the first Scene between the Wives, and in all *Ford's* part of the first Scene between him and *Falstaffe.* This is not said in the least with a design to derogate from *Shakespear's* merit, who performed more than any one else could have done in so short a time. In the alteration I have endeavoured to Correct the foresaid Errours. (pp. 279-80)

> *John Dennis, "A Large Account of the Taste in Poetry (1702)," in his* The Critical Works of John Dennis: 1692-1711, *Vol. I, edited by Edward Niles Hooker, The Johns Hopkins University Press, 1939, pp. 279-95.*

## NICHOLAS ROWE   (essay date 1709)

[*Rowe was the editor of the first critical edition of Shakespeare's plays (1709) and the author of the first authoritative Shakespeare biography. He believed that Shakespeare had not read classical Greek and Roman playwrights and was thus unaware of classical rules of dramaturgy. Unlike most other early eighteenth-century critics, Rowe postulated that had Shakespeare been constrained by Neoclassical standards, his plays might not have embodied "that Fire, impetuosity, and even beautiful Extravagance which we admire in Shakespeare." The excerpt below is taken from the preface to his 1709 edition of Shakespeare's works. Rowe is the first commentator to record the tradition that Queen Elizabeth specifically commanded Shakespeare to write a play showing Falstaff "in Love" and that he obliged her by composing* The Merry Wives of Windsor. *Rowe also identifies the process by which Ford is cured "of his unreasonable jealousy" as the fulcrum of the dramatic action. He praises the play as a whole, particularly lauding the variety and opposition of the "Humours" represented in the various characters.*]

Queen *Elizabeth* had several of [Shakespeare's] Plays Acted before her, and without doubt gave him many gracious Marks of her Favour. . . . She was so well pleas'd with that admirable Character of *Falstaff,* in the two Parts of *Henry* the Fourth, that she commanded him to continue it for one Play more, and to shew him in Love. This is said to be the Occasion of his

Writing *The Merry Wives of Windsor.* How well she was obey'd, the Play it self is an admirable Proof. (pp. viii-ix)

[In] *The Merry Wives of Windsor,* [Shakespeare] has made [Falstaff] a Dear-stealer, that he might at the same time remember his *Warwickshire* Prosecutor, under the Name of Justice *Shallow;* he has given him very near the same Coat of Arms which *Dugdale,* in his Antiquities of that County, describes for a Family there, and makes the *Welsh* Parson descant very pleasantly upon 'em. That whole Play is admirable; the Humours are various and well oppos'd; the main Design, which is to cure *Ford* of his unreasonable Jealousie, is extremely well conducted. (pp. xviii-xix)

> *Nicholas Rowe, in his* Some Account of the Life of Mr. William Shakespear, The Augustan Reprint Society, 1948, 1x p.

## [CHARLES GILDON]   (essay date 1710)

[*Gildon was the first critic to write an extended commentary on the entire Shakespearean dramatic canon. Like many other Neoclassicists, he regarded Shakespeare as an imaginative playwright who nevertheless lacked knowledge of the dramatic "rules" necessary for correct writing. In the following excerpt, taken from his "Remarks on the Plays of Shakespear" (1710), Gildon focuses on the structure of* The Merry Wives of Windsor. *He asserts that the "chief* Plot *or* Walk" *concerns the exposure of Falstaff's absurd attempt to woo two women simultaneously and "the under-Plot or Second Walk" centers on the successful deception carried out by Anne Page and Fenton. Gildon praises the play for its taut construction, noting especially the way in which Shakespeare incorporated secondary characters into the two central actions and concluding that, except for the Latin lesson in Act IV, Scene i, "the least incident . . . cannot well be left out without leaving a Gap in the Plot and Connection of the Play."*]

There are two *Walks* in this Play but much better join'd, connected and incorporated, than in any Play, that I remember, either in *Latin* or *English.* The chief *Plot* or *Walk,* is that of exposing the Character of Sir *John Falstaff* for his ridiculous Amours, or Attempt of two Women at once, when by Years and other Defects he cou'd be agreeable to neither, as Mrs. *Page* and the rest tell him on the Discovery in the fifth Act. . . . (pp. 285-86)

[The] *under-Plot* or second Walk is join'd in the Conclusion; for Mrs. *Ann Page,* Mr. *Page's* handsome Daughter is in Love with Mr. *Fenton,* a well-bred Gentleman, and of Quality superior to *Page,* tho' he had been a little wild, and a Companion of the Prince, by which he had something run his Estate aground, and for that Reason rejected by *Page* and his Wife. . . . [But] the young Lady loving *Fenton* deceives both Father and Mother, to obey both which she had promis'd, goes and is marry'd to her Beloved, which Discovery coming on that of Sir *John's* concludes the Play.

All the other Persons of the *Drama* are plainly join'd to and depending on those two *Walks,* and their incorporating them into the Plot seems very well contriv'd. The Quarrel betwixt Sir *John* and Justice *Shallow* occasions Sir *Hugh's* Proposal of a Mediation, and the Match betwixt Mr. *Slender* and Mrs. *Anne Page.* This brings Mr. *Page* and Sir *John* out of Mr. *Page's* House, where the Motion is made, and approv'd, and all invited in to Dinner, where all the Principal Characters of both Walks are brought acquainted with each other. The Comical Duel, is likewise to Effect the *Plot;* for Sir *Hugh* sends to the Doctor's House-keeper to assist his Friend *Slender* in his Amour she being intimately acquainted with Mother and

Daughter. This Messenger is intercepted by the Doctor, on which he sends the Priest a Challenge; which produces the Comical Scene of both their Passions, and Preparations for Fighting. In short the least Incident of the Play, except Mrs. *Pages* and her Son's Confabulation with Sir *Hugh* his Master, cannot well be left out without leaving a Gap in the Plot and Connection of the Play.

I Confess, that the Unities of Time, Place, and Action are not exactly observ'd according to the Rule and Practice of the *Antients*, yet as they are now manag'd among us; they may well pass. The Time is not above two Days and a half at most; the Place *Windsor*, and the Adjacent Fields and Places. The Action is visibly double, but that it is in all the Comedies of *Terence*.

The first Act shows all the principal Characters except the two *Fords;* prepares all the Business of the Play, and enters a little into the Action, in the two Letters sent by Sir *John*, and the Match Propos'd by Sir *Hugh*, and the Doctors Challenge to the Welsh Levite. So that it is an exact *Protasis* or *Prologue*. The *Episode* begins with the second Act, and carries all on to the *fifth;* where the *Exode* is in the Discovery and punishment of the Old Letcher; and the disappointment of a forc'd Match in *Fenton*'s Marrying Mrs. *Anne Page*. Mrs. *Fords* Resentment of Sir *Johns* Letter puts her and Mrs. *Page* on the Revenge of the Affront, and that Revenge furnishes the Intrigue or Episodical Turns of the Play.

The Information of *Pistol* and *Nim* prepares, and rouses *Ford*'s Jealousie, admirably and with a great deal of Art and Nature. Nor can any thing be more ridiculous, and entertaining, than the Scenes betwixt *Ford* under the Name of *Broom* and Sir *John*.

Upon the whole I think it is pretty plain, that nothing can be more agreeable to *Aristotles* definition of *Comedy;* for he says 'tis an Imitation of the *Worst Sort*, and that in *Ridicule;* it having thus all the Parts both of Quality and Quantity.

But to make the Parts of Quality more plain it wou'd be necessary to speak of the Humours; yet that wou'd be too tedious, as well, as unnecessary, being so many and yet so various, and so plainly distinguish'd from each other, that there is no need to point out Particulars. I shall only give you what Mr. *Dryden* says of the Character of *Falstaff* in his Essay on Dramatic Poetry [see excerpt above, 1668].—Falstaff *is the best of Comic Characters—there are* (says he) *many Men resembling him—old, fat, merry, cowardly, drunken, amorous, vain and lying:* and the Duke of *Buckingham* confirms it in this Verse

> *But* Falstaff *seems inimitable yet.*

*Fords*, is an excellent Character of a Politic, cautious, jealous Coxcomb; and all his Endeavours at the cautious and cunning Management of the Discovery of his Doubts and Fears, involves him the more, and makes him the more ridiculous; for the Conferences he has with Sir *John*, confirm him in his Suspicions, and his Disappointments expose his Folly.

The *Fairys* in the fifth Act makes a Handsome Complement to the Queen, in her Palace of *Windsor*, who had oblig'd him to write a Play of Sir *John Falstaff* in Love, and which I am very well assured he perform'd in a Fortnight; a prodigious Thing, when all is so well contriv'd, and carry'd on without the least Confusion. (pp. 288-91)

[Charles Gildon], "Remarks on the Plays of Shake-spear," in The Works of Mr. William Shakespear,

Vol. 7, 1710. Reprint by AMS Press, Inc., 1967, pp. 285-91.

### JOHN POTTER   (essay date 1772)

[Potter was an English miscellaneous writer whose Shakespearean criticism was originally published as a series of theatrical reviews in divers newspapers and subsequently reissued in his The Theatrical Review; or, New Companion to the Playhouse (1772). In the excerpt below from that work, the critic praises The Merry Wives of Windsor, calling it "the most perfect of all [Shakespeare's] Dramatic Pieces in the Comic way." He particularly notes its highly finished characters, skillfully constructed plots, and wit suited to virtue. Potter is also the first commentator to laud the merry wives themselves as entertaining, spirited characters.]

[The Merry Wives of Windsor] is generally allowed to be the most perfect of all [Shakespeare's] Dramatic Pieces in the Comic way. Even *Dryden*, who was not fond of praising other Writers, acknowledges it to be exactly formed [see excerpt above, 1679]. And surely nothing can be a more convincing proof of the force of this great Writer's Genius, or how capable he was of executing any hint given him, than the Piece now before us? Which is as perfect in its kind as any thing to be met with in our own or any other Language. This will appear the more extraordinary if we consider that it was written before a taste for Regularity was established in this Nation. A more perfect set of high-finished Characters was never exhibited in any Play. The double Plot is admirably contrived, for the under Plot is not only finely connected with the principal one and employs the same persons, but it occupies the intervals of the main action and is brought to a conclusion at the same time; which ought always to be the case, though it has been neglected by many of our best Dramatic Writers.—We have here a proof that Wit and Sprightliness are better suited to a virtuous than a vicious Character, and nothing can be more highly entertaining than the conduct of Mrs. *Ford* and Mrs. *Page*, two Ladies not more remarkable for mirth and spirit, than for the strictest purity of manners. (pp. 442-43)

John Potter, in an extract from Shakespeare, the Critical Heritage: 1765-1774, Vol. 5, edited by Brian Vickers, Routledge & Kegan Paul, 1979, pp. 442-43.

### SAMUEL JOHNSON   (essay date 1773)

[Johnson has long held an important place in the history of Shakespearean criticism. He is considered the foremost representative of modern English Neoclassicism and is credited by some literary historians with freeing Shakespeare from the strictures of the three unities valued by strict Neoclassicists: that dramas should have a single setting, take place in less than twenty-four hours, and have a causally connected plot. More recent scholars portray him as a critic who was able to synthesize existing critical theory rather than as an innovative theoretician. Johnson was a master of Augustan prose style and a personality who dominated the literary world of his epoch. In the following excerpt, taken from an edition of The Plays of William Shakespeare (1773) which he edited with George Steevens, Johnson is the first to argue that Queen Elizabeth's command to see Falstaff in love was impossible to fulfill, for "Falstaff could not love, but by ceasing to be Falstaff," and he notes that throughout The Merry Wives of Windsor the knight is motivated not by love but by avarice. Further, he judges the Falstaff of this play as less entertaining than that of 1 and 2 Henry IV and generally faults the progress of the dramatic action. But Johnson also remarks on Shakespeare's masterful use of language in The Merry Wives of Windsor and concludes that its

*dramatic powers are so great that most readers and audiences
"think it too soon at an end."*]

Of [*The Merry Wives of Windsor*] there is a tradition preserved
by Mr. Rowe, that it was written at the command of Queen
Elizabeth, who was so delighted with the character of Falstaff,
that she wished it to be diffused through more plays [see excerpt
above, 1709]; but suspecting that it might pall by continued
uniformity, directed the poet to diversify his manner, by shewing him in love. No task is harder than that of writing to the
ideas of another. Shakespeare knew what the queen, if the
story be true, seems not to have known, that by any real passion
of tenderness, the selfish craft, the careless jollity, and the lazy
luxury of Falstaff must have suffered so much abatement, that
little of his former cast would have remained. Falstaff could
not love, but by ceasing to be Falstaff. He could only counterfeit love, and his professions could be prompted, not by the
hope of pleasure, but of money. Thus the poet approached as
near as he could to the work enjoined him; yet having perhaps
in the former plays completed his own idea, seems not to have
been able to give Falstaff all his former power of entertainment.

This comedy is remarkable for the variety and number of the
personages, who exhibit more characters appropriated and dis-
criminated, than perhaps can be found in any other play.

Whether Shakespeare was the first that produced upon the
English stage the effect of language distorted and depraved by
provincial or foreign pronunciation, I cannot certainly decide.
This mode of forming ridiculous characters can confer praise
only on him, who originally discovered it, for it requires not
much of either wit or judgment: its success must be derived
almost wholly from the player, but its power in a skilful mouth,
even he that despises it, is unable to resist.

The conduct of this drama is deficient; the action begins and
ends often before the conclusion, and the different parts might
change places without inconvenience; but its general power,
that power by which all works of genius shall finally be tried,
is such, that perhaps it never yet had reader or spectator, who
did not think it too soon at an end. (p. 341)

> Samuel Johnson, "Notes on Shakespeare's Plays:
> 'The Merry Wives of Windsor'," in his The Yale
> Edition of the Works of Samuel Johnson: Johnson
> on Shakespeare, Vol. VII, edited by Arthur Sherbo,
> Yale University Press, 1968, pp. 327-41.

## AUGUST WILHELM SCHLEGEL (essay date 1811)

[*A prominent German Romantic critic, Schlegel holds a key place
in the history of Shakespeare's reputation in European criticism.
His translations of thirteen of the plays are still considered the
best German editions of Shakespeare. Schlegel was also a leading
spokesman for the Romantic movement, which permanently overthrew the Neoclassical contention that Shakespeare was a child
of nature whose plays lacked artistic form. In the excerpt below
from his* Lectures on Dramatic Art and Literature *(1811), Schlegel
comments on the tradition that Queen Elizabeth commanded
Shakespeare to compose a play showing Falstaff in love. Judging
that the knight could not conceivably be portrayed as being in
love, but only as simulating that emotion, the critic argues that
the most significant improbability in* The Merry Wives of Windsor
*is that Falstaff "can believe himself qualified to inspire a pas-
sion." Schlegel further claims that although the repeated dupings
of the knight give us a "less favorable opinion of his shrewdness"
than do* 1 and 2 Henry IV, *the scenes featuring the results of
these deceptions are "droll beyond all description." Finally, he
contends that the play approaches the "species of pure Comedy"*

*more than any other of Shakespeare's plays, and he praises the
final scene not only for its depiction of the ultimate affront to
Falstaff, but also for the way in which the intrigue of Anne Page
and Fenton is concluded "in a most ingenious manner."*]

[*The Merry Wives of Windsor*] is said to have been composed
by Shakspeare, in compliance with the request of Queen Elizabeth, who admired the character of Falstaff, and wished to
see him exhibited once more, and in love [see excerpt above
by Nicholas Rowe, 1709]. In love, properly speaking, Falstaff
could not be; but for other purposes he could pretend to be so,
and at all events imagine that he was the object of love. In the
present piece accordingly he pays his court, as a favoured
Knight, to two married ladies, who lay their heads together
and agree to listen apparently to his addresses, for the sake of
making him the butt of their just ridicule. The whole plan of
the intrigue is therefore derived from the ordinary circle of
Comedy, but yet richly and artificially interwoven with another
love affair. The circumstance which has been so much admired
in Molière's *School of Women* [1662], that a jealous individual
should be made the constant confidant of his rival's progress,
had previously been introduced into [*The Merry Wives of Windsor*], and certainly with much more probability. I would not,
however, be understood as maintaining that it was the original
invention of Shakspeare: it is one of those circumstances which
must almost be considered as part of the common stock of
Comedy, and everything depends on the delicacy and humour
with which it is used. That Falstaff should fall so repeatedly
into the snare gives us a less favourable opinion of his shrewdness than [*1 and 2 Henry IV*] had led us to form; still it will
not be thought improbable, if once we admit the probability
of the first infatuation on which the whole piece is founded,
namely, that he can believe himself qualified to inspire a passion. This leads him, notwithstanding his age, his corpulency,
and his dislike of personal inconveniences and dangers, to
venture on an enterprise which requires the boldness and activity of youth; and the situations occasioned by this infatuation
are droll beyond all description. Of all Shakspeare's pieces,
this approaches the nearest to the species of pure Comedy: it
is exclusively confined to the English manners of the day, and
to the domestic relations; the characters are almost all comic,
and the dialogue, with the exception of a couple of short love
scenes, is written in prose. But we see that it was a point of
principle with Shakspeare to make none of his compositions a
mere imitation of the prosaic world, and to strip them of all
poetical decoration: accordingly he has elevated the conclusion
of the comedy by a wonderful intermixture, which suited the
place where it was probably first represented. A popular superstition is made the means of a fanciful mystification of
Falstaff; disguised as the Ghost of a Hunter who, with ragged
horns, wanders about in the woods of Windsor, he is to wait
for his frolicsome mistress; in this plight he is surprised by a
chorus of boys and girls disguised like fairies, who, agreeably
to the popular belief, are holding their midnight dances, and
who sing a merry song as they pinch and torture him. This is
the last affront put upon poor Falstaff; and with this contrivance the conclusion of the second love affair is made in a most
ingenious manner to depend. (pp. 427-28)

> August Wilhelm Schlegel, "Criticisms on Shake-
> speare's Historical Dramas," in his A Course of
> Lectures on Dramatic Art and Literature, edited by
> A. J. W. Morrison, translated by John Black, revised
> edition, 1846. Reprint by AMS Press, Inc., 1965,
> pp. 414-45.

## WILLIAM HAZLITT   (essay date 1817)

[*Hazlitt is considered a leading Shakespearean critic of the English Romantic movement. A prolific essayist and critic on a wide range of subjects, Hazlitt remarked in the preface to his* Characters of Shakespear's Plays, *first published in 1817, that he was inspired by the German critic August Wilhelm Schlegel and was determined to supplant what he considered the pernicious influence of Samuel Johnson's Shakespearean criticism. Hazlitt's commentary is typically Romantic in its emphasis on character studies, and his interpretations of Shakespeare are frequently descriptive, rather than analytical. In the following excerpt, taken from the work cited above, Hazlitt asserts that in* The Merry Wives of Windsor *Falstaff's "wit and eloquence have left him"; like most critics, he rates the knight in this play inferior to the figure of Falstaff in* 1 *and* 2 Henry IV. *Similarly, the critic maintains that Nym, Bardolph, Pistol, and Shallow are pale representations of their originals in* 1 *and* 2 Henry IV, *but he generally praises the characterization of the other dramatic figures. Hazlitt is the first commentator to remark on Shakespeare's depiction of Slender, whom he describes as "a very potent piece of imbecility" and "the only first-rate character in the play."*]

*The Merry Wives of Windsor* is no doubt a very amusing play, with a great deal of humour, character, and nature in it: but we should have liked it much better, if any one else had been the hero of it, instead of Falstaff. We could have been contented

*Act III. Scene i. Slender, Shallow, Evans, Page, Caius, and Host. Frontispiece to the Rowe edition (1709). By permission of the Folger Shakespeare Library.*

if Shakespear had not been "commanded to shew the knight in love." Wits and philosophers, for the most part, do not shine in that character; and Sir John himself, by no means, comes off with flying colours. Many people complain of the degradation and insults to which Don Quixote is so frequently exposed in his various adventures. But what are the unconscious indignities which he suffers compared with the sensible mortifications which Falstaff is made to bring upon himself? What are the blows and buffetings which the Don receives from the staves of the Yanguesian carriers or from Sancho Panza's more hard-hearted hands, compared with the contamination of the buck-basket, the disguise of the fat woman of Brentford, and the horns of Herne the hunter, which are discovered on Sir John's head? In reading the play, we indeed wish him well through all these discomfitures, but it would have been as well if he had not got into them. Falstaff in the *Merry Wives of Windsor* is not the man he was in the two parts of *Henry IV.* His wit and eloquence have left him. Instead of making a butt of others, he is made a butt of by them. Neither is there a single particle of love in him to excuse his follies: he is merely a designing, bare-faced knave, and an unsuccessful one. The scene with Ford as Master Brook, and that with Simple, Slender's man, who comes to ask after the Wise Woman, are almost the only ones in which his old intellectual ascendancy appears. He is like a person recalled to the stage to perform an unaccustomed and ungracious part; and in which we perceive only "some faint sparks of those flashes of merriment, that were wont to set the hearers in a roar" [*Hamlet,* V. i. 190-91]. But the single scene with Doll Tearsheet, or Mrs. Quickly's account of his desiring "to eat some of housewife Keach's prawns," and telling her "to be no more so familiarity with such people" [*2 Henry IV,* II. i. 99-100], is worth the whole of the *Merry Wives of Windsor* put together. Ford's jealousy, which is the main spring of the comic incidents, is certainly very well managed. Page, on the contrary, appears to be somewhat uxorious in his disposition; and we have pretty plain indications of the effect of the characters of the husbands on the different degrees of fidelity in their wives. Mrs. Quickly makes a very lively go-between, both between Falstaff and his Dulcineas, and Anne Page and her lovers, and seems in the latter case so intent on her own interest as totally to overlook the intentions of her employers. Her master, Dr. Caius, the Frenchman, and her fellow-servant Jack Rugby, are very completely described. This last-mentioned person is rather quaintly commended by Mrs. Quickly as "an honest, willing, kind fellow, as ever servant shall come in house withal, and I warrant you, no tell-tale, nor no breed-bate; his worst fault is, that he is given to prayer; he is something peevish that way; but nobody but has his fault." The Welch parson, Sir Hugh Evans . . . is an excellent character in all respects. He is as respectable as he is laughable. He has "very good discretions, and very odd humours" [I. i. 44]. The duel-scene with Caius gives him an opportunity to shew his "cholers and his tremblings of mind" [III. i. 11-12], his valour and his melancholy, in an irresistible manner. In the dialogue, which at his mother's request he holds with his pupil, William Page, to shew his progress in learning, it is hard to say whether the simplicity of the master or the scholar is the greatest. Nym, Bardolph, and Pistol, are but the shadows of what they were; and Justice Shallow himself has little of his consequence left. But his cousin, Slender, makes up for the deficiency. He is a very potent piece of imbecility. In him the pretensions of the worthy Gloucestershire family are well kept up, and immortalised. He and his friend Sackerson and his book of songs and his love of Anne Page and his having nothing to say to her can never be forgotten. It is the only first-rate character in the play: but it is in that class. Shakespear is the only writer who was as great in describing weakness as strength. (pp. 250-52)

William Hazlitt, " 'The Merry Wives of Windsor'," in his Characters of Shakespear's Plays, 1817. Reprint by E. P. Dutton & Co., 1906, pp. 250-52.

## HERMANN ULRICI (essay date 1839)

[*A German scholar, Ulrici was a professor of philosophy and the author of works on Greek poetry and Shakespeare. The following excerpt is from an English translation of his* Über Shakespeares dramatische Kunst, und sein Verhältniss zu Calderon und Göthe, *a work first published in 1839. This study exemplifies the "philosophical criticism" developed in Germany during the nineteenth century. The immediate sources for Ulrici's critical approach appear to be August Wilhelm Schlegel's conception of the play as an organic, interconnected whole and Georg Wilhelm Friedrich Hegel's view of drama as an embodiment of the conflict of historical forces and ideas. Unlike his fellow German Shakespearean critic G. G. Gervinus, Ulrici sought to develop a specifically Christian aesthetics, but one which, as he carefully points out in the introduction to the work mentioned above, in no way intrudes on "that unity of idea, which preeminently constitutes a work of art a living creation in the world of beauty." In his commentary below, Ulrici is the first critic to demonstrate the significance of the satirical elements in* The Merry Wives of Windsor. *Stating that the object of the play "is not so much the exhibition of human life from its comic aspect, as a satirical exhibition of the comic itself," he contends that Falstaff, as the embodiment of the comic principle, is the central focus of Shakespeare's satire; but he also notes that other characters in the play are similarly "cheated and laughed at in the very point* where, according to their own *conceit, they are strongest and most infallible." The difference between Falstaff and the others, Ulrici argues, is that the knight is the only one who recognizes and acknowledges his frailties and weaknesses. Ulrici is also the earliest critic to stress the importance of the repeated distinctions made in the play "between the knightly and the burgher classes," asserting that these serve to emphasize Shakespeare's ridicule of the remnants of the chivalric convention that had survived into the Elizabethan age.*]

[It] is obvious that [Falstaff] could never be, as his royal admirer wished to see him—in love. The very wish is a satire, since it supposes as real what his very nature renders radically impossible. It reveals at once the hollowness of his whole being. Deep affection of any kind soever must in Falstaff's sight have been a mere mockery, and consequently the satirical element is by no means put aside, if, as is actually the case, the love of the old sinner be merely put on, and a mere pretext to cover his designs on the flesh-pots of the worthy citizens, whose wives he is courting. For it is impossible to suppose for a moment, that Falstaff, so conscious as he is of his own figure and personality, could ever hope to awaken reciprocal affection, or to succeed with any woman. He was no longer Falstaff if he could entertain such an idea for an instant; his wit and acuteness must have left him [see excerpt above by William Hazlitt, 1817], and he was a changed character from what he appeared in *Henry the Fourth*. As, then, the poet has taken for the ground-work of his drama this arbitrary and impossible hypothesis, he has abandoned the objectivity of perception and representation, and has adopted a purely subjective tendency, which, in so far as ridicule is its object, terminates in satire.

To portray a comic character—the pure creation of the poet's fancy—without sacrificing aught of its ideal personality and general significance, and yet with such vitality and perfect verisimilitude that it should be fitted to become the subject of a satirical comedy, is an achievement in which no genius less than Shakspeare could ever have succeeded. For poetry, when it exhibits its own artistic creations, and not real characters, in the mirror of satire, necessarily sinks into mere travestie whenever these poetical personages are unable to put in any claim to the truth of reality. To pass, too, from the objectivity of the original representation into the subjective tendency of satire, must inevitably disturb the poetic effect wherever the satire is not skilfully concealed. All turns upon this; and this Shakspeare has fully effected. For the ridicule is derived from the reflection, that Falstaff is wholly incapable of love, whether real or pretended, which, however, exists solely in the spectators' minds, without being ever presented objectively in the drama itself. And although the knight is somewhat roughly handled, and his evil designs and practices openly put to shame and confusion, he nevertheless comes off the best of all the dramatic personages. For in all of them,—the jealous Ford, the empty Shallow, the lank silly Slender, the dull unspiritual Welsh Parson, the vain and absurd French Doctor, the foolish Page, and his no less foolish wife, who deceive each other in the hope of carrying their own plans of forcing their daughter into an unnatural marriage, and are both at last deceived as easily as the babbling host is cheated out of his horses,—in all these adversaries Falstaff has to do with less perversity and folly no doubt, but yet with less also of shrewdness and self-knowledge. All alike are rendered ridiculous by the disgraceful failure of their own designs; all participate in the same fate of human frailty which overtakes Falstaff; but their fall is the heavier, because they are not so conscious of their own weakness as he is. It could not but be so, for Falstaff's character is, as it were, the concentration and living presence of the comic view; and however absurd, therefore, he may be made to look, yet as the embodied principle of Comedy he necessarily places all the others in a still more ridiculous light.

To comprise in a few words the ground-idea of this remarkable comedy: its object is not so much the exhibition of human life from its comic aspect, as a satirical exhibition of the comic itself, in order to ridicule the comic by the means of comedy. And this it accomplishes by reflection within itself, by which it recognises its own comic nature, and makes itself the mockery which others make of it. . . . [The] *Merry Wives of Windsor* becomes also a satire on the wisdom of man, who in spite of his boasted clearness, through the height of sin and wickedness to which he is subject in this life, falls into error and mistake—unconsciously into unconsciousness.

But even when viewed from another aspect, the present piece appears equally of a satirical cast. I think Shakspeare intended it as a fine and delicate ridicule of chivalry generally, but especially of the particular form it had assumed in his own day. . . . [*The Merry Wives of Windsor*] bears throughout a decided stamp of Shakespeare's own age; but for Page's incidental mention of Prince Henry, we could not fail to take its whole physiognomy for that which England bore under the virgin Queen, for whose special gratification the piece was written. Further, it is equally impossible to misunderstand the stress which is laid upon the distinction between the knightly and the burgher classes. Falstaff prides himself on his knighthood; he thinks he is doing an honour to the citizens by condescending to seduce their wives, and by it accounts for the ease with which he gains admission to their houses. Justice Shallow, and his cousin Slender too, with amusing vanity, cannot sufficiently publish the fact that they too possess a scrap of knighthood; and they appear in this respect as pendants to Falstaff. The trait too of the host being cheated of his horses by the noble Germans, who pretend to be going to court, and the laughable duel between the parson and the doctor, are not without their deep meaning. The burgher class takes an ill revenge on Falstaff's chivalry, and knighthood looks no where more pitiable than among the foul linen in the buck-basket, or when soundly beaten as the old woman of Brainford, or punished and tortured to death as the spectre of the wood. In short, we cannot fail to see in these three traits so many metaphorical lashes of satire on the chivalry of his day.

The preceding remarks sufficiently evince, that the leading idea is to be found, variously modified, in the other characters, and also in the chief springs of the action. With Falstaff, in short, all the others are cheated and laughed at *in the very point* where, according to their own *conceit,* they are strongest and most infallible: Justice Shallow in his pride of place and nobility; young Slender in his knighthood and loveableness; Mr. and Mrs. Page in their wise plans for their daughter; Ford in his jealous rule of his wife and house; the host in his boasted prudence and cunning; and lastly, the parson and the doctor, in their prejudice and testiness. The whole piece is nothing but mutual banter and over-reaching. Fundamentally, all are the laughing-stocks of chance and their own weaknesses; their plans and designs either come to nothing of themselves, or else are frustrated by hazard and intrigue, and at last, against their will and without their knowledge, the rational and right are brought about. Lastly, the reasons which induced Shakspeare to give so fantastic a termination to a piece which is so obviously a comedy of intrigue—a point which has hitherto remained unexplained—appear to me to be drawn from the subordinate satirical view, and partly from the agreement of such a close with the fundamental idea, so far as the ridicule of comedy, even in its fantastic form, preys on itself. For it is clear that the fantastic, in such sorry imitation as Falstaff and the Welsh parson could give of it, could not but make itself ridiculous. (pp. 329-33)

> *Hermann Ulrici, "Criticisms of Shakspeare's Dramas: 'Merry Wives of Windsor'—'Troilus and Cressida'," in his* Shakspeare's Dramatic Art: And His Relation to Calderon and Goethe, *translated by Rev. A. J. W. Morrison, Chapman, Brothers, 1846, pp. 323-41.*

## HARTLEY COLERIDGE   (essay date 1849?)

[*Hartley Coleridge, the eldest son of Samuel Taylor Coleridge, was a minor English poet and essayist. The following excerpt is taken from a collection of his poems, criticism, and marginal notations assembled by his brother Derwent after Hartley's death in 1849 and published as* Essays and Marginalia *(1851). Although he judges* The Merry Wives of Windsor *"exceedingly diverting," Coleridge shares the view of several earlier critics that Falstaff could not be portrayed as being in love. In fact, he contends, Queen Elizabeth's wish to see Falstaff in the role of lover "proves her to have been, as she was, a gross-minded old baggage." Coleridge is the first commentator to assert that the nature of Ford's jealousy is inappropriately serious for a comic drama.*]

This play was a task. . . . That Queen Bess should have desired to see Falstaff making love proves her to have been, as she was, a gross-minded old baggage. Shakspeare has evaded the difficulty with great skill. He knew that Falstaff could not be in love; and has mixed but a little, a very little *pruritus* [sexual excitement] with his fortune-hunting courtship. But the Falstaff of the *Merry Wives* is not the Falstaff of *Henry the Fourth*. It is a big-bellied impostor, assuming his name and style, or at

best it is Falstaff in dotage. The Mrs. Quickly of Windsor is not mine Hostess of the Boar's Head; but she is a very pleasant, busy, good-natured, unprincipled old woman, whom it is impossible to be angry with. Shallow should not have left his seat in Gloucestershire and his magisterial duties. Ford's jealousy is of too serious a complexion for the rest of the play. The merry wives are a delightful pair. Methinks I see them, with their comely middle-aged visages, their dainty white ruffs and toys, their half witchlike conic hats, their full farthingales, their neat though not over-slim waists, their housewifely keys, their girdles, their sly laughing looks, their apple-red cheeks, their brows, the lines whereon look more like the work of mirth than years. And sweet Anne Page—she is a pretty little creature whom one would like to take on one's knee. And poor Slender, how pathetically he fancies himself into love; how tearfully laughable he is in his disappointment, and how painfully ludicrous in his punctilio; how delightful in his valour! How finely he sets forth his achievement to pretty Anne!—"I have seen Sackerson loose" [I. i. 294-95]. Othello could not brag more amorously. Parson Hugh is a noble Cambro-Briton, but Doctor Caius is rather so-so. Mine Host of the Garter is evidently a portrait. The plot is rather farcical; but no matter, it is exceedingly diverting. (pp. 133-34)

> *Hartley Coleridge, "Notes on Shakspeare," in his* Essays and Marginalia, Vol. II, *edited by Derwent Coleridge, Edward Moxon, 1851, pp. 129-200.*

## G. G. GERVINUS   (essay date 1849-50)

[*One of the most widely read Shakespearean critics of the latter half of the nineteenth century, the German critic Gervinus was praised by such eminent contemporaries as Edward Dowden, F. J. Furnivall, and James Russell Lowell; however, he is little known in the English-speaking world today. Like his predecessor Hermann Ulrici, Gervinus wrote in the tradition of the "philosophical criticism" developed in Germany in the mid-nineteenth century. Under the influence of August Wilhelm Schlegel's literary theory and Georg Wilhelm Friedrich Hegel's philosophy, such German critics as Gervinus tended to focus their analyses around a search for the literary work's organic unity and ethical import. Gervinus believed that Shakespeare's works contained a rational ethical system independent of any religion—in contrast to Ulrici, for whom Shakespeare's morality was basically Christian. In the following excerpt from his* Shakespeare Commentaries, *originally published in German in 1849-50, Gervinus is the first to assert that* The Merry Wives of Windsor *provides the audience with ethical instruction, together with its "merry pleasantry." Noting that in* 1 *and* 2 Henry IV *the surpassing wit of Falstaff makes him attractive despite his morally reprehensible behavior, the critic argues that in this play Shakespeare "wished to remove him entirely from our esteem," accomplishing this by divesting him of intellectual acuity so that we can no longer overlook his intrinsic vanity and egotism. Gervinus contends that other characters in the play who seek to achieve their goals by devious rather than by simple and open means similarly have their schemes defeated, and he holds that the various intrigues in* The Merry Wives of Windsor *all demonstrate this ethical proposition: "Unclouded honest sense is always superior to base passion."*]

In the year 1702 the *Merry Wives of Windsor*, which was much liked in Charles II.'s time, was remodelled by John Dennis into a piece entitled 'the Comical Gallant.' In his dedication he says that Shakespeare's play was written at the desire of Queen Elizabeth, and in the short time indeed of fourteen days [see excerpt above, 1702]. Rowe added to this tradition the circumstance that her desire had been to see Falstaff in love [see excerpt above, 1709]. This tradition has in it something so credible that even the severest of the English critics do not venture to disregard it. It may be alleged in *favour* of its correctness that among all the plays of Shakespeare's riper period this is by far the least important. It is designed without any deeper background, without any merit of idea, without pathetic elevation, and without serious passages; it is almost entirely written in prose; it is the only piece of the poet's in which the plot decidedly outweighs the characterisation, the only one which moves in the stratum of plain, common, and homely society. It may be alleged *against* the tradition that the piece appears to be written with the stated object of being a counterpart to *Henry V.*, and in evident continuation of the contrast in the moral development of Falstaff and Henry, which the poet had already begun in the second part of *Henry IV.* (pp. 377-78)

[In the second part of *Henry IV.*] Shakespeare separated the prince and Falstaff outwardly, and led them inwardly by different paths. He intended again to bring forward Falstaff in *Henry V.*, but . . . he changed his mind. He made the prince in *Henry V.* accomplish for himself his royal campaign and his noble conquest of love, and then to this heroic play he placed in opposition one of a simple homely character, in which Falstaff follows out his old purse-stealing habits in a new form of wooing. He saw himself, however, obliged to place this adventure of Falstaff's previous to Henry's accession to the throne and Falstaff's disgrace, because he must have felt that after this glaring fall, in all the incorrigibleness and decrepitude of his paralytic age, Falstaff must necessarily have been ruined mentally and physically. But he exhibited him as separated from the prince, removed from the ennobling presence of that witty society, wholly abandoned to himself, and sinking to a greater degree than Henry rose; at last even, hardly conceivable as it may appear, utterly fallen in his own estimation. If it is possible to point out this ever increasing decline in Falstaff just as plainly as the growing greatness of Henry, there can be no doubt that this piece was written as a counterpart to *Henry V.*, whether any inducement on the part of the queen may have been furnished or not.

Henry as prince and king, with the most splendid objects for his ambition before him, performed the highest actions of renunciation and self-privation which human power can win from the soul, and his finest deeds and the glory of them he cast from himself upon others, upon visible mortals or invisible powers. Falstaff we have seen throughout turning to the lowest objects of covetousness and concupiscence. His mental power was subordinate to his physical impulses and necessities, every passion was in their service; in [*The Merry Wives of Windsor*] even that of love, which in all instances is enlivened by some spiritual spark, but by him is only feigned and pretended for a material purpose. His perfect selfishness referred the whole world and all creatures in it to himself alone, and to the advantage he could draw from them; it appropriated everything to itself, according to his theory of the natural right of animals, without a sense of the rights and possessions of others; it endeavoured to place the basest qualities in a good light, and to stamp cowardice as heroic courage. This egotism had its serious and harmful side, which exhibited Falstaff as the enemy and destroyer of society; it had also its laughable side, which placed him in the first rank of what they call good companions. Both sides of this self-love, the harmful and the ridiculous, we find united in our present play in those wooings and in that kind of love of which alone he was susceptible. He falls in with two homely simple citizens' wives in Windsor. They afford him a free kind of conversation and a merry humour; this is

sufficient for him to look upon them as of the same metal as the women of his former intercourse. He wooes them in disbelief of their morality, and, when he appears to succeed, he believes in his own attractiveness. He aims not at love; he thinks only on artifices for improving his condition. Both the wives keep the keys of the rich gold-coffers of their husbands; only for this reason does he admire women thus far from young, one of whom has already a marriageable daughter; he intends to make them his 'East and West Indies, and to trade to them both' [I. iii. 71-2]. He believes not in honesty; he looks down contemptuously with his knightly pride on the burgher husbands; they are dace of another kind, which the pike endeavours to snap at in a new manner. It is even too dishonourable for Pistol and Nym to play the pander for so ridiculous a wooer; they had before been always *subject* to Falstaff's honour and conscience, but now he is more coarse in feeling than they, and only when these 'baboons' and rogues venture to rebuke him with their *own* reputation are his feelings roused. 'It is as much as he can do,' he says to Pistol, 'to keep the terms of his honour precise.' He himself sometimes, 'hiding his honour in his necessity, is fain to shuffle and to lurch,' and yet Pistol will 'ensconce his rags' and coarseness under the shelter of his honour against him. We must now observe how he keeps the terms of his honour precise in the transaction which he is contriving. He so far cleverly begins it, that he comes forward to the honest burghers' wives at least in an honest tone; he is not inclined for fulsome flattery; he conceals this behind a masculine nature which does not admit of it. But at the same time he is so careless in his gentlemanliness, that he sends the same letter to both the women. The success which it meets with transports him, but it also deprives him of his senses; his sudden self-complacency makes him quite blind. After his vanity has led him to the monstrous idea of considering himself an object of love, nothing is impossible to him. He accepts all the gross flatteries of Master Brook as pure coin; he does not suffer himself to become suspicious by the strangest commission; he thinks the woman in love with him, though he hears that she is inflexibly honourable towards an ordinary well-grown man. Vanity and pride make him imprudently candid to this stranger, who, it is true, pays him. He has retained his well-known shamelessness which belongs to this candour, but at the same time his judgment forsakes him. Twice he allows himself in the grossest manner to be cheated, bathed, and beaten, without being in the least more heedful of a third trap laid for him; although he said, after the first trick, that if they served him such another, he would have his 'brains taken out and buttered and given to a dog' [III. iv. 7-8]. The wanton women have conspired against him, his despised servants also, and his page is bribed; though many unequal powers are in arms against him, he surrenders himself to the very weakest, when he has once stumbled over his self-love. Confusion, blows, vapour-baths, and cold baths, loss of money, pinches and burnings, the horns which he had designed for others— all return upon his own head; the consciousness of his guilt, the sudden fascination of his judgment, drive him at the last adventure to believe in and to fear even fairies; he mistakes even the voice of the parson Evans, and thinks him a Welsh fairy! When all is at length unriddled to him, the man who never could attain to a knowledge of himself is ashamed even to self-contempt. When he is thus degraded before himself and in his own judgment, Shakespeare might have hoped to direct the judgment of his spectators with respect to this character more in accordance with his own view. But morally this would have been impossible. On this point he had long ago so sunk that he would not have been perplexed even by the perception that it was just honesty and integrity which had outwitted him. That they all at length assail him, and with the most shocking expressions call him intolerable, old, cold, slanderous, wicked, and given to fornication, all this might not have made him think worse of himself. But on the side of his wit, an impression could still be made upon him. This was the gift by which he felt himself superior to blockheads and equal with the clever. On this very point, which corrupted our own judgment, our judgment was to be rectified; and while the poet lowered him in our estimation in this last recommendatory point, he gave us the surest token that he wished to remove him entirely from our esteem. And thus is it with Falstaff in this play. All become thoroughly weary of him, and when he has lost his last attraction they cast him away. He had thought neither caution nor wit necessary to meet the burghers' honesty and ignorance, and he is bamboozled by both. He is obliged to acknowledge himself that 'wit may be made a Jack-a-Lent, when 'tis upon ill employment' [V. v. 126-28]; the crafty wit is made 'an ox and an ass,' the robber is fleeced. It grieves him that ignorance itself is 'a plummet' over him. It grieves him still more that such a simple schoolmaster as the Welshman Evans, who is as ignorant as his childish scholars, should make a fool of him. He finds that his star has forsaken him; *'this is enough to be the decay of lust and late-walking through the realm!'* [V. v. 143-45]. Thus degraded before himself, he seems so now not only to his companions, but to the reader and the spectator also. The poet has thus gained his end. Hazlitt, the great admirer of this character, now perceives in Falstaff nothing more than a shameless and moreover unsuccessful intriguer, whom wit and words have forsaken; he is, he says, no longer the same man [see excerpt above, 1817]. But we have pointed out the same motives in this as in the former Falstaff; the former was rather never the man which Hazlitt took him to be.

It was unquestionably Shakespeare's intention to repeat here the moral lesson which he had placed in the second part of *Henry IV.* and in *Henry V.* He had probably observed effects of his *Henry IV.* on the stage which did not please him; he therefore set forth in *Henry V.* the glaring example of punishment in Bardolph and Nym, and here he degrades the fat Falstaff in the highest point of his distinction, that is, in his wit. Possibly enough, Shakespeare himself saw, in actual life, effects produced by this play which startled him and made him speak thus forcibly. For we are well aware that the scenes which he depicted in *Henry IV.* were in his time not foreign to reality; and that under Elizabeth's rule brawlers were the order of the day, who staked their honour in fighting and quarrelling; lads who styled themselves, like Poins, proper fellows of their hands, when, in Bardolph's technical expression, they 'cozened' on the highway vagabonds who lived on the industry of others, who turned night into day, sought good company in drinking and playing, and bravery in daring and swearing. There appeared in consequence on the stage numbers of those plays of the later school, which entirely consisted of intrigues, bantering, cheating, and jokes of a rude and repulsive nature, the subjects for which moved in the stratum of English burgher life, and represented a very loose morality. It was probably in opposition to these that Shakespeare emphasized so strongly the moral tendency of this play, as far as was practicable with retaining the merry pleasantry of the comedy. The honest citizens' wives in Windsor are quite beside themselves at the impudent and shameless wooing of the bulky courtier; they are incensed at the bad opinion which he has of honourable matrons; they almost begin to doubt whether in their honesty they may not have made a mistake. Their mutual thought is to revenge themselves on him; they would teach him

to know 'turtles from jays' [III. iii. 42]; yet they have also a scruple as to playing any trick which comes too near their honour. Great emphasis is laid throughout on honest knavery, in contrast to Falstaff's knavery. A wife, say the two women, may be merry and yet honest too. . . . That the tricks played upon Falstaff were not only 'admirable pleasures' but *'honest knaveries'* [IV. iv. 80, 81] can alone move the plain, true, timid, and pious pastor to take pleasure in them. This simple but honest knavery celebrates its victory throughout over cunning and presumption. The crafty self-loving dig the pit and fall into it themselves; it is dug too strangely wide even for the simple, because self-conceited cunning estimates too lightly its opponent honesty. These words may be regarded as the soul of the play. It is a reflection to be drawn from no other of Shakespeare's dramas, but only from this play of intrigue. All the underplot of the piece relates to this point and to this lesson. The cunning host—a boaster full of mockery and tricks, who considers himself a great politician and Machiavellian—teases the wavering, fencing Dr. Caius and the pedantic Welshman Evans; the same vexation befalls him as Falstaff, that the simple men, who cannot even speak English, combine against him, and cheat the crafty man about his horses. The jealous Ford gives away money and name, and places the honour of his house at stake, only to learn more certainly the supposed treachery of his wife; the eavesdropper hears not of his innocent better half, but of his own shame, and suffers torments himself in return for those which he would have prepared for the envied unsuspecting Page and his innocent wife. In Page's house again other tricks are devised. Husband and wife conspire against each other and against the happiness of their innocent daughter, to whom the one wishes to give an awkward simpleton for a husband, and the other an odd fellow; mutually they fall into the snares laid for them, and Fenton brings home the bride who has committed a 'holy offence,' since marriages are settled in Heaven, and wives are not, like land, to be purchased by money. Alike in all these corresponding affairs does business seek to ensnare honesty—cunning, simplicity—jealousy, innocence—and avarice, the inoffensive nature; and their evil design reverts upon themselves. Unclouded honest sense is always superior to base passion. And this moral, which links together these four intrigues, will be found, if we consider the piece from an ethical point of view (for the sake of its principal character and its development), to have a special reference to Falstaff's position and character. The selfishness which we exhibited as the soul of Falstaff's nature appears at its highest climax when, opposed to the virtue and simplicity which are its usual prey, in its vain security it considers the more subtle means of ensnaring as no longer necessary, and is thus ensnared in a gross trap. An egotist like Falstaff can suffer no severer defeat than from the honesty in which he does not believe, and from the ignorance which he does not esteem. The more ridiculous side of self-love is, therefore, in this play subjected to a ridiculous tragic-comic fall, which, as regards time and the development of the plot, precedes the serious comic-tragic fall which meets Falstaff on the accession of the king, when the serious and mischievous side of his self-love was just on the point of a dangerous triumph. (pp. 379-85)

G. G. Gervinus, "Second Period of Shakespeare's Dramatic Poetry: 'The Merry Wives of Windsor'," in his Shakespeare Commentaries, translated by F. E. Bunnètt, revised edition, 1877. Reprint by AMS Press Inc., 1971, pp. 377-85.

**REV. H. N. HUDSON** (essay date 1872)

*[Hudson was a nineteenth-century American clergyman and literary scholar whose Harvard edition of Shakespeare's works,*

*Act III. Scene iii. Mistress Page, Falstaff, and Mistress Ford. Frontispiece to the Hanmer edition by Francis Hayman (1744). By permission of the Folger Shakespeare Library.*

*published in twenty volumes between 1880 and 1881, contributed substantially to the growth of Shakespeare's popularity in America. He also wrote two critical works on Shakespeare, one a collection of lectures, the other—the more successful—a biographical and critical study entitled* Shakespeare: His Life, Art, and Characters *(1872), from which the following excerpt is taken. Hudson offers a generally sympathetic appraisal of the character of Falstaff in* The Merry Wives of Windsor, *stating that "we can scarce help pitying" him even as we recognize that he himself is largely responsible for his "shames and failures." The critic further notes that, like Falstaff, other prominent figures in the play suffer disappointment as their schemes go awry, but he contends that Falstaff "is the only one of them that rises by falling, and extracts grace out of his disgraces." Indeed, Hudson expresses some dissatisfaction over Falstaff's victimization by his "merry persecutors," for he believes they are unworthy to "thrive at his expense."*]

As a specimen of pure comedy, *The Merry Wives of Windsor* by general concession stands unrivalled. I say *pure* comedy, for it has no such interminglings of high poetry and serious passion as mark the Poet's best comedies, and give them a semi-tragic cast. This play is not only full of ludicrous situations and predicaments, but is also rich and varied in comic characterization. Even Falstaff apart, who is an inexhaustible storehouse of laughter-moving preparations, there is comic matter enough in the characters and doings of the other persons to

make the play a perpetual diversion. Though historically connected with the reign of Henry the Fourth, the manners and humours of the scene are those of the Poet's own time; and in this respect we need but compare it with Ben Jonson's *Every Man in his Humour,* to see "how much easier it was to vanquish the rest of Europe than to contend with Shakespeare."

The action of the piece proceeds throughout by intrigue; that is, a complication of cross-purposes wherein the several persons strive to outwit and circumvent one another. And the stratagems all have the appropriate merit of causing a pleasant surprise, and a perplexity that is grateful, because it stops short of confusion; while the awkward and grotesque predicaments, into which the persons are thrown by their mutual crossing and tripping, hold attention on the alert, and keep the spirits in a frolic. Yet the laughable proceedings of the scene are all easy and free; that is, the comic situations are ingenious without being at all forced; the ingenuity being hidden in the naturalness with which every thing comes to pass. The play well illustrates, too, though in its own peculiar sort, the general order and method of Shakespeare's art; the surrounding parts falling in with the central one, and the subordinate plots drawing, as by a secret impulse, into harmony with the leading plot. For instance, while Falstaff undergoes repeated collapses from a hero into a butt, that others may laugh at his expense; the Welsh Parson and the French Doctor are also baulked of their revenge, just as they are getting over the preliminary pains and vexations; and, while pluming themselves with anticipated honours, are suddenly deplumed into "vlouting-stogs" [III. i. 117-18]: Page, too, and his wife no sooner begin to exult in their success than they are taken down by the thrift of a counter stratagem, and left to the double shame of ignobly failing in an ignoble undertaking: and Ford's jealousy, again, is made to scourge himself with the very whip he has twisted for the scourging of its object. Thus all the more prominent persons have to chew the ashes of disappointment in turn; their plans being thwarted, and themselves made ridiculous, just as they are on the point of grasping their several fruitions. Falstaff, indeed, is the only one of them that rises by falling, and extracts grace out of his disgraces. For in him the grotesque and ludicrous is evermore laughing and chuckling over itself: he makes comedies extempore out of his own shames and infirmities; and is himself the most delighted spectator of the scenes in which he figures as chief actor.

This observation and enjoyment of the comical as displayed in himself, which forms one of Sir John's leading traits, and explains much in him that were else inexplicable, is here seen however labouring under something of an eclipse. The truth is, he is plainly out of his sphere; and he shows a strange lapse from his wonted sagacity in getting where he is: the good sense so conspicuous in his behaviour on other occasions ought to have kept him from supposing for a moment that he could inspire the passion of love in such a place; nor . . . does it seem likely that the Poet would have shown him thus, but that he were moved thereto by something outside of his own mind. For of love in any right or even decent sense Sir John is essentially incapable. And Shakespeare evidently so regarded him: he therefore had no alternative but either to commit a gross breach of decorum or else to make the hero unsuccessful,—an alternative in which the moral sanity of his genius left him no choice. So that in undertaking the part of a lover the man must needs be a mark of interest chiefly for what is practised upon him. For, if we may believe Hazlitt, "wits and philosophers seldom shine in that character"; and, whether this be true or not, it is certain that "Sir John by no means comes off with flying colours'' [see excerpt above, 1817]. In fact, he is here the dupe and victim of his own heroism, and provokes laughter much more by what he suffers than by what he does. (pp. 301-03)

On the whole, this bringing-forth of Sir John rather for exposure than for exhibition is not altogether grateful to those whom he has so often made to "laugh and grow fat." Though he still gives us wholesome shakings, we feel that it costs him too much: the rare exhilaration he affords us elsewhere, and even here, invests him with a sort of humorous reverence; insomuch that we can scarce help pitying even while we approve his merited, yet hardly merited, shames and failures. Especially it touches us something hard that one so wit-proud as Sir John should be thus dejected, and put to the mortification of owning that "ignorance itself is a plummet o'er me" [V. v. 163]; of having to "stand at the taunt of one that makes fritters of English" [V. v. 142-43]; and of asking, "Have I laid my brain in the sun, and dried it, that it wants matter to prevent so gross o'er-reaching as this?" [V. v. 135-37] and we would fain make out some excuse for him on the score of these slips having occurred at a time in his life when experience had not yet disciplined away the natural vanity which may sometimes lead a man of genius to fancy himself an object of the tender passion. And we are the more disposed to judge leniently of Falstaff, inasmuch as his merry persecutors are but a sort of decorous, respectable, commonplace people, who borrow their chief importance from the victim of their mischievous sport; and if they are not so bad as to make us wish him success, neither are they so good that we like to see them thrive at his expense. (p. 304)

> Rev. H. N. Hudson, "Shakespeare's Characters: 'The Merry Wives of Windsor'," in his Shakespeare: His Life, Art, and Characters, Vol. I, *fourth revised edition, Ginn & Company, 1872, pp. 297-313.*

## KARL KAUTSKY   (essay date 1888)

[*Kautsky was a prominent German political theoretician who played a leading role in the development of international socialism. Modern scholars point out that, despite Kautsky's adherence to Marxism, his interpretation of history is more comparable to social Darwinism than to the revolutionary views of Karl Marx. The following excerpt is taken from a section of his* Thomas More and His Utopia *(1888), in which Kautsky offers an account of the socioeconomic changes that were occurring throughout Europe during the sixteenth century. He points to several examples from literature of that era which reflect the struggle of peasants, clergy, and minor nobility to adjust to the emergence of the new middle class as capitalism replaced feudalism as the principal means of economic production. Kautsky contends that Sir John Falstaff is an archetypal example of the satirized penurious knight and that, for all its "rollicking humour,"* The Merry Wives of Windsor *accurately describes what Shakespeare observed happening in Elizabethan England: "the struggle between the decaying knighthood . . . and the aspiring middle class." Although he is not the earliest critic to comment on the distinctions made in* The Merry Wives of Windsor *between the knightly and middle classes, Kautsky is the first to view the play as a reflection of Elizabethan social conflict.*]

The keynote of the sixteenth century is the death-grapple of feudalism with nascent capitalism. It bears the impress of both modes of production, and constitutes a strange mixture of the two. (p. 4)

The adaptation of the lesser nobles to the new mode of production was, of course, no more effected without severe con-

vulsions than were the other social transformations of the Reformation period. The knighthood strove obstinately to maintain its independence, which, however, was only possible if the feudal mode of production should survive in its original form. Moreover, the knighthood adopted the needs which the development of commodity production awakened among the ruling classes; the demands made by the knighthood upon life became greater as the possibility of satisfying them upon the basis of the feudal mode of production diminished.

The contrast between desires and capabilities in the knighthood became more and more pronounced and formed one of the peculiarities of the beginnings of the new age. The contrast often assumed a tragic form, but it did not seem so to urban literature which acclaimed the new money power. The knight, with the monk and the peasant, was the representative of the old feudal mode of production. Each of these three classes was hated and despised by the population of the great towns in which intellectual life was concentrated. But there was nothing hypocritical about the middle class while it was revolutionary, and moral indignation was the weapon it most rarely used. It fought its opponents with satire and mockery. The stupid peasant, the fat parson, the proud beggarly knight are among the favourite figures of the literature of the Renaissance and its offshoots.

We meet them first in Italy, where the new mode of production developed the earliest, but soon these figures were familiar in the literature of all Europe. From the *Decameron* (which appeared about 1352) of Boccaccio to *Don Quixote* (which appeared in 1604) there extended a long series of poems in which now the one, now the other, sometimes all three, of the aforesaid classes were held up to ridicule.

The greater part of this literature is now forgotten. Two figures among the many which formed the mocking epitaph of the knighthood are, however, still known to everybody: they are the immortal Don Quixote and Falstaff.

The *Merry Wives of Windsor* (written 1602) appears now to most readers as a very harmless comedy, but it typifies a bitter class struggle for all the rollicking humour which marks it. Whether Shakespeare pursued a political tendency in the comedy we do not know, but he described what he saw, the struggle between the decaying knighthood, which would not adapt itself to the bourgeois mould, and the aspiring middle class, whose women were wiser and braver than the knights without fear and reproach. (pp. 32-3)

> Karl Kautsky, "The Rise of Capitalism and of the Modern State" and "Landed Property," in his Thomas More and His Utopia, *translated by H. J. Stenning, A. & C. Black, Ltd., 1927, pp. 4-20, 21-33.*

## DENTON J. SNIDER   (essay date 1890?)

[*Snider was an American scholar, philosopher, and poet who closely followed the precepts of the German philosopher Georg Wilhelm Friedrich Hegel and contributed greatly to the dissemination of his dialectical philosophy in America. Snider's critical writings include studies on Homer, Dante, and Goethe, as well as Shakespeare. Like Hermann Ulrici and G. G. Gervinus, Snider sought for the dramatic unity and ethical import in Shakespeare's plays, but he presented a more rigorous Hegelian interpretation than those two German philosophical critics. In the introduction to his three-volume work* The Shakespearian Drama: A Commentary *(1887-90), Snider states that Shakespeare's plays present various ethical principles which, in their differences, come into "Dramatic Collision," but are ultimately resolved and brought into harmony. He claims that these collisions can be traced in the plays' various "Dramatic Threads" of action and thought, which together form a "Dramatic Movement," and that the analysis of these threads and movements—"the structural elements of the drama"—reveal the organic unity of Shakespeare's art. Snider observes two basic movements in the tragedies—guilt and retribution—and three in the comedies—separation, mediation, and return. In the following excerpt, taken from the final volume of the above mentioned work, Snider is principally concerned with the movement of the dramatic action of* The Merry Wives of Windsor, *beginning with the initial conflicts in the Family caused by Falstaff's and Ford's assaults on "the honor of married life" and the implicit attack on "the honor of love" by the parents of Anne Page. He contends that the mediation of these conflicts by Mistress Ford and Mistress Page, Anne Page, and even Mistress Quickly follows Shakespeare's usual pattern of assigning the role of mediator to female characters, and thus "the four women of Windsor, though humble, show their kinship to Shakespeare's grand dramatic queens." The reconciliation in the final scene of the play reflects the structural unity of the dramatic design, Snider argues, for the final tricking of Falstaff becomes, as well, the means by which Ford is cured of his unreasonable jealousy and Anne and Fenton are united. Snider is also one of the first commentators to call attention to linguistic elements in* The Merry Wives of Windsor, *commenting that the dramatist's use of prose and "perverted human speech" is highly appropriate to the spirit of caricature which pervades the play. Finally, he identifies sensuality as the knight's principal trait, and he maintains that at the conclusion of the play Sir John sees the inadequacy of his wit and cunning and the folly of his lust, even to the extent of articulating repentance—which "may last for a time."]*

There is more philological fun in [*The Merry Wives of Windsor*] than in any other work of Shakespeare. Language, the outer garment of thought, is distorted and torn, in order to make a comic drapery suitable to the characters. Most of the important persons in *Merry Wives* have some linguistic peculiarity, more or less pronounced; Sir John himself sets off the same tendency by turning critic of his mother tongue. Two foreigners, a Frenchman and a Welchman, are introduced, talking in a dialect which may well be able "to fright English out of his wits" [II. i. 138-39]. In a different manner, Mrs. Quickly, though a native, "hacks our English" [III. i. 77-8] to very shreds. Ancient Pistol is full of theatrical bombast; Corporal Nym is overmastered by his one word, "humors;" mine Host of the Garter has his characteristic appellative, "bully rook." Linguistic oddities Shakespeare has employed elsewhere, but never so many as in the present instance; the play is a curiosity of perverted human speech. In consonance with the spirit of the entire drama, language itself is turned into a caricature of language, and the people speak not merely their own character, but their own jargon. The result is, the piece, though humorous, is prose and must be written in prose. With a true instinct, and in perfect accord with the subject, the poet has employed less verse than in any other of his works. The minimum of meter and maximum of caricature very properly go together.

Usually, though not always in Shakespeare's comedies, prose is spoken by the characters with English names, and is reserved for burlesque and rollicking broad humor, while poetry, with its elevated passion, is spoken by persons with Italian or Romanic names. But in *Merry Wives* there is not an Italian name, though an Italian source has been found for some of its incidents; one stray French character is the Romanic contribution, and that is stranded in England and is caricatured. The setting and atmosphere of the play are purely English; there is through it a dash of English scenery with park, town, river, mead, and with a certain breeziness of the country. English jollity, too, we see throughout; merry England is here embodied, with its

types in the merry wives, and in the men quite as merry. The world has turned to an English holiday, in whose pastimes business, work, the earnest ends of life have vanished. Yet not all England is here, but only the well-fed middle class of the country; the high and the low, the aristocracy and the populace are absent; the court and city appear faintly in the distance. On account of these narrow limits which exclude the refined and elevated part of the social system, the broad comic vein can be indulged in, and the picture, in many of its shades, turns a caricature.

English we find it in another sense; there is plenty of good eating and drinking in the play, to which no human being still in the bonds of the flesh ought to make objection. The drama at once finds "dinner on the table" [I. i. 261], whereof the attraction is stated, "a hot venison pasty" [I. i. 195], and the wine has been brought in already with which the attempt is made to "drink down all unkindness" [I. i. 196-97]—a thing which in thirsty throats requires quite a river of liquid. As the play begins with eating, so it ends with eating; thus says Page, comforting the Fat Knight: "Yet be cheerful, Knight; thou shalt eat a posset to-night at my house, where I will desire thee to laugh at my wife that now laughs at thee" [V. v. 170-72]. So eating is the grand peace-maker. But what shall we say to the drinking, with Falstaff as hero? The center of Windsor is the tavern, the Garter, from which the influences radiate through the whole action. Fat, round, red-faced, merry English people are all the characters apparently, except one, Slender, who is ridiculed and nick-named because he is not like the rest; the national consciousness seems reflected in the fact that he is slender in mind, since he is slender in body. A lean man probably had a small chance of appreciation in Windsor. In this respect, too, the Fat Knight is the hero of the piece and gives tone to it throughout, by his ponderosity; verily he is the bearer, the grand embodiment of eating and drinking. For once we see that the poet has given over to his realistic tendency an entire drama, and allowed his idealism to be utterly swept out of the field.

Like all the comedies of Shakespeare, this play rests on Mediation, which is brought about mainly by the women. As in the instances of Portia, Rosalind, Hermione [in *The Merchant of Venice, As You Like It,* and *The Winter's Tale,* respectively], and many others, the poet makes his leading female characters mediatorial, though their texture in the present case be slighter than usual. The merry wives not only maintain their honor against Falstaff, but to a degree, they mediate him; that is, they unmask and punish him, and bring him to repentance, which at least is uttered by him, and may last for a time. A husband is also cured of jealousy by their comic penalty. Anne Page, too, mediates her love conflict against father and mother. Even Mrs. Quickly has a mediatorial function, that of go-between and match-maker, wherein the high vocation falls down to caricature. So the four women of Windsor, though humble, show their kinship to Shakespeare's grand dramatic queens. Mediation now drops into the realm of low comedy, though it preserves its genuine spirit in an arabesque of laughter. (pp. 144-48)

For comic incident, [*The Merry Wives of Windsor*] can hardly be surpassed; the tricks and schemes follow in quick succession, and with increasing interest to the close; the action is both rapid and diversified. A spirit of rollicking humor pervades the whole work—wit, caricature, and, sometimes, perhaps a touch of satire, are not wanting. The persons who participate in its scenes are of ample number, and of sufficient variety; there is no dullness or tediousness, though Falstaff is deceived thrice in quite the same manner. But the weak side of this drama is generally considered to be its characterization; the Fat Knight, who is the center of interest, has descended somewhat from his former high pedestal; the other characters are sketches, outlines, even caricatures—that is, the shapes here are not so fully individualized into human beings as is usual with the Poet; the chief stress seems to be laid upon movement and diversity. But there is a unity of theme and structure which places upon this drama the stamp of Shakespeare, who can be more truly detected by his dramatic architecture than by his characterization.

Casting a look at the external grouping, we observe that there are, in the main, four sets of people who are brought together. One is the Welsh parson and his foolish associates, Shallow and Slender; another is the two families of Windsor, which furnish the Merry Wives; the third is Sir John Falstaff and his boon companions, to whom mine Host of the Garter may be added; the fourth is Doctor Caius and his household. Fenton stands outside of them all, and is of a different mould. But the internal movement of the play does not run in these grooves; the groups just mentioned will separate and coalesce again, according to the necessity of the idea which is to be embodied. This demands mainly two threads, though somewhat complicated—that of Falstaff and his adventures, and that of Mistress Anne Page and her suitors. Dropping, therefore, the merely external side of the drama, we may proceed to develop its inner structure along with its thought and characters.

The action lies wholly in the realm of the Family, of which relation there are presented two phases—that after marriage, and that before marriage. In the first case an assault is made upon the marital bond—from without by incontinence, and from within by jealousy; in the person of the wife the integrity of domestic life is attacked, both by the libertine and by the husband. In the second case there is a violation of the fundamental condition of marriage on the part of both father and mother, who disregard the right of love in the person of their daughter. Such is the double wrong which the course of the drama must now overcome in a twofold manner. On the one hand the foolish voluptuary, as well as the jealous husband, must meet with a comic retribution for their deeds, and on the other hand the choice of the maiden must be shown triumphant against the will of the parents. Mrs. Ford and Mistress Anne Page are the heroines; the former maintains the honor of married life against a double assault, the latter maintains the honor of love against a double assault. Both, therefore, in their different spheres, uphold the essential principle of the Family against the various colliding obstacles. Thus the action starts with violation, and passes through conflict to triumph and ultimate unity in the domestic relation.

The structure of the play can be seen best by dividing it into three movements, since the division into acts is made according to theatrical requirements, and seldom corresponds to the demands of thought. The first thread of the first movement has for its central figure Sir John Falstaff, who is here shown in his transition from thief to lover. He—together with his companions, Bardolph, Nym, and Pistol—is in conflict with Shallow and Slender, who have been robbed and otherwise abused by the roguish set. Sir Hugh Evans (the Welsh Parson) and Page (the Windsor burgher) are the peace-makers. But from this occupation Sir John soon passes to love-making; he becomes infatuated with the notion that two married women, Mrs. Ford and Mrs. Page, are enamored of his portly person.

The second thread has for its central figure Mistress Anne Page, who finds herself besieged by three suitors—the simpleton Slender, the fantastic Doctor Caius, and the sensible youth Fenton. From the rivalry of the first two lovers springs a duel—a challenge is sent by the French Doctor to the Welsh Parson. The second movement has also two threads, the first of which gives the adventures of Falstaff in his new occupation; he will continue to make advances to the Merry Wives, who will trick him twice, and thereby punish him—he will be cast into the Thames as dirty linen, and beaten as the old Witch of Brentford. Running parallel to the designs of the Fat Knight are the exploits of Ford, the jealous husband, who is also deluded and punished for his foolish suspicion. The second thread continues the story of Mistress Anne Page and her three lovers—one of whom, Slender, has the consent of the father; another, the French Doctor, has the support of the mother; the third, Fenton, has the powerful assistance of Mistress Anne herself. There results a conspiracy of each against the others—who the winner will be can not be told till the end of the play. An undercurrent belonging here is the duel, which terminates in a practical joke played upon the combatants by the Host of the Garter, who afterwards has his trick brought home to himself. The third movement brings together the two previous threads—the third punishment of Falstaff is made the means for the solution of the conflict between the suitors; the schemes of both parents are defeated by the daughter, and she is joined in marriage to Fenton, who alone possesses her heart. Reciprocal affection must overcome all obstacles, as it is the true basis of the Family.

The first movement, as usual in Shakespeare's comedies, portrays the wrong, the violation, which produces a tension, or possibly a disruption in the Family. Some breach in the Ethical World must be shown, in order to reveal the healing process of time's wounds. In the present instance, as before stated, the violation is double, against the marital and the ante-marital bond. Upon the former a double assault is made, that of incontinence and of jealousy; upon the latter a fourfold attack we witness, from father, mother, matchmaker and parson. (pp. 150-55)

Falstaff assails two married women, and thus seeks to destroy the domestic bond already established; the parents of Mistress Anne Page violate the right of their daughter in disregarding her love, and thus they sap the foundation of marriage. Both parties, therefore, are in collision with the domestic institution, yet in very different degrees—the one party attacks it as realized, hence becomes criminal, and should be punished; the other party attempts to thwart its true realization by their individual ends, and hence, must be foiled in their endeavor.

The second movement is essentially mediatorial; its process is to teach the old lecher a lesson, which will turn him from his evil ways—a lesson in which the jealous husband participates. Anne Page, too, shows herself an accomplished mediator of her own conflict. All these women are equal to the emergency, both in punishing the wrong and in vindicating the right, of the Family. Even Mrs. Quickly, the fraud and caricature of mediation, seems to attain her object, which is money. (pp. 161-62)

The third movement recounts the complete reconciliation of all the colliding elements. Two tricks are not enough to disillusion Falstaff, so strongly intrenched in him are his self-conceit and his salacity; the bait of temptation is flung before his eyes a third time, and he grasps for it, but the Devil will not allow him to sin. The grossest trick of all is played upon him, he is reached through his superstition in spite of his wit;

he loses his vanity and sees that lechery leads to folly. The story of Falstaff's final deception is made the means of settling the struggle among the suitors of Anne Page; thus the two threads run together in a common solution and need not be separately developed. (pp. 166-67)

But what shall be said of the character of Falstaff as shown in this play? He is portrayed in love, but his love is mere sensuality. Its nature can be easily inferred from the fact that it is called forth by two married women. But there is added his desire for money; he tries to reach the husband's purse through the wife, and, at the same time, takes the gains of a procurer. Still, all his cash is spent for bodily gratification, and we come back to sensuality as his fundamental trait. The comic element of his portraiture consists in his retributive deception; his passion spreads the net in which he is caught. He is outwitted at his own game, tricked with his own cunning; his fine-spun intrigue simply entangles himself. But the personal trait which gave him most pleasure was his cunning, and, hence, he does not hesitate to attempt carrying out his monstrous scheme. Bitter is his confession: "See now how wit may be made a Jack-a-lent when 'tis upon ill employment" [V. v. 126-28]. It is, indeed, his deepest humiliation that his cunning has been unable to save him from this supreme disgrace. "Have I laid my brain in the sun and dried it that it wants matter to prevent so gross o'er-reaching as this?" [V. v. 135-37]. It has all been done, too, by rude country bumpkins, men and women, honest people, but merry. He belongs, in this play at least, to Involuntary Comedy of Character; he pursues an utter delusion without knowing it; the solution is that he be brought to a complete consciousness of what he has been doing, and of the absurd nature of his conduct. This is the comic retribution which here overtakes him. Nor does he fail to declare the moral of his story: "This is enough to be the decay of lust and late walking through the realm" [V. v. 143-45].

Thus the two groups have removed the obstacles which stood in the way of the Family, and harmony has been attained. The Merry Wives have vindicated their integrity and punished the aggressors; particularly Mrs. Ford is the strong character who has defended her domestic honor against the assaults from within and from without. Mistress Anne Page has triumphed over the schemes of her parents, and is joined in wedlock to the chosen one of her heart. In both cases—before and after marriage—the principle of the Family is victorious. (pp. 168-70)

> *Denton J. Snider, "'Merry Wives of Windsor'," in his* The Shakespearian Drama, a Commentary: The Comedies, *Sigma Publishing Co., 1890? pp. 144-71.*

**GEORGE BRANDES** (essay date 1895-96)

[*Brandes was a prominent Danish scholar and literary critic. His* William Shakespeare *(1895-96) was translated into English in 1898 and widely read in both Germany and England. In the excerpt below from that work, Brandes remarks on the almost unbelievable stupidity Falstaff displays throughout* The Merry Wives of Windsor *as he continually commits "afresh the same inconceivable blunders." The critic argues that Falstaff became the victim of Queen Elizabeth's "barbarous wish" to see him in love, for Shakespeare was unable to comply with her command without degrading the knight and making him almost wholly inconsistent with his representation in* 1 *and* 2 Henry IV. *Brandes further claims that* The Merry Wives of Windsor *is not only the most farcical of Shakespeare's comedies up to that time, but also, by virtue of its focus on the contemporary life of the English middle classes, the most "prosaic and bourgeois" of all Shakespeare's plays.*]

Old Queen Bess can scarcely have been a great judge of art, or she would not have conceived the extravagant notion of wanting to see Falstaff in love; she would have understood that if there was anything impossible to him it was this. She would also have realised that his figure was already a rounded whole and could not be reproduced. (p. 208)

The poet must have set himself unwillingly to the fulfilment of the "radiant queen's" barbarous wish, and tried to make the best of a bad business. He was compelled entirely to ruin his inimitable Falstaff, and degrade the fat knight into an ordinary avaricious, wine-bibbing, amatory old fool. . . .

As it amused the London populace to see kings and princes upon the stage, so it entertained the Queen and her court to have a glimpse into the daily life of the middle classes, so remote from their own, to look into their rooms, and hear their chat with the doctor and the parson, to see a picture of the prosperity and contentment which flourished at Windsor right under the windows of the Queen's summer residence, and to witness the downright virtue and merry humour of the red-cheeked, buxom townswomen. Thus was the keynote of the piece determined. Thus it became more prosaic and bourgeois than any other play of Shakespeare's. (p. 209)

Shakespeare has here woven together no fewer than three different actions—Falstaff's advances to the two Merry Wives, Mrs. Ford and Mrs. Page, and all the consequences of his ill-timed rendezvous; the rivalry between the foolish doctor, the imbecile Slender, and young Fenton for the hand of fair Anne Page; and finally, the burlesque duel between the Welsh priest and the French doctor, which is devised and set afoot by the jovial Windsor innkeeper.

Shakespeare has himself invented much more than usual of the complicated intrigue. (p. 210)

[But the] invention is not always very happy. For instance, it is a highly unpleasing and improbable touch that Ford, as Master Brook, should bribe Falstaff to procure him possession of the woman (his own wife) whom he affects to desire, and whom Falstaff also is pursuing. Ford's jealousy, moreover, is altogether too stupid and crude in its manifestations. But we have especially to deplore that the nature of the intrigue and the moral tendency to be impressed on the play should have made Falstaff, who used to be quickness and ingenuity personified, so preternaturally dense that his incessant defeats afford his opponents a very poor triumph.

He is ignorant of everything it would have been his interest to know, and he is perpetually committing afresh the same inconceivable blunders. It is foolish enough, in the first place, to write two identical love-letters to two women in the same little town, who, as he ought to know, are bosom friends. It is incredibly stupid of him to walk three times in succession straight into the coarse trap which they set for him; in doing so he betrays such a monstrous vanity that we find it impossible to recognise in him the ironical Falstaff of the Histories. It is inexpressibly guileless of him never to conceive the slightest suspicion of "Master Brook," who, being his only confidant, is therefore the only man who can have betrayed him to the husband. And finally, it is not only childish, but utterly inconsistent with the keen understanding of the earlier Falstaff, that he should believe in the supernatural nature of the beings who pinch him and burn him by night in the park.

On the other hand, the old high spirits and the old wit now and again flame forth in him, and a few of his speeches to

Shallow, to Pistol, to Bardolph and others are exceedingly amusing. He shows a touch of his old self when, after having been soused in the water along with the foul linen, he protests that a drowning is "a death that I abhor, for the water swells a man, and what a thing should I have been when I had been swelled!" [III. v. 15-17]. And he has a highly humorous outburst in the last act ... when he declares, "I think the devil will not have me damned, lest the oil that is in me should set hell on fire" [V. v. 34-5]. But what are these little flashes in comparison with the inexhaustible whimsicality of the true Falstaff!

The play is more consistently farcical than any earlier comedy of Shakespeare's, *The Taming of the Shrew* not excepted. The graceful and poetical passages are few. We have in Mr. and Mrs. Page a pleasant English middle-class couple; and though the young lovers, Fenton and Anne Page, have only one short scene together, they display in it some attractive qualities. Anne Page is an amiable middle-class girl of Shakespeare's day, one of the healthy and natural young women whom Wordsworth has celebrated in the nineteenth century. Fenton, who is said (though we cannot believe it) to have been at one time a comrade of Prince Hal and Poins, is certainly attached to her; but it is very characteristic that Shakespeare, with his keen sense for the value of money, sees nothing to object to in the fact that Fenton, as he frankly confesses, was first attracted to Anne by her wealth. This is the same trait which we found in another wooer, Bassanio [in *The Merchant of Venice*], of a few years earlier.

Finally, there is real poetry in the short fairy scene of the last act. The poet here takes his revenge for the prose to which he has so long been condemned. It is full of the aromatic woodscents of Windsor Park by night. What is altogether most valuable in *The Merry Wives* is its strong smack of the English soil. The play appeals to us, in spite of the drawbacks inseparable from a work hastily written to order, because the poet has here for once remained faithful to his own age and his own country, and has given us a picture of the contemporary middle-class, in its sturdy and honest worth, which even the atmosphere of farce cannot quite obscure. (pp. 210-12)

> George Brandes, "Elizabeth and Falstaff—'The Merry Wives of Windsor'—The Prosaic and Bourgeois Tone of the Piece—The Fairy Scenes," translated by William Archer, in his William Shakespeare, William Heinemann, 1920, pp. 208-12.

## FREDERICK S. BOAS   (essay date 1896)

[*Boas was a specialist in Elizabethan and Tudor drama who combined the biographical interest prevalent in the late nineteenth century with the historical approach that developed in the first decades of the twentieth century. His commentary thus reflects the important transition that occurred in Shakespearean criticism during this period. In the excerpt below from his* Shakspere and His Predecessors *(1896), Boas focuses on the character of Falstaff. He takes issue with G. G. Gervinus (1849-50) and contends that* The Merry Wives of Windsor *cannot be read as an attempt to divest the knight of the "distorting charms" he displayed in* 1 *and* 2 Henry IV *in order to convey moral and ethical instruction, for there are so many differences in the character of the histories from that of the comedy that his punishments in this play cannot be related to his misbehavior in the earlier ones. Yet Boas also maintains that commentators who have held that Sir John in* The Merry Wives of Windsor *bears little or no resemblance to the figure in* 1 *and* 2 Henry IV *have overlooked the consistency in his characterization in the three plays, including his courtly dis-*]

*dain for common citizens and the same "strange medley of refinement and vulgarity that flows from his lips." The critic judges that what is lacking in the Falstaff of* The Merry Wives of Windsor *is the ability to overwhelm the other dramatic figures with his powers of "fascination," and he concludes that the knight in this play is "Shakspere's literary crime; his caricature (for whatever reasons) of one of the mightiest of his own creations."*]

*The Merry Wives of Windsor* is an admirable farcical comedy, breezy in its movement, full of capital situations, and, at the same time, satisfying strict literary requirements with a skilfully interwoven major and minor plot. It deals purely with *bourgeois* life, and critics have seen in this an additional evidence that it was prepared for the special benefit of Elizabeth and her train, who would relish this vigorous sketch of middle-class society, with its manners and morals so entirely at variance with those of a refined and dissolute court. The allusions in Act V. to Windsor Castle, and to the chairs and insignia of the Knights of the Garter, seem even to suggest the scene of the first performance, though it is questionable whether Elizabethan gallants could have entirely enjoyed the spectacle of one of their own order, however degraded, suffering discomfiture at the hands of citizens' wives. Nor is it true to say that *The Merry Wives* is Shakspere's only play of middle-class life. *The Comedy of Errors,* in spite of its classical source and names, deals with exactly the same social grade; and indeed the two plays are akin in their unflagging bustle and wealth of humorous incident, which produce, besides other results, in one case the cure of a jealous wife, and in the other, of a jealous husband.

In itself the play offers few difficulties, but as soon as we begin to compare the Falstaff, who is the centre of its main plot, with the Falstaff of *Henry IV,* we are perplexed, not merely on matters of detail, but on the broad issue of the identity of the two characters. Hazlitt, Hartley Coleridge, [and] Hudson [see excerpts above, 1817, 1849, and 1872] ... concur in repudiating this identity, which other critics—among them Gervinus [see excerpt above, 1849-50] ...—unhesitatingly maintain, asserting that in *The Merry Wives* we see the climax of that degeneration in Sir John which had been going on during *Henry IV.* According to this view, *The Merry Wives of Windsor,* whether written at the Queen's request or not, is no accidental offshoot from the historical plays, but is an integral part of Shakspere's scheme, for whose fulfilment it was necessary, not only to cast round Henry V the true halo of heroism, but to strip Falstaff of that false halo which his wit had shed over his evil life. If this was Shakspere's aim, it must be admitted that he carried it through unflinchingly. (pp. 293-94)

But the very extremity of Falstaff's humiliation inevitably raises the question, Can this be the man who formerly triumphed over every foe, and was only crushed at the last by the irresistible weight of moral reality embodied in *Henry V*? The simplest and most attractive solution of the difficulty is that adopted by the critics who deny the identity of the two Falstaffs. But a minute comparison of the characters will scarcely sustain so sweeping a generalization. It is not only that the Sir John of *The Merry Wives* retains all the physical features of the earlier Sir John, nor that he displays the same sins of lust and greed. There is a more subtle affinity in the contempt of the courtier, however false to his own class-standard, for the citizen, the 'peasant, the mechanical salt-butter rogue' [II. ii. 278], and in the strange medley of refinement and vulgarity that flows from his lips. Do we not hear the voice of the old Sir John in the description of Mistress Page, the purse-bearer, 'a region in Guiana, all gold and bounty' [I. iii. 69], who 'examined my

*Act I. Scene i. Simple, Slender, and Anne Page. By Robert Smirke. The Department of Rare Books and Special Collections, The University of Michigan Library.*

parts with most judicious oeilliades: sometimes the beam of her view gilded my foot, sometimes my portly belly' [I. iii. 60-2]; or in the adroit compliments to Mistress Ford: 'Thou wouldst make an absolute courtier; and the firm fixture of thy foot would give an excellent motion to thy gait in a semi-circled farthingale' [III. iii. 62-4]? And have we not the same perverted scriptural and classical reminiscences, as in the account to 'Master Brook' of his second encounter with Ford; 'He beat me grievously in the shape of a woman; for in the shape of man, I fear not Goliah with a weaver's beam, because I know also life is a shuttle' [V. i. 20-3]; or when, horned as a stag, and waiting for Mistress Ford in Windsor Park, he invokes the assistance of Jove, who became a bull for the sake of Europa's love? In face of these and similar passages it is impossible to set down the Falstaff of *The Merry Wives* as merely 'a big-bellied impostor assuming the name and style' of the Falstaff of Eastcheap [see excerpt above by Hartley Coleridge, 1849]. Are we then to adopt the edifying view of the chief German critics, that here at last we see the true Falstaff, stript of the distorting haze which his humour had thrown round him, and that the object of the play is to show 'how wit may be made a Jack-a-Lent, when 'tis upon ill-employment' [V. v. 126-28]? But here again we meet with difficulties, for the two Falstaffs are at once the same and not the same. . . . [The] Sir John of Eastcheap was not in the strict sense either a liar or a coward; in the present play he is both. Formerly his humour had made its most brilliant strokes in

extricating him from apparently hopeless defeats; but now it forsakes him on every emergency, and delivers him into the hands of his enemies, to be misused in the grossest fashion. The erewhile unmatched gladiator in the combats of wit, the triumphant rival of Prince Hal and the Chief Justice, has forgotten the very elements of fence, and every puny whipster gets his sword. But it is neither moral nor intellectual inferiority that most completely sunders the earlier and the later Sir John. It might be urged that we merely see here completed the deterioration that had begun in *Henry IV,* Part II, though the change has become one of kind rather than of degree. But the crucial difference between the two Falstaffs goes deeper still, down to the very roots of personality. Out of every man there goes forth a 'virtue,' the product of his sum of qualities. The 'virtue' of the original Falstaff was *fascination,* depending indeed primarily on his wit, but almost equally on the peculiar balance of the other elements in his nature. This fascination, it should be observed, is as all-powerful in *Henry IV,* Part II, as it is in Part I, though it is exerted less over Prince Hal, and more over subordinate figures, like Mistress Quickly, Doll, and Shallow. But the Falstaff of *The Merry Wives* is absolutely devoid of this 'virtue.' In the very first scene, Shallow, who in *Henry IV* had begged Sir John to be his guest for another day, turns upon him with reproaches, and threatens to make a Star-chamber matter of his misdoings. Even his closest associates forsake him. Bardolph gladly leaves his service to become a tapster, and Nym and Pistol, in a sudden access of virtue, refuse to carry his letter to Mistress Ford. The Merry Wives do not see in him a seductive tempter against whose assaults virtue will have to arm herself in complete steel, but merely a gross compound of animalism, 'a whale, with so many tuns of oil in his belly' [II. i. 64-5], thrown ashore at Windsor. But the true Falstaff is no such mere monster of the slime. Mingled with his earthiness are the air and fire of genius, and had *he* been the wooer, Master Ford would have had real cause to tremble for his household honour, and would have had to defend it with finer weapons than a cudgel. It seems therefore impossible to uphold the judgement of the critics who see in the play a profound moral aim of exhibiting vice in its nakedness, stripped of distorting charms—and equally impossible to agree with those who applaud Shakspere for having, to all appearance, humoured Elizabeth's wish to see Falstaff in love, and yet made a lay-figure do duty for the knight whom he had already sent to 'Arthur's bosom' [*Henry V,* II. iii. 9-10]. The two Falstaffs are too different to suit the first theory, and too alike to suit the second. Rather it might be suggested that the Falstaff of *The Merry Wives of Windsor* is Shakspere's literary crime; his caricature (for whatever reasons) of one of the mightiest of his own creations. . . . (pp. 295-97)

*Frederick S. Boas, "The Golden Prime of Comedy," in his* Shakspere and His Predecessors, *Charles Scribner's Sons, 1896, pp. 292-343.*

## A. C. BRADLEY (essay date 1902)

*[Bradley was a major Shakespearean critic whose work culminated the method of character analysis initiated in the Romantic era. He is best known for his* Shakespearean Tragedy *(1904), a close analysis of* Hamlet, Othello, King Lear, *and* Macbeth. *Bradley concentrated on Shakespeare as a dramatist, and particularly on his characters, excluding not only the biographical questions so prominent in the works of his immediate predecessors but also the questions of poetic structure, symbolism, and thematics which became prominent in later criticism. He thus may be seen as a pivotal figure in the transition in Shakespearean studies from the*

nineteenth to the twentieth century. He has been a major target for critics reacting against Romantic criticism, but he has continued to be widely read to the present day. In the following excerpt from an essay first published in The Fortnightly Review, May 1, 1902, Bradley describes as "horrible" the series of tricks and indignities suffered by Falstaff in The Merry Wives of Windsor and asserts that the representation of the knight "repentant and didactic" at the close of the play is "worst of all." Like many critics before him, he contends that it was impossible for Shakespeare to show Falstaff in love, and he styles Sir John in this play as an "impostor" who should be viewed as a separate and distinct character from the Falstaff of 1 and 2 Henry IV.]

[Not] very long after [1 and 2 Henry IV. and Henry V.] were composed, Shakespeare wrote, and he afterwards revised, the very entertaining piece called The Merry Wives of Windsor. Perhaps his company wanted a new play on a sudden; or perhaps, as one would rather believe, the tradition may be true that Queen Elizabeth, delighted with the Falstaff scenes of Henry IV., expressed a wish to see the hero of them again, and to see him in love. Now it was no more possible for Shakespeare to show his own Falstaff in love than to turn twice two into five. But he could write in haste—the tradition says, in a fortnight—a comedy or farce differing from all his other plays in this, that its scene is laid in English middle-class life, and that it is prosaic almost to the end. And among the characters he could introduce a disreputable fat old knight with attendants, and could call them Falstaff, Bardolph, Pistol, and Nym. And he could represent this knight assailing, for financial purposes, the virtue of two matrons, and in the event baffled, duped, treated like dirty linen, beaten, burnt, pricked, mocked, insulted, and, worst of all, repentant and didactic. It is horrible. It is almost enough to convince one that Shakespeare himself could sanction the parody of Ophelia in the Two Noble Kinsmen. But it no more touches the real Falstaff than Ophelia is degraded by that parody. To picture the real Falstaff befooled like the Falstaff of the Merry Wives is like imagining Iago the gull of Roderigo, or Becky Sharp the dupe of Amelia Osborne [in William Thackeray's Vanity Fair]. Before he had been served the least of these tricks he would have had his brains taken out and buttered, and have given them to a dog for a New Year's gift. I quote the words of the impostor, for after all Shakespeare made him and gave to him a few sentences worthy of Falstaff himself. But they are only a few—one side of a sheet of notepaper would contain them. And yet critics have solemnly debated at what period in his life Sir John endured the gibes of Master Ford, and whether we should put this comedy between the two parts of Henry IV., or between the second of them and Henry V. And the Falstaff of the general reader, it is to be feared, is an impossible conglomerate of two distinct characters, while the Falstaff of the mere playgoer is certainly much more like the impostor than the true man. (pp. 247-48)

> A. C. Bradley, "The Rejection of Falstaff," in his Oxford Lectures on Poetry, Macmillan and Co., Limited, 1909, pp. 247-73.

## MRS. ROSA LEO GRINDON (essay date 1902)

[Grindon is the first to assert that The Merry Wives of Windsor is "a woman's play," noting that it is the female characters who are the principal agents of the dramatic action, "the ministers of justice, shaming and punishing wickedness and vice." She points to the differences between Mistress Ford and Mistress Page and contends that the former is the one who originates the schemes and the latter the one who attends to the details. Grindon admires the wives for their "tact and integrity," arguing that, as much as they delight in carrying out their plans, "yet deeper feelings are actuating them, and they stand for justice."]

"The Merry Wives of Windsor" is the only play that, so far as is known, was written by the Royal command, to amuse the Queen who would see Sir John Falstaff in love. What an opportunity for the master-dramatist and the master-courtier. Shakespere's homage to Royalty never fails; even his fictitious kings are hedged round with a rare divinity.

A direct command from a living Queen, the glorious Elizabeth, whom everyone delighted to honour, whom all the poets sang and whom the finest statesmen were proud to serve, would bring with it an inspiration of no mean quality. (pp. 7-8)

The title itself, "The Merry Wives of Windsor," was happily chosen, and indicates at the start that it is to be a woman's play. Shakespere makes no mistakes in his titles. The women will carry it all along the line, the women will be the ministers of justice, shaming and punishing wickedness and vice, while the one pure maiden, the "Pretty Virginity" of Windsor, the embodiment of the Virgin Queen herself, will hold her own and "be herself," as Fenton says, in spite of all the machinations of those about her. (pp. 9-10)

Both [Mistress Page and Mistress Ford] form a fine study in themselves. Shakespere has worked them up with great care, and the contrast in character of husbands and wives is one of the most natural things in the play. While Page is good-humoured and easy he shows little penetration or shrewdness—indeed there are many indications that he is somewhat obtuse. A keen-sighted, originating mind like that of his wife is required to balance the household. We can excuse his preference for Slender only on the ground that his "idiocy" is unnoticed.

In the Ford family it is the husband whose mind is ever on the alert; silent, brooding, and full of suspicion and jealousy. His description of his wife exactly fits himself—

> Then she plots, then she ruminates, then she
> devises; and what they think in their hearts they
> may effect, they will break their hearts, but
> they will effect.
>
> [II. ii. 305-08]
> (p. 27)

Mrs. Ford generally starts the ideas and Mrs. Page works out the details. Though they are such friends Mrs. Ford's character bears the closer investigation. Her language is better and she gets through the courting scene without a coarse word. Indeed an actress may take this famous scene on the stage in as refined a manner as she pleases; while coquetting and leading him on, she may still keep him at arm's length all the time, there is not a word set down for her that a Beatrice [in Much Ado about Nothing] may not utter, and the attitudes are in her own hands. After the second lesson has been successfully accomplished, there is a moment's pause in the mirth—just long enough to show that though they may enjoy the fun, yet deeper feelings are actuating them, and they stand for justice. (p. 28)

["The Merry Wives of Windsor"] is a woman's play, written for a woman, and emanating from a genius that knew as much of the womanhood of the world as he knew of its manhood. Falstaff's personality looms large on the horizon, and some can see nothing but Falstaff. The ton of corn that lies behind his ton of chaff may need looking for, but it will still be there when the chaff has been all blown away, and the tact and integrity of these Merry Wives will take firm hold as the years go by. (p. 44)

Mrs. Rosa Leo Grindon, in her In Praise of Shakespere's "Merry Wives of Windsor": An Essay in Exposition and Appreciation, Sherratt and Hughes, 1902, 46 p.

## E. K. CHAMBERS (essay date 1906)

[*Chambers occupies a transitional position in Shakespearean criticism, one which connects the biographical sketches and character analyses of the nineteenth century with the historical, technical, and textual criticism of the twentieth century. While a member of the education department at Oxford University, Chambers earned his reputation as a scholar with his multivolume works,* The Medieval Stage *(1903) and* The Elizabethan Stage *(1923), while he also edited* The Red Letter Shakespeare *(1904-08). Chambers investigated both the purpose and limitations of each dramatic genre as Shakespeare presented it and speculated on how the dramatist's work was influenced by contemporary historical issues and his own frame of mind. In the following excerpt from his introduction to the Red Letter edition of* The Merry Wives of Windsor *(1906), Chambers is the first critic to link the play with the medieval French verse form known as* fabliau, *whose principal characteristic is the satiric treatment of individual persons. He demonstrates that the realistic tone and manner of the play, as well as its elements of bawdy humor, are reminiscent of this earlier genre. Chambers also remarks on the sharp alteration in mood and dramatic treatment from the early scenes to the final episode of the drama, contending that the elements of romance in the forest of Windsor provide a "delightful contrast to the bustling realism which fills the rest of the play."*]

[*The Merry Wives of Windsor*] is admirably constructed, and moves, given competent interpreters, with astonishing vitality and go. . . . [The] two central scenes, wherein the buck-basket plays its immortal part, fully attain that vivacity of action which so much of Elizabethan comedy, depending as it is apt to do upon fashions of verbal fence, unfortunately misses. Its complexities of domestic intrigue almost make the piece a farce in the modern sense; but it answers more precisely to the older conception of the form which prevailed in fifteenth-century France. Such farce you may define, if you will, as acted *fabliau*. And of acted *fabliau*, *The Merry Wives* is the best English specimen, just as Chaucer's *Miller's Tale* and *Reeve's Tale* are the best English specimens of *fabliau* in narrative. It has all the well-known characteristics of the *genre;* the realistic portraiture of contemporary types; the frankness, not to say coarseness, of manners; the light esteem for the marriage-tie; the love of 'scoring off' someone, and by preference in a matter of venery. The fact that the someone is the man of rather better birth can only give an added spice to so *bourgeois* a literary type as the *fabliau* has always been. Nor was the victory of the 'wives' over the gentlemen a subject in any way likely to offend the susceptibilities of Elizabeth and the company at the Garter feast. The great nobles who filled the stalls of St George's Chapel were not likely to trouble themselves about the dignity of a Sir John Falstaff or a Justice Shallow. (pp. 169-70)

And for Shakespeare himself, the irrepressible poet, there is the wonderful forest scene at the end, with its delightful contrast to the bustling realism which fills the rest of the play. Out of the busy Windsor streets, with their eating and mirth and laughter, he steps into the dewy glades where the shadows of legendary oaks lie black across the white moonlight. A gross form wearing the horns and clanking the chains of Herne the Hunter lies prostrate in a ditch, while light-footed children flit amongst

the trees with torches that glimmer like fireflies. And for a moment the mockery and the malice give way to romance, as sweet Anne Page, eluding alike him who would take her in white and him who would take her in green, trips disguised in red to where the priest awaits her with young Master Fenton, who has kept company, it is whispered, with the wild prince and Poins, but is an honest lad for all that—''he capers, he dances, he has eyes of youth, he writes verses, he speaks holiday, he smells April and May'' [III. ii. 67-9]. This sudden shifting of the mood, even if it war against a formal unity, is not the least of Shakespeare's irregular and poignant charm. (p. 171)

E. K. Chambers, '' 'The Merry Wives of Windsor','' in his Shakespeare: A Survey, 1925. Reprint by Hill and Wang, 1958, pp. 164-71.

## H. B. CHARLTON (essay date 1935)

[*An English scholar, Charlton is best known for his* Shakespearian Tragedy *(1948) and* Shakespearian Comedy *(1938)—two important studies in which he argues that the proponents of New Criticism, particularly T. S. Eliot and I. A. Richards, were reducing Shakespeare's drama to its poetic elements and in the process losing sight of his characters. In his introduction to* Shakespearian Tragedy, *Charlton described himself as a ''devout'' follower of A. C. Bradley, and like his mentor he adopted a psychological, character-oriented approach to Shakespeare's work. In the following excerpt from an essay first published in the* Bulletin of the John Rylands Library *in 1935, Charlton maintains that Shakespeare became disillusioned with Falstaff as the ideal comic hero and represented him in* The Merry Wives of Windsor *as a ''contemptible caricature'' of the Sir John of* 1 Henry IV. *Arguing that throughout* 2 Henry IV *Falstaff appears to be increasingly overwhelmed by events and unable to exert his former superb mastery over them, the critic contends that the discrediting of the knight was complete before Shakespeare even began to compose* The Merry Wives of Windsor. *Charlton holds that his argument need not signify that the dramatist consciously intended to abase his comic hero, but he declares that the ''boisterous merriment of* The Merry Wives of Windsor *is a cynical revenge which Shakespeare took on the hitherto unsuspecting gaiety of his own creative exuberance.''*]

Shakespeare, so the story runs, was commanded by his Queen to resuscitate the corpse whose heart had been fracted and corroborate, and to show him in love. Shakespeare obeyed: and there can be no clearer evidence of his own rejection of Falstaff. The boisterous merriment of *The Merry Wives of Windsor* is a cynical revenge which Shakespeare took on the hitherto unsuspecting gaiety of his own creative exuberance. The Falstaff in it bears a name which masks the bitterness of its author's disillusionment. Any competent dramatist after Plautus could have followed the conventions of comedy, and shown a gross, fat, lascivious, old man ludicrously caught in the toils of his own lust. But for Shakespeare to call that old fat man Falstaff, that is the measure of his bitterness. (p. 31)

The masquerading figure in *The Merry Wives* is an old fat fellow whom all can gull to make a public sport. He himself knows how little of the old Sir John survives: it is even time that little were choked with a piece of toasted cheese. ''I have been transformed, and how my transformation hath been washed and cudgelled, they [his old associates at court] would melt me out of my fat drop by drop and liquor fisherman's boots with me: I warrant they would whip me with their fine wits till I were as crestfallen as a dried pear'' [IV. v. 95-100]. So far is he out at heels that he can only try to provide for himself by shifts and cony-catchings which he has no longer the genius to bring successfully off. He is encumbered with new afflictions. He carries his wine now only like a Flemish drunkard. Not only has he quaking fits of sheer fear, but he openly confesses his intolerable fright. His pride has gone: he himself broadcasts the story of his ignominy: "I knew not what 'twas to be beaten till lately" [V. i. 26]. (pp. 31-2)

Time and again, in *The Merry Wives,* some situation or another recalls by grotesque contrast the extent of Sir John's transformation. Think, for instance, of his impressive nonchalance in planning his own safety at Shrewsbury: "Hal, if thou see me down in the battle, and bestride me, so" [*1 Henry IV,* V. i. 121-22]: and set by its side his frenzy of fear when news of Ford's return renders him witless to plan anything and makes him appeal in a panic to the women to devise any sort of trick by which he may escape: "good hearts, devise something; any extremity rather than a mischief" [IV. ii. 73-4]. His counterfeits, too, are different. His *sang-froid* deceived Douglas into believing that he was dead enough to need no further killing [in Act V, scene iv of *1 Henry IV*]. But now, he counterfeits by a ludicrous disguise as an old woman merely to avoid a jealous husband . . . , and, by so doing, after heavy thwackings, a mere stroke of luck prevents his being set in the common stocks by a knave constable. How are the mighty fallen! He cannot indeed fall lower than he does when, to escape, not now a Douglas, but a band of children playing fairies, he lies down ostrich-wise, with eyes pressed close to the ground, oblivious altogether of the receipt of fern-seed he used to carry with him. "I'll wink and couch" [V. v. 48].

His wits have lost all their nimbleness. He no longer has the confidence that they will always be quick enough to bring him out of his scrapes. Gone is his old art of creeping into a halfpenny purse, into a pepper box, or slipping through a key-hole. Difficulties which he would formerly have welcomed with zest, no longer excite his exuberance: indeed mere news of them now distracts him. Worse still, his wit is so dulled that he does not even see his difficulties. "I do *begin* to perceive," he says—and that, after he has been fooled egregiously and often,—"I do *begin* to perceive that I am made an ass" [V. v. 119]. Truth is, they can fool him even as they wish; once, twice, three times running, he falls into their toils. Anybody can fool him: neither Mistress Page nor Mistress Ford ever for a moment imagines that he will be too clever for her—

> Devise but how you'll use him when he comes,
> And let us two devise to bring him thither.
>                                          [IV. iv. 26-7]

And these are just citizens' wives of Windsor. Even Pistol knows Mistress Quickly for a punk who is Cupid's carrier. But, of all dullards, Mistress Quickly can tell a tale well enough to gull Falstaff now. When such a go-between is amply adequate to overreach Sir John, he is indeed gone beyond recovery. There is scarcely a saving grace. He who had been a prince's confederate in highway escapades is now a receiver of the petty loot of pocket-picking and bag-snatching: a fan-handle now, no longer a king's exchequer: and all for fifteen pence. He shuffles, hedges, and lurches amongst a sordid gang of unconfinable baseness. Mean and low as his associates now are, he is on no better than an equal footing with them at best, and as often as not, they round on him and outdo him. With his one-time familiars, he had been Jack Falstaff, John with his brothers and sisters, but Sir John with all Europe. Now he is 'bully-rook' even with a provincial innkeeper. He is on entirely new terms with rascals like Pistol and Nym: "my honest lads,"

he must call them, to ward off their quips [I. iii. 38]. Not only have they the impudence to jibe at him; they have the audacity to defy him openly, and flatly refuse to do his bidding. In the end, two simple bourgeois and their wives, colleagued with a foolish doctor, a comic Welsh parson, and an innkeeper, can trample the once mighty Falstaff in Windsor's mud. (pp. 32-4)

But why this ruthless exposure, this almost malicious laceration of him who had once rejoiced the hearts of his author and of the rest of the world?

It might be, and has been, claimed that the original Falstaff overgrew his part, and had to be turned out of the cycle at the point when Hal became king. . . . Throughout the second *Henry IV* Falstaff is falling from Shakespeare's grace; by the end of the play, he has almost forced his author, though reluctantly, to face up to the situation. Falstaff has in fact displayed his inability to be what had seemed to be. He has disqualified himself as a comic hero. He has let Shakespeare down.

The figure which the dramatist's imagination had intuitively compounded, had seemed infinitely better provided than any of his predecessors with the gifts of the comic hero. With such a spirit, such a mind, such intuitions, and such an outlook on life, he appeared to bear within his own nature a complete guarantee of survival and of mastery of circumstance, the pledge of the perfect comic hero. But somehow or other, when the intoxication of creating him is momentarily quieter, hesitancies begin to obtrude and the processes of creation are different. The clogging becomes stronger. Falstaff must be cast off, as he is cast off at the end of the second *Henry IV*. But a pathetic hope persists, and is spoken in the Epilogue: it may still be possible to save Sir John: "our humble author will continue the story with Sir John in it, and make you merry with fair Katherine of France: where, for any thing I know, Falstaff shall die of a sweat, unless already a' be killed with your hard opinions" [*2 Henry IV,* Epilogue, 27-31]. But before the play with Katherine in it is written, the issue is settled. Falstaff is irrevocably discredited, fit for nothing more but Windsor forest.

This suggestion as to the decline and fall of Falstaff neither requires nor presupposes a conscious purpose in Shakespeare's reason. In the sheer abandon of his imaginative fervour, Falstaff and the circumstances he overcomes are projected by the unthinking zest of the author's imaginative apprehension, and shape themselves into the coherent universe which a play makes for itself. But at moments the world of his creation is threatened by the intrusion of circumstances which will have destroyed its validity if they should prove too much for Falstaff. And by no fetch of his imagination can he endow Falstaff with the aptitude to acquire his customary mastery over these intrusions: nor, springing as did Falstaff himself from his imagination, can they be dismissed more readily than can he. In the way in which, without deliberate judgment, an artist's creation of an image of life is satisfying, Falstaff had satisfied Shakespeare. Within the scope of worldly wisdom, which is the philosophy of comedy, Falstaff had seemed to justify entire trust. In this sense, Shakespeare believed in him; and Falstaff proved to be a god with feet of clay. Hence his bitter disillusionment and his willingness to call the contemptible caricature of *The Merry Wives* by the name of Sir John Falstaff. (pp. 34-6)

> *H. B. Charlton, in his* Falstaff, *Folcroft Library Editions, 1974, 44 p.*

## MARK VAN DOREN (essay date 1939)

[*Van Doren was a Pulitzer prize-winning poet, American educator, editor, and novelist. In the introduction to his* Shakespeare

*(1939), he states that he "ignored the biography of Shakespeare, the history and character of his time, the conventions of his theater, the works of his contemporaries" to concentrate on the interest of the plays and their relevance to the modern reader or spectator. In the following excerpt, Van Doren contends that* The Merry Wives of Windsor *lacks vigor and vitality, for although it evinces Shakespeare's dramatic talent and craftsmanship, it shows neither his genius nor "his love." The critic argues that this is reflected not only in the deplorable depiction of Falstaff as witless, but also in the inferior language of the knight's speeches. Remarking on the passages in which Falstaff's wit appears forced and his humor relies heavily on puns and "monstrous circumlocutions," Van Doren unfavorably compares these with the speeches of the Host of the Garter Inn. The critic describes the Host as the "one satisfactory person of the comedy" and praises the exuberance and forcefulness of his eloquence.]*

The Falstaff of "Henry IV" is missing from "The Merry Wives of Windsor," which is said to have been writtten for a queen who wanted to see the fat knight in love. The trouble is just there; he is in love with the merry wives—or with the plot to make them think he is—rather than with truth and existence, rather than with the merry lives he had been living when Shakespeare caught him in his comic prime. His ambition for Mistress Ford and Mistress Page, together with the delusions which it requires, fills all his mind; he has a single end in view, and believes he can attain it. He does not lose his belief until the last act, though to every other person in the play he has been a fool from the first. The old man who once had missed nothing now misses everything; he has toppled from his balance, he is unintelligent. Hitherto he had made a large world merry by playing the butt; here he makes a small one sad by being the butt of coarse-grained men and women who drag and buffet him about until the business grows as boring as a practical joke. His dignity was never touched in "Henry IV"; rather it increased with every exposure, for what exposed itself was his understanding. In "The Merry Wives" he has none to lose, being no longer a man of mind but a tub of meat to be bounced downstairs and thrown in the muddy river. Even the dull senses of Sir Hugh Evans can smell in him a man of middle-earth. And it is not until a few minutes from the final line that Falstaff sees he has been grossly over-reached. Then he utters the incredible sentence:

> I do begin to perceive that I am made an ass.
>
> [V. v. 119]

"I do begin to perceive." His perception had once been without beginning or end; or if there was a beginning it ran nimbly before that of the quickest eyes about him. No wonder he has to beg off at the close with three equally incredible words:

> I am dejected.
>
> [V. v. 162]

So will any audience be which remembers the chimes at midnight, Master Shallow.

Only the husk of Falstaff's voice is here. Shakespeare has written the part with great talent but without love. The long speeches, descriptive in most cases of mishaps by hamper and flood, are certainly very able, and a phrase in one of them, "I have a kind of alacrity in sinking" [III. v. 12-13], almost restores the man we knew. Nor has he dropped the habit of spilling his speech in short repeated units: "I warrant thee, nobody hears; mine own people, mine own people" [II. ii. 50-1]. The labor of composition, however, is often apparent in passages where Falstaff forces his wit. "No quips now, Pistol! Indeed, I am in the waist two yards about; but I am now about no waste, I am about thrift" [I. iii. 41-3]—the pun is poor, and furthermore Falstaff used to get on without puns, just as he used to manage an effect of verbal felicity without having to lug in monstrous circumlocutions like "pullet-sperm in my brewage" for "eggs in my sack" [III. v. 31-2]. Perhaps his best remark is a reference to the Welshman Evans as "one who makes fritters of English" [V. v. 143]. But that is because he retains something of his old interest in language; though it should be pointed out in passing that Falstaff would have been entertained by the fritters of a vastly better Welshman than Evans if he had lived to hear Fluellen in "Henry V." So for that matter with Pistol and Bardolph, who do not survive in "Henry V" with all of their old vigor, but who are happier there, along with the laconic Nym, than these poor pieces of them are in "The Merry Wives." Their betrayal of the fat jester whom once they feared and adored . . . is doubtless the clearest sign of their degradation—not in moral character, for they had none, but in that dramatic character which preserved them in their prime from the indignity of a descent to conventional comic devices. In their prime they lived for no other reason than that they were alive, and loved to come swaggering out of the darkness into lighted taverns. Here they exist simply to keep a comic machinery turning, as Mistress Quickly exists solely in the profession of go-between and tale-bearer. As for Master Shallow, we have one or two remnants of the well-starved justice: "Come, coz; come, coz; we stay for you. A word with you, coz; marry, this, coz" [I. i. 206-07]; and "Bodykins, Master Page, . . . we have some salt of our youth in us; we are the sons of women, Master Page" [II. iii. 44-9]. But the full music of his foolishness is missing too.

The one satisfactory person of the comedy is, perhaps naturally enough, a new one. Mine host of the Garter Inn comes bellowing into the dialogue with something like the primeval force his fellows formerly had. He wields a mad, winy (or is it beery) eloquence. He is a man of few words but he uses them over and over, mounting through repetitions of them to a preposterous peak of self-induced excitement. As his custom is in such cases, Shakespeare has hit upon a single word that will do the trick, and will seem to do it without any further effort on his part. The word is "bully."

> *Falstaff.* Mine host of the Garter!
> *Host.* What says my bully-rook? Speak scholarly and wisely.
> *Falstaff.* Truly, mine host, I must turn away some of my followers.
> *Host.* Discard, bully Hercules; cashier. Let them wag. Trot, trot.
> *Falstaff.* I sit at ten pounds a week.
> *Host.* Thou 'rt an emperor, Caesar, Keisar, and Pheezar. I will entertain Bardolph; he shall draw, he shall tap. Said I well, bully Hector?
> *Falstaff.* Do so, good mine host.
> *Host.* I have spoke; let him follow. Let me see thee froth and lime. I am at a word; follow.
>
> [I. iii. 1-15]

The dialogue is clearly mine host's, not Falstaff's. It is he that carries it away, for he is mad about words, he goes into ecstasies of epithet, he boils over into a foam of phrases. (pp. 136-39)

Master Fenton has eyes of youth and speaks in verses of the sweet Anne Page whom the action ushers into his arms at the end. But they are meager verses, like those in which she simpers her reciprocated love. It is not a comedy in which poetry would be expected, any more than comedy itself. After "The Comedy of Errors" it is Shakespeare's most heartless farce. And this is too bad, since it is his only citizen play, his one local and contemporary piece. In another mood he might have made much of Ford and Page, and of their wives who to our loss are here so coarse-grained, so monotonous and broad-hipped in their comic dialect.

> *Mrs. Ford.* "Boarding," call you it? I'll be
> sure to keep him above deck.
> *Mrs. Page.* So will I. If he come under my
> hatches, I'll never to sea again.
>
> [II. i. 90-3]

With craft and talent Shakespeare has supplied what the convention and a queen demanded. But his genius is not here, or his love. (pp. 139-40)

> *Mark Van Doren, " 'The Merry Wives of Windsor',"*
> *in his* Shakespeare, *Henry Holt and Company, 1939,*
> *pp. 136-40.*

## NORTHROP FRYE   (lecture date 1948)

[*Frye is considered one of the most important critics of the twentieth century and a leader of the anthropological or mythic approach to literature which gained prominence during the 1950s. As outlined in his seminal work* An Anatomy of Criticism *(1957), Frye views all literature as ultimately derived from certain myths or archetypes present in all cultures, and he therefore sees literary criticism as an unusual type of science in which the literary critic seeks to decode the mythic structure inherent in a work of art. Frye's intention was to formulate a method of literary interpretation more universal and exact than that suggested in other critical approaches, such as New Criticism, biographical criticism, or historical criticism—all of which he finds valuable, but also limited in application. As a Shakespearean critic, Frye has made his greatest contribution in the areas of the comedies and romances, especially with his definition of the three main phases of Shakespearean comic and romantic structure: the initial phase of "the anticomic society," "the phase of temporarily lost identity," and the establishment of a "new society" or "deliverance" through either marriage or self-knowledge. In the following excerpt, Frye becomes the first critic to link* The Merry Wives of Windsor *with traditional folk rituals. Comparing the vicissitudes of Falstaff to the banishment of the ceremonial figure who represents death or winter, and whose defeat signals the return of life and summer to the world, the critic notes that by undergoing extended torments Falstaff "had done about all that could reasonably be asked of any fertility spirit." Frye's brief remarks have served as an important point of departure for subsequent criticism of* The Merry Wives of Windsor. *The essay excerpted below was originally delivered as a lecture at the 1948 meeting of the English Institute.*]

[The tradition of comedy] established by Peele and developed by Lyly, Greene, and the masque writers, which uses themes from romance and folklore and avoids the comedy of manners, is the one followed by Shakespeare. These themes are largely medieval in origin, and derive, not from the mysteries or the moralities or the interludes, but from a fourth dramatic tradition. This is the drama of folk ritual, of the St. George play and the mummers' play, of the feast of the ass and the Boy Bishop, and of all the dramatic activity that punctuated the Christian calendar with the rituals of an immemorial paganism. We may call this the drama of the green world, and its theme is . . . the triumph of life over the waste land, the death and revival of the year impersonated by figures still human, and once divine as well. (p. 67)

The green world charges the comedies with a symbolism in which the comic resolution contains a suggestion of the old ritual pattern of the victory of summer over winter. . . . In *The Merry Wives of Windsor* there is an elaborate ritual of the defeat of winter, known to folklorists as "carrying out Death," of which Falstaff is the victim; and Falstaff must have felt that, after being thrown into the water, dressed up as a witch and beaten out of a house with curses, and finally supplied with a beast's head and singed with candles while he said, "Divide me like a brib'd buck, each a haunch" [V. v. 24], he had done about all that could reasonably be asked of any fertility spirit. (pp. 68-9)

> *Northrop Frye, "The Argument of Comedy," in* English Institute Essays, *1948, pp. 58-93.*

## DONALD A. STAUFFER   (essay date 1949)

[*In the excerpt below, Stauffer regards* The Merry Wives of Windsor *as a work of moral didacticism, revealing the dramatist's "natural and wholesome instincts." The central lesson, the critic argues, is that both Falstaff's avarice and lust and Ford's shameful jealousy must be punished, for "neither the leering lover nor the green-eyed husband deserves sympathy." Additionally, Stauffer maintains that the successful courtship of Anne Page and Fenton demonstrates Shakespeare's belief in a just proportion between "ideal, romantic, limitless love" and "social common sense."*]

At first glance it would appear odd that among Shakespeare's comedies, his farces should contain the most obvious moral lessons. Perhaps the spirit of farce is so simple that artistically it needs an equally simple moral to match. *The Merry Wives*

*Act I. Scene i. Anne Page and Slender. By R. P. Bonington.*

*of Windsor* organizes its gallery of town and country portraits and genre paintings about a plot. And the plot takes as theme the chastisement of those two renegades of love, Sir John Falstaff and Master Frank Ford. Shakespeare could not be more blunt in his analysis. The figure whom he here calls Falstaff is a mere mountain of greed for money and victuals. He interprets others through his single passion, and finds in Mistress Ford's smiles "the leer of invitation" [I. iii. 45-6] and in Mistress Page's good nature "the appetite of her eye" [I. iii. 66-7]. He will use their base desires as means to rifle their husbands' purses. "I will be cheaters to them both, and they shall be exchequers to me" [I. iii. 69-71]. Even his retainers, Pistol and Nym, see themselves as panders to base humours. Falstaff is triply a fool and knave in founding his plots on sensuality, in using lustful desires to further even more sordid and trivially base appetites, and in mistaking the character of the Windsor wives. Such badness, however it may be buttered with careless wit, must be trounced; and by the time Falstaff has undergone his third rough-and-tumble lesson, he is dejected deeper than any plummet.

If Falstaff is to be shown in love, if romantic love is equally impossible to the genuine Falstaff and to this weak imitation, and if this is to be a smacking farce, then horseplay must grow out of horn-play. Most theatres have found cuckoldry funny only when wives and lovers league against impotently raging and suspicious husbands. The health of Shakespeare's notions regarding married love (or more precisely, regarding the relations of sex to society) is marked by his almost invariable refusal to portray illicit or extra-marital love with any degree of sympathy. Love is loyalty. The two wives of Windsor, therefore, immediately indignant at Falstaff's advances, set out to avenge their sullied honor, though it is stained only in Falstaff's mind. "Against such lewdsters and their lechery" [V. iii. 21] no action is a betrayal. In the third and final chastisement of Falstaff, both wives and both husbands are in league to make a horned monster out of the fat knight who had tried to plant horns on the husbands' heads.

The husbands had not been privy to Falstaff's first two ignominies. In their own assured integrity the wives had felt it no less necessary to teach the jealous Ford how shameful his suspicions were. Other playwrights might point the moral of jealousy by punishing ungrounded suspicions through fulfilling them in reality. . . . Not so in Shakespeare. Jealousy is shamed by twice proving it to be groundless; then it is forgiven. Again, the impregnability of Shakespeare's natural and wholesome instincts has been made evident in this double moralizing—that neither the leering lover nor the green-eyed husband deserves sympathy. Mistress Ford, therefore, after the first successful lesson to her two refractory pupils, exults to her friend: "I know not which pleases me better, that my husband is deceived, or Sir John" [III. iii. 78-9]. And the two wives set merrily ahead in their second plot to try Ford's jealousy further, and to purge Falstaff's "dissolute disease" [III. iii. 191], which is such that a single dose will scarce prove effective. They must be certain that "The spirit of wantonness is sure scar'd out of him" [IV. ii. 209-10]. Yet since the rites of marriage and the rights of love are both on their husbands' side, the jealous Ford is at last received back repentant, and a period is brought to the jest, the husbands' feelings restored, by making Falstaff into "public sport" [IV. iv. 13].

In the sub-plot also, the woman in love, because she is constant and knows her own heart, is the rightful judge and contriver, as she is in all of Shakespeare's happy comedies. Once more

the theme of "Thou shalt not be covetous" is enforced. Mistress Page, dazzled by the supposed court connections of the well-moneyed French Doctor Caius, has chosen him for her daughter Anne; Master Page has settled on the awkward amateur athlete and tepid wooer Abraham Slender, also well-moneyed. But Anne sees through them both, and coolly judges her father's championing of Slender:

> O, what a world of vile ill-favour'd faults
> Looks handsome in three hundred pounds a year!
>
> [III. iv. 32-3]

Her choice is the young gallant Fenton. The love between Anne Page and Master Fenton is the standard for judgment; the ideal is the temperate, socially acknowledged, well proportioned, unforced union of independent spirits. Fenton looks forward "in the lawful name of marrying To give our hearts united ceremony" [IV. vi. 50-1]. (pp. 46-8)

The problem of proportion is, indeed, the moral problem of all comedy. Shakespeare, in his great comedies, continually confronts what is for him a basic issue: the reconcilement, or domestication, of ideal, romantic, limitless love with social common sense. He believes in both. In *The Merry Wives of Windsor,* farce and occasional-piece though it is, Cupid is essentially a "child of conscience; he makes restitution" [V. v. 28-9]. Even here the dramatist observes proportion, and although the only song in the play is over-sober in its attack on "sinful fantasy," "lust and luxury," the "bloody fire Kindled with unchaste desire," its last notes close with "candles and starlight and moonshine" [V. v. 93-6, 102]. (p. 49)

> *Donald A. Stauffer, "The School of Love," in his* Shakespeare's World of Images: The Development of His Moral Ideas, *W. W. Norton & Company, Inc., 1949, pp. 39-66.*

### JOHN RUSSELL BROWN   (essay date 1957)

[*In the following excerpt, taken from his* Shakespeare and His Comedies *(1957), Brown comments on "the interplay of appearance and reality" in* The Merry Wives of Windsor *and discusses the amateur performance acted out for the benefit of Falstaff in Act V, Scene v. Noting that most of the dramatic figures in the play mistakenly rely on their abilities to create or interpret appearances, the critic avers that the play-within-the-play at Herne's Oak represents the "culmination of a series of false confidences," merrily exposing the vanities and dangers inherent in pretense.*]

[In] *The Merry Wives of Windsor* Shakespeare . . . related farcical incidents to a play-within-the-play and again explored the interplay of appearance and reality.

Most of the *dramatis personae* of *The Merry Wives* are over-confident about appearances: Sir Hugh, Page, and Shallow forget that Slender's goodwill is not sufficient to enable him to play a lover's part; Sir Hugh and Dr Caius are ridiculous in any role because they are too confident of their ability to speak English; Ford prides himself on his perspicacity but the 'truth' he sees derives only from his own imagination. The merry wives themselves are adept as actors, but Mrs Ford too readily believes that Falstaff praises only her, and Mrs Page's device of a play at Herne's Oak fails in half its purpose because she presumes that only she can manipulate appearances. Falstaff is the prime actor in this play, but, too confident in his success in a lover's part, he is ducked, beaten, and publicly mocked for his pains. His confidence is never greater than in his last adventure; he recognizes the appropriateness of his absurd disguise of horns:

> Remember, Jove, thou wast a bull for thy Europa; ... O powerful love! that, in some respects, makes a beast a man, in some other, a man a beast. ...
>
> [V. v. 3, 4-6]

but he does not mind the indignity:

> When gods have hot backs, what shall poor men do? For me, I am here a Windsor stag; and the fattest, I think, i' the forest.
>
> [V. v. 11-13]

He is not in the least discountenanced when two ladies come to the *rendezvous;* he is happy to be divided between them and looks for their appreciation of his play-acting:

> Am I a woodman, ha? Speak I like Herne the hunter?
>
> [V. v. 27-8]

As always Falstaff is carried away by his apparent success and is ready to believe any fiction; he accepts Mrs Quickly and Pistol as fairies and is even in terror of the 'Welsh fairy'. He allows himself to be pinched for his 'corrupted heart' and crouches in fear as the fairies condemn 'lust and luxury', sins which we have seen him commit more in intention than in deed. When the fairies run off and he unmasks, he finds that he has been 'made an ass' in the eyes of those he had tried to deceive. But rather than give them the pleasure of thinking *they* have fooled him, he prefers to blame himself:

> ... the guiltiness of my mind, the sudden surprise of my powers, drove the grossness of the foppery into a received belief, in despite of the teeth of all rhyme and reason, that they were fairies.
>
> [V. v. 123-26]

He speaks all too truthfully, for the actors had condemned him for the fault that was, in fact, in his mind; his imagination had readily 'amended' the shadows:

> See now how wit may be made a Jack-a-Lent, when 'tis upon ill employment!
>
> [V. v. 126-28]

But before the night is out he has some comfort for those who had 'ta'en a special stand to strike' at him, find that their arrow has 'glanced' [V. v. 234-35] and the joke is on them as well. So they all go off to 'laugh this sport o'er by a country fire' [V. v. 242].

The play-within-the-play which concludes *The Merry Wives* ... shows the absurdity and the risk of acting a lie. It is the fantastic culmination of a series of false confidences—false in the creation and interpretation of appearances—and the contrasts which it invites us to make between the various characters suggest that without modesty, generosity, and a regard for love's truth, our dreams will never be given reality.

More than any other of Shakespeare's comedies, *The Merry Wives* aims at making a number of people look ridiculous, but its judgement is not simple. Shakespeare's use of the 'truth' of the theatre as an image for truth in the world has given a strange depth to this last scene. We laugh at Falstaff for the aptness of his role, for his confidence in his powers as an actor, and for his admission that the 'guiltiness' of his own mind has

led him to accept the appearance of reproof as a reality; but we have also seen Falstaff preparing for his performances with such a zest that it seems hard that he should be shown up before such an audience and by means of such unsuitable actors. But perhaps there is a double-edged humour in casting Mrs Quickly, Pistol, and Sir Hugh as fairies; not only is Falstaff fooled by the foolish, but the foolish succeed in unlikely roles. The fact that the fairies are solemn enough to speak the praise of the great Order of the Garter which was under the Queen's special patronage suggests that Shakespeare meant them to achieve an illusion which would not only convince Falstaff but also impress others. It is significant that they are all word perfect (the efforts of Sir Hugh, the play's producer, were far less successful when it came to teaching simple Latin) and that all goes to plan as far as reproving Falstaff is concerned. ... By assuming a hatred of 'sluts and sluttery' even these actors might have been acting a 'truth' which lay within them deep and half-forgotten.

And after the make-believe has been exposed, a way is suggested for making a profit out of the loss; if the actors are all ready to laugh at each other and at themselves, the human masquerade can always provide mutual, good-natured entertainment. (pp. 99-102)

> *John Russell Brown, ''Love's Truth and the Judgements of 'A Midsummer Night's Dream' and 'Much Ado About Nothing','' in his* Shakespeare and His Comedies, *second edition, Methuen & Co. Ltd., 1962, pp. 82-123.*

## BERTRAND EVANS (essay date 1960)

[*In two studies of Shakespearean drama,* Shakespeare's Comedies *(1960) and* Shakespeare's Tragic Practice *(1979), Evans examines what he calls Shakespeare's use of ''discrepant awarenesses.'' He claims that Shakespeare's dramatic technique makes extensive use of ''gaps'' between the different levels of awareness the characters and audience possess concerning the circumstances of the plot. Evans argues that the discrepant awarenesses of the dramatic figures in* The Merry Wives of Windsor *are the result not only of the dazzling array of ''practices and counter-practices'' of various characters, but also of an innate ''lack of perspective'' that disadvantages several of them. He contends that whereas Falstaff is deceived by others into misapprehensions of reality ''despite his wit,'' Ford's misperceptions are self-induced and ensue from his abnormal jealousy. Maintaining that* The Merry Wives of Windsor *manifests Shakespeare's incomparable dramatic artistry, the critic particularly praises the way in which the separate dramatic actions are drawn together in the final scene and contends that in no other play did the dramatist exhibit ''greater technical skill in composing a whole and single thing out of myriad and disparate parts.'' Like many commentators before him, Evans is pained by the depiction of Falstaff's degradation, and he argues that Shakespeare's unhappiness with Queen Elizabeth's command to show the fat knight in love led him to substitute Mrs. Quickly for Anne Page in the role of the queen of the fairies, thus offering ''a left-handed compliment'' to his sovereign.*]

A fundamental difference between *As You Like It* and *The Merry Wives of Windsor* appears in the fact that whereas in the one the brilliant Rosalind stands at the apex of the structure of awarenesses, in the other Mistress Quickly perches here. Serving as accomplice in the wives' multiple practices on Falstaff, managing a thriving personal enterprise at the expense of sweet Anne Page's three suitors, and at last—quite unexpectedly—serving as Queen of the Fairies in command of ouphes and elves at Herne's oak, 'that foolish carrion' [III. iii. 193] is *The Merry Wives of Windsor*'s nearest equivalent to Oberon,

Portia, Rosalind, Viola, Vincentio, and Prospero [in *A Midsummer Night's Dream, The Merchant of Venice, As You Like It, Twelfth Night, The Taming of the Shrew,* and *The Tempest,* respectively]. Between her peak and—in a startling inversion of their positions in *Henry IV*—Falstaff's nether depth range the other major participants without whose practices and counterpractices there would be neither action nor comic effects. (p. 98)

Eleven distinct practices, several of which run concurrently, inextricably bound with others yet whole in themselves, compose the material and the means of action and effect: that of Falstaff on the wives; that of Pistol and Nym on Falstaff in betraying him to Page and Ford; that of Mistress Quickly on Sir Hugh (acting for Slender, incapable of acting for himself), Caius, and Fenton in their respective suits to Anne; that of the wives on Falstaff, involving Mistress Quickly as go-between; that of the Host on Caius and Sir Hugh in appointing them different meeting places for a duel; that of Ford on Falstaff in posing as Master Brook; that of Sir Hugh and Caius on the Host in the affair of the 'Germans'; that of all Windsor on Falstaff in the affair of Herne's oak; that of Page on his wife in arranging for Anne to be taken by Slender; that of Mrs. Page on Page in arranging Anne's elopement with Caius; and, finally, that of Fenton on both husband and wife in stealing Anne for himself. This is the greatest accumulation of practices in any play of Shakespeare's except *Cymbeline.* (p. 99)

Nearly all its discrepancies in vision . . . result from activities of the many practisers. The two main gaps—that between the wives and Falstaff and that between Ford and Falstaff—are exploited, with shrewd variations on each occasion, three times each, the six scenes which exploit them constituting the principal action of the play. In one scene Falstaff is deceived by three persons in succession, each time with respect to a different fact of the complex situation. In five of the sixteen scenes whose business and effects are made by exploitation of discrepancies in awareness, not one participant commands a whole view of the situation. . . . In addition to the gaps created by the activities of practisers are others that result from the participants' native lack of perspective: both Caius and Sir Hugh are so made as to be deceived when no one is deceiving them; their outstanding scenes are those which exhibit their natural follies in situations in which they are also abused by practices. Though their individual idiosyncrasies differentiate them superficially from all other persons, these two are essentially of the race of Bottom, Dogberry, and Aguecheek [in *A Midsummer Night's Dream, Much Ado about Nothing,* and *Twelfth Night,* respectively]. Less conspicuously of this breed, but nevertheless of it also, is Shallow. . . . Not a blood brother but a cousin of the race is Slender, who, unlike Bottom, has a certain pitiful awareness despite a lack of brains. The one poignant note in the play is that sounded from time to time in the minor key, asserting Slender's humble worship of sweet Anne Page. . . . Slender has a corner somewhere in head or heart that knows Anne is not for him; his is the desire of the moth for the star—if the moth could also sense futility. Mistress Quickly, though she occupies a vantage-point higher than any other's, does so not by virtue of superior intellect but because circumstances make her an accomplice in the wives' practice at the same time she is the foxy-foolish proprietor of her own triple game: she simply holds a good place. Conversely, Falstaff, in *Henry IV* the supreme comic example of wit and circumspection, is here reduced by multiple practices mounted against him to a level from which he sees no more of the total reality than Caius and Sir Hugh. Deceived by all and deceiving

none, he holds the bottom despite his wit, as Mistress Quickly is hoisted to the top despite her lack of it. (pp. 99-100)

Act II, ii . . . opens with an elaborate machinery of exploitation. On the bottommost level—where he remains until the end of the play despite the fact that he himself devised the practice which set all in motion—stands Falstaff, triply abused, being ignorant that Nym and Pistol have betrayed him, that Ford intends to 'sound' him in the disguise of 'Master Brook', and that the wives have consulted against him. His own practice thus has been circumscribed from the moment he divulged it to Nym and Pistol, and his ignorance of this fact is the basic exploitable matter of the play until the final moments of Act V, when, having been pinched by fairies, he rises as from a long sleep: 'I do begin to perceive that I am made an ass' [V. v. 119]. On the level just above Falstaff's stands Ford: informed by Pistol that 'Sir John affects thy wife' [II. i. 111] and disguised also, he holds double advantage over Falstaff, who of course supposes himself to hold the advantage. But Ford is blind to his wife's staunch honesty and ignorant that she has devised her own means of dealing with Falstaff. His low place on the scale is not, therefore, due wholly to his ignorance of the practices against him. If these practices alone were responsible, Page should occupy the same low level, since he has learned from Nym as Ford from Pistol that Sir John 'loves your wife' [II. i. 132]. Ford stands lower because of the fault in his nature which makes him self-deceived as well as deceived; thus,

> I do not misdoubt my wife; but I would be loath
> to turn them together. A man may be too confident. I would have nothing lie on my head.
> I cannot be thus satisfied.
>
> [II. i. 185-88]

Page, however, not being self-deceived, is quite unaffected by the plots and counter-plots of Falstaff and Mrs. Page; thus Page:

> If he should intend this voyage towards my
> wife, I would turn her loose to him; and what
> he gets more of her than sharp words, let it lie
> on my head.
>
> [II. i. 181-84]

On the next level above stand the wives, aware of Falstaff's double-dealing, having 'consulted' about his letters, and possessed of shrewd advantage in their joint and secret practice on the knight. But their vision, too, is imperfect, since they are ignorant that Nym and Pistol have exposed Falstaff's device and that Ford, masquerading as 'Brook', has a jealous eye on the whole affair. Furthermore, perhaps because of their middle-aged vanity, they do not guess the true purpose of Falstaff's overture, but assume that he covets their persons: that their persons are in fact secondary, being his means to their husbands' purses, is Falstaff's own well-guarded secret, never discovered by husbands or wives. In this special sense, Falstaff out-tops them all even while he is the dupe of all: thus, in spite of the odds, Shakespeare preserves a shred of the old Falstaffian prestige.

Such is the disposition of awarenesses with respect to the principal action. The preparatory arrangement for the secondary action, the manoeuvring for the hand of Anne Page, is less elaborate but as firmly established. Caius and Sir Hugh hold the lowest level in this structure, being abused both by Mistress Quickly and by Shallow, the Host, and Page, who appoint them contrary places for their duel. Both Slender and Fenton escape the latter kind of abuse, but they also are abused by Mistress Quickly. Falstaff has no place in this arrangement. It is not until the final scene that his affair and that of Anne Page, which have moved along parallel lines through nearly five acts, at last converge.

Only Mistress Quickly, operating between the wives and Falstaff and between the jockeying suitors and Anne Page, commands a full view of both actions. She is the only person other than the wives who knows their game with Falstaff—and perhaps she perceives more clearly than they the deeper purpose of Falstaff's suit to them. At the same time, she is sole proprietor of a lucrative practice on the suitors. Her vision, it is true, lacks the perfection of ours: she knows nothing of 'Master Brook', and presumably she is ignorant of the Host's practice on Caius and Sir Hugh. But these matters are irrelevant; ignorance of them or of any other aspect of the complicated situation never exposes her to laughter. The pre-eminence of her position overlooking both major lines of action is appropriately signified when at last, as Fairy Queen, she presides over their convergence.

However otherwise *The Merry Wives of Windsor* may be inferior to *As You Like It* and *Twelfth Night*, one fact is evident: that no comedy exhibits a technically finer development of an initial, highly complex apparatus for subsequent exploitation. Uniquely here, Shakespeare defers all exploitation until the full structure has been erected; though five scenes are required for preparation, nothing moves until all is ready. Then, once begun, exploitation proceeds swiftly on the lines laid, with little need of further exposition. . . . *The Merry Wives of Windsor* makes no false starts, never needs to start anew, leaves nothing uncapitalized. . . . [Everything] that looks ahead goes ahead; no initial promise is unkept; all that has been marked for exploitation is exploited; the gaps opened between awarenesses during the first five scenes are kept open until the last measure of comic effect has been squeezed from them. (pp. 101-03)

In all scenes in which Falstaff appears the primary business is exploitation of the gap between his inferior and some superior awareness. Sometimes the superior awareness is ours alone; sometimes we share it with a participant. When Falstaff is shown with other persons who know less than we, but more than he, both discrepancies are exploited—but always Falstaff's ignorance furnishes the basic comic stuff. Thus in II. ii he appears three times in the inferior position, each time with a different person and with respect to a different part of the situation. First he rants at Pistol, ignorant that Pistol has already betrayed him to Ford: 'Go. A short knife and a thong! To your manor of Pickthatch! Go. You'll not bear a letter for me, you rogue!' [II. ii. 17-20]. 'I do relent,' says Pistol [II. ii. 30]—and says nothing of the betrayal, which is of course uppermost in both his mind and ours. Next Falstaff is interviewed by Mistress Quickly, as the wives' knowing emissary. Since Pistol is also present here, we are made to remember that Falstaff has already been exposed to Ford—hence his ignorance is touched from two sides at once: he knows neither that the wives are practising on him nor that Ford's eye is on him. Neither Mistress Quickly nor Pistol sees the situation in its entirety, as we do, each being ignorant of the other's secret; hence while a great gap stands between Falstaff's understanding and ours, lesser gaps stand also between the other participants' and ours.

Further, it is during this interview that Falstaff comes nearest to self-deception. 'Setting the attraction of my good parts aside

I have no other charms,' he boasts [II. ii. 105-06]; and, at the end of the meeting:

> Say'st thou so, old Jack? Go thy ways. I'll
> make more of the old body than I have done.
> Will they yet look after thee? Wilt thou, after
> the expense of so much money, be now a gainer?
> Good body, I thank thee.
>
> [II. ii. 138-42]

The Falstaff of *Henry IV*, blessed beyond all else with a true view of himself, would of course have known better; and it appears that though the new Falstaff comes dangerously close he does not even here quite sink among those who lack perspective on themselves. . . . Falstaff's expectations of the wives' persons and purses are first told to Pistol and Nym—and it was always his fashion to *boast* to his followers, and to Hal, even when he saw that no one really believed him. It is perhaps the old Falstaff who speaks here:

> O, she did so course o'er my exteriors with
> such a greedy intention, that the appetite of her
> eye did seem to scorch me up like a burning-
> glass!
>
> [I. iii. 65-7]

This, and the rest of it—'Page's wife . . . even now gave me good eyes too, examin'd my parts with most judicious oeillades: sometimes the beam of her view gilded my foot, sometimes my portly belly' [I. iii. 59-62]—is conscious bragging to an audience that must especially be impressed just now, when Falstaff, 'almost out at heels', must dismiss his followers. Never reluctant to undertake an enterprise—or at least to make a show of doing so—he writes letters to the wives: 'We will thrive, lads, we will thrive'' [I. iii. 74]. Whatever, if any, were his true expectations, they were evidently different from those that are aroused when Mistress Quickly reports that the wives dote on him and desire an immediate appointment. 'This news distracts me!' [II. ii. 134] he shouts. His surprise at the turn of events makes it plain that he is deceived, not self-deceived.

Falstaff's third interview, with Ford in the character of 'Brook', marks the true beginning of exploitation made possible by the earlier elaborate preparation. Here, though his position is inferior to Ford's, he remains deceived rather than self-deceived. Though victim of both Ford's and the wives' practices, he is less a victim of his own blindness than is Ford. Ford, holding advantage only in that he knows his own identity, is victim of that sometimes-tragic brand of self-deception, horn-madness, which blinds and nearly destroys Leontes of *A Winter's Tale* and does destroy Othello. With Ford, however, the consequence is only comic; nothing more serious results than spectacular flashes, when irony, darting about the heads of the deceived and the self-deceived, lights two gaps, that between us and Falstaff and that between us and Ford:

> *Fal.* Master Brook, I will first make bold with
> your money; next, give me your hand; and last,
> as I am a gentleman, you shall, if you will,
> enjoy Ford's wife.
> *Ford.* O good sir!
> *Fal.* I say you shall.
> *Ford.* Want no money, Sir John; you shall want
> none.
> *Fal.* Want no Mistress Ford, Master Brook, you
> shall want none.
>
> [II. ii. 252-61]

Irony, the most spectacular but not always the finest effect of exploitation of discrepant awarenesses, is the sole effect of this interview, as, indeed, it is of most scenes in *The Merry Wives of Windsor*. The conscious irony of Ford—'Do you know Ford, sir' [II. ii. 268-69]—flashes from the one side; the unconscious irony of Falstaff—'Hang him, poor cuckoldly knave! I know him not' [II. ii. 270-71]—flashes from the other: and arching above both is the brighter flash from our knowledge that the speakers are alike ignorant of the wives' game. Both men's ignorance is at once knowing and unknowing. Ford knows his own identity and knows Falstaff's ignorance of it, but is horn-mad, his jealousy groundless. Falstaff does not know Ford, does not know the wives' intent—but remains the witting rogue who for love of 'face' with others will boast of compassing anything: 'I will use her as the key of the cuckoldly rogue's coffer; and there's my harvest-home. . . . I will predominate over the peasant, and thou shalt lie with his wife' [II. ii. 273-75, 281-83]. (pp. 103-06)

Since the main action is shown in six scenes of the repeated duping of Falstaff, a major dramatic problem of *The Merry Wives of Windsor* was evidently that of achieving variation within repetition. The three interviews of Falstaff and 'Brook' are, respectively, preliminaries to the three scenes in which Falstaff is victimized twice by the wives and finally by all Windsor. Though he keeps Falstaff always at the bottom and though the results of exploitation during these scenes are always flashes of comic irony, Shakespeare finds variation most notably by shuffling the awarenesses above Falstaff's level. (p. 107)

All practices in the play that do not relate to Falstaff's affair relate to Anne's. Until the final scene, however, Anne herself plays no part in any intrigue, but is rather a destination than a participant. Until their convergence, the principal link between the two main lines is of course Mistress Quickly, at once the wives' instrument against Falstaff and proprietor of her own game with Anne's suitors, each of whom supposes that she uses her influence on Anne for him alone. Out of the lovers' competition grows Caius's challenge: 'You jack'nape, give-a this letter to Sir Hugh. By gar, it is a shallenge. I will cut his troat in de park' [I. iv. 107-09]. And out of this challenge grows the Host's practice on both Caius and Sir Hugh; thus Shallow to Page: 'Will you go with us to behold it? My merry host hath had the measuring of their weapons, and, I think, hath appointed them contrary places' [II. i. 206-09]. During two scenes thereafter (II. iii; III. i) the unawareness of Caius and Sir Hugh, each awaiting the other's arrival at a wrong meeting-place, is the exploitable matter. 'I pray you,' says Caius to the Host, Shallow, Slender, and Page, the Host's accomplices, 'bear witness that me have stay six or seven, two, tree hours for him, and he is no come' [II. iii. 35-7]. And while Caius waits in a field near Windsor, his rival waits in a field near Frogmore; thus Sir Hugh: 'How melancholies I am! I will knog his urinals about his knave's costard when I have good opportunities for the ork. Pless my soul!' [III. i. 13-16]. It is Sir Hugh who first perceives the hoax: 'Pray you, let us not be laughing-stocks to other men's humours' [III. i. 85-6]. Before the scene ends, the Host's victims are devising a practice for revenge. Thus even the practice against the Host, involving the 'cozen-germans' who make off with his horses and keep his rooms empty of guests for a week, stems from the affair of Anne Page, and, therefore, from Mrs. Quickly's practice.

It should be mentioned, of course, that though discrepancies in awareness are indispensable conditions of action and effect in the scenes that involve Sir Hugh and Caius, exploitation of these discrepancies is not the sole source of comic effect in these scenes. The situations in which Sir Hugh and Caius stand ignorant of what we know, and of what their pranksters know, serve primarily as frames to set off these eccentrics' natural follies—which manifest themselves most conspicuously as linguistic peculiarities. Unquestionably the special circumstances which surround the display of these peculiarities enhance their comic force; Caius and Sir Hugh are at their linguistic best when they are put upon, abused, angry: 'By gar, you are de coward, de Jack dog, John ape', for the one, and, for the other, 'Pless my soul, how full of chollors I am, and trempling of mind!' [III. i. 83-4, 11-12]. The dialectal eccentricities are themselves specific manifestations of native unawareness, like Bottom's hairy head. The two principal scenes which exhibit Caius and Sir Hugh thus exploit simultaneously their ignorance of situation and their native condition, of which their speech is the conspicuous outward sign.

So far as Falstaff's affair is concerned, there are to be only two levels of awareness in the final scene—that of Falstaff and that of 'half Windsor', which is also ours. If the action concerned merely the duping of Falstaff, it would be simpler than in either of the preceding assignation scenes, which involved four levels and, briefly, even five. Such simplicity would hardly serve for a final climactic scene, the less so since the duping of Falstaff has already been twice represented. What saves the third representation from anti-climactic repetition is the masterful fusion of the affairs of Falstaff and Anne.

That this is a superbly wrought fusion there can be no question. Shakespeare nowhere exhibits greater technical skill in composing a whole and single thing out of myriad and disparate parts. Anne's winning and Falstaff's conclusive duping meet in one design of action, over which presides a giddy Prospero, 'that foolish carrion', Mistress Quickly, as Fairy Queen. The care of the dramatist to pack our minds with preparatory information, to direct our gaze so that it will sweep every corner of the complex array of elements, and to prod our awareness so that it will not nod and miss something is noteworthy. . . . The eyes of 'half Windsor' are to be fixed on Falstaff—for 'half Windsor' knows nothing of what else is afoot. *But the dramatist fixes our own eyes on Anne Page.* We have seen Falstaff gulled and abused twice before, when his gulling was central; the variation of the pattern for the final scene is thus drastic and bold. We are to note Falstaff, of course, and all the 'urchins, ouphes, and fairies, green and white' [IV. iv. 50], but all this spectacle—the pageantry of fairies with song and dance, and the fat knight himself, disguised as Herne, with huge horns on his head—will appear in our perspective as setting for the main event, the elopement of Anne. (pp. 110-13)

We do not . . . go at once to the elaborately intertwined spectacle of Falstaff's duping and Anne's abduction, but are conducted by stages, through four quick scenes [in Act V] which together review yet again every aspect of the complex situation and make assurance not doubly but triply sure that nothing will escape our understanding. (p. 114)

Together the four scenes make Shakespeare's most elaborate set of directions for witnessing a single scene. So familiar have we been made in advance that the action itself may look like something already seen. But with every movement known beforehand, our minds are free to contemplate the complex crossplay of awarenesses for which the fantastic rout of fairies, ouphes, and elves, great and small, with their song and dance, is the setting. First comes Falstaff, entering on the midnight tolling of Windsor bell; appearing immediately after the four

*Act I. Scene iv. Rugby, Caius, Mistress Quickly, and Simple. By Robert Smirke. The Department of Rare Books and Special Collections, The University of Michigan Library.*

scenes that have gone over and over the situation, he stands in an appallingly un-Falstaffian light:

> Now, the hot-blooded gods assist me! Remember, Jove, thou wast a bull for thy Europa; love set on thy horns. O powerful love! that, in some respects, makes a beast a man, in some other, a man a beast. . . . Send me a cool rut-time, Jove. . . .
>
> [V. v. 2-6, 13-14]

The Falstaffian wit—'A fault done first in the form of a beast. O Jove, a beastly fault! And then another fault in the semblance of a fowl; think on't, Jove; a foul fault!' [V. ii. 8-11]—here equal to that which once delighted Prince Hal, strikes with an incongruous sound. To be compelled to display so fine a faculty in a moment when he is as unaware of his situation as a Bardolph, a Dogberry, or an Aguecheek: this is Falstaff's fate in *The Merry Wives of Windsor.* Magnificently self-aware, Falstaff was once Shakespeare's great example of the mind that most contrasts with the unknowing intellect of Bottom and his successors. And the quality of his wit never showed better than now, as he addresses the wives: 'Divide me like a brib'd buck, each a haunch. I will keep my sides to myself, my shoulders for the fellow of this walk, and my horns I bequeath your husbands' [V. v. 24-7]. And again, at the sound of the fairies' approach: 'I think the devil will not have me damn'd, lest the oil that's in me should set hell on fire; he would never else

cross me thus' [V. v. 34-6]. These are brilliant, even for Falstaff. But even while his wit shoots sparks and flashes as of old, every line he speaks betrays woeful ignorance of the immediate situation; and all the while he speaks the buck's horns atop his head render this same ignorance palpable. The ass's head on Bottom's shoulders signifies his native condition; the addition is not incongruous, being a projection of what is within. But Falstaff's horns are a monstrous contradiction. At the lowest point of his disgrace, as he lies flat, swarmed over by ouphes and elves, his wit flashes as of old: 'Heavens defend me from that Welsh fairy, lest he transform me to a piece of cheese!' [V. v. 81-2]. It is almost, but, alas, not quite, as if he saw through the whole trick and feigned ignorance to delight his tormentors, as he used to do with Hal. Indeed, when at last his disillusionment comes, Ford and the wives having cast their last barbs into his sides, he comes near to claiming as much: 'I was three or four times in the thought they were not fairies' [V. v. 121-22]. But he does not press the claim: 'See now how wit may be made a Jack-a-Lent, when 'tis upon ill employment!' [V. v. 126-28].

The worse employment, if legend is true, was neither Falstaff's nor Shakespeare's, but the Queen's. To be required to show Falstaff in love was to be required to make him somebody's fool. 'Who cannot be crush'd with a plot?' [IV. iii. 325] asks Parolles in *All's Well that Ends Well.* In *Much Ado about Nothing* Shakespeare had already put down with a plot, but not crushed, a fine pair of wits, Benedick and Beatrice. The answer to Parolles's question is that *even Falstaff can be crushed with a plot—if the Queen commands.* Indeed, had Elizabeth lived to order some special sequel to *The Tempest,* Shakespeare might have crushed Prospero himself. 'Have I laid my brain in the sun and dri'd it, that it wants matter to prevent so gross o'er-reaching as this?' [V. v. 135-37]. The crushing of Falstaff is a fault in nature. Shakespeare does his best to save him by preserving his native wit. Moreover, he has shrewdly saved the most dazzling display of this wit for those moments when the man is most deceived in his situation. But the Queen's terms—if there were such—were impossible: a wonderfully circumspect man, of great wit, who is exhibited in a moment of deep unawareness, cannot look other than foolish at last.

If the incongruous spectacle is painful to us, it must have been infinitely more so to Falstaff's creator. The fairies who pinch the great man fallen in Windsor Park are sometimes taken as a compliment to Queen Elizabeth; but it is possible to take them quite otherwise. Despite all the preparation the dramatist makes for the final scene—packing our minds with detail, conspicuously illuminating the several gaps between the participants' vision and ours, repeatedly reviewing each aspect of the situation, going over everything again and again—one monumental surprise looms up at last. It is one which could so easily have been avoided as to occasion suspicion that it may have been deliberate—and in that case it is the more conspicuous because it is one of very few surprises in all the plays. Sweet Anne Page was to have been Queen: her mother said so, her father said so, *even Fenton said so,* whose design capped those of the parents and who gave us the final word on the matter. Our minds were conditioned, our eyes trained to catch sight of this sweet girl; a rare one even among Shakespeare's heroines of comedy, 'loose enrob'd, / With ribands pendent, flaring 'bout her head' [IV. vi. 41-2], whether all in white, as her father planned, or quaint in green after her mother's wish, or in some other colour as her lover directed—but in any event presenting the Fairy Queen, exquisite compliment to a mortal one. Instead, suddenly and shockingly, leading a fairy rout that includes Sir Hugh as a Satyr, Pistol as Hobgoblin, and no telling what rabble else, appears that sly old schemer, ubiquitous busybody, double and triple dealer, Mistress Quickly. She it is who first directs the gang of ouphes to make Windsor Castle 'Worthy the owner, and the owner it' [V. v. 60]—an equivocal utterance—and then sets them at the torment of Falstaff, which but completes a humiliation that was inevitable from the moment it was commanded that he fall in love: 'About him, fairies; sing a scornful rhyme; / And, as you trip, still pinch him to your time' [V. v. 91-2].

The shock of seeing Mistress Quickly instead of Sweet Anne Page might have been avoided by but one sentence spoken by Fenton before the action. The dramatist's extraordinary care to inform us in advance of the action—indeed, to describe the whole scene in detail for us beforehand—argues against an oversight. Mistress Quickly can be only a deliberate surprise. Moreover, the pains taken in preparing the scene makes this surprise the more conspicuous—like something suddenly gone dreadfully wrong in a well-rehearsed and otherwise flawless performance. It is the more startling, finally, because it contradicts Shakespeare's regular method: there is only one other clearly deliberate surprise in all the plays, the restoration of Hermione in *The Winter's Tale*. Coming as such a surprise, in such a setting, Mistress Quickly, more hag than queen, may be taken as a left-handed compliment, well deserved by her who had condemned Falstaff, of the race of Rosalind and Prospero, to play the role of Bottom. (pp. 115-17)

> Bertrand Evans, "For the Love of Mockery: Approach to the Summit," in his Shakespeare's Comedies, *Oxford at the Clarendon Press, Oxford, 1960, pp. 68-117.*

## JOHN DOVER WILSON   (essay date 1962)

[*Dover Wilson was a highly regarded Shakespearean scholar who was involved in several aspects of Shakespeare studies. As an editor of the* New Cambridge Shakespeare, *he made numerous contributions to twentieth-century textual criticism of Shakespeare, making use of the scientific bibliography developed by W. W. Greg and Charlton Hinman. As a critic, Dover Wilson combines several contemporary approaches and does not fit easily into any one critical "school." He is concerned with character analysis in the tradition of A. C. Bradley; he delves into Elizabethan culture like the historical critics, but without their usual emphasis on hierarchy and the Great Chain of Being; and his interest in visualizing possible dramatic performances of the plays links him with his contemporary, Harley Granville-Barker. In the excerpt below, Dover Wilson focuses his critical interest on the secondary characters in* The Merry Wives of Windsor, *declaring—in his review of Mistress Quickly—that the essence of the play has been "overshadowed and obscured by the silly debate about the degradation of Falstaff." He views the work as "a comedy of humours, i.e. a collection of whimsical characters" in the Jonsonian dramatic mode, although differing greatly in spirit and treatment from that style, in that all the minor figures— with the exception of Pistol and Nym—are imbued with human qualities which evoke our sympathy as well as our laughter. The critic maintains that Shakespeare's treatment of these comic characters is "without bitterness, without malice, and without even a trace of contempt," and he views the play as consistently light-hearted and merry. Dover Wilson also hypothesizes that Shakespeare borrowed the plot, and perhaps some of the characters, from an earlier play by another dramatist.*]

[If], as the legend implies, Queen Bess, supposing that a play could be improvised as quickly as one of those masque-like entertainments to which she was so often invited by her noble

hosts on progress, only allowed something like a fortnight for the composition of the command performance—probably, as the finale of the play indicates, a performance at Windsor for some ceremony connected with the Order of the Garter—there is one way Shakespeare might have accomplished it without undue strain, viz. by going to work upon a play already in being and adapting it to the purpose. It is true that W. W. Greg, who has given us a masterly edition of the 1602 Quarto which is a memorized report of the full text by the actor who played the part of the Host on the stage, can find no evidence of a pre-Shakespearian play at the back of the Folio version [see Additional Bibliography]. Yet I find it difficult to understand a number of features except on the assumption that Shakespeare has been obliged, either single-handed or in collaboration, to foist the fat knight into a play in which originally he had no part. This seems evident from the opening scene, in which a great effort is made to link the play on to *Henry IV*, an effort which is scarcely maintained beyond that opening.

It is a promising enough beginning. Here we have Justice Shallow of Gloucestershire once again, furnished with Slender, a new cousin, even more exquisitely foolish than his other cousin, Master Justice Silence, and in a towering rage with Falstaff for deer-stealing in his park. Slender, who may have had an original in the old play, remains as the goose-like wooer of Mistress Anne Page, daughter of one of the citizens of Windsor, and the poaching incident gives Falstaff an opportunity for some of his accustomed effrontery; but nothing more is heard of it after the first scene, and old man Shallow drifts aimlessly through the rest of the play. He has served his turn, which was that of a hyphen between Falstaff as the Master of Revels and Falstaff as the slave of Venus.

Nor is it difficult, I feel, to dissect out an original self-complacent philanderer from beneath which Shakespeare has hastily—too hastily—endeavoured to conceal him. For after his insolence to Justice Shallow in the first scene, he is only fitfully the Falstaff we can recognize. (pp. 78-9)

The Falstaff of *The Merry Wives* is a sort of monster like the Mock-Turtle in *Alice in Wonderland;* his body, padded out with cushions, has the proportions of the beast he affects to be; but the calf's head that surmounts it discloses his true nature; while the tongue of this remarkable animal-compound speaks the dialect of both elements.

As for the irregular humorists Bardolph, Pistol and Nym, they are stage-figures introduced to remind the audience of the historical play of which *The Merry Wives* is but a pendant, and possess little life of their own. (p. 80)

Even more traditional is the part that Mistress Quickly plays. She is, of course, another hyphen-character with *Henry IV*. But it has often been noticed that she cannot be the same woman as the Hostess of the Boar's Head, Eastcheap, who marries Pistol in *Henry V*. For how came that presiding genius over Falstaff's revels in London to be house-keeper to a French doctor in Windsor? . . . And yet, though the two Quicklys are different women, they speak with the same voice. They *had* to, because Shakespeare was obliged to foster the illusion of their identity in order to keep open his line of communication with *Henry IV* and so help to conceal the trick of blowing-out a rather commonplace self-complacent philanderer to look like the great Sir John Falstaff.

Nevertheless how extraordinarily successful the whole transformation was! There are textual untidinesses and loose ends here and there which give proof of the haste with which the transaction was carried through—or . . . of successive revisions. But if the re-writing only took a fortnight, the eighteenth-century critic Gildon is justified in acclaiming it 'a prodigious thing, when all is so well contrived, and carried on without the least confusion' [see excerpt above, 1710]. The plot, of course, with its two strands, was ex hypothesi already there, together with the ranting Host, and, I suspect, the French doctor and the Welsh parson. (pp. 81-2)

Yet, much as I believe he owed to his unknown predecessor, Shakespeare's own contribution to the play was no small one. Besides Falstaff and the fantastics just mentioned he added Justice Shallow, his cousin Slender, and the three 'irregular humourists' Bardolph, Pistol and Nym from the *Henry IV* and *Henry V* underplots, to say nothing of disguising a garrulous old nurse of the original as Mistress Quickly. In a word he gave us a gallery of 'humorous' portraits without rival even in the comedies of Ben Jonson. (p. 83)

But [Shakespeare's] . . . chief contribution to this play, when all is said, is his unique comic spirit, the spirit of laughter without bitterness, without malice, without even a trace of contempt. Let us . . . look at one or two of the antics which he found when he came to the play or himself imported into it, and watch him at work falling in love with them and making us fall in love in our turn. And we will begin by carving the goose.

Master Slender is a *gull* (lit. = a gosling), one of the stock figures in Elizabethan drama. He is the witless counterpart, among the gentry, of the fool natural among clowns. Most stage-gulls are merely stupid puppets, for the utterance of inconsequent rubbish, laughing-stocks for the ridicule of all beholders. Like the rest of his kind, Slender is an imbecile and a poltroon. (p. 84)

But there is a great deal more in Slender than this. He has pride, pride in his uncle, the great Justice Shallow, 'A gentleman born, master parson', he boasts, 'who writes himself "Armigero", in any bill, warrant, quittance, or obligation—"Armigero!"'' [I. i. 8-11]. And pride in his own gentle birth. 'Go sirrah', he bids his servant Simple,

> for all you are my man, go wait upon my cousin
> Shallow. . . . A justice of peace sometime may
> be beholding to his friend, for a man: I keep
> but three men and a boy yet, till my mother be
> dead; but what though? yet I live like a poor
> gentleman born.
>
> [I. i. 271-76]

This last is enough by itself, to endear him to us, had he said nothing else in the play. In simple candour he has uttered the secret thoughts of many an heir that waits for his parents' shoes.

How human too is the strutting in his gait when he first encounters the destined lady! He will show her that he is not like other folk, and refuses to follow them in to dinner. He brags of his 'playing at sword and dagger with a master of fence' and of his delight in bear-baiting:

> SLENDER. Why do your dogs bark so? be there
> bears i' th' town?
> ANNE. I think there are, sir; I hear them talked
> of.

> SLENDER. I love the sport well; but I shall as
> soon quarrel at it as any man in England. *You*
> are afraid, if you see the bear loose, are you
> not?
> ANNE. Ay, indeed, sir.
> SLENDER. That's meat and drink to *me*, now.
> I have seen Sackerson loose twenty times, and
> have taken him by the chain; but I warrant you,
> the women have so cried and shrieked at it,
> that it passed: but women, indeed, cannot abide
> 'em; they are very ill-favoured rough things.
>
> [I. i. 286-99]

That should put her in her place, and show him for the he-man he is! And so, his little triumph over, she soon has him in to his dinner—and hers.

The ordeal of his life comes when he is put to the wooing of her. He has wit enough to realize something of what belongs to love, and has marked Anne Page before his uncle proposes the match: 'Mistress Anne Page?' he recollects, 'she has brown hair, and speaks small like a woman' [I. i. 47-8]. And when she appears before him, he longs for poetry like the approved lover—'I had rather than forty shillings I had my Book of Songs and Sonnets here' [I. i. 198-99]—an old-fashioned taste.

He gives her, too, what other men would call his heart: of that there can be no doubt. So love-struck is he, indeed, that he remains unconscious of all that happens between Sir Hugh Evans and Dr. Caius in Frogmore fields, and can only sigh at intervals, 'O, sweet Anne Page!' [III. i. 40, 70, 144], when he can be heard between their shouts. And yet, when he has to put the question, he is utterly at a loss, do what his uncle can to help him through with it:

> SHALLOW. She's coming; to her, coz. . . . O
> boy, thou hadst a father!
> SLENDER. I had a father, Mistress Anne. My
> uncle can tell you good jests of him; pray you,
> uncle, tell Mistress Anne the jest, how my fa-
> ther stole two geese out of a pen, good uncle.
> SHALLOW. Mistress Anne, my cousin loves you.
> SLENDER. Ay, that I do—as well as I love any
> woman in Gloucestershire. . . .
> ANNE. What is your will?
> SLENDER. My will! od's heartlings! that's a
> pretty jest, indeed. I ne'er made my will yet,
> I thank heaven! I am not such a sickly creature,
> I give heaven praise.
> ANNE. I mean, Master Shallow, what would
> you with me?
> SLENDER. Truly, for mine own part, I would
> little or nothing with you. . . . Your father and
> my uncle hath made motions: if it be my luck,
> so; if not, happy man be his dole! They can
> tell you how things go, better than I can; you
> may ask your father; here he comes.
>
> [III. iv. 36-44, 56-66]

It is a scene at which that hard-faced woman, Queen Elizabeth, must have laughed until the tears ran down her cheeks, as Shakespeare intended she should.

But did Shakespeare laugh when he wrote it? And may he not have guessed that some at least in the audience would find pity as well as laughter in their heart for his idiot boy, with the 'little whey-face' and the 'little yellow beard' [I. iv. 22-3]? 'A goose to say grace over', as 'Q' [Arthur Quiller-Couch] says [see Additional Bibliography], and the grace is, 'There, but for the grace of God, might go the wisest of us all.'

It is the same story with the other human oddities—we cannot help loving them, because their author so obviously did. Their chief comic function . . . is to 'hack our English' [III. i. 77-8]. There is for instance the Welsh parson, who when Anne Page is mentioned as a likely bride for Master Slender, delivers himself after this fashion:

> It is that fery person for all the 'orld, as just as you will desire, and seven hundred pounds of moneys, and gold, and silver, is her grand-sire, upon his death's bed—Got deliver to a joyful resurrections!—give, when she is able to overtake seventeen years old.
>
> [I. i. 49-54]

There is the French doctor, who murders the language in his own way: there is mine Host with his staccato manner of speech; there are Pistol and Nym, the former well described by Professor Willcock as 'a walking scarecrow of worn-out shreds and patches', the other a purveyor of the new-fangled jargon of the humours; there are Justice Shallow and nephew Slender, misusing the Queen's English in different fashions; lastly there is Mistress Quickly, who anticipates the malapropisms of Mrs. Malaprop [in Richard Brinsley Sheridan's *The Rivals*]. (pp. 85-7)

Evans's own peculiarities of speech are the more ludicrous that he is himself a schoolmaster, and a whole scene is devoted to a lesson in Latin grammar in which Master William Page is the victim. The name of the boy is, one likes to feel, significant. Little William Shakespeare had no doubt undergone similar examinations in his time, and been dismissed, if not with a threat of a birching, at least with a commendation upon his 'good sprag memory' [IV. i. 82].

But Evans is much more than a stupid old Welsh pedant. He has the vivacity which possesses all the characters in this rollicking play. And Shakespeare commends him to us by the little human touches which he confers upon him: How fond, for example, he is of his meals! 'The dinner is on the table', announces Mistress Anne at the end of I, i. 'My father desires your worships' company.' 'I will wait upon him, fair Mistress Anne', prounounces Shallow pompously. 'Od's plessed-will', exclaims Sir Hugh, briskly hurrying in; 'I will not be absence at the grace.' He is out again, before the repast is over, in order to dispatch Simple with a letter to Mistress Quickly. But he cuts his instructions short, because of what lies within, and so concludes: 'Be gone. I will make an end of my dinner; there's pippins and seese to come' [I. i. 261-65]. And when he is most ridiculous he is most human—as he waits trembling in Frogmore fields for his furious adversary and tries to pluck up heart by singing.

As for Mistress Quickly of *The Merry Wives,* she is surely one of the most precious characters in all Shakespeare, and would long ago have been recognized as such, had not the whole play (together with the personages in it) been overshadowed and obscured by the silly debate about the degradation of Falstaff. (p. 88)

[Mistress Quickly] is quite incapable of framing moral judgments or drawing moral distinctions. With a keen sense of the benison of the creature comforts—'we'll have a posset for't soon at night, in faith at the latter end of a sea-coal fire' [I. iv. 8-9] gives us her idea of bliss—she had that standard and no other in her estimates of other people. Her servant, John Rugby, she tells us, is

> an honest, willing, kind fellow, as ever servant shall come in house withal; and, I warrant you, no tell-tale nor no breed-bate; his worst fault is, that he is given to prayer: he is something peevish that way; but nobody but has his fault.
>
> [I. iv. 10-15]

Not that she is against prayer in itself, for those who can afford time for it: 'Let me tell you in your ear', she says to Falstaff of Mrs. Page,

> she's as fartuous a civil modest wife, and one, I tell you, that will not miss you morning nor evening prayer, as any is in Windsor, whoe'er be the other: and she bade me tell your worship that her husband is seldom from home, but she hopes there will come a time. . . . But Mistress Page would desire you to send her your little page, of all loves: her husband has a marvellous infection to the little page: and, truly, Master Page is an honest man: never a wife in Windsor leads a better life than she does: do what she will, say what she will, take all, pay all, go to bed when she list, rise when she list, all is as she will: and truly she deserves it; for if there be a kind woman in Windsor, she is one.
>
> [II. ii. 96-102, 113-21]

'Kindness', and a love of comfort especially when expressed in concrete form, are the only virtues she can understand. 'Now heaven send thee good fortune!' she exclaims as Fenton goes out after pressing money into her hand. 'A kind heart he hath: a woman would run through fire and water for such a kind heart' [III. iv. 101-04].

In short, from the standpoint of the Charity Organization Society and social reform generally, she is without moral fibre, a speck of dirt in the body politic, fit only for a 'clean-up'. . . . In the large chamber of Shakespeare's imagination, however, there was a warm corner for her and all her kind, warm enough to stir her blood and give her life and motion, for the delight of man as long as the English language, that she so deliciously mishandled, endures. And what a comment unexpressed, unconscious, but none the less pungent, she is on human society, now as well as then! For what are her muddled ideas about right and wrong but a reflection of the conflict between the ideals and the conduct of her betters? The gift of hypocrisy is beyond her, because she lacks the wit to draw the curtain of convention across the facts of life. She speaks as she finds.

Bergson defined comedy as a criticism in the name of society of characters which show 'a special lack of adaptability' to social conventions and intercourse. Shakespearian comedy is rather a criticism of society itself and its conventions from the point of view of beings who through lack of intellect or education or adaptability or because they are outcasts like Shylock, are not recognized as full members of society. It has in fact a much closer affinity with the novels of Dostoevsky (e.g. *The Idiot*) than with the plays of Molière or Ibsen, possessing as it does tragic implications. Yet there is nothing whatever tragic about *The Merry Wives*. The jealousy of Master Ford supplies the only serious note in it, and that is not taken seriously by anyone but himself. It is even more consistently light-hearted than the gay *Love's Labour's Lost,* since it contains no messenger of Death to convert hilarity into sobriety at the close of the play. From first to last, all is merry, as the title promises; and though the judicial Dr. Johnson pronounces 'the conduct' of the drama to be 'deficient', he is nevertheless compelled to add that

> its general power, that power by which all works of genius shall finally be tried, is such, that perhaps it never yet had reader or spectator who did not think it too soon at the end [see excerpt above, 1773].

Yet the play represents the nearest Shakespeare came to writing a comedy after the fashion of Ben Jonson. It is, indeed, often classed by critics with [Jonson's] *Every Man in his Humour* and Chapman's *Humourous Day's Mirth,* both of which were written about the same period. (pp. 89-91)

At first sight the similarity is somewhat striking: Like *Every Man in his Humour, The Merry Wives* is, as we have seen, a comedy of humours, i.e. a collection of whimsical characters. For example, there is little except mere oddity in the Host, Pistol, and Nym, and not much more in Evans and Caius. In fact, I do not know any other of Shakespeare's plays which contains so many purely stage figures. This may be due in part to Jonson's influence. It cannot, for example, be mere coincidence that Falstaff and his cronies are all labelled 'Irregular Humorists' in the list of characters printed at the end of *2 Henry IV* in the Folio. The description was clearly intended to recall Jonson's innovation, as was Nym's constantly ejaculated 'And that's the humour of it' in the play we are now dealing with.

But if these things show consciousness of Jonson, it is consciousness of a quizzical nature. For instance, Nym is probably deliberately introduced as a skit either on Jonson himself or on his mannerism. Thus if Shakespeare imitated Jonson he did so as much in mockery, gentle mockery, as in flattery. In any case the similarity between *The Wives* and the plays of Jonson's school is largely a formal one. In outlook and spirit it is totally unlike.

This is true not merely in the attitude of the dramatist towards his characters. Here the difference is well defined by Professor Gayley, who describes Jonson's plays as 'pure comedy of humours by way of ridicule', whereas *The Merry Wives* is a 'comedy of manners or humours, by way of exposition' [in *Representative English Comedies*]. Its fantastics are *revealed* to us in all their oddity and their foolishness. And those which do not quite come alive, like the Host and Caius, we take to our hearts because they breathe the same air as Slender and Mistress Quickly. Only Pistol and Nym seem to stand without the charmed circle—and that because I suggest they were meant to be stage-jokes rather than human characters.

Furthermore *The Merry Wives* has a romantic core, which the comedies of Jonson lack. Anne Page and young Fenton keep the love-motive central, and do much to keep the air of the play fresh from beginning to end. Still more do the references to the countryside. . . . It is one of the miracles of the great magician that this play which he made by a fortnight's work, probably upon a drama by some other dramatist, gives us a truer and more vivid picture of the life and doings of his own Stratford than anything else that has come down to us. (pp. 91-3)

All this is very remote from the London which is the scene of so many of Jonson's plays. And the finale in Windsor Park— how entirely un-Jonsonian! It has often been described as mere extravaganza. But it is no more so than the equally effective finale of *A Midsummer Night's Dream,* from which it is clearly in part borrowed. That the fairies here are not 'real fairies' is little to the point. For stage purposes they are 'real', and with their song and dance, their crowns of fire and their coloured ribbons, the choir of boys rounded off the evening of gaiety, at that first command performance, very delightfully. Indeed, it is all gaiety and delight from beginning to end. And the iniquities of Falstaff, once unmasked, confessed, and punished—with nothing more serious than pinching—are so far forgiven that he is invited by honest Master Page to 'a posset at my house, where I will desire thee to laugh at my wife, that now laughs at thee' [V. v. 171-72].

It is a posset-comedy, warm, domestic, exhilarating, a very cordial of merriment and good fellowship. (p. 93)

> John Dover Wilson, "'The Merry Wives of Windsor'," in his Shakespeare's Happy Comedies, Northwestern University Press, 1962, pp. 76-93.

### BRIAN VICKERS   (essay date 1968)

[*Vickers is the author of* The Artistry of Shakespeare's Prose *(1968) and editor of the six-volume* Shakespeare: The Critical Heritage *(1974-1981), a comprehensive collection of Shakespearean commentary from 1623 to 1801. In the following excerpt, Vickers analyzes Shakespeare's use of language in* The Merry Wives of Windsor *and asserts that the play exhibits "a virtuoso control of styles." Noting that most of the characters generally express themselves in unadorned, conversational prose speeches, the critic maintains that Shakespeare achieved a remarkable degree of differentiation among the minor characters by ascribing an idiosyncratic use of language to each. Vickers argues that Ford's insane suspiciousness is vividly conveyed through his rambling and disjointed prose style, and he judges that "the application of prose to such an intense and realistically developed emotional state is the major success of the play."*]

Our sense of the decline of Falstaff [in *The Merry Wives of Windsor*] is obviously conditioned by our knowledge of the *Henry IV* plays, and it is not to be explained by the traditional legend of the play being a special commission hastily turned out in a fortnight, for as Bertrand Evans has shown [see excerpt above, 1960] *The Merry Wives of Windsor* is carefully and ingeniously constructed, and one would suppose that if Shakespeare had been given an urgent job he would have found verse easier. The conception of Falstaff found here is necessitated by the plot, and any resistance or resilience on his part would have been fatal: he must be easily duped, as Ford is. These larger dramatic requirements determine the nature of the imagery applied to him and also affect the whole texture of the play's plot and its language: style is simply the final manifestation of larger dramatic issues. Shakespeare has decided to write a prose comedy, limiting his characters to the middle and lower classes, and only making an exception to the norm by using verse for situations of more dignity (such as the final stages of the play, in the masking and the tribute to the Queen) or more imagination (as with the love of Fenton and Nan). Given this social equality there can be no clown to entertain the nobility, and none of the witty aristocratic repartee: the characters are all bourgeois, and their language must be that of 'realistic' conversation, a plain style with little imagery and with no rhetorical structure.

The obvious danger is that all the characters will talk alike, and though some are set apart by other means—the superior intellectual status of the Wives is reflected in their use of imagery, as is Ford's abnormal condition—Shakespeare still has the problem of individualizing a great number of minor characters who are not just comic relief but are needed for the intricacies of the plot. He solves this problem by giving each of these characters a separate group of verbal *tics,* an individualizing group of oddities which are at the same time amusing (if one were to rewrite the play removing all distinctive signs it would be seen how much more than the individuality would be lost). The differentiation between characters is remarkably well done (as ever, Shakespeare specifically comments on what he is doing), and Pope's claim that given any speech he could assign it to the correct character is here literally true, for only two or three lines would be enough for us to distinguish between Shallow, Slender, Pistol, Quickly, Bardolph, Nym, Evans, the Host, Caius,—and of course, Falstaff.... Shakespeare's own development of language depended in part on the exercise of such verbal individualization, and it is an ability which he developed in prose long before he could in verse, albeit at a simpler and more schematic level. We may never regard *The Merry Wives of Windsor* with great relish, but we must concede that it shows a virtuoso control of styles.

Those characters already created in the other plays naturally retain their styles, although the humour is inevitably dissipated by being spread over five Acts. Shallow is at once introduced in his eternal relationship to Falstaff: 'if he were twenty Sir John Falstaffs, he shall not abuse Robert Shallow Esquire' [I. i. 2-4], and his repetitions are constant, sharper than ever as he stands on his dignity: 'He hath wronged me, indeed he hath, at a word he hath. Believe me Robert Shallow Esquire saith he is wronged' [I. i. 105-07]. Mistress Quickly malaprops as usual, with her 'allicholly', 'canaries', (for 'quandary'), 'speciously', and the fault is developed into a whole scene [IV. i] ... where her horrified comments on the grammar lesson ... are still amusing, as when William Page produces his 'genitive case plural':

> WILLIAM. Genitive horum, harum, horum.
> QUICKLY. Vengeance of Jenny's case! Fie on her! Never name her, child, if she be a whore.
>
> [IV. i. 61-3]

And as ever Shakespeare does not stop with the stylistic effect, but relates it to the characters involved, as with the following insight into Mistress Quickly's report on experience as she reproves the schoolmaster:

> You do ill to teach the child such words. He teaches him to hick and to hack; which they'll do fast enough of themselves, and to call horum; fie upon you!
>
> [IV. i. 65-8]

That is a tiny touch, but it shows Shakespeare's constant empathy, his re-creation of the personalities and attitudes of his characters. (pp. 141-43)

Nym is immediately recognized by his fondness for catchphrases, especially the word 'humour', which he uses in almost every speech he utters, from the first—'Slice, I say; pauca, pauca. Slice, that's my humour' [I. i. 132-33] to the last extraordinary solo:

> And this is true. I like not the humour of lying. He hath wronged me in some humours. I should have borne the humoured letter to her; but I have a sword, and it shall bite upon my ne-

*Act II. Scene i. Mistress Ford and Mistress Page. By M. W. Peters. The Department of Rare Books and Special Collections, The University of Michigan Library.*

cessity.... Adieu, I love not the humour of bread and cheese. And there's the humour of it. Adieu.

[II. i. 128-32, 135-37]

Page is given the comment here: 'The humour of it, quoth'a? Here's a fellow frights English out of his wits' [II. i. 138-39]. With his ominous military aggressiveness Nym is a sort of poor man's Pistol, and in his final speech he actually ascends to Pistolian verse. Another parallel to these braggarts is provided by the Host, who is bluff and aggressive: his favourite phrase 'bully' links him with Bottom, and he shares with other verbal warriors the inversion portentous: 'Bully Sir John! Speak from thy lungs military' [IV. v. 16-17]. In addition to this aspect of his character he is given remarkably urgent language (as if he were always in a state of emergency), using short excessively clipped phrases, scarcely six words at a time, as in his first speeches (by their words you shall know them, and in this play immediately):

> What says my bully-rook? Speak scholarly and wisely.... Discard, bully Hercules, cashier; let them wag; trot, trot.... Thou'rt an emperor, Caesar, Keisar, and Pheesar. I will entertain Bardolph; he shall tap; said I well, bully Hector?
>
> [I. iii. 1-11]

In addition to joining the military circle by his brusqueness, like almost everyone in the play he malaprops: 'For the which I will be thy adversary towards Anne Page' [II. iii. 94-5]. The English language takes quite a beating here, and even those who set up as correctors are themselves tainted: thus when Slender says that he is ready to marry Nan, 'that I am freely dissolved, and dissolutely' [I. i. 251-52], the schoolmaster Evans reproves him but makes a mistake or two himself: 'It is a fery discretion answer; save the fall is in the ort ''dissolutely''' [I. i. 253-54]. The effect, which was also seen in *A Midsummer Night's Dream*, is of the blind leading the blind. (pp. 144-45)

The largest of the characters from the lower world is of course Falstaff, but although we can perceive some of his old tricks they are now faded. Far from dominating repartee he becomes the butt, and of all people, of Pistol [I. iii. 32-76], though he gets some revenge later with a series of puns and abusive images [II. ii. 1-29]. His only piece of logic is a pathetically pale echo of his original sophistic comparison of his failings to Adam's:

> When gods have hot backs what shall poor men
> do?
>
> [V. v. 11-12]

But the echo only exposes more clearly his decline, and throughout the play he is cannon-fodder, helpless as a child—as he is made to say himself: 'Since I plucked geese, played truant, and whipped top, I knew not what 'twas to be beaten, till lately' [V. i. 24-6]. Easily deceived and humiliated by repetitive plots (perhaps the weakest aspect of the play is that he is made to fall into three traps running, without a moment's hesitation), Falstaff becomes the target for a series of predictable images, mostly from the women in the earlier part of the play: he is 'well-nigh worn to pieces with age', a 'Flemish drunkard' with 'guts made of puddings', a 'whale with so many tuns of oil in his belly', he is 'grease', this 'unwholesome humidity, this gross watery pumpion' [II. i. 21-2, 31-2, 64-5; III. iii. 40-1]—abuse which culminates in a set denunciation of him by Ford, Page, Mrs Page, and Evans: 'What, a hodge-pudding? A bag of flax?'—'A puffed man?'—'Old, cold, withered, and of intolerable entrails?' [V. v. 151-54]. No more one-sided scene of abuse has been written since the courtiers mocked the pageant in *Love's Labour's Lost*, especially Holofernes, and the formal nature of this railing is recognized in Falstaff's dejected comment: 'Well I am your theme. You have the start of me, I am dejected. . . . Use me as you will' [V. v. 160-64]. He is finally made to recognize himself as a passive butt, in an image which sums up the metaphors of hunting used for his pursuit: 'I am glad, though you have ta'en a special stand to strike at me, that your arrow hath glanced' [V. v. 233-34]—but it is like bear-baiting with a paralysed bear. Besides these external attacks, as the play develops he is made to use mocking images to describe himself, and whereas in *Henry IV* the same device suggested a strength which could afford to invoke its own weakness, here it is simply another wounding arrow. (pp. 147-48)

Despite the necessity of subordinating Falstaff to the general design of the play, we may nevertheless feel slightly resentful towards Shakespeare for having so consciously diminished and restrained that personality and power of wit. However there is some consolation in the presence of Ford, who is the centre of the imaginative exploration in this play. The presentation of Ford's mad jealousy is done partly through his images and partly through his syntax. Our awareness of his jealousy is established directly by the wives' comments but also by a revealing detail after Nym has delivered his 'humoured' announcement that Falstaff loves Mistress Ford. Page reacts naturally to Nym's ludicrous speech, Ford with growing jealousy:

> PAGE. I never heard such a drawling, affecting
> rogue.
> FORD. If I do find it—well.
> PAGE. I will not believe such a Cataian, though
> the priest o'th' town commended him for a true
> man.
> FORD. 'Twas a good sensible fellow—well.
>
> [II. i. 141-47]

By this contrast we see that Ford actually approves of Nym, being pleased to find confirmation for his jealousy, and for the rest of this scene he is set aside in his fixation ('A man may be too confident. I would have nothing lie on my head' [II. i. 186-87]). In the next scene he bribes Falstaff 'lay an amiable siege to the honesty of this Ford's wife' [II. ii. 234-35], and his dissimulation is also shown by his language which is now that fluent but anonymous type of prose which Shakespeare generally creates for courtiers, or for gentlemen retailing important news, with rather formal disjunctions and politely expanded imagery [II. ii. 160-251]. In reply Falstaff shows his to-be-expected confidence that his attractions will overpower her 'embattled' defences, and not knowing who this 'Master Brook' actually is, begins to abuse Ford in violent images:

> I will use her as the key of the cuckoldy rogue's
> coffer, and there's my harvest-home. . . . Hang
> him, mechanical salt-butter rogue, I will stare
> him out of his wits. I will awe him with my
> cudgel; it shall hang like a meteor o'er the cuck-
> old's horns.
>
> [II. ii. 273-75, 278-81]

This is a magnificent dramatic situation, and has been extremely well exploited, particularly with Falstaff's usual vaunting *in absentia* being most sharply undercut.

Ford responds in agony, at first in imagery: 'What a damned Epicurean rascal is this! My heart is ready to crack with impatience' [II. ii. 287-88], but as his passion grows it forces itself into hypnotized symmetries:

> My wife hath sent to him,
> the hour is fixed,
> the match is made.
>
> [II. ii. 289-90]

He catches up Falstaff's boasts in a still more rigid pattern:

> My bed shall be abused,
> my coffers ransacked,
> my reputation gnawn at . . . .
>
> [II. ii. 292-93]

The thought of the double abuse now bites him (two longer sentences linked by the like ending 'this wrong') and he thrusts both the names of devils and the proverbial infidelities of nations into the same angry mould. The structure becomes more intense still as he returns to his wife and to thoughts of revenge:

> Then she plots,
> then she ruminates,
> then she devises;

and what they think in their hearts they may effect;
    they will break their hearts but they will
effect.
Heaven be praised for my jealousy! Eleven o'clock the
hour.
    I will prevent this,
        detect my wife,
    be revenged on Falstaff,
        and laugh at Page.
I will about it; better three hours too soon
          than  a  minute too late.
Fie, fie, fie!
Cuckold, cuckold, cuckold!

                        [II. ii. 305-14]

The content alone of this speech would be enough to convey Ford's manic jealousy, but the force of his fragmented, self-hunted syntax and his incoherent repetitions—this is all immeasurably increased by the stiff obsessional mould which syntactical symmetry here assumes. (pp. 151-53)

After Shakespeare's brilliant application of prose and its detailed devices of imagery and symmetrical syntax to Ford's insane jealousy, it is a relief to read his lines when, having been purged for ever of his mad fit, he is raised to verse and to the first ennobling image of the play:

Pardon me, wife, henceforth do what thou wilt.
I rather will suspect the sun with cold,
Than thee with wantonness. Now doth thy honour stand,
In him that was of late an heretic,
As firm as faith.

                        [IV. iv. 6-9]

But nevertheless the application of prose to such an intense and realistically developed emotional state is the major success of the play, for despite Shakespeare's great ventriloquism in creating that host of minor figures, and despite his flexible use of rhetorical structure for the extreme poles of Falstaff's clumsy letter and his erotic apotheosis, it is in the creation of Ford that the development of his prose is greatest. Here for the first time, excluding a few speeches from Shylock, prose is used for a character and situation of some seriousness: of course Ford is also comic (perhaps more to the Elizabethans than to us) but he is not a clown, a wit, or a rogue, and the emotions he presents are deeper than anything yet given to prose. In this respect *The Merry Wives of Windsor* is an improvement on the *Henry IV* plays, and in an important direction. (pp. 155-56)

> Brian Vickers, "The World of Falstaff," in his The Artistry of Shakespeare's Prose, *Methuen & Co. Ltd., 1968, pp. 89-170.*

### MURIEL C. BRADBROOK (lecture date 1968)

[*Bradbrook is an English scholar especially noted for her commentary on the development of Elizabethan drama and poetry. In her Shakespearean criticism, she combines both biographical and historical research, paying particular attention to the stage conventions of Elizabethan and earlier periods. In the excerpt below, taken from a lecture delivered at Trinity College, Cambridge in 1968, Bradbrook focuses on the incomparable professional skills which enabled Shakespeare to compose* The Merry Wives of Windsor *according to the terms set by his sovereign, Queen Elizabeth. She hypothesizes that in order to accomplish the feat within a fortnight the dramatist synthesized elements from a variety of "theatrical genres," recreated some of his most popular comic characters in supporting roles for the resurrected Falstaff, and drew upon his intimate understanding of life in the provincial*

*town of Stratford-upon-Avon. The play's vivid portrayal of "small town society," Bradbrook contends, earns it not only the designation of "citizen comedy," but also high praise for the craftsmanship of its creator.*]

In conversation recently . . . W. H. Auden roundly asserted that *The Merry Wives* was Shakespeare's worst play. Perhaps this is understandable from a lyric poet—for this is the most prosaic drama Shakespeare wrote, rising only to very pedestrian verse. Its virtues are craft virtues. (p. 75)

I shall consider *The Merry Wives* as an example of craftsman's theatre—a special order carried out superbly with all the resources of a great playwright and a great company. The very early tradition that it was written in a fortnight at the command of Queen Elizabeth, who wished to see Falstaff in love, explains both the strength and the limitations of what is one of the most thoroughly professional jobs in the English theatre. (p. 76)

In this play, it may be hazarded, we see what Shakespeare did when pushed hard. He turned out, most supremely competently, a planned, tidy, lively serviceable play which enjoyed professional esteem throughout the seventeenth century, and which has held the stage continuously both in England and elsewhere. (pp. 76-7)

[As] a piece of craftsmanship it is the product of a successfully established theatre, and one that was increasingly independent of court favour, surviving on the demand of the common citizens for this form of entertainment. It was no longer necessary to hold the mirror up to courtly life; we have moved from the world of Castiglione and Sidney into the new century.

But the old mock-battle between actor and audience underlies the treatment of Falstaff; there is a kind of covert hostility that culminates in the folk-game which is also a court masque, the hunting of the 'male deer' at Herne the Hunter's oak.

The play opens with a walk-on of figures some of whom do not appear again, for Act I is a shew parade of rôles from the company's recent comic successes—Falstaff and his followers. (pp. 77-8)

In the parade come Shallow and his Wise Cousin, a new figure modelled on Andrew Aguecheek [in *Twelfth Night*], Pistol, Bardolph and Falstaff's Boy; Corporal Nym comes from *Henry V;* the company's Welshman had a part. What action there is in Act I concerns three men wooing a maid . . . and an absurd duel, both of which could be in the mind of the author from *Twelfth Night.*

At the beginning of Act II, the play suddenly bursts into life, as the confident and resourceful wives encounter each other with identical love letters. No woman can fail to feel flattered by a love letter and Mrs Page is at first amused—'What, have I 'scaped love letters in the holiday time of my beauty and am I now a subject for them? let me see' [II. i. 1-3]; but her indignation is roused by the attempt to carry her by storm and her dignity reasserts itself. Mistress Ford recognizes the social condescension implied and achieves an epigram; 'If I would but go to hell for an eternal moment or so, I might be knighted' [II. i. 49-50]. This hinted at the darkness of the act, and perhaps there is a naughty pun in *hell* for the wives are free-spoken. (p. 78)

Rejecting the courtly code of secrecy in favour of bourgeois solidarity, the two women jump to the unromantic truth when they compare the duplicate letters with those duplicate dedications with blank spaces for names, which needy authors hawked about among subscribers. Falstaff would put us two in the press, says Mistress Page, but 'I had as lief be a giantess and lie under Mount Pelion' [II. i. 79-80]. Other brisk and familiar comparisons confirm the spirit of the formidable pair, and establish them as successors to a long line of tradesmen's wives, going back through Lydgate's Christmas mumming of henpecked husbands to Mrs Noah. . . .

Once the main action of man wooing two women is set going, Falstaff's retinue disappears, Justice Shallow dwindles, peaks, and pines in the wings, the three men wooing Nan Page patter on in minor scenes as an underplot. (p. 79)

The wooing of Nan follows a traditional theme for citizen comedy. Shakespeare's old rival Greene had shewn an earl wooing the keeper's daughter at Fressingfield, with the Prince of Wales as rival (*Friar Bacon and Friar Bungay*). Shallow's opening complaint: 'Knight, you have beaten my men, killed my deer and broken open my lodge' is countered by Falstaff's cool taunt 'But not kissed your keeper's daughter? . . . I have done all this' [I. i. 111-12, 113, 115]. The zest of the hunt, the fast instinctive move of hounds on the scent, drives the play forward, though it is a human hunt up to the last scene where Falstaff impersonates the ghostly Hunter; then, he who boasted to give the horns becomes the hunted prey. Dragging a chain like a lugged bear he goes 'like Actaeon, he, with Ringwood at his heels' [II. i. 118], not only the ghost of the old hunter but the ghost of himself.

Wooing games and roving in the woods, the mad mistakes of a night, were a popular and traditonal subject for many plays, and here again the actors had as it were a craft model upon which basis they and their dramatist could work.

The humours of the wooers and the mad mistakings which surround Mistress Anne leave her cool and always ready to 'be herself' on her own terms. When Fenton admits that her father thinks his interest is mercenary and he loves her 'but as a property', Anne observes with penetrating candour 'Maybe he tells you true' [III. iv. 10, 11]. She remains outside the women's league (or should it be called the Women's Institute?) 'Never a woman in Windsor knows more of Anne's mind than I do,' boasts Mrs Quickly [I. iv. 127-29]—and that is precisely nothing. Anne has appealed in vain to her mother against being married to Caius, under the sexually vivid image of feeling herself a mere property, a target for country sportsmen to aim at:

> Alas, I had rather be set quick i' the earth,
> And bowl'd to death with turnips.
>
> [III. iv. 86-7]

Youth and age are in contest from the beginning and youth wins. The old man turned young by love is mocked; 'Youth in a basket!' snarls the furious Ford [IV. ii. 116-17] thinking he has found his victim, and at the end Falstaff is mocked as 'metamorphosed youth'. He in turn feels himself a cock-shy, beringed by little William and his shrill-voiced mates:

> See now how Wit may be made a Jack-a-Lent
> when 'tis upon ill employment!
>
> [V. v. 126-28]
> (pp. 82-3)

The original Falstaff of course could not be revived. He had developed, perhaps without conscious planning; his heart had been 'fracted and corroborate' [*Henry V*, II. i. 124] by Hal's denial of him. However in the world of the theatre, no death is final; the impossible but intensely flattering order was man-

fully obeyed. The players met their day, and fulfilled their service and humble duty. Falstaff was brought out of the wardrobe—tatters, padding and all—only to be dumped back into the property basket. For that most serviceable object at last came into its own—what is the buckbasket but the property basket with the contents of the players' wardrobe? . . .

The relish with which Falstaff recounts his adventure among the laundry is the relish of his creator at seeing the old rags come to life. Told first to Bardolph, then to the deluded husband, the narrative rings with the built-in irony of the Gadshill story. To Falstaff, however, it is by now all as good as a play, though broken off when 'we had embraced, kissed and as it were, spoken but the prologue of our comedy' [III. v. 73-5]. (p. 84)

In his transvestite rôle as Old Mother Prat, Falstaff gets the sort of beating that Evans was always promising unwilling scholars, but afterwards he boasts to the Host that an old woman 'hath taught me more wit than ever I learnt before in my life, and I paid nothing for it neither but was paid for my learning'; and to Ford, more openly, of his own histrionic skill 'my admirable dexterity of wit, my counterfeiting the action of an old woman', which delivered him from the cudgel and the stocks [IV. v. 59-62, 117-18]. The vivacity and creative zest of his tormentors has been stimulated also; they set on again. 'Come,' cries Mrs Page, 'to the forge with it then; shape it; I would not have things cool!' [IV. ii. 223-24].

These jests are the familiar stuff of classical comedy of Figaro and Goldoni's innkeeper. The story indeed has a long ancestry, mainly in Italian plays. . . . (p. 85)

The Italian works, and many of the English comedies derived from them with likenesses to Shakespeare shew one startling difference—

All are tales of *youthful* and *successful* adultery. None has more than one heroine; the cornuto may be an ancient professor, and the successful intruder one of his own undergraduates. This is the sort of comedy Falstaff imagines himself to be part of, with his scornful description of 'the peaking cornuto, her husband' [III. v. 70-1], and his own assumption of youthful energy. (p. 86)

In the forest scene it is, of course, Falstaff who is admitted to the order of Cornuto, by incorporation as it were. Draped in his leg chains, he also provides a kind of parody of the Garter ceremony.

The village mumming of the Hunting of the Wild Man, the old German folk-play, may lie at the back of the legend of Herne the Hunter; there is a cruel folk ritual here where the wild man is lured to death by a woman (a part played by another man in disguise). But at Windsor too there would be a theme of the transformation of Actaeon in the presence of Diana (Ovid was in Shakespeare's mind, as one or two phrases betray). Diana duly received her praise in the final masque: at one point Falstaff seems to dissolve the play world and speak directly to the original audience—the court, who are always just off-stage in the play, but who were actually in their seats in the auditorium:

> If it should come to the ears of the court how
> I have been transformed and how my transfor-
> mation hath been washed and cudgelled, how
> they would melt me out of my fat drop by drop
> and liquor fisherman's boots with me; I warrent

they would whip me with their fine wits till I
were as crestfallen as a dried pear.

[IV. v. 94-100]

So, in the final scene, imagination in chains stands under the
pelting invective of shrewd counting-house and pulpit in Puritan alliance:

MRS PAGE. Why, Sir John, do you think . . .
that the devil could ever have made you our
delight? . . .
FORD. One that is as slanderous as Satan?
PAGE. And as poor as Job?
FORD. And as wicked as his wife?
EVANS. And given to fornications and to taverns
and sack and wine and metheglins?

[V. v. 146, 149-50, 155-59]

The ingredients of the play [turn] out to be the old traditional
triumph of the women's league (the Hock Tuesday play), the
pastoral wooing of courtier and country beauty, the merry mistakings of Love in a Wood, and jealous Italian comedy, revised
to a moral English theme. There remains what might be called
the social comedy or comical history and here again Shakespeare has used and transformed an old stage convention.

In comical histories, the King always appears in festive association with his subjects, and often in disguise. . . . No monarch appears or is even mentioned in this play about Windsor
town—for the Queen had commanded it and was present at its
first performance.

'It was not for me to bandy compliments with my sovereign,'
said Dr Johnson on a like occasion; the great honour made any
intervention of royalty in the play unnecessary—except the
'reflector' rôle of the Fairy Queen in the mask. The most
graceful thing was for the players to keep within their own
sphere, and this was what happened. (pp. 86-8)

In this play, and in this play alone, we meet Shakespeare at
home. The occasion, the compliment, called out a modest civic
pride. Bernard Shaw was probably right, when he wrote *The
Dark Lady of the Sonnets,* in suggesting that William Shakespeare was rather proud of being the son of the High Bailiff
of Stratford.

We meet the whole of a small town society here; it is not just
sketched in by one or two figures, but presents the crowded
vivacity of a Breughel painting, with many little sideshows.
Of course this is a holiday society. Even little William is given
a holiday from school, the burghers spend their time in sports;
there are bears in the town.

Relations however are realistic, not idyllic. The play is solidly
and comfortably bourgeois; it belongs to the new society of
late Elizabethan times. Mistress Ford, when the court was at
Windsor, had been the subject of attention from 'Earls, nay
which is more, pensioners' [II. ii. 76-7] but she scorned them
all. Mistress Page leads a better life than any in Windsor: 'Do
what she will, say what she will, take all, pay all, go to bed
when she list, all is as she list' [II. ii. 117-20], according to
Mistress Quickly, who adds that she never misses morning and
evening prayer. (pp. 88-9)

This is a pious community, and Ford repents in the language
of religion—for which he is rebuked by the solider Page.

Now doth thine honour stand,
In him that was of late an heretic,
As firm as faith.

[IV. iv. 8-10]

Mistress Page not only appropriates Falstaff's last remaining
servant, but is inclined to bully the schoolmaster (under the
formula, well known to all instructors of youth, 'My husband
says . . .' [IV. i. 14]. She does most of the planning for the
Falstaff campaign, enlists Quickly, arranges times and seasons;
but Mistress Ford commands a deadly coolness of retort, appropriate to one who had domestic difficulties, that is just as
serviceable as Mrs Page's more authoritative dominance.

Three or four families in a country village is
the very thing to work on.

as a later comic artist counselled [Jane Austen in a letter to
Anna Austen, September 14, 1814]; the scene at Windsor is
very close to the scene at Stratford. . . . Here is Stratford on
Avon's open hospitality; the hard shrewd look cast at a stranger;
the small boy being led to school; the Welsh schoolmaster
(Shakespeare's master had been Thomas Jenkins); the distant
sound of barking dogs as the bearward leads in his blind shac-
kled charge. Ben Jonson knew the streets of London in this
way; what Shakespeare knew best of all was 'English verdure,
English culture, English comfort, under a sun bright, without
being oppressive'. There are no beggars, no handicraftsmen,
no Wart nor Bullcalf [in *2 Henry IV*]; only the upper crust of
small-town society, with its personal servants. (pp. 89-90)

*The Merry Wives of Windsor* gives, as no other citizen's comedy does, the feel of provincial society at a particular time;
there is an exact awareness of the attitudes and prejudices of
a prosperous, Protestant, moralizing citizenry that is almost
Jonsonian. For instance, Master Page rejecting the courtly suitor
of his well-endowed girl:

Not by my consent, I promise you. The gentleman is of no having . . . No, he shall not
knit a knot in his fortunes with the finger of
my substance. If he take her, let him take her
simply; the wealth I have waits on my consent
and my consent goes not that way.

[III. ii. 71-2, 74-8]

When a man is hard pushed, he will employ what is nearest
to hand and uppermost in his mind. (p. 90)

I would think that in this play, working at speed, Shakespeare
made use of a 'Factotum'—a roughly familiar shape, which
represented a speedy adaptation from stock. But I do not think
that he took an old play, whether the lost 'Jealous Comedy'
or the much more unlikely *Two Merry Women of Abingdon*
and rewrote it. . . . The process I envisage is something like
that Mrs Page suggests behind Falstaff's love letter:

I warrent he hath a thousand of these letters,
written with blank spaces for different names,
and these are of the second edition.

[II. i. 74-7]

Once however, the play developed, with the transvestite farce
of the Wives, other false starts were simply left uneliminated.
The play was designed to give a chance to all the company;
everyone had a good fat part. (pp. 95-6)

'Our fellow Shakespeare' provided the script; Burbage stepped
down from his Falstaffian eminence to be cozened by two
others; what came out was a synthesis of many theatrical genres
which we do not recognize because they no longer separately
exist.

Perhaps for once Shakespeare also took a quick look at the
work of Ben Jonson. If the play was celebrated throughout the

*Act III. Scene iii. Mistress Ford and Falstaff. By J. McL. Ralston. The Department of Rare Books and Special Collections, The University of Michigan Library.*

seventeenth century as being Shakespeare's only regular comedy, the only one to fulfil the classical unities, it is perhaps an ironic touch that in such circumstances he found they had their uses. All this adds up to the very best second-best Shakespeare—the side of him that was sometimes defeated by his imagination. *The Merry Wives* has the deceptive simplicity of the completely professional accomplishment. (p. 96)

> Muriel C. Bradbrook, "Royal Command: 'The Merry Wives of Windsor'," in her Shakespeare, the Craftsman: The Clark Lectures, 1968, 1969. Reprint by Cambridge University Press, 1979, pp. 75-96.

**JEANNE ADDISON ROBERTS** (essay date 1970)

[*In her discussion of* The Merry Wives of Windsor *excerpted below, Roberts demonstrates that Shakespeare's play is a comedy and not a farce, basing her assessment on three reasons: the drama champions the integrity of social institutions, its dramatic action follows a structural pattern of rational "cause and effect," and it offers a hopeful view of life. Just as Mistress Ford and Mistress Page serve as "defenders of the social order," the critic argues, Falstaff is the personification of the vices that undermine marriage and society. Roberts contends that Falstaff—initially motivated by greed, but also displaying increasing evidence of lust as the play progresses—represents "a sexual menace" who must be incapacitated. Noting that none of the other transgressors*

*in the play receives a similar measure of punishment, the critic compares Falstaff to a scapegoat figure "who must be sacrificed to restore the health of society." Indeed, Roberts maintains, at the conclusion of the ritual masque in the final scene of the play, the entire community appears released "from all its follies and anxieties" and* The Merry Wives of Windsor *ends with the harmonious spirit of accommodation that is characteristic of the "comedy of forgiveness." Roberts is the earliest commentator to offer an extended examination of ritualistic elements in the play.*]

Most modern critics who discuss Shakespeare's *The Merry Wives of Windsor* at all sooner or later describe it as farcical, or a farce. At best the terms are used with a note of condescension or apology, and at worst they are scathing. . . .

On the surface there is nothing surprising about considering *The Merry Wives* a farce. Its most memorable, most referred to, most illustrated scenes—Falstaff in the buck-basket, Falstaff horned as Herne the Hunter—involve visual, physical humor; its characters are recognizable types; the plot is rapid and artificially repetitious; the tone is joyously light-hearted. All this sounds to the modern ear like farce. And yet, the more we study the critical history of the play, the more uneasy we become about dismissing it as a farce. The modern attitude has by now become a habit which blinds us to much of the play's skillful design, genuine comic impact—even subtlety. Both in content and dramatic technique, if not in depth of characterization or poetry, *The Merry Wives* deserves, I believe, to be considered with such other plays of its probable period of composition as *The Merchant of Venice* and *Much Ado About Nothing* rather than with the more farcical *Comedy of Errors* and *The Taming of the Shrew* with which it is frequently associated. The play has a structural coherence and a social orientation which are fundamentally opposed to the spirit of farce. (p. 109)

Structure is, of course, closely related to the importance of action. . . . (p. 110)

[Both] early and modern critics have seen in *The Merry Wives* a play where plot and action are important. But for modern critics, this quality, far from eliciting praise, has demoted the play to farce or evoked the epithet ''non-Shakespearean.'' . . .

F. T. Bowers sees the emphasis on plot and the use of type characters as clearly identifying the play as farce [in his Introduction to *The Merry Wives of Windsor* (1963)]. R. B. Heilman, speaking generally [in ''The *Taming* Untamed; or, The Return of the Shrew''], lists the ''surface manifestations'' of farce as being ''hurly-burly theater, with much slapstick, roughhouse . . . pratfalls, general confusion, trickery, uproars, gags, practical jokes.'' Such description brings to mind immediately the dumping, beating, and pinching of Falstaff, the choleric rantings of Dr. Caius, the duel that is never fought, the post-horse plot, the multiplicity and rapid movement of characters—all of which seem to point toward farce. About one characteristic of farce, in fact, it seems to me that there can be no quarrel. From its earliest appearance as the interpolation of gags in religious drama, through its manifestation in the mute Harlequin in the *commedia dell'arte*, farce has always involved bodily and non-verbal humor. And insomuch as physical and non-verbal action are an important element in the continuous stage success of *The Merry Wives*, there can be no doubt that in this respect the play is farcical. Farcical, but not necessarily a farce.

It is important to distinguish here between stage business—admittedly often farcical—and plot. *The Merry Wives* has at least two plots, and their structures are of great interest. The main plot is farcical in subject matter, though not, I think, in treatment. *The Oxford Companion to the Theatre* defines a farce as a ''full-length play dealing with some absurd situation hinging generally on extramarital relations,'' and this does describe the action involving the title characters. The second plot, however, is typically comic, if we adopt the view that comedy is the celebration of the triumph of young love, the overthrow of the authority of the older generation and the acceptance by society of the new. There is the suggestion of a third plot in the affairs of the Host, Caius, Sir Hugh, Nym and Pistol. The various threads of the three plots are loosely interwoven until they come together in the last act. (p. 112)

Here at last, in the complex and artfully contrived plot, is the proof, one might suppose, that *The Merry Wives* is a comedy rather than a farce. But even on this there is no necessary agreement. . . . [Emphasis] on plot is taken as a sign of farce by modern critics. Heilman says that neatness of plot and mechanical action leading to symmetrical effects are typical of farce. Neatness and symmetry there certainly are in *The Merry Wives*. There are three suitors for the hand of Anne Page, and Mistress Quickly systematically encourages all three. Falstaff decides to send identical letters to Mistress Ford and Mistress Page, and their identical responses lead to his being trapped three times in the situation of a would-be adulterer. The body-

curer is balanced by the soul-curer. Both Master and Mistress Page decide at the same time on a secret marriage for their daughter, and both are disappointed. Both would-be suitors carry off boys instead of girls. It is like an elaborate ritual dance; and, as in any good dance, there is a little incidental variety. Mistress Ford is jealous and Master Page is not; Slender is shown wooing and Caius is not; however, the variations only emphasize the patterns, and it is obvious that symmetry is an important part of the method and meaning of the play. But then, is not symmetry important to the method and meaning of all drama? indeed of all art? (p. 113)

Symmetry is especially crucial to certain kinds of comedy, where effects depend on the arousal and manipulation of audience expectation, and where absurd repetition is frequently a vehicle of satire. But it is a mistake, I think, to identify symmetrical effect as a special characteristic, and not simply an instrument, of farce. Typically the symmetry of farce is saying that the world is absurd and that man is a ridiculous animal compulsively repeating meaningless configurations. The structure of *The Merry Wives* is saying rather that the world is patterned and the patterns have meaning. And the effect is not limited to this one play. Elaborate symmetry is a regular characteristic of Shakespearean comedy, at least through *Twelfth Night*. On the other hand, mechanical action, co-incidence, effects produced without developed motivation of character, and behavior persistent in the face of all probability are more properly associated with farce. Here the judging of *The Merry Wives* becomes a delicate matter.

The greatest improbability in the play is that Falstaff should be fooled three times by essentially the same device. If one can accept this—and Shakespeare makes it easier, as Bertrand Evans points out, by manipulating suspense and discrepant awarenesses in the second occurrence, and by focussing our attention on Anne Page in the third [see excerpt above, 1960]—the rest of the play becomes consistent and credible. There is nothing remarkable about Falstaff's being willing to exploit sex for money, in three men wanting to marry a rich beautiful girl, or in a perversely jealous husband wanting to discover what he believes to be the truth. And the action which grows out of these situations is not mechanical. Only Falstaff blindly repeats his folly. Sir Hugh and Dr. Caius discover that they have been tricked by the Host and conspire together for ''revenge.'' Ford discovers his error and reforms. (pp. 113-14)

Everything in the play is believably arranged by someone in it. Comic effects are achieved by the fact that all of the arrangers, except Anne Page, are ignorant of some essential fact. Betrand Evans is wrong, I think, in assigning Mistress Quickly the role of an all-knowing Portia or Rosalind. She knows no more than the wives in the Ford-Falstaff plot; and she is in fact ignorant of Anne Page's true affections, as we see when she says after her first interview with Fenton, ''But Anne loves him not . . .'' [I. iv. 163-64]. It is not Mistress Quickly but the Host who is Fenton's confidant on the night of the elopement. And it seems likely that Quickly only takes the role of the Fairy Queene at the end because the part must be taken by an actor who has established a ''female'' identity in the play, and no other such actor is available.

Bentley argues that in the world of farce co-incidence is taken for granted and mischief becomes fate [in his *The Life of the Drama*]. Thus the jealous husband arrives home by accident when the lover is being entertained by his wife. But in *The Merry Wives* the jealous husband arrives home because he has helped to plan the assignation. As Bertrand Evans points out, nearly everyone in the play is both deceiving and deceived. The Host aborts a duel by deceiving Caius and Evans but is in turn victimized by their plot. Falstaff is deceived by Ford but still gains a kind of superiority over him as he relates his "adventures" with his wife. The wives deceive Falstaff but are genuinely surprised at the actual arrival of Ford at the assignation when they had expected only to pretend he was coming. Fenton is deceived by Mistress Quickly, who takes his money while apparently doing nothing to advance his suit, but at the end he deceives everyone and triumphantly bears off Anne Page. Master and Mistress Page, Slender, and Caius plan to deceive each other but are deceived by Fenton and Anne.

Complex as it is, the structure of the play is obviously a simplification and ordering of life. It is not the random world of farce. It is a world of cause and effect, human interaction, and rational principle. One might note in passing that, though everyone in the play but the lovers is notably imperfect, the women are superior to the men in knowledge and capability. And, although no one person is in control, some beneficent force, perhaps even Queen Elizabeth herself presiding from the audience, is ordering this universe. If farce is absurd and ruled by whim, one is forced to conclude that . . . *The Merry Wives* is not farce but comedy.

There remains to be considered the question of characterization. Everyone has seen the characters of this play as varied and vivid, but it would be hard to deny that they are shallowly developed and superficially presented to the audience. The movement of the action is very rapid. Although there are a number of soliloquies, none of them is memorable as a subtle exploration of character. Their purpose is clearly either to advance the plot—as in the case of Mistress Page's reading of the letter from Falstaff—or to supply incidental humor or develop mood—as in the soliloquies of Falstaff. Most of the play is written in prose; and where there is poetry, it is usually flat and "unpoetic" in tone. There are no long, leisurely scenes which reveal the nuances of human interrelations. The main plot demands a husband, wife, and lover; and they are supplied, the two former in duplicate. The Anne Page plot demands parents, daughter, and suitor; and they are supplied, the latter in triplicate. Several characterizations—Nym and probably Caius and the Host—are determined by the vogue for humours in comedy. . . . The chief comic features of Caius and Sir Hugh are the result simply of their national origins.

Certainly these characters are types, but I would deny that this makes them farcical. (pp. 114-15)

[Early] and late critics agree that farce is drama of which the only purpose is to provoke laughter. Thus, those critics who have designated the play a farce are generally bound by definition to find it lacking in underlying significances. (p. 116)

The more one thinks of the moral design of the play, however, the more interesting it becomes. It is not simply an illustration of the poetic justice which one would expect Neo-classical critics to admire. In fact, Dennis tried to make the play conform more nearly to poetic justice. In his adaptation [1702] he substituted Ford for Falstaff in the final scene, thus ensuring that Ford be punished for his unreasonable jealousy and that Falstaff be saved from the final ignominy. But this was not Shakespeare's way.

His play, a true domestic drama, focussed on marriage—the problems of achieving it and the perils of maintaining it. The enemies of good marriage which he singles out are greed, lust, jealousy, and stupidity. Greed appears in two forms and pro-

vides a thematic link between the two plots: it is Falstaff's greed which motivates him to attempt to seduce the wives (though vanity and lust become operative later); and it is greed also, in a more innocuous-appearing form, which is Page's motive for desiring to marry his daughter to Slender. As Anne shrewdly observes, "a world of vile ill-favour'd faults / Looks handsome in three hundred pounds a year!" [III. iv. 32-3]. Interestingly Falstaff's greed is punished, not once but three times, while Page's, though of potentially more disastrous consequences, is disappointed but forgiven.

Similarly Falstaff's adulterous intentions and his developing lust, although they are hardly dangerous since they are instantly recognized and rejected, are thrice punished. Ford's jealousy, a really serious threat to happy marriage, involving blindness and breach of trust, goes unpunished except for his humiliation before his friends. An echo of the jealous theme appears in the sub-plot in Caius's hysterical challenge to Sir Hugh when he hears of a rival. As a husband he would be more jealous than Ford. His passion leads to mild humiliation; and his desires, like Page's, are ludicrously disappointed, but he is otherwise unscathed. Stupidity appears, alas, in the Falstaff of the main plot, in spite of his still-active wit, and is supremely developed in the poignantly unassuming Slender. Again the major deficiency of Slender is laughingly enjoyed, while Falstaff suffers the consequences of his fault.

Why should Falstaff bear so much and everyone else so little? It does begin to appear that non-rational, perhaps subconscious forces are at work in the play as well as clear-cut principles of cause and effect. Eric Bentley, who takes farce very seriously as a means of the emotional catharsis of suppressed aggression through laughter, contends that violence is the essence of farce. Conceivably there is some vicarious pleasure in the violence directed against Falstaff. Possibly some of the audience is in fact delighted by the exposing of the outrageously witty con-man who got away with so much in *Henry IV,* and now reveals himself as a stupid, vain, old man. Perhaps the furiously-offended critics who object so loudly are only a very vocal minority. But even if this is so, it does not explain the lenience in dealing with Ford or the other subtly diffused hostilities which are explored but never openly enjoyed.

Underlying hostilities there certainly are in this play. Most of them are generated by sexual feelings—a fact that should hardly surprise us in a play about marriage. It is sexual rivalry which leads to the attempted duel between Caius and Evans; it is sexual rivalry which motivates the struggle between Ford and Falstaff. And, interestingly enough, as Sherman Hawkins points out [in "The Two Worlds of Shakespearean Comedy"], some of the hostility is expressive of the war between the sexes. Mistress Page and Mistress Ford move with one accord, almost savagely, to be "revenged" on Falstaff; and Ford seems to get considerable pleasure from cudgelling the old "woman" of Brainford. Master and Mistress Page are rivals in their plans for their daughter. Mistress Ford gratuitously tricks her husband a second time with the buck basket, apparently enjoying his agonies; and he is almost sadistic in plotting to unmask his wife as an adulteress. Anne Page moves with all the cool clear-sightedness of Shaw's life-force to select her mate, blithely dismissing the ineffectual ardor of Slender, and protesting that rather than marry Caius she would be "set quick i' the earth / And bowl'd to death with turnips" [III. iv. 86-7].

Thus, sexual encounters may be fraught with dangers, fringed with resentments, and generative of hostilities, but these are not openly exploited as they are in farce. Shakespeare keeps these hostilities peripheral. They are safely suppressed by the general aura of good feeling; the need of society for the establishment and preservation of the family overrides the incidental feelings of the individuals. And what cruelty there is, is insulated by the sure sense that the audience has that what they see is all a game, that the limited characters before them cannot, in fact, feel much pain.

If there is a real satisfaction in violence in *The Merry Wives*, it is interesting to note that its source is exactly opposite to that which Bentley describes in farce. He argues that violence springs out of resentment against the repression imposed by society. Farce embodies, he says, the wish to damage the family and "desecrate the household gods." The forbidden delights of adultery are openly contemplated, and the mother-in-law is actually slapped. The reverse is true in the dominant themes of *The Merry Wives*. Although there are the casually-revealed social hostilities mentioned above, and although there may be some faint traces of good-natured satire against the follies of the churchman, the schoolmaster, and the doctor, the major emphases of the play specifically reinforce the middle-class social values of its participants. The chief enemy—personified by Falstaff, and defeated in the ruthless attack mounted against him—is not just adultery, but uncontrolled sex. The wives in this action become not merely women whose virtue has been affronted but defenders of the social order. The narrative becomes not so much moralistic as flatly descriptive. The sex drive is not so much "punished" as rechanneled.

An interpretation of this sort explains, I think, the puzzling identification of Falstaff with Actaeon, discussed by Geoffrey Bullough and John M. Steadman [see Additional Bibliography], and accounts for what seems to be an anticlimactic sequence in the defeats of Falstaff. Why should Falstaff, the fat, dissolute old knight, be associated with the young hunter, the nephew of Cadmus, who comes by accident upon Diana bathing, is changed to a stag and torn to pieces by his own dogs? Why should Actaeon be associated with adultery, and in what sense can he be seen as representing a moral lesson? It may be true that Actaeon came to be associated with adultery because of his horns, but neither he nor Falstaff fits as the prototype of the cuckold, the horned husband. Each represents rather a sexual menace, whose horns are a sign of sexual potency. Actaeon begins to grow his horns immediately upon seeing the naked body of Diana; Falstaff's develop more slowly, urged on by the desire to be revenged on Ford and by two unsuccessful encounters with the wives. The phallic significance of the horns is reinforced in Falstaff's heavily erotic soliloquy in the last scene where he refers to Jove as a bull on whom "love set . . . horns" [V. v. 4]. By this last scene Falstaff has become so eager that he prays to Jove for a "cool rut-time" lest he "piss his tallow" [(V. v. 14-15]. Whether or not there is a moral "sin" involved in the "horniness" of Actaeon or Falstaff is really irrelevant. The Elizabethans may have moralized the myth, and Shakespeare's fairies speak against "unchaste desire" [V. v. 96]; but the myth itself is purely descriptive of causes and effects. Actaeon simply happened to be in the wrong place at the wrong time. Ovid says specifically that not desert, but "cruell fortune . . . was the cause of . . . his smart" [in *The Metamorphoses*]. Falstaff's initial motivation in writing his letters, as we have seen, was greed. His lust develops later, and we see him as much pursued as pursuing. One might well even argue that the wives are guilty of entrapment. But the point is that both Actaeon and Falstaff become sexually threatening to the social order, and the order

does not tolerate such menaces. Actaeon is torn to pieces by dogs; Falstaff is symbolically castrated.

One wonders in reading *The Merry Wives* in the study, though not as one sees it on the stage, why Shakespeare chose the order that he did for the three humiliations of Falstaff. Being pinched by fairies seems something of an anti-climax after being thrown into the Thames with a basket of dirty linen, and beaten by a jealous husband. There is in the final episode a change in mood from the realistic to the fantastic as well as what seems a decrease in physical intensity. I would argue that the decrease in intensity is only seeming and not actual. Because the events of the final scene are ruthless and cruel, and because the play is a comedy, the action is quite literally masqued. The atmosphere is lightened by the pretense of unreality; the lecherous fat knight is balanced by the ideal of the Knights of the Garter. But what happens is clear.

Society has tried its usual methods for controlling illicit, threatening behavior. Rebirth and baptism—the expulsion from the buck-basket and the dip in the Thames—have failed. Physical punishment—the cudgelling by Ford—has failed. The only alternative is to incapacitate the offender. Lest there be any doubt, we have Mrs. Page's announcement that the group's objective is to "dis-horn the spirit" [IV. iv. 64].

"Dis-horning the spirit" means three things in this scene: 1) the removal of the sexual potency of Falstaff; 2) the transferral of this potency to Ford; 3) and the final exorcising of the specter of cuckoldry. The moment the pinching is finished, Falstaff becomes Fall-staff, the figure of impotence his very name suggests. . . . The horns should, I think, be removed from his head immediately. The stage directions do not make this clear, but the dialogue suggests it strongly. Mistress Page, forbidding her husband to carry the "jest" further, apparently holds up the horns, saying "Do not these fair yokes / Become the forest better than the town?" [V. v. 107-08] (i.e. unchecked sexuality is all right among animals but not in human society.) And in the next speech Ford jokingly shows the horns to "Master Brook." The final speech of the play, in which Ford says to Falstaff, "To Master Brook you yet shall hold your word; For he to-night shall lie with Mistress Ford" [V. v. 244-45] indicates that Ford means to make good use of his horn(s).

I would not rule out the likelihood that the horned Falstaff represents specifically adultery as well as sexual potency. Obviously the two are closely related, and the image of the horned man would surely have suggested cuckoldry to the audience. . . . The final scene of *The Merry Wives* represents then both the disarming of the threatener and the removal of the threat. Altogether a victory for middle-class morality.

The emotional effects of the action of *The Merry Wives* may be variously explained, but all the explanations point toward comedy rather than farce. It may be that Falstaff is the *pharmakos*, or scapegoat, who must be sacrificed to restore the health of society. This would explain the fact that only he suffers real punishment, and that his final punishment seems to release the group from all its follies and anxieties. . . . It may be that the play represents, as Frye suggests . . . , an "elaborate ritual of the defeat of winter" [see excerpt above, 1948]. . . . If this view is accepted, the play becomes a "festive comedy," appropriately designed for the season, if April 23, 1597 is indeed the date of the first performance.

One might also speculate that Shakespeare was contrasting in this work, as well as in *The Merchant of Venice, Much Ado About Nothing*, and *Measure for Measure*, notions of strict justice as opposed to mercy. In any case, the reconciliation and total harmony of the end suggest "comedy of forgiveness." One other element is clearly operative. The younger generation quietly but resolutely establishes a new social unit and overrules the edicts of its elders. (pp. 116-20)

Emotionally as well as rationally the effect then of *The Merry Wives* is that of comedy. We might say that farce is the exploitation of fears and resentments, conscious and unconscious—the fear that man is essentially only an animal, and that chance totally controls the universe; the resentment of the repressions and frustrations of a social order. Comedy, on the other hand, is the literary equivalent of the theology of hope. It reinforces our confidence in social forms, and asserts that there are orderly and beneficent forces at work in them, however weak, imperfect, and absurd or cruel the individual parts. The latter is an exact description of the tone of *The Merry Wives*. Farcical it is in some respects, . . . but we cannot achieve a full appreciation of the play by reducing it to a farce. More accurately we might describe it as a farcical, humorous, ironic, occasionally poetic, happy, festive middle-class comedy of forgiveness in prose. (pp. 120-21)

> *Jeanne Addison Roberts, "The Merry Wives: Suitably Shallow, but neither Simple nor Slender," in* Shakespeare Studies: An Annual Gathering of Research, Criticism, and Reviews, *Vol. VI, 1970, pp. 109-23.*

**RALPH BERRY** (essay date 1972)

[*Berry describes* The Merry Wives of Windsor *as a "brutal farce" in which the central motif of revenge evokes sadistic reactions from the audience, reflecting the hostility directed against Falstaff by the other characters. He notes that the citizens of Windsor do not shield or play up to Falstaff as Prince Hal did in* 1 *and* 2 Henry IV, *and he argues that this shift from cooperation to enmity has led commentators to the mistaken belief that Falstaff himself has changed. Berry judges that "if one were to take it at all seriously,"* The Merry Wives of Windsor *"would be a markedly unpleasant play."*]

A certain quality of brutality distinguishes *The Merry Wives of Windsor*. This derives from the circumstances of its composition: the old tale that the play was written upon demand within a short space of time is doubtless true, though one need not accept the Queen herself as the most exigent of the play's sponsors. It bears all the marks of rapid production, evident not so much in the loose ends and padding as in the forced and mechanical quality of the writing. The piece seems a by-product of Shakespeare's career, executed with professionalism but without inner commitment. (p. 146)

The main problem of the commission is clearly the handling of Falstaff. . . . It is commonly said that Falstaff is much changed, that the Falstaff of *Henry IV* would have penetrated the deceptions without difficulty. Now this view is odd, because by the end of *Henry IV, Part II* Falstaff is living in an advanced state of fantasy. He has erected his hopes into facts, precisely the situation of *The Merry Wives of Windsor*. What has changed is not Falstaff, but other people. The environment no longer cooperates with him. Hal, in the Gadshill-Boar's Head escapade [in *1 Henry IV*], is really an accomplice of Falstaff's, playing up to the old man. Elsewhere, as at Shrewsbury, Hal shields Falstaff from the consequences of his actions. The burghers of Windsor see matters differently. They, and not the declining Falstaff, make the play the brutal farce it is.

The idea of the play is revenge, a communal impulse of hostility directed toward a single target. The plot is a double revenge action. [Mistress Page's] "How shall I be revenged on him? for revenged I will be, as sure as his guts are made of puddings" [II. i. 30-1] is echoed by [Mistress Ford's] "How shall I be revenged on him?" [II. i. 66], the two uniting operatically in "Let's be revenged on him" [II. i. 93]. This move against Falstaff is preceded by Nym and Pistol's

> *Nym:* I have operations which be humors of revenge.
> *Pistol:* Wilt thou revenge?
>
> [I. iii. 89-91]

And so the combination against Falstaff is mounted. The play essentially consists of "operations which be humors of revenge" against Falstaff, the comic scapegoat. Thus the moment which, more than any other, projects the idea of the play, is its climax. The play's ikon is the prostrate Falstaff, circled around (like a covered wagon by Indians), derided, pinched, and burnt by his tormentors.

The revenge motif unleashes much sadism in the audience. If farce were not mechanical, it would be Theater of Cruelty; so the playwright has to maintain his dramatis personae, and the audience's reactions, under rigorous control. Falstaff aside, the most vulnerable person in this farce-world is Ford. He has to have a capacity for feeling pain, the plot demands it. The part offers something to the actor, and has been known to stand stereoscopically out of a production. But the soliloquies of the apprehensive cornuto are not allowed to generate more than laughter, the laughter of rejection. The other characters fit into a consistent pattern, that of limitation. They normally exhibit a single humor, a quirk of attitude and language. No illustration is required, but we ought to note the reduction of this approach to characterization: the foreigners. Sir Hugh and Dr. Caius are distinguished for little save their un-Englishness: their accents place them, account for them, define them. They *are* accents. The difference between Fluellen [*Henry V*] and Sir Hugh is the measure of serious drama, and farce. The audience enjoys total superiority over these puppets, and this superiority extends to the situations in which they are placed. Time and again the audience has the advantage over the participants, and this is most tellingly, perhaps, demonstrated in the scenes between Falstaff and Ford/Brook. Falstaff's gifts as a raconteur compose what may be termed the manifest humor of III, 5. The dynamism of the encounter is situational; Ford, converting his horror to solicitude, is in a memorable plight, and nothing in the play is funnier than Falstaff's parting "Adieu. You shall have her, Master Brook; Master Brook, you shall cuckold Ford" [III. v. 136-38]. At such moments the audience enjoys a huge triumph at the expense of the participants in the action. (pp. 146-49)

The quality of *The Merry Wives of Windsor* is perfectly expressed in its jokes. What *Pericles* is to myth, *The Merry Wives of Windsor* is to jokes; the piece is a Public Record Office of graffiti, a register of underground jokes. Some of them, naturally, are harmless enough; the name joke, for instance ("Alice Shortcake" [I. i. 204]), or Pistol's response to Falstaff's "My honest lads, I will tell you what I am about." "Two yards, and more" [I. iii. 38-40]. But the play offers an opportunity, unparalleled in Shakespeare, to discern the underground life of the nation, surfacing briefly like the turbid Fleet before resuming its subterranean flow. Here, for example, are the comic foreigners whose insecure command of language leads to a scatological pun. *Dr. Caius:* "If dere be one, or two, I shall make-a de turd" [III. iii. 236-37]. Here is that stock property of medical farce, or of farce containing a doctor, the bedpan joke:

> Host: Thou art a Castilian King-Urinal
>
> [II. iii. 33]
>
> Evans: I will knog his urinals about his knave's costard.
>
> [III. i. 13-14]

Here is the combination of malapropism and pun scatological, or pun sexual: Mistress Quickly reigns over these provinces of language. "She's as fartuous a civil modest wife" [II. ii. 97-8] instances the one. The other is richly elaborated in IV, 1, where the audience is invited to share the commentary of Mistress Quickly on the grammar lesson. She, for the moment, is the representative of the audience on the stage. Without her, someone might conceivably miss the point of

> Evans:      What is the focative case, William?
> William:   "O, vocativo, O."
> Evans:      Remember, William; focative is "caret."
>
> [IV. i. 50-3]

Any such strays are reintegrated into the community following Mistress Quickly's "And's that a good root" [IV. i. 54]. . . . A bawd's speciality is bawdry: and Mistress Quickly's function is to deliver it, whether knowingly or not. ("She does so take on with her men—they mistook their erection." "So did I mine," says Falstaff bitterly [III. v. 39-41].)

Inventive as some of the verbal humor is, most of the jokes exploit areas of stock response. The well-known addiction of the Irish to whiskey, and the Welsh to cheese, is faithfully noted. . . . Similarly, the Host's "bully-rook" and Nym's "humour" are a sort of inverted euphuism, a form of language that reduces all expression to a set mode. The Host has some feeling for language, but Nym's "humour" is pure catch-phrase, and Shakespeare milks it shamelessly in I, 3. The solecisms of the undereducated (Slender and Quickly), and the blunders of the foreigners are remorselessly detailed. Even the village idiot makes his contribution, through Simple's brief appearance. Double entendre reigns over all. The audience—whose faculties are less extended than in any other play in the canon—is consistently urged to celebrate its release from the standards normally operating in a Shakespeare comedy.

The jokes, the characters, and the action all express a central impulse: hostility governed by superiority. As is the audience to the mechanized puppets, so are the puppets to their target. And yet, Falstaff is not the only one to suffer, for the spirit of hostility, let loose in the play, turns round to strike back at its agents. The Host fools Sir Hugh and Dr. Caius, yet is robbed by the German confidence ring. Page deceives his wife concerning his daughter, yet is himself deceived by Fenton. Mistress Page triumphs over Falstaff, yet her plans for Anne are thwarted. Ford and his wife are presumably sufficiently paid by remaining married to each other; the record is fairly explicit on the matter. Everyone, it seems, is under-cut. So revenge becomes a kind of figure for the impulse of hostility that animates the play; and that impulse is satisfied, in the audience, by the downfall of the revengers, just as it is at the end of [Cyril Tourneur's] The Revenger's Tragedy. (That, too, is an essentially comic resolution.) The balancing, or compensation of hostile forces is well observed by Falstaff, speaking for the audience: "I am glad, though you have ta'en a special stand to strike at me, that your arrow hath glanced" [V. v. 234-35].

This kind of resolution is one of comedy's analogues to catharsis.

The festive ending of The Merry Wives of Windsor, therefore, is not a jovial drunkenness, a feeling of holiday repletion, but the satisfaction of contending forces finding an equilibrium. It is the ideal ending for what, if one were to take it at all seriously, would be a markedly unpleasant play. One imagines that Shakespeare laid down his pen with some relief, after disposing of this account of ignorant stereotypes clashing by night. There are times, certainly, when on the evidence here one could mistake Shakespeare's avocation for scriptwriter, rather than playwright. All the same, one comes away from The Merry Wives of Windsor with a feeling of enhanced respect for its author. Only a professional could have done it. (pp. 149-53)

> Ralph Berry, "The Revengers' Comedy," in his Shakespeare's Comedies: Explorations in Form, Princeton University Press, 1972, pp. 146-53.

## W. L. GODSHALK   (lecture date 1973)

[Godshalk identifies a structural pattern of "offense, revenge of punishment, . . . and reconciliation" in The Merry Wives of Windsor that shapes not only the central dramatic action, but several of the subplots as well. As both Falstaff and Ford undergo a course of purgation leading to enlightenment and regeneration, the critic maintains, each passes through a "symbolic transformation from man to beast" which mirrors the way in which their transgressions have led to their alienation from human society. Godshalk contends that their failure to understand and appreciate the "true worth" of others is the principal reason for their alienation. Commenting that several minor characters also misapprehend each other's value, the critic demonstrates that the feeling of estrangement in the play is heightened by repeated instances of failed verbal communication, and he concludes that throughout The Merry Wives of Windsor "linguistic alienation reflects the lack of moral understanding." This essay was first delivered as a lecture at the 1973 meeting of the Southeastern Renaissance Conference.]

[The Merry Wives of Windsor] needs not so much the apology of excuse as it does the apology of defense and explanation, for it is not so superficial and disunified as the critics would suggest. Shakespeare's grasp of his material is as firm here as it is in any of his comedies. (p. 98)

[The play] is largely unified by a series of comic revenges, in which illusion plays a dominant and varied role. Since the play is a comedy, revenge leads not to bloodshed, but to reconciliation, and the pattern of offence, revenge of punishment (either threatened or carried out), and reconciliation echoes through the play. It is announced in the first scene, where Falstaff's offence—"you have beaten my men, kill'd my deer, and broke open my lodge" [I. i. 111-112]—calls forth Shallow's vengeance—"I will make a Star Chamber matter of it" [I. i. 1-2]. If he were younger, Shallow suggests, "the sword should end it" [I. i. 40-1], in a duel. Although we may question Shallow's valour, Evans, Page, and the Host of the Garter keep the matter from becoming serious and bring about a reconciliation. "I would," says Page, "I could do a good office between you" [I. i. 99-100] and Evans offers to "make atonements and compromises" [I. i. 33-4].

The quarrel between Shallow and Falstaff is reflected in Slender's accusation of Falstaff's three followers: "Bardolph, Nym, and Pistol . . . carried me to the tavern and made me drunk, and afterward picked my pocket" [I. i. 125-27]. Both Falstaff and his men stand accused, but since this is the last time that we hear of the offences, we assume that Page's feast of hot venison pasty and wine leads to some sort of reconciliation.

The feast also leads to the major action, for it is at Page's love feast that Falstaff decides to try his fortune at seducing Mrs. Page and Mrs. Ford. Aimed at bringing about brotherly love between the contending parties, the feast serves to excite Falstaff's lust for the two wives and for their money, and the wrong he has done Shallow becomes a prelude to Falstaff's intended cony-catching. He will make another attempt at poaching deer/dear, and his attempt leads imaginatively to the deer hunting in the play's final scene.

Blinded by his own self-esteem, Falstaff deceives himself with the belief that the social kindnesses (and possibly the disbelieving stares) of Mrs. Ford and Mrs. Page mean more than they do. . . . The dissolute knight consequently determines to mend his fortunes by becoming the mutual lover of the wealthy middle-class ladies: "They shall be my East and West Indies, and I will trade to them both" [I. iii. 71-2], and he sends his young page as a "pinnace to these golden shores" [I. iii. 80]. His self-deception, his belief that his age and his obesity will allow him to be a dashing lover, leads directly to his attempt at deceiving the merry wives.

The two ladies react to Falstaff's identical love letters with the same question: "How shall I be reveng'd on him?" [II. i. 30],

Act III. Scene iii. Mistress Ford, Falstaff, Mistress Page, and Robin. By M. W. Peters. The Department of Rare Books and Special Collections, The University of Michigan Library.

. . . and they conspire to avenge the knight's offence against their middle-class morality: "Let's be reveng'd on him" [II. i. 93]. Their comic vengeance results in the triple "transformation" . . . of Falstaff into dirty linen, into the old witch of Brainford, and into Herne the Hunter. Carried to the Thames "in the name of foul clothes" [III. v. 99], he is changed into the dirty linen of the lecher he desires to be. Or perhaps he has befouled himself in another manner, as Mrs. Ford suggests: "I am half afraid he will have need of washing; so throwing him into the water will do him a benefit" [III. iii. 182-84]. Wearing the dress of Mother Pratt, he becomes both witch and effeminate man, for effeminacy, Elizabethans believed, was the result of giving oneself to lust. Last of all, dressed as Herne with horns and chains, he becomes a native English Actaeon, changed into a beast through the excess of his lusts. Each of the transformations in the revenge plot is symbolic, and by assuming the three roles, Falstaff loses first his dignity, second his masculinity, and finally his humanity. In his progression from man to beast, he is stifled, beaten, and burnt; he undergoes, in effect, a purgative course. (pp. 98-100)

In a way, Ford's actions [also] follow the pattern of offence, revenge, and reconciliation. However, the offence that Ford believes he has found does not in actuality exist: "Who says this is improvident jealousy? My wife hath sent to him, the hour is fix'd, the match is made. . . . See the hell of having a false woman!" [II. ii. 288-90, 291-92]. Motivated by the vengeful Pistol, Ford is as blind through self-deception as Falstaff, and his attempts to "be reveng'd" [II. ii. 310-11] are abortive and comic. He misses both chances to capture Falstaff and his wife in a compromising situation, and he literally becomes a *means* for the plots laid by Mrs. Page and his wife. It is not until he gains insight and learns the truth that he can participate with open eyes in the revenge scheme. In the end, he joins in the general reconciliation.

But, like Falstaff, Ford is more victim than victimizer. If Falstaff offends Mrs. Ford by his immoral letter, Ford offends her by his irrational jealousy, and her punishment of Falstaff becomes a punishment for her husband as well. "I know not," she confesses to Mrs. Page, "which pleases me better, that my husband is deceived, or Sir John" [III. iii. 178-79]. Her plots cut in both directions, and if she forces the knight into a strange series of metamorphoses, Ford must undergo a transformation to Mr. Brook, the man who is (both deceptively and actually) alienated from Mrs. Ford. He tells Falstaff: "I have pursu'd her as love hath pursued me, which hath been on the wing of all occasions. But whatsoever I have merited, either in my mind or in my means, meed, I am sure, I have received none, unless experience be a jewel" [II. ii. 200-04]. Although Ford does not realize the truth of his fabrication, "experience"—a true understanding of Mrs. Ford—will be the "jewel" that he gains through his transformation.

Moreover, Ford must undergo, like his antagonist, the symbolic transformation from man to beast. Pistol has warned him that he must prevent Falstaff, or "go thou, / Like Sir Actaeon he, with Ringwood at thy heels" [II. i. 117-18]. In the scene of comic madness which follows Falstaff's escape in the buck-basket, Ford announces: "I will proclaim myself what I am. . . . I'll be horn-mad" [III. v. 143-44, 152]. Both possible meanings of "horn-mad" are intended: "as mad as a beast" and "insane because of having become a cuckold." Ford considers himself a cuckold, but, ironically, he will proclaim himself not a cuckold, but a man who seems irrationally, and thus bestially, to desire horns. His metaphoric descent into the beast prefigures the final transformation of Falstaff into Herne-Actaeon. As Herne, Falstaff partakes of both kinds of horn-madness, for he is not only the figure of the lust-driven Actaeon, but the symbol of the cuckold, the deceived man. In his final transformation, Falstaff stands for both himself and Ford.

Having learned the truth about his wife—"I rather will suspect the sun with cold / Than thee with wantonness" [IV. iv. 7-8]—Ford is purged of his irrational jealousy and is reconciled to his wife. They reunite in the final punishment of Falstaff, where the fat knight, acting as a scapegoat, assumes the horns which Ford was mad to have, and the purgation of Falstaff becomes symbolic of Ford's comic regeneration. In the last scene, Ford emerges with a clear vision, helping to reconcile the Pages to their new son-in-law. He no longer has those "crotchets in [his] head" [II. i. 154-55].

Ford, then, fits into the offence-revenge-reconciliation pattern in an ironic way. Assigning himself the role of avenger, he becomes the offender who must be punished and purged so that he may be reconciled to his wife and to the rest of society. Ford and Falstaff are equally antagonists and fellow-conspirators; and in Falstaff's punishment, Ford participates, suffers, and is regenerated. In the end, the two reach an ironic reconciliation. Falstaff has promised the disguised Ford: "the conclusion shall be crowned with your enjoying her" [III. v. 135-36], and Ford reminds him in the play's last moment: "Sir John, / To Master Brook you yet shall hold your word, / For he to-night shall lie with Mistress Ford" [V. v. 244-45].

The basic pattern of action that we have followed in the main plot is mirrored in the subplot action involving Evans and Caius. The offence, like Falstaff's, derives from a letter, a letter concerned with the romantic quest for Anne Page. Here the revenge takes the form of an open duel; Caius sends his "shallenge" directly to Evans [I. iv. 108], and the arrangements are put into the ubiquitous hands of the Host of the Garter. Again, Page and the Host are on the committee of reconciliation, this time with Shallow making a third. Page once more offers "to do a good office" [III. i. 49], repeating his former words to Shallow, and the Host turns all into jest. Although we may wonder if Evans would ever have raised his sword against Caius, the Host has made certain that violence is averted. He emphasizes a cosmic, albeit comic, unity: "Give me thy hand, terrestrial! so. Give me thy hand, celestial! so" [III. i. 105-06]. The scene reflects the initial reconciliation of Falstaff and Shallow, and at the same time looks forward to the general reconciliation which ends the play.

Like its counterpart in the main action, the reconciliation of Evans and Caius also leads to further complications and another revenge plot. The Host has made a temporary peace, but he has inadvertently offended the Welshman and the Frenchman who, having been taken in and humiliated by the fast-talking Host, secretly plot their revenge. Although the horse-stealing plot is only sketched in with the barest details, the three German impostors in the employ of Evans and Caius are the most adept deceivers in the play.

The disguised, deceptive horse thieves bring us to one of the most important elements of this play: alienation, here a lack of knowledge and understanding of others. Evans and Caius, as foreigners, comically personify alienation, which is, as we have seen, a more serious matter in the central action. There is a failure in genuine communication, a lack of understanding which leads to the revenge plots. Both Ford and Falstaff offend because they are completely deceived about the nature of oth-

ers. In a sense, this lack of sensitivity about the true quality of others is the central concern of the play.

The concern with alienation is reflected in the verbal structure. Beginning with Slender's precarious vocabulary in the first scene, there is a pattern of verbal failure. "Sir, will you hear me?" Fenton asks his future father-in-law, and Mr. Page answers sternly, "No, good Master Fenton" [III. iv. 74]. Although Caius can certainly hear the ranting Host, he has no idea what he means. . . . Page comments that Nym is "a fellow" who "frights English out of his wits" [II. i. 138-39], and the Host, who speaks his own brand of Elizabethan nonsense, says that Caius and Evans "hack our English" [III. i. 77-8].

But perhaps the best example of how linguistic alienation reflects the lack of moral understanding is IV. i, where non-communication acts as a preface to Ford's blindness in the following scene. Evans questions young William while Mrs. Quickly listens and misunderstands. . . . The mistakes Mrs. Quickly makes with the language are precisely the mistakes Ford makes about his wife, and the innocent Latin is mistranslated in much the way that Falstaff indecently mistranslates Mrs. Ford. As Pistol comments, "He hath studied her well and translated her will—out of honesty into English" [I. iii. 49-50]. The problem with language reflects the larger problem of understanding, and both Ford and Falstaff must undergo a metaphoric education in "translation" before they are reintegrated into society. (pp. 103-07)

[The] play ends on the notes of union and adjusted values. The final emphasis is on the three qualities of reconciliation, understanding, and human worth. Ford accepts the true worth of his wife; if not completely converted to a new set of values, the Pages gracefully accept the *fait accompli*, and Fenton and Anne join the Fords in wedded happiness. The anti-Garter knight, Falstaff, is baffled, and the inverted values which he represented are subdued. We laugh tolerantly at the final dissidences and realize that, for the moment, they are simply part of the greater harmony celebrated by Shakespeare's comedy. (p. 108)

*W. L. Godshalk, "An Apology for 'The Merry Wives of Windsor'," in* Renaissance Papers 1973, *1973, pp. 97-108.*

### J. A. BRYANT, JR.   (essay date 1974)

[*Developing the suggestion first made by Northrop Frye (1948) that Falstaff resembles a sacrificial figure in folk ritual, Bryant traces the similarities between the three punishments inflicted on the fat knight and traditional fertility ceremonies discussed by cultural anthropologists. The critic contends that no regeneration follows the first two chastisements, but that Falstaff's final humiliation in Act V, Scene v of* The Merry Wives of Windsor *"suggests unmistakably the ancient castigation of the scapegoat" which results in the renewal of the community. Bryant also maintains that in their preoccupation with the financial implications of marriage the citizens of Windsor ignore its procreative purpose; Anne and Fenton triumph only because the reenactment of the scapegoat ritual offers a cover for their elopement. Thus, the critic concludes, Shakespeare's use of this ceremony serves not only to deepen the significance of the central Falstaff plot, but it also "provides the solution by which the oppressiveness of Windsor's old order can be relaxed and Windsor's winter made to give way to the interests of spring."*]

Shakespeare's remarkable manipulation of materials has produced in *The Merry Wives of Windsor* something that has a special kind of unity and occupies a central position not merely in the chronology of his works but in his growing awareness of the dimensions of the comic form.

The visible outline of *The Merry Wives* is provided by the Fenton-Anne plot, in which young love triumphs in good New Comedy fashion over a series of obstacles imposed by the girl's ambitious parents.... Laughter in this part of the play is provided by the plot itself as the details of it begin to mesh and satisfy our expectation, and by the series of farcelike episodes and embellishments: the fractured English of Parson Hugh and Dr. Caius, the absurd duel between these two that never comes off, the horse-stealing business, and the Latin lesson.

One should note that in the mechanics of the Fenton-Anne plot there is no specific need either for the Fords or for Falstaff. By putting only one wife in Windsor and no fat man at all Shakespeare could have resolved his plot in ways more conventional and far less improbable than the one he hit upon. For example, a parentally manipulated May Day with the inevitable backfire might have been a better ending for *The Merry Wives* had the fortunes of the young lovers in it been the main consideration. Undoubtedly, one reason for Shakespeare's choice of a nighttime episode in Windsor Park was the opportunity that setting provided for a joint conclusion with the Falstaff action, which is the trunk and life of the whole piece. If tradition be true, Shakespeare began with the need to exploit his fat man, and only to embellish that did he bring to life and adapt a supplementary frame plot derived from stereotyped Italianate versions of New Comedy. The ending appropriate to his central action luckily was good both for tricking the old and for pairing off the young. (pp. 296-97)

The Falstaff action also has affinities with New Comedy themes and characters; nevertheless, it is closer in point of evolutionary development to Old or Aristophanic Comedy and to the antecedents of that comedy. Such a relationship was noted briefly in 1948 by Northrop Frye, who wrote in an English Institute essay for that year that *The Merry Wives* contains "an elaborate ritual of the defeat of winter, known to folklorists as 'carrying out Death,' of which Falstaff is the victim" [see excerpt above, 1948]. To a generation brought up on Frazer and the Cambridge anthropologists the pertinence of such a remark—referring, one imagines, to Falstaff's series of humiliations—may have seemed self-evident; and perhaps it seemed so to Frye, who passed quickly on without bothering to probe further into the implications of what he had said. Yet the suggestion remains to tantalize knowledgeable readers. The resemblances between the first two humiliations of Falstaff and the European forms of "Carrying Out Death" are, of course, obvious to anyone who reads about the latter in Sir James G. Frazer's *The Golden Bough* or the works of such investigators as F. M. Cornford and Jane Harrison. Falstaff undergoes his first humiliation, we recall, when he escapes from Ford's house in a buck-basket full of dirty linen. He describes the indignity as follows:

> I suffered the pangs of three several deaths; first, an intolerable fright, to be detected with a jealous rotten bell-wether; next, to be compass'd, like a good bilbo, in the circumference of a peck, hilt to point, heel to head; and then, to be stopp'd in, like a strong distillation, with stinking clothes that fretted in their own grease. Think of that,—a man of my kidney,—think of that,—that am as subject to heat as butter; a man of continual dissolution and thaw,—it was a miracle to scape suffocation. And in the

> height of this bath, when I was more than half stew'd in grease, like a Dutch dish, to be thrown into the Thames, and cool'd, glowing hot, in that surge, like a horse-shoe; think of that,— hissing hot,—think of that, Master Brook.
> [III. v. 107-22]

Frazer records no observance in which laundry, as such, is used as part of a ceremony; but he gives several illustrations in which old and dirty clothing, symbolizing the ills of the community, is begged from house to house and thereafter draped upon a crude effigy of some kind, usually made of straw or birch twigs, to be carried through the town and eventually tossed into the river. (p. 297)

Falstaff's second humiliation even more closely resembles ritualistic practice, especially that of "Carrying Out Death" in other parts of central Europe; for this time he is dressed in the clothes of an old woman, reviled, beaten out of the house, and chased through the streets. This is suggestive of mid-Lent observances in parts of Silesia:

> In many places the grown girls with the help of the young men dress up a straw figure with women's clothes and carry it out of the village towards the setting sun. At the boundary they strip it of its clothes, tear it in pieces, and scatter the fragments about the fields. This is called "Burying Death." As they carry the image out, they sing that they are about to bury Death under an oak, that he may depart from the people ... [James Frazer, in *The Golden Bough*].

Neither of the pseudorituals in Shakespeare, however, proceeds to a proper conclusion. One of them ends simply as dirty linen in the river, and the other evaporates as soon as Falstaff has a chance to slip out of his disguise. In neither is Death carried out; and neither precipitates any kind of renewal, as practically all the genuine rituals of carrying out Death are expected to do.

Falstaff's third trial does have the efficacy of ritual, and that trial is suggestive of something far more ancient and more serious than the widespread forms of folk game that "Carrying Out Death" assumes in central and western Europe. In fact, Shakespeare, knowingly or unknowingly, seems to have arranged Falstaff's three humiliations in an order of increasing seriousness so that the whole series has the painful effect of stripping away one by one the layers of civility that normally shield the primitive nerve in our psyche and make the darker part of our humanity bearable. Thus, while we laugh at the spectacle of Falstaff in the forest, we may also shudder as we laugh; for this last humiliation, involving as it does the victim disguised as an animal and the people's participation in the punishment of that victim, suggests unmistakably the ancient castigation of the scapegoat, whereby an animal, or a man, or a man dressed as an animal was made to take upon himself and suffer for the sins of a whole community.

The term itself indicates the form of this ritual that is familiar to most of us: that is, the one using an actual goat and practiced by the ancient Jews on their Day of Atonement (Leviticus xvi. 8-22).... Shakespeare's last humiliation of Falstaff reached beyond any existing practice in Windsor, Warwickshire, or the rest of Europe to provide for the old fat man a punishment that was, at least in part, directed at the expulsion of evil which was not entirely of his own generating.

Falstaff's principal fault at the time of the play, aside from some petty poaching and keeping of disreputable company, is that age has caught up with him. "It is as much as I can do to keep the terms of my honour precise," he tells the recalcitrant Pistol. "Ay, I myself sometimes, leaving the fear of God on the left hand and hiding mine honour in my necessity, am fain to shuffle, to hedge, and to lurch" [II. ii. 21-5]. His instincts are now for survival only, and the objective of his assault on the wives of Windsor is not the satisfaction of lust but satisfaction of the belly. To everyone but Falstaff and Master Ford the whole business is a clear piece of senile folly; and even Falstaff himself is uneasy until Mistress Quickly relieves his anxiety with her false tales of the complaisance of the two women. Thus reassured, however, he is ripe to receive the fulsome flattery that Ford, disguised as Brook, heaps upon him: "You are a gentleman of excellent breeding, admirable discourse, of great admittance, authentic in your place and person, generally allow'd for your many war-like, court-like, and learned preparations" [II. ii. 225-29]. Finally, when Ford lays before him the temptation of tangible coin, Falstaff is completely undone and ready to believe almost anything. Even at this point, however, he sees himself only as a man of parts and undiminished vigor, not as a small-town lecher, the role in which Ford's jealousy flatteringly casts him. "Master Brook," he declares grandly (and gratefully for the last compliment), "thou shalt know I will predominate over the peasant, and thou shalt lie with his wife" [II. ii. 281-83].

For Ford, by contrast, everything is colored by the almost insane sexual jealousy through which he views his world. Folly of this kind is conventionally presented as laughable in comedy, and it is so presented here; but here . . . jealousy is given a dimension that renders it credible as well as funny. Mistress Ford warns us that her husband's problem is a recurring one even before he appears on the scene. "O, that my husband saw this letter!" she says in her first reference to him. "It would give eternal food to his jealousy" [II. i. 100-01]. Ford's behavior shortly thereafter in his encounter with informing Pistol and later in his interview with Falstaff leaves no doubt about the matter: Ford's mind leaps at the intimation of sex, and he is always prepared to suspect that his wife is indulging in it illicitly. Moreover, his malady is infectious or else it is endemic in Windsor; for both wives seem to be especially chagrined at receiving an attempt on their virtue that cannot possibly come to anything except embarrassment; and even Page, for all his counsels of moderation, declares in the end for appointing "a meeting for this old fat fellow, / Where we may take him and disgrace him for it" [IV. iv. 14-15]. Evans is speaking the truth when he observes, "You say he has been thrown in the rivers and has been grievously peaten as an old 'oman. . . . Methinks his flesh is punish'd; he shall have no desires" [IV. iv. 20-4]. Nevertheless, they proceed with the plan, burning and pinching him for the lust he never enjoyed, reviling him for being too old to make other men cuckolds . . . , and finally even dunning him for the twenty pounds that he has received from the jealous Ford disguised as Brook.

The irony of all this is that only the victimizers here are physically vigorous enough to be even partly guilty of the charges they are making; their victim is too old for the performance of sex and almost, but not quite, too old to be stirred by the recollection of it. Furthermore, he is far too clumsy to serve as a pander even for middle-aged lovers like the Fords. Falstaff's fundamental awareness of his inadequacies is painfully suggested in the feeble wit of the extravagant mock prayer that he makes in the Park just before his tormentors arrive:

The Windsor bell hath struck twelve; the minute draws on. Now, the hot-blooded gods assist me! Remember, Jove, thou wast a bull for thy Europa; love set on thy horns. O powerful love! that, in some respects, makes a beast a man, in some other, a man a beast. You were also, Jupiter, a swan for the love of Leda. O omnipotent love! how near the god drew to the complexion of a goose! A fault done first in the form of a beast. O Jove, a beastly fault! . . .

[V. v. 1-9]

Enlightenment follows shortly after this, and his overt confession comes only a hundred or so lines later: "I do begin to perceive that I am made an ass" [V. v. 119]. To this, Ford, with the figure of a discredited scapegoat standing before him, replies aptly, "Ay, and an ox too; both the proofs are extant" [V. v. 120].

One can say a number of things about Shakespeare's treatment of the scapegoat theme here. It is, of course, broadly funny in the childish, rough-and-tumble way that good folk art often is, and for this reason alone it enhances the value of the play. Moreover, once we recognize clearly the presence of the scapegoat theme in *The Merry Wives of Windsor*, we may discover suddenly that we have also sharpened our perception of less well-defined treatments of the same theme in other plays of Shakespeare—notably those in *The Merchant of Venice*, in *Twelfth Night*, and, as pointed out by C. L. Barber, in *Henry IV, Part I*. Most important, however, recognizing the scapegoat theme in *The Merry Wives* means finding a new dimension to the play, one of major significance without which it would remain merely the more or less effective farce that most critics have found it to be. In this regard, two additional sets of observations should be made. First, the Fenton-Anne plot, the New Comedy element of the piece, is stiffly regular by comparison with the Falstaff plot and chiefly funny in its farcing or episodic detail; furthermore, it generates no proper resolution of its own. Second, the Falstaff plot, set in motion early in Act I but developed independently throughout most of the play, converges with the Fenton-Anne plot at precisely that point at which the scapegoat theme emerges explicitly; and thus it is the Falstaff plot that provides the solution by which the oppressiveness of Windsor's old order can be relaxed and Windsor's winter made to give way to the interests of spring. The one plot complements the other; and fitted together in this ingenious fashion they create both an entertaining play and one that makes visible within its scope something of the whole evolution of comedy.

The plot of the young lovers, to be sure, has a movement in the direction of renewal; but that movement is one that promises only an escape for the young lovers—an elopement rather than the general and potentially joyous acceptance of an alteration in the balance of constituent elements in the community. Susanne Langer has characterized the feeling given by mature comedy as a renewed awareness of the impetus and flow, the continuing rhythm of human life; and she identifies the antagonist of comedy as the "World," meaning by that one of those artificial and temporary structures perpetually being established by the very same rhythm that promotes life's continuity [in *Feeling and Form*]. One function of the Fenton-Anne plot is to present concretely that rigidly established World, which collapses only with the sacrifice of Falstaff. As *The Merry Wives* begins, economic considerations in Windsor have temporarily replaced genetic ones. Pretty Anne Page is of marriageable age. She is virginal but conspicuously fertile, and the senior members of the community are mightily concerned to see that she is disposed of to their advantage. Justice Shallow, noting that she is heiress to seven hundred pounds in her own right in addition to whatever she may expect from her father, is seeking to pair her off with his simpleton of a nephew, Abraham Slender, whom he controls. Parson Hugh and the girl's father both support him in this, again for economic reasons. No one of the older generation, with the possible exception of the Host of the Garter Inn, seems to remember the primary purpose of such pairings or to be aware that matches for money are often of the kind that bring a community to extinction. Even Fenton admits that money has until recently been his own motive in seeking Anne's hand:

> . . . I will confess thy father's wealth
> Was the first motive that I woo'd thee, Anne;
> Yet, wooing thee, I found thee of more value
> Than stamps in gold or sums in sealed bags;
> And 'tis the very riches of thyself
> That now I aim at.
>
> [III. iv. 13-18]

In short, Windsor has for some time been shivering with the counsels and whispers of winter, old age, and death; and these must be "carried out" if Windsor is to survive for another cycle of life and living.

So it is that the business of Herne the Hunter, devised as the climax of a series of humiliations for a Falstaff who has been doing his feeble best to peddle love for money, fortuitously provides the appropriate screen behind which Anne's unwanted suitors can be matched with boys in female dress and Fenton and Anne triumphantly become man and wife. Monetary concerns are defeated, biology wins out, and the resulting unity of community and play, to say nothing of the play's measure as comedy, is reflected in the general mood of acceptance that this funny but painful event produces. The Pages, the Fords, and even Falstaff are moved to pronounce the unanticipated part of the outcome a good thing for all concerned. Falstaff with gratifying magnanimity—remarkable considering the pain and embarrassment his thankless role has caused him—says it best: "I am glad, though you have ta'en a special stand to strike at me, that your arrow hath glanc'd" [V. v. 234-35]. The round of confessions and acceptances at this point suggests that the spiritual ills of Windsor were perhaps never so grave as some of the early symptoms indicated; but suggestions like this are usually part of the reassurance that proper comedy, as distinguished from such special things as farce and satire, always provides. The Merry Wives of Windsor has at least this much—and it is a great deal—in common with the other proper comedies of Shakespeare; that is, it makes us once more see the mysterious terms on which we live, accept those terms, and once more concede that the game shall go on. (pp. 297-300)

*J. A. Bryant, Jr., "Falstaff and the Renewal of Windsor," in PMLA, 89, Vol. 89, No. 2, March, 1974, pp. 296-301.*

## WILLIAM CARROLL    (essay date 1977)

[*Carroll contends that a central thematic concern in The Merry Wives of Windsor is "the use and abuse of imagination" and that—through the complementary characters of Ford and Falstaff, the language of the play, and the intrigues devised by the wives—Shakespeare demonstrates the power of imagination to transform, enliven, and delude. Imagination inspires Falstaff and haunts Ford, the critic maintains, but the effect in both is social anarchy. Noting that language, too, may break away from a speaker's intended significance "to lead a wayward life of its own," Carroll examines the unintended richness and creativity in the puns and malapropisms of such characters as Nym, Mistress Quickly, and the Host of the Garter Inn. Finally, he compares the manipulation of illusion by Mistress Ford and Mistress Page as they vanquish Falstaff's threat to the community with the way in which a playwright shapes our perception of his dramatic world through similar tricks and deceptions, arguing that the play represents both "the equivocal, subversive power of imagination" and its capacity to enrich our lives.*]

[One] of the major subjects of [The Merry Wives of Windsor] is the use and abuse of imagination. In its relation of Ford to Falstaff, in its inventive verbal style, and in its metaphors of playacting, the play first qualifies and then vindicates the power of the imagination to shape, even to transform "reality," and identifies this power with the more obvious power that every dramatist wields. I believe these subjects of interest link the play with the mainstream of Shakespeare's work, and that the play's consignment to the backwaters of criticism has been unjust. To describe *Merry Wives* as a "farce," and have done with it, is not to see its most vigorous sources of life. For it is the equivocal, subversive power of imagination to which the play again and again returns. I intend to follow this power through three of its manifestations—Ford's relation to Falstaff, verbal style, metaphors of playacting—to its inevitable culmination in the exposure and ridicule of "this old fat fellow" [IV. iv. 14].

A shadow of his former self, the Falstaff we meet in *The Merry Wives of Windsor* does seem to be suffering from the effects of a spiritual and sexual diet that has been all too effective. Like the advertiser's "after" picture, he is now, as the Pages describe him, "Old, cold, withered" [V. v. 153]. The threat he supposedly offers to the honor of the merry wives is never convincing, and they easily overtake and outwit the once-nimble knight. (pp. 187-88)

It is made clear that Falstaff is a threat only to the extent that people think he is. And Ford is the only person in *Merry Wives* who considers him a threat. Falstaff has retained his girth—he is still a "hodge-pudding . . . a bag of flax" [V. v. 151]—but even Pistol and Nym are able to trick him now. Only Ford succumbs to him, and Ford's deception is self-induced. Falstaff becomes a grotesque incarnation of Ford's worst fears, a priapic bogeyman conjured up by a runaway imagination. Like Orgoglio in [Spenser's] *The Faerie Queene*, Falstaff is a decrepit windbag pumped up by his victim's error—by Ford's mania, what Evans terms his "fery fantastical humours and jealousies" [III. iii. 170-71]. When Ford's "humour" is exorcized and he comes to his senses, Falstaff is suddenly deflated. Even Mistress Page is contemptuous of Falstaff in reality: "Why, Sir John, do you think, though we would have thrust virtue out of our hearts by the head and shoulders, and have given ourselves without scruple to hell, that ever the devil could have made you our delight?" [V. v. 146-50]. But this, in fact, is what Ford as well as Falstaff has thought.

Recent critics of the play have stressed the ritual elements in it, and described Falstaff as a scapegoat figure, re-enacting a folk game Frazer called "Carrying Out Death" [in *The Golden Bough*]. Falstaff's general impotence, moreover, indicates that his final punishment is partly, as J. A. Bryant, Jr. has observed, "directed at the expulsion of evil which was not entirely of his own generating" [see excerpt above, 1974]. That is the very definition of the scapegoat's role—the embodiment of the sins or fears of the larger community, which will be purged when the scapegoat is driven off or sacrificed. Falstaff's role, as ever, leans toward allegory. The "reverend vice," "grey iniquity," and "father ruffian" of *I Henry IV* [II. iv. 453-54] attains the status of a full "devil" in Ford's mind, and the movement of *Merry Wives* indicates how it is Ford's mind that must be purged of a "devil" that the rest of society has presumably tamed and domesticated. (pp. 189-90)

Ford has all along had an unhealthy predisposition to "figures" and "imaginings," for his jealous "humour" slides all too easily into paranoia. When Ford and Page first hear of Falstaff's intentions toward their wives, their very different reactions are set in apposition:

> *Page.* If he [Falstaff] should intend this voyage toward my wife, I would turn her loose to him, and what he gets more of her than sharp words, let it lie on my head.
> *Ford.* I do not misdoubt my wife; but I would be loath to turn them together; a man may be too confident; I would have nothing lie on my head; I cannot be thus satisfied.
>
> [II. i. 181-88]

Page's loose style indicates a mind at ease. The "if" clause refers not even to his wife's infidelity, but to the issue of whether Falstaff has such intentions at all; his hortatory conclusion shows the extent of his confidence. Ford's paratactic nervousness, by contrast, jumps from assumption to assumption, as the hypothetical gives way to deluded declaratives,

*Act III. Scene iii. Falstaff, Mistress Page, and Mistress Ford. By H. Makart. The Department of Rare Books and Special Collections, The University of Michigan Library.*

and the feeble double negative "not misdoubt" emotionally betrays the logically positive affirmation. It is the prose equivalent to Leontes's anguished reflections in *The Winter's Tale*, especially the famous passage on "affection" . . . , or to Othello's agonized self-deceptions. Ford plays Iago to his own Othello: he's divided against himself. When Ford, disguised as his watery namesake Brook, makes his self-cuckolding proposal to Falstaff, all logic has been overturned. Even Falstaff proclaims, "Methinks you should prescribe to yourself very preposterously" [II. ii. 240-41], and the double irony of the situation reverberates at the deepest levels of the play.

Another index of Ford's susceptibility to delusion is found in the allusions to the "witch" of Brainford. The name of the town almost too obviously suggests the witch's origin in Ford's brain. To commonsensical Mistress Ford, this unseen woman is merely "My maid's aunt, the fat woman of Brainford" [IV. ii. 75-6]. Significantly, Falstaff, that other emanation of Ford's brain, is disguised in her clothing. Of all the characters in the play, only Ford believes her to be a witch. . . . When Ford does learn that "she" is in his house, he becomes more hysterical (it is only a matter of degree by now): "She comes of errands, does she? We are simple men; we do not know what's brought to pass under the profession of fortune-telling. She works by charms, by spells, by th' figure, and such daubery as this is, beyond our element; we know nothing. Come down, you witch, you hag, you; come down, I say!" [IV. ii. 173-79]. By beating Falstaff in the "witch's" clothing, Ford is cudgelling both phantoms of his brain at the same time, but his exorcism still has a further course to run.

Ford's encounter with the "witch" of Brainford marks an important turning point in *Merry Wives*. He rushes off stage in a frenzy, but when we next see him, just forty lines later, much has changed. His mania has vanished: "Pardon me, wife. Henceforth do what thou wilt: / I rather will suspect the sun with cold / Than thee with wantonness" [IV. iv. 6-8]. His conversion is only as arbitrary as his mania's initial cause, but there are also religious undertones when Ford describes his former self (already in the third person) as "him that was of late an heretic," but now "as firm as faith" [IV. iv. 9-10] in the belief of his wife's honor. Whatever happened offstage, it is clear that the encounter with the "witch" symbolized the extremity of Ford's delusion. The middle class of Windsor may have been more susceptible to such superstition—we have already heard Evans suggesting possession as the cause of Ford's mania—but the play has everywhere stressed that Ford is alone, and without foundation, in his beliefs. Even he questions at times the reality of his experiences. During the first search of his house, Ford says to his friends, "Gentleman, I have dreamed to-night; I'll tell you my dream. Here, here, here be my keys; ascend my chambers; search, seek, find out" [III. iii. 161-63]. And in a soliloquy after another visit, as "Brook," to Falstaff, Ford asks himself, "Hum! Ha! Is this a vision? Is this a dream? Do I sleep? Master Ford, awake; awake, Master Ford: there's a hole made in your best coat, Master Ford" [III. v. 139-42]. . . . Ford unwittingly reverses the terms of the customary distinction between dreaming and waking. While he believes himself to be "waking" to a new clarity and perception, Ford has only fallen deeper into "vision," a word with special resonance in *Merry Wives*. "Nightmare" might be the better term, however, since Ford's encounters with Falstaff become progressively more grotesque, and Falstaff's means of escape correspondingly more ludicrous.

With Ford about to enter the botched tryst, the "witch" Falstaff desperately seeks a hiding place: "What shall I do? I'll creep up into the chimney." To which Mistress Ford replies, "There they always use to discharge their birding-pieces. Creep into the kill-hole" [IV. ii. 55-8]. This exchange is a windfall for Freudian analysis. All of the hiding places which are suggested are dream-displaced images of the female sexual organs—"press, coffer, chest, trunk, well, vault." According to his wife, Ford "hath an abstract for the remembrance of such places and goes to them by his note" [IV. ii. 62-3]. Of course: where else does one go in a dream? This also suggests that Ford knows these places by book or rote rather than by experience. Mistress Ford concludes, "There is no hiding you [Falstaff] in the house" [IV. ii. 63-4]. Nor outside, either. The only way out for Falstaff is by sexual disguise, so that Ford's brain will not recognize its own creation; the female emanation temporarily displaces the male spectre. Succubus takes over for incubus, but the implications are the same. In his moment of greatest delusion, finally, just before he will beat Falstaff off the stage, Ford sarcastically addresses his wife: "Mistress Ford, the honest woman, the modest wife, the virtuous creature, that hath the jealous fool to her husband!" [IV. ii. 129-31]. The irony is severe, the inversion of values complete. After Ford paradoxically asserts that "my jealousy is reasonable" [IV. ii. 148-49], he rushes off stage and is converted. He is "awakened" from his dream-vision, control over his imagination restored. The sexual aberrations suggested by his "dream" have been curbed, safely confined again within the institution of marriage.

Ford may be in control of himself, but Falstaff, like Frankenstein's monster, is still on the loose, a too-visible reminder of folly and sexual license. . . . Falstaff continually reminds us of the animal nature of man—first as a presumably tumescent buck, later as a whimpering scapegoat. To catalogue all the animal imagery associated with Falstaff would be to stand like Adam naming the beasts, and it is already clear that Falstaff—"this whale," as Mistress Ford says, thrown "with so many tuns of oil in his belly, ashore at Windsor" [II. i. 64-5]—represents an aspect of man that Ford, for one, would prefer to suppress. No wonder that the quelling of Falstaff has so many primitive, even savage, undertones.

As an emblem and agent of wit, Falstaff also embodies the possibilities, often dangerous ones, of change and transformation. Circean elements—men changed into animals through appeals to their lower natures—represent the greatest threat, but more often there is simply a fear of disruption and change in Windsor. Ford has fallen away from an implied better self and must be brought back to it. Falstaff would overturn all sorts of social institutions, not the least of which is marriage, and must be brought to a halt. Above all, Falstaff is, in his own words, "a man of continual dissolution and thaw" [III. v. 116]—continually reinventing himself and redefining his relation to those around him. Eventually he will claim that he has "suffered more for their [the women's] sakes—more than the villainous inconstancy of man's disposition is able to bear" [IV. v. 108-09]. It is just this "inconstancy," Falstaff's natural condition, which is a threat to the rest of Windsor and which must be harnessed. Shapeshifting is bad form. (pp. 192-96)

But after, and only after, Ford's great awakening—when Falstaff's dream-like power vaporizes—Falstaff begins to fear his own metamorphosis. "I would all the world might be cozened," he says, "for I have been cozened and beaten too. If it should come to the ear of the court how I have been transformed, and how my transformation hath been washed and cudgelled, they would melt me out of my fat drop by drop, and liquor fishermen's boots with me" [IV. v. 94-9]. This

punishment is both comic and terrifying. Surrounded in the forest, Falstaff cowers in fear of still another kind of "dissolution": "Heavens defend me from that Welsh fairy, lest he transform me to a piece of cheese" [V. v. 81-2].

In one sense, such a transformation would be a desirable means of escape. Falstaff enters the final scene disguised as Herne the Hunter, *"wearing a buck's head"* [V. v. 1, s.d.], and he invokes the Ovidian tradition of metamorphosis to justify his condition: "Remember, Jove, thou wast a bull for thy Europa; love set on thy horns. O powerful love, that in some respects makes a beast a man; in some other, a man a beast. You were also, Jupiter, a swan for the love of Leda. O omnipotent love, how near the god drew to the complexion of a goose!" [V. v. 3-8]. This choric commentary reflects on much that has happened in the play, and looks back as well to such very different comedies of metamorphosis as *Love's Labour's Lost* and *A Midsummer Night's Dream*. "Powerful!" and "omnipotent" Love is the agent of change that has brought Falstaff to this ludicrous state, whereas the dark side of love—fanatic, hysterical jealousy—has induced Ford's mania and turned Falstaff into a monstrous projection of fear. Ford dropped to the animal when he temporarily lost his reason; when he regained it, Falstaff, the "man of middle earth" [V. v. 80], began to sink more and more quickly down the chain of being. "You may know by my size," he says, "that I have a kind of alacrity in sinking" [III. v. 12-13]. The two characters complement each other, like buckets in a pulley-well: one up, the other down. Falstaff embodies all the energy, vitality, and imagination which Ford has repressed and which therefore threatens him. Ford represents all the security, wealth, and success Falstaff has never achieved. (pp. 197-98)

The pattern of deception and delusion revealed in Ford's mania finds its counterpart in the language, the verbal usage of the play. If imagination can inspire Falstaff and haunt Ford, it can also reveal itself in the transformations, abuses, and phantoms of language. To the extent that Falstaff symbolizes this anarchic force as it seizes control of Ford, he must be curbed. The thrust of comedy is always towards social reintegration. But if the Windsorites condemn "visions" in general as unwholesome, they also recognize and express certain saving powers of imagination, most evident in the speech of verbal acrobats who usually teeter and fall but occasionally achieve a precarious victory.

To examine the style of the Windsorites is to discover that all of the characters possess some idiosyncratic verbal quirk, from Evans's comic mispronunications to Nym's tedious repetition of "humour" as an all-purpose grammatical makeshift. The Windsorites are also greatly concerned wih proper English usage. Broken accents, inkhornisms, and alien borrowings are as intensely disliked (though often secretly admired) as foreigners in any small town. Quickly anticipates that in Caius's great anger there will be "an old abusing of God's patience and the King's English" [I. iv. 5-6], while the Host urges the disarming of Caius and Evans, the French and Welsh combatants, with similar expectations: "Let them keep their limbs whole, and hack our English" [III. i. 77-8]. Falstaff, the master stylist, suspects that he may be finally undone by the verbal inadequacies of Evans, such as his mispronunciations of "cheese" and "butter": "'Seese' and 'putter'? Have I lived to stand at the taunt of one that makes fritters of English? This is enough to be the decay of lust and late-walking through the realm" [V. v. 142-45]. Somehow it doesn't seem right that such errant linguists should triumph over Falstaff.

Proper English means, for the Windsorites, not only a plain but a native style as well. The Host is particularly adept in using inflated diction to impress or confuse others.... Shakespeare satirizes the Host, who is pretentious about his verbal skills, by having him tricked by a Frenchman, a Welshman, and a crew of offstage "Germans." An ability to use lofty or Latinate diction is evidently no proof of a real capacity of imagination. Nym and Pistol serve, as they do in the Henriad, as additional comic indices, as practitioners of more extreme verbal abuse. Here is Nym's remarkable message to Page about Falstaff: "He loves your wife; there's the short and the long. My name is Corporal Nym; I speak, and I avouch; 'tis true: my name is Nym, and Falstaff loves your wife. Adieu. I love not the humour of bread and cheese. Adieu." Page's reaction is rightly one of astonishment: "The 'humour' of it, quoth 'a! Here's a fellow frights English out of his wits.... I never heard such a drawling, affecting rogue" [II. i. 131-39]. (pp. 200-01)

The pretentious stylists are finally shown to be deficient in imagination. But a genuine creative energy mysteriously inheres and thrives in the malaprops. Those who know what they mean but can't express it usually wind up saying two or three things simultaneously, and their language consequently possesses an unwitting richness. Caius, for example, joins Ford and Evans: "If there be one or two, I shall make-a the turd" [III. iii. 236-37], a statement whose truth cannot be challenged. Quickly is chief producer and consumer of what she calls "alligant terms" [II. ii. 68]. We have already heard her misuse of "erection," triggered, perhaps, by Falstaff's rejection of egg in his sack a few lines earlier: "I'll no pullet-sperm in my brewage" [III. v. 31-2]. Psychoanalysis has demonstrated how slips of the tongue release unconscious concerns, and of all the characters in the play Quickly is most likely to express what she least wants to admit. Mistress Page, Quickly wants to tell Falstaff, is virtuous: "let me tell you in your ear, she's as fartuous a civil modest wife, and one, I tell you, that will not miss you morning nor evening prayer, as any is in Windsor" [II. ii. 96-9]. Indeed, Quickly's errors are like those of Vladimir Nabokov's Pnin, whose "verbal vagaries," we are told, "add a new thrill to life. His mispronunciations are mythopeic. His slips of the tongue are oracular."

Quickly's most brilliant moment comes in the Latin lesson—a scene often considered an anomaly in the play but really the key to a central theme. As Evans leads Page's son William through Lilly's *Shorte Introduction of Grammar* (apparently), Quickly provides a malaprop commentary of increasing outlandishness. Dead Latin words gain a new life in her mouth, taking on complex English meanings, almost always sexual. Illiterate error is raised to the level of creative genius here. "Pulcher" [IV. i. 27], a word for beauty, is misheard as a slang term for "prostitute": "Polecats? There are fairer things than polecats, sure." (pp. 201-02)

As Evans goes on to ask about the "genitive case plural," the audience must sense linguistic disaster:

William.  Genitive *horum, harum, horum.*
Quickly.  Vengeance of Ginny's case; fie on her! Never name her, child, if she be a whore.
Evans.    For shame, 'oman.
Quickly.  You do ill to teach the child such words.— He teaches him to hick and to hack, which they'll do fast enough of themselves, and to call 'horum'—fie upon you!

                                [IV. i. 61-8]

Quickly's repressions bubble up so completely, so perfectly, that her self-betrayal must serve as a paradigm for all such creative error. Borrowing the grammatical "case" for possession, Quickly creates a whore (from "*horum*"), while "genitive" generates "Ginny." She has also misunderstood the word "case," hearing in it not the grammatical term but a slang word for the female sexual organ. Quickly has given "Ginny" not only a name but, considering her vocation, her most profitable possession as well. In her own mistaken way, Quickly has accomplished a kind of creation *ex nihilo* [out of nothing], a prototypical poetic act like that described by Theseus in *A Midsummer Night's Dream,* where

>     as imagination bodies forth
> The forms of things unknown, the poet's pen
> Turns them to shapes, and gives to airy nothing
> A local habitation and a name.

                                [V. i. 14-17]

Quickly thus provides a comic example of the dramatist's art, joining and twisting sounds to create a name and a character. The irony is that the character Quickly is herself a personified adverb, a part of speech given vigorous and unpredictable life. Meanwhile, Evans forges on with the Latin lesson, concluding with "your *quies,* your *quaes,* and your *quods*" [IV. i. 78], a whole new cornucopia of obscene puns.... Speechless for once, Quickly offers no running commentary. Instead, we have Mistress Page's startlingly deadpan conclusion: "He is a better scholar than I thought he was" [IV. i. 80-1]. (pp. 202-03)

The Windsorites consider themselves accomplished stylists, working imaginative effects with words. But words more often work against them. Language escapes the speaker's intended meaning and breaks free to lead a wayward life of its own. Punning is endemic to Windsor because words are slippery and the local inhabitants undermine their own pretensions:

Evans. *Pauca verba;* Sir John, good worts.
Falstaff. Good worts? Good cabbage!

                                [I. i. 120-21]

From conundrum to cabbage—this is the way words are declined at Windsor. When Evans enters later, expecting to fight Caius, he carries a sword in one hand and a Bible ... in the other. Shallow asks him, "What, the sword and the word? Do you study them both, Master Parson?" [III. i. 44-5]. Only a sibilant distinguishes words from swords, but both are double-edged. The recognition of their similarity, and the instinct to pun with them, marks a new stage in the corruption, but also in the enrichment, of language. It is but another sibilant's slide into "worts," and we have a miniature history of the Word since Babel—breaking down into babble, metamorphosing into weapons and plants, spawning and multiplying not to make communication more precise but to make it more complex, while at the same time making possible an almost limitless fertility.

When in doubt, however, the Windsorites prefer to use the words sanctioned by tradition, the moral sententiae and wisdom of the cliché, to guide their behavior—what the Host punningly calls "the proverbs and the no-verbs" [III. i. 105], that is, the do's and don't's of the bourgeois ethic. But imagination also springs forth through puns and malapropisms, as we have seen, generating a gallery of freaks and chimeras, and even the featherless biped "Ginny." Quickly's error is best understood, then, as a comic version of Ford's error about Falstaff; the identical power—of imagination gone unregulated—has led both to give "a local habitation and a name" to some murky aspect of their own minds. Both have unwittingly revealed sexual insecurities by the personifications they have projected, for "Ginny" and the "witch" of Brainford are finally sisters in the same family. Both Ford's and Quickly's delusions depend on an *a priori* expectation—he who looks for dirt will surely find it—and on a suspension of disbelief so total that they are both, as Evans says of Ford, "lunatics . . . mad as a mad dog" [IV. ii. 124-25]. Both succumb to a phantom created through language. The only comparable power, as we shall see next, is that of the theater, where "lunatics" (or poets) may literally enact their dreams.

Most of the Windsorites, particularly the merry wives, reveal unusual and unexpected talents in playacting and staging scenes. The language of the theater runs thoughout the play. (pp. 203-05)

The importance of playacting in *The Merry Wives of Windsor* may be seen in the recurrence of the word "plot," which generally means at this time both "plan" or "scheme" and, more specifically, the action of a play. Mistress Page promises her friend "I will lay a plot to try that, and we will yet have more tricks with Falstaff" [III. iii. 190-92], and Page later urges "let our plot go forward" [IV. iv. 12]. Such allusions point in two directions: inward, to the intersecting intrigues of the characters, and outward, to the audience, as an index of the play's awareness of its own theatricality. As we watch the characters being deceived by potent "visions," we recognize a similar deception operating upon us—more enjoyable, less threatening than the plot on stage, but equally illusory.

Each line of action in *Merry Wives* develops an "intrigue" plot which relies primarily on tricks and illusions. Ford disguises himself to dupe Falstaff. The Host gulls Evans and Caius but is deceived by them in turn. The Pages scheme against Fenton but he allies himself with the Host to trick the parents . . . and escape with Anne Page. Everyone in the play, it turns out, aims to gain some sort of "revenge" against somebody else. Chicanery is the *modus vivendi* in Windsor, and Nym speaks for all: "I have operations which be humours of revenge" [I. iii. 89-90]. The word "revenge" or its variants occurs ten times in the play. The ultimate recipient of all these revenge plots—the last man in line—is naturally Falstaff, who has deluded himself into believing that he is in complete control. His final humiliation acts as a lightning-rod to discharge the air of accumulated connivance and ill-will.

The merry wives are the most accomplished tricksters. In conducting their deceptions, they three times resort to play-acting and theatrical imagery so openly that their performances may fairly be termed plays-within-the-play. Before Falstaff's first visit to Mistress Ford, for example, stage properties like the buck-basket have been carefully arranged, John and Robert have been given their cues . . . , and Mistress Page instructed, on her "cue," to "act it." Her sudden entrance is blatantly melodramatic (just as Falstaff begins to achieve some success, or so he thinks): "O Mistress Ford, what have you done? You're shamed, you're overthrown, you're undone for ever!" [III. iii. 94-6]. . . . The wives put on a good show for Falstaff, who *"hides behind the arras"* [III. iii. 92, s.d.] and watches the action as we do. The wives draw out their plot to delicious length, finally stowing Falstaff in the basket and covering him with dirty linen, when to their surprise Ford does walk in. The claim used to deceive Falstaff—that Ford was coming "with all the officers in Windsor, to search for a gentleman that he says is here now in the house" [III. iii. 107-08]—turns out to be true. But the wives are not rattled; they know how to make chance and design cooperate in their plot, just as any good

dramatist does, and they proceed to incorporate Ford into their action. Mistress Page asks Mistress Ford, "Is there not a double excellency in this?" [III. iii. 176-77]. We could not agree more, and admire the way in which "illusion" has been momentarily shattered by "reality," but quickly reaffirms itself and makes the intrusion an element in an even larger design. The parallel is again to the course of Ford's "dream," as his delusions grow larger and larger until they incorporate a whole world of suspicions.

Falstaff's second visit to Mistress Ford (in IV, ii) follows the same curve of action as the first visit. Once more he is the hidden, duped audience (Mistress Ford tells Mistress Page to "speak louder" for his benefit [IV. ii. 16-17]), once again he is covered by clothes (this time dressed as the witch), and once again Ford unexpectedly appears. Again, the wives incorporate Ford's surprise entrance in their plot, and Ford goes off more deluded than ever. In both scenes, the wives show an ability to act and to improvise that is no less than professional. The final gulling of Falstaff, however, reveals the wives at their most ingenious, and confronts most directly the nature of illusion and its relation to the theatrical experience. A parallel to Ford's "dream" is apparent throughout.

The final "plot"—the third of the plays-within-the-play—begins with Ford's conversion, but the wives, as usual, have planned that too. Mistress Page then relates the "old tale" of "Herne the hunter," once a keeper in Windsor Forest. Like Puck in *A Midsummer Night's Dream*, he is a personification of natural disruption; legend has it that Herne,

> Doth all the winter-time, at still midnight,
> Walk round about an oak, with great ragg'd horns,
> And there he blasts the tree, and takes the cattle,
> And makes milch-kine yield blood, and shakes a chain
> In a most hideous and dreadful manner.
>
> [IV. iv. 30-4]

As preparations for re-enactment of the myth proceed on-stage, Quickly somehow convinces Falstaff off-stage to approach the wives again for the ritualistically inevitable third time. The Windsorites do not believe this myth, but they recognize its immense influence on older, more gullible times:

> . . . well you know
> The superstitious idle-headed eld
> Receiv'd, and did deliver to our age,
> This tale of Herne the hunter for a truth.
>
> [IV. iv. 35-8]

Ford, of course, is another "superstitious idle-headed" elder taking a theory for a truth. Moreover, Mistress Page's description of Herne sounds like the phantom of jealousy in Ford's brain—"hideous and dreadful," the horns an emblem of cuckoldry, possessing ("takes") others, destructive, thriving in darkness. Page goes on to extend the power of the myth down to the present age, including the audience itself: "Why, yet there want not many that do fear / In deep of night to walk by this Herne's oak" [IV. iv. 39-40]. (pp. 205-09)

Between the planning (IV, iv) and the enactment (V, v) of Falstaff's humiliation, a parallel sequence of intrigue deceptions takes place. In IV, v Evans and Caius play the merry wives to the Host's Falstaff, springing the trick of the stolen horses on him. In IV, vi Fenton conspires with the Host to foil at once Page's plot to marry Anne to Slender and Mistress Page's plot to marry her to Caius. Fenton will take advantage of the anticipated exposure of Falstaff, the "great scene" in which "my sweet Nan" will "present the Fairy Queen" [IV. vi. 17, 20]. For her part, Anne will switch disguises to foil her parents' plans. The green and white colors intended "to denote her" to Caius and Slender respectively will be given to others, and all but Fenton will be deceived by the false "token" [IV. vi. 39, 44].

All of this plotting immerses us in the language of semiology ("denote," "token," and, soon, "decipher"). The simple though convoluted schemes assume more profound connotations. What has been going on throughout *Merry Wives* is more than just another exploration of the familiar appearance/reality problem. Shakespeare confronts us, again and again, with the question of *how* we know—how we shape our world in perceiving it, and how that shaping in turn transforms us. The energy of imagination—the power to animate (Quickly's errors), to transform (Ford's mania), to deceive (the wives' plots)—is perhaps the deepest concern of the play, and this underlying seriousness should help us understand how *Merry Wives* is related to the plays that surround it in the canon.

The scene is set for Falstaff's final entrance. The amateur actors are concealed in the wings. Slender prepares himself, as best he can, to "decipher" [V. ii. 9] Anne's token. Ironically, his prepared "nay-word" or password is "mumbudget" [V. ii. 6]—a word "used of an inability or a refusal to speak." Falstaff, for one, is afraid to speak in the fairies' midst, and as he did in *Henry IV,* he falls to the ground and shams death when he sees them: "he that speaks to them shall die. / I'll wink and couch: no man their works must eye" [V. v. 47-8]. But the jig is finally up, and when Evans smells "a man of middle earth" [V. v. 80], the ritualistic "sacrifice" of Falstaff, the most famous scene in the play, begins in earnest. There is a strain of real cruelty in all the pinching and burning; referring to Falstaff as having "the flesh of a corrupted heart" [V. v. 87] is an excercise in rhetorical overkill. Yet the cruelty is mitigated by elements of ludicrous farce—it is Quickly, rather than Anne, who appears as a most unlikely "Fairy Queen," a bit of inspired casting that casts some doubt on the theory that this play was intended as a compliment to Elizabeth. (pp. 209-10)

The audience's reactions to the scene must be complex. Falstaff has had it coming, but the process of exposure seems too drawn-out, too painfully vengeful. The Fords and the Pages point out the moral and trumpet their own cleverness at excessive length. The initial suggestiveness of this final scene—the legend of the tree and the hunter, the costume, the people coming out from town to a forest setting, the note of communal preservation—all this, suggestive though it is, becomes unexpectedly explicit and harsh. This primitive impulse suggests that the Windsorites might be expelling something they really need.

At the end, once the truth about the fairies is revealed, Falstaff is puzzled. He attributes his deception to the ability of the imagination to suspend disbelief and accept stolen goods:

> And these are not fairies? I was three or four times in the thought they were not fairies; and yet the guiltiness of my mind, the sudden surprise of my powers, drove the grossness of the foppery into a received belief, in despite of the teeth of all rhyme and reason, that they were fairies. See now how wit may be made a Jack-a-Lent, when 'tis upon ill employment!
>
> [V. v. 121-28]

Ford has already been converted and "awakened" in the previous act, but Falstaff's admission provides the best commentary on Ford's mania as well as his own. A "received belief" in the shape of the outer world is a precarious thing, as everyone begins to realize. The grossness of foppery may lie just beneath the surface of plausibility. "Well, I am your theme" [V. v. 161] Falstaff admits. The remark is true in a double sense, for it refers both to the situation of the moment and, unwittingly, to his larger role in the play's critique of imagination. Several more received beliefs are quickly shattered when Slender and Caius return with boys rather than Anne, and the Pages are, for once, tricked when Fenton returns with their daughter as his wife.

The ritual of exorcism has been successful in that even Falstaff, the cause that wit is in other men, has learned how the imagination can be self-deceiving. But the Windsorites had specific targets in mind, not a general and complete condemnation of imagination—they have simply used fire to fight fire, after all. Evans directed one "fairy" to the proper subject:

> Go you, and where you find a maid
> That ere she sleep has thrice her prayers said
> Raise up the organs of her fantasy,
> Sleep she as sound as careless infancy;
> But those as sleep and think not on their sins,
> Pinch them, arms, legs, backs, shoulders, sides, and shins.
>
> [V. v. 49-54]

The organs of fantasy, as the double entendre suggests, are both the imagination and the genitals, and they have in different ways been central to the deception of both Ford and Falstaff. Only those who "sleep and think not on their sins" must be purged by the Windsorites, and by now the only character who qualifies is Falstaff. The emphasis on "prayer" seems in part a piece of orthodox dogma, and the Fairies' song makes the same point:

> Fie on sinful fantasy,
> Fie on lust and luxury!
> Lust is but a bloody fire,
> Kindled with unchaste desire,
> Fed in heart, whose flames aspire,
> As thoughts do blow them, higher and higher.
> Pinch him, fairies, mutually;
> Pinch him for his villainy.
>
> [V. v. 93-100]

There is some sense here in which "fantasy" (a word twice repeated in the final scene) is itself "sinful," for the "thoughts" which fan the flames of lust are as dangerous as the lust itself. More: they are its cause. Yet there is a larger issue of self-knowledge involved, one wider-reaching than the purely local concerns of the Windsorites. Those who "sleep and think not on their sins" are numerous, if we take the key terms of that expression more figuratively as well as in the narrower religious sense. Evans excepts only the innocent maid, whose "fantasy" will be raised up in a pleasing dream though "sleep she as sound as careless infancy." Just because she *is* careless in fancy, as the pun has it, her imagination is still uncorrupted. Anne knows her own heart, surely, and Fenton his, but (with the crucial exception of the wives) the other Windsorites and Falstaff have, like Lear, ever but slenderly known themselves. Each intrigue plot ends with a "discovery," a literal revelation which strips away pretense and unnecessary disguise. (pp. 210-12)

This final scene, as in most of Shakespeare's plays, begins to distance us from too close an involvement with the action. The patently mechanical resolution of the interlocking plots is deliberate, I think; the revelations fall into place just as each deceived person claims a victory for his point of view. But a more important technique distances us in this final scene: a sudden self-conscious reminder of artifice and theatricality. Slender was deceived by a costume; as Page tells him, he "took the wrong" [V. v. 189]:

> *Slender*. What need you tell me that? I think so, when I took a boy for a girl. If I had been married to him, for all he was in woman's apparel, I would not have had him.
>
> [V. v. 190-93]

Caius appears with a similar complaint:

> By gar, I am cozened: I ha' married *un garcon*, a boy; *un paysan*, by gar; a boy; it is not Anne Page; by gar, I am cozened.
>
> [V. v. 204-07]

But we have all been cozened, everyone in the audience has taken the wrong. Caius and Slender abruptly remind us that Anne *is* a boy—a boy-actor—and the paradox strikes us anew as Anne and Fenton enter immediately after Caius's and Slender's speeches. Both are boys, but we have accepted the illusion that one is not. If Falstaff can swallow for a "received belief" the premise that disguised children are fairies; if Ford can

*Act III. Scene iii. Mistress Ford, Mistress Page, and Falstaff. By W. H. Margetson.*

believe that Falstaff is a genuine sexual threat and that his wife is promiscuous; then the audience should not be surprised that we have succumbed to, even sought out, a comparable deceit, the temporary belief that a male actor is a girl named "Anne," or, more generally, that any actor "is" Falstaff. Although the willing suspension of disbelief is voluntary—dangerously self-induced, in Ford's case—it is never complete, and Shakespeare's audience, well trained by now by other Shakespearean reversals, must have enjoyed still another "double excellency" in the knowledge that the "girl," like the "witch" of Brainford, was also a phantom, that fictions and illusions mingle cheek by jowl with putative realities as "positive as the earth is firm" [III. ii. 48], to use Ford's expression.

Falstaff had made the grandiose, and mistaken, claim that his "admirable dexterity of wit," his uncanny "counterfeiting the action of an old woman" [IV. v. 117-18], had saved him from being set in the stocks for a witch (though it had also earned him a beating). The audience knows that Falstaff's wit was neither admirable nor particularly dexterous in that situation, and that the wives had suggested his disguise. No one would argue, either, that Falstaff's "counterfeiting" had been convincing. Ford, as usual, was the only gull; there are few other takers in this play for Falstaff's wooden nickels. But the character's failure is the author's triumph. Falstaff's "counterfeiting" reminds us, by way of contrast, of Shakespeare's. It is a special mark of the Falstaff of *Merry Wives*, in contrast to his predecessor in *I Henry IV*, that he is allowed to fail and not really recover; his wit can still transform the world, but the world shows more resistance to his force, and occasionally even overcomes him. Only a supremely confident playwright could risk showing so many warts on his audience's favorite character. If Shakespeare has not been granted full success in this effort, it may be because his readers now prefer to freeze Falstaff in his previous incarnation, having forgotten that he is "a man of continual dissolution and thaw."

To take a boy-actor for a girl, however, is small game compared to the much larger illusion which cozens us—the play itself, and the character of Falstaff, whose very being is a masterful "counterfeit," a triumph of the transforming imagination. Ford's runaway imagination, we saw, precipitated too total a division between "dream" and "reality"; he had even reversed the terms in his own mind, and could not control his responses to the world. Though his deception was extensive, Falstaff, at least, "three or four times" thought that they were *not* fairies that were pinching him, before he succumbed to the "received belief" that they were. The audience, if the production is a good one and if the actors are convincing, may in turn three or four times believe that Falstaff and Ford are "real," that they are alive to the point, not merely of suspended disbelief, but through to that mysterious, exhilarating realm of received, and enchanting, belief. And no one can ask for more than that. (pp. 212-15)

*William Carroll, "'A Received Belief: Imagination in 'The Merry Wives of Windsor',"* in Studies in Philology, *Vol. LXXIV, No. 2, April, 1977, pp. 186-215.*

**RONALD HUEBERT** (essay date 1977)

[*Suggesting that* The Merry Wives of Windsor *may be viewed as "sophisticated literary parody" of a variety of late sixteenth-century writers and dramatic conventions, Huebert identifies three levels of satire evident in the play: mock-heroic, burlesque, and self-parody. The critic finds evidence that Shakespeare was im-*

*itating for comic effect the works of Sidney, Lyly, Marlowe, and Ovid's* Metamorphoses, *inverting some of the very conventions of New Comedy which he had employed in his earlier comic dramas, and presenting Falstaff in this play as "a buffoon, or a parody of the trickster he once was."*]

*The Merry Wives* is, in part, a pastiche of quotations from and allusions to literary forms and fashions that had become *démodé* by the end of the sixteenth century. Many of the targets of parody have in fact been isolated; editors of the play point out miscellaneous borrowings from Sidney, Marlowe, Lyly, and from the standard Elizabethan translation of Ovid's *Metamorphoses.* . . . To interpret the play as sophisticated literary parody is at least one way of getting beyond the surface of slapstick and farce without completely muffling the spirit of riot and laughter at the centre of Shakespeare's design.

Falstaff's first attempt to seduce Mistress Ford amounts to a parody of the Petrarchan mode of lovemaking. He begins his assault with an apparent quotation from [Sir Philip Sidney's *Astrophil and Stella*]: "Have I caught thee, my heavenly jewel?" [III. iii. 43]. To glorify his title as a lover, Falstaff tries to capitalize on the similarities between his position and Astrophil's, for like Astrophil he is courting a woman who is married to a jealous husband. But, issuing from Falstaff's lips, the line trembles with absurdity: the speaker is no longer the superbly sensitive Elizabethan courtier, but a decayed and dissolute knight who has just been described by his supposed mistress as a "gross watery pumpion" [III. iii. 41]. Nor does Mistress Ford correspond to the Petrarchan pattern; she is neither the disdainful Stella nor the unapproachable ideal. Indeed, her middle-class common-sense immediately deflates Falstaff's courtly pretensions: "I your lady, Sir John?" she queries, "Alas, I should be a pitiful lady" [III. iii. 52-3]. There may well be a pun on "pitiful": on the one hand a bourgeois housewife is a poor substitute for a lady of genuine nobility; on the other hand Mistress Ford is full of pity for the fat knight, unlike the elevated mistresses of typical unrequited lovers.

In fact Falstaff's remark is not a quotation but a free rendering of the opening line from Astrophil's Second Song. The original reads as follows:

> Have I caught my heav'nly jewell,
> Teaching sleepe most faire to be?
> Now will I teach her that she,
> When she wakes, is too too cruell.

Falstaff makes two changes that appear to be trivial at first glance, but turn out to be crucial. He adds the pronoun "thee" and he makes "heavenly" trisyllabic. The result—"Have I caught thee, my heavenly jewel?"—is a major stylistic change. Sidney's extremely formal trochaic metre has become homespun prose in Falstaff's rendering. In Sidney's version no pronoun object is required, because Astrophil aspires to reach the high ideal which the beloved represents; in Shakespeare's parody Falstaff gives "caught" a more literal and physical meaning by adding an informal pronoun to stand for the object of his desires. The change in tone may also affect the flavour of the word "jewel." In the standard Petrarchan formula, "jewel" is the mark of absolute value; but in less elevated contexts, "jewel" can also be the treasure that virgins are supposed to guard against lecherous assailants. We do Falstaff no injustice to assume that he is aware of the sexual meaning of the word; in another courtship scene he picks up Mistress Ford's punning reference to himself as "my male deer" and promptly turns her into "My doe with the black scut" [V. v. 17-18].

*Astrophil and Stella* reaches something of an erotic climax in this Second Song, for it tells of the famous kiss which the lover steals from the sleeping mistress. Astrophil has been celebrating and pursuing Stella through the poetic maze of seventy-two sonnets before he gains his momentary reward. At once Stella awakens, frowns, and sends her lover into a paroxysm of anguish mingled with desire. Significantly, Falstaff chooses his Petrarchan conceit from the only passage in which Astrophil and Stella make physical contact. Unlike his more reticent model, Falstaff begins the matter of courtship by lunging *in medias res*. He has not been ardently pursuing his mistress in vain, and he has no intention of doing so; he does not wait until he finds her asleep before he dares to approach. And while Astrophil worries and frets about Stella's husband in the "Rich" sonnets (24, 35, 37), Falstaff disposes of the jealous husband without mental struggle. "Now shall I sin in my wish," he announces: "I would thy husband were dead" [III. iii. 49-50].

Falstaff's wooing of Mistress Ford, then, satisfies at least the minimum requirement of literary parody: it sets up an ironic relationship between the target of parody and its likeness or caricature. Indeed, the mental picture of Falstaff kneeling to his "pitiful lady" and reciting fragments of half-remembered Petrarchan poetry is a fairly close illustration of the best scholarly definition of parody. "We may define it," writes Gilbert Highet, "as imitation which, through distortion and exaggeration, evokes amusement, derision, and sometimes scorn" [in *The Anatomy of Satire*]. Falstaff's ridiculous Petrarchan stance, it must be admitted, evokes little "derision" or "scorn" because it belongs to a type of parody that generates primarily amusement. This first level of parody is known as the mock-heroic. . . . In Pope's brilliant phrase, the technique of mock-heroic is like "using a vast force to lift a *feather*" [in "Postscript" to the *Odyssey*]. The parodist suspects that the pretensions of his model are just a trifle absurd, and by pretending to reproduce the tone of his model in cold seriousness, he works the miracle that makes it "absurder than it was."

In *The Merry Wives* Falstaff's desire to repair his financial losses is the trivial thing which motivates the mighty cause of Petrarchan lovemaking. He must pretend to be in earnest, of course, or his plan will have no chance of success, so he lifts the feather of his desires with the vast force of courtly language. Even the letter which he sends simultaneously to Mistress Ford and Mistress Page shows Falstaff using high rhetorical devices for inconsequential purposes. Mistress Page is at first delighted by the euphuistic cadences which disguise and yet suggest the lover's wishes: "Ask me no reason why I love you; for though Love use Reason for his precision, he admits him not for his counsellor" [II. i. 4-6]. This artful aphorism is worthy of John Lyly both in style and sentiment; like the lovers in [Lyly's] *Euphues,* Falstaff gives a gracefully reasoned account of the unreasonable nature of love. The debate between love and reason is of course a favourite topic in Elizabethan sonnet sequences: in *Astrophil and Stella* a personified Reason eventually kneels to the bright beams of Stella's eyes and offers to prove "By reason good, good reason her to love" (Sonnet 10). This is the sort of casuistry that Falstaff has in mind when he calls reason the "precisian" but not the "counsellor" to love. The parody here runs so close to its model that like Mistress Page we may for a moment be in danger of missing the joke. But soon Falstaff distends the elegant parallelisms of his prose to include his real interests. "You love sack," the letter continues, "and so do I. Would you desire better sympathy?" [II. i. 8-10]. The stylistic surface of the letter cracks under the pressure of mockery; like his physical bulk, Falstaff's rhetoric shows "a kind of alacrity in sinking" [III. v. 12-13].

Falstaff is by no means alone in his use of the mock-heroic vein. Part of Ford's disguise consists in the language he uses, for whenever he poses as "Brook" he adopts the courtly idiom. In his first interview with Falstaff, "Brook" sounds a note of high sentence that might have come from his commonplace book:

Love like a shadow flies when substance love pursues;
Pursuing that that flies, and flying what pursues.
                                        [II. ii. 207-08]

The second line of this mock proverb is techically a specimen of *anti-metabole* (AB:BA). Decidedly formal repetition of this sort is both normal and mellifluous in the sonnet or in *Euphues*, but Ford's couplet limps rather badly ("that that") and comes to a halt with an identical rhyme. Perhaps Ford is in the same predicament as Slender, who dreads the thought of courting Anne Page without his "Book of Songs and Sonnets" [I. i. 199]. On the whole Master "Brook" manages a very credible imitation of the courtly style, though like Falstaff he is merely using the rhetoric of love to cloak his special interests. (pp. 137-40)

The second level of parody is the less congenial and more venomous form of attack known as burlesque. . . . The writer of burlesque is not content to manipulate the tone of his original by shifting the situation; he deflowers the language of his model with the unmistakable bludgeon of bathos. While mock-heroic parody pays at least the lefthanded compliment of bemused imitation, "a burlesque treats its subject with ridicule, vulgarity, distortion, and contempt" [Highet].

The purest example of burlesque in *The Merry Wives* is the scene in which Sir Hugh administers the melody of Latin grammar to young Master William while Mistress Quickly provides the *basso continuo*. Sir Hugh may well be consulting a grammar book in this scene, where, under the rubric "Numbres of Nounes," he could find the following instruction: "In Nounes be two numbres: the singular, and the plural. The Singular nūbre speaketh of one: as *Lapis*, a Stone. The plurall nūbre speaketh of mo then one: as *Lapides*, Stones." With wooden resolution the parson begins his questioning: "William, how many numbers is in nouns?" [IV. i. 21]. Then, "What is 'lapis,' William?" [IV. i. 31]. Master William provides the answers in the same mechanical way that Sir Hugh frames the questions, but not before Mistress Quickly has performed some imaginative scholarship of her own. She translates *pulcher* as "Polecats," and conjectures that "'Hang-hog' [*haec, hoc*] is Latin for bacon" [IV. i. 28, 48]. The scene reaches a climax in the genitive case plural, when William obligingly recites: "Genitivo, horum, harum, horum" [IV. i. 61]. This is too much for Mistress Quickly. "Vengeance of Jenny's case!" she cries; "fie on her! Never name here, child, if she be a whore" [IV. i. 62-3]. With her brilliant, unabashed vulgarity Mistress Quickly can say that generations of Elizabethan schoolboys must have wanted to say; as a result, the frail edifice of Sir Hugh's classical learning topples like a house of cards.

The primary target of Shakespeare's burlesque in *The Merry Wives* is an Elizabethan love tragedy, *Soliman and Perseda*, probably written by Thomas Kyd. This play contains just the sort of verbal bombast and strident rhetoric that helped to make [Kyd's] *The Spanish Tragedy* so susceptible to parody. (pp. 141-42)

There is considerable evidence to suggest that Shakespeare used scraps of *Soliman and Perseda* while working on several different plays, and indeed it has been remarked that Kyd's comic characters Piston and Basilisco may have contributed something to the creation of Pistol and Falstaff. But the relationship between Kyd's play and Shakespeare's can hardly be described with such usual terms as "influence" or "borrowing." Mistress Ford comes much closer to the truth when she coins a proverb that might be taken as a definition of burlesque: "they do no more adhere and keep pace together than the Hundredth Psalm to the tune of 'Greensleeves'" [II. i. 61-3]. Mistress Ford is speaking of the jarring incongruity between Falstaff's real character and his professed intentions, but her simile also describes the difference between the pomp and circumstance of tragedy and the inversion of tragedy through burlesque. It would be a pleasant exercise in absurdity to take Mistress Ford at her word; this would require locating the relevant Psalm ("All people that on earth do dwell") in the collection by Sternhold and Hopkins and singing it to the familiar and lascivious Elizabethan ballad tune. The magisterial tone of the Old Hundredth would then correspond to the high rhetoric of Kyd's tragedy, while the gay dance rhythms of "Greensleeves" might stand for Shakespeare's irreverent use of the stuff of tragedy. The metaphor holds true not only for the specific target of burlesque, but also for the broad class of revenge plays to which it belongs. As G. R. Hibbard has recently shown, many stages in the intrigue of *The Merry Wives* involve actions of revenge: Ford seeks revenge for his supposed cuckoldry, Caius and Evans form a pact to avenge the insults of the Host, and the merry wives themselves plot revenge against Falstaff. Add to this the fragments of rant that form the core of Pistol's vocabulary and *The Merry Wives* becomes, at one level, "a most consummate piece of burlesque" [G. R. Hibbard, in his introduction to *The Merry Wives of Windsor* (1973)].

The distinction between mock-heroic and burlesque has analytic validity only, and many of my examples very nearly straddle the imaginary boundary between the first two levels of parody. This means only that the two processes can operate simultaneously, just as magnification and reduction can have complementary functions in satire. Falstaff seldom soars to mock-heroic heights without the risk of falling into the vulgarisms of burlesque. In mock-heroic fashion he draws the traditional comparison between his mistress's eyes and the sun: "Sometimes the beam of her view gilded my foot, sometimes my portly belly" [I. iii. 61-2]. The reference to Falstaff's girth is sufficiently gross to move the conceit in the direction of burlesque, and Pistol's retort completes the descent: "Then did the sun on dunghill shine" [I. iii. 63]. Even this fragment of abuse contains mock-heroic pretensions, for it aspires to mimic the sententious wisdom of *Euphues:* "The Sun shineth upon the dungehill, and is not corrupted, the Diamond lyeth in the fire, and is not consumed, the Christall toucheth the Toade, and is not poysoned." Lyly's controlled comparison leads up to the maxim that a complete gentleman is never corrupted with lewdness, but in Pistol's quip such moral intentions have been left far behind. For the burlesquer the fun of the line is in telling Falstaff that his belly is "full of shit."

More significantly, mock-heroic and burlesque work together in Falstaff's scene as Herne the Hunter. As several critics have ably demonstrated, Shakespeare returns in this scene to his favourite mythological source-book, Ovid's *Metamorphoses*. Falstaff enters sporting a pair of antlers on his head. Then he calls himself "a Windsor stag; and the fattest, I think, i' the forest'' [V. v. 12-13]. By using mock-heroic strategy Shake-speare identifies Falstaff with Actaeon, who in Ovid's account is transformed into ''the shape of Stagge'' as punishment for watching Diana take her customary naked bath.

But if Herne the Hunter is Shakespeare's vehicle for a game of wit at Ovid's expense, he is also a heavier weapon in a more devastating attack. The target of burlesque in this case is, I believe, Marlowe's *Doctor Faustus*. Every Elizabethan the-atregoer would be familiar with the ominous scene in which Faustus meets his damnation. *''The clock strikes eleven''* as Faustus begins his soliloquy, and the last ''bare hour'' of life is relentlessly measured with knells of doom at half-past eleven and twelve. ''The Windsor bell hath struck twelve.'' Falstaff announces in the opening line of his parallel scene [V. v. 1]. If this implied stage-direction is honoured during the scene change, then the audience has already been prepared for a burlesque of the more serious damnation scene. Just as Faustus is carried away by a crew of devils at the end of his soliloquy, so Falstaff will be abused by a troop of fairies when his mid-night sports are done. And since Mephistophilis appears as the ring-leader of the devils, it is only appropriate to have Sir Hugh disguised as a satyr giving instructions to the fairy band. Faus-tus tries to repent in his last speech, and seeks to bargain his way out of eternal torment. ''O God,'' he prays:

> Let Faustus live in hell a thousand years,
> A hundred thousand, and at last be saved.

This is a cowardly retreat from his earlier resolution, and it echoes through Falstaff's corresponding rationalization. ''I think the devil will not have me damned,'' says a terrified Falstaff, ''lest the oil that's in me should set hell on fire'' [V. v. 34-6]. The argument is of course nonsensical, but hardly less im-pressive than the death-bed casuistries of the famous Witten-berg logician. Grasping at straws, Faustus remembers the pop-ular Pythagorean heresy of *metempsychosis*, and hopes a least that instead of being damned he may be transformed ''Into some brutish beast'' [V. ii. 173]. The burlesque version takes Faustus literally, for his namesake stands at stage centre with buck's horns on his head. Falstaff's address to Jove at the beginning of his scene as Herne becomes a travesty of Faustus' prayer: ''Remember, Jove, thou wast a bull for thy Europa: love set on thy horns. O powerful love, that in some respects makes a beast a man; in some other, a man a beast'' [V. v. 3-6]. Here the Pythagorean doctrine reaches complete absurd-ity; through the inversions of burlesque it is reduced to nothing more than another way of justifying the ''beastly fault'' of lust [V. v. 9].

If the classical allusions in this scene point to Ovid as the target of mock-heroic parody, the stage picture and accompanying effects would strongly suggest *Doctor Faustus* as the victim of burlesque. And once again Shakespeare has taken the trouble to prepare his spectators for the *coup de théâtre* [theatrical effect]. Early in the play Pistol throws out threatening re-minders of ''Mephistophilus'' [I. i. 130] and ''Lucifer'' [I. iii. 76]. The ridiculous adventure of the Duke of Germany comes to a close when Bardolph rushes on stage to tell the Host that ''three German devils, three Doctor Faustuses'' have cozened him of his horses [IV. v. 69-70]. And Mistress Page invites us to see the demonic significance of the adventure at Herne's Oak. ''No man means evil but the devil,'' she says, ''and we shall know him by his horns'' [V. ii. 12-14]. Such pointed remarks support the theatrical burlesque by conditioning au-dience response. And if further support is required, it comes from the broadly ironic relationship between the story of the

German doctor and the misadventures of the fat knight. Faustus is a ''wanton and lascivious'' man [II. i. 140] who covers his genuine lust with the mantle of learning and pays the price of damnation. Falstaff merely pretends to be a lecher; he dresses up his supposed lust in the disguise of courtly language; he is damned at last by a troop of village children masquerading as malevolent spirits.

Reflexive parody or self-parody is the third artistic strategy of *The Merry Wives*. Chaucer provides the defining model in this case; the complex and ironic contrast between *The Knight's Tale* and *The Miller's Tale* can hardly be described without recourse to ''self-parody'' or some equivalent term. Both tales set up love triangles in which two male rivals compete for the single available woman, but the gentle knights of the target story become the opportunistic clerks of the parody. (pp. 143-46)

The love plot of *The Merry Wives* belongs to the level of self-parody, for in the story of Fenton and Anne Page Shakespeare undercuts the conventions of New Comedy as he had used them in constructing plays like *The Two Gentlemen of Verona* and *A Midsummer Night's Dream*. ''The normal action'' of such comedies, in Northrop Frye's formula, ''is the effort of a young man to get possession of a young woman who is kept from him by various social barriers: her low birth, his minority or shortage of funds, parental opposition, the prior claims of a rival'' [in *A Natural Perspective*]. At first glance this looks like a fair description of the love affair between Fenton and Anne, but matters are by no means so simple. Fenton, for example, is hardly an ordinary young man. He appears to be a thoroughgoing prig for most of the play, perhaps because he speaks blank verse in a world where the customary idiom is prose. He admits that he was first attracted to Anne because of her money [III. iv. 13-14], and so becomes susceptible to the same charges of insincerity that are made against Falstaff. Page (the *senex* figure) objects to Fenton's candidacy on the grounds that he is too nobly born [III. ii. 73]; in itself this is a curious barrier, for the normal heavy fathers of Elizabethan comedy take pains to select husbands from the highest possible rank on the social scale. To make matters worse, Fenton is graceless enough to repeat the objection to Anne [III. iv. 4].

Mistress Quickly's lineage has been traced back to the *fantesca* of the *commedia dell'arte*, who of course belongs to the same family tree as the clever slave of New Comedy. But one need only compare the ''foolish carrion'' of *The Merry Wives* [III. iii. 193] to the legitimate maidservant Lucetta in *The Two Gentlemen of Verona* to realize that Mistress Quickly is an impostor. Despite her many claims to omniscience in matters of love, she has no knowledge whatever of ''Anne's mind'' [I. iv. 127]. She notices the wart above Fenton's eye, but fails to recognize it as the infallible mark of the true prince charming of New Comedy. She lacks even the instinctive sympathy which comic maidservants have for their charges, for she treats Anne like a piece of merchandise that must be turned into a quick profit before the inevitable bankruptcy of marriage. Yet, as soon as the love plot takes a turn for the better, Mistress Quickly is the first to take credit: ''This is my doing now. 'Nay,' said I, 'will you cast away your child on a fool, and a physician? Look on Master Fenton.' This is my doing'' [III. iv. 95-8]. Instead of convincing us that matters are secure in her com-petent hands, Mistress Quickly demonstrates only that she is shrewd enough to back the right horse after the betting has closed. As for her wit—another stock characteristic of the *fan-tesca*—Mistress Quickly has no more than the negative ca-pability of mismanaging language at least as badly as she mishandles events. Hers is one of the funniest parts in the play, precisely because she is not the typical maidservant of New Comedy but a ludicrous caricature of the species.

The usual procedure at the end of a New Comedy involves reconciliation and festivity; the hero is recognized by the older generation as a genuinely deserving lover, and the betrothal or marriage of hero and heroine is celebrated in a banquet, dance, or masque. In *The Merry Wives* the order of events is reversed. Page and Mistress Page sponsor the dance only because each remains convinced that one or other of the undesirable rivals will elope with their daughter. Instead of following the ordered formality of a betrothal ceremony, the festival turns into a chaotic series of mistaken identities from which only Fenton and Anne emerge undisturbed. The authority figures are at last forced to sanction a marriage conducted without their approval.

In Falstaff's humiliation by the fairies M. C. Bradbrook detects "a kind of parody of the Garter ceremony" [see excerpt above, 1968], while Geoffrey Bullough calls the fairy dance "almost a parody" of Shakespeare's earlier fairy world in *A Midsummer Night's Dream* [see Additional Bibliography]. Both suggestions point in the right direction. In her role as Fairy Queen, Mistress Quickly quotes the motto of the Knights of the Garter: "Honi soit qui mal y pense" [V. v. 69]. Such a sentiment is appropriate enough at the end of *Sir Gawain and the Green Knight*, where a series of chastity tests has purified the hero from corruption by carnal desire. In *The Merry Wives* the motto is spoken by the "punk" of the play [II. ii. 135] and applied to a "bag of flax" who has never been in any real danger of corruption through lust [V. v. 151]. Yet the fairies perform the required trial by ordeal, and when their tapers burn Falstaff's fingers the verdict is plain: "Corrupt, corrupt, and tainted in desire" [V. v. 90]. Since this is clearly an inaccurate result, the trial by fire must be a mock ordeal, and as Falstaff will soon remark, the fairies cannot be *real* otherworld creatures. "And these are not fairies?" he says as the truth dawns. "I was three or four times in the thought they were not fairies; and yet the guiltiness of my mind, the sudden surprise of my powers, drove the grossness of the foppery into a received belief" [V. v. 121-25]. Still, Falstaff is no more gullible than the usual audience of a New Comedy, when for instance they are asked to accept the fopperies of Puck and Oberon as received belief. Nor is he more gullible than Master Slender, who elopes with one of the fairies only to discover that "she's a great lubberly boy" [V. v. 184]; nor than Doctor Caius, who complains: "By gar, I am cozened—I ha' married un garçon" [V. v. 204-06]. This is our last laugh at the expense of New Comedy and its conventions; it is a parody of the world in which "Sebastian" can serve as page to Proteus [in *The Two Gentlemen of Verona*] and Orsino can fall in love with "Cesario" [in *Twelfth Night*]. And there is the additional wink at theatrical conventions, for of course the actor who marries Fenton sings in the same falsetto range as Slender's lubberly boy or the Doctor's "garçon."

The most prominent specimen of self-parody in the play is Falstaff himself. H. B. Charlton long ago identified the Falstaff of *The Merry Wives* as a "contemptible caricature" of his former self, while assuming that such a description implied also the artistic degradation that Bradley first outlined [see excerpts above, 1935 and 1902]. But if *The Merry Wives* functions as parody at a great many levels, then the weakness of its central character becomes in fact a strength of the play. It is true that the Falstaff of *The Merry Wives* falls into exactly the kinds of traps he would have cleverly avoided in the history

plays. In *2 Henry IV* he manages both the Hostess and Doll Tearsheet with the confidence of a man who knows his way around women; in *The Merry Wives* he is ludicrously vulnerable to any morsels of flattery that Mistress Quickly throws his way. In the bustle of historical events Falstaff acquires a considerable though fraudulent military reputation; at Windsor he cannot intimidate even his wretched followers. He is still a genius with words, but again in the spirit of parody most of his jokes recoil at length upon the inventor's head. After his escape from calamity disguised as the Witch of Brainford, for instance, Falstaff demonstrates his famous ability to save face by fabrication. "There was, mine Host, an old fat woman even now with me," he explains as soon as he has removed the opprobrious costume, "but she's gone" [IV. v. 24-5]. The story has grown into a demonstration of his agility by the time he tells it to Mistress Quickly: "But that my admirable dexterity of wit, my counterfeiting the action of an old woman, delivered me, the knave constable had set me i' the stocks, i' the common stocks, for a witch" [IV. v. 117-20]. The account he gives to "Brook" is closer to the truth, although he frames the story in language aimed at proving his staunch courage in the face of adversity. But at this point Falstaff does not realize that he is talking to the very man who has beaten him "grievously, in the shape of a woman" [V. i. 20-1], that he is playing into Ford's hands. What he lacks is the triumphant "instinct" which in *1 Henry IV* allows him to penetrate the disguise of the Lord's anointed. . . . In the history plays Falstaff as clown plays opposite a whole gallery of straight-men ranging from Hotspur to the Lord Chief Justice. In *The Merry Wives* he is still the clown; but he is also a buffoon, or a parody of the trickster he once was.

On the surface there would appear to be one major exception to the thesis I have tried to develop—the character of Master Ford. When he appears in disguise, Ford mimics the stance of the Petrarchan lover; but *in propria persona* [in his own nature], by the measurement of realism and the test of theatrical production, he is by far the most sympathetic character in the play. Yet every rule of comedy, old and new, would nominate Ford as the potential butt of sexual humour. As the jealous husband he has illustrious ancestors . . . , not to mention his many contemporaries and successors. The Italian tales and English jests which form the corpus of sources and analogues for the jealous husband plot all agree in two particulars: the husband invariably bears the stigma of cuckoldry and the brunt of comic abuse. Ford's position, then, even if not technically an instance of parody, amounts to at least a striking inversion of the rules of comedy. Perhaps this is the natural result of Shakespeare's technique elsewhere in the play: the effect of turning the normally serious characters upside down is to put the duped husband on his feet again as it were by default. Thus Ford's part in the play becomes a parody of the second remove. In creating a sympathetic jealous husband Shakespeare inverts the old ironies of the comic tradition. (pp. 146-49)

In the broadest thematic terms *The Merry Wives* is an elaborate game of "let's pretend." The dance of fairies which occupies such a strong climactic position at the end of the play brings together half Windsor in a pantomime of pretence. The village children disguise themselves as fairies, the Parson plays at being a satyr, Mistress Quickly is queen for a day, and Falstaff arrives in "the shape of Stagge." A usual, the play-within-the-play reflects the structure of the play as a whole, and it now becomes clear that every major character has been involved in a similar game of pretence, disguise, and deception. . . . Parody is the language of comic pretence. Its principles of imitation, distortion, and amusement imply that the parodist creates a language that for comic reasons pretends to be something it is not. The levels of parody in *The Merry Wives* generate part of the humour of the play, while the technique of parody itself corroborates the central theme of pretence. (pp. 149-50)

> Ronald Huebert, "Levels of Parody in 'The Merry
> Wives of Windsor'," in English Studies in Canada,
> Vol. III, No. 2, Summer, 1977, pp. 136-52.

### RICHARD F. HARDIN    (essay date 1978)

[*Hardin examines several variations on the theme of honor in* The Merry Wives of Windsor. *Falstaff, he asserts, is "the nemesis of honor," for his conduct is a profanation of his knightly vows and exemplifies the deterioration of the chivalric code; he adds, however, that Falstaff's attempt to compromise Mistress Ford and Mistress Page is only one of the "threats to feminine honor" that recur in the play. Hardin contends that Ford is equally guilty of believing that all women are "weak and faithless," thus dishonoring his wife by denying her personal integrity, and he maintains that the men all share the conviction that a young, marriageable woman can be treated as chattel. Although the marriage of Anne and Fenton represents an endorsement of personal honor, Hardin argues, it also underscores the view found throughout* The Merry Wives of Windsor *that an "aristocrat who expects to keep what remains of his family glory must deal with the Pages and Fords of the new order."*]

Shakespeare's opening dialogue often serves to foreshadow an important theme, and [*The Merry Wives of Windsor*] is no exception. Shallow, Slender, and Evans are talking about titles of honor—esquire, justice, keeper of the rolls, "armigero" or gentleman. A related topic is heraldry, the "luces" or pikes in Shallow's coat of arms: "The dozen white louses do become an old coat well; it agrees well, passant. It is a familiar beast to man, and signifies love" [I. i. 19-2!]. The ambiguity of luce-louse and coat-coot (the pun could have been made in Elizabethan English) typifies the problem of distinguishing between external honor and its true inward counterpart. Inheriting an old coat, a coot like Robert Shallow can acquire "honors"; the highest-ranking character in the play is the least honorable; on the other hand, commoners like Mistress Page and Ford have their only honor in virtue and a good name. "O woman," says Mrs. Ford with tongue in cheek, "if it were not for one trifling respect, I could come to such an honor! . . . If I would go to hell for an eternal moment or so, I could be knighted" [II. i. 44-5, 49-50]. The conflict between the two middle-aged women and the fat knight comically reenacts the encounter between the knight errant and the country maid, so familiar in the pastourelles of Shakespeare's century, and to some extent surviving in [Samuel Richardson's] *Pamela* and its offspring. In this play we can say that for the most part true honor eventually proves its worth over titled honor, although gentry is to some extent redeemed in the romantic plot of Anne Page and Fenton.

The first act seems constructed around particular threats to feminine honor, especially the threat of sexual union for the sake of wealth. It had never occurred to Slender to make overtures to Anne until he heard about her inheritance [II. i. 58-9]. Yet he still requires a go-between, as does Caius. The ambience of the brothel that Mistress Quickly imports from the history plays, and especially her role as intermediary—procuress, as it were, for Anne's three suitors and Falstaff—reduces the arranged marriage to a kind of prostitution. The first, second, and fourth scenes all disclose the threats to Anne's future, while

Scene Three reveals Falstaff's plot against the citizen's wives. Scene Four consists mostly of a burlesque on Mistress Quickly's honor, the concealed lover motif anticipating the women's jokes on Falstaff. Not until the end of this act is Fenton introduced, the character who comforts us with hope that the mercenary schemes for Anne's hand will miscarry.

Falstaff too has imported something from the history plays in his role as the nemesis of honor. To the extent that any character is shaped by the world of his play, the world of *Henry IV* is so vastly unlike that of *The Merry Wives* that we should not really expect to find the same character in Windsor—any more than Goneril [in *King Lear*] should turn up in *The Comedy of Errors*. The Henry plays are about honor in a world where the chivalric code has become bankrupt, ushering in a state of misrule parodied in the tavern scenes between Hal and Falstaff. The [Order of the] Garter itself is not immune to the assaults of Falstaff, who can tell Hal to "Hang thyself in thine own heir-apparent garters" [*1 Henry IV*, II. ii. 43-4]. Honor is a word, air, a mere scutcheon, runs the famous catechism; if it were not for his dishonorable attempts to filch honor (in stabbing dead Hotspur in the first, and in handing over the captive Coleville in the second part of *Henry IV*), such witty nihilism might carry the day. Falstaff is amusing and even admirable in a world of great hypocrites, but in Windsor the terms are reversed when he seeks to take advantage of a lesser, though not weaker, social class. Among the citizens he is nearly reduced to the stereotyped Vice figure from which he came. (pp. 144-45)

The imagery of hell and fire in the play frequently reminds us of the Vice or tavern-fellow devil behind the mask of Falstaff. Mrs. Ford plans to "entertain him with hope, till the wicked fire of lust have melted him in his own grease" [II. i. 68]. Falstaff imagines that Mrs. Page's eye "did seem to scorch me like a burning glass" [I. iii. 67], and he later tells Pistol, "I am damn'd in hell for swearing to gentlemen my friends, you were good soldiers" [II. ii. 10-11]. In Mrs. Ford's laundry basket he is "more than half stew'd in grease, like a Dutch dish," so that he is "thrown into the Thames, and cool'd, glowing hot" [III. v. 118-19, 119-20]. Earlier he had remarked that "if the bottom were as deep as hell, I should down" [III. v. 13-15]. Alone in Windsor Forest at night he thinks, "The devil will not have me damn'd, lest the oil that's in me should set hell on fire" [V. v. 34-5]. These images of the infernal are not intended to purge Windsor of vice in the purely Christian moral sense so much as to castigate dishonor to the chivalric code. . . . The painting of Falstaff's room with the story of the prodigal son [IV. v. 7-8] not only associates him with the Christian parable, but underscores his prodigality to the earthly vows of knighthood.

Ford's pummeling "the old woman of Brainsford" is to Mrs. Page a kind of exorcism: "I'll have the cudgel hallow'd and hung over the altar. . . . The spirit of wantonness is sure scared out of him. If the devil have him not in fee-simple, with fine and recovery, he will never, I think, in the way of waste, attempt us again" [IV. ii. 204-05, 209-12]. In fact, Falstaff had already been exorcised by immersion in water, the evil of dishonor to be washed away like the filth in Mrs. Page's laundry. Then follows the beating of the witch, a standard treatment accorded the possessed in Elizabethan Bedlam. Finally the erring knight-errant is arraigned and judged at midnight in the forest—"Corrupt, corrupt, and tainted in desire" [V. v. 90]. His fingers are burned with tapers, and the fairies pinch him while singing a ritual taunt, a "scornful rhyme" [V. v. 91] in

*Act IV. Scene i. Mistress Quickly, William, Mistress Page, and Evans. By Robert Smirke. The Department of Rare Books and Special Collections, The University of Michigan Library.*

the meter of the witches' chant in *Macbeth* [I. iii. 14ff. and IV. i. 1ff.]. Page's line, "No man means evil but the devil, and we shall know him by his horns" [V. ii. 12-14], prepares us for this ritual, the phrase "means evil" translating the "mal y pense" of the Garter motto. In the metaphor of the two chivalries the association of religion (the devil) with the Garter allusion represents a last judgment at the bar of honor. (pp. 145-46)

A special case of "thinking evil" is Ford, who Falstaff says has in him "the finest mad devil of jealousy . . . that ever governed frenzy" [V. i. 18-19]. His jealous soliloquies also reinforce the pattern of diabolic reference in the play:

> See the hell of having a false woman! My bed shall be abus'd, my coffers ransack'd, my reputation gnawn at, and I shall not only receive this villainous wrong, but stand under the adoption of abominable terms, and by him that does me this wrong. Terms! names! Amaimon sounds well; Lucifer well; Barbason well; yet they are the devil's additions, the names of fiends; but Cuckold! Wittol!—Cuckold! the devil himself hath not such a name.
>
> [II. ii. 291-300]

His wife and Page's "share damnation together" [III. ii. 39-40], and Page, appalled at his suspicions, asks, "What spirit, what

devil suggests this imagination?" [III. iii. 215-16]. Ford imagines Falstaff guided by a devil [III. v. 147-48], and when he thinks a second time that he has captured Falstaff, he cries out, "Now shall the devil be sham'd" [IV. ii. 119]. A character whose dark soul is simply a given in the play, Ford provides the sinister undertone that so often surfaces in Shakespeare's comedies—the disharmony between Adriana and her husband in *Comedy of Errors* or the conflict between father and daughter in *Midsummer Night's Dream*. And like Othello's, his fear of cuckoldry stems from his obsession with another variety of honor, "reputation."

These references to the devil echo older comic incidents in English religious drama, such as the binding-up or casting-out of Satan in the Corpus Christi plays; but they do not mean that we should read theology into *The Merry Wives*. The "religion" of this play is honor, as expressed in Ford's abashed confession when his wife has revealed her joke with Falstaff:

> Now doth thy honor stand
> In him that was of late an heretic,
> As firm as faith.
>
> [IV. iv. 8-9]

In the theology of honor, Ford's sin is mistrust and jealousy, heresies that should have been dispelled by the simple faith of married love. His earlier denial of his wife is likened to the heretic's denial of God, but the tenor of the play remains secular. As a natural virtue, honor occupies a middle place between earth and heaven. It is thus appropriate that the fairies carry out Falstaff's sentence . . . because they are natural spirits, already associated with chivalric honor in Spenser's great poem [*The Faerie Queene*]. (pp. 146-48)

Honor does not subsist in the material world; in this respect it resembles human love, as described in the proverb that Ford quotes: "Love like a shadow flies when substance love pursues, / Pursuing that that flies, and flying what pursues" [II. ii. 207-08]. Falstaff represents a caricature of honor, knighthood, tainted by "substance"; but the same taint almost prevails in Anne's parents' plans for her marriage. (p. 148)

Fenton is the logical choice for Anne, as the Host recognizes: "he writes verses, he speaks holiday, he smells April and May" [III. ii. 67-9]. Page has rejected him on the grounds of "substance": "The gentleman is of no having. . . . No, he shall not knit a knot in his fortunes with the finger of my substance" [III. ii. 71-2, 74-5]. In this scene, associating Fenton with Prince Hal's madcap days endows him with something of Hal's role as youth resisting the older generation's pressures for conformity. It is not only substance that alienates Page from Fenton, however; underlying this is his townsman's mistrust of the upper class, which in the arena of public honor parallels Ford's mistrust of his wife's personal honor. Fenton "is of too high a region, he knows too much," says Page [III. ii. 73-4]; and Fenton tells Anne that her father "doth object I am too great of birth" [III. iv. 4]. His elopement not only saves Anne from the miseries of enforced marriage, but effects a union of wealth and honor that will advance both Page's and Fenton's families, much like the union of Lacy and Rose in [Thomas Dekker's] *The Shoemaker's Holiday*.

In a play so much concerned with honor, it is not surprising that the plot is so heavily dependent upon revenge. The wives are of course the foremost exponents of revenge, the word itself occurring five times in the first hundred lines of Act Two, Scene One, where they first react to Falstaff's overtures. Mrs. Ford's revenge, however, is more complex than Mrs. Page's:

"O that my husband saw this letter! it would give eternal food to his jealousy" [II. i. 100-01]. The wives are thus managing two revenge plots simultaneously, enhanced by the way in which Ford's and Falstaff's self-gulling roles reinforce one another. In both cases what is most important about the women's schemes is that they undermine that conventional masculine sterotyping of women as weak and faithless, familiar in such poems as Donne's "Go and catch a falling star."

Falstaff's arrogance in reading this type into the wives needs no comment. Ford is perhaps a subtler case, sharing that fatal, almost metaphysical suspicion of women that we find in Hamlet, Othello, and Lear. In his first jealous tirade, he has no trouble moving from the singular to the plural third person (italics mine): "I will rather trust a Fleming with my butter, ... than my wife with herself. Then she plots, then she ruminates, then she devises; and what *they* think in their hearts they may effect, they will break their hearts but they will effect" [II. ii. 302-05]. The grammatical non-sequitur signals Ford's capitulation to received ideas—always a dangerous sign in Shakespeare—despite repeated assurances that all Windsor knows his wife to be honest [III. iii. 219-20]. Eventually this madness comes into the open, as Mrs. Page reports how he "rails against all married mankind" and "curses all Eve's daughters" [IV. ii. 23-4]. It is essential to realize that the second laundry basket scene is deliberately engineered by the women to embarrass Ford in front of his friends; they know beforehand that Ford has heard how Falstaff escaped the first time [IV. ii. 31-3]. The basket of dirty laundry, empty of grounds for suspicion, appropriately represents Ford's state of mind. Accordingly, the play manages to explode fashionable misogyny along with the myth that women of Anne's years can be sold to the highest bidder. The catalyst in this affirmation of woman's integrity is properly Mistress Quickly, who in her role in the history plays as well as her dubious relationship with Doctor Caius exemplifies the most abused class of women in society: hence she is both the message carrier in the wives' plot, and the Fairy Queen presiding over punishments of masculine impudence at the end.

The women's vow for revenge in the first scene of Act Two follows hard upon the opening of another revenge plot in the comedy, Caius' challenge to Parson Evans. This is something more than a burlesque upon French obsessions with the code of honor. The hostility between physician and parson mirrors the disjoining of the spiritual from the physical in the values of the main characters. In assigning his nationalities Shakespeare may have had in mind the Elizabethan caricature of the physicality of French behavior ... as contrasted to the Welsh penchant for things of the spirit world.... The cleavage between spirit and flesh underlies all the problems of honor in society—the requisite of "substance" in Anne's marriage, Falstaff's and Ford's pact of love for money, even Fenton's want of money, without which his honor cannot really be maintained. Shallow draws our attention to the rival doctor and parson as "curer of souls" and "curer of bodies" [II. iii. 39], as does the jocular Host ("Give me thy hand, terrestrial; so. Give me thy hand, celestial" [III. i. 105-06]). The reconciliation of terrestrial and celestial metaphorically clears the way for the vindication of honor in the main action of the play. (pp. 148-50)

It is sometimes forgotten that Shakespeare first used the name of Sir John Falstaff for the cowardly knight who deserts Talbot on the battlefield in *I Henry VI,* and from whose person, in this scene, Talbot rips the badge of the Garter. In Falstaff's

beginning is his end. With *The Merry Wives* Falstaff returns to Windsor in only a figurative sense, for that minor character bears little resemblance to his greater namesake. Still, in the comedy he reminds us of the vicissitudes which "the sacred name of knight" [*1 Henry VI,* IV. i. 40] has undergone since the reign of Edward III. The aristocrat who expects to keep what remains of his family glory must deal with the Pages and Fords of the new order, who will no longer grant him the advantage. The day of the citizen having arrived, if aristocratic honor is bankrupt, at least each man and woman can keep his personal honor intact. (p. 151)

Richard F. Hardin, "Honor Revenged: Falstaff's Fortunes and 'The Merry Wives of Windsor'," in Essays in Literature, *Vol. V. No. 2, Fall, 1978, pp. 143-52.*

## BARBARA FREEDMAN   (essay date 1981)

[*Focusing on our emotional responses to* The Merry Wives of Windsor *and the painful feelings evoked by the humiliation of Falstaff, Freedman views the play as a representation of human limitations generally and, more specifically, of the impending decline in physical and mental abilities that must be faced by middle-aged males. She avers that in his depiction of the repeated degradations of Falstaff Shakespeare is* "making us laugh at something essentially disturbing: an aggressive and yet guilty sense of sexuality" *which seeks punishment through the agency of the females who have been offended. Freedman regards Master Page as posessing a self-confident, nondestructive sense of male sexuality and as serving, through his* "commitment to a creed of communal trust, faith, and harmony," *the role of mediator between the inadequate old order of Windsor society and the chaotic forces which attack it. She postulates that* The Merry Wives of Windsor *is Shakespeare's comic treatment of many of the central issues of the later tragedies and holds that the final punishment of Falstaff is not a reenactment of a scapegoating ceremony, but* "a self-conscious and playful parody of that ritual."]

We can understand the nature and the history of the criticism on *The Merry Wives* as a series of attempts to come to terms with the disturbing response that the buffoon, and the punishment he requests, evokes. Critics are unanimous in their annoyance at Falstaff's buffoonery, in their disgust at his cruel punishment at Windsor Forest, and in their desire to look outside the text to explain away both these responses. (p. 163)

[One] means of avoiding the problem of Falstaff's buffoonery has been to moralize the issue. Either the community is to be blamed for unfair behavior, or Falstaff is to be blamed for his villainy in order for these critics to accept the play's action. Jeanne Addison Roberts' article, "Falstaff in Windsor Forest: Villain or Victim?" [see Additional Bibliography] bluntly states the moralizers' dilemma: "Is Falstaff ... a social menace who brings on himself a well-deserved punishment? Or is he a nearly-innocent victim, entrapped by the scheming wives and used by society for its own rather devious ends?" Roberts concludes that he is both and turns to historical parallels of scapegoating to explain the ambiguity of Falstaff's criminal status.

The view of Falstaff as scapegoat eludes the moralizers' dilemma in enabling us to see him as guilty and innocent at once, but it demands an identification with the wives, with their community, and with certain professed social aims that is problematic, if not impossible, given the way in which the play is written. The result is ... [another] means of evading our response to the play: focusing on historical situations which inform the play's pattern of events but which fail to explain Shakespeare's use of them. While vestiges of a primitive scapegoat ritual certainly loom large in *The Merry Wives*, the fact remains that the Falstaff of *The Merry Wives* is not a ritual scapegoat but a realistically drawn dramatic character with psychological validity. The wives who punish him are not "defenders of the social order" [see excerpt above by Jeanne Addison Roberts, 1970] but offended women with minds and plans of their own—both of which they refuse to share with the other members of their community. Even when the entire community is involved in Falstaff's punishment, and that is only one action in a much larger sequence of events, the punishment is not a ritual scapegoating but a self-conscious and playful parody of that ritual. Furthermore, Falstaff's humiliation in Windsor Forest is neither necessary nor successful in "purging" the Windsor community. The crisis of a manipulative view of others and of reality which plagues Windsor society is only "mythically" solved by the symbol of Fenton and Anne Page's freely willed marriage at the play's end; a tragicomic awareness of our inability to control the outcome of events, and our inability to stop trying to control events, is tellingly underlined by the fact of that wedding as well.

On the surface, the play reads as a citizen comedy: Falstaff is a threat to the community, and his punishment at the hands of the Windsor wives is merry, moral, and survival-oriented. Yet if we consider our emotional response to the play or attempt to understand what desires the author may be fulfilling through creating and sharing its core fantasy, there is a second possible view of the action. We don't—or I don't—always feel as if the wives simply represent the interests of a sane society. And Shakespeare apparently didn't either, for he has these wives doubt their own intentions and then protest far too much: "What think you?" Mrs. Ford asks Mrs. Page, "May we, with the warrant of womanhood and the witness of a good conscience, pursue him [Falstaff] with any further revenge?" [IV. ii. 206-08]. Mrs. Page's reply is a confident one: "The spirit of wantonness is, sure, scared out of him. If the devil have him not in fee simple . . . he will never, I think . . . attempt us again" [IV. ii. 209-12]. The wives then blithely forge ahead with a new plan to "still be the ministers" [IV. ii. 218-19] of Falstaff's punishment, rationalizing their action with such pithy couplets as "Against such lewdsters and their lechery / Those that betray them do no treachery" [V. iii. 21-2]. Their vindictive reaction to Falstaff's "love letter" is understandable the first time, but they feed his flattery and egg him on to future sexual transgressions most cruelly—and unnecessarily. Quite simply, the wives and their "sane community" do not provide ample motivation for this fantasy, and if we identify with them, we won't fully understand why Shakespeare was writing this play. Facts are facts. Shakespeare was interested, for some strange reason, in writing about clownish male sexual humiliation and punishment, in making us laugh at something essentially disturbing: an aggressive and yet guilty sense of sexuality. The play expresses an obvious pleasure in being caught, in being humiliated, in being punished for sexual transgressions. Perhaps if we consider the play as Falstaff's fantasy—a self-directed farce of repeated self-humiliations—we will be closer to the true spirit of the play.

Punishing Falstaff could have been a good deal more fun if *The Merry Wives* were written as traditonal farce. Central to that genre is a pattern of sexual transgression and punishment for that transgression which is usually well disguised. Insofar as farce, by definition, derives humor from absurd plot aggression directed against flat characters, it characteristically enables us to enjoy aggression whose cause and effect is denied. In *The Merry Wives*, however, we have a self-conscious use of farce for didactic aims: a self-conscious punishment for sexuality which is disturbing as much as it is humorous. . . . Punishing Falstaff may be fun at first, but without the disguises of traditional farce, it becomes serious business. By the second and third times around, as critics have noted, it becomes downright humiliating.

To understand the highly self-conscious, punitive view of sexuality in *Merry Wives*, it is useful to examine the play in the larger context of the plays Shakespeare wrote around the same time. It is enlightening, for example, to see how the play anticipates, and gives comic expression to, the same sexual conflicts that characterize such tragedies as *Othello* and *King Lear*. Common to Shakespeare's plays of this period is a focus on an aging male protagonist facing, or attempting to evade, a decrease in mental and physical agility, and facing, or attempting to evade, accompanying fantasies of emasculation and humiliation by women. Since there are two Lears and two Othellos, that there are two Falstaffs should not, perhaps, be so confusing; a play about Falstaff in love is a play about male sexuality in middle age, which for Shakespeare seems to connote a definite falling off from what one was before, a sense of impending impotence of mind and body. Shakespeare emphasizes Falstaff's decline by choosing to depict the comic defeat of a character with an established reputation for vitality, and by forcing him to acknowledge, early on in the play, a disturbing shift in the state of affairs and a need to adjust accordingly: "Well, sirs, I am almost out at heels," he complains to his men, adding: "There is no remedy—I must cony-catch, I must shift" [I. iii. 31, 33-4]. Shakespeare focuses on the onset of intellectual inadequacy when he has Falstaff repeatedly forget and need to be reminded of times and dates after demonstrating remarkable mental agility in the play's opening scene. But the comedy's major concern is with a sense of sexual inadequacy, a loss of manliness; hence, the majority of its plots concern impotent old men trying to prove their masculinity through foolishly conceived duels and even more foolishly conceived sexual liaisons, none of which comes to fruition.

One defense against this crisis is narcissistic self-aggrandizement, achieved through a costly dependence on external proofs of one's grandeur; this is most evident in the heroics of an Othello or a King Lear. *The Merry Wives* also begins with old men foolishly parading their official titles in a pathetic attempt to restore their shattered self-esteem. Falstaff's overblown self-image and subsequent downfall merely anticipate, in comic fashion, the hubris and destruction of the tragic heroes who are to follow. Unlike Lear, Falstaff manages to retain his preposterously grandiose self-image despite numerous humiliations, yet he does so only to be set up for repeated comic pratfalls.

A second defense characteristic of this crisis is a premature adjustment to declining powers in the form of a regression to an infantile posture of dependency upon woman. Lear would draw from Cordelia an absolute declaration of love so that he might comfortably fulfill his plans "to set my rest / On her kind nursery" [*King Lear*, I. i. 123-24]; without Desdemona, Othello's occupation is gone. Falstaff mirrors Lear in his wholly unrealistic plans to make a living off disinterested Windsor wives: "They shall be my East and West Indies, and I will trade to them both" [I. iii. 71-2]. Ford, like Othello and Lear, is plagued with unrealistic fantasies of possessiveness and fears of abandonment. In sum, *The Merry Wives* is a world of impotent old men wholly dependent upon asexual maternal figures of financial and emotional well-being—so much so that the primary action of the play is the devising of crafty plots whereby one can draw from these women one's sustenance.

As taking from woman in this play is imagined in terms of an infantile dependency on maternal figures, it is not surprising that sexuality is described in oral images. Eating seems to be the major preoccupation of Windsor society; everyone is always coming from or going to a dinner. And close analysis reveals that the Windsor characters' attitudes towards dining parallel their attitudes towards coupling in the play. Basically, there are two dominant attitudes towards eating and sexuality in *The Merry Wives*. The creed of comedy, and its ideal of sexuality, is the benevolent oral merger, based on trust in the other, and represented by Master Page. For Page, eating is sharing, being a Host is not losing oneself but finding oneself, creating harmony. Page speaks of "drink[ing] down all unkindness" [I. i. 196-97] and of making amends at the table; eating, for him, is a creative, restorative process. Correspondingly, Page is patient, trustful, and giving in his relationships with others, most obviously with his wife. The opposing creed of farce, and its view of sexuality, is the destructive oral merger, based on a distrustful compulsion greedily to devour or prey upon others, and a fear of like retribution for that sin. For Falstaff, eating is stealing, a sign of transgression which brings on punishment, a devouring which leads to being devoured. His monstrous size is our first clue to his greedy intent. In this play we first meet him eating stolen deer at Page's house; he soon attempts to steal Page's "dear," his wife, as well. Yet her desire appears to Falstaff to be as destructive and devouring as his own. He tells us that "she did so course o'er my exteriors with such a greedy intention that the appetite of her eye did seem to scorch me up like a burning-glass" [I. iii. 65-7]. Falstaff's burning by the Windsor fairies at the play's conclusion records the triumph of this maternal devouring. His hungry preying is similar to Ford's jealous possessiveness. The stealing and possessiveness are simply two sides of one coin, resulting from a sense of not having enough inside, and so being unable to give to others, and from a feeling that one must take in order to counteract what others take from one, in turn. Ford fears that everyone will steal from him, and yet so does Falstaff; they simply defend against that threat differently. In sum, if Page is the perfect host, Falstaff is the perfect parasite; their attitudes towards eating and sexuality correspond to these roles.

Hostile fantasies of hurting, preying upon, and devouring that which sustains one naturally call forth guilty fantasies of retribution. The parasitical Windsor males who would prey upon women are punished through sexual frustration, sexual humiliation, symbolic castration, and symbolic devouring. Quickly cruelly leads on Anne Page's suitors in the subplot, as the merry wives entice and frustrate Falstaff in the main plot. Anne's suitors are publicly humiliated by being led into abortive duels and, even worse, abortive marriages (being wed to "great lubberly boys" [V. v. 184]); Falstaff is humiliated by having his sexual desires and desirability mocked by the community. Falstaff's symbolic castration is discussed by Jeanne Roberts who notes that the community's aim, as described by Mrs. Page, is to "dis-horne the spirit" [IV. iv. 64]; Roberts also points out that the dialogue concerning the horns strongly suggests that Falstaff's horns are removed from his head by the community immediately [in her *Shakespeare's English Comedy;* see Additional Bibliography]. The symbolic devouring of Falstaff occurs in the greasy knight's public burning.

The traditional association of fire with a destructive devouring is already made by the community, who notes that "lust is but a bloody fire" [V. v. 95] and then burns Falstaff accordingly for it.

Yet farce provides a partial solution to this guilty attack on the self for destructive sexuality—a particular, defensive mode of dealing with guilty self-punishment. Unlike Lear, who is the passive victim of his daughter's cruel attacks, Falstaff unmans and humiliates himself. He is not only foolish to begin with, thereby already collaborating in the Windsor women's plot to punish him, but he plays the fool repeatedly, thereby helping it along. Whereas the tragic mode of heroic challenge and attack is followed by a martyred submission to persecutory fantasies, the farcical mode moves from mock transgression and self-emasculation through punishment to laughing forgiveness: the pattern of the buffoon. Falstaff dismisses his own train before the wives deceptively win away his page; Falstaff allows himself to be fooled without an Iago, although the women do egg him on in his self-flattery. Falstaff willingly dons Mother Prat's clothes in an attempt to avoid punishment, whereas Lear agonizes over the woman's tears that threaten his masculine self-image. As if to avoid punishment for womanish dependency, for an aggressive taking from woman, Falstaff becomes foolish woman, emasculates himself, and asks for ridicule and humiliation. In a sense, Falstaff takes the option that Lear couldn't and willingly plays the fool. (pp. 164-68)

Like the typical buffoon and comedian, Falstaff projects his own deficiencies onto others and then laughs at them for it; in this case, the Windsor elders are ridiculed for their impotence and parasitic behavior. But Falstaff seems especially concerned with attacking powerful maternal figures and then being discovered and humiliated by them. His dependence on and aggression toward women . . . are given expression through costume as well as through action. In a memorable scene between Falstaff and his alter ego, Master Ford, Falstaff dresses up as Mother Prat—by name a punitive maternal figure. Ford vents his anger at the old woman because of her fortune-telling, her alleged control over situations "beyond our element" about which "we know nothing" [IV. ii. 178]. Aggression against a punitive maternal figure is thus released by both men in this scene. But Falstaff's aggression toward women upon whom he is dependent and his curious desire to be punished for it are most obvious in his ridiculous plan of writing degrading love letters to a number of maternal figures in the community who are sure to see through him and make him suffer for his advances. The traditional clown and Falstaff set themselves up to be caught; being chased and beaten is the essence of farce action, and Falstaff's role is to be continually found out and humiliated for the same sin. (p. 170)

Why is this image of man, with his aggressive and yet guilty sense of sexuality, his focus on humiliation and abuse at the hands of woman, preoccupying Shakespeare between the writing of a *Twelfth Night* and a *Hamlet*? Or "why," as William Green asks us in his introduction to the Signet edition of the play, "when engrossed in writing romantic comedy . . . does [Shakespeare] suddenly backtrack to the farcical treatment of love that he successfully presented in *The Taming of the Shrew*?" The most prevalent philosophical concern in Shakespeare's plays of the time period is not with the potential, ever renewing accommodations and adjustments to life which comedy celebrates but with a tragic awareness of man's limitations. Throughout the plays is a disturbing sense of the impossibility of purposive language and action in a world of flux, created by man and sustained by his frail faith in himself and in others. This conflict is commonly expressed in the form of a triad. One term is an ideal world order, received from one's fathers, and often represented by them: a world that in each subsequent incarnation, is increasingly revealed to be less viable and less self-aware.... A recognition of its flaws is necessary but, ultimately, neither comforting nor useful; threatening to take its place is a world of chaos.... This is our second term, the chaotic world which Bolingbroke opened up like a Pandora's box [in *Richard II*].... In between the ideal and the real, the private and the public, the past and the present, is a mediator attempting to join the two; ... that mediator simply represents a makeshift, manmade order subject to constant attack from without and within, sustained only by human imagination, faith, and respect.

The problem of maintaining a makeshift, imaginative, communal order in the face of external attack and a loss of faith in a previous order is given comic expression in *The Merry Wives of Windsor*. Representing the old order in the form of its institutions of law and religion are the farcical Windsor elders. Threatening to replace them are the chaotic forces of power, will, and appetite, represented by the ridiculous buffoon Falstaff and his farcically swaggering crew. Shakespeare reenacts his tragic dilemma on the familiar testing ground of English soil, Windsor community—and on the familiar testing ground of English comedy as well. What sustains Windsor society is its commitment to the opposite of the manipulative, predatory, capitalistic behavior in which both parties engage—its commitment to a creed of communal trust, faith, and harmony, as represented by Master Page. The possibility of tragedy threatens, however, when Shakespeare rests an order, as he must, on imaginative grounds; trust implies mistrust, and every Page has its counterpart Ford in Shakespeare's works. Yet Ford is here linked with Falstaff; the miser becomes the thief's alterego, and through this identification, the threat that Ford presents can be safely overcome. After all, this is a comedy. What makes the play humorous is Shakespeare's portrayal of the Windsor elders in such a way that their impotence is comic rather than tragic, and his portrayal of the forces of chaos in terms of comic weaknesses as well. What makes the play comedy, rather than farce, is the addition of an alternative which has all the trappings of success, a mediating term with which we can identify and which will save the community. (pp. 170-72)

The ideal mean, a secure masculine sexual identity dependent upon the possibility of intimacy without self-destruction, a successful sense of being with and through others, is depicted in *The Merry Wives* in the confident relationship of the Pages. (p. 172)

*Barbara Freedman, "Falstaff's Punishment: Buffoonery as Defensive Posture in 'The Merry Wives of Windsor',"* in Shakespeare Studies: An Annual Gathering of Research, Criticism, and Reviews, *Vol. XIV, 1981, pp. 163-74.*

### MARILYN FRENCH  (essay date 1981)

[*French contends that "possession of property, possession of women, and fear of theft" are the central thematic issues in* The Merry Wives of Windsor. *As members of the aristocracy, she maintains, Falstaff and Fenton are the outsiders in this bourgeois society and are perceived by the Windsorites as challenging the legitimate, proprietary interests of the old order. Although Fenton succeeds in integrating himself into the community, French argues, Falstaff's acceptance is limited, because his lack of money*

*signifies a diminished status in a society where everyone views human relationships in terms of property and possession.*]

The setting [of *The Merry Wives of Windsor*] is bourgeois—settled, prosperous, and imbued with a moral complacency.... Its terms are overwhelmingly "masculine": the play opens with Shallow and Slender listing the former's claim to legitimacy in the form of titles and prerogatives, anciency of house, coats of arms. Because the characters are so foolish, this discussion acts to challenge the notion of legitimacy. Thus, as usual in Shakespeare, the opening of the play sets forth its terms: they seem familiar—legitimacy versus challenges to it. But in this case, the challenge arises (at first) not from outsiders, illegitimates, but in our minds, as a result of the inanity and self-satisfaction of the legitimates. There are further challenges quickly: Falstaff kills Shallow's deer, illegally; his men pick Slender's pockets. And we know by now that Slender is intending a kind of theft: he agrees to marry Anne Page for her money.

The major themes of the play are the cornerstones of bourgeois life: possession of property, possession of women, and fear of theft. There are two plots, each containing a stranger who is a down-at-heels aristocrat (foreigner) who is attempting to "steal" from the propertied men of Windsor. The action concerns the efforts of Falstaff and Fenton to get what they want, and the efforts of the Windsorites to thwart them. The outsiders are perceived as thieves, like the "Germans" who do steal the host's horses.

But in keeping with the suggestion that the legitimates are not any more legitimate than anyone else, the insiders are also busy thieving. The host cheats his customers; Mistress Quickly cheats anyone who will pay for her help; the host intends to cheat the "Germans" who cheat him first. Evans and Caius intend to duel over a piece of property neither of them owns—Anne Page—but are cozened by the host and cozen him in return. Slender and his adherents intend to cheat the Pages by offering a false devotion to Anne in return for her person and her property.

Falstaff, supposedly the major cozener, is cozened into giving money to Mistress Quickly, is cozened by the wives, and is betrayed by his own servants. Ford is cozened by Falstaff into paying for his own cozening. Both Pages cozen each other in their attempts to have Anne stolen away, but she and Fenton cozen them instead. Everyone in the play (except William) cozens, is cozened, or both.

For the most part, the disguises operate similarly—they fool the person who adopts the disguise. Both Falstaff and Ford become the victims of their own disguises.

*Merry Wives* is a play about property. One reason for its unpopularity may be that property is *all* it is about. Even the "feminine" elements of the play—chaste constancy in the wives, love in Anne, and Falstaff's outlaw feminine sexual rebellion—become mere counters in a conflict over property.

Falstaff is set up as an example of the outlaw feminine principle (as he is in the *Henry IV* plays). He wishes to undermine or challenge the established order: he has a reputation for drinking, sexual freedom, and petty crime. But very quickly, in this play, a different note enters: his intention in crime and cozening is not primarily the fun of it—it is for survival. He has an edge of desperation in this play that makes him at once more pathetic and less fun—because he is less free—than the Falstaff of the histories.

And here, his opposition to the established order is less a rebellion against its constrictions and hypocrisies, less based in a need to assert other values, than it is an effort, however odd, to win a place within it. He cheats and steals and strives to seduce in order to find a place within the society he is victimizing: he wants money to play the gentleman. Originally, he claims that his intention in attempting to seduce the wives is to get at their husbands' purses; but in his meeting with the wives, particularly that in the last scene, he expresses genuine desire for sexual or perhaps merely affectionate love. In his pathetic longing for esteem and affection, he is a sad scapegoat. He wants what everyone else in the play wants—and however unacceptable his means of attaining it, he is more morally acceptable than Mr. Ford. What keeps Sir John an outsider in Windsor, despite his status, is his lack of wealth.

The pathos built into his character world not preclude him from being a villain . . . if his goal were really what it seems—to destroy chaste constancy, the emblem of the feminine principle. But money values override everything in this world. The wives respond to his letters with an outrage similar to that one would feel at an attempted robbery. Their language and their behavior demonstrate that they, like their husbands, see their bodies and reputations as possessions of which Falstaff is trying to defraud them. Their revenge is motivated by the sense that in writing to them at all, he has stolen something from them, and it is

calculated in the same terms: they will lead him on until he is forced to pawn his horses to the host.

The host is jealous and possessive about his property; Caius is jealous and possessive about his house and closets; Ford is jealous and possessive about his wife. Page is jealous and possessive about his daughter, whom he sees as property to be disposed of as he chooses: Caius, Evans, and Slender see Anne the same way. (No wonder she speaks so little in the play.) Even Fenton confesses to her that his original intention in courting her was to gain control of her wealth.

Cuckoldry means something quite different to Mr. Ford than it does to Claudio in *Much Ado About Nothing,* or to Posthumus [in *Cymbeline*]. For them it is a failure of the pivot on which the rest of human life turns. For Mr. Ford it is theft: ''My bed shall be abus'd, my coffers ransack'd, my reputation gnawn at'' [II. ii. 292-93]. He is not concerned with his wife's affections, her relation with him. Nor is he primarily concerned with his reputation—he drags the whole community into his house to witness what he conceives of as *his* degradation. His fear of cuckoldry is a fear of theft. (pp. 106-08)

[Everyone] in the community except Anne Page and possibly Fenton, perceives all events in terms of money, possession, and theft. (p. 109)

*Act IV. Scene ii. Ford, Falstaff as an old woman, Mistress Page, and others. By James Durno. The Department of Rare Books and Special Collections, The University of Michigan Library.*

Fenton, who is in some ways Falstaff's other half, succeeds. He wins Anne Page and proves his love by marrying her even though her father has threatened to cut her off. Falstaff is another case. He is attacked because of his sexual improprieties, mainly, but there is only one value in this town, and Falstaff is no more of a threat to the property of its men than is the host. He is, at the conclusion, accepted as an "insider," but he cannot be an insider because he has no money. Falstaff is an eternal outsider; as a sexual threat he is a poor devil. Neither his defeat nor his acceptance is quite satisfying: a play about property is fun only when the cozeners win. (p. 110)

*Marilyn French, "Money," in her* Shakespeare's Division of Experience, Summit Books, 1981, pp. 100-10.

## JAN LAWSON HINELY   (essay date 1982)

[*In a departure from earlier assessments of Falstaff as a scapegoat figure, Hinely contends that the vices for which the knight is punished are "a reflection of the vanities and pretensions which afflict the society punishing him," thus are not strictly his alone. The festive ending of* The Merry Wives of Windsor *is unique, the critic argues, in that instead of merely portraying the reintegration of the scapegoat figure into the community after he has acknowledged and accepted his folly, it demonstrates how other errant individuals in that community achieve a parallel recognition of their own guilt, thus allowing a "full integration of comic scapegoat and society." Hinely also examines Falstaff's role in the play as alazon or "boasting impostor," whose conduct degrades the ideals of knighthood in general and of the Order of the Garter in particular. Demonstrating the similarities between the three degradations suffered by Falstaff and the ritual humiliations which actually accompanied the expulsion of a disgraced Garter Knight, the critic maintains that Elizabethan courtiers who viewed the play would not only recognize the resemblances, but might also consider whether the fat knight's reprehensible behavior served as a mirror of their own foolish vices.*]

Falstaff has his roots deep in the very genesis of comic form—in the complementary roles of alazon and pharmakos. He is the alazon, the boasting impostor, who lays claim to society's traditional rewards for heroic achievement—sexual prerogatives, feasting and wealth—on the basis of personal virtues he does not really possess. He is also the pharmakos, the scapegoat whose "guilty" nature is a reflection of the vanities and pretensions which afflict the society punishing him. His role of alazon connects him with the play's only other representative of the upper classes, Fenton, and, more significantly, with the recurring references to the anticipated court investiture of the Knights of the Garter; while his role of pharmakos is seen most clearly in his relationship to Ford, who is an obvious example of the ills afflicting the middle class society of Windsor.

Falstaff's knightly rank is crucial to his role as alazon in the action of the play. An awareness of Falstaff's standing as a courtier, a knight, and a one-time intimate of the great gives a decided edge of class consciousness to his exchanges with the other characters. The first scene shows us a Falstaff who lords it over citizens who have come heartily to resent him. Justice Shallow's opening remarks underline this clash of rank, "I will make a Star Chamber matter of it. If he were twenty Sir John Falstaffs, he shall not abuse Robert Shallow, esquire" [I. i. 1-4]. The following exchange between Slender and Shallow about the coat with the "dozen white luces" [I. i. 16], though it may have a now obscure topical reference, is, more significantly, Shallow's way of bolstering his courage for the coming confrontation with Falstaff. As he reminds all, he is a

"gentleman born" [I. i. 8-9] and has been for "three hundred years" [I. i. 13].

Despite this bravado, Shallow's grievances, "Knight, you have beaten my men, kill'd my deer, and broke open my lodge," are turned aside by "the knight Sir John" with an airy, "But not kiss'd your keeper's daughter?" [I. i. 111-12, 113]. To Shallow's assertion that "this shall be answer'd," he brazenly responds, "I will answer it straight: I have done all this. That is now answer'd" [I. i. 114-16]. Falstaff assures the angry Shallow that if he brings the matter before the king he will "be laugh'd at," and adds insult to the injury he has given the slender-witted Slender by inquiring, "Slender, I broke your head; what matter have you against me?" [I. i. 119, 121-22].

Because of his intervention, poor Slender's just complaints against the thieveries of Bardolph, Pistol, and Nym are overlooked, a miscarriage of justice that would have special meaning to the citizens of London who suffered not only from excesses of unruly courtiers but also from the fact that the nobility often interfered to save members of their retinues from deserved punishment by city officials. As Sir John later admits, in reproaching Pistol for disloyalty.

> I have been content, sir, you should lay my
> countenance to pawn. I have grated upon my
> good friends for three reprieves for you and
> your coach-fellow Nym; or else you had look'd
> through the grate, like a geminy of baboons.
>
> [II. ii. 5-9]

Falstaff's rank is also the one trump card he holds in his wooing of the merry wives. "I would thy husband were dead," he cajoles, "I'll speak it before the best lord, I would make thee my lady" [III. iii. 49-51]. Though Mistress Ford coyly denies her suitability for such a position, this possibility had occurred to her earlier. When she first told Mistress Page of her surprising wooer, Sir John's rank seemed the only attraction worth mention, "—if it were not for one trifling respect, I could come to such honor!"—"If I would but go to hell for an eternal moment or so, I could be knighted" [II. i. 44-5, 49-50].

This note is struck again by Ford in his disguise of Master Brook. "Brook" cannot win Ford's wife, but Falstaff, who is a "gentleman of excellent breeding, admirable discourse, of great admittance, authentic in [his] place and person," and "generally allow'd" for his "many war-like, court-like, and learned preparations," may well succeed [II. ii. 225-27, 227-29]. Although Ford is flattering Falstaff here for his own purposes, his jealousy has painted a picture of Falstaff as courtier, scholar, soldier, and knight which, in his own mind, gives a kind of credibility to his insane jealousy.

Falstaff's behavior to the citizens of Windsor, bad enough if seen as the actions of a mere fat con man, is made more serious by its juxtaposition with the coming investiture of new members into the Order of the Garter, England's highest order of knighthood. The ideals of the Order of the Garter, which was founded in response to a slur on a lady's reputation, clearly stand as a contrast to the behavior of Shakespeare's fat knight, who in the play itself is a Knight of the Garter, if only the Garter Inn. If this play was written specifically for the April 1597 celebration of the installation of Lord Hunsdon as a Knight of the Garter, certain aspects of Falstaff's behavior and punishment gain new significance. C. L. Barber has persuasively shown that Falstaff, in *Henry IV, I* and *II*, acts as a scapegoat whose sacrifice guarantees the preservation of courtly ideals [in *Shakespeare's Festive Comedies*]. In *The Merry Wives*,

Shakespeare pointedly connects this perversion with the standards of the Order of the Garter. (pp. 37-9)

Falstaff's punishments are clearly related to his status as degenerate Garter Knight. These punishments recall both general procedures associated with the loss of knighthood and the specific degradations prescribed for the removal of a disgraced Garter Knight. The first adventure of the "buck basket," where Falstaff, covered with "foul linen," is borne out on the shoulders of serving men and cast "in the muddy ditch close by Thames side" [III. iii. 15-16], seems a tongue-in-cheek allusion to this traditional ceremony . . . :

> First *Garter,* in his *Coat of Arms,* . . . reads aloud the *Instrument* for Publication of the *Knights Degradation. . . .*
>
> This being read, one of the *Heralds* deputed thereunto (a Ladder being raised to the backside of the convict *Knights Stall,* and he, in his *Coat of Arms,* placed there before hand) when *Garter* pronounceth the words, *Expelled and put from among the Arms,* Etc. takes his *Crest,* and violently casts it down into the *Choire,* and after that his *Banner* and *Sword,* and when the Publication is read out, all the *Officers of Arms* spurn the *Atchievements* out of the *Choire* into the Body of the *Church,* first the *Sword,* then the *Banner,* and last of all the *Crest,* so out of the *West-Door,* thence to the *Bridge,* and over into the *Ditch.*

Falstaff, covered with dirty linen instead of crests and banners, suffers in his own person the fate meted out to the disgraced knight's achievements. It is difficult to imagine that a courtly audience, particularly if assembled for the installation of new Garter members, would not recognize the joke involved.

Falstaff's second and third punishments, though not clearly related to the loss of the Garter, also seem related to rituals connected with the loss of knightly status. The second punishment is a combination of two traditional punishments marking a loss of manhood—to accept passively a sound beating and to be "transformed" into a woman. Though Falstaff complained loudly to Bardolph, Mistress Quickly and "Brooke" about his physical suffering in the buck basket, his response to the second adventure is one of shamed embarrassment which includes a recognition of the loss of heroic identity:

> If it should come to the ear of the court, how I have been transform'd, and how my transformation hath been wash'd and cudgell'd, they would melt me out of my fat drop by drop, and liquor fishermen's boots with me. I warrant they would whip me with their fine wits till I were as crestfall'n as a dried pear.
>
> [IV. v. 94-100]

These elements of public humiliation and ritualized loss of identity are significant aspects of the "disgracing of a corupt knight" as described by Sir William Segar, *The booke of honor and armes* (London, 1590). In a combination burial/christening ceremony the disgraced knight was led to a high stage where thirteen priests said prayers ordinarily used at burial services. There he was "peecemeale dispoyled . . . of all his Armes, as well offensive as defensive, which one after another were throwne to the ground." He was then "baptized" as "traitor," with a "Bason of gold or silver full of warme water," in the process

being denied the use of his right name. The last part of the ritual suggests Falstaff's third and final punishment. "Then with great ignomie he [the disgraced knight] was brought unto the Altar, and there laied groveling on the ground, and over him was read a Psalme full of curses." The curses sung over Falstaff are preceded by the "Faerie Queen's" verses in honor of the Order of the Garter. Though these lines, which strike a tone of solemnity not found elsewhere in the play, have sometimes been viewed as a topical interpolation interrupting the flow of action, they invoke the idealized standard of knighthood Falstaff has disgraced, and add a note of gravity to the unmasking of the impostor knight which lifts his punishment far beyond the level of farce.

In the context of the play Falstaff's "purification" seems a necessary prelude to the triumph of the only other character singled out for his higher social status, Fenton. Fenton's rank ("of too high a region"), his court associations, and his poverty have disqualified him as a suitor in the eyes of the distrustful Page [III. ii. 73]. Like Falstaff, Fenton has kept company with the "wild Prince and Poins" [III. ii. 72-3], and, like Falstaff, his wooing, at least initially, had a mercenary motive. But Fenton has come to love Anne for herself, and the Garter song, celebrating true nobility and order, vindicates Fenton and the ideal of knighthood as it condemns Falstaff and his misuse of knightly status.

From the perspective of the society viewing the play, particularly if this society was initially Elizabeth's court, Falstaff may act as a distorted but recognizable mirror of its own vices and follies. His arrogance, based on underestimating those of lesser rank, his cowardice, his prodigality, his false claims to honor—even his game of cuckolding citizens with attractive wives—were not uncommon to some members of the nobility. Within the middle-class context of the play itself, however, Falstaff's social position, which both isolates and magnifies his shortcomings, makes him the likely pharmakos for vices which have only incidental connection to his noble rank but which mirror the frailties of the bourgeois citizens of Windsor. Though the citizens attempt to treat Falstaff as an interloper, one whose alien presence is the source of disruption in an otherwise healthy society, both Falstaff and the villagers are guilty of egocentricity, an egocentricity most markedly shown in their attempts to abuse, for mercenary or selfish purposes, the forces of sexuality. Their actions are alike disruptive of social and natural harmony, and the play leads not only to Falstaff's exposure as a false knight but to Windsor's recognition of the guilt it shares with the scapegoat it has singled out for mockery.

The egocentricity which leads Falstaff to cast off Pistol and Nym and to pillage Shallow is most markedly shown in his plan to make love to the "merry wives" as a means of filling his purse. This plot, striking as it does at the sexual bond between man and wife, is a threat to the stability of Windsor society. It is a further abuse of healthy sexuality that Falstaff's interest in the two women is solely mercenary. To "Brook" he admits, "They say the jealous wittoly knave [Ford] hath messes of money, for the which his wife seems to me well-favor'd" [II. ii. 271-73]. That his interest can only be mercenary is further suggested by references to Falstaff's age and state of physical decay. Though in the last scene he mimics the role of a fertility deity, awaiting the two wives with "horns" erect, his total unfitness for this role is jeeringly emphasized by the assembled citizens: "Why, Sir John, do you think . . . that ever the devil could have made you our delight?" "What, a hodge pudding? A bag of flax?'' ''A puff'd man?'' ''Old, cold, wither'd, and of intolerable entrails?'' [V. v. 146-50, 151-54].

Falstaff's misuse of sexuality and his attempts to dupe others for his own purposes are traits shared by the very citizens who taunt him. Though critics have commented on the lively vigor of Windsor's community life, this vigor is not in itself a sign of health. The play overflows with comic ''practices'' and counter ''practices,'' all designed by citizens energetically engaged in vain efforts to get the better of their fellows. (pp. 42-3)

The plots and counterplots of the citizens, like Falstaff's thwarted endeavor, are primarily examples of abuses of natural sexuality, ranging from Ford's horn-mad jealousy of his wife to the concerted though contradictory efforts of the rest of the citizens to assist in the disposal of the seven hundred pounds and ''pretty virginity'' of nubile Anne Page. Shakespeare interweaves the traditional romantic comedy plot of young lovers overcoming rival suitors and parental disapproval with its opposite comic stereotype—the farce triangle of jealous husband, suspected wife, and illicit lover. But Shakespeare stands the later stereotype on its head by switching the parts—Falstaff, old, fat and out of condition, plays ''young'' Damon [in Virgil's *Eclogues*] to the vigorous Ford's ''old'' January [in Chaucer's ''The Merchant's Tale'']. The humor of the encounters between Ford and Falstaff is thus neatly balanced between Falstaff's vanity and Ford's blindness, but the effect is to emphasize the unhealthy excesses of Ford's sexual jealousy. (p. 43)

The last scene, surely one of the richest in Shakespearean comedy, masterfully draws together the dominant threads of the play. Through the ritual punishment of Falstaff as alazon-pharmakos, the exposure of the ''imposter'' knight is linked to the overthrow of the forces of egocentricity and sterile sexuality. This expulsion of hostile forces is countered, as in the most basic traditions of Aristophanic comedy, by the invocation of the positive natural and social forces of true knighthood, fertility, and mutuality.

Falstaff's appearance in this scene, ''with a buck's head upon him,'' is resonant in connotations. He is half-man, half-beast, his horns, like Actaeon's, symbolizing both sexual potency (''Remember, Jove, thou wast a bull for thy Europa, love set on thy horns'') and cuckoldom (''my horns I bequeath your husbands'') [V. v. 3-4, 26-7]. Falstaff's willingness to enact the nature-reviving role of fertility deity (''Let the sky rain potatoes; let it thunder to the tune of 'Green-sleeves,' hail kissing-comfits, and snow eringoes'') contains an intuitive acknowledgement of the primitive fate of such deities (''Divide me like a brib'd-buck, each a haunch'' [V. v. 19-20, 24]). On a less mythic level his buck's head aptly recalls the opening dispute with Shallow about the poached deer. Falstaff compares himself to a ''brib'd-buck,'' a stolen deer which must be hurriedly cut up after poaching.

The ''fairies'' torment Falstaff for his ''sinful fantasy'' and ''unchaste desire,'' but these crimes are not his alone. Our complex response to Falstaff's downfall is partially due to the coming together here of his dual roles: as alazon he *must* he exposed, as pharmakos his exposure makes us uncomfortable in direct proportion to the unawareness, on the part of his tormentors, of their complicity in his guilt. Falstaff suffers exposure, humiliation and defeat, but he neither withdraws nor is excluded from the festive society of the play's conclusion. Traditionally the comic scapegoat, after his downfall, may be invited into the circle of festive celebrants. Page, indeed, makes such an invitation, an echo of his premature first act attempt to reconcile the knight and society. But Page's invitation is made from a false sense of his own superiority, ''Yet be cheerful, knight. Thou shalt eat a posset to-night at my house, where I will desire thee to laugh at my wife, that now laughs at thee'' [V. v. 170-72], and Shakespeare postpones the resolution until all the erring characters are made aware of their own vulnerability to ridicule. Shakespeare varies his traditional comic form by inviting his festive society into the scapegoat's circle of discomfiture.

Evans reminds Ford of his flawed nature by telling him that he must ''leave [his] jealousies'' even as he tells Falstaff to ''leave'' his ''desires'' [V. v. 132, 130]. Sir Hugh himself, who has taken an overzealous interest in Anne's wooing, appears costumed as a horned satyr, a visual reminder that Falstaff's errors are reflected in the society that has singled him out for chastisement. Falstaff's salutary disappointment in ''love'' is shared by the play's other false suitors, for while he is pinched and burned by the troop of children, the true lovers escape and Caius and Slender are fobbed off with adolescent boys. Caius even marries his before he discovers his error. Both Page and his wife have their share in this lesson. By working against the natural desires of their daughter and at cross purposes they have opened the way for the union of Anne and Fenton, and they must suffer not only Fenton's success but his just rebuke.

> You would have married her most shamefully,
> Where there was no proportion held in love. . . .
> Th' offense is holy that she hath committed,
> And this deceit loses the name of craft,
> Of disobedience, or unduteous title,
> Since therein she doth evitate and shun
> A thousand irreligious cursed hours
> Which forced marriage would have brought upon her.
>                                    [V. v. 221-22, 225-30]

Finally, Falstaff casts off his roles of alazon and pharmakos by, ironically, accepting them. By acknowledging his folly he overcomes it and leaves it behind. He admits that he was deceived partly because of ''the guiltiness of my mind,'' and even pauses to moralize upon his downfall, ''See now how wit may be made Jack-a-Lent, when 'tis upon ill employment!'' [V. v. 123, 126-28]. This gain of self-knowledge releases him from the role of alazon as his growing awareness of the complete events of the night releases him from the solitary position of pharmakos. Shakespeare gives Falstaff the last laugh, ''I am glad, though you have ta'en a special stand to strike at me, that your arrow hath glanc'd'' [V. v. 234-35]. Falstaff's final joke, ''When night-dogs run, all sorts of deer are chas'd,'' recalls his original crime against Shallow, his pursuit of the ''female deer,'' and his own enactment of the hunted stag, and rejoices in the fact that those who hunted him were blind to the other game afoot [V. v. 238]. Mistress Page's third and last invitation to Falstaff tacitly acknowledges that all have been the objects as well as the instigators of mirth, ''let us every one go home, / And laugh this sport o'er by a country fire— / Sir John and all'' [V. v. 241-43]. And the last words in the play are Ford's ironic compliment to Falstaff's unintentional success in restoring sexual harmony and social balance to Windsor, ''Sir John, / To Master Brook you yet shall hold your word, / For he to-night shall lie with Mistress Ford'' [V. v. 244-46]. (pp. 46-8)

Shakespeare's comic scapegoats are all, to some extent, combinations of the roles of alazon and pharmakos; they are all initially differentiated from the rest of society by external traits, particularly social class; and audience response to the endings of Shakespeare's comedies is shaped to a large extent by the successful exposure and education of the alazon/pharmakos figure and by his reintegration into an enlightened society. (p. 48)

Shakespeare's comedies move toward integration between the comic scapegoat and his society, but, in part because of the combination of the alazon/pharmakos roles, this integration is not easily achieved. To cast off the role of alazon the comic scapegoat must be exposed to himself and come to terms with his true identity. But the scapegoat can not, alone, cast off the role of pharmakos. The society which casts him out must take him back, and this is achieved only when the society admits its own participation in the guilt of the pharmakos. (p. 50)

Only in *The Merry Wives* do we find the mutual acceptance of faults which permits the full integration of comic scapegoat and society. Falstaff accepts his humiliation at the hands of the citizens of Windsor; the citizens accept the truth that they share Falstaff's human follies and that this bond is more important than the factors which separate them. The tone of social harmony and festivity achieved at the end of *The Merry Wives* is, one feels, the most characteristic tone of the endings of Shakespearean comedy. This tone is relatively easy to achieve when the comic follies of a society are spread more evenly over its members, as in *Midsummer Night's Dream* and *As You Like It*. When the follies are more concentrated in a scapegoat figure, the comedy moves toward satire, toward rejection rather than integration. It is surely additional proof of the inclusiveness of Shakespeare's comic spirit that of all the plays containing a comic scapegoat, the play containing his most elaborate treatment of this figure is also the one which ends on the clearest note of acceptance and integration. (p. 52)

> *Jan Lawson Hinely, "Comic Scapegoats and the Falstaff of 'The Merry Wives of Windsor'," in* Shakespeare Studies: An Annual Gathering of Research, Criticism, and Reviews, *Vol. XV, 1982, pp. 37-54.*

## ANNE BARTON  (essay date 1985)

[*Barton rejects the view of earlier critics who have discovered a pattern of ritual renewal in* The Merry Wives of Windsor *and have compared Falstaff's punishment to the sacrifice of a scapegoat figure. In her estimation, Windsor is essentially "sound, stable, and remarkably well defined" and does not need to undergo a ritualistic cleansing, for despite minor flaws, it upholds the traditional Shakespearean comic values of marriage and an established, cohesive community. Barton argues that this setting is inimical to Falstaff and represents "the polar opposite" of the London locale where the knight thrived in* 1 Henry IV. *Noting that in* 1 *and* 2 Henry IV *Falstaff functions as "a truth-teller" who "qualifies and questions certain limiting and dangerous assumptions that society is prone to make," Barton maintains that Sir John not only has no similar function in* The Merry Wives, *but that he occupies no influential position at all in the Windsor community.*]

Falstaff is one of the most memorable embodiments of a comic type stretching back to Aristophanes. But Shakespeare seems to have found it possible to realize this character fully only within the context of English history, and not within that of comedy, his expected and proper domain.

The Falstaff of *The Merry Wives of Windsor* is not, of course, in love. If that was what Elizabeth demanded, she was not obeyed. In effect, Falstaff treats Alice Ford and Margaret Page as he treats Mistress Quickly in *2 Henry IV*. His sexual adventurism, including the promise of marriage at some indefinite future date, is fundamentally an attempt by him to raise cash. In Eastcheap this works brilliantly; in Windsor it does not. Falstaff descends upon this little, bourgeois society in much the same way that he fastens upon the rural Gloucestershire of Justice Shallow [in *2 Henry IV*]. He is a predatory intruder from a more sophisticated world, a visitor who means to ingratiate himself and then bleed the environment that gives him temporary shelter. But where Gloucestershire is unsuspecting and acquiescent, Windsor not only resists but unites to dismember the outsider. The problem (pace Bradley [see excerpt above, 1902]) would seem to be not so much that Falstaff is an altered character in *The Merry Wives of Windsor* as that Windsor is, by nature, a place he does not understand and in which he cannot thrive. Although Fenton is accused of having "kept company with the wild Prince and Poins" [III. ii. 72-3], and Falstaff is joined at Windsor by several characters—Shallow, Mistress Quickly, Pistol, Bardolph, and Nym—who also share his life in *1* and *2 Henry IV*, or *Henry V*, the world here is unequivocally comical, not historical. And the norms of Shakespearean comedy are even more destructive to Falstaffian values than the Lord Chief Justice, the grinning honors of Shrewsbury, or the cold blood of Prince John.

C. L. Barber excluded *The Merry Wives of Windsor* from his brilliant account of Falstaff as Carnival, the festive lord of the histories who must be defeated when he seeks to set up his holiday license on an everyday basis. Subsequent writers have often found this omission puzzling, arguing that *The Merry Wives of Windsor* is surely a festive comedy in precisely Barber's terms: a play in which the entire community finally bands together to sacrifice an aging fertility god in preparation for a seasonal return to order and normality. Barber's instincts, characteristically, were right. *The Merry Wives of Windsor* is not properly or primarily a festive comedy. Its ritual patterns, where they exist at all, lie deep below the surface and cannot be made to control the movement and atmosphere of the play. (pp. 132-33)

In its characteristic movement "through release to clarification," as C. L. Barber defined it [in *Shakespeare's Festive Comedy*], Shakespearean comedy often depends upon the agency of one or more intruders from a different world. *The Comedy of Errors, The Taming of the Shrew, Love's Labour's Lost, Much Ado About Nothing,* and *Twelfth Night* all begin with the arrival in a settled community of strangers whose presence will radically alter that community's allegiances and normal way of life. Although, initially, the newcomers cause a certain amount of disruption, and even pain, the society that assimilates them by the end of the play is invariably happier and more firmly based than the one which existed at the beginning. This is partly because it has freed itself from various weaknesses and affectations, especially in the area of sexual relationships, and also because the strangers have precipitated one or more marriages that we welcome and believe to be good.

*The Merry Wives of Windsor* presents a highly individual variation on this basic pattern. Most successful productions of the play within recent years have been comparatively realistic in style, stressing the particularity and completeness of the play's picture of contemporary, small-town life. This seems right. Windsor itself, as a corporate entity, is the true protagonist of the comedy, not Falstaff, the shadowy young lovers, or even the merry wives themselves, who uphold its values so well. This is why seemingly irrelevant details, such as young William's grapple with Latin grammar, Mistress Quickly's itemization of her household responsibilities, or Slender's exercise of his prerogative as a "distinguished" visitor to give the town's children a "playing-day" [IV. i. 9], are in fact central. Children, adolescents, mature married couples, bachelor members of the professional classes, servants, and postmaster's boys: only the very old are excluded from the panorama of life at Windsor. It seems significant that unlike any other heroine in Shakespearean comedy (except Marina in *Pericles* and Perdita in *The Winter's Tale,* where the circumstances are very special), Anne Page is actually provided with a mother. This is very much a family play.

The community at Windsor has its flaws and delusions, notably the way the Pages try to dispose of their daughter in marriage, and the causeless jealousy of Ford, but at heart it is sound, stable, and remarkably well defined.... [It] represents the polar opposite of Falstaff's Eastcheap world, which is one of rootless individuals, separated from their family contexts and sometimes, like Prince Hal, in active rebellion against them. The Boar's Head, as Hal rather unkindly puts it, is Falstaff's customary sty, and the place from which he gathers strength.... The London tavern is Falstaff's real home and it, by definition, is the place of irresponsibility, an artificial society whose components are in a continual state of flux. (pp. 142-43)

Although the Garter Inn is an establishment more respectable than the Boar's Head, it is nonetheless a slightly suspect and dangerous enclave in the center of Windsor. This is because its function, in large part, is to harbor outsiders, transients who may benefit but who also may harm the community on the edges of which they exist.

As it happens, it is one of Windsor's strengths as a society that it is remarkably inclusive and willing to absorb foreign elements. Neither Sir Hugh Evans, its parson and schoolmaster, nor its local doctor, Caius, are indigenous to the place—as their accents continually declare. But, whenever it was that they arrived, they have become fully accepted and indeed leading members of the community. Mistress Quickly, on a humbler level, appears to have acclimatized herself equally successfully, and Pistol seems, at least for a time, to be following in her footsteps. There are limits, however, to what this society is willing to embrace, particularly when its provenance is the Inn. As Page's favored suitor for the hand of Anne, Slender (together with his servant Simple and his uncle Shallow) is an innocuous and welcome visitor. Falstaff, and those other dimly glimpsed strangers who also book rooms at the Garter, some of them pursuing mysterious business at Court, are another matter. Whether or not Fenton actually lodges at the Garter during his visits to Windsor is unclear; he is, however, closely associated with its host.

A cheerful, exuberant figure, the "ranting" and "merry" Host of the Garter [II. i. 189, 207] possesses a linguistic extravagance that serves to link him significantly with Falstaff, his paying guest. Far more comprehensible verbally than Pistol, he is nonetheless given to larding his discourse with references to cavaleiros and bully-rooks, Ethiopians, Anthropophaginians, Ephesians, and Bohemian-Tartars.... His motives in deceiving Caius and Evans as to the place of their potentially fatal encounter are far more benevolent than those of Sir Toby Belch in stage managing the duel between Caesario and Sir Andrew Aguecheek in *Twelfth Night.* Toby's doubledealing is

chastized by Sebastian, Viola's twin. The Host, far less deservedly, incurs the ire of both Caius and Evans, the two touchy men he has prevented (at the expense of a modicum of their social dignity) from trying to kill one another without cause. Because Windsor's doctor and its parson abruptly join forces in a revenge action against the "mad host" [III. i. 112], he finds himself, at the end, missing three of his best horses. This part of the plot is puzzlingly sketchy and incomplete, but it looks very much as though Shakespeare were insisting upon a certain distrust, and even resentment, of the freewheeling comic innkeeper: a man whose allegiances, by temperament, as well as by the nature of his trade, are more fluid and dangerous than those of the solid citizens of the town.

Significantly, the Host is not present in Windsor Great Park in act 5, when the community bands together to humiliate Falstaff, the interloper who spurns marriage and an establishment, and makes taverns and inns his home. As it happens, Fenton requires the Host's services elsewhere, arrranging his clandestine union with Anne Page. It is interesting, however, that he should not apparently have been invited to join the Page family, the Fords, Shallow, Slender, Caius, Evans, Pistol, Mistress Quickly, and the children of Windsor around the blasted oak. Equally telling is the fact that it should be the Host to whom Fenton appeals after all the young man's attempts to obtain Anne Page with her parent's consent—the method approved of in Windsor—have failed. As a kind of stationmaster, whose professional duty it is to meet incoming and departing trains, the Host has tolerated and even enjoyed Falstaff, turning a tolerant eye on his faults, and relieving the drain on his finances by providing his follower, Bardolph, with employment at the Garter. Fenton, however, is the man who will recompense the Host for his stolen horses (doubtless out of Anne Page's dowry), and through whom he will be associated with the winning side at the end of the play.

For all his greed and riot, his selfishness and occasional brutality, Falstaff does function in the histories as a truth-teller, a man who presents a genuinely alternative point of view. Among people half-crazed (as Hotspur is) by the thirst for honor and personal glory, cold, unfeeling politicians such as Prince John and, to some extent, Hal himself, joyless officers of the law, and monstrous egotists such as Worcester and Northumberland who shelter (as Falstaff does not) behind an affectation of high principle, Shakespeare's sensual pacifist comes to operate to some extent like his remote ancestor, the Aristophanic hero. He qualifies and questions certain limiting and dangerous assumptions that society is prone to make, without forgetting for a moment that he himself is a rogue. (pp. 143-45)

In *The Merry Wives of Windsor,* on the other hand, Falstaff never functions in this way. That Ford should finally be enlightened as to the folly of suspecting a good and chaste wife of trying to cuckold him is obviously a good thing. Falstaff's role, however, in bringing this about is inadvertent. Indeed, the discovery is one that runs counter not only to his own personal wishes in the matter but, more importantly, to his characteristic attitudes and ways of thinking. The fact is, that although Windsor is certainly not perfect, its faults are not of a kind which render it vulnerable to Falstaff's particular kind of dissent. It is young Fenton, the former prodigal, who emerges at the end to remind Windsor of certain youthful impulses and prerogatives that it was in danger of forgetting, redressing an imperiled balance by restoring the community to its own best self. He needs the help of the Host, at last, to accomplish this, but his own future will not lie in inns or taverns. Fenton's

*Act V. Scene v. Mistress Page, Falstaff, and Mistress Ford.
By Robert Smirke.*

deceit, as he says tellingly, "loses the name of craft," because it has been committed genuinely in the interests of love, and because it honors that ideal of true, as opposed to "forced marriage" [V. v. 226, 230] upon which life in Windsor—and in Shakespearean comedy generally—relies. Both Fenton and Falstaff go home from Windsor Park to Page's house to "laugh this sport o'er by a country fire" with the others [V. v. 242]. Fenton, however, is not only a victor but a man who has won a wife and acceptance in a comic community whose values he has not only respected but actually helped to keep in repair. Falstaff, by contrast, the failed hero of a different kind of comedy, will have no option tomorrow but to move on. (p. 145)

*Anne Barton, "Falstaff and the Comic Community,"
in* Shakespeare's "Rough Magic": Renaissance Essays in Honor of C. L. Barber, *edited by Peter Erickson and Coppélia Kahn, University of Deleware Press, 1985, pp. 131-48.*

**PETER ERICKSON**   (lecture date 1986)

[*Erickson analyzes the way in which* The Merry Wives of Windsor *dramatizes the conflicts between men and women and between different social classes, concluding that while the class struggle is resolved in favor of the aristocracy, there is no parallel "restoration of male control" and the play ends on a note of "residual male discontent." The triumph of the aristocracy, the critic contends, is represented by the marriage of Anne Page to Fenton*

*and the passing of her wealth into his control, and it is underscored by the participation of the middle class Windsorites in the Order of the Garter masque in Act V, Scene v. Erickson argues that by virtue of having the country folk celebrate the courtly values of the Order "all classes are subsumed in a celebration of national identity that is aristocratic rather than egalitarian in orientation." Noting that "the play cannot reaffirm class hierarchy without also affirming female power in the Queen," the critic argues that Shakespeare reveals in this play his distrust of the cult of Elizabeth, uneasiness with the idea that her power may be extended to other women, and resentment that a patriarchal society should be ruled by a woman. Erickson's essay was originally delivered as a lecture at the World Shakespeare Congress in West Berlin in April, 1986.*]

As the title acknowledges, the most striking thing about [*The Merry Wives of Windsor*] is the role of the wives, whom Muriel Bradbrook sees as "the women's league" [see excerpt above, 1968]. Their power is consciously presented as a direct challenge to orthodox sexual politics: "Why, I'll exhibit a bill in the parliament for the putting down of men" [II. i. 29-30]. . . .

The prevention of an orthodox patriarchal ending by pervasive female domination in this play should not, however, be construed as protofeminist insight or sympathy. . . . The wives by and large retain the dominant power position but this does not make Shakespeare a feminist before his time or the play a liberated, protected cultural space. Rather, we confront the paradox that the women's superior power is granted, yet the play's spirit is not progressive. . . .

The present study of *The Merry Wives of Windsor* focuses on class and gender as the two crucial ideological strands in the play. If one believes that Shakespeare gives a progressive valuation to both elements, then the play becomes a positive celebration of female, middle-class power. This is a reading I oppose. I shall argue on the contrary that both class and gender are strongly marked by a conservative valence: neither supports an enlightened egalitarian image of the play. Moreover, the two terms are in conflict rather than alignment with each other. Insofar as the play dissolves class antagonism, the resulting reconciliation cannot be seen as a democratic-spirited leveling. Instead, the class harmony represented by the bourgeois townsfolk's participation and absorption in the aristocratic rites of the Order of the Garter promotes the royal power of "our radiant Queen" [V. v. 46] and thus ratifies, while palliating, the existing class structure. Queen Elizabeth did cultivate an authentic popular touch, but this was used for conservative political ends; *The Merry Wives of Windsor* replicates this process. The underlying critical uneasiness in the play involves misogynist discomfort with Elizabeth's gender, not the injustice of class divisions.

In order to investigate the ideology of *The Merry Wives of Windsor*, it is necessary to reopen two basic questions. Is the community dramatized within the play a healthy one? And since, given their central roles, the first question cannot be answered without considering the status of the wives, we must also ask: is the wives' behavior an essentially positive communal resource? The standard position is most eloquently represented by Anne Barton [see excerpt above, 1985], who, while conceding that the society of *The Merry Wives of Windsor* is not perfect, nonetheless finds it fundamentally sound:

> Most successful productions of the play within recent years have been comparatively realistic in style, stressing the particularity and completeness of the play's picture of contemporary, small-town life. This seems right. Windsor it-

self, a corporate entity, is the true protagonist of the comedy, not Falstaff, the shadowy young lovers, or even the merry wives themselves, who uphold its values so well.... The community at Windsor has its flaws and delusions ... but at heart it is sound, stable, and remarkably well defined.

Though appealing, this sanguine view encourages a sentimentality that obviates the need for detailed close examination of how the society operates. But the play communicates disparity between the characters' activity and the overworked stock vocabulary they use to describe it. The constant offhand recourse to "sport" and "jest" as catch-all terms to cover a multitude of volatile, sharply posed issues including money, courtship, violence and deception puts on display a terminology so thin that it becomes conspicuously inadequate and question-begging. The tension between verbal self-justification and potentially unsavory action is manifested, for example, in Evans' avid plotting: "it is admirable pleasures and fery honest knaveries" [IV. iv. 80-1]. The blunt word "knaveries" pulls uneasily against the profession of honesty, retroactively qualifying the assertion about the admirableness of the pleasures.

The society of the play exhibits a pervasive pattern for dealing with conflict: characters promote an imbalance between conflict and reconciliation by stimulating conflict as much as possible, while making rhetorical exhortations to peace after things have gone too far.... [The] entire Windsor group, from the miscellany of minor characters to the wives at the apex, shares a common mode of social interchange which cannot be ascribed to harmless, inconsequential farce because Shakespeare's characterization of their collective social action cuts too deeply.

The play immediately introduces the motif of conflict by opening in the midst of Shallow's angry outburst: "Sir Hugh, persuade me not: I will make a Star Chamber matter of it" [I. i. 1-2]. Not until well into the first scene, at lines [I. i. 105-06], is the referent of "it" specified by Shallow's clearcut accusation in direct confrontation with Falstaff. In the meantime, since unclarified bones of contention allow one to bark louder and longer, we are made to feel that the theme is generalized contention for its own sake and to notice that prolonged conflict invites mediation. For it is Evans, in his role as mediator, who is highlighted here: "If Sir John Falstaff have committed disparagements unto you, I am of the church and will be glad to do my benevolence, to make atonements and compromises between you" [I. i. 30-4]. The nature of the reconciliation Evans effects is subsequently shown to be permanent postponement of a resolution....

Evans' approach allows Shallow to overlook the conflict with Falstaff because his discretion includes a proposed new plot that deflects attention away from the initial problem:

> It is petter that friends is the sword, and end
> it; and there is also another device in my prain,
> which peradventure prings good discretions with
> it. There is Anne Page, which is daughter to
> Master Thomas Page, which is pretty virginity.
>
> [I. i. 42-6]

Shallow needs laughably little persuasion to take up the suggestion that he turn to the more profitable business of advancing his nephew's courtship of Page's well-dowered daughter. The pattern of problem-solving established here in relatively transparent form involves the substitution of a diversionary plot for the original difficulty; but since the new plot leads to new contention this pattern becomes an endless, potentially vicious cycle with a tendency to escalate....

This trend of bypassing problems in favor of involvement in further plotting becomes more serious when it extends to a major character such as Ford. The trivial, freefloating violence that hovers around the minor characters is, in the character of Ford, brought to frightening psychological concentration. Though he does not have Othello's capacity to destroy because the balance of power here favors the women, Ford's compressurized vulnerability to suspicion—"Well, I hope it be no so" [II. i. 109]—suggests Othello's simmering jealousy, as does Ford's need to "torture my wife" [III. ii. 40-1]. This context makes it impossible to respond to the climactic moment of violence when Ford releases his frustration through beating a woman as mere slapstick. The old woman of Brainford occasions the uninhibited expression of Ford's anxiety about women in general: "We are simple men ... we know nothing" [IV. ii. 174, 178]. The symbolic woman he attacks is actually the disguised Falstaff, yet this fact does not undercut the seriousness of Ford's genuine distress but rather doubles male exposure and humiliation since Ford's and Falstaff's delusions about women are simultaneously punished.

The crucial question is whether this scene serves as the exorcism that enables Ford's change of heart, as the negative precondition of his positive conversion:

> Pardon me, wife. Henceforth do what thou wilt;
> I rather will suspect the sun with cold
> Than thee with wantonness; now doth thy honour stand,
> In him that was of late an heretic,
> As firm as faith.
>
> [IV. iv. 6-10]

This passage is less of a resolution than it may appear, as Page's immediately following response to Ford's religiosity signals: "'Tis well, 'tis well; no more. / Be not as extreme in submission / As in offence. / But let our plot go forward" [IV. iv. 10-12]. Consistent with the rest of the play, the standard paradigm of reconciliation—eager participation in a fresh plot as a means of avoiding difficult issues—is enacted by Page's hasty change of subject. In shifting to the ongoing sport, he buries his telling glance at Ford's problematic "submission" and the unresolved tension between inequality and mutuality in gender relations. What particularly gives Ford's confession of faith the aspect of premature closure is his subsequent compulsive taunting of Falstaff throughout the play's final scene. Though others participate in the strenuous scapegoating of Falstaff, Ford is conspicuous in his need to rub it in:

> Now, sir, who's a cuckold now? Master Brook,
> Falstaff's a knave, a cuckoldly knave; here are
> his horns, Master Brook; and, Master Brook,
> he hath enjoyed nothing of Ford's but his buck-
> basket, his cudgel, and twenty pounds of his
> money, which must be paid to Master Brook;
> his horses are arrested for it, Master Brook.
>
> [V. v. 109-15]

Ford's gloating effort to deny his own disgrace in the Master Brook role rings false, but, when Evans reminds him, Ford cannot gracefully accept the point:

> Evans.   And leave your jealousies too, I pray you.
> Ford.    I will never mistrust my wife again, till thou
>          art able to woo her in good English.
>
> [V. v. 132-34]

Ford's revenge against Falstaff conforms to the general social pattern of evasion through plotting; his particular evasiveness calls into question the newfound harmony with his wife, suggesting that bad feeling remains which must be released indirectly in this unbecoming fashion.

Despite their assertions of moral impunity, the wives too participate in the shared ethic of manipulative plotting: they are not above it but rather its most successful and sophisticated embodiment. Their strategy with Falstaff of "leading him on with a fine-baited delay" [II. i. 95-6] corresponds to the host's method of egging on Evans and Caius while stopping just short of consummation. From the outset, the wives are concerned to absolve their behavior from association with the nasty side of plotting, as though aware their actions needed defending: "Nay, I will consent to any villainy against him that may not sully the chariness of our honesty" [II. i. 99-101]. In the formulation that echoes the play's title, the wives boldly insist on the compatibility of villainy and honesty:

> We'll leave a proof, by that which we will do,
> Wives may be merry and yet honest too.
> We do not act that often jest and laugh;
> 'Tis old, but true: 'Still swine eats all the draff'.
>
> [IV. ii. 104-07]

The weight in this patly aphoristic, rhyming format falls on "merry," which, like Evans' elliptical and flexible use of "discretion," functions as an all-purpose euphemism for attractions of plotting that can neither be candidly acknowledged nor clearly defined.

As the wives seek a plot to bring the plotting to a stop—"there would be no period to the jest . . ." [IV. ii. 221-22], their self-justification becomes both more pressing—"What think you: may we, with the warrant of womanhood and the witness of a good conscience, pursue him with any further revenge?" [IV. ii. 206-08]—and more gnomic—"Against such lewdsters and their lechery / Those that betray them do no treachery" [V. iii. 21-2]. Like other characters, the wives evade difficult questions by rushing on to new action: "Come, to the forge with it, then; shape it: I would not have things cool" [IV. ii. 223-24].

Ultimately the women's power is qualified when Fenton, in secretly marrying Anne Page against her parents' wishes, beats Mrs. Page at her own game: "Th' offence is holy that she hath committed, / And this deceit loses the name of craft" [V. v. 225-26]. Fenton's use of moral position to deny craft mirrors the wives' own rhetorical method. His sanctimonious tone, however, conveys not Fenton's victory as superior moral hero but rather the mutual exposure of the wives and Fenton—the exposure of the whole social system of plotting in which . . . all the characters are engaged. Plotting may be seen as endemic to comedy and this generic argument used as a self-sufficient aesthetic explanation that makes it unnecessary to recognize the political and social implications of plotting. But a cultural study of Elizabethan theater must examine all the dramatic forms and not restrict political analysis to the more "serious" genres of the history play and tragedy. Shakespeare's comedies also perform cultural work in their period, and in the case of *The Merry Wives of Windsor* Fenton's class significance is a crucial indicator of the nature of this work.

The play's class dynamic can be represented in three principal ways: as the victory of a bourgeois solidarity over the aristocratic court, as the reconciliation of the best of both bourgeois and aristocratic worlds, or as the consolidation of aristocratic

power through a populist approach. The first version is suggested by the wives' repeated triumph over Falstaff, in which rural bourgeois values defeat the corrupted court symbolized by Falstaff's ill-earned knighthood. Prominent as the Falstaff episodes are however, the play's overall design depends on the pairing and counterpointing of Falstaff with Fenton. The latter's climactic success checks and even reverses the straightforward reading of simple middle-class victory. What Falstaff loses, Fenton recuperates. By providing a clear contrast with Falstaff's aristocratic imposture, Fenton enacts the rehabilitation and vindication of true aristocracy. Since Fenton reinstates aristocratic integrity, Falstaff becomes a parodic scapegoat who carries the burden of court courruption and who is easily sacrificed to dispel resentment towards it.

The play is surprisingly explicit in its expression of the potential for class anatagonism. Fenton, like Prince Hal, is in need of reformation because of "My riots past, my wild societies" [III. iv. 8], while the class-conscious Page adamantly rejects him as his daughter's suitor: "He is of too high a region; he knows too much. He shall not knit a knot in his fortunes with the finger of my substance" [III. ii. 73-5]. This class conflict is averted by the correction of both Fenton's profligacy and of Page's provincialism and economic tightness. In particular, the sensitive issue of money is mediated through the medium of love. Fenton's sincerity in transmuting his financial interest into authentic feeling must be articulated:

> Albeit I will confess thy father's wealth
> Was the first motive that I woo'd thee, Anne,
> Yet, wooing thee, I found thee of more value
> Than stamps in gold or sums in sealed bags;
> And 'tis the very riches of thyself
> That I now aim at.
>
> [III. iv. 13-18]

Thus an idealized vision of love underwrites an idealized view of class reconciliation and national unity.

This reading of class as class harmony does not yield an accurate account, however. The marriage between Fenton and Ann Page symbolizes the synthesis of aristocratic status and bourgeois wealth, but the strength of this cultural system is that it allows the redistribution of wealth upwards and hence the revitalization of the aristocratic class. This result implies a third reading of class: the play resolves class tension in a way that favors aristocratic interests. This is not cynically to discredit Fenton's profession of love nor to disallow the emotional content of the love; Fenton's personal sincerity is not at issue. Rather, it is a question of showing that larger social forces operate through their love, of explaining the obvious paradox that Fenton's need for money—his "first motive"—is satisfied through the ideal of love that requires him to eschew it. Fenton's final declaration of the sacredness of love, for example, by no means excludes financial considerations. He reckons with and protects against the possibility of Anne's disinheritance by denying that her elopement constitutes "unduteous title" [V. v. 227]. Ford's blunt follow-up keeps the economic dimension of love in the fore: "Money buys lands, and wives are sold by fate" [V. v. 233].

The marriage works not only to transfer financial resources from the bourgeois to the aristocracy but also to transfer control out of female and into male hands. Unlike her mother, Anne succeeds in "alter[ing] the article of [her] gentry" [II. i. 53]. But, also unlike mother, she defers to her husband (if not to her father). Anne is no Portia to Fenton's Bassanio [in *The*

*Merchant of Venice*]. Class synthesis is purchased at the price of diminution of female power in the next generation.

The argument that the play supports aristocratic power does not rest on the single character of Fenton, for the force of aristocratic culture is represented in ways that escape character analysis. One reason the assessment of community in this play has been so difficult is a particular stress on the uniqueness of its location in Windsor. One can make Windsor emblematic of a rural bourgeois enclave and stronghold in opposition to the urban court, and one can enlist the resemblances of Windsor to Stratford and thus to the whole ethos of Shakespeare's native Warwickshire to prove his sympathy for this interpretation. Yet Windsor has a double class meaning because of the location there of Saint George's Chapel. As Quickly's allusion—"When the court lay at Windsor" [II. ii. 61-2]—reminds us and as the later invocation of the Order of the Garter dramatizes, the court is literally present in Windsor because the chapel is a focal point for Garter ritual. . . .

The Garter chapel evokes the institution of royal progresses that brought the London-based court out into the country and, as a pastoral environment, Windsor provides a green world for the masque celebrating the Garter ideal of aristocratic chivalry. . . .

As deployed in this play, both general pastoral convention and the specific Garter masque are courtly forms that convey and reinforce courtly stances and values. Through these forms a strong court presence pervades the play, deeply shaping the actions of its middle-class characters. The class transformations enabled by Renaissance pastoral negotiate class difference by circumventing the lower-class perspective it seemingly evokes. The motif of the courtier as shepherd, for example, allows the upper class to play at lower-class roles while making the lower class express aristocratic preoccupations and thus deflecting and neutralizing the potential disruptiveness of a genuinely different point of view. The bourgeois country folk who perform the Garter masque in *The Merry Wives of Windsor* are, like shepherds, made to speak and identify with courtly values. The final scene becomes the occasion for the convergence of classes in the sense that all classes are subsumed in a celebration of national identity that is aristocratic rather than egalitarian in orientation. . . .

Fenton's triumph in the final scene sets a limit to the wives' power, a limit that specifically signals the reimposition of an aristocratic framework. However, Fenton's successful completion of his quest for Anne Page does not have the conclusive, definitive impact that might be expected. In particular, there is no clearcut restoration of male control. Fenton is, in his turn, implicitly outflanked and counterbalanced because ultimate authority is vested in a woman, the "radiant Queen" [V. v. 46] whose position as head of the Order of the Garter the play conspicuously remarks.

The affirmation of aristocracy that puts the rural bourgeois wives in their place leads to the female power at a higher level, at the apex of the political system. This raises the possibility of a latent cross-class link between the wives and Elizabeth. Elizabethan culture hedged the Queen's power by defining her as an exception to normal definitions of gender. But Shakespeare's jocularity in *The Merry Wives of Windsor* plays out and defends against an anxious suspicion that Elizabeth may not be exceptional at all if her power extends to ordinary women. . . .

Though the wives are not an exact analogue of the queen, there are strong connections between the wives' marital chastity, which is figured in the penultimate scene as Diana's attack on Actaeon, and the queen's mythologized virginity. Emphasizing the power of female purity and integrity, the Diana image is apt for Elizabeth, but, in spite of their married status, the wives are also cast in this role through their punishment of Falstaff. . . . [The] power of the wives and Elizabeth coincides in a political Petrarchism whose logic of control requires that amorous invitation—Falstaff's "leer of invitation" [I. iii. 45-6] and "tempest of provocation" [V. v. 21]—first be set in motion in order that desire can then be prohibited. . . . The play reproduces and magnifies the pattern of provocation, deferral, prohibition and frustration found in the cult of Elizabeth and the styles of courtship it activated.

The motif of courtship, as developed in *The Merry Wives of Windsor,* plays up the feeling that the woman is unapproachable. Despite coaching Slender remains ineffectual through two painfully comic wooing scenes, while Falstaff, who as a well-versed courtier is fully prepared to devote himself not only to "the simple office of love" but also to "all the accoutrement, complement, and ceremony of it" [IV. ii. 4, 5-6], fares no better. Like an extravagant Petrarchan lover, Falstaff undergoes the "suffering" inflicted by the tyrannical beloved. With his irrepressible body and his inexhaustible inflated lyricism, Falstaff keeps going back for more but never gets further than "the prologue" [III. v. 74]. . . .

But the play's most convincing image of lack of fulfillment is Ford's. His long speech as the disguised Brook is not simply a clever fiction designed for Falstaff because it carries a deeper ring of actual fantasy suggested by his confessional pose that "I shall discover a thing to you, wherein I must very much lay open mine own imperfection" [II. ii. 183-85]:

> I have long loved her and, I protest to you,
> bestowed much on her; followed her with a
> doting observance; engrossed opportunities to
> meet her; fee'd every slight occasion that could
> but niggardly give me sight of her . . . But
> whatsoever I have merited, either in my mind
> or in my means, meed I am sure I have received
> none, unless experience be a jewel, that I have
> purchased at an infinite rate. . .
>
> [II. ii. 194-98, 202-05]

This passage gives full expression to the disappointment men may feel when they experience love as a Petrarchan game controlled by women; Ford's delusion about his wife suggests a male pathology induced in part by a court culture in which a Queen does rely on deferred sexuality to maintain power. Given the problem that the inaccessible lady "is too bright to be looked against" [II. ii. 244-45], the only recourse Ford can imagine is her degradation [II. ii. 245-51], a plot which the wives handily transform into his self-degradation, followed eventually by an idealized submission. This sequence releases a sexual discomfort that the play's conclusion does not entirely anull.

So great is Ford's alienation that he casts doubt on the wives' heterosexual desire—"I think, if your husbands were dead, you two would marry" [III. ii. 14-15]. As though in reaction against his sense of a powerful female bond that excludes him, he fashions a male counterbond by entering into a series of secret rendezvous with Falstaff. His physical contact with the transvestized Falstaff provides a literal image of Ford's equivocal sexuality, an image reinforced by the pairing of Evans and Caius with transvestite boys in the last scene. The play's final words are given to Ford, whose triumphant declaration— "Sir John, / To Master Brook you yet shall hold your word, / For he to-night shall lie with Mistress Ford" [V. v. 243-45]— presents heterosexual satisfaction as a shaky male boast that retains the triangle with its male bond; Falstaff, it appears, is necessary to Ford's imagined sexual happiness. Ford's off-key tone continues to convey consternation even when he wins. The spirit of Ford's concluding remark prevents the adoption of the view that the dramatic action is simply the operation of a basically healthy society that restores anxiety-free marital love.

The critic who finds defects in characters at the end of a comedy is apt to be accused of his or her own character defects—to wit, a deficient sense of humor. But the deficiency lies in the concept of humor as free-spirited pure fun. . . . The pressures on Ford's character that make us laugh are symptomatic of a larger discomfort that goes beyond individual character analysis to structural ambiguity in the culture, an ambiguity that here specifically involves the tension between class and gender and the paradox that the play cannot reaffirm class hierarchy without also affirming female power in the Queen. The two elements of class and gender form an unstable mix that gives the play's ending its unresolved, ambivalent quality. . . .

In *The Merry Wives of Windsor*, female power is duly acknowledged but subject to residual male discontent. In the culture at large, Leicester's relations with the Queen and, more strikingly, Essex's open revolt provide evidence of male frustration with female rule. Male protest in *The Merry Wives of Windsor* is, by contrast, muted and covert, but Shakespeare nonetheless gainsays the official line of the cult of Elizabeth.

> Peter Erickson, "The Order of the Garter, The Cult of Elizabeth, and Class/Gender Tension in 'The Merry Wives of Windsor','' in Subversion, Recuperation, Rehearsal: The Ideological Function of the Shakespearean Text, *edited by Jean E. Howard and Marion O'Connor, to be published by Methuen & Co. Ltd., 1987.*

## ADDITIONAL BIBLIOGRAPHY

Baldwin, T. W. *"The Merry Wives of Windsor."* In his *On the Literary Genetics of Shakspere's Plays: 1592-1594*, pp. 447-71. Urbana: University of Illinois Press, 1959.

   A detailed analysis of the origins in earlier English and Italian plays of certain dramatic elements in *The Merry Wives of Windsor*. Baldwin examines the play's structure and finds analogues in other Shakespearean comedies, namely *Love's Labour's Lost, A Midsummer Night's Dream, The Two Gentlemen of Verona,* and *The Comedy of Errors*.

Bennett, A. L. "The Sources of Shakespeare's *Merry Wives*." *Renaissance Quarterly* XXIII, No. 4 (Winter 1970): 429-33.

   Suggests Nicholas Udall's *Ralph Roister Doister* (1552) as one of the principal sources for the main plot of *The Merry Wives of Windsor*.

Bracy, William. *"The Merry Wives of Windsor": The History and Transmission of Shakespeare's Text*. University of Missouri Studies, vol. XXV, no. 1. Columbia: Curators of the University of Missouri, 1952, 154 p.

   A comprehensive textual study which argues that the 1602 Quarto of *The Merry Wives of Windsor* is a coherent abridgement of Shakespeare's original play. Bracy also addresses textual biblio-

graphic problems associated with the transmission of the quarto and Folio texts.

Bullough, Geoffrey. "Introduction to *The Merry Wives of Windsor*." In his *Narrative and Dramatic Sources of Shakespeare*, Vol. II, pp. 3-18. London: Routledge and Kegan Paul, 1958.

   A comprehensive discussion of the probable sources of *The Merry Wives of Windsor*, including works of Ser Giovanni Fiorentino, G. F. Straparola, Richard Tarlton, and Barnaby Riche, and Shakespeare's use of them. Bullough also cites several English analogues which may be "possible Shakespearian sources."

Campbell, Oscar James. "The Italianate Background of *The Merry Wives of Windsor*." In *Essays and Studies in English and Comparative Literature: By Members of the English Department of the University of Michigan*, pp. 81-117. Ann Arbor: University of Michigan Press, 1932.

   Attempts to form "a fair idea of the nature of *The Jealous Comedy*" by tracing the recurrence of certain dramatic features in Italian commedia dell'arte, Italianate comedies in England, and academic or university plays composed in the last thirty years of the sixteenth century. Campbell maintains that *The Jealous Comedy* was "hastily revised" by Shakespeare between 1598 and 1601 and became *The Merry Wives of Windsor*.

Craig, Hardin. "The End of the Century." In his *An Interpretation of Shakespeare*, pp. 154-77. New York: Dryden Press, 1948.

   Argues that *The Merry Wives of Windsor* was evidently written in great haste and that the character of Falstaff was inserted into an already existing work by another dramatist. Craig judges that it is "a play touched with Shakespeare's finest comic genius and yet a hasty piece of work and not completely his."

Crofts, J. *Shakespeare and the Post Horses: A New Study of "The Merry Wives of Windsor."* Bristol, England: J. W. Arrowsmith, 1937, 231 p.

   An exhaustive analysis of the implications of topical allusions in the play upon the quarto and Folio texts of *The Merry Wives of Windsor*. Crofts postulates that Shakespeare borrowed heavily from an earlier play by an unknown dramatist in order to complete the writing of *The Merry Wives* in two weeks, and that after the first performance in May, 1597, he continued the process of revision, expanding the play and making it more suitable for the public stage. While the 1602 Quarto is a memorial reconstruction of the play as it was first performed for a private audience, Crofts argues, the Folio version represents a revised text which the First Folio editors discovered among Shakespeare's papers.

Draper, John W. *Stratford to Dogberry: Studies in Shakespeare's Earlier Plays*. Pittsburgh: University of Pittsburgh Press, 1961, 320 p.

   A collection of essays written from a historical perspective. Draper's work includes chapters on Falstaff and such secondary characters from *The Merry Wives of Windsor* as Shallow, Robin, and Nym.

Felheim, Marvin, and Traci, Philip. "Realism in *The Merry Wives of Windsor*." *Ball State University Forum* XXII, No. 1 (Winter 1981): 52-9.

   Examines realistic elements in *The Merry Wives of Windsor*, including the characters' use of language, their employment of written communications, and the attitudes they express toward love and money. Felheim and Traci argue that the "large admixture of realism" raises the play above the level of farce and enhances its portrayal of the middle class's emergence into political prominence.

Fleay, Frederick Gard. *A Chronicle History of the Life and Work of William Shakespeare: Player, Poet, and Playmaker*. London: John C. Nimmo, 1886, 364 p.

   One of the earliest claims that *The Merry Wives of Windsor* is an adaptation of an earlier play, the *Jealous Comedy* (1592). Fleay argues that the 1602 Quarto was printed from "a partly revised prompter's copy" of the *Jealous Comedy* that the acting company no longer needed once Shakespeare had completed his revision for a court performance in 1600.

Fleissner, Robert F. "The Malleable Knight and the Unfettered Friar: *The Merry Wives of Windsor* and Boccaccio." *Shakespeare Studies* XI (1978): 77-93.

    Proposes that Shakespeare borrowed important elements from the Second Tale of the Fourth Day of Boccaccio's *Decameron* for use in *The Merry Wives of Windsor*. Fleissner demonstrates the many parallels between the two works and emphasizes the similarities between Shakespeare's Falstaff and Boccaccio's Friar Alberto, especially "the water episodes, the use of multiple disguises, and the comic humiliations" common to both.

Gianakaris, C. J. "Folk Ritual as Comic Catharsis and *The Merry Wives of Windsor*." *Mississippi Folklore Register* X, No. 2 (Fall 1976): 138-53.

    An anthropological and psychoanalytic study of the scapegoat figure in comedy and, in particular, *The Merry Wives of Windsor*. Gianakaris demonstrates that Shakespeare's use of "folklore patterns" helps to bridge the gap between his dramatically created world and the audience's real world.

Gilbert, Allan. "*The Merry Wives of Windsor*." In his *The Principles and Practices of Criticism: "Othello," "The Merry Wives," "Hamlet*," pp. 67-93. Detroit: Wayne State University Press, 1959.

    An extended comparison of the character of Falstaff in *1* and *2 Henry IV* and in *The Merry Wives of Windsor*. Gilbert contends that comedy requires the punishment of villainous behavior, or at least the extraction of repentance from the miscreant, and he asserts that any "objection to Falstaff's defeat in *The Merry Wives* is . . . an objection to the very nature of comic drama."

Green, William. *Shakespeare's "Merry Wives of Windsor."* Princeton, N.J.: Princeton University Press, 1962, 239 p.

    Examines the events surrounding the play's composition and how these events shaped the text. Green offers a hypothetical reconstruction of the play's composition and supporting arguments for Lesie Hotson's proposal that *The Merry Wives* was first performed on April 23, 1597 (see entry below). Green's important study touches on the major textual issues connected with the play.

Greg, W. W. Introduction to *Shakespeare's Merry Wives of Windsor: 1602*, edited by W. W. Greg, pp. vii-xliv. Oxford: At the Clarendon Press, 1910.

    An analysis of the relationship between the 1602 Quarto and the First Folio versions of *The Merry Wives of Windsor*. Greg maintains that the Folio text was set from an authentic playhouse copy and that the quarto text represents a memorial reconstruction by an actor who had played the Host of the Garter Inn.

Haller, Eleanor Jean. "The Realism of the Merry Wives." *West Virginia University Studies III: Philological Papers* 2 (May 1937): 32-8.

    Analyzes the characters of Mistress Ford and Mistress Page in terms of Elizabethan expectations of women as mothers, wives, and lovers. Haller asserts that the characters' behavior in these roles is very realistic and representative of contemporary attitudes, noting particularly that in their relations with their husbands their actions are consonant with "the Elizabethan conception of feminine frailty and the actuality of women's independence."

Hotson, Leslie. *Shakespeare versus Shallow*. London: Nonesuch Press, 1931, 375 p.

    Earliest contention that the first performance of *The Merry Wives of Windsor* was given on April 23, 1597, at the palace at Westminster as part of a Feast of the Order of the Garter. Important in Hotson's determination of this date is his proposed identification of two individuals whom Shakespeare was satirizing in the characters of Shallow and Slender.

Leggatt, Alexander. "The Comedy of Intrigue: Adultery." In his *Citizen Comedy in the Age of Shakespeare*, pp. 125-49. Toronto: University of Toronto Press, 1973.

    Emphasizes the balance that Shakespeare maintained between moral seriousness and light-handed judgment of his characters in *The Merry Wives of Windsor*. Leggatt maintains that the play is Shakespeare's only experiment in writing in the genre known as "citizen comedy."

Lewis, Marjorie Dunlavy. "The Ingenious Compliment: Consideration of Some Devices and Episodes in *The Merry Wives of Windsor*." In *Studies in Medieval, Renaissance, and American Literature: A Festschrift*, edited by Betsy Feagan Colquitt, pp. 64-72. Fort Worth: Texas Christian University Press, 1971.

    Argues that *The Merry Wives of Windsor* "celebrates the virtues of gentility and chivalry" intrinsic in "the real gentlemen of the audience" attending its first performance by ridiculing the absurd pretensions of several characters in the play. Lewis maintains that a "motif of quarreling pretenders to gentility" recurs throughout the play and is especially evident in the posturing of Caius and Evans as they ape the ritual of formal combat.

Long, John H. "Another Masque for *The Merry Wives of Windsor*." *Shakespeare Quarterly* III, No. 1 (January 1952): 39-43.

    Argues that the 1602 Quarto version of the masque in Act V, Scene v of *The Merry Wives of Windsor* is "dramatically more apt" than the Folio masque and thus ought to replace it in modern editions of the play. Describing the Folio masque as "ornate, courtly, somewhat stilted" and the quarto version as "light, genial, satirical, and rather vulgar," Long maintains that the latter is more consistent with the remainder of the play, as well as being less prone to textual problems, confusions, and inconsistencies.

Murry, John Middleton. "The Creation of Falstaff." In his *Discoveries: Essays in Literary Criticism*, pp. 223-62. London: W. Collins Sons & Co., 1924.

    Argues that if *The Merry Wives of Windsor* is evaluated on its own merits it will be seen as "a most excellent play," particularly for its vivid evocation of the English countryside. Murry finds plausible the tradition that the play was written by royal command and in a very short period of time, for this would help to explain, he contends, why Shakespeare was "sick to death" of Falstaff by the time he came to write *Henry V*.

Nosworthy, J. M. *Shakespeare's Occasional Plays: Their Origin and Transmission*. London: Edward Arnold, 1965, 238 p.

    Devotes three chapters to an analysis of the discrepacies between the Folio and quarto versions of *The Merry Wives of Windsor*. Nosworthy hypothesizes that the quarto text is based on the foul papers of a lost domestic comedy, perhaps Henry Porter's *The Two Merry Women of Abingdon*, which Shakespeare used as a source for his own play and on which he had inscribed marginal notations for the changes he would make in the original. The Folio text reflects, Nosworthy contends, the final result of Shakespeare's revision or adaptation of the preexisting play.

Ogburn, Vincent H. "*The Merry Wives* Quarto: A Farce Interlude." *PMLA* LVII, No. 3 (September 1942): 654-60.

    Maintains that the 1602 Quarto of *The Merry Wives of Windsor* was based on a revised text by an unknown author who shortened the original play and accentuated its vulgar elements to make it more suitable for performance as an interlude. Ogburn argues that the compression, quickened pace, and scant number of "character-revealing speeches" found in the 1602 version are typical of a farce interlude and would have made it more appealing to an audience especially receptive to this form of comedy.

Oliver, H. J. Introduction to *The Merry Wives of Windsor*, by William Shakespeare, edited by H. J. Oliver, pp. vii-lxxix. The New Arden Edition of the Works of William Shakespeare, edited by Harold F. Brooks and Harold Jenkins. London: Methuen and Co., 1971.

    A comprehensive treatment of the major issues associated with *The Merry Wives of Windsor*. Oliver examines the relationship between the Folio and quarto texts, literary sources and analogues, the occasion of the play's composition, and possible instances of personal satire; he also provides a valuable and thorough critical commentary on the play.

Pollard, A. W., and Wilson, J. Dover. "The 'Stolne and Surreptitious' Shakespearian Texts." *Times Literary Supplement*, No. 916 (7 August 1919): 420.

    Contends that members of Shakespeare's company hastily revised and adapted an earlier play known as the *Jealous Comedy* (1592) in response to the royal command to produce a work showing

Falstaff in love. Pollard and Dover Wilson claim that Shakespeare is the author of the initial scene of *The Merry Wives of Windsor* and added "a few more touches here and there," but that otherwise the play is the work of "one or more collaborators." They further maintain that the pirated text used for the 1602 Quarto was based upon an abridged version (1593) of the *Jealous Comedy*, to which the pirate added what he could recall of the 1598 performances he had witnessed. The absence of stage directions and the "patent imperfections" in the First Folio text of *The Merry Wives of Windsor*, they hypothesize, may indicate that the Folio editors had "no clean copy" of the play to work from, and thus had to rely solely on surviving players' parts.

Q[uiller-Couch, Arthur]. Introduction to *The Merry Wives of Windsor*, by William Shakespeare, edited by Arthur Quiller-Couch and John Dover Wilson, pp. vii-xxxix. Cambridge: Cambridge University Press, 1921.

Explores the transmission of and relation between the texts of the Folio and 1602 Quarto, possible dates of composition, topical allusions, the tradition of Queen Elizabeth's commission, and the problematic internal time frame of *The Merry Wives of Windsor*. Quiller-Couch regards the play as a hasty improvisation upon an earlier comedy. He also offers commentary on various characters, judging that Shakespeare has "overcharged" the play with eccentric figures, "for the Queen's merriment, no doubt."

Reik, Theodor. "Comedy of Intrigue." In his *The Secret Self: Psychoanalytic Experiences in Life and Literature*, pp. 63-75. New York: Farrar, Straus and Young, 1953.

Focuses on "the unconscious content and intent" of the three humiliations suffered by Falstaff in *The Merry Wives of Windsor*. Arguing that each of these humiliations unconsciously represents the disappointments and disillusions that Shakespeare experienced in his boyhood relationship with his mother, Reik theorizes that repressed childhood memories might have been evoked in Shakespeare by the contradictory emotions of obedience and reluctance with which he regarded his commission from Queen Elizabeth.

Roberts, Jeanne Addison. "*The Merry Wives of Windsor* as a Hallowe'en Play." *Shakespeare Survey* 25 (1972): 107-12.

Associates the mood of *The Merry Wives of Windsor* with the decline of the year and the final heyday of the lord of misrule and his mischievous spirits. Roberts regards the scapegoating of Falstaff as necessary for the community's return to normalcy, but also "disturbing" because of its irrationality. She argues that if this play is read between the two parts of *Henry IV*, it becomes a foreshadowing of the rejection of Falstaff at the close of *2 Henry IV*, when a new generation supplants the old.

———. "Falstaff in Windsor Forest: Villain or Victim." *Shakespeare Quarterly* XXVI, No. 1 (Winter 1975): 8-15.

Asserts that in *The Merry Wives of Windsor* Falstaff is both a "social menace" who merits the punishment he receives and "a nearly-innocent victim" who is tricked and exploited by the citizens of Windsor. Roberts focuses on the last scene of the play and demonstrates the way in which Shakespeare sustains the audience's ambiguous response to Falstaff until the very close, when our estimation of the fat knight "as victim subtly overshadows any sense of his villainy."

———. *Shakespeare's English Comedy: "The Merry Wives of Windsor" in Context*. Lincoln: University of Nebraska Press, 1979, 169 p.

Discusses the major issues connected with *The Merry Wives of Windsor*, including text, date, and source material, and includes a comprehensive survey of the criticism of the character of Falstaff. Although Roberts allows that the play is "in some ways unique," she also connects it with other Shakespeare plays—histories as well as comedies—through its imagery, themes, and symbolism.

Robertson, J. M. *The Problem of "The Merry Wives of Windsor."* London: Chatto and Windus, 1918, 32 p.

Disintegrationist theory of the authorship of *The Merry Wives of Windsor* which proposes that Shakespeare had only a minor role in its composition. Robertson contends that the original version of the play was drafted in 1593 by another writer and that Shakespeare "did but insert the best of the comic matter." About 1598, the critic holds, the earlier play was revised and expanded; in Robertson's opinion, Shakespeare "did some work" on this revision, but the "chief reviser" was George Chapman.

Steadman, John M. "Falstaff as Actaeon: A Dramatic Emblem." *Shakespeare Quarterly* XIV, No. 3 (Summer 1963): 231-44.

Argues that the striking similarities between Falstaff's disguise in Act V, Scene v and Renaissance portraits of Ovid's mythic hunter Actaeon were intended to emphasize that the knight was being exposed and humiliated for his lechery. Two other classical exemplars of the punishment of excessive love, Steadman notes, were Virgil—who suffered confinement in a basket—and Hercules—who was made to wear women's clothing; each of Falstaff's three humiliations, he contends, links him with a stock example of "the corrupting effects of lust."

# Romeo and Juliet

**DATE:** Textual scholars generally agree that Shakespeare composed *Romeo and Juliet* sometime between 1595 and 1596, with the earlier year being the most frequently cited date. Yet, some critics have argued that the play was written as early as 1591. Those opting for the 1591 date base their conclusion on the Nurse's reference at I. iii. 23 to an earthquake, "now eleven years" past, stating that Shakespeare was here alluding to the earthquake in London on April 6, 1580. However, as the New Arden editor Brian Gibbons has pointed out (see Additional Bibliography), there were a number of earthquakes in England between 1580 and 1590, thus making it impossible to determine which, if any, Shakespeare had in mind. In the face of such insubstantial evidence, most authorities consider the later date of 1595 the more convincing of the two. In support of this assessment, they cite the play's similarities to other of the so-called lyrical works known to have been written between 1595 and 1596, such as *A Midsummer Night's Dream* and *Richard II;* they also note the reference to Lord Hunsdon's Men as the performing company on the title page of the First Quarto (Q1), published early in 1597, claiming that since Shakespeare's troop of actors was under the patronage of Lord Hunsdon only between July 1596 and March 17, 1597, *Romeo and Juliet* was probably written shortly before this period.

**TEXT:** Shakespeare's tragedy was first published in QUARTO form sometime before March of 1597 and reads on its title page: "An excellent conceited Tragedie of Romeo and Iuliet, as it hath been often (with great applause) plaid publiquely by the Right Honourable the L. of Hunsdon his Seruants." A Second Quarto (Q2) of the play appeared in 1599, claiming on the title page that it was "Newly Corrected, augmented and amended." The text of Q1 is now generally regarded as a BAD QUARTO, based on a MEMORIAL RECONSTRUCTION by a reporter or one or more actors who had appeared in what seems to be an abridged version of the tragedy. Q1 contains about 700 lines less than Q2; it also demonstrates numerous instances of corruption, such as the omission of key passages, the presence of garbled lines, and an inconsistency in speech headings. Q2, on the other hand, is considered authoritative, although it too shows signs of corruption, including certain anomalies and inconsistencies in the text. There has been much speculation over the copy on which the Second Quarto is based. One theory suggests that Q2, except for certain isolated lines derived from Q1, was printed directly from Shakespeare's FOUL PAPERS—an assessment which, if true, would account for the inconsistencies in the text, since these could easily by explained as errors in Shakespeare's uncorrected manuscript. This is essentially the view of Brian Gibbons, who maintains in his edition of *Romeo and Juliet* that in only one extended passage did the COMPOSITOR of Q2 refer to the earlier quarto, probably because of some obscurity or deficiency in the author's manuscript. The other theory, first proposed by J. Dover Wilson in 1955 (see Additional Bibliography) and again by him and George Ian Duthie in their Cambridge edition of the play, claims that Q2 was based on an exemplar of Q1, corrected and annotated by a scribe who had collated it with Shakespeare's own manuscript. The anomalies in the Second Quarto peculiar to an author's uncorrected manuscript, both Dover Wilson and Duthie argued, are in fact inadvertent errors of the scribe in charge of collating the texts.

*Romeo and Juliet* was subsequently published in three other quarto editions between 1609 and 1637. These "derivative editions," as Gibbons has called them, differ from the principal quartos (Q1 and Q2) in two ways: one, they include new errors on the part of the respective compositors; two, they all include attempted corrections done apparently without authority, initiated either by the compositor or the editor. *Romeo and Juliet* was also published in the FIRST FOLIO of 1623, which most scholars maintain was based principally on the Third Quarto of 1609, although it contains a number of passages that follow Q4, published in 1622.

**SOURCES:** Arthur Brooke's poem *The Tragicall Historye of Romeus and Juliet* (1562) stands as the only direct source for Shakespeare's play. However, the Romeo and Juliet legend goes far back in history and was retold by a number of European writers whose stories Shakespeare may have encountered in the original language or in English translation. The first known work with many of the features of *Romeo and Juliet* is the thirty-third tale in Masuccio Salernitano's *Cinquante Novelle* (1476), which presents the misfortunes of a pair of star-crossed lovers and incorporates the device of feigned death to avoid an undesirable marriage. Another version was that of Luigi da

Porto in his *Istoria Novellamente Ritrovata di due Nobili Amanti* (c. 1530). Da Porto's was the first to set the action in Verona, to name the lovers Romeo and Giulietta, and to present as a central incident the feud between the families of the Montecchi and Capelletti. His story also includes a Friar Lorenzo, a Mercuccio, a Thebaldo, and the Conte di Lodrone—the equivalent of Shakespeare's Paris. MATTEO BANDELLO next retold the story in his *Novelle* (1554), which was later translated into English by William Painter and included in his collection *The Palace of Pleasure* (1566). Bandello's tale places further emphasis on Romeo's initial melancholy and on the family feud; it also includes for the first time the character of the Nurse and a figure corresponding to Shakespeare's Benvolio. Bandello's narrative served as the source for Pierre Boaistuau's French translation in 1559, which in turn was adapted by Brooke in his English poem. Boaistuau made some significant alterations to Bandello's story that can also be found in Brooke and, consequently, in Shakespeare. For example, Romeo's visit to the apothecary is described in detail; in the tomb scene, the hero dies before Juliet awakens; the friar encourages Juliet to flee the tomb, then himself runs away when he hears the voices of the approaching citizens; and last, the heroine stabs herself to death with Romeo's dagger.

Despite the close similarities of Shakespeare's *Romeo and Juliet* and Brooke's poem—indeed, Shakespeare's play follows its source not only in incident, but also in wording at many points—there are some significant differences as well. Of these, scholars note, the foremost are Shakespeare's development of the character of Mercutio, his compression of time in the history of events, and his subtle reworking of the fatalistic touches so recurrent in Brooke's verse tale. Whereas Mercutio is barely mentioned in the poem, Shakespeare gives the character a life and personality of his own, providing us with an obvious contrast to Romeo's love-sick persona in the early stages of the drama. Shakespeare, too, reduces Brooke's history of love from a number of months to just a few days, adding to the sense of haste and impending doom, as well as protecting his lovers from an impression of immoral or clandestine behavior—something Brooke's hero and heroine never overcome. And although fate appears to play as prominent a role in Shakespeare's drama as in Brooke's poem, the intent in *Romeo and Juliet* is much less certain, balanced as it is against other suggestions, such as the lovers' reckless disregard of moderation, the possibility of divine intervention, and even the unassailable fact of blind chance.

*CRITICAL HISTORY:* Although critics have found fault with certain aspects of *Romeo and Juliet,* most consider it among the worthiest of Shakespeare's early works; in fact, some have even praised it as the first successful modern tragedy of young love and have noted its influence on the subsequent development of English drama. Despite its critical shortcomings, the play remains one of the most popular in the canon, and its depiction of innocent love thwarted by hate and misfortune has aroused the sympathy of generations of readers and spectators. According to the twentieth-century critic John Erskine, Shakespeare gave the legend a universal appeal by transforming it from a tragedy of two young lovers into "the tragedy of young love." Commentary on the play has focused on a variety of issues, but none so significant as the question of Shakespeare's tragic design. Was the dramatist presenting here a history of young love at odds with fate or misfortune? Or was he dramatizing the tragic end of all human passion that disregards moderation and seeks only its own intense gratification, regardless of the cost? Yet, a third reading claims that the play

enacts a retributive and providential pattern, the lovers serving as the instruments by which divine will both punishes and reconciles the feuding families, thus restoring harmony to Verona's disrupted society. Critics have debated this issue through two centuries and continue to disagree. Recently, scholars have tended to postulate that Shakespeare incorporated the possibility of all three interpretations in his tragedy; proponents of this view generally suggest, as a few earlier critics did, that although fate or divine will plays a role in reconciling the families through the lovers' sacrifice, neither Romeo nor Juliet can be absolved of contributing to their own tragic end. Other important issues in the criticism of *Romeo and Juliet* include Shakespeare's characterization, especially Friar Lawrence and his function in the play; the dramatist's adaptation of his source material; the propriety of the Romeo-Rosaline affair; the success or failure of Shakespeare's work as tragic dramaturgy; the play's language and imagery, especially its emphasis on contradiction, opposition, and paradox; the relation of the love-death or *Liebestod* motif to the lovers' ordeal; and the question of the hero and heroine's maturation throughout the course of the drama.

There is little known commentary on *Romeo and Juliet* in the seventeenth century. Besides Samuel Pepys unfavorable reference to the play in his diary entry for March 1, 1662, the only other comment is the often quoted remark of John Dryden, who praised Mercutio as demonstrating "the best" of Shakespeare's skill and declared, on the basis of a rumor, that Shakespeare had to kill the character "to prevent being kill'd by him," a point disputed by many subsequent critics. More substantial reactions to the play were offered in the eighteenth century. Nicholas Rowe was the first to comment on the "Design" or theme of *Romeo and Juliet,* which he stated "is plainly the Punishment of [the] two Families for the unreasonable Feuds and Animosities that had been so long kept up between 'em." Although lauding the compassion *Romeo and Juliet* "raises," Charles Gildon disparaged its violation of probability and naturalness. He was also the first to remark on Shakespeare's language in the drama, specifically, the balcony scene in II. ii., which he considered "corrupted" by Shakespeare's reading of Petrarch. Near the middle of the century, Charlotte Lennox discussed the playwright's adaptation of his sources in *Romeo and Juliet,* noting that the tragedy is not based on what she calls the original Italian story, but is worked from an English translation or from Pierre Boaistuau's French version. Like Gildon, Henry Home emphasized Shakespeare's failure to adhere to the rules of tragic dramaturgy in the play, asserting that such tragedies "of the pathetic kind," to the extent that they depict the sufferings of characters due to accidents of fate, should always end on a "fortunate" note, which Shakespeare's drama fails to do. Samuel Johnson, on the other hand, found much to admire in *Romeo and Juliet;* he called the play "one of the most pleasing of [Shakespeare's] performances" and praised, especially, the probability of events as required by the rules of tragedy. Johnson also disagreed with Dryden's claim that Mercutio should have been kept alive until the play's end. Returning to the question of Shakespeare's tragic design in *Romeo and Juliet,* Elizabeth Griffith stated that the tragedy is meant to demonstrate, through the deaths of "the unhappy lovers," a moral against such reckless venturing and "unweighed engagement," thus becoming the first critic to place the tragic responsibility squarely on the hero and heroine, and not on fate.

Three issues dominated nineteenth-century criticism of *Romeo and Juliet:* the question of Friar Lawrence's role in the play, the propriety of the Romeo-Rosaline affair, and the nature of Shakespeare's tragic design. However, other concerns—such as the dramatist's use of language and imagery—also received considerable attention.

At the beginning of the century, Charles Dibdin commented on David Garrick's alterations of *Romeo and Juliet* in a recent production of the play, agreeing with all of the changes except for one, the deletion of Romeo's initial affair with Rosaline. Dibdin argued that this episode was not a lapse on Shakespeare's part but was necessary to the play, in that it contributes to the "awful grandeur" of the plot and theme as well as to the sense of reckless love we see later in Romeo's relationship with Juliet. This issue was taken up again by such subsequent critics as Anna Brownell Jameson, Samuel Taylor Coleridge, Hermann Ulrici, and Denton J. Snider. Jameson declared that the affair with Rosaline, "far from prejudicing us against Romeo," actually "adds a fresh stroke of truth to the portrait of the lover." Like Jameson, Coleridge maintained that the opening affair demonstrates "the fineness of [Shakespeare's] insight into the nature of the passions." Ulrici contended that Romeo's love-sickness is essential to a proper understanding of the hero's character, besides offering a contrast with his later, more sincere love for Juliet. Near the close of the century, Snider offered the strongest argument yet in support of the Romeo-Rosaline affair, concluding that it directs our attention toward "the true motive for the tragic termination of the action."

The concern among nineteenth-century commentators over Shakespeare's principal theme in *Romeo and Juliet* was often linked with the question of Friar Lawrence's role in the play—in short, was he or was he not the dramatist's spokesman in his frequent admonition of the lovers for their reckless behavior. Those who argued that the protagonists are responsible for their tragic deaths usually emphasized Friar Lawrence's importance to this moral design, while those who considered the catastrophe beyond Romeo and Juliet's control disputed his so-called choric function, if they discussed the character at all. Still, others regarded the play as more symbolic and universal in its conflict between love and fate, offering in the process little analysis of any of the characters. Dibdin described Shakespeare's central theme as a "solemn warning" to the Montague and Capulet families, by the sacrifice of their children, "of the horrid effects of domestic enmity." August Wilhelm Schlegel, on the other hand, saw in the play "a picture of love and its pitiable fate," though he added that even in death the young lovers transcend despair. Ulrici disagreed with Schlegel's reading of the tragedy, claiming that love is not Shakespeare's central theme but only the efficient means of his story. The critic averred that the primary purpose of the play's tragic action is to resolve the contradiction in its double vision of the protagonists' love—the view that the lovers' passion is purifying and, at the same time, dangerous in its exclusiveness, since it disturbs "the internal harmony of the moral powers." Interestingly, Ulrici also disputed the friar's choric significance in the drama, stating that Paris provides a truer reflection of Shakespeare's design, to the extent that his "flat, dull, and heartless conception of love" demonstrates its own obvious inadequacy when compared to the passion of Romeo and Juliet. In an assessment similar to Ulrici's, G. G. Gervinus maintained that Shakespeare was here concerned with the nature of intense, sexual passion, such as that of the lovers, and the paradox that such extreme passion can ennoble individuals while it can also carry "man beyond himself and his natural limits," thus destroying him. However, unlike Ulrici, Gervinus regarded the friar as Shakespeare's spokesman in the play, adding that the

lovers, and not fate, bring about the final tragic events through their rash behavior. The French critic Alfred Mézières also stressed Friar Lawrence's importance in *Romeo and Juliet*, claiming that his philosophy of moderation "is but the judgment which the poet pronounces from the background of the tragedy." Edward Dowden took issue with Gervinus's claim that the friar serves a choric function in *Romeo and Juliet* and, as such, expresses Shakespeare's own ethical ideas. According to Dowden, the lovers' ordeal is not meant to provide us with a just moral, such as the friar's warning of the dangers of immoderation, but demonstrates "that every strong emotion which exalts and quickens the inner life of man at the same time exposes the outer life of accident and circumstance to increased risk." In a structural analysis of the drama, Denton J. Snider asserted that Romeo and Juliet's love for each other, despite its attractiveness, exceeds all natural and social limitations, thereby sacrificing reason, utility, and self-control, and eventually destroying the lovers. Snider regarded the friar's philosophy of moderation as the play's moral, but he also identified as a central, unifying theme the conflict between love and fate, in which "the individual is the merest instrument, ready to be sacrificed without the least hesitation." Snider's apparent combination of readings here, wherein both fate and the lovers are held accountable for the tragic conclusion, foreshadowed similar approaches by such twentieth-century critics as Franklin M. Dickey, Douglas L. Peterson, Marilyn L. Williamson, and Frederick Kiefer. A final comment from the nineteenth century concerning Shakespeare's theme was voiced by Frederick S. Boas, who, like Dowden, disagreed with Gervinus's assessment of the friar's choric function in the play. For Boas, Shakespeare nowhere censures the love of Romeo and Juliet, but demonstrates instead that "the ecstasies of love are brief and brittle" in the face of destiny.

The lyrical and stylized nature of the language in *Romeo and Juliet* has also been addressed by many nineteenth-century critics. The noted French novelist and essayist Châteaubriand provided some brief, unfavorable comments on Shakespeare's form of expression in the play, which he described as frequently "inflated," "distorted," and "eminently wanting in simplicity." He cited in particular Romeo's account of the apothecary in Act V, Scene i as support for his assessment. Schlegel, however, praised the lyrical beauty of *Romeo and Juliet* and noted, especially, the skill with which Shakespeare combined various contrasts and oppositions into a unified whole. Jameson commended the romantic poetry "interfused through all the characters," and Coleridge focused on the stylized verse in the so-called lamentations scene (IV. v.), which he regarded as "excusable," though he added that it is difficult to determine how we are to react to the various outbursts of grief in this episode. Like Châteaubriand, Henry Hallam disparaged the poetic language in Shakespeare's tragedy—the numerous conceits, "frigid metaphors," and "incongruous conceptions," all of which, he claimed, "interfere with the very emotion the poet would excite." Besides discussing the thematics of *Romeo and Juliet*, Gervinus was also the first critic to examine Shakespeare's use of such traditional verse forms as the sonnet, the epithalamium or nuptial poem, and the dawn-song to enhance the lyrical quality of his play. M. Guizot, like Hallam and Châteaubriand, faulted the language with which Shakespeare expressed the lovers' passion, asserting that it is "often factitious, laden with developments and ornaments . . . which do not flow naturally from the lips of a dramatic personage." And Algernon Charles Swinburne maintained that "the whole heart or spirit of *Romeo and Juliet* . . . is distilled" in two scenes: the garden scene following the Capulet feast and the parting balcony scene in Act III. According to Swinburne, these two episodes express emotions in simple, accessible language, while the remainder of the play is often extravagant, evidencing "the tentative uncertain grasp of a stripling giant."

Shakespeare's language in *Romeo and Juliet* and the question of tragic responsibility continued to dominate twentieth-century criticism of the play. However, other issues also received serious consideration. These include Shakespeare's mixture of comic and tragic elements; the role of contradiction, opposition, and paradox in the tragedy; the importance of the love-death or *Liebestod* motif; the maturation of the lovers; the medieval influence on Shakespeare's tragic design; and the question of whether the play fails or succeeds as tragedy.

Near the turn of the century, Richard G. Moulton disputed those commentators who discerned "folly" in the behavior of the lovers. He emphasized the role of Accident as well as Destiny and countered the view that the friar's message of moderation is meant as a judgment against the hero and heroine's youthful passion, noting that Friar Lawrence himself contributes to the final catastrophe. Similar assessments of the play were variously proposed by such later critics as E. K. Chambers, Elmer Edgar Stoll, H. B. Charlton, George Ian Duthie, John Lawlor, and Susan Snyder. In a biographical reading of *Romeo and Juliet*, Chambers argued that the tragedy's central concern is the conflict between love and destiny, and he further ridiculed the idea that Friar Lawrence is Shakespeare's mouthpiece in the play. Chambers called such an interpretation "a singularly futile one," in that "both the love and the love's disaster are presented as things entirely beyond the power of their puppets to cause or cure by any deliberate act or abstention of their own." Stoll maintained that Shakespeare was not concerned here with providing motives for his characters' actions, but instead was intent on dramatizing a certain, established pattern, freely borrowing conventions from romantic tradition in order to give his drama shape and direction. According to the critic, *Romeo and Juliet* depicts the ageless conflict between ideal, passionate love and destiny. Stoll also averred that Friar Lawrence is a chorus figure "only in so far as his moralizings and warnings have the effect of misgivings and forebodings, which contribute to the suspense." In one of the most influential studies of *Romeo and Juliet* in the twentieth century, Charlton labelled the play a failed experiment in tragedy. Like Chambers, he argued that its central theme is the conflict between love and fate, but concluded that neither fate nor the feud adequately sustains the tragic outcome as it stands. According to Charlton, the feud seems out of place in the play's world and lacks the conviction to compel the lovers' sacrifice; and the notion of fate, at least by the time Shakespeare wrote *Romeo and Juliet*, "was no longer a deity strong enough to carry the responsibility of a tragic universe." Charlton's assessment was essentially repeated by Duthie, who regarded the play as a medieval *de casibus* tragedy pitting fortune or fate against the happiness of the lovers; but Duthie added that Shakespeare failed to sustain this tragic design in two significant ways: one, by making both the feud and the powers of fate unconvincing; and two, by providing frequent suggestions throughout that the lovers themselves are flawed and therefore equally responsible for their deaths. Like Duthie, Lawlor compared *Romeo and Juliet* to what he called the medieval *tragedie*—a literary form popular during the Middle Ages which depicts an unfortunate hero's gradual recognition of a greater good beyond this world as a result of his sufferings. And in a brief comment on the play's central theme, Susan Snyder concluded that *Romeo and Juliet* is a tragedy of "milieu," one of

the few Shakespearean works which demonstrate that "it is not what you are that counts, but the world you live in."

The second leading interpretation of *Romeo and Juliet*—namely, that the tragedy dramatizes foremost the punishment and reconciliation of the feuding families through the deaths of their children—was iterated by such twentieth-century critics as Stopford A. Brooke, Bertrand Evans, Harold S. Wilson, Irving Ribner, and Paul N. Siegel. In his essay of 1905, Brooke contended that the feud between the families is the central event in *Romeo and Juliet*, adding that Shakespeare here depicts the process by which "Justice" achieves harmony through the sacrifice of the innocent lovers. In one of the more atypical readings of *Romeo and Juliet*, Evans asserted that fate achieves a reconciliation of the families "through the common human condition of not knowing"—in other words, through the inability of the characters involved to decipher false appearances and recognize the true meaning of events. Wilson echoed Brooke's assessment and concluded that the deaths of Romeo and Juliet are in no way retributive for their past actions, but serve only to secure the reconciliation of the feuding families. However, like Charlton and Duthie, Wilson noted that Shakespeare marred this design by making the hero and heroine so attractive that the audience terminates its interest once they are dead, thus missing the culmination of the play in the resolution of the feud. Ribner posited a more religious reading of *Romeo and Juliet*; he maintained that the tragedy is explicitly Christian, depicting the operation of divine providence as it sacrifices the lovers in order to reconcile the warring families—in Ribner's words, to reestablish "God's harmonious order" and "a rebirth of love." Siegel, too, found a definite Christian philosophy in the play, but he asserted that Shakespeare combined this teaching with the medieval concept of "the religion of love," a doctrine which held that "Love is a god in supreme control over human beings" and that faithfulness in love, even to the point of death, was the greatest human virtue. According to Siegel, Shakespeare transformed this idea "into a complexly unified attitude," demonstrating that cosmic love manifests itself through sexual love to conquer "strife and disorder in society."

The third principal reading of *Romeo and Juliet*, which regards the tragic catastrophe as primarily the result of the lovers' intense passion, received considerable support in the twentieth century. In relation to this, Friar Lawrence's importance as Shakespeare's spokesman in the play also found endorsement among many modern critics. Writing in 1913, Brander Matthews commented on the often-noted shortcomings in Shakespeare's drama, such as the detention of Friar John, claiming that these so-called faults are merely minor lapses and that the play as a whole is more classically tragic than critics give credit. For, according to Matthews, not fate but the characters themselves contribute to the final catastrophe by being intolerant of opposition and determined to do what they have decided, "regardless of the consequences." Near the mid-way point of the century, E. C. Pettet offered one of the most unfavorable assessments of Romeo written thus far, claiming that although the hero matures before his death, his behavior throughout the play is presented by Shakespeare as unhealthy and reckless. In addition, Pettet argued that Friar Lawrence represents the reproving voice of Shakespeare, though he cautioned against viewing the friar as a chorus figure "in the formal Greek sense of the word." On a related matter, Pettet maintained, unlike Matthews, that *Romeo and Juliet* is not a tragedy in a strict definition of the term, since "the catastrophe depends on chance, the undelivered letter of Friar Lawrence." In a discussion of

Shakespeare's language, M. C. Bradbrook also commented on *Romeo and Juliet*'s "governing idea," which she identified in the friar's philosophy of moderation, saying that such intense passion as the lovers share can only be destructive. Two other important essays on this theme were offered in the 1960s by Robert O. Evans and Roy W. Battenhouse. Evans declared that it is misleading to view *Romeo and Juliet* as a tragedy of fate, for although destiny does play a role in the drama, the catastrophe is brought about by the characters' own decisions and actions. Significantly, Evans averred that the lovers' tragic flaw resides not in their overly sensuous natures, as many critics have maintained, but in "the great powers of their intellects combined with the higher parts of [their] souls." Like Irving Ribner, Battenhouse discerned an explicit Christian philosophy in Shakespeare's tragedy, though unlike Ribner he argued that the lovers' reckless behavior and the tragic conclusion are intimately related, for both the hero and heroine seek an idolatrous and narcissistic form of passion which ultimately undermines the Christian, communal aspect of love and, as such, leads only to despair.

Since the late 1950s, a handful of critics have noted many unanswered questions in the three leading interpretations of *Romeo and Juliet,* taken individually, and have thus attempted to synthesize aspects from each. Franklin M. Dickey was the first to do so, claiming that Shakespeare's play is "a carefully wrought tragedy which balances hatred against love and which makes fortune the agent of divine justice without absolving anyone from his responsibility for the tragic conclusion." Thus, according to Dickey, divine will, fortune, and the lovers' intense passion are not separable, opposing elements, but interrelated forces which equally contribute to Shakespeare's tragic design. In a similar assessment, Douglas L. Peterson argued that although it is true that divine will has brought Romeo and Juliet together for the purpose of ending the family feud, the lovers are "nevertheless free to choose the means by which they fulfill what Providence has ordained." For Peterson, Romeo and Juliet can either follow the guidance of reason and divine powers throughout their ordeal, thus restoring order "through the normal operation of the laws of nature," or they can yield to blind passion and achieve harmony "through violence, retribution, and purgation." It is this latter course, the critic concluded, which the lovers follow at every crucial moment. Most recently, Marilyn L. Williamson, Frederick Kiefer, and Northrop Frye have all proposed various interpretations of *Romeo and Juliet* which synthesize what were once viewed as opposing elements. Williamson, in an attempt to reconcile the conflicting readings of the play, declared that fate is not the tragic force behind events, since Romeo actually desires death even before he meets and falls in love with Juliet; but, the critic added, the family feud contributes to the final catastrophe to the extent that it fosters Romeo's wish for self-destruction in the first place. In an examination of the medieval influence on *Romeo and Juliet,* Kiefer noted how Shakespeare balances the lovers' view of events as fortuitous or accidental with the friar's—and to a lesser extent, the prince's—sense of divine retribution, concluding that neither view is meant to obliterate the other, but that both are purposely juxtaposed. Thus, Kiefer proclaimed, Shakespeare in this tragedy recognizes both the protagonists' responsibility for the tragic events and "the awesome power of hostile circumstance." Frye emphasized the importance of the feud, saying that without it the tragedy would not exist; but he added that reducing the tragic force of the drama to this one element leaves much unaccounted for, especially the "greater mysteries in things" necessary to the full tragic effect. This sense of greater mystery Frye identified in the image of the lovers as sacrificial victims, who in their quest for an ideal love demonstrate the maxim that "nothing that breaks through the barriers of ordinary experience can remain in the world of ordinary experience."

Other critical issues related to the question of Shakespeare's tragic design in *Romeo and Juliet* include the maturation of the lovers, the medieval influence on the play, the importance of the love-death motif, and Shakespeare's mixture of comic and tragic elements.

The effect of the lovers' ordeal as a maturing experience in the play was first given serious consideration by Harley Granville-Barker. In a general character analysis of Romeo and Juliet, Granville-Barker noted how the hero, especially, evolves throughout the play, undergoing a maturation until he accepts his fate with tragic dignity and learns to love deeply despite the consequences. Concerning Juliet, the critic asserted that although she, too, matures as a result of her ordeal, "she has not grown older as Romeo has, nor risen to an impersonal dignity of sorrow." As mentioned above, E. C. Pettet also commented on Romeo's maturation, but unlike Granville-Barker he maintained that though the hero does develop, with respect to his love for Juliet, he remains an impetuous figure in the play. As part of his Christian reading of *Romeo and Juliet,* Irving Ribner stressed the spiritual education of both the hero and heroine throughout their ordeal, which he stated is especially apparent in their eventual recognition and acceptance of the sad part they must play in God's plan. John Vyvyan presented one of the most exhaustive investigations into Romeo's spiritual development; he regarded the tragedy as an allegory of love, depicting the hero's gradual transformation into spiritual consciousness, whereby he forsakes his old, conventional, and mistaken view of love for a more exalted, religious, and Platonic awareness. Also as outlined above, John Lawlor paid particular attention to the maturation of Romeo and Juliet as part of Shakespeare's adaptation of the medieval *tragedie,* stating that this is best exemplified in the language of the lovers, which comes to accommodate contradiction, paradox, and ambiguity, even transforming the world in which they live. Lastly, Derick R. C. Marsh further noted the favorable development of the hero and heroine as a result of their experience, asserting that in their ultimate sacrifice to preserve their union they "establish a quality of love, of life intensely lived, that becomes its own value."

The medieval influence on Shakespeare's *Romeo and Juliet* has been discerned most often in the play's tragic design. For example, George Ian Duthie argued that the drama is modeled on the medieval *de casibus* tragedy and depicts fate or fortune endowing the young lovers with happiness only to "cast them down to sorrow and to ruin." As mentioned above, Paul N. Siegel averred that the doctrine of "the religion of love," popularized during the Middle Ages, had a profound influence on Shakespeare's tragedy. Like Duthie, Lawlor identified the medieval *tragedie* convention as the ultimate source for the lovers' descent from happiness to despair. In the present decade, both Frederick Kiefer and Northrop Frye have further defined this medieval influence: Kiefer discussed Shakespeare's adaptation in *Romeo and Juliet* of "the Love-Fortune-Death topos" popular during the Middle Ages and throughout Elizabeth's reign; Frye, on the other hand, was concerned with the three forms of the medieval courtly love tradition presented in Shakespeare's tragedy: first, "the orthodox Petrarchan convention in Romeo's professed love for Rosaline"; second, the more serious love between the hero and heroine; and third,

Mercutio's and the Nurse's "more cynical and ribald perspective."

The significance of the love-death pattern in *Romeo and Juliet*—also referred to as the *amour-passion* or *Liebestod* myth—was not suggested until the 1950s; but it has since become one of the more prevalent issues in commentary on the tragedy, especially as it is identified with Shakespeare's use of contradiction and paradox in both the language and structure of his play. Writing in 1956, Denis de Rougemont was the first critic to relate *Romeo and Juliet* to what he termed the *amour-passion* myth in European literature. His suggestion, though brief, attracted the interest of such later critics as M. M. Mahood, Robert O. Evans, Roy W. Battenhouse, James L. Calderwood, and Coppélia Kahn. After noting the numerous similarities in Shakespeare's tragedy and the *amour-passion* myth discussed by de Rougemont, Mahood claimed that the play conflicts with this convention in several important ways. Foremost, she argued, is the fact that the lovers' behavior throughout their ordeal is not governed by a death-wish, as is the case in the *amour-passion* or *Liebestod* myth, but by a desire to survive and live together. Evans, too, proclaimed that Shakespeare was more his own mythmaker than a spokesman for existing conventions, noting how the dramatist combined ingredients from *amour-passion*—such as mystical passion and impious license—with "the great theme of marriage for love" and a more rational attitude of the hero and heroine towards their love than the intense eroticism prevalent in the myth. Battenhouse linked Romeo's courtly love expression, which he considered a "false religion," with the *amour-passion* or *Liebestod* myth noted by these earlier critics, stating that, like these forms of passion, it is intrinsically destructive, pagan in its idealistic eroticism, and nontranscendent. In an examination of the conflict between public and private language in *Romeo and Juliet*, Calderwood compared the lovers' gradual movement toward death—which he described as the ultimate silence and, as such, the purest form of love's expression which the hero and heroine have sought throughout their brief relationship—to the *Liebestod* myth in its similar reconciliation of these opposing phenomena. Kahn discussed how the lovers' final union in death is actually a triumph over Verona's paternal society, which, in her assessment, inhibits normal sexual development and promotes a violent, self-destructive attitude among its members.

Shakespeare's mixture of comedy and tragedy in *Romeo and Juliet* was first given serious consideration by Harry Levin in 1960. Levin, whose principal concern was the importance of antithesis and paradox in the play, noted that the most obvious example of this drama of contradiction is Shakespeare's use of comic conventions in what turns out to be a very tragic work. This issue was subsequently discussed by John Wain, Susan Snyder, and Rosalie L. Colie. In a brief analysis of why *Romeo and Juliet* fails as a tragedy, Wain stressed the fact that the play "is in essence a comedy that turns out tragically," adding that it proceeds as it does for no apparent reason other than Shakespeare's desire to write a tragedy. Like Wain, Snyder contended that the play is indeed a comedy transformed into its opposite, maintaining that the opening acts show all the usual markings of comic dramaturgy, but that, with the death of Mercutio, the remaining acts turn toward the tragic mode. And Colie focused on the techniques with which Shakespeare successfully adapted the theme of love, traditionally a comic concern exclusively, into the tragic story of Romeo and Juliet.

Undoubtedly the most pervasive concern in twentieth-century commentary on *Romeo and Juliet*, after the issue of the tragedy's central theme, is Shakespeare's use of language and imagery, especially his depiction of contradiction, opposition, and paradox in the play. Although the language and rhetoric interested scholars as early as Charles Gildon in the eighteenth century, it was not until the 1930s and later that commentators began to recognize the importance of the characters' expressions to both the structure and thematics of the drama. In her study of 1935, Caroline F. E. Spurgeon was the first critic to analyze the imagery in *Romeo and Juliet* and to emphasize the contrast between the lovers' frequent allusions to starlight, sunlight, and moonlight in their assessment of each other's beauty, and their perception of the world around them in the antithetical terms of darkness, night, clouds, and mist. M. C. Bradbrook commented on the abundance of rhetorical language in *Romeo and Juliet*, which is so pervasive, in her opinion, that entire passages or scenes in the play "are emptied of all feeling." Wolfgang Clemen asserted that Shakespeare's use of imagery in *Romeo and Juliet* is more adept than in his earlier works and demonstrates a greater understanding of dramatic poetry. Significantly, Clemen also argued that the juxtaposition of conventional and natural styles in the tragedy was intended by Shakespeare and serves a dramatic function. In a frequently cited study, Mahood examined the lovers' wordplay and noted how it contributes to our admiration of their passion. She was also among the earliest critics to stress the importance of opposition and antithesis to the structure of Shakespeare's play. Focusing on the differences between Shakespeare's early and mature tragedies, R. F. Hill contended that the frequent use of rhetorical language in *Romeo and Juliet* was intended not, as in the case of the previous plays, to create a "poetic reality," but to imitate "the language of imaginary feelings which are later to be contrasted with true feelings." In another influential study of the language in the play, Harry Levin investigated Shakespeare's use of reduplication, contrariety, antithesis, and paradox both within the language and as an integral part of the drama's structure. He further emphasized how the lovers stand out "against this insistence upon polarity . . . , the one organic relation amid an overplus of stylized expressions and attitudes." As previously mentioned, John Lawlor linked the spiritual maturation of the hero and heroine with their newfound ability to accommodate contradiction, paradox, and ambiguity in their expressions of love. Although more concerned with the construction of *Romeo and Juliet*, Stephen A. Shapiro noted the manner in which Shakespeare juxtaposed elements in specific scenes to convey "ironic or dramatic reversals." In fact, he argued, the meaning of the tragedy is expressed through just such "contraries and contradictions" as he examined.

Other important essays on the language of *Romeo and Juliet* include those by Winifred Nowottny, David Laird, Nicholas Brooke, Norman Rabkin, James L. Calderwood, and Rosalie L. Colie. Nowottny discussed Shakespeare's adaptation of the sonnet tradition, demonstrating how the stylized, Petrarchan mode apparent in the lovers' expressions helps to universalize their experience and to convey the exalted, ennobling nature of their love. Focusing on the language and attitudes of the characters in both the public and private worlds of *Romeo and Juliet*, Laird emphasized two points: one, that the determination with which Romeo and Juliet "act out their love and assert its value beyond time" forces the public world of Verona—which is blinded by habit and "conventional response"—"to acknowledge what it could not see"; and two, that as the lovers "expose the fatal inadequacy" of Verona's conventional behavior, the demands of that public world provoke them "to an awareness quite different from that fostered by their dream of romantic fulfillment'' expressed early in the play. The critic also identified in the later authentic and personal utterances of the lovers an ability to transcend the ambiguities and contradictions of life, as well as a willingness to accommodate ''disparate aspects of existence.'' Brooke asserted that in this tragedy Shakespeare employed stylized poetry to enshrine, ''as no other form of utterance could, the profoundest imaginative values in the play,'' while at the same time forcing us to recognize the central paradox of the action—the ''death-marked love'' of the protagonists. He added that ''the tragic conception implied'' is not a personal one, but is more universal, suggesting that ''the finest of human experiences have inherent limitations, regardless of who embodies them,'' an assessment similar to that voiced in the nineteenth century by Edward Dowden. Reviewing the scene in which the Capulets mourn over Juliet's apparent death (IV. v.), Rabkin declared that the artificial language in this and other episodes of the play is part of Shakespeare's purposeful design, indicating an insincerity of feeling when contrasted with those scenes which are more genuinely emotive. The critic linked this stylistic technique with the play's tragic theme, maintaining that the oxymora and paradox which were once part of Romeo's affected poise eventually become the definitive expressions ''of things as they are,'' since his and Juliet's love finds ultimate satisfaction not in life but only in death. Like Laird, Calderwood emphasized the contrast between the public and private worlds of *Romeo and Juliet*, claiming that a central conflict in the play is that between the lovers' desire to develop a pure and personal language to express their love and the reality that language, as a public commodity, can never adequately denote the private world of feelings. More recently, Colie investigated Shakespeare's extensive use of the sonnet or Petrarchan tradition in order to invest his love theme with tragic seriousness and dignity. She also noted the numerous instances in *Romeo and Juliet* where this sonnet rhetoric informs, even shapes, the action, adding that the stylized language appears as frequently in the later scenes—where the expression of love is supposedly more sincere, less ornamental—as in the early ones.

What is apparent from the centuries of commentary on *Romeo and Juliet* is that the tragedy has interested critics as much as it has attracted both readers and spectators to its moving story of ill-fated love. Although scholars often disagree as to the play's principal merits—and faults—none would deny its importance to Shakespeare's development as a tragic dramatist. Yet, many critical issues continue to plague those who would label it an unqualified success, not the least of which is the question of Shakespeare's tragic design. Twentieth-century commentators, especially since the 1950s, have shifted from a focus on the play's moral significance to a study of its rhetoric and language, claiming in the process that the meaning of the tragedy is intimately linked with these elements. This approach has proven quite fruitful and won much support, but it nonetheless has never eclipsed the problem of Shakespeare's tragic conception and the manner in which this issue has divided critics throughout history, ultimately detracting from any assessment of the play as a successfully integrated work. Perhaps, as many scholars indicate, this question can never be resolved; indeed, for some it is just this uneasy alliance in *Romeo and Juliet* of fate, fortune, and tragic guilt that makes it so critically appealing. In the words of the noted Shakespearean critic G. Blakemore Evans: ''That [Shakespeare] juxtaposes these concepts instead of fusing them, as he is able to do in his later major tragedies, may indeed be recognized as a sign of immaturity and inexperience, but it should also be admitted that

the play succeeds because of, not despite, what critics have described as Shakespeare's 'confusion'.''

---

## SAMUEL PEPYS (diary date 1662)

[*A diversified background of travel, intellectual pursuits, and public office gave Pepys the opportunity to be a close observer of his society. His unique* Diary *is an unreserved study of the affairs and customs of his time. His personal revelations create a document of unusual psychological interest as well as providing a history of the Restoration theater. In the following excerpt from his diary entry of March 1, 1662, Pepys mentions a performance of* Romeo and Juliet *he attended and refers to the play as ''the worst that ever I heard in my life.''*]

[I went to] the Opera, and there saw ''Romeo and Juliet,'' the first time it was ever acted, but it is a play of itself the worst that ever I heard in my life. . . .

> *Samuel Pepys, in a diary entry of March 1, 1662, in* The Shakspere Allusion-Book: A Collection of Allusions to Shakspere from 1591-1700, Vol. II, *edited by John Munro, revised edition, 1932. Reprint by Books for Libraries Press, 1970; distributed by Arno Press, Inc., p. 90.*

## JOHN DRYDEN (essay date 1672)

[*Dryden, the leading poet and playwright of Restoration England, helped formulate the Neoclassical view of Shakespeare as an irregular genius whose native talent overcame his ignorance of the proper ''rules'' and language for serious drama. He was also instrumental in establishing Shakespeare's reputation as the foremost English dramatist, and his assessment of Shakespeare's works influenced critics well into the following century. In the following excerpt, Dryden asserts that in the character of Mercutio, Shakespeare ''show'd the best of his skill,'' and he recounts the rumor that Shakespeare had to kill Mercutio ''to prevent being kill'd by him.'' Dryden's assessment of Shakespeare's handling of Mercutio was frequently debated in subsequent commentary on* Romeo and Juliet. *The following excerpt is taken from an essay originally published in 1672 with Dryden's play* The Conquest of Granada by the Spaniards.]

Shakespear show'd the best of his skill in his *Mercutio*, and he said himself, that he was forc'd to kill him in the third Act, to prevent being kill'd by him. But, for my part, I cannot find he was so dangerous a person: I see nothing in him but what was so exceeding harmless, that he might have liv'd to the end of the Play, and dy'd in his bed, without offence to any man.

> *John Dryden, in an extract from* The Shakspere Allusion-Book: A Collection of Allusions to Shakspere from 1591-1700, Vol. II, *edited by John Munro, revised edition, 1932. Reprint by Books for Libraries Press, 1970; distributed by Arno Press, Inc., p. 176.*

## NICHOLAS ROWE (essay date 1709)

[*Rowe was the editor of the first critical edition of Shakespeare's plays (1709) and the author of the first authoritative Shakespeare biography. In the excerpt below, he is the earliest critic to comment on the ''Design'' or theme of* Romeo and Juliet, *which he states ''is plainly the Punishment of [the] two Families for the unreasonable Feuds and Animosities that had been so long kept up between 'em.''*]

The Design in *Romeo and Juliet,* is plainly the Punishment of [the] two Families, for the unreasonable Feuds and Animosities that had been so long kept up between 'em, and occasion'd the Effusion of so much Blood. In the management of this Story, [Shakespeare] has shewn something wonderfully Tender and Passionate in the Love-part, and very Pitiful in the Distress. (p. xxxi)

> *Nicholas Rowe, "Some Account of the Life, &c. of Mr. William Shakespear," in* The Works of Mr. William Shakespear, Vol. 1, *edited by Nicholas Rowe, 1709. Reprint by AMS Press, Inc., 1967, pp. iii-xl.*

### [CHARLES GILDON]   (essay date 1710)

[*Gildon was the first critic to write an extended commentary on the entire Shakespearean dramatic canon. Like many other Neoclassicists, he regarded Shakespeare as an imaginative playwright who nevertheless frequently violated the dramatic "rules" necessary for correct writing. In the following excerpt from his "Remarks on the Plays of Shakespear" (1710), Gildon both praises* Romeo and Juliet *for the compassion it "raises" and disparages its violation of probability and naturalness. This is especially evident in his comments on the first balcony scene (II. ii.), which he states is "corrupted" by Shakespeare's reading of Petrarch, yet pleases us with its "pure unsophisticated Nature."*]

Tho' this Play have no less, than five or six Murthers, yet they are nothing akin to those of [*Titus Andronicus*], these, for the most Part, are the Effect of Heat and Passion, and by Way of Duels, which Custom has given a sort of Reputation to, as being upon the Square. If therefore they are faulty, they yet are of that Nature, that we pity, because every Gentleman is liable to fall into that by the Necessity of Custom. Tho' this Fable is far from Dramatic Perfection, yet it undeniably raises Compassion in the later Scenes.

There are in it many Beauties of the Manners and Sentiments, and Diction. The Character of *Mercutio* is pleasant and uniform; that of *Tybalt* always *equal;* as indeed they all are; the Nurse is a true Comic Character, tho' some of our *Chit-chat* Poets would look on it as Farce or low Comedy. (pp. 369-70)

Whether Passion be so pregnant of Similes as *Romeo* and *Juliet* every where give us, I dare not determine, since to say that all they speak is not natural, wou'd be to provoke too many, that admire it as the Soul of Love. . . .

The Scene betwixt *Romeo* and *Juliet* when he is in the Garden, and she at her Window, tho' it contain many things, that will not join with Probability, and tho' perhaps *Shakespear* like *Cowly* was a little corrupted by reading *Petrarch,* that modern Debaucher of Poetry into *Conceits,* and *Conundrums;* yet the Fancy . . . is every where so fine, and Nature so agreeably painted, that we are pleas'd with the very *Fucus,* and perswade our selves that it is pure unsophisticated Nature. . . . (p. 371)

> [*Charles Gildon*], *"Remarks on the Plays of Shakespear," in* The Works of Mr. William Shakespear, *Vol. 7, 1710. Reprint by AMS Press, Inc., 1967, pp. 257-444.*

### [CHARLOTTE LENNOX]   (essay date 1753)

[*Lennox was an eighteenth-century novelist and Shakespearean scholar who compiled* Shakespear Illustrated *(1753-54), a three-volume edition of translated texts of the sources used by Shakespeare in twenty-two of his plays, including some analyses of the ways in which he adapted these sources. In the following excerpt*

*from the first volume of that work, Lennox is the earliest critic to argue that Shakespeare did not base* Romeo and Juliet *on Bandello's Ninth Novel—what she calls the original Italian story— but worked from an English translation or from Pierre Boaistuau's French version. She points to evidence throughout Shakespeare's play that recalls Boaistuau's story, rather than Bandello's, claiming that though* Romeo and Juliet *is "a very affecting Tragedy," Shakespeare would have composed yet a better play had he had access to the Italian version.*]

On the Incidents in the [Ninth Novel of Bandello], *Shakespear* has formed the fable of his *Romeo* and *Juliet,* one of the most regular of all his Tragedies. . . . [Yet] I think it will not be difficult to prove, or at least to make it appear highly probable, that he never saw, and did not understand the Original, but copied from a *French* Translation extant in his Time; or, what is equally probable, from an *English* Translation of that *French* one, both very bad, in some Places rather paraphrased than translated; in others, the Author's Sense absolutely mistaken, many Circumstances injudiciously added, and many more altered for the worse, or wholly omitted. The Story of *Romeo* and *Juliet* may be found translated in a Book, entituled, *Histoires Tragiques extraictes des Oeuvres de Bandel* [by Pierre Boaistuau]. . . . A literal Translation of this Story, from the *French,* is in the second Tome of the *Palace of Pleasure. . . ,* translated into *English* by *William Painter,* from several *Greek, Latin, Spanish* and *Italian* Authors. . . . (pp. 89-90)

Had *Shakespear* ever seen the original Novel in *Bandello,* he would have been sensible that the Translation of it is extremely bad: That he did not see it, must be owing to nothing else than his not understanding *Italian;* for can it be supposed, that having resolved to write a Tragedy upon the Subject of an *Italian* Story, he would rather chuse to copy from a bad Translation of that Story, than follow the Original.

This Supposition would be as absurd as to imagine a Man would slake his Thirst with the muddy Waters of a polluted Stream, when the clear Spring, from whence it issues, is within his Reach. That *Shakespear* consulted the Translator, appears from his having followed him in all the Alterations he has made in the Original; some few of which I shall take notice of, and shew that in some Places he has not only taken Circumstances from the Translator, but also made Use of his Thoughts and Expressions. (p. 90)

The Translator makes *Juliet,* upon hearing that her Cousin is slain by *Romeo,* break into Complaints and Reproaches against her Husband, and after she has for some Time given a Loose to her Resentment, her returning Tenderness for *Romeo* forces her to repent of the injurious Words which, in the first Emotions of her Grief and Rage, she had uttered against him; she condemns herself for her too hasty Censure, and begs Pardon of the absent *Romeo* for her unkind Reproaches.

There is not the least Foundation for all this in the Original. *Bandello* every where shews *Juliet* so much engrossed by her extreme Passion for *Romeo,* that all other Affections, all Tyes of Consanguinity, all filial Duty and Obedience is swallowed up in the Immensity of her Love; and therefore when the News of *Tibbald*'s Death and *Romeo*'s Banishment is brought to her at the same Time, she does not weep for the Death of her Cousin, but for the Banishment of her Husband. (p. 91)

[*Juliet*'s] superior Affecion for *Romeo* is also painted by *Shakespear* in that Speech wherein she laments his Banishment, and acknowledges it is a greater Misfortune to her than the Death of all her Relations would be; but both these Circumstances the Translator has in common with *Bandello*: He differs from him in making *Juliet* complain of her Husband's Cruelty in killing her Cousin, and *Shakespear* has exactly followed that Hint. (p. 92)

In *Bandello*, the Friar, who is sent with the Letters to *Romeo*, is detained at a Monastery in *Mantua*: The Translator makes him be stopped at his own Convent in *Verona*; which last is followed by *Shakespear*.

There is no Mention made in the Original of the Apothecary, of whom *Romeo* buys the Poison; there we are only told that he had mortal Drugs in his Possession, which was given him by a *Spoletto* Mountebank in *Mantua*, long before.

The Translator makes him walk through the Streets in *Mantua* in order to find a Person that would sell him such a Composition, and accordingly he goes into the Shop of an Apothecary, whose Poverty is observable from the miserable Furniture of it; and he for a Bribe of fifty Ducats furnishes him with a strong Poison.

*Shakespear* has not only copied this Circumstance from the Translator, but also borrowed some Hints from him in his celebrated Description of the miserable Shop.

These few Instances are sufficient to prove that *Shakespear* took the Incidents on which he has founded his Tragedy of *Romeo* and *Juliet* from the Translation; and consequently that he did not peruse, because he did not understand, the original *Italian*.

His Management of the Tomb Scene, and the Death of the two Lovers, is entirely copied from the Translator, who differs greatly from the Original in those Circumstances. The plain and simple Narration of that melancholy Event in *Bandello* is more natural, more pathetic, and fitter to excite the Passions of Pity and Terror, than the Catastrophe of the Tragedy, as managed by *Shakespear*, who has kept close by the Translator.

In *Bandello*, when *Pietro* informs his Master of *Juliet*'s Death, Astonishment and Grief for some Moments deprive him of Speech; recovering a little, he breaks into Complaints and Self-Reproaches; then, wild with Despair, he flies to his Sword, and endeavours to kill himself, but being prevented by his Servant, he sinks into an Excess of silent Sorrow, and, while he weeps, calmly deliberates on the Means he should use to die in the Monument with *Juliet*.

The Translator makes *Romeo*, upon receiveing the fatal News, resolve immediately to poison himself; and for that Purpose *Romeo* dissembles his Affliction, and tells his Servant he will go and walk about the Streets of *Mantua* to divert himself; but his real Design is to procure some Poison, which having purchased of a poor Apothecary, he goes immediately to *Verona*.

*Shakespear* has here copied the Translator exactly, and makes *Romeo* in the Midst of his Affliction for the Death of his Wife, and while the horrible Design of killing himself was forming in his Mind, give a ludicrous Detail of the miserable Furniture of a poor Apothecary's Shop; a Description, however beautiful in itself, is here so ill timed, and so inconsistent with the Condition and Circumstances of the Speaker, that we cannot help being shocked at the Absurdity, though we admire the Beauty of the Imagination.

There appears so much Contrivance and Method in *Romeo*'s Design of buying Poison, and going to *Verona* to drink it in the Monument of his Wife, that he might expire near her, that we can hardly suppose it to be the spontaneous Effect of a sudden and furious Transport of Grief. In the Original therefore

we see him not taking this Resolution till the first violent Sallies of his Sorrow are abated; till after, in a sudden Transport of Despair, he had ineffectually endeavoured to fall upon his Sword; but while he forms that fatally regulated Design, he is dissolved in Tears, and plunged in a calm and silent Excess of Sorrow. (pp. 93-5)

*Romeo*, in the *French* and *English* Translations, dies before *Juliet* awakes, and the Friar and *Peter* enter the monument the same Moment that he expires; then *Juliet* awaking, they press her to leave the Monument, but she refusing, and they both being alarmed at the Approach of some Soldiers, cowardly run away, and *Juliet*, left alone, stabs herself with a Dagger.

*Shakespear* has copied all these Circumstances from the Translator. *Romeo* dies in the Play before *Juliet* awakes; the Friar fearing to be discovered by the Watch, as he calls it, but there is no such Establishment in any of the cities of *Italy*, presses her to leave the monument; she refuses; he runs away; and she stabs herself with *Romeo's* Dagger.

In *Bandello*, while the dying Husband is holding her lifeless Body, as he supposes, in his Arms, and shedding his last Tears for her Death, she awakes; she opens her Eyes, gazes on him, and entreats him to carry her out of the Monument.

*Romeo* is for some Moments lost in a Transport of Surprize and Joy to see her alive, but reflecting that he is poisoned, that he must shortly die and leave her, his Agonies return with double Force: How pathetically does he complain of his miserable Destiny! With what tender Extasy does he congratulate her Return to Life! With what affecting Sorrow lament his approaching Death, which must tear him from her! nor is the Astonishment, the Grief, and wild Despair of the wretched *Juliet* less beautifully imagined. (pp. 97-8)

Had *Shakespear* ever seen the *Italian* Author, these striking Beauties would not have escaped him; and, if by copying the Translation only, he has given us a very affecting Tragedy, what might we not have expected, had he drawn his Hints from the beautiful Original. (p. 99)

There is not one Incident of *Shakespear*'s Invention in his Play of *Romeo* and *Juliet*, except the Death of *Paris* by *Romeo*: This Character might have been very well spared in the Drama; his Appearance is of little Use, and his Death of still less, except to divert our Compassion from the two principal Persons in the Play, whose Deaths make up the Catastrophe of the Tragedy.

*Paris* seems only introduced to fall by the Hands of *Romeo*; and why must our Compassion of the unfortunate *Romeo* be suspended by the undeserved Fate of *Paris*? What Necessity is there for making *Romeo*, who is all along represented as an amiable and virtuous Character, imbrue his Hands in the Blood of an innocent Youth, (whose Death is of no Consequence) just before he expires?

This Incident, however, is the only one of the Poet's Invention throughout the Play: The Fable and all the Characters, except *Mercutio*, were formed to his Hands. (pp. 99-100)

[*Charlotte Lennox*], "Observations on the Use Shakespear Has Made of the Foregoing Novel in His Tragedy of 'Romeo and Juliet'," in her Shakespear Illustrated; or, the Novels and Histories, on Which the Plays of Shakespear Are Founded, Vol. I, 1753. Reprint by AMS Press, Inc., 1973, pp. 89-100.

## HENRY HOME, LORD KAMES   (essay date 1762)

[*Home disputes Shakespeare's adherence to the rules of tragic dramaturgy in* Romeo and Juliet, *asserting that such tragedies "of the pathetic kind," to the extent that they depict the sufferings of characters due to the accidents of fate, should always end on a "fortunate" note, which Shakespeare's play fails to do.*]

[Subjects] fitted for the theatre, are not in such plenty as to make us reject innocent misfortunes which rouse our sympathy, tho' they inculcate no moral. With respect indeed to subjects of that kind, it may be doubted, whether the conclusion ought not always to be fortunate. Where a person of integrity is represented as suffering to the end under misfortunes purely accidental, we depart discontented, and with some obscure sense of injustice: for seldom is man so submissive to Providence, as not to revolt against the tyranny and vexations of blind chance; he will be tempted to say, This ought not to be. Chance, giving an impression of anarchy and misrule, produces always a damp upon the mind. I give for an example the *Romeo and Juliet* of Shakespear, where the fatal catastrophe is occasioned by Friar Laurence's coming to the monument a minute too late: we are vexed at the unlucky chance, and go away dissatisfied. Such impressions, which ought not to be cherished, are a sufficient reason for excluding stories of that kind from the theatre. (pp. 380-81)

> *Henry Home, Lord Kames, "Beauty of Language: Versification," in* Elements of Criticism, *Vol. II, 1762. Reprint by Garland Publishing, Inc., 1971, pp. 353-463.*

## SAMUEL JOHNSON   (essay date 1765)

[*Johnson has long held an important place in the history of Shakespearean criticism. He is considered the foremost representative of moderate English Neoclassicism and is credited by some literary historians with freeing Shakespeare from the strictures of the three unities valued by strict Neoclassicists: that dramas should have a single setting, take place in less than twenty-four hours, and have a causally connected plot. More recent scholars portray him as a critic who was able to synthesize existing critical theory rather than as an innovative theoretician. Johnson was a master of Augustan prose style and a personality who dominated the literary world of his epoch. In the following excerpt, originally published as an endnote to* Romeo and Juliet *in his 1765 edition of Shakespeare's plays, Johnson considers the tragedy "one of the most pleasing of [Shakespeare's] performances," praising its various incidents, the "affecting" catastrophe, and the probability of events required by the rules of tragic dramaturgy. He also mentions John Dryden's comment on Mercutio (see excerpt above, 1672), disagreeing with that critic's claim that the young wit should have been allowed to live on until the play's end.*]

[*Romeo and Juliet*] is one of the most pleasing of our author's performances. The scenes are busy and various, the incidents numerous and important, the catastrophe irresistibly affecting, and the process of the action carried on with such probability, at least with such congruity to popular opinions, as tragedy requires.

Here is one of the few attempts of Shakespeare to exhibit the conversation of gentlemen, to represent the airy sprightliness of juvenile elegance. Mr. Dryden mentions a tradition, which might easily reach his time, of a declaration made by Shakespeare, that "he was obliged to kill Mercutio in the third act, lest he should have been killed by him" [see excerpt above, 1672]. Yet he thinks him "no such formidable person, but that he might have lived through the play, and died in his bed,"

without danger to a poet. Dryden well knew, had he been in quest of truth, that, in a pointed sentence, more regard is commonly had to the words than thought, and that it is very seldom to be rigorously understood. Mercutio's wit, gaiety and courage, will always procure him friends that wish him a longer life but his death is not precipitated, he has lived out the time allotted him in the construction of the play; nor do I doubt the ability of Shakespeare to have continued his existence, though some of his sallies are perhaps out of the reach of Dryden; whose genius was not very fertile of merriment, nor ductile to humour, but acute, argumentative, comprehensive, and sublime.

The Nurse is one of the characters in which the authour delighted: he has, with great subtilty of distinction, drawn her at once loquacious and secret, obsequious and insolent, trusty and dishonest.

His comick scenes are happily wrought, but his pathetick strains are always polluted with some unexpected depravations. His persons, however distressed, "have a conceit left them in their misery, a miserable conceit" [John Dryden, in his preface to *Fables Ancient and Modern*]. (pp. 956-57)

> *Samuel Johnson, "Notes on Shakespeare's Plays: 'Romeo and Juliet'," in his* The Yale Edition of the Works of Samuel Johnson: Johnson on Shakespeare, *Vol. VIII, edited by Arthur Sherbo, Yale University Press, 1968, pp. 939-57.*

## ELIZABETH GRIFFITH   (essay date 1775)

[*Griffith exemplifies the seventeenth- and eighteenth-century preoccupation with searching through Shakespeare's plays for set speeches and passages that could be read out of dramatic context for their own sake. Griffith, however, avoided the more usual practice of collecting and commenting on poetic "beauties" and concentrated instead on the "moral" subjects treated in the text. Concerning* Romeo and Juliet, *Griffith states that "were it my province to have selected the poetical beauties of [Shakespeare], there are few of his Plays that would have furnished me more amply than this." She adds, however, that with respect to Shakespeare's dialogue and plot there is little for moral evaluation, concluding that* Romeo and Juliet *simply demonstrates, through the tragic catastrophe of "the unhappy lovers," a moral against such reckless venturing and "unweighed engagement" as the characters undertake. Thus, Griffith is the first critic to suggest that the tragedy of* Romeo and Juliet *resides within the lovers themselves, and not within the realm of fate.*]

Were it my province to have selected the poetical beauties of [Shakespeare], there are few of his Plays that would have furnished me more amply than [*Romeo and Juliet*]. The language abounds with tenderness and delicacy, and seems to breathe the soul of youthful fondness; but neither the fable nor the dialogue can afford much assistance toward my present purpose; as the first is founded on a vicious prejudice unknown to the liberal minds of Britons, that of entailing family feuds and resentments down from generation to generation; and the second, as far, at least, as the lovers are concerned, though poetical and refined, is dictated more by passion than by sentiment.

But as my young Readers might not forgive my passing over this Play unnoticed, I shall just observe, that the catastrophe of the unhappy lovers seems intended as a kind of moral, as well as poetical justice, for their having ventured upon an unweighed engagement together, without the concurrence and consent of their parents. (p. 497)

*Elizabeth Griffith, "'Romeo and Juliet'," in her* The
Morality of Shakespeare's Drama Illustrated, *1775.
Reprint by Frank Cass & Co. Ltd., 1971, pp. 495-99.*

## THOMAS WARTON  (essay date 1781)

[*Warton asserts that Shakespeare, "misled" by Arthur Brooke's
poem, fails to include in his tragedy "a most affecting scene"
present in the Italian versions of the story, namely, Juliet's awakening before Romeo dies from taking poison. This departure from
his source plays, as well as Shakespeare's presentation of the
Romeo-Rosaline affair, received much attention in nineteenth-
century commentary on* Romeo and Juliet.]

It is evident from a coincidence of absurdities and an identity
of phraseology, that [Arthur Brooke's *The Tragicall Hystory
of Romeus and Juliet*] was Shakespeare's original, and not the
meagre outline which appears in Painter.... [The] original
writer of this story was Luigi da Porto, a gentleman of Verona,
who died in 1529. His narrative appeared at Venice in 1535,
under the title of *La Giulietta*, and was soon afterwards adopted
by Bandello. Shakespeare, misled by the English poem, missed
the opportunity of introducing a most affecting scene by the
natural and obvious conclusion of the story. In Luigi's novel,
Juliet awakes from her trance in the tomb before the death of
Romeo. (pp. 471-72)

*Thomas Warton, "Translation of Italian Novels," in
his* The History of English Poetry: From the Close
of the Eleventh to the Commencement of the Eighteenth Century, *Vol. III, J. Dodsley, 1781, pp. 461-89.*

## CHARLES DIBDIN  (essay date 1800)

[*Dibdin initially comments on David Garrick's alterations of Romeo and Juliet in his production of the play, stating that these
changes were "judiciously done" and not excessive, though he
also maintains that the Romeo-Rosaline affair, which Garrick
deleted, contributes to the "awful grandeur" of Shakespeare's
plot and to a principal theme of the play. This theme Dibdin
describes as a "solemn warning" to the Montague and Capulet
families, by the sacrifice of their children, "of the horrid effects
of domestic enmity." Dibdin is also the first commentator to note
that "Romeo's amorous apostacy" with Rosaline, as he calls it,
contributes to the sense of reckless love we see later in his relationship with Juliet. In addition, the critic remarks on Shakespeare's characterization of Friar Lawrence, the Nurse, and Mercutio. He disagrees with John Dryden's assertion that Shakespeare
should have let Mercutio live until the end of the play (see excerpt
above, 1672), stating that the dramatist rightfully disposed of him
as he did in order that the audience may view "with additional
horror" the grave consequences of the family disputes.*]

*Romeo and Juliet* is best known by that copy of it which is
generally performed, and in which GARRICK has very judiciously done little more than make SHAKESPEAR alter his own
play, fitting the catastrophe to the original invention of the
novelist. The two grand points that GARRICK, by the advice of
his friends, has insisted on, are the expunging the idea of
ROSALIND, and ROMEO's sudden inconstancy on the first
impression of JULIET's superior beauty, and heightening the
catastrophe, by ROMEO's first swallowing the poison, then in
the extacy of finding JULIET survive, forgetting the desperate
act he had committed, and flattering himself with a delusive
hope of future happiness, and, again, the astonishment and
delight of JULIET at recovering her lover, all which is instantly
damped by a discovery that her fallacious hopes are to be but
momentary.

It must be confessed these alterations are more admissable by
common auditors, than the incidents as they originally stood;
not that they were forced or unnatural before, for violent love
breeds with it inconstancy, because it is always inconsiderate.... (pp. 43-4)

But this does not seem to be all that SHAKESPEAR intended in
ROMEO's amorous apostacy. He has appeared to insist upon
this incident to give an awful grandeur to his plot, the great
drift of which is, and this has been but little considered, the
solemn warning to MONTAGUE and CAPULET, by the dreadful
sacrifice of their children, and in them to all other parents, of
the horrid effects of domestic enmity.

To bring about this great and important end, is ROMEO made
inconstant; is JULIET, who had been taught all her life to hate
the MONTAGUES, made as suddenly to fall in love with her
mortal enemy; or, as she describes it, her only love sprung
from her only hate. These circumstances discover a depth, a
solidity of which SHAKESPEAR is oftener capable than suspected. This love, so born, he contrives with the pen of a poet
and the hand of a master, in various ways and by various
degrees, to warm and encourage, till he makes even the Friar
consent to the union of the lovers, which it was positively his
duty not to do, from a reflection that Providence, from this
fortunate event, might so open the eyes of the parents to the
folly and injustice of their mutual and long-existing animosity,
"to turn their houses' rancour to pure love" [II. iii. 92]. (pp. 44-5)

Meritorious punishment has been clearly with [Shakespeare]
his decided drift. Even the lovers tender, delicate, and honourable as they are, merit punishment; for their conduct is
thoughtlessly a deviation from the very principles they profess;
it is born of imprudence, and nursed by deceit; and, in this
point of view, it is better that ROMEO should have been inconstant, and JULIET at least capricious.

Nay, the imprudence of the Friar, with all his wisdom and
sagacity, is most admirably thrown in. Having in one instance,
from the best motives in the world, done a positive wrong he
is obliged to persist, still comforting himself with the purity
of his intentions. He becomes the honourable pander of the
lovers, he leagues with a chattering and perfidious servant,
whose honesty he fears, and whose servility he ought to distrust. Instead of wisely attempting to apply a solid remedy,
instead of manfully stepping forward and avowing the marriage
of ROMEO and JULIET, at the moment she is menaced with the
hand of PARIS, and attemting, through the mediation of the
Prince, to bring about a reconciliation between the two families;
he, timid, irresolute, and one would almost think vain of his
judgment in the conduct of intrigue, advises a desperate and
unwise means, not to bring about any wished for end, but to
procrastinate and put off the evil day at the hazard of accumulated mischief.

The sum of his danger is by this time so ascertained that he
has cut off his own retreat. He, therefore, makes another confident in FRIAR JOHN, employs him to carry a letter, which
miscarrying, he seizes his iron crow and romantically undertakes himself to release JULIET from the vault of her ancestors.
All this folly is he guilty of, and yet you pity and almost admire
him from beginning to end; but remember it is impossible to
commend him, and this is the nice distinction SHAKESPEAR has
so well drawn; pointing out, that in the best and the wisest, a
single deviation from the path of rectitude must lead to remorse
and may, perhaps, to punishment.

As to the character of MERCUTIO, concerning which so much has been said and written, SHAKESPEAR has certainly introduced it to give fresh force to the colouring his main design. He represents this young officer as an elegant man, a complete gentleman, and an accomplished wit, and that the characters in the play, and the spectators at it, may look with additional horror at the family disputes of the MONTAGUES and the CAPULETS, he is lost, to one, at a time of life when his brilliant talents and engaging manners are at their height, and, therefore, ardently cherished by his friends, and, to the other, at the moment he has become their delight and admiration.

In the face of DRYDEN [see excerpt above, 1672] . . . , I look upon this to have been SHAKESPEAR's sole motive for killing MERCUTIO so early in the play. It had been said by the critics that SHAKESPEAR had so surpassed his own expectation in the character of MERCUTIO that he killed him in the third act, lest, had he continued him, he should have been killed by him; and this DRYDEN has affected to smile at, under an idea that he was "no such formidable person, for that he might have lived through the play and died in his bed without any danger to a poet."

This tradition, and this declaration are equally wrong. The trait of MERCUTIO's death, in the manner we witness it, is, for the reasons I have given above, a most affecting circumstance, and that SHAKESPEAR could not have carried on this character to the end of ten plays with the same force and spirit is ridiculous to assert. On the other hand; that DRYDEN, who was all candour and full of judgment, should think so indifferently of the wit of MERCUTIO, is not very easily understood, even with Dr. Johnson's mode of accounting for it, who says that, in this remark, "DRYDEN was not in quest of truth," and that "the sallies of MERCUTIO were beyond his reach" [see excerpt above, 1765], for no man searched more after truth than DRYDEN, and he has given sufficient proof in his own admirable writings that the higher the sallies of any wit were elevated they would the more easily come in contact with his genius.

But to put aside the curious question of whether or not SHAKESPEAR created a personage and then was so terrified at his formidable appearance, that he watched an opportunity and gave him an unlucky blow under ROMEO's arm for fear of worse consequences to himself; that great judge of nature, who violated propriety much seldomer than has been generally admitted, had a motive for bringing about this premature death which does not seem to have been noticed.

ROMEO, having killed TIBALT, it would have been mainfest injustice in the Duke not to have taken "the forfeit life of ROMEO" had he not qualified his sentence of banishment with describing TIBALT's crime to have been worse than ROMEO's. SHAKESPEAR, therefore, makes MERCUTIO the Duke's relation; "who, as his blood has issued from MERCUTIO's wounds," whose life ROMEO endeavoured to save, sees the crime in a much more heinous light in TIBALT than in ROMEO, and, therefore, when MONTAGUE pleads for his son saying that "he but took the forfeit of TIBALT," the discrimination of banishment is correctly consistent. Thus in perfect consonance to dramatic construction, a subordinate character is disposed of to give better opportunity of keeping a principal character in the fore ground; and this I believe is a rational way of accounting for this mighty circumstance which has created so much cavil than to suppose, admirable as the character of MERCUTIO is, that SHAKESPEAR was at all afraid of continuing it to the end with encreased warmth, had propriety warranted this necessity.

Before we leave *Romeo and Juliet*, we must not forget to notice the Nurse; a sort of character in which SHAKESPEAR took particular delight, because he delighted in every thing that was natural. He has made this talkative old woman full of self importance, and, therefore, she is permitted to take liberties which no other description of servants would dare to do; but having given her all the low and corrupted cunning of a thorough paced mercenary domestic, from her own depravity of mind and liquorish vanity, she endeavours to seduce that beauty and innocence which is the constant theme of her praise; and having persuaded her into something more than imprudence in her marriage with ROMEO, to avert the consequences, she does not hesitate to devise an infamous method of compounding the business by her marriage, nevertheless, with PARIS.

Thus she is possessed of cunning which is counteracted by her ignorance, thus she insinuates herself into the secrets of her young lady to gain over her an insolent ascendancy, and thus, a stranger to the gratitude due to her benefactors, she abuses that indulgence, and betrays that confidence of which they themselves ought to have known her unworthy.

There cannot be a properer lesson to parents and children than this. Half, perhaps nine-tenths of the various instances of family misery happen through the improper confidence placed in servants; and thus SHAKESPEAR has made this nurse, who after all may be in great measure excused on the score of pampered indulgence which she ignorantly takes to herself as her right, and implicit reliance which gives her a reprehensible importance, an instrument to shew by what natural degrees the smallest neglect of prudence in parents may produce the most fatal consequence to their children, and how a deviation of prudence in children may prove a source of misery and regret to their parents.

Thus is is impossible to blame any thing in the conduct or construction of this play. It is in vain to say that tragedy and comedy are unnaturally blended together, for the reverse is the fact. The story is purely domestic; and familiar circumstances, however productive in the end of distress and misery, ought not to be treated otherwise than as SHAKESPEAR has treated them, nay, in this play particularly, he has managed the comic part with a most happy judgment; for, as the play advances and the interest it is intended to create becomes more and more important, the comic characters drop off and leave the mind at leisure, without mixture or interruption, to attend to the plot as it approaches to, perhaps, the most interesting catastrophe ever represented to an audience; and here we have another proof of the great propriety of SHAKESPEAR's killing MERCUTIO in the third act. (pp. 45-52)

> *Charles Dibdin, "Shakespear's Plays," in* A Complete History of the English Stage, Vol. III, *1800. Reprint by Garland Publishing, Inc., 1970, pp. 30-65.*

### CHÂTEAUBRIAND (essay date 1801)

[*In the following excerpt, the noted French novelist and essayist Châteaubriand comments generally on Shakespeare's form of expression, which he states is frequently "inflated," "distorted," and "eminently wanting in simplicity." In support of this claim, he points to Romeo's description of the apothecary in Act V, Scene i of* Romeo and Juliet. *Châteaubriand's comments were originally published in 1801 in his* Mélanges Littéraires.]

[The] admirers of the tragic and comic genius of [Shakespeare] seem to me to be much deceived when they applaud the *naturalness of his style*. Shakespeare is natural in his sentiments and ideas, never in his expressions, except in those fine scenes where his genius rises to its highest flight; yet in those very scenes his language is often affected; he has all the faults of the Italian writers of his time; he is eminently wanting in simplicity. His descriptions are inflated, distorted; they betray the badly-educated man, who, not knowing the gender, nor the accent, not the exact meaning of words, introduces poetic expressions at hap-hazard into the most trivial situations. Who can repress a groan at the sight of an enlightened nation, that counts among its critics a Pope and an Addison, going into raptures over the description of an Apothecary in *Romeo and Juliet*? It is the most hideous and disgusting burlesque. True it is that a flash of lightning illumines it, as in all Shakespeare's shadows. Romeo utters a reflection on the unfortunate wretch who clings so closely to life burdened though he be with every wretchedness. It is the same sentiment that Homer, with so much *naïveté*, puts in the mouth of Achilles, in Hades: 'I would rather be the slave, on the earth, to a poor laborer, with scanty means of living, than to reign a sovereign in the empire of shades.' (pp. 432-33)

> *Châteaubriand, in an extract, translated by A. L. Wister, in* A New Variorum Edition of Shakespeare: Romeo and Juliet, Vol. 1, *edited by Horace Howard Furness, J. B. Lippincott Company, 1871, pp. 432-33.*

## AUGUST WILHELM SCHLEGEL   (essay date 1811)

[*A prominent German Romantic critic, Schlegel holds a key place in the history of Shakespeare's reputation in European criticism. His translations of thirteen of the plays are still considered the best German editions of Shakespeare. Schlegel was also a leading spokesman for the Romantic movement, which permanently overthrew the Neoclassical contention that Shakespeare was a child of nature whose plays lacked artistic form. In the excerpt below, taken from his* A Course of Lectures on Dramatic Art and Literature, *originally published in German in 1811, Schlegel stresses the lyrical beauty of* Romeo and Juliet, *describing the play as "a picture of love and its pitiable fate." But Schlegel adds that even in death the young lovers transcend despair, "for their love survives them, and by their death they have obtained an endless triumph over every separating power." The critic concludes with a comment on Shakespeare's mixture of contrasts and oppositions in* Romeo and Juliet, *an issue that continues to dominate twentieth-century assessments of the play.*]

*Romeo and Juliet* is a picture of love and its pitable fate, in a world whose atmosphere is too sharp for this the tenderest blossom of human life. Two beings created for each other feel mutual love at the first glance; every consideration disappears before the irresistible impulse to live in one another; under circumstances hostile in the highest degree to their union, they unite themselves by a secret marriage, relying simply on the protection of an invisible power. Untoward incidents following in rapid succession, their heroic constancy is within a few days put to the proof, till, forcibly separated from each other, by a voluntary death they are united in the grave to meet again in another world. All this is to be found in the beautiful story which Shakspeare has not invented, and which, however simply told, will always excite a tender sympathy: but it was reserved for Shakspeare to join in one ideal picture purity of heart with warmth of imagination; sweetness and dignity of manners with passionate intensity of feeling. Under his handling, it has become a glorious song of praise on that inexpressible feeling which ennobles the soul and gives to it its highest sublimity, and which elevates even the senses into soul, while at the same time it is a melancholy elegy on its inherent

and imparted frailty; it is at once the apotheosis and the obsequies of love. It appears here a heavenly spark, that, as it descends to the earth, is converted into the lightning flash, which almost in the same moment sets on fire and consumes the mortal being on whom it lights. All that is most intoxicating in the odour of a southern spring,—all that is languishing in the song of the nightingale, or voluptuous in the first opening of the rose, all alike breathe forth from this poem. But even more rapidly than the earliest blossoms of youth and beauty decay, does from the first timidly-bold declaration and modest return of love hurry on to the most unlimited passion, to an irrevocable union; and then hastens, amidst alternating storms of rapture and despair, to the fate of the two lovers, who yet appear enviable in their hard lot, for their love survives them, and by their death they have obtained an endless triumph over every separating power. The sweetest and the bitterest love and hatred, festive rejoicings and dark forebodings, tender embraces and sepulchral horrors, the fulness of life and self-annihilation, are here all brought close to each other; and yet these contrasts are so blended into a unity of impression, that the echo which the whole leaves behind in the mind resembles a single but endless sigh. (pp. 400-01)

> *August Wilhelm Schlegel, "Criticisms on Shakspeare's Tragedies," in his* A Course of Lectures on Dramatic Art and Literature, *edited by Rev. A. J. W. Morrison, translated by John Black, revised edition, 1846. Reprint by AMS Press, Inc., 1965, pp. 400-13.*

## WILLIAM HAZLITT   (essay date 1817)

[*Hazlitt is considered a leading Shakespearean critic of the English Romantic movement. A prolific essayist and critic on a wide range of subjects, Hazlitt remarked in the preface to his* Characters of Shakespear's Plays, *first published in 1817, that he was inspired by the German critic August Wilhelm Schlegel, and was determined to supplant what he considered the pernicious influence of Samuel Johnson's Shakespearean criticism. Hazlitt's criticism is typically Romantic in its emphasis on character studies. His experience as a drama critic was an important factor in shaping his descriptive, as opposed to analytical, interpretations of Shakespeare. In his commentary on* Romeo and Juliet, *taken from the work mentioned above, Hazlitt praises the play's lyrical, romantic, and sensual qualities, claiming that nothing in the relationship of the young lovers is "of a sickly and sentimental cast," but that their love affair "speaks the very soul of pleasure, the high and healthy pulse of the passions." The critic offers further analysis of the hero and heroine, and he claims that in its mixture of young and old, its conflicting views of love and sexual relationships,* Romeo and Juliet *"presents a beautiful* coup-d'oeil *of the progress of human life."*]

It has been said of *Romeo and Juliet* by a great critic, that "whatever is most intoxicating in the odour of a southern spring, languishing in the song of the nightingale, or voluptuous in the first opening of the rose, is to be found in this poem" [see excerpt above by August Wilhelm Schlegel, 1811]. The description is true; and yet it does not answer to our idea of the play. For if it has the sweetness of the rose, it has its freshness too; if it has the languor of the nightingale's song, it has also its giddy transport; if it has the softness of a southern spring, it is as glowing and as bright. There is nothing of a sickly and sentimental cast. Romeo and Juliet are in love, but they are not love-sick. Every thing speaks the very soul of pleasure, the high and healthy pulse of the passions: the heart beats, the blood circulates and mantles throughout. Their courtship is not an insipid interchange of sentiments lip-deep, learnt at second-hand from poems and plays,—made up of beauties of the most shadowy kind . . . , of evanescent smiles, and sighs that breathe not, of delicacy that shrinks from the touch, and feebleness that scarce supports itself, an elaborate vacuity of thought, and an artificial dearth of sense, spirit, truth, and nature! It is the reverse of all this. It is Shakespear all over, and Shakespear when he was young.

We have heard it objected to *Romeo and Juliet,* that it is founded on an idle passion between a boy and a girl, who have scarcely seen and can have but little sympathy or rational esteem for one another, who have had no experience of the good or ills of life, and whose raptures or despair must be therefore equally groundless and fantastical. Whoever objects to the youth of the parties in this play as ''to unripe and crude'' to pluck the sweets of love, and wishes to see a first-love carried on into a good old age, and the passions taken at the rebound, when their force is spent, may find all this done in the *Stranger* and in other German plays, where they do things by contraries, and transpose nature to inspire sentiment and create philosophy. Shakespear proceeded in a more straight-forward, and, we think, effectual way. He did not endeavour to extract beauty from wrinkles, or the wild throb of passion from the last expiring sigh of indifference. . . . It was not his way. But he has given a picture of human life, such as it is in the order of nature. He has founded the passion of the two lovers not on the pleasures they had experienced, but on all the pleasures they had *not* experienced. All that was to come of life was theirs. At that untried source of promised happiness they slaked their thirst, and the first eager draught made them drunk with love and joy. They were in full possession of their senses and their affections. Their hopes were of air, their desires of fire. Youth is the season of love, because the heart is then first melted in tenderness from the touch of novelty, and kindled to rapture, for it knows no end of its enjoyments or its wishes. Desire has no limit but itself. Passion, the love and expectation of pleasure, is infinite, extravagant, inexhaustible, till experience comes to check and kill it. Juliet exclaims on her first interview with Romeo—

> My bounty is as boundless as the sea,
> My love as deep.
>
> [II. ii. 133-34]

And why should it not? What was to hinder the thrilling tide of pleasure, which had just gushed from her heart, from flowing on without stint or measure, but experience which she was yet without? What was to abate the transport of the first sweet sense of pleasure, which her heart and her senses had just tasted, but indifference which she was yet a stranger to? What was there to check the ardour of hope, of faith, of constancy, just rising in her breast, but disappointment which she had not yet felt? As are the desires and the hopes of youthful passion, such is the keenness of its disappointments, and their baleful effect. Such is the transition in this play from the highest bliss to the lowest despair, from the nuptial couch to an untimely grave. The only evil that even in apprehension befalls the two lovers is the loss of the greatest possible felicity; yet this loss is fatal to both, for they had rather part with life than bear the thought of surviving all that had made life dear to them. In all this, Shakespear has but followed nature, which existed in his time, as well as now. The modern philosophy, which reduces the whole theory of the mind to habitual impressions, and leaves the natural impulses of passion and imagination out of the account, had not then been discovered; or if it had, would have been little calculated for the uses of poetry. (pp. 83-5)

This play presents a beautiful *coup-d'oeil* of the progress of human life. In thought it occupies years, and embraces the circle of the affections from childhood to old age. Juliet has become a great girl, a young woman since we first remember her a little thing in the idle prattle of the nurse. Lady Capulet was about her age when she became a mother, and old Capulet somewhat impatiently tells his younger visitors,

> I've seen the day,
> That I have worn a visor, and could tell
> A whispering tale in a fair lady's ear,
> Such as would please: 'tis gone, 'tis gone, 'tis gone.
>
> [I. v. 21-4]

Thus one period of life makes way for the following, and one generation pushes another off the stage. One of the most striking passages to shew the intense feeling of youth in this play is Capulet's invitation to Paris to visit his entertainment.

> At my poor house, look to behold this night
> Earth-treading stars that make dark heav'n light;
> Such comfort as do lusty young men feel
> When well-apparel'd April on the heel
> Of limping winter treads, even such delight
> Among fresh female-buds shall you this night
> Inherit at my house.
>
> [I. ii. 24-30]

The feelings of youth and of the spring are here blended together like the breath of opening flowers. Images of vernal beauty appear to have floated before the author's mind, in writing this poem, in profusion. Here is another of exquisite beauty, brought in more by accident than by necessity. Montague declares of his son smit with a hopeless passion, which he will not reveal—

> But he, his own affection's counsellor,
> Is to himself so secret and so close,
> So far from sounding and discovery,
> As is the bud bit with an envious worm,
> Ere he can spread his sweet leaves to the air,
> Or dedicate his beauty to the sun.
>
> [I. i. 147-53]

This casual description is as full of passionate beauty as when Romeo dwells in frantic fondness on ''the white wonder of his Juliet's hand.'' The reader may, if he pleases, contrast the exquisite pastoral simplicity of the above lines with the gorgeous description of Juliet when Romeo first sees her at her father's house, surrounded by company and artificial splendour.

> What lady's that which doth enrich the hand
> Of yonder knight?
> O she doth teach the torches to burn bright;
> Her beauty hangs upon the cheek of night
> Like a rich jewel in an Æthiop's ear.
>
> [I. v. 41-6]
> (pp. 86-8)

Speaking of *Romeo and Juliet,* [Schlegel] says, ''It was reserved for Shakespeare to unite purity of heart and the glow of imagination, sweetness and dignity of manners and passionate violence, in one ideal picture.'' The character [of Juliet] is indeed one of perfect truth and sweetness. It has nothing forward, nothing coy, nothing affected or coquettish about it;— it is a pure effusion of nature. It is as frank as it is modest, for it has no thought that it wishes to conceal. It reposes in conscious innocence on the strength of its affections. Its delicacy does not consist in coldness and reserve, but in combining warmth of imagination and tenderness of heart with the most voluptuous sensibility. Love is a gentle flame that rarifies and expands her whole being. (pp. 89-90)

The tragic part of this character is of a piece with the rest. It is the heroic founded on tenderness and delicacy. Of this kind are her resolution to follow the Friar's advice, and the conflict in her bosom between apprehension and love when she comes to take the sleeping poison. . . .

Romeo is Hamlet in love. There is the same rich exuberance of passion and sentiment in the one, that there is of thought and sentiment in the other. Both are absent and self-involved, both live out of themselves in a world of imagination. Hamlet is abstracted from every thing; Romeo is abstracted from every thing but his love, and lost in it. . . . He is himself only in his Juliet; she is his only reality, his heart's true home and idol. The rest of the world is to him a passing dream. (p. 90)

Romeo's passion for Juliet is not a first love: it succeeds and drives out his passion for another mistress, Rosaline, as the sun hides the stars. This is perhaps an artifice (not absolutely necessary) to give us a higher opinion of the lady, while the first absolute surrender of her heart to him enhances the richness of the prize. The commencement, progress, and ending of his second passion are however complete in themselves, not injured if they are not bettered by the first. The outline of the play is taken from an Italian novel; but the dramatic arrangement of the different scenes between the lovers, the more than dramatic interest in the progress of the story, the development of the characters with time and circumstances, just according to the degree and kind of interest excited, are not inferior to the expression of passion and nature. . . . Of the passionate scenes in this tragedy, that between the Friar and Romeo when he is told of his sentence of banishment, that between Juliet and the Nurse when she hears of it, and of the death of her cousin Tybalt (which bear no proportion in her mind, when passion after the first shock of surprise throws its weight into the scale of her affections) and the last scene at the tomb, are among the most natural and overpowering. In all of these it is not merely the force of any one passion that is given, but the slightest and most unlooked-for transitions from one to another, the mingling currents of every different feeling rising up and prevailing in turn, swayed by the mastermind of the poet, as the waves undulate beneath the gliding storm. (pp. 91-2)

The lines in [Romeo's] speech, describing the loveliness of Juliet, who is supposed to be dead [V. iii. 91-120], have been compared to those in which it is said of Cleopatra after her death, that she looked "as she would take another Antony in her strong toil of grace" [Antony and Cleopatra, V. ii. 347-48]; and a question has been stated which is the finest, that we do not pretend to decide. We can more easily decide between Shakespear and any other author, than between him and himself.—Shall we quote any more passages to shew his genius or the beauty of Romeo and Juliet? At that rate, we might quote the whole. (pp. 93-4)

William Hazlitt, "Characters of Shakespear's Plays: 'Romeo and Juliet'," in his Characters of Shakespear's Plays & Lectures on the English Poets, The Macmillan Company, 1903, pp. 83-94.

FRANZ HORN   (essay date 1823)

[Horn maintains, in an excerpt from Volume One of his Shakespeare's Schauspiele (1823), that the present ending in Romeo and Juliet is appropriate, and he considers mistaken the view that Shakespeare failed in not following his Italian sources by making Juliet awake after, rather than before Romeo dies. Such a scene, according to Horn, "would not be tragic, but an offensive piece of torture, irritating to the last degree."]

Some of the earlier critics [of Romeo and Juliet] have maintained that Shakespeare in the tomb-scene allows a very touching situation to escape him, for it is obvious enough that if Juliet had been made to awake just as Romeo took the poison, she might have had some very harrowing and effective talk with him. True, this is obvious enough, so obvious that for this very reason the true Poet scorned it.

Such a scene would not be tragic, but an offensive piece of torture, irritating to the last degree. Had the Poet aimed to gratify those readers who can never sup sufficiently on horrors, the proposed scene could have been got up with all the ease imaginable; nay, he could, of course, have had old Capulet, old Montague, the Prince and Friar Lawrence all die at the tomb, and then had an earthquake swallow up the entire city; it would have cost nothing but—ink. (p. 448)

Franz Horn, in an extract, translated by William Henry Furness, in A New Variorum Edition of Shakespeare: Romeo and Juliet, Vol. 1, edited by Horace Howard Furness, J. B. Lippincott Company, 1871, pp. 445-48.

ANNA BROWNELL JAMESON   (essay date 1833)

[Jameson was a well-known nineteenth-century essayist. Her essays and criticism span the end of the Romantic age and the beginning of Victorian realism, reflecting elements from both periods. She is best remembered for her study Shakspeare's Heroines (1833), which was originally published in a slightly different form in 1832 as Characteristics of Women: Moral, Poetical, and Historical. This work demonstrates both her historical interests and her sympathetic appreciation of Shakespeare's female characters. In the following excerpt from this study, Jameson offers the first in-depth analysis of Juliet. She describes the heroine as representing the idea of "love itself," this passion forming entirely her state of being and without which "she has no existence." Jameson also praises the romantic poetry "interfused through all the characters," and she comments on Romeo's previous love for Rosaline, claiming that "far from prejudicing us against Romeo" the affair "adds a fresh stroke of truth to the portrait of the lover." She concludes by examining the final scene of the play, saying that Shakespeare "has done well" ending the drama as he did.]

It is not without emotion that I attempt to touch on the character of Juliet. Such beautiful things have already been said of her— only to be exceeded in beauty by the subject that inspired them!—it is impossible to say anything better; but it is possible to say something more. Such, in fact, is the simplicity, the truth, and the loveliness of Juliet's character, that we are not at first aware of its complexity, its depth, and its variety. There is in it an intensity of passion, a singleness of purpose, an entireness, a completeness of effect, which we feel as a whole; and to attempt to analyse the impression thus conveyed at once to soul and sense is as if, while hanging over a half-blown rose, and revelling in its intoxicating perfume, we should pull it asunder, leaflet by leaflet, the better to display its bloom and fragrance. Yet how otherwise should we disclose the wonders of its formation, or do justice to the skill of the divine hand that hath thus fashioned it in its beauty? (pp. 85-6)

All Shakspeare's women, being essentially women, either love or have loved, or are capable of loving; but Juliet is love itself.

The passion is her state of being, and out of it she has no existence. It is the soul within her soul; the pulse within her heart; the life-blood along her veins.... (p. 86)

There was an Italian painter who said that the secret of all effect in colour consisted in white upon black, and black upon white. How perfectly did Shakspeare understand this secret of effect! and how beautifully has he exemplified it in Juliet!—

> So shows a snowy dove trooping with crows,
> As yonder lady o'er her fellows shows.
>
> [I. v. 48-9]

Thus she and her lover are in contrast with all around them. They are all love, surrounded with all hate; all harmony, surrounded with all discord; all pure nature, in the midst of polished and artificial life. Juliet, like Portia [in *The Merchant of Venice*], is the foster-child of opulence and splendour; she dwells in a fair city—she has been nurtured in a palace—she clasps her robe with jewels—she braids her hair with rainbow-tinted pearls; but in herself she has no more connection with the trappings around her than the lovely exotic transplanted from some Eden-like climate has with the carved and gilded conservatory which has reared and sheltered its luxuriant beauty.

But in this vivid impression of contrast there is nothing abrupt or harsh. A tissue of beautiful poetry weaves together the principal figures and the subordinate personages. The consistent truth of the costume, and the exquisite gradations of relief with which the most opposite hues are approximated, blend all into harmony.... The poetry, too, the richest that can possibly be conceived, is interfused through all the characters; the splendid imagery lavished upon all with the careless prodigality of genius; and the whole is lighted up into such a sunny brilliance of effect, as though Shakspeare had really transported himself into Italy and had drunk to intoxication of her genial atmosphere. How truly it has been said, that "although Romeo and Juliet are in love, they are not lovesick!" [see excerpt above by William Hazlitt, 1817]. What a false idea would anything of the mere whining amoroso give us of Romeo, such as he really is in Shakspeare—the noble, gallant, ardent, brave, and witty! And Juliet—with even less truth could the phrase or idea apply to her.... No, the whole sentiment of the play is of a far different cast. It is flushed with the genial spirit of the south: it tastes of youth, and of the essence of youth; of life, and of the very sap of life. We have indeed the struggle of love against evil destinies and a thorny world; the pain, the grief, the anguish, the terror, the despair; the aching adieu; the pang unutterable of parted affection; and rapture, truth, and tenderness trampled into an early grave: but still an Elysian grace lingers round the whole, and the blue sky of Italy bends over all!

In the delineation of that sentiment which forms the groundwork of the drama, nothing in fact can equal the power of the picture, but its inexpressible sweetness and its perfect grace: the passion which has taken possession of Juliet's whole soul has the force, the rapidity, the resistless violence of the torrent; but she is herself as "moving delicate," as fair, as soft, as flexible as the willow that bends over it, whose light leaves tremble even with the motion of the current which hurries beneath them. But at the same time that the pervading sentiment is never lost sight of, and is one and the same throughout, the individual part of the character in all its variety is developed, and marked with the nicest discrimination. For instance,—the simplicity of Juliet is very different from the simplicity of Miranda [in *The Tempest*]: her innocence is not the innocence

of a desert island. The energy she displays does not once remind us of the moral grandeur of Isabel [in *Measure for Measure*], or the intellectual power of Portia; it is founded in the strength of passion, not in the strength of character; it is accidental rather than inherent, rising with the tide of feeling or temper, and with it subsiding. Her romance is not the pastoral romance of Perdita [in *The Winter's Tale*], nor the fanciful romance of Viola [in *Twelfth Night*]: it is the romance of a tender heart and a poetical imagination. (pp. 87-9)

[Our] impression of Juliet's loveliness and sensibility is enhanced, when we find it overcoming in the bosom of Romeo a previous love for another. His visionary passion for the cold, inaccessible Rosalind forms but the prologue, the threshold, to the true, the real sentiment which succeeds to it. This incident, which is found in the original story, has been retained by Shakspeare with equal feeling and judgment; and far from being a fault in taste and sentiment, far from prejudicing us against Romeo, by casting on him, at the outset of the piece, the stigma of inconstancy, it becomes, if properly considered, a beauty in the drama, and adds a fresh stroke of truth to the portrait of the lover.... We must remember that in those times every young cavalier of any distinction devoted himself, at his first entrance into the world, to the service of some fair lady, who was selected to be his fancy's queen; and the more rigorous the beauty, and the more hopeless the love, the more honourable the slavery.... Romeo, then, is introduced to us with perfect truth of costume, as the thrall of a dreaming, fanciful passion, for the scornful Rosalind, who had forsworn to love; and on her charms and coldness, and on the power of love generally, he descants to his companions in pretty phrases, quite in the style and taste of the day... (pp. 95-6)

But when once he has beheld Juliet, and quaffed intoxicating draughts of hope and love from her soft glance, how all these airy fancies fade before the soul-absorbing reality! The lambent fire that played round his heart burns to that heart's very core. We no longer find him adorning his lamentations in picked phrases, or making a confidant of gay companions; he is no longer "for the numbers that Petrarch flowed in" [II. iv. 38-9]; but all is concentrated, earnest, rapturous, in the feeling and the expression. (p. 96)

His first passion is indulged as a waking dream, a reverie of the fancy; it is depressing, indolent, fantastic: his second elevates him to the third heaven, or hurries him to despair. It rushes to its object through all impediments; defies all dangers, and seeks at last a triumphant grave in the arms of her he so loved. Thus Romeo's previous attachment to Rosalind is so contrived as to exhibit to us another variety in that passion which is the subject of the poem, by showing us the distinction between the fancied and the real sentiment. It adds a deeper effect to the beauty of Juliet; it interests us in the commencement for the tender and romantic Romeo; and gives an individual reality to its character, by stamping him like an historical, as well as a dramatic portrait, with the very spirit of the age in which he lived. (p. 97)

In the extreme vivacity of her imagination, and its influence upon the action, the language, the sentiments of the drama, Juliet resembles Portia; but with this striking difference. In Portia, the imaginative power, though developed in a high degree, is so equally blended with the other intellectual and moral faculties, that it does not give us the idea of success. It is subject to her nobler reason; it adorns and heightens all her feelings; it does not overwhelm or mislead them. In Juliet, it is rather a part of her southern temperament, controlling and modifying the rest of her character; springing from her sensibility, hurried along by her passions, animating her joys, darkening her sorrows, exaggerating her terrors, and, in the end, overpowering her reason. With Juliet, imagination is, in the first instance, if not the source, the medium of passion; and passion again kindles her imagination. It is through the power of imagination that the eloquence of Juliet is so vividly poetical: that every feeling, every sentiment comes to her, clothed in the richest imagery, and is thus reflected from her mind to ours. The poetry is not here the mere adornment, the outward garnishing of the character; but its result, or, rather, blended with its essence. It is indivisible from it, and interfused through it like moonlight through the summer air. (pp. 102-03)

With regard to the termination of the play, which has been a subject of much critical argument, it is well known that Shakspeare, following the old English versions, has departed from the original story of Da Porta; and I am inclined to believe that Da Porta, in making Juliet waken from her trance while Romeo yet lives, and in his terrible final scene between the lovers, has himself departed from the old tradition, and, as a romance, has certainly improved it; but that which is effective in a narrative is not always calculated for the drama; and I cannot but agree with Schlegel, that Shakspeare has done well and wisely in adhering to the old story. Can we doubt for a moment that he who has given us the catastrophe of Othello, and the tempest scene in Lear, might also have adopted these additional circumstances of horror in the fate of the lovers, and have so treated them as to harrow up our very soul—had it been his object to do so? But apparently it was *not*.... [*Romeo and Juliet*] is in truth a tale of love and sorrow, not of anguish and terror. We behold the catastrophe afar off with scarcely a wish to avert it. Romeo and Juliet *must* die: their destiny is fulfilled: they have quaffed off the cup of life, with all its infinite of joys and agonies, in one intoxicating draught. What have they to do more upon this earth? Young, innocent, loving and beloved, they descend together into the tomb: but Shakspeare has made that tomb a shrine of martyred and sainted affection consecrated for the worship of all hearts—not a dark charnel-vault, haunted by spectres of pain, rage, and desperation. Romeo and Juliet are pictured lovely in death as in life . . . ; all pain is lost in the tenderness and poetic beauty of the picture. Romeo's last speech over his bride is not like the raving of a disappointed boy: in its deep pathos, its rapturous despair, its glowing imagery, there is the very luxury of life and love. (pp. 106-08)

The poem, which opened with the enmity of the two families, closes with their reconciliation over the breathless remains of their children; and no violent, frightful, or discordant feeling is suffered to mingle with that soft impression of melancholy left within the heart, and which Schlegel compares to one long, endless sigh [see excerpt above, 1811]. (pp. 108-09)

Anna Brownell Jameson, ''Juliet,'' in her Shakespeare's Heroines: Characteristics of Women, Moral, Practical, & Historical, *George Newnes, Limited, 1897, pp. 85-109.*

## SAMUEL TAYLOR COLERIDGE   (essay date 1834?)

[*Coleridge's lectures and writings on Shakespeare form a major chapter in the history of English Shakespearean criticism. As the channel for the critical ideas of the German Romantics and as an original interpreter of Shakespeare in the new spirit of Romanticism, Coleridge played a strategic role in overthrowing the last remains of the Neoclassical approach to Shakespeare and in establishing the modern view of the dramatist as a conscious artist and masterful portrayer of human character. Coleridge's remarks on Shakespeare come down to posterity largely as fragmentary notes, marginalia, and reports by auditors on the lectures, rather than in polished essays. Coleridge comments on a number of different aspects of* Romeo and Juliet. *He argues that ''the groundwork'' of the play ''is altogether in family life'' and that the feud is the source of all subsequent action. He then touches on the issue of Romeo's love for Rosaline and its effect on the hero's characterization. Coleridge next discusses the characters of the Nurse and Mercutio: he describes the former as ''the nearest of anything in Shakespeare to borrowing observation,'' the latter as ''the man of quality and the gentleman, with all its excellencies and all its faults.'' Last, the critic judges the so-called lamentations scene (IV. v.) ''excusable,'' but claims that it is difficult to determine how we are to react to the various outbursts of grief in this episode. Many subsequent critics, especially in the twentieth century, have evaluated this scene as a telling example of Shakespeare's manipulation of language in* Romeo and Juliet. *The date of the following excerpt is based on the year of Coleridge's death, since its time of composition remains in question.*]

[The] groundwork of [*Romeo and Juliet*] is altogether in family life, and the events of the play have their first origin in family-feuds. Filmy as are the eyes of party spirit, at once dim and truculent, still there is commonly some real or supposed object in view, or principle to be maintained—and tho' but equal to the twisted wires on the plate of rosin in the preparation for electrical pictures, it is still a guide in some degree, an assimilation to an outline; but in family quarrels, which have proved scarcely less injurious to states, wilfulness and precipitancy and passion from the mere habit and custom can alone be expected. With his accustomed judgement Shakespeare has begun by placing before us a lively picture of all the impulses of the play, like a prelude; and [as] human folly ever presents two sides, one for Heraclitus and one for Democritus, he has first given the laughable absurdity of the evil in the contagion of the servants. The domestic tale begins with domestic[s], that have so little to do that they are under the necessity of letting the superfluity of sensorial power fly off thro' the escape-valve of wit-combats and quarrelling with weapons of sharper edge, all in humble imitation of their masters. Yet there is a sort of unhired fidelity, an *our*-ishness about it that makes it rest pleasant on one's feelings. And all that follows to [the conclusion of the Prince's speech] is a motley dance of all ranks and ages to one tune, as if the horn of Huon had been playing. (p. 5)

If, as I believe from the internal evidence, this was one of Shakespeare's early dramas, it marks strongly the fineness of his insight into the nature of the passions that Romeo is introduced already love-bewildered. The necessity of loving creating an object for itself, etc.; and yet a difference there is, tho' to be known only by the perception. The difference in this respect between men and women—it would have displeased us that Juliet had been in love or fancied herself so. (p. 6)

The character of the Nurse [is] the nearest of anything in Shakespeare to borrowing observation. The reason is that, as in infancy and childhood, the individual in nature is a representative. Like larch trees, in describing one you generalize a grove. . . .

[Act I, Scene iv] introduces Mercutio to us. O how shall I describe that exquisite ebullience and overflow of youthful life, wafted on over the laughing wavelets of pleasure and prosperity, waves of the sea like a wanton beauty that distorted a face on which she saw her lover gazing enraptured, had wrinkled her surface in the triumph of its smoothness. Wit ever wakeful, fancy busy and procreative, courage, an easy mind that, without cares of its own, was at once disposed to laugh away those of others and yet be interested in them,—these and all congenial qualities, melting into the common copula of all, the man of quality and the gentleman, with all its excellencies and all its faults. (p. 7)

Something I must say on this scene [Act IV, Scene v]—yet without it the pathos would have been anticipated.

As the audience knew that Juliet is not dead, this scene is, perhaps, excusable. At all events, it is a strong warning to *minor* dramatists not to introduce at one time many different characters agitated by one and the same circumstance. It is difficult to understand what *effect,* whether that of pity or laughter, Shakespeare meant to produce—the occasion and the characteristic speeches are so little in harmony.... (p. 10)

> *Samuel Taylor Coleridge, "Notes on the Tragedies of Shakespeare: 'Romeo and Juliet',"* in his Shakespearean Criticism, Vol. 1, *edited by Thomas Middleton Raysor, second edition, Dutton, 1960, pp. 4-11.*

## JOHN QUINCY ADAMS   (essay date 1835)

[*Adams, the sixth President of the United States and an influential diplomat and congressman, was also an amateur literary scholar who wrote frequently on Shakespeare's plays. In the excerpt below, taken from an essay that originally appeared in the* New England Magazine *in December 1835, he applies the classic definition of tragedy to* Romeo and Juliet, *concluding that Shakespeare's play is a tragic work "of the highest order."*]

Tragedy, according to the admirable definition of Aristotle, is a poem imitative of human life, and the object of which is to purify the soul of the spectator by the agency of terror and pity. The terror is excited by the incidents of the story and the sufferings of the person represented; the pity, by the interest of sympathy with their characters. Terror and pity are moved by the mere aspect of human sufferings; but the sympathy is strong or weak, in proportion to the interest that we take in the *character* of the sufferer. With this definition of tragedy, "Romeo and Juliet" is a drama of the highest order. The incidents of terror and the sufferings of the principal persons of the drama arouse every sympathy of the soul, and the interest of sympathy with Juliet. She unites all the interest of ecstatic love, of unexampled calamity, and of the peculiar tenderness which the heart feels for innocence in childhood. (p. 222)

> *John Quincy Adams, "Misconceptions of Shakespeare, Upon the Stage,"* in Notes and Comments Upon Certain Plays and Actors of Shakespeare *by James Henry Hackett, third edition, Carleton, Publisher, 1864, pp. 217-28.*

## HENRY HALLAM   (essay date 1837-39)

[*Although he praises Shakespeare's unity of action in* Romeo and Juliet, *Hallam asserts that, among the dramatist's works, few "are more open to reasonable censure." Foremost of the play's shortcomings, the critic contends, is the overly poetic language—the numerous conceits, "frigid metaphors," and "incongruous conceptions"; all of this, Hallam states, interferes "with the very emotion the poet would excite."*]

The incidents in *Romeo and Juliet* are rapid, various, unintermitting in interest, sufficiently probable, and tending to the catastrophe. The most regular dramatist has hardly excelled one writing for an infant and barbarian stage. It is certain that the observation of the unity of time, which we find in this tragedy, unfashionable as the name of unity has become in our criticism, gives an intenseness of interest to the story, which is often diluted and dispersed in a dramatic history. No play of Shakspeare is more frequently represented, or honoured with more tears....

If from this praise of the fable we pass to other considerations, it will be more necessary to modify our eulogies.... [Few plays], if any, are more open to reasonable censure; and we are almost equally struck by its excellencies and its defects....

Madame de Staël has truly remarked, that in *Romeo and Juliet* we have, more than in any other tragedy, the mere passion of love; love, in all its vernal promise, full of hope and innocence, ardent beyond all restraint of reason, but tender as it is warm. The contrast between this impetuosity of delirious joy, in which the youthful lovers are first displayed, and the horrors of the last scene, throws a charm of deep melancholy over the whole. Once alone each of them, in these earlier moments, is touched by a presaging fear; it passes quickly away from them, but is not lost on the reader. To him there is a sound of despair in the wild effusions of their hope, and the madness of grief is mingled with the intoxication of their joy. And hence it is that, notwithstanding its many blemishes, we all read and witness this tragedy with delight. (p. 282)

The character of Romeo is one of excessive tenderness. His first passion for Rosaline, which no vulgar poet would have brought forward, serves to display a constitutional susceptibility. There is indeed so much of this in his deportment and language, that we might be in some danger of mistaking it for effeminacy, if the loss of his friend had not aroused his courage. It seems to have been necessary to keep down a little the other characters, that they might not overpower the principal one; and though we can by no means agree with Dryden, that if Shakspeare had not killed Mercutio, Mercutio would have killed him [see excerpt above, 1672], there might have been some danger of his killing Romeo. His brilliant vivacity shows the softness of the other a little to a disadvantage. Juliet is a child, whose intoxication in loving and being loved whirls away the little reason she may have possessed. It is however impossible, in my opinion, to place her among the great female characters of Shakspeare's creation. (pp. 282-83)

Of the language of this tragedy what shall we say? It contains passages that every one remembers, that are among the nobler efforts of Shakspeare's poetry, and many short and beautiful touches of his proverbial sweetness. Yet, on the other hand, the faults are in prodigious number. The conceits, the phrases that jar on the mind's ear, if I may use such an expression, and interfere with the very emotion the poet would excite, occur at least in the first three acts without intermission. It seems to have formed part of his conception of this youthful and ardent pair, that they should talk irrationally. The extravagance of their fancy, however, not only forgets reason, but wastes itself in frigid metaphors and incongruous conceptions; the tone of Romeo is that of the most bombastic common-place of gallantry, and the young lady differs only in being one degree more mad. The voice of virgin love has been counterfeited by the authors of many fictions; I know none who have thought the style of Juliet would represent it. Nor is this confined to the happier moments of their intercourse. False thoughts and misplaced phrases deform the whole of the third act. It may be added that, if not dramatic propriety, at least the interest of the character, is affected by some of Juliet's allusions. She seems indeed to have profited by the lessons and language of

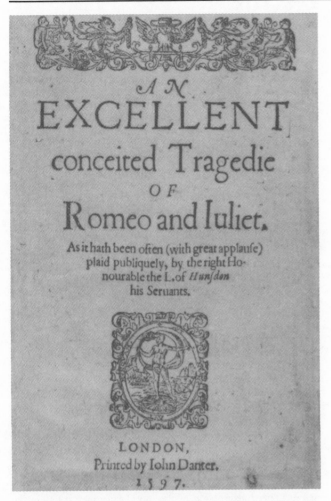

*Title page of the First Quarto of* Romeo and Juliet *(1597).*

her venerable guardian; and those who adopt the edifying principle of deducing a moral from all they read, may suppose that Shakspeare intended covertly to warn parents against the contaminating influence of such domestics. These censures apply chiefly to the first three acts; as the shadows deepen over the scene, the language assumes a tone more proportionate to the interest: many speeches are exquisitly beautiful; yet the tendency to quibbles is never wholly eradicated. (pp. 283-84)

> Henry Hallam, "History of Dramatic Literature from 1550 to 1600," in his Introduction to the Literature of Europe in the Fifteenth, Sixteenth, and Seventeenth Centuries, Vol. II, 1837-39. John Murray, 1905, pp. 249-87.

## HERMANN ULRICI (essay date 1847)

[*A German scholar, Ulrici was a professor of philosophy and the author of works on Greek poetry and Shakespeare. His study* Über Shakespeares dramatische Kunst, und sein Verhältniss zu Calderon und Göthe, *first published in 1839, exemplifies the "philosophical criticism" developed in Germany during the nineteenth century. The immediate sources for Ulrici's critical approach appear to be August Wilhelm Schlegel's conception of the play as an organic, interconnected whole and Georg Wilhelm Friedrich Hegel's view of drama as an embodiment of the conflict of historical forces and ideas. Unlike his fellow German Shakespearean*

*critic G. G. Gervinus, Ulrici sought to develop a specifically Christian aesthetics, but one which, as he carefully points out in the introduction to the work mentioned above, in no way intrudes on "that unity of idea, which preminently constitutes a work of art a living creation in the world of beauty." In the following excerpt from his* Shakespeare's dramatische Kunst-Geschichte und Chavakteristik des Shakspeareschen Dramas *(1847), Ulrici disputes August Wilhelm Schlegel's view that* Romeo and Juliet *is concerned primarily with the eternal and transitory qualities of love (see excerpt above, 1811), claiming instead that Shakespeare adopts love only as the foundation of his play, upon which he develops his theme of passion as a source of tragic pathos. Ulrici maintains that the purpose of the tragic action in* Romeo and Juliet *is to solve the contradiction in its double vision of the protagonists' love—the view that the lovers' passion is ennobling and purifying and, at the same time, dangerous in its exclusiveness, since it disturbs "the internal harmony of the moral powers." The critic avers that Shakespeare reconciles this contradiction and internal conflict through the deaths of the young lovers, which both "destroys the one-sidedness and immoderation of their reckless passion" and resolves the feud. Ulrici raises some other significant points as well; foremost among these are his claims that Friar Lawrence is not Shakespeare's spokesman in the play and that the Romeo-Rosaline affair is necessary to a proper understanding of the hero's character, besides offering a contrast with his later, more sincere love for Juliet.*]

"The ideal picture presented to us in 'Romeo and Juliet,'" says Schlegel, "is a glorious hymn of praise to that inexpressible feeling which ennobles the soul in the highest degree, and even changes the senses themselves into soul, but is at the same time a sad elegy upon its frailty, by reason of its very nature and of external circumstances . . ." [see excerpt above, 1811]. That the chief interest of this drama turns upon the loves of Romeo and Juliet, is self-evident. And yet I should not care to believe that the meaning and object of the whole was *only* to express the substance of what is eternal and transitory in love, *only* to represent the nature of love. In 'its very nature' love is by no means transitory, nor is it so by reason of 'external circumstances.' Moreover, to attain this end there would have been no necessity for the extensive apparatus, the quarrel and struggle between the two great families, the interference of the Prince, the participation of the whole community in the action. Love, as I think, rather forms but the ground upon which the poet here takes his stand, the central point of that side of human life which he wishes to describe. . . . He may conceive it thus: love, in the first place as the love of the betrothed, is the foundation of marriage, therefore of the family, and again of the state, consequently of the development and formation of the whole human race. It is, therefore, the central idea to which all life may be referred, and is, in reality, the highest and sublimest of what man possesses, for it is the source of all morality, of all beauty, of all human greatness. It is upon this foundation that Shakespeare raises his structure; from it he contemplates life and gives us a picture which becomes a tragedy because it is taken from the stand-point of the tragic conception of the world. In other words, the love of the betrothed is here but the material into which he breathes his breath, the breath of poetry, by working it into the picture of an aspect of life which is based upon the tragical view of life.

For this purpose Shakespeare raises love on to the sunny heights of the most glowing passion, and contrasts it with a hate equally passionate, thus making the nature of passion itself, passion in its two chief forms, the source of the tragic pathos; for love and hate are, so to speak, the two fundamental passions to which all others may be traced. Passion, however, according to the modern idea of tragedy, is a chief motive in tragic action;

for where its substance is great, noble and morally just—to which man, impelled by it, subjects all his powers and capabilities, his whole being and life—it is the expression of the highest dignity of human nature, of that ideal capability to be filled with enthusiasm for what is great, noble and beautiful, even to complete self-forgetfulness. But, in so far as man in passion—while aiming at the *one* great and beautiful object—not only forgets himself, but the general moral order of the world, and, in the pursuit of his own right, tramples upon the rights and duties of others, or, in so far as—blinded by it—he confounds the great and beautiful object about which he is wholly captivated, with the *enjoyment* which it affords *himself,* and seeks *his* own satisfaction only in the possession of it, regardless of the weal or woe of others—passion at the same time becomes the most pregnant expression of ethical weakness in the multifarious forms which it may assume, either as one-sidedness or limitation of the moral aim, or, as an error and perversity of judgment, or, again, as a weakness of will, or the want of consideration and self-control. (pp. 381-82)

Romeo's and Juliet's love is of an ideal beauty, the ethereal fire of two great, rich hearts, the tenderest and at once the firmest bond of two noble natures, which, as it were, are created for love and in their inmost nature destined for each other; the one beholding in the other its own more beautiful self, the embodied ideal of its deepest longings and strivings, the symbol of the highest ideal beauty.... This love becomes tragic, not, as might be supposed, in the antique sense—on account of its ideal beauty and greatness, through the envy of the immortal gods, or through the power of Nemesis, which threatens everything that is uncommon and extraordinary, nor from the prosaically correct, but unpoetical and ethically untrue reason, that love is but a special feeling ..., and that, therefore, it is not becoming in a man, at least, to be completely and wholly absorbed by it—but simply because from the very beginning, it was an overpowering and reckless passion as well.

This very passionateness is its poetry, its force and grandeur; quickened by its glowing warmth, the noble manliness of Romeo's character, and the lovely, tender womanliness of Juliet's nature, rapidly develop into full bloom; sustained by it, the two rise above all the petty, prosaic, selfish interests of love, and soar high above a common earthly existence, in the ether of the bright sphere of the ideal; steeled by it, they overcome the terrors of death, and in dying, put their seal upon the immortality of love, and sublimity of the struggling mind over suffering and ruin, the sovereignty of the realm of poetry over all hostile powers. But as, in consequence of this passion, they make the right of their love and sole, exclusive law of the world, their own good the general and sole good, and as they lose sight of the sanctity of the moral order of the world, so their passion, at the same time, is a rebellion against the prevailing power of the moral necessity; it separates itself from the organism of the whole; it, so to say, trespasses beyond the boundaries of the good and the beautiful, and by disturbing the internal harmony of the moral powers, involuntarily falls into the opposite domain. The lovers, by completing their union on their own responsibility against the will and knowledge of their parents, not only break through the barriers of custom and of tradition, but utterly destroy the bond, and injure the right of family relationship; they thereby offend a moral power which has the right—both internally and externally, to put itself on a perfect equality with their love. But their passion is mixed with the selfish instinct and desire of sensual enjoyment and personal gratification (as the second and third scenes of Act iii. distinctly prove). It is this element of selfishness—though

only a secondary, concealed and, it may be, natural element—that makes them lose that power of reflection and self-control, of which the great passion is not only capable, but by virtue of which alone it is able to accomplish what is great. This is why their passion degenerates into that blind fury, into which Romeo falls when—upon hearing that he is to be banished—he throws himself upon the ground, and is on the point of ruining all by a rash and senseless attempt at suicide. It is this same want of reflection and self-control that manifests itself in the inconsiderate haste with which Romeo throws himself between the swords of Mercutio and Tybalt, and thus having caused the death of the former, in a fierce single combat also gives the latter his death-blow; accordingly he himself lays the foundation of the tragic catastrophe. With the same inconsiderate haste, the same obstinate violence of mind, he rushes off to kill himself, upon hearing the accidental report of Juliet's death; he does not stay to receive a more accurate account, does not stay to ask Friar Laurence for further particulars, he merely follows the passionate impulse of the moment.

This reckless passion, this fatal vehemence of love is contrasted by a *hate* quite as passionate and as fatal. Hate is, as it were, but the reverse of love, the same passion in its negative force; the Nay which is directly contained in the Yea of love, and which expresses itself with the same energy against all that is hostile to it, as when asserting itself.... What [Shakspeare] had to do was to exhibit this correlation in the nature of love; and therefore he connects the passion of the lovers with an equally passionate hate which threatens their very existence. Their love has to overcome this hate and to assert itself in opposition to it; whether, and in what way their love conquers it, will be the test of their power and their right, the central and turning point of their fate. This explains the apparent contradiction that, from out of the very midst of the deadly enmity of the parents, there arises the consuming love of the children, extremes meet, not accidentally, but by reason of their inmost nature. The transgression of the moral law, which lies in the irreconcilable hatred of the parents, takes its revenge upon the children, and through them again upon the parents themselves. For the destructive element in hate exists also in love—in spite of the contradiction—for both are one in passion. Regarded in this light, even the foundation upon which the whole play is based manifests an internal necessity which determines its structure, and which has its seat in human nature itself.

This tragic contrariety is the key to the tragic action in all its essential features. The tragic conflict of the rights and duties is given: on the one side we have Romeo's and Juliet's love in the full justice of its ideal beauty, their marriage as a necessary demand of this love, not as a merely subjective, but as an objective *moral* necessity—for marriage ought to be desired where there is genuine and sincere love;—on the other side we have the equally justified right of the parents, the sacred sphere of the family bond, which cannot be broken with impunity. Accordingly, right and wrong are so interwoven with one another, that the right of the lovers is, at the same time, a wrong, their secret marriage both a moral and an immoral proceeding. The task of the tragic action is to solve this contradiction. (pp. 383-86)

As tragedy, according to Shakspeare's conception, stands in *direct* connection with the ethical laws of human life and the ethical motives of human destinies, so, that which in comedy appears to be the work of chance, of error and caprice, in tragedy appears as the result of an internal necessity. This is here shown by the principal events of the dramatic action. It is no matter of chance that Tybalt kills Mercutio, and Romeo Tybalt, but the unavoidable consequence, partly of the inconsiderate passionateness in Romeo's nature, partly of the prevailing hate between the two families. Both Mercutio and Tybalt are, therefore, by no means unnecessary, subordinate characters; the former in the cheerful levity of the coarse, quarrelsome, reckless humor—with which he, at the same time, counterbalances the dull seriousness of the passion which prevails all around, and relieves it of its oppressive weight—Tybalt in the blind, gloomy zeal of his savage nature—both are the active representatives of this party feud, which, as such, must inevitably express itself in murder and death. The calm, considerate Benvolio seeks in vain to extinguish the flames of the strife, but his function in the organism of the whole is to show that, in fact, it is inextinguishable; the two old men, Montague and Capulet—the actual originators of the feud—powerless and incapable of acting, yet for this very reason the more significant representatives of the invisible power of this hatred—are there, for no other purpose than to suffer and to reap the bloody harvest which they themselves had sown.

It is no mere chance that Romeo remains in the mistaken belief that Juliet is dead, or that the latter does not awake at least a few minutes sooner than she does, before Romeo has swallowed the poison. Friar Laurence's pious deception, which proceeded from the quiet solitude of philosophical enquiry, and his contemplative but loving view of things, cannot strike root on this unsteady, volcanic soil, amid the rushing torrent of such passions; such heterogeneous elements repel each other. As Romeo replies to the solaces of philosophy by attempting suicide, and as he casts off all reflection and consideration, he cannot, of course, be saved by the proferred help of considerate, meditative philosophy; it is the hand of that invisible divine power which guides the whole, which directs chance, and withholds Laurence's letter, in order that the tragic conflict may be solved in a truly tragic manner, in such a way that, at the same time, it is also conciliatory and elevating to the mind. (pp. 387-88)

As regards the characters, no one will deny, that in conception and treatment they entirely correspond with this internal necessity of the tragic action; the one is the direct result of the other. But as it is not my intention to enter very minutely into Shakspeare's skill in the delineation of characters. . . . I shall confine myself to some general remarks and to briefly defending Shakspeare against the unfounded censure which has been cast upon him, less in regard to the delineation, than in regard to the *choice* of his characters. Especial offence has been taken in this respect, at the person of the Nurse, at her equivocal stories and expressions her fondness for match-making, her fickleness and her entire want of character. . . . Schlegel . . . has made some excellent observations to justify the poet, but these, as it seems to me, do not hit the main point. At all events they do not decide the questions as to why this character—even though its truth to life and reality are undeniable—is conceived in this one light and in no other. In my opinion this seems to be a proof of Shakspeare's skill in furnishing a motive for every character, which skill has often been disputed, and certainly is often but very gently suggested by the poet. This lasciviousness, this delight in match-making, this eagerness to let her nurseling taste the pleasures of love as early as possible, this wantonness in the character of the Nurse—who takes the mother's place with Juliet, and has been her constant companion and attendant from infancy to girlhood—could not have remained without its influence upon Juliet's nature and the formation of her character; it partly, at

all events, accounts for her pining, longing for love, the impatience and the vehemence of the desire which so quickly leads the girl—still in the bud of maidenhood—into the arms of the lover, in utter disregard of the considerations due to her parents and family. The character of the Nurse, therefore, at the same time, casts a severe reproach upon Juliet's mother—obviously a proud, cold and hard hearted woman—who lets the Nurse fill her place, and consequently could not possibly have won her daughter's love and confidence.

Still less can I agree with the objection which supposes that Friar Laurence's undutiful compliance with the wishes of the lovers, is wanting in motive, unnatural and inconsistent with his character. Would Laurence's refusal have altered or improved the state of affairs? Would it have been able to cause the swelling torrent to return to its bed? Would not the passion of the lovers have rather taken illegally what was denied them by law? Laurence is portrayed quite in the spirit of the catholic clergy; as a father confessor, he is on intimate and familiar terms with the two lovers, he loves them himself with a paternal affection, and because he loves them he wishes to make them happy. Moreover, his heart is still warm enough to understand their glowing passion. This is why he unites them in marriage, this is why, after the proposal of Count Paris, he endeavours to save Juliet from the destructive anger of her parents; this is why he does not explain that she is already married, but recommends her that desperate 'remedy' which delivers her over to the grave. . . . Not only the happiness of the lovers, his own interests also, require that he should seek to save Juliet from despair and suicide by the 'desperate remedy.' Some critics have thought the good Friar a herald of the poet's intentions, through whose mouth Shakspeare is supposed to inform us that his poem is by no means a 'hymn of praise,' a 'deification' of love, but on the contrary, that it is meant, to show us that love is only a 'happy intoxication,' only a 'flower liked for its sweet smell, the poison of which, when taken as food, will work fatally upon the heart.' However, Friar Laurence is in reality not at all so prosaically wise and so good as his eulogisers suppose, he does not deny the ideal power and beauty of the love of Romeo and Juliet, nor the ethical rights of their love, otherwise he would not have married them—an action which directly contradicts his supposed disposition—he does not blame the passion itself, but merely its blind, immoderate vehemence. (pp. 388-91)

The intention, attributed to Shakspeare, is rather to be found in the character of Count Paris. It has been asked, what need is there, at all, for Count Paris and his love affair, and more particularly for the fight between him and Romeo? It is said that his death by the hand of the latter is obviously quite superfluous, wanting in motive, and as meaningless as a mere sensational scene. In answer to this it might at once be said, that nothing is superfluous that gives a clearer insight into the character of the principal hero, and that it must continue to be more fully and definitely unfolded throughout all the incidents of the action. But the chief reason for the death of the calm, cold, prosaic Count lies in his flat, dull and heartless conception of love, in his purposing to bargain with the parents for the beauty and amiability of their daughter—without first consulting the inclinations of her heart—in consideration of his rank, position and untried virtue. This is why the divine power of love, as it were, takes its revenge upon him; his manner of loving, therefore, forms the organic contrast of Romeo's and Juliet's passion; his fate is meant to show us that the poet, in representing the tragic fate of the great, beautiful and poetic passion, had no idea of speaking in behalf of common prose.

In a similar way Tybalt and Mercutio fall, not only as the victims to blind party feud, but also in consequence of their position to the fundamental idea of the whole. Mercutio, who does nothing but ridicule love, who fancies himself above it, and despises it as effeminate trifling, thereby as much offends the divine power of love . . . as does Tybalt the quarrelsome, the 'furious' and the revengeful, who in his uncouthness and savageness is incapable of entertaining the more tender emotions of the heart, and, accordingly, is equally at enmity with the ethical power of love. The same, lastly, applies in a still higher degree to the old Capulets and Montagues; hence they are even more severely punished by the tragic pathos than those who pay for their delusion with their lives.

Romeo and Juliet themselves are pre-eminently the vessels and instruments of this ruling power, this fatal power of love, and for the very reason they are the heroes of the drama, the bearers of the tragic pathos. Both are entirely absorbed in the one great, overwhelming passion; this passion not only forms and develops their character but is, as it were, itself their character, its development, is their life, their fate. Thus we find Romeo, immediately on his first appearance, absorbed in sentimental love for Rosaline. But this love is, in fact, *only* a sentimental fancy, only a desire and longing for love, not love itself; in this craving for love, which has complete possession of him, which urges and drives him onwards, he has made a mistake and taken the first beauty he met, not as the actual object of his love, but, so to say, as the representative, the symbol of the still unknown object of his ardent love. In order to give us a vivid picture of this thirst for love, this tendency of Romeo's whole nature towards being a hero in love, to give us an insight into his romantic character—which is a slave to imagination and emotion—and, on the other hand, to show us the difference between mere sentimental love and the true, genuine passion, between play and seriousness in love—which are so often confounded—the poet at first presents Romeo to us in that almost ludicrous form which is justly ridiculed by Mercutio. Rosaline's Romeo is a melancholy, heavy, idle dreamer, wholly absorbed in his own frosty reflections on the nature of love, which are more witty than true, and who tries to escape not only from the society of his fellow men but from his own self, so as, in solitude, amid sighs and tears, to build up another world and another self. Juliet's Romeo, on the other hand, is a cheerful, lively youth, of a sparkling mind and wit, still always reserved, it is true, and jealous of his blissful secret, but full of energy and vigour, all sinews on the stretch, every beat of his pulses a bold hope, an inspiring remembrance; he gives himself up to the world and is yet raised above it, he has the fulness of existence within his own breast and is nevertheless not satisfied;—the contrast cannot be greater. The former was the mere shadow of Romeo, an unfortunate gambler who has lost himself, an erring wanderer in search of his home; the latter is the true Romeo, who has found himself again in Juliet, and in her love first wins life and existence. For Juliet is Romeo in female form. Mrs. Jameson observes as ingeniously as correctly: 'All Shakspeare's women being essentially women, either love or have loved, or are capable of loving; but Juliet is love itself. The passion is her state of being, and out of it she has no existence' [see excerpt above, 1833]. (pp. 391-93)

Romeo's self also is nothing but love; each finds in the other only itself again. This unity of their inmost natures contains the sublime power as well as the ideal beauty of their love; their characters unfold all the wealth of their inner life in this unity, this double existence, and rises step by step with the course of the action, from the toying play of sentiment, through the manifold stages of feeling and emotion, soaring up to the sublime heights of tragic pathos, ever borne onwards by the waves of a glowing passion and an active, youthfully-enthusiastic imagination.

The peculiar colouring which Shakspeare has contrived to give his *diction* corresponds with the character of the two chief characters, with their lives and destinies, and consequently with the substance of the whole representation. The language, as it were, clothes the body of the drama like the wide-flowing garment of antique statues, which does not conceal the beauty of the bodily forms; but rather enhances and, as it were, multiplies them. It appears especially rich in youthful, flowery imagery, as appropriate as it is graceful, peculiarly elastic, pliant and melodious, full of lyrical elements, ever rising and swelling, and of the greatest vitality; it is an ethereal body in which all is pulsating, all nerves vibrating, now rocked in a smiling landscape by the balmy breezes of southern climes, now raised and carried along by the storm of passion and tragic pathos. But, inasmuch as the young and beautiful spirit of betrothed love pervades the whole, the language always flows along in the undulating line of beauty; even where the storm enters and waves rise, they do not break in sharp angles, but draw their deep furrows in round undulations.

The whole drama bears this same impress of youthful beauty in all its various parts. If 'Romeo and Juliet' be compared with Shakspeare's earlier dramas, with 'Titus Andronicus,' 'Henry VI.,' 'Richard III.,' which were written much about the same time, or with the later great tragedies of 'King Lear,' 'Othello,' 'Macbeth,' a striking contrast will become manifest. For while in these the action and tragic pathos seem placed in the hands of mature men, or of old but vigorous men, in the present case the heroes and bearers of the action, Romeo and Juliet, Tybalt, Mercutio, and Count Paris, are all persons in the bloom of youth. And while in the former cases the action, in the height of its development, presents us with almost nothing but scenes of horror and terror, in the present case it gives us nothing but pictures of grace and beauty; even the scene in the sepulchre containing the open coffin of the apparently dead Juliet, illuminated by Romeo's torch, is a picture surrounded by the charm of romantic beauty. And while in the former cases the tragic pathos appears carried to the climax of the terrible, the overwhelming, and the destructive, here it remains within the compass of beauty, and rises only up to a feeling of deep, intense sorrow. The lovely picture presented by the two lovers even in their death, softens the pain at their tragic end. Of all Shakspeare's tragedies, the one most closely akin to 'Romeo and Juliet' is his 'Hamlet;' but even here the hideous crime which forms the basis of the play and the horrible appearance of the ghost, obscure the ray of sweet beauty which is cast over 'Romeo and Juliet.'

This characteristic feature of beauty, this unison of peculiarly intense and tender harmony, which soothes all discords and lessens all harshness, is shown, lastly, also by the *composition* of the whole, which, in the genuine dramatic work of art naturally results from the choice of the characters, from the determination of their position in life, and from the development of the action in word and deed. For the composition, that is, the *form* of the artistic work which holds all the parts together, is, in fact, nothing but the harmonious co-operation of the constituent elements of the drama, that is, for developing and bringing into view the *idea* which forms its foundation. Shakspeare . . . is fond of exhibiting his leading thoughts in various ways and from different points of view. Thus, in the present case also, the fundamental idea is, as it were, carried out doubly, once thetically, by the main action in the loves of Romeo and Juliet, then antithetically by the secondary action, in the love of Count Paris for Juliet; directly and indirectly, however, in the characters, deeds and fortunes of all the other persons who take part in the action. For all, as we have seen, are placed in a definite relation to the tragic power of love which rules the whole, and assigns to them their parts, in accordance with their position. It is only at the end, at the catastrophe, that the idea of the whole bursts, so to speak, out of its enveloping calyx, and appears in the broad light of day as the fruit, the result of the represented action. The conclusion of the tragedy is the reconciliation of the tragic conflict, the solution of the contradiction into which the elements of the moral order of the universe have fallen with one another, owing to the weakness and delusion of its bearers. Romeo's and Juliet's love retains its right, but only in, and by death which destroys the selfishness of their desires and enjoyment, the one-sidedness and immoderation of their reckless passion, which injured the rights of others; in death, purified from the dross of earthly existence, they assume the glorified form of ideal beauty. Their love retains its right, for, in death the lovers are united *with* the sanction of their parents; the dissolving as well as assimilating power of death removes the contradiction of their existence, bursts the fetters which the party-feud placed around their loves, and melts the icy crust which had separated the hearts of the Capulets and Montagues; over their grave the furious party-feud ends in reconciliation and even resolves itself into love.

The fundamental idea of the whole, accordingly, is, we may say, the young man's view of life, but reflected within the tragic conception of the world. With him existence still turns entirely upon the love of his betrothed; his young and bold endeavour to open up the world for himself, and to conquer a place in it for himself, is concentrated in the possession of the woman he loves; she, whom his imagination has endowed with all heaven's gifts, is to him the living unity of all existence, the symbol, the personification of all bliss; to possess her, to lose her, is to him equivalent to life and death. The form, however, in which this love exhibits itself, in which its nature is conceived and its pathos passed through, is not only the most striking feature of a single character, but a pregnant expression of the character of all peoples and periods of civilization. Romeo's and Juliet's love is the poetic reflection of that conception which was peculiar to the spirt of modern Europe, more especially to the spirit which prevailed in Germany during the Middle Ages; it is the *romantic* form, the *romantic* idea of love. This sublime self-will, which risks all life for its union with the one individual, as if there existed nothing else in the world that was great, beautiful and amiable, is expressed in that boundless dignity and significance, which the modern view of life—in contrast to antiquity—attributes to the individual person, to man in his individuality. To exhibit the truth and everlastingness of this conception in tragic conflict with the weakness, one-sidedness and narrowness of human nature, but also in its tragic victory over all adverse and hostile forces, this is the true meaning, the ideal character of this tragedy of Shakspeare's, which is acknowledged to be one of the greatest masterpieces of dramatic art.

In conclusion let me add a few remarks in regard to the closing scene of the drama. It has been objected to, and sometimes altered or omitted, because it was supposed that Shakspeare had there offended the laws of dramatic art, insasmuch as,

instead of directly closing with the death of the lovers, he added a superfluous scene of explanation and enquiry which weakened the tragic impression. But is the scene merely one of explanation and enquiry? Has the tragedy no other object than of shaking the nerves of the spectators out of their ordinary state of lassitude, by scenes of murder and suicide? Would not the death of beauty, greatness and nobility leave the impression of a revolting murder, did it not, at the same time, express a soothing, elevating solace? And this solace, which is an element in the conception of tragic pathos—inasmuch as it also portrays human greatness and beauty in its purification, and hence in its true, ideal reality—sounds forth from this closing scene in the soft harmony of a calm, intense sadness, a harmony in which all harshness is resolved into sweet sound. The lovers have fallen victims to the hostile powers of their earthly existence, which check and combat all ideals; powers which oppose their union, partly from within, partly from without. But their love rises from the tomb pure and golden—like the Phœnix from the ashes—not only to obtain a happier existence in another world, but also to continue to live in this, and to prove its divine power in its victory over the grim hate which opposed it. No more significant, more exalting or more affecting funeral elegy can be conceived, than is here presented to the lovers—the victims of a high, noble and ideal striving—by the beautiful, deeply poetical drama. (pp. 393-97)

*Hermann Ulrici, "Romeo and Juliet," in his* Shakspeare's Dramatic Art: History and Character of Shakspeare's Plays, Vol. 1, *translated by L. Dora Schmitz, George Bell and Sons, 1876, pp. 381-97.*

## G. G. GERVINUS  (essay date 1849-50)

[*One of the most widely read Shakespearean critics of the latter half of the nineteenth century, the German critic Gervinus was praised by such eminent contemporaries as Edward Dowden, F. J. Furnivall, and James Russell Lowell; however, he is little known in the English-speaking world today. Like his predecessor Hermann Ulrici, Gervinus wrote in the tradition of the "philosophical criticism" developed in Germany in the mid-nineteenth century. Under the influence of August Wilhelm Schlegel's literary theory and Georg Wilhelm Friedrich Hegel's philosophy, such German critics as Gervinus tended to focus their analyses around a search for the literary work's organic unity and ethical import. Gervinus believed that Shakespeare's works contained a rational ethical system independent of any religion—in contrast to Ulrici, for whom Shakespeare's morality was basically Christian. In the following excerpt from his* Shakespeare (1849-50), *Gervinus focuses on two important aspects of* Romeo and Juliet: *its poetry and its central theme. He is the first critic to note that Shakespeare enhanced the lyric quality of his play through the use of such traditional verse forms as the sonnet, the epithalamium or nuptial poem, and the dawn-song. Regarding the play's central concern, Gervinus argues that Shakespeare is here preoccupied with the nature of intense, sexual passion, such as that of the lovers, and the paradox that such extreme passion can ennoble and purify individuals while it can also carry "man beyond himself and his natural limits," thus destroying him. Gervinus considers Friar Lawrence Shakespeare's mouthpiece within this tragic presentation of love, and he contends that fate has nothing to do with the events of the drama; all can be attributed to the rash behavior of the lovers, he adds, whose mutual need for a constant, true, and faithful love compels them towards a final union in death.*]

Every reader must feel that in *Romeo and Juliet*, in spite of the severe dramatic bearing of the whole, an essentially lyric character prevails in some parts. This lies in the nature of the subject. When the poet exhibits to us the love of Romeo and Juliet in collision with outward circumstances, he is throughout on dramatic ground; when he depicts the lovers in their happiness, in the idyllic peace of blissful union, he necessarily passes to lyric ground, where thoughts and feelings speak along, and not actions, such as the drama demands. There are in our present play three such passages of an essentially lyric nature: Romeo's declaration of love at the ball, Juliet's soliloquy at the beginning of the bridal-night, and the parting of the two on the succeeding morning. If in parts such as these, where the poet's great art for displaying character and motive found far less scope than in the dramatic and animated parts of the piece, he would maintain an equally high position, he must endeavour to give the greatest possible charm and value to his lyric expressions. This he did; it is to these very passages that every reader will always revert most readily. But while in these very passages he sought after the truest and fullest expression and the purest and most genuinely poetic form, we might point out an artifice . . . , or we might better say, a trick of nature . . . , which he employed in order to give these passages the deepest and most comprehensive background. In all three passages he has adhered to fixed lyric forms of poetry, each in harmony with the circumstances of the case, and well filled with the usual images and ideas of the respective styles. The three species we allude to are: the sonnet, the epithalamium or nuptial poem, and the dawn-song. . . . (pp. 205-06)

Romeo's declaration of love to Juliet at the ball is certainly not confined within the usual limits of a sonnet, yet in structure, tone and treatment it agrees with this form, or is derived from it. This style of lyric is devoted to love by Petrarca, of whom this play on love reminds us. Following his example, spiritual love alone in all its brightness and sacredness has been almost always celebrated in this style of poetry; never, with few exceptions, has the sensual aspect of love been sung in it. Yet every genuine heart-affection, when not arising from a mere intoxication of the senses, but taking hold of the spiritual and moral nature of the man, is in its beginning and origin ever of an entirely inward nature. A beautiful form may for the moment affect our senses, but it is only the whole being of a man that can enchain us lastingly, and the first conception of this being is ever purely spiritual. It is thus as judicious as it is true that in this first meeting, when the suitor approaches his beloved, like a holy shrine, with all the reverence of innocence, and avows his love with purely spiritual feeling, the poet has adhered to the canonical style of the lyric, as expressing the first pure emotions of love.

Juliet's soliloquy before the bridal-night . . . calls to mind the epithalamium, or nuptial poems of the age. The reader should read this wonderful passage, and the actress act it, with that exquisite feeling which moderates the audible words into silent thoughts. . . . Juliet, according to the ideas of those poems, supposes the presence of Love as understood; she designates him with the nickname of 'the run-away' . . . , which had belonged to him originally, because he was in the habit of running away from his mother. She longs for the night, when Romeo may leap to her arms unseen; 'even the run-away's eyes may wink' [III. ii. 6], she says; he may not, she means, fulfil his office of illuminating the bridal chamber, where in this case secrecy and darkness are enjoined. . . . The absence of the wedding feast, usual under happier auspices, leads Juliet naturally to these thoughts. No other voice sang to her the bridal song; she sings it, as it were, herself; and this casts a further melancholy charm over this passage, for the absence of the hymeneal feast was considered in olden times as an evil omen, and thus it proves to be here.

The scene of Romeo's interview by night with Juliet afforded the Italian novelists, after their rhetorical fashion, opportunity for lengthy speeches; Shakespeare draws over it the veil of chastity which never with him is wanting when required, and he permits us only to hear the echo of the happiness and the danger of the lovers. In this farewell scene there is no play of mind and ingenuity, as in the sonnet, but feelings and forebodings are at work; the sad gleams of the predicting heart shine through the gloom of a happy past, which the painful farewell of the present terminates. The poet's model in this scene . . . is a kind of dialogue poem, which took its rise at the time of the Minnesingers, and was designated the dawn-song. In England these dawn-songs were also in vogue. . . . The uniform purport of these songs is that two lovers, who visit each other by night for secret intercourse, appoint a watcher, who wakes them at dawn of day, when, unwilling to separate, they dispute between themselves or with the watchman as to whether the light proceeds from the sun or moon, and the waking song from the nightingale or the lark. The purport of this dialogue is of a similar character, though it indeed far surpasses every other dawn-song in poetic charm and merit.

Thus this tragedy, which in its mode of treatment has always been considered as the representative of all love-poetry, has in these passages formally admitted three principal styles, which may represent the erotic lyric. While it has profoundly made use of all that is most true and deep in the innermost nature of love, the poet has imbued himself also with those external forms which the human mind had long before created in this domain of poetry. He preferred rather not to be original than to misconceive the form suitable; he preferred to borrow the expression and the style which centuries long had fashioned and developed, for in this the very test of their genuineness and durability lay; and thus the lyric love-poetry of all ages is, as it were, recognised in the forms, images, and expressions employed in this tragedy of love. (pp. 206-08)

If we would now proceed to investigate the central point of the work, the poet, it seems to us, has afforded a twofold clue to it, with greater distinctness than is his wont. If we simply conceive the two principal figures in their disposition and circumstances, the idea of the whole becomes apparent of itself from the dispassionate consideration of the simple facts; the action alone and its motives do not suffer it to be mistaken. But besides this the poet has also by direct teaching given the clue which the reader or spectator might not have perhaps discovered from the motives and issue of the action. This twofold assistance, therefore, must guide us in our considerations; and we will first take the latter, which by a shorter path, though certainly with a more limited manner, accomplishes our purpose.

The oldest biblical story exhibits work and toil as a curse which is laid on the human race; if it be so, God has mixed with the bitter lot that which can sweeten it: true activity is just that which most ennobles the vocation of man, and which transforms the curse into the richest blessing. On the other hand, there are affections and passions given us to heighten our enjoyment of life; but pursued in an unfair degree, they transform their pleasure and blessing into curse and ruin. Of no truth is the world of actual experience so full, and to none does the poetry of Shakespeare more frequently and more expressively point.

Arthur Brooke, Shakespeare's immediate source for his drama, interspersed his narrative with the reflection that all that is most noble in man is produced by great passions; but that these incur the danger of carrying the man beyond himself and his natural limits, and thus of ruining him. In our drama the passion of love is depicted in this highest degree of attraction and might, affording at once the fullest testimony to its ennobling and to its destroying power. The poet has exhibited the good and bad attributes of this demon in that superior manner with which we are familiar in him, and with that noble ingenuousness and impartiality that render it impossible to say whether he may have thought more of the exalting power of love, or less of its debasing influence. He has depicted its pure and its dangerous effects, its natural nobleness and its inherent wiles, with such evenness of mind that we are struck with admiration at this mighty power, just as much as we are with wonder at the weakness into which it degenerates. There are but few persons who are capable of receiving the poet's view and of allowing his representation to influence them on both sides with equal power and with equal impartiality. Most men incline predominantly to one side only; readers of more sensual ardour regard the might of love in this couple as an ideal power, as a lawful and desirable authority; others of more moral severity look upon it as an excessive tyranny which has violently stifled all other inclinations and attractions.

Shakespeare has exhibited in this play the opposite extremes of all human passion, love and hate; and as in the *Midsummer-Night's Dream* the picture of maidenly discretion afforded a pleasing contrast to the intoxication of fickle sensual love, so here in the midst of the world agitated by love and hate he has placed Friar Laurence, whom experience, retirement, and age have deprived of inclination to either. He represents, as it were, the part of the chorus in this tragedy, and expresses the leading idea of the piece in all its fulness, namely, that excess in any enjoyment, however pure in itself, transforms its sweet into bitterness; that devotion to any single feeling, however noble, bespeaks its ascendancy; that this ascendancy moves the man and woman out of their natural spheres; that love can only be an accompaniment to life, and that it cannot completely fill out the life and business of the man especially; that in the full power of its first feeling it is a paroxysm of happiness, the very nature of which forbids its continuance in equal strength. . . . (pp. 210-11)

These ideas are placed by the poet in the lips of the wise Laurence in almost a moralising manner with gradually increasing emphasis, as if with the careful intention that no doubt should remain of his meaning. He utters them in his first soliloquy, under the simile of the vegetable world, which is occupying his attention; but he introduces them merely *instructively*, and as if without application; he expresses them *warningly* when he unites the lovers, and assists their union; and finally he repeats them *reprovingly* to Romeo in his cell, when he sees the latter 'dismembering' himself and his own work, and he predicts what the end will be. (pp. 211-12)

[Many critics] have opposed the moral which Friar Laurence draws from the story. Romeo's words of rebuff to the holy aged man, who with cold blood preaches morals and philosophy to the lover, those words: 'thou canst not speak of what thou dost not feel' [III. iii. 64], have been the guide of the Romanticists in their estimate of Laurence and his wisdom. That the words are spoken in the deepest distraction of a despairing man, whom defiance renders insusceptible of consolation, and passion incapable of all reflection, was never taken into consideration by them. And yet his Laurence is in this very scene neither delineated as a mechanical and pedantic moraliser, nor as a dry stoic. He has only too much sympathising regard for

the lovers, he enters upon a dangerous plan in order to secure their union, and the plan almost ruins himself. He attempts, indeed, to comfort this desponding man of love with the cordial of philosophy, but he devises also real means of consolation as good as any that *the lover himself* could have devised, and such indeed as he in his despairing defiance *could not have devised* for himself, and which not only comfort him, but for the moment cure him. Nor is it only the task of Laurence to reproach the foolish man, but even the nurse can do so, even his Juliet might do so. We err . . . in taking this pair as an ideal of virtue, but we err perhaps still more from the poet's aim in passionately siding with their passion. We have no choice left in that case but to blame the tragedist for unfair and unjust cruelty. For in their death following upon their life, we do not mean to say that Shakespeare made use of a narrow morality, that he allowed divinity and destiny to punish these mortals for the sake of this fault, just because an arbitrary law of custom or religion condemned it. Shakespeare's wise morality, if we may judge from those very sayings which he placed in the lips of Friar Laurence in that first soliloquy, knew of no such virtue and no such crime, warranting once for all reward or punishment. We have heard him affirm that from circumstance 'virtue itself turns vice,' and 'vice sometime's by action dignified' [II. iii. 21-2]; and as he here depicts a love which sprang from the purest and most innocent grounds, in its ascendancy, in its over-sensibility, and in its self-avenging degeneracy, he has elsewhere elevated that which we regard simply as sin into pardonable, aye, into great actions; for who would hesitate to break, like Jessica [in *The Merchant of Venice*], her filial piety; who would not wish to lie as Desdemona lies? Shakespeare recognises only human gifts and dispositions, and a human freedom, reason, and volition to use them well or ill, madly or with moderation. He recognises only a fate which the man forges for himself from this good or bad cause, although he may accuse the powers without him as its author, as Romeo does the 'inauspicious stars' [V. iii. 111]. With him, as throughout actual life, outward circumstances and inward character work one into the other with alternating effect; in this tragedy of love they mutually fashion each other, the one furthers the other, until at last the wheels of destiny and passion are driven into more violent collision, and the end is an overthrow.

Lingering thus on the moral idea of the play, and on the tragic conclusion to which this idea urges, it may appear as if the poet in delineating this rare love clung with greater stress to the severe judgment of the reflective mind than to the sympathy of the heart, and that he was too much inclined to do this for us to invest him with that strict impartiality which we have before extolled in him. But this reproach vanishes of itself if we carry our eye from the abstract contemplation to the action, from the bare isolated idea to the whole representation, to the living warmth and richness of the circumstances, the intricacies, the motives, and the characters. The idea which we have gathered from the didactic passages of the piece becomes more fully enlightened and enlivened in the consideration of the facts; not only does the moral of the action call forth the abstract idea, but the complete view of all co-operating circumstances, both within and without, challanges the heart and soul; the whole being of the spectator is called into judgment, not alone his head and mind. It is for this reason that the view of the action in all its completeness is ever the only accurate way of arriving at an understanding of one of our poet's plays.

We will now, following out our design, survey our drama also in this second manner, and study it in the broader and more varied aspect of its facts and acting characters. At the conclusion we shall arrive indeed at the same aim, but with our views much more enlarged and informed.

We see two youthful beings of the highest nobility of character and position, endowed with tender hearts and with all the sensual fire of a southern race, standing isolated in two families, who are excited to hatred and murder against each other, and repeatedly fill the town of Verona with blood and uproar. Upon the dark ground of the family hatred the two figures come out the more clearly. . . .

Romeo and Juliet share not the deadly hatred which divides their families; the harmlessness of their nature is alien to their wild spirit; much rather upon this same desolate soil a thirsting for love has grown in them to excess; this is more evidently displayed in Romeo, and less consciously so in Juliet, in the one excited rather in opposition to the contention raging in the streets, in the other arising from a secret repulse of those nearest to her in her home. The head of his enemies, the old Capulet himself, bears testimony of Romeo that 'Verona brags of him, to be a virtuous and well-governed youth' [I. v. 67-8]. However much, amid the increasing hindrances to the course of their love, a disproportion and excess of the powers of feeling and affection were developed rapidly and prematurely in both, the two characters were yet originally formed for a harmony of the life of mind and feeling, and rather for fervent and deep, than for excited and extravagant affection. It is no impulse of the senses, it is not even merely self-willed obstinacy which hurries them at last to ruin upon a hazardous and fatal path, but it is the impulse of a touching fidelity and constancy stretching beyond the limits of the grave. The quality of stubborn wilfulness which the friar blames in Romeo—a quality also apparent with womanly moderation in Juliet, when she opposes her parents' plan for her marriage—is certainly in both an heirloom of the hostile family spirit, but it is kept concealed by the peaceful influence of innate tenderness of feeling. It is excited in them only in unhappiness and under the pressure of insufferable circumstances; but even then in these harmless beings it is not pernicious to others, but its ruinous effects turn only against themselves. That which the friar calls 'grace' in the human being, by which outward and inward nobility in appearance and habits is intended, forms the essential nature of both; and if Romeo, according to the words of the friar, in misfortune and despair and under the influence of a defiant spirit, shames his shape, his love, and his wit—that is, all his endowments of person, mind, and heart—these endowments, these even usuriously measured gifts, still belong to his original nature, which appears in him, as in Juliet, in all its lustre when no outer circumstances cross and destroy the peace of their souls. (pp. 213-16)

Setting aside the later unravellings of the plot, the mixture of these beautiful and noble qualities of Romeo's nature with elements of evil is early apparent, even when he appears before us previous to his meeting with Juliet. This Romeo might be that servant of love, and our poem might be the volume spoken of in the *Two Gentlemen of Verona*, in which the writer says that 'love inhabits in the finest wits of all,' but also that 'by love the young and tender wit is turned to folly' [*Two Gentlemen of Verona*, I. i. 43-4, 47-8], and as the worm in the bud, is blasted. . . . The wise Friar Laurence perceived that 'affliction was enamoured' of the susceptible qualities of this deeply agitated and violent nature, and that he was 'wedded to calamity' [III. iii. 2-3]. Averse to the family feuds, he is early isolated and alienated from his own house. Oppressed by society re-

pugnant to him, the overflowing feeling is compressed within a bosom which finds no one in whom it may confide. Of refined mind, and of still more refined feelings, he repels relatives and friends who seek him, and is himself repulsed by a beloved one, for whom he entertains rather an ideal and imaginary affection. Reserved, disdainful of advice, melancholy, laconic, vague and subtle in his scanty words, he shuns the light, he is an interpreter of dreams, his disposition is foreboding, and his nature pregnant with fate. His parents stand aloof from him in a certain background of insignificance; he has no heartfelt association with his nearest relatives and friends. The peaceful, self-sufficient Benvolio, presuming upon a fancied influence over Romeo, is too far beneath him; Mercutio's is a nature too remote from his own. . . . Romeo feels himself little disposed to impart the silent joys and sorrows of his heart [to these two characters], and this constrained reserve works fatally upon his nature and upon his destiny. He entertains an affection, at the time we become acquainted with him, for one Rosaline, a being contrasted to his subsequent love, of Juno-like figure, fair, with black eyes, stronger physically and mentally than Juliet, a character not formed for ardent love, a niece of Capulet's, and a rejector of his suit. The vague necessity of his heart thus remains unsatisfied; he suffers . . . the vexing torments of a Tantalus, and the void experienced dries up his soul like a sponge. No wonder that he is subsequently overcome with the sudden intoxication of a nameless happiness, which too powerfully attacks this unfortified soul, sick as it is with longing and privation, and undermined by sorrow.

The Juliet, the heiress of the hostile house, who is to replace Rosaline, lives, unknown to him, in like sorrowful circumstances, though in womanly manner more careless of them. A tender being, small, of delicate frame—a bark not formed for severe shocks and storms—she lives in a domestic intercourse which unconsciously must be inwardly more repulsive to her than the casual intercourse with his friends can be to Romeo. Just as Romeo, when elevated by happiness and not depressed by morbid feelings, appears clever and acute enough, even showing himself in ready repartee equal or superior to Mercutio, so Juliet also possesses similar intellectual ability: an Italian girl, full of cunning self-command and quiet, steady behaviour, she is equally clever at evasion and dissimulation. She has inherited something of determination from her father; by her quick and witty replies she evades Count Paris; not without reason she is called by her father in his anger 'a choplogick' [III. v. 149]. How can she—with a mind so full of emotion, and a heart so tender, and with a nature evidencing an originally cheerful disposition—how can she find pleasure in her paternal home, a home at once dull, joyless, and quarrelsome? The old Capulet, her father (a masterly design of the poet's), is, like all passionate natures, a man of unequal temper, and fully calculated to explain the alternate outbursts and pauses in the discord between the houses. . . . The lady Capulet is at once a heartless and unimportant woman, who asks advice of her nurse, who in her daughter's extremest suffering coldly leaves her, and entertains the thought of poisoning Romeo, the murderer of Tybalt. The nurse Angelica, whose whole character is designed in Brooke's narrative, is therefore the real mistress of the house; she manages the mother, she assists the daughter, and fears not to cross the old man in his most violent anger. She is a talker with little modesty, a woman whose society was not likely to make a Diana of Juliet, an instructress without propriety, a confidant with no enduring fidelity, and Juliet at length suddenly rejects her. To these home surroundings may be added a conventional wooing of Count Paris, which for the first time obliges the innocent child to read her heart. Hitherto she had, at the most, experienced a sisterly inclination for her cousin Tybalt, as the least intolerable of the many unamiable beings who formed her society. But how little filial feeling united the daughter to the family is glaringly exhibited in that passage in which, even before she has experienced the worst treatment from her parents, the striking expression excapes her upon the death of this same Tybalt, that if it had been her parents' death, she would have mourned them only with 'modern lamentation.' (pp. 217-20)

[After] having become thus acquainted with these characters, we shall find, in sad succession, the fates of the lovers and of their houses intelligibly developed out of their own nature, and not out of the chance decrees of the goddess Fortune. Romeo certainly has nothing in his nature which would have actively kept up the strife of the families, but with his reserved temper he also certainly did nothing to relax it. This reserved nature now works in him afresh. Animated by his youthful happiness, he turns indeed suddenly as to a new life, and Mercutio is astonished at the ready wit of his melancholy friend; still his cheerful humour does not go so far as to dispose him to free communication. He hides his successful affection from his friends more carefully than his sorrow for Rosaline; this reserved enjoyment of requited love belongs in general but rarely to the man's nature and temper. His friends were unquestionably more worthy of his confidence than the nurse was of Juliet's; had he communicated his feelings to them, Mercutio would have avoided the wantonly sought combat with Tybalt; Romeo would not have killed Tybalt, and the first seed of the rapidly rising mischief would not have been sown. With considerate moderation Romeo has the prudence to avoid Tybalt, but not to forbear whispering a word in the ear of his friend; much less we may believe can he restrain the flaming fire of vengeance, when the triumphant murderer of his friend returns. When he has killed him, in his stubborn taciturn manner he compresses his complete expectation of a dreaded fate into the words, 'I am fortune's fool!' [III. i. 136] just as subsequently, after Juliet's death, he throws into one sentence his despair and defiance; a more open nature would have at both times avoided the extremity by communication. In him a hidden fire burns with a dangerous flame; his slight forebodings are fulfilled, not because a blind chance causes them to be realised, but because his fatal propensity urges him to rash deeds; he calls that fortune which is the work of his own nature. (p. 223)

If in the [aftermath of Tybalt's death] Romeo less deserved our approbation, [her betrothal to Paris] placed Juliet in the same position; if the man in the one lost his manly nature, Juliet in the other was carried out of her womanly sphere. Lately elevated by the happiness of Romeo's society, she had lost the delicate line of propriety within which her being moved. Even when her mother speaks of her design of causing Romeo to be poisoned, she plays too wantonly with her words, when she ought rather to have been full of care; and when her mother then announces to her the unasked-for husband, she has lost her former craftiness in delaying the marriage with a mild request or with a clever pretext; she is scornful towards her mother, straightforward and open to her father whose caprice and passion she provokes, and subsequently she trifles with confession and sacred things in a manner not altogether womanly. But in order that, even here, we should not lose our sympathy with this being, the catastrophe at the same time calls forth all the moral elevation of her nature. When she is abandoned by father and mother, and is at length heartlessly advised by her nurse to separate from Romeo, she throws off even this last support; she rises grandly above the 'ancient

damnation,' faithlessness, and perjury, and prefers to strike a death-blow to hand and heart than to turn with perfidious desertion to another. When obstacles cross love, it rises to its utmost height; when compulsion and force would annihilate it, faithfulness and constancy become the sole duty. And this it is which, in the midst of the tragic defeat of this love, glorifies its victory. If the lovers, full of sensual ardour, had once innocently aspired after happiness and enjoyment, they now, witout hesitation and with moral steadfastness, hastened towards the death which would inseparably unite them. Overexcited by the alternations of joy and sorrow, agitated by sleepless nights, rendered undutiful on the threshold of a forced marriage, no sooner is Juliet alone, than those sluices of her hopelessness are opened wide which previously womanly dissimulation had closed: she longs to die. But still not even now does she lose her womanly self-command. Her first course is to ask counsel of Friar Laurence; her ultimate design is suicide; her firm will calls the friar into its desperate counsels. It is a fearful adventure upon which Juliet unscrupulously resolves, although shortly before its execution womanly nature and timidity, after all the excitement endured, demand a natural tribute. But at the same time it is an ingeniously hazardous game, practicable to the circumspect Juliet, but not so to a man of such vast passions as Romeo. He had arranged with Laurence to receive intelligence by means of his man, but he had also promised Juliet to omit no opportunity of conveying his greetings to her; he had sent his servant also to Juliet. To such an extent does the impatience of love cross the unimpassioned hand of the trusted watcher over its fate. Balthazar comes with the sad tidings of Juliet's death; it falls upon the man, who in his solitary and fatal mood had, waking or asleep, dreamed and brooded only over death and poison. In the Italian tales, Romeo raves in a long speech; in Shakespeare, one sentence—'Is it even so? then I defy you, stars!' [V. i. 24] decides the rash, obstinate resolve, with the dumb despair of a nature inwardly tumultuous, such as we know Romeo's to have been. He defies the fate that would have helped him had he consented to its rule; he crosses it with the self-will of hardened defiance, which, once on the path of evil, only too readily rushes towards the utmost limit, as if delighting in self-annihilation. In this agitation of mind, Romeo, in a moral point of view, will scarcely appear to us any longer accountable. The strength of the impulse of love, which with overwhelming force made him seek for that final union with his Juliet, and the hearty fidelity with which, undoubtedly, he felt himself inviolably bound to follow his dead beloved one in her dread journey, excite in us only the one feeling of painful admiration. (pp. 225-27)

We cannot accuse any blind accident of fate, nor can we blame any arbitrary exercise of punishment on the part of the poet; it is this tumultuous nature alone, in the violence of one happy and yet fatal passion, which shatters the helm of its own preservation, and exercises justice upon itself. . . . Over the grave of this unbounded single love, general irreconcilable hate is extinguished, and peace is again restored to the families and to the town. Just as this vehemence of love could arise only amid the narrowing hate of the families, and amid the continual fear of disturbance, so the hate of the families seemed only able to be extinguished by the sacrifice of their noblest members. The exuberance of the love which killed them overflowed after their death, and the blood shed prepared the soil for reconciliation, which could not take root before. The happiness of their love was, as it says in the *Midsummer-Night's Dream*,

> momentary as a sound,
> Swift as a shadow, short as any dream:
> Brief as the lightning in the collied night,

That in a spleen, unfolds both heaven and earth,
And ere a man hath power to say,—Behold!
The jaws of darkness do devour it up;
        [*A Midsummer Night's Dream*, I. i. 143-48]

but in this lightning, the storm-laden air hanging over the state of Verona disburdened itself, and the last transient storm-cloud gave place to the first gleams of enduring brightness. (pp. 228-29)

> G. G. Gervinus, "Second Period of Shakespeare's Dramatic Poetry: 'Romeo and Juliet'," in his Shakespeare Commentaries, *translated by F. E. Bunnètt, revised edition, 1877. Reprint by AMS Press, Inc., 1971, pp. 204-29.*

## M. GUIZOT (essay date 1852)

[*Guizot discusses the contrast in* Romeo and Juliet *between "the depth of the feelings which the poet describes, and the form in which he expresses them." Although the critic admires Shakespeare's handling of the innocent and ideal love of the protagonists, he disparages the language in which he presents this passion, stating that "its expression is often factitious, laden with developments and ornaments . . . which do not flow naturally from the lips of a dramatic personage."*]

[Throughout "Romeo and Juliet"] Shakspeare has abandoned himself without constraint to that abundance of reflection and discourse which is one of the characteristics of his genius. Nowhere is the contrast more striking between the depth of the feelings which the poet describes, and the form in which he expresses them. Shakspeare excels in seeing our human feelings as they really exist in nature, without premeditation, without any labor of man upon himself, ingenuous and impetuous, mingled of good and evil, of vulgar instincts and sublime inspirations, just as the human soul is, in its primitive and spontaneous state. What can be more truthful than the love of Romeo and Juliet, so young, so ardent, so unreflecting, full at once of physical passion and of moral tenderness, without restraint, and yet without coarseness, because delicacy of heart ever combines with the transports of the senses! There is nothing subtle or factitious in it, and nothing cleverly arranged by the poet; it is neither the pure love of piously exalted imaginations, nor the licentious love of palled and perverted lives; it is love itself—love complete, involuntary and sovereign, as it bursts forth in early youth, in the heart of man, at once simple and diverse, as God made it. "Romeo and Juliet" is truly the tragedy of love, as "Othello" is that of jealousy, and "Macbeth" that of ambition. Each of the great dramas of Shakspeare is dedicated to one of the great feelings of humanity; and the feeling which pervades the drama is, in very reality, that which occupies and possesses the human soul when under its influence. Shakspeare omits, adds, and alters nothing; he brings it on the stage simply and boldly, in its energetic and complete truth.

Pass now from the substance to the form, and from the feeling itself to the language in which it is clothed by the poet; and observe the contrast! In proportion as the feeling is true and profoundly known and understood, its expression is often factitious, laden with developments and ornaments in which the mind of the poet takes delight, but which do not flow naturally from the lips of a dramatic personage. Of all Shakspeare's great dramas, "Romeo and Juliet" is, perhaps, the one in which this fault is most abundant. We might almost say that Shakspeare had attempted to imitate that copiousness of words,

and that verbose facility which, in literature as well as life, generally characterize the peoples of the South. He had certainly read, at least in translation, some of the Italian poets; and the innumerable subtleties interwoven, as it were, into the language of all the personages in "Romeo and Juliet," and the introduction of continual comparisons with the sun, the flowers, and the stars, though often brilliant and graceful, are evidently an imitation of the style of the sonnets, and a dept paid to local coloring. It is, perhaps, because the Italian sonnets almost always adopt a plaintive tone, that choice and exaggeration of language are particularly perceptible in the complaints of the two lovers. The expression of their brief happiness in, especially in the mouth of Juliet, of ravishing simplicity; and when they reach the final term of their destiny, when the poet enters upon the last scene of this mournful tragedy, he renounces all his attempts at imitation, and all his wittily wise reflections. His characters, who, says Johnson, "have a conceit left them in their misery," lose this peculiarity when misery has struck its heavy blows; the imagination ceases to play; passion itself no longer appears, unless united to solid, serious, and almost stern feelings; and that mistress, who was so eager for the joys of love, Juliet, when threatened in her conjugal fidelity, thinks of nothing but the fulfillment of her duties, and how she may remain without blemish the wife of her dear Romeo. What an admirable trait of moral sense and good sense is this in a genius devoted to the delineation of passion!

However, Shakspeare was mistaken when he thought that, by prodigality of reflections, imagery, and words, he was imitating Italy and her poets. At least he was not imitating the masters of Italian poetry, his equals, and the only ones who deserved his notice. Between them and him, the difference is immense and singular. It is in comprehension of the natural feelings that Shakspeare excels, and he depicts them with as much simplicity and truth of substance as he clothes them with affectation and sometimes whimsicality of language. It is, on the contrary, into these feelings themselves that the great Italian poets of the fourteenth century, and especially Petrarch, frequently introduce as much refinement and subtlety as elevation and grace; they alter and transform, according to their religious and moral beliefs, or even to their literary tastes, those instincts and passions of the human heart to which Shakspeare leaves their native physiognomy and liberty. What can be less similar than the love of Petrarch for Laura, and that of Juliet for Romeo? In compensation, the expression, in Petrarch, is almost always as natural as the feeling is refined; and whereas Shakspeare presents perfectly simple and true emotions beneath a strange and affected form, Petrarch lends to mystical, or at least singular and very restrained emotions, all the charm of a simple and pure form. (pp. 167-70)

I need not insist upon the comparison; who does not feel how much more simple and beautiful the form of expression is in Petrarch? It is the brilliant and flowing poetry of the South, beside the strong, rough, and vigorous imagination of the North. (p. 171)

Wherever they are not disfigured by conceits, the lines in "Romeo and Juliet" are perhaps the most graceful and brilliant that ever flowed from Shakspeare's pen. They are, for the most part, written in rhyme, another homage paid to Italian habits. (p. 173)

> M. Guizot, "'Romeo and Juliet'," in his Shakspeare and His Times, *Harper & Brothers, Publishers, 1852, pp. 161-73.*

## ALFRED MÉZIÈRES   (essay date 1860)

[*In the following excerpt from his* Shakspeare, ses oeuvres et ses critiques *(1860), Mézières praises Shakespeare's ability to sympathize with the plight of the young lovers in his play while at the same time provide "the calmest observation and analysis of the events which must needs be narrated in burning words." Mézières adds that the friar's philosophy of moderation "is but the judgement which the poet pronounces from the background of the tragedy."*]

Like a great poet who knows all the storms of youth and love, Shakespeare painted the lofty sentiments, the burning passions, the headlong actions, the countless joys and sorrows of which the tissue of [*Romeo and Juliet*] is woven. But he was not only the limner of the passions, he was their judge, and herein, perchance, lies the greatest wonder of his genius. There is nothing, in sooth, more difficult than to identify one's self, on the one hand, with characters hurried away by passion, while, on the other, the entire freedom of an impartial spectator is reserved for the calmest observation and analysis of the events which must needs be narrated in burning words. [Shakspeare] seems to share in all the illusion and enthusiasm of the lovers, and yet at the very instant that he is pouring forth like fire their intense emotion he fixes on them the calm gaze of a philosopher. The philosophy of the Friar is but the judgement which the poet pronounces from the background of the tragedy. When the Friar speaks we seem to hear the reflections which the poet is making aloud to himself as the play comes from his creative hands. Under the garb of the monk, [Shakspeare] communicates to us the results of his personal experience, and the conclusions to which the spectacle of the world has led him. He was profoundly versed in the study of human nature; he knew its weaknesses, its contradictions, its impatient desires, its rashness attended by boundless hope and followed by utter despair, its misfortunes whether merited or self-provoked; he knew the self-deception man so often practices; all this he knew, and yet the knowledge never lessens his indulgence or his sympathy for his fellow-creatures. He smiles at their folly, he is vexed at their weaknesses, and he sometimes sternly summons them back to their duties; but all the while he is full of compassion, extending the helping hand, and by wise counsels endeavouring to soften their lot. . . . *Romeo and Juliet* is a youthful work; if [Shakspeare] had written it later he would doubtless have lopped the *concetti* and the flowers of rhetoric, by he might perchance have drawn those passionate emotions with less ardor. Whoever touches the play under pretext of correcting it, cannot efface a blemish without erasing the brilliant colors of this youthful and burning poetry. (pp. 439-40)

*Alfred Mézières, in an extract, translated by A. L. Wister, in* A New Variorum Edition of Shakespeare: Romeo and Juliet, Vol. 1, *edited by Horace Howard Furness, J. B. Lippincott Company, 1871, pp. 439-40.*

## ALGERNON CHARLES SWINBURNE   (essay date 1880)

[*Swinburne was an English poet, dramatist, and critic who devoted much of his literary career to the study of Shakespeare and other Elizabethan writers. His three books on Shakespeare—*A Study of Shakespeare *(1880),* Shakespeare *(1909), and* Three Plays of Shakespeare *(1909)—all demonstrate his keen interest in Shakespeare's poetic talents and, especially, his major tragedies. Swinburne's literary commentary is frequently conveyed in a style that is markedly intense and effusive. In the following excerpt, the critic maintains that "the whole heart or spirit of* Romeo and Juliet *is summed up and distilled" in two scenes: the so-called garden scene following the Capulet feast and the parting*

*balcony scene in Act III. According to Swinburne, these two episodes express emotions in simple, accessible language, while the remainder of the play is often excessive or extravagant, evidencing "the tentative uncertain grasp of a stripling giant."*]

In two scenes we may say that the whole heart or spirit of *Romeo and Juliet* is summed up and distilled into perfect and pure expression; and these two are written in blank verse of equable and blameless melody. Outside the garden scene in the second act and the balcony scene in the third, there is much that is fanciful and graceful, much of elegiac pathos and fervid if fantastic passion; much also of superfluous rhetoric and (as it were) of wordy melody, which flows and foams hither and thither into something of extravagance and excess; but in these two there is no flaw, no outbreak, no superflux, and no failure. Throughout certain scenes of the third and fourth acts I think it may be reasonably and reverently allowed that the river of verse has broken its banks, not as yet through the force and weight of its gathering stream, but merely through the weakness of the barriers, or boundaries found insufficient to confine it. . . . It is in the scenes of vehement passion, of ardour and of agony, that we feel the comparative weakness of a yet ungrown hand, the tentative uncertain grasp of a stripling giant. The two utterly beautiful scenes are not of this kind; they deal with simple joy and with simple sorrow, with the gladness of meeting and the sadness of parting love; but between and behind them come scenes of more fierce emotion, full of surprise, of violence, of unrest; and with these the poet is not yet (if I dare say so) quite strong enough to deal. Apollo has not yet put on the sinews of Hercules. (pp. 35-7)

*Algernon Charles Swinburne, "First Period: Lyric and Fantastic," in his* A Study of Shakespeare, *R. Worthington, 1880, pp. 1-65.*

## EDWARD DOWDEN   (essay date 1881)

[*Dowden was an Irish critic and biographer whose* Shakspere: A Critical Study of His Mind and Art, *first published in 1875 and revised in 1881, was the leading example of the biographical criticism popular in the English-speaking world near the end of the nineteenth century. Biographical critics sought in the plays and poems a record of Shakespeare's personal development. As that approach gave way in the twentieth century to aesthetic theories with greater emphasis on the constructed, artificial nature of literary works, the biographical analysis of Dowden and other critics came to be regarded as limited and often misleading. In the following excerpt from the study mentioned above, Dowden disputes G. G. Gervinus's claim that Friar Lawrence represents a kind of chorus in* Romeo and Juliet *and, as such, expresses Shakespeare's own ethical ideas (see excerpt above, 1849-50). Instead, he argues that the friar is as "misled by error as well as the rest," noting that in all Shakespeare's works no one character is ever given an absolute vision of the truth. According to Dowden, the lovers' ordeal is not meant to provide us with a just moral, such as the friar's warning of the dangers of immoderation, but demonstrates "that every strong emotion which exalts and quickens the inner life of man at the same time exposes the outer life of accident and circumstance to increased risk."*]

It is impossible to agree with those critics, among others Gervinus, who represent the friar as a kind of chorus expressing Shakspere's own ethical ideas, and his opinions respecting the characters and action [of *Romeo and Juliet*]. It is not Shakspere's practice to expound the moralities of his artistic creations; nor does he ever, by means of a chorus, stand above and outside the men and women of his plays, who are bone of his bone, and flesh of his flesh. . . . No! Friar Laurence . . .

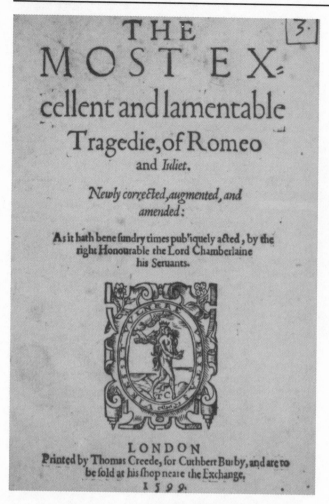

*Title page of the Second Quarto of* Romeo and Juliet *(1599).*

is moving in the cloud, and misled by error as well as the rest. Shakspere has never made the moderate, self-possessed, sedate person a final or absolute judge of the impulsive and the passionate. The one sees a side of truth which is unseen by the other; but to neither is the whole truth visible. The friar had supposed that by virtue of his prudence, his moderation, his sage counsels, his amiable sophistries, he could guide these two young, passionate lives, and do away the old tradition of enmity between the houses. There in the tomb of the Capulets is the return brought in by his investment of kindly scheming. Shakspere did not believe that the highest wisdom of human life was acquirable by mild, monastic meditation, and by gathering of simples in the coolness of the dawn. Friar Laurence too, old man, had his lesson to learn.

In accordance with his view that the friar represents the chorus in this tragedy, Gervinus discovers as the leading idea of the piece a lesson of moderation: the poet makes his confession that "excess in any enjoyment, however pure in itself, transforms its sweet into bitterness; that devotion to any single feeling, however noble, bespeaks its ascendency; that this ascendency moves the man and woman out of their natural spheres" [see excerpt above by G. G. Gervinus, 1849-50]. It is somewhat hard upon Shakspere to suppose that he secreted in each of his dramas a central idea for a German critic to discover. But if there be a central idea in *Romeo and Juliet*, can this be it? What! did Shakspere, then, mean that Romeo and Juliet

loved too well? That all would have been better if they had surrendered their lives each to the other less rapturously, less absolutely? At what precise point ought a discreet regard for another human soul to check itself and say, "Thus far towards complete union will I advance, but here it is prudent to stop?" (pp. 107-08)

No; this method of judging characters and actions by gross awards of pleasure and pain as measured by the senses does not interpret the ethics or the art of Shakspere or of any great poet. Shakspere was aware that every strong emotion which exalts and quickens the inner life of man at the same time exposes the outer life of accident and circumstance to increased risk. But the theme of tragedy, as conceived by the poet, is not material prosperity or failure; it is spiritual; fulfilment or failure of a destiny higher than that which is related to the art of getting on in life. To die, under certain conditions, may be a higher rapture than to live.

Shakspere did not intend that the feeling evoked by the last scene of this tragedy of *Romeo and Juliet* should be one of hopeless sorrow or despair in presence of failure, ruin, and miserable collapse. Juliet and Romeo, to whom Verona has been a harsh stepmother, have accomplished their lives. They loved perfectly. Romeo had attained to manhood. Juliet had suddenly blossomed into heroic womanhood. Through her, and through anguish and joy, her lover had emerged from the life of dream into the waking life of truth. Juliet had saved his soul; she had rescued him from abandonment to spurious feeling, from abandonment to morbid self-consciousness, and the enervating luxury of emotion for emotion's sake. What more was needed? And as secondary to all this, the enmity of the houses is appeased. Montague will raise in pure gold the statue of true and faithful Juliet; Capulet will place Romeo by her side. Their lives are accomplished; they go to take up their place in the large history of the world, which contains many such things. Shakspere in this last scene carries forward our imagination from the horror of the tomb to the better life of man, when such love as that of Juliet and Romeo will be publicly honored and remembered by a memorial all gold. (pp. 108-10)

*Edward Dowden, "The First and the Second Tragedy: 'Romeo and Juliet'; 'Hamlet'," in his* Shakspere: A Critical Study of His Mind and Art, *third edition, Harper & Brothers Publishers, 1881, pp. 84-143.*

## DENTON J. SNIDER  (essay date 1887)

*[Snider was an American scholar, philosopher, and poet who closely followed the precepts of the German philosopher Georg Wilhelm Friedrich Hegel and contributed greatly to the dissemination of his dialectical philosophy in America. Snider's critical writings include studies on Homer, Dante, and Goethe, as well as Shakespeare. Like Hermann Ulrici and G. G. Gervinus, Snider sought the dramatic unity and ethical import of Shakespeare's plays, but he presented a more rigorous Hegelian interpretation than either of these German philosophical critics. In the introduction to his three-volume work* The Shakespearian Drama: A Commentary *(1887-90), Snider states that Shakespeare's plays present various ethical principles which, in their differences, come into "Dramatic Collision," but are ultimately resolved and brought into harmony. He claims that these collisions can be traced in the plays' various "Dramatic Threads" of action and thought, which together form a "Dramatic Movement," and that the analysis of these threads and movements—"the structural elements of the drama"—reveal the organic unity of Shakespeare's art. Snider*

*observes two basic movements in the tragedies—guilt and retribution—and three in the comedies—separation, mediation, and return. In a structural analysis of* Romeo and Juliet, *in which he traces the play's various "movements" and "threads," Snider contends that Shakespeare's central, unifying theme is "love unconquerable by fate, whereof the individual is the merest instrument, ready to be sacrificed without the least hesitation." But he does not view Shakespeare's dramatization of this idea as something positive, asserting instead that Romeo and Juliet's love for each other, in its single-minded intensity, exceeds all natural and social limitations, sacrificing reason, utility, and self-control, and eventually destroys the lovers. Like many previous critics, Snider discerns the play's moral in the friar's philosophy of moderation. The critic also comments on Romeo's apparent fickleness in his love for Rosaline then Juliet, saying that his "transition" is not a "great blemish" on the work, but actually provides "the true motive for the tragic termination of the action." Lastly, he points out that Shakespeare's play does not end on a note of despair, but concludes with a brief opposite movement that depicts the reconciliation of the two houses as a result of the lovers' sacrifice.]*

[*Romeo and Juliet*] shows in many ways that it belongs to the youthful productions of Shakespeare. Its theme is the passion of youth; it has the wild freedom and intensity of youth. There is a lack of that severity of treatment which belongs to the later works of the Poet. There are important parts which are dismissed with an undue brevity and bareness of statement, and then again there are other parts developed at length which appear quite unnecessary to the action; there is often a sensuous fullness of delineation, and often an abstract meagerness; there are found the finest and purest bursts of poetry intermingled with frigid conceits and far-fetched antitheses. Everywhere in the drama can be noticed an inequality—an inequality in thought, in language, in the structure of the plot. Still, beneath all this play of caprice and irregularity there is felt to be a deep, pervading harmony throughout the entire work. The inequality seems to be the inequality of the subject—the inequality of youth, with its fitful, tempestuous passion. It has been well named the tragedy of love—love in all its conflicts, love in all its extravagance and volcanic tossings, love despised, and love triumphant. It portrays this passion boiling over with a fervor which sweeps down all traditional barriers—even the most deadly enmity—and which advances firmly to a struggle with death itself. The theme is, therefore, love unconquerable by fate, whereof the individual is the merest instrument, ready to be sacrificed without the least hesitation. Such is the feeling that warms this poem in every part—youthful love in the most glowing intensity; for it is just the intensity which characterizes the love of Romeo and Juliet above all other loves, and which prefers death to permanent separation.

At this point, then, lies the tragedy. Love, the emotion of the Family, in its excess destroys the Family; though it be the origin and bond of the domestic institution, it now assails and annihilates that institution. Love, in its very devotion, becomes narrow, even selfish, because it gives itself up to pure self-indulgence; it sacrifices its rational to its emotional element, and perishes along with the individual. The gratification of passion, even the passion of love, has in it the tragic germ, and may destroy itself along with the man who yields to it, like any other passionate excess. Romeo's love is high, noble, pure; it has no ulterior motive of gain, rank, or lust; still it is a story of uncontrolled self-indulgence. Love is his strength, and his weakness; in one sense he is heroic, marching boldly to death; in another sense he is unmanly, yielding to an emotion without any self-restraint.

Romeo thus is caught between the upper and the nether millstone of his passion, and is ground to death. Shakespeare often flings, as it were, his characters into the vortex of a self-destructive antithesis, which always lurks in the great deed and in the great passion; so, heroic natures, in their very mightiness, dash against their own fate and are tragic. . . . So these lovers, Romeo and Juliet, through love, really destroy love and themselves, for this life at least, and the poet has not united them beyond, though the reader may, if he chooses.

That Shakespeare was conscious of this principle, even in its abstract form, is shown by what he puts into the mouth of the Friar:

> For nought so vile that on the Earth doth live,
> But to the Earth some special good doth give;
> Nor aught so good but strained from that fair use,
> Revolts from true birth, stumbling on abuse.
> Virtue itself turns vice, being misapplied,
> And vice sometimes' by action dignified.
>
> [II. iii. 17-22]

Evil has in it the possibility of good, may be the means thereof, and the Friar will employ evil as the means of good, wherein he will himself commit an excess, and furnish an example to point his own moral. On the other hand, good, being strained, becomes evil. Here we see that the poet has been thinking deeply upon the ethical element in character as the basis of his tragedy; he states the counter-play of both evil and good into their opposites. Some may think that he was too young when this drama was written to have such thoughts; but really it betrays the youthful and immature artist to reveal his abstract principle of procedure. (pp. 36-9)

If we should connect the meaning of this drama with the life of the poet, we would say, that it is his youth's solution of emotion. This absorption of one's self in feeling, this yielding even to the sweetness of love, means tragedy, even when the love is pure; it drives the man against the restraint of institutions, if he has no self-restraint to start with. Emotion breaks forth into passion, which is destiny; thus it is written here. Shakespeare had in his heart this volcano of feeling, but he had also in his head the tragedy thereof; intense passion he shows, but shows it dashing itself to pieces against the walls of the Universe. In this Italian atmosphere, then, we feel the Teutonic current; and, in spite of its warm Southern tone, and color, and sympathy, the play reveals itself written by a Northerner and resting at last upon Northern consciousness. (pp. 40-1)

If we study the organism of [*Romeo and Juliet*], we find in it two essential Movements—two grand sweeps of the Ethical World, upon which the poet is wont to base ultimately the tragic action. The First Movement culminates in the union of Romeo and Juliet, and portrays the events and obstacles antecedent to that union; it shows the transition from the unrequited to the requited love of the hero, ending in marriage. But their union has produced a still deeper social disunion; the domestic concord of the pair has called up a more universal domestic discord. This Movement embraces the first two Acts. The Second Movement, including the other three Acts, will show the Ethical World purifying itself of the inner discord, by eliminating the lovers and reconciling the parents. Romeo does the deed of violence, the lovers are separated, and finally perish at the tomb of the Capulets. Their death mediates the hatred of their houses, harmony is restored to the troubled Veronese world, both in State and Family. Thus the entire action is a sweep into and out of a disordered social condition, compressed into a two hours' spectacle.

Such are the general Movements of the entire work; but through the whole action there run a certain number of Threads, which must be carefully distinguished. One of these Threads is the prince with his attendants, representing the State, which stands above all the conflicting elements and enforces their obedience to its commands. Its efforts are directed to keeping peace between the two hostile families, to securing, by its power, an external harmony and order; still, the enmity is so intense that upon slight provocation, it boils over, and bears down all authority. This Thread is the least prominent one in the play. . . . [It acts] in connection with the other two Threads, with which it is closely united. The first Thread, therefore, is the two houses, the Montagues and Capulets, with their respective adherents, both of which have one common trait—mutual hatred. The hostility between them is so deep-seated that it not only assails the higher authority of the State, as above mentioned, but also the Family, in such a manner that through this hate the Family turns against itself and assails its own existence, and, indeed, finally destroys itself in its children. Thus there is portrayed a double collision—the Family against itself and against the State. This Thread is the disturbing principle of the play; it disturbs both public order and domestic peace. The second Thread, however, is the most important one of the play—is, in fact, the play itself. It turns, not upon family hatred, but upon the opposite passion—love—which constitutes the basis of the Family. Its bearers are Romeo and Juliet, a Montague and a Capulet, whose union thus falls athwart the enmity of their houses, and is sought in vain to be reconciled with the same by Friar Laurence, the great mediator of the drama. Both, too, are brought into conflict with the suitor Paris, who is favored by the parents. Love thus is the source of manifold collisions, which the poet has taken the pains to portray fully. First comes the unrequited love of Romeo, in which the conflict is wholly subjective, in which the individual is struggling with his own passion. Then follows his requited love, which, however, has to endure a double collision from an external source—with the will of the parents of Juliet on the one hand, and with the suit of his rival, Paris, on the other. (pp. 48-50)

The first Movement begins with a tumult between the Montagues and Capulets, and its suppression by the State. The very first scene thus depicts the extent and the intensity of the hatred between the two houses; it reaches down to their servants, who are ready for a fight whenever they meet, and involves the relatives of both families, together with their respective adherents in the city. Order is trampled under foot, a violent struggle ensues in the streets, till the Prince, as the head of the State, has to appear for the purpose of vindicating authority and restoring peace. We are also told that these brawls have repeatedly taken place. Thus it is shown that the conflict between the hostile families is so violent and widespread that it assails the State and threatens the existence of public security. Such is the social background upon which the chief action of the play is to be portrayed. We see a hot emotional people, full of feuds and hate; here is passion which overbears all law. So it is with Romeo internally; as in the community reason cannot control feeling, so he has no rational self-control.

This world of strife and contradiction is, accordingly, an outer image of Romeo, who now appears in it, manifesting the full intensity of his love. He shuns society, seeks the covert of the wood, avoids daylight, desires not even to be seen. His passion is so strong that he cannot master himself; he sighs and weeps; he goes out of the way of everybody, in order not to expose his state of mind and to give full vent to his fancy and emotions.

His absorption is complete; he is so swallowed up in one individual of the opposite sex that he cuts himself off from all other relations of life—from father, mother, relatives, and friends. Thus the intensity of his love is the key-note of his character, and it is this intensity which will bring forth all the tragic consequences of the drama.

But his love is unrequited; he loves, and is not loved in return. Here we reach the cause of his strange demeanor and the source of all his affliction. There has arisen a struggle within his own bosom which he cannot allay. He gives expression to his conflicting emotions in language so strongly antithetic and contradictory that it often seems unnatural and frigid, yet it is only a highly-wrought picture of his own internal condition. (pp. 50-2)

Romeo's mind is in a state of contradiction; his language is in the same state. He feels at times that his condition and his words are humorous, and may excite a laugh; still the matter is no comedy to him. (p. 52)

The collision, so far, is purely subjective—in the breast of the individual; but, to produce a dramatic action, there must be a struggle with an external power, which the poet now prepares to introduce.

Hence we must pass to the love which is requited, and which brings him into collision with the hostile family. Romeo, in company with his friends, among whom is the gay scoffer, Mercutio, goes to a masquerade at the dwelling of Capulet, the mortal enemy of his house, evidently for the purpose of beholding the fair Rosaline. While there, he sees Juliet, and at once transfers to her all his passion. Indeed, its intensity is so great that he for the moment questions his former affection. This passage has been often construed as if Shakespeare meant to assert that Romeo's first love was only a fanciful delusion. How utterly aimless, how ridiculous, must this whole first Act then become! For we would seek in vain to find its object. The poet, if such were his meaning, would be simply denying his own work. These words of Romeo, are but the exaggerated expression of his present impulse. He passes to Juliet and talks with her; the language between them, though full of dark and far-fetched metaphor, is plain enough when supplemented with the look and the kiss. If he could not endure the previous struggle, what must become of him now? Juliet is also caught; her fervor seems equally great. Both have loved at first sight. Through all this volcanic might of passion the tragic end is peering, for separation now means death.

Thus Romeo *has* changed, notwithstanding his protestations to Benvolio. This transition is the central point of the whole first Movement of the play, and, indeed, gives the true motive for the tragic termination of the action. But it has been so generally misunderstood, according to our judgment of the drama, that the grounds for it require a full statement. It is declared that this sudden change from one individual to another is unnatural, and is, moreover, a great blemish in the work. The apparent lack of fidelity is said to give offense to our ethical feelings, and to destroy our respect for the hero. Also, Romeo seems now the most inconstant of lovers, but afterwards is faithful to death—which fact looks like an inconsistency in the character, and an unsolved contradiction in the play. The defenders of the poet have injured him more deeply than his assailants; they have defended his work by destroying it. The first love of Romeo, so fully detailed by the author, is pronounced to be no love—a mere caprice. But a careful view of the circumstances will show that this change is not only psychologically justifiable, but is the only adequate motive for the death of the lovers—that is, for the tragedy itself.

Romeo is consumed with the most ardent passion; its intensity is its great characteristic. He has given himself away, has made a complete sacrifice of his individuality, but there is no return for his devotion. This is the motive upon which the poet has laid the chief stress; the first love of Romeo was not reciprocated. The necessity of a corresponding passion is felt by everybody, though its logical basis is not usually thought of. Love is the surrender of the individual to one of the opposite sex, through the feelings. Each must find his or her emotional existence in the loved person; each must be only through the other. This mutual sacrifice of self on the part of both constitutes the unity and harmony of love. (pp. 52-5)

But let one side be wanting, the reciprocity is destroyed; there is the sacrifice without the compensation. The lover loses, for a time at least, his own individuality, as far as his emotion is concerned, without gaining another. Hence he is harrassed with an internal struggle, more or less severe according to the intensity of the passion.... In such a struggle a restoration may be, and usually is, brought about by the healing influence of time. But the sacrifice may be so complete, and the passion so intense, that recovery is extremely difficult by this means—nay, impossible. Then there is only one other way—change the object; find some new individual who will make the sacrifice. It is a matter of not uncommon experience that rejected lovers resort to these sudden transfers of affection; not from spite, however, as is often supposed, but from a real necessity. This sudden change of Romeo has the authority both of Shakespeare and of the legend from which he drew his materials; thus it is stamped, as completely as may be, with seal of Human Nature, by people and poet.

Such is the conflict in Romeo's bosom, and such is its solution. The fervor of his love does not permit him to recover himself; he, indeed, must change in order to get repose and harmonize the struggle. It is, therefore, not fickleness, but rather the permanence and strength of his passion, which causes its transference from Rosaline to Juliet. This change is grounded in the fact that his love is unrequited, and yet so intense that it must have an object—a corresponding sacrifice. He cannot retrace his steps. He is just seeking that which comes across his way in the form of Juliet, for Rosaline cannot now have any reality for him. The relief is instantaneous—he recovers himself at a bound. (pp. 55-6)

The intensity now reached by Romeo and Juliet is kept up by both throughout the play, and constitutes its great distinguishing feature; for the love of man and woman has here attained such a potence that neither can exist without the other. In the vast majority of mankind it never reaches quite so high a degree; it stops this side of death. And, indeed, it should never reach quite so high a degree, for thus it turns to guilt and prepares the tragic fate. Romeo and Juliet are devoted to one another as individuals, and not so much to the Family as an institution. Their love thus turns to an ethical violation, since it renders domestic life impossible if the one chance be lost. The rational object of marriage is for man to exist in the Family, which, if it cannot be reached through one person, must be sought through another. The Institution is higher than the Individual; but, in the present drama, the love of an individual assails the Family on its universal side; thus there must result a tragic termination. For, truly considered, love, which is the emotional ground of the Family, is here destroying the Family itself. Love thus

annihilates its own object, puts an end to itself; so do Romeo and Juliet, its bearers. (pp. 57-8)

The marriage of the lovers introduces us to the grand mediator of the play, Friar Laurence. We are ushered into his presence in the quiet of early morn. The holy man of contemplation is shown in all the surroundings; the very atmosphere breathes serenity and repose. His reflection leads him to consider the contradictions of nature and of mind; he notes that excess calls forth strife; virtue itself, being strained, turns to its opposite. Here is given the germ of his character. He recognizes the source of all conflict, and seeks the means of its reconciliation. He employs the religious form of expressing this contradiction—grace on the one hand, rude will on the other. Still, his more natural way of thinking is rather that of the moral philosopher than of the religious teacher. He has himself subordinated all the passions of the soul; his order indicates his exclusion from secular struggles; he stands in striking contrast to the passion-tossed world around him.... The Friar is the mediator of the whole community. The very intensity of their passions demands one who is without passion to direct, advise, and soothe. Romeo, we see, has been a frequent visitor; the Friar was his confidant when no one else was, and has already often calmed his excited feelings concerning Rosaline. Such is the beautiful character of the Friar, standing in the midst of this tempest passion, controlling, directing, pacifying it; for both love and hate seem equally ungovernable and destructive without his reconciling presence. He is represented as a profound observer of the natural proprieties of objects; hence he can provide a drug of such wonderful potency for Juliet. But his chief mental principle is the shunning of all extremes; and just here lies the basis of his deceptions, of the pious frauds which he practices. A rigid moralist he is not, and cannot be in consistency with his principle:

Virtue itself turns to vice, being misapplied.
[II. iii. 21]

As mediator, he has to smooth over difficulties and harmonize collisions; he cannot be hampered by moral punctilios at every step. He brushes them away; but still he seeks to be true to the highest end, and subordinate to it every minor scruple. It is to be noticed that all of Shakespeare's mediatorial characters have quite the same traits; they falsify and deceive, without the least hesitancy, in order to accomplish their important mediations. The Friar unites Romeo and Juliet in marriage, for this is the only solution; separation means death; religion adds its sanction to love, to the right of subjectivity, even against the consent of the parents; and the new family unites within itself the heirs of both the Capulets and the Montagues, whose ancient hatred must henceforth vanish in their descendants. Such a consummation is assuredly a great religious object.

Yet, just at this point, the Friar is caught in the net of his own principle. He carries his shunning of excess so far that he commits an excess, and in the very means of harmony he destroys harmony. He misapplies his virtue and it turns to vice. In employing deception, he lays himself open to the blow of Fate; the outside power will rush in and destroy his plan. Like Romeo, the Friar also has a passion—a love of subtle management, and this will prove fatal to his mediation, and almost fatal to him.... He, the thinker, knows of the danger of extremes, yet falls into an extreme, through his very cunning. The reconciliation is wrenched out of his hand by Destiny, who always finds it very hard to deal with truth, but very easy to deal with deception. (pp. 60-2)

Such is, in the main, the First Movement of the play culminating in the marriage of the lovers. But this marriage rests upon a volcano muttering underneath—the hate of the two houses. Will it break forth? The test is at once to be applied to Romeo; if he can contain himself, he may be saved, but he will have to manifest a quality which he has not hitherto shown. Here the Second Movement begins, which portrays the outburst sweeping on to separation and death of the lovers, to final reconciliation of the hostile families. The two previous Threads are continued.

Tybalt, the hottest head in the play—we wonder not that he dies so soon, but that he has lived so long, in that turbulent society—seems to have regarded the presence of a Montague at the masquerade as an audacious affront to his house. He seeks a quarrel with Romeo; but, for the latter, all enmity against the Capulets has vanished in his union with Juliet. Romeo quietly endures the insult of Tybalt, hate seems to be conquered by love, and we think that the young man is beyond the stroke of his destiny. But his friend, Mercutio, an outsider belonging to neither of the families, takes up the quarrel and is slain for his interference. The passionate reaction now comes over Romeo, hate shows itself stronger than love, and he slays Tybalt. So Romeo has not stood the test, which was to endure the family hate; just as little was he able to endure the first test, which was love unrequited. He is still Romeo, ruled by his passion, if not of love, then of hate. . . . Again the enmity of the two families has disturbed public order; the State appears, in the person of the Prince, and decrees the immediate banishment of Romeo, who has so deeply violated the principle of authority. (pp. 64-6)

Banishment is decreed; the unity of love must be violently torn asunder. The conduct and feelings of the lovers, which are now manifested, are in the most perfect consonance with their principle. Both think of death; loss of existence is preferable to the loss of union, so great is its intensity. They are brought forward in different scenes, but their pathos is quite the same. The tragic motive is again manifest—permanent separation means destruction. In the breast of Juliet, however, there is a double conflict—her dearest relative has been slain by her husband, and now that husband must leave her. . . . Juliet, in the beginning, thinks of the death of her cousin, Tybalt. Her family thus comes up first in her mind, and she curses Romeo. But soon the deeper principle manifests itself; that which rends her heart is the separation, and she says directly that she would rather endure the destruction of her whole family—Tybalt, father, and mother—than the banishment of her husband. Just as great is the desperation of Romeo. Again he must betake himself to the Friar, who will comfort him with "adversity's sweet milk, philosophy" [III. iii. 55], and will soothe his agitated soul— the true function of the religious mediator. The good monk adopts the only solution possible—the separation must not be permanent. Romeo can only be buoyed up with hope of a speedy return. This hope is furnished to him by the Friar. He is now prepared to endure the parting from Juliet, which accordingly takes place, and the separation is accomplished.

Let us now go back . . . and consider that part of the action which collides with this union, namely, the suit of Paris, supported by the consent of the parents. In the absence of Romeo, this part becomes the sole element of the drama, and Juliet has to support the struggle alone. Her fidelity is to be tried to the utmost. Afflictions will be laid upon her, increasing in intensity, till death; but she will never, for a moment, flinch in her devotion. The father, who previously asserted for his daughter the right of love, in true accord with the Shakespearian view, now changes his basis, and commands Juliet to marry Paris. This change lies in his impulsive, volatile nature, as far as the poet has given to it any motive. . . . Paris is pressing his suit; both the father and the mother of Juliet favor him; she resists. The result is that she is berated by her parents, and threatened with expulsion from home and with disinheritance. Here is the next affliction after the banishment of Romeo. The conflict between the right of love and the will of the parent is manifested in all its intensity, but she cannot yield. She resorts for comfort to the nurse, who knows of her love, and from whom she expects sympathy; but this last source, too, is cut off. The old woman advises her to submit, and cites every consideration but the right one, namely, love—which is the sole possible motive with Juliet. Thereupon she is done with the nurse; their friendly relation henceforth ceases, and the nurse disappears from every essential mediation of the play. (pp. 68-70)

As soon as the nurse gives this advice to abandon Romeo her mediatorial function ceases; the case is out of her reach. The Friar alone can understand and solve the difficulty. Accordingly Juliet betakes herself to his cell. At once she finds both sympathy and aid, for it is the character of the Friar to give complete validity to love. He is ready with a plan—she must drink off a liquor which produces the semblance of death, and be buried in the vault of her family, whither he and Romeo will come to her rescue. This means appears far-fetched and without adequate motive. Why could she have not gone directly to his cell and secreted herself, or have slipped off and hurried to Romeo at Mantua? Yet the design of the poet is manifest. Since he is portraying love in its highest intensity, he makes it endure every gradation of trial, and finally death itself. The most terrible thing to the human imagination is, probably, the idea of being buried alive, and shut up in a vault with dead bodies. But she, a tender girl, resolves to undergo what would make the heart of the most courageous man blench. It is the affliction next to death, yet love gives her the daring to endure. Read her soliloquy as she drinks off the contents of the vial. There she recounts the possibilities; imagination starts up the direst phantasms; madness stares her in the face; still, she will drink. This occurrence, therefore, is in perfect harmony with the spirit of the play. Before death, Juliet is brought to the tomb alive. It is one of the series of trials, increasing in pain and horror, in whose fire her love must be tested.

But just here incidents are portrayed for which it is extremely difficult to find any adequate justification. What necessity of exhibiting the sorrow of the parents over their child, whom they suppose to be dead—all of which must be a false pathos to the audience? The only excuse is, their grief is not very deep, and the cries of formal lamentation are made to sound hollow. Friar Laurence again appears in his true role of mediator and consoler, but his dissimulation now seriously impairs his high ethical character. Both the weeping of the parents and the deception of the Friar could have been here omitted without injury to the action, and to the decided advantage of thought and logical consistency. In fact, the entire drama has a certain natural fullness which makes it often vivid, but obscures its unity as a Whole. It lacks the more rigid adherence to a central thought found in the later works of the poet.

The conflict of Juliet with the will of her parents is thus met by the plan of the Friar, who protects her against her family as he protected Romeo against the authority of the State. Nothing now seems in the way of the speedy reunion of the separated lovers. Romeo is still in exile, filled with longings and anticipations of the time when he will be restored to his Juliet. His thoughts by day and his dreams by night have no other employment. Suddenly the terrible news arrives—Juliet is dead. His love is at once all ablaze; he will still be united with her, though in death. He resolves to set out immediately for home. But herein he disobeys the Friar, and acts without the latter's knowledge. Thus the Friar's plan is interfered with and destroyed. Romeo proceeds upon mistaken information, and the good monk fails in his scheme of reconcilement. (pp. 71-3)

Thus Romeo breaks down in his third great probation, as he did in the other two. He is the same in all, without self-control; he could not endure the unrequited love, could not endure the trial of family hate, could not endure for a moment the test of Juliet's death. Each time he calls down upon himself the blow of Fate increasing in might to the last, because he will not be a freeman; he indulges his emotion, which finds vent in fancy, and then his fancy runs uncontrolled to imagery. He is determined by judgement neither in his actions, nor in his metaphors. Still we must appreciate Romeo, he has an heroic side of character, he is a lover unto death; granted his weakness, he has in that weakness enough strength to be tragic.

In this respect Juliet is different, she is more self-centered, has reflection, and the power of self-suppression. She meets her trial, in the suit of Paris, with self-control, and with an artifice which we wonder at, not altogether admiringly. But in the presence of Romeo, she is transformed by his passion, even her speech and imagery become like his, and run a race with his extravagance. Her deepest trait is still devotion to her love, for the sake of which she employs deception, and thus exposes herself to stroke of Fate along with the Friar. Compared to her, Romeo is single-souled; she has doubleness, nay, duplicity; she can assume a character and play it, and what is more wonderful, meet her tragic situation with ambiguities of speech which become almost comic. Note the part she plays to her parents and to Paris, telling the truth in words, but in fact falsifying, or perchance dramatizing a disguise. Yet she is deeply in earnest, has the noblest end in view; but for this end she employs deception, in which Fate catches her; still when caught, she defies Fate, and triumphantly dies. (pp. 74-5)

Thus we see that the logical result of [the] feud has been the annihilation of the Family. Each house willed the destruction of the other, and therein the destruction of itself. For their conduct must return upon themselves, and the drama only portrays the manner of that return. Both families lose their children, their heirs, and, in their loss, must pass away forever. The Prince, too, suffers along with them, for "winking at the discords" [V. iii. 294], and he declares in the plainest terms, the great law of retribution by which all are punished.

We have now reached the termination of the purely tragic movement of the play, namely, the union of the lovers in death. Their last and greatest trial has been passed; both have remained true to love. Their tie was so strong, their oneness so complete, that they could not really exist as separate individuals. The grand object of the play has been frequently stated: it is to portray a love so intense that separation must cause death. But such a result is contrary to the common experience of mankind, and hence the poet seeks every possible means for manifesting the *intensity* of the passion. That it lay in the character of Romeo never to recover his individuality, after it was once surrendered to his affection, is shown in the First Movement of the play; the taking away of the loved object is literally the taking away of himself, so complete is his sacrifice. Juliet's passion is motived, both in kind and in degree, by that of

Romeo; her devotion must be as great as his. The Second Movement of the tragedy portrays the separation of the pair—at first supposed to be only temporary; but the moment Romeo, and afterwards Juliet, become possessed of the notion that the separation will be eternal, self-destruction is the logical necessity of their characters. It is indeed the tragedy of love. This coloring of intensity it keeps throughout, amid all its vagaries and excrescences. This is, in fact, the deep underlying unity of the work, whose power every one must feel. The guilt of the unhappy pair must be placed here, also, if we can predicate guilt of them, and certainly we must do so if we are able to justify the tragedy. The emotional nature of man must be controlled and subordinated to the rational principle, and, under no circumstances, can it have the right to utterly absorb and destroy individual existence.

At this point an opposite movement sets in for a short time— the reconciliation of the two hostile houses. The Prince insists upon it; the public order of the city has been violated; he has lost two kinsmen in the feud; he, too, has been punished in his family. But, more emphatically the poet insists upon it; he would have us see that such a visitation is not without its purpose in the plan of the world; it clears up, purifies, harmonizes. Shakespeare's tragic view is a glance into the providential order, and is a revelation thereof to men, showing the movement of a society into and out of a disrupted ethical condition. Tragedy with him means not death merely, but is a sacrifice; Shakespeare's tragedy is at bottom mediatorial, and reaches into the divine scheme of the world. The lovers, Romeo and Juliet, die, but their death has in it for the living a redemption. (pp. 76-8)

*Denton J. Snider, "'Romeo and Juliet'," in his* The Shakespearian Drama, a Commentary: The Tragedies, *Sigma Publishing Co., 1887, pp. 36-78.*

## FREDERICK S. BOAS (essay date 1896)

[*Boas was a specialist in Elizabethan and Tudor drama who combined the biographical interest prevalent in the late nineteenth century with the historical approach that developed in the first decades of the twentieth century. His commentary thus reflects the important transition that occurred in Shakespearean criticism during this period. Boas disputes G. G. Gervinus's claim that the friar's philosophy of moderation is the "keynote" of* Romeo and Juliet, *and that Shakespeare was therefore condemning the lovers for yielding to passion instead of being ruled by grace (see excerpt above, 1849-50). The critic maintains that Shakespeare nowhere censures the love of Romeo and Juliet, but demonstrates instead that "the ecstasies of love are brief and brittle" in the face of destiny.*]

Within the infant rind of this weak flower
Poison hath residence, and medicine power.
For this, being smelt, with that part cheers each part,
Being tasted, stays all senses with the heart.
Two such opposed Kings encamp them still
In man as well as herbs—grace and rude will,
And when the worser is predominant
Full soon the canker death eats up the plant....
[II. iii. 23-30]

Gervinus [finds] in these words the keynote of [*Romeo and Juliet*], and [looks] upon the Friar as playing the part of the classical chorus, which was the mouthpiece of the poet's own sentiments [see excerpt above, 1849-50]. Shakspere, according to this interpretation, censures the lovers for yielding to 'rude will' or passion instead of being regulated by 'grace' or gentle moderation. But adherents of the Romantic school from Schlegel onwards, have refused to see in the Friar's words anything more than a suitable dramatic utterance. The problem is, without doubt, perplexing. Though Shakspere never identifies himself absolutely with any single character, yet certain of his creations make the impression of representing him more fully than others, and it must be allowed that the hermit's moralizing phrases are introduced and repeated with what sounds like deliberate emphasis. But this doctrine of moderation in love is nowhere else found in Shakspere's writings. . . . Why then should Romeo and Juliet, the glowing creations of the dramatist's youth, alone be condemned out of his own mouth? There is another interpretation which in some degree reconciles the opposing views. All through the drama there runs the note of tragic predestination. It has had utterance from the lips of Romeo and Juliet, but merely as a vague presentiment. In the friar's mouth it naturally takes a moralizing form and is made the occasion of a sermon on man's unruliness. As the hero and heroine repeat time after time their apprehensions of evil to come, so, after his own fashion, does the Friar. Hence the prominence given to his warnings: they are part of the ever-swelling burden of the drama that the ecstasies of love are brief and brittle: they must not be simply set aside as prosy commonplaces, but they cannot be accepted as the full and final judgement upon love and life by Shakspere, the Shakspere of the Sonnets to Will. And indeed, if Romeo and Juliet, swayed by passion, become the victims of an ironical destiny, is this less true of the cautious Laurence with all his saws and maxims? Romeo bursts into the cell, his tongue on fire with the exciting news of his last night's fortunes. He cannot stop to give details, but blurts out breathlessly his main object:

> When, where, and how,
> We met, we wooed, and made exchange of vow
> I'll tell thee as we pass; but this I pray
> That thou consent to marry us to-day.
>
> [II. iii. 61-4]

The churchman blames the young waverer's precipitancy, but thinks to bring good out of evil: a match between a Montague and a Capulet may turn the households' rancour to pure love. Is not this amiable confidence as bitterly mocked by the sequel as the hopes of the wooers, who that very afternoon are made man and wife? The scene is brief but intensely significant. (pp. 206-07)

No *a priori* ideas that Shakspere is pre-eminently the poet of free will as opposed to necessity should prevent us recognizing that in *Romeo and Juliet,* following the steps of Brooke, and treating a characteristically mediaeval theme, he has given to Fate a prominence unique in his writings. The lovers have been 'star-crossed,' and in their 'misadventured piteous overthrows' [Prologue, 6, 7] they merit neither blame nor praise. Still less does Shakspere explicitly strike the transcendental note of the modern poet that 'Love is all, and Death is nought.' Yet he does not leave us bowed in barren sorrow. Over the dead bodies of their children, Montagu and Capulet clasp hands, and the family vendetta is stayed for ever. The love of 'true and faithful' [V. iii. 302] Juliet and her Romeo has been the love spoken of in *A Midsummer Night's Dream.*

> Swift as a shadow, short as any dream,
> Brief as the lightning in the collied night
> That, in a spleen, unfolds both heaven and earth,
> And ere a man hath power to say, Behold!
> The jaws of darkness do devour it up.
>
> [*A Midsummer Night's Dream,* I. i. 144-48]

But lightning, the elemental force, though it carry death and terror with it, purges and purifies the world's atmosphere. So is it with the equally elemental force of love. (p. 214)

> Frederick S. Boas, "Shakspere Italianate: 'Romeo and Juliet'—'The Merchant of Venice'," in his Shakspere and His Predecessors, *Charles Scribner's Sons, 1896, pp. 197-234.*

## RICHARD G. MOULTON   (essay date 1903)

[*Moulton avers that in* Romeo and Juliet *Shakespeare was not concerned with depicting the processes of moral retribution, as he had done in other plays, but was composing a tragedy of accident as well as destiny. The critic thus disagrees with those who discern "folly" in the behavior of the lovers, and he counters the view that the friar's message of moderation is meant as a condemnation of their passion, noting that Friar Lawrence's counsel itself contributes to the final catastrophe.*]

I believe that no mistake has done more to distort Shakespeare criticism than the assumption on the part of so many commentators that retribution is an invariable principle. Their favourite maxims are that the deed returns upon the doer, that character determines fate. But these specious principles need careful examination. If the meaning be merely this, that the deed often returns upon the doer, that character is one of the forces determining fate, then these are profound truths. But if, as is usually the case, there is the suggestion that such maxims embody invariable laws—that the deed always returns upon the doer, that character and nothing but character determines the fate of individuals—then the principles are false; false alike to life itself and to the reflection of life in poetry. (p. 46)

[One] of the principles underlying the exceptions to the universality of retribution, one of the forces that will be found to come between individual character and individual fate, is that which is expressed by the term Accident. I know that to many of my readers this word will be a stumblingblock; those especially who are new to ethical studies are apt to consider that their philosophical reputation will be compromised if they consent to recognise the possibility of accidents. But such a feeling rests upon a confusion between physics and morals. In the physical world, which is founded upon universality and the sum of things, we make it a preliminary axiom that every event has a cause, known or yet to be discovered. But in the world of morals, where individual responsibility comes in, it is obvious that events must happen to individuals the causes of which are outside individual control. (pp. 49-50)

The moral system of Shakespeare gives full recognition to accident as well as retribution; the interest of plot at one point is the moral satisfaction of nemesis, where we watch the sinner found out by his sin; it changes at another point to the not less moral sensation of pathos, our sympathy going out to the suffering which is independent of wrong doing. A notable illustration of the latter is the tragedy of *Romeo and Juliet.* In this play Shakespeare engages our sympathies for two young and attractive lives, and proceeds to bring down upon them wave after wave of calamity, which come upon them not as the result of what Romeo and Juliet have done, but from accident and circumstances not within their control. Instead of wrong and retribution, we have in this case innocence and pathos. Here however a misconception must be avoided. To say that Romeo and Juliet are innocent is not the same thing as to say that they are perfect. No one cares to discuss whether these young souls had not their full share of original sin; nor is it relevant to inquire whther two different persons in their situation might or might not have acted differently. The essential point is that in the providential dispensations of Shakespeare's story, the tragedy overwhelming the lovers is brought about, not by error on their part, but by circumstances outside their control, by what is to them external accident. (pp. 50-1)

In the dim background of the story, for those who care to look for it, may be seen a providence of retribution: evil has brought forth evil, where the feud of the parents has caused the death of the children. This retribution is seen balanced by its opposite, for the heroism of Juliet is a good that but brings forth evil. But in the foreground, at every turn of the movement, we see emphasised the strange work of providence by which accident mocks the best concerted schemes of man; pity, not terror, is the emotion of the poem. It is accident which has brought Romeo and Juliet together, and they have loved without sin; accident has converted Romeo's self-restraint into the entanglement of exile from his bride; the smallest of accidents has been sufficient to turn deep wisdom and devoted heroism into a tragedy that engulfs three innocent lives [Romeo, Juliet, and Paris].

There are certain passages of the play into which have been read suggestions of folly and its penalty, but which in truth are entirely in tune with the prevailing impression of irresistible circumstance. When Juliet says—

> I have no joy of this contract to-night;
> It is too rash, too unadvised, too sudden;
> Too like the lightning, which doth cease to be
> Ere one can say, 'It lightens':—
>
> [II. ii. 117-20]

and Romeo answers—

> I am afeard,
> Being in night, all this is but a dream,
> Too flattering-sweet to be substantial:—
> [II. ii. 139-41]

the two are not making confession of faulty rashness: it is only the common thought of new-born love, that it is too good to be true. Similarly, when the Friar says to Romeo—

> These violent delights have violent ends . . .
> Therefore love moderately;—
> [II. v. 9, 14]

he is not blaming, but fearing: his own action shows that this is the sense. The Friar justly rebukes the desperate fury of Romeo at the sentence of banishment; but this fault of Romeo does not affect the movement of events, for he does not act upon his fury, but on the contrary lays it aside, and submits to the counsel of his spiritual adviser—the counsel which eventually turns to his ruin.

On the other hand, it may be said that in this more than in any other play Shakespeare comes near to being a commentator on himself, and to giving us his own authority for the true interpretation. In the prologue it is the author who speaks: this opening of the plot exhibits, not sin and its consequences, but a suggestion of entangling circumstance; when he speaks of the "fatal loins" of the parents, the "star-cross'd lovers," and their "misadventured piteous overthrows" [Prologue, 5, 6, 7], Shakespeare is using the language of destiny and pathos. For what is spoken in the scenes the speakers alone are responsible; yet a succession of striking passages has the effect of carrying on the suggestion of the prologue—dramatic foreshadowings,

unconscious finger-pointings to the final tragedy, just like the shocks of omen that in ancient drama brought out the irony of fate. . . .

[In these passages] Destiny itself seems to be speaking through the lips of the dramatis personæ. In their more ordinary speech the personages of the play reiterate the one idea of fortune and fate. Romeo after the fall of Tybalt feels that he is "fortune's fool" [III. i. 136]. The Friar takes the same view:

> Romeo, come forth; come forth, thou fearful man:
> Affliction is enamour'd of thy parts,
> And thou art wedded to calamity:
>
> [III. iii. 1-3]

he sees in the banished husband a prodigy of ill luck, misfortune has fallen in love with him. Juliet feels the same burden of hostile fate:

> Alack, alack, that heaven should practice stratagems
> Upon so soft a subject as myself!
> [III. v. 209-10]

Romeo recognises the slain Paris as "one writ with me in sour misfortune's book" [V. iii. 82]; his last fatal act is a struggle "to shake the yoke of inauspicious stars from this world-wearied flesh" [V. iii. 111-12]. The wisdom of the Friar receives the detention of the messenger as "unhappy fortune" [V. ii. 17]; in the final issue of events he tremblingly feels how "an unkind hour is guilty of this lamentable chance," how "a greater power than we can contradict hath thwarted our intents" [V. iii. 145-46, 153-54]. The note struck by the prologue rings in the final couplet of the poem: no moral lesson is read, but the word pathos is found in its simple English equivalent—

> For never was a story of more WOE
> Than this of Juliet and her Romeo.
> [V. iii. 309-10]
> (pp. 61-4)

*Richard G. Moulton, "Innocence and Pathos: The Tragedy of 'Romeo and Juliet'," in his* The Moral System of Shakespeare: A Popular Illustration of Fiction as the Experimental Side of Philosophy, *The Macmillan Company, 1903, pp. 46-64.*

### E. K. CHAMBERS  (essay date 1904)

*[Chambers occupies a transitional position in Shakespearean criticism, one which connects the biographical sketches and character analyses of the nineteenth century with the historical, technical, and textual criticism of the twentieth century. While a member of the education department at Oxford University, Chambers earned his reputation as a scholar with his multivolume works,* The Medieval Stage *(1903) and* The Elizabethan Stage *(1923); he also edited* The Red Letter Shakespeare *(1904-08). Chambers investigated both the purpose and limitations of each dramatic genre as Shakespeare presented it and speculated on how the dramatist's work was influenced by contemporary historical issues and his own frame of mind. In the excerpt below, taken from his introduction to the 1904 Red Letter edition of* Romeo and Juliet, *Chambers postulates that Shakespeare's two early plays on love—*Romeo and Juliet *and* A Midsummer Night's Dream*—have an autobiographical basis, each reflecting the dramatist's own youthful experience of this passion. He notes that the comedy is the later of the two works, written when the "poignancy" of Shakespeare's love experience had faded and his sense of humor reasserted itself;* Romeo and Juliet, *however, was composed when Shakespeare still viewed love "in the distorted glass of his own unlucky experience." On other matters, Chambers regards the conflict between love and destiny as the central theme of the play,*

*and he disagrees with those critics who consider Friar Lawrence's philosophy of moderation Shakespeare's moral axiom, calling such a reading "a singularly futile one," in that "both the love and the love's disaster are presented as things entirely beyond the power of their puppets to cause or cure by any deliberate act or abstention of their own."*]

[*Romeo and Juliet*] is a tragedy of lyric emotion, not a tragedy of philosophic insight. The convention of star-crossed lovers is familiar to all romance; and what *Romeo and Juliet* claims to do is only to give this convention yet another new setting. In a different sense, of course, it is personal enough. Like all the plays of this period, it reflects something of that disturbance in Shakespeare's own emotional life, of which the more direct, although far from clear, record is in the *Sonnets*. Shakespeare has been, at the age of thirty or thereabouts, in love, and it has proved a rather serious matter. He has come through the fire and is more or less whole again, no doubt; but he still remains much preoccupied with his puzzling and not altogether satisfactory adventure. Both *A Midsummer Night's Dream* and *Romeo and Juliet* are attempts on the part of a reflective and youngish man to state life in terms of the force by which he has been nearly tripped up and is still obsessed. That the statement is a somewhat conventional one may perhaps be explained by the fact that many other youngish poets have shared the experiences by which it is prompted. Of course, the two plays differ entirely in their way of putting things. In *A Midsummer Night's Dream* the problem is seen from the comic point of view. Life as the sport of love is a bewildering fantasy, a game of hide and seek. But *A Midsummer Night's Dream* is an afterthought, written while the poignancy of the experience faded, and the sense of humour asserted itself. Certain elements of it seem like a deliberate travesty of *Romeo and Juliet*. The comic point of view is not wholly absent from the tragic and probably earlier play. It is embodied in the irony and the audacious license of Mercutio's talk. Love to Mercutio, as to the author of *A Midsummer Night's Dream*, is one of—

> The children of an idle brain,
> Begot of nothing but vain fantasy,
> Which is as thin of substance as the air.
>
> [I. iv. 97-9]

But it must be observed that the love at which Mercutio tilts is less the romantic passion which is the subject of the play, than the mere shadow and foil of that passion, the boyish fancy which occupies the unawakened heart before the true love comes. Rosaline must endure Mercutio's jesting, but Juliet is beyond its reach, and as the plot thickens, the jesting itself passes into tragedy, and Mercutio's voice is heard no more. Essentially the temper of *Romeo and Juliet* is a high and serious one. Love comes into life like a sword, touching here a man and there a woman, and scorching them with a terrible flame. The boy and girl lovers are doomed souls from the beginning. They are raised into the highest heaven, merely that an envious fate may pluck them down again. Love is a mighty power, but destiny is mightier still, and cruel. And the conflict of these Titanic forces, crushing the young lives between them, is the issue of the tragedy.

The pity and the terror of it are heightened by the rapidity of the action and by the presaging gloom which, in true Shakespearean fashion, hangs about its earlier moments. The oncoming of love is a sudden splendour, without help and without preparation. . . . Romeo has been an amorist, posing before the mirror of his own self-consciousness, with tears and sighs and early morning walks and an affectation of solitude and the

humorous night. He was for the numbers that Petrarch flowed in, has rhymed 'love' and 'dove,' and nick-named Cupid with paradox and artful phrase. All this has meant nothing; it has been but fantasy, born of leisure and the romantic imagination. With the first sight of Juliet all this vanishes. The pale hardhearted wench Rosaline becomes as though she were not. Romeo remains a poet still, with a turn for the romantic embroidery of his emotions which contrasts with the direct simplicity of Juliet's self-abandonment. But the quality of his poetry has changed; it has put off empty conceits, and at once rings out sincere in the magnificent and characteristically Elizabethan hyperbole of—

> O, she doth teach the torches to burn bright,
>
> [I. v. 44]

and in that exquisite image, remembered from a Stratford morning—

> So shows a snowy dove trooping with crows,
> As yonder lady o'er her fellows shows.
>
> [I. v. 48-9]
> (pp. 69-71)

But the shadow of the end is already upon it all. . . . There is one brief and memorable dialogue in the pauses of the dance, darkened almost immediately by the thought of the feud between the houses; one cool night of pomegranates and the moon and the soft Italian air. And then the blow falls with the death of Tybalt, and Juliet and her Romeo become the shuttlecocks of fate, which, as ever, finds battledores ready to hand in meaningless accident and human stupidity. The insolence of a hot-headed boy, the ambition of worldly parents, the blundering of a messenger, the tremors of an ancient friar; such are the instruments which bring about the catastrophe. But they are only the instruments. For Shakespeare, at this moment of his thought, things could not have ended otherwise. As he sees love, in the distorted glass of his own unlucky experience, it is of its essence that it should issue tragically. (pp. 72-3)

The intensity of such a tragedy as *Romeo and Juliet* is the result of concentration, and every element in the play, which does not directly bring the two lovers and their fate before the audience, none the less derives its meaning from its relation to the central theme. I have already pointed out how Romeo's earlier fancy for Rosaline serves as a foil for the real passion which was lying in wait for him, and how Mercutio voices the comic aspect of love in contrast to that tragic aspect which is here the dominant inspiration of the poet. Most of the other subordinate characters are designed to add to the significance of the background. They stand for readings of love different from that of the idealist. To Paris, as to Romeo himself in his unregenerate days, it is a sentimental exercise; to Juliet's parents, part of the customary business of a well-ordered and honourable family life; to the nurse, a gross affair of the physical senses. The dramatic function of the friar is perhaps a little more difficult to formulate. He has sometimes been taken as less an actor in the tragedy than its spectator and critic; a kind of chorus, whose business it is to fit it with a moral; and this is found in the speech in which he advises Romeo to 'love moderately,' because—

> These violent delights have violent ends.
>
> [II. v. 9]

Of such a theory it can only be said that, if it correctly expounds the moral of the play, this is a singularly futile one, since it must be obvious that both the love and the love's disaster are presented as things entirely beyond the power of their puppets to cause or cure by any deliberate act or abstention of their own. There is, of course, no reason whatever why there should be a moral at all. *Romeo and Juliet* is a tragedy, not a comedy; and the burden of a tragedy is always an emotion, not an idea. So far as it has ethics, they are implied, and do not call for deliberate statement. Moreover, the friar is by no means sufficiently detached from the action to be capable of being regarded as a mere chorus. It is, after all, the failure of his scheme which leads directly to the final woes. I take it that he is not so made a main agent without intention, and that the object is to increase the spectator's sense of an irresistible destiny warring against the lovers. The wisdom of age is no more able than the ardour of youth to withstand the courses of the stars.

Intense tragedy often ends upon a softened note. This is a matter of dramatic psychology. The overwrought nerves demand the cadence. One recalls the benison of the goddess at the end of the *Hippolytus,* and the exquisite close of the *Samson Agonistes.* . . . Similarly *Romeo and Juliet* finishes upon 'a glooming peace.' All is not matter for sorrow. There is an obvious gain to set against the loss in the reconciliation of the houses over the grave of the 'poor sacrifices of their enmity'' [V. iii. 304]. And also, surely, there is the consciousness that the splendour of love in life is not wholly obliterated, even when life and love are blotted out together. We have seen Romeo turned from a boy into a man by love, and the white-souled Juliet into a breathing, passionate, daring woman. The exaltation of this endures, so that after all it would seem as if it were love and not destiny that is the indomitable force. (pp. 73-6)

> E. K. Chambers, '' 'Romeo and Juliet','' in his *Shakespeare: A Survey, 1925. Reprint by Hill and Wang, 1958, pp. 68-76.*

## STOPFORD A. BROOKE (essay date 1905)

[*Brooke argues that the feud between the families is the central event in* Romeo and Juliet, *stating that the play depicts the process by which ''Justice'' achieves harmony and reconciliation through the sacrifice of the innocent lovers.*]

In the first four scenes [of *Romeo and Juliet*], so long and careful is [Shakespeare's] preparation, all the elements of a coming doom are contained and shaped—the ancient feud, deepening in hatred from generation to generation, the fiery Youth-in-arms of whom Tybalt is the concentration; the intense desire of loving in Romeo, which thinks it has found its true goal in Rosaline but has not, and which, therefore, leaps into it when it is found in Juliet; the innocence of Juliet whom Love has never touched, but who is all trembling for his coming; the statesman's anger of the Prince with the quarrel of the houses; and finally, the boredom of the people, whose quiet is disturbed, with the continual interruption of their business by the rioters—

> Clubs, bills, and partizans! Strike! beat them down!
> Down with the Capulets, down with the Montagues!
> [I. i. 73-4]

a cry which seems to ring through the whole play. It is impossible this should continue. Justice will settle it, or the common judgment of mankind will clear the way.

The quarrel of the houses is the cause of the tragedy, and Shakespeare develops it immediately. It begins with the servants in the street; it swells into a roar when the masters join in, when Tybalt adds to it his violent fury, when the citizens push in—till we see the whole street in multitudinous turmoil, and the old men as hot as the young. . . . Then, when the Prince enters, his stern blame of both parties fixes into clear form the main theme of the play. He collects together, in his indignant reproaches, the evils of the feud and the certainty of its punishment. We are again forced to feel that the over-ruling Justice which develops states will intervene. (pp. 35-6)

[By the end of *Romeo and Juliet,* Justice] has done her work. She has passed through a lake of innocent blood to her end. Tybalt, Mercutio, Paris, Romeo, Juliet, Lady Montague, have all died that she might punish the hate between the houses. Men recognise at last that a Power beyond them has been at work. 'A greater power,' cries the Friar to Juliet, 'than we can contradict hath thwarted our intents'' [V. iii. 153-54]. The Friar explains the work of Justice to the Prince; the Prince applies the punishment to the guilty—

> Where be these enemies? Capulet! Montague!
> See what a scourge is laid upon your hate,
> That heaven finds means to kill your joys with love;
> And I, for winking at your discords too,
> Have lost a brace of kinsmen; all are punish'd.
> [V. iii. 291-95]

The reconciliation follows. That is the aim of Justice. The long sore of the state is healed. But at what a price? We ask, was it just or needful to slay so many for this end? Could it not have been otherwise done? And Shakespeare, deeply convinced, even in his youth, of the irony of life, deeply affected by it as all his tragedies prove, has left us with that problem to solve, in this, the first of his tragedies; and has surrounded the problem with infinite pity and love, so that, if we are troubled, it may be angry, with the deeds of the gods, we are soothed and uplifted by our reverent admiration for humanity.

Shakespeare could not tell, nor can we, how otherwise it might have been shaped; but to be ignorant is not to be content. We are left by the problem in irritation. If the result the gods have brought about be good, the means they used seem clumsy, even cruel, and we do not understand. This is a problem which incessantly recurs in human life, and as Shakespeare represented human life, it passes like a questioning spirit through several of his plays. I do not believe that he began any play with the intention of placing it before us, much less of trying to solve it. But as he wrote on, the problem emerged under his hand, and he became aware of it. He must have thought about it, and there are passages in *Romeo and Juliet* which suggest such thinking, and such passages are more frequent in the after tragedies. But with that strange apartness of his from any personal share in human trouble, which is like that of a spirit outside humanity—all the more strange because he represented that trouble so vividly and felt for it so deeply—he does not attempt to solve or explain the problem. He contents himself with stating the course of events which constitute it, and with representing how human nature, specialised in distinct characters, feels when entangled in it.

This is his general way of creating, and it is the way of the great artist who sets forth things as they are, but neither analyses nor moralises them. But this does not prevent any dominant idea of the artist, such as might arise in his imagination from contemplation of his subject, pervading the whole of his work, even unconsciously arranging it and knitting it into unity. Such an idea seems to rule this play. It seems from the way the events are put by Shakespeare and their results worked out, that he conceived a Power behind the master-event who caused it and meant the conclusion to which it was brought. This Power might be called Destiny or Nemesis—terms continually used by writers on Shakespeare, but which seem to me to assume in his knowledge modes of thought of which he was unaware. What he does seem to think is; That, in the affairs of men, long-continued evil, such as the hatreds of the Montagues and Capulets or the Civil Wars in England, was certain to be tragically broken up by the suffering it caused, and to be dissolved in a reconciliation which should confess the evil and establish its opposite good; and that this was the work of a divine Justice which, through the course of affairs, made known that all hatreds—as in this case and in the Civil Wars—were against the Universe. We may call this Power Fate or Destiny. It is better to call it, as the Greek did, Justice. This is the idea which Shakespeare makes preside over *Romeo and Juliet,* and over the series of plays which culminates in *Richard III.* (pp. 63-5)

[In] *Romeo and Juliet* the work of Justice is done through the sorrow and death of the innocent, and the evil Justice attacks is destroyed through the sacrifice of the guiltless. Justice, as Shakespeare saw her, moving to issues which concern the whole, takes little note of the sufferings of individuals save to use them, if they are good and loving, for her great purposes, as if that were enough to make them not only acquiescent but happy. Romeo and Juliet, who are quite guiltless of the hatreds of their clans, and who embody the loving-kindness which would do away with them, are condemned to mortal pain and sorrow of death. Shakespeare accepted this apparent injustice as the work of Justice; and the impression made at the end upon us, which impression does not arise from the story itself, but steals into us from the whole work of Shakespeare on the story, is that Justice may have done right, though we do not understand her ways. The tender love of the two lovers and its beauty, seen in their suffering, awaken so much pity and love that the guilty are turned away from their evil hatreds, and the evil itself is destroyed. And with regard to the sufferers themselves, there is that—we feel with Shakespeare—in their pain and death which not only redeems and blesses the world they have left, but which also lifts them into that high region of the soul where suffering and death seem changed into joy and life. (pp. 67-8)

*Stopford A. Brooke, " 'Romeo and Juliet'," in his* On Ten Plays of Shakespeare, *1905. Reprint by Constable and Company Ltd., 1925, pp. 35-70.*

GEORGE PIERCE BAKER  (essay date 1907)

[*Baker is among the earliest critics to point out the shortcomings of* Romeo and Juliet *as a tragic drama. He maintains that the play would be a "perfect tragedy" were it not for one detail: the detention of Friar John and, as a result, Friar Lawrence's inability to reach Romeo with the information of his and Juliet's scheme. Baker concludes that this event in the play "is at the will of the dramatist, is melodrama, and it breaks the chain of circumstances necessary for perfect tragedy." Later commentators have devoted much critical attention to this apparent flaw in Shakespeare's tragic design, while others have identified more substantial problems in the play's tragic conception.*]

[The] play, before 1600, in which Shakespeare goes deepest into life on its serious side, is, except in one detail, perfect tragedy. I mean, of course, *Romeo and Juliet.* At the moment when it is necessary that Romeo shall have news that Juliet is waiting for him in the tomb of her fathers, the swift, relentless

logic of the play breaks down. Thus far everything that has happened has been an inevitable consequence of a secret marriage between the son and the daughter of two houses at deadly feud. Grant Tybalt's state of mind when Romeo and Juliet first meet, and that first meeting must sooner or later lead to bloodshed and tragic consequences. . . . [Notice], too, how carefully Shakespeare has motivated Romeo's relation to the killing of Tybalt so that his banishment, granted the earlier scenes, comes as something well-nigh inevitable. But what is it which prevents Romeo from getting the news that his wife is merely stupefied, not dead? Merely a device of the dramatist; there is no inevitableness in this whatever. Friar John, sent to Mantua with the letter from Friar Laurence, seeks a fellow-monk as companion, only to find himself in a plague-stricken house, whence the authorities will not allow him to come out till Romeo, warned by his servant, Balthasar, of the death of Juliet, has returned to Verona to die. That turn in the play is at the will of the dramatist, is melodrama, and it breaks the chain of circumstance necessary for perfect tragedy. (pp. 275-76)

*George Pierce Baker, "Tragedy," in his* The Development of Shakespeare as a Dramatist, *1907. Reprint by The Macmillan Company, 1914, pp. 255-85.*

BRANDER MATTHEWS  (essay date 1913)

[*Matthews touches on a number of different issues in* Romeo and Juliet. *Perhaps most significant is his claim that the play, despite its differences from the tragedies of the Greeks, is "in essential accord with the requirements of Aristotle" and his assertion that Friar John's detention, though an artistic fault, "is only a petty lapse from the inevitability of the tragedy, since we all know that the fate of the lovers is already sealed." On thematic concerns, Matthews avers that all the characters contribute to the final catastrophe, to the extent that each "is forthputting and intolerant of opposition, determined to do what he has decided, regardless of the consequences to others or to himself."*]

['Romeo and Juliet'] is not the loftiest or the mightiest effort of [Shakspere's] tragic genius; but it is the most universal in the wide appeal of its pathetic story. It is the eternal tale of youthful love rushing to its fate, a tale fiery with passion and yet chilly with the sense of impending doom. It is at once epic in its sweep, lyric in its fervor and dramatic in its intensity, with a pervading note of romance not surpassed in any of his later and greater tragedies. (pp. 102-03)

The popularity of 'Romeo and Juliet' with all sorts and conditions of men and in all parts of the modern world is evidence that in its composition the poet and the playwright worked in loyal collaboration. Sometimes Shakspere is happy-go-lucky in his plotting, as in 'King John'; and sometimes when he has put his structure together with cautious skill, as in the 'Comedy of Errors,' he is willing to rely mainly on the plot for the interest of his play. He does his best as poet and as playwright both only when his heart is in his work and when his interest is deeply aroused by his theme. Indeed, his effort seems to be in proportion to the attraction exerted on him by the subject he is at work on. He is often casual and careless in his choice of material, apparently taking whatever chances to be nearest at hand and descending to stories as unworthy of his genius as those which he borrowed later as the basis of 'All's Well that Ends Well' and 'Measure for Measure.' When the material he has accepted is not really worth while (as in these two so-called comedies), his artistic endeavor is relaxed and he fails to exert his full energy; he does what he has to do in the easiest way, moving along the line of least resistance and letting the unfortunate story construct itself as best it can.

It is only those pieces wherein he discovers a topic really stimulating to his imagination that demand his utmost endeavor; and it is only in such pieces that he is nerved to put forth his whole strength both as playwright and as poet. There are only half a dozen or half a score of these plays in which we can perceive the working of all his powers at their fullest possibilities; and in them alone do we see him taking the utmost pains, toiling over his technic, setting his characters firmly on their feet, and endowing them with exuberant vitality. When he is intensely interested in the theme of a play, tragic or comic, his energy kindles and he spares no trouble to present the story to most complete advantage and to get out of it all that can be expressed from it. (pp. 103-04)

That he should have attained an elevated standard on these occasions is more remarkable than that he should more often have fallen below it. Plays were then intended solely for the two hours' traffic of the stage; they were held up to the mark by no pressure of competent criticism; they could expect no supporting praise other than the plaudits of the theater. Shakspere had before him when he composed 'Romeo and Juliet' no model of tragedy to arouse his ambition to rivalry, and no competitor pressing close at his heels. To the Elizabethan playwright the stimulus to attain the highest plane of purely artistic excellence was never external; it had to be internal, within himself; it had to be aroused by his own interest in the alluring subject which had then captivated his ardent attention. When Shakspere has such a subject, as he had in 'Romeo and Juliet,' he works as one inspired, for his own sake, for his own delight in his sheer artistry, for the joy of the deed itself; and he achieves a technical beauty, a balanced proportion, a masterly structure, a massive movement, irresistible and inevitable, and a perfect harmony of the whole, such as can be matched only in the major plays of Sophocles and Molière.

It is quite possible that he builded better than he knew, and that he did not suspect the full value of what he was doing. He may not have been conscious that in 'Romeo and Juliet' he was creating the earliest model of English tragedy. He may have supposed that he was only putting on the stage in the fashion most likely to interest an Elizabethan audience, an Italian tale which had interested him. He may have intended only to prepare a novel in action and in dialogue, such as other playwrights were producing about that time. None the less he was able to give it a unity which no other playwright had striven for. Thereby he achieved a tragedy which, however different in its method from that of the Greeks, was in essential accord with the requirements of Aristotle. (pp. 104-05)

The action of 'Romeo and Juliet' is action and not narrative; it is serious and of a certain magnitude; it is complete, having a beginning, a middle and an end; and through pity and fear it effects the proper purgation of the emotions. We may go further and insist that it has also the unity which Aristotle demanded from Greek tragedy—not the pseudo-unities of Time and Place, which the Italian critics had falsely deduced from their misreading of Aristotle's treatise, but that unity of Action, of story, which is imperative in all the arts. And this tragedy of Shakspere's has also the equally important unity of tone which characterizes the greatest of Greek plays; all its episodes and all its figures are in unison with its theme; they are all coherent and consistent; they all serve to elucidate and to illuminate. (pp. 105-06)

*Act V. Scene iii. Romeo, Juliet, and Paris. Frontispiece to the Rowe edition (1709). By permission of the Folger Shakespeare Library.*

When we compare the masterly plot of 'Romeo and Juliet' with the fragmentary construction of the serious plays which had preceded it, we may be moved to wonder at the sudden development of Shakspere's structural skill. The explanation is to be found in the fact that he had exhibited the same kind of skill in two of his comedies. The principles of playmaking are the same in comedy and in tragedy, however different the ultimate effect may be. Shakspere had practised his hand in weaving the intricate imbroglio of the 'Comedy of Errors' and in combining the fantastic misadventures of the 'Midsummer Night's Dream'; and these experiences in the construction of comedy stood him in stead when he worked out the crescendo of tragic situations in 'Romeo and Juliet.' The results are as unlike as may be, but the method is identical; and admirable as is the mechanism of this first great tragedy, it is not better in its kind than the machinery which functions so felicitously in the 'Comedy of Errors.' Of course, there is not only the wide difference between tragedy and comedy, there is also the more important divergence due to the fact that the early farce has little or no other merit than the deft ingenuity of its plot, whereas the tragedy is dowered with poetry no less than with psychology, and its lovely story moves forward so smoothly that its artful mechanism is unsuspected until we set ourselves deliberately to spy out its secrets.

Shakspere reveals here a constructive skill, surpassing anything yet seen on the English stage, a dramaturgic dexterity he was to employ again later in a scant half-dozen of his succeeding tragedies. He is here dealing with one theme only, large enough to sustain a whole play without admixture of any subplot; and he is satisfied with his single story. He sees the full value of it, and he so handles it as to get out of it all possible effect. . . . He starts no false clues and he wastes no time in by-paths. He puts in no scene which can be spared and he omits no scene which is integral to the plot. He avoids all improbability, making clear the motive for every deed and every speech and making sure that this motive is not only plausible but immediately acceptable without a cavil or even consideration. All the characters move forward naturally, obeying the law of their own being, saying and doing exactly what they would naturally say and do. Every episode is tense with increasing suspense; and no episode is marred by the disconcerting shock of mere surprise. (pp. 107-09)

Our interest in a play when we see it presented in the theater is almost in proportion to the sharpness of the struggle which animates the story. To this sharpness is due the ease with which we can apprehend this conflict, and the sympathy thereby aroused, leading us to take sides with one or the other of the combatants. In 'Romeo and Juliet' hero and heroine alike, and to an equal degree, have wills of their own and know their own minds and are bent on having their own way. They are not only wilful, but headstrong, and so they rush straight to their doom. By their implacable purpose they sustain the action from the beginning to the end. Nor are hero and heroine alone in this characteristic. Capulet is a masterful man, insistent in coercion; he is the fit father for Juliet, and she is truly his daughter. Tybalt is equally impetuous in asserting himself, volcanic and irreconcilable. The Prince is firm in resolve and prompt in action. Even Friar Lawrence is unhesitating in the successive steps he takes in aid of the ill-starred lovers. Almost every character in the play is forthputting and intolerant of opposition, determined to do what he has decided, regardless of the consequences to others or to himself. (pp. 110-11)

Attention has here been directed to the articulation of the skeleton of the action, because it is the dexterous construction which supports the story and which is responsible for the enduring success of the play. Moreover, the construction is concealed from most of those who enjoy the tragedy by the beauty of the poetry and by the variety and veracity of the psychology. In no one of Shakspere's earlier plays had he peopled his plot with characters, all of them alive and all of them true to life. It is in this play that, for the first time, he exhibits his supreme power of endowing all his creatures with a vitality of their own. Even the relatively unimportant Benvolio is individual and indisputable; and even the pale profile of the Apothecary, seen only for an instant, etches itself on the memory.

As for the poetry in which the play is bathed, that needs no praise; it is patent to all who hear it. 'Romeo and Juliet' is a true poetic drama, because it is dramatic in theme and dramatic in treatment, as well as poetic in theme and poetic in treatment. . . . Juliet and Romeo phrase their passion in most exquisite and melodious verse, and yet they utter only what is exactly appropriate for them to utter. The emotions they express with all the luxuriance of poetry, the thoughts they put into into lines of undying felicity, are the very emotions and the very thoughts they would naturally declare if they were reduced to the bare prose of every-day life.

To say this is not to suggest that Shakspere is always faultless. 'Romeo and Juliet' was composed in his youthful immaturity when he was still subject to the influences of his epoch. There are speeches couched in that high-flown grandiloquence which was common in the stage-diction of the period. Even in certain of Romeo's own utterances (though only in the earlier episodes) we find merely fanciful phrases, far-fetched comparisons, conceit hunting, quite in the manner of the Elizabethan sonneteers. There is here an impression of mere cleverness for its own sake, perhaps not insincere, but suggesting a sentiment not so deeply felt that it could not be played with for the sheer pleasure of the playing. Even Juliet, when the Nurse tells her "he is dead" [III. ii. 37] and leaves her in doubt whether or not it is Romeo who has gone, at the very height of her anxiety, quibbles on *I* and *ay*, in the taste of the time, which seems to us now false to her surging emotion. The family lamentations over the supposed death of Juliet are artificial, antiphonal, almost operatic. The dialogue is sometimes self-conscious, and therefore to that extent undramatic; and it is sometimes stiff with rhetoric, and therefore to that extent frankly theatric. (pp. 114-15)

One flaw has been picked in the conduct of the plot—the non-delivery of Friar Lawrence's letter to Romeo in Mantua. This is purely the result of an accident; it is brought about by the long arm of coincidence rather than indicated by the finger of fate. It has been defended on the plea that accident is forever interfering in the affairs of men, and that in real life the unexpected is continually happening. To urge this is to confound the reality of nature with the reality of art. There is no advantage in denying that the reason why Romeo did not receive the letter in time is arbitrary; it is due to the direct intervention of the dramatist himself. But, after all, this is but a trifle; it is only a petty lapse from the inevitability of the tragedy, since we all know that the fate of the lovers is already sealed. Even if this letter had been delivered in time, some other stroke of ill fortune would have prevented Romeo's arrival in season to save Juliet's life. What had to be, had to be; and no one need cavil at the specific accident which brought about what was certain from the very beginning. Violent delights could have only a violent end. Shakspere cleverly conceals his employment of a casual accident by only telling us about it and by not showing us the actual interference with the messenger who bore it. On the stage, narrative makes little impression; and the specators keep in mind only what they have seen with their own eyes. (p. 116)

> *Brander Matthews, "'Romeo and Juliet'," in his* Shakspere as a Playwright, *Charles Scribner's Sons, 1913, pp. 102-16.*

## JOHN ERSKINE   (essay date 1916)

[*Considering what aspects of Shakespeare's version of the Romeo and Juliet story make it so universally appealing, Erskine maintains that Shakespeare broadened the effect of his tale by transforming it from a tragedy of two young lovers into "the tragedy of young love." The critic discusses Shakespeare's alteration of his sources to accomplish this end, concluding that perhaps the most significant change was the element of innocence he contributed the legend.*]

Even before Shakspere increased its beauty and widened its appeal, the tragedy of Romeo and Juliet was, if not a classic, at least a popular story. . . . Yet in no other version than Shakspere's did this love-story enjoy a much larger audience, or appeal to a much later time, than that which read it first. Every known form of it, from Masuccio to Brooke, contained some passing note, some temporary emphasis, which clearly enough, as we can see now, narrowed and shortened its fame.

If it is curious that a tale of such vitality should have waited so long for an adequate rendering, it is still more extraordinary that in order to transfigure it into a world poem Shakspere should have made so few and such simple changes. In one sense, of course, his changes and additions were large and momentous, for at a stroke he expressed adequately for the race what it had long tried in vain to say. But in another sense the changes were slight. In fact, 'Romeo and Juliet' illustrates better than some of his greater dramas the essentially corrective quality in Shakspere's genius—the gift for setting an old story right, for adjusting it to the criticism of facts, rather than for contriving novelties and surprises. It might be argued that this play, though in subject less complex and in many ways less profound, is a happier instance than even 'Hamlet' of his genius for revising the labored inventions of other men into an obvious immortality; for Hamlet, even when clarified in Shakspere's imagination, remains still a special case, arousing and baffling our curiosity, whereas the two lovers, as he drew them, illustrate a universal experience in a manner which, with all differences of time and of language, is still universally understood. (pp. 215-16)

It is natural to ask by what changes, however slight, was the story made to fit a universal experience. It is natural to ask also whether something besides Shakspere's genius did not contribute to the remarkable result; for if his genius alone had accomplished it, why is not 'Hamlet' or 'Lear' as germane to the Latin taste as 'Romeo and Juliet,' or why is not 'Romeo and Juliet' less intelligible to the northern mood? As he tells the story, it is far more simple than in the earlier versions; for this difference his dramatic instinct may entirely account. But the story is also far more innocent, and the characters are more pure; and this difference makes of the play an essentially new drama, in spite of its far-descended plot, for the innocence of the lovers appeals to certain emotions which the Italian or French Romeo and Juliet could hardly have aroused, and the appeal to these emotions has proved as effective in Italy and France as in England and Germany. To put the whole matter in a phrase, the story before Shakspere touched it was a tragedy which befell two young lovers; he made it the tragedy of young love.

We may see more clearly the direction in which Shakspere simplified his plot if we first observe the contradiction which appears in all the great tragedies of love. Hero and heroine are doomed to love at the cost of whatever sacrifice, yet in circumstances which forbid their loving. Out of much experience of what is typical in passion, the race has chosen to remember chiefly that where the union of hearts seems most imperative, the barriers to it seem insurmountable. (p. 217)

[In the story of] Romeo and Juliet the fated love meets the fatal barriers, though time has altered the terms of the paradox. Something more than youth and beauty or the fury of passion drew them to their doom. Before Shakspere told the story, men had learned a spiritual fineness in love; Dante and Petrarch, devoted to the memory of dead women, had conferred on the human passion a mood and a ritual that raised it to the dignity of a religion, so that after them any well nurtured lover, even in the midst of the Renaissance delight in the body, would hold as the best part of his ideal the marriage of true minds. In this harmony of soul Romeo and Juliet recognized their destiny. They loved at first sight, as we say; and though the philosopher

rightly reminds us now that in times when women were rarely seen and ordinarily not to be spoken to, people fell in love at first sight since they must fall in love somehow, yet the poet made something universal of that circumstance—with true lovers there seems to be no wooing, for they are mated ere they are born. The feud also, which was to defeat Romeo and Juliet with implacable hate, had been prepared for them before their birth. Their destiny was one passion, the obstacle to it was another. (p. 218)

An ancient hatred, a destined love—upon this irreconcilable conflict the poet focuses all the distracted interests of the story he inherited, and this concentration brings about his simplicity. To fill the tragedy with meaning for all young lovers, he had only to emphasize the estrangement of Romeo and Juliet from their environment; he therefore rearranged his material so as to bring out clearly three contrasts—the contrast of love with hate, of youth with age, of courtesy with vulgarity. The contrast with hate has often been analyzed, and it needs but a brief summary here. It shows itself in the old quarrel of the houses, so old that no one remembers how it began. The servants of the families fight in the streets till they become a public nuisance, yet the quarrel with them is mechanical. With Tybalt, however, it is quite conscious; the feud is stored up in him as pure venom, hate incarnate. As though to explain him, Shakspere makes the Capulets the quarrelsome family, whose hot temper and wilfulness center in this one unpleasant character. Juliet's sorrow for him is no deeper than kinship demands, and that her parents should think her to be grieving over his death is explicable only by their exaggerated clan loyalty. Yet though Shakspere clarifies the story by distinguishing between the temper of the families, he is too observing to set up an absolute or mechanical difference; he allows the Capulets, even Tybalt, a better self, a melting mood. To be sure, whether it is a servant or Tybalt himself, it is always a Capulet who begins the fight, whereas the Montagues, at least Romeo and Benvolio, are consistently for peace. Yet we too easily overlook the instances when the impulsive Capulets take a generous course. The one glimpse we have of the gentler Tybalt is, unfortunately for him, where few readers find it—in a silence. When he comes upon Romeo and challenges him to fight, angry because the Montague had dared to come uninvited to the Capulet banquet, the newly-married husband asks for his friendship instead of his hate, and Tybalt drops the quarrel. If Mercutio had not misunderstood Romeo's motive, and had not then provoked Tybalt on his own account, there might have been a chance of reconciliation. . . . Shakspere specifies also that it was old Capulet who first confessed himself wrong and asked forgiveness at the grave of his child. Yet with all these shadings of character, the poet manages to concentrate every degree of malevolence in an almost visible cloud of death, which shadows the story from beginning to end, and which is felt quite naturally in the dark metaphors of the dialog. 'My only love sprung from my only hate' [I. v. 138], says Juliet, when she learns who Romeo is. 'Where be these enemies?' [V. iii. 291] asks the Prince ironically at the end of the play, when the two fathers look down at their dead children.

The estrangement of the children from their parents, which is suggested in the contrast between love and hate, is indicated sharply in the contrast between youth and age. The lovers are young, and in the story as Shakspere tells it only the young can sympathize with them. It is probably far-fetched to think, with some readers, that the poet deliberately sounded the theme of youth in his metaphors, as he had sounded the theme of hate; it was probably in order to express Romeo's character rather than his own comment that he often gave the youthful lover a presentiment of evil, a sense of approaching death, which would seem but the humor of love melancholy did not the event give it tragic force. . . . It is probably due to the exigencies of the plot rather than to any purpose of symbolism that the poet lays so many scenes at dawn or in the morning hours. We first hear of the sentimental Romeo as haunting the woods at dawn. It is in the morning that the first fight occurs. Romeo seeks Friar Laurence in his cell at dawn; at dawn he leaves Juliet, who is then told she must marry Paris; at dawn she is found apparently dead; at dawn she and Romeo and Paris are found in the tomb. Yet if these many sunrises are implicit in the story, it is otherwise clear that Shakspere knew the dramatic importance of the youth of the lovers. 'Wert thou as young as I,' says Romeo to Friar Laurence, 'then mightst thou speak' [III. iii. 65-8]. Shakspere takes obvious pains to emphasize Juliet's youth by making her but fourteen years old, two years younger than she had been in earlier versions of the story; and he does more than name her years—he removes from her character every suggestion of experience with the world.

This morning-glamor in hero and heroine is set off by the age of their parents, age that has forgotten what love and youth are like. So violent has Shakspere made the contrast that the tale seems to be of grandparents and grandchildren. 'Old Montague,' as Capulet calls him, cannot guess what ails Romeo, nor can Lady Montague, although the malady is too obvious to younger eyes for Benvolio not to hit it in his first question. Neither parent has the son's confidence. Yet here again, as in the other contrast, Shakspere makes his general point clearer by distinguishing between the families. If the Montagues do not understand their son, at least they show for him a tender solicitude, which the Capulets never felt for Juliet. (pp. 219-22)

As though to emphasize these master themes, these contrasts of love with hate, of youth with age, Shakspere announces them together in one consecutive passage, in the scene of Capulet's feast. It is always unsafe to ascribe to deliberate intention in Shakspere what may be only a coincidence, and it is not necessary to suppose that here the poet is conscious of all the irony in his lines; but those lines would hardly have been written had he not imagined the story as in essence a conflict between love and its inhospitable environment, between the immediateness of youth and the forgetfulness of old age. Juliet's father, who represents Age, welcomes another Capulet to the feast, asks how long it is since they two were 'in a mask,' and is astounded to find it is thirty years; in other words, the dancing days of Juliet's father ended some sixteen years before she was born. Then follows the impassioned speech of Romeo, who in the double contrast represents Youth and Love; he has caught sight of Juliet, and his heart is lost. At once Tybalt speaks, the pursuing Hate—

> This, by his voice, should be a Montague.
> Fetch me my rapier, boy.
>
> [I. v. 54-5]

The inhospitality of environment has the effect of setting Romeo and Juliet off by themselves, in a kind of loneliness. At first we meet them in their proper society, surrounded with friends and relatives; but as the story proceeds they are estranged from their world. It is this common estrangement that makes them appeal to us as one character, as devoted to a single tragic fate. In a world such as theirs, of which the strongest principle is family pride, to become strange to one's own people is disaster enough, whether or not other sufferings

follow. Even if they had escaped successfully to Mantua, or to any place under heaven, their fate, so wrenched from its order, would have been tragic; so that it even seems a kind of saving from total wreck that, if they must die, they should die in the ancestral tomb, with the reconciled living and the unreconciled dead about them. Yet until that moment the effect of the story is to isolate them. (pp. 223-24)

[The Nurse] represents that third contrast which Shakspere's audience would feel more acutely perhaps than we do—she is too vulgar to understand love. She illustrates inversely, as it were, the troubadour doctrine which Dante among others bequeathed to the Renaissance, that love is identical with gentleness of heart. Her heart was warm but not gentle; the coarseness of its fibre is shown by the anecdotes she inflicts upon her mistress, and—most fatally—in the sort of advice she gives to Juliet. So long as that advice concerns Romeo, Juliet nobly misunderstands it, and takes the counsel of physical passion to be only a rude phrasing of her own pure desires; but when the nurse urges her to marry Paris, on the ground that a living husband is better than the dead or as good as dead, Juliet perceives that they talk different languages, and she confides in the nurse no more. . . . The change that Shakspere here made in Brooke's account has the effect of stressing vulgarity in the nurse, rather than immorality. . . . Juliet is angry with the old woman for advising her to consider Romeo a dead man, as legally he is, and to marry Paris. In Brooke's poem the nurse advised Juliet to marry Paris and at the same time encourage Romeo's love, if ever he should return, so that she might be provided with both a husband and a paramour.

These contrasts between love and hate, youth and age, gentleness and vulgarity, which serve to remove Romeo and Juliet from their environment, Shakspere found almost ready in his material; he had but to clarify and emphasize them. But by rearranging certain episodes in the older story, he managed to isolate the lovers further, in a more subtle way—he cut them off from their own past, as he had estranged them from their surroundings, and by so doing he increased the feeling that a single experience, a single moment of fate, draws them together. (pp. 225-27)

It was long ago observed that as soon as [Romeo] met Juliet he became another man, less sentimental, more mature. He certainly became a man of action, decisive, daring, and resolute, and his character was ennobled by love, yet he was but one man after all, and if he appears to change, it is only because the altered circumstances give us another view of him. It has been said, for example, that in his second love he ceases to be talkative, and no longer advertises his passion. Perhaps this new secrecy is somewhat due to the fact that his life now depends on it. But it is not clear that he ceases to be talkative; certainly he was always a trifler with words. Moreover, a careful reading of this play, even without other acquaintance with literary fashions in Elizabeth's reign, would show that the young Shakspere saw nothing amiss in elaborate wordplay. The wordplay of Romeo or of Juliet is not in Shakspere's eyes a fault, nor does the habit disappear as the story proceeds. The modern reader is perplexed by Romeo's puns as he grieves for Rosaline:

*Rom.*    Give me a torch: I am not for this ambling;
          Being but heavy, I will bear the light.
*Mercutio* Nay, gentle Romeo, we must have you
          dance.

*Rom.*     Not I, believe me: you have dancing shoes
             With nimble soles: I have a soul of lead
             So stakes me to the ground I cannot move.
*Mercutio*  You are a lover; borrow Cupid's wings,
             And soar with them above a common bound.
*Rom.*     I am too sore enpierced with his shaft
             To soar with his light feathers, and so bound.
             I cannot bound a pitch above dull woe.

                                [I. iv. 11-21]

But the reader will be no less perplexed when Romeo in the same manner grieves over his banishment from Juliet:

    More honorable state, more courtship lives
    In carrion-flies than Romeo: they may seize
    On the white wonder of dear Juliet's hand
    And steal immortal blessings from her lips,
    Who, even in pure and vestal modesty,
    Still blush, as thinking their own kisses sin;
    But Romeo may not; he is banished:
    Flies may do this, but I from this must fly.

                                [III. iii. 34-41]
                                (pp. 227-28)

The change that really transfigures Romeo is the terrible sincerity that overtakes him. All that he had said or been or done in unconscious trifling, fate now remembers against him in earnest, and brings to pass. 'I'll be a candle holder and look on' [I. iv. 38], he had said cheerfully enough when Rosaline declined his suit, with other hints that happiness in love is not for him. But life takes him at his word, the imagined tragedy comes true, the sentimental words become fatal. Our perception that he is caught between the passion and the obstacle, that he knows the reality and is doomed, turns our attention from the trivial to the heroic in him. We cannot even tease him for overconfidence in his first love. He had gone to the Capulet ball, at Benvolio's challenge, to prove that no woman more beautiful than Rosaline would be there. 'Thou canst not teach me to forget' [I. i. 237], he had sworn, yet within twenty-four hours he was saying—

    With Rosaline, my ghostly father? No;
    I have forgot the name, and that name's woe.

                                [II. iii. 45-6]

In a play of another key such boasting would not pass without remark; a Benedick or a Beatrice, so caught, must stand teasing. But here the sincerity is too deep. Careless words are overlooked in the tragic shadow, or are left for fate to comment on. (p. 229)

In Shakspere's simplification of his plot, he took it for granted . . . that his characters should have no escape. But a plot which allows hero and heroine no escape will interest us less in their conduct than in their feelings; for this reason the tragic love-stories, as we have described them, are naturally lyrical. They offer us sorrow or joy for its own sake; they give us the flavor of life in a noble and intense moment. Single passages of 'Romeo and Juliet' are famed for lyrical beauty, but we sometimes forget that the whole play, though written for the stage, is a lyric. As we read or see it, we live entirely in our emotions, and know what it is to be caught between the irresistible passion and the immovable obstacle. Did not our emotions occupy us fully, such a story would be baffling in the extreme; if we looked for that harvesting of the past which is the essence of drama, we might perceive it in the death of Mercutio or Tybalt, and in the banishment of Romeo, but not in the love story, which is the principal theme. The love between Romeo and

Juliet is the result of no past here revealed, nor is it in the logic of Juliet's heredity that she should be capable of love at all. Nor can we find in the story a prospect of destiny, the epic prospect; nor, if we adopted the old definition of epic which made it exhibit the will of the gods, can we make much of a divine will which contradicts itself. But it is significant that such questions are far from us while we read or see the play. In the presence of this tragedy we simply feel.

The feelings the play inspires in us indicate the innocence into which Shakspere transposed the story, and it is probably this innocence of feeling, more than the simplification of the plot, which made the play universal. The changes in the plot are important chiefly because they bring out new lights, new values, in the portrait of hero and heroine. In Brooke's poem Juliet was sophisticated, a 'wily wench,' who knew how to deceive her mother, and who after her marriage and Romeo's banishment encouraged Paris to make love to her. Her mother trusted neither her nor the nurse, but set another servant to watch them. In Brooke, Juliet is experienced and calculating; she knows all the symptoms of falling in love, so that she can diagnose her case, and provides herself with a reason for marrying Romeo if he can be got to propose—the hope that their union may end the feud. . . . In Brooke's poem and in other accounts of the story, Romeo too was less fine. He went to the Capulet feast, for example, not in defiance of his friend's advice to fall in love with another beauty, but actually in the hope of finding a substitute for his obdurate mistress; Shakspere made him an uncalculating lover, with delicacy of speech and manners. Perhaps inspired with Protestant overzeal, Brooke had hinted that Friar Laurence's retired cell, where Romeo and Juliet were married, had served the ghostly father in his youth for amorous adventures of his own; Shakspere imagined the Friar as noble and sincere. He also brought out, as we saw, the contrast between the age of the parents and the youth of the lovers; he brought out the contrast of the Friar's philosophy with Romeo's passion, of the nurse's vulgarity with Juliet's refinement; he gave the tone of destiny to the feud by introducing Tybalt early, at the moment when Romeo sees Juliet; he developed in Mercutio that gaiety which now reinforces in the story the atmosphere of youth, just as he increased the suddenness with which the lovers realized their passion, making them fall in love actually at first sight; and by crowding the action of the story into days instead of months, he set the whole tragedy in the abrupt, volcanic atmosphere of youthful romance.

These changes contribute to a wonderful purity of character and conduct—all the more wonderful since the play exhibits, along with its spiritual innocence, such a natural frankness towards the physical basis of love as a close study of the text makes even startling. Would Juliet be so specific in her thoughts? If so, what constitutes the immense gulf between her nature and that of the nurse? The difference is that Romeo and Juliet, speaking frankly of the body, think always of the soul; recognizing intuitively, as the philosopher says, that life 'is animal in its origin,' they feel as instinctively that it is 'spiritual in its possible fruits.' So they keep the beauty of this world before our eyes and ideal values in our thoughts—and to no other love-story can such praise be wholly given. (pp. 231-34)

*John Erskine, " 'Romeo and Juliet'," in* Shaksperian Studies, *edited by Brander Matthews and Ashley Horace Thorndike, 1916. Reprint by Russell & Russell, Inc., 1962, pp. 215-36.*

## HARLEY GRANVILLE-BARKER   (essay date 1930)

*[Granville-Barker was a noted actor, playwright, director, and critic. His work as a Shakespearean critic is at all times informed by his experience as a director, for he treats Shakespeare's plays not as works of literature better understood divorced from the theater, as did many Romantic critics, but as pieces meant for the stage. As a director, he emphasized simplicity in staging, set design, and costuming. He believed that elaborate scenery obscured the poetry which was of central importance to Shakespeare's plays. Granville-Barker also eschewed the approach of directors who scrupulously reconstructed a production based upon Elizabethan stage techniques; he felt that this, too, detracted from the play's meaning. In the following excerpt on* Romeo and Juliet, *drawn from a broader study in which the critic discusses such other issues as the action of the play, the question of act division, and specific staging problems, Granville-Barker offers a detailed analysis of the characters of Romeo and Juliet. He describes the hero as a figure who evolves throughout the play, who undergoes maturation until he comes to accept his fate with tragic dignity and learns to love deeply despite the consequences. Concerning Juliet, Granville-Barker asserts that hers is "a child's tragedy" and that "half its poignancy would be gone" if we were to forget her youthful years, especially in terms of her innocent impression of the world. Although the critic notes that Juliet matures, too, as a result of her ordeal, he adds that "she has not grown older as Romeo has, nor risen to an impersonal dignity of sorrow."]*

Romeo has been called an early study for Hamlet. It is true enough to be misleading. The many ideas that go to make up Hamlet will have seeded themselves from time to time in Shakespeare's imagination, sprouting a little, their full fruition delayed till the dominant idea ripened. . . . But Romeo is not a younger Hamlet in love, though Hamlet in love seem a disillusioned Romeo. The very likeness, moreover, is largely superficial, is a common likeness to many young men, who take life desperately seriously. The study of him is not plain sailing. If Hamlet's melancholy is of the soul, Romeo's was something of a pose; and there is Shakespeare's own present pose to account for, the convention of word-spinning and thought-spinning in which he cast much of the play, through which he broke more and more while he wrote it; there are, besides, the abundant remains of Brooke's *Romeus*. Romeo is in the making till the end; and he is made by fits and starts. Significant moments reveal him; but, looking back, one perceives screeds of the inessential, more heat than light in them. (pp. 51-2)

Decorative method allowed for, the Romeo of

> Why then, O brawling love! O loving hate!
> O anything of nothing first create!
> O heavy lightness! serious vanity!
> Misshapen chaos of well-seeming forms!
> Feather of lead, bright smoke, cold fire, sick health!
> Still-waking sleep, that is not what it is . . .
>
> [I. i. 176-81]

pictures an actual Romeo truly enough; and, if it seems to overcolour him, why, this Romeo was busy at the moment overcolouring himself. Yet amid all the phrase-mongering we may detect a phrase or two telling of a deeper misprison than the obduracy of Rosaline accounts for. The inconsequent

> Show me a mistress that is passing fair,
> What doth her beauty serve but as a note
> Where I may read who passed that passing fair? . . .
>
> [I. i. 234-36]

is very boyish cynicism, but it marks the unhappy nature. And Rosaline herself was a Capulet, it seems; so, had she smiled on him, his stars would still have been crossed. He is posing to himself certainly, more in love with love than with Rosaline, posing to his family and friends, and not at all displeased by their concern. But beneath all this, the mind that, as he passes with the Maskers and their festive drum to Capulet's feast,

> . . . misgives
> Some consequence yet hanging in the stars . . .
>
> [I. iv. 106-07]

shows the peculiar clarity which gives quality to a man, marks him off from the happy-go-lucky crowd, and will at a crisis compel him to face his fate. By a few touches, then, and in a melody of speech that is all his own, he is set before us, a tragic figure from the first.

He sees Juliet. Shakespeare insists on the youth of the two, and more than once on their innocence, their purity—his as well as hers. It is not purposelessly that he is given the Dian-like Rosaline for a first love; nor that his first words to Juliet, as he touches her finger tips, are

> If I profane with my unworthiest hand
> This holy shrine . . .
>
> [I. v. 93-4]

nor that their first exchange is in the pretty formality of a sonnet, the kiss with which it ends half jest, half sacrament. But their fate is sealed by it, there and then. They cannot speak again, for Lady Capulet calls Juliet away; and Benvolio, ever cautious, urges Romeo out of danger before there may be question of unmasking and discovery. Not before he has accepted his fate, though, and she hers—for better, for worse, without doubt, question, or hesitation! He (if we are to note niceties) accepts it even more unquestioningly than she. But her cry when she first hears his name gives us early promise of the rebellious Juliet, the more reckless and desperate of the two.

They look into the abyss and then give no more heed to it. Virginal passion sweeps them aloft and away, and to its natural goal. What should hinder? Nothing in themselves, none of the misgiving that experience brings; and for counsellors they have Nurse and Friar, she conscienceless, he as little worldly as they. Juliet is no questioner, and Romeo's self-scrutinies are over. The balcony scene is like the singing of two birds; and its technical achievement lies in the sustaining at such length—with no story to tell, nor enlivening clash of character—of those simple antiphonies of joy.

Rosaline's adorer, aping disillusioned age, is hardly to be recognised in the boyishly, childishly happy Romeo that rushes to the Friar's cell. From there he goes to encounter Mercutio, still overflowing with spirits, apt for a bout of nonsense, victorious in it, too. From this and the meeting with the Nurse, back to the cell, to Juliet and the joining of their hands!

Note that the marriage and its consummation are quite simply thought of as one, by them and by the Friar. And fate accepts Romeo's challenge betimes.

> Do thou but close our hands with holy words,
> Then love devouring death do what he dare;
> It is enough I may but call her mine.
>
> [II. vi. 6-8]

It is of the essence of the tragedy that, for all their passionate haste, the blow should fall upon their happiness before it is complete, that they must consummate their marriage in sorrow.

And, in a sense, it is Romeo's ecstatic happiness that helps precipitate the blow. It lets him ignore Tybalt's insult:

> O sweet Juliet,
> Thy beauty hath made me effeminate,
> And in my temper softened valour's steel.
>
> [III. i. 113-15]

But, for all that, it has fired him to such manliness that he cannot endure the shame put upn him by Mercutio's death. Nothing is left now of the young Romeo, love-sick for Rosaline, and so disdainful of the family feud. His sudden hardihood is the complement to his chaffing high spirits of a few hours earlier; even as the grim

> This day's black fate on more days doth depend,
> This but begins the woe others must end
>
> [III. i. 119-20]

makes a counterpart to his confident challenge to fate to give him Juliet and do its worst after. He must seem of a higher stature as he stands over Tybalt's body, stern, fated, and passive to the next Capulet sword that offers, did not Benvolio force him away.

The hysterics of the next scene with the Friar, when he hears of his banishment, may seem as retrograde in character as they certainly are in dramatic method; but Shakespeare has taken the episode almost intact—and at one point all but word for word—from Brooke. And it does attune us . . . to the fortuitous disasters of the story. Then the tragic parting of the two echoes the happy wooing of the first balcony scene; and later in Mantua we find Shakespeare's Romeo, come to his full height.

Euphuism has all but vanished from the writing now. We have instead the dynamic phrase that can convey so much more than its plain meaning, can sum up in simplicity a ferment of emotion and thought.

> Is it even so? Then I defy you, stars! . . .
>
> [V. i. 24]

is his stark comment on the news of Juliet's death; but what could be more eloquent of the spirit struck dead by it? (pp. 52-6)

There follows the scene with the apothecary; its skeleton Brooke's, its clothing Shakespeare's, who employs it, not so much for the story's sake, as to give us, in repose, a picture of the Romeo his imagination has matured.

> How oft, when men are at the point of death
> Have they been merry! which their keepers call
> A lightning before death . . .
>
> [V. iii. 88-90]

he lets him say later. He does not make him merry; but he gives him here that strange sharp clarity of eye and mind which comes to a doomed man, a regard for little things when his own end means little to him. He brings him to a view of life far removed from that first boyish, selfish petulance, to a scornful contemplation of what men come to, who will not dare to throw with fate for happiness, and be content to lose rather than be denied. (pp. 56-7)

Life has broken him, and he in turn breaks all compact with life. . . . He knows that he sins in killing himself: very well, he will sin. He implores Paris not to provoke him; but, provoked, he slaughters him savagely. At last he is alone with his dead.

At this juncture we lose much by our illegitimate knowledge of the story's end, and actors, presuming on it, make matters worse. They apostrophise Paris and Tybalt and Juliet at their leisure. But the dramatic effect here lies in the chance that at any minute, as we legitimately know, Juliet may wake or Friar Laurence come; and it is Romeo's haste—of a piece with the rest of his rashness—which precipitates the final tragedy. (p. 57)

From the beginning so clearly imagined, passionately realised in the writing, deeply felt at the end; this Romeo, when he had achieved him, must have stood to Shakespeare as an assurance that he could now mould a tragic figure strong enough to carry a whole play whenever he might want to.

The first thing to mark about Juliet, for everything else depends on it, is that she is, to our thinking, a child. Whether she is Shakespeare's fourteen or Brooke's sixteen makes little difference; she is meant to be just about as young as she can be; and her actual age is trebly stressed. Her tragedy is a child's tragedy; half its poignancy would be gone otherwise. Her bold innocence is a child's, her simple trust in her Nurse; her passionate rage at the news of Tybalt's death is easily pardonable in a child, her terrors when she takes the potion are doubly dreadful as childish terrors. . . . Life to Juliet, as she glimpsed it around her, was half jungle in its savagery, half fairy tale; and its rarer gifts were fever to the blood. A most precocious young woman from our point of view, no doubt; but the narrower and intenser life of her time ripened emotion early.

Not that there is anything of the budding sensualist in her; for to be sensual is to be sluggish, not fevered. Her passion for Romeo is ruled by imagination. And were this not the true reading of it, Shakespeare would have been all but compelled, one may say, to make it so; doubly compelled. Of what avail else would be his poetry, and through what other medium could a boy-actress realise the part? The beauty of the girl's story, and its agonies too, have imagination for their fount. (pp. 58-60)

Her quick florescence into womanhood is the more vivid for its quiet prelude; for the obedient

> Madam, I am here.
> What is your will?
>
> [I. iii. 5-6]

when she first appears, for the listening to the Nurse's chatter, the borrowed dignity with which she caps her mother's snub that ends it, the simple

> It is an honour that I dreamed not of.
>
> [I. iii. 66]

with which she responds to the hint of the great match awaiting her, the listening to her mother's talk of it and the

> I'll look to like, if looking liking move;
> But no more deep will I endart mine eye,
> Than your consent gives strength to make it fly
>
> [I. iii. 97-9]

that seal our first impression of her. Where could one find a more biddable young lady?

What could one guess, either, from her first meeting with Romeo, from the demure game of équivoque she plays; though something shows, perhaps, in the little thrust of wit—

> You kiss by the book
>
> [I. v. 110]

—by which she evades the confession of a kiss returned. One moment later, though, there comes the first flash of the true Juliet; a revelation to herself, is it, as to us?

> My only love sprung from my only hate. . . .
>
> [I. v. 138]

And she stands, lost in amazement at this miracle that has been worked in her (even as Romeo will stand later lost in the horror of Tybalt's slaying), till the puzzled Nurse coaxes her away.

We next see her at her window. Yet again Shakespeare holds her silent a little, but for that one 'ay me' to tell us that now the still depths in her are brimming; when they brim over, again it is to herself she speaks. The scene is conventionalised to a degree, with its overheard soliloquies, its conceits, its lyric flow. It turns every exigency of stage and acting to account, and its very setting, which keeps the lovers apart, stimulates passionate expression and helps sustain it. . . . Modesty, boldness, shyness, passion, each and all shot through with innocence, chase their way through the girl's speech; and Romeo, himself all surrender, sings to her tune. Together, but still apart, this is their one hour of happiness, and she is enskied in it, even as he sees her there.

We find her next, two scenes later, impatient for the Nurse's return with news of him; and in reckless delight and quick imagery for its expression she rivals Romeo now—the Juliet that could stand so mute! Then comes the quiet moment of the marriage. Making her reverence to the Friar, she may seem still to be the self-contained young lady we first saw; but even in the few lines of formal speech we hear a stronger pulse-beat and a deeper tone. She stands, not timidly at all, but just a little awed upon the threshold of her womanhood.

After the tragic interval that sees Mercutio and Tybalt killed we find her alone again, and again her newly franchised self, expectant of happiness, pending the blow that is to kill it. (pp. 60-3)

Till now, we have seen Juliet at intervals; but with Romeo's farewell to her and his passing to Mantua she becomes for a space the sole centre of the play, while misfortune batters at her. In her helpless courage is the pathos, in her resolve from the first to kill herself sooner than yield—she is fourteen!—is the high heroism of the struggle. . . . Her mother repulses her, her Nurse betrays her; the trap is closing on her. She flies to the Friar. There is Paris himself; and for appearance sake she must stop and parley with him while he claims her with calm assurance as his wife, must let him kiss her, even! Back she flies again from the shaken old man, armed with the only aid he can give her, one little less desperate than the dagger that never leaves her. The time is so short; and, in her distraction—playing the hypocrite as she must, and over-playing it—she even contrives to make it shorter. It escapes her quite that she is now—and fatally—not following the Friar's directions. She easily hoodwinks her mother and her nurse; then, left alone, outfacing terror, she drinks the potion.

She wakes in the vault, hopefully, happily:

> O comfortable friar, where is my lord?
> I do remember well where I should be
> And there I am. Where is my Romeo?
>
> [V. iii. 148-50]

to have for all answer

> Thy husband in thy bosom there lies dead.
>
> [V. iii. 155]

and to see Friar Laurence—even he!—turn and desert her. Should we wonder at the scorn sounded in that

> Go, get thee hence, for I will not away. . . .
>
> [V. iii. 160]

Romeo's dagger is all she has left.

The simplest reason for Juliet's leave-taking of life being short is that Romeo's has been long. But, theatrical effect apart, the sudden brutal blow by which her childish faith in the 'comfortable Friar' is shattered, and her unquestioning choice of death, make a fitting end to the desperate confidence of her rush to escape from what is worse than death to her. In the unreflecting haste of it all lies her peculiar tragedy. One day a child, and the next a woman! But she has not grown older as Romeo has, nor risen to an impersonal dignity of sorrow. Shakespeare's women do not, for obvious reasons, so develop. They are vehicles of life, not of philosophy. Here is a life cut short in its brightness; and it is a cruel business, this slaughter of a child betrayed. (pp. 65-6)

> Harley Granville-Barker, "'Romeo and Juliet'," in his Preface to Shakespeare, second series, Sidgwick & Jackson, Ltd., 1930, pp. 1-66.

## CAROLINE F. E. SPURGEON (essay date 1935)

[Spurgeon's Shakespeare's Imagery and What It Tells Us (1935) inaugurated the "image-pattern analysis" method of studying Shakespeare's plays, one of the most widely used methods of the mid-twentieth century. In this work, she interprets the thematic structure of the plays through an examination of patterns in the imagery. Spurgeon also sought to learn about Shakespeare's personality from a study of his images, a course which few of her disciples followed. Since publication of her book, earlier works on image patterns in Shakespeare have been discovered, but none was so important in the history of Shakespearean criticism as Spurgeon's. In the following excerpt, Spurgeon is the first critic to analyze the imagery in Romeo and Juliet and assess its importance to the drama. She notes the numerous examples where the lovers comprehend each other's beauty in terms of starlight, sunlight, moonlight, lightning, and so on, and points out how they view the world around them in opposite terms of darkness, night, clouds, and mist. Because of the dominance of this imagery, Spurgeon suggests, Shakespeare must have viewed the story "in its swift and tragic beauty, as an almost blinding flash of light, suddenly ignited, and as swiftly quenched."]

In Romeo and Juliet the beauty and ardour of young love are seen by Shakespeare as the irradiating glory of sunlight and starlight in a dark world. The dominating image is light, every form and manifestation of it: the sun, moon, stars, fire, lightning, the flash of gunpowder, and the reflected light of beauty and of love; while by contrast we have night, darkness, clouds, rain, mist and smoke.

Each of the lovers thinks of the other as light; Romeo's overpowering impression when he first catches sight of Juliet on the fateful evening at the Capulets' ball is seen in his exclamation,

> O, she doth teach the torches to burn bright!
> It seems she hangs upon the cheek of night
> Like a rich jewel in an Ethiop's ear.
>
> [I. v. 44-6]

To Juliet, Romeo is 'day in night' [III. ii. 17]; to Romeo, Juliet is the sun rising from the east, and when they soar to love's ecstasy, each alike pictures the other as stars in heaven, shedding such brightness as puts to shame the heavenly bodies themselves.

The intensity of feeling in both lovers purges even the most highly affected and euphuistic conceits of their artificiality, and transforms them into the exquisite and passionate expression of love's rhapsody.

Thus Romeo plays with the old conceit that two of the fairest stars in heaven, having some business on earth, have entreated Juliet's eyes to take their place till they return, and he conjectures,

> What if her eyes were there, they in her head?
>
>                                            [II. ii. 18]

If so,

> The brightness of her cheek would shame those stars,
> As daylight doth a lamp;
>
>                                          [II. ii. 19-20]

and then comes the rush of feeling, the overpowering realisation and immortal expression of the transforming glory of love:

> her eyes in heaven
> Would through the airy region stream so bright
> That birds would sing and think it were not night.
>
>                                          [II. ii. 20-2]

And Juliet, in her invocation to night, using an even more extravagant conceit, such as Cowley or Cleveland at his wildest never exceeded, transmutes it into the perfect and natural expression of a girl whose lover to her not only radiates light, but is, indeed, very light itself:

> Give me my Romeo; and, when he shall die,
> Take him and cut him out in little stars,
> And he will make the face of heaven so fine,
> That all the world will be in love with night,
> And pay no worship to the garish sun.
>
>                                          [III. ii. 21-5]

Love is described by Romeo, before he knows what it really is, as

> a smoke raised with the fume of sighs;
> Being purged, a fire sparkling in lovers' eyes;
>
>                                          [I. i. 190-91]

and the messengers of love are pictured by Juliet, when she is chafing under the nurse'd delay, as one of the most exquisite effects in nature, seen especially on the English hills in spring— the swift, magical, transforming power of light:

> love's heralds [she cries] should be thoughts,
> Which ten times faster glide than the sun's beams,
> Driving back shadows over louring hills.
>
>                                          [II. v. 4-6]

The irradiating quality of the beauty of love is noticed by both lovers; by Juliet, in her first ecstasy, when she declares that lovers' 'own beauties' are sufficient light for them to see by [III. ii. 9], and, at the end, by Romeo, when, thinking her dead, he gazes on her and cries,

> her beauty makes
> This vault a feasting presence full of light.
>
>                                            [V. iii. 85-6]

There can be no question, I think, that Shakespeare saw the story, in its swift and tragic beauty, as an almost blinding flash of light, suddenly ignited, and as swiftly quenched. He quite deliberately compresses the action from over nine months to the almost incredibly short period of five days; so that the lovers meet on Sunday, are wedded on Monday, part at dawn on Tuesday and are reunited in death on the night of Thursday. The sensation of swiftness and brilliance, accompanied by danger and destruction, is accentuated again and again; by Juliet, when she avows their betrothal

> is too rash, too unadvised, too sudden,
> Too like the lightning, which doth cease to be
> Ere one can say 'It lightens';
>
>                                          [II. ii. 118-20]

and by Romeo and the friar, who instinctively make repeated use of the image of the quick destructive flash of gunpowder. Indeed the friar, in his well-known answer to Romeo's prayer for instant marriage, succinctly, in the last nine words, sums up the whole movement of the play:

> These violent delights have violent ends,
> And in their triumph die; like fire and powder
> Which as they kiss consume.
>
>                                           [II. vi. 9-11]

Even old Capulet, whom one does not think of as a poetical person, though he uses many images—some of great beauty— carries on the idea of light to represent love and youth and beauty, and of the clouding of the sun for grief and sorrow. He promises Paris that on the evening of the ball he shall see at his house

> Earth-treading stars that make dark heaven light;
>
>                                            [I. ii. 25]

and when he encounters Juliet weeping, as he thinks, for her cousin Tybalt's death, he clothes his comment in similar nature imagery of light quenched in darkness:

> When the sun sets, the air doth drizzle drew;
> But for the sunset of my brother's son
> It rains downright.
>
>                                          [III. v. 126-28]

In addition to this more definite symbolic imagery, we find that radiant light, sunshine, starlight, moonbeams, sunrise and sunset, the sparkle of fire, a meteor, candles, torches, quick-coming darkness, clouds, mist, rain and night, form a pictorial background, or running accompaniment, to the play, which augments unconsciously in us this same sensation.

We meet it at once in the prince's description of the attitude of the rival houses

> That quench the fire of your pernicious rage
> With purple fountains issuing from your veins;
>
>                                            [I. i. 84-5]

and later, in the talk of Benvolio and Montague about the rising sun, the dew and clouds, followed by Romeo's definition of love, Capulet's words just quoted, Benvolio's riming proverb about fire, the talk of Romeo and Mercutio about torches, candles, lights and lamps, the flashing lights and torches of the ball, four times accentuated, Romeo's conception of Juliet as a 'bright angel',

> As glorious to this night, . . .
> As is a winged messenger of heaven;
>
>                                           [II. ii. 27-8]

in the moonlight in the orchard, the sunrise Friar Lawrence watches from his cell, the sun clearing from heaven Romeo's sighs, the exquisite light and shadow swiftly chasing over Juliet's words in the orchard, the 'black fate' [III. i. 119] of the day on which Mercutio was killed, the 'fire-eyed fury' [III. i. 124] which leads Romeo to challenge Tybalt, their fight, to which they go 'like lightning' [III. i. 172], the sunset which Juliet so ardently desires to be swift 'and bring in cloudy night immediately' [III. ii. 4], the exquisite play of quivering light from darkness through dawn, till

> jocund day
> Stands tiptoe on the misty mountain tops,
>
> [III. v. 9-10]

which forms the theme of the lovers' parting song; and, at the last, in Romeo's anguished reply to Juliet, pointing the contrast between the coming day and their own great sorrow:

> More light and light: more dark and dark our woes!
>
> [III. v. 36]

And then, at the end, we see the darkness of the churchyard, lit by the glittering torch of Paris, quickly quenched; Romeo's arrival with his torch, the swift fight and death, the dark vault, which is not a grave but a lantern irradiated by Juliet's beauty, Romeo's grim jest on the 'lightning before death' [V. iii. 90], followed immediately by the self-slaughter of the 'star-crossed' lovers, the gathering together of the stricken mourners as the day breaks, and the 'glooming' peace of the overcast morning when

> The sun for sorrow will not show his head.
>
> [V. iii. 306]

Shakespeare's extraordinary susceptibility to suggestion and readiness to borrow are well exemplified in this running imagery. He took the idea from the last place we should expect, from the wooden doggerel of Arthur Brooke. . . . (pp. 310-15)

But although Shakespeare took the idea from his original, it scarcely needs saying that in taking it, he has transformed a few conventional and obvious similes of little poetic worth into a continuous and consistent running image of exquisite beauty, building up a definite picture and atmosphere of brilliance swiftly quenched, which powerfully affects the imagination of the reader. (pp. 315-16)

> Caroline F. E. Spurgeon, "Leading Motives in the Tragedies," in her Shakespeare's Imagery and What It Tells Us, 1935. Reprint by Cambridge at the University Press, 1971, pp. 309-56.

## ELMER EDGAR STOLL   (essay date 1937)

[Stoll was one of the earliest critics to attack the method of character analysis that had dominated nineteenth-century Shakespearean criticism. Instead, he maintained that Shakespeare was primarily a man of the professional theater and that his works had to be interpreted in the light of Elizabethan stage conventions and understood for their theatrical effects, rather than their psychological insight. Stoll has in turn been dispraised for seeing only one dimension of Shakespeare's art. In the following excerpt, Stoll refutes the psychological interpretation of Romeo and Juliet, claiming that critics err in seeking the "tragic fault" in the lovers that precipitates their deaths. According to Stoll, Shakespeare was not concerned here with providing motives for his characters' actions, but instead was intent on creating dramatic interest, borrowing certain conventions freely from romantic tradition in order to give his story shape and direction. Stoll thus considers

Romeo and Juliet Shakespeare's dramatization of the conflict between ideal, passionate love and destiny—a struggle between the lovers and the unlucky fate, symbolized by the family feud, in which they find themselves. The critic also disagrees that the friar is Shakespeare's mouthpiece in Romeo and Juliet, stating that he is a chorus figure "only in so far as his moralizings and warnings have the effect of misgivings and forebodings, which contribute to the suspense."]

Most of Shakespeare's lovers in tragedy could with propriety and without much change have been put into comedies, or at least into the romantic sort that Shakespeare nearly always wrote; and those in comedy could have been put into his tragedies. It is not so with Corneille or Racine, Jonson or Molière. In their comedies lovers betray some foible or affectation; in their tragedies, either a fault or a maladjustment. By those dramatists love is dramatized.

By Shakespeare, strictly speaking, it is not. The lovers are less closely implicated with the action, less complicated in themselves. The passion, or the soul that experiences it, is little analysed but is exhibited directly and as a whole; and still less than Shakespeare's other heroes and heroines are the lovers the authors of their own fortune or misfortune. The obstacles to their happiness are not internal, but are villains or enemies, relatives or rivals; they suffer from no inner maladjustments or misunderstandings, but only from those arising out of deception or slander, feigning or disguise. Their jealousy, when they have any—the heroines have none—is ordinarily not born in their bosoms, but injected into them, witness Othello, the Claudio of Much Ado, and Posthumus [in Cymbeline]. . . . Their coquetry is open and innocent, as Portia's is when she gives Bassanio reasons for delaying his choice [in The Merchant of Venice]; not deceitful or cruel, as Rosalind's is not when she peeps a little from under the veil of her disguise [in As You Like It]: it has the attraction, not of sophistication but of unsophistication, or if of coquetry, that which renounces itself, on Juliet's principle,

> Or if thou think'st I am too quickly won,
> I'll frown and be perverse and say thee nay,—
> So thou wilt woo; but else, not for the world.
>
> [II. ii. 95-7]

The only real coquette is Cressida, for Cleopatra is in love and has recourse to coquetry only as a lure. Shakespeare's comedy and tragedy alike are not studies, not human documents; and the passion, arising at first sight, is a simple reaction, to the woman's beauty or the man's noble mien. It is an affair of the imagination, not of the intellect, and, apparently, neither the result of a community of tastes or aspirations, on the one hand, nor the cause of a new envisagement of life or adjustment to it, on the other. In this respect, consequently, the plays are scarcely dramas. The passion is not pitted against others such as ambition or revenge; not brought into conflict with ideals such as honour, or with duties such as those to parents or society. It is generally both spontaneous and contagious, untroubled by fear or doubt or questioning. (pp. 1-3)

Now all this is true of Romeo and Juliet. . . . They fall in love at sight and for ever, and, in their own personal relations, are material only for poetry, not for psychology but for character-drawing. Their struggle is not with each other, nor within themselves, but only with their quarrelling families, against the stars. They do not misunderstand or deceive, allure or elude, suspect or tantalize, turn, naturally or unnaturally, from love to hatred or wreak themselves upon each other, as both in drama and in life lovers not uncommonly do; nor are they swayed or inwardly troubled by their inheritance of enmity, or by filial fealty, or for more than a moment by thoughts of a Capulet's blood on Romeo's hand. There is not even the veil of a disguise between them. . . . 'All for Love and The World Well Lost' might be the title, though in a different sense from Dryden's; and it is not their self-centred absorption and infatuation or any other internal entanglement that brings them to their death, but (the poet makes clear) the feud and destiny.

There is no tragic fault, or (as we shall see) none in the ordinary sense of the word. Certainly there is none of a social or psychological sort. The play itself, like most of Shakespeare's love stories, is conceived in terms not only of poetry but of romance, of *amor vincit omnia* [love conquers all]; and these young and tender things are no more to be judged for disobeying and deceiving their parents than Desdemona or Imogen [in *Othello* and *Cymbeline*], Florizel or Perdita [in *The Winter's Tale*], Ferdinand or Miranda [in *The Tempest*], who also do. . . . [In] so far as their recklessness occurs to us it is meant to redound to the lovers' credit. The point of the play—the wonder of the story—is, not how such a love can arise out of hatred and then triumph over it in death, but that it does. . . . I have little for theorists like Gervinus, who complains of Juliet's quibbling and prevaricating with her parents, and concealing her purposes, as she goes to confession, under the mask of piety [see excerpt above, 1849-50]. . . . If the Heidelberg professor, so widely read in literature, did not appreciate the romantic tradition, with its plenary indulgence of lovers, even from the times of the Greek romances, he ought, as a Teuton at least, to have remembered the source, the *Quelle*, an Italian novel, an English poem, famous in Shakespeare's day.

The social or ethical bias, however, now plays less part in the verdict than the psychological. For some critics the lovers, particularly Romeo, are *not* in equilibrium, and hence their fall. . . . Not only is there no suggestion that Romeo's passion is morbid, or that he is in himself unmanly; there is also in Shakespeare's dramaturgy generally, as in the ancient, no requirement that a man's death or ruin should proceed from an inner flaw. The motivation of the action, as in *Hamlet, Othello, King Lear,* and *Macbeth,* though not in *Coriolanus,* is more external. . . . [In all these tragedies] the presentation of character is poetical rather than psychological and ethical, as in Greek Tragedy, in Homer and Virgil, and these anxious searchings for a tragic sin are out of place. Above all is that true of such a story as this, and in the resistance of these lovers to their fate they are not really succumbing to it. In Mantua, after his banishment, Romeo has not been pining and moping, absence has not been a torment, and before he gets the news of his lady's death he has, throughout the day, been lifted above the ground with cheerful thoughts. His dream has seemed to him of good omen. But when that has by the news been made an ambiguous mockery, he at once cries out,

> Is it even so? Then I defy you, stars,
> [V. i. 24]

in the same spirit as when he looked at the body of Tybalt, whose cousin he had just married, and whose blood, for that reason, he had a moment before refused to shed. 'O, I am fortune's fool!' [III. i. 136]. And such he is now—though not altogether—a second time. Before that, on the point of marriage, he had cried,

> Then, love-devouring Death do what he dare,
> It is enough I may but call her mine.
> [II. vi. 7-8]

For in those days men really believed in fortune, in the stars, in Death with his pestilent scythe; and they did so all the more of course when in a tragedy.

That is not the language of weakness, though also not of reason and restraint: It is the lovers' youth that we must bear in memory, and their innocence, for both are heightened and emphasized; an we must equally bear in mind that the play is a poem. Juliet is fourteen, not sixteen as in the source, and Romeo is little more than a lad. In the poet's hands both are far less sophisticated and artful; and a contrast or opposition is kept before us (though always concretely) not only between love and hatred, youth and age (as Mr. Erskine notices [see excerpt above, 1916] but also between love and death. The struggle is only external, and the drama now and then verges upon the lyric . . . ; and not because there is anything wrong with them do the youth and maiden perish but only because 'love is strong as death,' and fate unfriendly. (pp. 3-8)

As a youth Romeo enjoys immunities; and one of these, at the outset, is that of being 'love-bewildered,' as Coleridge puts it [see excerpt above, 1834], in love with love in the distant and cruel shape of Rosaline. To this he proves his right, for once he sets eyes upon Juliet he is in love indeed and is himself again. The lovesickness, evidently, was transitory and normal. It is now in a different vein that he talks, not only to Juliet but (of every-day matters) to other people. He can jest again—lovesick lovers cannot—and more than hold his own at the game against Mercutio. . . . No longer does he pace under the sycamores by night or pen sonnets in a dark room by day. Here may seem to be an instance of a resultant adjustment to life such as I have to Shakespeare's lovers just denied; but it is rather a readjustment; and in any case it is not explained. . . . All there is to the present situation is that the youth had been healthy and lively enough before the recent perturbation, as appears not only from Mercutio's words but from the previous anxious comments of his parents, and now by a real solid love has been restored. He is no sentimentalist or philanderer. And surely it is no weakling . . . that avenges Mercutio or, still less, that, rising above the requirements of the punctilio, spares Tybalt when he challenges him before this. These high external obligations he unmistakably and gloriously heeds.

Dowden, who has admirably refuted the critics' dour morality, particularly that of Gervinus, is still troubled by their psychology [see excerpt above, 1881]. He does remember Romeo's youth but seems not fully to appreciate the naturalness and temporariness of his lovesickness. He compares him with Hamlet, and thinks his will is sapped, though by a different disease of soul. 'To him . . . emotion, apart from thought and apart from action, is an end in itself.' His is a serious condition, and while he is eventually cured by his real love for Juliet, he is not at once. No doubt Dowden is affected by the greater imaginativeness of Romeo's wooing than of Juliet's and by his lamentations in the Friar's cell. (pp. 8-10)

If Romeo be morbid, Juliet, who dies to join him, even as he has died to join her, must surely be the same; but of that, naturally enough, little has been said. If Juliet cannot pass the censor, who, pray can? Another charge, made by both the Germans and also the Swedes . . . , is that these Italian passions are unbalanced in another meaning of the word, that is, sensual; and here Juliet, in her frank and eager expectation of her wedding-night, bears the burden of reproach, though in so far as lack of acquaintance at the outset is also matter for deprecation, Romeo shares it. (p. 10)

[One] wonders at the critics' failure to remember early literature, particularly the romantic. In medieval and Renaissance story, whether verse or prose, epic, ballad, or drama, it is love at first sight generally, without regard to reason or prudence. Was Dante sensual? But it was so that he fell in love in the *Vita Nuova*, and how many words had he had with the maiden before she died? What, moreover, do these critics make of Shakespeare elsewhere? Are Rosalind, Viola, Olivia, Miranda, and their lovers, too, no better than they should be, no more respectable and continent, indeed, than the actors and actresses that ordinarily undertake to play them? As at least romantic poets know, extremes may meet, outwardly high romance is not far removed from folly, and Coleridge's ethereal Genevieve falls into her cavalier's arms without waiting for a proposal. To the casual onlooker, Romeo and Juliet may seem to love and marry as carelessly and unthinkingly as folk do at Hollywood or at college; but not to us, who know them. (pp. 11-12)

In drama, at any rate, if not in life, there is justification enough for this instantaneous and explosive temperament—in drama, which has no more than three or four hours at its disposal, above all the Elizabethan, which tells the whole story, not, like the modern, merely the last chapter, and, whether in tragedy or in comedy, often more stories than one. And what is as important, stories with action, incidents, and vicissitudes; the taste of the Elizabethan theatrical public, and (so far as we know) that of its most popular purveyor, not easily contenting itself . . . without plot or complication. Hence the need of the dramatist's availing himself of summary and compendious devices; and this of love at first sight, in *Romeo and Juliet, As You Like It,* the *Tempest,* in *Twelfth Night* thrice over, in *Much Ado* so far as Claudio is concerned, ties the knot of the complication and precipitates the action like another, that of slander, in *Othello, Much Ado, Cymbeline,* the underplot of *King Lear.* Both devices, like overhearing and soliloquy, disguise and mistaken identity, are short cuts, contrivances to that end highly desirable in drama—compression and intensity. Time in *Romeo and Juliet,* as in most of Shakespeare's love stories when compared with their sources, has been reduced by the dramatist from a stretch of months to one of days, in this to four—there, if nowhere else, are the trammels of psychology and realism flung aside! And if Romeo and Juliet, in a story which is also that of a feud and the Capulets' match-making, had been required to proceed properly and decorously through the psychologically and socially appropriate stages of acquaintance and a growing attachment, Juliet, indeed, would, like most flesh-and-blood Italian girls of her era, have been fast married to Paris before ever her heart had awakened. In the play as it is, compression permits of comprehension. Through the instantaneousness of the love-making, there are, on the same principle, both room and warrant for an in itself improbable number of external events and an in itself improbable range of internal development. In their three days the inexperienced pair grow up before us, to tragic stature. Juliet breaks away from the counsellor of her childhood and dares to take the potion, Romeo because of his love puts up with insults from Tybalt, despite his love avenges Mercutio, and either of them unhesitatingly has recourse to death in order to rejoin the other. And these doings are made plausible, not of course by analysis or adequate motivation, but . . . by the temper and utterance of the youth or the maiden, which harden and deepen without losing their identity.

The merely dramatic conventions and requirements, however, are here less significant than the narrative, which are older. . . .

*Act V. Scene iii. Paris and Romeo. Frontispiece to the Hanmer edition by Francis Hayman (1744). By permission of the Folger Shakespeare Library.*

[Love] at first sight began with the story of Adam and Eve, and the calumniator credited (very probably) even before Joseph and Potiphar, Bellerophon and Proetus. That in this particular story the romantic effect of such an emotional explosion, though on the stage naturally greater, had already proved striking, appears from the many versions before Shakespeare approached the subject. Even reading the *novella* or poem, the public had delighted in this angelical cry of love arising, unexpectedly and spontaneously, from out of the harsh tumult of quarrel, in defiance of death.

Moreover, the thing has actually happened, to folk quite above the cultural level of our first parents in the garden; this convention is not remote from reality: and in the case before us the only question should be whether it is made plausible. There is motivation, of a sort; yet here again there is little analysis and still less of novelty, but the summary method followed in Shakespeare's other love stories, and if this one does not satisfy Teutonic and Scandinavian rigour, I do not see how the others can. One of my students, with a German given name and a North-British surname, has, with the acuteness of the latter race and the laboriousness of the former, examined and tabulated the data in Shakespeare generally; and these turn out to be surprisingly like those in the medieval epic poets and troubadours and the Renaissance sonneteers. As already suggested, and as of such impetuosity could be expected, Shakespeare's heroes love their ladies for their beauty, pure and simple. When they go into detail, it is still a matter mainly of externals. Not the face but the white hand is most fondly dwelt upon. . . . After the hand in importance comes the breath; then the eyes; then the hair, nearly always golden; then the lips of coral and the voice of silver: all traditional enough. Sometimes the form, the carriage, and the gait are touched upon; and once love has its way, qualities and accomplishments, but in terms that might be duplicated everywhere in earlier poetry. . . . And what the women, for their part, admire in their lovers is beauty too—here again Shakespeare might be found insufficiently Nordic, and regrettably akin to Homer and Virgil, who take time and pains to tell us who were the handsomest warriors—but the ladies are still less original and analytical, though they pay more attention to form and bearing, less to curls and complexion, and for accomplishments and virtues prefer the martial and noble.

In short, the reasons for the love are as summary and traditional as the manner of its appearance; and in the play before us it is, again, by the heroine's beauty that the hero is captivated, even as in the medieval troubadours and romancers. At various times he momentarily praises her eyes, hand, cheek, and lips; but has nothing to say of her wit, wisdom, and chastity though he has had something to say of Rosaline's. There is no occasion, for he does not fall into discussion of her with Benvolio; but he might well have done so with the Friar as he informed him of the change, and the omission is only a clearer indication how little precise and fundamental motiving counts. We have seen already how love brings the pair to their death only as in a poem or fable, without psychological causation, and it is so that their love arises. In Shakespeare elsewhere, as in most other Elizabethan drama, love, like jealousy and villainy, is as sudden; and a good deal of the motiving is traditional and superficial, more narrative or epical than strictly dramatic. It is for the story, to get the action started, as in the present instance, or to keep it moving, as in that . . . of Romeo's and the whole Capulet family's precipitate conduct. It is pretty arbitrary, with little reason or provocation, though there may have been some in the source. (pp. 12-17)

What interests Shakespeare, and should interest us, is not so much the motives but what is moved; that is, the action, of which the characters are a part but not the source; the poem, which is not a study of the passions, but a presentation of a contrast or conflict between them and of the harmony in their effect upon us, and not much of any conflict within the single bosom, either, as it is with Corneille and Racine. For Romeo and Juliet the path is pretty straight and undeviating, still more so than for Othello, Lear, Hamlet, and Macbeth; all that the young man has to contend with is the hatred of the families, and the stars, which lend the feud the dignity of a fate. In the tragedy the quarrel plays a larger part than in the source; it is the fate-*motif,* and four times, at critical moments, it makes itself audible and visible—at the ball and at the deaths of the Prince's kinsman, of Mercutio and Tybalt, of Paris and the lovers—as the Ghost in *Hamlet* and the Weird Sisters in *Macbeth* do thrice. And to the ominous luminaries above Romeo lifts his eyes before he enters the ball-room, when he hears the news of Juliet's death, and before he dies himself. It is a simple and sensuous, imaginative and passionate effect at which the poet is aiming.

Romeo's love for Rosaline has long been taken to be an internal preparation; it is—for an external contrast and surprise. No doubt there is a psychological reality in the passing of a hopeless lovesickness, under the spell of a higher influence, into

love itself; but there is none in its doing this so completely and instantaneously, as the youth comes to the dance to see Rosaline, not, as in the source, to find a substitute for his obdurate mistress, but to prove her move beautiful than any. The contrast is external; there is no struggle or hesitation; to Rosaline, from now on, he gives not another thought. Instead of natural and psychological, gradual and probable, Romeo's falling in love is made the contrary; and this simply to produce the greater effect for Juliet's beauty and for the love that, without consideration of family, rank, or any other terrestrial concern, takes possession of both. The Rosaline affair has, further, the purely dramatic or poetic advantage of offering an interesting contrast between Romeo's demeanour now and before, and (with comic effect) between the past and the present connection, as Mercutio thinks him still in love with Rosaline or else no longer in love at all, or as the Friar, fearing the sleepless youth has passed the night with her, learns he would now be married to another:

> Holy Saint Francis, what a change is here!
>
> [II. iii. 65]

'Just what I expected,' he might have said, and either he or somebody else in the play should have said, if the psychological theory were sound.

It is a surprise for him, who does not and could not know the lovers and their feelings as we do; but, though of a different sort, it was meant to be a surprise for us in the first place. It is poetically, dramatically, not psychologically, that the characters are meant to interest us, even more than in Shakespeare generally; and as usually in Shakespeare's tragedy and even in comedy (witness Benedick and Beatrice), they do this more deeply because they are in a situation not wholly of their making. . . . It is contrary to psychology, contrary to nature, that in the presence of Juliet the romantic Romeo should forget Rosaline at once and for good and all; but that he should do so throws his love for Juliet into high relief.

The great emotional situation is what Shakespeare was seeking; and in this early and lesser tragedy Romeo is swept off his feet by love as, in the later ones, Othello, Posthumus, and Leontes are by jealousy, Macbeth by ambition, Hamlet by the Ghost's revelations and command, and Lear by thwarted paternal affection. And for the full impression we need—we must have—no analysis or previously indicated inclination, but a Romeo thinking, the moment before, of another woman when we hear him break out at the ball, at the sight of Juliet:

> O, she doth teach the torches to burn bright!
>
> [I. v. 44]

and we need a Juliet who has already averred that matrimony is an honour that she dreams not of, when she bids her Nurse

> Go ask his name.—If he be marrièd,
> My grave is like to be my wedding-bed . . .
>
> [I. V. 134-35]

a Juliet and a Romeo each aware, the moment after, that the other is an enemy. For the full impression, moreover, we need the traditional, the simple and sensuous motive of the maiden's beauty. With the full force of the impression a more spiritual motive, even could it here be adequately provided, would interfere.

And the emotional situation is justified or made acceptable, as often in Shakespeare, not by analysis and realism, but by stage management, by poetry, by the fitness of the situation in the world that the poet has created. Instead of a definite psychological transition from Rosaline to Juliet, there is, for plausibility's sake, a slight interval after Romeo's outcry (which the hero may be supposed to use for reflection and readjustment) bridged by the quarrel between the testy Tybalt and the hospitable Capulet; and instead of the long and tedious process of getting acquainted and making love, there is a wooing which is lifted above the level of life by rime and brought within the compass of a sonnet. . . . That the youth and the maiden should fall in love at sight is not out of keeping with their at once making the fact known to each other, with her doing more than the girl's ordinary share of the wooing and his forgetting Rosaline on the spot; with the thought of both that this is a matter of union or of death, in disregard of all prudential or practical considerations, in defiance of the stars; and with their high poetical ways of talking generally as well as the romantic incidents and setting-masques, balls, tempestuous quarrels and duels, endearments in the moonlight and bidding adieu at dawn, a wedding in a Friar's cell and a ladder to reach the wedding-bed, and thereupon the sleeping-potion, the burial alive to escape the accepted suitor, the reunion only in the grave. It is a thoroughly romantic world (though a more turbulent and passionate one), as in the *Midsummer Night's Dream, The Merchant of Venice, As You Like It, Twelfth Night,* and nearly all the rest, where more or less similarly the premature falling in love is made plausible. (pp. 18-23)

The method, then, is imaginative and immediate, impulsive and emotional, dramatic or at least structural and poetic, not (happily) psychological or sociological. The motives, in so far as there are any—Juliet's beauty and her particular features—are dwelt upon but to start the story and support the situation; and that the lovers are fitted for each other appears indirectly and incidentally—they themselves are not concerned about it—as with Benedick and Beatrice, Orlando and Rosalind, Florizel and Perdita, Ferdinand and Miranda. If not otherwise, by their fruits we know them,—health out of lovesickness, daring and resourcefulness out of inexperience. But the chief thing is that we should be made to feel the greatness of their love and then in each of them find warrant for it. . . . [We] must be impressed directly by Romeo's and Juliet's reality and charm; for ourselves we must be led to acknowledge that each is worth the winning; and in this play, as . . . in Shakespeare generally, that is done, again, not by analysis, but by poetry and the quality and individuality of their speech. (p. 24)

Certainly [*Romeo and Juliet*] would have been more logical and compact if, as one good critic would have it do, 'the same fatality which passes through Mercutio found its mark at last in hero and heroine' [Prosser Hall Frye, in his *Romance and Tragedy*], and thus their deaths were more directly and evidently the result of the quarrel. But for the Elizabethans and their age and, I fancy, for a goodly number of the unsophisticated even today, such a sociological study and demonstration would have been too tame and narrow, would not have offered sufficient emotional and poetic scope. The stars, though they may be taken for the Elizabethan equivalent of our modern 'environment,' 'society,' or 'heredity,' are really another matter. Those fateful orbs appear in the Prologue as presiding. It is of them that Romeo speaks in his foreboding as he goes to the ball; it is they, not human institutions or enmity, that he defies as he hears of her death; and it is their yoke that he shakes from his world-wearied flesh as he expires. This makes for compactness, though of a sort, to be sure, less logical and more external. . . . No doubt the quarrel might fittingly, and to our academic taste more dramatically, be now again at the

end the instrument of fate or fortune; but then the malign power of fate or fortune would be less apparent. That effect is necessary to provoke the hero's defiance; the hero's defiance is necessary to motive his headlong rush to death; his headlong rush to death, over every obstacle, including the body of Paris, is necessary to produce the tragic outcome and the emotional contrasts and explosions. The mere death of Juliet, without such irony and mockery, would lead as naturally to the hero's own, not 'tonight' but a day or a week hence—after she has wakened! As things are, moreover, to Romeo, to the poet and his audience, the feud and fate or fortune are nearly identical. Nearly all that is needed to justify any tragic conclusion is adequate preparation; and this has been provided not only in premonition but in fulfilment as, twice before, the feud has bloody consequences—by the deaths of the Prince's kinsman and of Mercutio and Tybalt. Fortune's fool he is now more than ever as the Friar's message fails to reach him, and as he kills himself, Juliet being still alive. (pp. 38-40)

If that is so, the rashness or impetuosity comes as a matter of course: without it the stars might lour but, not being defied, would bring down no disaster. . . . [This] particular sort of tragic fault, to be found in the heroes of other Shakespearean tragedies, such as *King Lear, Othello* and *Macbeth,* and in the ancient, such as the *Œdipus,* is often but a matter of tragic momentum. When the hero is positive, not negative, an actor, not merely a sufferer, and also virtuous and noble enough to keep our admiration and sympathy, how can he ordinarily come to grief at all if he be wholly prudent and discreet? In some measure, to be sure, for plausibility's sake, the tragic hero or heroine must be his or her own destiny, or seem to be so. Hence the Friar's moralizing about those stumbling who run fast, and on violent delights having violent ends. There he has a grain of justification—as Brabantio has when he warns Othello against the deceitfulness of Desdemona! . . . It is in the interest of drama that the Friar is permitted to have his say, his point of view; in some small part it is even in the interest of drama that this humdrum prudence is given expression; but when he bids the young pair 'love moderately,' he does not fill the role of a chorus, or else the poet's efforts to arouse our emotions and call forth our whole sympathy for them would be defeated. He is the chorus only in so far as his moralizings and warnings have the effect of misgivings and forebodings, which contribute to the suspense.

A fault, moreover, implies in the catastrophe an act of justice; and for a satisfaction of that sense within us there is no place in this romantic tragedy of fate, but only for pity—and sympathy. All that is needed is that the catastrophe should be plausible and harmonious, in keeping with both our sense of reality and the nature of tragedy; and such it is. If Romeo, and Juliet too, did nothing at all to bring fate down upon their heads, they would not be the vital and positive natures that they have hitherto seemed to be, and the play would not be a tragedy. But in the circumstances they are not to blame, nor are they morbid or unbalanced, and you will surely excuse me from stopping to consider any notion so irrelevant as that they are impulsive, uninhibited Italians. What, then, of Macbeth and his Lady, in their impetuosity, who are Scotch? *Highland* Scotch, I suppose, Gaels, not dour Presbyterian Saxons. What *is* to the point has been said of late, though perhaps less truly, of the great love-story of the eighteenth century: 'Tout est simple dans *Manon,* comme le malheur et le plaisir, la jeunesse et l'amour' ['Everything is simple in *Manon,* like sadness and pleasure, youth and love']. Here are psychology and realism, not the stars or fortune, as in *Romeo and Juliet.* This is a novel, and as M. Suarès observes, classical in form; the other, a tragedy and certainly romantic. But masterpieces of literary art—novel or drama, classical or romantic, prose or verse—partake of the nature of poetry, even as 'all art,' according to Pater, 'constantly aspires towards the condition of music.' All masterpieces of fiction are akin. And *Manon* too is a poem, a triumphal hymn of love.

This before us is a finer, loftier one, with intenser emotional effect and less admixture of human frailty. The characters are less substantial and true to life but more vivid and convincing in themselves. We see them and hear them, to adapt Mr. Eliot's words, if we do not, on second thoughts, understand them. The height and intensity of emotional effect, however, is especially owing to the finer and more compelling rhythm. This is not merely in the verse but in the structure of the fable. Three times the feud asserts itself with fateful consequences, three times Romeo remembers his baleful stars, and once their malign influence is touched upon in the prologue. And there are verbal echoes, in Romeo's repeated recognition of a fate impending and his figure of the pilot and his bark. But the main musical effect is in the fluctuation, the swell and subsidence, which cannot be attained within the close and sober limits of prose. Within this storm of passion and the resultant harmony of effect Romeo and Juliet keep their individuality, none the less real because they stand for love contending with hatred, none the less human because they are not adequately motived, all the more vivid because placed in a situation not of their own making but touched by poetic power. (pp. 40-4)

> Elmer Edgar Stoll, "Romeo and Juliet," in his Shakespeare's Young Lovers, *Oxford University Press*, 1937, pp. 1-44.

## MARK VAN DOREN   (essay date 1939)

[*Van Doren was a Pulitzer prize-winning poet, American educator, editor, and novelist. In the introduction to his* Shakespeare *(1939), he states that he "ignored the biography of Shakespeare, the history and character of his time, the conventions of his theater, the works of his contemporaries" to concentrate on the interest of the plays and their relevance to the modern reader or spectator. In the excerpt below, Van Doren discusses the various characters' attitudes towards love in* Romeo and Juliet, *noting, especially, the manner in which Shakespeare manages to set apart and heighten the romantic love of the hero and heroine.*]

One of the reasons for the fame of "Romeo and Juliet" is that it has so completely and clearly isolated the experience of romantic love. It has let such love speak for itself; and not alone in the celebrated wooing scenes, where the hero and heroine express themselves with a piercing directness, but indirectly also, and possibly with still greater power, in the whole play in so far as the whole play is built to be their foil. Their deep interest for us lies in their being alone in a world which does not understand them; and Shakespeare has devoted much attention to that world.

Its inhabitants talk only of love. The play is saturated with the subject. Yet there is always a wide difference between what the protagonists intend by the term and what is intended by others. The beginning dialogue by Sampson and Gregory, servants, is pornographic on the low level of puns about maidenheads, of horse-humor and hired-man wit. Mercutio will be more indecent . . . on the higher level of a gentleman's cynicism. Mercutio does not believe in love, as perhaps the servants clumsily do; he believes only in sex, and his excellent mind

has sharpened the distinction to a very dirty point. He drives hard against the sentiment that has softened his friend and rendered him unfit for the society of young men who really know the world. When Romeo with an effort matches one of his witticisms he is delighted:

> Now art thou sociable, now art thou Romeo,
> now art thou what thou art, by art as well as
> by nature.
>
>                              [II. iv. 89-91]

He thinks that Romeo has returned to the world of artful wit, by which he means cynical wit; he does not know that Romeo is still "dead" and "fishified," and that he himself will soon be mortally wounded under the arm of his friend—who, because love has stupefied him, will be capable of speaking the inane line, "I thought all for the best" [III. i. 104]. (pp. 70-1)

The older generation is another matter. Romeo and Juliet will have them with them to the end, and will be sadly misunderstood by them. The Capulets hold still another view of love. Their interest is in "good" marriages, in sensible choices. They are match-makers, and believe they know best how their daughter should be put to bed. This also is cynicism, though it be without pornography; at least the young heart of Juliet sees it so. Her father finds her sighs and tears merely ridiculous: "Evermore show'ring?" [III. v. 130]. She is "a wretched puling fool, a whining mammet" [III. v. 183-84], a silly girl who does not know what is good for her. Capulet is Shakespeare's first portrait in a long gallery of fussy, tetchy, stubborn, unteachable old men. . . . He is tart-tongued, breathy, wordy, pungent, and speaks with a naturalness unknown in Shakespeare's plays before this, a naturalness consisting in a perfect harmony between his phrasing and its rhythm:

> How how, how how, chop-logic! What is this?
> "Proud," and "I thank you," and "I thank you not;"
> And yet "not proud." Mistress minion, you,
> Thank me no thankings, nor proud me no prouds,
> But fettle your fine joints 'gainst Thursday next,
> To go with Paris to Saint Peter's Church,
> Or I will drag thee on a hurdle thither.
>
>                              [III. v. 149-55]
>                                 (pp. 71-2)

The Nurse, a member of the same generation, and in Juliet's crisis as much her enemy as either parent is, for she too urges the marriage with Paris [III. v. 212-25], adds to practicality a certain prurient interest in love-business, the details of which she mumbles toothlessly, reminiscently, with the indecency of age. Her famous speech concerning Juliet's age [I. iii. 12-57], which still exceeds the speeches of Capulet in the virtue of dramatic naturalness, runs on so long in spite of Lady Capulet's attempts to stop it because she has become fascinated with the memory of her husband's broad jest. . . . The Nurse's delight in the reminiscence is among other things lickerish, which the delight of Romeo and Juliet in their love never is, any more than it is prudent like the Capulets, or pornographic like Mercutio. Their delight is solemn, their behavior holy, and nothing is more natural than that in their first dialogue [I. v. 93-110] there should be talk of palmers, pilgrims, saints, and prayers.

It is of course another kind of holiness than that which appears in Friar Laurence, who nevertheless takes his own part in the endless conversation which the play weaves about the theme of love. The imagery of his first speech is by no accident erotic:

> I must up-fill this osier cage of ours
> With baleful weeds and precious-juiced flowers.
> The earth, that's nature's mother, is her tomb;
> What is her burying grave, that is her womb;
> And from her womb children of divers kind
> We sucking on her natural bosom find.
>
> [II. iii. 7-12]

The Friar is closer to the lovers in sympathy than any other person of the play. Yet this language is as alien to their mood as that of Capulet or the Nurse; or as Romeo's recent agitation over Rosaline is to his ecstasy with Juliet. The lovers are alone. Their condition is unique. Only by the audience is it understood. (pp. 72-4)

> Mark Van Doren, "Romeo and Juliet," in his Shakespeare, *Henry Holt and Company, 1939, pp. 65-75.*

### H. B. CHARLTON   (essay date 1948)

[*An English scholar, Charlton is best known for his* Shakespearian Comedy *(1938) and* Shakespearian Tragedy *(1948)—two important studies in which he argues that the proponents of New Criticism, particularly T. S. Eliot and I. A. Richards, were reducing Shakespeare's drama to its poetic elements and in the process losing sight of his characters. In his introduction to* Shakespearian Tragedy, *Charlton described himself as a "devout" follower of A. C. Bradley, and like his mentor he adopted a psychological, character-oriented approach to Shakespeare's work. Charlton's comments on* Romeo and Juliet *have significantly influenced subsequent criticism of the play and have frequently been cited. He contends that the tragedy was an experimental work on Shakespeare's part, claiming that it differs from his first tragedies—* Titus Andronicus, Richard III, *and* Richard II—*in that it deals with no historical material, depicts ordinary individuals, and—most importantly—treats the turmoils of love as its central theme. For Charlton, however, Shakespeare's experiment fails "as a pattern of the idea of tragedy," since neither the family feud nor fate or destiny, despite the dramatist's emphasis, adequately sustains the tragic outcome as it stands. According to the critic, the feud seems out of place in the play's world and lacks the conviction to compel the lovers' sacrifice; and the notion of fate, at least by the time Shakespeare wrote* Romeo and Juliet, *"was no longer a deity strong enough to carry the responsibility of a tragic universe." Charlton's essay on* Romeo and Juliet, *originally delivered as a lecture in 1939 (see Additional Bibliography), was significantly revised for inclusion in his 1948 study of Shakespeare's tragedies.*]

[Shakespeare's] *Titus Andronicus, Richard III* and *Richard II* belong in the main to [a] conventional pattern. They deal with historical material. Their heroes are of high rank and potent in determining the destiny of nations. The plot is never mainly a lovers' story, though a love-intrigue intrudes sporadically here and there within the major theme. But somehow the prescriptions had not produced the expected result. There was something unsatisfying in these plays as divinations of man's tragic lot. And so the conventions were jettisoned in *Romeo and Juliet.*

Shakespeare was casting in fresh directions to find the universality, the momentousness, and above all the inevitability of all-compelling tragedy. In particular, he was experimenting with a new propelling force, a new final sanction as the determinant energy, the *ultima ratio* of tragedy's inner world; and though *Romeo and Juliet* is set in a modern Christian country, with church and priest and full ecclesiastical institu-

tion, the whole universe of God's justice, vengeance and providence is discarded and rejected from the directing forces of the play's dramatic movement. In its place, there is a theatrical resuscitation of the half-barbarian, half-Roman deities of Fate and Fortune. (pp. 50-1)

Moreover the hero and the heroine, Romeo and Juliet, had none of the pomp of historic circumstance about them; they were socially of the minor aristocracy who were to stock Shakespeare's comedies, and their only political significance was an adventitious rôle in the civic disturbance of a small city-state. Romeo and Juliet were in effect just a boy and a girl in an novel; and as such they had no claim to the world's attention except through their passion and their fate.

To choose such folk as these for tragic heroes was aesthetically wellnigh an anarchist's gesture; and the dramatist provided a sort of programme-prologue to prompt the audience to see the play from the right point of view. In this play-bill the dramatist draws special attention to two features of his story. First, Verona was being torn by a terrible, bloodthirsty feud which no human endeavour had been able to settle; this was the direct cause of the death of the lovers, and but for those deaths it never would have been healed. Second, the course of the young lovers' lives is from the outset governed by a malignant destiny; fatal, star-crossed, death-marked, they are doomed to piteous destruction.

The intent of this emphasis is clear. The tale will end with the death of two ravishingly attractive young folk; and the dramatist must exonerate himself from all complicity in their murder, lest he be found guilty of pandering to a liking for a human shambles. He disowns responsibility and throws it on Destiny, Fate. The device is well warranted in the tragic tradition, and especially in its Senecan models. But whether, in fact, it succeeds is a matter for further consideration. The invocation of Fate is strengthened by the second feature scored heavily in the prologue, the feud. The feud is, so to speak, the means by which Fate acts. The feud is to provide the sense of immediate, and Fate that of ultimate, inevitability. For it may happen that, however the dramatist deploys his imaginative suggestions, he may fail to summon up a Fate sufficiently compelling to force itself upon the audience as unquestioned shaper of the tragic end. In such circumstance Romeo's and Juliet's death would be by mere chance, a gratuitous intervention by a dramatist exercising his homicidal proclivities for the joy of his audience. Hence the feud has a further function. It will be the dramatist's last plea for exculpation or for mercy; and it will allow his audience to absolve him or to forgive him without loss of its own 'philanthropy'; for through death came the healing of the feud, and with it, the removal of the threat to so many other lives.

It becomes, therefore, of critical importance to watch Shakespeare's handling of these two motives, Fate and Feud, to see how he fits them to fulfill their function, and to ask how far in fact they are adequate to the rôle they must perforce play. Both Fate and Feud, although absent as motives from the earliest European form of the Romeo and Juliet story, had grown variously in the successive tellings of the tale before it came to Broke. The general trend had been to magnify the virulence of the feud, and, even more notably, to swell the sententious apostrophising of Fate's malignity. (pp. 51-3)

So when Shakespeare took up the story, Broke had already sought to drench it in fatality. But since Shakespeare was a dramatist, he could not handle Fate and Feud as could a narrative poet. His feud will enter, not descriptively, but as action; and for fate he must depend on the sentiments of his characters and on an atmosphere generated by the sweep of the action. The feud may be deferred for a moment to watch Shakespeare's handling of Fate.

His most frequent device is to adapt what Broke's practice had been; instead of letting his persons declaim formally, as Broke's do, against the inconstancy of Fortune, he endows them with dramatic premonitions. Setting out for Capulet's ball, Romeo is suddenly sad:

> my mind misgives
> Some consequence, yet hanging in the stars,
> Shall bitterly begin his fearful date
> With this night's revels; and expire the term
> Of a despised life, clos'd in my breast,
> By some vile forfeit of untimely death:
> But he that hath the steerage of my course
> Direct my sail!
>
> [I. iv. 106-13]

As the lovers first declare their passion, Juliet begs Romeo not to swear, as if an oath might be an evil omen:

> I have no joy of this contract to-night:
> It is too rash, too unadvised, too sudden;
> Too like the lightning, which doth cease to be
> Ere one can say 'It lightens'.
>
> [II. ii. 117-20]

Romeo, involved in the fatal fight, cries 'O, I am fortune's fool!' [III. i. 136]. (pp. 54-5)

Besides these promptings of impending doom there are premonitions of a less direct kind. The friar fears the violence of the lover's passion:

> These violent delights have violent ends
> And in their triumph die, like fire and powder,
> Which as they kiss consume.
>
> [II. vi. 9-11]

Another source of omen in the play is the presaging of dreams. . . . There is much dreaming in *Romeo and Juliet*. Mercutio may mock at dreams as children of an idle brain, begot of nothing but vain phantasy. But when Romeo says he 'dream'd a dream to-night' [I. iv. 50], Mercutio's famous flight of fancy recalls the universal belief in dreams as foreshadowings of the future. Again Romeo dreams; this time, 'I dreamt my lady came and found me dead' [V. i. 6]. As his man Balthasar waits outside Juliet's tomb, he dreams that his master and another are fighting and the audience knows how accurately the dream mirrors the true facts.

But Shakespeare not only hangs omens thickly round his play. He gives to the action itself a quality apt to conjur the sense of relentless doom. It springs mainly from his compression of the time which the story stretches. In all earlier versions there is a much longer lapse. Romeo's wooing is prolonged over weeks before the secret wedding; then, after the wedding, there is an interval of three or four months before the slaying of Tybalt; and Romeo's exile lasts from Easter until a short time before mid-September when the marriage with Paris was at first planned to take place. But in Shakespeare all this is pressed into three or four days. The world seems for a moment to be caught up in the fierce play of furies revelling in some mad supernatural game.

But before asking whether the sense of an all-controlling Fate is made strong enough to fulfil its tragic purpose let us turn to the feud. Here Shakespeare's difficulties are even greater. Italian novelists of the quattro- or cinquecento, throwing their story back through two or three generations, might expect their readers easily to accept a fierce vendetta. But the Verona which Shakespeare depicts is a highly civilised world, with an intellectual and artistic culture and an implied social attainment altogether alien from the story of society in which a feud is a more or less natural manifestation of enmity. The border country of civilisation is the home of feuds, a region where social organisation is still of the clan, where the head of the family-clan is a strong despot, and where law has not progressed beyond the sort of wild justice of which one instrument is the feud. (pp. 55-6)

It was wellnigh impossible for Shakespeare to fit the blood-lust of a border feud into the social setting of his Verona. The heads of the rival houses are not at all the fierce chieftains who rule with ruthless despotism. When old Capulet, in fire-side gown, bustles to the scene of the fray and calls for his sword, his wife tells him bluntly that it is a crutch which an old man such as he should want, and not a weapon. Montague, too, spits a little verbal fire, but his wife plucks him by the arm, and tells him to calm down: 'thou shalt not stir one foot to seek a foe' [I. i. 80]. Indeed, these old men are almost comic figures, and especially Capulet. His querulous fussiness, his casual bonhomie, his almost senile humour and his childish irascibility hardly make him the pattern of a clan chieftain. Even his domestics put him in his place:

> Go, you cot-quean, go,
> Get you to bed; faith, you'll be sick to-morrow
> For this night's watching,
>
> [IV. iv. 6-8]

the Nurse tells him; and the picture is filled in his wife's reminder that she has put a stop to his 'mouse-hunting'. There is of course the prince's word that

> Three civil brawls, bred of an airy word,
> By thee, old Capulet, and Montague,
> Have thrice disturb'd the quiet of our streets.
>
> [I. i. 89-91]

But these brawls bred of an airy word are no manifestations of a really ungovernable feud. When Montague and Capulet are bound by the prince to keep the peace, old Capulet himself says

> 'tis not hard, I think,
> For men so old as we to keep the peace
>
> [I. ii. 2-3]

and there is a general feeling that the old quarrel has run its course. (pp. 56-7)

Moreover, the rival houses have mutual friends. Mercutio, Montague Romeo's close acquaintance, is an invited guest at the Capulets' ball. Stranger still, so is Romeo's cruel lady, Rosaline, who in the invitation is addressed as Capulet's cousin. It is odd that Romeo's love for her, since she was a Capulet, had given him no qualms on the score of the feud. When Romeo is persuaded to go gate-crashing to the ball because Rosaline will be there, there is no talk at all of its being a hazardous undertaking. Safety will require, if even so much, no more than a mask. On the way to the ball, as talk is running gaily, there is still no mention of danger involved. Indeed, the feud is almost a dead letter so far. The son of the Montague does not know what the Capulet daughter looks like, nor she what he is like. The traditional hatred survives only in one or two high-spirited, hot-blooded scions on either side, and in the kitchen-folk. Tybalt alone resents Romeo's presence at the ball, yet it is easy for all to recognise him; and because Tybalt feels Romeo's coming to be an insult, he seeks him out next day to challenge him, so providing the immediate occasion of the new outburst. Naturally, once blood is roused again, and murder done, the ancient rancour springs up with new life. Even Lady Capulet has comically Machiavellian plans for having Romeo poisoned in Mantua. But prior to this the evidences of the feud are so unsubstantial that the forebodings of Romeo and Juliet, discovering each other's name, seem prompted more by fate than feud. There will, of course, be family difficulties; but the friar marries them without a hesitating qualm, feeling that such a union is bound to be accepted eventually by the parents, who will thus be brought to amity.

The most remarkable episode, however, is still to be named. When Tybalt discovers Romeo at the ball, infuriated he rushes to Capulet with the news. But Capulet, in his festive mood, is pleasantly interested, saying that Romeo is reputed to be good-looking and quite a pleasant boy. He tells Tybalt to calm himself, to remember his manners, and to treat Romeo properly. . . . When Tybalt is reluctant, old Capulet is annoyed and testily tells him to stop being a saucy youngster. . . . (pp. 58-9)

This is a scene which sticks in the memory; for here the dramatist, unencumbered by a story, is interpolating a lively scene in his own kind, a vignette of two very amusing people in an amusing situation. But it is unfortunate for the feud that this episode takes so well. For clearly old Capulet is unwilling to let the feud interrupt a dance; and a quarrel which is of less moment than a galliard is being appeased at an extravagant price, if the price is the death of two such delightful creatures as Romeo and Juliet;

> their parents' rage,
> Which, but their children's end, naught could remove,
>                                        [Prologue, 10-11]

loses all its plausibility. A feud like this will not serve as the bribe it was meant to be; it is no atonement for the death of the lovers. Nor, indeed, is it coherent and impressive enough as part of the plot to propel the sweep of necessity in the sequence of events. If the tragedy is to march relentlessly to its end, leaving no flaw in the sense of inevitability which it seeks to prompt, it clearly must depend for that indispensable tragic impression not on its feud, but on its scattered suggestions of doom and of malignant fate. And, as has been seen, Shakespeare harps frequently on this theme.

But how far can a Roman sense of Fate be made real for a modern audience? . . . The forms and the phrases by which these powers had been invoked were a traditional part in the inheritance of the Senecan drama which came to sixteenth-century Europe. Fortuna, Fatum, Fata, Parcae: all were firmly established in its *dramatis personae*. Moreover their rôle in Virgilian theocracy was familiar to all with but a little Latin. . . . (pp. 60-1)

But with what conviction could a sixteenth-century spectator take over these ancient figures? Even the human beings of an old mythology may lose their compelling power; 'what's Hecuba to him, or he to Hecuba?' [*Hamlet*, II. ii. 559]. But the gods are in a much worse case; pagan, they had faded before the God of the Christians: *Vicisti, Galilæe!* Fate was no longer a deity strong enough to carry the responsibility of a tragic

universe; at most, it could intervene casually as pure luck, and bad luck as a motive turns tragedy to mere chance. (p. 61)

Is then Shakespeare's *Romeo and Juliet* an unsuccessful experiment? To say so may seem not only profane but foolish. In its own day, as the dog's-eared Bodley Folio shows, and ever since, it has been one of Shakespeare's most preferred plays. It is indeed rich in spells of its own. But as a pattern of the idea of tragedy, it is a failure. Even Shakespeare appears to have felt that, as an experiment, it had disappointed him. At all events, he abandoned tragedy for the next few years and gave himself to history and to comedy; and even afterwards, he fought shy of the simple theme of love, and of the love of anybody less than a great political figure as the main matter for his tragedies.

Nevertheless it is obvious that neither sadism nor masochism is remotely conscious in our appreciation of *Romeo and Juliet*, nor is our 'philanthropy' offended by it. But the achievement is due to the magic of Shakespeare's poetic genius and to the intermittent force of his dramatic power rather than to his grasp of the foundations of tragedy.

There is no need here to follow the meetings of Romeo and Juliet through the play, and to recall the spell of Shakespeare's poetry as it transports us along the rushing stream of the lovers' passion, from its sudden outbreak to its consummation in death. . . . Shakespeare, divining their naked passion, lifts them above the world and out of life by the mere force of it. It is the sheer might of poetry. Dramatically, however, he has subsidiary resources. He has Mercutio and the Nurse.

Shakespeare's Mercutio has the gay poise and the rippling wit of the man of the world. By temperament he is irrepressible and merry; his charm is infectious. His speech runs freely between fancies of exquisite delicacy and the coarser fringe of wordly humour; and he has the sensitiveness of sympathetic fellowship. Such a man, if any at all, might have understood the depth of Romeo's love for Juliet. But the *camraderie* and the worldly *savoir-faire* of Mercutio give him no inkling of the nature of Romeo's passion. The love of Romeo and Juliet is beyond the ken of their friends; it belongs to a world which is not their world; and so the passing of Romeo and Juliet is not as other deaths are in their impact on our sentiments.

Similarly, too, the Nurse. She is Shakespeare's greatest debt to Broke, in whose poem she plays a curiously unexpected and yet incongruously entertaining part. She is the one great addition which Broke made to the saga. She is garrulous, worldly, coarse, vulgar, and babblingly given to reminiscence stuffed with native animal humour and self-assurance. Shakespeare gladly borrowed her, and so gave his Juliet for her most intimate domestic companion a gross worldly creature who talks much of love and never means anything beyond sensuality. Like Romeo's, Juliet's love is completely unintelligible to the people in her familiar circle. To her nurse, love is animal lust. To her father, who has been a 'mouse-hunter' in his time, and to her mother, it is merely a social institution, a worldly arrangement in a very wordly world. This earth, it would seem, has no place for passion like Romeo's and Juliet's. And so, stirred to sympathy by Shakespeare's poetic power, we tolerate, perhaps even approve, their death. At least for the moment.

But tragedy lives not only for its own moment, nor by long 'suspensions of disbelief'. There is the inevitable afterthought and all its 'obstinate questionings'. Our sentiments were but momentarily gratified. And finally our deeper consciousness protests. Shakespeare has but conquered us by a trick: the experiment carries him no nearer to the heart of tragedy. (pp. 61-3)

   *H. B. Charlton, "Experiment and Interregnum: 'Romeo and Juliet', 'King John', 'Julius Caesar'," in his* Shakespearian Tragedy, *Cambridge at the University Press, 1948, pp. 49-82.*

## E. C. PETTET (essay date 1949)

[*Although Pettet agrees that Romeo matures into an ideal romantic lover before his death, he contends that the hero remains a target of Shakespeare's criticism throughout* Romeo and Juliet. *According to the critic, Shakespeare perceived in the lover an unhealthy, reckless attitude towards life, even during those moments when he is most in love with and committed to Juliet. In this respect, Pettet perceives in Friar Lawrence the reproving voice of Shakespeare, though he cautions that such a character "may have a choric function" without being a chorus "in the formal Greek sense of the word." Also important in Pettet's essay is his claim that* Romeo and Juliet *is not a tragedy in a strict definition of the term, since "the catastrophe depends on chance, the undelivered letter of Friar Lawrence."*]

*Romeo and Juliet*, written about the same time as *A Midsummer Night's Dream*, falls naturally into [a] discussion of Shakespeare's attitude towards romantic love, for though conventionally described as a tragedy, two-thirds of it belongs unmistakably to the world of the comedies. Certainly, apart from its *dénouement*, it is both in spirit and substance as much a comedy as *Much Ado About Nothing*. Moreover, its main theme is love, and the forms of love represented have much to do with the romantic ideal.

In the first place, the Romeo of the opening act is a portrait and—as far as we can be definite about these matters of impression—almost certainly a caricature of the typical romantic lover. He is introduced to us indirectly through the account of his companion, Benvolio, who relates how he has seen Romeo in the early morning seeking the solitude of a nearby wood. Romeo's father describes other familiar symptoms: his son weeps and sighs; he locks himself up in his room during the daytime, making an artificial night for himself. (p. 114)

When Romeo himself appears, all that he says and does only adds to the outlines of the caricature. He is woefully sad; desperate to madness. He rails (but a willing slave) against the torment of love; and he is utterly hopeless, out of favour, for his Rosaline is of course one of the proud and scornful fair ones. . . . (p. 115)

To deepen the lines of exaggeration and caricature Shakespeare invests Romeo's speech with all the conventional rhetoric of contemporary love-poetry. He habitually talks in oxymoron, hyperbole and extravagant conceit, and he is always close to the sonnet vein. On one occasion Shakespeare actually gives him a sonnet sestet to speak, while his first words to Juliet form a sonnet in the pseudo-religious style, in the recitation of which Juliet joins.

All this strained and sham-poetic artificiality of speech can have but one effect, which Shakespeare certainly intended: we are convinced of the utter shallowness of Romeo's believed passion for Rosaline. Even before Friar Lawrence reminds us, we realise that it is mere 'doting'.

But, though Juliet shares the speaking of the 'If I profane with my unworthiest hand' sonnet [I. v. 93-107] she is no Rosaline. Refracted to us at first through the memories of the nurse— memories of suckling, of childish, innocently indecent remarks—an earthiness that surrounds but does not sully Juliet— she is a spontaneous, passionate child of nature, whose speech and heart are always one. She is not ignorant of the conventional frowns and perverseness of the lady of romantic love; indeed she protests that she would have aped that style had not Romeo caught her unawares:

> I should have been more strange, I must confess,
> But that thou overheard'st, ere I was ware,
> My true love's passion.
>
>          [II. ii. 102-04]

But one is certain she would never have been able to keep up this demureness and make-believe for long.

Meeting such a woman, falling in love with her at first sight, Romeo experiences real passion for the first time, and the experience transforms his whole being, indeed turns him from a caricature into a human being. There is scarcely a single correspondence between the Romeo of the first act and the Romeo of the rest of the play, who is as unlike his prototype as the Falstaff of *Henry IV* is unlike the Falstaff of *The Merry Wives*. His speech (usually a significant index of Shakespeare's characters) is completely changed as we can realise at once if we compare such lines as

> O, she doth teach the torches to shine bright!
> It seems she hangs upon the cheek of night
> Like a rich pearl in an Ethiope's ear;
> Beauty too rich for use, for earth too dear!
>
>          [I. v. 44-7]

with

> O, she is rich in beauty, only poor,
> That when she dies with beauty dies her store.
>
>          [I. 215-16]

This is not to deny the considerable amount of conceit and hyperbole in Romeo's courtship of Juliet; nor can we make an exception of such lines as those in the first quotation on the grounds that Romeo has still not completely shaken off his old self, since such artifice is found everywhere, even in the superb aubade that he speaks with Juliet. But this artifice is no longer frigid or perfunctory; and it is rarely conventional. It is, we are convinced, a lyrical fervour that flames from deep and genuine love.

This initial caricature of Romeo, and his transformation, certainly show that by the time Shakespeare wrote this play (1595?) he was able to regard the conventional lover of the romantic school with complete detachment; also that he realised the conventions and poetry of the romantic tradition did not correspond with the realities of human passion. But is this all?

To make any sort of answer to this question we must recognise that while the Romeo of the last four acts is no longer the lover of contemporary sonnet and Petrarchian love-poetry, he is certainly a type, one of the supreme types, of the more modern ideal of the 'romantic' lover. His characteristic mood is emotional, ecstatic, unanalytical, and, therefore, uncomplicated; he prefers death to separation from Juliet; and love is his chief, if not his only value. For love he is prepared to sacrifice everything.

Now the play cannot be described as a tragedy of this ideal. Strictly speaking—and certainly if we take Shakespeare's other tragedies as a criterion—we cannot admit *Romeo and Juliet* as a tragedy at all, for the catastrophe depends on chance, the undelivered letter of Friar Lawrence. Without that accident, all might have been well. But, even if we ignore this objection, we never feel, as we do in *Antony and Cleopatra*, that the element of unrestrained passion inherent in the romantic ideal is necessarily destructive and disruptive. True, there is a unique stress on doom in *Romeo and Juliet* and much play with pre-monition; but these are poetic and dramatic effects, something external and imposed that is not to be confused with the in-evitable tragedy that is within Antony and Cleopatra. The fun-damental theme of *Romeo and Juliet,* which is imaginative not moral, is the unending conflict between Eros (love and life) and the forces of death. This conflict is developed dramatically by the story of sexual love arising out of family feud, chal-lenging it, triumphing over it, and finally destroyed by it, and developed poetically by the powerful imagery of strife, con-trast, contradiction and paradox.

But does this mean that Shakespeare was completely uncritical of what has become the *modern* ideal of romantic love?

Our answer to this question must depend primarily on our conception of Friar Lawrence, and in particular on our inter-pretation of Act II, Scene iii.

Now there are two clear-cut and opposing attitudes to this character. The first, an emphatically moral one, was satisfac-torily stated by Gervinus. 'By Friar Lawrence who, as it were, represents the part of the chorus in this tragedy, the leading idea of the piece is expressed in all fulness . . . that excess in any enjoyment, however pure in itself, transforms its sweet into bitterness, that devotion to any single feeling, however noble, bespeaks its ascendancy . . .'' [see excerpt above, 1849-50]. (pp. 115-18)

Edward Dowden, on the other hand, would have nothing of these 'well-meant moralisings' of Gervinus. He flatly denied that Friar Lawrence is a chorus to the tragedy and regarded him as a type of interfering, middle-aged prudence—something of a milder, more gracious Polonius in fact [see excerpt above, 1881]. . . .

There is undoubtedly considerable force in these objections of Dowden. For instance, he is obviously right in insisting on the importance of Friar Lawrence as an actor in the drama and on the disastrous outcome of his hopeful attempt to reconcile the Capulet and Montague families. Again, as we have already said, it is a gross distortion of the play to turn it into some sort of moral drama and to argue that any ethical or philo-sophical idea embodied in Friar Lawrence is the 'leading idea of the piece'. But a character, active in the drama to some extent, may have a choric function without fulfilling the role of chorus in the formal Greek sense of the word. . . . (p. 118)

The central idea of Friar Lawrence's long soliloquy is definite enough and fairly expressed by Gervinus' paraphrase: that any single good, pursued blindly in isolation and to extremes, is dangerous and may, by a dialectical process, give rise to its opposite; that every virtue (including love by implication) has its particular good, but no more:

> For nought so vile that on the earth doth live
> But to the earth some special good doth give,
> Nor aught so good but strained from that fair use
> Revolts from true birth, stumbling on abuse:
> Virtue itself turns vice, being misapplied;
> And vice sometimes by action dignified.
>
> [II. iii. 17-22]

This same idea, it should be noticed, is repeated by Friar Lawrence, with an explicit reference to love, just before the marriage of Romeo and Juliet:

> These violent delights have violent ends
> And in their triumph die, like fire and powder,
> Which as they kiss consume: the sweetest honey
> Is loathsome in its own deliciousness
> And in the taste confounds the appetite.
>
> [II. vi. 9-13]

Of course, this soliloquy of Friar Lawrence is to a large extent simply a piece of dramatic artifice: it bridges the awkward interval between Romeo's exit at the end of the previous scene and his appearance in this, while its references to 'baleful weeds and precious-juiced flowers' [II. iii. 8] prepare us for some necessary business of the play that is to follow. But why the length of the soliloquy, why its grave, sincere accent (which is not to be compared with the platitudinous moralisings of Polonious in his 'Give thy thoughts no tongue' speech [*Hamlet,* I. iii. 59-80]) unless Shakespeare intended it as a significant comment—and a critical one—on the extravagance of the ro-mantic ideal?

But there is no need to leave this objection to Dowden's analysis in mid-air, suspended on an interrogation mark. A few scenes later, in the main current of the play, the attitudes of Romeo and Friar Lawrence are brought into direct conflict, and there can be no doubt which is presented to us in the more favourable light. We cannot, assuredly, be quite unsympathetic to Ro-meo's retort to the Friar's well-meaning words of comfort and wisdom when he is informed of his banishment:

> Heaven is here,
> Where Juliet lives; and every cat and dog
> And little mouse, every unworthy thing,
> Live here in heaven and may look on her;
> But Romeo may not.
>
> [III. iii. 29-33]

Philosophy may, as the Friar states, be adversity's sweet milk; our minds allow the proposition. But who ever drank that milk at the right time, in actual and felt adversity? It is the old, old story—the philosopher vainly attempting to assuage a grief he has never, and can never, feel himself; and part of us, rebellious always against the woes of life, applauds when Romeo cries out impatiently:

> Hang up philosophy!
> Unless philosophy can make a Juliet,
> Displant a town, reverse a prince's doom,
> It helps not, it prevails not: talk no more.
>
> [III. iii. 57-60]

This is the moment when we are inclined to agree with Dow-den's dismissal of Friar Lawrence as an 'amiable critic of life seen from the cloister' who 'does not understand life or hate or love'. Yet all this is merely a transient reaction. Our total impression of the scene is of an extravagant, pitiful, even ludicrous Romeo reduced to a state of emotional deliquescence like Troilus at the opening of *Troilus and Cressida*. He blub-bers, he rolls on the ground, he is hopeless and incapable of stirring a finger to help himself. And this is not the Romeo of the first act—pitiful and absurd in a different, a more callow way—but the grand romantic lover of the Balcony scene and, in a few hours, of the great dawn-farewell to Juliet. The Friar, on the other hand, is altogether admirable: he rises to and dominates the situation. His reproof of Romeo's unmanly despair and desperation, besides pulling Romeo together with the right sort of appeal, is entirely just, and without wasting words he maps out a practical and hopeful course of action for the lovers. By word and deed he completely refutes Dowden's interpretation of him, and Romeo, as always, except when he is grief-distraught, appreciates his sterling worth:

> But that a joy past joy calls out on me,
> It were a grief, so brief to part with thee.
>
> [III. iii. 173-74]

The sorry spectacle that Romeo, the romantic lover, makes of himself in this scene should not be regarded in isolation, for it points directly forward to the catastrophe. Admittedly, he does not bear the responsibility for that catastrophe that Othello and Anthony bear for the disasters in which they are overwhelmed. But if the efficient cause of the catastrophe in *Romeo and Juliet* is an accident, this catastrophe is hastened by Romeo himself who, when he hears the false report of Juliet's death, reveals the same weaknesses that he had shown when Friar Lawrence had informed him of his banishment—reckless impulsiveness, an incapacity to think, and a despair that turns instantly to thoughts of suicide. But this time there is no Friar Lawrence to stand beside him, and he perishes miserably. (pp. 118-21)

> *E. C. Pettet, "Shakespeare's Detachment from Romance," in his* Shakespeare and the Romance Tradition, *1949. Reprint by Haskell House Publishers Ltd., 1976, pp. 101-35.*

### DONALD A. STAUFFER (essay date 1949)

[*Stauffer avers that Shakespeare was apparently undecided if Romeo and Juliet was to be a tragedy of fate concerning social evil, or a tragedy of character, in which the lovers suffer and die as a result of their own shortcomings. Because of this, he concludes, the play fails "as serious tragedy." However, Stauffer commends* Romeo and Juliet *for its presentation of "the purity and intensity of ideal love."*]

Among the enemies that beset the course of true love, Shakespeare in *A Midsummer Night's Dream* realizes momentarily, with a poignancy that almost destroys the dream itself, that the most dangerous enemy is Time. Seeking some source of belief that will not alter, Shakespeare has settled upon love, which he often equates with faith or loyalty. Yet how can its truth be sealed unalterably, if the moving finger of Time has the power to mar, to alter, or to destroy? . . . The quality of Time that Shakespeare feels most piercingly is [its] power, helped by its servants Opportunity and Oblivion, to blot and spoil and change whatever is noble and dignified. If brevity is the soul of wit, it is also the foe of worth. The ideal good can be changed only for the worse by Time, if Time has power at all. (p. 53)

In Lysander's lines in *A Midsummer Night's Dream,* Time the quick murderer is etched in stiletto strokes as the destroyer of true love:

> War, death, or sickness did lay siege to it,
> Making it momentany as a sound,
> Swift as a shadow, short as any dream,
> Brief as the lightning in the collied night,
> That, in a spleen, unfolds both heaven and earth,
> And ere a man hath power to say 'Behold!'
> The jaws of darkness do devour it up:
> So quick bright things come to confusion.
>
> [I. i. 142-49]

Such a tragic thunderclap startles the moonlit landscapes and fantastic laughter of the midsummer night. To convey his vivid intuition of the place and duration of love in the dark world of time, Shakespeare finds the lightning-in-the-night adequate as the germinating and organizing symbol for *Romeo and Juliet.* The theme of love, which he expands in other keys in plays before and after, remains central, though now it is to be idealized in all seriousness. Yet since the dark shades of hate are here little more than the touches of an artist designed to set off the brilliant lightning flash of passion, *Romeo and Juliet* shows less the tragedy than the pathos of pure love: "So quick bright things come to confusion!" (p. 54)

Shakespeare was never more patently the schoolmaster than in his repeated moralizing that love must destroy hate: The prologue tells us that the misadventured piteous overthrows of the two lovers bury their parents' strife. Nothing could remove the continuance of their parents' rage except their children's end. The moral lesson is so shaped formally that it becomes the main theme of the drama: the opening scene stops the bitter feud temporarily; the middle act results in two deaths and the separation of the lovers when murderous quarreling breaks out again; the closing scene offers the sacrifice of innocents to wipe out in blood the cursed strife of the old partisans. Church and state combine at the end to arraign the hate-filled families. The Friar presents himself "both to impeach and purge" [V. iii. 226]. And the Prince of Verona speaks the ironic moral:

> Capulet, Montague,
> See what a scourge is laid upon your hate,
> That heaven finds means to kill your joys with love!
>
> [V. iii. 291-93]

"All are punish'd" [V. iii. 295]. Yet the houses are reconciled in clasped hands, and golden statues shall rise as memorials to these "Poor sacrifices of our enmity!" [V. iii. 304]. . . . Insofar as this play is a tragedy of fate—and Shakespeare sets up dozens of signposts pointing toward the foregone moral conclusion—all accidents and events work toward the final sacrifice. Romeo and Juliet are puppets, since the moral punishment of the raging clans becomes more powerful in proportion to the innocence and helplessness of the sacrifices. In no other play does Shakespeare envisage a general moral order operating with such inhuman, mechanical severity.

On the surface, social evil is castigated and purged by "Fate," which is an extra-human moral order. Yet in contrast to this often declared thesis, and by no means reconciled with it, Shakespeare intrudes a line of thinking which was to become central in his serious philosophy: that the causes of tragedy lie in the sufferers themselves. The doctrines of individual responsibility and of fate as a social Nemesis offer divergent motivations: this play may fail as serious tragedy because Shakespeare blurs the focus and never makes up his mind entirely as to who is being punished, and for what reason. Later he learned to carry differing hypotheses simultaneously, to suggest complex contradictory interactions convincingly; but that is not the effect of the double moral motivations in *Romeo and Juliet.*

The dangerous fault of the two lovers is their extreme rashness. The Friar chides his protégé's sudden haste: "Wisely, and slow. They stumble that run fast" [II. iii. 94-5]. He has rebuked him earlier "for doting, not for loving" [II. iii. 82]. An even in a love affair which he approves he will counsel Romeo to

> Love moderately: long love doth so;
> Too swift arrives as tardy as too slow. . . .
>
> [II. vi. 14-15]

If the theme of personal responsibility were not drowned out by the theme of fate, it might be argued that the lovers' deaths in the tomb are caused by Romeo's sudden decision to buy poison, and again by his immediate suicide when he mistakes Juliet's sleep for death. But this is quibbling with destiny.

It is not quibbling to point out Shakespeare's emphasis on their surging wrong-headed impulses midway in the drama, so much more cunningly wrought and convincing than the moral tags. Juliet, when she hears that her husband has killed her cousin Tybalt, at once breaks out in a paradoxical curse twelve times illustrated: "O serpent heart, hid with a flow'ring face!" [III. ii. 73]. True, she soon veers back to her loyalty, but fast running has led to stumbling at the start. In the preceding scene, Romeo has banished "respective lenity" to heaven and has embraced "fire-ey'd fury" [III. i. 123-24] to kill Tybalt. And in the succeeding scene, Romeo's passion turns him hysterical. . . . No less than in the hatred of brawling houses, then, "unreasonable fury" may be shown in love. And Shakespeare's own sounder moral sense answers the philosophy of this so-called "tragedy of fate" in the Friar's direct statement:

Why railest thou on thy birth, the heaven, and earth?
Since birth and heaven and earth, all three do meet
In thee at once; which thou at once wouldst lose.
          [III. iii. 119-21]

Man cannot evade his pilotage by proclaiming himself "fortune's fool" [III. i. 136].

Such are the moralizings in this play. They protest too much in words, attest too little in experience. The actual ethical energy of the drama resides in its realization of the purity and intensity of ideal love. Here there is no swerving. Both Romeo and Juliet are wholly devoted to their overpowering discovery: from the religious imagery of the wooing to the feasting imagery of the Capulet vault, when Romeo's wit plays its "lightning before death" [V. iii. 90], the power of love is idealized; and true love, as though it were a hyphenated compound, echoes through the play.

Shakespeare has found skill adequate to his ambition. Nothing but the finest part of pure love inhabits his scenes of romantic enchantment—the courtship at the ball, the moonlit wooing, the bridal night. He has intensified its purity by contrasting it with Romeo's first posings, with Capulet's bargainings and tantrums, with Mercutio's bawdry, with the Friar's benign philosophizing, and with the nurse's loose opportunism. He has shown that love makes lovers fearless. He sings its hymn in Juliet's epithalamium; and consecrates it as rising above life, in the successive draughts, of sleep and of death, which each lover drinks to the other. (pp. 55-8)

Above all, he has brought out the pathos of love by violent contrasts. Time hurries all things away, and in the lightning imagery the kiss and the consummation are as fire and powder. Frail love, surrounded by disasters, becomes a thing of light in blackness, itself "like a rich jewel in an Ethiop's ear" [I. v. 46]. All is loneliness: Juliet is deserted by her father, then by her mother, then by her nurse, until she is left only with the power to die, or to consign herself to the horrible vault. Romeo is exiled—and indeed through the middle scenes "banished! banished!" beats like a pulse. Desperate and exiled, love knows only enemies, ranging from the vulgar nurse to "love-devouring death" [II. vi. 7] itself.

The secret of the play is that the deaths of the lovers are *not* the result of the hatred between the houses, nor of any other cause except love itself, which seeks in death its own restoring cordial. Love conquers death even more surely than it conquers hate. It sweeps aside all accidents, so that fate itself seems powerless. Time is conquered, in that first stirring of a belief that Shakespeare came later to trust completely: that the intensity of an emotion towers above its temporal duration or success. . . . [This] sense of triumph descends upon the play from a love so straight, so simple, and so certain that its very bravery transforms death and time and hatred—yes, and the accidents of Fate—into insubstantial shadows. The quick bright things remain shining and alive. (pp. 58-9)

> Donald A. Stauffer, "The School of Love," in his Shakespeare's World of Images: The Development of His Moral Ideas, W. W. Norton & Company, Inc., 1949, pp. 39-66.

**BERTRAND EVANS** (essay date 1950)

[*In two studies of Shakespearean drama,* Shakespeare's Comedies *(1960) and* Shakespeare's Tragic Practice *(1979), Evans examines what he calls Shakespeare's use of "discrepant awarenesses." He claims that Shakespeare's dramatic technique makes extensive use of "gaps" between the different levels of awareness the characters and audience possess concerning the circumstances of the plot. In the following excerpt, Evans disagrees with two negative critical reactions to* Romeo and Juliet: *he maintains that Friar Lawrence's final speech (V. iii. 229-69) is, after all, necessary, and that the accident of Friar John's detention does not spoil* Romeo and Juliet's *tragic construction. According to the critic, there is a way to view the play which "alters the appearance of both the accident and the speech by being faithful to the facts"— namely, an interpretation that acknowledges each character's unawareness of the relevant circumstances. Thus, Evans calls* Romeo and Juliet—*even more than* Othello—"*a tragedy of unawareness," one in which fate achieves its desired ends "through the common human condition of not knowing." In light of this reading, the critic disputes these so-called failures in the play, claiming that the friar's final speech is necessary for both the characters and for us, since "the full tragic force requires not only that these persons learn of the roles they have played but that we be permitted to look on when they grasp the meaning of their past actions." And the accident of Friar John's detention upon which the tragedy has been faulted, Evans adds, is actually irrelevent, since the link between the catastrophe and preceding events "is not the friar's failure to reach Mantua—a negative thing—but Balthasar's success," which serves to keep Romeo misinformed and unaware of the truth.*]

Critical comment on *Romeo and Juliet* in the past hundred and seventy-five years has made two of Shakespeare's alleged errors in that play loom above all others. These I shall call the trespasses of Friars Laurence and John: Friar Laurence, it is said, talks too much and thus detains the final curtain; Friar John enters a house suspected of contagion and, much too conveniently, *is* detained. My general purpose here is to examine the two problems within a single frame, for I believe they must be so reviewed if the validity of long-standing charges is to be fully tested. Furthermore, although the incident of Friar John is the graver "fault," my review of that problem is undertaken in part as a means of approach to the lesser "fault," the speech of Friar Laurence. Refined, then, my primary purpose is to focus some more light on the latter problem. (p. 841)

Friar John's detention remains one of the greatest embarrassments in Shakespeare. Othello's handkerchief can be waved boldly, like a flag, in spite of Rymer, because "there's magic in it." The improbability of Lear's opening folly can be convincingly diminished on the grounds that the real arrangements for division of the kingdom were drawn before the scene opens. The portly sails can draw safe home to harbor the very last of Antonio's lost argosies because that is the way of things in the world of comedy. *Titus Andronicus* ceases to embarrass those who prove to themselves that Shakespeare must not have written it. But Friar John's detention remains an unsightly fact that must be apologized for, grieved over, elaborately evaded, minimized, blamed on Brooke, or, all else failing, confessed as irredeemable.

George Pierce Baker's statement represents one widespread attitude:

> At the moment when it is necessary that Romeo shall have news that Juliet is waiting for him in the tomb of her fathers, the swift, relentless logic of the play breaks down. . . . What is it which prevents Romeo from getting the news that his wife is merely stupified, not dead? Merely a device of the dramatist; there is no inevitableness in this whatever. . . . That turn [the detention] is at the will of the dramatist, is melodrama, and it breaks the chain of circumstance necessary for perfect tragedy [see excerpt above, 1907]. . . .

In this view, which now prevails, *Romeo and Juliet* is not tragedy, and the reason is the accident of Friar John's detention.

At the other extreme, many critics have beaten a path which widely skirts the problem of the accident, demonstrating that the play *is* tragedy by shifting responsibility for the catastrophe away from the accident and placing it, as firmly as their prose can, on the character of Romeo, or, less frequently, on both lovers. The view is represented by the remarks of Gervinus:

> In him [Romeo] a hidden fire burns with a dangerous flame; his slight forebodings are fulfilled, not because a blind chance causes them to be realized, but because his fatal propensity urges him to rash deeds; he calls that fortune which is the work of his own nature. . . . We cannot accuse any blind accident of fate, nor can we blame any arbitrary exercise of punishment on the part of the poet; it is Romeo's tumultuous nature alone [which] exercises justice upon itself [see excerpt above, 1849-50].

Between the extremes of bold admission that the accident ruins the tragedy and complete dismissal of its importance lies such a middle position as that which is best represented by Brander Matthews' words:

> But, after all, this is but a trifle; it is only a petty lapse from the inevitability of the tragedy, since we all know that the fate of the lovers is already sealed. Even if this letter had been delivered in time, some other stroke of ill fortune would have prevented Romeo's arrival in season to save Juliet's life. What had to be had to be; and no one need cavil at the specific accident which brought about what was certain from the very beginning. Violent delights could have only a violent end [see excerpt above, 1913]. . . .

Evidence abounds that critics have come reluctantly to their task of dealing with Friar John. The fact of the accident has embarrassed them even to the point that some have invented strange interpretations of the causes of the catastrophe to avoid the need of mentioning the accident. . . . But the general dismay on this point is understandable, for critics have loved *Romeo and Juliet*, even as audiences have loved it. Nearly all extended discussions of the play begin as eulogies, only to turn, half way through, upon a "but," followed by some painful remarks on Friar John. Brander Matthews seems desperate in his remarks, which follow several pages of high praise. Hazelton Spencer admits the defect bravely, but only after he has given the play rare encomiums [see Additional Bibliography]. Baker's famous comments on the dramatic structure up to the point of the accident make it plain that he sees in the opening acts the nonpareil of craftsmanship.

In one view, then, *Romeo and Juliet* is a beautiful drama of youthful love, but a failure in tragedy because the catastrophe hinges on the one accident. In the other, which may have been adopted less under the influence of Aristotle than in the need to avoid speaking harshly of a well-loved work, the play is a tragedy in which the catastrophe is inevitable because the lovers, one or the other, or both, possess a tragic flaw.

The two views are at such variance as to make it unlikely both should be true. My belief is that the pattern of the tragedy Shakespeare wrote is not accurately mirrored in either. Although the second view causes the problem of Friar John to vanish, the feat is achieved by legerdemain; however well or ill the tragic-flaw explanation fits the four greatest tragedies, it does not fit this one at all. It is inapplicable to the facts of the play as the play is written, and rather than resort to this means of blotting out Friar John's detention one would probably do better to confess that the accident spoils the tragedy. Furthermore, neither view sheds light on the problem of Friar Laurence's speech, which must indeed appear repetitious and long, an unfortunate necessity at best, in either.

There is, however, another way to look at the tragedy which, besides being faithful to the facts and showing the accident in another light, markedly alters the appearance of the Friar's speech. Or, more emphatically, this view alters the appearance of both the accident and the speech by being faithful to the facts.

We can best lead to this view by examining the situation that exists immediately before the Friar speaks. Here the people of Verona find results which some of them have caused, but by actions whose significance no one of them has wholly comprehended, and, indeed, of which several of the chief contributors to the catastrophe have been wholly unaware. The lovers lie warm and dead with Paris beside them in the tomb. For the audience, which has had full vision of all events from the beginning, this spectacle holds no mystery. But the Prince, the feuding families, and the citizens come upon the scene from outside, as from another world—like Fortinbras, say, upon the destruction which ends *Hamlet,* with no more knowledge than he of what has happened. The spectacle shows no causes, but only effects. We miss the full force of the tragedy if in the clarity of our own vision we forget that the Prince and his subjects have no vision at all.

That Shakespeare meant the audience to mark the bewilderment of the participants and to remember the breadth of the gulf which lies between its own and the participants' understanding is evinced by the dramatist's underscoring. The fifty lines that precede the Friar's narration of the events *as he knows them* strike a single note, too insistent to go unheard. The first man from "outside," the Chief Watchman, strikes it first:

> . . . here lies the County slain;
> And Juliet, bleeding, *warm,* and *newly dead,*
> Who here hath lain *this two days buried.*
>
> [V. iii. 174-76]

To him, not us, Juliet's warmth in death is a phenomenon; he sends others to tell the Prince and the families, and then, as he continues, his remark pointedly reminds the audience of the gap between the spectators' and the participants' visions:

> *We* see the ground whereon these woes do lie,
> But the true ground of all these piteous woes
> *We* cannot without circumstance descry. . . .
>
> [V. iii. 179-81]

The inexplicable fact of three bodies lies before the Prince, the families, and the citizens. The Prince makes a demand that must prove vain: "Search, seek, and *know how* this foul murder comes" [V. iii. 198]. The consternation of all is epitomized in the remarks of the fathers at this point. Capulet can only fumble, not even guess what events have led to this pass:

> This dagger has mista'en, for lo, his house
> Is empty on the back of Montague,
> And is missheathed in my daughter's bosom!
>
> [V. iii. 203-05]

Montague, who has besides lost his wife overnight, cannot do even so much; for him, the causes of the spectacle are not merely unknown but unimaginable. . . . The bewildered out-cries are at last silenced by a second command from the Prince, a command which might be also the dramatist's reminder to those who have had the godlike privilege of watching the action from the beginning that what they know fully the participants do not know at all:

> Seal up the mouth of outrage for awhile,
> Till we can clear these ambiguities
> And know their spring, their head, their true descent.
>
> [V. iii. 216-18]

Who killed Romeo and Juliet and Paris? It is their question, and none among them possesses more than pieces of the an-swer; when these pieces shall have been fitted together, there will yet be no whole. The Prince and the families know literally nothing of the cause; with a sense of shock one may realize in this moment that Montague does not even know that Romeo had been in love with Rosaline: thus widely is his knowledge separated from ours. The Friar knows most; yet the whole of his knowledge, as that is revealed in the disputed recapitulation, includes in fact only fragments of the concatenation of events which produced the catastrophe. And even after his story has been supplemented by the scraps of information held with no sense of their meaning by Balthasar and Paris' page, the gulf lies wide between the total understanding of the characters and that of the audience. Upon our awareness that this gulf remains, depends something of our experience of the full tragic force of the play.

Specifically, Friar Laurence tells the other characters these facts, of which until now they were ignorant: (1) that Romeo and Juliet were married; (2) that Juliet grieved for Romeo, not Tybalt; (3) that he (Laurence) gave Juliet a trance-producing potion; (4) that his letter advising Romeo of this action was delayed by accident; (5) that on his arrival at the tomb Romeo and Paris were dead; (6) that Juliet killed herself when she

found Romeo dead. . . . One fact that he does not reveal is how Romeo came to be in the tomb. His silence is for good reason—for the same reason that, as we shall see, is key to the pattern of the tragedy: he does not know. Another fact on which he is silent for the same reason is how Paris came to be there. No passages in the play hint more boldly at the line of "true descent" than do those in which Balthasar and the page con-tribute these missing bits of information. "He came with flow-ers to strew his lady's grave" [V. iii. 281], the page says innocently—not knowing, of course, that Juliet was not "his" (Paris') lady, but Romeo's; and he continues,

> And bid me stand aloof, and so I did.
> Anon comes one with light to ope the tomb;
> And by-and-by my master drew on him;
> And then I ran away to call the watch.
>
> [V. iii. 282-85]

To him this action had been shadow-play by dim light, such action as might happen in a dream. To Balthasar, whose lot it is to speak a line of more terrible significance, "I brought my master news of Juliet's death" [V. iii. 272], the same action had indeed appeared as a dream:

> As I did sleep under this yew tree here,
> I dreamt my master and another fought,
> And that my master slew him.
>
> [V. iii. 137-39]

Pieced together, the words of the Friar and the servants clear away the most immediate ambiguities for the surviving partic-ipants, and they enable the Prince to say,

> See what a scourge is laid upon your hate,
> That Heaven finds means to kill your joys with love!
>
> [V. iii. 292-93]

To that extent the vision of all has been widened, and the reconciliation is made possible. Yet they are only the obvious questions that are thus answered. Fate, the Prologue told us, destroyed the lovers in order to end the feud. "Heaven finds means," the Prince knows to say at the last, and so both spectators and participants know that the first cause of the catastrophe was the feud, which had prompted Fate to "find means." The ultimate responsibility for the deaths, then, be-longs to the feudists themselves; all this is clear to both spec-tators and participants: we have Shakespeare's words in the Prologue, and the participants have the Prince's at the end, and the two agree.

But though it is unmistakable that Fate used the deaths of the lovers as means to end the feud, it is not made clear to the participants what means Fate used to kill the lovers. No par-ticipant can describe those means wholly. . . . [It] is evident that the whole truth of just how Heaven found means to kill their joys, of what these means were, must remain mystery. Their wisest cannot trace the details of that true descent which is thrice demanded by the Prince; neither can all, combining the pieces of their information, reconstruct the whole pattern.

We, however, are spectators, and we should be able to take up the Prince's challenge, to describe the means in full of Fate's working to the deaths of Romeo and Juliet. Yet, as the rep-resentative critical statements set down at the first of this paper make evident, we have not described them. We have said (1) that the accident of the detention was the means, or (2) that defects in the lovers' characters were the means. Or, worse, with Brander Matthews in a desperate moment, we have claimed both accident and "violent delights" as the means, and then

*Act I. Scene v. Romeo, Juliet, Nurse, Benvolio, Mercutio, Tybalt, and others. By William Miller. The Department of Rare Books and Special Collections, The University of Michigan Library.*

dismissed both as "trifles" anyway, because "we all know that the fate of the lovers is already sealed," and "what had to be had to be." It is sure enough that Fate wrought the end: the Prologue tells us so. But a tragic dramatist cannot simply announce that "Fate did it" and thereby have a tragedy, nor can a critic excuse him if he stops on that plea, or defend him by making the plea for him. If "Fate did it," yet the dramatist must show how Fate worked. Plead Fate as he may, he has no inevitability and no tragedy if he neglects to show that. It is impossible that Shakespeare, even the "apprentice" Shakespeare of *Romeo and Juliet,* if one thinks of him so, should have been ignorant of this obvious necessity. If we find such level of incompetence in Shakespeare unbelievable, our task is plain enough: it is to expose the pattern of the operations of Fate as Shakespeare drew the pattern, and the place to find this is in the play.

Brooke, it may be said, left Shakespeare free to devise the pattern of Fate's working. Brooke, by my count, uses the word "Fortune" forty times. He makes clear that the catastrophe came about because of the feud, but his repetition of "Fortune" adds at last only to the verdict, "It happened because of Fortune," not to "How Fortune made it happen." All that Brooke had told, Shakespeare tells in his Prologue; but he is then left to show how Fate worked, which is the business of the play itself. The dramatist might have chosen to show Fate working

through a human villain, planted among the feudists to deceive and destroy them. He did not so choose: there is no villain in *Romeo and Juliet.* He might have shown Fate directing men to their dooms by means of oracles, witches, or other supernatural agents used to make contact with mortals. He might even have chosen a more direct intervention of Fate in the affairs of men, a flashing blow straight out of the heavens. The play shows that he chose none of these means.

It is the heavy underscoring of the fact that at the end of the play the survivors cannot discover, in all its details, the exact pattern of events that killed Romeo and Juliet that suggests the means of Fate's working. Earlier in this paper I have insisted, for I believe Shakespeare insisted, that the final hundred and forty lines of the play are dominated by two facts: the fact of the bewilderment of the participants, and the fact of the wide gap that lies between our clear understanding of the situation then existing and their bewilderment. What is suggested is that the very bewilderment which is here overwhelming is itself related to the means by which Fate wrought the catastrophe; indeed, that the means by which this bewilderment mounted to the proportions which characterize it in the tomb scene are identical with the means by which the catastrophe was brought about—that is, with the means by which Fate worked, or the line of "true descent."

More than any other of Shakespeare's—even more than *Othello,* as a count of pertinent data shows—*Romeo and Juliet* is a tragedy of unawareness. Fate, or Heaven, as the Prince calls it, or the "greater power" [V. iii. 153], as the Friar calls it, working out its purpose without the use of either a human villain or a supernatural agent sent to intervene in mortal affairs, operates through the common human condition of not knowing. Participants in the action, some of them in parts that are minor and seem insignificant, contribute one by one the indispensable stitches which make the pattern, and contribute them not knowing; that is to say, they act when they do not know the truth of the situation in which they act, this truth being known, however, to us who are spectators. . . . In the line of true descent, which is in fact the *way* Fate worked, neither Romeo's "wild-eyed fury" [III. i. 124] nor the accidental detention of Friar John looms so large as the positive actions of those who do what they do in moments of ignorance of the situation which then exists. It is these actions, I believe, that we must re-examine to expose the pattern of the tragedy.

Although the feud named in the Prologue has long existed, the tragic pattern with which we are concerned as spectators is shown to begin in the first scene of the play. Critics have admired this scene, noting the efficiency of the exposition which brings us into the feud even as we are learning of it. But more is here than masterful exposition. . . . [The opening action of the Capulet and Montague servants] is of a kind with actions which follow, through which are made the essential contributions to the tragic outcome. The unawareness of the servants here differs in degree, rather than in kind, from the unawareness of situation in which later Capulet, for example, acts. The difference is that when this initial action takes place no fully developed situation as yet exists, whereas in Capulet's later moments of decision and action a fully developed situation does exist, of which Capulet is unaware. However, we know that an enveloping situation exists when the servants act, for we heard in Shakespeare's Prologue a clear warning that what immediately follows will exhibit Fate at work. Sampson and Gregory, Abram and Balthasar intend no injury to the children of their respective masters. When they act, they cannot possibly guess the consequences of their actions. Furthermore, they cannot and do not ever know either how they contributed or *that* they contributed to the final catastrophe. If they are present in the last scene of the play—and certainly they should be present among the citizens who view the spectacle and wonder how it came to be—they cannot connect any act of theirs with this end. When the time has come to view the bodies in the tomb, the pattern, as we have already seen, has been obscured by its own darkness, and the participants can only gape as Friar Laurence, himself shaken by the knowledge of his unawareness, diffuses just light enough to enable recognition, among the survivors, of the most obvious means. The many particular acts, inconspicuous as they seemed trivial to the actors, though in fact indispensable in the full pattern, are gone and irrecoverable.

The servants are the first, then, to act in a situation of which they know less than we know. The next, as Fate proceeds, is Tybalt. Hot-headed and arrogant, Tybalt might have attacked Benvolio merely because of hot-headedness and arrogance. These are not his reasons, however, as Shakespeare wrote the scene. Before Tybalt appears, Shakespeare has made Benvolio cry, "Put up your swords. You know not what you do" [I. i. 65]. Benvolio tries to stop the fight, and the audience is made to understand his motive. Only thereafter does Tybalt enter, with his cry, " . . . art thou drawn among these heartless hinds?"

[I. i. 66]. It is useless to deny that Tybalt is itching for a fight; the next line suggests that, once his sword is out, no reason will quiet him until he has given some blows. Nevertheless, as Shakespeare arranged the scene, Tybalt's intervention occurred because of his unawareness of Benvolio's motive, known to us. And with Tybalt's intervention the flare-up spreads; the edict of the Prince temporarily ends the incident:

> If ever you disturb our streets again
> Your lives shall pay the forfeit of the peace. . . .
>
> [I. i. 96-7]

[One] effect of the incident is the bottling up of Tybalt's wrath, later to explode and draw the first blood. But of equal importance here is the fact that the Prince's statement is public and therefore the more binding. The force of the first brawl as an incident in the tragedy falls most heavily when next the streets are disturbed—that is, in the hot noontide scene where Mercutio and Tybalt die. Justice calls at that time—if the entire circumstance, from the beginning to that point, were known to the participants as fully as it is known to the audience—for Romeo's exoneration, and there is evidence throughout the scene of Shakespeare's intention to imply that in ordinary circumstances the Prince would have freed Romeo. But justice is deflected by the Prince's obligation to his earlier edict, "If ever you disturb our streets again," and so, though the doom threatened is softened, it is not disregarded; Romeo is neither freed nor executed, but banished.

Twice in the first scene, then, Shakespeare has shown Fate operating through the unawareness of participants, and each time he has marked the means of Fate's operation. Before the end of the scene, and still before the lovers have met, two additional persons contribute to the pattern; these are Rosaline and Benvolio.

The function of Rosaline and the dramatic purpose of introducing Romeo in love have often been discussed, and it is hardly relevant to repeat the discussion. Yet no critic, to my knowledge, has suggested that Rosaline, however innocently, contributes a stitch to the fatal pattern. Rosaline speaks no word that we hear, and she is glimpsed but once, ambiguously then, among the other beauties at the Capulet feast. What link joins this voiceless and almost bodiless creation to the bloody spectacle that ends the tragedy? Not so much by doing as merely by being, Rosaline is as vital a part of the pattern as Capulet himself; without her the end could not have been brought about as Shakespeare showed it to be brought about. There might have been another and better way; but Shakespeare used Rosaline, or, more precisely, showed that Fate used Rosaline, as it used the servants, Tybalt, and others.

What Shakespeare makes clear is that had there been no Rosaline, Romeo would not have gone to the Capulet ball. Miserably in love and glorying in his misery, he bids Benvolio, "O, teach me how I should forget to think!" And Benvolio, "Examine other beauties" [I. i. 226, 228]. At the end of the first scene the motivation is underscored with a challenge and an acceptance:

> Rom. . . . Thou canst not teach me to forget.
> Ben. I'll pay that doctrine, or else die in debt
>
> [I. i. 237-38]

When soon thereafter Romeo finds Rosaline's name among those invited to the Capulets, he resolves to go, not, indeed, for Benvolio's urging, but "to rejoice in splendour of my own" [I. ii. 101]. In short, he goes to see Rosaline. Of all this,

Rosaline is and remains forever unaware. If she is present at the end, nothing in Friar Laurence's speech can enable her to recognize the fact that Fate worked to this conclusion through her.

Benvolio's usefulness to Fate at this point lies in his preparation of Romeo's mind to seize the opportunity which comes shortly thereafter. This opportunity is brought by another casual participant—nearly as casual as Rosaline. The illiterate servant sent by old Capulet to deliver the invitations is and remains as unaware as Rosaline that he has been useful to Fate. Asked to read the list, Romeo discovers the name of Rosaline. On his own initiative—and the line underscores again the way of Fate's working—the servant bids Romeo, " . . . if you be not of the house of Montague, I pray come and crush a cup of wine" [I. ii. 80]. We know, of course, more than the servant knows, and we watch him walk away blissfully ignorant, even as he must remain at the end though Friar Laurence will then have spoken forty lines in order to divulge all of the means of Fate's working that are known to him.

The actions that occur in the first four scenes of the play are of course preliminary. The situation proper begins with the meeting of Romeo and Juliet. (pp. 843-54)

Up to the meeting of the lovers, it is the Prologue on which Shakespeare relies to give the spectators a margin of knowledge. With the meeting of the lovers, however, the situation proper comes into being, and thereafter the audience is omniscient because it is omnipresent; at the same time, the narrowness of the participants' vision becomes increasingly conspicuous. If the fact is discernible that in the preliminary action Shakespeare showed Fate to be working through the human condition of not knowing, it is vividly marked through the scenes that follow. With the situation laid open to our own vision, and with the limits of each character's knowledge as sharply defined, we recognize immediately any action that is performed in unawareness of the situation known to us, viewing the whole from our Olympian vantage point.

The condition of unawareness prevails in the moment of the first meeting. Romeo and Juliet love before either knows the identity of the other. The servant's "I know not" [I. v. 43], in answer to Romeo's question, seems significantly placed: it directly precedes Romeo's speech in which, at the end, he privately seals his devotion. Shakespeare's paralleling of the lovers' reactions when each learns the name of the other signifies the way of Fate's operations as sharply as did, earlier, Benvolio's cry to the fighting servants, "You know not what you do." . . . One may argue, but pointlessly, that Romeo and Juliet would have fallen in love at this meeting even though each knew at first sight the identity of the other. That, however, was not Shakespeare's way of writing the scene. As the lines are written, it appears that Shakespeare meant to show that in this critical moment Fate, proceeding to the end promised in the Prologue, takes advantage of each lover's unawareness of the identity of the other.

After this meeting, the cloud of not knowing, increasing in density, blurs the vision of the participants even to blindness; the vision of the spectators, on the contrary, becomes wider and clearer, so that it takes in not only the participants in their changing situation but also, as my purpose is to show, the cloud itself that blinds them. Repeatedly, as we shall observe, while the rift widens between the knowledge that belongs to the participants and that which belongs to us, the dramatist

marks the cleavage and thus reminds us of the nature of the pattern being woven.

The widening of this gulf is signalized, for instance, by the conversation of Benvolio and Mercutio at the opening of Act II. "Blind is his love" [II. i. 32], says Mercutio, and perhaps that is true; but it is truer that Mercutio is blind, for he has conjured Romeo "by Rosaline's bright eye" [II. i. 17], and we realize suddenly that neither he nor Benvolio knows that Romeo has forgotten Rosaline. When next the three friends meet [II. iv. 36ff.] Romeo and Mercutio engage in the familiar verbal play, and Romeo defeats his brilliant companion. . . . Of the reason for Romeo's change of spirit—his arrangement to marry Juliet—Mercutio, of course, knows nothing. No serious consequence follows Mercutio's unawareness of the situation in these incidents, which serve primarily as preparation: twice we are shown that Mercutio knows nothing of Romeo's matters. But the third meeting of the friends comes (III, i), and this time Fate strikes through the open channel we have twice seen. Though the day is hot and both Mercutio and Tybalt are quarrelsome, heat is not the indispensable condition here. That condition is Mercutio's and Tybalt's unawareness that Romeo and Juliet are married. "I see thou knowest me not" [III. i. 65], Romeo replies to Tybalt, and no more does Mercutio know him as Tybalt's cousin of an hour. "Vile submission!" [III. i. 73] is therefore Mercutio's judgment on Romeo's refusal to fight, and out of this judgment, pronounced in darkness, in this instance darkness in the blaze of noon, comes death for Mercutio and Tybalt, neither of whom learns the truth of the situation in which he died.

Thus the power at work, striking through the channel of men's unawareness of the situation which exists when they act, has engineered the first fatalities. These deaths are important in the tragedy; indeed, it is usual to view them as the climax which seals the doom of the lovers. Yet they are themselves effects rather than causes; the means by which they were brought about, rather than the deaths themselves, are the essentials in the tragic pattern. Violence and bloodshed are shocking and memorable; hence the deaths of Mercutio and Tybalt divert attention from the means by which these deaths occurred, and that is to say, from the *how* of Fate's working.

So too the causes of the decisions and actions of Capulet, whose contributions to the ultimate catastrophe we now examine, are more relevant than his deeds to the study of the means of Fate's working. Some critics have oversimplified Capulet, naming him a tyrannical father, a type individualized, if at all, only by his senility. The marks of type are apparent, certainly, and the sudden and wide variations of his moods suggest senility. Yet there are two facts, one often forgotten or avoided, the other, to my knowledge, never stated, that must figure in an analysis of Juliet's father if that analysis is to throw light on the manner of Fate's working. The first is the fact of his love for his daughter, a love that includes deep concern for her well-being. . . . The second fact is that, although certain of Capulet's actions are indeed indispensable links that lead to his daughter's death, these without exception are performed in that same condition of unawareness which is the environment of all the key actions and judgments along the line of descent.

That the "greater power" works through Capulet's character—of senile, tyrannical father, if one will—toward dire consequence to his daughter is true; but it does so only in situations of which it is impossible for Capulet, *senile or no*, to see the truth as the spectators see it. What is most significant, I believe, is that the dramatist has taken pains to show that Capulet is a devoted father who would not knowingly act against his daughter. It cannot, then, be said that Capulet does as he does in a given situation because he is as he is and that the result is Juliet's death. It must rather be said that in a given situation *of which he knows nothing* he does as he does and that the consequence is Juliet's death. Had he our vision, yet acted as he acts, he would be villainous, and the pattern of the tragedy would be different. But judgment of his actions must not be blind to his blindness; this considered, he is blameless, as are the others whose actions nevertheless kill the lovers. (pp. 854-57)

Paris' contribution to the tragic pattern is like Capulet's in that it is both indispensable and wholly unwitting. Tybalt is dead early in the third act, and thereafter Paris shares with Capulet the opprobrium of the spectator, who feels a rising resentment against those whose actions menace the lovers. The presence of Paris is from the first an unrelenting pain, remembered, thrust out of the upper consciousness, and still remembered in the dread that it will break out anew. Paris' suit precipitates the events which lead on to catastrophe. But for it, the Friar would not be driven upon his "desperate remedy" [IV. i. 69]. But for it, Romeo might wait in Mantua until the Friar can find a time.

> To blaze your marriage, reconcile your friends,
> Beg pardon of the Prince, and call thee back....
>
> [III. iii. 151-52]

On this reasonable expectation Romeo leaves the Friar's cell and goes to take leave of his wife. But it is in the next scene that Capulet makes his "desperate tender," the menace of Paris becomes a throbbing reality, and the hope of the lovers is destroyed as it is born—though destroyed unknown to them. (p. 858)

Shakespeare could have made Paris a scoundrel, proper for our anger. That he did not, but made him impeccable in manner and being, seems to me significant. The ill that Paris does can come only through his unawareness. Shakespeare might have shown Fate working through another Paris in another way, and perhaps that way would have been better, perhaps worse; in any event, another way would have been out of harmony with the rest of the tragic pattern. So Paris, like the others, is made one whose only harm can be unwitting.

A final action of the same kind completes the pattern—and it is not that action which is alleged to mar the tragedy, the detention of Friar John. It is that by which Balthasar contributes to the end. When the closing events are viewed against the pattern we have traced, Friar John's accident proves unimportant, even irrelevant. This event is not of a kind with those which have made the pattern to this point, nor is its irrelevance a blemish in the structure: there was no need for the dramatist to make the manner of Friar John's detention accord with the manner of Fate's working throughout the play, for the incident is not part of the pattern.

The indispensable stitch between Capulet's "We'll to church tomorrow" [IV. ii. 37] and Romeo's suicide, which ends the pattern, is not the Friar's failure to reach Mantua—a negative thing—but Balthasar's success—a positive one. The obvious answers to two questions show that this is fact: First, what would have happened had there been no incident of Friar John at all? The answer is certain: the suicide of Romeo, just as it stands. Second, what would have resulted had there been no Balthasar? Shakespeare wrote this answer, when he made it plain that Friar John returns to Friar Laurence in time for the latter to reach Juliet's tomb before she wakes. Friar Laurence says,

> Now must I to the monument alone.
> Within this three hours will fair Juliet wake.
>
> [V. ii. 24-5]

That the Friar found three hours sufficient to reach the tomb is proved by the plain fact that when Juliet wakes he *is* beside her. Had there been no Balthasar, the Friar would have found Juliet just waking, and he could then actually have done just what he had planned to do as he began his dash to the tomb— "... keep her at my cell till Romeo come—Poor living corse, clos'd in a dead man's tomb" [V. ii. 29-30].

The episode of Friar John, then, falls outside the pattern. But if it is irrelevant, why did Shakespeare include it? And why does it not *seem* irrelevant—for indeed most critics have found it anything but so. We can answer by noting how Shakespeare introduces the episode. In giving Juliet the potion, Friar Laurence makes this promise:

> ... against thou shalt awake,
> Shall Romeo by my letters know our drift;
> And hither shall he come; and he and I
> Will watch thy waking....
>
> [IV. i. 113-16]

The plan was devised as a comfort, naturally and plausibly, to Juliet, who must take a mysterious compound and wake in a fearful place. When the Friar learns that his letter has failed, his distress is for the promise he had made: "She will beshrew me much that Romeo / Hath had no notice of these accidents" [V. ii. 26-7]. Unaware of Balthasar's action, he suspects no greater harm than the breaking of his promise, that Juliet will wake to find only him beside her; and but for Balthasar, all would have been so. *It is Balthasar's action, not Friar John's, that needs to be and is consonant with the tragic pattern.* (pp. 860-61)

We now return to the situation which exists when Friar Laurence begins to speak, and to those survivors who gape. Their need at this moment is enlightenment, first, because they are thunderstruck, and, second, because among them are some who were the means to the end they stare on. Who among them can trace the whole pattern of events? The Friar's words enable some who have served Fate to recognize their connection with the catastrophe, though imperfectly. Thus in the Friar's speech are these special words for the Prince:

> ... their stol'n marriage day
> Was Tybalt's doomsday....
>
> [V. iii. 233-34]

Let the Prince now remember and reassess that situation in which he pronounced his sentence of banishment.... To omit the Friar's speech would be to deny us contemplation of the Prince's thoughts in this instant; and that would be to lose one of the rarest experiences the tragedy affords. But the Friar has not ended; for Capulet are these:

> ... not for Tybalt, Juliet pin'd
>
> [V. iii. 236]

Let Capulet now, we being by, review the justice of his ultimatum: "... hang, beg, starve, die in the streets..." [III.

v. 192]. And for Balthasar—though even now the Friar is unaware that they are for him—are these terrible words:

> Then gave I her . . .
> A sleeping potion. . . .
>                          [V. iii. 243-44]

Let Balthasar's loyal eyes start from their spheres in his memory of the words he spoke to his master: "I saw her laid low . . ." [V. i. 20].

Conspicuous in the Friar's speech is mention of Friar John:

> But he which bore my letter, Friar John,
> Was stay'd by accident, and yesternight
> Return'd my letter back.
>                          [V. iii. 250-52]

These lines magnify the seeming importance of the accident, since Friar Laurence himself thus appears to attribute the catastrophe to this cause. But when he speaks these lines, *the Friar does not yet know* of Balthasar's action which had brought Romeo to the tomb. Hence the lines are really but another manifestation of the condition of unawareness which has prevailed from the thumb-biting scene to this. . . . Had the Friar known, when he began to speak, what then was known to Balthasar alone of the living, he would have had no cause even to mention Friar John; for he would then have known that only two facts were pertinent: that he had arrived in time to save Juliet, but that Romeo had already been killed by Balthasar's false word.

Because the persons who gape at the scene of catastrophe are—with others now dead—the very ones who have caused it, experience of the full tragic force requires not only that these persons learn of the rôles they have played but that we be permitted to look on when they grasp the meaning of their past actions. The Friar's speech provides this opportunity, and that is one reason I find it indispensable. (pp. 862-64)

Yet this is only half of the reason for the Friar's speech; the other half is subtle, but, I believe, in view of the pattern of the tragedy as Shakespeare designed it, intended by the dramatist. Contemplation reminds us that not every actor present in the final scene is enabled by the Friar's words to glimpse, however remotely, his connection with the lovers' deaths. What the Friar knows to say is a scrappy and inadequate tale; of the close details of Fate's working he knows nothing. Those persons, of course, who have been not only participants in the fatal events but their victims too—the dead ones—cannot hear with ears of flesh even this poor reconstruction of the events by which they died. Pain of a kind proper to tragedy lies in our reflection that of the four whose bodies are here none died aware of the situation as it really was. Add to these Mercutio, whose body is elsewhere, and all five youths, one may say, died "not knowing": Mercutio not knowing why Romeo would neither fight nor allow him to fight without interference; Tybalt not knowing that Romeo is his cousin of an hour, dearly bound; Paris not knowing it is a husband whom he would apprehend; Romeo not knowing why his wife's cheek is crimson; Juliet not knowing why her husband died. So much for these, who cannot ever be informed, even though the Friar who speaks over them enjoyed our full vision and spoke as many lines to reconstruct the pattern as I have used.

Yet Rosaline, the thumb-biters, the illiterate servant, and Benvolio are presumably present at the last, alive, awake, and staring as the Friar exposes such fragments as he possesses. So much is his vision narrower than ours that his forty lines

cannot compel any of these to glimpse the causal connection between themselves and the scene before them. Their minds are as far beyond the reach of the Friar's review as the dead ones' minds are beyond the reach of any earthly review. Our knowledge of the shares these have had in this tale of woe is therefore locked in us unrelieved; and the pain left with us marks our awareness of the brevity—the irremediable fact of the brevity—of Friar Laurence. (pp. 864-65)

> *Bertrand Evans, "The Brevity of Friar Laurence," in* PMLA, 65, *Vol. LXV, No. 2, March, 1950, pp. 841-65.*

## WOLFGANG CLEMEN (essay date 1951)

[*A German Shakespearean scholar, Clemen was among the first critics to consider Shakespeare's imagery an integral part of the development of his dramatic art. J. Dover Wilson described Clemen's method as focusing on "the form and significance of particular images or groups of images in their context of the passages, speech or play in which they occur." This approach is quite different from that of the other leading image-pattern analyst, Caroline F. E. Spurgeon, whose work is more statistical in method and partly biographical in aim. Clemen examines Shakespeare's adept use of imagery in* Romeo and Juliet, *noting that although his language still contains many instances of the decorative style of his earlier plays, it also demonstrates a more dramatic use of poetry. The critic especially praises Shakespeare's talent, beginning to develop in this work, for uniting images closely to character and situation. Significantly, Clemen also argues that the juxtaposition of conventional and natural styles in* Romeo and Juliet *was intended by Shakespeare and serves a dramatic function. The following excerpt was originally published in Clemen's* The Development of Shakespeare's Imagery *in 1951.*]

In Shakespeare's work, conventional style and a freer, more spontaneous mode of expression are not opposite poles which may be definitely assigned to different periods. It is impossible to say that with a certain play, the conventional style comes to an end, and that from then on, a new style exclusively prevails. There are many transitions and interrelationships, and in some plays which stand at the turning-point between the young and the mature Shakespeare, the most traditional and conventional wording is to be found together with a direct and surprising new language which allows us to divine the Shakespeare of the great tragedies. *Romeo and Juliet* is the best example of this co-existence of two styles. (p. 63)

On the whole it may be said, that the first scenes of *Romeo and Juliet* strike us as being more conventional in tone and diction than the later ones. The blank-verse, too, is handled more conventionally here than in the later parts of the play. It may very well be that this is intentional. For the nearer the play advances towards its tragic culmination, the less powerful and significant becomes the conventional world from which the two lovers have freed themselves by accepting their fate. This transition of style has not, of course, been worked out consistently. The rhetoric and the declamatory style never quite vanish, and are certainly not meant to disappear entirely. Their persistence, however, may set off better those passages (more frequent in the last acts), in which we find a new simplicity and poignant directness of diction, as in Romeo's famous line, "Is it even so? Then I defy you, stars!" [V. i. 24]. This manner of placing significant moments and passages into fuller relief, by contrasting them with very different stylistic patterns has been most effectively used by Shakespeare throughout the whole play. It is interesting to trace this art of contrast in the use of imagery; it accounts not only for many subtle dramatic effects, but also for several juxtapositions which appear odd at first sight, but become clear when judged from the context.

That the same characters speak in this play, now in a very conventional, now in quite a new and different manner, may best be seen with Romeo. It is he who (besides Juliet and the nurse) is most often able to rise above the level of flowery or witty, conventional phrases (as in the balcony scene and in the garden scene). But, on the other hand, he is just as much confined to this conventional mode as all the others. If we look closer, however, we see that this change in diction in Romeo is not the result of chance but rather of a change in his mood. Before Romeo has met Juliet, he still finds pleasure in polished and witty dialogue with Benvolio, speaks of "love" in the usual stereotyped phrases, using in his speech, apart from metaphors, a great variety of other figures which contribute to the artificiality of his whole utterance at this stage of the play. (pp. 64-5)

But this same Romeo speaks a new language in those two scenes with Juliet, which stand out from the drama like unforgettable peaks: the garden scene and the balcony scene. Here two characters meet who no longer carry on coquetry with elegant conceits on "love" but who are passionately in love with one another and give direct expression to their love. The fact that, in *Romeo and Juliet*, Shakespeare shaped human love for the first time in *timeless* form gives this play an important position not only in his own development, but also in the history of the Elizabethan drama. This fundamental experience of deep and passionate love is at the very base of the whole drama; in these two scenes it finds its most genuine expression. For these scenes bring the secret converse of the lovers, freed from their conventional environment and from distraction, but at one with the heart of nature. The warmth and tenderness of these scenes raises the language to a poetic height and richness unmatched in Shakespeare's work and the imagery displays a complexity surpassing everything hitherto found:

> O, speak again, bright angel! for thou art
> As glorious to this night, being o'er my head,
> As is a winged messenger of heaven
> Unto the white-upturned wondering eyes
> Of mortals that fall back to gaze on him
> When he bestrides the lazy-pacing clouds
> And sails upon the bosom of the air.
>
> [II. ii. 26-32]

Judged by its style, this is indeed still descriptive, meticulously handled imagery, rich in epithets. But the way this image is connected with the situation and the characters is new; it springs wholly from the situation and contains nothing extraneous, whereas up to this point, the images had been illustrated by comparisons from other spheres. Now the situation is itself of such a metaphorical nature, that it permits an organic growth of the image; Romeo stands below in the dark garden, above which slow-sailing clouds move in a star-strewn sky (all this is conjured up by his words!); Juliet appears above at the window. Romeo must lift his eyes, just as one must glance upward in order to perceive the heavenly bodies (the white-upturned eyes are his own eyes). When, in the first lines, the eyes of the beloved appear to Romeo as "two of the fairest stars in all the heaven" [II. ii. 15], then this is no conventional phrase but is based on the reality of the moment, on the fact that he has raised his eyes to heaven and to Juliet at the same time. And when Juliet now appears to him—in the image quoted—as "winged messenger of heaven", this, too, results from the metaphorical character of the situation itself. So ev-

erything in this image has a double function: the clouds and the heavenly *messengers* may be reality, and at the same time they are symbols. The deeply organic nature of this image is to be seen also in the fact that is coincides as a poetic, enhancing element with Romeo's ecstatically uplifted mind. Its inspiration belongs to this moment and to no other; this symbolical moment gave Romeo's words the power to rise above the levels of expression hitherto achieved. In this image three functions merge, which we usually meet separately: it is the enhanced expression of Romeo's own nature, it characterizes Juliet (light, the most important symbol for her, occurs here), and it fills the night with clouds and stars, thus creating atmosphere.

In this scene, it must be admitted, there are still many themes of imagery which appear unoriginal, culled perhaps from the stock-motifs of Elizabethan poetry. . . . Still the tenderness and intensity of the feeling which pulses through this whole scene can occasionally permit so worn a comparison as that of love to the deepest ocean to appear in a wording whose simple straightforwardness makes us wholly forget the conventionality of the image, such as Juliet's:

> My bounty is as boundless as the sea,
> My love as deep; the more I give to thee,
> The more I have, for both are infinite.
>
> [II. ii. 133-35]

The transition we perceive in *Romeo and Juliet* cannot therefore adequately be described as a transition from "conventional" to "natural" speech. For Shakespeare does not simply abandon the language of conceit or the use of artificial and highly elaborated imagery. The change lies rather in the different impression these passages make on us. For they strike us as being more natural, more spontaneous. And this is due to their being more closely adapted to the situation and to the moment. They convince us because we feel the intense emotion that is expressed by them, and we now believe the characters who utter such language. (pp. 66-8)

In the development of imagery, the garden scene and the balcony scene are of importance, because it is here for the first time that "nature-imagery" derives from the characters as their own expression of mood. Romeo and Juliet deliver no excursive speeches, they utter merely their own being and their love for one another, but their words reveal the beauty of nature, the background to that wonderful night. On the other hand, this fusing of the nature-images with nature itself is perfect and complete only because Romeo and Juliet themselves have a personal relationship to the powers of night. A few lines from Juliet's monologue at the opening of the second scene of the third act may serve as example:

> Come, civil night,
> Thou sober-suited matron, all in black,
> And learn me how to lose a winning match,
> Play'd for a pair of stainless maidenhoods:
> Hood my unmann'd blood, bating in my cheeks,
> With thy black mantle; till strange love, grown bold,
> Think true love acted simple modesty.
> Come, night; come, Romeo; come, thou day in night;
> For thou wilt lie upon the wings of night
> Whiter than new snow on a raven's back.
> Come, gentle night, come, loving, black-brow'd
>   night, . . .
>
> [III. ii. 10-20]

Here the night is no longer something detached and extraneous, it appears as Juliet's ally, which she longs for and summons like a human being. The appeal to the night, recurring in this monologue four times, like the theme of a fugue, is intimately associated with the whole of Juliet's speech. The apostrophe of a personified element of nature is indeed a rhetorical artifice and a proven device, but how has convention once again been quickened with throbbing life and made to fit new aims! This great art of Shakespeare's of blending outer nature with the inner spirit of his characters, finds clear expression in the parting scene of the lovers (III. v.). Here the dawning day becomes to them a symbol of parting; but this interrelationship needs no artful constructions in expression, because the situation is so chosen that nature enters naturally and organically into the lovers' dialogue.

In *Romeo and Juliet* Shakespeare employed a special artifice by means of which the atmosphere of nature, though itself a symbol, is introduced in an organic manner. As Caroline Spurgeon was the first to show [see excerpt above, 1935], the two lovers appear to each other as light against a dark background, and all these light-images, in which sun, moon, the stars, lightning, heaven, day and night figure, thus aid in spreading over the whole play and intensive atmosphere of free nature. In the later tragedies we shall find in great perfection this art of characterization through images, whereby a particular atmosphere may be lent to the play. (pp. 71-2)

Thus *Romeo and Juliet* shows at several points how Shakespeare produces a closer harmony between the imagery and the characters, between the inner and outer situation and the theme of the play. But even here, we have not yet what we should call "dramatic" imagery. With its rich poetic decoration, its abundance of epithets, its personifications, the imagery is still predominantly of a descriptive character. Thus the long description of Queen Mab [I. iv. 53-95] appears as an extra-dramatic moment in the structure of the play. Less interrupting, but also exemplifying the tendency to elaborate, are the description of the effect which the poison will have upon Juliet [IV. i. 95-106] and the description of the apothecary and his dwelling by Romeo [V. i. 37-55]. In *Romeo and Juliet* Shakespeare is still writing in a style which leaves nothing unsaid. This tendency towards complete representation, clarification, amplification and description is nevertheless favourable to the development of a poetic diction of great wealth and colour in which the metaphorical element can freely unfold. For, compared to earlier plays, we find in *Romeo and Juliet* an increase of metaphors used where formerly a conceit or an elaborate comparison would have been inserted. These, it is true, have not yet disappeared, but the growing predilection for metaphors seems significant and suggests the way Shakespeare will go. Viewed from this angle, too, *Romeo and Juliet* appears as a play of transition. (pp. 72-3)

Wolfgang Clemen, " '*Romeo and Juliet*'," in his The Development of Shakespeare's Imagery, *Methuen and Co. Ltd., 1951, pp. 63-73.*

## M. C. BRADBROOK (essay date 1951)

[*Bradbrook is an English scholar noted especially for her commentary on the development of Elizabethan drama and poetry. In her Shakespearean criticism, she combines both biographical and historical research, paying particular attention to the stage conventions of Elizabethan and earlier periods. Her Shakespeare and Elizabethan Poetry (1951) is a comprehensive work which relates Shakespeare's poetry to that of George Chapman, Christopher Marlowe, Edmund Spenser, and Philip Sydney, and describes the evolution of Shakespeare's verse. In the following excerpt, Brad-*

*brook notes the abundance of rhetorical language in* Romeo and Juliet, *so much, in her opinion, that entire passages or scenes in the play "are emptied of all feeling." She also comments on the drama's "governing idea," identifying it in the friar's philosophy of moderation. In her words, "such intensity of living must be destructive." Bradbrook therefore views fate and the family feud as only "the efficient causes" of the tragedy, the dramatic cause centered squarely on the lovers themselves.*]

Parts of [*Romeo and Juliet*] are in a manner so rhetorical that they are emptied of all feeling. Romeo like Titus moralizes on a fly at the height of his laments. The modern actress can put across Juliet's reception of the news of Tybalt's murder only by treating it as an outburst of hysterics, which is certainly not how it would originally have been delivered.

> O serpent heart, hid with a flowring face,
> Did ever dragon keepe so faire a Cave? . . .
> Dove-feathr'd Raven, wolvish-ravening lambe,
> Despised substance of divinest show!
> Just opposite to what thou justly seemst,
> A damned saint, an honourable villaine.
>
> [III. ii. 72-9]

Here is a dramatic presentation of that moment of confusion which in *The Rape of Lucrece* and other early work is merely elaborated. . . . Throughout *Romeo and Juliet* there are plain traces of *Titus* and *Lucrece*—the sharp contrast of brilliant light and deep darkness, the metaphor of beauty as a triumphant conqueror, marvellously revived as Romeo gazes upon the face he thinks is dead and ironically recognizes life without knowing what he says:

> O my Love, my Wife,
> Death, that hath suckt the Honey of thy breath,
> Hath had no power yet upon thy beautie:
> Thou are not conquer'd: beauties ensign yet
> Is Crimson in thy lips and in thy cheekes,
> And Deaths pale flag is not advanced there
>
> [V. iii. 91-6]

The skeleton which Juliet sees as she drinks the potion is the commonest of medieval symbols, but it is horribly envisaged by Romeo as 'amorous'. The lights and feasting of the early scenes, the processions, the sudden sharp bouts of fighting, are on the other hand purely dramatic. This play as Granville Barker noted calls for more sheer acting than any of the previous plays had done. When Romeo hears of Juliet's death he has only a few words. The rest is left to the actor. This was an innovation and to an audience must have felt extremely poignant. It was a new way of appealing to their sympathy. What happened in *Romeo and Juliet* is that Shakespeare became a dramatic poet. Mercutio and the Nurse are conceived from the inside: yet they are dramatic characters in the full sense, placed and detached as the hero and heroine are not. Both are comic: both have one scene that is deadly serious. Angelica has the exuberance of the flesh, the natural speech of Mrs. Quickly [in *Henry IV* and *The Merry Wives of Windsor*]— Juliet's weaning is as good as Falstaff's proposal. She has the shameless amoral opportunism of Sir John Falstaff himself— who was rejected by his nursling for precisely the same *reason* though in a different manner from the 'Ancient damnation!' [III. v. 234] which follows her sudden unconscious betrayal of Juliet. . . . Mercutio is a more subtle and more complex character, yet his 'cause' of being is to serve as foil to Romeo in a multiplicity of ways: his frank bawdry is a contrast, his quick wit a messmate, and his violent, pitiful, unnecessary death a foreshadowing of the hero's. The speed of the story, which all critics remark upon, and which is Shakespeare's own invention, is essential to the governing Idea. 'These violent delights have violent ends' [II. vi. 9] says the Friar. The quenched torch, the meteor gliding through the night, the wedding cheer changed to a burial feast, all are embodiments of the same theme.

> Come what sorrow can.
> It cannot countervaile the exchange of joy
> That one short minute gives me in her sight:
> Doe thou but close our hands with holy words,
> Then love-devouring death doe what he dare,
> It is inough I may but call her mine.
>
> [II. vi. 3-8]

These words of Romeo define the inward meaning of the tragedy. Fate and the feud may be the efficient causes which determine the cruel end of the star-crossed lovers; that which redeems it from mere cruelty is the sense that all

> quick bright things come to confusion—
> [*A Midsummer Night's Dream*, I. i. 149]

that such intensity of living must be destructive. Put in terms of character, both Romeo and Juliet are too impulsive to live safely in the electric atmosphere that surrounds them; put in terms of action, the speed of the plot carries everything along at such a pace that we feel the momentum cannot be checked; at this pace the smallest accident is fatal, the merest rub of circumstance will throw a life away. All of which Shakespeare has built up from a lumbering and sentimental love-poem. The invention in the Elizabethan sense, the discovery of relations between different realms of imagination—which put Queen Mab into the mouth of the blunt Mercutio, and was soon to put her in the arms of Bottom [in *A Midsummer Night's Dream*]—shows the kind of daring that is possible only by a happy marriage of instinct and skill. It is notable that in taking such a story as *Romeo and Juliet* at all, Shakespeare was flouting convention. Tragedies dealt with the falls of princes and the fate of kingdoms, they were moreover bound to be true stories, and their theme should be a high and lofty one. Shakespeare stooped to be popular. He threw away the dignified apostrophes of Fate, Hell, Vengeance, which he had used so profusely before. He threw away the rule of kingdoms and took a simple love story. The contrast of the bridal bed and the grave is almost the kind of thing that might have been found in a ballad. The story is more like *Clerk Saunders* than any previous tragedy of the English stage. It was overwhelmingly successful; but quite as sharp a defiance to contemporary notions of decorum as *Hero and Leander*.

The feud, the efficient cause of the lovers' deaths, is by no means unimportant, and Shakespeare stressed it both at the beginning and at the end. It makes all the violence natural. In so far as this is a tragedy in the newspaper sense, the feud provides all the motives. It is probably not more dangerous than the feuds which broke out between the followers of Ralegh and Essex at court. The Earl of Oxford's quarrel with Sidney might very well have ended as Tybalt's quarrel did. Life was cheap in Elizabethan London, though not perhaps as cheap as in Italy; but the situation would be familiar in kind if not in degree. It is worth noting how the code works in detail. Old Capulet will not tolerate Tybalt's attempt to start a quarrel at the feast. It is under his roof; and he will not have his guests—even an uninvited Montague—insulted, and his household disturbed in a merrymaking at which nobility are present. Yet he

is quite ready to join in a street brawl himself if his wife did not mock him out of it.

In such matters a character may be realistically drawn, yet at another moment he may lapse into something near moral heraldry. All the fighting, the comedy, the stagecraft, are concentrated upon one end: throwing into sharper relief the love of Romeo and Juliet. It was the orchard scene which the young Inns of Court men learnt by heart . . . It is the final scene, in which Juliet's words

> My grave is like to be my bridal bed
>
> [I. v. 135]

are fulfilled before the spectator's eyes, that is dramatically the most subtle and poetically the most moving. The manipulation of suspense in this scene, the echoes of the first meeting in the 'feasting presence' [V. iii. 86], the contrast between Romeo's *canzone* [song] and Juliet's quick sharp action, are in keeping because Shakespeare has abandoned his models and taken simply and solely to writing like himself.

The theme in general was that of the age. There never was a period in which more love-poetry appeared. The sonnet sequences, many of them written earlier no doubt, were pouring from the press. Ovidian Romances, Heroical Epistles, lyrics of all kinds abounded. So far as the subject went, Shakespeare swam with the stream. . . . [Romeo and Juliet] exist only as lovers, only in the relation of love. Society is outside. 'Call me but Love and I'll be new-baptised' [II. ii. 50] cries Romeo: he is Everyman in Love and though Verona and the feud, the Nurse and Mercutio exist as supporters to the star-crossed lovers, the play's core and heart is a love-duet. In courtly poetry there is always the chorus. The Elizabethans would, then, have seen *Romeo and Juliet* as 'an amorous tragi-comedy' if any Polonius [in *Hamlet*] had essayed its classification. They would have recognized—though for different reasons than the modern ones—that it was not a full tragedy. They might have been content to agree that *Measure for Measure*, when it appeared, was the more tragical of the two, dealing with the high and grave matter of Justice and Mercy, in terms more lofty. Claudio's vision of death and judgment is more serious than the skeleton who keeps his 'feasting presence' in a grave.

Above all, the theme of love was 'comical' for the Elizabethan. The course of true love never did run smooth; personal affection was bound to cut across social exigencies among great ones. . . . They took it as unquestioned presupposition that the odds were heavy against Hero being anything but a nun, Criseyde being anything but a middle-class young woman and Troilus out of her sphere. In real life, Juliet was married to Paris. Nevertheless young love will not obey an old decree. In stealing a marriage, Romeo and Juliet, like Florizel and Perdita [in *The Winter's Tale*], justified the rebellious blood among the auditory; they would have this extra claim upon the sympathy of youth. Society is flouted and takes revenge; yet the lovers' deaths heal the feud which caused them. (pp. 116-22)

> *M. C. Bradbrook, "Moral Heraldry: 'Titus Andronicus', 'Rape of Lucrece', 'Romeo and Juliet'," in her* Shakespeare and Elizabethan Poetry: A Study of His Earlier Work in Relation to the Poetry of the Time, *Chatto & Windus, 1951, pp. 104-22.*

## GEORGE IAN DUTHIE (essay date 1953)

[*In the following excerpt from his 1953 introduction to the Cambridge edition of* Romeo and Juliet, *Duthie states that Shake-*

*speare's play is modeled on the medieval* de casibus *tragedy and depicts fate or fortune endowing the young lovers with happiness only to "cast them down to sorrow and to ruin." The critic adds, however, that Shakespeare modified this tragic rendering of his lovers' ordeal by placing it within the larger context of the family feud and by making the lovers' deaths the source of the final reconciliation. But Duthie declares that Shakespeare failed to sustain this tragic design in two significant ways: one, by making both the feud and the powers of fate in the play unconvincing, almost arbitrary; and two, by providing frequent suggestions throughout that the lovers themselves are flawed and, as such, equally responsible for their deaths.]*

Romeo and Juliet are 'star-crossed'. Again and again the dialogue brings out the theme of the malignant influence of the stars on human beings. From quite early in the play we have the expression of premonitions of unhappy doom. The lovers are the predestined victims of a malicious Fate. Fortune is against them. The stars, or Fate, or Destiny, or Fortune, or whatever other specific name may be applied to the cosmic force with which we are concerned, brings the lovers together, gives them supreme happiness and self-fulfillment for a short time, and then casts them down to destruction. The spectator or reader is aware of a devastating sense of waste, and he reacts to the spectacle of the destruction of the lovers with a feeling of deep pity. Their doom is pathetic.

Fate works against the lovers in diverse ways. It works against them by arranging that they are placed in a context of family hostility. It works against them by contriving a deadly series of accidents and coincidences. It works against them through character-flaws in friends and associates of theirs.

The play is full of accident, coincidence, chance. If Friar Lawrence's letter to Romeo had reached Romeo at the time when the Friar was entitled to suppose it would—had not Friar John been unexpectedly detained in a house in Verona suspected of harbouring the plague—then all might have been different. This is but one of the sequence of chance happenings which extends throughout the play. Shakespeare does not want us to think of these 'accidents' as merely fortuitous. We cannot avoid the impression that he asks us to think of them as intentionally arranged by Fate. Fate deliberately works against the lovers by this means.

And then we have the family feud. Romeo with friends, masked, presents himself at Capulet's ball. Old Capulet himself is only too ready to forget the feud, only too ready to take the maskers' visit as a compliment (as normally, in any given case, it would be taken). Tybalt hot-headedly objects. Capulet wisely pacifies Tybalt, albeit with difficulty. But Tybalt's rancour outlasts the evening. He seeks out Romeo, intent on avenging what he takes to be a slight on his family's 'honour'. Romeo (with good enough reason, in all conscience) will not fight. Mercutio—ignorant of Romeo's love for Juliet, and thus failing to understand Romeo's attitude—assails Tybalt. This results in Mercutio's death; and then Romeo must needs avenge it. Tybalt dies. Romeo is banished. Had Romeo not been banished, the final catastrophe might never have taken place.

Fate is here operating against Romeo and Juliet through the fact that Tybalt and Mercutio have false ideals, false values. Tybalt is a man whose values are similar to those of Hotspur in *Henry IV*. He is obsessed with the notion of 'honour', but it is not honour in the best sense; it is a mistaken view of honour, and it leads him into conduct which is contrary to reason. Mercutio has essentially the same mistaken sense of honour. (pp. xvii-xviii)

Fate works against the lovers by means of the feud, by means of accident and coincidence, and by means of character-flaws in others. But are the lovers themselves in any way responsible for their own doom? Is there any error in their own behaviour, any fault or faults in their own characters, which may be regarded as at least partially responsible for their unhappy end?

From time to time the dialogue invites us to consider the question, are the lovers too rash, impetuous, reckless? Friar Lawrence thinks they are. Or at any rate he feels that they must be counselled not to be.

> Wisely and slow. They stumble that run fast.
>
>                                            [II. iii. 94-5]

> These violent delights have violent ends, . . .
> Therefore love moderately; long love doth so:
> Too swift arrives as tardy as too slow.
>
>                                            [II. vi. 9, 14-15]

The Friar is a very worthy man. But surely we must hesitate long before accepting his viewpoint in these passages as being that of Shakespeare. The Friar is prudent; he is worldly-wise. He knows what will work and what will not work. Furthermore, we must do him the justice of noting that he is, with genuine religious fervour, anxious to press the claims of the spirit against those of the flesh. But our general impression of the play as a whole forbids us to take the Friar's views as being those which Shakespeare wants to be accepted as valid. We cannot think that Shakespeare wants us to blame these two incomparable young people as being over-hasty; we cannot think that Shakespeare wants us to believe that it would have been better for them, fundamentally, if they had been more prudent, more coolly calculating. We cannot think that Shakespeare wants us to take the Friar's words as indicating the true standard by which we must judge these golden young people. One may, in one's own philosophy, value divine love as infinitely finer than human love. One may, in one's own philosophy, feel that reason, moderation, should prevail over feeling and passion. But surely, if one accepts the assumptions that Shakespeare seems to be implying in this play—if, in other words, one tries to fathom Shakespeare's intentions—one must ask what this well-meaning but dull, timid and unimaginative cleric knows of the ecstasies of a sublime passion which the play, even if it succeeds in doing nothing else, certainly succeeds in glorifying magnificently.

It may, however, be pointed out that it is not only Friar Lawrence who brings up the notion of rashness, Juliet herself says to Romeo—

>             Although I joy in thee,
> I have no joy of this contract tonight:
> It is too rash, too unadvised, too sudden,
> Too like the lightning, which doth cease to be
> Ere one cay say 'It lightens'.
>
>                                            [II. ii. 116-20]

This is one of those touches of premonition by which Shakespeare, as noted above, helps to paint in the atmosphere of Fate, of oncoming doom, which overhangs the play. But we are not to suppose that Juliet intends it seriously herself or to take it as anything more than a momentary superstitious utterance of a young girl who, having suddenly discovered supreme happiness, is, for a second or two, half-afraid that her happiness is too great to last. (pp. xix-xxi)

Is Romeo to be blamed for over-hastiness in buying the poison? Is he to be blamed for over-hastiness in committing his suicide?

There is nothing blameworthy about his believing Balthasar's report of Juliet's 'death'. Romeo has no reason to doubt the news. And later, when he sees Juliet in the tomb, she certainly seems to be dead. It would be quite ridiculous to blame him for supposing that in fact she is dead. And, since he has, from his first view of her, regarded her as his whole life, how can he be blamed by anyone of good will for killing himself in the belief that she is dead? There is nothing that we can hold against him here unless we insist on the (admitted) validity of moral conceptions that have no meaning for Shakespeare in this play, such as that under no circumstances should a man end his own life, or unless we press the claims of prudent scepticism to the point of insisting that a man is culpable if he accepts a report from his faithful servant without verifying it, or if, seeing his loved one lying motionless in a sepulchre, he fails to say to himself that perhaps, despite appearances, she is not dead at all and that perhaps, after all, he had better wait and see. It is true that when he learns of Juliet's 'death' from Balthasar Romeo looks 'pale and wild' [V. i. 28]. There is emotional unbalance. But, thinking of the magnitude of the blow he has sustained, how can we blame him?

We do not say that there are no character-flaws in hero and heroine. On the contrary, there are, as we shall see later. But it is not part of the basic design of the story of the lovers that spectator or reader should regard their fate as directly caused, even partly, by their own character-flaws.

It seems quite clear that the tragic design which Shakespeare intends to embody in the story of the lovers is a design very popular in the Middle Ages—the conception of tragedy as consisting of the malignant operation of Fate, or Fortune, against human beings, these human beings in no way deserving their doom. . . . While the falls of illustrious men exercised . . . great appeal, writers sometimes turned to the stories of people not of the very highest social eminence, and to private rather than public life. The Troilus and Cressida story is a case in point; and indeed Mr Nevill Coghill has declared that 'the most pervasive influence, one which gave Shakespeare the definable form of tragedy that we see in *Romeo and Juliet,* came from *Troilus and Criseyde'.* (pp. xxi-xxiii)

As regards the story of the lovers, then, Shakespeare intends to follow the traditional pattern of the tragedy of Fate or Fortune or Destiny or the Stars, which endow human beings with great happiness (sometimes it is worldly success, power, empire, riches: here it is emotional and spiritual self-fulfilment), and then cast them down to sorrow and to ruin. Their fall is not their own fault. They are the helpless victims of a malevolent, or at least capricious, universal force. The philosophy underlying this conception of tragedy is a profoundly pessimistic philosophy.

But the play deals not only with the lovers but also with the families.

The play ends with a reconciliation between the two warring families; and it is with the families that it begins—

> Two households, both alike in dignity,
>     In fair Verona, where we lay our scene,
> From ancient grudge break to new mutiny,
>     Where civil blood makes civil hands unclean.
>                                         [Prologue, 1-4]

The lovers are set in this context; and the Prologue indicates that, in the all-embracing pattern of the play, the fate of the lovers is meant to be regarded as subsidiary to the fate of the families. The lovers have 'misadventured piteous overthrows' [Prologue, 7], but the final significance of these is that they bury the strife of the parents. The lovers die and must be buried. They are innocent victims, and we feel a sense of pathos. But at the same time the families' strife dies and is buried, and we feel that in the future all is going to be well in Verona. We have, fundamentally, a happy ending, though it is purchased at a sad cost.

If the play concerned nothing but the 'misadventured piteous overthrows' of the two young people who are the innocent victims of a malignant Fate, then we should have to say that it embodied a tragic design that Shakespeare never attempted again. In *King Lear* there is a point at which the Earl of Gloucester declares that

> As flies to wanton boys are we to the gods,
> They kill us for their sport.
>                                 [*King Lear,* IV. i. 36-7]

But this is not the final message with which Shakespeare leaves us at the end of *King Lear.* If, in *Romeo and Juliet,* we think of the lovers' story by itself, we shall no doubt feel that that *is* his final message here. That pessimistic message is, in fact, the message of any writer who sets out to deal *simpliciter* with the theme of Fortune's wheel or with the theme of the malignant stars which ruin men for no reason connected with justice. That theme had been dealt with by many writers before Shakespeare's time, and he was fully aware of it. But in this play, handling that theme, he wanted it to fall into place as part of another theme.

The two great protagonists of the drama are the two families. They belong to the same city, and they should, in the light of a moral law that we can all accept, be bound together in a relationship of affection and cooperation. Actually they are at daggers drawn. The families sin, then: and they do so before the hero and heroine are even born. It is a case of 'ancient grudge'. The hero and heroine, living in this context, are brought to a fatal doom which they themselves do not deserve. But their fate brings the two families together, the feud comes to an end, and the future of Verona looks bright. Society is redeemed through suffering and loss. The families are punished for their sin by the loss of their brightest scions. The final message, then, is that the gods are just (punishing the families as they do), and also that the gods are charitable in the highest sense, wishing to replace hate with love in the world. It takes the sacrifice of the innocent to purge the guilty of their sin and to turn strife into amity. But at least the sacrifice of the innocent is contrived in a total design which is ultimately regulated by both justice and mercy, in due proportion, in the forces which run the universe.

How far was Shakespeare successful in the carrying out of this design? The answer must be: (i) what he actually accomplished is very fine—the play is deservedly one of the most perennially popular of his works; but (ii) he did not quite succeed in doing what he set out to do, so that, in fact, as Professor Charlton has said, the play 'as a pattern of the idea of tragedy . . . is a failure' [see excerpt above, 1948].

The story of the two families is vitally important to the intended design, and that of the two lovers is only part of that design: yet, while the design is clearly perceptible, it seems defective, inasmuch as most of the dramatist's attention is concentrated on the lovers, his attention to the families frequently (though not invariably) appearing to be somewhat perfunctory. Thus, while the dramatist is trying to convey a certain great tragic conception (which points forward to his maturity), he succeeds, with many readers, in conveying with full conviction only a fragment of that conception—conveys in fact an impression of tragedy different from that which he finally wanted to convey. The play does not fail because it lacks design. The reason why it fails, to the extent it does, is that the author is profoundly interested in parts of the design, and he is not nearly so much interested in other parts of the design. And so the structure is lop-sided.

Two aspects of this failure which have been noted by critics may be mentioned here. One has been noted by Professor Charlton, the other by Professor Stauffer [see excerpt above, 1949].

Professor Charlton feels, and others feel with him, that, while wishing the idea of Fate and the plot-element of the feud to be vitally important components of the design exercising an overwhelming compulsion upon the lovers, Shakespeare has in fact made the feud quite unconvincing and has made of the conception of Fate nothing more important than a matter of sheer bad luck.

In this connexion we must, of course, avoid making the elementary mistake of treating partially non-naturalistic drama as if it were meant to be completely naturalistic. Consider the following point. When Romeo falls in love with Juliet, Shakespeare certainly means us to think, right away, of the feud as the only obstacle in the way of the lover's happiness. But before he fell in love with Juliet Romeo was, or thought he was, in love with Rosaline. It is a critical commonplace that Shakespeare wants us to contrast Romeo's love of Juliet with his earlier love of Rosaline. In the one case Romeo is, to use a convenient cliché, in love with being in love. His feeling for Rosaline, while quite sincere, is not deep, not fundamental. He is going through a fashionable stage of youthful development, thinking, behaving, and speaking in accordance with the well-established conventions that the fashion dictated. In the other case he really is in love, if any man in literature ever was. The distinction is clear. But, in successfully making this distinction, Shakespeare ignores a point which, in the light of a strictly naturalistic interpretation, may well seem to involve unfortunate inconsistency. Romeo's love-affair with Rosaline meets with frustration. Romeo is a Montague, Rosaline a Capulet. But his frustration is not caused thereby. One may wonder why. If the feud stands in the way of his love of Juliet, why did it not stand in the way of his love of Rosaline? It did not: or, if it did, Shakespeare makes nothing of the point. What, he tells us, actually stands in the way of Romeo's success with Rosaline is her ideal of celibacy.... But our point is this—that a naturalistic critic may say, on the one hand, that there is an inconsistency here which is an artistic blot on the play, or he may say, on the other hand, that we cannot be expected to take the feud very seriously since it seems to have been no obstacle as regards Romeo's first love-affair. To both criticisms the reply must be that Shakespeare's plays are liable to be only partly naturalistic, and that one should always be on one's guard against applying to them critical criteria which are irrelevant to them.

Nevertheless, allowing for all this, Professor Charlton is right. Our first view of the feud on the stage involves nothing more impressive than a vulgar brawl amongst servants, some at least of whom behave in a distinctly unvalorous and ignoble manner. And then we have the heads of the houses coming in and appearing rather ridiculous. Capulet, attired in a dressing-gown, calls for an absurdly obsolete weapon, and we enjoy his wife's

delightful tartness—'A crutch, a crutch! Why call you for a sword?' [I. i. 76-7]. Montague's wife treats her lord similarly. It all seems rather trivial, rather silly. Professor Charlton notes this, and he feels that the feud is not presented by Shakespeare in such a way as to seem to be a force, working against the lovers, as terrible and as serious as the author apparently wanted it to seem. Admittedly there are places where it at least nearly seems to be such a force. But Shakespeare does not sustain the idea throughout with full conviction.

Now for the point made by Professor Stauffer. Though, as we have said, it was no part of Shakespeare's consciously intended dramatic design that the hero or heroine should be held even partially responsible for their own doom owing to any character-flaws, that is not the end of the matter.

Indubitable weaknesses of character they have, and Shakespeare does not spare them in pointing these out. When the Friar tells him that he is banished, Romeo rants hysterically. He grovels on the floor. He well deserves the rebuke of the Nurse—'Stand up, stand up, stand an you be a man' [III. iii. 88]. Indeed, he shows 'the unreasonable fury of a beast' [III. iii. 111]. He behaves contemptibly. His conduct is infantile. And it must be noted, too, with however much regret, that Juliet is capable of behaving in a similar manner, though this is not shown on the stage.... They are two very fine young people, certainly: but both of them are lacking, at certain points, in mature poise and balance. They are young: they are immature. Thus, while we cannot see that these defects contribute directly and demonstrably to their doom, there they are, and Shakespeare emphasizes them; so that we are left wondering what place, if any, they are supposed to have in the dramatic

*Act I. Scene v. Romeo, Juliet, and others. By J. Pawsey.*

design. And though some critics pretend to reconcile their apparent inconsistency or obscurity, it can hardly be denied that it spells some degree of failure on Shakespeare's part. . . . The truth is, Shakespeare was thinking predominantly in terms of the medieval tragedy of Fortune; but the idea of the hero as partially responsible for his own fate, through defects in himself, an idea to become fundamental in later tragedies, was also present at the back of his mind. He seems to be wanting to bring this idea to the fore at certain points; but he does not succeed in accommodating it to the other theme in a convincing manner. What we actually have then is a drama of Fate involving the destruction of two innocent victims who have defects of character which are not properly worked into the pattern.

But if Shakespeare failed in these ways, wherein consists the success of the play? For, admitting that 'as a pattern of the idea of tragedy it is a failure', the fact remains that in some way or ways it is a resplendent success, being indeed one of the best-loved and most frequently quoted of the author's works.

The answer is that while the play is in certain important respects a dramatic failure, it is a great poetic success. The thing that most powerfully impressed Shakespeare's imagination as he worked on *Romeo and Juliet* was the emotional richness of the lovers' feeling for each other, and he expresses this in lines of incomparable poetic beauty. . . . In fact the impression that remains longest in our minds after witnessing or reading the play is not an impression depending on the tragic design that Shakespeare obviously intended to produce. What remains longest in our minds is the feeling that Death has no power to destroy the beauty or the power of the feelings of the lovers for each other. What is totally successful in this play is the poetry which expresses these feelings. . . . The expression of the hero's love for the heroine, and of hers for him, is but a part of the fabric of the play. But it is the part that Shakespeare realizes most glowingly; and this was no doubt the reason which led the novelist George Moore to declare, not only that the play is an 'exquisite love-song', but that it is 'no more than a love-song in dialogue'. Had this verdict been presented to Shakespeare himself, he would have had to say, if he accepted it, that he had failed in his artistic intentions. But at any rate, if he failed in these, he certainly succeeded in something else—in that part of his design which, to all spectators and readers since his time, has mattered above all else. (pp. xxiii-xxxiii)

> *George Ian Duthie, in an introduction to* Romeo & Juliet *by William Shakespeare, Cambridge at the University Press, 1955, pp. xi-xxxvii.*

## DENIS DE ROUGEMONT    (essay date 1956)

[*The following excerpt is drawn from a general investigation of the* amour-passion *myth and its presence in works of literature throughout history. De Rougemont's commentary on* Romeo and Juliet, *though brief, is important as the first such analysis to relate Shakespeare's play to this myth. The* amour-passion *tradition in literature presents love as an emotion nurtured by the obstacles put in its way, death being the ultimate obstacle towards which the lovers move and, by dying, render their passion eternal.*]

We know almost nothing about Shakespeare—but he has left us *A Midsummer Night's Dream.* It has been alleged that he was a Roman Catholic—but *Romeo and Juliet* is the one courtly tragedy, as well as the most magnificant resuscitation of the [*amour-passion*] myth that the world was to be given till Wagner wrote and composed his *Tristan.* (p. 190)

In the margin of the religious disputes of the sixteenth century, which caused the ancient heresies to be wrapped in an ever greater darkness, the tragedy of the *Veronese Lovers* tears aside the veil for an instant and leaves in our eyes the negative record of a flash, 'the black Sun of Melancholy'. Sprung up out of the depths of a spirit avid of transfiguring torments, out of the abysmal night in which the lightning flash of love plays now and then on features motionless and fascinating—that *our own self* of horror and divinity to which the most splendid poems of Europe are addressed—resurrected all of a sudden in its full stature, as though stunned by its provocative youth and drunk with rhetoric, on the threshold of the Mantuan tomb here once again the myth stands forth in the glow of a torch which is being held aloft by Romeo.

Juliet rests, put to sleep by the potion. The son of Montague enters, and he speaks.

> How oft when men are at the point of death,
> Haue they beene merrie? Which their Keepers call
> A lightning before death. Oh how may I
> Call this a lightning? O my Loue, my Wife,
> Death that hath suckt the honey of thy breath,
> Hath had no power yet vpon thy Beautie.
> Thou art not conquer'd; Beauties ensigne yet
> Is Crymson in thy lips, and in thy cheekes,
> And Deaths pale flaggs not aduanced there.
>
>       . . . Ah deare Juliet:
> Why art thou yet so faire? I will belieue,
> Shall I belieue? that vnsubstantiall death is amorous?
> And that the leane abhorred Monster keepes
> Thee here in darke to be his Paramour?
> For feare of that, I still will stay with thee,
> And neuer from this Pallace of dym night
> Depart againe: heere, here will I remaine,
> With Wormes that are thy Chambermaides: O here
> Will I set up my euerlasting rest:
> And shake the yoke of inauspicious starres
> From this world-wearied flesh: Eyes looke your last,
> Armes take your last embrace: And lips, O you
> The doores of breath, seale with a righteous kisse
> A dateless bargaine to ingrossing death:
> Come bitter conduct, come vnsauoury guide,
> Thou desperate Pilot, now at once run on
> The dashing Rocks, thy Sea-sick wearie Barke:
>
> Here's to my Loue.
>
>            (*Drinks.*)
>       O true Appothecary:
> Thy drugs are quicke. Thus with a kisse I die.
>              [V. iii. 88-96, 101-20]

Death's *consolamentum* [consolation] has sealed the one kind of marriage that Eros was ever able to wish for. Once more there comes a profane 'dawn', and once more the world goes on again. Restored to his strict reign, the Prince declares:

> A glooming peace this morning with it brings. . . .
> Go hence, to haue more talke of these sad things.
>              [V. iii. 305, 307]
>              (pp. 190-91)

> *Denis de Rougemont, " 'Romeo and Juliet', and then Milton," in his* Passion and Society, *translated by Montgomery Belgion, revised edition, Faber & Faber Limited, 1956, pp. 189-93.*

**FRANKLIN M. DICKEY**  (essay date 1957)

[*Dickey is the first critic to synthesize the two conflicting interpretations of* Romeo and Juliet *as a tragedy of fate and a tragedy of character. According to Dickey, Shakespeare's play is "a carefully wrought tragedy which balances hatred against love and which makes fortune the agent of divine justice without absolving anyone from his responsibility for the tragic conclusion." Thus, the critic argues, divine will, fortune, and the lovers' intense passion are not separable, opposing elements, but interrelated forces which equally contribute to Shakespeare's tragic design.*]

*Romeo and Juliet,* above everything a play of love, is also a play of hatred and of the mysterious ways of fortune. Although love in the first part of the play amuses us, in the end we pity the unhappy fate of young lovers, a fate which critics find embarrassingly fortuitous or, in the Aristotelian sense, unnecessary, the accident of chance to which all human life is subject. Despite the compelling poetry of the play and Shakespeare's skill at creating the illusion of tragedy, the play is said to succeed "by a trick—" [see excerpt above by H. B. Charlton, 1949]. . . . Romeo and Juliet die, critics often tell us, only as the result of a series of mistakes and misunderstandings. In this light the lovers' death is pathetic rather than really tragic.

Critics are also embarrassed by Shakespeare's paradoxical treatment of the three great themes of the tragedy. On the one hand it can be demonstrated that the catastrophe develops from faults of character: Romeo's impetuous nature leads him to despair and die. On the other hand the text also gives us reason to believe that the love of Romeo and Juliet comes to a terrible end because of the hatred between the two families. And yet a third view makes fate the main cause of the final disaster: Romeo and Juliet had to die because they were "star-cross'd."

The seeming conflict of these themes and the division among critics has given support to the belief that Shakespeare reveals no consistently moral view of the universe in this tragedy but gives us a slice of life without comment, standing apart from the great guiding ethos which dominates both Tudor philosophy and literary criticism. If the play has any final meaning it is to be found in the passionate rhetoric of love with which Shakespeare expresses his own youthful ardor.

Against these prevailing views the following chapters propose that *Romeo and Juliet* is a true mirror of the Elizabethan concept of a moral universe although Shakespeare does not preach morality. Judged by Elizabethan standards, the play is not merely a gorgeous and entertaining melodrama but a carefully wrought tragedy which balances hatred against love and which makes fortune the agent of divine justice without absolving anyone from his responsibility for the tragic conclusion. Unlike his source Shakespeare attempts a solution to the problem of evil by fitting the power of fortune into the scheme of universal order. Although Shakespeare's viewpoint is not Greek, Romeo like Orestes is an agent of God's justice but remains responsible for his own doom. (pp. 63-4)

One of the most solid features in the unchanging ground of Shakespeare is the belief in a just Providence. Mysterious as the ways of this Providence are, the pattern remains visible. Although the innocent suffer, the guilty are always punished. Not fate but the corrupt will makes men the agents of their own destruction. . . .

There is no blind fate in Shakespearean tragedy nor in the Elizabethan universe. Behind what looked like chance stood God in control of his creation. Fortune was a figure of speech devised by men to explain the inexplicable operations of the Deity. . . . (p. 91)

[A] belief in individual responsibility forms the philosophical background of mature Elizabethan tragedy. The Renaissance God used fortune as the instrument of his vengeance. In Shakespeare the wayward passions of men subject them to the whims of fate. Thus Hamlet, praising Horatio, equates fortune and the will:

> blest are those
> Whose blood and judgement are so well commingled,
> That they are not a pipe for Fortune's finger
> To sound what stop she please. Give me that man
> That is not passion's slave, and I will wear him
> In my heart's core. . . .
>
> [*Hamlet*, III. ii. 68-73]

While viewing drama, especially *Romeo and Juliet,* we often respond passionately as the doomed heroes respond, and this is, as critics have always known, one of the secrets of tragic catharsis. But beneath these passions the ground bass of an unshakable system continues to move, adding harmonies which we who have rejected that ethic no longer hear. Tragic tension results from the contest between human passion and will which work with and against fate in the elaborate Elizabethan harmony.

This *condition humaine* helps to explain what otherwise are glaring faults in the progress of *Romeo and Juliet*. Shakespeare has promised us at the very beginning that we are to see a pair of star-crossed lovers. Romeo himself first dreads the influence of the stars and then curses them for his misfortune. Both he and Juliet have forebodings of the sorrow to come. Again and again the characters gropingly predict the course of the future. Accident and coincidence add to our feeling that blind fate dominates the action.

But to offset this feeling Shakespeare has provided two commentators to remind us that the terrible things we have seen are all the work of divine justice. When Friar Laurence cries,

> A greater power than we can contradict
> Hath thwarted our intents . . .
>
> [V. iii. 153-54]

it seems most natural to suppose that the holy Friar is invoking God rather than blind fate, for he has denied that fate is the cause of Romeo's wretchedness. Earlier he has warned frantic Romeo that his fortune depended upon his own virtue and moderation, that the man who flies in the face of fortune is to blame for his own misery. . . . And when he discovers Juliet in the tomb, we learn that he has begged her to come forth

> And bear this work of heaven with patience.
>
> [V. iii. 261]

According to the Friar Romeo's actions must determine his ultimate felicity or doom, and yet at the end he finds Romeo's death to be the "work of heaven." It would seem that . . . the Friar does not dissociate human actions and the power of fortune which represents God's will.

The second commentator Shakespeare gives us to point up the meaning of the tragedy is Prince Escalus, who at the ending of the play and at the point of greatest emphasis, sums up the significance of all that has happened:

> See, what a scourge is laid upon your hate,
> That Heaven finds means to kill your joys with love.
>
> [V. iii. 292-93]

After hearing these words and contemplating the evenhanded justice which has leveled parent with parent, child with child, and friend with friend, would not the audience sensitive to providential fortune and its use in tragedy understand without any tedious explication that fortune has operated here to punish sin and that this avenging fortune is the work of heaven? Such an audience would not have stuck at applying pitiful Rosamond's words to the lovers [from Samuel Daniel's *The Complaint of Rosamond*],

> fate is not prevented, though foreknown,
> For that must hap, decreed by heavenly powers
> Who work our fall yet make the fault still ours.

In *Romeo and Juliet* then fortune may be considered not the prime mover but the agent of a higher power. If fortune is not the independent cause of the catastrophe, then we must look behind fortune for the actions which set it in motion. Friar Laurence warns Romeo that his own folly in love will doom him. Prince Escalus, speaking as chorus, attributes the tragedy to hate. Both are right, for it is the collision of these passions which dooms the lovers.

Of these two forces love overshadows the other dramatically, since it is the passion of the protagonists and since Shakespeare has lavished his most moving poetry upon the love scenes. But the fact remains that this is not a play centered on one passion but a play of carefully opposed passions. The prologue informs us that we are to see a drama of love and hate. Hatred is the first passion to threaten tragedy in the comic opening of the play; hatred brings about the actual climax of the action, Mercutio's death; and hatred is the theme which Shakespeare introduces with love at the end of the play to explain the workings of fate.

The theme of hatred involves more than the opposition of two private families; because of the street brawls, because of the murderous intrigues of the two opposed parties, it involves the whole state. Romeo and Juliet, whose love would unite the two houses, are forced apart by the quarrel which they seek to avoid. Thus the love story in the play, as in *Antony and Cleopatra* and *Troilus and Cressida,* is more than a tale of love, and the problems of the play are not only ethical but in the broadest sense political. (pp. 92-5)

Thus although our main interest is in Shakespeare's handling of love, we must also inquire into Shakespeare's use of the complementary theme of hatred. *Romeo and Juliet* is built about two passions traditionally opposed, and the interweaving of these two themes, . . . adds to the peculiar irony which pervades the play. (p. 96)

The full power of hatred comes out . . . in Escalus's speech which sums up the meaning of the action. He calls the miserable fathers from the crowd:

> Capulet! Montague!
> See, what a scourge is laid upon you hate,
> That Heaven finds means to kill your joys with love.
> An I for winking at your discords too
> Have lost a brace of kinsmen. All are punish'd.
> [V. iii. 291-95]

This speech does not make sense unless we take into account the close interaction of fate, hatred, and love in the play.

Escalus's gloomy judgments give us a true criticism of the whole tragedy. The phrase "your joys" must refer to the lovers, the hope of each of the two warring houses. Their death

through love is the punishment of heaven, working through fate, upon the families who have carried on the feud. (p. 100)

When we look back over the course of hatred, we see the truth of Escalus's sentence, "All are punish'd." Fate has worked to produce an evenhanded justice. The force of Mercutio's dying imprecation on the houses appears at the end of the tragedy in the mysterious death of Lady Montague on the night of her son's suicide. Her death, Shakespeare's additon to his source as are the deaths of Paris and Mercutio, evens the score between the families. Partisan pays for partisan and kinsman for kinsman. Just as love holds families and nations and indeed the whole universe together, so hatred breaks up families, destroys commonwealths, and, represented by Satan, constantly works to unframe God's whole handiwork. It is precise and ironical justice that quenches the one passion by means of its opposite. *Romeo and Juliet,* no less than Shakespeare's mature tragedies, celebrates the great vision of order by which the English Renaissance still lives. (p. 101)

The play is uniquely constructed in that the same passions which make us tearful or indignant before the action ends, do amuse us with little interruption for almost half the acting time. Even the events leading up to Mercutio's death promise comedy rather than tragedy, and it must have startled the first audience to see laughter so quickly turn to mourning. Yet the play is an exceptionally powerful tragedy, even if it sometimes embarrasses critics. Where the first half delights us with love comedy, the last three short acts explore the tragic potentialities of young love. Fortune and hatred threaten to turn the lovers' bliss to ashes, but the immediate cause of their unhappy deaths is Romeo's headlong fury and blind despair. Thus in both the beginning of the play and at the end Shakespeare's view of love remains sound philosophically and dramatically. (p. 102)

Throughout *Romeo and Juliet* Romeo is precipitate in love. Juliet, who loves as faithfully, is much less subject to the gusts of passion which blind Romeo. Romeo never examines the consequence of his actions, but Juliet fears that their love may be "too rash, too unadvis'd, too sudden" [II. ii. 118]. Romeo never shares Juliet's insight. After they have pledged love at Juliet's window, his only concern is that the love he feels seems too delightful to be true. It is Juliet not Romeo who thinks practically of arranging for marriage and who remembers to ask what time she is to send her messenger in the morning.

On Romeo's inability to control either his passionate love or his passionate grief, his death and Juliet's depend. The boundless love which Romeo felt at the sight of Juliet turns as suddenly to despair, just as any well-versed Renaissance philosopher might have predicted, for the man in the grip of one passion was easily swayed by another. (pp. 105-06)

Romeo therefore is a tragic hero like Othello in that he is responsible for his own chain of passionate actions. When we first see him he is already stricken with love. This first love is comic, but nevertheless it is a real attack of the sickness of love, as his father makes clear when he complains that Romeo's humor will turn "Black and portentous" [I. i. 141] unless checked.

Since the man stricken with passion could not readily defend himself against new onslaughts of passion, Romeo's sudden passionate about-face when he sees Juliet would have seemed realistic to an Elizabethan audience. Romeo's transports for Juliet differ from his first melancholy because she returns his affection. For a time he is cured and conducts himself so reasonably that even Mercutio comments on the change in his temper.

But with Mercutio's death Romeo casts aside all reason and begins a chain of passionate action which leads to death. Rejecting the reasonable conduct with which he had first answered his enemy, he attacks and kills Tybalt. It would certainly have spoiled the play for Romeo to have waited for the law to punish Tybalt, but the fact remains that this reasonable action would have turned tragedy into comedy. In this choice between reasonable and passionate action lies one great difference between the genres. Forgiveness produces the happy ending of comedy; revenge produces the catastrophe of tragedy.

Romeo's next passionate mistake is to fall into frantic despair after the Prince sentences him to banishment. When Romeo cries out against his lot, Friar Laurence, the consistent voice of moderation and wisdom, warns him that he is truly unfortunate only in giving way to uncontrolled grief.

The next step in Romeo's march to destruction is his sudden and complete despair when he learns that Juliet is dead. The direct result of Romeo's frenzied desire to kill himself is his killing of Paris, an incident which Shakespeare adds, like the death of Lady Montague and the death of Mercutio, to his source. Thus Brooke's Romeus dies with less on his conscience than does Shakespeare's hero. In Brooke Romeus kills Tybalt only to save his own life, not to revenge a friend, and at the end of the play dies guiltless of any additional blood save his own. In our play, however, Shakespeare is careful to make Romeo guilty of sinful action under the influence of passion, while at the same time making us sympathize with Romeo's agonies of despair. In his encounter with Paris Romeo announces both his own mad desperation and the fact that in bringing the chain of passionate folly to its close, he puts one more sin upon his head.

Romeo's last passion-blinded act is to kill himself just before Juliet awakes, and her suicide may be thought of as the direct result of his. Although Shakespeare does not preach, the Elizabethan audience would have realized that in his fury Romeo has committed the ultimate sin. (pp. 114-16)

[The] tragedy of Romeo and Juliet is a true tragedy, preserving the ambiguous feelings of pity and terror which produce catharsis. Romeo remains a free agent even though he scarce knows what he does. Those who allowed passion to carry reason headlong were guilty of the very fault that Elizabethan ethics were designed to prevent. It is exactly because love could unseat the reason that few men who loved excessively could look forward to a virtuous life and a happy death. (p. 116)

Does this mean that . . . the spectators in [Shakespeare's] day, or that Shakespeare himself, looked upon the play as an edifying lesson in how not to conduct oneself in love? I hardly think so. The pattern of the action, given shape by Friar Laurence's warnings, Mercutio's satiric ebullience, and the Prince's scattered judgments, revolves around two of the most attractive young lovers in all literature. But the patterns of moral responsibility are necessary to give the action its perspective, and it is these patterns of the destructive as well as the creative force of love and the dependence of fate upon the passionate will which most contemporary criticism neglects or denies. We, who have moved so far from Shakespeare's world, need to be reminded of these things. They would have touched his audience far more deeply than they touch us today. (p. 117)

*Franklin M. Dickey, in his* Not Wisely but Too Well: Shakespeare's Love Tragedies, *1957. Reprint by The Huntington Library, 1966, 205 p.*

## HAROLD S. WILSON   (essay date 1957)

[*Wilson regards* Romeo and Juliet *as a tragedy of fate in which the deaths of the young lovers are in no way retributive for their past actions, but serve to secure the reconciliation of the feuding families. Wilson argues, however, that Shakespeare marred this design by making his hero and heroine so attractive that the audience terminates its interest once they are dead, thus missing the culmination of the play in the resolution of the feud.*]

The tragic conception of *Romeo and Juliet* is simply stated for us in the opening sonnet-prologue. By thus announcing his theme and describing the central action, Shakespeare prepares us for the method he will follow throughout the play. We are to watch a sequence of events as they move towards the catastrophe in the full knowledge that they are tragic, that the tragic culmination is somehow inevitable. The tragic effect is to be one of anticipation and its realization. The Greek tragedians, and their imitator Seneca whom Shakespeare knew better, could count on their audiences' familiarity with the story of the play. Shakespeare uses his opening prologue in *Romeo and Juliet* to establish the same condition.

The action concerns not simply two lovers but two families. An ancient feud breaks forth anew, involving in its course two lovers whose destiny it is to be sacrificed to the healing of their families' strife, "which, but their children's end, naught could remove" [Prologue, 11]. The pathos is that the lovers' sacrifice is inescapable; their love is "death-mark'd"; they are "star-cross'd" [Prologue, 9, 6], fated to die in the fifth act. But the tragic outcome is not quite unrelieved. There is to be a kind of reconciliation at the end, though we are not to expect a "happy" ending. Thus carefully are we prepared to understand and anticipate the ensuing action.

This method of foreshadowing the outcome is carried through the play, in the premonitions and misgivings of the two lovers. "I dreamt a dream tonight" [I. iv. 50], says Romeo, as he goes with Benvolio and Mercutio towards the Capulet party. Mercutio at once takes him up, rallies him, makes his melancholy remark the occasion of his elaborate fancy of Queen Mab. Yet as Benvolio tries to hurry them on: "Supper is done, and we shall come too late!" Romeo reflects,

> I fear, too early; for my mind misgives
> Some consequence, yet hanging in the stars,
> Shall bitterly begin his fearful date
> With this night's revels and expire the term
> Of a despised life, clos'd in my breast,
> By some vile forfeit of untimely death.
> But he that hath the steerage of my course
> Direct my sail! On, lusty gentlemen!
> [I. iv. 105-13]

As we are later to realize, Romeo's foreboding is all too well justified. Ere another day passes, Romeo will have loved another maiden than the lady Rosaline who now has all his thoughts; he will have married Juliet, anticipating only happiness; but Mercutio will be slain by Tybalt, Tybalt slain by Romeo, Romeo banished from Verona; and the lives of Romeo and Juliet will be eventually sacrificed. (pp. 19-20)

All of these echoes and foreshadowings emphasize and reemphasize a single theme, a single conception: the seemingly inscrutable necessity of the whole action, a necessity imposed by some power greater than men. (p. 22)

The play culminates with the reconciliation of the rival houses, as the prologue states. Old Capulet and Montague, confronted by the terrible results of their hatred in the deaths of their children, are at length brought to recognize their responsibility. The Prince sums it up:

> See what a scourge is laid upon your hate,
> That heaven finds means to kill your joys with love;
> And I, for winking at your discords too,
> Have lost a brace of kinsmen; all are punish'd.
>
> [V. iii. 292-95]

The parents are truly penitent, and from this time forth, we are to understand, their hatred was turned to love.

The importance of this ending in Shakespeare's design may be seen by contrasting the culmination of the story in his principal source, Arthur Brooke's poem called *Romeus and Juliet*. In Brooke's version, the various instruments of the outcome—the apothecary who sold Romeo the poison, the Nurse, the Friar—are punished or pardoned, but neither the parents nor the enmity of the two houses is even mentioned in censure. Shakespeare's revision of Brooke's ending and his different emphasis are eloquent of his different conception of the point of the tale.

From another point of view, we may test the importance Shakespeare must have attached to the idea the play is designed to express by observing the very arbitrariness with which he manipulates not merely the plot but the characterizations as well, in the interest of working out his total design. The arbitrary insistence upon ironic coincidence in the successive stages of the action is evident. But equally arbitrary is the lack of coherent motivation in Friar Laurence's crucial role. Granted that Friar Laurence is timid and unworldly, and proud of his herbalist's resources, besides; he is still an odd kind of spiritual adviser, without confidence in his authority with the two families, and, we must surely add, without elementary common sense. In real life, any man of sense in Friar Laurence's position would have reflected that the proposed marriage of Juliet with Paris was impossible. Juliet was already married to Romeo. And he would have used this circumstance to force a reconciliation upon the two families—a motive which he professed in marrying the young people in the first place. It is evident that he could count upon the Prince's support in thus seeking to reconcile the feud, and Romeo's pardon, and his own, would easily follow upon the achieving of this worthy end.

This sort of speculation is obviously not relevant to the play as we have it; for such a solution would have given comedy, and Shakespeare was here intent upon tragedy. We must allow the author such arbitrary means; the tragic idea, and the tragic effect, are more important than any mere question of psychological verisimilitude. In observing the arbitrariness of the contrivance, however, we are able to gauge the more accurately the author's central concern. It is with the idea of the play, and the artificial means are an index of the length he is prepared to go in expressing it. Shakespeare neither blames Friar Laurence for his romantic folly, nor allows the common sense solution of the lovers' difficulties to occur to him or to them; and we must not consider that any such point is worth making in our criticism of the play except in so far as our consideration of it may help us the better to understand what the play is about.

If the cumulatively parallel episodes of *Romeo and Juliet* may be called the warp of the play's structural design, the woof is a series of contrasts. It is a drama of youth pitted against age, as Granville Barker has noted [see excerpt above, 1930]. Correspondingly, youth stands for love, and age for continuing hate. Most fundamental of all is the contrast, which is not fully revealed until the end, of accident and design.

Arthur Brooke's *Romeus and Juliet* is a translated version of a familiar folk-tale rather clumsily worked up as a popular romance in Pierre Boaistuau's *Histoires tragiques;* in Brooke's version, as in Boaistuau's, the ironic succession of reversals is attributed casually to "Fortune"—the customary resource of the romancer intent only upon the turns of his plot. Shakespeare more ambitiously undertook to comprehend the relations of chance and destiny in his tragic design.

Carefully, then, the responsibility of the lovers for their catastrophe, in Shakespeare's play, is minimized, as it is not in Brooke's version. The fact of the feud is emphasized at the outset, and the involvement of Romeo and Juliet is not only innocent but against their will. Even in the catastrophe itself, their self-destruction is hardly more than their assent to compelling circumstance. Romeo, it is true, buys poison to unite himself with Juliet in the grave; but before he reaches the tomb, Paris intervenes to seal with his death the one chance of Romeo's pausing in his resolve. Granville Barker oddly remarks that Paris's death "is wanton and serves little purpose." Actually, it is calculated to enhance our sense of the pressure of circumstance upon Romeo. He was distraught before he met Paris at the tomb of Juliet, but not utterly desperate, perhaps. Now, with the blood of Paris upon his hands (again contrary to his will and his anguished protest), he has no remaining ground of hope, no reason to delay his purpose. The death of Paris at Romeo's hands is Shakespeare's own addition to the story and hence an especially significant clue to his conception. It is another irony that prepares us for the most poignant irony of all, as Romeo, in his rapt intentness upon joining Juliet in the grave, fails to interpret aright the signs of returning animation in the sleeping girl. . . . Juliet, as she plunges the knife in her breast, thinks only of joining her lover. Shakespeare, of course, is not excusing their self-destruction; but it is no part of his design to blame them. Their deaths are a *donnée* of the story; the point of it lies elsewhere than in their responsibility.

The blame lies with the families, with the elders. But what of the role of chance, of the fate which so evidently has crossed the love of Romeo and Juliet from beginning to end? They fell in love by accident. Romeo went to the Capulet party expecting to indulge his unrequited passion for Rosaline; Juliet came for the express purpose of seeing and learning to love the County Paris. Amid their later difficulties, if Friar John had been able to deliver Friar Laurence's letter; if Friar Laurence had thought to use Balthazar as his messenger, as he first proposed to do [III. iii. 169-71], or if Balthazar too had been delayed; if Friar Laurence, even had been a little quicker in getting to Juliet's tomb—if anyone of these possibilities had occurred, the outcome might have been very different. We are meant to reflect upon this chain of seeming accidents, for they are prominently displayed.

Here, then, in the play as we have it, is the design—an arbitrary one, to be sure—of "a greater power than we can contradict" [V. iii. 153], that finds means to humble the rival houses "with love." It is a stern conception of Providence, to the working of whose purposes human beings are blind, which fulfils the moral law that the hatred of the elders shall be visited upon the children—"poor sacrifices of our enmity" [V. iii. 304], as Capulet describes them—yet whose power turns hatred in the end to love. The design of the tragedy has been a Christian moral, implicit but still sufficiently manifest to the thoughtful. Herein lies the rationale of the play's structure. The three entrances of the Prince mark the three stages of the action intended to show a chain of seeming accidents issuing in a moral design adumbrated in the sonnet-prologue, implicit from the beginning. The final entrance of the Prince marks the logical climax of a tightly built narrative scheme. This concluding stage of the action reveals, in recapitulation, the significance of the whole design, a design in which the catastrophic deaths of the lovers contribute but a part; the punishment of the elders, and still more their reconciliation, complete the pattern.

But if the logical climax of the play's conception lies in this denouement, the emotional climax comes before, with the deaths of Romeo and Juliet. In this, the world's favourite love story, Shakespeare has endowed his young lovers with all the riches of his earlier lyrical style, with the music of his sonnets which echoes through the play; and he has given them a grace and a purity of motive, in keeping with his larger design, that ensures our complete sympathy from beginning to end. As we follow their story, we cannot help taking sides with them against the elders—against the blind selfishness and perversity of their parents, against the stupid animality, however amusing, of the Nurse, against the absurd ineptitude of Friar Laurence; and as we see them hasten unwittingly to their destruction, we can only pity their youth, their innocence, and their ill luck. They themselves have no awareness of a tragic misstep, of a price justly exacted for human pride or folly, and neither have we: their story is full of pathos, but it has in itself little or nothing of tragic grandeur.

The tragic irony of the story, as Shakespeare tells it, lies in the blindness of the elders to the consequences of their hatred until it is too late, in the reversal brought about by the power greater than they. Yet despite the dramatist's eforts to direct our attention to this larger significance of the action—through the prologue and the structural foreshadowing of his whole scheme; through the chain of unlucky coincidences and arbitrary motives; through the reiteration of the theme of fortune and ill chance and fate—our feelings remain linked with the story of the lovers throughout the play; and audiences and actors alike notoriously feel that with the deaths of Romeo and Juliet the interest of the play is at an end, that the subsequent explanations are prolix and anticlimactic and may well be abridged. This feeling is manifestly contrary to what the dramatist aimed at, but he himself is chiefly responsible for our feeling, in having made his young lovers the centre of our regard.

Thus the play misses its full unity of effect because our sympathies are exhausted before the tragic design is complete. The story of a young and idealistic love thwarted is not enough to make a great tragedy; but Shakespeare, trying to place it within a grander conception, has not been able to achieve a larger unity. There is no failure in any detail of execution, and the conception of the play as a whole is worked out with remarkable regularity and precision. But the love story is not quite harmonious with the larger conception; our sympathies do not culminate in this larger conception; they culminate in pity for the lovers. The awe that we should feel as well is not inherent in their story but is indicated (rather than effected) in what seems to us like an epilogue; it is something explained to us at the end rather than rendered immediately dramatic and com-

pelling as the heart of the design. Shakespeare never made this particular mistake again; and we must surely add that, even though he overreaches himself in his play, he yet enchants us with the beauty of what he holds in his grasp.

Even this judgment, perhaps, is too rigorous. If *Romeo and Juliet* is deficient by the severest standard—by the standard of Shakespeare's own later achievements in tragedy—it yet remains one of the loveliest of all his works. And if we consider it not too closely but as we yield ourselves to its lyrical appeal in the theatre, we may find therein a sufficient argument of its unity. The lines from sonnet CXVI . . . :

> Love's not Time's fool, though rosy lips and cheeks
> Within his bending sickle's compass come;
> Love alters not with his brief hours and weeks,
> But bears it out even to the edge of doom,

commemorate the most lasting impression the play leaves with us, the impression of its imperishable beauty. We distinguish between the transitory life and fortunes of Romeo and Juliet and their love, which remains ideal, and, in a sense, beyond the reach of fortune or death. It is not their love that is blighted, after all, but their lives. The tragic episode of their lives may thus be seen as participating in the "Divine Comedy"; and, fundamentally, this is what we recognize as we are moved by their story. (pp. 25-31)

*Harold S. Wilson, "Thesis: 'Romeo and Juliet' and 'Hamlet'," in his* On the Design of Shakespearian Tragedy, *University of Toronto Press, 1957, pp. 19-51.*

## M. M. MAHOOD   (essay date 1957)

[*Mahood emphasizes the numerous similarities in* Romeo and Juliet *and the* Liebestod *or amour-passion myth discussed by Denis de Rougemont (1956), but she claims that the play conflicts with this myth in several ways. Foremost, she argues, is that although* Romeo and Juliet *contains the wordplay peculiar to amour-passion—such as the allusions to love as war, idolatry, and sickness—the distribution of this wordplay demonstrates that the protagonists' love for each other is "something quite different." Mahood perhaps best identifies this difference in the lovers' behavior throughout the play, which she says is not governed by a death-wish, as in the* Liebestod, *but by a desire to live together.*]

*Romeo and Juliet* is one of Shakespeare's most punning plays; even a really conservative count yields a hundred and seventy-five quibbles. Critics who find this levity unseemly excuse it by murmuring, with the Bad Quarto Capulet, that 'youth's a jolly thing' even in a tragedy. Yet Shakespeare was over thirty, with a good deal of dramatic writing already to his credit, when *Romeo and Juliet* was first performed. He knew what he was about in his wordplay, which is as functional here as in any of his later tragedies. It holds together the play's imagery in a rich pattern and gives an outlet to the tumultuous feelings of the central characters. By its proleptic second and third meanings it serves to sharpen the play's dramatic irony. Above all, it clarifies the conflict of incompatible truths and helps to establish their final equipoise.

Shakespeare's sonnet-prologue offers us a tale of star-crossed lovers and 'The *fearful passage* of their *death-markt* loue' [Prologue, 9]. *Death-marked* can mean 'marked out for (or by) death; fore-doomed'. If, however, we take *passage* in the sense of a voyage (and this sub-meaning prompts *trafficque* in the twelfth line) as well as a course of events, *death-marked* recalls the 'euer fixed marke' of Sonnet 116 and the sea-mark of Othello's utmost sail [*Othello*, V. ii. 268], and suggests the meaning 'With death as their objective'. The two meanings of *fearful* increase the line's oscillation; the meaning 'frightened' makes the lovers helpless, but they are not necessarily so if the word means 'fearsome' and so suggests that we, the audience, are awe-struck by their undertaking. These ambiguities pose the play's fundamental question at the outset: is its ending frustration or fulfilment? Does Death choose the lovers or do they elect to die? This question emerges from the language of the play itself and thus differs from the conventional, superimposed problem: is *Romeo and Juliet* a tragedy of Character or of Fate? which can be answered only by a neglect or distortion of the play as a dramatic experience. To blame or excuse the lovers' impetuosity and the connivance of others is to return to Arthur Broke's disapproval of unhonest desire, stolen contrasts, drunken gossips and auricular confession. Recent critics have, I believe, come nearer to defining the play's experience when they have stressed the *Liebestod* of the ending and suggested that the love of Romeo and Juliet is the tragic passion that seeks its own destruction. Certainly nearly all the elements of the *amour-passion* myth as it has been defined by Denis de Rougemont are present in the play [see excerpt above, 1956]. The love of Romeo and Juliet is immediate, violent and final. In the voyage imagery of the play they abandon themselves to a rudderless course that must end in shipwreck.... The obstacle which is a feature of the *amour-passion* legend is partly external, the family feud; but is partly a sword of the lovers' own tempering since, unlike earlier tellers of the story, Shakespeare leaves us with no explanation of why Romeo did not put Juliet on his horse and make for Mantua. A *leitmotiv* of the play is Death as Juliet's bridegroom; it first appears when Juliet sends to find Romeo's name: 'if he be married, My graue is like to be my wedding bed' [I. v. 134-35]. At the news of Romeo's banishment Juliet cries 'And death not Romeo, take my maiden head' [III. ii. 137], and she begs her mother, rather than compel her to marry Paris, to 'make the Bridall bed In that dim Monument where Tibalt lies' [III. v. 200-01]. The theme grows too persistent to be mere dramatic irony:

> O sonne, the night before thy wedding day
> Hath death laine with thy wife, there she lies,
> Flower as she was, deflowred by him,
> Death is my sonne in law, death is my heire.
> My daughter he hath wedded.
>
> [IV. v. 35-9]

Romeo, gazing at the supposedly dead Juliet, could well believe

> that vnsubstantiall death is amorous,
> And that the leane abhorred monster keepes
> Thee here in darke to be his parramour.
>
> [V. iii. 103-05]

Most significant of all, there is Juliet's final cry:

> O *happy* dagger
> This is thy sheath, there rust and let me *dye*.
>
> [V. iii. 169-70]

where *happy* implies not only 'fortunate to me in being ready to my hand' but also 'successful, fortunate in itself' and so suggests a further quibble on *die*. Death has long been Romeo's rival and enjoys Juliet at the last.

In all these aspects *Romeo and Juliet* appears the classic literary statement of the *Liebestod* myth in which (we are told) we seek the satisfaction of our forbidden desires; forbidden, according to Freud, because *amour-passion* is inimical to the Race, ac-

cording to de Rougemont because it is contrary to the Faith. Shakespeare's story conflicts, however, with the traditional myth at several points. Tragic love is always adulterous. Romeo and Juliet marry, and Juliet's agony of mind at the prospect of being married to Paris is in part a concern for her marriage vow: 'My husband is on earth, my faith in heauen' [III. v. 205]. Again, Romeo faces capture and death, Juliet the horror of being entombed alive, not because they want to die but because they want to live together. These woes are to serve them for sweet discourses in their time to come. In contrast to this, the wish-fulfilment of the *Liebestod* is accomplished only by the story of a suicide pact. (pp. 56-8)

The real objection to reading *Romeo and Juliet* as the *Liebestod* myth in dramatic form is that it is anachronistic to align the play with pure myths like that of Orpheus and Eurydice or with the modern restatement of such myths by Anouilh and Cocteau. Shakespeare's intention in writing the play was not that of the post-Freud playwright who finds in a high tale of love and death the objective correlative to his own emotions and those of his audience. We may guess that the story afforded Shakespeare an excited pleasure of recognition because it made explicit a psychological experience; but he did not, on the strength of that recognition, decide to write a play about the death wish.... Shakespeare believed his lovers to be historical people. He read and retold their adventures with the detached judgment we accord history as well as with the implicated excitement we feel for myth. The story is both near and remote; it goes on all the time in ourselves, but its events belong also to distant Verona in the dog days when the mad blood is stirred to passion and violence. The resultant friction between history and myth, between the story and the fable, kindles the play into great drama. When we explore the language of *Romeo and Juliet* we find that both its wordplay and its imagery abound in those concepts of love as a war, a religion, a malady, which de Rougemont has suggested as the essence of *amour-passion*. If the play were pure myth, the fictionalising of a psychological event, all these elements would combine in a single statement of our desire for a tragic love. But because the play is also an exciting story about people whose objective existence we accept during the two hours' traffic of the stage, these images and quibbles are dramatically 'placed'; to ascertain Shakespeare's intentions in using them we need to see which characters are made to speak them and how they are distributed over the course of the action.

Act I begins with some heavy-witted punning from Sampson and Gregory—a kind of verbal tuning-up which quickens our ear for the great music to come. The jests soon broaden. This is one of Shakespeare's most bawdy plays, but the bawdy has always a dramatic function. Here its purpose is to make explicit, at the beginning of this love tragedy, one possible relationship between man and woman: a brutal male dominance expressed in sadistic quibbles. After the brawl has been quelled, the mood of the scene alters ...; Romeo himself appears and expresses, in the numbers that Petrarch flowed in, the contrary relationship of the sexes: man's courtly subjection to women's tyranny. Rosaline is a saint, and by his quibbles upon theological terms Romeo shows himself a devotee of the Religion of Love.... It is characteristic of this love learnt by rote from the sonnet writers that Romeo should combine images and puns which suggest this slave-like devotion to his mistress with others that imply a masterful attack on her chastity. Love is a man of war in such phrases as 'th' incounter of assailing eies' [I. i. 213] which, added to the aggressive wordplay of Sampson and Gregory and to the paradox of 'ô brawling loue, ô louing hate' [I. i. 176], reinforce the theme of ambivalence, the *odi-et-amo* duality of passion.

All the Petrarchan and anti-Petrarchan conventions are thus presented to us in this first scene: love as malady, as worship, as war, as conquest. They are presented, however, with an exaggeration that suggests Romeo is already aware of his own absurdity and is 'posing at posing'. 'Where shall we dine?' [I. i. 173] is a most unlover-like question which gives the show away; and Benvolio's use of 'in sadnesse' implies that he knows Romeo's infatuation to be nine parts show. Romeo is in fact ready to be weaned from Rosaline, and the scene ends with a proleptic pun that threatens the overthrow of this textbook language of love. (pp. 59-61)

Love in Verona may be a cult, a quest or a madness. Marriage is a business arrangement. Old Capulet's insistence to Paris, in the next scene, that Juliet must make her own choice, is belied by later events. Juliet is an heiress, and her father does not intend to enrich any but a husband of his own choosing:

> *Earth* hath swallowed all my hopes but she,
> Shees the hopefull Lady of my *earth*.
>
> [I. ii. 14-15]

This quibbling distinction between *earth* as the grave and *earth* as lands . . . is confounded when Juliet's hopes of happiness end in the Capulets' tomb. (p. 61)

The ball scene at Capulet's house is prologued by a revealing punning-match between Romeo and Mercutio. Romeo's lumbering puns are the wordplay of courtly love: the other masquers have nimble soles, he has a soul of lead: he is too bound to earth to bound, too sore from Cupid's darts to soar in the dance. Mercutio's levity, on the other hand, is heightened by his bawdy quibbles. Mercutio appears in early versions of the tale as what is significantly known as a ladykiller, and his dramatic purpose at this moment of the play is to oppose a cynical and aggressive idea of sex to Romeo's love-idolatry and so sharpen the contrast already made in the opening scene. Yet just as Romeo's touch of self-parody then showed him to be ready for a more adult love, so Mercutio's Queen Mab speech implies that his cynicism does not express the whole of his temperament. The falsity of both cynicism and idolatry, already felt to be inadequate by those who hold these concepts, is to be exposed by the love between Romeo and Juliet. (pp. 61-2)

For the ball scene, Shakespeare deploys his resources of stagecraft and poetry in a passage of brilliant dramatic counterpoint. Our attention is divided, during the dance, between the reminiscences of the two old Capulets . . . and the rapt figure of Romeo who is watching Juliet. Nothing is lost by this, since the talk of the two pantaloons is mere inanity. We are only aware that it has to do with the passage of years too uneventful to be numbered, so that twenty-five is confused with thirty; simultaneously we share with Romeo a timeless minute that cannot be reckoned by the clock. Yet the old men's presence is a threat as well as a dramatic contrast. They have masqued and loved in their day, but ''tis gone, 'tis gone, 'tis gone' [I. v. 24].

Romeo's first appraisal of Juliet's beauty is rich not only in its unforgettable images but also in the subtlety of its wordplay. Hers is a 'Bewtie too rich for vse, for earth too deare' [I. v. 47]. When we recall that *use* means 'employment', 'interest' and 'wear and tear' that *earth* means both 'mortal life' and 'the grave', that *dear* can be either 'cherished' or 'costly' and

that there is possibly a play upon *beauty* and *booty* . . . , the line's range of meanings becomes very wide indeed. Over and above the contrast between her family's valuation of her as sound stock in the marriage market and Romeo's estimate that she is beyond all price, the words contain a self-contradictory dramatic irony. Juliet's beauty is too rich for use in the sense that it will be laid in the tomb after a brief enjoyment; but for that very reason it will never be faded and worn. And if she is *not* too dear for earth since Romeo's love is powerless to keep her out of the tomb, it is true that she is too rare a creature for mortal life. Not all these meanings are consciously present to the audience, but beneath the conscious level they connect with later images and quibbles and are thus brought into play before the tragedy is over.

The counterpoint of the scene is sustained as Romeo moves towards his new love against the discordant hate and rage of her cousin. Tybalt rushes from the room, threatening to convert seeming sweet to bitter gall, at the moment Romeo touches Juliet's hand. The lovers meet and salute each other in a sonnet full of conceits and quibbles on the Religion of Love. . . . for the place is public and they must disguise their feelings beneath a social persiflage. The real strength of those feelings erupts in Romeo's pun—'O *deare* account!'—and in Juliet's paradox—'My only loue sprung from my only hate' [I. v. 118, 138]—when each learns the other's identity, and the elements of youth and experience, love and hate, which have been kept apart throughout the scene, are abruptly juxtaposed. Then the torches are extinguished and the scene ends with a phrase of exquisite irony, when the Nurse speaks to Juliet as to a tired child after a party: 'Come lets away, the strangers all are gone' [I. v. 144]. Romeo is no longer a stranger and Juliet no longer a child.

A quibbling sonnet on love between enemies and some of Mercutio's ribald jests separate this scene from that in Capulet's orchard. It is as if we must be reminded of the social and sexual strife before we hear Romeo and Juliet declare the perfect harmony of their feelings for each other. At first Romeo seems still to speak the language of idolatry, but the 'winged messenger of heauen' [II. ii. 28] belongs to a different order of imagination from the faded conceits of his devotion to Rosaline. The worn commonplaces of courtship are swept aside by Juliet's frankness. One of the few quibbles in the scene is on *frank* in the meanings of 'generous' and 'candid, open', and it introduces Juliet's boldest and most beautiful avowal of her feelings:

> *Rom.* O wilt thou leaue me so vnsatisfied?
> *Iul.*  What satisfaction canst thou haue to night?
> *Rom.* Th' exchange of thy loues faithful vow for
>        mine.
> *Iul.*  I gaue thee mine before thou didst request it:
>        And yet I would it were to giue againe.
> *Rom.* Woldst thou withdraw it, for what purpose loue?
> *Iul.*  But to be franke and giue it thee againe,
>        And yet I wish but for the thing I haue,
>        My bountie is as boundlesse as the sea,
>        My loue as deepe, the more I giue to thee
>        The more I haue, for both are infinite.
>
> [II. ii. 125-35]

Thus the distribution of wordplay upon the concepts of love-war, love-idolatry, love-sickness, serves to show that the feelings of Romeo and Juliet for each other are something quite different from the *amour-passion* in which de Rougemont finds all these disorders. For Romeo doting upon Rosaline, love was a malady and a religion; for Mercutio it is sheer lunacy . . . or a brutal conquest with no quarter given. All these notions are incomplete and immature compared to the reality. When Romeo meets Mercutio the next morning a second quibbling-match ensues in which the bawdy expressive of love-war and love-madness is all Mercutio's. Romeo's puns, if silly, are gay and spontaneous in comparison with his laboured conceits on the previous evening. Then, as he explained to Benvolio, he was not himself, not Romeo. Now Mercutio cries: 'now art thou sociable, now art thou Romeo' [II. iv. 89-90]. In fact Romeo and Juliet have experienced a self-discovery. Like Donne's happy lovers, they 'possess one world, each hath one and is one' [in his "The Good-Morrow"]; a world poles apart from the Nirvana quested by romantic love. The play is a tragedy, not because the love of Romeo for Juliet is in its nature tragic, but because the ending achieves the equilibrium of great tragedy. The final victory of time and society over the lovers is counterpoised by the knowledge that it is, in a sense, *their* victory; a victory not only over time and society which would have made them old and worldly in the end (whereas their deaths heal the social wound), but over the most insidious enemy of love, the inner hostility that 'builds a Hell in Heaven's despite' and which threatens in the broad jests of Mercutio. For we believe in the uniqueness of Romeo's and Juliet's experience at the same time as we know it to be, like other sublunary things, neither perfect nor permanent. If our distress and satisfaction are caught up in the fine balance of great tragedy at the end of the play, it is because, throughout, the wordplay and imagery, the conduct of the action and the grouping of characters contribute to that balance. The lovers' confidence is both heightened and menaced by a worldly wisdom, cynicism and resignation which, for the reason that candle-holders see more of the game, we are not able to repudiate as easily as they can do. (pp. 62-5)

> M. M. Mahood, "'Romeo and Juliet'," in her *Shakespeare's Wordplay, Methuen & Co Ltd., 1957, pp. 56-72.*

**R. F. HILL** (essay date 1958)

[*In an unexcerpted portion of his essay on Shakespeare's early tragedies, Hill contends that one of the major differences of these works from the later, mature tragedies is the frequent use of rhetorical language or "figures," especially at moments of intense emotion. As outlined in the excerpt below, the critic states that by the time Shakespeare came to write* Romeo and Juliet *he was moving away from the rhetorical tradition towards his mature, naturalistic style; yet, Hill identifies numerous instances in the play where Shakespeare falls back on this method. The critic adds, however, that here the dramatist adopts this style not, as in the early plays, to create a "poetic reality," but deliberately to imitate "the language of imaginary feelings which are later to be contrasted with true feelings."*]

The study of rhetorical tragedy has important consequences for the criticism of *Romeo and Juliet.* Although this play and *Richard II* are sometimes linked together as a part of Shakespeare's lyric phase, the resemblances of style are superficial. The language of *Richard II* is considered, ceremonious, whereas that of *Romeo and Juliet* is altogether lighter and more spontaneous. There is less application of conventional rhetoric to express idea, and a greater immediacy of imagery. Figures of repetition are used more loosely, and closely approximate to

the repetitions of natural speech. Juliet's prothalamium [III. ii. 1-31] is at once poetic, rhetorical, and conversational:

> Come, night, come Romeo, come, thou day in night;
> For thou wilt lie upon the wings of night
> Whiter than new snow on a raven's back. . . .
>
> [III. ii. 17-19]

Thought controls imagery and rhythm, creating poetry which can flow unobtrusively into the conversation which follows. Unfortunately the naturalism of this poetry is not sustained, for we are shortly jolted up against the artificial diction of rhetorical tragedy. In her passion of grief, Juliet puns violently upon "I", and a little later indulges in a spate of conventional love-paradoxes ("Beautiful tyrant! fiend angelical", etc. [III. ii. 75ff.]). These passages express mental disturbance in a manner suited to tragedy of which *Richard II* is the type. They cannot accord with the inwardness and movement of her cry:

> Give me my Romeo; and when he shall die,
> Take him and cut him out in little stars,
> And he will make the face of heaven so fine,
> That all the world will be in love with night,
> And pay no worship to the garish sun.
>
> [III. ii. 21-5]

In this incompatibility can be seen the foundation upon which must be built any criticism of the play. In *Romeo and Juliet* must be recognised two tragic styles operating side by side.

Romeo's final soliloquy is true to the rhetorical convention which requires exaltation of sentiment and diction at the moment of death, but the language is a miraculous blend of considered rhetoric and spontaneous imagery, the first strains of the tragic music to come. Although the soliloquy contains many ordinarily stiff rhetorical figures . . . , passion gives them life, and the sense of their formality is lost in the dazzle of,

> her beauty makes
> This vault a feasting presence full of light.
>
> [V. iii. 85-6]

> O, here
> Will I set up my everlasting rest,
> And shake the yoke of inauspicious stars
> From this world-wearied flesh.
>
> [V. iii. 109-12]

Such glowing imagery conveys to the audience what no mere weight of rhetorical ornament could have done.

This soliloquy shows a greater complexity of language than Juliet's prothalamium; yet neither is characterized by the balanced rhythms, antitheses, and rigid iterative tricks in which consists the artificiality of *Richard II*. Their lines, for the most part, have a natural movement which allows them to exist in the same world as Peter and the Nurse. Nothing could be more palpable than the aches and pains of the intractable old Nurse:

> O God's lady dear!
> Are you so hot? marry, come up, I trow;
> Is this the poultice for my aching bones?
>
> [II. v. 61-3]

The conversation in this scene and elsewhere in the play is in a high degree naturalistic but artistically acceptable in poetic drama provided that the dramatist eschews stylized diction. At the beginning of this scene Juliet's speech, with the exception of the final couplet, has the variable cadence of verse unhindered by heavy rhetoric. From it we pass easily to conversation.

*Romeo and Juliet* is pivotal in the development of Shakespeare's tragic style. On the one hand, it contains vestiges of the early manner with its ornate diction and rhetorical modes of expressing emotion; on the other hand, the seeds of the mature tragic style are present in the mixture of serious and comic elements, in the strong characterization, in verisimilitude of speech, and in the deep-searching imagery. Characterization and naturalism are breaking through conventions. Rhetorical language, no longer a continuous medium, is used intermittently for special effects. Particularly interesting in this respect is the second part of the opening scene, where Benvolio converses with the Montagues and afterwards with Romeo. Love is the theme, love dissected, defined, not felt. And the language is as artificial as the passion. Instead of creating, as in *Richard II*, a world of poetic reality, rhetoric becomes the language of imaginary feelings which are later to be contrasted with true feelings. Romeo's paradoxes [I. i. 176-81] express no more than the conventional lover's pains. The vexation of words which had emotional potency in rhetorical tragedy is rendered impotent by contrast with the real language of passion.

This all too brief criticism of *Romeo and Juliet* cannot be concluded without reference to the style of the lamentations poured forth by the Capulets over the supposed dead body of Juliet [IV. v. 17-64]. It is entirely a rhetorical expression of grief and as such strikes a false note in the naturalism of this tragedy. It is full of silly iterations, and is precisely the kind of ridiculous outcry which Shakespeare burlesqued in the "very tragical mirth" of *Pyramus and Thisbe* [*A Midsummer Night's Dream*, V. i. 57]. "O love! O life! not life, but love in death!" cries Paris, and Capulet echoes him mechanically, "O child! O child! my soul, and not my child!" [IV. v. 58, 62]. This figure of rhetoric (epanorthosis or metanoia) is more expressive of grief even in the notorious lines from *The Spanish Tragedy*, and the dolorous clamor of Othello shows the device fully articulate:

> If she come in, she'll sure speak to my wife:
> My wife! my wife! what wife? I have no wife.
> O, insupportable!
>
> [*Othello*, V. ii. 97]

What then are we to think of this episode from *Romeo and Juliet*? Is it just another indication of Shakespeare's unconscious vacillation between the rhetorical and the naturalistic? Or is it that in the mid-'nineties he knew no method other than the rhetorical of expressing this full-throated lamentation? Alternatively is it intentional? Did Shakespeare intend us to look beyond these suits of woe to the emotional void within? This last, I feel, is the true explanation. The Capulets had treated their daughter as little more than a chattel to be disposed of in the interests of profit and prestige. Paris was the conventional lover acting always like the man of wax he was so aptly termed. The Nurse evinced no personal affection for Juliet, and her gross mind could have no communion with the singleness and totality of Juliet's love. What had this quartet to do with deep sorrow? Shakespeare accordingly showed the hollowness of their feelings in their stylized, over-emphatic speech. For pathos he substituted bathos, achieved most simply by setting exaggerated rhetoric in the midst of a basically naturalistic treatment. Just so did Rosaline know that Romeo's love "did read by rote that could not spell" [II. iii. 88].

With *Romeo and Juliet* rhetorical tragedy is at an end. It had carried Shakespeare through his 'prentice years and enabled him to flex his muscles and fathom his own powers. It was, however, a form too narrow to contain his wide ranging imag-

ination, too artificial for the expression of tragic ideas no longer merely traditional but afire with personal doubts and convictions. In his mature tragedies Shakespeare never entirely abandoned the early formality; with it he mingled an informality, creating a medium of immeasurable range. Ritual and realism were married. The poet could glance from heaven to earth, from philosophic abstraction to the lowest passion, without incongruity. (pp. 466-68)

R. F. Hill, "Shakespeare's Early Tragic Mode," in *Shakespeare Quarterly*, Vol. IX, No. 4, Autumn, 1958, pp. 455-69.

## IRVING RIBNER (essay date 1959)

[*Ribner maintains that* Romeo and Juliet *depicts something more profound than a "tragedy of fate" or a tragedy of retribution in which the young lovers are punished for their lawless passion. According to him, the play is explicitly Christian, demonstrating the operation of divine providence as it sacrifices Romeo and Juliet in order to reconcile the feuding families—in Ribner's words, to reestablish "God's harmonious order" and "a rebirth of love." The critic emphasizes the hero and heroine's maturation throughout this ordeal, especially as they come to recognize and accept their part in this cosmic plan.*]

Critics have usually regarded Shakespeare's *Romeo and Juliet* as . . . a Senecan tragedy of inexorable fate; some have emphasized the sinfulness of the young lovers. We cannot deny the role of fate and accident in Shakespeare's play; it is established in the prologue and it runs as a constant theme through all five acts. We would not expect this to be otherwise, for this was the formula with which Shakespeare began. But Shakespeare's play is far more than a tragedy of fate. It is, moreover, not at all a story of just deserts visited upon young sinners, although some critics have found it so. The fate that destroys Romeo and Juliet is not an arbitrary, capricious force any more than it is the inexorable agent of nemesis, which in Senecan tragedy executed retribution for sin. Shakespeare's play is cast in a more profoundly Christian context than [this] . . . ; the "greater power than we can contradict" [V. iii. 153] is divine providence, guiding the affairs of men in accordance with a plan which is merciful as well as just. Out of the evil of the family feud—a corruption of God's harmonious order—must come a rebirth of love, and the lives of Romeo and Juliet are directed and controlled so that by their deaths the social order will be cleansed and restored to harmony. Shakespeare uses the story of the lovers to explore the operation of divine providence, the meaning of a fate which in the ordinary affairs of life will sometimes frustrate our most careful plans. . . . It is in Shakespeare's departure from the Senecan tradition he inherited that the particular significance of *Romeo and Juliet* as tragedy lies. Here we see him groping for a tragic design to embody a view of life far more significant and meaningful than what the Senecan stereotypes could afford. (pp. 273-74)

In [the] emphasis upon youth which runs throughout Shakespeare's play, but which is not so evident in his source, we may find a clue to the philosophical pattern Shakespeare imposed upon Senecan tradition. Romeo and Juliet are children born into a world already full of an ancient evil not of their own making. The feud is emphasized in the opening lines of the prologue, and in the opening scene of the play—before either hero or heroine is introduced—the feud is portrayed in all its ramifications, corrupting the social order from the lowliest serving man up to the prince himself, for just as it breeds household rancor, it disturbs also the very government of Verona.

There is a universality in this situation. Romeo and Juliet epitomize the role in life of all men and women, for every being who is born, as the Renaissance saw it, is born into a world in which evil waits to destroy him, and he marches steadily towards an inexorable death. It is a world, moreover, in which his plans, no matter how virtuous, may always be frustrated by accident and by the caprice of a seemingly malignant fate. It is this universality that gives the play its stature as tragedy, for Romeo and Juliet in a sense become prototypes of everyman and everywoman. They attempt to find happiness in a world full of evil, to destroy evil by means of love, for with Friar Lawrence they see their marriage as the termination of the feud, but evil in the world cannot be destroyed; their fate cannot be escaped, and thus, like all men and women, they suffer and die. This is the life journey of all, but Shakespeare's play asserts that man need not despair, for he is a creature of reason with the grace of God to guide him, and through his encounter with evil he may learn the nature of evil and discover what it means to be a man. The ultimate message of Renaissance tragedy is that through suffering man grows and matures until he is able to meet his necessary fate with a calm acceptance of the will of God. The tragic vision and the religious vision spring ultimately out of the same human needs and aspirations.

Shakespeare saw in the legend of Romeo and Juliet a story which illustrated neither retribution for sin nor the working out of a blind inexorable Senecan fatalism. He saw a story that might be used to portray the maturation of youth through suffering and death. *Romeo and Juliet* may thus be called an "education" play, drawing upon the established morality tradition of such plays as *Nice Wanton* and *Lusty Juventus*. Romeo and Juliet learn the fundamental lessons of tragedy; the meaning of human life and death. Their education can culminate only in death and then rebirth in a world in which evil has no place. We can thus see Shakespeare in this play combining a story already cast for him in Senecan mold with a quite alien medieval dramatic tradition, which in its origins was based upon peculiarly Christian assumptions.

Romeo and Juliet are foolish, of course. They are hasty and precipitous and they make many mistakes, but to speak of a "tragic flaw" in either of them is to lead to endless absurdity. The impetuosity, haste, and carelessness of the lovers are the universal attributes of youth. Their shortcomings are what make them the ordinary representatives of humanity that this type of play must have as its tragic protagonists. Their errors, moreover, are all committed with a virtuous end in view, the same end that leads the wise and mature Friar Lawrence to marry them in spite of the dangers he sees both to them and to his own position. Unlike a later Othello or Macbeth, they are guilty of no deliberate choice of evil.

Both Romeo and Juliet mature greatly as the play unfolds, but to demonstrate the particular progress of the human life journey, Shakespeare concentrates upon Romeo. The exigencies of drama required that he concentrate upon one figure, and Romeo, of course, was the natural one. The Renaissance generally held that woman's powers of reason were somewhat less than those of man, and the design of the play called for a free-willed rational acceptance of the Christian stoic view of life to which Romeo comes at the end of the play.

How can a man live in a world in which evil lurks on every side and in which the inevitable end of all man's worldly aspirations must be death, a world in which the cold necessity of Fortune cannot be avoided? The Renaissance had a very simple answer which it carried over from the consolation philosophy of the Middle Ages, itself a Christian adaptation of the classical creed of Stoicism. Good and evil are in the world together, but the entire universe is ruled by a benevolent God whose plan is deliberate, meaningful, and ultimately good. The paradox of the fortunate fall taught that evil itself contributed to this ultimate good. Man, bearing the burden of original sin, had evil within him, but as the chosen creature of God, he had good also. When the evil within him predominated he was ruled by passion, but he had the gift of reason, which by proper exercise could always keep passion under control. Reason, of course, lay in an acceptance of the will of God. This central core of Renaissance belief is perfectly expressed by Friar Lawrence:

> For naught so vile that on the earth doth live
> But to the earth some special good doth give,
> Nor aught so good but, strain'd from that fair use
> Revolts from true birth, stumbling on abuse: . . .
> Two such opposed kings encamp them still
> In man as well as herbs, grace and rude will;
> And where the worser is predominant,
> Full soon the canker death eats up that plant.
>
> [II. iii. 17-20, 27-30]

Grace, of course, is reason, and rude will is passion. Man can live happily in the world if he allows his reason to guide his actions, to show him that the plan of the world essentially is good and just and that evil itself is designed to further the ends of a divine providence. With reason thus guiding him, man can become impervious to the blows of Fortune. He will accept his fate, whatever it may be, as contributing to a divine purpose beyond his comprehension but ultimately good and just. Through his encounter with evil Romeo learns to accept his fate in just such a manner.

We first meet Romeo as a lovesick boy assuming the conventional role of the melancholy lover, playing a game of courting a Capulet girl who he knows can never accede to his suit. We may well believe that it is because Rosaline is a Capulet that Romeo pursues her, and that because she knows the basic insincerity of his suit, she spurns him with her supposed vows of chastity. This is the boy Romeo, not yet ready to face the responsibilities of life, unaware of the real sorrows that are the lot of man, but playing with a make-believe sorrow that he enjoys to the fullest. We usually think that at his first sight of Juliet he abandons this childish pose and experiences true love. This may be so, for the dramatist is forced to work rapidly even at the expense of character consistency, but it is not really the sight of Juliet that causes him to change. It is his own precipitous act of leaping out from the dark beneath her window with his

> I take thee at thy word:
> Call me but love, and I'll be new baptized;
> Henceforth I never will be Romeo.
>
> [II. ii. 49-51]

With this hasty speech the game of make-believe love becomes no longer possible. The hasty act of impetuous youth is the means to maturity. Romeo must now face the realities of life with all its consequences both for good and evil. There may be a double meaning in that final line. Never again will he be the same Romeo who had pined for Rosaline. Juliet too can no longer be the same once she has poured her heart out into the night. She too must now face the world as it is. Her un-premeditated outpouring of her love parallels the precipitous speech of Romeo.

Like all young people, Romeo and Juliet are uncertain and hasty in their first encounters with the problems of reality. Their plans at best are foolish ones. The force of evil had already intruded into their world immediately following Romeo's first sight of Juliet. His first poetic rapture [I. v. 44-53] has been echoed by the harsh voice of Tybalt:

> This, by his voice, should be a Montague.
> Fetch me my rapier, boy.
>
>        [I. v. 54-5]

This is Shakespeare's unique poetic way of showing the ever-present juxtaposition of love and hate, good and evil. Before the marriage may be consummated, Romeo must now face this evil force in the world. He is not yet, however, able to accept it as he should. When Tybalt lies dead at his feet and a full awareness of what he has done comes upon him, Romeo cries out in despair: "O, I am fortune's fool" [III. i. 136]. This is a crucial line and all its implications must be understood. . . . When Romeo calls himself the "dupe" or "plaything" of Fortune, he is asserting a capricious, lawless Fortune, and thus he is denying the providence of God, of which in the Christian view Fortune was merely the agent. Romeo here sees the universe as a mindless chaos, without guiding plan; he is proclaiming a philosophy of despair. (pp. 274-79)

From this low point Romeo must make his slow journey to maturity, and Shakespeare shows his progression in three stages. First we find him in the friar's cell, weeping and wailing, beating his head upon the ground and offering to kill himself. This abject surrender to passion is the behavior not of a rational man but of a beast, as the friar declares:

> Hold thy desperate hand:
> Art thou a man? Thy form cries out thou art:
> Thy tears are womanish; thy wild acts denote
> The unreasonable fury of a beast.
>
>        [III. iii. 108-11]

Romeo's education now begins at the hands of Friar Lawrence, who in a lengthy speech [III. iii. 108-54] teaches him to make a virtue of necessity, that to rail on Fortune is foolish and fruitless, that careful reason will demonstrate to him that he is indeed far more fortunate than he might have been. When rather than kill himself he stops his weeping and goes to comfort Juliet, he has taken the first step toward maturity.

That his growth is a steady one from that point forward we may perceive from a bare hint as Romeo climbs from Juliet's window to be off for Mantua. "O, think'st thou we shall ever meet again?" [III. v. 51] asks Juliet, and Romeo replies:

> I doubt it not; and all these woes shall serve
> For sweet discourses in our time to come.
>
>        [III. v. 52-3]

What is significant here is that Romeo has thrown off despair and can face the future with some degree of hope in an ultimate providence. It is but the barest hint of a change in him, and we see no more of him until the beginning of Act V, where in Mantua we perceive by his first words that he is a new man entirely. All of Act IV had been devoted to Juliet. The dramatist has not had time to show in detail the growth of Romeo. The change must be made clear in Romeo's first speech, and it must be accepted by the audience as an accomplished fact. We

immediately sense a new serenity about him as he walks upon the stage at the beginning of Act V:

> My dreams presage some joyful news at hand:
> My bosom's lord sits lightly in his throne;
> And all this day an unaccustom'd spirit
> Lifts me above the ground with cheerful thoughts.
>
>        [V. i. 2-5]

He expects joyful tidings, but the news Balthazer brings is the most horrible of which he can conceive. Shakespeare gives his opening speech to Romeo, I believe, so that it may emphasize the shock of the news of Juliet's supposed death coming when happy news is expected, and in the face of this shock to illustrate the manner in which the new Romeo can receive the severest blow of which Fortune is capable.

The line with which Romeo answers his servant's dread report has been a troublesome one for editors [V. i. 24], and it may well be that this is one textual problem that can be resolved only in the light of the design for tragedy upon which the entire play is constructed. The bad quarto of 1597 reads:

> Is it euen so? then I defie my Starres.

The good quarto of 1599 reads:

> Is it in so? then I denie you starres.

The First Folio breaks the line in two:

> Is it euen so?
> Then I denie you Starres.
>
>        (pp. 280-82)

I should like to suggest that the second quarto reading is preferable. Not only does editorial consistency demand it, but it is, in fact, a far more meaningful line than the feeble reconstruction of it in the bad quarto. The design of the tragedy does not call at this point for a Byronic defiance of fate by Romeo, a daring of Fortune to pour its worst upon his head. . . . The design calls for an escape from Fortune's oppression through an acceptance of the order of the universe, and this meaning is implicit in "I denie you Starres."

We may ask first what the word "deny" means in the context in which Shakespeare here uses it. We do not have far to look, for in the second act we find a significant clue. Here Juliet speaks:

> O Romeo, Romeo! wherefore art thou Romeo?
> Deny thy father and refuse thy name.
>
>        [II. ii. 33-4]

She is asking wistfully that Romeo not be the son of his father, and her wish falls naturally into two parts: that he give up the name of his father and that he break the bond which ties him to his father. To "deny" his father is to negate the natural relationship of son to father, one, as the Renaissance saw it, of subjection and obedience. It is thus, in Shakespeare's sense, to cast off his father's authority, to refuse to be ruled by him. "I denie you starres," . . . is the very line with which Romeo attains the victory over circumstances which is the sign of the mature stoical man. It is probably the most crucial single line of the play. To deny one's stars is to throw off the control of a hostile fortune, just as a son might throw off the control of his father. To Renaissance man there was only one means by which this might be accomplished: by an acceptance of the way of the world as the will of God, and by a calm, fearless acceptance of death as the necessary and proper end of man, which releases him from all earthly evil and assures him of a

*Act II. Scene ii. Romeo and Juliet. By H. Hofmann. The Department of Rare Books and Special Collections, The University of Michigan Library.*

and a rebirth of good, a catharsis that would be well-nigh impossible were it bought with the souls as well as the lives of the young lovers. (pp. 282-84)

The world of *Romeo and Juliet* is a somber, realistic one in which youth is born into evil and must struggle against it ceaselessly until the conflict is ended by inevitable death. But Shakespeare's tragic vision is not one of resignation or despair; it is one of defiance and hope, of pride in those qualities of man that enable him to survive and achieve victory in such a world. . . . There is a design for tragedy in his early play, a conception of man's position in the universe to which character and event are designed by the artist to conform. There are, of course, inconsistencies in the design; Shakespeare has not yet been able entirely to escape the limitations imposed upon him by his sources, but we can nevertheless perceive, governing and shaping the matter that Shakespeare took from Arthur Brooke, the idea of tragedy as a portrait of man's journey from youth to maturity, encountering the evil in the world, learning to live with it, and achieving victory over it by death. Like the tragedies of Aeschylus, *Romeo and Juliet* proclaims also that man learns through suffering, but even more strongly than in Greek tragedy, there is affirmation in Shakespeare that the ultimate plan of the universe is good, for out of the suffering of individuals the social order is cleansed of evil. The deep-rooted family feud is finally brought to an end. (pp. 285-86)

> *Irving Ribner, ''Then I Denie You Starres: A Reading of 'Romeo and Juliet','' in* Studies in the English Renaissance Drama: In Memory of Karl Julius Holzknecht, *Josephine W. Bennett, Oscar Cargill, Vernon Hall, Jr., eds., New York University Press, 1959, pp. 269-86.*

**HARRY LEVIN**   (essay date 1960)

[*Levin focuses on Shakespeare's use of reduplication, contrariety, antithesis, and paradox in the early acts of* Romeo and Juliet, *both within the language and as an integral part of the structure of the play. The most obvious example of this drama of contradiction, the critic states, is the mixture of comic form and the tragic presentation of the lovers' ordeal. But Levin also perceives it in the play's antithetical structure, the consistent accumulation of pairings, the symmetry of the characters, and the reduplication of language, all of which progress toward a final harmony or synthesis in the last act. Levin further emphasizes how the lovers stand out ''against this insistence upon polarity . . . , the one organic relation amid an overplus of stylized expressions and attitudes.''*]

*Romeo and Juliet*, the most elaborate product of [Shakespeare's] so-called lyrical period, was his first successful experiment in tragedy. Because of that very success, it is hard for us to realize the full extent of its novelty, though scholarship has lately been reminding us of how it must have struck contemporaries. They would have been surprised, and possibly shocked, at seeing lovers taken so seriously. Legend, it had heretofore taken for granted, was the proper matter for serious drama; romance was the stuff of the comic stage. Romantic tragedy . . . was one of those contradictions in terms which Shakespeare seems to have delighted in resolving. His innovation might be described as transcending the usages of romantic comedy, which are therefore very much in evidence, particularly at the beginning. Subsequently, the leading characters acquire together a deeper dimension of feeling by expressly repudiating the artificial language they have talked and the superficial code they have lived by. . . . An index of this development is the incidence of rhyme, heavily concentrated

true felicity in heaven. For Romeo this will be reunion with Juliet.

It has been argued, of course, that since the Anglican church taught that the punishment for suicide was damnation, Romeo and Juliet in killing themselves are merely assuring the loss of their souls. We are not dealing here, however, with Shakespeare the theologian illustrating a text, but rather with Shakespeare the dramatist using symbolically a detail inherited from his sources in order to illustrate a greater and more significant truth. The Senecan tradition in which the story came down to Shakespeare endorsed suicide as a means of release from a world full of pain and as a means of expiation for complicity in the death of a loved one. It was in these terms that suicide was so essential a part of the Romeo and Juliet story. There was in the Renaissance, moreover, much respect for the classical notion of suicide as a noble act by which man fulfills his obligations and attains a higher good than life itself, and on the stage suicide was often portrayed in such terms. Only the most insensitive of critics could regard Romeo and Juliet as destined for damnation; their suicide, inherited by Shakespeare as an essential part of the story, must be regarded as a symbolic act of acceptance of inevitable death. Dramatically it is the most effective means by which such acceptance may be portrayed. The results of the act are not damnation, but instead, the destruction of evil by the ending of the feud. Out of the self-inflicted deaths of Romeo and Juliet come a reconciliation in the First Act, and its gradual replacement by a blank verse which is realistic or didactic with other speakers and unprecedentedly limpid and passionate with the lovers. (p. 6)

Comedy set the pattern of courtship, as formally embodied in a dance. The other *genre* of Shakespeare's earlier stagecraft, history, set the pattern of conflict, as formally embodied in a duel. *Romeo and Juliet* might also be characterized as an anti-revenge play, in which hostile emotions are finally pacified by the interplay of kindlier ones. Romeo sums it up in his prophetic oxymorons:

> Here's much to do with hate, but more with love.
> Why then, O brawling love! O loving hate!
> O anything, of nothing first create!
>
> [I. i. 175-77]

And Paris, true to type, waxes grandiose in lamenting Juliet:

> O love! O life! not life, but love in death!
>
> [IV. v. 58]

Here, if we catch the echo from Hieronimo's lament in [Thomas Kyd's] *The Spanish Tragedy*,

> O life! no life, but lively form of death,

we may well note that the use of antithesis, which is purely decorative with Kyd, is functional with Shakespeare. The contrarieties of his plot are reinforced on the plane of imagery by omnipresent reminders of light and darkness, youth and age, and many other antitheses subsumed by the all-embracing one of Eros and Thanatos, the *leitmotif* of the *Liebestod*, the myth of the tryst in the tomb. This attraction of ultimate opposites—which is succinctly implicit in the Elizabethan ambiguity of the verb *to die*—is generalized when the Friar rhymes "womb" with "tomb", and particularized when Romeo hails the latter place as "thou womb of death" [II. iii. 9-10; V. iii. 45]. Hence the "extremities" of the situation, as the Prologue to the Second Act announces, are tempered "with extreme sweet" [Prologue II, 14]. Those extremes begin to meet as soon as the initial prologue, in a sonnet disarmingly smooth, has set forth the feud between the two households, "Where civil blood makes civil hands unclean" [Prologue I, 4]. Elegant verse yields to vulgar prose, and to an immediate riot, as the servants precipitate a renewal—for the third time—of their masters' quarrel. The brawl of Act I is renewed again in the *contretemps* of Act III and completed by the swordplay of Act V. Between the street-scenes, with their clashing welter of citizens and officers, we shuttle through a series of interiors, in a flurry of domestic arrangements and family relationships. The house of the Capulets is the logical center of action, and Juliet's chamber its central sanctum. Consequently, the sphere of privacy encloses Acts II and IV, in contradistinction to the public issues raised by the alternating episodes. (pp. 6-7)

The alignment of the *dramatis personae* is as symmetrical as the antagonism they personify. It is not without relevance that the names of the feuding families, like the Christian names of the hero and heroine, are metrically interchangeable (though "Juliet" is more frequently a trochee than an amphimacer). Tybalt the Capulet is pitted against Benvolio the Montague in the first street-fight, which brings out—with parallel stage directions—the heads of both houses restrained by respective wives. Both the hero and heroine are paired with others, Rosaline and Paris, and admonished by elderly confidants, the Friar and the Nurse. Escalus, as Prince of Verona, occupies a superior and neutral position; yet, in the interchange of blood for blood, he loses "a brace of kinsman", Paris and Mercutio

[V. iii. 295]. Three times he must quell and sentence the rioters before he can pronounce the final sestet, restoring order to the city-state through the lovers' sacrifice. He effects the resolution by summoning the patriarchal enemies, from their opposite sides, to be reconciled. "Capulet, Montague," he sternly arraigns them, and the polysyllables are brought home by monosyllabics:

> See what a scourge is laid upon your hate
> That heaven finds means to kill your joys with love.
>
> [V. iii. 291-93]

The two-sided counterpoise of the dramatic structured is well matched by the dynamic symmetry of the antithetical style. One of its peculiarities, which surprisingly seems to have escaped the attention of commentators, is a habit of stressing a word by repeating within a line, a figure which may be classified in rhetoric as a kind of *ploce*. . . . Thus Montague and Capulet are accused of forcing their parties

> To wield old partisans in hands as old,
> Cank'red with peace, to part your cank'red hate.
>
> [I. i. 94-5]

This double instance, along with the wordplay on "cank'red," suggests the embattled atmosphere of partisanship through the halberds; and it is further emphasized in Benvolio's account of the fray:

> Came more and more, and fought on part and part.
>
> [I. i. 114]

The key words are not only doubled but affectionately intertwined, when Romeo confides to the Friar:

> As mine on hers, so hers is set on mine.
>
> [III. iii. 59]

Again, he conveys the idea of reciprocity by declaring that Juliet returns "grace for grace and love for love" [II. iii. 86]. The Friar's warning hints at poetic justice:

> These violent delights have violent ends.
>
> [II. vi. 9]

Similarly Mercutio, challenged by Tybalt, turns "point to point", and the Nurse finds Juliet—in *antimetabole*—"Blubb'ring and weeping, weeping and blubbering" [III. i. 160; III. ii. 87]. Statistics would prove illusory, because some repetitions are simply idiomatic, grammatical, or—in the case of old Capulet or the Nurse—colloquial. But it is significant that the play contains well over a hundred such lines, the largest number being in the First Act and scarcely any left over for the Fifth.

The significance of this tendency toward reduplication, both stylistic and structural, can perhaps be best understood in the light of Bergson's well-known theory of the comic: the imposition of geometrical form upon the living data of formless consciousness. The stylization of love, the constant pairing and counterbalancing, the *quid pro quo* of Capulet and Montague, seem mechanical and unnatural. (pp. 7-8)

Against this insistence upon polarity, at every level, the mutuality of the lovers stands out, the one organic relation amid an overplus of stylized expressions and attitudes. The naturalness of their diction is artfully gained . . . through a running critique of artificiality. In drawing a curtain over the consummation of their love, Shakespeare heralds it with a prothalamium and follows it with an epithalamium. Juliet's "Gallop apace, you fiery-footed steed" . . . is spoken "alone" but in breathless anticipation of a companion [III. ii. 1-31]. After having besought the day to end, the sequel to her solo is the duet in which she begs the night to continue. In the ensuing *débat* of the nightingale and the lark, a refinement upon the antiphonal song of the owl and the cuckoo in *Love's Labour's Lost,* Romeo more realistically discerns "the herald of the morn" [III. v. 6]. When Juliet reluctantly agrees, "More light and light it grows", he completes the paradox with a doubly reduplicating line:

> More light and light—more dark and dark our woes!
>
> [III. v. 35-6]

The precariousness of their union, formulated arithmetically by the Friar as "two in one" [II. vi. 37], is brought out by the terrible loneliness of Juliet's monologue upon taking the potion:

> My dismal scene I needs must act alone.
>
> [IV. iii. 19]

Her utter singleness, as an only child, is stressed by her father and mourned by her mother:

> But one, poor one, one poor and loving child.
>
> [IV. v. 46]

Tragedy tends to isolate where comedy brings together, to reveal the uniqueness of individuals rather than what they have in common with others. (p. 9)

The overriding pattern through which [Juliet] and Romeo have been trying to break—call it Fortune, the stars, or what you will—ends by closing in and breaking them; their private world disappears, and we are left in the social ambiance again. Capulet's house has been bustling with preparations for a wedding, the happy ending of comedy. The news of Juliet's death is not yet tragic because it is premature; but it introduces a peripety which will become the starting point for *Hamlet.*

> All things that we ordained festival
> Turn from their office to black funeral—
>
> [IV. v. 84-5]

the old man cries, and his litany if contraries is not less poignant because he has been so fond of playing the genial host:

> Our instruments to melancholy bells,
> Our wedding cheer to a sad burial feast;
> Our solemn hymns to sullen dirges change;
> Our bridal flowers serve for a buried corse;
> And all things change them to the contrary.
>
> [IV. v. 86-90]

His lamentation, in which he is joined by his wife, the Nurse, and Paris, reasserts the formalities by means of what is virtually an operatic quartet. Thereupon the music becomes explicit, when they leave the stage to the Musicians, who have walked on with the County Paris. Normally these three might play during the *entr'acte,* but Shakespeare has woven them into the dialogue terminating the Fourth Act. Though their art has the power of soothing the passions and thereby redressing grief, as the comic servant Peter reminds them with a quotation from Richard Edward's lyric *In Commendacion of Musicke,* he persists in his query: "Why 'silver sound'?" [IV. v. 129]. Their answers are those of mere hirelings, who can indifferently change their tune from a merry dump to a doleful one, so long as they are paid with coin of the realm. Yet Peter's riddle touches a deeper chord of correspondence, the interconnection between discord and harmony, between impulse and discipline. "Consort," which can denote a concert or a companionship,

can become the fighting word that motivates the unharmonious pricksong of the duellists [III. i. 46]. The "sweet division" of the lark sounds harsh and out of tune to Juliet, since it proclaims the lovers must be divided [III. v. 29]. Why "silver sound"? Because Romeo, in the orchard, has sworn by the moon

> That tips with silver all these fruit-tree tops.
>
> [II. ii. 108]

Because Shakespeare, transposing sights and sounds into words, has made us imagine:

> How silver-sweet sound lovers' tongues by night,
> Like softest music to attending ears!
>
> [II. ii. 165-66]
> (pp. 10-11)

*Harry Levin, "Form and Formality in 'Romeo and Juliet'," in* Shakespeare Quarterly, *Vol. XI, No. 1, Winter, 1960, pp. 3-11.*

## JOHN VYVYAN   (essay date 1960)

[*Vyvyan's essay is one of the most exhaustive investigations into Romeo's spiritual education through sexual love. In the excerpt below, Vyvyan argues that the tragedy exemplifies an allegorical presentation of love, depicting Romeo's gradual transformation, through the figure of Juliet, into spiritual consciousness, whereby he forsakes his old, conventional, and mistaken view of love for a more exalted, religious, and Platonic awarenesss. Thus, the critic considers the Romeo-Rosaline affair appropriate to Shakespeare's design. Although Vyvyan notes that by killing Tybalt Romeo fails to maintain his spiritual vision, he adds that in the final act the hero achieves a second "spiritual triumph," resolving the ancient grudge and affirming mutual forgiveness as humanity's saving attribute.*]

When we read Shakespeare's non-historical plays in the order in which he wrote them—as far as this is ascertainable—a thing that strikes us immediately about *Romeo and Juliet* is that for the first time Shakespeare is gripped by his story. He does not play with it: he matches its emotional impetus with his own. He follows his source—Brooke's poem, *The Tragicall Historye of Romeus and Juliet*—fairly closely, but increases its explosive power by compression. Our first feeling is that the tragedy of these lovers is like a ferment of new wine which bursts the old wineskins and is lost. Detailed allegory, being a work of the intellect, is not favoured by this uprush of emotion. Nevertheless, the Shakespearean parable is there.

The fact that in this play Shakespeare takes so much from Brooke provokes a general question. Are Shakespeare's borrowings to be discounted from the point of view of parable and plot? Are we to say, "he took this detail from so-and-so, and therefore he must not be given credit for the thought"? Or, on the other hand, should we maintain that Shakespeare was selective in his appropriations; that he took from his sources only what would fit into his own pattern; and that because this new context gives a new, or enhanced significance to the old ideas, they must therefore be accounted Shakespearean?

Fine critics could be cited in support of either contention. But if we were to press the first to logical finality, subtracting from Shakespeare every phrase and conception for which we would find a source, the outcome would be near disintegration. The plays would begin to look like rag-mats, stitched together out of innumerable pieces of ancient material. We are compelled to revolt against this grotesque conclusion. We know that poetry is not created in that way. But we cannot deny the bor-rowings; and if judgment is not to sink to the level of caprice, we must have some standard for assessing them.

Coleridge has been censured for giving *Shakespeare* the credit for showing Romeo ''love-bewildered'' by Rosaline before he meets Juliet [see excerpt above, 1834]. But the issue is not simple: Coleridge may be right. To depict the hero worshipping the mask, the picture, the shadow, the moon in water, before he unveils the reality is a part of the Shakespearean love-pattern; and if it had not been, or, at any rate, if it had conflicted with the pattern, we may reasonably suppose that Shakespeare would have rejected this element of Brooke's. By selecting it with deliberation, he makes it, from our standpoint, his own. Details that are used with allegorical consistency from play to play must, it seems to me, be treated as Shakespeare's, what-ever their source. Shakespeare was not a maker of rag-mats. But sometimes we may conceive of him as a jeweller, re-setting old gems into his own design. When we find a consistency in principles, then the origin of the illustrations that support them is of secondary importance. Naturally, however, marked de-viation from the source-story will merit special attention.

Shakespeare must have had a great determination to make people see, feel and understand the cause of the world's tragedy. Human life is never free from the threat of calamity. Why is this so? Can the curse be lifted? Shakespeare never ceased to wrestle with these problems, and to do his utmost to make his audience face and grasp what he believed to be the facts. . . . But the study of the disease held no morbid fascination for him, and he is not a whit less preoccupied with the remedy. . . . In *Romeo and Juliet,* his first deep analysis of tragedy, he is asking the audience to do much more than pity these lovers; he is urging and demanding that it shall exert its intelligence as well:

> Where be these enemies?—Capulet! Montague!
> See what a scourge is laid upon your hate—
>
> [V. iii. 291-92]

Shakespeare, according to his method, is making a closing demonstration, ''Look at the corpses in front of you—your own son and daughter! Why are they dead. For God's sake think!'' And he is requiring the audience to do the same—not merely to shudder at the scourge, but also to ponder the reasons for the reconciliation with which the play ends. Let us now turn to the prologue:

> Two households, both alike in dignity,
>    In fair Verona, where we lay our scene,
> From ancient grudge break to new mutiny,
>    Where civil blood makes civil hands unclean.
> From forth the fatal loins of these two foes
>    A pair of star-cross'd lovers take their life;
> Whose misadventured piteous overthrows
>    Do with their death bury their parents' strife.
>
> [Prologue, 1-8]

There is to be much of love, here, as well as of hate; and Shakespeare is intending to give us a wide view of both.

At the rise of the curtain, they are shown to us in the shape of the stupid brute. The serving-men of the house of Capulet have straightforward intentions with regard to all Montagues: they will murder the men and ravish the maids—hate and ''love'' in indistinguishable simplicity. But in this first scene, it is not so much the brutality as the stupidity that Shakespeare seems to find insufferable. We are never told the origin of the quarrel

between the Capulets and Montagues. None of the servants has any valid reason for hating anybody. It is just ''the ancient grudge'', purposely presented in terms general to humanity. If Shakespeare had laid bare the cause, he would doubtless have shown it to be as empty as the jealousy of Othello; and what he does present is senseless strife in which there are no winners. (pp. 141-45)

There is a lightning sketch, in the first scene, of a huge pan-orama from the grotesque to the divine. The fight [between the servants] is stopped, for a few moments, by Benvolio:

> Part, fools!
> Put up your swords; you know not what you do.
>
> [I. i. 64-5]

We cannot miss the echo from the Gospels. This senseless hate—the principle of hate—is leading to the crucifixion of love. Whether Brooke thought of it or not, Shakespeare is holding that conception in his mind. In *The Two Gentlemen of Verona,* we have been introduced to the theme of the effec-tiveness of love's self-sacrifice: Julia suffered both for and from her faithless lover; and because she did so, they regained their mutual joy. Mariana does the same for Angelo in *Measure for Measure*—it is one of Shakespeare's fundamental ideas. We are led to it again, in a wider context, here. When the reconciled enemies stand together in the last scene, their final reflection is not so much on the death as on the worth of Romeo and Juliet. . . . The stress, at the last, is on the value and effectiveness of love's sacrifice: it has ended ''the ancient grudge''. This is not a mere *coup de théâtre* [theatrical act]. Shakespeare has reached his conclusion by measured steps, and by the same gradation we must follow him.

I have already suggested that Coleridge may have been right—if not by argument, then by intuition—in giving Shakespeare the credit for making Romeo love-bewildered at the opening of the play. In establishing his hero's state of mind, Brooke or no Brooke, Shakespeare is conforming with his own method when he makes Romeo exclaim:

> I have lost myself; I am not here;
> This is not Romeo—
>
> [I. i. 197-98]

But it is Shakespeare, and at his most deliberate. He regularly shows the development of his characters to be a function of self-knowledge, or of self-discovery. And love and the self . . . are invariably linked and ultimately united. If Romeo has lost the reality of himself, then he has not found the reality of love. He is in the phase of shadow-worship, and is partly aware of it:

> These happy masks that kiss fair ladies' brows,
> Being black, put us in mind they hide the fair—
>
> [I. i. 230-31]

It is the familiar theme, ''Love doth approach disguised'', and there follows a lament for the lack of true love-sight that would pierce the disguise:

> Alas, that love, whose view is muffled still,
> Should without eyes see pathways to his will!
>
> [I. i. 171-72]

The pity is that they are the wrong pathways. At this phase, as Julia has told us, ''Love is a blinded god'' [*The Two Gen-tlemen of Verona,* IV. iv. 196]; but he receives his sight when the hero, allegorically speaking, recognizes the love-ideal in the heroine. . . . All these principles, which we have found enunciated elsewhere, are reaffirmed in Romeo—who, for the moment, "makes himself an artificial night" [I. i. 140]—and the only conclusion we can come to is that, whatever use Shakespeare made of Brooke, his own self-consistency is steadfast.

Romeo's love-bewilderment is further emphasized by his speechful of paradoxes . . . :

Why then, O brawling love! O loving hate!
O any thing, of nothing first created!
O heavy lightness! serious vanity!
Misshapen chaos of well-seeming forms!
Feather of lead, bright smoke, cold fire, sick health!
Still-waking sleep, that is not what it is!
This love feel I, that feel no love in this.
                              [I. i. 176-82]

That is the point: true love is not felt in this way. This is only a "fume of sighs", "moonshine in the water".

But Romeo is about to discover reality. As he and his friends stand outside the house of the Capulets, where he will have his first sight of Juliet, Benvolio says to him:

The date is out of such prolixity;
We'll have no Cupid hoodwink'd with a scarf—
                              [I. iv. 3-4]

They are discussing how they shall present themselves; but the double-meaning, here, is indubitable. The prolixity of paradox is done with. The time of muffled view and artificial night is over. Cupid is no longer to be hood-blind. All the emphasis is now upon clear sight, and the dissipation of vain fantasy. And Romeo confirms it when his eyes fall on Juliet:

For I ne'er saw true beauty till this night
                              [I. v. 53]

There comes a sound of muted thunder, a warning of the hate-storm that impends, in the muttered exchanges between Tybalt and Capulet. Then Tybalt leaves the hall. And Romeo speaks to Juliet.

If I profane with my unworthiest hand
This holy shrine, the gentle sin is this,
My lips, two blushing pilgrims, ready stand
To smooth that rough touch with a tender kiss.
JULIET: Good pilgrim, you do wrong your hand too much,
Which mannerly devotion shows in this;
For saints have hands that pilgrims' hands do touch,
And palm to palm is holy palmers' kiss.
ROMEO: Have not saints lips, and holy palmers too?
JULIET: Ay, pilgrim, lips that they must use in prayer.
ROMEO: O, then, dear saint, let lips do what hands do;
They pray, grant thou, lest faith turn to despair.
JULIET: Saints do not move, though grant for prayers' sake.
ROMEO: Then move not, while my prayers effect I take.
Thus from my lips, by thine, my sin is purged.
                              [I. v. 93-107]

This is a strange first conversation for a boy and a girl. Certainly, it is not Shakespeare's aim to mirror nature here. Do romance and poetry explain it fully? I hardly think so. The religious imagery is too insistent, too sustained. It suggests allegory. And that, in Shakespeare, means an underlying pattern that will be found elsewhere. Do we find it? The question needs only to be raised to be answered. We first remember

that Julia, planning her journey, says she will undertake it as a "true-devoted pilgrim":

And make a pastime of each weary step,
Till the last step have brought me to my love;
And there I'll rest, as after much turmoil,
A blessed soul doth in Elysium.
                 [The Two Gentlemen of Verona, II. vii. 35-8]

That pilgrimage could be a coincidence, although we are bound to pause over a metaphor so long sustained, and also to remember that the theme of love as religion was emphasized in Love's Labour's Lost. But it is Ophelia who dispels all doubt. The creation of Ophelia is nearly ten years later than that of Juliet. So it cannot be coincidental that she holds a key that will turn this lock:

How should I your true love know
From another one?
By his cockle hat and staff
And his sandal shoon.
                              [Hamlet, IV. v. 23-5]

We now see that it is nothing less than the distinguishing mark of the true lover that he should be a pilgrim. . . . No explanation of chance or poetry will account for ten years' consistency. That love is a pilgrimage to Elysium is a reiterated allegory in Shakespeare. (pp. 145-51)

It is important that we should feel quite sure that Shakespeare is following a love-pattern with full deliberation, because the allegory is sustained with a subtlety for which we need to be prepared. After his first meeting with Juliet, Romeo is more than romantically in love, he is spiritually altered. This is not a Shakespearean caprice, it has a literary background. And to this also it is essential that we should give full weight.

Romeo is now in a state that corresponds, but is not identical with that of Dante at the opening of the Vita Nuova. After his first sight of Beatrice, we may remember, Dante begins a new volume in the book of life, headed with a rubric saying, "Incipit vita nova" [Here begins a new life]. And thenceforward his love-development is traced, in religious language, to its culmination in paradise. The full sweep of Shakespeare's vision is not apparent until we have penetrated his allegories; but when we have done so, we find it is certainly not less that that of Dante. On the contrary . . . , the Shakespearen metaphysic is absolute. There are anticipations, and I make them to establish one point: the change in Romeo, although romantically presented, is philosophically conceived; and the birth of the new involves the death of the old. That is the fact which Mercutio is brought on to tell us, "The ape is dead!"

Mercutio, a mere name to Brooke, is all Shakespeare; and we must consider the purpose of his creation. He is dramatically valuable, but dramatic criticism is beyond the field of our enquiry. What is his place in the pattern? Clearly, he is at the mocking stage . . . and he does not live long enough to pass beyond it. His astringent wit—compared with the "deal of brine" that Romeo shed for Rosaline—is refreshing; but it is love-blindness none the less. He is in the condition Berowne was in, at the opening of Love's Labour's Lost:

—to study where I well may dine,
Or study where to meet some mistress fine—
                              [Love's Labour's Lost, I. i. 61, 63]

these desiderata being almost equally appreciated, with the dinner taking slight precedence of the mistress. . . . So thinks

Mercutio. And not having passed beyond that point himself, he cannot imagine that Romeo is much beyond it either: hence his conjuration of the ape, which fails to raise the familiar in his mistress' circle. (pp. 151-53)

Reality is an ambiguous word, and for the purposes of studying Shakespeare we must accept his definition. His philosophy, I believe, owes much to Plato. And Plato's famous comparison, in the seventh book of *The Republic,* of the objects that our physical senses perceive to mere shadows on the wall of a cave, is virtually Shakespearean. Throughout the plays, shadow, matter and appearance are contrasted with substance, spirit and reality as the lower world to the higher, earth to heaven. But there is no question, either in Shakespeare or in Plato, of the soul being perpetually chained in the cavern of shadows. At some time, as in a moment of new birth, it will emerge, look upon the world of light, and even make an attempt, which is of small avail, to explain its vision to those who are still immured. This moment of transition from the cave to the light, from the false to the true, is presented in Shakespearean allegory as the moment when the blinded love-god receives his sight. (pp. 153-54)

Mercutio's "Adam Cupid" is love in the hoodwinked phase of muffled view, but the work "Adam" remains a puzzle. It might be—though I will not press the suggestion—that there is a play here on the idea of the old Adam and the new, the man of earth and the man of spirit. At all events, Mercutio represents the one, and Romeo has a flash, before the tragedy closes in, of the vision appropriate to the other.

Mercutio makes his first appearance in the scene before Capulet's feast. At the feast, Romeo will receive his love-sight, and behold, as he tells us, "true beauty" for the first time. In contrast to this unveiling of reality, Mercutio delivers a very long speech about Queen Mab. She is our lady of illusion, bringing to everyone some insubstantial dream of his desire. She is the very quintessence of the phase of shadows. And after listening to forty-two lines about her, Romeo, who is so near to bidding her a last good-bye, has had enough:

> Peace, peace, Mercutio, peace!
> Thou talk'st of nothing.
>
> [I. iv. 95-6]

Mercutio will not be shut up, but he admits that he is talking about dreams:

> Which are the children of an idle brain,
> Begot of nothing but vain fantasy,
> Which is as thin of substance as the air,
> And more inconstant than the wind—
>
> [I. iv. 97-100]

There is a little more wind, and then Benvolio brings the speech to a stop, by making the point to which Shakespeare has been leading:

> This wind you talk of blows us from ourselves—
>
> [I. iv. 104]

Mercutio is silenced, for this scene. He has served his symbolic purpose. But whichever play we open, we shall find that, in some form or other, Shakespeare will face us with this antithesis: the realm of the fairies' midwife, full of teasing shadows and false shapes, and the reality that we must discover and be true to in ourselves. Very soon, Romeo will find his own self in Juliet's self. And, as Shakespeare makes beautifully plain, at that level of spirit they are one.

At the feast, Mercutio says nothing. But he comes into his own immediately after, with his conjuration speech. This is followed by the balcony scene between Romeo and Juliet, and the logic of the construction is now clear. The conjuration speech is to the balcony scene as the Queen Mab speech is to the feast—a contrast between two planes of consciousness. But this time the allegory is more enriched.

The feast is over. We are in a lane by the wall of Capulet's orchard. Romeo enters alone, and halts:

> Turn back, dull earth, and find thy centre out.
>
> [II. i. 2]

Then he climbs the wall and disappears. The words simply underline what we have already established—his conversion. Dull earth is to seek, at its centre, the essence of itself. Mercutio and Benvolio now come on; they are looking for Romeo, and Mercutio calls:

> Romeo! humours! madman! passion! lover!
> Appear thou in the likeness of a sigh:
> Speak but one rhyme and I am satisfied;
> Cry but "Ay me!" pronounce but "love" and "dove";
> Speak to my gossip Venus one fair word,
> One nickname for her publind son and heir,
> Young Adam Cupid—
> He heareth not, he stirreth not, he moveth not;
> The ape is dead—
>
> [II. i. 7-13, 15-16]

The Romeo they are looking for, in fact, exists no more. When we see how carefully Shakespeare has built up the allegory to this point, and how meticulously he continues it, we cannot doubt that "the ape" has this double meaning. Nor does he ever cease to regard as a proper study for mankind the antics of the ape-within: we meet the ape, again, in *Measure for Measure,* where the creature, in an angry mood,

> Plays such fantastic tricks before high heaven
> As make the angels weep—
>
> [II. ii. 121-22]

For Romeo, however, its lamentable love-tricks are now over—in that respect, his ape has had its day. But Mercutio continues in a fine simian style that might move the heavens to laughter. Not finding the body, he proceeds to conjure the spirit of the ape. . . . There follow some over-the-port witticisms about "his mistress' circle", and then Benvolio comes back to the theme of love's want of sight. Romeo, he says, has hidden himself among the trees:

> Blind is his love and best befits the dark.
>
> [II. i. 32]

The darkness is Benvolio's own, and it is dwelt on here for the greater glory of the light which will shine in the next scene—*ex tenebris lux* [out of darkness, light]. And for the same constructional reason, the creation of an awakening contrast, Mercutio finishes the picture of what Romeo is supposed to be doing:

> Now will he sit under a medlar-tree,
> And wish his mistress were that kind of fruit
> As maids call medlars when they laugh alone.
> O, Romeo, that she were, O, that she were
> An open et cetera, thou a poperin pear!
>
> [II. i. 34-8]

Witty, smutty—and immeasurably wide of the mark. Romeo is not under a medlar-tree; but in a few moments he will be under Juliet's balcony, and there breathe a wish far from the imaginings of Mercutio:

> O, speak again, bright angel! for thou art
> As glorious to this night, being o'er my head,
> As is a winged messenger of heaven
> Unto the white-upturned wondering eyes
> Of mortals, that fall back to gaze on him
> When he bestrides the lazy-pacing clouds
> And sails upon the bosom of the air.
>
> [II. ii. 26-32]

Not even Shakespeare could have contrived antitheses more arresting than the medlar-tree and Juliet's balcony, the poperin pear and love's pilgrim, who has come to the shrine of his own heart's saint—a place so beautiul that we know it must be holy.

There is not a metaphor in the balcony scene that recalls the cave of shadows—unless it is the exhortation to cast off the livery that is "sick and green": everything belongs to a new world of light. The east—the sun—the fairest stars of heaven—the airy region—the bright angel—the winged messenger: not one symbol of dull earth, which before was so insistent, every image is celestial.

If we are to pass beyond this, it can only be into the unity of spirit, or, in Platonic terms, of pure being. Words must falter here, and at last fail utterly. But Shakespeare carries us as far, perhaps, as language will reach in revealing the essence of the self as love. In his philosophy, to realize this and be true to it is to be perfect. It has been said that all art strains towards the free condition of music; and likewise, we may think, all love in Shakespeare, tends toward the union in essence of *The Phoenix and the Turtle*:

> Reason in itself confounded
> Saw division grow together—

And we are brought to the mystical paradox, where not merely language fails us, but conceptual thought. Shakespeare leads his lovers to the threshold of the knowledge of their spiritual identity, which is not, of course, any creation of their own: their love-sight simply shows them that it is.

Ideally, this should culminate in the mystic vision, or philosophic conclusion, of the unity of being, which other explorers—Heraclitus, Plotinus, and many in the Orient—have arrived at by different roads. That Shakespeare chose the path of love must be partly for reasons of temperament, but mainly because the Middle Ages, Neo-Platonism, and the Gospels had prepared his way. I am not, of course, suggesting that Romeo and Juliet here reach this absolute—there would have been no tragedy if they had. I wish to establish a direction. They are moving *towards* what Plato calls "the pure blaze of being", and the Shakespearean path to this is through the "mutual flame". (pp. 154-59)

Shakespeare's heroines lead the hero, if he will follow, to paradise and beyond it, as unerringly as Beatrice guided Dante; but they deliver no lectures; they are unconscious of their role; it is simply their nature, as love-symbols, to be the true beauty and to reveal it. In answer to Romeo's prayer to the "bright angel"—which, of course, she did not hear—Juliet gives him,

without knowing that she does so, Shakespeare's pass-key to self-knowledge:

> 'Tis but thy name that is my enemy;
> Thou art thyself—
> What's a Montague?
> What's in a name?
> —Romeo, doff thy name,
> And for thy name, which is no part of thee,
> Take all myself.
>
> [II. ii. 38-40, 43, 47-9]

She is speaking simply, out of her heart; but Shakespeare is speaking out of his philosophy. The mask, the favour, the jewel on the sleeve, the portrait—and now, the name. It is one more entry in the long list of disguises. . . . It was to find the centre, the essence of himself, that Romeo came here. And now he is being led towards the discovery that the centre is pure being, the essence love, and that his true self is also hers. This is presented to him as an exchange of selves in the communion of love. And ideally, this should culminate in the consciousness of the divine in all.

Romeo does not achieve this realization. But the ideal standard is in Shakespeare's mind; he is measuring his characters against it: and the degree by which they fall short of it is the measure of their tragedy. Romeo has been described as "Hamlet in love" [see excerpt above by William Hazlitt, 1817]. There are many resemblances between them which it would be confusing to examine here, but one is particularly relevant: each was near to being "man new made", and each of them failed at the last, or nearly the last test. But we must remember that they are being measured against a standard of perfection. In Shakespeare's view, it is not impossible to reach this standard—but it requires perfect constancy to love. And that means to face, in principle, the test of the Cross. If this is passed, there is an out-flow of "power divine", which is a saving grace to a wider sphere; and it is on the assumption that this spiritual power is paramount absolutely that Shakespeare resolves his tragedies. For these reasons, we may rightly speak of the religion of love in Shakespeare: the path goes all the way from the lowest consciousness to the highest; and it is not "the primrose path of dalliance", but the pilgrim's way. In moments of intensity when the parable is receiving special stress, Shakespeare uses religious imagery—sometimes classical, sometimes Christian; it may be Elysium and the oracle of Apollo, it may be heaven and the bright angel, each is holy, each brings the authentic message of the spirit.

So it is here. Romeo, who has been concealed, now steps forward and reveals himself to Juliet:

> Call me but love, and I'll be new baptized—
>
> [II. ii. 50]

This is one more careful contrast with the preceding scene: the medlar-tree and the balcony, the poperin pear and the pilgrim, and, now, the dead ape and the soul that is new baptized. "Adam Cupid" may or may not be a play on the idea of the old Adam and the new; but the scenes, in the sum of their effects, are set beside each other as earth to spirit. I know that some of my readers will be sceptical of my view of the philosophy implicit here; but I think everyone will grant that Shakespeare is aiming to present more than the romantic exchanges of two young people. At the least, a power is being generated that can, and in the end does, reconcile the Montagues with the Capulets. (pp. 159-61)

For the remainder of the act, Shakespeare follows his source fairly closely, except that he shortens the time. The most important divergence is that he makes Tybalt send a written challenge to Romeo's house. Romeo does not receive it, because he has gone straight from the balcony scene to Friar Laurence's cell. The friar, agreeing to marry the lovers in secret, indicates to us the plot's unfolding scope:

> For this alliance may so happy prove,
> To turn your households' rancour to pure love.
>
> [II. iii. 91-2]

This clearly fits Shakespeare's pattern—that the grace of love is a power effective in a widening sphere; but as it is in Brooke, we need not give Shakespeare special credit for it here. The clandestine marriage concludes the act and the protasis of the plot. In the third act, as usual, Black plays its trump card—the killing of Tybalt by Romeo. And although this is also in the source, Shakespeare reshapes the whole episode so characteristically that, for our present purpose, Brooke may be dismissed. The way in which this is handled is of great importance, not only to the present play, but to a general understanding of Shakespeare's conception of tragedy and its resolution.

In what may be called the dynamics of Shakespearean tragedy, "the ancient grudge" works like a monstrous pendulum of which the powerful swing does not diminish with the passage of time. It is not difficult to set this going, but it requires a superhuman exertion to bring it to a stop. Lacking this higher intervention, the revenge-sequence will continue in perpetuity, although it is frequently dignified with the names of law and justice. Shakespeare sees no hope whatever in retributive justice and the law that derives from it; and he therefore repudiates the old law in favour of the new. One thing only will bring the tragic pendulum to a standstill—an act of creative mercy. This is not at all the same thing as condoning the offence. It is an outflow of divine power which changes the offender, kills the enmity and leaves the enemy a living friend. (pp. 162-63)

But spiritual power has to be worked for; and in Shakespeare's philosophy, it can be acquired only through self-knowledge and constancy to love. The hero who can achieve and be true to these will save himself and others; he who cannot, is caught in an *ewige Runde*, on the unmanageable wheel of fate. In later plays, Shakespeare works these things out in detail; but we find a helpful sketch of them in the third act of *Romeo and Juliet*. (p. 163)

[If] we see that Shakespeare is measuring Romeo, in the third act, by the standard of the perfect man, we understand, first, that his test is a real and decisive one, and, second, that at this stage of his development failure was inevitable. Romeo comes on after Mercutio has begun to pick his quarrel with Tybalt, but before they have crossed swords. Tybalt then turns to Romeo and calls him a villain, to which he replies:

> Tybalt, the reason that I have to love thee
> Doth much excuse the appertaining rage
> To such a greeting: villain am I none;
> Therefore farewell; I see thou know'st me not.
> TYBALT: Boy, this shall not excuse the injuries
> That thou hast done me; therefore turn and draw.
> ROMEO: I do protest I never injured thee,
> But love thee better than thou canst devise,
> Till thou shalt know the reason of my love:
> And so, good Capulet, which name I tender
> As dearly as mine own, be satisfied.

At this, Mercutio breaks in:

> O calm, dishonourable, vile submission!—
> Tybalt, you rat-catcher, will you walk?
>
> [III. i. 62-75]

If we place this in a wider context of Shakespearean ideas, we see that more is involved than the plot of a particular play. Under great provocation, Romeo is maintaining constancy to love throughout a sphere of which Juliet is the centre. The circumference of this sphere is potentially infinite, although in practice it is variable. And it is the infinite possibility that gives spiritual meaning to Shakespeare's heroines as allegorical figures: they are revealers, as Beatrice was to Dante, of . . . the love-power that harmonizes all things and brings cosmos out of chaos. Consequently, when Prospero says to Ferdinand:

> —all thy vexations
> Were but my trials of thy love, and thou
> Hast strangely stood the test—
>
> [*The Tempest*, IV. i. 5-7]

he is stating a principle which enters into all Shakespearean temptation scenes. When the hero fails in them, he is invariably failing his highest self, which, for Shakespeare, is the same as failing love; and the consequence is a reversion to chaos, first in his own soul, and then in the world around him. It is this that gives a Judas-quality to the tragic heroes, and in some measure to all men until they are perfect—"man new made". Romeo, up to the point we have quoted him, has "strangely stood the test". Like Prospero himself, he has taken part with his "nobler reason" against fury. It may seem incredible to the audience that Romeo's effort to overcome evil with good would have proved effectual in the given situation; but the impulse of the audience does not constitute a philosophic judgment, and we are bound to infer, from Shakespeare's consistent ethic, that, as love has the power in principle to dissolve hate, it might have done so here. The scale is turned by the fatal intervention of Mercutio. (pp. 167-69)

Romeo's reaction to Mercutio's death seems almost inevitable; and in this, again, he resembles Hamlet. In both heroes, I suggest, Shakespeare is presenting the dilemma of the Christian soul poised—indeed, torn—between the ethic of the Old Testament and that of the New. Both of them, tested to breaking-point, revert to what is, according to the Old Law, justifiable and even obligatory vengeance. By that standard they are not wrong. But none the less, because they adopt it, all hope of achieving the freedom and power of the perfect man is lost, and "black fate" takes over the play. . . . Romeo is, one might say, deconverted. And in his outburst, Shakespeare presents to us, for the first time, his conception of the irrevocable moment in tragedy:

> Away to heaven, respective lenity,
> And fire-eyed fury be my conduct now!—
> Now, Tybalt, take the "villain" back again
> That late thou gavest me! for Mercutio's soul
> Is but a little way above our heads,
> Staying for thine to keep him company:
> Either thou, or I, or both, must go with him.
>
> [III. i. 123-29]

Black, with these words, plays its winning card of death. . . . [Romeo] falls, from near freedom, back into the vortex of fate. And as he looks at the dead body of Tybalt, Juliet's kinsman, he exclaims:

O, I am fortune's fool!

[III. i. 136]
(pp. 170-72)

In the fourth act, White—almost always in the form of the allegorical figure of Love—plays its highest card: win or lose, life or death, the game is decided. If the card Black played in the preceding act is unbeatable, Love is shown to us as pathetic, deserted and lost. Such is Ophelia, who is prominent in the fourth act, but helpless: she can only stir our sympathy, which is something; pray for mercy on every soul, which is more, and drown. Lady Macduff, the only good woman in *Macbeth*, is murdered with all her children in the fourth act; it is the martyrdom of love and the slaughter of the innocents; she is doomed and can do no more than suffer. In the fourth act of *Othello*, Emilia and Desdemona do their utmost by protest, appeal and supplication: it is unavailing. On the other hand, when the play is to end with the triumph of life, the action of Love initiates this trend in the fourth act. This is what Mariana does in *Measure for Measure*. Perdita is the incarnation of returning spring in *The Winter's Tale*. And Julia makes love's redeeming sacrifice in *The Two Gentlemen of Verona*.

It is therefore time for Juliet to take action. She goes to Friar Laurence and asks for his advice. With the threat of a forced marriage to Paris now added to her other woes, she is prepared to dare anything. . . . [The Friar] offers her the desperate remedy of simulated death, but adds:

If no inconstant toy nor womanish fear
Abate thy valour in the acting it.

[IV. i. 119-20]

Juliet's answer is emphatic:

Give me, give me! O, tell me not of fear!

[IV. i. 121]

This plan she follows faithfully—not without terror, but in spite of it; and the course of the action is now deflected, and largely determined by her decision.

Why does the plan fail? Why does the death-card played by Black in the third act win the game? On the surface, it appears to be due to pure chance: if the letter Friar Laurence sent to Romeo had been delivered, the lovers would have escaped together to Mantua, till the friar found a time:

To blaze your marriage, reconcile your friends,
Beg pardon of the prince, and call thee back
With twenty hundred thousand times more joy
Than thou went'st forth in lamentation—

[III. iii. 151-54]

This would have been the kind of life-ending that Shakespeare handles very well in other plays; and if it does not happen here, it will not be *only* because he is following Brooke. Shakespeare always adds his philosophic commentary to the stories he borrows, telling us why, according to his own system of ideas, they turn out as they do. In his view, there are stronger forces than mere chance working against the efforts of Friar Laurence and Juliet for love and life; and this outlook has a bearing on many other plays. (pp. 180-82)

But death is not the end of it for Shakespeare. He believes in immortality. And many times he makes the point that, in the deeper sense, death solves nothing: the hate-sequence is carried on just as relentlessly both in and from the world beyond. The whole action in *Hamlet* is precipitated by the ghost's demand for retributive justice—and his discarnate will drives the living

towards it, corpse by corpse, until his brother-enemy falls in the last blood-soaked scene. Shakespeare's ghosts do more than titillate the audience to agreeable horror; they are psychic forces that may dominate the play; and the crude incident of killing a character on the stage never removes him from the plot. . . . These ghosts are neither wraiths nor lookers-on; they are persisting powers, who have lost nothing but their bodies; and we are intended to sense their participation in the drama to the last act-drop. They are able to infect the living with the madness that precedes disaster. And when Juliet imagines herself regaining consciousness in the family vault, alone, she says:

O, if I wake, shall I not be distraught,
Environed with all these hideous fears?
And madly play with my forefathers' joints?
And pluck the mangled Tybalt from his shroud?
And, in this rage, with some great kinsman's bone,
As with a club, dash out my desperate brains?

[IV. iii. 49-54]

From Juliet's lips, the phrasing is unnatural, and the concluding action is impossible; but Shakespeare is making a point of some importance. He sees it as a general proposition that one consequence of the perpetuation of hate is that succeeding generations do, in effect, dash out their own and one another's brains with their great kinsmen's bones. Nor is that the worst of it. Although the revengeful dead will lend their bones for clubs, they have indirect control of more effective weapons. This brings us to the present instance. Romeo has already told us that Mercutio—from the other side of death—claimed Tybalt's life. In the speech of challenge, in which he dismisses lenity to heaven, he said:

—Mercutio's soul
Is but a little way above our heads,
Staying for thine to keep him company—

[III. i. 126-28]

Mercutio was not kept waiting long. But Tybalt, from the world beyond, claims a blood-sacrifice as well; and in view of Shakespeare's way with ghosts, we may take it that Juliet saw one, when she says:

O, look! methinks I see my cousin's ghost
Seeking out Romeo, that did spit his body
Upon a rapier's point:—stay, Tybalt, stay!

[IV. iii. 55-7]

Tybalt will not be stayed. He exacts payment to the uttermost farthing, and Romeo meets his own death in Tybalt's tomb. But there the curse is lifted. As Romeo is about to drink the poison, he says:

Tybalt, liest thou there in thy bloody sheet?
O, what more favour can I do to thee
Than with that hand that cut thy youth in twain
To sunder his that was thine enemy?
Forgive me, cousin!

[V. iii. 97-101]

That half-line, in Shakespeare's scheme of things, changes the tragedy to a spiritual triumph. Romeo pays his debt with constancy to love; and, therefore, there is an outflowing of grace which dissipates the ancient enmity. As he drains the bitter cup, he turns to Juliet:

Thus with a kiss I die.

[V. iii. 120]

And the grudge dies with him. Here is a last and supreme contrast between Mercutio and Romeo. Mercutio died with—"A plague on both your houses!" [III. i. 106]. Romeo dies with a benediction upon both. The one fanned the flames of hate: the other extinguishes them for ever. (pp. 182-84)

Romeo calls Juliet's tomb "a lantern"—meaning the structure on the summit of a building through which light flows: and from this there would seem to be only one inference that Shakespeare can have intended us to draw—it is in illumination that love's pilgrimage will end. In the course of it, there are inevitable errors. The death of Paris is the last of these. But it is clear that he is included in a reconciliation of souls; and that in a world beyond possessiveness and jealousy, his relation to Juliet—who is a revealer of the true Beauty—will be as perfect as that of Romeo himself. (p. 185)

The play ends with one of Shakespeare's most persistent themes: mutual forgiveness is essential. Whatever the past, it has to be accepted, in charity and humility, as a shared fate and a shared fault; on that basis, the future will be better—on any other, it is likely to be worse.

Whenever the Shakespearean hero is offered a choice between love and violence, the one is presented as creative and the other as destructive power. If he reverts to violence, there is a regression towards hell; if he is constant to love, through tests and temptations, there is a dramatic movement towards cosmos and heaven. He is not being measured by our habitual standard; but by one that, in Shakespeare's view, is appropriate to a "perfect man". (pp. 185-86)

> *John Vyvyan, " 'Romeo and Juliet'," in his* Shakespeare and the Rose of Love: A Study of the Early Plays in Relation to the Medieval Philosophy of Love, *Chatto & Windus, 1960, pp. 141-86.*

## PAUL N. SIEGEL (essay date 1961)

[*Siegel discusses the influence on* Romeo and Juliet *of "the religion of love," a doctrine passed on from the Middle Ages and adopted by many Elizabethan writers in their adaptations of the Italian novelle. This doctrine held that "Love is a god in supreme control over human beings" and that faithfulness in love, even to the point of death, was the highest virtue. Siegel asserts that Shakespeare transformed this idea "into a complexly unified attitude," demonstrating that cosmic love manifests itself through sexual love to conquer "strife and disorder in society." The critic thus contends that although hate kills the lovers, "the love of heaven, redressing order and restoring concord through the love of Romeo and Juliet, triumphs over the hate which has endangered the peace of Verona."*]

The long established traditional interpretation of *Romeo and Juliet* is that it is a drama of fate or of sheer misfortune in which the lovers are not at all responsible for the catastrophe they suffer. Recently, however, a number of scholars have argued that the Elizabethans, with their Christian background of thought, would have regarded the lovers as guilty sinners rather than as innocent victims. What has not been appreciated by either of these two groups of critics is that *Romeo and Juliet*, one of many Elizabethan adaptations of stories of disastrous love derived from Italian novelle, was affected by the manner in which these other adaptations used the ideas of the religion of love that persisted from the Middle Ages.

What had been an aristocratic cult became in the hands of the Elizabethan adapters of the Italian novelle a means of middle-class entertainment. To the straightforwardly realistic accounts of Boccaccio and Bandello, they added a further dash of spice and then a generous portion of moralization to give the mixture a properly medicinal flavor for an audience that thought of literature as a sugar-coated pill, increasing the amount of these ingredients already increased in intervening French translations. . . . In their stories dealing with love the reader could find sensational incidents providing gratifying thrills presented to him as moral instruction. Each of them proclaimed that passionate love brought destruction and death, but at the same time glorified this love and, in keeping with the doctrine of the religion of love, presented faithfulness in it as the highest virtue.

What is in the other Elizabethan works drawn from the Italian novelle a crudely mechanical mixture of a glorification of passionate love and a Christian moralistic condemnation of it is in Shakespeare's *Romeo and Juliet* a subtle blend of these two ingredients. In the other adaptations the author oscillates between frivolously inconsistent attitudes toward the lovers; in *Romeo and Juliet* these mutually contradictory attitudes are transformed into a complexly unified attitude. As in Shakespearian tragedy generally, perception of the hero's fatal lack of balance does not preclude admiration and sympathy. Moreover, the ideas of the religion of love and those of Christianity, instead of merely being placed in incongruous juxtaposition as in the other novella adaptations, are in *Romeo and Juliet* interwoven into a unified artistic pattern. Thus in the other adaptations the idea that Love is a god in supreme control over human beings and the idea that divine providence rules the affairs of men are juggled without rime or reason. In *Romeo and Juliet* the medieval and Renaissance concept that sexual love is a manifestation of the cosmic love of God, which holds together the universe in a chain of love and imposes order on it, acts as a nexus between the two doctrines. (pp. 371-72)

This is not to say that Shakespeare expressed a logically consistent outlook encompassing the ideas of both Christianity and the religion of love. He was concerned with artistic unity, not with logical unity. The ideas of the religion of love and those of Christianity not only work together; they also pull in opposite directions, creating a dramatic tension which is relieved only with the transcendence of love at the very end. According to a tenet of the medieval religion of love that continued to be expressed in the Elizabethan adaptations of novelle, joining the loved one in death qualifies the lover as one of Cupid's saints and ensures that the two meet in the "Paradise in which dwelt the god of love, and in which were reserved places for his disciples" [William G. Dodd, in his *Courtly Love in Chaucer and Gower*]. According to Christianity, suicide, unless repentance occurs between the act and death, ensures damnation. In *Romeo and Juliet*, unlike *Hamlet*, *Othello*, *Macbeth*, and *King Lear*, it is the lovers' paradise of the religion of love, not the after-life of Christian religion, which is adumbrated at the close of the tragedy. . . . If it seems strange that dramatic use of this tradition was accepted by the Christian Elizabethans, it should be remembered that it originated in the Christian Middle Ages. In this tradition, C. S. Lewis points out, love, at times "an escape from religion" and at other times "a rival religion", can also be "an extension of religion" and even a "combination" of all of these things [in his *The Allegory of Love*]. (pp. 372-73)

[In *Romeo and Juliet*] Friar Laurence supplies the moralizing with which the authors of the adaptations of novelle would garnish them. In Shakespeare, however, this moralizing is not extraneous to the work, although it does not contain within itself its complexity. Friar Laurence's comments concerning the conduct of Romeo are just and foreshadow the conclusion. His warnings about immoderateness and reckless abandon, in fact, only repeat the misgivings of Juliet at the time of their avowals of love:

> I have no joy of this contract to-night:
> It is too rash, too unadvised, too sudden;
> Too like the lightning, which doth cease to be
> Ere one can say "It lightens."
>
> [II. ii. 117-20]

It is not merely the failure of Friar John to get to Mantua, the last accident in a fatal chain of mishaps, that brings about the death of the lovers; it is the speed with which Romeo acts, a speed which distinguishes the lovers' action throughout. Romeo's drive to death in the last act is only the culmination of a drive which reaches its goal at the conclusion. The words "I long to die" [IV. i. 66], with which Juliet, threatening, knife in hand, to kill herself, impels Friar Laurence to his desperate strategem, express well the drive to death of the two lovers. Ready like half-cocked pistols to go off or, as Friar Laurence says of Romeo, "like powder in a skilless soldier's flask" [III. iii. 132;], they are prone to suicide. The hasty jumping to conclusions and the thoughts of death with which each responds to the initial disaster of Tybalt's death foreshadow the suicides as the result of misunderstanding at the end as surely as the frequently pointed out dreams, premonitions, references to death as a lover, and mentions of fate. Juliet, mistaking the Nurse's lamentations over Tybalt for an announcement of Romeo's death, exclaims: "Vile earth, to earth resign; end motion here; / And thou and Romeo press one heavy bier!" [III. ii. 59-60]. When Romeo will in fact be dead, having killed himself in the mistaken belief that she is dead, she will indeed join him to lie in one grave with him.

So too Romeo, overwhelmed at the thought of his banishment and mistaking the Nurse's description of Juliet's grief for an indication that she is sorrowing over Tybalt and has rejected him, is about to kill himself when Friar Laurence restrains him, reclaiming him from despair with a lengthy speech that contains some prophetic passages:

> Hold thy desperate hand:
> Art thou a man? . . .
> Thy wild acts denote
> The unreasonable fury of a beast. . . .
> Wilt thou slay thyself?
> And slay thy lady too that lives in thee,
> By doing damnèd hate upon thyself? . . .
> Take heed, take heed, for such die miserable.
> [III. ii. 108-09, 110-11, 116-18, 145]
> (pp. 380-81)

If, however, Friar Laurence's warning is prophetic, the intensity of the love of Romeo and Juliet is presented as its own justification. Their love is reckless, tending to destruction, but it is glorious. Each utterance of Friar Laurence is balanced by one of Romeo. We should not, with Dowden [see excerpt above, 1881], disregard those of Friar Laurence or, with Dickey [see excerpt above, 1957], disregard those of Romeo: both sets of utterances have validity. What in the other novella adaptations are two opposing views of love voiced by the author without regard for self-contradiction are here two views appropriately voiced by two dramatic characters, for each of whom the audience has sympathetic understanding.

Of the philosophical discussion of his situation in which Friar Laurence wishes to engage him Romeo says:

> Thou canst not speak of that thou doest not feel:
> Wert thou as young as I, Juliet thy love,
> An hour but married, Tybalt murdered,
> Doting like me and like me banished,
> Then mightst thou speak. . . .
>
> [III. iii. 64-8]

The advice of the philosopher is no doubt wise, but would he himself be able to follow it if he had the youthful heart of Romeo? If not, "hang up philosophy!" [III. iii. 57]. Philosophy is for the old, not for the young, who must follow the law of love taught to them by their hearts. The sensitive members of the Elizabethan audience would have looked upon the participants of this dialogue with a double vision. They would have been able to see Romeo through the eyes of Friar Laurence as a "fond mad man" "with his own tears made drunk" [III. iii. 52, 83], one who violated all the familiar preachings of the moral philosophers and the divines by permitting his passion to overcome his reason. At the same time, responding sympathetically to Romeo's statement of the familiar idea that love has an irresistible power over youth, they would also have been able to see Friar Laurence through his eyes as an old man incapable of genuinely entering into the feelings of the young.

Moreover, Romeo expresses not merely the power of the love glorified in the novelle but also its rewards. Side by side with Friar Laurence's adjuration that immoderate love must come to speedy destruction is Romeo's assertion, a kind of dedication to love made immediately before the sacrament of marriage is performed:

> Come what sorrow can,
> It cannot countervail the exchange of joy
> That one short minute gives me in her sight:
> Do thou but close our hands with holy words,
> Then love-devouring death do what he dare;
> It is enough I may but call her mine.
>
> [II. vi. 3-8]

If such love brings sorrow and death, it is nevertheless worth it.

Friar Laurence's own image captures the ambivalent feeling toward Romeo and Juliet's love projected by the play:

> These violent delights have violent ends
> And in their triumph die, like fire and powder,
> Which as they kiss consume.
>
> [II. vi. 9-11]

If this love is destructive, it is also ecstatic. Taken in conjunction with "kiss", "die" suggests the consummation of the sexual act which is one of the Elizabethan meanings of the word. Such violent delight may be short-lived, but its completion is a "triumph", a word that means not only "rapturous delight" but "splendor" and "victory." . . . Burning one's candle at both ends. Edna St. Vincent Millay found, make a lovely light; by the same token, bringing fire and gunpowder together makes a splendid explosion. (pp. 382-83)

Destructive as their love for each other is to the lovers, through it providence is shown as working out its own ends. But before we can discuss this aspect of *Romeo and Juliet*, we must first look at the history of the concept that sexual love is a manifestation of the all-pervading love of God, through which the universe is governed. (p. 383)

*Act II. Scene iv. Nurse and Peter. The Department of Rare Books and Special Collections, The University of Michigan Library.*

In poems written in the courtly love tradition the praise of sexual love as a manifestation of God's creative energy is unqualified; in other works the praise of sexual love among human beings is restricted to love within marriage. Common to both, however, is the idea that a cosmic love, permeating the universe and finding expression in sexual love, works against the chaos which would otherwise prevail. . . . The power of love holds together the universe, which is constantly threatening to get out of order. It brings about universal and social harmony, reconciling the elements, which would otherwise be at war with each other, and doing the same for men.

It is with the operation of the cosmic love in society, in other human relations as well as in sexual love, that we are here concerned. Since God loves, says Chaucer in his invocation to Venus in the proem to Book Three of *Troilus and Criseyde,* He will not refuse love to others. Love, the source of all happiness, animates all living things in their seasons and among human beings holds together in unity realm and household. This concept of love as the bond holding together human society as well as the universe itself was also expressed during the Renaissance.

Thus in Barnaby Googe's *Zodiac of Life* . . . , there is a passage beginning with the statement of the traditional themes of the universality of love among all creatures, which feel "Cupids flame"; of "loues assured knot", but for which "the worlde should straight be at an end, and the elements decay"; of the "principle of replenishment" by which "the loue of God, that all doth guide", maintains everlasting order by continuing the species despite the death of individuals. It then exalts peace

as ministering to the universal fecundity: "In time of peace do all things growe, and all things liuely be." (pp. 383-84)

*Romeo and Juliet* dramatizes this concept of a cosmic love manifesting itself through sexual love and working against strife and disorder in society. The love of Romeo and Juliet is opposed to the hate of their parents. Although the lightning power of their love helps to bring about their destruction, it is, after all, only the hatred existing between the two houses that makes fatal the magnetic attraction toward each other of the two young lovers. As in Shakespearian tragedy generally, although the hero contributes to his own disaster, the main cause of it lies outside of him. The lovers may be imprudent, but the parents are guilty. The swift and violent passion of Romeo and Juliet is the answering force to their parents' furious and violent hate. Hate kills the lovers, but love, the love of heaven, redressing order and restoring concord through the love of Romeo and Juliet, triumphs over the hate which has endangered the peace of Verona. (p. 385)

Romeo and Juliet fulfil their adverse destiny, but it is a destiny which serves the purpose of divine providence. "A greater power than we can contradict", Friar Laurence tells Juliet, "Hath thwarted our intents" [V. iii. 153-54], and in recounting to the Prince what had happened he reiterates his faith in God's mysterious ways: "I entreated her come forth, / And bear this work of heaven with patience" [V. iii. 260-61]. His faith is justified by the conclusion. Romeo and Juliet are, as Capulet says, the "poor sacrifices" of their parents' enmity, the tragic scapegoats through whom their parents expiate the sin of their vengefulness. . . . The death of the lovers, says the Prince, acting as a moralizing epilogue, is the awful retribution of heaven upon their feuding families:

> Capulet, Montague,
> See what a scourge is laid upon your hate,
> That heaven finds means to kill your joys with love!
> [V. iii. 291-93]

His words are rich in significance, bearing a number of meanings dependent on different meanings of the word "love": (1) see how heaven finds means to kill your happiness, punishing you through the love of your children; (2) see how heaven finds means to kill your happiness, punishing you while loving you; (3) see how heaven finds means to kill your happiness, punishing you while destroying your hate through the force of cosmic love.

If, however, *Romeo and Juliet* makes use of the reconciliation between Cupid and God that had been effected by having Cupid act as a minister of God in maintaining social harmony, it also makes use of the ancient conflict between Cupid and God. Most critics have observed that the love of Romeo and Juliet is transcendent in death. They have not observed however, how the ideas of the religion of love are used to gain this effect, and they have not seen the tension that was resolved by this transcendence of love.

We have seen the prophetic force of Friar Laurence's warning in the lines quoted earlier; this warning, however, is concerned not only with what will happen to Romeo here on earth. It is concerned also with what will happen to him after death. . . . Friar Laurence speaks of damnation. "Desperate" connoted to Elizabethans despair, a heinous sin. To die in despair—and this is what is implied by the phrase "die miserable"—is to ensure perdition. In committing suicide Romeo would do "damnèd hate" upon himself because suicide is an act of self-hatred that is damnable. . . . Is this warning of damnation prophetic? This is the question that hangs heavy over the last act. It is answered only with Romeo's final speech.

The act begins with Romeo's telling of the happy dream he has had, in which Juliet, finding him dead, "breathed such life with kisses in my lips" that he "revived, and was an emperor" [V. i. 8-9]. This dream is ironically false in accordance with the folk belief that dreams go by contraries. In another sense, however, it is profoundly true, for, as we shall see, it signifies the coming triumph of the lovers over death.

Immediately after Romeo tells of his dream of death and re-awakening, he receives the fatal misinformation of Juliet's death. The exclamation that he utters is a contrast to his ex-clamation over the corpse of Tybalt. No longer does he pas-sively accept himself as "fortune's fool" [III. i. 136]. "Is it even so? then I defy, you, stars!" [V. i. 24]. With the quiet strength of this line Romeo attains tragic heroism. He is no longer the helpless plaything of Fortune since he can by a single act deprive her of her power over him. Totally committed to love, he chooses death. But is he a tragic hero eternally doomed? His defiance of the stars could be taken as a rejection of the destiny which God has fixed and which operates through the celestial constellations. In this view, the traditional Christian view, by not accepting Juliet's death as the will of God and by determining to commit self-slaughter, he is damned. It could also be taken, however, as the expression of superiority over earthly mutability of one who, like the Christian saints, is renouncing the world. In this view, the view of the religion of love, by going to join Juliet, he is achieving martyrdom and gaining the paradise of true lovers.

The first way of regarding Romeo is suggested by Balthasar's entreaty "Have patience" [V. i. 27], which echoes Friar Laur-ence's adjuration "Be patient" [III. iii. 16]. "Patience" con-notes the Christian fortitude in accepting the evil of this world as serving God's purposes that is best exemplified by the con-duct of Christ and the saints. But Romeo's calmness, as Bal-thasar realizes, is in reality a controlled frenzy of despair that is revealed in his wild looks and that impels him to commit violence upon himself. (pp. 387-89)

The second way of regarding Romeo is suggested by his words to the apothecary:

> There is thy gold, worse poison to men's souls,
> Doing more murders in this loathsome world,
> Than these poor compounds that thou mayst not sell.
> I sell thee poison; thou hast sold me none.
> Farewell: buy food, and get thyself in flesh.
>
> [V. i. 80-4]

The "loathsome world" is here contemned in orthodox *de contemptu mundi* [contempt of the world] terms. The haggard apothecary represents that wretched poverty driven to sinful envy and repining against its lot attacked by Chaucer's Man of Law in the prologue to his tale and personified in *Impatient Poverty*. "The world is not thy friend nor the world's law" [V. i. 72], Romeo tells him. But the desperate apothecary, unlike the desperate Romeo, comes to terms with the world. He accepts gold, which is so frequently associated in the mo-rality plays with the things of this world and opposed to the things of the spirit. "Get thyself in flesh", Romeo tells him with contemptuous pity, as he himself rejects the world and the flesh. (p. 389)

We have here something of the same paradox that underlies Donne's "The Canonization", in which Donne, following his

custom of giving old ideas new twists, presents himself and his mistress as "unworldly lovers, love's saints", who, "like the holy anchorite," "have given up the world" and "win a better world by giving up this one". This paradox was prepared for in the first act. In their playful exchange at their first meeting, Romeo had addressed Juliet as "saint" and Juliet had addressed Romeo as "pilgrim", and Romeo had continued to call Juliet "saint" throughout the balcony scene. Looking up to her from below the window, he had imagined her a bright angel. She was, indeed, marked to be one of Cupid's saints, a martyr of love, and Romeo, a pilgrim of love, in finding her had been initiated into love's mystery.

When Romeo, however, warns Paris not to prevent him from doing what he has to do, his language once more suggests the view that he is a Christian sinner rather than Cupid's saint:

> Good gentle youth, tempt not a desperate man. . . .
>            I beseech thee, youth,
> Put not another sin upon my head,
> By urging me to fury: O, be gone!
> By heaven, I love thee better than myself;
> Stay not, be gone; live, and hereafter say,
> A madman's mercy bade thee run away.
>
> [V. iii. 59, 61-4, 66-7]

Romeo indeed speaks in the manner of a madman proceeding upon his purposes in the grip of a fixed idea but able at the same time to look upon himself from the outside and to observe his irrational behavior. He realizes that he is about to commit a sin and begs not to be compelled to add the sin of murder to that of suicide. He has come armed against himself, ready to do "damnèd hate" against himself, but in the midst of his "madness" he has the compassion for Paris to warn him not to interfere. Again, as in the Tybalt scene, he speaks to his antagonist of his love for him—and again, on being provoked by him, gives way to fury.

But on hearing Paris' dying words, "If thou be merciful, / Open the tomb, lay me with Juliet" [V. iii. 72-3], Romeo wakes as from a feverish dream:

> What said my man, when my betossèd soul
> Did not attend him as we rode? I think
> He told me Paris should have married Juliet:
> Said he not so? or did I dream so?
>
> [V. iii. 76-9]

Although Romeo remains steadfast in his purpose, he no longer proceeds in a frenzy but with meditative deliberation. He clasps Paris' hand in friendship and compassionately grants him his request. Lover, beloved, and rejected rival are to be united in the grave in a general reconciliation. Tybalt, whom Romeo perceives in the tome, shares in the reconciliation: "Forgive me, cousin!" [V. ii. 101]. Love finally conquers in this scene in more than one sense.

For Romeo's suicide is a triumph over death and fate as well as a defeat. Throughout the play there had been intimations of the conclusion in the images of death as a bridegroom taking Juliet. But now Romeo, thinking Juliet dead, says:

> Ah, dear Juliet,
> Why are thou yet so fair? shall I believe
> That unsubstantial death is amorous,
> And that the lean abhorrèd monster keeps

Thee here in dark to be his paramour?
For fear of that, I still will stay with thee;
And never from this palace of dim night,
Depart again.

                                 [V. iii. 101-08]

Death the conqueror has "not conquered" Juliet [V. iii. 94], for her beauty remains intact. Now, united with his wife in the "bed of death" [V. iii. 28], Romeo will deprive the grim skeleton who would be her lover of his prize. He and Juliet are, as it were, wedded again in their mutual renunciation of life, with the "bed of death" their marital bed. (pp. 389-91)

Romeo's words concerning his and Juliet's reunion and everlasting triumph over death must have suggested to the Elizabethan audience the paradise of lovers of religion of love. . . . Romeo makes use of the image of the princely court which recurs in descriptions of the paradise of love: the vault is "a feasting presence full of light" [V. iii. 86], the brilliantly lit presence chamber used by kings for state occasions. In the "palace of dim night" of the Capulet vault, it is intimated, Romeo is to be an emperor, as he has dreamed, with Juliet his ever-radiant bride. (p. 391)

Thus Shakespeare exploited imaginatively the concept of the lovers' paradise to further a feeling of reconciliation. This feeling of reconciliation, as we have seen, is also ministered to by a sense of the richness of the lives of Romeo and Juliet, brief as they were, by a sense of the inevitability of the catastrophe, given the reckless abandon of the lovers in their situation, and by the larger perception that their disastrous fate serves the end of providence. The feeling of reconciliation and indeed of exaltation at the close of the play does not, however, cause us to forget the tragic fact of the death of the two young people who have so deeply engaged our sympathies. For the glorification of the love of Romeo and Juliet involves a basic acceptance of this world, that acceptance which is necessary if suffering and death are to be tragically meaningful. (pp. 391-92)

> *Paul N. Siegel, "Christianity and the Religion of Love in 'Romeo and Juliet,'" in* Shakespeare Quarterly, *Vol. XII, No. 4, Autumn, 1961, pp. 371-92.*

## JOHN LAWLOR (essay date 1961)

[*Lawlor disagrees with the interpretation of* Romeo and Juliet *as either a "tragedy of fortune" or a "tragedy of character," relating it instead to what he calls the medieval* tragedie, *a literary form popular during the Middle Ages which depicts the protagonist as a victim of "forces beyond his control" who nonetheless recognizes a greater good beyond this world as a result of his sufferings. According to Lawlor, Shakespeare's* Romeo and Juliet *is an extension of this literary form, in that the lovers do not merely surrender to their destiny, as in the medieval* tragedie, *but willingly accept it and, therefore, triumph over death. In light of this reading, the critic considers the maturation of the hero and heroine in* Romeo and Juliet *a significant point, a process he states is best exemplified in the language of the lovers, which grows more and more to accommodate contradiction, paradox, and ambiguity, transforming the world and incapacitating time.*]

It is perhaps impossible to approach any play of Shakespeare's without strong, if latent, preconception; and this may be especially so with his first major incursion into tragedy. *Romeo and Juliet* is not Shakespeare's first attempt at tragic writing; but it is the first of his plays to excite and sustain any deep concern with humanity in the ills that befall it. This concern, however, it appears to be generally held, is other than that evoked by later tragedies; and since in them we have an insistent probing of the connections between what men are and what may befall them, it is easy to make a distinction between the tragedy of fortune and the tragedy of character; and, referring the first to a medieval inheritance, find in *Romeo and Juliet* an experiment, in greater or less degree unsuccessful, towards a second and greater mode. It is in these terms that G. I. Duthie, an editor of the *New Cambridge Shakespeare*, introduces the play [see excerpt above, 1953]. The feud between Montague and Capulet is 'quite unconvincing'; Fate is thus 'nothing more important than a matter of sheer bad luck'; and the protagonists have 'weaknesses of character' (principally a lack of 'mature poise and balance') which are yet not related to their doom. In this Duthie follows two principal critics, H. Charlton in the first point and D. Stauffer in the second [see excerpts above, 1948 and 1949]. 'What we actually have then,' he concludes, 'is a drama of Fate involving the destruction of two innocent victims who have defects of character which are not properly worked into the pattern.' . . . *Romeo and Juliet* may yet appear to be saved by its poetry: Shakespeare, though lacking a true 'grasp of the foundations of tragedy' [Charlton] is 'totally successful' in expressing the triumph of a love over which 'Death has no power' [Duthie]. It is a fair expression of the majority view: the dramatist has failed 'to convey a certain great tragic conception (which points forward to his maturity)'; and Duthie localizes that failure in an imperfect relation between the story of the two lovers, as embodying 'a certain well-known traditional conception of tragedy', and the story of the two families which prompts 'quite another conception of tragedy—a more deeply satisfying conception'. Much, evidently, depends on certain assumptions about the tragic. It will be best to begin with the 'traditional conception' inherited by the Elizabethan.

Medieval tragedy—it may make for clarity if it is called hereafter *tragedie*—is perhaps more often understood in terms of its characteristic working than its final effect. It is as though criticism of the more familiar kind if tragedy were to fasten wholly upon its mechanism—the 'passions' that 'spin the plot'—and ignore its distinctive effect upon the spectator. That effect is one in which apparent opposites are reconciled; a balance is struck between pity and terror, the logic of events and whatever we may mean by an inscrutable Fate—'the necessary' as opposed to 'the probable'. There is an end of any merely mechanistic notion (a quasi-causal relation between what men are and what may befall them) and, at the same time, of a wholly inscrutable Fate. It is a dual perception, affirming a system as finally mysterious while revealing it in part of its ordered working. Against this, *tragedie* is, from one point of view, less complex; it calls forth no dual perception, for it needs none. Its central truth is that Fortune knows nothing of human deserving. But her activities are not, in the end, inscrutable; for those who are minded to learn, a greater good is in prospect. Similarly, on the level of 'plot'—the sequence of events in the external world—*tragedie* may be said to have beginning and end, but no distinctive middle. The beginning is in 'prosperitee', a happiness unshadowed by imminent reversal; the end in apparent disaster, as unalterable as unpredictable. The formula, then, is simple; but the experience available to us in these terms is a more complex matter. It is certainly not 'profoundly pessimistic', as Duthie, following a general persuasion, would have us believe. Fortune's 'delight' in her operations is the illusion of the sufferer, clinging to his belief in a retributive justice and protesting, like Chaucer's Troilus, 'I have it nat deserved'. . . . [It] is in fact this universal misunderstanding of Fortune's operations which *tragedie* exists to challange, and to alter. When disaster has come in *tragedie*, we find man lamenting as uncovenanted the harm that has befallen him. . . . But the tragic design puts a period to fruitless lament: we may rise to an understanding that

> All is best, though we oft doubt,
> What th' unsearchable dispose
> Of highest wisdom brings about,
> And ever best found in the close.

The 'close' of *tragedie* enables the spectator to look beyond a limited time of inexplicable suffering to a happiness beyond time's reach. In the close, we, like Troilus, repair 'home'; another dimension of time, an eternal present, is entered upon in *tragedie*. . . . (pp. 123-25)

The aerial ascent of Troilus's spirit in the close of Chaucer's poem is appropriate to this order of exalted vision. It is the definitive experience of *tragedie*, corresponding to the *katharsis* of nemesis-type tragedy. Where such tragedy returns us to the real world, *tragedie* takes us beyond it. The important consideration is that the one is not an imperfect form of the other; where causal connection interests the Greek, what absorbs the medieval mind is the absence of a rationale in any terms less than an unsearchable Divine wisdom. Refused all proximate solutions, we must confront man as the patient of forces beyond his control. Through lesser disasters we are drawn to a greater good; and this, so far from being pessimistic, can touch the deeps of happiness—the landfall long postponed, and lately despaired of, is at last in view. . . . We shall go very far astray if we think of the 'tragedy of fortune' as pessimistic in giving an apparent victory to Death. Its distinctive capacity is in fact the awakening to understanding of a greater good. Not all the feeble *exempla* of mere reversal, the turning of her wheel by the strumpet Fortune, should distract us from this distinctive capacity of *tragedie* in the hands of a master-poet. (pp. 125-26)

That Death has no final power over the lovers of *Romeo and Juliet* is therefore not 'an impression' differing from 'the tragic design that Shakespeare obviously intended to produce' [Duthie]. Whatever may be discoverable about Shakespeare's intentions, it is wholly consistent with *tragedie* that out of evil comes not good merely but a greater good. What we see in the close of *Romeo and Juliet* is not simply a renewal of a pattern disturbed, but its re-ordering; life is not continued merely; it is regenerated. Only thus do we experience the quality of a 'Beauty too rich for use, for earth too dear' [I. v. 47]. It is earth, the realm of Fortune, that is the loser. We see it as 'unworthy' of the lovers, a world of 'less generous passions' [see the essay by Geoffrey Bullough cited in the Additional Bibliography]; so this love is placed, fittingly, at once beyond reach and beyond change. Shakespeare, in this at least, has not broken with but rather has reaffirmed the distinctive quality of *tragedie*. (p. 127)

The feud between Montague and Capulet is certainly introduced to us in undignified terms. Parallel with the vulgar delight of a serving-man in his master's quarrel is the senile eagerness of Capulet calling for his 'long sword', testily answered by his wife, 'A crutch, a crutch!' 'Old Montague', we are told, 'flourishes his blade in spite of me' [I. i. 75, 76, 77-78]. It is the very language of childish pique; and the foolishness of the whole proceeding is appropriately berated by the Prince. . . . But before the feud itself is dismissed as 'all . . . rather trivial, rather silly' [Duthie] we must place it in its full setting. There is not only the commonplace brawling of the servants and the

undignified caperings of the old men; there is also Tybalt's grim acceptance of the feud, and Mercutio's valiantly embracing it. We shall refer to the play of coincidence below; for the moment, the bearing of the feud on 'Fate' calls for some consideration. Romeo, we see, is placed in a world of untroubled assumptions; and it is these which, defining his situation, become the unalterable constraints upon him when he would pass beyond them. Thus, as to the point of honour, the behaviour expected of a young Montague, Romeo stands between the murderous Tybalt and the chivalrous Mercutio. It is a situation like that of Hamlet, opposed to the unhesitating vengefulness of Laertes, and put to shame at the sight of the honourable Fortinbras, whose example teaches what it is 'Rightly to be great' [*Hamlet*, IV. iv. 53]. At the turning-point for Romeo—as for Hamlet—the revenge code exacts obedience. But it is important not to mistake the desperate quality of Romeo's action. It is certainly not the dignified self-possession which we could infer from some critical accounts:

> Alive, in triumph! and Mercutio slain!
> Away to heaven, respective lenity,
> And fire-eyed fury be my conduct now! . . .
>
> [III. i. 122-24]

Romeo's is an honourable part, in taking it upon himself to requite a death incurred on his behalf. But the hot blood cannot be gainsaid; the rant of the revenge theme, though made appropriate to an honourable avenger, is still in sharpest contrast to the mild speech of the first encounter between Romeo and Tybalt; and now Romeo takes occasion to requite the insult ('villain') he had himself received. Romeo is indeed 'Fortune's fool': as his love for Juliet had raised him to a height far above 'respective lenity' (Capulet had been a name to tender as dearly as his own) so now he sinks—not to the level merely of the revenge-code, but to an offence against the Prince's law, a 'bandying in Verona streets' [III. i. 89]. Shakespeare has certainly made the feud undignified; but we must not miss the real point of its being so. After the first scene, with the Prince's angry intervention, 'honourable' courses can mean only public brawling. To say that Romeo disposes of Tybalt 'in the name of all that is manly and honest' [Peter Alexander, in his *A Shakespeare Primer*] is to ignore the higher understanding that had come to Romeo; and this, too, we must observe in its full setting.

The love which prompts this understanding in Romeo is a new thing in the world of the play. It differs, most obviously, from his own conventional passion for Rosaline and from Mercutio's light-hearted sensuality. But it differs, too, from everything else we see in Verona where 'love' is in question—from the attitudes of a masterful father; a match-making mother; a match-approving and therefore variable Nurse; a managing Friar, concerned to minimize risk and promote reconciliation; even—perhaps most of all—from the affections of a simple and likeable suitor, Paris. Every commentator has noticed that Shakespeare's Juliet is even younger than the Juliet of Brooke's poem. If we are to speak of maturity and immaturity, we must not fail to notice the decisive turning, in both Romeo and Juliet, away from the 'mature' viewpoints of all around them, to a new thing. The point of characterization will concern us below: for the moment, we must observe that whatever may be said of the opposition of the stars, the Fate which 'so enviously debars' this love is plainly evident in a world where love is known to the bystanders as many things—all different from the experience of love as we see it in the two central figures. In this respect at least *Romeo and Juliet* is true to a cardinal principal of Shakespearian drama—it might almost be called the authenticating mark of his authorship. Whatever is profoundly true (true in that mystery of things which the drama in part reveals) is always literally true, true in terms of unalterable human disposition. It is not merely that the one answers as a deeper echo to the other, the operations of a mysterious Fate giving an authoritative significance to mortal acts and entanglements. It is rather that, seeing more clearly into humanity we perceive both its unchanging limits and its incalculable possibilities; so that Fate and Chance become significant terms.

To this end, an initial 'immaturity' in the lovers is essential. In both we meet youth on the hither side of experience; and in Romeo, entirely subject to a hopeless love, we may see the false maturity in which all youthful inexperience would hide itself. Certainly, when we have heard his declaration of woeful love ('Mis-shapen chaos of well-seeming forms') we can echo his declaration: 'This is not Romeo, he's some other where' [I. i. 179, 198]. But when we see Romeo in torment at Friar Lawrence's cell (III. iii) we are not to assume that the antithetical flights in which he laments the sentence of banishment are a return to the first Romeo. His outcry parallels, as Miss Mahood has noted [see excerpt above, 1957], that in the preceding scene, where Juliet has fought against the belief that Romeo is slain; each episode must be placed among Shakespeare's 'first attempts to reveal a profound disturbance of mind by the use of quibbles.' . . . This is an 'immaturity' in the lovers, if we will; but it is also the dramatist's means of showing us the inadequacy of settled and ordered language . . . to deal with the bewildering reversals in which Romeo and Juliet find themselves. If the Friar must persist in speaking of what he cannot 'feel', this is the only language that the sufferers themselves can find to meet the first impact of disaster:

> Hath Romeo slain himself? Say thou but 'I',
> And that bare vowel 'I' shall poison more
> Than the death-darting *eye* of cockatrice:
> *I* am not *I,* if there be such an *I.* . . .
>
> [III. ii. 45-8]

Juliet's tormented iteration is perfectly consonant with Romeo's own anguish:

> Flies may do this, but I from this must fly. . . .
>
> [III. iii. 41]

It is a language which, embracing contradiction, is truer to reality than the single standpoints expressed by Nurse and Friar. (pp. 131-33)

Romeo, like Hamlet, is young, gifted, sensitive—and all but unequal to a situation which he cannot change. It is essential to our understanding that we see him grow from these beginnings to a final maturity which outsoars all else in the play. The gentleness proffered to Tybalt appears to Mercutio 'calm, dishonourable, vile submission' [III. i. 73], but it is a profounder quality than any yielding to 'honour's' demands. It is matched by the first forbearance shown to Paris at the tomb—

> By heaven, I love thee better than myself;
> For I come hither arm'd against myself—
>
> [V. iii. 64-5]

and by the noble epitaph for a fallen opponent seen as a fellow-victim,

> One writ with me in sour misfortune's book.
>
> [V. iii. 82]

Romeo has come to a maturity that is but a short time distant from his lying 'on the ground, with his own tears made drunk' [III. iii. 83]. These young lovers . . . grow to a final forgetfulness of self, Romeo obeys the Nurse's bidding to 'be a man' [III. iii. 88]: but the course taken by both the lovers is other than any the Nurse and the Friar can foresee in their concern with practical arrangements. . . . These two children, as the managing adults of their world see them, are, truly, innocents abroad. But they are quick to learn; in Romeo's attempted consolation of Juliet at their final leave-taking (III. v) we see the beginning of maturity in the man, while Juliet's improvised but spirited dissimulation of her true feelings (when reproved for grief by her mother [III. v.]) is evidence of her purpose, growing in its turn. Their love has been truly consummated; in the exchanges before parting there is a sharing of the burden of consolation. To this effect the earlier immaturity of the lovers is essential. We are to feel the prematurity of their love, their response to demands thrust upon them ahead of the ordinary process of time. (pp. 133-35)

The relation of the lovers' youth and thus unformed character to the process of time is vital, for it involves the great and challenging contrast between age without maturity and youth called to premature 'estate' (to use Friar Lawrence's word). The paradoxical, conceited poetry with which we begin—a poetry appropriate to 'immature' love, if we will—is essential to our understanding of the ends to which the lovers drive; for in that love-poetry the Elizabethan imagination had hitherto made its most frequent contact with the antithesis of change and permanence. It is, peculiarly, the subject of Renaissance poetry as a whole; for who but the poet can bind time—in the very act of declaring time's apparent victories? And for the dramatist, time is not so much a 'subject' as his essential medium. Before the play is done, the conventional antitheses of young love give place to 'the finest poetry which had yet been heard on the English stage' [see the essay by Kenneth Muir cited in the Additional Bibliography]. (p. 135)

The paradoxical nature of Elizabethan love-poetry is, as more than one critic has noted, peculiarly adaptable to a drama of sudden alternations. Thus, Bullough observes that Shakespeare 'modulates from the public to the private theme' when he 'makes Romeo's conventional passion express itself in contradictions and paradoxes suited to the pattern of the whole play.' . . . It is a fruitful remark. We may study these contradictions and paradoxes, evident in Shakespeare's general handling of his source-material, under several heads: as, contrast of tempo; the play of coincidence; and the conquering of all-conquering time (where, especially, the 'conceits' of traditional poetry are important). Only the outstanding instances can be noticed here; and we must add that the remarkable achievement in this early play is not the managing of striking moments but the unity of the whole. We have, in the end, to consider a balance which subsumes all antitheses.

The onward drive of events that concern the lovers, as against the slower pace of a world going about its habitual business—so that the nine months' action of Brooke's *Tragicall Historye* is crowded into a few days—is nowhere clearer than in the handling of the first three scenes of the play. As Bullough notes, by the end of I. iii both Romeo and Juliet are going to the ball—'one to see the woman he thinks he loves; the other to see . . . the man her parents want her to love. Both are soon to change.' . . . The second great instance of time-alteration is, of course, the brawl taking place between the marriage and its consummation (instead of 'a month or twain' afterwards).

It is an alteration which deepens a fundamental difference from Brooke's lovers. Their living together in clandestine happiness risks the reader's sympathy. . . . Shakespeare's Romeo and Juliet must consummate their marriage in the knowledge that the morning brings separation; and, as we have seen, the time that had moved too slowly now hastens against them, just as the coming of light in the world outside brings only darkness to the lovers in their private world. . . . (pp. 135-37)

The play of coincidence may be seen most clearly in the alterations that lead to the brawl and thus the banishment of Romeo and all that follows from it. Mercutio plays no part in the brawl in *The Tragicall Historye*. There it is a general encounter which Romeus, summoned by the uproar, endeavours to stop; and even when attacked by Tybalt he refuses to return the blow, appealing for Tybalt's 'helpe these folke to parte'. Only when Tybalt strikes again does Romeus slay him. That Shakespeare's Romeo is unable to stop a duel between Tybalt and Mercutio—for the code of honour is common ground between them—defines, as we have seen, his unique position. But that in the end we are back at worse than the beginning—the Mercutio who had avenged a laggard Romeo must himself be avenged—illustrates as nothing else could the turning of Fortune's wheel. It is futility upon futility, and Shakespeare has made accident—Romeo's entering upon the scene and then his thrusting between the contestants—play the decisive part. . . . [Shakespeare] knows when to make coincidence beautifully exact: as, the entire naturalness of Juliet meeting Paris at Friar Lawrence's cell, when she has come there to seek a means of escaping marriage with him; or the father's natural delight in her apparent submission which causes him to advance the date of the wedding—so that Friar Lawrence, that exponent of 'Wisely and slow', must act in haste, while for Juliet there can be no postponement of decision; and, in the end, the coming of Paris to the tomb, which ratifies in death a love as disinterested as Romeo's own, bringing a worthy guest to a vault made 'a feasting presence full of light' [V. iii. 86].

Shakespeare's wordplay gives us the most direct approach to that conquering of time which is at the play's centre. The ambiguities which we may be tempted to pass over as mere conceits have their own contribution to make. Thus, Romeo's language in the orchard at sight of Juliet 'above' plays delightedly with the impossible, that which is contrary to nature:

> her eyes in heaven
> Would through the airy region stream so bright
> That birds would sing and think it were not night.
>
> [II. ii. 20-2]

It is a passage which, as Miss Mahood has noted, is parallel with Juliet's apostrophe to night:

> Give me my Romeo; and, when he shall die,
> Take him and cut him out in little stars,
> And he will make the face of heaven so fine
> That all the world will be in love with night
> And pay no worship to the garish sun.
>
> [III. ii. 21-5]

The love of Romeo and Juliet is in fact to transform the world they live in—but only when the order of time is not arrested or inverted but made powerless. That Death has no final power over the lovers is the great truth to which we are directed by their own rapturous hyperboles and by the central fact of their love, its freedom from any taint of the merely clandestine—which derives immediately from its swiftness and brevity. . . . In the 'fearful passage' of this 'death-mark'd love' we can

therefore see and accept apparent opposites; and this acceptance is required from the outset, where both 'fearful' and 'death-mark'd' mean, not only 'pathetic' and 'doomed', but also 'terrifying' and 'deathward bound', journeying to Death as to a destination [Mahood].

In this, *Romeo and Juliet* fulfills an essential condition of all experience which warrants the term 'tragic', no matter what the special design and scope of the tragic form attempted. Whether 'tragedy' of *tragedie* in the major distinction discussed earlier, all must turn on the spectator perceiving not one meaning preponderating over its opposite, but both present, the more vividly for their interaction, in an experience where understanding can be full since intervention, the imaginative taking of sides, is totally inhibited. In tragedy of the causal-connective kind, opposites are transcended in an experience which is accepted as 'thus, and only thus' in its working. In *tragedie* these ordinary opposites yield before a greater good. The situation that we encounter in *Romeo and Juliet* is big with promise in the Shakespearian imagination—man caught in a world that tolerates no questions, knowing only reasons for actions. . . . *Romeo and Juliet*, like *Richard II*, offers a meeting-place of the old *tragedie* of ineluctable doom and a newer thing—the plain truth that man will not willingly relinquish his transitory happiness. . . . The tragedy must drive to man's dispossession, his being 'eased With being nothing' [*Richard II*, V. v. 40-1]; but then we may see a final triumph. The real significance of 'character' in such a drama is not in terms of 'flaws', nor in any more general emphasis upon casual connection (as the 'impetuosity' of the lovers in *Romeo and Juliet*). It is rather in the intensity of contrast between initial immaturity and the prematurity forced upon the protagonists. In that light we see man confronting and in the end dominating the ends to which he is brought—not by a fighting withdrawal but by accepting and going to meet his destiny. The 'ripeness' or readiness, especially as it is manifest between fellow-sufferers in the bond of love, is all. If that tie holds, Death is robbed of the greater glory; the ending is triumph, a transcending the limits of mortality by holding fast, in a union of suffering, to what is best in the mortal condition.

If this is the shape of tragedy in some early works of Shakespeare, including *Romeo and Juliet*, what status shall we accord it in the whole body of Shakespearian insights? In *A Midsummer Night's Dream*, following hard upon *Romeo and Juliet*, the story of Pyramus and Thisbe affords 'very tragical mirth'. The 'concord of this discord' [V. i. 60] is to be found in belated reconciliation, with Bottom starting up from the grave to assure us that

> the wall is down that parted their fathers.
> [*A Midsummer Night's Dream*, V. i. 351-52]

Does Shakespeare's mature vision, in comedy and tragedy alike, leave aside the striking fiction of reconciliation purchased by death, to dwell upon the sober truth that

> Love, friendship, charity, are subjects all
> To envious and calumniating time?
> [*Troilus and Cressida*, III. iii. 173-74]
>                                                                      (pp. 137-40)

If we seek the line of development from *Romeo and Juliet* we may find it not in the later tragedies but in the antitype of *tragedie*, those last plays of Shakespeare where the scope of accident includes the truth of fortunate accident, so that ancient wrongs are righted and the old make way for newness of life in the young; where fulfilment is achieved in this world and not in a region beyond the stars, even death itself being can-celled and the exile returned to his native land; where all, in fine, is subject to a Time which is not envious or calumniating but, joining with mortal designs, 'Goes upright with his car-riage' [*The Tempest*, V. i. 3]. . . . [In] both *Romeo and Juliet* and the last plays there is evident an Elizabethan poet's sense of paradox, of inherent impossibility only to be cancelled when love is triumphant. Romeo's boast—'love-devouring death do what he dare . . .' [II. vi. 7]—and Juliet's defiance of time are not tragic errors. They are not less than statements of the incompatibility between man and time when man would reach beyond time. We must not let our preconceptions blind us to the real drift and emphasis in Shakespeare, more particularly when there are involved ideas of drama and poetry with which we are relatively unfamiliar. That theme of reconciliation which is strongest and most constant of all in Shakespeare has a higher place in the Elizabethan imagination than we ordinarily may be prepared to allow.

The poetry which, in tragedy and romance alike, expresses these values, is fully charged with oblique meaning. Shake-speare's Friar Lawrence expatiating on the properties of herbs goes beyond the text Brooke has written for him, a simple discourse upon the right and wrong uses of knowledge, to the nature of man, himself the subject of contending forces of 'grace and rude will' [II. ii. 28]. In doing so, Friar Lawrence speaks more than he knows. His herbs will, in the event, lie in no separate and opposed categories; but, like the Apothe-cary's poison, they will at once heal and destroy. Friar Law-rence's is a world of firmly distinct properties. In this he is like Perdita of *The Winter's Tale*, another who discourses upon Nature's gifts of the earth: and it is a similar irony that the case for crossing these categories, by grafting different stocks, is something Perdita indignantly refuses while it is yet the destiny to which she must be brought, in a final order of reconciliation where all distinction between natural and arti-ficial disappears in an art which 'itself is nature' [*The Winter's Tale*, IV. iv. 97]. For the true placing of *Romeo and Juliet* we must look to Shakespeare's whole development, including those romances which offer a final check to any merely 'connective' drama; and which, allowing a free play of apparent opposites, exhibit the full context in which we are to place Elizabethan exploration of what man is and what may befall him. Shake-speare's course is not simple, but it is distinctive. Rejecting the stereotype of cruel Fortune's blows—man as merely the weak subject of heaven's stratagems—he reinvests *tragedie* with the sense of greater good. But it is a profound fidelity to the fact which places the attainment of that good on the further side of life. Man must be forcibly dispossessed before he can discover a power of bearing it out even to the edge of doom. Love is then transcendent, itself a 'Beauty too rich for use, for earth too dear' [I. v. 47]. Manifestly, such a climax is a triumph of poetic drama; the lovers outsoar the shadow of our night. The last act of this play, standing on the eve of the tragic sequence that begins with *Julius Caesar*, is surpassed in in-tensity only by the close of *Antony and Cleopatra*, where that sequence ends. But there, as here, we see that the drama is dependent on no mere fiction. The lovers purchase a final unity at the only true cost; and it is a cost exacted from them by the onward drive of events. If we can lay aside our preconceived notions alike of the 'tragedy of character' and the 'tragedy of fortune' we may see that *Romeo and Juliet* is profoundly con-sistent with the longer run of the Shakespearian imagination. (pp. 141-43)

John Lawlor, " 'Romeo and Juliet'," in Early Shake-speare, *Stratford-Upon-Avon Studies, No. 3*, Edward Arnold (Publishers) Ltd., 1961, pp. 123-44.

## NORMAN N. HOLLAND (essay date 1963)

[*Holland offers a psychoanalytic interpretation of the dream re-lated by Romeo in Act V, Scene i. Acknowledging the problems inherent in analyzing the invented dreams of literature, Holland deciphers Romeo's dream at various levels of meaning, noting the common element of wish-fulfillment at each level. For ex-ample, he emphasizes how the dream enables Romeo to overcome his separation from Juliet; how it rewards his romantic behavior by making him an "emperor," while in real life such behavior made him "a stateless outcast"; how it provides him with the power of a father-emperor he so obviously lacked in Verona; and, at its deepest level of sexual meaning, how it endows Romeo with unlimited sexual ability and transforms his impending death into a new birth. Holland adds, however, that such a reading of Ro-meo's dream would remain mere "psychological curio" if we cannot apply it in an assessment of the play as a whole. This he does by emphasizing the role of dreams and dreaming in* Romeo and Juliet *and by pointing out the motif of reversal uniting all the elements of the drama. The essay excerpted below was originally published in 1963.*]

"Invented dreams can be interpreted in the same way as real ones." That statement of Freud's seems natural enough, I sup-pose, once we have gotten used to the idea of a continuum between the making of dreams in sleep and the processes of waking creativity. Yet, from a literary point of view, it remains an astonishing statement. A real dream preserves sleep, ex-presses a wish, and fulfills it in fantasy; its form and content are biologically and psychologically determined in the mind of the dreamer. A dream in literature, however, serves typically to give a prophecy or insight, to introduce a symbol or theme, or any of a dozen purposes quite alien to those of a real dream. Unlike a real dream, an invented dream is determined not by the wishes of the "dreamer," or only secondarily and indirectly so, but by the author's imagination. Yet, Freud insists, invented dreams can be interpreted like real ones—as though a realism forced itself willy-nilly on a writer once he decided to invent a dream for one of his characters, surely a very odd idea. (p. 43)

One of the least conspicuous of the invented dreams in literature is Romeo's three-line recounting of a dream just before he learns of Juliet's supposed death. A tidy little dream, it raises precisely the question of realism involved. That is, *Romeo and Juliet* is a highly stylized play, not formally realistic (in Ian Watt's sense) like a modern novel . . . where an invented dream would indeed be likely to resemble a real one. Rather, *Romeo and Juliet* gives us a pair of teen-agers capable of composing (jointly!) an impromptu sonnet as they meet. It is hardly likely so talented a poet as Romeo would content himself with a mere ordinary dream. He tells it, in any case, in iambic pentameters, and few psychoanalysts, I expect, are lucky enough to have such poetic patients.

Nevertheless, according to Freud, we can consider such a dream realistically. To do so, however, we will need to know its background. We must establish both the context in which the dreamer dreamed the dream and a timetable of the events which may appear in it as day-residue.

Considered realistically, our dreamer finds himself in a cultural situation which puts a premium on aggressive, hostile behavior. The cultural group with which he is most closely identified is preoccupied with sex, but rather as a topic for amusement, as something fit for servants, crude, low, funny. Romeo is exactly and squarely on the outs with this cultural pattern. A rather dreamy character, he seems to care only for romantic love, not for the fighting, quarreling, and fornication which are the local amusements in Verona. And his friends, Benvolio and Mercutio, and his mentor, Friar Laurence, ridicule and criticize him for this dreamy, romantic quality.

Romeo dreamed the dream in question on a Tuesday night. As of Sunday morning, he was in love with Rosaline, who, unfortunately for him, had taken a vow of chastity. Sunday night, he crashed the Capulets' party where he met Juliet and promptly fell in love with her. Knowing that their families would disapprove of the match, he and Juliet plan to marry secretly the next day, Monday. They do so, but on his way home from this secret marriage ceremony, Monday afternoon, Romeo fails to avoid a fight with one of his wife's relatives, kills him, and as a result is banished. He stays around long enough, however, to consummate the marriage on Monday night, and he makes his getaway Tuesday morning.

On Tuesday night, he has this dream:

> If I may trust the flattering truth of sleep,
> My dreams presage some joyful news at hand:
> My bosom's lord sits lightly in his throne;
> And all this day an unaccustom'd spirit
> Lifts me above the ground with cheerful thoughts.
> *I dreamt my lady came and found me dead;*
> Strange dream, that gives a dead man leave to think!
> *And breath'd such life with kisses in my lips,*
> *That I reviv'd, and was an emperor.*
> Ah me! how sweet is love itself possess'd,
> When but love's shadows are so rich in joy!
>
> [V. i. 1-11]

At this point his servant turns up, and Romeo cries:

> News from Verona! How now, Balthasar!
> Dost thou not bring me letters from the friar?
> How doth my lady? Is my father well?
> How fares my Juliet?
>
> [V. i. 12-15]

Balthasar tells him of Juliet's supposed death, and, after one more request, "Hast thou no letters to me from the friar?" Romeo resolves—

> Well, Juliet, I will lie with thee tonight.
> Let's see for means: O mischief! thou art swift
> To enter in the thoughts of desperate men.
> I do remember an apothecary, . . .
>
> [V. i. 34-7]

And the tragedy proceeds to its medicinal catastrophe.

The normal way to interpret a dream is through the dreamer's free associations, but in trying to interpret an invented dream, we, of course, cannot have Romeo's associations. In such a case, Freud . . . suggests, "We shall have to content ourselves with referring to his impressions, and we may very tentatively put our associations in place of his." Dr. Robert Fliess in *The Revival of Interest in the Dream* notes that an analyst can contribute, independently of the dreamer's associating, two elements to the interpretation of a dream: (1) associations known to the analyst which the dreamer—for whatever reason—may not supply; (2) the interpretation of symbolism.

Romeo's dream seems to have almost all the properties a dream could have. For one thing, it is prophetic, but in a special way. As any good Elizabethan could have told Romeo, the "flattering truth of sleep" is likely to be just that. Since Romeo has had a joyful dream, he should be on the lookout for trouble, but Romeo is foolish in this as in most other things; and, in Act V, we find him drinking the poison he has bought from

the apothecary—he dies, saying, "Thus with a kiss I die" [V. iii. 120], an exact reversal of the dream. And Juliet, when she wakes up in the tomb, tries to kiss poison from Romeo's lips, another reversal of the dream-image in which she breathed life into his lips.

The dream is also a wish-fulfillment in the most simple, direct sense. That is, the dream enables Romeo to have Juliet with him, instead of her being in Verona while he is in Mantua. The dream makes him an important, powerful man—an emperor—who would outrank not only the two fathers whose enmity has interfered with his love, but also the Prince who has banished him. The dream is a wish-fulfillment in yet another sense: it is precisely because of his romantic behavior that Romeo becomes an emperor (Juliet breathes "*such life*" in his lips "that I revived and was an emperor"), a reversal of the real situation where it is precisely Romeo's romantic love that has turned him into a stateless outcast. The dream is also a sleep-preserving dream in the sense that it gives a substitute awakening ("I revived and was an emperor") instead of letting Romeo actually wake up from what must be quite disturbing dream-thoughts: the dread of his death, the separation from Juliet, thoughts of his own helpless situation. (pp. 44-6)

Freud suggests that the emperor in a dream is likely to symbolize the father, which entitles us to guess that the new life which Romeo takes involves some kind of identification with the father or replacing of him. Perhaps, in view of the fact that Romeo has just consummated his marriage, there is a wish quite literally to do what fathers do. Yet, we should remember that both the women Romeo loves during the course of the play, Rosaline and Juliet, are taboo—Rosaline because she has taken a vow of chastity; Juliet because she is a Capulet. It would seem that Romeo is drawn to women who are forbidden to him, either by a vowed-to God or his father's feud. In this context, Romeo's being found dead in the dream becomes the price he pays for equaling or becoming his father, for his relationship with Juliet, for having—and being had by—a forbidden woman.

Yet his being dead is a price both paid and unpaid by the dream, for "I revived." In terms of associations, Romeo's first thought when his servant arrives is of the friar, whom Romeo usually calls in the play "My ghostly father," "holy father" [II. iii. 45; IV. i. 37]. Further, once this servant has told him of Juliet's death, Romeo has a real "free association."

> Let's see for means: O mischief! thou art swift
> To enter in the thoughts of desperate men.
> I do remember an apothecary. . . .
>
> [V. i. 35-7]

In the context of the play as a whole, the apothecary is an "unholy father," the friar's opposite number: both men are poor; both are associated with herbs; each gives a lover "poison." In effect, Romeo, after he has recounted the dream, submits himself to these two fathers (as well as his real one: "Is my father well?" he asks his servant). Before recounting the dream, he has said, "My bosom's lord sits lightly in his throne." "Bosom's lord" literally means the heart (or perhaps Cupid), but the phrasing "lord" hints (like "emperor") at a father—the heart as "king of the organs." In effect, before recounting the dream, Romeo had shaken off his father; the dream enabled him to wear his father's domination "lightly," he having, through his dreamed death, paid (and unpaid) the price of sexually "becoming a man."

Freud points out that "judgments made *after waking* upon a dream that has been remembered, and the feelings called up in us by the reproduction of such a dream, form part, to a great extent, of the latent content of the dream and are to be included in its interpretation." In this dream, Romeo interrupts his account of it to comment that it is a "strange dream." He speaks of it beforehand as "the flattering truth of sleep" and afterward as "love's shadows." Freud suggests that when we come across this kind of discounting or ridicule of one's own dream, it leads back to a motif of criticism or ridicule in the dream-thoughts. And Romeo had indeed been criticized and ridiculed for being a romantic, dreamy individual (most notably by Mercutio, but also by Benvolio and his parents). The dream reverses this criticism; Romeo himself becomes the ridiculing critic.

Another quality of the dream is its "thinness," its abstract quality, the lack of sensory detail or imagery. "My lady," "such life," "revived," are all rather abstract words and phrases. "Was an emperor" has no supporting detail. This thinness suggests (to me, at least) almost a reluctance to dream, an alliance of the dream-work with the ridiculing motif, as though the dream itself embodied a wish not to dream. The thinness, in effect, fulfills Romeo's wish that he were not such a dreamy person, as does his waking judgment that his own dream was "strange" and the fact that he wakes up in the dream.

Surely, though, it must be an important part of the underlying dream-thoughts that this young man, who had been a virgin as of Monday afternoon . . . , consummated his marriage on Monday night. In describing the dream, Romeo says,

> . . . all this day an unaccustomed spirit
> Lifts me above the ground with cheerful thoughts,
>
> [V. i. 4-5]

almost as though his association to the dream, his reaction to it, were itself a kind of flying dream, as though in some sense . . . the dream signified an erection. Perhaps, then, the dream involves a body-penis symbol, where the idea, "I revived and was an emperor," suggests the penis arising in an erection to its all-powerful state. "My bosom's lord sits lightly in his throne." In such a case, the kisses which breathe life into the body-penis might suggest the act of love, which so far from exhausting this inexperienced lover, gives his body-penis new life. This symbolism might seem crude indeed were there not a considerable basis for it in the play.

In a rather crucial scene, the one in which Romeo learns that he is being banished, he collapses. The bawdy Nurse looks at him lying on the ground and says,

> Stand up, stand up: stand, an you be a man:
> For Juliet's sake, for her sake, rise and stand;
> Why should you fall into so deep an O?
>
> [III. iii. 88-90]

This should all be taken as double-entendre, the standing up standing for an erection, the "O" a quite explicit and conscious symbol for a vagina about which a number of jokes were made in this play and others. Romeo has fallen into it, and he should stand up again. Later, almost the last words that Juliet says to Romeo as he leaves after their wedding-night are:

> Methinks I see thee, now thou art so low,
> As one dead in the bottom of a tomb.
>
> [III. v. 55-6]

This, after their wedding-night, echoes not only the body-penis symbolism, but also the symbol of sexual consummation as a

falling or dying, repeated over and over again in this tragedy of a "death-marked love." Earlier, for example, the friar has said,

> The earth that's nature's mother is her tomb.
> What is her burying grave, that is her womb.
>
> [II. iii. 9-10]

This same "womb-tomb" equation occurs in Romeo's line as he plans suicide immediately after recounting the dream: "Well, Juliet, I will lie with thee tonight." Again, in the final scene, Romeo looks at Juliet's tomb and speaks of it as

> Thou detestable maw, thou womb of death,
> Gorg'd with the dearest morsel of the earth, . . .
>
> [V. iii. 45-6]

His linking of womb and tomb and maw or mouth reminds us that there is a considerable oral element in Romeo's dream. A mother is an obvious person for giving life into the lips of an infant, and Romeo's term, "my lady," for Juliet could refer to his mother as well as to his later love. In other words, we could say that Romeo's dream represents still another kind of reversal. The dream of his own death reverses his coming death and turns Romeo into one newly born, receiving life (milk) in his lips. (pp. 47-50)

In short, Romeo's dream can be analyzed with all the armamentarium of modern psychoanalytic dream-interpretation—it is as real a dream as a dream can be, although it occurs in one of the most formal, stylized, and artificial of Shakespeare's plays. And this is the paradox of literary realism, that highly realistic events can exist in the highly formal, unreal atmosphere of a work of art: an imaginary garden with real toads in it, as though an early creative movement toward shaping and order were canceled by a subsequent impulse toward verisimilitude. (p. 50)

Yet it seems doubtful that any audience but one composed entirely of psychoanalytic critics would respond, consciously or unconsciously, to Romeo's dream in terms so elaborate and complicated as these. Realistic Romeo's dreams may be, but surely not *this* realistic.

But equally sure, the psychoanalytic critic is entitled to his response just as much as the more conventional critic of, say, imagery is entitled to his Byzantine web woven of dozens of half-lines in subtle warp and woof. And surely the average playgoer is entitled to his response, innocent of all such subtleties, either psychoanalytic or imagistic. These responses are all legitimate, and yet, clearly, some responses must not be. There must be (to borrow a term from Ernst Kris) "stringencies" which define and limit in such analyses as this one what is idiosyncratic to the critic and what is "in the play." (p. 51)

The ingenious excursions of critics psychoanalytic, historical, or imagistic must at some point return and touch the base of text. That is vague—a more exact and convenient test is to see whether the psychological description of the character (or event) can be phrased in words that can apply to the total work, be they ordinarily critical language or the technical terms of psychoanalysis.

For example, in this paper, it is a little silly to analyze Romeo's dream and come up with an interpretation that it represents a wish for unlimited sexual potency. Such a statement, by itself, has no bearing on the tragedy; it is simply a psychological curio. What would save this paper would be a final paragraph or two stating the psychology of Romeo's dream in words that can also describe the play as a whole.

In *Romeo and Juliet* as a whole, dream, as such, is an important concern, most obviously in Mercutio's "Queen Mab" speech with its view of dreams as wish-fulfilling fantasies. Further, to some extent, the entire relationship of Romeo and Juliet is treated as a dream. Their affair mostly takes place a night . . . , and the love of Romeo and Juliet has no place in the gray morning on which the Montagues and Capulets make up. The analysis of Romeo's dream as wish-fulfilling is not at all inappropriate to the role of dreams in *Romeo and Juliet* as "the flattering truth of sleep."

There is, however, another way in which even a very elaborate account of Romeo's dream in psychoanalytic terms returns to the play as a whole. Romeo's dream prophesies (by reversal) his own death, "Thus with a kiss I die." It is also a wish-fulfillment which reverses his present precarious and loveless situation: he becomes an "emperor," a father, reversing his usual passivity. By his remarks on his own dream, he becomes himself the ridiculing critic of his own passivity and dreamless, again, a wishful reversal of his usual situation. In terms of sexual symbolism, his dream gives him an inexhaustible potency, in which intercourse simply produces new erections—presumably a reversal of his behavior on the wedding night. Finally, at the deepest level, the dream turns Romeo's own death into being newly born. He is the emperor-child-father whose mother thrusts life into his lips. In short, at every level, the dream operates by the process of reversal. It is a dream, we could say, about the power of dreams to reverse. And such an understanding must accord even with the innocent theatergoer's: to him, too, this happy dream, coming as it does just before Romeo learns of his love's death, must seem a reversal.

But the tragedy as a whole—its psychological effect—is also a reversal, for what is *Romeo and Juliet* but the most exquisite expression of the child's inverted wish for love, "Wait till I'm gone. *Then* they'll be sorry." And all through the tragedy we find oxymora and reversals. . . . The action of the tragedy is the young love of Romeo and Juliet reversing their families' old hate. "My only love, sprung from my only hate!" [I. v. 138] says Juliet, and then, at the end,

> Capulet, Montague,
> See what scourge is laid upon your hate,
> That heaven finds means to kill your joys with love.
>
> [V. iii. 291-93]

Love springs from hate; then the love of Romeo and Juliet reverses the families' hate. The action of the tragedy is itself a reversal; its psychological effect on the audience is as well. In short, then, that one term brings into meaningful interplay Romeo's tragedy, Romeo's audience, Romeo's dream—and the reversal worked in this essay. (pp. 51-3)

> *Norman N. Holland, "Romeo's Dream and the Paradox of Literary Realism," in* The Design Within: Psychoanalytic Approaches to Shakespeare, *edited by M. D. Faber, Science House, 1970, pp. 43-54.*

## STEPHEN A. SHAPIRO    (essay date 1964)

[*Shapiro suggests that Act II, Scene vi and Act III, Scene i in* Romeo and Juliet, *as well as the friar's speech at II. iii. 9-10, serve as key points which guide our interpretation of the play—the two scenes by the manner in which "they embody ironic or dramatic reversals" and juxtapose the union and separation of* the lovers, the friar's speech by the way in which it harmonizes such opposite concepts as "womb" and "tomb." In fact, Shapiro argues, the meaning of Shakespeare's play is conveyed through just such "contraries and contradictions" as these. Noting the various, simultaneous ways we react to Romeo and Juliet's love, the critic concludes that "contraries, reversals, and transformations" in the play are ultimately meant to reflect "a dynamic image of the impulsive-inhibited ambivalence of the human psyche itself"—the fact that "every human action is the mate, the father, the child of its contrary."*]

Act II, scene vi, and Act III, scene i, constitute the geographical center of *Romeo and Juliet*. The former scene ends with Friar Laurence hurrying to "incorporate two in one" [II. v. 37], to marry Romeo and Juliet. The latter scene embraces Romeo's slaying of Tybalt, an act which divides the lovers just as they are becoming united. Both scenes embody ironic or dramatic reversals. By concentrating on the reversals in these two scenes, I believe that much can be learned about both the structure and the meaning of the entire play.

By the end of Act II Friar Laurence, despite his counsel of moderation, is forced to "make short work" [II. v. 35] of the marriage of Romeo and Juliet. Thus, despite his knowledge that "they stumble that run fast" [II. iii. 94], the Friar begins to run, becomes involved in the relentless acceleration of events, acts contrary to the way in which he would choose to act. He exits with Romeo and Juliet, who are ecstatic over "this dear encounter" [III. v. 29]. The Friar's final words, "two in one," are left hanging in the air at the end of the scene. The next scene contradicts these words by ending with Romeo's banishment. But the words will have complex reverberations. For though Romeo and Juliet are divided, they become reunited, and their deaths incorporate two feuding families into one peaceful commonwealth.

Act III opens with Mercutio upbraiding the peaceful Benvolio for being a hot man to quarrel. The contrary of this situation is immediately asserted when Tybalt enters. Mercutio responds to Tybalt's "a word with one of you," with "make it a word and a blow." [II. i. 38, 40] Then Romeo enters, encountering Tybalt's hate with its contrary, love. But shortly thereafter, Romeo's love is transformed into its opposite by Tybalt's murder of Mercutio—a deathblow delivered under Romeo's peacemaking arm. It is important to note that Mercutio dies because he willingly involves himself in the feud between the Montagues and the Capulets. However, after he is stabbed by Tybalt, he three times cries, "A plague o' both your houses!" [III. i. 91, 99-100, 106]. And his dying gasp is "—your houses!"

It is not accidental that Mercutio's outcries come at the exact center of the play. "A plague o' both your houses!" is both a judgment and a prophecy, as well as a curse. Through the repetition of this line Mercutio rises almost physically above the action of the play. And as this line sounds and resounds, one begins to realize that the whole play pivots on it. For up to Mercutio's death *Romeo and Juliet* is a romantic comedy. After it, it becomes a tragedy. The comic brawl that opened the play has been transformed by death. (p. 498)

A moment later, Romeo kills Tybalt, and is exiled. The Romeo that begged Tybalt and Mercutio to "forbear this outrage" [III. i. 87] has committed that outrage. Like Friar Laurence, who counsels slowness, like Mercutio, who counselled peace, Romeo has advised one thing and enacted its opposite. The pressure of events forces all three men to reverse themselves. But do these contraries function within the pattern of a larger series of reversals and transformations? The "Prologue" indicates that they do.

> From forth the fatal loins of these two foes
>   A pair of star-cross'd lovers take their life;
> Whose misadventur'd piteous overthrows
>   Do with their death bury their parents' strife.
>                                      [Prologue, 5-8]

The play seems to be governed by the sacrificial deaths of Romeo and Juliet which reverse their parents' hate.

On another level, the language of the play deals in contraries, as Romeo's "Feather of lead, bright smoke, cold fire, sick health" speech [I. i. 180] attests. Juliet also explores contraries, calling Romeo:

> Beautiful tyrant! fiend angelical!
> Dove-feather'd raven! wolfish-ravening lamb!
> Despised substance of divinest show!
> Just opposite to what thou justly seem'st;
> A damned saint, an honourable villain! . . .
>                                      [III. ii. 75-9]

[Though] many critics have remarked about the various contraries and contrasts to be found in *Romeo and Juliet,* no one has yet attempted to explore their function in terms of the total meaning of the play.

It is my contention that the play "means" primarily through its contraries and contradictions. One is virtually forced to this conclusion, for either/or interpretations tend to be unsatisfactory because they ignore large sections of the play. H. L. Mencken was perhaps the first to suggest that *Romeo and Juliet* is a grotesque parody of romantic love. It is undeniable that elements of parody are to be found in the play—such as the exaggerated "O, O, O" grief patterns in Act IV, scene v, and perhaps even Juliet's melodramatic soliloquy on her forthcoming immolation. But one cannot ignore the fact that, as witnessed by all of Shakespeare's comedies, Shakespeare did not believe that romantic love was absurd, but rather that it could have a kind of religious value. At the same time, however, one cannot go to the other extreme and simply affirm that Romeo and Juliet are heroic figures. For the elements of parody cannot be ignored. Romeo and Juliet are immature, even absurd in their immaturity. . . . And there is something about the love of these two adolescents that is even more ambiguous than their immaturity.

The "Prologue" tells us that the love of Romeo and Juliet is "death-mark'd"—presumably because of the enmity of their parents and the disposition of the stars. But, though fortune plays a key role in this drama, Shakespeare also conceives of fate in terms of character. One of the first things we learn about Romeo is that he

> Shuts up his windows, locks fair daylight out,
> And makes himself an artificial night.
> Black and portentous must this humour prove . . .
>                                      [I. i. 139-41]

Even before he meets Juliet, Romeo seeks darkness. And his misgiving that his "despised life" will end in "untimely death" [I. iv. 110, 111], is certainly more immediately connected to his character, his desire to die, than to any medieval tradition. Shakespeare has anticipated one of the most paradoxical and profound insights of psychoanalysis: a man is as much re-

sponsible for what is done to him as for what he does. Fortune, what happens to one, and fate, what one is, fuse.

Is it not strange that when Romeo first arrived in Mantua, before he heard of Juliet's death, he thought of deadly poisons [V. i. 49-53]? Is it not disturbing that Juliet, after hearing of Romeo's banishment, resolves:

> I'll to the friar, to know his remedy:
> If all else fail, myself have power to die,
>                                      [III. v. 241-42]

instead of resolving to find Romeo and live? One begins to suspect that when Juliet threatens the friar: "I long to die, / If what thou speak'st speak not of remedy." [IV. i. 66], she longs more for death than for remedy.

However, one cannot quite conclude that when Romeo kills Tybalt, honorably revenging Mercutio's death, and cries "O! I am Fortune's fool" [III. i. 136], he is merely rationalizing. Nothing is simple in Shakespeare. If fortune fuses with fate on the one hand, it fuses with Providence on the other. Romeo *is* "Fortune's fool." But in *Romeo and Juliet,* fortune is not fickle but purposeful. . . . [It] operates not only to destroy Romeo and Juliet but also to reconcile the Montagues and Capulets. Thus Friar Laurence's lines:

> The earth that's nature's mother is her tomb;
> What is her burying grave that is her womb . . .
>                                      [II. iii. 9-10]

with their sense of harmonized contraries, may provide a "key" to the meaning of the play. They certainly symbolize the action of the play. The parents of the lovers are in a sense their tomb. But out of the tomb of the lovers, reconciliation, if not new life, is born. The "plague" that Mercutio wishes on the two houses becomes actualized as the deaths of Romeo and Juliet, but becomes partially transformed into a kind of blessing. However, the disproportion between what has been gained and what lost may indicate that there is irony in the reconciliation scene.

This ambiguous and perhaps unsatisfying scene returns us to the ambiguous nature of the love shared or indulged in by the protagonists. By suggesting that Romeo and Juliet desire to die, I am not necessarily concluding that this makes them simply an object of satire. The desire for perfect love, or perfect anything else, is fundamentally an unrealizable one—in life as we know it. But the desire for an endless and perfect night of love seems to be a constituent of the human personality, compounded of the will to die and the will to return to the womb. The fact that Romeo and Juliet, like Tristan and Isolde, hate the day and cherish the night is profoundly symbolic. A love like their love cannot live in the daylight world of prose. Thus their love has both a positive and a negative pole, and our response to it must be an ambivalent one. Romeo and Juliet have achieved something beyond the ability of Mercutio or the Nurse or the Friar or the parents to conceive. They have achieved perfect communion, total absorption of self in the other. We cannot help responding to this rare consummation. But its price is death, the extinction of the individual personality.

Tragedies of the greatest magnitude are rituals by self-destruction. The protagonists are sacrificed to "save" the audience. That is the meaning of catharsis. One is purged through tragedy of the desire to destroy oneself by an excess of desire, by monomania, by the unleashed forces of the id. In *Romeo and Juliet* Shakespeare offers us the opportunity both to participate in the love of Romeo and Juliet, to sympathize with it, to

*Act II. Scene vi. Juliet, Romeo, and Friar Lawrence. By H. W. Bunbury.*

vicariously gratify our own desire for it, and simultaneously to react against it.

The function of the contraries and reversals in *Romeo and Juliet* is to sustain what Simon O. Lesser terms *"a sense of the opposite."* The play possesses what Lesser calls "the sublime ambivalence of great narrative art." We are constantly aware of the double face of the action. When old Capulet laments:

> All things that we ordained festival,
> Turn from their office to black funeral;
> Our instruments to melancholy bells,
> Our wedding cheer to a sad burial feast,
> Our solemn hymns to sullen dirges change,
> Our bridal flowers serve for a buried corse,
> And all things change them to the contrary,
>
> [IV. v. 84-90]

he is saying more than he knows. For not only has he changed *his* complexion, not only is he grieving for a live daughter, not only is it his doing that has made a funeral of a festival, but the entire play is an expression of things changing to their contraries. Hasting lovers are transformed into statues; feuding fathers become friends; a moderation-counselling friar becomes the most extreme stumbler of all; fickle fortune becomes purposeful; life-giving, light-giving love radiates darkness and death; the deaths of the lovers produce a kind of birth by ending civil strife. In Friar Laurence's terms:

> The earth that's nature's mother is her tomb;
> What is her burying grave that is her womb . . .
>
> [II. iii. 9-10]

*Romeo and Juliet*, in its contraries, reversals, and transformations, furnishes us with a dynamic image of the impulsive-inhibited ambivalence of the human psyche itself. Every human action is the mate, the father, the child, of its contrary. (pp. 498-501)

> *Stephen A. Shapiro, " 'Romeo and Juliet': Reversals, Contraries, Transformations, and Ambivalence," in* College English, *Vol. 25, No. 7, April, 1964, pp. 498-501.*

**TOM F. DRIVER**   (essay date 1964)

[*Driver briefly examines the ways in which Shakespeare compressed the action in* Romeo and Juliet, *which the critic claims contribute not only to the sense of "real" events on the stage, but also further the theme of thoughtless "rapidity" in the play.*]

In *Romeo and Juliet* the young Shakespeare learned the craft of creating on stage the illusion of passing time. The Prologue is a kind of author's pledge that we are to see something that really happened. At least, and for technique it amounts to the same thing, it *could* have happened.

> Two households, both alike in dignity,
> In fair Verona, where we lay our scene,
> From ancient grudge break to new mutiny,
> Where civil blood makes civil hands unclean.
>
> [Prologue, 1-4]

The story is further summarized, and the Prologue ends with this couplet:

> The which if you with patient ears attend,
> What here shall miss, our toil shall strive to mend.
>
> [Prologue, 13-14]

Once such a beginning is made, the author is under obligation to be as faithful to the clock as possible. He must show one thing happening after another, according to its proper time, and he must keep the audience informed as to how the clock and the calendar are turning. Shakespeare was well aware of the obligation. *Romeo and Juliet* contains no less than 103 references to the time of the action—that is, 103 references which inform the audience what day things take place, what time of day it is, what time some earlier action happened, when something later will happen, etc. In every case but one Shakespeare was thoroughly consistent.

It is not enough, however, for the dramatist to be consistent. He also must be able to make us believe that in the short time we sit in the theater the whole action he describes can take place. He must compress the action of his story into the length of a theatrical performance. (p. 364)

Faced with a dramatic necessity, Shakespeare decided to make capital of it. If he has much business to set forth in a short time he will write a play about the shortness of time. . . . No little part of the attraction of the play is due to this frank exploitation of a dramatic necessity.

> Come, Montague; for thou art early up
> To see thy son and heir more early down.
>
> [V. iii. 208-09]

In addition to the 103 chronological references noted above, the play contains 51 references to the idea of speed and rapidity of movement.

I shall mention only briefly the two ways by which Shakespeare has achieved the uncommonly tight compression of action in this play. His first stratagem was to shorten the length of the action, as found in his source, from nine months to four or five days. With this he achieved two results: he heightened the sense of "o'er hasty" action considerably, and he enabled himself more easily to appear to account for all the "real" time in the story. He did not, of course, account for every hour, but he came nearer to a correspondence between stage time and "real" time.

His second stratagem was to make very short scenes on the stage account for comparatively long periods of "real" time. This effect, which has been called "double" time, was mastered by Shakespeare in the course of writing *Romeo and Juliet*. The play has two notable scenes in this respect: I. v, the feast at Capulet's house, and V. iii, the final scene. In both, the technique is to focus attention upon a series of small scenes within the major scene, one after another, so that we are forgetful of the clock, and then to tell us at the end that so-and-so-much time has gone by. Because the story has advanced, we are willing to believe the clock did also.

So much for the problem of compressing "real" time into stage time and for Shakespeare's use of the resulting rapidity as a theme in his play. There remains a further complexity owing to the drama's being a performed art. That is the problem of tempo. The sense of rapidity in the movement of the action must be varied. The play must have a rhythm different from the movement of the clock, however that clock may have been accelerated. There must be a fast and slow, and that fast and slow will account for much of the subtle form which the play assumes under the hand of the dramatist. Here is a major difference between art and life. In life, time is constant. The dull days last as long as the eventful ones, if not longer. In a drama time speeds up or slows down according to the meaning of the action. The excitement of dramatic art lies very largely in the tension thus established between chronological tempo and artistic, or dramatic, tempo.

Roughly speaking, *Romeo and Juliet* has four periods or phases—two fast and two slow. It opens in a slow time. True, there is a street fight to begin with; but that is in the nature of a curtain-raiser skillfully used to set the situation. Basically, the first period is the "Rosaline phase", and it moves as languidly as Romeo's mooning. The second period, of very swift action, begins to accelerate in I. iii with talk of Paris as a husband. It rushes headlong, with only momentary pauses, through love, courtship, and marriage until Tybalt is impetuously slain. Here there is a pause, while the audience waits with Juliet to see what will happen, and while Friar Laurence cautions Romeo to be patient until he can "find a time" to set matters straight. It is important to notice that this pause accounts for only a very small period of "real" time. The pause is purely psychological—or rather, dramatic. In the midst of it Shakespeare prepares to accelerate the action once more by inserting between two of the lovers' *andante* scenes the very remarkable *staccato* scene iv of Act III, in which Capulet arranges with Paris for Juliet's marriage. In this short scene of 35 lines there are no less than 15 specific references to time and haste. The scene is all about how soon the marriage can take place—counterpoint to the mood of the lovers, who would turn the morning lark into a nightingale. In the final phase of the play, speed takes over again and we rush to the catastrophe.

It is in the last phase that the most interesting relations between dramatic rhythm and chronological clarity may be seen. Two or three days of "real" time are required to pass in order to make sense of the action: Romeo must be exiled, Friar Laurence must put his plan for Juliet's false death into effect, messengers must travel, family must grieve, and a funeral be held. But the drama, once Juliet takes the sleeping potion, requires a swift conclusion. Therefore, after that event, references to exact time, which hitherto have been profuse, almost entirely disappear from the text. There is no way for an audience to know when any of the scenes in Act V begins. There are no clues as to what day it is, let alone what time of day, until line 176 of scene iii, when the Watch informs us that Juliet has been buried two days. The vagueness is deliberate. The "real" time is comparatively long, but the play wants to move swiftly. Therefore the audience is given an *impression* of speed, but specific time references are withheld.

The foregoing remarks should make it clear that in such a play as *Romeo and Juliet*, where the story demands a setting more or less realistic, Shakespeare strings his art between two poles: on one side, accurate imitation of what would really happen; on the other, bold shaping of events into an aesthetic pattern. We may say that the play results from a tension between these

SHAKESPEAREAN CRITICISM, Vol. 5

two. The actual technique is to move from one to the other. Tension, however, expresses our *feeling* about the play. Imagination and reality seem to be combined in a system of stresses and strains. Time is real, and to imitate action is to imitate time. But there is also in men a capacity for transcending time, which the playwright-artist and his audience know well. Time and its events alone do not produce an action; the imagination, transcending but not escaping time, may do so. (pp. 364-66)

Tom F. Driver, "The Shakespearian Clock: Time and the Vision of Reality in 'Romeo and Juliet' and 'The Tempest'," in Shakespeare Quarterly, Vol. XV, No. 4, Autumn, 1964, pp. 363-70.

## DAVID LAIRD (essay date 1964)

[*Focusing on the language and behavior of the characters in both the public and private worlds of* Romeo and Juliet, *Laird demonstrates two points: one, that the determination with which Romeo and Juliet "act out their love and assert its value beyond time" forces the public world of Verona—which is "blinded by habit and convention"—"to acknowledge what it could not see"; and two, that as the lovers "expose the fatal inadequacy" of Verona's conventional behavior, the "insistent demands of [that] public world provoke Romeo and Juliet to an awareness quite different from that fostered by their dream of romantic fulfillment" expressed early in the play. The critic also discerns in the later authentic and personal utterances of the lovers an ability to transcend the ambiguities and contradictions of life, as well as a willingness to accommodate "disparate aspects of existence."*]

"Humours! madman! passion! lover!" cries Mercutio to Romeo hiding in the shadows of Capulet's moonlit orchard.

> Appear thou in the likeness of a sigh:
> Speak but one rhyme, and I am satisfied;
> Cry but 'Ay me!' pronounce but 'love' and 'dove'....
> [II. i. 7-10]

When Mercutio particularizes the characteristics of the conventional lover, he mocks the disguises of love, the feigned passions and the twisted syntax of patterned artifice, the numbers and conceits "that Petrarch flowed in" [II. iv. 39]. When love is war, Mercutio refuses to fight: "Romeo, goodnight. I'll to my truckle-bed; / This field-bed is too cold for me to sleep" [II. i. 39-40]. His decision points a direction that some recent criticism has taken. After noting the play's obvious features, its conventions of behavior and utterance . . . , some critics are quite willing to abandon Romeo to what we are told is but a Petrarchan adventure. They are inclined to echo Mercutio's impatience with the idealization of romantic love and its patterned articulation.

But that opinion does not carry us far if we wish to follow Shakespeare's handling of conventional literary materials in the organization of the total work. The artificial style and the view of life it expresses develop a major theme of which Mercutio's satire is a partial reflection rather than a final summary. In its structural function, patterned artifice is one means of defining a dramatic truth—the frailty of human perception. No less important to that definition are the rigid patterns of social behavior which shape the public lives of Montague and Capulet. Concerned more with the social than with the literary face of convention, Mercutio pricks the forms by which men endeavor to escape the burden of perception. If he jokes about love, he jokes about family honor and the codes of civility. He lampoons the fine manners of fashionable young men—Romeo in the role of a Petrarchan poseur who loves by rhyme

and number, Tybalt in the guise of a "courageous captain of complements" who "fights by the book of arithmetic" [II. iv. 20; III. i. 102]. Mercutio tries to unmask the errors and distortions which endanger the private world of the youthful lovers and the public world of their embittered families. The full purpose of his satire becomes clear in the larger framework of the play when we realize that it is Romeo and Juliet who are uniquely capable of that unmasking.

The insistent demands of the public world provoke Romeo and Juliet to an awareness quite different from that fostered by their dream of romantic fulfilment. And the firm purpose with which they act out their love and assert its value beyond time and mortality forces that world to acknowledge what it could not see, blinded by habit and custom, betrayed by that folly-prone simplification and distortion of reality which, in the terms the play sets up, is conventional response. That is the first point I would like to develop. . . . A second is that, as Romeo and Juliet expose the fatal inadequacy of conventional response, they renounce implicitly the poetic conventions which give to their earlier utterances that charm and innocent unreality which Mercutio scorns. Patterned artifice first wears the colors of romantic illusion, but, subsequently, it sets the limits of perception in the public world. When Paris and Prince Escalus open and close the final scene, their words fall within the formal pattern of a sestet. Against that background of conventional lament and in striking contrast to it, the last speeches of Romeo and Juliet display a new-minted rhetoric. A stylistic innovation carries a more complex awareness breaking in upon the leading characters; it permits them to define their own truth with luminous certitude and authenticity.

Through the first three acts, Shakespeare uses conventional poetic forms to shape the dramatic interplay between the youthful lovers and to set them apart from a collection of characters in whom the most obvious quality is a habit of contention—habit keeps alive a quarrel whose original cause has long been forgotten. The sonnet shared by Romeo and Juliet at their first meeting at Capulet's party pulls away from the harsher forms of response to which other characters resort. The sonnet develops the familiar Petrarchan conceit linking love and religion. . . . The Religion of Love is essential to the design of [John Donne's] "The Canonization," which takes as its basic image the process by which a person is proved before an ecclesiastical court to be a saint.

> We can dye by it, if not live by love,
> And if unfit for tombes and hearse
> Our legend bee, it will be fit for verse
> And if no peece of Chronicle wee prove,
> We'll build in sonnets pretty roomes.

But Romeo and Juliet are not long for sonnets' pretty rooms. Romeo plays for the hand of Juliet against the immediate background of Tybalt's violent outburst that he must avenge the insult a Montague gives by appearing at Capulet's feast. We infer from the simple contrasts the scene articulates that the conventions of love will be challenged by the conventions of family honor. The joy with which Romeo and Juliet sound the words of love fades before a deepening sense of the inappropriateness of that love. With shocked surprise the lovers glimpse a contradiction they cannot fully comprehend. Their bewilderment is expressed in a series of oxymora with which the scene ends—Romeo's "O dear account! my life is my foe's debt" [I. v. 118], and Juliet's "My only love sprung from my only hate!" [I. v. 138]. The figure bears upon the argument or dialectic of the action by formalizing the relation of different and conflicting values. Through most of the play Romeo and Juliet are buffeted by the opposing claims of private and public worlds. The ritual or symbolic action of the private world is the masque; of the public world, the duel. The alternating movement within the rhythmic scheme of the whole play and the supporting contrasts in tone and imagery reproduce that basic polarity. Groping for definition, Romeo and Juliet fall back upon the inadequate terms of generalized and conventional paradox. The easy generality of their stylized formulation suggests that what they see is limited and superficial. The lovers have yet to acquire the power and means to temper "extremities with extreme sweet" [Prologue II, 14].

In response to those "extremities," Romeo and Juliet move between hope and despair. In the garden scene of Act II, hope is in the ascendant; the wish becomes the reality as if Mercutio's Queen Mab, who "gallops night by night / Through lovers' brains, and then they dream of love" [I. iv. 70-1], were with them, though they do not wait for sleep to dream. Their profession of love captures a springlike freshness, the charm of play, a game in which the young people make their own rules and no one keeps the score. In the play world of love, social identities can be forsworn:

> Deny thy father and refuse thy name;
> Or, if thou wilt not, be but sworn my love,
> And I'll no longer be a Capulet. . . .
> 'Tis but thy name that is my enemy;
> Thou art thyself, though not a Montague.
> What's Montague? . . .
> O, be some other name!
> What's in a name? that which we call a rose
> By any other name would smell as sweet;
> So Romeo would, were he not Romeo call'd,
> Retain that dear perfection which he owes
> Without that title. Romeo, doff thy name,
> And for thy name which is no part of thee
> Take all myself.
>
> [II. ii. 34-49]

Romeo quickly agrees . . . , but asks how he is to identify himself without a name. The love-religion metaphor introduced in the sonnet of Act I appears again.

> By a name
> I know not how to tell thee who I am:
> My name, dear saint, is hateful to myself,
> Because it is an enemy to thee;
> Had I it written, I would tear the word.
>
> [II. ii. 53-7]

Imagining themselves free from the entangling web of family feud and ancient hate, they see themselves no longer Montague and Capulet but new-baptized in the name of love [II. ii. 50]. Romeo's profession of love is unconditional—less obviously literary than his exaggerated vows of love to Rosaline; still the hyperboles and wordplay of the love convention weave its texture. . . . Juliet bring Romeo's verbal excursions to what would seem to her a more fitting destination—marriage. Her apology for undecorated truth evokes a gentle pathos:

> But trust me, gentleman, I'll prove more true
> Than those that have more cunning to be strange.
> I should have been more strange, I must confess. . . .
>
> [II. ii. 100-02]

Juliet distrusts the easy speed with which the lovers vault in words the social barriers that would separate them: "It is too rash, too unadvised, too sudden; / Too like the lightning, which doth cease to be / Ere one can say 'It lightens'" [II. ii. 118-20]. . . . [Her] fears foreshadow the shattering jolts of subsequent discovery.

The controlling idea of Acts III and IV is the discovery by Romeo and Juliet of the threats and denials to which their love is increasingly exposed and before which it is so peculiarly vulnerable. They feel with increasing force the pressures of social discord which in their youthful dream of love they had only dimly sensed and partially acknowledge. Now their claim to independence is tried by Tybalt and Capulet, spokesman of the public world. Romeo's trial comes in Act III through his encounter with Tybalt. When he ignores Tybalt's challenge, Mercutio fights. Romeo is caught in a shifting web of loyalties and obligations. He becomes a reluctant actor in a public show of honor. Juliet's trial comes in Acts III and IV. Confronted with her father's demand that she marry Paris, she feigns death. For her, the trial is even more severe than for Romeo. . . . The movement of the play is unmistakable. The harmonies of romantic illusion celebrated in Act II are shattered in Acts III and IV by the angry outcries of Tybalt and Capulet. In the last act Romeo and Juliet resolve all discord and prove their love no "hollow perjury" [III. iii. 128].

In Act V Romeo and Juliet move beyond the patterns of behavior and response with which they identify themselves early in the play. Experience brings new mastery and control. Earlier, when Romeo, hearing of the Prince's sentence of banishment, writhes in a spasm of empty phrases, Friar Laurence charges that "Thy noble shape is but a form of wax / Digressing from the valour of a man" [III. iii. 126-27]. The tendency to mask the dramatic situation in verbal extravagance is absent from Romeo's quiet acceptance of the news of Juliet's supposed death: "Is it even so? then I defy you, stars!" [V. i. 24]; "Well, Juliet, I will lie with thee to-night" [V. i. 34]. The economy and precision of language in these speeches, in sharp contrast with the artificiality of earlier utterances, reveals a wiser and less youthful Romeo. But the "strained touches" of rhetoric, disappearing from Romeo's language, continue to mark the language of the public world. At the Capulet tomb, Paris speaks a conventional lament, a sestet with four lines alternately rhymed followed by a concluding couplet complete with familiar wordplay and decorative conceits: the bridal bed becomes the grave canopied with dust and stones. Paris vows to visit the tomb each night and to water its flowers with his tears. Patterned artifice, which defined the illusions of romantic love, now suggests the limitations of conventional response and behavior in the public world. (pp. 204-10)

In the last scene language serves new purposes. In the speeches of Romeo and Juliet, it is no longer deliberately conventional and artificial. The formalized and predictable patterns which blur or soften the immediate dramatic situation have disappeared. An integral part of action, language now concentrates and intensifies the complex interplay of character and situation. In the certainty of their belief, the lovers momentarily transform the commonplace world. Recalling their first meeting at Capulet's party where Juliet taught the torches to burn bright, Romeo's language strikes a subtle mood of hopeful wonder and surprise against a darker knowledge of inevitable defeat. That double sense of renewal and extinction is mysteriously revealed in the succession of images which flash a final and ambiguous illumination. Juliet's grave is an end and a beginning; "thou womb of death" [V. iii. 45], a place of renewal. A new rhetoric develops genuine conviction. Romeo pledges himself as forfeit in "a dateless bargain to engrossing death!" [V. iii. 115]. Death's attempted ravishment of life becomes the referent of a daring metaphor capable of engaging the imagination at many different levels.

> Death, that hath suck'd the honey of thy breath,
> Hath had no power yet upon thy beauty:
> Thou art not conquer'd. . . .
>
> [V. iii. 92-4]

[This metaphor] prepares for that precise matching of image and idea which evokes simultaneously the sensuous and the transcendental aspects of love. Within that context, Romeo's final lines, remaining eloquently simple, "true plain words," move at several levels of signification.

> O true apothecary!
> Thy drugs are quick. Thus with a kiss I die.
>
> [V. iii. 119-20]

The apothecary is true because (1) he has told the truth about the drug and (2) he is true to his profession in ministering to Romeo's pain. The drug kills and renews—"Thy drugs are quick"—fast to kill and, at the same time, lively or life-giving. Juliet's final speech catches up that double meaning as she chides Romeo for his thoughtlessness in leaving none of the poison for her. His departure has been too sudden; he has not provided for Juliet, left alone to face "the terror of the place" [IV. iii. 38].

> O churl! drunk all, and left no friendly drop
> To help me after? I will kiss thy lips;
> Haply some poison yet doth hang on them,
> To make me die with a restorative.
>
> [V. iii. 163-66]
> (pp. 210-11)

Without the poison, Juliet seizes upon Romeo's dagger: "O happy dagger! / This is thy sheath; there rust, and let me die" [V. iii. 169-70]. That the dagger is happy implies, of course, that Juliet is fortunate it is at hand, ready for use. She is impatient for death as the cry of the watch announces an intruder. It is happy, too, in that it is the instrument which brings happiness absolutely—it puts Juliet beyond the pain of life without Romeo. A second meaning is imposed upon the lines by "sheath" and "die." In Elizabethan English, the verb "to die" can mean to consummate sexual passion, a meaning which has figured in the earlier "To make me die with a restorative." Here that reading of "die" draws immediate contextual support from the sexual implication of "dagger" and from the anatomical meaning of "sheath." . . . Thus Juliet's death becomes, metaphorically, the fulfilment of love. Again the yoking in metaphor of such disparate aspects of experience intensifies the pathos and irony of Juliet's plight. There is the acknowledgment of the reality of death—and, at the same time, the defiant assertion of reunion in death—of the triumph of love over time and mortality. We are made to see the lovers as victims and as victors, as destroyed by death and proved by death. And if we see more than the lovers see, we are made to believe in what they do see and feel through the power of vivid image and metaphor to astonish and convince. In the last act of *Romeo and Juliet*, Shakespeare moves beyond the standardized patterns of Elizabethan love poetry to anticipate that intensification and compression of language so characteristic of the great tragedies. In this early tragedy, he begins to adapt and enlarge the available conventions of Elizabethan drama and poetry.

But there is yet another level of meaning working through Juliet's final speech. It reveals the lovers' achievement in relation to that basic opposition between public and private worlds which frames the action. "O happy dagger! / This is thy sheath; there rust, and let me die" . . . brings those conflicting worlds into surprising juxtaposition and builds to a final reconciliation. The dagger as symbol of civil strife and family feud has been put away. The lovers have brought an end to social violence and division; their violent end becomes an end to violence. That meaning is caught up some thirty lines later by the bereaved Capulet:

> This dagger hath mista'en,—for, lo, his house
> Is empty on the back of Montague,—
> And it mis-sheathed in my daughter's bosom!
>
> [V. iii. 203-05]

A Montague's dagger is mis-sheathed. ("His house is empty on the back of Montague" not only describes the empty sheath, but also implies the ruined fortunes of the house of Montague—both wife and son are dead.) Romeo and Juliet are now seen as participants in a grotesque ritual enactment of the family feud—a Capulet disarms a Montague, a Montague's dagger kills a Capulet. The angry boasts of opposing families have been fulfilled. It remains for Montague and Capulet to undergo the agony of doubt. A dim perception of the actual and limiting conditions of life wakes a sense of human community: "Where be these enemies? Capulet! Montague!" [V. iii. 291]. A disenchanted public world discovers the fatal extravagance of habit and custom:

> See, what a scourge is laid upon your hate,
> That heaven finds means to kill your joys with love.
> And I for winking at your discords too
> Have lost a brace of kinsmen: all are punish'd.
>
> [V. iii. 292-95]

Montague and Capulet are reconciled: "Give me thy hand: / This is my daughter's jointure, for no more / Can I demand" [V. iii. 296-98]. Ironically, what the public world has denied in life, it will celebrate in art; it will raise Juliet's statue in pure gold and "As rich shall Romeo's by his lady's lie; / Poor sacrifices of our enmity!" [V. iii. 303-04].

Through the final scene and particularly as the Prince speaks the sestet with which the play ends, we are made to feel the fatal inadequacy of conventional response. Habit is a deadener and habit has here taken its toll. We acknowledge an inevitable sacrifice to the folly of blind habit, uncritical conformity, and easy routine. Our hold on reality is never very great, and it is only with considerable effort that we are brought to extend that hold. In *Romeo and Juliet* a complex image of reality eclipses our simplified and distorted notions about reality in what is certainly a function of tragic theater. (pp. 211-13)

> *David Laird, "The Generation of Style in 'Romeo and Juliet'," in* The Journal of English and Germanic Philology, *Vol. LXIII, No. 2, April, 1964, pp. 204-13.*

## WINIFRED NOWOTTNY (lecture date 1964)

[*In the following excerpt from a lecture given at University College, London, in 1964, Nowottny examines Shakespeare's adaptation of the sonnet tradition in* Romeo and Juliet, *noting how the stylized, Petrarchan mode apparent in the lovers' expressions provided Shakespeare with the means to universalize their experience and to convey the exalted, ennobling nature of their love. Nowottny also comments on the play's central theme, contending* that *"it is the development of the feud, not the characters of the lovers, which destroys them."*]

A carping tone is sometimes taken towards [*Romeo and Juliet*]. Sometimes it is said to be hardly tragic, since death comes about by a train of circumstances rather than from character; hardly about good and evil; in parts comic; much of it exuberant, much ecstatic. Even the love, some say, is often as extravagant in its expression as it is beautiful. Altogether, a young man's tragedy, and 'immature'.

But Shakespeare was, to the best of our knowledge, in his thirties when he wrote it. And surely it is about young lovers not as they see themselves, but as a man of that age sees them—hence the comedy, the deliberate stress on the lovers' violent heedlessness, and the appreciation of the high style in which the young live. There is one moment in the play when the dangerous insolence of young men is perfectly caught—when Mercutio takes on Tybalt with 'Tybalt, you rat-catcher, will you walk?' [III. i. 75]. The courting of danger, the quick sense of honour, and the swagger, are all there, and it is this moment in which the avalanche of the tragedy begins to move. The young fight and love and die in style—extravagantly, in hot blood, with folly and self-sacrifice and beautiful nonsense streaming from them in a non-stop glory. One has to have stopped being young to see how wonderful and dangerous this is.

Brought to the bar of criticism, the play will seem short of tragic only if we prescribe what a tragedy must be; for instance, that it must be about moral choice. As to its language, this will seem extravagant only if we demand that Romeo and Juliet should be less extravagant in feeling than they are, and that they should talk language such as men and women do use when they are not in love and not living in the sixteenth century. (p. 49)

It might be objected that an elaborate style will do for a sonneteer but not for a dramatist. There is, however, very good reason why Romeo the lover, and Juliet, too, should talk like a sonneteer. The play was written in the heyday of the sonnet, and the language of the sonnet was the language of love. The kind of love Petrarch had celebrated was often regarded as an experience which lifted a man above himself, as an exaltation of the spirit so spectacular that only religious experience could compete with it for intensity. It would hardly have been possible for Shakespeare, writing about idealistic passion at a time when the sonnet vogue was at its height, to ignore the sonneteers' language for it.

And, indeed, the convention was very useful for his purposes. The fact that it was, at this time, so highly developed, made it possible for him to present the experience of his hero and heroine in language which could claim to be universal; it is the language of lovers in general, not of Romeo and Juliet in particular; they do not need individual characters in order to be able to speak as they do. None the less, they are sufficiently individualized, within the world of the play itself, by the fact that to be in their state of mind is to be in a world of one's own. Their world, to Mercutio, is absurd; it is a closed world to the Nurse; it is a world Capulet has no time for, and one of whose wilfulness the Friar disapproves. This contrast between the world of lovers and the world of other people is itself a universal feature of the experience of being in love, and the plot of the play gives a dramatic heightening to this universal fact by placing this love in the midst of a feud between the lovers' families, so that it is the development of the feud, not the characters of the lovers, which destroys them. The plot itself makes a clear statement about the violent discrepancy between lovers and the world about them; to have individualized Romeo and Juliet would have blurred the clarity of this statement.

Shakespeare surmounts the difficulty of the second-hand character of this language by opening the play with a Romeo who talks at second hand himself, and later discovers the meaning of the language he has used. Romeo at first fancies himself in love with Rosaline and defines himself as a lover by a long tirade [I. i. 182-200], cast in the mould of that definition of love which comes at the climax of Petrarch's *Triumph of Love* . . . ; some of Petrarch's phrases recur, and the passages resemble one another in their use of a sustained barrage of contradictions declaring the contradictory nature of love. On seeing Juliet, he forswears his love for Rosaline:

> Did my heart love till now? forswear it, sight!
> For I ne'er saw true beauty till this night.
>
> [I. v. 52-3]

But his repudiation of his mistake is itself put in the conventional terms of a debate between heart and eye; the false object may have given place to the true one, but the language of love remains the same. So, when he speaks to Juliet for the first time, the dialogue of their encounter is cast in the sonnet form.

Shakespeare's debt to Petrarch and his imitators is not confined to formal and stylized passages; we can see it even at the height of the drama:

> Death, that hath suck'd the honey of thy breath,
> Hath had no power yet upon thy beauty:
> Thou art not conquer'd; beauty's ensign yet
> Is crimson in thy lips and in thy cheeks,
> And death's pale flag is not advanced there.
>
> [V. iii. 92-6]

This wonderful passage probably derives from the opening passage of Petrarch's *Triumph of Fame*. . . . Romeo's words as he takes the fatal potion,

> Thou desperate pilot, now at once run on
> The dashing rocks thy sea-sick weary bark!
>
> [V. iii. 117-18]

contain a famous Petrarchanism, the storm-tossed bark as an image for the unhappy lover—an image which Shakespeare used in his own sonnet, *Let me not to the marriage of true minds*, where he says that love "is the star to every wandering bark' [Sonnet 116].

The Petrarchan convention afforded such a variety of resources that it enabled Shakespeare, whilst avoiding monotony and disharmony alike, to maintain the pitch of lyrical utterance throughout a story which moves with such rapidity from one entranced moment to another—first sight, first exchange of words, first meeting in secret, first avowal, parting, reunion, marriage. And, of course, he does much to tie this language to immediate dramatic reality. For instance, the imagery of the lady as a source of light, so frequent in Petrarch, is used in the play in contexts where this imagery appears to be prompted by the immediate situation: Romeo meets Juliet by torchlight at the Capulets' feast, and 'she doth teach the torches to burn bright' [I. v. 44]; he sees a light at her window, and this suggests that 'It is the east, and Juliet is the sun' [II. ii. 3]; when she appears, above him, she is not merely an angel, but an angel seen by one who falls back to look with 'white-upturned wondering eyes' [II. ii. 29]. The nightingale, again, is traditional enough for lovers, but in the play Juliet will have it that the lark is the nightingale, and Romeo is content to agree, though it might mean his death if he were found. So Petrarchanism gives Shakespeare a repertoire of resources, which his own sense of fit language for particular situations enables him to treat selectively, and to put in a convincing relation to the immediate context of the drama.

I have dwelt on the influence of this literary tradition not only to justify the language of the play but also to indicate where we may look if we need anything external to tell us where Shakespeare thought the tragedy of it really lies. In his own sonnets the great theme is that 'every thing that grows / Holds in perfection but a little moment' [Sonnet 15]. 'This thought', he said in his sonnets, 'is as a death, which cannot choose / But weep to have that which it fears to lose' [Sonnet 64]. His first really tragic drama is constructed as a series of brief perfections, each moment perfect because it is the first—until that one of them which is the last. The play needs no insight, in order to make it tragic, deeper than this, its chief insight; one so important to Shakespeare that it spills over into *A Midsummer Night's Dream*, where Lysander says that true love, exposed always to difference of blood, to war, death and sickness, is

> Swift as a shadow, short as any dream;
> Brief as the lightning in the collied night,

(we remember Juliet's 'Too like the lightning, which doth cease to be / Ere one can say "It lightens"' [II. ii. 119-20])—

> That, in a spleen, unfolds both heaven and earth,
> And ere a man hath power to say "Behold!"
> The jaws of darkness do devour it up:
> So quick bright things come to confusion.
> [*A Midsummer Night's Dream*, I. i. 144-49]

To this [Hermia] replies, '. . . it is a customary cross' [I. i. 153]. It is, in short, a tragic aspect of the general human lot. It is no small part of the greatness of Shakespeare's first real tragedy, as of his later ones, that the tragedy lies essentially in the condition of man, not of particular men.

In later plays, the surface of the dialogue is less obviously encrusted with items transferred from a non-dramatic literature. But the endeavour to transfer the essence of other literature to the dramatic form is a feature of Shakespeare's work not confined to *Romeo and Juliet*. It is characteristic of his genius that he *was* able to devise a dramatic form for that view of life of which the Renaissance sonnet at its best had proved itself to be the ideal means of expression. This penetration into the very essence of another literature enabled Shakespeare throughout his career to realize the potential of the major conventions he inherited. *Romeo and Juliet,* if only because its indebtedness is so obvious, reminds us that Shakespeare drew strength from a literary heritage which was not England's alone. We may say of Shakespeare's tragedies that though their birthplace was England, their conception was in the literature of Greece and Rome and the European Renaissance. (pp. 50-4)

> Winifred Nowottny, "Shakespeare's Tragedies," in *Shakespeare's World, edited by James Sutherland and Joel Hurstfield, Edward Arnold (Publishers) Ltd., 1964, pp. 48-78.*

## JOHN WAIN   (essay date 1964)

[*Wain offers additional support for the idea that* Romeo and Juliet *fails as a tragedy—in his opinion because its materials are not inherently tragic. He maintains that the play "is in essence a comedy that turns out tragically," adding that it proceeds as it does for no apparent reason other than Shakespeare's desire to write a tragedy.*]

*Romeo and Juliet* is a mediaeval fate-tragedy. As such it can have no deep psychological interest. The impression it makes is one of pure pathos. 'Never was a story of more woe Than this of Juliet and her Romeo' [V. iii. 309-10]. And since everyone is responsive to pathos, it has always been a favourite on the stage. Shakespeare is still growing; he will do far greater things soon. But within its limitations, *Romeo and Juliet* is as perfectly achieved as anything in his work. It is a flawless little jewel of a play. It has the clear, bright colours, the blend of freshness and formality, of an illuminated manuscript. The eagerness and innocence of the young lovers is captured in words that are uncomplicated and memorable, and verse that chimes with a fresh, springy rhythm.

Not that this play is without indications of the more intricate richness that is to come. In the figure of the Nurse, we are already entering the area of mature Shakespearean realism. She is a sketch for Falstaff [in *Henry IV* and *The Merry Wives of Windsor*]; Romeo is a sketch for Hamlet. There is a morbid, self-wounding streak in the young man's nature that marks the dawn of Shakespeare's interest in characters of this type. After his impulsive killing of Tybalt, Romeo gives way to suicidal despair and tries to stab himself in the presence of Friar Laurence. This hot rashness recalls Hamlet's stabbing of Polonius, or his leaping into the grave with Laertes. And the Friar restrains him with a vehement rebuke that foreshadows some of Hamlet's reproaches against himself. (p. 106)

But where *Hamlet* takes us—albeit stumblingly—into purely tragic territory, the psychological premises of *Romeo and Juliet* are those of the early comedies. Characteristically, those comedies concern themselves with the inborn, unargued stupidity of older people and the life-affirming gaiety and resourcefulness of young ones. The lovers thread their way through obstacles set up by middle-aged vanity and impercipience. Parents are stupid and do not know what is best for their children or themselves: that is a *donnée* and does not have to be justified. *Romeo and Juliet* is in essence a comedy that turns out tragically. That is, it begins with the materials for a comedy—the stupid parental generation, the instant attraction of the young lovers, the quick surface life of street fights, masked balls and comic servants. But this material is blighted. Its gaiety and good fortune are drained away by the fact—also a *donnée*—that the lovers are 'star-crossed'. It is, to that extent, arbitrarily shaped. It is a tragedy because Shakespeare decided to sit down and write a tragedy. It does not build with inherently tragic materials. Where the comedies celebrate order by moving from disharmony to harmony, this play moves from surface disharmony to an almost achieved surface harmony, before being dashed by a blow from its author's fist into fundamental, irremediable disaster.

To put it another way, the form of *Romeo and Juliet* is that of a shattered minuet. The two lovers first come together in a dance (Act I, Scene v), and it is noteworthy that the first words they address to each other are in the form of a sonnet. A dance; a sonnet; these are symbols of a formal, contained wholeness. This wholeness is already threatened. Tybalt has recognized Romeo; and, though his demand for instant combat has been restrained by his host (a rare case of the older generation's being wiser than the younger), he is glowering and planning revenge. The worm is already in the fruit. But the nature of the worm is not explored. The characters move in a certain pattern because the author has decided on that pattern. Romeo and Juliet are all ardour and constancy, their families are all hatred and pride; no one's motives are mixed, and there are no question marks. After the tragedy the survivors are shocked into dropping their vendetta, and Montague and Capulet are united in grief. Once again, there are no question marks. Nothing made them enemies except the clash of their own wills, and nothing is needed to make them brothers except a change of heart.

A good many years went by before Shakespeare again handled this theme of lovers pushed apart by the world. When he did, he was deep in his tragic period, and had long since left behind the simpler notion that suffering is caused solely by the willed actions of human beings. If it were, people would only have to stop behaving tiresomely and paradise would arrive at once. (pp. 107-08)

> *John Wain, "Lovers Apart," in his* The Living World of Shakespeare: A Playgoer's Guide, *St. Martin's Press, 1964, pp. 104-41.*

## NORMAN N. HOLLAND    (essay date 1965)

[*Holland argues that the critic today is faced with a contradictory dilemma with respect to Shakespeare's works—namely, whether to accept the characters in the plays as "real," as people to be identified with, or whether to regard them merely as artifices of the dramatic world. Holland states that logically "it simply does not make sense to treat literary characters as real people," but he demonstrates nonetheless—through an examination of Mercutio in* Romeo and Juliet—*that it is still legitimate, indeed necessary to the enjoyment of dramatic art, to reconstruct a character's personality as if it were real. With this in mind, the critic claims that Mercutio is an individual who fears any emotion over which he has no control, such as love, and thus projects a "screen" of wordplay and "artificial gestures" against such normal human feelings. Holland discerns the same situation echoed in the play itself, where a highly stylized, artificial structure struggles to contain the tragic, emotional love of Romeo and Juliet, and he considers this tension "between verbal formality and raw emotion" the ultimate of "a whole series of formalized opposites" conveyed throughout the play.*]

When we pay tribute to [Shakespeare], we celebrate an imagination with a magnificent capacity for uniting things: the two traditions of his own day, popular and courtly; the most primitive functions of the human mind and the most intellectual—though every poet does that. More important for crossing centuries, he was able to span realism and nonrealism, "true things" and "their mock'ries" [*Henry V*, Prologue IV, 53]. That is, Shakespeare could transmute his own realistic experience localized in space and time, by somehow informing it with a nonrealistic, unlocalized significance. So informed, his characters from the sixteenth century can become part of the realistic experience of others four centuries later in states unborn and accents yet unknown. But how? How, despite the appalling weight of respectability and three centuries of criticism, indeed, an entire industry, can Shakespeare still appeal to an audience that has never seen or heard Shakespeare before? The Central Park Shakespeares are the obvious case in point. (p. 3)

[This] company traveled around the city playing in the small parks of Queens or the Bronx or, even, I suspect, Staten Island. They were playing to audiences many of whom had never seen a live actor before, most of whom had never seen Shakespeare before, and all of whom must have found such matters as

doublet, rapier, and the Elizabethan world picture as foreign as armadillos. They were, nevertheless, excited, pleased, identifying audiences who unabashedly rooted for the characters they liked. Especially enthusiastic, according to the *New Yorker*, were the grandmothers on their campstools. Quite delighted by Mercutio at a moment when he was playfully slapping the Nurse's backside, one elderly lady leaned to her neighbor and stage-whispered, "Like mine own son the dentist. A real chektah!"

Shakespeare, I think, would have been pleased, but most of his twentieth-century critics would not. The lady shows the same bridging quality we admire in Shakespeare himself—in her phrase, "a real character," she has managed to put back together something our century of critics has pulled apart, namely, the Shakespearean character. (pp. 3-4)

[Most neoclassical] critics held that Shakespeare's characters were like, or, for all practical purposes, the same as, real people. A minor, but earliest example is Margaret Cavendish describing in 1664 how "he Presents Passions so Naturally, and Misfortunes so Probably, as he Peirces the Souls of his Readers with such a True Sense and Feeling thereof, that it Forces Tears through their Eyes, and almost Perswades them, they are Really Actors, or at least Present at those Tragedies." Dennis and Rymer and Voltaire took the contrary view, but the main line of English critics came out resoundingly for the realism of Shakespeare's characters: Dryden, Pope, Lord Kames, and that most devious of critics, Dr. Johnson—"*Shakespeare* has no heroes: his scenes are occupied only by men, who act and speak as the reader thinks that he should himself have spoken or acted on the same occasion."

When, however, we turn from Johnson to Morgann, a dozen years later, we make a decisive shift into truly Romantic criticism of Shakespeare. That is, neoclassic critics like Johnson stressed our identification with the character, but Morgann saw the Shakespearean character as an historical being outside ourselves:

> He boldly makes a character act and speak from those parts of the composition, which are *inferred* only, and not distinctly shewn. This produces a wonderful effect: it seems to carry us beyond the poet to nature itself. . . . It may be fit [therefore] to consider them [the characters] rather as Historic than Dramatic beings; and, when occasion requires, to account for their conduct from the whole of character, from general principles, from latent motives, and from policies not avowed.

This historical externalization, looking at the events described by the text rather than the text itself, became the Romantic approach to Shakespeare. We see it in Goethe's remarks on *Hamlet* in 1795, in almost all of Coleridge's Shakespeare criticism, much of Hazlitt's, and on through the century in the effusions of Mrs. Jameson, Victor Hugo, Pushkin, or Swinburne. The culminating figure is, of course, Bradley. (pp. 4-5)

With one important exception (the psychoanalytic critics), twentieth-century criticism has turned its back on Bradley and all his works. Though, oddly enough, Edgar Allan Poe was the first to rebel against the nineteenth-century view and insist that Shakespeare's characters should not be treated as real people, the *locus classicus* for this point of view is L. C. Knight's 1933 essay, "How Many Children Had Lady Macbeth?" He took the basic twentieth-century position: the main business of the critic is to examine the words on the page and "'character'—like 'plot,' 'rhythm,' 'construction,' and all our other critical counters—is merely an abstraction from the total response in the mind of the reader or spectator, brought into being by written or spoken words" and entitled to no separate validity. Although Kenneth Burke, Kenneth Muir, Edmund Wilson, C. S. Lewis, F. R. Leavis, and many others take roughly the same view of Shakespeare, the most explicit anti-character Shakespearean is, of course, G. Wilson Knight: "The persons, ultimately, are not human at all, but purely symbols of a poetic vision." Furthermore, in a rare instance of critical and scholarly congeniality, the critics have received aid and comfort from those of the persuasion of Professor E. E. Stoll who have shown how unrealistic Shakespeare's theater and conventions were—as a matter of historical fact. Essentially, the new and neo-new critics are insisting on the formal nature of a work of art, and they deny the reality of character not just in Shakespeare's plays but in all kinds of fictions. . . . (pp. 5-6)

We have come, then, to an impasse. The old critics say we must think of Shakespeare's characters as real people; the new critics say we must not. Logically, we cannot have it both ways, and logic comes down squarely against treating the characters as real.

Literary characters exist in the contrived, shaped world of a work of art. Real people live in the unshaped world of everyday reality. It makes little sense to apply psychological concepts (Morgann's "general principles" of human nature) taken from the disorderly everyday world to a quite different world shaped by theme and form. In fact, literary characters are so shaped by the world in which they exist they cannot even be moved from book to book or play to play. . . . Even similar characters created by the same author face trouble moving from one work to another. Falstaff [in *Henry IV* and *The Merry Wives of Windsor*] would bulk too large in the romantic and pastoral world of *The Winter's Tale*, while Autolycus [in *The Winter's Tale*] with his ribbons and laces could hardly parade on the field at Shrewsbury or masquerade as Mother Prat of Brainford. If even such adaptable con men as Falstaff and Autolycus cannot move from one Shakespearean play to another, it seems to make still less sense to apply to both of them concepts of human nature from still a third world in which neither of them could be, namely, the real world.

Logically, it simply does not make sense to treat literary characters as real people. But does logic govern here? Or experience? H. L. Mencken had the answer. Because he was famous as an atheist, people liked to badger him on the subject, and one day a reporter asked him if he believed in infant baptism. Replied Mencken, "Believe in it? Hell, I've *seen* it!" And much the same thing is true of character analysis. Logically it is unsupportable, but I have seen, by the dozens, psychoanalytic studies which diagnose Shakespeare's characters as though they were real people on the couch or in clinic; and these studies, even when they are contradictory, give ample, more than ample, evidence from the plays themselves. The psychoanalytic critics are indeed applying psychological concepts from the world of everyday reality to characters who exist in a wholly different kind of world—it should not work, but it does. I have even done it myself by analyzing Romeo's little three-line dream as though it had been dreamed by a real young man who had lost his virginity the night before [see excerpt above, 1963]. In fact, some of the elements in the dream led me beyond the sacrosanct words-on-the-page to infer in the discredited

manner of Morgann certain things about the wedding night, though Shakespeare himself had tactfully drawn across them the curtain of the upper stage. (pp. 6-7)

The wise man chooses to make [characters] real, for how else could he experience the play, except by relating himself to [those] on the stage as people that he has known or been? From the lines we are hearing, we re-create the characters, the words on the page controlling and shaping the characters we create. Then, as in that writers' cliché, the characters "take on a life of their own," and they in turn shape and inform the words on the page. In short, we are not quasi-scientific observers of a phenomenon outside ourselves, historical as the Romantic critics would have it, or the words-on-the-page as the New Critic would have it. Rather, we are involved with the text and it with us in a way that demands the description of a harshly scientific word: feedback. We and the words-on-the-page bind ourselves in the literary transaction, a process as mutual as any bargain. Once we accept this bridge, namely, that we in the audience make the characters real, we are in a position to see how a character like Mercutio can be both realistic and, as Wilson Knight would have him, "purely symbol[ic] of a poetic vision."

At first glance, Mercutio is outrageously unrealistic. I have known a lot of witty and literary people, and never have I known anyone who was as fluent in blank verse as Mercutio or who could while away the hours of an adolescent evening by coming up *ad lib* with something like the Queen Mab speech. But I have known many people like Mercutio in other ways. He is the classic joker: he pours out a perfect stream of puns, rhymes, and cheerful obscenities. I have known people like that, and so I suspect have you—and so has Romeo, for he recognizes Mercutio as a type: "He jests at scars that never felt a wound" [II. ii. 1]. But what type?

We can tell from the kind of joke he makes. He aims his wit at Tybalt's Italianate duello, a "new form," like the pose of courtly love, Romeo's initial "groaning" toward Rosaline which also draws Mercutio's fire. He can speak of "my gossip Venus" and "young Abraham Cupid" [II. i. 11, 13]; he can accuse Romeo of thinking Laura a kitchen-wench, "Dido a dowdy, Cleopatra a gypsy, Helen and Hero hildings and harlots, Thisbe a grey eye or so, but not to the purpose" [II. iv. 41-3]. (pp. 9-10)

And yet, even as he tears down the gods and goddesses of others, he wishes himself to soar. In the very first words we hear him speak, he urges Romeo, who says he is feeling heavy, "Nay, gentle Romeo, we must have you dance" [I. iv. 13], and he urges him to "borrow Cupid's wings and soar with them above a common bound," to "beat love down" [I. iv. 17-18, 28] as he himself does. The epitaph Benvolio gives him is all too fitting:

> That gallant spirit hath aspired the clouds
> Which too untimely here did scorn the earth.
>
> [III. i. 117-18]
> (p. 10)

Mercutio's jokes, then, do two things. First, they attack the high and formal. For example, though he is invited to the Capulets' ball, he chooses instead to crash. Yet, even as he puts aside the formal invitation, he dons a mask to disguise himself, another kind of formality. The pattern of Mercutio's wit, then, is that he pulls down the imposing forms and idols of others but, second, he sets up in their high place his own artificial gestures—puns, rhymes, jokes, set speeches, and other masks. He attacks in others his own chief trait, and we can guess his reason—a sense of his own insufficiency. He calls his mask,

> A visor for a visor! What care I
> What curious eye shall quote deformities?
> Here are the beetle brows shall blush for me.
>
> [I. iv. 30-2]

Mercutio's wit follows the school of Hobbes or Kenneth Burke: "sudden glory arising from some sudden conception of some eminency in ourselves, by comparison with the infirmity of others or with our own formerly".... Laughter, Hobbes goes on, "is incident most to them that are conscious of the fewest abilities in themselves; who are forced to keep themselves in their own favour by observing the imperfections of other men."

As for Mercutio's sense of his own insufficiency, we can guess—again, from a heavily realistic point of view—its roots in childhood. They show in the speech where Mercutio conjures up the spirit of the absent Romeo, in the process making some grandly obscene remarks about Rosaline. The peaceful Benvolio remonstrates, "Thou wilt anger him" [II. i. 22]. Not so, says Mercutio.

> This cannot anger him. 'Twould anger him
> To raise a spirit in his mistress' circle
> Of some strange nature, letting it there stand
> Till she had laid it and conjured it down.
> That were some spite; my invocation
> Is fair and honest: in his mistress' name,
> I conjure only but to raise up him.
>
> [II. i. 23-9]

It was Romeo's "calm, dishonourable, vile submission" [III. i. 73], literally his 'putting himself under' that so infuriated Mercutio; and there is a grim irony in his being killed "under" Romeo's arm. Raising up seems to represent for Mercutio a child's ithyphallic notion of virility; being laid—down—its opposite, and so his defense is:

> If love be rough with you, be rough with love.
> Prick love for pricking, and you beat love down.
>
> [I. iv. 27-8]

The best defense is a good offense. Romeo says, "He jests at scars that never felt a wound," but we could with a more sophisticated psychology paraphase him: He jests at scars that fears to feel a wound—a certain kind of wound, the kind that comes from real love that would lay him low, make him undergo a submission like Romeo's. Mercutio's bawdry serves to keep him a noncombatant in the wars of love; it enables him to make allies of his companions, notably Romeo, against his own emotions—as he says, after a wit-sally, "Why, is this not better now than groaning for love?" [II. iv. 88-9]. Not for Mercutio is that entrance into the tomb or womb or maw which is Romeo's dark, sexual fate.

Whether we re-create Mercutio psychoanalytically or in the simpler and more loving way of the grandmotherly lady in the park, he can become the most realistic of real characters. He is a bit "thin"—that is, he does not have the great variety of traits a real person has, but what traits he does have are real enough. I have known him, I have even been him, warding off the dangers of emotion with a smokescreen of words.... Yet I find this man I have known or been in the most formal, artificial, and stylized of Shakespeare's plays: truly an imaginary garden with a real toad in it. I find in my own response the paradox or impasse between, on the one hand, Shake-

speare's seventeenth-, eighteenth-, and nineteenth-century critics and, on the other, his twentieth-century critics with their antirealistic view of character.

Shakespeare's modern critics turned away from character to imagery, and if we take off our ninteenth-century spectacles, the set of images that first strikes the eye consists of what Professor Harry Levin has called "formality" [see excerpt above, 1960]: the ceremonies, such as the Capulets' ball, the marriage of Romeo and Juliet, the Prince's decrees, or Juliet's funeral; the images of books, reading and writing, or words ("A rose by any other name would smell as sweet" [II. ii. 43-4]) and even letters of the alphabet—the two the play toys with are "R" and "I" which, by some strange coincidence, happen to be (in Elizabethan orthography) the initials of the two lovers. It is a pretty device, entirely too pretty and artificial. One senses in the tragedy as a whole a tension between this formality and the raw emotions of love and hate seething beneath its surfaces.

In other words, the whole work of art uses the same defense that the individual character does. Just as Mercutio puts up words as a screen against emotions that might wound, so the tragedy as a whole poises against the love of Romeo and Juliet the names Montague and Capulet or that other word that has "no end, no limit, measure, bound," the Prince's word "banished" [III. ii. 125]. As always in tragedy, the defense fails. There is a return of the repressed, love bursts through, and the tragic catastrophe follows. Romeo and Juliet's love undermines the words "Montague," "Capulet," "banished," just as Mercutio's jokes do not keep him from being laid low by Tybalt's "envious thrust."

This tension between verbal formality and raw emotion, however, makes but one in a whole series of formalized opposites into which the images of the tragedy divide: love-hate, old-young, male-female, water-fire, night-day, long-short, sweet-sour, vice-virtue, and even dog-cat. In the movement of the play as a whole, the tragic catastrophe comes when these opposites engulf each other, when the hate of the old Montagues and Capulets entombs the love of Romeo and Juliet, and when their love breaks down the families' hate:

> These violent delights have violent ends
> And in their triumph die, like fire and powder,
> Which, as they kiss, consume.
>
> [II. v. 9-11]

What is true of the play as a whole holds true for Mercutio in particular. He tries to pull down to earth the idolatries of others and set his own formalities on high. But just the opposite happens to him in this play of opposites. He is brought low by "a braggart, a rogue, a villain that fights by the book of arithmetic" and a friend who "kiss[es] by th' book" [III. i. 102; I. v. 110]. And even as he is made "a grave man," "worms' meat" [III. i. 98, 107] his spirit "has aspired the clouds." So in the tragedy as a whole: as the Prince tells old Montague at the end:

> Come, Montague; for thou art early up
> To see they son and heir more early down.
>
> [V. iii. 208-09]

As the lovers sink down into the tomb, so old Montague and Capulet promise to "raise" their statues in gold.

Pulling down the formalities of others to set up one's own, the two key elements in Mercutio's realistic character pervade the nonrealistic play. Or perhaps we should put it the other way around: the key themes of the play, the collapse of opposites, particularly verbal formality as against emotion, have shaped the naturalistic character of Mercutio. Each informs and creates the other. In short, we have found our bridge between the seventeenth, eighteenth, and nineteenth centuries' realistic view of Shakespeare's characters and our own view of the play as a "poetic construct."

From the words on the page so important in modern objective or formalist criticism, we have managed to cross by way of our subjective re-creation of the play to the Romantic sense of the tragedy as an external quasi-historical reality. In effect, we have found a bridge, but we never lost one. All we needed to do was to look not just at what the play brings to us, but also at what we bring to the play. The bridge was always there, in the human psyche, our own, but more to the point, Shakespeare's. He could create a thing of formal beauty that would nevertheless evoke from all of us, groundlings at the Globe or grandmothers in the Bronx, our deepest selves. This is the creative gift, the heart of the mystery. The poet informs realism with nonrealism and nonrealism with realism and so moves from his own unique and local experience to ours equally unique and local. Both are "solely singular for the singleness" [II. iv. 65-6], but the poet can bridge from himself to us by finding in his own realistic experience timeless and universal form— or, if not timeless, at least a form for the celebration of which, four hundred years is all too short a date. (pp. 10-14)

> Norman N. Holland, "Mercutio, Mine Own Son the Dentist," in Essays on Shakespeare, edited by Gordon Ross Smith, The Pennsylvania State University Press, University Park, 1965, pp. 3-14.

## NICHOLAS BROOKE (essay date 1965)

[Brooke avers that such early works by Shakespeare as Titus Andronicus and Romeo and Juliet are "conscious experiments in poetic drama," incorporating techniques that the playwright employed in his earlier nondramatic poems and reflecting "the highly sophisticated tradition of the Elizabethan poetic." He demonstrates that in Romeo and Juliet Shakespeare uses stylized poetry to enshrine, "as no other form of utterance could, the profoundest imaginative values in the play," while at the same time forcing us to recognize the central paradox of the action—the "death-marked love" of the protagonists. Brooke concludes that the "tragic conception implied" is not a personal one, "moralizing on the lovers' juvenile impatience," but is more universal, suggesting that "the finest of human experiences have inherent limitations, regardless of who embodies them."]

The differences between Shakespeare's earliest tragedies are so striking as to suggest a deliberate, formal distinction between different modes of tragedy: the historical-political in Richard III, the Roman (Senecan and Ovidian) in Titus Adronicus, and the romance in Romeo and Juliet. This deliberation extends, I think, to the obvious stylistic differences between the plays, and a clue to its character may be found in their different relationships to Shakespeare's non-dramatic poems. Titus abounds in parallels with his Ovidian narratives, Venus and Adonis and The Rape of Lucrece, whereas Romeo echoes the sonnets, and actually employs sonnet form both for the chorus and for the climax of Act I. The implication is that these plays are conscious experiments in poetic drama, conceived in the highly sophisticated tradition of Elizabethan poetic, the formal ordering of figures, emblems, and language which governs the variety and range of The Faerie Queene; and thus, in one

aspect, they may be seen as dramatic explorations of the poetic forms on which they draw. (p. 243)

Unlike Titus, Romeo and Juliet has retained its popularity on the stage, though frequently given, until quite recently, in "improved" versions. This popularity rests firmly enough on the romantic idealism of the lovers and the earthy comedy of the Nurse and old Capulet. Seen thus, the play has an apparently simple outline, and it may seem perverse to suggest that it is too simple to be true; yet it is obvious that the romance can be accepted at a magazine level that is not really superior to the horror-film aspect of Titus. Recognition of human bestiality was unpopular for two and a half centuries before the revelations of Belsen and Auschwitz; sentimental romance, however, flourished throughout that period. To put the point in a different way, one can say that either Romeo and Juliet is concerned with a more complex view of experience, or that a great deal of the play is at best unnecessary, at worst irrelevant.

Symmetry of structure is as evident here as in Titus (or, of course, Richard III). The opening and closing acts are governed by a very marked formality, suspending the play between the ceremonial of the sonnet encounter at the dance and the ritualized ceremony of death in the tomb. This ceremonial stress tends to give the play the over-all quality of a stately dance, a secular erotic ritual appropriately inclined to formal rhyme-patterns in its verse; and the ending is commonly felt, I think, to be effective rather in the way of spectacular ballet than of tragic drama. By contrast, the central climaxes of the play round which these ceremonies are balanced are very markedly unceremonial: the marriage is off-stage and unimportant, the consummation clandestine, and Mercutio's death scene is not allowed the dignity of verse. Structural formality is again echoed in the staging, most obviously in the dance of Act I, scene v, and probably in the placing of Juliet's table-tomb in the same discovery-space which had earlier held her bed—a visual juxtaposition which points the fulfilment of the Prologue's anticipation of a death-marked love.

The Prologue, and periodic echoes of it in the first two acts, are an insistent part of the formal structure, and they can seem uncomfortably blatant in anticipation of tragic themes—the family feud, the star-crossed lovers, and so on. Their insistence, however, has to be set against the fact that without them we should certainly feel a predominant tone of comedy, and be ill-prepared for the change of key in Act III. From the trivial prose of Samson and Gregory, through the mock-devotion of Romeo for Rosaline and the earthy humor of the Nurse, to the skeptical laughter of Mercutio and the diminutive malice of Queen Mab, there is little to suggest that the end will be in tears rather than laughter. Without the direct statements we could almost believe ourselves watching a sequel to The Two Gentlemen of Verona. Almost, though not quite, for there are serious suggestions in the lightest passages, and in the first scene these emerge through a rapid development not only of stage action but also of rhythm and seriousness in the mode of utterance. Bawdy prose yields to Benvolio's first introduction of blank verse: "Put up your swords; you know not what you do" [I. i. 65]; and that in turn gives way to the fully heroic tone of the Prince's rebuke to the assembled cast. This is not necessarily a tragic pitch, but it is certainly serious; and its seriousness emerging from the seemingly comic intensifies the thematic relevance of even the bawdiest punning about death and love:

> GREGORY. Drawn thy tool; here comes two of
> the house of Montagues.

SAMPSON. My naked weapon is out: quarrel; I
will back thee.

                                              [I. i. 31-4]

Pun and paradox, light or ominous, govern an exceptional
proportion of this play; they derive from the tradition of comedy, and of Elizabethan love poetry such as Chapman's *Shadow
of Night,* and the sonnet sequences. This play is much an
exploration of that tradition as *Titus* was of the Ovidian narrative. Love may be cruel-kind, absurd-beautiful, trivial-seri-
ous, earthy-divine, life-death, and so on; and these possibilities
are pursued through a multiplicity of detail focusing on the
central paradox of "death-marked love," through the structural
interaction of comic and tragic tones, as well as the contrast
of the casual, clandestine, accidental with the purposive implications of the formal and ceremonial. The insistence on wit
and wordplay continually reminds us of the non-dramatic tradition, and has . . . the consequence of formal detachment, of
reminding us that we are critical spectators, not participants.
(pp. 250-52)

The decisive shift from comedy to tragedy is achieved in Mercutio's death, which is simultaneously the extreme demonstration of the serious emerging from the trivial. Act III, scene
i, develops a lightness of touch which has already been conspicuous through most of Act II; the scuffle of Tybalt and
Mercutio appears casual and unimportant, and its devastating
result is scarcely apparent to the actors themselves:

> ROMEO. Courage, man; the hurt cannot be much.
> MERCUTIO. No, 'tis not so deep as a well, nor
> so wide as a church door, but 'tis enough, 'twill
> serve. Ask for me tomorrow and you shall find
> me a grave man.
>
>                                          [III. i. 95-8]

The justly celebrated pun marks the play's most directly moving moment as a transition to gravity; and at the same time
uses the plainness of prose to expose Romeo's unperceptiveness
and the shocking inadequacy of his later "I thought all for the
best" [III. i. 104]. The fanciful and poetic world of love is,
with Romeo, reproved by the prosaic event of death, as poetry
is apt to be reproved by reality (as Keats repeatedly affirmed).
The effect of this scene is very like the intrusion of death in
the last act of *Love's Labour's Lost* and, placed centrally, it
challenges the whole direction of the play. The poetic romance
must ultimately be fulfilled in a poetic death, but the "beauty"
of that will have to be established against not only the earthiness
of the Nurse or old Capulet but also the sharper sense of cold
reality here as Mercutio dies the way men do die—prosaically,
accidentally, irrelevantly, absurdly.

In short, either the poetic structure must prove capable of sustaining this shock, or be exposed as trivial prettiness. One may
feel that neither is quite the final situation, but the best of the
play is to make us recognize both. This is not, of course, the
first time that Romeo is reproved. When their joint sonnet has
celebrated the first moment of mutual recognition, his attempt
to extend the tone beyond the completion of the form is met
by Juliet's "You kiss by th' book" [I. v. 110]; and more
disturbingly, in Act II, scene ii, he never matches Juliet's
frankness, so his efforts to substitute vows for confidence are
repeatedly criticized [II. ii. 107ff]. Against this kind of thing,
the bawdy incredulity of Mercutio is most welcome. But the
critical interaction is two-way: Mercutio points the absurdity
of sonneteers, but he has no perception of the values they can
really represent. In Act II, scene iv, his mockery assumes that

Romeo has been to bed with Rosaline, and the double mistake—that it was not Rosaline, and not to bed—emphasizes
the ignorance that limits Mercutio's vision.

On the likeness and difference of comic and serious values
Shakespeare provides a commentary in set-speeches which
reinterpret emblems in a mode directly comparable with that
of *Titus Andronicus.* The comic view of love personified in
Mercutio is epitomized in his speech in Act I, scene iv, about
Queen Mab, the diminutive wagoner who whips her steeds
through the night to feed men's dreams of sex, wealth, and
power, cheating them with fear, blisters, and unwanted preg-
nancy. The same emblems of night figures in the radically
contrasting speech with which Juliet opens Act III, scene ii:

> Gallop apace, you fiery-footed steeds,
> Towards Phoebus' lodging! Such a waggoner
> As Phaëton would whip you to the west
> And bring in cloudy night immediately.
>
>                                          [III. ii. 1-4]

Juliet's night, as vast and momentous as Mercutio's was minute
and trivial, is no less a setting where love and lust are at their
climax indistinguishable: "civic night" is again the madam of
a brothel hooding the virgin's unmanned blood

> With thy black mantle till strange love, grown bold,
> Think true love acted simple modesty.
>
>                                          [III. ii. 15-16]

The speech echoes Queen Mab in more than Juliet's discovery
that she must be a prostitute in order to be a wife; the emblems
of night include the predatory and destructive raven:

> Come, Night! Come, Romeo! Come, thou day in night;
> For thou wilt lie upon the wings of night
> Whiter than snow upon a raven's back.
> Come, gentle Night; come, loving, black-browed Night:
> Give me my Romeo; and, when he shall die,
> Take him and cut him out in little stars. . . .
>
>                                          [III. ii. 17-22]

The familiar pun on death as orgasm is used to focus an association in "Night" between love and actual death, and so
suggest a rendering of "death-marked love," which is, as I
take it, the play's profoundest paradox. This is the particular
concern of Act III, where the sequence of scenes is very clearly
established to bring death and love to an intertwined climax.
The initial projection of a new tone is provided by the shock
of Mercutio's death; Juliet's soliloquy follows that, but is not
a consequence because she is not yet aware of what has happened. The contrast between her speech and "Queen Mab"
depends first on the experience of the love scenes in Act II,
of which Mercutio remained for ever unaware; but our attention
is sharpened by the sense of death, and though Juliet's desire
is not here stimulated by it, the consummation in Act III, scene
v, is achieved in the knowledge of its immanence. This sequence therefore associates their love with death without any
confusing suggestion of necrophilia (which we may feel later).
Nevertheless, the association is so strong that it seems only a
slight variation on her earlier longings when Juliet says:

> Come, cords; come, Nurse: I'll to my wedding bed,
> And death, not Romeo, take my maidenhead!
>
>                                          [III. ii. 136-37]

She later displays impatient desire for her mock death at the
Friar's hands in charnel-house images [IV. i. 77-88], and finally in

Give me, give me! O tell not me of fear!
[V. i. 121]

she grasps the poison that leads her into the tomb, where the mock death gives place to the ceremonial suicides in Act V, as the mock love and official coming-of-age in Act I had yielded to the ceremony of actual passion.

The significant point in this is that the desire of Juliet and Romeo moves without interval from love to death; and we are not allowed to think it could be otherwise, since its core is found in the emblems of night which exclude the ordinary and productive light of day. Remarkable as the love poetry of the play is, especially Juliet's "Gallop apace," it is as remarkable for what it is not. It contains no suggestion at all of continuity in life, no equivalent even of the fertile mud of the Nile; and though Juliet is compared to a flower occasionally, it is to be nipped by frost, not to fructify. Their love is, in fact, contrasted with much that is most vital in the play: the Nurse, Mercutio, the old Capulets. In all of these the stuff of life is earthy, bawdy, comic, certainly thoughtless, and impatient; in many respects it seems only a cheapened version of what the lovers can show, but it has a continuing warmth and resilence that is reassuring and utterly in contrast to the glory of Romeo and Juliet. This very vitality, in Capulet's impatience, precipitates disaster. It is the play's characteristically paradoxical suggestion that this sense of life is entirely alien to the romantic vision of love, and that each criticizes the other. The ecstatic love-death experience becomes unreal fantasy against this other; this becomes tawdry set against Beauty's ensign and Death's pale

*Act III. Scene v. Romeo, Juliet, and Nurse. By J. F. Rigaud.*

flag. As much as Mercutio can mock the absurdities of sonnet love, Juliet in turn can denounce her Nurse's exposed shallowness, "Ancient damnation" [III. v. 235ff.]. The formal poetry of the play enshrines, as no other form of utterance could, the profoundest imaginative values in the play; but it forces us to see that a shrine is a place of death. In so far as love has this absoluteness, it is absolute for death. Hemingway's admirers often compare his novels with *Romeo and Juliet;* and it is true of *A Farewell to Arms* or *For Whom the Bell Tolls* that one feels that the necessity for death as the end derives, not from the narrative circumstances, but from the fragile romanticism of the love itself. Shakespeare, unlike Hemingway, establishes this limitation as part of the substance of the play. However early in his output, this is a play *about* immaturity rather than an immature play. (pp. 252-56)

Both [*Titus Andronicus* and *Romeo and Juliet*] employ the formal achievements of Elizabethan verse to expound a spectacle of human experience from which we are in a measure detached by the formality of staging and utterance. Both contrast this with an emergent vitality of an alien kind: Aaron, or the Nurse. It is obvious that the range of utterance and perception is wider in *Romeo,* and that we may respond more easily to a play where our sympathy can be continued to the end. Yet the last act of *Romeo* often baffles that sympathy— for good reason—and the effort that is sometimes made to view the tragedy in straightforwardly personal terms, moralizing on the lovers' juvenile impatience, can never be more than partially convincing because the play is composed, like *Titus,* as much as a spectacle of human experience as a plea for individual pathos. The tragic conception implied is that the finest of human experiences have inherent limitations, regardless of who embodies them. Romantic love is a lightning before death; the dignity of Roman nobility is founded on barbarous bestiality. A sense of individual personality is present, of course, in both plays; but the generic condition dominates. Both plays are immensely ambitious, overcrowded, experimental; when they were written it was not just in poetry that they surpassed their predecessors . . . : in range and control of dramatic idea and language they are both achievements far beyond any other dramatist of the time. (p. 256)

Nicholas Brooke, "The Tragic Spectacle in 'Titus Andronicus' and 'Romeo and Juliet'," in Shakespeare, the Tragedies: A Collection of Critical Essays, *edited by Clifford Leech, The University of Chicago Press, 1965, pp. 243-56.*

**ROBERT O. EVANS**  (essay date 1966)

[*Evans suggests that the fundamental question of* Romeo and Juliet *"is not whether this is a tragedy arising from the characterization Shakespeare invented or one brought about largely by fortuitous circumstances," but "whether the ending is one of frustration or fulfillment." For Evans, it is one of fulfillment, an assessment he bases on Shakespeare's development of character in the play. According to the critic, it is misleading to view* Romeo and Juliet *as "a tragedy of fate," for although destiny does play a role in the drama, the catastrophe is brought about by the characters' own decisions and actions. Evans contends, however, that the lovers' tragic flaw resides not in their overly sensuous natures, as many critics have maintained, but in "the great powers of their intellects combined with the higher parts of [their] souls." The critic also comments on the* amour-passion *and* Liebestod *myths and their relevancy to* Romeo and Juliet.]

It has been said that [*Romeo and Juliet*] is not entirely successful as tragedy, though a good performance contradicts that contention. Nevertheless, careful students of the play find faults with both the plot and characterization. For example, Romeo and Juliet are both too young and . . . perhaps too ordinary for ideal tragic figures. For some critics accident too often seems to intervene in the development of the action. But, when we leave the theatre, we discover that we have experienced to the fullest the cup of tragedy.

Accordingly, it would seem the fundamental question of the play is not whether this is a tragedy arising from the characterization Shakespeare invented or one brought about largely by fortuitous circumstances. The fundamental question of the play, I believe, is really whether the ending is one of frustration or fulfillment, and, depending on how we answer it, whether the play will seem adequately tragic or a partial failure. Moreover, as M. M. Mahood says when [she] is discussing this point, "this question emerges from the language of the play itself and thus differs from the conventional, superimposed problem: is *Romeo and Juliet* a tragedy of character or fate?" [see excerpt above, 1957].

If the ending is one of fulfillment, as I contend, it must arise primarily from the development of character. One can have tragedy arising through the intervention of some outside force, as in classical drama. But an ending that suggests eternal fulfillment through the compulsions working within two personalities does not make plausible an assertion that the ending is produced by accident. Fulfillment surely suggests planned development. To say so certainly does not mean that we ought to ignore the role of fate in *Romeo and Juliet*, but here fate is moving within the characters. For example, the letter from Friar Laurence to Romeo in Mantua is, one might say, almost fatally delayed, thereby permitting the tragic action to proceed. But it is what Romeo is moved to do, not the delay of the letter, that has a fatal quality. It is not even certain that had he received the letter the outcome would have been altered. We have no idea how well Friar Laurence informed him. In any case the role of these drives from within is not equivalent to that of the gods in classical tragedy.

Critics who have thought the play was a tragedy of fate, though, are not perhaps entirely at fault; Shakespeare himself encouraged that opinion in the prefatory sonnet by calling the lovers "star-crossed." To us that term means fated—arising entirely from outside forces. It has not been suggested that Shakespeare might have been deliberately misleading us a little or even that the term might have a slightly ironic flavor, but if we consider the development of the action we must see the fateful quality that comes not from the stars but from *within* the two lovers. Although the two appear at last to move inexorably toward the tomb, the audience does not gaze awe-stricken and horror-bound, as in some Greek dramas, at a god-determined progression toward death. Even in the sonnet, if we consider the whole line, "A pair of star-crossed lovers take their life" [Prologue, 6] . . . , Shakespeare does not quite indicate that conclusion. Their stars do cross, and Romeo and Juliet fall in love and eventually die. On the surface at least we seem to be hearing that fate will intervene in the course of the love affair. But the sonnet also could mean just that they were destined to meet and fall in love—not destined by the gods to fall in love and accordingly die.

Their love was the cause of their deaths, but the sonnet does not quite say that. It only announces that they *take* their lives, indicating how they were to die, not why. The line does not say they *lose* their lives. If it did the role of fate would be emphasized. It does not even say their lives were *taken* from

them, though that would alter the meaning and require further explanation. Shakespeare through his choice of verbs seems deliberately to have altered the fatal aspect, or at least to have constructed an ambiguity. . . . An ambiguity about the inevitability of the outcome of the play, even so early in the prefatory sonnet, is as it should be, for we discover as the play progresses that there is no force greater than the love within them driving Romeo and Juliet to their deaths.

Shakespeare suggests that Romeo and Juliet are perhaps being driven towards their deaths by a romantic love that is fast becoming an all-consuming passion. That is part of a paradox that creates depth in what is after all a fairly simple story. But passion, no matter how strong it becomes, never does consume them; there is always a strong element of rationality to their love.

Though Shakespeare does not completely resolve this paradox for us, there are other ways of considering the matter that may shed some additional light. One may examine, for example, the philosophical concepts used in the play. Shakespeare understood well the medieval view of man as a rung on the hierarchical ladder of the universe. There man's place was determined or ordained by God, but within the limits of his human nature man was allowed to exercise a certain degree of freedom. Perhaps Shakespeare also felt that there is a contradiction inherent in that metaphysic. He must have been aware of even more extravagant, more paradoxical, Renaissance opinions. There is reason to believe that he sometimes leaned in their direction. . . . To the medieval mind man's abilities were limited; it was possible for man to become a saint but never an angel. The Renaissance, without discovering many solutions, questioned all such bounds. Anything seemed possible. It is hardly necessary to demonstrate that Shakespeare was attracted by this idea, for on it he founded the character of Prospero in *The Tempest*, long after he had considered it in *Romeo and Juliet*.

Equally available to the writer of the Renaissance was the Calvinistic view that man's ultimate spiritual course was predetermined. Such a position is antithetical to the doctrine of free will, but that seldom stopped the Renaissance thinker from considering both, even considering them together. This paradox was, perhaps unconsciously, exploited in *Romeo and Juliet*. There instead of emphasizing the inevitability of the action, Shakespeare pitted his attractive young lovers against the hard-bitten adult world of Verona and, if the game was to be worth the candle, gave them at least an outside chance to win happiness. In a sense they might shape their own destinies. But great love, grand passion, if often destructive to lovers' hopes in this world, may bring fulfillment at least in the next. The lovers may also have a part in the resolution of other issues, by bringing, for example, the feuding families to a truce at the end of the play. At the end war had apparently won; the lovers were dead. But in another way war itself was overcome. That is clear even if we do not think of a fulfillment beyond the grave.

There are also other, more complex matters at stake in the play. It might not be inconsistent with Renaissance psychology . . . to view the ending as having arisen from an excess in the appetitive portions of the souls of Romeo and Juliet. Indeed the humours employed in the play sometimes quite strongly create that impression. The play is often very earthy and sensual; the hero and heroine quite often indulge in bawdy language. Romeo in the earlier affair with Rosaline seems as much motivated by pure sexuality as Euphues in *The Anatomy of*

*Wit*. And a little later, his attraction for Juliet, who indicates from the beginning that she will not resist, arises from the same source in his nature. His feelings for Juliet are at first the same as they were for Rosaline, though they are soon to run much deeper. It is Juliet who thinks of marriage and honor, not Romeo. . . . [She] encourages him as her suitor not simply because she is a well-bred young lady whose *bel accueil* [gracious welcome] is extended to all her acquaintances, but because Romeo arouses a deep, passionate response in her nature. It is not his name that matters, we are told in the famous passage, but his person. I am afraid we invariably interpret that passage with reference to the feud, meaning that Juliet wished Romeo might cease to be a Montague so that courtship could proceed. But there is a deeper sense to the words that is quite as important. It is not who Romeo is, in terms of the age-old marriage game, but what he is that matters. He is an extremely attractive young man worthy of her passion which has been aroused in spite of the conventions of Veronese society. Nevertheless, Shakespeare did not move from such considerations to the writing of an *exemplum* in which two delightful young persons were punished for an excess of sensuality. If that had been his intention, why trouble to bring up the question of marriage at all? He treated excessive sensuality directly in *Troilus and Cressida*, but *Romeo and Juliet* was not conceived to be that kind of play.

It is possible to argue for an even subtler interpretation of the psychology of the play, that the lovers were punished for permitting their wills to usurp the functions of their reason. The two arguments are closely related. And Juliet is decidedly a girl of strong will; early in the play she made up her mind not to marry Paris no matter what her parents wished. If she could not marry Romeo, then she would die. But Shakespeare's sympathies and those of the audience are certainly with Juliet. Despite the show of independence, her attack on the conventional, she remains throughout the play a very rational girl. In her first scene she tells Romeo, "You kiss by the book" [I. v. 110]. There is a point at which a young girl with a sound head understands that the flirtation has gone far enough. It is not Juliet who is the irrational, headstrong one, but, we see as the play progresses, her father, old Capulet, who assumes one of the least sympathetic roles in Shakespeare. Like Brabantio in *Othello* or, in a lighter vein, like Polonius in *Hamlet*, the heavy father in Shakespeare is usually doomed.

Sensuality, which at one stage seems to detract from the play's tragic quality, is later shown to be a necessary ingredient of grand passion. Shortly, as love becomes great passion, it adds to the characterization. Shakespeare exploited that idea fully in *Antony and Cleopatra*. To Anthony, Cleopatra's kiss was worth a battle or a kingdom, even the greatest kingdom the world had known, and to Cleopatra, Antony's love aroused immortal longings. Neither Antony, an old rake, far worse than Shakespeare painted him if we are to believe Plutarch and Cicero, nor Cleopatra, an infamous courtezan, to speak of her kindly, are very appropriate subjects for great tragedy, at least not in an Aristotelian sense, but Shakespeare made them so by the complicated process of refining their language and forcing us to accept as elevating their grand passion. *Romeo and Juliet* in this sense was the proving ground for the later play. Romeo and Juliet are not the prince and princess of Verona, though they are far better people than Antony and Cleopatra. They are really rather ordinary youngsters from good, Veronese households, neither more nor less important than many others one might find at the Capulet ball. They are too young and too attractive to treat with anything less than full sympathy, and

had circumstances been different to start with, had their families been at peace and no unforeseen accidents occurred, they might have loved and wed and lived unnoticed happily ever after. Perhaps that was what Shakespeare meant to imply at the beginning of the play by mixing his genres, for the first two acts of *Romeo and Juliet* are romantic comedy. But Romeo and Juliet are raised to tragic stature, magically perhaps, but by the means Shakespeare had to work with at the time. One of these was to persuade his audience that grand passion was indeed an elevating and ennobling emotion. Another was to place in the mouths of the hero and heroine some of the most beautiful and lyrical language ever written. Still another was to emphasize the rationality of the lovers through their mastery of rhetoric. These matters . . . make it difficult for us to believe that Romeo and Juliet were punished for a tragic flaw that arose from an excess of sensuality, an imbalance in the appetitive portions of their souls.

As hard as it is to decide where the ending of the play lies in the spectrum between frustration and fulfillment, the close observer of Shakespeare's technique may find something overt to encourage the possibility of fulfillment. Shakespeare liked to mirror the macrocosm in the microcosm, to utilize to the fullest the doctrine of correspondences at all levels of the play. In fact *Romeo and Juliet* particularly exemplifies this technique elsewhere. The love affair for Romeo and Juliet is certainly fulfilling; the play reaches its apex at the consummation scene. It would be unusual for Shakespeare to contradict the tone of the play at its ending. If that were what he intended, there would be something wrong with the harmonics of correspondence, something so wrong that it would have disturbed an Elizabethan audience, although perhaps not a modern audience brought up on a different literature and serving a different ethic. But this argument cannot prove the case one way or the other; it only suggests that we examine the play thoroughly.

To some extent that has already been done. Some discerning, modern interpretations of the play, based on the *Liebestod* theme, attempt to persuade us that the ending is truly one of fulfillment. Such speculations are attractive and their conclusions generally correct, although the evidence cited sometimes appears inconclusive. The victory of love over death that we think we find in the play, at least in terms of ordinary events, appears to depend not so much on what the lovers say and do on the stage as it does on the erection of gold monuments to their memory by the bereaved parents, after Romeo and Juliet have ceased to exist as characters in the drama. If the intention to immortalize the lovers in gold (surely the statues never appeared on stage) symbolizes the eternal victory of love over death, it comes almost as an afterthought. But of course the primary purpose of the monuments was to signify peace brought about by union of the feuding families; they serve to settle the second theme of the play, that of war and violence, of injustice in the adult world. Consequently Shakespeare arranged the play so that the feud occupies our final attention. It was desirable to dispel the intensity of emotion after the death of the lovers, but he could not have done otherwise. The lovers had to die to bring the warring factions together. But does that really matter? Which theme serves which? The lovers are sacrificed for peace in the greater society of Verona, but the play is essentially a love story, not the story of a disarmament conference. Shakespeare could not have turned the play into comedy by settling the feud in a different manner, for after the death of Tybalt a marriage would hardly be enough to atone for the bloodletting. He might, however, have deemphasized the reconciliation of the families at the end by confining it to a few lines and omitting reference to the statues. But would not that have compromised his intention? It is proper for love, especially tragic love, to bring about peace. There may be a little thematic confusion at the end of the play, but the theatre-goer feels instinctively that the ending is appropriate. There may even be in it a hint of the peace of God that passeth understanding, but Shakespeare was content, I believe, to leave us with the understanding that the play is essentially about love. His aim was truer in *Antony and Cleopatra*, but he did not miss the mark by far in *Romeo and Juliet*.

It is also enlightening to consider *Romeo and Juliet* in terms of an *amour-passion* myth, as Denis de Rougemont has developed it. According to him *Romeo and Juliet* is the most important resuscitation of the *Tristan and Iseult* myth before Wagner [see excerpt above, 1956], but he acknowledges that not quite all of the elements of grand passion found in the archetype are present in Shakespeare. Useful as this kind of criticism is, it is perhaps just as easy to think of Shakespeare as his own mythmaker, for he has created a peculiarly Shakespearean version of grand passion (dependent very likely on Spenser's *Faerie Queene*) which incorporates such disparate elements as the *hochste Lust* [extreme pleasure] of *Tristan* with the great theme of marriage for love, which occupies a prominent position in *Romeo and Juliet* and in some of the earlier romantic comedies (especially *A Midsummer Night's Dream*). . . . (pp. 87-96)

It is not certain that the combination of these elements Shakespeare invented for *Romeo and Juliet* quite suited him or even that he took such matters as seriously as we do. When he came to examine them again in *Antony and Cleopatra*, he altered the mixture, omitting entirely the concept of marriage for love; in fact he parodied that theme from *Romeo and Juliet* in the relationship between Antony and Octavia. And he added another ingredient that appears only in embryo in *Romeo and Juliet*, the longing for the eternal. Cleopatra combines what Baudelaire was to call *le gout de l'eternal* [the relish for the eternal] with *hochste Lust*. Her most famous line is that spoken on the monument when she decides to follow Antony, "I have immortal longings in me" [*Antony and Cleopatra*, V. ii. 280-81]. Juliet only faintly suggests such things when she says that if she cannot marry Romeo death must take her maidenhead, or later when she handles the dagger with which she will extinguish her life. (pp. 96-7)

How does diction lend force to this view of *Romeo and Juliet*? Precisely because so many of the devices of rhetoric that Shakespeare uses serve to emphasize the development of character in the drama. It is important, for instance, to understand Friar Laurence's role in the play, especially as Shakespeare altered his character from the prototype he found in his source. And it is important to understand the sort of play Shakespeare was writing, and an understanding of the friar's role should assist us in making that kind of judgment. It is necessary to realize that Romeo and Juliet retain to a great extent their rationality even in the throes of the greatest passion in English literature. And the devices of rhetoric help to establish these judgments.

It has been suggested the psychology of the play encourages the opinion that Romeo and Juliet suffer from a flaw of excess passion. Certainly they are passionate lovers, but that is not why they are tragic. Their tragedy arises because they are also intellectuals, brought to their dreadful end through the development of their characters as they struggle with a grand emotion. If Shakespeare seemed ambivalent in combining fate and character or with regard to the elements of grand passion, he

did manage to leave us a tragedy of grand passion ending with a touch of exaltation. Romeo and Juliet love each other erotically and are willing to surrender the world as they know it for love. The terms of the myth are those de Rougemont suggests, but there is something beyond that, something that is not developed in *Tristan*, a passion of intellectuals that cannot be divorced from reason and spirit. Antony and Cleopatra are different. They are crafty, practical people who have somehow become involved in a passion beyond their control. Because they are the triple pillar of the ancient world and the exotic queen of Egypt, of whom no man can find surfeit, whom even "the holy priests bless when she is riggish" [*Antony and Cleopatra*, II. ii. 238-39], they fall far and tragically. But Romeo and Juliet must rest their claims on their attractiveness as young people and on the great powers of their intellects combined with the higher parts of the soul, powers that are so often demonstrated in the rhetoric of the play. Therein lies their ability to lose their lives and leave us with the suggestion that perhaps by doing so they found them.

Denis de Rougemont lists marriage for love, mystical passion, and impious license as three principal ingredients of eroticism, conceived as an answer to the Christian doctrine forbidding sensuality of any kind. The first two of these are obviously prominent in *Romeo and Juliet*, and perhaps the last is there too, if we consider secret marriage to be an impious license. Such marriage had been expressly forbidden by the Council of Trent. Juliet is especially filled with mystical passion, almost from the first moment she sees Romeo, but in the balcony scene she retains her rationality. Though transported by love, she remains a miracle of wit and reason—and rhetoric—and though it comes as an afterthought she does not fail to make it clear to Romeo that her intention is strictly marriage. Thus, as Shakespeare refines and idealizes passion, and synthesizes it on the model Spenser left him, the lovers are made great enough for serious tragedy. Sensual attraction becomes *fino amore* [fine love]. Shakespeare was working with a very daring conception, which goes a long way, I think, towards explaining why *Romeo and Juliet* is such a rhetorical play.

I am not convinced that *Romeo and Juliet* was entirely clear to the Elizabethan audience, but probably it seemed clearer to them than it does to us because they understood much better then we do the devices employed in it. Whether they thought the ending was satisfactory, whether for them the play ended on a note of frustration or fulfillment, we shall never really know. But after all, the best test of the play is the theatre, where it has survived as vital, meaningful repertoire for centuries. (pp. 97-9)

> *Robert O. Evans, in his* The Osier Cage: Rhetorical Devices in "Romeo & Juliet," *University of Kentucky Press, 1966, 108 p.*

## DOUGLAS L. PETERSON   (essay date 1966)

[*Peterson synthesizes the two leading interpretations of* Romeo and Juliet *as a tragedy of fate and a tragedy of character. He maintains that although it is true that divine providence has brought Romeo and Juliet together for the purpose of ending the family feud, the lovers are "nevertheless free to choose the means by which they fulfill what Providence has ordained." Peterson states that they can follow the guidance of reason and the divine throughout their ordeal, thus restoring order "through the normal operation of the laws of nature," or they can yield to blind passion and achieve harmony "through violence, retribution, and pur-*

*gation." It is the latter course, the critic claims, which the lovers follow at every crucial moment.]*

The major interpretive problem presented by *Romeo and Juliet* is that of determining who or what is finally responsible for the calamity that overtakes the young lovers. The evidence seems contradictory. The allusion in the Prologue to the lovers as "star-crossed," the extent to which chance seems to conspire against them (especially after Romeo has slain Tybalt), and the premonitions of disaster experienced by both lovers seem to indicate that the play is fatalistic, perhaps even, as one commentator has argued, a tragedy of "astrological determinism" [see essay by J. W. Draper cited in the Additional Bibliography]. On the other hand, there is a good deal of evidence throughout the play which points to defects of character as the determining cause of the catastrophe: the lovers' rashness in love and their desperation in the face of adversity (each threatens suicide when learning of Romeo's exile) are forcibly identified as sinful by Friar Laurence.

This apparently conflicting evidence has led some commentators to conclude that the play is defective—the work of an immature dramatist who has "failed to convey a certain tragic conception which points toward his maturity" [see excerpt above by John Lawlor, 1961]. (pp. 33-4)

But the inadequacy has been ours, not Shakespeare's. Whatever else in the play may suggest immaturity—the mannered courtly dialogue, the lack of depth in characterization, and a degree of inflexibility in the pentameter line—it discloses a tragic conception that is fully worked out and which looks forward to the mature tragedies, to *Hamlet,* especially. The contradictions attributed to Shakespeare are very much in evidence in Arthur Brooke's narrative, and it is certain from the ways in which Shakespeare replotted his source that he was quite aware of them. In place of Brooke's Fortune and her wheel, Shakespeare introduces Providence and the Renaissance idea of order; in place of Brooke's victims of Fortune, whose love at first sight was a "mischief" brewed by the whimsical goddess, Shakespeare introduces the only children of the feuding families, whose destiny is to end the feud and thus to restore civic order in Verona.

"The time is out of joint" in Verona just as surely as it is in Hamlet's Denmark, and the lovers, like Hamlet, are "born to set it right" [*Hamlet,* I. v. 188, 189]. They are "star-crossed" in a quite literal sense: Providence, having decreed that they will settle the feud, has selected the stars as the agency through which its determination will be effected. Once they meet, they will be powerfully attracted to each other. But it does not follow that since their love at first sight is providentially ordained, they are deprived of freedom of choice, or that their deaths are inevitable as the only means of restoring civic order. How they manage their affections, once they have met—hence how they will fulfill their destiny—will be up to them.

That the stars could influence though not directly determine choice is common Renaissance doctrine. Jack Cade, in *The Mirror for Magistrates,* observes:

> It may be well that planets do incline,
> And our complexions move our minds to ill;
> But such is reason that they bring to fine
> No work unaided by our lust and will.

It is the physical nature of man, and hence the passions, that are subject to astrological influence. His reason is free. The doctrine is stated more fully by George Wither. . . .

> . . . We know (and often feele) that from above
> The *Planets* have, on us, an *Influence;*
> And, that our Bodies varie, as they move.
>   Moreover, *Holy Writ* inferres, that these
> Have some such pow'r; ev'n in those Places, where
> It names *Orion,* and the *Pleiades;*
> Which, *Starres* of much inferiour *Nature* are.
>   Yet, hence conclude not, therefore, that the *Minde*
> Is by the *Starres* constrained to obey
> Their *influence;* or, so by them inclin'd
> That, by no meanes resist the same we may.
> For, though they forme the *Bodies* temp'rature,
> (And though the *Minde* inclineth after that)
> by *Grace,* another *Temper* we procure,
> Which guides the *Motions* of *Supposed Fate.*
> The *Soule of Man* is nobler than the *Sphæres;*
> And, if it gaine the Place which may be had,
> Not here alone on Earth, the Rule it beares,
> But, is the *Lord,* of all that *God* hath made.
>   Be *wise in him;* and, if just cause there bee,
>   The *Sunne* and *Moone,* shall stand and wayt on
>   thee. . . .

The stars may influence the mind and therefore choice, but only indirectly and only to the extent that man allows his mind to "incline after" the body, whose "temp'rature" is affected by their influence. (pp. 34-6)

Once [the lovers] meet they may surrender to passion, following its dictates . . . by choice; or they may temper it as, in fact, Friar Laurence recommends in [II. iii. 94]. Whichever they choose, their love, decreed by Providence and initiated by the stars, will be the means of reconciling the feuding families and restoring order in Verona. What Providence has decreed is irrevocable; but how the decree is fulfilled—whether order will be restored through the normal operation of the laws of nature or through violence, retribution, and purgation—will be up to them.

The choice of means confronting Romeo and Juliet is not confined to a single occasion. Rather, they are given a series of opportunities for choice. Each time they choose wrongly they make their situation more difficult, but—and the dramatic tension in the play is lost unless the audience realizes this—even as late as Romeo's return from exile it is possible for the play to end happily with the peaceful reconciliation of the feuding families. Up to the moment of Romeo's suicide Providence is sympathetic with the young lovers; on each occasion that they have the responsibility of choice, Providence offers them counsel, either directly through premonition or through Friar Laurence. If they will listen, if they will be properly guided, they will emerge safely from even the worst of their troubles.

The first occasion for choice occurs in the fourth scene of the first act. Mercutio, Benvolio, and Romeo are about to proceed to the Capulet ball when Romeo announces his reluctance. "'Tis no wit to go" [I. iv. 49], he says; and when Mercutio asks him why, he discloses that he has had a dream warning him of the grave dangers to be risked by going. Mercutio meets his concern with a scoff and attributes dreams in general to the imagination. But Romeo is unmoved. He is convinced that dreamers "do dream things true" [I. iv. 52].

>         . . . my mind misgives
> Some consequence, yet hanging in the stars,
> Shall bitterly begin his fearful date

With this night's revels, and expire the term
Of a despised life closed in my breast
By some vile forfeit of untimely death.

[I. iv. 106-11]

But his decision is to ignore the premonition and proceed to
the ball:

But He that hath the steerage of my course
Direct my sail! On, lusty gentlemen.

[I. iv. 112-13]

The premonition whose authenticity is borne out by the fact
that Romeo's decision to ignore it initiates a series of events
ending in his death, like those omens preceding Caesar's death,
is unmistakably a warning from Providence. The time is not
appropriate for the stars to exert their influence. To ignore the
premonition is, in short, to invite the consequences specified
in it.

It is obvious, then, that the "He" in line 112 is not, as most
editors have assumed, a reference to God, since Romeo's decision ignores a warning that can only have God as its source.
In the terms of the nautical metaphor, "He that hath the steerage of my course / Direct my sail!", Romeo is rejecting the
course charted by God as pilot. Romeo's decision is therefore
in no sense an expression of faith in a special "divinity that
shapes our ends, / rough-hew them how we will" [*Hamlet*, V.
ii. 10-11]. It is an expression of a reckless indifference. He is
a victim of unrequited love. Rosaline will have nothing to do
with him. Melancholy has made him indifferent, careless of
who will assume the charting of his course.

The identity of the "pilot" to whom Romeo entrusts his future
is no mystery. It is Cupid. Romeo had agreed originally to
Benvolio's suggestion to attend the ball only because it would
allow him the opportunity to "rejoice" in Rosaline's incomparable beauty [I. ii. 100-01]. It is Cupid who guides him to
the Capulet entertainment, and it will be Cupid who continues
to chart his course after he meets Juliet. (pp. 37-8)

The next occasion for choice occurs in II. iii, when Romeo
must decide between satisfying the urgency of his passion though
a secret marriage or proceeding "wisely and slow" [II. iii.
94], as his spiritual adviser counsels. Laurence's remarks about
the "opposed kings," "grace and rude will," which reside
"in man as well as herbs" [II. iii. 27, 28] remind the audience
of the ethical principle in terms of which Romeo's ardor is to
be judged. His passion, tempered, is a good; but left uncontrolled it is poisonous and self-destructive. Laurence is reluctant
to believe that Romeo's love for Juliet is any more authentic
than his infatuation for Rosaline has been, but he sees, and
correctly, that it can be a means of ending the feud. . . . Romeo's passion is neither good nor evil; rationally ordered it
will be a good and, furthermore, may have the virtue of turning
family rancor to love. But it is evident from Romeo's insistence
upon an immediate secret marriage, depsite the Friar's warning,
that Cupid is still steering Romeo's course.

The alternatives available to Romeo and Juliet that have been
identified in II. iii, reasonable caution and reckless haste, are
reintroduced in II. vi, the scene in which Laurence reluctantly
agrees to their secret marriage. The Friar's opening lines indicate his fear of what the consequences may be:

So smile the Heavens upon this holy act
That afterhours with sorrow chide us not!

[II. vi. 1-2]

He knows that "violent delights have violent ends" [II. vi.
9], but a secret and hasty marriage is better than fornication. . . . This scene, ending with the lovers and the Friar setting
out to church and followed by a time lapse during which the
marriage takes place and is consummated, concludes what
Shakespeare has plotted as a distinct and complete action. It
began when Romeo ignored a providential warning and recklessly gave the "steerage" of his course over to Cupid. As a
consequence he has met Juliet and thus come prematurely under
the influence of the stars. Faced now with the alternatives of
allowing Cupid to continue to direct his course or of accepting
Laurence as a new helmsman, he settles for Cupid. He will
marry Juliet immediately to satisfy his desire.

Up to now Providence has seemingly favored the lovers. They
are about to be married, and they will consummate the marriage
that night. But Romeo has ignored a divine warning, and Juliet
has ignored her own sound judgment:

I have no joy of this contract night,
It is too rash, too unadvised, too sudden.

[II., ii. 117-18]

Both have ignored the advice of Friar Laurence. Having committed themselves to passion, they will have to endure the
consequences; and order in Verona will have to be restored by
other than rational means.

The two ways recognized in the Renaissance by which Providence gains its ends are identified by Thomas Browne as the
"ordinary and open" and the "obscure" ways. The operation
of the laws of nature, he says, constitute the "ordinary way";
the other way men call fortune. . . . By rejecting reason the
lovers have rejected "the ordinary and open way" of fulfilling
their destiny and chosen, in effect, the "obscure" way. They
will discover in it that they are beset by chance and accident.

But if the new action begun in III. i, following the marriage,
is dominated by what seems to be chance, the lovers' responsibility is not diminished. They still have the opportunity for
decisions which will directly affect the manner in which they
accomplish what Providence has ordained.

The first opportunity for decision in the new action is presented
to Romeo just after Tybalt has killed Mercutio. It is an ironical
accident that Romeo should have inadvertently given Tybalt
the opportunity to kill Mercutio when in the role of peacemaker
he stepped between the two swordsmen. Now it is up to him
to decide whether to honor Escalus' directive to the feuding
families . . . or to satisfy the code of revenge. Again he allows
passion to direct his decision:

Away to Heaven, respective lenity,
And fire-eyed fury be my conduct now!

[III. i. 123-24]

He is, of course, not responsible for Mercutio's death, but by
defying Escalus' edict and slaying Tybalt he becomes responsible for the consequences resulting from Tybalt's death. Furthermore, in accusing Fortune for what has happened ("O, I
am fortune's fool!") [III. i. 136] he is guilty of impatience,
and impatience is blasphemy. (pp. 39-42)

From the time that Romeo kills Tybalt to the end of the play,
the lovers are faced with mounting adversity in which chance
is notoriously conspicuous. How they endure adversity will
now determine how they fulfill their destiny as agents of Providence. If their faith is strong enough . . . they may escape
calamity, unite the families, and live happily as man and wife.

Again it is the Friar who, in counseling Romeo, discloses the doctrine that is essential to the correct interpretation of the action. His instructions to Romeo on how to accept exile might have come from any of a number of texts on Christian patience. His opening lines,

> Romeo, come forth, come forth, thou fearful man.
> Affliction is enamored of they parts,
> And thou art wedded to calamity,
>
> [III. iii. 1-3]

are not merely indulgence in an idle conceit. The amorous figure is based upon a commonplace of Renaissance consolatory literature: *affliction is proof of God's love.* . . . But Romeo is unwilling to take the helm of his ship from the pilot to whom he had originally surrendered it. When Laurence offers him "Adversity's sweet milk, philosophy" [III. iii. 55], he throws himself on the ground, tears his hair, and finally, learning of how Juliet has received the news of Tybalt's death, draws his sword to commit suicide. It is only after the Friar, confronted by the threat of the unpardonable sin, has given Romeo *secular* or *wordly* cause for hope that he pulls himself together. His sin, so identified by the Friar, is despair—an insufficient faith in the ways of God to man.

Romeo's reaction to the news of his exile is paralleled by Juliet's reaction to the same news in [III. ii. 97ff], as the Nurse points out in her comparison of their despair in [III. iii. 84-7]. It is also paralleled by Juliet's tearful reaction to her father's decision that she will marry Paris. . . . The Friar, again faced with a potential suicide, is forced to the extreme plan of deception involving the trance-inducing herb. In this instance the end justifies the means: the prevention of suicide justifies deception. The strategy misfires because of what again appears to be a sheer accident. An important letter does not get delivered.

But again it is Romeo, not Fortune or Providence, who is responsible for the ensuing consequences. Once more he fails to meet adversity as he should. He despairs, again ignoring a reassuring premonition and Balthazar's advice to control himself. The final act opens with Romeo's disclosure that he has had another dream. . . . The news which Romeo then receives of Juliet's death seemingly contradicts the assurance of the dream that all will work out well. The dream seems in fact to be a cruel joke until we realize that it is a veiled assurance by Providence that the news he is about to receive is misleading, that death may be only apparent. The situation in the dream is of course reversed—"I dreamed my lady came and found me dead" [V. i. 6]—but the essential fact is there, and Romeo ponders it momentarily: "Strange dream, that gives a dead man leave to think!" [V. i. 7]. If he had taken the premonition to heart, either of two things might have happened. He might not have taken the news of Juliet's death as final and therefore not have rushed out to buy the poison; or, after returning to Verona and finding her apparently dead, he might have remembered the dream and the feelings of reassurance it had given him and perhaps have awakened her, as she in the dream had awakened him, with a kiss.

In any event, his reaction to the letter is indefensible. Balthazar advises him to be patient. . . . But he remains desperate, buys the poison, and rushes back to Verona. Even a few minutes' delay and he might have returned to find Juliet awakening. But he is impatient; he sees suicide as the only release from his

"world-wearied flesh" [V. iii. 112]. His last words are to invoke again the pilot to whom he has entrusted his course:

> Come, bitter conduct, some unsavory guide!
> Thou desperate pilot, now at once run on
> The dashing rocks thy seasick weary bark.
>
> [V. iii. 116-18]

Again, when Romeo has most need of a seasoned and resolute pilot, he allows a love grown desperate to end his voyage on the rocks of despair.

It is impossible, therefore, to maintain the romantic view of Romeo's suicide, and of Juliet's which immediately follows, as a beautiful sacrifice on the altar of innocent, ideal love. The families for their disruption of civic order, Tybalt and Mercutio for their impetuosity, Escalus for his "winking . . . at discord" [V. iii. 294], and Friar Laurence for his assuming that a happy reconciliation of the feuding families might be accomplished through untempered passion—all must share in the blame for the lovers' "misadventured piteous overthrows" [Prologue, 7]. But the lovers themselves must bear the final blame. Destined to end the "ancient grudge," they are nevertheless free to choose the means by which they fulfill what Providence has ordained. Repeatedly, they reject divine and rational guidance, following passion as their blind pilot instead, until, finally, they take their own lives, fulfilling what Providence has ordained—but only in a final act of irrational and unpardonable defiance. (pp. 42-6)

> *Douglas L. Peterson, "'Romeo and Juliet' and the Art of Moral Navigation," in* Pacific Coast Studies in Shakespeare, *edited by Waldo F. McNeir and Thelma N. Greenfield, University of Oregon Books, 1966, pp. 33-46.*

## WARREN D. SMITH (essay date 1967)

[*Smith asserts that the central concern of* Romeo and Juliet *is not the reconciliation of the feuding families, which many critics, he notes, have found unsatisfactory, but is "the immortality of the lovers." He points to a number of scenes and references in the play—most importantly, Romeo's dream at the beginning of Act V, Scene i—which establish the Christian belief in death as the provider of immortality. In light of this, Smith argues that Romeo's dream is significant, to the extent that it helps us recognize in the final moments of the play that "the hero does revive spiritually after Juliet's kisses, and that he becomes an 'emperor' by the side of his deathless bride."*]

The central idea of [*Romeo and Juliet*] may be embodied in the opening soliloquy of Act V, delivered by Romeo, who is in banishment at Mantua. The hero has had his final dream, a joyous one, which he describes to the audience with feelings of exultation:

> If I may trust the flattering truth of sleep,
> My dreams presage some joyful news at hand.
> My bosom's lord sits lightly in his throne,
> And all this day an unaccustom'd spirit
> Lifts me above the ground with cheerful thoughts.
> I dreamt my lady came and found me dead
> (Strange dream that gives a dead man leave to think!)
> And breath'd such life with kisses in my lips
> That I reviv'd and was an emperor.
>
> [V. i. 1-9]

The usual criticism is that the dream contains almost brutal irony: not only at the end of the speech does Balthasar enter with the unwelcome news of Juliet's 'death', but also, though in the tomb the lady does come and breathe kisses in the dead hero's lips, he is not revived and she kills herself shortly thereafter. Yet, as everyone has noticed, the other dreams and premonitions in the drama (as in all the other plays of Shakespeare) do come true. Contrary to the majority opinion, I believe that the final dream of Romeo also comes true symbolically, that the hero does revive spiritually after Juliet's kisses, and that he becomes an 'emperor' by the side of his deathless bride. For though hitherto it has passed unheeded, there is adequate preparation in earlier parts of the text for the metaphysical nature of the conclusion.

The germ of the conception, as I see it, lies in the exchange of speeches between Juliet's Nurse and Romeo in Act II . . . :

> Nurse   Doth not rosemary and Romeo begin both with a letter?
> Romeo   Ay, nurse; what of that? Both with an R.
> Nurse   . . . she hath the prettiest sententious of it, of you and rosemary, that it would do you good to hear it.
>
>                      [II. iv. 206-08, 211-12]

The only other time the word *rosemary* enters the dialogue is in Act IV, in Friar Laurence's attempt to still the grief of the Capulets, who are mourning Juliet's 'death':

> Dry up your tears and stick your rosemary
> On this fair corse, and, as the custom is,
> In all her best array bear her to church.
>
>                            [IV. v. 79-81]

The second reference to the term, unlike the first, is fortunately noted in the *Variorum* [edition of the play]. 'This plant was used in various ways at funerals. Being an evergreen, it was regarded as an emblem of immortality.' It would seem strange that Juliet would couple in her aphorism the name of the plant with that of Romeo were it not for the fact that rosemary in Elizabethan times was what Philip Williams calls 'paradoxical', in that it was employed at weddings as well as at funerals. Juliet, of course, is thinking consciously of the approaching wedding, but she is really referring, whether she knows it or not, to the symbol not only of marriage but also of immortality. And the hero's reference to being revived from death by his lady's kisses, when set against the sententiousness of the words *rosemary* and *Romeo* in combination, would appear to form a pattern. The pattern is anticipated by several other interesting references in the text. Probably of greatest import is something Friar Laurence says in soliloquy upon his first entrance. After having mentioned the herbs he has been gathering in the early morning dew, the Friar delivers a couplet that seems to be undramatic as well as paradoxical in nature: 'The earth that's nature's mother is her tomb. / What is her burying grave, that is her womb' [II. iii. 9-10]. Harry Levin remarks upon the antithetical rhyme 'tomb-womb' and the paradoxical epithet used by Romeo [V. iii. 45] when he hails the Capulet tomb as 'thou womb of death' in discussing what he calls the 'contrarities' of the plot in *Romeo and Juliet* [see excerpt above, 1960]. Since the audience knows from the Prologue onward that the lovers are destined to die, it would appear that the most likely dramatic excuse for the Friar's statement that what is nature's burying ground is also her 'womb' and Romeo's connotation of Juliet's tomb as a 'womb of death' is the implanting in the consciousness the Christian ideal of the resurrection of the souls of the protagonists after death. The earliest reference to the Christian paradox of death and life is given

by Juliet, innocently enough, after she has fallen in love with Romeo at the Capulet Ball. Having requested the Nurse to find out the name of her lover, she says, in an aside, 'If he be married / My grave is like to be my wedding bed' [I. v. 134-35]. The paradox is echoed by Lady Capulet, in disgust at Juliet's refusal to take advantage of the offer of marriage from Paris, 'I would the fool were married to her grave!' [III. v. 140]. It is reiterated again when Juliet asks her mother to delay the wedding with Paris for a month, a week, 'Or if you do not, make the bridal bed / In that dim monument where Tybalt lies' [III. v. 200-01]. The irony of all three speeches is trenchant. If Romeo's dream has meaning beyond its literal sense and the symbolic force of *rosemary* is felt by the audience, Juliet's grave does figuratively become her 'wedding bed'. (pp. 579-80)

[My] impression that the plot establishes the immortality of the lovers, their remarriage in heaven with consummation in the grave, is not based solely on passages like those quoted above. Significant to me also is the emphasis upon wedding regalia in the scene in which Juliet is discovered unconscious. . . . The Friar had told the girl that after she took the potion, 'In thy best robes uncovered on the bier / Thou shalt be borne to that same ancient vault / Where all the kindred of the Capulets lie' [IV. i. 110-12]. Surely the Friar's admonition to the grieving parents, 'and, as the custom is, / In all her best array bear her to church' [IV. v. 80-1] does not imply that Juliet is to appear in a shroud. That the 'funeral' is performed in wedding regalia is further implied in the lament of Lord Capulet: 'Our bridal flowers serve for a buried corse; / And all things change them to the contrary [IV. v. 89-90]. Thus, later, when Romeo enters the tomb, he must encounter his young wife dressed in her best array and bedecked with bridal flowers, ready, as it were, for their ultimate wedding. Additional emphasis on the conception of immortality predicted in Romeo's final dream may be indicated in the two references to yew trees in the final scene, one by Paris and the other by Balthasar, in the outer graveyard, for yew trees, also being evergreen, may, like rosemary, be a symbol of the after-life.

But if, as seems to be the case, the dramatist expends a significant part of his artistry on implanting in the minds of the audience the immortality of the lovers, what place in the drama is to be given to what is often said to be the central theme, the feud and the reconciliation, referred to in the Prologue and emphasized at the end of the play? The function of both is but to emphasize the really basic motif. In sharp contrast to the love of Romeo and Juliet, which is both heavenly and eternal, the feud is both mundane and transient. Its initial manifestation is ignominious, what with the puns of Samson and Gregory, the biting of the thumb, the bickering over which side the law might be on, the cowardice of all four menials, the absurdity of old Capulet's calling for a sword instead of a crutch. In contrast to the exalted orchard scenes between the lovers, the feud is trivial indeed. Even the choler of Tybalt and the pride of Mercutio are placed on a decidedly lower plane than the soaring lyricism of the love scenes. Moreover, since no cause for the feud is mentioned throughout the play, it lacks motivation, and, as has often been noted, the two protagonists appear to be almost oblivious of its existence.

The reconciliation scene, on the other hand, may at first seem to be more difficult to relegate to a secondary role. The play does not end, as simply by closing the inner-stage curtain over the mouth of the 'tomb' it readily could have been made to, with the suicide of Juliet, but rather with the two heads of the feuding families shaking hands and promising to erect gold statues in memory of each other's deceased progeny. But it has not been noticed that though Shakespeare makes the effigies gold, the source of the play, Brooke's poem, speaks only of marble. The reason for the change has nothing to do with the glorification of the reconciliation, as might be suspected, but rather with a significant speech in an earlier scene, Romeo's admonition to the apothecary after the purchase of the vial of poison:

> There is thy gold—worse poison to men's souls,
> Doing more murther in this loathsome world,
> Than these poor compounds that thou mayst not sell.
> I sell thee poison; thou hast sold me none.
>
> [V. i. 80-3]

Thus we are informed outright how low the hero evaluates gold before the feuding parents decide to use it in memory of their dead children. (pp. 581-82)

Much conjecture has been made about the purpose of the Friar's recapitulation, which runs on for some forty lines after he has promised to be 'brief', of everything the audience already knows. Granville Barker thinks it is a decided blemish on the play but probably necessary to the theme of burying the parents' strife; Bertrand Evans believes that for some reason the Prince, the Montagues, and the Capulets (as well as the audience) had to be enlightened about the circumstances of the death of the lovers [see excerpt above, 1950], and A. C. Sprague sees in the passage the necessary transition from the tragic outcome to its interpretation [see Additional Bibliography]. But Evans . . . admits that the Friar really doesn't tell us anything of much importance, that even after the story has been supplemented by the scraps of information 'held with no sense of their meaning by Balthasar and Paris' page, the gulf lies wide between the total understanding of the characters and that of the audience'. Exactly. I am convinced that the speech is not intended to be enlightening, indeed, not even interesting, to the audience. The attention of the audience is very likely not supposed to focus on the weary recapitulation of Laurence but rather on the lovers concealed from view behind the closed inner-stage curtain. The same device had been employed earlier in the play (III. 4), when, as Granville Barker has noted, the attention of the audience was made to wander to the closed curtain of the balcony inner stage (or chamber), behind which bride and groom were consummating their marriage (immediately before the famous 'nightingale-lark' scene), while mundane arrangements for the wedding of Juliet to Paris were being made by the unsuspecting Capulets below. Again, as in front of the curtain mundane arrangements are being made, this time for the erection of statues in the gold that Romeo holds in such contempt, behind the curtain a marriage is being consummated. For neither reader nor spectator leaves the play with the sensation of having been uplifted by the reconciliation of the two old men before the tomb of their children. Our concentration has been fixed by the dialogue and events on the consummation of the love of the two young protagonists, in the grave as well as in the marriage chamber.

As the play closes, Prince Escalus makes the interesting remark, 'A glooming peace this morning with it brings. / The sun for sorrow will not show his head' [V. iii. 305-06]. The failure of the morning sun to shine may be, of course, merely a device to intensify the tragic gloom, but I suspect it has meaning more profound. First of all, the absence of sunrise at the end of the drama is an ironic reminder of the foolhardy habit of the Romeo who moped with love-sickness for Rosaline by penning himself in his chamber at sunrise, shutting his

windows, and locking 'fair daylight out' [I. i. 139]. But more significant, all through the love scenes there has been emphasis on the stars and on night. The lovers first meet at night, they have their initial tryst, in the orchard, at night, they consummate their marriage at night, and finally they die together at night. The preference of the lovers for night is most memorably expressed in the beautiful hymn to marriage of Juliet as she impatiently awaits the setting of the sun and the approach of her bridegroom. . . . That the sun fails to shine at the close of the play is after all in harmony with Juliet's prediction concerning the death of Romeo:

> . . . and, when he shall die,
> Take him and cut him out in little stars,
> And he will make the face of heaven so fine
> That all the world will be in love with night
> And pay no worship to the garish sun.
>
> [III. ii. 21-5]

Romeo, in his turn, has no need of daylight. To him Juliet is the sun, and the 'triumphant' grave is as a lantern with his bride's beauty making the vault 'a feasting presence full of light' [V. iii. 83-6].

Immediately before Juliet awakes and breathes kisses into the lips of Romeo, Balthasar recounts the nature of his dream to Friar Laurence: 'As I did sleep under this yew-tree here, / I dreamt my master and another fought, / And that my master slew him' [V. iii. 137-39]—a dream which, as the Friar quickly discovers, has come true. The device appears to have little purpose other than to prepare the audience directly to believe in the validity of Romeo's dream. As almost immediately after Romeo kisses Juliet she revives, so, I think we can assume from the evidence, after she kisses him he revives, and, as his dream had predicted, is an 'emperor'. As the two lovers together pass on to eternal bliss, they need not golden statues nor the golden rays of morning sunlight. The lark will part them nevermore—it is the nightingale, and not the lark, that sings them to their rest. (pp. 582-83)

*Warren D. Smith, "Romeo's Final Dream," in* The Modern Language Review, *Vol. 62, No. 4, October, 1967, pp. 579-83.*

## NORMAN RABKIN (essay date 1967)

[*Rabkin declares that the seeming irregularity of the language and style of* Romeo and Juliet *is not evidence of artistic failure, but is part of Shakespeare's purposeful design. The critic points specifically to the scene in which the Capulets mourn over Juliet's apparent death (IV. v.) as a telling example—when compared with the following scene in which Romeo reacts to the news—of the dramatist's use of similar poetic forms with different results, the one episode appearing artificial, insincere, the other genuinely emotive. Rabkin links this stylistic technique with the play's tragic theme, maintaining that the oxymora and paradox which were once a self-conscious poise for Romeo eventually become the definitive expression "of things as they are." In short, according to the critic, both the hero and heroine come to realize the paradoxical nature of their love, which can find its ultimate satisfaction not in life but only in death.*]

Two aspects of *Romeo and Juliet* most trouble critics who see it as deeply flawed: its structure as tragedy and its style. Numerous critics, even when enthusiastically praising the play, confess to what Duthie calls "some degree of failure on Shakespeare's part" in making clear what kind of tragedy he is attempting to write [see excerpt above, 1953]. It is easy enough to locate the problem. The Prologue tells us that *Romeo and Juliet* is to be a tragedy of "star-crossed lovers," and Romeo on the verge of seeing Juliet for the first time discovers that his

> mind misgives
> Some consequences yet hanging in the stars,
> Shall bitterly begin his fearful date
> With this night's revels and expire the term
> Of a despised life closed in my breast
> By some vile forfeit of untimely death.
>
> [I. iv. 106-11]

Much in the play suggests that its tragedy is one of fate. But, as critics repeatedly observe, the sense of fatality is undercut by a series of accidents which remind us more of capricious fortune than of the nemesis of the Greeks: Capulet's impulsive decision to advance the date of the wedding, the detainment of Friar John, Romeo's chance meeting with Tybalt, Friar Laurence's failure to get to the tomb before Romeo. . . . Moreover, tragedies in which fate is dominant generally move us by demonstrating that it operates at the center of character; yet, as Duthie puts it once again, the "defects" in Romeo and Juliet which "contribute directly and demonstrably to their doom"— their lack of "mature poise and balance," their impetuous youth, their tendency at moments to blubber and weep—are scarcely worthy of the dignity of tragedy and operate at cross-purposes with what the play would seem to be claiming as tragic, and with Friar Laurence's rather tedious rehearsal at the end of the accidents that have brought about the catastrophe. If *Hamlet* and *Othello* are tragedies whose force emanates from the fact that the heroes are brought down by faults of character which we have been led to understand as supreme virtues, then *Romeo and Juliet* does not immediately strike us as belonging to their company. And the burden of the action that frames the mishaps of the lovers, the suggestion that the protagonists have contributed their deaths as a sacrificial offering to heal the civil strife of Verona, has little to do with the central action.

The difficulties of the style are perhaps even more readily seen. Many passages belong to the body of Shakespeare's most successful poetry, and few readers would fail to agree that *Romeo and Juliet* is his first poetic masterpiece. Yet the style is uneven. . . . [One] will find in *Romeo and Juliet* examples of Shakespeare's early, declamatory style, heavy on simile and merely decorative imagery, and of his mature style, in which metaphors more tersely embody complex ideas and no image seems extrinsic to the action; Wolfgang Clemen concludes that this stylistic unevenness, like other elements of the play, marks *Romeo and Juliet* as a "play of transition" [see excerpt above, 1951]. Few mature plays of Shakespeare show such a variety of styles as are comprehended here. (pp. 164-66)

But to recognize the variety of styles is only to begin to consider the question of style in the play. . . . Surely it is not bardolatry to suggest that in a play whose every line reflects an intense concern with language Shakespeare knew that he was making Mercutio's language very different from Capulet's, and the Nurse's from Paris', or that, as Clemen and most other critics . . . have been quick to perceive, Romeo and Juliet themselves mature linguistically in most remarkable fashion as the tragedy moves towards its catastrophe. Undeniably there is a good deal of irregularity in the style; but the more one studies the play the more reluctant one becomes to state categorically that any element of style is the result of Shakespeare's failure to revise an early state of his manuscript or to take advantage everywhere in the play of the maturity that some of the speeches

and scenes immediately manifest. It might be valuable to recall that the plays most probably contemporary with *Romeo and Juliet* are *Richard II* and *A Midsummer Night's Dream*, and that its immediate predecessor is *Love's Labour's Lost*. I suspect that most readers, asked to identify the plays in which Shakespeare most self-consciously experiments with style and relates the problem of style—what characters do with language—to their themes, would choose these very plays. Only by responding with sensitive awareness to the variations in style, and to pondering what they tell us, can we fully understand *Romeo and Juliet*.

Consider together two facts about *Romeo and Juliet*. First, the play is extraordinarily rich, even for Shakespeare, in poetic devices that call our attention to themselves. This is true not merely of the speeches critics are tempted to reject as immature, but of every part of the play. . . . Second, and paradoxically, the play itself makes us respond to certain stylized speeches as too artificial and to others as genuine and powerfully effective poetry. Were *Romeo and Juliet* as homogeneous in tone as *Titus Andronicus*, we should regard as harmonious parts of a stylized whole those passages that strike us now as excessive. What makes us respond to certain speeches as if they were natural utterances, so that we are scarcely aware of "style" when we hear them, is the staginess of others. The inconsistency of style in *Romeo and Juliet* directs our intense response to its most powerful language, and that forces us to attend to its meaning.

Consider one scene, that in which Juliet's family circle discovers her apparent death (IV. v). (pp. 166-68)

Opening the scene with the Nurse's characteristic chatter, which disjointedly reflects her amusing and touching love of Juliet and her pleasure in bawdy, Shakespeare resumes the tone of earthy commonplace present whenever she or Mercutio is on stage. As she realizes why she cannot awaken Juliet, she responds in a series of cries whose words hardly matter, and when Lady Capulet answers her summons the Nurse cannot even find words to tell her what has happened. Lady Capulet's first reaction is equally direct:

> O me, O me! My child, my only life,
> Revive, look up, or I will die with thee!
> Help, help! Call help.
>
> [IV. v. 19-21]

In the moment of her first shock Juliet's mother expresses with the economy of a single outcry her full understanding of what she has seen.

Upon entering her husband does the same; against the background of two lines of imageless blank verse spoken by Juliet's mother and her Nurse, in which five beats out of ten fall on the word "dead," a heretofore verbose Capulet reacts with a clinically precise description of his drugged daughter, and then with something new, a poetic image which arises from the physical fact of her coldness:

> Death lies on her like an untimely frost
> Upon the sweetest flower of all the field.
>
> [IV. v. 28-9]

These lines operate with all the force that poetry is capable of: They make us understand the poignant alacrity with which untimely death destroys what is delicate, beautiful, dear, and young. In this brilliant and classical image Capulet would seem to have said all that can be said, and as his wife and the Nurse continue to wail in conventional phrases—using language as a simple outlet for emotions they seem incapable of expressing, as Capulet has done—he declares that he too has been made inarticulate by death. But Shakespeare has not finished with our emotions, for now the wedding party arrives. The staggered entrances enable us to watch each character respond serially to the same shocking news, and Capulet answers the Friar's ironic greeting with a poetic reflection on the implications of the image he introduced a moment earlier. The speech is as spare as those that follow it are prolix. It states a series of simple and terrible truths, whose accuracy we fully realize only by our response to the entire play. Death is Juliet's groom; the young dead, there is no life for the old; if Juliet is a flower and has married Death, then death has deflowered her (how different this is from the innocent puns on coal-collier-choler-collar of the opening scene or the self-conscious quibbles in which Rosaline's lover indulged); if Juliet has married Death, Death is, as Capulet recognizes when again he begins to think about himself, his son-in-law, and as the possessor of an old man who has no more reason to live the heir of an inheritance that makes a mockery of lesser dowries. The end of Capulet's speech is a lyrical paradox which the alliteration of "leave" and "life" and "living" emphasizes, and its last phrase, "living, all is Death's" [IV. v. 40] is in its context both a freshly stated reminder of what we know most painfully and an incisive summary of what the tragedy is insisting that we feel (even though, of course, Juliet is not really dead).

But now a new movement begins in the scene. As Paris, whose love for Juliet not only has failed to move us before, but has constituted a fatal obstacle to the hopes of the protagonists, demands that we sympathize with his woes too, we may recall that Juliet is not yet dead. Lady Capulet's next speech touchingly reveals that she has heard nothing but her own grief, for it takes off from her last line, "o woful time" [IV. v. 30], spoken before Paris and the Friar arrived. . . . The detachment that we may be beginning to feel from the grief of the characters on stage grows more marked now in the next four speeches, and it does so because Shakespeare wants it to do so. Like Lady Capulet, the Nurse picks up where she left off in "o lamentable day!" [IV. v. 30]; but unlike Lady Capulet's speech, her own is thoroughly inadequate to communicate her grief, rather telling us that she is unhappy than compelling us to share her sorrow. . . . In its symmetry and artifice her speech reflects not a spontaneous outcry of grief, but an unsuccessful attempt—compared with what we have heard a moment earlier from Capulet—to find a rhetoric that will do justice to what she is feeling. . . . Paris' speech is even more distressing, for its manner, cataloguing and repetitious, is an awkward reprise of the Nurse's speech. Its last line, "O love! O life! Not life, but love in death!" [IV. v. 58], jars in a new way, for it is a parody of one of the most frequently parodied lines in *The Spanish Tragedy,* "O life! no life, but lively form of death." Paris' style is the style of Bottom's Pyramus recognizing the remains of his lady love. If we have any doubts about Shakespeare's intention here, we need only listen to the next and last speech in the strange litany as Capulet, beginning like Paris with a string of past participles, once again parodies Hieronymo: "O child! O child! my soul, and not my child!" [IV. v. 62]. Ironically it is Capulet, whose first speeches in this scene so moved us, who calls forth the Friar's reproach for futile and self-pitying lamentation.

Even the Friar, however, is not spared. We are grateful for his interruption of a series of speeches which are awakening in us more embarrassment than sympathy, but as he continues he falls into rhymed sententiae, cant formulae which we expect of his stock role but which no more satisfy us as adequately embodying what is happening on the stage than what they interrupt. A lesser dramatist might have used the speeches I have been running down to move his audience within a context whose style never admitted of the possibility of better things, as Kyd employed similar rhetoric to extort tears from his audience. But Shakespeare has established a context in which the norm represented by such speeches rings false.

Why does he do so? Because, though he wants us to feel the impact of the event on Juliet's parents, the tragedy is not theirs but Romeo's, and it is his response we must feel most deeply. Thus the scene we have been examining is followed by a brief interlude in which the musicians banter with one another, so that grief will not be laid ineffectively on grief, and so that the illusion of passing time may be conveyed more easily, and then immediately the action moves to Mantua where Romeo hears Balthasar's report of the catastrophe . . . :

How now, Balthasar!
Dost thou not bring me letters from the friar?
How doth my lady? Is my father well?
How fares my Juliet? That I ask again;
For nothing can be ill, if she be well.
   *Balthasar.* Then she is well, and nothing can be ill:
Her body sleeps in Capels' monument,
And her immortal part with angels lives.
I saw her laid low in her kindred's vault,
And presently took post to tell it you:
O, pardon me for bringing these ill news,
Since you did leave it for my office, sir.
   *Romeo.* Is it even so? then I defy you, stars!
Thou know'st my lodging: get me ink and paper,
And hire post-horses; I will hence to-night.
*Balthasar.* I do beseech you, sir, have patience.
Your looks are pale and wild, and do import
Some misadventure.
   *Romeo.*             Tush, thou art deceived:
Leave me, and do the thing I bid thee do.
Hast thou no letters to me from the friar?
   *Balthasar.* No, my good lord.
   *Romeo.*           No matter: get thee gone,
And hire those horses; I'll be with thee straight.
           [*Exit* Balthasar]
Well, Juliet, I will lie with thee to-night.
Let's see for means. . . .

              [V. i. 12-35]
              (pp. 170-75)

Now, tough-minded men do not customarily address the stars, and presumably few lovers even in Shakespeare's day would receive such news in Romeo's manner. But in the context established by the previous scene, his language conveys the illusion that it is not poetry but rather the direct utterance of the heart. He can deny Balthasar's worried description of his "pale and wild" looks; he does not need to call attention to a grief which is fully expressed in his immediate decision to die, couched in a laconic and powerful image that recalls the irony of Capulet's picture of Death as Juliet's husband: "Well, Juliet, I will lie with thee to-night." Like the Capulet of the preceding scene's opening, Romeo talks for the remainder of this speech in precise images evocative of a physical reality which tells us all we need to know to feel with him. His apothecary is as powerful an allegorization of death as Spenser ever achieved; yet it is simultaneously a disciplined and economical description of the world that our eyes see. Linked to an unblinking resolve really to die, it is more moving than all the protestations of Juliet's family circle that their lives are finished when in fact it is quite clear that their grief has not driven them to the death they apostrophize so repetitiously. Repeatedly Shakespeare has signaled to us that lamentations such as the Capulets' are inadequate: Capulet's resolve, soon broken, to say no more, the Friar's stern admonition to the grieving family, and Romeo's refusal to indulge in that ululation that Balthasar invites unmistakably ask us to contrast the styles we have witnessed.

Stylistic criticism such as this marks all of *Romeo and Juliet*. More trope-ridden than many of the nondramatic sonnets, the prologue employs alliteration, metonymy, paronomasia, antithesis, personification, and paradox, and the action opens with a punning match between servants. The play's rhetoric is continuously exuberant. Yet it is subject to almost constant reproach. Romeo first appears on the stage—having already been described in terms that present him as comically acting out the clichés of Petrarchan sonnets—spouting rhymed oxymora about love, and Benvolio promptly mocks him now as Mercutio will in subsequent scenes. The Nurse (I. iii.) punctures Lady Capulet's elaborate conceit of Paris as a "book of love, this unbound lover" [I. iii. 87] with the more prosaic (though witty and therefore still rhetorical) reminder that "women grow by men" [III. i. 95], opposing as Mercutio constantly does the realities of sexual love to verbal idealizations; the paradoxical realism of Mercutio's fantasy about Queen Mab—a classic exercise in the device of pseudomenos, precise in every whimsical detail—provides striking contrast to the loose verbosity of Romeo's laments. Friar Laurence, unable to understand the drift of Romeo's fanciful circumlocutions about his meeting with Juliet, urges him to "be plain, good son, and homely in thy drift; / Riddling confession finds but riddling shrift" [II. iii. 55-6]. . . . Mercutio, insistent to his last breath on semantic accuracy, counters Romeo's consolation that his wound cannot hurt much with a characteristic reminder, moving as a revelation of his steadfastness to himself and significant for the play at large, that facts matter more than formulations:

> No, 'tis not so deep as a well, nor so wide as a church door; but 'tis enough, 'twill serve.
>
> [III. i. 96-7]

Not the least power of these words, followed by a pun on "grave," is the fact that they recall another speech, of a very different order, to which we have already responded as a similar statement of fact that moves us and that reflects upon the entire play, Juliet's avowal of love for Romeo:

> My bounty is as boundless as the sea,
> My love as deep; the more I give to thee,
> The more I have, for both are infinite.
>
> [II. ii. 133-35]

And in contemplating these speeches, so far from one another, yet so hauntingly linked by their metaphors of deepness, we may begin to understand why Shakespeare has so made us concentrate on the problem of style in *Romeo and Juliet*. I have already recalled the commonplace that Romeo matures in his speech as the play develops. Of such speech as he utters in Mantua and afterwards he is not capable in the early action of Verona. . . . In the strings of oxymora [of Romeo's early speeches] we discover the self-conscious rhetorician exploring his subject, creating his argument through ingenuity and exuberant inventiveness. In the last speeches we perceive another kind of force, which we are compelled to recognize as heartfelt. Romeo does not search for verbal formulations, but finds them

implicit in the situation. . . . [The] imagery of Romeo's last speeches develops literally from his understanding of an actual situation; in context such poetry is not decorative, but rather the only satisfactory expression of things as they are and as they are felt. (pp. 175-79)

Yet in one crucial respect these two kinds of poetry are similar: They are founded on paradox. The paradoxes are not of the lovers' seeking, but tragically built into the experience to which they surrender themselves. Oxymoron is not simply a rhetorical device; it is a definition of their lives. Like Romeo, Juliet knows it from the start:

> My only love sprung from my only hate!
> Too early seen unknown, and known too late!
> Prodigious birth of love it is to me,
> That I must love a loathed enemy.
>
> [I. v. 138-41]

Love between the children of enemies is paradoxical; even more so is a love that finds its marriage only in death. Such paradox emerges not from the inventive mind of a sonnet-fed young man, turned in upon himself and delighting in the ambiguities of emotions simultaneously bitter and sweet, but from the actual confrontation of a reality that destroys in creating. We might consider the paradoxes of *Romeo and Juliet* from yet another angle. Throughout the first half of the play, as, among other critics, Harry Levin has argued in his indispensable study [see excerpt above, 1960], Romeo's idealization of romantic love is polarized against the naturalism of Mercutio and the Nurse (Levin notes that the Nurse's role gains force from her "natural" connection to Juliet as her wet-nurse). It is equally significant that the Nurse's role is of a different order in the second half, where it is her well-wishing advice to leave bad enough alone and later her pathetic grief that are set in counterpoint to Juliet's resolve; and that Mercutio, the voice of earthy realism and common sense about love, is killed at the play's center. In the first half of the tragedy Mercutio is opposed to a lover fixed on a sterile and virginal affection for a mistress who will have none of him; Romeo refuses to recognize the physical fact of love on which his friend constantly insists. But in the second half, Romeo is married and no longer needs Mercutio's bawdy instruction in the full meaning of his love. By the time of Mercutio's death Romeo has learned to salt his idealism with Mercutio's awareness of the reality of the flesh. But he has learned more than Mercutio knows, for he comes simultaneously to understand the full spirituality of his love for Juliet: He knows that it can find its ultimate satisfaction not in the vigorous life that Mercutio so poignantly embodies, but only in death. Having led us to reject wanton Petrarchism, Shakespeare thus brings us to affirm the existential antinomies from which Petrarch drew his true power.

Talking about style we have come back to character, and thus again to the problem of *Romeo and Juliet* as tragedy. The quality of Romeo's speech changes, as we have seen . . . , but the real change is that—except for some lapses—from the moment he falls in love with Juliet until he dies, Romeo's speech is bound to action. For Rosaline he "live[s] dead," he says [I. i. 224], and we do not believe him; for Juliet he dies. For Rosaline he turns the day into artificial night; but he can see Juliet only at night, when she "is the sun" [II. ii. 3]; day brings about the event that drives him from her, and at the end he must lie with her in a dark vault which "her beauty makes . . . a feasting presence full of light" [V. iii. 85-6]. Romeo and Juliet have given themselves over to passion. That passion is, as always in Shakespeare, thoughtless, impetuous, destructive, against all the advice of their elders to go "wisely and slow" because "they stumble that run fast" [II. iii. 94]; and it is what makes them the emblem of love. We have heard constant warnings against the amorous and paradoxical world of words which the lovers inhabit, but come at last to admire their paradoxes as wiser than the words of caution. Similarly we watch them warned by the commonsensical Nurse and by Friar Laurence, even once by Juliet herself in urging Romeo not to swear oaths . . . but we come to prize them as they prize each other, for the absoluteness of their passion. If Shakespeare has compressed a narrative which took months into a play which spans five days, if he has risked a growth in character that on reflection might seem to us to require more than even months, he has done so for a reason.

No critic's formulation could more accurately convey what I am talking about than Juliet's epithalamion, perhaps the most magnificent piece of poetry in the play, spoken at the center of the tragedy [III. ii. 1-31]. . . . As fanciful as any other passage in the play, it is nonetheless more precise than even Juliet knows. The night for which she longs is that long night in which she and Romeo will find that escape from a constantly interfering daylight world toward which they are rapidly being driven. Like the sonnet in which the lovers first woo one another, Juliet's invocation suggests her fealty to a religion of love, a religion set against that other represented by Friar Laurence, whose cautioning seems irrelevant and whose ministra-

tions result only in killing the lovers. The generation of parents preaches moderation; Lady Capulet's advice to Juliet not to weep excessively (for Tybalt, she thinks) reminds us of Claudius' advice to his nephew. But here as in *Hamlet* Shakespeare teaches us that in the consuming fire of passion there is something more compelling than men of moderation ever imagine. Only annihilation can do full justice to such longings as Romeo and Juliet share. Theirs is not a love of propagation and domestic contentment, but rather a yearning for a transformation of the world that will correspond to their inner state. Anything but death would be a betrayal of that love.

Thus we feel at the end of *Romeo and Juliet* as we do at the end of every Shakespearean tragedy: We have watched not the process of nemesis, or of fortune, or of retribution, but rather the playing out of an awesome dialectic in which what is most worth prizing in the hero is set complementarily against the wisdom that the world for good reason advises. The play's expressed judgment is against impetuosity and irrationality as destructive, but the valuation it implies is a judgment in favor of precisely these qualities as the foundation and essence of a transcendent love. Juliet's wedding invocation to the friendly night and Romeo's love of night and blackness suggest their growing up, as we have seen, to a view of love which simultaneously incorporates and refutes Mercutio's; Romeo's rejection of a chaste interest in Rosaline for a love that is of the body as well as of the soul leads ironically to his fulfillment in a death which does not merely happen to him, but which he chooses, and which means a good deal more than it did in Brooke's tragedy of fortune that served Shakespeare as source. Were love simple—were it not, to recall the myth Shakespeare set out in *Venus and Adonis,* the cursed mingling of two unreconcilable worlds, two kinds of experience, two opposed drives—we could find Romeo and his bride either right or wrong. But in a universe whose values are always complementary there is no such simple judgment to be made. . . . From one point of view Romeo and Juliet lose all; from another they gain all that there is to be gained. Unlike the paradoxes the early Romeo seeks out, the antinomies of love are woven, as he learns, into the fabric of a universe which can be comprehended only by a complementary vision. The problem is eros; its form is Shakespearean. (pp. 179-84)

> *Norman Rabkin, "Eros and Death," in his* Shakespeare and the Common Understanding, *The Free Press, 1967, pp. 150-91.*

*Act III. Scene v. Romeo and Juliet. By Frank Dicksee.*

### ROY W. BATTENHOUSE (essay date 1969)

[*Battenhouse is well known for his studies of religion and literature and for his theory that Shakespeare's works embody a specifically Christian world view. In the following excerpt, he asserts that the sentimental view of Romeo and Juliet as not responsible for their tragic deaths is unsatisfactory, claiming instead that the lovers' behavior and the final catastrophe are intimately connected, for both the hero and heroine seek an idolatrous and narcissistic form of passion which ultimately undermines the Christian, communal aspect of love. Battenhouse especially notes Romeo's fatal tendency to "mask" the sinful nature of his passion for Juliet in religious imagery; he states that this attitude towards their love is essentially no different from his initial affection for Rosaline, adding that it is but one more instance of the courtly love tradition that permeates Verona and binds its citizens to a "false religion." Battenhouse further links this courtly view of love to the* amour-passion *and* Liebestod *myths noted by earlier critics, stating that, like these forms of passion, it is intrinsically destructive, pagan in its idealistic eroticism, and nontranscendent.*]

From a traditional Christian point of view suicide is always sinful, except when the consequence of a special command from God (as in Samson's case), or when the mind is deranged, as is plainly the case in Ophelia's death. Does a play such as *Romeo and Juliet* imply this same general judgment? Does its structure suggest that its author was understanding the tragedy from a Christian point of view? This is a lively issue in Shakespeare criticism, and one which can properly challenge our careful analysis. If we are to deal with it, however, we must consider the suicide of the lovers in its full dramatic context, in which it arises as the culmination of the whole action of the story and not as an isolated episode. Further, we need not suppose that Shakespeare's intent is to moralize—in any case, not on the literal suicide, which may be (as for Cleopatra) merely the consequence of a prior and more basic sin. As a playwright of tragedy, Shakespeare is seeking, we may assume, to exercise and purge our pity and fear by what he reveals. His aim is not to blame but, as artist, to imitate action while including the action's moral quality in the imitation. What must concern us, then, is the poetic diction and symbolism through which that moral quality is revealed. (pp. 102-03)

The romantic reading of *Romeo and Juliet,* which prevails even in recent commentary, holds that the lovers are flawless victims of circumstances, or mischance, or a malign fate. G. I. Duthie, for instance, takes this view in his edition of the play [see excerpt above, 1953]. After debating whether the lovers are in any way responsible for their doom, he concludes that it is "not part of the basic design" that we should regard their fate "as directly caused, even partly, by their own character flaws." There is nothing we can hold against Romeo, he believes, unless we insist on "the (admitted) validity of moral conceptions that have no meaning for Shakespeare in this play." How can we blame Romeo, he asks, for killing himself on believing Juliet dead, "since he has, from his first vision of her, regarded her as his whole life"?

This critic's own final clause, however, can be our clue to Shakespeare's answer. That is, Romeo's regard for Juliet as his "whole life" is at the root of the tragedy, because of the idolatry and self-deception involved in such an attitude. The lovers idolize each other, and in doing so make a religion of their passion. The first clear signal of this fact comes at a point structurally important in every Shakespearean tragedy, the end of Act I. Here, in a love duet antiphonally sung, Romeo casts himself in the role of a pilgrim visiting his "saint" Juliet and seeking as the "fine" of his devotion—that is, both as its "end" and as its penitential "satisfaction"—a kiss at her "holy shrine" [I. v. 93 ff]. Juliet is in a mood sympathetic to this imaginary saint worship. She asks for service in the form of prayers to herself, since "Saints do not move, though grant for prayers' sake" [I. v. 105]. Already in imagination she is here eternizing herself as an immovable deity, foreshadowing dramatically her role in the tomb in Act V. In kissing her, Romeo sees his kiss as a prayer, and her lips as a purging absolution: "Then move not while my prayer's effect I take. / Thus from my lips by thine my sin is purged" [I. v. 106-07]. But at this point, half breaking the spell, comes the wit commentary of a more realistic logic:

JUL.     Then have my lips the sin that they have took.
ROM.     Sin from my lips? Oh, trespass sweetly urged!
         Give me my sin again.
JUL.                You kiss by the book.
                                            [I. v. 108-10]

By what "book" have they kissed? The context of a worship involving secret "sin" suggests the Book of Courtly Love. Is this perhaps Verona's code-book for courtesy and "mannerly" love? (pp. 103-04)

Romeo [takes] his religious conceits seriously. He continues them in his sighs to "dear saint" and "fair saint" in the orchard scene, when he has "night's cloak" to hide him and Juliet has "the mask of night" [II. ii. 55, 61, 75, 85] to screen her blushes. Benvolio, who has followed Romeo as far as the orchard wall, has commented: "Blind is his love, and best befits the dark" [II. i. 32]. Although Benvolio at this point does not know of Romeo's new mistress, his comment seems applicable beyond his immediate ken. Romeo has entered this orchard, as he entered the earlier party, as an interloper self-invited. Yet we see him translating his action in terms of sacred vocation, even though he is half-aware of its mundane aspect as a venturing for "merchandise." His quest has had its start, perhaps emblematically, in his being able to read "the letters and the language" [I. ii. 61] of a guest list. May Shakespeare be suggesting, figuratively, that Romeo is a superficial reader of love's *letters*—one who impetuously turns their meaning into the "trespass sweetly urged" of his fashionable sonneteering?

Metaphors of book and reading in connection with love are recurrent in the play. Romeo's love, the Friar remarks [II. iii. 88], "did read by rote and could not spell." The Friar here has in mind Romeo's rumored love for Rosaline; yet his comment may be, for Shakespeare, equally pertinent to the love Romeo has begun to devote to Juliet. And meanwhile we have witnessed an earlier scene which turns about the theme of Juliet's "reading." We have overheard Lady Capulet (in I. iii.) instructing Juliet in the ritual of love quest: she is to "read o'er" the volume of a "face" at a nighttime feast, to find out what her "liking" is [I. iii. 81 ff.]. In this "precious book of love," Lady Capulet goes on to say, Juliet will discover an "unbound" lover, who lacks only a "cover" to beautify him. Obviously this metaphor involves wordplay: by Lady Capulet at a social level ("unbound" meaning "bachelor"); but by Shakespeare, no doubt, at two further levels—the sexual ("unbound" meaning "naked"), and the moral ("unbound" in the sense of "irresponsible," a lover who needs the cover of some disguise or "mask" for his self-abandonment).

The book of love, evidently, has lurking ambiguities. For who is this prospective lover? Lady Capulet has in mind the "valiant Paris," kinsman to Verona's prince. But she is unaware of another lover of more bookish face, the legendary Paris who may be hidden in Verona's Romeo. Will not Juliet, by her liking for this secret lover, become the "face" that launches Romeo's ship on dangerous seas? We will hear of the dashing rocks which Romeo as voyager welcomes and dares [V. iii. 118], because he thinks to find "immortal blessing" [III. iii. 37] in Juliet's kiss—as did the ancient Paris (or Marlowe's Faustus) in Helen's. Juliet is idolized as Romeo's sole "Heaven"—once he has ignored his own mind's premonitory warning of the dire consequences that may lurk in the "night's revels" at Capulet's house. Rashly he entrusts the "steerage of my course" to a nameless "He" [I. iv. 112], who is later identified by allusion as the blind god, Cupid [II. ii. 80-1]. This is courtly love's hidden story, which Lady Capulet does not realize may lie in the "book" Juliet will read. (pp. 105-06)

The book by which Romeo loves, and Juliet too, teaches "faith" and pilgrimage. We have noted this language in the sonnet of [I. v. 93], and its significance is later highlighted when Mercutio calls Romeo a "Young Abraham Cupid" [II. i. 13]. Abraham is the Bible's paradigm for a pilgrim of faith. But there is a Shakespearean irony in associating his name with Cupid. For in what sense are Cupid's devotees like Abraham? Are they not blind versions of Abraham? Cupidinous lovers, as the play will indicate, are led by a faith—in glories of the "eye," the "I," and the "aye" (that shadow-trinity on which Shakespeare puns in [III. ii. 45-50]); and by a hope—of the promised land of a dark orchard and its bitter-sweet fruit; and by a love—of passion itself as "death-devouring." Are not these the shadow-virtues of a false religion? (p. 107)

In obedience to *eros* and *liebestod,* Romeo can overleap walls, alike mural and moral. Significantly, he is ready from the start to put off his Christian name at Juliet's suggestion.

> I take thee at thy word.
> Call me but love, and I'll be new baptised.
> Henceforth I never will be Romeo.
>
> [II. ii. 49-51]

Elizabethan auditors, if witty enough to recall their theology's association of rebaptism with Anabaptist heresy, may well have been startled by Romeo's vow here. Juliet herself is startled a bit: "What *man* art thou that, thus *bescreened in night,* / So *stumblest* on my counsel" [II. ii. 52-3]. I have italicized the *sententia* I think Shakespeare is conveying. Juliet, of course, understands only the literal sense of her words. She is intuitive enough, however, to sense an impropriety when Romeo goes on to offer to swear by the moon. She edits out the inconstant moon, asking Romeo to swear rather by "thy gracious self, / Which is the god of my idolatry" [II. ii. 113-14]. But is this revised oath any less auspicious of tragedy?

A moment later, Juliet's native intuition warns her that her contract has been "too unadvised," too much like lightning, and without joy. But then, reaching for some cover for her love, she rushes into her plan for a secret marriage. In Act III, similarly, she can recognize but suppress her glimpse of Romeo as "beautiful tyrant," and thus can turn to naming him, without shame, her "true knight." (pp. 107-08)

In Juliet's epithalamium, sung in solitude and not as a community hymeneal, we find numerous half-submerged images of Blind Cupid. Here at the center of the play (III. ii), Shakespeare by his motifs is enlightening his audience as to the "dark" nature of the lovers' love:

> Spread thy close curtain, love-performing night,
> That runaways' eyes may wink, and Romeo
> Leap to these arms, untalked of and unseen.
> Lovers can see to do their amorous rites
> By their own beauties; or, if love be blind,
> It best agrees with night.
>
> [III. ii. 5-10]

Curtaining night, runaways' eyes, an "unseen" lover welcomed with a winking leap—these are the images by which Juliet invokes a blind love, that she may learn "how to lose a winning match" [III. ii. 12]. The winning "match" that is lost in being won is more than sexual in its range of connotation. It suggests, morally, the Pyrrhic victory in which the play will end, and also carries wordplay on "match"—in the triple sense of "paired" lovers, love as a "game," and a putting of "fire" to the powder which (so Friar Laurence has remarked [II. vi. 10-11]) will "consume with a kiss" and in its triumph die, like a flash in the night.... This is a love which worships face. It also harbors a death wish, in its long-

ings for a cosmic immortality. But the immortality of stellification, obviously, is paganism's substitute for Christian transcendence. What it transcends is not sin and sorrow, which it secretly loves, but instead human community and life itself. True, Juliet's and Romeo's love is no crude sensualism; it is an idealistic eroticism. Yet it truncates both Platonic and Christian mysticism by lacking the final goal of Plato's *eros,* union with an invisible beauty; and it is notably devoid of the gift of Christian *agape,* which finds fulfilment in actions of caretaking and husbandry.

It is significant, I think, that when the lovers part in the morning after their night of love, neither one of them so much as suggests that, instead of parting, they go together to Mantua. Juliet had pled to go with Romeo in Arthur Brooke's version of the story; but to Shakespeare any such concern for the daytime needs of the fellow lover seemed improbable for the kind of love his drama is presenting. He therefore beautifies the lovers' parting, instead, with a day-song which scholarship can trace to models in the cult literature of courtly love.... [Denis de Rougemont] noted as typical features of this love the following: a twin narcissism in the lovers; their half-conscious wish for suffering and death; their secret need for some "obstruction" to the course of their love in order to stimulate *askesis;* the motif of love as religion and as war; and the story-motif of a love-potion as an alibi for passion. Finding these features in Tristan and Iseult, he pointed to Romeo and Juliet as exhibiting a similar pattern [see excerpt above, 1956]. Miss Mahood, in following up this lead, has traced in Shakespeare's play the *leitmotiv* of Death as bridegroom, and has noted also the ambiguity in the Prologue's reference to the "death-marked love" of Romeo and Juliet [see excerpt above, 1957]. This phrase can mean either a love "marked out for death," foredoomed; or it can mean a love which takes death as "its objective," its seamark in sailing. The first meaning suggests helpless lovers; the second suggests lovers who elect to die. Romantic readers of the play, by taking the upper side of the phrase, have supposed the Prologue to refer to some thwarting by malignant stars. But why not the undermeaning, that the lovers have their stars crossed—that is, they sail by a mistaken light?

The whole texture of the play, it seems to me, carries a tension between these two perspectives. The first represents the surface sense by which the lovers interpret their doom. The second reveals a deeper truth which they fugitively glimpse and ignore, but which a sophisticated audience can see full well by attending to their actions and to Shakespeare's diction. Many auditors may miss seeing it, of course, while the play is in motion. Yet they can have second thoughts when remembering the play's accumulative design—the figural content which haunts the literal. (pp. 108-10)

Many interpreters of Act I have supposed a radical change in Romeo when he first meets Juliet. In his mooning over Rosaline they recognize all the symptoms of a post-Petrarchan lovesickness, but imagine that all this is cured when he finds "real" love. Actually, however, what he discovered was but another object of worship, a Juliet-"sun" instead of coldly Diana-like Rosaline. Whereas Rosaline would not "ope her lap to saintseducing gold" [I. i. 214], Juliet reciprocates Romeo's love. Through this experience he becomes more sociable. Yet the change merely accords with Benvolio's recipe:

> Tut, man, one fire burns out another's burning.
> One pain is lessened by another's anguish.
> Turn giddy, and be holp by backward turning,

One desperate grief cures with another's languish.
Take thou some new infection to thy eye,
And the rank poison of the old will die.
                                                        [I. ii. 45-50]

With Juliet, Romeo has a new "infection." It represents, in fact, a turning "backward"—to a clandestine love, which socially is "giddy." But is it not the same "religion of mine eye" as was affirmed in [I. ii. 88]? (p. 111)

Juliet is "as much in love" as Romeo. Mercutio, who does not know this, is nevertheless not wrong, symbolically speaking, when he associates Romeo's beloved with Dido, Cleopatra, Helen, and Thisbe. All are types of tragic amour-passion. Of Dido's secret love with Aeneas, Virgil had written: "she calls it marriage and with that name veils her sin". . . . Juliet veils hers with the outward form of a marriage rite by Friar Laurence, but in a context having little or none of the inward purpose a church marriage should signify. Essentially, hers is a Carthaginian type of love, only more youthful than Dido's. (p. 112)

Why, incidentally, has Shakespeare invented Mercutio, out of little but a name in Brooke's account? Does Mercutio function in the play, as some commentators feel, as the scoffing sensualist who sets off by contrast the idealistic love of Romeo? Or is he the pure poet of the Queen Mab speech, which other readers adore for its soaring imagination? Perhaps he is something of both; but how exactly? . . .

Basically, I would suggest, Shakespeare is using Mercutio as a kind of internal chorus, by whom Romeo's love is being assessed with a two-sided realism. One side is the ethical realism of the speech on Queen Mab (I. iv). Note that under all the delicate fancy with which this Queen is described, she is also called a "hag." She is the midwife of earthly dreams—making lawyers dream on fees, ladies on kisses, and a soldier on the cutting of throats. And she elicits these dreams, we are told, by a touch of moonshine, spider web, and film. Surely this speech is more than decorative. Shakespeare through Mercutio is here defining Verona's courtly world, by telling us the nature of the "fairy" who captivates human beings to the service of cupidity in its many forms. At the same time it lends irony to Mercutio's character, in that he does nothing to use his wisdom toward curbing his own "vain fantasy" for quarreling. (p. 113)

Mercutio is as fatalistic about his own "humour" as about the humour of the madman-lover which he recognizes in Romeo. His fatalism, in fact, is analogous to Romeo's; and so is his fashion-mongering sword play. He is, so to speak, a bolder and more worldly version of Romeo. Just as he knows that lovers (including Romeo) are victims of a hag-fairy, so also he knows, and wittily says just before his Queen Mab speech, that Romeo's love is a sexual game. And since Mercutio's scenes of jesting are by Shakespeare sandwiched before and after Romeo's scenes of lovemaking to Juliet, hints are thereby offered to the audience that Romeo's "idealistic" love is, after all, grounded in bewitching dream on the one hand and idle sport, wild-goose chase, on the other. (p. 114)

But Mercutio is also important, thematically, in pointing up the analogy between love song and dueling. Tybalt, he says, "fights as you sing prick song" [II. iv. 20-1]. By thus linking love duet with duelling, Mercutio prepares the audience for Romeo's shift from the one to the other. Implicit here is the idea that these are but the two sides of one coin: fashionable quarreling and courtly romancing are polar activities. . . . As

polar forms of "Serious vanity," they are rooted in a dialectic I have already noted; namely, that a religion of the "eye" is paradoxically also a religion of the "I"—that is, of self-esteem. Hence when Romeo feels his reputation at stake, after his naive efforts at peacemaking between Tybalt and Mercutio have miscarried and disgraced him, he can rush to meet Tybalt with a "fire-eyed fury" that actually outdoes Tybalt's. Shakespeare, in order to bring out this point of Romeo's concern for self-esteem, has had to change Brooke's version, in which Romeo fought solely for physical self-defense.

In Act V, for the same reason, Shakespeare again departs from Brooke by adding Romeo's slaying of Paris. This later episode clinches the thematic paradox of "brawling love," along with the moral paradox of "sin" committed out of devotion to a "face" supposed heavenly. No wonder there is so much oxymoron in the rhetoric of this drama; it highlights the pointedly foolish behavior of the lovers. (pp. 114-15)

The action of Romeo's visit to the tomb is shaped by Shakespeare as a kind of upside-down analogy to the Easter story. To the sepulchre of his beloved, Romeo hastens with mattock and crowbar to force open the "jaws" of death, that he may there set up his "everlasting rest" [V. iii. 47, 110] with worms! He comes, by torchlight, to engage in what Paris rightly calls "unhallowed toil" [V. iii. 54]. He slays Paris for attempting to stop him, then prepares himself for a "dateless bargain to engrossing death" [V. iii. 115]. Hailing Juliet's beauty as a feast of light, he raises and drinks his cup of poison—a kind of blind *figura* of the Christian Mass. Since in the time scheme of the play it is now Thursday night, we recognize here a celebration which travesties the Thursday Last Supper of Christ. Romeo's rite climaxes a religion of love which has transcended reason—but by plunging into desperate dream. His devotion to *eros* has become a shadow-aping of *agape*. (p. 115)

[*Romeo and Juliet* ends] with Capulet and Montague burying their feud with a handshake. This gesture is noble; yet its motive may be little more than their instinctual desire for a self-rehabilitation in the public eye. Their Prince has just moralized the calamity as a punishment by Heaven on their hate. Understandably, they respond with shows of love to cover their disgrace. But we note that no tears are shed (even though Romeo's mother has been shedding them, and in fact has died of grief during the night). And there is an unmistakable undertone of rivalry, with a tinge even of commercialism, as the fathers contend in promising statues of gold in honor of their dead children. May Shakespeare be suggesting here a ceremony by which Verona is canonizing new household gods, to minister henceforth to the city's religion of the eye? (p. 117)

Although Verona achieves a temporary peace through the "Poor sacrifices" it makes, we may doubt that these will suffice for a long-lasting peace. (Bandello in his account remarks that the peace did not last any great while afterwards.) There has been attained, as the play's Prologue promised, a burying of strife—but not of the human proclivity to one-up-manship. It is the Earthly City's peace, useful for its moment of civil agreement, yet far short of a heavenly peace, which St. Augustine had described as a "most harmonious fellowship in the enjoyment of God and of one another in God."

The "golden story" of I. iii. 92 has thus come to its close, with little real self-discovery by Verona's participants in the drama. We may note that Prince Escalus, while politely including himself in the dictum "All are punished," does so in a glancing way which deflects the major blame on others—

"And I, for winking at *your* discords . . ." [V. iii. 294 ff.]. The phrase almost praises, indirectly, his own good nature. But did he, in fact, wink at discords? That is scarcely the impression he has given in the play's opening scene. There he thundered at them and threatened death to future brawlers. What he has chiefly winked at, we may say, is his true duty as a ruler, his duty to work out a reconciliation by group conference. He has substituted, like a policeman, a few separate summonses for laying down the law:

> You, Capulet, shall go along with me,
> And, Montague, come you this afternoon.
>
> [I. i. 99-100]

Thus the antagonists are never brought together in his chamber, but instead Escalus has paraded his own authority in the public eye—as he does again at the end of the play. This has been substituted, moreover, for any genuine policing of the streets—with the result that Romeo, and later Paris, get themselves into trouble through benevolently but unwisely undertaking to do the Prince's work for him, when undeputized they try to arrest a brawler.

In Act III, the Prince's only other appearance, he has blinked at Benvolio's testimony and swept under the rug the question of justice. Here his primary concerns were to placate Lady Capulet's demand for revenge and at the same time to display himself as merciful through reducing his edict of death to mere banishment—which of course simply shoved the genuine problem out of sight, and prevented discovery of the secret marriage which, had it been revealed, could immediately have ended the civic problem by reconciling the houses. . . . Shakespeare's view is given us indirectly through the Friar's comment that the Prince has "rushed aside the law" [III. iii. 26]. We may miss seeing and seizing the import of this remark because (by the dramatist's irony) the Prince's act is being accounted praiseworthy by the Friar, who foolishly is telling Romeo: "This is dear mercy and thou see'st it not" [III. iii. 28]. Actually, it is dear in the sense of *costly* to the state and to that general welfare which both a Prince and a Friar should be guarding. Yet no one in Verona perceives the falseness of the "mercy" here practiced. Even we of the audience, if we are to catch the point, need the help of Shakespeare's latent wordplay on *dear* and on *see'st, seiz'st* and *ceased*. The play through its diction is challenging us to see into the tragedy's enigma, so that *we* may cease to be blind.

Shakespeare's Escalus all along has been practicing a patchwork politics in place of true statesmanship. We need to recognize that in this respect he is a blind and tragic ruler, just as Friar Laurence, Verona's other official guardian of community welfare, is equally so and for the same reason, namely, a lapsing into pretentious devices out of a kind of vanity for feeling important, while neglecting thereby the heart of his responsibility. Moreover, these two heads of church and state have never conferred on community problems. Each has preferred doing things on his own. And this isolation of role (a strangely absolute separation of church and state) is reflected in analogous forms of individualism all the way down the social scale. Self-glory, by inducing mischances, is a basic cause of tragedy in Verona; and it is not eradicated even at the end.

Does Friar Laurence achieve humility, finally, when under arrest? Note the evasiveness of his plea: "And *if* aught in this / Miscarried by my fault, let my old life / Be sacrificed . . ." [V. iii. 266-68]. Even in this very speech there are the twin faults of self-pity and of a winking at his own cowardice in

having fled. Moreover, his recital of events distorts by suppressing telltale details. When he reports that "a noise did scare me from the tomb" [V. iii. 262], he omits to say that this noise came from the watch, whom he knew to be approaching. Thus he evades seeing and admitting that what scared him, really, was not the "noise" but the prospect of loss of reputation if arrested. Similarly, when he reports that Juliet "would not go with me" [V. iii. 263], he is omitting to confess that he had first proposed to "dispose" of her in a sisterhood, and then had disposed of his own responsibilities of "brotherhood" by forsaking her. It is all very analogous to Romeo's behavior: he too had fled, not taking Juliet with him when he left Verona, and never thinking to stay by her side and confess to the authorities his guilty secret. "Discovery" on the part of the chief persons in a Shakespearean tragedy seems to be limited, usually, to the discovery of being trapped by some mischance or fate, with little or no accompanying perception of how one's own moral fault has led him into the trap. The human proclivity for evasion is the drama's covert truth. Friar Laurence can mention in his report . . . "their stol'n marriage day" [V. iii. 233], yet fail to infer from this his own complicity in thievishness. (pp. 118-20)

The interpretation I [am] giving of the Friar differs both from the usual romantic one and also from the "Elizabethan" one proposed by Franklin Dickey [see excerpt above, 1957]. Dickey would see in Friar Laurence a "consistent voice of moderation and wisdom" opposing the gusts of passion in Romeo, and would argue that Romeo's "disregard of the Friar's reasonable counsels" dooms the lovers. He calls Laurence, therefore, "a true chorus whose words give the necessary moral base from which to judge the tragedy." I accept the view that the Friar is a kind of chorus, but am concerned to point out how inconsistent and tragic his choral "wisdom" is. It miscounsels Romeo, and later Juliet, by ignoring the Christian standard incumbent upon all clergymen and especially Franciscans. When, for instance, the Friar upbraids Romeo for "hollow perjury" to "Thy dear love sworn" [II. iii. 128], he is thinking only of Juliet and quite overlooking the "dear love" to which every Christian swears allegiance at baptism, and which every Franciscan binds himself to practice. The Friar's very perspective here is a perjury to his Ordination vow. Or, again, when at the mock funeral for Juliet the Friar moralizes to the parents,

> Oh, in this love, you love your child so ill
> That you run mad . . .
>
> [IV. v. 75-6]

is there not dramatic irony in that he himself, by his ill love for their child, is now running mad with pretenses for his own face-saving? (p. 124)

The Friar's advice-giving in general, throughout the play, is further and finally analogized by Shakespeare, I think, to the "musty seeds" and "skins / Of ill shaped fishes" which "make up a show" [V. i. 46, 43-4, 48] on the shelves of the Mantuan apothecary. These metaphors are marvellously apt, when one considers how basic to Christian teaching are the symbols of "seed" and "fish"—they virtually define the Christian vocation, which in Friar Laurence has become "musty" and mere "skin" of ill shape. The whole eleven-line passage describing the apothecary's shop [V. i. 38-48] is much more than picturesque local color. It serves as a dramatically distanced mirror of the other druggist in the play, Friar Laurence—as if the telltale relics of his Verona world were here collected in a Mantuan archeological museum. Laurence, like his Mantuan counterpart, is stocked with "simples" which witness to a beggarly destitution—in his case, however, a destitution not financial but moral. (p. 125)

The poverty of Shakespeare's Friar is a poverty in respect to the mysteries of gospel. Like the sentimentalists at Calvary, who offered as a medicine for anguish a sponge of vinegar and gall, Friar Laurence has given Juliet an escape drug. He has thus neglected Holy Communion—that is, the pastoral wisdom this sacrament implies, the "cure" whose mystery should constitute his priestly vocation. By a substituting of magic flask for holy cup, he has induced a mock sacrifice by Juliet, a disingenuous "two days buried" [V. iii. 176]. Indeed, its forty-two hours of artificial sleep is but a false and shadow-parallel to Christ's salvific forty hours in the region of the dead. The Friar's preaching, moreover, has substituted the theme of moderation for that of rectification—as if a less excessive doting were the chief need of the lovers. What they more basically need, however, is an "ordinate" love, freed of idolatry, a love which would give each created thing only its proper due in the total hierarchy of goods and values. This the Friar does not see, partly because he is misled by his ambition for the fame of peacemaker. (pp. 125-26)

The full meaning of *Romeo and Juliet,* I have been contending, is to be found only through weighing its symbolism and total logic. The perspective of the Prologues, for instance, represents only the limited vision of Verona's citizenry as voiced by this chorus. The focus of the initial Prologue is on the play's official moral, whose latent ambiguities are left unexplored. Its purpose is to engage our sympathy and prompt our pity and fear. But then, while our spellbound emotions are being exercised within this frame, the dramatist weaves into the action archetypal echoes, through wordplay and emblematic scenes, which offer for our intellect a deeper significance whenever (either during or after our moment in the theatre) we are ready to decipher it. This deeper meaning, in one sense, is simply Brooke's "moral" reimagined in a more sophisticated, unpropagandistic way. In another sense, however, it is purely intellectual: a recognition of the wonderful mock analogy to Christian story which is provided us in the storybook of Cupid's saints. How marvellously their religion of love unintentionally mimics a Christian love of religion! From this recognition, there can then arise for us a moral which is not didactic but confessional: "There but for the grace of God go I."

We can say this because our emotional response has undergone a progress in the course of the play, a movement toward catharsis. The catharsis is achieved, it seems to me, by the drama's eliciting of our emotion at two levels. Most immediate is the appeal to our instinctual sympathy for the lovers, especially through a rhetoric of romance which lures us to identify ourselves with their feelings and outlook. To some extent every auditor is caught up in fearing the external obstacles which the lovers fear, and in pitying their suffering from what seem traps of circumstance. This naive response (typical of teenagers, but felt also by older auditors, for whom it indulges a nostalgic reliving of youthful dreams) takes on an intensification through the accumulating mishaps which entangle the story's beautiful and gifted protagonists, until finally the disaster of their death brings to rest our pity and fear in a resigned acceptance of the hard fact of human mortality. But all this while the dramatist has also been challenging a deeper level of our emotions—our half-conscious fear for the rashness in such a love and our pity for the desperation in its courage. It is this second level of emotion which is (or can be on later reflection) enlightened by the ironies built into the drama. Through these our penchant

for a self-identification with the lovers is progressively brought under judgment by insight. And our insight feeds in us a pity which becomes compassion, and a fear which begins to dread death less than what now can be recognized as its moral cause, namely, a blind love. A pity and fear of this kind, if heretofore neglected or atrophied in us, is given opportunity to revive and mature. Thus our emotions acquire a better health. For while at a surface level the acted out tragedy has been permitting us to expend vicariously our unexamined sentimentality, at another level it has been awakening in us more enlightened forms of emotion—experienced by each auditor, however, only insofar as his attention is well tuned and using a good antenna. The dialectic between the two levels I take to be the purgative process of the play. (pp. 127-29)

*Roy W. Battenhouse, "In Search of an Adequate Perspective," in his* Shakespearean Tragedy: Its Art and Its Christian Premises, *Indiana University Press, 1969, pp. 45-130.*

## SUSAN SNYDER   (essay date 1970)

[*Snyder contends that* Romeo and Juliet *is essentially a comedy transformed into a tragedy, noting that the opening acts of the play show all the usual markings of the comic structure, but that—with the death of Mercutio—the remaining acts turn toward the tragic mode. Snyder also comments on the play's center of interest, concluding that Shakespeare's stress here on the dramatic "milieu" demonstrates "for this once in Shakespearean tragedy, it is not what you are that counts, but the world you live in."*]

*Romeo and Juliet* is different from Shakespeare's other tragedies in that it becomes, rather than is, tragic. Other tragedies have reversals, but in *Romeo and Juliet* the reversal is so radical as to constitute a change of genre: the action and the characters begin in familiar comic patterns, and are then transformed—or discarded—to compose the pattern of tragedy.

Comedy and tragedy, being opposed ways of apprehending the real world, project their own opposing worlds. The tragic world is governed by inevitability, and its highest value is personal integrity. In the comic world 'evitability' is assumed; instead of heroic or obstinate adherence to a single course, comedy endorses opportunistic shifts and realistic accommodations as means to an end of new social health. The differing laws of comedy and tragedy point to opposed concepts of law itself. Law in the comic world is extrinsic, imposed on society *en masse.* Its source there is usually human, so that law may either be stretched ingeniously to suit the characters' ends, or flouted, or even annulled by benevolent rulers. . . . But in the tragic world law is inherent: imposed by the individual's own nature, it may direct him to a conflict with the larger patterns of law inherent in his universe. The large pattern may be divine, as it generally is in Greek tragedy, or it may be natural and social, as in *Macbeth* and *King Lear.* Tragic law cannot be altered; it does no good to tell destruction to stop breeding destruction, or to tell gods or human individuals to stop being themselves.

In these opposed worlds our sense of time and its value also differs. The action of comedy may be quickly paced, but we know that it is moving towards a conclusion of 'all the time in the world'. The events of tragedy, on the other hand, acquire urgency in their uniqueness and their irrevocability: they will never happen again, and one by one they move the hero closer to the end of his own time in death. In comedy short-term urgencies are played against a dominant expansiveness, while in tragedy a sense that time is limited and precious grows with our perception of an inevitable outcome. (pp. 391-92)

Romeo and Juliet, young and in love and defiant of obstacles, are attuned to the basic movement of the comic game toward social regeneration. But they are not successful: the game turns into a sacrifice, and the favoured lovers become its marked victims. This shift is illuminated by a study of the play's two worlds and some secondary characters who help to define them.

If we divide the play at Mercutio's death, the death that generates all those that follow, it becomes apparent that the play's movement up to this point is essentially comic. With the usual intrigues and go-betweens, the lovers overcome obstacles in a move toward marriage. This personal action is set in a broader social context, so that the marriage promises not only private satisfaction but renewed social unity:

> For this alliance may so happy prove
> To turn your households' rancour to pure love.
>
> [II. iii. 91-2]

The state that requires this cure is set out in the first scene. The Verona of the Montague-Capulet feud is like the typical starting point of the kind of comedy described by Northrop Frye [in his *Anatomy of Criticism*]: 'a society controlled by habit, ritual bondage, arbitrary law and the older characters.' Even the scene's formal balletic structure, a series of matched representatives of the warring families entering on cue, conveys the inflexibility of this society, the arbitrary division that limits freedom of action.

The feud itself seems more a matter of mechanical reflex than of deeply felt hatred. As H. B. Charlton has noted, its presentation here has a comic aspect [see excerpt above, 1948]. The 'parents' rage' that sounds so ominous in the Prologue becomes in representation an irascible humour: two old men claw at one another only to be dragged back by their wives and scolded by their Prince. Charlton found the play flawed by this failure to plant the seeds of tragedy, but the treatment of the feud makes good sense if Shakespeare is playing on *comic* expectations.

Other aspects of this initial world of *Romeo and Juliet* suggests comedy. Its characters are the minor aristocracy and servants familiar in comedies, concerned not with wars and the fate of kingdoms but with arranging marriages and managing the kitchen. More important, it is a world of possibilities, with Capulet's feast represented to the young men as a field of choice. 'Hear all, all see', says Capulet to Paris, 'And like her most whose merit most shall be' [I. ii. 30-1]. 'Go thither', Benvolio tells Romeo, 'and with unattainted eye / Compare her face with some that I shall show . . .' [I. ii. 85-6] and Rosaline will be forgotten for some more approachable beauty. (pp. 392-93)

Violence and disaster are not absent, of course, but they are unrealized threats. The feast yields a kind of comic emblem when Tybalt's potential violence is rendered harmless by Capulet's festive accommodation.

> Therefore be patient, take no note of him.
> It is my will; the which if thou respect,
> Show a fair presence and put off these frowns,
> An ill-beseeming semblance for a feast.
>
> [I. v. 71-4]

This overruling of Tybalt is significant, for Tybalt is a recognizably tragic character, the only one in this part of the play. He alone takes the feud seriously: It is his inner law, the

propeller of his fiery nature. He speaks habitually in the tragic rhetoric of honour and death:

> What, dares the slave
> Come hither, cover'd with an antic face,
> To fleer and scorn at our solemnity?
> Now by the stock and honour of my kin,
> To strike him dead I hold it not a sin.
>
> [I. v. 55-9]

Tybalt's single set of absolutes cuts him off from a whole rhetorical range available to the other young men of the play: lyric love, witty fooling, friendly conversation. Ironically, his imperatives come to dominate the play's world only when he himself departs from it. While he is alive, Tybalt is an alien.

In a similar manner, the passing fears of calamity voiced by Romeo, Juliet, and Friar Laurence are not allowed to dominate this atmosphere. If the love of Romeo and Juliet is already imaged as a flash of light swallowed by darkness (an image invoking inexorable natural law), it is also expressed as a sea venture, which suggests luck and skill set against natural hazards, chance seized joyously as an opportunity for action. 'Direct my sail', Romeo tells his captain Fortune; but soon he feels himself in command:

> I am no pilot; yet, wert thou as far
> As that vast shore wash'd with the farthest sea,
> I would adventure for such merchandise.
>
> [II. ii. 82-4]

The spirit is Bassanio's as he adventures for Portia [in *The Merchant of Venice*], a Jason voyaging in quest of the Golden Fleece. (pp. 394-95)

[But] Mercutio's death intervenes to transform this world of exhilarating venture. Mercutio has been almost the incarnation of comic atmosphere. He is the best of game-players, endlessly inventive, full of quick moves and counter-moves. Speech for him is a constant play on multiple possibilities: puns abound because two or three meanings are more fun than one, and Queen Mab brings dreams not only to lovers like Romeo but to courtiers, lawyers, parsons, soldiers, maids. These have nothing to do with the case at hand—Romeo's premonition—but Mercutio is not bound by events. They are merely points of departure for his expansive wit. In Mercutio's sudden, violent end, Shakespeare makes the birth of a tragedy coincide exactly with the symbolic death of comedy. The element of freedom and play dies with him, and where many courses were open before, now there seems only one. Romeo sees at once that an irreversible process has begun:

> This day's black fate on moe days doth depend [hang over],
> This but begins the woe others must end.
>
> [III. i. 119-20]

It is the first sign in the play's dialogue pointing unambiguously to tragic causation. Romeo's future action is now determined: he *must* kill Tybalt, he *must* run away, he is fortune's fool.

This helplessness is the most striking quality of the second, tragic world of *Romeo and Juliet*. That is, the temper of the new world is largely a function of onrushing events. Under pressure of events, the feud turns from farce to fate, from tit for tat to blood for blood. Lawless as it is in the Prince's eyes, the feud is dramatically the law in *Romeo and Juliet*. Previously external and avoidable, it has now moved inside Romeo to become his personal law. . . . Even outside the main chain of vengeance, the world is suddenly full of imperatives: against his will Friar John is detained at the monastery, and against his will the Apothecary sells poison to Romeo. Urgency becomes the norm as nights run into mornings in continuous action and the characters seem never to sleep. The new world finds its emblem not in the aborted attack but in the aborted feast. As Tybalt's violence was out of tune with the Capulet feast in Act II, so in Acts III and IV the projected wedding is made grotesque when Shakespeare insistently links it with death. Preparations for the feast parallel those of the first part, so as to underline the contrast when

> All things that we ordained festival
> Turn from their office to black funeral—
> Our instruments to melancholy bells,
> Our wedding cheer to a sad burial feast.
>
> [IV. v. 84-7]

I have been treating these two worlds as consistent wholes in order to bring out their opposition, but I do not wish to deny dramatic unity to *Romeo and Juliet*. Shakespeare was writing one play, not two, and in spite of the prominence of the turning point we are aware that premonitions of disaster precede the death of Mercutio and that hopes for avoiding it continue until near the play's conclusion. The world-shift that converts Romeo and Juliet from instinctive winners into sacrificial victims is thus a gradual one. In this connection the careers of two secondary characters, Friar Laurence and the Nurse, are instructive.

In being and action these two belong to the comic vision. Friar Laurence is one of a whole series of Shakespearean manipulators and stage-managers, those wise and benevolent figures who direct the action of others, arrange edifying tableaux, and resolve intricate public and private problems. . . . Such figures are frequent in comedy but not in tragedy, where the future is not manipulable. The Friar's aims are those implicit in the play's comic movement, an inviolable union for Romeo and Juliet and an end to the families' feud.

The Nurse's goal is less lofty, but equally appropriate to comedy. She wants Juliet married—to anyone. Her preoccupation with marriage and breeding is as indiscriminate as the life force itself. But she conveys no sense of urgency in all this. Rather, her garrulity assumes that limitless time that frames the comic world but not the tragic. In this sense her circumlocutions and digressions are analogous to Mercutio's witty flights and to Friar Laurence's counsels of patience. The leisurely time assumptions of the Friar and the Nurse contrast with the lovers' impatience, creating at first the normal counterpoint of comedy and later a radical split that points us, with the lovers, directly to tragedy.

For what place can these two have in the new world brought into being by Mercutio's death, the world of limited time, no effective choice, no escape? In a sense, though, they define and sharpen the tragedy by their very failure to find a place in the dramatic progress, by their growing estrangement from the true springs of the action. 'Be patient', Friar Laurence tells the banished Romeo, 'for the world is broad and wide' [III. iii. 16]. But the roominess he assumes in both time and space simply does not exist for Romeo. His time has been constricted into a chain of days working out a 'black fate', and he sees no world outside the walls of Verona [III. iii. 17].

Comic adaptability again confronts tragic integrity when Juliet is faced with a similarly intolerable situation—she is ordered to marry Paris—and turns to her Nurse for counsel as Romeo

does to the Friar. The Nurse replies with the traditional worldly wisdom of comedy. Romeo has been banished and Paris is very presentable. Adjust yourself to the new situation. (pp. 395-98)

But such advice has become irrelevant, even shocking, in this context. There was no sense of jar when Benvolio, a spokesman for accommodation like the Nurse and the Friar, earlier advised Romeo to substitute a possible for an impossible love. True, the Nurse is urging violation of the marriage vows; but Romeo was also sworn to Rosaline, and for Juliet the marriage vow is a seal on the integrity of her love for Romeo, not a separate issue. The parallel points up the progress of tragedy, for while Benvolio's advice sounded sensible and was in fact unintentionally carried out by Romeo, the course of action outlined by the Nurse is unthinkable to the audience as well as Juliet. The memory of the lovers' dawn parting that began this scene is too strong. Juliet and the Nurse no longer speak the same language, and estrangement is inevitable. 'Thou and my bosom henceforth shall be twain', Juliet vows privately. Like the death of Mercutio, Juliet's rejection of her old confidante has symbolic overtones. The possibilities of comedy have again been presented only to be discarded.

Both Romeo and Juliet have now cast off their comic companions and the alternate modes of being that they represented. But there is one last hope for comedy. If the lovers will not adjust to the situation, perhaps the situation can be adjusted to the lovers. This is usual comic solution, and we have at hand the usual manipulator to engineer it.

The Friar's failure to bring off that solution is the fianl definition of the tragic world of the play. Time is the villain. Time in comedy generally works for regeneration and reconciliation, but in tragedy it propels the protagonists to destruction; there is not enough of it, or it goes wrong somehow. The Friar does his best: he makes more than one plan to avert catastrophe. The first, typically, is patience and a broader field of action. Romeo must go to Mantua and wait

> till we can find a time
> To blaze your marriage, reconcile your friends,
> Beg pardon of the Prince, and call thee back . . .
>
> [III. iii. 150-52]

It is a good enough plan, for life if not for drama, but it depends on 'finding a time'. As it turns out, events move too quickly for the Friar, and the hasty preparations for Juliet's marriage to Paris leave no time for cooling tempers and reconciliations.

His second plan is an attempt to *gain* time, to create the necessary freedom through a faked death. This is, of course, another comic formula; Shakespeare's later uses of it are all in comedies. . . . [Friar Laurence] does not hope that Juliet's death will dissolve the families' hatreds but only that it will give Romeo a chance to come and carry her off. . . . [But] Romeo's man is quicker with the news of Juliet's death than poor Friar John with the news of the deception. Romeo himself beats Friar Laurence to the Capulets' tomb. The onrushing tragic action quite literally outstrips the slower steps of accommodation before our eyes. The Friar arrives too late to prevent one half of the tragic conclusion, and his essential estrangement is only emphasised when he seeks to avert the other half by sending Juliet to a nunnery. It is the last alternative to be suggested. Juliet quietly rejects the possibility of adjustment and continuing life: 'Go, get thee hence, for I will not away' [V. iii. 160].

The Nurse and the Friar illustrate a basic principle of the operation of comedy in tragedy, which might be called the principle of irrelevance. In tragedy we are tuned to the extraordinary. *Romeo and Juliet* gives us this extraordinary centre not so much in the two individuals as in the love itself, its intensity and integrity. Our apprehension of this intensity and integrity comes gradually, through the cumulative effect of the lovers' lyric encounters and the increasing urgency of events, but also through the growing irrelevance of the comic characters. (pp. 398-400)

After *Romeo and Juliet* Shakespeare never returned to the comedy-into-tragedy formula, although the canon has several examples of potential tragedy converted into comedy. There is a kind of short comic movement in *Othello*, encompassing the successful love of Othello and Desdemona and their safe arrival in Cyprus, but comedy is not in control even in the first act. Iago's malevolence has begun the play, and our sense of obstacles overcome (Desdemona's father, the perils of the sea) is shadowed by his insistent presence. The act ends with the birth of his next plot.

It is not only the shift from comedy to tragedy that sets *Romeo and Juliet* apart from the other Shakespeare tragedies. Critics have often noted, sometimes disapprovingly, that external fate rather than character is the principal determiner of the tragic outcome. For Shakespeare, tragedy is usually a matter of both character and circumstance, a fatal interaction of man and moment. But in this play, although the central characters have their weaknesses, their destruction does not really stem from these weaknesses. One may agree with Friar Laurence that Romeo is rash, but it is not his rashness that propels him into the tragic chain of events but an opposite quality. In the crucial duel between Mercutio and Tybalt, Romeo tries to make peace. Ironically, this very intervention contributes to Mercutio's death. . . . If Shakespeare wanted to implicate Romeo's rashness in his fate, this scene is handled with unbelievable ineptness. Judging from the resultant effect, what he wanted to convey was an ironic dissociation between character and the direction of events.

Perhaps this same purpose dictated the elaborate introduction of comic elements before the characters are pushed into the opposed conditions of tragedy. Stress on milieu tends to downgrade the importance of individual temperament and motivation. For this once in Shakesperian tragedy, it is not what you are that counts, but the world you live in. (pp. 400-01)

> Susan Snyder, "'Romeo and Juliet': Comedy into Tragedy," in Essays in Criticism, Vol. XX, No. 4, October, 1970, pp. 391-402.

## JAMES L. CALDERWOOD (essay date 1971)

[*Calderwood has examined what he calls Shakespeare's "metadrama" in two studies,* Shakespearean Metadrama *(1971) and* Metadrama in Shakespeare's Henriad *(1979). In the introduction to his earlier book, Calderwood claims that Shakespeare's plays are not only concerned with various moral, social, and political themes, but are also self-reflexively concerned with dramatic art itself— "its materials, its media of language and theater, its generic forms and conventions, its relationship to truth and the social order." In the following excerpt from* Shakespearean Metadrama, *the critic argues that a central conflict in* Romeo and Juliet *is that between the lovers' desire to develop a pure and personal language to express their love and the reality that language is a public commodity which, as such, can never adequately denote the private world of feelings. An extreme example of the falsity*]

*of speech, Calderwood contends, is Romeo's initial Petrarchan mode of expression, which Juliet immediately reacts against as meaningless and impersonal. Despite their efforts, Calderwood concludes, Romeo and Juliet fail to purify and personalize language, to redefine reality according to their own verbal requirements, for reality and its terms of reference "remain intransigently themselves" and relentlessly intrude on the lovers' privacy. Calderwood also comments on the protagonists' gradual movement toward death, which he describes as the ultimate silence and the perfect communion they have sought throughout their brief relationship, and he compares this to the* Liebestod *myth identified in the play by earlier critics.*]

As an indirect entry to *Romeo and Juliet* let me dwell for a moment on Shakespeare's management of vows, since vows are especially good indices of a dramatist's conception of language in addition to having a strong bearing on character, motive, even dramatic form. In *Titus Andronicus* Shakespeare saw in the vow a formal principle of Senecan revenge tragedy. Out of the chaos of his material the dramatist contrives a teleology in which the vow serves as a structural promise to be redeemed by a culminating act of vengeance. (p. 85)

Vows are equally significant in *Love's Labour's Lost*. In vowing themselves to the life of Academe the scholars rely on the autonomy of words, not as they function in society but as defined, purified, and sworn to by themselves. So constituted, words will suppress nature in the form of the scholars' own "affections" and "the huge army of the world's desires" (primarily women) [*Love's Labour's Lost*, I. i. 9-10]. Since a purely private verbal world is impossible, their fragile fortress of words collapses before the assaulting army of the world's desires marching in petticoats from France. The scholars then scatter a second set of vows during their Muscovite wooing scene, each to the wrong lady, the disastrous effect of which suggests that if words may be overvalued through private hoarding they may also be undervalued through promiscuous spending. Behind the surface plight of laboring lovers hiding behind words and then distributing them wildly in all directions stands the poet's metadramatic plight as he tries to arbitrate between the individual and private needs of his art on the one hand and the all-too-public and debased nature of the language in which his art must be cast. (p. 86)

It is generally supposed that *Titus Andronicus* preceded *Love's Labour's Lost*, and if so then the comedy may be seen as a reaction to the would-be tragedy, a recoiling from violent action, contrived plots, and stage sensationalism. The result is a purely verbal, plotless, essentially nondramatic work. Since it is also generally supposed that *Love's Labour's Lost* preceded *Romeo and Juliet* perhaps the latter can be considered in some degree at least as a response to the issues dealt with in the comic play. The marriage of the hero and heroine for instance would seem to acquire special significance in view of the conspicuous non-marriage of the lovers in the earlier play. In *Love's Labour's Lost* marriage was conceived of as the proper terminus of dramatic form, where the play ought to but perversely refuses to end, and as the product of a true language. Neither form nor language is discovered, however, and we are left with a mannered, courtly play of words illustrating its author's astonishing virtuosity but also, as he himself underscores by thrusting Mercade into the nonaction, a certain glib and glittering superficiality. The truth of the feelings is first suppressed by words and later distorted and obscured by them. As the purgative punishments of the scholars imply, the poet's language must somehow incorporate inner truth and outer reality, the mystery of love and such bleak facts of nature as time, suffering, death.

These then are the major metadramatic issues, at least on the side of language, confronting Shakespeare as he turns to *Romeo and Juliet*. From the problem of language he moves on in this play to the problem of dramatic form. But first let us focus on language and particularly on the balcony scene of 2.2 where vows again come into prominence. The place to begin is of course Juliet's famous complaint against the tyranny of names:

> 'Tis but thy name that is my enemy;
> Thou art thyself though not a Montague.
> What's Montague? It is nor hand nor foot
> Nor arm nor face nor any other part
> Belonging to a man. O be some other name!
> What's in a name? That which we call a rose
> By any other word would smell as sweet.
> So Romeo would, were he not Romeo called,
> Retain that dear perfection which he owes
> Without that title. Romeo, doff thy name,
> And for thy name, which is no part of thee,
> Take all myself.
>
> [II. ii. 38-49]

Here and more widely throughout the play, brilliantly figured in the implicit metaphor of family and relatives, verbal nominalism is equated with a kind of social personalism. That is, in her anxiety to circumvent the opposition of their relatives Juliet would reject all relations and find ultimate truth in the haecceity, thisness, or as she puts it "dear perfection" of a totally unaffiliated Romeo. In the same way nominalism rejects the family or tribal relations of words in their more universal and abstract forms and situates verbal truth in the concrete and particular terms that seem most closely tied to the unique, unrelated, and hence true objects of which reality is composed. Juliet's nominalism here is a position with which the poet can readily sympathize, because words come to the poet as Romeo comes to Juliet, trailing dark clouds of a prior public identity. Romeo comes to Juliet not merely from the streets of Verona and the house of Montague but from the shallows of Petrarchan love dotage as well, since he begins this play as Berowne ended his [in *Love's Labour's Lost*], an unrequited wooer of "Rosaline" (who is appropriately no more than a "name" in *Romeo and Juliet*). Juliet's verbal program is roughly analogous to that of the scholars of Navarre when they sought to establish their Academe. Where they tried to seal themselves off from the outside world by founding an elite society on a private language, Juliet seeks to go even further, to rename or even "de-name" in the interests of purifying a Romeo who has been abroad with his pseudo-love. (Of course Juliet does not know about Rosaline, but Shakespeare does, and thus has Juliet repudiate Petrarchan "form," "strangeness," and "cunning" a bit further on.)

Romeo is more than willing to be renamed—

> Call me but love and I'll be new baptized;
> Henceforth I never will be Romeo
>
> [II. ii. 50-1]

—but his language throughout the scene betrays him. Like Berowne, who prematurely thought himself cured of the Petrarchan style, Romeo still has "a trick / Of the old rage" [*Love's Labour's Lost*, V. ii. 416-17]. It reveals itself most obviously when he begins keening vows:

> Lady, by yonder blessed moon I vow
> That tips with silver all these fruit-tree tops—

> JULIET. O swear not by the moon, the inconstant moon
> That monthly changes in her circled orb,
> Lest that thy love prove likewise variable.
>    ROMEO. What shall I swear by?
> JULIET.                        Do not swear at all.
> Or, if thou wilt, swear by thy gracious self,
> Which is the god of my idolatry,
> And I'll believe thee.
>    ROMEO.            If my heart's dear love—
>    JULIET. Well, do not swear. Although I joy in thee,
> I have no joy of this contract tonight.
> It is too rash, too unadvised, too sudden,
> Too like the lightning, which does cease to be
> Ere one can say it lightens.
>
> [II. ii. 107-20]
> (pp. 86-9)

Like the scholars of Navarre in their wooing phase ("O who can give an oath?" [*Love's Labour's Lost,* IV. iii. 246]) Romeo is a ready spender of words and, also like them, naively trustful that vows can trace around lovers a magic circle to hold the devilish world at bay. But like the French ladies Juliet has a maturer conception of the laws of verbal contract and the power of their magic. Her rejection of the "inconstant moon" as a third party to the contract and her apprehensions about the rash, unadvised, and oversudden enlarge the more immediate threat of the feuding families to include all that is dangerously unstable beyond the periphery of private feeling. But she is also unsure of Romeo's love, which is available to her only as it is given shape in his language. Instinctively she distrusts his *style,* as Shakespeare forces us to notice by having her twice interrupt him as he cranks up his rhetorical engines in preparation for Petrarchan flights. Throughout this scene, and the play for that matter, it is Romeo's speech that soars airily and often vacuously. Juliet's, though hardly leaden, is more earthbound. She is not opposed to vows entirely—though her nominalism inevitably tends in that direction—but seeks a true language in which they may be expressed. Thus when Romeo selects the moon as a symbol of purity to swear by, she, recognizing the pseudo-purity of his own Petrarchan style, reminds him that the moon is also a symbol of inconstancy. Not the purling phrases rising easily to the lips of a thousand dandies with well-hinged knees but the genuine custom-made article is what she seeks. (p. 90)

[Unfortunately] Romeo, who would forge a binding verbal contract, is himself bound to the book of form. . . . Romeo not only kisses "by the book" [I. v. 110] but trumpets vows by the book of Petrarchan form. Juliet admits that she *could* play at Petrarchanism and that to do so might even invest her behavior with an appearance of mature reserve that her forthrightness of feeling makes her seem without. But even if a bit fondly, she specializes in truth, not form, and so concludes "but farewell compliment! / Dost thou love me?" [II. ii. 89-90]. Truly virginal, she recoils from the potential contamination of vows loosely and grandiloquently untethered: "Well, do not swear." Do not swear, do not even speak—that is the end of the nominalistic line because even at their best words cannot perfectly reflect the autonomous individuality of objects, or in this case of genuine love. Seeking an ideal communion of love at a level beyond idle breath, Juliet would purify words quite out of existence and reduce dialogue to an exchange of intuition and sheer feeling—a marriage of true minds accomplished without the connective medium of language.

If we set Juliet's remarks on names in a literary perspective instead of a general nominalistic one they might be taken to suggest an extreme toward which the lyric impulse sometimes tends, that is an ineffable purity. . . . Etymologically, though not always in practice, lyric aspires to the condition of music, seeking to purify noise into melody and sometimes even . . . to a point beyond sound, to stillness. Similarly as regards time and motion, lyric would discover a terminal rest, a retreat from the hurly-burly of action and consequences where thought and feeling crystallize in an expressive stasis. Murray Krieger has demonstrated the apt ambiguity of the word "still" to express in terms of motion the ever-moving fixity of poetry as it sets progressive experience within a transfixing form or, in Yeatsian language, unites the dancer with the dance. In talking about *Romeo and Juliet,* however, we need to enlarge on the ambiguities of stillness by adding silence to the ever-neverness of motion since Juliet, as we have seen, would reduce love's dialogue to a silent communion of unique, inexpressible feeling.

Shakespeare, it is time to say, is abundantly aware how foolish such a *reductio ad silentium* must be from the standpoint of the poet. However intense his own longing to attain a purity out of the swing of speech—and it seems to me considerably so—he knows with Mallarmé that poetry is written with words, not ideas, and especially not ideas before which the poet must become breathless with adoration. If Juliet's view were to prevail the play would turn mute and time stand still. . . . Drama would dissolve into lyric and lyric would dissolve into a silent center of inexpressible love surrounded by the cacophony of the street scenes, the nurse's babble and Mercutio's bawdry, the expostulations of Capulet, and the intoned *sententia* of Friar Laurence.

The plight of the poet who would retreat within lyric to a purer wordlessness is humorously illustrated when Juliet, after appropriately hearing "some noise within" and retiring briefly to investigate, returns to the balcony and cannot momentarily locate Romeo:

> JULIET. Hist! Romeo, hist! O for a falconer's voice
> To lure this tassel-gentle back again!
> Bondage is hoarse, and may not speak aloud,
> Else would I tear the cave where Echo lies
> And make her airy tongue more hoarse than mine
> With repetition of my Romeo's name.
> Romeo!
>
> [II. ii. 158-63]

If "Necessity" as Berowne said could make the scholars "all forsworn / Three thousand times within this three years' space" [*Love's Labour's Lost,* I. i. 149-50], it can also make a sorely frustrated Juliet acknowledge the indispensability of names within a little more than a hundred lines of her great protest against them. In that brief space the tyrannous "bondage" of verbal categories (locking the free spirit of reality into claustrophobic linguistic cells) metamorphoses into its opposite, the "bondage" that prevents Juliet from giving full free voice to that most useful category "Romeo." For the lovers and for the poet Shakespeare the notion of establishing communion on a plane of feeling transcending the imperfections of speech is "but a dream / Too flattering-sweet to be substantial" [II. ii. 140-41]. Not only must the lovers rely on names for the rudiments of communication, but their love itself becomes a great name-singing celebration:

> ROMEO. It is my soul that calls upon my name.
> How silver-sweet sound lovers' tongues by night,
> Like softest music to attending ears!
>
> [II. ii. 164-66]

> JULIET.      . . . and every tongue that speaks
> But Romeo's name speaks heavenly eloquence.
>
> [III. ii. 32-3]

That Juliet somewhat humorously belies herself in this last quotation, finding a "heavenly eloquence" in the name she earlier thought inimical to their love, is in keeping with a play that seems founded on the principle of the oxymoron: she wants, it seems, a "nameless naming." The paradox metadramatically reflects the difficulty of Shakespeare's own situation as he wrestles in this play with the slipperiest of antagonists, verbal purity, against whom even he may be overmatched. It is a contest waged between every poet and language, and it ends for better or worse in a compromise somewhere between the private dream and the public fact. The contest is the more arduous for being conducted within the ring of drama where the impulse to verbal purity takes the form of lyric, which retards, as opposed to action, which impels. (pp. 91-4)

If one charted the private/public range of language in *Romeo and Juliet,* at the furthest private extreme would come "silence," a nominalistic tendency so rigorous as to still speech entirely. Obviously since we do have a script for the play this extreme does not become manifest, except at those moments during performances when the lovers exchange prolonged glances and wordless sighs. Still at this end of the chart would appear the lovers' language within the orchard—self-cherishing, insular, answerable only to private feeling. At the extreme public end of the chart opposite silence is noise, disturbance, disquiet—the "airy word" of the opening scene which the Prince says has "thrice disturbed the quiet of our streets" [I. i. 89, 91] with civil brawls. (The Prince is significantly more concerned with "peace" as quiet than as cessation of hostilities; the greatest threat to the play is sheer noise, its consistent goal harmonic sound.) Also at this end of the scale despite its affectation of privacy and purity is Romeo's Petrarchan language, full of sighs, show, and manner, and far too "airy" in its own way, as Juliet instantly perceives, to substantialize love in any genuine form. Here too, though antagonistic to Romeo's Petrarchanism, is Mercutio's ribald wordplay, as amusingly impure verbally as the sensuality it dotes on is in comparison to Romeo and Juliet's love.

One would also expect to place Friar Laurence's "holy words" within the public sphere since it is through the public institutions of church and marriage, by having "Holy Church incorporate two in one" [II. vi. 87], that the friar hopes to reunite the oppugnant families. That would seem an ideal union, the private bond of love becoming a public bond of marriage sealing the families, because although love itself may be a fine and private thing marriage is by nature public. Its function is to translate private feeling into the received language of society and so give public residence to what may otherwise be simply emotional vagrancy—unpropertied, subjective, and strange. This love, we know, transcends all that. But nonetheless the wedding *is* private, and the marriage it begets remains so. Consecrated by holy words, the lovers' vows bind them to one another (suggesting that the language of love's communion so absent from *Love's Labour's Lost* has been discovered) but in this private union they remain divorced from the wider social context into which genuine marriage would incorporate them.

Their love then is translated into a language that goes unheard beyond the narrow circle formed by themselves, the friar, and later the nurse. Alone in the privacy of his cell Friar Laurence can celebrate the sacrament of Communion, can give quiet voice to *the* Word (Logos), and have its spiritual benefits circulate among all men. But he cannot do so with the sacrament of marriage. If marriage is to be the medium of a secular, familial communion, its sacramental language must be heard by the fallen families it would save, and in that regard the friar's words are as inaudible as those of the lovers. The most obvious symbol of the friar's inability to give public circulation to his own and the lovers' language is his short-circuited letter to Romeo in Mantua. Like Romeo when he leaves the orchard haven for the brawling streets, the friar's words—surrogates for the lovers' words—run afoul of the "infectious pestilence" of the outside world [V. ii. 10]. . . . Despite his intentions then Friar Laurence is less a mediator between private and public spheres than a religious version of the private—his rather monastic celibacy suggesting an analogue to the withdrawn lyric adoration of the lovers. Only when the lovers are dead and he Horatio-like tells their story does the friar finally marry them to the social order and bind the families as he had hoped.

Through neither family nor church can love makes its way into the social context, nor through a third major institution, the state. As a political entity the Veronese state is elusive to the vanishing point; its dramatic form is simply the voice of the Prince, quite literally his sentences. In the opening scene ("hear the sentence of your moved prince" [I. i. 88]) he decrees death to anyone who breaks the peace, and in 3.1 he pronounces sentence on Romeo. . . . From one standpoint the princely word is not good since the peace it ordained is subsequently broken and the banished [Romeo] returns; from another it is, since Mercutio and Tybalt die for their offense and Romeo for his (the Prince had said "when [Romeo's] found that hour is his last," and so it is—[III. i. 195]). The political word clearly has its limits—as when the citizen, unaware that Tybalt is dead, cries "Up, sir, go with me. / I charge thee in the Prince's name, obey" [III. i. 139-40]—but it also has its sovereignty, as Juliet laments:

"Romeo is banished!" To speak that word
Is father, mother, Tybalt, Romeo, Juliet,
All slain, all dead. "Romeo is banished!"
There is no end, no limit, measure, bound,
In that word's death; no words can that woe sound.
[III. ii. 122-26]

If the Prince's word cannot spring the dead to life and duty as the citizen demanded, it can afflict the living with death.

The major emphasis in 3.2 and 3.3, in which the word "banished" is repeated nineteen times, is to force on the lovers the antinominalist realization that although as Juliet said a name is "nor hand nor foot / Nor arm nor face nor any other part / Belonging to a man," even so airily universal a verb as "banished" can permanently still all those moving parts. . . . If the language of love is inaudible to society, the language of society is deafening to the lovers. From such clangor the only final escape is to the quiet of the grave.

"Banished" is the severing word that immediately threatens and finally destroys the communion of love since because of it the lovers are forced to communicate through society by means of the friar's message, and that is precisely what they cannot do. Only in a state of lyric seclusion hermetically sealed off from the plague-stricken world outside can their language retain its expressive purity. But the lovers cannot remain forever in the orchard, much as they would like to, and the poet cannot escape the fact that whereas his art is private, wrought in his own stylistic image . . . , his linguistic medium itself is intransigently public. As part of the vulgar tongue the words

he would adopt are contaminated by ill usage, by an ever-present epidemic of imprecision, banality, lies, false rhetoric, jargon, true rhetoric, sentimentality, and solecisms, and by more localized historical plagues such as Petrarchanism, Euphuism, inkhorn neologisms, television commercials, social scientese, and beat or hippie nonspeak. Like Juliet on first confronting Romeo, the poet wants to compel words to abandon their corrupt public identities and submit to his cleansing rebaptism. (pp. 94-8)

This account of things is perhaps unduly metaphoric and a bit confusing as regards Romeo, whose verbal status is rather ambiguous. His Petrarchan style is impure, as underscored by Juliet's stylistic objections, because in the context of the play it comes from that extramural world outside the orchard. That is not to say that the sonnets of Wyatt, Sidney, Spenser, or Petrarch himself exhibit corrupt language. It is to say that the Petrarchan *style* has a public existence outside individual Petrarchan poems and that in Shakespeare's time . . . it stood for a debased literary currency. Paradoxically at least some of this impurity derives from the fact that the Petrarchan style aspires to pure poetry and in so aspiring becomes an airy, hyperbolic, mechanically artificial expression of unfelt and undiscriminating feelings. In this sense it is too pure . . . , and when the too pure becomes too popular it turns impure, an infectious blight on the literary landscape.

From this excessive purity excessively available, Juliet recoils, seeking like Shakespeare a more individual style, a more genuine purity. But neither Juliet nor Shakespeare fully succeeds in the attempt to forge a new and authentic idiom. We are clearly asked to regard the movement from Romeo-Rosaline to Romeo-Juliet as an advance from Petrarchan dotage to true romantic love. And surely in large degree it is—after all, this love seals its bond in marriage and bears it out even to and beyond the edge of doom. Granted, and yet I doubt that either we or Shakespeare can rest fully at ease with the lovers' style. The trouble is that the old Romeo is imperfectly killed off; the ape is not really dead—too much of his Petrarchan manner and language live on in him; and Juliet, despite her anti-Petrarchan bias, too readily quickens to the invitations of his style. Her better speeches are resistance pieces that gain eloquence in the process of denying the power of speech itself, most notably in the balcony scene. . . . But if the worth of private feeling cannot be assessed in the crude countinghouse of language, Juliet seems not always aware of it. This is most noticeable when on learning that Romeo has killed Tybalt her feelings swing from love to dismay:

O serpent heart hid with a flowering face!
Did ever dragon keep so fair a cave?
Beautiful tyrant! Fiend angelical!
Dove-feathered raven! Wolvish ravening lamb!
Despised substance of divinest show!
[III. ii. 73-7]
(pp. 98-9)

It is wonderfully fitting that Juliet should register the shock to private feeling by adopting Romeo's Petrarchan oxymorons . . . at the exact moment when her loyalties turn in the antinominalist direction of "family" (she grieves not for Tybalt the unique but for Tybalt the cousin). She quickly recovers from this style and feeling, as does their love in general, but in the remainder of the scene her style (like Romeo's in 3.3) keeps shrilling upward into a mannered hysteria in which conceit, less rich in matter than in words, brags of its ornament, not

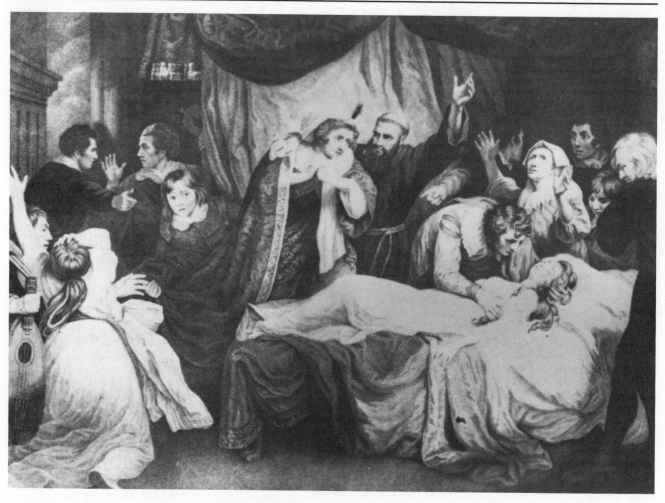

*Act IV. Scene v. Lady Capulet, Friar Lawrence, Paris, Nurse, Juliet, Capulet, and others. By John Opie. The Department of Rare Books and Special Collections, The University of Michigan Library.*

its substance. Bathos is now their medium, and their verbal excesses are defended on the authority of unique feeling:

> ROMEO. Thou canst not speak of that thou dost not
> feel.
> Wert thou as young as I, Juliet thy love,
> An hour but married, Tybalt murdered,
> Doting like me and like me banished,
> Then mightst thou speak, then mightst thou tear thy hair
> And fall upon the ground as I do now,
> Taking the measure of an unmade grave.
>
> [III. iii. 64-70]

Such claims disarm criticism—ours I suppose as well as that of the friar, who must be wincing at the amount of hypothesis required to put him in the position of youth and love. No one denies the validity and intensity of the feeling, but of course a riot of feeling need not necessitate a riot of language and premature measurements of graves that look suspiciously like cribs. Romeo rejects all discipline that originates beyond self, whether moral, social, or stylistic. In effect he repudiates the world, and so hastens logically on to the notion of suicide. When Friar Laurence, harried back and forth across the room by the banging of the world at his door and the blubbering of a Romeo who would dissolve all connections with the world, cries in exasperation "What simpleness is this!" [III. iii. 77]

his choice of the noun is perfect, for in the unblended simpleness of Romeo the man of unique feelings there is indeed at this point great silliness. However, Romeo is not altogether as pure in his simpleness as he would like. . . . To become pure "Romeo" and extirpate his connections with everything beyond self he would destroy "Montague," the "vile part" of him in which the world has staked its claim. But as the friar points out, the dagger that pierces Montague pierces Romeo as well:

> Why rail'st thou on thy birth, the heaven, and earth?
> Since birth and heaven and earth all three do meet
> In thee at once, which thou at once wouldst lose.
>
> [III. iii. 119-21]

So far as I can see there is small evidence that Romeo absorbs much of the friar's lesson. For him there remains no world beyond the walls of Juliet's garden, where the lovers still strive to meet with all the nominalistic singularity of their Edenic forebears. Their lamentations in 3.2 and 3.3 are only a more strident stylistic version of their speech in 3.5. In this the last scene in which they engage in genuine dialogue before the destructive force of the word "banished" takes its full toll, we see the lyric imagination desperately seeking to impose its own truth on the world of fact and sunrise:

JULIET. Wilt thou be gone? It is not yet near day.
It was the nightingale and not the lark
That pierced the fearful hollow of thine ear.
Nightly she sings on yond pomegranate tree.
Believe me, love, it was the nightingale.

[III. v. 1-5]

And again:

JULIET. Yond light is not daylight, I know it, I—
It is some meteor that the sun exhales
To be to thee this night a torchbearer
And light thee on thy way to Mantua.

[III. v. 12-15]

In line with her nominalistic "A rose by any other word" Juliet would rebaptize Nature, transforming lark and daylight into nightingale and meteor to the end that time stand still. Romeo allows himself to be persuaded that "it is not day," but as soon as he does so Juliet's lyric preoccupation is gone: "It is, it is! Hie hence, be gone, away!" [III. v. 26-7]. As it operates in the wide world, language may be less pure than the lovers would wish, but it stands for a view of reality that neither lover nor poet can safely ignore. Time, light, larks, and the usual terms for them remain intransigently themselves, answerable to their public definitions. The lover who withdraws entirely from the world into an autistic domain of feeling must pay for his pleasure with his life, as Romeo would were he to remain in the orchard. By the same token the poet who reshapes language in the exclusive light of his own designs, turning his back on his audience and creating not a truly individual but merely a unqiue style, must pay for his eccentric pleasures with his poetic life. There is no great danger of that here since the trouble with the lovers' style is not eccentricity but conventionality. The purity it aspires to, like that of the Petrarchanism to which it is uncomfortably akin, is too easily come by. And judging their language this way, I should be quick to add—that is, grading it down for poetic diction and a superabundance of rhetorical figures—is not to impose on the play a modern bias against rhetoric but to accept the implications of the play itself and to honor Shakespeare's own standards, which are implicit in his gradual estrangement over the years from an enameled, repetitive, lyrical style in favor of one that is concentrated, complex, and dramatic.

It would seem then that in *Romeo and Juliet* Shakespeare has encountered but by no means resolved the poet's dilemma. No doubt he must often have known perfectly well where he wanted poetically to go and yet could not get there, and knew that too. On the authority of the play's structure we can assume that he wanted to get from Rosaline to Juliet, from pure poetry to a viable poetic purity, but that he did not complete the journey in satisfactory style. That he realized this seems evident from the care he has taken to protectively enclose the lovers' poetic purity. Robert Penn Warren has shrewdly argued that the "impure poetry" of Mercutio and the nurse—poetry, that is, that reflects the impurity of life itself by means of wit, irony, logical contradictions, jagged rhythms, unpoetic diction, and so forth—provides a stylistic context in which we can more readily accept the too pure poetry of the lovers [see Additional Bibliography]. Warren assumes in other words that the impure poetry in the play functions much as William Empson claims comic subplots function, as lightning rods to divert the audience's potentially dyslogistic reactions away from the vulnerable high seriousness of the main plot (main style). The implication is that Shakespeare is trying to have it both ways at once, that like Juliet asking for an "unnamed naming" in the balcony scene he asks

us to accept the authenticity of a style that he himself knows is too pure and therefore needful of protection. From this perspective one sees that in stacking the literary deck against the lovers—by providing the stylistic opposition of Mercutio and the nurse and the environmental opposition of the feuding families, of fate, coincidences, and mistimings—Shakespeare has actually stacked it in their favor. (pp. 100-03)

The argument made here in terms of style can be extended to character and genre also, for the lovers themselves, no less than their style, are too pure and they acquire in the minds of too many readers an unearned tragic stature. Even though the play rejects uniqueness Shakespeare has nominalistically bleached from Romeo and Juliet most of the impurities that rub off on man by virtue of his public contacts. They simply have no public contacts. Despite the importance of family, they are essentially unrelated, meeting as isolated individuals rather than (like Antony and Cleopatra) as complex human beings with social, political, religious, and even national allegiances and responsibilities to contend with. Insufficiently endowed with complexity, with the self-division that complexity makes possible, and with the self-perceptiveness that such division makes possible, they become a study in victimage and sacrifice, not tragedy. Their experience portrays not the erosion within but the clash without, and the lot harries them toward lamentation instead of vision. One of the major ironies of the final scene in the tomb is that for all its imagery of radiance the illumination is entirely outside Romeo, kindled by torches and Juliet's beauty, not by a self-reflective consciousness. (pp. 103-04)

In Shakespeare's protection of the lovers Mercutio plays a crucial role, for although Juliet rejects the false purity of Romeo's Petrarchan style she never has to encounter the rich impurity of Mercutio's speech. And it is Mercutio who seems the genuine threat. The nurse's style is abundantly impure, but that is all it is, whereas Mercutio can deliver pure poetry impurely. In his much-admired, much-maligned Queen Mab speech, which looks so suspiciously and conspicuously irrelevant to the main issues of the play, Mercutio turns pure poetry back on itself. Even while presenting a lengthy illustration of pure poetry he defines it as a product of fancy and foolishness airily roaming like Queen Mab herself through dreaming minds, to which it offers substitute gratifications that have no direct bearing on reality—on real courtier's real curtsies and suits, on lawyer's stunning fees, ladies' kisses, parsons' benefices, soldiers' battles. "Peace, Mercutio, peace!" Romeo cries. "Thou talk'st of nothing" [I. iv. 95-6]. But because Mercutio can talk of something as well as nothing, because he can deal in both pure and impure styles, he is given a tough and enduring eloquence that makes the nurse, mired in the language of sensual expedience, seem gross and Romeo callow. (pp. 104-05)

Entering the orchard where felt experience is sovereign, Romeo can dismiss Mercutio's extramural ribaldry about Rosaline with a famous line—"He jests at scars that never felt a wound" [II. ii. 1]. When the wound is in the other chest though, Romeo must play straight man to more famous lines:

ROMEO. Courage, man, the hurt cannot be much.
MERCUTIO. No, 'tis not so deep as a well nor so wide
as a church door, but 'tis enough, 'twill serve.

[III. i. 95-7]

This asks to be compared to the lovers' style. They repeatedly claim that language is too shallow a thing to reach into the deeps of private feeling, but their own verbal practice is hardly consistent with such a claim. Whenever their feelings are touched, torrents follow.... It is in this context of grotesque verbal posturing, where convulsions of speech coalesce with tantrums of feeling, that Mercutio's words on death acquire a quiet and sustained eloquence. It is those words ironically that best fulfill the stylistic requirements of Juliet's early nominalism. The uniquely felt inner "hurt" Mercutio does not try directly to define, thus avoiding the risks of hyperbole and general verbal inflation that prey on the speech of the lovers when they reflect on *their* wounds. The private feeling that's past the size of speech is suggested only obliquely, in terms of the size of the physical "hurt," and even then by saying not what it is but what it is not. Here in the plain style is functional language, language that like the wound itself is content to be "enough," to "serve" rather than run riot. In general then it is the mixed tones of Mercutio's speech that the lovers most need to incorporate into their own style. But Shakespeare has kept Mercutio permanently stationed on the outer side of the orchard wall, as oblivious to the existence of their love as they are to him.

The public world is too crass and bellicose to assimilate the private truth of love, and Mercutio is a good instance of the fact that there are public truths that the lovers cannot assimilate. Given two such disjunctive languages, only mutual injury remains possible. The lovers' language fails when it seeks to make its way by means of Father John through the plague-ridden world beyond the orchard. Love's feelings hold constant, but during the reunion in the tomb the dialogue of love dissolves into lyric monologues heard only by the speaker. One further step remains. The purity of their love (figured after Romeo's departure in Juliet's resistance to marrying Paris) is reasserted in a second marriage ceremony that is even more private than the first:

> ROMEO. Arms, take your last embrace. And lips, O you
> The doors of breath, seal with a righteous kiss
> A dateless bargain to engrossing death!
>
> [V. iii. 113-15]

In this final contract the breath of lyric speech and the breath of life are simultaneously expended to seal an endless bond with silence. So too with Juliet, who retreats into a remoter stillness as the noise of the outside world rushes toward her:

> Yea, noise? Then I'll be brief. O happy dagger!
> This is thy sheath. There rest and let me die.
>
> [V. iii. 169-70]

As the *Liebestod* stressed by Denis de Rougemont and others [see excerpt above, 1956], Romeo and Juliet's love has been a flight from the frustrations of life toward the consummations of the grave. Similarly, as *Liebestille* their linguistic style has been a flight from noise toward a silence beyond speech. The silence is at last achieved and with it an expressiveness that extends their own bond of feeling outward. For embraced in and by death their still figures bespeak the truth of their love to the wondering representatives of the social order gathered in the tomb, and do so with such persuasiveness that it transforms those random and rancorous individuals into a genuine community united in sorrow and sympathy. The cost, however, runs high. What is purchased is in the Prince's apt phrase a "glooming peace"—peace as public amity has been bought by the sacrifice of the lovers to the peace of an enduring but eloquent stillness. (pp. 105-07)

*James L. Calderwood, "'Romeo and Juliet': A Formal Dwelling," in his* Shakespearean Metadrama: The Argument of the Play in Titus Andronicus, Loves Labour's Lost, Romeo and Juliet, A Midsummer Night's Dream, and Richard II, *University of Minnesota Press, Minneapolis, 1971, pp. 85-119.*

## M. D. FABER   (essay date 1972)

[*Faber offers a psychoanalytic reading of* Romeo and Juliet, *claiming that in this work Shakespeare depicts the suicides of the hero and heroine as a result of their resisting and threatening society. According to the critic, the Capulet and Montague households each embodies a narcissistic and incestuous self-love that prohibits its youthful members from satisfying his or her erotic impulses in the normal manner—with an individual outside the family unit. He notes that both Romeo and Juliet desperately seek to break free from this unhealthy Oedipal situation by establishing a nonincestuous relationship, but their attempt is "fated" to fail because they must rely on the antagonistic society "to provide them with an opportunity to do what [that] society does not want them to do." Furthermore, Faber maintains that it is not only the external opposition of their society with which the lovers have to contend, but "they must also cope with their own inner deficiency, their own inner lack of control that compounds their difficulties and may be traced to their social models."*]

*Romeo and Juliet* offers us a spectacle of suicide—suicide brought about by the blocking or thwarting of the adolescent's attempt to transfer his libidinal energies to a nonincestuous object and to achieve thereby one of life's major separations, the separation of the sexually mature child from the parent. On the other side of this psychological coin is, of course, reunion; that is to say, separation from the parent is accomplished through attachment to a parental substitute. In the union of young lovers there is a kind of magical reunion with the lost, or relinquished, object. But Shakespeare's play differentiates itself from other artistic treatments of this problem by diffusing the oppositional force that produces the life-destroying trauma. In Sophocles' Antigone, for example, Haemon's attempt to unite with the heroine is blocked by a single individual, his father, Creon. In *Romeo and Juliet* we have to reckon not only upon individual fathers but upon entire families, indeed, upon an entire society. Accordingly, I believe it will be possible to discover in Shakespeare's tragedy a particular syndrome leading to the suicidal behavior of youth. Our introduction to Romeo comes largely through the mouth of his father. Shortly after the termination of the swordplay that opens the tragedy, Montague describes for us the manner in which his adolescent son walks about during the night, "augmenting" the "fresh morning's dew" with "tear," and "Adding to clouds more clouds with his deep sighs" [I. i. 132ff.].... Prompted by his emerging sexuality to separate himself from the objects of his prepubescent years, Romeo spends much of his time "away from home"; and when he is home, he shuts his parents out, negates them, even obliterates them, a behavior that causes him to suffer, at the deepest emotional level, the anguish of their loss. Romeo attempts to offset this loss by finding his way toward a substitute object, for the concomitant inverse of his need to withdraw from the parents is his need to merge, or to unite, with someone else. In the play's first scene we discover him directing this need toward the inaccessible and highly idealized Rosalind, an obvious maternal surrogate who is, by virtue of her announced and voluntary inaccessibility, too closely associated with the mother in Romeo's mind to constitute a serious choice. What this means, of course, is that Romeo, at the very commencement of the play, is not quite ready to make his emotional separation in earnest, that he is rationalizing defensively the persistence of his Oedipal longing, as well as the intensity of his anguish over the loss of his earliest objects, by pining and sighing for a woman with whom he has never spoken or even been close. When he spies Juliet, however, the emotional event he has long been on the verge of suddenly takes place in actuality. As I see it, no further explanation of love at first sight is required, at least in this play. Romeo's need for a genuine, nonincestuous relationship has long been close to the surface, and he relinquishes his disingenuous hopes for the inaccessible Rosalind when this need fully and powerfully emerges at the Capulet's ball.

As we have suggested, Romeo finds it extremely difficult to gratify this need because of the family feud that stands at the center of the play and comprises an integral part of the tragedy's psychological dynamics. *Romeo and Juliet* presents us with five kinds of love. First, there is the love we know commonly as lust, the physical desire of one member of the species for another. We find the most memorable expression of this love in the bawdy talk of the low characters, such as Gregory and Sampson, as well as in the good-humored cynicism of Mercutio. Second, there is the love we know commonly as friendship and associate readily with the bond that unites such characters as Romeo and Mercutio. Third, there is the romantic love of Romeo and Juliet, love that consists in both mental and physical cathexes rooted in the Oedipal syndrome and is most likely to occur during the onset of adolescence and early adulthood, in a word, the love that "makes the world go 'round." Fourth, there is the intrafamilial love of the Montagues and Capulets that we sometimes connect with the word "togetherness," love that exists between father and son, mother and daughter, brother and sister, cousin and cousin, etc. Finally, there is the love we commonly think of as brotherly or fraternal, love of one man for another, love that ostensibly unites whole communities, love that exists outside the home, love that we ordinarily associate with words like "caritas" or "Christian," love most obviously connected in this play with the character of Friar Laurence. What I want to stress here is Shakespeare's dramatic interest in the readiness with which all of these loves can transform themselves into hates, into hostile, aggressive behavior capable of disrupting the civil order and provoking all manner of disastrous deeds. In fact, I would maintain that such transformation is Shakespeare's overriding concern in the play, and from a psychological standpoint, the drama's predominant thesis. (pp. 169-71)

It is with regard to [the family feud], which bears so importantly upon the suicides of Romeo and Juliet, that the play's preoccupation with the transformation of instinct directs our attention to a crucial psychological fact: the behavior of the Montagues toward the Capulets is an expression not only of the Montagues' hatred of the Capulets, but of the Montagues' *love of themselves,* of the Montagues' narcissism: conversely, the Capulets' hatred of the Montagues is integrally bound up with their own self-love. *Romeo and Juliet,* in other words, announces that narcissistic love, love that is devoid of the fraternal element associated with the figure of Friar Laurence, is ultimately unsatisfactory; it is rooted as much in a negative as in a positive mind-set and will cause its bearer sufficient discontentment to drive him, finally, to outwardly directed aggresssive behavior. Narcissism, Shakespeare realized, is a condition that affects not only individuals but the larger societal units that are comprised of individuals, and he realized, too, that narcissism is best expressed as an interest in the self that derives not from a genuine, healthy self-cathexis but from an inability to direct one's love toward others. Further, narcissistic love at the intrafamilial level is ultimately *dangerous,* unnatural love that discourages the tendency of the individual member of the family to extend himself away from the objects close to him toward other objects with whom he might enjoy guilt-free interaction. Such love encourages the individual either to become overly involved with incestuous objects or to attach himself to objects selected by the parents, that is, objects that constitute an extension of the parents, that are intrafamilial and incestuous. Accordingly, we would expect the Montagues and the Capulets to be discontented "unto themselves," to harbor profoundly ambivalent feelings toward their own kinsmen as well as toward their enemies, and finally, to produce children who struggle with powerful incestuous urges, and who are more or less unhappy.

We are now in a position to better understand the extremity of Romeo's behavior, his intense withdrawal, his weeping, his sighing, his initial involvement with an obvious Oedipal substitute, his fantasies of disaster (I, iv), his suicidal bent (III, iii), and, most important, the depth of his need for Juliet, his absolute dependence upon her love. As for Juliet herself, I would underscore her intense love for her cousin Tybalt (III, ii) and, in a play that continually juxtaposes death and love, her dreadful, anxiety-provoking fantasy of lying with Tybalt in the family tomb, of "plucking" him from his "shroud" after having "played" with the "joints" of her "forefathers," of dashing out her brains with her "kinsman's bone" [IV. iii. 51ff.]. I would also underscore the eagerness of her parents to marry her to an object of *their choice,* Paris, and to display profound, almost murderous dissatisfaction when Juliet appears unwilling to comply with their desires (III, v). Most of all, I would emphasize the distance between Juliet and her mother, the coldness with which her mother treats her (I, iii), her pathetic attempt to offset her mother's ambivalence by transforming her nurse into a parental substitute—crucial psychological facts that help us to appreciate the intensity of Juliet's need for Romeo and her absolute dependence upon his love. The danger of incest, the tendency toward regressive Oedipal and pre-Oedipal attachments, the ambivalence of the parents toward the child, the child's inordinate need for erotic involvement, as well as his absolute, life-and-death dependence upon the lover who offers him an opportunity to escape the narcissistic, incestuous home: these are the products of intrafamilial self-love that isolates and insulates the Montagues and the Capulets and easily transforms itself into hostile, murderous behavior that destroys the civil order of Verona.

*Romeo and Juliet* is centrally concerned with the manner in which the love of the hero and heroine can serve as a natural, emotional bridge between the contending families. In other words, because the shift of object cathexis during the adolescent years is ideally away from family members and toward the extrafamilial lover, who may recall the parents but is nevertheless distinct from them, Romeo and Juliet, by virtue of their love, contain the potential for moving the insulated families away from their narcissistic position toward a position that would permit the expression of the fifth kind of love we mentioned, the brotherly or Christian love associated with Friar Laurence and essential to the maintenance of a civilized community. This is why Friar Laurence is so interested in the love of Romeo and Juliet, why he spies in their love a possible cure for the bloody civil war that rages within the walls of Verona. Let me make three points here. First, while we may feel that a civilized community can be based upon a psychology that does not include an emotional bond between its members that is most conveniently described as charity, Shakespeare did not believe it, and neither did Freud. Both men believed that the bond that ultimately held the group—and the society—together was grounded in mankind's erotic energy. Shakespeare spoke simply of love; Freud spoke of sublimated libido; nevertheless . . . , they had the same thing in mind. Second, when Friar Laurence turns to the love of Romeo and Juliet as a possible bridge between the feuding households, he does so under the assumption that intrafamilial affection can follow a kinsman as he moves toward the member of another family, in this case a hated family. There is no guarantee that it will, but so desperate is the situation in Verona, and so grieved is the Christian Friar at what is happening there, that he decides to rely upon the method of bridging that has proved in the past to be a powerful socializing force. This brings me to my third point, which is more crucial than the first two. To speak of the bloody civil war that rages in Verona, to speak of the savage or uncivilized condition that prevails there, to bear in mind that this condition springs largely from narcissistic intrafamilial love that encourages intrafamilial libidinal cathexes, to recognize that Romeo and Juliet are attempting by their love to move away from unsatisfactory familial involvements that have already created within them an inordinate need for affection, and further, to recall that Friar Laurence, the play's civilizing or Christianizing force, connects the love of Romeo and Juliet with the savagery of the feuding families, is to appreciate that Verona is in the process of regressing to a kind of tribal, pre-Christian state and that the major horror of such a regression is the horror of incest. One can hardly miss the irony. Not only are Romeo and Juliet the products of the very society they must cure and therefore capable of damaging their own cause, but they must rely upon their society to provide them with an opportunity to do what their society does not want them to do. In other words, the nonincestuous seeds of renewal are destined, or, to use one of the play's favorite words, "fated" to spill and to die.

By virtue of their interminable quarrel, the Montagues and Capulets fail to support the lovers in their attempt to separate from incestuous objects. Romeo and Juliet are striving to unite in a world that is against them, for the most part. In terms of the protagonists' subsequent self-murders the significance of this fact must not be overlooked. Even adolescents who are supported and encouraged by their family and society often find it difficult and sometimes impossible to accomplish the interpersonal and biological transition with which they are confronted. But we must not regard Verona as an oppositional force that impinges upon the lovers only from without; Romeo and Juliet must struggle with deleterious societal influences, including influences that undermine the fulfillment of their wishes from within too. . . . Not only must Romeo and Juliet cope in an external way with the hostility of their families, they must also cope with their own inner deficiency, their own inner lack of control that compounds their difficulties and may be traced to their societal models. Verona, in its violence, moral confusion (even the nurse suggests that Juliet commit bigamy), passionate, unthinking impulsivity and tendency toward regressive methods of coping, has been unable to provide hero and heroine with safe, firm internal guides capable of steadily governing their passage toward separation and nonincestuous union. In almost every scene of the play Romeo reveals the immaturity of his ego development; when he is under particular stress in Act III, Scene iii, which follows hard upon Tybalt's murder, only the Friar's controlling influence prevents him from impulsively stabbing himself to death. Although Juliet appears on occasion to possess an ego somewhat more mature

than her lover's, she too gravitates toward suicidal behavior when she discovers herself in a complicated situation [IV. i. 50ff.]. Much of the fantasy material she brings forth when she is about to drink the Friar's potion and be taken to the family vault (IV, iii) is, as we suggested earlier, strikingly related to the problem of impulse control. What determines the "fate" of Romeo and Juliet in the universe of this play is a single psychological continuum encompassing both societal and intrapsychic forces. Hero and heroine do not simply act in Verona; they act there in response to crucial developmental influences that manifest themselves in current behavioral patterns.

Romeo's dream is a key to the play, as well as a valuable source of insight into the motivational dynamics of Romeo's self-murder. Just before Balthasar erroneously informs him of Juliet's sudden death, Romeo, exiled in Mantua, describes for the audience's benefit a nocturnal fantasy that goes as follows:

> I dreamed my lady came and found me dead—
> Strange dream, that gives a dead man leave to think!—
> And breathed such life with kisses in my lips
> That I revived and was an emperor. . . .

> [V. i. 6-9]

What is particularly important [here] is Romeo's fantasy of taking "such life" from the kiss of his beloved that he not only escapes death-banishment, but returns to the world of the living as an "emperor." When seen in the motivational context of the drama as a whole, this fantasy enables us to grasp the essence of a specific emotional syndrome leading to the suicide of youth.

For Romeo the emperor image is inextricably bound up with the problem of control and has social as well as intrapsychic significance, in line with our earlier contention that what shapes the destiny of characters in this play must be seen as a single, psychological continuum encompassing both societal and intrapsychic forces. Psychoanalysis has long recognized the way in which the image of the king or emperor is associated with the image of the individual father at the primary level. But what *Romeo and Juliet* so vividly demonstrates, and what Romeo apprehends in his wish-fulfilling dream, is the degree to which this association is grounded in fact as well as fantasy. In other words, what happens in the social arena, associated with and controlled by the "emperor," is largely dependent upon what happens within the family and the individual, the moral units upon which society is based. When Romeo dreams of being an emperor, he dreams of being an authority figure with controlling powers over himself and his individual destiny, a dream influenced by his acutal inability to govern himself under stress; on the other hand—and this is the clearest and most crucial interpretation—he also dreams of being an authority figure with controlling power over his chaotic society, over the fathers of that society, in short, over Verona, which is preventing him from making the normal transition from an incestuous to a nonincestuous object so that he might become a father himself. This is, of course, why it is Juliet who breathes "such life" into his lips, for it is Juliet who embodies his desire to separate from the controlling influences of his childhood and to unite with an extrafamilial sexual object that would allow him to approximate the ego ideal through the possession of what the ego ideal most obviously possesses, a wife. Romeo's use of the word "life" in this dream carries with it the connotations of (1) separation-reunion and (2) growth; accordingly, his use of the word "dead" expresses an arrest of the personality. Immediately after Romeo has told us of his dream, Balthasar enters with news of Juliet's death. "Her body sleeps in Capels' monument'' [V. i. 18], he says, playing inadvertently upon the metaphoric base of Romeo's dream and thereby keeping that dream in the forefront of our minds. Having digested Balthasar's message, Romeo decides to commit suicide, crying, in one of the drama's most revealing lines, ''Is it e'en so? Then I defy you, stars!'' [V. i. 24]. Now, when we consider Romeo's dream of becoming an emperor in conjunction with his unforgettable outcry against the stars, we recognize something important to our understanding of the emotional predicament in which Romeo discovers himself at his point in the action, namely, that he does not understand the source of his troubles at the conscious level and, as a result, does not know where to direct his aggression. What Romeo should be crying here is, ''Then I defy you, families,'' or, ''Then I defy you, Verona.'' In other words, at this juncture he should manifest an urge to rebel against the irresponsible society that stands behind his difficulties, not against the stars that stand far out in space. But because Romeo is himself a fully integrated member of the society against which he should be rebelling, he is unable to find his way toward a meaningfully focused, directed gesture of defiance. In Sophocles' Antigone Haemon, the adolescent son of the king, finds himself in difficulties similar to Romeo's; Haemon is able to focus his rebellion—albeit unsuccessfully—upon a tangible, explicit oppositional force, his father. In Shakespeare's play, by contrast, there is no model against which the hero can strive, because Verona, with its tendency toward intrafamilial, narcissistic love, has itself become the arresting, castrating, oppositional force. Romeo cannot meaningfully rebel because he cannot see where to rebel. Or, to put it another way, he cannot rebel because the object of his rebellion has come to be equated with the perceptual psychological universe in which he dwells and out of which he cannot get. Hence his pathetic cry, ''I defy you, stars,'' in which he attempts to displace his enormous anger, his enormous frustration and defiance, upon a set of remote celestial objects. Hence, too, his pathetic dream in which, as we have said, he magically becomes the controller of the whole society, all men, everything; for only as such an omnipotent controller would Romeo be able to make the normal transition from the incestuous to the nonincestuous object, the transition which usually involves a struggle with the father, as in Antigone, but in this play has come to involve a struggle with overpowering societal forces that have succeeded to the father's oppositional role. Thus Shakespeare's employment of stars, fortune, destiny in Romeo and Juliet is ultimately ironic, designed to impress on us that the adolescent's fate is bound up with the psychology of his parents and his society. (pp. 172-78)

Moments before he commits suicide, Romeo murders the innocent Paris, an action that constitutes, of course, the perfect expression of Romeo's desperation, his rage, his inability to control his enormous aggressive energies that cannot discover an appropriate object of discharge. Moreover, the slaying of Paris reminds us (1) that Romeo's psychology during the play's last moments is as murderous as it is suicidal and (2) that Romeo's suicide may well turn out to be psychologically very close to murder. Indeed, I maintain that at the deepest unconscious level Romeo harbors two fundamental desires as he goes about the business of taking his own life. The first of these is to reunite with his beloved, his nonincestuous maternal substitute from whom he has been abruptly severed. . . . On the other hand, Romeo, in his rage, anguish, and frustration at being blocked, stymied, abused, and rendered impotent, wants to murder the world and his parents as part of that world. His earlier wish to become the world's controller is transformed by his frustration and bereavement into his final wish to become

the world's destroyer. But because he cannot consciously pinpoint the ultimate source of his anguish or see that his narcissistic culture stands behind his terrible predicament, Romeo is still talking ineffectually about the stars as he comes to dispatch himself. . . . Thus the anger toward the world, and toward the parents as part of that world, is not provided with an appropriate channel of expression and is ultimately turned back upon the self.

Juliet's suicide lacks this murderous element. Awakening in the vault to find her lover dead beside her, Juliet's only desire is to get out of a world in which Romeo no longer dwells and which harbors the terrifying prospect of incestuous involvement. In other words, Juliet's conspicuous haste to follow Romeo in death is predicated not only on her emotional investment in him, her absolute dependence upon his love; it is also predicated on her fear of closeness in the family vault to the incestuous objects of her childhood, most notably Tybalt. To find Romeo dead in that place is overwhelming to her because it is that place which signifies the nightmarish, intrafamilial love-death from which Juliet has struggled to escape in her nonincestuous involvement with Romeo. Again, Juliet's haste reflects the failure of her narcissistic world to provide her with an atmosphere of succorance and support, to nourish her in her need for growth and separation. From every conceivable angle, the world of Verona has become for Juliet a place to leave.

Romeo and Juliet, then, presents us with the breakdown of an entire social order, a breakdown that engenders problems of growth and separation in its adolescent young. The narcissistically diseased city of Verona is actually destroying its children, driving them to carry the seeds of renewal, the promise of growth and nonincestuous involvement, into the very tomb that contains the children's forebears. Again, Shakespeare's tragedy demonstrates how a grievous social problem may impinge itself upon the adolescent who is striving to separate from incestuous objects and cause him to look out upon a hopeless, hostile world that he cannot regard as a matrix of possibility, a world that seems fixed against him, destined to frustrate and thwart him. With such a mind-set the adolescent hardly knows where to direct his aggression when he discovers himself in a crisis situation. What can one do when one is wounded still again in a world that appears to be unalterably set against the fulfillment of one's aims? Whether it happens in Shakespeare's Verona or in Harlem, the suicide of youth may constitute an attempt to explode a world that strives in its pathogenic blindness to frustrate and abuse its sons and daughters as they try to become fathers and mothers themselves. Most of all, Romeo and Juliet focuses for us the emotional difficulties that result when the young person is unable to see what opposes him. When, because of anxiety or plain incomprehension, he cannot discover the forces that are making his life unbearable, when he cannot rebel in an explicit, meaningful fashion against the influences that are damaging his cause, the adolescent is apt to perceive a malevolent intention in the world. Such a perception, especially if it is combined with the loss of the nonincestuous object who represents separation, growth, and autonomy, may well produce suicidal or murderous behavior. (pp. 179-80)

*M. D. Faber, ''The Adolescent Suicides of Romeo and Juliet,'' in* The Psychoanalytic Review, *Vol. 59, No. 2, Summer, 1972, pp. 169-81.*

**ROSALIE L. COLIE** (essay date 1974)

[*Colie examines the manner in which Shakespeare took the theme of love, traditionally a comic concern exclusively, and dramatized*

With *Romeo and Juliet,* its plot deriving from a sad and rather sordid novella, Shakespeare attempted his first love-tragedy. How did an ambitious and experimental author go about this task? First of all, he drew upon types officially "comic," types which had already colonized the prose narratives of the Renaissance. He peopled his play in a perfectly familiar way, with figures from the comic cast: the young girl; her suitor (*adulescens amans* [adolescent lover]), whom her father does not favor; another *adulescens* (County Paris), whom the father approves; a father, *senex,* who becomes, naturally, *senex iratus* [angry old man] when crossed by his daughter; a nurse, not only the customary *nutrix* but a particular subtype, *nutrix garrula* [garrulous nurse]. Our hero is accompanied by a friend, indeed by two friends, Benvolio and Mercutio; in a comedy, for symmetry, presumably Juliet would have had two schoolfellows with her, to be disposed of at the play's end to the two young men. Here, though, she is unaccompanied; and because the play is a tragedy, Mercutio can be killed off and Benvolio fall out of the play without our wondering why or lamenting the absence of appropriate girls to be given away to Romeo's "extra" friends.

Comedies take place in cities; this tragedy is very city-bound; even Friar Lawrence's cell is within walking distance of the famous two houses. When Romeo flees Verona, he does not take to the woods, as a proper romance-hero might have been expected to do (and as Orlando does [in *As You Like It*]), but settles in nearby Mantua, to outwait, as he hopes, his troubles. As befits a comic city-scene, we have splendid servants of different sorts, baiting each other and irritating as well as serving their betters, providing relief for what turns out to be a very grim sequence of actions.

So far, so good; but how to turn the play into a tragedy of love? What language, for example, to use? From the first spoken words of *Romeo and Juliet,* the Chorus' speech in sonnet-form, we are directed to a major source for the play's language, the sonnet tradition, from which, as we see at once, Romeo had drunk deep; like the young men at Navarre's court [in *Love's Labour's Lost*], Romeo knew the literary modes of the Renaissance young gentleman. Critics of the play speak again and again of the sonnets in the play itself; sometimes even a full fourteen lines spoken by a speaker alone or by two speakers in consort—the great sonnet exchange between Romeo and Juliet at their meeting is a sign both of their rhetorical sophistication and of their union with one another. Some of the sonnets have an extra quatrain or even sestet; once an octave stands alone, several times a sestet stands alone. All this sonnet-formality must draw our attention to what the playwright was up to—that is, his deepening of events by a language habitually associated with a particular kind of high-minded and devoted love. By his borrowing of devices and language from another genre for his tragedy, he cues us to the kind of love involved in his play. Of all the lyric forms, indeed of all the literary forms, of love, the sonnet-sequence honors the profound seriousness of the emotion: love is central to the life and existence of the sonnet-persona, who gives himself over to the delicious

exigencies of his condition, which he celebrates with all the force of his soul and of his poetical powers. As more transitory love-lyrics do not, the sonnet-sequence also provides opportunities for deep and faceted self-examination, as the sonneteer considers and reconsiders his ever-changing emotional state, recording as carefully as possible his perceptions of his own shifting progress and regress along his path.

We are introduced to Romeo, typed as a melancholy lover before he appears onstage, who enters speaking "distractedly" in the proper Petrarchan rhetoric of oxymoron. He runs through the rhetorical exercises of the love-poet with extraordinary facility. He sets his own text—"Here's much to do with hate, but more with love" [I. i. 175]—and amplifies it:

Why then, O brawling love! O loving hate!
O anything, of nothing first create!
O heavy lightness! serious vanity!
Mis-shapen chaos of well-seeming forms!
Feather of lead, bright smoke, cold fire, sick health!
Still-waking sleep, that is not what it is!
This love feel I, that feel no love in this.

[I. i. 176-82]

Shortly after this comical though splendid display of his reading in Petrarchan figure, Romeo defines love, in the manner, says one French theorist, of the *blason,* or (as English critics tended to say) of the definition:

Love is a smoke rais'd with the fume of sighs;
Being purg'd, a fire sparkling in lovers' eyes;
Being vex'd, a sea nourish'd with loving tears.
What is it else? A madness most discreet,
A choking gall, and a preserving sweet.

[I. i. 190-94]

He runs through the repertory—the oxymora, so casually tossed off, the variations upon a hundred sonnets in the official mode. His *epideixis* [scenic display] is clear—"Why then," and "What is it else?" introduce a spate of words in the right key, uttered by an energetic youth creating his own role according to the best literary models. (pp. 136-38)

[What] we are asked to see in this Romeo is the lover by the book, the lover *too* decorous, who adopts the Petrarchan role and lives it to the utmost—in his rhyme, in his solitary nightlife, in the moping melancholy that so worries his mother. And Romeo sticks to the rules of his loving: when Benvolio urges him to Capulet's feast, hoping that he will there find another lady to fall in love with, Romeo is shocked—but in a sestet:

When the devout religion of mine eye
Maintains such falsehood, then turn tears to fires;
And these, who, often drown'd, could never die,
Transparent heretics, be burnt for liars!
One fairer than my love! The all-seeing sun
Ne'er saw her match since first the world begun.

[I. ii. 88-93]

Romeo's hyperbolical fidelity leaves much to be desired, since he falls in love with Juliet the instant he claps eye on her and rhymes his new love at once, in familiar language most beautifully disposed:

O, she doth teach the torches to burn bright!
It seems she hangs upon the cheek of night
As a rich jewel in an Ethiop's ear. . . .

[I. v. 44-6]

and on and on, to

> Did my heart love till now? Forswear it, sight;
> For I ne'er saw true beauty till this night.
>
> [I. v. 52-3]

Both Romeo and Juliet are quick at this kind of language: their sonnet, with its "extra" quatrain at the end, spoken in turn by the two of them, is a marvelous sublimation of the witty exchange of young people meeting and trying each other out. (pp. 139-40)

Mercutio offers a critical voice against Romeo's softer one: as the young men go to the dance, Mercutio teases Romeo, challenging him to exchanges of wit much like those to which Benvolio had earlier challenged Romeo. All three young men knew their rhetorical alternatives and chose their styles freely: Mercutio mocks Romeo in terms of his love-learned language:

> Romeo! humours! madman! passion! lover!
> Appear thou in the likeness of a sigh;
> Speak but one rhyme and I am satisfied;
> Cry but "Ay me!" pronounce but "love" and
>     "dove" . . .
>
> [II. i. 7-10]

to pass on to a wonderfully punning salaciousness about the true purpose of loving. Mercutio provides at these points an Ovidian voice, that of the high-spirited libertine whose awareness of the physical delights of love balance the sweetness, the near-namby-pambyness of the Petrarchan traditional language. In his later exchange with Mercutio, Romeo answers in kind, thereby convincing his friend that he is once more "sociable," which is to say, out of love and a sane man again. Romeo has altered his decorum, as Mercutio notes—"Thy wit is a very bitter sweeting; it is a most sharp sauce" [II. i. 79-80]—from his melancholy sonneteering to the man-about-town, man-among-men style of the epigrammatist. . . . And this of course is what fools Mercutio into believing that his friend has fallen out of love, for no man in the lover's pose can make the jests of II. iv. about sexuality. We of course know better: Romeo is finally and at last in love—and, dutiful to convention, has fallen in at first sight. This prescription of love's proper origin is written into the action, given reality, unmetaphored, in the scene at the feast: both young people recognize, too, what is happening to them, though they obey the rules of courteous wordplay, which detonates their passion, as well as observing the rules of courtly loving.

Romeo by no means abandons sonnet-language because he has in fact fallen truly in love—again and again in his speeches to and about Juliet, conventional sonnet-topics turn up. To his new love, seen at her window, he offers the conventional likeness of eyes to stars. . . . He borrows other stock-elements from the sonneteer; in the orchard he wishes to be a glove on her hand to feel her cheek leaning against that hand, in Mantua he wishes to be a mouse, the humblest beast about the house, so as to catch sight of Juliet in Verona. Again, he combines two common sonnet-images, that of the lover as skipper and that of the lady as merchandise, in three pretty lines:

> I am no pilot; yet, wert thou as far
> As that vast shore wash'd with the farthest sea,
> I should adventure for such merchandise.
>
> [II. ii. 82-4]

As critics are fond of saying, Juliet's language is less artificial than Romeo's, which seems to point to her greater simplicity in love than his, to her greater realism about their situation than his. But she too has had her training in the love-rhetoric: her Romeo will "lie upon the wings of night / Whiter than new snow on the raven's back" [III. ii. 18-19]. She too can pursue a conceit to its ultimate, absurd conclusions:

> when he shall die,
> Take him and cut him out in little stars,
> And he will make the face of heaven so fine
> That all the world will be in love with night,
> And pay no worship to the garish sun.
>
> [III. ii. 21-5]
> (pp. 140-42)

When the Nurse comes in with the news of Tybalt's death at Romeo's hands, Juliet bursts into oxymoron, violently denouncing her lover in a passage as rhetorically extreme as anything Romeo had uttered in his period of self-persuaded, false love:

> O serpent heart, hid with a flow'ring face!
> Did ever dragon keep so fair a cave?
> Beautiful tyrant! fiend angelical!
> Dove-feather'd raven! wolfish-ravening lamb!
> Despised substance of divinest show!
>
> [III. ii. 73-7]

On she goes, in this language, until her reason returns to remind her that of the two, she would far rather have lost Tybalt than Romeo. With that realization, she returns to the simpler poetry more characteristic of her utterance. It may be, as Levin has suggested, that Juliet's linguistic extravagance marks her estrangement from Romeo—certainly it marks her loss of herself in passionate outrage; on the other hand, the images she uses in this passage are linked both to those she had earlier used to try to express her large love for Romeo, and to those he used of her. Even here, the conjunction between the lovers is maintained in their language.

As we look back over the lovers' utterance, we can see very plainly the problem of expression: petrarchan language, *the* vehicle for amorous emotion, can be used merely as the cliché which Mercutio and Benvolio criticize; or, it can be earned by a lover's experience of the profound oppositions to which that rhetoric of oxymoron points. When Romeo and Juliet seek to express their feelings' force, they return constantly to petrarchanisms hallowed with use—but, having watched their development as lovers, an audience can accept as valid the language upon which they must fall back. When Romeo readies himself to die, he does so in the proper sonnet-imagery, to which he has earlier had recourse—

> Thou desperate pilot, now at once run on
> The dashing rocks thy sea-sick weary bark.
>
> [V. iii. 117-18]
> (pp. 142-43)

[One] might note a general feature of this play, of which the *aubade* [in Act III, Scene v] is a splendid example: it is full of set-pieces of different kinds. Lady Capulet and the Nurse speak a duet about the County Paris's charms; at Juliet's supposed death, Lord and Lady Capulet, the Nurse, and Paris utter a quartet. There are many double exchanges—Juliet's sonnet-exchange with Romeo at the dance, Romeo's exchanges with Benvolio and Mercutio, Juliet's stichomythy with Paris at Friar Lawrence's cell. Arias as well: Juliet's great prothalamic invocation to night, with its Ovidian echoes, "Gallop apace, you fiery-footed steeds" [III. ii. 1], her schematic meditation on death and the charnel-house just before she takes the drug;

Mercutio's inventions on the subject of dreams. The effect of these passages is greatly to draw our attention to the poetry of this play, to the evocativeness of its language, but also to do something else, risky in a play though ideal in a lyric, to arrest the action for the sake of poetic display.

When we look at the play from some distance and in terms of fairly stock rhetorical patterns, we can see how formalized, how static, much of its organization is, how dependent upon tableaux and set-pieces. The Chorus begins the play with his sonnet, then one party enters, then the other (from, we presume, "houses" demarcated in the stage-architecture). The two parties engage in a mock-version of the vendetta which, with Tybalt's entrance onstage, quickly transforms the action into real violence, and ends with the Prince's order for the maintenance of peace. At the play's end, one party enters to lament the death of a child, then the other, lamenting the death of the other child; both parties stand to hear Friar Lawrence's unraveling of the plot and the Prince's strictures. Each bereaved father promises the other, appropriately, a sepulchral statue of his child in commemoration of child, of love, and of the ultimate sad settlement of the long feud. With a final moralizing sestet, the Prince, a dignified *deus ex machina,* ends the action altogether. The lyric interludes, so important to the tone and psychology of the whole play, are of a piece with the pageant-like dramaturgy. Though they reveal the conditions of the speaker's mind, they do so in language rather dictated by the situation than obedient to the complexity of the plot, character, or action. The language loosens itself in many ways from the sonnet-substance from which it draws so much, but in *Romeo and Juliet* it is never so free as in *Othello,* where the same body of conventional language is managed to fit the characters' and the plots' needs without drawing undue attention to itself.

*Romeo and Juliet* is in many ways an apprentice-play: there the poet first met the real problems involved in turning lyrical love into tragedy. The Chorus must tell us at the outset that these lovers are star-crossed, and, in case we should forget that this is so, Romeo says later, rather awkwardly, "my mind misgives / Some consequence, yet hanging in the stars, / Shall bitterly begin his fearful date / With this night's revels" [I. iv. 106-09]. Friar Lawrence's *sententiae* reinforce the notion of rash haste, but they do not increase our sense of tempo—rather, in the way of *sententiae,* they do just the opposite. Rash haste and star-crossing are the rigid *donnée* of the action, which we are not invited to question or to consider. Love is unhappy, deeply-felt, beautifully expressed; youth is wasted at the behest of irrational old age, but the involvements of tragic behavior have not found their language in this play, although the spectacular oppositions of the petrarchan rhetoric have been enlarged into plot, as well as into the emotional and social structure of the play.

All the same, *Romeo and Juliet* makes some marvelous technical manipulations. One of the most pleasurable, for me, of Shakespeare's many talents is his "unmetaphoring" of literary devices, his sinking of the conventions back into what, he somehow persuades us, is "reality," his trick of making a verbal convention part of the scene, the action, or the psychology of the play itself. Love-at-first-sight is here made to seem entirely natural, set against the artificiality and unreality of Romeo's self-made love for Rosaline; its conventionality is forgotten as it is unmetaphored by action. Again, the *aubade* is indeed a dawn-song sung after a night of love, when the lovers must part, but a dawn-song of peculiar poignancy and relevance because of the way in which these lovers must part

on this particular day. Another brilliant, natural unmetaphoring is the *hortus conclusus* [enclosed garden], which by metaphoric convention a virgin is, and where also pure love naturally dwells, according to the Song of Songs and a host of subsequent poems and romances. Juliet's balcony simply opens upon such an orchard, a garden enclosed, into which Romeo finds out the way. The virgin is, and is in, a walled garden: the walls of that garden are to be breached by a true lover, as Romeo leaps into the orchard.

Still more important is the much-noticed manipulation of light and dark in the play; for Romeo and Juliet, ordinary life is reversed, with darkness the only safe time, when love between them is really possible. They meet at night, their marriage lasts one night, until light parts them. When they finally come together, it is at night in a tomb, which becomes their tomb in actuality. (pp. 143-46)

The common juxtaposition and contrast of love and war are also involved in *Romeo and Juliet,* though not as simile merely. In Verona, love emerges as involved with warfare: the love of Romeo and Juliet is set in contrast to brawling and feud, but its poignancy comes from the bitterness of the unexplained vendetta. In their lives the lovers speak for peace and reconciliation and at their death are turned into symbols of that reconciliation, into sepulchral statues. Love and war are both real enough, but they do not and cannot coexist in this play's world: the one destroys the other. The conjunction of love and death, commonly linked in the metaphors of lyrical tradition, make this play unmistakably non-comic; death is the link between the love-theme and the war-theme, the irreversible piece of action that stamps the play as tragic. Still, Romeo and Juliet die as much by accident as Pyramus and Thisbe do, to whose story the narrative of their death owes much. Indeed, the lovers are preserved in a nearly Ovidian way, not as plants, but in an *ecphrasis,* as memorial statues exemplifying a specific lesson to future generations. (p. 146)

> *Rosalie L. Colie, " 'Othello' and the Problematics of Love," in her* Shakespeare's Living Art, *Princeton University Press, 1974, pp. 135-67.*

## CLIFFORD LEECH   (essay date 1976)

[*Leech, an Elizabethan drama scholar, edited* The Two Noble Kinsmen *and* The Two Gentlemen of Verona, *and produced numerous studies of the plays of Shakespeare and his contemporaries, including* Shakespeare's Tragedies and Other Studies in Seventeenth Century Drama *(1950),* Shakespeare: The Chronicles *(1962), and* "Twelfth Night" and Shakespearian Comedy *(1965). In the following excerpt, Leech considers the shortcomings of* Romeo and Juliet *as a tragedy. He argues that Shakespeare's play reflects "an ultimate withdrawal from the tragic" in two significant ways: first, in its inclusion of a final "moral" which suggests that the lovers' deaths will atone for or reconcile the feuding families' mutual hate; second, and more damaging, in its casual treatment of fate as somewhat responsible for the tragic catastrophe. Leech also regards as undermining the play's claim to tragedy Shakespeare's refusal to confront evil in his central characters and his "facile" use of mystery.*]

[*Romeo and Juliet* concludes with] a kind of "happy ending." The feud will be ended, the lovers will be remembered. We may be reminded of the commonplace utterance that we have two deaths: the moment of actual ceasing to be, and the moment when the last person who remembers us dies. These lovers have their being enshrined in a famous play. So they are remembered in perpetuity, and their lives, according to the play itself, will be recorded in their statues. Certainly this is a sad affair, like that of Paolo and Francesca in *The Divine Comedy*. But we may ask, is it tragic?

Tragedy seems to demand a figure or figures that represent us in our ultimate recognition of evil. We need to feel that such figures are our kin, privileged to be chosen for the representative role and coming to the destruction that we necessarily anticipate for ourselves. The boy and girl figures in *Romeo and Juliet* are perhaps acceptable as appropriate representatives for humankind: after all, they do grow up. What worries us more, I think, in trying to see this play as fully achieved "tragedy," is the speech of the Duke at the end, which suggests that some atonement will be made through the reconciliation of the Montague and Capulet families. We are bound to ask "Is this enough?" It appears to be offered as such, but we remember that the finest among Verona's people are dead.

Shakespearean tragedy commonly ends with a suggestion of a return to normality, to peace. Fortinbras will rule in Denmark, Malcolm in Scotland, Iago will be put out of the way. But these later tragedies leave us with a doubt whether the peace is other than a second-best, whether indeed it is in man's power ever to put things right. In *Romeo and Juliet* the ending of the feud is laboriously spelled out.

But there is also the matter of Fate and Chance. Romeo kills Paris: at first glance that was a quite fortuitous happening. Paris was a good man, devoted to Juliet, who unfortunately got in the way of Romeo's approach to Juliet's tomb. At this point Romeo's doom is sealed: he might kill Tybalt and get away with it; he could not get away with killing an innocent Paris, who was moreover the Prince's kinsman. Now it is inevitable that he will die, whatever the moment of Juliet's awakening. There is indeed a "star-cross'd" pattern for the lovers, there is no way out for Romeo once he has come back to Verona. But perhaps Paris's important function in the last scene is not sufficiently brought out: the spectator may feel that there is simple chance operating in Romeo's arrival before Juliet wakes, in his killing himself a moment too early, in the Friar's belated arrival. Later I must return to the matter of the play's references to the "stars": for the moment I merely want to refer to the fact that tragedy can hardly be dependent on "bad luck."

Even so, though simple chance will not do, we may say that tragedy properly exists only when its events defy reason. The Friar thought the marriage of the young lovers might bring the feud to an end, and that was a reasonable assumption. Ironically, it did end the feud but at the expense of Romeo's and Juliet's lives, at the expense too of Mercutio's, Tybalt's, and Lady Montague's lives. The element of *non sequitur* in the train of events common to tragedy—despite the fact that, with one part of our minds, we see the operation of "probability or necessity," as Aristotle has it—is well described by Laurens van der Post in his novel *The Hunter and the Whale:*

> I was too young at the time to realise that tragedy is not tragedy if one finds reason or meaning in it. It becomes then, I was yet to learn, a darker form of this infinitely mysterious matter of luck. It is sheer tragedy only if it is without discernible sense or motivation.

We may balk at "luck," as I have already suggested, but "mysterious" is right indeed (as Bradley splendidly urged on us in the First Lecture of *Shakespearean Tragedy*), for what "sense" or "motivation" does there seem to be in tragedy's

gods? The sense of mystery is not, however, firmly posited in *Romeo and Juliet*. Rather, it is laboriously suggested that the Montagues and the Capulets have been taught a lesson in a particularly hard way.

Thus we have several reasons to query the play's achievement in the tragic kind. Do the lovers take on themselves the status of major figures in a celebration of a general human woe? Is the ending, with its promise of reconciliation, appropriate to tragic writing? We have seen that the lovers grow up, and they give us the impression of justifying human life, in their best moments, more than most people do. But the suggestion that their deaths will atone, will bring peace back, seems nugatory: no man's death brings peace, not even Christ's—or the Unknown Soldier's. The play could still end tragically if we were left with the impression that the survivors were merely doing what they could to go on living in an impoverished world: we have that in *Hamlet* and the later tragedies too. Here the laboriousness with which Shakespeare recapitulates all the events known to us, in the Friar's long speech, is surely an indication of an ultimate withdrawal from the tragic: the speech is too much like a preacher's résumé of the events on which a moral lesson will be based. We can accept Edgar's long account of Gloucester's death in *King Lear,* because we need a moment of recession before the tragedy's last phase, where we shall see Lear and Cordelia dead, and because no moral lesson is drawn from Gloucester's death; but at the end of this earlier play, when Romeo and Juliet have already eloquently died, we are with difficulty responsive to the long reiteration of all we have long known through the play's action.

Shakespeare has not here achieved the sense of an ultimate confrontation with evil, or the sense that the tragic figure ultimately and fully recognizes what his situation is. Romeo and Juliet die, more or less content with death as a second best to living together. Montague and Capulet shake hands, and do what is possible to atone. The lovers have the illusion of continuing to be together—an illusion to some extent imposed on the audience. The old men feel a personal guilt, not a realization of a general sickness in man's estate. But perhaps only Lear and Macbeth and Timon came to that realization.

We can understand why Shakespeare abandoned tragedy for some years after this play. It had proved possible for him to touch on the tragic idea in his English histories, making them approach, but only approach, the idea of humanity's representative being given over to destruction, as with the faulty Richard II, the saintly Henry VI, the deeply guilty yet none the less sharply human Richard III. He had given his theater a flawed yet impressive Titus Andronicus and in the same play an Aaron given almost wholly to evil but obstinately alive. But in these plays the main drive is not tragic. The histories rely on the sixteenth-century chronicles, *Titus* on that tradition of grotesque legend that came from both Seneca and Ovid. The past was to be relived and celebrated in the histories; *Titus* was more of a literary exercise in antique horror than a play embodying a direct reference to the general human condition. In *Romeo and Juliet* Shakespeare for the first time essayed tragedy proper—that is, by wanting to bring the play's events into relation to things as they truly are—and he used a tale often told but belonging to recent times and concerned with people whom the spectators were to feel as very much their own kin. He may well have been particularly attracted to the story he found in Brooke's poem for the very reason that its figures and events did not have the authority of history and belonged to the comparatively small world of Verona. No major change in the political order can result from what happens in this play's action. No individual figure presented here is truly given over to evil. Without any precedents to guide him, he aimed at writing about eloquent but otherwise ordinary young people in love and about their equally ordinary friends and families. Only Mercutio has something daemonic in him, in the sense that his quality of life transcends the normal level of being. (pp. 68-71)

[If] Shakespeare had no useful dramatic precedents in this task, he had a manifold heritage of ideas about the nature of love; and many parts of that heritage show themselves in the play. The immoderateness and rashness that the Friar rebukes seem, on the one hand, to lead—in the fashion of a moral play—to the lovers' destruction. On the other hand, not only is our sympathy aroused but we are made to feel that what Romeo and Juliet achieve may be a finer thing than is otherwise to be found in Verona. Both views are strongly conveyed, and either of them might effectively dominate the play. Of course, they could coexist and interpenetrate—as they were to do so much later in *Antony and Cleopatra*—but here they seem to alternate, and to be finally both pushed into the background in the long insistence that the feud will end because of the lovers' deaths. The "moral" is thus finally inverted: the lovers' sequence of errors has culminated in the error of suicide, but now we are made to turn to their parents' error and to the consolation that Romeo and Juliet will be remembered through their golden statues. And it is difficult for us to get interested in these statues, or to take much joy in the feud's ending.

Yet the deepest cause of uneasiness in our response to the play is, I believe, to be found in the relation of the story to the idea of the universe that is posited. We are told in the Prologue of "star-cross'd lovers," and there are after that many references to the "stars." So there is a sense of "doom" here, but we are never fully told what is implied. Many coincidences operate: Romeo meets Tybalt just at the wrong moment; the Friar's message to Romeo about Juliet's alleged death goes astray; Romeo arrives at the tomb just before Juliet awakens; the Friar comes too late. I have already drawn attention to Shakespeare's device by which Romeo has to kill Paris, so that, even if he had arrived at the right time, there would have been no way out for him. We may feel that a similar sequence of chances operates in *Hamlet:* if Hamlet had not killed Polonius in a scared moment, if he had not had his father's seal with him on the voyage to England, if he had not managed to escape on the hospitable pirates' ship, if the foils had not been exchanged in the fencing bout with Laertes, if Gertrude had not drunk from the poisoned cup, things might indeed not have been disposed so as to lead him to Claudius's killing at the moment when it actually occurred. Even so, we can feel that, after all, the end would have been much as it is. Hamlet was a man in love with death, far more in love with death than with killing: we may say that only in the moment of death's imminence was he fully alive, freed from inhibition, able to kill Claudius: somehow or other, whatever the chances, this play demanded a final confrontation between the uncle-father and nephew-son. In *Romeo and Juliet,* on the other hand, we could imagine things working out better: the lovers are doomed only by the words of Prologue, not by anything inherent in their situation. It is not, as it is in Hardy's novels, that we have a sense of a fully adverse "President of the immortals": there is rather an insufficient consideration of what is implied by the "stars." Of course, in *King Lear,* in all later Shakespearean tragedy, there is a sense of an ultimate mystery in the universe: "Is there any cause in nature that makes these hard hearts?" [*King Lear,* III. vi. 77-8] Lear asks in his con-

dition of most extreme distress. Bradley recognized that this mystery was inherent in the idea of tragedy, as is implied too in the passage from Laurens van der Post I have already quoted. But in *Romeo and Juliet* there is no sense of the mystery being confronted: rather it is merely posited in a facile way, so that we have to accept the lovers' deaths as the mere result of the will of the "stars" (the astrological implication is just too easy), and then we are exhorted to see this as leading to a reconciliation between the families.

The final "moral" of the play, as we have seen, is applied only to Old Montague and Old Capulet: they have done evil in allowing the feud to go on, and have paid for it in the deaths of their children and of Lady Montague. But, largely because Romeo and Juliet are never blamed, the children themselves stand outside the framework of moral drama. They have, albeit imperfectly, grown up into the world of tragedy, where the moral law is not a thing of great moment. They have been

*Romeo's description of the apothecary and his shop, Act V. Scene i. By Henry Fuseli. The Department of Rare Books and Special Collections, The University of Michigan Library.*

sacrificed on the altar of man's guilt, have become the victims of our own outrageousness, have given us some relief because they have died and we still for a time continue living. . . . To that extent, *Romeo and Juliet* is "tragic" in a way we can fully recognize. But its long-drawn-out ending, after the lovers are dead, with the pressing home of the moral that their deaths will bring peace, runs contrary to the notion of tragedy. (pp. 72-3)

When Shakespeare wrote "love-tragedy" again, in *Othello* and in *Antony and Cleopatra,* he showed that love may be a positive good but that it was simultaneously destructive and that its dramatic presentation gave no manumission from error to those who contemplated the destruction and continued to live. Nowhere, I think, does he suggest that love is other than a condition for wonder, however much he makes fun of it. But in his mature years he sees it as not only a destructive force but as in no way affording a means of reform. That *Romeo and Juliet* is a "moral tragedy"—which, I have strenuously urged, is a contradiction in terms—is evident enough. It is above all the casualness of the play's cosmology that prevents us from seeing it as tragedy fully achieved: we have seen the need for a fuller appreciation of the mystery. As with *Titus Andronicus,* the nearest play to *Romeo and Juliet* overtly assuming a tragic guise in the chronology of Shakespeare's works, the march toward disaster is too manifestly a literary device. At this stage in his career Shakespeare had not worked as free from the sixteenth-century moral play as Marlowe had done in *Tamburlaine, Faustus,* and *Edward II.* (p. 73)

> Clifford Leech, "The Moral Tragedy of 'Romeo and Juliet'," in English Renaissance Drama: Essays in Honor of Madeleine Doran & Mark Eccles, *Standish Henning, Robert Kimbrough, Richard Knowles, eds., Southern Illinois University Press, 1976, pp. 59-75.*

## DERICK R. C. MARSH (essay date 1976)

[*Marsh attempts to define the tragic basis of* Romeo and Juliet, *noting that both the Aristotelean tragedy of character and the medieval model of the operation of fate "in some greater pattern of divine purpose" fail to account adequately for all the events in the play. Instead, he regards* Romeo and Juliet *as a tragedy of "first love" pitted against the destructive force of time. Marsh contends that although Shakespeare demonstrates in this work the impermanence of "intense sexual attraction," the love of Romeo and Juliet "wins a victory over time," to the extent that the family feud and what he calls "bad luck" protect it from time's decay in death. However, he adds, the lovers are also defeated, "since such a victory can only be won out of time." Marsh further comments on the maturation of the hero and heroine through their ordeal, stating that in their ultimate sacrifice to preserve their union they "establish a quality of love, of life intensely lived, that becomes its own value."*]

Too rigid a definition of what tragedy ought to be is one important reason, it seems to me, why a good deal of adverse criticism has been directed at *Romeo and Juliet:* it has been attacked primarily for being an immature or defective tragedy. The dangers of such an approach can readily be seen in some of the criticism of the play written in the first half of our century. By asking the wrong questions, some able critics have blinded themselves to those qualities that are there.

There may be some excuse for looking for signs of immaturity, for this is an early play. . . . Of the other plays that can be called tragedies, only *Richard III* and *Titus Andronicus* are reckoned to be earlier. It is followed by *Richard II* and is

clearly linked by similarities of theme and style with the Sonnets, with *A Midsummer Night's Dream* and with *Love's Labour's Lost.* If it is noticed that the play shares with these other works a concern with the clash between love and time, with the intense and potentially delusive nature of passion, and, particularly with *Love's Labour's Lost,* an awareness of the difficulty of finding a mode of expression that is adequate to communicate an intensely felt emotion, in a society where not only expression but feeling as well is threatened with restriction by convention, then its real nature is more likely to be recognised. Perhaps most of all we need to recognise in it an obvious and exuberant interest in language, not so much for its own sake, as has sometimes been claimed, but because this youthful energy and vitality itself reflects and comments on the central love situation. (pp. 46-7)

More recently, critics have been more prepared to accept [*Romeo and Juliet*] on its own terms; it is not as great a play as *Hamlet* or *King Lear,* but it is an excellent play of its kind, and one that has its own very important place in the Shakespearean canon. For this is Shakespeare's account of the nature of young love, of its intensity and of its terrifying vulnerability. It is his first taking up and working out of some of those hints which we have seen in the comedies, the suggestion that no lovers can feel themselves wholly secure from the world around them or from the dangers within them. In the comedies, such threats are averted, sometimes by good management, sometimes by sheer good luck. Here, though these lovers lack nothing in strength and sincerity and passion, the luck runs against them, and they are destroyed. Romeo and Juliet, particularly Juliet, are not without those qualities of wit and intelligent self-awareness the comedies show as necessary for the success of a love relationship, but these qualities are given little chance to develop or endure. Within four days Romeo and Juliet meet, fall in love, marry, part and die: there is no time for slow ripening. What their bad luck robs them of most of all is time; because their love is the all-consuming passion of first love, they have the illusion that they are independent of time, but, in the constantly repeated paradox of the Sonnets, time is both love's creator and its destroyer. Love cannot exist out of time, but once brought into being, it can only be destroyed:

> Ruin hath taught me thus to ruminate,
> That Time will come and take my love away.
>
> [Sonnet 64]

It is thus the common fate that Romeo and Juliet endure, but it is given terrible dramatic emphasis by the swiftness with which they are destroyed. Yet if this is a tragedy, it is a tragedy of a very special kind, for I believe that this play cannot satisfactorily be accounted for either as what might be called an Aristotelian tragedy, whether successful or not, or a tragedy on the medieval pattern. Romeo and Juliet do not hold important positions in their society, the plot does not arise directly from their characters, and while it may comprise a significant action in Aristotle's sense, it depends too much on chance and coincidence to conform to his requirements. The medieval definition of tragedy as an unexpected fall from prosperity into misery, produced by the operation of fate, the revolution of fortune's wheel, may be nearer to the mark, as Professor Dickey suggests [see excerpt above, 1957], but even the more complex kind of medieval tragedy, where the human suffering produced by unrestrained passion leads to some moral enlightenment, and is thus included in some greater pattern of divine purpose, leaves too much in this play unaccounted for.

For one thing, the action is so fiercely short, and so shot through with foreboding, that the description of an unexpected fall from prosperity to misery hardly seems to fit the case, and most important of all, attention is concentrated so firmly on the lovers themselves that it is very difficult to see the play as a whole as an example of the way that fortune fulfils God's purpose by turning men's eyes from this world to the next. It is true that even if we are unwilling to feel particularly directed towards a criticism of the excessive passion of the lovers, there is the moral issue of the feud, the external force directly responsible for five of the six deaths in the play, which is only healed over the lovers' grave, but it seems hardly justifiable to see the story of the lovers as labouring to this end. Their love, as the Prologue informs us, and as we are constantly reminded in the course of the play, is foredoomed, yet the final catastrophe depends on a remarkable number of coincidences and mischances. There is the servant who brings the invitation to the Capulet ball to a party of Montagues for interpretation, the intervention of Mercutio in the quarrel between his friend and Tybalt, Romeo's well-meaning obstruction, which causes Mercutio's death and consequently Tybalt's. After Romeo's banishment, there is the delay in the delivery of Friar Lawrence's message explaining the stratagem, the Friar's own failure to arrive at the tomb in time, and the final desperate bad luck of Juliet's awakening only moments too late to save Romeo's life and her own. If this is a tragedy that depends on a strong line of causality, it is a very badly constructed one indeed, for none of these accidents seems necessarily a result of some strength or flaw in hero's or heroine's character. In spite of Professor Dickey's careful study, I feel that the brevity of time spanned by the play, and the extreme ill-luck, both serve the purpose of directing our sympathy, and in the end our admiration, towards the lovers, whose death is seen as a sort of triumph over time, as well as a defeat. And this emphasis on bad luck makes the lovers' choices seem all the more audacious. (pp. 48-50)

[*Romeo and Juliet*] concerns itself with the nature of a particular kind of love, first love, that intense sexual attraction that by its very nature cannot long remain as it is. In the ordinary course of life, this change is accepted because it is inevitable; either the love withers away, or changes into some other kind of love, of equal or perhaps even greater value, but different in kind. In this play, it is protected from change, heightened and intensified by the sense of doom that pervades the play, but for that very reason, immune to time's decay, because neither we nor the lovers are ever allowed to believe that their love can last long enough to exhaust its first intensity. In that sense their love wins a victory over time, but since such a victory can only be won out of time, the love must end in death; in this sense it is self-defeating.

This love, seen against the background of hostility that the feud provides, is the subject of the play, which within the situation the feud creates is concerned with the effects of the intensity of their passion on the lovers themselves, in particular with the way in which their discovery of each other gives a sense of purpose and meaning to two young people who have, when the play opens, hardly yet begun to live. There is abundant evidence that Romeo, in love with love in his relationship with Rosaline, is looking for such a purpose: he so absolutely finds one in his love for Juliet that the boy who lay blubbering on the floor of Friar Lawrence's cell is at the play's end a man who takes the decision for life or death with a mature sense of responsibility and certainty. Juliet, not yet 14 . . . , starts as a girl who regards marriage as 'an honour / That I dream not

of' [I. iii. 66]; within a few days she has become a woman who, quite alone, can choose to risk death, and face the most terrifying implications of that choice, rather than contemplate life without her husband. The lovers themselves have neither the time nor the inclination to attempt to come to terms with the hostility and lack of understanding of their world: its hostility becomes the occasion for the destruction of their love, but that love is doomed by its very nature, for as we are reminded by the chain of images of lightning, fire, and gunpowder which runs through the whole play, love of this intensity is a consuming passion which cannot last. Shakespeare heightens its intensity, and its poignancy, by keeping us constantly aware that it will be cut off, constantly aware that though the lovers may love in interludes in a world seemingly released from time, as in the moment when they meet, or in the single night they spend together, even they themselves are made aware that their only real release from time is in death. They are defeated, as all who love must ultimately be defeated, by their own mortality, but by being prepared to die for each other Romeo and Juliet establish a quality of love, of life intensely lived, that becomes its own value. They choose to die . . . because each knows that he or she cannot live without the other, and knows this as a simple, literal truth, to be acted on at the first opportunity.

If the play is seen in this way, many of the objections and criticisms that have been directed at it lose much of their force. In any case the finding of wholesale weaknesses, even in an early play, is something that ought to make any critic reconsider the basis of his own reading, for it is always necessary in a play by Shakespeare to look for an organisation that will include in an harmonious whole as many of the play's characteristics as possible. This is not to argue that everything in all the plays is carried out with equal success, for to expect even Shakespeare always to maintain his own highest standards would be absurd. But without wanting to seem idolatrous, it does seem to me that we ought to regard with some suspicion a reading which finds radical flaws in the organisation of a play's material. The point of any scene or incident can generally be discovered, even if on some occasions we feel that the intention has not been perfectly realised. . . . [If] the shortness of the time spanned by *Romeo and Juliet* is seen both as an expansion of the moment of falling in love, and at the same time as a means of intensification of that love, seen as a maturing force, then many of the charges of inadequacy, of faultiness of plot and extravagance of language that have been directed at the play fall away. This remains true even though, in the special circumstances in which the lovers find themselves, the only operation of that maturity is to choose to live no longer. (pp. 50-2)

*Derick R. C. Marsh, '''Romeo and Juliet','' in his* Passion Lends Them Power: A Study of Shakespeare's Love Tragedies, *Barnes & Noble Books, 1976, pp. 46-88.*

## COPPÉLIA KAHN (essay date 1977-78)

[*Kahn avers that "the feud in a realistic social sense is the primary tragic force" in* Romeo and Juliet, *not because it serves as an "agent of fate," as many critics have argued, but because it is "an extreme and peculiar expression of [Verona's] patriarchal society, which Shakespeare shows to be tragically self-destructive." Kahn maintains that the feud forces Verona's sons and daughters to ally themselves with their own paternal households in opposition to any other household, thereby thwarting any allegiance outside the family. It also inhibits normal sexual devel-*

*opment by leading the sons to participate in a kind of rite of passage which promotes "phallic violence on behalf of [the] fathers." The critic also discusses how the love-death resolution in Act V of Romeo and Juliet corresponds to this pattern, claiming that the lovers' quest for an eternal union in death is a triumph over Verona's self-destructive society.]*

*Romeo and Juliet* is about a pair of adolescents trying to grow up. Growing up requires that they separate themselves from their parents by forming an intimate bond with one of the opposite sex which supersedes filial bonds. This, broadly, is an essential task of adolescence, in Renaissance England and Italy as in America today, and the play is particularly concerned with the social milieu in which these adolescent lovers grow up—a patriarchal milieu as English as it is Italian. I shall argue that the feud in a realistic social sense is the primary tragic force in the play—not the feud as agent of fate, but the feud as an extreme and peculiar expression of patriarchal society, which Shakespeare shows to be tragically self-destructive. The feud is the deadly *rite-de-passage* which promotes masculinity at the price of life. Undeniably, the feud is bound up with a pervasive *sense* of fatedness, but that sense finds its objective correlative in the dynamics of the feud and of the society in which it is embedded. As Harold Goddard says,

> The fathers are the stars and the stars are the fathers in the sense that the fathers stand for the accumulated experience of the past, for tradition, for authority, and hence for the two most potent forces that mold and so impart 'destiny' to the child's life . . . heredity and training. The hatred of the hostile houses in *Romeo and Juliet* is an inheritance that every member of these families is born into as truly as he is born with the name Capulet or Montague [see Additional Bibliography].

That inheritance makes Romeo and Juliet tragic figures because it denies their natural needs and desires as youth; Of course, they also display the faults of youth; its self-absorption and reckless extremism, its headlong surrender to eros. But it is the feud which fosters the rash, choleric impulsiveness typical of youth by offering a permanent invitation to and outlet for violence.

The feud is first referred to in the play as "their parents' strife and their parents' rage" [Prologue, 8, 10] and it is clear that the fathers, not their children, are responsible for its continuance. Instead of providing social channels and moral guidance by which the energies of youth can be rendered beneficial to themselves and society, the Montagues and the Capulets make weak gestures toward civil peace while participating emotionally in the feud as much as their children do. While they fail to exercise authority over the younger generation in the streets, they wield it selfishly and stubbornly in the home. So many of the faults of character which critics have found in Romeo and Juliet are shared by their parents that the play cannot be viewed as a tragedy of character in the Aristotelian sense, in which the tragedy results because the hero and the heroine fail to "love moderately." Rather, the feud's ambiance of hot temper permeates age as well as youth; viewed from the standpoint of Prince Escalus who embodies the law, it is Montague and Capulet who are childishly refractory.

In the course of the action, Romeo and Juliet create and try to preserve new identities as adults apart from the feud, but it blocks their every attempt. Metaphorically, it devours them in the "detestable maw" of the Capulets' monument, a symbol of the patriarchy's destructive power over its children. Thus both the structure and the texture of the play suggest a critique of the patriarchal attitudes expressed through the feud, which makes "tragic scapegoats" of Romeo and Juliet.

Specifically, for the sons and daughters of Verona the feud constitutes socialization into patriarchal roles in two ways. First, it reinforces their identities as sons and daughters by allying them with their paternal household against another paternal household, thus polarizing all their social relations, particularly their marital choices, in terms of filial allegiance. They are constantly called upon to define themselves in terms of their families and to defend their families. Second, the feud provides a "Psycho-sexual moratorium" for the sons [Erik Erikson, in his "The Problem of Ego Identity"], an activity in which they prove themselves men by phallic violence on behalf of their fathers, instead of by courtship and sexual experimentation which would lead toward marriage and separation from the paternal house. It fosters in them the fear and scorn of women, associating women with effeminacy and emasculation, while it links sexual intercourse with aggression and violence against women, rather than pleasure and love. Structurally, the play's design reflects the prominence of the feud. It erupts in three scenes at the beginning, middle, and end (I. i, III. i, V. iii) which deliberately echo each other, and the peripeteia [reversal], at which Romeo's and Juliet's fortunes change decisively for the worse, occurs exactly in the middle when Romeo kills Tybalt, an action which poses the two conflicting definitions of manhood between which Romeo must make his tragic choice.

It has been noted that *Romeo and Juliet* is a domestic tragedy but not that its milieu is distinctly patriarchal as well as domestic. Much of it takes place within the Capulet household and Capulet's role as *paterfamilias* [father and head of household] is apparent from the first scene in which his servants behave as members of his extended family, as *famuli* rather than employees. That household is a charming place: protected and spacious, plentiful with servants, food, light, and heat, bustling with festivity, intimate and informal even on great occasions, with a cosy familiarity between master and servant. In nice contrast to it stands the play's other dominant milieu, the streets of Verona. It is there that those fighting the feud are defined as men, in contrast to those who would rather love than fight, who in terms of the feud are less than men. Gregory and Sampson ape the machismo of their masters, seeking insults on the slightest pretext so that they may prove their valor. In their blind adherence to a groundless "ancient grudge," they are parodies of the feuding gentry. But in Shakespeare's day, as servants they would be regarded as their master's "children" in more than figurative sense, owing not just work but loyalty and obedience to their employers as legitimate members of the household ranking immediately below its children. As male servants their position resembles that of the sons bound by their honors to fight for their families' names. Most importantly, their obvious phallic competitiveness in being quick to anger at an insult to their status or manhood, and quick to draw their swords and fight, shades into phallic competitiveness in sex as well. . . . In [the opening] scene and elsewhere, the many puns on "stand" as standing one's ground in fighting and as erection attest that fighting in the feud demonstrates virility as well as valor. Sampson and Gregory also imply that they consider it their prerogative as men to take women by force as a way of demonstrating their superiority to the Montagues:

... women, being the weaker vessels, are ever thrust to the wall. Therefore I will push Montague's men from the wall and thrust his maids to the wall. ... When I have fought with the men, I will be civil with the maids—I will cut off their heads ... the heads of the maids or their maidenheads. Take it in what sense thou wilt [I. i. 15-18, 22-3, 25-6].

As the fighting escalates, finally Capulet and Montague themselves become involved, Capulet calling for a sword he is too infirm to wield effectively, simply because Montague, he claims, "flourishes his blade in spite of me" [I. i. 78]. With the neat twist of making the masters parody the men who have been parodying them, the fighting ends as the Prince enters. At the cost of civil peace, all have asserted their claims to manhood through the feud.

Tybalt makes a memorable entrance in this first scene. Refusing to believe Benvolio's assertion that his sword is drawn only to separate the fighting servants, he immediately dares him to defend himself. To Tybalt, a sword can only mean a challenge to fight, and peace is just a word. ... In the first two acts, Shakespeare contrasts Tybalt and Romeo in terms of their responses to the feud so as to intensify the conflict Romeo faces in Act III when he must choose between being a man in the sanctioned public way, by drawing a sword upon an insult, or being a man in a novel and private way: by reposing an inner confidence in his secret identity as Juliet's husband.

In Act III, the fight begins when Tybalt is effectively baited by Mercutio's punning insults; from Mercutio's opening badinage with Benvolio, it is evident that he too is spoiling for a fight, though he is content to let the weapons be words. But words on the hot mid-day streets of Verona are effectively the same as blows which must be answered by the drawing of a sword. When Romeo arrives, Tybalt calls him "my man," "a villain," and "boy" [III. i. 56, 61, 66], all terms which simultaneously impugn his birth and honor as well as his manhood. Mercutio made words blows, but Romeo tries to do just the opposite, by oblique protestations of love to Tybalt, which must seem quite mysterious to him if he listens to them at all. ... Romeo's puns of peacemaking fail where Mercutio's puns of hostility succeeded all too well. Only one kind of rigid, simple language, based on the stark polarities Capulet-Montague, man-boy, is understood in the feud. No wonder Mercutio terms Romeo's response a "calm, dishonorable, vile submission" [III. i. 73] and draws on Tybalt: Romeo has allowed a Capulet to insult his name, his paternal heritage, his manhood, without fighting for them. ... When Mercutio in effect fights for him and dies, the shame of having allowed his friend to answer the challenge which according to the code of manly honor, he should have answered, overcomes Romeo. He momentarily turns against Juliet, the source of his new identity, and sees her as Mercutio sees all women:

> O sweet Juliet,
> Thy beauty hath made me effeminate,
> And in my temper soft'ned valor's steel!
>
> [III. i. 113-15]

In that moment, caught between his radically new identity as Juliet's husband, which has made him responsible (he thinks) for his friend's death, and his previous traditional identity as the scion of the house of Montague, he resumes the latter and murders Tybalt. (pp. 5-8)

Among the young bloods serving as foils for Romeo, Benvolio represents the total sublimation of virile energy into peacemaking, agape instead of eros; Tybalt, such energy channeled directly and exclusively into aggression; and Mercutio, its attempted sublimation into fancy and wit. (Romeo and Paris seek manhood through love rather than through fighting, but are finally impelled by the feud to fight each other.) That Mercutio pursues the feud though he is neither Montague nor Capulet suggests that feuding has become the normal social pursuit for young men in Verona. Through his abundant risqué wit, he suggests its psychological function for them, as a definition of manhood. Love is only manly, he hints, if it is aggressive and violent and consists of subjugating, rather than being subjugated by women:

> If love be rough with you, be rough with love;
> Prick love for pricking, and you beat love down.
>
> [I. iv. 27-8]
> (p. 9)

Mercutio mocks not merely the futile, enfeebling kind of love Romeo feels for Rosaline, but all love. Moreover, his volley of sexual innuendo serves as the equivalent of both fighting and love. In its playful way, his speech is as aggressive as fighting, and while speech establishes his claim to virility, at the same time it marks his distance from women. ... Mercutio would rather fight than talk, but he would rather talk than love, which brings us to his justly famed utterance, the Queen Mab speech. Like so much in this play, it incorporates opposites. While it is surely a set-piece set apart, it is also highly characteristic of Mercutio, in its luxuriant repleteness of images and rippling mockery. While it purports to belittle dreamers for the shallowness of the wishes their dreams fulfill, it sketches the world of which the dreamers dream with loving accuracy, sweetmeats, tithe pigs, horses' manes and all. In service to the purest fancy, it portrays Mab's coach and accoutrements with workmanlike precision. It pretends to tell us dreams are "nothing but vain fantasy" [I. iv. 98] but this pose is belied by the speaker's intense awareness that real people do dream of real things. In short, Mercutio's defense against dreams gives evidence of this own urge to dream, but it also reveals his fear of giving in to the seething nighttime world of unconscious desires associated with the feminine; he prefers the broad daylight world of men fighting and jesting. Significantly, his catalogue of dreamers ends with a reference to the feminine mystery of birth, and an implied analogy between the birth of children from the womb and the birth of dreams from "an idle brain." He would like to think that women's powers, and desires for women, are as bodiless and inconsequential as the dreams to which they give rise. ... But Mercutio protests too much; the same defensiveness underlies his fancy as his bawdy. Puns and wordplay, the staple of his bawdy, figure prominently in dreams, as Freud so amply shows; relying on an accidental similarity of sound, they disguise a repressed impulse while giving voice to it.

In the feud names, the signs of patriarchal authority and allegiance, are calls to arms, and words are blows. As Romeo and Juliet struggle to free themselves from the feud, their effort at first takes the form of creating new names for themselves to reflect their new identities. ... Juliet's extended meditation on Romeo's name in the balcony scene begins with her recognition that for Romeo to refuse his name—to separate himself from the feud—he would have to deny his father [II. ii. 34], and moves from this unlikely alternative to her own fanciful effort to detach the man from the name, and their love from the social reality in which it is embedded: "'Tis but thy name that is my enemy. / Thou art thyself, though not a Montague" [II. ii. 38-9]. Through the irony of Juliet's casual "but thy name," Shakespeare suggests both that it is impossible for Romeo to separate himself from his public identity as a Montague, and that his public identity is nonetheless extraneous and accidental, no part of what he really is. The Romeo already transfigured by his love for Juliet is a different person and his name should reflect it. The exchange which Juliet proposes hints at this:

> Romeo, doff thy name;
> And for they name, which is no part of thee,
> Take all myself.
>
> [II. ii. 47-9]

In fact, his new identity as a man is to be based on this allegiance to her as her husband, and not on his allegiance to his father. In the wedding scene, Romeo says with his desperate faith, "It is enough I may but call her mine" [II. vi. 8], an ironic allusion to the fact that though she now has taken his surname in marriage, all he really can do is "call" her his, for the feud will not allow their new identities as husband and wife to become publicly known, as is all too apparent when Romeo's veiled references to Tybalt's name as one which he tenders as dearly as his go uncomprehended in Act III.

Later, bemoaning his banishment in Friar Lawrence's cell, Romeo curses his name and offers literally to cut it out of his body as though it were merely physical and its hateful consequences could be amputated. Symbolically, he is trying to castrate himself; as a consequence of the feud he cannot happily be a man either by fighting for his name and family or by loving Juliet. Banished and apart from her, he feels, he will have no identity, and nothing to live for. His obsession with his name at this point recalls Juliet's "'Tis but thy name that is my enemy." In the early moments of their love, both of them seek to mold social reality to their changed perceptions and desires by manipulating the verbal signifiers of that reality. But between Romeo's banishment and their deaths, both learn in different ways that not the word but the spirit can change reality. Juliet becomes a woman and Romeo a man not through changing a name but by action undertaken in a transformed sense of the self requiring courage and independence. (pp. 9-11)

In patriarchal Verona, men bear names and stand to fight for them; women, "the weaker vessels," bear children and "fall backward" to conceive them, as the Nurse's husband once told the young Juliet. It is appropriate that Juliet's growing up is hastened and intensified by having to resist the marriage arranged for her by her father, while Romeo's is precipitated by having to fight for the honor of his father's house. Unlike its sons, Verona's daughters have, in effect, no adolescence, no sanctioned period of experiment with adult identities or activities. Lady Capulet regards motherhood as the proper termination of childhood for a girl, for she says to Juliet,

> Younger than you,
> Here in Verona, ladies of esteem,
> Are made already mothers.
>
> [I. iii. 69-71]

and recalls that she herself was a mother when she was about her daughter's age. Capulet is more cautious at first: "Too soon marred are those so early made" [I. ii. 13], he says, perhaps meaning the pregnancies are more likely to be difficult for women in early adolescence than for those even slightly older. But the pun in the succeeding lines reveals another concern besides this one:

> Earth hath swallowed all my hopes but she;
> She is the hopeful lady of my earth.
>
> [I. ii. 14-15]

Fille de terre is the French term for heiress, and Capulet wants to be sure that his daughter will not only survive motherhood, but produce healthy heirs for him as well.

Capulet's sudden determination to marry Juliet to Paris comes partly from a heightened sense of mortality which, when it is introduced in the first act, mellows his character attractively:

> Welcome, gentlemen! I have seen the day
> That I have worn a visor and could tell
> A whispering tale in a fair lady's ear,
> Such as would please. 'Tis gone, 'tis gone, 'tis gone.
>
> [I. v. 21-4]

But he cannot give up claim on youth so easily as these words imply. When he meets with Paris again after Tybalt's death, it is he who calls the young man back, with a "desperate tender" inspired by the thought that he, no less than his young nephew, was "born to die" [III. iv. 12, 4]. Better to insure the safe passage of his property to an heir now, while he lives, than in an uncertain future. . . . For him, the wedding constitutes the promise that his line will continue, though his own time end soon. Shakespeare depicts Capulet's motives for forcing the hasty marriage with broad sympathy in this regard, but he spares the anxious old man no tolerance in the scene in which Juliet refuses to marry Paris. (pp. 12-13)

Romeo finds a surrogate father outside that system, in Friar Lawrence, and in fact never appears onstage with his parents. Juliet on the other hand, always appears within her father's household until the last scene in the tomb. Lodged in the bosom of the family, she has two mothers, the Nurse as well as her real one. With regard to Juliet, the Nurse is the opposite of what the Friar is for Romeo—a surrogate mother within the patriarchal family, but one who is, finally, of little help in assisting Juliet in her passage from child to woman. She embodies the female self molded devotedly to the female's family role. The only history she knows is that of birth, suckling, weaning, and marriage; for her, earthquakes are less cataclysmic than these turning points of growth. She and Juliet enter the play simultaneously in a scene in which she has almost all the lines and Juliet less than ten, a disproportion which might be considered representative of the force of tradition weighing on the heroine.

The Nurse's longest speech ends with the telling of an anecdote [I. iii. 35-48] which she subsequently repeats twice. It is perfectly in character: trivial, conventional, full of good humor but lacking in wit. And yet it masterfully epitomizes the way in which woman's subjugation to her role as wife and mother, in the patriarchal setting, is made to seem integral with nature itself. . . . (p. 14)

Against this conception of femininity, in which women are married too young to understand their sexuality as anything but passive participation in a vast biological cycle through childbearing, Shakespeare places Juliet's unconventional, fully conscious and willed giving of herself to Romeo. Harry Levin has pointed out how the lovers move from conventional formality to a simple, organic expressiveness which is contrasted with the rigid, arbitrary polarization of lanuage and life in Verona [see excerpt above, 1960]. Juliet initiates this departure in the balcony scene by answering Romeo's conceits, "love's light wings" and "night's cloak" [II. ii. 66, 75] with a directness highly original in the context:

> Dost thou love me? I know thou wilt say "Ay";
> And I will take thy word.
>
> [II. ii. 90-1]

Free from the accepted forms in more than a stylistic sense, she pledges her love, discourages Romeo from stereotyped love-vows, and spurs him to make arrangements for their wedding. As she awaits their consummation, the terms in which she envisions losing her virginity parody the terms of male competition, the sense of love as a contest in which men must beat down women or be beaten by them:

> Come, civil night,
> Thou sober-suited matron all in black
> And learn me how to lose a winning match,
> Played for a pair of stainless maidenhoods.
>
> [III. ii. 10-13]

She knows and values her "affections and warm youthful blood" [II. v. 12], but she has yet to learn the cost of such blithe individuality in the tradition-bound world of Verona. When the Nurse tells her that Romeo has killed Tybalt, she falls suddenly into a rant condemning him, in the same kind of trite oxymorons characteristic of Romeo's speech before they met . . . ; such language in this context reflects the automatic thinking of the feud, which puts everything in terms of a Capulet-Montague dichotomy. But she drops this theme when a word from the Nurse reminds her that she now owes her loyalty to Romeo rather than to the house of Capulet:

> NURSE. Will you speak well of him that killed your
> 　　cousin?
> JULIET. Shall I speak ill of him that is my husband?
> 　　Ah, poor my lord, what tongue shall smooth thy
> 　　name,
> 　　When I, thy three-hours' wife, have mangled it?
>
> [III. ii. 96-9]

Romeo's "name" in the sense of his identity as well as his reputation now rests not on his loyalty to the Montagues but on Juliet's loyalty to him and their reciprocal identities as husband and wife apart from either house. (pp. 15-16)

In this play ordered by antitheses on so many levels, the all-embracing opposition of Eros and Thanatos seems to drive the plot along. The lovers want to live in union; the death-dealing feud opposes their desire. The tragic conclusion, however, effects a complete turnabout in this clearcut opposition between love and death, for in the lovers' suicides love and death merge. Romeo and Juliet die as an act of love, in a spiritualized acting out of the ancient pun. Furthermore, the final scene plays off against each other two opposing views of the lovers' deaths: that they are consumed and destroyed by the fued, and that they rise above it, united in death. I shall now explore the ambivalence of this conclusion in an attempt to show how it reflects the play's concern with coming of age in the patriarchal family. (pp. 16-17)

The setting and action of the final scene are meant to remind us of the hostile social climate in which the lovers have had to act. It begins on a bittersweet note as the dull and proper Paris approaches to perform his mangled rites, recapitulating wedding in funeral with the flowers so easily symbolic of a young and beautiful maiden, and reminiscent of her expected defloration in marriage. By paralleling the successive entrances

of Paris and Romeo, one who has had no part in the feud, the other who has paid so much for resisting it, both of whom love Juliet, Shakespeare suggests the feud's indifferent power over youth. Each character comes in with the properties appropriate to his task, and enjoins the servant accompanying him to "stand aloof." Their ensuing sword-fight is subtly designed to recall the previous eruptions of the feud and to suggest that it is a man-made cycle of recurrent violence. Paris' challenge to Romeo . . . recalls Tybalt's behavior at the Capulets' ball, when he assumed Romeo's very presence to be an insult, and in Act III, when he deliberately sought Romeo out to get satisfaction for that insult. Romeo responds to Paris as he did to Tybalt, first by hinting cryptically at his true purpose in phrases echoing those he spoke in Act III:

> By heaven, I love thee better than myself,
> For I come hither armed against myself. . . .
>
> [V. iii. 64-5]

Then once more he gives in to "fire-eyed fury" when Paris continues to provoke him, and in a gesture all too familiar by now, draws his sword.

Shakespeare prepares us well before this final scene for its grim variations on the Friar's association of womb and tomb. Juliet's moving soliloquy on her fears of waking alone in the family monument amplifies its fitness as a symbol of the power of the family, inheritance, and tradition over her and Romeo. . . . In a "dismal scene" indeed, she envisions herself first driven mad by fear, desecrating [her ancestors'] bones by playing with them, and then using the bones against herself to dash her brains out. This waking dream, like all the dreams recounted in this play, holds psychological truth; it bespeaks Juliet's knowledge that in loving Romeo she has broken a taboo as forceful as that against harming the sacred relics of her ancestors, and her fear of being punished for the offense by the ancestors themselves—with their very bones.

As Romeo forces his way into the monument, he pictures it both as a monstrous mouth devouring Juliet and himself and as a womb:

> Thou detestable maw, thou womb of death,
> Gorged with the dearest morsel of the earth,
> Thus I enforce thy rotten jaws to open,
> And in despite I'll cram thee with more food.
>
> [V. iii. 45-8]

When the Friar hastens toward the monument a few minutes later, his exclamation further extends the meanings connected with it:

> Alack, alack, what blood is this, which stains
> The stony entrance to this sepulcher?
>
> [V. iii. 140-41]

The blood-spattered entrance to the tomb which has been figured as a womb recalls both a defloration or initiation into sexuality, and a birth. Juliet's wedding bed is her grave, as premonitions had warned her, and three young men, two of them her bridegrooms, all killed as a result of the feud, share it with her. The birth which takes place in this "womb" is perversely a birth into death, a stifling return to the tomb of the fathers, not the second birth of adolescence, the birth of an adult self, which the lovers strove for.

But the second part of the scene, comprising Romeo's death speech, the Friar's entrance and hasty departure, and Juliet's death speech, offers a different interpretation. Imagery and action combine to assert that death is a transcendent form of sexual consummation, and further, that it is rebirth into a higher stage of existence—the counterpart of an adulthood never fully achieved in life. That Shakespeare will have it both ways at once is perfectly in keeping with a play about adolescence in that it reflects the typical conflict of that period, which Bruno Bettelheim describes as "the striving for independence and self-assertion, and the opposite tendency, to remain safely at home, tied to the parents." It is also similar to the ambivalent ending of *Venus and Adonis*, another work about youth and love, in which Venus' long-striven-for possession of Adonis takes the form of the total absorption of each person in the other, at the price of Adonis' death.

It might be argued that Romeo and Juliet will their love-deaths in simple error, caused by the mere chance of Brother John's failure to reach Romeo with the news of Juliet's feigned death, and that chance is fate's instrument. But the poetic consistency and force with which their belief in death as consummation is carried out, by means of the extended play of words and actions on dying as orgasm, outweighs the sense of chance or of fate. The equation of loving with dying is introduced early, and most often dying is linked to the feud, for instance in Juliet's reference to grave and wedding bed in Act I, scene 5, re-stated in the wedding scene. Romeo's banishment produces an explosion of remarks linking wedding bed with tomb and Romeo as bridegroom with death. The Friar's potion inducing a simulated death on the day of Juliet's wedding with Paris titillates us further with ironic conjunctions of death and marriage. But when Romeo declares, the instant after he learns of Juliet's supposed death, "Is it e'en so? Then I defy you, stars!" [V. i. 24], the context in which we have been led to understand and expect the lovers' death is transformed. Romeo no longer conceives his course of action as a way of circumventing the feud, which now has no importance for him. Rather, he wills his death as a means to permanent union with Juliet. When he says, in the same tone of desperate but unshakable resolve, "Well, Juliet, I will lie with thee tonight" [V. i. 34], as her lover and bridegroom he assumes his role in the love-death so amply foreshadowed, but that love-death is not merely fated; it is willed. It is the lovers' triumphant assertion over the impoverished and destructive world which has kept them apart. (pp. 17-19)

Shakespeare fills Romeo's last speech with the imagery of life's richness: the gloomy vault is "a feasting presence full of light" [V. iii. 86], and Juliet's lips and cheeks are crimson with vitality. His last lines, "O true apothecary! / Thy drugs are quick. Thus with a kiss I die" [V. iii. 119-20], bring together the idea of death as sexual consummation and as rebirth. Similarly, Juliet kisses the poison on his lips and calls it "a restorative." They have come of age by a means different than the rites of passage, phallic violence and adolescent motherhood, typical for youth in Verona. Romeo's death in the Capulets' (not his own fathers') tomb reverses the traditional passage of the female over to the male house in marriage and betokens his refusal to follow the code of his fathers, while it is Juliet, not Romeo, who boldly uses his dagger, against herself. (p. 20)

> Coppélia Kahn, "Coming of Age in Verona," in Modern Language Studies, *Vol. VIII, No. 1, Winter, 1977-78, pp. 5-22.*

## MARILYN L. WILLIAMSON (essay date 1981)

[*Williamson proposes a reading of* Romeo and Juliet *to resolve the opposing interpretations of the play as a tragedy of fate and*

*a tragedy of character. She maintains that death is a self-fulfilled prophecy for Romeo, for the hero desires death even before he meets Juliet, and thus fate is not the tragic force in the play. She adds that the feud contributes to the final catastrophe only to the extent that it fosters Romeo's wish for self-destruction in the first place.*]

Critics and playgoers have assumed that Romeo's suicide is motivated entirely by his unwillingness to live without Juliet. Yet the play reveals that he whose name is a word for lover seems more faithful to his commitment to death than he is to any living woman—Rosaline or Juliet. Even as he moves from infatuation with Rosaline to his intense passion for Juliet, Romeo makes two constant assumptions about his life. One is that his destiny is beyond his control, that he can do little to change the course of his life; the other is that he will meet an early death. Romeo expresses these feelings early in the play and, whatever his sexual impulses, he remains true to these premises throughout the action. He expresses both ideas as the group of young madcaps make their way to Capulets' feast:

> my mind misgives
> Some consequence, yet hanging in the stars,
> Shall bitterly begin his fearful date
> With this night's revels and expire the term
> Of a despised life, closed in my breast,
> By some vile forfeit of untimely death.
> But he that hath the steerage of my course
> Direct my sail! On, lusty gentlemen!
>
> [I. iv. 106-13]

Nothing apparent in the scene that precedes this declaration accounts for it—nothing except Romeo's mention that he has had a dream, and Mercutio's interruption of Romeo's telling of it with the long, witty Queen Mab speech. As Norman Holland has said, Mercutio is a character who likes to avoid emotion by talking endlessly [see excerpt above, 1965], and so what we may have in this speech is Romeo's expression of the emotions his dream evoked despite the elaborate diversion of his companion. (p. 129)

Romeo's feelings about his prospective marriage to Juliet conform to his assumption that he will meet an early death. His statement about his love for Juliet inspires a moralistic reply from Friar Laurence, and Romeo insists,

> But come what sorrow can,
> It cannot countervail the exchange of joy
> That one short minute gives me in her sight.
> Do thou but close our hands with holy words,
> Then love-devouring death do what he dare—
> It is enough I may but call her mine.
>
> [II. vi. 3-8]

Strange words from a lusty, youthful bridegroom! Romeo's assumption is that his life is going to be short and that marrying Juliet perfects it before it is cut off, but as we have seen in the earlier statement he predicted his own early death before he met and loved Juliet. (pp. 129-30)

Romeo's reaction to his banishment also presupposes that he is meant for an early death. After killing Tybalt his attitude intensifies, and he becomes active in his pursuit of death, first verbally and then in deed. When the Prince banishes Romeo, Shakespeare makes clear that the youth's reaction of calling banishment death and his total despair at the sentence are strange attitudes in the face of events. But despite the Friar's urgings, Romeo falls down, as he says, "upon the ground, as I do now / Taking the measure of an unmade grave" [III. iii. 69-70].

During this scene Friar Laurence's arguments show that Romeo's reaction to his banishment does not make sense, even when it comes from a young love, who might be partially mad anyway. . . . It is only the presence of the Friar and the Nurse which prevents Romeo's taking his life before the consummation of his marriage to Juliet.

On the morning after the wedding night, Romeo's behavior about being discovered still in Verona fits with his attitudes in general: it is a compound of staginess and assertions about a willingness to die. When Juliet cannot believe that dawn has really come and pleads with him to remain with her, he replies, "Let me be ta'en, let me be put to death. / . . . I have more care to stay than will to go. / Come, death, and welcome! Juliet wills it so" [III. v. 17,23-24]. With a healthy reaction to their predicament, Juliet exclaims "Hie hence, be gone, away!" [III. v. 26].

Similarly, the next time we see Romeo, he is meditating about a dream of his own death and contemplation of the dream gives him pleasure:

> My dreams presage some joyful news at hand. . . .
> I dreamt my lady came and found me dead
> (Strange dream that gives a dead man leave to think!)
> And breathed such life with kisses in my lips
> That I revived and was an emperor.
>
> [V. i. 2, 6-9]

As soon as he hears from Balthasar that Juliet lies in the Capulet tomb, Romeo recalls his thoughts when seeing the apothecary and his shop, where he purchases the fatal dram; we should note that Romeo has had this fantasy *before* he believed that Juliet has died:

> Noting this penury, to myself I said,
> 'An if a man did need a poison now
> Whose sale is present death in Mantua,
> Here lives a caitiff wretch would sell it him.'
> Oh, this same thought did but forerun my need,
> And this same needy man must sell it me.
>
> [V. i. 49-54]

His unwillingness to look into circumstances and his headlong pursuit of suicide demonstrate that his assumptions about his life and death have been made before the immediate events of the play take place.

This sense is sustained when we discover that just as he is about to take poison, he uses the same image of the pilot he had used earlier in the Queen Mab scene: "Come, bitter conduct; come, unsavoury guide! / Thou desperate pilot, now at once run on / The dashing rocks thy seasick weary bark!" [V. iii. 116-18]. The repetition, which has been noted by commentators on *Romeo and Juliet* without attributing a significance to it, suggests that Romeo's suicide fulfills a pattern to which Juliet is both necessary and accidental: if she had not been the inspiration, there would have been some other. This interpretation is plausible for two reasons: first, because Romeo uses the pilot image and speaks of an early death before he has ever met Juliet, and second, because of the headlong speed with which he acts throughout the play, a speed which Juliet and Friar Laurence comment upon but can do little to retard. Romeo's actions therefore seem less choices than compulsions, and we understand the full meaning of the pilot image in his sense of not being able to control his actions as expressed in the Queen Mab scene. It is not fate but his own automatic

response which makes Romeo feel that he cannot control his life (pp. 130-32)

The play shows Romeo as a person who could credibly be self-destructive. Before we see him onstage, he is described by his father as depressed, withdrawn, and seeking dark privacy. . . . Although the play—especially through Mercutio—invites us to see Romeo's depression over his unrequited love for Rosaline as largely comic, his state of mind fits with his other actions so that we may not entirely dismiss it. That is, though we may not take very seriously the love Romeo feels for Rosaline, we may believe that the frustrating relationship feeds a real despair which Romeo feels.

His choice of love objects is also significant in fulfilling his self-ordained destiny: the first is unattainable and the second the daughter of his family's mortal enemy. Both can tend to bring self-destructive consequences; not necessarily, but the probability is high. When he discovers Juliet's identity, Romeo acknowledges this fact: "Is she a Capulet? / O dear account! My life is my foe's debt" [I. v. 117-18]. The commutation of Romeo's sentence by the Prince is a device by which Shakespeare demonstrates that a series of human—all too human—decisions, and not fate or the stars, account for the tragic ends of Romeo, Juliet, and Paris. No sooner has Romeo heard of the Prince's mercy in banishing him than he attempts suicide, as we have seen. In case the audience might be persuaded to sympathize unthinkingly with Romeo's extreme action, Shakespeare provides the Friar and the Nurse to comment on his attitudes. We are also not allowed to believe that his youth is solely responsible for Romeo's suicidal impulses, as Juliet shows none of the tendencies he displays. Although she says several times that she does not want to live without Romeo and determines to kill herself rather than commit bigamy, she hasks Friar Laurence's aid before taking her life, an action which she sees as a last resort. Shakespeare also gives her two important fantasies in which she expresses a healthy fear of death [at IV. 1. 77-8 and IV. iii. 14-58]. Finally she decides to die only a moment before she stabs herself, having been left alone in the tomb by Friar Laurence.

The apothecary too contrasts with Romeo in his attitude toward death. When he tells Romeo that selling poison is a capital offense in Mantua, Romeo can hardly understand his reluctance to risk his life in view of his miserable condition: "Art thou so bare and full of wretchedness / And fearest to die?" [V. i. 68-9]. The apothecary's reasonable fear even in his state sets off Romeo's casual attitude vividly, for neither has the world as his friend; yet the apothecary's hesitation shows the automatic behavior of Romeo for what it is. Thus Romeo's haste in procuring poison after hearing the news from Verona—without consulting Friar Laurence—his meditation about poison earlier, and his headlong rush back to Verona, all bespeak a drive to self-annihilation. What, he would ask us, could Friar Laurence tell him? Everything, we answer, who are privy to the trick of the potion. And, as if all this were not enough, he assures the outcome by killing Paris, an action that might seem necessary because of Romeo's desperate intention and unlawful presence in Verona, but which also conclusively determines his fate as twice a murderer. After this action, Romeo has only to greet death cheerfully. He cannot, Hamlet-like, let Paris administer the fatal blow; rather, like Cleopatra, he must die triumphantly for love. (pp. 132-34)

Although Juliet may be accidental to Romeo's suicide, his relationship to her certainly changes his attitude toward death, as well as the immediate motivation for his suicide. During the time in which he was infatuated with Rosaline, he was, as we have seen, withdrawn into darkness. As soon as he sees Juliet, his whole world lights up, especially at night. . . . [Death] which before might have come as a result of depression now is associated with joy, as in his dream of death in Mantua:

> If I may trust the flattering truth of sleep,
> My dreams presage some joyful news at hand.
> My bosom's lord sits lightly in his throne,
> And all this day an unaccustomed spirit
> Lifts me above the ground with cheerful thoughts.
>
> [V. i. 1-5]

This could be the euphoria of the confirmed suicide who senses that the time to end his life is close, but in Romeo's case it seems to be the result of dreaming of Juliet: "how sweet is love itself possessed" [V. i. 10]. Romeo's life, as he tells Friar Laurence, has been perfected by his relationship with Juliet, who fulfills the ideal on which he doted earlier and also returns his love. His death becomes lying with Juliet and taking the poison is a salute to her: "Here's to my love" [V.iii.119]. His relationship to Juliet forms Romeo's imagination about the state of death: he dreams, we recall, that Juliet revives him with kisses and he is an emperor. It is noticeable that Romeo's identification of love and death and his good spirits begin after his marriage with Juliet is consummated; he does not have these feelings in Friar Laurence's cell after killing Tybalt.

Even if this argument has been convincing, there are two questions which remain to be answered. The first is why Romeo would make such an assumption about his life in the first place. I believe the answer lies in the feud which permeates the existence of virtually all the nobility of Verona. Although the feud has been occasionally been discounted as a real factor in *Romeo and Juliet*, there is evidence that Shakespeare portrays Verona as a city in which violent tempers seethe beneath surface gentility, especially among young men. . . . We are left little doubt that the feud is not only active but a serious problem for the city when Prince Escalus exclaims:

> Three civil brawls, bred of an airy word
> By thee, old Capulet, and Montague,
> Have thrice disturbed the quiet of our streets . . .
> If ever you disturb our streets again,
> Your lives shall pay the forfeit of the peace.
>
> [I. 1. 89-91, 96-7]

As the only male heir to one of the disputant houses, Romeo would live with the risk of an early death. The aggressive Tybalt seeks the opportunity to challenge him for coming to the Capulets' feast and would have disrupted the gathering with another brawl, had not old Capulet's sense of hospitality—and doubtless the warning of the Prince—prevailed. Later when Romeo climbs the wall into the Capulets' orchard, Juliet is fearful that her kinsmen will murder him: "The orchard walls are high and hard to climb / And the place death, considering who thou art, / If any of my kinsmen find thee here" [II. ii. 63-5]. Romeo's self-destructive impulses can easily be understood in the violent atmosphere of his society. The guilt derived from the killing can account for some of the fulfillment Romeo finds in death. His marriage to Juliet gives him the momentary impulse to stop the killing, but when this fails, he becomes a desperate man, as he tells Paris, and he overdetermines his self-execution. (pp. 134-36)

Our second question has to be, "What difference does it make?" What does it matter that Romeo is suicidal? The answer lies in the debate about whether *Romeo and Juliet* is a tragedy of

fate, as implied by both the prologue and the concluding lines of the play, or one in which the lovers are largely responsible for their own destinies. The present interpretation resolves this issue, for it allows us to say that the feud has contributed to Romeo's action in a way that compels his death and thus motivates Juliet's as well. In this reading the lovers *are* responsible for their decisions and actions, though the feud is presumed to have a powerful influence on Romeo.

This approach not only resolves a much debated problem of interpretation of *Romeo and Juliet* but also reveals that the play is less simple than critics have assumed. . . . Romeo can no longer be seen as a simple character motivated by love and crushed by external forces. On the other hand, critics who would make Romeo and Juliet responsible have not convinced their readers, either. Thus, I believe that this reading, which accounts for the feud in its complicated effect on the psyche of Romeo, answers both sides of the long-standing dilemma. The lovers are responsible for their actions, but Romeo's actions have been determined by an early decision for death which he has made apparently as the result of the violence and guilt with which the feud has surrounded him. (pp. 136-37)

> Marilyn L. Williamson, "Romeo and Death," in *Shakespeare Studies: An Annual Gathering of Research, Criticism, and Reviews, Vol. XIV, 1981, pp. 129-37.*

## FREDERICK KIEFER (essay date 1983)

[*Kiefer examines Shakespeare's adaptation in* Romeo and Juliet *of "the Love-Fortune-Death topos" popular during the Middle Ages and the Renaissance, comparing it at several points to Thomas Kyd's personification of this rhetorical pattern in his play* Soliman and Perseda. *He maintains that this "tripartite cluster of symbols is articulated chiefly by the lovers," who consistently view themselves as the helpless victims of these three forces, and he notes how Shakespeare shapes his play by emphasizing the references to Love at the beginning, Fortune at the middle, and Death at the end. Kiefer also asserts that Shakespeare balances the lovers' view of events as fortuitous or accidental with the friar's—and to a lesser extent, the prince's—sense of divine retribution, concluding that neither view is meant to obliterate the other, but that both are juxtaposed. Therefore, the critic proclaims, Shakespeare in this play recognizes both the protagonists' responsibility for the tragic events and "the awesome power of hostile circumstance."*]

The tragedy of love, pioneered by Wilmot and further developed by Kyd [in his *Soliman and Perseda*], reached an apotheosis of sorts in *Romeo and Juliet*. . . . Shakespeare conveys, as no English dramatist had before, the intensity of youthful passion. Through the language, the pace of the action, and the sheer attractiveness of the lovers, he engages the audience immediately and powerfully. At the same time, however, Shakespeare applies conventions which impose a pattern upon the violent, brawling story. As Nicholas Brooke observes, *Romeo and Juliet* "in many ways seems to be a formal exercise in romantic tragedy, given the kind of overt formality of structure and verse which rather suggests the order of a stately dance" [see excerpt above, 1965]. This formal quality, achieved in *Soliman and Perseda* by the chorus, is created here in part by Shakespeare's adoption of the Love-Fortune-Death topos.

Love, Fortune, and Death do not, of course, take the form of actual characters in *Romeo and Juliet*: they are refined into a sophisticated imagistic motif. Frequently on the minds and lips of the characters, the three are variously invoked, petitioned, and decried. References to each personification, however, instead of appearing consistently throughout Shakespeare's plays, are clustered at those points where they are most appropriate to the mood and the dramatic action.

Cupid, or Love, figures most prominently in the first two acts, in which are dramatized Romeo's infatuation with Rosaline, his meeting with Juliet, and their falling in love. These are not merely fleeting references but detailed allusions that have an almost pictorial quality. In the first scene, for instance, Romeo envisages the weapons of Cupid when he says of Rosaline:

> she'll not be hit
> With Cupid's arrow, she hath Dian's wit;
> And in strong proof of chastity well arm'd,
> From Love's weak childish bow she lives uncharm'd.
>
> [I. i. 208-11]

Benvolio too calls to mind the accouterments found in iconographic representations of Cupid when he remarks comically, "We'll have no Cupid hoodwink'd with a scarf, / Bearing a Tartar's painted bow of lath, / Scaring the ladies like a cowkeeper" [I. iv. 4-6]. Mercutio mentions still another feature of Cupid's appearance when he bids Romeo "borrow Cupid's wings, / And soar with them above a common bound" [I. iv. 17-18]. . . . Juliet envisions both Cupid and Venus in vivid terms when she contemplates her wedding night:

> Love's heralds should be thoughts,
> Which ten times faster glides than the sun's beams,
> Driving back shadows over low'ring hills;
> Therefore do nimble-pinion'd doves draw Love,
> And therefore hath the wind-swift Cupid wings.
>
> [II. v. 4-8]

Collectively, these evocations of Cupid's (and Venus') appearance build up an elaborate mental image of the force that Kyd had personified and placed on state in *Soliman and Perseda*.

Toward the end of the second act, Love gives way to Fortune in prominence. The references are not so elaborate or numerous as those to Cupid, but they appear at important turning points of the story. For example, when Romeo kills Tybalt and thereby precipitates his banishment from Verona, he cries, "O, I am fortune's fool!" [III. i. 136]. And at the lovers' parting, Juliet entreats the favor of Fortune:

> O Fortune, Fortune, all men call thee fickle;
> If thou are fickle, what dost thou with him
> That is renowm'd for faith? Be fickle, Fortune:
> For then I hope thou wilt not keep him long,
> But send him back.
>
> [III. v. 60-4]

Chance continues to play a major role in the remainder of the drama, as Friar John is detained by quarantine, Romeo meets Paris at the tomb, Friar Lawrence arrives late at the tomb, and Juliet fails to awaken until Romeo is already dead. References to hap, accident, adventure, and mischance abound. Explicit mention of Fortune, however, is confined chiefly to the middle act of the play where she looms largest in the minds of the lovers.

The third member of the trio, although not entirely absent earlier in the play, predominates in the latter part of *Romeo and Juliet*. There, as the lovers' happiness is thwarted, Death assumes ever more authority. Juliet anticipates Death's victories when, after Tybalt's death, she says, "Come, cords,

come, nurse, I'll to my wedding-bed, / And death, not Romeo, take my maidenhead!" [III. ii. 136-37]. Later Romeo entreats Death too: "Come, death, and welcome! Juliet wills it so" [III. v. 24]. A more elaborate evocation of Death is that spoken by Capulet. Witnessing the effect of the potion upon his daughter, he says, "Death lies on her like an untimely frost / Upon the sweetest flower of all the field" [IV. v. 28-9]. And, turning to Paris, he adds,

> O son, the night before thy wedding-day
> Hath Death lain with thy wife. There she lies,
> Flower as she was, deflowered by him.
>
> [IV. v. 35-7].

The references to Death multiply as Romeo and Juliet approach their end. At the tomb Romeo conjures up the image of Death when he addresses his wife's form, "Death, that hath suck'd the honey of thy breath, / Hath had no power yet upon thy beauty" [V. iii. 92-3], and when he asks,

> Shall I believe
> That unsubstantial Death is amorous,
> And that the lean abhorred monster keeps
> Thee here in dark to be his paramour?
>
> [V. iii. 102-05]

Such allusions, in the aggregate, paint a vivid picture of Death, the lover and destroyer.

The inspiration for Shakespeare's personification of Love, Fortune, and Death may have come from his chief source, Arthur Brooke's *Tragicall Historye of Romeus and Juliet . . .* , itself an adaptation of Continental novelle. But it seems unlikely that Brooke alone prompted the poetic rendering of Love, Fortune, and Death in the play, for although he personifies all three in the poem, one of these predominates. Brooke creates a Dame Fortune whose hegemony over human affairs is unchallenged and whose authority is recognized by all of her subjects. Shakespeare, however, does not emulate Brooke's example; some figures in *Romeo and Juliet* acknowledge Fortune's sovereignty while others do not. Moreover, Shakespeare confines explicit reference to Fortune principally to the middle section of the play. He thus greatly diminishes the prominence enjoyed by Fortune in *Romeus and Juliet*. At the same time, he increases the prominence of Love and Death, who in Brooke's poem receive scant attention. As a consequence of these modifications, Love, Fortune, and Death attain a roughly co-equal status.

In his diminution of Brooke's omnipresent Fortune and in his enlargement of Love and Death, Shakespeare may well have been influenced by the chorus in *Soliman and Perseda*. . . . It is, however, also possible that, like Kyd, Shakespeare was inspired not merely by a single work but by the larger literary and iconographic tradition which had long given representation to Love, Fortune, and Death.

One of the most impressive contributions to that tradition is *La Danse aux aveugles,* a poem by Pierre Michault which recounts a man's journey through a series of gardens wherein Love, Fortune, and Death preside. A fifteenth-century manuscript of Michault's work contains an illumination that bears an interesting imagistic parallel to Shakespeare's play. The design presents a landscape which the viewer sees through three arches, connected one to another. In the compartment formed by the arch on the left, Cupid holds his bow and arrow; in the center, Fortune sits besides her turning wheel; and, on the right, Death rides his ox and brandishes his spear. In this portrayal the artist has sought to depict the essential narrative structure of the poem—the itinerary of the protagonist as he moves through a series of gardens. The poem and painting have, in addition, a more universal application, for they express the history of anyone who experiences love, adversity, and finally death. Indeed, the progress of Romeo and Juliet, as they move from the felicity of courtship to disastrous mischance and thence to their demise, may be said to match that of Michault's protagonist. In his tragedy Shakespeare, of course, paints no literal picture. But by clustering the references to Love, Fortune, and Death successively at the beginning, middle, and end of the play, he establishes an imagistic background against which the lovers move. In a sense, then, Shakespeare creates the dramatic counterpart of a triptych. And by so doing he subordinates the unruly phenomena of passion, accident, and sudden death to a formal pattern, familiar and explicable.

This is not to say that the triptych dominates the play in the same way as the chorus in *Soliman and Perseda*, for Shakespeare's tripartite cluster of symbols is articulated chiefly by the lovers. Other characters see other forces at work. Thus instead of perceiving the hand of Love, Fortune, or Death in what befalls the lovers, the Friar and the Prince offer a more orthodox explanation. The Friar may, like the lovers, experience accident, chance, coincidence. He may even perceive in these phenomena evidence of divine intervention; at the tomb he says, "A greater power than we can contradict / Hath thwarted our intents" [V. iii. 153-54]. However, the Friar—although speaking at one point of "unhappy fortune" (in the sense of "condition")—by his references to heaven attests to his faith in the Christian deity. If Romeo and Juliet believe their travail to be undeserved, Friar Lawrence regards adversity as the fate of the heedless. If they are bewildered by their experience and look outward for some explanation, he looks inward to discern the connection between human wrongdoing and divine displeasure. . . . Similarly, at the conclusion of the play, the Prince gives support to the notion of providential design when he tells the feuding families: "Capulet! Montague! / See what a scourge is laid upon your hate, / That heaven finds means to kill your joys with love" [V. iii. 291-93]. Through the character of the Friar and, to a lesser extent, the Prince, *Romeo and Juliet* is touched, if only lightly, by the moralism that dominates [Robert Wilmont's] *Gismond of Salerne*. Interestingly, it is Shakespeare who emphasizes the retributive element of the story; Brooke, despite the harsh tone of his Preface, portrays the lovers in a very sympathetic manner.

How are we to reconcile the viewpoint of the lovers with that of the authority figures? H. B. Charlton suggests, in effect, that we discount the latter: "the whole universe of God's justice, vengeance and providence is discarded and rejected from the directing forces of the play's dramatic movement. In its place, there is a theatrical resuscitation of the half-barbarian, half-Roman deities of Fate and Fortune" [see excerpt above, 1948]. Franklin M. Dickey, by contrast, would subordinate the vision of the lovers to that of the Friar and the Prince: "In *Romeo and Juliet* . . . fortune may be considered not the prime mover but the agent of a higher power [see excerpt above, 1959] . . . Neither of these interpretations, on reflection, seems very satisfactory. Romeo and Juliet go to their deaths convinced that they are the victims of a cruel world. Their suicides scarcely betoken faith in divine plan. Nor do the authority figures, for their part, claim that Fortune serves providence; they are in fact silent about Dame Fortune. What Shakespeare does is neither to assign Fortune the role of executrix (as Dickey suggests) nor to banish providence from the play (Charlton). The

playwright chooses a less rigid course. He allows the lovers to express an outlook appropriate to their youth, inexperience, and passion; in their world, as they see it, Dame Fortune wields great power. At the same time, the Friar and the Prince express a view consistent with their age, wisdom, and social station. Their assertion of providential design does not obliterate the lovers' view; nor does the lovers' obliterate theirs. The two are juxtaposed.

By allowing the characters to conceive of their milieu in sharply individualized fashion, Shakespeare creates a dramatic world of much greater complexity than that envisioned by his predecessors. Such complexity would probably have been impossible had Shakespeare emulated Kyd and imposed upon the play a chorus consisting of machinators. The author of *Soliman and Perseda* . . . seeks to create a world in which the lovers are doomed to stumble from crisis to crisis. By contrast, Shakespeare fashions characters who possess a far larger measure of autonomy. He affirms their power of choice and their accountability for their actions. Such a dramatist would naturally find the personified characters less useful than Kyd, for the direct, explicit authority exercised by Love, Fortune, and Death would necessarily undercut the independence of the human characters. And Shakespeare does not envision Romeo and Juliet merely as helpless victims of a cosmic game. At the same time, he recognizes the awesome power of hostile circumstance, for he portrays with sensitivity the lovers who believe themselves to be the victims of Love, Fortune, and Death. By combining at once the lovers' lamentations and the Friar's admonitions, Shakespeare strikes a balance between individual responsibility and external compulsion.

Shakespeare's Love, Fortune, and Death may lack the intrinsic interest of Kyd's choral figures, who exert an immediate appeal by virtue of their physical presence and contentiousness. But the personifications of *Romeo and Juliet* ably serve the artistic purposes of the dramatist. After all, for Shakespeare the topos is less a means of achieving striking theatrical effect than of creating a richly varied dramatic texture. And as expressions of the characters' attitudes and personalities, Love, Fortune, and Death effectively suggest the diversity of human experience; by making implicit what Kyd renders explicitly, Shakespeare conveys the lovers' sense of doom without requiring the audience to accept Love, Fortune, and Death as the sole arbiters of human destiny. Shakespeare's treatment of the topos also permits a more subtle delineation of Love, Fortune, and Death themselves. For if he gives them a less concrete form than does his predecessor, Shakespeare nevertheless preserves something that Kyd, by his theatricality, sacrifices: the essential mystery of the forces personified. (pp. 176-82)

> *Frederick Kiefer, "The Tragedy of Love," in his* Fortune and Elizabethan Tragedy, *The Huntington Library, 1983, pp. 158-92.*

## NORTHROP FRYE (essay date 1986)

[*Frye is considered one of the most important critics of the twentieth century and a leader of the anthropological or mythic approach to literature which gained prominence during the 1950s. As outlined in his seminal work* An Anatomy of Criticism (1957), *Frye views all literature as ultimately derived from certain myths or archetypes present in all cultures, and he therefore sees literary criticism as an unusual type of science in which the literary critic seeks only to decode the mythic structure inherent in a work of art. Frye's intention is to formulate a method of literary interpretation more universal and exact than that suggested in other critical approaches, such as New Criticism, biographical criticism, or historical criticism—all of which he finds valuable, but also limited in application. As a Shakespearean critic, Frye has made his greatest contribution in the area of the comedies and romances, especially with his definition of the three main phases of Shakespearean comic and romantic structure: the initial phase of "the anticomic society," "the phase of temporarily lost identity," and the establishment of a "new society" or "deliverance" through either marriage or self-knowledge. In his comments on* Romeo and Juliet, *Frye discusses the play's adaptation of the Courtly Love tradition popular during the Middle Ages, claiming that it depicts three forms of the convention: first, "the orthodox Petrarchan convention in Romeo's professed love for Rosaline"; second, the more serious love between the hero and heroine, "for which the only honourable resolution was marriage"; and third, Mercutio's and the Nurse's "more cynical and ribald perspective." The critic also notes how Shakespeare dramatizes through the language of the lovers the love-death or* Liebestod *motif central to the tragedy, and he postulates near the end of his essay on the continuing debate over* Romeo and Juliet's *tragic design. Frye concludes that although the tragedy would not exist without the feud, there is something not accounted for in this strict, causal reading—namely, the "greater mysteries in things" necessary to the tragic spirit. He finds this sense in the image of the lovers as sacrificial victims, who in their quest for an ideal love demonstrate the maxim that "nothing that breaks through the barriers of ordinary experience can remain in the world of ordinary experience."*]

*Romeo and Juliet* is a love story, but in Shakespeare's day love included many complex rituals. Early in the Middle Ages a cult had developed called Courtly Love, which focussed on a curious etiquette that became a kind of parody of Christian experience. Someone might be going about his business, congratulating himself on not being caught in the trap of a love affair, when suddenly the God of Love, Eros or Cupid, angry at being left out of things, forces him to fall in love with a woman. The falling in love is involuntary and instantaneous, no more "romantic," in the usual sense, then getting shot with a bullet. It's never gradual: "Who ever loved that loved not at first sight?" says Marlowe, in a line that Shakespeare quotes in *As You Like It*. From that time on, the lover is a slave of the God of Love, whose will is embodied in his mistress, and he is bound to do whatever she wants.

This cult of love was not originally linked to marriage. Marriage was a relationship in which the man had all the effective authority, even if his wife was (as she usually was) his social equal. The conventional role of the Courtly Love mistress was to be proud, disdainful and "cruel," repelling all advances from her lover. The frustration this caused drove the lover into poetry, and the theme of the poetry was the cruelty of the mistress and the despair and supplications of the lover. It's good psychology that a creative impulse to write poetry can arise from sexual frustration, and Elizabethan poets almost invariably were or pretended to be submerged in unhappy love, and writing for that reason.

Back in the thirteenth century, we have Dante, whose life was totally changed by seeing Beatrice at her father's home when he was nine years old. He devoted the rest of his life to her, even though he survived her by many years. But he had no further relations with her, certainly no sexual relations, and his devotion to her had nothing to do with his marrying someone else and fathering four children. His successor in poetry was Petrarch, whose mistress, also out of reach, was Laura, and it was Petrarch who popularized the convention in sixteenth-century England. In the 1590s, when the vogue was at its height, enormous piles of sonnets more or less imitating Petrarch were

being written. By Shakespeare's time the convention had become more middle-class, was much more frequently linked to eventual marriage, and the more overtly sexual aspects of such relationships were more fully explored. So "love" in *Romeo and Juliet* covers three different forms of a convention. First, the orthodox Petrarchan convention in Romeo's professed love for Rosaline at the beginning of the play. Second, the less sublimated love for which the only honourable resolution was marriage, represented by the main theme of the play. Third, the more cynical and ribald perspective that we get in Mercutio's comments, and perhaps those of the Nurse as well.

On the principle that life imitates art, Romeo has thrown himself, before the play begins, into a love affair with someone called Rosaline, whom we never see (except that she was at Capulet's party, where she must have wondered painfully what had happened to Romeo), and who tried to live up to the proud and disdainful role that the convention required. So Romeo made the conventional responses: he went around with his clothes untidy, hardly heard what was said to him, wrote poetry, talked endlessly about the cruelty of his mistress, wept and kept "adding to clouds more clouds with his deep sighs" [I. i. 133]. In short, he was afflicted with love melancholy, and we remember that melancholy in Shakespeare's time was a physical as well as an emotional disturbance. More simply, he was something of a mooning bore, his love affair a kind of pedantry, like Tybalt's fighting by the book of arithmetic. Juliet, to her disgust, is compelled to adopt some of the same coy and aloof attitude in her edgy dialogue with Paris in Friar Laurence's cell.

It's obvious that there was no sexual relationship between Romeo and Rosaline, a fact that would have disappointed Mercutio, who takes it for granted that Romeo has spent the night of what we now call the "balcony scene" in Rosaline's arms. Romeo enters the play practically unconscious that he has walked in on the aftermath of a dangerous brawl, and then starts explaining to Benvolio how firm and unyielding his attachment to Rosaline is, even though Rosaline, playing along as best she could, has told him that she has sworn to "live chaste." The dialogue between Romeo and Benvolio seems to us a curiously long one, for the amount said in it, but it's essential to round out the situation Romeo has put himself in.

I said that the Courtly Love convention used an elaborate and detailed parody, or counterpart, of the language of religion. The mistress was a "saint"; the "god" supplicated with so many prayers and tears was Eros or Cupid, the God of Love; "atheists" were people who didn't believe in the convention; and "heretics" were those who didn't keep to the rules. Benvolio suggests that Romeo might get Rosaline into better perspective if he'd compare her with a few other young women, and Romeo answers:

> When the devout religion of mine eye
> Maintains such falsehood, then turn tears to fires;
> And these, who, often drowned, could never die,
> Transparent heretics, be burnt for liars! . . .
>
> [I. ii. 88-91]

However, Romeo takes Benvolio's advice, goes to the Capulet party, sees Juliet, and the "real thing" hits him. Of course, the "real thing" is as much a convention, at least within the framework of the play, as its predecessor, but its effects on both Romeo and Juliet are very different. (pp. 19-22)

[Concerning] the effects of love on the two main characters, the most dramatic change is in their command of language.

*Act V. Scene iii. Friar Lawrence, Romeo, Juliet, and Paris. By James Northcote. The Department of Rare Books and Special Collections, The University of Michigan Library.*

Before she sees Romeo we hear Juliet making proper-young-lady noises like, "It is an honour that I dream not of" [I. iii. 66] ("it" being her marriage to Paris). After she sees Romeo, she's talking like this:

> Gallop apace, you fiery-footed steeds,
> Towards Phoebus' lodging! Such a wagoner
> As Phaëton would whip you to the west
> And bring in cloudy night immediately.
>
> [III. ii. 1-4]

It appears that Juliet, for all her tender years and sheltered life, has had a considerably better education than simply a technical training to be a wife and mother. The point is that it would never have occurred to her to make use of her education in her speech in the way she does here without the stimulus of her love.

As for Romeo, when we first meet him he's at the stage where he hardly knows what he's saying until he hears himself saying it. We don't hear any of the poetry he wrote about Rosaline (unless the "religion of mine eye" lyric I quoted from a moment ago belongs to it), and something tells us that we could do without most of it. But after he meets Juliet he turns out, to Mercutio's astonishment and delight, to be full of wit and repartee. "Now art thou what thou art, by art as well as by

nature" [II. iv. 90-1], Mercutio says, and even Mercutio knows nothing of the miraculous duets with Juliet in the great "balcony scene" and its successor. When he visits Friar Laurence, the Friar sees him approaching and feels rather apprehensive, thinking, "Oh no, not Rosaline again," and is considerably startled to hear Romeo saying, in effect, "Who's Rosaline?" More important, especially after Juliet also visits him, he realizes that two young people he has previously thought of as rather nice children have suddenly turned into adults, and are speaking with adult authority. He is bound to respect this, and besides, he sees an excellent chance of ending the feud by marrying them and presenting their furious parents with a *fait accompli*.

After disaster strikes with the death of Tybalt and the Prince's edict of banishment, we get very long speeches from both the lovers and from Friar Laurence. The rationale of the Friar's speech is simple enough: Romeo thinks of suicide, and the Friar immediately delivers an involved summary of his situation, trying to show that he could be a lot worse off. The speech is organized on lines of formal rhetoric, and is built up in a series of triads. The point of the length of the speech is its irony: the Friar is steadily adding to Romeo's despair while he is giving reasons why he should cool it. With Romeo and Juliet, the reason for the loosening of rhetorical control is subtler. Take Juliet:

Hath Romeo slain himself? Say thou but "I,"
And that bare vowel "I" shall poison more
Than the death-darting eye of cockatrice.
I am not I, if there be such an "I"
Or those eyes' shot that makes the answer "I."

[III. ii. 45-9]

It all turns on puns, of course, on "I," "Ay" (meaning yes,
and often spelled "I" at the time), and "eye." But she's not
"playing" with words: she's shredding them to bits in an agony
of frustration and despair. The powerful explosion of words
has nowhere to go, and simply disintegrates. Some critics will
tell you that this is *Shakespeare* being immature and uncertain
of his verbal powers, because, after looking up the probable
dates, they find it's an "early play." Don't believe them. It
is true that the earlier plays depend on formal rhetorical figures
much more than the later ones: it doesn't follow that the use
of such figures is immature. (pp. 24-6)

It is through the language, and the imagery the language uses,
that we understand how the *Liebestod* of Romeo and Juliet,
their great love and their tragic death, are bound up together
as two aspects of the same thing. . . . Soon after Romeo comes
in, we hear him talking like this:

Here's much to do with hate, but more with love.
Why then, O brawling love! O loving hate!
O anything, of nothing first create!

[I. i. 175-77]

The figure he is using is the oxymoron or paradoxical union
of opposites: obviously the right kind of figure for this play,
though Romeo is still in his Rosaline trance and is not being
very cogent. From there we go on to Friar Laurence's wonderfully concentrated image of

fire and powder
Which, as they kiss, consume,

[II. vi. 10-11]

with its half-concealed pun on "consummation," and to Juliet's

Too like the lightning, which doth cease to be
Ere one can say it lightens.

[II. ii. 119-20]

suggesting that their first glimpse of one another determined
their deaths as well as their love.

The love-death identity of contrasts expands into the imagery
of day and night. The great love scenes begin with Juliet hanging upon the cheek of night and end with the macabre horrors
of the Capulet tomb, where we reluctantly can't believe Romeo
when he says:

For here lies Juliet, and her beauty makes
This vault a feasting presence full of light.

[V. iii. 85-6]

The character who makes the most impressive entrances in the
play is a character we never see, the sun. The sun is greeted
by Friar Laurence as the sober light that does away with the
drunken darkness, but the Friar is speaking out of his own
temperament, and there are many other aspects of the light and
dark contrast. In the dialogue of Romeo and Juliet, the bird of
darkness, the nightingale, symbolizes the desire of the lovers
to remain with each other, and the bird of dawn, the lark, the
need to preserve their safety. When the sun rises, "The day
is hot, the Capulets abroad" [III. i. 2], and the energy of youth

and love wears itself out in scrambling over the blockades of
reality.

The light and dark imagery comes into powerful focus with
Mercutio's speech on Queen Mab. Queen Mab, Mercutio tells
us, is the instigator of dreams, and Mercutio takes what we
would call a very Freudian approach to dreams: they are primarily wish-fulfilment fantasies.

And in this state she gallops night by night
Through lovers' brains, and then they dream of love.

[I. iv. 70-1]

But such dreams are an inseparable mixture of illusion and a
reality profounder than the ordinary realities of the day. When
we wake we carry into the daylight world, without realizing
it, the feelings engendered by the dream, the irrational and
absurd conviction that the world as we want it to be has its
own reality, and perhaps is what could be there instead. Both
the lovers carry on an inner debate in which one voice tells
them that they are embarking on a dangerous illusion, and
another says that they must embark on it anyway whatever the
dangers, because by doing so they are martyrs, or witnesses,
to an order of things that matters more than the sunlit reality.
Romeo says:

O blessèd, blessèd night! I am afeard,
Being in night, all this is but a dream,
Too flattering-sweet to be substantial.

[II. ii. 139-41]

Perhaps so, but so much the worse for the substantial, as far
as Romeo's actions are concerned.

Who or what is responsible for a tragedy that kills half a dozen
people, at least four of them young and very attractive people?
The feud, of course, but in this play there doesn't seem to be
the clearly marked villain that we find in so many tragedies.
We can point to Iago in *Othello* and say that if it hadn't been
for that awful man there'd have been no tragedy at all. But
the harried and conscientious Prince, the kindly and pious Friar
Laurence, the quite likable old buffer Capulet: these are a long
way from being villainous. Tybalt comes closest, but Tybalt
is a villain only by virtue of his position in the plot. According
to his own code—admittedly a code open to criticism—he is
a man of honour, and there is no reason to suppose him capable
of the kind of malice or treachery that we find in Iago or in
Edmund in *King Lear*. He may not even be inherently more
quarrelsome or spoiling for a fight than Mercutio. Juliet seems
to like him, if not as devoted to his memory as her parents
think. Setting Tybalt aside, there is still some mystery about
the fact that so bloody a mess comes out of the actions of what
seem to be, taken one by one, a fairly decent lot of human
beings. (pp. 26-8)

The question of the source of the tragic action is bound up
with another question: why is the story of the tragic love and
death of Romeo and Juliet one of the world's best-loved stories?
Mainly, we think, because of Shakespeare's word magic. . . .
There's something about the story itself that can take any amount
of mistreatment from stupid producing and bad casting. I've
seen a performance with a middle-aged and corseted Juliet who
could have thrown Romeo over her shoulder and walked to
Mantua with him, and yet the audience was in tears at the end.
The original writer is not the writer who thinks up a new story—
there aren't any new stories, really—but the writer who tells
one of the world's great stories in a new way. (p. 29)

In this play we often hear about a kind of fatality at work in the action, usually linked with the stars. As early as the Prologue we hear about "star-crossed lovers" [Prologue, 6], and Romeo speaks, not of the feud, but of "some consequence still hanging in the stars" when he feels a portent of disaster. Astrology . . . was taken quite seriously then, but here it seems only part of a network of unlucky timing that's working against the lovers. Romeo gets to see Juliet because of the sheer chance that the Capulet servant sent out to deliver the invitations to the party can't read, and comes to him for help. There's the letter from Friar Laurence in Verona to Friar John in Mantua, which by accident doesn't get to him, and another hitch in timing destroys Friar Laurence's elaborate plan that starts with Juliet's sleeping potion. If we feel that Friar Laurence is being meddlesome in interfering in the action as he does, that's partly because he's in a tragedy and his schemes are bound to fail. In *Much Ado about Nothing* there's also a friar with a very similar scheme for the heroine of that play, but his scheme is successful because the play he's in is a comedy.

But when we have a quite reasonable explanation for the tragedy, the feud between the families, why do we need to bring in the stars and such? The Prologue, even before the play starts, suggests that the feud demands lives to feed on, and sooner or later will get them:

And the continuance of their parents' rage,
Which, but their children's end, nought could remove.
[Prologue, 10-11]

The answer, or part of the answer, begins with the fact that we shouldn't assume that tragedy is something needing an explanation. Tragedy represents something bigger in the total scheme of things than all possible explanations combined. All we can say—and it's a good deal—is that there'd have been no tragedy without the feud. (pp. 30-1)

Tragedy always has an ironic side, and that means that the audience usually knows more about what's happening or going to happen than the characters do. But tragedy also has a heroic side, and again the audience usually sees that more clearly than the characters. Juliet's parents don't really know who Juliet is: we're the ones who have a rather better idea. Notice Capulet's phrase, "Poor sacrifices of our enmity!" [V. iii. 304]. Romeo and Juliet are sacrificial victims, and the ancient rule about sacrifice was that the victim had to be perfect and without blemish. The core of reality in this was the sense that nothing perfect or without blemish can stay that way in this world, and should be offered up to another world before it deteriorates. That principle belongs to a still larger one: nothing that breaks through the barriers of ordinary experience can remain in the world of ordinary experience. One of the first things Romeo says of Juliet is: "Beauty too rich for use, for earth too dear!" [I. v. 47]. But more than beauty is involved: their kind of passion would soon burn up the world of heavy fathers and snarling Tybalts and gabby Nurses if it stayed there. Our perception of this helps us to accept the play as a whole, instead of feeling only that a great love went wrong. It didn't go wrong: it went only where it could, out. It always was, as we say, out of this world.

That's why the tragedy is not exhausted by pointing to its obvious cause in the feud. We need suggestions of greater mysteries in things: we need the yoke of inauspicious stars and the vision of Queen Mab and her midget team riding across the earth like the apocalyptic horsemen. These things don't explain anything, but they help to light up the heroic vision in

tragedy, which we see so briefly before it goes. It takes the greatest rhetoric of the greatest poets to bring us a vision of the tragic heroic, and such rhetoric doesn't make us miserable but exhilarated, not crushed but enlarged in spirit. (pp. 32-3)

> *Northrop Frye, "'Romeo and Juliet'," in his* Northrop Frye on Shakespeare, *edited by Robert Sandler, Yale University Press, 1986, pp. 15-33.*

---

## ADDITIONAL BIBLIOGRAPHY

Allen, N. B. "*Romeo and Juliet* Further Restored." *Modern Language Notes* LIV, No. 2 (February 1939): 85-92.
> Emphasizes the potential dangers of using Q1 as an authoritative text of *Romeo and Juliet*. Allen contends that the First Quarto "should be resorted to only when Q2 . . . is unintelligible," and not when a Q1 reading is "slightly smoother metrically or because we like it better."

Baldwin, T. W. "*Romeo and Juliet*." In his *Shakspere's Five-Act Structure: Shakspere's Early Plays on the Background of Renaissance Theories of Five-Act Structure from 1470*, pp. 742-48. Urbana: The University of Illinois Press, 1947.
> Argues that, because of its five-act structure, *Romeo and Juliet* demonstrates that Shakespeare was well aware of classical tragic form. Baldwin notes that Shakespeare's play, like Terence's models, follows a three-part movement over five acts: Acts I and II develop what he calls the *protasis*; Acts III and IV depict the *epitasis*; and Act V establishes the *catastrophe* and the end of the drama.

Bergeron, David M. "Sickness in *Romeo and Juliet*." *CLA Journal* XX, No. 1 (March 1977): 356-64.
> A detailed analysis of the imagery of sickness, disease, and remedy in *Romeo and Juliet* and how it contributes to the tragic structure of the play.

Berman, Ronald. "The Two Orders of *Romeo and Juliet*." *Moderna Sprak* LXIV, No. 3 (1970): 244-52.
> An act-by-act summary of the manner in which Shakespeare uses imagery of the heavens to suggest the two orders of reality depicted in *Romeo and Juliet*: "the human scene . . . shadowed against an immense and unyielding cosmic backdrop." Berman calls *Romeo and Juliet* "an existential tragedy," in that "it persists in comparing the permanence of the cosmic world with the temporality of the human world."

Bond, Ronald B. "Love and Lust in *Romeo and Juliet*." *Wascana Review* 15, No. 2 (Fall 1980): 22-31.
> Asserts that the process of Romeo and Juliet's love follows the pattern of the *gradus amoris*, "the steps toward illicit love which involve a succession of senses." According to Bond, the lovers never achieve that transcendent passion many critics have maintained they do, but remain "rapturously devoted to the flesh."

Bonnard, Georges A. "*Romeo and Juliet*: A Possible Significance?" *The Review of English Studies* n.s. II, No. 8 (October 1951): 319-27.
> Focuses on Shakespeare's major changes of Brooke's *Romeus and Juliet*, arguing that the dramatist undertook these alterations in order "to endow his play with some significance, . . . to give it, if possible, the dignity of true tragedy." These changes, according to Bonnard, transformed *Romeo and Juliet* into a play based on the eternal conflict between love and hate.

Bowling, Lawrence Edward. "The Thematic Framework of *Romeo and Juliet*." *PMLA* LXIV, No. 1 (March 1949): 208-20.
> Maintains that the central, unifying theme in *Romeo and Juliet* is that of the "wholeness and complexity of things, in contrast with a partial and simple view." Bowling identifies this theme in the wisdom of Friar Lawrence, in the gradual maturation of the characters, and in Shakespeare's numerous use of puns in the play, which demonstrates that even words possess multiple layers of meaning.

Brodwin, Leonora Leet. "The Classic Pattern of Courtly Love Tragedy: *Romeo and Juliet*." In her *Elizabethan Love Tragedy: 1587-1625*, pp. 44-64. New York: New York University Press, 1971.
Discusses generally the courtly love tradition in Elizabethan tragedy, then examines Shakespeare's adaptation of this convention in *Romeo and Juliet*, offering an act-by-act account of the ways in which the lovers both follow and qualify the standard attitudes of protagonists in courtly love tragedies.

Bulgin, Randolph M. "Dramatic Imagery in Shakespeare: *Romeo and Juliet*." *Shenandoah* XI, No. 1 (Autumn 1959): 23-38.
Examines the imagery in *Romeo and Juliet* and demonstrates how it both satisfies and fails to satisfy, at various points in the play, the "two great tests of imagery in drama"—namely, "economy of statement" and "a relation to the dramatic whole."

Bullough, Geoffrey. "*Romeo and Juliet*: Introduction." In *Narrative and Dramatic Sources of Shakespeare, Vol. I: Early Comedies, Poems, "Romeo and Juliet*," edited by Geoffrey Bullough, pp. 269-83. London: Routledge and Kegan Paul, 1957.
A comprehensive discussion of the sources for Shakespeare's *Romeo and Juliet*. Bullough also offers a reprinting of Arthur Brooke's *The Tragicall Historye of Romeus and Juliet*.

Cain, H. Edward. "*Romeo and Juliet*: A Reinterpretation." *Shakespeare Association Bulletin* XXII, No. 4 (October 1947): 163-92.
Reviews the sixteenth-century writings on human passion by Sir Thomas More, Pierre de la Primaudaye, Edmund Spenser, and Arthur Brooke—in his *Romeus and Juliet*—and contends that Shakespeare's *Romeo and Juliet* is "a study of the passion of anger" written from a Christian perspective.

Carroll, William C. "'We were born to die': *Romeo and Juliet*." *Comparative Drama* 15, No. 1 (Spring 1981): 54-71.
Asserts that *Romeo and Juliet* dramatizes the idea of the medieval morality plays that life is a pilgrimage or journey whose end "determines the shape of the journey itself." According to Carroll, "Shakespeare investigates this teleological puzzle in which the lovers' foreknown end colors the nature of their journey, continually darkening our belief in their potential and actual happiness." The critic also regards as emblematic the three scenes in which Romeo and Juliet appear alone—the two balcony scenes and the final tomb scene—and claims that these are meant to symbolize the "Three Ages of Man": courtship, sexual completion, and death.

Chang, Joseph S. M. J. "The Language of Paradox in *Romeo and Juliet*." *Shakespeare Studies* III (1967): 22-42.
Contends that the instances of Petrarchan polarities and oxymora in *Romeo and Juliet* are indications of Shakespeare's thematic concern in the play, namely, "the irreconcilable oppositions of love, or, indeed, of life itself."

Chapman, Raymond. "Double Time in *Romeo and Juliet*." *The Modern Language Review* XLIV, No. 3 (July 1949): 372-74.
Examines Shakespeare's use of "double time" in *Romeo and Juliet*. Chapman argues that beneath the very specific presentation of time in the play there are "suggestions of a longer time."

Charlton, H. B. *"Romeo and Juliet" as an Experimental Tragedy*. London: The British Academy, 1939, 45 p.
A more diverse and comprehensive treatment of his essay later published in his *Shakespearian Tragedy* (see excerpt above, 1948). Charlton discusses the Elizabethan concept of tragic drama and the various versions of the Romeo and Juliet story, then offers his theory why Shakespeare's play fails according to the tragic pattern it seeks to develop.

Cox, Marjorie Kolb. "Adolescent Processes in *Romeo and Juliet*." *The Psychoanalytic Review* 63, No. 3 (Fall 1976): 379-92.
Revises M. D. Faber's reading of *Romeo and Juliet* (see excerpt above, 1972) and claims that Shakespeare's work is a tragedy of adolescence, in which both the young and the older generation of authority fail to deal constructively with the coming of age of the characters.

Craig, Hardin. "The Beginnings: *Romeo and Juliet*." In his *An Interpretation of Shakespeare*, pp. 41-6. New York: The Citadel Press, 1948.
Refers to *Romeo and Juliet* as a tragedy of youth, in that it demonstrates "the wrongs that guiltless youth forever suffers from the wickedness of the organized society into which it is born." Craig adds, however, that the hero and heroine are not merely martyrs, but that they, too, participate in their personal tragedies.

Dowden, Edward. *"Romeo and Juliet."* In his *Transcripts and Studies*, pp. 378-430. London: Kegan Paul, Trench, Trubner & Co., 1910.
Summarizes the plots of the various retellings of the Romeo and Juliet story, then offers a detailed reconstruction of Shakespeare's play, focusing especially on the characters.

Draper, J. W. "Shakespeare's 'Star-Crossed Lovers'." *The Review of English Studies* 15, No. 57 (January 1939): 16-34.
Examines the theories of astrology prevalent during Shakespeare's lifetime, especially the Elizabethans' belief in the relation between the constellations and planets and human personality, to determine why the characters of *Romeo and Juliet* behave as they do.

———. "The Date of *Romeo and Juliet*." *The Review of English Studies* 25, No. 97 (January 1949): 55-7.
Computes a composition date for *Romeo and Juliet* of July 11-15, 1596, based on the explicit astrological references in the play.

———. "Patterns of Style in *Romeo and Juliet*." In his *Stratford to Dogberry: Studies in Shakespeare's Earlier Plays*, pp. 101-16. Pittsburgh: University of Pittsburgh Press, 1961.
Explores Shakespeare's use of the various figures of rhetoric in *Romeo and Juliet* and discusses how these patterns of speech contribute to the play's characterization, plot, tempo, and so on.

Durrant, G. H. "What's in a Name: A Discussion of *Romeo and Juliet*." *Theoria*, No. 8 (1956): 23-36.
A review of the seminal interpretations of *Romeo and Juliet* set in the context of a dialogue between a lecturer and his students.

Duthie, G. I. "The Text of Shakespeare's *Romeo and Juliet*." In *Studies in Bibliography: Papers of the Bibliographical Society of the University of Virginia, Volume Four, 1951-1952*, edited by Fredson Bowers, pp. 3-29. Charlottesville: Bibliographical Society of the University of Virginia, 1951.
Assesses the relationship of the Q1 and Q2 texts of *Romeo and Juliet* in an effort to determine to what extent the later quarto is based on the earlier.

Earl, A. J. "*Romeo and Juliet* and the Elizabethan Sonnets." *English* XXVII, Nos. 128 and 129 (Summer-Autumn 1978): 99-119.
Identifies the dominant qualities of Petrarchan poetry and reviews how the tradition of Petrarch was established in England, and eventually in Shakespeare. Earl then considers certain passages in *Romeo and Juliet* in light of the principal elements of Petrarchan love poetry previously discussed.

Edwards, Philip. "The Declaration of Love." In *Shakespeare's Styles: Essays in Honour of Kenneth Muir*, edited by Philip Edwards, Inga-Stina Ewbank, and G. K. Hunter, pp. 39-50. Cambridge: Cambridge University Press, 1980.
Examines Romeo's misuse of language and, more importantly, Juliet's distrust of her lover's hyperbolic vows in the marriage scene of Act II, Scene vi and the balcony scene of Act II, Scene ii.

Evans, G. Blakemore. Introduction to *Romeo and Juliet*, by William Shakespeare, edited by G. Blakemore Evans, pp. 1-48. Cambridge: Cambridge University Press, 1984.
General introduction which covers such issues as date, sources and structure, language, characters, and the tragic design of *Romeo and Juliet*. Evans also provides a survey of the play's major stage productions throughout history.

Gibbons, Brian. Introduction to *Romeo and Juliet*, by William Shakespeare, edited by Brian Gibbons, pp. 1-77. The New Arden Shakespeare, edited by Harold F. Brooks, Harold Jenkins, and Brian Morris. London and New York: Methuen, 1980.

A comprehensive examination of such issues as the date, text, and sources of *Romeo and Juliet*. Gibbons also offers an analysis of the play's language and other critical concerns.

Goddard, Harold C. *"Romeo and Juliet."* In his *The Meaning of Shakespeare*, pp. 117-39. Chicago: The University of Chicago Press, 1951.

 Deals primarily with Mercutio and the Nurse and their relation to the lovers' tragedy. Goddard adds commentary on a number of other issues: the role of fate in the play, Romeo's inability to follow the example of Juliet's ''boundless love'' in the face of Tybalt's challenge, and the lovers' subsequent deaths.

Hamilton, A. C. "The Resolution of the Early Period: *Romeo and Juliet.*" In his *The Early Shakespeare*, pp. 203-15. San Marino, Calif.: The Huntington Library, 1967.

 Places *Romeo and Juliet* in the context of Shakespeare's early plays, stating that it ''does not suggest or anticipate the later tragedies as much as it completes a pattern set up by the early plays.'' Hamilton especially notes *Romeo and Juliet*'s affinity with the early comedies in its ''affirmation of love . . . against the reality of death,'' although here that theme is treated tragically rather than comically.

Harrison, G. B. *"Romeo and Juliet."* In his *Shakespeare's Tragedies*, pp. 47-64. London: Routledge & Kegan Paul, 1951.

 Reviews the progression of events in *Romeo and Juliet* and examines the skillful manner in which Shakespeare developed his characters and sustained his plot. Harrison contends that ''more than any other single play *Romeo and Juliet* was responsible for the sudden flowering of English drama in the last decade of the sixteenth century and the first of the seventeenth.''

Hartley, Lodwick. "'Mercy but Murders': A Subtheme in *Romeo and Juliet.*" *Papers on English Language and Literature* 1, No. 4 (Autumn 1965): 259-64.

 Considers the misuse of authority an important subtheme in *Romeo and Juliet*. Hartley argues that the prince's failure to administer civic justice faithfully precipitates the final catastrophe and results in more innocent deaths.

Hudson, H. N. "Tragedies: *Romeo and Juliet.*" In his *Shakespeare: His Life, Art, and Characters*, Vol. II, rev. ed., pp. 203-28. Boston: Ginn & Co., 1872.

 Analysis of the principal characters in *Romeo and Juliet*. Hudson also briefly discusses what he considers the central theme of the play, namely, that nature, despite the efforts of humanity, will always break through the artificial restraints of society and exert her force.

Hunter, G. K. "Shakespeare's Earliest Tragedies: 'Titus Andronicus' and 'Romeo and Juliet'.'' *Shakespeare Survey* 27 (1974): 1-9.

 Compares Shakespeare's two earliest tragedies, focusing especially on their similar structures and their respective treatments of the theme of warring families.

Johnson, Robert Carl. "Four Young Men." *The University Review* XXXVI, No. 2 (December 1969): 141-47.

 Demonstrates how Shakespeare uses such secondary characters as Benvolio, Tybalt, Paris, and Mercutio to influence the tragedy of the young lovers and to further emphasize that the catastrophe is the result of the characters' ignorance, and not fate.

Kermode, Frank. Introduction to *Romeo and Juliet*, by William Shakespeare, edited by Frank Kermode, pp. 1055-57. The Riverside Shakespeare, edited by G. Blakemore Evans. Boston: Houghton Mifflin Co., 1974.

 Discusses date, text, source questions and reviews the principal critical issues in the play.

Levenson, Jill L. "The Definition of Love: Shakespeare's Phrasing in *Romeo and Juliet.*" *Shakespeare Studies* XV (1982): 21-36.

 A detailed examination of Shakespeare's use of Petrarchan imagery and stylistic devices in *Romeo and Juliet*. Levenson is concerned with the manner in which Shakespeare employs these ''Petrarchan *topoi*'' in various scenes and achieves different re-

sults in each case. According to the the critic, ''this early tragedy investigates the very stuff of amatory poetry, placing its components . . . in a wide variety of contexts to test their flexibility and compass.''

Link, Frederick M. "*Romeo and Juliet:* Character and Tragedy." *Boston University Studies in English* 1 (1955): 9-19.

 Reviews the various interpretations of *Romeo and Juliet* and argues that there is yet another reading possible. Link postulates, but does not develop, the idea that *Romeo and Juliet* presents ''two contradictory readings of reality which coexist without resolution in the text of the play.''

Maginn, William. "Characters in the Plays: Romeo." In *The Shakespeare Papers of the Late William Maginn*, edited by Shelton Mackenzie, pp. 67-84. New York: Redfield, 1856.

 Considers Romeo an unlucky person whose every good intention turns against him and causes some catastrophe. Maginn also focuses on the change of Romeo's language once he falls in love with Juliet.

McArthur, Herbert. "Romeo's Loquacious Friend." *Shakespeare Quarterly* X, No. 1 (Winter 1959): 35-44.

 Reviews the various interpretations of the character of Mercutio, from John Dryden (see excerpt above, 1672) to Robert Penn Warren (see entry below).

McLuskie, Kathleen E. "Shakespeare's 'Earth-Treading Stars': The Image of the Masque in 'Romeo and Juliet'." *Shakespeare Survey* 24 (1971): 63-9.

 Discusses the dramatic importance of the Capulet feast in Act I, Scene v and notes the recurring imagery of masques throughout the play.

Moisan, Thomas. "Rhetoric and the Rehearsal of Death: The 'Lamentations' Scene in *Romeo and Juliet.*" *Shakespeare Quarterly* 34, No. 4 (Winter 1983): 389-404.

 Closely analyzes the so-called lamentations scene in Act IV, Scene v of *Romeo and Juliet*. Moisan focuses on the rhetorical, stylized responses of the Capulet family to Juliet's apparent death, claiming that these speeches are interesting not for what they demonstrate about the limitations of language, but for what they do not say in regard to Juliet's death and the emotional effect of such an event. For Moisan, each of the lamenting characters is actually more concerned with his or her reaction to the spectacle of death than to the value of the deceased person herself, an attitude that distances the individual, through language, from the harsh reality of personal loss.

Moore, Olin H. *The Legend of Romeo and Juliet*. Columbus: The Ohio State University Press, 1950, 167 p.

 Traces the Romeo and Juliet legend throughout history and the story's various adaptations in the works leading to Shakespeare's play.

Muir, Kenneth. "Early Plays: *Romeo and Juliet.*" In his *The Sources of Shakespeare's Plays*, pp. 38-46. New Haven: Yale University Press, 1978.

 Examines Shakespeare's adaptation of Arthur Brooke's story and notes other possible influences on *Romeo and Juliet*, specifically, Philip Sydney.

Nevo, Ruth. "Tragic Form in *Romeo and Juliet.*" *Studies in English Literature: 1500-1900* IX, No. 2 (Spring 1969): 241-58.

 Contends that the tragedy of *Romeo and Juliet* is not based on a providential view of life, as voiced by Friar Lawrence, or a fatalistic-stoic view, as adopted by Romeo, but is a more complex pattern consisting of various factors, including the characters' inability to penetrate appearances and the lovers' embodiment of the forces ''whose collision provides the dynamic of the action.''

Nosworthy, J. M. "The Two Angry Families of Verona." *Shakespeare Quarterly* II, No. 3 (July 1952): 219-26.

 Postulates that Henry Porter's comedy, *The Two Angry Women of Abington*, is a possible source for Shakespeare's play.

Parsons, Philip. "Shakespeare and the Mask." *Shakespeare Survey* 16 (1963): 121-31.

> Demonstrates how Shakespeare's use of the mask or black visor in *Romeo and Juliet* corresponds to larger elements and themes in the play. Parsons also claims that Romeo's wearing of the mask before the Capulet feast signals an important moment in the drama, that crucial point when the hero is about to abandon his former identity and fulfill a new one in his union with Juliet.

Pettet, E. C. "The Imagery of *Romeo and Juliet*." *English* VIII, No. 45 (1950): 121-26.

> Examines the recurring references to fate and destiny in *Romeo and Juliet*, Shakespeare's use of star imagery, and the central motif of "the eternal struggle between eros . . . and the forces of death"—an idea that finds its clearest expression in the play's imagery of "strife, contrast, contradiction, and paradox."

Robertson, J. M. "*Romeo and Juliet*." In his *The Shakespeare Canon, Part III*, pp. 113-201. London: George Routledge & Sons, 1925.

> Theorizes that *Romeo and Juliet* was actually written by one of Shakespeare's predecessors, such as Robert Greene, Thomas Kyd, or Christopher Marlowe, and that Shakespeare merely revised or adapted this existing work.

Rozett, Martha Tuck. "The Comic Structures of Tragic Endings: The Suicide Scenes in *Romeo and Juliet* and *Antony and Cleopatra*." *Shakespeare Quarterly* 36, No. 2 (Summer 1985): 152-64.

> Discusses the presence of comic elements and devices in *Romeo and Juliet*, especially the convention of "feigned death," which Rozett asserts Shakespeare used in only five other romances and comedies and one other tragedy—*Antony and Cleopatra*.

Seward, James H. *Tragic Vision in "Romeo and Juliet."* Washington, D.C.: Consortium Press, 1973, 234 p.

> Reviews the "psycho-moral commonplaces" of Shakespeare's age in order to add credence to the view that Romeo and Juliet "bring destruction upon themselves through their own willful surrender to an unlawful passion." Seward maintains that such an assessment does not necessarily contradict our admiration of the lovers, but simply recognizes—as Shakespeare's Elizabethan audience would have recognized—that though their love is attractive it gradually succumbs to self-loving and self-indulgence at the expense of their higher natures.

Smith, Marion Bodwell. "The War of the Elements: Imagery in *Romeo and Juliet*." In her *Dualities in Shakespeare*, pp. 79-109. Toronto: University of Toronto Press, 1966.

> A detailed study of the imagery in *Romeo and Juliet*, especially those images drawn from the four elements of nature. Smith argues that the tragedy depicts the process of the natural world in which order is "established or restored through conflict."

Smith, Robert Metcalf. "Three Interpretations of *Romeo and Juliet*." *Shakespeare Association Bulletin* XXIII, No. 2 (April 1948): 60-77.

> Summarizes the three principal interpretations of *Romeo and Juliet* as 1) a tragedy of social justice; 2) a tragedy of character or poetic justice; and 3) a tragedy of fate or fortune. Smith points out the shortcomings of each of these readings, then argues that Shakespeare purposely incorporated the possibility of all three interpretations in his play.

Spencer, Hazelton. "Trial Flights in Tragedy: The Tragedy of *Romeo and Juliet*." In his *The Art and Life of William Shakespeare*, pp. 214-23. New York: Harcourt, Brace and Co., 1940.

> Covers date, text, source questions, focusing especially on Shakespeare's principal alterations of his source material. Spencer also discusses some of the more notable productions of *Romeo and Juliet*.

Sprague, Arthur Colby. *Shakespeare and the Audience: A Study in the Technique of Exposition*. Cambridge: Harvard University Press, 1935, 327 p.

> Passing references to *Romeo and Juliet* throughout, including one sustained comment on Friar Lawrence's final exposition in Act V, Scene ii. Sprague contends that the friar's speech here, though repetitive and undramatic, is necessary, since it provides a transition from the tragic catastrophe to its proper interpretation.

Stevens, Martin. "Juliet's Nurse: Love's Herald." *Papers on Language and Literature* 2, No. 3 (Summer 1966): 195-206.

> Traces the Nurse's role in *Romeo and Juliet* to that of the Roman *balia*, or comic messenger.

Stirling, Brents. "'They stumble that run fast'." In his *Unity in Shakespearian Tragedy: The Interplay of Theme and Character*, pp. 10-25. New York: Gordian Press, 1966.

> A detailed study of the "haste theme" in *Romeo and Juliet* and its "consistent expression . . . through character, choric commentary, and action."

Tanselle, G. Thomas. "Time in *Romeo and Juliet*." *Shakespeare Quarterly* XV, No. 4 (Autumn 1964): 349-61.

> Examines Shakespeare's use of time in *Romeo and Juliet* to draw attention to the lovers' impetuosity and to contribute to the sense of foreboding and the light/dark imagery in the play.

Utterback, Raymond V. "The Death of Mercutio." *Shakespeare Quarterly* XXIV, No. 2 (Spring 1973): 105-16.

> Analyzes Mercutio's death scene (III. i.) and its significance in *Romeo and Juliet*.

Villarejo, Oscar M. "Shakespeare's 'Romeo and Juliet': Its Spanish Source." *Shakespeare Survey* 20 (1967): 95-105.

> Contends that Lope de Vega's *Castlevines y Monteses* was a source for Shakespeare's *Romeo and Juliet*.

Warren, Robert Penn. "Pure and Impure Poetry." In his *Selected Essays*, pp. 3-31. New York: Random House, 1942.

> Discusses the lyrical poetry of the first balcony scene in *Romeo and Juliet* (II. ii.) and claims that the bawdy wit of Mercutio and the realism of the Nurse—in short, the "impure" poetic context—enhance the purity of the lovers' exchanges.

Wells, Stanley. "Juliet's Nurse: The Uses of Inconsequentiality." In *Shakespeare's Styles: Essays in Honour of Kenneth Muir*, edited by Philip Edwards, Inga-Stina Ewbank, and G. K. Hunter, pp. 51-66. Cambridge: Cambridge University Press, 1980.

> Identifies new techniques in Shakespeare's art in the Nurse's speech at I. iii. 11-59. Wells then demonstrates how this speech functions in the play as an aspect of Shakespeare's dramatic style.

Wilson, J. Dover. "The New Way with Shakespeare's Texts, II: Recent Work on the Text of *Romeo and Juliet*." *Shakespeare Survey* 8 (1955): 81-99.

> Contends that the Second Quarto of *Romeo and Juliet* is based entirely on a copy of Q1 corrected by a scribe who had access to Shakespeare's foul papers.

# Appendix

The following is a listing of all books used in Volume 5 of *Shakespearean Criticism*. Included in this list are all reprint rights and acknowledgments for those essays for which permission was obtained. Every effort has been made to trace copyright, but if omissions have been made, please let us know.

**THE EXCERPTS IN SC, VOLUME 5, WERE REPRINTED FROM THE FOLLOWING PERIODICALS:**

*The Atlantic Monthly*, v. LV, March, 1885.

*Bentley's Miscellany*, v. I, June, 1837.

*Bulletin of The John Rylands Library*, v. 19, January, 1935.

*College English*, v. 25, April, 1964. Copyright © 1964 by the National Council of Teachers of English. Reprinted by permission of the publisher.

*Criticism*, v. XVII, Fall, 1975 for "The Courtship of Katherine and the Second Tetralogy" by Marilyn L. Williamson. Copyright 1975, Wayne State University Press. Reprinted by permission of the publisher and the author.

*ELH*, v. 38, March, 1971. Reprinted by permission of the publisher.

*English Institute Essays*, 1948 for "The Argument of Comedy" by Northrop Frye. Copyright 1949, renewed 1977, Columbia University Press, New York. Reprinted by permission of the publisher and the author.

*The English Review*, v. XXIX, July, 1919.

*English Studies in Canada*, v. III, Summer, 1977 for "Levels of Parody in 'The Merry Wives of Windsor'" by Ronald Huebert. © Association of Canadian University Teachers of English 1977. Reprinted by permission of the publisher and the author.

*Essays in Criticism*, v. XX, October, 1970 for "'Romeo and Juliet': Comedy into Tragedy" by Susan Snyder. Reprinted by permission of the Editors of *Essays in Criticism* and the author.

*Essays in Literature*, v. V, Fall, 1978. Copyright 1978 by Western Illinois University. Reprinted by permission of the publisher.

*The Fortnightly Review*, v. LXXVII, May, 1902.

*The Huntington Library Bulletin*, n. 8, October, 1935.

583

**THE EXCERPTS IN SC, VOLUME 5, WERE REPRINTED FROM THE FOLLOWING BOOKS:**

Baker, George Pierce. From *The Development of Shakespeare as a Dramatist*. The Macmillan Company, 1907.

Barton, Anne. From ''Falstaff and the Comic Community,'' in *Shakespeare's ''Rough Magic'': Renaissance Essays in Honor of C. L. Barber*. Edited by Peter Erickson and Coppélia Kahn. University of Delaware Press, 1985. © 1985 by Associated University Presses, Inc. Reprinted by permission of the publisher.

Battenhouse, Roy W. From '''Henry V' as Heroic Comedy,'' in *Essays on Shakespeare and Elizabethan Drama in Honor of Hardin Craig*. Edited by Richard Hosley. University of Missouri Press, 1962. Copyright © 1962 by the Curators of the University of Missouri. Reprinted by permission of the publisher.

Battenhouse, Roy W. From *Shakespearean Tragedy: Its Art and Its Christian Premises*. Indiana University Press, 1969. Copyright © 1969 by Indiana University Press. All rights reserved. Reprinted by permission of the author.

Berry, Ralph. From *Shakespeare's Comedies: Explorations in Form*. Princeton University Press, 1972. Copyright © 1972 by Princeton University Press. All rights reserved. Reprinted with permission of the publisher.

Boas, Frederick S. From *Shakspere and His Predecessors*. Charles Scribner's Sons, 1896.

Bradbrook, Muriel C. From *Shakespeare, the Craftsman: The Clark Lectures, 1968*. Chatto & Windus, 1969. © M. C. Bradbrook 1969. Reprinted by permission of the author and Chatto & Windus.

Bradbrook, M. C. From *Shakespeare and Elizabethan Poetry: A Study of His Earlier Work in Relation to the Poetry of the Time*. Chatto & Windus, 1951.

Bradby, G. F. From *Short Studies in Shakespeare*. John Murray, 1929.

Brandes, George. From *William Shakespeare: A Critical Study*. Translated by William Archer. William Heinemann, 1898.

Brooke, Nicholas. From ''The Tragic Spectacle in 'Titus Andronicus' and 'Romeo and Juliet','' in *Shakespeare, the Tragedies: A Collection of Critical Essays*. Edited by Clifford Leech. University of Chicago Press, 1965. © 1965 by The University of Chicago. All rights reserved. Reprinted by permission of the publisher.

Brooke, Stopford A. From *On Ten Plays of Shakespeare*. A. Constable & Co., 1905.

Brooke, Stopford A. From *Ten More Plays of Shakespeare*. Constable and Company, Ltd., 1913.

Brown, John Russell. From *Shakespeare and His Comedies*. Methuen & Co. Ltd., 1957.

Bush, Geoffrey. From *Shakespeare and the Natural Condition*. Cambridge, Mass.: Harvard University Press, 1956. Copyright © 1956 by the President and Fellows of Harvard College. Renewed 1984 by Geoffrey Bush. Excerpted by permission of the publishers.

Calderwood, James L. From *Metadrama in Shakespeare's Henriad: ''Richard II'' to ''Henry V.''* University of California Press, 1979. Copyright © 1979 by The Regents of the University of California. Reprinted by permission of the publisher.

Calderwood, James L. From *Shakespearean Metadrama: The Argument of the Play in Titus Andronicus, Loves Labour's Lost, Romeo and Juliet, A Midsummer Night's Dream, and Richard II*, University of Minnesota Press, Minneapolis, 1971. © copyright 1971 by the University of Minnesota. All rights reserved. Reprinted by permission of the publisher.

Carlyle, Thomas. From *On Heroes, Hero-Worship and the Heroic in History*. Chapman & Hall, Limited, 1840.

Chambers, E. K. From *Shakespeare: A Survey*. Sidgwick & Jackson, Ltd., 1925.

Charlton, H. B. From *Shakespeare, Politics and Politicians*. The English Association, Pamphlet No. 72, 1929.

Charlton, H. B. From *Shakespearian Tragedy*. Cambridge at the University Press, 1948.

Châteaubriand. From an extract, translated by Mrs. A. L. Wister, in *A New Variorum Edition of Shakespeare: Romeo and Juliet, Vol. 1*. Edited by Horace Howard Furness. J. B. Lippincott Company, 1871.

Clarke, Charles Cowden. From *Shakespeare-Characters: Chiefly Those Subordinate*. Smith, Elder, & Co., 1863.

Clemen, Wolfgang H. From *The Development of Shakespeare's Imagery*. Methuen & Co. Ltd., 1951.

Coleridge, Hartley. From *Essays and Marginalia, Vol. II*. Edited by Derwent Coleridge. Edward Moxon, 1851.

Coleridge, Samuel Taylor. From *Shakespearean Criticism, Vol. 1*. Edited by Thomas Middleton Raysor. Cambridge, Mass.: Harvard University Press, 1930.

Colie, Rosalie L. From *Shakespeare's Living Art*. Princeton University Press, 1974. Copyright © 1974 by Princeton University Press. All rights reserved. Reprinted with permission of the publisher.

Collier, Jeremy. From *A Short View of the Immorality and Profaneness of the English Stage*. S. Keble, 1698.

Crane, Milton. From *Shakespeare's Prose*. The University of Chicago Press, 1951.

Cumberland, Richard. From *The Observer: Being a Collection of Moral, Literary and Familiar Essays, Vols. II & III*. C. Dilly, 1786.

Cunliffe, John William. From ''The Character of 'Henry V' as Prince and King,'' in *Shaksperian Studies*. Edited by Brander Matthews and Ashley Horace Thorndike. Columbia University Press, 1916.

Daniel, George. From remarks in *As You Like It: A Comedy*. By William Shakespeare. G. H. Davidson, 1829.

De Rougemont, Denis. From *Love in the Western World*. Translated by Montgomery Belgion. Revised edition. Pantheon, 1956. © 1956 by Pantheon Books, Inc. Renewed 1984 by Random House, Inc. All rights reserved. Reprinted by permission of Pantheon Books, a Division of Random House, Inc.

Dennis, John. From *The Comical Gallant; or, The Amours of Sir John Falstaff: A Comedy*, N. p., 1702.

Dibdin, Charles. From *A Complete History of the English Stage, Vol. III*. Charles Dibdin, 1800.

Dickey, Franklin M. From *Not Wisely but Too Well: Shakespeare's Love Tragedies*. The Huntington Library, 1957.

Dowden, Edward. From *Shakspere: A Critical Study of His Mind and Art*. Third edition. Harper & Brothers Publishers, 1881.

Dryden, John. From *The Conquest of Granada by the Spaniards*. H. Herringman, 1672.

Dryden, John. From *Of Dramatick Poesie, an Essay*. H. Herringman, 1668.

Dryden, John. From a preface to *Troilus and Cressida; or, Truth Found Too Late*. By William Shakespeare. Abel Swall, Jacob Tonson, 1679.

Duthie, George Ian. From an introduction to *Romeo & Juliet*. By William Shakespeare. Cambridge at the University Press, 1955.

Ellis-Fermor, Una. From *The Frontiers of Drama*. Methuen & Co. Ltd., 1945.

Erickson, Peter. From *Patriarchal Structure in Shakespeare's Drama*. University of California Press, 1985. Copyright © 1985 by The Regents of the University of California. Reprinted by permission of the publisher.

Erickson, Peter. From ''The Order of the Garter, The Cult of Elizabeth, and Class/ Gender Tension in 'The Merry Wives of Windsor',' in *Subversion, Recuperation, Rehearsal: The Ideological Function of the Shakespearean Text*. Edited by Jean E. Howard and Marion O'Connor. Methuen, 1987. Reprinted by permission of Methuen & Co., Ltd.

Erskine, John. From '' 'Romeo and Juliet',' in *Shaksperian Studies*. Edited by Brander Matthews and Ashley Horace Thorndike. Columbia University Press, 1916.

Evans, Bertrand. From *Shakespeare's Comedies*. Oxford at the Clarendon Press, Oxford, 1960. © Oxford University Press 1960. Reprinted by permission of the publisher.

Evans, Robert O. From *The Osier Cage: Rhetorical Devices in ''Romeo & Juliet.''* University of Kentucky Press, 1966. Copyright © 1966 by the University Press of Kentucky. Reprinted by permission of the publisher.

Farmer, Richard. From *An Essay on the Learning of Shakespeare*. W. Thurlbourn & J. Woodyer, 1767.

Faucit, Helena, Lady Martin. From *On Some of Shakespeare's Female Characters*. Fifth edition. William Blackwood and Sons, 1893.

French, Marilyn. From *Shakespeare's Division of Experience*. Summit Books, 1981. Copyright © 1981 by Marilyn French. All rights reserved. Reprinted by permission of Summit Books, a division of Simon & Schuster, Inc.

Frye, Northrop. From *Fools of Time: Studies in Shakespearean Tragedy*. University of Toronto Press, 1967. © University of Toronto Press 1967. Reprinted by permission of the publisher.

Frye, Northrop. From *Northrop Frye on Shakespeare*. Edited by Robert Sandler. Yale University Press, 1986. © Northrop Frye 1986. All rights reserved. Reprinted by permission of the publisher.

Furness, Horace Howard. From "Duration of the Action," in *A New Variorium Edition of Shakespeare: As You Like It, Vol. 8*. Edited by Horace Howard Furness. J. B. Lippincott & Company, 1890.

Gardner, Helen. From "'As You Like It'," in *More Talking of Shakespeare*. Edited by John Garrett. Longmans, Green, 1959. Copyright © 1959 Longmans, Green & Co. Ltd. and the author.

Gentleman, Francis. From an introduction to "King Henry V" in *Bell's Edition of Shakespeare's Plays, Vol. IV*. John Bell, 1774.

Gentleman, Francis. From *The Dramatic Censor; or, Critical Companion, Vol. I*. J. Bell, 1770.

Gervinus, G. G. From *Shakespeare Commentaries*. Translated by F. E. Bunnètt. Revised edition. Smith, Elder, & Co., 1877.

Gildon, Charles. From "Remarks on the Plays of Shakespear," in *The Works of Mr. William Shakespear, Vol. 7*. E. Curll and E. Sanger, 1710.

Goddard, Harold C. From *The Meaning of Shakespeare*. University of Chicago Press, 1951. Copyright 1951 by The University of Chicago. Renewed 1979 by Margaret G. Holt and Eleanor G. Worthen. All rights reserved. Reprinted by permission of the publisher.

Granville-Barker, Harley. From "From 'Henry V' to 'Hamlet'," in *Aspects of Shakespeare: Being British Academy Lectures*. Oxford at the Clarendon Press, Oxford, 1933.

Granville-Barker, Harley. From *Prefaces to Shakespeare, second series*. Sidgwick & Jackson, Ltd., 1930.

Greg, Walter W. From *Pastoral Poetry & Pastoral Drama*. A. H. Bullen, 1906.

Griffith, Elizabeth. From *The Morality of Shakespeare's Drama Illustrated*. T. Cadell, 1775.

Grindon, Rosa Leo. From *In Praise of Shakespere's "Merry Wives of Windsor": An Essay in Exposition and Appreciation*. Sherratt and Hughes, 1902.

Guizot, M. From *Shakspeare and His Times*. Harper & Brothers, Publishers, 1852.

Hallam, Henry. From *Introduction to the Literature of Europe in the Fifteenth, Sixteenth, and Seventeenth Centuries, 4 vols*. J. Murray, 1837-39.

Hanmer, Sir Thomas. From *The Works of Mr. William Shakespear: Comedies, Vol. 1*. Edited by Sir Thomas Hanmer. N.p., 1743.

Hazlitt, William. From *Characters of Shakespear's Plays*. R. Hunter, 1817.

Holland, Norman N. From "Mercutio, Mine Own Son the Dentist," in *Essays on Shakespeare*. Edited by Gordon Ross Smith. The Pennsylvania State University Press, University Park, 1965. Copyright © 1965 by The Pennsylvania State University. All rights reserved. Reprinted by permission of the publisher.

Home, Henry, Lord Kames. From *Elements of Criticism, Vol. II*. N.p., 1762.

Horn, Franz. From an extract, translated by William Henry Furness, in *A New Variorum Edition of Shakespeare: Romeo and Juliet, Vol. I*. Edited by Horace Howard Furness, J. B. Lippincott Company, 1871.

Hudson, Rev. H. N. From *Shakespeare: His Life, Art, and Characters, Vol. I*. Fourth revised edition. Ginn & Company, 1872.

Hunter, G. K. From *William Shakespeare, the Later Comedies: A Midsummer-Night's Dream, Much Ado About Nothing, As You Like It, Twelfth Night*. The British Council, 1962. © Profile Books Ltd. 1962. Reprinted by permission of Profile Books Limited.

Hurd, Richard. From *The Works of Richard Hurd, Vol. I.* T. Cadell and W. Davies, 1811.

Jameson, Anna Brownell. From *Characteristics of Women: Moral, Poetical, and Historical.* Second edition. N.p., 1833.

Johnson, Samuel. From *The Plays of William Shakespeare.* Edited by Samuel Johnson. J. & R. Tonson, 1765.

Johnson, Samuel. From notes on ''The Merry Wives of Windsor,'' in *The Plays of William Shakespeare, Vol. I.* Edited by Samuel Johnson and George Steevens, C. Bathurst, 1773.

Kautsky, Karl. From *Thomas More and His Utopia.* Translated by H. J. Stenning. A. & C. Black, Ltd., 1927.

Kiefer, Frederick. From *Fortune and Elizabethan Tragedy.* Huntington Library, 1983. Copyright 1983 by The Huntington Library. Reprinted by permission of the publisher.

Knight, Charles. From *Studies of Shakspere.* Charles Knight, 1849.

Kott, Jan. From *Shakespeare, Our Contemporary.* Translated by Boleslaw Taborski. New edition. Anchor Books, 1966. Originally published as *Szkice o Szekspirze.* Panstwowy Instytut Wydawniczy, 1961. Copyright © 1964 by Panstwowe Wydawnictwo Naukowe. Copyright © 1964, 1965, 1966 by Doubleday & Company, Inc. Reprinted by permission of Doubleday & Company, Inc. In Canada by Jan Kott.

Langbaine, Gerard. From *An Account of the English Dramatick Poets.* G. West and H. Clements, 1691.

Krieger, Elliot. From *A Marxist Study of Shakespeare's Comedies.* Barnes & Noble, 1979, Macmillan, 1979. © Elliot Krieger 1979. All rights reserved. Reprinted by permission of Barnes & Noble Books, a Division of Littlefield, Adams & Co., Inc. In Canada by Macmillan, London and Basingstoke.

Lawlor, John. From '''Romeo and Juliet','' in *Early Shakespeare,* Stratford-Upon-Avon Studies, No. 3. Arnold, 1961. © Edward Arnold (Publishers) Ltd. 1961. Reprinted by permission of the publisher.

Leech, Clifford. From ''The Moral Tragedy of 'Romeo and Juliet','' in *English Renaissance Drama: Essays in Honor of Madeleine Doran & Mark Eccles.* Standish Henning, Robert Kimbrough, Richard Knowles, eds. Southern Illinois University Press, 1976. Copyright © 1976 by Southern Illinois University Press. All rights reserved. Reprinted by permission of the publisher.

Leggatt, Alexander. From *Shakespeare's Comedy of Love.* Methuen, 1974. © 1973 Alexander Leggatt. All rights reserved. Reprinted by permission of Methuen & Co. Ltd.

Lennox, Charlotte. From *Shakespear Illustrated; or, the Novels and Histories, on Which the Plays of Shakespear Are Founded, Vol. I.* A. Millar, 1753.

Lennox, Charlotte. From *Shakespear Illustrated; or, the Novels and Histories, on Which the Plays of Shakespear Are Founded, Vol. III.* A. Millar, 1754.

Lloyd, William Watkiss. From *The Dramatic Works of William Shakespeare.* Bell & Daldy, 1856.

Mahood, M. M. From *Shakespeare's Wordplay.* Methuen & Co. Ltd., 1957.

Marsh, Derick R. C. From *Passion Lends Them Power: A Study of Shakespeare's Love Tragedies.* Barnes & Noble, 1976. © Derick R. C. Marsh 1976. All rights reserved. Reprinted by permission of Barnes & Noble Books, a Division of Littlefield, Adams & Co., Inc.

Masefield, John. From *William Shakespeare.* Henry Holt and Company, 1911.

Matthews, Brander. From *Shakspere as a Playwright.* Charles Scribner's Sons, 1913. Copyright, 1913, by Charles Scribner's Sons. Renewed 1941 by Nelson Macy, Jr. Reprinted with the permission of Charles Scribner's Sons.

Mézières, Alfred. From an extract, translated by Mrs. A. L. Wister, in *A New Variorum Edition of Shakespeare: Romeo and Juliet, Vol. I.* Edited by Horace Howard Furness. J. B. Lippincott Company, 1871.

Moulton, Richard G. From *The Moral System of Shakespeare: A Popular Illustration of Fiction as the Experimental Side of Philosophy.* The Macmillan Company, 1903.

Muir, Kenneth. From *Shakespeare's Comic Sequence.* Barnes & Noble, 1979. Copyright © 1979 by Liverpool University Press. All rights reserved. Reprinted by permission of Barnes & Noble Books, a Division of Littlefield, Adams & Co., Inc.

Nowottny, Winifred. From ''Shakespeare's Tragedies,'' in *Shakespeare's World.* Edited by James Sutherland and Joel Hurstfield. Arnold, 1964. © Edward Arnold (Publishers) Ltd. 1964. Reprinted by permission of the publisher.

Ornstein, Robert. From *A Kingdom for a Stage: The Achievement of Shakespeare's History Plays*. Cambridge, Mass.: Harvard University Press, 1972. Copyright © 1972 by the President and Fellows of Harvard College. All rights reserved. Reprinted by permission of the author.

Parrott, Thomas Marc. From *Shakespearean Comedy*. Oxford University Press, 1949. Copyright 1949 by Thomas Marc Parrott. Renewed 1976 by Frances M. Walters. Reprinted by permission of the Literary Estate of Thomas Marc Parrott.

Pepys, Samuel. From *Diary and Correspondence of Samuel Pepys, 6 Vols*. Edited by Mynors Bright. N.p., 1875-79.

Pepys, Samuel. From *The Diary of Samuel Pepys, Vol. 1*. Edited by Henry B. Wheatley. G. Bell and Sons, Ltd., 1924.

Peterson, Douglas L. From "'Romeo and Juliet' and the Art of Moral Navigation," in *Pacific Coast Studies in Shakespeare*. Edited by Waldo F. McNeir and Thelma N. Greenfield. University of Oregon Books, 1966. Copyright © 1966 University of Oregon Books. Reprinted by permission of the publisher.

Pettet, E. C. From *Shakespeare and the Romance Tradition*. Staples Press, 1949.

Phialas, Peter G. From *Shakespeare's Romantic Comedies: The Development of Their Form and Meaning*. University of North Carolina Press, 1966. Copyright © 1966 by The University of North Carolina Press. Reprinted by permission of the publisher and the author.

Pope, Alexander. From a footnote in *The Works of Mr. William Shakespear: Historical Plays, Vol. III*. Edited by Alexander Pope. Jacob Tonson, 1723.

Priestly, J. B. From *The English Comic Characters*. Dodd, Mead and Company, 1925.

Potter, John. From *The Theatrical Review; or, New Companion to the Playhouse*. S. Crowder, 1772.

Prior, Moody E. From *The Drama of Power: Studies in Shakespeare's History Plays*. Northwestern University Press, 1973. Copyright © 1973 by Moody E. Prior. All rights reserved. Reprinted by permission of Northwestern University Press, Evanston, IL.

Quiller-Couch, Sir Arthur. From *Notes on Shakespeare's Workmanship*. Holt, 1917. Copyright 1917 by Henry Holt and Company. Renewed 1946 by Louise Amelia Quiller-Couch. Reprinted by permission of the Literary Estate of Sir Arthur Quiller-Couch.

Rabkin, Norman. From *Shakespeare and the Common Understanding*. The Free Press, 1967. Copyright © 1967 by The Free Press, a Division of Macmillan Publishing Company. All rights reserved. Reprinted by permission of the author.

Ribner, Irving. From "Then I Denie You Starres: A Reading of 'Romeo and Juliet'," in *Studies in the English Renaissance Drama: In Memory of Karl Julius Holzknecht*. Josephine W. Bennett, Oscar Cargill, Vernon Hall, Jr., eds. New York University Press, 1959. Copyright © 1959 by New York University. Reprinted by permission of the publisher.

Richardson, William. From *A Philosophical Analysis and Illustration of Some of Shakespeare's Remarkable Characters*. Revised edition. J. Murray, 1780.

Richmond, H. M. From *Shakespeare's Political Plays*. Random House, 1967. Copyright © 1967 by Random House, Inc. All rights reserved. Reprinted by permission of the author.

Richmond, Hugh M. From *Shakespeare's Sexual Comedy: A Mirror for Lovers*. The Bobbs-Merrill Company, Inc., 1971. Copyright © 1971 Macmillan Publishing Company. Reprinted by permission of the author.

Riemer, A. P. From *Antic Fables: Patterns of Evasion in Shakespeare's Comedies,* St. Martin's Press, 1980, Manchester University Press, 1980. © A. P. Riemer 1980. All rights reserved. Reprinted by permission of St. Martin's Press, Inc. In Canada by Manchester University Press.

Rowe, Nicholas. From "Some Account of the Life, & c. of Mr. William Shakespear," in *The Works of Mr. William Shakespear Vol. 1*. Edited by Nicholas Rowe. Jacob Tonson, 1709.

Schlegel, August Wilhelm. From *A Course of Lectures on Dramatic Art and Literature*. Edited by Rev. A. J. W. Morrison, translated by John Black. Revised edition. Henry G. Bohn, 1846.

Sen Gupta, S. C. From *Shakespearian Comedy*. Oxford University Press, Indian Branch, 1950.

Shaw, Bernard. From *Dramatic Opinions and Essays with an Apology, Vol. 2*. Brentano's 1906.

Snider, Denton J. From *The Shakespearian Drama, a Commentary: The Comedies*. Sigma Publishing Co., 1890?

Snider, Denton J. From *The Shakespearian Drama, a Commentary: The Histories*. Sigma Publishing Co., 1890.

Snider, Denton J. From *The Shakespearian Drama, a Commentary: The Tragedies*. Sigma Publishing Co., 1887.

Spurgeon, Caroline F. E. From *Shakespeare's Imagery and What It Tells Us*. Cambridge at the University Press, 1935.

Stauffer, Donald A. From *Shakespeare's World of Images: The Development of His Moral Ideas*. Norton, 1949. Copyright 1949 by W. W. Norton & Company, Inc. Copyright renewed 1977 by Ruth M. Stauffer. Reprinted by permission of W. W. Norton & Company, Inc.

Stoll, Elmer Edgar. From *Poets and Playwrights: Shakespeare, Jonson, Spenser, Milton*. The University of Minnesota Press, 1930. Copyright, 1930, by The University of Minnesota. Renewed 1958 by Elmer Edgar Stoll. All rights reserved. Reprinted by permission of the publisher.

Stoll, Elmer Edgar. From *Shakespeare's Young Lovers*. Oxford University Press, 1937.

Swinburne, Algernon Charles. From *A Study of Shakespeare*. R. Worthington, 1880.

Swinden, Patrick. From *An Introduction to Shakespeare's Comedies*. Barnes & Noble, 1973, Macmillan, 1973. © Patrick Swinden 1973. All rights reserved. Reprinted by permission of Barnes & Noble Books, a Division of Littlefield, Adams & Co., Inc. In Canada by Macmillan, London and Basingstoke.

Taine, Hippolyte A. From *History of English Literature, Vol. I*. Translated by H. van Laun. Grosset & Dunlap, Publishers, 1908.

Thayer, C. G. From *Shakespearean Politics: Government and Misgovernment in the Great Histories*. Ohio University Press, 1983. © copyright 1983 by C. G. Thayer. All rights reserved. Reprinted by permission of Ohio University Press, Athens.

Theobald, Lewis. From *Shakespeare Restored or, a Specimen of the Many Errors as Well Committed, as Unamended by Mr. Pope*. J. Woodman and D. Lyon, 1726.

Tillyard, E. M. W. From *Shakespeare's History Plays*. Chatto & Windus, 1944. © 1944 by Chatto & Windus. Copyright renewed © 1971 by Stephen Tillyard, Mrs. V. Sankaran and Mrs. A. Ahlers. Reprinted by permission of the Literary Estate of E. M. W. Tillyard and Chatto & Windus.

Ulrici, Hermann. From *Shakspeare's Dramatic Art: And His Relation to Calderon and Goethe*. Translated by Rev. A. J. W. Morrison. Chapman, Brothers, 1846.

Ulrici, Hermann. From *Shakspeare's Dramatic Art: History and Character of Shakspeare's Plays, Vol. I*. Translated by L. Dora Schmitz. George Bell and Sons, 1876.

Van Doren, Mark. From *Shakespeare*. Henry Holt and Company, 1939.

Vickers, Brian. From *The Artistry of Shakespeare's Prose*. Methuen, 1968. © 1968 Brian Vickers. Reprinted by permission of Methuen & Co. Ltd.

Vyvyan, John. From *Shakespeare and the Rose of Love: A Study of the Early Plays in Relation to the Medieval Philosophy of Love*. Chatto & Windus, 1960. © John Vyvyan 1960. Reprinted by permission of the Tessa Sayle Agency.

Wain, John. From *The Living World of Shakespeare: A Playgoer's Guide*. St. Martin's Press, 1964. Copyright © John Wain 1964. Reprinted by permission of St. Martin's Press, Inc. In Canada by Curtis Brown on behalf of the author.

Walter, J. H. From an introduction to *''King Henry V''*. By William Shakespeare, edited by J. H. Walter. Methuen & Co. Ltd., 1954.

Warburton, William. From *The Works of Shakespeare, 8 Vols*. By William Shakespeare, edited by William Warburton. J. and P. Knapton, 1747.

Warton, Thomas. From *The History of English Poetry: From the Close of the Eleventh to the Commencement of the Eighteenth Century, Vol. III*. J. Dodsley, 1781.

Welsford, Enid. From *The Fool: His Social and Literary History*. Faber & Faber, 1935.

Whiter, Walter. From *A Specimen of a Commentary on Shakespeare*. T. Cadell, 1794.

Williams, Charles. From '' 'Henry V','' in *Shakespeare Criticism: 1919-1935*. Edited by Anne Bradby Ridler. Oxford University Press, London, 1936.

Wilson, Harold S. From *On the Design of Shakespearian Tragedy*. University of Toronto Press, 1957.

Wilson, John Dover. From an introduction to *King Henry V*. By William Shakespeare, edited by John Dover Wilson. Cambridge at the University Press.

Wilson, John Dover. From *Shakespeare's Happy Comedies*. Faber and Faber, 1962. © 1962 by John Dover Wilson. Reprinted by permission of Faber and Faber Ltd.

Winny, James. From *The Player King: A Theme of Shakespeare's Histories*. Chatto & Windus, 1968. © James Winny 1968. Reprinted by permission of the author.

Yeats, W. B. From *Ideas of Good and Evil*. A. H. Bullen, 1903.

Young, David. From *The Heart's Forest: A Study of Shakespeare's Pastoral Plays*. Yale University Press, 1972. Copyright © 1972 by Yale University. All rights reserved. Reprinted by permission of the publisher.

Zimbardo, Rose A. From ''The Formalism of 'Henry V','' in *Shakespeare Encomium*. Edited by Anne Paolucci. City College, 1964. Copyright © The City College of The City University of New York 1964. Reprinted by permission of the publisher.

# Glossary

**APOCRYPHA:** A term applied to those plays which have, at one time or another, been ascribed to Shakespeare, but which are outside the canon of the thirty-seven dramas generally accepted as authentic. The second issue of the THIRD FOLIO included seven plays not among the other thirty-six of the FIRST FOLIO: *Pericles, The London Prodigal, Thomas Lord Cromwell, Sir John Oldcastle, The Puritan, A Yorkshire Tragedy,* and *Locrine.* These seven were also included in the FOURTH FOLIO, but of them only *Pericles* is judged to be the work of Shakespeare. Four other plays that were entered in the STATIONERS' REGISTER in the seventeenth century listed Shakespeare as either an author or coauthor: *The Two Noble Kinsmen* (1634), *Cardenio* (1653), *Henry I* and *Henry II* (1653), and *The Birth of Merlin* (1662); only *The Two Noble Kinsmen* is thought to be, at least in part, written by Shakespeare, although *Cardenio*—whose text is lost—may also have been by him. Scholars have judged that there is strong internal evidence indicating Shakespeare's hand in two other works, *Sir Thomas More* and *Edward III.* Among other titles that have been ascribed to Shakespeare but are generally regarded as spurious are: *The Troublesome Reign of King John, Arden of Feversham, Fair Em, The Merry Devil of Edmonton, Mucedorus, The Second Maiden's Tragedy,* and *Edmund Ironside.*

**ASSEMBLED TEXTS:** The theory of assembled texts, first proposed by Edmond Malone in the eighteenth century and later popularized by John Dover Wilson, maintains that some of the plays in the FIRST FOLIO were reconstructed for the COMPOSITOR by integrating each actor's part with the plot or abstract of the play. According to Dover Wilson, this reconstruction was done only for those plays which had not been previously published in QUARTO editions and which had no company PROMPT-BOOKS in existence, a list he limits to three of Shakespeare's works: *The Two Gentlemen of Verona, The Merry Wives of Windsor,* and *The Winter's Tale.*

**BAD QUARTOS:** A name attributed to a group of early editions of Shakespeare's plays which, because of irregularities, omissions, misspellings, and interpolations not found in later QUARTO or FOLIO versions of the same plays, are considered unauthorized publications of Shakespeare's work. The term was first used by the twentieth-century bibliographical scholar A. W. Pollard and has been applied to as many as ten plays: The First Quartos of *Romeo and Juliet, Hamlet, Henry V,* and *The Merry Wives of Windsor; The First Part of the Contention betwixt the two famous Houses of Yorke and Lancaster* and *The True Tragedy of Richard Duke of Yorke,* originally thought to have been sources for Shakespeare's *2* and *3 Henry VI,* but now generally regarded as bad quartos of those plays; the so-called "Pied Bull" quarto of *King Lear;* the 1609 edition of *Pericles; The Troublesome Reign of King John,* believed to be a bad quarto of *King John,* and *The Taming of a Shrew,* which some critics contend is a bad quarto of Shakespeare's Shrew drama. The primary distinction of the bad quartos is the high degree of TEXTUAL CORRUPTION apparent in the texts, a fact scholars have attributed to either one of two theories: some have argued that each quarto was composed from a stenographer's report, in which an agent for the printer was employed to surreptitiously transcribe the play during a performance; others have held the more popular explanation that the questionable texts were based on MEMORIAL RECONSTRUCTIONS by one or more actors who had performed in the plays.

**BANDELLO, MATTEO:** (b. 1480? - d. 1561) Italian novelist and poet who was also a churchman, diplomat, and soldier. His literary reputation is principally based on the *Novelle,* a collection of 214 tragic, romantic, and historical tales derived from a variety of material from antiquity to the Renaissance. Many of the stories in the *Novelle* are coarse and lewd in their presentation of love, reflecting Bandello's secular interests rather than his clerical role. Together with the dedications to friends and patrons that accompany the individual stories, the *Novelle* conveys a vivid sense of historical events and personalities of the Renaissance. Several translations and adaptations appeared in the third quarter of the sixteenth century, most notably in French by Francois Belleforest and Pierre Boaistuau and in English by William Painter and Geoffrey Fenton.

**BLACKFRIARS THEATRE:** The Blackfriars Theatre, so named because it was located in the London precinct of Blackfriars, was originally part of a large monastary leased to Richard Farrant, Master of the Children of Windsor, in 1576 for the purpose of staging children's plays. It was acquired in 1596 by James Burbage, who tried to convert the property into a professional theater, but was thwarted in his attempt by surrounding residents. After Burbage died, the Blackfriars was taken over by his son, Richard, who circumvented the objections of his neighbors and, emulating the tactics of Farrant's children's company, staged both children's and adult plays under the guise of a private house, rather than a public theater. This arrangement lasted for five years until, in 1605, the adult company was suspended by King James I for its performance of the satire *Eastward Ho!* Shortly thereafter, the children's company was also suppressed for performing George Chapman's *Conspiracy and Tragedy of Charles Duke of Byron.* In 1608, Burbage organized a new group of directors consisting of his brother Cuthbert and several leading players of the KING'S MEN, including Shakespeare, John Heminge, Henry Condell, and William Sly. These "housekeepers," as they were called, for they shared no profits accruing to the actors, arranged to have the Blackfriars used by the King's Men alternately with the GLOBE THEATRE, an arrangement that lasted from the autumn of 1609 to 1642. Because it was a private house, and therefore smaller than the public theaters of London at that time, the Blackfriars set a higher price for tickets and, as such, attracted a sophisticated and aristocratic audience. Also, through its years of operation as a children's theater, the Blackfriars developed a certain taste in its patrons—one which appreciated music, dance, and masque in a dramatic piece, as well as elements of suspense, reconciliation, and rebirth. Many critics attribute the nature of Shakespeare's final romances to the possibility that he wrote the plays with this new audience foremost in mind.

**BOOKKEEPER:** Also considered the bookholder or prompter, the bookkeeper was a member of an Elizabethan acting company who maintained custody of the PROMPT-BOOKS, or texts of the plays. Many scholars believe that the bookkeeper also acted as the prompter during any performances, much as a stage manager would do today; however, other literary historians claim that another official satisfied this function. In addition to the above duties, the bookkeeper obtained a license for each play, deleted from the dramatist's manuscript anything offensive before it was submitted to the government censor, assembled copies of the players' individual parts from the company prompt-book, and drew up the "plot" of each work, that is, an abstract of the action of the play emphasizing stage directions.

COMPOSITOR: The name given to the typesetter in a printing shop. Since the growth of textual criticism in modern Shakespearean scholarship, the habits and idiosyncrasies of the individual compositors of Shakespeare's plays have attracted extensive study, particularly with respect to those works that demonstrate substantial evidence of TEXTUAL CORRUPTION. Elizabethan compositors set their type by hand, one letter at a time, a practice that made it difficult to sustain a sense of the text and which often resulted in a number of meaningless passages in books. Also, the lack of uniform spelling rules prior to the eighteenth century meant that each compositor was free to spell a given word according to his personal predilection. Because of this, scholars have been able to identify an individual compositor's share of a printed text by isolating his spelling habits and idiosyncrasies.

EMENDATION: A term often used in textual criticism, emendation is a conjectural correction of a word or phrase in a Shakespearean text proposed by an editor in an effort to restore a line's original meaning. Because many of Shakespeare's plays were carelessly printed, there exist a large number of errors in the early editions which textual scholars through the centuries have tried to correct. Some of the errors—those based on obvious misprints—have been easily emended, but other more formidable TEXTUAL CORRUPTIONS remain open to dispute and have solicited a variety of corrections. Perhaps the two most famous of these are the lines in *Henry V* (II. iii. 16-17) and *Hamlet* (I. ii. 129).

FAIR COPY A term often applied by Elizabethan writers and theater professionals to describe the corrected copy of an author's manuscript submitted to an acting company. According to available evidence, a dramatist would presumably produce a rough copy of a play, also known as the author's FOUL PAPERS, which would be corrected and revised either by himself or by a professional scribe at a later date. Eventually, the fair copy of a play would be modified by a BOOKKEEPER or prompter to include notes for properties, stage directions, and so on, and then be transcribed into the company's PROMPT-BOOK.

FIRST FOLIO: The earliest collected edition of Shakespeare's plays, edited by his fellow-actors John Heminge and Henry Condell and published near the end of 1623. The First Folio contains thirty-six plays, exactly half of which had never been previously published. Although this edition is considered authoritative for a number of Shakespeare's plays, recent textual scholarship tends to undermine this authority in calling for a broader consideration of all previous versions of a Shakespearean drama in conjunction with the Folio text.

FOLIO: The name given to a book made up of sheets folded once to form two leaves of equal size, or four pages, typically 11 to 16 inches in height and 8 to 11 inches in width.

FOURTH FOLIO: The fourth collected edition of Shakespeare's plays, published in 1685. This, the last of the FOLIO editions of Shakespeare's dramas, included a notable amount of TEXTUAL CORRUPTION and modernization—751 editorial changes in all, most designed to make the text easier to read.

**FOUL PAPERS:** The term given to an author's original, uncorrected manuscript, containing the primary text of a play with the author's insertions and deletions. Presumably, the foul papers would be transcribed onto clean sheets for the use of the acting company which had purchased the play; this transcribed and corrected manuscript was called a FAIR COPY. Available evidence indicates that some of Shakespeare's early QUARTOS were printed directly from his foul papers, a circumstance which would, if true, explain the frequent errors and inconsistencies in these texts. Among the quartos alleged to be derived from Shakespeare's foul papers are the First Quartos of *Much Ado about Nothing, A Midsummer Night's Dream, Love's Labour's Lost, Richard II,* and *1* and *2 Henry IV;* among the FIRST FOLIO editions are *The Comedy of Errors, The Taming of the Shrew,* and *Coriolanus.*

**GLOBE THEATRE:** Constructed in 1599 on Bankside across the Thames from the City of London, the Globe was destroyed by fire in 1613, rebuilt the following year, and finally razed in 1644. Accounts of the fire indicate that it was built of timber with a thatched roof, and sixteenth-century maps of Bankside show it was a polygonal building, but no other evidence exists describing its structure and design. From what is known of similar public theaters of the day, such as the Fortune and the Swan, it is conjectured that the Globe contained a three-tiered gallery along its interior perimeter, that a roof extended over a portion of the three-storied stage and galleries, and that the lowest level of the stage was in the form of an apron extending out among the audience in the yard. Further, there is speculation that the Globe probably included a tiring room or backstage space, that the first two stories contained inner stages that were curtained and recessed, that the third story sometimes served as a musicians' gallery, and that beneath the flat roof, which was also known as "the heavens," machinery was stored for raising and lowering theatrical apparatus. It is generally believed that the interior of the Globe was circular and that it could accommodate an audience of approximately two thousand people, both in its three galleries and the yard. The theater was used solely by the LORD CHAMBERLAIN'S MEN, later known as the KING'S MEN, who performed there throughout the year until 1609, when the company alternated performances at the fully-enclosed BLACKFRIARS THEATRE in months of inclement weather.

**HALL (or HALLE), EDWARD:** (b. 1498? - d. 1547) English historian whose *The Union of the Noble and Illustre Famelies of Lancastre and York* (1542; enlarged in 1548 and 1550) chronicles the period from the death of Richard II through the reign of Henry VIII. Morally didactic in his approach, Hall shaped his material to demonstrate the disasters that ensue from civil wars and insurrection against monarchs. He traced through the dynastic conflicts during the reigns of Henry VI and Richard III a pattern of cause and effect in which a long chain of crimes and divine retribution was ended by the accession of Henry VII to the English throne. Hall's eye-witness account of the pageantry and festivities of the court of Henry VIII is remarkable for its vivacity and embellished language. His heavy bias on the side of Protestantism and defense of Henry VIII's actions against the Roman Church led to the prohibition of his work by Queen Mary in 1555, but his interpretation of the War of the Roses was adopted by all subsequent Tudor historians. Hall's influence on Shakespeare is most evident in the English history plays.

**HOLINSHED, RAPHAEL:** (d. 1580?) English writer and editor whose *Chronicles of England, Scotlande, and Irelande* (1577; enlarged in 1587) traced the legends and history of Britain from Noah and the flood to the mid-sixteenth century. The *Chronicles* reveal a Protestant bias and depict the history of the British monarchy in terms of the "Tudor myth," which claimed that Henry VI's usurpation of the crown from Richard II set off a chain of disasters and civil strife which culminated in the reign of Henry VI and continued until the accession to the throne of Henry VII, who, through his marriage to Elizabeth of York, united the two feuding houses of Lancaster and York and brought harmony and peace to England. Holinshed was the principal author of the *Chronicles,* being responsible for the "Historie of England," but he collaborated with William Harrison—who wrote the "Description of England," a vivid account of six-teenth-century customs and daily life—and Richard Stanyhurst and Edward Campion, who together wrote the "Description of Ireland." "The History and Description of Scotland" and the "History of Ireland" were translations or adaptations of the work of earlier historians and writers. The *Chronicles* were immediately successful, in part because of the easily accessible style in which they were composed and because their patriotic celebration of British history was compatible with the rise of nationalistic fervor in Elizabethan England. As in the case of EDWARD HALL, Holinshed's influence on Shakespeare is most evident in the English history plays.

**INNS OF COURT:** Four colleges of law located in the City of London—Gray's Inn, the Middle Temple, the Inner Temple, and Lincoln's Inn. In the sixteenth and seventeenth centuries, the Inns were not only academic institutions, but were also regarded as finishing schools for gentlemen, providing their students with instruction in music, dance, and other social accomplishments. Interest in the drama ran high in these communities; in addition to producing their own plays, masques, and revels, members would occasionally employ professional acting companies, such as the LORD CHAMBERLAIN'S MEN and the KING'S MEN, for private performances at the Inns. Existing evidence indicates that at least two of Shakespeare's plays were first performed at the Inns: *The Comedy of Errors* and *Twelfth Night.*

**KING'S MEN:** An acting company formerly known as the LORD CHAMBERLAIN'S MEN. On May 19, 1603, shortly after his accession to the English throne, James I granted the company a royal patent, and its name was altered to reflect the King's direct patronage. At that date, members who shared in the profits of the company included Shakespeare, Richard Burbage, John Heminge, Henry Condell, Augustine Phillips, William Sly, and Robert Armin. Records of the Court indicate that this was the most favored acting company in the Jacobean era, averaging a dozen performances there each year during that period. In addition to public performances at the GLOBE THEATRE in the spring and autumn, the King's Men played at the private BLACKFRIARS THEATRE in winter and for evening performances. Because of the recurring plague in London from 1603 onward, theatrical companies like the King's Men spent the summer months touring and giving performances in the provinces. Besides the work of Shakespeare, the King's Men's repertoire included plays by Ben Jonson, Francis Beaumont and John Fletcher, Thomas Dekker, and Cyril Tourneur. The company continued to flourish until 1642, when by Act of Parliament all dramatic performances were suppressed.

**LORD ADMIRAL'S MEN:** An acting company formed in 1576-77 under the patronage of Charles Howard, Earl of Nottingham. From its inception to 1585 the company was known as the Lord Howard's Men, from 1585 to 1603 as the Lord Admiral's Men, from 1604 to 1612 as Prince Henry's Men, and from 1613 to 1625 as the Palsgrave's Men. They were the principal rivals of the LORD CHAMBERLAIN'S MEN; occasionally, from 1594 to 1612, these two troupes were the only companies authorized to perform in London. The company's chief player was Edward Alleyn, an actor of comparable distinction with Richard Burbage of the Lord Chamberlain's Men. From 1591 the company performed at the ROSE THEATRE, moving to the Fortune Theatre in 1600. The detailed financial records of Philip Henslowe, who acted as the company's landlord and financier from 1594 until his death in 1616, indicate that an extensive list of dramatists wrote for the troupe throughout its existence, including Christopher Marlowe, Ben Jonson, George Chapman, Anthony Munday, Henry Chettle, Michael Drayton, Thomas Dekker, and William Rowley.

**LORD CHAMBERLAIN'S MEN:** An acting company formed in 1594 under the patronage of Henry Carey, Lord Hunsdon, who was the Queen's Chamberlain from 1585 until his death in 1596. From

1596 to 1597, the company's benefactor was Lord Hunsdon's son, George Carey, and they were known as Hunsdon's Men until the younger Carey was appointed to his late father's office, when the troupe once again became officially the Lord Chamberlain's Men. The members of the company included Shakespeare, Will Kempe—the famous 'clown' and the most popular actor of his time—, Richard Burbage—the renowned tragedian—, and John Heminge, who served as business manager for the company. In 1594 they began performing at the Theatre and the Cross Key's Inn, moving to the Swan on Bankside in 1596 when the City Corporation banned the public presentation of plays within the limits of the City of London. In 1599 some members of the company financed the building of the GLOBE THEATRE and thus the majority became "sharers," not only in the actors' portion of the profits, but in the theatre owners' allotment as well. This economic independence was an important element in the unusual stability of their association. They became the foremost London company, performing at Court on thirty-two occasions between 1594 and 1603, whereas their chief rivals, the LORD ADMIRAL'S MEN, made twenty appearances at Court during that period. No detailed records exist of the plays that were in their repertoire. Ben Jonson wrote several of his dramas for the Lord Chamberlain's Men, but the company's success is largely attributable to the fact that, after joining them in 1594, Shakespeare wrote for no other company.

**MEMORIAL RECONSTRUCTION:** One hypothesis used to explain the texts of the so-called BAD-QUARTOS. Scholars have theorized that one or more actors who had appeared in a Shakespearean play attempted to reconstruct from personal memory the text of that drama. Inevitably, there would be lapses of recall with resultant errors and deviations from the original play. Characteristics of these corrupt "reported texts" include the transposition of phrases or entire speeches, the substitution of new language, omission of dramatically significant material, and abridgements of extended passages. It has been speculated that memorial reconstructions were produced by companies touring the provinces whose PROMPT-BOOKS remained in London, or by actors who sold the pirated versions to printers. W. W. Greg, in his examination of the bad quarto of *The Merry Wives of Windsor,* was the first scholar to employ the term.

**MERES, FRANCIS:** (b. 1565 - d. 1647) English cleric and schoolmaster whose *Palladis Tamia, Wit's Treasury* (1598) has played a valuable role in determining the dates of several of Shakespeare's plays and poems. The work is a collection of observations and commentary on a wide range of subjects, including religion, moral philosophy, and the arts. In a section entitled "A Comparative discourse on our English Poets with the Greeke, Latine, and Italian Poets," Meres compared Shakespeare's work favorably with that of OVID, PLAUTUS, and SENECA and listed the titles of six of his tragedies, six comedies, and two poems, thus establishing that these works were composed no later than 1598. Meres also praised Shakespeare as "the most excellent" of contemporary writers for the stage and remarked that, in addition to his published poetry, he had written some "sugred sonnets" which were circulated among a group of his "private friends."

**MIRROR FOR MAGISTRATES, A:** A collection of dramatic monologues in which the ghosts of eminent historical figures lament the sins or fatal flaws that led to their downfalls. Individually and collectively, the stories depict the evils of rebellion against divinely constituted authority, the obligation of rulers to God and their subjects, and the inconstancy of Fortune's favor. William Baldwin edited the first edition (1559) and wrote many of the tales, with the collaboration of George Ferrers and six other authors. Subsequently, six editions appeared by 1610, in which a score of contributors presented the first-person narrative complaints of some one hundred heroic personages, from King Albanact of Scotland to Cardinal Wolsey and Queen Elizabeth. The first edition to include Thomas Sackville's *Induction* (1563) is the most notable; Sackville's description of the poet's descent into hell and his encounters with allegorical figures, such as Remorse, Revenge, Famine, and War, is generally considered the most poetically meritorious work in the collection. With respect to Shakespeare, scholars claim that elements from *A Mirror for Magistrates* are most apparent in the history plays on the two Richards and on Henry IV and Henry VI.

OCTAVO: The term applied to a book made up of sheets of paper folded three times to form eight leaves of equal size, or sixteen pages. The dimensions of a folded octavo page may range from 6 to 11 inches in height and 4 to 7½ inches in width.

OVID [PUBLIUS OVIDIUS NASO]: (b. 43 B.C. - d. 18 A.D.) Roman poet who was extremely popular during his lifetime and who greatly affected the subsequent development of Latin poetry; he also deeply influenced European art and literature. Ovid's erotic poetry is molded in elegaic couplets, a highly artificial form which he reshaped by means of a graceful and fluent style. These erotic poems—*Amores, Heroides, Ars amatoria,* and *Remedia amoris*—are concerned with love and amorous intrigue, depicting these themes in an amoral fashion that some critics have considered licentious. Ovid's *Metamorphoses,* written in rapidly flowing hexameters, presents some 250 stories from Greek and Roman legends that depict various kinds of transformations, from the tale of primeval chaos to the apotheosis of Julius Caesar into a celestial body. *Metamorphoses* is a superbly unified work, demonstrating Ovid's supreme skills in narration and description and his ingenuity in linking a wide variety of sources into a masterly presentation of classical myth. His brilliance of invention, fluency of style, and vivid descriptions were highly praised in the Renaissance, and familiarity with his work was considered an essential part of a formal education. Ovid has been cited as a source for many of Shakespeare's plays, including *The Merry Wives of Windsor, A Midsummer Night's Dream, The Tempest, Titus Andronicus, Troilus and Cressida,* and *The Winter's Tale.*

PLAUTUS, TITUS MACCIUS: (b. 254? - d. 184 B.C.) The most prominent Roman dramatist of the Republic and early Empire. The esteem and unrivaled popularity he earned from his contemporaries have been ratified by scholars and dramatists of the past five hundred years. Many playwrights from the sixteenth to the twentieth century have chosen his works, particularly *Amphitruo, Aulularia, Captivi, Menaechmi, Miles Gloriosus, Mostellaria,* and *Trinummus,* as models for their own. Plautus adapted characters, plots, and settings from Greek drama, combined these with elements from Roman farce and satire, and introduced into his plays incongruous contemporary allusions, plays upon words, and colloquial and newly coined language. His dramatic style is further characterized by extensive use of song and music, alliteration and assonance, and variations in metrical language to emphasize differences in character and mood. His employment of stock character types, the intrigues and confusions of his plots, and the exuberance and vigor of his comic spirit were especially celebrated by his English Renaissance audience. The plays of Shakespeare that are most indebted to Plautus include *The Comedy of Errors, The Taming of the Shrew, The Merry Wives of Windsor, The Two Gentlemen of Verona, Romeo and Juliet,* and *All's Well That Ends Well.* His influence can also be noted in such Shakespearean characters as Don Armado (*Love's Labour's Lost*), Parolles (*All's Well That Ends Well*), and Falstaff (*Henry IV* and *The Merry Wives of Windsor*).

PLUTARCH: (b. 46? - d. 120? A.D.) Greek biographer and essayist whose work constitutes a faithful record of the historical tradition, moral views, and ethical judgments of second century A.C. Graeco-Roman culture. His *Parallel Lives*—translated into English by Sir Thomas North and published in 1579 as *The Lives of the Noble Grecianes and Romans compared together*—was one of the most widely read works of antiquity from the sixteenth to the nineteenth century. In this work, Plutarch was principally concerned with portraying the personal character and individual actions of the statesmen, soldiers, legislators, and orators who were his subjects, and through his warm and lively style with instructing as well as entertaining his readers. His portrayal of these classical figures as exemplars of virtue or vice and his emphasis on the successive turns of Fortune's wheel in the lives of great men were in close harmony with the Elizabethan worldview. His miscellaneous writings on religion, ethics, literature, science, and politics, collected under the general title of *Moralia,* were important models for sixteenth- and seventeenth-century essayists. Plutarch is considered a major source for Shakespeare's *Julius Caesar, Antony and Cleopatra,* and *Coriolanus,* and a minor source for *A Midsummer Night's Dream* and *Timon of Athens.*

PRINTER'S COPY: The manuscript or printed text of a work which the compositor uses to set type pages. The nature of the copy available to the early printers of Shakespeare's plays is important in assessing how closely these editions adhere to the original writings. Bibliographical scholars have identified a number of forms available to printers in Shakespeare's time: the author's FOUL PAPERS; a FAIR COPY prepared either by the author or a scribe; partially annotated foul papers or a fair copy that included prompt notes; private copies, prepared by a scribe for an individual outside the acting company; the company's PROMPT-BOOK; scribal transcripts of a prompt-book; a stenographer's report made by someone who had attended an actual performance; earlier printed editions of the work, with or without additional insertions provided by the author, a scribe, or the preparer of a prompt-book; a transcript of a MEMORIAL RECONSTRUCTION of the work; and an ASSEMBLED TEXT.

PROMPT-BOOK: Acting version of a play, usually transcribed from the playwright's FOUL PAPERS by a scribe or the dramatist himself. This copy, or "book," was then presented to the Master of the Revels, the official censor and authorizer of plays. Upon approving its contents, he would license the play for performance and endorse the text as the "allowed book" of the play. A prompt-book represents an alteration or modification of the dramatist's original manuscript. It generally contains detailed stage directions, including cues for music, off-stage noises, and the entries and exits of principal characters, indications of stage properties to be used, and other annotations to assist the prompter during an actual performance. The prompt-book version was frequently shorter than the original manuscript, for cuts would be made in terms of minor characters or dramatic incidents to suit the resources of the acting company. Printed editions of plays were sometimes based on prompt-books.

QUARTO: The term applies to a book made up of sheets of paper folded twice to form four leaves of equal size, or eight pages. A quarto page may range in size from 8½ inches to 12½ inches in height and 6¾ to 10 inches in width.

ROSE THEATRE: Built in 1587 by Philip Henslowe, the Rose was constructed of timber on a brick foundation, with exterior walls of lath and plaster and a roof of thatch. Its location on Bankside—across the Thames River from the City of London—established this area as a new site for public theaters. Its circular design included a yard, galleries, a tiring house, and "heavens." A half-dozen acting companies played there, the most important being the LORD ADMIRAL'S MEN, the chief rival to the LORD CHAMBERLAIN'S MEN, who performed at the Rose from 1594 to 1600, when they moved to the new Fortune Theatre constructed by Henslowe in Finsbury, north of the City of London. Among the dramatists employed by Henslowe at the Rose were Thomas Kyd, Christopher Marlowe, Shakespeare, Robert Greene, Ben Jonson, Michael Drayton, George Chapman, Thomas Dekker, and John Webster. The building was razed in 1606.

**SECOND FOLIO:** The second collected edition of Shakespeare's plays, published in 1632. While it is essentially a reprint of the FIRST FOLIO, more than fifteen hundred changes were made to modernize spelling and to correct stage directions and proper names.

**SENECA, LUCIUS ANNAEUS:** (b. 4? B.C. - d. 65 A.D.) Roman philosopher, statesman, dramatist, and orator who was one of the major writers of the first century A.D. and who had a profound influence on Latin and European literature. His philosophical essays castigating vice and teaching Stoic resignation were esteemed by the medieval Latin Church, whose members regarded him as a great moral teacher. His nine tragedies—*Hercules Furens, Thyestes, Phoen-issae, Phaedra, Oedipus, Troades, Medea, Agamemnon,* and *Hercules Oetaeus*—were trans-lated into English in 1581 and exerted a strong influence over sixteenth-century English dramatists. Seneca's plays were composed for reading or reciting rather than for performing on the stage, and they evince little attention to character or motive. Written in a declamatory rhetorical style, their function was to instruct on the disastrous consequences of uncontrolled passion and political tyranny. Distinctive features of Senecan tragedy include sensationalism and intense emotionalism, the depiction of wicked acts and retribution, adultery and unnatural sexuality, murder and revenge, and the representation of supernatural beings. Shakespeare's use of Seneca can be discerned most readily in such plays as *King John*, the histories from *Henry VI* to *Richard III, Antony and Cleopatra, Titus Andronicus, Julius Caesar, Hamlet,* and *Macbeth*.

**STATIONERS' REGISTER:** A ledger book in which were entered the titles of works to be printed and published. The Register was maintained by the Stationers' Company, an association of those who manufactured and those who sold books. In Tudor England, the Company had a virtual monopoly—aside from the university presses—on printing works written throughout the coun-try. Having obtained a license authorizing the printing of a work, a member of the Company would pay a fee to enter the book in the Register, thereby securing the sole right to print or sell that book. Many registered texts were acquired by questionable means and many plays were published whose titles were not entered in the records of the Company. However, the Stationers' Register is one of the most important documents for scholars investigating the literature of that period.

**TEXTUAL CORRUPTION:** A phrase signifying the alterations that may occur as an author's original text is transmitted through the subsequent stages of preparation for performance and printing. In cases where the PRINTER'S COPY was not an author's FAIR COPY, the text may contain unin-telligible language, mislineations, omissions, repetitious lines, transposed verse and prose speeches, inaccurate speech headings, and defective rhymes. Through their investigation of the nature of the copy from which a COMPOSITOR set his type, textual scholars attempt to restore the text and construct a version that is closest to the author's original manuscript.

**THIRD FOLIO:** The third collected edition of Shakespeare's plays, published in 1663. Essentially a reprint of the SECOND FOLIO, it contains some corrections to that text and some errors not found in earlier editions. The Third Folio was reprinted in 1664 and included "seven Playes, never before Printed in Folio." One of these seven—*Pericles*—has been accepted as Shakespeare's work, but the other six are considered apocryphal (see APOCRYPHA).

**VARIORUM:** An edition of a literary work which includes notes and commentary by previous editors and scholars. The First Variorum of Shakespeare's works was published in 1803. Edited by Isaac Reed, it was based on George Steevens's four eighteenth-century editions and includes extensive material from Samuel Johnson's edition of 1765, together with essays by Edmund Malone, George Chalmers, and Richard Farmer. The Second Variorum is a reprint of the First, and it was published in 1813. The Third Variorum is frequently referred to as the Boswell-Malone edition. Containing prefaces from most of the eighteenth-century editions of Shakespeare's work, as well as the poems and sonnets, which Steevens and Reed omitted, the Third Variorum was published in 1821. Edited by James Boswell the younger and based on the scholarship of Malone, it includes such a wealth of material that it is generally regarded as the most important complete edition of the works of Shakespeare. The Fourth Variorum, known as the "New Variorum," was begun by Horace Howard Furness in 1871. Upon his death, his son, Horace Howard Furness, Jr., assumed the editorship, and subsequently—in 1936—a committee of the Modern Language Association of America took on the editorship. The Fourth Variorum is a vast work, containing annotations, textual notes, and excerpts from eminent commentators throughout the history of Shakespearean criticism.

# Cumulative Index to Topics

[The Cumulative Index to Topics identifies the principal topics of debate in the criticism of each play. The topics are arranged alphabetically; page references indicate the beginning page number of those excerpts offering substantial commentary on that topic.]

Topic Index

Topic Index

# Cumulative Index to Critics

**Critic Index**